10th International Workshop on Semantic Evaluation (SemEval 2016)

San Diego, California, USA
16 - 17 June 2016

Volume 1 of 2

ISBN: 978-1-5108-2607-6

10th International Workshop on Semantic Evaluation (SemEval 2016)

San Diego, California, USA
16 - 17 June 2016

Volume 1 of 2

SemEval-2016

The 10th International Workshop on Semantic Evaluation

Proceedings of the Workshop

June 16-17, 2016
San Diego, California, USA

Welcome to SemEval-2016

The Semantic Evaluation (SemEval) series of workshops focuses on the evaluation and comparison of systems that can analyse diverse semantic phenomena in text with the aim of extending the current state of the art in semantic analysis and creating high quality annotated datasets in a range of increasingly challenging problems in natural language semantics. SemEval provides an exciting forum for researchers to propose challenging research problems in semantics and to build systems/techniques to address such research problems.

SemEval-2016 is the tenth workshop in the series of International Workshops on Semantic Evaluation Exercises. The first three workshops, SensEval-1 (1998), SensEval-2 (2001), and SensEval-3 (2004), focused on word sense disambiguation, each time growing in the number of languages offered, in the number of tasks, and also in the number of participating teams. In 2007, the workshop was renamed to SemEval, and the subsequent SemEval workshops evolved to include semantic analysis tasks beyond word sense disambiguation. In 2012, SemEval turned into a yearly event. It currently runs every year, but on a two-year cycle, i.e., the tasks for SemEval-2016 were proposed in 2015.

SemEval-2016 was co-located with the 2016 Conference of the North American Chapter of the Association for Computational Linguistics: Human Language Technologies (NAACL-HLT'2016) in San Diego, California. It included the following 14 shared tasks organized in five tracks:

- Text Similarity and Question Answering Track

    - Task 1: Semantic Textual Similarity: A Unified Framework for Semantic Processing and Evaluation
    - Task 2: Interpretable Semantic Textual Similarity
    - Task 3: Community Question Answering

- Sentiment Analysis Track

    - Task 4: Sentiment Analysis in Twitter
    - Task 5: Aspect-Based Sentiment Analysis
    - Task 6: Detecting Stance in Tweets
    - Task 7: Determining Sentiment Intensity of English and Arabic Phrases

- Semantic Parsing Track

    - Task 8: Meaning Representation Parsing
    - Task 9: Chinese Semantic Dependency Parsing

- Semantic Analysis Track

    - Task 10: Detecting Minimal Semantic Units and their Meanings
    - Task 11: Complex Word Identification
    - Task 12: Clinical TempEval

- Semantic Taxonomy Track

    – Task 13: TExEval-2 – Taxonomy Extraction
    – Task 14: Semantic Taxonomy Enrichment

This volume contains both Task Description papers that describe each of the above tasks and System Description papers that describe the systems that participated in the above tasks. A total of 14 task description papers and 198 system description papers are included in this volume.

We are grateful to all task organisers as well as the large number of participants whose enthusiastic participation has made SemEval once again a successful event. We are thankful to the task organisers who also served as area chairs, and to task organisers and participants who reviewed paper submissions. These proceedings have greatly benefited from their detailed and thoughtful feedback. We also thank the NAACL 2016 conference organizers for their support. Finally, we most gratefully acknowledge the support of our sponsor, the ACL Special Interest Group on the Lexicon (SIGLEX).

The SemEval-2016 organizers,
Steven Bethard, Daniel Cer, Marine Carpuat, David Jurgens, Preslav Nakov and Torsten Zesch

Organizers:

Steven Bethard, University of Alabama at Birmingham
Daniel Cer, Google
Marine Carpuat, University of Maryland
David Jurgens, Stanford University
Preslav Nakov, Qatar Computing Research Institute, HBKU
Torsten Zesch, University of Duisburg-Essen

Steering Committee:

Eneko Agirre, University of the Basque Country (UPV/EHU)
Niranjan Balasubramanian, Stony Brook University
Timothy Baldwin, The University of Melbourne
Svetla Boytcheva, Bulgarian Academy of Sciences, IICT
Tommaso Caselli, VU Amsterdam
Kevin Cohen, Computational Bioscience Program, U. Colorado School of Medicine
Gerard de Melo, Tsinghua University
Mona Diab, GWU
Anna Divoli, Pingar Research
Nadir Durrani, QCRI
Judith Eckle-Kohler, Technische Universität Darmstadt
Stefano Faralli, University of Mannheim
Dimitris Galanis, Institute for Language and Speech Processing, Athena Research Center
Francisco Guzmán, Qatar Computing Research Institute
Nizar Habash, New York University Abu Dhabi
Valia Kordoni, Humboldt-Universität zu Berlin
Zornitsa Kozareva, Yahoo!
Maria Liakata, University of Warwick
Wei Lu, Singapore University of Technology and Design
Lluís Màrquez, Qatar Computing Research Institute
Vivi Nastase, University of Heidelberg
Ani Nenkova, University of Pennsylvania
Stephan Oepen, Universitetet i Oslo
Sebastian Padó, Stuttgart University
Haris Papageorgiou, Institute for Language and Speech Processing ILSP/ ATHENA R.C.
Marius Pasca, Google
Ted Pedersen, University of Minnesota, Duluth
Marco Pennacchiotti, eBay Inc
Mohammad Taher Pilehvar, University of Cambridge
Sameer Pradhan, cemantix.org
Carlos Ramisch, LIF, Aix-Marseille Université
Alan Ritter, The Ohio State University
Sara Rosenthal, Columbia University

Irene Russo, ILC CNR
Derek Ruths, McGill University
Hassan Sajjad, Qatar Computing Research Institute
Fabrizio Sebastiani Qatar Computing Research Institute,
Veselin Stoyanov, Facebook
Carlo Strapparava, FBK-irst
Mihai Surdeanu, University of Arizona
Stan Szpakowicz, EECS, University of Ottawa
Irina Temnikova, Qatar Computing Research Institute, HBKU
Tony Veale, University College Dublin
Marilyn Walker, University of California Santa Cruz
Diarmuid Ó Séaghdha, Apple

Table of Contents

Workshop Program

16 Jun 2016

09:00–09:15 **Welcome**

Opening Remarks
SemEval organizers

09:15–10:30 **Sentiment Analysis**

09:15–09:30 *SemEval-2016 Task 4: Sentiment Analysis in Twitter*
Preslav Nakov, Alan Ritter, Sara Rosenthal, Fabrizio Sebastiani and Veselin Stoyanov

09:30–09:45 *SemEval-2016 Task 5: Aspect Based Sentiment Analysis*
Maria Pontiki, Dimitris Galanis, Haris Papageorgiou, Ion Androutsopoulos, Suresh Manandhar, Mohammad AL-Smadi, Mahmoud Al-Ayyoub, Yanyan Zhao, Bing Qin, Orphee De Clercq, Veronique Hoste, Marianna Apidianaki, Xavier Tannier, Natalia Loukachevitch, Evgeniy Kotelnikov, Núria Bel, Salud María Jiménez-Zafra and Gülşen Eryiğit

09:45–10:00 *SemEval-2016 Task 6: Detecting Stance in Tweets*
Saif Mohammad, Svetlana Kiritchenko, Parinaz Sobhani, Xiaodan Zhu and Colin Cherry

10:00–10:15 *SemEval-2016 Task 7: Determining Sentiment Intensity of English and Arabic Phrases*
Svetlana Kiritchenko, Saif Mohammad and Mohammad Salameh

10:15–10:30 *Sentiment Analysis Discussion*
Task Organizers

10:30–11:00 ***Coffee Break***

11:00–12:30   Poster Session: Sentiment Analysis

MITRE at SemEval-2016 Task 6: Transfer Learning for Stance Detection
Guido Zarrella and Amy Marsh

TakeLab at SemEval-2016 Task 6: Stance Classification in Tweets Using a Genetic Algorithm Based Ensemble
Martin Tutek, Ivan Sekulic, Paula Gombar, Ivan Paljak, Filip Culinovic, Filip Boltuzic, Mladen Karan, Domagoj Alagić and Jan Šnajder

LSIS at SemEval-2016 Task 7: Using Web Search Engines for English and Arabic Unsupervised Sentiment Intensity Prediction
Amal Htait, Sebastien Fournier and Patrice Bellot

iLab-Edinburgh at SemEval-2016 Task 7: A Hybrid Approach for Determining Sentiment Intensity of Arabic Twitter Phrases
Eshrag Refaee and Verena Rieser

UWB at SemEval-2016 Task 7: Novel Method for Automatic Sentiment Intensity Determination
Ladislav Lenc, Pavel Král and Václav Rajtmajer

NileTMRG at SemEval-2016 Task 7: Deriving Prior Polarities for Arabic Sentiment Terms
Samhaa R. El-Beltagy

ECNU at SemEval-2016 Task 7: An Enhanced Supervised Learning Method for Lexicon Sentiment Intensity Ranking
Feixiang Wang, Zhihua Zhang and Man Lan

12:30–02:00   *Lunch*

02:00–03:30   Textual Similarity, Question Answering and Semantic Analysis

02:00–02:15   *SemEval-2016 Task 1: Semantic Textual Similarity, Monolingual and Cross-Lingual Evaluation*
Eneko Agirre, Carmen Banea, Daniel Cer, Mona Diab, Aitor Gonzalez-Agirre, Rada Mihalcea, German Rigau and Janyce Wiebe

02:15–02:30   *SemEval-2016 Task 2: Interpretable Semantic Textual Similarity*
Eneko Agirre, Aitor Gonzalez-Agirre, Inigo Lopez-Gazpio, Montse Maritxalar, German Rigau and Larraitz Uria

02:30–02:45   *SemEval-2016 Task 3: Community Question Answering*
Preslav Nakov, Lluís Màrquez, Alessandro Moschitti, Walid Magdy, Hamdy Mubarak, abed Alhakim Freihat, Jim Glass and Bilal Randeree

02:45–03:00   *SemEval-2016 Task 10: Detecting Minimal Semantic Units and their Meanings (DiMSUM)*
Nathan Schneider, Dirk Hovy, Anders Johannsen and Marine Carpuat

03:00–03:15   *SemEval 2016 Task 11: Complex Word Identification*
Gustavo Paetzold and Lucia Specia

03:15–03:30   *Textual Similarity and Question Answering Discussion*
Task Organizers

03:30–04:00   *Coffee Break*

04:00–05:30   Poster Session: Textual Similarity, and Question Answering

17 Jun 2016

09:00–10:30 Perspectives

09:00–09:30   *SemEval-2017 Preview*
SemEval organizers

09:30–10:30   *Invited Talk*

10:30–11:00   *Coffee Break*

11:00–12:30   Semantic Analysis, Semantic Parsing and Semantic Taxonomy

11:00–11:15   *SemEval-2016 Task 12: Clinical TempEval*
Steven Bethard, Guergana Savova, Wei-Te Chen, Leon Derczynski, James Puste-jovsky and Marc Verhagen

11:15–11:30   *SemEval-2016 Task 8: Meaning Representation Parsing*
Jonathan May

11:30–11:45   *SemEval-2016 Task 9: Chinese Semantic Dependency Parsing*
Wanxiang Che, Yanqiu Shao, Ting Liu and Yu Ding

11:45–12:00   *SemEval-2016 Task 13: Taxonomy Extraction Evaluation (TExEval-2)*
Georgeta Bordea, Els Lefever and Paul Buitelaar

12:00–12:15   *SemEval-2016 Task 14: Semantic Taxonomy Enrichment*
David Jurgens and Mohammad Taher Pilehvar

12:30–02:00   *Lunch*

02:00–03:30   **Best Of SemEval**

02:00–02:15   *UMD-TTIC-UW at SemEval-2016 Task 1: Attention-Based Multi-Perspective Convolutional Neural Networks for Textual Similarity Measurement*
Hua He, John Wieting, Kevin Gimpel, Jinfeng Rao and Jimmy Lin

02:15–02:30   *Inspire at SemEval-2016 Task 2: Interpretable Semantic Textual Similarity Alignment based on Answer Set Programming*
Mishal Kazmi and Peter Schüller

02:30–02:45   *KeLP at SemEval-2016 Task 3: Learning Semantic Relations between Questions and Answers*
Simone Filice, Danilo Croce, Alessandro Moschitti and Roberto Basili

02:45–03:00   *SwissCheese at SemEval-2016 Task 4: Sentiment Classification Using an Ensemble of Convolutional Neural Networks with Distant Supervision*
Jan Deriu, Maurice Gonzenbach, Fatih Uzdilli, Aurelien Lucchi, Valeria De Luca and Martin Jaggi

03:00–03:15   *IIT-TUDA at SemEval-2016 Task 5: Beyond Sentiment Lexicon: Combining Domain Dependency and Distributional Semantics Features for Aspect Based Sentiment Analysis*
Ayush Kumar, Sarah Kohail, Amit Kumar, Asif Ekbal and Chris Biemann

03:15–03:30   *LIMSI-COT at SemEval-2016 Task 12: Temporal relation identification using a pipeline of classifiers*
Julien Tourille, Olivier Ferret, Aurélie Névéol and Xavier Tannier

03:30–04:00   *Coffee Break*

04:00–05:30   **Poster Session: Semantic Analysis, Parsing, and Taxonomy**

RIGA at SemEval-2016 Task 8: Impact of Smatch Extensions and Character-Level Neural Translation on AMR Parsing Accuracy
Guntis Barzdins and Didzis Gosko

DynamicPower at SemEval-2016 Task 8: Processing syntactic parse trees with a Dynamic Semantics core
Alastair Butler

M2L at SemEval-2016 Task 8: AMR Parsing with Neural Networks
Yevgeniy Puzikov, Daisuke Kawahara and Sadao Kurohashi

ICL-HD at SemEval-2016 Task 8: Meaning Representation Parsing - Augmenting AMR Parsing with a Preposition Semantic Role Labeling Neural Network
Lauritz Brandt, David Grimm, Mengfei Zhou and Yannick Versley

UCL+Sheffield at SemEval-2016 Task 8: Imitation learning for AMR parsing with an alpha-bound
James Goodman, Andreas Vlachos and Jason Naradowsky

CAMR at SemEval-2016 Task 8: An Extended Transition-based AMR Parser
Chuan Wang, Sameer Pradhan, Xiaoman Pan, Heng Ji and Nianwen Xue

The Meaning Factory at SemEval-2016 Task 8: Producing AMRs with Boxer
Johannes Bjerva, Johan Bos and Hessel Haagsma

UofR at SemEval-2016 Task 8: Learning Synchronous Hyperedge Replacement Grammar for AMR Parsing
Xiaochang Peng and Daniel Gildea

CLIP@UMD at SemEval-2016 Task 8: Parser for Abstract Meaning Representation using Learning to Search
Sudha Rao, Yogarshi Vyas, Hal Daumé III and Philip Resnik

SemEval-2016 Task 4: Sentiment Analysis in Twitter

Preslav Nakov♣, Alan Ritter◇, Sara Rosenthal♡, Fabrizio Sebastiani♣,* Veselin Stoyanov♠
♣Qatar Computing Research Institute, Hamad bin Khalifa University, Qatar
◇Department of Computer Science and Engineering, The Ohio State University, USA
♡IBM Watson Health Research, USA
♠Johns Hopkins University, USA

Abstract

This paper discusses the fourth year of the "Sentiment Analysis in Twitter Task". SemEval-2016 Task 4 comprises five subtasks, three of which represent a significant departure from previous editions. The first two subtasks are reruns from prior years and ask to predict the overall sentiment, and the sentiment towards a topic in a tweet. The three new subtasks focus on two variants of the basic "sentiment classification in Twitter" task. The first variant adopts a five-point scale, which confers an *ordinal* character to the classification task. The second variant focuses on the correct estimation of the prevalence of each class of interest, a task which has been called *quantification* in the supervised learning literature. The task continues to be very popular, attracting a total of 43 teams.

1 Introduction

Sentiment classification is the task of detecting whether a textual item (e.g., a product review, a blog post, an editorial, etc.) expresses a POSITIVE or a NEGATIVE opinion in general or about a given entity, e.g., a product, a person, a political party, or a policy. Sentiment classification has become a ubiquitous enabling technology in the Twittersphere. Classifying tweets according to sentiment has many applications in political science, social sciences, market research, and many others (Martínez-Cámara et al., 2014; Mejova et al., 2015).

As a testament to the prominence of research on sentiment analysis in Twitter, the tweet sentiment classification (TSC) task has attracted the highest number of participants in the last three SemEval campaigns (Nakov et al., 2013; Rosenthal et al., 2014; Rosenthal et al., 2015; Nakov et al., 2016b).

Previous editions of the SemEval task involved binary (POSITIVE vs. NEGATIVE) or *single-label multi-class* classification (SLMC) when a NEUTRAL[1] class is added (POSITIVE vs. NEGATIVE vs. NEUTRAL). SemEval-2016 Task 4 represents a significant departure from these previous editions. Although two of the subtasks (Subtasks A and B) are reincarnations of previous editions (SLMC classification for Subtask A, binary classification for Subtask B), SemEval-2016 Task 4 introduces two completely new problems, taken individually (Subtasks C and D) and in combination (Subtask E):

1.1 Ordinal Classification

We replace the two- or three-point scale with a five-point scale {HIGHLYPOSITIVE, POSITIVE, NEUTRAL, NEGATIVE, HIGHLYNEGATIVE}, which is now ubiquitous in the corporate world where human ratings are involved: e.g., Amazon, TripAdvisor, and Yelp, all use a five-point scale for rating sentiment towards products, hotels, and restaurants.

Moving from a categorical two/three-point scale to an ordered five-point scale means, in machine learning terms, moving from binary to *ordinal classification* (a.k.a. *ordinal regression*).

---

*Fabrizio Sebastiani is currently on leave from Consiglio Nazionale delle Ricerche, Italy.

[1]We merged OBJECTIVE under NEUTRAL, as previous attempts to have annotators distinguish between the two have consistently resulted in very low inter-annotator agreement.

Proceedings of SemEval-2016, pages 1–18,
San Diego, California, June 16-17, 2016. ©2016 Association for Computational Linguistics

1.2 Quantification

We replace classification with *quantification*, i.e., supervised class prevalence estimation. With regard to Twitter, hardly anyone is interested in whether *a specific person* has a positive or a negative view of the topic. Rather, applications look at estimating the *prevalence* of positive and negative tweets about a given topic. Most (if not all) tweet sentiment classification studies conducted within political science (Borge-Holthoefer et al., 2015; Kaya et al., 2013; Marchetti-Bowick and Chambers, 2012), economics (Bollen et al., 2011; O'Connor et al., 2010), social science (Dodds et al., 2011), and market research (Burton and Soboleva, 2011; Qureshi et al., 2013), use Twitter with an interest in aggregate data and *not* in individual classifications.

Estimating prevalences (more generally, estimating the *distribution* of the classes in a set of unlabelled items) by leveraging training data is called *quantification* in data mining and related fields. Previous work has argued that quantification is not a mere byproduct of classification, since (a) a good classifier is not necessarily a good quantifier, and vice versa, see, e.g., (Forman, 2008); (b) quantification requires evaluation measures different from classification. Quantification-specific learning approaches have been proposed over the years; Sections 2 and 5 of (Esuli and Sebastiani, 2015) contain several pointers to such literature.

Note that, in Subtasks B to E, tweets come labelled with the *topic* they are about and participants need not classify whether a tweet is about a given topic. A topic can be anything that people express opinions about; for example, a product (e.g., iPhone6), a political candidate (e.g., Hillary Clinton), a policy (e.g., Obamacare), an event (e.g., the Pope's visit to Palestine), etc.

The rest of the paper is structured as follows. In Section 2, we give a general overview of SemEval-2016 Task 4 and the five subtasks. Section 3 focuses on the datasets, and on the data generation procedure. In Section 4, we describe in detail the evaluation measures for each subtask. Section 5 discusses the results of the evaluation and the techniques and tools that the top-ranked participants used. Section 6 concludes, discussing the lessons learned and some possible ideas for a followup at SemEval-2017.

2 Task Definition

SemEval-2016 Task 4 consists of five subtasks:

1. **Subtask A:** Given a tweet, predict whether it is of positive, negative, or neutral sentiment.

2. **Subtask B:** Given a tweet known to be about a given topic, predict whether it conveys a positive or a negative sentiment towards the topic.

3. **Subtask C:** Given a tweet known to be about a given topic, estimate the sentiment it conveys towards the topic on a five-point scale ranging from HIGHLYNEGATIVE to HIGHLYPOSITIVE.

4. **Subtask D:** Given a set of tweets known to be about a given topic, estimate the distribution of the tweets in the POSITIVE and NEGATIVE classes.

5. **Subtask E:** Given a set of tweets known to be about a given topic, estimate the distribution of the tweets across the five classes of a five-point scale, ranging from HIGHLYNEGATIVE to HIGHLYPOSITIVE.

Subtask A is a rerun – it was present in all three previous editions of the task. In the 2013-2015 editions, it was known as Subtask B.[2] We ran it again this year because it was the most popular subtask in the three previous task editions. It was the most popular subtask this year as well – see Section 5.

Subtask B is a variant of SemEval-2015 Task 10 Subtask C (Rosenthal et al., 2015; Nakov et al., 2016b), with POSITIVE, NEUTRAL, and NEGATIVE as the classification labels.

Subtask E is similar to SemEval-2015 Task 10 Subtask D, which consisted of the following problem: *Given a set of messages on a given topic from the same period of time, classify the overall sentiment towards the topic in these messages as strongly positive, weakly positive, neutral, weakly negative, or strongly negative.* Note that in SemEval-2015 Task 10 Subtask D, exactly one of the five classes had to be chosen, while in our Subtask E, a distribution across the five classes has to be estimated.

---

[2]Note that we retired the expression-level subtask A, which was present in SemEval 2013–2015 (Nakov et al., 2013; Rosenthal et al., 2014; Rosenthal et al., 2015; Nakov et al., 2016b).

As per the above discussion, Subtasks B to E are new. Conceptually, they form a 2×2 matrix, as shown in Table 1, where the rows indicate the *goal* of the task (classification vs. quantification) and the columns indicate the *granularity* of the task (two- vs. five-point scale).

		Granularity	
		Two-point (binary)	Five-point (ordinal)
Goal	Classification	Subtask B	Subtask C
	Quantification	Subtask D	Subtask E

Table 1: A 2×2 matrix summarizing the similarities and the differences between Subtasks B-E.

3   Datasets

In this section, we describe the process of collection and annotation of the training, development and testing tweets for all five subtasks. We dub this dataset the *Tweet 2016* dataset in order to distinguish it from datasets generated in previous editions of the task.

3.1   Tweet Collection

We provided the datasets from the previous editions[3] (see Table 2) of this task (Nakov et al., 2013; Rosenthal et al., 2014; Rosenthal et al., 2015; Nakov et al., 2016b) for training and development. In addition we created new training and testing datasets.

Dataset	POSITIVE	NEGATIVE	NEUTRAL	Total
Twitter2013-train	3,662	1,466	4,600	9,728
Twitter2013-dev	575	340	739	1,654
Twitter2013-test	1,572	601	1,640	3,813
SMS2013-test	492	394	1,207	2,093
Twitter2014-test	982	202	669	1,853
Twitter2014-sarcasm	33	40	13	86
LiveJournal2014-test	427	304	411	1,142
Twitter2015-test	1,040	365	987	2,392

Table 2: Statistics about data from the 2013-2015 editions of the SemEval task on Sentiment Analysis in Twitter, which could be used for training and development for SemEval-2016 Task 4.

---

[3]For Subtask A, we did not allow training on the testing datasets from 2013–2015, as we used them for progress testing.

We employed the following annotation procedure. As in previous years, we first gathered tweets that express sentiment about popular topics. For this purpose, we extracted named entities from millions of tweets, using a Twitter-tuned named entity recognition system (Ritter et al., 2011). The collected tweets were greatly skewed towards the neutral class. In order to reduce the class imbalance, we removed those that contained no sentiment-bearing words. We used SentiWordNet 3.0 (Baccianella et al., 2010) as a repository of sentiment words. Any word listed in SentiWordNet 3.0 with at least one sense having a positive or a negative sentiment score greater than 0.3 was considered sentiment-bearing.[4]

The training and development tweets were collected from July to October 2015. The test tweets were collected from October to December 2015. We used the public streaming Twitter API to download the tweets.[5]

We then manually filtered the resulting tweets to obtain a set of 200 meaningful topics with at least 100 tweets each (after filtering out near-duplicates). We excluded topics that were incomprehensible, ambiguous (e.g., *Barcelona*, which is the name both of a city and of a sports team), or too general (e.g., *Paris*, which is the name of a big city). We then discarded tweets that were just mentioning the topic but were not really about the topic.

Note that the topics in the training and in the test sets do not overlap, i.e., the test set consists of tweets about topics different from the topics the training and development tweets are about.

3.2   Annotation

The 2016 data consisted of four parts: TRAIN (for training models), DEV (for tuning models), DEVTEST (for development-time evaluation), and TEST (for the official evaluation). The first three datasets were annotated using Amazon's Mechanical Turk, while the TEST dataset was annotated on CrowdFlower.

---

[4]Filtering based on an existing lexicon does bias the dataset to some degree; however, the text still contains sentiment expressions outside those in the lexicon.

[5]We distributed the datasets to the task participants in a similar way: we only released the annotations and the tweet IDs, and the participants had to download the actual tweets by themselves via the API, for which we provided a script: `https://github.com/aritter/twitter_download`

Instructions: Given a Twitter message and a topic, identify whether the message is highly positive, positive, neutral, negative, or highly negative (a) in general and (b) with respect to the provided topic. If a tweet is sarcastic, please select the checkbox "The tweet is sarcastic". Please read the examples and the invalid responses before beginning if this is the first time you are working on this HIT.

Sentence: **We're excited to announce that AC/DC tribute band Big Jack will take the main stage at Fall Jam on Sunday September 27th!**

Overall, the tweet is ○ Highly Positive ○ Positive ○ Neutral ○ Negative ○ Highly Negative
The sentiment towards the topic **ac/dc** is ○ Highly Positive ○ Positive ○ Neutral ○ Negative ○ Highly Negative
☐ The tweet is sarcastic.

Figure 1: The instructions provided to the Mechanical Turk annotators, followed by a screenshot.

Annotation with Amazon's Mechanical Turk. A Human Intelligence Task (HIT) consisted of providing all required annotations for a given tweet message. In order to qualify to work on our HITs, a Mechanical Turk annotator (a.k.a. "Turker") had to have an approval rate greater than 95% and to have completed at least 50 approved HITs. Each HIT was carried out by five Turkers and consisted of five tweets to be annotated. A Turker had to indicate the overall polarity of the tweet message (on a five-point scale) as well as the overall polarity of the message towards the given target topic (again, on a five-point scale). The annotation instructions along with an example are shown in Figure 1. We made available to the Turkers several additional examples, which are shown in Table 3.

We rejected HITs with the following problems:

- one or more responses do not have the overall sentiment marked;

- one or more responses do not have the sentiment towards the topic marked;

- one or more responses appear to be randomly selected.

Annotation with CrowdFlower. We annotated the TEST data using CrowdFlower, as it allows better quality control of the annotations across a number of dimensions. Most importantly, it allows us to find and exclude unreliable annotators based on hidden tests, which we created starting with the highest-confidence and highest-agreement annotations from Mechanical Turk. We added some more tests manually. Otherwise, we setup the annotation task giving exactly the same instructions and examples as in Mechanical Turk.

Consolidation of annotations. In previous years, we used majority voting to select the true label (and discarded cases where a majority had not emerged, which amounted to about 50% of the tweets). As this year we have a five-point scale, where the expected agreement is lower, we used a two-step procedure. If three out of the five annotators agreed on a label, we accepted the label. Otherwise, we first mapped the categorical labels to the integer values $-2, -1, 0, 1, 2$. Then we calculated the average, and finally we mapped that average to the closest integer value. In order to counter-balance the tendency of the average to stay away from -2 and 2, and also to prefer 0, we did not use rounding at ± 0.5 and ± 1.5, but at ± 0.4 and ± 1.4 instead.

To give the reader an idea about the degree of agreement, we will look at the TEST dataset as an example. It included 20,632 tweets. For 2,760, all five annotators assigned the same value, and for another 9,944 there was a majority value. For the remaining 7,928 cases, we had to perform averaging as described above.

The consolidated statistics from the five annotators on a three-point scale for Subtask A are shown in Table 4. Note that, for consistency, we annotated the data for Subtask A on a five-point scale, which we then converted to a three-point scale.

The topic annotations on a two-point scale for Subtasks B and D are shown in Table 5, while those on a five-point scale for Subtasks C and E are in Table 6. Note that, as for Subtask A, the two-point scale annotation counts for Subtasks B and D derive from summing the POSITIVEs with the HIGH-LYPOSITIVEs, and the NEGATIVEs with the HIGH-LYNEGATIVEs from Table 6; moreover, this time we also remove the NEUTRALs.

Tweet	Overall Sentiment	Topic Sentiment
Why would you still wear shorts when it's this cold?! I love how Britain see's a bit of sun and they're like 'OOOH LET'S STRIP!	POSITIVE	Britain: NEGATIVE
Saturday without Leeds United is like Sunday dinner it doesn't feel normal at all (Ryan)	NEGATIVE	Leeds United: HIGHLYPOSITIVE
Who are you tomorrow? Will you make me smile or just bring me sorrow? #HottieOfTheWeek Demi Lovato	NEUTRAL	Demi Lovato: POSITIVE

Table 3: List of example tweets and annotations that were provided to the annotators.

	POSITIVE	NEUTRAL	NEGATIVE	Total
TRAIN	3,094	863	2,043	6,000
DEV	844	765	391	2,000
DEVTEST	994	681	325	2,000
TEST	7,059	10,342	3,231	20,632

Table 4: 2016 data statistics (Subtask A).

	Topics	POSITIVE	NEGATIVE	Total
TRAIN	60	3,591	755	4,346
DEV	20	986	339	1,325
DEVTEST	20	1,153	264	1,417
TEST	100	8,212	2,339	10,551

Table 5: 2016 data statistics (Subtasks B and D).

	Topics	HIGHLYPOSITIVE	POSITIVE	NEUTRAL	NEGATIVE	HIGHLYNEGATIVE	Total
TRAIN	60	437	3,154	1,654	668	87	6,000
DEV	20	53	933	675	296	43	2,000
DEVTEST	20	148	1,005	583	233	31	2,000
TEST	100	382	7,830	10,081	2,201	138	20,632

Table 6: 2016 data statistics (Subtasks C and E).

As we use the same test tweets for all subtasks, the submission of results by participating teams was subdivided in two stages: (*i*) participants had to submit results for Subtasks A, C, E, and (*ii*) only after the submission deadline for A, C, E had passed, we distributed to participants the unlabelled test data for Subtasks B and D.

Otherwise, since for Subtasks B and D we filter out the NEUTRALs, we would have leaked information about which the NEUTRALs are, and this information could have been used in Subtasks C and E.

Finally, as the same tweets can be selected for different topics, we ended up with some duplicates; arguably, these are true duplicates for Subtask A only, as for the other subtasks the topics still differ. This includes 25 duplicates in TRAIN, 3 in DEV, 2 in DEVTEST, and 116 in TEST. There is a larger number in TEST, as TEST is about twice as large as TRAIN, DEV, and DEVTEST combined. This is because we wanted a large TEST set with 100 topics and 200 tweets per topic on average for Subtasks C and E.

4 Evaluation Measures

This section discuss the evaluation measures for the five subtasks of our SemEval-2016 Task 4. A document describing the evaluation measures in detail[6] (Nakov et al., 2016a), and a scoring software implementing all the five "official" measures, were made available to the participants via the task website together with the training data.[7]

For Subtasks B to E, the datasets are each subdivided into a number of "topics", and the subtask needs to be carried out independently for each topic. As a result, each of the evaluation measures will be "macroaveraged" across the topics, i.e., we compute the measure individually for each topic, and we then average the results across the topics.

---

[6] http://alt.qcri.org/semeval2016/task4/

[7] An earlier version of the scoring script contained a bug, to the effect that for Subtask B it was computing F_1^{PN}, and not ρ^{PN}. This was detected only after the submissions were closed, which means that participants to Subtask B who used the scoring system (and not their own implementation of ρ^{PN}) for parameter optimization, may have been penalized in the ranking as a result.

4.1 Subtask A: Message polarity classification

Subtask A is a *single-label multi-class* (SLMC) classification task. Each tweet must be classified as belonging to exactly one of the following three classes C={POSITIVE, NEUTRAL, NEGATIVE}.

We adopt the same evaluation measure as the 2013-2015 editions of this subtask, F_1^{PN}:

$$F_1^{PN} = \frac{F_1^P + F_1^N}{2} \qquad (1)$$

F_1^P is the F_1 score for the POSITIVE class:

$$F_1^P = \frac{2\pi^P \rho^P}{\pi^P + \rho^P} \qquad (2)$$

Here, π^P and ρ^P denote precision and recall for the POSITIVE class, respectively:

$$\pi^P = \frac{PP}{PP + PU + PN} \qquad (3)$$

$$\rho^P = \frac{PP}{PP + UP + NP} \qquad (4)$$

where PP, UP, NP, PU, PN are the cells of the confusion matrix shown in Table 7.

	Gold Standard		
	POSITIVE	NEUTRAL	NEGATIVE
Predicted POSITIVE	PP	PU	PN
NEUTRAL	UP	UU	UN
NEGATIVE	NP	NU	NN

Table 7: The confusion matrix for Subtask A. Cell XY stands for "the number of tweets that the classifier labeled X and the gold standard labells as Y". P, U, N stand for POSITIVE, NEUTRAL, NEGATIVE, respectively.

F_1^N is defined analogously, and the measure we finally adopt is F_1^{PN} as from Equation 1.

4.2 Subtask B: Tweet classification according to a two-point scale

Subtask B is a *binary classification* task. Each tweet must be classified as either POSITIVE or NEGATIVE.

For this subtask we adopt *macroaveraged recall*:

$$\rho^{PN} = \frac{1}{2}(\rho^P + \rho^N)$$
$$= \frac{1}{2}\left(\frac{PP}{PP + NP} + \frac{NN}{NN + PN}\right) \qquad (5)$$

In the above formula, ρ^P and ρ^N are the positive and the negative class recall, respectively. Note that U terms are entirely missing in Equation 5; this is because we do not have the NEUTRAL class for SemEval-2016 Task 4, subtask A.

ρ^{PN} ranges in $[0, 1]$, where a value of 1 is achieved only by the perfect classifier (i.e., the classifier that correctly classifies all items), a value of 0 is achieved only by the perverse classifier (the classifier that misclassifies all items), while 0.5 is both (*i*) the value obtained by a trivial classifier (i.e., the classifier that assigns all tweets to the same class – be it POSITIVE or NEGATIVE), and (*ii*) the expected value of a random classifier. The advantage of ρ^{PN} over "standard" accuracy is that it is more robust to class imbalance. The accuracy of the majority-class classifier is the relative frequency (aka "prevalence") of the majority class, that may be much higher than 0.5 if the test set is imbalanced. Standard F_1 is also sensitive to class imbalance for the same reason. Another advantage of ρ^{PN} over F_1 is that ρ^{PN} is invariant with respect to switching POSITIVE with NEGATIVE, while F_1 is not. See (Sebastiani, 2015) for more details on ρ^{PN}.

As we noted before, the training dataset, the development dataset, and the test dataset are each subdivided into a number of topics, and Subtask B needs to be carried out independently for each topic. As a result, the evaluation measures discussed in this section are computed individually for each topic, and the results are then averaged across topics to yield the final score.

4.3 Subtask C: Tweet classification according to a five-point scale

Subtask C is an *ordinal classification* (OC – also known as *ordinal regression*) task, in which each tweet must be classified into exactly one of the classes in C={HIGHLYPOSITIVE, POSITIVE, NEUTRAL, NEGATIVE, HIGHLYNEGATIVE}, represented in our dataset by numbers in $\{+2, +1, 0, -1, -2\}$, with a total order defined on C. The essential difference between SLMC (see Section 4.1 above) and OC is that not all mistakes weigh equally in the latter. For example, misclassifying a HIGHLYNEGATIVE example as HIGHLYPOSITIVE is a bigger mistake than misclassifying it as NEGATIVE or NEUTRAL.

As our evaluation measure, we use *macroaveraged mean absolute error* (MAE^M):

$$MAE^M(h, Te) = \frac{1}{|\mathcal{C}|} \sum_{j=1}^{|\mathcal{C}|} \frac{1}{|Te_j|} \sum_{\mathbf{x}_i \in Te_j} |h(\mathbf{x}_i) - y_i|$$

where y_i denotes the true label of item $\mathbf{x}_i$, $h(\mathbf{x}_i)$ is its predicted label, Te_j denotes the set of test documents whose true class is c_j, $|h(\mathbf{x}_i) - y_i|$ denotes the "distance" between classes $h(\mathbf{x}_i)$ and y_i (e.g., the distance between HIGHLYPOSITIVE and NEGATIVE is 3), and the "M" superscript indicates "macroaveraging".

The advantage of MAE^M over "standard" mean absolute error, which is defined as:

$$MAE^\mu(h, Te) = \frac{1}{|Te|} \sum_{\mathbf{x}_i \in Te} |h(\mathbf{x}_i) - y_i| \quad (6)$$

is that it is robust to class imbalance (which is useful, given the imbalanced nature of our dataset). On perfectly balanced datasets MAE^M and MAE^μ are equivalent.

Unlike the measures discussed in Sections 4.1 and 4.2, MAE^M is a measure of error, and not accuracy, and thus lower values are better. See (Baccianella et al., 2009) for more detail on MAE^M.

Similarly to Subtask B, Subtask C needs to be carried out independently for each topic. As a result, MAE^M is computed individually for each topic, and the results are then averaged across all topics to yield the final score.

4.4 Subtask D: Tweet quantification according to a two-point scale

Subtask D also assumes a *binary quantification* setup, in which each tweet is classified as POSITIVE or NEGATIVE. The task is to compute an estimate $\hat{p}(c_j)$ of the relative frequency (in the test set) of each of the classes.

The difference between binary classification (as from Section 4.2) and binary quantification is that errors of different polarity (e.g., a false positive and a false negative for the same class) can compensate each other in the latter. Quantification is thus a more lenient task since a perfect classifier is also a perfect quantifier, but a perfect quantifier is not necessarily a perfect classifier.

We adopt *normalized cross-entropy*, better known as *Kullback-Leibler Divergence* (KLD). KLD was proposed as a quantification measure in (Forman, 2005), and is defined as follows:

$$KLD(\hat{p}, p, \mathcal{C}) = \sum_{c_j \in \mathcal{C}} p(c_j) \log_e \frac{p(c_j)}{\hat{p}(c_j)} \quad (7)$$

KLD is a measure of the error made in estimating a true distribution p over a set $\mathcal{C}$ of classes by means of a predicted distribution $\hat{p}$. Like MAE^M in Section 4.3, KLD is a measure of error, which means that lower values are better. KLD ranges between 0 (best) and $+\infty$ (worst).

Note that the upper bound of KLD is not finite since Equation 7 has predicted prevalences, and not true prevalences, at the denominator: that is, by making a predicted prevalence $\hat{p}(c_j)$ infinitely small we can make KLD infinitely large. To solve this problem, in computing KLD we smooth both $p(c_j)$ and $\hat{p}(c_j)$ via additive smoothing, i.e.,

$$\begin{aligned} p^s(c_j) &= \frac{p(c_j) + \epsilon}{(\sum_{c_j \in \mathcal{C}} p(c_j)) + \epsilon \cdot |\mathcal{C}|} \\ &= \frac{p(c_j) + \epsilon}{1 + \epsilon \cdot |\mathcal{C}|} \end{aligned} \quad (8)$$

where $p^s(c_j)$ denotes the smoothed version of $p(c_j)$ and the denominator is just a normalizer (same for the $\hat{p}^s(c_j)$'s); the quantity $\epsilon = \frac{1}{2 \cdot |Te|}$ is used as a smoothing factor, where Te denotes the test set.

The smoothed versions of $p(c_j)$ and $\hat{p}(c_j)$ are used in place of their original versions in Equation 7; as a result, KLD is always defined and still returns a value of 0 when p and $\hat{p}$ coincide.

KLD is computed individually for each topic, and the results are averaged to yield the final score.

4.5 Subtask E: Tweet quantification according to a five-point scale

Subtask E is an *ordinal quantification* (OQ) task, in which (as in OC) each tweet belongs exactly to one of the classes in $\mathcal{C}$={HIGHLYPOSITIVE, POSITIVE, NEUTRAL, NEGATIVE, HIGHLYNEGATIVE}, where there is a total order on $\mathcal{C}$. As in binary quantification, the task is to compute an estimate $\hat{p}(c_j)$ of the relative frequency $p(c_j)$ in the test tweets of all the classes $c_j \in \mathcal{C}$.

The measure we adopt for OQ is the *Earth Mover's Distance* (Rubner et al., 2000) (also known as the *Vaseršteĭn metric* (Rüschendorf, 2001)), a measure well-known in the field of computer vision. EMD is currently the only known measure for ordinal quantification. It is defined for the general case in which a distance $d(c', c'')$ is defined for each $c', c'' \in \mathcal{C}$. When there is a total order on the classes in $\mathcal{C}$ and $d(c_i, c_{i+1}) = 1$ for all $i \in \{1, ..., (\mathcal{C} - 1)\}$ (as in our application), the Earth Mover's Distance is defined as

$$EMD(\hat{p}, p) = \sum_{j=1}^{|\mathcal{C}|-1} |\sum_{i=1}^{j} \hat{p}(c_i) - \sum_{i=1}^{j} p(c_i)| \quad (9)$$

and can be computed in $|\mathcal{C}|$ steps from the estimated and true class prevalences.

Like KLD in Section 4.4, EMD is a measure of error, so lower values are better; EMD ranges between 0 (best) and $|\mathcal{C}| - 1$ (worst). See (Esuli and Sebastiani, 2010) for more details on EMD.

As before, EMD is computed individually for each topic, and the results are then averaged across all topics to yield the final score.

5 Participants and Results

A total of 43 teams (see Table 15 at the end of the paper) participated in SemEval-2016 Task 4, representing 25 countries; the country with the highest participation was China (5 teams), followed by Italy, Spain, and USA (4 teams each). The subtask with the highest participation was Subtask A (34 teams), followed by Subtask B (19 teams), Subtask D (14 teams), Subtask C (11 teams), and Subtask E (10 teams).

It was not surprising that Subtask A proved to be the most popular – it was a rerun from previous years; conversely, none among Subtasks B to E had previously been offered in precisely the same form. Quantification-related subtasks (D and E) generated 24 participations altogether, while subtasks with an ordinal nature (C and E) attracted 21 participations. Only three teams participated in all five subtasks; conversely, no less than 23 teams took part in one subtask only (with a few exceptions, Subtask A). Many teams that participated in more than one subtask used essentially the same system for all of them, with little tuning to the specifics of each subtask.

Few trends stand out among the participating systems. In terms of the supervised learning methods used, there is a clear dominance of methods based on deep learning, including convolutional neural networks and recurrent neural networks (and, in particular, long short-term memory networks); the software libraries for deep learning most frequently used by the participants are Theano and Keras. Conversely, kernel machines seem to be less frequently used than in the past, and the use of learning methods other than the ones mentioned above is scarce.

The use of distant supervision is ubiquitous; this is natural, since there is an abundance of freely available tweets labelled according to sentiment (possibly with silver labels only, e.g., emoticons), and it is intuitive that their use as additional training data could be helpful. Another ubiquitous technique is the use of word embeddings, usually generated via either word2vec (Mikolov et al., 2013) or GloVe (Pennington et al., 2014); most authors seem to use general-purpose, pre-trained embeddings, while some authors also use customized word embeddings, trained either on the Tweet 2016 dataset or on tweet datasets of some sort.

Nothing radically new seems to have emerged with respect to text preprocessing; as in previous editions of this task, participants use a mix of by now obvious techniques, such as negation scope detection, elongation normalization, detection of amplifiers and diminishers, plus the usual extraction of word n-grams, character n-grams, and POS n-grams. The use of sentiment lexicons (alone or in combination with each other; general-purpose or Twitter-specific) is obviously still frequent.

In the next five subsections, we discuss the results of the participating systems in the five subtasks, focusing on the techniques and tools that the top-ranked participants have used. We also focus on how the participants tailored (if at all) their approach to the specific subtask. When discussing a specific subtask, we will adopt the convention of adding to a team name a subscript which indicates the position in the ranking for that subtask that the team obtained; e.g., when discussing Subtask E, "Finki$_2$" indicates team "Finki, which placed 2nd in the ranking for Subtask E". The papers describing the participants' approach are quoted in Table 15.

5.1 Subtask A: Message polarity classification

Table 8 ranks the systems submitted by the 34 teams who participated in Subtask A "Message Polarity Classification" in terms of the official measure F_1^{PN}. We further show the result for two other measures, ρ^{PN} (the measure that we adopted for Subtask B) and accuracy ($Acc = \frac{TP+TN}{TP+TN+FP+FN}$). We also report the result for a baseline classifier that assigns to each tweet the POSITIVE class. For Subtask A evaluated using F_1^{PN}, this is the equivalent of the majority class classifier for (binary or SLMC) classification evaluated via vanilla accuracy, i.e., this is the "smartest" among the trivial policies that attempt to maximize F_1^{PN}.

#	System	F_1^{PN}	ρ^{PN}	Acc
1	SwissCheese	0.633_1	0.667_2	0.646_1
2	SENSEI-LIF	0.630_2	0.670_1	0.617_7
3	UNIMELB	0.617_3	0.641_5	0.616_8
4	INESC-ID	0.610_4	0.662_3	0.600_{10}
5	aueb.twitter.sentiment	0.605_5	0.644_4	0.629_6
6	SentiSys	0.598_6	0.641_5	0.609_9
7	I2RNTU	0.596_7	0.637_7	0.593_{12}
8	INSIGHT-1	0.593_8	0.616_{11}	0.635_5
9	TwiSE	0.586_9	0.598_{16}	0.528_{24}
10	ECNU (*)	0.585_{10}	0.617_{10}	0.571_{16}
11	NTNUSentEval	0.583_{11}	0.619_8	0.643_2
12	MDSENT	0.580_{12}	0.592_{18}	0.545_{20}
	CUFE	0.580_{12}	0.619_8	0.637_4
14	THUIR	0.576_{14}	0.605_{15}	0.596_{11}
	PUT	0.576_{14}	0.607_{13}	0.584_{14}
16	LYS	0.575_{16}	0.615_{12}	0.585_{13}
17	IIP	0.574_{17}	0.579_{19}	0.537_{23}
18	UniPI	0.571_{18}	0.607_{13}	0.639_3
19	DIEGOLab16 (*)	0.554_{19}	0.593_{17}	0.549_{19}
20	GTI	0.539_{20}	0.557_{21}	0.518_{26}
21	OPAL	0.505_{21}	0.560_{20}	0.541_{22}
22	DSIC-ELIRF	0.502_{22}	0.511_{25}	0.513_{27}
23	UofL	0.499_{23}	0.537_{22}	0.572_{15}
	ELiRF	0.499_{23}	0.516_{24}	0.543_{21}
25	ISTI-CNR	0.494_{25}	0.529_{23}	0.567_{17}
26	SteM	0.478_{26}	0.496_{27}	0.452_{31}
27	Tweester	0.455_{27}	0.503_{26}	0.523_{25}
28	Minions	0.415_{28}	0.485_{28}	0.556_{18}
29	Aicyber	0.402_{29}	0.457_{29}	0.506_{28}
30	mib	0.401_{30}	0.438_{30}	0.480_{29}
31	VCU-TSA	0.372_{31}	0.390_{32}	0.382_{32}
32	SentimentalITists	0.339_{32}	0.424_{31}	0.480_{29}
33	WR	0.330_{33}	0.333_{34}	0.298_{34}
34	CICBUAPnlp	0.303_{34}	0.377_{33}	0.374_{33}
	Baseline	0.255	0.333	0.342

Table 8: Results for Subtask A "Message Polarity Classification" on the Tweet 2016 dataset. The systems are ordered by their F_1^{PN} score. In each column the rankings according to the corresponding measure are indicated with a subscript. Teams marked as "(*)" are late submitters, i.e., their original submission was deemed irregular by the organizers, and a revised submission was entered after the deadline.

All 34 participating systems were able to outperform the baseline on all three measures, with the exception of one system that scored below the baseline on Acc. The top-scoring team (SwissCheese$_1$) used an ensemble of convolutional neural networks, differing in their choice of filter shapes, pooling shapes and usage of hidden layers. Word embeddings generated via word2vec were also used, and the neural networks were trained by using distant supervision. Out of the 10 top-ranked teams, 5 teams (SwissCheese$_1$, SENSEI-LIF$_2$, UNIMELB$_3$, INESC-ID$_4$, INSIGHT-1$_8$) used deep NNs of some sort, and 7 teams (SwissCheese$_1$, SENSEI-LIF$_2$, UNIMELB$_3$, INESC-ID$_4$, aueb.twitter.sentiment$_5$, I2RNTU$_7$, INSIGHT-1$_8$) used either general-purpose or task-specific word embeddings, generated via word2vec or GloVe.

Historical results. We also tested the participating systems on the test sets from the three previous editions of this subtask. Participants were not allowed to use these test sets for training. Results (measured on F_1^{PN}) are reported in Table 9. The top-performing systems on Tweet 2016 are also top-ranked on the test datasets from previous years. There is a general pattern: the top-ranked system in year x outperforms the top-ranked system in year $(x-1)$ on the official dataset of year $(x-1)$. Top-ranked systems tend to use approaches that are universally strong, even when tested on out-of-domain test sets such as SMS, LiveJournal, or sarcastic tweets (yet, for sarcastic tweets, there are larger differences in rank compared to systems rankings on Tweet 2016). It is unclear where improvements come from: (a) the additional training data that we made available this year (in addition to Tweet-train-2013, which was used in 2013–2015), thus effectively doubling the amount of training data, or (b) because of advancement of learning methods.

We further look at the top scores achieved by any system in the period 2013–2016. The results are shown in Table 10. Interestingly, the results for a test set improve in the second year it is used (i.e., the year after it was used as an official test set) by 1–3 points absolute, but then do not improve further and stay stable, or can even decrease a bit. This might be due to participants optimizing their systems primarily on the test set from the preceding year.

#	System	2013		2014			2015	2016
		Tweet	SMS	Tweet	Tweet sarcasm	Live-Journal	Tweet	Tweet
1	SwissCheese	0.700_4	0.637_2	0.716_4	0.566_1	0.695_7	0.671_1	$\mathbf{0.633_1}$
2	SENSEI-LIF	0.706_3	0.634_3	0.744_1	0.467_8	0.741_1	0.662_2	$\mathbf{0.630_2}$
3	UNIMELB	0.687_6	0.593_9	0.706_6	0.449_{11}	0.683_9	0.651_4	$\mathbf{0.617_3}$
4	INESC-ID	0.723_1	0.609_6	0.727_2	0.554_2	0.702_4	0.657_3	$\mathbf{0.610_4}$
5	aueb.twitter.sentiment	0.666_7	0.618_5	0.708_5	0.410_{17}	0.695_7	0.623_7	$\mathbf{0.605_5}$
6	SentiSys	0.714_2	0.633_4	0.723_3	0.515_4	0.726_2	0.644_5	$\mathbf{0.598_6}$
7	I2RNTU	0.693_5	0.597_7	0.680_7	0.469_6	0.696_6	0.638_6	$\mathbf{0.596_7}$
8	INSIGHT-1	0.602_{16}	0.582_{12}	0.644_{15}	0.391_{23}	0.559_{23}	0.595_{16}	$\mathbf{0.593_8}$
9	TwiSE	0.610_{15}	0.540_{16}	0.645_{13}	0.450_{10}	0.649_{13}	0.621_8	$\mathbf{0.586_9}$
10	ECNU (*)	0.643_9	0.593_9	0.662_8	0.425_{14}	0.663_{10}	0.606_{11}	$\mathbf{0.585_{10}}$
11	NTNUSentEval	0.623_{11}	0.641_1	0.651_{10}	0.427_{13}	0.719_3	0.599_{13}	$\mathbf{0.583_{11}}$
12	MDSENT	0.589_{19}	0.509_{20}	0.587_{20}	0.386_{24}	0.606_{18}	0.593_{17}	$\mathbf{0.580_{12}}$
	CUFE	0.642_{10}	0.596_8	0.662_8	0.466_9	0.697_5	0.598_{14}	$\mathbf{0.580_{12}}$
14	THUIR	0.616_{12}	0.575_{14}	0.648_{11}	0.399_{20}	0.640_{15}	0.617_{10}	$\mathbf{0.576_{14}}$
	PUT	0.565_{21}	0.511_{19}	0.614_{19}	0.360_{27}	0.648_{14}	0.597_{15}	$\mathbf{0.576_{14}}$
16	LYS	0.650_8	0.579_{13}	0.647_{12}	0.407_{18}	0.655_{11}	0.603_{12}	$\mathbf{0.575_{16}}$
17	IIP	0.598_{17}	0.465_{23}	0.645_{13}	0.405_{19}	0.640_{15}	0.619_9	$\mathbf{0.574_{17}}$
18	UniPI	0.592_{18}	0.585_{11}	0.627_{17}	0.381_{25}	0.654_{12}	0.586_{18}	$\mathbf{0.571_{18}}$
19	DIEGOLab16 (*)	0.611_{14}	0.506_{21}	0.618_{18}	0.497_5	0.594_{20}	0.584_{19}	$\mathbf{0.554_{19}}$
20	GTI	0.612_{13}	0.524_{17}	0.639_{16}	0.468_7	0.623_{17}	0.584_{19}	$\mathbf{0.539_{20}}$
21	OPAL	0.567_{20}	0.562_{15}	0.556_{23}	0.395_{21}	0.593_{21}	0.531_{21}	$\mathbf{0.505_{21}}$
22	DSIC-ELIRF	0.494_{25}	0.404_{26}	0.546_{26}	0.342_{29}	0.517_{24}	0.531_{21}	$\mathbf{0.502_{22}}$
23	UofL	0.490_{26}	0.443_{24}	0.547_{25}	0.372_{26}	0.574_{22}	0.502_{25}	$\mathbf{0.499_{23}}$
	ELiRF	0.462_{28}	0.408_{25}	0.514_{28}	0.310_{33}	0.493_{25}	0.493_{26}	$\mathbf{0.499_{23}}$
25	ISTI-CNR	0.538_{22}	0.492_{22}	0.572_{21}	0.327_{30}	0.598_{19}	0.508_{24}	$\mathbf{0.494_{25}}$
26	SteM	0.518_{23}	0.315_{29}	0.571_{22}	0.320_{32}	0.405_{28}	0.517_{23}	$\mathbf{0.478_{26}}$
27	Tweester	0.506_{24}	0.340_{28}	0.529_{27}	0.540_3	0.379_{29}	0.479_{28}	$\mathbf{0.455_{27}}$
28	Minions	0.489_{27}	0.521_{18}	0.554_{24}	0.420_{16}	0.475_{26}	0.481_{27}	$\mathbf{0.415_{28}}$
29	Aicyber	0.418_{29}	0.361_{27}	0.457_{29}	0.326_{31}	0.440_{27}	0.432_{29}	$\mathbf{0.402_{29}}$
30	mib	0.394_{30}	0.310_{30}	0.415_{31}	0.352_{28}	0.359_{31}	0.413_{31}	$\mathbf{0.401_{30}}$
31	VCU-TSA	0.383_{31}	0.307_{31}	0.444_{30}	0.425_{14}	0.336_{32}	0.416_{30}	$\mathbf{0.372_{31}}$
32	SentimentalITists	0.339_{33}	0.238_{33}	0.393_{32}	0.288_{34}	0.323_{34}	0.343_{33}	$\mathbf{0.339_{32}}$
33	WR	0.355_{32}	0.284_{32}	0.393_{32}	0.430_{12}	0.366_{30}	0.377_{32}	$\mathbf{0.330_{33}}$
34	CICBUAPnlp	0.193_{34}	0.193_{34}	0.335_{34}	0.393_{22}	0.326_{33}	0.303_{34}	$\mathbf{0.303_{34}}$

Table 9: Historical results for Subtask A "Message Polarity Classification". The systems are ordered by their score on the Tweet 2016 dataset; the rankings on the individual datasets are indicated with a subscript. The meaning of "(*)" is as in Table 8.

5.2 Subtask B: Tweet classification according to a two-point scale

Table 11 ranks the 19 teams who participated in Subtask B "Tweet classification according to a two-point scale" in terms of the official measure ρ^{PN}. Two other measures are reported, F_1^{PN} (the measure adopted for Subtask A) and accuracy (Acc). We also report the result of a baseline that assigns to each tweet the positive class. This is the "smartest" among the trivial policies that attempt to maximize ρ^{PN}. This baseline always returns $\rho^{PN} = 0.500$.

Note however that this is also (*i*) the value returned by the classifier that assigns to each tweet the negative class, and (*ii*) the expected value returned by the random classifier; for more details see (Sebastiani, 2015, Section 5), where ρ^{PN} is called K.

The top-scoring team (Tweester[1]) used a combination of convolutional neural networks, topic modeling, and word embeddings generated via word2vec. Similar to Subtask A, the main trend among all participants is the widespread use of deep learning techniques.

Year	2013		2014			2015	2016
	Tweet	SMS	Tweet	Tweet sarcasm	Live-Journal	Tweet	Tweet
Best in 2016	0.723	0.641	0.744	0.566	0.741	0.671	0.633
Best in 2015	0.728	0.685	0.744	0.591	0.753	0.648	–
Best in 2014	0.721	0.703	0.710	0.582	0.748	–	–
Best in 2013	0.690	0.685	–	–	–	–	–

Table 10: Historical results for the best systems for Subtask A "Message Polarity Classification" over the years 2013–2016.

#	System	ρ^{PN}	F_1^{PN}	Acc
1	Tweester	0.797_1	0.799_1	0.862_3
2	LYS	0.791_2	0.720_{10}	0.762_{17}
3	thecerealkiller	0.784_3	0.762_5	0.823_9
4	ECNU (*)	0.768_4	0.770_4	0.843_5
5	INSIGHT-1	0.767_5	0.786_3	0.864_2
6	PUT	0.763_6	0.732_8	0.794_{14}
7	UNIMELB	0.758_7	0.788_2	0.870_1
8	TwiSE	0.756_8	0.752_6	0.826_8
9	GTI	0.736_9	0.731_9	0.811_{11}
10	Finki	0.720_{10}	0.748_7	0.848_4
11	pkudblab	0.689_{11}	0.716_{11}	0.832_7
12	CUFE	0.679_{12}	0.708_{12}	0.834_6
13	ISTI-CNR	0.671_{13}	0.690_{13}	0.811_{11}
14	SwissCheese	0.648_{14}	0.674_{14}	0.820_{10}
15	SentimentalITists	0.624_{15}	0.643_{15}	0.802_{13}
16	PotTS	0.618_{16}	0.610_{17}	0.712_{18}
17	OPAL	0.616_{17}	0.633_{16}	0.792_{15}
18	WR	0.522_{18}	0.502_{18}	0.577_{19}
19	VCU-TSA	0.502_{19}	0.448_{19}	0.775_{16}
	Baseline	0.500	0.438	0.778

Table 11: Results for Subtask B "Tweet classification according to a two-point scale" on the Tweet 2016 dataset. The systems are ordered by their ρ^{PN} score (higher is better). The meaning of "(*)" is as in Table 8.

Out of the 10 top-ranked participating teams, 5 teams (Tweester$_1$, LYS$_2$, INSIGHT-1$_5$, UNIMELB$_7$, Finki$_{10}$) used convolutional neural networks; 3 teams (thecerealkiller$_3$, UNIMELB$_7$, Finki$_{10}$) submitted systems using recurrent neural networks; and 7 teams (Tweester$_1$, LYS$_2$, INSIGHT-1$_5$, UNIMELB$_7$, Finki$_{10}$) incorporated in their participating systems either general-purpose or task-specific word embeddings (generated via toolkits such as GloVe or word2vec).

Conversely, the use of classifiers such as support vector machines, which were dominant until a few years ago, seems to have decreased, with only one team (TwiSE$_8$) in the top 10 using them.

5.3 Subtask C: Tweet classification according to a five-point scale

Table 12 ranks the 11 teams who participated in Subtask C "Tweet classification according to a five-point scale" in terms of the official measure MAE^M; we also show MAE^μ (see Equation 6). We also report the result of a baseline system that assigns to each tweet the middle class (i.e., NEUTRAL); for ordinal classification evaluated via MAE^M, this is the majority-class classifier for (binary or SLMC) classification evaluated via vanilla accuracy, i.e., this is (Baccianella et al., 2009) the "smartest" among the trivial policies that attempt to maximize MAE^M.

#	System	MAE^M	MAE^μ
1	TwiSE	0.719_1	0.632_5
2	ECNU (*)	0.806_2	0.726_8
3	PUT	0.860_3	0.773_9
4	LYS	0.864_4	0.694_7
5	Finki	0.869_5	0.672_6
6	INSIGHT-1	1.006_6	0.607_3
7	ISTI-CNR	1.074_7	0.580_1
8	YZU-NLP	1.111_8	0.588_2
9	SentimentalITists	1.148_9	0.625_4
10	PotTS	1.237_{10}	0.860_{10}
11	pkudblab	1.697_{11}	1.300_{11}
	Baseline	1.200	0.537

Table 12: Results for Subtask C "Tweet classification according to a five-point scale" on the Tweet 2016 dataset. The systems are ordered by their MAE^M score (lower is better). The meaning of "(*)" is as in Table 8.

The top-scoring team (TwiSE$_1$) used a single-label multi-class classifier to classify the tweets according to their overall polarity. In particular, they used logistic regression that minimizes the multinomial loss across the classes, with weights to cope with class imbalance. Note that they ignored the given topics altogether.

#	System	KLD	AE	RAE
1	Finki	$\mathbf{0.034}_1$	0.074_1	0.707_3
2	LYS	$\mathbf{0.053}_2$	0.099_4	0.844_5
	TwiSE	$\mathbf{0.053}_2$	0.101_5	0.864_6
4	INSIGHT-1	$\mathbf{0.054}_4$	0.085_2	0.423_1
5	GTI	$\mathbf{0.055}_5$	0.104_6	1.200_{10}
	QCRI	$\mathbf{0.055}_5$	0.095_3	0.864_6
7	NRU-HSE	$\mathbf{0.084}_7$	0.120_8	0.767_4
8	PotTS	$\mathbf{0.094}_8$	0.150_{12}	1.838_{12}
9	pkudblab	$\mathbf{0.099}_9$	0.109_7	0.947_8
10	ECNU (*)	$\mathbf{0.121}_{10}$	0.148_{11}	1.171_9
11	ISTI-CNR	$\mathbf{0.127}_{11}$	0.147_9	1.371_{11}
12	SwissCheese	$\mathbf{0.191}_{12}$	0.147_9	0.638_2
13	UDLAP	$\mathbf{0.261}_{13}$	0.274_{13}	2.973_{13}
14	HSENN	$\mathbf{0.399}_{14}$	0.336_{14}	3.930_{14}
	Baseline$_1$	$\mathbf{0.175}$	0.184	2.110
	Baseline$_2$	$\mathbf{0.887}$	0.242	1.155

Table 13: Results for Subtask D "Tweet quantification according to a two-point scale" on the Tweet 2016 dataset. The systems are ordered by their KLD score (lower is better). The meaning of "(*)" is as in Table 8.

Only 2 of the 11 participating teams tuned their systems to exploit the ordinal (as opposed to binary, or single-label multi-class) nature of this subtask. The two teams who did exploit the ordinal nature of the problem are PUT$_3$, which uses an ensemble of ordinal regression approaches, and ISTI-CNR$_7$, which uses a tree-based approach to ordinal regression. All other teams used general-purpose approaches for single-label multi-class classification, in many cases relying (as for Subtask B) on convolutional neural networks, recurrent neural networks, and word embeddings.

5.4 Subtask D: Tweet quantification according to a two-point scale

Table 13 ranks the 14 teams who participated in Subtask D "Tweet quantification according to a two-point scale" on the official measure KLD. Two other measures are reported, *absolute error* (AE):

$$AE(p, \hat{p}, \mathcal{C}) = \frac{1}{|\mathcal{C}|} \sum_{c \in \mathcal{C}} |\hat{p}(c) - p(c)| \qquad (10)$$

and *relative absolute error* (RAE):

$$RAE(p, \hat{p}, \mathcal{C}) = \frac{1}{|\mathcal{C}|} \sum_{c \in \mathcal{C}} \frac{|\hat{p}(c) - p(c)|}{p(c)} \qquad (11)$$

where the notation is the same as in Equation 7.

We also report the result of a "maximum likelihood" baseline system (dubbed Baseline$_1$). This system assigns to each test topic the distribution of the training tweets (the union of TRAIN, DEV, DEVTEST) across the classes. This is the "smartest" among the trivial policies that attempt to maximize KLD. We also report the result of a further (less smart) baseline system (dubbed Baseline$_2$), i.e., one that assigns a prevalence of 1 to the majority class (which happens to be the POSITIVE class) and a prevalence of 0 to the other class.

The top-scoring team (Finki$_1$) adopts an approach based on "classify and count", a classification-oriented (instead of quantification-oriented) approach, using recurrent and convolutional neural networks, and GloVe word embeddings.

Indeed, only 5 of the 14 participating teams tuned their systems to the fact that it deals with quantification (as opposed to classification). Among the teams who do rely on quantification-oriented approaches, teams LYS$_2$ and HSENN$_{14}$ used an existing structured prediction method that directly optimizes KLD; teams QCRI$_5$ and ISTI-CNR$_{11}$ use existing probabilistic quantification methods; team NRU-HSE$_7$ uses an existing iterative quantification method based on cost-sensitive learning. Interestingly, team TwiSE$_2$ uses a "classify and count" approach after comparing it with a quantification-oriented method (similar to the one used by teams LYS$_2$ and HSENN$_{14}$) on the development set, and concluding that the former works better than the latter. All other teams used "classify and count" approaches, mostly based on convolutional neural networks and word embeddings.

5.5 Subtask E: Tweet quantification according to a five-point scale

Table 14 lists the results obtained by the 10 participating teams on Subtask E "Tweet quantification according to a five-point scale". We also report the result of a "maximum likelihood" baseline system (dubbed Baseline$_1$), i.e., one that assigns to each test topic the same distribution, namely the distribution of the training tweets (the union of TRAIN, DEV, DEVTEST) across the classes; this is the "smartest" among the trivial policies (i.e., those that do not require any genuine work) that attempt to maximize EMD.

We further report the result of less smart baseline system (dubbed Baseline$_2$) – one that assigns a prevalence of 1 to the majority class (which coincides with the POSITIVE class) and a prevalence of 0 to all other classes.

#	System	EMD
1	QCRI	0.243_1
2	Finki	0.316_2
3	pkudblab	0.331_3
4	NRU-HSE	0.334_4
5	ECNU (*)	0.341_5
6	ISTI-CNR	0.358_6
7	LYS	0.360_7
8	INSIGHT-1	0.366_8
9	HSENN	0.545_9
10	PotTS	0.818_{10}
	Baseline$_1$	0.474
	Baseline$_2$	0.734

Table 14: Results for Subtask E "Tweet quantification according to a five-point scale" on the Tweet 2016 dataset. The systems are ordered by their EMD score (lower is better). The meaning of "(*)" is as in Table 8.

Only 3 of the 10 participants tuned their systems to the specific characteristics of this subtask, i.e., to the fact that it deals with quantification (as opposed to classification) *and* to the fact that it has an ordinal (as opposed to binary) nature.

In particular, the top-scoring team (QCRI$_1$) used a novel algorithm explicitly designed for ordinal quantification, that leverages an ordinal hierarchy of binary probabilistic quantifiers.

Team NRU-HSE$_4$ uses an existing quantification approach based on cost-sensitive learning, and adapted it to the ordinal case.

Team ISTI-CNR$_6$ instead used a novel adaptation to quantification of a tree-based approach to ordinal regression.

Teams LYS$_7$ and HSENN$_9$ also used an existing quantification approach, but did not exploit the ordinal nature of the problem.

The other teams mostly used approaches based on "classify and count" (see Section 5.4), and viewed the problem as single-label multi-class (instead of ordinal) classification; some of these teams (notably, team Finki$_2$) obtained very good results, which testifies to the quality of the (general-purpose) features and learning algorithm they used.

6 Conclusion and Future Work

We described SemEval-2016 Task 4 "Sentiment Analysis in Twitter", which included five subtasks including three that represent a significant departure from previous editions. The three new subtasks focused, individually or in combination, on two variants of the basic "sentiment classification in Twitter" task that had not been previously explored within SemEval. The first variant adopts a five-point scale, which confers an *ordinal* character to the classification task. The second variant focuses on the correct estimation of the prevalence of each class of interest, a task which has been called *quantification* in the supervised learning literature. In contrast, previous years' subtasks have focused on the correct labeling of individual tweets. As in previous years (2013–2015), the 2016 task was very popular and attracted a total of 43 teams.

A general trend that emerges from SemEval-2016 Task 4 is that most teams who were ranked at the top in the various subtasks used deep learning, including convolutional NNs, recurrent NNs, and (general-purpose or task-specific) word embeddings. In many cases, the use of these techniques allowed the teams using them to obtain good scores even without tuning their system to the specifics of the subtask at hand, e.g., even without exploiting the ordinal nature of the subtask – for Subtasks C and E – or the quantification-related nature of the subtask – for Subtasks D and E. Conversely, several teams that have indeed tuned their system to the specifics of the subtask at hand, but have not used deep learning techniques, have performed less satisfactorily. This is a further confirmation of the power of deep learning techniques for tweet sentiment analysis.

Concerning Subtasks D and E, if quantification-based subtasks are proposed again, we think it might be a good idea to generate, for each test topic t_i, multiple "artificial" test topics $t_i^1, t_i^2, ...$, where class prevalences are altered with respect to the ones of t_i by means of selectively removing from t_i tweets belonging to a certain class. In this way, the evaluation can take into consideration (*i*) class prevalences in the test set and (*ii*) levels of distribution drift (i.e., of the divergence of the test distribution from the training distribution) that are not present in the "naturally occurring" data.

By varying the amount of removed tweets at will, one may obtain *many* test topics, thus augmenting the magnitude of the experimentation at will while at the same time keeping constant the amount of manual annotation needed.

In terms of possible follow-ups of this task, it might be interesting to have a subtask whose goal is to distinguish tweets that are NEUTRAL about the topic (i.e., do not express any opinion about the topic) from tweets that express a FAIR opinion (i.e., lukewarm, intermediate between POSITIVE and NEGATIVE) about the topic.

Another possibility is to have a multi-lingual tweet sentiment classification subtask, where training examples are provided for the same topic for two languages (e.g., English and Arabic), and where participants can improve their performance on one language by leveraging the training examples for the other language via transfer learning. Alternatively, it might be interesting to include a cross-lingual tweet sentiment classification subtask, where training examples are provided for a given language (e.g., English) but not for the other (e.g., Arabic); the second language could be also a surprise language, which could be announced at the last moment.

References

Omar Abdelwahab and Adel Elmaghraby. 2016. UofL at SemEval-2016 Task 4: Multi domain word2vec for Twitter sentiment classification. In *Proceedings of the 10th International Workshop on Semantic Evaluation (SemEval 2016)*, San Diego, US.

Ramón Astudillo and Silvio Amir. 2016. INESC-ID at SemEval-2016 Task 4: Reducing the problem of out-of-embedding words. In *Proceedings of the 10th International Workshop on Semantic Evaluation (SemEval 2016)*, San Diego, US.

Giuseppe Attardi and Daniele Sartiano. 2016. UniPI at SemEval-2016 Task 4: Convolutional neural networks for sentiment classification. In *Proceedings of the 10th International Workshop on Semantic Evaluation (SemEval 2016)*, San Diego, US.

Stefano Baccianella, Andrea Esuli, and Fabrizio Sebastiani. 2009. Evaluation measures for ordinal regression. In *Proceedings of the 9th IEEE International Conference on Intelligent Systems Design and Applications (ISDA 2009)*, pages 283–287, Pisa, IT.

Stefano Baccianella, Andrea Esuli, and Fabrizio Sebastiani. 2010. SentiWordNet 3.0: An enhanced lexical resource for sentiment analysis and opinion mining. In *Proceedings of the 7th Conference on Language Resources and Evaluation (LREC 2010)*, Valletta, MT.

Alexandra Balahur. 2016. OPAL at SemEval-2016 Task 4: the Challenge of Porting a Sentiment Analysis System to the "Real" World. In *Proceedings of the 10th International Workshop on Semantic Evaluation (SemEval 2016)*, San Diego, US.

Georgios Balikas and Massih-Reza Amini. 2016. TwiSE at SemEval-2016 Task 4: Twitter sentiment classification. In *Proceedings of the 10th International Workshop on Semantic Evaluation (SemEval 2016)*, San Diego, US.

Johan Bollen, Huina Mao, and Xiao-Jun Zeng. 2011. Twitter mood predicts the stock market. *Journal of Computational Science*, 2(1):1–8.

Javier Borge-Holthoefer, Walid Magdy, Kareem Darwish, and Ingmar Weber. 2015. Content and network dynamics behind Egyptian political polarization on Twitter. In *Proceedings of the 18th ACM Conference on Computer Supported Cooperative Work and Social Computing (CSCW 2015)*, pages 700–711, Vancouver, CA.

Gerard Briones and Kasun Amarasinghe. 2016. VCU-TSA at SemEval-2016 Task 4: Sentiment analysis in Twitter. In *Proceedings of the 10th International Workshop on Semantic Evaluation (SemEval 2016)*, San Diego, US.

S. Burton and A. Soboleva. 2011. Interactive or reactive? Marketing with Twitter. *Journal of Consumer Marketing*, 28(7):491–499.

Esteban Castillo, Ofelia Cervantes, Darnes Vilariño, and David Báez. 2016. UDLAP at SemEval-2016 Task 4: Sentiment quantification using a graph based representation. In *Proceedings of the 10th International Workshop on Semantic Evaluation (SemEval 2016)*, San Diego, US.

Calin-Cristian Ciubotariu, Marius-Valentin Hrisca, Mihail Gliga, Diana Darabana, Diana Trandabat, and Adrian Iftene. 2016. Minions at SemEval-2016 Task 4: Or how to boost a student's self esteem. In *Proceedings of the 10th International Workshop on Semantic Evaluation (SemEval 2016)*, San Diego, US.

Vittoria Cozza and Marinella Petrocchi. 2016. mib at SemEval-2016 Task 4: Exploiting lexicon based features for sentiment analysis in Twitter. In *Proceedings of the 10th International Workshop on Semantic Evaluation (SemEval 2016)*, San Diego, US.

Giovanni Da San Martino, Wei Gao, and Fabrizio Sebastiani. 2016. QCRI at SemEval-2016 Task 4: Probabilistic methods for binary and ordinal quantification. In *Proceedings of the 10th International Workshop on Semantic Evaluation (SemEval 2016)*, San Diego, US. Forthcoming.

Jan Deriu, Maurice Gonzenbach, Fatih Uzdilli, Aurelien Lucchi, Valeria De Luca, and Martin Jaggi. 2016. SwissCheese at SemEval-2016 Task 4: Sentiment classification using an ensemble of convolutional neural networks with distant supervision. In *Proceedings of the 10th International Workshop on Semantic Evaluation (SemEval 2016)*, San Diego, US.

Peter S. Dodds, Kameron D. Harris, Isabel M. Kloumann, Catherine A. Bliss, and Christopher M. Danforth. 2011. Temporal patterns of happiness and information in a global social network: Hedonometrics and Twitter. *PLoS ONE*, 6(12).

Steven Du and Xi Zhang. 2016. Aicyber at SemEval-2016 Task 4: i-vector based sentence representation. In *Proceedings of the 10th International Workshop on Semantic Evaluation (SemEval 2016)*, San Diego, US.

Andrea Esuli and Fabrizio Sebastiani. 2010. Sentiment quantification. *IEEE Intelligent Systems*, 25(4):72–75.

Andrea Esuli and Fabrizio Sebastiani. 2015. Optimizing text quantifiers for multivariate loss functions. *ACM Transactions on Knowledge Discovery and Data*, 9(4):Article 27.

Andrea Esuli. 2016. ISTI-CNR at SemEval-2016 Task 4: Quantification on an ordinal scale. In *Proceedings of the 10th International Workshop on Semantic Evaluation (SemEval 2016)*, San Diego, US.

Cosmin Florean, Oana Bejenaru, Eduard Apostol, Octavian Ciobanu, Adrian Iftene, and Diana Trandabat. 2016. SentimentalITists at SemEval-2016 Task 4: Building a Twitter sentiment analyzer in your backyard. In *Proceedings of the 10th International Workshop on Semantic Evaluation (SemEval 2016)*, San Diego, US.

George Forman. 2005. Counting positives accurately despite inaccurate classification. In *Proceedings of the 16th European Conference on Machine Learning (ECML 2005)*, pages 564–575, Porto, PT.

George Forman. 2008. Quantifying counts and costs via classification. *Data Mining and Knowledge Discovery*, 17(2):164–206.

Jasper Friedrichs. 2016. IIP at SemEval-2016 Task 4: Prioritizing classes in ensemble classification for sentiment analysis of tweets. In *Proceedings of the 10th International Workshop on Semantic Evaluation (SemEval 2016)*, San Diego, US.

Hang Gao and Tim Oates. 2016. MDSENT at SemEval-2016 Task 4: Supervised system for message polarity classification. In *Proceedings of the 10th International Workshop on Semantic Evaluation (SemEval 2016)*, San Diego, US.

Stavros Giorgis, Apostolos Rousas, John Pavlopoulos, Prodromos Malakasiotis, and Ion Androutsopoulos. 2016. aueb.twitter.sentiment at SemEval-2016 Task 4: A weighted ensemble of SVMs for Twitter sentiment analysis. In *Proceedings of the 10th International Workshop on Semantic Evaluation (SemEval 2016)*, San Diego, US.

Helena Gomez, Darnes Vilariño, Grigori Sidorov, and David Pinto Avendaño. 2016. CICBUAPnlp at SemEval-2016 Task 4: Discovering Twitter polarity using enhanced embeddings. In *Proceedings of the 10th International Workshop on Semantic Evaluation (SemEval 2016)*, San Diego, US.

Hussam Hamdan. 2016. SentiSys at SemEval-2016 Task 4: Feature-based system for sentiment analysis in Twitter. In *Proceedings of the 10th International Workshop on Semantic Evaluation (SemEval 2016)*, San Diego, US.

Yunchao He, Liang-Chih Yu, Chin-Sheng Yang, K. Robert Lai, and Weiyi Liu. 2016. YZU-NLP at SemEval-2016 Task 4: Ordinal sentiment classification using a recurrent convolutional network. In *Proceedings of the 10th International Workshop on Semantic Evaluation (SemEval 2016)*, San Diego, US.

Brage Ekroll Jahren, Valerij Fredriksen, Björn Gambäck, and Lars Bungum. 2016. NTNUSentEval at SemEval-2016 Task 4: Combining general classifiers for fast Twitter sentiment analysis. In *Proceedings of the 10th International Workshop on Semantic Evaluation (SemEval 2016)*, San Diego, US.

Jonathan Juncal-Martínez, Tamara Álvarez-López, Milagros Fernández-Gavilanes, Enrique Costa-Montenegro, and Francisco Javier González-Castaño. 2016. GTI at SemEval-2016 Task 4: Training a naive Bayes classifier using features of an unsupervised system. In *Proceedings of the 10th International Workshop on Semantic Evaluation (SemEval 2016)*, San Diego, US.

Nikolay Karpov, Alexander Porshnev, and Kirill Rudakov. 2016. NRU-HSE at SemEval-2016 Task 4: The open quantification library with two iterative methods. In *Proceedings of the 10th International Workshop on Semantic Evaluation (SemEval 2016)*, San Diego, US.

Mesut Kaya, Guven Fidan, and Ismail Hakki Toroslu. 2013. Transfer learning using Twitter data for improving sentiment classification of Turkish political news. In *Proceedings of the 28th International Symposium on Computer and Information Sciences (ISCIS 2013)*, pages 139–148, Paris, FR.

Mateusz Lango, Dariusz Brzezinski, and Jerzy Stefanowski. 2016. PUT at SemEval-2016 Task 4: The ABC of Twitter sentiment analysis. In *Proceedings of the 10th International Workshop on Semantic Evaluation (SemEval 2016)*, San Diego, US.

Micol Marchetti-Bowick and Nathanael Chambers. 2012. Learning for microblogs with distant supervision: Political forecasting with Twitter. In *Proceedings of the 13th Conference of the European Chapter of the Association for Computational Linguistics (EACL 2012)*, pages 603–612, Avignon, FR.

Eugenio Martínez-Cámara, Maria Teresa Martín-Valdivia, Luis Alfonso Ureña López, and Arturo Montejo Ráez. 2014. Sentiment analysis in Twitter. *Natural Language Engineering*, 20(1):1–28.

Yelena Mejova, Ingmar Weber, and Michael W. Macy, editors. 2015. *Twitter: A Digital Socioscope*. Cambridge University Press, Cambridge, UK.

Tomas Mikolov, Wen-Tau Yih, and Geoffrey Zweig. 2013. Linguistic Regularities in Continuous Space Word Representations. In *Proceedings of the 2013 Conference of the North American Chapter of the Association for Computational Linguistics (NAACL 2013)*, pages 746–751, Atlanta, US.

Victor Martinez Morant, Lluís-F. Hurtado, and Ferran Pla. 2016. DSIC-ELIRF at SemEval-2016 Task 4: Message polarity classification in Twitter using a support vector machine approach. In *Proceedings of the 10th International Workshop on Semantic Evaluation (SemEval 2016)*, San Diego, US.

Mahmoud Nabil, Amir Atyia, and Mohamed Aly. 2016. CUFE at SemEval-2016 Task 4: A gated recurrent model for sentiment classification. In *Proceedings of the 10th International Workshop on Semantic Evaluation (SemEval 2016)*, San Diego, US.

Preslav Nakov, Sara Rosenthal, Zornitsa Kozareva, Veselin Stoyanov, Alan Ritter, and Theresa Wilson. 2013. SemEval-2013 Task 2: Sentiment analysis in Twitter. In *Proceedings of the 7th International Workshop on Semantic Evaluation (SemEval 2013)*, pages 312–320, Atlanta, US.

Preslav Nakov, Alan Ritter, Sara Rosenthal, Fabrizio Sebastiani, and Veselin Stoyanov. 2016a. Evaluation measures for the SemEval-2016 Task 4 "Sentiment analysis in Twitter". Available from http://alt.qcri.org/semeval2016/task4/.

Preslav Nakov, Sara Rosenthal, Svetlana Kiritchenko, Saif M. Mohammad, Zornitsa Kozareva, Alan Ritter, Veselin Stoyanov, and Xiaodan Zhu. 2016b. Developing a successful SemEval task in sentiment analysis of Twitter and other social media texts. *Language Resources and Evaluation*, 50(1):35–65.

Brendan O'Connor, Ramnath Balasubramanyan, Bryan R. Routledge, and Noah A. Smith. 2010. From tweets to polls: Linking text sentiment to public opinion time series. In *Proceedings of the 4th AAAI Conference on Weblogs and Social Media (ICWSM 2010)*, Washington, US.

Elisavet Palogiannidi, Athanasia Kolovou, Fenia Christopoulou, Filippos Kokkinos, Elias Iosif, Nikolaos Malandrakis, Haris Papageorgiou, Shrikanth Narayanan, and Alexandros Potamianos. 2016. Tweester at SemEval-2016 Task 4: Sentiment analysis in Twitter using semantic-affective model adaptation. In *Proceedings of the 10th International Workshop on Semantic Evaluation (SemEval 2016)*, San Diego, US.

Jeffrey Pennington, Richard Socher, and Christopher D. Manning. 2014. GloVe: Global vectors for word representation. In *Proceedings of the Conference on Empirical Methods in Natural Language Processing (EMNLP 2014)*, pages 1532–1543, Doha, QA.

Muhammad A. Qureshi, Colm O'Riordan, and Gabriella Pasi. 2013. Clustering with error estimation for monitoring reputation of companies on Twitter. In *Proceedings of the 9th Asia Information Retrieval Societies Conference (AIRS 2013)*, pages 170–180, Singapore, SN.

Stefan Räbiger, Mishal Kazmi, Yücel Saygın, Peter Schüller, and Myra Spiliopoulou. 2016. SteM at SemEval-2016 Task 4: Applying active learning to improve sentiment classification. In *Proceedings of the 10th International Workshop on Semantic Evaluation (SemEval 2016)*, San Diego, US.

Alan Ritter, Sam Clark, and Oren Etzioni. 2011. Named entity recognition in tweets: An experimental study. In *Proceedings of the Conference on Empirical Methods in Natural Language Processing (EMNLP 2011)*, pages 1524–1534, Edinburgh, UK.

Sara Rosenthal, Alan Ritter, Preslav Nakov, and Veselin Stoyanov. 2014. SemEval-2014 Task 9: Sentiment analysis in Twitter. In *Proceedings of the 8th International Workshop on Semantic Evaluation (SemEval 2014)*, pages 73–80, Dublin, IE.

Sara Rosenthal, Preslav Nakov, Svetlana Kiritchenko, Saif Mohammad, Alan Ritter, and Veselin Stoyanov. 2015. SemEval-2015 Task 10: Sentiment analysis in Twitter. In *Proceedings of the 9th International Workshop on Semantic Evaluation (SemEval 2015)*, pages 451–463, Denver, US.

Mickael Rouvier and Benoit Favre. 2016. SENSEI-LIF at SemEval-2016 Task 4: Polarity embedding fusion for robust sentiment analysis. In *Proceedings of the 10th International Workshop on Semantic Evaluation (SemEval 2016)*, San Diego, US.

Yossi Rubner, Carlo Tomasi, and Leonidas J. Guibas. 2000. The Earth Mover's Distance as a metric for image retrieval. *International Journal of Computer Vision*, 40(2):99–121.

Sebastian Ruder, Parsa Ghaffari, and John G. Breslin. 2016. INSIGHT-1 at SemEval-2016 Task 4: Convolutional Neural Networks for Sentiment Classification and Quantification. In *Proceedings of the 10th International Workshop on Semantic Evaluation (SemEval 2016)*, San Diego, US.

Ludger Rüschendorf. 2001. Wasserstein metric. In Michiel Hazewinkel, editor, *Encyclopaedia of Mathematics*. Kluwer Academic Publishers, Dordrecht, NL.

Abeed Sarker. 2016. DIEGOLab16 at SemEval-2016 Task 4: Sentiment analysis in Twitter using centroids, clusters, and sentiment lexicons. In *Proceedings of the 10th International Workshop on Semantic Evaluation (SemEval 2016)*, San Diego, US.

Fabrizio Sebastiani. 2015. An axiomatically derived measure for the evaluation of classification algorithms. In *Proceedings of the 5th ACM International Conference on the Theory of Information Retrieval (ICTIR 2015)*, pages 11–20, Northampton, US.

Uladzimir Sidarenka. 2016. PotTS at SemEval-2016 Task 4: Sentiment analysis of Twitter using character-level convolutional neural networks. In *Proceedings of the 10th International Workshop on Semantic Evaluation (SemEval 2016)*, San Diego, US.

Dario Stojanovski, Gjorgji Strezoski, Gjorgji Madjarov, and Ivica Dimitrovski. 2016. Finki at SemEval-2016 Task 4: Deep learning architecture for Twitter sentiment analysis. In *Proceedings of the 10th International Workshop on Semantic Evaluation (SemEval 2016)*, San Diego, US.

David Vilares, Yerai Doval, Miguel A. Alonso, and Carlos Gómez-Rodríguez. 2016. LYS at SemEval-2016 Task 4: Exploiting neural activation values for Twitter sentiment classification and quantification. In *Proceedings of the 10th International Workshop on Semantic Evaluation (SemEval 2016)*, San Diego, US.

Steven Xu, HuiZhi Liang, and Tim Baldwin. 2016. UNIMELB at SemEval-2016 Task 4: An ensemble of neural networks and a word2vec based model for sentiment classification. In *Proceedings of the 10th International Workshop on Semantic Evaluation (SemEval 2016)*, San Diego, US.

Vikrant Yadav. 2016. thecerealkiller at SemEval-2016 Task 4: Deep learning based system for classifying sentiment of tweets on two point scale. In *Proceedings of the 10th International Workshop on Semantic Evaluation (SemEval 2016)*, San Diego, US.

Zhengchen Zhang, Chen Zhang, Dongyan Huang, Wu Fuxiang, Weisi Lin, and Minghui Dong. 2016. I2RNTU at SemEval-2016 Task 4: Classifier fusion for polarity classification in Twitter. In *Proceedings of the 10th International Workshop on Semantic Evaluation (SemEval 2016)*, San Diego, US.

Yunxiao Zhou, Zhihua Zhang, and Man Lan. 2016. ECNU at SemEval-2016 Task 4: An empirical investigation of traditional NLP features and word embedding features for sentence-level and topic-level sentiment analysis in Twitter. In *Proceedings of the 10th International Workshop on Semantic Evaluation (SemEval 2016)*, San Diego, US.

Subtasks	Team ID	Affiliation	Nation	Paper
A	Aicyber	Aicyber.com	Singapore; China	(Du and Zhang, 2016)
A	aueb.twitter.sentiment	Department of Informatics, Athens University of Economics and Business	Greece	(Giorgis et al., 2016)
A	CICBUAPnlp	Instituto Politècnico Nacional Benemèrita Universidad Autonoma de Puebla	Mexico	(Gomez et al., 2016)
A B	CUFE	Cairo University	Egypt	(Nabil et al., 2016)
A	DIEGOLab16	Arizona State University	USA	(Sarker, 2016)
A	DSIC-ELIRF	Universitat Politècnica de València	Spain	(Morant et al., 2016)
A B C D E	ECNU	East China Normal University	China	(Zhou et al., 2016)
A	ELiRF	Universitat Politècnica de València	Spain	
B C D E	Finki	Saints Cyril and Methodius University, Skopje	Macedonia	(Stojanovski et al., 2016)
A B D	GTI	AtlantTIC Centre, University of Vigo	Spain	(Juncal-Martínez et al., 2016)
D E	HSENN	National Research University Higher School of Economics	Russia	
A	I2RNTU	Institute for Infocomm Research, A*STAR School of Computer Engineering, Nanyang Technological University	Singapore	(Zhang et al., 2016)
A	IIP	Infosys Limited	India	(Friedrichs, 2016)
A	INESC-ID	INESC-ID, Lisboa Instituto Superior Técnico, Universidade de Lisboa	Portugal	(Astudillo and Amir, 2016)
A B C D E	INSIGHT-1	INSIGHT Research Centre, National University of Ireland, Galway AYLIEN Inc.	Ireland	(Ruder et al., 2016)
A B C D E	LYS	Universidade da Coruña Universidade de Vigo	Spain	(Vilares et al., 2016)
A	MDSENT	University of Maryland Baltimore County	USA	(Gao and Oates, 2016)
A	mib	Istituto di Informatica e Telematica, Consiglio Nazionale delle Ricerche	Italy	(Cozza and Petrocchi, 2016)
A	Minions	University of Iasi	Romania	(Ciubotariu et al., 2016)
A B C D E	ISTI-CNR	Istituto di Scienza e Tecnologie dell'Informazione, Consiglio Nazionale delle Ricerche	Italy	(Esuli, 2016)
D E	NRU-HSE	National Research University Higher School of Economics	Russia	(Karpov et al., 2016)
A	NTNUSentEval	Norwegian University of Science and Technology	Norway	(Jahren et al., 2016)
A B	OPAL	European Commission Joint Research Centre	Italy	(Balahur, 2016)
B C D E	pkudblab	Peking University	China	
B C D E	PotTS	University of Potsdam Retresco GmbH	Germany	(Sidarenka, 2016)
A B C	PUT	Poznan University of Technology	Poland	(Lango et al., 2016)
D E	QCRI (**)	Qatar Computing Research Institute	Qatar	(Da San Martino et al., 2016)
A	SENSEI-LIF	Aix-Marseille University - CNRS - LIF	France	(Rouvier and Favre, 2016)
A B C	SentimentalITists	University of Iasi	Romania	(Florean et al., 2016)
A	SentiSys	Aix-Marseille University	France	(Hamdan, 2016)
A	SteM	Sabanci University Marmara University Otto-von-Guericke University Magdeburg	Turkey Germany	(Räbiger et al., 2016)
A B D	SwissCheese	ETH Zürich	Switzerland	(Deriu et al., 2016)
B	thecerealkiller	Amazon.in	India	(Yadav, 2016)
A	THUIR	Tsinghua University	China	
A B	Tweester	School of ECE, National Technical University of Athens School of ECE, Technical University of Crete Department of Informatics, University of Athens Signal Analysis and Interpretation Laboratory (SAIL) Institute for Language & Speech Processing - ILSP	Greece	(Palogiannidi et al., 2016)
A B C D	TwiSE	University of Grenoble-Alpes	France	(Balikas and Amini, 2016)
D	UDLAP	Universidad de las Américas Puebla (UDLAP)	Mexico	(Castillo et al., 2016)
A B	UNIMELB	University of Melbourne	Australia	(Xu et al., 2016)
A	UniPI	Università di Pisa	Italy	(Attardi and Sartiano, 2016)
A	UofL	University of Louisville	USA	(Abdelwahab and Elmaghraby, 2016)
A B	VCU-TSA	Virginia Commonwealth University	USA	(Briones and Amarasinghe, 2016)
A B	WR	WR	Hong Kong	
C	YZU-NLP	Yuan Ze University, Taoyuan Yunnan University, Kunming	Taiwan China	(He et al., 2016)
34 19 11 14 10	Total			

Table 15: Participating teams (Column 2), their affiliation (Column 3) and nationality (Column 4), the subtasks they have participated in (Column 1), and the paper they have contributed (Column 5). Teams whose "Affiliation" column is typeset on more that one row include researchers with different affiliations. Teams marked with a (**) include some of the SemEval 2016 Task 4 organizers. An empty entry for the "Paper" column indicates that the team have not contributed a system description paper.

SemEval-2016 Task 5: Aspect Based Sentiment Analysis

Maria Pontiki[*1], **Dimitrios Galanis**[1], **Haris Papageorgiou**[1], **Ion Androutsopoulos**[1,2],
Suresh Manandhar[3], **Mohammad AL-Smadi**[4], **Mahmoud Al-Ayyoub**[4], **Yanyan Zhao**[5],
Bing Qin[5], **Orphée De Clercq**[6], **Véronique Hoste**[6], **Marianna Apidianaki**[7],
Xavier Tannier[7], **Natalia Loukachevitch**[8], **Evgeny Kotelnikov**[9],
Nuria Bel[10], **Salud María Jiménez-Zafra**[11], **Gülşen Eryiğit**[12]

[1]Institute for Language and Speech Processing, Athena R.C., Athens, Greece,
[2]Dept. of Informatics, Athens University of Economics and Business, Greece,
[3]Dept. of Computer Science, University of York, UK,
[4]Computer Science Dept., Jordan University of Science and Technology Irbid, Jordan,
[5]Harbin Institute of Technology, Harbin, Heilongjiang, P.R. China,
[6]LT3, Ghent University, Ghent, Belgium,
[7]LIMSI, CNRS, Univ. Paris-Sud, Université Paris-Saclay, Orsay, France,
[8]Lomonosov Moscow State University, Moscow, Russian Federation,
[9]Vyatka State University, Kirov, Russian Federation,
[10]Universitat Pompeu Fabra, Barcelona, Spain,
[11]Dept. of Computer Science, Universidad de Jaén, Spain,
[12]Dept. of Computer Engineering, Istanbul Technical University, Turkey

Abstract

This paper describes the SemEval 2016 shared task on Aspect Based Sentiment Analysis (ABSA), a continuation of the respective tasks of 2014 and 2015. In its third year, the task provided 19 training and 20 testing datasets for 8 languages and 7 domains, as well as a common evaluation procedure. From these datasets, 25 were for sentence-level and 14 for text-level ABSA; the latter was introduced for the first time as a subtask in SemEval. The task attracted 245 submissions from 29 teams.

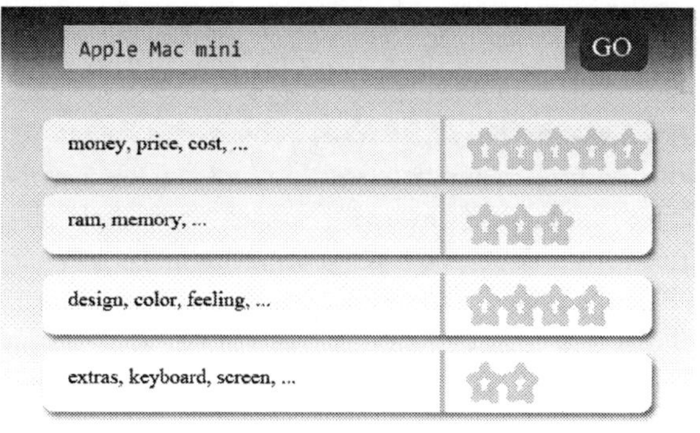

Figure 1: Table summarizing the average sentiment for each aspect of an entity.

1 Introduction

Many consumers use the Web to share their experiences about products, services or travel destinations (Yoo and Gretzel, 2008). Online opinionated texts (e.g., reviews, tweets) are important for consumer decision making (Chevalier and Mayzlin, 2006) and constitute a source of valuable customer feedback that can help companies to measure satisfaction and improve their products or services. In this setting, Aspect Based Sentiment Analysis (ABSA) - i.e., mining opinions from text about specific entities and their aspects (Liu, 2012) - can provide valuable insights to both consumers and businesses. An ABSA method can analyze large amounts of unstructured texts and extract (coarse- or fine-grained) information not included in the user ratings that are available in some review sites (e.g., Fig. 1).

Sentiment Analysis (SA) touches every aspect (e.g., entity recognition, coreference resolution, negation handling) of Natural Language Processing (Liu, 2012) and as Cambria et al. (2013) mention *"it requires a deep understanding of the explicit and implicit, regular and irregular, and syntactic and semantic language rules"*. Within the last few years several SA-related shared tasks have been organized in the context of workshops and conferences focus-

---

*Corresponding author: mpontiki@ilsp.gr.

19

Proceedings of SemEval-2016, pages 19–30,
San Diego, California, June 16-17, 2016. ©2016 Association for Computational Linguistics

ing on somewhat different research problems (Seki et al., 2007; Seki et al., 2008; Seki et al., 2010; Mitchell, 2013; Nakov et al., 2013; Rosenthal et al., 2014; Pontiki et al., 2014; Rosenthal et al., 2015; Ghosh et al., 2015; Pontiki et al., 2015; Mohammad et al., 2016; Recupero and Cambria, 2014; Ruppenhofer et al., 2014; Loukachevitch et al., 2015). Such competitions provide training datasets and the opportunity for direct comparison of different approaches on common test sets.

Currently, most of the available SA-related datasets, whether released in the context of shared tasks or not (Socher et al., 2013; Ganu et al., 2009), are monolingual and usually focus on English texts. Multilingual datasets (Klinger and Cimiano, 2014; Jiménez-Zafra et al., 2015) provide additional benefits enabling the development and testing of cross-lingual methods (Lambert, 2015). Following this direction, this year the SemEval ABSA task provided datasets in a variety of languages.

ABSA was introduced as a shared task for the first time in the context of SemEval in 2014; SemEval-2014 Task 4[1] (SE-ABSA14) provided datasets of English reviews annotated at the sentence level with aspect terms (e.g., "mouse", "pizza") and their polarity for the laptop and restaurant domains, as well as coarser aspect categories (e.g., "FOOD") and their polarity only for restaurants (Pontiki et al., 2014). SemEval-2015 Task 12[2] (SE-ABSA15) built upon SE-ABSA14 and consolidated its subtasks into a unified framework in which all the identified constituents of the expressed opinions (i.e., aspects, opinion target expressions and sentiment polarities) meet a set of guidelines and are linked to each other within sentence-level tuples (Pontiki et al., 2015). These tuples are important since they indicate the part of text within which a specific opinion is expressed. However, a user might also be interested in the overall rating of the text towards a particular aspect. Such ratings can be used to estimate the mean sentiment per aspect from multiple reviews (McAuley et al., 2012). Therefore, in addition to sentence-level annotations, SE-ABSA16[3] accommodated also text-level ABSA annotations and provided the respective training and testing data. Furthermore, the SE-ABSA15 annotation framework was extended to new domains and applied to languages other than English (Arabic, Chinese, Dutch, French, Russian, Spanish, and Turkish).

The remainder of this paper is organized as follows: the task set-up is described in Section 2. Section 3 provides information about the datasets and the annotation process, while Section 4 presents the evaluation measures and the baselines. General information about participation in the task is provided in Section 5. The evaluation scores of the participating systems are presented and discussed in Section 6. The paper concludes with an overall assessment of the task.

2   Task Description

The SE-ABSA16 task consisted of the following subtasks and slots. Participants were free to choose the subtasks, slots, domains and languages they wished to participate in.

Subtask 1 (SB1): Sentence-level ABSA. Given an opinionated text about a target entity, identify all the opinion tuples with the following types (tuple slots) of information:

- **Slot1: Aspect Category**. Identification of the entity E and attribute A pairs towards which an opinion is expressed in a given sentence. E and A should be chosen from predefined inventories[4] of entity types (e.g., "RESTAURANT", "FOOD") and attribute labels (e.g., "PRICE", "QUALITY").

- **Slot2: Opinion Target Expression (OTE)**. Extraction of the linguistic expression used in the given text to refer to the reviewed entity E of each E#A pair. The OTE is defined by its starting and ending offsets. When there is no explicit mention of the entity, the slot takes the value "NULL". The identification of Slot2 values was required only in the restaurants, hotels, museums and telecommunications domains.

- **Slot3: Sentiment Polarity**. Each identified E#A pair has to be assigned one of the following polarity labels: "positive", "negative", "neutral" (mildly positive or mildly negative).

---

[1]http://alt.qcri.org/semeval2014/task4/
[2]http://alt.qcri.org/semeval2015/task12/
[3]http://alt.qcri.org/semeval2016/task5/

[4]The full inventories of the aspect category labels for each domain are provided in Appendix A.

Lang.	Domain	Subtask	Train			Test		
			#Texts	#Sent.	#Tuples	#Texts	#Sent.	#Tuples
EN	REST	SB1	350	2000	2507	90	676	859
EN	REST	SB2	335	1950	1435	90	676	404
EN	LAPT	SB1	450	2500	2909	80	808	801
EN	LAPT	SB2	395	2375	2082	80	808	545
AR	HOTE	SB1	1839	4802	10509	452	1227	2604
AR	HOTE	SB2	1839	4802	8757	452	1227	2158
CH	PHNS	SB1	140	6330	1333	60	3191	529
CH	CAME	SB1	140	5784	1259	60	2256	481
DU	REST	SB1	300	1711	1860	100	575	613
DU	REST	SB2	300	1711	1247	100	575	381
DU	PHNS	SB1	200	1389	1393	70	308	396
FR	REST	SB1	335	1733	2530	120	696	954
FR	MUSE	SB3	-	-	-	162	686	891
RU	REST	SB1	302	3490	4022	103	1209	1300
RU	REST	SB2	302	3490	1545	103	1209	500
ES	REST	SB1	627	2070	2720	286	881	1072
ES	REST	SB2	627	2070	2121	286	881	881
TU	REST	SB1	300	1104	1535	39	144	159
TU	REST	SB2	300	1104	972	39	144	108
TU	TELC	SB1	-	3000	4082	-	310	336

Table 1: Datasets provided for SE-ABSA16.

An example of opinion tuples with Slot1-3 values from the restaurants domain is shown below: *"Their sake list was extensive, but we were looking for Purple Haze, which wasn't listed but made for us upon request!"* → {cat: "DRINKS#STYLE_OPTIONS", trg: "sake list", fr: "6", to: "15", pol: "positive"}, {cat: "SERVICE#GENERAL", trg: "NULL", fr: "0", to: "0", pol: "positive"}. The variable *cat* indicates the aspect category (Slot1), *pol* the polarity (Slot3), and *trg* the OTE (Slot2); fr, to are the starting/ending offsets of OTE.

Subtask 2 (SB2): Text-level ABSA. Given a customer review about a target entity, the goal was to identify a set of {*cat*, *pol*} tuples that summarize the opinions expressed in the review. *cat* can be assigned the same values as in SB1 (E#A tuple), while *pol* can be set to "positive", "negative", "neutral", or "conflict". For example, for the review text *The So called laptop Runs to Slow and I hate it! Do not buy it! It is the worst laptop ever "*, a system should return the following opinion tuples: {cat: "LAPTOP#GENERAL", pol: "negative"}, {cat: "LAPTOP#OPERATION_PERFORMANCE", pol: "negative"} .

Subtask 3 (SB3): Out-of-domain ABSA. In SB3 participants had the opportunity to test their systems in domains for which no training data was made available; the domains remained unknown until the start of the evaluation period. Test data for SB3 were provided only for the museums domain in French.

3 Datasets

3.1 Data Collection and Annotation

A total of 39 datasets were provided in the context of the SE-ABSA16 task; 19 for training and 20 for testing. The texts were from 7 domains and 8 languages; English (EN), Arabic (AR), Chinese (CH), Dutch (DU), French (FR), Russian (RU), Spanish (ES) and Turkish (TU). The datasets for the domains of restaurants (REST), laptops (LAPT), mobile phones (PHNS), digital cameras (CAME), hotels (HOTE) and museums (MUSE) consist of customer reviews, whilst the telecommunication domain (TELC) data consists of tweets. A total of 70790 manually annotated ABSA tuples were provided for training and testing; 47654 sentence-level annotations (SB1) in 8 languages for 7 domains, and 23136 text-level annotations (SB2) in 6 languages for 3 domains. Table 1 provides more information on the distribution of texts, sentences and annotated tuples per dataset.

The REST, HOTE, and LAPT datasets were annotated

at the sentence-level (SB1) following the respective annotation schemas of SE-ABSA15 (Pontiki et al., 2015). Below are examples[5] of annotated sentences for the aspect category "SERVICE#GENERAL" in EN (1), DU (2), FR (3), RU (4), ES (5), and TU (6) for the REST domain and in AR (7) for the HOTE domain:

1. Service was slow, but the people were friendly. → {trg: "Service", pol: "negative"}, {trg: "people", pol: "positive"}

2. Snelle bediening en vriendelijk personeel moet ook gemeld worden!! → {trg: "bediening", pol: "positive"}, {trg: "personeel", pol: "positive"}

3. Le service est impeccable, personnel agréable. → {trg: "service", pol: "positive"}, {trg: "personnel", pol: "positive"}

4. Про сервис ничего негативного не скажешь-быстро подходят, все улябаются, подходят спрашивают, всё ли нравится. → {trg: "сервис", pol: "neutral" }

5. También la rapidez en el servicio. → {trg: "servicio", pol: "positive" }

6. Servisi hızlı valesi var. → {trg: "Servisi", pol: "positive"}

7. .. الخدمة جيدة جدا و سريعة → {trg: "الخدمة" , pol: "positive"}

The LAPT annotation schema was extended to two other domains of consumer electronics, CAME and PHNS. Examples of annotated sentences in the LAPT (EN), PHNS (DU and CH) and CAME (CH) domains are shown below:

1. It is extremely portable and easily connects to WIFI at the library and elsewhere. → {cat: "LAPTOP#PORTABILITY", pol: "positive"} , {cat: "LAPTOP#CONNECTIVITY", pol: "positive"}

2. Apps starten snel op en werken vlot, internet gaat prima. → {cat: "SOFTWARE#OPERATION_PERFORMANCE", pol: "positive"}, {cat: "PHONE#CONNECTIVITY", pol: "positive"}

3. 当然屏幕这么好 →{cat: "DISPLAY#QUALITY", pol: "positive"}

4. 更轻便的机身也便于携带。→ {cat: "CAMERA# PORTABILITY", pol: "positive"}

In addition, the SE-ABSA15 framework was extended to two new domains for which annotation guidelines were compiled: TELC for TU and MUSE for FR. Below are two examples:

1. #Internet kopuyor sürekli :(@turkcell → {cat: "INTERNET#COVERAGE", trg: "Internet", pol: "positive"}

2. 5€ pour les étudiants, ça vaut le coup. → {cat: "MUSEUM#PRICES", "NULL", "positive"}

The text-level (SB2) annotation task was based on the sentence-level annotations; given a customer review about a target entity (e.g., a restaurant) that included sentence-level annotations of ABSA tuples, the goal was to identify a set of {cat, pol} tuples that summarize the opinions expressed in it. This was not a simple summation/aggregation of the sentence-level annotations since an aspect may be discussed with different sentiment in different parts of the review. In such cases the dominant sentiment had to be identified. In case of conflicting opinions where the dominant sentiment was not clear, the "conflict" label was assigned. In addition, each review was assigned an overall sentiment label about the target entity (e.g., "RESTAURANT#GENERAL", "LAPTOP#GENERAL"), even if it was not included in the sentence-level annotations.

3.2 Annotation Process

All datasets for each language were prepared by one or more research groups as shown in Table 2. The EN, DU, FR, RU and ES datasets were annotated using BRAT (Stenetorp et al., 2012), a web-based annotation tool, which was configured appropriately for the needs of the task. The TU datasets were annotated using a customized version of TURKSENT (Eryigit et al., 2013), a sentiment annotation tool for social media. For the AR and the CH data in-house tools[6] were used.

<hr>

[5]The offsets of the opinion target expressions are omitted.

[6]The AR annotation tool was developed by the technical team of the Advanced Arabic Text Mining group at Jordan University of Science and Technology. The CH tool was developed by the Research Center for Social Computing and Information Retrieval at Harbin Institute of Technology.

Lang.	Research team(s)
English	Institute for Language and Speech Processing, Athena R.C., Athens, Greece Dept. of Informatics, Athens University of Economics and Business, Greece
Arabic	Computer Science Dept., Jordan University of Science and Technology Irbid, Jordan
Chinese	Harbin Institute of Technology, Harbin, Heilongjiang, P.R. China
Dutch	LT3, Ghent University, Ghent, Belgium
French	LIMSI, CNRS, Univ. Paris-Sud, Université Paris-Saclay, Orsay, France
Russian	Lomonosov Moscow State University, Moscow, Russian Federation Vyatka State University, Kirov, Russian Federation
Spanish	Universitat Pompeu Fabra, Barcelona, Spain SINAI, Universidad de Jaén, Spain
Turkish	Dept. of Computer Engineering, Istanbul Technical University, Turkey Turkcell Global Bilgi, Turkey

Table 2: Research teams that contributed to the creation of the datasets for each language.

Below are some further details about the annotation process for each language.

English. The SE-ABSA15 (Pontiki et al., 2015) training and test datasets (with some minor corrections) were merged and provided for training (REST and LAPT domains). New data was collected and annotated from scratch for testing. In a first phase, the REST test data was annotated by an experienced[7] linguist (annotator A), and the LAPT data by 5 undergraduate computer science students. The resulting annotations for both domains were then inspected and corrected (if needed) by a second expert linguist, one of the task organizers (annotator B). Borderline cases were resolved collaboratively by annotators A and B.

Arabic. The HOTE dataset was annotated in repeated cycles. In a first phase, the data was annotated by three native Arabic speakers, all with a computer science background; then the output was validated by a senior researcher, one of the task organizers. If needed (e.g. when inconsistencies were found) they were given back to the annotators.

Chinese. The datasets presented by Zhao et al. (2015) were re-annotated by three native Chinese speakers according to the SE-ABSA16 annotation schema and were provided for training and testing (PHNS and CAME domains).

Dutch. The REST and PHNS datasets (De Clercq and Hoste, 2016) were initially annotated by a trained linguist, native speaker of Dutch. Then, the output was verified by another Dutch linguist and disagreements were resolved between them. Fi-

nally, the task organizers inspected collaboratively all the annotated data and corrections were made when needed.

French. The train (REST) and test (REST, MUSE) datasets were annotated from scratch by a linguist, native speaker of French. When the annotator was not confident, a decision was made collaboratively with the organizers. In a second phase, the task organizers checked all the annotations for mistakes and inconsistencies and corrected them, when necessary. For more information on the French datasets consult Apidianaki et al. (2016).

Russian. The REST datasets of the SentiRuEval-2015 task (Loukachevitch et al., 2015) were automatically converted to the SE-ABSA16 annotation schema; then a linguist, native speaker of Russian, checked them and added missing information. Finally, the datasets were inspected by a second linguist annotator (also native speaker of Russian) for mistakes and inconsistencies, which were resolved along with one of the task organizers.

Spanish. Initially, 50 texts (134 sentences) from the whole available data were annotated by 4 annotators. The inter-anotator agreement (IAA) in terms of F-1 was 91% for the identification of OTE, 88% for the aspect category detection (E#A pair), and 80% for opinion tuples extraction (E#A, OTE, polarity). Provided that the IAA was substantially high for all slots, the rest of the data was divided into 4 parts and each one was annotated by a different native Spanish speakers (2 linguists and 2 software engineers). Subsequently, the resulting annotations were validated and corrected (if needed) by the task organizers.

---

[7]Also annotator for SE-ABSA14 and 15.

Turkish. The TELC dataset was based on the data used in (Yıldırım et al., 2015), while the REST dataset was created from scratch. Both datasets were annotated simultaneously by two linguists. Then, one of the organizers validated/inspected the resulting annotations and corrected them when needed.

3.3 Datasets Format and Availability

Similarly to SE-ABSA14 and SE-ABSA15, the datasets[8] of SE-ABSA16 were provided in an XML format and they are available under specific license terms through META-SHARE[9], a repository devoted to the sharing and dissemination of language resources (Piperidis, 2012).

4 Evaluation Measures and Baselines

The evaluation ran in two phases. In the first phase (Phase A), the participants were asked to return separately the aspect categories (Slot1), the OTEs (Slot2), and the {Slot1, Slot2} tuples for SB1. For SB2 the respective text-level categories had to be identified. In the second phase (Phase B), the gold annotations for the test sets of Phase A were provided and participants had to return the respective sentiment polarity values (Slot3). Similarly to SE-ABSA15, F-1 scores were calculated for Slot1, Slot2 and {Slot1, Slot2} tuples, by comparing the annotations that a system returned to the gold annotations (using micro-averaging). For Slot1 evaluation, duplicate occurrences of categories were ignored in both SB1 and SB2. For Slot2, the calculation for each sentence considered only distinct targets and discarded "NULL" targets, since they do not correspond to explicit mentions. To evaluate sentiment polarity classification (Slot3) in Phase B, we calculated the accuracy of each system, defined as the number of correctly predicted polarity labels of the (gold) aspect categories, divided by the total number of the gold aspect categories. Furthermore, we implemented and provided baselines for all slots of SB1 and SB2. In particular, the SE-ABSA15 baselines that were implemented for the English language

(Pontiki et al., 2015), were adapted for the other languages by using appropriate stopword lists and tokenization functions. The baselines are briefly discussed below:

SB1-Slot1: For category (E#A) extraction, a Support Vector Machine (SVM) with a linear kernel is trained. In particular, n unigram features are extracted from the respective sentence of each tuple that is encountered in the training data. The category value (e.g., "SERVICE#GENERAL") of the tuple is used as the correct label of the feature vector. Similarly, for each test sentence s, a feature vector is built and the trained SVM is used to predict the probabilities of assigning each possible category to s (e.g., {"SERVICE#GENERAL", 0.2}, {"RESTAURANT#GENERAL", 0.4}. Then, a threshold[10] t is used to decide which of the categories will be assigned[11] to s. As features, we use the 1,000 most frequent unigrams of the training data excluding stopwords.

SB1-Slot2: The baseline uses the training reviews to create for each category c (e.g., "SERVICE#GENERAL") a list of OTEs (e.g., "SERVICE#GENERAL" $\rightarrow$ {"staff", "waiter"}). These are extracted from the (training) opinion tuples whose category value is c. Then, given a test sentence s and an assigned category c, the baseline finds in s the first occurrence of each OTE of c's list. The OTE slot is filled with the first of the target occurrences found in s. If no target occurrences are found, the slot is assigned the value "NULL".

SB1-Slot3: For polarity prediction we trained a SVM classifier with a linear kernel. Again, as in Slot1, n unigram features are extracted from the respective sentence of each tuple of the training data. In addition, an integer-valued feature[12] that indicates the category of the tuple is used. The correct label for the extracted training feature vector is the corresponding polarity value (e.g., "positive"). Then, for each tuple {category, OTE} of a test sentence s, a feature vector is built and classified using the trained SVM.

SB2-Slot1: The sentence-level tuples returned by the SB1 baseline are copied to the text level and duplicates are removed.

---

[8]The data are available at: `http://metashare.ilsp.gr:8080/repository/search/?q=semeval+2016`

[9]META-SHARE (`http://www.metashare.org/`) was implemented in the framework of the META-NET Network of Excellence (`http://www.meta-net.eu/`).

[10]The threshold t was set to 0.2 for all datasets.

[11]We use the −b 1 option of LibSVM to obtain probabilities.

[12]Each E#A pair has been assigned a distinct integer value.

Lang./ Dom.	Slot1 F-1	Slot2 F-1	{Slot1,Slot2} F-1	Slot3 Acc.
EN/ REST	NLANG./U/73.031	NLANG./U/72.34	NLANG./U/52.607	XRCE/C/88.126
	NileT./U/72.886	AUEB-./U/70.441	XRCE/C/48.891	IIT-T./U/86.729
	BUTkn./U/72.396	UWB/U/67.089	NLANG./C/45.724	NileT./U/85.448
	AUEB-./U/71.537	UWB/C/66.906	TGB/C/43.081*	IHS-R./U/83.935
	BUTkn./C/71.494	GTI/U/66.553	bunji/U/41.113	ECNU/U/83.586
	SYSU/U/70.869	Senti./C/66.545	UWB/C/41.108	AUEB-./U/83.236
	XRCE/C/68.701	bunji/C/64.882	UWB/U/41.088	INSIG./U/82.072
	UWB/U/68.203	NLANG./C/63.861	DMIS/U/39.796	UWB/C/81.839
	INSIG./U/68.108	DMIS/C/63.495	DMIS/C/38.976	UWB/U/81.723
	ESI/U/67.979	XRCE/C/61.98	**basel.**/C/37.795	SeemGo/C/81.141
	UWB/C/67.817	AUEB-./C/61.552	IHS-R./U/35.608	bunji/U/81.024
	GTI/U/67.714	UWate./U/57.067	IHS-R./U/34.864	TGB/C/80.908*
	AUEB-./C/67.35	KnowC./U/56.816*	UWate./U/34.536	ECNU/C/80.559
	NLANG./C/65.563	TGB/C/55.054*	SeemGo/U/30.667	UWate./U/80.326
	LeeHu./C/65.455	BUAP/U/50.253	BUAP/U/18.428	INSIG./C/80.21
	TGB/C/63.919*	**basel.**/C/44.071		DMIS/C/79.977
	IIT-T./U/63.051	IHS-R./U/43.808		DMIS/U/79.627
	DMIS/U/62.583	IIT-T./U/42.603		IHS-R./U/78.696
	DMIS/C/61.754	SeemGo/U/34.332		Senti./U/78.114
	IIT-T./C/61.227			LeeHu./C/78.114
	bunji/U/60.145			**basel.**/C/76.484
	basel./C/59.928			bunji/C/76.251
	UFAL/U/59.3			SeemGo/U/72.992
	INSIG./C/58.303			AKTSKI/U/71.711
	IHS-R./U/55.034			COMMI./C/70.547
	IHS-R./U/53.149			SNLP/U/69.965
	SeemGo/U/50.737			GTI/U/69.965
	UWate./U/49.73			CENNL./C/63.912
	CENNL./C/40.578			BUAP/U/60.885
	BUAP/U/37.29			

Table 3: English REST results for SB1.

SB2-Slot3: For each text-level aspect category c the baseline traverses the predicted sentence-level tuples of the same category returned by the respective SB1 baseline and counts the polarity labels (positive, negative, neutral). Finally, the polarity label with the highest frequency is assigned to the text-level category c. If there are no sentence-level tuples for the same c, the polarity label is determined based on all tuples regardless of c.

The baseline systems and evaluation scripts are implemented in Java and are available for download from the SE-ABSA16 website[13]. The LibSVM package[14] (Chang and Lin, 2011) is used for SVM training and prediction. The scores of the baselines in the test datasets are presented in Section 6 along with the system scores.

5 Participation

The task attracted in total 245 submissions from 29 teams. The majority of the submissions (216 runs) were for SB1. The newly introduced SB2 attracted 29 submissions from 5 teams in 2 languages (EN and SP). Most of the submissions (168) were runs for the REST domain. This was expected, mainly for two reasons; first, the REST classification schema is less fine-grained (complex) compared to the other domains (e.g., LAPT). Secondly, this domain was supported for 6 languages enabling also multilingual or language-agnostic approaches. The remaining submissions were distributed as follows: 54 in LAPT, 12 in PHNS, 7 in CAME and 4 in HOTE.

---

[13]http://alt.qcri.org/semeval2016/task5/index.php?id=data-and-tools

[14]http://www.csie.ntu.edu.tw/~cjlin/libsvm/

Lang./ Dom.	Slot1 F-1	Slot2 F-1	{Slot1,Slot2} F-1	Slot3 Acc.
ES/ REST	GTI/U/70.588 GTI/C/70.027 TGB/C/63.551* UWB/C/61.968 INSIG./C/61.37 IIT-T./U/59.899 IIT-T./C/59.062 UFAL/U/58.81 **basel.**/C/54.686	GTI/C/68.515 GTI/U/68.387 IIT-T./U/64.338 TGB/C/55.764* **basel.**/C/51.914	TGB/C/41.219* **basel.**/C/36.379	IIT-T./U/83.582 TGB/C/82.09* UWB/C/81.343 INSIG./C/79.571 **basel.**/C/77.799
FR/ REST	XRCE/C/61.207 IIT-T./U/57.875 IIT-T./C/57.033 INSIG./C/53.592 **basel.**/C/52.609 UFAL/U/49.928	IIT-T./U/66.667 XRCE/C/65.316 **basel.**/C/45.455	XRCE/C/47.721 **basel.**/C/33.017	XRCE/C/78.826 UWB/C/75.262 UWB/C/74.319 INSIG./C/73.166 IIT-T./U/72.222 **basel.**/C/67.4
RU/ REST	UFAL/U/64.825 INSIG./C/62.802 IIT-T./C/62.689 IIT-T./C/58.196 **basel.**/C/55.882 Danii./C/39.601 Danii./U/38.692	**basel.**/C/49.308 Danii./U/33.472 Danii./C/30.618	**basel.**/C/39.441 Danii./U/22.591 Danii./C/22.107	MayAnd/U/77.923 INSIG./C/75.077 IIT-T./U/73.615 Danii./U/73.308 Danii./C/72.538 **basel.**/C/71
DU/ REST	TGB/C/60.153* INSIG./C/56 IIT-T./U/55.247 IIT-T./C/54.98 UFAL/U/53.876 **basel.**/C/42.816	IIT-T./U/56.986 TGB/C/51.775* **basel.**/C/50.64	TGB/C/45.167* **basel.**/C/30.916	TGB/C/77.814* IIT-T./U/76.998 INSIG./C/75.041 **basel.**/C/69.331
TU/ REST	UFAL/U/61.029 **basel.**/C/58.896 IIT-T./U/56.627 IIT-T./C/55.728 INSIG./C/49.123	**basel.**/C/41.86	**basel.**/C/28.152	IIT-T./U/84.277 INSIG./C/74.214 **basel.**/C/72.327
AR/ HOTE	INSIG./C/52.114 UFAL/U/47.302 **basel.**/C/40.336	**basel.**/C/30.978	**basel.**/C/18.806	INSIG./C/82.719 IIT-T./U/81.72 **basel.**/C/76.421

Table 4: REST and HOTE results for SB1.

An interesting observation is that, unlike SE-ABSA15, Slot1 (aspect category detection) attracted significantly more submissions than Slot2 (OTE extraction); this may indicate a shift towards concept-level approaches. Regarding participation per language, the majority of the submissions (156/245) were for EN; see more information in Table 5. Most teams (20) submitted results only for one language (18 for EN and 2 for RU). Of the remaining teams, 3 submitted results for 2 languages, 5 teams submitted results for 3-7 languages, while only one team participated in all languages.

6 Evaluation Results

The evaluation results are presented in Tables 3 (SB1: REST-EN), 4 (SB1: REST-ES, FR, RU, DU, TU & HOTE-AR), 6 (SB1: LAPT, CAME, PHNS), and 7 (SB2)[15]. Each participating team was allowed to submit up to two runs per slot and domain in each phase; one constrained (C), where only the provided training data could be used, and one unconstrained (U), where other resources (e.g., publicly available

[15]No submissions were made for SB3-MUSE-FR & SB1-TELC-TU.

Language	Teams	Submissions
English	27	156
Arabic	3	4
Chinese	3	14
Dutch	4	16
French	5	13
Russian	5	15
Spanish	6	21
Turkish	3	6
All	29	245

Table 5: Number of participating teams and submitted runs per language.

lexica) and additional data of any kind could be used for training. In the latter case, the teams had to report the resources used. Delayed submissions (i.e., runs submitted after the deadline and the release of the gold annotations) are marked with "*".

As revealed by the results, in both SB1 and SB2 the majority of the systems surpassed the baseline by a small or large margin and, as expected, the unconstrained systems achieved better results than the constrained ones. In SB1, the teams with the highest scores for Slot1 and Slot2 achieved similar F-1 scores (see Table 3) in most cases (e.g., EN/REST, ES/REST, DU/REST, FR/REST), which shows that the two slots have a similar level of difficulty. However, as expected, the {Slot1, Slot2} scores were significantly lower since the linking of the target expressions to the corresponding aspects is also required. The highest scores in SB1 for all slots (Slot1, Slot2, {Slot1, Slot2}, Slot3) were achieved in the EN/REST; this is probably due to the high participation and to the lower complexity of the REST annotation schema compared to the other domains. If we compare the results for SB1 and SB2, we notice that the SB2 scores for Slot1 are significantly higher (e.g., EN/LAPT, EN/REST, ES/REST) even though the respective annotations are for the same (or almost the same) set of texts. This is due to the fact that it is easier to identify whether a whole text discusses an aspect c than finding all the sentences in the text discussing c. On the other hand, for Slot3, the SB2 scores are lower (e.g., EN/REST, ES/REST, RU/REST, EN/LAPT) than the respective SB1 scores. This is mainly because an aspect may be discussed at different points in a text and often with different sentiment. In such cases a system has to identify the dominant sentiment, which

Lang./ Dom.	Slot1 F-1	Slot3 Acc.
EN/ LAPT	NLANG./U/51.937	IIT-T./U/82.772
	AUEB-./U/49.105	INSIG./U/78.402
	SYSU/U/49.076	ECNU/U/78.152
	BUTkn./U/48.396	IHS-R./U/77.903
	UWB/C/47.891	NileT./U/77.403
	BUTkn./C/47.527	AUEB-./U/76.904
	UWB/U/47.258	LeeHu./C/75.905
	NileT./U/47.196	Senti./U/74.282
	NLANG./C/46.728	INSIG./C/74.282
	INSIG./U/45.863	UWB/C/73.783
	AUEB-./C/45.629	UWB/U/73.783
	IIT-T./U/43.913	SeemGo/C/72.16
	LeeHu./C/43.754	UWate./U/71.286
	IIT-T./C/42.609	bunji/C/70.287
	SeemGo/U/41.499	bunji/U/70.162
	INSIG./C/41.458	ECNU/C/70.037
	bunji/U/39.586	**basel.**/C/70.037
	IHS-R./U/39.024	COMMI./C/67.541
	basel./C/37.481	GTI/U/67.291
	UFAL/U/26.984	BUAP/U/62.797
	CENNL./C/26.908	CENNL./C/59.925
	BUAP/U/26.787	SeemGo/U/40.824
CH/ CAME	UWB/C/36.345	SeemGo/C/80.457
	INSIG./C/25.581	INSIG./C/78.17
	basel./C/18.434	UWB/C/77.755
	SeemGo/U/17.757	**basel.**/C/74.428
		SeemGo/U/73.181
CH/ PHNS	UWB/C/22.548	SeemGo/C/73.346
	basel./C/17.03	INSIG./C/72.401
	INSIG./C/16.286	UWB/C/72.023
	SeemGo/U/10.43	**basel.**/C/70.132
		SeemGo/U/65.406
DU/ PHNS	INSIG./C/45.551	INSIG./C/83.333
	IIT-T./U/45.443	IIT-T./U/82.576
	IIT-T./C/45.047	**basel.**/C/80.808
	basel./C/33.55	

Table 6: LAPT, CAME, and PHNS results for SB1.

usually is not trivial.

7 Conclusions

In its third year, the SemEval ABSA task provided 19 training and 20 testing datasets, from 7 domains and 8 languages, attracting 245 submissions from 29 teams. The use of the same annotation guidelines for domains addressed in different languages gives the opportunity to experiment also with cross-lingual or language-agnostic approaches. In addition, SE-ABSA16 included for the first time a text-

Lang./ Dom.	Slot1 F-1	Slot3 Acc.
EN/ REST	GTI/U/83.995 UWB/C/80.965 UWB/U/80.163 bunji/U/79.777 **basel.**/C/78.711 SYSU/U/68.841 SYSU/U/68.841	UWB/U/81.931 ECNU/U/81.436 UWB/C/80.941 ECNU/C/78.713 **basel.**/C/74.257 bunji/U/70.545 bunji/C/66.584 GTI/U/64.109
ES/ REST	GTI/C/84.192 GTI/U/84.044 **basel.**/C/74.548 UWB/C/73.657	UWB/C/77.185 **basel.**/C/74.548
RU/ REST	**basel.**/C/84.792	**basel.**/C/70.6
RU/ REST	**basel.**/C/84.792	**basel.**/C/70.6
DU/ REST	**basel.**/C/70.323	**basel.**/C/73.228
TU/ REST	**basel.**/C/72.642	**basel.**/C/57.407
AR/ HOTE	**basel.**/C/42.757	**basel.**/C/73.216
EN/ LAPT	UWB/C/60.45 UWB/U/59.721 bunji/U/54.723 **basel.**/C/52.685 SYSU/U/48.889 SYSU/U/48.889	ECNU/U/75.046 UWB/U/75.046 UWB/C/74.495 **basel.**/C/73.028 ECNU/C/67.523 bunji/C/62.202 bunji/U/60 GTI/U/58.349

Table 7: Results for SB2.

level subtask. Future work will address the creation of datasets in more languages and domains and the enrichment of the annotation schemas with other types of SA-related information like topics, events and figures of speech (e.g., irony, metaphor).

Acknowledgments

The authors are grateful to all the annotators and contributors for their valuable support to the task: Konstantina Papanikolaou, Juli Bakagianni, Omar Qwasmeh, Nesreen Alqasem, Areen Magableh, Saja Alzoubi, Bashar Talafha, Zekui Li, Binbin Li, Shengqiu Li, Aaron Gevaert, Els Lefever, Cécile Richart, Pavel Blinov, Maria Shatalova, M. Teresa Martín-Valdivia, Pilar Santolaria, Fatih Samet Çetin, Ezgi Yıldırım, Can Özbey, Leonidas Valavanis, Stavros Giorgis, Dionysios Xenos, Panos Theodorakakos, and Apostolos Rousas. The work described in this paper is partially funded by the projects EOX GR07/3712 and "Research Programs for Excellence 2014-2016 / CitySense-ATHENA R.I.C.". The Arabic track was partially supported by the Jordan University of Science and Technology, Research Grant Number: 20150164. The Dutch track has been partly funded by the PARIS project (IWT-SBO-Nr. 110067). The French track was partially supported by the French National Research Agency under project ANR-12-CORD-0015/TransRead. The Russian track was partially supported by the Russian Foundation for Basic Research (RFBR) according to the research projects No. 14-07-00682a, 16-07-00342a, and No. 16-37-00311mol_a. The Spanish track has been partially supported by a grant from the Ministerio de Educación, Cultura y Deporte (MECD - scholarship FPU014/00983) and REDES project (TIN2015-65136-C2-1-R) from the Ministerio de Economía y Competitividad. The Turkish track was partially supported by TUBITAK-TEYDEB (The Scientific and Technological Research Council of Turkey – Technology and Innovation Funding Programs Directorate) project (grant number: 3140671).

References

Marianna Apidianaki, Xavier Tannier, and Cécile Richart. 2016. A Dataset for Aspect-Based Sentiment Analysis in French. In *Proceedings of the International Conference on Language Resources and Evaluation*.

Erik Cambria, Björn W. Schuller, Yunqing Xia, and Catherine Havasi. 2013. New Avenues in Opinion Mining and Sentiment Analysis. *IEEE Intelligent Systems*, 28(2):15–21.

Chih-Chung Chang and Chih-Jen Lin. 2011. LIBSVM: A library for support vector machines. *ACM TIST*, 2(3):27.

Judith Chevalier and Dina Mayzlin. 2006. The effect of word of mouth on sales: Online book reviews. *J. Marketing Res*, pages 345–354.

Orphée De Clercq and Véronique Hoste. 2016. Rude waiter but mouthwatering pastries! An exploratory study into Dutch Aspect-Based Sentiment Analysis. In *Proceedings of the 10th International Conference on Language Resources and Evaluation*.

Gülsen Eryigit, Fatih Samet Cetin, Meltem Yanık, Turkcell Global Bilgi, Tanel Temel, and Ilyas Ciçekli.

2013. TURKSENT: A Sentiment Annotation Tool for Social Media. In *Proceedings of the 7th Linguistic Annotation Workshop and Interoperability with Discourse*.

Gayatree Ganu, Noemie Elhadad, and Amélie Marian. 2009. Beyond the Stars: Improving Rating Predictions using Review Text Content. In *Proceedings of WebDB*.

Aniruddha Ghosh, Guofu Li, Tony Veale, Paolo Rosso, Ekaterina Shutova, John Barnden, and Antonio Reyes. 2015. SemEval-2015 Task 11: Sentiment Analysis of Figurative Language in Twitter. In *Proceedings of the 9th International Workshop on Semantic Evaluation*, Denver, Colorado.

Salud M. Jiménez-Zafra, Giacomo Berardi, Andrea Esuli, Diego Marcheggiani, María Teresa Martín-Valdivia, and Alejandro Moreo Fernández. 2015. A Multilingual Annotated Dataset for Aspect-Oriented Opinion Mining. In *Proceedings of Empirical Methods in Natural Language Processing*, pages 2533–2538.

Roman Klinger and Philipp Cimiano. 2014. The USAGE Review Corpus for Fine Grained Multi Lingual Opinion Analysis. In *Proceedings of the Ninth International Conference on Language Resources and Evaluation*, Reykjavik, Iceland.

Patrik Lambert. 2015. Aspect-Level Cross-lingual Sentiment Classification with Constrained SMT. In *Proceedings of the Association for Computational Linguistics and the International Joint Conference on Natural Language Processing, 2015, Beijing, China*, pages 781–787.

Bing Liu. 2012. *Sentiment Analysis and Opinion Mining*. Synthesis Lectures on Human Language Technologies. Morgan & Claypool Publishers.

Natalia Loukachevitch, Pavel Blinov, Evgeny Kotelnikov, Yulia Rubtsova, Vladimir Ivanov, and Elena Tutubalina. 2015. SentiRuEval: Testing Object-oriented Sentiment Analysis Systems in Russian. In *Proceedings of International Conference Dialog*.

Julian J. McAuley, Jure Leskovec, and Dan Jurafsky. 2012. Learning Attitudes and Attributes from Multiaspect Reviews. In *12th IEEE International Conference on Data Mining, ICDM 2012, Brussels, Belgium, December 10-13, 2012*, pages 1020–1025.

Margaret Mitchell. 2013. Overview of the TAC2013 Knowledge Base Population Evaluation English Sentiment Slot Filling. In *Proceedings of the 6th Text Analysis Conference, Gaithersburg, Maryland, USA*.

Saif M Mohammad, Svetlana Kiritchenko, Parinaz Sobhani, Xiaodan Zhu, and Colin Cherry. 2016. SemEval-2016 Task 6: Detecting Stance in Tweets. In *Proceedings of the 10th International Workshop on Semantic Evaluation*, San Diego, California.

Preslav Nakov, Sara Rosenthal, Zornitsa Kozareva, Veselin Stoyanov, Alan Ritter, and Theresa Wilson. 2013. SemEval-2013 Task 2: Sentiment Analysis in Twitter. In *Proceedings of the 7th International Workshop on Semantic Evaluation*, Atlanta, Georgia.

Stelios Piperidis. 2012. The META-SHARE Language Resources Sharing Infrastructure: Principles, Challenges, Solutions. In *Proceedings of the 8th International Conference on Language Resources and Evaluation*.

Maria Pontiki, Dimitrios Galanis, John Pavlopoulos, Harris Papageorgiou, Ion Androutsopoulos, and Suresh Manandhar. 2014. SemEval-2014 Task 4: Aspect Based Sentiment Analysis. In *Proceedings of the 8th International Workshop on Semantic Evaluation*, Dublin, Ireland.

Maria Pontiki, Dimitrios Galanis, Harris Papageorgiou, Suresh Manandhar, and Ion Androutsopoulos. 2015. SemEval-2015 Task 12: Aspect Based Sentiment Analysis. In *Proceedings of the 9th International Workshop on Semantic Evaluation*, Denver, Colorado.

Diego Reforgiato Recupero and Erik Cambria. 2014. Eswc'14 challenge on concept-level sentiment analysis. In *Semantic Web Evaluation Challenge - SemWebEval 2014 at ESWC 2014, Anissaras, Crete, Greece*, pages 3–20.

Sara Rosenthal, Alan Ritter, Preslav Nakov, and Veselin Stoyanov. 2014. SemEval-2014 Task 4: Sentiment Analysis in Twitter. In *Proceedings of the 8th International Workshop on Semantic Evaluation*, Dublin, Ireland.

Sara Rosenthal, Preslav Nakov, Svetlana Kiritchenko, Saif M Mohammad, Alan Ritter, and Veselin Stoyanov. 2015. SemEval-2015 Task 10: Sentiment Analysis in Twitter. In *Proceedings of the 9th International Workshop on Semantic Evaluation*, Denver, Colorado.

Josef Ruppenhofer, Roman Klinger, Julia Maria Struß, Jonathan Sonntag, and Michael Wiegand. 2014. IGGSA Shared Tasks on German Sentiment Analysis (GESTALT). In *Workshop Proceedings of the 12th Edition of the KONVENS Conference*, pages 164–173.

Yohei Seki, David Kirk Evans, Lun-Wei Ku, Hsin-Hsi Chen, Noriko Kando, and Chin-Yew Lin. 2007. Overview of Opinion Analysis Pilot Task at NTCIR-6. In *Proceedings of the 6th NTCIR Workshop, Tokyo, Japan*.

Yohei Seki, David Kirk Evans, Lun-Wei Ku, Le Sun, Hsin-Hsi Chen, and Noriko Kando. 2008. Overview of Multilingual Opinion Analysis Task at NTCIR-7. In *Proceedings of the 7th NTCIR Workshop, Tokyo, Japan*.

Yohei Seki, Lun-Wei Ku, Le Sun, Hsin-Hsi Chen, and Noriko Kando. 2010. Overview of Multilingual Opinion Analysis Task at NTCIR-8: A Step Toward Cross

Lingual Opinion Analysis. In *Proceedings of the 8th NTCIR Workshop, Tokyo, Japan*, pages 209–220.

Richard Socher, Alex Perelygin, Jean Wu, Jason Chuang, Christopher D. Manning, Andrew Y. Ng, and Christopher Potts. 2013. Recursive Deep Models for Semantic Compositionality Over a Sentiment Treebank. In *Proceedings of Empirical Methods in Natural Language Processing*, pages 1631–1642, Stroudsburg, PA.

Pontus Stenetorp, Sampo Pyysalo, Goran Topic, Tomoko Ohta, Sophia Ananiadou, and Jun'ichi Tsujii. 2012. BRAT: A Web-based Tool for NLP-Assisted Text Annotation. In *Proceedings of the European Chapter of the Association for Computational Linguistics*, pages 102–107.

Ezgi Yıldırım, Fatih Samet Çetin, Gülşen Eryiğit, and Tanel Temel. 2015. The impact of nlp on turkish sentiment analysis. *TÜRKİYE BİLİŞİM VAKFI BİLGİSAYAR BİLİMLERI ve MÜHENDİSLİĞİ DERGİSİ*, 7(1 (Basılı 8).

Kyung Hyan Yoo and Ulrike Gretzel. 2008. What Motivates Consumers to Write Online Travel Reviews? *J. of IT & Tourism*, 10(4):283–295.

Yanyan Zhao, Bing Qin, and Ting Liu. 2015. Creating a Fine-Grained Corpus for Chinese Sentiment Analysis. *IEEE Intelligent Systems*, 30(1):36–43.

Appendix A. Aspect inventories for all domains

Entity Labels
LAPTOP, DISPLAY, KEYBOARD, MOUSE, MOTHERBOARD, CPU, FANS_COOLING, PORTS, MEMORY, POWER_SUPPLY OPTICAL_DRIVES, BATTERY, GRAPHICS, HARD_DISK, MULTIMEDIA_DEVICES, HARDWARE, SOFTWARE, OS, WARRANTY, SHIPPING, SUPPORT, COMPANY
Attribute Labels
GENERAL, PRICE, QUALITY, DESIGN_FEATURES, OPERATION_PERFORMANCE, USABILITY, PORTABILITY, CONNECTIVITY, MISCELLANEOUS

Table 8: Laptops.

Entity Labels
PHONE, DISPLAY, KEYBOARD, CPU, PORTS, MEMORY, POWER_SUPPLY, HARD_DISK, MULTIMEDIA_DEVICES, BATTERY, HARDWARE, SOFTWARE, OS, WARRANTY, SHIPPING, SUPPORT, COMPANY
Attribute Labels
Same as in Laptops (Table 8) with the exception of PORTABILITY that is included in the DESIGN_FEATURES label and does not apply as a separate attribute type.

Table 9: Mobile Phones.

Entity Labels
CAMERA, DISPLAY, KEYBOARD, CPU, PORTS, MEMORY, POWER_SUPPLY, BATTERY, MULTIMEDIA_DEVICES, HARDWARE, SOFTWARE, OS, WARRANTY, SHIPPING, SUPPORT, COMPANY, LENS, PHOTO, FOCUS
Attribute Labels
Same as in Laptops (Table 8).

Table 10: Digital Cameras.

Entity Labels
RESTAURANT, FOOD, DRINKS, AMBIENCE, SERVICE, LOCATION
Attribute Labels
GENERAL, PRICES, QUALITY, STYLE_OPTIONS, MISCELLANEOUS

Table 11: Restaurants.

Entity Labels
HOTEL, ROOMS, FACILITIES, ROOM_AMENITIES, SERVICE, LOCATION, FOOD_DRINKS
Attribute Labels
GENERAL, PRICE, COMFORT, CLEANLINESS, QUALITY, STYLE_OPTIONS, DESIGN_FEATURES, MISCELLANEOUS

Table 12: Hotels.

Entity Labels
TELECOM OPERATOR, DEVICE, INTERNET, CUSTOMER_SERVICES, APPLICATION_SERVICE
Attribute Labels
GENERAL, PRICE_INVOICE, COVERAGE, SPEED, CAMPAIGN_ADVERTISEMENT, MISCELLANEOUS

Table 13: Telecommunications.

Entity Labels
MUSEUM, COLLECTIONS, FACILITIES, SERVICE, TOUR_GUIDING, LOCATION
Attribute Labels
GENERAL, PRICES, COMFORT, ACTIVITIES, ARCHITECTURE, INTEREST, SET UP, MISCELLANEOUS

Table 14: Museums.

SemEval-2016 Task 6: Detecting Stance in Tweets

Saif M. Mohammad
National Research Council Canada
saif.mohammad@nrc-cnrc.gc.ca

Svetlana Kiritchenko
National Research Council Canada
svetlana.kiritchenko@nrc-cnrc.gc.ca

Parinaz Sobhani
University of Ottawa
psobh090@uottawa.ca

Xiaodan Zhu
National Research Council Canada
xiaodan.zhu@nrc-cnrc.gc.ca

Colin Cherry
National Research Council Canada
colin.cherry@nrc-cnrc.gc.ca

Abstract

Here for the first time we present a shared task on detecting stance from tweets: given a tweet and a target entity (person, organization, etc.), automatic natural language systems must determine whether the tweeter is in favor of the given target, against the given target, or whether neither inference is likely. The target of interest may or may not be referred to in the tweet, and it may or may not be the target of opinion. Two tasks are proposed. Task A is a traditional supervised classification task where 70% of the annotated data for a target is used as training and the rest for testing. For Task B, we use as test data all of the instances for a new target (not used in task A) and no training data is provided. Our shared task received submissions from 19 teams for Task A and from 9 teams for Task B. The highest classification F-score obtained was 67.82 for Task A and 56.28 for Task B. However, systems found it markedly more difficult to infer stance towards the target of interest from tweets that express opinion towards another entity.

1 Introduction

Stance detection is the task of automatically determining from text whether the author of the text is in favor of, against, or neutral towards a proposition or target. The target may be a person, an organization, a government policy, a movement, a product, etc. For example, one can infer from Barack Obama's speeches that he is in favor of stricter gun laws in the US. Similarly, people often express stance towards various target entities through posts on online forums, blogs, Twitter, Youtube, Instagram, etc. Automatically detecting stance has widespread applications in information retrieval, text summarization, and textual entailment.

The task we explore is formulated as follows: given a tweet text and a target entity (person, organization, movement, policy, etc.), automatic natural language systems must determine whether the tweeter is in favor of the given target, against the given target, or whether neither inference is likely. For example, consider the target–tweet pair:

> Target: legalization of abortion (1)
> Tweet: *The pregnant are more than walking incubators, and have rights!*

We can deduce from the tweet that the tweeter is likely in favor of the target.[1]

We annotated 4870 English tweets for stance towards six commonly known targets in the United States. The data corresponding to five of the targets ('Atheism', 'Climate Change is a Real Concern', 'Feminist Movement', 'Hillary Clinton', and 'Legalization of Abortion') was used in a standard supervised stance detection task – *Task A*. About 70% of the tweets per target were used for training and the remaining for testing. All of the data corresponding to the target 'Donald Trump' was used as test set in a separate task – *Task B*. No training data labeled with stance towards 'Donald Trump' was provided. However, participants were free to use data from Task A to develop their models for Task B.

---

[1]Note that we use 'tweet' to refer to the text of the tweet and not to its meta-information. In our annotation task, we asked respondents to label for stance towards a given target based on the tweet text alone. However, automatic systems may benefit from exploiting tweet meta-information.

31

Proceedings of SemEval-2016, pages 31–41,
San Diego, California, June 16-17, 2016. ©2016 Association for Computational Linguistics

Task A received submissions from 19 teams, wherein the highest classification F-score obtained was 67.82. Task B, which is particularly challenging due to lack of training data, received submissions from 9 teams wherein the highest classification F-score obtained was 56.28. The best performing systems used standard text classification features such as those drawn from n-grams, word vectors, and sentiment lexicons. Some teams drew additional gains from noisy stance-labeled data created using distant supervision techniques. A large number of teams used word embeddings and some used deep neural networks such as RNNs and convolutional neural nets. Nonetheless, for Task A, none of these systems surpassed a baseline SVM classifier that uses word and character n-grams as features (Mohammad et al., 2016b). Further, results are markedly worse for instances where the target of interest is not the target of opinion.

More gains can be expected in the future on both tasks, as researchers better understand this new task and data. All of the data, an interactive visualization of the data, and the evaluation scripts are available on the task website as well as the homepage for this Stance project.[2]

2 Subtleties of Stance Detection

In the sub-sections below we discuss some of the nuances of stance detection, including a discussion on neutral stance and the relationship between stance and sentiment.

2.1 Neutral Stance

The classification task formulated here does not include an explicit neutral class. The lack of evidence for 'favor' or 'against' does not imply that the tweeter is neutral towards the target. It may just be that one cannot deduce stance from the tweet. In fact, this is fairly common. On the other hand, the number of tweets from which we can infer neutral stance is expected to be small. An example is shown below:

> Target: Hillary Clinton   (2)
> Tweet: *Hillary Clinton has some strengths and some weaknesses.*

Thus, even though we obtain annotations for neutral stance, we eventually merge all classes other than 'favor' and 'against' into one 'neither' class.

2.2 Stance and Sentiment

Stance detection is related to, but different from, sentiment analysis. Sentiment analysis tasks are usually formulated as: determining whether a piece of text is positive, negative, or neutral, OR determining from text the speaker's opinion and the target of the opinion (the entity towards which opinion is expressed). However, in stance detection, systems are to determine favorability towards a given (pre-chosen) target of interest. The target of interest may not be explicitly mentioned in the text and it may not be the target of opinion in the text. For example, consider the target–tweet pair below:

> Target: Donald Trump   (3)
> Tweet: *Jeb Bush is the only sane candidate in this republican lineup.*

The target of opinion in the tweet is Jeb Bush, but the given target of interest is Donald Trump. Nonetheless, we can infer that the tweeter is likely to be unfavorable towards Donald Trump. Also note that in stance detection, the target can be expressed in different ways which impacts whether the instance is labeled favour or against. For example, the target in example 1 could have been phrased as 'pro-life movement', in which case the correct label for that instance is 'against'. Also, the same stance (favour or against) towards a given target can be deduced from positive tweets and negative tweets. See Mohammad et al. (2016b) for a quantitative exploration of this interaction between stance and sentiment.

3 A Dataset for Stance from Tweets

The stance annotations we use are described in detail in Mohammad et al. (2016a). The same dataset was subsequently also annotated for target of opinion and sentiment (in addition to stance towards a given target) (Mohammad et al., 2016b). These additional annotations are not part of the SemEval-2016 competition, but are made available for future research. We summarize below all relevant details for this shared task: how we compiled a set of tweets and targets for stance annotation (Section 3.1), the questionnaire and crowdsourcing setup used for stance annotation (Section 3.2), and an analysis of the stance annotations (Section 3.3).

---

[2]http://alt.qcri.org/semeval2016/task6/
http://www.saifmohammad.com/WebPages/StanceDataset.htm

3.1 Selecting the Tweet–Target Pairs

We wanted to create a dataset of stance-labeled tweet–target pairs with the following properties:

1: The tweet and target are commonly understood by a wide number of people in the US. (The data was also eventually annotated for stance by respondents living in the US.)

2: There must be a significant amount of data for the three classes: favor, against, and neither.

3: Apart from tweets that explicitly mention the target, the dataset should include a significant number of tweets that express opinion towards the target without referring to it by name.

4: Apart from tweets that express opinion towards the target, the dataset should include a significant number of tweets in which the target of opinion is different from the given target of interest. Downstream applications often require stance towards particular pre-chosen targets of interest (for example, a company might be interested in stance towards its product). Having data where the target of opinion is some other entity (for example, a competitor's product) helps test how well stance detection systems can cope with such instances.

To help with Property 1, the authors of this paper compiled a list of target entities commonly known in the United States. (See Table 1 for the list.)

We created a small list of hashtags, which we will call *query hashtags*, that people use when tweeting about the targets. We split these hashtags into three categories: (1) *favor hashtags*: expected to occur in tweets expressing favorable stance towards the target (for example, *#Hillary4President*), (2) *against hashtags:* expected to occur in tweets expressing opposition to the target (for example, *#HillNo*), and (3) *stance-ambiguous hashtags:* expected to occur in tweets about the target, but are not explicitly indicative of stance (for example, *#Hillary2016*). Next, we polled the Twitter API to collect over two million tweets containing these query hashtags. We discarded retweets and tweets with URLs. We kept only those tweets where the query hashtags appeared at the end. We removed the query hashtags from the tweets to exclude obvious cues for the classification task. Since we only select tweets that have the query

hashtag at the end, removing them from the tweet often still results in text that is understandable and grammatical.

Note that the presence of a stance-indicative hashtag is not a guarantee that the tweet will have the same stance.[3] Further, removal of query hashtags may result in a tweet that no longer expresses the same stance as with the query hashtag. Thus we manually annotate the tweet–target pairs after the pre-processing described above. For each target, we sampled an equal number of tweets pertaining to the favor hashtags, the against hashtags, and the stance-ambiguous hashtags—up to 1000 tweets at most per target. This helps in obtaining a sufficient number of tweets pertaining to each of the stance categories (Property 2). Properties 3 and 4 are addressed to some extent by the fact that removing the query hashtag can sometimes result in tweets that do not explicitly mention the target. Consider:

Target: Hillary Clinton   (4)
Tweet: *Benghazi must be answered for #Jeb16*

The query hashtags '#HillNo' was removed from the original tweet, leaving no mention of Hillary Clinton. Yet there is sufficient evidence (through references to Benghazi and #Jeb16) that the tweeter is likely against Hillary Clinton. Further, conceptual targets such as 'legalization of abortion' (much more so than person-name targets) have many instances where the target is not explicitly mentioned.

3.2 Stance Annotation

The core instructions given to annotators for determining stance are shown below.[4] Additional descriptions within each option (not shown here) make clear that stance can be expressed in many different ways, for example by explicitly supporting or opposing the target, by supporting an entity aligned with or opposed to the target, by re-tweeting somebody else's tweet, etc.

Target of Interest: [target entity]
Tweet: [tweet with query hashtag removed]

Q: From reading the tweet, which of the options below is most likely to be true about the tweeter's stance or outlook towards the target:

---

[3]A tweet that has a seemingly favorable hashtag may in fact oppose the target; and this is not uncommon. Similarly unfavorable hashtags may occur in tweets that favor the target.

[4]The full set of instructions is made available on the shared task website (http://alt.qcri.org/semeval2016/task6/).

33

1. We can infer from the tweet that the tweeter supports the target
2. We can infer from the tweet that the tweeter is against the target
3. We can infer from the tweet that the tweeter has a neutral stance towards the target
4. There is no clue in the tweet to reveal the stance of the tweeter towards the target (support/against/neutral)

Each of the tweet–target pairs selected for annotation was uploaded on CrowdFlower for annotation with the questionnaire shown above.[5] Each instance was annotated by at least eight respondents.

3.3 Analysis of Stance Annotations

The number of instances that were marked as neutral stance (option 3) was less than 1%. Thus we merged options 3 and 4 into one 'neither in favor nor against' option ('neither' for short). The inter-annotator agreement was 73.1%. These statistics are for the complete annotated dataset, which include instances that were genuinely difficult to annotate for stance (possibly because the tweets were too ungrammatical or vague) and/or instances that received poor annotations from the crowd workers (possibly because the particular annotator did not understand the tweet or its context). We selected instances with agreement equal to or greater than 60% (at least 5 out of 8 annotators must agree) to create the test and training sets for this task.[6] We will refer to this dataset as the *Stance Dataset*. The inter-annotator agreement on this set is 81.85%. The rest of the instances are kept aside for future investigation. We partitioned the Stance Dataset into training and test sets based on the timestamps of the tweets. All annotated tweets were ordered by their timestamps, and the first 70% of the tweets formed the training set and the last 30% formed the test set. Table 1 shows the number and distribution of instances in the Stance Dataset.

Inspection of the data revealed that often the target is not directly mentioned, and yet stance towards the target was determined by the annotators. About 30% of the 'Hillary Clinton' instances and 65% of the 'Legalization of Abortion' instances were found to

be of this kind—they did not mention 'Hillary' or 'Clinton' and did not mention 'abortion', 'pro-life', and 'pro-choice', respectively (case insensitive; with or without hashtag; with or without hyphen). Examples (1) and (4) shown earlier are instances of this, and are taken from our dataset.

An interactive visualization of the Stance Dataset that shows various statistics about the data is available at the task website. Note that it also shows sentiment and target of opinion annotations (in addition to stance). Clicking on various visualization elements filters the data. For example, clicking on 'Feminism' and 'Favor' will show information pertaining to only those tweets that express favor towards feminism. One can also use the check boxes on the left to view only test or training data, or data on particular targets.

4 Task Setup: Automatic Stance Classification

The Stance Dataset was partitioned so as to be used in two tasks described in the subsections below: Task A (supervised framework) and Task B (weakly supervised framework). Participants could provide submissions for either one of the tasks, or both tasks. Both tasks required classification of tweet–target pairs into exactly one of three classes:

- Favor: We can infer from the tweet that the tweeter supports the target (e.g., directly or indirectly by supporting someone/something, by opposing or criticizing someone/something opposed to the target, or by echoing the stance of somebody else).

- Against: We can infer from the tweet that the tweeter is against the target (e.g., directly or indirectly by opposing or criticizing someone/something, by supporting someone/something opposed to the target, or by echoing the stance of somebody else).

- Neither: none of the above.

4.1 Task A: Supervised Framework

This task tested stance towards five targets: 'Atheism', 'Climate Change is a Real Concern', 'Feminist Movement', 'Hillary Clinton', and 'Legalization of Abortion'. Participants were provided

---

[5]http://www.crowdflower.com

[6]The 60% threshold is somewhat arbitrary, but it seemed appropriate in terms of balancing quality and quantity.

| | | | **% of instances in Train** | | | | **% of instances in Test** | | |
Target	# total	# train	favor	against	neither	# test	favor	against	neither
Data for Task A									
Atheism	733	513	17.9	59.3	22.8	220	14.5	72.7	12.7
Climate Change is Concern	564	395	53.7	3.8	42.5	169	72.8	6.5	20.7
Feminist Movement	949	664	31.6	49.4	19.0	285	20.4	64.2	15.4
Hillary Clinton	984	689	17.1	57.0	25.8	295	15.3	58.3	26.4
Legalization of Abortion	933	653	18.5	54.4	27.1	280	16.4	67.5	16.1
All	4163	2914	25.8	47.9	26.3	1249	24.3	57.3	18.4
Data for Task B									
Donald Trump	707	0	-	-	-	707	20.93	42.29	36.78

Table 1: Distribution of instances in the Stance Train and Test sets for Task A and Task B.

with 2,914 labeled training data instances for the five targets. The test data included 1,249 instances.

4.2 Task B: Weakly Supervised Framework

This task tested stance towards one target 'Donald Trump' in 707 tweets. Participants were not provided with any training data for this target. They were given about 78,000 tweets associated with 'Donald Trump' to various degrees – the *domain corpus*, but these tweets were not labeled for stance. These tweets were gathered by polling Twitter for hashtags associated with Donald Trump.

4.3 Common Evaluation Metric for Both Task A and Task B

We used the macro-average of the F1-score for 'favor' and the F1-score for 'against' as the bottom-line evaluation metric.

$$F_{avg} = \frac{F_{favor} + F_{against}}{2} \tag{1}$$

where F_{favor} and $F_{against}$ are calculated as shown below:

$$F_{favor} = \frac{2P_{favor}R_{favor}}{P_{favor}+R_{favor}} \tag{2}$$

$$F_{against} = \frac{2P_{against}R_{against}}{P_{against}+R_{against}} \tag{3}$$

Note that the evaluation measure does not disregard the 'neither' class. By taking the average F-score for only the 'favor' and 'against' classes, we treat 'neither' as a class that is not of interest—or 'negative' class in Information Retrieval (IR) terms. Falsely labeling negative class instances still adversely affects the scores of this metric. If one uses simple accuracy as the evaluation metric, and if the negative class is very dominant (as is the case in IR), then simply labeling every instance with the negative class will obtain very high scores.

If one randomly accesses tweets, then the probability that one can infer 'favor' or 'against' stance towards a pre-chosen target of interest is small. This has motivated the IR-like metric used in this competition, even though we worked hard to have marked amounts of 'favor' and 'against' data in our training and test sets. This metric is also similar to how sentiment prediction was evaluated in recent SemEval competitions.

This evaluation metric can be seen as a micro-average of F-scores across targets (F-microT). Alternatively, one could determine the mean of the F_{avg} scores for each of the targets—the macro average across targets (F-macroT). Even though not the official competition metric, the F-macroT can easily be determined from the per-target F_{avg} scores shown in the result tables of Section 5.

The participants were provided with an evaluation script so that they could check the format of their submission and determine performance when gold labels were available.

5 Systems and Results for Task A

We now discuss various baseline systems and the official submissions to Task A.

5.1 Task A Baselines

Table 2 presents the results obtained with several baseline classifiers first presented in (Mohammad et al., 2016b). Since the baseline system was developed by some of the organizers of this task, it was

		Overall		Atheism	Climate	Feminism	Hillary	Abortion
Team	F_{favour}	$F_{against}$	F_{avg}	F_{avg}	F_{avg}	F_{avg}	F_{avg}	F_{avg}
Baselines								
Majority class	52.01	**78.44**	65.22	42.11	42.12	39.10	36.83	40.30
SVM-unigrams	54.49	72.13	63.31	53.25	38.39	55.65	57.02	60.09
SVM-ngrams	**62.98**	74.98	**68.98**	**65.19**	42.35	**57.46**	**58.63**	**66.42**
SVM-ngrams-comb	54.11	70.01	62.06	53.27	**47.76**	52.82	56.50	63.71
Participating Teams								
MITRE	59.32	**76.33**	**67.82**	61.47	41.63	**62.09**	57.67	57.28
pkudblab	**61.98**	72.67	67.33	63.34	52.69	51.33	64.41	61.09
TakeLab	60.93	72.73	66.83	**67.25**	41.25	53.01	**67.12**	61.38
PKULCWM	56.96	74.55	65.76	56.39	40.39	51.32	62.26	61.56
ECNU	60.55	70.54	65.55	61.97	41.32	56.21	57.85	61.25
CU-GWU	54.99	72.21	63.60	55.68	39.41	53.88	51.19	59.38
IUCL-RF	52.61	74.59	63.60	57.93	39.06	51.06	49.84	57.61
DeepStance	58.44	68.65	63.54	52.90	40.40	52.34	55.35	**63.32**
UWB	57.41	69.42	63.42	57.88	46.90	51.82	59.82	61.98
IDI@NTNU	58.97	65.97	62.47	59.59	**54.86**	48.59	57.89	54.47
Tohoku	49.25	75.18	62.21	58.90	39.51	52.41	39.81	37.75
ltl.uni-due	48.71	74.75	61.73	52.47	35.50	55.12	44.23	57.25
LitisMind	50.67	72.20	61.44	52.36	39.15	57.16	42.08	45.88
JU_NLP	46.68	74.53	60.60	38.99	42.60	45.65	50.25	41.83
NEUSA	49.03	71.20	60.12	48.90	41.95	52.14	48.53	61.89
nldsucsc	50.90	67.81	59.36	57.19	42.10	48.97	57.27	61.66
WFU/TNT	47.55	70.89	59.22	46.16	42.07	47.91	45.88	45.34
INESC-ID	50.58	64.57	57.58	52.67	44.92	49.00	50.64	49.93
Thomson Reuters	30.16	62.23	46.19	44.79	35.86	39.37	34.98	38.89

Table 2: Results for Task A, reporting the official competition metric as 'Overall F_{avg}', along with F_{favor} and $F_{against}$ over all targets and F_{avg} for each individual target. The highest scores in each column among the baselines and among the participating systems are shown in bold.

not entered as part of the official competition.
Baselines:

1. *Majority class*: a classifier that simply labels every instance with the majority class ('favor' or 'against') for the corresponding target;

2. *SVM-unigrams*: five SVM classifiers (one per target) trained on the corresponding training set for the target using word unigram features;

3. *SVM-ngrams*: five SVM classifiers (one per target) trained on the corresponding training set for the target using word n-grams (1-, 2-, and 3-gram) and character n-grams (2-, 3-, 4-, and 5-gram) features;

4. *SVM-ngrams-comb*: one SVM classifier trained on the combined (all 5 targets) training set using word n-grams (1-, 2-, and 3-gram) and character n-grams (2-, 3-, 4-, and 5-gram) features.

The SVM parameters were tuned using 5-fold cross-validation on the training data. The first three columns of the table show the official competition metric (Overall F_{avg}) along with the two components that are averaged to obtain it (F_{favor} and $F_{against}$). The next five columns describe per-target results—the official metric as calculated over each of the targets individually.

Observe that the Overall F_{avg} for the Majority class baseline is very high. This is mostly due to the differences in the class distributions for the five targets: for most of the targets the majority of the instances are labeled as 'against' whereas for target 'Climate Change is a Real Concern' most of the data are labeled as 'favor'. Therefore, the F-scores for the classes 'favor' and 'against' are more balanced over all targets than for just one target.

We can see that a supervised classifier using unigram features alone produces results markedly

	Opinion Towards		All
Team	Target	Other	
Baselines			
Majority class	71.27	41.33	65.22
SVM-unigrams	69.39	38.96	63.31
SVM-ngrams	**74.54**	**43.20**	**68.98**
SVM-ngrams-comb	66.60	38.05	62.06
Participating Teams			
MITRE	72.49	44.48	**67.82**
pkudblab	71.07	**46.66**	67.33
TakeLab	**73.66**	37.47	66.83
PKULCWM	70.62	45.89	65.76
ECNU	70.29	44.25	65.55
CU-GWU	67.89	45.28	63.60
IUCL-RF	67.77	41.96	63.60
DeepStance	67.81	44.00	63.54
UWB	67.60	44.54	63.42
IDI@NTNU	66.25	42.26	62.47
Tohoku	66.44	44.09	62.21
ltl.uni-due	67.23	42.45	61.73
LitisMind	66.42	41.27	61.44
JU_NLP	62.55	49.34	60.60
NEUSA	65.39	39.48	60.12
nldsucsc	65.71	34.64	59.36
WFU/TNT	67.28	34.89	59.22
INESC-ID	63.99	36.63	57.58
Thomson Reuters	49.98	32.43	46.19

Table 3: Results for Task A (the official competition metric F_{avg}) on different subsets of the test data. The highest scores in each column among the baselines and among the participating systems are shown in bold.

above the majority baseline for most of the targets. Furthermore, employing higher-order n-gram features results in substantial improvements for all targets as well as for the Overall F_{avg}. Training separate classifiers for each target seems a better solution than training a single classifier for all targets even though the combined classifier has access to significantly more data. As expected, the words and concepts used in tweets corresponding to the stance categories do not generalize well across the targets. However, there is one exception: the results for 'Climate Change' improve by over 5% when the combined classifier has access to the training data for other targets. This is probably because it has access to more balanced dataset and more representative instances for 'against' class. Most teams chose to train separate classifiers for different targets.

5.2 Task A Participating Stance Systems

Nineteen teams competed in Task A on supervised stance detection. Table 2 shows each team's performance, both in aggregate and in terms of individual targets. Teams are sorted in terms of their performance according to the official metric. The best results obtained by a participating system was an Overall F_{avg} of 67.82 by *MITRE*. Their approach employed two recurrent neural network (RNN) classifiers: the first was trained to predict task-relevant hashtags on a very large unlabeled Twitter corpus. This network was used to initialize a second RNN classifier, which was trained with the provided Task A data. However, this result is not higher than the SVM-ngrams baseline.

In general, per-target results are lower than the Overall F_{avg}. This is likely due to the fact that it is easier to balance 'favor' and 'against' classes over all targets than it is for exactly one target. That is, when dealing with all targets, one can use the natural abundance of tweets in favor of concern over climate change to balance against the fact that many of the other targets have a high proportion of tweets against them. Most systems were optimized for the competition metric, which allows cross-target balancing, and thus would naturally perform worse on per-target metrics. *IDI@NTNU* is an interesting exception, as their submission focused on the 'Climate Change' target, and they did succeed in producing the best result for that target.

We also calculated Task A results on two subsets of the test set: (1) a subset where opinion is expressed towards the target, (2) a subset where opinion is expressed towards some other entity. Table 3 shows these results. It also shows results on the complete test set (All), for easy reference. Observe that the stance task is markedly more difficult when stance is to be inferred from a tweet expressing opinion about some other entity (and not the target of interest). This is not surprising because it is a more challenging task, and because there has been very little work on this in the past.

5.3 Discussion

Most teams used standard text classification features such as n-grams and word embedding vectors, as well as standard sentiment analysis features such as those drawn from sentiment lexicons (Kiritchenko et al., 2014b). Some teams polled Twitter for stance-bearing hashtags, creating additional noisy stance data. Three teams tried variants of this strategy: *MITRE*, *DeepStance* and *nldsucsc*. These teams are distributed somewhat evenly throughout the standings, and although *MITRE* did use extra data in its top-placing entry, *pkudblab* achieved nearly the same score with only the provided data.

Another possible differentiator would be the use of continuous word representations, derived either from extremely large sources such as Google News, directly from Twitter corpora, or as a by-product of training a neural network classifier. Nine of the nineteen entries used some form of word embedding, including the top three entries, but *PKULCWM*'s fourth place result shows that it is possible to do well with a more traditional approach that relies instead on Twitter-specific linguistic pre-processing. Along these lines, it is worth noting that both *MITRE* and *pkudblab* reflect knowledge-light approaches to the problem, each relying minimally on linguistic processing and external lexicons.

Seven of the nineteen submissions made extensive use of publicly-available sentiment and emotion lexicons such as the NRC Emotion Lexicon (Mohammad and Turney, 2010), Hu and Liu Lexicon (Hu and Liu, 2004), MPQA Subjectivity Lexicon (Wilson et al., 2005), and NRC Hashtag Lexicons (Kiritchenko et al., 2014b).

Recall that the SVM-ngrams baseline also performed very well, using only word and character n-grams in its classifiers. This helps emphasize the fact that for this young task, the community is still a long way from an established set of best practices.

6 Systems and Results for Task B

The sub-sections below discuss baselines and official submissions to Task B. Recall, that the test data for Task B is for the target 'Donald Trump', and no training data for this target was provided.

6.1 Task B Baselines

We calculated two baselines listed below:

1. *Majority class*: a classifier that simply labels every instance with the majority class ('favor' or 'against') for the corresponding target;

Team	F_{favor}	$F_{against}$	F_{avg}
Baselines			
Majority class	0.00	59.44	29.72
SVM-ngrams-comb	18.42	38.45	28.43
Participating Teams			
pkudblab	**57.39**	55.17	**56.28**
LitisMind	30.04	**59.28**	44.66
INF-UFRGS	32.56	52.09	42.32
UWB	34.26	49.78	42.02
ECNU	17.96	50.20	34.08
USFD	10.93	54.46	32.70
Thomson Reuters	14.39	50.39	32.39
ltl.uni-due	46.56	05.71	26.14
NEUSA	16.59	34.87	25.73

Table 4: Results for Task B, reporting the official competition metric as F_{avg}, along with F_{favor} and $F_{against}$. The highest score in each column is shown in bold.

2. *SVM-ngrams-comb*: one SVM classifier trained on the combined (all 5 targets) Task A training set, using word n-grams (1-, 2-, and 3-gram) and character n-grams (2-, 3-, 4-, and 5-gram) features.

The results are presented in Table 4. Note that the class distribution for the target 'Donald Trump' is more balanced. Therefore, the F_{avg} for the Majority baseline for this target is much lower than the corresponding values for other targets. Yet, the combined classifier trained on other targets could not beat the Majority baseline on this test set.

6.2 Task B Participating Stance Systems

Nine teams competed in Task B. Table 4 shows each team's performance. Teams are sorted in terms of their performance according to the official metric. The best results obtained by a participating system was an F_{avg} of 56.28 by *pkudblab*. They used a rule-based annotation of the domain corpus to train a deep convolutional neural network to differentiate 'favour' from 'against' instances. At test time, they combined their network's output with rules to produce predictions that include the 'neither' class.

In general, results for Task B are lower than those for Task A as one would expect, as we remove the benefit of direct supervision. However, they are perhaps not as low as we might have expected, with the best result of 56.28 actually beating the best result for the supervised 'Climate Change' task (54.86).

	Opinion Towards		**All**
Team	Target	Other	
Baselines			
Majority class	35.20	25.52	29.72
SVM-ngrams-comb	31.39	20.13	28.43
Participating Teams			
pkudblab	**67.19**	25.77	**56.28**
LitisMind	51.60	**29.50**	44.66
INF-UFRGS	50.04	22.66	42.32
UWB	50.62	25.02	42.02
ECNU	40.66	19.14	34.08
USFD	38.87	22.80	32.70
Thomson Reuters	38.06	22.60	32.39
ltl.uni-due	34.16	4.69	26.14
NEUSA	28.86	18.35	25.73

Table 5: Results for Task B (the official competition metric F_{avg}) on different subsets of the test data. The highest score in each column is shown in bold.

Table 5 shows results for Task B on subsets of the test set where opinion is expressed towards the target of interest and towards some other entity. Observe that here too results are markedly lower when stance is to be inferred from a tweet expressing opinion about some other entity (and not the target of interest).

6.3 Discussion

Some teams did very well detecting tweets in favor of Trump (*ltl.uni-due*), with most of the others performing best on tweets against Trump. This makes sense, as 'against' tweets made up the bulk of the Trump dataset. The top team, *pkudblab*, was the only one to successfully balance these two goals, achieving the best F_{favor} score and the second-best $F_{against}$ score.

The Task B teams varied wildly in terms of approaches to this problem. The top three teams all took the approach of producing noisy labels, with *pkudblab* using keyword rules, *LitisMind* using hashtag rules on external data, and *INF-UFRGS* using a combination of rules and third-party sentiment classifiers. However, we were pleased to see other teams attempting to generalize the supervised data from Task A in interesting ways, either using rules or multi-stage classifiers to bridge the target gap. We are optimistic that there is much interesting follow-up work yet to come on this task.

Further details on the submissions can be found

in the system description papers published in the SemEval-2016 proceedings, including papers by Elfardy and Diab (2016) for *CU-GWU*, Dias and Becker (2016) for *INF-URGS*, Patra et al. (2016) for *JU_NLP*, Wojatzki and Zesch (2016) for *ltl.uni-due*, Zarrella and Marsh (2016) for *MITRE*, Misra et al. (2016) for *nldsucsc*, Wei et al. (2016) for *pkudblab*, Tutek et al. (2016) for *TakeLab*, Yuki et al. (2016) for *Tohoku*, and Augenstein et al. (2016) for *USFD*.

7 Related Work

Past work on stance detection includes that by Somasundaran and Wiebe (2010), Anand et al. (2011), Faulkner (2014), Rajadesingan and Liu (2014), Djemili et al. (2014), Boltuzic and Šnajder (2014), Conrad et al. (2012), Sridhar et al. (2014), Rajadesingan and Liu (2014), and Sobhani et al. (2015). There is a vast amount of work in sentiment analysis of tweets, and we refer the reader to surveys (Pang and Lee, 2008; Liu and Zhang, 2012; Mohammad, 2015) and proceedings of recent shared task competitions (Wilson et al., 2013; Mohammad et al., 2013; Rosenthal et al., 2015). See Pontiki et al. (2014), Pontiki et al. (2015), and Kiritchenko et al. (2014a) for tasks and systems on aspect based sentiment analysis, where the goal is to determine sentiment towards aspects of a product such as speed of processor and screen resolution of a cell phone.

8 Conclusions and Future Work

We described a new shared task on detecting stance towards pre-chosen targets of interest from tweets. We formulated two tasks: a traditional supervised task where labeled training data for the test data targets is made available (Task A) and a more challenging formulation where no labeled data pertaining to the test data targets is available (Task B). We received 19 submissions for Task A and 9 for Task B, with systems utilizing a wide array of features and resources. Stance detection, especially as formulated for Task B, is still in its infancy, and we hope that the dataset made available as part of this task will foster further research not only on stance detection as proposed here, but also for related tasks such as exploring the different ways in which stance is conveyed, and how the distribution of stance towards a target changes over time.

Acknowledgment

Annotations of the Stance Dataset were funded by the National Research Council of Canada.

References

Pranav Anand, Marilyn Walker, Rob Abbott, Jean E Fox Tree, Robeson Bowmani, and Michael Minor. 2011. Cats rule and dogs drool!: Classifying stance in online debate. In *Proceedings of the 2nd workshop on computational approaches to subjectivity and sentiment analysis*, pages 1–9.

Isabelle Augenstein, Andreas Vlachos, and Kalina Bontcheva. 2016. USFD at SemEval-2016 Task 6: Any-Target Stance Detection on Twitter with Autoencoders. In *Proceedings of the International Workshop on Semantic Evaluation*, SemEval '16, San Diego, California, June.

Filip Boltuzic and Jan Šnajder. 2014. Back up your stance: Recognizing arguments in online discussions. In *Proceedings of the First Workshop on Argumentation Mining*, pages 49–58.

Alexander Conrad, Janyce Wiebe, and Rebecca Hwa. 2012. Recognizing arguing subjectivity and argument tags. In *Proceedings of the Workshop on Extra-Propositional Aspects of Meaning in Computational Linguistics*, pages 80–88.

Marcelo Dias and Karin Becker. 2016. INF-UFRGS-OPINION-MINING at SemEval-2016 Task 6: Automatic Generation of a Training Corpus for Unsupervised Identification of Stance in Tweets. In *Proceedings of the International Workshop on Semantic Evaluation*, SemEval '16, San Diego, California, June.

Sarah Djemili, Julien Longhi, Claudia Marinica, Dimitris Kotzinos, and Georges-Elia Sarfati. 2014. What does Twitter have to say about ideology? In *Proceedings of the Natural Language Processing for Computer-Mediated Communication/Social Media-Pre-conference workshop at Konvens*.

Heba Elfardy and Mona Diab. 2016. CU-GWU at SemEval-2016 Task 6: Perspective at SemEval-2016 Task 6: Ideological Stance Detection in Informal Text. In *Proceedings of the International Workshop on Semantic Evaluation*, SemEval '16, San Diego, California, June.

Adam Faulkner. 2014. Automated classification of stance in student essays: An approach using stance target information and the Wikipedia link-based measure. In *Proceedings of the Twenty-Seventh International Flairs Conference*.

Minqing Hu and Bing Liu. 2004. Mining and summarizing customer reviews. In *Proceedings of the tenth ACM SIGKDD international conference on Knowledge discovery and data mining*, pages 168–177.

Svetlana Kiritchenko, Xiaodan Zhu, Colin Cherry, and Saif M. Mohammad. 2014a. NRC-Canada-2014: Detecting aspects and sentiment in customer reviews. In *Proceedings of the International Workshop on Semantic Evaluation*, SemEval '14, Dublin, Ireland, August.

Svetlana Kiritchenko, Xiaodan Zhu, and Saif M. Mohammad. 2014b. Sentiment analysis of short informal texts. *Journal of Artificial Intelligence Research*, 50:723–762.

Bing Liu and Lei Zhang. 2012. A survey of opinion mining and sentiment analysis. In Charu C. Aggarwal and ChengXiang Zhai, editors, *Mining Text Data*, pages 415–463. Springer US.

Amita Misra, Brian Ecker, Theodore Handleman, Nicolas Hahn, and Marilyn Walker. 2016. nldsucsc at SemEval-2016 Task 6: A Semi-Supervised Approach to Detecting Stance in Tweets. In *Proceedings of the International Workshop on Semantic Evaluation*, SemEval '16, San Diego, California, June.

Saif M Mohammad and Peter D Turney. 2010. Emotions evoked by common words and phrases: Using Mechanical Turk to create an emotion lexicon. In *Proceedings of the NAACL HLT 2010 Workshop on Computational Approaches to Analysis and Generation of Emotion in Text*, pages 26–34.

Saif Mohammad, Svetlana Kiritchenko, and Xiaodan Zhu. 2013. NRC-Canada: Building the state-of-the-art in sentiment analysis of tweets. In *Proceedings of the International Workshop on Semantic Evaluation*, SemEval '13, Atlanta, Georgia, USA, June.

Saif M. Mohammad, Svetlana Kiritchenko, Parinaz Sobhani, Xiaodan Zhu, and Colin Cherry. 2016a. A dataset for detecting stance in tweets. In *Proceedings of 10th edition of the the Language Resources and Evaluation Conference (LREC)*, Portorož, Slovenia.

Saif M. Mohammad, Parinaz Sobhani, and Svetlana Kiritchenko. 2016b. Stance and sentiment in tweets. *Special Section of the ACM Transactions on Internet Technology on Argumentation in Social Media*, Submitted.

Saif M Mohammad. 2015. Sentiment analysis: Detecting valence, emotions, and other affectual states from text.

Bo Pang and Lillian Lee. 2008. Opinion mining and sentiment analysis. *Foundations and Trends in Information Retrieval*, 2(1–2):1–135.

Braja Gopal Patra, Dipankar Das, and Sivaji Bandyopadhyay. 2016. JU_NLP at SemEval-2016 Task 6: Detecting Stance in Tweets using Support Vector Machines. In *Proceedings of the International Workshop on Semantic Evaluation*, SemEval '16, San Diego, California, June.

Maria Pontiki, Dimitrios Galanis, John Pavlopoulos, Harris Papageorgiou, Ion Androutsopoulos, and Suresh Manandhar. 2014. SemEval-2014 Task 4: Aspect based sentiment analysis. In *Proceedings of the International Workshop on Semantic Evaluation*, SemEval '14, Dublin, Ireland, August.

Maria Pontiki, Dimitrios Galanis, Haris Papageogiou, Suresh Manandhar, and Ion Androutsopoulos. 2015. SemEval-2015 Task 12: Aspect based sentiment analysis. In *Proceedings of the International Workshop on Semantic Evaluation*, SemEval '15, Denver, Colorado.

Ashwin Rajadesingan and Huan Liu. 2014. Identifying users with opposing opinions in Twitter debates. In *Proceedings of the Conference on Social Computing, Behavioral-Cultural Modeling and Prediction*, pages 153–160, Washington, DC, USA.

Sara Rosenthal, Preslav Nakov, Svetlana Kiritchenko, Saif M Mohammad, Alan Ritter, and Veselin Stoyanov. 2015. Semeval-2015 Task 10: Sentiment analysis in Twitter. In *Proceedings of the 9th International Workshop on Semantic Evaluations*.

Parinaz Sobhani, Diana Inkpen, and Stan Matwin. 2015. From argumentation mining to stance classification. In *Proceedings of the Workshop on Argumentation Mining*, pages 67–77, Denver, Colorado, USA.

Swapna Somasundaran and Janyce Wiebe. 2010. Recognizing stances in ideological on-line debates. In *Proceedings of the NAACL HLT 2010 Workshop on Computational Approaches to Analysis and Generation of Emotion in Text*, pages 116–124.

Dhanya Sridhar, Lise Getoor, and Marilyn Walker. 2014. Collective stance classification of posts in online debate forums. *Proceedings of the Association for Computational Linguistics*, page 109.

Martin Tutek, Ivan Sekulić, Paula Gombar, Ivan Paljak, Filip Čulinović, Filip Boltužić, Mladen Karan, Domagoj Alagić, and Jan Šnajder. 2016. TakeLab at SemEval-2016 Task 6: Stance Classification in Tweets Using a Genetic Algorithm Based Ensemble. In *Proceedings of the International Workshop on Semantic Evaluation*, SemEval '16, San Diego, California, June.

Wan Wei, Xiao Zhang, Xuqin Liu, Wei Chen, and Tengjiao Wang. 2016. pkudblab at SemEval-2016 Task 6: A Specific Convolutional Neural Network System for Effective Stance Detection. In *Proceedings of the International Workshop on Semantic Evaluation*, SemEval '16, San Diego, California, June.

Theresa Wilson, Janyce Wiebe, and Paul Hoffmann. 2005. Recognizing contextual polarity in phrase-level sentiment analysis. In *Proceedings of the Conference on Human Language Technology and Empirical Methods in Natural Language Processing*, pages 347–354, Vancouver, British Columbia, Canada.

Theresa Wilson, Zornitsa Kozareva, Preslav Nakov, Sara Rosenthal, Veselin Stoyanov, and Alan Ritter. 2013. SemEval-2013 Task 2: Sentiment analysis in Twitter. In *Proceedings of the International Workshop on Semantic Evaluation*, SemEval '13, Atlanta, Georgia, USA, June.

Michael Wojatzki and Torsten Zesch. 2016. ltl.uni-due at SemEval-2016 Task 6: Stance Detection in Social Media Using Stacked Classifiers. In *Proceedings of the International Workshop on Semantic Evaluation*, SemEval '16, San Diego, California, June.

Igarashi Yuki, Komatsu Hiroya, Kobayashi Sosuke, Okazaki Naoaki, and Inui Kentaro. 2016. Tohoku at SemEval-2016 Task 6: Feature-based Model versus Convolutional Neural Network for Stance Detection. In *Proceedings of the International Workshop on Semantic Evaluation*, SemEval '16, San Diego, California, June.

Guido Zarrella and Amy Marsh. 2016. MITRE at SemEval-2016 Task 6: Transfer Learning for Stance Detection. In *Proceedings of the International Workshop on Semantic Evaluation*, SemEval '16, San Diego, California, June.

SemEval-2016 Task 7: Determining Sentiment Intensity
of English and Arabic Phrases

Svetlana Kiritchenko and **Saif M. Mohammad**
National Research Council Canada
svetlana.kiritchenko@nrc-cnrc.gc.ca
saif.mohammad@nrc-cnrc.gc.ca

Mohammad Salameh
University of Alberta
msalameh@ualberta.ca

Abstract

We present a shared task on automatically determining sentiment intensity of a word or a phrase. The words and phrases are taken from three domains: general English, English Twitter, and Arabic Twitter. The phrases include those composed of negators, modals, and degree adverbs as well as phrases formed by words with opposing polarities. For each of the three domains, we assembled the datasets that include multi-word phrases and their constituent words, both manually annotated for real-valued sentiment intensity scores. The three datasets were presented as the test sets for three separate tasks (each focusing on a specific domain). Five teams submitted nine system outputs for the three tasks. All datasets created for this shared task are freely available to the research community.

1 Introduction

Words have prior associations with sentiment. For example, *honest* and *competent* are associated with positive sentiment, whereas *dishonest* and *dull* are associated with negative sentiment. Further, the degree of positivity (or negativity), also referred to as intensity, can vary. For example, most people will agree that *succeed* is more positive (or less negative) than *improve*, and *fail* is more negative (or less positive) than *setback*. We present a shared task where automatic systems are asked to predict a prior sentiment intensity score for a word or a phrase. The words and phrases are taken from three domains: general English, English Twitter, and Arabic Twitter.

For each domain, a separate task with its own development and test sets was set up. The phrases include those composed of negators (e.g., *nothing wrong*), modals (e.g., *might be fun*), and degree adverbs (e.g., *fairly important*) as well as phrases formed by words with opposing polarities (e.g., *lazy sundays*).

Lists of words and their associated sentiment are commonly referred to as *sentiment lexicons*. They are used in sentiment analysis. For example, a number of unsupervised classifiers rely primarily on sentiment lexicons to determine whether a piece of text is positive or negative. Supervised classifiers also often use features drawn from sentiment lexicons (Mohammad et al., 2013; Pontiki et al., 2014). Sentiment lexicons are also beneficial in stance detection (Mohammad et al., 2016a; Mohammad et al., 2016b), literary analysis (Hartner, 2013; Kleres, 2011; Mohammad, 2012), and for detecting personality traits (Minamikawa and Yokoyama, 2011; Mohammad and Kiritchenko, 2015).

Existing manually created sentiment lexicons tend to provide only lists of positive and negative words (Hu and Liu, 2004; Wilson et al., 2005; Mohammad and Turney, 2013). The coarse-grained distinctions may be less useful in downstream applications than having access to fine-grained (real-valued) sentiment association scores. Most of the existing sentiment resources are available only for English. Non-English resources are scarce and often based on automatic translation of the English lexicons (Abdul-Mageed and Diab, 2014; Eskander and Rambow, 2015). Manually created sentiment lexicons usually include only single words. Yet, the sentiment of a phrase can differ markedly from the

Proceedings of SemEval-2016, pages 42–51,
San Diego, California, June 16-17, 2016. ©2016 Association for Computational Linguistics

sentiment of its constituent words. Sentiment composition is the determining of sentiment of a multi-word linguistic unit, such as a phrase or a sentence, from its constituents. Lexicons that include sentiment associations for phrases and their constituents are useful in studying sentiment composition. We refer to them as *sentiment composition lexicons.*

Automatically created lexicons often have real-valued sentiment association scores, have a high coverage, can include longer phrases, and can easily be collected for a specific domain. However, due to the lack of manually annotated real-valued sentiment lexicons the quality of automatic lexicons are often assessed only extrinsically through their use in sentence-level sentiment prediction. In this shared task, we intrinsically evaluate automatic methods that estimate sentiment association scores for terms in English and Arabic. For this, we assembled three datasets of phrases and their constituent single words manually annotated for sentiment with real-valued scores (Kiritchenko and Mohammad, 2016a; Kiritchenko and Mohammad, 2016c).

We first introduced this task as part of the SemEval-2015 Task 10 'Sentiment Analysis in Twitter' Subtask E (Rosenthal et al., 2015). The 2015 test set was restricted to English single words and simple two-word negated expressions commonly found in tweets. This year (2016), we broadened the scope of the task and included three different domains. Furthermore, we shifted the focus from single words to longer, more complex phrases to explore sentiment composition.

Five teams submitted nine system outputs for the three tasks. All submitted outputs correlated strongly with the gold term rankings (Kendall's rank correlation above 0.35). The best results on all tasks were achieved with supervised methods by exploiting a variety of sentiment resources. The highest rank correlation was obtained by team *ECNU* on the General English test set ($\tau = 0.7$). On the other two domains, the results were lower (τ of 0.4-0.5).

All datasets created as part of this shared task are freely available through the task website.[1] For ease of exploration, we also created online interactive visualizations for the two English datasets.[2]

---

[1] http://alt.qcri.org/semeval2016/task7/
[2] http://www.saifmohammad.com/WebPages/SCL.html

2 Task Description

The task is formulated as follows: given a list of terms (single words and multi-word phrases), an automatic system needs to provide a score between 0 and 1 that is indicative of the term's strength of association with positive sentiment. A score of 1 indicates maximum association with positive sentiment (or least association with negative sentiment) and a score of 0 indicates least association with positive sentiment (or maximum association with negative sentiment). If a term is more positive than another, then it should have a higher score than the other.

There are three tasks, one for each of the three domains:

- **General English Sentiment Modifiers Set:** This dataset comprises English single words and multi-word phrases from the general domain. The phrases are formed by combining a word and a modifier, where a modifier is a negator, an auxilary verb, a degree adverb, or a combination of those, for example, *would be very easy*, *did not harm*, and *would have been nice*. The single word terms are chosen from the set of words that are part of the multi-word phrases, for example, *easy*, *harm*, and *nice*.

- **English Twitter Mixed Polarity Set:** This dataset focuses on English phrases made up of opposing polarity terms, for example, phrases such as *lazy sundays*, *best winter break*, *happy accident* and *couldn't stop smiling*. The dataset also includes single word terms (as separate entries). These terms are chosen from the set of words that are part of the multi-word phrases. The multi-word phrases and single-word terms are drawn from a corpus of tweets, and include a small number of hashtag words (e.g., *#wantit*) and creatively spelled words (e.g., *plssss*). However, a majority of the terms are those that one would use in everyday English.

- **Arabic Twitter Set:** This dataset includes single words and phrases commonly found in Arabic tweets. The phrases in this set are formed only by combining a negator and a word.

Teams could participate in any one, two, or all three tasks; however, only one submission was al-

Task	Total	Development set			Test set		
		words	phrases	all	words	phrases	all
General English Sentiment Modifiers	2,999	101	99	200	1,330	1,469	2,799
English Twitter Mixed Polarity	1,269	60	140	200	358	711	1,069
Arabic Twitter	1,366	167	33	200	1,001	165	1,166

Table 1: The number of single-word and multi-word terms in the development and test sets.

lowed per task. For each task, the above description and a development set (200 terms) were provided to the participants in advance; there were no training sets. The three test sets, one for each task, were released at the start of the evaluation period. The test sets and the development sets have no terms in common. The participants were allowed to use the development sets in any way (for example, for tuning or training), and they were allowed to use any additional manually or automatically generated resources.

In 2015, the task was set up similarly (Rosenthal et al., 2015). Single words and multi-word phrases from English Twitter comprised the development and test sets (1,515 terms in total). The phrases were simple two-word negated expressions (e.g., *cant waitttt*). Participants were allowed to use these datasets for the development of their systems.

3 Datasets of English and Arabic Terms Annotated for Sentiment Intensity

The three datasets, General English Sentiment Modifiers Set, English Twitter Mixed Polarity Set, and Arabic Twitter Set, were created through manual annotation using an annotation scheme known as Best–Worst Scaling (described below in Section 3.1). The terms for each set (domain) were chosen as described in Sections 3.2, 3.3, and 3.4, respectively. Note that the exact sources of data and the term selection procedures were not known to the participants. The total number of words and phrases included in each of the datasets can be found in Table 1. Table 2 shows a few example entries from each set.

3.1 Best–Worst Scaling Method of Annotation

Best–Worst Scaling (BWS), also sometimes referred to as Maximum Difference Scaling (MaxDiff), is an annotation scheme that exploits the comparative approach to annotation (Louviere and Woodworth,

Dataset	Sentiment
Term	**score**
General English Sentiment Modifiers Set	
favor	0.826
would be very easy	0.715
did not harm	0.597
increasingly difficult	0.208
severe	0.083
English Twitter Mixed Polarity Set	
best winter break	0.922
breaking free	0.586
isn't long enough	0.406
breaking	0.250
heart breaking moment	0.102
Arabic Twitter Set	
مجد (glory)	0.931
#السعادة_الزوجية# (marital happiness)	0.900
يقين# (certainty)	0.738
لا امكن (not possible)	0.300
ارهاب (terrorism)	0.056

Table 2: Examples of entries with real-valued sentiment scores from the three datasets.

1990; Cohen, 2003; Louviere et al., 2015). Annotators are given four items (4-tuple) and asked which item is the Best (highest in terms of the property of interest) and which is the Worst (least in terms of the property of interest). These annotations can then be easily converted into real-valued scores of association between the items and the property, which eventually allows for creating a ranked list of items as per their association with the property of interest. The Best–Worst Scaling method has been shown to produce reliable annotations of terms for sentiment (Kiritchenko and Mohammad, 2016a).

Given n terms to be annotated, the first step is to randomly sample this set (with replacement) to obtain sets of four terms each, *4-tuples*, that satisfy the following criteria:

1. no two 4-tuples have the same four terms;

2. no two terms within a 4-tuple are identical;

3. each term in the term list appears approximately in the same number of 4-tuples;

4. each pair of terms appears approximately in the same number of 4-tuples.

The terms for the three tasks were annotated separately. For each task, $2 \times n$ 4-tuples were generated, where n is the total number of terms in the task.

Next, the sets of 4-tuples were annotated through a crowdsourcing platform, CrowdFlower. The annotators were presented with four terms at a time, and asked which term is the most positive (or least negative) and which is the most negative (or least positive). Below is an example annotation question.[3] (The Arabic data was annotated through a similar questionnaire in Arabic.)

Focus terms:
1. shameless self promotion   2. happy tears   3. hug
4. major pain

Q1: Identify the term that is associated with the most amount of positive sentiment (or least amount of negative sentiment) – **the most positive term**:
   1. shameless self promotion
   2. happy tears
   3. hug
   4. major pain

Q2: Identify the term that is associated with the most amount of negative sentiment (or least amount of positive sentiment) – **the most negative term**:
   1. shameless self promotion
   2. happy tears
   3. hug
   4. major pain

Each 4-tuple was annotated by at least eight respondents. Let *majority answer* refer to the option most chosen for a question. For all three datasets, at least 80% of the responses matched the majority answer.

The responses were then translated into real-valued scores and also a ranking of terms by sentiment for all the terms through a simple counting procedure: For each term, its score is calculated as the percentage of times the term was chosen as the most positive minus the percentage of times the term was chosen as the most negative (Orme, 2009; Flynn

and Marley, 2014). For this competition, we converted the scores into the range from 0 (the least positive) to 1 (the most positive). The resulting rankings constituted the gold annotations for the three datasets. Finally, random samples of 200 terms from each dataset with the corresponding gold annotations were released to the participants as development sets for the three tasks. The rest of the terms were kept as test sets.

3.2 General English Sentiment Modifiers Dataset

The terms for this dataset were taken from the Sentiment Composition Lexicon for Negators, Modals, and Degree Adverbs (SCL-NMA) (Kiritchenko and Mohammad, 2016b).[4] SCL-NMA includes all 1,621 positive and negative words from Osgood's seminal study on word meaning (Osgood et al., 1957) available in General Inquirer (Stone et al., 1966). In addition, it includes 1,586 high-frequency phrases formed by the Osgood words in combination with simple negators such as *no*, *don't*, and *never*, modals such as *can*, *might*, and *should*, or degree adverbs such as *very* and *fairly*.[5] The eligible adverbs were chosen manually from adverbs that appeared in combination with an Osgood word at least ten times in the British National Corpus (BNC)[6]. Each phrase includes at least one modal, one negator, or one adverb; a phrase can include several modifiers (e.g., *would be very happy*). Sixty-four different (single or multi-word) modifiers were used in the dataset.

For this shared task, we removed terms that were used in the SemEval-2015 dataset. The final SemEval-2016 General English Sentiment Modifiers dataset contains 2,999 terms.

3.3 English Twitter Mixed Polarity Dataset

The terms for this dataset were taken in part from the *Sentiment Composition Lexicon for Opposing Polarity Phrases (SCL-OPP)* (Kiritchenko and Moham-

---

[3]The full sets of instructions for both English and Arabic datasets are available on the shared task website: http://alt.qcri.org/semeval2016/task7/

[4]www.saifmohammad.com/WebPages/SCL.html#NMA

[5]The complete lists of negators, modals, and degree adverbs used in this dataset are available on the task website: http://alt.qcri.org/semeval2016/task7/

[6]The British National Corpus, version 3 (BNC XML Edition). 2007. Distributed by Oxford University Computing Services on behalf of the BNC Consortium. URL: http://www.natcorp.ox.ac.uk/

mad, 2016c).[7] SCL-OPP was created as follows. We polled the Twitter API (from 2013 to 2015) to collect a corpus of tweets that contain emoticons: ':)' or ':('. From this corpus, we selected bigrams and trigrams that had at least one positive word and at least one negative word. The polarity labels (positive or negative) of the words were determined by simple look-up in existing sentiment lexicons: Hu and Liu lexicon (Hu and Liu, 2004), NRC Emotion lexicon (Mohammad and Turney, 2013), MPQA lexicon (Wilson et al., 2005), and NRC's Twitter-specific lexicon (Kiritchenko et al., 2014).[8] Apart from the requirement of having at least one positive and at least one negative word, an n-gram must satisfy the following criteria:

- the n-gram must have a clear meaning on its own, (for example, the n-gram should not start or end with '*or*', '*and*', etc.);

- the n-gram should not include a named entity;

- the n-gram should not include obscene language.

In addition, we ensured that there was a good variety of phrases—for example, even though there were a large number of bigrams of the form *super w*, where *w* is a negative adjective, only a small number of such bigrams were included. Finally, we aimed to achieve a good spread in terms of degree of sentiment association (from very negative terms to very positive terms, and all the degrees of polarity in between). For this, we estimated the sentiment score of each phrase using an automatic PMI-based method described in (Kiritchenko et al., 2014). Then, the full range of sentiment values was divided into 5 bins, and approximately the same number of terms were selected from each bin.[9]

In total, 851 n-grams (bigrams and trigrams) were selected. We also chose for annotation all unigrams that appeared in the selected set of bigrams and trigrams. There were 810 such unigrams.

When selecting the terms, we used sentiment associations obtained from both manual and automatic lexicons. As a result, some unigrams had erroneous sentiment associations. After manually annotating the full set of 1,661 terms (that include unigrams, bigrams, and trigrams), we found that 114 bigrams and 161 trigrams had all their comprising unigrams of the same polarity. These 275 n-grams were discarded from SCL-OPP but are included in this task dataset. Further, for this task we removed terms that were used in the SemEval-2015 dataset or in the General English set. The final SemEval-2016 English Twitter Mixed Polarity dataset contains 1,269 terms.

3.4 Arabic Twitter Dataset

Mohammad et al. (2015) automatically generated three high-coverage sentiment lexicons from Arabic tweets using hashtags and emoticons: Arabic Emoticon Lexicon, Arabic Hashtag Lexicon, and Dialectal Arabic Hashtag Lexicon.[10] In addition to Modern Standard Arabic (MSA), these three lexicons comprise terms in Dialectal Arabic as well as hashtagged compound words, e.g., ‏#السعادة_الزوجية‏ (#MaritalHappiness), which do not usually appear in manually created lexicons. Apart from unigrams, they also include entries for bigrams. From these lexicons, we selected single words as well as bigrams representing negated expressions in the form of '*negator w*', where *negator* is a negation trigger from a list of 16 common Arabic negation words.[11] Words used in negated expressions, but missing from the original list were also included. The selected terms satisfied the following criteria:

- the terms must occur frequently in tweets;

- the terms should not be highly ambiguous.

We also wanted the set of terms as a whole to have these properties:

- the set should have a good spread in terms of degree of sentiment association (from very

---

[7]www.saifmohammad.com/WebPages/SCL.html#OPP

[8]If a word was marked with conflicting polarity in two lexicons, then that word was not considered as positive or negative. For example, the word *defeat* is marked as positive in Hu and Liu lexicon and marked as negative in MPQA; therefore, we did not select any phrases with this word.

[9]Fewer terms were selected from the middle bin that contained phrases with very weak association to sentiment (e.g., phrases like *cancer foundation*, *fair game*, and *a long nap*).

[10]http://saifmohammad.com/WebPages/ArabicSA.html

[11]The complete list of Arabic negators is available on the task website: http://alt.qcri.org/semeval2016/task7/

Team ID	Affiliation
ECNU (Wang et al., 2016)	East China Normal University, China
iLab-Edinburgh (Refaee and Rieser, 2016)	Heriot-Watt University, UK
LSIS (Htait et al., 2016)	Aix-Marseille University, France
NileTMRG (El-Beltagy, 2016a)	Nile University, Egypt
UWB (Lenc et al., 2016)	University of West Bohemia, Czech Republic

Table 3: The participated teams and their affiliations.

negative terms to very positive terms, and all the degrees of polarity in between);

- the set should include both standard and dialectal Arabic, Romanized words, misspellings, hashtags, and other categories frequently used in Twitter. (We chose not to include URLs, user mentions, named entities, and obscene terms.)

The final SemEval-2016 Arabic Twitter dataset contains 1,366 terms.

4 Evaluation

Sentiment association scores are most meaningful when compared to each other; they indicate which term is more positive than the other. Therefore, the automatic systems were evaluated in terms of their abilities to correctly *rank* the terms by the degree of sentiment association.

For each task, the predicted sentiment intensity scores submitted by the participated systems were evaluated by first ranking the terms according to the proposed sentiment scores and then comparing this ranked list to the gold rankings. We used Kendall's rank correlation coefficient (Kendall's τ) as the official evaluation metric to determine the similarity between the ranked lists (Kendall, 1938):

$$\tau = \frac{c - d}{n(n-1)/2}$$

where c is the number of concordant pairs, i.e., pairs of terms w_i and w_j for which both the gold ranked list and the predicted ranked list agree (either both lists rank w_i higher than w_j or both lists rank w_i lower than w_j); d is the number of discordant pairs, i.e., pairs of terms w_i and w_j for which the gold ranked list and the predicted ranked list disagree (one list ranks w_i higher than w_j and the other list ranks w_i lower than w_j); and n is the total number of terms. If any list ranks two terms w_i and w_j the same, this pair of terms is considered neither concordant nor discordant. The values of Kendall's τ range from -1 to 1.

We also calculated scores for Spearman's rank correlation (Spearman, 1904), as an additional (unofficial) metric.

5 Participated Systems

There were nine submissions from five teams—three submissions for each task. The team affiliations are shown in Table 3.

Tables 4 and 5 summarize the approaches and resources used by the participants in the (two) English and (one) Arabic tasks, respectively. Most teams applied supervised approaches and trained regression classifiers using a variety of features. Team *ECNU* treated the task as a rank prediction task instead of regression and trained a pair-wise ranking model with the Random Forest algorithm.

The development data available for each task was used as the training data by some teams. However, these data were limited (200 instances per task); therefore, other manually labeled resources were also explored. One commonly used resource was the LabMT lexicon—a set of over 100,000 frequent single words from 10 languages, including English and Arabic (about 10,000 words in each language), manually annotated for happiness through Mechanical Turk (Dodds et al., 2011; Dodds et al., 2015). For the Arabic task, two teams took advantage of the Arabic Twitter corpus collected by Refaee and Rieser (2014). The features employed include sentiment scores obtained from different sentiment lexicons, general and sentiment-specific word embeddings, pointwise mutual information (PMI) scores between terms (single words and multi-word phrases) and sentiment classes, as well as lists of negators, intensifiers, and diminishers.

Team name	Supervision	Algorithm	Training data	Sentiment lexicons used	External corpora and other resources used
ECNU	supervised	Random Forest	LabMT, dev. data	Hu and Liu, MPQA	1.6M tweets (with emoticons)
LSIS	unsupervised	PMI	-	NRC Emoticon, SentiWordNet, MPQA	10K tweets (with manually annotated sentiment phrases)
UWB	supervised	Gaussian regression	dev. data	AFINN, JRC	pre-trained word2vec embeddings, pre-trained sentiment classifier

Table 4: Summary of the approaches for the two English-language tasks.

Team name	Supervision	Algorithm	Training data	Sentiment lexicons used	External corpora and other resources used
iLab-Edinburgh	supervised	linear regress., manual rules	LabMT, Arabic Twitter corpus	ArabSenti, MPQA, Dialectal Arabic	9K tweets (manually labeled for sentiment)
LSIS	unsupervised	PMI	-	NRC Emotion	12K tweets (manually labeled for sentiment), 63K book reviews (5-star ratings)
NileTMRG	supervised	regression, PMI	dev. data, Arabic Twitter corpus	NileULex	250K tweets (unlabeled), pre-trained sentiment classifier

Table 5: Summary of the approaches for the Arabic-language task.

Only one team, *LSIS*, employed an unsupervised approach to all three tasks. To predict a sentiment intensity score for a term, they used the following three sources: existing sentiment lexicons, PMI scores between terms and sentiment classes computed on sentiment-annotated corpora, and PMI scores between terms and words *poor* and *excellent* computed on Google search results.

All teams heavily relied on existing sentiment lexicons: AFINN (Nielsen, 2011), ArabSenti (Abdul-Mageed et al., 2011), Hu and Liu (Hu and Liu, 2004), Dialectal Arabic Lexicon (Refaee and Rieser, 2014), JRC (Steinberger et al., 2012), MPQA (Wilson et al., 2005), NRC Emoticon (a.k.a. Sentiment140) (Kiritchenko et al., 2014), NRC Emotion (Mohammad and Turney, 2013), NileULex (El-Beltagy, 2016b), and SentiWordNet (Esuli and Sebastiani, 2006). (Note that even though the NRC Emotion Lexicon was created for English terms, its translations in close to 40 languages, including Arabic, are available.[12])

<hr>

[12]http://saifmohammad.com/WebPages/NRC-Emotion-Lexicon.htm

6 Results

The results for the three tasks are presented in Tables 6, 7, and 8. Team *ECNU* showed the best performance in both English-language tasks. In the Arabic task, the best performing system was developed by *iLab-Edinburgh*.

A few observations can be made from the results:

- On all three datasets, the team rankings based on the two metrics, Kendall's τ and Spearman's ρ, are the same.

- For most of the teams, the results obtained on the General English Sentiment Modifiers set are markedly higher than the results obtained on the other datasets.

- The English Twitter Mixed Polarity set proved to be a challenging task for all teams. We have further analyzed regularities present in different kinds of mixed polarity phrases and concluded that for most phrases the sentiment of the phrase cannot be reliably predicted only from the parts of speech and polarities of their

48

Team	Overall		Single words		Multi-word phrases	
	Kendall's τ	Spearman's ρ	Kendall's τ	Spearman's ρ	Kendall's τ	Spearman's ρ
ECNU	**0.704**	0.863	0.734	0.884	0.686	0.845
UWB	0.659	0.854	0.644	0.846	0.657	0.849
LSIS	0.350	0.508	0.421	0.599	0.324	0.462

Table 6: Results for **General English Sentiment Modifiers** test set. The systems are ordered by their overall Kendall's τ score, which was the official competition metric. The highest score is shown in bold.

Team	Overall		Single words		Multi-word phrases	
	Kendall's τ	Spearman's ρ	Kendall's τ	Spearman's ρ	Kendall's τ	Spearman's ρ
ECNU	**0.523**	0.674	0.601	0.747	0.494	0.646
LSIS	0.422	0.591	0.384	0.543	0.423	0.593
UWB	0.414	0.578	0.564	0.752	0.366	0.524

Table 7: Results for **English Twitter Mixed Polarity** test set. The systems are ordered by their overall Kendall's τ score, which was the official competition metric. The highest score is shown in bold.

Team	Overall		Single words		Multi-word phrases	
	Kendall's τ	Spearman's ρ	Kendall's τ	Spearman's ρ	Kendall's τ	Spearman's ρ
iLab-Edinburgh	**0.536**	0.680	0.592	0.739	-0.046	-0.069
NileTMRG	0.475	0.658	0.510	0.701	0.078	0.118
LSIS	0.424	0.583	0.478	0.646	0.059	0.088

Table 8: Results for **Arabic Twitter** test set. The systems are ordered by their overall Kendall's τ score, which was the official competition metric. The highest score is shown in bold.

constituent words (Kiritchenko and Moham-mad, 2016d). For example, a positive adjective and a negative noun can form either a positive phrase (e.g., *happy tears*) or a negative phrase (e.g., *great loss*).

- The results achieved on the Arabic Twitter test set are substantially lower than the results achieved on a similar English Twitter data used in the 2015 competition.

- For most teams, the results obtained on single words are noticeably higher than the corresponding results on multi-word phrases. This is especially apparent on the Arabic Twitter data. The possible reason for this outcome is the lack of sufficient training data for phrases; none of the existing manually created English or Arabic real-valued sentiment lexicons provide annotations for multi-word phrases.

Overall, we observe strong correlations between the predicted and gold term rankings for terms in the general English domain as well as for single words in the other two domains. However, for multi-word phrases in the English Mixed Polarity set and Ara-bic Twitter set the correlations are markedly weaker, especially for the Arabic language. We hope that the availability of these datasets will foster further research towards automatic methods for sentiment composition in English and other languages.

7 Conclusions

We have created three sentiment composition lexicons that provide real-valued sentiment association scores for multi-word phrases and their constituent single words in three domains: the General English Sentiment Modifiers Set, the English Twitter Mixed Polarity Set, and the Arabic Twitter Set. The terms were annotated manually using the Best–Worst Scaling method of annotation. We included phrases composed of negators, modals, and degree adverbs—categories known to be challenging for sentiment analysis. Furthermore, we included phrases formed by words with opposing polarities. As future work, we would like to extend the task to cover more domains (e.g., biomedical, legal) and more languages. All datasets are freely available to the research community.

References

Muhammad Abdul-Mageed and Mona Diab. 2014. SANA: A large scale multi-genre, multi-dialect lexicon for Arabic subjectivity and sentiment analysis. In *Proceedings of the Language Resources and Evaluation Conference (LREC)*.

Muhammad Abdul-Mageed, Mona T. Diab, and Mohammed Korayem. 2011. Subjectivity and sentiment analysis of Modern Standard Arabic. In *Proceedings of the 49th Annual Meeting of the Association for Computational Linguistics (ACL)*, pages 587–591.

Steven H. Cohen. 2003. Maximum difference scaling: Improved measures of importance and preference for segmentation. Sawtooth Software, Inc.

Peter Sheridan Dodds, Kameron Decker Harris, Isabel M. Kloumann, Catherine A. Bliss, and Christopher M. Danforth. 2011. Temporal patterns of happiness and information in a global social network: Hedonometrics and Twitter. *PloS One*, 6(12):e26752.

Peter Sheridan Dodds, Eric M. Clark, Suma Desu, Morgan R. Frank, Andrew J. Reagan, Jake Ryland Williams, Lewis Mitchell, Kameron Decker Harris, Isabel M. Kloumann, James P. Bagrow, et al. 2015. Human language reveals a universal positivity bias. *Proceedings of the National Academy of Sciences*, 112(8):2389–2394.

Samhaa R. El-Beltagy. 2016a. NileTMGR at SemEval-2016 Task 7: Deriving prior polarities for Arabic sentiment terms. In *Proceedings of the International Workshop on Semantic Evaluation (SemEval)*.

Samhaa R. El-Beltagy. 2016b. NileULex: A phrase and word level sentiment lexicon for Egyptian and Modern Standard Arabic. In *Proceedings of the International Conference on Language Resources and Evaluation (LREC)*.

Ramy Eskander and Owen Rambow. 2015. SLSA: A sentiment lexicon for Standard Arabic. In *Proceedings of the 2015 Conference on Empirical Methods in Natural Language Processing (EMNLP)*, pages 2545–2550, Lisbon, Portugal.

Andrea Esuli and Fabrizio Sebastiani. 2006. SENTI-WORDNET: A publicly available lexical resource for opinion mining. In *Proceedings of the 5th Conference on Language Resources and Evaluation (LREC)*, pages 417–422.

T. N. Flynn and A. A. J. Marley. 2014. Best-worst scaling: theory and methods. In Stephane Hess and Andrew Daly, editors, *Handbook of Choice Modelling*, pages 178–201. Edward Elgar Publishing.

Marcus Hartner. 2013. The lingering after-effects in the reader's mind – an investigation into the affective dimension of literary reading. *Journal of Literary Theory Online*.

Amal Htait, Sebastien Fournier, and Patrice Bellot. 2016. LSIS at SemEval-2016 Task 7: Using web search engines for English and Arabic unsupervised sentiment intensity prediction. In *Proceedings of the International Workshop on Semantic Evaluation (SemEval)*.

Minqing Hu and Bing Liu. 2004. Mining and summarizing customer reviews. In *Proceedings of the 10th ACM SIGKDD International Conference on Knowledge Discovery and Data Mining (KDD)*, pages 168–177, New York, NY, USA.

Maurice G. Kendall. 1938. A new measure of rank correlation. *Biometrika*, pages 81–93.

Svetlana Kiritchenko and Saif M. Mohammad. 2016a. Capturing reliable fine-grained sentiment associations by crowdsourcing and best–worst scaling. In *Proceedings of The 15th Annual Conference of the North American Chapter of the Association for Computational Linguistics: Human Language Technologies (NAACL)*, San Diego, California.

Svetlana Kiritchenko and Saif M. Mohammad. 2016b. The effect of negators, modals, and degree adverbs on sentiment composition. In *Proceedings of the Workshop on Computational Approaches to Subjectivity, Sentiment and Social Media Analysis (WASSA)*.

Svetlana Kiritchenko and Saif M. Mohammad. 2016c. Happy accident: A sentiment composition lexicon for opposing polarity phrases. In *Proceedings of the International Conference on Language Resources and Evaluation (LREC)*.

Svetlana Kiritchenko and Saif M. Mohammad. 2016d. Sentiment composition of words with opposing polarities. In *Proceedings of The 15th Annual Conference of the North American Chapter of the Association for Computational Linguistics: Human Language Technologies (NAACL)*, San Diego, California.

Svetlana Kiritchenko, Xiaodan Zhu, and Saif M. Mohammad. 2014. Sentiment analysis of short informal texts. *Journal of Artificial Intelligence Research*, 50:723–762.

Jochen Kleres. 2011. Emotions and narrative analysis: A methodological approach. *Journal for the Theory of Social Behaviour*, 41(2):182–202.

Ladislav Lenc, Pavel Krl, and Vclav Rajtmajer. 2016. UWB at SemEval-2016 Task 7 : Novel method for automatic sentiment intensity determination. In *Proceedings of the International Workshop on Semantic Evaluation (SemEval)*.

Jordan J. Louviere and George G. Woodworth. 1990. Best-worst analysis. Working Paper. Department of Marketing and Economic Analysis, University of Alberta.

Jordan J. Louviere, Terry N. Flynn, and A. A. J. Marley. 2015. *Best-Worst Scaling: Theory, Methods and Applications*. Cambridge University Press.

Atsunori Minamikawa and Hiroyuki Yokoyama. 2011. Personality estimation based on weblog text classification. In *Modern Approaches in Applied Intelligence*, pages 89–97. Springer.

Saif M. Mohammad and Svetlana Kiritchenko. 2015. Using hashtags to capture fine emotion categories from tweets. *Computational Intelligence*, 31(2):301–326.

Saif M. Mohammad and Peter D. Turney. 2013. Crowdsourcing a word–emotion association lexicon. *Computational Intelligence*, 29(3):436–465.

Saif M. Mohammad, Svetlana Kiritchenko, and Xiaodan Zhu. 2013. NRC-Canada: Building the state-of-the-art in sentiment analysis of tweets. In *Proceedings of the International Workshop on Semantic Evaluation (SemEval)*, Atlanta, Georgia, USA, June.

Saif M Mohammad, Mohammad Salameh, and Svetlana Kiritchenko. 2015. How translation alters sentiment. *Journal of Artificial Intelligence Research*, 55:95–130.

Saif M. Mohammad, Svetlana Kiritchenko, Parinaz Sobhani, Xiaodan Zhu, and Colin Cherry. 2016a. A dataset for detecting stance in tweets. In *Proceedings of 10th edition of the the Language Resources and Evaluation Conference (LREC)*, Portorož, Slovenia.

Saif M. Mohammad, Parinaz Sobhani, and Svetlana Kiritchenko. 2016b. Stance and sentiment in tweets. *Special Section of the ACM Transactions on Internet Technology on Argumentation in Social Media*, Submitted.

Saif M Mohammad. 2012. From once upon a time to happily ever after: Tracking emotions in mail and books. *Decision Support Systems*, 53(4):730–741.

Finn Årup Nielsen. 2011. A new ANEW: Evaluation of a word list for sentiment analysis in microblogs. In *Proceedings of the ESWC-2011 Workshop on 'Making Sense of Microposts': Big things come in small packages*, pages 93–98.

Bryan Orme. 2009. Maxdiff analysis: Simple counting, individual-level logit, and HB. Sawtooth Software, Inc.

Charles E Osgood, George J Suci, and Percy Tannenbaum. 1957. *The measurement of meaning*. University of Illinois Press.

Maria Pontiki, Harris Papageorgiou, Dimitrios Galanis, Ion Androutsopoulos, John Pavlopoulos, and Suresh Manandhar. 2014. SemEval-2014 Task 4: Aspect based sentiment analysis. In *Proceedings of the 8th International Workshop on Semantic Evaluation (SemEval)*, Dublin, Ireland.

Eshrag Refaee and Verena Rieser. 2014. An Arabic Twitter corpus for subjectivity and sentiment analysis. In *Proceedings of the 9th International Conference on Language Resources and Evaluation (LREC)*.

Eshrag Refaee and Verena Rieser. 2016. iLab-Edinburgh at SemEval-2016 Task 7: A hybrid approach for determining sentiment intensity of Arabic Twitter phrases.

In *Proceedings of the International Workshop on Semantic Evaluation (SemEval)*.

Sara Rosenthal, Preslav Nakov, Svetlana Kiritchenko, Saif Mohammad, Alan Ritter, and Veselin Stoyanov. 2015. SemEval-2015 Task 10: Sentiment analysis in Twitter. In *Proceedings of the 9th International Workshop on Semantic Evaluation (SemEval)*, pages 450–462, Denver, Colorado.

Charles Spearman. 1904. The proof and measurement of association between two things. *The American Journal of Psychology*, 15(1):72–101.

Josef Steinberger, Mohamed Ebrahim, Maud Ehrmann, Ali Hurriyetoglu, Mijail Kabadjov, Polina Lenkova, Ralf Steinberger, Hristo Tanev, Silvia Vázquez, and Vanni Zavarella. 2012. Creating sentiment dictionaries via triangulation. *Decision Support Systems*, 53(4):689–694.

Philip Stone, Dexter C. Dunphy, Marshall S. Smith, Daniel M. Ogilvie, and associates. 1966. *The General Inquirer: A Computer Approach to Content Analysis*. The MIT Press.

Feixiang Wang, Zhihua Zhang, and Man Lan. 2016. ECNU at SemEval-2016 Task 7: An enhanced supervised learning method for lexicon sentiment intensity ranking. In *Proceedings of the International Workshop on Semantic Evaluation (SemEval)*.

Theresa Wilson, Janyce Wiebe, and Paul Hoffmann. 2005. Recognizing contextual polarity in phrase-level sentiment analysis. In *Proceedings of the Conference on Human Language Technology and Empirical Methods in Natural Language Processing*, pages 347–354, Stroudsburg, PA, USA.

CUFE at SemEval-2016 Task 4: A Gated Recurrent Model for Sentiment Classification

Mahmoud Nabil[1], Mohamed Aly[2] and Amir F. Atiya[3]

[1,2,3]Computer Engineering, Cairo University, Egypt
[2]Visual Computing Center, KAUST, KSA
[1]*mah.nabil@cu.edu.eg*
[2]*mohamed@mohamedaly.info*
[3]*amir@alumni.caltech.edu*

Abstract

In this paper we describe a deep learning system that has been built for SemEval 2016 Task4 (Subtask A and B). In this work we trained a Gated Recurrent Unit (GRU) neural network model on top of two sets of word embeddings: (a) general word embeddings generated from unsupervised neural language model; and (b) task specific word embeddings generated from supervised neural language model that was trained to classify tweets into positive and negative categories. We also added a method for analyzing and splitting multi-words hashtags and appending them to the tweet body before feeding it to our model. Our models achieved 0.58 F1-measure for Subtask A (ranked 12/34) and 0.679 Recall for Subtask B (ranked 12/19).

1 Introduction

Twitter is a huge microbloging service with more than 500 million tweets per day[1] from different locations in the world and in different languages. This large, continuous, and dynamically updated content is considered a valuable resource for researchers. However many issues should be taken into account while dealing with tweets, namely: (1) informal language used by the users; (2) spelling errors; (3) text in the tweet may be referring to images, videos, or external URLs; (4) emoticons; (5) hashtags used (combining more than one word as a single word); (6) usernames used to call or notify other users; (7) spam or irrelevant tweets; and (8) character limit for a tweet to 140 characters. This poses many challenges when analyzing tweets for natural language processing tasks. In this paper we describe our system used for SemEval 2016 (Nakov et al., 2016b) Subtasks A and B. Subtask A (Message Polarity Classification) requires classifying a tweet's sentiment as positive; negative; or neutral,. Subtask B (Tweet classification according to a two-point scale) requires classifying a tweet's sentiment given a topic as positive or negative. Our system uses a GRU neural network model (Bahdanau et al., 2014) with one hidden layer on top of two sets of word embeddings that are slightly fine-tuned on each training set (see Fig. 1). The first set of word embeddings is considered as general purpose embeddings and was obtained by training *word2vec* (Mikolov et al., 2013) on 20.5 million tweets that we crawled for this purpose. The second set of word embeddings is considered as task specific set, and was obtained by training on a supervised sentiment analysis dataset using another GRU model. We also added a method for analyzing multi-words hashtags by splitting them and appending them to the body of the tweet before feeding it to the GRU model. In our experiments we tried both keeping the word embeddings static during the training or fine-tuning them and reported the result for each experiment. We achieved 0.58 F1-measure for Subtask A (ranked 12/34) and 0.679 Recall for Subtask B (ranked 12/19).

2 Related Work

A considerable amount of research has been done to address the problem of sentiment analysis for

---

[1]`http://internetlivestats.com/`
`twitter-statistics/`

Proceedings of SemEval-2016, pages 52–57,
San Diego, California, June 16-17, 2016. ©2016 Association for Computational Linguistics

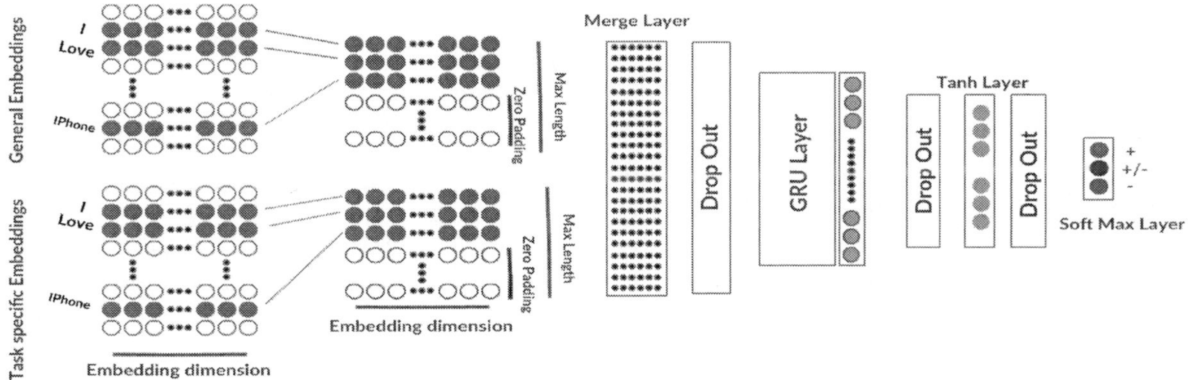

Figure 1: The architecture of the GRU deep Learning model

social content. Nevertheless, most of the state-of-the-art systems still extensively depends on feature engineering, hand coded features, and linguistic resources. Recently, deep learning model gained much attention in sentence text classification inspired from computer vision and speech recognition tasks. Indeed, two of the top four performing systems from SemEval 2015 used deep learning models. (Severyn and Moschitti, 2015) used a Convolution Neural Network (CNN) on top of skip-gram model word embeddings trained on 50 million unsupervised tweets. In (Astudillo et al., 2015) the author built a model that uses skip-gram word embeddings trained on 52 million unsupervised tweets then they project these embeddings into a small subspace, finally they used a non-linear model that maps the embedding subspace to the classification space. In (Kim, 2014) the author presented a series of CNN experiments for sentence classification where static and fine-tuned word embeddings were used. Also the author proposed an architecture modification that allow the use of both task-specific and static vectors. In (Lai et al., 2015) the author proposed a recurrent convolutional neural network for text classification. Finally regarding feature engineering methods, (Büchner and Stein, 2015) the top performing team in SemEval 2015, used an ensemble learning approach that averages the confidence scores of four classifiers. The model uses a large set of linguistic resources and hand coded features.

3 System Description

Fig 1 shows the architecture of our deep learning model. The core of our network is a GRU layer, which we chose because (1) it is more computational efficient than Convolutional Neural Network (CNN) models (Lai et al., 2015) that we experimented with but were much slower; (2) it can capture long semantic patterns without tuning the model parameter, unlike CNN models where the model depends on the length of the convolutional feature maps for capturing long patterns; (3) it achieved superior performance to CNNs in our experiments.

Our network architecture is composed of a word embeddings layer, a merge layer, dropout layers, a GRU layer, a hyperbolic tangent *tanh* layer, and a soft-max classification layer. In the following we give a brief description of the main components of the architecture.

3.1 Embedding Layer

This is the first layer in the network where each tweet is treated as a sequence of words $w_1, w_2...w_S$ of length S, where S is the maximum tweet length. We set S to 40 as the length of any tweet is limited to 140 character. We used zero padding while dealing with short tweets. Each word w_i is represented by two embedding vectors $w_{i_1}, w_{i_2} \in R^d$ where d is the embedding dimension, and according to (Astudillo et al., 2015) setting d to 200 is a good choice with respect to the performance and the computation efficiency. w_{i_1} is considered a general-purpose embedding vector while w_{i_2} is considered a task-specific embedding vector. We performed the following steps to initialize both types of word embeddings:

1. For the general word embeddings we collected about 40M tweets using twitter streaming API over a period of two month (Dec. 2015 and Jan. 2016). We used three criteria while collecting the tweets: (a) they contain at least one emoticon in a set of happy and sad emoticons like ':)' ,':(', ':D' ... etc. (Go et al., 2009); (b) hash tags collected from SemEval 2016 data set; (c) hash tags collected from SemEval 2013 data set. After preparing the tweets as described in Section 4 and removing retweets we ended up with about 19 million tweet. We also appended 1.5 million tweets from *Sentiment140* (Go et al., 2009) corpus after preparation so we end up with about 20.5 million tweet. To train the general embeddings we used *word2vec* (Mikolov et al., 2013) neural language model skipgram model with window size 5, negative sampling and filtered out words with frequency less than 5.

2. For the task specific word embeddings we used semi-supervised 1.5 million tweets from *sentiment140* corpus, where each tweet is tagged either positive or negative according to the tweet's sentiment . Then we applied another GRU model similar to Fig 1 with a modification to the soft-max layer for the purpose of the two classes classification and with random initialized embeddings that are fine-tuned during the training. We used the resulting fine-tuned embeddings as task-specific since they contain contextual semantic meaning from the training process.

3.2 Merge Layer

The purpose of this layer is to concatenate the two types of word embeddings used in the previous layer in order to form a sequence of length $2S$ that can be used in the following GRU layer.

3.3 Dropout Layers

The purpose of this layer is to prevent the previous layer from overfitting (Srivastava et al., 2014) where some units are randomly dropped during training so the regularization of these units is improved.

3.4 GRU Layer

This is the core layer in our model which takes an input sequence of length $2S$ words each having dimension d (i.e. input dimension is $2Sd$) . The gated recurrent network proposed in (Bahdanau et al., 2014) is a recurrent neural network (a neural network with feedback connection, see (Atiya and Parlos, 2000)) where the activation h_t^j of the neural unit j at time t is a linear interpolation between the previous activation h_{t-1}^j at time $t-1$ and the candidate activation $\tilde{h}_t^j$ (Chung et al., 2014):

$$h_t^j = (1-z_t^j)h_{t-1}^j + z_t^j \tilde{h}_t^j$$

where z_t^j is the *update gate* that determines how much the unit updates its content, and $\tilde{h}_t^j$ is the newly computed candidate state.

3.5 Tanh Layer

The purpose of this layer is to allow the neural network to make complex decisions by learning non-linear classification boundaries. Although the *tanh* function takes more training time than the Rectified Linear Units (ReLU), *tanh* gives more accurate results in our experiments.

3.6 Soft-Max Layer

This is last layer in our network where the output of the tanh layer is fed to a fully connected soft-max layer. This layer calculates the classes probability distribution.

$$P(y = c \,|\, x, b) = \frac{\exp\left(w_c^T x + b_c\right)}{\sum_{k=1}^{K} \exp\left(w_k^T x + b_k\right)}$$

where c is the target class, x is the output from the previous layer, w_k and b_k are the weight and the bias of class k, and K is the total number of classes. The difference between the architecture used for Subtask A and Subtask B is in this layer, where for Subtask A three neurons were used (i.e. $K = 3$) while for Subtask B only two neurons were used (i.e. $K = 2$).

4 Data Preparation

All the data used either for training the word embeddings or for training the sentiment classification model undergoes the following preprocessing steps:

Pattern	Examples	Normalization
Usernames	@user1, @user2	_UserName_
Happy emotions	:), :-), :=)	:)
Sad emotions	:(, :-(, :=(	:(
Laugh emotions	:D, :-D, :=D	:D
Kiss emotions	:-*, :*, :-)*	_KISS_
Surprise emotions	:O, :-o	:o
Tongue emotions	:P, :p	:p
Numbers	123	_NUM_
URLs	www.google.com	_URL_
Topic (Subtask B only)	Microsoft	_Entity_

Table 1: Normalization Patterns

1. Using NLTK twitter tokenizer[2] to tokenize each tweet.

2. Using hand-coded tokenization regex to split the following suffixes: 's, 've, 't , 're, 'd, 'll.

3. Using the patterns described in Table 1 to normalize each tweet.

4. Adding `_StartToken_` and `_EndToken_` at the beginning and the ending of each tweet.

5. Splitting multi-word hashtags as explained below.

Consider the following tweet *"Thinking of reverting back to 8.1 or 7. #Windows10Fail"*. The sentiment of the tweet is clearly negative and the simplest way to give the correct tag is by looking at the word "Fail" in the hashtag "#Windows10Fail". For this reason we added a depth first search dictionary method in order to infer the location of spaces inside each hashtag in the tweet and append the result tokens to the tweet's end. We used 125k words dictionary[3] collected from Wikipedia. In the given example, we first lower the hashtag case, remove numbers and underscores from the hashtag then we apply our method to split the hashtag this results in two tokens "windows" and "fail". Hence, we append these two tokens to the end of the tweet and the normal preparation steps continue. After the preparation the tweet will look like *"_StartToken_ Thinking of reverting back to _NUM_ or _NUM_ #Windows10Fail. windows fail _EndToken_"*.

Dataset	all	pos.	neg.	neut.
train-A	12886	5651	1967	5268
dev-A	3222	1395	462	1365
train-B	6324	5059	1265	-
dev-B	1265	1059	206	-

Table 2: Tweets distribution for Subtask A and B

Dataset	Subtask A	Subtask B
GRU-static	0.635	0.826
GRU-fine-tuned	0.639	0.829
GRU-fine-tuned + Split Hashtag	**0.642**	**0.830**

Table 3: Development results for Subtask A and B. **Note**: average F1-mesure for positive and negative classes is used for Subtask A, while the average recall is used for Subtask B.

5 Experiments

In order to train and test our model for Subtask A, we used the dataset provided for SemEval-2016 Task 4 and SemEval-2013 Task 2. We obtained 8,978 from the first dataset and 7,130 from the second, the remaining tweets were not available. So, we ended up with a dataset of 16,108 tweets. Regarding Subtask B we obtained 6,324 from SemEval-2016 provided dataset. We partitioned both datasets into train and development portions of ratio 8:2. Table 2 shows the distribution of tweets for both Subtasks.

For optimizing our network weights we used Adam (Kingma and Ba, 2014), a new and computationally efficient stochastic optimization method. All the experiments have been developed using Keras[4] deep learning library with Theano[5] backend and with CUDA enabled. The model was trained using the default parameters for Adam optimizer, and we tried either to keep the weights of embedding layer static or slightly fine-tune them by using a dropout probability equal to 0.9. Table 3 shows our results on the development part of the data set for Subtask A and B where we report the official performance measure for both subtasks (Nakov et al., 2016a). From 3 the results it is shown that fine-tuning word embeddings with hashtags splitting gives the best results on the development set. All our experiments were performed on a machine with Intel Core i7-4770 CPU @ 3.40GHz (8 cores), 16GB

Dataset	Baseline	F-measure (Old)	F-measure (New)
Tweet-2013	0.292	0.642	0.665
SMS-2013	0.190	0.596	0.665
Tweet-2014	0.346	0.662	0.676
Tweet-sarcasm	0.277	0.466	0.477
Live-Journal	0.272	0.697	0.631
Tweet-2015	0.303	0.598	0.624
Tweet-2016	0.255	0.580	0.608

Table 4: Results for Subtask A on different SemEval datasets.

Dataset	Baseline	Recall (Old)	Recall (New)
Tweet-2016	0.389	0.679	0.767

Table 5: Result for Subtask B on SemEval 2016 dataset.

of RAM and GeForce GT 640 GPU. Table 4 shows our individual results on different SemEval datasets. Table 5 shows our results for Subtask B. From the results and our rank in both Subtasks, we noticed that our system was not satisfactory compared to other teams this was due to the following reasons:

1. We used the development set to validate our model in order to find the best learning parameters, However we mistakenly used the learning accuracy to find the optimal learning parameters especially the number of the training epochs. This significantly affected our rank based on the official performance measure. Table 4 and Table 5 show the old and the new results after fixing this bug.

2. Most of the participating teams in this year competition used deep learning models and they used huge datasets (more than 50M tweets) to train and refine word embeddings according to the emotions of the tweet. However, we only used 1.5M from *sentiment140* corpus to generate task-specific embeddings.

3. The model used for generating the task-specific embeddings for Subtask A should be trained on three classes not only two (positive, negative, and neutral) where if the tweet contains positive emotions like ":)" should be positive, if it contains negative emotions like ":(" should be negative, and if it contains both or none it should be neutral.

6   Conclusion

In this paper, we presented our deep learning model used for SemEval2016 Task4 (Subtasks A and B).

The model uses a gated recurrent layer as a core layer on top of two types of word embeddings (general-purpose and task-specific). Also we described our steps in generating both types word embeddings and how we prepared the dataset used especially when dealing with multi-words hashtags. The system ranked 12th on Subtask A and 12th for Subtask B.

Acknowledgments

This work has been funded by ITIDA's ITAC project number CFP65.

References

Ramon F Astudillo, Silvio Amir, Wang Ling, Bruno Martins, Mário Silva, Isabel Trancoso, and Rua Alves Redol. 2015. Inesc-id: Sentiment analysis without hand-coded features or liguistic resources using embedding subspaces. *SemEval-2015*, page 652.

Amir F Atiya and Alexander G Parlos. 2000. New results on recurrent network training: unifying the algorithms and accelerating convergence. *Neural Networks, IEEE Transactions on*, 11(3):697–709.

Dzmitry Bahdanau, Kyunghyun Cho, and Yoshua Bengio. 2014. Neural machine translation by jointly learning to align and translate. *arXiv preprint arXiv:1409.0473*.

Matthias Hagen Martin Potthast Michel Büchner and Benno Stein. 2015. Webis: An ensemble for twitter sentiment detection. *SemEval-2015*, page 582.

Junyoung Chung, Caglar Gulcehre, KyungHyun Cho, and Yoshua Bengio. 2014. Empirical evaluation of gated recurrent neural networks on sequence modeling. *arXiv preprint arXiv:1412.3555*.

Alec Go, Richa Bhayani, and Lei Huang. 2009. Twitter sentiment classification using distant supervision. *CS224N Project Report, Stanford*, 1:12.

Yoon Kim. 2014. Convolutional neural networks for sentence classification. *arXiv preprint arXiv:1408.5882*.

Diederik Kingma and Jimmy Ba. 2014. Adam: A method for stochastic optimization. *arXiv preprint arXiv:1412.6980*.

Siwei Lai, Liheng Xu, Kang Liu, and Jun Zhao. 2015. Recurrent convolutional neural networks for text classification. In *AAAI*, pages 2267–2273.

Tomas Mikolov, Kai Chen, Greg Corrado, and Jeffrey Dean. 2013. Efficient estimation of word representations in vector space. *arXiv preprint arXiv:1301.3781*.

Preslav Nakov, Alan Ritter, Sara Rosenthal, Fabrizio Sebastiani, and Veselin Stoyanov. 2016a. Evaluation
measures for the semeval-2016 task 4 sentiment analysis in twitter (draft: Version 1.1).

Preslav Nakov, Alan Ritter, Sara Rosenthal, Veselin Stoyanov, and Fabrizio Sebastiani. 2016b. SemEval-2016
task 4: Sentiment analysis in Twitter. In *Proceedings
of the 10th International Workshop on Semantic Evaluation (SemEval 2016)*, San Diego, California, June.
Association for Computational Linguistics.

Aliaksei Severyn and Alessandro Moschitti. 2015.
Unitn: Training deep convolutional neural network for
twitter sentiment classification. In *Proceedings of the
9th International Workshop on Semantic Evaluation
(SemEval 2015), Association for Computational Linguistics, Denver, Colorado*, pages 464–469.

Nitish Srivastava, Geoffrey Hinton, Alex Krizhevsky,
Ilya Sutskever, and Ruslan Salakhutdinov. 2014.
Dropout: A simple way to prevent neural networks
from overfitting. *The Journal of Machine Learning
Research*, 15(1):1929–1958.

QCRI at SemEval-2016 Task 4:
Probabilistic Methods for Binary and Ordinal Quantification

Giovanni Da San Martino, Wei Gao, Fabrizio Sebastiani[*]
Qatar Computing Research Institute
Hamad bin Khalifa University
PO Box 5825, Doha, Qatar
Email: {gmartino,wgao,fsebastiani}@qf.org.qa

Abstract

We describe the systems we have used for participating in Subtasks D (binary quantification) and E (ordinal quantification) of SemEval-2016 Task 4 "Sentiment Analysis in Twitter". The binary quantification system uses a "Probabilistic Classify and Count" (PCC) approach that leverages the calibrated probabilities obtained from the output of an SVM. The ordinal quantification approach uses an ordinal tree of PCC binary quantifiers, where the tree is generated via a splitting criterion that minimizes the ordinal quantification loss.

1 Introduction

This document describes the systems we have used for participating in Subtasks D (binary quantification) and E (ordinal quantification) of SemEval-2016 Task 4 "Sentiment Analysis in Twitter". In the runs we have submitted no training data was used other than the officially provided ones (indeed, the only "external" data used were the sentiment lexicons mentioned in Section 2).

Like a classification system, a system for performing quantification consists of two main components: (i) an algorithm for converting the objects of interest (tweets, in our case) into vectorial representations that can be interpreted both by the learning algorithm and, once it has been trained, by the quantifier itself, and (ii) an algorithm for training quantifiers from vectorial representations of training ob-

jects. Section 2 will be devoted to discussing component (i), while Sections 3 and 4 will be devoted to discussing the two learning algorithms we have deployed for the two tasks.

2 Features for detecting tweet sentiment

As in (Gao and Sebastiani, 2015; Gao and Sebastiani, 2016), for building vectorial representations of tweets we have followed the approach discussed in (Kiritchenko et al., 2014, Section 5.2.1), since the representations presented therein are those used in the systems that performed best at both the SemEval 2013 (Mohammad et al., 2013) and SemEval 2014 (Zhu et al., 2014) tweet sentiment classification shared tasks.

The text is preprocessed by normalizing URLs and mentions of users to the constants `http://someurl` and `@someuser`, resp., after which tokenisation and POS tagging is performed. The binary features used (i.e., features denoting presence or absence in the tweet) include word n-grams, for $n \in \{1, 2, 3, 4\}$, and character n-grams, for $n \in \{3, 4, 5\}$, whether the last token contains an exclamation and/or a question mark, whether the last token is a positive or a negative emoticon and, for each of the 1000 word clusters produced with the CMU Twitter NLP tool[1], whether any token from the cluster is present. Integer-valued features include the number of all-caps tokens, the number of tokens for each POS tag, the number of hashtags, the number of negated contexts, the number of sequences of exclamation and/or question marks, and the number of elongated words (e.g., `coooooool`).

---

[*]Fabrizio Sebastiani is currently on leave from Consiglio Nazionale delle Ricerche, Italy.

[1]`http://www.ark.cs.cmu.edu/TweetNLP/`

Proceedings of SemEval-2016, pages 58–63,
San Diego, California, June 16-17, 2016. ©2016 Association for Computational Linguistics

A key addition to the above is represented by features derived from both automatically generated and manually generated sentiment lexicons; for these features, we use the same sentiment lexicons as used in (Kiritchenko et al., 2014), which are all publicly available. We omit further details concerning our vectorial representations (and, in particular, how the sentiment lexicons contribute to them), both for brevity reasons and because these vectorial representations are not the central focus of this paper; the interested reader is invited to consult (Kiritchenko et al., 2014, Section 5.2.1) for details.

3 Subtask D: Tweet quantification according to a two-point scale

For the binary quantification task, we have performed a thorough set of preliminary experiments using 8 quantification methods from the literature, i.e., Classify and Count (CC), Probabilistic Classify and Count (PCC) (Bella et al., 2010), Adjusted Classify and Count (ACC) (Gart and Buck, 1966), Probabilistic Adjusted Classify and Count (PACC) (Bella et al., 2010), Expectation Maximization for Quantification (EMQ) (Saerens et al., 2002), SVMs optimized for KLD (SVM(KLD)) (Esuli and Sebastiani, 2015), SVMs optimized for $NKLD$ (SVM(NKLD)) (Esuli and Sebastiani, 2014), and SVMs optimized for Q (SVM(Q)) (Barranquero et al., 2015).

All 8 methods are described in detail in (Gao and Sebastiani, 2016), where we test them on a ternary[2] tweet sentiment quantification task using 11 datasets and 6 evaluation measures. The aim of (Gao and Sebastiani, 2016) was to test whether the conclusions drawn from a previous experiment (Esuli and Sebastiani, 2015), where quantification was according to topic and where texts were significantly longer than tweets, were confirmed also in a context in which quantification is according to sentiment and the items are significantly shorter.

The preliminary experiments we performed for the present work were carried out by training our models on TRAIN+DEV and testing on DEVTEST. For the first 5 methods mentioned at the beginning of this section we make use of a standard SVM with a linear kernel, in the implementation made available in the LIBSVM system[3] (Chang and Lin, 2011). For the other 3 methods we make use of an SVM for structured output prediction, in the implementation made available in the SVM-perf system[4] (Joachims, 2005). For all 8 methods we optimize the C parameter (which sets the tradeoff between the training error and the margin) directly on DEVTEST by performing a grid search on all values of type 10^x with $x \in \{-6, ..., 7\}$; we instead leave the other parameters at their default value. The PCC, PACC, EMQ methods require the classifier to also generate posterior probabilities; since SVMs do not natively generate posterior probabilities, for these three methods we use the $-b$ option of LIBSVM, which converts the scores originally generated by SVMs into posterior probabilities according to the algorithm of (Wu et al., 2004).

The results of these preliminary experiments, which are reported in Table 1, indicated PCC as the best performer. These experiments by and large confirmed the results of (Gao and Sebastiani, 2016), where PCC was the best performer for 34 of the 66 combinations of 11 datasets $\times$ 6 evaluation measures. Instead, for none of the 66 combinations SVM(KLD), which had been the best performer in the experiments of (Esuli and Sebastiani, 2015) (where it also outperformed PCC), was the best performer. In (Gao and Sebastiani, 2016) we conjectured that this difference may be due to the fact that in quantification by sentiment, class prevalences tend to be fairly high ($>$ .10), and that the experiments of (Esuli and Sebastiani, 2015) mostly concerned classes with low prevalence ($<$ .10) or very low prevalence ($<$ .01), which tend to be the norm in classification by topic.

As a result of all this, in this work we decided to use PCC; Section 3.1 describes the PCC method in detail.

---

[2]Differently from the present task, the datasets we used in (Gao and Sebastiani, 2016) also used the Neutral class.

[3]LIBSVM is available from `http://www.csie.ntu.edu.tw/~cjlin/libsvm/`

[4]SVM-perf is available from `http://svmlight.joachims.org/svm_struct.html` . The modules that customize it to KLD and $NKLD$ were made available by Andrea Esuli, while the module that customizes it to Q was made available by José Barranquero.

Table 1: Results of our preliminary experiments for 8 quantification methods. The 2nd column indicates accuracy as measured via KLD (lower values are better), while the 3rd column indicates the value of the C parameter used, and which had proved optimal when training on TRAIN+DEV and testing on DEVTEST; **boldface** indicates the best performer.

	KLD	C
CC	0.0528275	0.00001
PCC	**0.0278864**	0.000001
ACC	0.0844489	0.0001
PACC	0.0509028	0.0001
EMQ	0.2215310	0.001
SVM(KLD)	0.0356832	0.001
SVM(NKLD)	0.1415660	0.001
SVM(Q)	0.0989133	0.1

3.1 Probabilistic Classify and Count (PCC)

The PCC method, originally introduced in (Bella et al., 2010), consists in generating a classifier from Tr, classifying the objects in Te, and computing $p_{Te}(c)$ as the *expected* fraction of objects predicted to belong to c. If by $p(c|\mathbf{x})$ we indicate the posterior probability, i.e., the probability of membership in c of test object $\mathbf{x}$ as estimated by the classifier, and by $E[x]$ we indicate the expected value of x, this corresponds to computing

$$\hat{p}_{Te}^{PCC}(c) = E[p_{Te}(\hat{c})]$$
$$= \frac{1}{|Te|} \sum_{\mathbf{x} \in Te} p(c|\mathbf{x}) \quad (1)$$

where $\hat{p}_S^M(c)$ indicates the prevalence of class c in set S as estimated via method M (the "hat" symbol indicates estimation). The rationale of PCC is that posterior probabilities contain richer information than binary decisions, which are usually obtained from posterior probabilities by thresholding.

For our final run, we have retrained the system on TRAIN+DEV+DEVTEST, using the parameter values which had performed best on DEVTEST in the preliminary experiments. On the official test set (Nakov et al., 2016) we obtained a KLD score of 0.055, and thus ranked 5th in a set of 14 participating teams.

4 Subtask E: Tweet quantification according to a five-point scale

Our goal in tackling the ordinal quantification task has been to devise a new learning algorithm for ordinal quantification. We decided to aim for an algorithm that (a) leverages the information inherent in the class ordering, and (b) performs quantification according to the *Probabilistic Classify and Count* (PCC) method ((Bella et al., 2010) – see also (Gao and Sebastiani, 2016, §4.2)), since this has proven the best-performing method in the tweet quantification experiments of (Gao and Sebastiani, 2016).

Ordinal quantification will be tackled by arranging the classes in the totally ordered set $\mathcal{C} = \{c_1, ..., c_{|\mathcal{C}|}\}$ into a binary tree. Given any $j \in \{1, \ldots, (|\mathcal{C}|-1)\}$, $\mathcal{C}_j = \{c_1, \ldots, c_j\}$ will be called a *prefix* of $\mathcal{C}$, and $\overline{\mathcal{C}}_j = \{c_{j+1}, \ldots, c_{|\mathcal{C}|}\}$ will be called a *suffix* of $\mathcal{C}$. Given any $j \in \{1, \ldots, (|\mathcal{C}| - 1)\}$ and a set S of items labeled according to $\mathcal{C}$, by $\underline{S}_j$ we denote the set of items in S whose class is in $\mathcal{C}_j$, and by $\overline{S}_j$ we denote the set of items in S whose class is in $\overline{\mathcal{C}}_j$.

4.1 Generating a quantification tree

The algorithm for training a quantification tree is described in concise form as Algorithm 1, and goes as follows. Assume we have a training set Tr and a held-out validation set Va of items labelled according to $\mathcal{C}$.

The first step (Line 3) consists in training $(|\mathcal{C}|-1)$ binary classifiers h_j, for $j \in \{1, \ldots, (|\mathcal{C}| - 1)\}$. Each of these classifiers must discriminate between $\mathcal{C}_j$ and $\overline{\mathcal{C}}_j$; for training h_j we will take the items in $\underline{Tr}_j$ as the negative training examples and the items in $\overline{Tr}_j$ as the positive training examples. We require that these classifiers, aside from taking binary decisions (i.e., predicting if a test item is in $\mathcal{C}_j$ or in $\overline{\mathcal{C}}_j$), also output posterior probabilities, i.e., probabilities $p(\mathcal{C}_j|\mathbf{x})$ and $p(\overline{\mathcal{C}}_j|\mathbf{x}) = (1 - p(\mathcal{C}_j|\mathbf{x}))$, where $p(c|\mathbf{x})$ indicates the probability of membership in c of test object $\mathbf{x}$ as estimated by the classifier[5].

The second step (Line 5) is building the ordinal quantification (binary) tree. In order to do this,

---

[5] If the classifier only returns confidence scores that are not probabilities (as is the case with many non-probabilistic classifiers), the former must be converted into true probabilities. If the score is a monotonically increasing function of the classifier's confidence in the fact that the object belongs to the class, the conversion may be obtained by applying a logistic function. *Well-calibrated* probabilities (defined as the probabilities such that the prevalence $p_S(c)$ of a class c in a set S is equal to $\sum_{\mathbf{x} \in S} p(c|\mathbf{x})$) may be obtained by using a *generalized* logistic function; see e.g., (Berardi et al., 2015, Section 4.4) for details.

```
1  Function GenerateTree (C, Tr, Va);
   /* Generates the quantification tree
      */
   Input  : Ordered set C = {c_1, ..., c_{|C|}};
            Set Tr of labelled items;
            Set Va of labelled items;
   Output: Quantification tree T_C.
2  for j ∈ {1, ..., (|C| − 1)} do
3  |   Train classifier h_j from Tr_j and Tr_j;
4  end
5  T_C ← Tree(C, {h_j}, Va);
6  return T_C;

7  Function Tree (C, H_C, Va);
   /* Recursive subroutine for
      generating the quantification tree
      */
   Input  : Ordered set C = {c_1, ..., c_{|C|}} of classes;
            Set of classifiers H_C = {h_1, ..., h_{(|C|−1)}};
   Output: Quantification tree T_C.
8  if C = {c} then
9  |   Generate a leaf node T_c;
10 |   return T_c;
11 else
12 |   h_t ← arg min_{h_j ∈ H_C} KLD(p, p̂, h_j, Va);
13 |   Generate a node T_C and associate h_t to it;
14 |   H'_C ← {h_1, ..., h_{(t−1)}};
15 |   H''_C ← {h_{(t+1)}, ..., h_{(|C|−1)}};
16 |   LChild(T_C) ← Tree(C_t, H'_C, Va);
17 |   RChild(T_C) ← Tree(C_t, H''_C, Va);
18 |   return T_C;
19 end
```

Algorithm 1: Function GenerateTree for generating an ordinal quantification tree.

among the classifiers h_j we pick the one (let us assume it is h_t) that displays the highest quantification accuracy (Line 12) on the validation set Va, and we place it at the root of the binary tree. We then repeat the process recursively on the left and on the right branches of the binary tree (Lines 14 to 17), thus building a fully grown quantification tree. Quantification is performed according to the PCC method described in Section 3.1. We measure the quantification accuracy of classifier h_j via *Kullback-Leibler Divergence (KLD)*, defined as

$$KLD(p, \hat{p}, h_j, S) = \sum_{c \in C} p_S(c) \log \frac{p_S(c)}{\hat{p}_S(c)} \qquad (2)$$

where $\hat{p}$ is the distribution estimated via PCC using the posterior probabilities generated by h_j.

4.2 Estimating class prevalences via an ordinal quantification tree

The algorithm for estimating class prevalences by using an ordinal quantification tree is described in concise form as Algorithm 2, and goes as follows. Essentially, for each item $\mathbf{x} \in Te$ and for each class $c \in C$, we compute (Line 6) the posterior probability $p(c|\mathbf{x})$; the estimate $\hat{p}_{Te}(c)$ is computed as the average, across all $\mathbf{x} \in Te$, of $p(c|\mathbf{x})$. The posterior probability $p(c|\mathbf{x})$ is computed in a recursive, hierarchical way (Lines 13 to 18), i.e., as the probability that the binary classifiers that lie on the path from the root to leaf c, would classify item $\mathbf{x}$ exactly in leaf c (i.e., that they would route $\mathbf{x}$ exactly to leaf c). This probability is computed as the product of the posterior probabilities returned by the classifiers that lie on the path from the root to leaf c.

An example quantification tree for a set of $|C| = 6$ classes is displayed in Figure 1; for brevity, classes are represented by natural numbers, the total order defined on them is the order defined on the natural numbers, and sets of classes are represented by sequences of natural numbers. Note that, as exemplified in Figure 1, our algorithm generates trees for which (a) there is a 1-to-1 correspondence between classes and leaves of the tree, (b) leaves are ordered left to right in the same order of the classes in C, and (c) each internal node represents a decision between a suffix and a prefix of C.

Point (c) is interesting, and deserves some discussion. Indeed, internal node "1234 vs. 56" is trained by using items labelled as 1, or 2, or 3, or 4 as negative examples and items labelled as 5, or 6 as positive examples; however, by looking at Figure 1, it would seem intuitive that items labelled as 6 should *not* be used, since the node is root to a subtree where class 6 is not an option anymore. The reason why we do use items labelled as 6 (which is the reason the node is labelled "1234 vs. 56" and not "1234 vs. 5") is that, during the classification stage, the classifier associated with the node might be asked to classify an item whose true label is 6, and which has thus been misclassified up higher in the tree. In this case, it would be important that this item be classified as 5, since this minimizes the contribution of this item to misclassification error; and the likelihood that this happens is increased if the classifier is trained to choose

```
 1  Function QuantifyViaHierarchicalPCC (Te, Tc);
       /* Estimates class prevalences on Te
          using the quantification tree */
    Input  : Unlabelled set Te;
             Quantification tree Tc;
    Output: Estimates p̂(c) for all c ∈ C;
 2  for c ∈ C do
 3  |   p̂(c) ← 0
 4  end
 5  for x ∈ Te do
 6  |   CPost(x, Tc, 1); /* Compute the {p(c|x)}
 7  |   for c ∈ C do
 8  |   |   p̂(c) ← p̂(c) + p(c|x)/|Te|;
 9  |   end
10  end
11  return {p̂(c)}

12  Procedure CPost (x, Tc, SubP);
       /* Recursive subroutine for computing
          all the posteriors {p(c|x)} */
    Input  : Unlabelled item x;
             Quantification tree Tc;
             Probability SubP of current subtree;
    Output: Posteriors {p(c|x)};
13  if Tc = {c} then
       /* Tc is a leaf, labelled by class
          c */
14  |   p(c|x) ← SubP;
15  else
16  |   CPost(x, LChild(Tc), p(Ct|x) · SubP);
17  |   CPost(x, RChild(Tc), p(C̄t|x) · SubP);
       /* p(Ct|x) and p(C̄t|x) are the
          posteriors returned by the
          classifier associated with the
          root of Tc  */
18  end
```

Algorithm 2: Function QuantifyViaHierarchicalPCC for estimating prevalences via an ordinal quantification tree.

between 1234 and 56, rather than between 1234 and 5.

Note also that this is one aspect for which our algorithm is a true *ordinal* classification algorithm; if there were no order defined on the classes this policy would make no sense.

A second reason why our algorithm is an inherently ordinal quantification algorithm is that the groups of classes (such as 1234 and 56) between which a binary classifier needs to discriminate are

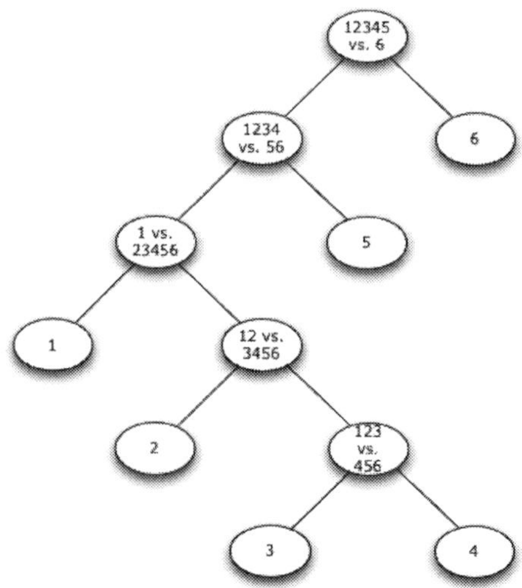

Figure 1: An example ordinal quantification tree.

groups of classes that are *contiguous* in the order defined on C. It is because of this contiguity that the structure of the trees we generate makes sense: if, say, classes $\{1, ..., 6\}$ represent degrees of positivity of product reviews, with 1 representing most negative and 6 representing most positive, the group 56 may be taken to represent the positive reviews (to different degrees), while 1234 may be taken to represent the reviews that are not positive; a group such as, say, 256, would instead be very hard to interpret, since it is formed of non-contiguous classes that have little in common with each other.

Finally, we remark that our ordinal quantification algorithm does not depend on the fact that PCC is the chosen quantification method, and could be adapted to work with other such methods, such as e.g., SVM(KLD). Indeed, if SVM(KLD) is the chosen quantification method, in Algorithm 1 we only need to change the learning method we use (Line 3), and change the recursive subroutine CPost (Lines 12 to 17) in such a way that, by recursively making binary choices down the tree, it picks exactly one out of the $|C|$ leaf classes instead of computing the posterior probabilities for all of them[6].

---

[6]The code that implements the PCC method for binary quantification, and our method for ordinal quantification, is available from http://alt.qcri.org/tools/quantification/

4.2.1 Our run

In our preliminary run over the DEVTEST set, our system obtained an EMD value of 0.210; for obtaining this, the optimization of the C parameter (see Section 3.1) was carried out using EMD as a criterion, i.e., the parameter that yielded the best EMD value on DEVTEST was chosen. For comparison, we also run on DEVTEST a baseline multiclass PCC system, i.e, one which performs quantification according to the PCC method and does not take the order on the classes into account; the baseline system, after parameter optimization, obtained an EMD value of 0.222, with a 5.64% deterioration over our system. As a result, we decided to tackle the unlabelled set with our system as described in Sections 4.1 and 4.2. Note that, unlike for Subtask D, in Subtask E we did not have a range of other datasets to perform preliminary experiments with; as a result, the only choice that could make sense here was using the system which had performed best on DEVTEST.

On the official test set (Nakov et al., 2016) we obtained an EMD score of 0.243, ranking 1st in a set of 10 participating systems, with a high margin over the other ones (systems from rank 2 to rank 8 obtained EMD scores between 0.316 and 0.366).

References

José Barranquero, Jorge Díez, and Juan José del Coz. 2015. Quantification-oriented learning based on reliable classifiers. *Pattern Recognition*, 48(2):591–604.

Antonio Bella, Cèsar Ferri, José Hernández-Orallo, and María José Ramírez-Quintana. 2010. Quantification via probability estimators. In *Proceedings of the 11th IEEE International Conference on Data Mining (ICDM 2010)*, pages 737–742, Sydney, AU.

Giacomo Berardi, Andrea Esuli, and Fabrizio Sebastiani. 2015. Utility-theoretic ranking for semi-automated text classification. *ACM Transactions on Knowledge Discovery from Data*, 10(1):Article 6.

Chih-Chung Chang and Chih-Jen Lin. 2011. LIBSVM: A library for support vector machines. *ACM Transactions on Intelligent Systems and Technology*, 2(3):Article 27.

Andrea Esuli and Fabrizio Sebastiani. 2014. Explicit loss minimization in quantification applications (preliminary draft). Presented at the *8th International Workshop on Information Filtering and Retrieval (DART 2014)*, Pisa, IT.

Andrea Esuli and Fabrizio Sebastiani. 2015. Optimizing text quantifiers for multivariate loss functions. *ACM Transactions on Knowledge Discovery and Data*, 9(4):Article 27.

Wei Gao and Fabrizio Sebastiani. 2015. Tweet sentiment: From classification to quantification. In *Proceedings of the 7th International Conference on Advances in Social Network Analysis and Mining (ASONAM 2015)*, pages 97–104, Paris, FR.

Wei Gao and Fabrizio Sebastiani. 2016. From classification to quantification in tweet sentiment analysis. *Social Network Analysis and Mining*. Forthcoming.

John J. Gart and Alfred A. Buck. 1966. Comparison of a screening test and a reference test in epidemiologic studies: II. A probabilistic model for the comparison of diagnostic tests. *American Journal of Epidemiology*, 83(3):593–602.

Thorsten Joachims. 2005. A support vector method for multivariate performance measures. In *Proceedings of the 22nd International Conference on Machine Learning (ICML 2005)*, pages 377–384, Bonn, DE.

Svetlana Kiritchenko, Xiaodan Zhu, and Saif M. Mohammad. 2014. Sentiment analysis of short informal texts. *Journal of Artificial Intelligence Research*, 50:723–762.

Saif M. Mohammad, Svetlana Kiritchenko, and Xiaodan Zhu. 2013. NRC-Canada: Building the state-of-the-art in sentiment analysis of tweets. In *Proceedings of the 7th International Workshop on Semantic Evaluation (SemEval 2013)*, pages 321–327, Atlanta, US.

Preslav Nakov, Alan Ritter, Sara Rosenthal, Fabrizio Sebastiani, and Veselin Stoyanov. 2016. SemEval-2016 Task 4: Sentiment analysis in Twitter. In *Proceedings of the 10th International Workshop on Semantic Evaluation (SemEval 2016)*, San Diego, US. Forthcoming.

Marco Saerens, Patrice Latinne, and Christine Decaestecker. 2002. Adjusting the outputs of a classifier to new a priori probabilities: A simple procedure. *Neural Computation*, 14(1):21–41.

Ting-Fan Wu, Chih-Jen Lin, and Ruby C. Weng. 2004. Probability estimates for multi-class classification by pairwise coupling. *Journal of Machine Learning Research*, 5:975–1005.

Xiaodan Zhu, Svetlana Kiritchenko, and Saif M. Mohammad. 2014. NRC-Canada-2014: Recent improvements in the sentiment analysis of tweets. In *Proceedings of the 8th International Workshop on Semantic Evaluation (SemEval 2014)*, pages 443–447, Dublin, IE.

SteM at SemEval-2016 Task 4: Applying Active Learning to Improve Sentiment Classification

Stefan Räbiger[a], **Mishal Kazmi**[a], **Yücel Saygın**[a], **Peter Schüller**[b], **Myra Spiliopoulou**[c]

[a]Sabanci University, Istanbul, Turkey
[b]Marmara University, Istanbul, Turkey
[c]Otto-von-Guericke University, Magdeburg, Germany
`{stefan,mishalkazmi,ysaygin}@sabanciuniv.edu`
`peter.schuller@marmara.edu.tr`
`myra@iti.cs.uni-magdeburg.de`

Abstract

This paper describes our approach to the SemEval 2016 task 4, "Sentiment Analysis in Twitter", where we participated in subtask A. Our system relies on AlchemyAPI and SentiWordNet to create 43 features based on which we select a feature subset as final representation. Active Learning then filters out noisy tweets from the provided training set, leaving a smaller set of only 900 tweets which we use for training a Multinomial Naive Bayes classifier to predict the labels of the test set with an F1 score of 0.478.

1 Introduction

Gaining an overview of opinions on recent events or trends is an appealing feature of Twitter. For example, receiving real-time feedback from the public about a politician's speech provides insights to media for the latest polls, analysts and interested individuals including the politician herself. However, detecting tweet sentiment still poses a challenge due to the frequent use of informal language, acronyms, neologisms which constantly change, and the shortness of tweets, which are limited to 140 characters.

SemEval's subtask 4A (Nakov et al., 2016) deals with the sentiment classification of single tweets into one of the classes "positive", "neutral" or "negative". Concretely a training set of 5481 tweets and a development set comprising 1799 tweets was given, and the sentiment of 32009 tweets in a test set had to be predicted and was evaluated using F1-score. The distribution of labels for the given datasets is depicted in Table 1. Tweets with positive polarity

outnumber the other two classes and the least number of instances is available for negative tweets. Initially, the organizers provided 6000 tweets for the training set and 2000 tweets for the development set, but only the tweet IDs were released to abide by the Twitter terms of agreement. By the time we downloaded the data, around 10% of the tweets (519 in the training set, 201 in the test set) were not available anymore. For further details about the labeling process and the datasets see (Nakov et al., 2016).

Lexicon-based approaches have done very well in this competition over the past years, i.e, the winners of the years 2013-2015 (Mohammad et al., 2013; Miura et al., 2014; Hagen et al., 2015) relied heavily on them. Our goal is to explore alternatives and to complement lexicon-based strategies. The SteM system performs preprocessing, including canonicalization of tweets, and based on that we extract 43 features as our representation, some features are based on AlchemyAPI[1] and SentiWordNet (Esuli and Sebastiani, 2006). We choose 28 of the features as final representation and learn three classifiers based on different subsets of these 28 features. We refer to the latter as *feature subspaces* or *subspaces* hereafter. However, independently of the subspace we use, we face the fact that tweet datasets inherently contain noise and all subspaces will - to a greater or lesser extend- be affected by this noise. To alleviate this problem, we propose to concentrate on only few of the labeled tweets, those likely to be most discriminative. To this purpose, we use Active Learning (AL) (Settles, 2012), as explained in Section 6. For AL, we set up a "budget", translating

---

[1]`http://www.alchemyapi.com`

Proceedings of SemEval-2016, pages 64–70,
San Diego, California, June 16-17, 2016. ©2016 Association for Computational Linguistics

Dataset	Total	Pos	Neu	Neg
Train	5481	2817	1882	782
Dev	1799	755	685	359

Table 1: Distribution of sentiment labels in the datasets.

Slang	c'mon	l8r	FB
Replacement	come on	later	Facebook

Table 2: Examplary slang words to be replaced by our lexicon.

to the maximum number of tweets, for which labels are requested. The term "budget" is motivated by the fact that labeling is a costly human activity. In our study, this budget is set to 900. On those 900 tweet we learn a classifier for each of the three feature subspaces to predict the labels of the test set.

The remainder of this paper is organized according to the pipeline of the SteM system. Section 2 explains preprocessing steps, Section 3 describes our features, Section 4 describes how we select our feature subset for the final representation, Section 5 gives details about learning the classifiers on the different subsets, Section 6 describes our Active Learning component, and Section 7 outlines the experiments we performed to select the best model for the competition.

2 Preprocessing

We note that while preprocessing tweets, we also extract related features. These features are described in the next section.

Removing URLs, mentions and replacing slang, abbreviations: we first remove Twitter handles (@username) and URLs. We remove dates and numbers with regular expressions and canonicalize common abbreviations, slang and negations using a lexicon we assembled from online resources.[2] Our list of negations encompasses: don't, mustn't, shouldn't, isn't, aren't, wasn't, weren't, not, couldn't, won't, can't, wouldn't. We replace these with the respective formal forms and we do the same for their apostrophe-free forms (e.g., 'cant'), which are more likely to occur in hashtags. In total we use 114 abbreviations, some are shown in Table 2.

Spelling correction: the remaining unknown words are replaced by the most likely alternative according to the PyEnchant dictionary.[3]

Splitting hashtags into words: instead of remov-

ing hashtags, we chunk them as follows. If a hashtag is comprised of a single word that exists in our dictionary, we only remove the hashtag symbol. In case of camel case hashtags (#HelloWorld), we split the words on the respective transitions from upper to lower case or vice versa. Otherwise we try to recover the multiple words in the following manner. If a hashtag contains less than 22 characters, we apply an exhaustive search to find a combination of words that all exist in a dictionary. For hashtags longer than 22 characters the exhaustive approach takes too long (about 10s), hence we opt for a greedy algorithm instead: we start at the end of the hashtag and traverse to the front trying to find the longest words that are found in a dictionary. In case not all parts can be resolved, we only keep the existing words and discard the remainder. Furthermore we remove emoticons and replace elongated characters by a single occurrence, e.g., wooooooow $\rightarrow$ wow.

Determine POS tags: on the resulting canonicalized text, we determine part-of-speech (POS) tags using the Stanford POS tagger (Manning et al., 2014). Finally we eliminate any punctuation.

Discard unbiased polarity words: since some of the words in the training corpus are uniformly distributed across the three labels, encountering such words in any tweet does not allow us to learn anything about the overall tweet sentiment. Hence, we compile a list of these words and exclude them when calculating tweet polarities. We detect such words with the help of categorical proportional difference (CPD) (Simeon and Hilderman, 2008) which describes how much a word w contributes to distinguishing the different classes. It is calculated as $CPD_w = |A - B|/(A + B)$, where A corresponds to the occurrences of the word w.r.t. one of the three classes, while B denotes the number of occurrences of the word in the remaining two classes. After computing this value for all three classes separately, the maximum value is chosen as a result. High values close to 1 indicate a strong bias towards one of the classes, while a value close to 0 signals that w is almost uniformly distributed. If this value is below

---

a fixed threshold of 0.6 we exclude the word from sentiment computation. Large CPD values indicate that a word occurs frequently with a specific class, while low values signal no particular association of the word with any class. Note that we consider only the absolute value of the enumerator in our equation, similar to (O'Keefe and Koprinska, 2009), while this is not the case in the original paper. The reason is that the direction of the association of a word with a class is not important to us.

3 Extracted features

In this section we describe the extracted features and motivate our choice. Table 3 presents an overview of the 43 extracted features. Column 'Used' lists the features that comprise our final representation after feature subset selection which is described in Section 4. We explain our reasoning for the different feature subspaces (column 'Subspace') in Section 5.

Since emoticons correlate with sentiment, we exploit this knowledge in our features. To do so, we create a lexicon encompassing 81 common positive and negative emoticons based on Wikipedia. We manually labeled these emoticons as either expressing positive or negative sentiment. While preprocessing we extract the respective emoticon features $1 - 2$. We assign features $3 - 4$ into the same category, as all four of them are easy to identify in a tweet. Hashtags share a similar relationship with sentiment like emoticons, i.e., they correlate with the overall tweet sentiment (Mohammad, 2012). Thus, we extract the features $6 - 16$ describing the sentiment of hashtags. Exclamation marks also hint at amplified overall tweet sentiment which is covered by feature 17. The length of a tweet affects whether it contains sentiment: if tweets are longer, it is more likely they contain mixed polarity and hence it is more difficult to label them. Features $18 - 20$ deal with this issue. We expect that sentiment bearing tweets contain a different sentence parts composition which is reflected in the features $21 - 24$.

We query AlchemyAPI about sentiment to benefit from a system that is known to yield accurate results, for example for the task of extracting entity-level sentiment (Saif et al., 2012). Moreover, AlchemyAPI allows to retrieve sentiment on different levels of granularity for documents, e.g., for a whole tweet or for single entities within a tweet. Features $25 - 32$ describe the relevant sentiment information from this online resource. The remaining features $33 - 43$ address sentiment on the whole tweet.

Note that we normalize the features $6-8, 27, 33-35$ by taking their absolute values and limiting them to the interval $[0 \ldots 1]$. For extracting tweet and hashtag sentiment, we consider negations, diminishers ("a little") and intensifiers ("very") when summing up the polarity scores of the separate words. To account for the correlation of emoticons with the overall tweet sentiment, we eventually multiply the respective positive or negative overall tweet sentiment by 1.5 if emoticons are present. The resulting value is multiplied by $1.5 *$ the number of multiple exclamation marks if multiple exclamation marks exist in a sentence. We query SentiWordNet to determine word polarities in order to obtain a triple of positive, neutral and negative sentiment scores per word. This allows us to define positive/neutral/negative words according to its prevalent sentiment. Similarly, we express the overall tweet sentiment with a triple representing positive, neutral and negative polarity. Values close to 0 indicate that only little sentiment is contained in a tweet, while larger ones imply stronger sentiment. In case of negations, we employ a simple sliding windows approach to switch positive and negative sentiment of the four succeeding words. If tweets end with "not", e.g., "I like you - not", we also switch their overall sentiment as this is a common pattern in tweets indicating sarcasm. The sentiment of capitalized and elongated words is amplified. We consider a word elongated if the same letter occurs more than twice consecutively. In case of intensifiers and diminishers, the sentiment of the four succeeding words is increased in the former case by multiplying it by 1.5, and decreased in the latter one by multiplying the term by 0.5. However, if "a bit" is encountered, also the sentiment of the four preceding words is updated, e.g., "I like you a bit".

4 Selecting a feature subset

We first use Weka (Hall et al., 2009) to find an initially promising subset of features. For this purpose, we employ the WrapperSubsetEval method. That means, Multinomial Naive Bayes (MNB) is used

ID	Name	Description	Subspace	Used
1	Pos_emo	Number of positive emoticons	emoticons	yes
2	Neg_emo	Number of negative emoticons	emoticons	yes
3	Elongated	Number of elongated words	emoticons	no
4	Upper	Number of CAPITALIZED words	emoticons	no
5	has_ht	Does the tweet contain at least one hashtag?	hashtag	yes
6	neg_ht	Negative sentiment of hashtag	hashtag	no
7	neu_ht	Neutral sentiment of hashtag	hashtag	no
8	pos_ht	Positive sentiment of hashtag	hashtag	yes
9	neg_words_ht	Number of negative words in hashtag	hashtag	yes
10	neu_words_ht	Number of neutral words in hashtag	hashtag	yes
11	pos_words_ht	Number of positive words in hashtag	hashtag	yes
12	pol_words_ht	Number of polarity words in hashtag	hashtag	yes
13	negat_words_ht	Number of negation words in hashtag	hashtag	yes
14	neu_words_ht_sum	Sum of negative sentiment in hashtag	hashtag	no
15	pos_words_ht_sum	Sum of neutral sentiment in hashtag	hashtag	yes
16	pol_words_ht_sum	Sum of positive sentiment in hashtag	hashtag	yes
17	punct	Number of occurrences of '!', '??', '!?', '?!'	default	yes
18	start_len	Number of words before preprocessing	default	yes
19	end_len	Number of words after preprocessing	default	no
20	avg_len	Average number of words per sentence	default	no
21	adj_frac	Percentage of adjectives	default	yes
22	adv_frac	Percentage of adverbs	default	yes
23	v_frac	Percentage of verbs	default	no
24	nn_frac	Percentage of nouns	default	no
25	al_t_pol	Tweet polarity (AlchemyAPI)	default	no
26	al_t_type	Tweet polarity type (AlchemyAPI)	default	yes
27	al_e_pol	Average entity polarity (AlchemyAPI)	default	no
28	al_e_type	Median entity polarity type (AlchemyAPI)	default	yes
29	al_neg_e	Number of negative named entities (AlchemyAPI)	default	yes
30	al_neu_e	Number of neutral named entities (AlchemyAPI)	default	yes
31	al_pos_e	Number of positive named entities (AlchemyAPI)	default	yes
32	al_mixed	Does the tweet contain mixed sentiment? (AlchemyAPI)	default	yes
33	neg	Negative sentiment (SentiWordNet)	default	yes
34	neu	Neutral sentiment (SentiWordNet)	default	yes
35	pos	Positive sentiment (SentiWordNet)	default	yes
36	neg_words	Number of negative words (SentiWordNet)	default	yes
37	neu_words	Number of neutral words (SentiWordNet)	default	no
38	pos_words	Number of positive words (SentiWordNet)	default	yes
39	negat_words	Number of negation words (SentiWordNet)	default	no
40	pol_words	Number of polarity words (SentiWordNet)	default	yes
41	neg_words_sum	Sum of negative sentiment (SentiWordNet)	default	no
42	neu_words_sum	Sum of neutral sentiment (SentiWordNet)	default	no
43	pos_words_sum	Sum of positive sentiment (SentiWordNet)	default	yes

Table 3: Overview of our extracted features.

to compute F1-scores and with the help of 10-fold cross-validation on the training set the merit of different feature subsets is determined. This leaves us with a feature subset comprising 10 features. But we must consider the fact that we are using different feature subspaces as opposed to a single one for which Weka selected the features. Hence, our approach might benefit from other features not selected by Weka as well as some currently selected features could affect the performance of our system negatively. To investigate this, we work with SteM and perform 10-fold cross-validation on the training set to monitor effects on the F1-scores. We first try to reduce the feature subset determined by Weka further by removing features separately. This yields a feature subset encompassing 7 features. Now we add all features that Weka discarded separately back into SteM and observe the effects on the F1-scores. Following this procedure, we added 21 more features to our subset leading to the final tweet representation with 28 features. The list of used features is found in Column 'Used' in Table 3.

5   Learning a model

We employ Scikit-learn (Pedregosa et al., 2011) for building our classifiers. Since some of our features occur only in a small portion of the dataset, we build classifiers on different feature subspaces which we manually defined (column 'Subspace' in Table 3). Otherwise these underrepresented features would not be selected as informative features when removing noisy features during feature subset selection, although they actually help discriminate the different classes. For example, only 10-15% of the tweets in the training, development and test set contain hashtags. Likewise few tweets include emoticons. Hence, we consider *emoticons* and *hashtags* as separate feature subspaces. We learn in total three classifiers for three different subspaces: *default*, *default + emoticons*, *default + hashtags*. We choose MNB as our classifier as it is competitive with Logistic Regression and linear SVM and fast in learning models which allows us to carry out multiple experiments for quantifying the merit of different AL strategies, feature subsets, etc., as these experiments are time-consuming. With a similar reasoning we decide against ensemble methods for now as we first want to obtain reliable results for single classifiers before studying ensembles.

6   Active learning

AL is motivated well in (Settles, 2010): "The key idea behind *active learning* is that a machine learning algorithm can achieve greater accuracy with fewer training labels if it is allowed to choose the data from which it learns." In (Martineau et al., 2014), the authors apply AL to detect misclassified samples and let experts relabel those instances to reduce noise. We utilize AL in a similar fashion, but instead of relabeling tweets, we discard them. We set a fixed budget for the AL strategy, which indicates for how many tweets the classifer can use the label for training, after starting from a small seed set of labeled tweets.

As AL strategies we pick uncertainty sampling (UC) and certainty sampling (C) and choose MNB as classifier. We calculate certainty/uncertainty according to two different criteria, namely margin and confidence (Li et al., 2012). In margin-based UC the tweet with the highest margin is selected for labeling, while in confidence-based UC the instance with the least confidence is chosen. Contrary to UC, C always selects the tweet about which the classifier is most confident in case of confidence, or the tweet with the lowest margin respectively. We initialize the seed set with approximately the same number of tweets from all three classes where the tweets are chosen randomly per class. Whenever an AL strategy selects a tweet to be labeled, we reveal its actual label. To identify a fixed budget for our AL strategies, we test different configurations of budgets and seed set sizes on the training set. For each run we perform 10-fold cross validation and average results over three executions to account for chance and then the labels of the development set are predicted. As a baseline method we choose random sampling which selects arbitrary tweets to be labeled. After conducting multiple experiments, we find that initializing the seed set with 500 tweets, setting the budget to 400 tweets and choosing confidence-based UC yields the highest weighted F1-scores with $F1 = 0.48$. Our experimental evaluation of different AL methods is visualized in Figure 1 using a seed set with 500 tweets

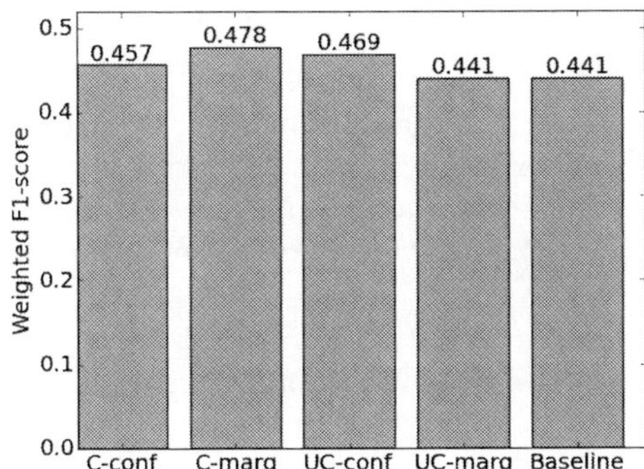

Figure 1: F1-scores on development set for different AL strategies with a seed set size of 500 tweets and a budget of 400 tweets.

Strategy	#Features	#Tweets	Dev
BL	8	5481	0.444
BL	8	900	0.466
SteM	43	5481	0.454
SteM	28	900	**0.473**

Table 4: Comparing F1-scores on development set using SteM and our baseline.

		Predicted		
		neg	neu	pos
	neg	181	93	85
Truth	neu	206	181	298
	pos	116	124	515

Table 5: Confusion matrix of SteM with 900 training instances.

and a budget of 400 tweets for which the strategies request the revealed labels. Although margin-based C seems to outperform confidence-based UC, we select the latter strategy. Tests on the development set using only the tweets selected by the respective AL strategies revealed that C achieved an F1-score of 0.30 while confidence-based UC achieved around 0.48. This inferiority of C on our data confirms reports from the literature, see e.g., (Kumar et al., 2010; Ambati et al., 2011).

7 Experiments

In this section we evaluate our approach on the development set as no labels for the test set are available. As AlchemyAPI is a full-fledged system, we use the 8 features extracted from it (Features $25 - 32$ in Table 3) as a baseline in our experiments to compare it with SteM using a) the full training set and b) the reduced tweets after performing confidence-based UC as explained in the previous section. We then reapply the learning procedure described in Section 5 to obtain our F1-scores. The results are depicted in Table 4. Initially, our system achieves an F1-score of 0.454 using all training instances. After selecting the 900 most informative tweets using confidence-based UC from the previous section, the score increases to 0.473. We observe a similar trend for our baseline and note that it is outperformed by SteM, although the margin shrinks when reducing the number of tweets in the training set. When analyzing the corresponding confusion matrix of SteM

with 900 tweets in Table 5, it becomes obvious that it fails to distinguish neutral sentiment from the remaining ones properly.

8 Conclusion and future work

In this paper we proposed SteM to predict tweet sentiment. After preprocessing, it extracts 43 features from tweets, selects 28 of these features as an appropriate subset to represent tweets for Multinomial Naive Bayes. One such classifier is trained for each of our three overlapping feature subspaces. To predict the labels of unknown instances, they are passed to the classifier that was trained on the respective feature subspace. Due to the noisy nature of labels in sentiment analysis, we select only few tweets for our training set by applying Active Learning. Despite utilizing only 26.3% (900 out of 5481) of the provided tweets for training, SteM outperforms an identical system trained on the full training set. Overall, our approach looks promising, but has room for improvement. Firstly, we plan to test our approach with ensembles and secondly, identify tweets with neutral sentiment more accurately. To this purpose, we plan to incorporate more features.

Acknowledgments

This work is partially supported by TUBITAK Grant 114E777.

References

Vamshi Ambati, Sanjika Hewavitharana, Stephan Vogel, and Jaime Carbonell. 2011. Active learning with multiple annotations for comparable data classification task. In *Proceedings of the 4th Workshop on Building and Using Comparable Corpora: Comparable Corpora and the Web*, pages 69–77. Association for Computational Linguistics.

Andrea Esuli and Fabrizio Sebastiani. 2006. Sentiwordnet: A publicly available lexical resource for opinion mining. In *In Proceedings of the 5th Conference on Language Resources and Evaluation (LREC06*, pages 417–422.

Matthias Hagen, Martin Potthast, Michael Büchner, and Benno Stein. 2015. Webis: An ensemble for twitter sentiment detection. In *Proceedings of the 9th International Workshop on Semantic Evaluation*, pages 582–589.

Mark Hall, Eibe Frank, Geoffrey Holmes, Bernhard Pfahringer, Peter Reutemann, and Ian H Witten. 2009. The weka data mining software: an update. *ACM SIGKDD explorations newsletter*, 11(1):10–18.

Mohit Kumar, Rayid Ghani, Mohak Shah, Jaime G Carbonell, and Alexander I Rudnicky. 2010. Empirical comparison of active learning strategies for handling temporal drift. *ACM Transactions on Embedded Computing Systems*, 9(4):161–168.

Shoushan Li, Shengfeng Ju, Guodong Zhou, and Xiaojun Li. 2012. Active learning for imbalanced sentiment classification. In *Proceedings of the 2012 Joint Conference on Empirical Methods in Natural Language Processing and Computational Natural Language Learning*, pages 139–148. Association for Computational Linguistics.

Christopher D Manning, Mihai Surdeanu, John Bauer, Jenny Rose Finkel, Steven Bethard, and David McClosky. 2014. The stanford corenlp natural language processing toolkit. In *ACL (System Demonstrations)*, pages 55–60.

Justin Martineau, Lu Chen, Doreen Cheng, and Amit Sheth. 2014. Active learning with efficient feature weighting methods for improving data quality and classification accuracy. In *Proceedings of the 52nd Annual Meeting of the Association for Computational Linguistics (Volume 1: Long Papers)*, pages 1104–1112, Baltimore, Maryland, June. Association for Computational Linguistics.

Yasuhide Miura, Shigeyuki Sakaki, Keigo Hattori, and Tomoko Ohkuma. 2014. Teamx: A sentiment analyzer with enhanced lexicon mapping and weighting scheme for unbalanced data. In *Proceedings of the 8th International Workshop on Semantic Evaluation (SemEval 2014)*, pages 628–632, Dublin, Ireland, August.

Association for Computational Linguistics and Dublin City University.

Saif M. Mohammad, Svetlana Kiritchenko, and Xiaodan Zhu. 2013. Nrc-canada: Building the state-of-the-art in sentiment analysis of tweets. In *Proceedings of the seventh international workshop on Semantic Evaluation Exercises (SemEval-2013)*, Atlanta, Georgia, USA, June.

Saif M Mohammad. 2012. # emotional tweets. In *Proceedings of the First Joint Conference on Lexical and Computational Semantics-Volume 1: Proceedings of the main conference and the shared task, and Volume 2: Proceedings of the Sixth International Workshop on Semantic Evaluation*, pages 246–255. Association for Computational Linguistics.

Preslav Nakov, Alan Ritter, Sara Rosenthal, Veselin Stoyanov, and Fabrizio Sebastiani. 2016. SemEval-2016 task 4: Sentiment analysis in Twitter. In *Proceedings of the 10th International Workshop on Semantic Evaluation (SemEval 2016)*. Association for Computational Linguistics.

Tim O'Keefe and Irena Koprinska. 2009. Feature selection and weighting methods in sentiment analysis. In *Proceedings of the 14th Australasian document computing symposium, Sydney*, pages 67–74. Citeseer.

F. Pedregosa, G. Varoquaux, A. Gramfort, V. Michel, B. Thirion, O. Grisel, M. Blondel, P. Prettenhofer, R. Weiss, V. Dubourg, J. Vanderplas, A. Passos, D. Cournapeau, M. Brucher, M. Perrot, and E. Duchesnay. 2011. Scikit-learn: Machine learning in Python. *Journal of Machine Learning Research*, 12:2825–2830.

Hassan Saif, Yulan He, and Harith Alani. 2012. Semantic sentiment analysis of twitter. In *The Semantic Web–ISWC 2012*, pages 508–524. Springer.

Burr Settles. 2010. Active learning literature survey. *University of Wisconsin, Madison*, 52(55-66):11.

Burr Settles. 2012. Active learning. *Synthesis Lectures on Artificial Intelligence and Machine Learning*, 6(1):1–114.

Mondelle Simeon and Robert Hilderman. 2008. Categorical proportional difference: A feature selection method for text categorization. In *Proceedings of the 7th Australasian Data Mining Conference-Volume 87*, pages 201–208. Australian Computer Society, Inc.

I2RNTU at SemEval-2016 Task 4: Classifier Fusion for Polarity Classification in Twitter

Zhengchen Zhang[1], Chen Zhang[2], Fuxiang Wu[3],
Dong-Yan Huang[1], Weisi Lin[2], Minghui Dong[1]

[1]Human Language Technology Department, Institute for Infocomm Research (I2R),
A*STAR, Singapore, 138632
[2]School of Computer Engineering, Nanyang Technological University,
50 Nanyang Avenue Singapore, 639798
[3]BeiHang University, Beijing, China, 100191
`huang@i2r.a-star.edu.sg`

Abstract

In this work, we apply classifier fusion to tweet polarity identification problem. The task is to predict whether the emotion hidden in a tweet is positive, neutral, or negative. An asymmetric SIMPLS (ASIMPLS) based classifier, which was proved to be able to identify the minority class well in imbalanced classification problems, is implemented. Word embedding is also employed as a new feature. For each word, we obtain three word embedding vectors on positive, neutral, and negative tweet sets respectively. These vectors are used as features in the ASIMPLS classifier. Another three state-of-the-art systems are implemented also, and these four systems are fused together to further boost the performance. The fusion system achieved 59.63% accuracy on the 2016 test set of SemEval2016 Task 4, Subtask A.

1 Introduction

The I2RNTU system works on the Subtask A: Message Polarity Classification in Twitter of SemEval-2016 Task 4: the Sentiment Analysis in Twitter (Nakov et al., 2016). The task is to predict whether a tweet is of positive, neutral, or negative sentiment. This task can be formulated as a multiclass classification problem, i.e., to classify a tweet into one of the three classes. We use the one-vs-rest strategy to solve the three-class classification problem. Given a tweet, a classifier generates three confidence scores about the tweet belonging to the three classes respectively. The predicted label is chosen based on the highest confidence score. Four classifiers are implemented in our work, and classifier fusion is used to improve the system performance.

Classifier fusion has been proved to be very powerful in classification problems. In SemEval-2015, a system named Webis won the first place in the message polarity classification subtask, which is subtask B of SemEval-2015 task 10 "Sentiment Analysis in Twitter" (Hagen et al., 2015). The authors reproduced four state-of-the-art twitter polarity prediction algorithms. Each algorithm generates three confidence scores for a tweet. The fusion system averages the scores generated by the four classifiers, and then predicts a label according to the highest average score. In the Speaker State Challenge of INTERSPEECH 2011, the method of fusing Asymmetric SIMPLS (ASIMPLS) and Support Vector Machines (SVMs) won the sleepiness sub-challenge (Huang et al., 2011). The asymmetric SIMPLS based classifier is shown to be able to generate a higher prediction accuracy for the class with small number of instances in the imbalanced classification problem, while SVMs are strong at predicting the class with majority number of instances. The fusion of these two types of methods could achieve a balance between favouring the majority class and the minority class. In the Music Information Retrieval Evaluation eXchange (MIREX 2013), the method of fusing SIMPLS and SuperFlux won the 3rd place on Audio Onset Detection subtask (Zhang et al., 2013). In the Emotion Recognition in the Wild Challenge (EmotiW2014), which aims to automatically classify the emotions acted by human subjects in video clips under real-world environment, the fusion of kernel SVM, logistic regression, and partial least squares (PLS) with different Riemannian ker-

Proceedings of SemEval-2016, pages 71–78,
San Diego, California, June 16-17, 2016. ©2016 Association for Computational Linguistics

nels won the first place of the competition (Liu et al., 2014). In this paper, we will take advantage of the classifier fusion again. We introduce the asymmetric SIMPLS based classifier to the tweet polarity classification problem, and combine it with other three of state-of-the-art classifiers. The fusion method is same with (Hagen et al., 2015).

The most popular features used in the tweet polarity classification problem are derived from sentiment lexicons (Rosenthal et al., 2015). Word embedding represents a word using a low dimensional vector which contains the syntactic and semantic meaning of the word. If we can enhance the sentiment information hidden in the vector, it may be a good feature for the task. Word embedding has been used in tweet sentiment analysis in (Zhang et al., 2015). The authors used the vectors with dimensionality of 300 trained by word2vec, which is publicly available on-line [1]. However, the vectors are trained using Google News. No emotional info was considered during the training. Also, the news articles are written in formal language. Many words appearing frequently in tweets such as 'goood' may not be included in the data set. In this paper, we train the word embedding on downloaded tweet data sets. Furthermore, we separate the tweet data set into three subsets named positive, neutral, and negative subsets respectively. For each word, three vectors are obtained. These vectors are used as features for the ASIMPLS classifier.

The papers of task description of SemEval (Rosenthal et al., 2015; Rosenthal et al., 2014; Nakov et al., 2013) may be the best material of understanding the related work of sentiment analysis in twitter. The classifiers used include SVM, maximum entropy, Conditional Random Fields (CRFs), deep neural networks, and linear regression etc. The most popular features are derived from sentiment lexicons. Bag-of-words, hashtags, and punctuations etc. are also used widely.

We will introduce the asymmetric SIMPLS classifier and the proposed word embedding feature in Section 2. The three state-of-the-art systems and the fusion method are described in Section 3. The experimental results are shown in Section 4. We conclude

our work in Section 5.

2 The Asymmetric SIMPLS (ASIMPLS) based classifier

2.1 The ASIMPLS algorithm

Partial Least Squares (PLS) has been introduced into classification problems in (Huang et al., 2011). SIMPLS is an efficient algorithm for PLS regression that calculates the PLS factors as linear combinations of the original variables (De Jong, 1993). Given two matrices $\mathbf{X} \in \mathbb{R}^{N \times M}$ with N samples and M dimensional features, and a label matrix $\mathbf{Y} \in \mathbb{R}^{N \times K}$. The SIMPLS algorithm aims to find a linear projection (De Jong, 1993)

$$\widehat{\mathbf{Y}} = \mathbf{XB} \tag{1}$$

For the bianry classification problems, $K = 1$. The solution is to extract the orthogonal factors of $\mathbf{X}$ and $\mathbf{Y}$ sequentially,

$$\mathbf{t}_a = \mathbf{X}_0 \mathbf{r}_a \tag{2}$$

and

$$\mathbf{u}_a = \mathbf{Y}_0 \mathbf{q}_a, a = 1, 2, ..., A \tag{3}$$

where $\mathbf{X}_0 = \mathbf{X} - \mathrm{mean}(\mathbf{X})$, $\mathbf{Y}_0 = \mathbf{Y} - \mathrm{mean}(\mathbf{Y})$, and $A \leq M$. The algorithm of extracting the parameters is shown in Algorithm 1 (De Jong, 1993; Huang et al., 2011; Zhang et al., 2013). It can be seen as the training algorithm of the ASIMPLS based classifier.

In the SIMPLS algorithm, a constrain is added that the scores $\mathbf{t}_i$ are orthogonal to each other, i.e., $\mathbf{t}_b' \mathbf{t}_a = 0$ for $a > b$. Also $\mathbf{t}_a$ is normalized by $\mathbf{t}_a = \mathbf{t}_a / \sqrt{\mathbf{t}_a' * \mathbf{t}_a}$. Then we have $\mathbf{T}'\mathbf{T} = \mathbf{I}$ where $\mathbf{T} = [\mathbf{t}_1, ..., \mathbf{t}_A]$. Hence,

$$\widehat{\mathbf{Y}}_0 = \mathbf{TT}'\mathbf{Y}_0 = \mathbf{X}_0\mathbf{RR}'\mathbf{X}_0'\mathbf{Y}_0 = \mathbf{X}_0\mathbf{RR}'\mathbf{S}_0 \tag{4}$$

We can write $\mathbf{B}$ in (1) as:

$$\mathbf{B} = \mathbf{R}(\mathbf{R}'\mathbf{S}_0) = \mathbf{R}(\mathbf{T}'\mathbf{Y}_0) = \mathbf{RQ}' \tag{5}$$

For a new feature matrix $\mathbf{X}^*$, the new projected matrix

$$\widehat{\mathbf{Y}}^* = \mathbf{X}_0^*\mathbf{B} \tag{6}$$

where $\mathbf{X}_0^* = \mathbf{X}^* - \mathrm{mean}(\mathbf{X}^*)$. The prediction can be written in another format (De Jong, 1993):

$$\mathbf{Y} = \sum_{i=1}^{A} \mathbf{b}_i \mathbf{t}_i^* \mathbf{q}_i' \tag{7}$$

---

[1]https://code.google.com/archive/p/word2vec/

Algorithm 1 Training procedure of SIMPLS
___
Input: Feature set $\mathbf{X}$, Label $\mathbf{y}$, and Number of components A

Variables: Projection matrix $\mathbf{R}$,
$\qquad$ score vectors $\mathbf{T}$ and $\mathbf{U}$,
$\qquad$ loading $\mathbf{P}$ and $\mathbf{Q}$

$\mathbf{R} = []; \mathbf{V} = []; \mathbf{Q} = []; \mathbf{T} = []; \mathbf{U} = [];$
$\mathbf{y} = [y_1, y_2, ..., y_N]'; \mathbf{X} = [\mathbf{x}_1, \mathbf{x}_2, \cdots, \mathbf{x}_N]'$
$\mathbf{y}_0 = \mathbf{y} - \text{mean}(\mathbf{y}); \mathbf{X}_0 = \mathbf{X} - \text{mean}(\mathbf{X});$
$\mathbf{S} = \mathbf{X}_0'\mathbf{y}_0$
for $i = 1$ to A **do**
$\quad \mathbf{q}_i = $ dominant eigenvectors of $\mathbf{S}'\mathbf{S}$
$\quad \mathbf{r}_i = \mathbf{S} * \mathbf{q}_i$
$\quad \mathbf{t}_i = \mathbf{X}_0 * \mathbf{r}_i$
$\quad \text{normt}_i = \text{SQRT}(\mathbf{t}_i'\mathbf{t}_i)$
$\quad \mathbf{t}_i = \mathbf{t}_i/\text{normt}_i$
$\quad \mathbf{r}_i = \mathbf{r}_i/\text{normt}_i$
$\quad \mathbf{p}_i = \mathbf{X}_0' * \mathbf{t}_i$
$\quad \mathbf{q}_i = \mathbf{y}_0^T * \mathbf{t}_i$
$\quad \mathbf{u}_i = \mathbf{y}_0 * \mathbf{q}_i$
$\quad \mathbf{v}_i = \mathbf{p}_i$
$\quad$ **if** $i > 1$ **then**
$\qquad \mathbf{v}_i = \mathbf{v}_i - \mathbf{V} * (\mathbf{V}' * \mathbf{p}_i)$
$\qquad \mathbf{u}_i = \mathbf{u}_i - \mathbf{T} * (\mathbf{T}' * \mathbf{u}_i)$
$\quad$ **end if**
$\quad \mathbf{v}_i = \mathbf{v}_i/\mathbf{SQRT}(\mathbf{v}_i' * \mathbf{v}_i)$
$\quad \mathbf{S} = \mathbf{S} - \mathbf{v}_i * (\mathbf{v}_i' * \mathbf{S})$
$\quad \mathbf{r}_i, \mathbf{t}_i, \mathbf{p}_i, \mathbf{q}_i, \mathbf{u}_i,$ and $\mathbf{v}_i$ into
$\quad \mathbf{R}, \mathbf{T}, \mathbf{P}, \mathbf{Q}, \mathbf{U},$ and $\mathbf{V}$, respectively.
end for
$\mathbf{B} = \mathbf{R} * \mathbf{Q}'$
___

Algorithm 2 To obtain new $\mathbf{T}$ in testing
___
Input: New feature matrix $\mathbf{X}$; projection matrix $\mathbf{R}$.
Output: New $\mathbf{T} = [\mathbf{t}_1^*, \mathbf{t}_2^*, ..., \mathbf{t}_A^*]$

$\mathbf{X}_0 = \mathbf{X} - \text{mean}(\mathbf{X})$
for $i = 1$ to A **do**
$\quad \mathbf{t}_i^* = \mathbf{X}_{i-1}\mathbf{r}_i;$
$\quad \mathbf{X}_i = \mathbf{X}_{i-1} - \mathbf{t}_i^*(\mathbf{t}_i^{*'}\mathbf{X}_{i-1})/(\mathbf{t}_i^{*'}\mathbf{t}_i^*);$
end for
___

where $\mathbf{b}_a = \mathbf{u}_a'\mathbf{t}_a/(\mathbf{t}_a'\mathbf{t}_a)$. The new $\mathbf{t}^*$ is calculated by Algorithm 2. For the classification problems, we need to predict the label of a sample

$$\hat{\mathbf{Y}} = \text{sign}(\sum_{i=1}^{A} \mathbf{b}_i\mathbf{t}_i^*\mathbf{q}_i') \tag{8}$$

$$= \text{sign}(\sum_{i=1}^{A} \mathbf{m}_i\mathbf{t}_i^*) \tag{9}$$

$$= \text{sign}(\mathbf{m} \cdot \mathbf{t}^*) \tag{10}$$

It can be observed that the label $\hat{\mathbf{Y}}$ is a function of the score vectors $\mathbf{t}^*$. If $\hat{\mathbf{Y}}$ and $\mathbf{t}$ were on a plane, the boundary would be a line passes the original point $(0,0)$. Suppose the original point is the center of the whole data set, which can be achieved by subtracting the mean of the data. When the number of instances of a class is much less than the other one, the original point will be far away from the center of the minority class, while near the center of the majority class. Hence, the line will pass cross the majority class. That is the reason that PLS based classifiers can detect the minority class well. However, the accuracy of majority class will decrease because the line cuts the majority class into two parts. The Asymmetric PLS classifier tries to move the line towards to the center of the minority class to make the boundary in the middle of the two classes (Huang et al., 2014). The distance moved is calculated on the first dimension of $\mathbf{T}$. The center points and the radii of positive and negative classes are estimated as in (11). Let the minority class be the positive class, and $index\_postive$ denotes the index of positive items in $\mathbf{Y}$. We use $\mathbf{t}_p = \mathbf{t}_1[index\_postive]$. Similarly, $\mathbf{t}_n = \mathbf{t}_1[index\_negative]$. The center points and the radii of the two classes are estimated by

$$\begin{aligned} rad_p &= std(\mathbf{t}_p) \\ rad_n &= std(\mathbf{t}_n) \\ cp_p &= mean(\mathbf{t}_p) \\ cp_n &= mean(\mathbf{t}_n) \end{aligned} \tag{11}$$

Then the distance should be moved is

$$distance = cp_p - (cp_p - cp_n) * \frac{rad_p}{rad_p + rad_n}$$

We move the line on the plane of **t**

$$\hat{\mathbf{Y}} = \text{sign}(\sum_{i=1}^{A} \mathbf{m}_i \mathbf{t}_i^*) - \mathbf{m}_1 * distance \qquad (12)$$

2.2 Features used in the ASIMPLS classifier

The features used in the ASIMPLS system are mainly adopted from the NRC-Canada (Mohammad et al., 2013) system. We will describe the features in detail in Section 3.1. In addition, we propose a type of word embedding based feature named emotional word embedding.

We assume that vectors obtained on pure positive/negative tweets are different from those obtained on the general text because the distribution of words are different. Hence, we collected three tweet sets on-line: positive, neutral, and negative. The twitter4j library [2] is used to collect the tweets. We collected a set of happy emoticons such as :), :D, :-), :o), :], :c), =], 8), =), :}, as well as a set of unhappy emoticons like :(, :-(, :c, :c, :[, :[, :{. We use them as keywords, and search tweets containing these emoticons. The tweets containing a happy emoticon are put into the positive set. Similarly, a tweet containing an unhappy emoticon is put into the negative set. For the neutral tweets, we search those containing keywords like sports, news, etc. This is a very simple rule to collect data sets. Noise will be introduced, and more filtering work shall be done in the future. Finally, we collect about 69 million positive tweets, 19 million neutral tweets, and 19 million negative tweets. The tweets are pre-processed by the CMU tweet NLP tools (Gimpel et al., 2011). We remove the @somebody tags and the hyper-links in the tweets. Three vectors are trained on the three data sets respectively for each word. The vectors are obtained using the open-source toolkit word2vec with negative sampler 10, window width 5, and vector dimension 100. The feature of a tweet is the mean value of the vectors of every word. These 300 dimensional features are put together with the other features to train the ASIMPLS classifier.

3   Reproduced Systems

With reference to the state-of-the-art system designed by team Webis (Hagen et al., 2015), we had

also incorporated three models out of four (those developed by team NRC-Canada, team GU-MLT-LT and team KLUE) into our own system. As proved by the outstanding performance of team Webis in SemEval-2015, each of the three systems employed a unique set of features that could complement each other and would help enhance the performance in the three-point scale tweets sentiment classification. Thus, we decide to keep most of the same set of features for each reimplemented model and use the same classifier, L2-regularized logistic regression, for the three reimplemented systems. In detail, we use the weka.classifiers.functions.LibLINEAR class. The SVM Type is set to be 0, and the Cost is set to be 0.05. The other parameters use default values. The preprocessing steps for all three implementations are similar, which involves converting all letters to lower case and removing all the URLs and user names. Each system is described shortly in the following subsections.

3.1   NRC-Canada

In the reimplementation of the model developed by team NRC-Canada (Mohammad et al., 2013), all preprocessed tweets are tokenized and POS-tagged with the Twitter NLP tool developed by Carnegie Mellon University (Gimpel et al., 2011). The model leverages a rich set of features. We had kept all the features. Firstly, **word N-grams** and **character N-grams** are used. Word N-grams include the existence of one to four contiguous sequences of tokens and non-contiguous ones. Character N-grams include the existence of three, four and five consecutive sequences of characters. Secondly, the number of words with **all capitalized letters** and the number of **hashtags** are included in the feature set. Thirdly, the feature set contains the number of times each **part-of-speech tag** occurred. Next, **punctuation marks** and **emoticons** are also part of the features, because the number of consecutive sequences of exclamation/question marks and the polarity of an emoticon in the tweets would help determine the overall sentiment. In addition, the number of **elongated words**, such as "youuuuuuu", and the number of **negations** are employed. As specified in (Pang et al., 2002), the negated context is part of a tweet that begins with a negation word, such as "not", and ends with a punctuation mark. With negation, the

---

sentiment expressed by a token will be reversed. We attach each token in a negated context with a suffix "NEG". Furthermore, with the Brown clustering method (Brown et al., 1992), 56,345,753 tweets by Owoputi (Owoputi et al., 2013) have been clustered into 1000 clusters. If the tokens belonging to these clusters were present in the tweets, these clusters would be included in the feature set. Lastly, three manually crafted and two automatically generated polarity dictionaries are used, i.e., the **NRC Emotion Lexicon** (Mohammad and Turney, 2010; Mohammad and Turney, 2013), **the MPQA Lexicon** (Wilson et al., 2005), **the Bing Liu Lexicon** (Hu and Liu, 2004), **Hashtag Sentiment Lexicon** and **sentiment140 Lexicon**.

3.2 GU-MLT-LT

For the system designed by team GU-MLT-LT (Günther and Furrer, 2013), the tokenization process is slightly different from that of NRC-Canada system. Besides tokenizing the original raw tweets, the letters of tweets are lowercased and these normalized tweets are tokenized. In addition, for all the elongated words shown in the aforementioned normalized tweets, such as "youuuu", repetitions of letters after the first one are removed. A new version of further normalized tweets are obtained and then tokenized. Team GU-MLT-LT employed a smaller set of features as compared to that of team NRC-Canada. Our team keeps some of the features original used by GU-MLT-LT in our reimplementation. Firstly, **unigrams and bigrams** are used. For bigrams, stop word tokens, such as "the", and punctuation tokens, such as ".", are removed. In addition, following the Porter stemmer algorithm (Porter, 1980), **the word stems** of the normalized tokens are included in the feature set. Moreover, the polarity dictionary used is **the Senti-WordNet** (Baccianella et al., 2010). Similar to that of team NRC-Canada, **clustering and negation** are also employed in the feature set.

3.3 KLUE

The tokenization process in the reimplementation of system designed by team KLUE (Proisl et al., 2013) is similar to that of team NRC-Canada. The features used by KLUE are quite different from those used by the other two teams. In order to complement the features of the other two systems, we keep most of the features used by team KLUE in our reimplementation. Firstly, **unigram and bigrams** are considered and their frequencies of occurrence serve as feature weights. In order to be counted as part of the feature set, the unigrams and bigrams should be present in at least five tweets. Secondly, **the total number of tokens per tweet** is also incorporated in the feature set. Furthermore, the polarity dictionary chosen is **AFINN-111 lexicon** (Nielsen, 2011) which contains a variety of words of degree from -5(very negative) to +5(very positive). The dictionary is used to extract features including **the frequencies of occurrence of positive and negative tokens, the total number of tokens that expressed one sentiment** as well as **the arithmetic mean of total sentiment scores per tweet**. Moreover, for **emoticons**, we adopt the manually crafted dictionary and its polarity scoring from Webis team and apply them in this reimplementation. Lastly, **negation** is considered for up to next three tokens or less for the case that the tweet ends within three tokens after the negated word and the sentiment scores for tokens up to a distance of at most 4 following the negated marker are reversed.

3.4 The fusion method

The four classifiers generate three confident scores $s_{pos}^i, s_{neu}^i, s_{neg}^i, i = 1, 2, 3, 4$ for each tweet respectively. We fuse the systems by summing these scores with a same weight. The final scores are $[\frac{1}{4}\sum_{i=1}^{4} s_{pos}^i, \frac{1}{4}\sum_{i=1}^{4} s_{neu}^i, \frac{1}{4}\sum_{i=1}^{4} s_{neg}^i]$. The predicted label is the index with the maximum score value.

We find that ASIMPLS does not perform well if the dimension of the features is much larger than the number of training samples. Unfortunately the features used in this task have more than 200 thousand dimensions, while we only have about 16 thousands training samples. Hence, the classifier fusion is used again. We split the features into 5 parts, e.g., the first 40 thousand dimensions of the features are used to train a ASIMPLS classifier. The second 40 thousand dimensions are used to train another one etc. The confidence scores of the 5 ASIMPLS classifiers are averaged to generate a new set of confidence scores. These scores are the output of the ASIMPLS system. We combine them with scores generated by other

	Training Set	Testing Set
2013	11338	3813
2014	0	1853
2016	5348	1704+1781
Total	16686	9151
After Preprocessing	16682	9146
Positive	6956	4153
Neutral	7166	3579
Negative	2560	1414

Table 1: Training and testing sets.

three systems as discussed above. For the ASIMPLS classifier, feature selection is an alternative way of improving system performance instead of classifier fusion, which will be tried in future work.

4   Experimental Results

Our training set is composed by the training and development set of SemEval-2013 as well as the training set of SemEval-2016. The testing set includes the development-test set of 2013 and 2014, as well as the development and development-test sets of 2016. The numbers of tweets in all data sets are shown in Table 1. We remove the tweets that only have @somebody or hyper-links. Hence, we have a total of 16682 tweets for training and 9146 tweets for testing after preprocessing. In both training and testing sets, there are much less number of negative tweets comparing to positive and neutral tweets. ASIMPLS may help improve the accuracy of negative tweets.

The experimental results are shown in Table 2. We list all the results of individual systems and the fusion results. In the table, the "Score" is the value obtained using the evaluation method of SemEval2016 Task 4 (Nakov et al., 2016). "Positive" means the accuracy of positive samples in the testing, i.e. $Positive = \frac{number\ of\ correct\ positive\ samples}{number\ of\ all\ positive\ samples}$. Similarly, "Negative" and "Neutral" denote the accuracies of negative as well as neutral samples respectively. "All Accuracy" means $\frac{number\ of\ all\ correct\ samples}{number\ of\ all\ testing\ samples}$. The results demonstrated that classifier fusion is able to generate better scores than individual classifiers. Fusing all systems obtained the best score 63.78. It is marginally higher than the score of fusing the first three systems 63.72. The score of the PLS system is worse than the other three systems. The reason may

be that the dimension of the features (more than 200 thousands) is even bigger than the number of training samples (about 16 thousands). The ASIMPLS classifier is not good at handling this type of data even we have used 5 subsystems to alleviate the influence of high dimensional features. Nonetheless, it obtained the highest accuracy of negative samples and the second-best accuracy of neutral samples. The positive accuracy is much worse than the other three classifiers. It indicates that the bias should be further adjusted in the future. The results of our submission are shown in Table 3. We obtained a score of 59.63 on the 2016 Tweet submission.

5   Conclusion

In this paper, we have applied classifier fusion to the sentiment analysis in twitter task. An ASIMPLS based classifier has been implemented, and has been combined with other three state-of-the-art methods. A new feature named emotional word embedding has been introduced, and has been used in the ASIMPLS based method. Experimental results demonstrated that the fusion is able to improve the system performance because it can combine the strengths of different classifiers. The ASIMPLS obtained a good minority class accuracy and a bad accuracy for the majority class. How to adjust the bias to improve the balance between these two classes is the future work.

References

Stefano Baccianella, Andrea Esuli, and Fabrizio Sebastiani. 2010. Sentiwordnet 3.0: An enhanced lexical resource for sentiment analysis and opinion mining. In *LREC*, volume 10, pages 2200–2204.

Peter F Brown, Peter V Desouza, Robert L Mercer, Vincent J Della Pietra, and Jenifer C Lai. 1992. Class-based n-gram models of natural language. *Computational linguistics*, 18(4):467–479.

Sijmen De Jong. 1993. Simpls: an alternative approach to partial least squares regression. *Chemometrics and intelligent laboratory systems*, 18(3):251–263.

Kevin Gimpel, Nathan Schneider, Brendan O'Connor, Dipanjan Das, Daniel Mills, Jacob Eisenstein, Michael Heilman, Dani Yogatama, Jeffrey Flanigan, and Noah A Smith. 2011. Part-of-speech tagging for twitter: Annotation, features, and experiments. In *Proceedings of the 49th Annual Meeting of the Association for Computational Linguistics: Human Language*

	NRC	GU-MLT-LT	KLUE	Fuse 3 methods	ASIMPLS	Fuse All
Score	61.48	62.30	61.55	63.72	57.49	**63.78**
Positive	71.18	**77.25**	70.29	74.57	56.85	74.52
Neutral	**53.93**	40.32	47.95	50.99	52.78	51.10
Negative	57.57	66.12	69.80	63.65	**75.60**	63.86
All Accuracy	62.32	61.08	61.47	63.66	58.16	**63.71**

Table 2: System performance.

2013		2014			2015	2016
Tweet	SMS	Tweet	Tweet sarcasm	Live Journal	Tweet	Tweet
69.27	59.66	68.02	46.93	69.63	63.80	59.63

Table 3: Submission results.

Technologies: short papers-Volume 2, pages 42–47. Association for Computational Linguistics.

Tobias Günther and Lenz Furrer. 2013. Gu-mlt-lt: Sentiment analysis of short messages using linguistic features and stochastic gradient descent.

Matthias Hagen, Martin Potthast, Michel Büchner, and Benno Stein. 2015. Webis: An ensemble for twitter sentiment detection. *SemEval-2015*, page 582.

Minqing Hu and Bing Liu. 2004. Mining and summarizing customer reviews. In *Proceedings of the tenth ACM SIGKDD international conference on Knowledge discovery and data mining*, pages 168–177. ACM.

Dong-yan Huang, Shuzhi Sam Ge, and Zhengchen Zhang. 2011. Speaker state classification based on fusion of asymmetric simpls and support vector machines. In *Twelfth Annual Conference of the International Speech Communication Association*.

Dong-Yan Huang, Zhengchen Zhang, and Shuzhi Sam Ge. 2014. Speaker state classification based on fusion of asymmetric simple partial least squares (simpls) and support vector machines. *Computer Speech & Language*, 28(2):392–419.

Mengyi Liu, Ruiping Wang, Shaoxin Li, Shiguang Shan, Zhiwu Huang, and Xilin Chen. 2014. Combining multiple kernel methods on riemannian manifold for emotion recognition in the wild. In *Proceedings of the 16th International Conference on Multimodal Interaction*, pages 494–501. ACM.

Saif M Mohammad and Peter D Turney. 2010. Emotions evoked by common words and phrases: Using mechanical turk to create an emotion lexicon. In *Proceedings of the NAACL HLT 2010 workshop on computational approaches to analysis and generation of emotion in text*, pages 26–34. Association for Computational Linguistics.

Saif M Mohammad and Peter D Turney. 2013. Crowdsourcing a word–emotion association lexicon. *Computational Intelligence*, 29(3):436–465.

Saif M Mohammad, Svetlana Kiritchenko, and Xiaodan Zhu. 2013. Nrc-canada: Building the state-of-the-art in sentiment analysis of tweets. *arXiv preprint arXiv:1308.6242*.

Preslav Nakov, Zornitsa Kozareva, Alan Ritter, Sara Rosenthal, Veselin Stoyanov, and Theresa Wilson. 2013. Semeval-2013 task 2: Sentiment analysis in twitter.

Preslav Nakov, Alan Ritter, Sara Rosenthal, Veselin Stoyanov, and Fabrizio Sebastiani. 2016. SemEval-2016 task 4: Sentiment analysis in Twitter. In *Proceedings of the 10th International Workshop on Semantic Evaluation (SemEval 2016)*, San Diego, California, June. Association for Computational Linguistics.

Finn Årup Nielsen. 2011. A new anew: Evaluation of a word list for sentiment analysis in microblogs. *arXiv preprint arXiv:1103.2903*.

Olutobi Owoputi, Brendan O'Connor, Chris Dyer, Kevin Gimpel, Nathan Schneider, and Noah A Smith. 2013. Improved part-of-speech tagging for online conversational text with word clusters. Association for Computational Linguistics.

Bo Pang, Lillian Lee, and Shivakumar Vaithyanathan. 2002. Thumbs up?: sentiment classification using machine learning techniques. In *Proceedings of the ACL-02 conference on Empirical methods in natural language processing-Volume 10*, pages 79–86. Association for Computational Linguistics.

Martin F Porter. 1980. An algorithm for suffix stripping. *Program*, 14(3):130–137.

Thomas Proisl, Paul Greiner, Stefan Evert, and Besim Kabashi. 2013. Klue: Simple and robust methods for polarity classification. In *Second Joint Conference on Lexical and Computational Semantics (* SEM)*, volume 2, pages 395–401.

Sara Rosenthal, Alan Ritter, Preslav Nakov, and Veselin Stoyanov. 2014. Semeval-2014 task 9: Sentiment analysis in twitter. In *Proceedings of the 8th International Workshop on Semantic Evaluation (SemEval 2014)*, pages 73–80.

Sara Rosenthal, Preslav Nakov, Svetlana Kiritchenko, Saif M Mohammad, Alan Ritter, and Veselin Stoyanov. 2015. Semeval-2015 task 10: Sentiment analysis in twitter. *Proceedings of SemEval-2015*.

Theresa Wilson, Janyce Wiebe, and Paul Hoffmann. 2005. Recognizing contextual polarity in phrase-level sentiment analysis. In *Proceedings of the conference on human language technology and empirical methods in natural language processing*, pages 347–354. Association for Computational Linguistics.

Zhengchen Zhang, Dong-yan Huang, Renbo Zhao, and Minghui Dong. 2013. Onset detection based on fusion of simpls and superflux. *Music Information Retrieval Evaluation eXchange (MIREX 2013)*.

Zhihua Zhang, Guoshun Wu, and Man Lan. 2015. Ecnu: Multi-level sentiment analysis on twitter using traditional linguistic features and word embedding features. *SemEval-2015*, page 561.

LyS at SemEval-2016 Task 4: Exploiting Neural Activation Values for Twitter Sentiment Classification and Quantification[*]

David Vilares[a], Yerai Doval[a,b], Miguel A. Alonso[a] and Carlos Gómez-Rodríguez[a]
[a]Grupo LyS, Departamento de Computación, Universidade da Coruña
Campus de A Coruña s/n, 15071, A Coruña, Spain
[b]Grupo COLE, Departamento de Informática,
E.S. de Enxeñaría Informática, Universidade de Vigo
Campus As Lagoas, 32004, Ourense, Spain
{david.vilares, yerai.doval, miguel.alonso, carlos.gomez}@udc.es

Abstract

In this paper we describe our deep learning approach for solving both two-, three- and five-class tweet polarity classification, and two- and five-class quantification. We first trained a convolutional neural network using pretrained Twitter word embeddings, so that we could extract the hidden activation values from the hidden layers once some input had been fed to the network. These values were then used as features for a support vector machine in both the classification and quantification subtasks, together with additional linguistic information in the former scenario. The results obtained for the classification subtasks show that this approach performs better than a single convolutional network, and for the quantification part it also yields good results. Official rankings locate us: 2nd (practically tied with 1st) for the binary classification task, 2nd for binary quantification and 4th (practically tied with 3rd) for the five-class polarity classification challenge.

1 Introduction

Opinion mining has become an important mechanism to monitor what people are saying about a variety of topics (Cambria et al., 2013). As an example, Thelwall et al. (2011) use SentiStrength to monitor popular events on Twitter (e.g. the Oscars, the SuperBowl), showing how these resonate among the public. In a similar line, Vilares et al. (2015) also use Twitter to measure the level of popularity of the main Spanish political leaders, proving that the results obtained by their systems are similar to the ones obtained by traditional polls.

Opinion mining on Twitter actually involves two different challenges: (1) analyzing the characteristics of individual tweets and (2) quantifying a given set of tweets so that useful statistics can be extracted. This paper describes our different models to overcome such challenges, using the SemEval 2016:Task 4 as the evaluation framework.

2 Sentiment Analysis in Twitter

The SemEval organization proposed two different types of challenges in its 2016 edition: (1) classification into two, three and five classes and (2) quantification into two and five categories. A detailed explanation of the task can be found in the description paper (Nakov et al., 2016). For all subtasks, three official splits are provided: training, development and development test sets. In this paper, we use the training and development sets for training, and the development test set for evaluation.[1]

2.1 Convolutional Neural Network

As a starting point, we train a deep neural network (DNN), in particular a convolutional neural network (CNN), following a similar configuration to the one

---

[*]This research is supported by the Ministerio de Economía y Competitividad (FFI2014-51978-C2). David Vilares is funded by the Ministerio de Educación, Cultura y Deporte (FPU13/01180). Yerai Doval is funded by the Ministerio de Economía y Competitividad (BES-2015-073768). Carlos Gómez-Rodríguez is funded by an Oportunius program grant (Xunta de Galicia).

[1]For classification into 3 polarities, we include the training set of SemEval 2013 as part of our training set and its development set as a part of our collection for tuning.

Proceedings of SemEval-2016, pages 79–84,
San Diego, California, June 16-17, 2016. ©2016 Association for Computational Linguistics

used by Severyn and Moschitti (2015). Figure 1 illustrates the topology of the CNN from where we will extract the hidden activation values.

2.1.1 Embeddings layer

Let w be a token of a vocabulary V, a word embedding is a distributed representation of that token as a low dimensional vector $v \in \mathbb{R}^n$. In that way, it is possible to create a matrix of embeddings, $E \in \mathbb{R}^{|V| \times n}$, to act as the input layer to the CNN. Particularly, we rely on a collection of Twitter word embeddings pretrained with Glove[2] (Pennington et al., 2014) with $|V| \approx 10^6$ and n=100.

Thus, given a tweet t=$[w_1, w_2, ..., w_t]$, after running our input layer we will obtain a matrix $T \in \mathbb{R}^{|t| \times n}$ that will serve as the input to the convolutional layer. Since tweets might have variable length, $|t|$ is set to 100, padding with zeros if the tweet is shorter and taking the first 100 words if it is longer. We have realized after the evaluation that this value might be not the best option for short texts, such as tweets, and we plan to optimize this parameter empirically. To avoid overfitting, we first apply dropout (Srivastava et al., 2014), which randomly sets to zero the activation values of x% of the neurons in a given layer (in this paper, $x = 50$).

2.1.2 Convolutional Layer

A convolutional layer exploits local correlations in the input data. In the case of text as input, this translates into extracting correlations between groups of word or character n-grams in a sentence. To do so, each hidden unit of the CNN will only respond (activate) to a specific continuous slice of the input text. This is implemented on `http://keras.io` using convolutional operations with m convolutional filters of width f separately applied to the input, obtaining m representations of this input usually known as feature maps.

Formally, let $T \in \mathbb{R}^{|t| \times n}$ be the matrix embedding for the tweet t and let $F \in \mathbb{R}^{f \times n}$ be a filter, the output of a wide convolution is a matrix $C \in \mathbb{R}^{m \times (|t|+f-1)}$, where each $c_i \in \mathbb{R}^{|t|+f-1}$ is defined as:

$$C_i = \sum_{j,k} T_{[i-f+1:i,:]} \otimes F \qquad (1)$$

____
[2]http://nlp.stanford.edu/data/glove.twitter.27B.zip

and where $\otimes$ is the element-wise multiplication, $1 < i < m$; and j and k are the rows and columns of the matrix $T_{[i-f+1:i,:]} \otimes F \in \mathbb{R}^{f \times n}$. The non valid rows of T ($T_{(i,:)}$ with $i < 0$) are set to zero.

Following Severyn and Moschitti (2015), in this paper we chose $f = 5$ and $m = 300$. We also rely on $ReLU(x) = max(0, x)$ as the non-linear activation function. To avoid overfitting we incorporate a L2 regularization of 0.0001. After that, a max pooling layer selects $max(ReLU(c_i))$ for each feature map.

2.1.3 Output layer

The output of the pooling layer is then passed to a fully connected layer ($\mathbb{R}^{100}$). We add again dropout (50%) and a ReLU as the activation function. Finally, an additional fully connected layer reduces the dimensionality of the input to fit the output (number of classes) and as the final step we apply a softmax function to make the final prediction.

2.1.4 Current limitations

Obtaining an accurate deep neural network can be a very slow process. Hyper-parameter engineering is often needed, but training a single DNN with its hyper-parameters can be painfully slow without enough computational resources. Additionally, *distant supervision* is also recommended to pretrain the network (Go et al., 2009; Severyn and Moschitti, 2015). These two issues act as limitations that we could not overcome at the moment. We did try pretraining, but at the moment, we did not achieve improvements over the CNN without pretraining. A preliminary analysis suggests that: (1) we need more tweets to exploit distant supervision, (2) fine hyper-parameter engineering needs to be explored to ensure that the fine-tuning on the labeled data does not completely overwrite what the network has already learned and (3), it is easy to collect tweets for analysis into 2 classes, but downloading non-noisy tweets for analysis into 3 and 5 classes is a more challenging issue.

In the following section we show how to exploit the hidden activation values of our deep learning model as part of a supervised system (Poria et al., 2015), when pretraining and fast hyper-parameter engineering are not feasible options.

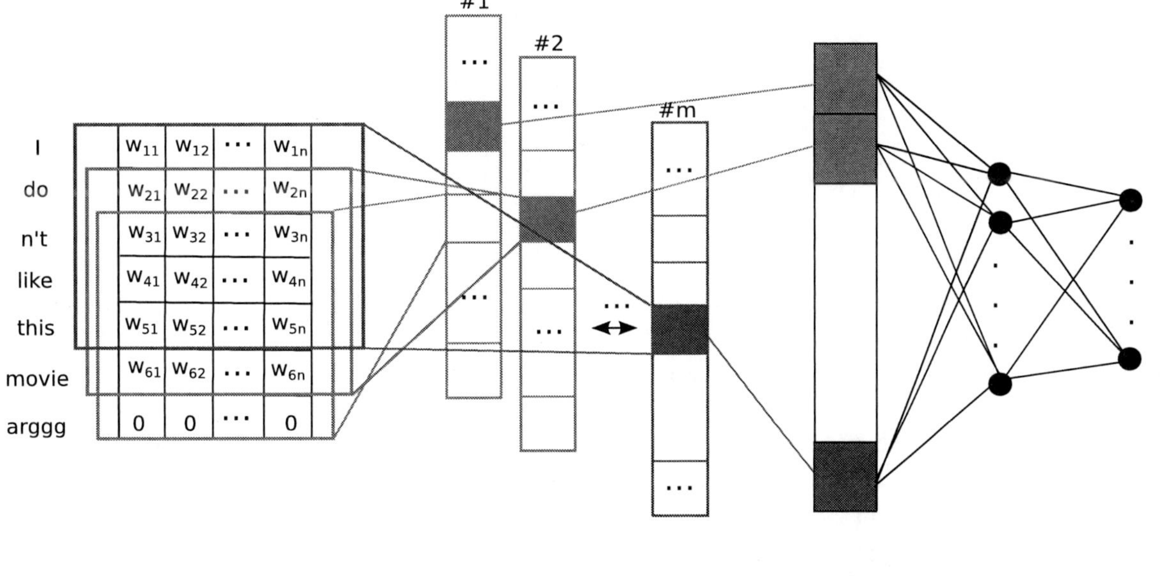

Figure 1: Topology of our CNN from where we will extract the neural activation values

2.2 Classification

Let $S=\{s_1, ..., s_n\}$ be a set of tweets and let $L=\{l_1, ..., l_n\}$ be a set of labels, the classification subtask can be defined as designing a hypothesis function $h_\Theta : S \rightarrow L$, where Θ denotes a set of features representing the texts. We build functions to solve classification into five (strong positive (P+), positive (P), neutral (NEU), negative (N) and strong negative (N+)), three (P, NEU and N) and two (P and N) classes. We rely on a support vector machine (SVM), in particular on a LibLinear (Fan et al., 2008) implementation with L2-regularization, to train our supervised model.[3] As features, we started testing some of those from of our last SemEval system (Vilares et al., 2014), using the total occurrence as the weighting factor. Information gain (IG) is used in all cases. Thus, before training our classifier we run an information gain algorithm to remove all irrelevant features, i.e. those where IG=0:

- *Words* (W): Each single word is considered as a feature to feed the supervised classifier.
- *Psychometric properties* (P): Features extracted from psychological properties coming from LIWC (Pennebaker et al., 2001) that relate

terms with psychometric properties (*e.g. anger* or *anxiety*) or topics (*e.g. family* or *religion*).

- *Part-of-speech tags* (T).

Additionally, this year we have included:

- *The last word of the tweet* (LW): The last term of each tweet is used as a separate feature.
- *The psychometric properties of the last word of the tweet* (LP).
- *Hidden activation values from the* CNN (HV): We take the hidden activation values of the last hidden layer.
- *Features extracted from sentiment dictionaries*: We extract the total, maximum, minimum and last sentiment score of a tweet from the Sentiment140 (Mohammad et al., 2013), Hu and Liu (2004) and Taboada et al. (2011) subjective lexica.

2.2.1 Experimental results

Table 1 shows the experimental results for classification into two classes obtained using the SVM with different feature sets and the CNN. The neural network outperforms most of the SVM approaches. Only when we combine a number of linguistic features with the hidden activation values and we

---

[3] We used Weka (Hall et al., 2009) to build the models.

Features	Recall-P	Recall-N	Macro avg. R
HV.P.D.LW.LP.FT*	0.721	0.803	**0.762**
HV.P.D.LW.LP.FT	0.856	0.581	0.719
HV	0.864	0.560	0.712
P	0.953	0.192	0.573
W	0.969	0.162	0.566
D	0.892	0.249	0.564
CNN	0.802	0.671	0.737

Table 1: Classification into two classes using the development test set 2016. We include feature models that include hidden activation values (HV), words (W), psychometric (P), sentiment dictionaries (D), last word of the tweet (LW) and last psychometric properties (LP). The dot indicates a model that combines those features. * indicates a model where the class weights have been tuned. We compared them against our CNN.

weight the classes, we obtain an improvement over the CNN. We believe that by applying fine hyper-parameter tuning on the CNN we will be able to further improve these results. Similar conclusions can be extracted from the classification into three classes, whose results are shown in Table 2. Finally, Table 3 details the results for the five categories classification subtask. In this case, the neural network does not perform as good as in previous scenarios.

Features	F1-P	F1-Neu	F1-N	Macro avg. F1
HV.P.FT.D.LW.LP*	0.676	0.520	0.538	0.598
HV.P.FT.D.LW.LP	0.664	0.565	0.483	0.576
HV	0.659	0.574	0.469	0.564
P	0.620	0.524	0.353	0.487
W	0.611	0.614	0.327	0.469
D	0.613	0.553	0.302	0.458
CNN	0.674	0.493	0.489	0.582

Table 2: Classification into three classes using both the development test set 2016 and the development set 2013. Macro-averaged F1-measure of positive and negative tweets is used to rank the models.

Features	F1-P+	F1-P	F1-Neu	F1-N	F1-N+	MAE
HV.P.FT.D.LW.LP*	0.277	0.621	0.439	0.296	0.237	**0.83**
HV.P.FT.D.LW.LP	0.098	0.689	0.439	0.304	0.063	0.93
HV	0.000	0.690	0.417	0.277	0.000	0.95
P	0.000	0.676	0.246	0.070	0.000	1.21
W	0.016	0.674	0.227	0.059	0.000	1.28
CNN	0.000	0.703	0.361	0.229	0.000	1.03

Table 3: Classification into five classes using the development test set 2016. Macro-averaged absolute error (MAE) is used to rank the models. F1-measure is used to show the performance over each class.

With respect to SVM-specific parameter optimiza-

tion, cost parameter (C) and class weigths (w):

- *2 classes*: C=0.005, $w_{negative}$=2.25 and $w_{positive}$=0.25.

- *3 classes*: C=0.0001, $w_{positive}$=0.5, $w_{neutral}$=0.4 and $w_{negative}$=2.

- *5 classes*: C=1, $w_{strong\ negative}$=5.5, $w_{negative}$=1, $w_{strong\ positive}$=1.5, $w_{positive}$=0.25 and $w_{neutral}$=0.5.

2.3 Quantification

For this task we are not interested in predicting the class of each individual instance of the dataset, as in classification tasks, but the relative frequency of each class in whole groups of instances; this is, the *class distribution*. In this context, models trained using loss functions well suited for classification are not necessarily good enough for quantification, as the loss function we need to optimize for has changed just in the same way as the aim of the task, in relation to a classification task (Barranquero et al., 2015).

The most simple approach to tackle this problem would be *Classify and Count* (CC) (Forman, 2008), which estimates the class frequencies counting the positive results of a classifier for each class over the total amount of input instances. Nevertheless, more specialized methods exist, such as the use of an SVM learning algorithm paired with a nonlinear loss function such as the *Kullback-Leibler Divergence* (KLD) (Esuli and Sebastiani, 2015), which we have used in this work thanks to the tool *SVM$_{perf}$* (Joachims, 2005) patched to work with KLD.[4]

The different feature sets tested for our quantification system were automatically obtained as the activation values from different layers of the convolutional network used in the classification subtasks of this workshop. The SVM model was trained with a linear kernel and no regularization bias, optimizing the KLD over the entire training dataset.

Finally, as our system deals specifically with binary quantification, we took a one-vs-all approach and trained multiple models to generalize the quantification process for n classes rather than just two

---

[4] http://hlt.isti.cnr.it/quantification/ .

(#) CNN layer	2 classes (KLD)	5 classes (EMD)
(4th) Max pooling	0.07	0.82
(5th) Linear	**0.06**	**0.55**
(6th) Dropout	**0.06**	**0.55**
(7th) ReLU	0.10	0.63
(8th) Linear	0.08	0.65
(9th) SoftMax	**0.06**	1.49
CC	0.26	2.10

Table 4: **Quantification into two and five classes** using the development test set 2016. Rows: CNN layer from where the activation values were extracted. The last one shows the CC baseline. Columns: system performance measured as KLD for two classes and Earth Mover's Distance (EMD) for five classes.

Test set	Subtask	Score	Ranking
Twitter 2016	A	0.575	(16/34)
Twitter 2016	**B**	**0.791**	**(2/19)**
Twitter 2016	**C**	**0.860**	**(4/11)**
Twitter 2016	**D**	**0.053**	**(2/14)**
Twitter 2016	E	0.360	(7/10)
Twitter 2013	A	0.650	(9/34)
SMS 2013	A	0.579	(13/34)
Twitter 2014	A	0.647	(13/34)
Twitter Sarcasm 2014	A	0.406	(18/34)
Live Journal 2014	A	0.655	(11/34)
Twitter 2015	A	0.603	(12/34)

Table 5: **Overall ranking** on the test sets following the official metric for each task.

classes. The results obtained later by these models were normalized so that relative frequencies sum up to one.

2.3.1 Experimental results

Results obtained using neural activation values chosen from particular layers of our convolutional network as features for the SVM can be found in Table 4. As our baseline, we performed a CC on the results obtained from the best classifiers from the classification subtasks.

3 Results on the gold test set

Table 5 shows the scores and rankings of our systems for each subtask, according to the official metrics used for each challenge. A detailed report of the results for all participants can be found at Nakov et al. (2016) and the official website.[5]

4 Conclusions

We have described our approach to tackle the classification and quantification challenges proposed at

---

[5]http://alt.qcri.org/semeval2016/task4/index.php?id=results

Task 4 of SemEval 2016: Sentiment Analysis in Twitter. Official rankings locate us in top positions for binary classification and quantification and also for the 5-class polarity classification challenge.

We first trained a convolutional neural network to address the classification challenge. Additionally, we used its hidden activation values as features to train support vector machines, both for classification and quantification tasks. In light of the results obtained, we can state that our convolutional network seems to be a good feature extractor for both of these tasks.

As future work, we plan to exploit new distributed representations of the input to improve the performance of our current model. For the quantification task, we are planning on extending our experiments to 8 other machine learning arquitectures, such as quantification trees (Milli et al., 2013) and different types of neural networks, and further exploring the feature domain using both handcrafted features and other continuous representation methods such as *doc2vec* (Le and Mikolov, 2014).

References

J. Barranquero, J. Díez, and J. J. del Coz. 2015. Quantification-oriented learning based on reliable classifiers. *Pattern Recognition*, 48(2):591–604.

E. Cambria, B. Schuller, Y. Xia, and C. Havasi. 2013. New avenues in opinion mining and sentiment analysis. *IEEE Intelligent Systems*, (2):15–21.

A. Esuli and F. Sebastiani. 2015. Optimizing text quantifiers for multivariate loss functions. *ACM Trans. Knowl. Discov. Data*, 9(4):27:1–27:27, June.

R. Fan, K. Chang, C. Hsieh, X. Wang, and C. Lin. 2008. LIBLINEAR: A library for large linear classification. *The Journal of Machine Learning Research*, 9:1871–1874.

G. Forman. 2008. Quantifying counts and costs via classification. *Data Min. Knowl. Discov.*, 17(2):164–206, October.

A. Go, R. Bhayani, and L. Huang. 2009. Twitter sentiment classification using distant supervision. *CS224N Project Report, Stanford*, 1:12.

M. Hall, E. Frank, G. Holmes, B. Pfahringer, P. Reutemann, and I. H. Witten. 2009. The WEKA data mining software: an update. *SIGKDD Explor. Newsl.*, 11(1):10–18, nov.

M. Hu and B. Liu. 2004. Mining and summarizing customer reviews. In *Proceedings of the tenth ACM*

SIGKDD international conference on Knowledge discovery and data mining, pages 168–177. ACM.

T. Joachims. 2005. A support vector method for multivariate performance measures. In *Proceedings of the 22nd International Conference on Machine Learning*, ICML '05, pages 377–384, New York, NY, USA. ACM.

Q. V. Le and T. Mikolov. 2014. Distributed representations of sentences and documents. *arXiv preprint arXiv:1405.4053*.

L. Milli, A. Monreale, G. Rossetti, F. Giannotti, D. Pedreschi, and F. Sebastiani. 2013. Quantification trees. In *Data Mining (ICDM), 2013 IEEE 13th International Conference on*, pages 528–536. IEEE.

S. M. Mohammad, S. Kiritchenko, and X. Zhu. 2013. NRC-Canada: Building the State-of-the-Art in Sentiment Analysis of Tweets. In *Proceedings of the seventh international workshop on Semantic Evaluation Exercises (SemEval-2013)*, Atlanta, Georgia, USA, June.

P. Nakov, A. Ritter, S. Rosenthal, V. Stoyanov, and F. Sebastiani. 2016. SemEval-2016 task 4: Sentiment analysis in Twitter. In *Proceedings of the 10th International Workshop on Semantic Evaluation (SemEval 2016)*, San Diego, California, June. Association for Computational Linguistics.

J. W. Pennebaker, M. E. Francis, and R. J. Booth. 2001. Linguistic inquiry and word count: LIWC 2001. *Mahway: Lawrence Erlbaum Associates*, page 71.

J. Pennington, R. Socher, and C. D Manning. 2014. Glove: Global Vectors for Word Representation. In *EMNLP*, volume 14, pages 1532–1543.

S. Poria, E. Cambria, and A. Gelbukh. 2015. Deep convolutional neural network textual features and multiple kernel learning for utterance-level multimodal sentiment analysis. In *Proceedings of EMNLP*, pages 2539–2544.

A Severyn and A Moschitti. 2015. UNITN: Training Deep Convolutional Neural Network for Twitter Sentiment Classification. In *Proceedings of the 9th International Workshop on Semantic Evaluation (SemEval 2015)*, pages 464–469, Denver, Colorado. Association for Computational Linguistics.

N. Srivastava, G. Hinton, A. Krizhevsky, I. Sutskever, and R. Salakhutdinov. 2014. Dropout: A simple way to prevent neural networks from overfitting. *The Journal of Machine Learning Research*, 15(1):1929–1958.

M. Taboada, J. Brooke, M. Tofiloski, K. Voll, and M. Stede. 2011. Lexicon-based methods for sentiment analysis. *Computational Linguistics*, 37(2):267–307.

M. Thelwall, K. Buckley, and G. Paltoglou. 2011. Sentiment in Twitter events. *J. Am. Soc. Inf. Sci. Technol.*, 62(2):406–418.

D. Vilares, M. Hermo, M. A. Alonso, C. Gómez-Rodríguez, and Y. Doval. 2014. LyS : Porting a Twitter Sentiment Analysis Approach from Spanish to English. In *Proceedings og The 8th InternationalWorkshop on Semantic Evaluation (SemEval 2014)*, number SemEval, pages 411–415.

D. Vilares, M. Thelwall, and M. A Alonso. 2015. The megaphone of the people? Spanish SentiStrength for real-time analysis of political tweets. *Journal of Information Science*, 41(6):799–813.

TwiSE at SemEval-2016 Task 4: Twitter Sentiment Classification

Georgios Balikas and **Massih-Reza Amini**
University of Grenoble-Alpes
`firstnane.lastname@imag.fr`

Abstract

This paper describes the participation of the team "TwiSE" in the SemEval 2016 challenge. Specifically, we participated in Task 4, namely "Sentiment Analysis in Twitter" for which we implemented sentiment classification systems for subtasks A, B, C and D. Our approach consists of two steps. In the first step, we generate and validate diverse feature sets for twitter sentiment evaluation, inspired by the work of participants of previous editions of such challenges. In the second step, we focus on the optimization of the evaluation measures of the different subtasks. To this end, we examine different learning strategies by validating them on the data provided by the task organisers. For our final submissions we used an ensemble learning approach (stacked generalization) for Subtask A and single linear models for the rest of the subtasks. In the official leaderboard we were ranked 9/35, 8/19, 1/11 and 2/14 for subtasks A, B, C and D respectively. The code can be found at `https://github.com/balikasg/SemEval2016-Twitter_Sentiment_Evaluation`.

1 Introduction

During the last decade, short-text communication forms, such as Twitter microblogging, have been widely adopted and have become ubiquitous. Using such forms of communication, users share a variety of information. However, information concerning one's sentiment on the world around her has attracted a lot of research interest (Nakov et al., 2016; Rosenthal et al., 2015).

Working with such short, informal text spans poses a number of different challenges to the Natural Language Processing (NLP) and Machine Learning (ML) communities. Those challenges arise from the vocabulary used (slang, abbreviations, emojis) (Maas et al., 2011), the short size, and the complex linguistic phenomena such as sarcasm (Rajadesingan et al., 2015) that often occur.

We present, here, our participation in Task 4 of SemEval 2016 (Nakov et al., 2016), namely Sentiment Analysis in Twitter. Task 4 comprised five different subtasks: Subtask A: Message Polarity Classification, Subtask B: Tweet classification according to a two-point scale, Subtask C: Tweet classification according to a five-point scale, Subtask D: Tweet quantification according to a two-point scale, and Subtask E: Tweet quantification according to a five-point scale. We participated in the first four subtasks under the team name "TwiSE" (<u>Twi</u>tter <u>S</u>entiment <u>E</u>valuation). Our work consists of two steps: the preprocessing and feature extraction step, where we implemented and tested different feature sets proposed by participants of the previous editions of SemEval challenges (Tang et al., 2014; Kiritchenko et al., 2014a), and the learning step, where we investigated and optimized the performance of different learning strategies for the SemEval subtasks. For Subtask A we submitted the output of a stacked generalization (Wolpert, 1992) ensemble learning approach using the probabilistic outputs of a set of linear models as base models, whereas for the rest of the subtasks we submitted the outputs of single models, such as Support Vector Machines and Logistic

Proceedings of SemEval-2016, pages 85–91,
San Diego, California, June 16-17, 2016. ©2016 Association for Computational Linguistics

Regression.[1]

The remainder of the paper is organised as follows: in Section 2 we describe the feature extraction and the feature transformations we used, in Section 3 we present the learning strategies we employed, in Section 4 we present a part of the in-house validation we performed to assess the models' performance, and finally, we conclude in Section 5 with remarks on our future work.

2 Feature Engineering

We present the details of the feature extraction and transformation mechanisms we used. Our approach is based on the traditional N-gram extraction and on the use of sentiment lexicons describing the sentiment polarity of unigrams and/or bigrams. For the data pre-processing, cleaning and tokenization[2] as well as for most of the learning steps, we used Python's Scikit-Learn (Pedregosa et al., 2011) and NLTK (Bird et al., 2009).

2.1 Feature Extraction

Similar to (Kiritchenko et al., 2014b) we extracted features based on the lexical content of each tweet and we also used sentiment-specific lexicons. The features extracted for each tweet include:

- N-grams with $N \in [1, 4]$, character grams of dimension $M \in [3, 5]$,

- # of exclamation marks, # of question marks, # of both exclamation and question marks,

- # of capitalized words and # of elongated words,

- # of negated contexts; negation also affected the N-grams features by transforming a word w in a negated context to w_NEG,

- # of positive emoticons, # of negative emoticons and a binary feature indicating if emoticons exist in a given tweet, and

- Part-of-speech (POS) tags (Gimpel et al., 2011) and their occurrences partitioned regarding the positive and negative contexts.

With regard to the sentiment lexicons, we used:

- manual sentiment lexicons: the Bing liu's lexicon (Hu and Liu, 2004), the NRC emotion lexicon (Mohammad and Turney, 2010), and the MPQA lexicon (Wilson et al., 2005),

- # of words in positive and negative context belonging to the word clusters provided by the CMU Twitter NLP tool[3]

- positional sentiment lexicons: sentiment 140 lexicon (Go et al., 2009) and the Hashtag Sentiment Lexicon (Kiritchenko et al., 2014b)

We make, here, more explixit the way we used the sentiment lexicons, using the Bing Liu's lexicon as an example. We treated the rest of the lexicons similarly. For each tweet, using the Bing Liu's lexicon we obtain a 104-dimensional vector. After tokenizing the tweet, we count how many words (i) in positive/negative contenxts belong to the positive/negative lexicons (4 features) and we repeat the process for the hashtags (4 features). To this point we have 8 features. We generate those 8 features for the lowercase words and the uppercase words. Finally, for each of the 24 POS tags the (Gimpel et al., 2011) tagger generates, we count how many words in positive/negative contenxts belong to the positive/negative lexicon. As a results, this generates $2 \times 8 + 24 \times 4 = 104$ features in total for each tweet.

For each tweet we also used the distributed representations provided by (Tang et al., 2014) using the min, max and average composition functions on the vector representations of the words of each tweet.

2.2 Feature Representation and Transformation

We describe the different representations of the extracted N-grams and character-grams we compared when optimizing our performance on each of the classification subtasks we participated. In the rest of this subsection we refer to both N-grams and

---

[1]To enable replicability we make the code we used available at `https://github.com/balikasg/SemEval2016-Twitter_Sentiment_Evaluation`.

[2]We adapted the tokenizer provided at `http://sentiment.christopherpotts.net/tokenizing.html`

[3]`http://www.cs.cmu.edu/~ark/TweetNLP/`

character-grams as words, in the general sense of letter strings. We evaluated two ways of representing such features: (i) a bag-of-words representation, that is for each tweet a sparse vector of dimension $|V|$ is generated, where $|V|$ is the vocabulary size, and (ii) a hashing function, that is a fast and space-efficient way of vectorizing features, i.e. turning arbitrary features into indices in a vector (Weinberger et al., 2009). We found that the performance using hashing representations was better. Hence, we opted for such representations and we tuned the size of the feature space for each subtask.

Concerning the transformation of the features of words, we compared the tf-idf weighing scheme and the α-power transformation. The latter, transforms each vector $x = (x_1, x_2, \ldots, x_d)$ to $x' = (x_1^\alpha, x_2^\alpha, \ldots, x_d^\alpha)$ (Jegou et al., 2012). The main intuition behind the α-power transformation is that it reduces the effect of the most common words. Note that this is also the rationale behind the *idf* weighting scheme. However, we obtained better results using the α-power transformation. Hence, we tuned α separately for each of the subtasks.

3   The Learning Step

Having the features extracted we experimented with several families of classifiers such as linear models, maximum-margin models, nearest neighbours approaches and trees. We evaluated their performance using the data provided by the organisers, which were already split in training, validation and testing parts. Table 1 shows information about the tweets we managed to download. From the early validation schemes, we found that the two most competitive models were Logistic Regression from the family of linear models, and Support Vector Machines (SVMs) from the family of maximum margin models. It is to be noted that this is in line with the previous research (Mohammad et al., 2013; Büchner and Stein, 2015).

3.1   Subtask A

Subtask A concerns a multiclass classification problem, where the general polarity of tweets has to be classified in one among three classes: "Positive", "Negative" and "Neutral", each denoting the tweet's overall polarity. The evaluation measure used for the subtask is the Macro-F_1 measure, calculated only for the Positive and Negative classes (Nakov et al., 2016).

Inspired by the wining system of SemEval 2015 Task 10 (Büchner and Stein, 2015) we decided to employ an ensemble learning approach. Hence, our goal is twofold: (i) to generate a set of models that perform well as individual models, and (ii) to select a subset of models of (i) that generate diverse outputs and to combine them using an ensemble learning step that would result in lower generalization error.

We trained four such models as base models. Their details are presented in Table 2. In the stacked generalization approach we employed, we found that by training the second level classifier on the probabilistic outputs, instead of the predictions of the base models, yields better results. Logistic Regression generates probabilities as its outputs. In the case of SVMs, we transformed the confidence scores into probabilities using two methods, after adapting them to the multiclass setting: the Platt's method (Platt and others, 1999) and the isotonic regression (Zadrozny and Elkan, 2002). To solve the optimization problems of SVMs we used the Liblinear solvers (Fan et al., 2008). For Logistic Regression we used either Liblinear or LBFGS, with the latter being a limited memory quasi Newton method for general unconstrained optimization problems (Yu et al., 2011). To attack the multiclass problem, we selected among the traditional one-vs-rest approach, the crammer-singer approach for SVMs (Crammer and Singer, 2002), or the multinomial approach for Logistic Regression (also known as MaxEnt classifier), where the multinomial loss is minimised across the entire probability distribution (Malouf, 2002).

For each of the four base models the tweets are represented by the complete feature set described in Section 2. For transforming the n-grams and character-grams, the value of $\alpha \in \{0.2, 0.4, 0.6, 0.8, 1\}$, the dimension of the space where the hashing function projects them, as well as the value of $\lambda \in \{10^{-7}, \ldots, 10^6\}$ that controls the importance of the regularization term in the SVM and Logistic regression optimization problems were selected by grid searching using 5-fold cross-validation on the training part of the provided data. We tuned each model independently before integrat-

	Train	Development	DevTest	Test
Subtask A	5,500	1,831	1,791	32,009
Subtask B & D	4,346	1,325	1,417	10,551
Subtask C & E	5,482	1,810	1,778	20,632

Table 1: Size of the data used for training and development purposes. We only relied on the SemEval 2016 datasets.

Algorithm	Multiclass approach	Optimizer	Probabilistic Outputs
SVMs	crammer-singer	Liblinear	isotonic regression
SVMs	crammer-singer	Liblinear	Platt's
Logistic Regression	one-vs-all	Liblinear	native
Logistic Regression	multinomial loss function	LBFGS	native

Table 2: Description of the base learners used in the stacked generalization approach.

ing it in the stacked generalization.

Having the fine-tuned probability estimates for each of the instances of the test sets and for each of the base learners, we trained a second layer classifier using those fine-grained outputs. For this, we used SVMs, using the crammer-singer approach for the multi-class problem, which yielded the best performance in our validation schemes. Also, since the classification problem is unbalanced in the sense that the three classes are not equally represented in the training data, we assigned weights to make the problem balanced. Those weights were inversely proportional to the class frequencies in the input data for each class.

3.2 Subtask B

Subtask B is a binary classification problem where given a tweet known to be about a given topic, one has to classify whether the tweet conveys a positive or a negative sentiment towards the topic. The evaluation measure proposed by the organisers for this subtask is macro-averaged recall (MaR) over the positive and negative class.

Our participation is based on a single model. We used SVMs with a linear kernel and the Liblinear optimizer. We used the full feature set described in Section 2, after excluding the distributed embeddings because in our local validation experiments we found that they actually hurt the performance. Similarly to subtask A and due to the unbalanced nature of the problem, we use weights for the classes of the problem. Note that we do not consider the topic of the tweet and we classify the tweet's overall polarity.

Hence, we ignore the case where the tweet consists of more than one parts, each expressing different polarities about different parts.

3.3 Subtask C

Subtask C concerns an ordinal classification problem. In the framework of this subtask, given a tweet known to be about a given topic, one has to estimate the sentiment conveyed by the tweet towards the topic on a five-point scale. Ordinal classification differs from standard multiclass classification in that the classes are ordered and the error takes into account this ordering so that not all mistakes weigh equally. In the tweet classification problem for instance, a classifier that would assign the class "1" to an instance belonging to class "2" will be less penalized compared to a classifier that will assign "-1" as the class . To this direction, the evaluation measure proposed by the organisers is the macroaveraged mean absolute error.

Similarly to Subtask B, we submitted the results of a single model and we classified the tweets according to their overall polarity ignoring the given topics. Instead of using one of the ordinal classification methods proposed in the bibliography, we use a standard multiclass approach. For that we use a Logistic Regression that minimizes the multinomial loss across the classes. Again, we use weights to cope with the unbalanced nature of our data. The distributed embeddings are excluded by the feature sets.

We elaborate here on our choice to use a conventional multiclass classification approach instead of an ordinal one. We evaluated a selection of methods described in (Pedregosa-Izquierdo, 2015) and in (Gutiérrez et al., 2015). In both cases, the results achieved with the multiclass methods were marginally better and for simplicity we opted for the multiclass methods. We believe that this is due to the nature of the problem: the feature sets and especially the fine-grained sentiment lexicons manage to encode the sentiment direction efficiently. Hence, assigning a class of completely opposite sentiment can only happen due to a complex linguistic phenomenon such as sarcasm. In the latter case, both methods may fail equally.

3.4 Subtask D

Subtask D is a binary quantification problem. In particular, given a set of tweets known to be about a given topic, one has to estimate the distribution of the tweets across the Positive and Negative classes. For instance, having 100 tweets about the new iPhone, one must estimate the fractions of the Positive and Negative tweets respectively. The organisers proposed a smoothed version of the Kullback-Leibler Divergence (KLD) as the subtask's evaluation measure.

We apply a classify and count approach for this task (Bella et al., 2010; Forman, 2008), that is we first classify each of the tweets and we then count the instances that belong to each class. To this end, we compare two approaches both trained on the features sets of Section 2 excluding the distributed representations: the standard multiclass SVM and a structure learning SVM that directly optimizes KLD (Esuli and Sebastiani, 2015). Again, our final submission uses the standard SVM with weights to cope with the imbalance problem as the model to classify the tweets. That is because the method of (Gao and Sebastiani, 2015) although competitive was outperformed in most of our local validation schemes.

4 The evaluation framework

Before reporting the scores we obtained, we elaborate on our validation strategy and the steps we used when tuning our models. in each of the subtasks we only used the data that were realised for the 2016 edition of the challenge. Our validation had the following steps:

	DevTest	Test	Rank
Subtask A	56.01	58.61	9/35
Subtask B	0.748	0.748	8/18
Subtask C	0.8121	0.72	1/11
Subtask D	0.00018	0.053	2/14

Table 3: The performance obtained on the "devtest" data and the SemEval 2016 Task 4 test data.

1. Training using the released training data,

2. validation on the validation data,

3. validation again, in the union of the devtest and trial data (when applicable), after retraining on training and validation data.

For each parameter, we selected its value by averaging the optimal parameters with respect to the output of the above-listed steps (2) and (3). It is to be noted, that we strictly relied on the data released as part of the 2016 edition of SemEval; we didn't use past data.

We now present the performance we achieved both in our local evaluation schemas and in the official results released by the challenge organisers. Table 3 presents the results we obtained in the "DevTest" part of the challenge dataset and the scores on the test data as they were released by the organisers. In the latter, we were ranked 9/35, 8/19, 1/11 and 2/14 for subtasks A, B, C and D respectively. Observe, that for subtasks A and B, using just the "devtest" part of the data as validation mechanism results in a quite accurate performance estimation.

5 Future Work

That was our first contact with the task of sentiment analysis and we achieved satisfactory results. We relied on features proposed in the framework of previous SemEval challenges and we investigated the performance of different classification algorithms.

In our future work we will investigate directions both in the feature engineering and in the algorithmic/learning part. Firstly, we aim to deal with tweets in a finer level of granularity. As discussed in Section 3, in each of the tasks we classified the overall polarity of the tweet, ignoring cases where the tweets were referring to two or more subjects. In the same line, we plan to improve our mechanism for handling negation. We have used a simple mechanism where a negative context is defined as the group of words after a negative word until a punctuation symbol. However, our error analysis revealed that punctuation is rarely used in tweets. Finally, we plan to investigate ways to integrate more data in our approaches, since we only used this edition's data.

The application of an ensemble learning approach, is a promising direction towards the short text sentiment evaluation. To this direction, we hope that an extensive error analysis process will help us identify better classification systems that when integrated in our ensemble (of subtask A) will reduce the generalization error.

Acknowledgments

We would like to thank the organisers of the Task 4 of SemEval 2016, for providing the data, the guidelines and the infrastructure. We would also like to thank the anonymous reviewers for their insightful comments.

References

[Bella et al.2010] Antonio Bella, Cesar Ferri, José Hernández-Orallo, and Maria Jose Ramirez-Quintana. 2010. Quantification via probability estimators. In *Data Mining (ICDM), 2010 IEEE 10th International Conference on*, pages 737–742. IEEE.

[Bird et al.2009] Steven Bird, Ewan Klein, and Edward Loper. 2009. *Natural Language Processing with Python*. O'Reilly Media.

[Büchner and Stein2015] Matthias Hagen Martin Potthast Michel Büchner and Benno Stein. 2015. Webis: An ensemble for twitter sentiment detection. *SemEval-2015*, page 582.

[Crammer and Singer2002] Koby Crammer and Yoram Singer. 2002. On the algorithmic implementation of multiclass kernel-based vector machines. *The Journal of Machine Learning Research*, 2:265–292.

[Esuli and Sebastiani2015] Andrea Esuli and Fabrizio Sebastiani. 2015. Optimizing text quantifiers for multivariate loss functions. *ACM Transactions on Knowledge Discovery from Data (TKDD)*, 9(4):27.

[Fan et al.2008] Rong-En Fan, Kai-Wei Chang, Cho-Jui Hsieh, Xiang-Rui Wang, and Chih-Jen Lin. 2008. Liblinear: A library for large linear classification. *The Journal of Machine Learning Research*, 9:1871–1874.

[Forman2008] George Forman. 2008. Quantifying counts and costs via classification. *Data Mining and Knowledge Discovery*, 17(2):164–206.

[Gao and Sebastiani2015] Wei Gao and Fabrizio Sebastiani. 2015. Tweet sentiment: From classification to quantification. In *Proceedings of the 2015 IEEE/ACM International Conference on Advances in Social Networks Analysis and Mining 2015*, pages 97–104. ACM.

[Gimpel et al.2011] Kevin Gimpel, Nathan Schneider, Brendan O'Connor, Dipanjan Das, Daniel Mills, Jacob Eisenstein, Michael Heilman, Dani Yogatama, Jeffrey Flanigan, and Noah A Smith. 2011. Part-of-speech tagging for twitter: Annotation, features, and experiments. In *Proceedings of the 49th Annual Meeting of the Association for Computational Linguistics: Human Language Technologies: short papers-Volume 2*, pages 42–47. Association for Computational Linguistics.

[Go et al.2009] Alec Go, Richa Bhayani, and Lei Huang. 2009. Twitter sentiment classification using distant supervision. *CS224N Project Report, Stanford*, 1:12.

[Gutiérrez et al.2015] P.A. Gutiérrez, M. Pérez-Ortiz, J. Sánchez-Monedero, F. Fernandez-Navarro, and C. Hervás-Martínez. 2015. Ordinal regression methods: survey and experimental study. *IEEE Transactions on Knowledge and Data Engineering*, Accepted.

[Hu and Liu2004] Minqing Hu and Bing Liu. 2004. Mining and summarizing customer reviews. In *Proceedings of the tenth ACM SIGKDD international conference on Knowledge discovery and data mining*, pages 168–177. ACM.

[Jegou et al.2012] H. Jegou, F. Perronnin, M. Douze, J. Sanchez, P. Perez, and C. Schmid. 2012. Aggregating local image descriptors into compact codes. *Pattern Analysis and Machine Intelligence, IEEE Transactions on*, 34(9):1704–1716, Sept.

[Kiritchenko et al.2014a] Svetlana Kiritchenko, Xiaodan Zhu, Colin Cherry, and Saif Mohammad. 2014a. Nrc-canada-2014: Detecting aspects and sentiment in customer reviews. In *Proceedings of the 8th International Workshop on Semantic Evaluation (SemEval 2014)*, pages 437–442. Association for Computational Linguistics and Dublin City University Dublin, Ireland.

[Kiritchenko et al.2014b] Svetlana Kiritchenko, Xiaodan Zhu, and Saif M Mohammad. 2014b. Sentiment analysis of short informal texts. *Journal of Artificial Intelligence Research*, pages 723–762.

[Maas et al.2011] Andrew L Maas, Andrew Y Ng, and Christopher Potts. 2011. Multi-dimensional sentiment analysis with learned representations.

[Malouf2002] Robert Malouf. 2002. A comparison of algorithms for maximum entropy parameter estimation. In *proceedings of the 6th conference on Natural language learning-Volume 20*, pages 1–7. Association for Computational Linguistics.

[Mohammad and Turney2010] Saif M Mohammad and Peter D Turney. 2010. Emotions evoked by common words and phrases: Using mechanical turk to create an emotion lexicon. In *Proceedings of the NAACL HLT 2010 workshop on computational approaches to analysis and generation of emotion in text*, pages 26–34. Association for Computational Linguistics.

[Mohammad et al.2013] Saif M Mohammad, Svetlana Kiritchenko, and Xiaodan Zhu. 2013. Nrc-canada: Building the state-of-the-art in sentiment analysis of tweets. *arXiv preprint arXiv:1308.6242.*

[Nakov et al.2016] Preslav Nakov, Alan Ritter, Sara Rosenthal, Veselin Stoyanov, and Fabrizio Sebastiani. 2016. SemEval-2016 task 4: Sentiment analysis in Twitter. In *Proceedings of the 10th International Workshop on Semantic Evaluation (SemEval 2016)*, San Diego, California, June. Association for Computational Linguistics.

[Pedregosa et al.2011] F. Pedregosa, G. Varoquaux, A. Gramfort, V. Michel, B. Thirion, O. Grisel, M. Blondel, P. Prettenhofer, R. Weiss, V. Dubourg, J. Vanderplas, A. Passos, D. Cournapeau, M. Brucher, M. Perrot, and E. Duchesnay. 2011. Scikit-learn: Machine learning in Python. *Journal of Machine Learning Research*, 12:2825–2830.

[Pedregosa-Izquierdo2015] Fabian Pedregosa-Izquierdo. 2015. *Feature extraction and supervised learning on fMRI: from practice to theory*. Ph.D. thesis, Université Pierre et Marie Curie.

[Platt and others1999] John Platt et al. 1999. Probabilistic outputs for support vector machines and comparisons to regularized likelihood methods. *Advances in large margin classifiers*, 10(3):61–74.

[Rajadesingan et al.2015] Ashwin Rajadesingan, Reza Zafarani, and Huan Liu. 2015. Sarcasm detection on twitter: A behavioral modeling approach. In *Proceedings of the Eighth ACM International Conference on Web Search and Data Mining*, pages 97–106. ACM.

[Rosenthal et al.2015] Sara Rosenthal, Preslav Nakov, Svetlana Kiritchenko, Saif M Mohammad, Alan Ritter, and Veselin Stoyanov. 2015. Semeval-2015 task 10: Sentiment analysis in twitter. *Proceedings of SemEval-2015.*

[Tang et al.2014] Duyu Tang, Furu Wei, Nan Yang, Ming Zhou, Ting Liu, and Bing Qin. 2014. Learning sentiment-specific word embedding for twitter sentiment classification. In *Proceedings of the 52nd Annual Meeting of the Association for Computational Linguistics (Volume 1: Long Papers)*, pages 1555–1565, Baltimore, Maryland, June. Association for Computational Linguistics.

[Weinberger et al.2009] Kilian Weinberger, Anirban Dasgupta, John Langford, Alex Smola, and Josh Attenberg. 2009. Feature hashing for large scale multitask learning. In *Proceedings of the 26th Annual International Conference on Machine Learning*, pages 1113–1120. ACM.

[Wilson et al.2005] Theresa Wilson, Janyce Wiebe, and Paul Hoffmann. 2005. Recognizing contextual polarity in phrase-level sentiment analysis. In *Proceedings of the conference on human language technology and empirical methods in natural language processing*, pages 347–354. Association for Computational Linguistics.

[Wolpert1992] David H Wolpert. 1992. Stacked generalization. *Neural networks*, 5(2):241–259.

[Yu et al.2011] Hsiang-Fu Yu, Fang-Lan Huang, and Chih-Jen Lin. 2011. Dual coordinate descent methods for logistic regression and maximum entropy models. *Machine Learning*, 85(1-2):41–75.

[Zadrozny and Elkan2002] Bianca Zadrozny and Charles Elkan. 2002. Transforming classifier scores into accurate multiclass probability estimates. In *Proceedings of the eighth ACM SIGKDD international conference on Knowledge discovery and data mining*, pages 694–699. ACM.

ISTI-CNR at SemEval-2016 Task 4: Quantification on an Ordinal Scale

Andrea Esuli

Istituto di Scienza e Tecnologia dell'Informazione "A. Faedo"
via G. Moruzzi, 1
56124, Pisa, ITALY
`andrea.esuli@isti.cnr.it`

Abstract

This paper details on the participation of ISTI-CNR to task 4 of Semeval 2016. Among the five subtasks, special attention has been paid to the five-point scale quantification subtask. The quantification method we propose is based on the observation that a standard document-by-document regression method usually has a bias towards assigning high prevalence labels. Our method models such bias with a linear model, in order to compensate it and to produce the quantification estimates.

1 Introduction

The participation of ISTI-CNR to task 4 of Semeval 2016 (Nakov et al., 2016) produced submissions for all the five proposed subtasks.

Submissions for subtasks A and B are based on a relatively typical machine learning pipeline, with B used as the base classification tool for subtask D, which uses a quantification via classification method. Subtask C uses an ordinal regression method, based on building a data-balanced tree of binary classifiers. The regression method of subtask C has been used as the base regression tool for the implementation of the quantification method for subtask E.

We propose a novel quantification method for subtask E, tweet quantification according to a five-point scale. The method stems from the intuition of measuring and compensating the bias a regression model may have for the labels with high prevalences.

All the code we produced for these tasks is mainly based on the scikit-learn python library (Pedregosa et al., 2011) and it is published under an open source license[1].

The next sections detail on the data and methods adopted to produce the five submissions.

2 Training data

The labeled training dataset has been downloaded using the tool suggested by the organizers[2]. Table 1 summarizes the total number of tweets available for download at the time of crawling (November 2015). The final number of tweets used to train the classifiers, or quantifiers, is 6223 for subtasks A, C and E, and 4475 for subtasks B and D.

A small number of tweets in the dataset appeared multiple times, some with conflicting labels. In the "train" data parts, for example, 25 tweets appeared twice for subtasks A, C, and E, six of them with conflicting labels for subtask A, and 14 with conflicting labels for subtasks C and E[3]. For subtasks B, D, the number of tweets appearing twice in training is 13, one of them with conflicting labels. Duplicate tweets have been reduced to a single instance and those with conflicting labels have been excluded from the dataset and from any analysis performed in this work.

---

[1] `https://github.com/aesuli/`
`semeval2016-task4`

[2] `https://github.com/aritter/twitter_`
`download`

[3] Subtask A uses a coarse-grained three-point scale, so it may happen that a conflicting '-1'/'-2' labeling of a tweet for subtasks C and E is reduced to a non-conflicting 'negative' labeling for subtask A.

Proceedings of SemEval-2016, pages 92–95,
San Diego, California, June 16-17, 2016. ©2016 Association for Computational Linguistics

subtask	set	labeled	downloaded
A	train	6000	3804
A	dev	2000	1229
A	devtest	2000	1190
A	*all*	10000	6223
C,E	train	6000	3804
C, E	dev	2000	1229
C, E	devtest	2000	1190
C, E	*all*	10000	6223
B, D	train	4346	2764
B, D	dev	1325	836
B, D	devtest	1417	875
B, D	*all*	7088	4475

Table 1: Number of tweets with labeling provided by the organizers and number of such tweets available for download at the time of crawling.

Training data for subtasks A and B has been enriched by adding 5331 positive and 5331 negative sentences extracted from movie reviews, which are part of the movie review dataset (Pang and Lee, 2005)[4]. Even though these sentences are domain-specific, they are deemed to contribute to the learning process by enriching the vocabulary of expressions used to denote positive and negative sentiments. The final training set for subtask A is thus composed of 16885 examples, and 15137 for subtask B.

2.1 Features

The transformation of each tweet into its vectorial representation uses a relatively simple processing. The text of each tweet is tokenized, stopwords are removed. Word bigrams and trigrams, and character fourgrams are added to representation. Regular expressions are used to detect mentions, hashtag, URLs, and emoticons, and metafeatures for each of these special type of information are added to the representation, e.g., if a tweet has two hashtags, the '_hashtag' feature with frequency two is added to the representation of the tweet. The vectors are weighted by $tf \cdot idf$. Feature selection based on $\chi2$ is used to retain only the x most informative features, with x determined for each subtask with a

---

[4]http://www.cs.cornell.edu/people/pabo/movie-review-data/

method	MAE^M
BBTOR	0.927
DDAG	1.227
SVORIM	1.066

Table 2: Subtask C: comparison of ordinal regression methods, based on 10-fold cross-validation on training data.

cross-validation on training data.

3 Subtasks A and B: classification

A linear SVM has been used for for both classification tasks: a simple binary classifier for subtask B, and three *one-vs-all* binary classifiers for subtask A. The value of the parameter C of the SVM has been determined with a cross-validation on training data.

4 Subtask C: regression

The *Balanced Binary Tree for Ordinal Regression* (BBTOR) method we designed for subtask C is based on building a tree of binary classifiers that recursively split the ordinal scale on the points of maximum balance in the number of training example assigned to the two sides of the binary classification problem.

For example, let's suppose to have a dataset with the following distribution of training examples: $|c_1| = 20$, $|c_2| = 10$, $|c_3| = 20$, $|c_4| = 30$, $|c_5| = 50$, where $|c_i| = n$ means that label c_i has n training examples. The first binary classifier learns to separate $\{c_1, c_2, c_3\}$ from $\{c_4, c_5\}$, given that the partion with 50 vs 80 training examples is the most balanced one[5]. Then two second-level binary classifiers are trained on the $\{c_1, c_2\}$ vs $\{c_3\}$ split and the $\{c_4\}$ vs $\{c_5\}$ split. The training is completed learning a $\{c_1\}$ vs $\{c_2\}$ classifier. A linear SVM is used to train the binary classifier, optimizing its C parameter with a cross-validation on training data.

This approach is in line with the proposal of *Data-Balanced Nested Dichotomies* of Dong et al. (2005) for multi-class problems, and extends it to consider the ordinal relations between labels. The method has been compared in cross-validation experiments on

---

[5]Note that also the $\{c_1, c_2, c_3.c_4\}$ from $\{c_5\}$ split produces an equivalent 80 vs 50 split. A second criterium is to prefer the splits in which also the number of labels is more balanced. In case of a tie also on the second criterium a random choice is made.

method	KLD
CC	0.742
ACC	0.756
PCC	0.230
PACC	0.319

Table 3: Subtask D: comparison of binary quantification methods, based on leave-one-topic-out validation on training data.

method	EMD
RC	0.547
ARC	0.374

Table 4: Subtask E: comparison of ordinal regression quantification methods, based on leave-one-topic-out validation on training data.

training data against other regression methods, i.e., SVORIM (Chu and Keerthi, 2007), based on linear regression, and DDAG (Aiolli et al., 2009), based on binary classifiers, and produced the best performance.

5 Subtask D: binary quantification

Four quantification methods based on classification have been compared, following the works of Forman (2008) and Bella et al. (2010). The four methods are: *classify and count* (CC), in which a classifier is applied to the test documents and the prevalences are determined by counting the documents assigned to each label; *adjusted classify and count* (ACC), in which the output of the CC method is corrected to take into account the bias in error towards one of the two labels the classifier may have; *probabilistic classify and count* (PCC) in which the contribution of each document to the counting is weighted on the confidence the classifier has on the assignment; *probabilistic adjusted classify and count* (PACC) which is the ACC method applied to the probabilistic model of PCC. From a cross validation on training data, in which each topic has been in turn used as test data and the remaining as training data, the PCC performed best and it was thus used for the final submission.

6 Subtask E: quantification on an ordinal scale

Two methods have been compared for subtask E. One is a simple *regress and count* (RC) method in which the BBTOR method used in subtask C is applied to documents of a topic and then the quantification values for the topic is determined by counting the number of documents assigned to each slot in the ordinal scale. We propose the *adjusted regress and count* (ARC) method, that is based on the intuition to measure, and compensate, the typical bias of regression methods to assign documents to the slots in the ordinal scale that have higher prevalences.

Let's denote the prevalences for a topic-label pair with $p_j(c_i)$, where j indicates a topic in the set of topics $\{t_1, \ldots, t_n\}$ and i a label in the set of ordered labels $\{c_1, \ldots, c_m\}$ that form the ordinal scale. On a given set of topics, the cumulative prevalence for each label is denoted as $P(c_i) = \sum_{j=1}^{n} p_j(c_i)$. Given a quantification method that produces estimations $\hat{p}_j(c_i)$, its cumulative prevalences are denoted as $\hat{P}(c_i) = \sum_{j=1}^{n} \hat{p}_j(c_i)$.

Under the hypothesis of a linear error model, knowing the estimate prevalences and the cumulative correct and estimate prevalences on a set of topics, the true prevalence for a topic can be determined as:

$$p_j(c_i) \simeq \frac{P(c_i)}{\hat{P}(c_i)} \hat{p}_j(c_i) = w_i \hat{p}_j(c_i) \qquad (1)$$

Note that the model uses a different linear correction weight $w_i = \frac{P(c_i)}{\hat{P}(c_i)}$ for each label c_i.

The correction value w_i cannot be determined on the test data, since $P(c_i)$ is unknown. Following the ACC method for binary quantification (Forman, 2008) that estimates its correction parameter on the training set, also the w_i values can be approximated on the training data using cross-validation, substituting w_i with the $w_i^{Tr} = \frac{P^{Tr}(c_i)}{\hat{P}^{Tr}(c_i)}$ value. In this way the ARC quantification estimate can be derived from the RC estimate using the formula :

$$\hat{p}_j^{\mathrm{ARC}}(c_i) = \frac{1}{Z_j} w_i^{Tr\mathrm{RC}} \hat{p}_j^{\mathrm{RC}}(c_i) \qquad (2)$$

where $Z_j = \sum_{i=1}^{m} \hat{p}_j^{\mathrm{ARC}}(c_i)$ is a normalization factor to guarantee that the prevalences for a topic sum up to one.

The ARC method produced a sensible improvement over RC on a leave-one-topic-out validation on training data as reported in Table 4.

7 Future work

The features extracted from text in these experiments are based on a traditional vector space model in which each distinct feature is a represented by a dedicated dimension in the vector space. The limited amount of training data, and the variety of topics, produces an effect of data sparsity, in which there is little overlap between features from training and test data. We plan to repeat the experiments using semantically-richer features based on the use of language models, which should improve the vectorial representations by projecting onto similar vectorial representations the features with similar semantic properties, thus reducing the effect of data sparsity.

The participation to subtask E resulted in a bias correction method, ARC, that performed well. ARC sensibly improved on the baseline produced by the direct use of the original regression method, the one used to produce the submission for subtask C, without correction. Future work will explore the use of the bias correction method in combination with other ordinal regression methods, either based on classification or linear regression.

A strong assumption of the ARC method is that the error on each label has a linear relation with respect to the prevalence. This assumption can be considered to hold locally, i.e., when the variation of prevalence for a label across topics is limited, while it is harder to consider it valid when prevalences varies a lot across topics. Future work will explore the use of more complex models, e.g., fitting the differences observed between $p_j(c_i)$ and $\hat{p}_j(c_i)$ on the training set using a polynomial model, instead of a single w_i weight.

References

Fabio Aiolli, Riccardo Cardin, Fabrizio Sebastiani, and Alessandro Sperduti. 2009. Preferential text classification: Learning algorithms and evaluation measures. *Information retrieval*, 12(5):559–580.

Antonio Bella, Cesar Ferri, José Hernández-Orallo, and Maria Jose Ramirez-Quintana. 2010. Quantification via probability estimators. In *Data Mining (ICDM), 2010 IEEE 10th International Conference on*, pages 737–742. IEEE.

Wei Chu and S Sathiya Keerthi. 2007. Support vector ordinal regression. *Neural computation*, 19(3):792–815.

Lin Dong, Eibe Frank, and Stefan Kramer, 2005. *Knowledge Discovery in Databases: PKDD 2005: 9th European Conference on Principles and Practice of Knowledge Discovery in Databases, Porto, Portugal, October 3-7, 2005. Proceedings*, chapter Ensembles of Balanced Nested Dichotomies for Multi-class Problems, pages 84–95. Springer Berlin Heidelberg, Berlin, Heidelberg.

George Forman. 2008. Quantifying counts and costs via classification. *Data Mining and Knowledge Discovery*, 17(2):164–206.

Preslav Nakov, Alan Ritter, Sara Rosenthal, Veselin Stoyanov, and Fabrizio Sebastiani. 2016. SemEval-2016 task 4: Sentiment analysis in Twitter. In *Proceedings of the 10th International Workshop on Semantic Evaluation*, SemEval '16, San Diego, California, June. Association for Computational Linguistics.

Bo Pang and Lillian Lee. 2005. Seeing stars: Exploiting class relationships for sentiment categorization with respect to rating scales. In *Proceedings of ACL*, pages 115–124.

F. Pedregosa, G. Varoquaux, A. Gramfort, V. Michel, B. Thirion, O. Grisel, M. Blondel, P. Prettenhofer, R. Weiss, V. Dubourg, J. Vanderplas, A. Passos, D. Cournapeau, M. Brucher, M. Perrot, and E. Duchesnay. 2011. Scikit-learn: Machine learning in Python. *Journal of Machine Learning Research*, 12:2825–2830.

aueb.twitter.sentiment at SemEval-2016 Task 4: A Weighted Ensemble of SVMs for Twitter Sentiment Analysis

Stavros Giorgis, Apostolos Rousas
John Pavlopoulos, Prodromos Malakasiotis and **Ion Androutsopoulos**
NLP Group, Department of Informatics
Athens University of Economics and Business, Greece
Patission 76, GR-104 34 Athens, Greece
http://nlp.cs.aueb.gr

Abstract

This paper describes the system with which we participated in SemEval-2016 Task 4 (Sentiment Analysis in Twitter) and specifically the Message Polarity Classification subtask. Our system is a weighted ensemble of two systems. The first one is based on a previous sentiment analysis system and uses manually crafted features. The second system of our ensemble uses features based on word embeddings. Our ensemble was ranked 5th among 34 teams. The source code of our system is publicly available.

1 Introduction

This paper describes the system with which we participated in SemEval-2016 Task 4 (Sentiment Analysis in Twitter) and specifically the Message Polarity Classification subtask (Nakov et al., 2016). In this subtask, each tweet is classified as expressing a positive, negative, or no opinion (neutral). Our system is a weighted ensemble of two systems. The first one is based on a previous sentiment analysis system (Karampatsis et al., 2014) and uses manually crafted features. The second system of our ensemble uses features based on word embeddings (Mikolov et al., 2013; Pennington et al., 2014). Our ensemble was ranked 5th among 34 teams.

Section 2 discusses the datasets we used to train and tune our ensemble. Sections 3 and 4 describe our ensemble and its performance respectively. Finally, Section 5 concludes and discusses future work.

2 Data

For system training and tuning we used 19,305 tweets from the 2016 datasets provided by the organisers of SemEval-2016 Task 4, as well as data from SemEval-2013 Task 2. Specifically, the datasets were:

- $TW_{train16}$: train data for SemEval-2016 Task 4,

- TW_{dev16} : development data for SemEval-2016 Task 4,

- $TW_{devtest16}$: dev-test data for SemEval-2016 Task 4,

- $TW_{train13}$: train data for SemEval-2013 Task 2,

- TW_{dev13} : development data for SemEval-2013 Task 2.

The organisers also provided 6,908 tweets from old SemEval data, to allow system evaluation during development. These data could not be used directly for training or tuning and were the following:

- $TW_{devtest13}$: dev-test data for SemEval-2013 Task 2,

- $TW_{devtest14}$: dev-test data for SemEval-2014 Task 9,

- $TW_{sarcasm14}$: tweets containing sarcasm,

- SMS_{13} : SMS messages from 2013,

- LJ_{14} : messages from Live Journal.

Proceedings of SemEval-2016, pages 96–99,
San Diego, California, June 16-17, 2016. ©2016 Association for Computational Linguistics

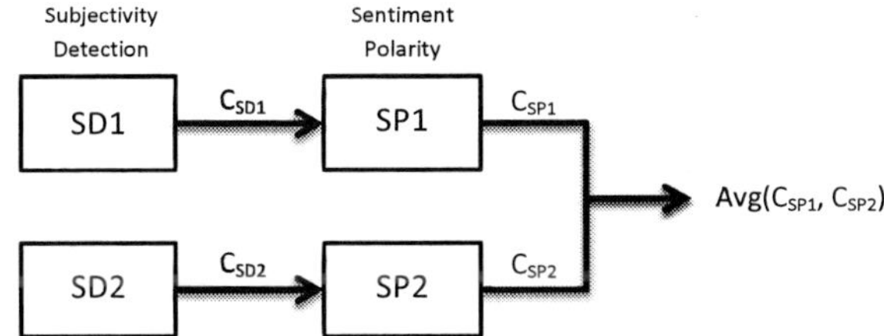

Figure 1: Ensemble of two sentiment polarity classifiers, SP1 and SP2, which are influenced by two subjectivity detection classifiers, SD1 and SD2, respectively.

3 System Overview

The main objective of SemEval-2016 Task 4 is to detect sentiment polarity, i.e., to identify whether a message (tweet) expresses positive, negative or no sentiment at all. We used a weighted ensemble of two sentiment polarity classifiers, namely SP1 and SP2 (Figure 1), each influenced by a subjectivity detection classifier, SD1 and SD2, respectively.

A correlation analysis between the confidence scores of SP1 and SP2 (C_{SP1} and C_{SP2} respectively) revealed that the two systems make different mistakes, which motivated combining them in an ensemble. Given a message and the confidence scores of the two systems (i.e., C_{SP1} and C_{SP2}), the ensemble computes a new confidence score for every sentiment label (C_{pos}, C_{neg} and C_{neu}) as follows:

$$C_{pos} = C_{SP1@pos} \cdot w_{pos} + C_{SP2@pos} \cdot (1 - w_{pos})$$

$$C_{neg} = C_{SP1@neg} \cdot w_{neg} + C_{SP2@neg} \cdot (1 - w_{neg})$$

$$C_{neu} = C_{SP1@neu} \cdot w_{neu} + C_{SP2@neu} \cdot (1 - w_{neu})$$

where w_{pos}, w_{neg}, w_{neu} are weights tuned on the development data. The sentiment with the highest confidence score is assigned to each tweet.[1]

Below, we describe the two Sentiment Polarity classifiers, along with the two subjectivity detection classifiers that influence them.

3.1 SP1 and SD1

First, each message is preprocessed by a a Twitter specific tokeniser and part-of-speech (POS) tagger (Owoputi et al., 2013) to obtain the tokens and

the corresponding POS tags, which are necessary for some features.[2] Then, we extract features, which can be categorized as follows:[3]

- features based on morphology,

- POS based features,

- sentiment lexicon based features,

- negation based features,

- features based on clusters of tweets.

We used a linear SVM classifier (Vapnik, 1998; Cristianini and Shawe-Taylor, 2000; Joachims, 2002) trained on three labels, namely, positive, negative and neutral.[4]

As already mentioned, SP1 is influenced by a subjectivity detection classifier called SD1. That is, SP1 uses as a feature the confidence score of SD1. SD1 is also a linear SVM classifier, which is trained on data of two labels, neutral and subjective (i.e., positive or negative).[5] The higher the confidence score of SD1 the more likely it is for the message to express sentiment (positive or negative). Apart from the score of SD1 (which was used by SP1), SP1 and SD1 used the same features.

3.2 SP2 and SD2

The second system of our ensemble uses word embeddings (Mikolov et al., 2013; Pennington et al., 2014). We use the centroid of the word embeddings of each tweet as the feature vector of the tweet. The centroid of a tweet (message) M is computed as follows:

$$\vec{M} = \frac{1}{|M|} \sum_{i=1}^{|M|} \vec{w_i}$$

---

[2] No lemmatization or stemming was used and tokens could be words, emoticons, hashtags, etc.

[3] All the features of SP1 are described in detail in a publicly available report, accompanying the source code of the system. The code and the report are available at `https://github.com/nlpaueb/aueb.twitter.sentiment`.

[4] We used the SVM implementation of Scikit Learn (Pedregosa et al., 2011; Fan et al., 2008). The same implementation was used for all our SVM classifiers. The optimal C value was found to be 0.00341, by using 5-fold cross validation on $\text{TW}_{train16}$.

[5] The optimal C value for SD1 was found to be 0.00195, by using 5-fold cross validation on $\text{TW}_{train16}$.

---

[1] Tuning led to $w_{pos} = w_{neg} = w_{neu} = 0.66$.

Test set	Score	Ranking
$\text{TW}_{devtest13}$	66.61%	9/34
SMS_{13}	61.77%	6/34
$\text{TW}_{devtest14}$	70.81%	7/34
$\text{TW}_{sarcasm14}$	41.00%	18/34
LJ_{14}	69.51%	8/34
TW_{15}	62.34%	7/34
TW_{16}	60.52%	5/34

Table 1: Rankings of our system

	Train data	Dev data	Tweet2016
Strict 2 stages	62.60%	58.50%	54.83% (19/34)
SP1 (with SD1)	68.00%	64.70%	59.40% (7/34)
SP2 (with SD2)	60.80%	59.00%	57.50% (15/34)
ENS	68.40%	65.80%	60.52% (5/34)

Table 2: Average $F1$ scores of SP1, SP2, ENS (our ensemble) and a strict two-stage system.

where $|M|$ is the number of tokens in M and $\vec{w_i}$ is the embedding of word w_i.[6] We used the 200-dimensional word vectors for Twitter produced by GloVe (Pennington et al., 2014).[7]

As with SP1, SP2 incorporates the confidence score of SD2 as a feature. SD2 is a classifier trained on neutral and subjective data (positive or negative), again with centroid feature vectors. Given a message M, the confidence score of SD2 for M was added as a feature to its centroid and the resulting 201-dimension feature vector was used as input to SP2.[8] SP2 was then trained on the same three classes as SP1 (positive, negative, neutral).[9]

4   Experiments & Discussion

Our system was ranked 5th among 34 teams.[10] All teams were ranked by their score on the Twitter2016 Task 4 test dataset. Table 1 shows our rankings on each dataset. Below we discuss the results of our ensemble and we show how the subjectivity detection classifiers affect our system.

---

[6]We allow multiple word occurrences in a sentence, while we ignore words without embeddings.

[7]The word vectors were pre-trained on a 2 billion tweets corpus. See http://nlp.stanford.edu/projects/glove/.

[8]The confidence scores of SD1 and SD2 were exponentially normalized (Bishop, 2006).

[9]The optimal C values were found to be 1.40688 for SD2 and 7.39618 for SP2, by using 5-fold cross validation.

[10]http://alt.qcri.org/semeval2016/task4/data/uploads/semeval2016_task4_results.pdf

A strict two-stage approach, like the one suggested by Karampatsis et al. (2014), discards messages the sentiment detection (SD) classifier (first stage) decides they do not express sentiment, and classifies the rest as positive or negative. However, errors of the first stage propagate to the second, thus, playing a significant role in overall performance. We extend their approach and attempt to use the results of a subjectivity detection stage in a less rigorous manner; i.e., as a confidence factor along with various other features. Recall that our SD1 is actually the first stage of the system of Karampatsis et al. (2014), and that we use the confidence of SD1 as feature of SP1. Table 2 shows that SP1 (with the confidence of SP1 as a feature) outperforms the strict two-stage approach by 4.57%, yielding an increase in the ranking by 12 positions. Another interesting observation is that SP2 (with the confidence of SD2 as a feature) achieves a score only 1.9% lower than SP1 (with SD1) yielding a ranking around the middle of the list. This is achieved by using only features based on word embeddings along with the confidence of SD2 and no sophisticated feature engineering at all. A final, and also very interesting observation is that when we use an ensemble of SP1 and SP2, the results improve yielding a 5th place in the ranking.

5   Conclusions and future work

In this paper we presented the system with which we participated in the Message Polarity Classification subtask of SemEval-2016 Task 4. We used a weighted ensemble of two systems each operating in two stages. In a first, subjectivity detection stage, each message is assigned a confidence score representing the probability that the message expresses an opinion. This probability is then used as a feature by a classifier that detects sentiment. We used two different systems, one based on previous work by Karampatsis et al. (2014) (SP1 with the confidences of SD1 as a feature) and a second system that represents the messages by the centroids of their word embeddings (SP2 with the confidence of SD2 as a feature). The two systems are then combined with a weighted linear ensemble scheme in order to get the final sentiment label. Our experiments show that using the confidence of the subjectivity detection stage as a feature instead of using a strict two-stage approach can lead to an improved performance. Also, the ensemble performs better than any of its two systems on their own.

Despite the encouraging results of our approach (5th among 34 participating teams), there is still much room for improvement. A better continuous space vector representation of the messages might improve SD2 and SP2. Much research has been conducted recently on obtaining better continuous space vector representations of sentences (Le and Mikolov, 2014; Kiros et al., 2015; Hill et al., 2016) instead of centroid vectors. Another direction for future work would be to investigate replacing the SVM classifiers by multilayer perceptrons, possibly on top of recurrent neural nets that would compute vector representations of sentences.

Acknowledgments

This work was carried out during the BSc projects of the first two authors, which were co-supervised by the other three authors.

References

C. M. Bishop. 2006. *Pattern Recognition and Machine Learning (Information Science and Statistics)*. Springer-Verlag New York, Inc.

N. Cristianini and J. Shawe-Taylor. 2000. *An Introduction to Support Vector Machines and Other Kernel-based Learning Methods*. Cambridge University Press.

R. E. Fan, K. W. Chang, C. J. Hsieh, X.-R. Wang, and C. J. Lin. 2008. Liblinear: A library for large linear classification. *The Journal of Machine Learning Research*, 9:1871–1874.

F. Hill, K. Cho, and A. Korhonen. 2016. Learning distributed representations of sentences from unlabelled data. *arXiv preprint arXiv:1602.03483*.

T. Joachims. 2002. *Learning to Classify Text Using Support Vector Machines: Methods, Theory, Algorithms*. Kluwer.

R. M. Karampatsis, J. Pavlopoulos, and P. Malakasiotis. 2014. AUEB: Two stage sentiment analysis of social network messages. In *Proceedings of the 8th International Workshop on Semantic Evaluation*, pages 114–118, Dublin, Ireland.

R. Kiros, Y. Zhu, R. Salakhutdinov, R. S. Zemel, A. Torralba, R. Urtasun, and S. Fidler. 2015. Skip-thought vectors. *arXiv preprint arXiv:1506.06726*.

Q. Le and T. Mikolov. 2014. Distributed representations of words and phrases. In *Proceedings of the 31th International Conference on Machine Learning*, pages 1188–1196, Beijing, China.

T. Mikolov, K. Chen, G. Corrado, and J. Dean. 2013. Efficient estimation of word representations in vector space. *arXiv preprint arXiv:1301.3781*.

P. Nakov, A. Ritter, S. Rosenthal, V. Stoyanov, and F. Sebastiani. 2016. SemEval-2016 task 4: Sentiment analysis in Twitter. In *Proceedings of the 10th International Workshop on Semantic Evaluation*, San Diego, California.

O. Owoputi, B. O'Connor, C. Dyer, K. Gimpel, N. Schneider, and N. A. Smith. 2013. Improved part-of-speech tagging for online conversational text with word clusters. In *Proceedings of the 2013 Conference of the North American Chapter of the Association for Computational Linguistics: Human Language Technologies*, pages 380–390, Atlanta, Georgia.

F. Pedregosa, G. Varoquaux, A. Gramfort, V. Michel, B. Thirion, O. Grisel, M. Blondel, P. Prettenhofer, R. Weiss, V. Dubourg, J. Vanderplas, A. Passos, D. Cournapeau, M. Brucher, M. Perrot, and E. Duchesnay. 2011. Scikit-learn: Machine learning in Python. *Journal of Machine Learning Research*, 12:2825–2830.

J. Pennington, R. Socher, and C. D. Manning. 2014. Glove: Global vectors for word representation. In *Proceedings of the 2014 Conference on Empirical Methods in Natural Language Processing*, pages 1532–1543, Doha, Qatar.

V. Vapnik. 1998. *Statistical learning theory*. John Wiley.

thecerealkiller at SemEval-2016 Task 4: Deep Learning based System for Classifying Sentiment of Tweets on Two Point Scale

Vikrant Yadav

Amazon.in

Hyderabad, India

vikrantiitr1@gmail.com

Abstract

In this paper, we propose a deep learning system for classification of tweets on a two-point scale. Our architecture consists of a multilayered recurrent neural network having gated recurrent units. The network is pre-trained with a weakly labeled dataset of tweets to learn the sentiment specific embeddings. Then it is fine tuned on the given training dataset of the task 4B in SemEval-2016. The network does very little pre-processing for raw tweets and no post-processing at all. The proposed system achieves 3rd rank on the leaderboard of task 4B.

1 Introduction

Task 4 of SemEval-2016 (Nakov et al., 2016) - Sentiment Analysis in Twitter- turned out to be the most popular task of SemEval-2016. Among its sub-tasks, sub-task B - Tweet classification according to a two-point scale - was the 2nd most popular sub-task. A total of 19 teams participated in it including ours.

In this paper, we propose a multilayerd RNN architecture for classifying tweets on a two-point scale, namely, positive and negative. We first pre-train the network with a weakly labeled corpus of tweets, where labels are assigned based on the sentiment of the emoticon present in the tweets. It helps the network to learn sentiment specific embeddings of the words in the tweet. The network is then fine-tuned on the dataset of tweets provided as part of the sub-task 4B along with the training and development dataset of SemEval-2013 task 2.

In the second section, we describe our architecture. In third section, we explain our approach to train the network. After that, we describe the experimental setup and statistical properties of the data used. In the end, we discuss our results on the test dataset. We stood 3rd on the final leaderboard for sub-task 4B.

2 Proposed System

In this section, we elaborate our proposed architecture. The network is fed pre-processed tweets as input and it predicts the binary label of the tweets. It has 3 RNN layers each with gated recurrent units. Then a sum layer is added to sum the hidden states of the last recurrent layer over time. After that, a dense layer is present followed by a single sigmoid unit.

Now, we describe the components of our architecture in brief.

2.1 Pre-processing

The tweets are pre-processed to remove any punctuation if present. All URLs are encoded into a URL token. All the user accounts mentioned in a tweet are encoded as USER token. The tweet is converted to lower-case before feeding to the network. Note that we don't remove any stop-words as they define useful relationships between words and phrases. This amount of pre-processing turned out to be sufficient for the network to learn useful semantic and sentiment specific word-embeddings.

Proceedings of SemEval-2016, pages 100–102,
San Diego, California, June 16-17, 2016. ©2016 Association for Computational Linguistics

2.2 Embedding layer

The embedding layer maps a sequence of words present in the input tweet to the corresponding fixed length real valued vectors. The fixed length d is called the dimension of the embeddings. The embedding layer keeps track of the mapping so that the correct embeddings gets updated while doing back-propagation of the errors.

2.3 Recurrent layers

Recurrent neural networks are proved to be useful in handling variable length sequences. A stacking of recurrent layers on the top of each other allows the semantic composition of representations of words and phrases over time. We use the same intuition in our architecture.

The embedding layer passes the embedding matrix to the first recurrent layer. Each layer takes into input an embedding matrix which it processes i.e. updates its hidden state over time. The hidden states are stored after each time-step and fed to the next layer as input. Thus, the last layer outputs a matrix of hidden states.

We prefer GRU(Gated Recurrent Unit) (Cho et al., 2014) compared to a vanilla RNN unit. A classic RNN is difficult to train, because the gradients either tend to vanish or explode (Bengio et al., 1994). A GRU unit takes care of this problem and is able to cope with vanishing or exploding gradients while capturing the information for longer periods of time.

2.4 Sum over time

This layer receives the time-distributed hidden state matrix of the last recurrent layer as input where the nth column describes the hidden state at nth time-step. It outputs a vector where the kth element is sum of the kth row in the hidden state matrix. This helps to combine the sentiment specific representation of the phrases so as to yield an aggregate representation.

2.5 Dense layer and output layer

The output of the sum layer is fully connected with the dense layer consisting of rectified linear units. The dense layer in turn is connected with the output sigmoid units which predicts the probability of assigning a positive or negative label for the input tweet.

3 Approach to Train the Network

In this section, we describe our choice of training algorithm and the regularization method.

3.1 Training algorithm

We use mini-batch gradient descent algorithm as our choice of training algorithm. We utilized two Nvidia GK104 series GPU hardware to make matrix-matrix multiplications efficient. A mini-batch size of 128 is chosen for pre-training the network. We use rmsprop as an update rule for the parameters, an optimizer which divides the gradient by an exponential moving average of its squares.

3.2 Regularization

We use dropout (Srivastava, 2013) as the regularizer to prevent our network from overfitting. Dropout selects a fraction of the hidden units at random and sets their output to zero and thus, prevents co-adaptation of the features. However, it is tricky to be applied in the RNN as it is capable of unsettling the recurrent connections and thus, interfere with our recurrent layer's ability of retaining information for longer periods of time.

We choose the approach proposed in (Zaremba et al., 2014) to apply dropout in our network where it is being applied between inter-layer connections instead of intra-layer connections. This doesnt interfere with the recurrent updates in a layer and helps prevent co-adaptation of the features at the same time.

3.3 Pre-training the network

The training dataset provided as part of sub-task 4B in Semeval-2016 contain very few samples to effectively train our deep architecture. Thus, we used a weakly labeled corpus of tweets, namely, Sentiment140 (Go et al., 2009), to pre-train our network so as to learn semantic and sentiment specific representation of words and phrases.

We take the learned weights of the trained network as it is and fine tune them on the provided training dataset of sub-task 4B along with training and development dataset of task 2 in SemEval-2013. The network uses validation scores as the metric to do an early-stop while training. Macro-averaged recall, the official scoring metric of sub-task 4B, was

Type	Dataset	Positives	Negatives
Training	Twitter'16 + Twitter'13	8250	2500
Testing	Twitter'16	8212	2337

Table 1: Statistical information of training and testing datasets.

Scoring-metric	Score	Best-score	Rank
AvgR	**0.784**	**0.797**	**3**
AvgF1	0.762	0.799	5
Accuracy	0.823	0.862	9

Table 2: Resulting scores on testing dataset. AvgR was the official scoring metric of the task 4B.

also used as the validation scoring metric.

4 Experiments

4.1 Experimental settings

The statistical properties of training and testing datasets are provided in Table 1.

For evaluation, we use official scoring metric of Semeval-2016 task 4B - macro-averaged recall - average of recalls for both positive and negative classes.

The chosen parameters of our network are as follows: the maximum input sequence length is set to 30, vocabulary size is 400000, dimensionality of word embedding (d) is 100, recurrent units hidden state vector size is 128, number of recurrent layers is 3, number of hidden unit in dense layer is 256 with relu activation. We used a dropout of 50% after each layer while training.

4.2 Results

Results are shown in Table 2.

Our system produces a macro-averaged recall of 0.784, while the best system scored 0.797. Our system's performance with other scoring metrics is also good, achieving 5th and 9th rank for macro-averaged F1 and accuracy metric, respectively.

Our architecture uses very little pre-processing compared to the other systems of Semeval-2016. It is able to capture useful semantic relationships and sentiment specific embeddings of words and phrases using just the raw tweets. It can be improved by adding handcrafted features such as topics, number of positive-negative lexicons, etc. which we would like to try in future.

5 Conclusion

In this paper, we proposed a deep learning system for sentiment classification of tweets on a two-point scale. Our architecture was able to capture complex semantic relationships between words and phrases of the input tweets to decide their final sentiment. We show how to pre-train and fine-tune a deep network like ours well from end-to-end using weakly supervised dataset. Our system used very little pre-processing before feeding the raw tweets to the network. In future, we would like to use handcrafted features in addition to the raw tweets to see if they improve the overall score.

References

Y. Bengio, P. Simard, and P. Frasconi. 1994. Learning long-term dependencies with gradient descent is difficult. *Trans. Neur. Netw.*, 5(2):157–166, March.

KyungHyun Cho, Bart van Merrienboer, Dzmitry Bahdanau, and Yoshua Bengio. 2014. On the properties of neural machine translation: Encoder-decoder approaches. *CoRR*, abs/1409.1259.

Alec Go, Richa Bhayani, and Lei Huang. 2009. Twitter sentiment classification using distant supervision. Technical report, Stanford University.

Preslav Nakov, Alan Ritter, Sara Rosenthal, Veselin Stoyanov, and Fabrizio Sebastiani. 2016. SemEval-2016 task 4: Sentiment analysis in Twitter. In *Proceedings of the 10th International Workshop on Semantic Evaluation*, SemEval '16, San Diego, California, June. Association for Computational Linguistics.

Nitin Srivastava. 2013. *Improving neural networks with dropout. PhD thesis.* University of Toronto.

Wojciech Zaremba, Ilya Sutskever, and Oriol Vinyals. 2014. Recurrent neural network regularization. *CoRR*, abs/1409.2329.

NTNUSentEval at SemEval-2016 Task 4:[*]
Combining General Classifiers for Fast Twitter Sentiment Analysis

Brage Ekroll Jahren　　**Valerij Fredriksen**　　**Björn Gambäck**　　**Lars Bungum**

Department of Computer and Information Science
Norwegian University of Science and Technology (NTNU)
Sem Sælands vei 7–9, NO–7491 Trondheim, Norway
{brageej,valerijf}@stud.ntnu.no {gamback,larsbun}@idi.ntnu.no

Abstract

The paper describes experiments on sentiment classification of microblog messages using an architecture allowing general machine learning classifiers to be combined either sequentially to form a multi-step classifier, or in parallel, creating an ensemble classifier. The system achieved very competitive results in the shared task on sentiment analysis in Twitter, in particular on non-Twitter social media data, that is, input it was not specifically tailored to.

1 Introduction

As a growing platform for people to express themselves on a global scale, Twitter has become exceedingly attractive as an information source. In addition to text, a tweet comes with metadata such as the sender's location and language, and hashtags, making it possible to quickly gather vast amounts of data regarding a specific product, person or event. With a working Twitter Sentiment Analysis system, companies could get a feel of what consumers think of their products, or politicians could estimate their popularity amongst Twitter users in specific regions.

However, tweets and other informal texts on social media are quite different from texts elsewhere. They are short in length and contain a lot of abbreviations, misspellings, Internet slang, and creative syntax. Although the relative occurrence of non-standard English syntax is fairly constant among many types of social media (Baldwin et al., 2013),

analysing such texts using traditional language processing systems can be problematic, primarily since the main common denominator of social media text is not that it is informal, but that it describes language in rapid change (Androutsopoulos, 2011; Eisenstein, 2013), so that resources targeted directly at social media language quickly become outdated.

Twitter Sentiment Analysis (TSA) has been a rapibly growing research area in recent years, and a typical approach to TSA has been identified, using a supervised machine learning strategy, consisting of three main steps: preprocessing, feature extraction and classifier training. Preprocessing is used in order to remove noise and standardize the tweet format, for example, by replacing or removing URLs. Desired features of the tweets are then extracted, such as sentiment scores using specific sentiment lexica or the occurrence of different emoticons. Finally, a classifier is trained on the extracted features.

Since the machine learning algorithms used commonly are supervised, sentiment-annotated data is a prerequisite for training — and the growth of the TSA research field can largely be attributed to the International Workshop on Semantic Evaluation (SemEval) having run shared tasks on this theme since 2013 (Wilson et al., 2013), annually producing new annotated data. The SemEval-2016 version (Task 4) of the TSA task and the data sets are described by Nakov et al. (2016). Here we will specifically address Subtask A, which is a 3-way sentiment polarity classification problem, attributing the labels 'positive', 'negative' or 'neutral' to tweets.

The rest of the paper is laid out as follows: Section 2 describes a general architecture for building

---

[*]Thanks to Mikael Brevik, Jørgen Faret, Johan Reitan and Øyvind Selmer for their work on two previous NTNU systems.

Proceedings of SemEval-2016, pages 103–108,
San Diego, California, June 16-17, 2016. ©2016 Association for Computational Linguistics

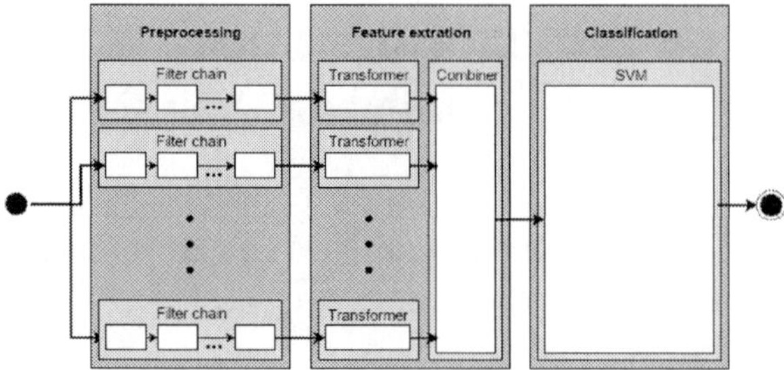

Figure 1: Overview of the core system architecture

Twitter sentiment classifiers, drawing on the experiences of developing two previous TSA systems (Selmer et al., 2013; Reitan et al., 2015). Section 3 reports the application of such a system ('NTNU-SentEval') to the SemEval data sets, while Section 4 points to ways that the results could be improved.

2 Sentiment Classifier Architecture

To solve the three-way sentiment classification task, a general multi-class classifier, *BaseClassifier*, was created. Utilizing a general methodology enables the combination of several BaseClassifiers in various ways, either sequentially to create a multi-step classifier, or in parallel, as a classifier ensemble.

The BaseClassifier consists of three steps: preprocessing, feature extraction, and then either classification or training. These are handled by a Pipeline object built in the Scikit-Learn Python machine learning library (Pedregosa et al., 2011). Scikit-Learn Transformer objects are used to extract or generate feature representations of the data. Figure 1 illustrates the overall architecture of the system. When creating a BaseClassifier instance, a set of parameters is specified, including the classification algorithm, the preprocessing functions to use, and options for each of the transformers. The preprocessing methods invoked depend on the transformers and the features they aim to extract.

2.1 Preprocessing

The preprocessing step modifies the raw tweets before they are passed to feature extraction: noise is filtered out and negation scope is detected. The filtering consists of a chain of simple methods using regular expressions. There are ten basic filters that can be invoked, six of which replace various twitter-specific objects with the empty string: emoticons, username

mentions, RT (retweet) tags, URLs, only hashtag signs (#), and hashtags (incl. the string following the sign). The other four filters transform uppercase characters to lowercase, remove non-alphabetic or space characters, limit the maximum repetitions of a single character to three, and perform tokenization using Pott's tweet tokenizer (Potts, 2011).

Negation detection uses a simple approach where n words appearing after a negation cue, but before the next punctuation mark, are marked as negated. The negation cues were adopted from Councill et al. (2010), supplemented by five common misspellings obtained by looking up each negation cue in TweetNLP's Twitter word cluster (Owoputi et al., 2013): *anit*, *couldnt*, *dnt*, *does'nt*, and *wont*.

2.2 Feature Extraction

The feature extraction is implemented as a Scikit-Learn Feature Union, which is a collection of independent transformers (feature extractors), that build a feature matrix for the classifier. Each feature is represented by a transformer. Eight such transformers have been implemented: two extract the number of *punctuations* (repeated alphabetical and grammatical signs) and the number of happy and sad *emoticons* found in the tweet. Two other transformers extract TF–IDF values for *word n-grams* and *character n-grams* using a bag-of-words vectorizer implementation, which is an extension of Scikit-Learn's default *TfidfVectorizer*.

A *part-of-speech* transformer uses the GATE TwitIE tagger (Derczynski et al., 2013) to assign part-of-speech tags to every token in the text; the tag occurrences are then counted and returned. A *word cluster* transformer counts the occurrences of different TweetNLP word clusters (Owoputi et al., 2013), that is, if a word in a tweet is a member of a cluster, a counter for that specific cluster is incremented.

The last two transformers are essentially lexical: the *VADER* transformer runs the lexicon-based social media sentiment analysis tool VADER (Hutto and Gilbert, 2014) and extracts its output. VADER (Valence Aware Dictionary and sEntiment Reasoner) goes beyond the bag-of-words model, taking into consideration word order and degree modifiers.

The *lexicon* transformer is a single transformer using a combination of six automatically and manually annotated prior polarity sentiment lexica. The automatically annotated lexica used are NRC Sentiment140 and HashtagSentiment (Kiritchenko et al., 2014), that contain sentiment scores for both unigrams and bigrams, where some are in a negated context. Similarly, two manually annotated lexica, AFINN (Nielsen, 2011) and NRC Emoticon (Mohammad and Turney, 2010), give a sentiment score for each word (AFINN) or each emoticon (NRC Emoticon). However, two further manually annotated lexica, MPQA (Wilson et al., 2005) and Bing Liu (Ding et al., 2008), do not list sentiment scores for words, but only whether a word contains positive or negative sentiment. For those two lexica, negative and positive word sentiments were mapped to the scores -1 or $+1$, respectively.

For all lexica, four different features were extracted from each tweet. Following Kiritchenko et al. (2014), the four features for manually annotated lexica are the sums of positive scores and of negative scores for words in both affirmative and negated contexts, while the four features for automatically annotated lexica comprise the number of unigrams or bigrams with sentiment score $\neq 0$, the sum of all sentiment scores, the highest sentiment score, and the score of the last unigram or bigram in the tweet.

2.3 Classification

After all desired features have been extracted, a BaseClassifier instance allows for the use of state-of-the-art classification algorithms such as Support Vector Machines (SVM), Naïve Bayes and Maximum Entropy (MaxEnt). Scikit-Learn includes a series of implementations of the SVM algorithm (Vapnik, 1995). The NTNUSentEval system uses the SVC variant, also known as C-Support SVM classifier since it is based on the idea of setting a constant C to penalize incorrectly classified instances. High C values create a narrower margin, enabling more elements to be correctly classified. However, this can lead to overfitting, so it is desirable to perform some kind of parameter optimization to find the best C value. For multi-class classification, Scikit-Learn uses a One-vs-One method with a run time complexity more than quadratic to the number of elements; however, this is not a problem for our relatively small (under 10,000 elements) datasets.

A single BaseClassifier acts as a one-step classifier, but by chaining BaseClassifiers sequentially,

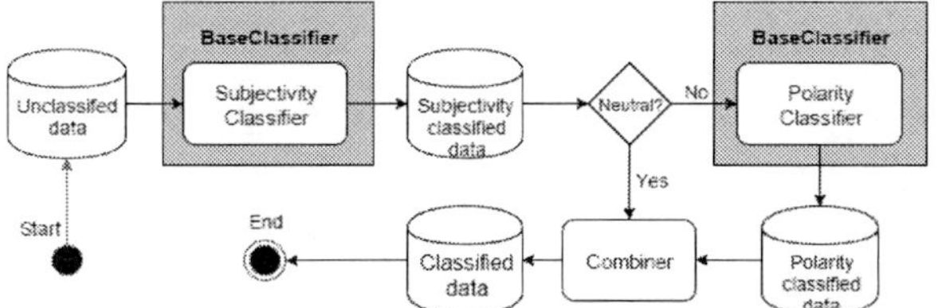

Figure 2: Data flow in the two-step classifier

a *multi-step classifier* can be created. Each classifier can be trained independently on different data, thereby learning a different classification function. Figure 2 illustrates how chaining two BaseClassifiers can create a two-step classifier. The first BaseClassifier is trained only on data labeled as subjective or objective, while the second BaseClassifier is trained only on subjective data, labeled positive or negative. When classifying, if the first BaseClassifier classifies an instance as subjective, the instance is forwarded to the second BaseClassifier to determine if it is positive or negative. The results from both classifiers are then combined and the final classification is returned.

By combining BaseClassifiers in parallel, an *ensemble of classifiers* can be created. Each of the classifiers is independent of the others and all classify the same instances. In the end, the classifiers vote to decide on the classification of an instance. Since the BaseClassifiers are so general, it is possible to create BaseClassifiers that extract different features, do different preprocessing, or use different classification algorithms — and then combine these to create an ensemble system.

2.4 Parameter Optimization

In order to find the optimal parameter values for the NTNUSentEval system, an extensive grid search was performed through the Scikit-Learn framework over all subsets of the training set (shuffled), using stratified 5-fold cross-validation and optimizing on F_1-score. During development we were able to find parameters that yielded better results on the complete test set than the parameters from the grid search. However, the optimal parameters are those that perform best on average, and using the parameters identified through development when presented with new data would most likely perform worse than using the parameters identified through grid search.

Feature	tokenize	lower_case	no_emotes	no_user	no_rt_tag	no_url	no_hashsign	no_hashtag	limit_chars	limit_repeat
Word n-grams			✓	✓	✓	✓		✓		
Char n-grams				✓	✓	✓	✓		✓	✓
Lexicon		✓		✓	✓	✓	✓		✓	✓
PoS Tagger	✓			✓	✓	✓		✓		
Word Clusters		✓		✓	✓	✓	✓			✓
Punctuation				✓		✓				
Emoticons						✓				
VADER				✓	✓	✓	✓			

Table 1: Preprocessing used by feature extractors

| Parameter | n-grams | | Lexicon |
	Word	Character	
n-range	$(1, 5)$	$(3, 6)$	N/A
use_idf	True	True	N/A
min_df	0.0	0.0	N/A
max_df	0.5	0.5	N/A
negation_length	4	None	-1

Table 2: Optimal parameter settings

As described in Section 2.2, a total of eight different feature extractors have been implemented, all of which can be enabled or disabled. Each feature extractor utilizes a specific preprocessor setting, as shown in Table 1. Further, there are three option settings for the SVM algorithm: type, kernel and C, which after grid search were set to SVC, Linear, and 0.1, respectively. In addition to the preprocessor options, there are eleven more feature extractor options, whose grid-searched optimal values are displayed in Table 2, where *n-range* gives the lower and upper n-gram sizes, *use_idf* enables Inverse Document Frequency weighting, *min_df* and *max_df* give the proportions of lowest resp. highest document frequency occurring terms to be excluded from the final vocabulary, and *negation_length* the maximum number of tokens inside a negation scope.

3 Experimental Results

The NTNUSentEval TSA system was trained on the Twitter training set (8,748 tweets), using the optimal parameters identified through grid search, and tested on the SemEval Twitter test sets from 2013 and 2014. The complete results on these test sets are shown in Table 4 below, while Nakov et al. (2016) give the results on all test sets, including the unknown 2016 tweet set, in terms of the official evaluation metric, F_1^{PN}, which is the average of the F1-scores on the negative and the positive tweets.

Notably, our system performed extremely well on the out-of-domain test sets (i.e., the non-Twitter data), being the best of all 34 participating systems on the 2013-SMS set (with a 0.641 F_1^{PN} score, compared to a 0.190 F_1^{PN} baseline), the 3rd on the 2014-Live-journal set ($F_1^{PN} = 0.719$, with a 0.272 baseline), and overall tied for first on the out-of-domain data, supporting our claim that the approach taken in itself is quite general. However, the lack of domain fine-tuning of the system showed in comparison to the best systems on Twitter data, with the NTNUSentEval system consistently placing 11–13 on the different test sets, including 11th on the 2016 set ($F_1^{PN} = 0.583$, with baseline 0.255).

3.1 Ablation Study

In order to detect the overall importance or impact each feature has, a simple ablation study was conducted by removing each feature in turn and checking how the performance of the system was affected. The results of this study are shown in Table 3.

Evidently, the single most important feature is Sentiment Lexica. On the 2013-test set, system accuracy is reduced from 0.7227 to 0.6945 when the feature is removed, while the effect of removing it when testing on the 2014 set is not as apparent. A possible reason for this difference may be that most of the sentiment lexica used were created at the same time as the 2013-test set, and they might thus better reflect the language in that period of time. As noted in Section 1, the language of social media is rapidly changing, so that a lexicon created in 2013 might have reduced value already for data collected a year later. This effect is also noticeable when testing the system on the 2014-test set, where the VADER Sentiment feature is the most important one, reducing the accuracy from 0.6905 to 0.6793 when being removed. On the 2013-test set, the VADER Sentiment feature, which was created in 2014, does not have the same impact, again indicating a change in how the language is used and that VADER might better reflect the Twitter language of 2014.

The second most important contribution comes from the n-gram features. The removal of both char-

Features	2013-test	2014-test
All	.7227	.6905
- Word n-grams	.7136	.6892
- Character n-grams	.7085	.6885
- Both n-grams	.7017	.6872
- Automatic Lexica	.7088	.6799
- Manual Lexica	.7085	.6938
- All Sentiment Lexica	.6945	.6826
- Word Clusters	.7166	.6872
- Part-of-Speech tag counts	.7159	.6865
- Punctuation counts	.7143	.6932
- Emoticons counts	.7156	.6918
- All counts	.7127	.6925
- VADER Sentiment	.7114	.6793

Table 3: Feature ablation study results (F_1-scores)

Data	Precision	Recall	F_1	Accuracy	Time
	1-step classifier				
2013	.7370	.6639	.6848	.7227	106.97
2014	.7031	.6619	.6691	.6905	53.01
	2-step classifier				
2013	.7278	.6526	.6729	.7172	118.36
2014	.7079	.6570	.6676	.6912	59.6
	1-step classifier with fast PoS tagging				
2013	.7364	.6639	.6846	.7221	80.13
2014	.7032	.6591	.6673	.6892	41.03

Table 4: Sentiment classifier performance

acter n-grams and word n-grams lead to a degradation in performance. On the 2013-test set the degradation in performance is quite significant, while on the 2014-test set the degradation is more subtle.

Another interesting result is the impact of the Emoticons and Punctuation count features. On the 2013-test set, removing them gives a slight reduction in performance, while on the 2014-test set we can observe a slight *increase* in performance. One possible reason for this could be that the way emoticons and punctuation are used in tweets changes over time, but the most likely cause is merely noise in the data. Although causing slightly increased or decreased performance, the individual count features do not significantly affect the overall results.

3.2 Architectural Experiments

Two instances of the BaseClassifier can be chained sequentially creating a 2-step classifier. Such a classifier was tested on the 2013 and 2014 test sets, as shown in Table 4. The 2-step classifier performs worse than the 1-step classifier on the 2013 set, while their performances on the 2014 set are comparable, so based on these results it is not clear that 1-step classification is better than 2-step.

The GATE TwitIE part-of-speech tagger uses an underlying model when tagging tweets. In addition to the standard best performing model, another high-speed model trading 2.5% token accuracy for half the tagging speed is available, and the results from testing BaseClassifier using the high-speed tagger model are also shown in Table 4. Although a slight reduction in performance can be observed compared to using the best tagger model, the high-speed model significantly reduced the total execution time, from 107 to 80 seconds on the 2013-test set and from 53 to 41 seconds on the 2014-test set.

4 Conclusion and Future Work

Drawing on the experiences from two previous Twitter Sentiment Analysis systems (Selmer et al., 2013; Reitan et al., 2015), a new TSA system was created using a simplified and generalised architecture, allowing for accurate and fast tweet classification.

As seen in the ablation study of Section 3.1, the Sentiment Lexica is the single most important feature, while also being one of the simplest: our implementation is based only on summing up the sentiment value of each word. A possible improvement would thus be to extract more information by considering the order of the words, part-of-speech tags, and degree modifiers, such as 'very', 'really' and 'somewhat', that can affect the sentiment value of the following word. These modifiers are currently not handled by the Sentiment Lexica extractor, yet they clearly carry a lot of sentiment weight.

Another interesting feature of lexicon-based systems is their good run-time performance, which is also confirmed in our system, where the lexicon feature extractor is one of the fastest feature extractors. This is a particularly important property for a TSA system to be useful in a real world setting, as the opinion mining accuracy confidence depends on the number of opinions examined.

References

Jannis Androutsopoulos. 2011. Language change and digital media: a review of conceptions and evidence. In Kristiansen and Coupland, editors, *Standard Languages and Language Standards in a Changing Europe*, pages 145–159. Novus, Oslo, Norway, February.

Timothy Baldwin, Paul Cook, Marco Lui, Andrew MacKinlay, and Li Wang. 2013. How noisy social media text, how diffrnt social media sources? In *6th International Joint Conference on Natural Language Processing*, pages 356–364, Nagoya, Japan, October.

Isaac G. Councill, Ryan McDonald, and Leonid Velikovich. 2010. What's great and what's not: learning to classify the scope of negation for improved sentiment analysis. In *48th Annual Meeting of the Association for Computational Linguistics*, pages 51–59, Uppsala, Sweden, July. ACL. Workshop on Negation and Speculation in Natural Language Processing.

Leon Derczynski, Alan Ritter, Sam Clark, and Kalina Bontcheva. 2013. Twitter part-of-speech tagging for all: Overcoming sparse and noisy data. In *9th International Conference on Recent Advances in Natural Language Processing*, pages 198–206, Hissar, Bulgaria, September.

Xiaowen Ding, Bing Liu, and Philip S. Yu. 2008. A holistic lexicon-based approach to opinion mining. In *2008 International Conference on Web Search and Data Mining*, pages 231–240, Stanford, California, February. ACM.

Jacob Eisenstein. 2013. What to do about bad language on the internet. In *2013 Conference of the North American Chapter of the Association for Computational Linguistics*, pages 359–369, Atlanta, Georgia, June.

C.J. Hutto and Eric Gilbert. 2014. VADER: A parsimonious rule-based model for sentiment analysis of social media text. In *8th International Conference on Weblogs and Social Media*, Ann Arbor, Michigan, June.

Svetlana Kiritchenko, Xiaodan Zhu, and Saif M. Mohammad. 2014. Sentiment analysis of short informal texts. *Journal of Artificial Intelligence Research*, 50:723–762, August.

Saif Mohammad and Peter Turney. 2010. Emotions evoked by common words and phrases: Using Mechanical Turk to create an emotion lexicon. In *2010 Conference of the North American Chapter of the Association for Computational Linguistics*, pages 26–34, Los Angeles, California, June. ACL. Workshop on Computational Approaches to Analysis and Generation of Emotion in Text.

Preslav Nakov, Alan Ritter, Sara Rosenthal, Fabrizio Sebastiani, and Veselin Stoyanov. 2016. SemEval-2016 Task 4: Sentiment analysis in Twitter. In *10th International Workshop on Semantic Evaluation*, San Diego, California, June. ACL.

Finn Årup Nielsen. 2011. A new ANEW: Evaluation of a word list for sentiment analysis in microblogs. In *1st Workshop on Making Sense of Microposts (#MSM2011)*, pages 93–98, Heraklion, Greece, May.

Olutobi Owoputi, Brendan O'Connor, Chris Dyer, Kevin Gimpel, Nathan Schneider, and Noah A. Smith. 2013. Improved part-of-speech tagging for online conversational text with word clusters. In *2013 Conference of the North American Chapter of the Association for Computational Linguistics*, pages 380–390, Atlanta, Georgia, June. ACL.

Fabian Pedregosa, Gaël Varoquaux, Alexandre Gramfort, Vincent Michel, Bertrand Thirion, Olivier Grisel, Mathieu Blondel, Peter Prettenhofer, Ron Weiss, Vincent Dubourg, Jake Vanderplas, Alexandre Passos, David Cournapeau, Matthieu Brucher, Matthieu Perrot, and Édouard Duchesnay. 2011. Scikit-learn: Machine learning in Python. *Journal of Machine Learning Research*, 12(1):2825–2830.

Christopher Potts. 2011. Sentiment symposium tutorial. In *Sentiment Analysis Symposium*, San Francisco, California, November. Alta Plana Corporation. `sentiment.christopherpotts.net/`

Johan Reitan, Jørgen Faret, Björn Gambäck, and Lars Bungum. 2015. Negation scope detection for Twitter sentiment analysis. In *2015 Conference on Empirical Methods in Natural Language Processing*, pages 99–108, Lisbon, Portugal, September. 6th Workshop on Computational Approaches to Subjectivity, Sentiment and Social Media Analysis.

Øyvind Selmer, Mikael Brevik, Björn Gambäck, and Lars Bungum. 2013. NTNU: Domain semi-independent short message sentiment classification. In *2nd Joint Conference on Lexical and Computational Semantics (*SEM), Vol. 2: 7th International Workshop on Semantic Evaluation*, pages 430–437, Atlanta, Georgia, June. ACL.

Vladimir N. Vapnik. 1995. *The Nature of Statistical Learning Theory*. Springer, New York, New York.

Theresa Wilson, Paul Hoffmann, Swapna Somasundaran, Jason Kessler, Janyce Wiebe, Yejin Choi, Claire Cardie, Ellen Riloff, and Siddharth Patwardhan. 2005. OpinionFinder: A system for subjectivity analysis. In *2005 Human Language Technology Conference and Conference on Empirical Methods in Natural Language Processing*, pages 34–35, Vancouver, British Columbia, October. ACL. Demonstration Abstracts.

Theresa Wilson, Zornitsa Kozareva, Preslav Nakov, Alan Ritter, Sara Rosenthal, and Veselin Stoyanov. 2013. SemEval-2013 Task 2: Sentiment analysis in Twitter. In *2nd Joint Conference on Lexical and Computational Semantics (*SEM), Vol. 2: 7th International Workshop on Semantic Evaluation*, Atlanta, Georgia, June. ACL.

UDLAP at SemEval-2016 Task 4: Sentiment Quantification Using a Graph Based Representation

Esteban Castillo[1], Ofelia Cervantes[1], Darnes Vilariño[2] and David Báez[1]

[1]Universidad de las Américas Puebla
Department of Computer Science, Electronics and Mechatronics, Mexico
`{esteban.castillojz, ofelia.cervantes, david.baez}@udlap.mx`

[2]Benemérita Universidad Autónoma de Puebla
Faculty of Computer Science, Mexico
`darnes@cs.buap.mx`

Abstract

We present an approach for tackling the tweet quantification problem in SemEval 2016. The approach is based on the creation of a co-occurrence graph per sentiment from the training dataset and a graph per topic from the test dataset with the aim of comparing each topic graph against the sentiment graphs and evaluate the similarity between them. A heuristic is applied on those similarities to calculate the percentage of positive and negative texts. The overall result obtained for the test dataset according to the proposed task score (KL divergence) is **0.261**, showing that the graph based representation and heuristic could be a way of quantifying the percentage of tweets that are positive and negative in a given set of texts about a topic.

1 Introduction

In the past decade, new forms of communication, such as microblogging and text messaging have emerged and become ubiquitous. There is no limit to the range of information conveyed by tweets and texts. These short messages are extensively used to **share opinions and sentiments** that people have about their topics of interest. Working with these informal text genres presents challenges for Natural Language Processing (NLP) beyond those encountered when working with more traditional text genres. Typically, this kind of texts are short and the language used is very informal. We can find creative spelling and punctuation, slang, new words, URLs, and genre-specific terminology and abbreviations that make their manipulation more challenging.

Representing that kind of text for automatically mining and understanding the opinions and sentiments that people communicate inside them has very recently become an attractive research topic (Pang and Lee, 2008). In this sense, the experiments reported in this paper were carried out in the framework of the SemEval 2016[1] (**Sem**antic **Eval**uation) which has created a series of tasks for sentiment analysis on Twitter (Nakov et al., 2016b). Among the proposed tasks we chose Task 4, subtask D which was named **tweet quantification according to a two-point scale** and was defined as follows: "Given a set of tweets known to be about a given topic, estimate the distribution of the tweets across the Positive and Negative classes". In order to solve this task we created an algorithm that builds up graphs to compare each topic against all possible sentiments for obtaining the polarity percentage of each one. The steps involved in our sentiment quantification process are then discussed in detail.

The rest of the paper is structured as follows: in Section 2 we present some related work found in the literature with respect to the quantification of sentiments in text documents. In Sections 3 to 5 the algorithm and the graph representation used to detect the percentage of texts for each sentiment are explained. In Section 6, the experimental results are presented and discussed. Finally, in Section 7 the conclusions as well as further work are described.

---

[1]http://alt.qcri.org/semeval2016/

109

Proceedings of SemEval-2016, pages 109–114,
San Diego, California, June 16-17, 2016. ©2016 Association for Computational Linguistics

Algorithm 1 Sentiment quantification process

Input:

/*Preprocess documents*/

$X = \{x_1, ..., x_m\}$ positive training docs.

$Y = \{y_1, ..., y_n\}$ negative training docs.

$Z = \{z_1, ..., z_s\}$ topic names

$DT = \{DT[z_1], ..., DT[z_s]\}$ test docs per topic.

Output:

/* Positive (p) and negative (n) polarity percentage for each topic*/

$PT = \{(p_1, n_1), ..., (p_s, n_s)\}$

Procedure:

/* Let $G_{Positive}$ and $G_{Negative}$ denote the graphs of the positive an negative documents created from X and Y*/

$G_{Positive}, G_{Negative}$

for each z_i in Z **do**

   /*Let G_{Topic} denote a topic graph created from $DT[z_i]$*/

   G_{Topic}

   /*Similarity between topic and sentiments, see algorithm 2*/

   $Sim_1 = Similarity(G_{Topic}, G_{Positive})$

   $Sim_2 = Similarity(G_{Topic}, G_{Negative})$

   /*Apply a heuristic*/

   if $Sim_1 > Sim_2$ **then**

      $PT[z_i] = (1 - Sim_1, Sim_1)$

   else

      $PT[z_i] = (Sim_2, 1 - Sim_2)$

   end if

end for

2 Related Work

There exist a number of works in literature associated to the automatic quantification of sentiments in documents. Some of these works have focused on the contribution of particular features, such as the use of the vocabulary to extract lexical elements associated to the documents (Kim and Hovy, 2006), the use of part-of-speech tag n-grams and syntactic phrase patterns (Esuli et al., 2010) to capture syntactic features of texts associated with a sentiment, the use of dictionaries and emoticons of positive and negative words (Go et al., 2009) as well as man-

ually and semiautomatically constructed syntactic and semantic phrase and lexicons (Gao and Sebastiani, 2015; Whitelaw et al., 2005).

On the other hand, many contributions focused on the use of structures to represent the features associated to a document like the frequency of occurrence vector (Manning et al., 2008; Balinsky et al., 2011) or the vectors that represent the presence or absence of features (Kiritchenko et al., 2014). But research works that use graph representations for texts in the context of sentiment quantification barely appear in the literature (Pinto et al., 2014; Poria et al., 2014). It has usually been proposed the concept of n-grams with a frequency of occurrence vector to solve it (Pang and Lee, 2008). However, there is still an enormous gap between this approach and the use of more detailed graph structures that represent in a natural way the lexical, semantic and stylistic features.

3 Sentiment Quantification

Algorithm 1 shows the steps involved in computing the percentage of positive and negative tweets for each topic in the test dataset (see section 6.1) considering the use of graphs to represent the word interaction for each sentiment in the training dataset and for each topic in the test dataset. The algorithm consists of five relevant stages:

1. Preprocess all documents in the dataset. This task includes elimination of punctuation symbols and all the elements that are not part of the ASCII encoding. Then, all the remaining words are changed to lowercase.

2. Create a graph for each sentiment using the **training** dataset documents (see Section 4).

3. Create a graph for each topic using the **test** dataset documents (see Section 4).

4. Compare each topic graph against the sentiment graphs and calculate the similarity score between both (see Section 5).

5. Compare those similarities and take the highest to use it as a base to calculate the quantification score for each sentiment in a topic, considering

that the sum of all percentages related to a topic must be equal to one[2].

4 Graph Based Representation

Among different proposals for mapping texts to graphs, the co-occurrence of words (Sonawane and Kulkarni, 2014; Balinsky et al., 2011) has become a simple but effective way to represent the relationship of one term over another one in texts where there is no syntactic order (usually social media texts like Twitter or SMS). Formally, the proposed co-occurrence graph used in the experiments is represented by $G = (V, E)$, where:

- $V = \{v_1, ..., v_n\}$ is a finite set of **vertices** that consists of the words contained in one or several texts.

- $E \subseteq V \times V$ is the finite set of **edges** which represent that two vertices are connected if their corresponding lexical units **co-occur within a window of maximum 2 words** in the text (at least once). We consider this type of window because it represents the natural relationship of words.

As an example, consider the following sentence ζ extracted from a text T in the dataset: "Axel Rose needs to just give up. Now. Not later, not soon, not tomorrow.", which after the preprocessing stage (see Section 3) would be as follows: "axel rose needs to just give up now not later not soon not tomorrow". Based on the proposed representation, preprocessed sentence ζ can be mapped to the co-occurrence graph shown in Figure 1.

5 Graph similarity

After having created the graph representation for each topic and sentiment in the dataset, the steps involved in computing the similarity score (Castillo et al., 2015) are shown in algorithm 2. The algorithm consists of four relevant stages:

1. Obtain all vertices (words) that share the topic graph as well as the sentiment graph.

2. Apply the Dice similarity measure (Montes et al., 2000; Adamic and Adar, 2003) for each

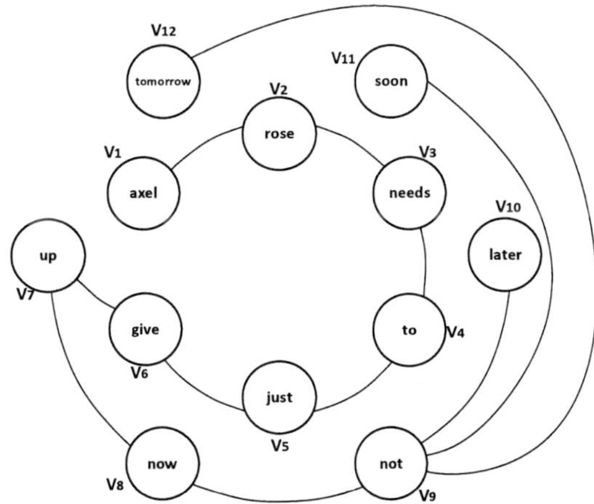

Figure 1: co-occurrence graph example.

graph, taking as input the shared vertices of the previous step and the graph to be analyzed. The result is a matrix that represents the similarity scores for each pair of input vertices, based on their connection patterns. Formally, Dice similarity calculates the similarity of two vertices (x, y) as twice the number of common neighbors (ngb) divided by the sum of the neighbors of the vertices (see equation 1).

$$Dice(x, y) = \frac{2 \, |ngb(x) \cap ngb(y)|}{|ngb(x)| + |ngb(y)|} \quad (1)$$

3. Obtain the upper triangular values for each matrix and use them to build a vector representation (Manning et al., 2008). The rest of the matrix values are not useful, because the main diagonal represents the similarity of an input vertex with itself and the lower triangular is the same as the upper one.

4. Apply the normalized Euclidean distance (Cancho, 2004) between the vector representing the topic and the vector representing a sentiment. The result is a value in the range of 0 to 1 that indicates how similar the two graphs are. The Euclidean distance of vector A and B is calculated using equation 2.

$$Euclidean(A, B) = \sqrt{\sum_{i=1}^{n} \frac{(A_i - B_i)^2}{n}} \quad (2)$$

---

[2]SemEval 2016 task 4, subtask D requirement.

Algorithm 2 Similarity between graphs

---
function Similarity(G_A, G_B)

/* Let $V(G_A)$ denote the set of vertices of graph G_A*/

$V(G_A)$

/* Let $V(G_B)$ denote the set of vertices of graph G_B*/

$V(G_B)$

/* Calculate the Intersection between graphs G_A and G_B*/

$I = V(G_A) \cap V(G_B)$

/* Apply Dice similarity for each pair of shared vertices in both graphs, see equation 1*/

$ResultMatrix_A = DiceSim(G_A, I)$

$ResultMatrix_B = DiceSim(G_B, I)$

/* Let $Vector_A$ denote the upper triangular values of $ResultMatrix_A$*/

$Vector_A$

/* Let $Vector_B$ denote the upper

/* triangular values of $ResultMatrix_B$*/

$Vector_B$

/* Apply the normalized Euclidean distance taking as input both vectors, see equation 2*/

$Result = Euclidean(Vector_A, Vector_B)$

return $Result$

end function

---

6 Experimental results

The results obtained with the proposed approach are discussed in this section. First, we describe the dataset used in the experiments and, thereafter, the results obtained.

6.1 Dataset

The document collection used in the experiments is a subset of the SemEval 2016 task 4 corpus (Nakov et al., 2016b), which includes, several text documents in English on different topics and genres. The dataset is divided in two groups:

- **Training documents:** It contains a set of topics each one with a set of known documents. For each document a label that indicates the polarity of the text (positive or negative) is assigned.

- **Test documents:** It contains a set of topics[3] each one with a set of known documents. In this case there is no label that indicates the polarity of the text. These documents are used to test our algorithm taking into account the writing style samples of the training documents.

In Table 1, main dataset features are shown, including the number of documents per topic for the training and test dataset.

Table 1: SemEval task 4 subtask D dataset features.

Feature	Training	Test
Type of documents	Tweet	Tweet
Number of documents	5205	10551
Number of topics	59	100
Number of documents per topic	70-100	60-250
Avg. words per document	68	52
Avg. words per sentence	5	5
Vocabulary size	6869	9732

6.2 Obtained results

In Table 2 we present results obtained with the test dataset considered in the SemEval 2016 task 4 subtask D. The results were evaluated according to the Kullback-Leibler Divergence (KLD), which is a measure of the error made in estimating a true distribution p over a set C of classes by means of a predicted distribution $\hat{p}$. KLD (Nakov et al., 2016a) is a measure of error, so lower values are better (see equation 3).

$$KLD(\hat{p}, p, C) = \sum_{c_j \in C} p(c_j) log \frac{p(c_j)}{\hat{p}(c_j)} \quad (3)$$

Table 2: Evaluation of the proposed algorithm using the test dataset.

System	KLD score
Competition, best result	0.034
UDLAP team	**0.261**
Competition, baseline 1	0.887
Competition, baseline 2	0.175

Taking into account obtained results, our approach performed above the baseline 1 and slightly

---

[3]Different from the training topics.

below baseline 2. We consider that these results were obtained even though the training corpus was very unbalanced (there were more positive texts than others) and there was a high difference between the vocabulary of the topics of the training and test datasets. The proposed algorithm showed an effective and relative fast way[4] (00:02:48 minutes) to get the percentage of positive and negative documents although it is necessary to perform different experiments using the proposed approach on a test dataset with more topics. Further analysis on the use of a co-occurrence graph and the similarity measure will allow us to find more accurate features that can be used for the sentiment quantification problem.

7 Conclusions

We have presented an approach that incorporates the use of a graph representation to solve the sentiment quantification problem (task 4 subtask D). The results obtained show a competitive performance that is above one of the baseline scores. However there is still a great challenge to improve the techniques for dealing with the quantification problem where the text could be smaller and there are different topics, each one with his own vocabulary. One of the contributions of this paper is that we proposed a graph based representation and a similarity measure for the quantification problem instead of using traditional classification techniques like a supervised learning method based on the extraction of stylistic features (Kharde and Sonawane, 2016). As further work we propose the following:

- Use different co-occurrence windows for modeling the text using a graph based representation.

- Experiment with other graph representations for texts that include alternative levels of language descriptions such as the use of sentence chunks, pragmatic sentences, etc (Mihalcea and Radev, 2011).

- Propose a similarity measure that uses the semantic information of a graph (Alvarez and Yan, 2011).

- Explore different techniques that can be used in the sentiment quantification problem (Pang and Lee, 2008).

- Compare the algorithm presented with other classical approaches like the use of stylistic features or the N-gram model (Stamatatos, 2008).

- Explore different supervised/unsupervised classification algorithms (Cook and Holder, 2000).

Acknowledgments

This work has been supported by the CONACYT grant with reference #373269/244898 and the CONACYT-PROINNOVA project no. 0198881.

References

Lada Adamic and Eytan Adar. 2003. Friends and neighbors on the web. *Social Networks*, 25(3):211–230.

Marco Alvarez and Changhui Yan. 2011. A graph-based semantic similarity measure for the gene ontology. *J. Bioinformatics and Computational Biology*, 9(6):681–695.

Helen Balinsky, Alexander Balinsky, and Steven Simske. 2011. Document sentences as a small world. In *SMC*, pages 2583–2588. IEEE.

Ramon Cancho. 2004. Euclidean distance between syntactically linked words. *Phys. Rev. E*, 70(5), nov.

Esteban Castillo, Ofelia Cervantes, Darnes Vilariño, and David Báez. 2015. Author verification using a graph-based representation. *International Journal of Computer Applications*, 123(14):1–8, August.

Diane Cook and Lawrence Holder. 2000. Graph-based data mining. *IEEE Intelligent Systems*, 15(2):32–41.

Andrea Esuli, Fabrizio Sebastiani, and Ahmed ABBASI. 2010. Sentiment quantification. *IEEE intelligent systems*, 25(4):72–79.

Wei Gao and Fabrizio Sebastiani. 2015. Tweet sentiment: From classification to quantification. In *Proceedings of the 2015 IEEE/ACM International Conference on Advances in Social Networks Analysis and Mining 2015*, pages 97–104. ACM.

A Go, L Huang, and R Bhayani. 2009. Sentiment analysis of twitter data. *Entropy*, 2009(June):17.

Vishal Kharde and Sheetal Sonawane. 2016. Sentiment analysis of twitter data : A survey of techniques. *CoRR*.

Soo-Min Kim and Eduard Hovy. 2006. Automatic identification of pro and con reasons in online reviews. In *Proceedings of the COLING/ACL Main Conference Poster Sessions*, pages 483–490.

---

[4]The execution runtime consider all the steps involved in algorithm 1.

Svetlana Kiritchenko, Xiaodan Zhu, and Saif Mohammad. 2014. Sentiment analysis of short informal texts.
J. Artif. Intell. Res. (JAIR), 50:723–762.

Christopher Manning, Prabhakar Raghavan, and Hinrich
Schütze. 2008. *Introduction to Information Retrieval*.
Cambridge University Press.

Rada Mihalcea and Dragomir Radev. 2011. *Graph-
based natural language processing and information
retrieval*. Cambridge University Press.

Manuel Montes, Aurelio López, and Alexander Gelbukh.
2000. Information retrieval with conceptual graph
matching. In *Lecture Notes in Computer Science*,
number 1873, pages 312–321. Springer-Verlag.

Preslav Nakov, Alan Ritter, Sara Rosenthal, Fabrizio Sebastiani, and Veselin Stoyanov. 2016a. Evaluation
measures for the semeval-2016 task 4 sentiment analysis in Twitter. In *Proceedings of the 10th International
Workshop on Semantic Evaluation*, SemEval '16, San
Diego, California, June. Association for Computational Linguistics.

Preslav Nakov, Alan Ritter, Sara Rosenthal, Veselin Stoyanov, and Fabrizio Sebastiani. 2016b. SemEval-2016
task 4: Sentiment analysis in Twitter. In *Proceedings
of the 10th International Workshop on Semantic Evaluation*, SemEval '16, San Diego, California, June. Association for Computational Linguistics.

Bo Pang and Lillian Lee. 2008. Opinion mining and
sentiment analysis. *Foundations and Trends in Information Retrieval*, 2(1-2):1–135.

David Pinto, Darnes Vilariño, Saul León, Miguel Jasso,
and Cupertino Lucero. 2014. Buap: Polarity classification of short texts. In *Proceedings of the 8th International Workshop on Semantic Evaluation (SemEval
2014)*, pages 154–159. Association for Computational
Linguistics and Dublin City University, August.

Soujanya Poria, Erik Cambria, Grégoire Winterstein,
and Guang-Bin Huang. 2014. Sentic patterns:
Dependency-based rules for concept-level sentiment
analysis. *Knowl.-Based Syst.*, 69:45–63.

S. S. Sonawane and P. A. Kulkarni. 2014. Article: Graph
based representation and analysis of text document: A
survey of techniques. *International Journal of Computer Applications*, 96(19):1–8, June.

Efstathios Stamatatos. 2008. Author identification: Using text sampling to handle the class imbalance problem. *Inf. Process. Manage.*, 44(2):790–799, mar.

Casey Whitelaw, Navendu Garg, and Shlomo Argamon.
2005. Using appraisal groups for sentiment analysis. In *Proceedings of the ACM SIGIR Conference
on Information and Knowledge Management (CIKM)*,
pages 625–631. ACM.

GTI at SemEval-2016 Task 4: Training a Naive Bayes Classifier using Features of an Unsupervised System

Jonathan Juncal-Martínez, Tamara Álvarez-López, Milagros Fernández-Gavilanes
Enrique Costa-Montenegro, Francisco Javier González-Castaño
GTI Research Group
AtlantTIC Centre, School of Telecommunication Engineering, University of Vigo
36310 Vigo, Spain
{jonijm, talvarez, milagros.fernandez, kike}@gti.uvigo.es,
javier@det.uvigo.es

Abstract

This paper presents the approach of the GTI Research Group to SemEval-2016 task 4 on Sentiment Analysis in Twitter, or more specifically, subtasks A (Message Polarity Classification), B (Tweet classification according to a two-point scale) and D (Tweet quantification according to a two-point scale). We followed a supervised approach based on the extraction of features by a dependency parsing-based approach using a sentiment lexicon and *Natural Language Processing* techniques.

1 Introduction

In recent years, research on the field of *Sentiment Analysis* (SA) has increased considerably, due to the growth of user content generated in social networks, blogs and other platforms on the Internet. These are considered valuable information for companies, which seek to know or even predict the acceptance of their products, to design their marketing campaigns more efficiently. One of these sources of information is Twitter, where users can write about any topic, using colloquial and compact language. As a consecuence, SA in Twitter is specially challenging, as opinions are expressed in one or two short sentences.

Many approaches have been proposed for SA, and can be roughly divided into two categories. The first one tries to capture and model linguistic knowledge through the use of dictionaries (Taboada et al., 2011) containing words that are tagged with their semantic orientation. These methods detect the words present in a text using different strategies involving lexics, syntax or semantics (Quinn et al., 2010). The other one is machine learning-based, which is currently the most predominant approach including supervised learning and deep learning. They widely use classifiers including *Support Vector Machines* (SVM), *Maximum Entropy Models* (MAXENT), and *Naive Bayes* classifiers. Most of the time, they are built from features of a *"bag of words"* representation (Pak and Paroubek, 2010).

Our group has participated in SemEval-2016 task 4 on Sentiment Analysis in Twitter, subtasks A (Message Polarity Classification), B (Tweet classification according to a two-point scale) and D (Tweet quantification according to a two-point scale) (Nakov et al., 2016b).

The remainder of this article is structured as follows: Section 2 presents in detail the system proposed for the performance of these subtasks, and Section 3 shows the results obtained and discusses them. Finally, Section 4 summarizes the main findings and conclusions.

2 System Overview

Our main objective was to create a supervised system using extracted features from an unsupervised system described in (Fernández-Gavilanes et al., 2015). This last approach comprises different processing stages, including the generation of sentiment lexicons, test preprocessing and the application of different methods for determining contextual polarity based on syntactical structure. This makes our approach robust in diverse contexts without the need for previous manual tagging of datasets. As we can decide independently which modules

115

Proceedings of SemEval-2016, pages 115–119,
San Diego, California, June 16-17, 2016. ©2016 Association for Computational Linguistics

of the unsupervised system to use or not, it was easy to extract different features from each one individually or together. Once extracted, classification was applied using *Weka* tool (Hall et al., 2009). This environment contains a collection of *machine learning-based* algorithms for data mining tasks, such as, classification, regression, clustering, association rules, and visualization. The new supervised system was built with a *Naive Bayes* classifier.

2.1 Modules combination features

The first extracted features of the unsupervised system were the different sentiment outputs of the modules combination. As mentioned before, modules can be enabled and disabled independently. With this feature, multiple sentiment outputs were obtained from these combinations.

The unsupervised system has four different modules ("*intensification treatment*" (I), "*negation treatment*" (N), "*polarity conflict treatment*" (C) and "*adversative/concessive clause treatment*" (A/CO)). In total, there were 14 possible combinations: one by one, combining pairs or groups of three of them, and all of them at once (the latter is the default output of the unsupervised system). In subtask A, each output obtained is defined by a sentiment value contained between three possible ones: *negative*, *neutral* or *positive*. However, in subtask B, the sentiment value obtained for each combination only can be contained between two possible ones: *negative* or *positive*. So, the result of each one of these 14 combinations was considered as a feature. All of them are defined in Table 1.

Combination	Subtask A	Subtask B
I		
N		
C		
A/CO		
I + N		
I + C	POSITIVE	POSITIVE
I + A/CO	NEGATIVE	NEGATIVE
N + C	NEUTRAL	
N + A/CO		
C + A/CO		
I + N + C		
I + N + A/CO		
N + C + A/CO		
ALL		

Table 1: Possible combinations of modules.

2.2 Individual modules features

In addition to the previous modules combination results extracted, other features were also extracted from each module independently. Each tweet was represented as a vector of generic and relational features. Generic features are those that are not related to a scope in a given tweet, and relational features represent the corresponding scope needed for each module. For example, in the negation module, the scope would begin in the unigram that caused the negation (the negator term itself), and would cover all affected unigrams in a branch of the dependencies tree, detected by its syntactic function. For this reason, both types of features can be distinguished. The option chosen to mark the scope was to use relational attributes. With them, unigram to unigram can be stored with all its associated features: such as it is an intensifier, a negator, a part of the scope of negation, etc.

Generic features: The first features introduced are not related to a scope, and involve:

- *Phrases*: the number of phrases of a particular tweet.

- *Adjectives*: the number of existing adjectives in a given tweet.

- *Common names*: the number of existing common names in a given tweet.

- *Verbs*: the number of existing verbs in a given tweet (except auxiliary verbs).

- *Positive/negative polarity unigrams*: the number of unigrams with positive/negative polarity in a given tweet.

- *Positive/negative emoticons*: the number of positive/negative emoticons (with positive/negative polarity) in a given tweet.

- *Positive/negative intensifications*: the number of positive/negative intensifications in a given tweet.

- *Unigrams*: all lemmas were considered (except *hashtag*, *mention*, *URL*, unigrams with numbers, unigrams with length 1 and punctuation marks).

116

Relational features: They can be defined as an array of features. Each unigram of a given tweet has assigned all the features defined in the relational, so it is easy to mark the scope of treatment of each of the separate modules. Then, all features introduced for each unigram in the relational are detailed.

- *Part of speech*: it can take one of the next five values: adjective, common name, verb, adverb or other.

- *Polarity value*: it can take one of the next seven values: negative +, negative, negative -, none, positive -, positive and positive +.

- *Is intensifier*: it indicates if an unigram is an intensifier. It can take one of the next five values: intensity - -, intensity -, none, intensity +, intensity + +.

- *Was intensified*: it indicates if an unigram was intensified. It can take one of the next seven values: negative +, negative, negative -, none, positive -, positive and positive +.

- *Conflict unigram*: it indicates if an unigram causes a polarity conflict, with its polarity converted to intensity. It can take one of the next five values: intensity - -, intensity -, none, intensity +, intensity + +.

- *Affected unigram*: it indicates when an unigram is affected by a conflict unigram, modifying its polarity value. It can take one of the next seven values: negative +, negative, negative -, none, positive -, positive and positive +.

- *Negator unigram*: it indicates when an unigram is a negator, modifying the polarity value of the subsequent unigrams. It can take one of the next two values: 0 if it isn't a negator or 1 if it is.

- *Negated unigram*: it indicates when an unigram is affected by a negator, modifying its polarity value. It can take one of the next seven values: negative +, negative, negative -, none, positive -, positive and positive +. This is the value contributed by that unigram in a negated branch of the dependencies tree (the scope).

2.3   Sentiment prediction

Once features were extracted, the next step was to create a model to predict sentiment in testing datasets. Previously, it was said that *Weka* contains a collection of machine learning algorithms for data mining tasks. Several algorithms were tested, such as *Support Vector Machines* (SVM) (Mullen and Collier, 2004), *Large-Scale Linear* (LIBLINEAR) (Fan et al., 2008) or *Hidden Markov Model* (HMM) (Soni and Sharaff, 2015), but the best results obtained were with *Naive Bayes* (Tan et al., 2009). Also, *10-fold cross-validation* was used to obtain the best classification model with the training dataset. Once all classification models were obtained, in subtask A the model with the best *F-measure* was selected, while in subtask B the selected model was the one with the best *recall* (R), as the organization proposed. For the subtask D, the subtask B results were taken into account.

A previous step before the selection of the best classification model is needed. Most algorithms do not accept as input relational attributes, so it was necessary to apply an unsupervised filter by attribute, *RELAGG*, both in training and test files. It processes all relational attributes that fall into the user defined range, making them nominal attributes. In *Naive Bayes* algorithm, the default settings were used, for both the training and the testing datasets, as they are defined in *Weka*. Finally, applying the best model for each subtask on the corresponding testing dataset, the final sentiment prediction for all tweets was obtained.

3   Experimental results

In this section, the conducted experiments for subtasks A, B and D are described. The experiments were carried out using the datasets provided by SemEval-2016 task organizers. These datasets are composed of texts extracted from Twitter, and in the case of the subtasks B and D, with a given topic. In subtask A, the number of tweets is 32009 and the performance of the system is measured by means of the *F-score*. In subtask B, the number of tweets is 10551 and the performance of the system is measured by means of the *macroaveraged recall*. Finally, in subtask D, as in subtask B, the number of tweets is 10551 (same dataset) but this time, the performance of the system is measured by means of the normalized cross-entropy, better known as *Kullback-Leibler Divergence* (KLD). In this last case, there is a minor modification in the formula, with a smoothed version of the originals $p(c_j)$ and $\hat{p}(c_j)$, and a smoothing factor ϵ. All of these measurements are described in (Nakov et al., 2016a).

Table 2 presents the overall scores for subtasks A, B and D, in their respective test sets: *F-measure*, *recall* and KLD, respectively. The third column shows the unsupervised approach results (UAR) and the fourth shows the supervised approach results (SAR) obtained this year.

	Test set	UAR	SAR
	Tw 2013	59.44%	61.17%
	SMS 2013	52.19%	52.38%
	Tw 2014	62.45%	63.90%
Subtask A	*TwS 2014*	46.77%	46.77%
	LJ 2014	61.16%	62.32%
	Tw 2015	57.64%	58.44%
	Tw 2016	53.17%	53.94%
Subtask B	*Tw 2016*	73.36%	73.60%

	Test set	UAR	SAR
Subtask D	*Tw 2016*	0.067	0.055

Table 2: Results of the approach for subtasks A, B and D. *Tw* refers to Twitter, *TwS* to Twitter Sarcasm and *LJ* to LiveJournal.

After performing several experiments on the training, development and development-test datasets provided by organizers, the neutral sentiment intervals were set to [-0.5, 0.5] for subtask A and [-0.05, 0.05] for subtask B (subtask D depends on subtask B). More specifically, in subtask A, our supervised approach was tested with SemEval-2014 development-test, SemEval-2015 development-test and 2016 development-test datasets provided; in subtask B, it was tested with 2016 development-test dataset; and for subtask D, the 2016 development-test dataset results in subtask B were taken into account. In development time, the improvement of our supervised system was between 1 and 3 % compared to our unsupervised system for subtasks A and B, and for subtask D a difference of -0.02 KLD.

In order to assess the improvement of our supervised system regarding our unsupervised system, a comparison is performed in the test sets of this year, as it can be seen in Table 2. With these results, we can say that the new approach, in most cases, improves the unsupervised system, between 0.19 and 1.73 % for subtask A and B (except in Twitter Sarcasm 2014), and a difference of -0.012 in subtask D.

4 Conclusion

This paper describes the participation of the GTI Research Group, AtlantTIC Centre, University of Vigo, in SemEval-2016 task 4: Sentiment Analysis in Twitter. The results were achieved using a supervised system with extracted features from an unsupervised system, described in (Fernández-Gavilanes et al., 2015). Table 3 shows the position of this approach in the ranking published for subtasks A, B and D for the datasets evaluated.

	Test set	Position
	Twitter 2013	13 / 34
	SMS 2013	17 / 34
	Twitter 2014	16 / 34
Subtask A	*Twitter Sarcasm 2014*	7 / 34
	LiveJournal 2014	17 / 34
	Twitter 2015	19 / 34
	Twitter2016	20 / 34
Subtask B	*Twitter 2016*	9 / 19
Subtask D	*Twitter 2016*	5 / 14

Table 3: Positions of the approach for subtasks A, B and D.

The unsupervised approach consists of sentiment propagation rules on dependencies where features were selected (as the different sentiment outputs of the modules combination), and a vector of generic (features not related to a scope in a given tweet) and relational (features extracted from the scope in each treatment performed in each module) features. The results denote a low/medium improvement in subtask A regarding the unsupervised system, and a low improvement in the subtask B (also reflected in the subtask D). Although the new approach is supervised, the fact of using only features of an unsupervised system makes it totally different from other approaches, and still has margin of improvement adding new external features.

Acknowledgments

This work was supported by the Spanish Government, co-financed by the European Regional Development Fund (ERDF) under project TACTICA.

References

Rong-En Fan, Kai-Wei Chang, Cho-Jui Hsieh, Xiang-Rui Wang, and Chih-Jen Lin. 2008. LIBLINEAR: A Library for Large Linear Classification. *J. Mach. Learn. Res.*, 9:1871–1874, June.

Milagros Fernández-Gavilanes, Tamara Álvarez López, Jonathan Juncal-Martínez, Enrique Costa-Montenegro, and Francisco Javier González-Castaño. 2015. GTI: An Unsupervised Approach for Sentiment Analysis in Twitter. In *Proceedings of the 9th International Workshop on Semantic Evaluation (SemEval 2015)*, pages 533–538, Denver, Colorado, June. Association for Computational Linguistics.

Mark Hall, Eibe Frank, Geoffrey Holmes, Bernhard Pfahringer, Peter Reutemann, and Ian H. Witten. 2009. The WEKA Data Mining Software: An Update. *SIGKDD Explor. Newsl.*, 11(1):10–18, November.

Tony Mullen and Nigel Collier. 2004. Sentiment Analysis using Support Vector Machines with Diverse Information Sources. In Dekang Lin and Dekai Wu, editors, *Proceedings of EMNLP 2004*, pages 412–418, Barcelona, Spain, July. Association for Computational Linguistics.

Preslav Nakov, Alan Ritter, Sara Rosenthal, Fabrizio Sebastiani, and Veselin Stoyanov. 2016a. Evaluation Measures for the Semeval-2016 task 4: Sentiment Analysis in Twitter (Draft: Version 1.12). In *Proceedings of the 10th International Workshop on Semantic Evaluation (SemEval 2016)*, San Diego, California, June. Association for Computational Linguistics.

Preslav Nakov, Alan Ritter, Sara Rosenthal, Veselin Stoyanov, and Fabrizio Sebastiani. 2016b. SemEval-2016 task 4: Sentiment Analysis in Twitter. In *Proceedings of the 10th International Workshop on Semantic Evaluation (SemEval 2016)*, San Diego, California, June. Association for Computational Linguistics.

Alexander Pak and Patrick Paroubek. 2010. Twitter as a corpus for sentiment analysis and opinion mining. In Nicoletta Calzolari (Conference Chair), Khalid Choukri, Bente Maegaard, Joseph Mariani, Jan Odijk, Stelios Piperidis, Mike Rosner, and Daniel Tapias, editors, *Proceedings of the Seventh International Conference on Language Resources and Evaluation (LREC'10)*, Valletta, Malta, may. European Language Resources Association (ELRA).

Kevin M. Quinn, Burt L. Monroe, Michael Colaresi, Michael H. Crespin, and Dragomir R. Radev. 2010. How to analyze political attention with minimal assumptions and costs. *American Journal of Political Science*, 54(1):209–228.

Swati Soni and Aakanksha Sharaff. 2015. Sentiment Analysis of Customer Reviews Based on Hidden Markov Model. In *Proceedings of the 2015 International Conference on Advanced Research in Computer Science Engineering & Technology (ICARCSET 2015)*, ICARCSET '15, pages 12:1–12:5, New York, NY, USA. ACM.

Maite Taboada, Julian Brooke, Milan Tofiloski, Kimberly Voll, and Manfred Stede. 2011. Lexicon-based methods for sentiment analysis. *Comput. Linguist.*, 37(2):267–307, June.

Songbo Tan, Xueqi Cheng, Yuefen Wang, and Hongbo Xu. 2009. Adapting Naive Bayes to Domain Adaptation for Sentiment Analysis. In *Proceedings of the 31th European Conference on IR Research on Advances in Information Retrieval*, ECIR '09, pages 337–349, Berlin, Heidelberg. Springer-Verlag.

Aicyber at SemEval-2016 Task 4: i-vector based sentence representation

Steven Du, Zhang Xi
www.aicyber.com
No. 39 Nanjing Road, Capitaland International Trade Center Block B 1604
Tianjin China
{steven,zhangxi}@aicyber.com

Abstract

This paper introduces aicyber's systems for SemEval 2016 , Task 4A. The first system is build on vector space model (VSM), the second system is build on a new framework to estimate sentence vector, it is inspired by the i-vector in speaker verification domain. Both systems are evaluated on SemEval 2016 (Task4A) as well as IMDB dataset. Evaluation results show that the i-vector based sentence vector is an alternative approach to present sentence.

1 Introduction

The SemEval 2016 Task 4 is sentiment analysis in tweets. The subtask, task A focused on classifying tweets into three classes: positive, negative or neutral sentiment (Nakov et al., 2016).

This paper will first presents the submitted system used by team aicyber. Then a new framework of estimating sentence vector will be introduced and evaluated.

2 The aicyber system

This section introduces the submitted system for team aicyber. The text data is first being processed by tweet tokenizer, emoticons are preserved as tokens. Bag-of-ngram feature is extracted and filtered by a TF-IDF (Salton, 1991) selection. Resulting feature dimension is around 3800, it is then reduced to 400 by truncated singular value decomposition (SVD) (Klema and Laub, 1980; Halko et al., 2009). This process is also known as Latent Semantic Analysis (LSA) or Vector Space Model (Turney and Pan-

tel, 2010). Finally a Linear Discriminant Analysis (LDA) classifier (Hastie et al., 2009) is trained to classify the test data.

The SemEval 2016 training dataset which contains 3887 tweets are selected to train the TF-IDF, SVD and LDA. Development dataset is used for tuning parameters and develop-test dataset are used for local testing.

Task A adopted Macro-F1 measure as evaluation metric (Nakov et al., 2016):

$$F_1^{PN} = \frac{F_1^{Pos} + F_1^{Neg}}{2} \tag{1}$$

The Macro-F1 for Aicyber system measured on development, develop-test and 2016 Tweet set, are respectively 0.4514, 0.4787 and 0.4024.

It is obvious that this classification problem has not been satisfactorily answered. One possible reason is the unbalanced training data causes system bias towards positive classes. There are 2101 positive, 1292 neutral but only 494 negative tweets.

Another reason is the size of labeled training set is too small,with only 3887 tweets, which could hardly cover a reasonable amount of words. As a result, the bag-of-ngarm features learned from this training set, could not generalized well. This motivate us to seeking alternative feature representation of tweet, that is sentence vector.

3 Sentence vector

(Le and Mikolov, 2014) proposed sentence vector or paragraph vector (PV) which could learn the continuous distributed vector representation for

Proceedings of SemEval-2016, pages 120–125,
San Diego, California, June 16-17, 2016. ©2016 Association for Computational Linguistics

text of variable-length and achieved promising result on movie review texts. It is inspired by word2vec (Mikolov et al., 2013) embedding which captures rich notions of semantic relatedness and constitutionality between words. (Mesnil et al., 2014) shows the ensemble of sentence vector, RNN language model (Mikolov et al., 2010) and NB SVM (Wang and Manning, 2012) achieved new state-of-the-art result.

(Dai et al., 2015) extends the study and provide a more thorough comparison of PV to other task such as document modeling. It concluded PV can effectively be used for measuring semantic similarity between long pieces of texts.

However such approach assume testing data is known during learning of vector representation. Access of testing data during training may not allowed for certain machine learning task, and it is not practical for real application.

Thus we would like to introduce a new approach to estimate sentence vector or PV for variable-length of texts from word embeddings by using i-vector framework.

3.1 i-vector framework in speech domain

i-vector (Dehak et al., 2011) is one of the dominant approaches in speaker verification (SV) research in the recent years. It projects variable length speech utterances into a fixed-size low-dimensional vector, namely i-vector. Its development advanced from traditional techniques such as the Gaussian Mixture Models (GMMs) (Rose and Reynolds, 1990; Reynolds and Rose, 1995) , adapted GMMs (Reynolds et al., 2000), GMM supervectors (Campbell et al., 2006) and Joint Factor Analysis (Kenny et al., 2007).

To understand i-vector, firstly we need to understand the speech data, the speech data is a sequence of frames. At each frame a fixed-size feature vector is extracted, such as MFCC (Davis and Mermelstein, 1980), with addition of dynamics features such as "delta" and "delta-delta" (Furui, 1986). Thus one utterance could be viewed as a list of continuous-valued vectors as shown in Fig.1. A large amount of utterances are used to train the background GMM in i-vector framework. Secondly we need to learn the supervector. Its aim was to convert a spoken utterance with arbitrary duration to a fixed length vec-

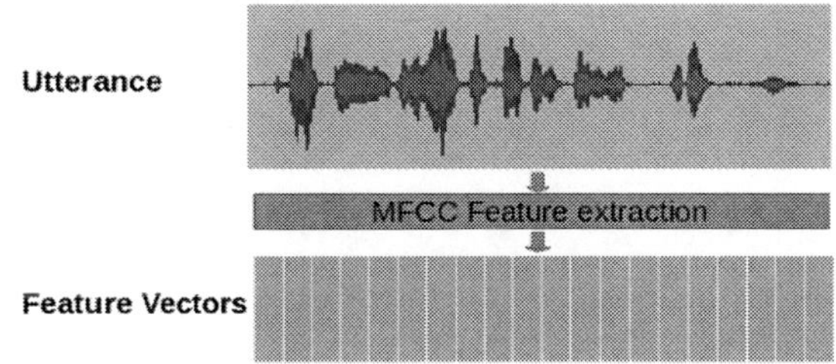

Figure 1: In i-vector framework of SV system, during data pre-processing, spoken utterance is presented as a list of feature vectors. A trained i-vector extractor could map utterances of various length into fixed-size vectors.

tor. The supervector mentioned here is specific to the GMM supervector constructed by stacking the means of the mixture components. For example, a GMM with 2048 components built on 60 dimensional feature vectors results a 122880 (2048*60) dimensional supervector. A review of GMM and supervector is presented in (Kinnunen and Li, 2010).

Given an utterance, its GMM supervector s can be represented as follows:

$$s = m + Tw \qquad (2)$$

where m denotes Universal Background Gaussian Mixture Model's (UBM) supervector, T is the total-variability matrix, which is used to represent the primary directions' variation across a large amount of training data. The coefficients w of this total variability is known as identity vector or simply i-vector.

Extraction of this i-vector can be done as follows (Given a SV system built on F dimensional MFCC features and UBM with C Gaussian components):

$$w = (I + T^t \Sigma^{-1} N T)^{-1} T^t \Sigma^{-1} A \qquad (3)$$

where I is $F \times F$ identity matrix, N is a $CF \times CF$ diagonal matrix whose diagonal blocks are $N_c I$(c=1,2,....C), and the supervector A is generated by the concatenation of the centralized first-order Baum-Welch statistics. Σ is the covariance matrix of the residual variability not captured by T. The i-vector's dimension is usually 400, much lower than that of supervectors. This thus allows the use of various techniques that were not practical in high dimensional space. To give a completed review of i-vector is out of scope of this paper, interested individuals are strongly encouraged to read (Kenny et al., 2008; Dehak et al., 2011).

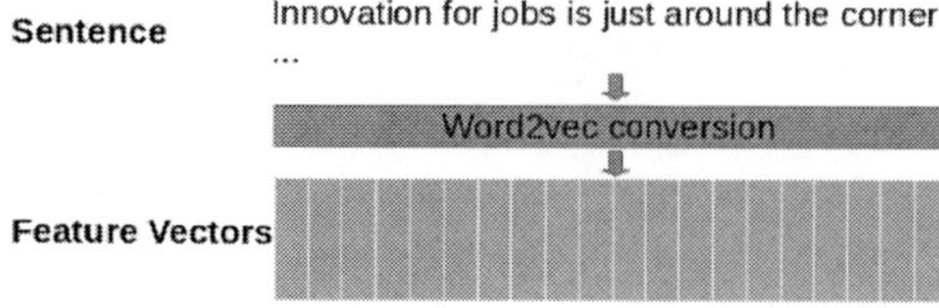

Figure 2: Data preprocessing of proposed NLP i-vector framework. Sentence is represented by its word embedding. A trained i-vector extractor could map sentence of arbitrary length into one fixed-size vector.

3.2 i-vector framework for Natural Language Processing task

(Shepstone et al., 2016) points out that *the central to computing the total variability matrix and i-vector extraction, is the computation of the posterior distribution for a latent variable conditioned on an observed feature sequence of an utterance.* In Natural Language Processing(NLP) when observations (words) could be represented as sequences of feature vectors, will the same methodology apply? This motivated us to bring i-vector from speech to NLP domain. Fig. 2 illustrates the fundamental principle of proposed i-vector framework for NLP task, where a sentence is represented through its word embedding during data preprocessing. Delta and delta-delta feature is added during training in order to capture the context information. Compare to Fig. 1 where spoken utterance is viewed as list of frame level MFCC feature vectors. The proposed i-vector framework replace MFCC features by word vectors, and trained using similar implementation as of speech data.

3.3 The implementation of i-vector framework

Many implementations of i-vector framework are developed recently, (Glembek et al., 2011) use standard GMM approach. (Snyder et al., 2015) incorporated time delayed deep neural network (TDNN) trained on speech recognition task into i-vector framework. A 50% relative improvement is obtained when TDNN instead of GMM is used to collect first-order Baum-Welch statistics. In this paper we use the light weighted conventional GMM approach for proof of concept purpose.

4 Experiment and evaluation

Training of i-vector system is in a completely unsupervised manner, it includes training of word2vec and training of i-vector extractor. Evaluation is done on IMDB similar to (Maas et al., 2011; Le and Mikolov, 2014; Mesnil et al., 2014) and SemEval 2016 Task4A.

4.1 Word2vec training

Word2vec training is done by using gensim [1]. Training dataset is selected from IMDB, it contains 25000 labeled training samples and 50000 unlabeled data, a total of 75000 movie reviews.

The training use a context window of 7, minimum word count of 10 and the resulting dimension of word vector is 20.

4.2 i-vector extractor training

Same data from word2vec training is used for i-vector extractor training. As illustrated in Fig 2, the data preprocessing involved word-to-vector conversion. Words that not appear in the word2vec model are ignored. Each review is treated as one sentence. The sentence is saved as list of word vectors, can be viewed as a $M \times 20$ matrix. Where M denotes number of words in that sentence.

The proposed i-vector extractor training system[2] is developed using the Kaldi Speech Recognition Toolkit (Povey et al., 2011)[3]. Feature used is a 60 dimensional features consisting of the 20 dimensional word vector and its delta, double delta. Mean and variance normalization is not applied. During training, a universal background model (UBM) with 2048 Gaussian mixture components is trained on 64000 sentences. Each Gaussian in UBM has a full covariance matrix. After UBM is trained, the total variability matrix is similar trained with all the 75000 sentences. Learned i-vector extractor is then used to estimate vectors for IMDB and SemEval 2016 dataset. The output dimension of i-vector is 200. Note that, test data of IMDB and all data in SemEval 2016 are not observed during training.

---

[1] http://radimrehurek.com/gensim/
[2] https://github.com/StevenLOL/aicyber_semeval_2016_ivector
[3] https://github.com/kaldi-asr/kaldi

System	Training Data	Accuracy (%)
State-of-the-art	train+test+unlabeled	**92.57**
Sentence Vectors	train+test+unlabeled	88.73
Aicyber's system	train	88.38
i-vector	train+unlabeled	**87.52**
i-vector+VSM	train+unlabeled	**89.94**

Table 1: Proposed i-vector based sentence vector evaluated on the IMDB dataset. It didn't beat the state-of-the-art, an ensemble of three sub systems.

4.3 Evaluation of proposed framework

The i-vector framework is first evaluated on the IMDB dataset then on the SemEval 2016 dataset.

4.3.1 Evaluation on IMDB

Evaluation metric is accuracy measured on IMDB database. Table 1 shows the performance of different systems. The current state-of-the-art system is an ensemble of RNN language model, sentence vectors and NB SVM, achieved 92.57% (Mesnil et al., 2014) testing accuracy. Sentence vector system is one of sub-system used in ensemble and achieved 88.73% accuracy alone. Aicyber's system is the same system mentioned in Section 2, a VSM approach, it obtained 88.38%. To make a fair comparison same type of classifier, LDA is used to train and classify i-vector system, a 87.52% accuracy is reported. Concatenation of i-vector and vector from VSM a 89.94% accuracy can be achieved.

4.3.2 Evaluation on SemEval 2016

Evaluation metric for SemEval 2016 task is Macro-F1 introduced in Equation 1. During evaluation period we validate the performance on development and develop-test dataset. Results as shown in Table 2 indicate i-vector system is worse than our baseline system. So we only submitted the baseline system.

4.4 Discussion

Judging from the IMDB evaluation, the idea of i-vector from speech domain is successfully applied for NLP task. Though it didn't beat the state-of-the-art, it is well-known that basic machine learning techniques can yield strong baselines (Wang and Manning, 2012) on this dataset.

Performance dropped in SemEval 2016 could due

System	Aicyber's system	i-vector system
Development (Macro-F1)	0.4514	0.3732
Development-test (Macro-F1)	0.4787	0.3814

Table 2: Proposed i-vector based sentence vector evaluated on the SemEval 2016 dataset. Aicyber's system is VSM approach and trained on 3887 tweets. The i-vector extractor learned from IMDB dataset and apply on SemEval data. The results show that the i-vector system could not beat our submitted system.

to data mis-match, the word2vec and i-vector extractor is trained on the movie review texts which are much longer, more formal than tweets and are of different vocabulary.

Further improvement can be made in the following aspects.

1. The word-to-vector conversion is done via word2vec, using of Glove word vectors (Pennington et al., 2014), either alone or as concatenation of two type of word vectors for system training is worth to explored.

2. Parameters in word2vec, GMM and i-vector training is not yet optimized to the task. For example, word vector is set to 20 dimensions which is much smaller than 300 dimensional Google word vector. Finding the best parameters will bring more insight of semantical meaning of sentence vector.

3. In this paper, the implementation of i-vector framework is a GMM based approach. Incorporating deep neural network (Snyder et al., 2015) or a Convolutional Neural Network (Kalchbrenner et al., 2014) for NLP task is worth to investigated.

5 Conclusion

This paper had presented a vector space model approach for team aicyber and a new idea of estimating sentence vector. Proposed i-vector framework had evaluated on SemEval 2016 as well as IMDB dataset. Result shows that the i-vector based sentence vector is an alternative approach to present sentence.

References

W. M. Campbell, D. E. Sturim, and D. A. Reynolds. 2006. Support vector machines using gmm supervectors for speaker verification. *IEEE Signal Processing Letters*, 13(5):308 – 311.

A. M. Dai, C. Olah, and Q. V. Le. 2015. Document Embedding with Paragraph Vectors. *ArXiv e-prints*, July.

S. B. Davis and Paul Mermelstein. 1980. Mermelstein, p.: Comparison of parametric representations for monosyllabic word recognition in continuously spoken sentences. ieee trans. acoust speech signal processing 28(4), 357-366. *IEEE Transactions on Acoustics Speech and Signal Processing*, 28(4):357–366.

N. Dehak, P. J. Kenny, R. Dehak, P. Dumouchel, and P. Ouellet. 2011. Front-end factor analysis for speaker verification. *IEEE Transactions on Audio Speech and Language Processing*, 19(4):788–798.

Sadaoki Furui. 1986. Speaker-independent isolated word recognition based on emphasized spectral dynamics. In *Acoustics, Speech, and Signal Processing, IEEE International Conference on ICASSP*, pages 1991–1994.

O. Glembek, L. Burget, P. Matejka, and M. Karafiat. 2011. Simplification and optimization of i-vector extraction. In *Acoustics, Speech and Signal Processing (ICASSP), 2011 IEEE International Conference on*, pages 4516 – 4519.

N. Halko, P. G. Martinsson, and J. A. Tropp. 2009. Finding structure with randomness: Probabilistic algorithms for constructing approximate matrix decompositions. *Siam Review*, 53(2):217–288.

T. Hastie, R. J. Tibshirani, and J. H. Friedman. 2009. The elements of statistical learning: Springer. *Chemistry International*, (6):91–108.

Nal Kalchbrenner, Edward Grefenstette, and Phil Blunsom. 2014. A convolutional neural network for modelling sentences. *Eprint Arxiv*, 1.

P. Kenny, G. Boulianne, P. Ouellet, and P. Dumouchel. 2007. Joint factor analysis versus eigenchannels in speaker recognition. *IEEE Transactions on Audio Speech and Language Processing*, 15(4):1435–1447.

P. Kenny, P. Ouellet, N. Dehak, V. Gupta, and P. Dumouchel. 2008. A study of inter-speaker variability in speaker verification. In *IEEE Trans. Audio, Speech and Language Processing*, pages 980 – 988.

Tomi Kinnunen and Haizhou Li. 2010. An overview of text-independent speaker recognition: From features to supervectors. *Speech Communication*, 52(1):1240.

V. Klema and A. J. Laub. 1980. The singular value decomposition: Its computation and some applications. *IEEE Transactions on Automatic Control*, 25(2):164–176.

Quoc V. Le and Tomas Mikolov. 2014. Distributed representations of sentences and documents. *Eprint Arxiv*, 4:1188–1196.

Andrew L. Maas, Raymond E. Daly, Peter T. Pham, Dan Huang, Andrew Y. Ng, and Christopher Potts. 2011. Learning word vectors for sentiment analysis. In *Proceedings of the 49th Annual Meeting of the Association for Computational Linguistics: Human Language Technologies - Volume 1*, pages 142–150.

Grégoire Mesnil, Tomas Mikolov, Marc'Aurelio Ranzato, and Yoshua Bengio. 2014. Ensemble of generative and discriminative techniques for sentiment analysis of movie reviews. *arXiv preprint arXiv:1412.5335*.

Tomas Mikolov, Martin Karafit, Lukas Burget, Jan Cernock, and Sanjeev Khudanpur. 2010. Recurrent neural network based language model. *Interspeech*, pages 1045–1048.

Tomas Mikolov, Ilya Sutskever, Kai Chen, Greg Corrado, and Jeffrey Dean. 2013. Distributed representations of words and phrases and their compositionality. *Advances in Neural Information Processing Systems*, 26:3111–3119.

Preslav Nakov, Alan Ritter, Sara Rosenthal, Veselin Stoyanov, and Fabrizio Sebastiani. 2016. SemEval-2016 task 4: Sentiment analysis in Twitter. In *Proceedings of the 10th International Workshop on Semantic Evaluation*, SemEval '16, San Diego, California, June. Association for Computational Linguistics.

Jeffrey Pennington, Richard Socher, and Christopher D Manning. 2014. Glove: Global vectors for word representation. In *EMNLP*, volume 14, pages 1532–1543.

Daniel Povey, Arnab Ghoshal, Gilles Boulianne, Luk Burget, Ondej Glembek, Nagendra Goel, Mirko Hannemann, Petr Motlek, Yanmin Qian, and Petr Schwarz. 2011. The kaldi speech recognition toolkit. *Idiap*.

D. A. Reynolds and R. C. Rose. 1995. Robust text-independent speaker identification using gaussian mixture speaker models. *IEEE Transactions on Speech and Audio Processing*, 3(1):72–83.

Douglas A. Reynolds, Thomas F. Quatieri, and Robert B. Dunn. 2000. Speaker verification using adapted gaussian mixture models. *Digital Signal Processing*, 10(1-3):19–41.

R. C. Rose and D. A. Reynolds. 1990. Text independent speaker identification using automatic acoustic segmentation. In *International Conference on Acoustics, Speech, and Signal Processing, Icassp*, pages 293 – 296.

Gerard Salton. 1991. Developments in automatic text retrieval. *Science*, 253(5023):974–980.

Sven Shepstone, Kong Aik Lee, Haizhou Li, Zheng-Hua Tan, and Soren Holdt Jensen. 2016. Total variability modeling using source-specific priors.

David Snyder, Daniel Garcia-Romero, and Daniel Povey. 2015. Time delay deep neural network-based universal background models for speaker recognition. ASRU.

Peter D. Turney and Patrick Pantel. 2010. From frequency to meaning: Vector space models of semantics. *Journal of Artificial Intelligence Research*, 37(4):141–188.

Sida Wang and Christopher D. Manning. 2012. Baselines and bigrams: simple, good sentiment and topic classification. In *Proceedings of the 50th Annual Meeting of the Association for Computational Linguistics: Short Papers - Volume 2*, pages 90–94.

PUT at SemEval-2016 Task 4: The ABC of Twitter Sentiment Analysis

Mateusz Lango and **Dariusz Brzezinski** and **Jerzy Stefanowski**
Institute of Computing Science, Poznan University of Technology
60-965 Poznań, Poland
{mlango,dbrzezinski,jstefanowski}@cs.put.edu.pl

Abstract

This paper describes a classification system that participated in SemEval-2016 Task 4: Sentiment Analysis in Twitter. The proposed approach competed in subtasks A, B, and C, which involved tweet polarity classification, tweet classification according to a two-point scale, and tweet classification according to a five-point scale. Our system is based on an ensemble consisting of Random Forests, SVMs, and Gradient Boosting Trees, and involves the use of a wide range of features including: n-grams, Brown clustering, sentiment lexicons, Wordnet, and part-of-speech tagging. The proposed system achieved 14th, 6th, and 3rd place in subtasks A, B, and C, respectively.

1 Introduction

In recent years, sentiment analysis (Liu, 2012) has become a common yardstick for many new text mining algorithms. This trend is a direct result of the rapid growth of social media, where users express their views and opinions regarding a wide range of topics. As a result, social networks like Twitter have become a crucial resource in product design, assessing marketing campaigns, and detecting news bursts (Liu, 2012; Mathioudakis and Koudas, 2010).

However, while the merits of resources such as Twitter are evident, there are several difficulties with the use of social media data. In contrast to classical sentiment analysis methods, which were originally designed for dealing with well-written product reviews, texts from social media often contain misspellings, letter substitutions, ambiguities, non-standard abbreviations, and improper use of gram-

mar (Sarker et al., 2015). Furthermore, resources such as Twitter generate thousands of new texts per second and introduce challenges characteristic for stream processing (Krempl et al., 2014). Moreover, the limited length of these texts makes classical n-gram feature vectors extremely sparse, which in turn hinders generalization abilities of classification algorithms. Finally, sentiments are usually unevenly distributed (Kiritchenko et al., 2014), resulting in class imbalance and, therefore, additional difficulties for classifiers (He and Garcia, 2009).

To promote research in this area, Task 4 of SemEval-2016 was devoted to sentiment analysis in Twitter. The task consisted of five subtasks involving standard classification, ordinal classification, and distribution estimation; for a more detailed description see (Nakov et al., 2016).

In this paper, we present our approach to learn a classification system which participated in subtasks A, B, and C of SemEval-2016 Sentiment Analysis in Twitter. The proposed approach combines Random Forests, Support Vector Machines, and Gradient Boosting Trees, trained on a wide range of lexical and semantic features including: n-grams, k-grams, Brown clustering, sentiment lexicons, Senti-WordNet, and part of speech tagged 1-grams. These components were carefully combined and optimized to create a separate version of the system for each of the tackled subtasks.

In the following sections, we describe each group of features used in our system. Moreover, we explain the details of the proposed classification algorithm with respect to each realized subtask. Finally, we conclude the paper with a discussion on the ob-

126

Proceedings of SemEval-2016, pages 126–132,
San Diego, California, June 16-17, 2016. ©2016 Association for Computational Linguistics

tained results, importance of each feature group, and possible lines of future research.

2 Basic Features

We briefly describe the features used in our system. The same set of developed features was used in all three subtasks our algorithms participated in. However, for some of the component classifiers we additionally performed feature selection using a filter method based on the F-statistic. Details on this subject will be discussed later.

2.1 Preprocessing

Prior to extracting features, we performed standard natural language processing procedures to clean the data. First, each tweet was tokenized into words, hashtags, punctuation marks, and special symbols. Next, tokens were lemmatized by NLTK Word-NetLemmatizer[1] to unify different versions of the same words. Subsequently, certain words were removed based on a hand-crafted stop list. Finally, certain symbols (urls, hashtags, numbers, percentages, prices, dates, hours) that occurred less than five times in the dataset were grouped according to their meaning, and those tokens that could not be grouped were removed from the training data.

2.2 Word n-grams

The first feature set consisted of word n-grams, i.e., sequences of n continuous words in a text segment. For our system, we generated 1-, 2-, 3-, 4-, and 5-grams based on all available tweet messages.

2.3 Negation n-grams

In addition to traditional n-grams, we also utilized n-grams in negation context (Remus, 2013). Negation n-grams are sequences of words that appear in a negated context. Negations were discovered based on "not" and "n't" tokens, and a negated context was defined as a set of words falling between a negation and a "terminal" punctuation symbol $\{., ;, , , !, ?\}$. We used 1- and 2-negation-grams in our system.

2.4 Character k-grams

Another group of features was created by generating character k-grams. Character k-grams were created by extracting sequences of k continuous characters from each word. To distinguish character-grams from word-grams, we will refer to character sequences as *k-grams*. We used 3-, 4-, and 5-character-grams as features.

2.5 POS 1-grams

Another set of n-grams was created by using a part-of-speech tagger. This approach combines words with the part of speech they represent, in an attempt to distinguish different meanings of the same word. In our system, we used the NLTK PerceprtronTagger[2] to add concatenated {word, part-of-speech} pairs as features.

2.6 Sentiment Lexicons

A major group of features used in our system was formed by sentiment scores, which were created by summing word-sentiment associations for a given tweet. More precisely, for each tweet we counted the number of words conveying each sentiment defined in a given lexicon. We used this procedure for four sentiment lexicons: the NRC emotion lexicon (Mohammad and Turney, 2013), Hu and Liu Opinion lexicon (Hu and Liu, 2004), the Multi-perspective Question Answering corpus (Wiebe et al., 2005), and SentiWordNet (Baccianella et al., 2010).

The NRC emotion lexicon is a list of words and their associations with eight emotions (anger, fear, anticipation, trust, surprise, sadness, joy, and disgust) and two sentiments (negative and positive). Combined this gives a total of ten real valued sentiment scores, which were added to our feature set.

The Opinion Lexicon, assembled by Hu and Liu, consists of two lists: one containing positive and one containing negative words. Because intensities of these two sentiments are not specified, we counted the occurrences of lexicon words in each tweet to create two sentiment scores.

The Multi-perspective Question Answering (MPQA) corpus contains four sentiment word lists: positive, negative, both, and neutral. As with the Opinion Lexicon, we counted the occurrences of each in-lexicon word to create four additional features.

Finally, the SentiWordNet is a sentiment tagged

---

[1] http://www.nltk.org/api/nltk.stem.html

[2] http://www.nltk.org/api/nltk.tag.html

wordnet. We used this network to find synsets (semantical equivalents) of words and used their sentiment scores as features.

2.7 Hashtag Lexicon

An interesting addition to the aforementioned word lexicons was the use of the NRC Hashtag Affirmative/Negated Context Sentiment Lexicon (Kiritchenko et al., 2014). This lexicon contains a real-valued sentiment score associated with single words and 2-grams designed specifically for Twitter. For each tweet we calculated the minimal, maximal, and mean sentiment score based on all words in a tweet.

2.8 Brown Clustering

Our final set of features was created using Brown clustering (Brown et al., 1992). Brown clustering is a form of hierarchical clustering of words based on the contexts in which they occur. We used a precompiled clustering of English tweets into 1000 clusters provided by Owoputi et al. (2013).

3 Classification

3.1 Multi-class classification (subtask A)

The goal of subtask A was to correctly classify tweets into three classes: positive, neutral, and negative. Macro-averaged F_1 score over the positive and negative class was used as an evaluation metric. The provided training set consisted of 5459 tweets[3] and the test set, which was used for internal model verification and validation, consisted of 1806 tweets.

Gradient Boosting Trees (Friedman, 2001) is a popular classifier which combines the idea of a boosting ensemble and gradient descent optimization. We have chosen it, because it proved to work well in many data mining competitions and on a variety of problems. GBT are also robust to very sparse features, which makes them a good choice for tweet classification.

In our system we used GBT with softmax as the loss function, the maximum depth of a single tree was set to 40 and no tree pruning was performed afterwards. To prevent overfitting the L2 regularization factor was added to the optimization func-

tion. Additionally, to increase the diversity of the model, each ensemble component was trained on a subset of features. Each subset was constructed using randomly chosen 40% of the features. Furthermore, each tree component was trained on a random sample of the training set which contained 80% of the examples.

From the training set 10% of examples were extracted to form a validation set. This additional dataset was used for verification of the early stopping condition. After learning every new tree, the performance of the whole classifier was verified on the validation set in terms of macro-averaged F_1 score. The lack of improvement during 30 iterations triggered the early stopping condition and terminated the ensemble construction. GBT was always fitted until the early stopping condition was met, without any constraint on the maximal number of ensemble components[4].

During initial experiments we discovered, that the classifier made wrong predictions on negative and neutral examples more often than on instances belonging to the positive class. The trained model suffered from class imbalance, which often leads to generalization problems of many classification techniques (He and Garcia, 2009). Indeed, the dataset in this subtask contains 2804 positive examples (51%) together with only 781 negative (14%) and 1874 neutral (34%) examples.

To overcome this problem, inspired by solutions in the field of cost-sensitive learning (He and Garcia, 2009), we assigned each instance a weight $w = 1/(c \cdot |C_i|)$ where $|C_i|$ is the number of examples belonging to the true class of the i-th example in the training set and c is the total number of classes (in this subtask $c = 3$). The use of such instance weights in the loss function ensures that each class is equally important for optimization, because the sums of example weights for each class are equal.

We also tested Random Forests (Breiman, 2001) and linear Support Vector Machines (Cortes and Vapnik, 1995) classifiers. As preliminary experiments showed that the performance of Random Forests and SVM was sensitive to the increasing number of features, we decided to carry out addi-

---

[3]The dataset provided by task organizers was a little bit bigger, but we report the number of tweets which we were able to download successfully.

[4]In practice we always set the maximum number of iterations to a big number (10000).

tional feature selection. Hence, we trained them on 5000 best features selected by the F value of ANOVA which improved micro-averaged F_1 and also had a positive influence on training time. The best results for Random Forest, according to macro-averaged F_1, were achieved when each leaf of a single tree was enforced to contain at least three examples, the number of trees was equal to 5000 and instance weighting (as described above) was used. Also SVM gave best results with instance weighting. Despite the fact that both Random Forests and SVMs achieved results that were a little worse than GBT (macro-averaged F_1 score was about 3% lower for both of them) we decided to use them to refine predictions of GBT.

Finally, our classification system is a heterogeneous multiple-classifier consisting of three different components: Random Forests, Gradient Boosting Trees, and Support Vector Machines. Each of them is trained on the same training set and the final classification of the ensemble is a result of simple majority voting. We use a well-known scikit-learn (Pedregosa et al., 2011) implementation of Random Forests, and SVMs in Python as well as a very effective Gradient Boosting Trees implementation from the XGBoost library[5].

3.2 Binary classification (subtask B)

The goal of subtask B also involved the classification of tweets, however, only two classes (positive and negative) were considered. Just as in subtask A, the dataset was highly imbalanced: only 17% (679) of examples were negative.

In subtask A we could not use more advanced methods for tackling class imbalance since most of them are designed for binary classification only. One of such techniques is Roughly Balanced Bagging (Hido et al., 2009), which proved to give the best results among extensions of bagging for class imbalance (Błaszczyński and Stefanowski, 2015).

RBBag learns each base classifier on a random sample of the training set and then the final class prediction is a result of averaging predictions of components. The main difference between classical bagging and RBBag is its specialized sampling scheme. First, the training set is divided into two

[5]https://github.com/dmlc/xgboost

subsets, each containing examples from only one class. From the subset containing minority examples, RBBag creates a classical bootstrap sample which contains N instances, where N is the number of minority examples in the training set. To this sample, M majority examples are added randomly where M is not the number of majority examples, but it is taken from a negative binomial distribution with parameters $p = 0.5$ and $n = N$.

We used Roughly Balanced Bagging with GBT as the base classifier. All parameters of GBT were set just like described in section 3.1, however during experiments different learning rates and regularization factors were selected. Additionally, RBBag was tested with 5, 7, 15 and 30 base classifiers, but the best results were obtained for 7 GBTs, which confirms earlier observations of Lango and Stefanowski (2015) that RBBag does not require many components to achieve good performance.

3.3 Ordinal classification (subtask C)

Subtask C concentrated on classifying tweets into 5 classes: very negative, negative, neutral, positive and very positive. Since the order in the classes is established, this subtask can be considered as an ordinal classification problem.

We implemented an ensemble algorithm described by Frank and Hall (2001), which decomposes ordinal classification into several binary classification problems. Each classifier is trained on the same training set, but the class label of every example is changed by the function $I(x_{class} > i)$ where $I()$ is an indicator function, x_{class} is a class of a given example and i is the reference class. The reference class for the first classifier is "very negative", for the second "negative" etc. Finally, we have four classifiers and each of them returns the likelihood of a positive response to the question "is the class of the analyzed example higher than the reference class". The final set of likelihoods can be easily transformed to the likelihood of every class.

Again, we used GBT as a base classifier with the same setup as described in section 3.1. However, we also tested linear SVM, Random Forests, Factorization Machines (Rendle, 2010) and transductive SVMs (Joachims, 1999). Linear SVM achieved results very similar to GBT in terms of macro-averaged mean absolute error (MAE^M). Despite this fact, during the analysis of responses of both classifiers on the test set, for several examples we discovered significant differences in responses (e.g. "very negative" vs "positive"). Since both models performed almost equally good and MAE^M highly punishes significant differences between classes on the ordinal scale, we decided to create a meta-classifier from these two models. In our ensemble the final prediction is an average of predictions of GBT and SVM-based models, which is rounded towards the decision of the GBT-based model (since its MAE^M score was a little higher).

4 Results and feature analysis

This section includes the experimental results of our system for all three sub-tasks. We present the scores and ranks achieved by our system followed by a discussion on the relative importance of the proposed features.

The evaluation metric was different in each subtask (Nakov et al., 2016). For subtask A, it was required to optimize the macro-averaged F_1-score (F_1^M) calculated over the positive and negative classes. In subtask B, the goal was to achieve a high macro-averaged recall (R^M), while subtask C took into account a macro-averaged mean absolute error (MAE^M). Table 4 presents the overall performance of our system.

Subtask	Metric	Our score	Best score	Rank
A	F_1^M	0.576	0.633	14
B	R^M	0.763	0.797	6
C	MAE^M	0.860	0.719	3

Table 1: Overall performance of the system.

We also performed an analysis of feature importance using one trained Gradient Boosting Trees classifier (GBT). For this classifier the feature importance can be easily measured by observing the increase of purity while performing splits on a particular feature, following an approach from (Breiman and Friedman, 1984).

In subtasks A and C we used a meta-classifier of many different algorithms, so the results would not accurately reflect the feature importance in the whole system. Hence, we decided to run this experiment on the dataset from subtask B only.

Table 2 presents 15 features with the highest relative importance in our classifier. The most important feature was the mean of word sentiments in a tweet according to the NRC Hashtag Lexicon (the maximum word sentiment on this lexicon is also pretty high in the ranking). Other lexicon features, based on the Opinion Lexicon and SentiWord-Net, also achieved high relative importance. Note that many features with high importance come from Brown clustering and k-grams.

In Table 3, we present results of feature importance aggregated in groups. The most important features are those created from character k-grams and their total relative importance is almost 70%. The contribution of features created from Brown clustering, negated n-grams and from n-grams with part-of-speech tags is also very significant. The importance of the rest of the features sums up to only 10%. The poor results of lexicon-based features can be justified by the fact that the number of features in these groups is very small (from 2 to 8 features).

Feature name	Rel. impor. [%]
NRC Hashtag Lexicon: mean	0.79
Brown cluster: 01110110	0.73
SentiWordNet: sum of negative	0.63
5 k-gram: "d &am"	0.55
Brown cluster: 1110011001111	0.49
NRC Hashtag Lexicon: max	0.48
Opinion Lexicon: negative	0.47
Brown cluster: 111101011101	0.42
3 k-gram "ok "	0.41
4 k-gram " nor"	0.40
Brown cluster: 0100100	0.38
3 k-gram " NY"	0.35
2 n-gram: not against	0.35
Brown cluster: 111101111100100	0.34
5 k-gram " Anth"	0.34

Table 2: Relative feature importances (%) of top 15 features.

For Random Forests and SVM we used feature selection according to the F-statistics. We analyzed how features selected by this approach relate to importances estimated by GBT.

Surprisingly, feature importances estimated by the F-statistic and GBT are quite coherent. Almost 80% of features selected by the F-statistic were character-grams, 12% of features were negated n-grams, and features from POS constituted 3,9% of all selected features. The main difference between these two methods is that the F-statistic selected

Feature group	Rel. impor. [%]
5 character-gram	26.03
4 character-gram	21.75
3 character-gram	21.74
Brown clusters	6.92
Negated 1-gram	6.62
1-gram + POS	4.24
Negated + 2-gram	3.48
1-gram	2.69
2-gram	1.87
NRC Hashtag Lexicon	1.49
SentiWordNet	1.00
NRC Lexicon	0.93
Opinion Lexicon	0.62
3-gram	0.34
MPQA corpus	0.25
4-gram	0.03

Table 3: Relative feature importances (%) for features groups.

only one feature from Brown clustering. However, once again simple n-grams were used very rarely (2% of all selected features). This result, together with earlier observations from importances estimated by GBT, seem to show that features created from character-grams are superior to those created by word-grams. It is also worth mentioning that the entire GBT model used only 3579 features, which is an indicator of its feature selection abilities.

5   Conclusions and Future Work

Our system achieved relatively good performance in SemEval-2016 Task 4: Sentiment Analysis in Twitter. Among 34 participants of subtask A we reached rank 14, we took 6th place among 19 competitors in subtask B, and won 3rd place in subtask C where 11 teams competed. The analysis of features used by our system shows that character-grams seem to perform better than word n-grams for Twitter's short-text messages. Furthermore, results obtained by Gradient Boosting Trees in our system confirmed good feature filtering capabilities of this algorithm.

One possible way to further improve our system could be to transfer features selected by GBT to other classifiers (e.g. SVM). Another possible line of the future research is the development of new features based on character-grams, such as negated character-grams or character-gram lexicons.

Acknowledgments

This research was partially funded by the Polish National Science Center under Grant No. DEC-2013/11/B/ST6/00963.

References

Stefano Baccianella, Andrea Esuli, and Fabrizio Sebastiani. 2010. Sentiwordnet 3.0: An enhanced lexical resource for sentiment analysis and opinion mining. In *Proceedings of the International Conference on Language Resources and Evaluation*.

Jerzy Błaszczyński and Jerzy Stefanowski. 2015. Neighbourhood sampling in bagging for imbalanced data. *Neurocomputing*, 150, Part B:529–542.

Leo Breiman and Jerome H. Friedman. 1984. *Classification and regression trees*. Chapman & Hall, New York.

Leo Breiman. 2001. Random forests. *Machine learning*, 45(1):5–32.

Peter F. Brown, Vincent J. Della Pietra, Peter V. de Souza, Jennifer C. Lai, and Robert L. Mercer. 1992. Class-based n-gram models of natural language. *Computational Linguistics*, 18(4):467–479.

Corinna Cortes and Vladimir Vapnik. 1995. Support vector machine. *Machine learning*, 20(3):273–297.

Eibe Frank and Mark Hall. 2001. A simple approach to ordinal classification. In *Proceedings of the 12th European Conference on Machine Learning*, pages 145–156.

Jerome H Friedman. 2001. Greedy function approximation: a gradient boosting machine. *Annals of statistics*, pages 1189–1232.

Haibo He and Edwardo A Garcia. 2009. Learning from imbalanced data. *Knowledge and Data Engineering, IEEE Transactions on*, 21(9):1263–1284.

Shohei Hido, Hisashi Kashima, and Yutaka Takahashi. 2009. Roughly balanced bagging for imbalanced data. *Statistical Analysis and Data Mining*, 2(5-6):412–426.

Minqing Hu and Bing Liu. 2004. Mining and summarizing customer reviews. In *Proceedings of the Tenth ACM SIGKDD International Conference on Knowledge Discovery and Data Mining*, pages 168–177.

Thorsten Joachims. 1999. Transductive inference for text classification using support vector machines. In *International Conference on Machine Learning (ICML)*, pages 200–209.

Svetlana Kiritchenko, Xiaodan Zhu, and Saif M. Mohammad. 2014. Sentiment analysis of short informal texts. *Journal of Artificial Intelligence Research*, 50:723–762.

Georg Krempl, Indrė Žliobaitė, Dariusz Brzezinski, Eyke Hüllermeier, Mark Last, Vincent Lemaire, Tino Noack, Ammar Shaker, Sonja Sievi, Myra Spiliopoulou, and Jerzy Stefanowski. 2014. Open challenges for data stream mining research. *SIGKDD Explorations*, 16(1):1–10.

Mateusz Lango and Jerzy Stefanowski. 2015. Applicability of roughly balanced bagging for complex imbalanced data. In *Proceedings of the 4th Workshop on New Frontiers in Mining Complex Patterns (NFMCP 2015)*, pages 62–73.

Bing Liu. 2012. *Sentiment Analysis and Opinion Mining*. Synthesis digital library of engineering and computer science. Morgan & Claypool.

Michael Mathioudakis and Nick Koudas. 2010. Twittermonitor: Trend detection over the twitter stream. In *Proceedings of the 2010 ACM SIGMOD International Conference on Management of Data*, pages 1155–1158.

Saif Mohammad and Peter D. Turney. 2013. Crowdsourcing a word-emotion association lexicon. *Computational Intelligence*, 29(3):436–465.

Preslav Nakov, Alan Ritter, Sara Rosenthal, Veselin Stoyanov, and Fabrizio Sebastiani. 2016. SemEval-2016 task 4: Sentiment analysis in Twitter. In *Proceedings of the 10th International Workshop on Semantic Evaluation*.

Olutobi Owoputi, Brendan O'Connor, Chris Dyer, Kevin Gimpel, Nathan Schneider, and Noah A. Smith. 2013. Improved part-of-speech tagging for online conversational text with word clusters. In *Proceedings of Human Language Technologies: Conference of the North American Chapter of the Association of Computational Linguistics*, pages 380–390.

F. Pedregosa, G. Varoquaux, A. Gramfort, V. Michel, B. Thirion, O. Grisel, M. Blondel, P. Prettenhofer, R. Weiss, V. Dubourg, J. Vanderplas, A. Passos, D. Cournapeau, M. Brucher, M. Perrot, and E. Duchesnay. 2011. Scikit-learn: Machine learning in Python. *Journal of Machine Learning Research*, 12:2825–2830.

Robert Remus. 2013. Modeling and representing negation in data-driven machine learning-based sentiment analysis. In *Proceedings of the First International Workshop on Emotion and Sentiment in Social and Expressive Media: approaches and perspectives from AI (ESSEM 2013)*, pages 22–33.

Steffen Rendle. 2010. Factorization machines. In *Proceedings of the 10th International Conference on Data Mining (ICDM)*, pages 995–1000.

Abeed Sarker, Azadeh Nikfarjam, Davy Weissenbacher, and Graciela Gonzalez. 2015. Diegolab: An approach for message-level sentiment classification in twitter. In *Proceedings of the 9th International Workshop on Semantic Evaluation*, pages 510–514.

Janyce Wiebe, Theresa Wilson, and Claire Cardie. 2005. Annotating expressions of opinions and emotions in language. *Language Resources and Evaluation*, 39(2-3):165–210.

MIB at SemEval-2016 Task 4a: Exploiting lexicon-based features for sentiment analysis in Twitter

Vittoria Cozza
IIT-CNR
Pisa Italy
`v.cozza@iit.cnr.it`

Marinella Petrocchi
IIT-CNR
Pisa Italy
`m.petrocchi@iit.cnr.it`

Abstract

This work presents our team solution for task 4a (Message Polarity Classification) at the SemEval 2016 challenge. Our experiments have been carried out over the Twitter dataset provided by the challenge. We follow a supervised approach, exploiting a SVM polynomial kernel classifier trained with the challenge data. The classifier takes as input advanced NLP features. This paper details the features and discusses the achieved results.

1 Introduction

Revealing the sentiment behind a text is motivated by several reasons, e.g., to figure out how many opinions on a certain topic are positive or negative. Also, it could be interesting to span positivity and negativity across a n-point scale. As an example, a five-point scale is now widespread in digital scenarios where human ratings are involved: Amazon, TripAdvisor, Yelp, and many others, adopt the scale for letting their users rating products and services.

Under the big hat of sentiment analysis (Liu, 2012), polarity recognition attempts to classify texts into positive or negative, while the rating inference task tries to identify different shades of positivity and negativity, e.g., from strongly-negative, to strongly-positive. There currently exists a number of popular challenges on the matter, as those included in the SemEval series on evaluations of computational semantic analysis systems[1]. Both polarity recognition and rating inference have been applied

---

[1] `https://en.wikipedia.org/wiki/SemEval`

to recommendation systems. Recently, Academia has been focusing on the feasibility to apply sentiment analysis tasks to very short and informal texts, such as tweets (see, e.g. (Rosenthal et al., 2015)).

This paper shows the description of the system that we have set up for participating into the Semeval 2016 challenge in (Nakov et al., 2016b), task 4a (Message Polarity Classification). We have adopted a supervised approach, a SVM polynomial kernel classifier trained with the data provided by the challenge, after extracting lexical and lexicon features from such data.

The paper is organised as follows. Next section briefly addresses related work in the area. Section 3 describes the features extracted from the training data. In Section 4, we present the results of our attempt to answer to the challenge. Finally, we give concluding remarks.

2 Related work

In the last recent years, the Semeval tasks series challenges the polarity evaluation of tweets. This represents a detachment from the traditional polarity detection task. Tweets usually features the use of an informal language, with mispellings, new words, urls, abbreviations and specific symbols (like RT for "re-tweet" and # for hashtags, which are a type of tagging for Twitter messages). Existing approaches and open issues on how to handle such new challenges are in related work like (Kouloumpis et al., 2011; Barbosa and Feng, 2010).

At the 2015 challenge (Rosenthal et al., 2015), the top scored systems were those using deep learning, i.e., semantic vector spaces for single words, used

Proceedings of SemEval-2016, pages 133–138,
San Diego, California, June 16-17, 2016. ©2016 Association for Computational Linguistics

as features in (Turney and Pantel, 2010). Other approaches, as (Basile and Novielli, 2015), exploited lexical and sentiment lexicon features to classify the sentiment of the tweet through machine learning.

In (Priyanka and Gupta, 2013), the authors also exploited different lexical and lexicon features for evaluating the sentiment of a review corpus. The current work inherits most of such features. While they used the lexicon SentiWordNet (Esuli and Sebastiani, 2006), we rely instead on two different ones, LabMT in (Dodds et al., 2011) and Sentic-Net3.0 presented in (Cambria et al., 2014).

All the above cited lexicons (Cambria et al., 2014; Esuli and Sebastiani, 2006; Dodds et al., 2011) are popular and extensively adopted lexicons for sentiment analysis tasks.

3 Sentiment analysis

The SemEval 2016 Sentiment Analysis challenge (Nakov et al., 2016b) requires the labelling of a test set of 28,481 tweets. In order to facilitate the application of supervised machine learning approaches, the challenge organisers provide the access to a gold dataset: a set of labeled tweets, where the labels - positive, negative or neutral - were manually assigned. In detail, the labeled dataset is divided in a training set of 4,000 tweets and a development set of 2,000 tweets. 340 tweets in the training data and 169 ones in the development data could have not be accessed, since such tweets were"Not Available" at crawling time. We rely on the provided labeled dataset (train + devel) in order to respectively train and evaluate a Support Vector Machine (SVM) classifier (Chang and Lin, 2011) to learn a model for automatic Sentiment Analysis on Twitter. We investigate four groups of features based on: keyword and micro-blogging characteristics, n-grams, negation, and sentiment lexicon.

After evaluating the feature set, we built a new classifier model for annotating the unlabeled test set provided by the challenge (prediction phase, see Figure 1). In this phase, we used as features the best combination of the features previously extracted (actually, all of them) and as the training corpus the overall labeled tweet data (devel+test). The results were not satisfactory, being our team ranked 30 (over 34 teams). The challenge results are reported

and discussed in (Nakov et al., 2016b).

In the following, we will detail the process of test cleaning and feature extractions. Then, we present our evaluation, which has been designed to test the efficacy of our feature set for sentiment analysis. Finally, we provide the results obtained at the challenge.

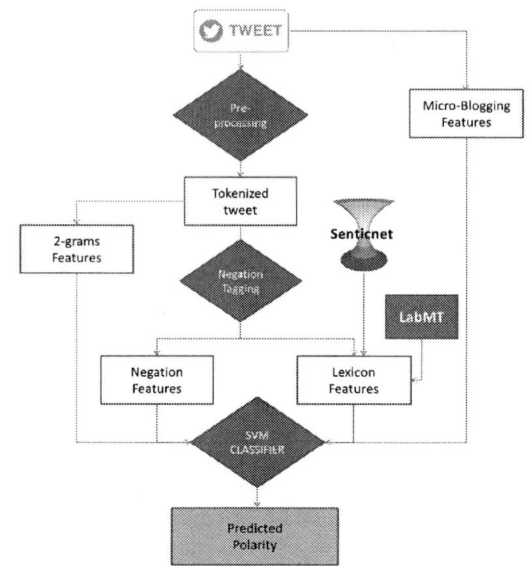

Figure 1: Sentiment analysis: Prediction phase

In the follwoing, we will use the following tweet as a running example.

> Happy hour at @Microsoft #msapc2015 with @sarah-vaughan and friends. Good luck for tomorrow's keynote `http://t.co/emvqoeRS6j`

3.1 Micro-blogging features

The microblogging features have been extracted from the tweet original text, without pre-processing it. We have defined such features with the aim of capturing some typical aspects of micro-blogging. These have been extracted by simply matching regular expressions. First of all, we have cleaned the text from the symbols of mentions "@" and hashtags "#", from urls, from emoticons. Indeed, their presence makes challenging to analyze the text with a traditional linguistic pipeline. Before deleting symbols, emoticons and urls, we have counted them, having as features:

- the number of hashtags;

- the number of mentions;

- the number of urls;

- EmoPos, i.e., the number of positive emoticons;

- EmoNeg, i.e., the number of negative emoticons;

Also, we have also focused on vowels repetitions, exclamations and question marks, introducing the following features:

- the number of vowels repetitions;

- the number of question marks and exclamation marks repetitions.

Concerning the marks, we consider a repetition when they are repeated more than once, as in "!!". Instead, we have considered a vowel as repeated when it occurs more than twice, as in "baaad". The positive and negative emoticons we considered are those on the Wikipedia's page[2].

3.2 Text pre-processing

In order to extract syntactic and semantic features from the text, we pre-processed it with the *Tanl pipeline* (Attardi et al., 2010), a suite of modules for text analytics and natural language processing, based on machine learning. Pre-processing has consisted in first dividing the text in sentences and then into the single word forms composing the sentence. Then, for each form, we have identified the lemma (when available) and the part of speech (POS). As an example, starting from the sentence *Happy hour at Microsoft msapc2015 with sarahvaughan and friends* in the above sample tweet, we obtain the annotation shown in Figure 2. The last column gives the part of speech that a word form yields in a sentence, according to the *Penn Treebank Project*[3].

The last phase of pre-processing is data cleaning. For each sentence, we removed conjunctions, number, determiners, pronouns, and punctuation (still relying on the Penn Treebank POS tags). For the remaining terms, we keep the lemma. Thus, the example sentence results in the following list of lemmas:

Form	Lemma	POS
Happy	happy	JJ
hour	hour	NN
at	at	IN
Microsoft	Microsoft	NNP
msapc2015	msapc2015	,
with	with	IN
sarahvaughan	sarahvaughan	NN
and	and	CC
friends	friend	NNS

Figure 2: Annotation with Tanl English Pipeline (http://tanl.di.unipi.it/en/)

(*happy, hour, microsoft, msapc2015, sarahvaughan, friend*).

In the following, we describe the features we have extracted from the pre-processed text. Among others, we inherit some of the features in (Priyanka and Gupta, 2013) and (Basile and Novielli, 2015), which face with sentiment analysis on Twitter.

3.3 n-grams features

Upon pre-processing, we have obtained a words vector representation of each tweet. Then, we have extracted n-grams, i.e., all the pairs of sequencing lemmas in the vector. As an over simplification, we have considered only the case of n=2. We thought this was reasonable, since tweets are short portions of text bounded to 140 characters. In the example sentence, some are (*happy-hour, hour-microsoft*).The 2-grams have been discretised into binary attributes representing their presence or not in the text. There are 1,237 unique 2-grams.

3.4 Negation-based features

Handling negations is an important step in sentiment analysis, as they can reverse the meaning of a sentence. Also, negations can often occur with sarcastic and ironic goals, which are quite difficult to detect. We consider 1-grams and we prefix them with P (N) when they are asserted (negated). To identify if the unigram appears in a negated scope, we have applied a rule-based approach[4]. The approach works as follows. Considering a negative sentiment tweet, like, e.g., *"It might be not nice but it's the reality.*, the "nice" unigram is in the scope of negation, and, thus, it will be labeled as N_nice. The "but" unigram changes again the scope, thus "reality" will be

---

[2] https://it.wikipedia.org/wiki/Emoticon
[3] https://www.ling.upenn.edu/courses/Fall_2003/ling001/penn_treebank_pos.html

[4] http://sentiment.christopherpotts.net/lingstruc.html#negation

labeled as P_reality.

We have identified the following features as suitable for handling negations:

- Unigrams with scope;

- Positiveterms: Number of lemmas with positive scope;

- Negativeterms: Number of lemmas with negative scope;

The first feature has been discretised into binary attributes representing the presence (or not) of the 1-gram. The number of unique unigrams (with scope) are 5,110.

3.5 Sentiment lexicon-based features

Several lexicons are available for sentiment analysis. In this work, we consider SenticNet 3.0 (Cambria et al., 2014) and the LabMT (Dodds et al., 2011).

SenticNet 3.0 is a large concept-level base of knowledge, assigning semantics, sentics, and polarity to 30,000 natural language concepts. In particular, polarity is a floating number between -1 (extreme negativity) and +1 (extreme positivity) [5]. We rely on SenticNet 3.0 to compute features based on polarity, according to the SenticNet lexicon:

- Min, max, average and standard deviation polarity of lemmas;

- PA Positive Asserted: number of lemmas with a positive polarity, e.g., "good";

- PN Positive Negated: number of lemmas with a positive polarity, but negated, e.g., "not good";

- NA Negative Asserted: n. lemmas with a negative polarity (e.g., "bad");

- NN Negative Negated: n. lemmas and with a negative polarity, and negated (e.g., "not bad").

To assign the polarity to "not good", we consider the polarity of "good" in the SenticNet lexicon (0.667) and we revert it, assigning -0.667.

Also, SenticNet provides the polarity score to complex expressions. As an example, the popular idiomatic expression "32 teeth" obtains a polarity score of 0.903. Thus, beside unigrams polarity

Class	Precision	Recall	F1
negative	0.16	0.17	0.16
neutral	0.46	0.27	0.34
positive	0.50	0.75	0.60
avg / total	0.42	0.43	0.51

Table 2: MIB results (Tweets 2016 - dev, all feats)

scores, we have also considered 2-grams polarity scores.

Since not all the lemmas in the dataset were covered by the SenticNet lexicon, we have enlarged the covering by relying on LabMT (Dodds et al., 2011). LabMT is a list of words, manually labeled with a sentiment score through crowdsourcing. In particular, we considered the happiness score. This value ranges over 1 and 9 (1 is very unhappy, while 9 absolutely happy). We have normalised such values to range over -1 and 1, using the linear function y=(x-5)/4.

4 Evaluation and results

We have preliminarily built a prediction model trained with the 2016 challenge data, in details we have used the train and the devel data, respectively for training and evaluation. The prediction model is based on an SVM linear kernel classifier. For the experiments, the classifier has been implemented through sklearn[6] in Python. We have used a linear classifier suitable for handling unbalanced data: SGDClassifier with default parameters[7]. The model exploits the four groups of features presented in Section 3. Upon extracting the features from the training dataset, we obtained 6,547 features. In the following, we will show some feature ablation experiments, each of them corresponds to remove one category of features from the full set. Results are in terms of Precision and Recall, see Table 1.

The features evaluation shows that we do not have a set of dominant features group, leading to a not satisfying discrimination among positive, negative, and neutral tweets. Ablation tests show that negation-based features are the most relevant ones. Polarity lexicon features are influential to identify the nega-

---

[5] http://sentic.net/

[6] http://scikit-learn.org/stable/
[7] http://scikit-learn.org/stable/
modules/generated/sklearn.linear_model.
SGDClassifier.html

System	Negative			Neutral			Positive			Average
	P	R	F1	P	R	F1	P	R	F1	F1
All but n-grams feats	0.33	0.24	0.28	0.45	0.22	0.30	0.41	0.72	0.53	0.38
All but negation-based feats	0.42	0.08	0.13	0.52	0.06	0.10	0.39	0.97	0.56	0.28
All but polarity lexicon feats	0.34	0.10	0.15	0.44	0.42	0.43	0.42	0.58	0.48	0.40

Table 1: Ablation tests

tive class, but, overall, less than we have expected.

In (Cozza et al., 2016), the authors have proposed a similar approach to the one here presented. The aim was to evaluate the sentiment of a large set of online reviews. In online reviews, the textual opinion is usually accompanied by a numerical score, and sentiment analysis could be a valid alley for identifying misalignment between the score and the satisfaction expressed in the text. Work in (Cozza et al., 2016) shows that the features' set was discriminant for evaluating the sentiment of the reviews. In part, this would support the thesis that standard sentiment analysis approaches are more suitable for "literary" texts than for short, informal texts featured by tweets.

It is worth noting that the lexicons we rely on are based on lemmas, while there exist other lexicons that consider also the part of speech, see, e.g., SentiWordNet (Esuli and Sebastiani, 2006). Let the reader consider the following tweet, from the SemEval 2016 training set:

> #OnThisDay1987 CBS records shipped out the largest pre-order in the company's history for Michael Jackson's album Bad `http://t.co/v4fkyOx2eW`

In this example, the word "Bad" should not be considered as a negative adjective, since it is an album name. However, in the current work, we have not discriminated between nouns and adjectives with same spelling.

4.1 Challenge results

The results over the challenge test set are available on the SemEval website[8], according to the challenge score system described in (Nakov et al., 2016a). Table 3 shows the comparison of our results with the ones of the winning team. In the submitted result, the classifier has been trained over the training + development dataset, annotated with the best combination of features, as analyzed before.

team	score
SwissCheese	63.301
MIB	40.10

Table 3: SemEval 2016 task 4a results (Tweet 2016)

5 Conclusions

The approach proposed in this work achieved unsatisfactory results. This was in part due to a data preprocessing phase and a feature extraction phase that do not consider characteristics intrinsic to microblogging. Indeed, we mostly dealt with tweets handling them as regular text. The challenge data have been preprocessed by supervised approached, where features have been extracted through a NLP pipeline, trained on newswire domain. Within our proposed features, the sentiment lexicon-based features has proved to work well. However, we believe their extraction could take advantage of the adoption of other lexicons, different to those we have relied on. Specifically, there exist lexicons trained over tweets, such as the NCR emotion lexicon (Mohammad and Turney, 2013). Finally, we expect that a better solution could be achieved by extending the approach to include features extracted by unsupervised approaches (word embeddings), or by adopting a deep learning classifier, instead of a linear one.

References

Giuseppe Attardi, Stefano Dei Rossi, and Maria Simi. 2010. The TANL pipeline. *Web Services and Processing Pipelines in HLT: Tool Evaluation, LR Production and Validation (LREC:WSSP)*.

Luciano Barbosa and Junlan Feng. 2010. Robust sentiment detection on Twitter from biased and noisy data. In *23rd International Conference on Computational Linguistics: Posters*, pages 36–44. Association for Computational Linguistics.

P. Basile and N. Novielli. 2015. UNIBA: Sentiment analysis of English tweets combining micro-blogging, lexicon and semantic features. In *9th International Work-*

---

shop on Semantic Evaluation (SemEval 2015), pages 595–600. Association for Computational Linguistics.

Erik Cambria, Daniel Olsher, and Dheeraj Rajagopal. 2014. SenticNet 3: a common and common-sense knowledge base for cognition-driven sentiment analysis. In *28th AAAI Conference on Artificial Intelligence*, pages 1515–1521.

Chih-Chung Chang and Chih-Jen Lin. 2011. LIBSVM: a library for support vector machines. *Transactions on Intelligent Systems and Technology (TIST)*, 2(3):27.

Vittoria Cozza, Marinella Petrocchi, and Angelo Spognardi. 2016. Write a number in letters: A study on text-score disagreement in online reviews.

Peter Sheridan Dodds, Kameron Decker Harris, Isabel M. Kloumann, Catherine A. Bliss, and Christopher M. Danforth. 2011. Temporal patterns of happiness and information in a global social network: Hedonometrics and twitter. *PLoS ONE*, 6(12):e26752, 12.

Andrea Esuli and Fabrizio Sebastiani. 2006. SENTIWORDNET: A publicly available lexical resource for opinion mining. In *5th Conference on Language Resources and Evaluation*, pages 417–422.

Efthymios Kouloumpis, Theresa Wilson, and Johanna Moore. 2011. Twitter sentiment analysis: The good the bad and the omg. In *AAAI Conference on Weblogs and Social*.

Bing Liu. 2012. *Sentiment Analysis and Opinion Mining*. Morgan & Claypool Publishers, May.

Saif M. Mohammad and Peter D. Turney. 2013. Crowdsourcing a word-emotion association lexicon. *Computational Intelligence*, 29(3):436–465.

Preslav Nakov, Alan Ritter, Sara Rosenthal, Fabrizio Sebastiani, and Veselin Stoyanov. 2016a. Evaluation measures for the semeval-2016 task 4 sentiment analysis in Twitter.

Preslav Nakov, Alan Ritter, Sara Rosenthal, Veselin Stoyanov, and Fabrizio Sebastiani. 2016b. SemEval-2016 task 4: Sentiment analysis in Twitter. In *Proceedings of the 10th International Workshop on Semantic Evaluation (SemEval 2016)*, San Diego, California, June. Association for Computational Linguistics.

C. Priyanka and D. Gupta. 2013. Identifying the best feature combination for sentiment analysis of customer reviews. In *Advances in Computing, Communications and Informatics (ICACCI)*, pages 102–108.

Sara Rosenthal, Preslav Nakov, Svetlana Kiritchenko, Saif Mohammad, Alan Ritter, and Veselin Stoyanov. 2015. SemEval-2015 task 10: Sentiment analysis in Twitter. In *9th International Workshop on Semantic Evaluation*, pages 451–463. Association for Computational Linguistics, June.

Peter D. Turney and Patrick Pantel. 2010. From frequency to meaning: Vector space models of semantics. *CoRR*, abs/1003.1141.

MDSENT at SemEval-2016 Task 4: A Supervised System for Message Polarity Classification

Hang Gao and **Tim Oates**
hanggao1@umbc.edu, oates@cs.umbc.edu
University of Maryland Baltimore County
11000 Hilltop Circlet
Baltimore, MD 21250, USA

Abstract

This paper describes our system submitted for the Sentiment Analysis in Twitter task of SemEval-2016, and specifically for the Message Polarity Classification subtask. We used a system that combines Convolutional Neural Networks and Logistic Regression for sentiment prediction, where the former makes use of embedding features while the later utilizes various features like lexicons and dictionaries.

1 Introduction

Recently, rapid growth of the amount of user-generated content on the web prompts increasing interest in research on sentiment analysis and opinion mining. A typical example is Twitter, where lots of users express feelings and opinions about various subjects. However, unlike traditional media, language used in social network services like Twitter is often informal, leading to new challenges to corresponding text analysis.

The SemEval-2016 Sentiment Analysis in Twitter task (SESA-16) is a task that focuses on the sentiment analysis of tweets. As a continuation of SemEval-2015 Task 10, SESA-16 introduces several new challenges, including the replacement of classification with quantification, movement from two/three-point scale to five-point scale, etc.

We participated in Subtask A of SESA-16, namely message polarity classification, a task that seeks to predict a sentiment label for some given text. We model the problem as a multi-class classification problem that combines the predictions given by two different classifiers: one is a Convolutional

Neural Network (CNN) and the other is Logistic Regression (LR). The former takes embedding-based features while the latter utilizes various features such as lexicons, dictionaries, etc.

The remainder of this paper is structured as follows. In Section 2, we describe our system in detail, including feature description and approaches. In Section 3, we list the details of datasets for the experiments, along with hyperparameter settings and training techniques. In Section 4, we report the experiment results and present the corresponding discussion.

2 System Description

Our system aims at predicting the sentiment of a given message, i.e., whether the message expresses positive, negative or neutral emotion. To achieve that, we adopt two separate classifiers, CNN and LR, designed to utilize different types of features. The final prediction for sentiment is a combination of predictions given by both classifiers.

2.1 Data Preprocessing

Tweets often include informal text, making it essential to preprocess tweets before they are fed to the system. However, we keep the preprocessing to a minimum by only removing URLs and @User tags. We then further tokenize and tag tweets with arktweetnlp (Gimpel et al., 2011). In addition, all tweets are lower-cased.

2.2 Logistic Regression

We use the LR classifier for features from sentiment lexicons and token clusters. We have used the fol-

Proceedings of SemEval-2016, pages 139–144,
San Diego, California, June 16-17, 2016. ©2016 Association for Computational Linguistics

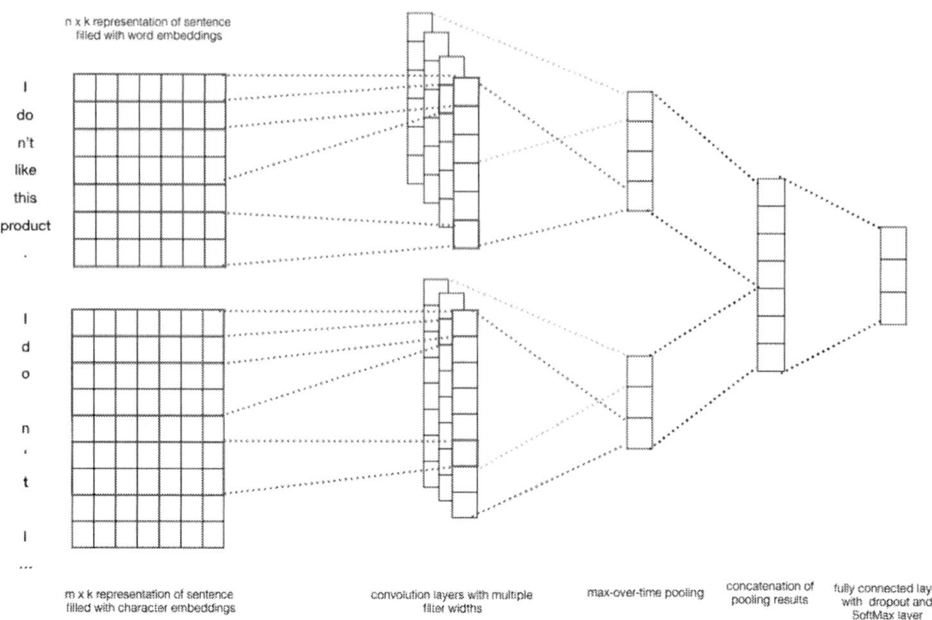

Figure 1: CNN architecture for an example with both word-based and character-based input maps.

lowing:

- **clusters**: 1000 token clusters provided by the CMU tweet NLP tool. These clusters are produced with the Brown clustering algorithm on 56 million English-language tweets.

- **manually-constructed sentiment lexicons**: NRC Emotion Lexicon (Mohammad and Turney, 2010), MPQA (Wilson et al., 2005), Bing Liu Lexicon (Hu and Liu, 2004) and AFINN-111 Lexicon (Nielsen, 2011).

- **automatically-constructed sentiment lexicons**: Hashtag Sentiment Lexicon and Sentiment140 Lexicon (Mohammad et al., 2013).

For the Sentiment140 Lexicon and Hashtag Sentiment Lexicon, we compute separate lexicon features for uni-grams and bi-grams, while for other Lexicons, only uni-gram lexicon features are produced. For each lexicon, let t be the token(uni-gram or bi-gram), p be the polarity and s be the score provided by the lexicon. We use the same features that are also adopted by the NRC-Canada system (Mohammad et al., 2013):

- the total count of tokens in a tweet with $s(t, p) > 0$.

- the total score of tokens in a tweet $\sum_w s(t, p)$.

- the maximum score of tokens in a tweet $\max_w s(t, p)$.

- the score of the last token in the tweet with $s(t, p) > 0$.

For each token, we also use features to describe whether it is present or absent in each of the 1000 token clusters. There are in total 1051 features for a tweet.

2.3 Convolutional Neural Network

Deep learning models have achieved remarkable results for various NLP tasks, with most of them based on embeddings that represent words, characters, etc. with vectors of real values. Some work on embeddings suggests that word vectors generated by some embedding algorithms preserve many linguistic regularities (Mikolov et al., 2013a).

Among the various deep learning models, we use Convolutional Neural Networks, which have already been used for sentiment classification with promising results (Kim, 2014). We show the network architecture in Figure 1.

In general, the architecture contains two separate CNNs: one is for word-based input maps while the other is for character-based input maps. In our system, an input map for a tweet is a stack of the embeddings of its words/characters w.r.t. their order in the tweet. We initialize word embeddings with the publicly available 300 dimension Google News embeddings trained with Word2Vec, but randomly initialize character embeddings with the same dimension. We fine tune both kinds of embeddings during the training procedure.

Each of the two separate CNNs has its own set of convolutional filters. We fix the width of all filters to be the same as the corresponding embedding dimension, but set their height according to predefined types of n-grams. For example, a filter for bi-grams on an input map constructed with 300 dimensional word embeddings will have shape (2, 300), where 2 is the height and 300 is the width. In other words, we use each filter to capture and extract features w.r.t. a specific type of n-gram from an input map.

The feature maps generated by a particular filter may have different shapes for different input maps, due to variable tweet lengths. Thus we adopt a pooling scheme called max-over-time pooling (Collobert et al., 2011), which captures the most important feature, i.e., the one with highest value, for each feature map. This pooling scheme naturally deals with the variable tweet length problem.

After pooling, we first generate a representation for each CNN by concatenating its own pooled features, and then form a final representation by concatenating the two separate representations. The final representation is then fed into a multi-layer perceptron (MLP) classifier for predictions.

2.3.1 Regularization

For regularization we employ dropout with a constraint on l_2-norms of the weight vectors (Hinton et al., 2012). The key idea of dropout is to prevent co-adaptation of feature detectors (hidden units) by randomly dropping out a portion of hidden units in the training procedure. At test time, the learned weight vectors are scaled according to the portion while no dropout is needed.

In addition to dropout, we constrain weight vectors by introducing an upper limit on their l_2-norms. That is, for a weight vector w, we rescale it to have $||w||_2 = l$, whenever it has $||w||_2 > l$, after gradient descent step.

2.4 Combination

We combine the predictions of the two classifiers in the form of a weighted summation. Given the prediction P_{LR} by Logistic Regression and the prediction P_{CNN} by the CNN, we introduce a scalar w, such that the final prediction is given as,

$$P_{final} = (1 - w)P_{LR} + wP_{CNN} \qquad (1)$$

In other words, let x be the input instance,

$$\begin{aligned} P_{final}(Y = y|x) = {} & wP_{CNN}(Y = y|x) \\ & + (1 - w)P_{LR}(Y = y|x) \end{aligned} \qquad (2)$$

We do not simply feed the features of LR along with the features generated by the CNN into a single classifier because they are naturally different. The features from LR are highly relevant with manually-created or automatically-generated dictionaries, scores, clusters, etc. They are a mixture of binary and real-value features with high variance. While for the CNN, the features are generated by convolutional kernels on distributed representations (embeddings), leading to strong correlation and relatively smaller variance. Our preliminary experiments show that by simply adding LR features to CNN features, the performance of our system does not increase, but drops.

3 Experiment

3.1 Datasets

We test our model on the SemEval-2016 benchmark dataset with two different settings. Setting 1 uses only the 2016 datasets while Setting 2 uses a combination of 2016 and 2013 datasets. We list the details of the two settings in Table 1.

For setting 2, the merge of two datasets is conducted w.r.t. the train/dev splits. Although we did

Settings	Train	Dev	Test
Setting 1	5975	1997	32009
Setting 2	12964	3100	32009

Table 1: Statistics of our two settings of datasets for experiments. Setting 1: a dataset with only the SemEval-2016 dataset. Setting 2: a dataset that is a combination of the SemEval-2016 and SemEval-2013 datasets. In Setting 2, the merge is conducted w.r.t. train/dev splits, with "Not Available" tweets removed.

		Actual		
		Pos	Neu	Neg
Predicted	Pos	PP	PU	PN
	Neu	UP	UU	UN
	Neg	NP	NU	NN

Table 2: The confusion matrix for Subtask A. Cell XY stands for "the number of tweets that were labeled as X and should have been labeled as Y", where P U N stand for Positive Neutral Negative, respectively.

not remove any "Not Available" tweets for setting 1, we found a relatively high amount of such tweets in the combined dataset, which may significantly influence the system performance, thus we removed all the "Not Available" tweets for setting 2.

3.2 Hyperparameters and Training

3.2.1 CNN

For both settings, we use rectified linear units. For the word-based CNN, we use filters of height 1,2,3,4, while for the character-based CNN, we use filters of height 3,4,5. And 100 feature maps are used for each filter. We also use a dropout rate of 0.5, l_2-norm constraint of 3, and mini-batch size of 50. These values were picked on the Dev dataset of Setting 1.

We perform early stop on dev datasets during training. We use Adadelta as the optimization algorithm (Zeiler, 2012).

3.2.2 LR

We use the publicly available tool LibLinear for LR training. The cost is set to be 0.5 with all other parameters assigned with default settings. The cost is chosen based on the Dev dataset of Setting 1.

3.2.3 Combination

The scalar w is picked via grid search on the Dev dataset for both settings. Because of the random initialization of weights and random shuffling of batches for the CNN during the training procedure, w is different for different runs. Thus we consider it as a weight to be trained with other weights.

3.3 Embeddings

It is popular to initialize word vectors with pre-trained embeddings obtained by some unsupervised algorithms trained over a large corpus to improve system performance (Kim, 2014) (Socher et al., 2011). We use the publicly available Word2Vec vectors trained on 100 billion words from Google News using the continuous bag-of-words architecture (Mikolov et al., 2013b) to initialize word embeddings, but randomly initialize character embeddings. All embeddings have dimensionality of 300. We also randomly initialize word embeddings that are not present in the vocabulary of those pre-trained word vectors.

4 Results and Discussion

The same evaluation measure as the one used in previous years is adopted, i.e.,

$$F_1^{PN} = \frac{F_1^{Pos} + F_1^{Neg}}{2} \qquad (3)$$

where F_1^{Pos} is defined as,

$$F_1^{Pos} = \frac{2\pi^{Pos}\rho^{Pos}}{\pi^{Pos} + \rho^{Pos}} \qquad (4)$$

with ρ^{Pos} defined as the precision of predicted positive tweets, i.e., the fraction of tweets predicted to be positive that are indeed positive,

$$\rho^{Pos} = \frac{PP}{PP + PU + PN} \qquad (5)$$

and π^{Pos} defined as the recall of predicted positive tweets, i.e., the fraction of positive tweets that are predicted to be such,

$$\pi^{Pos} = \frac{PP}{PP + UP + NP} \qquad (6)$$

where PP, PU, PN, UP, NP are defined in Table 2, a confusion matrix for Subtask A provided by (Nakov et al.,). F_1^{Neg} is defined similarly as F_1^{Pos}.

Rank	System	2013		2014			2015	2016
		Tweet	SMS	Tweet	Tweet sacasm	Live-Journal	Tweet	Tweet
1	SwissCheese	0.700_5	0.637_2	0.716_5	0.566_1	0.695_7	0.671_1	0.633_1
2	SENSEI-LIF	0.706_4	0.634_3	0.744_2	0.467_8	0.741_1	0.662_2	0.630_2
3	unimelb	0.687_7	0.593_9	0.706_7	0.449_{11}	0.683_9	0.651_4	0.617_3
4	INESC-ID	0.723_2	0.609_6	0.727_3	0.554_3	0.702_4	0.657_3	0.610_4
5	aueb*	0.666_8	0.618_5	0.708_6	0.410_{17}	0.695_7	0.623_7	0.605_5
6	SentiSys	0.714_3	0.633_4	0.723_4	0.515_5	0.726_2	0.644_5	0.598_6
7	I2RNTU	0.693_6	0.597_7	0.680_8	0.469_6	0.696_6	0.638_6	0.596_7
8	INSIGHT-1	0.602_{16}	0.582_{12}	0.644_{16}	0.391_{23}	0.559_{23}	0.595_{16}	0.593_8
9	twise	0.610_{15}	0.540_{17}	0.645_{14}	0.450_{10}	0.649_{13}	0.621_8	0.586_9
10	ECNU	0.643_{10}	0.593_9	0.662_9	0.425_{14}	0.663_{10}	0.606_{11}	0.585_{10}
11	NTNUSentEval	0.623_{12}	0.641_1	0.651_{11}	0.427_{13}	0.719_3	0.599_{13}	0.583_{11}
12	MDSENT	0.589_{19}	0.509_{21}	0.587_{20}	0.386_{24}	0.606_{19}	0.593_{18}	$\mathbf{0.580_{12}}$
12	CUFE	0.642_{11}	0.596_8	0.662_9	0.466_9	0.697_5	0.598_{14}	0.580_{12}
14	THUIR	0.616_{13}	0.575_{14}	0.648_{12}	0.399_{20}	0.640_{15}	0.617_{10}	0.576_{14}
14	PUT	0.565_{21}	0.511_{20}	0.614_{19}	0.360_{27}	0.648_{14}	0.597_{15}	0.576_{14}
-	MDSENT*	0.664_9	0.610_6	0.676_9	0.410_{17}	0.689_9	0.628_7	$\mathbf{0.601_6}$
	baseline	0.292	0.190	0.346	0.277	0.272	0.303	0.255

Table 3: Evaluation Results of the top 15 systems with ranks provided as subscripts. aueb* stands for "aueb.twitter.sentiment". Our model with setting 1 ranks 12th among 34 systems. We also show the evaluation results and our reported ranks of MDSENT with setting 2 among the 34 systems in MDSENT*.

Runs	Setting 1		Setting 2	
	w	F_1^{PN}	w	F_1^{PN}
Run 1	0.66	0.582	1.00	0.603
Run 2	0.81	0.583	1.00	0.604
Run 3	0.60	0.587	0.98	0.607
Run 4	0.60	0.591	0.97	0.603
Run 5	0.60	0.592	0.95	0.601
Average	0.654	0.587	0.98	0.604

Table 4: Statistics of 5 individual runs for both settings.

We show the evaluation results of our system in Table 3, along with the top 15 systems reported. Originally we tested the system with only setting 1 and it ranks 12th among 34 systems. However, we find the system with setting 1 perform poorly on older datasets, which may due to the lack of training data. Thus we then test our model with setting 2 and report ranks generated from the same list of evaluation results reported by the 34 systems. It is apparent that our system can benefit from more training data and shows significant performance improvement (rank 6th).

Another interesting observation is that when provided with large amounts of training data, the CNN itself can perform very well, with LR assigned a very small weight during the combination proce-dure. We further test this finding by making 5 individual runs for both settings and checking the combination scalar weight w and final evaluation score F_1^{PN}. We list corresponding results in Table 4. With more training data, w increased from an average of 0.654 to an average of 0.98, which is very close to 1, while the performance improved from an average of 0.587 to an average of 0.604. This suggests the possibility to use only deep learning techniques along with embeddings to achieve similar or even better performance than traditional systems that require a lot of human engineered features and knowledge bases.

Our future work includes finer-design of the CNN, e.g., performing two stages of classification: first for subjectivity detection and then for polarity classification. We will also seek the possibility of conducting unsupervised learning with the CNN, which allows us to make use of the large amount of tweets on the Internet. With such increased amount of training data, our system may further improve its performance.

References

Ronan Collobert, Jason Weston, Léon Bottou, Michael Karlen, Koray Kavukcuoglu, and Pavel Kuksa. 2011.

Natural language processing (almost) from scratch. *The Journal of Machine Learning Research*, 12:2493–2537.

Kevin Gimpel, Nathan Schneider, Brendan O'Connor, Dipanjan Das, Daniel Mills, Jacob Eisenstein, Michael Heilman, Dani Yogatama, Jeffrey Flanigan, and Noah A Smith. 2011. Part-of-speech tagging for twitter: Annotation, features, and experiments. In *Proceedings of the 49th Annual Meeting of the Association for Computational Linguistics: Human Language Technologies: short papers-Volume 2*, pages 42–47. Association for Computational Linguistics.

Geoffrey E Hinton, Nitish Srivastava, Alex Krizhevsky, Ilya Sutskever, and Ruslan R Salakhutdinov. 2012. Improving neural networks by preventing co-adaptation of feature detectors. *arXiv preprint arXiv:1207.0580*.

Minqing Hu and Bing Liu. 2004. Mining and summarizing customer reviews. In *Proceedings of the tenth ACM SIGKDD international conference on Knowledge discovery and data mining*, pages 168–177. ACM.

Yoon Kim. 2014. Convolutional neural networks for sentence classification. *arXiv preprint arXiv:1408.5882*.

Tomas Mikolov, Kai Chen, Greg Corrado, and Jeffrey Dean. 2013a. Efficient estimation of word representations in vector space. *arXiv preprint arXiv:1301.3781*.

Tomas Mikolov, Ilya Sutskever, Kai Chen, Greg S Corrado, and Jeff Dean. 2013b. Distributed representations of words and phrases and their compositionality. In *Advances in neural information processing systems*, pages 3111–3119.

Saif M Mohammad and Peter D Turney. 2010. Emotions evoked by common words and phrases: Using mechanical turk to create an emotion lexicon. In *Proceedings of the NAACL HLT 2010 workshop on computational approaches to analysis and generation of emotion in text*, pages 26–34. Association for Computational Linguistics.

Saif M Mohammad, Svetlana Kiritchenko, and Xiaodan Zhu. 2013. Nrc-canada: Building the state-of-the-art in sentiment analysis of tweets. *arXiv preprint arXiv:1308.6242*.

Preslav Nakov, Alan Ritter, Sara Rosenthal, Fabrizio Sebastiani, and Veselin Stoyanov. Evaluation measures for the semeval-2016 task 4 'sentiment analysis in twitter'(draft: Version 1.1).

Finn Årup Nielsen. 2011. A new anew: Evaluation of a word list for sentiment analysis in microblogs. *arXiv preprint arXiv:1103.2903*.

Richard Socher, Eric H Huang, Jeffrey Pennin, Christopher D Manning, and Andrew Y Ng. 2011. Dynamic pooling and unfolding recursive autoencoders for paraphrase detection. In *Advances in Neural Information Processing Systems*, pages 801–809.

Theresa Wilson, Janyce Wiebe, and Paul Hoffmann. 2005. Recognizing contextual polarity in phrase-level sentiment analysis. In *Proceedings of the conference on human language technology and empirical methods in natural language processing*, pages 347–354. Association for Computational Linguistics.

Matthew D Zeiler. 2012. Adadelta: an adaptive learning rate method. *arXiv preprint arXiv:1212.5701*.

CICBUAPnlp at SemEval-2016 Task 4-A: Discovering Twitter Polarity using Enhanced Embeddings

Helena Gómez-Adorno, Grigori Sidorov
Center for Computing Research
Instituto Politécnico Nacional
Av. Juan de Dios Bátiz
C.P. 07738, Mexico City, Mexico
`helena.adorno@gmail.com`
`sidorov@cic.ipn.mx`

Darnes Vilariño, David Pinto
Faculty of Computer Science
Benemérita Universidad Autónoma de Puebla
Av. San Claudio y 14 sur
C.P. 72570, Puebla, Mexico
`darnes@cs.buap.mx`
`dpinto@cs.buap.mx`

Abstract

This paper presents our approach for SemEval 2016 task 4: Sentiment Analysis in Twitter. We participated in Subtask A: Message Polarity Classification. The aim is to classify Twitter messages into positive, neutral, and negative polarity. We used a lexical resource for pre-processing of social media data and train a neural network model for feature representation. Our resource includes dictionaries of slang words, contractions, abbreviations, and emoticons commonly used in social media. For the classification process, we pass the features obtained in an unsupervised manner into an SVM classifier.

1 Introduction

In this paper, we describe our approach for the SemEval 2016 task 4 "Sentiment Analysis in Twitter" subtask A (Nakov et al., 2016), where the goal is to classify a tweet message as either positive, neutral, or negative. The main goal of our approach is to improve the feature representation obtained by a well-known neural network method–Doc2vec (Le and Mikolov, 2014), using dictionaries of abbreviations, contractions, slang words, and emoticons.

Approaches based on neural networks for unsupervised feature representation (or embeddings) often do not perform data cleaning (Le and Mikolov, 2014; Socher et al., 2011), considering that the network itself would solve the related problems. These approaches treat special characters such as ,.!?# and user mentions as a regular word (Le and Mikolov, 2014; Brigadir et al., 2014). Still, in some works

which use embeddings a basic data cleaning process (i.e., stopwords removal, URL filtering, and removal of rare terms) improves the feature representation and, consequently, the performance of the classification task (Yan et al., 2014; Rangarajan Sridhar, 2015; Jiang et al., 2014).

The problem with the content of social media messages is that they usually have a lot of non-standard language expressions (Pinto et al., 2012; Atkinson et al., 2013). Due to the short nature of the messages, most of the users use a large vocabulary of slang words, abbreviations, and emoticons (Das and Bandyopadhyay, 2011). Slang words are not considered as a part of the standard vocabulary of a language, and they are mostly used in informal messages, while abbreviations are shortened forms of a word or name that are used in order to replace the full forms. Emoticons usually convey the current feeling of the message writer.

For this task we propose a preprocessing phase using the dictionaries that we previously built for the task of Authorship Atribution (Posadas-Durán et al., 2015). These dictionaries are useful for pre-processing and cleaning messages obtained from several social networks, such as Facebook, Google+, Instagram, etc.

The rest of the paper is structured as follows. Section 2 describes related work. Section 3 introduces the social media lexical resource used for this work. Section 4 presents our proposed approach. Section 5 presents the evaluation of the task using the neural network based feature representation. Finally, Section 6 draws the conclusions from our experiments and points out the possible directions of future work.

145

Proceedings of SemEval-2016, pages 145–148,
San Diego, California, June 16-17, 2016. ©2016 Association for Computational Linguistics

2 Related Work

There are many works that tackle the problem of social media texts pre-processing (Baldwin, 2012; Clark and Araki, 2011; Das and Bandyopadhyay, 2011); however, to the best of our knowledge, the research based on neural network for feature representation did not consider the effect that data cleaning have on the quality of the representation (specially on social media data).

Several approaches have been proposed for vector-space distributed representations of words and phrases. These models are used mainly for predicting a word given a surrounding context. However, most of the authors indicate that distributed representations of words and phrases can also capture syntactic and semantic similarity or relatedness (Le and Mikolov, 2014; Socher et al., 2013; Mikolov et al., 2013). This particular behaviour makes these methods attractive to solve several NLP tasks, nevertheless, at the same time, it raises new issues, such as dealing with unnormalized texts, which are typically present in social media forums such as Twitter, Facebook, Instagram, among others. Researchers have proposed several pre-processing steps in order to overcome this issue, which led to an overall performance increase. Yan et al. (Yan et al., 2014) obtained almost 2% increase using standard NLP pre-processing, which consists in tokenization, lowercasing, removing stopwords and rare terms. Kumar et al. (Rangarajan Sridhar, 2015) focused on the spelling issues in social media messages, which includes repeated letters, omitted vowels, use of phonetic spellings, substitution of letters with numbers (typically syllables), use of shorthands and user created abbreviations for phrases. In a data-driven approach, Brigadir et al. (Brigadir et al., 2014) apply URL filtering combined with standard NLP preprocessing techniques.

3 Resources

We developed the dictionaries with the aim of preprocessing tweets for the author profiling task at PAN 2015 (Posadas-Durán et al., 2015). First, we reviewed the tweets present in the PAN corpus and found excessive use of shortened vocabulary, which can be divided into three categories: slang words, abbreviations, and contractions. Moreover, we came

Table 1: Number of entries of the English dictionary

Type of Dictionary	English
Abbreviations	1,346
Contractions	131
Slang words	1,249
Emoticons	482
Total	3,208

across a large number of emoticons, which are a typographic display of a facial representation.

The lexical resource was originally built for 4 languages, but for the purposes of this work we only use the English dictionary. The statistics for the English dictionary are presented in Table 1. The dictionaries are freely available on our website[1].

4 Approach to Sentiment Classification

From a machine learning point of view, the Message Polarity Classification task can be considered as a supervised multi-class classification problem, where a set of tweets $\mathbf{T} = \{t_1, t_2, \ldots, t_i\}$ is given, and each sample is assigned to one of the target classes $\{positive, negative, neutral\}$. So, the problem is to build a classifier F that assigns a sentiment class to unclassified tweets.

Since the tweets are very noisy, we perform the preprocessing over each dataset (train, unlabeled and test). In the preprocessing phase, we executed the following steps:

Expand slang words and abbreviations Not all tweets use slang words and abbreviation in the same way. There are Twitter users that do not use slang words and due to this reason we expanded all slang words and abbreviations with their full meaning using the dictionaries described in section 3.

Remove url ULR do not provide information about the sentiment of the tweet and because of this reason every ULR is removed from the text.

Remove hashtags symbols Hashtags in tweets carry useful information about the topic and

---

[1]`http://www.cic.ipn.mx/~sidorov/lexicon.zip`

polarity of the message. We only remove the hashtag symbol, keeping the words.

Remove emoticons In order to obtain a distributed representation of a tweet, we used only words and punctuation symbols. So, unlike traditional preprocessing for sentiment analysis we removed the emoticons from tweets by looking up in our emoticons dictionary.

For training, a vector representation of each tweet is obtained in an unsupervised manner by a neural network based model, i.e., $v^i = \{v_1, v_2, \ldots, v_j\}$ where v^i is the vector representation of the tweet t_i. In order to obtain the vector representation of the tweets, a neural network based distributed representation model is trained using the doc2vec algorithm (Le and Mikolov, 2014). It is an unsupervised algorithm that aggregates all the words in a sentence (of variable length) into a vector of fixed length. The algorithm takes into account the contexts of words, and it is able to capture the semantics of the input texts. We used a freely available implementation of doc2vec included in the *Gensim*[2] python module. The doc2vec model is trained with both labeled and unlabeled tweets in order to learn the distributed representation. The learned vector representations have 300 dimentions, we set the windows size to 3 and minimal word frequency is set to 2. Then, a classifier is trained using the vector representations of the labeled tweets. We perform the experiments with the SVM liblinear classifier (Fan et al., 2008), especifically the *LinearSVC* algorithm the implemented in the *Scikit Learn*[3] python module with default parameters.

For the evaluation, the vector representations of the test tweets are obtained retraining the doc2vec model built in the training stage, plus the test tweets. Finally, the vector representation of the tweets are passed to the SVM model in order to assign the corresponding polarity label to each tweet.

We used the train set of SemEval-2014 Task 9: Sentiment Analysis in Twitter - subtask B (Rosenthal et al., 2014), consisting of 6124 tweets (removing the tweets with the objective class). Besides, we

expanded the training set with some tweets of this year training set (the ones we could download) and with Stanford Sentiment Analysis Dataset (Go et al., 2009). So, in total we employed 11377 classified tweets for training. For the neural network based feature representation we used the 1.7 millons unlabeled tweets for training the Doc2Vec model.

5 Results

In this section we present the results obtained in the competition when various test datasets are used. The evaluation metric used in the competition is the macro-averaged F measure calculated over the positive and negative classes. Table 2 presents the overall performance of our approach for different datasets. It can be observed that our approach overcome the baseline for almost all datasets.

Table 2: Obtained results for 2016 Test and Progress

Year	Corpus	Ours	Baseline score
2013	Tweet	0.194	0.292
2014	SMS	0.193	0.190
	Tweet	0.335	0.346
	Tweet Sarcasm	0.393	0.277
	Live-Journal	0.326	0.272
2015	Tweet	0.303	0.303
2016	Tweet	0.303	0.255

6 Conclusions

We presented our results for sentiment analysis on Twitter. We rely on a supervised approach, which is based on top of a deep learning system enhanced with special preprocesing techniques using a lexical social media resource. We reported the overall accuracy for the sentiment classification task in three classes: positive, negative and neutral.

In the future, we will improve our preprocessing phase by removing the target mentions, numbers and repeated sequences of characters.

Acknowledgments

This work was done under the support of the "Red Temática en Tecnologías del Lenguaje", Mex-

---

[2]https://radimrehurek.com/gensim/
[3]http://scikit-learn.org/stable/index.html

ican Government (CONACYT project 240844, SNI, COFAA-IPN and SIP-IPN 20151406, 20161947).

References

John Atkinson, Alejandro Figueroa, and Claudio Pérez. 2013. A semantically-based lattice approach for assessing patterns in text mining tasks. *Computación y Sistemas*, 17(4):467–476.

Timothy Baldwin. 2012. Social media: Friend or foe of natural language processing? In *The 26th Pacific Asia Conference on Language, Information and Computation*, pages 58–59.

I. Brigadir, D. Greene, and P. Cunningham. 2014. Adaptive Representations for Tracking Breaking News on Twitter. *ArXiv e-prints*, March.

Eleanor Clark and Kenji Araki. 2011. Text normalization in social media: Progress, problems and applications for a pre-processing system of casual english. *Procedia - Social and Behavioral Sciences*, 27:2 – 11. Computational Linguistics and Related Fields.

Dipankar Das and Sivaji Bandyopadhyay. 2011. Document Level Emotion Tagging: Machine Learning and Resource Based Approach. *Computación y Sistemas*, 15:221 – 234.

Rong-En Fan, Kai-Wei Chang, Cho-Jui Hsieh, Xiang-Rui Wang, and Chih-Jen Lin. 2008. Liblinear: A library for large linear classification. *J. Mach. Learn. Res.*, 9:1871–1874, June.

Alec Go, Richa Bhayani, and Lei Huang. 2009. Twitter sentiment classification using distant supervision. *Processing*, pages 1–6.

Fei Jiang, Yiqun Liu, Huanbo Luan, Min Zhang, and Shaoping Ma. 2014. Microblog sentiment analysis with emoticon space model. In *Social Media Processing*, pages 76–87. Springer.

Quoc V Le and Tomas Mikolov. 2014. Distributed representations of sentences and documents. *arXiv preprint arXiv:1405.4053*.

Tomas Mikolov, Kai Chen, Greg Corrado, and Jeffrey Dean. 2013. Efficient estimation of word representations in vector space. *CoRR*, abs/1301.3781.

Preslav Nakov, Lluís Màrquez, Walid Magdy, Alessandro Moschitti, Jim Glass, and Bilal Randeree. 2016. SemEval-2016 task 3: Community question answering. In *Proceedings of the 10th International Workshop on Semantic Evaluation*, SemEval'16, San Diego, California, June. Association for Computational Linguistics.

David Pinto, Darnes Vilariño-Ayala, Yuridiana Alemán, Helena Gómez-Adorno, Nahun Loya, and Héctor Jiménez-Salazar. 2012. The soundex phonetic algorithm revisited for sms-based information retrieval. In *II Spanish Conference on Information Retrieval CERI 2012*.

Juan Pablo Posadas-Durán, Helena Gómez-Adorno, Ilia Markov, Grigori Sidorov, Ildar Z. Batyrshin, Alexander F. Gelbukh, and Obdulia Pichardo-Lagunas. 2015. Syntactic n-grams as features for the author profiling task: Notebook for PAN at CLEF 2015. In *Working Notes of CLEF 2015 - Conference and Labs of the Evaluation forum, Toulouse, France, September 8-11, 2015*.

Vivek Kumar Rangarajan Sridhar. 2015. Unsupervised text normalization using distributed representations of words and phrases. In *Proceedings of the 1st Workshop on Vector Space Modeling for Natural Language Processing*, pages 8–16, Denver, Colorado, June. Association for Computational Linguistics.

Sara Rosenthal, Alan Ritter, Preslav Nakov, and Veselin Stoyanov. 2014. Semeval-2014 task 9: Sentiment analysis in twitter. In *Proceedings of the 8th International Workshop on Semantic Evaluation (SemEval 2014)*, pages 73–80, Dublin, Ireland, August. Association for Computational Linguistics and Dublin City University.

Richard Socher, Cliff C Lin, Chris Manning, and Andrew Y Ng. 2011. Parsing natural scenes and natural language with recursive neural networks. In *Proceedings of the 28th international conference on machine learning (ICML-11)*, pages 129–136.

Richard Socher, Alex Perelygin, Jean Y. Wu, Jason Chuang, Christopher D. Manning, Andrew Y. Ng, and Christopher Potts. 2013. Recursive deep models for semantic compositionality over a sentiment treebank. In *Proceedings of the conference on empirical methods in natural language processing (EMNLP)*, volume 1631, page 1642.

Chunwei Yan, Fan Zhang, and Lian'en Huang. 2014. Drws: A model for learning distributed representations for words and sentences. In Duc-Nghia Pham and Seong-Bae Park, editors, *PRICAI 2014: Trends in Artificial Intelligence*, volume 8862 of *Lecture Notes in Computer Science*, pages 196–207. Springer International Publishing.

Finki at SemEval-2016 Task 4: Deep Learning Architecture for Twitter Sentiment Analysis

Dario Stojanovski, Gjorgji Strezoski, Gjorgji Madjarov, Ivica Dimitrovski

Faculty of Computer Science and Engineering

Ss. Cyril and Methodius University

Rugjer Boshkovikj 16 1000 Skopje, Republic of Macedonia

{stojanovski.dario, strezoski.g}@gmail.com

{gjorgji.madjarov, ivica.dimitrovski}@finki.ukim.mk

Abstract

In this paper, we present a novel deep learning architecture for sentiment analysis in Twitter messages. Our system **finki**, employs both convolutional and gated recurrent neural networks to obtain a more diverse tweet representation. The network is trained on top of GloVe word embeddings pre-trained on the Common Crawl dataset. Both neural networks are used to obtain a fixed length representation of variable sized tweets, and the concatenation of these vectors is supplied to a fully connected softmax layer with dropout regularization. The system is evaluated on benchmark datasets from the Sentiment Analysis in Twitter task of the SemEval 2016 challenge where our model achieves best and second highest results on the 2-point and 5-point quantification subtasks respectively. Despite not relying on any hand-crafted features, our system manages the second highest average rank on the considered subtasks.

1 Introduction

Twitter sentiment analysis is an area of Natural Language Processing (NLP) dealing with the classification of sentiment polarity in Twitter messages. Most of the approaches to this problem are generally based on hand crafted features and sentiment lexicons (Mohammad et al., 2013; Pak and Paroubek, 2010). These features are then used as input to classifying algorithms such as, Support Vector Machines (SVM) and naive Bayes classifier. However, such approaches require extensive domain knowledge, are laborious to define, and can lead to incomplete or over-specific features.

Deep learning methods for sentiment analysis, on the other hand, handle the feature extraction automatically which provides for robustness and adaptability. Notably, most popular deep learning methods are convolutional neural networks (CNN), which have been shown to achieve state-of-the-art results (Kim, 2014; dos Santos and Gatti, 2014), though some works propose different models such as Recursive Neural Tensor Network (Socher et al., 2013).

Recurrent neural networks (RNN) are intuitive architectures for NLP as they inherently take into account the ordering of words in the text as opposed to CNNs which take only a small limited context window. However, to our knowledge, these networks have not been applied to sentiment analysis in Twitter messages. Le et al. (Le and Zuidema, 2015) report state-of-the-art results with Long Short Term Memory (LSTM) networks on binary and fine-grained classification on the Stanford Sentiment Treebank dataset.

In this paper, we present a novel deep learning architecture for sentiment classification and quantification in Twitter messages. The model consists of a convolutional and a gated recurrent neural network (GRNN). Both neural networks are used to model a suitable representation of a tweet. The feature representations output from the networks are fused and fed to a standard softmax regression classifier. The system leverages unsupervised pre-training of word embeddings. For this, we utilize the publicly available GloVe[1] word embeddings (Pennington et al., 2014), specifically ones trained on the Common

---

[1]http://nlp.stanford.edu/projects/glove

Proceedings of SemEval-2016, pages 149–154,

San Diego, California, June 16-17, 2016. ©2016 Association for Computational Linguistics

Crawl dataset. In previous work (Stojanovski et al., 2015), we have experimented with multiple filters with additional window sizes of 4 and 5 and we leave such system implementation for future work.

We evaluate our deep learning system on four out of five subtasks of the Sentiment Analysis in Twitter task (Task 4) (Nakov et al., 2016) as part of the SemEval 2016 challenge. We competed in the 2-point and 5-point classification and quantification. Our model achieves high results on the quantification subtasks, getting second place on Subtask E and attaining the best score on Subtask D.

2   Deep learning architecture

The proposed model for sentiment analysis in this paper, consists of two neural networks. The first is a convolutional neural network with a single filter with windows size of 3. The second part of the architecture is a gated recurrent neural network. The system architecture is presented in Figure 1. The model is implemented using the Keras[2] library for deep learning on a Theano backend.

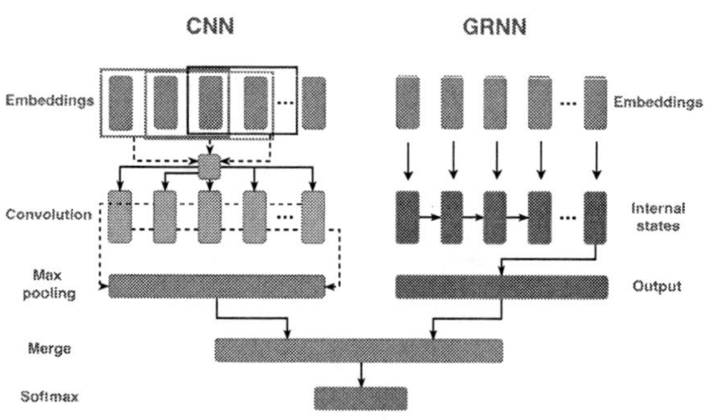

Figure 1: Deep neural network architecture.

2.1   Preprocessing

Twitter constraints tweet length to a maximum of 140 characters. Consequently, users are forced to find new and unpredictable ways of expressing themselves. Determining sentiment in these circumstances is very challenging and, as a result, we apply some preprocessing steps in order to clean tweets from unnecessary information. All URLs and HTML entities are removed from the tweets

[2]http://keras.io

along with punctuation with the exception of question and exclamation marks. Emoticons and Twitter specifics such as hashtags are kept in their original form, unlike user mentions, which are completely removed. We also lowercase all words. Additionally, each appearance of an elongated word is shortened to a maximum of three character repetitions. Since all tweets are in relation to some topic, and the model has to determine the overall sentiment for the quantification tasks, we decided to replace words matching the tweet topic with generic tokens.

2.2   Pre-trained word embeddings

Each word or token that is a part of a tweet is first mapped to an appropriate distributional feature representation, also known as word embedding. Before training, we define the so called lookup table, where each word is associated with the corresponding feature representation. For the purposes of this work, we utilize the publicly available GloVe embeddings, pre-trained on the Common Crawl dataset with a dimensionality of 300. We choose these over the GloVe embeddings trained on Twitter data because of the higher dimensionality, considerably larger training corpus and vocabulary of unique words.

For words in the dataset not present in the lookup table, we use random initialization of word embeddings. However, despite their effectiveness in encoding syntactic and semantic regularities of words, they are oblivious to the words' sentiment characteristics. To counteract this, word embeddings are continuously updated during network training by back-propagating the classification errors. Therefore, sentiment regularities are being encoded in the feature representation.

2.3   Convolutional neural network

One component of our architecture is a convolutional neural network for feature extraction of Twitter messages. Dealing with variable sized text is inherently built into CNNs. Additionally, these networks, to some extent, take into account the ordering of the words and the context each word appears in. Unlike applications of CNNs in image processing, we only employ one convolutional and max pooling layer. The convolutional layer is used to extract local features around each word window, while the max pooling layer is used to extract the most important features in the feature map.

Let's consider a tweet t with length of n tokens. Because of the sliding window manner in which the filters are applied, we apply appropriate padding at the beginning and at the end of the tweet. Padding length is defined as $h/2$ where h is the window size of the filter. Before we apply the convolutional operation, each word is mapped to its corresponding word embedding. A tweet is represented as a concatenation of these word embeddings, $t = [w_1, w_2, \ldots, w_n]$, where w_i is the word embedding for the i-th word in the tweet and $w_i \in R^{300}$.

In this work, we only use a single filter with window size of 3. As tweets are limited in length, smaller window sizes are more favorable in contrast to larger ones. The network learns a filter W_c and a bias term for the filter. The convolutional operation is applied to every possible window of words and as a result a feature x_i is produced. We can formally express the operation as:

$$x_i = f(W_c \cdot t_{i:i+h-1} + b_c), \tag{1}$$

where $t_{i:i+h-1}$ is the concatenation of word vectors from position i to position $i + h - 1$, while $f(\cdot)$ is an activation function. In this work, we choose the hard rectified linear activation function. Each of the produced features are used to generate a feature map

$$x = [x_1, x_2 \ldots x_{n-h+1}]. \tag{2}$$

Then, the max-over-time pooling operation is applied over the feature map, which takes the maximum value $\hat{x} = max\{x\}$. The max pooling layer outputs a fixed sized vector with a predefined dimensionality.

2.4 Gated recurrent neural network

The accompanying part of the CNN in our deep learning architecture is a gated recurrent neural network. RNNs make use of sequential data. They perform the same task for every element in a sequence with the output being dependent on previous computations. These networks compute hidden states and each hidden state depends on its predecessor. They can also be seen as having a memory compo-nent, enabling them to look back arbitrarily in the sequence of words.

RNNs suffer from the exploding and vanishing gradient problem. There are two proposed methods for overcoming this issue: the LSTM networks (Hochreiter and Schmidhuber, 1997) and the Gated Recurrent Unit (Chung et al., 2014). We decided to use GRU because of the fewer model parameters, potentially needing less data to generalize and enabling faster training. GRU has gating units that modulate the flow of information inside the unit. The activation s_t^j of the GRU at time t is a linear interpolation between the previous activation s_{t-1}^j and the candidate activation $\hat{s}_t^j$:

$$s_t^j = (1 - z_t^j)s_{t-1}^j + z_t^j \hat{s}_t^j, \tag{3}$$

where an update gate z_t^j decides how much the unit updates its activation or content. The update gate is computed as:

$$z_t^j = \sigma(W_z x_t + U_z s_{t-1})^j. \tag{4}$$

where σ is a logistic sigmoid function. The GRU unlike LSTM has no mechanism to control the degree to which it exposes its state and exposes the whole state each time. The candidate activation is computed as:

$$\hat{s}_t^j = tanh(W x_t + U(r_t \odot s_{t-1}))^j, \tag{5}$$

where r_t is a set of reset gates and $\odot$ is an element-wise multiplication. The reset gate is computed as:

$$r_t^j = \sigma(W_r x_t + U_r s_{t-1})^j. \tag{6}$$

This network also produces a fixed vector which is necessary in our model.

2.5 Network fusion

The outputs from both networks are concatenated to form a single feature vector. This vector is then fed to a fully connected softmax layer. The softmax regression classifier gives probability distribution over the labels in the output space. The label having the highest probability is chosen as the final prediction.

	Positive	Negative	Total
Train	7374	2542	9916
Dev	1009	234	1243
Test	8202	2331	10535

Table 1: Dataset label distribution for Subtasks B and D.

	VN	N	Neu	P	VP	Total
Train	107	871	2083	3654	419	7134
Dev	28	200	520	835	191	1774
Test	138	2201	10081	7830	382	20632

Table 2: Dataset label distribution for Subtasks C and E. (N - negative, VN - very negative, Neu - neutral, VP - very positive, P - positive)

2.6 Regularization and model parameters

Due to the high number of parameters being learned, deep learning methods suffer from overfitting. To counteract this issue, we utilize dropout regularization (Srivastava et al., 2014), which randomly drops a proportion of hidden units in each iteration of network training. The dropout parameter is set to 0.25. The output size of the convolutional network and the GRU network is set to 100. The network is trained using stochastic gradient descent over shuffled mini-batches using the RMSprop (Tieleman and Hinton, 2012) update rule.

3 Experiments and results

3.1 Dataset

We train our model on the benchmark datasets provided by the SemEval challenge. However, due to deletion or changed privacy settings, we were not able to retrieve all tweets. For the 2-point classification and quantification we used the datasets from SemEval 2016 and we apply the topic preprocessing step previously mentioned. Moreover, we use positive and negative tweets from previous editions of the challenge to additionally refine our model in spite of the fact that these tweets are not labeled with the related topic.

For the 5-point classification and quantification, we only used the dataset from this year's edition of SemEval. The model is trained on the provided training and development sets while as validation set we use the provided devtest set. The testing sets are also provided by the SemEval challenge without the need to download the specific tweets. The distribution of the sentiment labels in both datasets are provided in Table 1 and Table 2.

3.2 Results

The performance our model achieves and the official ranking are provided in Table 3. The systems are ranked by the macroaveraged recall for the Subtask B where higher scores are better. On the other subtasks, systems are ranked by the error functions where lower scores are better. From the obtained results, we can see that our system notably performs best on the quantification subtasks.

The merging of the networks provides better performance over their distinctive versions for the quantification tasks. Separately, the CNN and GRNN achieve KLD scores of 0.045 and 0.035 on Subtask D respectively, while only managing 0.761 and 0.632 for the EMD score on Subtask E. On Subtask C, the model surpasses the CNN, which attains a MAE^M score of 0.92, but fails in comparison to the GRNN which gets 0.812. On Subtask B, both networks achieve comparable accuracy and F1 score in comparison to our proposed model, but gain better results on the recall measure, improving the performance by $\sim$ 5 points.

For Subtask B, our model performs best according to the accuracy measure, being ranked 4th. According to the average recall and F1 score, the model does not achieve notable performance although it produces significant improvement over baseline scores, especially for the AvgF1 measure. For the 5-point classification, our model again obtains average performances when compared against other teams.

Concerning Subtask D, our deep learning system produces best KLD score and also a considerable improvement over baseline scores on all three measures. Furthermore, the system gains high results on the 5-point quantification subtask as well, being

Measure	Baseline	Score	Rank
Acc	0.778	0.848	4
AvgF1	0.438	0.748	7
AvgR	0.5	0.72	10
MAE^{μ}	0.537	0.672	6
MAE^{M}	1.2	0.869	5
AE	0.184	0.074	1
RAE	2.11	0.707	3
KLD	0.175	0.034	1
EMD	0.474	0.316	2
AvgRank			4.5

Table 3: Results and ranks for Subtask B, C, D and E respectively

ranked second. Our model averages a score of 4.3 on the all scores for each subtask, while averaging 4.5 on the main scores. The proposed method of our team is one of the most robust out of all other teams, as it manages second highest average rank on the considered subtasks.

4 Conclusion

In this paper, we presented a novel deep learning model for sentiment classification of Twitter messages. We proposed a fusion of CNN and GRNN for extracting features from Twitter messages and a softmax layer for generating class predictions. The deep neural network is trained on top of GloVe word embeddings pre-trained on the Common Crawl dataset. The model effectiveness is evaluated on the Sentiment Analysis in Twitter task from SemEval 2016 where our system achieved second best average rank on the 2-point and 5-point classification and quantification subtasks, testifying for its robustness.

Although our model achieved high results, there is room for improvement. For future work, we would like to pre-train word embeddings on a large set of distantly labeled tweets. Additionally, it would be interesting to see the effects of using bi-directional GRNN.

Acknowledgments

We would like to acknowledge the support of the European Commission through the project MAES-TRA Learning from Massive, Incompletely annotated, and Structured Data (Grant number ICT-2013-612944).

References

Junyoung Chung, Caglar Gulcehre, KyungHyun Cho, and Yoshua Bengio. 2014. Empirical evaluation of gated recurrent neural networks on sequence modeling. *arXiv preprint arXiv:1412.3555*.

Cícero Nogueira dos Santos and Maira Gatti. 2014. Deep convolutional neural networks for sentiment analysis of short texts. In *COLING*, pages 69–78.

Sepp Hochreiter and Jürgen Schmidhuber. 1997. Long short-term memory. *Neural computation*, 9(8):1735–1780.

Yoon Kim. 2014. Convolutional neural networks for sentence classification. *arXiv preprint arXiv:1408.5882*.

Phong Le and Willem Zuidema. 2015. Compositional distributional semantics with long short term memory. *arXiv preprint arXiv:1503.02510*.

Saif M Mohammad, Svetlana Kiritchenko, and Xiaodan Zhu. 2013. Nrc-canada: Building the state-of-the-art in sentiment analysis of tweets. *arXiv preprint arXiv:1308.6242*.

Preslav Nakov, Alan Ritter, Sara Rosenthal, Veselin Stoyanov, and Fabrizio Sebastiani. 2016. SemEval-2016 task 4: Sentiment analysis in Twitter. In *Proceedings of the 10th International Workshop on Semantic Evaluation*, SemEval '16, San Diego, California, June. Association for Computational Linguistics.

Alexander Pak and Patrick Paroubek. 2010. Twitter as a corpus for sentiment analysis and opinion mining. In *LREc*, volume 10, pages 1320–1326.

Jeffrey Pennington, Richard Socher, and Christopher D. Manning. 2014. Glove: Global vectors for word representation. In *Empirical Methods in Natural Language Processing (EMNLP)*, pages 1532–1543.

Richard Socher, Alex Perelygin, Jean Y Wu, Jason Chuang, Christopher D Manning, Andrew Y Ng, and Christopher Potts. 2013. Recursive deep models for semantic compositionality over a sentiment treebank. In *Proceedings of the conference on empirical methods in natural language processing (EMNLP)*, volume 1631, page 1642. Citeseer.

Nitish Srivastava, Geoffrey Hinton, Alex Krizhevsky, Ilya Sutskever, and Ruslan Salakhutdinov. 2014. Dropout: A simple way to prevent neural networks from overfitting. *The Journal of Machine Learning Research*, 15(1):1929–1958.

Dario Stojanovski, Gjorgji Strezoski, Gjorgji Madjarov, and Ivica Dimitrovski. 2015. Twitter sentiment analysis using deep convolutional neural network. In *Hybrid Artificial Intelligent Systems*, pages 726–737. Springer.

Tijmen Tieleman and Geoffrey Hinton. 2012. Lecture 6.5-rmsprop: Divide the gradient by a running average of its recent magnitude. *COURSERA: Neural Networks for Machine Learning*, 4:2.

Tweester at SemEval-2016 Task 4: Sentiment Analysis in Twitter using Semantic-Affective Model Adaptation

Elisavet Palogiannidi[2,3,1], Athanasia Kolovou[4,1], Fenia Christopoulou[1],
Filippos Kokkinos[1], Elias Iosif[1,3], Nikolaos Malandrakis[5], Harris Papageorgiou[3],
Shrikanth Narayanan[5,6], Alexandros Potamianos[1,3,6]

[1] School of ECE, National Technical University of Athens, Zografou 15780, Athens, Greece
[2] School of ECE, Technical University of Crete, Chania 73100, Crete, Greece
[3] "Athena" Research and Innovation Center, Maroussi 15125, Athens, Greece
[4] Department of Informatics, University of Athens, Athens, Greece
[5] Signal Analysis and Interpretation Laboratory (SAIL), USC, Los Angeles, CA 90089, USA
[6] Behavioral Informatix, Los Angeles, CA 90089, USA

`epalogiannidi@isc.tuc.gr, akolovou@di.uoa.gr, el10136@mail.ntua.gr`
`el11142@mail.ntua.gr, iosife@central.ntua.gr, malandra@usc.edu`
`xaris@ilsp.athena-innovation.gr, shri@sipi.usc.edu, potam@central.ntua.gr`

Abstract

We describe our submission to SemEval2016 Task 4: Sentiment Analysis in Twitter. The proposed system ranked first for the sub-task B. Our system comprises of multiple independent models such as neural networks, semantic-affective models and topic modeling that are combined in a probabilistic way. The novelty of the system is the employment of a topic modeling approach in order to adapt the semantic-affective space for each tweet. In addition, significant enhancements were made in the main system dealing with the data pre-processing and feature extraction including the employment of word embeddings. Each model is used to predict a tweet's sentiment (positive, negative or neutral) and a late fusion scheme is adopted for the final decision.

1 Introduction

Nowadays, the usage of social networks such as Twitter dominates the daily communication of hundreds of millions of people around the world. People often share opinions and express their feelings about various topics through social networks. Tasks such as opinion mining and sentiment analysis (Pang and Lee, 2008) have become very popular, since they can capture a large portion of the public opinion.

The sentiment analysis of tweets was applied in various domains, such as commerce (Jansen et al., 2009), disaster management (Verma et al., 2011) or health (Chew and Eysenbach, 2010). This task is especially challenging due to the terse and informal writing style, the semantic diversity of content, as well as the often "unconventional" grammar and orthography. Many computational systems like those submitted to SemEval 2015 Task 10 (Rosenthal et al., 2015) incorporate bag-of-words models with Twitter-specific features like hashtags and emoticons (Davidov et al., 2010; Büchner and Stein, 2015). Word embeddings obtained from large amounts of tweets are used under the scope of an unsupervised approach for sentiment analysis (Astudillo et al., 2015). Additionally, deep learning models have recently become very popular for Twitter sentiment analysis (Severyn and Moschitti, 2015). Topic modeling approaches for sentiment analysis can also be found in literature, e.g., (Mei et al., 2007; Lin and He, 2009; Lu et al., 2011; Alam et al., 2016; Rao, 2016)

In this paper, we present systems submitted to the SemEval 2016 Task 4 (Nakov et al., 2016) that deal with the sentiment analysis of tweets on the sentence level. The submitted systems are based on the fusion of the different classifiers. Specifically, 1) we enhanced the system submitted by Malandrakis et al. (2014) to the SemEval 2014 Task 9 (Rosenthal et al., 2014), 2) we used the open-source system submitted by Büchner and Stein (2015) to the SemEval 2015 Task 10 (Rosenthal et al., 2015), 3) we trained a convolutional neural network on a large amount of unlabelled Twitter data, 4) we developed a system

Proceedings of SemEval-2016, pages 155–163,
San Diego, California, June 16-17, 2016. ©2016 Association for Computational Linguistics

based on topic modeling and 5) we trained a classifier using word embeddings as features. Our system was submitted on two subtasks, namely subtask A (message polarity classification) and subtask B (tweet classification according to a two-point scale) and ranked in the fifth[1] and the first place, respectively.

2 System Description

2.1 Baseline

The baseline system is an enhanced version of the system submitted by Malandrakis et al. (2014) to the SemEval 2014 Task 9 (Rosenthal et al., 2014). The major changes include the different manipulation of hasgatags, muliword expressions and the affective features as well as the incorporation of new features. A plethora of features is extracted, the majority of which are affective. The feature extraction is performed at the tweet, suffix and prefix level. Assume the following tweet: *"Lol Red Sox just slid through 3rd base #out"* (tweet level). A window applied at the beginning estimates the prefix e.g., *"Lol Red Sox"* (prefix level) and a window at the end of the tweet estimates the suffix *"3rd base #out"* (suffix level).

2.1.1 Affective features

The baseline is based on affective features derived from the semantic-affective model proposed by Malandrakis et al. (2013). The semantic-affective model relies on the assumption that semantic similarity implies affective similarity (Malandrakis et al., 2013). First, a semantic model is built and then affective ratings are estimated for unknown tokens exploiting the affective ratings of semantically similar words. It is applicable both to single words or short multiword expression as shown below:

$$\hat{v}(t_j) = \alpha_0 + \sum_{i=1}^{N} \alpha_i v(w_i) S(t_j, w_i), \qquad (1)$$

where t_j is the unknown lexical token, $w_{1..N}$ are the seed words, $v(w_i)$, α_i are the affective rating and the weight corresponding to the word w_i and $S(\cdot)$ is the semantic similarity metric between two tokens. The

semantic model was built as shown in (Palogiannidi et al., 2015) using word-level contextual feature vectors and adopting a scheme based on mutual information for feature weighting. The dimensionality of the affective features was reduced by retaining only the polarity features (instead of using additional affective dimensions, like arousal and dominance). Affective lexica were created using a generic corpus (116M sentences) (Iosif et al., 2016) and a Twitter corpus (115M tweets) created for the purpose of our submission. In the former case task-independent affective ratings are estimated. Task-dependent affective ratings can be estimated by keeping domain-specific sentences in the generic corpus. A language model was built using domain relevant sentences and then the top 30% of the most relevant entries of the generic corpus were selected[2].

Affective features were also derived through semantic models that were built from corpora that were collected based on the topic modeling approach described in Section 2.2. **Third party affective lexica** were also used. Affin (Nielsen, 2011) contains discrete polarity ratings in the range $[-5, 5]$, nrc, nrctag (Mohammad et al., 2013) contain continuous polarity ratings for tokens, generated from a collection of tweets that include a positive or a negative word hashtag.

2.1.2 Tokenization

Based on the assumption that **hashtags** in different positions in a tweet may have different semantic interpretation, the tweets are transformed as follows: if a hashtag occurs at the end of the tweet it is assumed to convey semantic information. Otherwise, the hashtag is treated as a word or possibly a union of words. In the latter case, only the corresponding word is kept (e.g., "#moon is so beautiful tonight" → "moon is so beautiful tonight", but "What a beautiful night under the moonlight #romantic" is preserved as is). A hashtag that contains a union of words is expanded, e.g., #Hockeyisback → Hockey is back. Hashtags were expanded using the Viterbi algorithm (Forney and David, 1973) exploiting n-gram datasets. The n-gram dataset

---

[1]The actual performance of the system is different from the official results due to an erroneous submission.

[2]Perplexity filtering was used in order to estimate the relevance of a sentence to the language model while 30% was selected to be the most appropriate percentage over other percentages that were examined.

we used is a concatenation of the Google n-gram corpus that contains 1 trillion tokens from publicly accessible web pages (Brants and Franz, 2006) and an n-gram corpus based on 75 million English tweets (Herdağdelen, 2013). The absolute and relative frequencies of hashtags to be expanded were also used as features, as well as the indicators (binary features) that a tweet contains hashtags that require expansion. **POS-tagging / Tokenization** was then performed using the ARK NLP tweeter tagger (Owoputi et al., 2013), a Twitter-specific tagger. A tweet contains single words or emoticons and punctuations or multiword expressions. **Multiword expressions (MWE)** are non-compositional expressions that are processed as a single token. They were detected using the Gensim library (Řehůřek and Sojka, 2010) and they were added to the affective lexica.

Some parts of the tweets may be crucial for the correct understanding of its affective meaning. We assume that such parts, are the prefix, the suffix and the negated parts. **Negations** were detected using the list proposed by Potts (2011). When a negation token is detected, the tokens that follow are marked as negated until a punctuation mark is reached. Then, feature extraction is applied on the negated part of the tweet. **Windows** are used for splitting a tweet into prefix and suffix attempting to estimate the cognitive dissonance phenomenon that is associated with sarcasm, irony and humour (Reyes et al., 2012). The suffix is extracted by applying windows that keep the 20%, 50% and 70% of tokens that occur at the end of the tweet. Feature extraction is performed for both suffixes and prefixes.

2.1.3 Word2vec features

In addition to the use of semantic similarity features as in (Malandrakis et al., 2014), we use semantic representations, i.e., word embeddings that are utilized for the semantic similarity estimation, i.e., the $S(\cdot)$ in (1). **Word embedding features** were derived using word2vec (Mikolov et al., 2013), representing each word as a 300-D vector. Since tweet-level features are required, for each tweet a 300-D vector is generated by averaging the corresponding vectors of the constituent words.

2.1.4 Additional features

Additional features based on characters and subjectivity lexica were used. Character features include the absolute and relative frequencies of selected characters. The selected characters are the **capitalized** letters, the **punctuation** marks, the **emoticons** as well as characters **repetitions** , i.e., at least three same successive characters in a word. **Subjectivity** features were also extracted based on the subjectivity lexicon of (Wilson et al., 2005). Specifically, the absolute and the relative frequencies of the strong positive/negative and weak positive/negative words were used as features.

2.1.5 Statistics extraction

The statistics of the token-level polarity features were estimated in order to extract tweet-level features. The following statistics were computed: length (cardinality), min, max, max amplitude, sum, average, range (max minus min), standard deviation and variance. Normalized versions of the same statistics were also calculated.

2.2 Topic Modeling

Topic modeling is a method for discovering "topics" that occur in collections of documents. Typically, multiple topics are present in a document. The most widely used topic modeling approach is the Latent Dirichlet Allocation (LDA) (Blei et al., 2003) which is based on Latent Semantic Analysis (LSA) (Deerwester, 1988) and probabilistic Latent Semantic Analysis (pLSA) (Hofmann, 2000). Here, we used topic modeling in order to adapt the semantic space on each tweet. In essence, the corpus was split in a probabilistic way based on the detected topics and then a semantic model was built for each subcorpus. Since this technique is probabilistic, each corpus sentence can belong to each revealed topic with a given probability. Then, clusters of sentences per topic were created by classifying each sentence to the most probable topic. A semantic model was built for each cluster, using word2vec (Mikolov et al., 2013). A mixture of the semantic models, weighted by the topic posteriors is used for the estimation of tweet's semantic similarities, e.g., $S(\cdot)$ in (1).

2.3 Convolutional Neural Network

A deep convolutional neural network (CNN) was also developed. The neural network's architecture is inspired by sentence classification tasks (Collobert et al., 2011; Kalchbrenner et al., 2014; Kim, 2014). Each tweet is represented by a "sentence" matrix $\mathbf{S}$ that is created as follows. First, each word is represented as a 300-D vector using word2vec, and then, the word vectors are concatenated as follows: $\mathbf{S} = W_1 \oplus W_2 \oplus W_3 \oplus \cdots \oplus W_n., S \in \mathbb{R}^{d \times n}$, where $\oplus$ indicates the concatenation operation. Each column i of $\mathbf{S}$ is a vector $W \in \mathbb{R}^d$ that corresponds to the ith word of the tweet. This way the sequence of the words in the tweet is kept. In order to preserve the same length for all tweets, zero padding was applied concatenating zero word vectors until the length n of the longest tweet is reached. The size of $\mathbf{S}$ is $d \times n$, where d is the dimension of the word embedding and n is the length of the longest tweet. The matrix $\mathbf{S}$ is the input to the network, where a convolution operation is applied between $\mathbf{S}$ and a kernel $F \in \mathbb{R}^{d \times m}$. The width m was set to 5 and the parameters of the model, i.e., the values of the kernel, the size of the sliding window h are learned. The result of the convolutional layer is a vector $c \in \mathbb{R}^{n-m+1}$ (Kim, 2014). In fact, the convolution network uses multiple kernels with varying sliding windows and generates multiple features. These features are the inputs to the next layer which selects the maximum value of each feature by applying a max-over-time pooling operation (max-pooling layer) (Collobert et al., 2011). Next, the output of the max-pooling layer is passed to a dropout layer (Srivastava et al., 2014). A softmax layer that classifies each test instance to one of the possible classes is the final step.

2.4 Word2vec System

Based on the assumption that similarity of meaning implies affective similarity (Malandrakis et al., 2013) we build a system that relies exclusively on tweets' semantic representation. Specifically, word2vec was applied over large text corpora in order to compute the semantic representations of words (formulated as vectors). Then, the vectors of each tweet's constituent words were averaged in order to create a single vector. These vectors were used for training a random forest classifier.

2.5 Webis

The Webis open-source system (Büchner and Stein, 2015) that was submitted on (Rosenthal et al., 2015) is the ensemble of different subsystems that ranked at the top of Semeval 2013, Semeval 2014 Sentiment Analysis tasks (Nakov et al., 2013; Rosenthal et al., 2014). The following systems were combined in a late fusion scheme, based on the mean posterior probabilities: 1) NRC-Canada (Mohammad et al., 2013) is based on morphological, linguistic and polarity features, 2) GU-MLT-LT (Günther and Furrer, 2013) trains a linear classifier by stochastic gradient descent which uses social media specific text preprocessing and linguistic features, 3) KLUE (Proisl et al., 2013) employs a Maximum Entropy classifier with bag-of-words models, sentiment, emoticons and internet slang abbreviations features, 4) TeamX (Miura et al., 2014) is similar to NRC-Canada but uses more lexicon-based features and handles the unbalance distribution of tweets' sentiment by adopting a weighting scheme to bias the output.

2.6 Fusion of the systems

The motivation behind the development of various systems for sentiment classification is that different systems may capture different aspects of the sentiment, and by combining them we can predict more accurately the sentiment of tweets. The system architecture including the fusion scheme is summarized in the figure below.

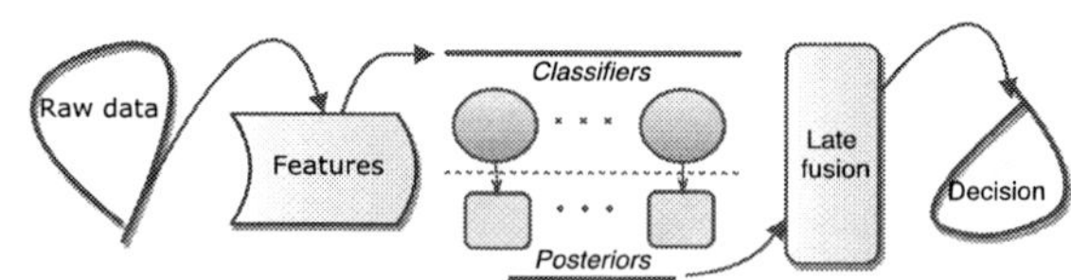

Figure 1: System Architecture.

As shown in Figure 1, the various classifiers were trained with features extracted from Twitter datasets and their posterior probabilities were combined in a late fusion scheme. Various techniques can be used for the late fusion of classifiers, e.g., voting-based (Tulyakov et al., 2008) methods, multi-classifiers fusion that use posteriors as features for training a new classifier (Kittler et al., 1998; Gutierrez et al., 2016)

| | Datasets | | | | | | |
| System | 2013 | | 2014 | | | 2015 | 2016 |
	SMS	Twitter	LiveJour.	Twitter	TwitterSarcasm	Twitter	Twitter
W-CNN-B-W2V	0.547	0.704	0.687	0.715	0.455	0.658	0.608
W-TM-B*-W2V	0.610	0.704	0.705	0.718	0.473	0.638	0.611
W-CNN-B*-W2V	0.593	0.716	0.707	0.721	0.485	0.643	0.614
W-B*-CNN	0.635	0.717	0.725	0.720	0.508	0.645	**0.618**
W-B*-W2V	0.632	0.711	0.732	0.727	0.468	0.640	**0.624**

Table 1: Macro-averaged F-score for subtask A and various system combinations. The submitted system is highlighted in grey.

NRC	GU-MLT-LT	TeamX	Klue	Baseline	Topic Modeling	CNN	AvgR	AvgF1
AvgR								
0.709	0.712	0.712	0.737	**0.821**	0.753	0.752		
√	√	√	√	√	√	√	**0.803**	**0.808**
×	×	×	×	√	√	√	0.818	0.793
√	√	√	√	×	√	√	0.765	0.781
√	√	√	√	√	×	√	0.780	0.790
√	√	√	√	√	√	×	0.798	0.801
√	√	√	×	√	√	×	0.797	0.799
×	×	×	×	√	×	√	**0.827**	0.789
×	√	×	√	√	√	√	**0.824**	**0.805**

Table 2: Macro-averaged recall and F1 for subtask B, for a 2016 test twitter dataset. The submitted system is highlighted in grey.

or algebraic combinations (Kittler et al., 1998). Algebraic combinations are based on operations such as mean, median, product, max or min.

3 Experimental Procedure and Results

3.1 Data

We trained our systems using both general purpose and Twitter data. We used a large generic corpus that contains 116M sentences (G-116M). The dataset was created by posing queries on a web search engine and aggregating the resulting snippets. A Twitter specific dataset was also created collecting 115M tweets (T-115M). We also used the training data provided by SemEval 2016 for subtasks A and B (Sem/A-2016, Sem/B-2016), as well as training data from the corresponding task of SemEval 2013 (Sem-2013). We also used ANEW (Bradley and Lang, 1999) for bootstrapping the affective lexicon expansion process.

3.2 Systems

The following subsystems were combined for the subtask A: Baseline (B), CNN, Word2vec system (W2V) and Webis (W). Baseline and Webis were trained on the concatenation of Sem/A-2016 and Sem-2013. A two-stage feature selection was applied, the first one took place on each feature set separately and the second to the combined feature set of the first stage. Finally, a Naive Bayes tree classifier was trained. Affective features derived by the topic modeling approach were also incorporated. The word vectors that are required for the CNN are derived from different corpora, i.e., the combination of a Google News dataset and the T-115M corpus. Specifically, for each word in the tweet, the word vector extracted from the latter corpus is used only if the word doesn't exist in the former corpus. The vectors of OOV words are initialized randomly from a uniform distribution. For the word2vec-based system we trained a random forest classifier with 100 trees using 300-D feature vectors on the concatenation of Sem/A-2016 and Sem-2013. We experimented with various fusion schemes and system combinations. The mean algebraic fusion scheme was selected for the reported results.

The submission for the subtask B includes the following systems: Baseline (B*), Topic Modeling (TM) and three Webis subsystems, i.e., NRC-Canada, GU-MLT-LT and Team X. The Baseline ($B^\star$) and the selected Webis systems were trained on the Sem/B-2016 dataset. Both feature selection and the classification of $B^\star$ are similar to the Baseline that was used in subtask A. The difference between B and $B^\star$ is that the former, in contrast to the second, includes affective features extracted through the approach based on topic modeling. The topic modeling system applies the LDA algorithm on the G-116M, using 16 topics[3]. Then, affective ratings are estimated and they are used in order to train a Naive Bayes tree classifier. Similarly to subtask A, a mean algebraic fusion scheme was selected for combining the systems.

3.3 Results

The developed systems for subtask A classify each tweet in one out of three sentiment classes (positive vs. negative vs. neutral), however the performance of the model is measured taking into consideration only the performance on the two polarity classes, i.e., positive and negative. The macro-averaged F-score of the positive and negative classes $F_1^{PN} = \frac{F_1^{Pos}+F_1^{Neg}}{2}$ is reported in Table 1 for various datasets. In the first column the integrated systems are presented, while the submitted system is highlighted with grey color. Our system ranked fifth, while experimenting with different system combinations we can climb up to the third position.

Subtask B is a binary classification task (positive vs. negative). Macro-averaged recall $p^{PN} = \frac{p^{Pos}+p^{Neg}}{2}$, $p^{PN} \in [0,1]$ and macro-averaged F-score are reported in Table 2 for various system combinations. The systems and their macro-averaged recall are listed in the first and second row of the table, respectively. The reported scores were derived by the test tweets of 2016 that belong to specific topics. Each row that follows indicates a unique combination and the submitted system is highlighted with grey color. In the case that all the available systems are combined, the marco-averaged recall (AvgR) is 0.803 and macro-averaged F-score (AvgF1) is 0.808. The combinations that follow contain a subset of the systems (the selected systems are

---

[3]The number of topics derived after the conduction of experiments on a news headlines dataset.

denoted with $\sqrt{}$ and the omitted systems with $\times$). The baseline was proved to be the most robust system achieving the highest performance among the others and higher performance than the submitted system (0.797). When using all the subsystems but one, performance decreases except in the case that the Webis system is omitted, then AvgR increased to 0.818. The highest performance drop is achieved when the baseline system is omitted. Investigating more combination schemes AvgR rises to 0.827. The combination of CNN, TM and $B^\star$ with two of the best Webis systems yields robust performance with AvgR and AvgF1 0.824 and 0.805, respectively.

4 Conclusions

We presented a system for the sentiment classification of tweets for the SemEval 2016 Task 4: Sentiment analysis in Twitter. We participated in subtasks A and B and we won subtask B. We developed various systems including a CNN and a topic modeling approach for the adaptation of the semantic space to each tweet. Regarding task A, the submitted system was ranked between the fifth and third position. The performance for subtask B can be higher (up to +3% compared to the submitted system) for various system combinations. Future work will focus on the fusion of the systems as well as their enhancement in order to achieve higher performance to the three-point scale sentiment classification.

Acknowledgements: Elisavet Palogiannidi, Elias Iosif and Alexandros Potamianos were partially funded by the SpeDial project supported by the EU Seventh Framework Programme (FP7), grant number 611396 and the BabyRobot project supported by the EU Horizon 2020 Programme, grant number: 687831.

References

Md. H. Alam, W. Ryu, and S. Lee. 2016. Joint Multi-grain Topic Sentiment: Modeling Semantic Aspects for Online Reviews. *Information Sciences*, 339:206–223.

R. Astudillo, S. Amir, W. Ling, B. Martins, M. J. Silva, and I. Trancoso. 2015. INESC-ID: Sentiment Analysis without Hand-Coded Features or Linguistic Resources using Embedding Subspaces. In *Proc. of the 9th International Workshop on Semantic Evaluation (SemEval)*, pages 652–656.

D. M. Blei, A. Y. Ng, and M. I. Jordan. 2003. Latent Dirichlet Allocation. *The Journal of Machine Learning Reasearch*, 3:993–1022.

M. Bradley and P. Lang. 1999. Affective norms for English words (ANEW): Instruction Manual and Affective Ratings. Technical report.

T. Brants and A. Franz. 2006. Web 1T 5-gram corpus Version 1. Technical report, Google Research.

M. Büchner and B. Stein. 2015. Webis: An Ensemble for Twitter Sentiment Detection. In *Proc. of the 9th International Workshop on Semantic Evaluation (SemEval)*, pages 582–589.

C. Chew and G. Eysenbach. 2010. Pandemics in the age of Twitter: content analysis of Tweets during the 2009 H1N1 outbreak. *PloS ONE*, 5(11):1–13.

R. Collobert, J. Weston, L. Bottou, M. Karlen, K. Kavukcuoglu, and P. Kuksa. 2011. Natural language processing (almost) from scratch. *The Journal of Machine Learning Research*, 12:2493–2537.

D. Davidov, O. Tsur, and A. Rappoport. 2010. Enhanced sentiment learning using twitter hashtags and smileys. In *Proc. of Conference on Computational Linguistics (Coling)*, pages 241–249.

S. Deerwester. 1988. Improving Information Retrieval with Latent Semantic Indexing. In *Proc. of the 51st Annual Meeting of the American Society for Information Science and Technology (ASIS&T)*, pages 36–40.

J. Forney and G. David. 1973. The Viterbi algorithm. *In Proceedings of the IEEE*, 61(3):268–278.

T. Günther and L. Furrer. 2013. GU-MLT-LT: Sentiment analysis of short messages using linguistic features and stochastic gradient descent. In

Proc. of the 7th International Workshop on Semantic Evaluation (SemEval), pages 328–332.

P. A. Gutierrez, M. Perez-Ortiz, J. Sanchez-Monedero, F. Fernandez-Navarro, and C. Hervas-Martinez. 2016. Ordinal regression methods: survey and experimental study. *IEEE Transactions on Knowledge and Data Engineering*, 28(1):127–146.

A. Herdağdelen. 2013. Twitter n-gram corpus with demographic metadata. *Language Resources and Evaluation*, 47(4):1127–1147.

T. Hofmann. 2000. Learning the similarity of documents: An information-geometric approach to document retrieval and categorization. In *Proc. of Conference on Advances in Neural Information Processing Systems (NIPS)*, pages 914–920.

E. Iosif, S. Georgiladakis, and A. Potamianos. 2016. Cognitively Motivated Distributional Representations of Meaning. In *Proc. of the Language Resources and Evaluation Conference (LREC)*.

B. J. Jansen, M. Zhang, K. Sobel, and A. Chowdury. 2009. Twitter power: Tweets as electronic word of mouth. *Journal of the American Society for Information Science and Technology*, 60(11):2169–2188.

N. Kalchbrenner, E. Grefenstette, and P. Blunsom. 2014. A Convolutional Neural Network for Modelling Sentences. In *Proc. of the 52nd Annual Meeting of the Association for Computational Linguistics*, pages 655–665.

Y. Kim. 2014. Convolutional Neural Networks for Sentence Classification. In *Proc. of the Conference on Empirical Methods in Natural Language Processing (EMNLP)*, pages 1746–1751.

J. Kittler, M. Hatef, R. PW Duin, and J. Matas. 1998. On combining classifiers. *IEEE Transactions on Pattern Analysis and Machine Intelligence*, 20(3):226–239.

C. Lin and Y. He. 2009. Joint sentiment/topic model for sentiment analysis. In *Proc. of the 18th Conference on Information and Knowledge Management (CIKM)*, pages 375–384.

B. Lu, M. Ott, C. Cardie, and B. K. Tsou. 2011. Multi-aspect sentiment analysis with topic models. In *Proc. of International Conference on Data Mining Workshops (ICDMW)*, pages 81–88. IEEE.

N. Malandrakis, A. Potamianos, E. Iosif, and S. Narayanan. 2013. Distributional semantic models for affective text analysis. *IEEE Transactions on Audio, Speech and Language Processing*, 21(11):2379–2392.

N. Malandrakis, M. Falcone, C. Vaz, J. Bisogni, A. Potamianos, and S. Narayanan. 2014. SAIL: Sentiment Analysis using Semantic Similarity and Contrast Features. In *Proc. of the 8th International Workshop on Semantic Evaluation (SemEval)*, pages 512–516.

Q. Mei, X. Ling, M. Wondra, H. Su, and C. Zhai. 2007. Topic sentiment mixture: modeling facets and opinions in weblogs. In *Proc. of the 16th International Conference on World Wide Web (ICWWW)*, pages 171–180.

T. Mikolov, I. Sutskever, K. Chen, G. S. Corrado, and J. Dean. 2013. Distributed representations of words and phrases and their compositionality. In *Proc of. Advances in Neural Information Processing systems (NIPS)*, pages 3111–3119.

Y. Miura, S. Sakaki, K. Hattori, and T. Ohkuma. 2014. TeamX: A sentiment analyzer with enhanced lexicon mapping and weighting scheme for unbalanced data. In *Proc. of the 8th International Workshop on Semantic Evaluation (SemEval)*, pages 628–632.

S. M. Mohammad, S. Kiritchenko, and X. Zhu. 2013. NRC-Canada: Building the State-of-the-Art in Sentiment Analysis of Tweets. In *Proc. of the 7th International Workshop on Semantic Evaluation (SemEval)*, pages 321–327.

P. Nakov, Z. Kozareva, A. Ritter, S. Rosenthal, V. Stoyanov, and T. Wilson. 2013. Semeval-2013 Task 2: Sentiment Analysis in Twitter. In *Proc. of the 7th International Workshop on Semantic Evaluation (SemEval)*, pages 312–320.

P. Nakov, A. Ritter, S. Rosenthal, V. Stoyanovand, and F. Sebastiani. 2016. SemEval-2016 task 4: Sentiment Analysis in Twitter. In *Proc. of the 10th International Workshop on Semantic Evaluation (SemEval)*.

F. Å. Nielsen. 2011. A new ANEW: Evaluation of a word list for sentiment analysis in microblogs. In *Proc. of the ESWC Workshop on Making Sense of Microposts*, pages 93–98.

O. Owoputi, C. Dyer, K. Gimpel, N. Schneider, and N. A. Smith. 2013. Improved part-of-speech tagging for online conversational text with word clusters. In *Proc. of North American Chapter of the Association for Computational Linguistics (NAACL)*.

E. Palogiannidi, E. Iosif, P. Koutsakis, and A. Potamianos. 2015. Valence, Arousal and Dominance Estimation for English, German, Greek, Portuguese and Spanish Lexica using Semantic Models. In *Proc. of Interspeech*, pages 1527–1531.

B. Pang and L. Lee. 2008. Opinion mining and Sentiment analysis. *Foundations and trends in information retrieval*, 2(1-2):1–135.

C. Potts. 2011. Sentiment symposium tutorial. In *Proc. of Sentiment Symposium Tutorial*.

T. Proisl, P. Greiner, S. Evert, and B. Kabashi. 2013. KLUE: Simple and Robust methods for polarity classification. In *Proc. of the 7th International Workshop on Semantic Evaluation (SemEval)*, pages 395–401.

Y. Rao. 2016. Contextual Sentiment Topic Model for Adaptive Social Emotion Classification. *IEEE Intelligent Systems*, 31(1):41–47.

R. Řehůřek and P. Sojka. 2010. Software Framework for Topic Modelling with Large Corpora. In *Proc. of the Language Resources and Evaluation Conference (LREC) Workshop on New Challenges for NLP Frameworks*, pages 45–50.

A. Reyes, P. Rosso, and D. Buscaldi. 2012. From humor recognition to irony detection: The figurative language of social media. *Data & Knowledge Engineering*, 74:1–12.

S. Rosenthal, A. Ritter, P. Nakov, and V. Stoyanov. 2014. Semeval-2014 Task 9: Sentiment Analysis in Twitter. In *Proc. of the 8th International Workshop on Semantic Evaluation (SemEval)*, pages 73–80.

S. Rosenthal, P. Nakov, S. Kiritchenko, S. M. Mohammad, A. Ritter, and V. Stoyanov. 2015. Semeval-2015 Task 10: Sentiment Analysis in Twitter. In *Proc. of the 9th International Workshop on Semantic Evaluation (SemEval)*, pages 451–463.

A. Severyn and A. Moschitti. 2015. UNITN: Training deep convolutional neural network for Twitter sentiment classification. In *Proc. of the 9th International Workshop on Semantic Evaluation (SemEval)*, pages 464–469.

N. Srivastava, G. Hinton, A. Krizhevsky, I. Sutskever, and R. Salakhutdinov. 2014. Dropout: A simple way to prevent neural networks from overfitting. *The Journal of Machine Learning Research*, 15(1):1929–1958.

S. Tulyakov, S. Jaeger, V. Govindaraju, and D. Doermann. 2008. Review of classifier combination methods. In *Machine Learning in Document Analysis and Recognition*, pages 361–386.

S. Verma, S. Vieweg, W. J Corvey, L. Palen, J. H Martin, M. Palmer, A. Schram, and K. M. Anderson. 2011. Natural Language Processing to the Rescue? Extracting "Situational Awareness" Tweets During Mass Emergency. In *Proc. of the 5th International Conference on Web and Social Media (ICWSM)*.

T. Wilson, J. Wiebe, and P. Hoffmann. 2005. Recognizing contextual polarity in phrase-level sentiment analysis. In *Proc. of the Conference on Human Language Technology and Empirical Methods in Natural Language Processing (HLT/EMNLP)*, pages 347–354.

UofL at SemEval-2016 Task 4: Multi Domain word2vec for Twitter Sentiment Classification

Omar Abdelwahab, Adel Elmaghraby
Computer Science and Engineering
University of Louisville, Louisville, KY
`{omar.abdelwahab,adel}@louisville.edu`

Abstract

In this paper, we present a transfer learning system for twitter sentiment classification and compare its performance using different feature sets that include different word representation vectors. We utilized data from a different source domain to increase the performance of our system in the target domain. Our approach was based on training various word2vec models on data from the source and target domains combined, then using these models to calculate the average word vector of all the word vectors in a tweet observation, then input the average word vector as a feature to our classifiers for training. We further developed one doc2vec model that was trained on the positive, negative and neutral tweets in the target domain only. We then used these models in calculating the average word vector for every tweet in the training set as a preprocessing step. The final evaluation results show that our approach gave a prediction accuracy on the Twitter2016 test dataset that outperformed two teams that were among the top 10 in terms of AvgF1 scores.

1 Introduction

Twitter sentiment analysis deals with classifying the polarity of a tweet as positive or negative or neutral. We have participated in Semeval 2016 Twitter Sentiment Analysis subtask-A. Where we had to predict the polarity of a whole tweet rather than part of a tweet. We have started off with feature engineering and data preprocessing. Then we have divided our task into five classification tasks. Then we worked on creating our feature sets that we later used to select the best classifier/feature set combination for each classification task as will be explained further in the paper.

In section 2 we explain our transfer learning approach, system components, data preprocessing, aggregation approach, word2vec training and doc2vec training. In section 3, we present our experiments. Then in section 4, we review and discuss our results. Finally in section 5, we make conclusions and outline some future work.

2 Transfer Learning Approach

Our transfer learning approach was based on using data from an additional source domain to supplement the provided target domain twitter data to train our word2vec models. The resultant models were later used in calculating the average word2vec vector of each tweet in our twitter training set as will be explained in section 2.4. We have also developed four binary classifiers and one arbiter three class label classifier. The four binary classifiers as well as the fifth arbiter classifier were a combination of logistic regression and SVM classifiers as we will show in the following sections.

2.1 System Components and Data Sets

In this section, we will specify the system components that were used in predicting the final results that we have submitted to SEMEVAL Task number 4. We have trained six word2vec models that will be discussed in more detail in section 2.4.

After training our word2vec models, we have selected five classifiers based on experimentation results using the preprocessed combined Rosenthal et al. (2015) and Nakov et al. (2016) semeval training twitter data set.

164

Proceedings of SemEval-2016, pages 164–170,
San Diego, California, June 16-17, 2016. ©2016 Association for Computational Linguistics

Two SVM classifiers, one for classifying positive and negative tweets was trained on positive and negative tweets. The second was for classifying between negative and non-negative tweets and it was trained on negative and non-negative tweets. In addition, we have trained three Logistic Regression classifiers, one for classifying between positive, neutral sentiments and it was trained on positive and neutral tweets.

While the second classifier was trained on negative, neutral tweets for classifying between negative and neutral polarities. The third logistic regression classifier was for classifying between positive, negative, neutral tweets and it was trained on positive, negative and neutral tweets. Different sets of features were used with each classifier as we will discuss in section 2.3.

As mentioned earlier, we have combined the 2015 Semeval twitter sentiment analysis subtask B's training set and the 2016 Semeval twitter sentiment analysis subtask A's training set into one training set of 11,798 tweets named full_training_set. We then combined the Guestrin et al. (2015) amazon baby toys product reviews data set (source domain) which were around 150,000 reviews with the full_training_set to build our word2vec models. On the other hand, we used the full_training_set to train our doc2vec model as will be explained in section 2.5. After training our word2vec and doc2vec models, the full_training_set was preprocessed for training our five classifiers mentioned above.

The validation set used for every classifier in the ensemble had the same characteristics of the training set. For example, since the positive/negative classifier was trained on positive and negative tweets, its validation set contained positive and negative tweets only.

Finally, the output of our five classifiers is aggregated to produce the final system output as discussed in section 2.3.

2.2 Preprocessing and Feature Engineering

Before we have trained any of our classifiers, we have started with preprocessing our training data. Keeping in mind that any preprocessing we performed on the training set was applied on the test set. We started with the following preprocessing steps:

- Removed character repetitions by removing the character repetitions that could distract our classifiers. For example a word like LOOOOOOOL is replaced with LOL.

- Replaced patterns by replacing words like 'won't' with 'will not', 'can't' with 'cannot'. 're' with 'are', etc.

- Converted tweets to lower case by converting upper case characters to lower case.

- Replaced website links with URL so links to websites that start with www.* or http?://* were replaced with URL symbol.

- Converted @username to AT_USER by replacing @username instances found in tweets with AT_USER for our classifiers to easily identify that a user is being referenced.

- Removed additional white spaces in order to remove any noise that might affect our classifiers' performance.

- Replaced hash tags and removed stop words. As we replaced hash tags with the same word without the hash. For example, #fun is replaced with fun. As hash tags can give useful information. Also stop words are removed.

- Replaced Non-Alphabets and question words with space. Then we replaced numbers with $NUM symbol.

- Performed stemming and lemmatization using porter stemmer and WordNet lemmatizer class in the NLTK library.

- We used Bing Liu et al. (2004) positive-word and negative-word lexicons that contained a list of thousands of words associated with positive sentiment and negative sentiment. We replaced positive words with $po and negative words with $ne. We also used the NRC Unigram lexicon that helped us in replacing words that are more likely to give a positive sentiment with 'HAPO' and words that will more likely result in a negative sentiment with 'HANE'.

- The source domain data was preprocessed in the same way the target domain data (tweets) were preprocessed. However, the source domain data were only used in training the word2vec and doc2vec models.

- After finishing with the initial preprocessing steps discussed previously, the training set and the validation set were parsed into Graphlab Sframes for further manipulation.

- Then the Unigrams, bigrams and trigrams of every tweet in the training set were calculated and stored in additional columns in the same Sframe.

- Furthermore, the TFIDF of every tweet was calculated and stored in a new column.

- The six trained word2vec models that will be discussed in section 2.4 were each used in calculating the word vectors of each word in a tweet observation in the training set.

- Afterwards, the word vectors generated by each word2vec model were later averaged to get six averaged word vectors for every tweet in the training set. These average vectors were later saved in columns named w2v_vectors_pos_neg, w2v_vectors_pos_neutral, w2v_vectors_neutral_neg, w2v_vectors_pos_ornot, w2v_vectors_neg_ornot, w2v_vectors_neutral_ornot which were later used as features to our classifiers.

2.3 Features used and Aggregation

We have categorized our feature sets into four categories. There are different feature sets in each category. The first category is called feature category 1 that includes only base features tfidf, unigram, bigram, and trigrams. Then a second category containing the base as well as word2vec vectors and it's called feature category 2. Then a third feature category that contains base features in addition to doc2vec vectors only named feature category 3. Finally, a fourth category that contains base features, word2vec vectors, and doc2vec vectors is called feature category 4.

The features included in every feature set is presented in Appendix A while the feature sets in each category is shown in Appendix B.

When it came to aggregating the predictions from the four binary classifiers, we gave the highest priority to the neg_ornot classifier. As it had a reasonably high accuracy in discriminating between negative and non-negative tweets on the validation set. Therefore if the neg_ornot classifier classifies a tweet as negative, the final output of the system will be negative. However, if it classifies a tweet as non-negative, a majority vote is taken between the other three remaining binary classifiers. If two classifiers classify a tweet as positive, then the final system output will be positive, similarly if two classifiers classify a tweet as neutral, then the final system prediction is neutral, and likewise if two classifiers agree that a tweet is negative then the final sentiment output is negative. In the case when we get a tie from the other three classifiers and the neg_ornot classifier classifies a tweet as non-negative, then the fifth arbiter three class label classifier is deployed to give the final classification output of the system.

2.4 Word2Vec

When Training our word2vec models for our final system, we used the continuous bag-of-words architecture. We combined positive amazon reviews and positive tweets into one file and named it pos_text, then combined the negative tweets and negative amazon reviews into a second file named neg_text, and similarly we combined the neutral amazon reviews with the neutral tweets in a third file named neutral_txt. Our first word2vec_pos_neg model was trained on the pos_text and neg_text files.

While, the word2vec_pos_neutral model was trained on the pos_text and neutral_text. Then the word2vec_neg_neutral model was trained on the neg_text and neutral_text. Furthermore, the other three word2vec models were trained to be used to distinguish between negative and nonnegative tweets, positive and non-positive tweets, neutral and non-neutral tweets using pos_text, neg_text and neutral_text files. The word2vec_neg_ornot model was trained on the neg_text, and non_neg_text (pos_text and neutral_text combined). Also, word2vec_pos_ornot model was trained on the pos_text and non_pos_text (neg_text and neu-

Classification	Clas-sifier	Feature Set	Cate-gory	Accu-racy
Neg-Nonnega-tive	SVM	6	2	0.894
Neg-Neutral	LR	7	3	0.778
Pos-neg	SVM	8	4	0.851
pos-neg-neutral	LR	12	4	0.610
Pos-Neutral	LR	2	2	0.713

Table 1: Final classifier/feature set combinations selected.

tral_text combined). Lastly, word2vec_neutral_or-not was trained on neutral_text and non_neu-tral_text (pos_text and neg_text combined).

2.5   Paragraph Vector

We have trained a doc2vec model on all the positive, negative and neutral tweets in the training set to test whether paragraph vectors would improve fscores and prediction accuracies on the validation set. After building our doc2vec distributed memory model, we used it in inferring the tweet vector of every tweet in the training set and stored the result in the 'vectors_doc2vec_tweetsonly_dm' column. Column vectors_doc2vec_tweetsonly_dm is then added as a feature to our feature sets shown in Appendix A.

3   Experiments

We have carried out a number of experiments to help in selecting the feature sets to use for each classifier as well as which classifier type (SVM or Logistic Regression or boosted trees) to use for every binary classification and for the arbiter classifier.

Appendix C contains a flowchart describing the system structure. The flowchart illustrates our system's sentiment prediction process.

Table 2.0 shows the validation prediction accuracies for each binary classifier and on the arbiter classifier when varying the feature set. The feature set, classifier combination was selected based on the combination that yielded the best validation prediction accuracies. However, when evaluating our whole system or our final system output, we use fscore as a measure of system performance and not the test set prediction accuracy.

We have set class weights to auto in all classifiers we trained to help protecting against data imbalance which would lead to misleading results.

	Classifier	Feature Set	Accuracy
negative-notnegative	SVM	Feature Set 6	**0.89382**
	LR	Feature Set 9	0.87354
	SVM	Feature Set 1	0.87309
	LR	Feature Set 1	0.87156
	SVM	Feature Set 9	0.87022
	LR	Feature Set 6	0.86688
	LR	Feature Set 7	0.85667
	SVM	Feature Set 7	0.85503
neg-neutral	LR	Feature Set 7	**0.77817**
	LR	Feature Set 10	0.77432
	SVM	Feature Set 7	0.77113
	SVM	Feature Set 3	0.75102
	SVM	Feature Set 10	0.75097
	LR	Feature Set 1	0.74909
	SVM	Feature Set 1	0.74182
	LR	Feature Set 3	0.73878
pos-neg	SVM	Feature set 8	**0.85058**
	SVM	Feature Set 2	0.84890
	LR	Feature Set 2	0.82418
	LR	Feature set 8	0.82184
	LR	Feature Set 7	0.74869
	SVM	Feature Set 7	0.74607
	LR	Feature Set 1	0.73469
	SVM	Feature Set 1	0.72886
pos-neg-neutral	LR	Feature Set 12	**0.60966**
	LR	Feature Set 5	0.60686
	BoostedTrees	Feature Set 1	0.60613
	BoostedTrees	Feature Set 7	0.60232
	BoostedTrees	Feature Set 5	0.60081
	LR	Feature Set 7	0.57907
	BoostedTrees	Feature Set 12	0.56137
	LR	Feature Set 1	0.55799
pos-neutral	LR	Feature Set 4	**0.71325**
	SVM	Feature Set 4	0.70602
	SVM	Feature Set 1	0.68333
	LR	Feature Set 1	0.67619
	SVM	Feature Set 7	0.66508
	SVM	Feature Set 11	0.66180
	LR	Feature Set 7	0.66033
	LR	Feature Set 11	0.65693

Table 2: Validation Accuracy for different classifier/Feature Set combinations.

Starting System Fscore on the test set	0.26
Final system Fscore on the test set	0.51

Table 3: Fscore of the whole system when using the least performing classifier/feature set combinations and when using the best performing classifier/feature set combination.

4   Results and Analysis

Table 3 shows the least Fscore of the system we started with (features set 1 for all classifiers in the system) and the final system fscore before submission on our test set. We used fscore as the overall system performance measure and not the system accuracy. However, we have put the validation accuracy as the top classifier/feature set combination selection criteria for the individual classifiers in our system while setting class weights to auto in all of our classifiers in our system. It is clear from Table 1.0 that feature categories 2 and 4 were associated with the best performing classifiers. As mentioned earlier feature category 2 uses word vectors in addition to the base features in feature set 1. While feature category 4 uses word vectors and paragraph vectors with feature set 1. Which indicates that the addition of paragraph vectors with word2vec vectors gave best validation accuracies with the positive/negative and the pos/neg/neutral classifiers. However, it did not give the best validation accuracies with the positive/neutral and negative/nonnegative classifiers. As Feature category 2 that uses word vectors with feature set 1 gave the best validation accuracies with the positive/neutral and the negative/nonnegative classifiers. Finally, using only paragraph vectors with feature set 1 yielded the best validation accuracy with the negative/neutral classifier. Even though our doc2vec model was only trained on data from the target domain (tweets), it managed to give slightly better validation accuracy than when using word2vec vectors trained on the source (amazon reviews) and target (tweets) domains combined. Nonetheless, for positive/negative, positive/neutral, negative/nonnegative, positive/negative/neutral classification using word2vec vectors that were generated by our word2vec models trained on the source and target domains combined gave better validation set accuracies than when using only the doc2vec vectors generated by our doc2vec model that was trained on the full_training_set (tweets) with feature set 1 only. Since Le et al. (2014) concluded that paragraph vectors are competitive with the state of the art word representation methods. We inferred based on our results that combining the source and target data to train our word2vec models would give better results than when training them only on the target data. Thus the external source data helped in building word2vec models that gave us more powerful features when compared to those generated by doc2vec (paragraph vector) models trained only on the target data (tweets in full_training_set).

5   Conclusion

Our approach resulted in higher prediction accuracies on the 2016 twitter test data set outperforming eight teams that had better AvgF1scores. Two of the eight teams were in the top 10 in terms of AvgF1scores. In the future, we will focus more on cross domain word representation as illustrated in Bollegala et al. (2015) for improving our transfer learning approach.

References

Bing Liu and Minqing Hu. 2004. *Mining and Summarizing Customer Reviews*. In Proceedings of KDD'04, August 22-25, 2004, Seattle, Washington, USA.

Quoc Le and Tomas Mikolov. 2014. *Distributed Representations of Sentences and Documents*. Proceedings of the 31st International Conference on Machine Learning, Beijing, China.

Danushka Bollegala, Takanori Maehara, and Ken-ichi Kawarabayashi. 2015. *Unsupervised Cross-Domain Word Representation Learning*. In Proceedings of the 53rd Annual Meeting of the Association for Computational Linguistics and the 7th International Joint Conference on Natural Language Processing, Beijing, China.

Carlos Guestrin, and Emily Fox. 2015. *Machine Learning Foundations: A Case Study Approach*. By the University of Washington on Coursera, Seattle, WA.

Sara Rosenthal, Preslav Nakov, Svetlana Kiritchenko, Saif M Mohammad, Alan Ritter, and Veselin Stoyanov. 2015. SemEval-2015 Task 10: Sentiment Analysis in Twitter. *In Proceedings of the 9th International Workshop on Semantic Evaluation (SemEval 2015)*. Association for Computational Linguistics, Denver, Colorado.

Preslav Nakov, Alan Ritter, Sara Rosenthal, Veselin Stoyanov and Fabrizio Sebastiani. 2016. SemEval-

2016 Task 4: Sentiment Analysis in Twitter. *In Proceedings of the 10th International Workshop on Semantic Evaluation (SemEval 2016)*. Association for Computational Linguistics, San Diego, California.

Appendix A. Feature Sets.

The following table shows the contents of each feature Set referenced above.

Set	Features included
1	['tfidf','1gram features','2gram features','3gram features']
2	['tfidf','1gram features','2gram features','3gram features','w2v_vectors_pos_neg','w2v_vectors_pos_neutral','w2v_vectors_pos_ornot','w2v_vectors_neg_ornot']
3	['tfidf','1gram features','2gram features','3gram features','w2v_vectors_neutral_neg','w2v_vectors_neg_ornot','w2v_vectors_neutral_ornot']
4	['tfidf','1gram features','2gram features','3gram features','w2v_vectors_pos_neutral','w2v_vectors_pos_ornot','w2v_vectors_neutral_ornot']
5	['tfidf','1gram features','2gram features','3gram features','w2v_vectors_neg_ornot','w2v_vectors_pos_neg','w2v_vectors_pos_neutral','w2v_vectors_neutral_neg','w2v_vectors_pos_ornot','w2v_vectors_neutral_ornot']
6	['tfidf','1gram features','2gram features','3gram features','w2v_vectors_neg_ornot']
7	['tfidf','1gram features','2gram features','3gram features','vectors_doc2vec_tweetsonly_dm']
8	['tfidf','1gram features','2gram features','3gram features','w2v_vectors_pos_neg','w2v_vectors_pos_neutral','w2v_vectors_pos_ornot','w2v_vectors_neg_ornot','vectors_doc2vec_tweetsonly_dm']
9	['tfidf','1gram features','2gram features','3gram features','w2v_vectors_neg_ornot','vectors_doc2vec_tweetsonly_dm']
10	['tfidf','1gram features','2gram features','3gram features','w2v_vectors_neutral_neg','w2v_vectors_neg_ornot','w2v_vectors_neutral_ornot','vectors_doc2vec_tweetsonly_dm']
11	['tfidf','1gram features','2gram features','3gram features','w2v_vectors_pos_neutral','w2v_vectors_pos_ornot','w2v_vectors_neutral_ornot','vectors_doc2vec_tweetsonly_dm']
12	['tfidf','1gram features','2gram features','3gram features','w2v_vectors_neg_ornot','w2v_vectors_pos_neg','w2v_vectors_pos_neutral','w2v_vectors_neutral_neg','w2v_vectors_pos_ornot','w2v_vectors_neutral_ornot','vectors_doc2vec_tweetsonly_dm']

Appendix B. Feature Categories.

The following table shows mapping of feature sets to categories.

Feature Sets	Feature Category
1	1
2, 3,4,5,6	2
7	3
8, 9,10,11,12	4

Appendix C. System Flowchart.

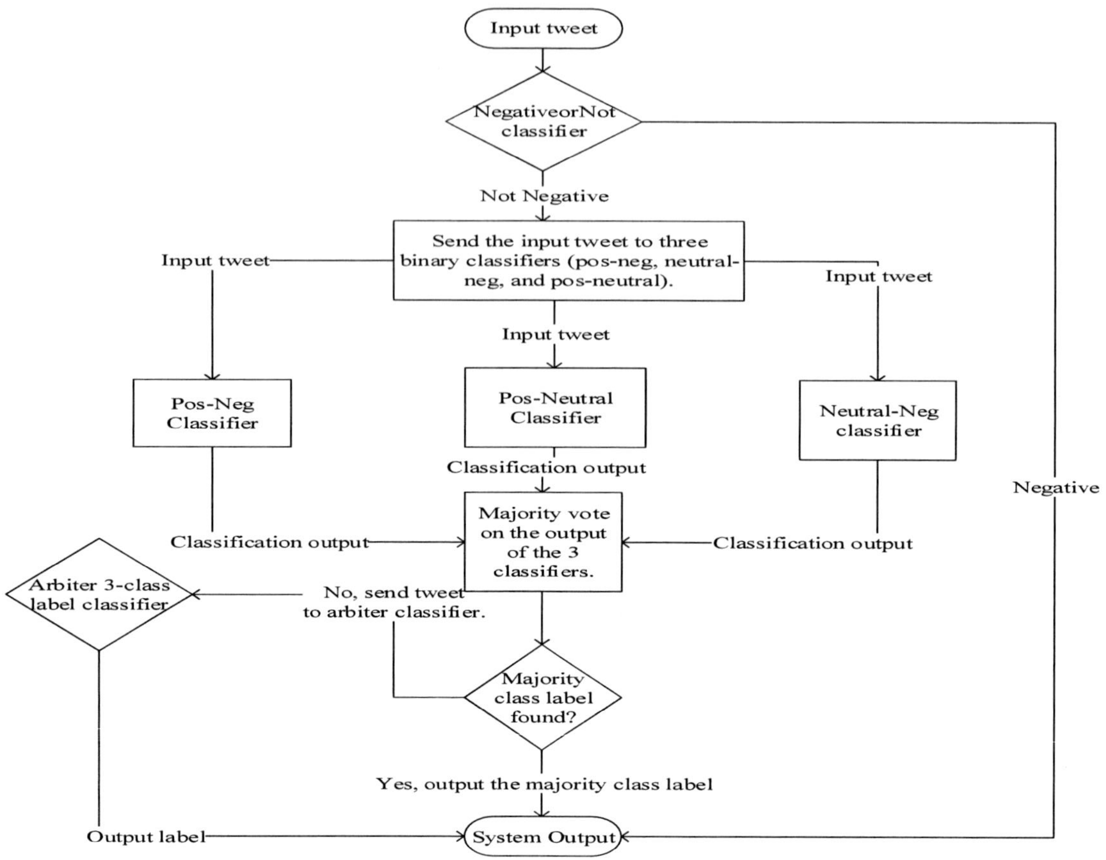

NRU-HSE at SemEval-2016 Task 4: Comparative Analysis of Two Iterative Methods Using Quantification Library

Nikolay Karpov, Alexander Porshnev, Kirill Rudakov

National Research University Higher School of Economics
25/12 Bolshaja Pecherskaja str. 603155
Nizhny Novgorod, Russia
{nkarpov, aporshnev}@hse.ru, rudakovkirillx@gmail.com

Abstract

In many areas, such as social science, politics or market research, people need to track sentiment and their changes over time. For sentiment analysis in this field it is more important to correctly estimate proportions of each sentiment expressed in the set of documents (quantification task) than to accurately estimate sentiment of a particular document (classification). Basically, our study was aimed to analyze the effectiveness of two iterative quantification techniques and to compare their effectiveness with baseline methods. All the techniques are evaluated using a set of synthesized data and the SemEval-2016 Task4 dataset. We made the quantification methods from this paper available as a Python open source library. The results of comparison and possible limitations of the quantification techniques are discussed.

1 Introduction

In many areas, such as customer-relationship management or opinion mining, people need to track changes over time and measure proportions of documents expressing different sentiments. In these situations, the task of accurate categorization of each document is replaced by the task of providing accurate proportions of documents from each class (quantification). George Forman suggested defining the 'quantification task' as finding the best estimate for the amount of cases in each class in a test set, using a training set with substantially different class distribution (Forman, 2008).

Application of the quantification approach in opinion mining (Esuli et al., 2010), network-behavior analysis (Tang et al., 2010), word-sense disambiguation (Chan and Ng, 2006), remote sensing (Guerrero-Curieses et al., 2009), quality control (Sánchez et al., 2008), monitoring support-call logs (Forman et al., 2006) and credit scoring (Hand and others, 2006) showed high performance even with a relatively small training set.

Although quantification techniques are able to provide accurate sentiment analysis of proportions in situations of distribution drift, the question of optimal technique for analysis of tweets still raises a lot of questions. It is worth mentioning that sentiment analysis of tweets presents additional challenges to natural language processing, because of the small amount of text (less than 140 characters in each document), usage of creative spelling (e.g. "happpyyy", "some1 yg bner2 tulus"), abbreviations (such as "wth" or "lol"), informal constructions ("hahahaha yava quiet so !ma I m bored av even home nw") and hashtags (BREAKING: US GDP growth is back! #kidding), which are a type of tagging for Twitter messages.

In our paper we used several quantification methods mentioned in literature as the best ones and evaluated them by comparing their effectiveness with one another and with baseline methods.

The paper is organized as follows. In Section 2, we first look at the notation, then we briefly overview six methods to solve the quantification problem. Section 3 describes two datasets we use in our research. Section 4 describes the results of our experiments, while Section 5 concludes the work defining open research issues for further investigation.

2 Quantification Methods

In this section we describe the methods used to handle changes in class distribution.

First, let us give some definition of notation.

X: vector representation of observation x;

$C = \{c_1, \ldots, c_n\}$: classes of observations, where n is the number of classes;

$p_S(c)$: a true prior probability (aka "prevalence" of class c in the set S;

$\hat{p}_S(c_j)$: estimated prevalence of c_j using the set S;

$\hat{p}_S^M(c_j)$: estimated $\hat{p}_S(c_j)$ obtained via method M;

171

Proceedings of SemEval-2016, pages 171–177,
San Diego, California, June 16-17, 2016. ©2016 Association for Computational Linguistics

$p(c_j /x)$: a posteriori probabilitiesto classify an observation x to the class c_j;

$TRAIN, TEST$: training and test sets of observations, respectively;

$TEST_c$: a subset of $TEST$ set where each observation falls within class c;

$TEST\_CD = \{p_{TEST}(c_i)\}$; $i=\overline{1,n}$: class probability distribution of the test set;

$TRAIN\_CD = \{p_{TRAIN}(c_i)\}$; $i=\overline{1,n}$: class probability distribution of the training set;

The problem we study has some training set, which provides us with a set of labeled examples – TRAIN, with class distribution TRAIN_CD. At some point the distribution of data changes to a new, but unknown class distribution – TEST_CD, and this distribution provides a set of unlabeled examples – TEST. Given this terminology, we can state our quantification problem more precisely.

2.1 Classify and Count

The first approach provides information about proportions of document in each class just by classification of each document. In this case, the process starts with training the best available classifier, applying it to the test set and counting the amount of documents in each class. Forman named this obvious approach as Classify and Count (CC) (Forman, 2008).

The observed count P of positives from the classifier will include both true positives and false positives, P = TP + FP, as characterized by the standard 2 × 2 confusion matrix.

Classifier Predictions:

Actual\Prediction	P_	N_
P	TP	FN
N	FP	TN

2.2 Adjusted Classify and Count

Adjusted Classify and Count (ACC – aka the "confusion matrix model" quantification method (Forman, 2005) consists of six steps:

1. training a binary classifier on the entire training set
2. estimating its characteristics via many-fold cross-validation (tpr = TP/P and fpr = FP/N)
3. applying the classifier to the test set
4. counting the number of test cases on which the classifier outputs positives
5. estimating the true percentage of positives via Equation (1)

$$\hat{p}^{ACC}(c) = \frac{\hat{p}_{cc}(c) - fpr(c)}{tpr(c) - fpr(c)} \qquad (1)$$

6. clipping the output to the feasible range.

As mentioned by Forman, the performance of the ACC method degrades severely in the situation of a highly imbalanced training sample. If one of the classes is rare in the training set, the classifier will learn not to vote for this class because of tpr = 0%. Small denominator ($tpr - fpr$) in Equation (1) makes the quotient highly sensitive in the estimation of tpr or fpr, and this leads to low quantification accuracy especially at the small training sets with high class imbalance (Forman et al., 2006).

2.3 Probabilistic Classify and Count

The Probabilistic Classify and Count (PCC) method differs from the CC algorithm by counting the expected share of positive predicted documents, i.e. the probability of membership in class c of observation x_i after classifying documents in the TEST set.

$$\hat{p}_{TEST}^{PCC}(c) = \frac{\sum_{x_i \in TEST} p(c|x_i)}{|TEST|} \qquad (2)$$

2.4 Probabilistic Adjusted Classify and Count

The central idea of the Probabilistic Adjusted Classify and Count (PACC) algorithm is evidently to combine two algorithms above – ACC and PCC. $\hat{p}_{cc}(c)$, $fpr(c)$, $tpr(c)$ should be replaced by their expected values, i.e.

$$\hat{p}^{CC}(c) \sim \hat{p}^{PCC}(c),$$

$$tpr(c) \sim E\{tpr(c)\},$$

$$fpr(c) \sim E\{fpr(c)\},$$

where

$$E\{tpr(c)\} = \frac{\sum_{x_i \in TEST_c} p(c|x_i)}{|TEST_c|}$$

$$E\{fpr(c)\} = \frac{\sum_{x_i \in TEST_{\bar{c}}} p(c|x_i)}{|TEST_{\bar{c}}|}$$

then the form of the PACC is

$$\hat{p}^{PACC}(c) = \frac{\hat{p}^{PCC}(c) - E\{fpr(c)\}}{E\{tpr(c)\} - E\{fpr(c)\}} \qquad (3)$$

2.5 Expectation Maximization

A simple procedure to adjust the outputs of a classifier to a new a priori probability is described in the study by (Saerens et al., 2002).

$$p(c_j/x_k) = \frac{\frac{p\,TEST(c_j)}{p\,TRAIN(c_j)}\hat{p}(c_j/x_k)}{\sum_{i=1}^{n}\frac{p\,TEST(c_i)}{p\,TRAIN(c_i)}\hat{p}(c_i/x_k)} \qquad (4)$$

It is important that authors suggest using not only the well-known formula (4) to compute the corrected a posteriori probabilities, but also an iterative procedure to adjust the outputs of the trained classier with respect to these new a priori probabilities, without having to refit the model, even when these probabilities are not known in advance.

To make the Expectation Maximization (EM) method clear, we specify its algorithm in Figure1 using a pseudo-code. The algorithm begins with counting start values for class probability distribution, using labels on the training set TRAIN (line 1), builds an initial classifier C_i from the TRAIN set (line 2) and classifies each item in the unlabeled TEST set (line3), where the `classify` functions return the a posteriori probabilities (`TEST_prob`) for the specified datasets. The algorithm then iterates in lines 4-9 until the maximum number of iterations (`maxIterations`) is reached. In this loop, the algorithm first uses the previous a posteriori probabilities TEST_prob to estimate a new a priori probability (line 6). Then, in line 7, a posteriori probabilities are computed using Equation (4). Finally, once the loop terminates, the last posteriori probabilities returns (line 9).

```
EM (TRAIN, TEST)
1.TEST_CD = prevalence(TRAIN)
2. C_i = build_clf(TRAIN)
3. TEST_prob = classify(C_i, TEST)
4. for (i=1; i<maxIterations; i++)
5. {
6.  TEST_CD = prevalence(TEST_prob)
7.  TEST_prob = bayes(TEST_CD, TEST_prob)
8. }
9. return TEST_CD
```
Figure 1: Pseudo-code for the EM algorithm.

To build a classifier in the function `build_clf`, we use support vector machines (SVM) with linear kernel.

2.6 Iterative Class Distribution Estimation

Another interesting method is iterative cost-sensitive class distribution estimation (CDEIterate) described in the study by (Xue and Weiss, 2009).

The main idea of this method is to retrain a classifier at each iteration, where the iterations progressively improve the quantification accuracy of performing the «classify and count» method via the generated cost-sensitive classifiers.

For the CDE-based method, the final prevalence is induced from the TRAIN labeled set with the cost of classes COST. The COST value is computed with Equation (5), utilizing the class distribution calculated during the previous step TEST_CD. For each iteration, we recalculate:

$$COST = \frac{TEST\_CD}{TRAIN\_CD} \qquad (5)$$

The CDEIterate algorithm is specified in Figure 2, using the pseudo-code. The algorithm begins with counting the class distribution TRAIN_CD for training labels TRAIN (line 1). Then it builds an initial classifier C_i from the TRAIN set (line 2). In a loop, this algorithm uses the previous classifier C_i to classify the unlabeled TEST set by estimating a posterior probability TEST_prob for each item in a test set (line 5). Then, in line 6, the a priory probability distribution is computed and the cost ratio information is updated (line 7). In line 8, a new cost-sensitive classifier C_i is generated using the TRAIN set with the updated cost ratioCOST. The algorithm then iterates in lines 4-9 until the maximum number of iterations (`maxIterations`) is reached. Finally, once the loop terminates, the last a priory probability distribution of classes is returned TEST_CD (line 10).

```
CDEIterate (TRAIN, TEST, COST_start)
1.TRAIN_CD = prevalence(TRAIN)
2. C_i = build_clf(TRAIN, COST_start)
3. for (i=1; i<maxIterations; i++)
4. {
5.  TEST_prob= classify(C_i, TEST)
6.  TEST_CD = prevalence(TEST_prob)
7.  COST = TEST_CD/TRAIN_CD
8.C_i = build_clf(TRAIN, COST)
9. }
10. return TEST_CD
```
Figure 2: Pseudo-code for the CDE-Iterate algorithm.

To build a cost-sensitive classifier in the function `build_clf`, we tried a few ones and chose a fast logistic regression classifier.

We did not find any open library where baseline quantification methods were implemented. We, therefore, shared all the algorithms, which we had programmed using the Python language, on the Github repository[1]. We believe that this library can help pool information on quantification.

3 Experiment Methodology

This section describes our experimental setup. It describes the datasets we use, the specific experiments we run and the classifier induction algorithm we employ.

3.1 Simulations on Artificial Data

We present a simple experiment that illustrates the efficiency of iterative adjustment of the a priori probabilities.

---

[1]https://github.com/Arctickirillas/Rubrication

We use random sample generators from SkiKit-Learn Library to build artificial datasets of controlled size and complexity[2]. For each dataset we generate 10,000 records with 10 features. Figure 3 exemplifies 2 features of a dataset with two classes.

The initial prevalence for classes c_1 and c_2 was equal ($p_{train}(c_1) = p_{train}(c_2) = 0.5$). The total set randomly splits into two subsets: 25% training set, 75% test set. For the training set, the class distribution remains unchanged. For the test set, we vary prevalence value $p_{test}(c_1)$ from 0.05 to 0.95.

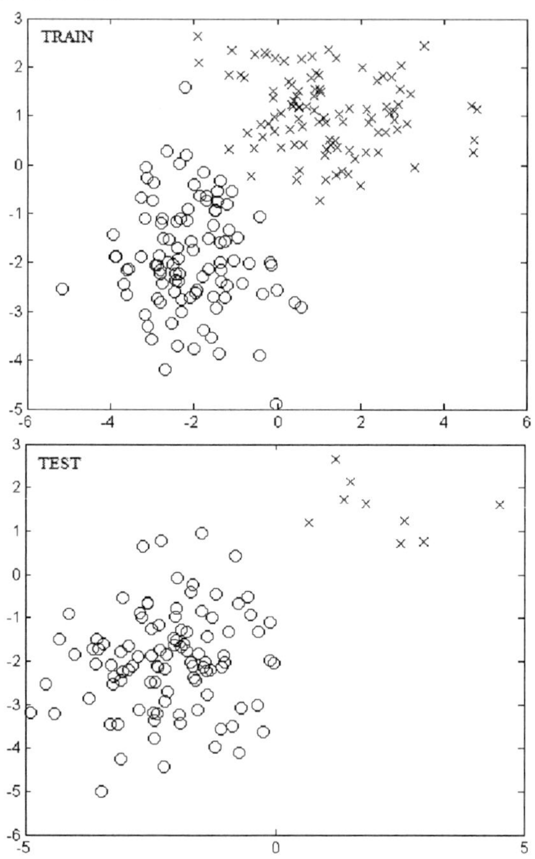

Figure 3: An example of TRAIN and TEST dataset items with TRAIN_CD = {0.5, 0.5} and TEST_CD = {0.1, 0.9} respectively (generated with 2 features).

For each prevalence value we generate a hundred different test sets. Therefore, nineteen hundred replications of the following experimental design are applied.

We used a Kullback-Leibler Divergence (KLD) between the true class prevalence and the predicted class prevalence as a quality evaluation metrics for quantifiers.

3.2 Test Dataset

To evaluate the algorithms on the real data, we participated in the SemEval-2016 Task 4 called "Sentiment Analysis in Twitter". Its dataset consists of Twitter messages (aka observations) divided into several topics. Task 4 consists of five subtasks, but we only participated in subtasks D and E: tweet quantification according to a two-point scale and five-point scale, respectively. These subtasks are evaluated independently for different topics, and the final result is counted as an average of evaluation measure out of all the topics (Nakov et al., 2016).

The organizers provide a default split of the data into training, development and development-time testing datasets. The algorithms evaluation is performed using these subsets. The training subset is used as a TRAIN set, development and development-time testing subsets are used as a TEST set.

Since observation x in this dataset is a message written in a natural language, we first need to transform it to the vector representation X. Based on a study by (Gao and Sebastiani, 2015), we choose the following components of the feature vector:

- TFIDF for word n-grams with n varying from 1 to 4

- TFIDF character n-grams where n varies from 3 to 5.

Feature vector is extracted with a Scikit_Learn tool[3]. We also perform data preprocessing .Several text patterns (e.g. links, emoticons, numbers) were replaced with their substitutes. For word n-grams we apply lemmatization using WordNetLemmatizer.

It is interesting to characterize messages using the SentiWordNet library. For each token x_i in document X we obtain its polarity value from the SentiWordNet. First, we recognize the part of speech using a speech tagger from the NLTK library (Bird et al., 2009). Second, we get the SentiWordNet first polarity value for this token using the part of speech information.

We used polarity values to extend vector representation of documents in two ways: first we simply calculate the polarity score as a sum of positive minus a sum of negative polarity values and add this feature to the vector representation of a document. Second, we calculate the sum of positive polarities and the sum of negative

---

[2]http://scikit-learn.org/stable/modules/generated/sklearn.datasets.make_classification.html

[3]http://scikit-learn.org/stable/modules/generated/sklearn.feature_extraction.text.TfidfVectorizer.html

polarities and add these two features to the vector representation of a document.

The metrics that we use to evaluate the classifier performance are described in (Nakov et al., 2016) and are not described here.

4 Experiment Results

We apply six quantification methods mentioned above in Section 2: CC, PCC, ACC, PACC, EM, CDEIterate and compare them.

4.1 Synthesized Data

First, we applied CC, PCC, ACC, PACC, EM and CDEIterate algorithms to generated data described in Section 3.1. Synthesized data allows us to perform a comparative analysis of these quantification methods with different amount of distribution drift.

In Figure3, which demonstrates the means and standard deviation values of the evaluation measure – Kullback-Leibler Divergence (KLD), each point is obtained by averaging over one hundred generated datasets with different prevalence.

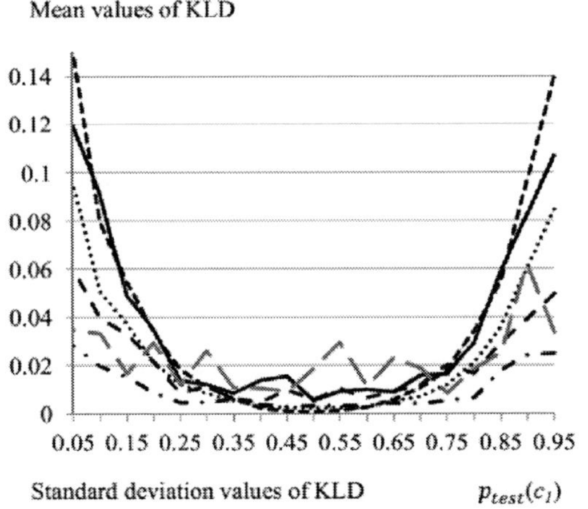

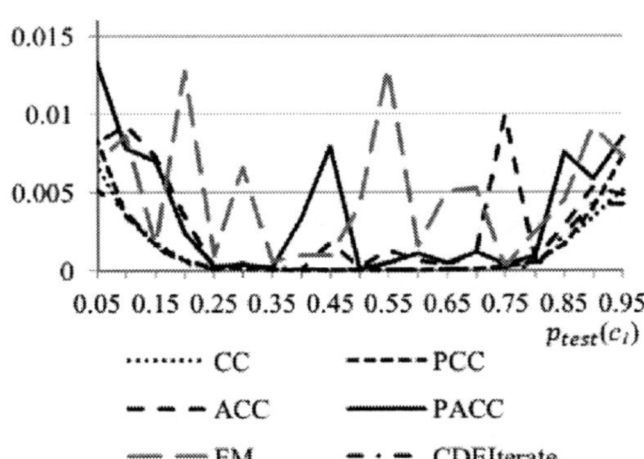

Figure 4: Mean and standard deviation values of Kullback-Leibler Divergence for different distribution drifts in the TEST set on the linear scale.

It is obvious from Figure 4 that the CDEIterate approach shows the lowest KLD mean values when a distribution drift is relatively large. A standard deviation value for the CDEIterate method remains the smallest one among all possible distribution drifts.

On the contrary, the EM approach shows very unstable results. Sometimes the EM algorithm converges far from the real value. Its standard deviation displays the same unstable behavior.

For more careful consideration, let us show its functions in the logarithmic scale in Figure 5.

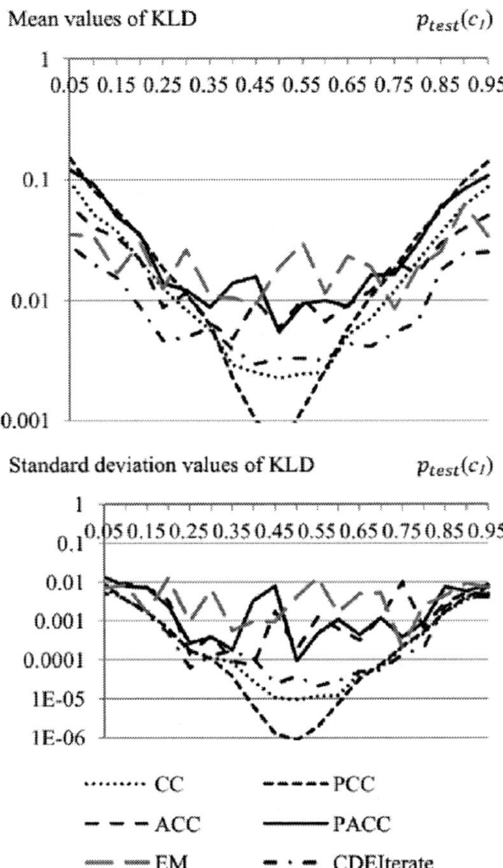

Figure 5: Mean and standard deviation values of Kullback-Leibler Divergence for different distribution drifts in the TEST set on the logarithmic scale.

When distribution changes from the starting value $p_{train}(c) = 0.5$ by less than 0.1, the simple methods like CC and PCC show better performance (lower KLD).

4.2 Test Data

We noticed that CDEIterate methods sometimes converge to different values, if an algorithm starts iteration from a different starting point. To support this, we add the `COST_start` variable to the algorithm shown in Figure 2. The first starting point is a priori probability distribution of a training set. Therefore, for the starting iteration we assume TEST_CD to equal TRAIN_CD. The second starting point is when TEST_CD is uniformly distributed. This case is labeled as CDEIterate_U. In the previous Section 4.1, these two starting points were actually the same.

Method	Quantification accuracy measure
CC	0.102469788749
ACC	0.192896311253
PCC	0.24076249451
PACC	0.23644037492
EM	0.24076249451
CDEIterate	0.101057466171
CDEIterate_U	0.0886349793929

Table1: Comparison of methods on test sample with a two-point scale (SemEval-2016 Task4 Subtask D).

Method	Quantification accuracy measure
CC	0.940764808798
ACC	0.878280429893
PCC	1.02616631747
PACC	1.04546915144
EM	1.12790745311
CDEIterate	0.538279399063
CDEIterate_U	0.536691406139

Table 2: Comparison of methods ontest sample with a five-point scale (SemEval-2016 Task4 Subtask E).

CDEIterate_U approach showed the best accuracy on the testing set among others with both five-point and two-point scales.

SentiWordNet is usually regarded as an important source of information about word sentiment (Baccianella et al., 2010; Esuli and Sebastiani, 2006). In our comparison, we add the sum of positive scores and the sum of negative scores of each word as two additional features to the feature vector. Only the first meaning, according to the recognized part of speech, was used. The quantification methods remain the same. The results provided in Table 3, show that the new features increase quantification accuracy for CC, ACC, but surprisingly decrease it for PCC, PACC, EM, CDEIterate and CDEIterate-U.

Method	Quantification accuracy measure
CC	0.868282929268
ACC	0.861784553862
PCC	1.05532269963
PACC	1.0731851762
EM	1.11319538187
CDEIterate	0.58872710467
CDEIterate_U	0.587811269105

Table 3: Comparison of methods on test sample with a five-point scale with additional SentiWordNet features (SemEval-2016 Task4 Subtask E).

We explain this behavior as follows: simple algorithms cannot adjust to the whole singularity and such additional features increase dimension and, thereby, accuracy. In a more complex case, the classifier extracts information from features more efficiently. Additional information about polarity scores leads to algorithm overtraining. We can guess that, as tweets contain creative spelling and abbreviation common in Twitter (like "lol", not presented in SentiWordNet), the existence of character n-grams contains more specific information than polarity scores of selected, properly written words. Therefore, we exclude SentiWordNet features from the final feature vector.

5 Conclusion and future work

The aim of this research was to perform comparative analysis of different approaches of state-of-the-art quantification techniques.

For tweet quantification on a five-point scale (Subtask E) and a two-point scale (Subtask D), the best performance was demonstrated by the adopted iterative method proposed by (Xue and Weiss, 2009), based on the iterative procedure with the cost-sensitive supervise learner. All the algorithms mentioned in the article, are available on the Github repository[4].

In our future work, we are planning to move in two directions. First, we plan to extend the vector of features used for representation of documents. Second, we want to add more quantification methods to our open source library.

Acknowledgments

The reported study was funded by RFBR under research Project No. 16-06-00184 A.

References

Stefano Baccianella, Andrea Esuli, and Fabrizio Sebastiani. 2010. SentiWordNet 3.0: An Enhanced Lexical Resource for Sentiment Analysis and Opinion Mining. In *LREC*, volume 10, pages 2200–2204.

Steven Bird, Ewan Klein, and Edward Loper. 2009. *Natural language processing with Python*. O'Reilly Media, Inc.

Yee Seng Chan and Hwee Tou Ng. 2006. Estimating class priors in domain adaptation for word sense disambiguation. In *Proceedings of the 21st International Conference on Computational Linguistics and the 44th an-*

---

[4]https://github.com/Arctickirillas/Rubrication

nual meeting of the Association for Computational Linguistics, pages 89–96. Association for Computational Linguistics.

Andrea Esuli and Fabrizio Sebastiani. 2006. Sentiwordnet: A publicly available lexical resource for opinion mining. In *Proceedings of LREC*, volume 6, pages 417–422. Citeseer.

Andrea Esuli, Fabrizio Sebastiani, and Ahmed ABBASI. 2010. Sentiment quantification. *IEEE intelligent systems*, 25(4):72–79.

George Forman. 2005. Counting positives accurately despite inaccurate classification. In *Machine Learning: ECML 2005*, pages 564–575. Springer. bibtex: forman2005counting.

George Forman. 2008. Quantifying counts and costs via classification. *Data Mining and Knowledge Discovery*, 17(2):164–206, June.

George Forman, Evan Kirshenbaum, and Jaap Suermondt. 2006. Pragmatic text mining: minimizing human effort to quantify many issues in call logs. In *Proceedings of the 12th ACM SIGKDD international conference on Knowledge discovery and data mining*, pages 852–861. ACM.

Wei Gao and Fabrizio Sebastiani. 2015. Tweet Sentiment: From Classification to Quantification. In *Proceedings of the 2015 IEEE/ACM International Conference on Advances in Social Networks Analysis and Mining 2015*, pages 97–104. ACM. bibtex: gao2015tweet.

A. Guerrero-Curieses, R. Alaiz-Rodriguez, and J. Cid-Sueiro. 2009. Cost-sensitive and modular land-cover classification based on posterior probability estimates. *International Journal of Remote Sensing*, 30(22):5877–5899.

David J. Hand and others. 2006. Classifier technology and the illusion of progress. *Statistical science*, 21(1):1–14.

Preslav Nakov, Alan Ritter, Sara Rosenthal, Veselin Stoyanov, and Fabrizio Sebastiani. 2016. SemEval-2016 Task 4: Sentiment Analysis in Twitter. In *Proceedings of the 10th International Workshop on Semantic Evaluation (SemEval 2016)*, San Diego, California, June. Association for Computational Linguistics. bibtex: SemEval:2016:task4.

Marco Saerens, Patrice Latinne, and Christine Decaestecker. 2002. Adjusting the outputs of a classifier to new a priori probabilities: a simple procedure. *Neural computation*, 14(1):21–41. bibtex: saerens2002adjusting.

Lidia Sánchez, Víctor González, Enrique Alegre, and Rocío Alaiz. 2008. Classification and quantification based on image analysis for sperm samples with uncertain damaged/intact cell proportions. In *Image Analysis and Recognition*, pages 827–836. Springer.

Lei Tang, Huiji Gao, and Huan Liu. 2010. Network quantification despite biased labels. In *Proceedings of the Eighth Workshop on Mining and Learning with Graphs*, pages 147–154. ACM.

Jack Chongjie Xue and Gary M Weiss. 2009. Quantification and semi-supervised classification methods for handling changes in class distribution. In *Proceedings of the 15th ACM SIGKDD international conference on Knowledge discovery and data mining*, pages 897–906. ACM. bibtex: xue2009quantification.

INSIGHT-1 at SemEval-2016 Task 4: Convolutional Neural Networks for Sentiment Classification and Quantification

Sebastian Ruder[12]   **Parsa Ghaffari[2]**   **John G. Breslin[1]**

[1]Insight Centre for Data Analytics
National University of Ireland, Galway
`firstname.lastname@insight-centre.org`

[2]Aylien Ltd.
Dublin, Ireland
`firstname@aylien.com`

Abstract

This paper describes our deep learning-based approach to sentiment analysis in Twitter as part of SemEval-2016 Task 4. We use a convolutional neural network to determine sentiment and participate in all subtasks, i.e. two-point, three-point, and five-point scale sentiment classification and two-point and five-point scale sentiment quantification. We achieve competitive results for two-point scale sentiment classification and quantification, ranking fifth and a close fourth (third and second by alternative metrics) respectively despite using only pre-trained embeddings that contain no sentiment information. We achieve good performance on three-point scale sentiment classification, ranking eighth out of 35, while performing poorly on five-point scale sentiment classification and quantification. An error analysis reveals that this is due to low expressiveness of the model to capture negative sentiment as well as an inability to take into account ordinal information. We propose improvements in order to address these and other issues.

1 Introduction

Social media allows hundreds of millions of people to interact and engage with each other, while expressing their thoughts about the things that move them. Sentiment analysis (Pang and Lee, 2008) allows us to gain insights about opinions towards persons, objects, and events in the public eye and is used nowadays to gauge public opinion towards companies or products, to analyze customer satisfaction, and to detect trends.

Its immediacy allowed Twitter to become an important platform for expressing opinions and public discourse, while the accessibility of large quantities of data in turn made it the focal point of social media sentiment analysis research.

Recently, deep learning-based approaches have demonstrated remarkable results for text classification and sentiment analysis (Kim, 2014) and have performed well for phrase-level and message-level sentiment classification (Severyn and Moschitti, 2015).

Past SemEval competitions in Twitter sentiment analysis (Rosenthal et al., 2014; Rosenthal et al., 2015) have contributed to shape research in this field. SemEval-2016 Task 4 (Nakov et al., 2016) is no exception, as it introduces both quantification and five-point-scale classification tasks, neither of which have been tackled with deep learning-based approaches before.

We apply our deep learning-based model for sentiment analysis to all subtasks of SemEval-2016 Task 4: three-point scale message polarity classification (subtask A), two-point and five-point scale topic sentiment classification (subtasks B and C respectively), and two-point and five-point scale topic sentiment quantification (subtasks D and E respectively).

Our model achieves excellent results for subtasks B and D, ranks competitively for subtask A, while performing poorly for subtasks C and E. We perform an error analysis of our model to obtain a better understanding of strengths and weaknesses of a deep learning-based approach particularly for these new tasks and subsequently propose improvements.

Proceedings of SemEval-2016, pages 178–182,
San Diego, California, June 16-17, 2016. ©2016 Association for Computational Linguistics

2 Related work

Deep-learning based approaches have recently dominated the state-of-the-art in sentiment analysis. Kim (2014) uses a one-layer convolutional neural network to achieve top performance on various sentiment analysis datasets, demonstrating the utility of pre-trained embeddings.

State-of-the-art models in Twitter sentiment analysis leverage large amounts of data accessible on Twitter to further enhance their embeddings by treating smileys as noisy labels (Go et al., 2009): Tang et al. (2014) learn sentiment-specific word embeddings from such distantly supervised data and use these as features for supervised classification, while Severyn and Moschitti (2015) use distantly supervised data to fine-tune the embeddings of a convolutional neural network.

In contrast, we observe distantly supervised data not to be as important for some tasks as long as sufficient training data is available.

3 Model

The model architecture we use is an extension of the CNN structure used by Collobert et al. (2011).

The model takes as input a text, which is padded to length n. We represent the text as a concatenation of its word embeddings $x_{1:n}$ where $x_i \in \mathbb{R}^k$ is the k-dimensional vector of the i-th word in the text.

The convolutional layer slides filters of different window sizes over the word embeddings. Each filter with weights $w \in \mathbb{R}^{hk}$ generates a new feature c_i for a window of h words according to the following operation:

$$c_i = f(w \cdot x_{i:i+h-1} + b) \qquad (1)$$

Note that $b \in \mathbb{R}$ is a bias term and f is a non-linear function, ReLU (Nair and Hinton, 2010) in our case. The application of the filter over each possible window of h words or characters in the sentence produces the following feature map:

$$c = [c_1, c_2, ..., c_{n-h+1}] \qquad (2)$$

Max-over-time pooling in turn condenses this feature vector to its most important feature by taking its maximum value and naturally deals with variable input lengths.

A final softmax layer takes the concatenation of the maximum values of the feature maps produced by all filters and outputs a probability distribution over all output classes.

4 Methodology

4.1 Datasets

For every subtask, the organizers provide a training, development, and development test set for training and tuning. We use the concatenation of the training and development test set for each subtask for training and use the development set for validation.

Additionally, the organizers make training and development data from SemEval-2013 and trial data from 2016 available that can be used for training and tuning for subtask A and subtasks B, C, D, and E respectively. We experiment with adding these datasets to the respective subtask. Interestingly, adding them slightly increases loss on the validation set, while providing a significant performance boost on past development test sets, which we view as a proxy for performance on the 2016 test set. For this reason, we include these datasets for training of all our models.

We notably do not select the model that achieves the lowest loss on the validation set, but choose the one that maximizes the F_1^{PN} score, i.e. the arithmetic mean of the F_1 of positive and negative tweets, which has historically been used to evaluate the SemEval message polarity classification subtask. We observe that the lowest loss does not necessarily lead to the lowest F_1^{PN}, as it does not include F_1 of neutral tweets.

4.2 Pre-processing

For pre-processing, we use a script adapted from the pre-processing script[1] used for training GloVe vectors (Pennington et al., 2014). Besides normalizing urls and mentions, we notably normalize happy and sad smileys, extract hashtags, and insert tags for repeated, elongated, and all caps characters.

4.3 Word embeddings

Past research (Kim, 2014; Severyn and Moschitti, 2015) found a good initialization of word embed-

---

[1] http://nlp.stanford.edu/projects/glove/ preprocess-twitter.rb

dings to be crucial in training an accurate sentiment model.

We thus evaluate the following evaluation schemes: random initialization, initialization using pre-trained GloVe vectors, fine-tuning pre-trained embeddings on a distantly supervised corpus (Severyn and Moschitti, 2015), and fine-tuning pre-trained embeddings on 40k tweets with crowd-sourced Twitter annotations. Perhaps counter-intuitively, we find that fine-tuning embeddings on a distantly supervised or crowd-sourced corpus does not improve performance on past development test sets when including the additionally provided data for training. We hypothesize that additional training data facilitates learning of the underlying semantics, thereby reducing the need for sentiment-specific embeddings. Our scores partially echo this theory.

For this reason, we initialize our word embeddings simply with 200-dimensional GloVe vectors trained on 2B tweets. Word embeddings for unknown words are initialized randomly.

4.4 Hyperparameters and pre-processing

We tune hyperparameters over a wide range of values via random search on the validation set. We find that the following hyperparameters, which are similar to ones used by Kim (2014), yield the best performance across all subtasks: mini-batch size of 10, maximum sentence length of 50 tokens, word embedding size of 200 dimensions, dropout rate of 0.3, l_2 regularization of 0.01, filter lengths of 3, 4, and 5 with 100 filter maps each.

We train for 15 epochs using mini-batch stochastic gradient descent, the Adadelta update rule (Zeiler, 2012), and early stopping.

4.5 Task adaptation and quantification

To adapt our model to the different tasks, we simply adjust the number of output neurons to conform to the scale used in the task at hand (two-point scale in subtasks B and D, three-point scale in subtask A, five-point scale in subtasks C and E).

We perform a simple quantification for subtasks D and E by aggregating the classified tweets for each topic and reporting their distribution across sentiments. We would thus expect our results on subtasks B and D and results on subtasks C and E to be closely correlated.

Metric	Our score	Best score	Rank
F_1^{PN}	**0.593**	**0.633**	**8/34**
R^{PN}	0.616	0.670	12/34
Acc^{PN}	0.635	0.646	5/34

Table 1: Our score and rank for subtask A for each metric compared to the best team's score (results for official metric in bold).

	2013		2014			2015
	TW	SMS	TW	TW /s	LJ	TW
+	72.49	66.73	76.84	64.52	69.08	65.56
-	47.97	49.65	51.95	13.64	50.00	53.00
=	67.53	77.83	65.51	45.71	67.28	65.23

Table 2: F_1 scores of our model for positive, negative, and neutral tweets for each progress dataset of subtask A. TW: Tweet. /s: sarcasm. LJ: Live Journal. +: positive. -: negative. =: neutral.

5 Evaluation

We report results of our model in Tables 1 and 2 (subtask A), Table 3 (subtask B), Tables 5 and 6 (subtask C), Table 4 (subtask D), and Table 7 (subtask E). For some subtasks, the organizers make available alternative metrics. We observe that the choice of the scoring metric influences results considerably, with our system always placing higher if ranked by one of the alternative metrics.

Subtask A. We obtain competitive performance on subtask A in Table 1. Analysis of results on the progress test sets in Table 2 reveals that our system achieves competitive F_1 scores for positive and neutral tweets, but only low F_1 scores for negative tweets due to low recall. This is mirrored in Table 1, where we rank higher for accuracy than for recall. The scoring metric for subtask A, F_1^{POS} accentuates F_1 for positive and negative tweets, thereby ignoring our good performance on neutral tweets and leading to only mediocre ranks on the progress test sets for our system.

Subtasks B and D. We achieve a competitive fifth rank for subtask B by the official recall metric in Table 3. However, ranked by F_1 (as in subtask A), we place third – and second if ranked by accuracy. Similarly, for subtask D, we rank fourth (with a differential of 0.001 to the second rank) by KLD, but second and first if ranked by AE and RAE respectively. Jointly, these results demonstrate that classifi-

Metric	Our score	Best score	Rank
R	**0.767**	**0.797**	**5/19**
F_1	0.786	0.799	3/19
Acc	0.864	0.870	2/19

Table 3: Our score and rank for subtask B for each metric compared to the best team's score (results for official metric in bold).

Metric	Our score	Best score	Rank
KLD	**0.054**	**0.034**	**4/14**
AE	0.085	0.074	2/14
RAE	0.423	0.423	1/14

Table 4: Our score and rank for subtask D for each metric compared to the best team's score (results for official metric in bold).

cation performance is a good indicator for quantification without using any more sophisticated quantification methods. These results are in line with past research (Kim, 2014) showcasing that even a conceptually simple neural network-based approach can achieve excellent results given enough training data per class. These results also highlight that embeddings trained using distant supervision, which should be particularly helpful for this task as they are fine-tuned using the same classes, i.e. positive and negative, are not necessary given enough data.

Subtasks C and E. We achieve mediocre results for subtask C in Table 5, only ranking sixth – however, placing third by the alternative metric. Similarly, we only achieve an unsatisfactory eighth rank for subtask E in Table 7. An error analysis for subtask C in Table 6 reveals that the model is able to differentiate between neutral, positive, and very positive tweets with good accuracy. However, similarly to results in subtask A, we find that it lacks expressiveness for negative sentiment and completely fails to capture very negative tweets due to their low number in the training data. Additionally, it is unable to take into account sentiment order to reduce error for very positive and very negative tweets.

Metric	Our score	Best score	Rank
MAE^M	**1.006**	**0.719**	**6/11**
MAE^μ	0.607	0.580	3/11

Table 5: Our score and rank for subtask C for each metric compared to the best team's score (results for official metric in bold).

Sentiment	-2	-1	0	1	2
MAE^M	2.09	1.29	0.78	0.17	0.71

Table 6: Macro-averaged mean absolute error (MAE^M) of our model for each sentiment class for subtask C. Lower error is better.

Metric	Our score	Best score	Rank
EMD	**0.366**	**0.243**	**8/10**

Table 7: Our score and rank for subtask E compared to the best team's score.

5.1 Improvements

We propose different improvements to enable the model to better deal with some of the encountered challenges.

Negative sentiment. The easiest way to enable our model to better capture negative sentiment is to include more negative tweets in the training data. Additionally, using distantly supervised data for fine-tuning embeddings would likely have helped to mitigate this deficit. In order to allow the model to better differentiate between different sentiments on a five-point scale, it would be interesting to evaluate ways to create a more fine-grained distantly supervised corpus using e.g. a wider range of smileys and emoticons or certain hashtags indicating a high degree of elation or distress.

Ordinal classification. Instead of treating all classes as independent, we can enable the model to take into account ordinal information by simply modifying the labels as in (Cheng et al., 2008). A more sophisticated approach would organically integrate label-dependence into the network.

Quantification. Instead of deriving the topic-level sentiment distribution by predicting tweet-level sentiment, we can directly minimize the Kullback-Leibler divergence for each topic. If the feedback from optimizing this objective proves to be too indirect to provide sufficient signals, we can jointly optimize tweet-level as well as topic-level sentiment as in (Kotzias, 2015).

6 Conclusion

In this paper, we have presented our deep learning-based approach to Twitter sentiment analysis for two-point, three-point, and five-point scale sentiment classification and two-point and five-point scale sentiment quantification. We reviewed the different aspects we took into consideration in creating our model. We rank fifth and a close fourth (third and second by alternative metrics) on two-point scale classification and quantification despite using only pre-trained embeddings that contain no sentiment information. We analysed our weaker performance on three-point scale sentiment classification and five-point scale sentiment classification and quantification and found that the model lacks expressiveness to capture negative sentiment and is unable to take into account class order. Finally, we proposed improvements to resolve these deficits.

Acknowledgments

This project has emanated from research conducted with the financial support of the Irish Research Council (IRC) under Grant Number EBPPG/2014/30 and with Aylien Ltd. as Enterprise Partner. This publication has emanated from research supported in part by a research grant from Science Foundation Ireland (SFI) under Grant Number SFI/12/RC/2289.

References

Jianlin Cheng Jianlin Cheng, Zheng Wang Zheng Wang, and G. Pollastri. 2008. A neural network approach to ordinal regression. *2008 IEEE International Joint Conference on Neural Networks (IEEE World Congress on Computational Intelligence)*.

Ronan Collobert, Jason Weston, Leon Bottou, Michael Karlen, Koray Kavukcuoglu, and Pavel Kuksa. 2011. Natural Language Processing (almost) from Scratch. *Journal of Machine Learning Research*, 12(Aug):2493–2537.

Alec Go, Richa Bhayani, and Lei Huang. 2009. Twitter Sentiment Classification using Distant Supervision. *Processing*, 150(12):1–6.

Yoon Kim. 2014. Convolutional Neural Networks for Sentence Classification. *Proceedings of the Conference on Empirical Methods in Natural Language Processing*, pages 1746–1751.

Dimitrios Kotzias. 2015. From Group to Individual Labels using Deep Features.

Vinod Nair and Geoffrey E Hinton. 2010. Rectified Linear Units Improve Restricted Boltzmann Machines. *Proceedings of the 27th International Conference on Machine Learning*, (3):807–814.

Preslav Nakov, Alan Ritter, Sara Rosenthal, Veselin Stoyanov, and Fabrizio Sebastiani. 2016. SemEval-2016 Task 4: Sentiment Analysis in Twitter. In *Proceedings of the 10th International Workshop on Semantic Evaluation*, San Diego, California. Association for Computational Linguistics.

Bo Pang and Lillian Lee. 2008. Opinion Mining and Sentiment Analysis. *Foundations and trends in information retrieval*, 2(1-2):1–135.

Jeffrey Pennington, Richard Socher, and Christopher D Manning. 2014. Glove: Global Vectors for Word Representation. *Proceedings of the 2014 Conference on Empirical Methods in Natural Language Processing*, pages 1532–1543.

Sara Rosenthal, Alan Ritter, Preslav Nakov, and Veselin Stoyanov. 2014. SemEval-2014 Task 9: Sentiment Analysis in Twitter. *Proceedings of the 8th International Workshop on Semantic Evaluation (SemEval 2014)*, (SemEval):73–80.

Sara Rosenthal, Preslav Nakov, Svetlana Kiritchenko, Saif M Mohammad, Alan Ritter, and Veselin Stoyanov. 2015. SemEval-2015 Task 10: Sentiment Analysis in Twitter. *Proceedings of the 9th International Workshop on Semantic Evaluation (SemEval 2015)*, (SemEval):451–463.

Aliaksei Severyn and Alessandro Moschitti. 2015. UNITN : Training Deep Convolutional Neural Network for Twitter Sentiment Classification. (SemEval):464–469.

Duyu Tang, Furu Wei, Nan Yang, Ming Zhou, Ting Liu, and Bing Qin. 2014. Learning Sentiment-Specific Word Embedding. *Proceedings of the 52nd Annual Meeting of the Association for Computational Linguistics*, 1:1555–1565.

Matthew D. Zeiler. 2012. ADADELTA: An Adaptive Learning Rate Method.

UNIMELB at SemEval-2016 Tasks 4A and 4B: An Ensemble of Neural Networks and a Word2Vec Based Model for Sentiment Classification

XingYi Xu   **HuiZhi Liang**   **Timothy Baldwin**

Department of Computing and Information Systems
The University of Melbourne VIC 3010, Australia
stevenxxiu@gmail.com   oklianghuizi@gmail.com   tb@ldwin.net

Abstract

This paper describes our sentiment classification system for microblog-sized documents, and documents where a topic is present. The system consists of a soft-voting ensemble of a `word2vec` language model adapted to classification, a convolutional neural network (CNN), and a long-short term memory network (LSTM). Our main contribution consists of a way to introduce topic information into this model, by concatenating a topic embedding, consisting of the averaged word embedding for that topic, to each word embedding vector in our neural networks. When we apply our models to SemEval 2016 Task 4 subtasks A and B, we demonstrate that the ensemble performed better than any single classifier, and our method of including topic information achieves a substantial performance gain. According to results on the official test sets, our model ranked 3rd for F^{PN} in the message-only subtask A (among 34 teams) and 1st for accuracy on the topic-dependent subtask B (among 19 teams).

1 Introduction

The rapid growth of user-generated content, much of which is sentiment-laden, has fueled an interest in sentiment analysis (Pang and Lee, 2008; Liu, 2010). One popular form of sentiment analysis involves classifying a document into discrete classes, depending on whether it expresses positive or negative sentiment (or neither). The classification can also be dependent upon a particular topic. In this work, we describe the method we used for the sentiment classification of tweets, with or without a topic.

Our approach to the document classification task consists of an ensemble of 3 classifiers via soft-voting, 2 of which are neural network models. One is the convolutional neural network (CNN) architecture of Kim (2014), and another is a Long Short Term Memory (LSTM)-based network (Hochreiter and Schmidhuber, 1997). Both were first tuned on a distant-labelled data set. The third classifier adapted `word2vec` to output classification probabilities using Bayes' formula, a slightly modified version of Taddy (2015). Despite the `word2vec` classifier being intended as a baseline, and having a small weight in the ensemble, it proved crucial for the ensemble to work well. To adapt our models to the case where a topic is present, in the neural network models, we concatenated the embedding vectors for each word with a topic embedding, which consisted of the element-wise average of all word vectors in a particular topic.

We applied our approach to SemEval 2016 Task 4, including the message-only subtask (Task A) and the topic-dependent subtask (Task B) (Nakov et al., to appear). Our model ranked third for F^{PN} in the message-only subtask A (among 34 teams) and first for accuracy[1] on the topic-dependent subtask B (among 19 teams).

---

[1] There were some issues surrounding the evaluation metrics. We only got 7th for ρ^{PN} and 2nd for F^{PN} officially, but when we retrained our model using ρ^{PN} as the subtask intended, we place first across all metrics.

Proceedings of SemEval-2016, pages 183–189,
San Diego, California, June 16-17, 2016. ©2016 Association for Computational Linguistics

The source code for our approach is available at `https://github.com/stevenxxiu/senti`.

2 Models

We now describe the classifiers we used in detail, our ensemble method, and our motivations behind choosing these classifiers.

2.1 Convolutional neural network

We used the dynamic architecture of Kim (2014) for our convolutional neural network. This consists of a single 1-d convolution layer with a non-linearity, a max-pooling layer, a dropout layer, and a softmax classification layer.

This model was chosen since it was a good performer empirically. However, due to max-pooling, this model is essentially a bag-of-phrases model, which ignores important ordering information if the tweet contains a long argument, or 2 sentences. We now give a review of the layers used.

2.1.1 Word embedding layer

The input to the model is a document, treated as a sequence of words. Each word can possibly be represented by a vector of occurrences, a vector of counts, or a vector of features. A vector of learnt, instead of hand-crafted features, is also called a word embedding. This tends to have dimensionality $d \ll |V|$, the vocabulary size. Hence the vectors are dense, which allows us to learn more functions of features with limited data.

Given an embedding of dimension d, $W_{\text{emb}} \in \mathbf{R}^{d \times |V|}$, we mapped map each document s to a matrix $W_{\text{emb},s} \in \mathbf{R}^{d \times |s|}$, with each word corresponding to a row vector in the order they appear in. W_{emb} can be trained.

2.1.2 1-d convolution layer

A 1-d convolution layer aims to extract patterns useful for classification, by sliding a fixed-length filter along the input. The convolution operation for an input matrix $S \in \mathbf{R}^{d \times |s|}$ and a single filter $F \in \mathbf{R}^{d \times m}$ of width m creates a feature $y_{\text{conv}} \in \mathbf{R}^{|s|+m-1}$ by:

$$y_{\text{conv},i} = \sum_{k,j} (S_{[:,i:i+m-1]} \odot F)_{k,j} + b_{\text{conv}}$$

where $\odot$ is element-wise multiplication, and b_{conv} is a bias. There are typically $n > 1$ filters, which by stacking the feature vectors, results in $Y_{\text{conv}} \in \mathbf{R}^{n \times (|s|+m-1)}$. Each filter has its own separate bias.

We used a common modification to the filter sliding, by padding the document embedding matrix with $m - 1$ zeroes on its top and bottom. This is done so that every word in the document is covered by m filters.

2.1.3 Max pooling layer

There may be very few phrases targeted by a feature map in the document. For this reason, we only need to know if the desired feature is present in the document, which can be obtained by taking the maximum. Formally, we obtain a vector $d \in \mathbf{R}^n$, such that:

$$y_{\text{pool},i} = \max_j Y_{\text{conv},i,j}$$

2.1.4 Softmax layer

To convert our features into classification probabilities, we first use a dense layer, defined by:

$$y_{\text{dense}} = W_{\text{dense}} \cdot y_{\text{pool}} + b_{\text{dense}}$$

with a softmax activation function:

$$\text{softmax}(x)_i = \frac{e^{x_i}}{\sum_i e^{x_i}}$$

such that the output dimension is the same as the number of classes. Note that output values are non-negative and sum to 1, which form a discrete probability distribution.

2.1.5 Regularization

To regularize our CNN model, dropout (Srivastava et al., 2014) is used after the max pooling layer. Intuitively, dropout assumes that we can still obtain a reasonable classification even when some of the features are dropped. To do this, each dimension is randomly set to 0 using a Bernoulli distribution $B(p)$. In order to have the training and testing to be of the same order, the test outputs can be scaled by p.

The softmax layer for the CNN model also uses a form of empirical Bayes regularization, where each row of W_{soft} is restricted using an ℓ_2

norm, by re-normalizing the vector if the norm threshold is exceeded.

2.2 Long short term memory network

We used an LSTM for our recurrent architecture, which consisted of an embedding layer, LSTM layer, and a softmax classification layer.

A recurrent neural network is a neural network designed for sequential problems. Even simple RNNs are Turing complete, and they can theoretically obtain information from the entire sequence instead of only an unordered bag of phrases. But finding good architectures which can capture this and training them can be difficult. Indeed, there were many instances where our LSTM failed to capture important ordering information. We now give a brief review of the LSTM.

Given an input sequence $x = [x_1, \ldots, x_T]$, a recurrent network defines an internal state function f_c and an output function f_y to iterate over x, so that at time step t:

$$c_t = f_c(x_t, y_{t-1}, c_{t-1})$$
$$y_t = f_y(x_t, y_{t-1}, c_t)$$

where c_0 and y_0 are initial bias states. The simplest RNN, where:

$$f_y(x_t, y_{t-1}, c_t) \;=\; \tanh\!\left(W \cdot \begin{bmatrix} x_t \\ y_{t-1} \end{bmatrix}\right)$$

suffers from the gradient vanishing and exploding problem (Hochreiter and Schmidhuber, 1997). In particular, products of saturated tanh activations can vanish the gradient, and products of W can vanish or explode the gradient.

The LSTM is a way to remedy this (Hochreiter and Schmidhuber, 1997). It sets:

$$i_t = \sigma_i(W_{xi}x_t + W_{hi}h_{t-1} + w_{ci} \odot c_{t-1} + b_i)$$
$$f_t = \sigma_f(W_{xf}x_t + W_{hf}h_{t-1} + w_{cf} \odot c_{t-1} + b_f)$$
$$c_t = f_t \odot c_{t-1} + i_t \odot \sigma_c(W_{xc}x_t + W_{hc}h_{t-1} + b_c)$$
$$y_t = \sigma_o(W_{xo}x_t + W_{ho}h_{t-1} + w_{co} \odot c_t + b_o) \odot \sigma_h(c_t)$$

Here, $W_{\bullet}$ is made up of weights; i_t, f_t, c_t, y_t are the input gates, forget gates, cell states and output states. Cell states have an identity activation function. The gradient will not vanish if input x_i needs to be carried to x_j, since this can only happen when the forget gates are near 1. However, gradient explosion can still be present. We use the common approach of cutting off gradients above a threshold for the gradients inside $\sigma_i, \sigma_f, \sigma_c, \sigma_o$.

To use the LSTM, we first used a document embedding matrix in the same manner as our convolutional neural network architecture. This was fed into to an LSTM layer. The output for the final timestep of the LSTM layer was then fed into a final softmax layer with the appropriate output size for classification.

We also experimented with a similar and commonly used network, the Gated Recurrent Network (GRU), but it was not used due to lower results compared to the LSTM.

2.3 word2vec Bayes

Our word2vec Bayes model is our baseline model, and described in Taddy (2015), with the inclusion of a class prior. Taddy (2015) uses Bayes formula to compute the probabilities of a document belonging to a sentiment class. Given a document d, its words $\{w\}_i$, label y, Bayes formula is:

$$p(y|d) = \frac{p(d|y)p(y)}{p(d)}$$

For classification problems, we can ignore $p(d)$ since d is fixed. $p(d|y)$ is estimated by first training word2vec on a subset of the corpus with label y, then using the skipgram objective composite likelihood as an approximation:

$$\log p(d|y) \approx \sum_{s \in d} \sum_{j=1}^{|s|} \sum_{k=1}^{|s|} 1_{1 \leq |k-j| \leq b} \log p(w_k|w_j, y)$$

We estimated $p(y)$ via class frequencies, i.e. the MLE for the categorical distribution, compared to Taddy (2015), who used the discrete uniform prior.

This model was chosen since it provides a reasonable baseline, and also appears to be independent enough from our neural networks to provide a performance gain in the ensemble. The word2vec based model benefits from being a semi-supervised method, but it also loses ordering information outside a word's context window, and the prediction of neighboring words also ignores distance to that word. The limited amount of data for each class is also an issue.

2.4 Ensemble

If the errors made by each classifier are independent enough, then combining them in an ensemble can reduce the overall error rate. We used soft voting as a method to combine the outputs of the above classifiers. We define soft voting as:

$$y_{\text{vote}} = \sum_i w_i y_i, \text{ s.t. } \sum_i w_i = 1, \forall i : w_i \geq 0$$

where y_i is the output of classifier i.

3 Topic dependent models

To adapt our neural networks to topic-dependent sentiment classification, in our neural network models, we augmented each embedding vector by concatenating it with a topic embedding. The motivation behind this approach is to allow the model to interpret each word to be within the context of some topic.

Our topic embeddings were obtained by the element-wise average of word embeddings for each word in that topic. We found that empirically, this is a simple yet effective way of achieving a document embedding. When used directly as a feature vector in logistic regression for sentiment analysis, we have found this to outperform methods described in Le and Mikolov (2014).

Word embeddings of dimension $d = 300$ pretrained over Google News were used directly, without any further tuning. Words in the tweet which were not present in this pretrained embedding were ignored.

4 Experiments and evaluation

We evaluated our models on SemEval 2016 Task 4 subtask A, the message-only subtask, and subtask B, the topic-dependent subtask.

4.1 Data

Task A consisted of 3 sentiment classes — POSITIVE, NEUTRAL and NEGATIVE — whilst Task B consisted of 2 sentiment classes — POSITIVE and NEGATIVE. We only managed to download 90% of the entire set of tweets for the 2016 SemEval data, due to tweets becoming "not available". In addition to the Twitter data for 2016, for Task A we also used training data from SemEval 2016 Task 10. The data is summarized in Table 1.

To pretrain our network using distant learning (described below), we took a random sample of 10M English tweets from a 5.3TB Twitter dataset crawled from 18 June to 4 Dec, 2014 using the Twitter Trending API. We then processed tweets with a regular expression: tweets which contained emoticons like *:)* were considered POSITIVE, while those which contained emoticons like *:(* were considered NEGATIVE; tweets which contained both positive and negative emoticons, or others emoticons such as *:—*, were ignored. We extracted 1M tweets each for the POSITIVE and NEGATIVE classes.

4.2 Evaluation

Evaluation consisted of accuracy, macro-averaged F_1 across the POSITIVE and NEGATIVE classes, which we denote F^{PN}, and macro-averaged recall across the POSITIVE and NEGATIVE classes, which we denote ρ^{PN}.

4.3 Preprocessing

All methods use the same preprocessing. We normalized the tweets by first replacing URLs with *_url* and author methods such as *@Ladiibubblezz* with *_author*. Casing was preserved, as the pretrained `word2vec` vectors included casing. The tweets were tokenized using `twokenize`, with *it's* being split into *it* and *'s*.

4.4 Training and hyperparameters

4.4.1 Neural networks

For both our models, we initialized W_{emb} to word embeddings pretrained using `word2vec`'s skip-gram model (Mikolov et al., 2013) on the Google News corpus, where $d = 300$. Unknown words were drawn from $U[-0.25, 0.25]$ to match the variance of the pretrained vectors. For the CNN model, we also stripped words so all documents had a length ≤ 56.

Datset	A total	A used	B total	B used
Twitter 2016-train	6000	5465	4346	3941
		(+11340)		
Twitter 2016-dev	2000	1829	1325	1210
Twitter 2016-test	2000	1807	1417	1270

Table 1: Semeval-2016 data. The NEGATIVE : NEUTRAL : POSITIVE split was $16 : 42 : 42$ for all of 2016 Task A used. The NEGATIVE : POSITIVE split was $19 : 81$ for all of 2016 Task B used.

For our CNN, we used used 3 1-d convolutions, with filter sizes of $3, 4, 5$, each with 100 filters. Our dropout rate was 0.5, and our ℓ_2 norm restriction was 3. For our LSTM, we used a cell dimension size of 300, and our activations were chosen empirically to be $\sigma_i = \sigma_f = \sigma_o =$ sigmoid, $\sigma_c = \tanh$, our gradient cutoff was 100.

To train our neural networks, we used cross entropy loss and minibatch gradient descent with a batch size of 64. For our CNN, we used the adadelta (Zeiler, 2012) gradient descent method with the default settings. For our LSTM, we used the rmsprop gradient descent method with a learning rate of 0.01.

Due to limited training data, we can use distant learning (Severyn and Moschitti, 2015), by initializing the weights of our neural networks by first training them on a silver standard data set (generated using Twitter emoticons which we describe below), then tuning them further on the gold standard data set (Severyn and Moschitti, 2015). However, we did not use this for our topic-dependent models, as there was no performance gain.

We split the distant data into 10^4 tweets per epoch, and took the best epoch on the validation set as the initial weights, using F^{PN} as our scoring metric. We repeatedly iterated over the SemEval data with 10^3 tweets per epoch for 10^2 epochs, and again took the best epoch on the validation set as the final weights.

4.4.2 `word2vec` Bayes

Gensim (Řehůřek and Sojka, 2010) was used to train the word embeddings and obtain $p(d|y)$. We used the skipgram objective, with a embedding dimension of 100, window size of 10, hierarchical softmax with 5 samples, 20 training iterations, no frequent word cutoff, and a sam-

Dataset	F^{PN}
Twitter 2013	0.687_7
Twitter 2014	0.706_7
Twitter 2015	0.650_4
Twitter 2016	0.617_3
Twitter Sarcasm 2014	0.449_{11}
SMS 2013	0.593_{10}
LiveJournal 2014	0.683_9

Table 2: Official test scores and ranks for Task A.

Dataset	Val metric	ρ^{PN}	F^{PN}	Acc
Twitter 2016	F^{PN}	0.758_7	0.788_2	0.870_1
Twitter 2016	ρ^{PN}	0.807_1	0.806_1	0.867_1

Table 3: Test scores and ranks for Task B. The official run incorrectly used F^{PN} as the validation metric.

ple coefficient of 0.

4.4.3 Soft voting

To find w_i, we first relaxed the sum condition of w_i by setting $w_1 = 1$ and noting that $\max_k y_{vote,i,k}$ is invariant under scaling. We then used the L-BFGS-B algorithm, with initial weights of 1, combined with basin-hopping for 1000 iterations. We optimized for accuracy, since this most-consistently improved results.

5 Results

The official evaluation results are shown in Table 2 and Table 3. The results for Task A suggest that our models are overfitting. Our best position was achieved on the Twitter 2016 dataset, and indeed, this is what our parameters were chosen on.

Our own evaluation of our different classifiers, using Twitter 2016-test, is shown in Table 4 and

Model	Accuracy	F^{PN}
soft voting all	0.5772	0.6000
lstm	0.5379	0.5869
soft voting cnn + lstm	0.5606	0.5848
cnn	0.5612	0.5841
word2vec Bayes	0.5130	0.4983

Table 4: Results for Task A, sorted by F^{PN}.

Model	Accuracy	ρ^{PN}
soft voting all	0.8008	0.7849
soft voting cnn + lstm	0.7976	0.7846
cnn topic	0.8047	0.7762
lstm topic	0.6756	0.7494
cnn	0.8354	0.7253
word2vec Bayes	0.7654	0.7138
lstm	0.8118	0.6916

Table 5: Results for Task B, sorted by ρ^{PN}. The dashed line separates topic models from message-only models. The lstm topic model has poorer accuracy due to being optimized on ρ^{PN}.

Table 5. Taking into account all evaluation metrics, we can see that in both tasks, our CNN outperforms our LSTM, in Task A slightly and in Task B substantially. The word2vec Bayes model is worse than both, moreso in Task B.

Soft voting outperforms all classifiers, showing that there is some independence amongst the errors made. In Task A, there appears to be more correlation between the CNN and LSTM classifiers, as excluding the word2vec Bayes model reduces the performance. In Task B, the word2vec Bayes model appears to perform too poorly to provide a marked benefit.

From Table 5 we can see that the inclusion of topic information provides a substantial boost to both of our neural networks. This shows that our method of incorporating topic information is a useful way of modifying neural networks, and provides a strong baseline for alternative ways of doing this.

6 Conclusions

We described our ensemble approach to sentiment analysis both the task of topic-dependent document classification and document classification by itself. We gave a detailed description of how to modify our classifiers to be topic-dependent. The results show that ensembles can work for neural nets, and that our way of including topics achieves performance gains, and forms a good basis for future research in this area.

References

[Hochreiter and Schmidhuber1997] Sepp Hochreiter and Jürgen Schmidhuber. 1997. Long short-term memory. *Neural computation*, 9(8):1735–1780.

[Kim2014] Yoon Kim. 2014. Convolutional neural networks for sentence classification. In *Proceedings of the 2014 Conference on Empirical Methods in Natural Language Processing (EMNLP)*, pages 1746–1751, Doha, Qatar.

[Le and Mikolov2014] Quoc V. Le and Tomas Mikolov. 2014. Distributed representations of sentences and documents. In *arXiv preprint arXiv:1405.4053*.

[Liu2010] Bing Liu. 2010. Sentiment analysis and subjectivity. In Nitin Indurkhya and Fred J. Damerau, editors, *Handbook of Natural Language Processing*. Chapman & Hall/CRC, Boca Raton, USA, 2nd edition.

[Mikolov et al.2013] Tomas Mikolov, Ilya Sutskever, Kai Chen, Greg S. Corrado, and Jeff Dean. 2013. Distributed representations of words and phrases and their compositionality. In *Advances in neural information processing systems*, pages 3111–3119.

[Nakov et al.to appear] Preslav Nakov, Alan Ritter, Sara Rosenthal, Veselin Stoyanov, and Fabrizio Sebastiani. to appear. SemEval-2016 Task 4: Sentiment analysis in Twitter. In *Proceedings of the 10th International Workshop on Semantic Evaluation (SemEval 2016)*, San Diego, USA.

[Pang and Lee2008] Bo Pang and Lillian Lee. 2008. Opinion mining and sentiment analysis. *Foundations and trends in information retrieval*, 2(1-2):1–135.

[Řehůřek and Sojka2010] Radim Řehůřek and Petr Sojka. 2010. Software framework for topic modelling with large corpora. In *Proceedings of the LREC 2010 Workshop on New Challenges for NLP Frameworks*, pages 45–50, Valletta, Malta. ELRA. http://is.muni.cz/publication/884893/en.

[Severyn and Moschitti2015] Aliaksei Severyn and Alessandro Moschitti. 2015. UNITN: Training deep convolutional neural network for Twitter sentiment classification. In *Proceedings of the 9th*

International Workshop on Semantic Evaluation (SemEval), pages 464–469, Denver, USA.

[Srivastava et al.2014] Nitish Srivastava, Geoffrey Hinton, Alex Krizhevsky, Ilya Sutskever, and Ruslan Salakhutdinov. 2014. Dropout: A simple way to prevent neural networks from overfitting. *The Journal of Machine Learning Research*, 15(1):1929–1958.

[Taddy2015] Matt Taddy. 2015. Document classification by inversion of distributed language representations. In *arXiv:1504.07295 [cs, stat]*.

[Zeiler2012] Matthew D. Zeiler. 2012. ADADELTA: An adaptive learning rate method. *arXiv preprint arXiv:1212.5701*.

SentiSys at SemEval-2016 Task 4: Feature-Based System for Sentiment Analysis in Twitter

Hussam Hamdan
Aix-Marseille University
hamdan.hussam@gmail.com

Abstract

This paper describes our sentiment analysis system which has been built for Sentiment Analysis in Twitter Task of SemEval-2016. We have used a Logistic Regression classifier with different groups of features. This system is an improvement to our previous system Lsislif in Semeval-2015 after removing some features and adding new features extracted from a new automatic constructed sentiment lexicon.

1 Introduction

Sentiment analysis in Twitter is different from document level sentiment analysis. Normally, in document level, each document is classified as positive or negative, the document is long enough to obtain a good representation using only the existing words (bag-of-words). For example, in movie reviews we can get f-score of 85% using bag-of-words representation with SVM classifier while in Twitter it is about 60% according to our experiments in previous SemEval workshops. This lower performance in Twitter domain is not surprising if we know the limitations of such task when applied to Twitter:

- The size of a tweet is limited to 140 characters which leads to sparseness where the tweets do not provide enough word co-occurrence.

- The informal language and non-standard expressions.

- The numerous spelling errors.

For dealing with the previous limitations, we have decided to extend the bag-of-words representation. Therefore, many group of features have been extracted. Uni-gram, bi-gram and 3-grams of words features to capture the text of tweet and the context. Negation features to handle the negated context. Sentiment lexicons features can help the classification because it contains positive and negative words which can add a useful information about the polarity of a tweet, they also contain a lot of terms which may not appear in the training data which can be very useful. Semantic features as Brown clusters can also give a rich representation which can be useful for reducing the sparsity.

For evaluating our system, we have participated in SemEval-2016 competition for sentiment analysis in Twitter (message polarity subtask A)[1] (Nakov et al., 2016). Our system has been ranked six over 34, this system is derived from our previous system LsisLif which has been ranked third in SemEval-2015.

The rest of this chapter is organized as follows. Section 2 presents the problem formulation. Section 3 gives an overview of our proposed approach. The features we extracted for training the classifier are presented in Section 4. Our experiments are described in Section 5. The related work is presented in Section 6. The conclusion and future work are presented in Section 7.

2 Problem Formulation

Let $T = t_1, t_2, .., t_n$ be a collection of n tweets. Each tweet t_i will be represented by a subset of all

---

[1]http://alt.qcri.org/semeval2016/task4/

Proceedings of SemEval-2016, pages 190–197,
San Diego, California, June 16-17, 2016. ©2016 Association for Computational Linguistics

possible features $F = f_1, f_2, .., f_m$ that can appear in t_i. The features can be single words, bigrams, n-grams, stemmed words or other syntactic or semantic features. If a feature f_i exists in a tweet t_j, the tweet can be represented as a vector of weighted features $t_j = (w_1, w_2, .., w_m)$ where w_i is the weight of the feature f_i in the tweet t_j. w_i can represent the presence or absence of the feature or the frequency or any other function of the feature frequency in the tweet.

Let us have three classes $C = c_1, c_2, c_3$ where c_1 represents the negative class, c_2 the neutral class and c_3 the positive class. Our task is to assign each tweet t_j to a class c_i.

3 Overview of the Proposed Approach

Our proposed approach for sentiment polarity classification consists of three steps:

1. We tokenize each tweet to get the feature space which contains the words, punctuations and emoticons that appear in the tweets.

2. We extend the feature space by extracting some features using different resources (Sentiment lexicons, Twitter dictionary) and some semantic features.

3. We train a supervised classifier to get a trained model in order to predict the sentiment of the new tweets.

The next section describes the features we have extracted.

4 Feature Extraction

Before extracting the features, we should tokenize the tweet. Tokenization is a challenging problem for Twitter text. Happytokenizer[2] is the tokenizer which we used. It can capture the words, emoticons and punctuations. For example, for this tweet:

"RT @ #happyfuncoding: this is a typical Twitter tweet :-)"

It returns the following terms:

{rt, @, #happyfuncoding, :, this, is, a, typical, twitter, tweet, :-)}

We also replaced each web link by the word *url* and each user name by *uuser*. Then, several groups of features have been extracted to improve the bag-of-words representation.

4.1 Word ngrams

Unigram, bigram and 3-gram are extracted for each term in the tweet without any stemming or stopword removing, all terms with occurrence less than 3 are removed from the feature space. Therefore, for this tweet:

"i'am going to chapel hill on sat. :)"

The feature vector produced by this group of feature will be:

{"i'm", 'going', 'to', 'chapel', 'hill', 'on', 'sat', '.', ':)', "i'm going", 'going to', 'to chapel', 'chapel hill', 'hill on', 'on sat', 'sat .', '. :)', "i'm going to", 'going to chapel', 'to chapel hill', 'chapel hill on', 'hill on sat', 'on sat .', 'sat . :)'}.

4.2 Negation Features

The rule-based algorithm presented in Christopher Potts' Sentiment Symposium Tutorial[3] is implemented. This algorithm appends a negation suffix to all words that appear within a negation scope which is determined by a negation key and a punctuation or a connector belonging to [",", ";", ".", "!", "?", "but", "—", "so"]. All the negated words are added to the feature space. For example, for this tweet:

"I'am not happy"

The feature vector generated by the words n-gram features with negation features is:

{"i'am", 'not', 'happy_Neg', 'happy', "i'am not", 'not happy', "i'am not happy"}

happy_NEG is added by the negation features while the others are the ngrams features. Obviously, we have chosen to add the negated feature to the vector without removing the original feature *happy*.

4.3 Twitter Dictionary

We constructed a dictionary for the abbreviations and the slang words used in Twitter in order to overcome the ambiguity of these terms which may increase the similarity between two similar tweets written in two different ways. This dictionary maps

---

[2]http://sentiment.christopherpotts.net/tokenizing.html

[3]http://sentiment.christopherpotts.net/lingstruc.html

certain Twitter expressions and emotion icons to their meaning or their corresponding sentiment. It contains about 125 terms collected from different pages on the Web. Table 1 shows a part of the dictionary.

Twitter expression	Meaning
:)	veryhappy
:)	veryhappy
b/c	Because
FWIW	For what it's worth
Gr8	Great
IMHO	In my honest opinion or in my humble opinion
J/K	Just kidding
LOL	Laughing out loud funny
OMG	Oh my God
PLZ	Please
ROFL	Rolling on the floor laughing
RTHX	Thanks for the retweet
hahaha	laughing funny
wow	amazing surprised

Table 1: A part of Twitter dictionary.

All terms presented in a tweet and in the Twitter dictionary are mapped to their corresponding terms in the dictionary and added to the feature space. For this tweet: "i'am going to chapel hill on sat. :)", the term *veryhappy* will be added to the tweet vector because the emoticon *:)* will be replaced by *veryhappy* as indicated in the dictionary.

4.4 Semantic Features

The semantic representation of a text may bring some important hidden information, which may result in a better document representation and a better classification system. Usually, the semantic features can help to overcome the problem of spareness in short text. Externally resources may be important to get such representation.

4.4.1 Brown Dictionary Features

From over 56 million English tweets (837 million tokens), 1000 hierarchical clusters have been constructed over 217 thousand words (Owoputi et al., 2013). Table 2 shows an example of five clusters.

Cluster	Top words (by frequency)
A1	lmao lmfao lmaoo lmaooo hahahahaha lool ctfu rofl loool lmfaoo lmfaooo lmaoooo lmbo lololol
A2	haha hahaha hehe hahahaha hahah aha hehehe ahaha hah hahahah kk hahaa ahah
A3	yes yep yup nope yess yesss yessss ofcourse yeap likewise yepp yesh yw yuup yus
A4	yeah yea nah naw yeahh nooo yeh noo noooo yeaa ikr nvm yeahhh nahh nooooo
A5	smh jk #fail #random #fact smfh #smh #winning #realtalk smdh #dead #justsaying

Table 2: Example Twitter word clusters: we list the most probable words, starting with the most probable, in descending order.

Note that in cluster A1, the term lololol (an extension of lol for "laughing out loud") is grouped with a large number of laughter acronyms.

Each word in the text is mapped to its cluster in Brown dictionary, 1000 features are added to feature space where each feature represents the number of words in the text belonging to each cluster.

4.5 Sentiment Lexicons

The system extracts four features from the manual constructed lexicons and six features from the automatic ones. For each sentence the number of positive words, the number of negative ones, the number of positive words divided by the number of negative ones and the polarity of the last word are extracted from manual constructed lexicons. In addition to the sum of the positive scores and the sum of the negative scores from the automatic constructed lexicons.

The manual lexicons are: MPQA Subjectivity Lexicon[4] and Bing Liu Lexicon[5]. The automatic ones are: NRC Hashtag Sentiment Lexicon and our lexicon based on natural entropy measure (Hamdan et al., 2015c).

Thus, this feature group adds 20 features to the tweet vector, some of this features are integer numbers others are floats. The lexicons which we used are the following:

4.5.1 Manually Constructed Sentiment Lexicons

Two manual constructed lexicons have been exploited:

1. **MPQA Subjectivity Lexicon**
   Multi-Perspective Question Answering Subjectivity Lexicon is maintained by (Wilson et al., 2005), a lexicon of over 8,000 subjectivity single-word clues, each clue is classified as positive or negative. This is a fragment illustrating this lexicon structure:

Strength	Length	Word	Part-of-speech	Stemmed	priorpolarity
weaksubj	1	abandoned	adj	n	negative
weaksubj	1	abandonment	noun	n	negative
weaksubj	1	abandon	verb	y	negative

2. **Bing Liu Lexicon**
   A list of positive and negative opinion words or sentiment words for English (around 6800

---

[4]http://mpqa.cs.pitt.edu/lexicons/subj_lexicon/
[5]http://www.cs.uic.edu/ liub/FBS/sentiment-analysis.html#lexicon

words). This list was compiled over many years starting from this paper (Hu and Liu, 2004a). These are the first three words in each class of this lexicon:

Positive	Negative
abound	abnormal
abounds	abolish
abundance	abominable

4.5.2 Automatic Constructed Sentiment Lexicons

Three automatic constructed lexicon have been exploited:

1. **NRC Hashtag Sentiment Lexicon**
   NRC Hashtag Sentiment Lexicon (Mohammad, 2012) contains tweet terms with scores, positive score indicates association with positive sentiment, whereas negative score indicates association with negative sentiment. It has entries for 54,129 unigrams and 316,531 bigrams; the scores were computed using PMI over corpus of tweets. Here are the first and the last three lines of the unigrams NRC lexicon file:

Term	Score	#positive	#negative
#fabulous	7.526	2301	2
#excellent	7.247	2612	3
#superb	7.199	1660	2
ipad2	-6.615	1	1205
#dreadful	-6.764	1	1398
#unacceptable	-6.925	2	3284

Score is a real number indicates the sentiment score. *#positive* is the number of times the term co-occurred with a positive marker such as a positive emoticon or a positive hashtag. *#negative* is the number of times the term co-occurred with a negative marker such as a negative emoticon or a negative hashtag.

4.6 Our Sentiment Lexicon

PMI metric has been widely used to compute the semantic orientation of words in order to construct the automatic lexicons. Sentiment140 lexicon is constructed using semantic orientation on Sentiment140 corpus (Go et al., 2009), a collection of 1.6 million tweets that contain positive and negative emoticons [6]. But this corpus is a balanced corpus, it contains the same number of positive and negative tweets. Therefore, semantic orientation can be rewritten as following:

$$SO(w) = PMI(w, +) - PMI(w, -) = log(\frac{p(w,+)}{p(w).p(+)}) - log(\frac{p(w,-)}{p(w).p(-)}) \tag{1}$$

As $p(+) = p(-) = 0.5$ in the balanced corpus:

$$So(w) = 1 + log(p(+|w)) - 1 - log(p(-|w)) = log(a/c) \tag{2}$$

where + stands for the positive class, - stands for negative class, a is the number of documents containing the word w in the positive class, c is the number of documents containing the word w in the negative class. Thus, the semantic orientation is positive if a>c else it is negative. We should note that the probability of the classes does not affect the final semantic orientation score, therefore we propose another metric which depends on the distribution of the word over the classes which seems more relevant in the balanced corpus.

We constructed a lexicon from sentiment140 corpus, we calculated Natural Entropy (ne) score for each term in this manner:

$$ne(w) = 1 - (-(p(+|w).log(p(+|w)) - p(-|w).log(p(-|w)))) \tag{3}$$

where

$p(+|w)$: The probability of the positive class given the word w.

$p(-|w)$: The probability of the negative class given the word w.

The more uneven the distribution of documents where a term occurs, the larger the Natural Entropy of this term is. Thus, the entropy of the term can express the uncertainty of the classes given the term. One minus this degree of uncertainty boosts the terms that unevenly distributed between the two classes (Wu and Gu, 2014). *ne* score is always between 0 and 1, and it assigns a high score for the words unevenly distributed over the classes, but it cannot discriminate the positive words from the negative ones. Therefore, we have used the a and c for discriminating the positive words from the negative ones; if a>c then the word is considered positive else it is considered negative.

---

[6]http://help.sentiment140.com/for-students

Using this lexicon instead of sentiment140 can improve the performance of a state-of-the-art sentiment classifier as shown in (Hamdan et al., 2015c).

5 Experiments and Results

5.1 Twitter Dataset

Twitter datasets have been provided by SemEval organizers since 2013 for message polarity classification subtask of sentiment analysis in Twitter (Nakov et al., 2013). The participants have been provided with training tweets annotated positive, negative or neutral. In addition to a script for downloading the tweets. After executing the given script, we got the whole training dataset which consists of 9684 tweets. The organizers have also provided a development set containing 1654 tweets for tuning a machine learner. Table 3 shows the distribution of each label in each dataset.

Data	All	Positive	Negative	Neutral
train	9684	3640	1458	4586
dev	1654	739	340	575
test-2016	-	-	-	-

Table 3: Sentiment labels distribution in the training, testing and development datasets in Twitter.

5.2 Experiment Setup

We trained the L1-regularized logistic regression classifier implemented in LIBLINEAR (Fan et al., 2008), we had also tested L2 regularization technique but it gives less performance than L1. The classifier is trained on the training dataset using the features in the previous section with the three polarities (positive, negative, and neutral) as labels. A weighting schema is adapted for each class, we use the weighting option $-w_i$ which enables a use of different cost parameter C for different classes. Since the training data is unbalanced, this weighting schema adjusts the probability of each label. Thus, we tuned the classifier in adjusting the cost parameter C of logistic regression, weight w_{pos} of positive class and weight w_{neg} of negative class. We used the development set for tuning the three parameters, all combinations of C in range [0.1 .. 4] by step of 0.1, w_{pos} in range [1 .. 8] by step of 0.1, w_{neg} in range [1 .. 8] by step of 0.1 are tested. The combination

C=0.3, w_{pos}=7.6, w_{neg}=5.2 have given the best F1-score for the development set and therefore it was selected for our experiments on test set 2016.

5.3 Results

The evaluation score used by the task organizers was the averaged F1-score of the positive and negative classes. In the SemEval-2016 competition, our submission is ranked six (59.8%) over 34 submissions while it was ranked third in SemEval-2015.

Table 4 shows the results of our experiments after removing a feature group at each run for the four test set 2016.

Run	Test-2016
All features	59.8
all-lexicons	56.9
all-ngram	58.1
all-brown	58.4

Table 4: The F1 score for each run, All features run exploits all features while the others remove a feature group at each run lexicons, n-gram and brown cluster, respectively.

The results show that the sentiment lexicons features are the most important ones which conforms with the conclusion in different studies (Hamdan et al., 2015c; Mohammad et al., 2013) .

6 Related Work

There are two principally different approaches to opinion mining: lexicon-based and supervised. The lexicon-based approach goes from the word level in order to constitute the polarity of the text. This approach depends on a sentiment lexicon to get the word polarity score. While the supervised approach goes from the text level and learn a model which assigns a polarity score to the whole text, this approach needs a labeled corpus to learn the model.

6.1 Lexicon-Based Approach

Lexicon-based approaches decide the polarity of a document based on sentiment lexicons. The sentiment of a text is a function of the common words between the text and the sentiment lexicons.

Much of the first lexicon-based research has focused on using adjectives as indicators of the semantic orientation of text (Hatzivassiloglou and McKeown, 1997; Hu and Liu, 2004b). (Taboada et al., 2011) proposed another function called SO-CAL (Semantic Orientation CALculator) which uses dictionaries of words annotated with their semantic orientation (polarity and strength), and incorporates intensification and negation.

Thus, the sentiment lexicon is the most important part of this approach. Three different ways can be used to construct such lexicons: Manual Approach, Dictionary-Based Approach and Corpus-Based Approach.

6.2 Supervised Approach

The supervised approach is a machine learning approach. Sentiment classification can be seen as a text classification problem (Pang et al., 2002; Liu, 2012).

The research papers in sentiment classification have mainly focused on the two steps: document representation and classification methods.

While some papers have extended the bag-of-word representation by adding different types of features (Pang et al., 2002; Mohammad et al., 2013; Hamdan et al., 2013; Hamdan et al., 2015c), others have proposed different weighting schemas to weight the features such as PMI, Information Gain and chi-square χ^2 (Martineau and Finin, 2009; Paltoglou and Thelwall, 2010; Deng et al., 2014). Recently, after the success of deep learning techniques in many classification systems, several studies have learned the features instead of extracting them (Socher et al., 2013; Severyn and Moschitti, 2015).

The work of (Pang et al., 2002) was the first to apply this approach to classify the movie reviews into two classes positive or negative. They tested several classifiers (Naive Bayes, SVM, Maximum entropy) with several features.

Later on, many studies have proposed different features and some feature selection methods to choose the best feature set. Many features have been exploited :

- Terms and their weights: The features are the unigrams or n-grams with the associated frequency or weight given by a weighting schema like TF-IDF or PMI.

- Part of Speech (POS): The words can indicate different sentiment according to their parts of speech (POS). Some papers treated the adjectives as special features.

- Sentiment Lexicons: The words and expressions which express an opinion have been used to add additional features as the number of positive and negative terms.

- Sentiment Shifters: The terms that are used to change the sentiment orientation, from positive to negative or vice versa such as *not* and *never*. Taking into account these features can improve the sentiment classification.

- Semantic Features: The named entities, concepts and topics have been extracted to get the semantic of the text.

Many systems which have worked on feature extraction have achieved a state-of-the-art performance in many competitions like SemEval[7]. For example, (Mohammad et al., 2013) used SVM model with several types of features including terms, POS and sentiment lexicons in Twitter data set. (Hamdan et al., 2015a; Hamdan et al., 2015c; Hamdan et al., 2015b) have also proved the importance of feature extraction with logistic regression classifier in Twitter and reviews of restaurants and laptops. They extracted terms, sentiment lexicon and some semantic features like topics. And (Hamdan et al., 2013) has proposed to extract the concepts from DBPedia.

Recently, some research papers have applied deep learning techniques to sentiment classification. (Socher et al., 2013) proposed to use recursive neural network to capture the compositionality in the phrases, (Tang et al., 2014) combined the hand-crafted features with learned features. They used neural network for learning sentiment-specific word embedding, then they combined hand-crafted features with these word embedding to produce a state-of-the-art system in sentiment analysis in Twitter. (Kim, 2014) proposed a simple convolutional neural network with one layer of convolution which performs remarkably well. Their results add to the well-established evidence that unsupervised pre-training of word vectors is an important ingredient in deep learning for Natural language processing.

---

[7]https://www.cs.york.ac.uk/semeval-2013/task2.html

7 Conclusion and Future Work

In this paper, we tested the impact of combining several groups of features on the sentiment classification of tweets. A logistic regression classifier with weighting schema was used, the sentiment lexicon-based features seem to get the most influential effect with the combination.

As the sentiment lexicons features seem to be so important in sentiment classification, we think that it is important to orient our future work on this direction. Improving the automatic construction of sentiment lexicons may lead to an important improvement on sentiment classification. For example, taking the context in the consideration may help such process. Another important direction is using deep learning techniques which have recently proved their performance in several studies. Thus, we can learn the features instead of extracting them.

References

Zhi-Hong Deng, Kun-Hu Luo, and Hong-Liang Yu. 2014. A study of supervised term weighting scheme for sentiment analysis. *Expert Systems with Applications*, 41(7):3506 – 3513.

Rong-En Fan, Kai-Wei Chang, Cho-Jui Hsieh, Xiang-Rui Wang, and Chih-Jen Lin. 2008. LIBLINEAR: A Library for Large Linear Classification. *Journal of Machine Learning Research*, 9:1871–1874.

Alec Go, Richa Bhayani, and Lei Huang. 2009. Twitter Sentiment Classification using Distant Supervision. *Processing*, pages 1–6.

Hussam Hamdan, FrÃ©dÃ©ric Bechet, and Patrice Bellot. 2013. Experiments with DBpedia, WordNet and SentiWordNet as resources for sentiment analysis in micro-blogging. In *International Workshop on Semantic Evaluation SemEval-2013 (NAACL Workshop)*, Atlanta, Georgia (USA), April.

Hussam Hamdan, Patrice Bellot, and Frederic Bechet. 2015a. Lsislif: CRF and Logistic Regression for Opinion Target Extraction and Sentiment Polarity Analysis. In *Proceedings of the 9th International Workshop on Semantic Evaluation (SemEval 2015)*, pages 753–758, Denver, Colorado, June. Association for Computational Linguistics.

Hussam Hamdan, Patrice Bellot, and Frederic Bechet. 2015b. Lsislif: Feature Extraction and Label Weighting for Sentiment Analysis in Twitter. In *Proceedings of the 9th International Workshop on Semantic Evaluation (SemEval 2015)*, pages 568–573, Denver, Colorado, June. Association for Computational Linguistics.

Hussam Hamdan, Patrice Bellot, and Frederic Bechet. 2015c. Sentiment Lexicon-Based Features for Sentiment Analysis in Short Text. In *Proceeding of the 16th International Conference on Intelligent Text Processing and Computational Linguistics*, Cairo, Egypt.

Vasileios Hatzivassiloglou and Kathleen R. McKeown. 1997. Predicting the Semantic Orientation of Adjectives. In *Proceedings of the Eighth Conference on European Chapter of the Association for Computational Linguistics*, EACL '97, pages 174–181, Stroudsburg, PA, USA. Association for Computational Linguistics.

Minqing Hu and Bing Liu. 2004a. Mining and Summarizing Customer Reviews. In *Proceedings of the Tenth ACM SIGKDD International Conference on Knowledge Discovery and Data Mining*, KDD '04, pages 168–177, New York, NY, USA. ACM.

Minqing Hu and Bing Liu. 2004b. Mining and Summarizing Customer Reviews. In *Proceedings of the Tenth ACM SIGKDD International Conference on Knowledge Discovery and Data Mining*, KDD '04, pages 168–177, New York, NY, USA. ACM.

Yoon Kim. 2014. Convolutional Neural Networks for Sentence Classification. *CoRR*, abs/1408.5882.

Bing Liu. 2012. *Sentiment Analysis and Opinion Mining*. Synthesis Lectures on Human Language Technologies. Morgan & Claypool Publishers.

Justin Martineau and Tim Finin. 2009. Delta TFIDF: An Improved Feature Space for Sentiment Analysis. In *ICWSM*.

Saif M. Mohammad, Svetlana Kiritchenko, and Xiaodan Zhu. 2013. NRCCanada: Building the State-of-the-Art in Sentiment Analysis of Tweets. In *Proceedings of the International Workshop on Semantic Evaluation, SemEval '13*.

Saif Mohammad. 2012. #Emotional Tweets. In **SEM 2012: The First Joint Conference on Lexical and Computational Semantics – Volume 1: Proceedings of the main conference and the shared task, and Volume 2: Proceedings of the Sixth International Workshop on Semantic Evaluation (SemEval 2012)*, pages 246–255, Montréal, Canada, June. Association for Computational Linguistics.

Preslav Nakov, Sara Rosenthal, Zornitsa Kozareva, Veselin Stoyanov, Alan Ritter, and Theresa Wilson. 2013. SemEval-2013 Task 2: Sentiment Analysis in Twitter. In *Second Joint Conference on Lexical and Computational Semantics (*SEM), Volume 2: Proceedings of the Seventh International Workshop on Semantic Evaluation (SemEval 2013)*, pages 312–320, Atlanta, Georgia, USA, June. Association for Computational Linguistics.

Preslav Nakov, Alan Ritter, Sara Rosenthal, Fabrizio Sebastiani, and Veselin Stoyanov. 2016. SemEval-2016 Task 4: Sentiment Analysis in Twitter. In *Proceedings of the 10th International Workshop on Semantic Evaluation*, SemEval '2016. Association for Computational Linguistics, June.

Olutobi Owoputi, Brendan O'Connor, Chris Dyer, Kevin Gimpel, Nathan Schneider, and Noah A Smith. 2013. Improved part-of-speech tagging for online conversational text with word clusters. In *Proceedings of NAACL-HLT*, pages 380–390.

Georgios Paltoglou and Mike Thelwall. 2010. A Study of Information Retrieval Weighting Schemes for Sentiment Analysis. In *Proceedings of the 48th Annual Meeting of the Association for Computational Linguistics*, ACL '10, pages 1386–1395, Stroudsburg, PA, USA. Association for Computational Linguistics.

Bo Pang, Lillian Lee, and Shivakumar Vaithyanathan. 2002. Thumbs Up?: Sentiment Classification Using Machine Learning Techniques. In *Proceedings of the ACL-02 Conference on Empirical Methods in Natural Language Processing - Volume 10*, EMNLP '02, pages 79–86, Stroudsburg, PA, USA. Association for Computational Linguistics.

Aliaksei Severyn and Alessandro Moschitti. 2015. UNITN: Training Deep Convolutional Neural Network for Twitter Sentiment Classification. In *Proceedings of the 9th International Workshop on Semantic Evaluation (SemEval 2015)*, pages 464–469, Denver, Colorado, June. Association for Computational Linguistics.

Richard Socher, Alex Perelygin, Jean Y Wu, Jason Chuang, Christopher D Manning, Andrew Y Ng, and Christopher Potts Potts. 2013. Recursive Deep Models for Semantic Compositionality Over a Sentiment Treebank. In *EMNLP*.

Maite Taboada, Julian Brooke, Milan Tofiloski, Kimberly Voll, and Manfred Stede. 2011. Lexicon-based Methods for Sentiment Analysis. *Comput. Linguist.*, 37(2):267–307, June.

Duyu Tang, Furu Wei, Nan Yang, Ming Zhou, Ting Liu, and Bing Qin. 2014. Learning Sentiment-Specific Word Embedding for Twitter Sentiment Classification. In *Proceedings of the 52nd Annual Meeting of the Association for Computational Linguistics (Volume 1: Long Papers)*, pages 1555–1565, Baltimore, Maryland, June. Association for Computational Linguistics.

Theresa Wilson, Paul Hoffmann, Swapna Somasundaran, Jason Kessler, Janyce Wiebe, Yejin Choi, Claire Cardie, Ellen Riloff, and Siddharth Patwardhan. 2005. OpinionFinder: A System for Subjectivity Analysis. In *Proceedings of HLT/EMNLP on Interactive Demonstrations*, HLT-Demo '05, pages 34–35, Stroudsburg, PA, USA. Association for Computational Linguistics.

Haibing Wu and Xiaodong Gu. 2014. Reducing Over-Weighting in Supervised Term Weighting for Sentiment Analysis. In *COLING 2014, 25th International Conference on Computational Linguistics, Proceedings of the Conference: Technical Papers, August 23-29, 2014, Dublin, Ireland*, pages 1322–1330.

DSIC-ELIRF at SemEval-2016 Task 4: Message Polarity Classification in Twitter using a Support Vector Machine Approach

Víctor Martínez   Ferran Pla   LLuís-F. Hurtado
Universitat Politècnica de València
Camí de Vera s/n, 46022 València
`{vmartinez2,fpla,lhurtado}@dsic.upv.es`

Abstract

This paper contains the description of our participation at task 4 (sub-task A, Message Polarity Classification) of SemEval-2016. Our proposed system consists mainly of three steps. Firstly, the preprocessing step includes the tokenization and identification of special elements including URLs, hashtags, user mentions and emoticons. The second step aims at selecting and extracting the feature set. Finally, a supervised approach, in particular a Support Vector Machine has been applied to tackle the classification problem.

1 Introduction

In the last few years, Twitter has become a source of a huge amount of information which introduces endless possibilities of research in the field of Sentiment Analysis. Sentiment Analysis, also called Opinion Mining, is a research area within Natural Language Processing whose aim is to identify the underlying emotion of a certain document, sentence or aspect (Liu, 2012). As a case in point, Opinion Mining has been applied for recognizing reviews as recommended or not recommended (Turney, 2002) and for generating aspect-based summaries (Hu and Liu, 2004).

The goal of SemEval-2016 task 4 (Nakov et al., 2016) consists of categorizing tweets as positive, negative or neutral concerning the opinion that a user holds with regard to a certain topic. One issue to take into consiteration is that the language adopted in Social Media, especially in Twitter, needs to be treated differently than normalized language due to the use of specific characteristics such as users, hashtags, emoticons and slang as well as some linguistic phenomena including sarcasm and irony.

Our system is closely related to (Giménez et al., 2015). Section 2 describes the proposed method which consists mainly of three steps. Firstly, the preprocessing step includes the tokenization and identification of special elements including URLs, hashtags, user mentions and emoticons. The second step aims at selecting and extracting the feature set. Finally, a supervised approach such as Support Vector Machine (SVM) has been applied to tackle the classification problem. In section 3, the experiments carried out are described. Finally, section 4 discusses the results obtained for the different experiments in the tuning phase and in the official competition.

2 System Overview

In this section, we describe the steps carried out in this work to achieve the results obtained in Semeval 2016. In this approach, a matrix of ocurrences, in which tweets are represented as rows and features as columns, normalized by tf-idf was used to represent whether a certain feature appears or not in a tweet.

2.1 Preprocessing

After fetching all the data from Twitter, our corpus needs to be preprocessed. As Twitter makes an extensive use of emoticons, URLs and concrete elements such as @User mentions and #hashtags, some regex are utilized to substitute these mentioned elements of special interest by labels of the form <URL>, <HASH>, <USER>and <EMOTICON>that let us count the amount of ap-

198

Proceedings of SemEval-2016, pages 198–201,
San Diego, California, June 16-17, 2016. ©2016 Association for Computational Linguistics

pearances in a certain tweet. Indeed, after tokenizing the tweet, punctuation and stop words are removed.

2.2 Feature Set

In this paper, the following features have been tried out althought not all were included for the final submision: see section 4

N-grams at word-level were selected ranging from 1-grams to 6-grams. These were combined in the experimentation process.

Skip-grams at the word level with 2 words and 1 gap between them. As an example, "What an amazing film" will generate the following list of skip-grams [("What","amazing"),("an","film")]

K most frequent Skip-grams. This feature takes the k-most frequent Skip-grams and discards the other ones which are under the k threshold.

Lexicons

1. Jeffrey (Hu and Liu, 2004): This lexicon contains two sets of words: a positive and a negative word set. From this lexicon we obtain two scores coming from the addition of the positive words appering in a tweet and, likewise, from the addition of the negative words.

2. NRC Emotion Lexicon (Mohammad and Turney, 2013): This lexicon contains a set of words and a value (0 or 1) expressing whether a word is associated to a certain emotion such as anger, anticipation, disgust, fear, joy, sadness, surprise and sad.

Twitter Features. The way of expressing ideas in Twitter as in other social networks differs from the language used in formal writing. That is why we should capture the peculiarities about this language that could be useful for identifying the polarity of a tweet in certain situations.

- **Elongated Words** We count the number of elongated words. For instance, "I love you sooooo much".

- **ALL CAPS** We count the number of words in upper case.

- **#Hashtags**. We count the number of hashtags in a tweet.

Finally, a **tf-idf** normalization was applied in all the selected features.

2.3 Classification

In this work, we classified the tweets polarity using a SVM formalism. An implementation using regularized linear models with stochastic gradient descent (SGD) learning is provided by the scikit-learn toolkit (Pedregosa et al., 2011).

3 Experiments

In this section, we expose the experiments carried out. Every experiment applies the preprocessing explained in section 2.1. The dataset used to conduct the experimentation was the one adopted on SemEval-2013 task 2 subtask B (Nakov et al., 2013). Indeed, all the experimentation applies a linear SVM as a classifier. The following lines express the features implemented in the most successful experiments.

- **Experiment 1**
  - Unigrams and Bigrams
  - Jeffrey's Lexicon.

- **Experiment 2**
  - 1-6 grams
  - Jeffrey's Lexicon.

- **Experiment 3**
  - Unigrams
  - Jeffrey's Lexicon.
  - Skip-grams

- **Experiment 4**
  - Unigrams
  - Jeffrey's Lexicon.
  - 100-most frequent Skip-grams

- **Experiment 5**
  - Unigrams and Bigrams
  - Jeffrey's and NRC Emotion Lexicons.

- **Experiment 6**
  - Unigrams and Bigrams
  - Jeffrey's and NRC Emotion Lexicons.
  - All Twitter Features

- **Experiment 7**

Experiment	$F1_{pos}$	$F1_{neg}$	$(F1_{pos} + F1_{neg}) / 2$
1	0.6913	0.5593	0.6253
2	0.6383	0.5548	0.6180
3	0.6860	0.5458	0.6159
4	0.6851	0.5603	0.6227
5	**0.6973**	**0.5824**	**0.6399**
6	0.6197	0.3516	0.4857
7	0.5906	0.3262	0.4584
8	0.5807	0.3306	0.4556
9	0.6215	0.2840	0.4527

Table 1: Results. SemEval-2013 Dataset.

 – Unigrams and Bigrams

 – Jeffrey's and NRC Emotion Lexicons.

 – #Hashtags

• **Experiment 8**

 – Unigrams and Bigrams

 – Jeffrey's and NRC Emotion Lexicons.

 – ALLCAPS

• **Experiment 9**

 – Unigrams and Bigrams

 – Jeffrey's and NRC Emotion Lexicons.

 – Elongated Words

4 Results

This section summarizes the results of the tuning phase. As we can see in Table 1, the best approach is the one used in experiment 5 which uses only unigrams, bigrams and both lexicons. This fact shows the importance of unigrams and bigrams as well as the relevance of using lexicons which can improve considerably a message polarity classification model. Moreover, using n-grams larger than bigrams (6-grams in our experiments) can introduce noise in the model.

As we can see in Table 1, Twitter features decrease the performance of the classification. In experiment 6, we use all Twitter features together which leads us to a decreasing of $(F1_{pos}+F1_{neg})/2$ from 0.6399 to 0.4857. Likewise, the results of experiments 7, 8 and 9 which use Twitter features individually show a diminution of similar magnitude in the evaluation measure $(F1_{pos}+F1_{neg})/2$.

4.1 N-grams vs Skip-grams

In this work, we presented Skip-grams as an alternative to N-grams and we see that N-grams performed slightly better than Skip-grams. However, this difference in the performance is not statistically significant and can vary between different corpora. In addition, experiment 4 includes a variation taking only the one hundred most frequent Skip-grams. The comparison between experiment 3 and 4 shows that using the most frequent Skip-grams leads to better results than using all the Skip-grams generated.

4.2 Competition Results

For the competition, the model used in experiment 5 which outperformed the others in the tuning phase was submitted. This model consists of unigrams, bigrams and both lexicons (Jeffrey and NRC emotion lexicon). In the official rank our system achieved the 22nd out of 34 teams.

Acknowledgments

This work has been partially funded by the project ASLP-MULAN: Audio, Speech and Language Processing for Multimedia Analytics (Spanish MINECO TIN2014-54288-C4-3-R).

References

Mayte Giménez, Pla Ferran, and Lluís-F. Hurtado. 2015. Elirf: A support vector machine approach for sentiment analysis tasks in twitter at semeval-2015. In *In Proceedings of the 9th International Workshop on Semantic Evaluation (SemEval 2015)*, pages 574—-581. Association for Computational Linguistics.

Minqing Hu and Bing Liu. 2004. Mining and summarizing customer reviews. In *Proceedings of the tenth ACM SIGKDD international conference on Knowledge discovery and data mining*, pages 168–177. ACM.

Bing Liu. 2012. Sentiment analysis and opinion mining. *Synthesis lectures on human language technologies*, 5(1):1–167.

Saif M Mohammad and Peter D Turney. 2013. Nrc emotion lexicon. Technical report, NRC Technical Report.

Preslav Nakov, Zornitsa Kozareva, Alan Ritter, Sara Rosenthal, Veselin Stoyanov, and Theresa Wilson. 2013. Semeval-2013 task 2: Sentiment analysis in twitter.

Preslav Nakov, Alan Ritter, Sara Rosenthal, Veselin Stoyanov, and Fabrizio Sebastiani. 2016. SemEval-2016 task 4: Sentiment analysis in Twitter. In *Proceedings of the 10th International Workshop on Semantic Evaluation*, SemEval '16, San Diego, California, June. Association for Computational Linguistics.

Fabian Pedregosa, Gaël Varoquaux, Alexandre Gramfort, Vincent Michel, Bertrand Thirion, Olivier Grisel, Mathieu Blondel, Peter Prettenhofer, Ron Weiss, Vincent Dubourg, et al. 2011. Scikit-learn: Machine learning in python. *The Journal of Machine Learning Research*, 12:2825–2830.

Peter D Turney. 2002. Thumbs up or thumbs down?: semantic orientation applied to unsupervised classification of reviews. In *Proceedings of the 40th annual meeting on association for computational linguistics*, pages 417–424. Association for Computational Linguistics.

SENSEI-LIF at SemEval-2016 Task 4: Polarity embedding fusion for robust sentiment analysis

Mickael Rouvier
Aix-Marseille Université
CNRS, LIF UMR 7279
13000, Marseille, France
mickael.rouvier@lif.univ-mrs.fr

Benoit Favre
Aix-Marseille Université
CNRS, LIF UMR 7279
13000, Marseille, France
benoit.favre@lif.univ-mrs.fr

Abstract

This paper describes the system developed at LIF for the SemEval-2016 evaluation campaign. The goal of Task 4.A was to identify sentiment polarity in tweets. The system extends the Convolutional Neural Networks (CNN) state of the art approach. We initialize the input representations with embeddings trained on different units: lexical, part-of-speech, and sentiment embeddings. Neural networks for each input space are trained separately, and then the representations extracted from their hidden layers are concatenated as input of a fusion neural network. The system ranked 2nd at SemEval-2016 and obtained an average F1 of 63.0%.

1 Introduction

This paper describes the system developed at LIF for the SemEval-2016 sentiment analysis evaluation task (Nakov et al., 2016). The goal of our participation was to apply approaches developed for the European FP7 project SENSEI [1] based on the study of human conversations according to feelings, opinions, emotions of the participants, in corpora such as transcripts of telephone speech and web comments.

We have participated in Subtask A: sentiment analysis at the message level. It consists in determining the message polarity of each tweet in the test set. The sentiment polarity classification task is set as a three-class problem: positive, negative and neutral.

The sentiment analysis task is often modeled as a classification problem which relies on features extracted from the text in order to feed a classifier. Recent work has shown that Convolutional Neural Networks (CNN) using word representations as input are well suited for sentence classification problems (Kim, 2014) and have been shown to produce state-of-the-art results for sentiment polarity classification (Tang et al., 2014a; Severyn and Moschitti, 2015). Pre-trained word embeddings are used to initialize the word representations, which are then taken as input of a text CNN.

Our approach consists in learning polarity classifiers for three types of embeddings, based on the same CNN architecture. Each set of word embedding models the tweet according to a different point of view: lexical, part-of-speech and sentiment. A final fusion step is applied, based on concatenating the hidden layers of the CNNs and training a deep neural network for the fusion.

Our contributions are as follows:

- We extend the deep CNN architecture proposed in (Poria et al., 2015) and introduce lexical information similar to (Ebert et al., 2015).

- We introduce **polarity embeddings**, tweet representations extracted from the hidden layer of CNNs with different word embeddings as input.

- We fuse polarity embeddings by concatenating them and feeding them to a neural network trained on the final task.

- The source code of our system, the models trained for the evaluation, and the corpus collected for creating word embeddings are made

---

[1] http://www.sensei-conversation.eu/

Proceedings of SemEval-2016, pages 202–208,
San Diego, California, June 16-17, 2016. ©2016 Association for Computational Linguistics

available to the community to help future research [2].

The paper is structured as follows. Section 2 presents the system architecture. Section 3 reviews the implementation details. Then we detail the different word embeddings and other features used in our system (Section 4). Results and discussion appear in Section 5.

2 Polarity embeddings

Deep learning models have been shown to produce state-of-the-art performance in various domains (vision, speech, etc...). Convolutional Neural Networks (CNN) represent one of the most used deep learning model in computer vision (LeCun and Bengio, 1995). Recent work has shown that CNNs are also well suited for sentence classification problems and can produce state-of-the-art results (Tang et al., 2014a; Severyn and Moschitti, 2015). The difference between CNNs applied to computer vision and their equivalent in NLP lies in the input dimensionality and format. In computer vision, inputs are usually single-channel (eg. grayscale) or multi-channel (eg. RGB) 2D or 3D matrices, usually of constant dimension. In sentence classification, each input consists of a sequence of words of variable length. Each word w is represented with a n-dimensional vector (word embedding) e_w of constant size. All the word representations are then concatenated in their respective order and padded with zero-vectors to a fixed length (maximum possible length of the sentence).

Word embeddings are an approach for distributional semantics which represents words as vectors of real numbers. Such representation has useful clustering properties, since it groups together words that are semantically and syntactically similar (Mikolov et al., 2013). For example, the word "coffee" and "tea" will be very close in the created space. The goal is to use these features as input to a CNN classifier. However, with the sentiment analysis task in mind, typical word embeddings extracted from lexical context might not be the most accurate because antonyms tend to be placed at the same location in the created space. As exemplified in Table 1, "good" and "bad" occur in similar con-

texts, and therefore obtain very similar representations. In addition, the model does not differentiate the senses of a word and creates a representation close to the most used sense in the training data. In order to tackle the representation robustness problem, we propose to extract word embeddings with different training regimes, and fuse their contribution to the system.

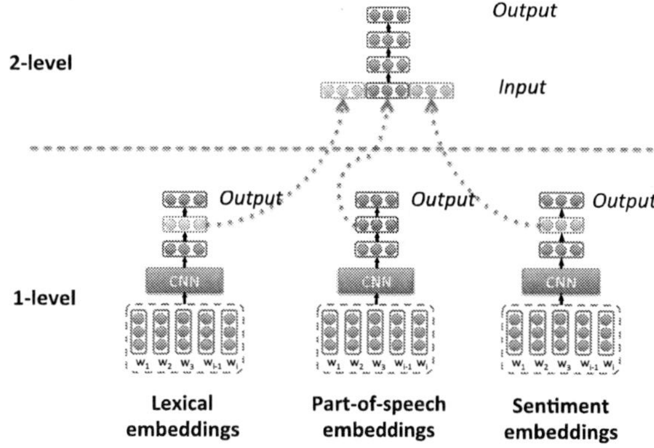

Figure 1: Overview of the sentiment embedding fusion approach. In a first level, different word representations are used to train CNNs to predict sentiment polarity, in the second level, representations extracted at hidden layers are concatenated and fed to a final classifier.

There are two approaches commonly used for fusion: early and late fusion. Late fusion considers that the different systems are independent by first applying classification separately on each system and then merging the output using a high-level classifier. Unfortunately, the classifier cannot model the correlations among modalities. The early fusion approach tackles this problem by learning features and class relationships to model the interaction between modalities. While late fusion cannot benefit from different system feature correlations, early fusion requires lots of training data.

In previous work (Rouvier et al., 2015), we have proposed a new fusion framework called embedding fusion which consists in concatenating hidden layers of subsystems trained independently, and input them to an other classifier trained to the actual task targets. This embedding fusion approach goes beyond late fusion and overcomes most of the problems linked to early fusion.

In this paper, we apply the embedding fusion to

---

[2]http://www.github.com/mrouvier/SemEval2016

Lexical		Part-of-speech		Sentiment	
good	**bad**	**good**	**bad**	**good**	**bad**
great	good	great	good	great	terrible
bad	terrible	bad	terrible	goid	horrible
goid	baaad	nice	horrible	nice	shitty
gpod	horrible	gd	shitty	goood	crappy
gud	lousy	goid	crappy	gpod	sucky
decent	shitty	decent	baaaad	gd	lousy
agood	crappy	goos	lousy	fantastic	horrid
goood	sucky	grest	sucky	wonderful	stupid
terrible	horible	guid	fickle-minded	gud	:/
gr8	horrid	goo	baaaaad	bad	sucks

Table 1: Closest words to "good" and "bad" according to different regimes for creating word embeddings: lexical, part-of-speech and sentiment (described later in the paper).

the sentiment polarity prediction task, with a two-level architecture (Figure 1). Given a tweet, the first level extracts input representations based different word embeddings. These embeddings are fed to a CNN with n-gram filters (from 1 to 5). The CNN is followed by a series of fully connected hidden layers which are trained to predict the target (sentiment polarity). Three different sets of word embeddings are used: lexical embeddings, joint lexical-part-of-speech embeddings, and joint lexical-sentiment embeddings. The training procedure for the embeddings is explained in the following sections.

The second level inputs the concatenation of the last hidden layer resulting from each input representation, which we call **polarity embeddings**. This representation is fed to fully connected hidden layers, and also trained to predict the polarity target. This method allows us to take advantage of both early and late fusion at the same time, which brings an improvement in term of performance over merging the decisions of the independent neural networks.

3 Implementation details

The proposed architecture relies on word embeddings as word representation as well as sentiment polarity lexicon features, concatenated to the word representation. An alternative to word-level features captured by CNNs is to extract sentence-level features in order to model global evidence in the tweet. In order to incorporate this source of information into the system, a classical MLP with one hidden layer is trained to predict sentiment polarity from a set of sentence-level features and its hidden layer is

concatenated to the other polarity embeddings and fed to the second-level MLP. The CNN and MLP are trained jointly.

The final complete architecture including CNNs and the sentence-level MLP, presented in Figure 2, is based on a single convolutional layer followed by a max-over-time pooling layer (Collobert et al., 2011) and two fully-connected layers. In order to learn this kind of model there are two soft-max fully connected layers. The first one is connected to the pooling layer and the second one at the end of fully-connected layer.

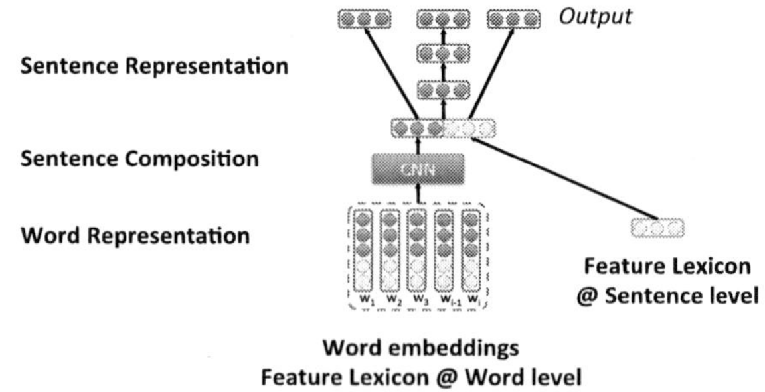

Figure 2: Actual CNN architecture: word representations are concatenated with lexicon features, and sentence-level lexicon features are concatenated with the polarity embeddings, and also trained to predict polarity targets on its own.

The parameters of our model were chosen so as to maximize performance on the development set: the width of the convolution filters is set to 5 and the number of convolutional feature maps is 500. We use ReLU activation functions and a simple max-pooling. The two fully connected hidden-layers are of size 512. For each layer, a standard dropout of 0.4 (40 % of the neurons are disabled in each iteration) is used. The back-propagation algorithm used for training is Adadelta. In our experiments we observed that the weight initialization of the convolution layer can lead to high variation in term of performance. Therefore, we trained 20 models and selected the one that obtained the best results on the development corpus.

In the second part of the system which inputs polarity embeddings and predicts polarity targets, the DNN is composed of two 512-dimensional hidden layers. The non-linearity of the hidden layers is corrected by a ReLU function.

4   Input features

4.1   Word embeddings

We propose to make use of word embeddings trained under different regimes, in order to capture different aspects of the relation between words so that it might benefit the polarity classifier. Three representations are explored.

Lexical embeddings: these embeddings are obtained with the classical skipgram model from (Mikolov et al., 2013). The representation is created by using the hidden layer of a linear neural network to predict a context window from a central word. For a given context $w_{i-2} \ldots w_{i+2}$, the input to the model is w_i, and the output could be w_{i-2}, w_{i-1}, w_{i+1}, w_{i+2}. This method typically extracts a representation which both covers syntax and semantics, to some extent.

Part-of-speech embeddings: as stated earlier, the lexical model cannot distinguish between the senses of words and creates a single representation per word form. For example, the word "apple" receives an embedding that is a mixture of its different contextual senses: fruit, company... A lot of sophisticated approaches have been proposed to tackle the problem (Guo et al., 2014; Neelakantan et al., 2015; Huang et al., 2012), by considering senses as latent variables during training, or by conditionning the training documents on topic distributions. In our system we follow a very simple approach which creates joint embeddings for words and their part of speech. Thus, for con-

text $w_{i-2} \ldots w_{i+2}$ tagged with the part-of-speech sequence $p_{i-2} \ldots p_{i+2}$ the input to the model is (w_i, p_i) and the output is (w_{i-2}, p_{i-2}), (w_{i-1}, p_{i-1}), $(w_{i+1} : p_{i+1})$, (w_{i+2}, p_{i+2}).

Sentiment embeddings: another problem with the basic skipgram approach (lexical embeddings) is that the model ignores the sentiment polarity of the words. As a result, words with opposite polarity, such as "good" and "bad", are mapped into close vectors. In (Tang et al., 2014b), the authors propose to tackle this problem so that sentiment information is encoded in the continuous representation of words. They propose to create a neural network that predicts two tasks: the context of the word and the sentiment label of the whole sentence. Since it is expensive to manually label sentences with a polarity label, the authors propose to use tweets that contain emoticons and rely on the polarity of the emoticon to label the sentences. As they report that best performance is obtained by weighting both tasks equivalently, the model is the same as for lexical embeddings, except that the predicted context is formed of (word, sentiment) couples. For example, if s is the polarity of the sentence where the context $w_{i-2} \ldots w_{i+2}$ is extracted, the model gets w_i as input and has to predict $(w_{i-2}, s), (w_{i-1}, s), (w_{i+1}, s), (w_{i+2}, s)$.

4.2   Sentiment lexicon features

Word representations are learned from distributional information of words in large corpora. Although such statistics are semantically informative, they disregard the valuable information that is contained in manually curated sentiment lexicons. In (Ebert et al., 2015), the authors propose to incorporate knowledge from semantic lexicons at the word level. The goal is to extract features based on the overlap between words in the input and sentiment lexicons, and stack these features to the word embedding.

We create two such features per word per lexicon. Both are binary indicators of positive and negative polarity of that word in the lexicons. The lexicons for this feature type are MPQA (Wiebe et al., 2005), Opinion lexicon (Hu and Liu, 2004), and NRC Emotion lexicon (Mohammad and Turney, 2013). The NRC lexicons provide a score for each word instead of just a label. We replace the binary indicators by the scores.

4.3 Sentence-level features

The following features are extracted at sentence level and used for training the sentence-level MLP:

- **Lexicons**: frequency of lemmas that are matched in MPQA (Wiebe et al., 2005), Opinion Lexicon (Hu and Liu, 2004) and NRC Emotion lexicon (Mohammad and Turney, 2013).
- **Emoticons**: number of emoticons that are grouped in positive, negative and neutral categories.
- **All-caps**: number of words in all-caps
- **Elongated units**: number of words in which characters are repeated more than twice (for example: looooool)
- **Punctuation**: number of contiguous sequences of period, exclamation mark and question mark.

5 Experiments

5.1 Pre-processing

A step of pre-processing is applied to every tweet in the corpus:

- **Character encoding:** every tweet is encoded in UTF-8
- **XML Entities:** all the XML entities are converted back to characters
- **Lowercase:** all the characters are converted in lowercase
- **Lengthening:** character lengthening consists in repeating several times a character in a word. It is used in social media as a method to emphasize a fact. This extension is often correlated with the expression of sentiment. If a character is repeated more than three times, we reduce it to three characters. For example, "looool" is replaced by "loool".
- **Tokenization:** tokenization is performed by splitting a sentence in pre-lexical units. We used the tokenizer from the macaon toolchain (Nasr et al., 2011). It is based on a regular grammar that defines a set of types of atoms. A lexical analyzer detects the character sequences (in terms of the grammar) and combines them as a type. We added the atoms for detecting smileys, hashtags and users names (atoms specific to tweets).

- **Map generic words:** The hashtags, numbers and usertags are mapped to generic tokens.

5.2 Corpus

We use the train and dev corpora from Twitter'13 to 16 for training and Twitter'16-dev as a development set. Note that we were unable to download all the training and development data because some tweets were deleted or not available due to modified authorization status. The datasets are summarized in Table 3:

Corpus	Positive	Negative	Neutral	Total
Train	7.727	2.916	7.837	18.480
Dev	884	279	616	1.779

Table 3: Statistics of the successfully downloaded part of the SemEval 2016 Twitter sentiment classification dataset.

5.3 Word embedding training

To train the word embeddings, we have created a unannotated corpus of sentiment bearing tweets in English. These tweets were recovered on the Twitter platform by searching for emotion keywords (from the sentiment lexicons) and unigrams, bigrams and trigrams extracted from the SemEval training corpus. This corpus consists of about 90 million tweets. A sub-corpus of about 20 million tweets containing at least one emoticon is used for training the sentiment embeddings. Both corpora are made available [3].

In our experiments, lexical embeddings and part-of-speech embeddings are estimated using the word2vec toolkit (Mikolov et al., 2013). Sentiment embeddings are estimated using word2vecf. This toolkit allows to replace linear bag-of-word contexts with arbitrary features. The embeddings are trained using the skipgram approach with a window of size 3 and 5 iterations. The dimension of the embeddings is fixed to 100. Part-of-speech tagging is performed with Tweet NLP (Owoputi et al., 2013; Gimpel et al., 2011).

5.4 Results

Overall performance: The evaluation metric used in the competition is the macro-averaged F-measure calculated over the positive and negative categories. Table 4 presents the overall performance of our system. It achieved the second rank on the Twitter 2016

---

[3] http://www.github.com/mrouvier/SemEval2016

Feature set	Lexical	Part-of-speech	Sentiment	SENSEI-LIF
all features	61.3	62.0	62.3	63.0
w/o word level lexicon	61.7 (+0.4)	62.4 (+0.4)	61.6 (**-0.7**)	63.2 (+0.2)
w/o sentence level lexicon	60.7 (**-0.6**)	61.1 (**-0.9**)	62.0 (**-0.3**)	62.6 (**-0.4**)
w/o both lexicon	61.0 (**-0.3**)	61.4 (**-0.6**)	61.8 (**-0.5**)	62.8 (**-0.2**)
w/o word embeddings	58.4 (**-2.9**)	59.1 (**-2.9**)	59.6 (**-2.7**)	59.6 (**-3.4**)

Table 2: Ablation experiment: macro-averaged F-scores obtained on the Twitter 2016 test sets with each of the feature groups removed.

data among 34 teams. The system proved to generalize well to other types of short informal texts; it ranked first and third respectively on the two out-of-domain datasets: Live Journal 2014 and SMS 2013.

Corpus	SENSEI-LIF	Rank
Twt2013	70.6	3
SMS2013	63.4	3
Twt2014	74.4	1
TwtSarc2014	46.7	8
LvJn2014	74.1	1
Twt2015	66.2	2
Twt2016	63.0	2

Table 4: Overall performance of the SENSEI-LIF sentiment analysis systems.

Contribution of features: Table 2 presents the results of ablation experiments on the Twitter 2016 test set. *SENSEI-LIF* is the system which participated to the evaluation campaign. We present the results of three contrastive systems: *Lexical, Part-of-speech* and *Sentiment*. These systems are based on the CNN classifier prior to the concatenation of the hidden layers. They use only one set of word embeddings without any kind of fusion.

The different features used in our system are: lexicon features and word embeddings. The ablation of lexicon features removes the lexicon features at the word and sentence level. The ablation of word embeddings feature consists in randomly initializing the word representations.

We observe that the most influential features are word embeddings. They provide a gain of 3.4 points. The main advantage of word embeddings is to learn unsupervised representations on very large corpora which capture general semantic properties. The last most important features are lexicon features. We observe that word level lexicon features are not relevant and tend to degrade the performance of the *SENSEI-LIF* system on the Twitter 2016 dataset.

Impact of fusion: Table 5 presents the results us-

ing different kinds of fusion: early, late and embedding fusion. We observe that early fusion obtains the worse results. We think that is due to the small training corpus used. Embedding fusion obtains the bests results on the Twitter 2016 dataset, but more generally late and embedding fusions obtain very close results on the other datasets.

Corpus	Early	Late	Embedding
Twt2013	69.4	70.4	**70.6**
SMS2013	62.6	**63.7**	63.4
Twt2014	73.4	74.3	**74.4**
TwtSarc2014	46.2	44.7	**46.7**
LvJn2014	74.3	**74.4**	74.1
Twt2015	64.1	**66.8**	66.2
Twt2016	61.6	62.8	**63.0**

Table 5: Overall performance using different methods of fusion: early, late and embedding fusion.

6 Conclusions

This paper describes the LIF participation at SemEval 2016. Our approach consists in learning polarity classifiers for three types of embeddings, based on the same CNN architecture. Each set of word embeddings models the tweet according to a different point of view: lexical, part-of-speech and sentiment. A final fusion step is applied, based on concatenating the hidden layers of the CNNs and training a deep neural network for the fusion. The fusion system ranked 2nd at the SemEval-2016 evaluation campaign.

Acknowledgments

The research leading to these results has received funding from the European Union - Seventh Framework Programme (FP7/2007-2013) under grant agreement 610916 SENSEI [4]. The Tesla K40 used for this research was donated by the NVIDIA Corporation.

---

[4]http://www.sensei-conversation.eu

References

Ronan Collobert, Jason Weston, Léon Bottou, Michael Karlen, Koray Kavukcuoglu, and Pavel Kuksa. 2011. Natural language processing (almost) from scratch. *JMLR*, 12:2493–2537.

Sebastian Ebert, Ngoc Thang Vu, and Hinrich Schütze. 2015. A linguistically informed convolutional neural network. In *Computational Approaches to Subjectivity, Sentimant and Social Media Analysis WASSA*, page 109.

Kevin Gimpel, Nathan Schneider, Brendan O'Connor, Dipanjan Das, Daniel Mills, Jacob Eisenstein, Michael Heilman, Dani Yogatama, Jeffrey Flanigan, and Noah A Smith. 2011. Part-of-speech tagging for twitter: Annotation, features, and experiments. In *Proceedings of the 49th Annual Meeting of the Association for Computational Linguistics: Human Language Technologies: short papers-Volume 2*, pages 42–47. Association for Computational Linguistics.

Jiang Guo, Wanxiang Che, Haifeng Wang, and Ting Liu. 2014. Learning sense-specific word embeddings by exploiting bilingual resources. In *COLING*, pages 497–507.

Minqing Hu and Bing Liu. 2004. Mining and summarizing customer reviews. In *SIGKDD*, pages 168–177.

Eric H Huang, Richard Socher, Christopher D Manning, and Andrew Y Ng. 2012. Improving word representations via global context and multiple word prototypes. In *Proceedings of the 50th Annual Meeting of the Association for Computational Linguistics: Long Papers-Volume 1*, pages 873–882. Association for Computational Linguistics.

Yoon Kim. 2014. Convolutional neural networks for sentence classification. *arXiv preprint arXiv:1408.5882*.

Yann LeCun and Yoshua Bengio. 1995. Convolutional networks for images, speech, and time series. *The handbook of brain theory and neural networks*, 3361(10).

Tomas Mikolov, Kai Chen, Greg Corrado, and Jeffrey Dean. 2013. Efficient estimation of word representations in vector space. *arXiv preprint arXiv:1301.3781*.

Saif M Mohammad and Peter D Turney. 2013. Nrc emotion lexicon. Technical report, NRC Technical Report.

Preslav Nakov, Alan Ritter, Sara Rosenthal, Veselin Stoyanov, and Fabrizio Sebastiani. 2016. SemEval-2016 task 4: Sentiment analysis in Twitter. In *Proceedings of the 10th International Workshop on Semantic Evaluation*, SemEval '16, San Diego, California, June. Association for Computational Linguistics.

Alexis Nasr, Frédéric Béchet, Jean-François Rey, Benoît Favre, and Joseph Le Roux. 2011. Macaon: An nlp tool suite for processing word lattices. In *ACL*, pages 86–91.

Arvind Neelakantan, Jeevan Shankar, Alexandre Passos, and Andrew McCallum. 2015. Efficient non-parametric estimation of multiple embeddings per word in vector space. *arXiv preprint arXiv:1504.06654*.

Olutobi Owoputi, Brendan O'Connor, Chris Dyer, Kevin Gimpel, Nathan Schneider, and Noah A Smith. 2013. Improved part-of-speech tagging for online conversational text with word clusters. Association for Computational Linguistics.

Soujanya Poria, Erik Cambria, and Alexander Gelbukh. 2015. Deep convolutional neural network textual features and multiple kernel learning for utterance-level multimodal sentiment analysis. In *Proceedings of EMNLP*, pages 2539–2544.

Mickael Rouvier, Sebastien Delecraz, Benoit Favre, Meriem Bendris, and Frederic Bechet. 2015. Multimodal embedding fusion for robust speaker role recognition in video broadcast. In *ASRU*.

Aliaksei Severyn and Alessandro Moschitti. 2015. Unitn: Training deep convolutional neural network for twitter sentiment classification. In *Proceedings of the 9th International Workshop on Semantic Evaluation (SemEval 2015), Association for Computational Linguistics, Denver, Colorado*, pages 464–469.

Duyu Tang, Furu Wei, Bing Qin, Ting Liu, and Ming Zhou. 2014a. Coooolll: A deep learning system for twitter sentiment classification. In *Proceedings of the 8th International Workshop on Semantic Evaluation (SemEval 2014)*, pages 208–212.

Duyu Tang, Furu Wei, Nan Yang, Ming Zhou, Ting Liu, and Bing Qin. 2014b. Learning sentiment-specific word embedding for twitter sentiment classification. In *ACL (1)*, pages 1555–1565.

Janyce Wiebe, Theresa Wilson, and Claire Cardie. 2005. Annotating expressions of opinions and emotions in language. *Language resources and evaluation*, 39(2-3):165–210.

DiegoLab16 at SemEval-2016 Task 4: Sentiment Analysis in Twitter using Centroids, Clusters, and Sentiment Lexicons

Abeed Sarker and Graciela Gonzalez
Department of Biomedical Informatics
Arizona State University
Scottsdale, AZ 85259, USA
`{abeed.sarker,graciela.gonzalez}@asu.edu`

Abstract

We present our supervised sentiment classification system which competed in SemEval-2016 Task 4: Sentiment Analysis in Twitter. Our system employs a Support Vector Machine (SVM) classifier trained using a number of features including n-grams, synset expansions, various sentiment scores, word clusters, and term centroids. Using weighted SVMs, to address the issue of class imbalance, our system obtains positive class F-scores of 0.694 and 0.650, and negative class F-scores of 0.391 and 0.493 over the training and test sets, respectively.

1 Introduction

Social media has evolved into a data source that is massive and growing rapidly. One of the most popular micro-blogging social networks, for example, is Twitter, which has over 645,750,000 users, and grows by an estimated 135,000 users every day, generating 9,100 tweets per second.[1] Users tend to use social networks to broadcast the latest events, and also to share personal opinions and experiences. Therefore, social media has become a focal point for data science research, and social media data is being actively used to perform a range of tasks from personalized advertising to public health monitoring and surveillance (Sarker et al., 2015a). Because of its importance and promise, social media data

has been the subject of recent large-scale annotation projects, and shared tasks have been designed around social media for solving problems in complex domains (*e.g.*, Sarker *et al.* (2016a)) While the benefits of using a resource such as Twitter include large volumes of data and direct access to end-user sentiments, there are several obstacles associated with the use of social media data. These include the use of non-standard terminologies, misspellings, short and ambiguous posts, and data imbalance, to name a few.

In this paper, we present a supervised learning approach, using Support Vector Machines (SVMs) for the task of automatic sentiment classification of Twitter posts. Our system participated in the SemEval-2016 task *Sentiment Analysis in Twitter*, and is an extension of our system for SemEval2015 (Sarker et al., 2015b). The goal of the task was to automatically classify the polarity of a Twitter post into one of three predefined categories— positive, negative and neutral. In our approach, we apply a small set of carefully extracted lexical, semantic, and distributional features. The features are used to train a SVM learner, and the issue of data imbalance is addressed by using distinct weights for each of the three classes. The results of our system are promising, with positive class F-scores of 0.694 and 0.650, and negative class F-scores of 0.391 and 0.493 over the training and test sets, respectively.

2 Related Work

Following the pioneering work on sentiment analysis by Pang *et. al.* (2002), similar research has been carried out under various umbrella terms such as: se-

---

[1] `http://www.statisticbrain.com/twitter-statistics/` Accessed on: 23rd December, 2015.

Proceedings of SemEval-2016, pages 209–214,
San Diego, California, June 16-17, 2016. ©2016 Association for Computational Linguistics

mantic orientation (Turney, 2002), opinion mining (Pang and Lee, 2008), polarity classification (Sarker et al., 2013), and many more. Pang *et al.* (2002) utilized machine learning models to predict sentiments in text, and their approach showed that SVM classifiers trained using bag-of-words features produced promising results. Similar approaches have been applied to texts of various granularities— documents, sentences, and phrases.

Due to the availability of vast amounts of data, there has been growing interest in utilizing social media mining for obtaining information directly from users (Liu and Zhang, 2012). However, social media sources, such as Twitter posts, present various natural language processing (NLP) and machine learning challenges. The NLP challenges arise from factors, such as, the use of informal language, frequent misspellings, creative phrases and words, abbreviations, short text lengths and others. From the perspective of machine learning, some of the key challenges include data imbalance, noise, and feature sparseness. In recent research, these challenges have received significant attention (Jansen et al., 2009; Barbosa and Feng, 2010; Davidov et al., 2010; Kouloumpis et al., 2011; Sarker and Gonzalez, 2014; Sarker et al., 2016b).

3   Methods

3.1   Data

Our training and test data consists of the data made available for SemEval 2016 task 4, and additional eligible training data from past Semeval sentiment analysis tasks. Each instance of the data set made available consisted of a tweet ID, a user ID, and a sentiment category for the tweet. For training, we downloaded all the annotated tweets that were publicly available at the time of development of the system. We obtained all the training and devtest set tweets, and also the training sets from past SemEval tasks. In total, we used over 19,000 unique tweets for training. The data is heavily imbalanced with particularly small number of negative instances.

3.2   Features

We derive a set of lexical, semantic, and distributional features from the training data. Brief descriptions are provided below. Some of these features

were used in our 2015 submission to the SemEval sentiment analysis task (Sarker et al., 2015b). In short: we have removed uninformative features such as syntactic parses of tweets, and have added features learned using distributional semantics-oriented techniques.

3.2.1   Preprocessing

We perform standard preprocessing such as tokenization, lowercasing and stemming of all the terms using the Porter stemmer[2] (Porter, 1980). Our preliminary investigations suggested that stop words can play a positive effect on classifier performances by their presence in word 2-grams and 3-grams; so, we do not remove stop words from the texts.

3.2.2   N-grams

Our first feature set consists of word n-grams. A word n-gram is a sequence of contiguous n words in a text segment, and this feature enables us to represent a document using the union of its terms. We use 1-, 2-, and 3-grams as features.

3.2.3   Synset

It has been shown in past research that certain terms, because of their prior polarities, play important roles in determining the polarities of sentences (Sarker et al., 2013). Certain adjectives, and sometimes nouns and verbs, or their synonyms, are almost invariably associated with positive or non-positive polarities. For each adjective, noun or verb in a tweet, we use WordNet[3] to identify the synonyms of that term and add the synonymous terms as features.

3.2.4   Sentiment Scores

We assign three sets of scores to sentences based on three different measures of sentiment. For the first set of scores, we used the positive and negative terms list from Hu and Bing (2004). For each tweet, the numbers of positive and negative terms are counted and divided by the total number of tokens in the tweet to generate two scores.

For the second sentiment feature, we incorporate a score that attempts to represent the general sentiment of a tweet using the prior polarities of its terms.

---

[2]We use the implementation provided by the NLTK toolkit http://www.nltk.org/.

[3]http://wordnet.princeton.edu/. Accessed on December 13, 2015.

Each word-POS pair in a comment is assigned a score and the overall score assigned to the comment is equal to the sum of all the individual term-POS sentiment scores divided by the length of the sentence in words. For term-POS pairs with multiple senses, the score for the most common sense is chosen. To obtain a score for each term, we use the lexicon proposed by Guerini *et al.* (2013) . The lexicon contains approximately 155,000 English words associated with a sentiment score between -1 and 1. The overall score a sentence receives is therefore a floating point number with the range [-1:1].

For the last set of scores in this set, we used the Multi-Perspective Question Answering (MPQA) subjectivity lexicon (Wiebe et al., 2005). In the lexicon, tokens are assigned a polarity (positive/negative), and a strength for the subjectivity (weak/strong). We assign a score of -1 to a token for having negative subjectivity, and +1 for having positive subjectivity. Tokens having weak subjectivity are multiplied with 0.5, and the total subjectivity score of the tweet is divided by the number of tokens to generate the final score.

3.2.5   Word Cluster Features

Our past research shows that incorporating word cluster features improve classification accuracy (Nikfarjam et al., 2014). These clusters are generated from vector representations of words, which are learned from large, unlabeled data sets. For our word clusters, the vector representations were learned from over 56 million tweets, using a Hidden Markov Model-based algorithm that partitions words into a base set of 1000 clusters, and induces a hierarchy among those 1000 clusters (Owoputi et al., 2012). To generate features from these clusters, for each tweet, we identify the cluster number of each token, and use all the cluster numbers in a bag-of-words manner. Thus, every tweet is represented with a set of cluster numbers, with semantically similar tokens having the same cluster number. More information about generating the embeddings can be found in the related papers (Bengio et al., 2003; Turian et al., 2010; Mikolov et al., 2013).

3.2.6   Centroid Features

We collected a large set of automatically 'annotated' sentiment corpus (Go et al., 2009). Using the negative and positive polarity tweets separately, we generated two distributional semantics models using the Word2Vec tool.[4] We then applied K-means clustering to the two distributional models to generate 100 clusters each. Finally, we compute the centroid vectors for each of the clusters in the two sets.

Two feature vectors are generated from each tweet based on these centroid vectors. For each tweet, the centroid of the tweet is computed by averaging the individual word vectors in the tweet. The cosine similarities of the tweet centroid are then computed with each of the two sets of 100 centroid vectors. The vectors of similarities are then used as features. Our intuition is that these vectors will indicate similarities of tweets with posts of negative or positive sentiments.

3.2.7   Structural Features

We use a set of features which represent simple structural properties of the tweets. These include: length, number of sentences, and average sentence length.

3.3   Classification

Using the abovementioned features, we trained SVM classifiers for the classification task. The performance of SVMs can vary significantly based on the kernel and specific parameter values. For our work, based on past research on this type of data, we used the RBF kernel. We computed optimal values for the *cost* and γ parameters via grid-search and 10-fold cross validation over the training set. To address the problem of data imbalance, we utilized the weighted SVM feature of the LibSVM library (Chang and Lin, 2011), and we attempted to find optimal values for the weights in the same way using 10-fold cross validation over the training set. We found that $cost = 64.0$, $\gamma = 0.0$, $\omega_1 = 1.2$, and $\omega_2 = 2.6$ to produce the best results, where ω_1 and ω_2 are the weights for the positive and negative classes, respectively.

4   Results

Table 1 presents the performance of our system on the training and test data sets. The table presents the

---

[4]https://code.google.com/archive/p/word2vec/. Accessed Feb-22-2016.

positive and negative class F-scores for the system, and the average of the two scores— the metric that is used for ranking systems in the SemEval evaluations for this task. The training set results are obtained via training on the training set and evaluating on the devtest set. The test results are the final SemEval results.

Data set	Positive F-score (P)	Negative F-score (N)	$\frac{P+N}{2}$
Training	0.694	0.391	0.542
Test	0.650	0.493	0.571

Table 1: Classification results for the DIEGOLab16 system over the training and test sets.

4.1   Feature Analysis

To assess the contribution of each feature towards the final score, we performed leave-one-out feature and single feature experiments. Tables 2 and 3 show the $\frac{P+N}{2}$ values for the training and the test sets for the two set of experiments. The first row of the tables present the results when all the features are used, and the following rows show the results when a specific feature is removed or when a single feature is used. The tables suggest that almost all the features play important roles in classification. As shown in Table 3, n-grams, word clusters, and centroids give the highest classification scores when employed individually. Table 2 illustrates similar information, by showing which features cause the largest drops in performance when removed. For all the other feature sets, the drops in the evaluation scores shown in Table 3 are very low, meaning that their contribution to the final evaluation score is quite limited. The experiments suggest that the classifier settings (*i.e.*, the parameter values and the class weights) play a more important role in our final approach, as greater deviations from the scores presented can be achieved by fine tuning the parameter values than by adding, removing, or modifying the feature sets. Further experimentation is required to identify useful features and to configure existing features to be more effective.

Feature removed	$\frac{P+N}{2}$
None	0.542
N-grams	0.540
Synsets	0.553
Sentiment Scores	0.540
Word Clusters	0.515
Centroids	0.527
Other	0.541

Table 2: Leave-one-out $\frac{P+N}{2}$ feature scores for the training and test sets.

Feature	$\frac{P+N}{2}$
All	0.542
N-grams	0.515
Synsets	0.494
Sentiment Scores	0.472
Word Clusters	0.531
Centroids	0.535
Other	0.254

Table 3: Single feature $\frac{P+N}{2}$ scores for the training and test sets.

5   Conclusions and Future Work

Our system achieved moderate performance on the SemEval sentiment analysis task utilizing very basic settings. The F-scores were particularly low for the negative class, which can be attributed to the class imbalance. Considering that the performance of our system was achieved by very basic settings, there is promise of better performance via the utilization of feature generation and engineering techniques.

We have several planned future tasks to improve the classification performance on this data set, and for social media based sentiment analysis in general. Following on from our past work on social media data (Sarker and Gonzalez, 2014; Sarker et al., 2016b), our primary goal to improve performance in the future is to employ preprocessing techniques that can normalize the texts and better prepare them for the feature generation stage. We will also attempt to optimize our distributional semantics models further.

Acknowledgments

This work was supported by NIH National Library of Medicine under grant number NIH NLM 1R01LM011176. The content is solely the responsibility of the authors and does not necessarily represent the official views of the NLM or NIH.

References

Luciano Barbosa and Junlan Feng. 2010. Robust Sentiment Detection on Twitter from Biased and Noisy Data. In *Proceedings of COLING*, pages 36–44.

Yoshua Bengio, Réjean Ducharme, Pascal Vincent, and Christian Jauvin. 2003. A Neural Probabilistic Language Model. *Journal of Machine Learning Research*, 3:1137–1155.

Chih-Chung Chang and Chih-Jen Lin. 2011. LIBSVM: A library for support vector machines. *ACM Transactions on Intelligent Systems and Technology*, 2:27:1–27:27. Software available at http://www.csie.ntu.edu.tw/~cjlin/libsvm.

Dmitry Davidov, Oren Tsur, and Ari Rappoport. 2010. Enhanced Sentiment Learning Using Twitter Hashtags and Smileys. In *Proceedings of COLING*, pages 241–249.

Alec Go, Richa Bhayani, and Lei Huang. 2009. Twitter Sentiment Classification using Distant Supervision. https://www-cs.stanford.edu/people/alecmgo/papers/TwitterDistantSupervision09.pdf.

Marco Guerini, Lorenzo Gatti, and Marco Turchi. 2013. Sentiment Analysis: How to Derive Prior Polarities from SentiWordNet. In *Proceedings of Empirical Methods in Natural Language Processing (EMNLP)*, pages 1259–1269.

Minqing Hu and Bing. 2004. "mining and summarizing customer reviews". In *Proceedings of the ACM SIGKDD International Conference on Knowledge Discovery and Data Mining*.

Bernard J Jansen, Mimi Zhang, Kate Sobel, and Abdur Chowdury. 2009. Twitter Power: Tweets as Electronic Word of Mouth. *Journal of the American Society for Information Science and Technology*, 60(11):2169–2188.

Efthymios Kouloumpis, Theresa Wilson, and Johanna Moore. 2011. Twitter Sentiment Analysis: The Good the Bad and the OMG! In *Proceedings of the Fifth International AAAI Conference on Weblogs and Social Media*.

Bing Liu and Lei Zhang. 2012. A survey of opinion mining and sentiment analysis. In Charu C. Aggarwal and ChengXiang Zhai, editors, *Mining Text Data*, pages 415–463.

Tomas Mikolov, Kai Chen, Greg Corrado, and Jeffrey Dean. 2013. Efficient Estimation of Word Representations in Vector Space. arXiv:1301.3781v3.

Azadeh Nikfarjam, Abeed Sarker, Karen O'Connor, Rachel Ginn, and Graciela Gonzalez. 2014. Pharmacovigilance from social media: mining adverse drug reaction mentions using sequence labeling with word embedding cluster features. *Journal of the American Medical Informatics Association (JAMIA)*.

Olutobi Owoputi, Brendan O'Connor, Chris Dyer Kevin Gimpel, and Nathan Schneider. 2012. Part-of-Speech Tagging for Twitter: Word Clusters and Other Advances. Technical report, School of Computer Science, Carnegie Mellon University.

Bo Pang and Lillian Lee. 2008. Opinion Mining and Sentiment Analysis. *Foundations and Trends in Information Retrieval*, 2(1):1–135.

Bo Pang, Lillian Lee, and Shivakumar Vaithyanathan. 2002. Thumbs up? Sentiment Classification using Machine Learning Techniques. In *Proceedings of the ACL conference on Empirical Methods in Natural Language Processing (EMNLP)*, pages 79–86.

Martin F. Porter. 1980. An algorithm for suffix stripping. *Program*, 14(3):130–137.

Abeed Sarker and Graciela Gonzalez. 2014. Portable Automatic Text Classification for Adverse Drug Reaction Detection via Multi-corpus Training. *Journal of Biomedical Informatics*.

Abeed Sarker, Diego Molla, and Cecile Paris. 2013. Automatic Prediction of Evidence-based Recommendations via Sentence-level Polarity Classification. In *Proceedings of the International Joint Conference on Natural Language Processing (IJCNLP)*, pages 712–718.

Abeed Sarker, Rachel Ginn, Azadeh Nikfarjam, Karen O'Connor, Karen Smith, Swetha Jayaraman, Tejaswi Upadhaya, and Graciela Gonzalez. 2015a. Utilizing social media data for pharmacovigilance: A review. *Journal of Biomedical Informatics*, 54:202–212.

Abeed Sarker, Azadeh Nikfarjam, Davy Weissenbacher, and Graciela Gonzalez. 2015b. Diegolab: An approach for message-level sentiment classification in twitter. In *Proceedings of the 9th International Workshop on Semantic Evaluation (SemEval 2015)*, pages 510–514, Denver, Colorado, June. Association for Computational Linguistics.

Abeed Sarker, Azadeh Nikfarjam, and Graciela Gonzalez. 2016a. Social Media Mining Shared Task Workshop. In *Proceedings of the Pacific Symposium on Biocomputing*.

Abeed Sarker, Karen O'Connor, Rachel Ginn, Matthew Scotch, Karen Smith, Dan Malone, and Graciela Gonzalez. 2016b. Social media mining for toxicovigilance: Automatic monitoring of prescription medication abuse from twitter. *Drug Safety*, 39(3):231–240.

Joseph Turian, Lev Ratinov, and Yoshua Bengio. 2010. Word representations: A simple and general method for semi-supervised learning. In *Proceedings of the 48th Annual Meeting of the Association for Computational Linguistics*, pages 384–394.

Peter Turney. 2002. Thumbs up or thumbs down? Semantic orientation applied to unsupervised classification of reviews. In *Proceedings of ACL-02, 40th Annual Meeting of the Association for Computational Linguistics*, pages 417–424.

Janyce Wiebe, Theresa Wilson, and Claire Cardie. 2005. Annotating expressions opinion and emotion in language. *Language Resources and Evaluation*, 39:165–210.

VCU-TSA at Semeval-2016 Task 4: Sentiment Analysis in Twitter

Gerard Briones and **Kasun Amarasinghe** and **Bridget T. McInnes, PhD.**
Department of Computer Science
Virginia Commonwealth University
Richmond, VA, 23284, USA
{brioinesgc, amarasinghek, btmcinnes}vcu.edu

Abstract

The aim of this paper is to produce a methodology for analyzing sentiments of selected Twitter messages, better known as Tweets. This project elaborates on two experiments carried out to analyze the sentiment of Tweets from SemEval-2016 Task 4 Subtask A and Subtask B. Our method is built from a simple unigram model baseline with three main feature enhancements incorporated into the model: 1) emoticon retention, 2) word stemming, and 3) token saliency calculation. Our results indicate an increase in classification accuracy with the addition of emoticon retention and word stemming, while token saliency shows mixed performance. These results elucidate a possible classification feature model that could aid in the sentiment analysis of Twitter feeds and other microblogging environments.

1 Introduction

Twitter is a widely used microblogging environment which serves as a medium to share opinions on various events and products. Because of this, analyzing Twitter has the potential to reveal opinions of the general public regarding these topics. However, mining the content of Twitter messages is a challenging task due to a multitude of reasons, such as the shortness of the posted content and the informal and unstructured nature of the language used. The aim of this study is to produce a methodology for analyzing sentiments of selected Twitter messages, better known as Tweets. This project elaborates on two experiments carried out to analyze the sentiment

of Tweets, namely, Subtask A and Subtask B from SemEval-2016 Task 4 (Nakov et al., 2016).

Subtask A: Message Polarity Classification. The goal of this subtask was to predict a given Tweet's sentiment from three classes: 1) positive, 2) neutral, or 3) negative.

Subtask B: Tweet classification according to a two-point scale. The goal of this subtask was to classify a given Tweet's sentiment towards a given topic. The sentiments were limited to positive and negative, unlike Subtask A.

2 Method

We viewed both tasks as classification problems. We represented the Tweets in a statistical feature matrix and performed the classification using supervised machine learning classification algorithms. Several different feature vectors were experimented with and the same set of feature vectors were applied to both Subtask A and Subtask B.

2.1 Feature Vectors

Our methods consume Tweet data and output a matrix where each row represents a Tweet and each column represents a feature. The values in this matrix are the frequency of appearance of a feature in the Tweet. As reference for the rest of the project, please note that $n\text{-}grams$ are a continuous set of n terms in a document. Thus, when n=1, we are representing a unigram, or a single word; when n=2, we are representing a bigram, or a pair of words, and so on. We evaluated unigram, bigram and trigram models, but discuss only the unigram model. The bigram and trigram models results showed to be less effective.

Proceedings of SemEval-2016, pages 215–219,
San Diego, California, June 16-17, 2016. ©2016 Association for Computational Linguistics

2.1.1 Unigram Model

As a baseline, a unigram model was used as the primary feature vector. The unigram model consists of several one-state finite automatas, splitting the probabilities of different features in a context. The probability of occurrence for each feature is independent. In our project, each word in a Tweet represents a feature.

For the first step of creating the unigram feature vector, numbers and special characters were removed from each Tweet, since they carry little information when taken out of context. The Tweets were then converted to all lower case to reduce the dimensionality of the data, whereby different users' capitalization does not factor in as a new, separate feature. Next, the Tweets were tokenized by breaking up the messages into single word units that each represent a unique feature. All stop words were then removed from these token sets. Stop words, such as "the" and "a", are the most commonly occurring words in a language and are considered to carry little to no information due to their high frequency of appearance (Yao and Ze-wen, 2011). Their presence in the dataset has the potential of adversely affecting the classification results. The most frequent words in the dataset were then identified based on a specified frequency threshold, filtering out all tokens that appeared less than the threshold. This was done to reduce the size of the resultant feature vector and identify the most general set of terms that represents the dataset.

2.1.2 Unigram model with feature reduction through stemming

In addition to the baseline methodology, we applied a technique known as stemming, which reduces words to their basic forms. This process combines words with similar basic forms, for example the words "running" and "ran" are reduced to the base form of "run," thus reducing the overall feature count and increasing the co-occurrence count.

2.1.3 Unigram model with feature enhancement through emoticon retention

One of the disadvantages of removing special characters from the Tweets was that the emoticons, text representations of emotions, were lost. Emoticons are good indicators of expression and emotion,

and are frequently used in Tweets. We again performed the steps in the previous methods, but before the removal of special characters from the Tweet, we implemented a series of regular expressions to capture a specific set of emoticons and convert them into unique key words.

2.1.4 Unigram model with word saliency statistics

The saliency, or quality, of the terms in the unigram model were calculated using the Term Frequency - Inverse Document Frequency (TF-IDF) score. The values of the matrix were modified to the TF-IDF score through the equations below.

$$TF(\text{Tweet, term}) = \frac{\text{frequencyOfTerm(Tweet)}}{\text{totalTerms(Tweet)}} \tag{1}$$

$$IDF(\text{term}) = \log \frac{\text{totalDocuments}}{\text{numDocumentsContaining(term)}} \tag{2}$$

$$TF\text{-}IDF(\text{Tweet, term}) = TF(\text{Tweet, term}) \cdot IDF(\text{term}) \tag{3}$$

3 Classification

Once the feature vectors were created, the final step of classification was accomplished using supervised machine learning algorithms. In the presented methodology, classification was carried out using single classifiers as well as multiple classifiers. As a reminder, Subtask A is a three class problem, while Subtask B is a two class problem.

3.1 Single Classifier

For this classification method, only a single classifier was used to perform the classification. The feature vector of a Tweet was used as input and the classifier returned the predicted sentiment class for that Tweet.

3.2 Multiple Classifiers

For this classification method, multiple classifiers were utilized to produce the final sentiment class of the Tweet based on a voting system. Each classifier is given a single vote and performs the classification of the Tweet on its own; casting its vote for which classification should be assigned for that Tweet. The predicted class with the majority of votes is then assigned as the class for that Tweet. We refer to this process as *voting*.

4 Data

The SemEval-2016 (Nakov et al., 2016) training datasets were used for both tasks. The datasets consisted of Tweets with pre-labeled sentiments. Table 1 and Table 2 show the class distributions of the training data.

Table 1: Dataset for Subtask A

# of Tweets	*Pos*	*Neu*	*Neg*
705	345 (48.93%)	164	196

Table 2: Dataset for Subtask B

# of Tweets	Topics	*Pos*	*Neg*
3890	59	3215 (82.64%)	675

5 Implementation Specifics

This section discusses the parameters and assumptions made in the implementation of our systems. Our system is freely available for download [1].

5.1 Feature Vector Creation

For the feature vector creation, the stemming process was carried out using the Porter stemmer (Porter, 1997) supplied in the Natural Language Toolkit (NLTK) (Loper and Bird, 2002) platform [2]. The stop word list was manually created and is freely available in our package. The emoticons were retained by converting them to unique tokens using regular expressions. Table 3 shows the emoticons used by the system and their conversion.

For our implementation, we used a frequency threshold of five to filter our features. This parameter was determined during initial development of the system by evaluating several thresholds using 10-fold cross validation over the training data.

5.2 Classifiers

Three classifiers were tested for both subtasks. Subtask A utilized the Naive Bayes Multinomial, Naive Bayes, and J48 decision tree classifiers. Similarly,

---

[1]https://github.com/gerardBriones/twitter-sentiment-analysis
[2]http://www.nltk.org/

Table 3: Emoticons

smileEmoticon	:)
frownEmoticon	: (
winkEmoticon	;)
tongueEmoticon	: P
concernEmoticon	: /
grinEmoticon	: D
mirrorGrinEmoticon	D :
winkGrinEmoticon	; D
surpriseEmoticon	: O
tearSmileEmoticon	:')
tearFrownEmoticon	:' (

Subtask B used the Naive Bayes, J48 decision tree, and Support Vector Machine classifiers. These classifiers were used individually as well as with voting. All classifiers were implemented using the open source, freely available Weka (Hall et al., 2009) data mining package [3]. We used Weka's default learning parameters in our experiments.

6 Results

Table 4 shows the overall accuracies acquired by the different classifiers tested for Subtask A. We chose to use a baseline of a unigram model with the frequency threshold set to one. The Naive Bayes Multinomial classifier produced the highest results for Subtask A from the classifiers tested. Further, the enhancements done to the unigram model did not yield a significant increase of accuracy in our tests. The highest accuracy was achieved with the basic unigram model in conjunction with the Naive Bayes Multinomial classifier. With that being said, the basic unigram model with a frequency threshold of five was able to outperform our selected baseline.

Table 5 illustrates the overall accuracies obtained for Subtask B. We swapped the Naive Bayes Multinomial classifier with the Support Vector Machines classifier due to our use of the Tweet's topic as categorical data. The SVM classifier produced the highest overall results. Further, all classifiers except for Naive Bayes performed better than the baseline. Voting did not perform as well with the J48 and SVM algorithms, but still outperformed Naive Bayes. Our highest accuracy was achieved using the unigram model with stemming as features into the SVM classifier.

---

[3]http://www.cs.waikato.ac.nz/ml/weka/index.html

Table 4: Overall classification accuracies for Subtask A

	Uni	Uni + Stem	Uni+ Stem + Emot	Uni + Stem + Emot + TF-IDF
NBM	0.577	0.572	0.569	0.557
NB	0.550	0.539	0.540	0.552
J48	0.516	0.549	0.552	0.515
Voting	0.569	0.566	0.562	0.533

Table 5: Overall classification accuracies for Subtask B

	Uni	Uni + Stem	Uni+ Stem + Emot	Uni + Stem + Emot + TF-IDF
NBM	0.692	0.674	0.674	0.612
J48	0.864	0.870	0.870	0.872
SVM	0.879	0.881	0.881	0.870
Voting	0.867	0.865	0.863	0.876

Table 6 shows the results using our unigram, stemming, emoticon retention, and TF-IDF methodology on Subtask A. Our average F1 and average recall scores are higher than the baseline, with our accuracy score having a smaller, but still noticeable increase.

Table 6: Final Evaluation Results for Subtask A

#	System	AvgF1	AvgR	Acc
1	SwissCheese	0.633	0.667	0.646
2	SENSEI-LIF	0.630	0.670	0.617
3	unimelb	0.617	0.641	0.616
4	INESC-ID	0.610	0.663	0.600
5	aueb.twitter.sentiment	0.605	0.644	0.629
31	VCU-TSA	0.372	0.390	0.382
35	baseline (positive)	0.255	0.333	0.342

Table 7 shows the results using our unigram, stemming, emoticon retention, and TF-IDF methodology on Subtask B. Our average F1 and average recall scores are slightly better than the baseline, while our accuracy also slightly decreased.

Table 7: Final Evaluation Results for Subtask B

#	System	AvgF1	AvgR	Acc
1	Tweester	0.797	0.799	0.862
2	LYS	0.791	0.720	0.762
3	thecerealkiller	0.784	0.762	0.823
4	ECNU	0.768	0.770	0.843
5	INSIGHT-1	0.767	0.786	0.864
19	VCU-TSA	0.502	0.448	0.775
20	baseline (positive)	0.500	0.438	0.778

7 Discussion and Future Work

In this paper, we present a method to predict the sentiment of Twitter feeds. We evaluated using a unigram model with three feature modifications: (1) stemming, (2) emoticon retention, and (3) word saliency. These modifications were applied to the unigram model and consumed with machine learning algorithms from the Weka datamining package. The results showed that using a unigram model with a frequency threshold of five in conjunction with the Naive Bayes Multinomial classifiers obtained the highest accuracy for Subtask A, and the unigram model with stemming in combination with the Support Vector Machine classifier achieved the highest accuracy for Subtask B.

Analysis of the results showed that the unstructured nature of word spelling may have played a role in our relatively low accuracies, causing multiple features to be seen as unique, when in actuality they should in fact map to the same feature. We also believe that the mixed results from the inclusion of the TF-IDF score is due in part to the heavily skewed nature of the data. In both Subtask A and Subtask B, the training data was mostly comprised of positively tagged sentiments, overwhelming the other classifications.

In the future, we plan to explore incorporating synonym set evaluations, acronym expansion, and spelling correction to aid in feature reduction. Efforts will also be made to include more contextual information, like sentiment lexicon, and to explore other multiple classifier methods, such as co-training.

References

Mark Hall, Eibe Frank, Geoffrey Holmes, Bernhard Pfahringer, Peter Reutemann, and Ian H. Witten. 2009. The weka data mining software: An update. *SIGKDD Explor. Newsl.*, 11(1):10–18, November.

Edward Loper and Steven Bird. 2002. Nltk: The natural language toolkit. In *Proceedings of the ACL-02 Workshop on Effective Tools and Methodologies for Teaching Natural Language Processing and Computational Linguistics - Volume 1*, ETMTNLP '02, pages 63–70, Stroudsburg, PA, USA. Association for Computational Linguistics.

Preslav Nakov, Alan Ritter, Sara Rosenthal, Veselin Stoyanov, and Fabrizio Sebastiani. 2016. SemEval-2016 task 4: Sentiment analysis in Twitter. In *Proceedings of the 10th International Workshop on Semantic Evaluation*, SemEval '16, San Diego, California, June. Association for Computational Linguistics.

M. F. Porter. 1997. Readings in information retrieval. chapter An Algorithm for Suffix Stripping, pages 313–316. Morgan Kaufmann Publishers Inc., San Francisco, CA, USA.

Zhou Yao and Cao Ze-wen. 2011. Research on the construction and filter method of stop-word list in text preprocessing. In *Intelligent Computation Technology and Automation (ICICTA), 2011 International Conference on*, volume 1, pages 217–221. IEEE.

UniPI at SemEval-2016 Task 4: Convolutional Neural Networks for Sentiment Classification

Giuseppe Attardi, Daniele Sartiano
Dipartimento di Informatica
Università di Pisa
Italy
{attardi,sartiano}@di.unipi.it

Abstract

The paper describes our submission to the task on Sentiment Analysis on Twitter at SemEval 2016. The approach is based on a Deep Learning architecture using convolutional neural networks. The approach used only word embeddings as features. The submission used embeddings created from a corpus of news articles. We report on further experiments using embeddings built for a corpus of tweets as well as sentiment specific word embeddings obtained by distant supervision.

1 Introduction

Up until recently, the typical approaches to sentiment analysis of tweets were based on classifiers trained using several hand-crafted features, in particular lexicons of words with an assigned polarity value. At the SemEval 2015 task 10 on Sentiment Analysis of Twitter (Rosenthal et al., 2015), most systems relied on features derived from sentiment lexicons. Other important features included bag-of-words features, hash-tags, handling of negation, word shape and punctuation features, elongated words, etc. Moreover, tweet pre-processing and normalization were an important part of the processing pipeline.

Quite significantly, the top scoring system in subtask A: Phrase-Level Polarity (Moschitti and Severyn, 2015) was instead based on the use of a convolutional neural network, which used word embeddings as its only features. Word embeddings were created by unsupervised learning from a collection of 50 million tweets, using the SkipGram model by Mikolov et al, (2013). The tweets used for training were collected by querying the Twitter API on the presence of a set of emoticons representing positive or negative sentiment. The winning team achieved an F1 of 84.79 on the Twitter2015 test set. The team participated with a similar approach also to subtask B: Message-Level Polarity, achieving the second best score with an F1 of 64.59. The fourth F1 score of 64.17 was achieved also by a system exploiting word embeddings by INESC-ID. The top scoring system instead consisted in an ensemble combining four Twitter sentiment classification approaches that participated in previous editions, with an F1 of 64.84.

We decided to explore a similar approach for tackling SemEval 2016 task 4 on Sentiment Analysis in Twitter (Nakov et al., 2016).

2 Approach

The classifier is based on a Deep Learning architecture consisting of the following layers:

1. a lookup layer for word embeddings
2. a convolutional layer with relu activation
3. a maxpooling layer
4. a dropout layer
5. a linear layer with tanh activation
6. a softmax layer

Proceedings of SemEval-2016, pages 220–224,
San Diego, California, June 16-17, 2016. ©2016 Association for Computational Linguistics

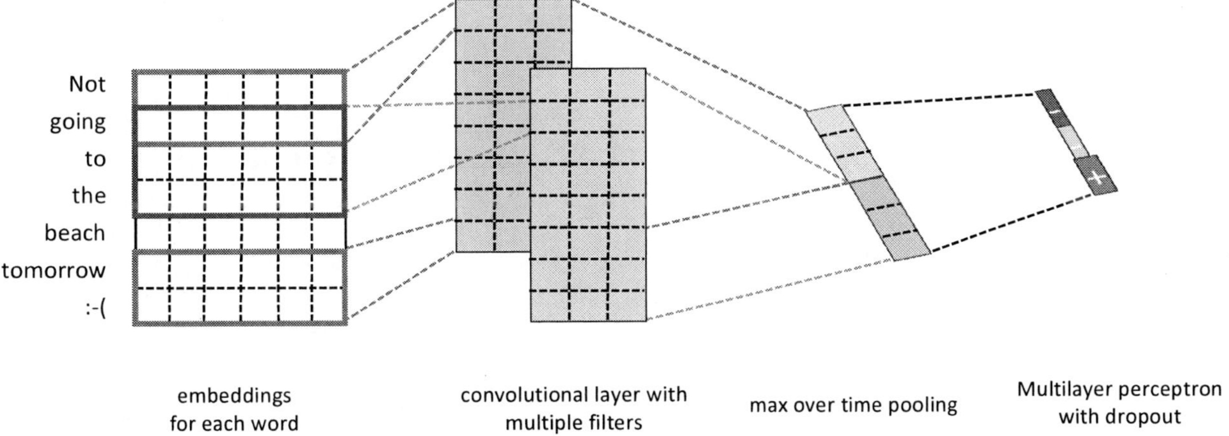

Figure 1. Architecture of the Deep Learning classifier.

The architecture is illustrated in Figure 1. The first layer looks up the embedding for words, i.e. vectors in $\mathbb{R}^d$. In our experiments we set $d = 300$. The convolutional layer consists of multiple convolutional filters of sliding windows of various sizes. These are then combined through a max-pooling layer and then passed through a multilayer perceptron with dropout.

A sentence s is represented by a sentence matrix S, where each row S_i corresponds to the embedding for the i-th word in a sentence (in the figure the matrix S is transposed).

A convolution operation involves a filter $F \in \mathbb{R}^{h,d}$, which is applied to sliding windows of size h words to produce a feature map. A feature c_i is obtained by applying the filter to a window of words $S_{i:i+h-1}$ as:

$$c_i = f(F \otimes S_{i:i+h-1} + b)$$

where $\otimes$ is the Frobenius matrix product, $b \in \mathbb{R}$ is a bias term and f is a non-linear activation function such as the hyperbolic tangent. The filter is applied to each possible window of words in the sentence to produce a feature map $c \in \mathbb{R}^{n-h+1}$, where n is the length of the sentence (padded as necessary).

Several filters F_k are used each with its own filter width h_k.

Max-pooling is applied to the feature maps produced by the filters obtaining a single vector that forms the input to an MLP with a dropout layer. Dropout is used to prevents co-adaptation of hidden units by setting to zero with probability p a portion of the hidden units during forward propagation.

We preprocessed the tweets using the Tanl pipeline (Attardi, 2010) for performing Sentence Splitting and applying a tweet tokenizer capable of recognizing mentions, hashtags and emoticons. All mentions were replaced by @user, all URL were replaced by http://URL. All sentences are padded to the same length in order to enable processing mini-batches in parallel using CUDA matrix operations.

For training we used the training and development set from SemEval 2013 task 10 and from SemEval 2016.

The code for the DL classifier is written in Theano and is available on GitHub[1]. The implementation is derived from the one developed by Yoon Kim for the paper (Kim, 2014), and provides the ability to configure parameters and settings of the network, as well as to control the use of cross-validation.

The network is implemented by a class `Con-vNet` that extends the `MLPDropout` class from `https://github.com/mdenil/dropout`.

Training is done by mean of ASGD with updated performed with Adadelta (Zeiler, 2012).

```
class ConvNet(MLPDropout):
    def __init__(self, U, height,
        width, filter_ws,
        conv_non_linear,
        feature_maps, output_units,
        batch_size, dropout_rates,
        activations)
```

---

[1] https://github.com/attardi/CNN_sentence

	2013		2014			2015	2016 Tweet	
	Tweet	SMS	Tweet	Sarcasm	Live-Journal	Tweet	Avg F1	Acc
SwissCheese	0.700_5	0.637_2	0.716_2	$\mathbf{0.566_1}$	0.695_7	$\mathbf{0.671_1}$	$\mathbf{0.633_1}$	$\mathbf{0.646_1}$
UniPI	0.592_{18}	0.585_{11}	0.627_{18}	0.381_{25}	0.654_{12}	0.586_{19}	0.571_{18}	0.639_3
UniPI SWE	0.642	0.606	0.684	0.481	0.668	0.635	0.592	0.652

Table 1. Official results of our submission compared to the top one, and an unofficial run.

where:

U: embedding matrix

height: sentence length

width: word vector dimension

filter_ws: filter window sizes

conv_activation: activation function of the convolutional layer (default relu)

feature_maps: number of feature maps (per filter window)

output_units: number of output variables

batch_size: size of the mini-batches

droput_rates: probability for the dropout laye

activations: the activation functions for each layer in the MLP

3 Experiments

The settings for the experiment were the following: word embeddings of 300 dimensions from a Google News corpus[2], filters of size 7,7,7 each with a 100 feature maps, dropout rate 0.5, MLP hidden units 100, batch size 50, adadelta decay 0.95, convolutional layer activation relu, training epochs 25.

For choosing the setting of our single submission, we took into account the suggestion from the experiments carried out by Zhang and Wallace. (2015).

The experiments were run on a linux server with an nVIDIA Tesla K40 accelerated GPU.

4 Results

The official submission achieved result presented in Table 1, compared to the top scoring system, as well as with an unofficial run using SWE (Sentiment Specific Word Embeddings) as described later.

A remarkable aspect of the submission is the fact that the accuracy on the 2016 Tweet jumps from the 18th position to third place.

In order to analyze this phenomenon, we present the breakdown of score among the three categories.

This is the breakdown of the scores of our official submission:

UniPI	Prec.	Rec.	F1
positive	69.50	63.97	66.62
negative	48.77	55.73	52.02
neutral	67.68	68.11	67.68
Avg F1			59.32
Accuracy			64.62

Table 2. Detailed scores of UniPI official submission.

Details of the evaluation of the top scoring system:

SwissCheese	Prec.	Rec.	F1
positive	67.48	74.14	70.66
negative	53.26	67.86	59.68
neutral	71.47	59.51	64.94
Avg F1			**65.17**
Accuracy			64.62

Table 3. Detailed scores of top submission for Task 4, subtask A.

After submission we performed further experiments, summarized in the following tables, which report the micro average F1 over the whole test set.

The experiments used embeddings from a corpus of 35 million tweets, and the whole training set, including the 10% that was held out for the 10-fold cross validation in the submission. A run with the same hyper-parameters obtained a slight improvement:

UniPI 2	Prec.	Rec.	F1
positive	76.86	56.87	65.37
negative	47.70	63.07	54.32
neutral	66.52	72.45	69.36
Avg F1			59.85
Accuracy			65.30

Table 4. Unofficial run using the full training set and embeddings from a corpus of 35 million tweets.

Using instead a set of filters of sizes 3,5,7,7, improved further, achieving an unofficial best accuracy score:

---

[2] https://code.google.com/archive/p/word2vec/

UniPI 3	Prec.	Rec.	F1
positive	70.88	65.35	68.00
negative	50.29	58.93	54.27
neutral	68.02	68.12	68.07
Avg F1			61.14
Accuracy			**65.64**

Table 5. Unofficial run using embeddings from tweets and filters of sizes 3,5,7,7.

The good F1 score on the neutral category seems to indicate that there is a certain degree of confusion between the two other categories.

We tested also filters of sizes 3,4,5,6,7,7,7 and 10 filters of size 7, with no overall improvements.

A more interesting experiment was the use of sentiment specific word embeddings (SWE), which encode sentiment information in the continuous representation of words. We incorporated sentiment polarity from the SemEval training corpus into the embeddings built from the corpus of 35 million of tweets, by using the technique by Tang et al. (2014), and implemented in DeepNL[3] (Attardi, 2015). A neural network with a suitable loss function provides the supervision for transferring the sentiment polarity of text (e.g. sentences or tweets) to the embeddings from generic tweets.

Training the same convolutional network with filters of size 3,5,7,7 using these sentiment specific word embeddings, produced an overall improvement that lead to an Avg F1 on Tweets 2016 of 0.595, and in detail:

UniPI SWE	Prec.	Rec.	F1
positive	68.87	68.38	68.62
negative	49.49	60.02	54.25
neutral	69.07	64.50	66.70
Avg F1			61.44
Accuracy			65.18

Table 6. Run using SWE and filters of size 3,5,7,7.

In order to compare the approach by Moschitti and Severyn (2015), which is quite similar to ours, we tested the code that Severyn kindly provided us. The experiment was run in a similar configuration, using filters of size 3,5,7,7 and also using the sentiment specific embeddings. Contrary to (Moschitti and Severyn, 2015), which used a feature map of a larger size (300), in our experiments we could not see particular benefits in increasing the feature map.

---

[3] https://github.com/attardi/deepnl

Moschitti and Severyn had used their own embeddings, created by distant supervision on a corpus of 50 million tweets that they collected, hence the comparison can only be considered indicative.

MS-2015	Prec.	Rec.	F1
Positive	68.03	61.73	64.73
negative	49.29	42.06	45.39
neutral	57.17	66.13	61.33
Avg F1			55.06
Accuracy			59.85

Table 7. Test performed using the code by Moschitti&Severyn for SemEval 2015.

5 Conclusions

The submission confirmed the effectiveness of convolutional neural networks in the task of tweet sentiment classification. Our systems achieved good precision scores and the third best accuracy score, achieving an overall above average official score.

After submission experiments showed a good ability in separating neutral tweets from the others, with an F1 of 70 on neutral tweets, and a good precision on positive tweets, while the recall on negative tweets was low. The use of sentiment specific word embeddings seems a promising approach for overcoming this problem.

Both the code for the classifier and for computing the sentiment specific embeddings are available on GitHub.

Acknowledgments

We grateful acknowledge the support of the University of Pisa through project PRA.
We gratefully acknowledge the support by NVIDIA Corporation with a donation of the Tesla K40 GPU used in the experiments.

References

Giuseppe Attardi, Stefano Dei Rossi, Maria Simi. 2010, The Tanl pipeline. Proc. of LREC Workshop on WSPP, Malta, 2010.

Giuseppe Attardi. 2015. DeepNL: a Deep Learning NLP pipeline. Workshop on Vector Space Modeling for NLP. Proc. of NAACL HLT 2015, Denver, Colorado (June 5, 2015).

Ramón Astudillo, Silvio Amir, Wang Ling, Bruno Martins, Mario J. Silva and Isabel Trancoso. 2015. INESC-ID: Sentiment Analysis without Hand-Coded

Features or Linguistic Resources using Embedding Subspaces. *Proceedings of the 9th International Workshop on Semantic Evaluation* (SemEval 2015). Denver, Colorado, Association for Computational Linguistics.

Yoon Kim. 2014. Convolutional Neural Networks for Sentence Classification. Proceedings of EMNLP 2014.

Tomas Mikolov, Ilya Sutskever, Kai Chen, Greg S Corrado, and Jeff Dean. 2013. Distributed representations of words and phrases and their compositionality. In *Advances in Neural Information Processing Systems 26*, pages 3111–3119.

Preslav Nakov, Alan Ritter, Sara Rosenthal, Fabrizio Sebastiani, Veselin Stoyanov. 2016. SemEval-2016 Task 3: Sentiment Analysis in Twitter. Proceedings of *of the 10th International Workshop on Semantic Evaluation* (SemEval 2016). ACL.

Aliaksei Severyn and Alessandro Moschitti. 2015. UNITN: Training Deep Convolutional Neural Network for Twitter Sentiment Classification. *Proceedings of the 9th International Workshop on Semantic Evaluation* (SemEval 2015). Denver, Colorado, Association for Computational Linguistics.

Sara Rosenthal, Preslav Nakov, Svetlana Kiritchenko, Saif Mohammad, Alan Ritter and Veselin Stoyanov. 2015. SemEval-2015 Task 10: Sentiment Analysis in Twitter. *Proceedings of the 9th International Workshop on Semantic Evaluation* (SemEval 2015). Denver, Colorado, Association for Computational Linguistics.

D. Tang, F. Wei, N. Yang, M. Zhou, T. Liu, and B. Qin. 2014. Learning Sentiment-Specific Word Embedding for Twitter Sentiment Classification. In ACL, pp. 1555-1565.

Matthew D. Zeiler. 2012. ADADELTA: An Adaptive Learning Rate Method. CoRR, vol. abs/1212.5701, http://arxiv.org/abs/1212.5701.

Ye Zhang and Byron Wallace. 2015. A Sensitivity Analysis of (and Practitioners' Guide to) Convolutional Neural Networks for Sentence Classification. CoRR, vol. abs/1510.03820, http://arxiv.org/abs/1510.03820

IIP at SemEval-2016 Task 4: Prioritizing Classes in Ensemble Classification for Sentiment Analysis of Tweets

Jasper Friedrichs

Infosys Limited

7707 Gateway Boulevard

Newark, CA 94560, USA

`jasper_friedrichs@infosys.com`

Abstract

This paper describes the submission of team IIP in SemEval-2016 Task 4 Subtask A. The presented system is a novel weighted sum ensemble approach for sentiment analysis of short informal texts. The ensemble combines member classifiers that output classification confidence metrics. For the ensemble classification decision the members are combined by weights. In the presented approach the weights are derived to prioritize specific classes in multi-class classification. The presented results confirm that this improves results for the prioritized classes. The official task submission achieved a macro-averaged negative positive F1 of 57.4%. Post submission changes resulted in a F1 score of 60.2%. The evaluation also shows that the system outperforms other ensemble methods.

1 Introduction

The SemEval workshops offer the opportunity to compete across a variety of natural language processing tasks. The SemEval-2016 Task 4 Subtask A targets message polarity classification of tweets (Nakov et al., 2016). The polarity can be negative, neutral or positive while the submissions are ranked omitting performance on the neutral class. In practical use cases some classes of a multi-classification problem might be deemed more important than others. For example some work looks explicitly at negative sentiment (Tetlock, 2007).

Combining diverse methods has shown success in sentiment analysis. The combination of machine learners and opinion lexicons has resulted in some of the best submissions in previous SemEval competitions (Kiritchenko et al., 2014; Miura et al., 2014). Along the line of combining different methods, ensemble approaches have also shown top results in previous runs of this task. Both ensembles of a small number of sophisticated systems (Hagen et al., 2015) as well as large numbers of simpler approaches have been evaluated (Wicentowski, 2015). Ensemble classification with regard to combining different machine learners and feature spaces has previously been evaluated extensively for document level sentiment classification (Xia et al., 2011). In that context, weighted sum ensemble methods have shown the best performance.

This paper describes a weighted sum ensemble that prioritizes some classes in multi-class classification. Results compare the system against two baselines. One baseline is the equivalent approach without prioritizing classes, while the other is an unweighted combination of ensemble members. Naive Bayes and logistic regression classifiers are explored as members across a variety of feature spaces. These classifiers are know to perform differently (Ng and Jordan, 2002). The presented results show:

1. The presented approach successfully prioritizes classes in a multi-class classification problem.

2. The ensemble method outperforms individual members and the baseline ensembles.

The system description will start by a brief outline of the evaluation data. Then the ensemble members are described before the ensemble method is detailed. Finally, the results on all SemEval test sets allow an assessment of the approach and future work.

Proceedings of SemEval-2016, pages 225–229,

San Diego, California, June 16-17, 2016. ©2016 Association for Computational Linguistics

Twitter Corpus	Pos.	Neg.	Neu.	Total
2013-train (A)	2869	1077	3733	7679
2013-dev (A,C)	459	258	569	1286
2013-test	1571	601	1637	3813
2014-test	978	200	668	1853
2015-test	1038	365	987	2392
2016-train (A)	2483	678	1625	4796
2016-dev (A,B,C)	669	319	611	1595
2016-devtest (A,B,C)	786	254	548	1588
2016-test	7060	3231	10342	20633

Table 1: SemEval data subsets as well as the full 2016 training set (A), submission (B) and post-submission (C) development data.

2 Data

Training data for this approach is constrained to data provided through the SemEval competitions. Table 1 shows the evaluation data used in the approach. This is a subset of the original data, as some tweets were unavailable when querying the Twitter API. The test data corresponds to the data used in the official task ranking (Nakov et al., 2016).

3 Ensemble Members

The ensemble members are the basic exchangeable building blocks of this approach. In this work Naive Bayes and logistic regression are chosen as differently performing members.

3.1 Naive Bayes

The Naive Bayes classifier is based on the Bayes theorem. The assumption that features are statistically independent might seem too naive. However, this approach often performs surprisingly well. The implementation uses the multinomial Naive Bayes classifier of the datumbox library[1].

3.2 Logistic Regression and Opinion Lexicons

Logistic regression is the second classification approach for ensemble members. Input for this method are text features, as well as scores from five opinion lexicons. Three lexicons have been created automatically from large corpora, namely SentiWordNet (Baccianella et al., 2010), NRC Hashtag Sentiment Lexicon and Sentiment140 Lexicon (Kiritchenko et al., 2014). Bing Liu's Opinion Lexicon (Hu and

Liu, 2004) was created manually and a fifth lexicon was created automatically and then curated manually. For each lexicon, the two sums over all negative as well as positive opinion scores corresponding to unigrams or lemmas in a message are added as features. The implementation uses the logistic regression classifier available in LIBLINEAR (Fan et al., 2008).

3.3 Feature Extraction

User names, URLs and retweet handles are removed before feature extraction. Part-of-speech tags of the CMU ARK Tagger (Owoputi et al., 2013) are used for truecasing if words in a tweet are mostly lowercase or mostly capitalized. ClearNLP (now NLP4J[2]) is used for tokenization, part-of-speech tagging and dependency parsing (Choi and Mccallum, 2013; Choi, 2016). Feature inputs for the classifiers are bag-of-words of unigrams (*uni*), part-of-speech tags (*pos*), bigrams (*bi*), dependency pairs (*dp*) (Xia et al., 2011) and brown clusters (*cl*) (Owoputi et al., 2013). In this work a classifier only ever uses one of the different text feature sets.

4 Ensemble

Ensemble methods combine a set of multiple member classifiers. These members can be various classifiers of different methods and different feature sets. Individual classifiers output a classification decision or a classification score for each class.

In the context of this approach classification scores are required for all ensemble members. These scores $o_{ki} \geq 0$ for every class $i \in C$ and every member classifier $k \in M$ are assumed to be normalized,

$$\sum_{i=1}^{C} o_{ki} = 1. \quad (1)$$

The score o_{ki} can be interpreted as a probability or confidence measure of classifier k for class i.

A basic score based classification method would be to derive the classification decision from the sum over all scores. The highest accumulated class sum would determine the decision, as in

$$\arg\max_{i \in C} \sum_{k=1}^{M} o_{ki}. \quad (2)$$

---

[1]https://github.com/datumbox/datumbox-framework

[2]https://github.com/emorynlp/nlp4j

Instead the approach uses a weighted sum, with a weight w_{ki} for every classifier k and every class i. Differentiating weights by class represents a finer grained weighting scheme than only differentiating by classifier. The ensemble output is determined by

$$\arg\max_{i \in C} \sum_{k=1}^{M} w_{ki} o_{ki}, \tag{3}$$

as the class with the highest weighted sum. The essential aspect of a weighed ensemble approach then is how the weights are calculated. The following sections describe optimization conditions that can be used to calculate weights.

4.1 Standard Weight Optimization

A weighted sum ensemble attempts to improve classification by weighing the class scores of individual members. Weights can be calculated based on a gold dataset where the class scores o_{ki} and the correct gold label g are known.

The decision function (3) is based on the maximal weighted sum of scores. It is straight forward that a lower difference between weighted sums of different classes is more prone to an erroneous decision through inaccuracies. Thus an intuitive condition for optimal weights could be to maximize the difference between the weighted sum for the correct class and all sums of incorrect classes. For every known gold label g and the corresponding scores o_{kg} the conditions would be

$$\sum_{k=1}^{M} w_{kg} o_{kg} - w_{kj} o_{kj} = |M|, \tag{4}$$

for all labels besides the gold label, $j \in C \backslash \{g\}$. The unweighted sum of classification scores was defined equal one for a single classifier (1). This would also be the maximal difference in case of one classifier. Consequently, the conditions for maximal difference between weighted sum scores over the classifier set M are set equal to the cardinality of the set.

4.2 Prioritizing Weight Optimization

In contrast to the previously introduced weight optimization conditions the following conditions aim to prioritize valid classification of some classes over others. Low priority classes are defined by the set

$L \subseteq C$. This also defines the priority classes as $P = C \backslash L$.

The approach does not aim to improve the ensemble classification across low priority classes L. For a low priority label $l \in L$ the weights are fixed to

$$w_{kl} = 1. \tag{5}$$

Based on this, the standard weight conditions (4) for any low priority gold label $g \in L$ and all priority labels $p \in P$ are rephrased as

$$\sum_{k=1}^{M} w_{kp} o_{kp} = -|M| + \sum_{k=1}^{M} o_{kg} \leq 0. \tag{6}$$

This is problematic because the unweighted sum over scores is positive by definition, since scores can't be negative. However, the derivation shows that the priority weights w_{kp} would be conditioned to change this sum to negative in favor of low-priority classification decisions. This is a contradiction to the concept of priority classes. The conditions (6) for any low priority gold label $g \in L$ and all priority labels $p \in P$ are relaxed to

$$\sum_{k=1}^{M} w_{kp} o_{kp} = 0. \tag{7}$$

This can be understood as a lower bound for priority weights. Priority weights are also still conditioned to improve priority classification decisions as per the standard conditions (4) for any $g \in P$.

Based on the gold dataset the conditions for low priority gold labels (7) and for priority gold labels (4) form an overdetermined system of equations. The solution to this are the priority weights optimized to improve the decision of the ensemble approach. The weights are calculated by solving the conditions as a least squares problem. This requires gold labels from a development dataset different from classifier training data.

5 Results

The following section compares results of the introduced approach against the ensemble members and two baseline ensemble methods. The results for Naive Bayes and logistic regression ensemble members on different feature spaces as well as the results for the ensembles are presented in the following.

Test, weight data	Sum			IIP std			IIP prio		
	uni-bi	uni-bi-cl	all	uni-bi	uni-bi-cl	all	uni-bi	uni-bi-cl	all
2013-test, B	55.5	56.8	55.7	55.1	55.4	53.7	**60.5**	**60.5**	59.8
2014-test, B	61.6	62.9	61.3	59.5	60.5	59.4	65.3	**65.9**	64.5
2015-test, B	57.4	59.4	58.3	58.5	57.6	56.8	**63.3**	62.9	61.0
2016-test, B	56.1	58.0	56.6	55.0	56.0	55.4	58.3	**58.7**	57.4*
2013-test, C	55.5	56.8	55.7	59.7	59.4	59.7	63.6	64.3	**64.6**
2014-test, C	61.6	62.9	61.3	64.7	66.1	65.3	68.0	**69.9**	68.5
2015-test, C	57.4	59.4	58.3	60.7	62.3	61.3	64.1	**66.2**	65.5
2016-test, C	56.1	58.0	56.6	58.2	59.0	58.8	59.4	**60.2**	59.5

Table 2: Macro-averaged positive negative F1 [%] for all test data sets across three ensemble methods and three member sets. Set *all* corresponds to all classifier, feature combinations evaluated for 2016-test data in Table 3. Ensemble members were trained on the full 2016 training set (A) while ensemble weights were optimized on 2016 (B) and 2013/2016 development sets (C, Table 1).

2016-test	uni	pos	bi	dp	cl
NB	54.5	30.3	40.7	37.6	**54.4**
LR	55.5	53.5	52.0	52.7	**57.6**

Table 3: Macro-averaged positive negative F1 [%] for ensemble members of 2016-test on full 2016 training set (A, Table 1).

Table 3 shows the results for Naive Bayes (*NB*) and logistic regression (*LR*) ensemble members. For both classification approaches brown clusters (*cl*) show the best performance.

Table 2 shows results for three ensemble approaches and three sets of members. The *Sum* columns show results for an unweighted sum over contributing classifier scores, as in (2). *IIP std* is a weighted sum approach with standard weight optimization as in (4). *IIP prio* adds the priority condition (7) with positive and negative as priority classes.

The bottom result set for weight optimization on 2013 and 2016 development data shows substantially better results than the top one, where weights were optimized on 2016 development data. While the weighted sum approach is of course unaffected by this, this holds true for all ensemble member sets in the weighted sum ensembles.

Across both result sets the *IIP prio* ensemble always outperforms the other two baseline ensemble methods. The standard ensemble which does not prioritize classes *IIP std* outperforms the sum baseline in the bottom result set but often does not in the top one. For all ensemble approaches the member sets of classifiers for unigram, bigram and cluster feature spaces usually show the best results.

The system for the official submission ∗ used all members with priority weight optimization, obtain-ing a macro-averaged F1 of 57.4%. Though this outperforms the equivalent baseline ensembles it performs on a similar level as the best logistic regression member in Table 3. In contrast the best *IIP prio* result used unigram, bigram and cluster members in an ensemble optimized for 2013 and 2016 development data, achieving a macro-averaged F1 of 60.2%.

6 Conclusion

This paper presented two methods for weighted sum ensemble classification. The introduced class prioritizing method outperformed the standard method in all evaluations. Furthermore, the results show that the class prioritizing weight ensemble method usually outperformed the basic sum ensemble approach substantially. This shows that combining different classifiers across various feature spaces while prioritizing some classes in multi-class classification works well with the presented system.

The results varied significantly depending on the data used for optimizing weights. Optimization on a more diverse data set showed better performance. Questions of domain dependence and over-fitting need to be explored further. With the modular nature of an ensemble a variety of classifiers and features are left to be evaluated in the context of this approach.

Acknowledgments

The author is grateful for the opportunity to contribute the implementation of this approach to NLP4J[3].

---

[3] https://github.com/emorynlp/nlp4j

References

Stefano Baccianella, Andrea Esuli, and Fabrizio Sebastiani. 2010. Sentiwordnet 3.0: An enhanced lexical resource for sentiment analysis and opinion mining. In *in Proc. of LREC*.

Jinho D. Choi and Andrew Mccallum. 2013. Transition-based dependency parsing with selectional branching. In *In Proceedings of the 51st Annual Meeting of the Association for Computational Linguistics (ACL 2013)*.

Jinho D. Choi. 2016. Dynamic feature induction: The last gist to the state-of-the-art. In *Proceedings of the 54th Annual Meeting of the Association for Computational Linguistics (NAACL 2016)*.

Rong-En Fan, Kai-Wei Chang, Cho-Jui Hsieh, Xiang-Rui Wang, and Chih-Jen Lin. 2008. LIBLINEAR: A library for large linear classification. *Journal of Machine Learning Research*, 9:1871–1874.

Matthias Hagen, Martin Potthast, Michel Bchner, and Benno Stein. 2015. Webis: an ensemble for twitter sentiment detection. In *Proceedings of the 9th International Workshop on Semantic Evaluation (SemEval 2015*, pages 582–589. Association for Computational Linguistics, June.

Minqing Hu and Bing Liu. 2004. Mining and summarizing customer reviews. In *Proceedings of the Tenth ACM SIGKDD International Conference on Knowledge Discovery and Data Mining*, KDD '04, pages 168–177, New York, NY, USA. ACM.

Svetlana Kiritchenko, Xiaodan Zhu, and Saif M. Mohammad. 2014. Sentiment analysis of short informal texts. *J. Artif. Intell. Res. (JAIR)*, 50:723–762.

Yasuhide Miura, Shigeyuki Sakaki, Keigo Hattori, and Tomoko Ohkuma. 2014. Teamx: A sentiment analyzer with enhanced lexicon mapping and weighting scheme for unbalanced data. In *Proceedings of the 8th International Workshop on Semantic Evaluation (SemEval 2014)*, pages 628–632, Dublin, Ireland, August. Association for Computational Linguistics and Dublin City University.

Preslav Nakov, Alan Ritter, Sara Rosenthal, Veselin Stoyanov, and Fabrizio Sebastiani. 2016. SemEval-2016 task 4: Sentiment analysis in Twitter. In *Proceedings of the 10th International Workshop on Semantic Evaluation (SemEval 2016)*, San Diego, California, June. Association for Computational Linguistics.

Andrew Y. Ng and Michael I. Jordan. 2002. On discriminative vs. generative classifiers: A comparison of logistic regression and naive bayes. In T. G. Dietterich, S. Becker, and Z. Ghahramani, editors, *Advances in Neural Information Processing Systems 14*, pages 841–848. MIT Press.

Olutobi Owoputi, Chris Dyer, Kevin Gimpel, Nathan Schneider, and Noah A. Smith. 2013. Improved part-of-speech tagging for online conversational text with word clusters. In *In Proceedings of NAACL*.

Paul C. Tetlock. 2007. Giving Content to Investor Sentiment: The Role of Media in the Stock Market. *Journal of Finance*, 62(3):1139–1168, 06.

Richard Wicentowski. 2015. Swatcs65: Sentiment classification using an ensemble of class projects. In *Proceedings of the 9th International Workshop on Semantic Evaluation (SemEval 2015)*, pages 631–635, Denver, Colorado, June. Association for Computational Linguistics.

Rui Xia, Chengqing Zong, and Shoushan Li. 2011. Ensemble of feature sets and classification algorithms for sentiment classification. *Inf. Sci.*, 181(6):1138–1152, March.

PotTS at SemEval-2016 Task 4: Sentiment Analysis of Twitter Using Character-level Convolutional Neural Networks.

Uladzimir Sidarenka

Applied Computational Linguistics/FSP Cognitive Science
University of Potsdam
Karl-Liebknecht Straße 24-25
14476 Potsdam
`sidarenk@uni-potsdam.de`

Abstract

This paper presents an alternative approach to polarity and intensity classification of sentiments in microblogs. In contrast to previous works, which either relied on carefully designed hand-crafted feature sets or automatically derived neural embeddings for words, our method harnesses character embeddings as its main input units. We obtain task-specific vector representations of characters by training a deep multi-layer convolutional neural network on the labeled dataset provided to the participants of the SemEval-2016 Shared Task 4 (Sentiment Analysis in Twitter; Nakov et al., 2016b) and subsequently evaluate our classifiers on subtasks B (two-way polarity classification) and C (joint five-way prediction of polarity and intensity) of this competition. Our first system, which uses three manifold convolution sets followed by four non-linear layers, ranks 16 in the former track; while our second network, which consists of a single convolutional filter set followed by a highway layer and three non-linearities with linear mappings in-between, attains the 10-th place on subtask C.[1]

1 Introduction

Sentiment analysis (SA) – a field of knowledge which deals with the analysis of people's opinions, sentiments, evaluations, appraisals, attitudes, and emotions towards particular entities mentioned in discourse (Liu, 2012) – is commonly considered to be one of the most challenging, competitive, but at the same time utmost necessary areas of research in modern computational linguistics.

Unfortunately, despite numerous notable advances in recent years (e.g., Breck et al., 2007; Yessenalina and Cardie, 2011; Socher et al., 2011), many of the challenges in the opinion mining field, such as domain adaptation or analysis of noisy texts, still pose considerable difficulties to researchers. In this respect, rapidly evaluating and comparing different approaches to solving these problems in a controlled environment – like the one provided for the SemEval task (Nakov et al., 2016b) – is of crucial importance for finding the best possible way of mastering them.

We also pursue this goal in the present paper by investigating whether one of the newest machine learning trends – the use of deep neural networks (DNNs) with small receptive fields – would be a viable solution for improving state-of-the-art results in sentiment analysis of Twitter.

After a brief summary of related work in Section 2, we present the architectures of our networks and describe the training procedure we used for them in Section 3. Since we applied two different DNN topologies to subtasks B and C, we make a cross-comparison of both systems and evaluate the role of the preprocessing steps in the next-to-last section. Finally, in Section 5, we draw conclusions from our experiments and make further suggestions for future research.

2 Related Work

Since its presumably first official mention by Nasukawa and Yi in 2003 (cf. Liu, 2012), sentiment analysis has constantly attracted the attention of re-

---

[1]The source code of our implementation is freely available online at `https://github.com/WladimirSidorenko/SemEval-2016/`

Proceedings of SemEval-2016, pages 230–237,
San Diego, California, June 16-17, 2016. ©2016 Association for Computational Linguistics

searchers. Though earlier works on opinion mining were primarily concerned with the analysis of narratives (Wiebe, 1994) or newspaper articles (Wiebe et al., 2003), the explosive emergence of social media (SM) services in the mid-2000s has brought about a dramatic focus change in this field.

A particularly important role in this regard was played by Twitter – a popular microblogging service first introduced by Jack Dorsey in 2006 (Dorsey, 2006). The sudden availability of huge amounts of data combined with the presence of all possible social and national groups on this stream rapidly gave rise to a plethora of scientific studies. Notable examples of these were the works conducted by Go et al. (2009) and Pak and Paroubek (2010), who obtained their corpora using distant supervision and subsequently trained several classifiers on these data; Kouloumpis et al. (2011), who trained an AdaBoost system on the Edinburgh Twitter corpus[2]; and Agarwal et al. (2011), who proposed tree-kernel methods for doing message-level sentiment analysis of tweets.

Eventually, with the introduction of the SemEval corpus (Nakov et al., 2013), a great deal of automatic systems and resources have appeared on the scene. Though most of these systems typically rely on traditional supervised classification methods, such as SVM (Mohammad et al., 2013; Becker et al., 2013) or logistic regression (Hamdan et al., 2015; Plotnikova et al., 2015), in recent years, the deep learning (DL) tsunami (Manning, 2015) has also started hitting the shores of this "battlefield".

In this paper we investigate whether one of the newest lines of research in DL – the use of character-level deep neural networks (charDNNs) – would be a perspective way for addressing the sentiment analysis task on Twitter as well.

Introduced by Sutskever et al. (2011), char-DNNs have already proved their efficiency for a variety of NLP applications, including part-of-speech tagging (dos Santos and Zadrozny, 2014), named-entity recognition (dos Santos and Guimarães, 2015), and general language modeling (Kim et al., 2015; Józefowicz et al., 2016). We hypothesized that the reduced feature sparsity of this approach, its lower susceptibility to informal spellings, and the shift of

the main discriminative classification power from input units to transformation layers would make it suitable for doing opinion mining on Twitter as well.

3 Method

To test our conjectures, we downloaded the training and development data provided by the organizers of the SemEval-2016 Task 4 (Sentiment Analysis in Twitter; Nakov et al., 2016b). Due to dynamic changes of this content, we were only able to retrieve a total of 5,178 messages for subtasks B and D (two-way polarity classification) and 7,335 microblogs for subtasks C and E (joint five-way prediction of polarity and intensity).

We deliberately refused to do any heavy-weight NLP preprocessing of these data to check whether the applied DL method alone would suffice to get acceptable results. In order to facilitate the training and reduce the variance of the learned weights though, we applied a shallow normalization of the input by lower-casing messages' strings and filtering out stop words before passing the tweets to the classifiers.

As stop words we considered all auxiliary verbs (e.g., *be*, *have*, *do*) and auxiliary parts of speech (prepositions, articles, particles, and conjunctions) up to a few exceptions – we kept the negations and words that potentially could inverse the polarity of opinions, e.g., *without*, *but*, and *however*. Furthermore, we also removed hyperlinks, digits, retweets, @-mentions, common temporal expressions, and mentions of tweets' topics, since all of these elements were a priori guaranteed to be objective. An example of such preprocessed microblog is provided below:

EXAMPLE 3.1.
  Original: *Going to MetLife tomorrow but not to see the boys is a weird feeling*
  Normalized: *but not see boys weird feeling*

3.1 Adversarial Convolutional Networks (Subtasks B and D)

We then defined a multi-layer deep convolutional network for subtasks B and D as follows:

At the initial step, we map the input characters to their appropriate embeddings, obtaining an input matrix $E \in \mathbb{R}^{n \times m}$, where n stands for the length of

---

[2] `http://demeter.inf.ed.ac.uk`

the input instance, and m denotes the dimensionality of the embedding space (specifically, we use $m = 32$).

Next, three sets of convolutional filters – positive (+), negative (−), and shifter (x) convolutions – are applied to the input matrix E. Each of these sets in turn consists of three subsets: one subset with 4 filters of width 3, another subset comprising 8 filters of width 4, and, finally, a third subset having 12 filters of width 5.[3]

Each subset filter F forms a matrix $\mathbb{R}^{w \times m}$ with the number of rows w corresponding to the filter width and the number of columns m being equal to the embedding dimensionality as above. A subset of filters S_w^p for $p \in \{+, -, \text{x}\}$ is then naturally represented as a tensor $\mathbb{R}^{c \times w \times m}$, where c is the number of filters with the given width w.

We apply the usual convolution operation with max-pooling over time for each filter, getting an output vector $\vec{v}_{S_w^p} \in \mathbb{R}^c$ for each subset. All output vectors $\vec{v}_{S_*^p}$ of the same subset are then concatenated into one vector $\vec{v}_{S^p} = [\vec{v}_{S_3^p}, \vec{v}_{S_4^p}, \vec{v}_{S_5^p}]$ of size $4 + 8 + 12 = 24$.

The results of the three sets are subsequently joined using the following equation:

$$\vec{v}_{conv} = \text{sig}(\vec{v}_{S+} - \vec{v}_{S-}) \odot \tanh(\vec{v}_{S\text{x}}),$$

where $\vec{v}_{S+}, \vec{v}_{S-}$, and $\vec{v}_{S\text{x}}$ mean the output vectors for the positive, negative, and shifter sets respectively, and $\odot$ denotes the Hadamard product.

The motivation behind this choice of unification function is that we first want to obtain the difference between the positive and negative predictions (thus $\vec{v}_{S+} - \vec{v}_{S-}$), then map this difference to the range $[0, 1]$ (therefore the sigmoid), and finally either inverse or dampen these results depending on the output of the shifter layer, whose values are guaranteed to be in the range $[-1, 1]$ thanks to tanh. Since we simultaneously apply competing convolutions to the same input, we call this layer "adversarial" as all of its components have different opinions regarding the final outcome.

After obtaining $\vec{v}_{conv}$, we consecutively use three non-linear transformations (linear rectification, hy-

---

[3]By simultaneously applying multiple filter sets of different width to the same input, we hoped to improve the precision-recall trade-off, getting more accurate outputs from wider filters while reducing their sparsity with narrower kernels.

perbolic tangent, and sigmoid function) with linear modifications in-between:

$$\vec{v}_{relu} = \text{relu}(\vec{v}_{conv} \cdot M_{relu} + \vec{b}_{relu}),$$
$$\vec{v}_{tanh} = \tanh(\vec{v}_{relu} \cdot M_{tanh} + \vec{b}_{tanh}),$$
$$\vec{v}_{sig} = \text{sig}(\vec{v}_{tanh} \cdot M_{sig} + \vec{b}_{sig}).$$

In this equation, M_{relu}, M_{tanh}, and $M_{sig} \in \mathbb{R}^{24 \times 24}$ stand for the linear transform matrices, and $\vec{b}_{relu}, \vec{b}_{tanh}, \vec{b}_{sig} \in \mathbb{R}^{24}$ represent the usual bias terms. With this combination, we hope to first prune unreliable input signals by using a hard rectifying linear unit (Jarrett et al., 2009) and then gain more discriminative power by successively applying tanh and sig, thus funneling the input to increasingly smaller ranges: $[-1, 1]$ in the case of tanh, and $[0, 1]$ in the case of sigmoid.

At the last stage, after applying a binomial dropout mask with $p = 0.5$ to the $\vec{v}_{sig}$ vector (Srivastava et al., 2014), we compute the final prediction as:

$$y' = \begin{cases} 1, & \text{if } \text{sig}(\sum \vec{v}_{sig} \cdot M_{pred} + \vec{b}_{pred}) \geq 0.5 \\ 0, & \text{otherwise,} \end{cases}$$
$$\tag{1}$$

where $M_{pred} \in \mathbb{R}^{24 \times 2}$ and $\vec{b}_{pred} \in \mathbb{R}^2$ stand for the transformation matrix and bias term respectively, and the summation runs over the two elements of the resulting $\mathbb{R}^2$ vector.

To train our classifier, we normally define the cost function as:

$$cost = \sum_i y_i * (1 - y_i') + (1 - y_i) * y_i', \tag{2}$$

where y_i denotes the gold category of the i-th training instance and y_i' stands for its predicted class, and optimize this function using RMSProp (Tieleman and Hinton, 2012).

3.2 Highway Convolutional Networks (Subtasks C and E)

A slightly different model was used for subtasks C and E:

In contrast to the previous two-way classification network, we only use one set of convolutions with 4 filters of width 3, 16 filters of width 4, and 24 filters of width 5, and the number of dimensions of the

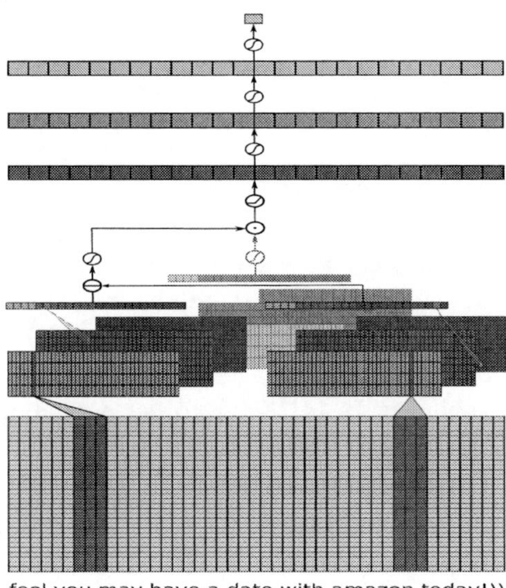

(a) Adversarial network used for subtasks B and D.

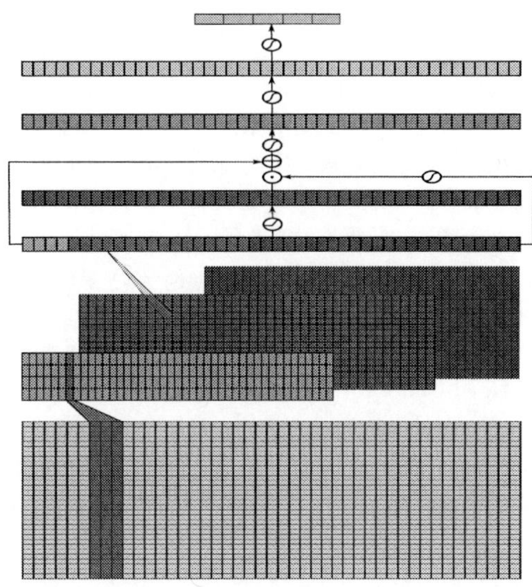

(b) Highway network used for subtasks C and E.

Figure 1: Network architectures.

resulting $\vec{v}_{conv}$ vector being equal to 44 instead of 24.

After normally computing and max-pooling the convolutions, we pass the output convolution vector through a highway layer (Srivastava et al., 2015) in addition to using relu, i.e.:

$$\vec{v}_{hw_{trans}} = \mathrm{sig}(\vec{v}_{conv} \cdot M_{hw_{trans}} + \vec{b}_{hw_{trans}}),$$
$$\vec{v}_{hw_{carry}} = \vec{v}_{conv} \odot (1 - \vec{v}_{hw_{trans}}),$$
$$\vec{v}_{relu'} = \mathrm{relu}(\vec{v}_{conv} \cdot M_{conv'} + \vec{b}_{conv'}),$$
$$\vec{v}_{relu} = \mathrm{sig}(\vec{v}_{relu'} \odot \vec{v}_{hw_{trans}} + \vec{v}_{hw_{carry}}).$$

The rest of the network is organized the same way as in the previous model, up to the final layer. Since this task involves multivariate classification, instead of computing the sigmoid of the sum as in Equation 1, we obtain a softmax vector $\vec{v}_\sigma \in \mathbb{R}^5$ and consider the argmax value of this vector as the predicted class:

$$\vec{v}_\sigma = \sigma(\vec{v}_{sig} \cdot M_\sigma + \vec{b}_\sigma)$$
$$y' = \mathrm{argmax}(\vec{v}_\sigma)$$

The corresponding cost function is appropriately defined as:

$$cost = \sum_i -\ln \vec{v}_\sigma[y_i] + \ell_2 * \sum_p \|p\|^2 + \ell_3 * (y_i - y_i')^2,$$

where $\vec{v}_\sigma[y_i]$ means the probability value for the gold class in the $\vec{v}_\sigma$ vector, ℓ_2 and ℓ_3 are constants (we use $\ell_2 = 1\mathrm{e}^{-5}$ and $\ell_3 = 3\mathrm{e}^{-4}$), p's denote the training parameters of the model, and $(y_i - y_i')^2$ stand for the squared difference between the numerical values of the predicted and gold classes.

In this task, we opted for the L_2 regularization instead of using dropout, since we found it working slightly better on the development set, though the differences between the two methods were not very big, and the derivative computation with dropout was significantly faster.

3.3 Initialization and Training

Because initialization has a crucial impact on the results of deep learning approaches (Sutskever et al., 2011), we did not rely on purely random weights but used the uniform He method (He et al., 2015) for initially setting the embeddings, convolutional filters, and bias terms instead. The inter-layer transformations were set to orthogonal matrices to ensure their full rank.

Additionally, to guarantee that each preceding network stage came maximally prepared and provided best possible output to its successors, after

233

adding each new intermediate layer, we temporarily short-circuited it to the final output node(s) and pre-trained this abridged network for 5 epochs, removing the short-circuit connections afterwards. The final training then took 50 epochs with each epoch lasting for 35 iterations over the provided training data.

Since our models appeared to be very susceptible to imbalanced classes, we subsampled the training data by getting $\min(1.1 * n_{min}, n_c)$ samples for each distinct gold category c, where n_{min} is the number of instances of the rarest class in the corpus, and n_c denotes the number of training examples belonging to the c-th class. This subset was resampled anew for each subsequent training epoch.

Finally, to steer our networks towards recognizing correct features, we randomly added additional training instances from two established sentiment lexica: Subjectivity Clues (Wilson et al., 2005) and NRC Hashtag Affirmative Context Sentiment Lexicon (Kiritchenko et al., 2014). To that end, we drew n binary random numbers for each polarity class in the corpus from a binomial distribution $B(n, 0.1)$, where n stands for the total size of the generated training set, and added a uniformly chosen term from either lexica whenever the sampled value was equal to one. In the same way, we randomly (with the probability $B(m, 0.15)$, where m means the number of matches) replaced occurrences of terms from the lexica in the training tweets with other uniformly drawn lexicon items.

4   Evaluation

To train our final model, we used both training and development data provided by the organizers, setting aside 15 percent of the samples drawn in each epoch for evaluation and using the remaining 85 percent for optimizing the networks' weights.

We obtained the final classifier by choosing the network state that produced the best task-specific score on the set-aside part of the corpus during the training. For this purpose, in each training iteration, we estimated the *macroaveraged recall* ρ^{PN} on the evaluation set for subtask B:

$$\rho^{PN} = \frac{\rho^{Pos} + \rho^{Neg}}{2},$$

and computed the *macroaveraged mean absolute error* measure MAE^M (cf. Nakov et al., 2016a) to select a model for track C :

$$MAE^M(h, Te) = \frac{1}{|\mathcal{C}|} \sum_{j=1}^{|\mathcal{C}|} \frac{1}{|Te_j|} \sum_{x \in Te_j} |h(x_i) - y_i|$$

The resulting models were then used in both classification and quantification subtasks of the SemEval competition, i.e., we used the adversarial network with the maximum ρ^{PN} score observed during the training to generate the output for tracks B and D and applied the highway classifier with the minimum achieved MAE^M rate to get predictions for subtasks C and E.[4] The scores of the final evaluation on the official test set are shown in Table 1.

Since many of our parameter and design choices were made empirically by analyzing systems' errors at each development step, we decided to recheck whether these decisions were still optimal for the final configuration. To that end, we re-evaluated the effects of the preprocessing steps by temporarily switching off lower-casing and stop word filtering, and also estimated the impact of the network structure by applying the model architecture used for subtask B to the five-way prediction task, and vice versa using the highway network for the binary classification. The output layers, costs, and regularization functions of these two approaches were also swapped in these experiments when applied to different objectives.

Because re-running the complete training from scratch was relatively expensive (taking eight to ten hours on our machine), we reduced the number of training epochs by a factor of five, but tested each configuration thrice in order to overcome the random factors in the He initialization. The arithmetic mean and standard deviation (with $N = 2$) of these three outcomes for each setting are also provided in the table.

As can be seen from the results, running fewer training epochs does not notably harm the final prediction quality for the binary task. On the contrary, it might even lead to some improvements for the adversarial network. We explain this effect by the fact that the model selected during the shorter training had a lower score on the evaluation set than the network state chosen during 50 epochs. Nevertheless,

---

[4] We used the official aggregating scripts to generate the results for the quantification tasks.

Training Configuration	$\rho^{PN} \wedge$ (Subtask B)	$MAE^M \vee$ (Subtask C)
Adversarial[1/5,cs]	$61.34^{\pm 1.24}$	$1.3^{\pm 0.05}$
Adversarial[1/5,sw]	$58.64^{\pm 0.8}$	$1.3^{\pm 0.05}$
Adversarial[1/5]	$61.9^{\pm 0.66}$	$1.37^{\pm 0.03}$
Adversarial	61.8	n/a
Highway[1/5,cs]	$59.87^{\pm 0.79}$	$1.26^{\pm 0.01}$
Highway[1/5,sw]	$60.35^{\pm 1.5}$	$1.23^{\pm 0.05}$
Highway[1/5]	$62.05^{\pm 0.75}$	$1.3^{\pm 0.04}$
Highway	n/a	1.24

Table 1: Results of the adversarial and highway networks with different preprocessing steps on Subtasks B and C. ($\wedge$ – *higher is better*; $\vee$ – *lower is better*; [1/5] – *using 1/5 of training epochs*; [cs] – *preserving the character case*; [sw] – *keeping stop words*)

despite its worse evaluation results, this first configuration was more able to fit the test data than the second system, which apparently overfitted the set-aside part of the corpus.

Furthermore, we also can observe a mixed effect of the normalization on the two tasks: while keeping stop words and preserving character case deteriorates the results for the binary classification, abandoning any preprocessing steps turns out to be a more favorable solution when doing five-way prediction. The reasons for such different behavior are presumably twofold: *a)* the character case by itself might serve as a good indicator of sentiment intensity but be rather irrelevant to expressing its polarity, and *b)* the number of training instances might have become scarce as the number of possible gold classes in the corpus increased.

Finally, one also can see that the highway network performs slightly better on both subtasks (two- and five-way) than its adversarial counterpart when used with shorter training. In this case, we assume that the swapping of the regularization and cost functions has hidden the distinctions of the two networks at their initial layers, since, in our earlier experiments, we did observe better results for the two-way classification with the adversarial structure.

5 Discussion and Conclusion

Unfortunately, despite our seemingly sound theoretical assumptions set forth at the beginning, relying on character embeddings as input did not work out in practice at the end. Our adversarial system was only ranked fourth to last on subtask B, and the highway

network attained the second to last place in track C. However, knowing this outcome in advance was not possible without trying out these approaches first.

In order to make a retrospective error analysis, we computed the correlation coefficients between the character n-grams occurring in the training data and their gold classes, also comparing these figures with the corresponding numbers obtained on the test set. The results of this comparison are shown in Table 2.

3 chars	ρ_{train}	ρ_{test}	4 chars	ρ_{train}	ρ_{test}	5 chars	ρ_{train}	ρ_{test}
urk	0.128	0.039	turk	0.14	0.036	_turk	0.127	0.036
pol	0.125	0.069	fail	0.124	0.038	_trum	0.122	0.055
why	0.112	0.083	rkey	0.112	0.036	urkey	0.117	0.036
ion	0.106	0.024	rump	0.112	0.067	turke	0.117	0.036
_no	0.105	0.109	urke	0.108	0.036	trump	0.112	0.067
tio	0.104	0.006	_ame	0.107	0.047	rump_	0.103	0.059
ate	0.104	0.031	_pol	0.105	0.063	rkey_	0.101	0.036
hy_	0.103	0.9	why_	0.105	0.085	_not	0.097	0.1
ot_	0.102	0.071	trum	0.104	0.054	_poll	0.096	0.026
isi	0.097	0.075	tion	0.104	0.006	amend	0.096	0.062

Table 2: Top-10 character n-grams from the training data and their correlation coefficients with the negative class on the training (ρ_{train}) and test sets (ρ_{test}) of subtask B.

As can be seen from the table, the most reliable classification traits that could have been learned during the training are very specific to their respective topics – in particular, *Trump* and *Turkey* appear to be very negatively biased terms. This effect becomes even more evident as the length of the character n-grams increases. The reason why we did not pre-filter these substrings in the preprocessing was that the respective topics of these messages were specified as *donald trump* and *erdogan*, but we only removed exact topic matches from tweets.

Due to this evident topic susceptibility, as a possible way to improve our results, we could imagine the inclusion of more training data. Applying ensemble approaches, as it was done by the top-scoring systems this year, could also be a perspective direction to go. We would, however, advise the reader from further experimenting with network architectures (at least when training on the original SemEval dataset only), since both the recursive (RNTN, Socher et al., 2012) and recurrent variants (LSTM, Hochreiter and Schmidhuber, 1997) of neural classifiers were found to perform worse in our experiments than the feed-forward structure we described.

References

Apoorv Agarwal, Boyi Xie, Ilia Vovsha, Owen Rambow, and Rebecca Passonneau. 2011. Sentiment Analysis of Twitter Data. In *Proceedings of the Workshop on Languages in Social Media*, LSM '11, pages 30–38, Stroudsburg, PA, USA. Association for Computational Linguistics.

Lee Becker, George Erhart, David Skiba, and Valentine Matula. 2013. AVAYA: Sentiment Analysis on Twitter with Self-Training and Polarity Lexicon Expansion. In *Second Joint Conference on Lexical and Computational Semantics (*SEM), Volume 2: Proceedings of the Seventh International Workshop on Semantic Evaluation (SemEval 2013)*, pages 333–340, Atlanta, Georgia, USA, June. Association for Computational Linguistics.

Eric Breck, Yejin Choi, and Claire Cardie. 2007. Identifying expressions of opinion in context. In Manuela M. Veloso, editor, *IJCAI 2007, Proceedings of the 20th International Joint Conference on Artificial Intelligence, Hyderabad, India, January 6-12, 2007*, pages 2683–2688.

Jack Dorsey. 2006. just setting up my twttr.

Cícero Nogueira dos Santos and Victor Guimarães. 2015. Boosting named entity recognition with neural character embeddings. *CoRR*, abs/1505.05008.

Cícero Nogueira dos Santos and Bianca Zadrozny. 2014. Learning character-level representations for part-of-speech tagging. In *Proceedings of the 31th International Conference on Machine Learning, ICML 2014, Beijing, China, 21-26 June 2014*, volume 32 of *JMLR Proceedings*, pages 1818–1826. JMLR.org.

Alec Go, Richa Bhayani, and Lei Huang. 2009. Twitter Sentiment Classification using Distant Supervision. *Technical report*, pages 1–6.

Hussam Hamdan, Patrice Bellot, and Frederic Bechet. 2015. Lsislif: Feature Extraction and Label Weighting for Sentiment Analysis in Twitter. In *Proceedings of the 9th International Workshop on Semantic Evaluation (SemEval 2015)*, pages 568–573, Denver, Colorado, June. Association for Computational Linguistics.

Kaiming He, Xiangyu Zhang, Shaoqing Ren, and Jian Sun. 2015. Delving deep into rectifiers: Surpassing human-level performance on imagenet classification. *CoRR*, abs/1502.01852.

Sepp Hochreiter and Jürgen Schmidhuber. 1997. Long short-term memory. *Neural Computation*, 9(8):1735–1780.

Kevin Jarrett, Koray Kavukcuoglu, Marc'Aurelio Ranzato, and Yann LeCun. 2009. What is the best multistage architecture for object recognition? In *IEEE 12th International Conference on Computer Vision, ICCV 2009, Kyoto, Japan, September 27 - October 4, 2009*, pages 2146–2153. IEEE.

Rafal Józefowicz, Oriol Vinyals, Mike Schuster, Noam Shazeer, and Yonghui Wu. 2016. Exploring the limits of language modeling. *CoRR*, abs/1602.02410.

Yoon Kim, Yacine Jernite, David Sontag, and Alexander M. Rush. 2015. Character-aware neural language models. *CoRR*, abs/1508.06615.

Svetlana Kiritchenko, Xiaodan Zhu, and Saif M. Mohammad. 2014. Sentiment analysis of short informal texts. *J. Artif. Intell. Res. (JAIR)*, 50:723–762.

Efthymios Kouloumpis, Theresa Wilson, and Johanna D. Moore. 2011. Twitter Sentiment Analysis: The Good the Bad and the OMG! In Lada A. Adamic, Ricardo A. Baeza-Yates, and Scott Counts, editors, *Proceedings of the Fifth International Conference on Weblogs and Social Media, Barcelona, Catalonia, Spain, July 17-21, 2011*. The AAAI Press.

Bing Liu. 2012. *Sentiment Analysis and Opinion Mining*. Synthesis Lectures on Human Language Technologies. Morgan & Claypool Publishers.

Christopher D. Manning. 2015. Computational linguistics and deep learning. *Computational Linguistics*, 41(4):701–707.

Saif M. Mohammad, Svetlana Kiritchenko, and Xiaodan Zhu. 2013. NRC-Canada: Building the State-of-the-Art in Sentiment Analysis of Tweets. *CoRR*, abs/1308.6242.

Preslav Nakov, Sara Rosenthal, Zornitsa Kozareva, Veselin Stoyanov, Alan Ritter, and Theresa Wilson. 2013. SemEval-2013 Task 2: Sentiment Analysis in Twitter. In *Second Joint Conference on Lexical and Computational Semantics (*SEM), Volume 2: Proceedings of the Seventh International Workshop on Semantic Evaluation (SemEval 2013)*, pages 312–320, Atlanta, Georgia, USA, June. Association for Computational Linguistics.

Preslav Nakov, Alan Ritter, Sara Rosenthal, Fabrizio Sebastiani, and Veselin Stoyanov. 2016a. Evaluation measures for the SemEval-2016 task 4: "sentiment analysis in Twitter".

Preslav Nakov, Alan Ritter, Sara Rosenthal, Veselin Stoyanov, and Fabrizio Sebastiani. 2016b. SemEval-2016 task 4: Sentiment analysis in Twitter. In *Proceedings of the 10th International Workshop on Semantic Evaluation (SemEval 2016)*, San Diego, California, June. Association for Computational Linguistics.

Alexander Pak and Patrick Paroubek. 2010. Twitter as a Corpus for Sentiment Analysis and Opinion Mining. In Nicoletta Calzolari, Khalid Choukri, Bente Maegaard, Joseph Mariani, Jan Odijk, Stelios Piperidis, Mike Rosner, and Daniel Tapias, editors, *Proceedings of the International Conference on Language Resources and Evaluation, LREC 2010, 17-23 May 2010,*

Valletta, Malta. European Language Resources Association.

Nataliia Plotnikova, Micha Kohl, Kevin Volkert, Stefan Evert, Andreas Lerner, Natalie Dykes, and Heiko Ermer. 2015. KLUEless: Polarity Classification and Association. In *Proceedings of the 9th International Workshop on Semantic Evaluation (SemEval 2015)*, pages 619–625, Denver, Colorado, June. Association for Computational Linguistics.

Richard Socher, Jeffrey Pennington, Eric H. Huang, Andrew Y. Ng, and Christopher D. Manning. 2011. Semi-supervised recursive autoencoders for predicting sentiment distributions. In *Proceedings of the 2011 Conference on Empirical Methods in Natural Language Processing, EMNLP 2011, 27-31 July 2011, John McIntyre Conference Centre, Edinburgh, UK, A meeting of SIGDAT, a Special Interest Group of the ACL*, pages 151–161. ACL.

Richard Socher, Brody Huval, Christopher D. Manning, and Andrew Y. Ng. 2012. Semantic compositionality through recursive matrix-vector spaces. In Jun'ichi Tsujii, James Henderson, and Marius Pasca, editors, *Proceedings of the 2012 Joint Conference on Empirical Methods in Natural Language Processing and Computational Natural Language Learning, EMNLP-CoNLL 2012, July 12-14, 2012, Jeju Island, Korea*, pages 1201–1211. ACL.

Nitish Srivastava, Geoffrey E. Hinton, Alex Krizhevsky, Ilya Sutskever, and Ruslan Salakhutdinov. 2014. Dropout: a simple way to prevent neural networks from overfitting. *Journal of Machine Learning Research*, 15(1):1929–1958.

Rupesh Kumar Srivastava, Klaus Greff, and Jürgen Schmidhuber. 2015. Highway networks. *CoRR*, abs/1505.00387.

Ilya Sutskever, James Martens, and Geoffrey E. Hinton. 2011. Generating text with recurrent neural networks. In Lise Getoor and Tobias Scheffer, editors, *Proceedings of the 28th International Conference on Machine Learning, ICML 2011, Bellevue, Washington, USA, June 28 - July 2, 2011*, pages 1017–1024. Omnipress.

T. Tieleman and G. Hinton. 2012. Lecture 6.5—RmsProp: Divide the gradient by a running average of its recent magnitude. COURSERA: Neural Networks for Machine Learning.

Janyce Wiebe, Eric Breck, Chris Buckley, Claire Cardie, Paul Davis, Bruce Fraser, Diane J. Litman, David R. Pierce, Ellen Riloff, Theresa Wilson, David S. Day, and Mark T. Maybury. 2003. Recognizing and organizing opinions expressed in the world press. In Mark T. Maybury, editor, *New Directions in Question Answering, Papers from 2003 AAAI Spring Symposium, Stanford University, Stanford, CA, USA*, pages 12–19. AAAI Press.

Janyce Wiebe. 1994. Tracking point of view in narrative. *Computational Linguistics*, 20(2):233–287.

Theresa Wilson, Janyce Wiebe, and Paul Hoffmann. 2005. Recognizing contextual polarity in phrase-level sentiment analysis. In *HLT/EMNLP 2005, Human Language Technology Conference and Conference on Empirical Methods in Natural Language Processing, Proceedings of the Conference, 6-8 October 2005, Vancouver, British Columbia, Canada*. The Association for Computational Linguistics.

Ainur Yessenalina and Claire Cardie. 2011. Compositional matrix-space models for sentiment analysis. In *Proceedings of the 2011 Conference on Empirical Methods in Natural Language Processing, EMNLP 2011, 27-31 July 2011, John McIntyre Conference Centre, Edinburgh, UK, A meeting of SIGDAT, a Special Interest Group of the ACL*, pages 172–182.

INESC-ID at SemEval-2016 Task 4-A: Reducing the Problem of Out-of-Embedding Words

Silvio Amir, Ramon F. Astudillo, Wang Ling, Mário J. Silva, Isabel Trancoso
Instituto de Engenharia de Sistemas e Computadores Investigação e Desenvolvimento
Rua Alves Redol 9
Lisbon, Portugal
`{samir,ramon.astudillo,wlin,mjs,isabel.trancoso}@inesc-id.pt`

Abstract

We present the INESC-ID system for the 2016 edition of SemEval Twitter Sentiment Analysis shared task (subtask 4-A). The system was based on the Non-Linear Sub-space Embedding (NLSE) model developed for last year's competition. This model trains a projection of pre-trained embeddings into a small sub-space using the supervised data available. Despite its simplicity, the system attained performances comparable to the best systems of last edition with no need for feature engineering. One limitation of this model was the assumption that a pre-trained embedding was available for every word. In this paper, we investigated different strategies to overcome this limitation by exploiting character-level embeddings and learning representations for out-of-embedding vocabulary words. The resulting approach outperforms our previous model by a relatively small margin, while still attaining strong results and a consistent good performance across all the evaluation datasets.

1 Introduction

Pre-trained word embeddings provide a simple means to attain semi-supervised learning in Natural Language Processing (NLP) tasks (Collobert et al., 2011). They can be trained with large amounts of unsupervised data and be fine tuned as the initial building block of a semi-supervised system. However, in domains with a significant number of typos, use of slang and abbreviations, such as social media, the high number of singletons leads to a poor fine tuning of the embeddings. In previous work,

we addressed this by learning a projection of the embeddings into a small sub-space (Astudillo et al., 2015b). This allowed us to attain representations also for Out-Of-Vocabulary (OOV) words, provided that embeddings for those words are available. However, even if the embeddings are estimated from large amounts of unlabeled text, in noisy domains, such as Twitter, a significant number of words will not be seen and therefore will not have an embedding. We refer to those words as the Out-of-Embedding Vocabulary (OOEV).

In this paper, we focus on the problem of obtaining good representations for OOEV words. We experimented with character to word models (C2W) and investigated different strategies for initializing and updating OOEVs from the available training data. The best results were attained by using the labeled data to perform small updates to these representations in the first few epochs of training. The resulting system outperforms that of the previous evaluation, although by a small margin. It ranks fourth in the 2016 evaluation with a consistently high performance in all years.

2 NLSE Model Overview

In this section, we briefly review the approach introduced in the 2015 evaluation (Astudillo et al., 2015a). For a particular regression or classification task, only a subset of all the latent aspects captured by the word embeddings will be useful. Therefore, instead of updating the embeddings directly with the available labeled data, we estimate a projection of these embeddings into a low dimensional sub-space. This simple method brings two fundamental advan-

Proceedings of SemEval-2016, pages 238–242,
San Diego, California, June 16-17, 2016. ©2016 Association for Computational Linguistics

tages. Firstly, the lower dimensional embeddings require fewer parameters fitting the complexity of the target task and the available training data. Secondly, the learned projection can be used to adapt the representations for all words with an embedding, even if they do not occur in the labeled dataset.

Assuming we are given a matrix of pre-trained embeddings, where each column represents a word from a vocabulary $\mathcal{V}$, let such matrix be denoted by $\mathbf{E} \in \mathbb{R}^{e \times |\mathcal{V}|}$, where e is the number of latent dimensions. We define the adapted embedding matrix as the factorization $\mathbf{S} \cdot \mathbf{E}$, where $\mathbf{S} \in \mathbb{R}^{s \times e}$, with $s \ll e$. The parameters of matrix $\mathbf{S}$ are estimated using the labeled dataset, while $\mathbf{E}$ is kept fixed. In other words, we determine the optimal projection of the embedding matrix $\mathbf{E}$ into a sub-space of dimension s. In what follows, we will refer to this approach as Non-Linear Sub-space Embedding (NLSE) model.

The NLSE can be interpreted as a simple feed-forward neural network model (Rumelhart et al., 1985) with one single hidden layer utilizing the embedding sub-space approach. Let

$$\mathbf{m} = [\mathbf{w}_1 \cdots \mathbf{w}_n] \tag{1}$$

denote a message of n words. Each column $\mathbf{w} \in \{0, 1\}^{v \times 1}$ of $\mathbf{m}$ represents a word in one-hot form, that is, a vector of zeros of the size of the vocabulary v with a 1 on the i-th entry of the vector. Let y denote a categorical random variable over K classes. The NLSE model, estimates the probability of each possible category $y = k \in K$ given a message $\mathbf{m}$ as

$$p(y = k|\mathbf{m}; \theta) \propto \exp\left(\mathbf{Y}_k \cdot \mathbf{h} \cdot \mathbf{1}\right) \tag{2}$$

with parameters $\theta = \{\mathbf{S}, \mathbf{Y}\}$. Here, $\mathbf{h} \in [0, 1]^{e \times n}$ are the activations of the hidden layer for each word, given by

$$\mathbf{h} = \sigma\left(\mathbf{S} \cdot \mathbf{E} \cdot \mathbf{m}\right) \tag{3}$$

where $\sigma()$ is a sigmoid function acting on each element of the matrix. The matrix $\mathbf{Y} \in \mathbb{R}^{3 \times s}$ maps the embedding sub-space to the classification space and $\mathbf{1} \in \mathbf{1}^{n \times 1}$ is a matrix of ones that sums the scores for all words together, prior to normalization. This is equivalent to a bag-of-words assumption. Finally, the model computes a probability distribution over the K classes, using the *softmax* function.

3 Out-of-Embedding Vocabulary Words

Despite the fact that word embeddings are typically estimated from very large amounts of unlabeled data, it is often the case that a number of words appearing on the training or test sets are not present on the unlabeled corpus. These words will not be represented in $\mathbf{E}$. This problem is even more significant in social media environments like Twitter, where there is a significant lexical variation and where novel words, expressions and slang can be introduced over time. In Table 1, we show the percentage of OOV and OOEV words on each Twitter dataset.

The näive way of dealing with this issue, is to simply set the embeddings of unknown words to zero, essentially ignoring them. As will see later, a better approach is to treat these words as model parameters and use the training signal to learn a better representation for them.

3.1 Character-level Embeddings

One natural way of avoiding OOEV in neural network models, is to learn character-level embeddings and define a composition function to combine them into word representations, thus obtaining representations for any given word.

We experimented using *C2W*, a simple compositional model for learning word representations, from character embeddings. Given a word w, the *C2W* model generates a set of character n-grams $\{c_1, \ldots, c_m\}$, and projects each n-gram c_i into a vector $\mathbf{e}_{c_i} \in \mathbb{R}^d$, where d is the number of latent dimensions. The individual character representations are then combined to obtain a fixed-size representation for word w as $\mathbf{e}_w = \mathbf{e}_{c_1} \oplus \ldots \oplus \mathbf{e}_{c_m}$, where $\oplus$ denotes pointwise sum. These word representations can be used as the input to a standard neural language model where the parameters are estimated from unlabeled data by learning to predict words within a context.

3.2 Mapping *C2W* to *SSG* Embeddings

Unfortunately the *C2W* embeddings performed very poorly in our model. Therefore, to have embeddings for all the words we employed an approach similar to (Mikolov et al., 2013). We learn a mapping between the embedding spaces induced by *C2W* and

	2013	2014	2015	2016
OOV	70.9%	37.9%	39.3%	65.1%
OOEV	15.0%	11.2%	11.5%	22%
OOV & OOEV	14.8%	11.0%	11.3%	21.8%

Table 1: Out Of Vocabulary (OOV) and Ouf Of Embedding Vocabulary (OOEV) statistics for the different SemEval Task4-B datasets. Embeddings reported are the Structured Skipgram embeddings used in the experiments.

System	2013	2014	2015
2015 hyperparameters	0.618	0.646	0.591
+lower neutral cost	0.706	0.702	0.669
+shuffle per epoch	0.723	0.721	0.649
+update OOEVs 2 iter	0.725	0.729	0.657
Best SemEval 2015	0.722	0.727	0.652

Table 2: Effect of the improvements on the NLSE model.

Structured Skip-Gram embeddings (SSG) (Ling et al., 2015), allowing us compute an approximate SSG embedding for all the words. To this end, we first obtained $\mathcal{C}$, the set of words present in the two embeddings spaces. Then, we learned a linear map $\mathbf{T}$ by solving for the following objective:

$$\mathbf{T} \leftarrow \underset{\mathbf{T}}{\operatorname{argmin}} \sum_{w \in \mathcal{C}} ||\mathbf{T} \cdot \mathbf{c}_w - \mathbf{s}_w||^2 \qquad (4)$$

where, $\mathbf{c}_w$ denotes the $C2W$ embedding for word w and $\mathbf{s}_w$ denotes the SSG embedding for word w. This mapping, was then used to compute a SSG embeddings for each OOEV as $\mathbf{s}_{w'} = \mathbf{T} \cdot \mathbf{c}_{w'}$.

3.3 Partial Update of Embeddings during Training

Given the small amount of supervised data, directly updating the embeddings with the SemEval train set leads to very poor results. It is however possible to update only the OOEV words present in the training set simultaneously to the computation of the subspace (Astudillo et al., 2015a). To obtain positive results with this approach, it was also necessary to reduce the effect of training by lowering the learning rate to 0.001 and updating the embeddings only in the first two iterations.

4 Main Improvements over the 2015 NLSE

One complication with Twitter-based evaluations is the need of the participant to retrieve the tweets themselves, since some of the tweets may no longer be available. The INESC-ID system presented in 2015 employed a train set of 8604 tweets, considerably smaller than the original dataset (with 11328 tweets). For this edition, it was possible to get ahold of the full dataset, as utilized by Severyn and Moschitti (2015). For reproducibility and comparison purposes our systems this year were developed with this dataset.

The system presented in 2015 was very simple both in its structure and the number hyperparameters. Furthermore, tunning and selection of candidate systems was also performed without automatic grid-search. It was therefore expected that our previous setup would outright produce better results by training on a larger dataset. Disappointingly, this was not the case. In fact, the NLSE optimized for the 2015 competition seemed to be sitting on a local optimum that was difficult to come out from. To overcome this problem, we introduced two modifications in the training procedure[1]. The NLSE is trained by minimizing the negative log-likelihood. This cost function is sub-optimal taking into account the evaluation metric, as it weights equally positive, negative and neutral predictions. A simple improvement over this cost is an asymmetric weighting that penalizes the predictions of neutral tweets. This was incorporated as a multiplicative factor on the log-likelihood of values $4/3$, $4/3$ and $1/3$ for the positive, negative and neutral classes, respectively. To reduce the risk of getting trapped into a local minimum, the train data was shuffled before each training epoch. The asymmetric cost and randomization led to a slower, less consistent convergence. For this reason the number of iterations was increased from 8 to 12. The learning rate was changed from 0.01 to 0.005. Table 2 shows the effect of the improvements on the submitted system.

After introducing these two improvements, we investigated different methods to address the problem of OOEV as described in the previous sec-

---

[1] After paper revision the model in `https://github.com/ramon-astudillo/NLSE` will be updated to reflect the new system.

tion. Namely those exploiting *C2W* embeddings, mapping *C2W* embeddings to *SSG* embeddings and training the embeddings for OOEVs. The results of these strategies are displayed in Table 3.

System	2013	2014	2015	2016
baseline	0.721	0.721	0.649	0.609
C2W embeddings	0.659	0.689	0.613	0.543
C2W → *SSG*	**0.724**	0.715	0.652	**0.613**
update OOEVs 2 iter	0.723	**0.728**	**0.656**	0.610

Table 3: Comparision of strategies to address the problem of OOEV

5   The Submitted System

As mentioned in the previous section, the system submitted is an improvement over our 2015 system (Astudillo et al., 2015b). It therefore shares the same training characteristics as the previous model. The 52 million tweets used by Owoputi et al. (2013) and the tokenizer described in the same work were used to train the word embeddings *Structured Skip-Gram* (SSG). For this submission, the *C2W* embeddings were also trained using a publicly available toolkit[2]. For the annotated SemEval training data, the messages were previously pre-processed as follows: lower-casing, replacing Twitter user mentions and URLs with special tokens and reducing any character repetition to at most 3 characters. Following Astudillo et al. (2015a), we used embeddings with 600 dimensions and set the sub-space size to 10 dimensions.

To train the model, the development set was split into 80% for parameter learning and 20% for model evaluation and selection, maintaining the original relative class proportions in each set. The weights were all randomly initialized uniformly with ranges of $[-0.001, 0.001]$, $[-0.1, 0.1]$ and $[-0.7, 0.7]$ for the OOEVs, subspace and classification layers respectively. The training procedure entailed minimizing the negative log-likelihood over the training data with respect to the parameters, using standard Stochastic Gradient Descent (Rumelhart et al., 1985) with a fixed learning rate of 0.005 and mini-batch of size 1, i.e., updating the weights after each message was processed. We reshuffled the training

---
[2]https://github.com/wlin12/wang2vec

System	2013	2014	2015	2016	Avg
SwissCheese	0.700_5	0.716_5	0.671_1	0.633_1	0.680_2
SENSEI-LIF	0.706_4	0.744_2	0.662_2	0.630_2	0.686_1
unimelb	0.687_7	0.706_7	0.651_4	0.617_3	0.665_4
INESC-ID	0.723_2	0.727_3	0.657_3	0.610_4	0.679_3
aueb	0.666_8	0.708_6	0.623_7	0.605_5	0.651_5

Table 4: Official test-set results for the top five systems in SemEval 2016 Task 4-B. Subscript number indicates position in general ranking.

examples after each training epoch and performed model selection by early stopping after 12 iterations. The candidate for submission was manually selected by observing the performance across 2013, 2014 and 2015 datasets. Priority was given to models that presented a consistent high performance in all the datasets. In retrospect, this was most probably a suboptimal decision judging from the evaluation results.

Table 4 displays the performance for the top 5 systems in SemEval 2016 task 4-B (Nakov et al., 2016). The NLSE system (labeled INESC-ID) ranks forth with a stable performance across all years. The results are particularly strong for 2013 with a difference of 0.017 points over the next best performing system on the top five. This is consistent with the divide noticed during system selection between performance in 2013 and 2015. High-performing systems in 2014, and particularly in 2013, do not appear to be equally performing in recent years.

6   Conclusions

We presented the INESC-ID system for the SemEval 2016 task 4-A, built on top of the successful Non-Linear Subspace Embedding model. We found that training with a larger dataset required a more careful procedure to avoid overfitting. Reproducing the best results obtained in SemEval 2015 required shuffling the data before each training epoch and adapting the cost function to better reflect the evaluation metric.

To address the problem of out-of-embedding words, we tried to introduce character-level embeddings in our model but found these to be detrimental. We obtained better results by learning embeddings for these words during the training. Even though the performance gains were not very pronounced, our system still attained very strong results across all the evaluation datasets.

Acknowledgments

This work was partially supported by Fundação para a Ciência e Tecnologia (FCT), through contracts UID/CEC/50021/2013, EXCL/EEI-ESS/0257/2012 (DataStorm), grant number SFRH/BPD/68428/2010 and Ph.D. scholarship SFRH/BD/89020/2012.

References

Ramón Astudillo, Silvio Amir, Wang Ling, Mario Silva, and Isabel Trancoso. 2015a. Learning word representations from scarce and noisy data with embedding subspaces. In *Proceedings of the 53rd Annual Meeting of the Association for Computational Linguistics and the 7th International Joint Conference on Natural Language Processing (Volume 1: Long Papers)*, pages 1074–1084, Beijing, China, July. Association for Computational Linguistics.

Ramon F. Astudillo, Silvio Amir, Wang Ling, Bruno Martins, Mário Silva, and Isabel Trancoso. 2015b. Inesc-id: Sentiment analysis without hand-coded features or liguistic resources using embedding subspaces. In *Proceedings of the 9th International Workshop on Semantic Evaluation*, SemEval '2015, Denver, Colorado, June. Association for Computational Linguistics.

Ronan Collobert, Jason Weston, Léon Bottou, Michael Karlen, Koray Kavukcuoglu, and Pavel Kuksa. 2011. Natural language processing (almost) from scratch. *The Journal of Machine Learning Research*, 12:2493–2537.

Wang Ling, Chris Dyer, Alan Black, and Isabel Trancoso. 2015. Two/too simple adaptations of word2vec for syntax problems. In *Proceedings of the 2015 Conference of the North American Chapter of the Association for Computational Linguistics: Human Language Technologies*. Association for Computational Linguistics.

Tomas Mikolov, Quoc V Le, and Ilya Sutskever. 2013. Exploiting similarities among languages for machine translation. *arXiv preprint arXiv:1309.4168*.

Preslav Nakov, Alan Ritter, Sara Rosenthal, Veselin Stoyanov, and Fabrizio Sebastiani. 2016. SemEval-2016 task 4: Sentiment analysis in Twitter. In *Proceedings of the 10th International Workshop on Semantic Evaluation (SemEval 2016)*.

Olutobi Owoputi, Chris Dyer, Kevin Gimpel, Nathan Schneider, and Noah A. Smith. 2013. Improved part-of-speech tagging for online conversational text with word clusters. In *In Proceedings of NAACL*.

David E Rumelhart, Geoffrey E Hinton, and Ronald J Williams. 1985. Learning internal representations by error propagation. Technical report, DTIC Document.

Aliaksei Severyn and Alessandro Moschitti. 2015. Unitn: Training deep convolutional neural network for twitter sentiment classification. In *Proceedings of the 9th International Workshop on Semantic Evaluation*, SemEval '2015, Denver, Colorado, June. Association for Computational Linguistics.

SentimentalITsts at SemEval-2016 Task 4:
building a Twitter sentiment analyzer in your backyard

Cosmin Florean, Oana Bejenaru, Eduard Apostol, Octavian Ciobanu,
Adrian Iftene and Diana Trandabăţ
University "Alexandru Ioan Cuza" of Iaşi, Romania
`{cosmin.florean, oana.bejenaru, eduard.apostol, octavian.ciobanu,`
`adiftene, dtrandabat}@info.uaic.ro`

Abstract

The paper presents the system developed by the *SentimentalITsts* team for the participation in Semeval-2016 task 4, in the subtasks A, B and C. The developed system uses off the shelf solutions for the development of a quick sentiment analyzer for tweets. However, the lack of any syntactic or semantic information resulted in performances lower than those of other teams.

1 Introduction

Slowly but surely, social media replaced the tradicional sources of information: people's need to be constantly updated changed our behavior from buying a newspaper or watching TV, to using a Facebook or Twitter account to visualize, in a customizable manner, the day's hottest news, with the bonus of being able to also comment on them.

Social media sites gained their popularity due to the "freedom" of expression they induce in people's mind: being able to post real time messages about your opinions on whatever topic you come across, discuss political and social decisions, complain, express gratitude or exchange impressions about products you use in everyday life.

Texts shared through social media applications offer us the information that we need: for example, the reviews of a product provide us useful information about its advantages and disadvantages, while the text of an advertisement invites us to eat at the new Chinese restaurant in town.

As huge amounts of texts become available through social media, a challenging task concerns the organization and processing of this information to extract knowledge. Natural language processing tools trained on large news corpora have usually problems when applied to unstandardized social media inputs, mainly due to the fact that social media content can appear in various forms (Becker et al., 2012), from photos and video updates to news, offers and literary works, and various informal formats.

Twitter is micro-blogging platform where people can send messages to one or multiple users, follow friends and read messages without much difficulty. Twitter messages, commonly known as tweets, are limited to 140 characters, and frequently include hashtags (labels which should make it easier for users to find messages with similar content), all in one making Twitter analysis charming.

Out of the 5 subtasks of Semeval-2016 task 4, the *SentimentalITsts* participated in subtask A: Message Polarity Classification , subtask B Tweet classification according to a two-point scale and subtask C Tweet classification according to a five-point scale. Subtask A asked to classify a given tweet in three categories: positive, negative or neutral, according to the identified sentiment (Nakov et al., 2016). The tweet was known to be about a specific topic (by topic is meant anything people usually express opinions about on social networks: a product, a political candidate, a policy, an event, etc.) and the topic was given by the task organizers. Subtask B is a two-scale sentiment classification task, where tweets need to be identified as

Proceedings of SemEval-2016, pages 243–246,
San Diego, California, June 16-17, 2016. ©2016 Association for Computational Linguistics

positive or negative. Subtask C is a refinement of the previous subtasks, demanding a five-point scale: very positive, positive, neutral, negative, very negative. A five-point scale is now ubiquitous in the corporate world where human ratings are involved; e.g., Amazon, TripAdvisor, Yelp, and many others, all use a five-point scale for their reviews.

The remaining of this paper is structured as follow: Section 2 provided an overview of the state of the art applications the team has considered for sentiment analysis of social media, Section 3 presents the method used by the *SentimentalITsts* to develop their own sentiment analyzer, Section 4 offers some not official results used in analyzing the system's performance, before the final section drawing conclusions and further directions.

2 State of the art

Specific processing tools (such as POS taggers or anaphora resolution systems), score a higher performance if used on the same text type as the ones they were trained on. In other words, we will have better results if using a POS tagger trained on news corpora to analyze news texts, rather than speech transcripts.

Thus, the short dimension of tweets and their creative informal spelling have raised a new set of challenges to the natural language processing field. How to handle such challenges so as to automatically mine and understand the opinions and sentiments that people are communicating has been the subject of several research (Jansen et al., 2009; Barbosa and Feng, 2010; Bifet and Frank, 2010; Davidov et al., 2010; O'Connor et al., 2010; Pak and Paroubek, 2010; Tumasjen et al., 2010; Kouloumpis et al., 2011; Russell 2013; Pang et el., 2002).

A list of functional applications developed until now on Sentiment Analysis and API's that have a great success over the internet is presented below:

Sentiment140[1] (formerly known as "Twitter Sentiment") allows the discovery of the sentiment associated to a brand, product, or topic on Twitter. The API (Go et al., 2009) uses a maximum entropy classifier, trained on a set of automatically extract-ed tweets. The training corpus of 1.600.000 tweets is created relying on the use of emoticons (tweets with happy smileys suggest a positive contents, while tweets with sad/anger smileys refer to negative contents). The API lets users classify tweets and integrate sentiment analysis functionality into their own websites or applications, using RESTful calls and responses formatted in JSON.

Werfamous[2] is another webservice offering a sentiment search ability for a user selected term.

Sentiment Analysis with Python NLTK Text Classification*:* It can classify the text introduced on one of three groups: positive, negative or neutral. Using hierarchical classification neutrality is determined first, and sentiment polarity is determined second, but only if the text is not neutral. The NLTK Trainer is used to train classifiers for the sentiments based on twitter sentiment or movie reviews. NLTK[3] (Bird et al., 2009) is a leading platform for building Python programs to work with human language data. It provides easy-to-use interfaces to over 50 corpora and lexical resources such as WordNet, along with a suite of text processing libraries for classification, tokenization, stemming, tagging, parsing, and semantic reasoning, etc.

DatumBox[4]: an OpenSource API that allows users to access the web services offered by DatumBox. This services include Sentiment Analysis on any post using a 3 point scale considering that the topic of the post is given.

AlchemyAPI[5] (Turian, 2013) launched in 2009, is a company that uses machine learning (specifically deep learning) to do natural language processing (specifically semantic text analysis including sentiment analysis) and computer vision (face detection and recognition) for its clients both over the cloud and on-premises.

LexAlytics[6] is a web platform for media monitoring, offering nice visualization tools and powerful document processing capabilities.

For the Semeval-2016 participation, the *SentimentalITsts* team has used a self-trained Naive

[1] http://help.sentiment140.com/home

[2] http://werfamous.com/
[3] http://www.nltk.org/
[4] http://www.datumbox.com/
[5] http://www.alchemyapi.com/
[6] https://www.lexalytics.com/

Bayes classifiers, combined with the existing Alchemy-API for the cases where the classifier's output score was below an empirically established threshold.

3 Architecture

Building a Social Media Monitoring tool requires at least 2 modules: one that evaluates how many people are influenced by the campaign and one that finds out what people think about the brand.

For the second tool, being able to evaluate the opinion of the users is not a trivial matter. Evaluating their opinions requires performing Sentiment Analysis, which is the task of automatically identifying the polarity, the subjectivity and the emotional states of a particular document or sentence. It requires Machine Learning and Natural Language Processing techniques.

The reminder of this section will present a short description of the classes and objects used for the development of the three systems which participated in SemEval subtasks A, B and C. The architecture for the three systems was similar, the main difference being the way Naïve Bayes classifiers were trained: for 2, 3 or 5 classes, respectively. The training instances were obtained from the train and development corpora offered by the organizers of the SemEval-2016 task, and the internal evaluation was performed on the test development data.

- NaiveBayes Class
  ○ main part of the Text Classifier
  ○ implements methods such as train() and predict() that are responsible for training a classifier and using it for predictions
  ○ use external methods to preprocess and tokenize the document before training

- NaiveBayesKnowledgeBase Object
  ○ output of training which stores all the necessary information and probabilities used by the classifier

- Document Object
  ○ training and prediction texts in the implementation are internally stored as Document Objects
  ○ stores all the tokens of the document, their statistics and target classification of the document

- FeatureStats Object
  ○ stores several statistics that are generated during the Feature Extraction phase.

- FeatureExtraction Class
  ○ calculates internally several of the statistics that are actually required by the classification algorithm in the later stage, and all these stats are cached and returned in a FeatureStats Object to avoid their recalculation.

- TextTokenizer Class
  ○ simple text tokenization class, responsible for preprocessing: cleaning and tokenizing the original texts, removing special symbols, identifying and annotating hashtags and smileys, standardizing word with repeated letters, and converting them into Document objects.

Similar to (Go et al, 2009 and Pang et al., 2002), the Naïve Bayes classifiers were trained using the following features: tokenized unigrams, emoticons, hashtags.

4 Non-official error analysis

In order to check the system's weakness and straightness, an internal evaluation was performed before the official evaluation, for each substask.

When analyzing the errors found in the classification for subtask A (Fig.1), one can easily note that the system is positive-biased, i.e. it gave too many positive answers. Thus, out of the 29% of negative instances wrongly classified, 77% were classified as positive, while 23 as neutral. Similarly, for the neutral instances in gold which were misclassified, 89% were identified as positive, and 11% as negative.

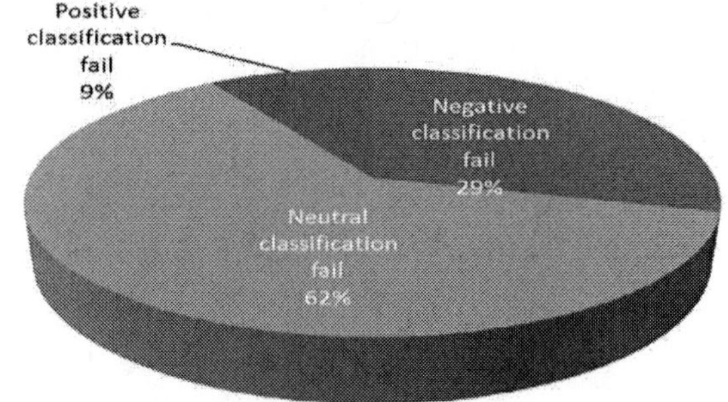

Figure 1. Internal evaluation for three-point scale error cases

For subtask B, the most misclassified category was the negative one. Table 1 presents the confusion matrix for the two categories. It is worth noticing that the system developed for subtask B is significantly better than the one for subtask A, according to our internal evaluation.

	Negative	Positive
Negative	81,14	18,86
Positive	3,40	96,60

Table 1. Confusion matrix for the five-scale task, evaluated on test development data

For subtask C, the system was biased towards the neutral classification. Thus, in case of doubt or when no other classification goes beyond a confidence score, the neutral classification was selected. The error matrix is presented in table 2.

	Very neg.	Very pos.	Pos.	Neutr.	Neg.
Very neg.	88,31	0,00	6,68	5,01	0,00
Very pos.	0,00	65,10	32,32	2,29	0,29
Pos.	4,39	0,00	62,42	30,72	2,47
Neutr.	0,00	0,00	62,14	36,27	1,59
Neg.	0,00	0,00	32,73	12,90	54,37

Table 2. Confusion matrix for the five-scale task, evaluated on test development data

5 Official evaluation and discussions

The official evaluation placed the *SentimentalITsts* on the 32nd place for subtask A (see table 3 for details of performances on each dataset). For subtask B, the team was placed 15th out of 19th, and for subtask C the official classification was at rank 9 out of 11 (see for details Nakov et al., 2016).

SentimentalITsts	2013		2014				
	Tweet	SMS	Tweet	Tweet sarcsm	Live Journal	2015 tweet	2016 Tweet
	0.33	0.23	0.39	0.28	0.32	0.34	0.33

Table 3. Official results for the SentimentalITsts team, task A

In this version of the system, no syntactic or semantic information was used. Similarly, hashtags or smileys, although they seemed useful in initial tests, ultimately showed that they bring more noise than relevant information, and were thus removed from the message files.

References

Barbosa, L. and Feng, J. (2010). *Robust sentiment detection on twitter from biased and noisy data*. Proceedings of Coling 2010 .

Bifet, A. and Frank, E. (2010). *Sentiment knowledge discovery in twitter streaming data*. Proceedings of 14th Int. Conference on Discovery Science.

Bird Steven, Klein E., Loper E., (2009) *Natural Language Processing with Python*, O'Reilly Media.

Davidov, D., Tsur, O., Rappoport, A. (2010). *Enhanced sentiment learning using twitter hashtags and smileys*. Proceedings of Coling 2010.

Go A., Bhayani R., Huang. L. (2009) Twitter Sentiment Classification using Distant Supervision, *Technical Report*.

Jansen, B.J., Zhang, M., Sobel, K., Chowdury, A. (2009). *Twitter power: Tweets as electronic word of mouth*. Journal of the American Society for Information Science and Technology 60(11):2169-2188.

Kouloumpis, E., Wilson, T., and Moore, J. (2011). *Twitter Sentiment Analysis: The Good the Bad and the OMG!* Proceedings of ICWSM. 2011

MA Russell (2013) Mining the Social Web: Data Mining Facebook, Twitter, LinkedIn, Google+, GitHub, and More.

Nakov P., Ritter A., Rosenthal S., Stoyanov V., Sebastiani F.(2016) *SemEval-2016 Task 4: Sentiment Analysis in Twitter*, Proc. of SemEval '16.

O'Connor, B., Balasubramanyan, R., Routledge, B., and Smith, N. 2010. From tweets to polls: Linking text sentiment to public opinion time series. Proceedings of ICWSM.

Pak, A. and Paroubek, P. 2010. *Twitter as a corpus for sentiment analysis and opinion mining*. Proceedings of LREC 2010.

Pang, Bo, Lillian Lee, and Shivakumar Vaithyanathan. (2002) "Thumbs up?: sentiment classification using machine learning techniques." Proceedings of EMNLP, pp. 79-86.

Tumasjan, A., Sprenger, T.O., Sandner, P., Welpe, I. (2010). Predicting elections with twitter: What 140 characters reveal about political sentiment. Proceedings of ICWSM 2010.

Turian Joseph, (2013) *Using AlchemyAPI for Enterprise-Grade Text Analysis*, PhD Thesis.

Minions at SemEval-2016 Task 4:
or how to build a sentiment analyzer using off-the-shelf resources?

Călin-Cristian Ciubotariu, Marius-Valentin Hrişca, Mihail Gliga, Diana Darabană,
Diana Trandabăţ and Adrian Iftene

University "Alexandru Ioan Cuza" of Iaşi, Romania

`{calin.ciubotariu, marius.hrisca, mihail.gliga, diana.darabana,`
`diana.trandabat, adiftene}@info.uaic.ro`

Abstract

Minions, a team formed of first year students in the Master of Computational Linguistics, started the participation at Semeval-2016 as a semester project, aiming to build a model for analyzing and classifying "tweets" into positive, neutral and negative, according to the evoked sentiment, while getting familiar with Natural Language Processing tools and methods. Therefore, the backbone of our sentiment analyzer consists in several off-the-shelf, freely available resources, enhanced with a classifier trained on the SemEval-2016 data.

1 Introduction

Texts live around us just as we live around them. At any instant, there are texts that people write, share, use to get informed, etc. (starting with an advertisement heard on the radio every morning and finishing with the contract of sale signed before a notary). Combining this with the concept of language economy (or the principle of least effort) – a tendency shared by all humans – consisting in minimizing the needed amount of effort to achieve the maximum result, it is no wonder why the social media, with its short, informal and context-dependent texts, achieved such a high popularity.

SemEval-2016 task 4 had several subtasks, but since our team consists mainly of members beginning to learn about Natural Language Processing, we only felt comfortable in participating in Subtask A. This subtask involved the classification of a message polarity, i.e. classify a given tweet in three categories: positive, negative or neutral, according to the identified sentiment (Nakov et al., 2016).

The remaining of this paper is structured as follows: Section 2 provides an overview of available online applications for analyzing social media sentiments; Section 3 presents our own sentiment analyzer, before the final section presenting the evaluation of the system and drawing some conclusions.

2 State of the art

Specific processing tools (such as POS taggers or anaphora resolution systems), score a higher performance if used on the same text type as the ones they were trained on. In other words, we will have better results if using a POS tagger trained on news corpora to analyze news texts, rather than speech transcripts.

Thus, the short dimension of tweets and their creative informal spelling have raised a new set of challenges to the natural language processing field. How to handle such challenges while automatically mining and understanding the opinions and sentiments that people are communicating has been the subject of several research (Jansen et al., 2009; Barbosa and Feng, 2010; Bifet and Frank, 2010; Davidov et al., 2010; O'Connor et al., 2010; Pak and Paroubek, 2010; Tumasjan et al., 2010; Kouloumpis et al., 2011).

We have investigated existing online applications for sentiment extraction of social media from Twitter, briefly discussed below, and integrated some of them in our sentiment analyzer.

Proceedings of SemEval-2016, pages 247–250,
San Diego, California, June 16-17, 2016. ©2016 Association for Computational Linguistics

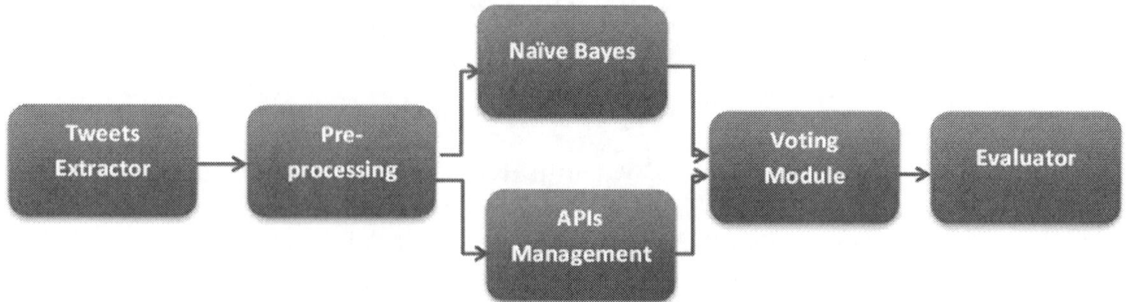

Figure 1. Diagram of our tweet sentiment analyzer

Trackur[1] is an online application, allowing the display of opinions on a particular search criterion, trained on datasets from various social networks such as Facebook, Google Plus, Instagram, etc.

Social Mention[2] application monitors over 100 social networks, blogs or forums such as Twitter, Facebook, Youtube, Digg, Google, etc. in an attempt to identify emerging hot topics.

AlchemyAPI[3] (Turian, 2013), provider of artificial intelligence cloud services, offers multiple modes of sentiment analysis: document-level, entity-level, and keyword-level sentiment mining is provided, in addition to support for advanced features such as negation handling, sentiment amplifiers / diminishers, slang, and typos, all based on the company's deep-learning classifier, trained on an impressive social media corpus.

Sentiment140[4] (formerly known as "Twitter Sentiment") allows the discovery of the sentiment associated to a brand, product, or topic on Twitter. It uses a maximum entropy classifier, trained on a set of automatically extracted tweets. The training corpus of 1.600.000 tweets was created relying solely on the use of emoticons (tweets with happy smileys suggest a positive contents, while tweets with sad/anger smileys refer to negative contents). The API lets users classify tweets and integrate sentiment analysis functionality into their own websites or applications, using RESTful calls and responses formatted in JSON.

NLTK[5] (Bird et al., 2009) is a platform for building Python programs to work with human language data. It provides easy-to-use interfaces to over 50 corpora and lexical resources (including WordNet), along with a suite of text processing libraries for classification, tokenization, stemming, tagging, parsing, and semantic reasoning, etc.

After analyzing the available applications for sentiment analysis, we decided to build our own analyzer based on several existing services (Alchemy, Sentiment 140 and NLTK's Sentiment analyzer), enhanced with a Naïve Bayes classifier trained on the SemEval-2016 data.

3 System Architecture

The system developed for SemEval-2016 can be divided in the following modules:

1. ***Tweets Extractor***: a module which extracts tweets based on a list of ID's provided by the task organizers;
2. ***Pre-processing***: cleaning operations needed to remove from tweets symbols unsupported by the sentiment analysis services;
3. ***APIs Management***: development of a web service able to manage the calls to the three sentiment analysis APIs: Alchemy, Sentiment 140, NLTK;
4. ***Naïve Bayes Classifier***: trains a Naïve Bayes classifier from the NLTK toolkit for identification of positive, negative and neutral sentiments.

---

[1] http://www.trackur.com/about-trackur

[2] http://socialmention.com/

[3] http://www.alchemyapi.com/

[4] http://help.sentiment140.com/home

---

[5] http://www.nltk.org/

5. ***Voting Module*** receives sentiment scores from the three APIs and decides, in case of mismatch, which one to further obey;

6. ***Evaluator***: Analysis the output file and creates statistics used to improve the system's performances.

The system's architecture is presented in figure 1 above and the modules are discussed in more details in the next subsections.

3.1 Tweet Extractor

This module receives as input a set of tweets IDs and extracts the text of tweets using Twitter API. One of the challenges with regard to this module was to overcome the limitations set by the Twitter API (a limit of 100 tweets in a response for any request). Therefore, the tweet extractor has a parameter that allows us to specify the frequency of crawling. We found that an interval of 2 minutes is a reasonable polling parameter.

Several tweet IDs returned errors when processing, the content of the tweets being no longer available. For example, for the train data, out of the 6000 ID's, 632 were not found.

3.2 Pre-processing

After obtaining the texts from tweets, a cleaning phase was performed, in order to standardize the data. Thus, regular expressions have been built to: convert the texts to lowercase, discard words shorter than two characters, remove special diacritic signs, URLs, as well as symbols unsupported by the sentiment analyzers' APIs (such as "?"). Users often include Twitter usernames in their tweets in order to direct their messages, using the @ symbol before the username (e.g. @radut), therefore a regex replaces all words that start with the @ symbol. Another modification proved to significantly reduce feature space, inspired by (Pang et al., 2002), is removing duplicated vowels in the middle of the words (e.g. cooooool). Any letter occurring more than two times in a row is replaced with exactly two occurrences.

3.3 APIs Management

This module was intended to manage the calls to the sentiment analysis APIs used in this project:

Alchemy, Sentiment 140 and NLTK's Sentiment analyzer.

3.4 Naïve Bayes Classifier

Similar to (Go et al, 2009 and Pang et al., 2002), we trained a Naïve Bayes classifier, using the NLTK's training facility, with the following features: tokenized unigrams, emoticons, hashtags. We used the train and development data made available by the SemEval-2016 organizers for training.

Ultimately, our internal evaluation on test development data from the SemEval-2016 competition revealed the fact that our Naïve Bayes classifier was introducing more errors than correct cases, most probably due to a bug. We therefore introduced a parameter allowing us to run the system with a customized series of analyzers. For the submitted runs, we only considered the outputs of the three sentiment analysis APIs.

3.5 Voting Module and Evaluator

These modules are used to analyze the output of the sentiment analysis APIs aiming to identify, in case different labels are issued, which sentiment analyzer is most reliable. The Evaluator outputs a set of statistics using the test development data provided by the SemEval-2016 organizers.

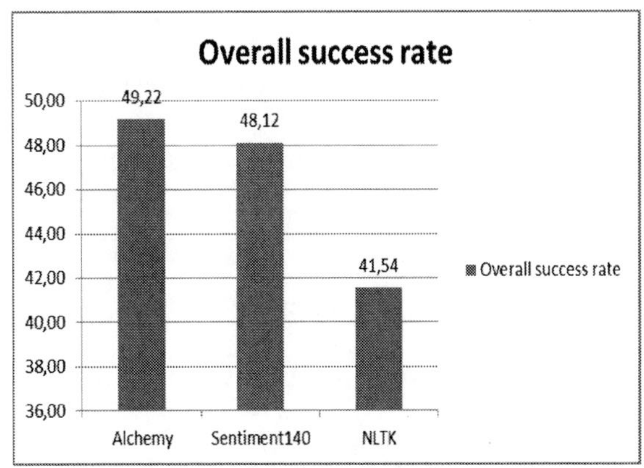

Figure 2. Comparison between the three sentiment identification services

Thus, this module checks how many agreements/disagreements are found in the results offered by different sentiment analyzers (see figure 2 for an overview and figure 3 for a detailed analysis of matched labels). We found that in only 14.9% of the cases, all three services gave the same good result. For 9.4% of the cases, the three services gave similar label, but failed to find the good one. Out of these situations, almost 14% were mislabeled negative cases, and only 1.5% mislabeled positive tweets.

However, in 30.6% of the cases, two of the services gave the same label, the good one and in 78% of cases at least one classifier gave the right answer.

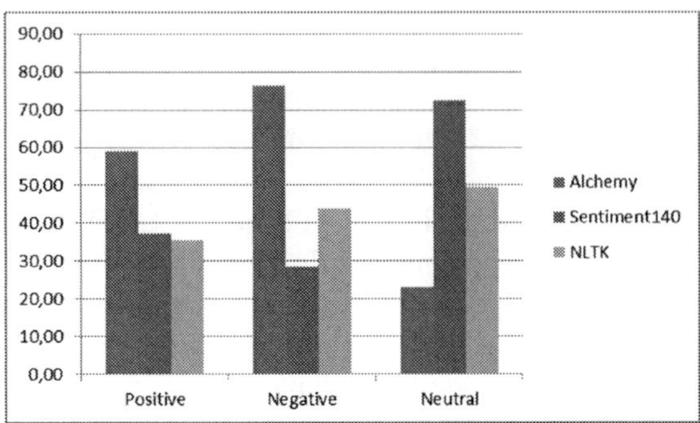

Figure 3. Percentage of correctly identified sentiments on SemEval-2016 training data

These analyses lead us to the decision to implement a simple voting module, which is based on the following empirically derived rules:

- If at least two services give the same label, this label is chosen;
- Otherwise, based on the internal evaluation (see figure 3), the priority was given as follows:
    o if Alchemy gives a negative result, select it;
    o else if Sentiment140 gave a neutral result, select it;
    o otherwise, if Alchemy gave a positive result, select it,
    o otherwise select the neutral label.

4 Official evaluation and discussions

The official evaluation (Nakov et al., 2016), presented in table 1, placed our system on the 28th place (out of 34 places).

Minions	2013		2014				
	Tweet	SMS	Tweet	Tweet sarcsm	Live Journal	2015 tweet	2016 Tweet
	0.48	0.52	0.55	0.42	0.47	0.48	0.41

Table 1 Official results for the Minions team

In this version of the system, we did not used part-of-speeches, since initial tests showed that in this configuration, they bring more noise than relevant information, conclusion shared (for part-of-speeches) also by (Pang et al., 2002). However, as further improvements, we intend to lemmatize the tweets before feeding them to our classifier, and use an external dictionary of sentiment valences in the voting module, to enhance our system's performance.

References

Barbosa, L. and Feng, J. (2010). *Robust sentiment detection on twitter from biased and noisy data*. Proceedings of Coling 2010 .

Bifet, A. and Frank, E. (2010). *Sentiment knowledge discovery in twitter streaming data*. Proceedings of 14th Int. Conference on Discovery Science.

Bird Steven, Klein E., Loper E., (2009) *Natural Language Processing with Python*, O'Reilly Media.

Davidov, D., Tsur, O., Rappoport, A. (2010). *Enhanced sentiment learning using twitter hashtags and smileys*. Proceedings of Coling 2010.

Go A., Bhayani R., Huang. L. (2009) Twitter Sentiment Classification using Distant Supervision, *Technical Report*.

Jansen, B.J., Zhang, M., Sobel, K., Chowdury, A. (2009). *Twitter power: Tweets as electronic word of mouth*. Journal of the American Society for Information Science and Technology 60(11):2169-2188.

Kouloumpis, E., Wilson, T., and Moore, J. (2011). *Twitter Sentiment Analysis: The Good the Bad and the OMG*! Proceedings of ICWSM. 2011

Nakov P., Ritter A., Rosenthal S., Stoyanov V., Sebastiani F.(2016) *SemEval-2016 Task 4: Sentiment Analysis in Twitter*, Proc. of SemEval '16.

O'Connor, B., Balasubramanyan, R., Routledge, B., and Smith, N. 2010. From tweets to polls: Linking text sentiment to public opinion time series. Proceedings of ICWSM.

Pak, A. and Paroubek, P. 2010. *Twitter as a corpus for sentiment analysis and opinion mining*. Proceedings of LREC 2010.

Pang, Bo, Lillian Lee, and Shivakumar Vaithyanathan. (2002) "Thumbs up?: sentiment classification using machine learning techniques." Proceedings of EMNLP, pp. 79-86.

Tumasjan, A., Sprenger, T.O., Sandner, P., Welpe, I. (2010). *Predicting elections with twitter: What 140 characters reveal about political sentiment*. Proceedings of ICWSM 2010.

Turian Joseph, (2013) *Using AlchemyAPI for Enterprise-Grade Text Analysis*, PhD Thesis.

YZU-NLP Team at SemEval-2016 Task 4: Ordinal Sentiment Classification Using a Recurrent Convolutional Network

Yunchao He[2,3,4], Liang-Chih Yu[1,3], Chin-Sheng Yang[1,3], K. Robert Lai[2,3], Weiyi Liu[4]
[1]Department of Information Management, Yuan Ze University, Taiwan
[2]Department of Computer Science & Engineering, Yuan Ze University, Taiwan
[3]Innovation Center for Big Data and Digital Convergence, Yuan Ze University, Taiwan
[4]School of Information Science and Engineering, Yunnan University, Yunnan, P.R. China

Abstract

Sentiment analysis of tweets has attracted considerable attention recently for potential use in commercial and public sector applications. Typical sentiment analysis classifies the sentiment of sentences into several discrete classes (e.g., positive and negative). The aim of Task 4 subtask C of SemEval-2016 is to classify the sentiment of tweets into an ordinal five-point scale. In this paper, we present a system that uses word embeddings and recurrent convolutional networks to complete the competition task. The word embeddings provide a continuous vector representation of words for the recurrent convolutional network to use in building sentence vectors for multi-point classification. The proposed method ranked second among eleven teams in terms of micro-averaged MAE (mean absolute error) and eighth for macro-averaged MAE.

1 Introduction

Sentiment analysis seeks to detect and analyze sentiment within texts. Following the rapid increase of user generated content in the form of social media, sentiment analysis has attracted considerable interest. Typical approaches to sentiment analysis classify the sentiment of a sentence into several discrete classes such as positive and negative polarities, or six basic emotions: anger, happiness, fear, sadness, disgust and surprise (Ekman, 1992). Based on this representation, various techniques have been investigated including supervised learning and lexicon-based approaches. Supervised learning approaches require training data for sentiment classification (Go et al., 2009; Yu et al., 2009; Saif et al., 2016), while lexicon-based approaches do not require training data but use a sentiment lexicon to determine the overall sentiment of a sentence (Liu, 2010; Hu et al., 2013).

A five-point scale (Nakov et al., 2016) is also a popular way to evaluate sentiment. Many companies, such as Amazon, Google, and Alibaba all use a multi-point scale to evaluate product or APP reviews. Unlike typical classification approaches, ordinal classification can assign different ratings (e.g., *very negative, negative, neutral, positive* and *very positive*) according to sentiment strength (Taboada et al., 2011; Li et al., 2011; Yu et al., 2013; Wang and Ester, 2014).

Task 4 subtask C of SemEval-2016 seeks to classify the sentiment of tweets into an ordinal five-point scale. This paper presents a system that uses word embeddings (Mikolov et al., 2013) and recurrent convolutional networks to this end. The word embeddings can capture both semantic and syntactic information of words to provide a continuous vector representation of those words. These word vectors are then used to build sentence vectors through a recurrent convolutional neural network. For multi-point classification, we discretize the continuous sentiment intensity to a five partitions of equal intervals.

The proposed recurrent convolutional network consists of two parts: a convolutional neural network (CNN) (LeCun et al., 1990) on the bottom to reduce the dimension of a sentence matrix, fol-

Proceedings of SemEval-2016, pages 251–255,
San Diego, California, June 16-17, 2016. ©2016 Association for Computational Linguistics

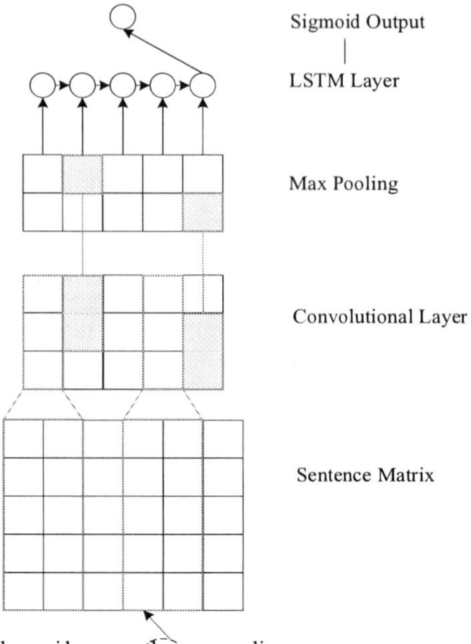

Figure 1: System architecture of the proposed CNN-LSTM model.

lowed by a long short-term memory (LSTM) (Hochreiter et al., 1997) layer to form the sentence representation, and a linear regression layer on the top to fit the sentiment intensity of sentences. The details of the CNN, LSTM and their combination are described in the following section.

2 Combining LSTM and CNN for Ordinal Classification

Ordinal classification of sentiment aims at classifying the sentence into ordinal discrete values according to their sentiment intensity. Figure 1 shows the system architecture of the proposed CNN-LSTM model for ordinal classification. In the bottom layer, the word vectors of vocabulary words are first trained from a large corpus using word embeddings. For each given sentence, a sentence vector is then built based on the word vectors of words in the sentences, which is further transformed into a matrix representation. The sentence matrix is sequentially passed through a convolutional layer and max pooling layer for multi-point classification. Unlike a conventional LSTM model which directly uses word embeddings as input, the proposed model takes uses outputs from a single-layer CNN with max pooling.

2.1 Convolutional Neural Network

In our model, the input of the LSTM layer is an output from the CNN. CNNs have achieved the state-of-the-art results in computer vision applications, and also have been shown to be effective for various NLP applications (Krizhevsky et al., 2012; Kim, 2014; Ma et al., 2015). The CNN architecture used for our tasks is described as follows.

Let V denote the vocabulary of words, while d denotes the dimensionality of word vectors, and $S \in R^{d \times n}$ denotes the sentence matrix built by concatenating the word vectors occurring in the sentences. Suppose that the sentence T is made up of a sequence of words $[d_1, d_2, ..., d_n]$, where n is the length of sentence T. Then the representation of T is given by the matrix $S^T \in R^{d \times n}$, where the j-th column corresponds to the embeddings for word d_j. Note that for batch processing we the zero-pad sentence matrix S^T so that the number of columns is a constant (equal to the max length of sentences) for all sentences in the corpus.

We apply a narrow convolution between S^T and a filter $F \in R^{d \times w}$ of a width w. We then add a bias term and apply a nonlinearity function to obtain a feature map $f^T \in R^{n-w+1}$. The i-th element of f^T is given by:

$$f^T[i] = relu(<S^T[:, i:i+w-1], F> +b) \qquad (1)$$

where $S^T[:, i:i+w-1]$ is the i-to-$(i+w-1)$-th column of S^T and $<A, B>=Trace(A \cdot B^T)$ is the Frobenius inner product.

The feature maps are input into a max pooling layer to capture the most salient feature (i.e., the one with the highest value) for a given filter. Filter operation is useful for determining the n-grams, where the size of the n-gram corresponds to the filter length.

The above description uses just one filter matrix to generate one feature. In practice, the proposed convolutional layer uses multiple filters in parallel to obtain the feature vectors.

2.2 Recurrent Neural Network

A recurrent neural network (RNN) architecture particularly suited for modelling sequence phenomena (Sak et al., 2014; Zhou et al. 2015). At each time step t, the RNN takes the input vector x_t

Name	# Tweets released	# Tweets used	# Top-ics	Avg. Length
Gold Train	6,000	5,346	60	19.49
Gold Dev	2,000	1,795	20	19.58
Gold Devtest	2,000	1,781	20	19.69
Test	20,632	20,632	100	19.62

Table 1: Summary of data statistics.

Name	# (-2)	# (-1)	# (0)	# (1)	# (2)
Gold Train	87	668	1654	3154	437
Gold Dev	43	296	675	933	53
Gold Devtest	31	233	583	1005	148

Table 2: Distributions of sentiment ratings. # (n) denotes the number of tweets annotated with a rating of n in the range of [-2, -1, ..., 2], corresponding to *Strongly Negative, Negative, Negative or Neutral, Positive, Strongly Positive,* respectively.

and the hidden state vector h_{t-1} to produce the next hidden state h_t by applying the following recursive operation:

$$h_t = f(Wx_t + Uh_{t-1} + b) \qquad (2)$$

Here W, U, b are the parameters of an affine transformation and f is an element-wise nonlinearity function. In theory, the RNN can summarize all historical information up to time t with the hidden state h_t. In practice, however, a vanilla RNN has difficulty learning long-term dependencies due to the vanishing gradient problem, as the gradient decreases exponentially with the number of network layers and the front layer trains very slowly.

Approaches have been developed to deal with vanishing gradient problem, and certain types of RNNs (like LSTM, GRU) are specially designed to get around them. LSTM (Hochreiter et al., 1997) addresses the problem of learning long-term dependencies by augmenting the RNN with a gating mechanism. To illustrate this, the following formulas show how a LSTM calculates a hidden state h_t.

$$i_t = \sigma(W^i x_t + U^i h_{t-1} + b^i)$$
$$f_t = \sigma(W^f x_t + U^f h_{t-1} + b^f)$$
$$o_t = \sigma(W^o x_t + U^o h_{t-1} + b^o)$$
$$g_t = \tanh(W^g x_t + U^g h_{t-1} + b^g) \qquad (3)$$
$$c_t = f_t \circ c_{t-1} + i_t \circ g_t$$
$$h_t = o_t \circ \tanh(c_t)$$

Here $\sigma(\cdot)$ and $\tanh(\cdot)$ are the element-wise sigmoid and hyperbolic tangent functions, $\circ$ is the element-wise multiplication operator, and i_t, f_t, o_t are called the *input, forget* and *output* gates respectively. All the gates have the same dimension d_s, which is equal to the size of hidden state, and c_0, h_0 are initialized to zero vectors at $t=1$. c_t is the internal memory of the unit, which could be regarded as how we want to combine previous memory and the new input.

The gating mechanism allows LSTM to model long-term dependencies. By learning the parameters W^j, U^j, b^j for $j \in \{i, f, o, g\}$, the network learns how its memory cells should behave.

3 Experiments and Evaluation

Dataset. We evaluated the proposed CNN-LSTM model by submitting the results to the SemEval-2016 Task 4 subtask. The statistics of the dataset used in this competition are summarized in Table 1. As the original tweets may be removed by Twitter users themselves, we can just download a part of the data in gold training, gold development, and gold development-test dataset. The distribution of sentiment labels shown in Table 2 shows data imbalance. Most of the data were annotated in [-1, 0, 1] labels, and only a few were annotated *Very Negative* (-2) or *Very Positive* (2).

Implementation details. As mentioned earlier, the proposed method consists of word embeddings and a recurrent convolutional network. Both parts may have their own parameters for optimization. For word embeddings, we used popular pre-trained word vectors from GloVe (Pennington et al., 2014). GloVe is an unsupervised learning algorithm for learning word representation. Training is performed on aggregated global word co-occurrence statistics from a large corpus, and the resulting representation showcases interesting linear substructures in the word vector space. They provide pre-trained word vectors trained on 840B tokens from common crawls and have a length of 300.

Although the pre-trained word embeddings can capture important semantic and syntactic in-

	MAE^{μ}	MAE^{M}
Scores	0.588	1.111
Rank	2	8

Table 3: Results of the proposed CNN-LSTM model for SemEval-2016 Task 4 Subtask C.

	Devtest Set		Test Set	
	MAE^{μ}	MAE^{M}	MAE^{μ}	MAE^{M}
CNN	0.656	0.992	0.534	0.939
CNN-LSTM	0.590	0.974	0.588	1.111

Table 4: Results of CNN-LSTM and CNN alone.

formation of words, they are not sufficient to capture sentiment behaviors in texts. To further improve word embeddings to capture sentiment information, we trained our recurrent convolutional network using an additional dataset from the Vader corpus (Hutto et al., 2014). It contains 4,000 tweets pulled from Twitter's public timeline, independently annotated by 20 human raters with sentiment ratings in a range of [-4, 4]. We discretized the continuous human-assigned ratings of [-4, 4] to discrete numbers [-2, -1, …, 2] to make them compatible with the task context.

The hyper-parameters of the network are chosen based on the performance on the development-test data. We use: rectified linear units (ReLU), filter windows (w) of 3 with 64 feature maps, dropout rate (p) of 0.25, pool length of 2, and mini-bath size of 16. *Adagrad* update rule is used to automatically tune the learning rate, and micro-averaged *MAE* is used as the loss function. Early stop mechanism is used to avoid overfitting. The activation function in the top layer is a sigmoid function, which scales each sentiment intensity to the range 0 to 1. These continuous intensity scores are transformed into a five-point scale through the cut-offs: [0, 0.2], (0.2, 0.4], (0.4, 0.6], (0.6, 0.8], (0.8, 1.0] for strongly negative, negative, negative or neutral, positive, strongly positive, respectively.

Evaluation metrics. SemEval-2016 Task 4 subtask C published the results for all participants using both macro-averaged mean absolute error (MAE^{M}) and micro-averaged mean absolute error (MAE^{μ}) (Nakov et al., 2015). The MAE^{M} is defined as:

$$MAE^{M}(h,Te) = \frac{1}{|C|}\sum_{j=1}^{|C|}\frac{1}{|Te_j|}\sum_{X_i \in Te_j}|h(X_i) - y_i| \quad (4)$$

where y_i denotes the true label of X_i, $h(X_i)$ denotes the predicted label, and Te_j denotes the set of test documents whose true class is c_j. The MAE^{μ} is defined as:

$$MAE^{\mu}(h,Te) = \frac{1}{|Te|}\sum_{X_i \in Te}|h(X_i) - y_i| \quad (5)$$

Compared to the micro-averaged MAE^{μ}, the macro-averaged MAE^{M} is more appropriate to measure the classification robustness of systems for imbalanced data.

Results. A total of eleven teams participated in subtask C. Table 3 shows the results of the proposed CNN-LSTM model for both MAE^{μ} and MAE^{M}. The proposed method ranked second for MAE^{μ} and eighth for MAE^{M}. The results of MAE^{μ} and MAE^{M} are inconsistent because we used a standard *MAE* as the loss function for model training and did not consider the imbalanced sentiment labels. Therefore, our model yielded better performance on MAE^{μ} than on MAE^{M}.

Table 4 shows the experimental results after the release of test set ratings. We found that the CNN-LSTM achieved better performance on the development test set than the test set. Conversely, the CNN alone yielded better performance on the test data than the development-test set.

4 Conclusions

This study presents a deep learning approach to classifying tweets into a five-point scale. The proposed model combines the convolutional neural networks and long short-term memory networks. To better capture the sentiment aspect of words, we further tuned our model using an additional sentiment corpus. Experimental results show that the proposed method archived good performance on the micro-averaged *MAE*.

Future work will focus on exploring more effective features and machine learning methods to improve classification performance for both micro- and macro-averaged *MAE*.

Acknowledgments

This work was supported by the Ministry of Science and Technology, Taiwan, ROC, under Grant No. NSC102-2221-E-155-029-MY3 and MOST 104-3315-E-155-002.

References

Paul Ekman. 1992. An argument for basic emotions. *Cognition and Emotion*, 6(3-4), 169-200.

Alex Go, Richa Bhayani, and Lei Huang. 2009. Twitter sentiment classification using distant supervision. In *CS224N Project Report*, Stanford.

Sepp Hochreiter and Jürgen Schmidhuber. 1997. Long short-term memory. *Neural computation*, 9(8), 1735-1780.

Xia Hu, Jiliang Tang, Huiji Gao, and Huan Liu. 2013. Unsupervised sentiment analysis with emotional signals. In *Proceedings of the 22nd international conference on World Wide Web*, pages 607-618.

Clayton J. Hutto, and Eric Gilbert. 2014. Vader: A parsimonious rule-based model for sentiment analysis of social media text. In *Proceedings of the Eighth International AAAI Conference on Weblogs and Social Media*.

Yoon Kim. 2014. Convolutional neural networks for sentence classification. In *EMNLP*, pages 1746–1751, Doha, Qatar.

Alex Krizhevsky, Ilya Sutskever, and Geoffrey E. Hinton. 2012. Imagenet classification with deep convolutional neural networks. In *Advances in neural information processing systems*, pages 1097-1105.

B. B. LeCun, John S. Denker, D. Henderson, Richard E. Howard, W. Hubbard, and Lawrence D. Jackel. 1990. Handwritten digit recognition with a back-propagation network. In *Advances in neural information processing systems*.

Fangtao Li, Nathan Liu, Hongwei Jin, Kai Zhao, Qiang Yang, and Xiaoyan Zhu. 2011. Incorporating reviewer and product information for review rating prediction. In *Proceedings of the 22nd International Joint Conference on Artificial Intelligence (IJCAI-11)*, pages 1820-1825.

Bing Liu. 2010. Sentiment Analysis and Subjectivity. *Handbook of natural language processing*, 2, 627-666.

Mingbo Ma, Liang Huang, Bing Xiang, and Bowen Zhou. 2015. Dependency-based Convolutional Neural Networks for Sentence Embedding. In *Proceedings of the 53rd Annual Meeting of the Association for Computational Linguistics (ACL-15)*, pages 174–179.

Tomas Mikolov, Ilya Sutskever, Kai Chen, Greg S. Corrado, and Jeff Dean. 2013. Distributed representations of words and phrases and their compositionality. In *Advances in neural information processing systems*, pages 3111-3119.

Preslav Nakov, Alan Ritter, Sara Rosenthal, Fabrizio Sebastiani, and Veselin Stoyanov. 2015. Evaluation Measures for the SemEval-2016 Task 4 "Sentiment Analysis in Twitter" (Draft: Version 1.1).

Preslav Nakov, Alan Ritter, Sara Rosenthal, Veselin Stoyanov, and Fabrizio Sebastiani. 2016. SemEval-2016 Task 4: Sentiment Analysis in Twitter. In *Proceedings of the 10th International Workshop on Semantic Evaluation, Association for Computational Linguistics*. San Diego, California.

Jeffrey Pennington, Richard Socher, and Christopher D. Manning. 2014. Glove: Global Vectors for Word Representation. In *Proceedings of the 2014 Conference on Empirical Methods on Natural Language Processing (EMNLP-14)*, pages 1532-1543.

Hasim Sak, Andrew W. Senior, and Françoise Beaufays. 2014. Long short-term memory recurrent neural network architectures for large scale acoustic modeling. In *Proceedings of INTERSPEECH-14*, pages 338-342.

Hassan Saif, Yulan He, Miriam Fernandez, and Harith Alani. 2016. Contextual semantics for sentiment analysis of Twitter. *Information Processing & Management*, 52(1), 5-19.

Maite Taboada, Julian Brooke, Milan Tofiloski, Kimberly Voll, and Manfred Stede. 2011. Lexicon-based methods for sentiment analysis. *Computational Linguistics*, 37(2):267-307.

Hao Wang and Martin Ester. 2014. A sentiment-aligned topic model for product aspect rating prediction. In *Proceedings of the 2014 Conference on Empirical Methods in Natural Language Processing (EMNLP-14)*, pages 1192-1202.

Jie Zhou and Wei Xu. 2015. End-to-end learning of semantic role labeling using recurrent neural networks. In *Proceedings of the 53rd Annual Meeting of the Association for Computational Linguistics (ACL-15)*, pages 1127–1137.

Liang-Chih Yu, Wu, Jheng-Long Wu, Pei-Chann Chang, and Hsuan-Shou Chu. 2013. Using a contextual entropy model to expand emotion words and their intensity for the sentiment classification of stock market news. *Knowledge-based Systems*. 41:89-97.

Liang-Chih Yu, Chung-Hsien Wu, and Fong-Lin Jang. 2009. Psychiatric document retrieval using a discourse-aware model. *Artificial Intelligence*, 173(7-8): 817-829.

ECNU at SemEval-2016 Task 4: An Empirical Investigation of Traditional NLP Features and Word Embedding Features for Sentence-level and Topic-level Sentiment Analysis in Twitter

Yunxiao Zhou[1], Zhihua Zhang[1], Man Lan[1,2*]
[1]Department of Computer Science and Technology,
East China Normal University, Shanghai, P.R.China
[2]Shanghai Key Laboratory of Multidimensional Information Processing
{10122130215, 51131201039}@ecnu.cn, mlan@cs.ecnu.edu.cn*

Abstract

This paper reports our submissions to Task 4, i.e., Sentiment Analysis in Twitter (SAT), in SemEval 2016, which consists of five subtasks grouped into two levels: (1) sentence level, i.e., message polarity classification (subtask A), and (2) topic level, i.e., tweet classification and quantification according to two-point scale (subtask B and D) or five-point scale (subtask C and E). We participated in all these five subtasks. To address these subtasks, we investigated several traditional Natural Language Processing (NLP) features including sentiment lexicon, linguistic and domain specific features, and word embedding features together with supervised machine learning methods. Officially released results showed that our systems rank above average.

1 Introduction

In recent years, with the emergence of social media, more and more users have shared and obtained information through microblogging websites, such as Twitter. As a result, a huge amount of available data attracts a lot of researchers. SemEval 2016 provides such a universal platform for researchers to explore in the task of Sentiment Analysis in Twitter (Nakov et al., 2016) (Task 4), which includes five subtasks grouped into two levels, i.e., sentence level and topic level. Subtask A is a sentence level task aiming at sentiment polarity classification of the whole tweet. The other four subtasks are at topic level, i.e., given one topic, the sentiment polarity of tweets are classified or assigned by a two-point scale (i.e., subtask

B and D) and by a five-point scale (i.e., subtask C and E). Specifically, subtask B is to identify the sentiment polarity label (i.e, *Positive* and *Negative*) of tweets with respect to the given topic while subtask D aims at estimating the sentiment distribution of tweets with respect to the given topic. Both subtask B and D are on a two-point scale. The purposes of subtask C and E are similar with that of subtask B and D, except for using a five-point scale, that is, the class labels are of 5 values, i.e, 2, 1, 0, -1 and -2 representing *Very Positive*, *Positive*, *Neutral*, *Negative* and *Very Negative*.

Given the character limitations on tweets, sentiment orientation classification on tweets can be regarded as a sentence-level sentiment analysis. Many researchers focus on feature engineering to improve the performance of SAT. For example, (Turian et al., 2010; Liu, 2012; Zhang et al., 2006) showed that one-hot representation on n-gram features is a relatively strong baseline. Furthermore, (Mohammad et al., 2013) proposed a state-of-the-art model which implemented several sentiment lexicons and a variety of manual features. Apart from the traditional methods, more and more researchers have paid their attention to use deep learning methods. Word embedding is one of such methods, where each word is represented as a continuous, low-dimension vector and has been applied into NLP tasks as a critical and fundamental step. Commonly, there are several types of word embedding models, e.g., Bengio proposed a *Neural Probabilistic Language Model (NNLM)* in (Bengio et al., 2003) to learn distributed representation for each word and Mikolov simplified the structure of *NNLM* and presented t-

256

Proceedings of SemEval-2016, pages 256–261,
San Diego, California, June 16-17, 2016. ©2016 Association for Computational Linguistics

wo efficient log-linear models in (Mikolov et al., 2013). Moreover, (Zhang and Lan, 2015; Tang et al., 2014) further proposed learning sentiment-based word embeddings to settle SAT. Meanwhile, topic-based opinion always adheres on certain words or phrases rather than whole tweet. To address topic-based SAT, (Wang et al., 2011) used the hashtag information, (Lin and He, 2009) utilized the topic model to extract topic information from tweets and (Zhang et al., 2015) picked out related words rather than all words in whole tweet as pending words for consequential feature extraction.

Previous work showed that feature engineering has a significant impact on this task. Thus, in this work, we presented multiple types of traditional NLP features to perform SAT, e.g., sentiment lexicon features (e.g., *MPQA, IMDB, Bing Liu opinion lexicon*, etc), linguistic features (e.g., negations, n-gram at the word level and character level, etc) and tweet specific features (e.g., emoticons, capital words, elongated words, hashtags, etc,). Besides, the word embedding features were adopted. We also performed a series of experiments to select effective feature subsets and supervised machine learning algorithms with optimal parameters.

The rest of this paper is organized as follows. Section 2 describes our system framework including preprocessing, feature engineering, evaluation metrics, etc. The experiments are reported in Section 3. Finally, this work is concluded in Section 4.

2 System Description

2.1 Data Preprocessing

With the aid of approximate $5,000$ abbreviations and slangs collected from Internet, we converted the informal writing into regular forms, e.g., *"asap"* replaced by *"as soon as possible"*, *"3q"* replaced by *"thank you"*, etc. And we recovered the elongated words to their original forms, e.g., *"soooooo"* to *"so"*. Finally, the processed data was performed for tokenization, POS tagging and parsing by using *CMU Parsing tools* (Owoputi et al., 2013).

2.2 Feature Engineering

We used four types of features, i.e, linguistic features (e.g., negations, n-gram, etc), tweet specific features (e.g., emoticons, all-caps, hashtags, etc),

sentiment lexicon features (the score calculated from eight sentiment lexicons) and word embedding features.

2.2.1 Linguistic Features:

- *Character n-grams:* The character-level n-grams are used, where $n = \{3, 4, 5\}$.

- *Word n-grams:* The word-level *unigrams, bigrams, trigrams* and *4-grams* are adopted.

- *POS:* The absolute frequency of each part-of-speech tag is recorded.

- *Negation:* Negation in a message always reverses its sentiment orientation. We collected 29 negations from Internet and recorded the frequency of negations in the whole tweet.

- *Cluster:* The *CMU TweetParser tool* provides $1,000$ token clusters produced with the Brown clustering algorithm on 56 million English language tweets. We recorded the existence of tokens in tweets with respect to these $1,000$ clusters.

- *Dependency triple:* The dependency tree is generated by *Stanford Parser tool* and each tweet contains several dependency triples (e.g., *relation(government, dependent)*). We used a binary feature to record if a dependency triple is present or absent in a tweet.

2.2.2 Tweet Specific Features:

- *Punctuation:* Punctuation marks (e.g, exclamation mark (!) and question mark (?)) usually indicate the strength of sentiment. Therefore, we recorded the numbers of these marks in isolation and in combination. Besides, the position of punctuation in tweet is also an important clue for sentiment, thus we used a binary feature to indicate whether it is the last token of tweet.

- *All-caps:* The number of words in uppercase is recorded.

- *Hashtag:* We recorded the number of hashtags in the tweet.

- *Emoticon:* We collected 67 emoticons from Internet and this feature type records the number of positive and negative emoticons respectively. Moreover, two binary values are to record whether the last token is a positive or negative emoticon respectively.

- *Elongated:* It indicates the number of elongated words in the raw text of tweet.

2.2.3 Sentiment Lexicon Features (SentiLexi):

We employed the following eight sentiment lexicons to extract sentiment lexicon features: *Bing Liu lexicon*[1], *General Inquirer lexicon*[2], *AFINN*[3], *IMDB*[4], *MPQA*[5], *NRC Emotion Sentiment Lexicon*[6], *NRC Hashtag Sentiment Lexicon*[7], and *NRC Sentiment140 Lexicon*[8]. Generally, we transformed the scores of all words in all sentiment lexicons to the range of -1 to 1, where the positive number indicates positive sentiment and the minus sign denotes negative sentiment.

The following six scores are calculated on the whole data for each sentiment lexicon: (1) the ratio of positive words to all words, (2) the ratio of negative words to all words, (3) the maximum sentiment score, (4) the minimum sentiment score, (5) the sum of sentiment scores, and (6) the sentiment score of the last word in tweet. If a word does not exist in one sentiment lexicon, its corresponding score is set to 0.

2.2.4 Word Embedding Features:

In this work, we employed three different types of word vectors. The general word vectors are trained by Google on huge amount of News, which is a different domain from Twitter. The other two sentiment word vectors are both trained on tweets but using different methods. The purpose of this feature type is to examine the effects of word embedding and sentiment word embedding on performance.

- *General Word Vector (GeneralW2V):* We adopted the *word2vec* tool[9] to obtain word vectors with the dimensionality of 300 (i.e., *GeneralW2V*), trained on 100 billion words from Google News.

- *Sentiment Word Vector (SWV):* (Zhang and Lan, 2015) proposed a *Combined-Sentiment Word Embedding Model* to learn sentiment word vectors (*SWV*) for sentiment analysis task. In this work, we learn *SWV* on *NRC140 tweet corpus*(Go et al., 2009), where the corpus is made up of 1.6 million tweets (0.8 million positive and 0.8 million negative). The vector dimension is set as 100.

- *Sentiment-specific Word Embedding (SSWE):* Similar with *SWV*, the sentiment-specific word embedding model proposed by (Tang et al., 2014) used a multi-hidden-layers neural network to train *SSWE* with dimensionality of 50.

To convert the above word vectors into a sentence vector, we simply adopted the *min, max* and *average* operations. Obviously, this combination strategy neglects the word sequence in tweet but it is simple and straightforward. As a result, the final sentence vector $V(s)$ was concatenated by $V_{min}(s)$, $V_{max}(s)$ and $V_{average}(s)$.

2.3 Evaluation Metrics

For subtask A, we used the macro-averaged F score of positive and negative classes (i.e., $F_{macro} = \frac{F_{pos}+F_{neg}}{2}$) to evaluate the performance. Subtask B and D just contain positive and negative labels. The official metric for subtask B is *macro-averaged recall* among positive and negative (i.e., $R_{macro} = \frac{R_{Pos}+R_{Neg}}{2}$). As for subtask D, it is *Kullback-Leibler Divergence* (KLD) among distributions of two classes (i.e., $KLD(pos, neg) = \sum_{c_j \in pos,neg} P(c_j) \cdot log\frac{P(c_j)}{\hat{P}(c_j)}$, where P denotes the probability of predicted label and $\hat{P}$ is the probability of gold label). There are 5 classes existing in subtask C and E, and

---

[1] http://www.cs.uic.edu/liub/FBS/sentiment-analysis.html#lexicon

[2] http://www.wjh.harvard.edu/inquirer/homecat.htm

[3] http://www2.imm.dtu.dk/pubdb/views/publication_details.php?id=6010

[4] http://anthology.aclweb.org//S/S13/S13-2.pdf#page=444

[5] http://mpqa.cs.pitt.edu/

[6] http://www.saifmohammad.com/WebPages/lexicons.html

[7] http://www.umiacs.umd.edu/saif/WebDocs/NRC-Hashtag-Sentiment-Lexicon-v0.1.zip

[8] http://help.sentiment140.com/for-students/

[9] https://code.google.com/archive/p/word2vec

the organizers adopted *Macroaveraged Mean Absolute Error* (i.e., MAE^M) and *Earth Mover's Distance* (EMD) among 5 predefined classes for two subtasks respectively, where the detail information of two metrics for evaluation is described in the official document available on the website[10].

3 Experiments

3.1 Datasets

Since only tweet IDs are provided by organizers, different participants may collect different numbers of tweets due to missing tweets or system errors. Subtask B and D are of the same data set. And subtask C and E share one common data set. The statistics of all datasets for these subtasks are shown in Tables 1, 2, and 3, respectively.

For subtask A, the training data set consists of four parts which are shown in Table 1, i.e., $2013train$, $2013dev$, $2016train$ and $2016dev$. The data set $2013train$ means SemEval-2013 Task 2 training data set (Nakov et al., 2013), and the following data sets are named in the same way. Actually, in consideration of the difference of polarity distribution between data set $2016devtest$ and $2013\&2014test$, we just adopted $2016devtest$ as development data. For subtask B, C, D and E, the data is divided into many topic sets.

	dataset	Positive	Negative	Neutral	Total
train	2013train	3,250(37%)	1,276(15%)	4,151(48%)	8,677
	2013dev	575(35%)	340(20%)	739(46%)	1,654
	2016train	2,839(51%)	787(14%)	1,892(34%)	5,518
	2016dev	772(42%)	359(20%)	702(38%)	1,833
dev	2016devtest	886(49%)	287(16%)	626(35%)	1,799
	2013&2014test	5,078(40%)	2,142(16%)	5,580(44%)	12,800
test	2016test	7,059(34%)	3,231(16%)	10,342(50%)	20,632

Table 1: Statistics of data sets in training (train), development (dev), test (test) data for subtask A.

dataset	Positive	Negative	Total
train	4,191(81%)	997(19%)	5,188
dev	1,027(81%)	238(19%)	1,265
test	8,212(78%)	2,339(22%)	10,551

Table 2: Statistics of data sets in training, development, test data for subtask B and D.

3.2 Experiments on Training Data

In order to improve the performance of sentiment analysis, we performed feature selection experi-

[10]http://alt.qcri.org/semeval2016/task4/data/uploads/eval.pdf

dataset	2	1	0	-1	-2	Total
train	475(6%)	3,815(50%)	2,295(30%)	906(12%)	120(2%)	7,611
dev	123(7%)	900(50%)	535(30%)	211(12%)	29(1%)	1,798
test	382(2%)	7,830(38%)	10,081(49%)	2,201(10%)	138(1%)	20,632

Table 3: Statistics of data sets in training, development, test set for subtask C and E.

ments on all subtasks and the optimum feature sets are shown in Table 4. From Table 4, it is interesting to find that: (1) Negation features and tweet specific features such as emoticon and all-caps make contributions to almost all subtasks. (2) The feature set with the best performance of subtask B is not quite beneficial for subtask D even though they have the same data set, perhaps because of the essential difference between binary classification and binary quantification: in the latter, errors of different polarity compensate each other. The similar observation is found in subtask C and E. (3) The sentiment lexicon features make contributions to performance improvement of subtask A, B and C, but are not quite useful for subtask D and E. A possible reason is that the latter two subtasks focus on quantification analysis while the sentiment lexicon only contains sentiment orientation rather than sentiment strength. (4) The word embedding features are not as effective as expected. It maybe because we obtained sentence vectors by the simplest combination method described above, which does not take into account contextual information and semantic relations among words.

Besides, since subtask B, C, D and E focus on topic-level sentiment analysis, we tried to extract features from related words rather than whole tweet. But the preliminary experimental results showed that extracting features from related words underperformed the latter strategy for extracting features. The possible reason is that in many cases a tweet only has one single sentiment polarity. Thus the sentiment polarity of sentence can always represent that of topic and extracting features from the related words may drop important information.

3.3 Learning Algorithm

For these subtasks, we examined several supervised machine learning classification algorithms with different parameters (e.g., Logistic Regression with $c=\{0.1, 1\}$, Support Vector Machine with $kernel=\{linear, rbf\}$, $c=\{0.01, 0.1, 1\}$, Random

Features		Subtask A (F_{macro})	Subtask B (R_{macro})	Subtask C (MAE^M)	Subtask D(KLD)	Subtask E (EMD)
SentiLexi	Sentiment Lexicon	√	√	√		
Linguistic	Unigram		√			√
	Bigram		√			
	Trigram	√	√		√	
	4-gram	√				
	3-char			√	√	
	4-char			√	√	√
	5-char		√			
	POS	√				
	Negation	√	√	√	√	√
	Cluster		√			
	Dependency Triple			√	√	√
Tweet-specific	All-caps	√	√	√	√	√
	Elongated		√		√	
	Punctuation	√			√	
	Emoticon		√	√	√	√
	Hashtag	√				
Word Embedding	GoogleW2V	√	√			
	SWV	√				
	SSWE		√			
Results		0.63	0.82	0.87	0.01	0.03

Table 4: Results of feature selection experiments for subtask A, B, C, D and E in terms of the corresponding evaluation metrics on the training data, where √ indicates this feature was employed in the corresponding subtask system.

Forest with $n=\{20, 50, 100, 400, 1000, 2000\}$, SGD with $loss=\{hinge, log\}$, etc). Finally, Logistic Regression with $c = 1$ implemented in *Liblinear*[11] was adopted for all five subtasks for its good performance in preliminary experiments.

3.4 Results on Test Data

Based on the optimum feature sets shown in Table 4 and configuration of classifiers described above, we trained separate models for each subtask.

Subtask	System	Score
	ECNU	0.585(10)
A	SwissCheese	0.633(1)
	SENSEI-LIF	0.630(2)
	ECNU	0.768(4)
B	Tweester	0.797(1)
	LYS	0.791(2)
	ECNU	0.806(2)
C	twise	0.719(1)
	PUT	0.860(3)
	ECNU	0.121(10)
D	finki	0.034(1)
	LYS	0.053(2)
	ECNU	0.341(5)
E	QCRI	0.243(1)
	finki	0.316(2)

Table 5: Performance of our systems and the top-ranked systems on all five subtasks. The numbers in the brackets are the official ranking.

Table 5 shows the results of our systems and the top-ranked systems on all five subtasks. Our systems ranked $10th$ out of 34 submissions for sub-task A, $4th/19$ for subtask B, $2nd/11$ for subtask C, $10th/14$ for subtask D and $5th/10$ for subtask E. Compared with the top ranked systems, there is much room for improvement in our work. Although word embedding features were adopted in this work, we used the simplest combination method to convert word vectors to sentence vectors. The effective convolution method is expected to be able to improve the performance of sentiment analysis.

4 Conclusion

In this paper, we extracted several traditional NLP features(e.g., linguistic features, tweet specific features, etc) and word embedding features from whole tweet and constructed classifiers using supervised machine learning algorithms to accomplish sentiment analysis towards sentence level(i.e., subtask A) and topic level(i.e., subtask B, C, D and E). Word embedding features are not as effective as expected since the way of using these features are quite simple and naive, thus it is too hasty to make a conclusion that the word embedding features make marginal contribution. In future work, we consider to focus on developing advanced convolution neural network to model sentence with the aid of sentiment word vector.

Acknowledgements

This research is supported by grants from Science and Technology Commission of Shanghai Municipality (14DZ2260800 and 15ZR1410700), Shanghai Collaborative Innovation Center of Trustworthy

---

[11] https://www.csie.ntu.edu.tw/ cjlin/liblinear/

Software for Internet of Things (ZF1213).

References

Yoshua Bengio, Réjean Ducharme, Pascal Vincent, and Christian Janvin. 2003. A neural probabilistic language model. *The Journal of Machine Learning Research*, 3:1137–1155.

Alec Go, Richa Bhayani, and Lei Huang. 2009. Twitter sentiment classification using distant supervision. *CS224N Project Report, Stanford*, pages 1–12.

Chenghua Lin and Yulan He. 2009. Joint sentiment/topic model for sentiment analysis. In *Proceedings of the 18th ACM conference on Information and knowledge management*, pages 375–384. ACM.

Bing Liu. 2012. Sentiment analysis and opinion mining. *Synthesis Lectures on Human Language Technologies*, 5(1):1–167.

Tomas Mikolov, Kai Chen, Greg Corrado, and Jeffrey Dean. 2013. Efficient estimation of word representations in vector space. *arXiv preprint arXiv:1301.3781*.

Saif Mohammad, Svetlana Kiritchenko, and Xiaodan Zhu. 2013. NRC-Canada: Building the state-of-the-art in sentiment analysis of tweets. In *Second Joint Conference on Lexical and Computational Semantics (*SEM), Volume 2: Proceedings of the Seventh International Workshop on Semantic Evaluation (SemEval 2013)*, pages 321–327, Atlanta, Georgia, USA, June.

Preslav Nakov, Sara Rosenthal, Zornitsa Kozareva, Veselin Stoyanov, Alan Ritter, and Theresa Wilson. 2013. SemEval-2013 Task 2: Sentiment analysis in Twitter. In *Second Joint Conference on Lexical and Computational Semantics (*SEM), Volume 2: Proceedings of the Seventh International Workshop on Semantic Evaluation (SemEval 2013)*, pages 312–320, Atlanta, Georgia, USA, June.

Preslav Nakov, Alan Ritter, Sara Rosenthal, Veselin Stoyanov, and Fabrizio Sebastiani. 2016. SemEval-2016 task 4: Sentiment analysis in Twitter. In *Proceedings of the 10th International Workshop on Semantic Evaluation*, SemEval '16, San Diego, California, June. Association for Computational Linguistics.

Olutobi Owoputi, Brendan O'Connor, Chris Dyer, Kevin Gimpel, Nathan Schneider, and Noah A Smith. 2013. Improved part-of-speech tagging for online conversational text with word clusters. In *HLT-NAACL*, pages 380–390.

Duyu Tang, Furu Wei, Nan Yang, Ming Zhou, Ting Liu, and Bing Qin. 2014. Learning sentiment-specific word embedding for twitter sentiment classification. In *The Annual Meeting of the Association for Computational Linguistics*, pages 1555–1565.

Joseph Turian, Lev Ratinov, and Yoshua Bengio. 2010. Word representations: a simple and general method for semi-supervised learning. In *The Annual Meeting of the Association for Computational Linguistics*, pages 384–394. Association for Computational Linguistics.

Xiaolong Wang, Furu Wei, Xiaohua Liu, Ming Zhou, and Ming Zhang. 2011. Topic sentiment analysis in Twitter: a graph-based hashtag sentiment classification approach. In *Proceedings of the 20th ACM international conference on Information and knowledge management*, pages 1031–1040.

Zhihua Zhang and Man Lan. 2015. Learning sentiment-inherent word embedding for word-level and sentence-level sentiment analysis. In *2015 International Conference on Asian Language Processing, IALP*.

Kuo Zhang, Hui Xu, Jie Tang, and Juanzi Li. 2006. Keyword extraction using support vector machine. In *Advances in Web-Age Information Management*, pages 85–96. Springer.

Zhihua Zhang, Guoshun Wu, and Man Lan. 2015. Ecnu: Multi-level sentiment analysis on twitter using traditional linguistic features and word embedding features. In *Proceedings of the 9th International Workshop on Semantic Evaluation (SemEval 2015)*, pages 561–567, Denver, Colorado, June. Association for Computational Linguistics.

OPAL at SemEval-2016 Task 4: the Challenge of Porting a Sentiment Analysis System to the "Real" World

Alexandra Balahur

European Commission Joint Research Centre
Institute for the Protection and Security of the Citizen
Via E. Fermi 2749, 21027 Ispra (VA), Italy
alexandra.balahur@jrc.ec.europa.eu

Abstract

Sentiment analysis has become a well-established task in Natural Language Processing. As such, a high variety of methods have been proposed to tackle it, for different types of texts, text levels, languages, domains and formality levels. Although state-of-the-art systems have obtained promising results, a big challenge that still remains is to port the systems to the "real world" – i.e. to implement systems that are running around the clock, dealing with information of heterogeneous nature, from different domains, written in different styles and diverse in formality levels. The present paper describes our efforts to implement such a system, using a variety of strategies to homogenize the input and comparing various approaches to tackle the task. Specifically, we are tackling the task using two different approaches: a) one that is unsupervised, based on dictionaries of sentiment-bearing words and heuristics to compute final polarity of the text considered; b) the second, supervised, trained on previously annotated data from different domains. For both approaches, the data is first normalized and the slang is replaced with its expanded version.

1 Introduction

Sentiment analysis is the task in Natural Language Processing (NLP) that deals with classifying opinions according to the polarity of the sentiment they express. Due to the large quantities of user-generated online contents available on different Internet sites (forums, social networks, blogs, review sites, microblogs, etc.) and the possible value they can have for different domains (Marketing, e-Rulemaking, Political Science, etc.), Sentiment Analysis has become a very popular task in the field in the past decade.

As such, a high variety of methods have been proposed to tackle it, for different types of texts, text levels, languages, domains and formality levels. Although state of the art systems have obtained promising results (most of all in priory defined datasets – domains, languages, styles, formality levels), a big challenge that still remains is to port the systems to the "real world" – i.e. systems that are running around the clock, dealing with information of heterogeneous nature, from different domains, written in different styles and diverse in formality levels.

The present paper describes our efforts to build such a system. The challenge is not straightforward to tackle, as this entails building a system that is: a) on the one hand, robust enough to obtain similar levels of performance across domains, languages, text types and formality levels; b) on the other hand, flexible enough to treat all these types of texts. Further on, this entails that such a system must have components to treat the input to make it as homogeneous as possible, so as it can be treated in an equal way (POS-tagging, lemmatizing, syntactic parsing, etc.). The methods employed have to be general enough so that they can be used for as many different languages as possible. This is especially difficult, since there are languages that are under-resourced and have little tools available (i.e. it is not possible to perform accurate syntactic

Proceedings of SemEval-2016, pages 262–265,
San Diego, California, June 16-17, 2016. ©2016 Association for Computational Linguistics

parsing in all languages, lemmatizing is more diffi-cult for some languages than others, etc.).

In order to address these issues, we proposed two approaches, which we plan to eventually combine in a unique system. The first approach is based on knowledge, taken from dictionaries of sentiment-bearing words. A variant of this system is imple-mented in-house to compute the tonality of entity mentions in the news. The second is based on su-pervised learning and is implemented in a system we are currently running in-house to classify the sentiment of tweets on different subjects. A model is trained on a set of input data and is subsequently used to classify new examples. The next sections detail on the implementation of the two methods.

2   State of the art and related approach-es.

As far as tweet processing and sentiment analysis in tweets is concerned, Go et al. (2009) pioneered research proposing the use of emoticons (e.g. ":)", ":(", etc.) as markers of positive and negative tweets. Read (2005) employed this method to generate a corpus of positive tweets, with positive emoticons ":)", and negative tweets with negative emoticons ":(". Pak and Paroubek (2010) also generated a corpus of tweets for sentiment analysis, by selecting positive and negative tweets based on the presence of specific emoticons. These approaches employed different supervised approaches for sentiment analysis, using n-grams as features. Zhang et al. (2011) employ a hybrid approach, combining supervised learn-ing with the knowledge on sentiment-bearing words, which they extract from the DAL sentiment dictionary (Whissell, 1989). The authors conclude that the most important features are those corresponding to sentiment-bearing words. Finally, (Jiang et al., 2011) classify sen-timent expressed on previously-given "targets" in tweets adding the context of the tweet to increase the text length.

The approaches employed are based on the system we developed in (Balahur et al., 2010) and (Balahur, 2013).

3   OPAL: Approaches in SemEval 2016 Task 4 A and B

The OPAL system participated in SemEval in Task 4, subtasks A and B.
In subtask A, the method employed was based on sen-timent dictionaries and rules to compute the final polari-ty of the tweets.

In subtask B, the system was trained on the training data provided by the organizers using SVM and uni- and bigrams.

Before applying each of the two approaches, the texts were pre-processed in order to be transformed from informal to formal language, to be treated by traditional text processing methods. Additionally, the words are matched against our in-house (Balahur et al., 2010)[1] sentiment and modifier dictionaries.

In the next subsections, we detail the steps, methods and resources employed.

3.1. Text Pre-processing

- **Multiple punctuation sign identification.** In the first step of the preprocessing, we detect repetitions of punctuation signs (``.", ``!" and ``?"). Multiple consecutive punctuation signs are replaced with the labels ``multistop", for the fullstops, ``multiexclamation" in the case of exclamation sign and ``multiquestion" for the question mark and spaces before and after. The entire context before the punctuation sign, up until the previous punctuation sign, is marked as "intensifier".

- **Emoticon replacement.** In the second step of the preprocessing, we employ the annotated list of emoticons from SentiStrength[2] and match the content of the tweets against this list. The emoticons found are replaced with their polari-ty score from this resource.

- **Lower casing and tokenization.** Further on, the tweets are lower cased and split into tokens, based on spaces and punctuation signs.

- **Slang replacement.** In order to be able to in-clude the semantics of the expressions fre-quently used in Social Media, we employed the list of slang expressions from the Urban Dic-tionary[3] and other two slang dictionaries dedi-cated sites[4].

- **Word normalization.** In the next step, we match the tokens against entries in Roget's Thesaurus. If no match is found, repeated let-ters are sequentially reduced to two or one until a match is found in the dictionary (e.g. "greeeeat" becomes "greeeat", "greeat" and fi-nally "great"). The words used in this way are replaced with "intensifier" plus original word as matched from Roget's Thesaurus.

---

[1] The dictionaries were obtained by mixing three existing re-sources that have proven to be most precise, although with less recall as others: General Inquirer, LIWC and MicroWNOp.
[2] http://sentistrength.wlv.ac.uk/
[3] http://www.urbandictionary.com/
[4] www.noslang.com/dictionary, www.smsslang.com

- **Affect word matching.** Further on, the tokens in the tweet are matched against the in-house produced lexicon based on three different sentiment dictionaries: General Inquirer, LIWC and MicroWNOp and split into four different categories ("positive", "high positive", "negative" and "high negative"). Matched words are replaced with their sentiment label - i.e. "positive", "negative", "hpositive" and "hnegative".
- **Modifier word matching.** Similar to the previous step, we employ a list of expressions that negate, intensify or diminish the intensity of the sentiment expressed to detect such words in the tweets. If such a word is matched, it is replaced with "negator", "intensifier" or "diminisher", respectively.
- **User and topic labeling.** Finally, the users mentioned in the tweet, which are marked with "@", are replaced with "PERSON" and the topics which the tweet refers to (marked with "#") are replaced with "TOPIC".

3.2. OPAL Task 4 A

In subtask A, the participating systems were supposed to classify a set of tweets in three classes, according to the polarity of the sentiment they conveyed: positive, negative or neutral.

To tackle this task, we used an unsupervised method, based on the identified sentiment words and modifiers. Each of the sentiment words was mapped to four categories, which were given different scores: positive (1), negative (-1), high positive (4) and high negative (-4). The dictionaries have been previously built and the process is described by Balahur et al. (2010). It is based on *WordNet Affect* (Strapparava and Valitutti, 2004), *SentiWordNet* (Esuli and Sebastiani, 2006), *MicroWNOp* (Cerini et al, 2007) and an in-house built resource entitled *JRC Tonality*. This resource has also been used to create the multilingual tonality dictionaries described by Steinberger et al. (2011) and are also implemented in the Europe Media Monitor system. Subsequently, in a window of 6 words around the identified sentiment-bearing token, the following rules were applied:

- When an "intensifier" was present, the value was multiplied with 1.5.
- When a "diminisher" was identified, the value was multiplied with 0.5.
- When a "negator" was identified, the value was multiplied with -1.

Finally, the partial scores obtained for the sentiment contexts were added and normalized by the number of contexts. A positive score led to the text being classified as "positive", a negative score to its being classified as "negative" and a score of 0 labeled as "neutral".

3.3. OPAL Task 4 B

In subtask B, the participating systems were tasked to classify a set of tweets in two classes: positive or negative.

In this task, we employed supervised learning using Support Vector Machines Sequential Minimal Optimization (Platt, 1998) with a binomial kernel, employing boolean features - the presence or absence of unigrams and bigrams determined from the training data (tweets that were previously preprocessed as described above) that appeared at least twice. Bigrams are used especially to spot the influence of modifiers (negations, intensifiers, diminishers) on the polarity of the sentiment-bearing words. We trained and tested the approach using the Weka data mining software[5], on the data provided for training by the organizers.

4   Evaluation

In the SemEval 2016 Task 4, the OPAL system obtained the following results (Nakov et al., 2016):

In subtask A, 0.50521 average F1, 0.56020 average Recall and 0.54122 accuracy.

In subtask B, OPAL scored 0.61617 average Recall, 0.63316 average F1 and 0.79215 accuracy.

5   Conclusions and Future Work

In this paper, we presented the two approaches to classify tweets according to their polarity, being simple enough to be ported to different languages, domains and deal with documents written in different styles and diverse in formality levels. The performance levels are promising given the simplicity of the implementations. As such, our next challenge resides in adding and evaluating new and simple processing components that can be added for specific languages and domains, in order to increase the classification performance while at the same time keeping the wide usability and reliability of the system.

References

1. Balahur, A. (2013). Sentiment analysis in social media texts. Proceedings of the 4th workshop on Computational Approaches to Subjectivity, Sentiment and Social Media Analysis, pp. 120-128, Association for Computational Linguistics.

2. Balahur, A., Steinberger, R., Kabadjov, M., Zavarella, V., Van Der Goot, Halkia, M.,

---

[5] http://www.cs.waikato.ac.nz/ml/weka/

Pouliquen, B. Belyaeva, J. (2010) Sentiment Analysis in the News, Proceedings of the 7th International Conference on Language Resources and Evaluation (LREC'2010), pp. 2216-2220. Valletta, Malta, 19-21 May 2010.

3. Cerini, S. , V. Compagnoni, A. Demontis, M. Formentelli and G. Gandini. (2007). Language resources and linguistic theory: Typology, second language acquisition, English linguistics, chapter Micro-WNOp: A gold standard for the evaluation of automatically compiled lexical resources for opinion mining. Franco Angeli Editore, Milano, IT. 2007.

4. Esuli, A. and Sebastiani, F. (2006). Sentiwordnet: A publicly available resource for opinion mining. In Proceedings of the 6th International Conference on Language Resources and Evaluation. ELRA.

5. Go, A., Richa Bhayani, and Lei Huang (2009). Twitter sentiment classification using distant supervision. Processing, pages 1–6.

6. Jiang, L., Mo Yu, Ming Zhou, Xiaohua Liu, and Tiejun Zhao (2011). Target-dependent twitter sentiment classification. In Proceedings of the 49th Annual Meeting of the Association for Computational Linguistics: Human Language Technologies – Volume 1, HLT '11, pages 151–160, Stroudsburg, PA, USA. Association for Computational Linguistics.

7. Nakov, P., Ritter, A., Rosenthal, S., Sebastiani, F., Stoyanov, V. (2016) SemEval-2016 Task 4: Sentiment Analysis in Twitter. Proceedings of SemEval 2016, San Diego, USA, 2016.

8. Pak, A. and Patrick Paroubek (2010). Twitter as a corpus for sentiment analysis and opinion mining. In Nicoletta Calzolari (Conference Chair), Khalid Choukri, Bente Maegaard, Joseph Mariani, Jan Odijk, Stelios Piperidis, Mike Rosner, and Daniel Tapias, editors, Proceedings of the Seventh conference on International Language Resources and Evaluation (LREC'10), Valletta, Malta; ELRA, may. European Language Resources Association, pp. 19-21.

9. Platt, J. (1999). Fast training of support vector machines using sequential minimal optimization. In Advances in kernel methods, Eds. Bernhard Schölkopf, Christopher J. C. Burges, Alexander J. Smola, ISBN 0-262-19416-3, pp. 185-208, MIT Press.

10. Platt, J. C. (1999). Fast training of support vector machines using sequential minimal optimization. MIT Press, Cambridge, MA, USA, pp. 185–208. URL http://dl.acm.org/citation.cfm?id=299094.299105

11. Read, J. (2005). Using emoticons to reduce dependency in machine learning techniques for sentiment classification. In Proceedings of the ACL Student Research Workshop, ACL student '05, pages 43–48, Stroudsburg, PA, USA. Association for Computational Linguistics.

12. Steinberger, J., Lenkova, P., Kabadjov, M., Steinberger, R., Van Der Goot, E. (2011) Multilingual Entity-Centered Sentiment Analysis Evaluated by Parallel Corpora. In Proceedings of the conference on Recent Advances in Natural Language Processing (RANLP 2011), pages 770-775.

13. Strapparava, C. and Valitutti, A. (2004) WordNet-Affect: an affective extension of WordNet. In Proceedings of the 4th International Conference on Language Resources and Evaluation (LREC 2004), Lisbon, May 2004, pp. 1083-1086.

Know-Center at SemEval-2016 Task 5:
Using Word Vectors with Typed Dependencies
for Opinion Target Expression Extraction

Stefan Falk
Know-Center GmbH
Inffeldgasse 13
Graz, 8010, Austria

Andi Rexha
Know-Center GmbH
Inffeldgasse 13
Graz, 8010, Austria

Roman Kern
Know-Center GmbH
Inffeldgasse 13
Graz, 8010, Austria

sfalk@know-center.at arexha@know-center.at rkern@know-center.at

Abstract

This paper describes our participation in SemEval-2016 Task 5 for Subtask 1, Slot 2. The challenge demands to find domain specific target expressions on sentence level that refer to reviewed entities. The detection of target words is achieved by using word vectors and their grammatical dependency relationships to classify each word in a sentence into *target* or *non-target*. A heuristic based function then expands the classified target words to the whole target phrase. Our system achieved an F1 score of 56.816% for this task.

1 Introduction

Nowadays, modern technologies allow us to collect customer reviews and opinions in a way that changed the sheer amount of information available to us. For that matter the requirement to extract useful knowledge from this data rose up to a point where machine learning algorithms can help to accomplish this much faster and easier than humanly possible. Natural language processing (NLP) emerges as an interfacing tool between human natural language and many technical fields such as machine learning and information extraction.

This article describes our approach towards Opinion Target Expression (OTE) extraction as defined by Task 5 for Subtask 1, Slot 2 of the SemEval-2016 (Pontiki et al., 2016) challenge. The core goal behind Slot 2 in Subtask 1 of Task 5 is to extract consecutive words which, by means of a natural language, represent the opinion target expression. The opinion target expression is that part of a sentence which stands for the entity towards which an opinion is being expressed. An example could be the word *"waitress"* in the sentence *"The waitress was very nice and courteous the entire evening."*.

The evaluation for Slot 2 fell into evaluation phase A, where provided systems were tested in order to return a list of target expressions for each given sentence in a review text. Each target expression was an annotation composed of the index of the starting and end character of the particular expression as well as its corresponding character string.

For our system we decided to used word vectors (Mikolov et al., 2013a; Mikolov et al., 2013b). Word vectors (Bengio et al., 2003) are distributed representations which are designed to carry contextual information of words if their training meets certain criteria. We also used typed grammatical dependencies to extract structural information from sentences. Furthermore we used a sentiment parser to determine the polarity of words.

2 External Resources

Our system uses Stanford dependencies (Chen and Manning, 2014) and utilizes the Stanford Sentiment Treebank (Socher et al., 2013) for sentiment word detection.

3 System for Slot 2: Opinion Target Extraction

For the Opinion Target Extraction (OTE) task, in order to extract different features, we followed a supervised approach. We train and test different combinations of these features first at the word level and

Proceedings of SemEval-2016, pages 266–270,
San Diego, California, June 16-17, 2016. ©2016 Association for Computational Linguistics

following on the provided training data[1] on sentence level before using our classifier for the final evaluation. There are two essential steps performed by our system to correctly annotate opinion target expressions.

1. Classify each word of a sentence as either *target* or *non-target*

2. Given each *target* word, find the full target phrase

For classification we use a L2-regularized L2-loss support vector dual classification[2] provided by the LIBLINEAR (Fan et al., 2008) library. In the second step we use heuristics, based on observations and statistical information we extracted from the training data. They key obversvation is that target expressions are usually composed of noun phrases and/or proper nouns. In all trials we allow only certain Part of Speech (PoS) tags for target words which are NN, NNS, NNP, NNPS and FW from the Penn Treebank (Marcus et al., 1993) listed in Table1.

PoS-Tag	Name
NN	Noun, singular or mass
NNS	Noun, plural
NNP	Proper noun, singular
NNPS	Proper noun, plural
FW	Foreign word

Table 1: Used PoS-Tags and their meaning according to the Penn Treebank.

4 Features

In this section we describe the different set of features we evaluated and how they can be extracted.

4.1 Token

We obtain tokens by using the Stanford Parser and extract all tokens from the available reviews used for training. We are then able to use tokens as a feature for the classifier.

4.2 Word Vector Feature

As another feature for words we are using the pre-trained word vectors of Google News dataset[3]. Each word vector is a 300-dimensional, real-valued vector.

4.3 Combined Typed Dependencies Feature

Using Stanford dependencies, we extract for each word in a sentence its typed dependencies to other words in the sentence.

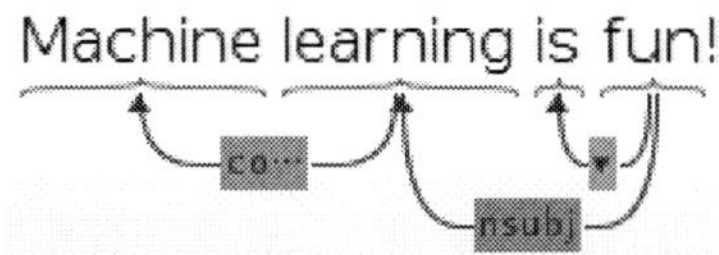

Figure 1: Shown are typed dependencies from Stanford dependencies visualized with grammarscope.

Given the sentence *"Machine learning is fun!"*, the feature for *"learning"* is `compound;nsubj` which are the present relations for this word. We extract all typed dependency combinations from all provided words in the training set and use these in a Bag of Words (BoW) sparse vector model. In order to normalize this feature we order the relations alphabetically and remove duplicates. For example `det;amod;amod` gets normalized to `amod;det`.

4.4 Individual Typed Dependencies Feature

Another approach is to look at the dependencies individually. We use the set of present grammatical relations as feature vector and set corresponding fields to 1 if the word does own such a relation and 0 otherwise. We are testing the two possible options of *directed* and *undirected* dependencies to see if this additional information has an impact on the end result. A short overview of a textual representation of these features can be seen in Table 2.

4.4.1 Undirected

In the undirected approach we extract the relations of each word from the data and use the resulting set of *present* relations as feature vector. From the training set we extracted 105 different undirected relations. Here the directional information of the grammatical dependency is lost.

4.4.2 Directed

For the directed approach we preserve the direction in terms of *incoming* or *outgoing* relations for each grammatical relation. As an example, the word

---

[1] Using the English data set
[2] Implementation of a Support Vector Regression Machine
[3] `https://code.google.com/archive/p/word2vec/`

"learning" from Figure 1 has an outgoing relation `compound+` and an incoming relation `nsubj-` where + depicts the outgoing relation and − the incoming respectively. This way we found 164 different relations in the training set.

Typed Dependency Features		
Directed	**Word**	**Feature**
no	*learning*	`coumpund;subj;`
yes	*learning*	`coumpund-;subj+;`

Table 2: The table shows two example of *undirected* and *directed* typed dependency features for the word *"learning"* in the sentence *"Machine learning is fun!"*.

4.5 Sentimend Dependency Feature

For a given word we determine whether it has a grammatical relation to a sentiment word. A sentiment word is a word that can have a positive or negative meaning for example *"breathtaking"* in *"The food was breathtaking!"*. We are not considering a directional approach which makes this a binary feature.

5 Results

This section describes the results we achieved on the restaurant domain of the SemEval-2016 aspect based sentiment analysis (ABSA) on Task 5, Slot 2. It also explains how we trained and tested our system only on the provided training data.

5.1 Word-Level Feature Evaluation

We determine how well our different features are performing by splitting the train data available and using 80% training and 20% test data. In Table 3 the performance on the *target*-word class of the individual features are shown depicting the performance of classifying single words as targets or non-targets.

The results for the similarly token-based approach outperforms the other approaches. The weighted average for *Token* settles at 0.696 and very similar *Token + combined typed dependencies* at 0.697. None of the word vector approaches outperforms these two.

5.2 Testing Features

To test our features we use the same training/testing split of the SemEval-2016 training data and utilize

it to train the classifier and run the SemEval-2016 evaluation tool respectively. In order to annotate the Opinion Target Expressions (OTE) our system first classifies single tokens of a sentence into *target* or *non-target* and further tries to complete the target expression. The completion of the target expression is heuristic based and looks at existing incoming or outgoing *compound* relations using Stanford dependencies (Chen and Manning, 2014). Each compound relation is added to the target phrase and correspondingly extended.

Evaluation class: target-word			
Feature	**Prec.**	**Rec.**	**F1 score**
			wt. avg.
Token	0.649	0.749	0.696
+ comb. typed dep.	0.657	0.741	0.697
w2v	0.595	0.649	0.621
+ comb. typed dep.	0.610	0.696	0.650
+ indiv. typed dep.			
undirected	0.595	0.587	0.591
undir. + sentiment	0.587	0.598	0.592
directed	0.568	0.674	0.617
dir. + sentiment	0.574	0.679	0.622

Table 3: The resulting F1 scores for the *target*-word class using different features on word-level over a 80/20 training/test split of the provided training data.

Feature	**Prec.**	**Rec.**	**F1 score**
Token	0.498	0.488	0.493
+ comb. typed dep.	0.460	0.433	0.446
w2v	0.484	0.598	0.535
+ comb. typed dep.	0.498	0.520	0.509
+ indiv. typed dep.			
undirected	0.482	0.550	0.513
undir. + sentiment	0.466	0.552	0.505
directed	0.465	0.623	0.532
dir. + sentiment	0.465	0.625	0.533

Table 4: Shown are evaluation F1 scores given by the SemEval-2016 evaluation tool for different features and feature combinations used for training on a 80/20 training/test split of the provided training data.

In Table 4 we can see the results for the evaluation. It shows that despite having a better result on word-level, the token-based approach falls behind the word vector approach. It is interesting to see, that adding the *undirected* grammatical relations as feature does not improve the F1 score but performs even worse than the pure *w2v* approach. However, taking *directed* dependencies into account does improve the results again. We can see that for directed dependencies the recall improves but in contradiction the precision declines resulting in a higher missclassification rate and thus in a lower F1 score than we were hoping to see.

5.3 Official Evaluation Results: Restaurant domain

Our submitted system is using the individual (directed) typed dependencies and the sentiment information combined with word vectors as features. The official results for participating *unconstrained* systems for Slot 2: Opinion Target Extraction can be seen in Table 5. The table shows the F1-score for all participating *unconstrained* systems. Our system was able to outperform the baseline and a few others. Considering only unconstrained systems, Know-Center reached rank 6 out of 10 (excluding the baseline results).

System	F1 score
NLANGP	72.340%
AUEB.	70.441%
UWB	67.089%
GTI	66.553%
bunji	64.882%
Know-Center	**56.816%**
BUAP	50.253%
Baseline	44.071%
IHS-R.	43.808%
IIT-T.	42.603%
SeemGo	34.323%

Table 5: Shown are the official evaluation results for Subtask 1, Slot 2 of Task 5 from the SemEval-2016 challenge for the Restaurant domain. The table shows only results for *unconstrained* systems.

6 Conclusions and Future Work

In this paper, we presented our approach for SemEval-2016 Task 5 for Subtask 1, Slot 2 in order to introduce ourselves to this particular evaluation task. Our solution might have potential for improvement and might be able to reach a much better ranking than what it achieved in the course of this challenge. Therefore, we will continue our work by focusing on finding the correct target phrase annotation given one or more target words. A drawback of our solution is the heuristic based selection of the *full* target phrase and we are curious about how we can improve our results with more sophisticated techniques for target phrase labelling.

Acknowledgments

The Know-Center GmbH Graz is funded within the Austrian COMET Program - Competence Centers for Excellent Technologies - under the auspices of the Austrian Federal Ministry of Transport, Innovation and Technology, the Austrian Federal Ministry of Economy, Family and Youth and by the State of Styria. COMET is managed by the Austrian Research Promotion Agency FFG.

References

Yoshua Bengio, Réjean Ducharme, Pascal Vincent, and Christian Janvin. 2003. A neural probabilistic language model. *J. Mach. Learn. Res.*, 3:1137–1155, March.

Danqi Chen and Christopher Manning. 2014. A Fast and Accurate Dependency Parser using Neural Networks. In *Proceedings of the 2014 Conference on Empirical Methods in Natural Language Processing (EMNLP)*, pages 740–750, Doha, Qatar, October. Association for Computational Linguistics.

Rong-En Fan, Kai-Wei Chang, Cho-Jui Hsieh, Xiang-Rui Wang, and Chih-Jen Lin. 2008. LIBLINEAR: A library for large linear classification. *Journal of Machine Learning Research*, 9:1871–1874.

Mitchell P. Marcus, Beatrice Santorini, and Mary Ann Marcinkiewicz. 1993. Building a large annotated corpus of english: The penn treebank. *COMPUTATIONAL LINGUISTICS*, 19(2):313–330.

Tomas Mikolov, Kai Chen, Greg Corrado, and Jeffrey Dean. 2013a. Efficient estimation of word representations in vector space. *CoRR*, abs/1301.3781.

Tomas Mikolov, Ilya Sutskever, Kai Chen, Greg Corrado, and Jeffrey Dean. 2013b. Distributed representations of words and phrases and their compositionality. *CoRR*, abs/1310.4546.

Maria Pontiki, Dimitrios Galanis, Haris Papageorgiou, Ion Androutsopoulos, Suresh Manandhar, Mohammad AL-Smadi, Mahmoud Al-Ayyoub, Yanyan Zhao, Bing Qin, Orphée De Clercq, Véronique Hoste, Marianna Apidianaki, Xavier Tannier, Natalia Loukachevitch, Evgeny Kotelnikov, Nuria Bel, Salud María Jiménez-Zafra, and Gülşen Eryiğit. 2016. SemEval-2016 task 5: Aspect based sentiment analysis. In *Proceedings of the 10th International Workshop on Semantic Evaluation*, SemEval '16, San Diego, California, June. Association for Computational Linguistics.

Richard Socher, Alex Perelygin, Jean Wu, Jason Chuang, Christopher D. Manning, Andrew Y. Ng, and Christopher Potts. 2013. Recursive deep models for semantic compositionality over a sentiment treebank. In *Proceedings of the 2013 Conference on Empirical Methods in Natural Language Processing*, pages 1631–1642, Stroudsburg, PA, October. Association for Computational Linguistics.

NileTMRG at SemEval-2016 Task 5: Deep Convolutional Neural Networks for Aspect Category and Sentiment Extraction

Talaat Khalil and **Samhaa R. El-Beltagy**

Center for informatics sciences

Nile University

Giza, Egypt

t.maher@nu.edu.eg, samhaa@computer.org

Abstract

This paper describes our participation in the SemEval-2016 task 5, Aspect Based Sentiment Analysis (ABSA). We participated in two slots in the sentence level ABSA (Subtask 1) namely: aspect category extraction (Slot 1) and sentiment polarity extraction (Slot 3) in English Restaurants and Laptops reviews. For Slot 1, we applied different models for each domain. In the restaurants domain, we used an ensemble classifier for each aspect which is a combination of a Convolutional Neural Network (CNN) classifier initialized with pre-trained word vectors, and a Support Vector Machine (SVM) classifier based on the bag of words model. For the Laptops domain, we used only one CNN classifier that predicts the aspects based on a probability threshold. For Slot 3, we incorporated domain and aspect knowledge in one ensemble CNN classifier initialized with fine-tuned word vectors and used it in both domains. In the Restaurants domain, our system achieved the 2nd and the 3rd places in Slot 1 and Slot 3 respectively. However, we ranked the 8th in Slot 1 and the 5th in Slot 3 in the Laptops domain. Our extended experiments show our system could have ranked 2nd in the Laptops domain in Slot 1 and Slot 3, had we followed the same approach we followed in the Restaurants domain in slot 1 and trained each domain separately in Slot 3.

1 Introduction

Due to the increasing numbers of user generated reviews written every day within e-commerce websites, a great interest has been shown in the sentiment analysis research community to build intelligent systems that can accurately tackle the task of sentiment analysis in these reviews.

In this context, the SemEval-2016 ABSA, task 5[1], Subtask 1 addresses a number of research problems related to this topic, including building systems that are able to extract aspect categories (Slot 1) and determine the sentiment polarity towards each aspect in each sentence (Slot-3) which were the two slots in which we participated.

The best results for Slot 1 in SemEval-2015 (Pontiki et al., 2015), were achieved by the NLANGP team (Toh and Su, 2015). The team tackled the problem by modeling it as a multi-class classification problem with binary classifiers for each aspect. They used a neural network with one hidden layer and features based on word n-grams, brown and k-means word clusters from Amazon and Yelp datasets and parsing features. For Slot 3, the best results were achieved by the Sentiue team (Saias, 2015) who used a Maximum Entropy classifier with domain and aspect features and features based on word n-grams, lemmas, negation terms, exclamation and question marks, sentiment lexicons, and POS tags.

---

[1] http://alt.qcri.org/semeval2016/task5/

271

Proceedings of SemEval-2016, pages 271–276,

San Diego, California, June 16-17, 2016. ©2016 Association for Computational Linguistics

This year, when addressing Slot 1, we participated with a system that can extract aspects in English reviews in the two domains that the task provided test sets for, namely: restaurants (REST) and laptops (LAPT). For the restaurants domain we treated the problem as a multi-class classification problem using an ensemble binary classifier for each aspect which is a combination of a Support Vector Machine (SVM) (Cortes and Vapnik, 1995) classifier and a Convolutional Neural Network (CNN). While the SVM classifier features were based on a Bag of words model, the CNN classifier was initialized with pre-trained word vectors based on the architecture proposed by Kim (2014). For the Laptops domain, we used one CNN classifier that outputs probability scores for each aspect, then a threshold was applied so that only outputs with scores higher than that threshold were predicted as aspects.

For Slot 3, we incorporated domain and aspect information in one ensemble classifier consisting of three CNNs trained using the whole training data provided in both domains and initialized with word vectors that were fine-tuned using training examples collected in a semi supervised way by the same CNN architecture as in an earlier phase.

The rest of this paper is organized as follows: section 2, describes the system architecture and settings, while section 3, presents and discusses our system performance and evaluation. Finally, section 4 concludes the paper and presents some ideas for potential future work.

2   System Details

To train our models, we depended mainly on the official training data provided by the SemEval-2016 task organizers. Furthermore, for choosing the best parameters and architectures, we used the SemEval-2015 (Pontiki, et al., 2015) training set for training and SemEval-2015 test set as a validation set. The validation set was used to choose the best model for each domain and to tune the network hyperparameters. In aspect category extraction (Slot 1), we used only the training data, however we considered our submission as an unconstrained one because we initialized our models using pre-trained publicly available word vectors[2] trained on a subset of Google news using the word2vec model (Mikolov,

et al., 2013). For polarity extraction (Slot 3), we used additional external examples for training and fine-tuning the word vectors from the Yelp Academic Dataset[3] and Amazon electronics reviews (Jo, 2011).

In the next subsections, we discuss the used CNN architecture as it's involved in all of our models. Then we discuss each model in detail.

2.1   Convolutional Neural Network architecture

Our CNN implementation is based on the architecture proposed by Kim (2014). In this model, each sentence is represented as a concatenation of all its word vectors which can be described using Equation (1),

$$x_{1:n} = x_1 \oplus x_2 \oplus \ldots x_n \tag{1}$$

where $x_i \in \mathbb{R}^k$ is a k dimensional word vector for the ith word in the sentence, $\oplus$ is the concatenation operator, and $x_{1:n}$ is the model input vector, which is the concatenated word vectors of the sentence from the first word to the nth word, where n is the number of words in the sentence.

A convolution filter w of width h words is then applied to the input vector to produce new features by simply taking the dot product between the filter and the corresponding input vector slice, then adding a bias factor b, and finally applying the non-linearity function f. The filter is then shifted by one word and applied again to produce the next feature until we reach the end of the input vector. This operation is clarified in Equation (2),

$$c_i = f(w \cdot x_{i:i+h-1} + b) \tag{2}$$

where c_i is the generated feature resulting from applying the filter w on the input vector slice from the start of word i to the end of word $i + h - 1$.

As a result of the convolution operation, a feature map $c \in \mathbb{R}^{n-h+1}$ is generated where:

$$c = [c_1, c_2, \ldots, c_{n-h+1}] \tag{3}$$

A max-pooling operation (Collobert et al., 2011) is then applied to the feature map vector c by only taking the maximum value $\hat{c} = \max\{c\}$ and considering it as a hidden layer feature generated from the corresponding convolution filter.

Since one feature is not enough to represent the needed knowledge, the process is repeated several

---

[2] https://code.google.com/archive/p/word2vec/

[3] https://www.yelp.com/dataset_challenge/

272

times using different filters and different filter widths. These features form a hidden layer, which is followed by a Softmax layer that outputs prediction probabilities for each output class.

To prevent overfitting to the training data, we employed 'dropout' on the hidden layer and constrained its weights by l_2-norms (Hinton, et al., 2012). This was done by randomly dropping some of the hidden layer units by a probability rate p while training to prevent over adaptation to certain units. We also applied a constraint on the l_2-norms, by rescaling the weights connecting the hidden layer and the output layer such that they are limited by an upper limit s after each update step.

For training, the backpropagation algorithm (Rumelhart, et al., 1986) was applied and the network weights were updated using mini-batch stochastic gradient descent with the Adadelta update rule (Zeiler, 2012), which considers a separate adaptive update rate for each weight. As will be detailed in the following subsections, we have mostly employed Static-CNN, where initialized input vectors are kept as is. However, there were cases where we also employed Dynamic-CNN. In Dynamic-CNN, input vectors are updated for optimizing the network.

For choosing the CNN hyperparameters, we started by using the ones which were validated by Kim (2014) and then we tried different values on our validation set. We ended up by choosing convolution filter window widths (h) of 3, 4, and 5 with 100 feature maps for each width. We used the rectified linear units as a non-linearity activation function, which simply outputs the maximum of zero and the input value. We set the dropout rate (p) to 0.5 and the l_2 maximum value (s) to 3. We set the number of optimization iterations over the whole data (epochs) and the mini-batch size to 25 except for the official Laptops aspect extraction model (LAEM), where the values were set to 100 and 50 accordingly.

2.2 Restaurants Aspect Extraction Model (RAEM)

To extract aspect categories for the restaurants domain, we dealt with the problem as a multi-class classification problem where we have a binary ensemble classifier for each of the 12 aspects, trained on the aspect data against all other aspects' data (one vs all strategy).

This ensemble classifier is a combination of two classifiers; one Static-CNN classifier initialized using the Google news word vectors, and one SVM classifier which was trained using word unigram counts weighted by the inverse word frequencies in the training data (IDF) (Salton and Buckley, 1988). Vectors for words that had no corresponding entry in the Google news vectors, were set to zeros. The model predicts the aspect if any of the two classifiers predicts it.

The SVM classifier had a high precision on the validation set but a very low recall. Using it as part of our ensemble thus increased the total F-Score on the validation set.

2.3 Laptops Aspect Extraction Model (LAEM)

To extract aspects from laptop reviews, we used a Static-CNN classifier with 81 output nodes representing all the aspects found in the Laptops training set. At test time, the classifier predicts the aspect if its output nodes' probability score exceeds a certain threshold.

To choose the best threshold, we tried different values on our validation set and found out that a threshold value of 0.18 performed best, followed by 0.16 which was slightly less in terms of the total F-Score. We preferred to use 0.16 as a threshold to prevent choosing a value resulting from overfitting on the validation set.

We chose to use this model for the laptops domain as using the alternative one vs all strategy needed 81 classifiers to be trained which is computationally slower during training and testing. The one classifier model also performed slightly better on the validation set at the chosen threshold. As we show in the extended experiments section (section 3.2), this was not the best strategy in approaching this problem.

2.4 The Sentiment Extraction Model (SEM)

For Slot 3, an ensemble model was used for both domains. This model counts votes from three classifiers and predicts the class which has the maximum number of votes from the three classes namely: the positive (Pos), the negative (Neg), and the neutral (Neu).

Data Domain	Positive Sentences	Negative Sentences
Amazon Dataset	50,000	18,326
Yelp Restaurants	50,000	50,000
Yelp Computers	1974	2230
Yelp Electronics	3478	2226

Table 1: Fine-tuning data distribution.

Data Domain	Neutral Example	Negative Examples
Amazon Dataset	22	2
Yelp Restaurants Dataset	78	24

Table 2: Hand labeled data distribution.

We adopted this voting criterion as it yielded slightly better results on the validation set. Each one of the three classifiers is similar to the one which was discussed in section 2.1 with a slight variation resulting from incorporating domain and aspect knowledge into the CNN model. This incorporation was done by introducing new binary features to the hidden layer of the CNN. The new features indicate the presence or the absence of a certain aspect or domain in a given sentence.

The problem with a word vector is that it represents a word by its semantic meaning captured through its context while the sentiments are not captured directly. To tackle this problem, we trained a Dynamic-CNN on sentences tokenized from the Yelp academic dataset reviews in restaurants, computers and electronics domains as well as data obtained from electronics and laptop reviews from Amazon. We employed a distant supervision method where five star review sentences are considered to be positive, while the one star ones are considered to be negative. We could not apply the same method for getting neutral sentences because we noticed that the three stars reviews can be mainly a combination of positive and negative sentences rather than neutral ones. Using these reviews could simply introduce more noise. A number of sentences were then sampled randomly from these reviews and used for fine-tuning the word vectors. Domain features were added when possible, otherwise they were set to zeros. The distribution of this collected dataset over the polarity labels and domains is clarified in Table 1.

Model	Domain	P	R	F
RAEM (Official)	REST	72.69	73.08	72.88
RAEM without SVM	REST	76.76	68.91	72.62
LAEM (Official)	LAPT	44.25	50.56	47.19
RAEM	LAPT	59.44	45.3	51.42
RAEM without SVM	LAPT	63.27	39.67	48.76

Table 3: Results for Slot 1 in terms of precision, recall, and F-Score.

Model	Domain	Pos-F	Neg-F	Neu-F	Acc.
SEM (Official)	REST	91.63	75.44	32.73	85.44
Domain Specific SEM	REST	91.25	74.94	32.73	85.09
SEM (Official)	LAPT	83.55	72.95	8.00	77.40
Domain Specific SEM	LAPT	84.85	73.65	11.76	78.65

Table 4: Results for Slot 3 in terms of positive, negative, neutral F-Score and accuracy.

After tuning the word vectors, three Static-CNNs with incorporated domain and aspect features were initialized with them, with random weights initializations, and trained on the whole training data from both domains in addition to 310 hand labeled examples which we added as an attempt to balance the training set label distribution across the two tackled domains (REST and LAPT) and to increase the number of the neutral labels as there were very few of them in the official training set compared to the other two polarities. The distribution of the hand labeled examples is shown in Table 2.

3 Evaluation and Results

In this section we discuss our official scores in the SemEval-2016 ABSA task. Furthermore, we present other experiments that were not officially submitted, but which provide insights regarding the adopted models as well as better performance for the laptops domain, than what was submitted.

3.1 Official Participations

For the aspect category extraction task (Slot 1), our RAEM model achieved the 2nd place out of 30 teams in the restaurants domain, with an F-Score of 72.886 which is only 0.145 less than what was achieved by the best performer. In the laptops domain, our LAEM model ranked the 8th amongst the 22 participating teams with an F-Score of 47.196. The detailed results in terms of precession, recall, and F-Score are shown in Table 3.

For the sentiment extraction task (Slot 3), we ranked 3rd and 5th in the restaurants and the laptops domains with accuracy scores of 85.448 and 77.403 respectively. The official evaluation accuracies and the per-class F-Scores are shown in Table 4. It can be deduced from the F-Scores that the number of training examples per class matters as the positive F-Score is always the best, followed by the negative and the neutral is always the worst which is a real reflection of the bias of the official training data distribution and the fine-tuning data.

3.2 Extended Experiments

In addition to the official submissions, we ran some additional experiments that were evaluated using the official scripts provided by the task organizers.

For Slot 1, given that the RAEM model achieved a good result in the restaurants domain, we decided to train this model on the laptops data. The resulting model achieved an F-score of 51.42 which would have put the system in 2nd place. We also experimented using the RAEM model without using the SVM classifier and reported that in Table 3 which shows that it contributed to enhancing the recall especially in the laptops domain. However, the RAEM system on its own, seems to perform relatively well even without the help of the SVM.

For Slot 3, we conducted two other experiments in which we used the fine-tuned word vectors to initialize two different ensemble classifiers like the one which was described in the SEM. However, here we separated the data so that we there is one classifier per domain. This provided better results in the laptops domain which would have ranked as the 2nd best performer, but decreased the accuracy slightly in the restaurants domain as shown in Table 4 as Domain Specific SEM.

4 Conclusions

In this paper, we presented models for extracting aspects and their corresponding sentiment polarities from user reviews in SemEval-2016, task 5. The proposed models achieved comparable scores to state of the art results on the test set without any feature engineering efforts.

Our experiments show that the best performance in the aspect category extraction task can be achieved by using one binary classifier per aspect following the one vs all strategy. For the sentiment extraction task, our results show that after fine tuning the word vectors, it is better to train a separate classifier for each domain.

We believe that bigger and more class balanced training and fine-tuning datasets can boost the results as it was clear that the classes' distributions are reflected in the testing results. We used fine-tuned word vectors for training the CNN model used for sentiment determination, initializing its weights randomly. In the future we plan investigating using the weights of the CNN that was used to fine tune the word vectors to initialize the second CNN used for sentiment classification. We expect that this might have a positive impact on the performance of the classifier, but this remains to be tested.

References

Collobert, R., Weston, J., Bottou, L., Karlen, M., Kavukcuoglu, K., & Kuksa, P. (2011). Natural Language Processing (almost) from Scratch. *Journal of Machine Learning Research*, *12*(Aug), 2493–2537. http://doi.org/10.1145/2347736.2347755

Cortes, C., & Vapnik, V. (1995). Support-Vector Networks. *Machine Learning*, *20*, 273–297.

Hinton, G. E., Srivastava, N., Krizhevsky, A., Sutskever, I., & Salakhutdinov, R. R. (2012). Improving neural networks by preventing co-adaptation of feature detectors. *arXiv: 1207.0580*, 1–18. http://doi.org/arXiv:1207.0580

Jo, Y. (2011). Aspect and Sentiment Unification Model for Online Review Analysis. *Proceedings of the Fourth ACM International Conference on Web Search and Data Mining*, 815–824. http://doi.org/10.1145/1935826.1935932

Kim, Y. (2014). Convolutional Neural Networks for Sentence Classification. *Proceedings of the 2014 Conference on Empirical Methods in Natural Language Processing (EMNLP 2014)*, 1746–1751. Retrieved from

http://emnlp2014.org/papers/pdf/EMNLP2014181
.pdf

Maria Pontiki, Dimitrios Galanis, Haris Papageorgiou, Suresh Manandhar, and I. A. (2015). SemEval-2015 Task 12: Aspect Based Sentiment Analysis. In *Proceedings of the 9th International Workshop on Semantic Evaluation (SemEval 2015), Denver, Colorado.* (pp. 486–495). Denver, Colorado.

Mikolov, T., Sutskever, I., Chen, K., Corrado, G., & Dean, J. (2013). Distributed Representations of Words and Phrases and their Compositionality.

Rumelhart, D. E., Hinton, G. E., & Williams, R. J. (1986). Learning representations by back-propagating errors. *Nature, 323*(6088), 533–536. http://doi.org/10.1038/323533a0

Saias, J. (2015). Sentiue: Target and Aspect based Sentiment Analysis in SemEval-2015 Task 12. In *Proceedings of the 9th International Workshop on Semantic Evaluation* (pp. 767–771). Denver, Colorado.

Salton, G., & Buckley, C. (1988). Term-weighting Approaches in Automatic Text Retrieval. *Information Processing and Management, 24*(5), 513–523.

Toh, Z., & Su, J. (2015). NLANGP: Supervised Machine Learning System for Aspect Category Classification and Opinion Target Extraction. In *Proceedings of the 9th International Workshop on Semantic Evaluation* (pp. 496–501).

Zeiler, M. D. (2012). ADADELTA: An Adaptive Learning Rate Method. *arXiv*, 6. Retrieved from http://arxiv.org/abs/1212.5701

XRCE at SemEval-2016 Task 5: Feedbacked Ensemble Modelling on Syntactico-Semantic Knowledge for Aspect Based Sentiment Analysis

Caroline Brun and **Julien Perez** and **Claude Roux**
Xerox Research Centre Europe
6, chemin de Maupertuis
38240 Meylan, France
`{caroline.brun, julien.perez, claude.roux}@xrce.xerox.com`

Abstract

This paper presents our contribution to the SemEval 2016 task 5: Aspect-Based Sentiment Analysis. We have addressed Subtask 1 for the restaurant domain, in English and French, which implies opinion target expression detection, aspect category and polarity classification. We describe the different components of the system, based on composite models combining sophisticated linguistic features with Machine Learning algorithms, and report the results obtained for both languages.

1 Introduction and Related Work

Sentiment Analysis is an important topic in natural language processing, and Aspect Based Sentiment Analysis (ABSA), i.e. detection of sentiments expressed on different aspects of a given entity, constitute a very interesting but quite challenging task (Liu, 2012; Ganu et al., 2009). ABSA is a task first introduced at SemEval in 2014 (Pontiki et al., 2014), continued in 2015 (Pontiki et al., 2015) and now, in 2016 (Pontiki et al., 2016). Our team has participated to the first edition, with good results on the restaurant domain (Brun et al., 2014) and decided to reiterate the participation in 2016, on the same domain but on English and French, as the challenge has become multilingual. While relatively similar, the task has evolved since 2014: aspect targets and categories are annotated together instead of separately; only opinionated terms (Opinion Target Expressions, OTE) are annotated, and aspect categories are finer grained (12 classes instead of 5), which makes the subtasks even more challenging.

In the previous challenges, most systems, including ours, use state-of-the art machine learning algorithms such as SVMs (Wagner et al., 2014; Kiritchenko et al., 2014; Brun et al., 2014; Brychcín et al., 2014) or CRFs (Toh and Wang, 2014; Hamdan et al., 2015), with lexical information, bigrams and POS as features. In 2014, (Kiritchenko et al., 2014) had particularly good results on aspect category and aspect polarity detection, using SVMs combined with rich linguistic features including dependency parsing. In 2015, the system presented by (Saias, 2015) reported the best result for polarity classification, using a maximum entropy classifier, having bag-of-words, lemmas, bigrams after verbs, and punctuation based features, along with sentiment lexicon-based features. Our system shares whith these ones the use of syntactic features to address the different ABSA tasks.

For the present challenge, we addressed substask 1, which implies target terms detection, aspect category and polarity classification. In the remaining of the paper, we describe the different components of our system which combine rich linguistic features and machine learning algorithms (CRF, Ensemble models for classification). We then present and discuss our results on the different subtasks. We finally conclude and propose future directions.

2 System Description

We present here the different components of our system, dedicated to linguistic feature extraction, sequence labeling and classification.

Proceedings of SemEval-2016, pages 277–281,
San Diego, California, June 16-17, 2016. ©2016 Association for Computational Linguistics

2.1 Linguistic Feature Factory

We use a robust syntactic parser (XIP (Ait-Mokhtar et al., 2002)) as one of the fundamental components of our system. This parser provides a full processing chain including tokenization, morpho-syntactic analysis, POS tagging, Named Entity Detection, chunking and finally, extraction of dependency relations such as subject, object and modifiers. This robust parser has been already used for the Aspect Based Sentiment Analysis of SemEval 14 (Brun et al., 2014). We have designed and adapted a semantic extraction component that extracts semantic information about aspect targets and their polarities on top of the parser described before. For this task, syntactic dependencies, lexical information about word polarities and semantic classes, sub-categorization information are all combined within the parser to extract semantic relations associated to aspect targets. We already have developed a component that extracts sentiment relations (see (Brun, 2011) for the complete description of this component), taking into account contexts and scope of the polar predicates. This semantic component makes use of a polar lexicon associating polarities (only positive and negative) to words, and a semantic lexicon associating lexical semantic features (FOOD, DRINK, AMBIENCE, SERVICE, RESTAURANT, PRICE, STYLE) to words. For the present challenge, we used the English and French version of the grammars, and complemented the existing domain lexicons with lexical information extracted from the training corpus.

We use this parser as a "feature factory", that outputs linguistic features which can feed the various Machine Learning algorithms we applied to the ABSA tasks[1], that are described afterwards.

2.2 Domain Term detection using CRF

Conditional Random Fields (CRF) (Lafferty et al., 2001) is a popular class of statistical modelling for sequence labeling, which can be applied to term detection. For this specific task, we used CRFsuite[2] (Okazaki, 2007), which provides a cross-validation

---

[1]**Important note**: as we use this proprietary parser for our experiments, and for reproducibility concerns, we have released our feature datasets both for train and test, on English and French, for the different slots at this url: http://semeval2016.xrce.xerox.com/

[2]http://www.chokkan.org/software/crfsuite

mechanism, to detect the terms and categories in the different sentences. The CRF model was trained with some traditional features such as POS, lemma, surface form, and the presence of uppercase letters for instance. However, we also used the output of the XIP parser to detect if a word was in a particular syntactic construction such as attribute, coordination or object dependencies. The parser also supplies lexico-semantic information, for instance if a given noun phrase is related to food or to service, also integrated into the list of features. Finally, we used as feature whether a word was detected as being part of a sentiment analysis structure. We then combined the features from the three previous and the three next words in order to train our system within a window of seven words. Thus, the CRF model was trained over a mixture of word forms and syntax. Since CRFsuite provides a cross-validation scheme, we applied a 10 fold cross validation, which displayed a consistent F-measure of 85 over the English training set and the French training set.

2.3 Inference models

In this section, the different aspects of the decision model are presented. Based on the rich linguistic representation produced for the different tasks, a feedbacked loop of classification has been developed. Indeed, in order to highlight the most efficient linguistic features, we developed a simple framework of feedback generation for assisting feature definition and selection.

2.3.1 Feedbacked Ensemble Models

In order to address aspect category and polarity classification, an interactive feedbacked ensemble method pipeline has been designed to cope with the strong sparsity nature of the data. Indeed, figure 1 details the overall dynamic of the model. First, the feature set associated with the considered term is defined. Then, in order to cope with sparsity truncated singular value decomposition (Hansen, 1986) can be performed on the original set of features then a one-versus-all Elastic Net regression model (Zou and Hastie, 2003) is used to infer the target concept, in our case category and polarity. The advantage of Elastic Net is that it explicitly defines a trade-off between L1-norm and L2-norm type of regularization. As an output of the model learning task, a model representation and cross-validation scores are provided in order to allow for improvement of the feature set used as decision support, enabling a formal error analysis of such model. As feedbacked interaction, statistics informing of the relevance of the sentence features estimated during crossvalidation but also recurrent errors occuring in crossvalidation have been used as evidence in order to enhanced the linguistic representation of the sentences.

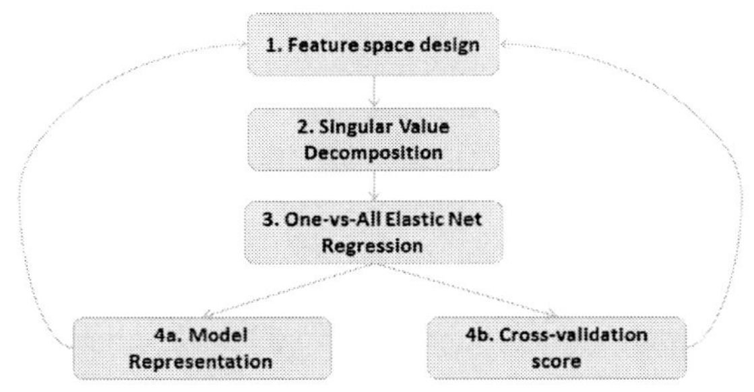

Figure 1: Ensemble Modeling Process for ABSA

This pipeline is applied to the different classification tasks described below.

2.3.2 Aspect Category Classification

For the restaurant domain, 12 semantic categories are covering the aspects (food#quality, food#style_options, food#prices, drinks#quality, drinks#style_options, drinks#prices, location#general, restaurant#general, restaurant#misc, restaurant#prices, service#general and ambience#general), into which explicit and implicit aspect targets have to be classified. Classification into aspect categories is done in two steps: the first step classifies aspect terms (explicit targets), which have been detected by the CRF model presented in section 2.2 into one or more aspect category; then a second classification step is applied to classify sentences into aspect categories, to cover the cases of implicit targets (i.e. "NULL" targets).

(1) Aspect term classification into aspect categories: to achieve this task we used a precise extraction of features that are relevant for a given term in a given sentence, knowing that several terms can be present in the same sentence. We apply a term centric feature extraction, i.e. for a given term, features are: lexical semantic features associated to the term by the parser (FOOD, SERVICE); bigrams and trigrams involving the term; all syntactic dependencies (subject, object, modifier, attribute,...) involving the term. In other words, a term, i.e. a node in the dependency graph, is represented by the information captured by the arcs connecting this specific node to other nodes of the graph. The classification models presented in section 2.3.1 output the list of aspect categories together with their probabilities: we systematically associate the class of highest probability to a term detected by the CRF, and then associate additional categories whenever this probability is above a certain threshold; the threshold for these additional categories for a term was selected by cross-validation on the training corpora.

(2) Sentence classification into aspect categories: for this purpose, we used the same set of features as previously but at sentence level (i.e. not restricted to a given term). The classification models associate the potential sentence level aspect categories together with their probabilities; we annotate at sentence level (i.e. NULL annotation) if and only if the probability is above a given threshold, also calculated by cross-validation on the training corpora.

2.3.3 Polarity Classification

Opinion has to be classified with the three following polarities: positive, negative or neutral. We applied a similar strategy as for the aspect categories classification, i.e. classify the detected terms using a term-centric feature representation and then classify the sentences. We use the same pipeline as previously but in this case, we associate the highest polarity probability to the term or the sentence, ignoring the few cases presenting a mixed polarity (i.e. both positive and negative). Features are extracted the same way, but we add the aspect category detected previously as a feature for polarity classification. We also delexicalized the features, replacing a term by its generic aspect category (e.g. "staff" is replaced by "SERVICE", "sushi" is replaced by "FOOD", etc.), since our parser associates lexical semantic information to the domain terms.

3 Evaluation

Tables 1 and 2 report the results obtained on the 4 slots for English and French.

Our system performs target term classification, using a term centric representation, which proba-

	XRCE	Baseline	Rank
S1: Categories (F-1)	68.701	59.928	7/29
S2: Targets (F-1)	61.98	44.071	10/18
S12: Tuples (F-1)	48.891	37.795	2/14
S3: Polarity (Acc.)	**88.126**	76.484	1/28

Table 1: Results on English for the restaurant domain

	XRCE	Baseline	Rank
S1: Categories (F-1)	**61.207**	52.609	1/5
S2: Targets (F-1)	65.316	45.455	2/2
S12: Tuples (F-1)	47.721	33.017	1/1
S3: Polarity (Acc.)	**78.826**	67.4	1/5

Table 2: Results on French for the restaurant domain

bly explain the relatively good results we get on slot 12, <categories,target> tuples. It also explains the less good results on slot 1 for English, for which a sentence level classification would probably have been a better strategy. Results of the CRF on slot 2 are somehow disappointing, but analyzing the errors shows that we may have used a too large feature window (-3, +3) that could have resulted to an overfitting behaviour. Reducing the window to (-2, +2) improves the results: for slot 2, the F-1 reaches 67.883 for English and 68.533 for French; for slot 12, the F-1 reaches 53.364 for English, and 49.182 for French.

There are significant differences in term of performances between the two languages: for aspect category detection, the lower results for French are partly due to the smaller coverage of the lexical semantic information inthe lexicon. For aspect polarity, most of the errors we've detected on English and French are misclassification of neutral utterances. This is due to the limited proportion of neutral cases in the training corpus (4% in English and 6% in French), and also to the fact that our polarity lexicons focus primarily on positive and negative vocabulary. This has a greater impact on the results for French, since the test corpus has a more balanced repartition of polarities.

In conclusion, the most encouraging result is that the system ranked first on polarity detection both for French and English. It tends to show that the combination of term-oriented and sentence-oriented classification performs well for polarity inference.

4   Conclusion

In this paper, we present a composite method based on ensemble modelling combined with rich linguistic features including lexical semantic information and syntactico-semantic dependencies to address aspect based category and polarity classification. We have also designed a target term recognizer using CRFs. Classification is performed at two levels : term level, for which we extract a set of term-centric features and sentence level, for which we extract sentence-based features, to adress the cases where there is no explicit mention of a term (i.e. "NULL"). We have participated to the SemEval 2016 ABSA subtask 1, for English and French, in the restaurant domain, on slots 1, 2, 12, and 3. The system obtained very satisfying results for category detection in French (slot 1), and for slot 12 in English. But the best performances are achieved on polarity detection, since the system ends up first for both languages on slot 3: first among 28 submissions for English, and first among 5 submissions for French. Further directions of investigation will focus on two aspects. On one hand, we plan to investigate methods to decrease the level of supervision of the system (Broß, 2013), and on the other hand, we plan to extend to other languages and domains, via domain adaptation methods.

Acknowledgements

We would like to warmly thank the SemEval 2016 Task 5 organizers and the French dataset support team for their support.

References

Salah Ait-Mokhtar, Jean-Pierre Chanod, and Claude Roux. 2002. Robustness beyond shallowness: incremental deep parsing. *Natural Language Engineering*, 8(2-3):121–144.

Jurgen Broß. 2013. *Aspect-Oriented Sentiment Analysis of Customer Reviews Using Distant Supervision Techniques*. Ph.D. thesis, Freie Universit"at Berlin, Berlin, Germany, 7.

Caroline Brun, Diana Nicoleta Popa, and Claude Roux. 2014. Xrce: Hybrid classification for aspect-based sentiment analysis. In *Proceedings of the 8th International Workshop on Semantic Evaluation (SemEval 2014)*, pages 838–842, Dublin, Ireland, August. Association for Computational Linguistics and Dublin City University.

Caroline Brun. 2011. Detecting opinions using deep syntactic analysis. In Galia Angelova, Kalina Bontcheva, Ruslan Mitkov, and Nicolas Nicolov, editors, *RANLP*, pages 392–398. RANLP 2011.

Tomáš Brychcín, Michal Konkol, and Josef Steinberger. 2014. Uwb: Machine learning approach to aspect-based sentiment analysis. In *Proceedings of the 8th International Workshop on Semantic Evaluation (SemEval 2014)*, pages 817–822, Dublin, Ireland, August. Association for Computational Linguistics and Dublin City University.

G. Ganu, N. Elhadad, and A. Marian. 2009. Beyond the stars: Improving rating predictions using review text content. In *Proceedings of the 12th International Workshop on the Web and Databases*, Providence, Rhode Island.

Hussam Hamdan, Patrice Bellot, and Frederic Bechet. 2015. Lsislif: Crf and logistic regression for opinion target extraction and sentiment polarity analysis. In *Proceedings of the 9th International Workshop on Semantic Evaluation (SemEval 2015)*, pages 753–758, Denver, Colorado, June. Association for Computational Linguistics.

Per C Hansen. 1986. The truncated svd as a method for regularization. Technical report, Stanford University, Stanford, CA, USA.

Svetlana Kiritchenko, Xiaodan Zhu, Colin Cherry, and Saif Mohammad. 2014. Nrc-canada-2014: Detecting aspects and sentiment in customer reviews. In *Proceedings of the 8th International Workshop on Semantic Evaluation (SemEval 2014)*, pages 437–442, Dublin, Ireland, August. Association for Computational Linguistics and Dublin City University.

John D. Lafferty, Andrew McCallum, and Fernando C. N. Pereira. 2001. Conditional random fields: Probabilistic models for segmenting and labeling sequence data. In *Proceedings of the Eighteenth International Conference on Machine Learning*, ICML '01, pages 282–289, San Francisco, CA, USA. Morgan Kaufmann Publishers Inc.

Bing Liu. 2012. *Sentiment Analysis and Opinion Mining*. Synthesis Lectures on Human Language Technologies. Morgan & Claypool Publishers.

Naoaki Okazaki. 2007. Crfsuite: a fast implementation of conditional random fields (crfs).

Maria Pontiki, Dimitrios Galanis, John Pavlopoulos, Harris Papageorgiou, Ion Androutsopoulos, and Suresh Manandhar. 2014. Semeval-2014 task 4: Aspect based sentiment analysis. In *International Workshop on Semantic Evaluation (SemEval)*.

Maria Pontiki, Dimitris Galanis, Haris Papageorgiou, Suresh Manandhar, and Ion Androutsopoulos. 2015.

Semeval-2015 task 12: Aspect based sentiment analysis. In *Proceedings of the 9th International Workshop on Semantic Evaluation (SemEval 2015)*, pages 486–495, Denver, Colorado, June. Association for Computational Linguistics.

Maria Pontiki, Dimitrios Galanis, Haris Papageorgiou, Ion Androutsopoulos, Suresh Manandhar, Mohammad AL-Smadi, Mahmoud Al-Ayyoub, Yanyan Zhao, Bing Qin, Orphée De Clercq, Véronique Hoste, Marianna Apidianaki, Xavier Tannier, Natalia Loukachevitch, Evgeny Kotelnikov, Nuria Bel, Salud María Jiménez-Zafra, and Gülşen Eryiğit. 2016. SemEval-2016 task 5: Aspect based sentiment analysis. In *Proceedings of the 10th International Workshop on Semantic Evaluation*, SemEval '16, San Diego, California, June. Association for Computational Linguistics.

José Saias. 2015. Sentiue: Target and aspect based sentiment analysis in semeval-2015 task 12. In *Proceedings of the 9th International Workshop on Semantic Evaluation (SemEval 2015)*, pages 767–771, Denver, Colorado, June. Association for Computational Linguistics.

Zhiqiang Toh and Wenting Wang. 2014. Dlirec: Aspect term extraction and term polarity classification system. In *Proceedings of the 8th International Workshop on Semantic Evaluation (SemEval 2014)*, pages 235–240, Dublin, Ireland, August. Association for Computational Linguistics and Dublin City University.

Joachim Wagner, Piyush Arora, Santiago Cortes, Utsab Barman, Dasha Bogdanova, Jennifer Foster, and Lamia Tounsi. 2014. Dcu: Aspect-based polarity classification for semeval task 4. In *Proceedings of the 8th International Workshop on Semantic Evaluation (SemEval 2014)*, pages 392–397, Dublin, Ireland, August. Association for Computational Linguistics and Dublin City University.

H. Zou and T. Hastie. 2003. Regularization and variable selection via the elastic net. *Journal of the Royal Statistical Society: Series B (Statistical Methodology)*, 67(2):301–320.

NLANGP at SemEval-2016 Task 5: Improving Aspect Based Sentiment Analysis using Neural Network Features

Zhiqiang Toh
Institute for Infocomm Research
1 Fusionopolis Way
Singapore 138632
ztoh@i2r.a-star.edu.sg

Jian Su
Institute for Infocomm Research
1 Fusionopolis Way
Singapore 138632
sujian@i2r.a-star.edu.sg

Abstract

This paper describes our system submitted to Aspect Based Sentiment Analysis Task 5 of SemEval-2016. Our system consists of two components: binary classifiers trained using single layer feedforward network for aspect category classification (Slot 1), and sequential labeling classifiers for opinion target extraction (Slot 2). Besides extracting a variety of lexicon features, syntactic features, and cluster features, we explore the use of deep learning systems to provide additional neural network features. Our system achieves the best performances on the English datasets, ranking 1st for four evaluations (Slot 1 for both restaurant and laptop domains, Slot 2, and Slot 1 & 2).

1 Introduction

Sentiment analysis and opinion mining have gained increasing interests in recent years due to the continuous growing of user-generated content on the Internet. Traditionally, the primary focus of the research has been on the detection of the overall sentiment of a sentence or paragraph. However, such approach is unable to handle conflicting sentiment for different aspects of the same entity. Hence, a more fine-grained approach, known as Aspect-Based Sentiment Analysis (ABSA), is proposed. The goal is to correctly identify the aspects of entities and the polarity expressed for each aspect.

The SemEval-2016 Aspect Based Sentiment Analysis (SE-ABSA16) task is a continuation of the same task in 2015 (Pontiki et al., 2015). Besides sentence-level ABSA (Subtask 1), it provides datasets to allow participants to work on text-level ABSA (Subtask 2). In addition, additional datasets in languages other than English are available (Pontiki et al., 2016).

We participate in Subtask 1 of SE-ABSA16, where we submitted results for Slot 1 (aspect category classification), Slot 2 (opinion target extraction), and Slot 1 & 2 (assessing whether a system correctly identifies both Slot 1 and Slot 2) for the English datasets.

Our work is based on our previous machine learning system described in Toh and Su (2015), enhanced using additional features learned from neural networks. For Slot 1, we treat the problem as a multi-class classification problem where aspect categories are predicted via a set of binary classifiers. The one-vs-all strategy is used to train a binary classifier for each category found in the training data. Each classifier is trained using a single layer feedforward network. We enhance the system by adding neural network features learned from a Deep Convolutional Neural Network system. For Slot 2, we treat the problem as a sequential labeling task, where sequential labeling classifiers are trained using Conditional Random Fields (CRF). The output of a Recurrent Neural Network system is used as additional features. To generate Slot 1 & 2 predictions, the predictions of Slot 1 and Slot 2 are combined.

The remainder of this paper is organized as follows. In Section 2, the features used in our system are described. Section 3 presents the detailed machine learning approaches. Section 4 and Section 5 show the official evaluation results and feature ablation results respectively. Finally, Section 6 summa-

Proceedings of SemEval-2016, pages 282–288,
San Diego, California, June 16-17, 2016. ©2016 Association for Computational Linguistics

rizes our work.

2 Features

Our system used a variety of features which are briefly described in the following subsections. Most of the features used are the same as the features used in Toh and Su (2015).

2.1 Word

Each word in a sentence is used as a feature. Additional word context is used for different slots: for Slot 1, all word bigram context found in a sentence are also used; for Slot 2, the previous word and next word context are also used.

2.2 Name List

Two name lists of opinion targets are generated from the training data of the restaurant domain. One list contains opinion targets that frequently occur in the training data. The other list contains words that often occur as part of an opinion target in the training data.

2.3 Head Word

For each word, the head word is extracted from the sentence parse tree and is used as a feature.

2.4 Word Embeddings

Word embeddings have shown previously to be beneficial to opinion target extraction, requiring only minimal feature engineering effort (Liu et al., 2015). We trained word embeddings from two unlabeled datasets: the Multi-Domain Sentiment Dataset containing product reviews from Amazon (Blitzer et al., 2007)[1], and the user reviews found in the Yelp Phoenix Academic Dataset[2]. Additional word embeddings are also generated from the concatenation of the above two datasets.

Two different approaches are used to train the word embeddings. The first approach uses the gensim[3] implementation of the word2vec tool (Mikolov et al., 2013)[4]. We experiment with different vector sizes, window sizes, minimum occurrences and subsampling thresholds.

The second approach uses the GloVe tool (Pennington et al., 2014)[5]. By varying the minimum count, window size and vector size, different embedding files are generated. The best embedding files to use are selected using 5-fold cross validation.

2.5 Word Cluster

We further processed the embedding files described in Section 2.4 by generating K-means clusters from them. Specifically, the K-means clusters are generated using the K-means implementation of Apache Spark MLlib[6]. Different cluster sizes are tried out and the best cluster files are selected using 5-fold cross validation.

2.6 Double Propagation Name List

Besides using the training data to generate name lists, we used the unsupervised Double Propagation (DP) algorithm (Qiu et al., 2011) to generate candidate opinion targets and collect them into a list. We adjust the logical rules stated in Liu et al. (2013) to derive our own propagation rules written in Prolog. The SWI-Prolog[7] is used as the solver. One issue with our rules is that it can only identify single-word targets. Thus, we check each identified target and include any consecutive noun words right before the target.

3 Approaches

This section describes our approaches used to generate the predictions for the different slots. The machine learning system is based on our previous work (Toh and Su, 2015) and is extended to use additional neural network features.

3.1 Aspect Category Classification (Slot 1)

For each category found in the training data, a binary classifier is trained using the Vowpal Wabbit tool[8], which provides the implementation of the single layer feedforward network algorithm that we use.

Besides using the features reported previously, we enhance our existing system by using additional features from a deep learning system described below.

---

[1]http://www.cs.jhu.edu/ mdredze/datasets/sentiment/
[2]http://www.yelp.com/dataset_challenge/
[3]https://radimrehurek.com/gensim/
[4]https://code.google.com/archive/p/word2vec/

[5]http://nlp.stanford.edu/projects/glove/
[6]http://spark.apache.org/mllib/
[7]http://www.swi-prolog.org/
[8]https://github.com/JohnLangford/vowpal_wabbit/wiki

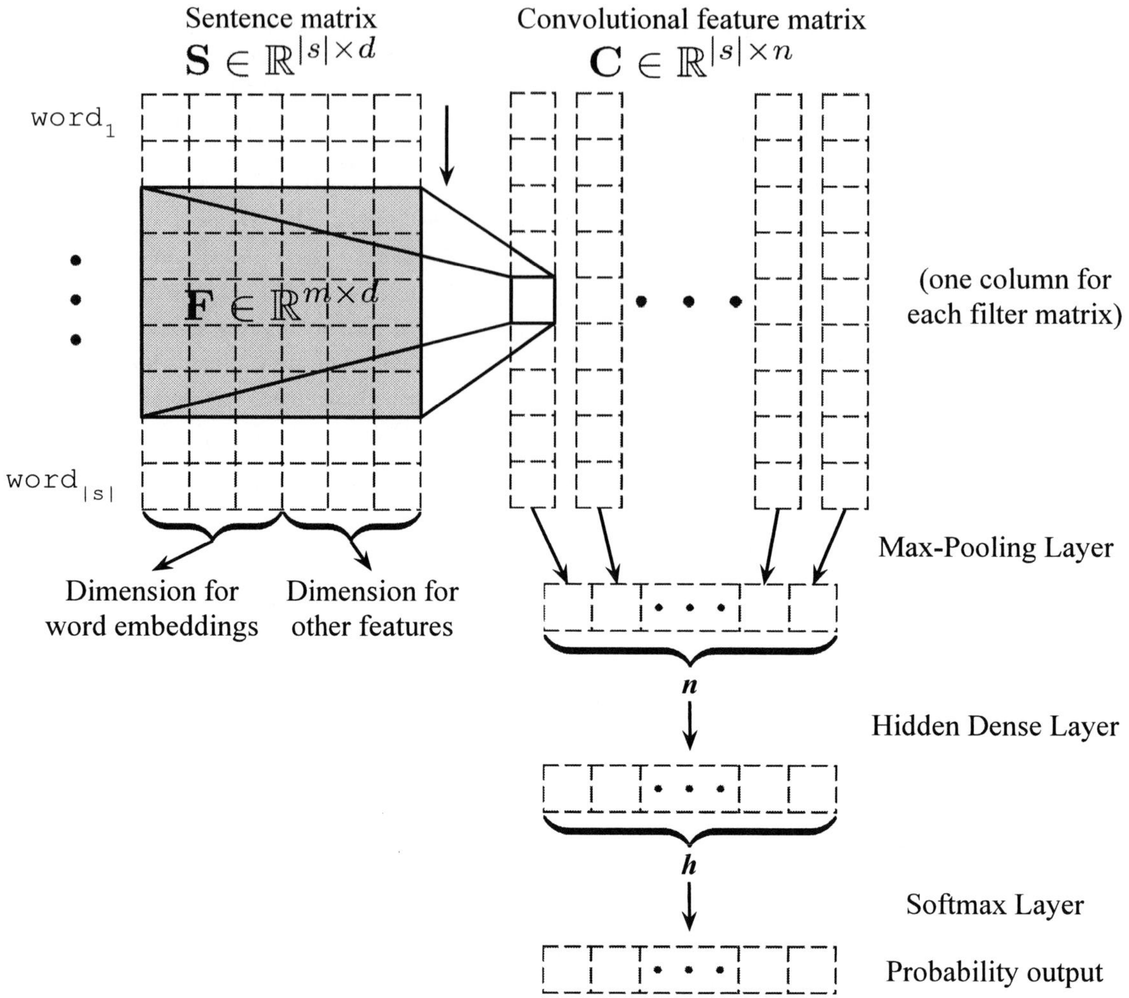

Figure 1: The architecture of our Convolutional Neural Network.

The deep learning system is based on the Deep Convolutional Neural Network (CNN) architecture described in Severyn and Moschitti (2015). The architecture we use is shown in Figure 1.

A sentence matrix $\mathbf{S} \in \mathbb{R}^{|s| \times d}$ is built for each input sentence s, where each row i is a vector representation of the word i in the sentence. The sentence length $|s|$ is fixed to the maximum sentence length of the dataset so that all sentence matrices have the same dimensions. (Shorter sentences are padded with row vectors of 0s accordingly.) Each row vector of the sentence matrix is made up of columns corresponding to different input features (e.g. word embedding feature, name list feature, etc.) concate-

nated together [9].

The input sentence matrix $\mathbf{S}$ is then passed through a series of network layer transformations, described in the following subsections.

3.1.1 Convolutional Layer

We apply a convolution operation between the input sentence matrix $\mathbf{S}$ and a filter matrix $\mathbf{F} \in \mathbb{R}^{m \times d}$ of context window size m, resulting in a column vector $\mathbf{c} \in \mathbb{R}^{|s|}$. The filter matrix $\mathbf{F}$ will slide (with a stride of 1) along the row dimension of $\mathbf{S}$, generating a value for each word in the sentence. Instead of a single filter matrix, n filter matrices are applied to

---

[9]Categorical features are converted to one-hot encodings.

the sentence matrix $\mathbf{S}$, resulting in a convolutional feature matrix $\mathbf{C} \in \mathbb{R}^{|s| \times n}$.

To learn non-linear decision boundaries, each element of $\mathbf{C}$ passes through the hyperbolic tangent *tanh* activation function.

3.1.2 Max-Pooling Layer

The output matrix $\mathbf{C}$ is then passed to the max-pooling layer. This layer will return the maximum value of each column.

3.1.3 Hidden Dense Layer

A hidden dense layer with h hidden units is applied to the output of the pooling layer, using Rectified Linear Unit (ReLU) as the activation function.

3.1.4 Softmax Layer

A softmax layer receives the output of the previous dense layer and computes probability distribution over the possible categories. We include an additional category "NIL" for the case where the sentence contains no aspect category. Since a sentence may contain more than one category, we output the categories whose output probability value is greater than a threshold t.

3.1.5 Network Training and Regularization

The stochastic gradient descent (SGD) algorithm is used to train the CNN network, using the back-propagation algorithm to compute the gradients. We run SGD for e epochs, where a batch size of b sentences is used. The categorical cross-entropy is used as the loss function. To prevent overfitting, the loss function is augmented with a L2 regularization term (l_2) for the parameters of the network. The Adadelta update function (with a specific decay rate ρ and constant ϵ) is used to control the learning rate.

The specific values used for the hyperparameters of the network are tuned using 5-fold cross-validation. The context window size m is set to 5. The number of filter matrices n is set to 300. The probability threshold t is set to 0.2. The number of hidden units h is set to 100. The number of epochs e is set to 50 and 100 for the restaurant and laptop domain respectively. The L2 regularization term l_2 is set to 0.01. The Adadelta decay rate ρ and constant ϵ is set to 0.95 and $1e^{-6}$ respectively.

Restaurant	
Feature	F1
Word[†]	0.6432
+ Head Word	0.6558
+ Name List[†]	0.6670
+ Word Cluster	0.7128
+ CNN Probabilities	0.7510
CNN System	0.7333

Laptop	
Feature	F1
Word[†]	0.5178
+ Head Word[†]	0.5358
+ Word Cluster	0.5463
+ CNN Probabilities	0.5983
CNN System	0.5693

Table 1: Experimental results of 5-fold cross-validation for Slot 1. Besides using the feature stated in the current row, features stated in all previous rows are also used. [†] indicates features used in constrained systems.

3.2 Slot 1 Features

Besides the features described in Section 2, the probability output of the CNN system is used as additional features to our multi-class classification system. The CNN system is trained on the following input features: Word Embeddings, Name List (only for the restaurant domain) and Word Cluster.

We performed 5-fold cross-validation experiments to obtain performances of the system after adding each feature group. Table 1 shows the experimental results.

We also include the 5-fold cross-validation performances if we only use the CNN system output for evaluation (last row). For both domains, the CNN system achieves better performances than the multi-class classification system without the neural network features.

However, the best performances are achieved when we used the CNN probability output as additional features to the multi-class classification system. This suggests our approach of combining two different machine learning systems is a feasible approach for the task.

3.3 Opinion Target Extraction (Slot 2)

We treat opinion target extraction as a sequential labeling task. The sequential labeling classifiers are trained using Conditional Random Fields (CRF). Such approach is similar to previous work that achieves state-of-the-art performances (Toh and Su, 2015). The implementation of CRF is provided by the CRFsuite tool (Okazaki, 2007).

Similar to our previous work, for different evaluations involving Slot 2, we train different models. For Slot 1 & 2 evaluation (multi setting), the explicit opinion targets may be classified under more than one category. Thus, a separate CRF model is trained for each category C found in the training data, where each model is trained using the corresponding BIO labels: "B-C", "I-C" and "O" (corresponding to start of an opinion target, continuation of an opinion target and outside respectively).

For Slot 2 evaluation (single setting), only the target span is required. Thus, all categories are collapsed into a single category (e.g. "TARGET"). A single CRF model is trained using the labels "B-TARGET", "I-TARGET" and "O".

We also enhance our existing CRF system by using the output of a Recurrent Neural Network (RNN) system as additional features.

Specifically, we implement the Bidirectional Elman-type RNN model described in Liu et al. (2015)[10]. Such a model allows long-range dependencies from the future as well as from the past to be captured, which are beneficial for sequential labeling tasks. The last layer of the model is a fully connected softmax layer to allow the model to output probabilities.

3.3.1 Network Training and Regularization

The RNN network is trained using SGD for 20 epochs, using Nesterov momentum with a learning rate of 0.05 and momentum of 0.9 and a batch size of 100 sentences. The categorical cross-entropy is used as the loss function, with L2 penalty of 0.01 for regularization. The number of hidden cell units for both directions is set to 250.

---

[10]Only a single RNN model is trained with all categories collapsed into a single category.

Restaurant (**multi**)	
Feature	F1
Word[†]	.4413
+ Name List[†]	.5672
+ Word Cluster	.5877
+ RNN Probabilities	0.6285

Restaurant (**single**)	
Feature	F1
Word[†]	0.6151
+ Name List[†]	0.6768
+ DP Name List	0.6992
+ Word Cluster	0.7162
+ RNN Probabilities	0.7390
RNN System	0.7190

Table 2: Experimental results of 5-fold cross-validation for Slot 2. Besides using the feature stated in the current row, features stated in all previous rows are also used. **multi**: Performances of Slot 2 for Slot 1 & 2 evaluation (ignoring NULL targets). **single**: Performances of Slot 2 for Slot 2 evaluation. [†] indicates features used in constrained systems.

3.4 Slot 2 Features

Besides the features described in Section 2, the probability output of the RNN system is used as additional features to our CRF system. The RNN system is trained on the following input features: Word Embeddings, Name List and Word Cluster.

We performed 5-fold cross-validation experiments to obtain performances of the system after adding each feature group. Table 2 shows the experimental results. We tune the system for two different settings: Slot 2 predictions used for Slot 1 & 2 evaluation (multi setting), and Slot 2 predictions used for Slot 2 evaluation (single setting).

3.4.1 Slot 1 & 2

To generate the predictions for Slot 1 & 2 evaluation, we combine Slot 1 and Slot 2 predictions together. First, we use all Slot 2 predictions used for Slot 1 & 2 evaluation (multi setting). This covers the cases for explicit targets. To include NULL targets, we check the Slot 1 predictions for categories that are not found in the Slot 2 predictions above. These categories are assumed to belong to NULL targets.

		Slot 1								
		Restaurant					Laptop			
System	Type	Rank	P	R	F1	Type	Rank	P	R	F1
NLANGP (U)	U	1	0.7245	0.7362	0.7303	U	1	0.5685	0.4781	0.5194
NLANGP (C)	C	14	0.6454	0.6662	0.6556	C	9	0.4897	0.4468	0.4673
1st	U	1	0.7245	0.7362	0.7303	U	1	0.5685	0.4781	0.5194
2nd	U	2	0.7269	0.7308	0.7289	U	2	0.4560	0.5319	0.4910
3rd	U	3	0.7011	0.7483	0.7240	U	3	0.5000	0.4819	0.4908
Baseline	C	–	0.5419	0.6703	0.5993	C	–	0.4592	0.3166	0.3748

		Slot 2					Slot 1 & 2			
		Restaurant								
System	Type	Rank	P	R	F1	Type	Rank	P	R	F1
NLANGP (U)	U	1	0.7549	0.6944	0.7234	U	1	0.5295	0.5227	0.5261
NLANGP (C)	C	8	0.7256	0.5703	0.6386	C	3	0.4667	0.4482	0.4572
1st	U	1	0.7549	0.6944	0.7234	U	1	0.5295	0.5227	0.5261
2nd	U	2	0.7182	0.6912	0.7044	C	2	0.4901	0.4878	0.4889
3rd	U	3	0.7510	0.6062	0.6709	C	3	0.4667	0.4482	0.4572
Baseline	C	–	0.5142	0.3856	0.4407	C	–	0.3656	0.3912	0.3780

Table 3: Official results for our system, top three performing systems and baselines.

4 Results

We participated in both unconstrained and constrained settings for the English datasets. Table 3 presents the official results of our submission. For comparison, the top three performing systems and baseline results are included (Pontiki et al., 2016).

As shown from the table, our system is ranked 1st for all four evaluations we participated (Slot 1 for both restaurant and laptop domains, Slot 2 and Slot 1 & 2 for the English datasets). Similar to previous observation, the constrained systems achieved lower results than the corresponding unconstrained systems, demonstrating the use of external resources are helpful for the task.

5 Feature Ablation

The feature ablation experimental results are shown in Table 4 (Slot 1) and Table 5 (Slot 2). The neural network features contributed the most performance gains. However, using the Name List and Word Cluster features do not seem to be particularly effective on the testing data: There are negligible or negative performance gains for Slot 1. As these two features are also used in the CNN system, it may be redundant to include them again in the multi-class classification system. In addition, the neural network features may have become the dominant features during training, affecting the usefulness of other features.

Further investigation may be needed to identify better ways of combining the different machine learning systems together. For example, instead of adding neural network probability output to our multi-class classification system, we could instead add our classifier probability output as additional features to our CNN system.

6 Conclusion

In this paper, we describe our system used in classifying aspect categories (Slot 1) and extracting opinion targets (Slot 2). We explore the use of deep learning systems to provide additional neural network features to our existing system. Our system is ranked 1st in the four evaluations on the English datasets. In future, we hope to perform better feature engineering and explore how our deep learning systems can be further enhanced for the task.

Restaurant		
Feature	F1	Loss
All features	0.7303	–
- Word	0.7228	0.0075
- Head Word	0.7291	0.0012
- Name List	0.7314	-0.0011
- Word Cluster	0.7251	0.0052
- CNN Probabilities	0.6937	0.0366

Laptop		
Feature	F1	Loss
All features	0.5194	–
- Word	0.5082	0.0112
- Head Word	0.5282	-0.0088
- Word Cluster	0.5189	0.0005
- CNN Probabilities	0.4955	0.0239

Table 4: Results of ablation experiments on the testing data for Slot 1. The columns are the resulting F1 measure and F1 loss after removing a single feature group.

Restaurant		
Feature	F1	Loss
All features	0.7234	–
- Word	0.6907	0.0327
- Name List	0.6977	0.0257
- DP Name List	0.6957	0.0278
- Word Cluster	0.7086	0.0148
- RNN Probabilities	0.6813	0.0421

Table 5: Results of ablation experiments on the testing data for Slot 2. The columns are the resulting F1 measure and F1 loss after removing a single feature group.

References

John Blitzer, Mark Dredze, and Fernando Pereira. 2007. Biographies, Bollywood, Boom-boxes and Blenders: Domain Adaptation for Sentiment Classification. In *Proceedings of the 45th Annual Meeting of the Association of Computational Linguistics*, pages 440–447, Prague, Czech Republic, June. Association for Computational Linguistics.

Qian Liu, Zhiqiang Gao, Bing Liu, and Yuanlin Zhang. 2013. A Logic Programming Approach to Aspect Extraction in Opinion Mining. In *Proceedings of the 2013 IEEE/WIC/ACM International Joint Conferences on Web Intelligence (WI) and Intelligent Agent Technologies (IAT) - Volume 01*, WI-IAT '13, pages 276–283.

Pengfei Liu, Shafiq Joty, and Helen Meng. 2015. Fine-grained Opinion Mining with Recurrent Neural Networks and Word Embeddings. In *Proceedings of the 2015 Conference on Empirical Methods in Natural Language Processing*, Lisbon, Portugal, September.

Tomas Mikolov, Wen-tau Yih, and Geoffrey Zweig. 2013. Linguistic Regularities in Continuous Space Word Representations. In *Proceedings of the 2013 Conference of the North American Chapter of the Association for Computational Linguistics: Human Language Technologies*, Atlanta, Georgia, June.

Naoaki Okazaki. 2007. CRFsuite: a fast implementation of Conditional Random Fields (CRFs).

Jeffrey Pennington, Richard Socher, and Christopher Manning. 2014. Glove: Global Vectors for Word Representation. In *Proceedings of the 2014 Conference on Empirical Methods in Natural Language Processing (EMNLP)*, Doha, Qatar, October.

Maria Pontiki, Dimitris Galanis, Haris Papageorgiou, Suresh Manandhar, and Ion Androutsopoulos. 2015. SemEval-2015 Task 12: Aspect Based Sentiment Analysis. In *Proceedings of the 9th International Workshop on Semantic Evaluation (SemEval 2015)*, Denver, Colorado, June.

Maria Pontiki, Dimitrios Galanis, Haris Papageorgiou, Ion Androutsopoulos, Suresh Manandhar, Mohammad AL-Smadi, Mahmoud Al-Ayyoub, Yanyan Zhao, Bing Qin, Orphée De Clercq, Véronique Hoste, Marianna Apidianaki, Xavier Tannier, Natalia Loukachevitch, Evgeny Kotelnikov, Nuria Bel, Salud María Jiménez-Zafra, and Gülşen Eryiğit. 2016. SemEval-2016 Task 5: Aspect Based Sentiment Analysis. In *Proceedings of the 10th International Workshop on Semantic Evaluation*, SemEval '16, San Diego, California, June.

Guang Qiu, Bing Liu, Jiajun Bu, and Chun Chen. 2011. Opinion Word Expansion and Target Extraction through Double Propagation. *Computational Linguistics*, 37(1):9–27.

Aliaksei Severyn and Alessandro Moschitti. 2015. UNITN: Training Deep Convolutional Neural Network for Twitter Sentiment Classification. In *Proceedings of the 9th International Workshop on Semantic Evaluation (SemEval 2015)*, Denver, Colorado, June.

Zhiqiang Toh and Jian Su. 2015. NLANGP: Supervised Machine Learning System for Aspect Category Classification and Opinion Target Extraction. In *Proceedings of the 9th International Workshop on Semantic Evaluation (SemEval 2015)*, Denver, Colorado, June.

bunji at SemEval-2016 Task 5: Neural and Syntactic Models of Entity-Attribute Relationship for Aspect-based Sentiment Analysis

Toshihiko Yanase, Kohsuke Yanai, Misa Sato, Toshinori Miyoshi, Yoshiki Niwa
Research & Development Group, Hitachi, Ltd.
{toshihiko.yanase.gm, kohsuke.yanai.cs, misa.sato.mw,
toshinori.miyoshi.pd, yoshiki.niwa.tx}@hitachi.com

Abstract

This paper describes a sentiment analysis system developed by the bunji team in SemEval-2016 Task 5. In this task, we estimate the sentimental polarity of a given entity-attribute (E#A) pair in a sentence. Our approach is to estimate the relationship between target entities and sentimental expressions. We use two different methods to estimate the relationship. The first one is based on a neural attention model that learns relations between tokens and E#A pairs through backpropagation. The second one is based on a rule-based system that examines several verb-centric relations related to E#A pairs. We confirmed the effectiveness of the proposed methods in a target estimation task and a polarity estimation task in the restaurant domain, while our overall ranks were modest.

1 Introduction

Sentiment analysis is an important technology for understanding users' intentions from review texts. Such technologies are also useful for argumentation mining because it is necessary for readers to capture targets of interest and their polarities (Sato et al., 2015). Shared tasks of aspect-based sentiment analysis (ABSA) in SemEval provide a test bed for fine-grained analysis of sentiment polarities (Pontiki et al., 2014; Pontiki et al., 2015; Pontiki et al., 2016).

We participate in all four slots (Slot 1, 2, 1 & 2, and 3) of the restaurant domain and laptop domain in English. We focus on two types of models to capture the entity-attribute relationship, especially in Slot 2

and Slot 3. The first one is a neural network based model. The second one is a rule-based approach.

Now, we explain the problem settings of the slots and our approaches. The following is an example of sentences that provide positive opinions to the FOOD#QUALITY aspect: Pizza here is good.

Slot 1 is an extraction of all aspects mentioned in a sentence. In this example, the goal is to choose FOOD#QUALITY among many other aspects. We formulate the problem as a multi-label classification problem and use a neural network-based model. Slot 2 is an extraction of opinion target expressions. The expected output is "Pizza" in the above example. We use a pattern matching based approach and focus on gathering resources such as dictionaries. For Slot 1 & 2, we simply combine the prediction results of Slot 1 and Slot 2. Slot 3 is an estimation of sentiment polarities. In this example, we estimate the polarity of this sentence from the aspect of FOOD#QUALITY. For Slot 3, we take two approaches. The first approach is a neural attention model (Luong et al., 2015) that considers the entity attention (FOOD) and attribute attention (QUALITY) of each token. The second approach is a pattern matching-based model that examines the relationship between "Pizza" and "good" that is also used in Slot 2.

The remainder of this paper is structured as follows: In Section 2, we describe our system of phase A. In Section 3, we explain our system of phase B. Finally, Section 4 summarizes our work.

Proceedings of SemEval-2016, pages 289–295,
San Diego, California, June 16-17, 2016. ©2016 Association for Computational Linguistics

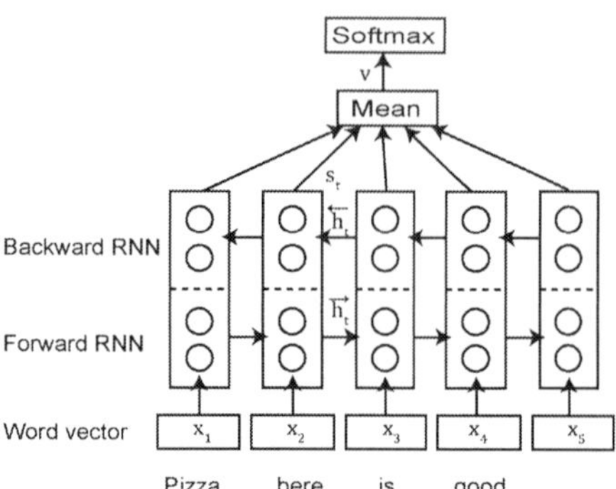

Figure 1: Structure of a neural network for Slot 1.

2 System Description of Phase A

2.1 Slot 1: Aspect Category

We formulate Slot 1 as a multi-label classification problem. In this problem, an entity-attribute pair is considered as a label. We use a neural model to solve this problem. The model is illustrated in Figure 1. Given a sequence of word vectors $X = (\mathbf{x}_1, \mathbf{x}_2, ..., \mathbf{x}_T)$, this model calculates a vector $\mathbf{y}$ whose element represents probability of each label as:

$$\mathbf{y} = f(X). \qquad (1)$$

At first, we apply Stanford Core NLP (Manning et al., 2014) to each document to obtain word sequences. Then, we use word embedding generated by Skip-gram with Negative Sampling (Mikolov et al., 2013) to convert words into word vectors. Three hundred dimensional vectors trained with Google News Corpus [1] are used in Slot 1.

Then, a word vector sequence X is inputted to a recurrent neural network (RNN). The RNN calculates an output vector $\mathbf{s}_t$ for each $\mathbf{x}_t$ as:

$$\mathbf{s}_t, \mathbf{h}_t = g(\mathbf{x}_t, \mathbf{h}_{t-1}), \qquad (2)$$

where $\mathbf{h}_t$ denotes a hidden state of the RNN at position t. We use Long Short-Term Memory (LSTM) (Sak et al., 2014) and Gated Recurrent Unit (GRU) (Cho et al., 2014) as implementations of RNN units.

We use a bi-directional RNN (BiRNN) (Schuster and Paliwal, 1997) in order to consider both forward context and backward context. A BiRNN consists of

[1] Word embedding is available at https://code.google.com/archive/p/word2vec/

a forward RNN that processes tokens from head to tail and a backward RNN that processes tokens from tail to head. We concatenate forward output $\overrightarrow{\mathbf{s}_t}$ and backward output $\overleftarrow{\mathbf{s}_t}$ into $\mathbf{s}_t$.

The sentence vector $\mathbf{v}$ is then computed as a mean of RNN outputs $\mathbf{s}_t$:

$$\mathbf{v} = \frac{1}{T} \sum_{t=1}^{T} \mathbf{s}_t. \qquad (3)$$

Finally, the probabilities in $\mathbf{y}$ are calculated by using a single layered perceptron:

$$\mathbf{y} = \mathrm{softmax}(\tanh(W\mathbf{v} + \mathbf{b})), \qquad (4)$$

where W, $\mathbf{b}$ denote a weight matrix and a bias vector, respectively.

We determine that a sentence contains the i-th aspect if its output y_i is greater than a threshold θ. The threshold θ is determined by using development data that is randomly sampled from training data.

We modify aspect names to a suitable format for our neural model. Low-frequency aspects in training datasets are replaced by a new aspect "OTHER". The most common 10 aspects are preserved in the restaurant domain; the most common 16 aspects are preserved in the laptop domain. "NONE" labels are assigned to sentences that do not have any labels. The probability $\mathbf{y_i}$ in an example of a training dataset is defined as $y_i = 1/k$ when a target sentence has the i-th aspect and a total of k aspects, otherwise $y_i = 0$.

We train the model by using backpropagation. The loss is calculated by using cross entropy. We use a minibatch stochastic gradient descent (SGD) algorithm together with an AdaGrad optimizer (Duchi et al., 2011). We add Dropout (Srivastava et al., 2014) layers to the input and output of the RNN. We clip the gradient norm when it exceeds 5.0 to improve the stability of training. The model parameters and θ are trained by the training dataset of the ABSA 2015, and the hyperparameters are tuned by test dataset of the ABSA 2015. We use random sampling to tune the hyperparameters. The best settings are shown in Table 1. We implement our neural systems by using Tensorflow (Abadi et al., 2015).

2.2 Slot 2: Opinion Target Expression

In Slot 2, we extract text spans corresponding to target entities. The procedure of our proposed method

Parameter	REST	LAPT
Dropout p_k	0.8	0.3
Learning rate	0.945	0.374
hidden unit size	128	64
minibatch size	20	20
max epochs	100	840
cell	LSTM	GRU
max token num	40	50
threshold	0.048	0.11

Table 1: Hyperparameter setting for Slot 1. p_k denotes a ratio to keep values in a Dropout layer.

is as follows:

1. Creating dictionaries of food names and drink names by extracting targets in a training dataset,
2. Collecting food names and drink names in Knowledge Base and adding them to dictionaries,
3. Applying dictionary matching to sentences in a test dataset,
4. Extracting restaurant names by using syntactic rules, and
5. Checking relationship between targets extracted by step 3 and step 4 and attribute expressions.

Three key features of our method are the dictionary creation in step 2, the syntactic rules in step 4, and the estimation of the entity-attribute relationship in step 5.

Dictionary Creation

Coverage of dictionaries is crucial to improve recall metrics. In the training dataset, we observe various instances of FOOD entities such as bread, focaccia and gazpacho. Therefore, we try to import world knowledge written in Knowledge Base. We use DBpedia [2] as Knowledge Base to expand the dictionaries. We write a SPARQL query to retrieve labels (rdfs:label) of entities as dictionary entries. First we prepare a list of target types. For examples, we use http://dbpedia.org/ontology/Food and http://dbpedia.org/ontology/Fish as types of FOOD entities. We also prepare a list of types to be ignored such as "dbo:Beverage". Names of DRINK are also retrieved in the same manner as FOOD.

[2]http://wiki.dbpedia.org/

Domain	Team	Precision	Recall	F1
REST	bunji	48.86	78.20	60.14
	baseline	54.19	67.03	59.93
	Ranked 1st	72.45	73.62	73.03
LAPT	bunji	44.09	35.92	39.59
	baseline	45.92	31.66	37.48
	Ranked 1st	56.85	47.81	51.94

Table 2: Official results of Subtask 1 Slot 1

Domain	Team	Precision	Recall	F1
REST	bunji	62.61	67.32	64.88
	baseline	51.42	38.56	44.07
	Ranked 1st	75.49	69.44	72.34

Table 3: Official results of Subtask 1 Slot 2

Restaurant Name Extraction

We use syntactic rules to extract restaurant names. We define a set of verb-centric rules such as "A1 visited A2" where A1 is a subject, and A2 is an object. A2 is likely to be restaurant names. We manually create 15 rules from training data.

Entity-Attribute Relationship Estimation

We observe entities not related to sentimental expressions in dictionary-match results, which decrease precision scores. Therefore, we filter entities related to sentiment expressions. We use the same method as that in Slot 3.

2.3 Results

Table 2 shows the results of Slot 1. Our system marked the highest recall score among all of the teams in the restaurant domain, while our precision score is lower than that of the baseline system. This is partly because of the determination of threshold values that may be overfitted to the development sets. One possible solution is to use cross validation to estimate more reliable threshold values.

Table 3 shows the results of Slot 2. We can observe improvement of both the precision score and the recall score from those of the baseline system. The recall score is comparable to that of the ranked 1st team, while there is much room for improvement of the precision scores.

Table 4 shows the results of Slot 1 & 2. We can observe the similar tendency to Slot 1's results because we simply merged the results of Slot 1 and Slot 2, and Slot 1 performs worse than Slot 2.

Domain	Team	Precision	Recall	F1
REST	bunji	35.41	49.01	41.11
	baseline	36.56	39.12	37.80
	Ranked 1st	52.95	52.27	52.61

Table 4: Official results of Subtask 1 Slot 1 & 2

Domain	Team	Precision	Recall	F1
REST	bunji	72.71	88.37	79.78
	baseline	90.65	69.55	78.71
	Ranked 1st	87.00	81.19	83.99
LAPT	bunji	66.84	46.32	54.72
	baseline	86.55	37.86	52.68
	Ranked 1st	72.49	51.83	60.45

Table 5: Official results of Subtask 2 Slot 1

Table 5 shows the results of Slot 1 of Subtask 2. We merge the sentence-wise results into document-wise results.

3 System Description of Phase B

3.1 Slot 3: Sentiment Polarity

Neural Approach

Our method is inspired by a Deep Learning method proposed by Wang and Liu (Wang and Liu, 2015). They used estimated probabilities of Slot 1 as weights of a target entity-attribute pair, and then they inputted weighted tokens to a convolutional neural network. Instead of probabilities of Slot 1, we directly calculate entity attention and attribute attention at each token by using a neural attention model (Luong et al., 2015). The model is illustrated in Figure 2. We calculate a vector $\mathbf{y}_p$ that represents probabilities of polarities (positive, negative,

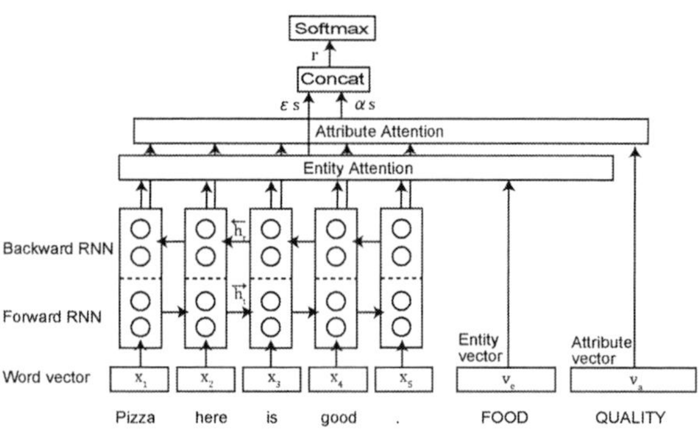

Figure 2: Structure of a neural network for Slot 3.

and neutral) as:

$$\mathbf{y}_p = f(X, \mathbf{v}_e, \mathbf{v}_a), \tag{5}$$

where $\mathbf{v}_e$ and $\mathbf{v}_a$ denote vectors corresponding to a target entity and a target attribute. At first we calculate RNN outputs $\mathbf{s}_t$ with Eq. 2 similarly to Slot 1. Then, attention weights for both entity and attribute are computed at attention layers. An entity-attention layer calculates weights ε_t at position t. At each position, e_t is computed to measure the relationship between $\mathbf{s}_t$ and $\mathbf{v}_e$:

$$e_t = \mathbf{v}_e^{\mathrm{T}} W_e \mathbf{s}_t. \tag{6}$$

Then, we transform the scale of e_t and obtain an entity-attention weight ε_t as:

$$\varepsilon_t = \frac{\exp(e_t)}{\sum_j \exp(e_j)}. \tag{7}$$

Similarly, the attribute attention layer has weights α_t at position t as follows:

$$a_t = \mathbf{v}_a^{\mathrm{T}} W_a \mathbf{s}_t, \tag{8}$$

$$\alpha_t = \frac{\exp(a_t)}{\sum_j \exp(a_j)}. \tag{9}$$

Then, we calculate a sentence vector $\mathbf{r}$ that is a weighted sum of RNN output with entity attention weights and attribute attention weights as:

$$\mathbf{r} = \sum_t (\alpha_t \mathbf{s}_t \| \varepsilon_t \mathbf{s}_t), \tag{10}$$

where $\|$ denotes a concatenation operator that creates a vector in $\mathbb{R}^{2d}$ from two vectors in $\mathbb{R}^d$.

Finally, we calculate $\mathbf{y}_p$ by using a single layered perceptron:

$$\mathbf{y}_p = \mathrm{softmax}(\tanh(W_p \mathbf{r} + \mathbf{b}_p)). \tag{11}$$

We train the Slot 3 model by using backpropagation. We use a minibatch stochastic gradient descent (SGD) algorithm together with the ADAM optimizer (Kingma and Ba, 2015). Hyperparameters are tuned similarly to Slot 1. The hyperparameter settings in Slot 3 are shown in Table 6. We add Dropout (Srivastava et al., 2014) layers to the input and output of the RNN. We also apply L2-regularization to two attention layers and a softmax

Parameter	REST (U)	REST (C)	LAPT (C)
Dropout p_k	0.9	0.9	0.9
Learning rate	1.7×10^{-3}	1.4×10^{-3}	5.8×10^{-4}
RNN state size	64	128	64
minibatch size	16	32	16
max epochs	12	19	6
L2 coef	1.9×10^{-4}	1.9×10^{-4}	3.3×10^{-4}

Table 6: Hyperparameter setting for Slot 3. p_k denotes a ratio to keep values in a Dropout layer.

Domain	Team	C/U	Accuracy
REST	bunji(neural)	U	81.02
	bunji(neural)	C	76.25
	baseline	C	76.48
	Ranked 1st	U	88.13
LAPT	bunji(rel)	U	70.16
	bunji(neural)	C	70.29
	baseline	C	70.04
	Ranked 1st	U	82.77

Table 7: Official results of Subtask 1 Slot 3. (neural) and (rel) denote the neural approach and the relation-feature approach, respectively.

layer. The attention unit size is 300. In an unconstrained setting, we use the same word embedding that has 300 dimensional vectors as Slot 1. In a constrained setting, we use 128-dimensional vectors that are initialized by uniform distribution. We clip the gradient norm when it exceeds 5.0 to improve stability of training. We set the maximum token length as 40. Initial values of entity vectors are created by averaging word vectors in sentences that have target entities. Attribute vectors are also initialized in the same manner as the entity vectors.

Relation-Features Approach

This approach trains a linear classifier using relations of a given entity and a given attribute as features. In the first step, we annotate the following 11 annotations of relations to all documents:

believe Showing someone's belief such as "X likes Y" and "X avoids Y",

significant Showing X's significance such as "X is impressive" and "X is terrible",

require Showing requirement such as "X needs Y",

equivalent Showing X is equivalent to Y, such as "X viewed Y" and "X regarded Y",

include Showing inclusion or possession such as "X has Y" and "X equips Y".

contrast Comparing X with Y such as "Y is ... than X" and "Y is ... compared to X",

affect Showing X affects Y such as "X increases Y" and "X causes Y",

state Showing statement such as "X doubts that Y",

negation Showing negations such as "not X" and "no X",

shift Reversing X's polarity such as "X ban" and "X shortage", and

absolutize Fixing polarity of X such as "X problem" and "X risk".

These annotations were originally developed for an argument-generation system (Sato et al., 2015).

In the second step, we identify an entity expression and an attribute expression that correspond to a given entity-attribute pair. We use a simple dictionary-matching approach. In the restaurant domain, we use a given target annotation as an entity expression. In the laptop domain, we prepare a list of entities extracted from a training dataset. For both domains, we create an attribute dictionary. Entries of the dictionary are manually extracted from training datasets. Then, we assign a sentimental polarity (positive, negative, or neutral) to each entry.

In the third step, we create features for a linear classifier. Those features are generated by combining annotations to capture various relations of a target entity-attribute pair. For example, we examine whether an affect annotation is negated or not and whether a target entity is a subject of an affect annotation or an object.

Finally, we classify a sentimental polarity by using a linear classifier. We use a linear SVM in scikit-learn (Pedregosa et al., 2011) as an implementation of the classifier, on the parameter C = 0.1, loss = squared_epsilon_insensitive, and penalty = l2.

3.2 Results

Table 7 shows the results for Slot 3. We select a suitable method from the neural method and the rule-based method for each domain by comparing scores in the ABSA15 dataset. In the restaurant domain, we can observe that the proposed method improves the accuracy by 10 percentage points compared with the baseline system.

We merged sentence-wise estimation and created document-wise estimation. We gathered polarities of an entity-attribute pair. If a result was both positive and negative, then we judged it as conflicting. Table 8 shows the results for Subtask 2. We can see

Domain	Team	C/U	Accuracy
REST	bunji(neural)	U	70.54
	bunji(neural)	C	66.58
	baseline	C	74.26
	Ranked 1st	U	81.93
LAPT	bunji(rel)	U	60.00
	bunji(neural)	C	62.20
	baseline	C	73.03
	Ranked 1st	U	75.05

Table 8: Official results of Subtask 2 Slot 3. (neural) and (rel) denote the neural approach and the relation-feature approach, respectively.

a similar tendency to the results in Subtask 1.

4 Conclusions

In this paper, we described the participation of the bunji team in SemEval-2016. We used both a neural approach and a rule-based approach to model an entity-attribute relationship. We confirmed the effectiveness of the proposed methods in a target estimation task and a polarity estimation task in the restaurant domain, while our overall ranks were modest.

As a future work, we plan to investigate network structures that are simple enough to be trained with a relatively small dataset. For the rule-based system, we plan to add more rules to improve precision scores.

References

Martín Abadi, Ashish Agarwal, Paul Barham, Eugene Brevdo, Zhifeng Chen, Craig Citro, Greg S. Corrado, Andy Davis, Jeffrey Dean, Matthieu Devin, Sanjay Ghemawat, Ian Goodfellow, Andrew Harp, Geoffrey Irving, Michael Isard, Yangqing Jia, Rafal Jozefowicz, Lukasz Kaiser, Manjunath Kudlur, Josh Levenberg, Dan Mané, Rajat Monga, Sherry Moore, Derek Murray, Chris Olah, Mike Schuster, Jonathon Shlens, Benoit Steiner, Ilya Sutskever, Kunal Talwar, Paul Tucker, Vincent Vanhoucke, Vijay Vasudevan, Fernanda Viégas, Oriol Vinyals, Pete Warden, Martin Wattenberg, Martin Wicke, Yuan Yu, and Xiaoqiang Zheng. 2015. TensorFlow: Large-scale machine learning on heterogeneous systems. Software available from tensorflow.org.

Kyunghyun Cho, Bart van Merrienboer, Caglar Gulcehre, Dzmitry Bahdanau, Fethi Bougares, Holger Schwenk, and Yoshua Bengio. 2014. Learning phrase representations using rnn encoder–decoder for statistical machine translation. In *Proceedings of the 2014 Conference on Empirical Methods in Natural Language Processing (EMNLP)*, pages 1724–1734.

John Duchi, Elad Hazan, and Yoram Singer. 2011. Adaptive subgradient methods for online learning and stochastic optimization. *J. Mach. Learn. Res.*, 12:2121–2159.

Diederik Kingma and Jimmy Ba. 2015. Adam: A method for stochastic optimization. *The International Conference on Learning Representations (ICLR)*.

Thang Luong, Hieu Pham, and Christopher D. Manning. 2015. Effective approaches to attention-based neural machine translation. In *Proceedings of the 2015 Conference on Empirical Methods in Natural Language Processing*, pages 1412–1421.

Christopher D. Manning, Mihai Surdeanu, John Bauer, Jenny Finkel, Steven J. Bethard, and David McClosky. 2014. The Stanford CoreNLP natural language processing toolkit. In *Proceedings of 52nd Annual Meeting of the Association for Computational Linguistics: System Demonstrations*, pages 55–60.

Tomas Mikolov, Kai Chen, Greg Corrado, and Jeffrey Dean. 2013. Efficient estimation of word representations in vector space. *Proceedings of Workshop at International Conference on Learning Representations*.

Fabian Pedregosa, Gaël Varoquaux, Alexandre Gramfort, Vincent Michel, Bertrand Thirion, Olivier Grisel, Mathieu Blondel, Peter Prettenhofer, Ron Weiss, Vincent Dubourg, Jake Vanderplas, Alexandre Passos, David Cournapeau, Matthieu Brucher, Matthieu Perrot, and Édouard Duchesnay. 2011. Scikit-learn: Machine learning in Python. *Journal of Machine Learning Research*, 12:2825–2830.

Maria Pontiki, Dimitris Galanis, John Pavlopoulos, Harris Papageorgiou, Ion Androutsopoulos, and Suresh Manandhar. 2014. Semeval-2014 task 4: Aspect based sentiment analysis. In *Proceedings of the 8th International Workshop on Semantic Evaluation (SemEval 2014)*, pages 27–35.

Maria Pontiki, Dimitris Galanis, Haris Papageorgiou, Suresh Manandhar, and Ion Androutsopoulos. 2015. Semeval-2015 task 12: Aspect based sentiment analysis. In *Proceedings of the 9th International Workshop on Semantic Evaluation (SemEval 2015)*, pages 486–495.

Maria Pontiki, Dimitrios Galanis, Haris Papageorgiou, Ion Androutsopoulos, Suresh Manandhar, Mohammad AL-Smadi, Mahmoud Al-Ayyoub, Yanyan Zhao, Bing Qin, Orphée De Clercq, Véronique Hoste, Marianna Apidianaki, Xavier Tannier, Natalia Loukachevitch, Evgeny Kotelnikov, Nuria Bel, Salud María Jiménez-Zafra, and Gülşen Eryiğit. 2016. SemEval-2016 task

5: Aspect based sentiment analysis. In *Proceedings of the 10th International Workshop on Semantic Evaluation*, SemEval '16.

Hasim Sak, Andrew W. Senior, and Françoise Beaufays. 2014. Long short-term memory based recurrent neural network architectures for large vocabulary speech recognition. *INTERSPEECH*, abs/1402.1128:338–342.

Misa Sato, Kohsuke Yanai, Toshinori Miyoshi, Toshihiko Yanase, Makoto Iwayama, Qinghua Sun, and Yoshiki Niwa. 2015. End-to-end argument generation system in debating. In *Proceedings of ACL-IJCNLP 2015 System Demonstrations*, pages 109–114.

Mike Schuster and Kuldip K. Paliwal. 1997. Bidirectional recurrent neural networks. *IEEE TRANSACTIONS ON SIGNAL PROCESSING*, 45(11):2673–2681.

Nitish Srivastava, Geoffrey Hinton, Alex Krizhevsky, Ilya Sutskever, and Ruslan Salakhutdinov. 2014. Dropout: A simple way to prevent neural networks from overfitting. *Journal of Machine Learning Research*, 15:1929–1958.

Bo Wang and Min Liu. 2015. Deep learning for aspect-based sentiment analysis. *Reports for CS224d, Stanford University*.

IHS-RD-Belarus at SemEval-2016 Task 5:
Detecting Sentiment Polarity Using the Heatmap of Sentence

Maryna Chernyshevich
IHS Inc. / IHS Global Belarus
131 Starovilenskaya St
220123, Minsk, Belarus
{Marina.Chernyshevich}@ihs.com

Abstract

This paper describes the system submitted by IHS-RD-Belarus team for the sentiment detection polarity subtask on Aspect Based Sentiment Analysis task at the SemEval 2016 workshop on semantic evaluation. We developed a system based on artificial neural network to detect the sentiment polarity of opinions. Evaluation on the test data set showed that our system achieved the F-score of 0.83 for restaurants domain (rank 4 out of 28 submissions) and F-score of 0.78 for laptops domain (rank 4 out of 21 submissions).

1 Introduction

Social media texts found in user review services have a great data-mining potential, as they offer real-time data that can be useful to monitor public opinion on brands, products, events, etc.

Most of recent approaches to sentiment analysis task are based on bag-of-words features, syntactic dependency features, out-of-domain and domain-specific sentiment lexicons, to train an supervised model that predicts the polarity of each given term or aspect category. This approach is very popular but it relies on heavy pre-processing of the data which involves careful choosing of the right features, empirical thresholds and intuitive analysis of the training set (Brun et al., 2014, Saias, 2015).

In this paper, we present an approach to the opinion polarity detection task based on an artificial neural network and sentiment orientation score of words.

2 Task description

The SemEval-2016 shared task on Aspect based Sentiment Analysis focuses on identifying the Opinion target expressions (OTE), the Aspect categories and the sentiment expressed towards each OTE or Aspect category.

The main focus of this paper is polarity subtasks, such as OTE polarity in restaurant subject domain and Aspect category polarity in laptop subject domain.

In the OTE polarity subtask, the input consists of a review sentence and the set of terms or aspect categories. The expected output is a polarity label (positive, negative or neutral) for each of the associated terms or aspect categories.

For example, the system should determine the polarity of *fajitas* and s*alads* in the following sentence: *I hated their fajitas, but their salads were great.*

As for the Aspect category polarity, the task is more complicated. In the following sentence, the system has to determine the polarity of display quality (DISPLAY#QUALITY) and display usability (DISPLAY#USABILITY): *The display has a great resolution but has difficulty always seeing the small print.*

The task organizers provided a dataset of customer reviews with manually annotated opinion targets: 2500 sentences for laptop domain and 2000 sentences for restaurant domain.

Evaluation was to be carried out according to Precision, Recall and F1 metrics.

Proceedings of SemEval-2016, pages 296–300,
San Diego, California, June 16-17, 2016. ©2016 Association for Computational Linguistics

3 System description

The central idea behind our system is the visualization of sentiment orientation in a word sequence using heatmap, that highlights regions with higher or lower "temperature". The "temperature" of a word is its sentiment polarity, positive or negative, and the intensity is calculated based on sentiment orientation score of word.

3.1 Sentiment orientation lexicon

Sentiment orientation score indicates the strength of association of words (w) with positive (pr) and negative (nr) reviews. Following Turney and Littman (2003), we calculated SO as the difference using Pointwise Mutual Information (PMI) measures:

$$SO(w) = PMI(w, pr) - PMI(w, nr)$$

SO score is positive when the word or phrase tends to occur mostly in positive reviews and negative when the word occurs more often in negative reviews. The magnitude indicates the degree of association.

We followed the lexicon-generation approach proposed by Kiritchenko et al. (Kiritchenko et al., 2014) and when generating the sentiment lexicons we distinguished the terms appearing in negated and affirmative contexts. Sentiment scores were then calculated separately for these two types of contexts.

We created uni-, bi- and tri-gram lexicons based on Yelp restaurant reviews and Amazon reviews.

3.2 Sentiment orientation score

The final SO score of n-gram in a sentence can be affected by some neighbour terms, such as valence shifters and intensifiers (Kennedy and Inkpen, 2006). We created short wordlists and tuned final SO score of n-gram if words from these lists were found in term context.

3.2.1 Valence shifters

Valence shifters are terms that can change the semantic orientation of another term, for example, combining positively valenced words with a nega-

tion flips the positive orientation to a negative orientation. The most important shifters are negations such as *not, never, none, nobody*, etc. (Polanyi and Zaenen, 2004).

As it was mentioned above we included negations, such as *not* and *never*, as n-gram postfix into lexicons. If the n-gram in negative context is not found in lexicon or its raw frequency in review corpus is less than 5, the final SO score is calculated based on calculation rules showed in table 1.

These negation rules are designed in order to improve the sentiment text analysis and are based on simple assumption: the negation flips positive the valence of a word to a negative with the same strength, but the negation doesn't flip the valence of a negative word, it rather reduces its strength.

SO of word	calculation rule	Example
positive SO	SO=pos_SO * -1	SO(love) = +2.6 SO(not love) = -2.6
negative SO	SO=neg_SO * 0.5	SO(hate) = -2.2 SO(not hate) = -1.1

Table 1: SO calculation rules in negative context.

3.2.2 Intensifiers

Intensifiers are terms that change the degree of the expressed sentiment. For example, in the sentence *"The waterfly cases are very good."*, the term *very good* is more positive together than just *good* alone. So to calculate the final SO score we multiply sentiment score of n-gram by 3.

On another side, in the sentence *"The waterfly cases are barely good."*, the term *barely* makes this statement less positive. We created 4 lists of intensifiers of different intensity of affecting the final SO score of n-gram.

3.2.3 Unreality and conditionality

A sentence in reviews can express not only a real user experience, but also an unreal opinion, for example a wish, *"I should have bought something better."* or *"The laptop may be better"*. We collected all surface patterns which can express unreality or conditionality. The SO of all positive n-grams in unreal context is flipped to negative with the same strength. The SO of negative n-grams is not changed.

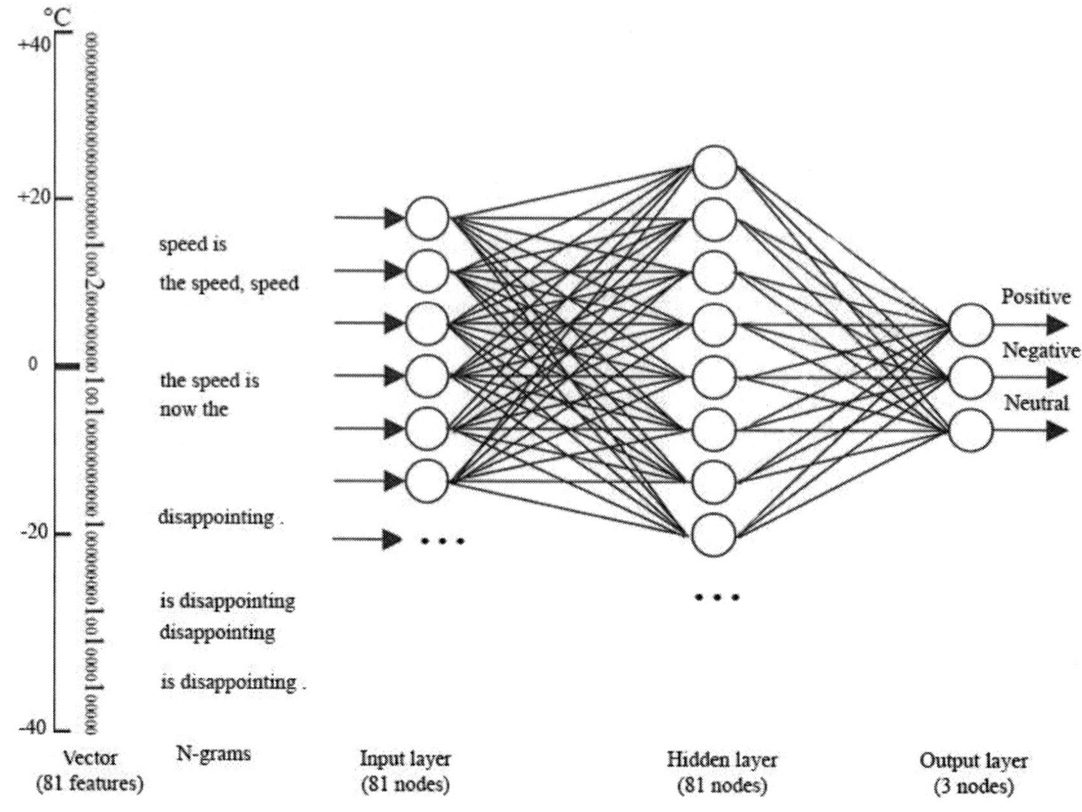

Fig. 1: System architecture

3.3 Neural network architecture

A fully connected multilayer neural network with back-propagation is applied. The network, illustrated in Fig. 1, contains 3 layers:

- input with 81 nodes - one for each feature presenting "temperature" range;
- hidden layer with 80 nodes - each node in the input layer is connected to each node of the hidden layer;
- output layer with 3 nodes - one for each of 3 classes.

As the activation function the sigmoid function is used. We apply dropout to our hidden layers, as described in Srivastava et al. (Srivastava et al., 2014), to prevent network overfitting.

The network architecture is implemented on Keras[1], which is an effective deep learning framework implementation in python.

---

[1] http://keras.io/

At the first step, we detect the context of opinion target expressions or category. If the sentence has only one opinion target, the term context will include all words from the beginning to the end of the sentence. If the sentence has many targets, the context will include all words surrounding the term enclosed between two separators. As a separator we consider all punctuation marks, the next opinion target, the end and the beginning of the sentence. In the laptops subtask we had to detect polarity of the category that is not bounded to any word in the sentence. That is why we considered the whole sentence as context for every aspect category.

For training, each term context was represented as a vector of 81 features that resembles the scale of "temperature" from -40 (very negative) to 40 (very positive). Each word according to its SO score was placed on this scale. The value of a feature means the number of words within this range of sentiment orientation.

Table 2 illustrates a set of n-grams with their final SO scores and "temperature" extracted from the sentence *"Now the speed is disappointing"*.

	n-gram	SO score	°C
Uni-grams	disappointing	-3.0	-30
	speed	+1.0	+10
Bi-grams	is disappointing	-2.7	-27
	disappointing .	-1.7	-17
	now the	-0.4	-4
	the speed	+1.0	+10
	speed is	+1.4	+14
Tri-grams	is disappointing .	-3.5	-35
	the speed is	-0.1	-1

Table 2: SO scores of n-grams

The number of training epochs is set to 2. More epochs would lead to overfitting because the training set that is relatively small.

4 Results and further work

The 3-fold cross-validation procedure was used to test the system performance. It uses 66% of the data to train and the remaining 33% to assess the accuracy. This is repeated 3 times with a different 33% left. Table 3 represents the results.

	restaurants	laptops
total accuracy	**0.82838934**	**0.8030438**
F1 positive	0.882567	0.8479
F1 negative	0.762167	0.796867
F1 neutral	0.0	0.0

Table 3: 3-fold cross-validation results

The results on the official test set are given in Table 4. They are similar to our best results attained during the developments stage.

	restaurants	laptops
total accuracy	**0.8393481**	**0.7790262**
F1 positive	0.9078	0.8308
F1 negative	0.753	0.7588
F1 neutral	0.0	0.0

Table 4: Official results

On both sets our system did not recognize neutral (mildly positive or mildly negative sentiment) sentiments, although we used 3 classes classification. The reason is the low number of neutral sentiments in the annotated corpus.

As a future work, we intend to develop more complex artificial neural network architecture and try to use review-long memory about the polarity of previous targets. Also we are going to investigate the influence of words with extremely high or low sentiment orientation score on the SO scores of neighbouring words.

5 Conclusion

We have presented a simple neural network architecture that predicts polarity of word sequence based the heatmap of sentence that highlights regions with higher or lower sentiment intensity. We submitted runs corresponding to the slot3 subtasks, obtaining competitive results. Our submission was ranked 4th out of 28 submissions for restaurants domain and 4th out of 21 submissions for laptops domain.

References

Alfred. V. Aho and Jeffrey D. Ullman. 1972. *The Theory of Parsing, Translation and Compiling, volume 1.* Prentice-Hall, Englewood Cliffs, NJ.

Caroline Brun, Diana Nicoleta Popa, Claude Roux. 2014. *XRCE: Hybrid Classification for Aspect-based Sentiment Analysis.* in Proceedings of the eight international workshop on Semantic Evaluation Exercises (SemEval-2014), August 2014, Dublin, Ireland.

Kennedy, A. and D. Inkpen. 2006. *Sentiment Classification of Movie Reviews using Contextual Valence Shifters.* Computational Intelligence, vol.22(2), pp.110-125, 2006.

José Saias. 2015. *Sentiue: Target and Aspect based Sentiment Analysis in SemEval-2015 Task 12.* In Proceedings of the 9th International Workshop on Semantic Evaluation (SemEval 2015), Denver, Colorado.

Livia Polanyi and Annie Zaenen. *Contextual valence shifters.* In Proceedings of the AAAI Symposium on Exploring Attitude and Affect in Text: Theories and Applications (published as AAAI technical report SS-04-07), 2004.

Maria Pontiki, Dimitrios Galanis, Haris Papageorgiou, Ion Androutsopoulos, Suresh Manandhar, Mohammad AL-Smadi, Mahmoud Al-Ayyoub, Yanyan Zhao, Bing Qin, Orphée De Clercq, Véronique Hoste, Marianna Apidianaki, Xavier Tannier, Natalia Loukachevitch, Evgeny Kotelnikov, Nuria Bel, Salud María Jiménez Zafra, and Gülşen Eryiğit. 2016. *SemEval-2016 Task 5: Aspect Based Sentiment Analysis.* In Proceedings of the 10th International Workshop on Semantic Evaluation, SemEval '16, San Diego, California, June 2016. Association for Computational Linguistics.

Svetlana Kiritchenko, Xiaodan Zhu, Colin Cherry, and Saif M. Mohammad. 2014. *NRC-Canada-2014: De-*

tecting Aspects and Sentiment in Customer Reviews. in Proceedings of the eight international workshop on Semantic Evaluation Exercises (SemEval-2014), August 2014, Dublin, Ireland.

Srivastava. N, Hinton, G, Krizhevsky, A, Sutskever, I, Salakhutdinov, R. *Dropout: A Simple Way to Prevent Neural Networks from Overfitting.* Journal of Machine Learning Research 15, 2014

BUTknot at SemEval-2016 Task 5: Supervised Machine Learning with Term Substitution Approach in Aspect Category Detection

Jakub Macháček

Brno University of Technology,
Faculty of Information Technology,
IT4Innovations Centre of Excellence
Božetěchova 2, 612 66 Brno, Czech Republic
`qmachacek@stud.fit.vutbr.cz`

Abstract

This paper describes an approach used to solve *Aspect Category Detection* (Subtask 1, Slot 1) of *SemEval 2016* Task 5. The core of the presented system is based on *Supervised machine learning* using bigram *bag-of-words* model. The performance is enhanced by several pre-processing methods, most importantly by a term substitution technique. The system has reached a very good performance in comparison with other submitted systems.

1 Introduction

As the Internet more and more becomes the means of expressing opinions about various subjects, the need to effectively process those opinions (subjective information) is becoming more and more important. Many companies around the world are now interested in gathering public opinion and performing strategic moves accordingly. Thus, *Sentiment Analysis* (also known as *Opinion mining*) has become an important area of interest.

Existing systems performing sentiment analysis usually only predict polarity of a given sentiment. While this can be sufficient in a lot of cases, sometimes we wish to analyze opinions about different aspects of the same entity. This task is known as *Aspect-based Sentiment Analysis*.

SemEval 2016 Task 5 (Pontiki et al., 2016) consists of three subtasks. The first subtask is about sentence-level sentiment analysis and is divided into three slots: *Aspect Category Detection*, *Opinion Target Expression* and *Sentiment Polarity Detection*.

There are multiple distinct domains in which participants were given the opportunity to test their systems. Each domain was available for one of the following languages: Arabic, Chinese, Dutch, English, French, Russian, Spanish and Turkish.

For all domains, there is a limited, known in advance, list of entities and aspects the system should recognize. Each entity can be associated with only certain aspect(s). The set of all possible entity-aspect pairs is also limited and known in advance.

Each submitted system could run in two modes: *Constrained* (using no external data sources like lexicons or additional training sets) and *Unconstrained* (no data source restriction).

The system I propose is focused on *Aspect Category Detection* only, i.e. it only predicts which aspects of a given entity a given sentiment has opinions about. I decided to participate in the English language, for which two domains were available: restaurant and laptop reviews. There were 12 entity-aspect pairs for the restaurants domain and over 80 for the laptops domain.

2 Approach

My approach was inspired by the NLANGP system (Toh and Su, 2015) which achieved excellent results in *SemEval 2015* (Pontiki et al., 2015) with a straightforward solution.

I model the task as a *multi-label* classification with *binary relevance* transformation, where labels correspond to the entity-aspect pairs. All train and test sentences are pre-processed (see Section 2.2). Words from each sentence are used as individual binary features of that sentence. For each entity-aspect

301

Proceedings of SemEval-2016, pages 301–305,
San Diego, California, June 16-17, 2016. ©2016 Association for Computational Linguistics

pair, all training sentences are used as positive or negative examples of that entity-aspect pair.

Vowpal Wabbit[1], a supervised machine learning tool, is used to train the resulting binary classifiers. More precisely, a variant of *online gradient descent* algorithm is used to perform *logistic regression* with *squared cost function*.

2.1 Model properties

It has been observed that the model offers higher accuracy if bigrams are allowed in VW. However, additional raising the n of VW's n-gram feature is counterproductive. Allowing skips inside bigrams also does not help. For the RESTAU-RANT#MISCELLANEOUS aspect category, however, setting $n = 5$ seemed to be a better choice. The system has generally unsatisfying score of predicting aspect categories associated with the MIS-CELLANEOUS attribute. Setting $n > 2$ did not improve the accuracy for any other aspect category.

I have also tuned VW's *learning rate* and a threshold T for comparing probabilities returned from VW's classifiers. When it predicts that a sentiment has opinion(s) about an aspect category C with the probability of P, the system drops the prediction iff $P < T$. Table 1 shows the tuned properties.

Domain	Restaurants	Laptops
Learning rate	0.41	0.38
Prediction threshold T	0.40	0.34

Table 1: Tuned learning rate and the prediction threshold

2.2 Text pre-processing

The initial text pre-processing step consists of removing the punctuation from each sentence and converting all characters to lower case. *Stanford CoreNLP*[2] is used to tokenize each sentence, *lemmatize* all words and also extract their *part of speech* (*POS*).

2.2.1 Filtering words

The POS tags are useful to estimate how much important given words are in terms of aspect category detection. The system does not introduce the tags to the machine learning algorithm, but it uses each tag to consider removing the corresponding

---

[1]https://github.com/JohnLangford/vowpal_wabbit/wiki
[2]Homepage: http://stanfordnlp.github.io/CoreNLP/

Food	Service	Opinion	Laptop
pizza	staff	good	computer
sauce	clerk	average	machine
entree	she	terrific	notebook
hot dog	friendly	disappointing	netbook
croquette	attentive	poor	desktop
...	...	...	...

Table 2: Example term lists compilation

word from its sentence. Also, some words are removed regardless of their POS.

An automated experiment over the oficial training set has been implemented to produce a POS filter and a list of stop words, for each domain separately. Both features are included in the constrained mode.

The experiment showed that for the restaurants domain, it was not demonstrably beneficial to remove any word based on its POS. On the other hand, it generated a list of tags for the laptops domain.

The lists of stop words that the experiment produced were surprisingly small. It seemed there were just few high frequency words which were irrelevant in the learning process.

2.2.2 Term groups

As a part of the pre-processing phase, a simple substitution system has been implemented to support machine learning. When multiple n-grams have roughly the same meaning, or they are related in a certain way, it is often beneficial if classifiers do not distinguish between them. A set of n-gram (term) lists in the fashion depicted in Table 2 has been manually compiled. Presence of the listed terms is then checked in each sentence and if found, each occurrence is replaced by its representative. Terms are always compared by their lemmas. The lists have been compiled by applying the following:

1. For each entity and attribute independently, only those sentences from the train dataset that contain the entity or attribute were selected. Then all unigrams from the sentences were sorted by number of occurrences. The most frequent words were manually checked, one by one, and the ones closely related to a particular entity or attribute were added to the respective lists.

2. In case of the restaurants domain, opinion targets from the train datasets were also extracted. This resulted in much shorter lists of high precision terms. All terms could be therefore individually checked in a reasonable time. Again, terms closely related to an entity or attribute were added to the respective lists. Some *n*-grams were split into multiple pieces, e.g. *lava cake dessert* → {*lava cake, dessert*}.

3. While performing the preceding two methods, I also noticed that some terms played a certain role in aspect category detection even if they were not associated with just a single entity or attribute but rather a set of them. This, for example, included opinion words (indicating attributes GENERAL and QUALITY) and words describing problems (e.g. *fail, problematic, blue screen* – indicating attributes OPERATION_PERFORMANCE, QUALITY and possibly some other).

The following methods for extending the lists were also used but they are not applied in the constrained mode:

4. For some specific words (e.g. adjectives expressing food taste), an online dictionary[3] has been used to search for their synonyms and the term lists have been manually appended with suitable words.

5. Several lists of words publicly available on the Internet have also been included:

- Food: http://eatingatoz.com/food-list/ and https://www.atkins.com/how-it-works/atkins-20/phase-1/low-carb-foods; both lists have been manually checked and some misleading items removed (mostly words related to drinks)
- Drinks: http://cocktails.lovetoknow.com/ List_of_Popular_Cocktails and others compiled manually
- Laptop manufacturers: https://en.wikipedia.org/wiki/List_of_laptop _brands_and_manufacturers#Major_brands

---

- Laptop series: manually extracted names of laptop series available at https://en.wikipedia.org/wiki/Asus#Laptops, https://en.wikipedia.org/wiki/List_of_Hewlett-Packard_products#Business_notebooks and http://www.acer.com/ac/en/US/content/ models/laptops
- Processors: manually extracted names of CPU series from Wikipedia pages https://en.wikipedia.org/wiki/ List_of_AMD_microprocessors and https://en.wikipedia.org/wiki/List_of_Intel _microprocessors
- Operation systems: manually extracted names of mainstream Linux distributions from the list published at https://en.wikipedia.org/wiki/List_of_ Linux_distributions
- Screen resolution names: https://en.wikipedia.org/wiki/Display_ resolution#Common_display_resolutions

2.2.3 Other pre-processing steps

The system also tries to improve its accuracy by replacing all numbers by the word *number*. Numbers preceded by a currency symbol ($, €, £) are replaced with the word *price* (which then indicates the PRICES attribute).

Words containing both alpha and numeric characters are replaced with the word *model* as it was observed that in most cases, such words represent particular model names (e.g. *i7, G73JH-x3, d620*). This seemed to be helpful notably in the laptops domain.

The system removes all words shorter than two characters. It is important to note that this step comes after removing all non-alphanumeric characters. This means words like *w/* are eventually removed.

The system also neutralizes consecutive letters which effectively replaces words like *waay* or *waaaaaay* by the word *way*.

2.3 Prediction post-processing

The presence of previously detected opinion words indicates the QUALITY and GENERAL attributes. The corresponding aspect categories are correctly

Domain	Rest	Lapt
Basic text pre-processing	63.9	49.6
Bigrams	65.3	50.1
Minimal word length	65.7	50.7
Lemmatization	65.8	50.7
Consecutive letters neutralization	65.8	
Prices recognition	66.1	50.9
Numbers+models recognition	66.2	51.0
POS filter		52.4
Stop words	66.4	52.4
Prediction post-processing	68.0	
Term groups (constrained)	71.6	53.5
Term groups (unconstrained)	72.1	53.8

Table 3: The F-measure in percentage using 4-fold cross validation over the training sets. Each row represents the system's accuracy when the corresponding technique and all those from previous rows are enabled. The prediction threshold, as well as VW's learning rate, is always optimized. Missing values represent unused techniques.

Domain	Restaurants		Laptops	
Mode	C	U	C	U
1st place	**71.494**	73.031	47.891	51.937
2nd place	68.701	72.886	**47.527**	49.105
3rd place	67.817	**72.396**	46.728	49.076
4th place	67.350	71.537	45.629	**48.396**
5th place	65.563	**71.494**	43.754	47.891

Table 4: Rankings in ACD (slot 1) of the Subtask 1. The F-score of the submitted systems is represented in percentage. Results of my system are highlighted in bold-faced font. C stands for the constrained and U for the unconstrained mode.

predicted by VW only in cases in which the opinion words are directly preceded or followed by words indicating entities (i.e. they make up bigrams). When these words are separated by one or more other words, no aspect category is predicted. For this reason, the system always looks for an entity-related word which is closest to the opinion word and still not farther than four skips. If such word is found, the corresponding aspect category is additionally predicted. The same process is repeated with the PRICES attribute with the difference that when no suitable entity is found, RESTAURANT#PRICES is predicted. The system does no post-processing in the laptops domain.

3 Results

All techniques and features described in Section 2 have been tuned separately for each domain using *4-fold cross* validation. Table 3 displays the reached accuracy.

The tuned system has been trained using the official training sets containing 2000 and 2500 sentences in the restaurants and laptops domains respectively. The test sets consisted of 676 sentences in the restaurants domain and 808 sentences in the laptops domain.

The system achieved very good results, especially in the restaurants domain where it ranked *third* in the unconstrained mode, falling behind the winner only by 0.635%, and *first* in the constrained mode. Table 4 shows the F-score of the top five systems in each domain and mode. The best accuracy in the unconstrained mode has been reached in both domains by the NLANGP team which has ranked first also in SemEval 2015.

4 Conclusion

This paper described my approach to aspect category detection. The presented system has ranked as one of the most accurate in this task. As I have never contributed to the field of aspect-based sentiment analysis (and SA generally) before, I find my results more than satisfactory.

The system has an advantage of its relatively high adaptability to work with previously unseen domains. All techniques except the term groups and the prediction post-processing can be tuned automatically with no additional manual help needed. Multilinguality is limited by the used lemmatizer(s) but since lemmatization offers just a mild increase in accuracy, it is possible to omit it when working with unsupported languages.

The system does not take review context of input sentences into consideration. In my future work I would like to remove this flaw. The term groups described in Section 2.2.2 will be significantly improved by extending them and creating new groups for other important terms.

Acknowledgments

This work was supported by the H2020 project *MixedEmotions*, grant agreement No. 644632.

References

Everton Alvares Cherman, Maria Carolina Monard, and Jean Metz. 2011. Multi-label problem transformation methods: a case study. *CLEI Electronic Journal*, 14(1).

José Saias. 2015. Sentiue: Target and Aspect based Sentiment Analysis in SemEval-2015 Task 12. In *Proceedings of the 9th International Workshop on Semantic Evaluation (SemEval 2015)*, Denver, Colorado.

Satarupa Guha, Aditya Joshi, and Vasudeva Varma. 2015. SIEL: Aspect Based Sentiment Analysis in Reviews. In *Proceedings of the 9th International Workshop on Semantic Evaluation (SemEval 2015)*, Denver, Colorado.

Minqing Hu and Bing Liu. 2004. Mining and Summarizing Customer Reviews. In *Proceedings of the Tenth ACM SIGKDD International Conference on Knowledge Discovery and Data Mining*. Seattle, Washington, USA.

John Pavlopoulos. 2014. *Aspect based sentiment analysis*. PhD thesis, Dept. of Informatics, Athens University of Economics and Business, Greece.

Maria Pontiki, Dimitrios Galanis, Haris Papageorgiou, Suresh Manandhar, and Ion Androutsopoulos. 2015. SemEval-2015 Task 12: Aspect Based Sentiment Analysis. In *Proceedings of the 9th International Workshop on Semantic Evaluation (SemEval 2015)*, Denver, Colorado.

Maria Pontiki, Dimitrios Galanis, Haris Papageorgiou, Ion Androutsopoulos, Suresh Manandhar, Mohammad AL-Smadi, Mahmoud Al-Ayyoub, Yanyan Zhao, Bing Qin, Orphée De Clercq, Véronique Hoste, Marianna Apidianaki, Xavier Tannier, Natalia Loukachevitch, Evgeny Kotelnikov, Nuria Bel, Salud María Jiménez-Zafra, and Gülşen Eryiğit. 2016. SemEval-2016 task 5: Aspect based sentiment analysis. In *Proceedings of the 10th International Workshop on Semantic Evaluation*, SemEval '16, San Diego, California, June. Association for Computational Linguistics.

Hassan Saif, Miriam Fernandez, Yulan He, and Harith Alani. 2014. On Stopwords, Filtering and Data Sparsity for Sentiment Analysis of Twitter. *Ninth International Conference on Language Resources and Evaluation*, pages 810–817.

Zhiqiang Toh and Jian Su. 2015. NLANGP: Supervised Machine Learning System for Aspect Category Classification and Opinion Target Extraction. In *Proceedings of the 9th International Workshop on Semantic Evaluation (SemEval 2015)*, Denver, Colorado.

Bo Wang and Min Liu. 2015. Deep Learning for Aspect-Based Sentiment Analysis.

Lei Zhang and Bing Liu. 2014. Aspect and Entity Extraction for Opinion Mining. In *Data Mining and Knowledge Discovery for Big Data: Methodologies, Challenges, and Opportunities*. Springer.

GTI at SemEval-2016 Task 5: SVM and CRF for Aspect Detection and Unsupervised Aspect-Based Sentiment Analysis

Tamara Álvarez-López, Jonathan Juncal-Martínez, Milagros Fernández-Gavilanes
Enrique Costa-Montenegro, Francisco Javier González-Castaño
GTI Research Group
AtlantTIC Centre, School of Telecommunication Engineering, University of Vigo
36310 Vigo, Spain
`{talvarez, jonijm, milagros.fernandez, kike}@gti.uvigo.es,`
`javier@det.uvigo.es`

Abstract

This paper describes in detail the approach carried out by the GTI research group for SemEval 2016 Task 5: Aspect-Based Sentiment Analysis, for the different subtasks proposed, as well as languages and dataset contexts. In particular, we developed a system for category detection based on SVM. Then for the opinion target detection task we developed a system based on CRFs. Both are built for restaurants domain in English and Spanish languages. Finally for aspect-based sentiment analysis we carried out an unsupervised approach based on lexicons and syntactic dependencies, in English language for laptops and restaurants domains.

1 Introduction

In the last years, with the growth of Internet, people use it as a means of expressing their opinions and experiences about several subjects. That is the reason why there is a great amount of user generated information available online, through many different platforms, such as blogs, social networks, etc. This information became very valuable for companies, politicians, etc., who are interested in what users say about them or their products. Due to this, Sentiment Analysis (SA) techniques have attracted the interest of researches, trying to process all this amount of information by means of usually supervised methods based on classifiers.

Most of these researches focus on extracting the sentiment of a whole review or text (Liu, 2012). This is enough for many applications and purposes. However, sometimes there is a need for analysing the text in a deeper way, at entity or aspect level. For example, a review in the restaurants domain can include different opinions about different aspects, such as the service or the food quality, so it is interesting to distinguish the different opinions for each of these aspects. This is the reason why some studies emerged about the so-called aspect-based sentiment analysis (Marcheggiani et al., 2014; Lu et al., 2011).

Hence this is the subject of the task 5 of the SemEval 2016 (Pontiki et al., 2016), divided into different subtasks. Groups are asked to detect aspect categories in a review or sentence, which are predefined for each domain and formed by an entity and an attribute. Then, there is a subtask which consists of detecting the opinion target expression, which are related to the categories found. Finally, aspect-based sentiment analysis is required for one of the subtasks, associating a polarity, which can be positive, negative or neutral, to each of the categories found in the sentence or review. Datasets in different languages and domains are available for proving the approaches.

The remainder of this paper is structured as follows. In Section 2 we make a description of the system developed for all the subtasks. Section 3 contains the results of all the different subtasks, as well as detailed scores for each slot. Finally, in section 4 we summarize the main aspects of our system and extract some final conclusions.

2 System Overview

In this section we make a brief description of the system submitted for the different subtasks. We presented our submission for English restaurants

Proceedings of SemEval-2016, pages 306–311,
San Diego, California, June 16-17, 2016. ©2016 Association for Computational Linguistics

dataset for subtask 1, slots 1, 2 and 3, and subtask 2, slots 1 and 3. For English laptops dataset we sent a submission for subtasks 1 and 2 only in slot 3. Then, the system was also developed for Spanish language and restaurants dataset in subtasks 1, slots 1 and 2 and subtask 2, slot 1. In the next subsections we describe the different stages carried out for obtaining all the different results.

2.1 Preprocessing

As a first step for all the subtasks, each preprocessed social media review must first be broken into tokens, in order to derive the syntactic context. Part-of-speech (POS) tagging and lemmatization are performed to ensure that all the inflected forms of a word are covered. In the case of English, Stanford Tagger is applied due to its better results, however it does not provide lemmatization. That is why using the resulting form and tag, lemma is extracted by means of Freeling Tagger (Atserias et al., 2006; Padró and Stanilovsky, 2012). On the other hand, for Spanish language only Freeling Tagger is used. Freeling is a library that provides multiple languages among which are English and Spanish. Food and drinks recognition is also performed, based on dictionaries [1], in order to identify words referring to those topics for the subsequent processing of the sentences.

POS tagging allows the identification of lexical items that can contribute to the correct recognition of targets in a message. These items are namely adjectives, adverbs, verbs and nouns. The lemmatized and POS-annotated messages are fed to a parser that transforms the output of the tagger into a full parse tree. Finally, the tree is converted to dependencies, and the functions are annotated. The entire process is performed by means of Freeling Parser (Padró and Stanilovsky, 2012).

2.2 Subtask 1: Sentence-level Aspect-Based Sentiment Analysis (ABSA)

This subtask contains different slots, having participated in three of them, which are slot 1, slot 2 and slot 3. The system for Spanish and English language is exactly the same for both slots 1 and 2.

2.2.1 Slot 1 Aspect category detection

The aim of this task is to assign to each sentence a category, which is a tuple (entity, attribute), from a given set of 12 different predefined categories. To do this, we used a linear SVM classifier combined with word lists. These word lists are created from the training file provided by the organization, which was composed of 2000 sentences, grouped in 350 reviews. Different datasets were provided for several languages and topics. Our system was developed for restaurants dataset, both in English and Spanish.

The library libsvm (Chang and Lin, 2011) was used to implement the SVM classifier, using the following features for each sentence:

- Words: those words appearing in the sentence, which are nouns, verbs or adjectives are extracted.

- Lemmas: lemmas from nouns, verbs and adjectives are selected.

- POS tags: part of speech from nouns, verbs and adjectives in the sentence.

- Bigrams: all the bigrams found in the sentence.

We developed 12 different binary classifiers, one for each possible category. If the output of one classifier for a particular sentence is "1", then we add the related category to the sentence. If more than one category is found for the same sentence, we add all of them to the list of categories. After this, the outputs are improved by means of our word lists, as we can see in Algorithm 1, executed for each sentence. The word lists were created automatically from the training file, extracting all the nouns and adjectives appearing in sentences from the same category, and manually filtered later in order to remove noisy items. Six different lists are composed, containing terms related to: ambience, service, prices, quality, style options and location.

The inputs defined for the following algorithm are the list of categories obtained from SVM for each sentence (CList(s)) and the six word lists created previously. The output is the new list per sentence, containing the old categories from SVM and the new ones added.

Algorithm 1: Combining SVM outputs with word lists for a sentence s.

Input: CList(s), ambienceL, serviceL, locationL, pricesL, qualityL, styleL

Output: newList(s)

```
 1  newList(s) = CList(s);
 2  foreach unigram(s) do
 3      if unigram(s) ∈ ambienceL then
 4          newList(s) = newList(s) ∪ {AMBIENCE#GENERAL}
 5      end
 6      if unigram(s) ∈ serviceL then
 7          newList(s) = newList(s) ∪ {SERVICE#GENERAL}
 8      end
 9      if unigram(s) ∈ locationL then
10          newList(s) = newList(s) ∪ {LOCATION#GENERAL}
11      end
12      if unigram(s) ∈ pricesL then
13          if FOOD#A ∈ CList(s) then
14              newList(s) = newList(s) ∪ {FOOD#PRICES}
15          else
16              if DRINKS#A ∈ CList(s) then
17                  newList(s) = newList(s) ∪ {DRINKS#PRICES}
18              else
19                  newList(s) = newList(s) ∪ {RESTAURANT#PRICES}
20              end
21          end
22      end
23      if unigram(s) ∈ qualityL then
24          if DRINKS#A ∈ CList(s) then
25              newList(s) = newList(s) ∪ {DRINKS#QUALITY}
26          else
27              newList(s) = newList(s) ∪ {FOOD#QUALITY}
28          end
29      end
30      if unigram(s) ∈ styleL then
31          if DRINKS#A ∈ CList(s) then
32              newList(s) = newList(s) ∪ {DRINKS#STYLEOPTIONS}
33          else
34              newList(s) = newList(s) ∪ {FOOD#STYLEOPTIONS}
35          end
36      end
37  end
```

2.2.2 Slot 2 Opinion target expression

For this slot, teams were asked to extract the exact expressions or words in the sentence, in which an opinion is expressed. The implementation for this slot is made by means of CRFs, using CRF++ tool (Kudo, 2005) and the training file provided for building the model. A training file is needed to build as input for the CRF, whose structure is as follows. In the first column, all the words for every sentence are written, then in the second column, the corresponding lemma. The third column represents the tag and the last one represents if the word is an aspect or not or if it is included in a multiword aspect. Then for creating the model we take into account all these features, as well as all the possible bigrams in each sentence. In the output, if no target is found, no opinion is returned for that sentence.

2.2.3 Slot 3 Sentiment polarity

This slot is implemented only for English language, both restaurants and laptops datasets. Our system is fully unsupervised, this can explain the low results obtained for this slot. An adjustment was made to the system already implemented for sentiment analysis in the whole sentence, which was presented in Semeval 2015, task 10: sentiment analysis in Twitter (Fernández-Gavilanes et al., 2015), which was also unsupervised. For this dataset, a new polarity lexicon was generated automatically from the training dataset, applying a polarity rank algorithm, as explained in the mentioned article. Then, it was merged with SOCAL (Taboada et al., 2011) and AFINN (Nielsen, 2011) lexicons, which are general context ones, by applying an average for those words which appeared in more than one of them.

Our system for the restaurant dataset implements the following syntactic rules:

- If there is no opinion or only one target expression in the sentence, the system automatically takes the polarity of the whole sentence and assign it to all the categories which appear in this sentence.

- If there is only one different target expression but appearing more than once, we check if there is an adversative clause in the sentence built with "but" particle. If not, we also take the polarity of the whole sentence for all the opinions. If the previous condition is fulfilled, we will take the polarity of the first clause of the sentence, which is the piece of sentence placed before the "but" and then apply a polarity linear system, which consists of summing up all the polarities found in the dictionary created. For the next opinions which have the same target, we will follow the same procedure but with the piece of sentence after the "but". For this linear approach, we take negations in account only for adjectives, flipping the polarity of the adjectives which come inmediately after a negation particle, as "no" or "not".

- When there are several different opinion targets, we split the sentence to detect the scope of each target and apply the same linear polarity algorithm explained in the previous point. To detect the scope of the target, we take the words which appear before and after the target, splitting by punctuation marks (";", ",", ".", "?", "!", "-").

For the laptops dataset, since there are no opinion target expressions, we take the polarity of the whole sentence to assign the polarity of each category.

2.3 Subtask 2: Text-level ABSA

Subtask 2 is similar to subtask 1, but instead of implementing aspect detection at sentence-level, it is performed at text-level. Participants are asked to implement slots 1 and 3 for this subtask. We participate in slot 1 for Spanish and English language, following the same procedure for both. Slot 3 is just implemented for English language for restaurants and laptops datasets.

2.3.1 Slot 1 Aspect category detection

Once we performed aspect category detection at sentence-level, we use this output as input for text-level detection. All the categories found are grouped at sentence-level and added all of them at review-level. Besides this, if RESTAURANT#GENERAL is not explicitly assigned to any sentence of the review, we add it anyway.

2.3.2 Slot 3 Sentiment polarity

Similarly to slot 1, we use the output from subtask 1 slot 3 as input for this slot. All the polarities found are again grouped for all the sentences contained in the review and added them to text-level. If there are different polarities for the same category, some rules are applied: if polarities are negative and neutral, negative is finally assigned; if there are positive and neutral opinions, positive polarity is assigned; if there are positive and negative opinions for the same category, the tag "conflict" is assigned to that category at review-level.

Moreover, as RESTAURANT#GENERAL is compulsory for every review, if no sentence has this category assigned, we take into account all the polarities of the other categories found and then assign the polarity for this category. Again, if there are different polarities containing positive and negative, "conflict" tag is assigned. The same process is followed for laptops dataset, with the LAPTOPS#GENERAL category.

3 Experimental Results

In this section, we describe the experiments carried out for the different subtasks and slots and the datasets provided by the organization. These datasets are composed of several reviews, splitted in sentences, for restaurants and laptops topics. The performance of slots 1 and 2, for both subtasks, are measured by means of the F-score, while slot 3 is evaluated by means of the accuracy.

Table 1 represents the precision, recall and F-score obtained for restaurants datasets and all the slots submitted. For English language, an unconstrained system was presented, while for Spanish language both constrained and unconstrained systems were submitted. The constrained approaches do not need any external resources, but only the training files provided, while in the unconstrained ones, food and drinks lexicon was used in the pre-processing step for identifying different foods and drinks.

It can be seen that there is not much difference between constrained and unconstrained systems for Spanish language, so we can assume that the recognition of different names of foods or drinks does not increase the knowledge of the classifiers, perform-

		Prec.	Rec.	F
EN - U	Subt1-Slot1	72.14	63.79	67.71
	Subt1-Slot2	69.45	63.89	66.55
	Subt2-Slot1	87.00	81.19	83.99
SP - U	Subt1-Slot1	74.82	66.80	70.59
	Subt1-Slot2	69.94	66.90	68.39
	Subt2-Slot1	86.31	81.89	84.04
SP - C	Subt1-Slot1	74.59	65.98	70.02
	Subt1-Slot2	69.45	67.60	68.51
	Subt2-Slot1	86.63	81.89	84.19

Table 1: Measures for restaurants dataset, slots 1 and 2.

ing almost equally. Moreover, we can state that our system perfoms as well for English as for Spanish language.

In Table 2, the detailed scores for slot 3 are shown in English language, for restaurants dataset, likewise in Table 3 for laptops dataset.

		Prec.	Rec.	F	Acc.
Subt1	P	84.66	76.76	80.52	
	N	60.5	59.31	59.9	69.96
	NEU	10.48	25.00	14.77	
Subt2	P	87.2	76.22	81.34	
	N	62.75	38.1	47.41	64.11
	NEU	18.18	8.7	11.76	
	CONFL.	7.61	63.64	13.59	

Table 2: Detailed scores for slot 3, restaurants dataset in English language.

		Prec.	Rec.	F	Acc.
Subt1	P	68.78	87.94	77.19	
	N	63.39	42.34	50.77	67.29
	NEU	0	0	0	
Subt2	P	74.64	76.63	75.62	
	N	60.81	27.78	38.14	58.35
	NEU	12.12	12.9	12.5	
	CONFL.	10.99	71.43	19.05	

Table 3: Detailed scores for slot 3, laptops dataset in English language.

As it can be seen in Table 2 and Table 3, the results obtained for the sentiment slot are not quite competitive with the other teams. This can be due to the fact that our system is fully unsupervised, while the others are usually supervised systems, based on training. Moreover, we performed a simple adaptation from our original system, made for sentiment analysis in Twitter, presented to SemEval 2015, so there is still a lot of improvement on this field.

4 Conclusions

This paper describes the participation of the GTI group, AtlantTIC Research Center, University of Vigo, in the SemEval 2016, Task 5: Aspect-Based Sentiment Analysis. We developed a supervised system based on SVM classifiers for category detection, and CRFs for opinion target detection. Then, for the aspect-based sentiment analysis we submitted a fully unsupervised system, based on syntactic dependencies and context-based polarity lexicons.

Test sets				Position
EN	REST	Subtask1	Slot1	*10/20*
			Slot2	*4/15*
			Slot3	*19/20*
		Subtask2	Slot1	*1/3*
			Slot3	*4/4*
	LAPT	Subtask1	Slot3	*14/15*
		Subtask2	Slot3	*4/4*
SP	REST	Subtask1	Slot1	*1/6*
			Slot2	*1/3*
		Subtask2	Slot1	*1/2*

Table 4: Position of our approach in the different datasets and subtasks submitted, according to the results published by the organisation.

As we can see in Table 4, competitive results were obtained for aspect and category detection, being in first position for Spanish language, both in subtask 1 and subtask 2. Moreover, in subtask 2, which is aspect detection at review level, we also achieved the first position for English language in restaurants datasets. However, our system did not perform as well as expected in slot 3, maybe due to the fact of the lack of supervision for our model. It results not competitive against other supervised approaches, although its main advantage is that there is no need of training sets, which is time and resource consuming in order to manually tag them.

Acknowledgments

This work was supported by the Spanish Government, co-financed by the European Regional Development Fund (ERDF) under project TACTICA.

References

Jordi Atserias, Bernardino Casas, Elisabet Comelles, Meritxell González, Lluís Padró, and Muntsa Padró.

2006. Freeling 1.3: Syntactic and semantic services in an open-source nlp library. In *Proceedings of LREC*, volume 6, pages 48–55.

Chih-Chung Chang and Chih-Jen Lin. 2011. Libsvm: a library for support vector machines. *ACM Transactions on Intelligent Systems and Technology (TIST)*, 2(3):27.

Milagros Fernández-Gavilanes, Tamara Álvarez López, Jonathan Juncal-Martínez, Enrique Costa-Montenegro, and Francisco Javier González-Castaño. 2015. GTI: An Unsupervised Approach for Sentiment Analysis in Twitter. In *Proceedings of the 9th International Workshop on Semantic Evaluation (SemEval 2015)*, pages 533–538, Denver, Colorado, June. Association for Computational Linguistics.

Taku Kudo. 2005. Crf++: Yet another crf toolkit. *Software available at http://crfpp. sourceforge. net*.

Bing Liu. 2012. Sentiment analysis and opinion mining. *Synthesis lectures on human language technologies*, 5(1):1–167.

Bin Lu, Myle Ott, Claire Cardie, and Benjamin K Tsou. 2011. Multi-aspect sentiment analysis with topic models. In *Data Mining Workshops (ICDMW), 2011 IEEE 11th International Conference on*, pages 81–88. IEEE.

Diego Marcheggiani, Oscar Täckström, Andrea Esuli, and Fabrizio Sebastiani. 2014. Hierarchical multi-label conditional random fields for aspect-oriented opinion mining. In *Advances in Information Retrieval*, pages 273–285. Springer.

Finn Årup Nielsen. 2011. A new anew: Evaluation of a word list for sentiment analysis in microblogs. *arXiv preprint arXiv:1103.2903*.

Lluís Padró and Evgeny Stanilovsky. 2012. Freeling 3.0: Towards wider multilinguality. In *LREC2012*.

Maria Pontiki, Dimitrios Galanis, Haris Papageorgiou, Ion Androutsopoulos, Suresh Manandhar, Mohammad AL-Smadi, Mahmoud Al-Ayyoub, Yanyan Zhao, Bing Qin, Orphée De Clercq, Véronique Hoste, Marianna Apidianaki, Xavier Tannier, Natalia Loukachevitch, Evgeny Kotelnikov, Nuria Bel, Salud María Jiménez-Zafra, and Gülşen Eryiğit. 2016. SemEval-2016 Task 5: Aspect Based Sentiment Analysis. In *Proceedings of the 10th International Workshop on Semantic Evaluation*, SemEval '16, San Diego, California, June 2016. Association for Computational Linguistics.

Maite Taboada, Julian Brooke, Milan Tofiloski, Kimberly Voll, and Manfred Stede. 2011. Lexicon-based methods for sentiment analysis. *Computational linguistics*, 37(2):267–307.

AUEB-ABSA at SemEval-2016 Task 5: Ensembles of Classifiers and Embeddings for Aspect Based Sentiment Analysis

Dionysios Xenos, Panagiotis Theodorakakos, John Pavlopoulos,
Prodromos Malakasiotis and **Ion Androutsopoulos**
NLP Group, Department of Informatics
Athens University of Economics and Business
Patission 76, GR-104 34 Athens, Greece
`http://nlp.cs.aueb.gr`

Abstract

This paper describes our submissions to the Aspect Based Sentiment Analysis task of SemEval-2016. For Aspect Category Detection (Subtask1/Slot1), we used multiple ensembles, based on Support Vector Machine classifiers. For Opinion Target Expression extraction (Subtask1/Slot2), we used a sequence labeling approach with Conditional Random Fields. For Polarity Detection (Subtask1/Slot3), we used an ensemble of two supervised classifiers, one based on hand crafted features and one based on word embeddings. Our systems were ranked in the top 6 positions in all the tasks we participated. The source code of our systems is publicly available.

1 Introduction

The amount of user-generated content on the web has grown rapidly in recent years, leading to increased interest in sentiment analysis and, more generally, opinion mining. The task of Aspect Based Sentiment Analysis of SemEval-2014 (SE-ABSA14) and SemEval-2015 (SE-ABSA15) was concerned with identifying the aspects of given target entities and extracting the sentiment expressed towards each aspect (Pontiki et al., 2014; Pontiki et al., 2015). The task of Aspect Based Sentiment Analysis of SemEval-2016 (SE-ABSA16) is a continuation of those tasks (Pontiki et al., 2016). We participated in Aspect Category Detection (ACD, Subtask1/Slot1), Opinion Target Expression (OTE, Subtask1/Slot2), and Polarity Detection (PD, Subtask1/Slot3).

In ACD, we participated in the English language, for both Laptops and Restaurants, submitting both constrained and unconstrained systems. Our constrained system used only the provided training data for the corresponding domain. Features were extracted from lexicons created from the training data. One Support Vector Machine (SVM) classifier (Vapnik and Vapnik, 1998) was trained for each Entity and Attribute category (called E and A respectively). Our unconstrained system used word embeddings as additional resources (Mikolov et al., 2013). For each category (E or A), we used an ensemble of two systems: our constrained system and one new system, which was based on word embeddings.

In OTE, we participated with both a constrained and an unconstrained system.[1] The task is to identify aspects of given target entities. We addressed the problem as a sequential labeling task (Toh and Wang, 2014), assigning one label to each word in a sentence, indicating whether the word was an aspect term or not. In this task, we used Conditional Random Fields (Lafferty et al., 2001). Similarly to ACD, our unconstrained system differed in that it also used word embeddings as features.

In PD, we participated only with an unconstrained system, in both domains, in the English language. We used an ensemble of two classifiers. The first classifier used hand crafted features and sentiment lexicons with scores. The second classifier was based on IDF-weighted centroids of the word embeddings of each sentence (Kosmopoulos et al., 2015).

The remainder of this paper is structured as follows. In Section 2, we describe our systems in detail, including data preprocessing and feature de-

---

[1] Only the restaurants domain was available in OTE.

312

Proceedings of SemEval-2016, pages 312–317,
San Diego, California, June 16-17, 2016. ©2016 Association for Computational Linguistics

scriptions. In Sections 3 and 4, we present our official results and experiments, respectively. Finally, Section 5 summarizes our work and proposes future directions.

2   Systems

All our submissions used supervised learning. In Restaurants, the training data were 350 reviews (2,000 sentences), annotated with 2,499 aspects and their polarities. Each aspect consists of one Entity (E) and one Attribute of E (A), thus, forming an E#A pair. The sentiment polarity of any aspect may be positive, negative or neutral. Included, were also annotations for linguistic expressions, called Opinion Target Expressions (OTE), indicating the origin of each E. For example, in "The food was well prepared and the service impeccable." there were two annotations:

- 1st OTE: "food" offsets: 4 to 8

    - category: FOOD#QUALITY
    - polarity: positive

- 2nd OTE: "service" offsets: 35 to 42

    - category: SERVICE#GENERAL
    - polarity: positive

In Laptops, the training data were 450 reviews (2,500 sentences), annotated with 2,923 {E#A, Polarity} labels. In this domain, no OTE annotations were included.

As a preprocessing step, we excluded sentences with no opinion tuples and sentences labeled as "Out of Scope".[2] All the features and hyper-parameter values used are described in a publicly available report, along with the source code of our systems.[3]

2.1   Aspect Category Detection

In Aspect Category Detection (ACD), each aspect E#A (e.g., FOOD#PRICE) in a sentence should be discovered. The possible E and A labels were predefined; thus, we considered this to be a classification task.

Constrained ACD system

One Support Vector Machine (SVM) classifier was trained for each predefined E and A, based on lexicons created from the training data.[4] [5] The lexicons assigned scores to unigrams (stemmed and unstemmed) and bigrams (stemmed, unstemmed or using only POS tag bigrams). For each unigram or bigram, we computed its Precision, Recall and F1 over the training data, following the work of Karampatsis et al. (2014). We used the average, median, maximum, and minimum values for each score (Precision, Recall, F1) and for each lexicon (stemmed unigrams, unstemmed unigrams, stemmed, unstemmed, POS tag bigrams), thus, yielding 12 features per lexicon and 60 features overall.

One Support Vector Machine (SVM) classifier was trained for each E and A label, yielding 11 classifiers for Restaurants and 31 for Laptops. Given a new text, the confidence scores of all the classifiers were examined and the Es and As of the classifiers whose confidence exceeded a threshold were used to form the E#A aspects.[6] All the possible E#A combinations are formed, provided that they appeared at least once in the training data. Thus, assuming that the classifiers of |E| entities and |A| attributes exceeded the threshold, we form at most |E| · |A| aspects.

Following the work of Hsu et al. (2010), we used a 5-fold cross validation on the training data for tuning and we performed a loose grid search, followed by a fine grid search. During the loose grid search, various kernels were examined (i.e., Linear, Sigmoid, Polynomial and RBF) and hyper-parameter values were searched with a big step and in a big range of values. During the fine grid search, the best kernel of the loose grid search was used and hyper-parameter values were searched with a smaller step in a much smaller range of values.

Unconstrained ACD system

Our unconstrained system was based on multiple ensembles, one for each E and A combination encountered in our training data. Each ensemble

---

[2]Sentences including opinions that can not be described by the SE-ABSA16 annotation schema, are "Out of Scope".

[3]https://github.com/nlpaueb/aueb-absa

[4]Lexicons were created only for tokens that appeared more than 2 times in the training dataset, for each E and A category.

[5]http://scikit-learn.org/stable/

[6]The threshold was manually fixed to 0.4.

returned the linear combination of the confidence scores of two systems.[7] The first system in each ensemble was the corresponding constrained system. The second system in each ensemble was a system based on word embeddings (Mikolov et al., 2013).

We used the Amazon product review data to produce word embeddings and Inverse Document Frequency (IDF) scores (McAuley et al., 2015).[8] Word embeddings were produced, with 200 dimensions and the skip-gram model, using Gensim.[9] Then, following the work of Kosmopoulos et al. (2015), for each sentence s_i in our data, we computed its centroid $c(s_i)$ as follows:

$$c(s_i) = \frac{\sum_{j=1}^{|V|} e_j \cdot TF(w_j, s_i) \cdot IDF(w_j)}{\sum_{i=1}^{|V|} TF(w_j, s_i) \cdot IDF(w_i)}$$

where $|V|$ is the size of the vocabulary, e_j is the embedding of word w_j, $TF(w_j, s_i)$ is the Boolean term frequency of w_j in sentence s_i, and $IDF(w_j)$ is the IDF score of w_j. Preliminary experiments in both domains, with IDF scores and term frequency (Boolean or not) scores, showed that the use of Boolean term frequency scores along with IDF scores was better than any other combination.

We normalized each centroid using L2 normalization and we computed the cosine similarity between the centroid of the sentence and the word embedding of the label of each possible E or A. The final feature vector of each unconstrained E or A classifier (2nd classifier in each ensemble) is produced by concatenating all the cosine scores and the normalized centroid. We trained one SVM classifier per E and A, yielding 11 unconstrained classifiers for Restaurants and 31 for Laptops, as already noted. All the unconstrained classifiers were tuned similarly to our constrained classifiers.

In a final step, our unconstrained system returns one score per E and A, which is the linear combination of the confidence scores of the constrained and unconstrained classifiers in the corresponding

ensemble. Similarly to our constrained system, E#A aspects are then returned.

2.2 Opinion Target Expression

Opinion Target Expression is addressed as a sequential labeling problem. Each word in a sentence is assigned the label "B" to indicate the start of an aspect term, "I" to indicate the continuation of an aspect term, and "O" if the token is not an aspect term.

Both our constrained and unconstrained systems use Conditional Random Fields (CRF) (Lafferty et al., 2001).[10] However, our unconstrained system extends our constrained one, by incorporating more features. The features used in each system are discussed below.

Constrained OTE system

The features of our constrained system are the following:

- Morphological (Boolean), about the current token:

  - Capital first letter
  - All letters in capitals
  - Only digits
  - Existence of punctuation mark
  - Other

- Lexicon-based (one-hot)

  - POS tags (both of current token and context)
  - Word affixes (prefixes and suffixes) of the current token
  - Aspect terms

For features based on lexicons, we used the training data to form lists of POS tags, word affixes of various lengths (prefixes and suffixes of length 1, 2 and 3 characters) and aspect terms. Then, we formed a single one-hot vector (i.e., a vector of 0's and a single 1) per list, indicating which member of the list the token being examined corresponds to. We used 5 vectors for the POS based features (one for the current token and 4 for the context; two on the left and two on the right), 6 vectors for features based on word affixes (prefixes and affixes of one, two and

---

[7]The weights of the two confidence scores were set to 0.5, i.e. we used the average of the two scores. Other weighs were also examined, but they did not lead to better performance.

[8]We used the files for individual product categories from the Amazon product data corpus, which had duplicate item reviews removed (http://jmcauley.ucsd.edu/data/amazon/).

[9]https://radimrehurek.com/gensim/

[10]https://pystruct.github.io/index.html

314

three letters) and 1 vector for aspect terms seen in the training data. Finally, we concatenated the vectors and the Boolean features to yield one overall feature vector.

Unconstrained OTE system

Our unconstrained system extends our constrained system by incorporating the following features:

- Word embedding of the current token

- Word embeddings of the context

For each word, we compute its embedding and incorporate it to our constrained system's feature vector. Word embeddings were calculated as in Section 2.1; each word corresponds to a 200-dimensional embedding. We also incorporate features for the word's context. We compute the embeddings of the words in a 5-context window (i.e., two words on the left and two on the right) and concatenate them to a 1000-dimensional vector.

If a word from the context had no embedding, we replaced it by the previous (for left context) or next (for right context) word that had an embedding. Also, in order to cope with missing words at the beginning and the end of a sentence, we introduced four special tokens, for the first two and the last two words of the sentence. The respective tokens were positioned before and after each sentence of the Amazon product reviews corpus, before producing word embeddings.

2.3 Polarity Detection

The objective of Polarity Detection (PD) was to detect the correct sentiment label for each aspect E#A in a sentence; possible sentiment labels were positive, negative and neutral (i.e., mildly positive or negative). Sentences could contain multiple aspects; e.g., the sentence "Excellent food, although the interior could use some help." contains two aspects; "FOOD#QUALITY" and "AMBIENCE#GENERAL", which should be labeled positive and negative respectively.

We used an Ensemble of two Multi-class Logistic Regression (LR) classifiers, trained with different sets of features. Each classifier yields one confidence sentiment (for each E#A) per sentiment label.

Then, for each sentiment label, our ensemble computes a linear combination of the corresponding two scores of the classifiers and the label with the highest combined score is returned.[11]

We describe below the feature sets of the two LR classifiers, LRI and LRII.

LR I PD classifier

In LRI, we used 50 hand crafted features, which could be categorized by nature:

- Morphological (Karampatsis et al., 2014)

    - frequency based (number of exclamation and question marks, etc.)
    - Boolean based (exclamation or question mark in the end of the sentence, etc.)

- POS based (number of nouns, adjectives, verbs and adverbs) (Karampatsis et al., 2014)

- E#A based (number of aspects and bags of entities and attributes)

- Sentiment lexicons

    - AFINN[12]
    - Hu & Liu[13]
    - NRC[14]

For features based on sentiment lexicons, besides the already given word scores, we compute new scores, which are relative to our data. Following the work of Karampatsis et al. (2014), we computed Precision and $F1$ scores per sentiment label, for each word in the lexicon and for each POS bigram (i.e., two sequential part of speech tags).

To take into consideration negation phenomena, we used the negation lexicon compiled by Zhang et al. (2014). If a negation word precedes a word in a lexicon, we reverse the word's score sign; i.e., positive becomes negative and vice versa. Also, we make special use of words only in upper case. If a word in upper case exists in a lexicon we multiply

---

[11] We used the average of the two scores in practice.

[12] http://www2.imm.dtu.dk/pubdb/views/publication_details.php?id=6010, AFINN-111

[13] http://github.com/woodrad/Twitter-Sentiment-Mining/tree/master

[14] http://saifmohammad.com/WebPages/NRC-Emotion-Lexicon.htm

Domain	Precision	Recall	F-measure	Rank
Restaurants (U)	67.75%	75.77%	71.54%	4th/30
Restaurants (C)	64.22%	70.79%	67.35%	4th/12
Laptops (U)	45.60%	53.19%	49.10%	2nd/22
Laptops (C)	40.69%	51.94%	45.63%	4th/9

Table 1: AUEB-ABSA's evaluation in Aspect Category Detection. The first column shows the domain and the run (C for constrained and U for unconstrained). The last column shows the rank of our system.

Domain	Precision	Recall	F-measure	Rank
Restaurants (U)	71.82%	69.12%	70.44%	2nd/19
Restaurants (C)	64.35%	58.99%	61.55%	6th/8

Table 2: AUEB-ABSA's evaluation in Opinion Target Expression.

its score, in order to make it more significant.[15] The resulting feature vector is normalized to [0,1] with the Euclidean norm.

LR II PD classifier

The second PD classifier uses the centroid of the word embeddings of each sentence as features. The centroids are compiled as in Section 2.1, but without the IDF scores in the denominator.[16] Words without embeddings or IDF scores are ignored when computing the centroids. The same applies to words with IDF scores below a given threshold.[17] Word embeddings are normalized with the Euclidean norm.

3 Results

Table 1 shows the results of our Aspect Category Detection (ACD) system. In Restaurants, our unconstrained ACD system was ranked 4th among 30 submissions. Our constrained ACD system was also ranked 4th, but amongst 12 submissions. In Laptops, our unconstrained ACD system was ranked 2nd among 22 submissions and our constrained one was ranked 4th among 9 submissions.

Table 2 shows the results of our Opinion Target Expression (OTE) system. Our unconstrained OTE system was ranked 2nd out of 19 submissions, while our constrained OTE system was ranked 6th out of 8 submissions.

---

[15]Here, we arbitrarily tripled the score

[16]Our experiments have shown that removing the IDF from the denominator improves the performance of LRII

[17]The threshold was set to 0.5, which led to best results on the validation data.

Domain	Accuracy	Rank
Restaurants (U)	83.24%	6th/28
Laptops (U)	76.90%	6th/21

Table 3: AUEB-ABSA's evaluation on Polarity Detection.

Table 3 shows the evaluation of our PD system (unconstrained only). We were ranked 6th out of 28 submissions in Restaurants and 6th out of 21 submissions in Laptops.

4 Experiments & Discussion

As described in Section 2.1, our unconstrained ACD system used an ensemble of two systems, one based on word embeddings and one based on features calculated only on the training data. Preliminary experiments showed that the ensemble is better than each system alone and better than a single system combining all the features of the two systems.

In the same task, experiments in the domain of Restaurants showed that there is no important difference between having one classifier for each possible E#A label, and having separate classifiers for each E and each A label. However, in Laptops, the latter approach led to slightly better results and, hence, it was preferred.

In the task of OTE, our constrained system is below the median participant (6th out of 8 submissions). However, when extended with features based on word embeddings (our unconstrained system), its performance is outstanding (2nd out of 19 submissions).

It is also worth noting that, in preliminary experiments for OTE, the use of a context vector (i.e., concatenated embeddings of words in a 5-context window of the word in question) gave far better results than using the centroid of these word embeddings.

System	Restaurants	Laptops
LRI (hand crafted)	80.71% (12th)	73.92% (9th)
LRII (embeddings)	74.94% (22th)	73.12% (11th)
Ensemble	**83.24% (6th)**	**76.90% (6th)**

Table 4: Accuracy of our submitted PD ensemble and its two subsystems, LRI (feature based) and LRII (based on word embeddings). In parentheses are estimated ranks of the two subsystems and the official rank of our ensemble.

For PD, we performed some post-experiments on the gold test data. As can be seen in Table 4, our ensemble, which is our final PD system, outperforms its two subsystems, both in Restaurants (2.5% - 8.3%) and Laptops (3%-3.8%). Also, post-experiments showed that the negation lexicon improved the Accuracy of our ensemble by 0.5% in Restaurants and 1% in Laptops.

5 Conclusions and future work

We presented our approach to sentence level Aspect Based Sentiment Analysis (SE-ABSA16), which includes the subtasks of Aspect Category Detection (ACD), Opinion Target Expression (OTE) and Polarity Detection (PD). We observed and showed in post-experiments the benefits of using word embeddings and ensembles. The source code of our systems is publicly available. Future work includes the incorporation of neural networks in our ensembles.

Acknowledgments

This work was carried out during the BSc projects of the first two authors, which were co-supervised by the other three authors.

References

C. Hsu and C. Chang. 2010. A practical guide to support vector classification. Technical report, Department of Computer Science, National Taiwan University.

R. M. Karampatsis, J. Pavlopoulos, and P. Malakasiotis. 2014. Aueb: Two stage sentiment analysis of social network messages. In *Proceedings of SemEval 2014, at COLING 2014*, pages 114–118, Dublin, Ireland.

A. Kosmopoulos, I. Androutsopoulos, and G. Paliouras. 2015. Biomedical semantic indexing using dense word vectors in bioasq. *Journal of Biomedical Semantics, supplement on Semantics-Enabled Biomedical Information Retrieval*, pages 5–7.

J. D. Lafferty, A. McCallum, and F. C. N. Pereira. 2001. Conditional random fields: Probabilistic models for segmenting and labeling sequence data. In *Proceedings of the 18th ICML*, pages 282–289, San Francisco, CA, USA.

J. McAuley, R. Pandey, and J.Leskovec. 2015. Inferring networks of substitutable and complementary products. In *Proceedings of the 21th ACM SIGKDD*, pages 785–794.

T. Mikolov, I. Sutskever, G. S. Corrado K. Chen, and J. Dean. 2013. Distributed representations of words and phrases and their compositionality. In *Proceedings of NIPS 2013*, pages 3111–3119.

M. Pontiki, D. Galanis, J. Pavlopoulos, H. Papageorgiou, I. Androutsopoulos, and S. Manandhar. 2014. Semeval-2014 task 4: Aspect based sentiment analysis. In *Proceedings of SemEval 2014*, pages 27–35, Dublin, Ireland.

M. Pontiki, D. Galanis, H. Papageogiou, S. Manandhar, and I. Androutsopoulos. 2015. Semeval-2015 task 12: Aspect based sentiment analysis. In *Proceedings of SemEval 2015*, pages 27–35, Denver, Colorado.

Maria Pontiki, Dimitrios Galanis, Haris Papageorgiou, Ion Androutsopoulos, Suresh Manandhar, Mohammad AL-Smadi, Mahmoud Al-Ayyoub, Yanyan Zhao, Bing Qin, Orphée De Clercq, Véronique Hoste, Marianna Apidianaki, Xavier Tannier, Natalia Loukachevitch, Evgeny Kotelnikov, Nuria Bel, Salud María Jiménez-Zafra, and Gülşen Eryiğit. 2016. Semeval-2016 task 5: Aspect based sentiment analysis. In *Proceedings of SemEval 2016*, San Diego, California.

Z. Toh and W. Wang. 2014. Dlirec: Aspect term extraction and term polarity classification system. In *Proceedings of SemEval 2014*, pages 235–240, Dublin, Ireland.

V. N. Vapnik and V. Vapnik. 1998. *Statistical learning theory*, volume 1. Wiley New York.

F. Zhang, Z. Zhang, and M. Lan. 2014. Ecnu: A combination method and multiple features for aspect extraction and sentiment polarity classification. In *Proceedings of SemEval 2014*, pages 252–258, Dublin, Ireland.

AKTSKI at SemEval-2016 Task 5: Aspect Based Sentiment Analysis for Consumer Reviews

Shubham Pateria and **Prafulla Kumar Choubey**

System Software Division

Samsung R and D Institute India Bangalore Pvt Ltd

Bangalore, Karanataka, India -560037

`s.pateria, prafulla.ch@samsung.com`

Abstract

This paper describes the polarity classification system designed for participation in SemEval-2016 Task 5 - ABSA. The aim is to determine the sentiment polarity expressed towards certain aspect within a consumer review. Our system is based on supervised learning using Support Vector Machine (SVM). We use standard features for basic classification model. On top this, we include rules to check precedent polarity sequence. This approach is experimental.

1 Introduction

In the consumer-focused markets today, understanding opinions expressed on the online platforms or review portals is of key essence for the businesses. Statistical or Machine learning methods and Natural Language Processing are now being widely applied to extract important information or patterns from the opinion data. A review statement may have a mix of sentiments towards different aspects. For e.g., consider *the food and ambiance at xyz hotel were extraordinary, as expected. However, the waiters seemed rude*. Here, the main entity of review is a 'hotel'. Henceforth, we will refer to such main entity as *global item*. However, there is no definite overall sentiment expressed towards the *global item*. Different sentiments are expressed towards *food* and *ambiance* aspects (extraordinary: positive) and towards the aspect of service (*waiters*, rude: negative). Thus, it is important to approach sentiment detection as an aspect-based problem.

The SemEval-2016 Task 5 - Aspect Based Sentiment Analysis (ABSA) focuses on this problem (Pontiki et al., 2016). This task is a continuation from SemEval-2015 ABSA task (Pontiki et al., 2015). The task was organized across different domains and languages. We participated in Restaurant domain in English language. The focus of our system is polarity detection and not aspect extraction. Thus, we use dataset in which aspects are already known.

To develop our system, we have used standard features for basic model and also rules to check effect of precedent-polarity sequence pattern on polarity to be predicted. We focus on experimenting with sequence pattern. The system is described in Section 3. Pre-processing is described in Sub-section 3.1. selected features are discussed in Sub-section 3.2 and sequence pattern discussed in Sub-section 3.3. In section 4, we discuss the analysis and evaluation results for our system.

2 Related Work

Aspect-based sentiment analysis has been a subject of some interesting works so far. (McAuley et al., 2012) employ topic modeling paradigm to address this problem. Deep Learning has also been explored in this area, such as by (Wang and Liu, 2015). They used Convolutional Neural Network for aspect-based analysis of SemEval-2015 ABSA data and reported performance comparable to top systems of the 2015 task. Previously, the system by (Kiritchenko et al., 2014) achieved the best performance in Polarity Detection task in SemEval-2014. They used various innovative linguistic features, publicly available sentiment lexicon corpora and automatically generated polarity lexicons. In

318

Proceedings of SemEval-2016, pages 318–324,

San Diego, California, June 16-17, 2016. ©2016 Association for Computational Linguistics

Semeval-2015, SENTIUE system by (Saias, 2015) provided remarkable results. They used wide range of features such as Bag-of-Words, negation words, bigram after negation, polarity inversion, polarized terms in last 5 tokens, publicly available lexicons etc. They used MALLET[1] with Maximum Entropy classifier.

3 Classification System

Our system uses Support Vector Machine (SVM) with Radial Basis Function (RBF) kernel as classifier. The scikit-learn SVM implementation has been used (Pedregosa et al., 2011). This classifier is trained using dataset provided by task organizers. This dataset consists of several reviews, each with a unique review ID (rID). Each review consists of several sentences. A sentence may have single or multiple aspects. Sentences under same rID express sentiment towards the same *global item*. In our case, the *global item* is some *restaurant*. The data are parsed into following format:
{Review(rID) {Sentence1 aspect1:(target, category, polarity, from, to)}, {Sentence2 aspect1:(target, category, polarity, from, to)}, ..., {SentenceN aspect1:(target, category, polarity, from to) ... aspectM:(target, category, polarity, from, to)} }.

Here, Review(rID) is just one instance out of several such reviews. (target, category, polarity, from, to) are values belonging to an aspect of a sentence. Polarity values are *positive*, *negative* or *neutral*. SentenceN is an example of a sentence which contains multiple aspects. The test data are also parsed in the same format except that polarity values are not provided. Henceforth, (target, category, polarity, from, to) will be referred to as (tar, cat, p, f, t) for simplicity.

To develop our system, we have used NLTK package (Loper and Bird, 2002) in Python with resources such as WordNet package[2], SentiWordNet, Bing Liu's opinion lexicon and MPQA subjectivity lexicon[3].

---

[1]MAchine Learning for LanguagE Toolkit (McCallum and Kachites, 2002)

[2]Princeton University "About WordNet." WordNet. Princeton University. 2010. <http://wordnet.princeton.edu>

[3]Bing Liu's lexicon (Liu et al., 2005; Liu, 2012), SentiWord-Net (Esuli and Sebastiani, 2010), MPQA subjectivity clues

3.1 Pre-processing

Consider following sentence,
Chow fun was dry; pork shu mai was more than usually greasy and had to share a table with loud and rude family[4]

For this sentence, we have following (tar, cat, p, f, t) values:
target="Chow fun", category="FOOD#QUALITY", polarity="negative", from="0", to="8"; target="pork shu mai", category="FOOD#QUALITY", polarity="negative", from="18", to="30"; target="NULL", category="RESTAURANT#MISCELLANEOUS", polarity="negative", from="0", to="0"

Here, from-to values provide the location of *tar* within the sentence.

Based on the observation made on the provided dataset, we hypothesize that only the terms related to *tar* affect the aspect-polarity *p*. In the example above, only "more than usually greasy" is relevant for "pork shu mai". Thus, first we decompose any {SentenceX aspect1:(tar, cat, p, f, t) ... aspectM:(tar, cat, p, f, t)} into {SubSent1 aspect1:(tar, cat, p, f, t), ..., SubSentM aspectM:(tar, cat, p, f, t)}, where M is greater than or equal to 1 and SentenceX is any sentence with aspect values assigned to it.

For decomposition, we first use Stanford Dependency Parser (de Marneffe et al., 2006) to obtain a dependency graph of SentenceX. Using the obtained graph, we choose terms in SentenceX which are more closely related to *tar* terms. For e.g., in *the staff acted like we were imposing on them and they were very rude*, the underlined terms are related in the dependency graph. Here, *tar* is 'staff'. SubSent for any *tar* can be formed using only such related terms.

SubSent formation is not straightforward when *tar* is NULL. We use self-generated *tar* values in such cases. Our intuition is that the terms express-

---

(Wiebe et al., 2005). Bing Liu's lexicons and SentiWordnet are available as part of NLTK package. Bing Liu's lexicons and MPQA are binary, i.e., they simply classify words or terms as positive or negative. SentiWordNet provides a range of positive and negative scores for terms.

[4]This sentence, and all sentences henceforth, are taken from training dataset.

ing sentiment should be related to a noun or pronoun subject (for instance, "loud" and "rude" related to *family*). Thus, after eliminating all SubSent for non-NULL *tar*, sentiment terms in the remaining sentence are identified by looking-up terms in the lexicon corpora. Then, a noun or pronoun related (in dependency graph) to identified terms is considered as *tar*. Since the *global item* is restaurant, if 'food', 'drinks', 'service', 'waiter', 'price', 'staff' or 'ambiance' are present, they are preferably considered as *tar*. Also, 'they', 'she' and 'he' are frequently used to refer to service staff in the provided dataset. Hence, these terms are also preferred as *tar*.

After decomposing, we filter-out stop words selected from NLTK's stop word list. Numbers and symbols (except '!') are also filtered-out using regular expression.

3.2 Features

Following basic features have been used in our model:

1. **Sentiment lexicons** - Separate features for Bing Liu's (binary), MPQA (binary) and SentiWordNet (range of scores).
   Presence of negation terms : The scores of sentiment lexicons are modified according to negation (e.g., 'not', 'didn't', 'don't' etc.). Bing Liu and MPQA features are simply reversed (pos $\rightarrow$ neg, neg $\rightarrow$ pos). For SentiWordnet features, negation is made in proportion to the scores. For e.g., a word like 'extraordinary' having higher positive score is less affected by negation compared to a word like 'good' having lower positive score. We use a simple scheme for score modification: pos = pos + $\frac{(neg-pos)}{2}$ and neg = neg + $\frac{(pos-neg)}{2}$. Here, pos and neg are positive and negative lexicon scores of a term, receptively. A significant work on negation problem has been done by (Zhu et al., 2014). They provide several methods to perform shifting of sentiment scores.

2. **Uni-grams and Bi-grams** extracted from each SubSent.

3. **Self-generated list of neutral terms** - Based on observation made on provided training dataset, we found that following terms frequently occur in "neutral" polarity SubSent(s): 'average', 'normal', 'simple', 'okay', 'ok', 'not great', 'nothing great', 'moderate', 'typical', 'alright', 'fair', 'mediocre', 'just', 'fine', 'not too good', 'good enough'
   These terms and phrases do not necessarily fall in positive or negative category of lexicon features. Hence, these are used as separate uni-grams. Terms in a phrase like 'not too good' are concatenated as 'not0too0good'.

4. **Punctuation** like '!'. In the training dataset, this punctuation mostly co-occurs with positive polarity. Hence, the occurrence of the punctuation is checked.

5. **Keywords associated with specific aspect category** - There are a total of 12 aspect-categories (*cat*) such as FOOD#QUALITY, FOOD#PRICES, RESTAURANT#GENERAL, SERVICE#GENERAL etc. in the provided dataset. For a specific *cat*, there could be keywords which, when co-occurring with the *cat*, express some sentiment. For e.g., high and low are generic terms but for FOOD#PRICES they can indicate a polar sentiment. We divide the dataset into 12 documents, one for each *cat*. Then, we identify keywords based on Term Frequency - Inverse Document Frequency (TF-IDF) scores. The frequently occurring terms are added to a keyword list. Frequency thresholds of min:0.3 & max:0.8 are used. Total 12 keyword lists are obtained, one for each *cat*. Then, for each {SubSent aspect:(tar, cat, p, f, t)}, we check for presence of keywords corresponding to *cat* in SubSent. If found, the keywords are used as new uni-gram features.

These are the features used for basic classification model. In the next sub-section, we describe inclusion of sequence pattern.

3.3 Using precedent polarity sequence (experimental)

Following observations are made on the provided training dataset:
1. In majority of the cases, the sentences under the

same rID exhibit similar sentiment. In other words, polarity values $\{p_1, p_2, ..., p_N\}$, under same rID, are equal. Henceforth, we will refer to this as *Flow*.

2. There are sentences where the polarity values change, i.e., p_i is not equal to p_{i-1}, under same rID. Henceforth, we will refer to this as *Trans* (transition). *Trans* instances may be identified by explicit contrast terms present around *tar*. The common contrast terms found in the dataset are: 'but', 'however', 'though', 'tho', 'although', 'yet', 'except'

For instance, *The decor is right tho...but they REALLY need to clean that vent in the ceiling...its quite un-appetizing, and kills your effort to make this place look sleek and modern*

target="place" polarity="negative"; target="decor" polarity="positive"; target="vent" polarity="negative"

However, this does not imply that a contrast term is always present when *Trans* happens.

Exploiting the '*Flow or Trans*' patterns can help address ambiguity. This is the main reason for including sequence pattern. Consider following sentence:

The manager came to the table and said we can do what we want, so we paid for what we did enjoy, the drinks and appetizers.

For a classifier, the sentiment expressed towards 'manager' may be ambiguous. Our basic model classifies this as *neutral*, while the true polarity is *negative*. However, if we take previous sentence in consideration - *The level of rudeness was preposterous* - the state of mind of the reviewer becomes more clear.

Based on this observation, we hypothesize that, under same review (rID), precedent polarity outcome affects current polarity outcome, either by *Flow* or *Trans*, given certain conditions. (Vanzo et al., 2014) propose a context-based model for sentiment analysis of tweets, on similar lines. They use sequence of tweets to build Conversational context, hashtags to build Topical context and also use Markovian approach.

We describe our methods to account for *Flow* or *Trans* here.

Method1: We use new set of features instead of basic feature-set discussed in sub-section 3.2. First, we generate the features representing conditions for *Flow* or *Trans*. We use two conditions for our model - contrast keywords and sentiment keywords - present in a SubSent. The training dataset is divided into 3 sub-sets according to polarity labels. Then, we search for sentiment terms belonging to one of the lexicon corpora, sentiment terms with negation terms (bi-grams and tri-grams) and terms belonging to our neutral word list. A new dictionary D is created with these terms. Moreover, TF-IDF based selection is performed on the 3 sub-sets (or documents). Frequency thresholds are min:0.3 & max:0.8. This ensures inclusion of any frequent keywords which are not already a member of D. Then, for a $SubSent_i$, feature set $X_i = \{posD, negD, neutD, cont\}_i$ is generated. Here, *posD*: terms in a SubSent belonging to positive section of D; *negD*: terms in a SubSent belonging to negative section of D; *neutD*: terms in a SubSent belonging to neutral section of D; *cont*: contrast terms in SubSent.

Separate sentiment classes have been used here to let the classifier learn how strongly a SubSent is inclined towards any particular sentiment type. The classifier should learn that if such inclination is strong, then ambiguity is low. So, effect of previous SubSent should also be low.

New input feature-set corresponding to $SubSent_i$ is $\mathbf{X(i)} = \{X_i, X_{i-1}, X_{i-2}\}$, plus, selective features from sub-section 3.2. For initial two SubSent(s) under a rID, X_{i-2} or both X_{i-1} and X_{i-2} are empty. We do not use n-gram and neutral word features because terms are now selected from D. Punctuation is ignored since its effect is minimal (Table 1). *cat* specific keywords are included because they are extracted using different document-types. Lexicon scores are also included to capture sentiment strength. The same SVM-RBF classifier is then trained with $\mathbf{X}$ to predict polarities. For test data, same dictionary D is used to generate new features.

Method2: This method is along the lines of auto-regression[5]. However, polarity sequence is not a strict time-series. Hence, we devise our mathematical model with necessary considerations. A first set of predicted polarities $P_1 = \{p_{11}, p_{12}, ..., p_{1k}\}$ are obtained using SVM-RBF with all of the basic

---

[5] <http://paulbourke.net/miscellaneous/ar/>

features from sub-section 3.2. Polarities are mapped as {*positive, negative, neutral*} → {1,-1,0}. The aim is to obtain final predictions, $P_2 = \{p_{21}, p_{22}, ..., p_{2k}\}$. Feature-set $X_i = \{posD_i, negD_i, neutD_i, cont_i\}$ for $SubSent_i$ of test data is obtained using D. However, we do not predict using these features. The *Flow* or *Trans* effect is directly calculated using P_1 values. For each $SubSent_i$, we define following values:

s_i^p : positive vote. This is initialized by *0*, then incremented by *+1* for first term found in $posD_i$ and by *+0.5* for every next term in $posD_i$,

s_i^n : negative vote. This is initialized by *0*, then incremented by *-1* for first term found in $negD_i$ and by *-0.5* for every next term in $negD_i$,

s_i^o : neutral vote. This is initialized by *0.4* (s_{imin}^o), then incremented by $(1-s_i^o)/4$ for every term found in $neutD_i$, keeping the value below 1.

c_i : contrast vote. This is initialized by *+1*; assigned $c_i = 2$, if $cont_i$ is not empty,

w_i : aggregate voting weight. This is calculated as, $w_i = |p_{1i}|(|(p_{1i}+1)/2|(2s_i^p + s_i^n) + |(p_{1i}-1)/2|(s_i^p + 2s_i^n) + s_{imin}^o) + ||p_{1i}|-1|s_i^o$,

Since, a SubSent must express some sentiment, we assume a basic neutral characteristic in each SubSent. Hence, s_{imin}^o is added.

We define a function $g(w,p) = |w|(p + ||p|-1|)$. Then, using these parameters we calculate a weighted effect, $\hat{p}(i)$, for polarity as,

$E_i = g(w_{i-1},p_{1,i-1})+\sum_{r=l}^{r=i-1}(c_r/c_{r-1})g(w_{r-1},p_{1,r-1})$,

$E_{i(avg)} = E_i/(1+\sum_{r=l}^{r=i-1}(c_r/c_{r-1}))$,

$\hat{p}(i) = g(w_i,p_{1i}) + E_{i(avg)}/2c_i$.

The increment and assignment values have been chosen after experimenting with different values. Also, for our model, $l = i-2$ works best. Effect value E_i captures the effect of precedent polarities. The effect of a polarity value $p_{1,i-2}$ should be amplified with respect to $p_{1,i-1}$ if $p_{1,i-1}$ came by contrast and reduced if $p_{1,i-2}$ itself came by contrast. Hence, $p_{1,i-2}$ is multiplied with c_{i-1}/c_{i-2}. Finally, the average effect $E_{i(avg)}$ should be reduced if current $SubSent_i$ has explicit contrast terms. Hence, the division by $2c_i$. Then, if $\hat{p}(i)<0$, $p_{2i} = -1$; if $\hat{p}(i)>1$, $p_{2i} = 1$; otherwise, $p_{2i} = 0$.

These equations are tuned based on observations made on training data. More generic and robust equations need to be formed. This needs further investigation.

Features	Accuracy
n-grams only	0.61 (+/- 0.04)
lexicons-with-negation (lx) only	0.64 (+/- 0.06)
n-grams + lx	0.69 (+/- 0.05)
n-grams + lx + neutral terms (nt)	0.71 (+/- 0.04)
n-grams + lx + nt + punctuation	0.71 (+/- 0.05)
n-grams + lx + nt + keywords (kw)	0.75 (+/- 0.04)
Method1 + n-grams + lx + nt + kw	0.79 (+/- 0.04)
Method1 + lx + kw	0.80 (+/- 0.04)
Method2	0.82 (+/- 0.04)

Table 1: Model performance on training dataset.

4 Analysis and Evaluation Results

4.1 Analysis using training data

The analysis of our system on training data is provided in Table 1. SVM-RBF with parameters : [C=100, kernel='rbf', gamma = 0.001] is used (same for evaluation/test). Parameters are obtained using grid search. The accuracy scores are obtained using 10-fold cross-validation from scikit-learn (Pedregosa et al., 2011). N-grams obtained using dependency relation with aspect-target are base features. Lexicons are essential to capture sentiment types and scores. However, we found that there were some terms occurring in neutral sentences which were not listed in lexicon corpora. Hence, we generated our own list of neutral words. Punctuation (!) has negligible effect on the performance. Including aspect-category keywords improves accuracy. As discussed earlier, keywords are required to include terms that express some opinion specific to a category. These are the only basic features used. On top of this, we include polarity sequence pattern. It can be seen that Method2 provides better result than Method1 by a slight margin only. Method2 may not be necessarily better, but we prefer using it. It theoretically permits using more than one precedent polarities in the sequence, if required, without involving complex features; only the summation series needs to be expanded as we go along a polarity sequence. Method2 is used in final Evaluation model.

Due to time constraint, we focus more on inclusion of polarity sequence pattern instead of engineering better features or classifier ensemble.

System	Accuracy	Ratio	Rank
AKTSKI	0.717	616/859	24
Highest1 : XRCE	0.881	757/859	1
Highest2 : IIT-TUDA	0.867	745/859	2
Baseline	0.764	657/859	21

Table 2: Evaluation results. Ratio is no. of correct predictions/total no. of aspects. Accuracy values are on scale of 0 to 1.

Score	System1	System2	System3
Accuracy	0.668	0.702	0.717
Precision	0.480	0.510	0.500
Recall	0.482	0.500	0.506

Table 3: Comparative performance. System1: without sequence pattern, System2: using Method1, System3: Using Method2. Accuracy values are on scale of 0 to 1.

4.2 Evaluation result

The result of evaluation is provided in Table 2. There were 676 sentences in the evaluation (test) data and 859 instances of aspect values (tar, cat, f, t). The polarity values had to be predicted. The system predictions were evaluated against gold labels by the organizers. There were total 30 submissions in polarity detection task for Restaurant domain and English language. This included multiple submissions from single teams as well. Relative performance of our system was poor. This may be attributed to less effort invested on improving classifier model (using ensembles, or otherwise) or on using more robust features. We also suspect that {posD, negD, neutD, cont} features may be biased towards training data as the keyword dictionary D was generated on the full training dataset before evaluation. Moreover, Method2 is tuned using training data and expected to perform weaker on unseen datasets.

4.3 Further evaluation on gold-labeled data

We did further evaluation of our system after release of gold-labeled test data. This was aimed at checking the effect of using sequence pattern. The results are provided in Table 3. The accuracy obtained against gold labels without using sequence pattern was 0.668. By using Method1, the accuracy increased to 0.702. With Method2, the accuracy obtained was 0.717. These are small increments. Also, the method has obvious caveats as mentioned above. So, the usage of sequence pattern needs to be improved by more research.

5 Conclusion

We submitted unconstrained system for sentiment polarity detection. The system was unconstrained in the sense that it used several external resources for feature generation. Apart from standard features, we experimented with polarity sequence pattern. This approach provides slight improvement in prediction accuracy as checked on evaluation data. However, for any serious purpose, this approach requires deeper investigation. Our next step would be to devise more robust feature-extraction to handle polarity sequence patterns. Moreover, this approach needs to be tested on broader datasets. We will also explore using sequence pattern with multi-class Platt Scaling (Zadrozny and Elkan, 2002) or ensemble models to check performance.

References

Marie-Catherine de Marneffe, Bill MacCartney, and Christopher D. Manning. 2006. Generating typed dependency parses from phrase structure parses. In *Proceedings of the fifth international conference on Language Resources and Evaluation (LREC)*.

Stefano Baccianella Andrea Esuli and Fabrizio Sebastiani. 2010. Sentiwordnet 3.0: An enhanced lexical resource for sentiment analysis and opinion mining. In *Proceedings of the 9th international conference on Language Resources and Evaluation (LREC)*.

Svetlana Kiritchenko, Xiaodan Zhu, Colin Cherry, and Saif Mohammad. 2014. Nrc-canada-2014: Detecting aspects and sentiment in customer reviews. In *Proceedings of the 8th International Workshop on Semantic Evaluation (SemEval 2014)*, pages 437 – 442. Association for Computational Linguistics.

Bing Liu, Minqing Hu, and Junsheng Cheng. 2005. Opinion observer: Analyzing and comparing opinions on the web. In *In Proceedings of the 14th International World Wide Web conference*.

Bing Liu. 2012. *Sentiment Analysis and Opinion Mining*. Synthesis Lectures on Human Language Technologies.

Edward Loper and Steven Bird. 2002. Nltk: The natural language toolkit. In *Proceedings of the ACL Workshop on Effective Tools and Methodologies for Teaching Natural Language Processing and Computational*

Linguistics. Philadelphia: Association for Computational Linguistics. Association for Computational Linguistics.

Julian McAuley, Jure Leskovec, and Dan Jurafsky. 2012. Learning attitudes and attributes from multi-aspect reviews. In *Proceedings of the 12th IEEE International Conference on Data Mining*, Brussels, Belgium. IEEE Computer Society.

McCallum and Andrew Kachites. 2002. *MALLET: A Machine Learning for Language Toolkit.*

F. Pedregosa, G. Varoquaux, A. Gramfort, V. Michel, B. Thirion, O. Grisel, M. Blondel, P. Prettenhofer, R. Weiss, V. Dubourg, J. Vanderplas, A. Passos, D. Cournapeau, M. Brucher, M. Perrot, and E. Duchesnay. 2011. Scikit-learn: Machine learning in Python. *Journal of Machine Learning Research*, 12:2825 – 2830.

Maria Pontiki, Dimitrios Galanis, Haris Papageorgiou, Ion Androutsopoulos, and Suresh Manandhar. 2015. SemEval-2015 task 12: Aspect based sentiment analysis. In *Proceedings of the 9th International Workshop on Semantic Evaluation*, SemEval '15, pages 486 – 495. Association for Computational Linguistics.

Maria Pontiki, Dimitrios Galanis, Haris Papageorgiou, Ion Androutsopoulos, Suresh Manandhar, Mohammad AL-Smadi, Mahmoud Al-Ayyoub, Yanyan Zhao, Bing Qin, Orphée De Clercq, Véronique Hoste, Marianna Apidianaki, Xavier Tannier, Natalia Loukachevitch, Evgeny Kotelnikov, Nuria Bel, Salud Maria Jiménez-Zafra, and Gülşen Eryiğit. 2016. SemEval-2016 task 5: Aspect based sentiment analysis. In *Proceedings of the 10th International Workshop on Semantic Evaluation*, SemEval '16, San Diego, California, June. Association for Computational Linguistics.

Josê Saias. 2015. Sentiue: Target and aspect based sentiment analysis in semeval-2015 task 12. In *Proceedings of the 9th International Workshop on Semantic Evaluation (SemEval 2015)*, pages 767 – 771.

Andrea Vanzo, Danilo Croce, and Roberto Basili. 2014. A context-based model for sentiment analysis in twitter. In *Proceedings of COLING 2014, the 25th International Conference on Computational Linguistics*, pages 2345–2354, Dublin, Ireland, August. Association for Computational Linguistics.

Bo Wang and Min Liu. 2015. *Deep Learning For Aspect-Based Sentiment Analysis*. Stanford University report, https://cs224d.stanford.edu/reports/WangBo.pdf.

Janyce Wiebe, Theresa Wilson, and Claire Cardie. 2005. *Annotating expressions of opinions and emotions in language*. Language Resources and Evaluation.

Bianca Zadrozny and Charles Elkan. 2002. Transforming classifier scores into accurate multiclass probability estimates. In *Proceedings of the 8th ACM SIGKDD Conference on Knowledge Discovery and Data Mining*, Alberta, Canada.

Xiaodan Zhu, Hongyu Guo, Saif Mohammad, and Svetlana Kiritchenko. 2014. An empirical study on the effect of negation words on sentiment. In *Proceedings of the 52nd Annual Meeting of the Association for Computational Linguistics*, pages 304 – 313. Association for Computational Linguistics.

MayAnd at SemEval-2016 Task 5: Syntactic and word2vec-based Approach to Aspect-based Polarity Detection in Russian

Vladimir Mayorov and **Ivan Andrianov**
Institute for System Programming of the Russian Academy of Sciences
25 Alexander Solzhenitsyn Street
Moscow, Russia
`vmayorov@ispras.ru, ivan.andrianov@ispras.ru`

Abstract

This paper describes aspect-based polarity detection system for Russian, used in aspect-based sentiment analysis task (ABSA) of SemEval-2016 (Task 5, subtask 1, slot 3). The system consists of two independent classifiers: for opinion target expressions and for implicit opinion target mentions. We introduce a set of standard unigram features together with more sophisticated ones: based on sentence syntactic structure and based on lemmas vector representation.

Being applied to Russian restaurant reviews, our system achieved best quality among four participants.

1 Introduction

Aspect-based sentiment analysis task (ABSA) drew much attention with the growth of Internet retail sites and facilities for customers to make a free text product review. ABSA systems allow businesses to track reputation of their products even more granularly than before: per aspect. At the same time, customers can be provided with per-aspect sentiment summaries of reviews about concurrent products to simplify their choice.

SemEval-2016 Task 5 (ABSA) organizers (Pontiki et al., 2016) proposed two subtasks: Sentence-level ABSA and Text-level ABSA. First subtask was split to three slots: Aspect Category Detection, Opinion Target Expression, Sentiment Polarity. Training data for the task were available for various languages (English, Russian, etc.) and domains (restaurants, laptops, etc.).

Slot 3 can be described as follows: given a set of reviews labeled with OTEs (opinion target expressions: start-end-entity-attribute quadruples) determine a polarity label for each OTE: positive, negative, neutral (mildly positive or mildly negative sentiment). Additionally polarity labels should be computed for entity-attribute pairs assigned to reviews sentences.

This paper describes our team participation in slot 3 evaluation for Russian language Restaurant domain. The rest of the article is structured as follows: section 2 mentions some recent approaches to aspect-based polarity detection task, section 3 contains our system description, section 4 provides our system evaluation results.

2 Related work

According to (Andrianov et al., 2015), aspect-based polarity detection methods can be divided to three categories: classifier-based (Zhang and Lan, 2015; Hamdan et al., 2015; Blinov and Kotelnikov, 2015), neural network-based (Tarasov, 2015) and unsupervised (García Pablos et al., 2015). Most promising approaches according to recent evaluations results (Pontiki et al., 2015; Loukachevitch et al., 2015) are classifier-based methods, especially semi-supervised ones which bring "external knowledge" (word2vec (Mikolov et al., 2013), Brown clusters (Brown et al., 1992), polarity lexicons (Baccianella et al., 2010; Wilson et al., 2005)) into the table. Semi-supervised techniques become extremely useful due to lack of labeled data for the aspect-based sentiment analysis task in general and polarity detection subtask in particular.

Proceedings of SemEval-2016, pages 325–329,
San Diego, California, June 16-17, 2016. ©2016 Association for Computational Linguistics

3 System Description

Our aspect-based polarity detection system consists of two independent parts: OTE polarity classifier and implicit entity mention polarity classifier. Both parts are based on linear SVM with L2 regularization for three classes: positive, negative, neutral (available training set contains the only conflict polarity label, thus it is ignored).

At first, we preprocess review using Texterra (Turdakov et al., 2014) system. We perform tokenization, part of speech tagging, lemmatization and syntactic parsing for each review sentence.

All used features can be grouped to several classes:

- opinion target features;

- sentence-level lexical features;

- syntactic-level features.

Some most valuable features are based on word vector representation obtained by word2vec. For word2vec training we used 40140 unlabeled reviews from restoclub[1] resource. All word2vec models were trained with same dimensionality (100) and same window size (10). We tried word2vec with different input data preprocessing approaches: without preprocessing, with lowercased words and with lemmatized words. The last one demonstrates the best result on 8-fold cross-validation (see section 4 for details).

The rest of this section describes each group of features in details.

3.1 Opinion Target Features

Initially we tried to train separate SVM classifiers for each entity-aspect pair. Unfortunately training data contains just a few examples of certain entity-attribute pairs (e.g., *DRINKS#PRICES* are presented in training data only 17 times). Moreover, we suspect that different entities can share most part of sentiment vocabulary for some attributes (e.g., quality).

So, we decided to use a single SVM classifier for all entity-aspect labels and to extract two additional features: opinion target entity label and opinion target attribute label. These features are used in both system parts.

---

[1]www.restoclub.ru

3.2 Sentence-level Features

As implicit entity mention has no boundaries, we use the whole sentence to extract its features. We use a number of common features, usually exploited in NLP tasks: sentence word unigrams, sentence lemma unigrams, part of speech tag of each word in sentence. Moreover we use frequency of punctuation token unigrams in sentence as a feature.

Described features group is used for implicit entity mention polarity classifier as well as for OTE polarity classifier, because of slight quality improvement.

For OTE polarity classification information about entity mention is also used: we utilize vector representations of lemmatized sentence words. We extract lemmas in window of size 5 (5 words to the left and 5 words to the right from OTE), map them to vector representations and concatenate these representations.

3.3 Syntactic-level features

Figure 1: Syntactic dependency parsing for review sentence "I would like to mention very nice table appointments."

OTE polarity classifier exploits a number of syntactic-level features. Our basic assumption is that OTE polarity is closely related to some dependent words (especially adjectives), which may express sentiment. Our system uses Texterra syntactic dependency parser to produce syntactic tree of input sentence.

Each OTE should match subtree in syntactic tree, which is treated as a single node. In case OTE is not a subtree, syntactic-level features for classifi-

Data source	Preprocessing	Accuracy	Positive F1	Negative F1	Neutral F1
Wikipedia	–	0.8095	0.8907	0.5615	0.2766
	lowercase	0.8089	0.8909	0.5515	0.2820
	lemmatization	0.8113	0.8928	0.5566	0.2930
Restoclub	–	0.8137	0.8937	0.5700	0.2906
	lowercase	0.8158	0.8955	0.5662	0.3086
	lemmatization	**0.8189**	**0.8966**	**0.5817**	**0.3271**

Table 1: 8-fold cross-validation with different word2vec training settings

cation are abandoned. For instance, Figure 1 depicts syntactic tree extracted from review sentence "I would like to mention very nice table appointments.". Opinion target expression "Table appointments" is a subtree, so it is treated as a single node.

We start from using OTE parent words as features: we extract a chain of parent words for given OTE (up to 3 words), and use their lemmas vector representations as features. In example syntactic tree (Figure 1) there are two parent words: "otmetit'" at depth 1 and "hochu" at depth 2.

Additionally we use syntactic children chains to extract some relevant features. For each word dependent on OTE (in parent-child chains of length up to 2) we use syntactic relations path conjoint with word form, lemma and lemma vector representation as features. In example (Figure 1) syntactic children words are "krasivuju" with relations path "attributive" and "ochen'" with relations path "attributive-restrictive".

4 Evaluation

4.1 word2vec Training Settings

During system development we tried several word2vec models trained with different settings. We varied data sources (Russian Wikipedia and restaurant reviews obtained from restoclub.ru) and data preprocessing (without preprocessing, lowercased words and lemmatized words). We experimented with 8-fold cross-validation on training data. The best result was obtained with restoclub.ru data source and lemmatization preprocessing (see Table 1).

4.2 Features Impact

In this section we try to evaluate each feature group impact. We test quality of our system with all de-

scribed features on test data (using gold labels provided by organizers after evaluation) and using 8-fold cross-validation on train data (as we did before evaluation). Then we consecutively test our system without some group of features. Test results are presented in Table 2.

Features	cv on train data	on test data
All	**0.8189**	0.7808
All - opinion target	0.8128 (-0.0061)	**0.7923 (+0.0123)**
All - sentence-level	0.7793 (-0.0396)	0.7038 (-0.0770)
All - syntactic	0.8142 (-0.0047)	0.7777 (-0.0031)
All - word2vec	0.8029 (-0.0160)	0.7661 (-0.0147)

Table 2: Features impact evaluation. Accuracy score of the system with various features sets

In spite of the fact that word lemmas vector representation features are present in sentence-level and syntactic features groups, we additionally test these features impact separately.

As it could be seen, most significant feature groups are sentence level features and lemma vector representation features. However, large impact of sentence-level features group is explained with the fact that implicit entity mention polarity classifier uses a few additional features, and when we don't use sentence-level features it uses only opinion target features. If we test OTE polarity classifier separately, we obtain 0.8115 accuracy score without sentence-level features versus 0.8287 with all features on cross-validation (0.0172 impact) and 0.7746 versus 0.7860 on test data (0.0114 impact).

4.3 Evaluation Results

The official results are presented in Table 3. Our system (MayAnd) official result differs from result presented in Table 2 due to regrettable inadvertence with training dataset. Our system was trained on initially published data instead of revised dataset that had been published later. Table 2 reflects actual quality of our system (trained on the latest published dataset).

System name	Result (Accuracy)
MayAnd	**0.7792**
INSIG.	0.7508
IIT-T.	0.7362
Danii.	0.7331
baseline	*0.7100*

Table 3: Evaluation official results

5 Conclusion

Aspect-based sentiment analysis task and polarity detection subtask are still at their early days. Current methods are not able to significantly overcome trivial baselines. The following directions of future work can be recommended: collecting more reviews for various languages and domains to improve quality of unsupervised techniques like word2vec; development of sentiment lexicons for non-English languages and various domains.

Acknowledgments

This work has been supported by the RFBR grant No. 15-37-20375.

References

Ivan Andrianov, Vladimir Mayorov, and Denis Turdakov. 2015. Modern approaches to aspect-based sentiment analysis. In *Proceedings of the Institute for System Programming*, volume 27, pages 5–22.

Stefano Baccianella, Andrea Esuli, and Fabrizio Sebastiani. 2010. Sentiwordnet 3.0: An enhanced lexical resource for sentiment analysis and opinion mining. In *LREC*, volume 10, pages 2200–2204.

Pavel Blinov and Evgeny Kotelnikov. 2015. Semantic similarity for aspect-based sentiment analysis. In *Proceedings of the 21st International Conference on Computational Linguistics Dialog-2015*, volume 2, pages 36–45.

Peter F Brown, Peter V deSouza, Robert L Mercer, Vincent J Della Pietra, and Jenifer C Lai. 1992. Class-based n-gram models of natural language. *Computational linguistics*, 18(4):467–479.

Aitor García Pablos, Montse Cuadros, and German Rigau. 2015. V3: Unsupervised aspect based sentiment analysis for semeval2015 task 12. In *Proceedings of the 9th International Workshop on Semantic Evaluation (SemEval 2015)*, pages 714–718, Denver, Colorado, June. Association for Computational Linguistics.

Hussam Hamdan, Patrice Bellot, and Frederic Bechet. 2015. Lsislif: Crf and logistic regression for opinion target extraction and sentiment polarity analysis. In *Proceedings of the 9th International Workshop on Semantic Evaluation (SemEval 2015)*, pages 753–758, Denver, Colorado, June. Association for Computational Linguistics.

Natalia Loukachevitch, Pavel Blinov, Evgeny Kotelnikov, Yuliya Rubtsova, Vladimir Ivanov, and Elena Tutubalina. 2015. Sentirueval: testing object-oriented sentiment analysis systems in russian. In *Proceedings of the 21st International Conference on Computational Linguistics Dialog-2015*, volume 2, pages 12–24.

Tomas Mikolov, Kai Chen, Greg Corrado, and Jeffrey Dean. 2013. Efficient estimation of word representations in vector space. *arXiv preprint arXiv:1301.3781*.

Maria Pontiki, Dimitris Galanis, Haris Papageorgiou, Suresh Manandhar, and Ion Androutsopoulos. 2015. Semeval-2015 task 12: Aspect based sentiment analysis. In *Proceedings of the 9th International Workshop on Semantic Evaluation (SemEval 2015)*, pages 486–495, Denver, Colorado, June. Association for Computational Linguistics.

Maria Pontiki, Dimitrios Galanis, Haris Papageorgiou, Ion Androutsopoulos, Suresh Manandhar, Mohammad AL-Smadi, Mahmoud Al-Ayyoub, Yanyan Zhao, Bing Qin, Orphée De Clercq, Véronique Hoste, Marianna Apidianaki, Xavier Tannier, Natalia Loukachevitch, Evgeny Kotelnikov, Nuria Bel, Salud María Jiménez-Zafra, and Gülşen Eryiğit. 2016. SemEval-2016 task 5: Aspect based sentiment analysis. In *Proceedings of the 10th International Workshop on Semantic Evaluation*, SemEval '16, San Diego, California, June. Association for Computational Linguistics.

Dmitriy Tarasov. 2015. Deep recurrent neural networks for multiple language aspect-based sentiment analysis of user reviews. In *Proceedings of the 21st International Conference on Computational Linguistics Dialog-2015*, volume 2, pages 77–88.

Denis Turdakov, Nikita Astrakhantsev, Yaroslav Nedumov, Andrey Sysoev, Ivan Andrianov, Vladimir Mayorov, Denis Fedorenko, Anton Korshunov, and Sergey Kuznetsov. 2014. Texterra: A framework for text analysis. *Programming and Computer Software*, 40(5):288–295.

Theresa Wilson, Janyce Wiebe, and Paul Hoffmann. 2005. Recognizing contextual polarity in phrase-level sentiment analysis. In *Proceedings of the conference on human language technology and empirical methods in natural language processing*, pages 347–354. Association for Computational Linguistics.

Zhihua Zhang and Man Lan. 2015. Ecnu: Extracting effective features from multiple sequential sentences for target-dependent sentiment analysis in reviews. In *Proceedings of the 9th International Workshop on Semantic Evaluation (SemEval 2015)*, pages 736–741, Denver, Colorado, June. Association for Computational Linguistics.

INSIGHT-1 at SemEval-2016 Task 5: Deep Learning for Multilingual Aspect-based Sentiment Analysis

Sebastian Ruder[12]   **Parsa Ghaffari**[2]   **John G. Breslin**[1]

[1]Insight Centre for Data Analytics
National University of Ireland, Galway
`firstname.lastname@insight-centre.org`

[2]Aylien Ltd.
Dublin, Ireland
`firstname@aylien.com`

Abstract

This paper describes our deep learning-based approach to multilingual aspect-based sentiment analysis as part of Se-mEval 2016 Task 5. We use a convolutional neural network (CNN) for both aspect extraction and aspect-based sentiment analysis. We cast aspect extraction as a multi-label classification problem, outputting probabilities over aspects parameterized by a threshold. To determine the sentiment towards an aspect, we concatenate an aspect vector with every word embedding and apply a convolution over it. Our constrained system (unconstrained for English) achieves competitive results across all languages and domains, placing first or second in 5 and 7 out of 11 language-domain pairs for aspect category detection (slot 1) and sentiment polarity (slot 3) respectively, thereby demonstrating the viability of a deep learning-based approach for multilingual aspect-based sentiment analysis.

1   Introduction

With access to the Internet becoming more prevalent, an inreasing number of people express their opinions online in a plethora of lan-guages. Sentiment analysis (Liu, 2012) enables us to derive shallow insights from these opinions related to their overall polarity. Often, however, e.g. in reviews, people do not express their opinion towards the entity as a whole, but refer to specific aspects such as the service in a restaurant.

Aspect-based sentiment analysis allows us to go deeper and determine sentiment towards such aspects of an entity. Past research in aspect-based sentiment analysis has largely fo-cused on the English language, while SemEval 2016 Task 5 (Pontiki et al., 2016) for the first time provides a forum for multilingual aspect-based sentiment analysis.

Recently, deep learning-based approaches have demonstrated remarkable results for text classification and sentiment analysis (Kim, 2014). A cascade of non-linearities allows them to model complex functions such as sentiment compositionality, while their ability to process raw signals renders them language and domain independent. In spite of these factors, they have largely gone untested for aspect-based senti-ment analysis, particularly in the multilingual setting.

In this paper, we introduce our deep-learning

Proceedings of SemEval-2016, pages 330–336,
San Diego, California, June 16-17, 2016. ©2016 Association for Computational Linguistics

based approach to aspect-based sentiment analysis as part of our participation in SemEval-2016 Task 5 Aspect-based Sentiment Analysis Slot 1 (Aspect Category Detection) and Slot 3 (Sentiment Polarity) .

2 Related work

Aspect-based sentiment analysis is traditionally split into an aspect extraction and a sentiment analysis subtask.

Previous approaches to aspect extraction framed the task as a multiclass classification problem and relied mostly on CRS that leveraged a plethora of common features, e.g. NER, POS tagging, parsing, semantic analysis, bag-of-words, as well as domain-dependent ones, such as word clusters learnt from Amazon and Yelp data, while previous sentiment analysis approaches have used different classifiers with a wide range of features based on n-grams, POS, negation words, and a large array of sentiment lexica (Pontiki et al., 2014; Pontiki et al., 2015).

Past deep learning-based approaches have focused mostly on the sentiment analysis subtask: Tang et al. (2015) use a target-dependent LSTM to determine sentiment towards a target word, while Nguyen and Shirai (2015) use a recursive neural network that leverages both constituency as well as dependency trees.

In contrast to previous approaches, our model neither relies on expensive feature engineering, availability of a parser, nor positional information, but solely on a language's input signals.

3 Model

The model architecture we use is an extension of the CNN structure used by Collobert et al. (2011), which has been successfully used by many others (Kim, 2014).

The model takes as input a text, which is padded to length n. We represent the text as a concatenation of its word embeddings $x_{1:n}$ where $x_i \in \mathbb{R}^k$ is the k-dimensional vector of the i-th word in the text.

The convolutional layer slides filters of different window sizes over the input embeddings. Each filter with weights $w \in \mathbb{R}^{hk}$ generates a new feature c_i for a window of h words according to the following operation:

$$c_i = f(w \cdot x_{i:i+h-1} + b) \tag{1}$$

Note that $b \in \mathbb{R}$ is a bias term and f is a non-linear function, ReLU (Nair and Hinton, 2010) in our case. The application of the filter over each possible window of h words or characters in the sentence produces the following feature map:

$$c = [c_1, c_2, ..., c_{n-h+1}] \tag{2}$$

Max-over-time pooling in turn condenses this feature vector to its most important feature by taking its maximum value and naturally deals with variable input lengths.

A final softmax layer takes the concatenation of the maximum values of the feature maps produced by all filters and outputs a probability distribution over all output classes.

4 Methodology

4.1 Preprocessing

We lower-case and tokenize the corpus, where applicable, keeping the 10,000 most frequent words as the vocabulary for each language and domain. For Chinese, in preparation for the previous step, we additionally segment the corpus using the `mmseg` Python library.

4.2 Hyperparameters

We randomly split off 20% of each training data set as a validation set. We use this to optimize

Listing 1: Example sentence with aspect and sentiment annotations for the English laptops domain.

```
1 <sentence id="347:0">
2     <text>I bought it for really cheap also and its AMAZING.</text>
3     <Opinions>
4         <Opinion category="LAPTOP#PRICE" polarity="positive"/>
5         <Opinion category="LAPTOP#GENERAL" polarity="positive"/>
6     </Opinions>
7 </sentence>
```

hyperparameters via random search over a wide range of values.

For both tasks and all languages and domains, we use the following hyperparameters, which are similar to those reported by Kim (2014): mini-batch size of 10, maximum sentence length of 100 tokens, word embedding size of 300, dropout rate of 0.5, and 100 filter maps. We use filter lengths of 3, 4, and 5, and of 4, 5, and 6 for aspect extraction and aspect-based sentiment analysis respectively since these produced good results for the respective task.

English word embeddings are initialized with 300-dimensional GloVe vectors (Pennington et al., 2014) trained on 840B tokens of the Common Crawl corpus for the unconstrained submission. Word embeddings for the constrained submission, for all other languages, as well as for words not present in the pre-trained set of words are initialized randomly.

We train for 15 epochs using mini-batch stochastic gradient descent, the Adadelta update rule (Zeiler, 2012), and early stopping.

4.3 Aspect Category Detection

To extract aspects, e.g. `LAPTOP#PRICE` and `LAPTOP#GENERAL` from sentences as in Listing 1, we cast aspect extraction as a multi-label classification problem and train a convolutional neural network (CNN) to output probability distributions over aspects, minimizing the cross-entropy loss. To model multi-label output as a probability distribution, we define an aspect a's probability p given a sentence s as $p(a|s) = 1/n$ if a appears in s and s contains n aspects, otherwise $p(a|s) = 0$. We define a threshold f and discard all aspects with $p(a|s) < f$. After training, we select f maximizing the F1 score on the validation set.

We observe that aspect distributions vary significantly depending on the domain and language. For instance, the English laptops domain contains 82 aspects, while the restaurants domain only contains 13 aspects.

In every domain, we thus replace all aspects that occur less than 5 times with an `OTHER` aspect.[1] E.g. this produces 51 aspects covering 98% of occurrences and all 13 aspects for the English laptops and restaurants domain respectively. For instance, in the English laptops domain, aspects such as `HARDWARE#MISCELLANEOUS` and `BATTERY#USABILITY`, which occur less than 5 times are replaced with `OTHER` during training. We add a `NONE` aspect to each sentence containing no aspect to enable the CNN

---

[1] We found that replacing all aspects with fewer than 5 occurrences yields the best trade-off between accuracy and recall.

to make no aspect prediction. During inference, every time the model predicts OTHER, the most frequent aspect replaced by OTHER for each domain is output instead. For the English laptops domain, this can be one of several aspects, e.g. SOFTWARE#QUALITY occurring four times. Finally, we discard all predicted NONE aspects.

We experimented with producing representations for the preceding and subsequent sentence to take context information into account, but this did not improve results.

4.4 Sentiment Polarity

For aspect-based sentiment analysis, we feed the aspect vector together with the word embeddings of the input sentence into a CNN. To obtain the aspect vector, we follow an approach similar to the one used by Socher et al. (2013) to represent named entities: We split each aspect into its constituent tokens, e.g. RESTAURANT#GENERAL → *restaurant, general*. We embed the tokens of all aspects in an embedding space. We then look up the embedding of each of the tokens and average them to retrieve the aspect vector. This way, the model should learn that aspects sharing the same entity, e.g. *restaurant* are correlated without the need to train several tiered models to classify between entities (*restaurant*) and attributes (*general*).

For aspect-based sentiment analysis in the English language, we embed aspect tokens in the same embedding space as word tokens to exploit the semantics of pre-trained embeddings. For all other languages, we keep the embedding spaces separate, as aspect tokens are in English and word tokens are in the respective languages. Translating aspect tokens into the source language did not provide any benefits, but the use of pre-trained embeddings in the source language could ameliorate this.

We have experimented with different variants of adding aspect embeddings to our model: We evaluated summation, concatenation, and multiplication of word vectors and aspect vectors before the convolution, and multiplication and concatenation of the max-pooled sentence vector and the aspect vector after the convolution. We find that concatenating each word vector with the aspect vector before the convolution yields the best results.

To summarize, for the sentence in Listing 1 and the aspect LAPTOP#PRICE, our model first pads the input sentence, then looks up the embeddings of each of the input words. It creates the aspect vector by splitting LAPTOP#PRICE into the aspect tokens *laptop* and *price*. For these, it looks up the embeddings in the aspect embedding space (which is the same as for word embeddings for English) and averages both embeddings. The resulting aspect vector is then concatenated with each word vector, which are then concatenated to produce a 100x600 sentence matrix. Convolutions, max-pooling and softmax are applied to this matrix as described in section 3.

We observe for some languages an incremental performance improvement when using additional average-pooling as reported by Tang et al. (2014). We further note that simply using a low-dimensional embedding space to embed aspects leads to superior results on a few occasions when no pre-trained word embeddings are used.

5 Evaluation

We have participated for all domains and languages in Slot 1: Aspect Category Detection and Slot 3: Sentiment Polarity. We report results for aspect extraction in Table 1 and results for aspect-based sentiment analysis in Table 2.

Lg.	Dom.	F1	Top F1	R.
EN	REST	68.108 U 58.303 C	73.031	9/30
SP	REST	61.370	70.588	5/9
FR	REST	53.592	61.207	4/6
RU	REST	62.802	64.825	2/7
DU	REST	56.000	60.153	2/6
TU	REST	49.123	61.029	5/5
AR	HOTE	52.114	52.114	1/3
EN	LAPT	45.863 U 41.458 C	51.937	10/22
DU	PHNS	45.551	45.551	1/4
CH	CAME	25.581	36.345	2/4
CH	PHNS	16.286	22.548	3/4

Table 1: F1 and rank of our system for aspect extraction for each language and domain in comparison to the best system. Lg.: Language. Dom.: Domain. R.: Rank. EN: English. SP: Spanish. FR: French. RU: Russian. TU: Turkish. AR: Arabic. DU: Dutch. CH: Chinese. REST: Restaurants. HOTE: Hotels. LAPT: Laptops. PHNS: Phones. CAME: Cameras. U: Unconstrained submission. C: Constrained submission.

5.1 Aspect Category Detection

Despite using only the input sentence as data, our system is able to achieve competitive performance for multilingual aspect extraction, placing first or second in 5 out of 11 language-domain pairs. However, for English, Spanish, French, and Turkish, the differential with regard to the best performing system still remains large. We observe that initializing the system with general-purpose pre-trained embeddings provides a significant performance boost, which is most pronounced in the English restaurants domain.

Consequently, we hypothesize that the most straightforward way to overcome this performance differential is to initialize the system with embeddings trained on a large mono-lingual corpus in the target language. Incorporating domain information used by best-performing systems (Pontiki et al., 2015) by pre-training on a large in-domain corpus such as the dataset released as part of the Yelp Dataset Challenge[2] should further improve results.

The multi-label condition is currently enforced only after prediction through the application of a threshold, which may potentially discard promising aspects or retain erroneous ones, while the current normalization of aspect probabilities might lead to the loss of signals. To make the model more robust, the multi-label condition can be integrated more naturally into the architecture, e.g. by adapting the error function and using a trainable thresholding function as in (Zhang et al., 2006).

5.2 Sentiment Polarity

We report convincing results for multilingual aspect-based sentiment analysis, placing first or second for 7 out of 11 language-domain pairs. Again, the difference in performance compared to the best-performing system is largest for English, Spanish, French, and Turkish. To mitigate this, pre-trained word embeddings as described in 5.1 can be used.

However, without relying on dependency and constituency trees (Nguyen and Shirai, 2015) or positional information (Tang et al., 2015), the model falls short of being able to reliably triangulate aspects, particularly in sentences with opposing sentiments toward different aspects. Simply concatenating each word vector with the aspect vector does not seem to provide the model with enough expressiveness to model truly aspect-dependent sentiment. Training the model to associate different surface forms with their aspect instantiations should help to ame-

---

[2]https://www.yelp.com/dataset_challenge

Lg.	Dom.	Acc.	Top Acc.	R.
EN	REST	82.072 **U** 80.210 **C**	88.126	7/28
SP	REST	79.571	83.582	4/5
FR	REST	73.166	78.826	4/6
RU	REST	75.077	77.923	2/6
DU	REST	75.041	77.814	3/4
TU	REST	74.214	84.277	2/3
AR	HOTE	82.719	82.719	1/3
EN	LAPT	78.402 **U** 74.282 **C**	82.772	2/21
DU	PHNS	83.333	83.333	1/3
CH	CAME	78.170	80.457	2/5
CH	PHNS	72.401	73.346	2/5

Table 2: Accuracy and rank of our system for aspect-based for each language and domain in comparison to the best system. For legend, refer to Table 1.

liorate this.

6 Conclusion

In this paper, we have presented a deep learning-based approach to aspect-based sentiment analysis, which employs a convolutional neural network for aspect extraction and sentiment analysis as part of our submission to SemEval-2016 Task 5. We have demonstrated convincing results in the multilingual setting, which is particularly appropriate for neural networks due to their language and domain independence. We have evaluated our model, outlining weaknesses and potential future improvements.

Acknowledgments

This project has emanated from research conducted with the financial support of the Irish Research Council (IRC) under Grant Number EBPPG/2014/30 and with Aylien Ltd. as Enterprise Partner. This publication has emanated from research supported in part by a research grant from Science Foundation Ireland (SFI) under Grant Number SFI/12/RC/2289.

References

Ronan Collobert, Jason Weston, Leon Bottou, Michael Karlen, Koray Kavukcuoglu, and Pavel Kuksa. 2011. Natural Language Processing (almost) from Scratch. *Journal of Machine Learning Research*, 12(Aug):2493–2537.

Yoon Kim. 2014. Convolutional Neural Networks for Sentence Classification. *Proceedings of the Conference on Empirical Methods in Natural Language Processing*, pages 1746–1751.

Bing Liu. 2012. Sentiment Analysis and Opinion Mining. *Synthesis Lectures on Human Language Technologies*, 5(1):1–167.

Vinod Nair and Geoffrey E Hinton. 2010. Rectified Linear Units Improve Restricted Boltzmann Machines. *Proceedings of the 27th International Conference on Machine Learning*, (3):807–814.

Thien Hai Nguyen and Kiyoaki Shirai. 2015. PhraseRNN : Phrase Recursive Neural Network for Aspect-based Sentiment Analysis. (September):2509–2514.

Jeffrey Pennington, Richard Socher, and Christopher D Manning. 2014. Glove: Global Vectors for Word Representation. *Proceedings of the 2014 Conference on Empirical Methods in Natural Language Processing*, pages 1532–1543.

Maria Pontiki, Dimitrios Galanis, John Pavlopoulos, Haris Papageorgiou, Ion Androutsopoulos, and Suresh Manandhar. 2014. SemEval-2014 Task 4: Aspect Based Sentiment Analysis. *Proceedings of the 8th International Workshop on Semantic Evaluation (SemEval 2014)*, pages 27–35.

Maria Pontiki, Dimitris Galanis, Haris Papageorgiou, Suresh Manandhar, and Ion Androutsopoulos. 2015. SemEval-2015 Task 12: Aspect Based Sentiment Analysis. *Proceedings of the 9th International Workshop on Semantic Evaluation (SemEval 2015)*, pages 486–495.

Maria Pontiki, Dimitrios Galanis, Haris Papageorgiou, Ion Androutsopoulos, Suresh Manandhar,

Mohammad AL-Smadi, Mahmoud Al-Ayyoub, Yanyan Zhao, Bing Qin, Orphée De Clercq, Véronique Hoste, Marianna Apidianaki, Xavier Tannier, Natalia Loukachevitch, Evgeny Kotelnikov, Nuria Bel, Salud María Jiménez-Zafra, and Gülşen Eryiğit. 2016. SemEval-2016 Task 5: Aspect-Based Sentiment Analysis. In *Proceedings of the 10th International Workshop on Semantic Evaluation*, San Diego, California. Association for Computational Linguistics.

Richard Socher, Danqi Chen, Christopher D. Manning, and Andrew Y. Ng. 2013. Reasoning With Neural Tensor Networks for Knowledge Base Completion. *Proceedings of the Advances in Neural Information Processing Systems 26 (NIPS 2013)*, pages 1–10.

Duyu Tang, Furu Wei, Nan Yang, Ming Zhou, Ting Liu, and Bing Qin. 2014. Learning Sentiment-Specific Word Embedding. *Proceedings of the 52nd Annual Meeting of the Association for Computational Linguistics*, 1:1555–1565.

Duyu Tang, Bing Qin, Xiaocheng Feng, and Ting Liu. 2015. Target-Dependent Sentiment Classification with Long Short Term Memory. *arXiv preprint arXiv:1512.01100*.

Matthew D. Zeiler. 2012. ADADELTA: An Adaptive Learning Rate Method. *arXiv preprint arXiv:1212.5701*.

Min-ling Zhang, Zhi-hua Zhou, and Senior Member. 2006. Multilabel Neural Networks with Applications to Functional Genomics and Text Categorization. *IEEE Transactions on Knowledge and Data Engineering*, 18(10):1338–1351.

TGB at SemEval-2016 Task 5: Multi-Lingual Constraint System for Aspect Based Sentiment Analysis

Fatih Samet Çetin
Istanbul Technical University
cetinfatih@itu.edu.tr

Ezgi Yıldırım
Istanbul Technical University
yildirimez@itu.edu.tr

Can Özbey
Turkcell Global Bilgi
canozbeycan@gmail.com

Gülşen Eryiğit
Istanbul Technical University
gulsen.cebiroglu@itu.edu.tr

Abstract

This paper gives the description of the TGB system submitted to the Aspect Based Sentiment Analysis Task of SemEval-2016 (Task 5). The system is built on linear binary classifiers for aspect category classification (Slot 1), on lexicon-based detection for opinion target expressions extraction (Slot 2), and on linear multi-class classifiers for sentiment polarity detection (Slot 3). We conducted several different approaches for feature selection to improve classification performance on both Slot 1 and Slot 3. Our proposed methods are easily adaptable to all languages and domains since they are built as constrained systems which do not use any additional resources other than the provided datasets and which uses standard preprocessing methods.

1 Introduction

Since Web 2.0 and social media platforms have become popular in recent times, the amount of accessible text data has shown rapid increase. The manual analysis of this huge amount of data is almost impossible to accomplish in a reasonable time, thus automatic sentiment analysis and opinion mining have turned into a significant requirement for companies. The most of earlier studies conducted in this area were generally focused on document level (Yıldırım, et al., 2015; Pang, et al., 2002; Esuli & Sebastiani, 2006) until the recognition of that different opinions can exist in the same sentence or paragraphs. Another disadvantage of general sentiment analysis approaches is the disability to match the sentiment polarities to the target entities. Therefore, this type of analysis becomes insufficient for deep understanding of opinions about products and features. The most commonly referenced study (Liu, 2012) on Aspect-Based Sentiment Analysis (ABSA) discusses the problem as extracting the tuples including multiple opinions.. The need for a detailed sentiment analysis with respect to specific target entities has given birth to ABSA. In International Workshop on Semantic Evaluation (SemEval), a shared task called Aspect-based Sentiment Analysis has been actualized since 2014 (Pontiki, et al., 2014; Pontiki, et al., 2015; Pontiki, et al., 2016). In this year's task, the data is annotated at both sentential and textual levels with reference to predefined domain-dependent aspect categories. For more information and details about the aspect categories consult (Pontiki et al., 2016). The task description (SemEval, 2016) provides regulations as to how these categories should be determined.

This paper presents our system prepared for ABSA 2016. It covers 3 different languages, namely, English, Spanish and Dutch. The system has multi-lingual capabilities giving nearly con-

Proceedings of SemEval-2016, pages 337–341,
San Diego, California, June 16-17, 2016. ©2016 Association for Computational Linguistics

sistent performances for each language. Our proposed methods are easily adaptable to all languages due to their multi-lingual nature by switching language codes for stemming phase. Considering the individual tasks, we have applied specific methods for each characteristic problem. In order to accomplish the task, we used different approaches for different slots. In order to find aspect category (Slot 1), we used a multi classifier approach which uses textual and probabilistic features. A lexicon based approach is chosen to extract the opinion target expressions (OTE) (Slot 2). We used a linear classifier which utilizes aspect category, aspect attribute and OTE features as well as textual features to detect the sentiment class for an opinion tuple (Slot 3).

2 System Description

In this section we present our aspect based sentiment analysis system. The system is experimented on the Restaurant datasets. Our submission is composed of the experiments on three languages; English, Dutch and Spanish. English dataset consists of 300 reviews and 2000 sentences, Spanish dataset has 627 reviews and 2070 sentences, and Dutch dataset contains 300 reviews and 1722 sentences.

The following preprocessing steps are used in all datasets:

- Removing html codes/URLs
- Tokenization
- Stemming

Sentences are tokenized and analyzed with Apache Lucene (Foundation, 2016) Analyzers which contains different types of operations. These operations are tokenization, filtering and transforming. In this system, we have used Standard Lucene Tokenizer for tokenization. Afterwards, we applied lowercase transformation on top of the previous step. In the following stage stemming is applied to all tokens using Snowball stemmer (Porter, 2001). An applied version of Snowball stemmer is already presented in the Lucene project. Finally, Lucene Shingle Filter is used to extract unigram and bigram features. In all of the introduced methods, we used these unigrams and bigrams (of the word stems in the datasets) as textual features,.

For the classification task, we use logistic regression from LIBLINEAR (Fan, 2008-9) classification library. LIBLINEAR is an open source library for large-scale linear classification (Fan, 2008-9). It provides easy-to-use command-line tools and library calls for users and developers.

We have implemented a generic framework to make text classification on LIBLINEAR library. Our framework basically provides an infrastructure to developers for building custom preprocessing steps and classification systems. Developers only need to be aware of framework's interfaces and Lucene Analyzers.

2.1 Aspect Category Classification (Slot 1)

In order to detect aspect categories, we used a two-layered approach. First layer consists of one-vs-all binary classifiers for the detection of each different aspect entity (E) and aspect attribute (A). This first layer is used to obtain the possibilities of an instance to belong to the corresponding classes (entity or attribute). The obtained probabilities will be further used in the second layer for the ultimate classification.

In the first layer, according to the instances available in different training sets (for each different language), at most 11 distinct binary classifiers are independently trained. For instance representation, we use unigram and bigram features occurring in the training sets.

Features	Instance
Textual Features 1	1
⋮	⋮
Textual Features n	0
FOOD	0,45
DRINKS	0,33
SERVICE	0,41
AMBIENCE	0,65
LOCATION	0,17
RESTAURANT	0,75
GENERAL	0,5
PRICES	0,33
QUALITY	0,65
STYLE&OPTIONS	0,67
MISCELLANEOUS	0,85
CLASS	AMBIENCE#GENERAL

Table 1: Feature representation of ultimate classifier

In the second layer, we construct an ultimate classifier which uses additional features extracted from the first layer's output. These are entity and attribute labels used as real-valued features (as opposed to the binary unigram and bigram textual features). This feature representation is depicted in Table 1. The probabilities from the previous layer are assigned as values for these features. The ultimate classifier is trained in order to produce aspect categories (E#A) that are composed of both entity and attribute label. Architectural model of the proposed method can be seen in Figure 1.

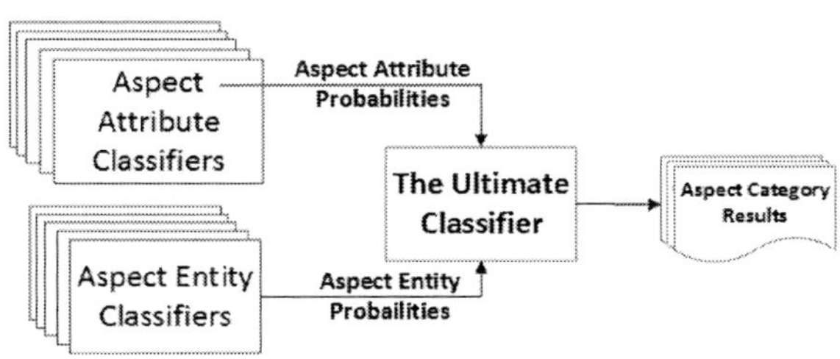

Figure 1: Slot 1 System Architecture

2.2   Opinion Target Extraction (Slot 2)

In opinion target extraction task, we basically follow the baseline opinion target extraction (OTE) procedure proposed in SemEval ABSA 2016 shared task with some changes and assumptions over it.

First, we extracted all opinion targets of each E#A pair from the training set, then used them to check if an opinion target is matched when a new sentence is examined during testing. If an opinion target is detected and the E#A pair of sentence is identical with the E#A pair of stored opinion target, this opinion target is assigned to the sentence. While we are extracting opinion targets from the training data, we applied different preprocessing steps composed of only lowercasing and asciiification. However, in some cases many different opinion targets are found to be related to the same E#A pair. In these situations, we applied different approaches to choose the most suitable opinion target from all possible candidates.

Our first assumption is that if an opinion target already contains another one in itself (as a sub-unit), the longer one should be the specialized version of the same opinion target and assumed to be the most proper indication of the relevant opinion target. For instance, *"traditional dishes"* is better than only *"dishes"* while it contains the subsequent.

Even if we aimed to singularize extracted opinion targets with the first assumption, it is still possible to end up with several opinion candidates after this reduction method. Therefore, we applied some secondary approaches to singularize them. First, we experimented with utilizing the frequencies of opinion targets for each E#A pair. For instance, if "pasta" and "spaghetti" are detected as possible opinion targets of a sentence, and "pasta" is more frequent than "spaghetti" for "FOOD#PRICE" pair, "pasta" is preferred in this scenario. Second, we examined the selection of the longest opinion target from all candidates for the same E#A pair because of the similar assumption to the first one: the longer, the better. well decorated and lighted place" is a better choice than "charming place".

After we evaluated the success of our assumptions, we found the best results by selecting the first inclusive opinion targets, and later the longer ones if still necessary.

2.3   Slot 1&2

To generate the predictions for Slot 1&2, we combine Slot 1 predictions with that of Slot 2. In this phase, instead of using gold E#A pair annotations to match them to opinion target expressions as we did in the Slot 2 prediction phase, we directly utilize the predictions of Slot 1. If any of the predictions of Slot 1 cannot be linked to any opinion targets, we assigned a NULL expression to these opinion targets.

2.4   Polarity Detection (Slot 3)

For sentiment polarity detection, gold standard aspect category and aspect terms are provided in the training sets. Therefore, the problem is to find and fill the sentiment polarity of each opinion tuple. We use a single classifier approach for solving the problem. Our classifier is able to determine the polarity class of the tuple from three types of polarity. Polarity classes are "positive", "negative" and "neutral".

We use textual as well as the features obtained from the previous aspect category detection phase. In other words aspect entity, aspect attribute and aspect terms are also placed in the feature representation of the train set. Each of the aspect entity, aspect attributes and aspect terms are represented with binary features. Therefore, 6 additional features for aspect entity, 5 additional features for aspect attribute and additional OTE features of the number of unique opinion targets in dataset are used in our feature representation. While producing feature value set for an instance, values are assigned according to the feature existence in the instance. The mentioned features can be shown in Table 2. After the feature representation, a single classifier is trained using the Logistic Regression algorithm.

Features	Instance
Textual Features 1	1
⋮	⋮
Textual Features n	0
ENTITY-FOOD	1
ENTITY-DRINKS	0
ENTITY-SERVICE	0
ENTITY-AMBIENCE	0
ENTITY-LOCATION	0
ENTITY-RESTAURANT	0
ATTRIBUTE-GENERAL	0
ATTRIBUTE-PRICES	0
ATTRIBUTE-QUALITY	1
ATTRIBUTE-STYLE&OPTIONS	0
ATTRIBUTE-MISCELLANEOUS	0
TERM-expensive	0
TERM-wine list	0
TERM-restaurant	0
TERM-delicious	1
⋮	⋮
TERM-price	0
CLASS	positive

Table 2: Slot 3 feature representation

3   Results

We submitted our constrained system predictions to all slots of Subtask 1 for the restaurant domain. Since we use a common method for each language, we expected to have similar results for each language. According to the results of the task's evaluation, this expectation seems to be satisfied. Except for the English dataset, we highly ranked for all slots and languages that we've applied. In Dutch dataset, our Slot 1, Slot 1&2 and Slot 3 results are the best one and we obtained the second rank for Slot 2.

However, we would like to emphasize that the best result for Slot 2 is obtained by an unconstrained system. So, we may say that our system provides successful results for constrained systems. We attained similar successful results also in the Spanish dataset especially among constrained systems. In the English dataset we obtained fourth best score among thirty constrained system for Slot 3 and third best score for Slot 1&2.

TEAM	C/U	F-1
TGB	C	60.153
INSIG.	C	56
IIT-T.	U	55.247
IIT-T.	C	54.98
UFAL	U	53.876
baseline	C	42.816

Table 3: Dutch dataset- Slot 1 results table

TEAM	C/U	F-1
TGB	C	77.814
IIT-T.	U	76.998
INSIG.	C	75.041
basel.	C	69.331

Table 4: Dutch dataset – Slot 3 results table

TEAM	C/U	F-1
IIT-T.	U	83.582
TGB	C	82.09
UWB	C	81.343
INSIG.	C	79.571
basel.	C	77.799

Table 5: Spanish dataset – Slot 3 results table

TEAM	C/U	F-1
NLANGP	U	52.607
XRCE	C	48.891
NLANGP	C	45.724
TGB	C	43.081
bunji	U	41.113
UWB	C	41.108
UWB	U	41.088
⋮	⋮	⋮

Table 6: English dataset - Slot1&2 results table

4   Conclusion

In this paper, we show our experiments and approaches on aspect category classification and sentiment polarity detection using supervised machine learning methods and opinion target extraction using lexicon based approaches. For these problems, we used only the supplied resources by the shared task committee. We built well-performed multi-lingual systems which do not require additional resources and special manipulations for different languages and domains except only stemmers for the preprocessing stage. By the successful data preparation and feature extraction methods, our system gives reasonable results on aspect category classification and sentiment polarity prediction of sentences and detection of related opinion expressions if in question.

Acknowledgments

This work is accomplished as a part of a TUBITAK-TEYDEB (The Scientific and Technological Research Council of Turkey - Technology and Innovation Funding Programs Directorate) project (grant number: 3140671) in "Turkcell Global Bilgi" Information Technology Department.

References

Esuli, A., & Sebastiani, F. (2006). Sentiwordnet: A publicly available lexical resource for opinion mining. *Proceedings of LREC*, (pp. 417-422).

Fan, R. E. (2008-9). LIBLINEAR: A library for large linear classification. *The Journal of Machine Learning Research*, 1871-1874.

Foundation, A. S. (2016). *Lucene*. Retrieved from Apache Lucene: https://lucene.apache.org/

Liu, B. (2012). Sentiment analysis and opinion mining. *Synthesis lectures on human language technologies*, 1-167.

Pang, B., Lee, L., & Vaithyanathan., S. (2002). Thumbs up?: sentiment classification using machine learning techniques. *Proceedings of the ACL-02 conference on Empirical methods in natural language processing-Volume 10* (pp. 79-86). Association for Computational Linguistic.

Pontiki, M., Galanis, D., Papageorgiou, H., Androutsopoulos, I., Manandhar, S., AL-Smadi, M., Al-Ayyoub, M., Zhao, Y., Qin, B., De Clercq, O., Hoste, V., Apidianaki, M., Tannier, X., Loukachevitch, N., Kotelnikov, E., Bel, N., Zafra, S., Eryiğit, G. (2016). SemEval-2016 Task 5: Aspect Based Sentiment Analysis. *In Proceedings of the 10th International Workshop on Semantic Evaluation*. San Diego: Association for Computational Linguistics.

Pontiki, M., Galanis, D., Papageorgiou, H., Manandhar, S., & Androutsopoulos, I. (2015). Semeval-2015 task 12: Aspect based sentiment analysis. *In Proceedings of the 9th International Workshop on Semantic Evaluation* (pp. 486-495). Association for Computational Linguistics.

Pontiki, M., Galanis, D., Pavlopoulos, J., Papageorgiou, H., Androutsopoulos, I., & Manandhar, S. (2014). Semeval-2014 task 4: Aspect based sentiment analysis. *international workshop on semantic evaluation (SemEval 2014)*, (pp. 27-35).

Porter, M. F. (2001). Snowball: A language for stemming algorithms.

SemEval. (2016). *SemEval-2016 Task 5*. Retrieved from SemEval: http://alt.qcri.org/semeval2016/task5/

Yıldırım, E., Çetin, F. S., Eryiğit, G., & Temel, T. (2015). The impact of NLP on Turkish sentiment analysis. *TÜRKİYE BİLİŞİM VAKFI BİLGİSAYAR BİLİMLERİ ve MÜHENDİSLİĞİ DERGİSİ*.

UWB at SemEval-2016 Task 5: Aspect Based Sentiment Analysis

Tomáš Hercig[†‡], Tomáš Brychcín[‡], Lukáš Svoboda[†‡] and Michal Konkol[†‡]
[†] Department of Computer Science and Engineering, Faculty of Applied Sciences,
University of West Bohemia, Univerzitní 8, 306 14 Plzeň, Czech Republic
[‡] NTIS – New Technologies for the Information Society, Faculty of Applied Sciences,
University of West Bohemia, Technická 8, 306 14 Plzeň, Czech Republic
`tigi@kiv.zcu.cz`   `brychcin@kiv.zcu.cz`

`svobikl@kiv.zcu.cz`   `konkol@kiv.zcu.cz`

Abstract

This paper describes our system used in the Aspect Based Sentiment Analysis (ABSA) task of SemEval 2016. Our system uses Maximum Entropy classifier for the aspect category detection and for the sentiment polarity task. Conditional Random Fields (CRF) are used for opinion target extraction. We achieve state-of-the-art results in 9 experiments among the constrained systems and in 2 experiments among the unconstrained systems.

1 Introduction

The goal of Aspect Based Sentiment Analysis (ABSA) is to identify the aspects of a given target entity and estimate the sentiment polarity for each mentioned aspect. In recent years the aspect-based sentiment analysis has undergone rapid development mainly because of competitive tasks such as SemEval 2014 (Pontiki et al., 2014) and SemEval 2015 (Pontiki et al., 2015). The highest ranking participants are for SemEval 2014 (Kiritchenko et al., 2014; Brun et al., 2014; Castellucci et al., 2014; Toh and Wang, 2014; Wagner et al., 2014; Brychcín et al., 2014) and for SemEval 2015 (Saias, 2015; Toh and Su, 2015a; San Vicente et al., 2015; Zhang and Lan, 2015).

In the current ABSA task - SemEval 2016 task 5 (Pontiki et al., 2016) has attracted 29 participating teams competing in 40 different experiments among 8 languages. The task has three subtasks: Sentence-level (SB1), Text-level (SB2) and Out-of-domain ABSA (SB3). The subtasks are further divided into three slots:

- 1) Aspect Category Detection – the category consists of an entity and attribute (E#A) pair.

- 2) Opinion Target Expression (OTE)

- 3) Sentiment Polarity (positive, negative, neutral, and for SB2 conflict)

In phase A we solved slots 1 and 2. In phase B we were given the results for slots 1 and 2 and solved slot 3. We participate in 19 experiments including Chinese, English, French, and Spanish.

2 System Description

Our approach to the ABSA task is based on supervised Machine Learning. Detailed description for each experiment can be found in Section 2.2 and Section 2.3.

2.1 Features

Our system combines a large number of features to achieve competitive results. In this section we will describe the features in detail.

2.1.1 Semantics Features

We use semantics models to derive word clusters from unlabeled datasets. Similarly to (Toh and Su, 2015b) we use the `Amazon` product reviews from (Blitzer et al., 2007) and the user reviews from the `Yelp` Phoenix Academic Dataset[1] to create semantic word clusters. Additionally, we use a review `Opentable` dataset[2]. In this paper we consider the following semantics models.

---

[1] `https://www.yelp.com/dataset_challenge`
[2] downloaded from `http://opentable.com`

Proceedings of SemEval-2016, pages 342–349,
San Diego, California, June 16-17, 2016. ©2016 Association for Computational Linguistics

	Dimension	**Window**	**Iterations**
GloVe	300	10	100
CBOW	300	10	100
LDA	–	sentence	1000

Table 1: Model settings.

Global Vectors (GloVe) (Pennington et al., 2014) use the ratios of the word–word co-occurrence probabilities to encode the meanings of words.

Continuous Bag-of-Words (CBOW) (Mikolov et al., 2013) is model based on Neural Network Language Model (NNLM) that tries to predict the current word using a small context window around the word.

Latent Dirichlet Allocation (LDA) (Blei et al., 2003) discovers the hidden topics in text. We experiment with 50, 100, 200, 300, 400, and 500 topics.

The settings of the GloVe and CBOW models reflect the results of these methods in their original publications (Pennington et al., 2014; Mikolov et al., 2013). The detailed settings of all these methods are shown in Table 1.

We used the GloVe implementation provided on the official website[3], CBOW model uses the Word2Vec[4] implementation and the LDA implementation comes from the MALLET (McCallum, 2002) software package.

CLUTO software package (Karypis, 2003) is used for words clustering with the k-means algorithm and cosine similarity metric. All vector space models in this paper cluster the word vectors into four different numbers of clusters: 100, 500, 1000, and 5000.

The following features are based on the word clusters created using the semantic models.

Clusters (C) – The occurrence of a cluster at a given position.

Bag of Clusters (BoC) – The occurrence of a cluster in the context window.

Cluster Bigrams (CB) – The occurrence of cluster bigram at a given position.

[3]http://nlp.stanford.edu/projects/glove
[4]https://code.google.com/p/word2vec

Bag of Cluster Bigrams (BoCB) – The occurrence of cluster bigram in the context window.

2.1.2 Constrained Features

Affixes (A) – Affix (length 2-4 characters) of a word at a given position with a frequency > 5.

Aspect Category (AC) – extracted aspect category. We use separately the entity, attribute, and the E#A pair.

Aspect Target (AT) – listed aspect target.

Bag of Words (BoW) – The occurrence of a word in the context window.

Bag of Words filtered by POS (BoW-POS) – The occurrence of a word in the context window filtered by POS tags.

Bag of Bigrams (BoB) – The occurrence of a bigram in the context window.

Bag of Words around Verb (5V) – Bag of 5 words before verb and a bag of 5 words after verb.

Bag of 5 Words at the Beginning of Sentence (5sS) – Bag of 5 words at the beginning of a sentence.

Bag of 5 Words at the End of Sentence (5eS) – Bag of 5 words at the end of a sentence.

Bag of Head Words (BoHW) – bag of extracted head words from the sentence parse tree.

Emoticons (E) We used a list of positive and negative emoticons (Montejo-Ráez et al., 2012). The feature captures the presence of an emoticon within the text.

Head Word (HW) – extracted head word from the sentence parse tree.

Character N-gram (ChN) – The occurrence of character n-gram at a given position.

Learned Target Dictionary (LTD) – presence of a word from learned[5] dictionary of aspect terms.

Learned Target Dictionary by Category (LTD-C) – presence of a word from the learned dictionary[5] of aspect terms grouped by category.

[5]from training data

N-gram (N) – The occurrence of n-gram in the context window.

N-gram Shape (NSh) – The occurrence of word shape n-gram in the context window. We consider unigrams with frequency >5 and bigrams, trigrams with frequency > 20.

Paragraph Vectors (P2Vec) is an unsupervised method of learning text representation (Le and Mikolov, 2014). Resulting feature vector has a fixed dimension while the input text can be of any length. The model is trained on the *One billion word benchmark* presented in (Chelba et al., 2013), resulting vectors[6] are used as features for a sentence. We use the implementation by Řehůřek and Sojka (2010).

POS N-gram (POS-N) – The occurrence of POS n-gram in the context window.

Punctuation (P) – The occurrence of a question mark, an exclamation mark or at least two dots in the context window.

Skip-bigram (SkB) – Instead of using sequences of adjacent words (n-grams) we used skip-grams (Guthrie et al., 2006; Reyes et al., 2013), which skip over arbitrary gaps. We consider skip-bigrams with 2 to 5 word skips and remove skip-grams with a frequency ≤ 5.

Target Bag of Words (T-BoW) – BoW containing parent, siblings, and children of the target from the sentence parse tree.

TF-IDF (TF-IDF) – Term frequency - inverse document frequency of a word computed from the training data.

Verb Bag of Tags (V-BoT) – Bag of syntactic dependency tags of parent, siblings, and children of the verb from the sentence parse tree.

Verb Bag of Words (V-BoW) – Bag of words for parent, siblings, and children of the verb from the sentence parse tree.

---

[6] Vector dimension has been set to 300.

Word Shape (WSh) – we assign words into one of 24 classes[7] similar to the function specified in (Bikel et al., 1997).

Words (W) – The occurrence of word at a given position (e.g. previous word).

2.1.3 Unconstrained Features

Dictionary (DL) – presence of a word from dictionary extracted from the Annotation Guidelines for Laptops.

Dictionary (DR) – presence of a word from dictionary extracted from the Annotation Guidelines for Restaurants.

Enchanted Dictionary (ED) – presence of a word from a dictionary extracted from website[8].

Group of Words from ED (EDG) – presence of any word from a group from the ED dictionary.

Dictionary of Negative Words (ND) – presence of any negative word from the negative words list[9].

Sentiment (S) – this is a union of features dealing with sentiment. It consists of *BoG* features where the groups correspond to various sentiment lexicons. We used the following lexicon resources: Affinity lexicon (Nielsen, 2011), Senticon (Cruz et al., 2014), dictionaries from (Steinberger et al., 2012), MICRO-WNOP (Cerini et al., 2007), and the list of positive or negative opinion words from (Liu et al., 2005). Additional feature includes the output of Stanford CoreNLP (Manning et al., 2014) v3.6 sentiment analysis package by (Socher et al., 2013).

2.2 Phase A

Sentence-level Category (SB1, slot 1) We use maximum entropy classifier for all classes. Then a threshold t is used to decide which categories will be assigned by the classifier.

---

[7] We use edu.stanford.nlp.process.WordShapeClassifier with the WORDSHAPECHRIS1 setting.

[8] http://www.enchantedlearning.com/wordlist/

[9] http://dreference.blogspot.cz/2010/05/negative-ve-words-adjectives-list-for.html

Chinese We used identical features for both domains (*BoB, BoHW, BoW, ChN, N*), where *ChN* ranges from unigram to 4-gram and *ChN* with frequency < 20 are removed and *N* ranges from unigram to trigram and *ChN* with frequency < 10 are removed. The threshold was set to $t = 0.1$.

Spanish For Spanish we used the following features: *5V, 5eS, BoB, BoHW, BoW, BoW-POS, ChN, V-BoT*, where *5V* considers only adjective, adverb, and noun, *5eS* considers adjectives and adverbs with frequency > 5, *ChN* ranges from unigram to 4-gram and *ChN* with frequency < 20 are removed, *BoW-POS* is used separately for adverbs, nouns, verbs, and a union of adjectives, adverbs, nouns, and verbs, *V-BoT* is used separately for adverbs, nouns, and a union of adjectives and adverbs while reducing feature space by 50 occurrences. The threshold was set to $t = 0.2$.

English English features employ lemmatization. The threshold was set to $t = 0.14$. Common features for all experiments in this task are *5V, 5eS, BoB, BoHW, BoW, BoW-POS, P, TF-IDF, V-BoT*, where *5V* considers only adjective, adverb, and noun, *5eS* filters only adjective and adverb, *BoW-POS* contains adjectives, adverbs, nouns, and verbs, *V-BoT* filters adjectives and adverbs with frequency > 20.

The unconstrained model for the Laptops domain additionally uses *BoC, BoCB, DL, ED, P2Vec BoC* and *BoCB* include the GloVe and CBOW models computed on the Amazon dataset.

The constrained model for the restaurant domain additionally uses *5sS, ChN, LTD, LTD-C, P2Vec 5sS* filters only adjective and adverb, *ChN* in this case means character unigrams with frequency > 5. This model also considers separate *BoW-POS* features for groups for adverbs, nouns and verbs.

The unconstrained model for the restaurant domain uses *BoC, BoCB, DR, LDA, ND, NSh* on top of the previously listed features for the constrained model.

BoC and *BoCB* include the GloVe, CBOW, and LDA models computed on the Yelp dataset and CBOW model computed on the Opentable dataset.

Sentence-level Target (SB1, slot 2) Similarly to (Brychcín et al., 2014), we have decided to use Conditional Random Fields (CRF) (Lafferty et al., 2001)

to solve this subtask. The context for this task is defined as a five word window centred at the currently processed word. English features for this subtask employ lemmatization.

The baseline feature set consists of *A, BoB, BoW-POS, HW, LTD, LTD-C, N, POS-N, V-BoT, W, WSh*. *BoW-POS* contains adjectives, adverbs, nouns, verbs, and a union of adverbs and nouns. We consider *POS-N* with frequency > 10. *V-BoT* includes adverbs, nouns, and a union of adjectives, adverbs, nouns, and verbs.

In the unconstrained model, we extend this with the semantic features *C, CB* (created using the CBOW model computed on the opentable dataset) and with lexicons *DR, EDG*.

Sentence level Category & Target (SB1, slot 1&2) We firstly assign targets as described above and then combine them with the best five candidates for aspect category[10]. We also add aspect categories without target. This produces too many combinations thus we need to filter the unlikely opinions. We remove the opinions without target in a sentence where the aspect category is already present with a target. When there is only one target and one aspect category in a sentence we combine them into a single opinion.

Text-level Category (SB2, slot 1) We used the baseline algorithm: the predicted sentence-level tuples (SB1, slot 1) are copied to text-level and duplicates are removed.

2.3 Phase B

Sentence level Sentiment Polarity (SB1, slot 3) Our sentiment polarity detection is based on the Maximum Entropy classifier, which works very well in many NLP tasks, including document-level sentiment analysis (Habernal et al., 2014).

Chinese We used identical features for both domains (*5V, 5eS, 5sS, AC, BoB, BoHW, BoW, BoW-POS, ChN, N, NSh, P, SkB, V-BoT, V-BoW*), where *5V* considers adjectives and adverbs with frequency > 5, *5eS* and *5sS* contain adjectives, adverbs, nouns, and verbs, *BoW-POS* is used separately for adjectives and adverbs, *ChN* ranges from unigram to 5-

---

[10]We use the same settings and approach as in the sentence-level category detection (SB1 slot 1).

gram and *ChN* with frequency < 5 are removed, *N* ranges from unigram to 5-gram and *ChN* with frequency < 2 are removed, *V-BoT* is used separately for verbs, and a union of adjectives and adverbs, *V-BoW* is used separately for adjectives, adverbs, verbs, a union of adjectives and adverbs and a union of adjectives, adverbs, nouns, and verbs, while reducing feature space by 2 occurrences.

French We employ lemmatization for French. The first constrained model includes the following features: *AC, BoB, BoHW, BoW, BoW-POS, ChN, LTD, LTD-C, N, NSh, P, SkB, V-BoT*, where *BoW-POS* is used separately for adjectives, adverbs and a union of adjectives, adverbs, nouns, and verbs, *ChN* ranges from unigram to 5-gram and *ChN* with frequency $\leq$ 5 are removed, *N* ranges from unigram to 5-gram and *N* with frequency < 2 are removed, *V-BoT* is used separately for verbs, and a union of adjectives and adverbs.

The second constrained model additionally uses *5V, 5eS, 5sS, AT, T-Bow, V-BoW*, where *5V* considers only adjective and adverb, *5eS, 5sS* considers adjective, adverb, noun, and verb, *T-BoW* is used for adjectives, adverbs, nouns, and verbs, *V-BoW* is used separately for adjectives, adverbs, verbs, a union of adjectives and adverbs and a union of adjectives, adverbs, nouns, and verbs, while reducing feature space by 2 occurrences.

Spanish We employ lemmatization for Spanish. We used the following features: *5V, 5eS, AC, BoB, BoHW, BoW, BoW-POS, E, ChN, LTD, LTD-C, N, NSh, P, SkB, T-Bow, V-BoT, V-BoW*, where *5V* considers only adjective and adverb, *5eS* considers adjective, adverb, noun, and verb, *BoW-POS* is used separately for adjectives, adverbs, *ChN* ranges from unigram to 5-gram and *ChN* with frequency $\leq$ 5 are removed, *N* ranges from unigram to 5-gram and *N* with frequency < 2 are removed, *T-BoW* is used for adjectives, adverbs, nouns, and verbs, *V-BoT* is used separately for verbs, and a union of adjectives and adverbs, *V-BoW* is used separately for adjectives, adverbs, verbs, a union of adjectives and adverbs and a union of adjectives, adverbs, nouns, and verbs, while reducing feature space by 2 occurrences.

English We use lemmatization in this subtask. Common features for all experiments in this task

are *5V, 5eS, 5sS, AC, AT, BoB, BoHW, BoW, BoW-POS, E, ChN, LTD, LTD-C, N, NSh, P, SkB, V-BoT, V-BoW*, where *5V* considers adjectives and adverbs, *5eS, 5sS* consists of adjectives, adverbs, nouns, and verbs, , *BoW-POS* contains adjectives and adverbs, *N* ranges from unigram to 5-gram and *N* with frequency < 2 are removed, *V-BoT* is used separately for verbs, and a union of adjectives and adverbs, *V-BoW* is used separately for adjectives, adverbs, verbs, a union of adjectives and adverbs and a union of adjectives, adverbs, nouns, and verbs, while reducing feature space by 2 occurrences.

The unconstrained model for the Laptops domain additionally uses *BoC, BoCB, ED, S BoC* and *BoCB* include the `GloVe` and `CBOW` models computed on the `Amazon` dataset.

The constrained model for the restaurant domain additionally uses *T-Bow, TF-IDF*, where *T-BoW* is used for adjectives, adverbs, nouns, and verbs.

The unconstrained model for the restaurant domain uses *BoC, BoCB, ED, ND, S* on top of the previously listed features for the constrained model.

BoC and *BoCB* include the `GloVe` and `CBOW` models computed on the `Yelp` dataset and `CBOW` model computed on the `Opentable` dataset.

Text-level Sentiment Polarity (SB2, slot 3) The baseline algorithm traverses the predicted sentence-level tuples of the same category and counts the respective polarity labels (positive, negative or neutral). Finally, the polarity label with the highest frequency is assigned to the text-level category. If there are not any sentence-level tuples of the same category the polarity label is determined based on all tuples regardless of the category.

Our improved algorithm contains an additional step, that assigns polarity for cases (categories) with more than one sentence-level polarity labels. The resulting polarity is determined by the following algorithm:

```
if(catPolarity == lastPolarity){
  assign lastPolarity;
}else if(catPolarity == entPolarity){
  assign entPolarity;
}else{
  assign CONFLICT;
}
```

where `catPolarity` is the polarity label with the highest frequency for the given category

Domain	Lang	Subtask	Constrained				Unconstrained			
			Category		Sentiment		Category		Sentiment	
			Rank	$F_1[\%]$	Rank	$ACC[\%]$	Rank	$F_1[\%]$	Rank	$ACC[\%]$
Restaurants	EN	SB1	3.	67.8	2.	81.8	8.	68.2	9.	81.7
Laptops	EN	SB1	1.	47.9	3.	73.8	7.	47.3	10.	73.8
Restaurants	EN	SB2	1.	81.0	1.	80.9	3.	80.2	1.	81.9
Laptops	EN	SB2	1.	60.5	1.	74.5	2.	59.7	1. - 2.	75.0
Restaurants	FR	SB1	–	–	2.	75.3	–	–	–	–
Cameras	CH	SB1	1.	36.3	3.	77.8	–	–	–	–
Phones	CH	SB1	1.	22.5	3.	72.0	–	–	–	–
Restaurants	SP	SB1	3.	62.0	2.	81.3	–	–	–	–
Restaurants	SP	SB2	3.	73.7	1.	77.2	–	–	–	–
			Target		Category & Target		Target		Category & Target	
			Rank	$F_1[\%]$	Rank	$F_1[\%]$	Rank	$F_1[\%]$	Rank	$F_1[\%]$
Restaurants	EN	SB1	1.	66.9	4.	41.1	3.	67.1	6.	41.1

Table 2: Achieved ranks and results (in %) by UWB for all submitted systems.

(E#A touple), `entPolarity` is the polarity label with the highest frequency for the entity E and `lastPolarity` is the last seen polarity label for the given category. This follows our believe that the last polarity tends to reflect the final sentiment (opinion) toward the aspect category.

2.4 System Settings

For all experiments we use Brainy (Konkol, 2014) machine learning library.

Data preprocessing includes lower-casing and in some cases lemmatization.

We utilize parse trees, lemmatization and POS tags from the Stanford CoreNLP (Manning et al., 2014) v3.6 framework. We chose it because it has support for Chinese, English, French, and Spanish.

3 Results and Discussion

As shown in the Table 2 we achieved very satisfactory results especially for the constrained experiments.

In the English sentence level Laptops domain our constrained method was slightly better than the unconstrained one (by 0.6%). We believe this is not a significant deviation.

The baseline algorithm for text-level category (SB2, slot 1)[11] achieves an F_1 score of 96.08% on the Laptops domain and 97.07% on the Restaurants domain for English. When we add the corresponding general class for the given domain (e.g. `RESTAURANT#GENERAL` and `LAPTOP#GENERAL`) the algorithm achieves an F_1 score of 96.87% on the Laptops domain and 99.75% on the Restaurants domain for English.

The baseline algorithm for text-level sentiment polarity (SB2, slot 3)[11] achieves an Accuracy of 86.8% on the Laptops domain and 89.6% on the Restaurants domain for English, while the improved algorithm achieves an Accuracy of 94.5% on the Laptops domain and 97.3% on the Restaurants domain for English.

4 Conclusion

We competed in 19 constrained experiments and won 9 of them. In the other 10 cases we have reached at worst the 4th place. Our unconstrained systems participated in 10 experiments and achieved 5 ranks ranging from the 1st to 3rd place.

In the future we aim to explore the benefits of using neural networks for sentiment analysis.

Acknowledgements

This work was supported by the project LO1506 of the Czech Ministry of Education, Youth and Sports and by Grant No. SGS-2016-018 Data and Software Engineering for Advanced Applications. Computational resources were provided by the CESNET LM2015042 and the CERIT Scientific Cloud LM2015085, provided under the programme "Projects of Large Research, Development, and Innovations Infrastructures".

---

[11]Using the sentence-level gold test data.

References

Daniel M Bikel, Scott Miller, Richard Schwartz, and Ralph Weischedel. 1997. Nymble: a high-performance learning name-finder. In *Proceedings of the fifth conference on Applied natural language processing*, pages 194–201. Association for Computational Linguistics.

D. M. Blei, A. Y. Ng, M. I. Jordan, and J. Lafferty. 2003. Latent Dirichlet allocation. *Journal of Machine Learning Research*, 3:2003.

John Blitzer, Mark Dredze, Fernando Pereira, et al. 2007. Biographies, bollywood, boom-boxes and blenders: Domain adaptation for sentiment classification. In *ACL*, volume 7, pages 440–447.

Caroline Brun, Diana Nicoleta Popa, and Claude Roux. 2014. XRCE: Hybrid classification for aspect-based sentiment analysis. In *Proceedings of the 8th International Workshop on Semantic Evaluation (SemEval 2014)*, pages 838–842, Dublin, Ireland, August. Association for Computational Linguistics.

Tomáš Brychcín, Michal Konkol, and Josef Steinberger. 2014. UWB: Machine learning approach to aspect-based sentiment analysis. In *Proceedings of the 8th International Workshop on Semantic Evaluation (SemEval 2014)*, pages 817–822. Association for Computational Linguistics.

Giuseppe Castellucci, Simone Filice, Danilo Croce, and Roberto Basili. 2014. UNITOR: Aspect based sentiment analysis with structured learning. In *Proceedings of the 8th International Workshop on Semantic Evaluation (SemEval 2014)*, pages 761–767, Dublin, Ireland, August. Association for Computational Linguistics.

Sabrina Cerini, Valentina Compagnoni, Alice Demontis, Maicol Formentelli, and G Gandini. 2007. Micro-WNOp: A gold standard for the evaluation of automatically compiled lexical resources for opinion mining. *Language resources and linguistic theory: Typology, second language acquisition, English linguistics*, pages 200–210.

Ciprian Chelba, Tomas Mikolov, Mike Schuster, Qi Ge, Thorsten Brants, Phillipp Koehn, and Tony Robinson. 2013. One billion word benchmark for measuring progress in statistical language modeling. *arXiv preprint arXiv:1312.3005*.

Fermín L Cruz, José A Troyano, Beatriz Pontes, and F Javier Ortega. 2014. Building layered, multilingual sentiment lexicons at synset and lemma levels. *Expert Systems with Applications*, 41(13):5984–5994.

David Guthrie, Ben Allison, Wei Liu, Louise Guthrie, and Yorick Wilks. 2006. A closer look at skip-gram modelling. In *Proceedings of the 5th international Conference on Language Resources and Evaluation (LREC-2006)*, pages 1–4.

Ivan Habernal, Tomáš Ptáček, and Josef Steinberger. 2014. Supervised sentiment analysis in Czech social media. *Information Processing & Management*, 50(5):693–707.

G. Karypis. 2003. CLUTO—A clustering toolkit.

Svetlana Kiritchenko, Xiaodan Zhu, Colin Cherry, and Saif Mohammad. 2014. NRC-Canada-2014: Detecting aspects and sentiment in customer reviews. In *Proceedings of the 8th International Workshop on Semantic Evaluation (SemEval 2014)*, pages 437–442, Dublin, Ireland, August. Association for Computational Linguistics.

Michal Konkol. 2014. Brainy: A machine learning library. In Leszek Rutkowski, Marcin Korytkowski, Rafa Scherer, Ryszard Tadeusiewicz, Lotfi A. Zadeh, and Jacek M. Zurada, editors, *Artificial Intelligence and Soft Computing*, volume 8468 of *Lecture Notes in Computer Science*. Springer-Verlag, Berlin.

John Lafferty, Andrew McCallum, and Fernando Pereira. 2001. Conditional random fields: Probabilistic models for segmenting and labeling sequence data. In *Proceedings of International Conference on Machine Learning*.

Quoc V. Le and Tomas Mikolov. 2014. Distributed representations of sentences and documents. In *Proceedings of the 31th International Conference on Machine Learning, ICML 2014, Beijing, China, 21-26 June 2014*, pages 1188–1196.

Bing Liu, Minqing Hu, and Junsheng Cheng. 2005. Opinion observer: analyzing and comparing opinions on the web. In *Proceedings of the 14th international conference on World Wide Web*, pages 342–351. ACM.

Christopher D. Manning, Mihai Surdeanu, John Bauer, Jenny Finkel, Steven J. Bethard, and David McClosky. 2014. The Stanford CoreNLP natural language processing toolkit. In *Association for Computational Linguistics (ACL) System Demonstrations*, pages 55–60.

Andrew Kachites McCallum. 2002. MALLET: A machine learning for language toolkit.

Tomas Mikolov, Kai Chen, Greg Corrado, and Jeffrey Dean. 2013. Efficient estimation of word representations in vector space. arXiv preprint arXiv:1301.3781.

A. Montejo-Ráez, E. Martínez-Cámara, M. T. Martín-Valdivia, and L. A. Ureña López. 2012. Random walk weighting over sentiwordnet for sentiment polarity detection on twitter. In *Proceedings of the 3rd Workshop in Computational Approaches to Subjectivity and Sentiment Analysis*, WASSA '12, pages 3–10, Stroudsburg, PA, USA. Association for Computational Linguistics.

Finn Årup Nielsen. 2011. A new ANEW: Evaluation of a word list for sentiment analysis in microblogs. In

Proceedings of the ESWC2011 Workshop on 'Making Sense of Microposts': Big things come in small packages. 93-98.

Jeffrey Pennington, Richard Socher, and Christopher D Manning. 2014. Glove: Global vectors for word representation. In *Proceedings of the 2014 Conference on Empirical Methods in Natural Language Processing (EMNLP)*, pages 1532–1543.

Maria Pontiki, Dimitris Galanis, John Pavlopoulos, Harris Papageorgiou, Ion Androutsopoulos, and Suresh Manandhar. 2014. SemEval-2014 Task 4: Aspect based sentiment analysis. In *Proceedings of the 8th International Workshop on Semantic Evaluation (SemEval 2014)*, pages 27–35, Dublin, Ireland, August. Association for Computational Linguistics and Dublin City University.

Maria Pontiki, Dimitrios Galanis, Haris Papageorgiou, Suresh Manandhar, and Ion Androutsopoulos. 2015. Semeval-2015 task 12: Aspect based sentiment analysis. In *Proceedings of the 9th International Workshop on Semantic Evaluation (SemEval 2015), Association for Computational Linguistics, Denver, Colorado*, pages 486–495.

Maria Pontiki, Dimitrios Galanis, Haris Papageorgiou, Ion Androutsopoulos, Suresh Manandhar, Mohammad AL-Smadi, Mahmoud Al-Ayyoub, Yanyan Zhao, Bing Qin, Orphée De Clercq, Véronique Hoste, Marianna Apidianaki, Xavier Tannier, Natalia Loukachevitch, Evgeny Kotelnikov, Nuria Bel, Salud María Jiménez-Zafra, and Gülşen Eryiğit. 2016. SemEval-2016 task 5: Aspect based sentiment analysis. In *Proceedings of the 10th International Workshop on Semantic Evaluation*, SemEval '16, San Diego, California, June. Association for Computational Linguistics.

Radim Řehůřek and Petr Sojka. 2010. Software Framework for Topic Modelling with Large Corpora. In *Proceedings of the LREC 2010 Workshop on New Challenges for NLP Frameworks*, pages 45–50, Valletta, Malta, May. ELRA. `http://is.muni.cz/publication/884893/en`.

Antonio Reyes, Paolo Rosso, and Tony Veale. 2013. A multidimensional approach for detecting irony in twitter. *Language Resources and Evaluation*, 47(1):239–268.

José Saias. 2015. Sentiue: Target and aspect based sentiment analysis in semeval-2015 task 12. Association for Computational Linguistics.

Inaki San Vicente, Xabier Saralegi, Rodrigo Agerri, and Donostia-San Sebastián. 2015. Elixa: A modular and flexible absa platform. *SemEval-2015*, page 748.

Richard Socher, Alex Perelygin, Jean Y Wu, Jason Chuang, Christopher D Manning, Andrew Y Ng, and Christopher Potts. 2013. Recursive deep models for semantic compositionality over a sentiment treebank.

In *Proceedings of the conference on empirical methods in natural language processing (EMNLP)*, volume 1631, page 1642. Citeseer.

Josef Steinberger, Mohamed Ebrahim, Maud Ehrmann, Ali Hurriyetoglu, Mijail Kabadjov, Polina Lenkova, Ralf Steinberger, Hristo Tanev, Silvia Vzquez, and Vanni Zavarella. 2012. Creating sentiment dictionaries via triangulation. *Decision Support Systems*, 53(4):689 – 694.

Zhiqiang Toh and Jian Su. 2015a. Nlangp: Supervised machine learning system for aspect category classification and opinion target extraction.

Zhiqiang Toh and Jian Su. 2015b. NLANGP: Supervised Machine Learning System for Aspect Category Classification and Opinion Target Extraction. In *Proceedings of the 9th International Workshop on Semantic Evaluation (SemEval 2015)*, pages 496–501, Denver, Colorado, June. Association for Computational Linguistics.

Zhiqiang Toh and Wenting Wang. 2014. DLIREC: Aspect term extraction and term polarity classification system. In *Proceedings of the 8th International Workshop on Semantic Evaluation (SemEval 2014)*, pages 235–240, Dublin, Ireland, August. Association for Computational Linguistics.

Joachim Wagner, Piyush Arora, Santiago Cortes, Utsab Barman, Dasha Bogdanova, Jennifer Foster, and Lamia Tounsi. 2014. DCU: Aspect-based polarity classification for SemEval Task 4. In *Proceedings of the 8th International Workshop on Semantic Evaluation (SemEval 2014)*, pages 223–229, Dublin, Ireland, August. Association for Computational Linguistics.

Zhihua Zhang and Man Lan. 2015. Ecnu: Extracting effective features from multiple sequential sentences for target-dependent sentiment analysis in reviews. *SemEval-2015*, page 736.

SentiSys at SemEval-2016 Task 5: Opinion Target Extraction and Sentiment Polarity Detection

Hussam Hamdan
Aix-Marseille University
hamdan.hussam@gmail.com

Abstract

This paper describes our contribution in Opinion Target Extraction and Sentiment Polarity sub-tasks of SemEval 2016 ABSA task. A Conditional Random Field model has been adopted for opinion target extraction. A Logistic Regression model with a weighting schema of positive and negative labels has been used for sentiment polarity. Our submission for opinion target extraction is ranked second among the constrained systems which do not use additional resources and sixth over 19 submissions among the constrained and unconstrained systems in English restaurant reviews. Our submission for Sentiment Polarity is ranked eighth over 22 submissions on the laptop reviews.

1 Introduction

Classifying opinion texts at document or sentence levels is not sufficient for applications which need to identify the opinion targets. Even if the document is about one entity, many applications need to determine the opinion about each aspect of the entity. A user may express a positive opinion towards a restaurant, but he may have a negative opinion towards some aspects as the ambiance. Therefore, we need to identify the aspects and determine whether the sentiment is positive, negative or neutral towards each one. This task is called Aspect-Based Sentiment Analysis or Feature-Based opinion mining as called in the early work (Hu and Liu, 2004). Aspect-Based Sentiment Analysis is composed of four subtasks:

1. Opinion Target Expression Extraction

   Opinion Target Expression is a linguistic expression used in a given text to refer to an aspect of the reviewed entity. This subtask aims at identifying all the aspect terms present in a given set of sentences with pre-identified entities such as restaurants, laptops. An opinion target names a particular aspect of the target entity. For example:

   > "I liked the service and the staff, but not the food"
   > "The hard disk is very noisy"

   The *service*, *staff* and *food* are opinion target expressions. *hard disk* is multi-word opinion target expression which will be treated as a single term.

2. Aspect Sentiment Detection

   Each identified opinion target has to be assigned to one of the following polarity labels: positive, negative or neutral.

   For example:

   > Input: "I hated their fajitas, but their salads were great"

   > Output: {fajitas: negative, salads: positive}

3. Aspect Category Detection

   This subtask aims at identifying the aspect categories discussed in a given sentence from a predefined set of aspect categories such as

350

Proceedings of SemEval-2016, pages 350–355,
San Diego, California, June 16-17, 2016. ©2016 Association for Computational Linguistics

price and food. Aspect categories are typically coarser than the opinion targets, and they do not necessarily occur as terms in a given sentence.

For example, given the set of aspect categories of restaurant entity {food, service, price, ambiance}:

"The restaurant was too expensive"

The aspect category is {price}.

"The restaurant was expensive, but the menu was great"

The aspect categories are {price, food}.

4. Aspect Category Polarity

Given a set of pre-identified aspect categories such as {food, price}, this subtask aims at determining the polarity of each aspect category. For example:

"The restaurant was too expensive"

{price: negative}

"The restaurant was expensive, but the menu was great"

{price: negative, food: positive}

In this paper, we focus on Opinion Target Extraction (OTE) and Sentiment Polarity towards a target or a category. The description of each subtask is provided by ABSA organizers (Pontiki et al., 2016). For OTE, a CRF model is proposed with several groups of features including syntactic and lexical features. For polarity detection, a logistic regression classifier is trained with the weighting schema for positive and negative labels and several groups of features are extracted including lexical, syntactic, semantic and sentiment lexicon features.

The rest of this paper is organised as follows. Section 2 outlines existing work in target extraction and polarity detection. Section 3 describes our system for opinion target extraction. Polarity detection is presented in Section 4. Section 5 shows the conclusion and the future work.

2   Related Work

Aspect-Based Sentiment Analysis consists of several subtasks. Some studies have proposed different methods for aspect detection and sentiment polarity analysis, others have proposed joint models in order to obtain the aspect and their polarities from the same model, these last models are generally unsupervised.

The early work on opinion target detection from on-line reviews presented by (Hu and Liu, 2004) used association rule mining based on Apriori algorithm (Agrawal and Srikant, 1994) to extract frequent noun phrases as product features. For polarity detection, they used two seed sets of 30 positive and negative adjectives, then WordNet has been used to find and add the synonyms of the seed words. Infrequent product features or opinion targets had been processed by finding the noun related to an opinionated word.

Opinion Digger (Moghaddam and Ester, 2010) also used the Apriori algorithm to extract the frequent opinion targets. The kNN algorithm is applied to estimate the aspect rating scaling from 1 to 5 stands for (Excellent, Good, Average, Poor, Terrible).

Supervised methods use normally Conditional Random Fields (CRF) or Hidden Markov models (HMM). (Jin and Ho, 2009) applied a HMM model to extract opinion targets using the words and their part-of-speech tags in order to learn a model, then unsupervised algorithm for determining the opinion targets polarity using the nearest opinion word to the opinion target and taking into account the polarity reversal words (such as not).

A CRF model was used by (Jakob and Gurevych, 2010) with the following features: tokens, POS tags, syntactic dependency (if the opinion target has a relation with the opinionated word), word distance (the distance between the word in the closest noun phrase and the opinionated word), and opinion sentences (each token in the sentence containing an opinionated expression is labeled by this feature), the input of this method is also the opinionated expressions, they use these expressions for predicting the opinion target polarity using dependency parsing for retrieving the pair target-expression from the training set. (Hamdan et al., 2014; Hamdan et al.,

2015a) also applied a CRF model with different features .

Unsupervised methods based on LDA (Latent Dirichlet allocation) have been proposed. (Brody and Elhadad, 2010) used LDA to figure out the opinion targets, determined the number of topics by applying a clustering method, then they used a similar method proposed by (Hatzivassiloglou and McKeown, 1997) to extract the conjunctive adjectives, but not the disjunctive due to the specificity of the domain.

(Lin et al., 2012) proposed Joint model of Sentiment and Topic (JST) which extends the state-of-the-art topic model (LDA) by adding a sentiment layer, this model is fully unsupervised and it can detect sentiment and topic simultaneously.

(Wei and Gulla, 2010) modeled the hierarchical relation between product aspects. They defined Sentiment Ontology Tree (SOT) to formulate the knowledge of hierarchical relationships among product attributes and tackled the problem of sentiment analysis as a hierarchical classification problem. Unsupervised hierarchical aspect Sentiment model (HASM) was proposed by (Kim et al., 2013) to discover a hierarchical structure of aspect-based sentiments from unlabeled online reviews.

3 Opinion Target Expression (OTE)

The objective of opinion target extraction is to extract all opinion target expressions in a restaurant review, opinion target could be a word or multiple words. This extraction consists of the following steps:

1. Review Segmentation

   This step segments each review into sentences. In restaurant dataset, we already have the sentences.

2. Sentence Tokenizing

   Each sentence is tokenized to get the terms. One can consider the spaces as separators or use a more complex tokenizer. We tokenize each sentence using NTLK tokenizer[1] which extracts the words, numbers and punctuations.

3. Sentence Tagging

   Each term in the sentence should be tagged in order to be presented to a tagging classifier. We choose the IOB notation for representing each sentence in the review. Therefore, we distinguish the terms at the Beginning, the Inside and the Outside of opinion target expression. For example, for the following review sentence:

   "But the staff was so horrible to us."

   Where *staff* is opinion target. The tag of each term will be:

   But:O the:O staff:B was:O so:O horrible:O
   to:O us:O.

4. Feature Extraction

   This is the main step of opinion target extraction. For representing each term, we extract the following features:

   - The term itself.
   - POS: We use NLTK parser[2] to attach a part of speech tag to each term.
   - word shape: the shape of each character in the word (capital letter, small letter, digit, punctuation, other symbol)
   - word type: the type of the word (uppercase, digit, symbol, combination)
   - Prefixes (all prefixes having length between one to four).
   - Suffixes (all suffixes having length between one to four).
   - Stop word: if the word is a stop word or not.

   In addition to the previous features, we extract for each term the following features:

   - The two preceding and three subsequent terms of the actual term.
   - The value of each two successive features in the the range -2,2 (the previous and subsequent two terms of actual term) for the following features: term, word POS, word

---

[1]http://www.nltk.org/api/nltk.tokenize.html

[2]http://www.nltk.org/book/ch05.html

shape, word type. For example, for POS feature we extract:

pos[-2]—pos[-1]=DT—JJ
pos[-1]—pos[0]=JJ—NN
pos[0]—pos[1]=NN—,
pos[1]—pos[2]=,—C

- We also extract the value of each three successive features in the the range -1,1 for the two features: term POS and term. For example, for the feature *term* we extract:
term[-2]—term[-1]—term[0]=a—good—place
term[-1]—term[0]—term[1]=good—place—,

5. Training Method

we have used a Conditional Random Fields (CRF) which receives the feature representation of each term in each sentence and builds a tagging model in order to use it for predicting the tags of the new sentences.

3.1 Experiments

The data set is extracted from restaurant reviews, provided by SemEval 2016 ABSA organisers (Pontiki et al., 2016) where each review is composed of several sentences and each sentence may contain several OTEs. CRFsuite tool is used for this experiment. This tool is fast in training and tagging (Okazaki, 2007).

Our submission is ranked second among the constrained systems and sixth over all 19 systems with the F1 score. Table 2 shows the result of our system.

Experiment	F1 Score
Our System	66.545
Baseline	44.071

Table 1. The results of OTE slot.

4 Sentiment Polarity

For a given set of aspect terms within a sentence, we determine whether the polarity of each aspect term is positive, negative or neutral. For example, the system should extract the polarity of `fajitas` and *salads* in the following sentence: *"I hated their fajitas, but their salads were great"*, fajitas: negative and salads: positive.

This sub-task can be seen as sentence level or phrase level sentiment Analysis. We should determine the polarity, which could be positive, negative, neutral. We use the system described by (Hamdan et al., 2015b). Thus,We propose to use a logistic regression classifier with weighting schema of positive and negative labels with the following features:

- Word n-grams Features

Unigrams and bigrams are extracted for each word in the text without any stemming or stop-word removing, all terms with occurrence less than 3 are removed from the feature space.

- Sentiment Lexicon-based Features

The system extracts four features from the manually constructed lexicons (Bing Liu Lexicon (Hu and Liu, 2004) and MPQA subjectivity Lexicon (Wilson et al., 2005)) and six features from the automatic ones (NRC Hashtag Sentiment Lexicon (Mohammad, 2012), Sentiment Lexicon (Hamdan et al., 2015b)). For each text the number of positive words, the number of negative ones, the number of positive words divided by the number of negative ones and the polarity of the last word are extracted from manual constructed lexicons. In addition to the sum of the positive scores and the sum of the negative scores from the automatic constructed lexicons.

- Negation Features

The rule-based algorithm presented in Christopher Potts' Sentiment Symposium Tutorial is implemented. This algorithm appends a negation suffix to all words that appear within a negation scope which is determined by the negation key and a certain punctuation. All these words are added to the feature space.

- Brown Cluster Features

Each word in the text is mapped to its cluster in Brown clusters, 1000 features are added to feature space where each feature represents the number of words in the text mapped to each cluster. The 1000 clusters is provided in Twitter Word Clusters of CMU ARK group which were constructed from approximately 56 million tweets.

- Category Feature

We also added the category of each OTE as a feature to the feature space.

4.1 Experiments

We trained a L1-regularized Logistic regression classifier implemented in LIBLINEAR, which has given good results in several papers (Hamdan et al., 2015b) (Hamdan et al., 2015a). The classifier is trained on the training data set using the previous features with the three polarities (positive, negative, and neutral) as labels. A weighting schema is adapted for each class, we use the weighting option *-wi* which enables a use of different cost parameter *C* for different classes. Since the training data is unbalanced, this weighting schema adjusts the probability of each label. Thus we tuned the classifier in adjusting the cost parameter *C* of Logistic Regression, weight w_{pos} of positive class and weight w_{neg} of negative class.

We used the 1/10 of training data set for tuning the three parameters in Laptop reviews, all combinations of C in range 0.1 to to 4 by step 0.1, w_{pos} in range 1 to 8 by step 0.1, w_{neg} in range 1 to 8 by step 0.1 are tested. The combination *C*=0.3, textitw_{pos}=1.2, w_{neg}=1.9 have been chosen. Table 2 shows the results of our system on the Laptop data set. Our system is ranked eighth over 22 submissions.

Experiment	Accuracy
Laptops	
Our system	74.282
Baseline	44.071

Table 2. Results of sentiment polarity in laptops reviews.

5 Conclusion

We have built two systems for opinion target extraction of restaurant data set, and sentiment polarity analysis for laptops. We have used supervised tagger for OTE, trained a CRF model with several features. A Logistic regression classifier is used for sentiment polarity where we adopted a weighting schema.

References

Agrawal, R. and Srikant, R. (1994). Fast Algorithms for Mining Association Rules in Large Databases. In *Proceedings of the 20th International Conference on Very Large Data Bases*, VLDB '94, pages 487–499, San Francisco, CA, USA. Morgan Kaufmann Publishers Inc.

Brody, S. and Elhadad, N. (2010). An Unsupervised Aspect-sentiment Model for Online Reviews. In *Human Language Technologies: The 2010 Annual Conference of the North American Chapter of the Association for Computational Linguistics*, HLT '10, pages 804–812, Stroudsburg, PA, USA. Association for Computational Linguistics.

Hamdan, H., Bellot, P., and Bechet, F. (2014). Supervised Methods for Aspect-Based Sentiment Analysis. In *Proceedings of the Eighth International Workshop on Semantic Evaluation (SemEval 2014)*.

Hamdan, H., Bellot, P., and Bechet, F. (2015a). Lsislif: CRF and Logistic Regression for Opinion Target Extraction and Sentiment Polarity Analysis. In *Proceedings of the 9th International Workshop on Semantic Evaluation (SemEval 2015)*, pages 753–758, Denver, Colorado. Association for Computational Linguistics.

Hamdan, H., Bellot, P., and Bechet, F. (2015b). Sentiment Lexicon-Based Features for Sentiment Analysis in Short Text. In *Proceeding of the 16th International Conference on Intelligent Text Processing and Computational Linguistics*, Cairo, Egypt.

Hatzivassiloglou, V. and McKeown, K. R. (1997). Predicting the Semantic Orientation of Adjectives. In *Proceedings of the Eighth Conference on European Chapter of the Association for Computational Linguistics*, EACL '97, pages 174–181, Stroudsburg, PA, USA. Association for Computational Linguistics.

Hu, M. and Liu, B. (2004). Mining and Summarizing Customer Reviews. In *Proceedings of the Tenth ACM SIGKDD International Conference on Knowledge Discovery and Data Mining*, KDD '04, pages 168–177, New York, NY, USA. ACM.

Jakob, N. and Gurevych, I. (2010). Extracting Opinion Targets in a Single- and Cross-domain Setting with Conditional Random Fields. In *Proceedings of the 2010 Conference on Empirical Methods in Natural Language Processing*, EMNLP '10, pages 1035–1045, Stroudsburg, PA, USA. Association for Computational Linguistics.

Jin, W. and Ho, H. H. (2009). A Novel Lexicalized HMM-based Learning Framework for Web Opinion miningNOTE FROM ACM: A Joint ACM Conference Committee Has Determined That the Authors of This Article Violated ACM's Publication Policy on Simultaneous Submissions. Therefore ACM Has Shut off

Access to This Paper. In *Proceedings of the 26th Annual International Conference on Machine Learning*, ICML '09, pages 465–472, New York, NY, USA. ACM.

Kim, S., Zhang, J., Chen, Z., Oh, A., and Liu, S. (2013). A Hierarchical Aspect-Sentiment Model for Online Reviews. In *Proceedings of The Twenty-Seventh AAAI Conference on Artificial Intelligence (AAAI-13)*. AAAI.

Lin, C., He, Y., Everson, R., and Ruger, S. (2012). Weakly Supervised Joint Sentiment-Topic Detection from Text. *IEEE Trans. on Knowl. and Data Eng.*, 24(6):1134–1145.

Moghaddam, S. and Ester, M. (2010). Opinion Digger: An Unsupervised Opinion Miner from Unstructured Product Reviews. In *Proceedings of the 19th ACM International Conference on Information and Knowledge Management*, CIKM '10, pages 1825–1828, New York, NY, USA. ACM.

Mohammad, S. (2012). #Emotional Tweets. In **SEM 2012: The First Joint Conference on Lexical and Computational Semantics – Volume 1: Proceedings of the main conference and the shared task, and Volume 2: Proceedings of the Sixth International Workshop on Semantic Evaluation (SemEval 2012)*, pages 246–255, Montréal, Canada. Association for Computational Linguistics.

Okazaki, N. (2007). *CRFsuite: a fast implementation of Conditional Random Fields (CRFs)*.

Pontiki, M., Galanis, D., Papageorgiou, H., Androutsopoulos, I., Manandhar, S., AL-Smadi, M., Al-Ayyoub, M., Zhao, Y., Qin, B., Clercq, O. D., Hoste, V., Apidianaki, M., Tannier, X., Loukachevitch, N., Kotelnikov, E., Bel, N., Jimenez-Zafra, S. M., and Eryigit, G. (2016). SemEval-2016 task 5: Aspect based sentiment analysis. In *Proceedings of the 10th International Workshop on Semantic Evaluation*, SemEval '16, San Diego, California. Association for Computational Linguistics.

Wei, W. and Gulla, J. A. (2010). Sentiment learning on product reviews via sentiment ontology tree. In *Proceedings of the 48th Annual Meeting of the ACL*, pages 404–413. ACL.

Wilson, T., Hoffmann, P., Somasundaran, S., Kessler, J., Wiebe, J., Choi, Y., Cardie, C., Riloff, E., and Patwardhan, S. (2005). OpinionFinder: A System for Subjectivity Analysis. In *Proceedings of HLT/EMNLP on Interactive Demonstrations*, HLT-Demo '05, pages 34–35, Stroudsburg, PA, USA. Association for Computational Linguistics.

COMMIT at SemEval-2016 Task 5: Sentiment Analysis with Rhetorical Structure Theory

Kim Schouten and **Flavius Frasincar**
Erasmus University Rotterdam
P.O. Box 1738, NL-3000 DR Rotterdam, the Netherlands

Abstract

This paper reports our submission to the Aspect-Based Sentiment Analysis task of SemEval 2016. It covers the prediction of sentiment for a given set of aspects (e.g., subtask 1, slot 2) for the English language using discourse analysis. To that end, a discourse parser implementing the Rhetorical Structure Theory is employed and the resulting information is used to determine the context of each aspect, as well as to compute the expressed sentiment in that context by weighing the discourse relations between words. While discourse analysis yields high level linguistic information that can be used to better predict sentiment, the proposed algorithm does not yet stack up to the high-performing machine learning approaches that are commonly exploited for this task.

1 Introduction

With sentiment analysis being at the forefront of research, many avenues are explored to find that one new algorithm that will outperform all others. This drive towards excellence is of no surprise given the high practical value this type of algorithms have and the added value they can yield for businesses and consumers alike. This is especially true for aspect-level sentiment analysis, where sentiment scores are assigned, not to a document or sentence, but to the various characteristics, or aspects, of the entity under consideration. Such a fine-grained analysis of, for instance, products or services, can provide many useful insights into consumer thinking.

The majority of the algorithms for aspect-level sentiment analysis is centered around the use of a machine learning classifier and involves tasks such as feature construction and parameter estimation. While the past has shown that this kind of algorithms have strong performance, other directions are also explored (Schouten and Frasincar, 2016). One of these is the concept-driven approach (Cambria et al., 2015), which functions at the semantic level, built upon a layer of natural language processing components. Another direction, which is the research we describe here, is using discourse analysis to improve sentiment classification.

Discourse analysis looks at how the various text segments interact with each other. For example, in *"So even though this laptop is ugly, bulky and way overpriced, I still like it."*, the first half of the sentence gives an explanation for the second part of the sentence. As illustrated in the above example, knowing which parts of the text are ancillary and which parts of the text form the core of the sentence can play a vital role in classifying sentiment. In this case, the sentiment for the laptop in general is positive, even though all of the discussed aspects are negative. Rhetorical Structure Theory (RST) (Mann and Thompson, 1988) describes the various discourse units and their relations, and multiple RST parsers exist that can extract these discourse elements (Marcu, 1997; Surdeanu et al., 2015).

This research shows how one can use RST to classify aspect sentiment. The basic principles of RST are explained in Section 2. The following section showcases some related work on RST, while Section 4 describes how our pipeline is set up. The algorithm

Proceedings of SemEval-2016, pages 356–360,
San Diego, California, June 16-17, 2016. ©2016 Association for Computational Linguistics

is evaluated in Section 5, followed by conclusions and future work in Section 6.

2   Rhetorical Structure Theory

When performing an RST analysis, the text is first split into clauses, which are called elementary discourse units (EDUs). These clauses form the basic building blocks of the discourse tree. The RST parser then postulates relations between the EDUs, selecting them from a predefined list of discourse relations. There are two basic types of relations: mononuclear and multinuclear relations. The former connects two discourse elements where one element is supporting the other, whereas the latter connects two or more discourse elements that do not have such a clear division of roles. For example, in *'I've only had mine a day but I'm already used to it...'*, the part before 'but' is ancillary and is called the satellite. It supports the second clause, which is called the nucleus, by setting up a contrast. An example of a multinuclear relation is *'It is in the best condition and has a really high quality.'* In this sentence, both elements are nuclei since none of them is specifically supporting the other and they are on the same level instead. EDUs that are linked by a discourse relation together form a new clause that can be linked to another clause again. In this way, a hierarchical structure, which is called the discourse tree, can be formed that spans a whole document. In Figure 1, the discourse tree is shown for the following example.

> 'Being a PC user my whole life, it's taking
> a bit of time to adapt to the OS of a Mac
> but I 'm finding my way around.'

3   Related Work

One of the first approaches that applies RST to sentiment analysis is (Taboada et al., 2008). This work suggests to rank words within a satellite EDU differently from words that are within a nucleus EDU. Even such a simple use of discourse information already leads to a higher performance of their framework. Note that because only EDUs are used, this method only exploits information from the leafs of the discourse tree.

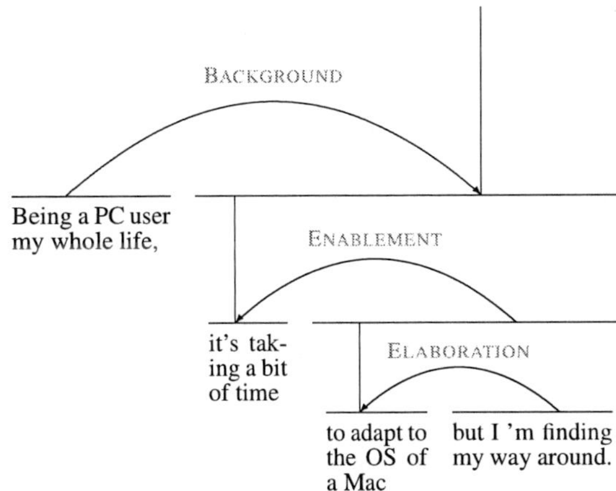

Figure 1: Full discourse tree of a simple review sentence (the curved lines denote a mononuclear relation between a nucleus and a satellite).

This is also true for the approach taken in (Heerschop et al., 2011), which uses the same split between words in a nucleus or words in a satellite. Additionally, they take the rhetorical relations these EDUs are in, into account. One of the outcomes of this research is that certain relations are more important for sentiment analysis than others. Hence, words that are in a EDU with an important relation should have a higher influence on the sentiment analysis than others. Another interesting idea was that some EDUs are in a contrasting relation and sentiment scores for words in these EDUs should be negated or flipped. In the described experiments, F_1 increased with 15% compared to a baseline because of the exploitation of discourse information. Note that this approach performs sentiment analysis at the sentence level, while we are applying discourse analysis for aspect-level sentiment analysis.

Being closer to aspect-level, the method described in (Zirn et al., 2011) applies RST at the sub-sentence or clause level embedding it inside a Markov Logic Chain. The research mainly focuses on finding relations that negate the sentiment of a certain clause since this has a high impact on the total sentiment score. Compared to a Support Vector Machine baseline, the employed model shows a significant improvement.

4   Framework

In order to apply RST for aspect-level sentiment analysis, the discourse context of an aspect has to be defined first, since this varies from aspect to aspect. Fortunately, we can exploit the discourse tree to select the relevant parts of the text with respect to a given aspect. Knowing the relevant parts of the sentence, the sentiment can be computed by having different weights on the various discourse relations and multiplying the sentiment scores for individual words through the relevant parts of the discourse tree, aggregating the partial scores to one final score that determines the sentiment class.

The first step consists of finding the leaf node(s) in the discourse tree that cover a given aspect. For explicit aspects, the exact position within the sentence is known (i.e., with the `from` and `to` values), so determining the relevant EDU is straightforward. Sometimes, an aspect spans multiple EDUs. This is the case for some explicit aspects and for all implicit aspects, since the latter do not have a specific target (i.e., `target` is NULL and `from` and `to` are zero). When multiple EDUs are returned by this step, the following steps are performed for each EDU, and the final results are aggregated at the end.

Since satellites are complementing the information presented in the nuclei, it stands to reason that, when determining the sentiment of an aspect that is described in a nucleus, we also utilize the information in the satellite that supports that nucleus. On the other hand, when an aspect is described in a satellite, we do not need to include the information of its nucleus since nuclei do not add information to satellites. This information asymmetry helps us to define the context of an aspect. We can look at the discourse tree and, starting at the leaf containing the aspect, move up the tree. As long as we are encountering nuclei we need to go higher because the related satellites need to be included in the context. Hence, as soon as we arrive at a satellite node, that node will be the root of the context tree, since its related nucleus does not need to be included because of the reasons specified before. For the example in Figure 1, since the aspect 'OS' is in a nucleus, we go up to include its elaborating satellite, thereby arriving in a satellite node. Since the first encountered satellite node will be the root node of the context tree, we will not move up the discourse tree any further.

With the context tree available, each word is assigned a sentiment score, using the Stanford Sentiment Tool (Socher et al., 2013). The sentiment values are then combined using Formula 1.

$$sent(s_i) = \sum_{t_j \in s_i} sent(t_j) \times \prod_{r_n \in P_{s_i}} w_{r_n}, \forall s_i \in S_a.$$

(1)

where S_a is the set of leaf nodes of the context tree for aspect a, $sent(s_i)$ is the sentiment score corresponding to leaf node $s_i \in S$, and P_{s_i} denotes all edges on the path from the root node of the context tree to leaf node s_i. Furthermore, $sent(t_j)$ is the sentiment score for word $t_j \in s_i$ and w_{r_n} denotes the weight associated with the rhetorical role of edge r_n. These weights are obtained by running a Genetic Algorithm, optimizing for accuracy.

In the final step, all of the $sent(s_i)$ values for a given aspect are added to arrive at a final sentiment score for each aspect, as shown in Formula 2.

$$sent(s_a) = \sum_{s_i \in S_a} sent(s_i)$$

(2)

To map the sentiment score of an aspect to a class label, we use a threshold ϵ to make the distinction between positive and negative classes. As suggested in (Heerschop et al., 2011), we compute the average sentiment score for all aspects that are positive as well as for all aspects that are negative. The ϵ threshold is then set as the mean of those two values. This helps to avoid the sentiment bias in reviews. Note than in its current form, the algorithm is only capable of assigning a positive or a negative sentiment class to an aspect. Hence all neutral aspects will be misclassified.

Implementation Notes

The above framework is implemented using the Stanford CoreNLP (Manning et al., 2014) pipeline, including the already mentioned sentiment component (Socher et al., 2013), together with the CLU-LAB (Surdeanu et al., 2015) discourse parser.

5 Evaluation

The evaluation is performed on a previously unseen test set by the organizers of the task. For a description of the used data sets, we refer to the task description paper (Pontiki et al., 2016). The results of this evaluation are shown in Table 1. The proposed algorithm is limited to predicting the senti-

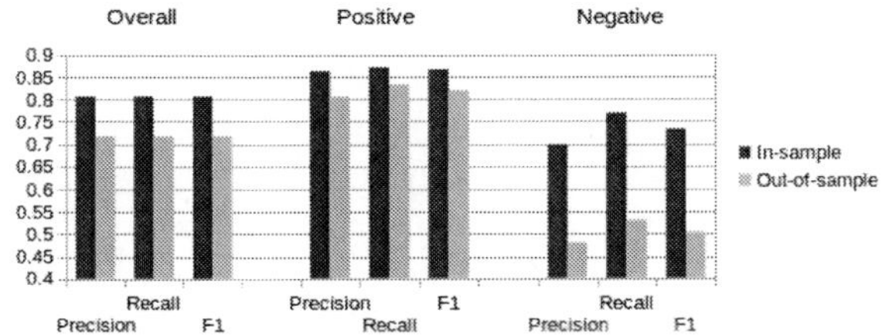

Figure 2: Results on the restaurants data, specified per sentiment class.

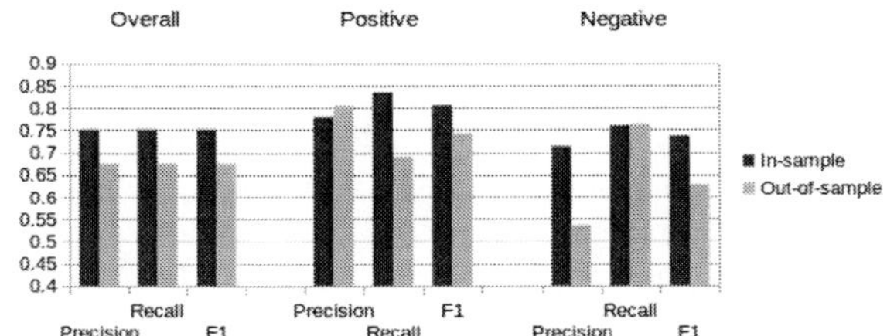

Figure 3: Results on the laptops data, specified per sentiment class.

ment value only (i.e., slot 3 for subtask 1) and only operates on English.

	Restaurants	Laptops
In-sample	79.1%	77.3%
10-fold cross-validation	76.1%	71.8%
Official test data	71.8%	67.5%

Table 1: Results of the proposed algorithm on the two considered datasets. Note that the official results on the restaurant data set are slightly higher than in the official ranking due to a few parsing errors with HTML entities in the submitted file.

As can be seen in Table 1, the algorithm suffers from overfitting, which is caused by optimizing the weights of the various RST relation types. Interestingly, the positive class of the restaurants dataset appears to be unaffected by this overfitting, as its performance on the cross-validated training data is only 2% lower than the in-sample accuracy. This is in stark contrast to the negative class, which suffers a sharp decrease in performance when going from in-sample to cross-validation. However, even comparing the cross-validation results with the test data shows a gap in performance. This can be due to a number of reasons, where it is most likely that the test data is slightly different in terms of language usage than the training data.

Looking at the precision and recall scores for the positive and negative class in Figures 2 and 3, we can see that on the restaurants data, the negative class is poorly predicted, with both a low precision and a low recall. The positive class, however, is performing only slightly worse than on the training data, with the biggest hit taken on the precision. For the laptops data, the situation is different. Here, both the positive and the negative class have a slightly higher recall than precision on the training data. Looking the test data, however, shows that the algorithm predicts too many negative aspects, as the precision for the negative class plummets, but the recall stays roughly the same. For the positive class, the reverse is true: since it only predicts positive in a limited number of cases, the precision is high, but recall is much lower than on the training data.

Negative comments are more difficult to find, as evidenced by the shown performance scores, because of the greater range of expressions used for negative expressions. For example, besides using words with a known negative sentiment, people can express themselves using sarcasm or by describing some aspect and letting the reader conclude that that is sub-par.

6   Conclusions

This research shows how Rhetorical Structure Theory (RST) can be used for aspect-level sentiment analysis. Using discourse information when determining sentiment allows certain parts of the text to be stressed while others can be diminished in influence with respect to the sentiment computation. Optimizing the weights of the various relations with a Genetic Algorithm unfortunately leads to overfitting, reducing its effectiveness. Furthermore, we hypothesize that the rather straightforward way of multiplying sentiment through the context tree might be too simplistic. Hence, our suggestions for future work are to limit overfitting of the relation weights and to look for a more sophisticated approach to combining the sentiment scores within the context tree. A good avenue for future research is to investigate the dependence of RST methods on language usage, since the laptop data and restaurant data show such a different result when comparing in-sample and out-of-sample performance. Determining the context tree is also a subject for future research, as we have not yet tried a full range of possibilities. Last, embedding the discourse information in a classifier like Support Vector Machines is worthy of investigation to see the effect of combining high level linguistic information with the power of statistical inference.

Acknowledgments

The authors are supported by the Dutch national program COMMIT

References

Erik Cambria, Soujanya Poria, Federica Bisio, Rajiv Bajpai, and Iti Chaturvedi. 2015. The CLSA model: A novel framework for concept-level sentiment analysis. In *16th International Conference on Computational Linguistics and Intelligent Text Processing (CICLing 2015) (Part II)*, pages 3–22.

Bas Heerschop, Frank Goossen, Alexander Hogenboom, Flavius Frasincar, Uzay Kaymak, and Franciska de Jong. 2011. Polarity analysis of texts using discourse structure. In *Proceedings of the 20th ACM International Conference on Information and Knowledge Management (CIKM, 2011)*, pages 1061–1070. ACM.

William C Mann and Sandra A Thompson. 1988. Rhetorical structure theory: Toward a functional theory of text organization. *Text-Interdisciplinary Journal for the Study of Discourse*, 8(3):243–281.

Christopher D. Manning, Mihai Surdeanu, John Bauer, Jenny Finkel, Steven J. Bethard, and David McClosky. 2014. The Stanford CoreNLP natural language processing toolkit. In *Proceedings of 52nd Annual Meeting of the Association for Computational Linguistics: System Demonstrations*, pages 55–60. Association for Computational Linguistics.

Daniel Marcu. 1997. The rhetorical parsing of natural language texts. In *Proceedings of the Eighth Conference on European Chapter of the Association for Computational Linguistics (EACL 1997)*, pages 96–103. Association for Computational Linguistics.

Maria Pontiki, Dimitrios Galanis, Haris Papageorgiou, Ion Androutsopoulos, Suresh Manandhar, Mohammad Al-Smadi, Mahmoud Al-Ayyoub, Yanyan Zhao, Bing Qin, Orphée De Clercq, Véronique Hoste, Marianna Apidianaki, Xavier Tannier, Natalia Loukachevitch, Evgeny Kotelnikov, Nuria Bel, Salud María Jiménez-Zafra, and Gülşen Eryiğit. 2016. SemEval-2016 task 5: Aspect based sentiment analysis. In *Proceedings of the 10th International Workshop on Semantic Evaluation*, SemEval '16, San Diego, California, June. Association for Computational Linguistics.

Kim Schouten and Flavius Frasincar. 2016. Survey on aspect-level sentiment analysis. *IEEE Transactions on Knowledge and Data Engineering*, 28(3):813–830.

Richard Socher, Alex Perelygin, Jean Wu, Jason Chuang, Christopher D. Manning, Andrew Ng, and Christopher Potts. 2013. Recursive deep models for semantic compositionality over a sentiment treebank. In *Proceedings of the 2013 Conference on Empirical Methods in Natural Language Processing (EMNLP 2013)*, pages 1631–1642. Association for Computational Linguistics.

Mihai Surdeanu, Thomas Hicks, and Marco A. Valenzuela-Escárcega. 2015. Two practical rhetorical structure theory parsers. In *Proceedings of the 2015 Conference of the North American Chapter of the Association for Computational Linguistics - Human Language Technologies (NAACL HLT 2015): Software Demonstrations*.

Maite Taboada, Kimberly Voll, and Julian Brooke. 2008. Extracting sentiment as a function of discourse structure and topicality. Technical Report TR 2008-20, Simon Fraser University School of Computing Science.

Cäcilia Zirn, Mathias Niepert, Heiner Stuckenschmidt, and Michael Strube. 2011. Fine-grained sentiment analysis with structural features. In *5th International Joint Conference on Natural Language Processing (IJCNLP 2011)*, pages 336–344. Association for Computational Linguistics.

ECNU at SemEval-2016 Task 5: Extracting Effective Features from Relevant Fragments in Sentence for Aspect-Based Sentiment Analysis in Reviews

Mengxiao Jiang[1], Zhihua Zhang[1], Man Lan[1,2]*
[1]Department of Computer Science and Technology,
East China Normal University, Shanghai, P.R.China
[2]Shanghai Key Laboratory of Multidimensional Information Processing
{51151201080, 51131201039}@ecnu.cn, mlan@cs.ecnu.edu.cn*

Abstract

This paper describes our systems submitted to the Sentence-level and Text-level Aspect-Based Sentiment Analysis (ABSA) task (i.e., Task 5) in SemEval-2016. The task involves two phases, namely, Aspect Detection phase and Sentiment Polarity Classification phase. We participated in the second phase of both subtasks in laptop and restaurant domains, which focuses on the sentiment analysis based on the given aspect. In this task, we extracted four types of features (i.e., Sentiment Lexicon Features, Linguistic Features, Topic Model Features and Word2vec Feature) from certain fragments related to aspect rather than the whole sentence. Then the proposed features are fed into supervised classifiers for sentiment analysis. Our submissions rank above average.

1 Introduction

Aspect-Based Sentiment Analysis task (ABSA), i.e., task 5 in SemEval-2016, is an interesting task, which focuses on the sentiment analysis based on the target and certain categories. The organizers set up three subtasks, i.e., Sentence-level ABSA (i.e, Subtask 1), Text-level ABSA (i.e., Subtask 2), and Out-of domain ABSA (i.e., Subtask 3). For subtask 1 and 2, the training data in each domain is provided, while no labeled data is provided for subtask 3. Given an opinionated document in a domain, both subtask 1 and subtask 2 are grouped into two phases, i.e., Aspect Detection phase and Sentiment Polarity Classification phase. We participated in the second phase

of these two subtasks, aiming to identify the sentiment polarity for each given aspect which is made up of $<E\#A, OTE>$ in two domains.

Specifically, for Sentence-level ABSA, focusing on identifying all the opinion tuples (i.e., $<E\#A, OTE, polarity>$) in each sentence of the reviews, the Aspect Detection phase contains two slots. The Slot1 is to identify every entity (i.e., E) and attribute (i.e., A) pair (also named as category, e.g., *RESTAURANT-PRICES*) according to given sentence, and the Slot2 focuses on detecting Opinion Target Expression (i.e., *OTE* or target in short). For example, in *"Pizza here is consistently good"*, the participants are required to recognize *Pizza* as *OTE* and *FOOD#QUALITY* as *E#A*. The second phase, i.e., Sentiment Polarity Classification (Slot3), is to determine the sentiment polarity (i.e., positive, negative, or neutral) for each aspect (i.e., $<E\#A, OTE>$). As for Text-level ABSA, aiming at identifying the opinion tuples (i.e., $<E\#A, polarity>$) expressed in each review, the Aspect Detection phase is to identify the *E#A* pairs and the second phase is to assign the sentiment label (positive, negative, neutral or conflict) for each detected *E#A*. The conflict label is assigned when the dominant sentiment of the opinion is not clear.

In previous work, (Kim et al., 2013) presented a hierarchical aspect sentiment model to classify the polarity of aspect terms from unlabeled online reviews. (Jiménez-Zafra et al., 2015) proposed a syntactic approach for identifying the words that modify each aspect. (Branavan et al., 2009; He et al., 2012; Mei et al., 2007) used topic or category information. (Saias, 2015) used a 3-class classifier and

361

Proceedings of SemEval-2016, pages 361–366,
San Diego, California, June 16-17, 2016. ©2016 Association for Computational Linguistics

some handcrafted features to perform ABSA. (Lin and He, 2009; Jo and Oh, 2011) presented LDA-based models, which incorporated aspect and sentiment analysis together to model sentiments towards different aspects. Unlike these work, which try to extract features from the whole sentence, we propose a method which just takes certain fragments related to the given aspect from the sentence into consideration to perform feature engineering for the ABSA task.

The rest of this paper is structured as follows. In Section 2, we describe our system in details, including motivation, preprocessing, feature engineering, evaluation metric and algorithm, etc. Section 3 reports data sets, experiments and result discussion. Finally, Section 4 concludes our work.

2 System Description

2.1 Motivation

At sentence-level ABSA, generally, a review consists of several sentences and one single sentence may contain mixed opinion tuples (i.e., *<OTE, E#A, polarity >*) towards different *OTE* or *E#A*. The goal of our system is to identify the polarity for each opinion tuple. We found that the given aspect is just related to certain fragments in corresponding sentence. Therefore, in order to extract features from the relevant fragments, we proposed a two-step method to acquire potential words related to given aspect as pending words for future feature extraction. This approach consists of two steps, i.e., *Segmentation step*, which is to split each sentence into several fragments, and *Selection Step*, which selects out one or more fragments from sentence for each aspect.

Specifically, in the *Segmentation Step*, we used punctuation marks (i.e., $\{,.?!\}$) and conjunctions (i.e., $\{and, but\}$) to split the sentence into several *candidate fragments*. It is worth noting that the *OTE* is the entity or attribute words in reviews the users explicitly indicated. When there is no explicit mention of the entity, the *OTE* takes the value *NULL*. In restaurant domain, both *E#A* and *OTE* are provided in reviews, whereas only *E#A* are annotated and provided in the laptop domain, we assumed its *OTE* is *NULL*. Therefore, we adopted two strategies for *Selection Step*. In the case that the targets are provided,

we located the fragment which contains the target as *target fragment* and selected the words ranging from the prior *target fragment* (not include) to the current *target fragment* (included) as pending words. In another case that the targets are *NULL*, we automatically assigned a *target fragment* for it as follows. We firstly divided all sentences in training data into several subsets according to their attributes (i.e., *A* in E#A). If multiple attributes exist in the same sentence then the sentence is shared in corresponding subsets. Then we calculated the *tfidf* score for each word in each subset. Finally, we summed up the *tfidf* scores of all words in each fragment according to the attribute in given opinion. The fragment with top score is set as *target fragment*. After locating the *target fragment*, the approach to select the pending words is the same as the case that the targets are provided.

As for text-level ABSA, the opinion tuples (i.e., *<E#A, polarity>*) are endowed with each review rather than the sentence. Based on the statistic of the training data, we found that the labels of *E#A* in text-level are consistent with the most frequent polarity of the corresponding *E#A* in one review at sentence-level. Thus, for subtask 2 (i.e., text-level), we counted the number of positive, negative and neutral labels for each *E#A* in each review from the results of subtask 1. Then the most frequent polarity of each *E#A* is set as the label for corresponding *E#A* in each review in subtask 2.

For each domain, the participants are required to submit two runs, (1) *constrained:* only the provided data can be used; (2) *unconstrained:* any additional resources can be used. In this task, we adopted external resources, i.e., 8 sentiment lexicons and 100 billion words from Google News, to train the *Sentiment Lexicon* features and the *Word2vec* (Mikolov et al., 2013) feature. Thus, the difference between our two systems lies in these two features. For both systems, we also extracted many traditional types of features to build classifiers for classification.

2.2 Data Preprocessing

The original data is provided in XML format. So we first removed the XML tags from data and then transformed the abbreviations to their normal format. We used *Stanford Parser tools*[1] for tokenization, POS tagging and parsing. Then, the WordNet-based Lemmatizer implemented in NLTK[2] was adopted to lemmatize words to their base forms with the aid of their POS tags.

2.3 Feature Engineering

Four types of features extracted from the pending words are adopted to build the classifiers, i.e., Linguistic features, Sentiment Lexicon features, Topic Model features and Word2vec feature.

2.3.1 Linguistic Features

Word *N*-grams: For all pending words, after transforming them into lowercase, we extracted the unigram, bigram, trigram and 4-gram as word *N*-grams features.

Lemmatized Word *N*-grams:
Pending words were lemmatized by NLTK firstly, then we extracted four types of *N*-grams from the lemmatized form as Lemmatized Word *N*-grams, i.e., unigram_L, bigram_L, trigram_L and 4-gram_L.

Word Nchars: We recorded presence or absence of contiguous sequences of 3, 4, and 5 characters from pending words as *N-chars* features.

POS: We counted the number of nouns (the corresponding POS tags were *NN, NNP, NNS and NNPS*), verbs (*VB, VBD, VBG, VBN, VBP and VBZ*), adjectives (*JJ, JJR and JJS*) and adverbs (*RB, RBR and RBS*) in pending words as the pos feature.

Allcaps: It indicated the number of uppercase words in pending words.

Elongated: We recorded the number of the words contained the repeating characters (e.g., *slowwwwww*) as the elongated feature.

Punctuation: Customers often use exclamation mark (!) and question mark (?) to express surprise or emphasis, so we recorded the number of exclamation and question marks in pending words as the punctuation features.

Negation: Negation comprised various kinds of devices to reverse the truth value of a proposition, thus the identification of negations is very essential. In our work, we collected 29 negations from Internet and designed this binary feature to indicate whether there is negation in pending words.

2.3.2 Sentiment Lexicon Features

Giving the pending words, we first converted them into lowercase and then calculated five sentiment scores for each sentiment lexicon to construct *Sentiment Lexicon Features* (*SentiLexi*) (1) the ratio of positive words to pending words, (2) the ratio of negative words to pending words, (3) the maximum sentiment score, (4) the minimum sentiment score, (5) the sum of sentiment scores. We transformed the sentiment scores in all sentiment lexicons to the range of $[-1, 1]$, where "$-$" denotes negative sentiment. If the pending word does not exist in one sentiment lexicon, its corresponding score is set to zero. The following 8 sentiment lexicons are adopted in our systems: *Bing Liu opinion lexicon*[3], *General Inquirer lexicon*[4], *IMDB*[5], *MPQA*[6], *AFINN*[7], *SentiWordNet*[8], *NRC Hashtag Sentiment Lexicon*[9], *NRC Sentiment140 Lexicon*[10].

2.3.3 Topic Model Features

With the aid of *LDA-C tool*[11] with default parameter setting, we generate topic-related features from all training data as follows.

Sent2Topic: The *LDA* could generate the document distribution among predefined topics. We extracted this distribution as *Sent2Topic* feature.

Top Topic word (TopTopic): Since the topic probability of each word indicates its significance in corresponding topic, we set 20 topics and collect the top 25 words in each topic to build *TopTopic* feature.

2.3.4 Word2vec Feature

Google Word2vec (GoogleW2V): We used the publicly available *word2vec* tool[12] to get word vectors with dimensionality of 300, which is trained on 100 billion words from Google News as *GoogleW2V*.

---

[1]http://nlp.stanford.edu/software/lex-parser.shtml
[2]http://nltk.org

[3]http://www.cs.uic.edu/liub/FBS/sentiment-analysis.html#lexicon
[4]http://www.wjh.harvard.edu/inquirer/homecat.htm
[5]http://anthology.aclweb.org//S/S13/S13-2.pdf#page=444
[6]http://mpqa.cs.pitt.edu/
[7]http://www2.imm.dtu.dk/pubdb/views/publication_details.php?id=6010
[8]http://sentiwordnet.isti.cnr.it/
[9]http://www.umiacs.umd.edu/saif/WebDocs/NRC-Hashtag-Sentiment-Lexicon-v0.1.zip
[10]http://help.sentiment140.com/for-students/
[11]http://www.cs.princeton.edu/ blei/lda-c/
[12]https://code.google.com/archive/p/word2vec

2.4 Evaluation Measure and Algorithm

To evaluate the performance of different systems, the official evaluation measure *accuracy* is adopted. We employ the *Logistic Regression* algorithm with the default parameter implemented in *liblinear* tools[13] to build the classifiers for its good performance in our preliminary experiments. The 5-fold cross validation is adopted for system development.

3 Experiment

3.1 Datasets

In restaurant domain, the opinion tuple is composed of target, category and polarity (i.e., <OTE, E#A, Polarity>). And in laptop domain, the *OTE* is not taken into account in opinion tuple (i.e., <E#A, Polarity>). The restaurant domain contains 6 entities (e.g., *AMBIENCE, DRINKS, FOOD, RESTAURANT*, etc) and 5 attributes (i.e., *GENERAL, PRICES, STYLE_OPTIONS, QUALITY, PRICES*, etc). While in laptop, 22 entities (e.g., *BATTERY, SUPPORT, CPU, COMPANY*, etc.) and 9 attributes (e.g., *USABILITY, GENERAL, QUALITY*, etc) are tagged. Table 1 shows the statistics of the data sets used in our experiments.

Data	Reviews	Sentences	Opinions	Positive	Negative	Neutral	Conflict
Restaurant(SB1):							
train	350	2,000	2,506	1,657	751	98	0
test	90	676	859	611	204	44	0
Laptop(SB1):							
train	450	2,500	2,908	1,634	1,086	188	0
test	80	808	801	481	274	46	0
Restaurant(SB2):							
train	335	1,950	1,435	1012	327	55	41
test	90	676	404	286	84	23	11
Laptop(SB2):							
train	395	2,373	2,082	1,210	708	123	41
test	80	808	545	338	162	31	14

Table 1: Statistics of training and test dataset of two subtasks in laptop and restaurant domains. *Positive, Negative, Neural, Conflict* stand for the number of corresponding labels.

3.2 Experiments on Training data

For both laptop and restaurant domains, we adopted similar methods, i.e, employing rich features to build classifiers, and performed constrained systems and unconstrained systems respectively. Since *Sentiment lexicon* feature and *GoogleW2V* feature utilized the external data, we did not use these two types of features in the constrained system. As for

unconstrained systems, all features were employed. As for feature selection, a *hill climbing* algorithm is adopted to find out the contributions of different features, which is described as: keeping adding one type of feature at a time until no further improvement can be achieved. Table 2 shows the results of feature selection experiments for unconstrained and constrained systems in restaurant and laptop domains.

According to Table 2, it is interesting to find that (1) *3-char*, *4-char* and *negation* are beneficial to this task. The possible reason may be that there exists a lot of derivations in training data, e.g., *relax* and *relaxing*. Besides, the negator always reverses the sentiment polarity of corresponding review, which results in the good contribution of *negation* feature. (2) *SentiLexi* features are effective in two domains. In our preliminary experiments, we found that the *SentiLexi* features made great contribution to sentiment analysis task, which indicates that this type of features are indeed significant. (3) *POS* features are not quite effective in all systems. The possible reason may be that *POS* aims at identifying the subjective instances from objective ones, but the objective records just occupy a small proportion. (4) The majority of features are more valid in unconstrained system than that in constrained system. The possible reason may be that there are certain overlapped information between the *SentiLexi* features, the Word2vec feature and the other features.

In our preliminary experiments, we conducted the baseline system where features are extracted from the whole sentence without the consideration of *OTE* and *E#A*. The result showed that the method described in section 2.1 outperformed the baseline. Thus, we used the strategy that extracting features from certain relevant fragments rather than the whole sentence for this task.

3.3 Results and Discussion on test data

Using the optimum feature set shown in Table 2 and the algorithm described in section 2.4, we trained separate models for each domain and evaluated them against the test set in SemEval-2016 Task 5. For both subtask 1 and 2, we constructed 4 systems for unconstrained and constrained systems in restaurant and laptop domains respectively.

From the Table 3, we find that: (1) The uncon-

---

[13]https://www.csie.ntu.edu.tw/ cjlin/liblinear/

Features		Laptop Domain		Restaurant Domain	
		constrain	unconstrain	constrain	unconstrain
Linguistic	unigram		✓	✓	✓
	bigram		✓		
	trigram		✓		✓
	forgram		✓		✓
	unigram_L		✓		✓
	bigram_L		✓		✓
	trigram_L		✓		
	forgram_L		✓		
	trichar	✓	✓	✓	✓
	forchar	✓	✓	✓	
	fifchar		✓		
	POS				✓
	AllCaps		✓	✓	
	Elongated	✓	✓		✓
	Punctuation		✓		✓
	Negation	✓	✓	✓	✓
Sentiment Lexicon	SentiLexi	-	✓	-	✓
Topic Model	Sent2Topic			✓	
	TopTopic		✓		✓
GoogleW2V	GoogleW2V	-	✓	-	✓
Accuracy (%)		76.81	81.09	77.81	83.36

Table 2: Results of feature selection experiments for restaurant and laptop domains on training datasets.

strained system performed better than constrained system in both laptop and restaurant domains. This implicates that the *SentiLexi* feature and the *GoogleW2V* feature are effective for performance improvement in sentiment classification. (2) The accuracy in restaurant domain is higher than that in laptop. One reason may be that in laptop domain, the *OTE* are not provided.

Subtask	TeamID	Restaurant		Laptop	
		Con	Uncon	Con	Uncon
SB1	ECNU	80.559(5)	83.586(4)	70.037(6)	78.152(3)
	XRCE	88.126(1)	-	-	-
	LeeHu	-	-	75.905(1)	-
	IIT-T	-	86.729(1)	-	82.772(1)
SB2	ECNU	78.713(2)	81.436(2)	67.523(3)	75.046(1)
	UWB	80.941(1)	81.931(1)	74.495(1)	-

Table 3: Performance of our systems and the top-ranked systems for laptop and restaurant domains in terms of *Accuracy(%)* on test datasets. *Con* stands for *constrained* and *Uncon* represents *unconstrained*. The numbers in the brackets are the rankings on corresponding submissions.

4   Conclusion

In this paper, we extracted several types of features, i.e., *Linguistic* features, *SentiLexi* features, *Topic Model* features and *Word2vec* feature, and employed the Logistic Regression classifier to detect the sentiment polarity in given aspect for reviews. Moreover, we have demonstrated a two-step approach to acquire the pending words from the relevant fragments instead of the whole sentences for feature extraction. This enables the system to capture the relationship between the sentiment of the sentence and its opinion adherent. The results on test and training data showed the effectiveness of our method for the ABSA task. For the future work, it would be interesting to explore domain-specific sentiment lexicons to improve the performance and examine more advanced ways of using sentiment lexicons and word embedding features.

Acknowledgments

This research is supported by grants from Science and Technology Commission of Shanghai Municipality (14DZ2260800 and 15ZR1410700), Shanghai Collaborative Innovation Center of Trustworthy Software for Internet of Things (ZF1213).

References

SRK Branavan, Harr Chen, Jacob Eisenstein, and Regina Barzilay. 2009. Learning document-level semantic properties from free-text annotations. *Journal of Artificial Intelligence Research*, 34(2):569.

Yulan He, Chenghua Lin, Wei Gao, and Kam-Fai Wong. 2012. Tracking sentiment and topic dynamics from social media. In *Sixth International AAAI Conference on Weblogs and Social Media*.

Salud M. Jiménez-Zafra, Eugenio Martínez-Cámara, M. Teresa Martín-Valdivia, and L. Alfonso Ureña López. 2015. Sinai: Syntactic approach for aspect-based sentiment analysis. In *Proceedings of the 9th International Workshop on Semantic Evaluation (SemEval 2015)*, pages 730–735, Denver, Colorado, June. Association for Computational Linguistics.

Yohan Jo and Alice H Oh. 2011. Aspect and sentiment unification model for online review analysis. In *Proceedings of the 4th ACM international conference on Web search and data mining*, pages 815–824.

Suin Kim, Jianwen Zhang, Zheng Chen, Alice Oh, and Shixia Liu. 2013. A hierarchical aspect-sentiment model for online reviews. In *Proceedings of The Twenty-Seventh AAAI Conference on Artificial Intelligence (AAAI-13)*. AAAI, July.

Chenghua Lin and Yulan He. 2009. Joint sentiment/topic model for sentiment analysis. In *Proceedings of the 18th ACM conference on Information and knowledge management*, pages 375–384.

Qiaozhu Mei, Xu Ling, Matthew Wondra, Hang Su, and ChengXiang Zhai. 2007. Topic sentiment mixture: modeling facets and opinions in weblogs. In *Proceedings of the 16th international conference on WWW*, pages 171–180.

Tomas Mikolov, Ilya Sutskever, Kai Chen, Greg S Corrado, and Jeff Dean. 2013. Distributed representations of words and phrases and their compositionality. In C. J. C. Burges, L. Bottou, M. Welling, Z. Ghahramani, and K. Q. Weinberger, editors, *Advances in Neural Information Processing Systems 26*, pages 3111–3119. Curran Associates, Inc.

José Saias. 2015. Sentiue: Target and aspect based sentiment analysis in semeval-2015 task 12. In *Proceedings of the 9th International Workshop on Semantic Evaluation (SemEval 2015)*, pages 767–771, Denver, Colorado, June. Association for Computational Linguistics.

UFAL at SemEval-2016 Task 5:
Recurrent Neural Networks for Sentence Classification

Aleš Tamchyna and **Kateřina Veselovská**

Charles University in Prague, Faculty of Mathematics and Physics

Institute of Formal and Applied Linguistics

Malostranské náměstí 25, Prague, Czech Republic

`{tamchyna,veselovska}@ufal.mff.cuni.cz`

Abstract

This paper describes our system for aspect-based sentiment analysis (ABSA). We participate in Subtask 1 (sentence-level ABSA), focusing specifically on aspect category detection. We train a binary classifier for each category. This year's addition of multiple languages makes language-independent approaches attractive. We propose to utilize neural networks which should be capable of discovering linguistic patterns in the data automatically, thereby reducing the need for language-specific tools and feature engineering.

1 Introduction

Aspect-based sentiment analysis (ABSA) refers to the identification of specific entities and their aspects (aspect terms, opinion targets) in text and to the classification of their polarity. Typically, ABSA is applied to user reviews from various fields, such as consumer electronics, hotels or restaurants. In ABSA, we assume that the general target of evaluation has several aspects (e.g. food quality for restaurants) and we attempt to identify users' opinions on these individual aspects. Unlike the more general task of sentiment analysis where the goal would be to classify the polarity of entire sentences (or even whole reviews), in ABSA, we need to take a more fine-grained approach and consider also the internal structure of the given sentences.

As for the sentence-level ABSA, the aim is to identify all opinion tuples present in the sentence, taking into account the context of the whole review.

In our work, we focus on identifying aspect term categories; these are composed of entities (e.g. FOOD) and their attribute labels (e.g. QUALITY or PRICE). Both the entities and the attribute labels were assigned based on predefined inventories.

We apply our method on several languages covering the following domains:

- Arabic: hotels

- Dutch: restaurants

- English: consumer electronics and restaurants

- French: restaurants

- Russian: restaurants

- Spanish: restaurants

- Turkish: restaurants

Our submission was the best system for Russian and Turkish but did not achieve noteworthy results in other domains/languages.

2 Related Work

The previous results for different ABSA SemEval tasks are discussed in Pontiki et al. (2014) and Pontiki et al. (2015). So far, most researchers in the field have focused on traditional machine learning approaches, such as various probabilistic methods (see Agarwal and Mittal (2016)), and/or employed deterministic methods, e.g. subjectivity lexicons (Taboada et al., 2011). Because more languages were added this year, approaches such as neural networks, which require less language-specific data and engineering, become attractive.

Proceedings of SemEval-2016, pages 367–371,

San Diego, California, June 16-17, 2016. ©2016 Association for Computational Linguistics

Neural networks have been used for sentiment analysis. Particularly, in last year's SemEval Twitter sentiment classification task, several submissions applied convolutional networks (Toh and Su, 2015; Ebert et al., 2015). In our work, we use recurrent networks instead. Our motivation for this decision is that for aspect identification, syntactic relationships and long-distance dependencies may play a significant role and that such phenomena may be better modeled with a recurrent network. Furthermore, our recurrent network could easily be adapted to perform sequence labeling instead of sentence level classification – this would allow us to identify the exact position in the sentences where the aspect was mentioned.

3 System Description

Our system addresses Subtask 1 – sentence-level ABSA. Within the subtask, we focus on Slot 1, i.e. aspect category detection. For each sentence, our goal is to identify all aspect categories which are mentioned. Each category is composed of an entity E (e.g. FOOD or SERVICE) and its attribute A (e.g. QUALITY or PRICE). We do not decompose this definition and treat each category independently, effectively reducing the task to many binary classification subtasks (one for each E#A pair).

Each classifier in our system is a deep recurrent neural network with Long Short-Term memory cells (LSTM, Hochreiter and Schmidhuber (1997)). LSTMs have been designed to overcome the vanishing gradient problem present in standard recurrent neural networks. Their ability to remember information over many time steps should enable them to capture long-term dependencies in the data.

Our network encodes the input sentence word by word and at the end produces a binary classification decision based on the representation of the full sentence.

3.1 Word Representations

We represent each word (token) on the input by its pre-trained word embedding (and we do not further optimize the embeddings when training the network).

For each language, we use the current dump of

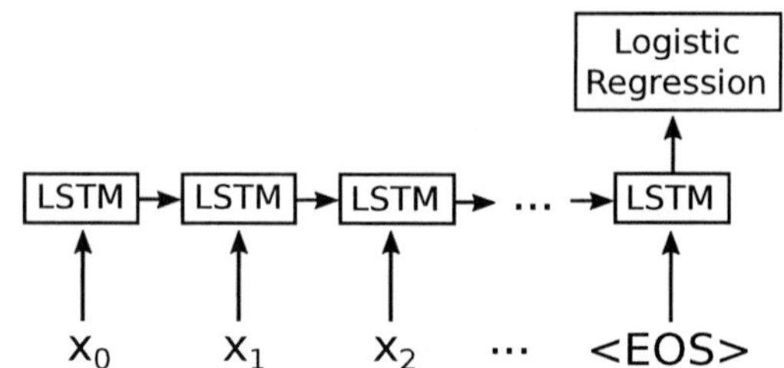

Figure 1: Architecture of our network (a single binary classifier).

Wikipedia[1] as training data for the word embeddings. We use WikiExtractor[2] to extract plain text from the dump. We run a sentence splitter and we tokenize the sentences. Table 1 shows statistics of the data for each language.

Language	Sentences (M)	Tokens (M)
English	97.0	2103
French	26.2	633
Spanish	20.5	505
Russian	18.9	347
Dutch	15.4	252
Turkish	3.9	60
Arabic	3.1	63

Table 1: Sizes of Wikipedia dumps for each language.

We train the representations using `word2vec`[3] with continuous bag of words as the underlying model. We set the embedding size to 200.

3.2 Network Architecture

Our network is essentially a deep LSTM encoder followed by a logistic regression layer with two output classes (neurons). For each sentence, we go over the input word by word and provide the embeddings of the tokens to the input layer. The hidden LSTM layers maintain a state at each step which encodes the (partial) sentence. After the final token, we input an artificial end-of-sentence token which signals the network to output a classification decision on the final layer. Depending on the activation of the

---

[1] `http://wikipedia.org/`, we retrieved the current dumps on January 6, 2016.

[2] `http://medialab.di.unipi.it/wiki/Wikipedia_Extractor`

[3] `https://code.google.com/archive/p/word2vec/`

two output neurons, we either classify the instance as positive (i.e. containing the given E#A pair) or negative.

Figure 1 shows an illustration of the architecture. We initially experimented with a single LSTM layer but stacking several layers lead to improved accuracy. All of the networks used in the final submission share an identical architecture consisting of an input layer (word2vec embeddings, size 200) followed by three LSTM layers (64, 32 and 32 cells) and the final layer with two neurons. We did not experiment with tuning a decision threshold; we simply assign the class (positive or negative) which has the higher probability according to the network. We implement the networks in Chainer,[4] an open-source framework for neural networks.

3.3 Training

We evaluated several optimization algorithms and found that Adam (Kingma and Ba, 2014) lead to the fastest convergence. We also use gradient clipping as described in Pascanu et al. (2012): when the L2 norm of the gradients increases over a given threshold (which we set to 1), gradients are rescaled to fit within that norm. We also found dropout (Srivastava et al., 2014) to improve the results and we utilize it in all LSTM layers with the probability set to 0.5.

When training, we use cross-validation and measure held-out accuracy to detect overfitting. We found that even though training error (almost) monotonically decreases, held-out performance tends to be rather unstable. Moreover, many classes are rare and the held-out set may therefore only contain a handful of positive instances. We were not able to mitigate this instability which made it difficult to choose the final model.

Nonetheless, we decide how many training iterations to run based on cross-validation; we measure the average f-measure over the folds for each iteration and then choose the iteration with the highest average.

4 Results

In this section, we present and discuss the obtained results. We compare a number of systems for each language and domain.

Official Baseline. We report the results of the official baseline (provided by the task organizers). The official baseline is an SVM classifier with bag-of-words features which assigns a positive label to a sentence if the predicted probability is above a certain threshold.

Baseline. We also implement our own baseline. We use a simple logistic regression model and, similarly to the submitted system, we train a binary classifier for each category. We only use bag of words as features; we do not include any other information (such as morphological analysis or subjectivity lexicon features). We use L2 regularization with weight 1 for all models. Our motivation for including this baseline is to provide a direct comparison with a simpler model trained in a similar way as the neural network.

Submitted. The system as submitted for the official evaluation. Due to the number of networks that we had to train, we were not able to fully optimize all of them before the submission deadline. In some cases, we therefore use models trained only on a handful of iterations over the training data.

Optimized. We report the results of the fully optimized system separately. These results were obtained after the deadline. In this case, all models were selected based on cross-validation as described in Section 3.3.

Best. To put the performance of our system into context of the state of the art, we also report the scores of the best system for each language and domain.

4.1 Discussion

We evaluate our system using the toolkit provided by the organizers of the task. Table 2 shows all our results. The best result for each data set (excluding the winning system) is marked in bold. Asterisks mark the cases where our system won.

Concerning baselines, we observe that our implementation is often substantially better than the official baseline. This does not hold for the restaurants domain in English and Turkish, and for laptops. For Turkish, we suspect that the size of the test set (144 sentences) plays a role – the scores can be unstable when test data is small. For laptops, we believe this can be attributed to the large number of possible categories in this domain; our classifiers do not use a

---

Domain, Language	Restaurants						Hotels	Laptops
	English	Spanish	French	Dutch	Russian	Turkish	Arabic	English
Off. Baseline	59.93	54.69	52.61	42.82	55.88	58.90	40.34	37.48
Baseline	58.05	**62.17**	**54.81**	54.71	60.75	34.41	49.43	35.08
Submitted	**59.30**	58.81	49.93	53.88	**64.83**	**61.03**	47.30	26.98
Optimized	58.40	58.54	50.84	**55.03**	60.19	56.54	**52.59**	**38.26**
Best	73.03	70.59	61.21	60.15	64.83*	61.03*	52.11	51.94

Table 2: F-measure of the baselines, the submitted system, the fully optimized system and the winning system for all domains and languages.

tuned threshold.

Our submitted systems do not always outperform the baselines. While we did win in Russian and Turkish, results in other data sets are less promising, with scores similar to the (stronger) baseline or even lower. This is a discouraging finding, especially considering the amount of additional data used in network training – word embeddings were trained on millions of sentences from Wikipedia.

However, we do observe some generalization in the outputs of the deep-learning models which is beyond the capabilities of the baseline models. For instance, our model correctly identifies the category FOOD#QUALITY in the sentence "Green Tea creme brulee is a must!", even though this dish is not mentioned in the training data.

Our *optimized* networks do not always perform better than the submitted systems. Considering that we trained the submitted networks with fewer iterations (due to time constraints), we suspect that even with our model selection based on cross validation, overfitting may still have affected the results.

Overall, there are several possible explanations for the weak performance. Due to significant domain mismatch between Wikipedia and the data sets for the task, the trained word embeddings may not be suitable.[5]

Overfitting, and more generally, suboptimal setting of model (hyper)parameters, also most likely play a role.

The system design may also be problematic: we build a relatively large number of completely independent models (each doing binary classification for a single category) even though it seems clear that some parameter sharing should be possible. This problem is particularly prominent in data sets with

a large number of possible classes, such as the laptop domain. In these cases, many E#A pairs are very rare. Because we do not decompose the entity and attribute and we train separate models, our classifiers only observe a handful of positive training instances, which results in very unreliable models.

5 Conclusion

We described our submission to the ABSA shared task. Our system won in two categories but overall does not outperform a simple baseline solution. We believe that more careful training of the networks is required and that we may need to revise the system design. On the other hand, the deep-learning model does show some generalization power, so this direction seems promising.

5.1 Future Work

In the future, we are planning to try other possible network architectures. In particular, instead of our many binary classifiers we could train a single network (for each language/domain) where the final layer would have as many neurons as there are categories. This could simplify the training and perhaps make the model more robust. Especially for domains with many possible sentence labels (such as laptops), this could improve the system performance.

A natural extension of this approach would be to design the network to predict the entity and attribute separately; this could also allow for some parameter sharing between different classes.

We would also like to further investigate the issue of hyperparameter tuning and model selection.

Finally, a direct comparison with convolutional networks could also be interesting.

---

⁵We would like to thank the reviewers for this observation.

370

Acknowledgements

This work was supported by the grant no. GA15-06894S of the Grant Agency of the Czech Republic.

References

Basant Agarwal and Namita Mittal. 2016. Machine learning approach for sentiment analysis. In *Prominent Feature Extraction for Sentiment Analysis*, pages 21–45. Springer.

Sebastian Ebert, Ngoc Thang Vu, and Hinrich Schütze. 2015. Cis-positive: A combination of convolutional neural networks and support vector machines for sentiment analysis in twitter. In *Proceedings of the 9th International Workshop on Semantic Evaluation (SemEval 2015)*, pages 527–532, Denver, Colorado, June. Association for Computational Linguistics.

Sepp Hochreiter and Jürgen Schmidhuber. 1997. Long short-term memory. *Neural Comput.*, 9(8):1735–1780, November.

Diederik P. Kingma and Jimmy Ba. 2014. Adam: A method for stochastic optimization. *CoRR*, abs/1412.6980.

Razvan Pascanu, Tomas Mikolov, and Yoshua Bengio. 2012. Understanding the exploding gradient problem. *CoRR*, abs/1211.5063.

Maria Pontiki, Dimitris Galanis, John Pavlopoulos, Harris Papageorgiou, Ion Androutsopoulos, and Suresh Manandhar. 2014. Semeval-2014 task 4: Aspect based sentiment analysis. In *Proceedings of the 8th international workshop on semantic evaluation (SemEval 2014)*, pages 27–35.

Maria Pontiki, Dimitrios Galanis, Haris Papageorgiou, Suresh Manandhar, and Ion Androutsopoulos. 2015. Semeval-2015 task 12: Aspect based sentiment analysis. In *Proceedings of the 9th International Workshop on Semantic Evaluation (SemEval 2015), Association for Computational Linguistics, Denver, Colorado*, pages 486–495.

Nitish Srivastava, Geoffrey Hinton, Alex Krizhevsky, Ilya Sutskever, and Ruslan Salakhutdinov. 2014. Dropout: A simple way to prevent neural networks from overfitting. *J. Mach. Learn. Res.*, 15(1):1929–1958, January.

Maite Taboada, Julian Brooke, Milan Tofiloski, Kimberly Voll, and Manfred Stede. 2011. Lexicon-based methods for sentiment analysis. *Comput. Linguist.*, 37(2):267–307, June.

Zhiqiang Toh and Jian Su. 2015. Nlangp: Supervised machine learning system for aspect category classification and opinion target extraction. In *Proceedings of the 9th International Workshop on Semantic Evaluation (SemEval 2015)*, pages 496–501, Denver, Colorado, June. Association for Computational Linguistics.

UWaterloo at SemEval-2016 Task 5: Minimally Supervised Approaches to Aspect-Based Sentiment Analysis

Olga Vechtomova and **Anni He**
University of Waterloo, Canada
{ovechtomova, anni.he}@uwaterloo.ca

Abstract

This paper describes our system for Aspect-Based Sentiment Analysis (ABSA), task 5 of SemEval 2016. To conduct sentence level ABSA, we employed minimally supervised approaches for each type of extracted information. The system uses Word2Vec to derive word semantic similarities, and relies on external review corpora as training data. The results of the 2016 evaluation are discussed and suggestions for improvements are given.

1 Introduction

In this paper, we describe our system for Aspect-Based Sentiment Analysis (ABSA), Task 5 of SemEval 2016. The task involves classifying consumer reviews into existing aspect category labels (slot 1), identifying the opinion target expression (OTE) corresponding to the aspect category label (slot 2), then assigning sentiment polarity expressed about the aspect category (slot 3). The aspect category (slot 1) consists of two parts: Entity (e.g. food, ambience, restaurant) and Attribute (e.g. price, quality).

Our system tackles the problem in three stages addressing each slot individually for the restaurant domain and laptop domain (slot 3 only). The strengths of the system include no lexicon resources and minimal amount of labeled corpora. For the aspect category identification and OTE extraction, the approach is semi-supervised utilizing Word2Vec models (Mikolov et al., 2013) to derive word semantic similarities. The lists of words ranked by their semantic similarities to each entity and each attribute are generated for the aspect category identification.

For the polarity assignment, we build from the approach of (Vechtomova et al., 2014) using corpora of consumer-rated electronics and restaurant reviews. The method does not require any sentiment labels at the word or sentence level or sentiment lexicons.

The paper describes each stage of the system in detail in section 2. In section 3, results of the system are presented and conclusions are drawn in section 4.

2 System Description

2.1 Corpora

At different stages of our system we used various resources we automatically generated from two corpora, described below. In both of these corpora we used only the original text of the review and the overall review ratings assigned by the consumer.

For the Restaurant domain, we used a corpus of 157,865 restaurant reviews from one of the major business review websites (Vechtomova, 2014). The collection contains reviews for 32,782 restaurants in the United States. The average number of words per review is 64.7. We will refer to this corpus as the Restaurant corpus throughout the paper.

For the Laptop domain, we used a subset of the Amazon corpus (Jindal and Liu, 2008), containing 138,504 reviews of products in the category Consumer Electronics. We will refer to this corpus as the CE corpus throughout the paper.

2.2 Aspect Category Detection

For this slot, the goal is to identify all entity and attribute pairs expressed by the given review sentence.

372

Proceedings of SemEval-2016, pages 372–377,
San Diego, California, June 16-17, 2016. ©2016 Association for Computational Linguistics

Prior to the two-stage entity and attribute identification pipeline, we obtain ranked lists of words for each entity type (entity ranked lists) and some of the attribute labels (attribute ranked lists). Extraction of OTEs by the process described in section 2.3 must be done prior to the feed into the category identification step.

We participated in Slot 1 in the Restaurant domain only. The entity ranked lists are generated from a Word2Vec model trained on the Restaurant corpus with a vocabulary size of 22118 words. The ranked lists are generated using a semi-supervised approach by using OTEs from the 2015 ABSA Restaurant training set as seed words. A list of top n similar words (n=500) is computed for each seed word by cosine similarity, then the lists are merged to form one ranked list per entity. The top n similar words parameter is chosen empirically to be sufficiently large relative to the vocabulary size in order to generate a fair-sized merged list. A weight of 5 is applied to the seed words to boost their rank in the merged list. The similarity scores in the merged lists are normalized to a range of [0,1]. When the entity ranked lists are utilized in the entity identification step, we apply a similarity threshold of 0.05 to discard any words below the threshold. The trained Word2Vec model only detects single words, therefore the ranked lists contain no multiword phrases.

The entity identification is based on the previously extracted OTEs for each review sentence and the generated entity ranked lists from Word2Vec. For each identified OTE of each sentence, its cosine similarity score is obtained from each entity ranked list. The entity with the highest similarity to the OTE is assigned. The OTE is further tokenized if it is a MWU. Each token goes through the same entity assignment as above, then the entity with the highest similarity is assigned to the entire MWU-OTE. If the OTE does not appear in any of the ranked lists, then the OTE is discarded, and no entity or attribute is assigned.

In order to identify the attribute component of the entity-attribute pair, we first generate a set of seed words from the ABSA 2015 training set. This process is done for each entity category that has more than one attribute (e.g. FOOD, DRINKS). For every entity-attribute pair (e.g. FOOD#PRICES) we parse all sentences in the training set that are labeled with this pair, and extract all words that have JJ (adjective) and VBN (verb, past participle) POS tags, have frequency greater than one, and have one of the following relationships with at least one noun or pronoun: adjectival modifier, relational clause modifier, nominal subject or passive nominal subject. These attribute seed words are then used to obtain a ranked list of words (attribute ranked list) using Word2Vec in a similar process as the entity ranked lists.

After an entity is identified, attributes are assigned based on the information from the review sentence. Each review sentence is tokenized, singularized with stop words removed. Intersection of all the tokens is computed with each attribute ranked list. The attribute with the highest similarity is assigned. If none of the ranked list attributes are assigned, then the attribute with the highest prior probability in the ABSA 2015 training set is assigned.

2.3 Extraction of Opinion Target Expressions

We approach the problem of opinion target extraction with a semi-supervised method. The opinion target expression (OTE) is Slot 2 in the ABSA task, and is only set for the Restaurant domain.

First, seed words are extracted for each Entity from the set of opinion target expressions in the ABSA 2015 training dataset. These are ranked by frequency, and top n are used. We evaluated different values for n, with 5 showing the best results on the ABSA 2015 test data. For each seed word we generate a ranked list of words using Word2Vec models, and create a merged entity ranked list as explained in Section 2.2.

The next stage in the OTE extraction process is identification of the boundaries of nominal multiword units (MWUs) representing OTEs in the sentences. We use an algorithm developed by (Vechtomova, 2014) that builds MWUs in a bottom-up manner. Each sentence in the dataset is parsed using Stanford dependency parser (De Marneffe et al., 2006). The process begins by identifying all single nouns, which are governors in at least one syntactic dependency relation. By following a set of syntactic rules, we merge each of these nouns with the adjacent words (e.g. adjectives, other nouns) in an iterative manner, one at a time. The merging proceeds in two stages: in the first stage, the algorithm iteratively merges pairs of words that have either adjectival modifier (e.g. salty fish), nominal compound modifier (e.g. garden salad), or possession modifier (e.g. Chef's choice) dependency relationship. In the second stage, it iteratively merges pairs of words that have a prepositional modifier (e.g. fish with rice) or a conjunct (e.g. fish and chips) relationship. In addition to applying syntactic rules, before each merge, the algorithm calculates Normalized Pointwise Mutual Information (NPMI) between two strings to be merged. Only if all the syntactic rules are satisfied and the NPMI is above the specified threshold, the two strings are merged. The algorithm is described in detail in (Vechtomova, 2014). The output of this stage is a set of nominal MWUs (which may include single nouns) for each sentence.

Finally, the system calculates a score for each MWU–Entity pair by summing the scores of the matching words in the corresponding entity ranked list. If an MWU has a score (s) of zero in all categories, it is discarded. If the score is $0 < s < 0.1$, the target is changed to NULL. If $s \geq 0.1$, it is retained as OTE.

2.4 Polarity Identification

We address the problem of polarity detection with an approach that only uses the texts of consumer reviews and overall review ratings assigned by consumers. The attractiveness of the method is that it does not require any sentiment lexicons or sentiment labels at the word or sentence levels. We extend a method described in (Vechtomova et al., 2014). Due to the growing popularity of online product/business reviewing, there exist vast repositories of reviews in many categories of consumer products and businesses. Most of the online review sites require users to rate products numerically on some scale (e.g. a 5-star rating scheme in Amazon). We leverage these resources in our methods. The Restaurant corpus that we used has ratings on a 10-point scale, while the CE corpus, on a 5-point scale. For the Restaurant domain we generate a set of negative reviews by pooling all reviews with ratings of 1 and 2, and a set of positive reviews by pooling all reviews with the rating of 10 from the Restaurant corpus. In the Laptop domain, reviews with ratings 1 and 2 were used for the negative set, while reviews with the rating of 5 for the positive set.

In summary, the process consists of the following

steps. First, two vectors of context features are created for each adjective or verb (w) that has a dependency relationship with a noun or personal pronoun. One vector $posV$ is built based on all occurrences of w in the positive set, and the second vector $negV$ is built based on its occurrences in the negative set. Next, polarity of the occurrence of w in a previously unseen sentence s is determined by building a vector $evalV$ based only on the context of w in s, and computing a pairwise similarity of $EvalV$ to $posV$ and $negV$.

In more detail, the following steps are performed on each of the two sets: positive and negative. Each sentence in a positive/negative set is processed by using a dependency parser in the Stanford CoreNLP package. In each sentence, we first locate all nouns or personal pronouns (n). Then, for each n, its dependency triples with adjectives and verbs (w) are extracted, where the dependency relation is either an adjectival modifier, nominal subject, passive nominal subject, direct object or relative clause modifier. An example of a dependency triple is *nsubj(pizza, hot)*, where pizza is a governor, while hot is a dependent. We also identify dependency relations of adjectival complements, clausal complements and open clause complements and merge them with the nominal subject relationship sharing the same verb, e.g. *nsubj(menu, looks)* and *acomp(looks, great)* are merged into *nsubj_acomp(menu, look_great)*.

We also created a set of rules to determine whether the context containing an instance of w is negated or not. For each occurrence of w the following information is recorded: negation ($1 - w$ is negated; $0 - w$ is not negated); dependency relation of w with n; w lemma (output by Stanford CoreNLP). These three pieces of information form a pattern p, e.g., "negation=0; amod; better". A context feature vector ($PosV$ and $NegV$) is built for each p, as follows: for each instance of w matching this pattern in the corpus (positive or negative, respectively) we extract all dependency relations containing it. Each of them is transformed into a context feature f of the form:"lemma; Part Of Speech (POS); dependency relation". For instance, if adjective "hot" occurs in a dependency triple *advmod(hot, too)*, the following feature is created to represent "too" and its syntactic role (adverbial modifier) with respect to "hot": "too, RB, advmod". We also build

Pattern	Context
NEGATION=0, nsubj, cold, JJ	also, RB, advmod
	be, VBZ, cop
	bread, NN, nsubj
	horrible, JJ, conj_and
	it, PRP, nsubj
	not, RB, conj_and
	particularly, RB, advmod
	quickly, RB, advmod
	tired, JJ, conj_and

Table 1: Example of a Pattern and its Context Features.

composite features by joining up to four dependency relations by traversing the dependency graph.

For each f we record its frequency of co-occurrence with p (used as TF in Eq. 1). Table 1 contains an example of a pattern and a subset of its context features. The same algorithm is used to build a feature vector ($EvalV$) for each pattern extracted from each sentence in the ABSA test dataset.

Next, for each pattern p found in the test sentence, we compute pairwise similarity between its $Eval_p$ vector and $posV_p$ and $negV_p$ respectively. For the purpose of computing similarity we evaluated two similarity functions: BM25 Query Adjusted Combined Weight (QACW) (Sparck Jones et al., 2000) and TF.IDF. QACW was first used to compute term-term similarity in (Vechtomova and Robertson, 2012). The $EvalV_p$ is treated as the query, while $posV_p$ and $negV_p$ as documents (V_p in Eq. 1)

$$Sim(EvalV_p, V_p) = \sum_{f=1}^{F} \frac{TF(k_1 + 1)}{K + TF} \times QTF \times IDF_f$$

(1)

Where: F – the number of features that $EvalV_p$ and V_p have in common; TF – frequency of feature f in V_p; QTF – frequency of feature f in $EvalV_p$; K = $k1((1b)+bDLAVDL)$; k_1 – feature frequency normalization factor; b – Vp length normalization factor; DL – number of features in V_p; $AVDL$ – average number of features in the vectors V for all patterns p in the training set (positive or negative). The b and k_1 parameters were set to 0.1 and 50 respectively, as these showed best performance on the ABSA 2016 Restaurant training dataset. The IDF (Inverse Document Frequency) of the feature f is calculated as $IDF_f = \log(N/n_f)$, where, n_f – number of vectors V in the training set (positive or negative) containing f; N – total number of vectors V in the training set.

Finally, if $Sim(EvalV_p, posV_p) > Sim(EvalV_p,$ $negV_p)$, we assign positive polarity to the given instance of p in the test sentence, otherwise, negative.

Polarity detection in ABSA is done as a Phase B evaluation, i.e. after the Phase A goldset (containing OTEs and Entity-Attribute pairs) is released. The next steps differ for the Restaurant and Laptop domains, since the former has OTEs, while the latter does not.

For the Restaurant domain, for each OTE in the goldset, the method determines the majority polarity based on all p that contain the OTE or any of its words if the OTE is an MWU. If there is equal number of positive and negative cases, then neutral polarity is assigned. If no word matching OTE or any of its constituents is found by our method, then average polarity is calculated based on the current sentence. This method was also used for cases with NULL OTEs. If no words have been extracted by our method for the given sentence, then average polarity based on the entire review is calculated.

For the Laptop domain, we tried two methods. In Method 1 (submitted), the average polarity is calculated based on the entire sentence, and if no opinion words have been extracted for the given sentence, then we assign the average polarity calculated based on the entire review. In Method 2, for each Entity type in the goldset (e.g. Battery, Memory) we first built a set of related words using Word2Vec given the entity name as the seed word. Top 500 words ranked by cosine similarity to the seed word were used. For each Entity-Attribute pair in each sentence of the Phase A goldset, we first determine if any opinion target extracted by our method matches a word in the ranked list for the corresponding entity. If it does, then we assign its polarity to the corresponding Entity-Attribute tuple(s) for that sentence. If no matching word for an entity is found, then we calculate polarity based on all words that did not match any other category. If no such words exist, we default to Method 1.

3 Results

In this section we present results of the runs on the ABSA 2016 training and test datasets.

Tables 2 through 6 show results for entity-attribute identification and OTE extraction. The training set performs better than the test set in all

Dataset	Precision	Recall	F-Measure
TRAIN 2016	0.5334	0.5168	0.5250
TEST 2016	0.4980	0.4966	0.4973

Table 2: Slot 1 (Aspect category) results (restaurant).

Dataset	Precision	Recall	F-Measure
TRAIN 2016	0.6331	0.6676	0.6499
TEST 2016	0.6100	0.6457	0.6273

Table 3: Slot 1 results (restaurant) evaluating on entity only.

Dataset	Precision	Recall	F-Measure
TRAIN 2016	0.4826	0.7143	0.5760
TEST 2016	0.4804	0.7026	0.5707

Table 5: Slot 2 (Opinion Target Expression) results (restaurant dataset).

Dataset	Precision	Recall	F-Measure
TRAIN 2016	0.3582	0.3934	0.3750
TEST 2016	0.3240	0.3667	0.3440

Table 6: : Slots 1&2 results (restaurant dataset).

three evaluations. This can be attributed to the fact that the entity/attribute ranked lists were built using Word2Vec models generated from the 2015 training set which is a subset of the 2016 training set.

Motivation of the ranked lists process stems from the minimal amount of annotated training data. It is hypothesized that the OTEs from the training data provide strong signals for entity labels. For example, if the OTE is "waiter", then the entity is most likely "SERVICE". Once the entity is identified, attribute labels are assigned using tokenized words in the sentence besides the OTE. It is thought that the other words in the sentences are better predictors for attribute labels. For example, the review sentence "the food was not worth the price" has OTE "food" and the entity-attribute label "FOOD#PRICES". The attribute label can easily be determined from the word price ranked at the top of the #PRICES attribute ranked list. There are several consequences impacting the performance of the system as a result of the two-stage design as explained below.

A comparison can be made between the results for entity-attribute pair identification (Table 2) and entity-only identification (Table 3) to show progression of the system performance between the two stages. The system performs more than 10% better in the entity-only case for both test and train datasets. This is expected because attribute identification using tokenized words as features from the review sentence is less reliable than using the OTE as a single feature.

Another weakness of the system is in the aspect category identification for NULL OTEs. The en-

tity/attribute ranked lists procedure is not designed for NULL targets due to the lack of OTEs. Currently the NULL target sentences require a different process whereby words in the sentence are tokenized and compared to both the entity ranked lists and attribute ranked lists to identify the label pair. The system evaluated without the NULL targets shows about a 4% improvement in F-measure for the test and train datasets. To improve the system, the NULL target aspect category identification may need to use additional features from the previous and following sentences of the review.

Table 5 shows the results of the evaluation for Slot 2 (OTE). While recall is good, the precision is not high. A better method of computing similarity between a candidate OTE and the Entity categories is needed. Also, a better method to detect NULL targets is needed. Out of 198 NULL OTEs in the test gold set, our method missed 164. As expected, the combined results of slots 1& 2 is rather poor as shown in Table 6.

Our approach to polarity identification showed promising results. QACW performed slightly better on both the training and test Restaurant datasets. As can be seen from Table 7, Method 1 in the laptop polarity task performed better than Method 2. This is likely due to the fact that using one word per entity as seed is not sufficient to generate a good set of entity-related words. In the future, it will be good to explore how to generate a better set of seed words semantically representing the entity.

In our submission for the Laptop Slot 3, we did not use features based on adjectival, clausal and open clausal complements merged with the nominal subject modifier, e.g. *nsubj_acomp(menu, look_great)* (for the description of features see Section 2.4). When we added these relations to the

Dataset	Precision	Recall	F-Measure
TRAIN 2016	0.5000	0.6616	0.5696
TEST 2016	0.4822	0.6273	0.5453

Table 4: Slot 1 results (restaurant) with NULL OTEs removed.

Dataset/Method	Accuracy
TRAIN 2016 – REST TF.IDF (submitted)	0.7801
TRAIN 2016 – REST QACW	0.7825
TEST 2016 – REST TF.IDF (submitted)	0.8033
TEST 2016 – REST QACW	0.8056
TRAIN 2016 – LAPT TF.IDF, Method 1	0.7417
TRAIN 2016 – LAPT TF.IDF, Method 2	0.7383
TEST 2016 – LAPT TF.IDF, Method 1 (submitted)	0.7129
TEST 2016 – LAPT TF.IDF, Method 2	0.7066

Table 7: Slot 3 (polarity) results.

Dataset/Method	Accuracy
TRAIN 2016 – LAPT TF.IDF Method 1	0.7634
TEST 2016 – LAPT TF.IDF Method 1	0.7316

Table 8: Slot 3(polarity) generated by adding adjectival, clausal and open clausal complements to the feature set.

feature set, the performance improved by 2.9% and 2.6% on the training and test datasets respectively (see Table 8).

One of the major reasons why the polarity method did not perform better is that we adapted a method that was designed for identifying two categories (positive and negative) to the ABSA task, which has three categories (positive, negative and neutral). This is evident when we break down the results by polarity category: the F-measure in the Restaurant domain for Positive, Negative and Neutral categories is 0.8815, 0.6439 and 0.1194 respectively. For the Laptop it is 0.8004, 0.5727 and 0 respectively. Further work is needed on better identification of neutral cases.

4 Conclusion

In this paper, we described our system for aspect-based sentiment analysis used for aspect category identification, extraction of opinion target expression and polarity identification. Our polarity identification method only leverages available consumer reviews with the associated overall review ratings assigned by the consumer. It does not require any sentiment lexicons or sentiment annotations in the texts of the reviews. The polarity identification and

OTE extraction showed promising results among other systems having performed within one percent of the mean scores of all participating systems in the restaurant and laptop domains. To advance our system, we identified weaknesses of the aspect category identification and hopeful next steps to improve the results by refined treatment of NULL target sentences.

References

Marie-Catherine De Marneffe, Bill MacCartney, Christopher D Manning, et al. 2006. Generating typed dependency parses from phrase structure parses. In *Proceedings of LREC*, volume 6, pages 449–454.

Nitin Jindal and Bing Liu. 2008. Opinion spam and analysis. In *Proceedings of the 2008 International Conference on Web Search and Data Mining*, pages 219–230. ACM.

Tomas Mikolov, Ilya Sutskever, Kai Chen, Greg S Corrado, and Jeff Dean. 2013. Distributed representations of words and phrases and their compositionality. In *Advances in neural information processing systems*, pages 3111–3119.

K Sparck Jones, Steve Walker, and Stephen E. Robertson. 2000. A probabilistic model of information retrieval: development and comparative experiments: Part 2. *Information Processing & Management*, 36(6):809–840.

Olga Vechtomova and Stephen E Robertson. 2012. A domain-independent approach to finding related entities. *Information Processing & Management*, 48(4):654–670.

Olga Vechtomova, Kaheer Suleman, and Jack Thomas. 2014. An information retrieval-based approach to determining contextual opinion polarity of words. In *Advances in Information Retrieval*, pages 553–559. Springer.

Olga Vechtomova. 2014. A method for automatic extraction of multiword units representing business aspects from user reviews. *Journal of the Association for Information Science and Technology*, 65(7):1463–1477.

INF-UFRGS-OPINION-MINING at SemEval-2016 Task 6: Automatic Generation of a Training Corpus for Unsupervised Identification of Stance in Tweets

Marcelo Dias and **Karin Becker**

Instituto de Informática (INF)
Universidade Federal do Rio Grande do Sul (UFRGS)
Porto Alegre, RS, Brazil
{marcelo.dias, karin.becker}@inf.ufrgs.br

Abstract

This paper describe a weakly supervised solution for detecting stance in tweets, submitted to the SemEval 2016 Stance Task. Our approach is based on the premise that stance can be exposed as positive or negative opinions, although not necessarily about the stance target itself. Our system receives as input n-grams representing opinion targets and common terms used to denote stance (e.g. hashtags), and use these features, together with the sentiment detection solutions, to automatically compose a large training corpus. Then, it applies a supervised learning algorithm to develop a stance prediction model.

1 Introduction

Sentiment analysis involves the automatic identification of opinions, feelings, evaluations, attitudes and emotions expressed by people in the written language. Popular lines of work in this field are opinion mining (Liu, 2012) and emotion mining (Mohammad, 2016). Stance detection is a less explored problem, addressed as part of SemEval-2016 (International Workshop on Semantic Evaluation 2016), Task 6[1]. Stance detection is defined in this task as the automatic determination from text whether its author is in favor of the given target, against the given target, or whether neither inference is likely.

The present work describes the solution developed for Task 6-b, which involves the unsupervised stance detection in tweets based solely in their content. The target is Donald Trump, a possible republican presidential candidate, for which two sets of

non-annotated tweets were supplied: a domain corpus with 78,156 tweets and a test corpus with 707 tweets for task evaluation purpose. Another set of annotated tweets for stance detection was available as part of Task 6-a (supervised stance detection), which included 639 tweets about another possible candidate, Hillary Clinton. We used this annotated data to develop the proposed method, due to the similarity of problems. Details of the Task 6 can be found at (Mohammad et al., 2016).

The identification of stance can be complex even for humans (Walker et al., 2012), and our strategy was to address it partly as an opinion mining problem. Stance can be exposed as positive or negative opinions, but not necessarily about the target of the stance problem. For instance, when the opinion target is a politician, the target may be his/her agenda for health or education, members of the same party, or opponents. In addition, stance detection faces challenges common to sentiment analysis in general, such as use of vocabulary and slang specific of the media, orthography errors, sarcasm, etc.

We developed a weakly supervised method for detecting stance in tweets. Our method requires some side-related targets and key stance n-grams, which are used, together with sentiment detection solutions, to automatically label tweets with regard to a stance. The automatically labeled tweets are then used to train a classifier to detect stance in tweets, resulting in a stance prediction model.

The remaining of the paper describes the obtained results, the proposed solution and the experiments developed.

---

[1]http://alt.qcri.org/semeval2016/task6/

Proceedings of SemEval-2016, pages 378–383,
San Diego, California, June 16-17, 2016. ©2016 Association for Computational Linguistics

	Predicted			
	Against	**Favor**	**None**	**Recall**
Against	206	44	49	68.90
Favor	94	42	12	28.38
None	192	24	44	16.92
Precision	41.87	38.18	41.90	
F-score	52.09	32.56	24.11	

Table 1: Trump Corpus: Confusion Matrix and Metrics

2 Results

Task 6-b evaluated the proposed solutions according to the mean F-score of *Against* and *Favor* stances, considering the test dataset. Among 9 participants, the solution proposed by our team was the second runner-up, with a mean F-score of 42.43. Table 1 displays the confusion matrix related to the test dataset, together with the respective precision, recall and F-score metrics. The precision obtained for all classes are relatively similar, ranging from 38.18% (*Favor*) to 41.9% (*None*). However, it is clear that our solution tends to classify instances as *Against*, which explains why only the recall of this stance displays a good value (68.9%).

These results can be explained by the fact that our approach is more effective in identifying *Against* tweets when they are related to Trump or related targets, but fails to recognize endorsements to Trump when they are expressed as criticisms to his opponents. In addition, our system relies on the identification of sentiment, and the performance for identification of negative sentiment was clearly superior, compared to the detection of positive and neutral tweets, as discussed in more detail in Section 4.2. The particularly low recall obtained for the *None* class, which assumes lack of sentiment, might have influenced the other results.

3 The Process

Our system was developed on the premise that the stance towards a politician could be detected by analysing opinions of people tweeting explicitly about him, his party, his supporters or opponents, as well as subjects that he endorses or criticizes. As a weakly supervised solution, our system receives as input n-grams representing opinion targets (e.g. variations on the name of Trump, or his opponents), and terms frequently used to denote stance (e.g. hashtags, derogatory terms). Tweets

expressing opinions according to these characteristics could be used to automatically compose a large training corpus for a supervised approach, such that a stance prediction model could be produced. This eliminates the burden of manual annotation.

For that purpose, we developed a process for automatically detecting stance in tweets that converts a stance detection problem into a polarity detection problem, according to the following steps:

1. Stance Features Identification;
2. Rule-based Automatic Annotation of a Training Corpus;
3. Creation of a Stance Prediction Model Using Supervised Learning;
4. Stance Prediction of Unlabeled Tweets.

3.1 Stance Features Identification

The first step in the process was to identify n-grams that typically would indicate a stance in the domain corpus. We developed a program to extract n-grams (uni-gram, bi-grams and tri-grams) from the domain corpus, and rank them by frequency. Then, we manually inspected the most frequent n-grams (top 200), selecting the ones that directly or indirectly were related to the stance target. We divided these n-grams into two categories: *side-related targets* and *stance keywords*. Side-related targets are expressions used as the target of an opinion. Variations of "Donald Trump" (e.g. "Donald", "Trump") and his party are examples of the Favor side, whereas variations of the name of his opponents (e.g. Hilary Clinton) and subjects that compose this political platform (e.g. immigrants) are instances of the Against side. Table 2 shows all the side-related targets selected for Trump.

Stance keyword n-grams consist of expressions that enable to assign a stance even when the opinion target is implicit. For example, the unigram "Apprentice", name of the TV show presented by Trump, was used in ironic tweets denoting an against stance about him, whereas the hashtag #stophillary would represent a favor stance towards Trump. Table 3 displays the stance all keyword n-grams selected for Trump.

3.2 Automatic labeling of a Training Corpus

The goal of this step is to automatically label tweets, so as to compose a training dataset to develop a

Side	Side Related Targets
FAVOR	realdonaldtrump, donaldtrump, donald trump, donald, trump, republican, republicans
AGAINST	hillaryclinton, hillary clinton, hilary clinton, hillary, hilary, clinton, clintons, hill, democrats, democrat, bill clinton, obama, mexicans, mexican, latino, latinos, elchapo, chapo, immigrant, immigrants, immigration, mexico

Table 2: Side Related Targets

Side	Key Stance N-grams
FAVOR	stop hillary, stophillary
AGAINST	love wins, lovewins, apprentice, dontvotefortrump, mr trump, racist

Table 3: Key Stance N-grams

Rule	Stance
1 - KEY-FAVOR Presence of a favor keyword n-gram with no against keyword n-gram	FAVOR
2 - KEY-AGAINST Presence of an against keyword n-gram with no favor keyword n-gram	AGAINST
3 - FAVOR-POSITIVE Presence of a favor-related side target with no against-related side target and positive tweet polarity	FAVOR
4 - FAVOR-NEGATIVE Presence of a favor-related side target with no against-related side target and negative tweet polarity	AGAINST
5 - AGAINST-POSITIVE Presence of a against side related target with no favor-related side target and positive tweet polarity	AGAINST
6 - AGAINST-NEGATIVE Presence of an against-related side target with no favor-related side target and negative tweet polarity	FAVOR
7 - NEUTRAL Neutral tweet polarity	NONE
Other cases	DISCARD TWEET

Table 4: Rules used for automatic labeling

stance prediction model using supervised learning. We devised a set of rules that represent our premise about opinions characterizing the stance, displayed in Table 4. Only clearly expressed stances are considered for the training dataset (FAVOR, AGAINST and NONE), otherwise they are disregarded.

Rules 1 and 2 assume the use of stance keywords to denote positive/negative opinions, whereas rules 3-6 consider the combination of a side-related target and the positive/negative polarity of the sentiment contained in the text. Rule 7 assumes that it is unlikely that tweets without sentiments represent a stance (NONE).

We developed a program to generate for each tweet of the corpus the following features:

- Presence of at least one favor stance keyword n-gram;
- Presence of at least one against stance keyword n-gram;
- Presence of at least one favor-related target n-gram;
- Presence of at least one against-related target n-gram;
- Tweet polarity;

The program scans all tweets in the domain corpus tweets, and generates a new dataset with these features. It verifies the presence of key stance n-grams and side related targets, and evaluates tweet polarity by submitting the tweet text to three sentiment analysis APIs. Once the stance features are generated for each tweet, the rules are applied. Tweets are included in the training corpus if rules 1,

2, 3, 4, 5, 6 or 7 hold, or discarded otherwise. The resulting training dataset is composed by the original tweet texts, and the label automatically assigned to the tweet.

With the goal of increasing the precision of tweet polarity identification, we combined the results of three off-the-shelf sentiment analysis APIs, namely HP Haven On Demand[2], IBM Alchemy[3] and Vivekn[4]. Each API returns the polarity property as a label (i.e. negative, positive or neutral) and the respective score property. The developed program first verifies if Haven's score and Alchemy's score are equal to zero, a condition that defines a tweet as neutral. Otherwise, the program combines the APIs by adding the three scores. The result is a negative tweet if the calculated value is negative, and positive otherwise. This particular combination was based on experiments on the use of these APIs, which are described in more details in Section 4.2.

Table 5 displays the distribution of tweets per rule considering both Trump and Hillary datasets. With regard to Trump corpus, although there were 78,156 tweets in the domain corpus supplied for the task,

---

[2]https://www.havenondemand.com/
[3]http://www.alchemyapi.com/
[4]http://sentiment.vivekn.com/docs/api/

Rule	Hillary	Trump
1 - KEY-FAVOR	10	1
2 - KEY-AGAINST	96	1,383
3 - FAVOR-POSITIVE	63	2,295
4 - FAVOR-NEGATIVE	127	7,369
5 - AGAINST-POSITIVE	6	0
6 - AGAINST-NEGATIVE	25	4
7 - NEUTRAL	41	2,201
Other cases	271	6,709
Total	**639**	**19,952**

Table 5: Domain Corpus Tweets X Rule

it was possible to apply the rules only to 19,952 tweets due to quota restrictions for the free usage of Alchemy. Most tweet labeled as *Against* were detected using Rules 4 and 2, whereas most *Favor* labels were assigned due to Rule 3. It is possible to see that most tweets in Trump's corpus were focused on Donald Trump himself and target representing support to him, and therefore, the bias related to opinions related to opposition targets, as represented by rules 5 and 6, could not be explored. The training sets resulting from application of the rules were unbalanced, with a dominance of *Against* instances. Hillary training set was composed of 229 *Against* (62%), 98 *Favor* (27%) and 41 *None* instances (11%). Trump training set was composed of 8,752 *Against* (66%), 2,300 *Favor* (17%) and 2,201 *None* instances (17%).

3.3 Creation of a Stance Prediction Model Using Supervised Learning

The goal of this step is to develop a stance predictive model by submitting the training dataset automatically labeled to a classification algorithm.

The training corpus generated in previous step is composed of the original tweet text and the stance label. We pre-processed the texts and submitted them to a classification algorithm for a three class problem: Favor, Against and None. We adopted the Weka platform (version 3.7.11) (Hall et al., 2009), and an SVM classification algorithm (SMO) available in this environment with the default parameters.

The following actions were performed during pre-processing: a) convert all tweet texts to lower case; b) replace all mentions for tweet profiles by the `"a_mention"` unigram, except those containing the text of a side-related target (e.g. "realdon-

		Predicted			
		Against	Favor	None	Recall
	Against	290	46	25	80.33
Actual	Favor	45	55	12	49.11
	None	113	23	30	18.07
	Precision	64.73	44.35	44.78	
	F-score	71.69	46.61	25.75	

Table 6: Hillary Corpus: Confusion Matrix and Metrics

aldtrump"); c) submit the text to the *Stringtoword-vector* function available in Weka for textual feature extraction and creation of the training dataset. We chose the following parameters for feature extraction: a) extraction of alphabetic unigrams and bigrams; b) removal of stopwords; c) no limitation on the number of n-grams extracted; and d) binary representation of features (i.e. presence or absence).

3.4 Stance Prediction of Unlabeled Tweets

The last step of the process is to predict the stance for any tweet, using the model trained in the previous step. For the Semeval task, we applied the predictive model to the provided test set, composed of 707 instances, obtaining the results displayed in Table 1.

As an experiment, we also tested the approach on the Hillary dataset provided in Task 6-a, but limited to the tweets that were discarded during the creation of the training set. The results are displayed in Table 6, which are significantly better, compared to Trump's. In both results, it is clear that performance for the *None* class is the weakest point of our solution. Very few neutral tweets are recognized as such (recall of 16.92% and 18.07% for the Trump and Hillary datasets, respectively), compromising the precision of both *Favor* and *Against* stances.

4 Experiments

We made two main experiments as the basis for the proposed solution: a) verification of the impact of proposed rules with regard to the performance of the predictive model, using the Hillary labeled dataset, and b) verification of the precision of the off-the-shelf sentiment detection APIs used. These are described in the remaining of this section.

Rules	Class	Automatic labeling			Predictive Model			Combined		
		Precision	Recall	F-score	Precision	Recall	F-score	Precision	Recall	F-score
(a) 1.2.7	Against	85.41	79.61	82.41	52.45	95.35	67.67	58.05	90.86	70.84
	Favor	40.00	33.33	36.36	0.00	0.00	0.00	40.00	3.57	6.55
	None	36.59	46.88	41.10	21.74	3.73	6.37	31.25	12.05	17.39
	Weighted Avg.	71.08	68.71	69.66	33.43	51.02	37.22	47.92	55.09	45.69
(b) 3.4.5.6.7	Against	78.20	66.24	71.72	58.30	70.59	63.86	65.26	68.70	66.94
	Favor	48.86	65.15	55.84	17.39	26.09	20.87	35.03	49.11	40.89
	None	36.59	38.46	37.50	50.82	24.41	32.98	45.10	27.71	**34.33**
	Weighted Avg.	64.62	61.83	62.63	50.79	49.60	48.21	54.72	54.62	53.90
(c) All rules	Against	81.22	77.18	79.15	47.49	86.67	61.36	64.73	80.33	**71.69**
	Favor	47.96	66.20	55.62	30.77	19.51	23.88	44.35	49.11	**46.61**
	None	36.59	26.79	30.93	57.69	13.64	22.06	44.78	18.07	25.75
	Weighted Avg.	68.01	67.39	67.27	49.10	46.87	39.74	55.98	58.68	**55.36**

Table 7: Experiments with Hillary dataset

4.1 Experiments on the Rules to Detect Stance

We experimentally developed our method using the Hillary labeled corpus provided for Task 6-a, given that both stance targets are politicians in campaign. To perform this test and assess the performance of our method, we automatically labeled the Hillary training corpus, and applied the predictive model only to the instances that were not filtered by any of the rules. Table 7 displays the results obtained according to the rules used to prepare the training dataset. We compared three different scenarios:

(a) Stance Keywords rules (rules 1 and 2) combined with the neutral rule (rule 7);
(b) Side-related target and polarity rules (3 to 7 rules);
(c) All rules;

We measured the precision, recall and F-measure of the instances that were included in the training dataset (columns *Automatic labeling*), predicted instances according to the trained model (columns *Predictive Model*), and the whole set of instances labeled either using the rules or the predictive model (columns *Combined*). Scores are detailed per class and weighted average.

With regard to automatic labeling, the best weighted F-score was obtained by the set of stance keyword rules (a), i.e. 69.66, despite the poor result for the *Favor* class. However, our objective was to improve detection of *Against* and *Favor* stances, even at the expense of a less favorable result for the *None* class. Thus the set of all rules (c), which presents the second better F-score, is more interest-ing because it yields good scores for both *Favor* and *Against* stances.

Considering the predictive model, even if the training set is less accurate using only the rules involving sentiment about a side-related target (b), the respective model yields more accurate predictions (i.e. weighted F-measure of 48.21%). However, considering the *Against* and *Favor* classes, again the set of all rules (c) produced a slightly better result.

Finally, when considering the combination of the instances labeled by the rules and the ones by the predictive model, the best results are displayed for the set of all rules (c), considering both the weighted F-measure, and the scores for the *Against* and *Favor* classes. Thus, the set of all rules presents more balanced results throughout the 2 phases of the process, yielding the best final result.

It should be noticed that the results summarized in Tables 1 and 6 for Trump and Hillary corpora, respectively, were produced differently. The test set provided for Task-b was labeled using the predictive model only, whereas the Hillary results were produced using the combined approach of rules and predictive model. Considering that Trump corpus was much bigger, compared to Hillary's, we assumed for the task that the results of the predictive model would be more accurate. By applying the combined approach over Trump test set instead, the result would be slightly better (43.8%, using the same evaluation criterion adopted for the task).

4.2 The Sentiment Analysis APIs

We started the development of our solution using only Haven On Demand API but, after some tests, we noticed issues on the precision of the polarity detection step, which is key in our process. Indeed, it can be seen in Table 5 that an elevated number of tweets is filtered by sentiment rules.

API	Class	Precision	Recall	F-Score
Alchemy	Negative	64.39	78.42	70.71
	Neutral	17.82	26.34	**21.26**
	Positive	39.23	15.89	22.62
Haven	Negative	46.42	51.28	48.73
	Neutral	16.84	17.20	17.02
	Positive	55.97	46.73	50.93
Vivekn	Negative	57.99	56.62	57.30
	Neutral	13.39	17.20	15.06
	Positive	36.20	31.46	33.67
Combination	Negative	64.84	78.42	**70.99**
	Neutral	31.46	15.05	20.36
	Positive	61.56	61.37	**61.47**

Table 8: APIs Comparison

Using a polarity annotated dataset also in the political domain[5] (Mohammad, 2016), we compared the performance of the 3 chosen APIs, and their combination. Results are displayed in Table 8. It can be seen that the best results for negative and neutral texts are yielded by Alchemy API, whereas Haven on Demand provides a better result for positive tweets. The major benefit obtained by the combination of the three APIs was a significant better performance with regard positive texts, given that the results for negative and neutral texts are quite similar to the use of Alchemy alone. These results reveal that all solutions perform better in the detection of negative sentiment.

The performance in sentiment identification seems to have a straightforward relationship with the results obtained in stance identification. According to Table 5, the rules that combine sentiment with Favor-related side are the most representative ones, not to mention that the only rule for identifying lack of stance is related to neutral sentiment. It is interesting to note that very similar figures can be found when we compare the F-measure of the *Combination* of solutions in Table 8, and the *Automatic labeling* scores obtained for the sentiment rules (b) in Table 7, particularly Negative/Against (70.99% and 71.72%), and Positive/Favor (61.47% and 55.84%) F-measure scores.

---

[5]http://www.purl.org/net/PoliticalTweets2012

5   Conclusions and Future Work

The results obtained by the participants of SemEval Task 6 reveal that stance identification is a hard problem, for which available solutions still need to evolve. For the non-supervised task, the best result achieved the mean F-score of 56.28%, which still is not a good performance in itself. The publication of the gold standard for the task, together with the labeled datasets available for Task 6-a, will allow us to improve the process, focusing mainly in strategies for increasing the performance with regard to the Favor and None stances. Among the strategies are the improvement of polarity detection for the positive and neutral classes, increasing the automatic generated training corpus by overcoming the dependency on Alchemy (subject to quota limitations), and the investigation of a revised set of rules. Another approach would be to label instances based on social information like Twitter profiles, and the exploration of conversation threads and the connections among profiles available in the Twitter platform. We also intend to test our process using other domain corpora to explore whether the approach adopted and its underlying premise can be generalized to stance identification on other subjects.

References

Mark Hall, Eibe Frank, Geoffrey Holmes, Bernhard Pfahringer, Peter Reutemann, and Ian H Witten. 2009. The weka data mining software: an update. *ACM SIGKDD explorations newsletter*, 11(1):10–18.

Bing Liu. 2012. Sentiment analysis and opinion mining. *Synthesis Lectures on Human Language Technologies*, 5(1):1–167.

Saif M. Mohammad, Svetlana Kiritchenko, Parinaz Sobhani, Xiaodan Zhu, and Colin Cherry. 2016. Semeval-2016 task 6: Detecting stance in tweets. In *Proceedings of the International Workshop on Semantic Evaluation*, SemEval '16, San Diego, California, June.

Saif M. Mohammad. 2016. Sentiment analysis: Detecting valence, emotions, and other affectual states from text. In Herb Meiselman, editor, *Emotion Measurement*. Elsevier.

Marilyn A Walker, Pranav Anand, Rob Abbott, Jean E Fox Tree, Craig Martell, and Joseph King. 2012. That is your evidence?: Classifying stance in online political debate. *Decision Support Systems*, 53(4):719–729.

pkudblab at SemEval-2016 Task 6 : A Specific Convolutional Neural Network System for Effective Stance Detection

Wan Wei, Xiao Zhang, Xuqin Liu, Wei Chen, Tengjiao Wang

Key Laboratory of High Confidence Software Technologies, Ministry of Education,
School of Electronics Engineering and Computer Science,
Peking University, Beijing 100871, China
{wanw, zxcs, xuqinliu, pekingchenwei, tjwang}@pku.edu.cn

Abstract

In this paper, we develop a convolutional neural network for stance detection in tweets. According to the official results, our system ranks 1st on subtask B (among 9 teams) and ranks 2nd on subtask A (among 19 teams) on the twitter test set of SemEval2016 Task 6. The main contribution of our work is as follows. We design a "vote scheme" for prediction instead of predicting when the accuracy of validation set reaches its maximum. Besides, we make some improvement on the specific subtasks. For subtask A, we separate datasets into five sub-datasets according to their targets, and train and test five separate models. For subtask B, we establish a two-class training dataset from the official domain corpus, and then modify the softmax layer to perform three-class classification. Our system can be easily re-implemented and optimized for other related tasks.

1 Introduction

There are several requirements for stance detecting applications on the internet. However it is unpractical for humans to classify massive amounts of tweets. Twitter stance detection aims to automatically determine the emotional tendency of tweets. To classify tweets polarity, mainstream approaches are based on Pang (Pang et al., 2002), like regression problem, using machine learning algorithm to build classifiers from tweets with manually annotated polarity to classify the polarity of a tweet(Jiang et al., 2011; Hu et al., 2013; Dong et al., 2014). In this direction, most studies focus on designing effective

features to obtain better classification performance (Pang and Lee, 2008; Liu, 2012; Murakami and Raymond, 2010). For example, Mohammad (Mohammad and Turney, 2013) implements some sentiment lexicons and several manually-selected features. To leverage massive tweets containing positive and negative emoticons for automatically feature learning, Tang (Tang et al., 2014) proposes to learn sentiment-specific word embedding. We transfer this method to detect tweets stance.

In this paper, we develop a specific convolutional neural network learning model for stance detection. Firstly, we learn word embedding from Google News database as the input of our system. Afterwards, we train the CNN model with the SemEval2016 Task 6 dataset. Finally, we design a "vote scheme" using the softmax results to predict the label of test set. We also make some task specific improvement. For subtask A, we separate datasets into five sub-dataset, and train and test five separate models. For subtask B, we establish a two-class training dataset from the official domain corpus based on several special expressions. We evaluate our deep learning system on the test set of SemEval2016 Task 6. Our system ranks 1st on subtask B and 2nd on subtask A. The good performance in the Task 6 evaluation verifies the effectiveness of our model and schemes.

2 Architecture overview

The architecture of our convolutional neural network is mainly inspired by the architecture proposed by Kim, which performs well and efficiently in sentence classification tasks (Kim, 2014). The reason

Proceedings of SemEval-2016, pages 384–388,
San Diego, California, June 16-17, 2016. ©2016 Association for Computational Linguistics

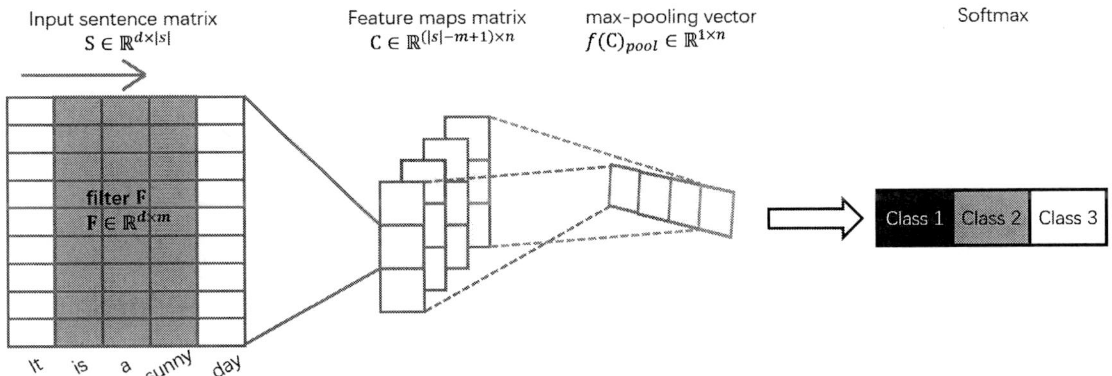

Figure 1: Main archtecture of our convolutional neural network.

why we base on Kim's model is that there is much in common between stance detection task and sentence classification task when the amount and the distribution of dataset is rather reasonable. Our architecture is shown on Fig. 1.

In the following, we give a brief introduction of the main components of our network architecture in the connecting order: look-up table, input matrix, convolutional layer, activation function, pooling layer and softmax layer. We also describe the approach to train this model.

2.1 Look-up table

Look-up table is a huge word embedding matrix. Each column of the table, which is d-dimensional, corresponds to a word. Word embedding in the look-up table are pre-trained vectors published by word2vec team (Mikolov et al., 2013)[1]. These vectors are trained on part of Google News dataset (about 100 billion words).

2.2 Input matrix

An input matrix S, $S \in \mathbb{R}^{d \times |s|}$, is the representation of an input sentence: $[w_1, w_2, ..., w_{|s|}]$. $|s|$ is the length of the sentence, w_i is the corresponding d-dimensional vector found in look-up table. If this word does not exist in the look-up table, make it a zero vector or a vector whose components are numbers randomly generated in a given range.

[1] https://code.google.com/archive/p/word2vec/

2.3 Convolutional layer

The goal of the convolutional layer is to extract patterns, so that some common abstractive representation can be found among the dataset. Pattern means specific sequential words in a sentence. Patterns can be extracted by different filter matrixes F which are discriminatively sensitive to different patterns.

More formally, the convolution operation $\odot$ between an input sentence matrix $S \in \mathbb{R}^{d \times |s|}$ and a filter $F \in \mathbb{R}^{d \times m}$, where m is an assigned width, is defined as follow:

$$c_i = \sum \left(S_{[:,i:i+m-1]} \odot F \right),$$

where $1 \leq i \leq |s| - m + 1$. $S_{[:,i:i+m-1]}$ is a matrix slice of size m along the columns and $\odot$ is the element-wise multiplication. Both S and F have the same d rows. As shown on Fig. 1, filter F slides along the column dimension of S generating vector c: $[c_1, c_2, ..., c_{|s|-m+1}]$, named feature map.

So far we have introduced how to compute a convolution between the input sentence matrix and a single filter. To get a richer representation of the dataset, we apply n filters on every input sentence matrix to compute feature maps matrix C, $C \in \mathbb{R}^{(|s|-m+1) \times n}$. Note that every input sentence matrix has a corresponding C matrix and every column of matrix C corresponds to a convolution result between a filter and this input sentence matrix.

In practice, we also add a bias vector $b \in \mathbb{R}^n$ to every row of matrix C element-wise to train a more appropriate model.

2.4 Activation function

To fit the non-linear boundaries better, convolutional layer is always followed by a non-linear activation function $f()$ in practice. $f()$ is applied element-wise on feature maps matrix C. Among the most popular choices of activation functions: sigmoid, tanh (hyperbolic tangent) and ReLU (rectified linear), we finally choose ReLU, since it is rather simple and sometimes more efficient[2].

2.5 Pooling layer

For the purpose of simplifying the information in the output from the convolutional layer (passed through the activation function), pooling layer is used. We adopt the max-pooling method, which is choosing the maximum value from every column of $f(C)$ ($f()$ is the ReLU operation), to form a condensed representation vector. More formally, after the max-pooling operation, $f(C) \in \mathbb{R}^{(|s|-m+1)\times n} \rightarrow pool(f(C)) \in \mathbb{R}^{1\times n}$, which is also shown on Fig. 1.

2.6 Output layer: softmax

The fully connected softmax layer is for classification. To a K-class dataset, the probability distribution of j-th class is as follows:

$$P(y = j|x, s, b) = \text{softmax}_j(x^T w + b)$$

$$= \frac{e^{x^T w_j + b_j}}{\sum_{k=1}^{K} e^{x^T w_k + b_k}},$$

where x is the input vector (the vector produced by pooling layer in our network), w_k and b_k, having the same dimensionality as the input vector x, are weight vector and bias vector of the k-th class respectively.

Softmax layer calculates the probability of each class and then chooses the class having the maximum value as the predict label.

2.7 Approach to train the network

The parameters trained by our network are as follows:

$$\theta = \{W; F; b; w_k; b_k\},$$

where W is the word embedding of all words in dataset, including those found in the look-up table and those randomly assigned; F is the set of all the filters; b is the bias vector in the convolutional layer; w_k and b_k are the weight and the bias vector of k-th class in the softmax layer.

We use backpropogation algorithm to optimize these parameters and we adopt Adadelta (Zeiler, 2012) update rule to automatically tune the learning rate. We also opt our network by another two methods: l2-norm regularization terms for the parameters to mitigate overfitting issues and dropout scheme (Srivastava et al., 2014), which is to set the chosen value zero, to prevent feature co-adaptation.

3 Improvement for stance detection

In this session, we briefly introduce our improvement on the CNN archtecture we described above. The improvement is task specific.

Vote scheme. We validate our model by cross validation method. For the models of subtask A and subtask B, we design ten parallel epochs, whose validation sets are randomly selected from the training set and non-overlap.

Different from general network, we design a "vote scheme" for prediction instead of predicting when the accuracy of validation set reaches its maximum. In each epoch, we choose some iterations deliberately to predict the test set. Then, when this epoch ends, for every sentence in the test set, we appoint the label which appears most frequently in these predictions as the result of this epoch. Finally, when ten epochs end, we vote within results of these ten epochs by the same method described above to determine the final labels.

By performing multiple times independently and voting twice, we get a rather robust mechanism for predicting.

"divide and conquer" scheme. For subtask A, we separate both training and test datasets respectively into five sub-datasets according to their targets, and then train and test five separate models with these divided datasets. The contrast experiment between this "divide and conquer" model and the model trained by the integral dataset is shown in Session 4.

"2-step" scheme. For subtask B, in the condition

---

[2] Rough experiment have been done on the training set with different activation functions, since these experiment are not that thoughtful, the result will not be shown in experiment session.

Corpus	Favor	Against	None	Total
Training Dataset				
Subtask A	753	1,394	766	2,913
Subtask A-Atheism	92	304	117	513
Subtask A-CC[1]	212	15	168	395
Subtask A-FM[2]	210	328	126	664
Subtask A-HC[3]	118	393	178	689
Subtask A-LofA[4]	121	354	177	652
Subtask B	2,562	3,418	—	5,980
Test Dataset				
Subtask A	304	715	230	1,249
Subtask A-Atheism	32	160	28	220
Subtask A-CC[1]	123	11	35	169
Subtask A-FM[2]	58	183	44	285
Subtask A-HC[3]	45	172	78	295
Subtask A-LofA[4]	46	189	45	280
Subtask B	148	299	260	707

[1] Target "Climate Change is a Real Concern".
[2] Target "Feminist Movement".
[3] Target "Hillary Clinton".
[4] Target "Legalization of Abortion".

Table 1: Task 6 dataset.

Corpus	"Divide"[1] Model	"Integral"[1] Model
subtask A-all	0.6733	0.6498
subtask A-Atheism[2]	0.6334	0.5652
subtask A-CC[2]	0.5269	0.5379
subtask A-FM[2]	0.5133	0.5377
subtask A-HC[2]	0.6441	0.6172
subtask A-LofA[2]	0.6109	0.6098

[1] Official metric: (F_favor + F_against) / 2.
[2] Abbreviation of targets. Those have been described in the footnote of Table 1.

Table 2: Contrast experiment results on subtask A. "Divide" refers that those results come from five separate model trained by five target corpus. "Integral" refers that those results come from one model trained by integral subtask A corpus.

that the official corpus is unlabeled whereas training set is necessary for our supervised model, we come up with a solution having two steps: 1. Build a two-class training dataset; 2. Modify the softmax layer to perform three-class classification on the two-class training dataset.

According to some expressions and hashtags revealing a distinct tendency, for example, "go trump" and "#MakeAmericaGreatAgain" reveal favor tendency whereas "idiot" and "fired" reveal against tendency, we finally establish a two-class training dataset, which has about 2000 favor tweets and about 3000 against tweets, from the domain corpus for subtask B (Mohammad et al., 2016). Then, we modify the softmax layer. For a test sentence, if the absolute value of the subtraction between the probability values of the two classes is less than a randomly selected real number $\alpha(\alpha \in [0.05, 0.1])$, predict this sentence as "None" stance. Otherwise, predict it the class having the greater probability value.

4 Experiments and evaluation

Dataset. For subtask A, the training set is the official training data for Task A (Mohammad et al., 2016). For subtask B, the training set is described in Session 3. Details about datasets are shown in Table 1.

Parameters setup. Word embedding matrix is described in Session 2.1, the dimensionality d is 300. We design three different width filters, 100 in width 3, 100 in width 4 and 100 in width 5, which means that there are 300 filters in total. We choose ReLU as activation function and we use max-pooling. L2-norm regularization term is set to 1e-6, the probability of dropout is set to 0.5. Bias vector b, as well as w_k and b_k in softmax layer are all set to zero vectors.

Test result. We perform contrast experiments on subtask A. The results of the "divide and conquer" model and its contrast integral model, as well as the five separate models are shown in Table 2. The description of these models is in Session 3. We can see from Table 2 that "divide and conquer" model does not always have a better performance. However, since the words using in the sentences which belong to the same target are expected to be more similar, the "divide" model still performs much better on some dataset (e.g. Atheism). The "divide and conquer" model is the one we submit for evaluation.

Official ranking. Part of the official rankings for both subtask A and B are summarized in Table 3. As we can see our model performs well on both subtasks. Our model ranks 2nd on subtask A, whose official metric is only 0.5% lower than the first team. On subtask B our model ranks 1st, and the official metric is 56.28%, about 10% higher than the second team.

Team	Official Metric[1]	Rank
Subtask A		
MITRE	0.6782	1
pkudblab	0.6733	2
TakeLab	0.6683	3
PKULCWM	0.6576	4
#Total teams: 19		
Subtask B		
pkudblab	0.5628	1
LitisMind	0.4466	2
INF-UFRGS -OPINION-MINING	0.4232	3
#Total teams: 9		

[1] Official metric: (F_favor + F_against) / 2.

Table 3: Part of the official result.

5 Conclusions

We develop a specific convolutional neural network system for detecting twitter stance in this paper. We give a detailed description of our model and specific adaptation for different subtasks. Among 28 submitted systems, our system obtains good rank on both subtask A and subtask B on the test set of SemEval2016 Task 6. Our system has good scalability for other related tasks.

6 Future work

Due to the tight schedule, there are still many aspects need to explore. For example, why the Google news word2vec performs well in this context? How much does this word embedding improve the score compared with randomly initial word embedding? Is the more suitble word embedding exists? What's more, the vote scheme is somewhat curt, we should do more experiment to validate its robustness. Our code is available in github for anyone who has a interest in further exploration[3].

References

Li Dong, Furu Wei, Chuanqi Tan, Duyu Tang, Ming Zhou, and Ke Xu. 2014. Adaptive recursive neural network for target-dependent twitter sentiment classification. In *ACL (2)*, pages 49–54.

Xia Hu, Jiliang Tang, Huiji Gao, and Huan Liu. 2013. Unsupervised sentiment analysis with emotional sig-

nals. In *Proceedings of the 22nd international conference on World Wide Web*, pages 607–618. International World Wide Web Conferences Steering Committee.

Long Jiang, Mo Yu, Ming Zhou, Xiaohua Liu, and Tiejun Zhao. 2011. Target-dependent twitter sentiment classification. In *Proceedings of the 49th Annual Meeting of the Association for Computational Linguistics: Human Language Technologies-Volume 1*, pages 151–160. Association for Computational Linguistics.

Yoon Kim. 2014. Convolutional neural networks for sentence classification. *arXiv preprint arXiv:1408.5882*.

Bing Liu. 2012. Sentiment analysis and opinion mining. *Synthesis lectures on human language technologies*, 5(1):1–167.

Tomas Mikolov, Kai Chen, Greg Corrado, and Jeffrey Dean. 2013. Efficient estimation of word representations in vector space. *arXiv preprint arXiv:1301.3781*.

Saif M Mohammad and Peter D Turney. 2013. Crowdsourcing a word–emotion association lexicon. *Computational Intelligence*, 29(3):436–465.

Saif M. Mohammad, Svetlana Kiritchenko, Parinaz Sobhani, Xiaodan Zhu, and Colin Cherry. 2016. Semeval-2016 task 6: Detecting stance in tweets. In *Proceedings of the International Workshop on Semantic Evaluation*, SemEval '16, San Diego, California, June.

Akiko Murakami and Rudy Raymond. 2010. Support or oppose?: classifying positions in online debates from reply activities and opinion expressions. In *Proceedings of the 23rd International Conference on Computational Linguistics: Posters*, pages 869–875. Association for Computational Linguistics.

Bo Pang and Lillian Lee. 2008. Opinion mining and sentiment analysis. *Foundations and trends in information retrieval*, 2(1-2):1–135.

Bo Pang, Lillian Lee, and Shivakumar Vaithyanathan. 2002. Thumbs up?: sentiment classification using machine learning techniques. In *Proceedings of the ACL-02 conference on Empirical methods in natural language processing-Volume 10*, pages 79–86. Association for Computational Linguistics.

Nitish Srivastava, Geoffrey Hinton, Alex Krizhevsky, Ilya Sutskever, and Ruslan Salakhutdinov. 2014. Dropout: A simple way to prevent neural networks from overfitting. *The Journal of Machine Learning Research*, 15(1):1929–1958.

Duyu Tang, Furu Wei, Nan Yang, Ming Zhou, Ting Liu, and Bing Qin. 2014. Learning sentiment-specific word embedding for twitter sentiment classification. In *ACL (1)*, pages 1555–1565.

Matthew D Zeiler. 2012. Adadelta: an adaptive learning rate method. *arXiv preprint arXiv:1212.5701*.

---

[3] https://github.com/nestle1993/SE16-Task6-Stance-Detection

USFD at SemEval-2016 Task 6: Any-Target Stance Detection on Twitter with Autoencoders

Isabelle Augenstein and **Andreas Vlachos** and **Kalina Bontcheva**
Department of Computer Science
University of Sheffield
i.augenstein@sheffield.ac.uk, a.vlachos@sheffield.ac.uk,
k.bontcheva@sheffield.ac.uk

Abstract

This paper describes the University of Sheffield's submission to the SemEval 2016 Twitter Stance Detection weakly supervised task (SemEval 2016 Task 6, Subtask B). In stance detection, the goal is to classify the stance of a tweet towards a target as "favor", "against", or "none". In Subtask B, the targets in the test data are different from the targets in the training data, thus rendering the task more challenging but also more realistic. To address the lack of target-specific training data, we use a large set of unlabelled tweets containing all targets and train a bag-of-words autoencoder to learn how to produce feature representations of tweets. These feature representations are then used to train a logistic regression classifier on labelled tweets, with additional features such as an indicator of whether the target is contained in the tweet. Our submitted run on the test data achieved an F1 of 0.3270.

1 Introduction

Stance detection is the task of assigning stance labels to a piece of text with respect to a topic, i.e. whether a piece of text is in favour of "abortion", neutral, or against. Previous work considered target-specific stance predictors in debates (Walker et al., 2012; Hasan and Ng, 2013) or news (Ferreira and Vlachos, 2016).

The variety of topics discussed on Twitter calls for developing methods that can generalise to any target, including targets not seen in the training data, which is the focus of Subtask B in Task 6 of SemEval 2016 (Mohammad et al., 2016). A further challenge is that the targets are not always mentioned in the tweets, which distinguishes this task from target-dependent sentiment analysis (Zhang et al., 2015; Zhang et al., 2016), and open-domain target-dependent sentiment analysis (Mitchell et al., 2013; Vo and Zhang, 2015).

The SemEval Stance Detection task is further related to that of textual entailment (Dagan et al., 2005; Bowman et al., 2015; Lendvai et al., 2016), i.e. we judge if a hypothesis (tweet in our task) entails, contradicts or is neutral towards a textual premise (target in our task). However, the premises in typical RTE datasets offer a richer context than the stance detection targets, i.e. they are full sentences instead of topic labels such as "atheism". Simple baselines such as textual overlap can achieve an F1 of >0.5 (Bowman et al., 2015), whereas for stance detection such baselines would not perform well, as the target is only mentioned in about half the tweets.

In our approach we learn a 3-way logistic regression classifier to perform stance detection. Apart from the standard bag-of-words features commonly used in sentiment analysis, we also use features from a trained bag-of-words autoencoder similar to the one used by Glorot et al. (2011). In our experiments we show that the bag-of-words autoencoder trained on a large amount of unlabelled tweets about the targets can help generalise to unseen targets better; on our development set it achieves an 8% increase over our best baseline. Further, tweets which contain the target are easier to classify correctly than tweets which do not contain the target. Such information can be useful for stance detection and we experiment with different ways of integrating it, finding that including a binary feature "targetContainedIn-

Proceedings of SemEval-2016, pages 389–393,
San Diego, California, June 16-17, 2016. ©2016 Association for Computational Linguistics

Tweet" outperforms including features extracted by applying the autoencoder to the target.

2 Method Description

At the core of our stance detection approach is a classifier trained on tweets stance-labelled with respect to a target. For this purpose we used the logistic regression classifier from scikit-learn with L2 regularisation (Pedregosa et al., 2011)[1]. In what follows we describe the various feature representations we used and the data pre-processing. Resources to reproduce our experiments are available on Github[2].

The stages of our approach are: a) unlabelled tweets about the targets; b) preprocess the data; c) train a bag-of-word autoencoder on all task data and unlabelled collected tweets, d) apply the autoencoder to all labelled training tweets to get a fixed-length feature vector; add a "does target appear in tweet" feature; and e) train a logistic regression model and apply it to the test tweets.

2.1 Autoencoder Training

After tweets are tokenised, a bag-of-word autoencoder is trained on them. To do so, a vocabulary of the 50000 most frequent words is constructed. The input to the autoencoder is a vector $input\_dim$ for each training example of size 50000. Each index i in $input\_dim[i]$ corresponds to a word in the vocabulary, $input\_dim[i]$ is 1 if the tweet contains the corresponding word in the vocabulary and 0 otherwise. During autoencoder training, an encoder, i.e. embedding function is learned which maps input of size $input\_dim$ to an embedding of size $output\_dim$, as well as a decoder which reconstructs the input. We apply the encoder to the training and test data to obtain features of size $output\_dim$ for supervised learning and disregard the decoder. While it would be possible to train an encoder which preserves word order, i.e. an LSTM (Li et al., 2015), we opt for a simpler bag-of-word autoencoder here, following Glorot et al. (2011).

The architecture of the autoencoder is as follows: $input\_dim$ is 50000, it has one hidden layer of dimensionality 100, and $output\_dim$ is of size 100. A dropout of 0.1 is added to the hidden layer (Srivastava et al., 2014). The autoencoder is trained with Adam (Kingma and Ba, 2014), using the learning rate 0.1, for 2600 iterations. In each iteration, 500 training examples are selected randomly.

Additional tweets are collected: 395212 tweets, tweeted between 18 November and 13 January, collected with the Twitter Keyword Search API[3] using up to two keywords per target (hillary, clinton, trump, climate, femini, aborti). Note that Twitter does not allow for regular expression search, so this is a free text search disregarding possible word boundaries.

2.2 Feature Extraction

The autoencoder is applied to the labelled data to get an 100-dimensional feature vector. For the final run, it was only applied to the tweets, but we also experiment with applying it to the target (see Section 3.2).

One additional binary feature is used for the final run, targetInTweet, which indicates if the name of the target is contained in the tweet. The following mapping was used for this purpose: 'Hillary Clinton' → 'hillary', 'clinton'; Donald Trump → 'trump'; 'Climate Change is a Real Concern' → 'climate'; 'Feminist Movement' → 'feminist', 'feminism'; 'Legalization of Abortion' → 'abortion', 'aborting'. Further features, which are not used for the final run, are discussed in Section 3.2.

2.3 Preprocessing

Twitter-based tokenisation is performed with twokenize[4]. Afterwards, tokens are normalised to lower case and stopwords are filtered, using the nltk[5] English stopword list, punctuation characters, plus Twitter-specific stopwords. The latter is manually created and consists of: "rt", "#semst", "thats", "im", "'s", "...", "via", "http". The first seven have to be an exact token match, the last one has to match the beginning of a token. Finally, phrases are detected, using an unsupervised method that creates 2-grams of commonly occurring expression such as "hillary clinton", "donald trump", "hate muslims"

---

[1] http://scikit-learn.org/stable/
    modules/generated/sklearn.linear_
    model.LogisticRegression.html
[2] http://github.com/sheffieldnlp/
    stance-semeval2016
[3] https://dev.twitter.com/rest/public/
    search
[4] https://github.com/leondz/twokenize
[5] http://www.nltk.org/

(Mikolov et al., 2013)[6]. The phrase detection model is trained on all tweets except the test tweets. At application time, if two subsequent tokens are identified as a phrase, those tokens are merged to one token (i.e. "donald", "trump" → "donald_trump").

3 Experiments

3.1 Experimental Setup

Our development setup is to train on all labelled tweets for the targets "Climate Change is a Real Concern", "Feminist Movement" and "Legalization of Abortion", then evaluate on "Hillary Clinton" tweets. The motivation for this is that Hillary Clinton is the most semantically related target to the Task B test target Donald Trump, since both entities are persons and politicians. For final submission we tuned all settings with this setup, then retrained on all data and applied the model to the test data.

3.2 Methods

Our goal is to determine if including the target is beneficial and if so, how best to include the it. To this end, the following features are evaluated:

- Aut-twe: the autoencoder is applied to the tweet only
- Aut-twe_tar: the autoencoder is applied to the tweet and the target, the target features are concatenated with the tweet features
- Aut-twe*tar: the autoencoder is applied to the tweet and the target, and the outer product of the tweet and target features is used
- InTwe: A boolean "targetInTweet" feature

We evaluate the impact of traditional sentiment analysis gazetteer features, extracted by assessing appearance of each word of the tweet in the gazetteers:

- Emo: emoticon recognition[7] One gazetteer/binary feature for each of: happy, sad, happy+sad, not_available
- Aff: WordNet Affect gazetteer features, one binary feature for each of: anger, disgust, fear, joy, sadness, surprise (Strapparava and Valitutti, 2004)[8]

---

[6] https://radimrehurek.com/gensim/models/phrases.html

[7] https://github.com/brendano/tweetmotif/blob/master/emoticons.py

[8] http://wndomains.fbk.eu/wnaffect.html

Method	Stance	P	R	F1
BoW	FAVOR	0.1587	0.1709	0.1646
	AGAINST	0.5544	0.4020	0.4661
	Macro			0.3153
BoW+inTwe	FAVOR	0.2278	0.1538	0.1837
	AGAINST	0.5545	0.5700	0.5621
	Macro			0.3729
Word2Vec	FAVOR	0.2647	0.0769	0.1192
	AGAINST	0.5179	0.2570	0.3435
	Macro			0.2314
Aut-twe	FAVOR	0.1538	0.1538	0.1538
	AGAINST	0.5680	0.7328	0.6400
	Macro			0.3969
Aut-twe_tar	FAVOR	0.1652	0.1624	0.1638
	AGAINST	0.5503	0.6539	0.5977
	Macro			0.3807
Aut-twe*tar	FAVOR	0.0000	0.0000	0.0000
	AGAINST	0.5712	1.0000	0.7271
	Macro			0.3636
Aut-twe+inTwe	FAVOR	0.2388	0.1368	0.1739
	AGAINST	0.5709	0.7684	0.6551
	Macro			0.4145
Aut-twe_tar+inTwe	FAVOR	0.1731	0.0769	0.1065
	AGAINST	0.5487	0.7888	0.6472
	Macro			0.3768
Aut-twe+inTwe+Emo	FAVOR	0.2063	0.1111	0.1444
	AGAINST	0.5733	0.7964	0.6667
	Macro			0.4056
Aut-twe+inTwe+Aff	FAVOR	0.2113	0.1282	0.1596
	AGAINST	0.5701	0.7964	0.6645
	Macro			0.4121

Table 1: Stance Detection results, reported on the development set. The best results are achieved with Aut-twe+inTwe.

In addition we experiment with substituting the bag of word autoencoder with a word2vec model trained on the same data. We trained a skip-gram model with a dimensionality of 300, 10 min words and a context of 10 with the gensim implementation of word2vec[9]. Word vectors are combined by multiplication to get a fixed-length sentence-level vector. We also report a bag-of-words baseline, which disregards the unlabelled data and extracts unigram and bigram bag-of-word features from the training data. For the word2vec models as well as the bag-of-words baseline, the same preprocessing as for the autoencoder approach is used.

4 Results

Results are reported in Tables 1 and 2 for all the experiments above, using the dev setup (Hillary Clinton) and the test setup (Donald Trump). Overall re-

---

[9] https://radimrehurek.com/gensim/models/word2vec.html

Method	Stance	P	R	F1
	FAVOR	0.2933	0.1486	0.1973
BoW	AGAINST	0.4116	0.6154	0.4933
	Macro			0.3453
	FAVOR	0.2308	0.0608	0.0963
BoW+inTwe	AGAINST	0.4121	0.7057	0.5203
	Macro			0.3083
	FAVOR	0.3500	0.0473	0.0833
Word2Vec	AGAINST	0.4155	0.8629	0.5609
	Macro			0.3221
	FAVOR	0.0889	0.0270	0.0415
Aut-twe	AGAINST	0.4266	0.8462	0.5673
	Macro			0.3044
	FAVOR	0.2273	0.0676	0.1042
Aut-twe_tar	AGAINST	0.4192	0.8161	0.5539
	Macro			0.3290
	FAVOR	0.0000	0.0000	0.0000
Aut-twe*tar	AGAINST	0.4229	1.0000	0.5944
	Macro F			0.2972
	FAVOR	0.2857	0.0676	0.1093
Aut-twe+inTwe	AGAINST	0.4087	0.8161	0.5446
	Macro			0.3270
	FAVOR	0.3077	0.0541	0.0920
Aut-twe_tar+inTwe	AGAINST	0.4250	0.8629	0.5695
	Macro			0.3307
	FAVOR	0.4762	0.0676	0.1183
Aut-twe+inTwe+Emo	AGAINST	0.4265	0.8829	0.5752
	Macro			0.3468
	FAVOR	0.2667	0.0541	0.0899
Aut-twe+inTwe+Aff	AGAINST	0.4107	0.8763	0.5592
	Macro			0.3246

Table 2: Stance Detection results, reported on official test. The submitted run is Aut-twe+InTwe.

inTwe	Stance	P	R	F1
	FAVOR	0.2830	0.1456	0.1923
Yes	AGAINST	0.7072	0.7237	0.7154
	Macro			0.4538
	FAVOR	0.0714	0.0714	0.0714
No	AGAINST	0.4361	0.8529	0.5771
	Macro			0.3243

Table 3: Stance Detection results, reported on dev, split by tweets containing the target and not containing the target. The run used is Aut-twe+inTwe.

inTwe	Stance	P	R	F1
	FAVOR	0.7778	0.0486	0.0915
Yes	AGAINST	0.5201	0.8931	0.6574
	Macro			0.3745
	FAVOR	0.0000	0.0000	0.0000
No	AGAINST	0.3333	0.8286	0.4754
	Macro			0.2377

Table 4: Stance Detection results, reported on test, split by tweets containing the target and not containing the target. The run used is Aut-twe+inTwe.

Adding autoencoder features for the target did not improve results for dev. For test, tweet features aggregated with target features slightly outperform target features on their own. As for traditional sentiment analysis features, Emo improves macro F1 for test, but not but dev, and Aff does not improve macro F1 for either of them.

5 Conclusions and Future Work

To conclude, we showed that it is important to detect if the target is mentioned in the tweet, and that a bag-of-word autoencoder can help to detect stance towards unseen targets. Further, developing a stance detection method for new targets without any labelled training data is challenging - we found that there are some discrepancies between what features perform well for a development versus a test set. In future work we will investigate how to better incorporate the target for stance detection, as this target-dependence is crucial in capturing that the same tweet can have different stance with respect to different targets that are not mentioned in the tweet.

Acknowledgments

This work was partially supported by the European Union, grant agreement No. 611233 PHEME[10].

[10]http://www.pheme.eu

sults for dev are significantly better than for test, and F1 for AGAINST is consistently higher than for FAVOR. Performance increases for test with respect to baselines are much smaller than for dev. The best results for the dev set are achieved with Aut-twe+inTwe, and it was chosen for the final run on the test set. However, the best results on the test set are achieved with Aut-twe+inTwe+Emo, which is almost on par with the BoW baseline.

The feature that contributes positively to both dev and test performance is inTwe. It was introduced because almost all tweets in the training data that contain the target either FAVOR or are AGAINST the target, but are rarely neutral towards the target. 363 out of 656 Hillary Clinton dev tweets contain the target, and 309 out of 689 Donald Trump test tweets contain the target. We observed that there is a significant difference in performance between tweets containing the target and tweets which do not contain the target (see Tables 3 and 4).

References

Samuel R. Bowman, Gabor Angeli, Christopher Potts, and Christopher D. Manning. 2015. A large annotated corpus for learning natural language inference. In *Proceedings of the 2015 Conference on Empirical Methods in Natural Language Processing*, pages 632–642, Lisbon, Portugal. Association for Computational Linguistics.

Ido Dagan, Oren Glickman, and Bernardo Magnini. 2005. The PASCAL Recognising Textual Entailment Challenge. In Joaquin Quionero Candela, Ido Dagan, Bernardo Magnini, and Florence d'Alch Buc, editors, *MLCW*, Lecture Notes in Computer Science, pages 177–190. Springer.

William Ferreira and Andreas Vlachos. 2016. Emergent: a novel data-set for stance classification. In *Proceedings of NAACL*.

Xavier Glorot, Antoine Bordes, and Yoshua Bengio. 2011. Domain Adaptation for Large-Scale Sentiment Classification: A Deep Learning Approach. In Lise Getoor and Tobias Scheffer, editors, *Proceedings of the 28th International Conference on Machine Learning (ICML-11)*, pages 513–520, New York, NY, USA. ACM.

Kazi Saidul Hasan and Vincent Ng. 2013. Stance Classification of Ideological Debates: Data, Models, Features, and Constraints. In *IJCNLP*, pages 1348–1356. Asian Federation of Natural Language Processing / ACL.

Diederik P. Kingma and Jimmy Ba. 2014. Adam: A Method for Stochastic Optimization. *CoRR*, abs/1412.6980.

Piroska Lendvai, Isabelle Augenstein, Kalina Bontcheva, and Thierry Declerck. 2016. Monolingual Social Media Datasets for Detecting Contradiction and Entailment. In *Proceedings of the 10th International Conference on Language Resources and Evaluation (LREC)*, Portorož, Slovenia. European Language Resources Association (ELRA).

Jiwei Li, Thang Luong, and Dan Jurafsky. 2015. A Hierarchical Neural Autoencoder for Paragraphs and Documents. In *Proceedings of the 53rd Annual Meeting of the Association for Computational Linguistics and the 7th International Joint Conference on Natural Language Processing (Volume 1: Long Papers)*, pages 1106–1115, Beijing, China. Association for Computational Linguistics.

Tomas Mikolov, Ilya Sutskever, Kai Chen, Greg S Corrado, and Jeff Dean. 2013. Distributed Representations of Words and Phrases and their Compositionality. In C.J.C. Burges, L. Bottou, M. Welling, Z. Ghahramani, and K.Q. Weinberger, editors, *Advances in Neural Information Processing Systems 26*, pages 3111–3119. Curran Associates, Inc.

Margaret Mitchell, Jacqui Aguilar, Theresa Wilson, and Benjamin Van Durme. 2013. Open Domain Targeted Sentiment. In *Proceedings of the 2013 Conference on Empirical Methods in Natural Language Processing*, pages 1643–1654, Seattle, Washington, USA. Association for Computational Linguistics.

Saif M. Mohammad, Svetlana Kiritchenko, Parinaz Sobhani, Xiaodan Zhu, and Colin Cherry. 2016. SemEval-2016 Task 6: Detecting stance in tweets. In *Proceedings of the International Workshop on Semantic Evaluation*, SemEval '16, San Diego, California.

F. Pedregosa, G. Varoquaux, A. Gramfort, V. Michel, B. Thirion, O. Grisel, M. Blondel, P. Prettenhofer, R. Weiss, V. Dubourg, J. Vanderplas, A. Passos, D. Cournapeau, M. Brucher, M. Perrot, and E. Duchesnay. 2011. Scikit-learn: Machine Learning in Python. *Journal of Machine Learning Research*, 12:2825–2830.

Nitish Srivastava, Geoffrey E. Hinton, Alex Krizhevsky, Ilya Sutskever, and Ruslan Salakhutdinov. 2014. Dropout: A Simple Way to Prevent Neural Networks from Overfitting. *Journal of Machine Learning Research*, 15(1):1929–1958.

Carlo Strapparava and Alessandro Valitutti. 2004. WordNet-Affect: An affective extension of WordNet. In *Proceedings of the 4th International Conference on Language Resources and Evaluation*, pages 1083–1086. ELRA.

Duy-Tin Vo and Yue Zhang. 2015. Target-Dependent Twitter Sentiment Classification with Rich Automatic Features. In Qiang Yang and Michael Wooldridge, editors, *IJCAI*, pages 1347–1353. AAAI Press.

Marilyn Walker, Pranav Anand, Rob Abbott, and Ricky Grant. 2012. Stance Classification using Dialogic Properties of Persuasion. In *Proceedings of the 2012 Conference of the North American Chapter of the Association for Computational Linguistics: Human Language Technologies*, pages 592–596.

Meishan Zhang, Yue Zhang, and Duy Tin Vo. 2015. Neural Networks for Open Domain Targeted Sentiment. In *Proceedings of the 2015 Conference on Empirical Methods in Natural Language Processing*, pages 612–621, Lisbon, Portugal. Association for Computational Linguistics.

Meishan Zhang, Yue Zhang, and Duy-Tin Vo. 2016. Gated Neural Networks for Targeted Sentiment Analysis. In *Proceedings of the Thirtieth AAAI Conference on Artificial Intelligence*, Phoenix, Arizona, USA. Association for the Advancement of Artificial Intelligence.

IUCL at SemEval-2016 Task 6:
An Ensemble Model for Stance Detection in Twitter

Can Liu, Wen Li, Bradford Demarest, Yue Chen, Sara Couture, Daniel Dakota,
Nikita Haduong, Noah Kaufman, Andrew Lamont, Manan Pancholi,
Kenneth Steimel, Sandra Kübler

Indiana University

{liucan,wl9,bdemares,yc59,scouture,ddakota,nhaduong,nokaufma,
alamont,mpanchol,ksteimel,skuebler}@indiana.edu

Abstract

We present the IUCL system, based on super-vised learning, for the shared task on stance detection. Our official submission, the random forest model, reaches a score of 63.60, and is ranked 6th out of 19 teams. We also use gradient boosting decision trees and SVM and merge all classifiers into an ensemble method. Our analysis shows that random forest is good at retrieving minority classes and gradient boosting majority classes. The strengths of different classifiers wrt. precision and recall complement each other in the ensemble.

1 Introduction

Stance detection is a difficult task since it often re-quires reasoning in order to determine whether an utterance is in favor of or against a specific issue. In the shared task (see Mohammad et al. (2016) for de-tails about the shared task), we interpret it as a vari-ant of sentiment analysis and adopt an approach that combines shallow lexical features with an ensemble of different supervised machine learning classifiers. Previous work has shown that using "arguing" fea-tures based on an arguing lexicon along with modal verbs and targets identified via syntactic rules (So-masundaran and Wiebe, 2010); finding polarized re-lations between aspects and topics (Somasundaran and Wiebe, 2009); adding semantic frames (Hasan and Ng, 2013) and contextual features (Anand et al., 2011) generally improve results. Since some of these features do not generalize across targets (Anand et al., 2011), and since we have an additional challenge in processing Twitter data, we rely on uni-gram features and word vectors. This means that our

approach is incapable of handling sarcasm or humor. Instead, it provides a robust basis on which we can later add more informative features.

Our approach consists of classifiers with a bag of words (unigrams) or with word vectors as features. We use three separate classifiers (SVMs, random forest, gradient boosting decision trees) and an en-semble classifier (TiMBL). Our official submission is the random forest classifier with word unigrams.

2 Methods

We use the data sets provided by the SemEval-2016 shared task 6 (Mohammad et al., 2016).

2.1 Preprocessing

Preprocessing mostly consists of tokenization. Dur-ing tokenization, we normalize capitalization, and all punctuation signs are separated except for @ and #, as these symbols indicate hashtags and handles. We extract frequency counts of each token in the en-tire corpus and in each stance (Favor, Against, None) per target for use in the feature selection process.

We experimented with TWEEBOPARSER (Kong et al., 2014), a dependency parser specifically de-signed for Twitter data, to extract dependency re-lations among words. We extract POS tags, multi-word expressions, and dependency triples from the parses. However, due to the feature sparsity, none of them improved over unigrams. Thus, they are not used in the final systems.

2.2 Features

One of the major decisions in developing a ma-chine learning system for stance detection lies in

394

Proceedings of SemEval-2016, pages 394–400,
San Diego, California, June 16-17, 2016. ©2016 Association for Computational Linguistics

Model	Features
GBDT	GloVe word vectors
random forest	unigrams + IG
SVM	unigrams + IG
ensembleG	three classifiers + global
ensembleNG	three classifiers only

Table 1: Summary of features for each model. The random forest model constitutes our official submission.

the choice of features and of feature representations. Detecting stance in political tweets can be regarded as a form of sentiment analysis for short text, and we assume that different stances of tweets are partially expressed by the choice of words. For example, not mentioning any words that express a polarized attitude indicates that a tweet is most likely a None stance. Tweets are relatively short documents, we use bag of words (unigrams) since in this case bigrams and trigrams are likely to be too sparse to be informative. Another possibility would be to follow approaches in sentiment analysis and use sentiment lexicons. However, such lexicons are normally general purpose resources, and domain specific information is not included. In contrast, we need such domain specific knowledge, for example to capture the fact that "dear lord" is an indication of a negative stance towards the target Atheism while it may have a different meaning when it occurs for the target Hillary Clinton. Since unigrams include a high number of irrelevant features and also constitute a rather impoverished representation, we use feature selection as well as word vectors in our experiments.

Table 1 summarizes the features used for each of our models. We use information gain (IG) for feature selection on unigrams. Global refers to global features (see section 2.2.3). The three classifiers are GBDT, random forest, and SVM; the ensemble uses their output (predicted label and its probability).

2.2.1 Feature Selection

There are issues resulting from the large number of bag-of-words features: 1) Not all words are good indicators for stance; some words occur evenly across the data set. 2) Rare words, which are less likely to occur in the test data, do not contribute much. To alleviate these problems, we perform feature selection using information gain (IG). IG esti-

mates the amount of information a word gives for the decision on the stance. We choose IG because it has been shown to be robust across different sentiment analysis data sets and across different skewing ratios, compared to other feature selection methods (Liu et al., 2014). Note that different from its use in decision trees, we use IG as an external filter to select a subset of features, before and independent of any classifiers.

2.2.2 Word Vector Features

One limitation of bag-of-words features is that they are very sparse, and they cannot handle out-of-vocabulary words properly. Since tweets are relatively short, and the amount of official training data is small, it is likely that the out-of-vocabulary rate is high. Thus we also build models using word vectors, which represent each word with a vector of continuous values. Word vectors have been shown to capture the similarity among words and thus alleviate data sparseness (Collobert et al., 2011).

We have experimented with two different word vector models, word2vec (Mikolov et al., 2013) and GloVe (Pennington et al., 2014). We have used the pre-trained word2vec obtained from the Google News dataset, which contains a 300-dimensional vector representation for 3 million words and phrases[1], and the pre-trained GloVe, which is obtained from 2 billion tweets and has a 250-dimensional vector representation for 1.2 million words and phrases[2].

To construct a representation for a tweet, we look up a word in the word vectors model, then average all vectors for words to produce a vector representation for the tweet. For example, to represent a 15 word tweet using word2vec, we first obtain a 300-dimensional vector for each word, then average all 15 vectors. This means that the word order is lost and the representation constitutes a "bag of vectors".

Comparing Word Vectors We have performed a comparison of both word vector variants in a 5-fold cross validation experiment on the training data. Table 2 summarizes the results. We can see that GloVe performs consistently better than word2vec except for Feminist where word2vec is 0.6% better than

---

[1] https://code.google.com/archive/p/word2vec/
[2] http://nlp.stanford.edu/projects/glove/

Target	Word2vec	GloVe
Abortion	61.4	62.4
Atheism	62.6	66.4
Climate	69.9	71.1
Feminist	53.8	53.2
Hillary	59.5	61.1

Table 2: Comparing word2vec and GloVe.

GloVe. We assume that this performance gap is mainly caused by the domain difference from which the word vectors are obtained: We used GloVe pre-trained on tweets and word2vec pre-trained on news. This leads to a higher number of out-of-vocabulary words for the word2vec model. In other words, GloVe provides a broader coverage for this data set.

2.2.3 Global Features

The bag-of-words features used in the classifiers (see section 3) assume that the words are considered independently. However, in many situations, it is the distributions of positively and negatively oriented words that determine the final stance of a tweet. A low coverage of words from these two distributions is a strong indicator for None stance as well. This is especially important for the ensemble classifier. For this reason, we have developed two additional features for the ensemble, which capture information from these two distributions: one feature for positive orientation and one for negative orientation. The feature is a numeric score, representing the association of a tweet with positive or negative stance respectively. The positive orientation is calculated based on the following equation:

$$score_T^{pos} = \frac{1}{|T|} \sum_{w \subset T} \frac{freq(w) \text{ in POS}}{\sum_{w' \subset V} freq(w') \text{ in POS}}$$

where T is a tweet, $|T|$ is the tweet length excluding stop words. V is the entire vocabulary. $Freq(w)$ is the frequency count of w in the following set. POS is the set of all positive tweets. This score measures for each word (its lemma) the association with positive stance, sums up all words in the tweet, and normalizes the score by the tweet length. The score for the negative orientation is calculated accordingly.

The None orientation is not calculated since it is already represented by the absence of positively or negatively oriented words. I.e., we assume that if a tweet has low positive and negative orientations, it indicates a None stance.

2.3 Adding Manually Annotated Data

We mined additional tweets for each of the five targets in Nov. 2015 by searching for hashtags relevant to the targets. These tweets are not included in the final systems since they increased the class imbalance. We will investigate better options for including the data in the future. Hashtags for Abortion include #abortion, #abortionrights, and #prolife; Atheism includes #atheism, #atheist, and #theist; Climate includes #actionclimate and #climatechange; Feminist includes #feminism, #feminist, #heforshe, and #womensrights; and Hillary includes #HillaryClinton.

Tweets were then annotated for stance, following the guidelines used for the annotation of the official shared task data[3]. Two annotators participated in the annotation process. The number of additional tweets ranged between 260 and 2,400 per target.

3 Classifiers

Since there is little research on determining the best fitting bias for stance detection, we explore three different classifiers for the stance classification, support vector machines (SVM), random forest, and gradient boosting decision trees (GBDT). For all three classifiers, we use the implementations in Scikit-Learn (Pedregosa et al., 2011).

We choose SVM because it is the most widely used machine learning model for text classification and sentiment analysis (e.g., (Pilászy, 2005)).

Additionally, it has been shown to be robust with high dimensional features (e.g., (Joachims, 1998)). Random forest is adopted because of its capability of reducing overfitting by performing sampling on data points and on feature subspaces. GBDT is selected because it works well with continuous numerical features such as word vectors.

We train individual classifiers for each target. Parameters are optimized in a 5-fold cross-validation over the training data. SVM and random forest are trained on different numbers of selected unigrams

---

[3]See `http://alt.qcri.org/semeval2016/task6/data/uploads/stance-question.pdf`.

for each target: 1,700 for Abortion, 1,535 for Atheism, 1,381 for Climate, 1,749 for Feminist, and 1,704 for Hillary. GBDT is trained on the word vectors: 300 dimensions for word2vec and 250 dimensions for GloVe. Additional experiments are performed with a standard feed-forward neural network on word vectors. These showed better performance on the training set for some targets, but overall, GBDT prove to be more reliable.

SVM Our initial experiments using cross validation on training data showed that linear kernel performed better than non-linear ones, and that the LinearSVC implementation (one-vs-rest strategy for multi-class) outperformed SVC (one-vs-one strategy). The optimal parameters differ for each target: 0.015-0.3 for the slack variable; standard hinge or squared hinge for the loss function; and L2 norm for the penalty term.

Random Forest The parameters for random forest are: 50, 70, or 90 for the number of trees; 500 or All for the number of features to consider when looking for the best split; 200, 500, or unlimited for the maximum depth of trees.

GBDT The gradient boosting decision trees (GBDT) classifier is used in combination with word vector features. Our initial experiments showed that GBDT handles word vector features better than SVM and random forest. The optimal parameter range for different targets are: 80-100 for number of estimators; 0.05-0.3 for learning rate; false for warm start; and 0.5-1.0 for subsample ratio.

Ensemble Classifier Since initial experiments with the three classifiers showed considerable differences across targets and stances, we investigate whether an ensemble classifier would benefit from aggregating their predictions. For the ensemble classifier, we choose a memory-based learner, TiMBL, because of the need to operate on a small set of rather abstract features: stance predictions and confidence scores from the three classifiers along with the global features (see section 2.2.3).

We use TiMBL (Daelemans et al., 2009) version 6.4.2, and perform 5-fold jackknifing to generate the training set for this ensemble classifier. Parameter optimization is performed on the five folds. The best parameters are different in each target: 7-29

Team	Official Metric
MITRE	67.82
IUCL-RF	63.60

Table 3: Official results of the IUCL-RF system in comparison to the best system.

Model	Official Metric
GBDT	*64.64*
Random Forest	63.60
SVM	61.93
EnsembleG	62.46
EnsembleNG	**66.14**

Table 4: Overall comparison of all IUCL systems. The best accuracy of an individual classifier is shown in italics, the best overall result in bold.

for the number of neighbors; default minority voting for class voting in most cases; Modified Value Distance, Jeffrey divergence, and cosine distance for distance metric; and gain ratio for feature weight in most cases.

4 Results

4.1 Official Result

Since the ensemble classifier was not completed in time for submission, we had to decide which individual classifier to submit. The random forest model is selected based on a five-fold cross validation on the training set. This system reaches a score of 63.60 (macro-averaged F), as shown in table 3, the sixth best result out of 19 participating systems. This result is approximately 4 percent points lower than that of the highest performing system.

4.2 Additional Results

4.2.1 Overview of All Classifiers

Table 4 shows the results of the three individual classifiers as well as of the two ensemble model variants, one combining only the individual classifiers' outputs (EnsembleNG), the other one (EnsembleG) including also the global features (see section 2.2.3). These results show that the GBDT approach using GloVe reaches the highest result (64.64) among the individual classifiers. The random forest classifier, which constitutes our official submission is about 1 percentage point lower (63.60), and the

| | Abortion | | | | | | | Atheism | | | | | | |
| | | | Favor | | Against | | None | | | | Favor | | Against | | None | |
Model	Acc	F	Prec	Rec	Prec	Rec	Prec	Rec	Acc	F	Prec	Rec	Prec	Rec	Prec	Rec
GBDT	*65.0*	53.6	52.6	21.7	75.6	77.2	38.2	57.8	67.3	56.4	37.0	31.2	82.3	75.6	37.0	60.7
RF	*65.0*	57.6	43.6	37.0	83.8	68.3	41.4	80.0	***70.5***	57.9	45.0	28.1	81.2	81.2	40.0	57.1
SVM	60.7	58.6	43.6	52.2	81.6	60.8	36.9	68.9	59.1	51.9	26.1	37.5	81.5	66.2	27.0	42.9
EnsembleG	62.9	46.3	55.6	10.9	75.1	73.5	37.2	71.1	69.1	45.9	50.0	6.2	76.1	85.6	36.1	46.4
EnsembleNG	**66.8**	60.2	50.0	39.1	80.2	73.0	43.1	68.9	69.1	50.6	57.1	12.5	74.0	88.7	28.6	21.4

| | Climate | | | | | | | Feminist | | | | | | |
| | | | Favor | | Against | | None | | | | Favor | | Against | | None | |
Model	Acc	F	Prec	Rec	Prec	Rec	Prec	Rec	Acc	F	Prec	Rec	Prec	Rec	Prec	Rec
GBDT	***72.8***	41.8	82.0	85.4	0.00	0.00	43.9	51.4	57.9	51.6	30.3	34.5	69.3	72.7	44.4	27.3
RF	68.0	39.1	82.7	74.0	0.00	0.00	40.7	68.6	57.2	51.1	31.1	39.7	73.9	61.7	46.6	61.4
SVM	68.6	39.8	79.7	79.7	0.00	0.00	39.1	51.4	55.4	54.6	33.9	67.2	76.5	55.2	47.4	40.9
EnsembleG	69.2	39.6	81.2	77.2	0.00	0.00	42.3	62.9	**65.6**	44.9	57.1	6.9	68.9	88.5	48.8	47.7
EnsembleNG	72.2	40.5	84.2	78.0	0.00	0.00	47.3	74.3	62.8	57.9	39.4	44.8	75.1	72.7	47.6	45.5

| | Hillary | | | | | | |
| | | | Favor | | Against | | None | |
Model	Acc	F	Prec	Rec	Prec	Rec	Prec	Rec
GBDT	64.4	48.7	40.0	13.3	66.0	93.6	63.9	29.5
RF	***70.2***	49.8	75.0	13.3	70.5	84.9	68.8	70.5
SVM	62.0	55.3	36.8	46.7	70.2	68.6	62.9	56.4
EnsembleG	63.4	44.1	100.0	8.9	66.0	79.1	55.3	60.3
EnsembleNG	67.8	51.6	80.0	17.8	71.1	77.3	60.2	75.6

Table 5: Detailed comparison. Best accuracies of individual classifiers are shown in italics, best overall results in bold. (F = macro-averaged F over Favor and Against; official score.)

SVM classifier is about 1.5 percentage points below that (61.93). A closer look at the ensemble variants shows that using the global features has a detrimental effect across all targets, most likely because this information is too coarse. The other ensemble classifier improves over GBDT by 1.5 percentage points (66.14). This shows that we can benefit from important information from all individual classifiers.

4.2.2 Further Analysis

While the official scorer averages the results over all five targets, we are interested in whether our classifiers show a stable performance across targets, and why the ensemble model benefits from combining all individual classifiers. For this reason, we modified the scorer so that it would calculate accuracy, precision, and recall for individual stances per target separately. The results are shown in table 5. The official metric is the macro-averaged F-measure on Favor and Against while accuracy is equivalent to the micro-averaged F-measure based on all classes.

The results show a more diverse picture: For the individual classifiers, GBDT reaches the highest ac-curacies for the targets Climate and Feminist, random forest for Atheism and Hillary, and they tie for Abortion. For the ensembles, the version without global features reaches higher accuracies for Abortion, Climate, and Hillary, the version with global features has a higher accuracy for Feminist, and they tie for Atheism.

EnsembleNG, which reaches the best score across all targets, only reaches the best score for two targets: Abortion and Feminist. It reaches lower results than the best individual classifier for 3 targets: Atheism, Climate, and Hillary. However, since the best results for the latter 3 targets are reached by different individual classifiers (random forest for Atheism and Hillary; GBDT for Climate), we assume that the ensemble provides the best compromise.

In order to obtain a better understanding of the differences in performance of classifiers across targets, we have analyzed the distribution of stances per target. Table 6 shows the distribution in training and test data. If we combine the information from table 5 with the stance distributions, we notice that a major advantage of the random forest classifier is its

Data Set	Stance	Abortion	Atheism	Climate	Feminist	Hillary
Train	Favor	18	18	54	32	17
	Against	55	59	4	49	57
	None	27	23	42	19	26
Test	Favor	17	14	73	20	15
	Against	67	73	7	64	58
	None	16	13	20	16	27

Table 6: Class distribution across targets in percentage.

high recall on the None stance, which is generally (one of) the minority class(es). For the second minority class (Favor for Abortion, Atheism, Hillary, and Feminist; and Against for Climate), the picture is less clear: For Climate, none of the classifiers manage to identify any of the Against tweets. For Abortion and Feminist, random forest also shows a high recall for Favor, but for Atheism and Hillary, its precision is considerably higher. In contrast, GBDT reaches a higher recall for the majority class (with Atheism as the only exception). SVM generally has precision and recall values between or below the other classifiers. The only exception is the target Feminist, where SVM reaches the highest precision for all three stances.

One hypothesis that could be drawn from the analysis above is that the GBDT model is better suited for finding examples of the majority classes while random forest is better at finding minority class examples. However, when we compare the targets Abortion and Atheism, the class distribution is similar, but the performance of the two classifiers is vastly different: For Abortion, GBDT reaches higher recall for the majority class (Against) and higher precision for Favor. For Atheism, it has a higher precision for the majority class and a higher recall for Favor. The reasons for these different behaviors need to be determined in future work.

5 Conclusion

In this shared task, we regard stance detection as a special case of sentiment analysis, using supervised classifiers and bag of unigrams and word vectors as features. Our submitted system is based on a random forest classifier because of its capability to handle overfitting and to generalize over the test data. Since the amount of available training data is small, random forest's ability to sample data points and fea-

ture subspaces reduces data sparsity. The submitted system has an official score of 63.60 and ranked 6th out of 19 teams.

We also experimented with other single models (SVM and GBDT) and with an ensemble model built on a memory-based classifier. The GBDT model using GloVe word vectors reaches a higher score of 64.64, which may be a result of the word vectors' capability to capture similarities among words, which helps in dealing with out-of-vocabulary words. The ensemble model that aggregates information from the three individual classifiers reaches the highest performance of 66.14. Our hypothesis is that different strengths (e.g., good performance for minority/majority classes) from individual models complement each other in the ensemble.

However a closer look at the performance of all classifiers and ensembles across individual targets shows that no system reaches consistently good results across all targets. The best performing ensemble (EnsembleNG) outperforms individual classifiers only for Abortion and Feminist; for the other targets, random forest or GBDT reach higher accuracies. Some of the variation in system performance can be explained by the class imbalance present in the data sets for the different targets, but further work is required to identify other factors.

Finally, it is worth pointing out that our approach to stance detection utilizes very surface oriented features. To boost performance, we may need to develop methods that incorporate inference, entailment, and world knowledge, for example, to handle cases such as "keep H. out of the white house".

Acknowledgement

This work is based on research supported by the U.S. Office of Naval Research (ONR) via grant #N00014-10-1-0140.

References

Pranav Anand, Marilyn Walker, Rob Abbott, Jean E Fox Tree, Robeson Bowmani, and Michael Minor. 2011. Cats rule and dogs drool!: Classifying stance in online debate. In *Proceedings of the 2nd Workshop on Computational Approaches to Subjectivity and Sentiment Analysis*, pages 1–9, Portland, OR.

Ronan Collobert, Jason Weston, Léon Bottou, Michael Karlen, Koray Kavukcuoglu, and Pavel Kuksa. 2011. Natural language processing (almost) from scratch. *Journal of Machine Learning Research*, 12:2493–2537.

Walter Daelemans, Jakub Zavrel, Ko van der Sloot, and Antal van den Bosch. 2009. TiMBL: Tilburg memory based learner – version 6.2 – reference guide. Technical Report ILK 09-01, Induction of Linguistic Knowledge, Computational Linguistics, Tilburg University.

Kazi Saidul Hasan and Vincent Ng. 2013. Stance classification of ideological debates: Data, models, features, and constraints. In *Proceedings of the Sixth International Joint Conference on Natural Language Processing (IJCLNP 2013)*, pages 1348–1356, Nagoya, Japan.

Thorsten Joachims. 1998. *Text Categorization with Support Vector Machines: Learning with Many Relevant Features*. Springer.

Lingpeng Kong, Nathan Schneider, Swabha Swayamdipta, Archna Bhatia, Chris Dyer, and Noah A Smith. 2014. A dependency parser for tweets. In *Proceedings of the 2014 Conference on Empirical Methods in Natural Language Processing (EMNLP 2014)*, pages 1001–1012, Doha, Qatar.

Can Liu, Sandra Kübler, and Ning Yu. 2014. Feature selection for highly skewed sentiment analysis tasks. In *Proceedings of the Second Workshop on Natural Language Processing for Social Media (SocialNLP)*, pages 2–11, Dublin, Ireland.

Tomas Mikolov, Kai Chen, Greg Corrado, and Jeffrey Dean. 2013. Efficient estimation of word representations in vector space. *arXiv preprint arXiv:1301.3781*.

Saif M. Mohammad, Svetlana Kiritchenko, Parinaz Sobhani, Xiaodan Zhu, and Colin Cherry. 2016. Semeval-2016 task 6: Detecting stance in tweets. In *Proceedings of the International Workshop on Semantic Evaluation*, SemEval'16, San Diego, CA, June.

Fabian Pedregosa, Gaël Varoquaux, Alexandre Gramfort, Vincent Michel, Bertrand Thirion, Olivier Grisel, Mathieu Blondel, Peter Prettenhofer, Ron Weiss, Vincent Dubourg, Jake Vanderplas, Alexandre Passos, David Cournapeau, Matthieu Brucher, Matthieu Perrot, and Édouard Duchesnay. 2011. Scikit-learn: Machine learning in Python. *Journal of Machine Learning Research*, 12:2825–2830.

Jeffrey Pennington, Richard Socher, and Christopher D Manning. 2014. GloVe: Global vectors for word representation. In *Proceedings of the 2014 Conference on Empirical Methods in Natural Language Processing (EMNLP)*, pages 1532–1543, Doha, Qatar.

István Pilászy. 2005. Text categorization and support vector machines. In *Proceedings of the 6th International Symposium of Hungarian Researchers on Computational Intelligence*, Budapest, Hungary.

Swapna Somasundaran and Janyce Wiebe. 2009. Recognizing stances in online debates. In *Proceedings of the Joint Conference of the 47th Annual Meeting of the ACL and the 4th International Joint Conference on Natural Language Processing of the AFNLP*, pages 226–234, Suntec, Singapore.

Swapna Somasundaran and Janyce Wiebe. 2010. Recognizing stances in ideological on-line debates. In *Proceedings of the NAACL HLT 2010 Workshop on Computational Approaches to Analysis and Generation of Emotion in Text*, pages 116–124, Los Angeles, CA.

Tohoku at SemEval-2016 Task 6: Feature-based Model versus Convolutional Neural Network for Stance Detection

Yuki Igarashi
Tohoku University
yuki.i@dc.tohoku.ac.jp

Hiroya Komatsu
Tohoku University
h-komatsu@ecei.tohoku.ac.jp

Sosuke Kobayashi
Tohoku University
sosuke.k@ecei.tohoku.ac.jp

Naoaki Okazaki
Tohoku University
okazaki@ecei.tohoku.ac.jp

Kentaro Inui
Tohoku University
inui@ecei.tohoku.ac.jp

Abstract

In this paper, we compare feature-based and Neural Network-based approaches on the supervised stance classification task for tweets in SemEval-2016 Task 6 Subtask A (Mohammad et al., 2016). In the feature-based approach, we use external resources such as lexicons and crawled texts. The Neural Network based approach employs Convolutional Neural Network (CNN). Our results show that the feature-based model outperformed the CNN model on the test data although the CNN model was better than the feature-based model in the cross validation on the training data.

1 Introduction

To solve supervised short text classification tasks, there are two major approaches; feature-based and Neural Network based approaches. In traditional feature-based approaches, we extract various features from a text. The features are usually constructed from n-grams (e.g., bigrams) of the texts and external resources such as lexicons and unlabeled corpora.

In Neural Network based approaches, a number of models for text classifications exist; for example, Feed-Forward Neural Network model using an average of embeddings of target word sequences as the input layer (Iyyer et al., 2015), Recursive Neural Network (Socher et al., 2011; Socher et al., 2013), and Convolutional Neural Network (CNN) (Johnson and Zhang, 2015; dos Santos and Gatti, 2014; Kim, 2014).

In this paper, we compare feature-based and Neural Network based approaches on the supervised stance classification task for tweets, SemEval-2016 Task 6 Subtask A (Mohammad et al., 2016). The feature-based approach classifies tweets using logistic regression model. The features are extracted using external knowledge such as SentiWordNet (Esuli and Sebastiani, 2006) and a collection of crawled tweets, in addition to unigrams or bigrams in the target tweet. For the Neural Network approach, we implement CNN based on Kim (2014). As the input embeddings, we use word embeddings trained by Continuous Bag-Of-Words (CBOW) model (Mikolov et al., 2013) on Wikipedia articles.

The experimental results show that the CNN based approach performed the best in the cross validation on the training data. However the tendency was opposite on the test data probably because the CNN model overfitted to the training data. In contrast, the feature-based approach was more robust, leveraging the external knowledge.

2 Datasets

We use the dataset of the SemEval-2016 Task 6 Subtask A, which is a supervised tweet classification task for five topics. There are three stances to classify; NONE, FAVOR, AGAINST. Table 1 shows the topics and distributions of the training data.

401

Topic	FAVOR	AGAINST	NONE
Atheism	92	304	117
Climate Change is a Real Concern	212	15	168
Feminist Movement	210	328	126
Hillary Clinton	112	361	166
Legalization of Abortion	105	334	164

Table 1: Distributions of the labels for each topics in the training data.

To classify tweets into their stances, we consider two configurations: *Three-way Polarity Classifier* which detects three stance labels at once, and a combination of *Topic Classifier* and *Two-way Polarity Classifier*. Topic Classifier judges the relevance of a tweet to the topic, in other words, whether a stance label is NONE or not (FAVOR/AGAINST). Two-way Polarity Classifier then labels FAVOR or AGAINST for tweets that were not judged as NONE by the Topic Classifier.

3 Feature-Based Approach

3.1 Preprocessing Tweets

We remove reply and mention expressions (@UserName) in tweets to prevent overfitting, and keep flags indicating whether tweets contain them or not. We also remove hashtags based on the following rules to prevent overfitting.

Rule 1. Hashtags embedded in the sentence with capitals or digits at non-inital letters
e.g., #WeLoveJapan, #Pray4all

Rule 2. Hashtags at the end of a tweet
e.g., #SemST, #2014, #LylicTweet

Rule 1 removes hashtags that are too long or unpopular. **Rule 2** removes hashtags that do not contain a stance. Remaining hashtags such as #hillary and #god may provide important features to detect the stances.

We also expand shortened forms such as "I'm" and "can't" based on simple rules. Finally, we obtain part-of-speech (POS) tags and dependency trees of tweets by using Stanford CoreNLP[1].

3.2 Features

Reply (R): If a tweet has a flag that indicates a reply or mention expression, we gener-

---

[1] http://stanfordnlp.github.io/CoreNLP/

Topic	Query	# tweets
Atheism	"atheism"	24124
Climate Change is a Real Concern	"climate", "climate change"	22703
Feminist Movement	"feminist", "feaminism", "feminist movement", "gender equality"	131677
Hillary Clinton	"hillary", "clinton", "hillary clinton"	980080
Legalization of Abortion	"abortion"	54846

Table 2: Crawled tweets used for HighPMI Features. This table shows search queries and the number of tweets we collected for each topic.

Topic	Keywords
Atheism	"atheism"
Climate Change is a Real Concern	"climate", "change"
Feminist Movement	"feminist", "feminism"
Hillary Clinton	"hillary", "clinton"
Legalization of Abortion	"abortion"

Table 3: Seed keywords for each topic for TargetSentiment and HighPMI features.

ate R=is_reply or R=is_mention as a feature. This feature may be effective because a reply or mention may provides a clue for detecting a stance.

BagOfWords (BoW): For detecting stances, words in a tweet are very informative. We include all unigrams of lemmas in a tweet as features. (e.g. BoW=think, BoW=not)

BagOfDependencies (BoD): Dependency relations such as adjectival modifier and negation are important for detecting stances. We include all dependency relations in a tweet as features. (e.g. BoD=hate=>i, BoD=like=>not)

BagOfPOSTag (BoP): We also extract features from POS tags. For example, if a tweet contains several interjections, the user probably has a negative opinion to the topic. We include all unigrams of POS tags in a tweet as features. (e.g. BoP=NOUN, BoP=UH)

SentiWordNet (SWN): Content words in a tweet may express some sentiment, which indicates stances and emotions of the user. We use SentiWordNet (Esuli and Sebastiani, 2006) for introducing sentiment of a word. It assigns positive/negative/objective scores to each word. In sentiment classification task, Pang et al. (2002) introduce SentiWordNet features. Following their work, we include sentiment polarity features for nouns, verbs,

Classifier	Atheism	ClimateChange is a Real concern	Feminist Movement	Hillary Clinton	Legalization Of Abortion	ALL topics
3-way Polarity	0.5314	0.5144	0.5735	0.5273	0.5277	0.6083
Topic + 2-way Polarity	**0.5327**	**0.5248**	**0.5860**	**0.5502**	**0.5290**	**0.6188**

Table 4: Comparison of 3-way Polarity Classifier with Topic + 2-way Polarity Classifier on 10-fold cross validation using the feature-based approach. The scores were measured in a macro average of micro-F1 scores of FAVOR and AGAINST for each topic and all topics.

Feature sets	Atheism	ClimateChange is a Real concern	Feminist Movement	Hillary Clinton	Legalization Of Abortion	ALL topics
ALL	0.5327	0.5248	0.5860	0.5502	0.5290	0.6188
- R	0.5373	0.5248	0.5776	0.5539	0.5349	0.6180
- BoW	0.5440	0.5248	**0.5936**	0.4927	0.5341	0.6185
- BoD	**0.5672**	0.5097	0.5895	**0.5561**	**0.5746**	**0.6276**
- BoP	0.5525	0.5248	0.5785	0.5527	0.5034	0.6169
- SWN	0.5357	0.5168	0.5760	0.5475	0.5308	0.6162
- SWS	0.5316	0.5248	0.5783	0.5520	0.5342	0.6174
- TS	0.5327	0.5248	0.5882	0.5502	0.5349	0.6200
- P	0.5360	0.5248	0.5834	0.5520	0.5406	0.6204
Best	0.5672	0.5642	0.5208	0.5883	0.5208	0.6297

Table 5: Ablation Test of Topic + 2-way Polarity Classifier on 10-fold cross validation using the feature-based approach. The scores were measured in a macro average of micro-F1 scores of FAVOR and AGAINST for each topic and all topics.

adjectives and adverbs in the tweet based on the following rules.

1. For a given word, look up the top item in SentiWordNet and obtain a negative and positive score of the word.

2. If the negative score is equal to the positive score, no features are generated.

3. If the negative score is larger than the positive score, generate a negative polarity feature, otherwise generate a positive polarity feature. (e.g. `SWN=love=>p, SWN=hate=>n`)

SentiWordSubject (SWS): This feature focuses on sentiment expressed by subjective pronouns such as "I" or "we", which may indicate emotions or stances of the user of a tweet. We obtain a sentiment polarity from the word modifying a subjective pronoun in a tweet, and include it as a feature. A sentiment polarity is obtained by SentiWordNet using the same rules for SWN features. (e.g. `SWS=I=love=>p, SWS=We=hate=>n`)

TargetSentiment (TS): We also consider sentiment or emotion for the topics. Jiang et al. (2011) add words modifying target words as features. Similarly, we extract words modifying target words in a tweet, and include sentiment polarity features using the same rules in SWN features.

We calculate similarities between words and seed keywords using word embeddings. If the similarity is higher than 0.7, we use it as the target word. Table 3 shows the seed keywords for each topic.

For example, given a tweet "We hate feminist", we extract "hate" that modifies the target word "feminist". Then we get a feature `TS=n` using the same rules in SWN features. (e.g. `TS=p, TS=n`)

HighPMI (P): We crawled tweets containing target words, and collected words cooccuring with seed keywords (Table 3) in all crawled tweets for each topic. Table 2 shows query words and the number of crawled tweets for each topic. Then we calculate Point-wise Mutual Information (PMI) for all words. If the word in a tweet is in top 300 of the PMI, we generate a feature. This feature detects a tweet containing words related to the topic. This feature may be effective to classify whether NONE or not. (e.g. `P=humanist, P=meninist`)

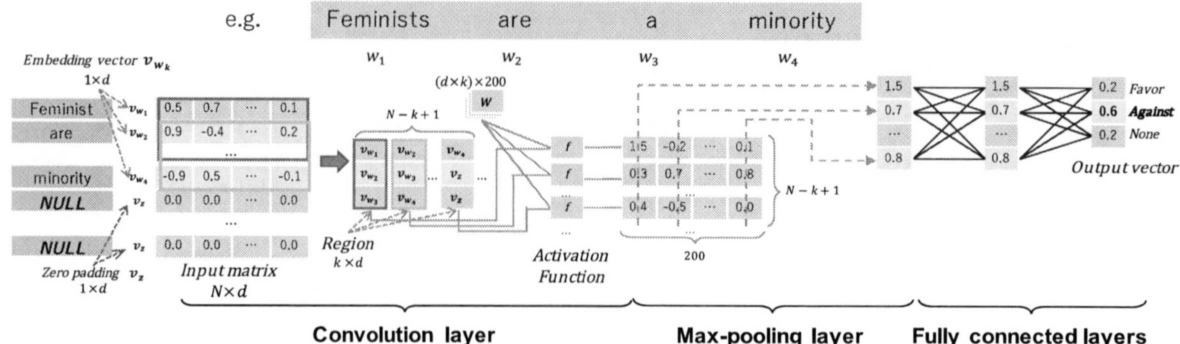

Figure 1: Overview of our CNN model.

3.3 Evaluation

3.3.1 Experimental Setups

We used L2 logistic regression as the classification algorithm, and measured the classification performance on 10-fold cross validation using the Classias package (Okazaki, 2009). We evaluated each model by a macro average of micro-F1 scores of FAVOR and AGAINST for each topic and all topics.

3.3.2 Comparison of Classifier Combinations

We compared Three-way Polarity Classifier with the combination of Topic Classifier and Two-way Polarity Classifier. Table 3.1 shows the performances of these two classifier configurations. We confirmed that the combination of Topic Classifier and Two-way Polarity Classifier outperformed Three-way Polarity Classifier. Therefore, we used the combination of Topic Classifier and Two-way Polarity Classifier hereafter.

3.3.3 Ablation Test

Through this experiment, we explore the contribution of individual features explained in Section 3.2. Table 5 shows the results of ablation tests. These results show that SWN features were the most effective to classify the stances. Sentiment of the tweet is one of the keys for stance classification. In contrast, BoD features degraded the classifier. We experimented further ablation tests with the feature set except for degraded features in the ablation test. These experiments revealed the best feature sets {**BoW, BoP, R, SWN, P**} (denoted 'Best' in Table 5).

4 CNN Based Approach

4.1 Method Overview

In recent years, Convolutional Neural Network (CNN) models have achieved remarkable results in various fields of research, such as computer vision and speech recognition. In the field of natural language processing, CNN models are also used for text classification tasks (Johnson and Zhang, 2015; dos Santos and Gatti, 2014), sentiment analysis (Kim, 2014), etc.

Following Kim (2014), we constructed CNN models to detect stances, as shown in Figure 1. They consist of one convolution layer with one max-pooling layer, and a three-layered feedforward network with softmax at the end to predict a distribution over classes. The convolution layer has 200 kernel windows whose sizes are $k \times d$, where k is the number of words in a window and d is the dimension size of the word embeddings. We denote an input tweet s as a sequence of words $\mathbf{w_1}, \mathbf{w_2}, ..., \mathbf{w_n}$, and their embeddings $\mathbf{v_{w_1}}, \mathbf{v_{w_2}}, ..., \mathbf{v_{w_n}}$. We use Chainer[2] for creating neural networks. To create a fixed-size input matrix for the implementation on Chainer, we added zero-padding vectors into the end of a sentence so that each input matrix will be $N \times d$ matrix, where N is the upper bound of the length of a sentence.

As we mentioned in Section 2, we consider both **Three-way Polarity Classifier** and a combination of **Topic Classifier** and **Two-way Polarity Classifier**. We also try to find out the best hyper parameter k and activation functions.

---

[2]http://chainer.org/

404

Classifier	Activation Functions		Atheism	Climate Change is a Real Concern	Feminist Movement	Hillary Clinton	Legalization of Abortion	Total
3-way	sig		**0.6770**	0.4118	0.5958	0.5681	0.4814	0.6664
	relu		0.6039	0.5186	0.6015	0.6098	0.5421	0.6647
Topic + 2-way	sig	sig	0.6751	0.4080	0.5969	0.6061	0.5528	0.6381
	relu	relu	0.5736	0.5710	0.5990	0.6391	0.5455	0.6365
	sig	relu	0.5826	**0.5774**	0.5974	**0.6402**	0.5425	**0.6713**
	relu	sig	0.6688	0.4017	**0.6005**	0.6090	**0.5612**	0.6398

Table 6: Comparison of 3-way Polarity Classifier with Topic + 2-way Polarity Classifier on 10-fold cross validation using CNN based approach. The scores were measured in a macro average of micro-F1 scores of FAVOR and AGAINST for each topic and all topics.

Kernel Size (k)	Atheism	Climate Change is a Real Concern	Feminist Movement	Hillary Clinton	Legalization of Abortion	ALL topics
2	**0.6390**	0.5743	0.6189	**0.6490**	**0.5611**	**0.6831**
3	0.5826	**0.5774**	0.5974	0.6402	0.5425	0.6713
4	0.5746	0.5746	**0.6276**	0.6354	0.5398	0.6755

Table 7: Tuning of window size per word k on 10-fold cross validation using CNN based approach. The scores were measured in a macro average of micro-F1 scores of FAVOR and AGAINST for each topic and all topics.

4.2 Experimental Setups

We trained 300 dimensional word embeddings using Word2Vec[3] with Wikipedia articles[4] (3950598 articles in total)[5]. We set N to 100, which exceeds the maximum length of all tweets. We use $(300 \times k) \times 200$ matrix as W and three fully connected layers that consist of 200-50-3 units (Three-way Polarity Classifier) or 200-50-2 units (Topic Classifier or Two-way Polarity Classifier).

We measured the performance on 10-fold cross validation. We evaluated each model by a macro average of micro-F1 scores of FAVOR and AGAINST for each topic and all topics.

4.3 Evaluation

4.3.1 Comparison of Classifier Combinations

We compared Three-way Polarity Classifier with the combination of Topic Classifier and Two-way Polarity Classifier with $k = 3$. We tried using all possible combinations of sigmoid and relu functions in the CNN models.

Table 6 shows the performances of the classifiers.

The table indicates that the combination of Topic Classifier and Two-way Polarity Classifier outperformed Three-way Polarity Classifier. We confirmed that the combination of these classifier has been found effective for not only the feature-based approach, but also for the CNN-based approach.

We also achieved the best score when we use sigmoid function for Topic Classifier and relu for Two-way Polarity Classifier.

4.3.2 Tuning of Window Size k

We searched for the best value of the hyperparameter k with the highest model in Section 4.3.1. Table 7 shows that the model obtained the highest score with window size $k = 2$. The results show that bigram is appropriate for stance detection on the training data.

4.3.3 Visualization of the CNN Model

In this section, we visualize the CNN model that achieved the highest score in Section 4.3.2. To visualize the CNN model, we define a *region score* as the number of dimensions that are selected by the max-pooling layer per region. Figure 2 shows a heat map reflecting the region score.

The figure provides several observations.

- Topic related words such as *movement* received a high score in both Topic classifier and Two-way Polarity Classifier. This shows that each

---

[3] https://code.google.com/archive/p/word2vec/

[4] https://dumps.wikimedia.org/enwiki/20151201/enwiki-20151201-pages-articles.xml.bz2

[5] We used the following options: `-size 300 -window 5 -sample 1e-4 -negative 5 -hs 0 -cbow 1 -iter 3`

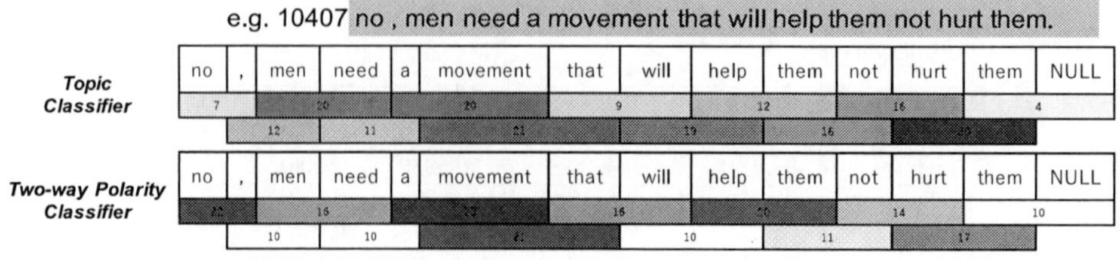

Figure 2: Visualization of the CNN model. A bigram region in deep color receives high *region score*, which indicates that the convolution layer highly focuses on the region.

Method	Train	Test					
	Total	Atheism	Climate Change is a Real Concern	Feminist Movement	Hillary Clinton	Legalization of Abortion	ALL topic
Feature-Best	0.6297	**0.5973**	0.3891	**0.5487**	**0.5360**	**0.5796**	**0.6426**
CNN-Best (Submission)	**0.6831**	0.5890	**0.3951**	0.5241	0.3981	0.3775	0.6221
Majority Baseline	0.5411	0.4210	0.4212	0.3910	0.3683	0.4030	0.6522

Table 8: Comparison of Feature-based Model and CNN Model on test data. The scores were measured in a macro average of micro-F1 scores of `FAVOR` and `AGAINST` for each topic and all topics.

CNN model automatically detects the topic words.

- Nouns, verbs and adjectives that appear in SentiWordNet received a higher score in both classifiers. In addition, their scores have some associations with cooccurrence with the topic word.

- Negation words such as *not* and *can't* received high scores in Polarity Classifier, but they received less scores in Topic Classifier.

5   Overall Results

We compared feature-based models with CNN models and the majority baseline in the test data. The feature-based models used Topic + Two-way Polarity Classifiers and the best feature sets mentioned in Section 3.3.3. The CNN models used Topic + Two-way Polarity Classifiers and the best hyperparameters mentioned in Section 4.3. The majority baseline labeled the test data as the stance that was most prevalent in the training data.

Table 8 shows a macro average of micro-F1 scores of `FAVOR` and `AGAINST` for two models in the test data and the cross validation results. As a comparison, we also show the majority baseline in Table 8.

We found that the feature-based model outperformed the CNN model in the test data, although the CNN model was better in the cross validation on the training data. We think that the feature-based model was more robust, including broad external knowledge such as SentiWordNet and crawled tweets. In contrast, the CNN model obtained a lower score on the test data than on the cross validation.

6   Conclusion

We compared the feature-based and the CNN based approaches on SemEval-2016 Task 6 Subtask A. The CNN based approach performed the best in the cross validation on the training data although the feature-based approach outperformed the CNN model on the test data. We also visualized the CNN model to reveal what was focused on. We found that the CNN model automatically detected the topic words and effective words to detect the stances.

Acknowledgments

We acknowledge the support of the Step-QI School program, Department of Information and Intelligent Systems, Tohoku University.

References

Cicero dos Santos and Maira Gatti. 2014. Deep convolutional neural networks for sentiment analysis of short texts. In *Proceedings of COLING 2014, the 25th In-*

ternational Conference on Computational Linguistics: Technical Papers, pages 69–78.

Andrea Esuli and Fabrizio Sebastiani. 2006. Sentiwordnet: A publicly available lexical resource for opinion mining. In *Proceedings of the 5th Conference on Language Resources and Evaluation*, pages 417–422.

Mohit Iyyer, Varun Manjunatha, Jordan Boyd-Graber, and Hal Daumé III. 2015. Deep unordered composition rivals syntactic methods for text classification. In *Proceedings of the 53rd Annual Meeting of the Association for Computational Linguistics and the 7th International Joint Conference on Natural Language Processing (Volume 1: Long Papers)*, pages 1681–1691.

Long Jiang, Mo Yu, Ming Zhou, Xiaohua Liu, and Tiejun Zhao. 2011. Target-dependent twitter sentiment classification. In *Proceedings of the 49th Annual Meeting of the Association for Computational Linguistics: Human Language Technologies - Volume 1*, HLT '11, pages 151–160.

Rie Johnson and Tong Zhang. 2015. Effective use of word order for text categorization with convolutional neural networks. In *NAACL HLT 2015, The 2015 Conference of the North American Chapter of the Association for Computational Linguistics: Human Language Technologies*, pages 103–112.

Yoon Kim. 2014. Convolutional neural networks for sentence classification. In *Proceedings of the 2014 Conference on Empirical Methods in Natural Language Processing (EMNLP)*, pages 1746–1751.

Tomas Mikolov, Kai Chen, Greg Corrado, and Jeffrey Dean. 2013. Efficient estimation of word representations in vector space. *CoRR*, abs/1301.3781.

Saif M. Mohammad, Svetlana Kiritchenko, Parinaz Sobhani, Xiaodan Zhu, and Colin Cherry. 2016. SemEval-2016 Task 6: Detecting stance in tweets. In *Proceedings of the International Workshop on Semantic Evaluation*, SemEval '16.

Naoaki Okazaki. 2009. Classias: a collection of machine-learning algorithms for classification.

Bo Pang, Lillian Lee, and Shivakumar Vaithyanathan. 2002. Thumbs up?: Sentiment classification using machine learning techniques. In *Proceedings of the ACL-02 Conference on Empirical Methods in Natural Language Processing - Volume 10*, EMNLP '02, pages 79–86.

Richard Socher, Jeffrey Pennington, Eric H. Huang, Andrew Y. Ng, and Christopher D. Manning. 2011. Semi-Supervised Recursive Autoencoders for Predicting Sentiment Distributions. In *Proceedings of the 2011 Conference on Empirical Methods in Natural Language Processing (EMNLP)*.

Richard Socher, Alex Perelygin, Jean Wu, Jason Chuang, Christopher D. Manning, Andrew Ng, and Christopher Potts. 2013. Recursive deep models for semantic compositionality over a sentiment treebank. In *Proceedings of the 2013 Conference on Empirical Methods in Natural Language Processing*, pages 1631–1642.

UWB at SemEval-2016 Task 6: Stance Detection

Peter Krejzl
University of West Bohemia
Faculty of Applied Sciences
Dept. of Computer Sci. and Eng.
Univerzitni 8, 30614 Pilsen
Czech Republic
pkrejzl@gmail.com

Josef Steinberger
University of West Bohemia
Faculty of Applied Sciences
NTIS Centre
Univerzitni 8, 30614 Pilsen
Czech Republic
jstein@kiv.zcu.cz

Abstract

This paper describes our system participating in the SemEval 2016 task: Detecting stance in Tweets. The goal was to identify whether the author of a tweet is in favor of the given target or against. Our approach is based on a maximum entropy classifier, which uses surface-level, sentiment and domain-specific features. We participated in both the supervised and weakly supervised subtasks and received promising results for most of the targets.

1 Introduction

Stance detection has been defined as automatically detecting whether the author of a piece of text is in favor of the given target or against it. In the third class, there are the cases, in which neither inference is likely. It can be viewed as a subtask of opinion mining and it stands next to the sentiment analysis. The significant difference is that in the case of sentiment analysis, systems determine whether a piece of text is positive, negative, or neutral. However, in stance detection, systems are to determine the author's favorability towards a given target and the target even may not be explicitly mentioned in the text. Moreover, the text may express positive opinion about an entity contained in the text, but one can also infer that the author is against the defined target (an entity or a topic). This makes the task more difficult, compared to the sentiment analysis, but it can often bring complementary information.

There are many applications which could benefit from the automatic stance detection, including information retrieval, textual entailment, or text summarization, in particular opinion summarization. Twitter was selected as the source of the text because of its popularity and because people express stance implicitly or explicitly there.

We first shortly introduce the task in Section 2 and the available dataset.[1] In Section 3, we describe our preprocessing, the implemented approach and system's features. It is followed by the setup for each analysed topic and a discussion of official results (Section 4).

2 Task Description

The **Detecting Stance in Tweets** task[2] (Mohammad et al., 2016) had two independent subtasks: supervised and weakly supervised stance identification.

The supervised task (subtask A) tested stance towards five targets: *Atheism, Climate Change is a Real Concern, Feminist Movement, Hillary Clinton,* and *Legalization of Abortion.* Participants were provided 2814 labeled training tweets for the five targets. An example tweet annotated as IN FAVOR: *These pics of #pornstars with/without makeup? Just perpetuating the myth that women need makeup to be considered pretty.* (the *Feminist Movement* target, ID: 1017).

A detailed distribution of stances for each target is given in Table 1. The distribution is not uniform and there is always a preference towards a certain stance (e.g., 59% tweets about *Atheism* are labelled as AGAINST).

---

[1] Details can be found in the overview paper (Mohammad et al., 2016).

[2] http://alt.qcri.org/semeval2016/task6/

Proceedings of SemEval-2016, pages 408–412,
San Diego, California, June 16-17, 2016. ©2016 Association for Computational Linguistics

It naturally reflects the real-world scenario, in which a majority of people tend to one of the stances. This is also depending on the source of the data. For example, in the case of *Legalization of Abortion*, we can assume that the distribution will be significantly different in religious communities than in atheistic communities.

For the weakly supervised task (subtask B), there were no labelled training data but participants could use a large number of tweets related to the single target: *Donald Trump*. Example: *There are so many reasons to dislike #HillaryClinton but Half Human and Half Orangutan #DonaldTrump takes it to next level.* (ID: 589371241204711424).

Due to Twitter legal requirements, the dataset for subtask B contained only tweet ids and participants had to download those tweets using the provided script. The dataset contains 78256 tweet ids generated by searching for the tags #DonaldTrump and #trump2016. Unfortunately, some of those tweets did not exist at the download time, as their authors removed them. Our dataset contained 69454 tweets.

Topic	FAV	AG	NONE	TOT
Atheism	92 (18%)	304 (59%)	117 (23%)	513
Climate Change is a Real Concern	212 (54%)	15 (4%)	168 (43%)	395
Feminist Movement	210 (32%)	328 (49%)	126 (19%)	664
Hillary Clinton	112 (18%)	361 (56%)	166 (26%)	639
Legalization of Abortion	105 (17%)	334 (55%)	164 (27%)	603

Table 1: Training data statistics. FAV = IN FAVOR, AG = AGAINST, and NONE = neither inference.

3 The Approach Overview

We decided to build a classical supervised learning system, in particular, we used a maximum entropy classifier (Loper et al., 2002). The classifier was trained separately for each topic. For the subtask B - weakly supervised system (*Donal Trump*) we used the *Hillary Clinton* training data, which we considered as the closest. We also added some enhancements we discuss later.

We first analysed hashtags in the training corpus. We automatically identified those that predict the stance well for each topic. These hashtags strongly correlate with one of the stance classes. For example, if the tweet contains hashtag *#benghazi* (the *Hillary Clinton* target), the stance is always AGAINST. We picked hashtags which appear at least in 10 tweets and at least 90% of these tweets are annotated with a particular stance.

The important hashtags are listed in Table 2.

We also gathered from Twitter additional data (via Twitter API) based on these automatically detected hashtags (#benghazi, #stophillary2016, etc.). This additional data was not used directly during the training phase but we created a set of dictionaries (ADSD) out of them.

Topic	Hashtag	Stance
Atheism	#freethinker	IN FAVOR
	#islam	AGAINST
Climate Change is a Real Concern	#climate	IN FAVOR
	#mission	IN FAVOR
	#peace	NONE
	#tip	IN FAVOR
Feminist Movement	#feminists	AGAINST
	#spankafeminist	AGAINST
Hillary Clinton	#benghazi	AGAINST
	#lol	AGAINST
	#stophillary2016	AGAINST
Legalization of Abortion	#alllivesmatter	AGAINST
	#ccot	AGAINST
	#prolifeyouth	AGAINST

Table 2: Hashtags analysis.

3.1 Preprocessing

Preprocessing starts the pipeline. Each of the following steps was applied to every tweet.

1. All URLs are replaced by keyword *URL*,

2. multiple exclamation marks are replaced by *MULTIPLEEXCLAMATIONS*,

3. mutiple question marks are replaced by *MULTIPLEQUESTIONMARKS*,

4. Twitter usernames like *@peter_krejzl* are replaced by *NAME*,

5. links to images (pic.twitter.com) are replaced by *IMGURL*,

6. hashtag *#sems* is removed,

7. initial tag *RT* is removed,

8. English stopwords are removed, [3]

9. only letters are preserved, the rest of the characters is removed,

10. for the *Donald Trump* target, we used training data from the *Hillary Clinton* target but we removed the following words from the tweets: *hillary, hilary, clinton.*

3.2 Features

A basic set of features was created from the preprocessed text. Unigrams perform quite well in the task (Somasundaran et al., 2009), so we used it as a baseline for all targets. The model is based on TF-IDF and uses not more than 750 features (first 750 words from the vocabulary). This is used for all five topics. Then, we implemented a set of other features that could be turned on or off for each topic.

We built a set of features from **hashtags** in Table 2. In maximum 50 unigram and bigram features were generated from the hashtags using the TF-IDF weighting.

Anand et al. (2011) showed that **initial n-grams** are useful features. Our system supports initial unigrams to initial trigrams, the maximum number is 50 features. However, from our experiments with the training dataset, we found useful only initial unigrams, and initial bigrams for the *Hillary Clinton* target (turned on for *Donald Trump* as well).

Another surface feature was **tweet length** (in words) after preprocessing.

Part-of-speech tags were generated from the preprocessed tweet and we built unigram and bigram data model using TF-IDF, limited to 50 features. [4]

General Inquirer (GI) [5] (General-Inquirer, 1966) provides dictionaries useful for example for sentiment analysis. We used a subset of the dictionary, in particular columns: *Positiv, Negativ, Hostile, Strong, Pleasure, Pain.*

---

[3]We used stopwords available in the *nltk.corpus* python library.

[4]We used *Nltk* part-of-speech tagger.

[5]http://www.wjh.harvard.edu/ inquirer/

Entity-centered sentiment dictionaries (ECSD): We used another resource borrowed from the sentiment analysis: dictionaries created mainly for the purpose of entity-related polarity detection (Steinberger et al., 2012). We used both the highly positive and positive terms[6] as IN FAVOR features and highly negative / negative terms as AGAINST features.

In some topics like *Legalization of abortion* or *Atheism* any **reference to a bible** (e.g., *Romans 12:2*) is also a very good indicator. We add additional binary feature based on the presence of a bible reference. [7]

Domain Stance Dictionary (DSD) Based on the training data analysis of each topic, we created a list of key words that tend to indicate a particular stance. We first generated a list of candidates: for each topic, we took words with ratio $frequency - in - topic/frequency - in - the - training - data > 0.6$ and $frequency - in - topic > 1$. If a word occurred at least 4 times more frequently in 'IN FAVOR' tweets than in 'AGAINST', it was added to the 'IN FAVOR' candidates' list. We repeated the same approach to produce 'AGAINST' candidates. The lists were then filtered manually and it resulted in strong stance-predictive keywords lists. All the lists together contain 221 words, an average list had 22 words. For instance, for the *Legalization of Abortion* topic, the following words or hashtags suggest the AGAINST stance: *unborn, womb, prolifegen, conception, precious, chooselife, kills, abortionismurder, destroys, itsnotonitsnotsafe, manslaughter, eliminated, cannibalism, heartbeat, ...* We used the number of words from each dictionary the tweets contain as features.

Additional Domain Stance Dictionary (ADSD): In the case of the *Legalization of Abortion* and *Hillary Clinton* topics, we created additional two dictionaries per topic. It was a similar exercise to DSD, but we used the additional tweets gathered through Twitter API as an input. For example, the AGAINST dictionary for *Hillary Clinton* contains: *attack, benghazihearings, blamed, blood, BloodOnHerHands, corrupt, irritated, Killary, ...*

---

[6]There are two levels of intensity for both polarities.

[7]Simple python regular expression `(\d+) : (\d+)`.

Both the DSD and ADSD dictionaries contain terms that strongly indicate a particular stance. They were used to modify the final output towards the particular stance and override the classifier result. For each tweet we count the number of words from each positive or negative DSD/ADSD. If there are more words from the positive dictionary then the whole tweet is deemed FAVOR and vice versa. If the counts of positive and negative words are equal then the override logic is not used. We also noticed (during the development phase) that the classifier was overridden only few times in the Task A, while more times in the Task B. We think it is due to the different training data used for the Donald Trump task.

4 Configuration and Results

During the development phase, we used 10-fold cross-validation to test all combinations of features. Each particular dataset was split randomly. For each experiment we measured average F1-score on IN FAVOR and AGAINST classes, the same metric as the official one (Mohammad et al., 2016). This way we identified an optimal set of features for each topic, listed in Table 3.

Topic	Features
Atheism	Unigrams, Bible reference, DSD
Climate	Unigrams, Hashtags, POS, DSD
Feminism	Unigrams, Hashtags, DSD
Hillary	Unigrams, Hashtags, Initial unigrams, Initial Bigrams, ECSD, DSD, DSDA
Abortion	Unigrams, Bible reference, DSD, DSDA
Trump	Unigrams, Hashtags, Initial Unigrams, Initial Bigrams, ECSD, DSD, DSDA

Table 3: Features per topic used for the submission.

Table 4 shows results on the development set. We reached the best improvement over the baseline for *Hillary Clinton*, followed by *Feminism* and *Atheism*. However, detecting a correct stance for these targets seemed to be the most difficult.

Official results of the SemEval task are summarized in Table 5. There were 19 participating systems for subtask A and 9 for subtask B. We per-

formed well for *Abortion* (2nd), *Climate* (3rd) and *Hillary Clinton* (4th) targets in comparison with the other participating systems, we received an average rank for *Atheism* and *Feminism*. The overall rank was 9th.

In the weakly supervised subtask (*Donald Trump*), we were ranked 4th, only the top system was significantly better. The difference between performances on the *Hillary Clinton* and *Donald Trump* topics (.5982 vs. .4202) indicate the difference in complexity between the subtasks.

It seems that although Clinton and Trump are competitors on political stage, Clinton's training data brought useful features for Trump as well (criticizing or praising a politician), although in many cases the overriding strategy corrected the classifier's prediction.

Topic	Baseline (unigrams)	Features (no override)	Features + override	Diff against baseline
Atheism	.5579	.6314	.6314	+13%
Climate	.6250	.6589	.6590	+5%
Feminism	.4722	.5424	.5443	+15%
Clinton	.4460	.5386	.5386	+21%
Abortion	.6250	.6749	.6749	+8%

Table 4: Development results per topic with features turned on/off (K-10 fold validation).

Topic	UWB (Rank)	Avg. system	Best system
Atheism	.5788 (8)	.5510	.6725
Climate	.4690 (3)	.4219	.5486
Feminism	.5182 (10)	.5155	.6209
Hillary	.5982 (4)	.5248	.6712
Abortion	.6198 (2)	.5472	.6332
Sub-task A	.6342 (9)	.6202	.6782
Sub-task B	.4202 (4)	.3737	.5628

Table 5: Official results of the SemEval task. There were 19 submissions for subtask A and 9 submissions for subtask B.

5   Conclusion

The paper describes our participation in the Tweets stance detection task of SemEval 2016. Our submission was based on a maximum entropy classifier with mainly surface-level, sentiment and domain-specific features. The system was among the top systems for three of the five targets from the supervised task. Without the labeled tweets, the weakly supervised scenario, our position was fourth (from nine). Currently, we investigate in more detail how to gather more training data automatically.

Acknowledgments

This work was supported by grant no. SGS-2013-029 Advanced computing and information systems and by project MediaGist, EU's FP7 People Programme (Marie Curie Actions), no. 630786.

References

Anand, P., Walker, M., Abbott, R., Tree, J. E. F., Bowmani, R., and Minor, M. 2011. Cats rule and dogs drool!: Classifying stance in online debate. In *Proceedings of WASSA'11*, ACL.

Mohammad, S., Kiritchenko, S., Sobhani, P., Zhu, X., and Cherry, C. 2016. Semeval-2016 task 6: Detecting stance in tweets. In *Proceedings of SemEval '16*, ACL.

Faulkner, A. 2014. Automated Classification of Stance in Student Essays: An Approach Using Stance Target Information and the Wikipedia Link-Based Measure. In *Proceedings of the Twenty-Seventh International Flairs Conference*, AAAI.

Schneider, J., Groza, T., Passant, A. 2014. A review of argumentation for the social semantic web. In *Semantic Web, 4(2)*, pages 159-218, IOS Press.

Hasan, K. S., and Ng, V. 2013. Stance classification of ideological debates: Data, models, features, and constraints. In *Proceedings of the Sixth International Joint Conference on Natural Language Processing*, pages 1348-1356, ACL.

Kiritchenko, S., Zhu, X., and Mohammad, S. 2014. Sentiment Analysis of Short Informal Texts. In *Journal of Artificial Intelligence Research, vol. 50*, pages 723-762, AAAI Press.

Loper, E. and Bird, S. 2002. NLTK: The Natural Language Toolkit In *Proceedings of the ACL Workshop on Effective Tools and Methodologies for Teaching Natural Language Processing and Computational Linguistics*, ACL.

Mohammad, S., Kiritchenko, S. and Zhu, X. 2013. NRC-Canada: Building the State-of-the-Art in Sentiment Analysis of Tweets. In *Proceedings of SemEval-2013*, ACL.

Kiritchenko, S., Zhu, X. and Mohammad, S. 2016. Sentiment Analysis: Detecting Valence, Emotions, and Other Affectual States from Text. In *Emotion Measurement*, Elsevier.

Mohammad, S., Kiritchenko, S. and Zhu, X. 2010. Support or Oppose? Classifying Positions in Online Debates from Reply Activities and Opinion Expressions. In *Proceedings of the International Conference on Computational Linguistics*, pages 869-875, ACL.

Rajadesingan, A. and Huan, L. 2014. Identifying Users with Opposing Opinions in Twitter Debates. Social Computing, Behavioral-Cultural Modeling and Prediction. In *Social Computing, Behavioral-Cultural Modeling and Prediction*, pages 153-160, Springer.

Recasens, M., Danescu-Niculescu-Mizil, C. and Jurafsky, D. 2013. Linguistic Models for Analyzing and Detecting Biased Language. In *Proceedings of ACL 2013*, pages 1650-1659, ACL.

Somasundaran, S. and Wiebe, J. 2009. Recognizing stances in online debates. In *Proceedings of the ACL/AFNLP*, pages 226-234, ACL.

Sridhar, D., Getoor, L. and Walker, M. 2014. Collective Stance Classification of Posts in Online Debate Forums. In *Proceedings of the Joint Workshop on Social Dynamics and Personal Attributes in Social Media* pages 109-117, ACL.

Steinberger, J., Lenkova, P., Ebrahim, M., Ehrmann, M., Hurriyetoglu, A., Kabadjov, M., Steinberger, R., Tanev, H., Zavarella, V. and Vazquez, S. 2012. Creating Sentiment Dictionaries via Triangulation. In *Decision Support 53(4)*, pages 689-694, Elsevier.

Stone, P., Dumphy, D., Smith, M., Ogilvie, D. 1966. The general inquirer: a computer approach to content analysis. In *M.I.T. studies in comparative politics*, M.I.T. Press.

Thomas, M., Pang, B., and Lee, L. 2006. Get out the vote: Determining support or opposition from Congressional floor-debate transcripts. In *Proceedings of EMNLP*, pages 327-335, ACL.

Walker, M. A., Anand, P., Abbott, R., and Grant, R. 2012. Stance classification using dialogic properties of persuasion. In *Proceedings of the NAACL/HLT*, pages 592-596, ACL.

Wyner, A., and Schneider, J.. 2012. Arguing from a Point of View. In *Proceedings of the First International Conference on Agreement Technologies*, CEUR.

DeepStance at SemEval-2016 Task 6: Detecting Stance in Tweets Using Character and Word-Level CNNs

Prashanth Vijayaraghavan, Ivan Sysoev, Soroush Vosoughi and Deb Roy

MIT Media Lab, Massachusetts Institute of Technology

Cambridge, MA 02139

`pralav@mit.edu, isysoev@mit.edu,`
`soroush@mit.edu, dkroy@media.mit.edu`

Abstract

This paper describes our approach for the *Detecting Stance in Tweets* task (SemEval-2016 Task 6). We utilized recent advances in short text categorization using deep learning to create word-level and character-level models. The choice between word-level and character-level models in each particular case was informed through validation performance. Our final system is a combination of classifiers using word-level or character-level models. We also employed novel data augmentation techniques to expand and diversify our training dataset, thus making our system more robust. Our system achieved a macro-average precision, recall and F1-scores of 0.67, 0.61 and 0.635 respectively.

1 Introduction

Stance detection is the task of automatically determining whether the authors of a text are against or in favour of a given target. For instance, take the following sentence: "It has been such a cold April, so much for global warming." This sentence's author is most likely against the concept of global warming (i.e., does not believe in it). The work presented here is specifically targeted towards detecting stance in tweets. The noisy and idiosyncratic nature of tweets make this a particularly hard task.

Automatic identification of stance in tweets has practical applications for a range of domains. For instance, it can be used as a sensor to measure the attitude of Twitter users on various issues, such as: political issues, candidates, brand names, TV shows, etc.

There has been extensive research done on modelling and automatic detection of stance in political arenas (e.g., debates) (Thomas et al., 2006) and on online forums (Somasundaran and Wiebe, 2009; Murakami and Raymond, 2010). However, as we alluded to earlier, the peculiar nature of tweets make techniques that have been developed for other platforms unsuitable. The field closest to this work is the field of Twitter sentiment classification, where the task is to detect the sentiment of a given tweet, usually as positive, negative, or neutral. Nonetheless, it is important to note that there are substantial differences between sentiment classification and stance detection. Sentiment classifiers determine the polarity of a given tweet, without considering any targets (see Vosoughi et al. (Vosoughi et al., 2015) for an example of a Twitter sentiment classifier). For instance, consider the tweet: "I love Donald Trump", this tweet has a positive sentiment, and the author of the tweet has a positive stance towards Donald Trump, but it can also be inferred that the author is most likely against or at best neutral towards Bernie Sanders. In this paper, we present a system for automatic detection of stance in Tweets.

2 Our Approach

We trained a different model for each of the five targets. Models for some of the targets used character-level convolutional neural networks(CNN), while other used word-level models. In one particular target (Hillary Clinton), a combination of character-level and word-level models was used. Though Character-level models are robust to the idiosyncratic and noisy nature of tweets, they require a larger dataset compared to word-level models. Our

413

Proceedings of SemEval-2016, pages 413–419,
San Diego, California, June 16-17, 2016. ©2016 Association for Computational Linguistics

choice between the models was informed by validation performance (as explained in section 5). The character and word-level models are explained in the section below.

2.1 Character-Level CNN Tweet Model

Character-level CNN (CharCNN) is a slight variant of the deep character level convolutional neural network introduced by Zhang et al (Zhang and LeCun, 2015), based on the success of CNNs in image recognition tasks (Girshick et al., 2014) (Hinton et al., 2012). In this model, we perform temporal (one-dimensional) convolutional and max-pooling operations. Given a discrete input function $f(x) \in [1, l] \mapsto \mathbb{R}$, a discrete kernel function $k(x) \in [1, m] \mapsto \mathbb{R}$ and stride s, the convolution $g(y) \in [1, (l - m + 1)/s] \mapsto \mathbb{R}$ between $k(x)$ and $f(x)$ and pooling operation $h(y) \in [1, (l - m + 1)/s] \mapsto \mathbb{R}$ of $f(x)$ is calculated as:

$$g(y) = \sum_{x=1}^{m} k(x) \cdot f(y \cdot s - x + c) \quad (1)$$

$$h(y) = max_{x=1}^{m} f(y \cdot s - x + c) \quad (2)$$

where $c = m - s + 1$ is an offset constant. In our implementation of the model, the stride s is set to 1.

This model is illustrated in Figure 1. We adapted this model for the size limit of tweets (140 characters). The character set includes English alphabets, numbers, special characters and unknown character. There are 70 characters in total, given below:

```
abcdefghijklmnopqrstuvw
xyz0123456789-,;.!?:'"/
\|_#$%&^*~`+-=<>()[]{}
```

Each character in the tweet can be encoded using one-hot vector $x_i \in \{0, 1\}^{70}$. Hence, a tweet is represented as a binary matrix $x_{1..150} \in \{0, 1\}^{150x70}$ with padding wherever necessary, where 150 is the maximum number of characters in a tweet plus padding and 70 is the size of the character set. Each tweet, in the form of a matrix, is now fed into a deep model consisting of four 1-d convolutional layers. A convolution operation employs a filter w, to extract l-gram character feature from a sliding window of l characters at the first layer and learns abstract textual features in the subsequent layers. This filter

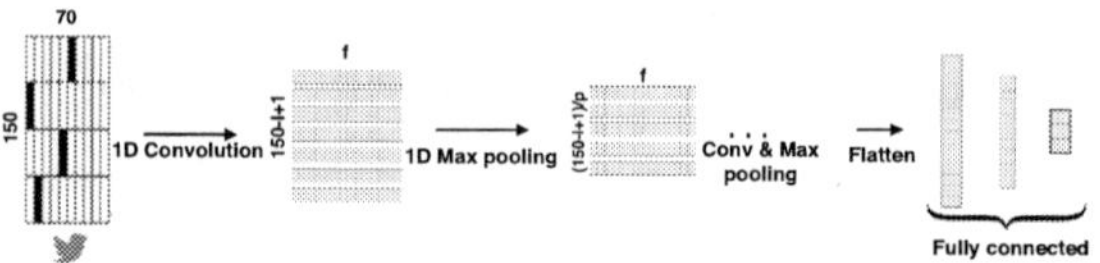

Figure 1: Illustration of CharCNN Model

w is applied across all possible windows of size l to produce a feature map. A sufficient number (f) of such filters are used to model the rich structures in the composition of characters. Generally, with tweet s, each element $c_i^{(h,F)}(s)$ of a feature map F at the layer h is generated by:

$$c_i^{(h,F)}(s) = g(w^{(h,F)} \odot \hat{c}_i^{(h-1)}(s) + b^{(h,F)}) \quad (3)$$

where $w^{(h,F)}$ is the filter associated with feature map F at layer h; $\hat{c}_i^{(h-1)}$ denotes the segment of output of layer $h-1$ for convolution at location i (where $\hat{c}_i^{(0)} = x_{i...i+l-1}$ — one-hot vectors of l characters from tweet s); $b^{(h,F)}$ is the bias associated with that filter at layer h; g is a rectified linear unit and $\odot$ is element-wise multiplication. The output of the convolutional layer $c^h(s)$ is a matrix, the columns of which are feature maps $c^{(h,F_k)}(s)|k \in 1..f$.

The output of the convolutional layer is followed by a 1-d max-overtime pooling operation (Collobert et al., 2011) over the feature map and selects the maximum value as the prominent feature from the current filter. Pooling size may vary at each layer (given by $p^{(h)}$ at layer h). The pooling operation shrinks the size of the feature representation and filters out trivial features like unnecessary combination of characters (in the initial layer). The window length l, number of filters f, pooling size p at each layer can vary for each classification task.

The output from the last convolutional layer is flattened and passed into a series of fully connected layers. The output of the final fully connected layer (sigmoid or softmax) gives a probability distribution over categories in our classification task. For regularization we apply a dropout (Hinton et al., 2012) mechanism after the first fully connected layer. This prevents co-adaptation of hidden units by randomly setting a proportion ρ of the hidden units to zero (Generally, we set $\rho = 0.5$). CharCNN can be robust to misspellings and noise, provided there is sufficiently large dataset to train the model.

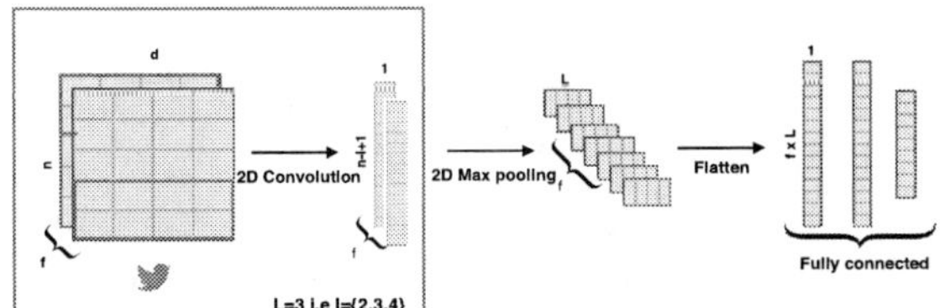

Figure 2: Illustration of Word-Embedding Convolutional Model

2.2 Convolutional Word-Embedding Model

The convolutional embedding model (see Figure 2) assigns a d dimensional vector to each of the n words of an input tweet resulting in a matrix of size $n \times d$. Each of these vectors are initialized with uniformly distributed random numbers i.e. $x_i \in \mathbb{R}^d$. The model, though randomly initialized, will eventually learn a look-up matrix $\mathbb{R}^{|V| \times d}$ where $|V|$ is the vocabulary size, which represents the word embedding for the words in the vocabulary.

A convolution layer is then applied to the $n \times d$ input tweet matrix, which takes into consideration all the successive windows of size l, sliding over the entire tweet. A filter $w \in \mathbb{R}^{h \times d}$ operates on the tweet to give a feature map $c \in \mathbb{R}^{n-l+1}$. We apply a max-pooling function (Collobert et al., 2011) of size $p = (n - l + 1)$ shrinking the size of the resultant matrix by p. In this model, we do not have several hierarchical convolutional layers - instead we apply convolution and max-pooling operations with f filters on the input tweet matrix for different window sizes (l).

The vector representations derived from various window sizes can be interpreted as prominent n-gram word features for the tweets. These features are concatenated to give a vector of size $f \times L$, where L is the number of different l values which is further compressed to a size k before passing it to a fully connected softmax or a sigmoid layer whose output is the probability distribution over different categories of our classification task.

3 Model Training

We trained the CharCNN model and the Word-Embedding convolutional model for different targets and selected the best model for each of them. In our task, the tweets are classified into three categories: Favor, Against, and None. We defined the ground truth vector p as a one-hot vector. The com-

monly used hyperparameters for the convolutional layers of our CharCNN are: $f = 256$, $l = 7$ (first two layers) and $l = 3$ (other 3 layers). The sizes of the fully connected layers in our CharCNN model are 1,024 and 512.

Similarly, the commonly used hyperparameters of the Convolutional Word-Embedding model are: $l = 2, 3, 4$, $f = 200$, $d = 300$, $k = 256$. Softmax layer takes the output from the penultimate layers of the corresponding models, thereby generating a distribution over the three classes in our task. The class with the maximum probability is the label for the given input tweet.

To learn the parameters of the model we minimize the cross-entropy loss as the training objective using the Adam Optimization algorithm (Kingma and Ba, 2014). It is given by

$$CrossEnt(p, q) = - \sum p(x) \log(q(x)) \quad (4)$$

where p is the true distribution (1-of-C representation of ground truth) and q is the output of the softmax. This, in turn, corresponds to computing the negative log-probability of the true class. Each of the classifiers were trained for approximately 8-10 epochs.

In order to deal with the imbalance in the data, we used a simple balancing technique: to choose a sample on each training step, we randomly picked a class and then randomly selected a tweet associated with this class.

4 Training Set Expansion

We expanded the training set by collecting additional tweets for each target-stance pair from the Twitter historical archives. To form a query for the historical API, we automatically selected 40 representative hashtags for each target-stance pair and manually filtered the resulting hashtags lists. The total amount of additional tweets was 1.7 million. Since number of collected tweets vastly exceeded the size of the official dataset, we decided to abstain from using the latter for training and instead use it for validation purposes. For some targets (mentioned in the section 5.2), we augmented the collected set with tweets obtained by replacing some words and phrases with similar ones, using Word2Vec.

4.1 Identifying Representative Hashtags

We found hashtags well-suited for forming a data expansion query. Hashtags are commonly used to represent a "topic" or "theme" of a tweet and thus often convey information of both the target and the stance (e.g. #stophillary2016).

We measured the strength of association between a hashtag and a particular target-stance pair by computing mutual information between them. More precisely, we defined two indicator variables for hashtag occurrences in tweets:

1. Whether the current hashtag is equal to the hashtag of interest.

2. Whether the tweet has the target and the stance of interest.

The mutual information between two random variables is computed as:

$$I(X, Y) = \sum_{x \in X, y \in Y} p(x, y) log \frac{p(x, y)}{p(x)p(y)} \qquad (5)$$

We estimate mutual information between our indicator variables using a Bayesian approach. We find the expected value of mutual information, assuming an uninformed Dirichlet prior on the joint distribution of the two variables. It can be approximately computed using the formula provided in (Hutter, 2002):

$$E[I] \approx \sum_{i,j \in \{0,1\}} \frac{n_{ij}}{n} log \frac{n_{ij}n}{n_{i+}n_{+j}} + \frac{0.5}{n} \qquad (6)$$

Where n_{ij} is the count of samples with indicator variables assuming values i and j respectively, corrected by a pseudo-count of 0.5; $n_{i+} = \sum_j n_{ij}$ and $n_{+j} = \sum_i n_{ij}$.

To get a more reliable estimation of hashtag frequencies for tweets unrelated to the targets, we collected a "background" sample of 1.2 million English-language tweets. We treated these tweets as having no stance in relation to any of the targets and used them in computation of the counts above.

For each target-stance pair, we selected 40 hashtags with highest mutual information for further manual filtering. Samples of selected hashtags can

be seen in Table 1. The manual filtering step was necessary, since the statistical association with a target-stance pair could only serve as a proxy for the fact that the tag explicitly expresses the target and the stance. For example, #tcot (standing for "top conservatives on Twitter") was highly associated with the stance "AGAINST" for the target "Climate Change is a Real Concern", but not explicitly expressing this stance. Although we did not make the identification of representative hashtags completely automatic, we found that hashtag filtering is a very manageable task for the annotator, taking only an hour of time for all five targets, making it an ideal place to introduce minimal human input.

$Target$	$FAVOR\ (F)$	$AGAINST\ (A)$
Abn.	#antichoice	#prolifeyouth
Ath.	#fuckreligion	#teamjesus
Cl. Ch.	#cfcc15	#carbontaxscam
Fem.	#yesallwomen	#gamergate
H. Cl.	#hillary4women	#nohillary2016

Table 1: Samples of representative hashtags

4.2 Collecting and Preprocessing Tweets

$Target$	$FAVOR\ (F)$	$AGAINST\ (A)$
Abortion	23,228	274,769
Atheism	3,041	551,193
Climate Change	355,763	60,238
Feminism	124,760	178,834
Hillary Clinton	40,060	82,294

Table 2: Number of collected tweets per target and stance

As can be seen in Table 2, the collected tweets are very unevenly distributed between target-stance pairs. There are two causes for this: the uneven distribution of different stances on Twitter in general, and uneven number of representative hashtags that we were able to associate with each target-stance pair. For instance, the pair "Climate Change is a Global Concern: AGAINST" was represented by only 15 tweets in the training data that was provided, limiting us to only two representative hashtags. Since our deep learning models require balanced amount of samples, we used the balancing technique described in the previous section.

To eliminate the possibility that resulting classifiers would only learn the hashtags in the query, we removed these hashtags from the majority of the collected tweets, keeping them only in 25% of the tweets.

4.3 Augmenting Data Using Word2Vec

Data augmentation techniques are widely used to enhance generalization of models with respect to input transformations that are known to not affect the output significantly. An example application of data augmentation in NLP can be found in (Zhang and LeCun, 2015), where they used thesaurus-based synonym replacement (WordNet (Fellbaum, 1998)) to generate additional training samples. We applied the technique used by Zhang et al (Zhang and Le-Cun, 2015) to our task, with the difference that we used Word2Vec (Mikolov et al., 2013) instead of a thesaurus to find similar words. The underlying intuition was that Word2Vec can provide better coverage for phrases related to our targets.

The algorithm of the data augmentation is as follows. At every step, we randomly selected a tweet from the non-augmented training set. We sampled a number r of words/phrases we would like to replace from a geometric distribution with parameter p. We then randomly sampled r words/phrases, that are part of the Word2Vec vocabulary from the current tweet. (if r was larger than number of available words/phrases n, we used $r \mod n$.) For each of these words/phrases, we retrieved a list of most similar ones in terms of cosine similarity of Word2Vec vectors. We ordered the list in decreasing order of similarity and truncated it to not include items with similarity less than threshold t. We then sampled index s of selected replacement from another geometric distribution with parameter q (again, we used modulo if s was too big). The original words/phrases were then replaced, and the tweet was added to the augmented dataset. The particular values of p, q and t were 0.5, 0.5 and 0.25 respectively. Using this method, we generated 500,000 extra tweets for each target-stance pair.

5 Evaluation

5.1 Baseline

To have a better sense of our approach's performance, we compared results against a simple baseline. We built a set of Naive Bayes classifiers using bag-of-word features and optimized their pa-

rameters using 20-fold cross validation on original training data. We experimented with different thresholds on word count for a word to be included into vocabulary. We also set up separate thresholds for hashtags and at-mentions. After selecting the most promising values of thresholds, priors and the smoothing parameter, we ran the Naive Bayes classifiers on the test data to obtain results shown in Table 3.

5.2 Validation Results

We trained the models using the collected dataset and validated them on the training set provided for the task. The validation results informed the choice between the word-level and the character-level classifiers for each target. Without Word2Vec augmentation, character-level classifier achieved the best performance only for the target "Feminist Movement". When Word2Vec augmentation was introduced, the character-level model achieved the best performance for the target "Climate Change" and the stance "FAVOR" of the target "Hillary Clinton". The word-level model performed better for the targets: "Legalization of Abortion", "Atheism" and the stance "AGAINST" of the target "Hillary Clinton". We were able to achieve better average performance for the target "Hillary Clinton" by combining character-level and word-level classifiers with a simple heuristic: whenever character-level model

Target	St.	Precision	Recall	F1
Abortion	F	0.44	0.35	0.39
Abortion	A	0.73	0.85	0.79
Atheism	F	0.34	0.28	0.31
Atheism	A	0.79	0.86	0.82
Clinton	F	0.42	0.22	0.29
Clinton	A	0.64	0.90	0.75
Climate	F	0.80	0.73	0.77
Climate	A	N/A	0	N/A
Feminism	F	0.24	0.64	0.35
Feminism	A	0.72	0.43	0.54
All	F	0.44	0.35	0.39
All	A	0.73	0.85	0.79
Macro-Avg	-	0.59	0.64	0.61

Table 3: Baseline performance (Naive Bayes classifiers, test data), St. - Stance

Target	St.	Precision (Word)	Recall (Word)	F1 (Word)	Precision (CharCNN)	Recall (CharCNN)	F1 (CharCNN)
Climate	A	**1.00**	0.27	0.42	0.55	**0.41**	**0.47**
Climate	F	**0.80**	0.67	0.73	0.69	**0.80**	**0.74**
Clinton	A	0.72	**0.83**	**0.77**	**0.76**	0.71	0.73
Clinton	F	**0.63**	0.11	0.18	0.54	**0.46**	**0.50**
Feminism	A	0.71	0.625	0.66	**0.73**	**0.64**	**0.68**
Feminism	F	0.51	0.38	0.44	**0.51**	**0.40**	**0.45**

Table 4: Performance of Word-Level Classifiers for Climate Change, Hillary Clinton and Feminist Movement.

predicts "AGAINST", use that decision, otherwise resort to the decision of word-level model.

Table 4 compares the performance of the character-level and word-level classifiers for the targets where character-level classifiers yielded an advantage. The macro-average F1 validation score was 0.65.

5.3 SemEval Competition Results

Our model was able to achieve a Macro F-score of 0.6354 (placing us eighth out of 19 teams), while the best performing model had a Macro F-score of 0.6782. Table 5 details results on the test data for each target and stance.

Target (rank)	St.	P	R	F1
Abn. (1)	F	0.54	0.67	0.60
	A	0.86	0.54	0.66
Ath. (12)	F	0.33	0.25	0.29
	A	0.82	0.73	0.77
H. Cl (9)	F	0.37	0.53	0.43
	A	0.68	0.66	0.67
Cl. Ch. (12)	F	0.80	0.82	0.81
	A	N/A	0	N/A
Fem. (8)	F	0.37	0.40	0.38
	A	0.79	0.58	0.67
All (8)	F	0.56	0.61	0.58
	A	0.78	0.61	0.68
Macro-Avg	-	0.67	0.61	0.635

Table 5: Results on test data, with rank out of the 19 teams.

6 Discussion and Future Work

An interesting result of our work was that given enough data, character-level models outperformed word-level models for tweet classification (with a dramatic improvement in case of "Hillary Clinton: FAVOR"). Due to the lack of data, it was necessary to resort to a data augmentation technique to generate sufficient amount and diversity of data for character-level model to show its advantage. Another interesting finding from our work is the suitability of word2vec-based substitution as a data augmentation technique. As far as we know, word2vec has not previously been used for data augmentation in this manner.

As can be seen in Table 5, our system did not perform too well for certain target-stance pairs (e.g., Atheism-Against). We hypothesize that the reason for this is the noise and the limited size of the collected training data. Thus, we believe that the performance of the system can be improved through better data expansion and cleaning techniques.

We see several avenues for future improvements. First, it might be beneficial to use unsupervised pre-training for our models (e.g., using autoencoders for Twitter (Vosoughi et al., 2016)). Second, data cleaning can potentially be improved using bootstrapping. This would entail using our current models (optimized for high precision) to gather cleaner data for the second tier of models. It could be repeated while validation performance improves. Finally, because of the constraints of this SemEval task, we did not manually select hashtags or terms commonly associated with target-stance pairs. Inclusion of such hashtags can potentially boost the quality of the dataset, leading to better performance of our models.

References

Ronan Collobert, Jason Weston, Léon Bottou, Michael Karlen, Koray Kavukcuoglu, and Pavel Kuksa. 2011.

Natural language processing (almost) from scratch. *The Journal of Machine Learning Research*, 12:2493–2537.

Christiane Fellbaum. 1998. *WordNet*. Wiley Online Library.

Ross Girshick, Jeff Donahue, Trevor Darrell, and Jitendra Malik. 2014. Rich feature hierarchies for accurate object detection and semantic segmentation. In *Proceedings of the IEEE conference on computer vision and pattern recognition*, pages 580–587.

Geoffrey E Hinton, Nitish Srivastava, Alex Krizhevsky, Ilya Sutskever, and Ruslan R Salakhutdinov. 2012. Improving neural networks by preventing co-adaptation of feature detectors. *arXiv preprint arXiv:1207.0580*.

Marcus Hutter. 2002. Distribution of mutual information. *Advances in neural information processing systems*, 1:399–406.

Diederik Kingma and Jimmy Ba. 2014. Adam: A method for stochastic optimization. *arXiv preprint arXiv:1412.6980*.

Tomas Mikolov, Ilya Sutskever, Kai Chen, Greg S Corrado, and Jeff Dean. 2013. Distributed representations of words and phrases and their compositionality. In *Advances in neural information processing systems*, pages 3111–3119.

Akiko Murakami and Rudy Raymond. 2010. Support or oppose?: classifying positions in online debates from reply activities and opinion expressions. In *Proceedings of the 23rd International Conference on Computational Linguistics: Posters*, pages 869–875. Association for Computational Linguistics.

Swapna Somasundaran and Janyce Wiebe. 2009. Recognizing stances in online debates. In *Proceedings of the Joint Conference of the 47th Annual Meeting of the ACL and the 4th International Joint Conference on Natural Language Processing of the AFNLP: Volume 1-Volume 1*, pages 226–234. Association for Computational Linguistics.

Matt Thomas, Bo Pang, and Lillian Lee. 2006. Get out the vote: Determining support or opposition from congressional floor-debate transcripts. In *Proceedings of the 2006 conference on empirical methods in natural language processing*, pages 327–335. Association for Computational Linguistics.

Soroush Vosoughi, Helen Zhou, and Deb Roy. 2015. Enhanced twitter sentiment classification using contextual information. In *6TH Workshop on Computational Approaches to Subjectivity, Sentiment and Social Media Analysis (WASSA 2015)*, page 16.

Soroush Vosoughi, Prashanth Vijayaraghavan, and Deb Roy. 2016. Tweet2vec: Learning tweet embeddings using character-level cnn-lstm encoder-decoder. In *Proceedings of the 39th International ACM SIGIR Conference on Research and Development in Informaion Retrieval*. ACM.

Xiang Zhang and Yann LeCun. 2015. Text understanding from scratch. *arXiv preprint arXiv:1502.01710*.

NLDS-UCSC at SemEval-2016 Task 6: A Semi-Supervised Approach to Detecting Stance in Tweets

Amita Misra, Brian Ecker, Theodore Handleman, Nicolas Hahn and **Marilyn Walker**
Natural Language and Dialogue Systems Lab
University of California, Santa Cruz
1156 N. High. SOE-3
Santa Cruz, California, 95064, USA
`amisra2|becker|thandlem|nhahn|mawalker@ucsc.edu`

Abstract

Stance classification aims to identify, for a particular issue under discussion, whether the speaker or author of a conversational turn has Pro (Favor) or Con (Against) stance on the issue. Detecting stance in tweets is a new task proposed for SemEval-2016 Task6, involving predicting stance for a dataset of tweets on the topics of abortion, atheism, climate change, feminism and Hillary Clinton. Given the small size of the dataset, our team created our own topic-specific training corpus by developing a set of high precision hashtags for each topic that were used to query the twitter API, with the aim of developing a large training corpus without additional human labeling of tweets for stance. The hashtags selected for each topic were predicted to be stance-bearing on their own. Experimental results demonstrate good performance for our features for opinion-target pairs based on generalizing dependency features using sentiment lexicons.

1 Introduction

Social media websites such as microblogs, weblogs, and discussion forums are used by millions of users to express their opinions on almost everything from brands, celebrities, and events to important social and political issues. In recent years, the microblogging service Twitter has emerged as one of the most popular and useful sources of user content, and recent research has begun to develop tools and computational models for tweet-level opinion and sentiment analysis. Stance classification aims to identify, for a particular issue under discussion, whether the

speaker or author of a conversational turn has a Pro (Favor) or Con (Against) stance on the issue (Somasundaran and Wiebe, 2009; Somasundaran and Wiebe, 2010; Walker et al., 2012c; Sridhar et al., 2015; Hasan and Ng, 2013).

Id	Tweet	Stance
T1	We are causing the ice masses of Earth to melt at an alarming rate.	FAVOR
T2	ONE Volcano emits more pollution than man has in our HISTORY!	AGAINST
T3	It's most exciting to witness a major development!	NONE
T4	The Weather app keeps taunting us with rain. #PNW #drought	NONE

Table 1: Example tweets with stance labels for the issue *Climate Change is a Real Concern*.

Detecting stance in tweets is a new task proposed for SemEval-2016 (Mohammad et al., 2016). The aim of the task is to determine user stance (FAVOR, AGAINST, or NONE) in a dataset of tweets on the five selected topics of abortion, atheism, climate change, feminism and Hillary Clinton. Consider the tweets in Table 1, which express stance toward the target issue *Climate Change is a Real Concern*. It can be inferred that the author of tweet **T1** is in favor of the target while the author of tweet **T2** is clearly against the target. However due to the brevity of tweets, there is not always sufficient information about the target to determine stance: in the case of tweet **T3**, we are unsure what *major development* the user is talking about. In the case of tweet **T4**, we know the user acknowledges the existence of a drought, but we do not know their stance on the issue of climate change solely based on this information. In such cases the stance of the tweets is labelled NONE for

420

this issue.

The task is nontrivial due to the challenges of the tweet genre. Tweets are often highly informal with language that is colorful and ungrammatical. They may also involve sarcasm, making opinion-mining tasks more challenging (Riloff et al., 2013; Reyes et al., 2012). Users may assert their stance using factual or emotional content, and due to their restricted length, tweets may not be well structured or coherent. As a result, NLP tools trained on well-structured text do not work well in Twitter (Dey and Haque, 2008), and new tools are constantly being developed (Qadir and Riloff, 2014; Kong et al., 2014; Han and Baldwin, 2011; Zhu et al., 2014).

Our approach to stance classification in tweets is primarily based on developing a suite of tools for processing Twitter that mirrors our previous work on stance classification in online forums (Walker et al., 2012c; Sridhar et al., 2015; Anand et al., 2011; Walker et al., 2012b; Misra and Walker, 2015). We develop generalized dependency features that capture expressed sentiment or attitude towards particular targets, using the Tweebo dependency parser (Kong et al., 2014). Given the small size of the official task dataset, we created our own topic-specific training corpus in a semi-supervised manner. We developed a set of high precision hashtags for each topic that were used to query the Twitter API in order to create a large training corpus without additional human labeling of tweets for stance. The hashtags and boolean combinations of hashatgs selected for each topic were predicted to be stance-bearing on their own. See Table 2.

There has been considerable previous work on stance classification in online forums and in congressional debates (Thomas et al., 2006; Burfoot et al., 2011; Somasundaran and Wiebe, 2009; Somasundaran and Wiebe, 2010; Walker et al., 2012c; Sridhar et al., 2015; Hasan and Ng, 2013; Boltuzic and Šnajder, 2014; Hasan and Ng, 2014). A number of these studies show that collective classification approaches perform well, and that the context (Walker et al., 2012c; Abbott et al., 2011), and meta information such as author constraints are useful for stance classification (Hassan et al., 2012; Hasan and Ng, 2014). Collective classification is not possible in the current task because the only information provided is the text of each individual

tweet. Inspired by earlier work (Joshi and Penstein-Rosé, 2009; Somasundaran and Wiebe, 2009; Somasundaran and Wiebe, 2010; Walker et al., 2012b), we apply a framework for developing features for opinion-target pairs based on generalized structural dependency features, using the LIWC dictionary as the basis for generalization (Pennebaker et al., 2001). We also develop features to capture domain knowledge using PMI values for topic n-grams in order to improve the recognition of tweets with the NONE stance. We describe our system and data in Sec. 2, our experimental set-up in Sec. 3, and our results and error analysis in Sec. 4. We conclude and discuss future directions in Sec. 5.

2 Data

The relatively small, unbalanced training set provided for the task introduced an interesting subtask for precise topic-oriented tweet collection without direct human annotation. Twitter hashtags provide a method for users to tag their own content by topic, and we exploit this self-annotation to collect a larger dataset for training by hand-selecting seed hashtags for both the FAVOR and AGAINST stances for each topic. We then query Twitter for tweets containing these hashtags using the API, and produce a training set from the results without further supervision. We treat the original SemEval dataset as development data, assuming it is similar to the SemEval test set.

When collecting data in this fashion, there are multiple factors that must be accounted for. These include the accuracy of labels, data uniformity and representativeness, and dataset size. The accuracy of our labels is directly related to the specificity of our hashtags. We perform a small evaluation of each hashtag added to our seed pool by checking it's accuracy on a subset of queried data by hand. With regard to data uniformity and representativeness, we want to ensure that our collected data is not too uniform as a large collection of very similar tweets provides little additional information, and we want to ensure that our data is representative of the actual SemEval data that may be produced from different preprocessing and collection techniques. We evaluate the uniformity and representativeness of our data in Sec. 4.

After we finish collecting data, we create bal-

Topic	Seed Hashtags		Tweets
	FAVOR	**AGAINST**	**#N**
Abortion	#ProChoice, #StandWithPP, #IStandWithPP, #RightTo-Choose	#ProLife, #UnbornLivesMatter, #DefundPP, #PrayToEndAbortion	22194
Atheism	#Awesome$\wedge$atheism, #AtheistVoter, #AntiReligion, #NotAfraidOfBurningInHell	#AntiAtheism, #HolyBible, #God, #PrayerWorks, #PraiseTheLord	11616
Climate Change	#DemandClimateAction, #SaveThePlanet, #ActOnClimate, #GlobalWarmingIsReal	#Lies$\wedge$climate, #Hoax$\wedge$climate, #GlobalWarmingIsALie, #Fraud$\wedge$climate	321
Feminism	#YayFeminism, #YesAllWomen $\wedge$ feminism, #FeministsAreBeautiful	#AntiFeminism, #AntiFeminist, #WomenAgainstFeminism	4446
Hillary Clinton	#ImWithHer, #HillYes, #ITrustHillary, #TeamHillary	#StopHillary, #OhHillNo, #HillNo, #HillaryForPrison, #WhyImNotVotingForHillary	8529

Table 2: Example hashtags and hashtag boolean combinations used to produce training data, and size of the resulting final balanced training dataset.

anced FAVOR, AGAINST, and NONE training sets for each topic. Tweets in the NONE class are collected from other topics or from a corpus of random tweets. A summary of the final seed hashtags and dataset sizes is shown in Table 2.

2.1 Data preprocessing

Since tweets can be noisy, uninformative, or ambiguously labeled, we apply the three filters below to get better quality tweets.

- *Duplicate removal*: Remove all tweets that have an 80% or greater overlap with another already included tweet.

- *Dictionary words*: Tweets with less than 4 dictionary words are excluded. Although this filter may not be appropriate for all tasks as Tweets may incorporate large amounts of non-dictionary slang, we observe that the SemEval training data has few instances that do not pass this test.

- *Favor and Against*: Remove tweets that have both FAVOR and AGAINST hashtags.

2.2 Data Normalization

Tweets can be noisy due to irregular words and other genre specific language. We preprocess all tweets as follows:

- *Repeated characters*: Replace a sequence of repeated characters by two characters. For example, convert "shooooooooot" to "shoot".

- *Lexical variation*: We used the Python Enchant dictionary to determine if a token is a dictionary word. If a token is not present in the dictionary then it is replaced by finding a possible lexical variant using the English Social Media Normalisation Lexicon (Han et al., 2012), for example, *"tmrrw"* is changed to *"tomorrow"*.

We use a part-of-speech tagger for tweets to perform tokenization and POS labelling (Gimpel et al., 2011). We also use TweeboParser, a dependency parser specifically designed for tweets, to parse each tweet (Kong et al., 2014).

Our data representation for the corpus keeps track of the original tweet, the normalization replacements, the POS tags, and the parses. Sec. 3 describes the features derived from these pre-processing steps that we also store in our corpus database, modelled after IAC 2.0. (Abbott et al., 2016).

3 Experimental Setup

We explored a large number of machine learning algorithms and feature combinations, using the automatically harvested tweets as training and the training set provided for the task as our development data to fit the parameters for the final submitted NLDS-UCSC system. Sec. 3.1 describes the feature sets created using the development set. To evaluate the effects of hashtags on the test set we explored two different ways to train the system. Table 4 presents the results on the test set with hashtags present in the dataset while Table 5 is the performance without hashtags.

Topic	Features	Feature Selection	F_score (evaluation metric)		
			favor	against	average
Abortion	unigram, bigram, dep, liwc_dep, opinion_dep	none	0.71	0.64	0.67
Atheism	unigram, bigram, dep, liwc_dep, opinion_dep	correlation	0.73	0.66	0.69
Climate Change	unigram, bigram, liwc_dep, opinion_dep, POS_bigram, POS_trigram, LIWC, high_pmi_n-gram_count, max_pmi, high_pmi_in_topic	gainratio	0.53	0.67	0.60
Feminism	unigram, bigram, dep, liwc_dep, opinion_dep, POS_bigram	correlation	0.55	0.57	0.56
Hillary Clinton	unigram	none	0.63	0.60	0.61

Table 3: Best performing model for each topic on Dev Set w/ hashtags, along with F-measure for favor, against, and their average.

Features	Abortion			Atheism			Climate Change			Feminism			Hillary Clinton		
	favor	against	avg	favor	against	avg	favor	against	avg	favor	against	avg	favor	against	avg
Unigram	0.55	0.72	0.63	0.51	0.77	0.64	0.61	0.22	0.41	0.33	0.64	0.49	0.42	0.73	0.57
All dependencies	0.48	0.68	0.58	0.41	0.76	0.59	0.55	0.16	0.36	0.35	0.61	0.48	0.40	0.66	0.52
POS n-gram	0.40	0.47	0.44	0.36	0.75	0.55	0.58	0.11	0.35	0.26	0.47	0.37	0.31	0.52	0.42
LIWC	0.42	0.44	0.43	0.36	0.66	0.51	0.59	0.18	0.38	0.28	0.49	0.39	0.28	0.42	0.35
PMI	0.40	0.65	0.52	0.32	0.58	0.45	0.52	0.12	0.32	0.30	0.49	0.39	0.1	0.49	0.30
Best model (Dev)	0.52	0.73	0.62	0.43	0.72	0.57	0.69	0.15	0.42	0.36	0.64	0.50	0.42	0.73	0.57

Table 4: Feature ablation w/ hashtags for each topic on Test Set, along with F-measure for favor, against, and their average.

3.1 Features

Unigrams and Bigrams: We extracted unigrams and bigrams from the preprocessed tweets. The useful unigrams are mainly hashtags. We used both stemmed and unstemmed ngrams.

POS bigrams and trigrams: The tweet part-of-speech tagger is used to perform tokenization and POS identification (Gimpel et al., 2011). We then extracted POS bigrams and trigrams as features.

LIWC: We derived features using the Linguistics Inquiry Word Count tool and use the count of words in each category as the feature value (Pennebaker et al., 2001).

Dependency: We used TweeboParser to extract dependency features. For a given tweet, TweeboParser predicts its syntactic structure, represented by unlabeled dependencies (Kong et al., 2014).

Generalized LIWC and Opinion Dependency: We created two kinds of generalized dependency features. Building on the idea that partially generalized dependencies are better than ungeneralized or completely generalized dependencies (Joshi and Penstein-Rosé, 2009), we leave one dependency element lexicalized and generalize the other to its LIWC category for LIWC dependency features. We follow a similar process to produce generalized opinion dependencies using AFINN lexicon and opinion-lexicon-English by (Hu and Liu) replacing one element of the dependency with its sentiment score and leaving the other element lexicalized (Hu and Liu, 2004; Nielsen, 2011). [1] [2]

Inspired by previous work on combining sentiment lexicons we used a combined sentiment score to denote the accuracy of a sentiment word rather than its strength. If dictionaries contradict one another on the sentiment polarity for a word, then the score is neutralized to zero. If a single dictionary lists the polarity word, but it is unlisted or neutral in the other dictionary, then the score is 1 in the direction of the polarity. If both dictionaries list a word with the same polarity, then the score is 2 in the direction of the polarity. After calculating the combined sentiment score, we check if either of the previous two words is listed as a negation by LIWC,

---

[1] `https://www.cs.uic.edu/ liub/FBS /sentiment-analysis.html`
[2] `http://neuro.imm.dtu.dk/wiki/AFINN`

and invert the polarity if a negation is found(Cho et al., 2013; Hasan and Ng, 2012).

Pointwise Mutual Information (PMI): For each topic, we calculate normalized pointwise mutual information over a combination of an extended version of IAC 2.0, a topic annotated database of posts from debate forums (Abbott et al., 2016; Walker et al., 2012a), and our own collected tweets for each topic. IAC 2.0 includes several topics that are in overlap with the topics in the current task.

We then create a pool of top-N percent PMI unigrams, bigrams, and trigrams for each topic and use the count of words in each tweet that are also in this pool as a feature. We also use the highest PMI value of an n-gram in each tweet as a feature.

4   Results

We ran experiments using the SemEval training as our development data with NaiveBayesMultinomial, SVM, and J48 from WEKA. We tried a large number of feature combinations w/ and w/out stemmed n-grams.

The best performing system ended up being different for each topic. Overall, NBM worked the best for all topics. Table 3 describes the system model submitted for each topic based on the results. The model that performed best on the dev set was used to report accuracies on the test set. We present the results on the test set in Table 4. The best performing model from the dev set for the topic of climate control shows a marginal but not significant improvement, and none of the features on their own could beat a unigram baseline for any topic. Since most of the hashatgs are unigrams, we hypothesize this may be due to presence of strong stance-bearing hashtags in the data. In order to assess the issue of strong stance-bearing hashtags still existing in the training data, we remove all hashtags from both the training data and test data and retrain classifiers. See Table 5. For the topic of abortion we see that the combined unigram, bigram, and dependency model now outperforms the unigram model, and the dependencies alone start to edge out an advantage as well, suggesting that it may be the case that strong stance-bearing hashtags distract from and disguise true performance of each feature and potentially the model as a whole.

Feature ablation results reveal that for the majority of the topics part-of-speech n-grams perform better than LIWC. This was surprising because LIWC was designed to capture emotional and psychological behavior in conversations, and because previous research on stance classification using debate forums shows LIWC categories can improve an n-gram baseline (Anand et al., 2011). This may be due to *sarcam and irony*, a frequent phenomena in twitter not captured by LIWC, but which may to some extent be captured by part-of-speech n-grams that reflect the use of adjectives and adverbs in sarcastic posts (Lukin and Walker, 2013; Reyes et al., 2012). Generalizing Twitter-specific dependency structures using LIWC and sentiment lexicons does however prove useful.

4.1   Learning Curves

To asses the usefulness of increasing our training set size we plot learning curves for each topic (abortion shown in Figure 1 and all others in appendix A). For each topic we plot the average f-measure (FAVOR, AGAINST) for a unigram baseline, dependency baseline, and best performing model on the dev set.

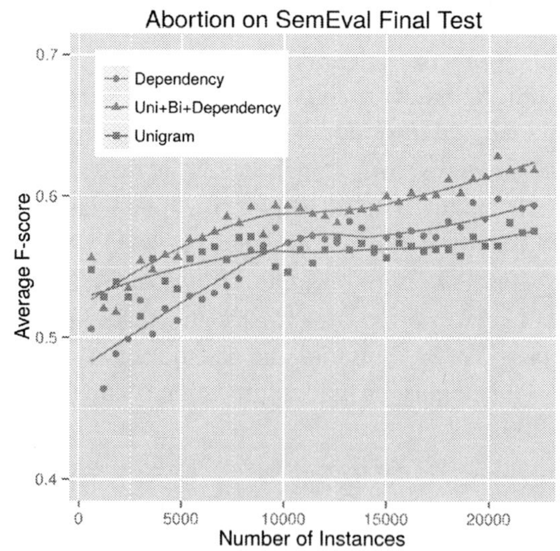

Figure 1:   Training set size vs average Fscore for abortion.

Figure 1 shows that the classifier for the abortion topic gains around 0.6 f-measure when increasing the number of instances from $5,000$ to $20,000$, and it continues to show promise for growth, especially

Features	Abortion			Atheism			Climate Change			Feminism			Hillary Clinton		
	favor	against	avg	favor	against	avg	favor	against	avg	favor	against	avg	favor	against	avg
unigram	0.50	0.70	0.60	0.49	0.77	0.63	0.62	0.20	0.41	0.32	0.63	0.47	0.35	0.67	0.51
All dependencies	0.50	0.71	0.61	0.41	0.77	0.59	0.63	0.12	0.38	0.36	0.62	0.49	0.40	0.68	0.54
POS	0.39	0.44	0.42	0.29	0.70	0.50	0.62	0.09	0.35	0.30	0.48	0.39	0.32	0.5	0.41
POS+Dep	.51	0.73	0.62	0.47	0.81	0.64	0.66	.09	0.38	0.32	0.61	0.46	0.42	0.69	0.56

Table 5: Tweets without hashtags on the Test set, along with F-measure for favor, against and their average.

in terms of the dependency and best model curves. We see a similar promise for growth in the model for Hillary Clinton in which dependencies have just passed unigrams. The differences in learning rate for each topic suggest that the precision of our stance-sided seed hashtags varies largely by topic because similar amounts of data provide less information gain, signaling the data may be of lower quality. In addition to extracting more data for each topic, it would also be helpful to refine our hashtag selection for topics such as atheism, where increase in training set size do not yield performance improvement.

5 Conclusion and Future work

We explore a semi-supervised approach to stance classification using stance-bearing hashtags and achieve reasonable accuracies on a hand-annotated test set. This suggests that our approach of querying using seed hashtags and using some heuristic filters to improve tweet quality may be promising for generating a large corpus of training data. It may also be useful in other domains where hand-annotated data does not exist and getting annotations is time consuming and costly effort. To determine the feasibility of using this semi-supervised data in other domains, we removed all the hashtags from the tweets and again compared the performance of our dependency and unigram features. Table 5 shows that these results look promising. In future work, we hope to use more intelligent features that may capture irony and sarcasm, and we plan to expand and refine our data collection process to account for the varying precision of stance-sided hashtags across topics.

6 Acknowledgments

We are thankful to Yanfei Tu for her help on the project. This work was supported by the Robust Intelligence Program of NSF under Award #IIS-1302668.

References

R Abbott, M Walker, J E. Fox Tree, Pranav Anand, Robeson Bowmani, and Joseph King. 2011. How can you say such things?!?: Recognizing Disagreement in Informal Political Argument. In *Proc of the ACL Workshop on Language and Social Media*.

R Abbott, B Ecker, P Anand, and M Walker. 2016. Internet argument corpus 2.0: An sql schema for dialogic social media and the corpora to go with it. In *Language Resources and Evaluation conf, LREC2016*.

P Anand, M Walker, R Abbott, J E. Fox Tree, Robeson Bowmani, and Michael Minor. 2011. Cats Rule and Dogs Drool: Classifying Stance in Online Debate. In *Proc of the ACL Workshop on Sentiment and Subjectivity*.

Filip Boltuzic and Jan Šnajder. 2014. Back up your stance: Recognizing arguments in online discussions. In *Proc of the First Workshop on Argumentation Mining*, pp 49–58.

Clinton Burfoot, Steven Bird, and Timothy Baldwin. 2011. Collective classification of congressional floor-debate transcripts. In *Association for Computational Linguistics (ACL)*, pp 1506–1515.

Heeryon Cho, Jong-Seok Lee, and Songkuk Kim. 2013. Enhancing lexicon-based review classification by merging and revising sentiment dictionaries. In *Sixth Inte Joint Conf on Natural Language Processing, IJCNLP 2013, 2013*, pp 463–470.

Lipika Dey and S K Mirajul Haque. 2008. Opinion mining from noisy text data. In *Proc of the Second Workshop on Analytics for Noisy Unstructured Text Data, AND '08*, pp 83–90, ACM.

Kevin Gimpel, Nathan Schneider, Brendan O'Connor, Dipanjan Das, Daniel Mills, Jacob Eisenstein, Michael Heilman, Dani Yogatama, Jeffrey Flanigan, and Noah A Smith. 2011. Part-of-speech tagging for twitter: Annotation, features, and experiments. In *Proc of the 49th Annual Meeting of the Assoc for Compu-*

tational Linguistics: Human Language Technologies: short papers-Volume 2, pp 42–47.

Bo Han and Timothy Baldwin. 2011. Lexical normalisation of short text messages: Makn sens a# twitter. In *Proc of the 49th Annual Meeting of the Association for Computational Linguistics: Human Language Technologies-Volume 1*, pp 368–378. Association for Computational Linguistics.

Bo Han, Paul Cook, and Timothy Baldwin. 2012. Automatically constructing a normalisation dictionary for microblogs. In *Proc of the 2012 Joint conf on Empirical Methods in Natural Language Processing and Computational Natural Language Learning*, EMNLP-CoNLL '12, pp 421–432.

Kazi Saidul Hasan and Vincent Ng. 2012. Predicting stance in ideological debate with rich linguistic knowledge. In *Proc of COLING 2012: Posters*, pp 451–460.

Kazi Saidul Hasan and Vincent Ng. 2013. Stance classification of ideological debates: Data, models, features, and constraints. page 1348–1356.

Kazi Saidul Hasan and Vincent Ng. 2014. Why are you taking this stance? identifying and classifying reasons in ideological debates. In *Proc of the Conf on Empirical Methods in Natural Language Processing*.

Ahmed Hassan, Amjad Abu-Jbara, and Dragomir Radev. 2012. Detecting subgroups in online discussions by modeling positive and negative relations among participants. In *Proc of the 2012 Joint Conf on Empirical Methods in Natural Language Processing and Computational Natural Language Learning*.

Minqing Hu and Bing Liu. 2004. Mining and summarizing customer reviews. In *Proc of the Tenth ACM SIGKDD International conf on Knowledge Discovery and Data Mining*, KDD '04, pp 168–177.

M. Joshi and C. Penstein-Rosé. 2009. Generalizing dependency features for opinion mining. In *Proc of the ACL-IJCNLP 2009 conf Short Papers*, pp 313–316.

Lingpeng Kong, Nathan Schneider, Swabha Swayamdipta, Archna Bhatia, Chris Dyer, and Noah A Smith. 2014. A dependency parser for tweets. In *In Proc. of EMNLP*. Citeseer.

Stephanie Lukin and Marilyn Walker. 2013. Really? well, Apparently bootstrapping improves the performance of sarcasm and nastiness classifiers for online dialogue. *NAACL 2013*, page 30.

Amita Misra and Marilyn A Walker. 2015. Topic independent identification of agreement and disagreement in social media dialogue. In *Proc of the SIGDIAL 2013 conf: The 15th Annual Meeting of the Special Interest Group on Discourse and Dialogue*.

Saif M. Mohammad, Svetlana Kiritchenko, Parinaz Sobhani, Xiaodan Zhu, and Colin Cherry. 2016. Semeval-2016 task 6: Detecting stance in tweets. In *Proc of the Inte Workshop on Semantic Evaluation*, SemEval.

Finn Årup Nielsen. 2011. A new ANEW: evaluation of a word list for sentiment analysis in microblogs. In Matthew Rowe, Milan Stankovic, Aba-Sah Dadzie, and Mariann Hardey, editors, *Proc of the ESWC2011 Workshop on 'Making Sense of Microposts': Big things come in small packages*, 718 of *CEUR Workshop Proc*, pp 93–98.

J. W. Pennebaker, L. E. Francis, and R. J. Booth, 2001. *LIWC: Linguistic Inquiry and Word Count*.

Ashequl Qadir and Ellen Riloff. 2014. Learning emotion indicators from tweets: Hashtags, hashtag patterns, and phrases. In *Proc of the conf on Empirical Methods in Natural Language Processing (EMNLP), Association for Computational Linguistics*, pp 1203–1209.

A. Reyes, P. Rosso, and D. Buscaldi. 2012. From humor recognition to irony detection: The figurative language of social media. *Data & Knowledge Engineering*.

Ellen Riloff, Ashequl Qadir, Prafulla Surve, Lalindra De Silva, Nathan Gilbert, and Ruihong Huang. 2013. Sarcasm as contrast between a positive sentiment and negative situation. In *Proc of the 2013 conf on Empirical Methods in Natural Language Processing*.

S. Somasundaran and J. Wiebe. 2009. Recognizing stances in online debates. In *Proc of the 47th Annual Meeting of the ACL*, pp 226–234.

S. Somasundaran and J. Wiebe. 2010. Recognizing stances in ideological on-line debates. In *Proc of the NAACL HLT 2010 Workshop on Computational Approaches to Analysis and Generation of Emotion in Text*, pp 116–124.

Dhanya Sridhar, James Foulds, Bert Huang, Lise Getoor, and Marilyn Walker. 2015. Joint models of disagreement and stance in online debate. In *Annual Meeting of the Ass for Computational Linguistics (ACL)*.

M. Thomas, B. Pang, and L. Lee. 2006. Get out the vote: Determining support or opposition from Congressional floor-debate transcripts. In *Proc of the 2006 conf on empirical methods in natural language processing*, pp 327–335.

Marilyn Walker, Pranav Anand, Robert Abbott, and Jean E. Fox Tree. 2012a. A corpus for research on deliberation and debate. In *Language Resources and Evaluation conf, LREC2012*.

Marilyn A Walker, Pranav Anand, Rob Abbott, Jean E Fox Tree, Craig Martell, and Joseph King. 2012b. That is your evidence?: Classifying stance in online political debate. *Decision Support Systems*, 53(4):719–729.

Marilyn A Walker, Pranav Anand, Robert Abbott, and Ricky Grant. 2012c. Stance classification using dialogic properties of persuasion. In *Proc of the 2012 conf of the North American Chapter of the Association for Computational Linguistics: Human Language Technologies*, pp 592–596.

Xiaodan Zhu, Svetlana Kiritchenko, and Saif M Mohammad. 2014. Nrc-canada-2014: Recent improvements in the sentiment analysis of tweets. In *Proc of the 8th Inter Workshop on Semantic Evaluation (SemEval 2014)*, pp 443–447.

A   Appendix: Learning Curves

Below we show the learning curves for each topic on the SemEval test data after removing hashtags from both the train and test sets. Climate change is excluded due to the small number of training instances. Each graph includes a line for unigrams, dependencies, and the best model on the dev set (unigrams are the best model for the Hillary Clinton topic).

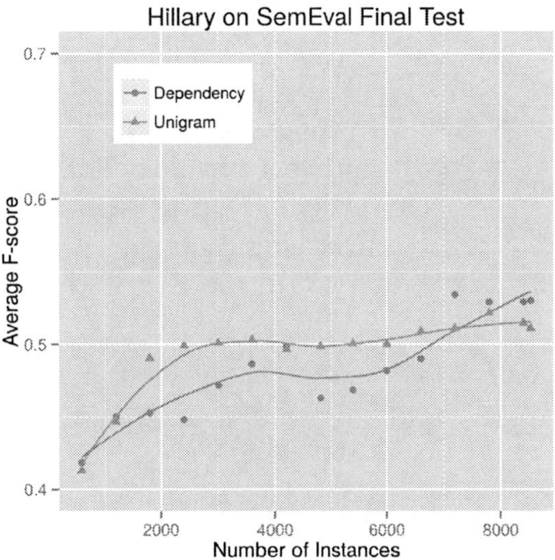

Figure 3: Training set size vs average Fscore for Hillary Clinton

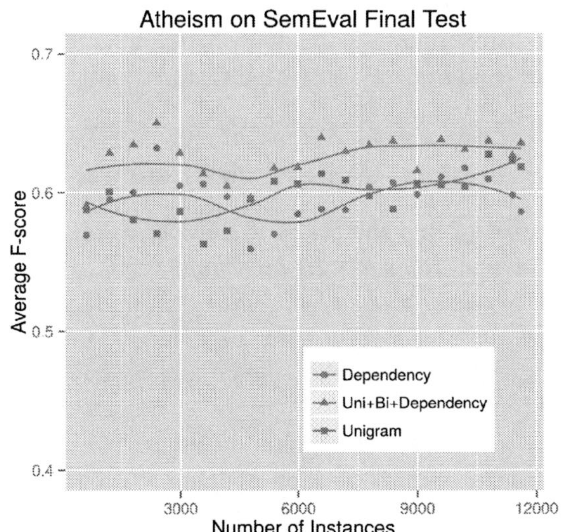

Figure 2: Training set size vs average Fscore for Atheism

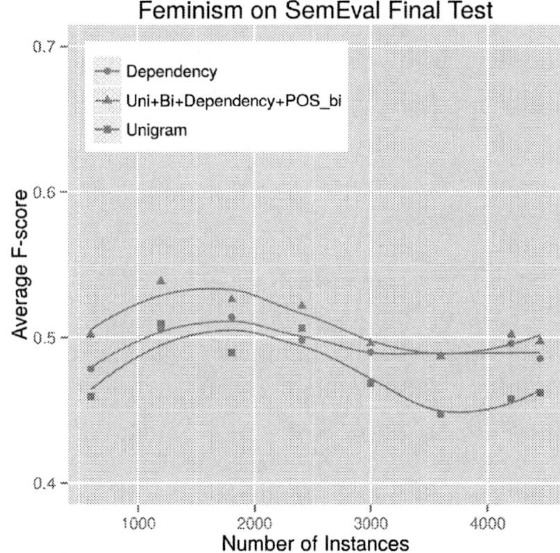

Figure 4: Training set size vs average Fscore for Feminism

ltl.uni-due at SemEval-2016 Task 6: Stance Detection in Social Media Using Stacked Classifiers

Michael Wojatzki
Language Technology Lab
University of Duisburg-Essen
Duisburg, Germany
michael.wojatzki@uni-due.de

Torsten Zesch
Language Technology Lab
University of Duisburg-Essen
Duisburg, Germany
torsten.zesch@uni-due.de

Abstract

In this paper, we describe our participation in the first shared task on automated stance detection (*SemEval 2016 Task 6*). We consider the task as a multidimensional classification problem and thus use a sequence of stacked classifiers. For subtask A, we utilize a rich feature set that does not rely on external information such as additional tweets or knowledge bases. For subtask B, we rely on the similarity of tweets in this task with tweets from subtask A in order to transfer the models learnt in subtask A.

1 Introduction

Stance-taking is an essential and frequently observed part of online debates and other related forms of social media interaction (Somasundaran and Wiebe, 2009; Anand et al., 2011). In the *SemEval 2016 Task 6: Detecting Stance in Tweets* (Mohammad et al., 2016), stance is defined relative to a given target like a politician or a controversial topic. A text can then either be in favor of the given target (FAVOR), or against it (AGAINST). As the dataset also contains texts without a stance, we additionally have to deal with the the the class NONE.

Being able to automatically detect and classify stance in social media is important for a deeper understanding of debates and would thus be a great tool for information seekers such as researchers, journalists, customers, users, companies, or governments. In addition, such analysis could help to create summaries, develop a deeper understanding of online debating behavior, identify social or political groups, or even adjust recommendations to users' standpoints (Anand et al., 2011; Sridhar et al., 2014; Boltuzic and Šnajder, 2014).

In the following, we describe our system for stance detection. We did not make use of any sources of external information such as additional tweets or stance knowledge bases, as our goal was to rely only on the provided training data. Since the task allowed just for one submission, we include some further analysis that will shed light on the usefulness and impact of the used features and parameters.

2 Subtask A – Supervised Framework

The goal of this subtask is to classify tweets about five targets: *Atheism, Climate Change is a Real Concern, Feminist Movement, Hillary Clinton,* and *Legalization of Abortion*. For each target, there are about 400-600 manually labeled tweets that can be used for training.

As the targets are quite different, we train a separate classifier for each of them. Additionally, we split the three-way classification into a stacked classification, in which we first classify whether the tweet contains any stance (classes FAVOR and AGAINST) or no stance at all (class NONE). In a second step, we classify the tweets labeled as containing a stance as FAVOR or AGAINST. This sequence of classifications is visualized in Figure 1.

All shown classifications are implemented using the DKPro TC framework[1] (Daxenberger et al., 2014) and utilize the integrated Weka SVM classifier.

---
[1] version 0.8.0-SNAPSHOT

Proceedings of SemEval-2016, pages 428–433,
San Diego, California, June 16-17, 2016. ©2016 Association for Computational Linguistics

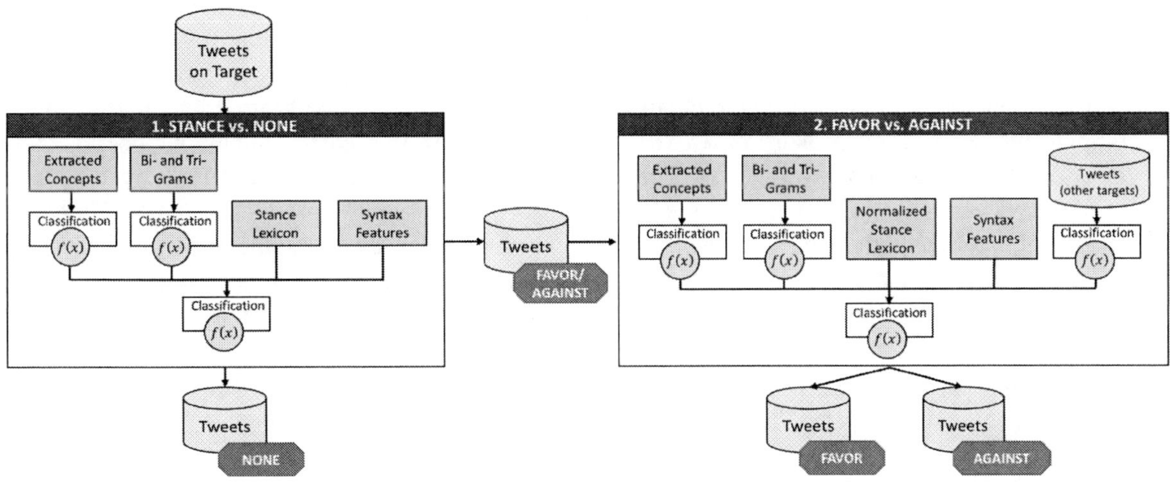

Figure 1: Overview on the sequence of stacked classifications that is used for the supervised setting (subtask A)

2.1 Preprocessing

We use the DKPro Core framework[2] (Eckart de Castilho and Gurevych, 2014) for preprocessing. We apply the twitter-specific tokenizer Twokenizer[3] (Gimpel et al., 2011), the DKPro default sentence splitter, and the Arktweet Pos tagger[4] (Gimpel et al., 2011).

As the Arktweet PoS tagger has a special tag for hashtags, even syntactically integrated hashtags like in *I like #Hillary !* would be assigned the tag *hashtag*. Since our feature set relies on the syntactic role of the used words (e.g. nouns as the subject or object of an proposition), we only keep hashtag labels that occur at the end of a tweet. For all other hashtags, we additionally apply the OpenNlp PoS tagger[5] and overwrite the hashtag label with the syntactic category.

Afterwards, we annotate a fixed set of negations (*not, no, none, nor, never, nobody, neither, nowhere*) including contractions such as *can't, aren't*. Finally, we annotate modal verbs (*can, could, may, might, must, shall, should, will, would*).

2.2 Features

Figure 1 shows that both classifications use roughly the same feature set. However, the FAVOR vs.

AGAINST classification additionally uses a feature that transfers models learnt from other targets. In the following, we describe all features in detail, explain how they may relate to stance taking language, and outline differences in both classifications.

N-Gram Features We use the 500 most frequent *bi-*and *trigrams* as binary features to capture expressions that are longer than single words. Thereby we want to approximate multi word expressions such as *climate change*. As the resulting 500 features would outnumber the other features, we use stacking to classify according to the n-gram features only and use the outcome as a single feature in the overall model. Note that we handle *unigrams* by using an automatically created stance lexicon.

Syntactic Features According to Faulkner (2014), the usage of conditional sentences and modal verbs may indicate stance taking behavior. Hence, we use the number of sentences starting with *if* and the occurrence of modal verbs as a feature. As stance-taking behavior may be indicated by the usage of exclamation- and question marks (Anand et al., 2011), we use as a feature the overall counts as well as the count of over-usage like *???* or *!?!*. Finally, we use as a feature the number of negation markers in a tweet.

Stance-lexicon Features For each target, we create a unigram stance lexicon by computing their statistical association with one of the outcome val-

---

[2]version 1.7.0
[3]version 0.3.2
[4]version 0.3.2
[5]*maxent* model in version 3.0.3

ues. This feature is inspired by the work of Somasundaran and Wiebe (2010) who use a subjectivity lexicon that was created by using the statistical association with negative and positive argumentation. We compute the association measure *gmean* (Evert, 2004) of every unigram towards the two poles (FAVOR/AGAINST or STANCE/NONE) and then use the difference between both values as the stance score s. The *gmean* association of a word x with a polarity class $+$ is computed as:

$$gmean_+(x) = \frac{c_+(x)}{\sqrt{c_+(x) \cdot c_-(x)}} \quad (1)$$

where $c_+(x)$ is the count of x in $+$ and $c_-(x)$ is the count of x in $-$. Based on the computed stance lexicon, we calculate the final polarity of as the normalized sum over the stance score s for each token in a tweet. In contrast to the mere use of *unigram* features the resulting lexicon has the advantage that it can distinguish between words that indicate stance with varying strengths.

As a defining feature of social media is the frequent usage of nonstandard spelling, we use text normalization in order to make this feature more robust. We first lowercase all tokens, remove @- and #-prefixes, and lemmatize plurals. For tokens that still do not appear in our stance lexicon, we compute the normalized *Levensthein* edit distance (implemented using the DKPro Similarity (Bär et al., 2013)) and use the largest score if the value is smaller than .15. However, the normalization is only applied for the STANCE vs. NONE classification, since we observed that even capitalization can be a signal for being in favor or against a certain target.

In addition to unigram stance lexicons, we create a hashtag stance lexicon by using the same methodology, but just considering the tokens with the hashtag PoS tag (see Section 2.1).

Concept Features When analyzing the data, we observed that each target is associated with a few concepts that are subject of a controversial debate. Whereas the stance lexicon models words that are highly associated with one class, these words are associated with both classes. Since they are used by authors of different stances, they can be be considered as being central for the debate. In order to retrieve the most central concepts, we select the top

12 nouns from each target. These candidates are then normalized (in the same fashion as described above) and cleaned for concepts that are not controversial (i.e. they are only used by authors with the same stance). For reasons of automation, no manual revision of concepts (e.g. handling words that are parts of multiword expressions such as *climate* and *change* or terms that are semantically related such as *feminist* and *feminism*) had been done. The remaining concepts are shown in Table 1.

For these concepts we learn, whether they express being in favor or against (respectively a stance at all) depending on their context. In order to model the context, the classifiers are equipped with n-gram features (*top 200 uni-, bi-, trigrams*). Finally, the prediction of these concept-classifiers is used as a feature.

Target Transfer Features Some targets appear to have a certain thematic overlap (e.g. there seems to be an overlap between *Legalization of Abortion* and *Feminist Movement* because both concern the rights of women). For example, consider a tweet about the target *Feminist Movement* that contains a stance towards abortion. If we want to classify the stance towards *Feminist Movement* it seems naturally to incorporate the stance towards abortion. This idea is modeled by applying models to a target that have been trained on a different target. The resulting classification is then used as a feature.

We only apply this feature if the tweet has a minimal topical overlap with one of the other targets domains. We found that on the training data, it works best if a tweet is related to a target if it contains one of the top 60 frequent nouns or named entities for some target domain (see also Section 3).

As shown in figure 1, this feature is only used for the AGAINST vs. FAVOR classification. On the training data, this feature only had an impact for the targets *Climate Change is a Real Concern*, *Hillary Clinton* and *Legalization of Abortion*. Thus, we only apply it for these targets on the test data, too.

2.3 Results

We report gained results on the provided test data using the official metric that is the macro-average of $F_1(\text{FAVOR})$ and $F_1(\text{AGAINST})$. As shown in the first row of Table 2, our system achieved a score of

Atheism	Climate Change	Feminist Movement	Hillary Clinton	Abortion
day	change	equality	campaign	abortion
death	climate	feminism	candidate	baby
faith	summer	feminist	country	body
god		gamergate	hillary	child
life		gender	hillaryclinton	choice
religion		male	president	life
		man	support	time
		rape	time	woman
		time	vote	
		woman	woman	

Table 1: Extracted concepts for which a separate classifier is trained

.62. This corresponds to rank 12 in the official ranking (Mohammad et al., 2016). The performance of our system varies significantly between the different targets. For instance, the difference between the classification of the target *Legalization of Abortion* and *Climate Change is a Real Concern* is about 20 percent points.

In order to analyze the impact of the used features, we conducted an ablation test. The results in Table 2 show that the stance lexicon is the only feature that has a significant impact on all targets. The concept features seem to be helpful for some targets. When training a model with only those two features, we reach a score of .65 (whole test data) compared to .62 when using all features.

3 Subtask B – Weakly Supervised Framework

There is no training data for subtask B, so this has to be tackled in an unsupervised or weakly supervised fashion. The target is *Donald Trump* and participants are provided with large corpus (about 78 000 tweets) of un-annotated tweets.

Our approach for task B works in two stages (in analogy to task A): First, in order to determine whether a tweet has any stance at all, we compare each tweet with the whole collection. We found on subtask A, that if one filters all tweets that do not contain one of the n most frequent nouns or named entities of the target, the majority of the remaining tweets have a stance. Of course, larger values for n will improve recall on the cost of precision. As the second classification (FAVOR vs. AGAINST)

depends on a high precision, we decided to use a threshold that assigns a higher weight to precision. We empirically found that $n = 60$ works well on subtask A. Tweets that are not similar are treated as NONE from here on.

Second, we select all targets (from Subtask A) that are most similar to a tweet. If a tweet is not similar to any target, we considered its stance as UNKNOWN from here on. If a target is selected, we use the model that has been trained on it to classify the tweet. This is the weakly-supervised part, as we apply a model that is trained on a different target.

There is one additional complication: One may argue that there is an inverse relationship between the stances of subtask A and the target *Donald Trump*. For instance, if a tweet is in favor of *Hillary Clinton*, there is a high likelihood that the tweet is implicitly against *Donald Trump*. A similar relation may be assumed for the other targets or at least for the majority of his supporters. Consequently, all classifications are inverted (AGAINST becomes FAVOR and FAVOR becomes AGAINST) and summed up. The final decision is then made on the majority vote. In case there are as much votes for FAVOR as for AGAINST we assume that the stance is UNKNOWN.

Results Our approach yields a score of .26 which corresponds to the 11th rank. However, this is inferior to the the performance of the base-rate (AGAINST) which is about .3. This suggests that the made assumptions (e.g. inverse relationship between stances of subtask A and B, majority vote of classifiers) are not optimal.

	All	Atheism	Climate Change	Feminist Movement	Hillary Clinton	Abortion
all features (SemEval Submission)	.62	.53	.36	.55	.44	.57
- stance lexicon	.54	.48	.29	.50	.41	.46
- concepts	.62	.52	.35	.54	.46	.58
- negation	.62	.55	.36	.55	.44	.57
- target transfer	.62	.53	.35	.55	.46	.58
- punctuation	.62	.56	.35	.55	.47	.57
- conditional sentences	.63	.58	.36	.55	.44	.60
- modal verbs	.63	.58	.36	.55	.44	.60
- n-grams	.64	.59	.38	.56	.51	.58

Table 2: Ablation test of the feature set on the test data

4   Conclusion

In this paper, we presented our approach on automated stance detection based on stacked classifications. We split the three-way classification into a first classifier deciding whether there is any stance at all, and a second classifier that only makes a decision about the polarity of a tweet with a stance. Overall, we found a significant variation in performance across the targets and even between train and test data. An ablation test shows that from our rich feature set, only the automatically derived *stance lexicon* feature has a significant impact.

In general, our system (as well as all other participating systems) leaves much room for improvement. Stance detection could probably benefit from more semantically oriented features that go beyond the surface form of words.

Acknowledgments

We would like to thank the the organizers of the SemEval task 6 for this interesting task and the three annonymous reviewers for their helpful comments. This work was supported by the Deutsche Forschungsgemeinschaft (DFG) under grant No. GRK 2167, Research Training Group "User-Centred Social Media".

References

Pranav Anand, Marilyn Walker, Rob Abbott, Jean E Fox Tree, Robeson Bowmani, and Michael Minor. 2011. Cats rule and dogs drool!: Classifying stance in on-line debate. In *Proceedings of the 2nd workshop on computational approaches to subjectivity and senti-ment analysis*, pages 1–9. Association for Computational Linguistics.

Daniel Bär, Torsten Zesch, and Iryna Gurevych. 2013. Dkpro similarity: An open source framework for text similarity. In *ACL (Conference System Demonstrations)*, pages 121–126.

Filip Boltuzic and Jan Šnajder. 2014. Back up your stance: Recognizing arguments in online discussions. In *Proceedings of the First Workshop on Argumentation Mining*, pages 49–58. Association for Computational Linguistics.

Johannes Daxenberger, Oliver Ferschke, Iryna Gurevych, and Torsten Zesch. 2014. Dkpro tc: A java-based framework for supervised learning experiments on textual data. In *Proceedings of 52nd Annual Meeting of the Association for Computational Linguistics: System Demonstrations*, pages 61–66, Baltimore, Maryland, June. Association for Computational Linguistics.

Richard Eckart de Castilho and Iryna Gurevych. 2014. A broad-coverage collection of portable nlp components for building shareable analysis pipelines. In *Proceedings of the Workshop on Open Infrastructures and Analysis Frameworks for HLT*, pages 1–11, Dublin, Ireland, August. Association for Computational Linguistics and Dublin City University.

Stefan Evert. 2004. *The Statistics of Word Cooccurrences: Word Pairs and Collocations*. Ph.D. thesis, IMS, University of Stuttgart.

Adam Faulkner. 2014. Automated classification of stance in student essays: An approach using stance target information and the wikipedia link-based measure. In *Proceedings of the 27th International Florida Artificial Intelligence Research Society Conference*, pages 174–179.

Kevin Gimpel, Nathan Schneider, Brendan O'Connor, Dipanjan Das, Daniel Mills, Jacob Eisenstein, Michael Heilman, Dani Yogatama, Jeffrey Flanigan, and Noah A Smith. 2011. Part-of-speech tagging for twitter: Annotation, features, and experiments. In *Pro-

ceedings of the 49th Annual Meeting of the Association for Computational Linguistics: Human Language Technologies: short papers-Volume 2, pages 42–47. Association for Computational Linguistics.

Saif M. Mohammad, Svetlana Kiritchenko, Parinaz Sobhani, Xiaodan Zhu, and Colin Cherry. 2016. Semeval-2016 task 6: Detecting stance in tweets. In *Proceedings of the International Workshop on Semantic Evaluation*, SemEval '16, San Diego, California, June.

Swapna Somasundaran and Janyce Wiebe. 2009. Recognizing stances in online debates. In *Proceedings of the Joint Conference of the 47th Annual Meeting of the ACL and the 4th International Joint Conference on Natural Language Processing of the AFNLP: Volume 1-Volume 1*, pages 226–234. Association for Computational Linguistics.

Swapna Somasundaran and Janyce Wiebe. 2010. Recognizing stances in ideological on-line debates. In *Proceedings of the NAACL HLT 2010 Workshop on Computational Approaches to Analysis and Generation of Emotion in Text*, pages 116–124. Association for Computational Linguistics.

Dhanya Sridhar, Lise Getoor, and Marilyn Walker. 2014. Collective stance classification of posts in online debate forums. *ACL Joint Workshop on Social Dynamics and Personal Attributes in Social Media*, page 109.

CU-GWU Perspective at SemEval-2016 Task 6: Ideological Stance Detection in Informal Text

Heba Elfardy
Department of Computer Science
Columbia University
New York, NY
heba@cs.columbia.edu

Mona Diab
Department of Computer Science
The George Washington University
Washington, DC
mtdiab@gwu.edu

Abstract

We present a supervised system that uses lexical, sentiment, semantic dictionaries and latent and frame semantic features to identify the stance of a tweeter towards an ideological target. We evaluate the performance of the proposed system on subtask A in SemEval-2016 Task 6: "Detecting Stance in Tweets". The system yields an average $F_{\beta=1}$ score of 63.6% on the task's test set and has been ranked the 6th by the task organizers out of 19 judged systems.

1 Introduction & Background

Automatically identifying a person's ideological stance (or perspective) from written text is quite a challenging research problem that finds applications spanning from enhancing advertisements targeting to planning political campaigns. From a computational viewpoint, perspective detection is closely related to subjectivity and sentiment analysis. A person's perspective normally influences his/her sentiment towards different topics or targets. Conversely identifying the sentiment of a person towards multiple targets can serve as a cue for identifying his/her perspective. While from a social-science viewpoint, the notion of "perspective" is related to the concept of "framing". Framing involves making some topics (or some aspects of the discussed topics) more prominent in order to promote the views and interpretations of the writer (communicator). The communicator can either make these framing decisions consciously or unconsciously (Entman, 1993).

In this paper, we present a system that employs lexical and semantic features to identify the stance of a person – "Favor", "Against" or "None"– on topics that are often backed up by one's ideology or belief system such as abortion, climate change and feminism. We evaluate the performance of the proposed system through the participation in Sub-Task A "Supervised Framework" of SemEval Task 6 "Detecting Stance in Tweets". (Mohammad et al., 2016)

We build on our previous work on automatic perspective detection (Elfardy et al., 2015) by exploring the use of sentiment, Linguistic Inquiry and Word Count (LIWC) dictionaries, frame and latent semantics in addition to standard lexical features to automatically classify a given tweet according to its stance on the topic of interest.

Most current computational linguistics research on supervised stance detection performs document (or post) level stance classification, whether binary or multiway and use a variety of lexical, syntactic and semantic features to identify the stance of a post towards a specific contentious topic/target such as the Israeli-Palestinian conflict, abortion, creationism, gun-rights, gay-rights, healthcare, legalization of marijuana and death penalty (Lin et al., 2006; Klebanov et al., 2010; Hasan and NG, 2012; Hasan and Ng, 2013; Somasundaran and Wiebe, 2010; Elfardy et al., 2015). For a detailed literature review, we direct the reader to our *Sem paper. (Elfardy et al., 2015)

2 Shared Task Description

SemEval Task 6 "Detecting Stance in Tweets" (Mohammad et al., 2016) aims at evaluating how well an automated system can identify the stance of a

434

Proceedings of SemEval-2016, pages 434–439,
San Diego, California, June 16-17, 2016. ©2016 Association for Computational Linguistics

	Training					Held-Out Test				
	Abortion	Atheism	Climate	Clinton	Feminism	Abortion	Atheism	Climate	Clinton	Feminism
Favor	105	92	212	112	210	46	32	123	45	58
Against	334	304	15	361	328	189	160	11	172	183
None	164	117	168	166	126	45	28	35	78	44
All	603	513	395	639	664	280	220	169	295	285

Table 1: Number of tweets per class in the training and test data.

tweeter on several contentious targets. Sub-Task A "Supervised Framework" of the task –in which we participate– focuses on five targets: "Atheism", "Climate Change is a Real Concern", "Feminist Movement", "Hillary Clinton", and "Legalization of Abortion". The training data has a total of 2,814 tweets and the test data has 1,249 tweets. While each tweet can have one of three class labels "Favor", "Against" or "None", the official metric calculates the performance of each system as the average $F_{\beta=1}$ score of the first two class labels only. Table 1 shows the distribution of the training and test data for each one of the five targets.

3 Approach

Our goal is to see how well lexical and semantic features can help in identifying the stance of a tweeter. We split the data into five subsets according to the target –"Atheism", "Climate Change is a Real Concern", "Feminist Movement", "Hillary Clinton", and "Legalization of Abortion'– and train a separate classifier for each one of these targets.

3.1 Lexical Features

For lexical features, we use standard n-grams. We apply basic preprocessing to the text by removing all punctuation and numbers and converting all words to lower case. Converting the text to lower case is intended to reduce the sparseness of the data while excluding the punctuation and number is meant to avoid overfitting the training data. We use n-grams having a length between 1 and 3 and exclude the ones that occur in only one training instance.

3.2 Latent Semantics

Latent Semantics map text from a high-dimensional space such as n-grams to a low-dimensional one such as topics. Most of these models assign a semantic profile to each given sentence (or document) by considering the observed words and assuming that each given document has a distribution over K topics. We apply Weighted Textual Matrix Factorization (WTMF) (Guo and Diab, 2012) to each tweet. The advantage WTMF offers –over standard topic models– is that in addition to modeling observed words, it models missing ones. WTMF defines missing words as the whole vocabulary of the training data minus the ones observed in the given tweet/post. Modeling missing words is particularly useful when the input is very short in length because in such case, only a limited context of observed words is present.

We use the distributable version of WTMF which is trained on WordNet (Fellbaum, 2010), Wiktionary definitions[1] and the Brown Corpus[2] and sets the number of topics (K) to 100.

3.3 Sentiment

As mentioned earlier, sentiment analysis is closely related to stance detection. The ideological stance of a person normally influences his/her sentiment towards different ideological topics. Accordingly we decide to identify the overall sentiment of each sentence in the given tweet and use this sentiment as a possible indicator of a tweeter's stance. Our assumption is that since tweets are inherently short in length, we can assume that the expressed sentiment targets the ideological topic the tweet is discussing. We use Stanford's sentiment analysis system (Socher et al., 2013) to identify the number of positive, negative and neutral sentences in a given tweet and use these three counts as features for our

---

[1] http://en.wiktionary.org
[2] http://en.wikipedia.org/wiki/Brown\
_Corpus

	Training					Held-Out Test				
	Abortion	Atheism	Climate	Clinton	Feminism	Abortion	Atheism	Climate	Clinton	Feminism
Feeling	8.93	5.83	7.56	8.58	10.21	7.45	6.31	6.43	11.45	7.32
Biological Pr.	2.81	4.08	12.85	4.68	5.41	3.55	4.5	8.77	4.04	5.92
Body	49.59	27.77	18.14	18.1	34.98	54.26	26.58	16.37	9.76	32.4
Health	12.07	8.74	6.05	6.55	12.31	11.7	6.76	6.43	3.7	13.94
Sexual	35.37	10.1	7.56	4.06	6.31	41.13	11.26	2.92	3.37	5.23
Ingestion	30.74	9.13	2.02	7.96	20.87	30.14	10.36	4.09	3.03	16.72
Relativity	1.32	3.5	5.29	2.03	4.05	1.06	1.8	5.85	2.02	4.88
Motion	73.39	76.5	84.89	73.17	69.97	71.99	73.87	83.04	73.74	73.17
Relativity	15.7	22.14	27.71	23.09	17.27	13.48	22.07	36.26	22.22	21.6
Space	48.93	54.37	59.45	46.96	46.1	50.35	50	60.82	44.78	46.34
Time	45.62	41.36	51.64	43.53	42.19	42.55	41.89	49.12	42.42	47.74
Work	16.2	20.39	25.94	30.42	20.42	16.31	21.62	21.64	34.01	14.98
Achievement	20.66	33.98	29.47	27.77	19.97	20.57	27.93	17.54	28.62	19.86
Leisure	6.61	11.65	9.82	10.76	21.92	10.28	13.51	8.77	9.76	17.77
Home	3.14	2.72	6.55	3.28	5.41	2.48	2.7	9.94	4.04	5.57
Money	7.27	6.41	8.82	11.08	7.81	6.38	4.95	14.62	10.44	8.01
Religion	15.7	64.27	7.05	3.28	6.46	14.18	68.02	1.75	6.4	4.18
Death	17.36	4.08	3.27	3.28	3.6	16.31	4.95	4.68	4.38	4.53
Assent	3.97	3.11	3.02	9.2	5.71	4.96	3.15	4.09	3.37	4.88

Table 2: Coverage of the used LIWC categories on the training and test sets of each target/domain

classifier.

3.4   Linguistic Inquiry & Word Count (LIWC)

LIWC (Tausczik and Pennebaker, 2010) uses a set of dictionaries to assign words in a given text to a set of psychologically meaningful categories such as death, science, emotion, space, family, swear words and many others. We apply LIWC to each given tweet in order to estimate the percentage of words belonging to each of the following categories:

Feeling, Biological Processes, Body, Health, Sexual, Ingestion, Relativity, Motion, Space, Time, Work, Achievement, Leisure, Home, Money, Religion, Death and Assent.

These categories convey the discussed topics in the given tweet. Table 2 shows the coverage of each of these categories. The coverage for each category corresponds to the percentage of tweets –out of all tweets– that have at least one word in this LIWC category. We calculate the coverage of the used LIWC categories on both the training and test sets for all five targets. By analyzing the numbers in Table 2, we find that "Atheism" dataset has the highest coverage for "Religion" category, "Abortion" has the highest coverage for "Death" category while "Cli-

mate Change" has the highest coverage for "Motion". Moreover for "Abortion", 25.8% of the tweets opposing it use words in the "death" category as opposed to only 8.6% for the tweets favoring the topic. For "Atheism", the use of "religion" category is high among both opposing and favoring tweets where 78.26% of the tweets that favor atheism use words in the "religion" category and 80.26% of the ones that oppose it use this category. While LIWC will potentially help in identifying the stance from which a given tweet or text in general is written, a main drawback to it is that it only performs a dictionary look-up on each word hence judging words in isolation of their context.

3.5   Frame Semantics

Frame semantics assemble the meanings of different elements in a given piece of text to model the meaning of the whole text (Baker et al., 1998). The basic semantic unit in frame semantics theory is the "frame". A frame is a conceptual structure that refers to a group of related concepts (or elements) where understanding one of these concepts requires an understanding of its whole structure. When any of these structures is present, it automatically triggers all of the other ones in the reader's mind (Fillmore, 2006). The word (or phrase) that triggers the

	Abortion	Atheism	Climate	Clinton	Feminism	All-Targets
Majority-BL	35.87	37.04	2.5	36	33	32.2
n-grams	58.04	**66.67**	40.48	**58.9**	47.82	62.39
WTMF	54.39	53.59	35	42.03	51.25	57.22
Sentiment	35.87	37.04	35	36	33	54.21
Frames	48.67	37.18	35.42	33.68	45.56	54.34
LIWC	35.29	36.11	34.48	36.36	33	53.36
Semantic	60.61	52.6	36.84	34.48	51.38	57.84
All	**66.06**	64.62	**41.46**	55.45	**51.58**	**63.98**

Table 3: Development Set Results (measured in average $F_{\beta=1}$ score of "Favor" and "Against" classes)

	Abortion	Atheism	Climate	Clinton	Feminism	All-Targets
Majority-BL	40.3	42.11	6.11	36.83	39.1	36.41
n-grams	57.43	54.98	36.71	51.59	48.37	60.41
WTMF	48.08	**57.73**	**39.83**	45.81	52.25	62.27
Semantic	57.25	48.77	39.48	39.89	**54.29**	63.1
All	**60.52**	56.39	38.89	**55.82**	51.93	**63.6**

Table 4: Held-Out Test Set Results (measured in average $F_{\beta=1}$ score of "Favor" and "Against" classes)

frame is called the "frame-target". For example, the target for the frame "Killing" can be any kill verb and the frame elements will include the killer and the victim.

We use SEMAFOR (Das et al., 2010; Chen et al., 2010), a publicly available frame-semantic parser, to identify all the semantic frames in each given tweet. For example, in the tweet *"Because I want young American women to be able to be proud of the 1st woman president."*, SEMAFOR identifies the following frames, *"Leadership Target:president"*, *"Capability Target:able"*, *"Origin Target:American"*, *"Desiring Target:want"*, *"People Target:women"* and *"Age Target:young"* . We create a list of all the frames that occur in the training data and use binary features to indicate the presence/absence of each of them in each given tweet. This set of features provides yet another abstraction in order to infer the topics discussed in the given text.

3.6 Classifier Training

Using WEKA toolkit (Hall et al., 2009) and the derived lexical and semantic features, we train an SVM classifier for each one of the five targets. We use a radial basis kernel and set the cost parameter C to 1.

4 Experiments & Results

For tuning, we split the training data for each target into two subsets: 90% training and 10% development. We evaluate different configurations of the proposed features on the development set and apply the ones that yield best tuning results to the held-out test set. Specifically we experiment with the following configurations: (1) Lexical Features (n-grams), (2) WTMF, (3) Sentiment, (4) Frames, (5) LIWC, (6) All Semantic features, (7) All features. We compare the proposed approach against a majority baseline which assigns all tweets to the most frequent class in the data ("Against"). Table 3 shows the results on the development set. N-grams outperform using any of the semantic features separately which is quite expected given how well n-grams generally perform on text classification tasks. Moreover WTMF outperforms all other semantic features except on "Climate Change" dataset. Overall we find "Climate Change" to show different trends and a much lower performance than those of the other four targets. We believe that this is attributed to the small size of this set and to its very skewed distribution. Only 3.8% of its tweets belong to "against" class which is the most frequent class in the whole dataset. Combining all semantic features yields better results than using any of them separately for three out of the five targets "Abortion", "Climate Change" and "Feminist Movement" while for the other two targets using WTMF only outperforms using the full set of semantic features. For the same two targets –"Atheism" and "Hillary Clinton"– using only n-grams outperforms combing n-grams with all-semantic features. Overall, combining lexical and semantic features yields the best results on the majority of tweets. Accordingly we used this setup in our official task submission.

We apply the top four development-set configurations –"n-grams", "WTMF", "all semantic" and "all features"– to the test set. Table 4 shows the held-out test results. While using the combination of lexical and all-semantic features yields best overall performance, using only the semantics features achieves close to best results. Additionally, using only WTMF yields best performance on two targets – "Atheism" and "Climate Change". We also find that while the best configuration for each target varies across the development and test sets, the best overall configuration for the majority of tweets remains the same.

5 Conclusion

In this paper, we explore the use of lexical and several semantic feature sets within a supervised framework to identify the stance of a tweet towards an ideological topic. We evaluate the performance of the proposed approach by participating in SemEval-2016 Task 6: "Detecting Stance in Tweets" which aims at identifying the stance of a given tweet towards five targets; "Abortion", "Atheism", "Climate Change", "Hillary Clinton" and "Feminist Movement". We find that WTMF, a latent semantics model that incorporates both observed and missing words, yields the best results among semantic features. Moreover, combining lexical and all semantic features results in the best performance.

References

Collin F Baker, Charles J Fillmore, and John B Lowe. 1998. The berkeley framenet project. In *Proceedings of the 17th international conference on Computational linguistics-Volume 1*. Association for Computational Linguistics.

Desai Chen, Nathan Schneider, Dipanjan Das, and Noah A Smith. 2010. Semafor: Frame argument resolution with log-linear models. In *Proceedings of the 5th international workshop on semantic evaluation*. Association for Computational Linguistics.

Dipanjan Das, Nathan Schneider, Desai Chen, and Noah A Smith. 2010. Semafor 1.0: A probabilistic frame-semantic parser. *Language Technologies Institute, School of Computer Science, Carnegie Mellon University*.

Heba Elfardy, Mona Diab, and Chris Callison-Burch. 2015. Ideological perspective detection using semantic features. *Lexical and Computational Semantics (* SEM 2015)*.

Robert M Entman. 1993. Framing: Toward clarification of a fractured paradigm. volume 43. Wiley Online Library.

Christiane Fellbaum. 2010. Wordnet: An electronic lexical database. 1998. *WordNet is available from http://www. cogsci. princeton. edu/wn*.

Charles J Fillmore. 2006. Frame semantics. *Cognitive linguistics: Basic readings*, 34.

Weiwei Guo and Mona Diab. 2012. Modeling sentences in the latent space. In *Proceedings of the 50th Annual Meeting of the Association for Computational Linguistics: Long Papers-Volume 1*, pages 864–872. Association for Computational Linguistics.

Mark Hall, Eibe Frank, Geoffrey Holmes, Bernhard Pfahringer, Peter Reutemann, and Ian H Witten. 2009. The weka data mining software: an update. *ACM SIGKDD Explorations Newsletter*, 11(1):10–18.

Kazi Saidul Hasan and Vincent NG. 2012. Predicting stance in ideological debate with rich linguistic knowledge. In *Proceedings of the 24th International Conference on Computational Linguistics*.

Kazi Saidul Hasan and Vincent Ng. 2013. Extra-linguistic constraints on stance recognition in ideological debates. In *Proceedings of the 51st Annual Meeting of the Association for Computational Linguistics*. Association for Computational Linguistics.

Beata Beigman Klebanov, Eyal Beigman, and Daniel Diermeier. 2010. Vocabulary choice as an indicator of perspective. In *ACL*, pages 253–257. Association for Computational Linguistics.

Wei-Hao Lin, Theresa Wilson, Janyce Wiebe, and Alexander Hauptmann. 2006. Which side are you on?: identifying perspectives at the document and sentence levels. In *Proceedings of the Tenth Conference on Computational Natural Language Learning*, pages 109–116. Association for Computational Linguistics.

Saif M. Mohammad, Svetlana Kiritchenko, Parinaz Sobhani, Xiaodan Zhu, and Colin Cherry. 2016. SemEval-2016 Task 6: Detecting stance in tweets. In *Proceedings of the International Workshop on Semantic Evaluation*, SemEval '16, June.

Richard Socher, Alex Perelygin, Jean Y Wu, Jason Chuang, Christopher D Manning, Andrew Y Ng, and Christopher Potts. 2013. Recursive deep models for semantic compositionality over a sentiment treebank. In *Proceedings of the conference on empirical methods in natural language processing (EMNLP)*, volume 1631. Citeseer.

Swapna Somasundaran and Janyce Wiebe. 2010. Recognizing stances in ideological online debates. In *Proceedings of the NAACL HLT 2010 Workshop on Computational Approaches to Analysis and Generation of Emotion in Text*, pages 116–124. Association for Computational Linguistics.

Yla R Tausczik and James W Pennebaker. 2010. The psychological meaning of words: Liwc and computerized text analysis methods. *Journal of language and social psychology*, 29(1).

JU_NLP at SemEval-2016 Task 6: Detecting Stance in Tweets using Support Vector Machines

Braja Gopal Patra, Dipankar Das, and **Sivaji Bandyopadhyay**
Department of Computer Science and Engineering, Jadavpur University
Kolkata, India
`{brajagopal.cse,dipankar.dipnil2005}@gmail.com`
`sivaji_cse_ju@yahoo.com`

Abstract

We describe the system submitted to the SemEval-2016 for detecting stance in tweets (Task 6, Subtask A). One of the main goals of stance detection is to automatically determine the stance of a tweet towards a specific target as 'FAVOR', 'AGAINST', or 'NONE'. We developed a supervised system using Support Vector Machines to identify the stance by analyzing various lexical and semantic features. The average F1 score achieved by our system is 60.60.

1 Introduction

Recent research in the areas of opinion mining and/or sentiment analysis on natural language texts is gaining importance due to various academic and commercial perspectives. One of the main reasons is that a vital amount of information can be obtained from text data that are available in the internet in forms of news, reviews, blogs, chats, and tweets.

Several experiments have been attempted in the field of sentiment analysis or opinion mining on user generated content or social media data till date (Patra et al., 2015). One of the main goals in such tasks is to assign polarities (positive or negative) to a piece of text. Identification of the writer's attitude towards a specific target, known as stance detection, is a relevant and challenging topic which has unduly been averted by most researchers (Mohammad et al., 2016). Lately it has become conventional that people express stance explicitly or implicitly in various microblogging sites.

Stance detection is the task of automatically determining from text whether the author is in favor of

the given target, against the given target, or whether neither inference is likely.[1] The stance detection can often bring complementary information to sentiment analysis, because we often care about the author's evaluative outlook towards specific targets and propositions rather than simply considering whether the speaker is angry or happy (Mohammad et al., 2016). Stance detection even becomes more difficult when it is performed on the short texts like tweets. The latter being an important sub-field of sentiment analysis/opinion mining. Automatic stance detection can be used in several applications such as information retrieval, text summarization, and textual entailment.

More recent approaches to stance detection have been performed using linguistic rules on *online debate dataset* (Somasundaran and Wiebe, 2009; Hasan and Ng, 2013; Sridhar et al., 2014) and *NPOV Corpus* from Wikipedia (Recasens et al., 2013). To the best of our knowledge, not much computational attempts have been performed on tweets for stance detection. It is also observed that both the supervised and unsupervised machine learning algorithms have been implemented for identifying the stance and several features like n-gram, frame semantic features, and dependency were used in stance detection tasks (Somasundaran and Wiebe, 2009; Anand et al., 2011; Sridhar et al., 2014).

We participated in the SemEval 2016-Task 6: Detecting Stance in Tweets.[1] The main goal of this task is to identify stance present in a tweet towards a specific target. For example, **Target** = '*Hillary Clinton*, **Tweet** = '*A Black President,Healthcare 4*

---

[1] http://alt.qcri.org/semeval2016/task6/

Proceedings of SemEval-2016, pages 440–444,
San Diego, California, June 16-17, 2016. ©2016 Association for Computational Linguistics

all, Marriage Equality...what's next?..a Woman President?!Damn RIGHT! #SCOTUS #MarriageEquality, **Stance** = *'FAVOR.* In the above example, the tweet is in favor of the target *"Hillary Clinton"*. In the test dataset, the targets of the corresponding tweets are given and we have to find out whether the stance towards the target is in 'FAVOR' or 'AGAINST' or 'NONE'.

There are two subtasks, in subtask A, we have to identify the stance towards a specific target whereas in subtask B, we have to identify the stance towards only one target *"Donald Trump"* using a large set of unlabeled tweets associated with the target. We have only participated in subtask A. Several lexical and semantic features are used to identify the stance towards a target. Support Vector Machines (SVM) is used for the classification purpose.

2   Dataset and Evaluation

The organizers provided the trial, training, and test dataset of 100, 2814, and 1249 tweets, respectively for detecting stance towards five targets namely *"Atheism"*, *"Climate Change is a Real Concern"*, *"Feminist Movement"*, *"Hillary Clinton"*, and *"Legalization of Abortion"*. All tweets in the dataset are annotated with stance ('FAVOR' or 'AGAINST' or 'NONE') towards the above mentioned targets. The stance *'NONE'* means the tweet is not in 'FAVOR' or 'AGAINST' of the target.

Systems were evaluated using the official metric calculated macro-average of two labels only, i.e. **F1 score** = (F-Score$_{FAVOR}$ + F-Score$_{AGAINST}$)/2.

3   System Framework

3.1   Features

In order to achieve good accuracy using machine learning algorithms, we need to have a good set of features. Based on the genre of tweet, we identified the following features as listed below.

3.1.1   Target Specific Words

Initially, an n-gram model was created to identify the target's presence in the tweet. But, we observed that the dimension as well as the sparsity of feature vectors were increased enormously. Thus, we created individual topic bags related to

	Topic	Word Bags	
	Bags	**Favor**	**Against**
A	311	69	210
C	129	63	42
F	95	72	49
H	73	40	31
L	101	44	59

Table 1: Statistics of the topic, favor, and against bags for five targets (A: Atheism, C: Climate Change is a Real Concern, F: Feminist Movement, H: Hillary Clinton, L: Legalization of Abortion)

each of the targets. Seed words related to the targets were populated using RitaWordNet.[2] Some handcrafted rules were implemented to find names in words and hashtags. For example, "Hillary" is present in "#HillaryClinton", then we considered "#HillaryClinton" in the topic bag "Hillary". Further, we checked the topic bags manually and removed some unrelated words collected using the WordNet. The detailed word level statistics of the topic bags are given in Table 1.

At first, we checked that whether a tweet contains any word from the corresponding target related topic bag or not. If no word is present, then we tagged that tweet as 'NONE' and no further processing is performed on that tweet. Further, this topic bags are used along with the dependency information.

3.1.2   Sentiment Words

We have used three lexicons namely SentiWordNet (Baccianella et al., 2010), NRC Emotion Lexicon (Mohammad and Turney, 2013), and NRC Hashtag Emotion Lexicon (Mohammad, 2012) for our experiments along with manually created lexicons for each of the targets. Moreover, two bags were created for each of the targets namely 'favor' and 'against' bags. Hashtags are also included in the above lexicons. The word level statistics of the 'favor' and 'against' bags are given in Table 1. We used the frequency of the sentiment words matched with the above sentiment or emotion lexicons as features. Again, we used these lexicons in the later experiments also.

---

[2]https://rednoise.org/rita/reference/RiWordNet.html

Parse

```
(ROOT
  (S
    (S
      (NP (NN @HillaryClinton) (NNS i))
      (VP (VBP am)
        (ADJP (JJ portuguese))))
    (CC and)
    (S
      (NP (FW i))
      (VP (VBP support)
        (NP (PRP$ your) (NN campaign))))
    (. !)))

(ROOT
  (INTJ (JJ Best) (NN luck) (. !)))
```

Universal dependencies

```
compound(i-2, @HillaryClinton-1)
nsubj(portuguese-4, i-2)
cop(portuguese-4, am-3)
root(ROOT-0, portuguese-4)
cc(portuguese-4, and-5)
nsubj(support-7, i-6)
conj(portuguese-4, support-7)
nmod:poss(campaign-9, your-8)
dobj(support-7, campaign-9)

amod(luck-2, Best-1)
root(ROOT-0, luck-2)
```

Figure 1: Dependency relations from Stanford Parser

3.1.3 Dependency Information

It is found in the literature that the dependency relations act as useful feature in sentiment analysis (Patra et al., 2014a; Patra et al., 2014b). Thus, we used the Stanford Parser[3] to get the dependency relations. We searched for the word pairs in dependency relations that consist of two component words, one of which is present in either 'favor' or 'against' bag, whereas the other one is present in SentiWordNet.

In the above Figure 1, we found a relation "dobj(support-7, campaign-9)". The word 'campaign' is present in the 'favor' bag for the target *"Hillary Clinton"* and the word 'support' is present in SentiWordNet as positive. This relation is considered as favor_positive type. Similarly, three other types namely favor_negative, against_positive, and against_negative were considered. The counts of each type are used as features.

Again, we identified the simple sentences based on the symbol "**(S**" or "**(ROOT**" in Figure 1. For

each of the simple sentences, we removed the stop-words (except the negation words) and identified the sentiment words using SentiWordNet. We applied some handcrafted rules given below. 1. Not + NEG = POS, 2. Not + POS = NEG, 3. POS + POS = POS, 4. NEG + NEG = NEG. If there are multiple positive words present in a simple sentence, we tagged it as positive. If there are only two sentiment words, one with positive and other as negative, we tagged the sentence as negative. It is observed that the frequency of the negative instances is much higher than the positive instances in the training data. Finally, we counted the number of positive and negative instances in a tweet and used as features.

3.2 Classification Framework

We used LibSVM, an variant of SVMs implemented in the Weka.[4] We performed the 10-fold cross validation on the training and trial dataset for all the targets using the above features. But, the system performance was observed as poor and the system achieves the average F1 score of 0.43. Again, we performed the 10-fold cross validation on the training and trial dataset for all the targets, separately. We calculated the average F1 score for each of the five targets and these are 0.46, 0.40, 0.48, 0.52, and 0.49 for "Atheism", "Climate Change is a Real Concern", "Feminist Movement", "Hillary Clinton", and "Legalization of Abortion", respectively. This yields an average F1 score of 0.47 for all the targets, which is higher than the F1 score achieved by the previous system. This motivates us to develop our final systems separately for each of the targets.

3.2.1 Results

The LibSVM based system achieved the maximum F-Score of 0.4668 and 0.7452 for the 'FAVOR' and 'AGAINST' classes, respectively as shown in Table 2. The system achieved the maximum average F1 score of 0.6060. Whereas, the team **MITRE** has achieved the first position with the maximum average F1 score of 0.6782.

The confusion matrix for our system is shown in Table 3. From the matrix, we observed that the system is biased towards the '*AGAINST*' stance (except "Climate Change is a Real Concern" target). The main reason may be the biasness in the

---

[3] http://stanfordnlp.github.io/CoreNLP/

[4] http://www.cs.waikato.ac.nz/ml/weka/

	Precision	Recall	F-Score
FAVOR	0.6687	0.3586	0.4668
AGAINST	0.7227	0.7692	0.7452

Table 2: System performance

			Predicted		
			A	**F**	**N**
Actual	**Atheism**	A	124	2	34
		F	25	0	7
		N	9	0	19
	Climate Change is a Real Concern	A	1	7	3
		F	21	92	10
		N	1	10	24
	Feminist Movement	A	145	12	26
		F	45	6	7
		N	9	2	33
	Hillary Clinton	A	135	15	22
		F	33	9	3
		N	21	1	56
	Legalization of Abortion	A	145	4	40
		F	35	2	9
		N	12	1	32

Table 3: Confusion Matrix of our System (A: Against, F: Favor, N: None)

training dataset as the number of instances for the '*AGAINST*' stance is maximum for all the targets (except "Climate Change is a Real Concern" target). Another reason may be the less number of training instances as we developed our system for each of the targets, separately.

4 Conclusion and Future Work

We presented a system for identifying the stance in tweets using dependency and semantic features. The maximum average F1 score of 0.6060 is achieved by the system using SVM classifier. The task stance detection on social media data is helpful for real life applications like political campaign and opinion poll.

In near future, we plan to use the TweeboParser,[5] as it works well for tweets as compared to the Stanford Parser. Another immediate goal is to increase the size of topic bags and sentiment lexicons related to each of the targets. We are also planing to use unsupervised approach and several machine learning algorithms for classifying the stance in near future.

Acknowledgments

The present work is supported by a grant from the project "CLIA System Phase II" funded by Department of Electronics and Information Technology (DeitY), Ministry of Communications and Information Technology (MCIT), Government of India. The first author is supported by "Visvesvaraya Ph.D. Fellowship" funded by DeitY, Government of India.

References

Pranav Anand, Marilyn Walker, Rob Abbott, Jean E. F. Tree, Robeson Bowmani, and Michael Minor. 2011. Cats rule and dogs drool!: Classifying stance in online debate. In *Proceedings of the 2nd workshop on computational approaches to subjectivity and sentiment analysis*, pages 1–9.

Stefano Baccianella, Andrea Esuli, and Fabrizio Sebastiani. 2010. Sentiwordnet 3.0: An enhanced lexical resource for sentiment analysis and opinion mining. In *Proceedings of 7th Language Resources and Evaluation Conference*, volume 10, pages 2200–2204.

Kazi S. Hasan and Vincent Ng. 2013. Stance classification of ideological debates: Data, models, features, and constraints. In *Proceedings of the 6th International Joint Conference on Natural Language Processing*, pages 1348–1356.

Saif M. Mohammad and Peter D. Turney. 2013. Crowdsourcing a word-emotion association lexicon. *Computational Intelligence*, 29(3):436–465.

Saif M. Mohammad, Svetlana Kiritchenko, Parinaz Sobhani, Xiaodan Zhu, and Colin Cherry. 2016. SemEval-2016 Task 6: Detecting stance in tweets. In *Proceedings of the International Workshop on Semantic Evaluation*, SemEval'16, San Diego, California.

Saif M. Mohammad. 2012. #emotional tweets. In **SEM 2012: The First Joint Conference on Lexical and Computational Semantics*, pages 246–255, Montréal, Canada, 7-8 June. Association for Computational Linguistics.

Braja G. Patra, Soumik Mandal, Dipankar Das, and Sivaji Bandyopadhyay. 2014a. Ju_cse: A conditional random field (crf) based approach to aspect based sentiment analysis. In *Proceedings of the 8th International Workshop on Semantic Evaluation (SemEval 2014)*, pages 370–374.

Braja G. Patra, Niloy Mukherjee, Arijit Das, Soumik Mandal, Dipankar Das, and Sivaji Bandyopadhyay.

---

[5] http://www.cs.cmu.edu/ ark/TweetNLP/

2014b. Identifying aspects and analyzing their sentiments from reviews. In *Proceedings of 13th Mexican International Conference on Artificial Intelligence (MICAI)*, pages 9–15. IEEE.

Braja G. Patra, Dipankar Das, Amitava Das, and Rajendra Prasath. 2015. Shared task on sentiment analysis in indian languages (sail) tweets-an overview. In *Proceedings of Mining Intelligence and Knowledge Exploration*, pages 650–655. Springer.

Marta Recasens, Cristian Danescu-Niculescu-Mizil, and Dan Jurafsky. 2013. Linguistic models for analyzing and detecting biased language. In *Proceedings of the 51th Annual Meeting of the ACL*, pages 1650–1659.

Swapna Somasundaran and Janyce Wiebe. 2009. Recognizing stances in online debates. In *Proceedings of the Joint Conference of the 47th Annual Meeting of the ACL and the 4th International Joint Conference on Natural Language Processing*, pages 226–234. Association for Computational Linguistics.

Dhanya Sridhar, Lise Getoor, and Marilyn Walker. 2014. Collective stance classification of posts in online debate forums. pages 109–117.

IDI@NTNU at SemEval-2016 Task 6: Detecting Stance in Tweets Using Shallow Features and GloVe Vectors for Word Representation

Henrik Bøhler and **Petter Fagerlund Asla** and **Erwin Marsi** and **Rune Sætre**
Norwegian University of Science and Technology
Sem Sælands vei 9
Trondheim, 7491, NORWAY
{henriboh,pettefas}@stud.ntnu.no, {emarsi,satre}@idi.ntnu.no

Abstract

This paper describes an approach to automatically detect stance in tweets by building a supervised system combining shallow features and pre-trained word vectors as word representation. The word vectors were obtained from several collections of large corpora using GloVe, an unsupervised learning algorithm. We created feature vectors by selecting the word vectors relevant to the data and summing them for each unique word. Combining multiple classifiers into a voting classifier, representing the best of both approaches, shows a significant improvement over the baseline system.

1 Introduction

This paper describes our submission to the SemEval 2016 competition Task 6A - *Detecting Stance in Tweets*. The goal of the task is to classify a tweet into one of the three classes – *against, favor* or *none* in regard to a certain topic. These classes represents the tweet's stance towards the given target.

Twitter, and other microblogging platforms, have in recent years become popular arenas to apply natural language processing tasks. One of the most popular tasks has been sentiment analysis. Stance detection differs from sentiment analysis because the sentiment of a text – generally positive or negative – does not necessarily agree with its stance regarding a certain topic of debate. For example, a tweet like "all those climate-deniers are morons" is negative in its overall sentiment, but positive with regard to the stance that climate change is a real concern. We refer the reader to the official SemEval 2016[1] website for a detailed task description.

Our approach to detect stance is based on shallow features (Kohlschütter et al., 2010; Hagen et al., 2015; Walker et al., 2012) and the use of GloVe word vectors (Pennington et al., 2014). During the development phase we explored several approaches by implementing features such as sentiment detection (Hutto and Gilbert, 2014), number of tokens and number of capital words. The experiments later in this paper show that not all features enhanced the performance of the implemented system.

The feature that turned out to boost performance the most, in combination with basic shallow features, was the use of pre-trained GloVe vectors (Pennington et al., 2014). The vector representations of tweets were created by summing the pre-trained word vectors for each unique word. No additional data was added to the training set used for our final submission, although we explored the possibility of gathering and automatically labelling additional tweets by using label propagation (Zhu and Ghahramani, 2002; Zhou et al., 2004). This did enhance our baseline system performance slightly, but not in combination with other features.

2 System description

To predict the stance in tweets we built a supervised machine learning system using the scikit-learn machine learning library (Pedregosa et al., 2011). Our system consists of a soft voting classifier that predicts the class label on the basis of the best re-

---

[1] http://alt.qcri.org/semeval2016/task6/

Proceedings of SemEval-2016, pages 445–450,
San Diego, California, June 16-17, 2016. ©2016 Association for Computational Linguistics

sults out of the three classifiers described in subsection 2.3.

2.1 Resources

Our system used a limited number of resources. It relies on the annotated training data consisting of 2814 tweets divided into five different topics: *Atheism, Climate Change is a Real Concern, Feminist Movement, Hillary Clinton*, and *Legalization of Abortion*. In addition, it uses pre-trained word vectors[2] created by Pennington et al. (2014).

2.1.1 Bootstrapping attempts

The labels for the climate change target showed a highly skewed distribution where only 3.8% were labelled *against*. Skewed data distributions in machine learning are a common problem. Monard and Batista (2002), Provost (2000) and Tang et al. (2009) discuss this problem and suggests several solutions, such as data under- and over-sampling. We did not have time to investigate the effects of these methods, but Elkan (2001) suggest that changing the balance of negative and positive training samples has little effect on learned classifiers.

In an attempt to even out the distribution of the climate change data, we searched for ways to add additional tweets. The most promising approach explored was label propagation (Zhu and Ghahramani, 2002; Zhou et al., 2004), a semi-supervised learning algorithm. Thousands of tweets were fetched based on the most common hashtags found in the climate topic data. We hand-picked a small portion of tweets that seemed relevant to the climate topic (e.g. same language and containing a statement). These tweets were then automatically labelled using label propagation. The label propagation was performed with a (small) representative sample of the labelled training data together with the collected, hand picked, unlabelled tweets. We found that adding more data to our system did not result in substantial improvement. An explanation could be that the gathered tweets were not meaningful enough to be effective. The additional data was therefore not used in subsequent experiments.

---

[2]http://nlp.stanford.edu/projects/glove/

2.2 Features

The submitted system used the following features, generated from the raw data supplied in the training set.

1. **Word bigrams:** All pairs of consecutive words
   - Punctuation ignored
2. **Character trigram:** All triples of consecutive characters
   - Punctuation ignored
   - Converted to lowercase
   - Ignored terms that had a document frequency strictly lower than 5 (cut-off)
3. **GloVe vectors:** Word embeddings for all words in a tweet
   - Punctuation ignored
   - Converted to lowercase
   - Removed stop words

In addition, we experimented with the following features, which were not included in the final system. They were left out as they did not improve the systems performance (section 3 will provide more details on this).

- **Negation:** Presence of negation in the sentence

- **Length of tweets:** Number of characters divided by the maximum length (140 characters)

- **Capital words:** Number of capital words in the tweet

- **Repeated punctuation:** Number of occurrences of non-single punctuation (e.g. !?)

- **Exclamation mark last:** Exclamation mark found last in non-single punctuation (e.g. ?!)

- **Lengthening of words:** Number of lengthened words (e.g. smoooth)

- **Sentiment:** Detecting sentiment in tweet using the Vader system (Hutto and Gilbert, 2014)

- **Number of tokens:** Count of total number of tokens in the tweet

2.2.1 GloVe

GloVe (Pennington et al., 2014) is an unsupervised
learning algorithm for obtaining vector representations of words. It creates word vectors based on the
distributional statistics of words, in particular how
frequently words co-occur within a certain window
in a large text corpus such as the Gigaword corpus (Parker et al., 2011). The resulting word vectors can be used to measure semantic similarity between word pairs, following the hypothesis that similar words tend to have similar distributions. The Euclidean or Cosine distance between two word vectors can thus be used as a measure of their semantic
similarity. For the word *frog*, for example, we can
find related words such as *frogs, toad, litoria, lepto-
dactylidae, rana, lizard, eleutherodactylu.*

In order to measure the semantic similarity between tweets, rather than isolated words, we needed
a way to obtain vector representations of documents.
Mitchell and Lapata (2010) looked at the possibility to use word vectors to represent the meaning of
word combinations in a vector space. They suggest,
among other things, to use vector composition, op-
erationalized in terms of additive (or multiplicative)
functions. Accordingly we created vector representations of tweets by combining the vectors of their
words. We used pre-trained word vectors created by
Pennington et al. (2014) trained on Wikipedia 2014
+ Gigaword 5[3] and Twitter data[4]. The word vectors
come in several versions with a different number of
dimensions (25, 50, 100, 200, 300) that supposedly
capture different granularities of meaning. The resulting features (from here on called GloVe features)
were obtained by summing the GloVe vectors, per
dimension, for all unique terms in a tweet.

2.3 Models

To detect stance we constructed separate models for
each of the five topics, each in the form of a soft
voting classifier from scikit-learn (Pedregosa et al.,
2011). The voting classifiers took input from the following three classifiers:

1. **Multinomial Naive Bayes** trained on word bigrams

2. **Multinomial Naive Bayes** trained on character
   trigrams

3. **Logistic Regression** trained on GloVe features

The soft voting classifier is – in contrast to a hard
voting classifier – able to exploit prediction probabilities from the separate classifiers. For each sample, the soft voting classifier predicts the class based
on the argmax of the sums of the predicted probabilities from the input classifiers.

In the task description it was stated that it was
not necessary to predict stance for every tweet in
the test set, leaving the uncertain ones with an *unknown* label. We decided to use a threshold value,
using the extracted probabilities, to prevent predictions with low confidence. Labels predicted with a
probability below the threshold were thus changed
into *unknown*. Details of the selection of the threshold value are presented at the end of section 4.

Due to the imbalanced distribution of labels in climate change data, our system had a low prediction
rate of *against* stances on this target. For that reason
we included a second slightly different model for
the climate change target. The difference between
the first and second model was that the second used
a hard (majority rule) voting classifier, which performed slightly better on the against labels in the
climate data. The combination of the two models
was implemented in a way such that for each of
the *against* predictions in the hard voting model, we
overwrote the soft model's prediction, labelling the
tweet *against*. Our submitted system thus consisted
of two models for predicting the climate class, giving a total of six models.

To summarize, the system contains six models,
where five of them consist of a soft voting classifier
with input from the three different classifiers introduced above. The sixth is a hard voting model that
supplements the soft voting model for the climate
change target.

3 Results on Development Data

To measure the system performance we conducted
multiple experiments using the training data to examine the effects of various shallow features and the
use of GloVe features with a varying number of dimensions. All experiments in this paper were conducted using stratified five-fold cross-validation and

---

[3]`http://nlp.stanford.edu/data/glove.6B.zip`
[4]`http://nlp.stanford.edu/data/glove.twitter.`
`27B.zip`

the results were measured with macro F-score based on precision and recall on the class labels *favor* and *against*. Our system used supervised machine learning algorithms supplied by the scikit-learn library (Pedregosa et al., 2011).

3.1 Baseline

The first experiment was set up to gain insight in the performance of different classifiers and their parameters. We chose a basic approach using only word unigrams (bag of words approach). The best of the resulting models was chosen as the baseline, serving as an indication of the performance of a simplistic system. The models were trained on the entire data set, not divided by individual targets. We chose to perform the experiment with two different Support Vector Machines (SVM) and one Naive Bayes (MNB) classifier with different parameters[5].

One of the hyperparameters we optimized was C, which is a regularization term for misclassifications of each sample. Higher values will do a better job correctly labelling the training data during training (smaller hyperplane margin), but are more likely to overfit. Conversely, lower values may have more misclassifications because it will ignore more outliers (larger hyperplane margin), but are less likely to overfit. We also used the *decision function shape* parameter to decide whether to use one-vs-one (*ovo*) or one-vs-rest (*ovr*) as decision function. *Ovo* constructs one classifier per pair of classes. At prediction time, a vote is performed and the class which receives the most votes is selected. The *ovr* strategy consist of fitting one classifier for each class. The table below displays the results from the experiments.

Classifiers	Parameter specification	Macro F
Multinomial NB	[alpha=0.01]	0.5513
SVM	[kernel='linear', C=0.37]	0.5701
LinearSVM	[kernel='linear', C=0.28]	**0.5819**

Table 1: Average macro F-scores from five-fold CV experiments with different classifiers on the entire training set.

LinearSVM scored highest and established the base-

---

[5]SVM with *kernel=[linear, rbf, poly]*, *C=numpy.logspace*(−3, 3, 50), *decision_function_shape=[ovo, ovr]* and LinearSVM with *C=numpy.logspace*(−3, 3, 50). MultinomialNB with *alpha=numpy.logspace*(−1, 1, 10)).

line with the macro F-score of 0.5819. However, the LinearSVM classifier was not beneficial in later experiments when trained individually per target[6] and therefore only used as a performance baseline.

3.2 Improved system

In the development phase, the data set was divided by the individual targets creating five respective data sets. The development experiments began by including more and more shallow features. We started off by applying various forms of n-grams (uni-, bi- and trigram of words and characters). The classifier that achieved the highest cross-validated macro F-score from these experiments was MNB using character trigram. The achieved score was 0.6290. The experiments continued by adding features (listed in section 2.2) to the MNB in addition to the character trigram feature. Results of these experiments can be seen in table 2.

Shallow Features	Macro F	Change
Trigram characters	0.6290	
.+negation	0.6308	(+ 0.0018)
.+length of tweets	0.6311	(+ 0.0003)
.+capital words	0.6313	(+ 0.0002)
.+non-single punctuation	0.6356	(+ 0.0043)
.+exclamation mark last	0.6358	(+ 0.0002)
.+lengthening words	**0.6360**	(+ 0.0002)
.+sentiment	0.6352	(- 0.0008)
.+number of tokens	0.6264	(- 0.0088)

Table 2: Average macro F-scores for different sets of shallow features from five-fold CV experiments with MNB classifier on the entire training set.

Table 2 shows that adding shallow features yielded only a slight increase in macro F-score from 0.6290 to 0.6360. Based on this, relatively small, improvement it is difficult to imply that the addition of features gave any substantial performance boost of the system.

3.3 Final system

Subsequent experiments tested the use of a Logistic Regression classifiers with GloVe feature vectors. We used pre-trained word vectors from

---

[6]Average macro F-score over all targets:
LinearSVM with word bigram: 0.4955.
LinearSVM with character trigram: 0.5970.
LinearSVM with shallow features: 0.5974

Features	Overall	std (σ)	Atheism	Climate	Feminism	Hillary	Abortion
Baseline	0.5819	0.0494	-	-	-	-	-
Best shallow features	0.6360	0.0891	0.6601	0.5923	0.6246	0.6022	0.7006
Glove features	0.6067	0.0722	0.6516	0.6256	0.5553	0.5898	0.6102
Glove + best shallow	0.6048	0.0659	0.5775	0.5604/0.6754	0.6291	0.5479	0.7088
Glove + n-gram	**0.6751**	0.0704	0.7055	0.6540/0.6404	0.6537	0.6427	0.7204

Table 3: Average macro F-scores, both overall and per target, for different combinations of feature sets from five-fold CV experiments on the entire training set. Baseline model was not trained per target, therefore no individual scores are available. Where two scores are listed, there were two models used (soft/hard voting).

different corpora with a various number of dimensions (*corpus sizes* $= [(6B\,tokens, 400K\,vocab),$ $(27B\,tokens, 1.2M\,vocab)]$ and *dimensions* $= [25, 50, 100, 200, 300]$). The various dimensions supposedly capture different granularities of meaning obtained from the corpora they were extracted from[7].

From table 3 we can observe that from the baseline score of 0.5819 the result increased to 0.6360 when applying the best shallow features. It also shows that using only the Logistic Regression classifier with GloVe vectors did not perform well. For this reason we decided to combine multiple classifiers. Initially we tried wrapping the Logistic Regression classifier and the MNB classifier from table 2 in a voting classifier. However, this new voting classifier did not improve the performance, instead a further drop in performance occurred. We later inspected the outcome of the combined classifiers when we reduced the feature set of the MNB classifier down to only applying versions of n-grams. This was more successful and our best result was achieved using the Logistic Regression classifier using GloVe features, MNB classifier using bigram words, and a MNB classifier with trigram characters wrapped inside a soft voting classifier. The final submission therefore included only n-gram features and the rest of the features were discarded. As seen in table 3 this scored 0.6751, which was a substantial improvement over the performance baseline.

---

[7]The final submission used the following word vectors: Atheism (*size*=6*B*, *dimension*=200), Climate Change (*size*=27*B*, *dimension*=200), Feminist Movement (*size*=27*B*, *dimension*=100), Hillary Clinton (*size*=27*B*, *dimension*=200), Legalization of Abortion (*size*=27*B*, *dimension*=100).

4 Results on Test Data

Our submitted approach achieved a macro F-score of **0.6247** on the test data, while the best system on task 6A achieved a score of 0.6782. After the gold labels were released, we ran the test ourselves in order to see how well we did on precision, recall, and F-score. Table 4 shows our final results. The high precision on the class *against* shows that predictions for this label were mostly correct, albeit with a relatively low recall.

Stance	Precision	Recall	F-score
Favor	0.5750	0.6053	0.5897
Against	0.8770	0.5287	0.6597
Overall macro F-score			0.6247

Table 4: Precision, recall and F-score of the official submission per class as well as overall macro F-score.

At the end of section 2.3, we mentioned that we established a threshold in our system. The threshold value was set at the last minute using a rule of thumb as we did not have time to perform experiments to determine the optimal setting, or even whether it was beneficial at all. Our intention was to use this approach only for the category *Climate Change is a Real Concern*, as this was the most skewed topic. However, by accident, it was applied to *all* topics. Comparing our best result in the development phase with the test result, we can observe a substantial drop in performance. This is a result of the threshold that was – by mistake – applied in all predictions. To measure how much this affected our system, we performed an overall test run where the threshold as used in the original submission was disregarded. This resulted in a macro F-score of 0.6660 - an increase of 0.0413 relative to our submission score. The threshold proved to have lowered the re-call for both *favor* and *against* and explains the low recall in the submitted system predictions.

Stance	Precision	Recall	F-score
Favor	0.5432	0.7237	0.6206
Against	0.8042	0.6378	0.7114
Overall macro F-score			0.6660

Table 5: Precision, recall and F-score of the submission without the applied threshold per class as well as overall macro F-score.

It is worth mentioning that even though the addi-tion of all shallow features gave poor results during development phase, it performed a lot better on the test data, scoring 0.6939.

5   Conclusion

This paper summarizes our system created for Sem-Eval 2016 task 6A - *Detecting Stance in Tweets*. Us-ing shallow features alone performed well, but com-bining shallow features and word embeddings cre-ated from GloVe word vectors increased the score substantially.

With this system we finished 10th as we were able to detect stance in tweets with a macro F-score of 0.6247 on the test data, whereas the best system in task 6A scored 0.6782. Post-analysis revealed that the application of an ad-hoc threshold to pre-vent low-confidence predictions was a mistake, re-sulting in a 0.0413 loss in overall macro F-score. The threshold should have been set using cross-validation, or even better, not at all.

References

Charles Elkan. 2001. The foundations of cost-sensitive learning. In *International joint conference on artificial intelligence*, volume 17, pages 973–978. LAWRENCE ERLBAUM ASSOCIATES LTD.

Matthias Hagen, Martin Potthast, Michel Büchner, and Benno Stein. 2015. Twitter sentiment detection via ensemble classification using averaged confidence scores. In *Advances in Information Retrieval*, pages 741–754. Springer.

Clayton J Hutto and Eric Gilbert. 2014. Vader: A par-simonious rule-based model for sentiment analysis of social media text. In *Eighth International Conference on Weblogs and Social Media (ICWSM-14)*, June.

Christian Kohlschütter, Peter Fankhauser, and Wolfgang Nejdl. 2010. Boilerplate detection using shallow text features. In *Proceedings of the third ACM inter-national conference on Web search and data mining*, pages 441–450. ACM.

Jeff Mitchell and Mirella Lapata. 2010. Composition in distributional models of semantics. *Cognitive science*, 34(8):1388–1429.

Maria Carolina Monard and Gustavo EAPA Batista. 2002. Learning with skewed class distributions. *Ad-vances in Logic, Artificial Intelligence, and Robotics: LAPTEC 2002*, 85:173.

Robert Parker, David Graff, Junbo Kong, Ke Chen, and Kazuaki Maeda. 2011. English gigaword fifth edition ldc2011t07. dvd. *Philadelphia: Linguistic Data Con-sortium.*

F. Pedregosa, G. Varoquaux, A. Gramfort, V. Michel, B. Thirion, O. Grisel, M. Blondel, P. Prettenhofer, R. Weiss, V. Dubourg, J. Vanderplas, A. Passos, D. Cournapeau, M. Brucher, M. Perrot, and E. Duches-nay. 2011. Scikit-learn: Machine learning in Python. *Journal of Machine Learning Research*, 12:2825–2830.

Jeffrey Pennington, Richard Socher, and Christopher D. Manning. 2014. Glove: Global vectors for word rep-resentation. In *Empirical Methods in Natural Lan-guage Processing (EMNLP)*, pages 1532–1543.

Foster Provost. 2000. Machine learning from imbal-anced data sets 101. In *Proceedings of the AAAI2000 workshop on imbalanced data sets*, pages 1–3.

Yuchun Tang, Yan-Qing Zhang, Nitesh V Chawla, and Sven Krasser. 2009. Svms modeling for highly im-balanced classification. *Systems, Man, and Cyber-netics, Part B: Cybernetics, IEEE Transactions on*, 39(1):281–288.

Marilyn A Walker, Pranav Anand, Rob Abbott, Jean E Fox Tree, Craig Martell, and Joseph King. 2012. That is your evidence?: Classifying stance in on-line political debate. *Decision Support Systems*, 53(4):719–729.

Dengyong Zhou, Olivier Bousquet, Thomas Navin Lal, Jason Weston, and Bernhard Schlkopf. 2004. Learn-ing with local and global consistency. In *Advances in Neural Information Processing Systems 16*, pages 321–328. MIT Press.

Xiaojin Zhu and Zoubin Ghahramani. 2002. Learning from labeled and unlabeled data with label propaga-tion. Technical report, Citeseer.

ECNU at SemEval-2016 Task 6: Relevant or Not? Supportive or Not? A Two-step Learning System for Automatic Detecting Stance in Tweets

Zhihua Zhang[1], Man Lan[1,2]*
[1]Department of Computer Science and Technology,
East China Normal University, Shanghai, P.R.China
[2]Shanghai Key Laboratory of Multidimensional Information Processing
`51131201039@ecnu.cn, mlan@cs.ecnu.edu.cn`*

Abstract

This paper describes our submissions to Task 6, i.e., Detecting Stance in Tweets, in SemEval 2016, which aims at detecting the stance of tweets towards given target. There are three stance labels: *Favor* (directly or indirectly by supporting given target), *Against* (directly or indirectly by opposing or criticizing given target), and *None* (none of the above). To address this task, we present a two-step learning system, which performs two steps, i.e., relevance detection and orientation detection, in a pipeline-based processing procedure. Our system ranked the 5th among 19 teams.

1 Introduction

Social platforms, such as *Twitter*, *Facebook*, etc., have attracted hundreds of millions of people to share and express their opinions or standpoints in the past few years. Promoted by that growth, researchers have been enthusiastic about mining useful information in these abundant free texts from social platform, such as stance detection. Determining the stance expressed in a post written for certain target is a relatively new task in sentiment analysis. Classifying stance involves identifying the target of the post and determining its sentiment orientation. The general researches just focus on detecting the stance of posts where the provided posts are relevant to the given target (Somasundaran et al., 2007; Somasundaran and Wiebe, 2010). Besides, the previous work usually aims at the posts collected from forums which have co-posts as reference (Murakami et al., 2007; Agrawal et al., 2003). Some approach-

es were adopted to settle stance detection, for example, Murakami and Agrawal detected the stance in the posts collected from forums and adopted co-posts as reference (Murakami et al., 2007; Agrawal et al., 2003).

The task of Detecting Stance in Tweets (DST) in SemEval 2016 aims at classifying the provided tweets into three stance classes, i.e., *Favor* (directly or indirectly by supporting given target), *Against* (directly or indirectly by opposing or criticizing given target) and *None* (none of the above) refer to a given target. The DST task consists of two subtasks which could be summarized as *supervised* subtask (i.e., subtask A) and *weakly supervised* subtask (i.e., subtask B). The supervised subtask is to test the stances of certain tweets towards five predefined targets with labeled training data, while the weak supervised subtask is to detect the stances of tweets towards one target with the aid of a mass of unlabeled training data.

Somasundaran showed that the stance classifier trained on unigram is a relatively strong baseline (Somasundaran and Wiebe, 2010). Based on Somasundaran and Wiebe's work, Anand augmented the *n*-gram features with several linguistic features (Anand et al., 2011). Except for feature engineering, many researchers focused on other methods to improve performance. For example, Murakami and Sridhar took the forward posts of current post into consideration (Murakami and Raymond, 2010; Sridhar et al., 2014). The previous works usually processed the posts with co-posts or some additional information, such as its author, writing timeline (Faulkner, 2014; Rajadesingan and Liu, 2014;

Proceedings of SemEval-2016, pages 451–457,
San Diego, California, June 16-17, 2016. ©2016 Association for Computational Linguistics

Hasan and Ng, 2013). Differ from these works, the DST focuses on classifying the stance of tweets into three classes, i.e., *Favor*, *Against* and *None*, rather than two classes. Moreover, the organizers did not provide the related information of tweet, such as author information. Thus, to address this task, we decomposed the stance detecting model into two parts, i.e., relevance detection and orientation detection, which aim at determining whether the tweet is relevant or irrelevant to the given target and whether the tweet is in favor of or against the given target. Since the given 6 targets belong to different types, e.g., *Hillary Clinton* and *Donald Trump* are about people, *Climate Change is a Real Concern* is a environmental topic, etc., considering the diversity of different targets, we built unique model for each target with different features. To achieve high performance, we proposed various features, e.g., *Linguistic Features*, *Topic Features*, *Word Vector Features*, *Similarity Features*, etc., to perform stance detection.

This paper is organized as follows. Section 2 reports our systems including preprocessing, feature engineering, evaluation metrics, etc. The data sets and experiments descriptions are shown in Section 3. Finally, we conclude this paper in Section 4.

2 System Description

To address these two subtasks, i.e., supervised framework and weakly supervised framework, we used the two-step model to classify certain tweets into 3 stance labels (i.e., *Favor, Against, None*). The first step (i.e., relevance detection) is to determine whether the tweet is relevant to the given target. The second step (i.e., orientation detection) aims at classifying whether the tweet is support for the given target. To improve the classification performance, we extract various types of features, such as linguistic features (e.g., *N-grams*, *N-chars*), similarity features (e.g., *cosine similarity*, *JSD similarity*), topic features (e.g., *sent2topic*, *top topic word*), sentiment lexicon features, etc. The difference of the methods to settle two subtasks is located in the different training data they used. For subtask A, we segmented the training data into 5 subsets according to the 5 predefined targets and trained two classifiers for each subset. Thus, for subtask A, our system consists of 10

classifiers and we conducted feature selection procedure for each classifier. As for subtask B, we combined all labeled data in subtask A as training data and constructed two classifiers to perform relevance detection and orientation detection.

2.1 Data Preprocessing

Due to the irregular writing form of tweets, we first convert the slangs or abbreviations to their formal forms with the aid of a pre-defined dictionary downloaded from Internet[1]. For example, we convert *"goooooood"* into *"good"*, *"gr8"* to *"great"*. The processed data is fed into *CMU TweetNLP tool* (Owoputi et al., 2013) to perform tokenization, POS tagging. Meanwhile, we employ *Stanford Parser tool* (Klein and Manning, 2003) and *LDA-C* (Blei et al., 2003) to implement dependency parsing and topic parsing respectively. Finally, the *NLTK tool* (Bird et al., 2009) is used to conduct lemmatization and stemming.

2.2 Feature Engineering

Since we decompose the stance detecting task into two steps, i.e., relevance detection and orientation detection, this task is related to similarity evaluation and stance orientation classification. Thus, we extract five types of features, i.e., *Traditional Linguistic Features*, *Similarity Features*, *Topic Features*, *Sentiment Lexicon Features*, *Tweet Specific Features* and *Word Vector Features*.

2.2.1 Traditional Linguistic Feature

N-grams: *N-grams* features are widely used in many NLP tasks. In this task, we extract *unigram*, *bigram*, *trigram* and *4-gram*.

N-chars: We record presence or absence of contiguous sequences of 3, 4, and 5 characters as *N-chars* features, i.e., *3-char, 4-char* and *5-char*.

Pos: There are total 23 types of pos tags collected in training data processed by *CMU TweetNLP tool*. We record the number of each pos tags as *Pos* features.

Cluster: The *CMU TweetParser tool* provides the token clusters produced with the Brown clustering algorithm on 56 million English language tweets. The 1, 000 clusters are served as *Cluster* features.

---

[1]This dictionary and the following Internet resources are available at https://github.com/haierlord/resource.git

Dependency: The dependency tree is generated by *Stanford Parser tool* and each tweet is represented as several triple (i.e., *relation(government, dependent)*). We extract three types of *Dependency* features: *relation-government (Rel-Gov)*, *government-dependent (Gov-Dep)*, *relation-government-dependent (Rel-Gov-Dep)*. The feature value is set as 1 or 0 if corresponding tuple is present or absent in tweet.

Top Tfidf Word (TopTfidf): We divide the labeled tweet datasets with *Favor* or *Against* stances into 5 subsets towards given targets and calculate the *tfidf* score for each word in 5 subsets separately. We collect the 20 words with top $tfidf$ scores in each subset and set binary feature value to indicate whether the corresponding word exists in current tweet as *TopTfidf* feature.

Punctuation: The numbers of exclamations (!) and questions (?) are also noted.

Negation: We collect 29 negations from Internet and designed binary feature to record if there is negation in tweet.

2.2.2 Topic Feature

We feed all training data into *LDA-C tool* to produce some topic-related information.

Sent2Topic: The *LDA* could generate the document distribution among predefined topics. We extract this distribution as *sent2topic* feature.

Word2Topic: Each word in input tweets could be expressed as the probabilities among topics. The *word2topic* feature is represented as the accumulation of the probability of corresponding topic of all word in single tweet.

Top Topic Word (TopTopic): Since the topic probability of each word indicates the significance for corresponding topic, thus we collect the top 20 words in each topic to build *TopTopic* feature.

2.2.3 Similarity Feature

Since we first determine whether the tweet is relevant to the given target, some similarity features are extracted to model the relevance detect classifier.

JSD Similarity (JSD): For each target, we collect the *Favor* and *Against* tweets to construct word distribution for different targets. Specifically, for subtask B, the tweets with *"#DonaldTrump"* are regarded as relevant record. For each tweet, we calcu-

late *Jensen-Shannon Divergence (JSD) similarity* of word distributions between current tweet and corresponding target, which denotes as follows:

$$JSD(S,T) = \frac{1}{2}KL(P_S\|Q) + \frac{1}{2}KL(P_T\|Q)$$

$$Q(w) = \frac{1}{2}(P_S(w) + P_T(w)) \tag{1}$$

$$KL(P\|Q) = \sum_{x \in X} P(x)\,log\frac{P(x)}{Q(x)}$$

where $KL(P\|Q)$ means the Kullback-Leibler divergence between distribution P and Q. Furthermore, we also take the distributions under lemmatization and stemming forms into consideration.

Cosine Similarity (Cosine): Similar with *JSD*, we obtain the word distributions among targets current tweet respectively. The cosine distance among two distributions is calculated as *Cosine Similarity* feature. For *Cosine Similarity*, we take lemmatization and stemming forms into account as well.

Overlap Similarity (Overlap): Overlap Similarity is a simple and effective similarity measure and calculated as follows:

$$Overlap\ Similarity = \frac{|A \cap B|}{|A|} \tag{2}$$

where where $|A \cap B|$ denotes the size of intersection of set A and set B and $|A|$ means the size of set A. Here, we treat the top $5/10/20$ most relevant words of corresponding target produced by the *LDA tool* as $|A|$ and the current tweet as $|B|$. Similar with *JSD* and *Cosine Similarity*, we also consider the lemmatization and stemming forms. Thus, final dimension of *Overlap Similarity* is 9.

ContainTopic: It indicates whether there is any intersection between target words and tweet.

2.2.4 Sentiment Lexicon Feature

We employ the following seven sentiment lexicons to extract sentimental lexicon (*SentiLexi*) features: *Bing Liu lexicon*[2], *General Inquirer lexicon*[3], *IMDB*[4], *MPQA*[5], *AFINN*[6], *NRC Hashtag Sentiment*

---

[2] http://www.cs.uic.edu/liub/FBS/sentiment-analysis.html#lexicon

[3] http://www.wjh.harvard.edu/inquirer/homecat.htm

[4] http://anthology.aclweb.org//S/S13/S13-2.pdf#page=444

[5] http://mpqa.cs.pitt.edu/

[6] http://www2.imm.dtu.dk/pubdb/views/publication_details.php?id=6010

Lexicon[7], and *NRC Sentiment140 Lexicon*[8]. Generally, we transform the scores of all words in all sentiment lexicons to the range of -1 to 1, where the minus sign denotes negative sentiment and the positive number indicates positive sentiment.

Given a tweet, we first convert it to lowercase. Then for each sentiment lexicon, we calculate the following five sentimental scores: (1) the ratio of positive words to all words, (2) the ratio of negative words to all words, (3) the maximum sentiment score, (4) the minimum sentiment score, (5) the sum of sentiment scores. If one word does not exist in one sentiment lexicon, its corresponding score is set to zero.

2.2.5 Tweet Specific Feature

AllCaps: It represents the number of words with uppercase letters.

Hashtag-Ngrams: The hashtag always carries significant information. Thus, we segment the hashtag to normal phrase and construct *Hash-unigram* and *Hash-bigram*.

Elongated: It indicates the number of words with one character repeated more than two times in raw tweet, e.g., *"gooooood"*.

Emoticon: We collect 69 emoticons from Internet and this binary feature records whether the corresponding emoticon is present in tweet.

2.2.6 Word Vector Feature

Word vector is a continuous-values representation of the word which usually carries important information. In this part, we utilize two types of word vector, i.e., general word vector, sentiment word vector.

General Word Vector (GoogleW2V): We used the publicly available *word2vec* tool[9] to get word vectors with dimensionality of 300, which is trained on 100 billion words from Google News as *general word vector*.

Sentiment Word Vector (SWV): Zhang proposed the *Combined-Sentiment Word Embedding Model* to settle sentiment analysis task (Zhang and Lan, 2015). In this work, we continue to use this mod-el to train the *sentiment word vector* with the aid of *NRC140 tweet corpus*(Go et al., 2009).

Since one tweet contains more than one word, we adopted simple *min, max, average* pooling strategies to obtain the text vector. Thus the final text vector $V(t)$ is concatenated by $V_{max}(t)$, $V_{min}(t)$ and $V_{average}(t)$.

2.3 Evaluation Metrics

For both subtask, we adopt the macro-averaged *F* score of *Favor* and *Against* stances (i.e., $F_{macro} = \frac{F_{Favor}+F_{Against}}{2}$) to evaluate the performance, which considers a sense of effectiveness on small classes. To estimate the system performance on training data, we employ $F_{macro} = \frac{F_{Relevant}+F_{Irrelevant}}{2}$ for step1 (i.e., relevance detection) and $F_{macro} = \frac{F_{Favor}+F_{Against}}{2}$ for step2 (i.e., orientation detection).

3 Experiments

3.1 Datasets

Target	Favor	Against	None	Total
subtask A:				
train:				
Hillary	118(17%)	393(57%)	178(26%)	689
Abortion	121(19%)	355(54%)	177(27%)	653
Atheism	92(18%)	304(59%)	117(23%)	513
Climate	212(54%)	15(4%)	168(42%)	395
Feminist	210(32%)	328(49%)	126(19%)	664
all	753(26%)	1,395(48%)	766(26%)	2,914
test:				
Atheism	32(14%)	160(73%)	28(13%)	220
Abortion	46(16%)	189(68%)	45(16%)	280
Hillary	45(15%)	172(58%)	78(27%)	295
Climate	123(73%)	11(6%)	35(21%)	169
Feminist	58(20%)	183(64%)	44(16%)	285
all	304(24%)	230(57%)	230(19%)	1,249
subtask B:				
train:				
Donald		-		68,984
test:				
Donald	148(21%)	299(42%)	260(37%)	707

Table 1: Statistics of data sets in training data for subtask A and B. (*Hillary, Abortion, Climate, Feminist* and *Donald* refer to *"Hillary Clinton"*, *"Legalization of Abortion"*, *"Climate Change is a Real Concern"* *"Feminist Movement"* and *"Donald Trump"* respectively.)

For subtask A, the organizer supplied all training data, which consists of 5 targets, i.e., *"Hillary*

---

[7]http://www.umiacs.umd.edu/saif/WebDocs/NRC-Hashtag-Sentiment-Lexicon-v0.1.zip
[8]http://help.sentiment140.com/for-students/
[9]https://code.google.com/archive/p/word2vec

"Clinton", "Legalization of Abortion", "Atheism", "Climate Change is a Real Concern" and "Feminist Movement". The statistics of datasets are listed in Table 1. For subtask B, the participants just received tweet ids and a script to collect data and the provided tweets have no labels. The distribution of test data of both subtasks is established in Table 1 as well.

3.2 Experiments on Training Data

3.2.1 Subtask A

To address this subtask A, we adopted a two-step method, which aims at determining whether the tweet is relevant to the given target and whether the tweet is support for the given target, respectively. Furthermore, considering the diversity of different targets, we separated the training data into 5 subsets according their targets and trained 5 models to to settle subtask A. For each target, we built two classifiers to perform stance detection. Thus, there are altogether 10 classifiers constructed for subtask A. In order to improve the performance of stance detection, we conducted feature selection procedure for every classifier. The 5-fold cross validation was performed for system development.

Since the majority of features are high dimensional and sparse, e.g., the dimensions of *4-char* and *5-char* in *Feminist* are $15,536$ and $26,658$ respectively, in our preliminary experiments for all five targets, we employed the *Logistic Regression* algorithm implemented in *liblinear tools*[10], which has good generalization for sparse data.

Table 2 shows the results of feature selection experiments for subtask A. For each target, the two columns, i.e., *Rel* and *Ori*, list the optimal feature sets for relevance detection step and orientation detection step, respectively. As for feature selection strategy, we adopted *hill climbing*: keeping adding one type feature at a time until no further improvement can be achieved. Due to page limitation, we only listed optimal feature types for each corresponding target.

From Table 2, it is interesting to find:

(1) The *Similarity Features* are effective to detect the stance regardless of the targets. Since almost half of training tweets are labeled as *None* records which

are not relevant to the given target, the *Similarity Features* are more adept at determining whether the tweet is related to the given target.

(2) The *Sentiment Lexicon* and *SWV* features are not quite effective as expected. Based on the observation on training data, we found that the *Favor* stance tweets not always directly express positive emotion and so are the *Against* tweets. For example, many tweeters usually support or against the target by commenting statements opposed to the given target rather than explicitly express their own opinions to the given target. Thus, it is hard to classify the tweet stance according to its sentiment polarity expressed in tweets alone. Furthermore, we also compared the output of feature selection procedure and the results using all features is much poorer than using optimal feature subsets (e.g., 57.81% vs 65.09% in *Hillary Clinton*), which shows that not all features are suitable for stance detection.

(3) The *Tweet Specific* features are beneficial to this task. It may be that the tweeters often use the emoticons (i.e., *Emoticon*), emphatic words (i.e., *Elongated*, *AllCaps*) to express their attitudes. Besides, the *hashtag* usually carries the main stance of the corresponding tweet.

We also performed preliminary experiments to tune parameters of classifier , e.g., the *penalty coefficient C*. Finally, the optimized configurations listed in Table 3 are adopted for subtask A test data.

3.2.2 Subtask B

As for subtask B, we did not construct extra system and just continued to use the method as subtask A. All labeled data of 5 targets in subtask A were used as training data for *Donald Trump* and two classifiers were built. The last two column in Table 2 shows the experiment results on training data for subtask B. The submitted system configuration is shown in Table 3.

Subtask	Target	Configuration	
		Step1	Step2
A	Hillary	LR, c=1	LR, c=2
	Abortion	LR, c=1	LR, c=2
	Atheism	LR, c=1	LR, c=0.5
	Climate	LR, c=1	LR, c=1
	Feminist	LR, c=5	LR, c=0.5
B	Donald	LR, c=1	LR, c=1

Table 3: System configurations for subtask A and B.

---

[10]https://www.csie.ntu.edu.tw/ cjlin/liblinear/

Feature (category)	Feature	Hillary Rel	Hillary Ori	Abortion Rel	Abortion Ori	Atheism Rel	Atheism Ori	Climate Rel	Climate Ori	Feminist Rel	Feminist Ori	All Rel	All Ori
												Subtask B	
Linguistic	unigram						✓						
	bigram					✓		✓		✓			
	trigram	✓	✓			✓		✓		✓	✓		
	4-gram					✓		✓		✓			
	3-char				✓			✓		✓	✓		
	4-char				✓						✓		
	5-char						✓				✓		
	Pos									✓			✓
	Negation	✓		✓				✓		✓	✓	✓	
	Cluster							✓			✓		
	Rel-Gov						✓	✓	✓		✓		
	Gov-Dep	✓		✓		✓		✓	✓	✓	✓		✓
	Rel-Gov-Dep							✓		✓			✓
	TopTfidf	✓		✓		✓		✓			✓	✓	✓
	Punctuation					✓		✓	✓	✓	✓	✓	✓
Topic	Sent2Topic				✓			✓		✓	✓		
	Word2Topic										✓		✓
	TopTopic			✓	✓	✓	✓	✓	✓	✓			✓
Similarity	JSD	✓		✓	✓	✓	✓	✓	✓			✓	✓
	Cosine			✓	✓	✓	✓	✓	✓		✓	✓	
	Overlap	✓	✓	✓		✓	✓	✓				✓	✓
	ContainTopic	✓		✓				✓				✓	✓
Sentiment Lexicon	SentiLexi												
Tweet	AllCaps		✓		✓	✓		✓		✓	✓	✓	
	Hashtag-unigram					✓		✓		✓	✓		✓
	Hashtag-bigram			✓				✓		✓	✓	✓	
	Elongated			✓		✓		✓		✓			✓
	Emoticon			✓	✓	✓		✓	✓	✓	✓	✓	
Word Vector	GoogleW2V		✓		✓	✓	✓	✓			✓		✓
	SWV								✓				
Steps Results ($F_{macro}\%$)		81.59	72.11	82.51	77.57	83.69	76.78	85.78	62.96	73.39	63.94	80.07	68.65
Final Results ($F_{macro}\%$)		65.09		71.42		73.75		56.22		61.58		63.34	

Table 2: Results of feature selection experiments for subtask A and subtask B. *Rel* and *Ori* stand for *relevance detection step* and *orientation detection step* respectively.

3.3 Results and Discussion

Using the optimum feature sets shown in Table 2 and configurations shown in Table 3, we constructed 10 classifiers for subtask A and 2 classifiers for subtask B and assessed them against the SemEval 2016 Task 6 test data. Table 4 lists the results of our systems and the top-ranked systems on test data provided by organizer for subtask A and B. In subtask A, our system ranked 5th out of 19 teams and in subtask B, the ranking is 5th/9.

Subtask	TeamID	Target	$F_{macro}(\%)$
A	ECNU(5)	Hillary	57.84
		Abortion	61.25
		Atheism	61.96
		Climate	41.32
		Feminist	56.20
		All	65.55
	MITRE(1)	All	67.82
	pkudblab(2)	All	67.33
B	ECNU(5)	Donald	34.08
	pkudblab(1)	Donald	56.28
	LitisMind(2)	Donald	44.66

Table 4: Performances of our systems and the top-ranked system for subtask A and B. *All* stands for the overall result for subtask A.

First, the results in Table 4 showed that our two-step system performed comparable to the best result in supervised framework (subtask A). It indicates that the proposed system and features are adept in detecting stance in tweet. However, compared with the results on training data, the results on test data are much poorer. The possible reason may be the difference between training data and test data. A further deep analysis will be done later.

Second, in subtask B, our system performed worse than the top results. The major reason lies in that we only adopted the same configuration tuned on training data and did not expanded the training data by adding unlabeled data.

4 Conclusion

In this paper, we decomposed the stance detection task into two steps, i.e., relevance detection and orientation detection, which aim at determining whether the tweet is relevant to the given target and whether the tweet is support for the given target. Considering the diversity of different targets, we built unique model for each target. Several types of features are proposed, for example, *Similarity Features*, *Linguistic Features*, *Topic Features*, etc. The experimental results on training and test data show that the proposed systems is suitable for stance detection. In future work, we consider to optimize the feature engineering to avoid overfitting.

Acknowledgments

This research is supported by grants from Science and Technology Commission of Shanghai Municipality (Grant No. 14DZ2260800 and 15ZR1410700), Shanghai Collaborative Innovation Center of Trustworthy Software for Internet of Things (ZF1213).

References

Rakesh Agrawal, Sridhar Rajagopalan, Ramakrishnan Srikant, and Yirong Xu. 2003. Mining newsgroups using networks arising from social behavior. In *Proceedings of the 12th international conference on World Wide Web*, pages 529–535. ACM.

Pranav Anand, Marilyn Walker, Rob Abbott, Jean E Fox Tree, Robeson Bowmani, and Michael Minor. 2011. Cats rule and dogs drool!: Classifying stance in online debate. In *Proceedings of the 2nd workshop on computational approaches to subjectivity and sentiment analysis*, pages 1–9. Association for Computational Linguistics.

Steven Bird, Ewan Klein, and Edward Loper. 2009. *Natural language processing with Python*. " O'Reilly Media, Inc.".

David M Blei, Andrew Y Ng, and Michael I Jordan. 2003. Latent dirichlet allocation. *the Journal of machine Learning research*, 3:993–1022.

Adam Faulkner. 2014. Automated classification of stance in student essays: An approach using stance target information and the wikipedia link-based measure. In *The Twenty-Seventh International Flairs Conference*.

Alec Go, Richa Bhayani, and Lei Huang. 2009. Twitter sentiment classification using distant supervision. *CS224N Project Report, Stanford*, pages 1–12.

Kazi Saidul Hasan and Vincent Ng. 2013. Stance classification of ideological debates: Data, models, features, and constraints. In *IJCNLP*, pages 1348–1356.

Dan Klein and Christopher D Manning. 2003. Accurate unlexicalized parsing. In *Proceedings of the 41st Annual Meeting on Association for Computational Linguistics-Volume 1*, pages 423–430. Association for Computational Linguistics.

Akiko Murakami and Rudy Raymond. 2010. Support or oppose?: classifying positions in online debates from reply activities and opinion expressions. In *Proceedings of the 23rd International Conference on Computational Linguistics: Posters*, pages 869–875. Association for Computational Linguistics.

Akiko Murakami, Tetsuya Nasukawa, Fusashi Nakamura, Hironori Takeuchi, Risa Nishiyama, Pnina Veisberg, and Hideo Watanabe. 2007. Innovation-jam: Analysis of online discussion records using text mining technology. In *International Workshop on Intercultual Collaboration 2007 (IWIC2007)*.

Olutobi Owoputi, Brendan O'Connor, Chris Dyer, Kevin Gimpel, Nathan Schneider, and Noah A Smith. 2013. Improved part-of-speech tagging for online conversational text with word clusters. In *HLT-NAACL*, pages 380–390.

Ashwin Rajadesingan and Huan Liu. 2014. Identifying users with opposing opinions in twitter debates. In *Social Computing, Behavioral-Cultural Modeling and Prediction*, pages 153–160. Springer.

Swapna Somasundaran and Janyce Wiebe. 2010. Recognizing stances in ideological on-line debates. In *Proceedings of the NAACL HLT 2010 Workshop on Computational Approaches to Analysis and Generation of Emotion in Text*, pages 116–124. Association for Computational Linguistics.

Swapna Somasundaran, Josef Ruppenhofer, and Janyce Wiebe. 2007. Detecting arguing and sentiment in meetings. In *Proceedings of the SIGdial Workshop on Discourse and Dialogue*, volume 6.

Dhanya Sridhar, Lise Getoor, and Marilyn Walker. 2014. Collective stance classification of posts in online debate forums. *ACL 2014*, page 109.

Zhihua Zhang and Man Lan. 2015. Learning sentiment-inherent word embedding for word-level and sentence-level sentiment analysis. In *2015 International Conference on Asian Language Processing, IALP*.

MITRE at SemEval-2016 Task 6: Transfer Learning for Stance Detection

Guido Zarrella and **Amy Marsh**
The MITRE Corporation
202 Burlington Road
Bedford, MA 01730-1420, USA
`jzarrella,amarsh@mitre.org`

Abstract

We describe MITRE's submission to the SemEval-2016 Task 6, Detecting Stance in Tweets. This effort achieved the top score in Task A on supervised stance detection, producing an average F1 score of 67.8 when assessing whether a tweet author was in favor or against a topic. We employed a recurrent neural network initialized with features learned via distant supervision on two large unlabeled datasets. We trained embeddings of words and phrases with the word2vec skip-gram method, then used those features to learn sentence representations via a hashtag prediction auxiliary task. These sentence vectors were then finetuned for stance detection on several hundred labeled examples. The result was a high performing system that used transfer learning to maximize the value of the available training data.

1 Introduction

This paper describes a system for performing automatic stance detection in social media messages. Our approach employs a recurrent neural network which was initialized from pre-trained features learned in successive attempts to encode world knowledge via weak external supervision.

Stance detection is the task of determining whether the author of a text is in favor or against a given topic, while rejecting texts in which neither inference is likely. This task is distinct from sentiment analysis in that an *in favor* or *against* stance can be measured independently of an author's emotional state. In stance detection we attempt to mea-

sure how an author's opinion is expressed in spontaneous, unstructured messages rather than the explicit prompts of formal opinion polls.

Declarations of stance are often couched in figurative language that can be difficult for machines to unravel. Consider the texts *We don't inherit the earth from our parents we borrow it from our children* and *Last time I checked, Al Gore is a politician, not a scientist*. To the human observer messages like these contain an interpretable stance relevant to the topic of climate change. But to understand rhetorical devices like sarcasm, irony, analogy, and metaphor, a reader often uses personal experience to infer broader context. For machines, matters are additionally complicated by use of informal vocabulary, grammar, and spelling. Furthermore, training data is often expensive or difficult to collect in bulk. These challenges motivated our efforts to seek transfer learning of broad world knowledge through feature pre-training using large unlabeled datasets.

2 Related Work

It is common for machine learning approaches to begin learning of any new task from scratch, for example by randomly initializing the parameters of a neural network. This disregards any knowledge gained by similar algorithms when solving previous tasks. Transfer learning approaches, on the other hand, store the knowledge gained in one context and apply it to different, related problems. This type of approach is particularly appealing when one lacks sufficient quantity of in-domain labeled training data, such as when there are only a few hundred known examples of a target.

Proceedings of SemEval-2016, pages 458–463,
San Diego, California, June 16-17, 2016. ©2016 Association for Computational Linguistics

One strategy for performing transfer learning is to train the parameters of a neural network on multiple tasks: first on an auxiliary task with plentiful data that allows the network to identify meaningful features present in the corpus, then a second time using actual task data to tune and exploit those features learned in the first pass.

Deep neural networks trained for image classification can be improved when initialized with features learned from distant tasks, for example Yosinski et al. (2014). In natural language processing domains, sentence representations learned on unlabeled data have been shown to be useful across a variety of classification and semantic similarity tasks (Kiros et al., 2015; Dai and Le, 2015; Hill et al., 2016). Weston et al. (2014) used a hashtag prediction task to learn sentence representations that improve a downstream content-based recommendation system.

Previous work in stance detection is significant (Mohammad, 2016), often with a focus on analysis of congressional debates or online forums (Thomas et al., 2006; Somasundaran and Wiebe, 2009; Murakami and Raymond, 2010; Walker et al., 2012) in which discourse and dialogue features offer clues for identifying oppositional speakers. Rajadesingan and Liu (2014) study stance detection in Twitter conversations and use a retweet-based label propagation approach. This objective of this work differs in that we attempt to detect an author's stance purely from analysis of the text of a single message.

3   Task and Evaluation

Detecting Stance in Tweets, Subtask A: Supervised Frameworks (Mohammad et al., 2016) was a shared task organized within SemEval-2016.

The task organizers provided training data in the form of 2,814 tweets covering five topics, with 395 to 664 tweets per topic. The organizers used crowdsourcing to manually annotate these tweets for stance. Class balance varied between topics, with some topics showing significant skew (e.g. *Climate Change is a Real Concern* with 4% AGAINST and 54% FAVOR) while others were more balanced (e.g. *Feminist Movement* with 49% AGAINST and 32% FAVOR). Approximately 74% of the provided tweets were judged to be either in favor or against,

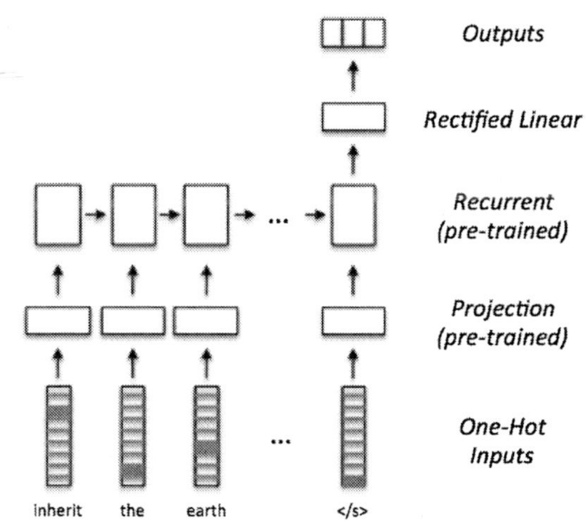

Figure 1: A recurrent neural network for stance detection.

while the remainder contained neither inference. An additional 1249 tweets with held-out labels were used as evaluation data. Systems were evaluated using the macro-average of F1-score(FAVOR) and F1-score(AGAINST) across all topics.

4   System Overview

We now describe an approach to stance detection that employs a recurrent neural network organized into four layers of weights (shown in Figure 1). Input tokens are encoded in a one-hot fashion, such that each token is represented by a sparse binary vector containing a single one-value at the index corresponding to the token's position in the vocabulary. A sequence of these inputs are projected through a 256-dimensional embedding layer, which feeds into a recurrent layer containing 128 Long Short-Term Memory (LSTM) units. The terminal output of this recurrent layer is densely connected to a 128-dimensional layer of Rectified Linear units trained with 90% dropout (Srivastava et al., 2014). Finally, this layer is fully connected to a three dimensional softmax layer in which each unit represents one of the output classes: *FAVOR*, *AGAINST*, or *NONE*.

This approach did not incorporate any manually engineered task-specific features or inputs relevant to the surface structure of the text. The only inputs to the network were the sequence of indices representing the identity of lowercased tokens (words or phrases) in the text. All feature pre-training was done using weak supervision from larger unlabeled text datasets, with a goal of automatically learning useful representations of words and input sequences.

4.1 Pre-Training the Projection Layer

The weights for the projection layer of the network were initialized from 256-dimensional word embeddings learned using the `word2vec` skip-gram (Mikolov et al., 2013a) algorithm. We sampled 218,179,858 tweets from Twitters public streaming API during 2015, and used this unlabeled data as our training corpus. Retweets, duplicates, and non-English messages were not included in this sample. Text was lowercased and tokenized to mimic the style of the task data. We then applied `word2phrase` (Mikolov et al., 2013b) twice consecutively to identify phrases comprised of up to four words, for example making a single token of the phrase *global climate change*.

We then trained 256-dimensional skip-gram embeddings for the 537,366 vocabulary items that appeared at least 100 times in our corpus, with a context window of 10 words and 15 negative samples per positive example. These hyperparameters were chosen in advance based on our prior experience in training embeddings for identifying word analogies and estimating semantic similarity of sentences. Out of vocabulary items were represented by the average of all in-vocabulary vectors.

Note that these projection layer weights were later tuned by backpropagation during training of the recurrent networks. Thus these initializations served to provide the RNNs with initial feature representations intended to capture the nuances of informal word usage observed in a large sample of text.

4.2 Pre-Training the Recurrent Layer

The second layer of our network was composed of 128 Long Short-Term Memory (LSTM) units (Hochreiter and Schmidhuber, 1997). This recurrent layer received as input a sequence of up to 30 embeddings, folding each into its hidden state in turn. It was initialized with weights that were pre-trained using the distant supervision of a hashtag prediction auxiliary task. In this manner the network learned distributed sentence representations from a dataset containing a broad array of stance declarations, rather than relying exclusively on the 2,814 explicitly labeled in-domain tweets.

We began by automatically identifying 197 hashtags with relevance to the topics under consideration, for example *#climatechange*, *#climatescam*, and *#gamergate*. These hashtags were selected on the basis of a nearest-neighbor search of the word embedding space. We queried the vector space using the embeddings of the topic titles, and selected the unique hashtags with high (top-50) cosine similarity. These selections varied greatly in frequency and task specificity, including a number of tags which were related to multiple topics and others which appeared ambiguously related. Half of the 40 most frequent tags in this list were related to the 2016 United States presidential elections. The final list of 197 relevant hashtags was held constant across all experiments.

We extracted 298,973 tweets containing at least one of these 197 hashtags from the 2015 corpus of 218 million English tweets. Text was lowercased, tokenized, and phrase chunked according with the preprocessing choices made during the training of word embeddings. If a tweet contained more than one hashtag, the most frequent tag was used as the prediction target. Tweets were then stripped of all hashtags, including both the correct hashtag and any additional hashtags appearing in the tweet.

This corpus was divided into a training set and development set using a 90/10 split. Each word in the tweet was converted into a vector using the word embeddings. The sequence of vector representations of the words in the tweet served as the input to a neural network with a 128-dimensional LSTM layer, followed by a dense softmax layer over the 197 possible candidate hashtags.

We trained the neural network with gradient descent using AdaDelta and categorical cross entropy minimization. Both the word embeddings and the recurrent layer were tuned during this process. Training continued until the accuracy on the development set reached its maximum, which took seven epochs. The final model correctly predicted development set hashtags with 42.6% accuracy.

5 Experiments

The system described in section 4 was designed to detect stances pertaining to a single topic. As such

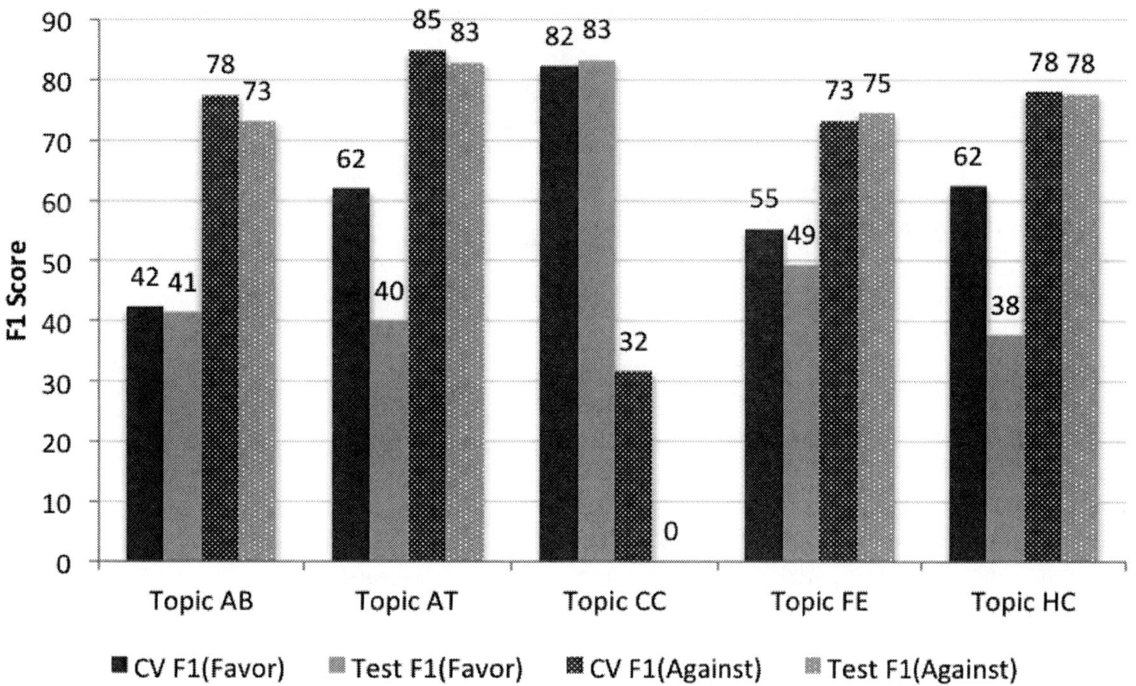

Figure 2: F1 scores for each topic and class on both cross-validation and test conditions.

we trained five distinct classifiers, one for each of the five topics under consideration in the evaluation. The embedding and recurrent layers of each classifier were initialized with the weights obtained from the pre-training process described above. The remainder of the weights were randomly initialized and the network was trained with stochastic gradient descent using a learning rate of 0.015 and momentum of 0.9. These networks were trained using a categorical cross-entropy loss function, with costs for each example weighted according to the prevalence of the class in the training data. This placed higher weight on rare classes. The recurrent networks were implemented using the `Keras` framework (Chollet, 2015).

The training data for each topic was shuffled and split into five chunks for cross-validation. The training process for a single topic's classifier therefore resulted in five distinct neural networks, each learning from 80% of the training data. These training set sizes ranged from 316 to 532 tweets. Each network was trained for 50 epochs, with early stopping to select the model with the best validation loss. Predictions from these five trained networks were used

to select a single class via majority vote at decode time.

Variants of this approach were considered as well. One variant used an identical framework with a recurrent layer initialized instead from a RNN trained on 6.5 million tweets containing the top 10,000 most frequent hashtags (as opposed to 197 topic-relevant hashtags). We also omitted the RNN pre-training altogether and randomly initialized the recurrent layer. These variants were not found to improve performance.

6   Results

Our submission achieved an average F1 score of 67.8 on the *FAVOR* and *AGAINST* classes of the held out test set, which contained tweets from all five topics. This was the top scoring system among the 19 entries submitted to the supervised stance detection shared task.

This same system had an average F1 of 71.1 in testing of the component systems using cross-validation on the training set, indicating a small amount of overfitting. Scores also varied moderately

461

across topics and classes (Figure 2).

One consistent observation across all topics was that the majority class, whether it was *FAVOR* or *AGAINST*, significantly outperformed the corresponding minority class. There was positive correlation ($R^2 = 0.67$) between the F1 score for a given class and the raw number of training examples representing that class.

The weight pre-training and initialization regimes that we applied improved performance relative to the tested alternatives. Entirely omitting pre-training of the recurrent layer (while keeping the projection layer pre-training) resulted in a drop of average F1 from 71.1 to 70.0 in 5-fold cross-validation. Meanwhile the RNN trained to select from among 10,000 popular hashtags led to an average F1 of 66.0, a relative reduction of 7.2% compared to the submission initialized from the RNN trained on 197 highly relevant hashtags.

7   Conclusion

We described a state-of-the-art system for automatically determining the stance of an author based on the content of a single tweet. This approach was able to maximize the value of limited training data by transferring features from other systems trained on large, unlabeled datasets.

Our results demonstrated that hashtag prediction and skip-gram tasks can result in pre-trained features that are useful for stance detection. The selection of domain-relevant hashtags appears to be a crucial aspect of this architecture, as experiments employing a larger collection of frequent hashtags resulted in significantly worse performance on the stance detection task.

Transfer learning does not completely eliminate the need for labeled in-domain training data. The most frequent stance classes uniformly outperformed the minority classes by all metrics. It is likely that stances which are rare in this training set are also proportionally absent from the larger unlabeled auxiliary hashtag task. Future experiments could investigate other techniques for identifying relevant hashtags, with a goal of maximizing the diversity of opinions represented in the auxiliary datasets.

Acknowledgments

This work was funded under the MITRE Innovation Program. Thanks to Spencer Marsh for his timely encouragement. Approved for Public Release; Distribution Unlimited: Case Number 16-1159.

References

Franois Chollet. 2015. Keras. `https://github.com/fchollet/keras`.

Andrew M Dai and Quoc V Le. 2015. Semi-supervised sequence learning. In *Advances in Neural Information Processing Systems*, pages 3061–3069.

Felix Hill, Kyunghyun Cho, and Anna Korhonen. 2016. Learning distributed representations of sentences from unlabelled data. *arXiv preprint arXiv:1602.03483*.

Sepp Hochreiter and Jürgen Schmidhuber. 1997. Long short-term memory. *Neural Computation*, 9(8):1735–1780, November.

Ryan Kiros, Yukun Zhu, Ruslan R Salakhutdinov, Richard Zemel, Raquel Urtasun, Antonio Torralba, and Sanja Fidler. 2015. Skip-thought vectors. In *Advances in Neural Information Processing Systems*, pages 3276–3284.

Tomas Mikolov, Kai Chen, Greg Corrado, and Jeffrey Dean. 2013a. Efficient estimation of word representations in vector space. *ICLR Workshop*.

Tomas Mikolov, Ilya Sutskever, Kai Chen, Greg S Corrado, and Jeff Dean. 2013b. Distributed representations of words and phrases and their compositionality. In *Advances in neural information processing systems*, pages 3111–3119.

Saif M. Mohammad, Svetlana Kiritchenko, Parinaz Sobhani, Xiaodan Zhu, and Colin Cherry. 2016. SemEval-2016 Task 6: Detecting stance in tweets. In *Proceedings of the International Workshop on Semantic Evaluation*, SemEval '16, San Diego, California, June.

Saif M. Mohammad. 2016. Sentiment analysis: Detecting valence, emotions, and other affectual states from text. In Herb Meiselman, editor, *Emotion Measurement*. Elsevier.

Akiko Murakami and Rudy Raymond. 2010. Support or oppose?: classifying positions in online debates from reply activities and opinion expressions. In *Proceedings of the 23rd International Conference on Computational Linguistics: Posters*, pages 869–875. Association for Computational Linguistics.

Ashwin Rajadesingan and Huan Liu. 2014. Identifying users with opposing opinions in twitter debates. In *Social Computing, Behavioral-Cultural Modeling and Prediction*, pages 153–160. Springer.

Swapna Somasundaran and Janyce Wiebe. 2009. Recognizing stances in online debates. In *Proceedings of the Joint Conference of the 47th Annual Meeting of the ACL and the 4th International Joint Conference on Natural Language Processing of the AFNLP: Volume 1-Volume 1*, pages 226–234. Association for Computational Linguistics.

Nitish Srivastava, Geoffrey Hinton, Alex Krizhevsky, Ilya Sutskever, and Ruslan Salakhutdinov. 2014. Dropout: A simple way to prevent neural networks from overfitting. *The Journal of Machine Learning Research*, 15(1):1929–1958.

Matt Thomas, Bo Pang, and Lillian Lee. 2006. Get out the vote: Determining support or opposition from congressional floor-debate transcripts. In *Proceedings of the 2006 conference on empirical methods in natural language processing*, pages 327–335. Association for Computational Linguistics.

Marilyn A Walker, Pranav Anand, Robert Abbott, and Ricky Grant. 2012. Stance classification using dialogic properties of persuasion. In *Proceedings of the 2012 Conference of the North American Chapter of the Association for Computational Linguistics: Human Language Technologies*, pages 592–596. Association for Computational Linguistics.

Jason Weston, Sumit Chopra, and Keith Adams. 2014. #tagspace: Semantic embeddings from hashtags. In *Proceedings of the 2014 Conference on Empirical Methods in Natural Language Processing, EMNLP 2014, October 25-29, 2014, Doha, Qatar, A meeting of SIGDAT, a Special Interest Group of the ACL*, pages 1822–1827.

Jason Yosinski, Jeff Clune, Yoshua Bengio, and Hod Lipson. 2014. How transferable are features in deep neural networks? In Z. Ghahramani, M. Welling, C. Cortes, N.d. Lawrence, and K.q. Weinberger, editors, *Advances in Neural Information Processing Systems 27*, pages 3320–3328. Curran Associates, Inc.

TakeLab at SemEval-2016 Task 6: Stance Classification in Tweets Using a Genetic Algorithm Based Ensemble

Martin Tutek, Ivan Sekulić, Paula Gombar, Ivan Paljak, Filip Čulinović,
Filip Boltužić, Mladen Karan, Domagoj Alagić, Jan Šnajder
University of Zagreb, Faculty of Electrical Engineering and Computing
Text Analysis and Knowledge Engineering Lab
Unska 3, 10000 Zagreb, Croatia
`name.surname@fer.hr`

Abstract

This paper describes our system for the detection of stances in tweets submitted to SemEval 2016 Task 6A. The system uses an ensemble of learning algorithms, fine-tuned using a genetic algorithm. We experiment with various off-the-shelf classifiers and build our model using standard lexical and a number of task-specific features. Our system ranked 3rd among the 19 systems submitted to this task.

1   Introduction

Stance is the overall position held by a person towards an object, idea, or proposition (Somasundaran and Wiebe, 2009). The task of stance detection – the automatic classification of stance expressed in text – has been attracting increasing interest, as it is of practical interest to many stakeholders, ranging from political bodies to companies. Most recent work focused on stance detection in online debates (Somasundaran and Wiebe, 2009; Somasundaran and Wiebe, 2010; Anand et al., 2011; Hasan and Ng, 2014; Sridhar et al., 2015).

Twitter is an outstanding platform for large-scale stance analysis. However, unlike in the case of dedicated online debate platforms, Twitter data is much less structured and dialogical. Furthermore, as pointed out by Rajadesingan and Liu (2014), processing of tweets poses specific challenges stemming from the high volume of data, brevity of messages, and the use of non-standard language.

In this paper, we describe a system for stance classification in tweets, with which we participated in the SemEval-2016 Task 6A. Given a tweet and the topic of the tweet (the *target*), the task was to predict the stance of the tweet author as either in FAVOR of the target, AGAINST it, or NONE. Our system relies on a supervised three-way classifier, using features standardly employed for stance classification and similar tasks, but also a number of task- and target-specific features. The gist of our approach was to start out with the entire "kitchen sink" of features, as well as a number of off-the-shelf classification algorithms, and then perform a comprehensive model optimization on a per-target basis. However, instead of relying on a single model for each target, we trained four different models and combined them into one classifier ensemble for each target using a genetic algorithm. Our system (TakeLab) ranked 3rd among the 19 systems submitted to the SemEval-2016 Task 6A.

2   Related Work

To the best of our knowledge, the only work to have addressed the stance classification in tweets is that of Rajadesingan and Liu (2014), who specifically tackle the data sparseness problem using a semi-supervised approach based on label propagation. Somasundaran and Wiebe (2009) and (2010) address stance detection in two-sided debates using supervised models with opinion-target pairs, as well as sentiment and argumentation trigger words as features. Anand et al. (2011) address the same domain, but also consider the dialogical properties of debates by identifying the rebuttals between posts, while Sridhar et al. (2015) consider the joint stance classification of posts and relations among them. Hasan and Ng (2014) combine stance classification with reason classification in a joint learning framework.

Proceedings of SemEval-2016, pages 464–468,
San Diego, California, June 16-17, 2016. ©2016 Association for Computational Linguistics

3 Model

We approach this task as a three-way multiclass supervised classification problem. We start off with a number of learning algorithms and also design a number of lexical and task-specific features. Subsequently, we reduce the algorithm and feature space by employing a series of optimization rounds. Finally, we train and fine-tune an ensemble of the chosen classifiers using a genetic algorithm. Following sections describe these steps in more detail.

3.1 Features

We first preprocess the data: we tokenize the tweets,[1] stem the resulting tokens, and finally eliminate the stop words using the NLTK toolkit (Bird et al., 2009). In some configurations, we use a sentiment lexicon compiled by Han and Baldwin (2011) to replace all positive and negative sentiment-bearing words with dummy labels POS and NEG, respectively.

We compute two types of features: lexical features and task-specific features. We compute the former after preprocessing and the latter before preprocessing the data. The lexical features are as follows:

- **Word features** – Word unigrams, bigrams, and trigrams, computed as (1) binary vectors, (2) count-based vectors, and (3) tf-idf-weighted vectors. We use a frequency cut-off of 2 and additionally filter based on class entropy with a cut-off set at 1.1;

- **Character features** – Character bigrams and trigrams, computed in the same manner as the word features;

- **Word embeddings** – A 300-dimensional distributional representation of the tweet obtained as as a weighted addition of the distributional vectors of the individual words. We use the freely available[2] skip-gram embeddings of Mikolov et al. (2013) and weight each vector based on the information content of the corresponding word, following Šarić et al. (2012).

We also used the following task-specific features:

- **Counting features** – The average word length, number of retweet symbols, number of hashes, number of emoticons, number of capitalized words, and the number of exclamation marks;

- **Repeated vowels** – Whether the tweet contains at least one sequence of the same vowel longer than two characters. This feature is often employed in Twitter sentiment analysis, e.g., in (Xu et al., 2015);

- **Number of misspelled words** – The number of misspelled words, determined using the freely-available PyEnchant spellchecking library;[3]

- **Scripture citation** – Our analysis of the dataset revealed that, for two out of five targets, namely *Atheism* and *Legalization of Abortion*, the users who quote the scriptures are by and large AGAINST the targets. To capture this regularity, we include a feature that checks whether the tweet matches some of the common scripture citation patterns, such as "*Rom. 14:17*" in "*RT @prayerbullets: Let the righteousness, peace, and joy of the kingdom be established in my life -Rom. 14:17*";

- **Hashtag splitting** – Our analysis also revealed that for some targets the hashtags are highly indicative of the stance. In some cases, however, a hashtag – although highly indicative – occurs quite rarely in the dataset. For example, in the tweet "*Rethink your beach clothes. Bc it may oppress some people!! #thisoppresseswomen*" the hashtag is fully indicative of the stance, but overall it occurs rarely. On the other hand, the unigram "oppress" and the bigram "oppress women" are rather frequent in the dataset and also indicative of the stance. To account for this, we split up each hashtag into its constituent words by employing a simple greedy procedure: we start from the end of the hashtag and work our way towards its start, always taking the longest possible word contained in the dictionary.

3.2 Model Optimization

Algorithm selection. We started off considering a number of different classification algorithms, implemented in the scikit-learn package (Pedregosa et al., 2011): Support Vector Machine (SVM), Random Forest (RF), Logistic Regression (LR), Gradient Boosting (GB), Multinomial Bayes (MB), Extra Trees (ET), and general stochastic gradient descent classifier (SGDC). We then fixed a baseline set of fea-

---

[1]http://sentiment.christopherpotts.net/code-data/happyfuntokenizing.py

[2]https://code.google.com/archive/p/word2vec/

[3]http://pythonhosted.org/pyenchant/

tures consisting of word unigrams and bigrams, and evaluated all the combinations of classifiers and text representations using a 3-fold cross-validation. We discarded the classifiers that performed considerably worse than the others, leaving us with four classifiers: RF, GB, LR, and SVM.

Ensemble learning. We decided to opt for an ensemble classifier using the four remaining algorithms, motivated by the fact that ensembles generally work better than their base learners as well as the fact that all of our algorithms performed comparably.

With this in mind, our next step was to optimize the hyperparameters of each of the four classifiers to have a fixed ensemble model. Since an exhaustive search would be too time-consuming, we arbitrarily fixed multiple feature sets and hyperparameter ranges.

We define the ensemble model as a linear combination of the output probabilities of the classifiers, and optimize its weights with respect to the F-score. A common way of building the ensemble is stacking, in which one uses the classifiers' predictions as inputs to a meta-level classifier. However, we decided not to use this approach as it would not allow us to optimize for the F-score. Instead, we used a genetic algorithm, which works with arbitrary objectives as fitness functions. As we optimize only four values, running time was not an issue.

We modeled the operators of the genetic algorithm as follows. We initialized the population of size 100 uniformly across the interval $[0, 1]$, and constrained the weights to the same interval by clipping. For crossover, we used tournament selection, randomly selecting three individuals from the population, replacing the worst of the three with the child of the remaining two. The crossover created a child by randomly selecting weights from either of the parents. We used mutation with random uniform noise from the interval $[-0.3, 0.3]$.

Feature selection. Lastly, we needed to find the best feature set for each target. We manually compiled a list of feature sets based on our experience with the task as well as intuition about which features work well in practice. We treated the ensemble as a single classifier, and all the constituents received the same feature sets as the input. However, instead of optimizing the score of the individual classifiers, we cross-validated the whole ensemble with respect to

the input features and the F-score, treating the genetic algorithm as a trainable classifier, with the stochastic search as an optimization algorithm.

4 Evaluation

4.1 Task Description

The dataset consisted of 2814 tweets in the train set and 1249 in the test set divided into five targets – *Atheism (ATH)*, *Climate Change is a Real Concern (CC)*, *Feminist Movement (FM)*, *Hillary Clinton (HC)*, and *Legalization of Abortion (LA)*. Possible stances were FAVOR, AGAINST, and NONE, where the latter served both as an indicator of a tweet not being related to the target (e.g., *"Pop may throw in the towel second half.."*), as well as the tweet being neutral towards the target (e.g., *"atheism involves what a person does or does not believe, agnosticism involves what a person does or does not know. #Waterford"*).

The official evaluation measure was the macro-average of F-score for FAVOR and AGAINST across all targets, meaning that weak F-score performance on an unbalanced label distribution for a target could be compensated for by the overall good performance on other targets. Note that the label NONE was ignored during the evaluation. Consequently, misclassifying FAVOR or AGAINST as NONE (or vice versa) was penalized less than misclassifying FAVOR as AGAINST (or vice versa).

Although the task can straightforwardly be approached as a three-way classification problem, it can also be framed as a two-step binary classification problem, first discriminating between NONE and FAVOR+AGAINST, and then between FAVOR and AGAINST. The potential benefit of the two-step approach is that the features may be separated more clearly between classes, while the downside is that the error propagates from the first to the second stage.

The ambiguity of the label NONE posed a problem in approaching the task as a two-step binary classification. The best accuracy on the first step (NONE vs. FAVOR and AGAINST) was around 70%, while the best classifiers reached about 80% accuracy in the second step (FAVOR vs. AGAINST), resulting in an overall much higher error rate than that of the three-way classification model.

4.2 Feature Analysis

As described in Section 3, we used an ensemble of classifiers fit by a genetic algorithm. One of the steps was to determine the best features for each target and for each classifier. For brevity, we provide just a part of the results of our feature analysis study in Table 1. We show the F-score for FAVOR and AGAINST for each target as well as the score across all targets. We consider the following ten feature groups (the first three are the groups used in the submitted system):

- **Group 1** – binary-weighted word unigrams, bigrams, and trigrams, as well as character trigrams and stylistic features (the first four task-specific features). This group was used for the ATH and LA targets;
- **Group 2** – POS/NEG labels, binary-weighted word unigrams, bigrams, and trigrams, character trigrams. This group was used for the CC and FM targets;
- **Group 3** – binary-weighted word unigrams, bigrams, and trigrams, as well as character trigrams, stylistic features, and word embeddings. This group was used for the HC target;
- **Group 4** – binary-weighted word unigrams;
- **Group 5** – word embeddings;
- **Group 6** – binary-weighted character trigrams, word embeddings;
- **Group 7** – frequency-weighted word unigrams and bigrams, character trigrams, stylistic features;
- **Group 8** – no stemming, binary-weighted word unigrams, bigrams, and trigrams, character trigrams, stylistic features;
- **Group 9** – no stemming, frequency-weighted word unigrams, bigrams, and trigrams, character trigrams, stylistic features;
- **Group 10** – frequency-weighted unigrams and bigrams, character trigrams.

4.3 Model Variants

In Table 2, we provide the performances (scored with the official evaluation metric) of the top three systems from the official run, namely MITRE, pkudblab, and TakeLab (our submission), as well as of the number of other model variants we produced. We include our single best performing classifier – the Random Forest classifier (Best single) and an ensemble where the output probabilities are simply averaged (Averag-

Group	ATH	CC	FM	HC	LA	All
1	**0.686**	0.712	0.645	0.638	0.660	**0.698**
2	0.669	**0.720**	**0.689**	0.621	0.658	0.694
3	0.676	0.706	0.654	0.643	0.645	0.689
4	0.673	0,707	0.654	**0.645**	0.636	0.694
5	0.655	0.706	0.659	0.628	0.649	0.692
6	0.672	0.719	0.657	0.631	0.634	0.697
7	0.660	0.719	0.664	0.636	0.655	0.693
8	0.655	0.715	0.655	0.639	0.611	0.692
9	0.672	0.718	0.660	0.618	0.640	0.695
10	0.656	0.714	0.655	0.628	**0.661**	0.690

Table 1: Feature analysis.

Team/model	F1-score
Optimistic	0.6956
MITRE	0.6782
pkudblab	0.6733
TakeLab*	0.6683
Majority vote	0.6522
Averaging	0.6331
Best single	0.6161

Table 2: Model performances (* marks our submitted model).

ing). Additionally, we include an optimistic variant of our best model (Optimistic), where the features and classifier hyperparameters are the same as in our submitted model, but we used the gold labeled test set as the validation set for the genetic algorithm. The result is a rough estimate of the upper-bound F-score of our submitted model on this dataset.

We also include a majority vote per target baseline model (Majority vote). The baseline yields an F-score of 0.6522, which surprisingly places it in the 6th place on the task leaderboard.

5 Conclusion

We described the stance classification system with which we participated in the SemEval-2016 Task 6A. Our system uses an ensemble of supervised classifiers, trained using a number of lexical and task-specific features, and optimized using a genetic algorithm. Our system ranked 3rd in the official evaluation run.

There are many possible directions for future work. One is to use the tweet data of users and their social network to augment the training data. Multitask learning might also be worth investigating, as some of the topics are semantically related. Furthermore, using external knowledge, such as searching the Wikipedia for keywords related to a topic, may be useful for identifying the tweets related to a topic.

References

Pranav Anand, Marilyn Walker, Rob Abbott, Jean E Fox Tree, Robeson Bowmani, and Michael Minor. 2011. Cats rule and dogs drool!: Classifying stance in online debate. In *Proceedings of the 2nd workshop on computational approaches to subjectivity and sentiment analysis*, pages 1–9. Association for Computational Linguistics.

Steven Bird, Ewan Klein, and Edward Loper. 2009. *Natural Language Processing with Python*. O'Reilly Media.

Bo Han and Timothy Baldwin. 2011. Lexical normalisation of short text messages: Makn sens # twitter. In *Proceedings of the 49th Annual Meeting of the Association for Computational Linguistics: Human Language Technologies*, volume 1, pages 368–378. Association for Computational Linguistics.

Kazi Saidul Hasan and Vincent Ng. 2014. Why are you taking this stance? Identifying and classifying reasons in ideological debates. In *Proceedings of the 2014 Conference on Empirical Methods in Natural Language Processing (EMNLP)*, pages 751–762. Association for Computational Linguistics.

Tomas Mikolov, Kai Chen, Greg Corrado, and Jeffrey Dean. 2013. Efficient estimation of word representations in vector space. *arXiv preprint arXiv:1301.3781*.

Fabian Pedregosa, Gaël Varoquaux, Alexandre Gramfort, Vincent Michel, Bertrand Thirion, Olivier Grisel, Mathieu Blondel, Peter Prettenhofer, Ron Weiss, Vincent Dubourg, et al. 2011. Scikit-learn: Machine learning in Python. *Journal of Machine Learning Research*, 12:2825–2830.

Ashwin Rajadesingan and Huan Liu. 2014. Identifying users with opposing opinions in twitter debates. In *Social Computing, Behavioral-Cultural Modeling and Prediction*, pages 153–160. Springer.

Frane Šarić, Goran Glavaš, Mladen Karan, Jan Šnajder, and Bojana Dalbelo Bašić. 2012. TakeLab: Systems for measuring semantic text similarity. In *Proceedings of the First Joint Conference on Lexical and Computational Semantics-Volume 1: Proceedings of the main conference and the shared task, and Volume 2: Proceedings of the Sixth International Workshop on Semantic Evaluation*, pages 441–448. Association for Computational Linguistics.

Swapna Somasundaran and Janyce Wiebe. 2009. Recognizing stances in online debates. In *Proceedings of the Joint Conference of the 47th Annual Meeting of the ACL and the 4th International Joint Conference on Natural Language Processing of the AFNLP: Volume 1-Volume 1*, pages 226–234. Association for Computational Linguistics.

Swapna Somasundaran and Janyce Wiebe. 2010. Recognizing stances in ideological on-line debates. In *Proceedings of the NAACL HLT 2010 Workshop on Computational Approaches to Analysis and Generation of Emotion in Text*, pages 116–124. Association for Computational Linguistics.

Dhanya Sridhar, James Foulds, Bert Huang, Lise Getoor, and Marilyn Walker. 2015. Joint models of disagreement and stance in online debate. In *Proceedings of the 53rd Annual Meeting of the Association for Computational Linguistics and the 7th International Joint Conference on Natural Language Processing*, pages 116–125. Association for Computational Linguistics.

Hongzhi Xu, Enrico Santus, Anna Laszlo, and Chu-Ren Huang. 2015. LLT-PolyU: Identifying sentiment intensity in ironic tweets. In *Proceedings of the 9th International Workshop on Semantic Evaluation (SemEval 2015)*, pages 673–678. Association for Computational Linguistics.

LSIS at SemEval-2016 Task 7: Using Web Search Engines for English and Arabic Unsupervised Sentiment Intensity Prediction

Amal Htait *,+
amal.htait@lsis.org
*Aix-Marseille University, CNRS
LSIS UMR 7296
13397, Marseille
France

Sebastien Fournier *,+
sebatien.fournier@lsis.org

Patrice Bellot *,+
patrice.bellot@lsis.org
+Aix-Marseille University, CNRS
CLEO OpenEdition UMS 3287
13451, Marseille
France

Abstract

In this paper, we present our contribution in SemEval2016 task7[1]: Determining Sentiment Intensity of English and Arabic Phrases, where we use web search engines for English and Arabic unsupervised sentiment intensity prediction. Our work is based, first, on a group of classic sentiment lexicons (e.g. Sentiment140 Lexicon, SentiWordNet). Second, on web search engines' ability to find the co-occurrence of sentences with predefined negative and positive words. The use of web search engines (e.g. Google Search API) enhance the results on phrases built from opposite polarity terms.

1 Introduction

A sentiment lexicon is a list of words and phrases, such as "excellent", "awful" and "not bad", each is being assigned with a positive or negative score reflecting its sentiment polarity and strength. Sentiment lexicon is crucial for sentiment analysis (or opining mining) as it provides rich sentiment information and forms the foundation of many sentiment analysis systems (Pang and Lee, 2008; Liu, 2012).

Sentence intensity is essential when we need to compare sentences having the same polarity orientation. It is expressed by words or phrases with different strengths. For example, the word "excellent" is stronger than "good". The sentiment words, like "good" and "bad", are used to express positive and negative sentiments. But also intensifier and diminisher words can change the degree of the expressed sentiment, an intensifier increases the intensity of a

positive or negative word like "very" and a diminisher decrease its intensity like "barely".

However, sentence intensity prediction of short sentences faces several challenges:

1. Due to the nature of the short sentence itself; the limited size of the sentences, the informal language of the content that may contain slang words and non-standard expressions (e.g. LOL instead of laughing out loud, greaaaaaat etc.), and the high level of noise due to the absence of spell checker tools.

2. Due to the sentiment lexicons not including all of the vocabulary needed, or may not be totally balanced between positive and negative sentences.

Our proposal is to:

1. Calculate the probability of positivity for the phrase in the sentiment lexicons, using the point-wise mutual information (PMI) (Cover et al., 1994).

2. When the phrase is not included in the sentiment lexicons, we use the web search engine to find probability of positivity for the phrase based on its co-occurrence near the word "excellent" and near the word "poor".

2 Related work

The sentiment words are the main factor for sentiment classification, by consequence sentiment words and phrases can be used for sentiment classification in an unsupervised method, a method that

---

[1] http://alt.qcri.org/semeval2016/task7/

Proceedings of SemEval-2016, pages 469–473,
San Diego, California, June 16-17, 2016. ©2016 Association for Computational Linguistics

can solve the problem of domain dependency and reduce the need for annotated training data. The method of Turney (2002) is such a technique. It performs classification based on fixed syntactic patterns that are usually used to express opinions. The syntactic patterns are formed based on part-of-speech (POS) tags, then the sentiment orientation (SO) of the patterns is calculated using the pointwise mutual information (PMI) measure. We renounced the use of syntactic patterns due to the majority of one word phrases in the competition files. Turney and Littman (2003) created two sets of prototypical polar words, one containing positive and another containing negative example words. To compute a new term's polarity, they used the point-wise mutual information (PMI) between that word and each of the prototypical sets (Lin, 1998). The same method was used by Kiritchenko et al. (2014), for the purpose of creating a large scale Twitter sentiment lexicons.

The work of Turney and Littman (2003) is the base of our approach, we use several available sentiment lexicons, and also we use web search engine for each phrase not included in those sentiment lexicons.

3   Difficulties Comparison in this task with languages: English and Arabic

Although the same method is applied for both languages: English and Arabic, the level of difficulty is different when treating both of them. On the resources level, for the English language, we can find many "free" and "available on-line" datasets of sentiment lexicons and labeled tweets (e.g. Sentiment140 with 1600k records). For the Arabic language, the resources are limited and our data-set of sentiment lexicons and labeled tweet is of 16K records only. On the language characters level, the Arabic language needed special treatment for the sentiment lexicons files, and for using the web search engines (e.g. using coding: UTF-8). On the language use and diversity level, there are 22 Arabic-speaking countries but the people of these countries speak their own "mutant-Arabic" languages (dialects), mostly influenced by other languages (e.g. French, English). Also most of the Arabic sentences are pronounced differently (due to accents) in these countries, and then written differently

on the social media.

4   Method

Our contribution is an unsupervised method with the use of web search engine as a way to maximize the chances of finding all the slang words, abbreviations, non-standard expressions that a classic corpora will not include.

The method is to calculate the sentiment score for a term w from the sentiment lexicons as shown in the Equation 1 (Kiritchenko et al., 2014):

$$SentSc(w) = PMI(w, pos) - PMI(w, neg) \quad (1)$$

PMI stands for pointwise mutual information, it measures the degree of statistical dependence between two terms. It is used in our work to calculate the degree of statistical dependence between a term and a class (negative or positive).

$$PMI(w, pos) = \log_2 \frac{freq(w, pos) \cdot N}{freq(w) \cdot freq(pos)} \quad (2)$$

Where $freq(w, pos)$ is the number of times a term w occurs as positive or in a positive tweet, $freq(w)$ is the total frequency of term w in sentiment lexicons and labeled tweets, $freq(pos)$ is the total number of positive terms in sentiment lexicons and labeled tweets, and N is the total number of terms in the data-set (Kiritchenko et al., 2014). $PMI(w, negative)$ is calculated similarly.

For the English language, we have done our testing using the below manual constructed sentiment lexicons:

1. Bing Liu Lexicon of Negative and postive words (Hu and Liu, 2004).
2. MPQA Subjectivity Lexicon, it is a Multi-Perspective Question Answering Subjectivity Lexicon (Wilson et al., 2005).

And the below automatic constructed sentiment lexicons:

3. Sentiment140 corpora containing tweets with positive or negative emoticons (Go et al., 2009).
4. NRC Hashtag Sentiment Lexicon (Mohammad and Turney, 2013).

5. SentiWordNet [2] (Baccianella et al., 2010), it is the result of automatically annotating all Word-Net synsets according to their degrees of positivity, negativity, and neutrality.

6. Sentiment words from the MPQA word list (Riloff et al., 2003; Wilson et al., 2005). We used the positive, negative words only.

7. And we also use the test file's data of Semeval-2013 Task2 (subtaskA) [3] with positive and negative annotated tweets.

And based on the test results, we used the sentiment lexicons 1,3,4,5 and 7 of the ones previously mentioned, which gave the best results.

For the Arabic language, we are using the below manual constructed sentiment lexicons:

1. Arabic Sentiment Tweets Dataset[4], a set of Arabic tweets containing over 10,000 entries.

2. Twitter data-set for Arabic Sentiment Analysis[5], 1000 positive tweets and 1000 negative ones on various topics such as: politics and arts.

3. LABR Lexicons[6].

4. NRC Hashtag Sentiment Lexicon in many languages (Mohammad and Turney, 2013).

The sentiment lexicons and labeled tweets we are taking as a base for our method do not include all the needed phrases and words. For example: the hashtag phrases (e.g. #live_love_laugh), the phrases with no space between the words (e.g. goodvibes), and in Arabic language the English words written in Arabic characters (e.g. cute written as كيوت).

To solve that issue, we use the web search engines to calculate the probability of using the phrase in a positive context, since the orientation of a phrase is negative if that phrase is more associated with the word "poor" and positive if it is more associated with the word "excellent". For that purpose we apply the Equation 3 for the sentiment orientation (SO) (Turney, 2002):

$$SO(p) = \log_2 \frac{hits(pNEAR"excellent") \cdot hits("poor")}{hits(pNEAR"poor") \cdot hits("excellent")} \quad (3)$$

Where $hits(x)$ is the number of pages returned from a search engine for a query based on the phrase used. For example, $hits('poor')$ represents the number of pages returned for the query 'poor'. When there are a phrase p and 'excellent' (or 'poor') connected by $NEAR$ operator, it is the co-occurrences of the phrase and 'excellent' (or 'poor') in same pages on a specified range of words (we choose the range of 10 words (Turney, 2002)). The SO values of the extracted phrase is considered as its sentiment intensity.

Since the main goal of SemEval2016 Task7 evaluation is the ranking of phrases provided according to their sentiment intensity, we are able to simplify the Equation 3 by removing the part shown in Equation 4, which is constant and will not effect the ranking. The final equation we use is Equation 5.

$$hits("poor")/hits("excellent") = 0.637 \quad (4)$$

$$SO(p) = \log_2 \frac{hits(pNEAR"excellent")}{hits(pNEAR"poor")} \quad (5)$$

For the Arabic language, we apply the same concept and equation, but we have to specify the words which once associated to a phrase, they make it more negative or more positive. We have done some tests, on a sample of 40 phrases from development data provided by SemEval-2016 Task7, using the translation of "poor" and "excellent" in Arabic (فقير, ممتاز). We had for many phrases the value of hits(p NEAR ممتاز) and hits(p NEAR فقير) equals to zero. Thus, we decided to choose a group of words that we find most sentimentally expressive:

1. Arabic Positive words:
رائع جميل أحسن أفضل فرح جيد ذكي

2. Arabic Negative words:
مخيف قبيح أسوأ غلط حزين سيئ غبي

We first tested our method using Bing Search Engine API[78]. But the use of the "near:" operator, to restrict the distance between search phrases, did not work as expected. For example when we search

---

[2] File:subjclueslen1-HLTEMNLP05.tff (http://www.cs.pitt.edu/mpqa/)

[3] https://www.cs.york.ac.uk/semeval-2013/task2/index.html

[4] http://www.mohamedaly.info/datasets/astd

[5] https://archive.ics.uci.edu

[6] http://www.mohamedaly.info/datasets/labr

[7] http://www.bing.com/toolbox/bingsearchapi

[8] Bing gives till 5,000 Transactions/month, set at 50 results per query, for free

Method	Kendall	Spearman
Google_Search_API	0.287	0.412
PMI_Sentiment_Lexicons	0.207	0.305

Table 1: Sample Eng. Test: Google Search API and Unsupervised PMI Sentiment Lexicons.

Method	Kendall	Spr.
PMI_Sentiment_Lexicons	0.443	0.620
PMI_Sent_Lex + Google_Search_API	0.452	0.631
Bing_Search_API	0.029	0.039

Table 2: Eng. Test: Bing Search API, Google Search API and PMI Sentiment Lexicons (Spr. as Spearman).

Method	Kendall	Spr.
PMI_Sentiment_Lexicons	0.417	0.584
PMI_Sent_Lex + Google_Search_API	0.402	0.561

Table 3: Arabic Test: Google Search API and PMI Sentiment Lexicons (Spr. as Spearman).

for the word "awesome" near the word "poor", at "near:5" we get 21360 results, and the same search with "near:10", although it should give larger number than the previous since we search in a wider range, it returns 21332 results. And we assume it is caused by the use limitation of Bing Search API, which as consequences gives bad results for the sentiment intensity prediction. Once applied on the test data provided by SemEval-2015 Task10 SubtaskE[9], it gives the below results reflecting the lack of correlation:

Kendall rank correlation coefficient: 0.029

Spearman rank correlation coefficient: 0.039

Then we applied our method using Google Search API[10]. We use it to return the number of documents containing the phrase of the query, within ten words of 'excellent' (or 'poor') in either order.

And as text prepossessing, we removed the hashtags (#) from the phrases, and we replaced the underscores (_) by spaces.

5 Experiments and Evaluations

We test our "English language system" using English test data provided by SemEval-2015 Task10 SubtaskE[11] (1315 of general English phrases). And since the use of Google Search API is limited by a number of queries by day, we tested Google Search API by a sample of 40 sentences from the test data file. As shown in Table 1, the Google Search API gives better results than the unsupervised PMI Sentiment Lexicons method alone.

In the Table 2 we have the results of the methods: PMI_Sentiment_Lexicons, PMI_Sentiment_Lexicons + Google_Search_API and Bing_Search_API, using English test data provided by SemEval-2015 Task10 SubtaskE. The best results are for "PMI_Sentiment_Lexicons + Google_Search_API" although the use of Google

Search API is applied on 5% only of the file's phrases (since those 5% were the only phrases not found in our data-set). And in case of no results returned from Google Search API, the phrase is classified Neutral and the value 0.5 is given as its sentiment intensity.

We test our "Arabic language system" using Arabic development data provided by SemEval-2016 Task7 (200 of Arabic phrases), where we used Google Search API on 20% of the phrases (since those 20% were not found in our data-set). The results are in Table 3. We can notice that the use of Google Search API did not increase the values and that would be due to our choice in Arabic positive and negative words included in the SO equation.

We apply the method with the higher score on the testing data provided by SemEval2016 task7[12]. A data-set was provided for each sub-task: the first sub-task's data-set contains 2799 single words and phrases of general English. The second sub-task's data-set contains 1069 English phrases of mixed polarity words (e.g. lazy Weekend). And the third data-set contains 1166 of single words and phrases commonly found in Arabic tweets. The results of the SemEval2016 Task7 are in Tables 4, 5 and 6. Compared to others teams' systems, which are based on supervised methods with extremely large training corporas (1.6M) or Deep-learning approaches, we can say that our system give good results for the mixed polarity English sub-task (since it has the second best result). Also in the Arabic phrases sub-task, we have interesting results since we applied the unsupervised PMI Sentiment Lexicons method only.

---

[9]http://alt.qcri.org/semeval2015/task10/

[10]https://developers.google.com/web-search/docs/

[11]http://alt.qcri.org/semeval2015/task10/

[12]http://alt.qcri.org/semeval2016/task7/

Team	Kendall	Spearman	Supervision
ECNU	0.704	0.863	Supervised
UWB	0.659	0.854	Supervised
LSIS	0.345	0.508	**Unsupervised**

Table 4: SemEval2016 Task7: General English Results.

Team	Kendall	Spearman	Supervision
ECNU	0.523	0.674	Supervised
LSIS	0.422	0.590	**Unsupervised**
UWB	0.414	0.578	Supervised

Table 5: SemEval2016 Task7: Mixed Polarity English Results.

Team	Kendall	Spearman	Supervision
iLab-Edinb.	0.536	0.680	Supervised
NileTMRG	0.475	0.658	Supervised
LSIS	0.424	0.583	**Unsupervised**

Table 6: SemEval2016 Task7: Arabic phrases Results.

6 Conclusion

In this paper, we present our contribution in SemEval2016 task7: Determining Sentiment Intensity of English and Arabic Phrases, where we use web search engines for English and Arabic unsupervised sentiment intensity prediction. Applying our system to the 3 sub-tasks, faced to other teams' systems based on supervised approaches with much higher costs than ours:

- For the General English sub-task, our system have modest but interesting results.

- For the Mixed Polarity English sub-task, our system results achieve the second place.

- For the Arabic phrases sub-task, our system have very interesting results since we applied the unsupervised method only.

Although the results are encouraging, further investigation is required, in both languages, concerning the choice of positive and negative words which once associated to a phrase, they make it more negative or more positive.

References

Stefano Baccianella, Andrea Esuli, and Fabrizio Sebastiani. 2010. SentiWordNet 3.0: An Enhanced Lexical Resource for Sentiment Analysis and Opinion Mining. *Proceedings of the Seventh International Conference on Language Resources and Evaluation (LREC'10)*, 0(January):2200–2204.

T M Cover, J A Thomas, and J Kieffer. 1994. *Elements of information theory.*

Alec Go, Richa Bhayani, and Lei Huang. 2009. Twitter Sentiment Classification using Distant Supervision. *Processing*, 150(12):1–6.

Minqing Hu and Bing Liu. 2004. Mining and summarizing customer reviews. *Proceedings of the 2004 ACM SIGKDD international conference on Knowledge discovery and data mining KDD 04*, 04:168.

Svetlana Kiritchenko, Xiaodan Zhu, and Saif M. Mohammad. 2014. Sentiment analysis of short informal texts. *Journal of Artificial Intelligence Research*, 50:723–762.

Dekang Lin. 1998. Automatic retrieval and clustering of similar words. *ACL '98 Proceedings of the 36th Annual Meeting of the Association for Computational Linguistics and 17th International Conference on Computational Linguistics*, pages 768–774.

Bing Liu. 2012. Sentiment Analysis and Opinion Mining. *Synthesis Lectures on Human Language Technologies*, 5(1):1–167.

Saif M. Mohammad and Peter D. Turney. 2013. Crowdsourcing a word-emotion association lexicon. *Computational Intelligence*, 29(3):436–465.

Bo Pang and Lillian Lee. 2008. Opinion Mining and Sentiment Analysis. *Foundations and Trends in Information Retrieval*, 2(12):1–135.

Ellen Riloff, Ellen Riloff, Janyce Wiebe, and Janyce Wiebe. 2003. Learning extraction patterns for subjective expressions. *Proceedings of the 2003 conference on Empirical methods in natural language processing*, pages 105–112.

Peter D Turney. 2002. Thumbs up or thumbs down? Semantic Orientation applied to Unsupervised Classification of Reviews. *Proceedings of the 40th Annual Meeting of the Association for Computational Linguistics (ACL)*, (July):417–424.

Theresa Wilson, Janyce Wiebe, and Paul Hoffmann. 2005. Recognizing contextual polarity in phrase-level sentiment analysis. In *HLT '05: Proceedings of the conference on Human Language Technology and Empirical Methods in Natural Language Processing*, pages 347–354, Morristown, NJ, USA. Association for Computational Linguistics.

iLab-Edinburgh at SemEval-2016 Task 7: A Hybrid Approach for Determining Sentiment Intensity of Arabic Twitter Phrases

Eshrag Refaee and **Verena Rieser**

Interaction Lab, School of Mathematical and Computer Sciences,
Heriot-Watt University,
EH14 4AS Edinburgh, United Kingdom.
`eaar1@hw.ac.uk, v.t.rieser@hw.ac.uk`

Abstract

This paper describes the iLab-Edinburgh Sentiment Analysis system, winner of the Arabic Twitter Task 7 in SemEval-2016. The system employs a hybrid approach of supervised learning and rule-based methods to predict a sentiment intensity (SI) score for a given Arabic Twitter phrase. First, the supervised method uses an ensemble of trained linear regression models to produce an initial SI score for each given text instance. Second, the resulting SI score is adjusted using a set of rules that exploit a number of publicly available sentiment lexica. The system demonstrates strong results of 0.536 Kendall score, ranking top in this task.

1 Introduction

Sentiment Analysis (SA) concerns the automatic extraction and classification of sentiment-related information from a given text instance (Thelwall et al., 2012). This is the first time SA on Arabic text is considered in an international competition, like SemEval. Most of previous work on SA is in English, but there have been recent attempts to address SA for Arabic, e.g. (Abdul-Mageed et al., 2012; Mourad and Darwish, 2013; Refaee and Rieser, 2014c; Refaee and Rieser, 2014b). Previous work in this area has mainly focused on identifying the sentiment polarity in a given tweet/phrase, whereas within SemEval-2016 Task 7, the task is to predict the Sentiment Intensity (SI) in Arabic tweets. That is, in addition to their prior association to a sentiment class, i.e. positive or negative, each text instance has an SI score that indicates the strength of its assigned sentiment on a scale from 0 to 1.

In this work, we use a combination of supervised learning and rule-based approaches, exploiting a number of publicly available sentiment lexica. We find that the quality (rather than quantity) of these lexica influence system performance for the supervised part of the system. Our best performing system demonstrates strong results of 0.536 Kendall score, ranking top in SemEval-2016 Task 7. This type of hybrid approach between rule-based and statistical methods has been demonstrated to be successful in other shared tasks, such as dialogue state tracking (Wang and Lemon, 2013).

2 Related Work

Research on predicting Sentiment Intensity in Arabic is still limited. For example, El-Beltagy and Ali (2013) built a sentiment lexicon in which each entry is manually assigned an SI score. Using this lexicon, they calculated the overall Sentiment Orientation for a set of Egyptian tweets by adding up the score of extracted positive/negative words. The authors observed a significant improvement of up to 20.6% in accuracy when exploiting the SI scores, as compared to results using a uniform weighting scheme, i.e. positive word= +1 and negative word= -1.

A recent effort by Eskander and Rambow (2015) presents a large-scale sentiment lexicon for Arabic called SLSA wherein each entry is associated with an SI score. The scores are assigned using a linking algorithm that links the English gloss of each Arabic entry to a synset from SentiWordNet (Esuli and Sebastiani, 2006), which is a large-scale sentiment lexicon for English with SI scores. SLSA

Proceedings of SemEval-2016, pages 474–480,
San Diego, California, June 16-17, 2016. ©2016 Association for Computational Linguistics

is publicly available, and contains up-to-date coverage with nearly 35k lemma. However, SLSA covers only Modern Standard Arabic (MSA), which differs substantially from Dialectal Arabic (DA) typically used in social media platforms (Habash et al., 2013).

Other work that built sentiment lexica for Arabic either includes SA labels without SI scores, e.g. (Abdul-Mageed et al., 2011), or suffers from having duplicated and inflected (surface form) entries, e.g. (Abdul-Mageed and Diab, 2014). Others have not been made publicly available yet, e.g. (Mahyoub et al., 2014).

In this work, we make use of publicly available SI lexica and also contribute to ongoing efforts in automatically creating SI lexica for Arabic.

3 Approach

The proposed system uses a hybrid approach of supervised learning and rules for determining the sentiment orientation and assigning an SI score for a given Arabic phrase (see Figure 1). The assigned scores are real-valued ranging from 0 to 1, with the interval $[0, 0.5]$ associated with negative sentiment and the interval $[0.5, 1]$ associated with positive sentiment.

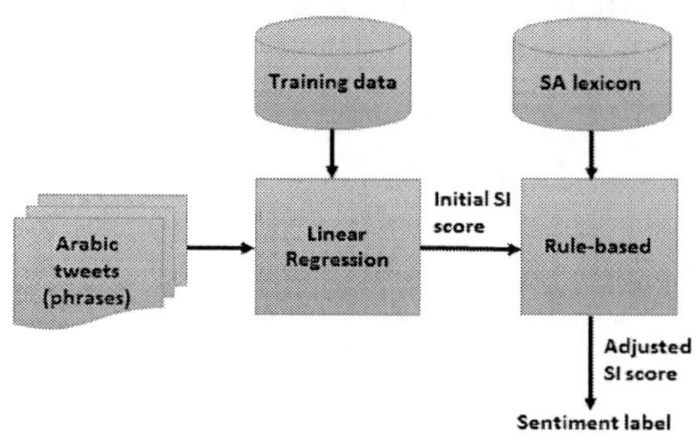

Figure 1: Hybrid system architecture.

3.1 Supervised Learning Component: Training LR models

The supervised part of the system uses Linear Regression (LR),[1] following Amir et al. (2015). To train the LR model, we use training data comprising publicly available sentiment lexica of positive/negative words along with their SI scores (training data-sets are described in section 4.1). We use word-lemma unigrams as features for training the LR models. The trained LR model is used to predict an initial SI score for each given text instance.

Training an LR model on thousands of data instances, such as those we used in our system to train the LR models (see section 4.1), can result in a significant increase in training time. For instance, we recorded a training time of more than 48 hours on a training-set of 10k instances (using a 64-bit operating system with 3.20 GHz, 48 core, 512GB RAM). Therefore, we experimented with several alternative settings. In our experiments, the best results (in terms of speed) are reached using a *bagging* method that generates multiple versions of a predictor, each of which is trained on a different sub-set of the learning data (Breiman, 1996). Each predictor produces a numerical value representing its prediction on a given test instance. The predictors are combined by averaging the output. In our experiments, we used an ensemble of 10 predictors, following (Banko and Brill, 2001), which produced a considerable reduction in training time (12.6 minutes to train an LR model using 10k instances).

3.2 Rule-based Component

In the second part of the system, the initial SI scores are passed to a rule-based component wherein a set of hand-crafted rules are applied to adjust the SI scores. The rules we use are inspired by those proposed by Taboada et al. (2011) and Thelwall et al. (2012) for lexicon-based SA. In particular, we use a combination of three publicly available sentiment lexica (see Section 4.2) [2] together with the following rules:

- Whenever a negative word from the combined lexicon (section 4.2) is detected, the SI score will be scaled towards negative $[0, 0.5]$.

- Same for positive words, except that the SI score will be scaled towards positive $[0.5, 1]$.

- If a negator is detected, the score will be shifted by a fixed amount, i.e. $+0.4/-0.4$. The

---

[1]We use WEKA's implementation of the LR scheme (Witten et al., 2013) with the default parameters configuration.

[2]Note that the sentiment lexica used in the 2nd phase are only associated with their sentiment labels, i.e. positive and negative, and are different from sentiment lexica used in the 1st phase of the system to train LR models.

only exception is when the SI score is between $[0.45, 0.55]$; then it will be considered neutral and will not be affected by negation.

- Finally, if no entries are found in the combined lexicon, then the final score will be the SI score initially assigned by the LR ensemble.

4 Data and Sentiment Lexica

4.1 Resources Used in the 1st Phase of the System: Training the LR Models

For the supervised LR models, we train with the following publicly available sentiment lexica that include SI scores. Note that the system that entered the competition only uses the labMT1.0 Sentiment Lexicon (see Section 6).

labMT1.0 Sentiment Lexicon: This is a compiled list of the most frequently-used 10k Arabic words from several resources including Twitter by Dodds et a. (2015). Each entry was manually annotated by 50 native speakers via Amazon MTurk using a nine-point-scale (1 very-negative/ 5 neutral/ 9 very-positive). We re-scale the manually assigned SI values to [0,1].

9k manually annotated Arabic Twitter data-set (Ar-tweet): This is a manually annotated and publicly available multi-dialect data-set of 9k Arabic tweets (Refaee and Rieser, 2014a). A feature vector representation of these tweets is created forming a list/lexicon of word-based unigrams. We add SI scores to this lexicon using an SVM classifier, following (Guyon et al., 2002). The classifier ranks the words according to how informative/useful they are for predicting the positive/negative label, see Table 1. Excluding words with a weight=0, the current list includes 9,785 words/features along with their weights/coefficients as assigned by the SVM classifier. Again, the SVM coefficients are re-scaled to [0,1].

SLSA v1.0 lexicon: This is a freely available sentiment lexicon for MSA (Eskander and Rambow, 2015). The lexicon is composed of nearly 35k entries annotated with their SI scores using a linking algorithm, as described in Section 2.

4.2 Resources Used in the 2nd Phase of the System: Rule-based Method

For the rule-based part of the system, the entries of the sentiment lexica do not need to be associated with SI scores. We therefore use a combination of the following resources:

ArabSenti sentiment lexicon: This is a freely available and manually annotated sentiment lexicon of 1,492 words that was created by Abdul-Mageed et al. (2011). Each entry is associated with a positive/negative sentiment label.

MPQA English sentiment lexicon: This is a manually annotated English lexicon that is created and made publicly available by Wilson et al. (2005). We automatically translate the lexicon (using Google Translate) and then manually filter it to remove irrelevant or no-sentiment-bearing words. The resultant lexicon includes 2,627 entries.

A manually annotated dialectal sentiment lexicon: This is a publicly available sentiment lexicon of 489 dialectal Arabic words. The lexicon is manually annotated by native speakers of Arabic (Refaee and Rieser, 2014a).[3]

4.3 Data Used for Developing and Evaluating the System

We use the data sets provided by SemEval Task 7.

SemEval'16 gold-standard development-set: This is a list of 200 instances (words/phrases taken from Arabic tweets) with their SI scores manually assigned. The entries can include negations. This set is used to evaluate different versions of the system.

SemEval'16 gold-standard test-set: This is a list of 1,166 instances (words/phrases taken from Arabic tweets) with their SI scores manually assigned. This data-set is used to evaluate the final system.

5 Data Pre-processing

We adopt a number of pre-processing techniques to tackle informality and alleviate the noise typically encountered in social media, following previous work, e.g. (Go et al., 2009; Bifet and Frank,

---

[3]The latter two lexica are available at: `http://goo.gl/qNLIZ2`

	Positive			Negative		
ID	**Arabic**	**English**	**SVM-weight**	**Arabic**	**English**	**SVM-weight**
1	مبروك	congratulations	0.7378	ابليس	devil	-0.0327
2	جميل	beautiful	0.6337	ارهَاب	terrorism	-0.5145
3	حلو	nice	0.5178	دمَار	destruction	-0.3653
4	ابدَاع	creative	0.4878	حقد	hatred	-0.3474
5	ابطَال	heros	0.0653	جحيم	hell	-0.3345

Table 1: Examples of the most predictive word uni-grams in the Ar-tweet data-set as evaluated by an SVM.

2010; Kouloumpis et al., 2011; Agarwal et al., 2011; Ahmed et al., 2013; Balahur et al., 2014; Rosenthal et al., 2014). The following procedures are applied to Ar-tweet (section 4.1) and SemEval's data-sets (section 4.3). Text lemmatisation is applied to all data described in section 4.

- **Normalising conventional symbols of Twitter:** this involves detecting entities like: #hashtags, @user-names, RT, and URLs; and replacing them by place-holders.

- **Normalising exchangeable Arabic letters**: mapping letters with various forms (i.e. *alef* and *yaa*) to their representative character.

- **Removing punctuations and normalising digits.**

- **Reducing emphasised words/expressive lengthening**: this involves normalising word-lengthening effects. In particular, a word that has a letter repeated subsequently more than 2 times will be reduced to 2 (e.g. *sadddd* is reduced to *sadd*).

- **Text lemmatisation:** we use lemmatised word-form to maximise coverage of the combined sentiment lexicon, following Taboada et al. (2011).[4]

6 Experiments and Results

We experimented using different combinations of lexical features (word-lemma unigrams) to train the LR models used in the 1st part of the system. The 2nd part is fixed throughout. Results are summarised in Table 2. The reported results are the final outcomes for the entire system, i.e. after adjusting IS

[4]For lemmatisation, we use a stat-of-the-art Arabic morphological analyser, namely MADAMIRA v1.0 (Pasha et al., 2014).

scores in phase 2. Overall, we recorded an average improvement of 14% for applying the 2nd phase of the system. We report on Kendall's rank correlation coefficient (τ) and Spearman's coefficient (ρ) to account for SI ordering. Further details of the task, data and competing systems can be found in the task description paper (Kiritchenko et al., 2016).

System 1: (*official submission to SemEval-16*) This version of the system attained the best performance at a Kendall score of 0.5362 using lexical features based on the LabMT lexicon. This version has entered the competition and won Task 7.

System 2: This version uses features based on the Ar-tweet lexicon, which have resulted in a significantly (p $<$0.05) lower performance as compared to LabMT at 0.0243 τ. A possible explanation for the performance variation is that the Ar-tweet lexicon is an auto-generated one. This auto-generation makes it prone to the inclusion of 'indirect' sentiment indicators (i.e. indicators which are merely inferred by the SVM model), because, for example, they are likely to appear in a negative political context. For instance, the SVM model assigned a strong negative weight of -0.78 for the feature *Bashar Al-Asad*, which is currently occurring in the context of the Syrian civil war. Thelwall et al. (2012) argue that such a feature can become outdated/irrelevant at a different point in time. Furthermore, human annotators, such as those recruited to annotate SemEval's test-set, are more likely to assign a neutral SI score to a feature like *Bashar Al-Asad*. In future, we will explore setting threshold values to filter features with lower SVM-weights as a mechanism to avoid the presence of indirect sentiment-bearing features.

System 3: Using SLSA, this version of the system is able to attain a comparable score to that recorded

System	Features	Kendall's τ coefficient	Spearman's ρ coefficient
1*	*labMT1.0*	**0.5362**	**0.67997**
2	Ar-tweet SVM-coeff.	0.0243	0.04329
3	SLSA	0.5244	0.65647
4	1 + 2	0.5261	0.66825
5	1 + 3	0.5256	0.67461
6	1 + 2 + 3	0.5141	0.66450

Table 2: Results on SemEval'16 gold-standard test-set using different lexical features for LR models. *System 1 entered the competition.

with LabMT. Although auto-generated (see section 4.1), SLSA is able to attain a Kendall score of up to 0.5244. SLSA has the advantage of being more than 3 times larger in size than LabMT (System 1) and Ar-tweet (System 2). In addition, the auto-generated SI scores in SLSA differs from the ones generated with SVM in Ar-tweet (System 2), as the former relies on linking Arabic entries to their corresponding English synset in SentiWordNet (Esuli and Sebastiani, 2006). Furthermore, being only based on MSA, SLSA can be assumed to be less noisy, especially when mapped to lemma-form, compared to slang and spelling variation in DA.

System 4: Combining LabMT and Ar-tweet has resulted in a comparable performance to System 3 at a Kendall score of 0.5261. However, this system is still not able to outperform that using LabMT on its own (see System 1). A possible explanation is that the presence of Ar-tweet results in introducing more noise than improving coverage of features (see System 2), resulting in slight degrading below the score attained by LabMT on its own (System 1).

System 5: Combining LabMT and SLSA has resulted in a slight improvement over using SLSA on its own, but still not competing with the performance of LabMT. However, when only considering phase 1 on its own, LabMT+SLSA performs best at a Kendall score of 0.377. In future work, we plan to investigate possible interactions between SLSA and the lexica used in phase 2.

System 6: Finally, combining all the training data still cannot reach the performance of LabMT on its own. It is also interesting to note that adding the auto-generated Ar-tweet caused a slight drop in Kendal score, compared to only using LabMT+SLSA (System 5).

7 Conclusion

This paper describes the iLab-Edinburgh Sentiment Analysis system, which is the top performing system of Arabic Twitter subtask for SemEval-2016 Task 7 (Kiritchenko et al., 2016). The aim of the task is to determine Sentiment Intensity for phrases taken from Arabic tweets. The proposed system consists of two phases: First, an ensemble of linear regression models are trained on lexicon-based word-lemma unigrams. Second, the SI scores are adjusted using a set of rules, leveraging pre-existing sentiment lexica. We experiment with different lexica for training the LR models. We find that the best results are attained using a manually annotated lexicon, labMT1.0 Sentiment Lexicon (Dodds et al., 2015). We also observe a drop in performance when adding features based on an auto-generated lexicon, which we attribute to noise. This highlights the need for high quality sentiment lexica for this task.

References

Muhammad Abdul-Mageed and Mona Diab. 2014. SANA: A large scale multi-genre, multi-dialect lexicon for Arabic subjectivity and sentiment analysis. In *Proceedings of the Language Resources and Evaluation Conference (LREC)*.

Muhammad Abdul-Mageed, Mona T. Diab, and Mohammed Korayem. 2011. Subjectivity and sentiment analysis of Modern Standard Arabic. In *Proceedings of the 49th Annual Meeting of the Association for Computational Linguistics: Human Language Technologies: short papers - Volume 2*, HLT '11, pages 587–591, Stroudsburg, PA, USA. Association for Computational Linguistics.

Muhammad Abdul-Mageed, Sandra Kuebler, and Mona Diab. 2012. SAMAR: A system for subjectivity and sentiment analysis of Arabic social media. In *Proceedings of the 3rd Workshop in Computational Ap-*

proaches to Subjectivity and Sentiment Analysis, pages 19–28. Association for Computational Linguistics.

Apoorv Agarwal, Boyi Xie, Ilia Vovsha, Owen Rambow, and Rebecca Passonneau. 2011. Sentiment analysis of Twitter data. In *Proceedings of the Workshop on Languages in Social Media*, pages 30–38. Association for Computational Linguistics.

Shehab Ahmed, Michel Pasquier, and Ghassan Qadah. 2013. Key issues in conducting sentiment analysis on Arabic social media text. In *Innovations in Information Technology (IIT), 2013 9th International Conference on*, pages 72–77. IEEE.

Silvio Amir, Wang Ling, Ramón Astudillo, Bruno Martins, Mario J. Silva, and Isabel Trancoso. 2015. INESC-ID: A regression model for large scale twitter sentiment lexicon induction. In *Proceedings of the 9th International Workshop on Semantic Evaluation (SemEval 2015)*, pages 613–618, Denver, Colorado, June. Association for Computational Linguistics.

Alexandra Balahur, Rada Mihalcea, and Andrés Montoyo. 2014. Computational approaches to subjectivity and sentiment analysis: Present and envisaged methods and applications. *Computer Speech & Language*, 28(1):1–6.

Michele Banko and Eric Brill. 2001. Scaling to very very large corpora for natural language disambiguation. In *Proceedings of the 39th annual meeting on association for computational linguistics*, pages 26–33. Association for Computational Linguistics.

Albert Bifet and Eibe Frank. 2010. Sentiment knowledge discovery in Twitter streaming data. In *Discovery Science*, pages 1–15. Springer.

Leo Breiman. 1996. Bagging predictors. *Machine learning*, 24(2):123–140.

Peter Sheridan Dodds, Eric M. Clark, Suma Desu, Morgan R. Frank, Andrew J. Reagan, Jake Ryland Williams, Lewis Mitchell, Kameron Decker Harris, Isabel M. Kloumann, James P. Bagrow, Karine Megerdoomian, Matthew T. McMahon, Brian F. Tivnan, and Christopher M. Danforth. 2015. Human language reveals a universal positivity bias. *Proceedings of the National Academy of Sciences*, 112(8):2389–2394.

Samhaa R El-Beltagy and Ahmad Ali. 2013. Open issues in the sentiment analysis of Arabic social media: A case study. In *Innovations in Information Technology (IIT), 2013 9th International Conference on*, pages 215–220. IEEE.

Ramy Eskander and Owen Rambow. 2015. SLSA: A sentiment lexicon for Standard Arabic. In *Proceedings of the 2015 Conference on Empirical Methods in Natural Language Processing*, pages 2545–2550, Lisbon, Portugal, September. Association for Computational Linguistics.

Andrea Esuli and Fabrizio Sebastiani. 2006. SentiWordNet: A publicly available lexical resource for opinion mining. In *Proceedings of LREC*, volume 6, pages 417–422.

Alec Go, Richa Bhayani, and Lei Huang. 2009. Twitter sentiment classification using distant supervision. *CS224N Project Report, Stanford*, pages 1–12.

Isabelle Guyon, Jason Weston, Stephen Barnhill, and Vladimir Vapnik. 2002. Gene selection for cancer classification using support vector machines. *Machine learning*, 46(1-3):389–422.

Nizar Habash, Ryan Roth, Owen Rambow, Ramy Eskander, and Nadi Tomeh. 2013. Morphological analysis and disambiguation for dialectal Arabic. In *HLT-NAACL*, pages 426–432.

Svetlana Kiritchenko, Saif M. Mohammad, and Mohammad Salameh. 2016. Semeval-2016 task 7: Determining sentiment intensity of English and Arabic Phrases. In *Proceedings of the International Workshop on Semantic Evaluation*, SemEval'16, San Diego, California, June.

Efthymios Kouloumpis, Theresa Wilson, and Johanna Moore. 2011. Twitter sentiment analysis: The good the bad and the OMG! *In Fifth International AAAI Conference on Weblogs and Social Media (ICWSM)*, 11:538–541.

Fawaz HH Mahyoub, Muazzam A Siddiqui, and Mohamed Y Dahab. 2014. Building an Arabic sentiment lexicon using semi-supervised learning. *Journal of King Saud University-Computer and Information Sciences*, 26(4):417–424.

Ahmed Mourad and Kareem Darwish. 2013. Subjectivity and sentiment analysis of Modern Standard Arabic and Arabic microblogs. *WASSA 2013*, page 55.

Arfath Pasha, Mohamed Al-Badrashiny, Mona Diab, Ahmed El Kholy, Ramy Eskander, Nizar Habash, Manoj Pooleery, Owen Rambow, and Ryan Roth. 2014. MADAMIRA: A fast, comprehensive tool for morphological analysis and disambiguation of Arabic. In *Proceedings of the Ninth International Conference on Language Resources and Evaluation (LREC'14)*, Reykjavik, Iceland, may. European Language Resources Association (ELRA).

Eshrag Refaee and Verena Rieser. 2014a. An Arabic twitter corpus for subjectivity and sentiment analysis. In *9th International Conference on Language Resources and Evaluation (LREC'14)*.

Eshrag Refaee and Verena Rieser. 2014b. Evaluating distant supervision for subjectivity and sentiment analysis on Arabic twitter feeds. In *Proceedings of the EMNLP 2014 Workshop on Arabic Natural Language Processing (ANLP)*.

Eshrag Refaee and Verena Rieser. 2014c. Subjectivity and sentiment analysis of Arabic twitter feeds with limited resources. In *Workshop on Free/Open-Source Arabic Corpora and Corpora Processing Tools (OS-ACT)*.

Sara Rosenthal, Preslav Nakov, Alan Ritter, and Veselin Stoyanov. 2014. Semeval-2014 task 9: Sentiment analysis in twitter. *Proc. SemEval*.

Maite Taboada, Julian Brooke, Milan Tofiloski, Kimberly Voll, and Manfred Stede. 2011. Lexicon-based methods for sentiment analysis. *Computational linguistics*, 37(2):267–307.

Mike Thelwall, Kevan Buckley, and Georgios Paltoglou. 2012. Sentiment strength detection for the social web. *Journal of the American Society for Information Science and Technology*, 63(1):163–173.

Zhuoran Wang and Oliver Lemon. 2013. A simple and generic belief tracking mechanism for the dialog state tracking challenge: On the believability of observed information. In *Proceedings of the SIGDIAL 2013 Conference*, page 423–432, Metz, France, August. ACL, Association for Computational Linguistics.

Theresa Wilson, Janyce Wiebe, and Paul Hoffmann. 2005. Recognizing contextual polarity in phrase-level sentiment analysis. In *Proceedings of the conference on human language technology and empirical methods in natural language processing*, pages 347–354. Association for Computational Linguistics.

Ian H Witten, Eibe Frank, and Mark A Hall. 2013. *Data Mining: Practical machine learning tools and techniques*. Morgan Kaufmann.

UWB at SemEval-2016 Task 7: Novel Method for Automatic Sentiment Intensity Determination

Ladislav Lenc, Pavel Král and **Václav Rajtmajer**
Dept. of Computer Science & Engineering
Faculty of Applied Sciences
University of West Bohemia
Plzeň, Czech Republic
{llenc,pkral,rajtmajv}@kiv.zcu.cz

Abstract

We present a novel method for determining sentiment intensity. The main goal is to assign a phrase a score from 0 to 1 which indicates the strength of its association with positive sentiment. The proposed model uses a rich set of features with Gaussian processes regression model that computes the final score. The system was evaluated on the data from 7th task of SemEval 2016. Our regression model trained on the development data reached Kendall rank correlation of 0.659 on general English phrases and 0.414 on English Twitter test data.

1 Introduction

A great part of today's communication takes place on the Internet. Many companies make their business on the Web, it is possible to read newspapers through this media, etc. All these topics are tightly connected with forums, reviews and comments where users express their opinions and feelings. This great amount of short messages is a very rich source of information. For example companies can survey how people appreciate their goods or services. Social media such as Twitter or Facebook can also provide large amount of data for opinion and sentiment analysis.

Sentiment analysis can be seen as a part of opinion mining that gives the affective part of an opinion (Kim and Hovy, 2004). The short texts are usually assigned either positive or negative sentiment (i.e. sentiment polarity). It can be done for example by text categorization techniques. The minimum

cuts are used for this task in (Pang and Lee, 2004). Another sentiment analysis approach based on Latent Dirichlet Allocation (LDA) is proposed in (Li et al., 2010).

Many researchers evaluate their approaches on movie or product reviews. Lately, with the boom of social networks, there are also applications that analyze sentiment on Twitter (Wang et al., 2011).

An important progress was made thanks to the SemEval workshop (Rosenthal et al., 2015) in a sentiment analysis task. The task of determining sentiment intensity was introduced as a part of SemEval 2015 task 10. The goal of this task is to associate a word (or a short phrase) with a score that indicates its sentiment level. A score of 1 means that the phrase is fully positive whereas 0 is assigned to negative ones. This approach allows much more fine-grained sentiment evaluation. This year, sentiment intensity determination is the objective of the task 7 (Kiritchenko et al., 2016) and aims at three separate datasets: General English phrases, English Twitter and Arabic Twitter.

An interesting method that uses no linguistic resources and is based on word embeddings was proposed in (Astudillo et al., 2015). The system reached Kendall rank correlation of 0.625 on the SemEval 2015 test data. Another successful system (Zhang et al., 2015) used sentiment lexicons and a regression model to determine the sentiment intensity.

The proposed system computes a rich set of features which are further used to train a regression model that computes the final sentiment intensity score. Four different types of features are proposed:

- lexicon based features;

481

Proceedings of SemEval-2016, pages 481–485,
San Diego, California, June 16-17, 2016. ©2016 Association for Computational Linguistics

List	hp	p	n	hn	int	inv	dim
Words	171	772	782	554	83	15	31

Table 1: Numbers of words in the JRC sentiment lexicon

- word2vec embeddings (Mikolov et al., 2013) based features;
- classifier based features;
- other features.

The paper is organized as follows. Section 2 describes the proposed system. Section 3 summarizes the experiments conducted with individual features and presents further the final results on the test data. Section 4 then concludes the paper and lists some perspectives for the future research.

2 Proposed System

The first part of this section is focused on the proposed features while the second one deals with the regression model.

The first group of the features used in the proposed system is built upon the sentiment lexicons.

2.1 Sentiment Lexicons

2.1.1 AFINN

AFINN 111 (Nielsen, 2011) contains 2,477 English words or 2-word phrases. All entries are associated with an integer value in the interval from -5 to 5.

Therefore, we have normalized these numbers to the interval $[0; 1]$.

2.1.2 JRC

This lexicon was created by using the approach proposed in (Steinberger et al., 2012). It contains four lists of words grouped according to their sentiment (*hp* - highly positive, *p* = positive, *n* = negative, *hn* = highly negative) and additional lists of intensifiers (*int*), inverters (*inv*) and diminishers (*dim*). Table 1 summarizes the numbers of words in these lists.

We have joined the four lists and associated all entries with vales 0, 0.25, 0.75 or 1 corresponding to its presence in the *hn*, *n*, *p* or *hp* list respectively.

2.1.3 SentiWordNet

SentiWordNet (SWN) is a large lexicon for sentiment analysis and opinion mining applica-

tions (Esuli and Sebastiani, 2006). We used the version 3.0 (Baccianella et al., 2010) which contains the results of automatic annotation of synsets from the WordNet dictionary. Each synset is annotated with three scores: *positivity*, *negativity* and *objectivity*. The sum of these three values is always equal to 1. Each word can have several entries for different meanings and for different Parts Of Speech (POS) tags.

To obtain one sentiment intensity value, we compute a score according to the Equation 1.

$$\frac{1}{P} \sum_{p=1}^{P} \sum_{m=1}^{M} \frac{1}{m}(Pos_{p,m} - Neg_{p,m}) \qquad (1)$$

where P is the number of POS tags that the word has entries for and M is the number of meanings that the word can have. $Pos{p,m}$ and $Neg{p,m}$ are the positivity and negativity word values with the given POS p and meaning m. The *objectivity* value was not used in this computation.

2.2 Features

We list below the features that we used to build our regression model. The features that are built upon the dictionaries (i.e. Direct search, W2V search and Rule based W2V search) are computed for each of the above described dictionaries.

1. **Direct search**: We search an intensity value of a particular word in the dictionary (if present, the result is its value, if not, the result is the neutral value 0.5). For multi-word phrases, we compute the arithmetic mean of all word values in the phrase.

2. **W2V search**: This approach is motivated by the assumption that semantically close words have often also similar sentiment (e.g. "nice" and "fine"). Of course, some exceptions can occur (e.g. "good" and "bad"), however we would like to minimize their impact by averaging a significant number of other close words.

   Word2vec is used to identify N semantically closest words from the dictionary for a word given. The resulting value is computed according to the Equation 2.

$$score = \frac{1}{KN} \sum_{k=1}^{K} \sum_{n=1}^{N} int(word_{k,n}) \qquad (2)$$

where K is the number of words in the analyzed phrase, N is the number of most similar words identified by word2vec and $int(word_{k,n})$ denotes the intensity value of n-*th* most similar word to the *k-th*. The intensity value is provided by a particular dictionary (described above).

3. **Rule based (rb) W2V search**: This feature computing approach is an extension of the previous one with two significant differences:

   - It first searches each word in the lists of diminishers, inverters and intensifiers. If the target word is not contained in these lists, we use word2vec and the dictionaries to compute the intensity (similarly as in the previous case).
   - The obtained value is further fine-tuned using three rules:
     - If the phrase contains a diminisher and is positive (intensity > 0.5), it is multiplied by a constant lesser than 1 (if negative, by a constant greater than 1)[1].
     - If the phrase contains an intensifier and is positive, it is multiplied by a constant greater than 1 (if negative by constant lesser than 1)[1].
     - If the phrase contains an inverter, its value is subtracted from 1.

4. **Classifier output**: We use the 5-level Stanford sentiment classifier proposed by Socher in (Socher et al., 2013). The classifier returns the probabilities of five labels. We compute the final sentiment intensity using a weighted sum of the probabilities with the following weights: -1,-0.5, 0, 0.5, 1 (1 for very positive phrases). This approach gives a value from the interval from -1 to 1 and it is thus normalized to the interval from 0 to 1.

5. **Other (simple) features**

   - **Word count**: number of words in a phrase
   - **Diminisher**: binary feature, 1 represents a presence of a diminisher (e.g. word "less")
   - **Inverter**: binary feature, 1 represents a presence of an inverter (e.g. word "not")
   - **Intensifier**: binary feature, 1 represents a presence of an intensifier (e.g. word "more")[2]

2.3 Regression Model

To combine the above described features and to obtain the final result we use a regression model. Because of our experience with the Weka package (Hall et al., 2009) we chose this tool for implementation. We did a comparison of several regression models that are implemented in this package and based on the experiments performed on the SemEval development data we chose Gaussian processes (Rasmussen, 2006) as a good candidate for creating the regression model.

3 Experimental Results

First, the development data containing 200 annotated words and phrases were provided for each subtask. The general English test dataset contains 2,799 words and phrases and the English Twitter dataset contains 1,069 phrases. All of the presented experiments are done on the general English test dataset. The testing gold data were not provided. Therefore, we have tuned our system on the development data as briefly presented below.

3.1 Results on General English Test Dataset

3.1.1 Performance of the Individual Features

We first use all proposed features (excluding binary and word count features) separately to check their individual performance. Table 2 shows the results of this experiment.

We have set the parameter $N = 16$ in the *W2V search* feature computing approach because this value gave the best results on the development data.

---

[1]Constant values were set experimentally on the development data to 0.85 and 1.15 respectively.

[2]The three last features are based on the lists provided by the JRC lexicon with a few words that were present in the development data and not in these lists.

Feature	Kendall	Spearman
AFINN direct search	0.435	0.560
JRC direct search	0.467	0.603
SWN direct search	0.438	0.617
AFINN W2V search	0.510	0.698
JRC W2V search	0.527	0.720
SWN W2V search	0.458	0.639
AFINN rb W2V	0.557	0.753
JRC rb W2V	0.541	0.726
SWN rb W2V	0.464	0.650
Classifier output	0.423	0.591

Table 2: Performance of the individual features on general English test dataset

Feature set	Kendall	Spearman
without SWN	**0.659**	**0.854**
without binary	0.630	0.831
all features	0.632	0.834

Table 3: Results of the regression model with the different feature sets on general English test dataset

We can conclude that the superior feature is *AFINN rb W2V* followed by *JRC rb W2V* and *JRC W2V search*. The other features have somewhat worse results but still might be usable in the final system.

3.1.2 Results of the Regression Model

Table 3 presents the results of the final regression model on general English test dataset. This model was trained on the development data. The bold-faced numbers indicate the results submitted to the SemEval. *Without SWN* means that we have used all the features except the three features based on the SWN dictionary. *Without binary* means that we have used all the features except the three binary features and the *word count* feature. Based on this experiment, we have decided not to use the SWN features in the submission because of its slightly lower performance on the development data. We have measured the performance on the development data using a ten fold cross-validation.

3.1.3 Comparison with the Top Three Teams

Table 4 shows the final results of the top three teams for the SemEval 2016 task 7 (general English subtask). This table shows that the performance of our system is close to the first one particularly when measured by Spearman correlation.

Team	Kendall	Spearman
ECNU	0.704	0.863
UWB (presented)	0.659	0.854
LSIS	0.350	0.508

Table 4: Comparison of the top three teams competing in SemEval 2016 task 7 general English subtask

Team	Kendall	Spearman
ECNU	0.523	0.674
LSIS	0.422	0.591
UWB (presented)	0.414	0.578

Table 5: Comparison of the top three teams competing in SemEval 2016 task 7 English Twitter subtask

3.2 Results on English Twitter

To show the robustness of our approach, we have evaluated the proposed model also on the English Twitter test data from the SemEval task 7. We did not use any tuning of the method for the rather specific data from Twitter. We just trained the model on the English Twitter development data and tested it on the test data. Table 5 shows the results of three best performing systems submitted to SemEval 2016 task 7, English Twitter subtask. The comparison shows that the performance is not far away from the two better systems.

4 Conclusion and Perspectives

We proposed a novel method for sentiment intensity determination. The method uses a rich set of features based on three sentiment lexicons, output of a sentiment classifier and binary features based on lists of modifiers. We first evaluated the features separately on the test data. Then we utilized a Gaussian processes regression model which combines the proposed features and computes the final sentiment intensity. The final system was submitted to the task 7 of the SemEval 2016 competition. The regression model trained on the SemEval development data reached Kendall rank correlation of 0.659 on general English phrases and 0.414 on English Twitter test data.

One perspective is using more sophisticated phrase parametrization. Another one is to prepare word embedding algorithm that groups together words with similar sentiment.

Acknowledgments

This work has been partly supported by the project LO1506 of the Czech Ministry of Education, Youth and Sports and by Grant No. SGS-2016-018 Data and Software Engineering for Advanced Applications.

References

Ramon F Astudillo, Silvio Amir, Wang Ling, Bruno Martins, Mário Silva, Isabel Trancoso, and Rua Alves Redol. 2015. Inesc-id: Sentiment analysis without hand-coded features or liguistic resources using embedding subspaces. *SemEval-2015*, page 652.

Stefano Baccianella, Andrea Esuli, and Fabrizio Sebastiani. 2010. Sentiwordnet 3.0: An enhanced lexical resource for sentiment analysis and opinion mining. In *LREC*, volume 10, pages 2200–2204.

Andrea Esuli and Fabrizio Sebastiani. 2006. Sentiwordnet: A publicly available lexical resource for opinion mining. In *Proceedings of LREC*, volume 6, pages 417–422. Citeseer.

Mark Hall, Eibe Frank, Geoffrey Holmes, Bernhard Pfahringer, Peter Reutemann, and Ian H Witten. 2009. The weka data mining software: an update. *ACM SIGKDD explorations newsletter*, 11(1):10–18.

Soo-Min Kim and Eduard Hovy. 2004. Determining the sentiment of opinions. In *Proceedings of the 20th international conference on Computational Linguistics*, page 1367. Association for Computational Linguistics.

Svetlana Kiritchenko, Saif M. Mohammad, and Mohammad Salameh. 2016. Semeval-2016 task 7: Determining sentiment intensity of english and arabic phrases. In *Proceedings of the International Workshop on Semantic Evaluation*, SemEval '16, San Diego, California, June.

Fangtao Li, Minlie Huang, and Xiaoyan Zhu. 2010. Sentiment analysis with global topics and local dependency. In *AAAI*, volume 10, pages 1371–1376.

Tomas Mikolov, Kai Chen, Greg Corrado, and Jeffrey Dean. 2013. Efficient estimation of word representations in vector space. *arXiv preprint arXiv:1301.3781*.

F. Å. Nielsen. 2011. Afinn, mar.

Bo Pang and Lillian Lee. 2004. A sentimental education: Sentiment analysis using subjectivity summarization based on minimum cuts. In *Proceedings of the 42nd annual meeting on Association for Computational Linguistics*, page 271. Association for Computational Linguistics.

Carl Edward Rasmussen. 2006. Gaussian processes for machine learning.

Sara Rosenthal, Preslav Nakov, Svetlana Kiritchenko, Saif M Mohammad, Alan Ritter, and Veselin Stoyanov. 2015. Semeval-2015 task 10: Sentiment analysis in twitter. *Proceedings of SemEval-2015*.

Richard Socher, Alex Perelygin, Jean Y Wu, Jason Chuang, Christopher D Manning, Andrew Y Ng, and Christopher Potts. 2013. Recursive deep models for semantic compositionality over a sentiment treebank. In *Proceedings of the conference on empirical methods in natural language processing (EMNLP)*, volume 1631, page 1642. Citeseer.

Josef Steinberger, Mohamed Ebrahim, Maud Ehrmann, Ali Hurriyetoglu, Mijail Kabadjov, Polina Lenkova, Ralf Steinberger, Hristo Tanev, Silvia Vázquez, and Vanni Zavarella. 2012. Creating sentiment dictionaries via triangulation. *Decision Support Systems*, 53(4):689–694.

Xiaolong Wang, Furu Wei, Xiaohua Liu, Ming Zhou, and Ming Zhang. 2011. Topic sentiment analysis in twitter: a graph-based hashtag sentiment classification approach. In *Proceedings of the 20th ACM international conference on Information and knowledge management*, pages 1031–1040. ACM.

Zhihua Zhang, Guoshun Wu, and Man Lan. 2015. Ecnu: Multi-level sentiment analysis on twitter using traditional linguistic features and word embedding features. *SemEval-2015*, page 561.

NileTMRG at SemEval-2016 Task 7: Deriving Prior Polarities for Arabic Sentiment Terms

Samhaa R. El-Beltagy

Center for Informatics Sciences

Nile University, Juhayna Square, Sheikh Zayed City

Giza, Egypt

samhaa@computer.org

Abstract

This paper presents a model that was developed to address SemEval Task 7: "Determining Sentiment Intensity of English and Arabic Phrases", with focus on 'Arabic Phrases'. The goal of this task is to determine the degree to which some given term is associated with positive sentiment. The underlying premise behind the model that we have adopted is that determining the context (positive or negative) in which a term usually occurs can determine its strength. Since the focus is on Twitter terms, Twitter was used to collect tweets for each term for which a strength value was to be derived. An Arabic sentiment analyzer, was then used to assign a polarity to each of these tweets, thus defining their context. We then experimented with normalized point wise mutual information with and without linear regression to assign intensity scores to input terms. The output of the model that we've adopted ranked at two out of the three presented systems for this task with a **Kendall** score of 0.475.

1 Introduction

During the past few years, interest in sentiment analysis has surged. Sentiment lexicons are often an essential component for building sentiment analysis systems. Entries in sentiment lexicons can vary significantly in terms of how strongly they reflect positive or negative sentiment. For example, while both the terms "good" and "amazing" reflect a positive sentiment, the term "amazing" is stronger and more positive than "good". In this paper, we address early work that has been conducted to determine the intensity of Arabic twitter sentiment terms with respect to positive sentiment. Since the desired task is to determine the "positive strength" of a word, the results can be interpreted as follows: the closer the term score is to 1, the stronger it is as a positive indicator; the closer it is to 0, the stronger it is as a negative indicator. Terms that can be used in both positive and negative contexts will usually fall somewhere in the middle.

While this task was introduced in SemEval--2015 as Task 10- sub-task E (Rosenthal et al. 2015) for English terms, this is the first time that it has been introduced for Arabic terms. Addressing this task for Arabic has to take place in the absence of many resources that are available for English. In this work we make of use an Arabic sentiment analyzer (El-Beltagy et al. 2016) that was developed by our team as well as of a sentiment lexicon that was also developed within by same team and which is publicly available for research purposes (El-Beltagy 2016).

The main idea behind this work is to try to collect a representative number of tweets for each term for which a strength value is to be derived and to then classify those tweets in terms of polarity. This

Proceedings of SemEval-2016, pages 486–490,

San Diego, California, June 16-17, 2016. ©2016 Association for Computational Linguistics

classification would then be used for calculating the co-relation between positive sentiments and the original terms using normalized point wise mutual information (nPMI) (Bouma 2009). However, as will be detailed in section3.1, there were cases when tweets were not available for input terms, or when they were too few. A small sample of development data was also supplied with the task. We have basically used this data set to test the developed model and to make adjustments when needed.

The rest of this paper is organized as follows: section 2 briefly outlines related work; section 3 provides an overview of the developed model, section 4 presents the evaluation results and future directions, while section 5 concludes this paper.

2   Related Work

Because sentiment lexicons are an integral part of many sentiment analysis systems, many such lexicons have been developed for the English language. The most commonly used English lexicons include: SentiWordNet (Baccianella et al. 2010), Bing Liu's opinion lexicon(Liu 2010), and the MPQA subjectivity lexicon (Wilson et al. 2005), Recently, Twitter specific lexicons have also come into existence and are increasing being used. These include the Hashtag Sentiment Lexicon and the Sentiment140 Lexicon (Mohammad et al. 2013) (Kiritchenko et al. 2014). However despite the availability of many English lexicons, only a few include a sentiment score, with work on automatically assigning such a score only recently starting to attract attention. This particular research area was introduced as a subtask in SemEval-2015- task10. The top performing team for this sub-task, employed word embeddings to train a logistic regression model for assigning scores to sentiment terms (Astudillo et al. 2015). The second best performing team, used 6 different sentiment lexicons to score input terms (2 manually created, and 4 automatically created). Basically, input terms were compared against entries in the lexicons. If a term was found in a manually constructed lexicon, it was assigned a value of 1 or -1, depending on its polarity. If it was found in any of the automatically created lexicons, it was assigned the score found in those lexicons. If it was not found in any of the used lexicons, it was assigned a default value (Hamdan et al. 2015).

Arabic lexicons are much more scarce than their English counterparts, and are often translated versions of an existing English lexicon. An example of this is the Arabic translated version of the NRC word emotion association lexicon (EmoLex) (Mohammad & Turney 2013).

There have been some attempts to assign scores to Arabic lexicon terms. (El-Beltagy & Ali 2013) presented a method for semi-automatically building a sentiment lexicon as well as two different approaches for assigning scores to sentiment terms. The authors also demonstrated that the introduction of sentiment scores can increase the accuracy of sentiment analysis. (Eskander & Rambow 2015) constructed a sentiment lexicon by devising a matching algorithm that tries to match entries in the lexicon of an Arabic morphological analyzer to entries in SentiWordNet (Baccianella et al. 2010). When a match is found, a link is created between the lexicon entry and the matching entry in SentiWordNet and the scores of the matching term in SentiWordNet are assigned to that entry.

3   Model Overview

In order to assign strength scores to a given list of terms (input terms), a number of steps are carried out. These steps can be summarized as follows:
1. Collect tweets for input terms
2. Classify and index collected tweets
3. Calculate a score for each term

Each of the above steps is explained in the following subsections.

3.1   Data Collection

Since the goal of our work was to try to determine the correlation between a given term and positive or negative sentiments, we had to obtain a representative set of tweets for each term. We have chosen to retrieve 500 tweets for each term using Twitter's search API (Twitter 2016). There were cases however, when the search API was unable to retrieve this number of tweets and cases where no tweets were retrieved at all.   It must also be noted that even though the flag that prevents retweets from being retrieved was set when invoking Twitter search, many tweets were in fact identical to other tweets in the tweet set. To eliminate those from the dataset, they were filtered out using the Jaccard similarity measure (Leskovec et al. 2014).

For cases when only very few tweets (less than 15) could be retrieved or when no tweets could be retrieved, an extra processing step was performed. In this step, a check was used to determine if the term in question was a hashtag. If it was, the hash symbol was removed from the term and so were any underscores. The resulting phrase was then used to query Twitter. If the term was not a hashtag or if the step just described also resulted in the retrieval of very few or no tweets, then the term was stemmed using a simple stemmer (El-Beltagy & Rafea 2011) and re-sent to Twitter as a query.

For the supplied 1166 test phrases in the Arabic set, 141 had to undergo these extra processing steps and 15 failed to return any tweets.

In total, approximately 249 K tweets were collected for deriving scores for the 1166 test phrases. This collection of tweets will henceforth be referred to as the twitter corpus.

3.2 Data Classification and Indexing

After carrying out the data collection step described in the previous section, each of the collected tweets was classified using the sentiment analyzer described in (El-Beltagy et al. 2016). The analyzer was built using a Complement Naïve Bayes classifier (Rennie et al. 2003) with a smoothing parameter of 1 and trained using 11,242 Arabic tweets of which 3759 were negative, 3725 were positive and 3758 were neutral. The prediction accuracy using 10 fold cross validation on this dataset was 79.4%. Complement Naïve Bayes was selected as a classifier based on the work presented in (Khalil et al. 2015).

Features related to the occurrence of positive and negative terms, were part of the feature-set used by the classifier. These features were determined using the NileULex sentiment lexicon (El-Beltagy 2016) which consists of 5953 single and compound MSA and Egyptian Arabic terms. The overlap between the input SemEval test set and NileULex was as follows: Out of the 1166 supplied test terms, 162 (13.8%) existed in the used lexicon, while 148(12.6%) hash-tagged terms, existed in the lexicon, but without the hashtag.

Some of the terms in both the development set and the test set, were negated. This was not really an issue when automatically assigning polarity labels, as the obtained label is one that it is relative to the entire phrase. What had to be handled however, were cases when the retrieved tweets included the negated form of a non-negated term. For example, when trying to assign a score to term "حلو", a tweet with the following text:

"@mention امسحي كلامك عن⃞علاقة مع احمد مش حلو
ها⃞حكي في حقها"

would be classified as negative. In cases like this, negative labels were converted to positive ones and vice versa.

Each polarity classified tweet was then indexed using the Lucene(Apache 2011) search engine. The index was used to store the body of the tweet, the polarity class of the tweet, and the search term that was used to retrieve the tweet.

3.3 Term Scoring

Following the indexing and classification step, it was easy to retrieve information needed to calculate the *normalized pmi* (*npmi*) scores for each term relative the positive class. So for each term $term_i$ in the list for which strength values are to be derived, equation 1 was applied to calculate its *npmi* value relative to positive (pos) sentiment.

$$npmi(term_i, pos) = \frac{pmi(term_i, pos)}{-\log p(term_i, pos)} \quad (1)$$

where

$$pmi(term_i, pos) = \log \frac{p(term_i, pos)}{p(term_i)p(pos)} \quad (2)$$

$$p(term_i) = \frac{\#\ of\ term_i\ in\ twitter\ corpus}{size\ of\ twitter\ corpus} \quad (3)$$

$$p(pos) = \frac{total\ number\ of\ positive\ tweets}{size\ of\ twitter\ corpus} \quad (4)$$

$$p(term_i, pos) = \frac{\#\ of\ pos\ term_i\ tweets}{size\ of\ twitter\ corpus} \quad (5)$$

To calculate the probability of the occurrence of the ith term in the test set ($p(term_i)$) in the twitter corpus, the number of tweets classified as neutral for this term ($term_i$) are subtracted from the total count of $term_i$ before applying equation 3. The total count of neutral tweets in the entire corpus is also subtracted from the size of the twitter corpus before applying equations 3 through 5.

Normalized point wise mutual information returns values in the range of [-1,1] where -1 indicates that a term would never occur with the positive class and 1, indicates that it always will. In our model, terms for which no tweets were retrieved received a *npmi* score of 0. The *nmpi* scores of terms that had to undergo extra processing as described in section 3.1 were penalized by multiplying their scores by a penalty factor <1. We have experimented with various factors using the development dataset, and ended up with 0.75 as a penalty factor.

We also experimented with two methods for re-scaling the *npmi* scores to values from 0 to 1. In the first model, we used the development dataset, which consisted of 200 terms, and then applied linear regression to map *npmi* scores to the gold standard scores. This linear regression model, was then applied on the scores of the supplied test set. In the second method, we applied simple re-scaling so that the scores would range from 0 to 1. When we experimented with both methods on the development dataset, simple re-scaling yielded slightly better results despite the fact that the regression model was built using that same set. Accordingly, the results that we've submitted, were the results obtained using simple rescaling rather the by applying linear regression.

4   Results and Discussion

Based on the results supplied by the organizers of the task, the presented approach ranked at number 2 as shown in **Table 1**.

Rank	Team name	(official metric) Kendall	Spearman
1	iLab-Edinburgh	0.5362	0.67997
2	NileTMRG	0.47515	0.65763
3	LSIS	0.42431	0.58299

Table 1:   Official results

We also ran the scoring script provided by the organizers on the results that were obtained using linear regression using the post submission test data with the gold labels. The results were as follows: **Kendall**: 0.47524, **Spearman:** 0.65756. The variation between these results and the submitted results are very minor.

By examining the results, it can be seen that the difference between our score and that achieved by the number 1 performer with respect to the Kendall metric is about 0.06. The difference in the Spearman metric is not quite as large. This difference as well as the score itself, suggests that there is still a need for improving this model.

The following points summarize some of the ideas that we plan on pursuing for improving this model:

1. Investigate alternative ways for handling the assignment of a score to terms for which no tweets were found.
2. Some terms had a higher percentage of duplicates than other in their tweet sets. Duplicate removal in cases like that resulted in those terms being under-represented. In the future, we intend to make sure that we get a pre-defined number of tweets for each term whenever possible.
3. We would like to repeat the experiment presented in this paper using tweets collected over a reasonable period of time, rather than in one go as we have done here. This should counter-act any time sensitivity issues for any given term.
4. We would like to examine the effect of replacing the sentiment analyzer for tweet labeling, with a method based on simple counting between the co-occurrence of the term for which we need to calculate a score, and known positive and negative terms.
5. Make better use of the existing lexicon as well as other available lexicons by experimenting with a similar approach to that presented in (Hamdan et al. 2015).

5   Conclusion

This paper presented the approach followed by NileTMRG for addressing Sem-Eval task 7, with respect to Arabic phrases. While the presented work shows promising results, further work is needed to improve its performance. In the previous section, we discussed several ideas that we believe might have a positive impact on the overall performance of the system.

Acknowledgments

The author wishes to thank the anonymous reviewers for their valuable feedback.

References

Apache, 2011. Lucene. Available at: http://lucene.apache.org/.

Astudillo, R.F. et al., 2015. INESC-ID: A Regression Model for Large Scale Twitter Sentiment Lexicon Induction. In *Proceedings of the 9th International Workshop on Semantic Evaluation (SemEval 2015)*. pp. 613–618. Available at: http://alt.qcri.org/semeval2015/cdrom/pdf/SemEval102.pdf.

Baccianella, S., Esuli, A. & Sebastiani, F., 2010. SentiWordNet 3.0: An Enhanced Lexical Resource for Sentiment Analysis and Opinion Mining. In *Proceedings of the Seventh International Conference on Language Resources and Evaluation (LREC'10)*. pp. 2200–2204.

Bouma, G., 2009. Normalized (Pointwise) Mutual Information in Collocation Extraction. In *the Biennial GSCL Conference*. pp. 31–40.

El-Beltagy, S.R. et al., 2016. Combining Lexical Features and a Supervised Learning Approach for Arabic Sentiment Analysis. In *CICLing 2016 - submitted*. Konya, Turkey.

El-Beltagy, S.R., 2016. NileULex: A Phrase and Word Level Sentiment Lexicon for Egyptian and Modern Standard Arabic. In *to appear in proceedings of LREC 2016*. Portorož , Slovenia.

El-Beltagy, S.R. & Ali, A., 2013. Open Issues in the Sentiment Analysis of Arabic Social Media : A Case Study. In *Proceedings of 9th the International Conference on Innovations and Information Technology (IIT2013)*. Al Ain, UAE.

El-Beltagy, S.R. & Rafea, A., 2011. An Accuracy Enhanced Light Stemmer for Arabic Text. *ACM Transactions on Speech and Language Processing*, 7(2), pp.2 – 23.

Eskander, R. & Rambow, O., 2015. SLSA: A Sentiment Lexicon for Standard Arabic. *Proceedings of the 2015 Conference on Empirical Methods in Natural Language Processing*, (September), pp.2545–2550. Available at: http://aclweb.org/anthology/D15-1304.

Hamdan, H., Bellot, P. & Bechet, F., 2015. lsislif: Feature extraction and label weighting for sentiment analysis in twitter. In *Proceedings of the 9th International Workshop on Semantic Evaluation*. pp. 568–573.

Khalil, T. et al., 2015. Which configuration works best? An experimental study on Supervised Arabic Twitter Sentiment Analysis. In *Proceedings of the First Conference on Arabic Computational Liguistics (ACLing 2015), co-located with CICLing 2015*. Cairo, Egypt, pp. 86–93.

Kiritchenko, S., Zhu, X. & Mohammad, S., 2014. Sentiment Analysis of Short Informal Texts. *Journal of Artificial Intelligence Research*, 50, pp.723–762.

Leskovec, J., Rajaraman, A. & Ullman, J.D., 2014. *Mining of Massive Datasets* 2 edition., Cambridge, UK: Cambridge University Press. Available at: http://ebooks.cambridge.org/ref/id/CBO978111390 58452.

Liu, B., 2010. Sentiment Analysis and Subjectivity. In N. I. and F. J. Damerau, ed. *Handbook of Natural Language Processing, Second Edition*.

Mohammad, S. & Turney, P., 2013. Crowdsourcing a Word-Emotion Association Lexicon. *Computational Intelligence*, 29(3), pp.436–465.

Mohammad, S.M., Kiritchenko, S. & Zhu, X., 2013. NRC-Canada: Building the State-of-the-Art in Sentiment Analysis of Tweets. In *Proceedings of the seventh international workshop on Semantic Evaluation Exercises (SemEval-2013)*. Atlanta, Georgia, USA.

Rennie, J.D.M. et al., 2003. Tackling the Poor Assumptions of Naive Bayes Text Classifiers. *Proceedings of the Twentieth International Conference on Machine Learning (ICML)-2003)*, 20(1973), pp.616–623.

Rosenthal, S. et al., 2015. SemEval-2015 Task 10: Sentiment Analysis in Twitter. In *Proceedings of the 9th International Workshop on Semantic Evaluation (SemEval 2015)*. pp. 451–463. Available at: http://alt.qcri.org/semeval2015/cdrom/pdf/SemEval078.pdf.

Twitter, 2016. Twitter Search API. Available at: https://dev.twitter.com/rest/public/search.

Wilson, T., Wiebe, J. & Hoffmann, P., 2005. Recognizing contextual polarity in phrase-level sentiment analysis. In *Proceedings of Human Language Technology Conference and Conference on Empirical Methods in Natural Language Processing (HLT/EMNLP)*. Vancouver, Canada, pp. 347–354.

ECNU at SemEval-2016 Task 7: An Enhanced Supervised Learning Method for Lexicon Sentiment Intensity Ranking

Feixiang Wang[1], Zhihua Zhang[1], Man Lan[1,2*]
[1]Department of Computer Science and Technology,
East China Normal University, Shanghai, P.R.China
[2]Shanghai Key Laboratory of Multidimensional Information Processing
51151201049@ecnu.cn, 51131201039@ecnu.cn, mlan@cs.ecnu.edu.cn*

Abstract

This paper describes our system submissions to task 7 in SemEval 2016, i.e., Determining Sentiment Intensity. We participated the first two subtasks in English, which are to predict the sentiment intensity of a word or a phrase in English Twitter and General English domains. To address this task, we present a supervised learning-to-rank system to predict the relevant scores, i.e., the strength associated with positive sentiment, for English words or phrases. Multiple linguistic and sentiment features are adopted, e.g., *Sentiment Lexicons, Sentiment Word Vectors, Word Vectors, Linguistic Features*, etc. Officially released results showed that our systems rank the 1st among all submissions in English, which proves the effectiveness of the proposed method.

1 Introduction

The study of sentiment analysis is increasingly drawing attention of Natural Language Processing (NLP). Many of the top performing sentiment analysis systems rely on sentiment lexicon (Tan et al., 2008; Na et al., 2009; Mohammad et al., 2013). A sentiment lexicon is a list of words and phrases, such as *"excellent", "awful"* and *"not bad"*, each of them is assigned with a positive or negative score reflecting its sentiment polarity and strength (Tang et al., 2014a). Higher scores indicate stronger sentiment strength. However, many existing manually generated sentiment lexicons consist of lexicons with only sentiment orientation rather than sentiment strength. For example, the words in *BL* (Ding et al., 2008) are generally divided to two classes, i.e.,

positive and negative. Although several sentiment lexicons have assigned discrete labels for terms, i.e., *strong* and *weak*, for example, MPQA (Wiebe et al., 2005), there is no continuous real-valued scores to indicate the intensity of sentiment so far.

The task of Determining Sentiment Intensity of English and Arabic Phrases intends to automatically create a sentiment lexicon with real-valued scores indicating the intensity of sentiment. The purpose of this task is to test the ability of an automatic system to predict a sentiment intensity score for a word or a phrase. Phrases include negators, modals, intensifiers, and diminishers. Given a list of terms, the participants are required to assign appropriate scores between 0 and 1, to indicate their strength of association with positive sentiment. The task contains three subtasks (the first two are in English and the third is in Arabic) and we participated the first two subtasks in English. The first General English Sentiment Modifiers Set contains phrases formed by a word and a modifier, where a modifier can be a negator, an auxiliary verb, a degree adverb, or even a combination of those above modifiers, e.g., *"would be very easy", "did not harm"*, and *"would have been nice"*. The second English Twitter Mixed Polarity Set contains phrases made up of opposite polarity terms, such as *"lazy sundays", "best winter break", "couldn't stop smiling"*, etc. The official evaluation measure is Kendall correlation coefficient (Lindskog et al., 2003).

In previous work, the task was treated as a regression problem, the word embedding is used as a feature (Amir et al., 2015). In addition, (Hamdan et al., 2015) adopted unsupervised approach by using

491

Proceedings of SemEval-2016, pages 491–496,
San Diego, California, June 16-17, 2016. ©2016 Association for Computational Linguistics

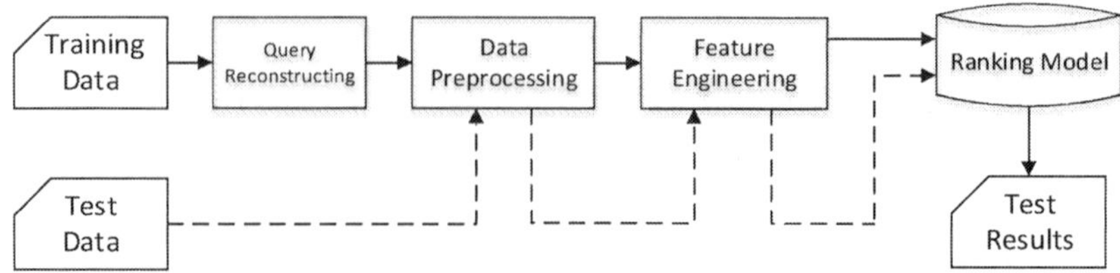

Figure 1: The framework of our proposed system.

several sentiment lexicons for computing the score for each twitter term and ranked them. In this paper, we treated this task as a ranking problem, and used pair-wise strategy to train the model.

The rest of the paper is organized as follows. Section 2 elaborates the procedure of query reconstruction, data preprocessing, feature engineering and the learning-to-rank model built in our systems. Section 3 describes the data sets and experiments. Finally, Section 4 concludes this work.

2 System Description

The purpose of this task is to predict the sentiment strength of given words or phrases, it is reasonable to regard the value of strength as the relevant score refer to positive polarity. Thus, to address the sentiment strength prediction task, we presented a supervised learning-to-rank system to predict the relevant score which interprets the strength associated with positive sentiment. Figure 1 depicts the architecture of our system, which contains four main modules, i.e., *Query Reconstruction*, *Data Preprocessing*, *Feature Engineering*, and *Ranking Model*. The diversity of methods for General English and English Twitter domains is located in the different training data.

2.1 Query Reconstruction

Since the sentiment strength task was treated as a ranking problem, we converted the provided training data into appropriate forms as the input of our ranking system in the first stage. In general, several queries were fed into the ranking system served as training data. In consideration of the provided training data is a word list ordered by the strength score associated with positive sentiment, we manually divided the word list into several *"queries"* and the words in each query were sorted by their corresponding scores. Specifically, the test data would

not be processed into *Query Reconstruction* module, because we considered all records in the test set as a unique query and the *Ranking Model* was used to predict their relevant scores.

2.2 Data Preprocessing

Due to the characteristic of training data in English Twitter domain, which consists of many informal words, such as *"waiiiiit"*, *"#happytweet"*, etc., we converted the irregular forms to normal forms. For example, the elongated word *"waiiiiit"* was transformed into *"wait"*, the hashtag *"#happytweet"* was converted into *"happy tweet"*. Then, we used the processed data to perform lemmatization and stemming to extract the further information with the aid of *NLTK tool*[1].

2.3 Feature Engineering

To address the sentiment strength task, we extracted features summarized as follows: *Sentiment Lexicon Features*, *Sentiment Word Vectors*, *Word Vectors*, and *Linguistic Features*.

2.3.1 Sentiment Lexicon Features

We employed the following seven sentiment lexicons to extract *Sentiment Lexicon Features*: *Bing Liu lexicon*[2], *General Inquirer lexicon*[3], *IMDB*[4], *MPQA*[5], *AFINN*[6], *NRC Hashtag Sentiment Lexicon*[7], and *NRC Sentiment140 Lexicon*[8]. Generally, we

---

[1] http://www.nltk.org/
[2] http://www.cs.uic.edu/liub/FBS/sentiment-analysis.html#lexicon
[3] http://www.wjh.harvard.edu/inquirer/homecat.htm
[4] http://anthology.aclweb.org//S/S13/S13-2.pdf#page=444
[5] http://mpqa.cs.pitt.edu/
[6] http://www2.imm.dtu.dk/pubdb/views/publication_details.php?id=6010
[7] http://www.umiacs.umd.edu/saif/WebDocs/NRC-Hashtag-Sentiment-Lexicon-v0.1.zip
[8] http://help.sentiment140.com/for-students/

transformed the sentiment orientation of all words in all sentiment lexicons into the range of -1 to 1, where the minus sign denotes negative sentiment and the positive number indicates positive sentiment.

We considered each term (consisting of phrases and words) in the provided data as a tuple. If one term contains a single word, the size of this tuple is 1. If one term is a phrase, e.g., *"happy accident"*, the tuple size is the count of words in the phrase (for *"happy accident"*, it is 2). Then, for each tuple, we concatenated the following sentimental scores extracted from each sentiment lexicon: (1) the maximum sentiment score of words, (2) the minimum sentiment score of words, (3) the sum of sentiment scores of all words. If one word does not exist in a sentiment lexicon, its corresponding score is set to 0. Specifically, if any negator, e.g.,*"not"*, exists in a tuple, we reverse its sentiment orientation.

Considering the diversity of word forms, we also extracted additional sentiment lexicon features about their lemmatization and stemming forms. The final sentiment lexicon representation of the i-th record $l_i \in \mathbb{R}^{n_l * n_s * t}$, where n_l is the number of sentiment lexicons (i.e.,7), n_s is set as 3 representing the three scores calculated according to the above rules, t is also set as 3 representing the three forms (i.e., original, lemmatization and stemming forms) of the word in the record.

2.3.2   Word Vectors

Word vector is a continuous-valued representation of the word which carries syntactic and semantic information. In this task, we adopted various *Word Vectors* as features. Since the task data contains phrases made up of more than one word, it is necessary to convert these word vectors into a phrase vector. Unlike previous work which summed up all words vectors to represent the phrase, we first check whether the phrase is present in training data or not. If a phrase is present in training data, we actually treat it as a single token and learn its vector based on the given word vector learning model. If it is a new phrase not existing in training data, we follow previous work and sum up all vectors of words in this phrase as a phrase vector.

In this part, we introduce two types of word vector which are adopted in our method, i.e., Traditional Word Vector and Sentiment Word Vector, which are described as follows:

Traditional Word Vectors:

- *GoogleW2V*: We used the publicly available *word2vec* tool[9] to get word vectors with dimensionality of 300, which were trained on 100 billion words from Google News as *GoogleW2V* feature.

- *GloveW2V*: The Glove(Pennington et al., 2014) rely on different assumptions about the relations between words within a context window. We used the available pre-trained word vector with dimensionality of 100 and trained on 2 billion tweets, which were supplied in *GloVe*[10] as *GloveW2V* feature.

- *NormalW2V*: We fed *NRC140 tweet corpus* into *word2vec tool* to build *NormalW2V* with dimensionality of 100.

- *NormalW2V_Multi*: To train specific word vectors (i.e., words and phrases) for this task, we preprocessed the *NRC140 corpus* by connecting words in the phrase appeared in training data to abtain a single token. The processed data were fed into word vector model to train *NormalW2V_Multi* with dimensionality of 100.

Sentiment Word Vectors: Since the above word vectors are trained based on the context, they are supposed to contain semantic and syntactic information. However, due to lack of sentiment information, these traditional word vectors may not be quite effective for sentiment analysis tasks. To address this issue, our previous work and other researchers has proposed methods to learn sentiment word vectors.

- *SWV*: In (Zhang and Lan, 2015) we proposed the *Combined-Sentiment Word Embedding Model* (i.e., *SWV-C*) to learn sentiment word vectors, which are confirmed to be helpful to settle sentiment analysis task. In this work, we used this model to train the *SWV* with the aid of *NRC140 tweet corpus* (Go et al., 2009), where the corpus is made up of 1.6 million positive tweets and 1.6 million negative tweets. The vector size is set as 100.

---

[9]https://code.google.com/archive/p/word2vec
[10]http://nlp.stanford.edu/projects/glove/

- *SWV_Multi*: Similar with *NormalW2V_Multi*, we used the *NRC140 corpus* as training corpus and reconstructed it to the task specific form. The processed corpus was employed as input of *SWV-C* model to generate *SWV_Multi* with dimensionality of 100.

- *SSWE*: The sentiment-specific word embeddings (*SSWE*) were proposed by (Tang et al., 2014b), which is quite similar to our idea in (Zhang and Lan, 2015) but differs in proposed models. This *SSWE* sentiment word embeddings were trained by using multi-hidden-layers neural network with vector size of 50.

2.3.3 Linguistic Features

- Negation: The sentiment polarity of word or phrase can be reversed by a modification of negation. Therefore, we collected 29 negations from Internet and we sign 1 or 0 to this binary feature if corresponding negation is present or absent in the pending word or phrase.

- Elongated: This feature represents if word or phrase with one character repeated more than twice, e.g.,*"lottttt"*.

2.4 Ranking Model

Different from the classification or regression methods, which focus on labeling the single record, the ranking method takes the relation between two arbitrary records associated with a query into consideration.

In this module, we used a supervised learning-to-rank approach to perform ranking. Generally, the mentioned approach can be divided into three groups: point-wise, pair-wise, and list-wise. We adopted the second strategy, i.e., pair-wise for our work. In pair-wise strategy, several record1-record2 pairs were constructed with a query and some records which were provided in advance. If record1 is more relevant than record2 in terms of the given query, this pair label will be set as 1, otherwise 0.

3 Experiments and Results

3.1 Datasets

This sentiment strength prediction task was severed as the subtask E of Sentiment Analysis on Tweet in SemEval 2015. Thus, the trial (i.e., 15*trial*) and test (i.e., 15*test*) data in SemEval 2015, which contained 200 and 1, 315 records separately, are integrated as training data for this task. The organizer provided 200 records as development data set for each domain (i.e., 16*trial_Twitter* and 16*trial_General*) and the labels are the same as before, where each record is labeled with a decimal in the range of 0 to 1 and the score is the strength associated with positive sentiment.

In consideration of the lack of training data, we expanded it with the Language Assessment by Mechanical Turk lexicon (i.e., *LabMT*) which automatically labeled by (Dodds et al., 2011). It contains 10, 222 words rated on a scale of 1(sad) to 9(happy). Note that the labels in the *LabMT* are different from the standard data, we converted the score to the scale of 0 to 1 by min-max normalization, i.e., $\frac{x-min}{max-min}$.

3.2 Evaluation Metrics

For this task, Kendall rank correlation coefficient (usually measures the association between two measured quantities) is used as the metric to compare the ranked lists. Besides, the scores for Spearman's Rank Correlation(a nonparametric measure of statistical dependence between two variables) is provided as well. The Kendall rank correlation coefficient is severed as the final official evaluation criteria.

3.3 Experiment on training data

As we described in 2.1, several operations should be conducted to transform the raw data form to accommodate the ranking system. Considering that the *LabMT* is a term list that has been automatically labeled, while the provided standard data is more precise, so we constructed each query in *LabMT* with 200 records. With regard to the provided standard data (i.e., 15*trial*, 15*test*), each query was made up of 20 records.

To construct training data for English Twitter domain, the *LabMT*, 15*train* and 15*test* were utilized, whereas the 16*trial_Twitter* was utilized as development data. Several types of features have been proposed in 2.3, in order to conduct feature selection, we adopted *hill climbing* which is described as: keeping adding one type of feature at a time until no further improvement can be achieved.

The system's diversity of two domains lies on

Feature		English Twitter	General English
Traditional W2V	GoogleW2V	√	
	NormalW2V	√	√
	NormalW2V_Multi		
	GloveW2V		√
Sentimental W2V	SWV	√	√
	SWV_Multi		√
	SSWE	√	√
Sentiment Lexicon	SentiLexi	√	√
Linguistic	Negation	√	√
	Emphasize	√	−
Ranking Results (Kendell/Sperman)		**59.83%/75.38%**	**71.67%/86.83%**
Regression Results (Kendall/Sperman)		57.80%/73.01%	70.50%/85.26%

Table 1: Results of feature selection experiments for Twitter English and General English domains.

the different training data we utilized: all tweet-related data were adopted in English Twitter, while the words and phrases with *hashtag*(#) or informal forms were removed for General English. Thus, the filtered data of *LabMT*, *15trial* and *15test* were severed as training data and the *16trial_General* were utilized as development data. The process of feature selection was similar with English Twitter domain except that the *Emphasize* feature was not used.

Table 1 shows the results of feature selection experiments on the development data, which lists the optimal feature sets of two domains.

From Table 1, it is interesting to find: (1) The *Sentiment Lexicon* features make a considerable contribution, because that the used sentiment lexicons contain sentiment information to some extent and its sentiment scores in lexicons are closely related to the strength associated with positive sentiment. For example, in *BL*, the scores of positive words are 1 and the negative words are represented as -1. (2) The *Linguistic* features (i.e., *Negation* and *Emphasize*) also contribute to performance. As for *Negation*, the possible reason may be that there are plentiful negators existed in training and development data and the emphatic words have similar situation. (3) The *NormalW2V* and *SWV* are both effective features for this task. In our further experiments which test the *SWV* and *NormalW2V* respectively, we found that *SWV* performs much better than *NormalW2V*, which showed that the *Combined Sentiment Word Vector Model* indeed captured sentiment information from abundant auto-labeled tweets. (4) The ranking based system outperforms the regression method, which indicates that it is convincing to regard this labeling task as a ranking problem. (5) Compared with the results on English Twitter domain, we notice that the performance is much better. Based on the observation on development data of two domains, we found that the phrases on English Twitter domain are made up of opposite polarity terms, e.g., *"happy accident"*, *"couldn't stop smiling"*, while the records in General English domain are much more ordinary. The diversity of data distribution results in the above mentioned gap.

3.4 System Configuration

We built two systems for the two subtasks. In our preliminary experiments, we examined several algorithms with different parameters implemented in *RankLib tool*[11], e.g., *Random Forest*, *RankNet*, *RankBoost*, and *ListNet*. According to the best performance in our experiments, we adopted *Random Forest* algorithm with parameters $tree = 5$, $bag = 100$ for English Twitter domain and $tree = 1$, $bag = 300$ for General English domain for our final submitted systems.

3.5 Results and Analysis

Table 2 lists the performances of our system and the top ranked system provided by organizer on test data.

The results in the Table 2 show that our system indeed performed well on sentiment strength prediction task regardless of domains, where the proposed system ranks 1st above both domains among all submissions. The results of test data are consistent with our experiment on training data, the performance on

---

[11]https://people.cs.umass.edu/ vdang/ranklib.html

English Twitter domain is worse than that on General English domain due to the data distribution.

Domain	Rank	TeamID	Kendall(%)	Sperman(%)
General	1	ECNU	**70.42**	**86.27**
	2	UWB	65.91	85.36
	3	LSIS	34.97	50.75
Twitter	1	ECNU	**52.31**	**67.40**
	2	LSIS	42.16	59.06
	3	UWB	41.38	57.82

Table 2: Performances of our systems and the top-ranked system for two domains. *General* and *Twitter* stand for *General English domain* and *English Twitter domain* respectively.

4 Conclusion

In this paper, we presented a supervised learning-to-rank system to predict the strength of positive sentiment associated with words and phrases. Multiple features, e.g., *Sentiment Lexicon, Sentiment Word Vectors, Word Vectors*, and *Linguistic Features*, were presented. We find that the *Sentiment Lexicon Features* and the *Sentiment Word Vectors* make contributions to performance improvement. However the phrase vector is not effective as expected and in future work it is interesting to explore more ways to represent phrase.

Acknowledgements

This research is supported by grants from Science and Technology Commission of Shanghai Municipality (14DZ2260800 and 15ZR1410700), Shanghai Collaborative Innovation Center of Trustworthy Software for Internet of Things (ZF1213).

References

Silvio Amir, Ramón Astudillo, Wang Ling, Bruno Martins, Mario J. Silva, and Isabel Trancoso. 2015. Inescid: A regression model for large scale twitter sentiment lexicon induction. In *SemEval 2015*, pages 613–618, Denver, Colorado, June. Association for Computational Linguistics.

Xiaowen Ding, Bing Liu, and Philip S Yu. 2008. A holistic lexicon-based approach to opinion mining. In *Proceedings of the 2008 International Conference on Web Search and Data Mining*, pages 231–240. ACM.

Peter Sheridan Dodds, Kameron Decker Harris, Isabel M Kloumann, Catherine A Bliss, and Christopher M Danforth. 2011. Temporal patterns of happiness and information in a global social network: Hedonometrics and twitter. *PloS one*, 6(12):e26752.

Alec Go, Richa Bhayani, and Lei Huang. 2009. Twitter sentiment classification using distant supervision. *CS224N Project Report, Stanford*, pages 1–12.

Hussam Hamdan, Patrice Bellot, and Frederic Bechet. 2015. Lsislif: Feature extraction and label weighting for sentiment analysis in twitter. In *Proceedings of the 9th International Workshop on Semantic Evaluation (SemEval 2015)*, pages 568–573, Denver, Colorado, June. Association for Computational Linguistics.

Filip Lindskog, Alexander Mcneil, and Uwe Schmock. 2003. *Kendall' s tau for elliptical distributions.* Springer.

Saif M Mohammad, Svetlana Kiritchenko, and Xiaodan Zhu. 2013. Nrc-canada: Building the state-of-the-art in sentiment analysis of tweets. *arXiv preprint arXiv:1308.6242*.

Seung-Hoon Na, Yeha Lee, Sang-Hyob Nam, and Jong-Hyeok Lee. 2009. Improving opinion retrieval based on query-specific sentiment lexicon. In *ECIR*, volume 9, pages 734–738. Springer.

Jeffrey Pennington, Richard Socher, and Christopher D Manning. 2014. Glove: Global vectors for word representation. In *EMNLP*, volume 14, pages 1532–1543.

Songbo Tan, Yuefen Wang, and Xueqi Cheng. 2008. Combining learn-based and lexicon-based techniques for sentiment detection without using labeled examples. In *Proceedings of the 31st annual international ACM SIGIR conference on Research and development in information retrieval*, pages 743–744. ACM.

Duyu Tang, Furu Wei, Bing Qin, Ming Zhou, and Ting Liu. 2014a. Building large-scale twitter-specific sentiment lexicon: A representation learning approach. In *Proceedings of COLING*, pages 172–182.

Duyu Tang, Furu Wei, Nan Yang, Ming Zhou, Ting Liu, and Bing Qin. 2014b. Learning sentiment-specific word embedding for twitter sentiment classification. In *The Annual Meeting of the Association for Computational Linguistics*, pages 1555–1565.

Janyce Wiebe, Theresa Wilson, and Claire Cardie. 2005. Annotating expressions of opinions and emotions in language. *Language resources and evaluation*, 39(2-3):165–210.

Zhihua Zhang and Man Lan. 2015. Learning sentiment-inherent word embedding for word-level and sentence-level sentiment analysis. In *2015 International Conference on Asian Language Processing, IALP*.

SemEval-2016 Task 1: Semantic Textual Similarity, Monolingual and Cross-Lingual Evaluation

Eneko Agirre[a], Carmen Banea[b], Daniel Cer[d], Mona Diab[e],
Aitor Gonzalez-Agirre[a], Rada Mihalcea[b], German Rigau[a], Janyce Wiebe[f]

[a]University of the Basque Country
Donostia, Basque Country

[b]University of Michigan
Ann Arbor, MI

[d]Google Inc.
Mountain View, CA

[e]George Washington University
Washington, DC

[f]University of Pittsburgh
Pittsburgh, PA

Abstract

Semantic Textual Similarity (STS) seeks to measure the degree of semantic equivalence between two snippets of text. Similarity is expressed on an ordinal scale that spans from semantic equivalence to complete unrelatedness. Intermediate values capture specifically defined levels of partial similarity. While prior evaluations constrained themselves to just monolingual snippets of text, the 2016 shared task includes a pilot subtask on computing semantic similarity on cross-lingual text snippets. This year's traditional monolingual subtask involves the evaluation of English text snippets from the following four domains: Plagiarism Detection, Post-Edited Machine Translations, Question-Answering and News Article Headlines. From the question-answering domain, we include both question-question and answer-answer pairs. The cross-lingual subtask provides paired Spanish-English text snippets drawn from the same sources as the English data as well as independently sampled news data. The English subtask attracted 43 participating teams producing 119 system submissions, while the cross-lingual Spanish-English pilot subtask attracted 10 teams resulting in 26 systems.

1 Introduction

Semantic Textual Similarity (STS) assesses the degree to which the underlying semantics of two segments of text are equivalent to each other. This assessment is performed using an ordinal scale that

---

The authors of this paper are listed in alphabetic order.

ranges from complete semantic equivalence to complete semantic dissimilarity. The intermediate levels capture specifically defined degrees of partial similarity, such as topicality or rough equivalence, but with differing details. The snippets being scored are approximately one sentence in length, with their assessment being performed outside of any contextualizing text. While STS has previously just involved judging text snippets that are written in the same language, this year's evaluation includes a pilot subtask on the evaluation of cross-lingual sentence pairs.

The systems and techniques explored as a part of STS have a broad range of applications including Machine Translation (MT), Summarization, Generation and Question Answering (QA). STS allows for the independent evaluation of methods for computing semantic similarity drawn from a diverse set of domains that would otherwise be only studied within a particular subfield of computational linguistics. Existing methods from a subfield that are found to perform well in a more general setting as well as novel techniques created specifically for STS may improve any natural language processing or language understanding application where knowing the similarity in meaning between two pieces of text is relevant to the behavior of the system.

Paraphrase detection and textual entailment are both highly related to STS. However, STS is more similar to paraphrase detection in that it defines a bi-directional relationship between the two snippets being assessed, rather than the non-symmetric propositional logic like relationship used in textual entailment (e.g., $P \rightarrow Q$ leaves $Q \rightarrow P$ unspecified). STS also expands the binary yes/no catego-

Proceedings of SemEval-2016, pages 497–511,
San Diego, California, June 16-17, 2016. ©2016 Association for Computational Linguistics

Score	English	Cross-lingual Spanish-English
5	*The two sentences are completely equivalent, as they mean the same thing.*	
	The bird is bathing in the sink. Birdie is washing itself in the water basin.	El pájaro se esta bañando en el lavabo. Birdie is washing itself in the water basin.
4	*The two sentences are mostly equivalent, but some unimportant details differ.*	
	In May 2010, the troops attempted to invade Kabul. The US army invaded Kabul on May 7th last year, 2010.	En mayo de 2010, las tropas intentaron invadir Kabul. The US army invaded Kabul on May 7th last year, 2010.
3	*The two sentences are roughly equivalent, but some important information differs/missing.*	
	John said he is considered a witness but not a suspect. "He is not a suspect anymore." John said.	John dijo que él es considerado como testigo, y no como sospechoso. "He is not a suspect anymore." John said.
2	*The two sentences are not equivalent, but share some details.*	
	They flew out of the nest in groups. They flew into the nest together.	Ellos volaron del nido en grupos. They flew into the nest together.
1	*The two sentences are not equivalent, but are on the same topic.*	
	The woman is playing the violin. The young lady enjoys listening to the guitar.	La mujer está tocando el violín. The young lady enjoys listening to the guitar.
0	*The two sentences are completely dissimilar.*	
	John went horse back riding at dawn with a whole group of friends. Sunrise at dawn is a magnificent view to take in if you wake up early enough for it.	Al amanecer, Juan se fue a montar a caballo con un grupo de amigos. Sunrise at dawn is a magnificent view to take in if you wake up early enough for it.

Table 1: Similarity scores with explanations and examples for the English and the cross-lingual Spanish-English subtasks.

rization of both paraphrase detection and textual entailment to a finer grained similarity scale. The additional degrees of similarity introduced by STS are directly relevant to many applications where intermediate levels of similarity are significant. For example, when evaluating machine translation system output, it is desirable to give credit for partial semantic equivalence to human reference translations. Similarly, a summarization system may prefer short segments of text with a rough meaning equivalence to longer segments with perfect semantic coverage.

STS is related to research into machine translation evaluation metrics. This subfield of machine translation investigates methods for replicating human judgements regarding the degree to which a translation generated by an machine translation system corresponds to a reference translation produced by a human translator. STS systems plausibly could be used as a drop-in replacement for existing translation evaluation metrics (e.g., BLEU, MEANT, ME-

TEOR, TER).[1] The cross-lingual STS subtask that is newly introduced this year is similarly related to machine translation quality estimation.

The STS shared task has been held annually since 2012, providing a venue for the evaluation of state-of-the-art algorithms and models (Agirre et al., 2012; Agirre et al., 2013; Agirre et al., 2014; Agirre et al., 2015). During this time, a diverse set of genres and data sources have been explored (i.a., news headlines, video and image descriptions, glosses from lexical resources including WordNet (Miller, 1995; Christiane Fellbaum, 1998), FrameNet (Baker et al., 1998), OntoNotes (Hovy et al., 2006), web discussion forums, and Q&A data sets). This year's

---

[1]Both monolingual and cross-lingual STS score what is referred to in the machine translation literature as adequacy and ignore fluency unless it obscures meaning. While popular machine translation evaluation techniques do not assess fluency independent from adequacy, it is possible that the deeper semantic assessment being performed by STS systems could benefit from being paired with a separate fluency module.

evaluation adds new data sets drawn from plagiarism detection and post-edited machine translations. We also introduce an evaluation set on Q&A forum question-question similarity and revisit news headlines and Q&A answer-answer similarity. The 2016 task includes both a traditional monolingual subtask with English data and a pilot cross-lingual subtask that pairs together Spanish and English texts.

2   Task Overview

STS presents participating systems with paired text snippets of approximately one sentence in length. The systems are then asked to return a numerical score indicating the degree of semantic similarity between the two snippets. Canonical STS scores fall on an ordinal scale with 6 specifically defined degrees of semantic similarity (see Table 1). While the underlying labels and their interpretation are ordinal, systems can provide real valued scores to indicate their semantic similarity prediction.

Participating systems are then evaluated based on the degree to which their predicted similarity scores correlate with STS human judgements. Algorithms are free to use any scale or range of values for the scores they return. They are not punished for outputting scores outside the range of the interpretable human annotated STS labels. This evaluation strategy is motivated by a desire to maximize the flexibility in the design of machine learning models and systems for STS. It reinforces the assumption that computing textual similarity is an enabling component for other natural language processing applications, rather than being an end in itself.

Table 1 illustrates the ordinal similarity scale the shared task uses. Both the English and the cross-lingual Spanish-English STS subtasks use a 6 point similarity scale. A similarity label of 0 means that two texts are completely dissimilar; this can be interpreted as two sentences with no overlap in their meanings. The next level up, a similarity label of 1, indicates that the two snippets are not equivalent but are topically related to each other. A label of 2 indicates that the two texts are still not equivalent but agree on some details of what is being said. The labels 3 and 4, both indicate that the two sentences are approximately equivalent. However, a score of 3 implies that there are some differences in important details, while a score of 4 indicates that the differing details are not important. The top score of 5, denotes that the two texts being evaluated have complete semantic equivalence.

In the context of the STS task, meaning equivalence is defined operationally as two snippets of text that mean the same thing when interpreted by a reasonable human judge. The operational approach to sentence level semantics was popularized by the recognizing textual entailment task (Dagan et al., 2010). It has the advantage that it allows the labeling of sentence pairs by human annotators without any training in formal semantics, while also being more useful and intuitive to work with for downstream systems. Beyond just sentence level semantics, the operationally defined STS labels also reflect both world knowledge and pragmatic phenomena.

As in prior years, 2016 shared task participants are allowed to make use of existing resources and tools (e.g., WordNet, Mikolov et al. (2013)'s word2vec). Participants are also allowed to make unsupervised use of arbitrary data sets, even if such data overlaps with the announced sources of the evaluation data.

3   English Subtask

The English subtask builds on four prior years of English STS tasks. Task participants are allowed to use all of the trial, train and evaluation sets released during prior years as training and development data. As shown in table 2, this provides 14,250 paired snippets with gold STS labels. The 2015 STS task annotated between 1,500 and 2,000 pairs per data set that were then filtered based on annotation agreement and to achieve better data set balance. The raw annotations were released after the evaluation, providing an additional 5,500 pairs with noisy STS annotations (8,500 total for 2015).[2]

The 2016 English evaluation data is partitioned into five individual evaluation sets: Headlines, Plagiarism, Postediting, Answer-Answer and Question-Question. Each evaluation set has between 209 to 254 pairs. Participants annotate a larger number of pairs for each dataset without knowledge of what pairs will be included in the final evaluation.

---

[2] Answers-forums: 2000; Answers-students: 1500; Belief: 2000; Headlines: 1500; Images: 1500.

year	dataset	pairs	source
2012	MSRpar	1500	newswire
2012	MSRvid	1500	videos
2012	OnWN	750	glosses
2012	SMTnews	750	WMT eval.
2012	SMTeuroparl	750	WMT eval.
2013	HDL	750	newswire
2013	FNWN	189	glosses
2013	OnWN	561	glosses
2013	SMT	750	MT eval.
2014	HDL	750	newswire headlines
2014	OnWN	750	glosses
2014	Deft-forum	450	forum posts
2014	Deft-news	300	news summary
2014	Images	750	image descriptions
2014	Tweet-news	750	tweet-news pairs
2015	HDL	750	newswire headlines
2015	Images	750	image descriptions
2015	Ans.-student	750	student answers
2015	Ans.-forum	375	Q&A forum answers
2015	Belief	375	committed belief
2016	HDL	249	newswire headlines
2016	Plagiarism	230	short-answer plag.
2016	Postediting	244	MT postedits
2016	Ans.-Ans.	254	Q&A forum answers
2016	Quest.-Quest.	209	Q&A forum questions

Table 2: English subtask: Train (2012, 2013, 2014, 2015) and test (2016) data sets.

3.1 Data Collection

The data for the English evaluation sets are collected from a diverse set of sources. Data sources are selected that correspond to potentially useful domains for application of the semantic similarity methods explored in STS systems. This section details the pair selection heuristics as well as the individual data sources we use for the evaluation sets.

3.1.1 Selection Heuristics

Unless otherwise noted, pairs are heuristically selected using a combination of lexical surface form and word embedding similarity between a candidate pair of text snippets. The heuristics are used to find pairs sharing some minimal level of either surface or embedding space similarity. An approximately equal number of candidate sentence pairs are produced using our lexical surface form and word embedding selection heuristics. Both heuristics make use of a Penn Treebank style tokenization of the text provided by CoreNLP (Manning et al., 2014).

year	dataset	pairs	source
2016	Trial	103	Sampled $\leq$ 2015 STS
2016	News	301	en-es news articles
2016	Multi-source	294	en news headlines, short-answer plag., MT postedits, Q&A forum answers, Q&A forum questions

Table 3: Spanish-English subtask: Trial and test data sets.

Surface Lexical Similarity Our surface form selection heuristic uses an information theoretic measure based on unigram overlap (Lin, 1998). As shown in equation (1), surface level lexical similarity between two snippets s_1 and s_2 is computed as a log probability weighted sum of the words common to both snippets divided by a log probability weighted sum of all the words in the two snippets.

$$\text{sim}_l(s_1, s_1) = \frac{2 \times \sum_{w \in s_1 \cap s_2} \log P(w)}{\sum_{w \in s_1} \log P(w) + \sum_{w \in s_2} \log P(w)} \quad (1)$$

Unigram probabilities are estimated over the evaluation set data sources and are computed without any smoothing.

Word Embedding Similarity As our second heuristic, we compute the cosine between a simple embedding space representation of the two text snippets. Equation (2) illustrates the construction of the snippet embedding space representation, $\mathbf{v}(s)$, as the sum of the embeddings for the individual words, $\mathbf{v}(w)$, in the snippet. The cosine similarity can then be computed as in equation (3).

$$\mathbf{v}(s) = \sum_{w \in s} \mathbf{v}(w) \quad (2)$$

$$\text{sim}_v(s_1, s_2) = \frac{\mathbf{v}(s_1)\mathbf{v}(s_2)}{||\mathbf{v}(s_1)||||\mathbf{v}(s_2)||} \quad (3)$$

Three hundred dimensional word embeddings are obtained by running the GloVe package (Pennington et al., 2014) with default parameters over all the data collected from the 2016 evaluation sources.[3]

---

[3]The evaluation source data contained only 10,352,554 tokens. This is small relative to the data sets used to train embedding space models that typically make use of $>$ 1B tokens. However, the resulting embeddings are found to be functionally

3.1.2 Newswire Headlines

The newswire headlines evaluational set is collected from the Europe Media Monitor (EMM) (Best et al., 2005) using the same extraction approach taken for STS 2015 (Agirre et al., 2015) over the date range July 28, 2014 to April 10, 2015. The EMM clusters identify related news stories. To construct the STS pairs, we extract 749 pairs of headlines that appear in same cluster and 749 pairs of headlines associated with stories that appear in different clusters. For both groups, we use a surface level string similarity metric found in the Perl package `String::Similarity` (Myers, 1986) to select an equal number of pairs with high and low surface similarity scores.

3.1.3 Plagiarism

The plagiarism evaluation set is based on Clough and Stevenson (2011)'s Corpus of Plagiarised Short Answers. This corpus provides a collection of short answers to computer science questions that exhibit varying degrees of plagiarism from related Wikipedia articles.[4] The short answers include text that was constructed by each of the following four strategies: 1) copying and pasting individual sentences from Wikipedia; 2) light revision of material copied from Wikipedia; 3) heavy revision of material from Wikipedia; 4) non-plagiarised answers produced without even looking at Wikipedia. This corpus is segmented into individual sentences using CoreNLP (Manning et al., 2014).

3.1.4 Postediting

The Specia (2011) EAMT 2011 corpus provides machine translations of French news data using the Moses machine translation system (Koehn et al., 2007) paired with postedited corrections of those translations.[5] The corrections were provided by human translators instructed to perform the minimum number of changes necessary to produce a publishable translation. STS pairs for this evaluation set are selected both using the surface form and embedding space pairing heuristics and by including the existing explicit pairs of each machine translation with its postedited correction.

3.1.5 Question-Question & Answer-Answer

The question-question and answer-answer evaluation sets are extracted from the Stack Exchange Data Dump (Stack Exchange, Inc., 2016). The data include long form Question-Answer pairs on a diverse set of topics ranging from highly technical areas such as programming, physics and mathematics to more casual topics like cooking and travel.

Pairs are constructed using questions and answers from the following less technical Stack Exchange sites: *academia, cooking, coffee, diy, english, fitness, health, history, lifehacks, linguistics, money, movies, music, outdoors, parenting, pets, politics, productivity, sports, travel, workplace* and *writers*. Since both the questions and answers are long form, often being a paragraph in length or longer, heuristics are used to select a one sentence summary of each question and answer. For questions, we use the title of the question when it ends in a question mark.[6] For answers, a one sentence summary of each question is constructed using LexRank (Erkan and Radev, 2004) as implemented by the Sumy[7] package.

4 Cross-lingual Subtask

The pilot cross-lingual subtask explores the expansion of STS to paired snippets of text in different languages. The 2016 shared task pairs snippets in Spanish and English, with each pair containing exactly one Spanish and one English member. A trial set of 103 pairs was released prior to the official evaluation window containing pairs of sentences randomly selected from prior English STS evaluations, but with one of the snippets being translated into Spanish by human translators.[8] The similarity scores associated with this set are taken from the manual STS annotations within the original English data.

---

useful for finding semantically similar text snippets that differ in surface form.

    [4]Questions: A. What is inheritance in object oriented programming?, B. Explain the PageRank algorithm that is used by the Google search engine, C. Explain the Vector Space Model that is used for Information Retrieval., D. Explain Bayes Theorem from probability theory, E. What is dynamic programming?

    [5]The corpus also includes English news data machine translated into Spanish and the postedited corrections of these translations. We use the English-Spanish data in the cross-lingual task.

    [6]Questions with titles not ending in a "?" are discarded.

    [7]`https://pypi.python.org/pypi/sumy`

    [8]SDL was used to translate the trial data set, `http://sdl.com`.

Task Instructions

Two snippets of text can mean the same thing even if they use very different words and phrases. Conversely, two texts that are superficially very similar in their word choice, phrasing and overall composition can have very different meanings.

For this task, you will compare two phrase or sentence length segments of text and select whether or not they have the same underlying meaning or message in terms of what they refer to, say or ask about the world.

For example, do both snippets refer to the exact same person, action, event, idea or thing? Or, are they similar but differ according to either large or small details?

Tips

- *Assign labels as precisely as possible according to the underlying meaning of the two snippets rather than their superficial similarities or differences.*
- Be careful of wording differences that have an important impact on what is being said or described.
- Ignore grammatical errors and awkward wordings as long as they do not obscure what is being conveyed.
- Avoid over labeling pairs with middle range scores such as "**(3) Roughly Equivalent**, ..." or "**(2) Not equivalent**, but share some details".
- Similarly, be careful of over reliance on extreme scores like "**(5) Completely equivalent**, ..." or "**(0) On different topics.**"

Hot Keys

To navigate this HIT more quickly and without using a mouse, try making use of the following hot keys:

`[tab]` Next Question, `[tab]`+`[shift]` Previous Question, `[up]` / `[down]` (arrow keys) Navigate Pair Meaning Similarity Scale

Figure 1: Annotation instructions for the STS English subtask.

Participants are allowed to use the labeled STS pairs from any of the prior STS evaluations. This includes STS pairs from all four prior years of the English STS subtasks as well as data from the 2014 and 2015 Spanish STS subtasks.

4.1 Data Collection

The cross-lingual evaluation data is partitioned into two evaluation sets: news and multi-source. The news data set is manually harvested from multilingual news sources, while the multi-source dataset is sampled from the same sources as the 2016 English data, with one of the snippets being translated into Spanish by human translators.[9] As shown in Table 3, the news set has 301 pairs, while the multi-source set has 294 pairs. For the news evaluation set, participants are provided with exactly the 301 pairs that will be used for the final evaluation. For the multi-source dataset, we take the same approach as the English subtask and release 2,973 pairs for annotation by participant systems, without providing information on what pairs will be included in the final evaluation.

4.1.1 Cross-lingual News

The cross-lingual news dataset is manually culled from less mainstream news sources such as Russia

Today[10], in order to pose a more natural challenge in terms of machine translation accuracy. Articles on the same or differing topics are collected, with particular effort being spent to find articles on the same or somewhat similar story (many times written by the same author in English and Spanish), that exhibit a natural writing pattern in each language by itself and do not amount to an exact translation. When compared across the two languages, such articles exhibit different sentence structure and length. Additional paragraphs are also included by the writer that would cater to the readers' interests. For example, in the case of articles written about the Mexican drug lord Joaquin "El Chapo" Guzman, who was recently captured, the English articles typically have less extraneous details, focusing more on facts, while the articles written in Spanish provide additional background information with more narrative. Such articles allow for the manual extraction of high quality pairs that enable a wider variety of testing scenarios: from exact translations, to paraphrases exhibiting a different sentence structure, to somewhat similar sentences, to sentences sharing common vocabulary but no topic similarity, and ultimately to completely unrelated sentences. This ensures that semantic similarity systems that rely heavily on lexical features (which have been also typically used in STS tasks to derive test and train datasets) are at

---

[9]The evaluation set was translated into Spanish by Gengo: `http://gengo.com/`

[10]English: `https://www.rt.com/`, Spanish: `https://actualidad.rt.com/`

a disadvantage, and rather systems that actually explore semantic information receive due credit.

4.1.2 Multi-source

The raw multi-source data sets annotated by participating systems are constructed by first sampling 250 pairs from each of the following four data sets from the English task: Answer-Answer, Plagiarism, Question-Question and Headlines. One sentence from each sampled pair is selected at random for translation into Spanish by human translators.[11] An additional 1973 pairs are drawn from the English-Spanish section of EAMT 2011. We include all pairings of English source sentences with their human post-edited Spanish translations, resulting in 1000 pairs. We also include pairings of English source sentences with their Spanish machine translations. This only produced an additional 973 pairs, since 27 of the pairs are already generated by human post-edited translations that exactly match their corresponding machine translations. The gold standard data are selected by randomly drawing 60 pairs belonging to each data set within the raw multi-source data, except for EMM where only 54 pairs were drawn.[12]

5 Annotation

Annotation of pairs with STS scores is performed using crowdsourcing on Amazon Mechanical Turk.[13] This section describes the templates and annotation parameters we use for the English and cross-lingual Spanish-English pairs, as well as how the gold standard annotations are computed from multiple annotations from crowd workers.

5.1 English Subtask

The annotation instructions for the English subtask are modified from prior years in order to accommodate the annotation of question-question pairs. Figure 1 illustrates the new instructions. References to *statements* are replaced with *snippets*. The new instructions remove the wording suggesting that anno-

tators "picture what is being described" and provide tips for navigating the annotation form quickly. The annotation form itself is also modified from prior years to make use of radio boxes to annotate the similarity scale rather than drop-down lists.

The English STS pairs are annotated in batches of 20 pairs. For each batch, annotators are paid $1 USD. Five annotations are collected per pair. Only workers with the MTurk *master* qualification are allowed to perform the annotation, a designation by the MTurk platform that statistical identifies workers who perform high quality work across a diverse set of MTurk tasks. Gold annotations are selected as the median value of the crowdsourced annotations after filtering out low quality annotators. We remove annotators with correlation scores < 0.80 using a simulated gold annotation computed by leaving out the annotations from the worker being evaluated. We also exclude all annotators with a kappa score $<$ 0.20 against the same simulated gold standard.

The official task evaluation data are selected from pairs having at least three remaining labels after excluding the low quality annotators. For each evaluation set, we attempt to select up to 42 pairs for each STS label. Preference was given to pairs with a higher number of STS labels matching the median label. After the final pairs are selected, they are spot checked with some of the pairs having their STS score corrected.

5.2 Cross-lingual Spanish-English Subtask

The Spanish-English pairs are annotated using a slightly modified template from the 2014 and 2015 Spanish STS subtask. Given the multilingual nature of the subtask, the guidelines consist of alternating instructions in either English or Spanish, in order to dissuade monolingual annotators from participating (see Figure 2). The template is also modified to use the same six point scale used by the English subtask, rather than the five point scale used in the Spanish subtasks in the past (which did not attempt to distinguish between differences in unimportant details). Judges are also presented with the cross-lingual example pairs and explanations listed on Table 1.

The cross-lingual pairs are annotated in batches of 7 pairs. Annotators are paid $0.30 USD per batch and each batch receives annotations from 5 workers. The annotations are restricted to workers who

---

[11]Inspection of the data suggests the translation service provider may have used a postediting based process.

[12]Our annotators work on batches of 7 pairs. Drawing 54 pairs from the EMM data results in a total number pairs that is cleanly divisible by 7.

[13]`https://www.mturk.com/`

Evaluación de similitud de texto en español y inglés

Se necesita conocimiento profundo de español y de inglés para completar esta tarea. / In depth knowledge of English and Spanish is needed to complete this task.

Dadas dos frases una en inglés y otra en español, la tarea consiste en cuantificar la similitud que tienen en significado entre ellas. The level of similarity should be expressed as a score between 0 and 5, where 0 reprents two sentences that are unrelated in meaning, and 5 indicates that the two sentences are perfect paraphrases of each other. Un HIT está formado por siete pares de frases.

Figure 2: Annotation instructions for the STS Spanish-English subtask.

have completed 500 HITs on the MTurk platform and have less than 10% of their lifetime annotations rejected. The gold standard is computed by averaging over the 5 annotations collected for each pair.

6   System Evaluation

This section reports the evaluation results for the 2016 STS English and cross-lingual Spanish-English subtasks.

6.1   Participation

Participating teams are allowed to submit up to three systems.[14] For the English subtask, there were 119 systems from 43 participating teams. The cross-lingual Spanish-English subtask saw 26 submissions from 10 teams. For the English subtask, this is a 45% increase in participating teams from 2015. The Spanish-English STS pilot subtask attracted approximately 53% more participants than the monolingual Spanish subtask organized in 2015.

6.2   Evaluation Metric

On each test set, systems are evaluated based on their Pearson correlation with the gold standard STS labels. The overall score for each system is computed as the average of the correlation values on the individual evaluation sets, weighted by the number of data points in each evaluation set.

6.3   Baseline

Similar to prior years, we include a baseline built using a very simple vector space representation. For this baseline, both text snippets in a pair are first tokenized by white-space. The snippets are then projected to a one-hot vector representation such that each dimension corresponds to a word observed in one of the snippets. If a word appears in a snippet one or more times, the corresponding dimension in the vector is set to one and is otherwise set to zero. The textual similarity score is then computed as the cosine between these vector representations of the two snippets.

6.4   English Subtask

The rankings for the English STS subtask are given in Tables 4 and 5. The baseline system ranked 100th. Table 6 provides the best and median scores for each of the individual evaluation sets as well as overall.[15] The table also provides the difference between the best and median scores to highlight the extent to which top scoring systems outperformed the typical level of performance achieved on each data set.

The best overall performance is obtained by Samsung Poland NLP Team's EN1 system, which achieves an overall correlation of 0.778 (Rychalska et al., 2016). This system also performs best on three out of the five individual evaluation sets: answer-answer, headlines, plagiarism. The EN1 system achieves competitive performance on the postediting data with a correlation score of 0.83516. The best system on the postediting data, RICOH's Run-n (Itoh, 2016), obtains a score of 0.867. Like all systems, EN1 struggles on the question-question data, achieving a correlation of 0.687. Another system submitted by the Samsung Poland NLP Team named

---

[14]For the English subtask, the SimiHawk team was granted permission to make 4 submissions as the team has 3 submissions using distinct machine learning models (feature engineered, LSTM, and Tree LSTM) and they asked to separately submit an ensemble of the three methods.

[15]The median scores reported here do not include late or corrected systems. The median scores for the on-time systems without corrections are: ALL 0.68923; plagiarism 0.78949; answer-answer 0.48018; postediting 0.81241; headlines 0.76439; question-question 0.57140.

Team	Run	ALL	Ans.-Ans.	HDL	Plagiarism	Postediting	Ques.-Ques.	Run Rank	Team Rank
Samsung Poland NLP Team	EN1	**0.77807**	**0.69235**	**0.82749**	**0.84138**	0.83516	0.68705	1	1
UWB	sup-general	0.75731	0.62148	0.81886	0.82355	0.82085	0.70199	2	2
MayoNLPTeam	Run3	0.75607	0.61426	0.77263	0.80500	0.84840	**0.74705**	3	3
Samsung Poland NLP Team	EN2	0.75468	**0.69235**	**0.82749**	0.81288	0.83516	0.58567	4	
NaCTeM	micro+macro	0.74865	0.60237	0.80460	0.81478	0.82858	0.69367	5	4
ECNU	S1-All	0.75079	0.56979	0.81214	0.82503	0.82342	0.73116	5*	4*
UMD-TTIC-UW	Run1	0.74201	0.66074	0.79457	0.81541	0.80939	0.61872	6	5
SimiHawk	Ensemble	0.73774	0.59237	0.81419	0.80566	0.82179	0.65048	7	6
MayoNLPTeam	Run2	0.73569	0.57739	0.75061	0.80068	0.82857	0.73035	8	
Samsung Poland NLP Team	AE	0.73566	0.65769	0.81801	0.81288	0.78849	0.58567	9	
DLS@CU	Run1	0.73563	0.55230	0.80079	0.82293	0.84258	0.65986	10	7
DLS@CU	Run3	0.73550	0.54528	0.80334	0.81949	0.84418	0.66657	11	
DTSim	Run1	0.73493	0.57805	0.81527	0.83757	0.82286	0.61428	12	8
NaCTeM	macro	0.73391	0.58484	0.79756	0.78949	0.82614	0.67039	13	
DLS@CU	Run2	0.73297	0.55992	0.80334	0.81227	0.84418	0.64234	14	
Stasis	xgboost	0.73050	0.50628	0.77824	0.82501	0.84861	0.70424	15	9
IHS-RD-Belarus	Run1	0.72966	0.55322	0.82419	0.82634	0.83761	0.59904	16	10
USFD	COMB-Features	0.72869	0.50850	0.82024	0.83828	0.79496	0.68926	17	11
USFD	CNN	0.72705	0.51096	0.81899	0.83427	0.79268	0.68551	18	
saarsheff	MT-Metrics-xgboost	0.72693	0.47716	0.78848	0.83212	0.84960	0.69815	19	12
MayoNLPTeam	Run1	0.72646	0.58873	0.73458	0.76887	0.85020	0.69306	20	
UWB	unsup	0.72622	0.64442	0.79352	0.82742	0.81209	0.53383	21	
UMD-TTIC-UW	Run2	0.72619	0.64427	0.78708	0.79894	0.79338	0.59468	22	
SERGIOJIMENEZ	Run2	0.72617	0.55257	0.78304	0.81505	0.81634	0.66630	23	13
IHS-RD-Belarus	Run2	0.72465	0.53722	0.82539	0.82558	0.83654	0.59072	24	
DTSim	Run3	0.72414	0.56189	0.81237	0.83239	0.81498	0.59103	25	
ECNU	U-SEVEN	0.72427	0.47748	0.76681	0.83013	0.84239	0.71914	25*	
SERGIOJIMENEZ	Run1	0.72411	0.50182	0.78646	0.83654	0.83638	0.66519	26	
NaCTeM	Micro	0.72361	0.55214	0.79143	0.83134	0.82660	0.61241	27	
SERGIOJIMENEZ	Run3	0.72215	0.49068	0.77725	0.82926	0.84807	0.67291	28	
DTSim	Run2	0.72016	0.55042	0.79499	0.82815	0.81508	0.60766	29	
DCU-SEManiacs	Fusion	0.71701	0.58328	0.76392	0.81386	0.84662	0.56576	30	14
DCU-SEManiacs	Synthetic	0.71334	0.68762	0.72227	0.81935	0.80900	0.50560	31	
RICOH	Run-b	0.71165	0.50871	0.78691	0.82661	0.86554	0.56245	32	15
ECNU	S2	0.71175	0.57158	0.79036	0.77338	0.74968	0.67635	32*	
HHU	Overlap	0.71134	0.50435	0.77406	0.83049	0.83846	0.60867	33	16
UMD-TTIC-UW	Run3	0.71112	0.64316	0.77801	0.78158	0.77786	0.55855	34	
University of Birmingham	CombineFeatures	0.70940	0.52460	0.81894	0.82066	0.81272	0.56040	35	17
University of Birmingham	MethodsFeatures	0.70911	0.52028	0.81894	0.81958	0.81333	0.56451	36	
SimiHawk	F	0.70647	0.44003	0.77109	0.81105	0.81600	0.71035	37	
UWB	sup-try	0.70542	0.53333	0.77846	0.74673	0.78507	0.68909	38	
Stasis	boostedtrees	0.70496	0.40791	0.77276	0.82903	0.84635	0.68359	39	
RICOH	Run-n	0.70467	0.50746	0.77409	0.82248	**0.86690**	0.54261	40	
Stasis	linear	0.70461	0.36929	0.76660	0.82730	0.83917	0.74615	41	
RICOH	Run-s	0.70420	0.51293	0.78000	0.82991	0.86252	0.52319	42	
University of Birmingham	CombineNoFeatures	0.70168	0.55217	0.82352	0.82406	0.80835	0.47904	43	
MathLingBudapest	Run1	0.70025	0.40540	0.81187	0.80752	0.83767	0.64712	44	18
ISCAS_NLP	S1	0.69996	0.49378	0.79763	0.81933	0.81185	0.57218	45	19
ISCAS_NLP	S3	0.69996	0.49378	0.79763	0.81933	0.81185	0.57218	46	
UNBNLP	Regression	0.69940	0.55254	0.71353	0.79769	0.81291	0.62037	47	20
DCU-SEManiacs	task-internal	0.69924	0.62702	0.71949	0.80783	0.80854	0.51580	48	
MathLingBudapest	Run2	0.69853	0.40540	0.80367	0.80752	0.83767	0.64712	49	
MathLingBudapest	Run3	0.69853	0.40540	0.80366	0.80752	0.83767	0.64712	50	
ISCAS_NLP	S2	0.69756	0.49651	0.79041	0.81214	0.81181	0.57181	51	
UNBNLP	Average	0.69635	0.58520	0.69006	0.78923	0.82540	0.58605	52	
NUIG-UNLP	m5all3	0.69528	0.40165	0.75400	0.80332	0.81606	0.72228	53	21
wolvesaar	xgboost	0.69471	0.49947	0.72410	0.79076	0.84093	0.62055	54	22
wolvesaar	lotsa-embeddings	0.69453	0.49415	0.71439	0.79655	0.83758	0.63509	55	
Meiji-WSL-A	Run1	0.69435	0.58260	0.74394	0.79234	0.85962	0.47030	56	23
saarsheff	MT-Metrics-boostedtrees	0.69259	0.37717	0.77183	0.81529	0.84528	0.66825	57	
wolvesaar	DLS-replica	0.69244	0.48799	0.71043	0.80605	0.84601	0.61515	58	
saarsheff	MT-Metrics-linear	0.68923	0.31539	0.76551	0.82063	0.83329	0.73987	59	
EECS	Run2	0.68430	0.48013	0.77891	0.76676	0.82965	0.55926	60	24
NUIG-UNLP	m5dom1	0.68368	0.41211	0.76778	0.75539	0.80086	0.69782	61	
EECS	Run3	0.67906	0.47818	0.77719	0.77266	0.83744	0.51840	62	
PKU	Run1	0.67852	0.47469	0.77881	0.77479	0.81472	0.54180	63	25
EECS	Run1	0.67711	0.48110	0.77739	0.76747	0.83270	0.51479	64	
PKU	Run2	0.67503	0.47444	0.77703	0.78119	0.83051	0.49892	65	
HHU	SameWordsNeuralNet	0.67502	0.42673	0.75536	0.79964	0.84514	0.54533	66	
PKU	Run3	0.67209	0.47271	0.77367	0.77580	0.81185	0.51611	67	
NSH	Run1	0.66181	0.39962	0.74549	0.80176	0.79540	0.57080	68	26
RTM	SVR	0.66847	0.44865	0.66338	0.80376	0.81327	0.62374	68*	26*
Meiji-WSL-A	Run2	0.65871	0.51675	0.58561	0.78700	0.81873	0.59035	69	
BIT	Align	0.65318	0.54530	0.78140	0.80473	0.79456	0.29972	70	27
UNBNLP	tf-idf	0.65271	0.45928	0.66593	0.75778	0.77204	0.61710	71	
UTA_MLNLP	100-1	0.64965	0.46391	0.74499	0.74003	0.71947	0.58083	72	28
RTM	FS+PLS-SVR	0.65237	0.35333	0.65294	0.80488	0.82304	0.64803	72*	
RTM	PLS-SVR	0.65182	0.34401	0.66051	0.80641	0.82314	0.64544	72*	
SimiHawk	LSTM	0.64840	0.44177	0.75703	0.71737	0.72317	0.60691	73	
BIT	VecSim	0.64661	0.48863	0.62804	0.80106	0.79544	0.51702	74	
NUIG-UNLP	m5dom2	0.64520	0.38303	0.76485	0.74351	0.76549	0.57263	75	

Table 4: STS 2016: English Rankings. Late or corrected systems are marked with a * symbol.

Team	Run	ALL	Ans.-Ans.	HDL	Plagiarism	Postediting	Ques.-Ques.	Run Rank	Team Rank
UTA_MLNLP	150-1	0.64500	0.43042	0.72133	0.71620	0.74471	0.62006	76	
SimiHawk	TreeLSTM	0.64140	0.52277	0.74083	0.67628	0.70655	0.55265	77	
NORMAS	SV-2	0.64078	0.36583	0.68864	0.74647	0.80234	0.61300	78	29
UTA_MLNLP	150-3	0.63698	0.41871	0.72485	0.70296	0.69652	0.65543	79	
LIPN-IIMAS	SOPA	0.63087	0.44901	0.62411	0.69109	0.79864	0.59779	80	30
NORMAS	ECV-3	0.63072	0.27637	0.72245	0.72496	0.79797	0.65312	81	
JUNITMZ	Backpropagation-1	0.62708	0.48023	0.70749	0.72075	0.77196	0.43751	82	31
NSH	Run2	0.62941	0.34172	0.74977	0.75858	0.82471	0.46548	82*	
LIPN-IIMAS	SOPA1000	0.62466	0.44893	0.59721	0.75936	0.76157	0.56285	83	
USFD	Word2Vec	0.62254	0.27675	0.64217	0.78755	0.75057	0.68833	84	
HHU	DeepLDA	0.62078	0.47211	0.58821	0.62503	0.84743	0.57099	85	
ASOBEK	T11	0.61782	0.52277	0.63741	0.78521	0.84245	0.26352	86	32
ASOBEK	M11	0.61430	0.47916	0.68652	0.77779	0.84089	0.24804	87	
LIPN-IIMAS	SOPA100	0.61321	0.43216	0.58499	0.74727	0.75560	0.55310	88	
Telkom University	WA	0.60912	0.28859	0.69988	0.69090	0.74654	0.64009	89	33
BIT	WeightedVecSim	0.59560	0.37565	0.55925	0.75594	0.77835	0.51643	90	
3CFEE	grumlp	0.59603	0.36521	0.72092	0.74210	0.76327	0.37179	90*	34*
ASOBEK	F1	0.59556	0.42692	0.67898	0.75717	0.81950	0.26181	91	
JUNITMZ	Recurrent-1	0.59493	0.44218	0.66120	0.73708	0.69279	0.43092	92	
VRep	withLeven	0.58292	0.30617	0.68745	0.69762	0.73033	0.49639	93	34
Meiji_WSL_teamC	Run1	0.58169	0.53250	0.64567	0.74233	0.54783	0.42797	94	35
JUNITMZ	FeedForward-1	0.58109	0.40859	0.66524	0.76752	0.66522	0.38711	95	
VRep	withStopRem	0.57805	0.29487	0.68185	0.69730	0.72966	0.49029	96	
VRep	noStopRem	0.55894	0.34684	0.67856	0.69768	0.74088	0.30908	97	
UNCC	Run-3	0.55789	0.31111	0.59592	0.64672	0.75544	0.48409	98	36
Telkom University	CS	0.51602	0.06623	0.72668	0.50534	0.73999	0.56194	99	
NORMAS	RF-1	0.50895	0.16095	0.58800	0.62134	0.72016	0.46743	100	
STS Organizers	*baseline*	0.51334	0.41133	0.54073	0.69601	0.82615	0.03844	100[†]	37[†]
meijiuniversity_teamb	4features_^LCS_pos	0.45748	0.26182	0.60223	0.55931	0.66989	0.16276	101	37
meijiuniversity_teamb	5features	0.45656	0.26498	0.60000	0.55231	0.66894	0.16518	102	
meijiuniversity_teamb	4features_^LCS	0.45621	0.26588	0.59868	0.55687	0.66690	0.16103	103	
Amrita_CEN	SEWE-2	0.40951	0.30309	0.43164	0.63336	0.66465	-0.03174	104	38
VENSESEVAL	Run1	0.44258	0.41932	0.62738	0.64538	0.27274	0.22581	104*	38*
UNCC	Run-1	0.40359	0.19537	0.49344	0.38881	0.59235	0.34548	105	
UNCC	Run-2	0.37956	0.18100	0.50924	0.26190	0.56176	0.38317	106	
WHU_NLP	CNN20	0.11100	-0.02488	0.16026	0.16854	0.24153	0.00176	107	39
3CFEE	bowkst	0.33174	0.20076	0.42288	0.50150	0.19111	0.35970	107*	
WHU_NLP	CNN10	0.09814	0.05402	0.19650	0.08949	0.16152	-0.02989	108	
DalGTM	Run1	0.05354	-0.00557	0.29896	-0.07016	-0.04933	0.08924	109	40
DalGTM	Run2	0.05136	-0.00810	0.28962	-0.07032	-0.04818	0.08987	110	
DalGTM	Run3	0.05027	-0.00780	0.28501	-0.07134	-0.05014	0.09223	111	
WHU_NLP	CNN5	0.04713	0.00041	0.13780	0.03264	0.12669	-0.08105	112	
IHS-RD-Belarus	Run3					0.83761		113	

Table 5: STS 2016: English Rankings (continued). As before, late or corrected systems are marked with a * symbol. The baseline run by the organizers is marked with a [†] symbol (at rank 100).

Evaluation Set	Best	Median	Δ
ALL	0.77807	0.69347	0.08460
Ans.-Ans.	0.69235	0.48067	0.21169
HDL	0.82749	0.76439	0.06311
Plagiarism	0.84138	0.79445	0.04694
Postediting	0.86690	0.81272	0.05418
Ques.-Ques.	0.74705	0.57673	0.17032

Table 6: Best and median scores by evaluation set for the English subtask as well as the difference between the two, Δ.

EN2 achieves the best correlation on the question-question data at 0.747.

The most difficult data sets this year are the two Q&A evaluation sets: answer-answer and question-question. Difficulty on the question-question data was expected as this is the first year that question-question pairs are formally included in the evaluation of STS systems.[16] Interestingly, the baseline system has particular problems on this data, achieving a correlation of only 0.038. This suggests that surface overlap features might be less informative on this data, possibly leading to prediction errors by the systems that include them. An answer-answer evaluation set was previously included in the 2015 STS task. Answer-answer data is included again in this year's evaluation specifically because of the poor performance observed on this type of data in 2015.

In Table 6, it can be seen that the difficult Q&A data sets are also the data sets that exhibit the biggest difference between the top performing system for that evaluation set and typical system performance, as capture by the median on the same data. For the easier data sets, news headlines, plagiarism, and postediting, there is only a relatively modest gap between the best system for that data set and typical system performance ranging from about 0.05 to 0.06. However, on the difficult Q&A data set the difference between the best system and typical systems jumps to 0.212 for answer-answer and 0.170 for question-question. This suggests these harder

---

[16]The pair selection criteria from prior years did not explicitly exclude the presence of questions or question-question pairs. Of the 19,189 raw pairs from prior English STS evaluations as trial, train or evaluation data, 831 (4.33%) of the pairs include a question mark within at least one member of the pair, while 319 of the pairs (1.66%) include a question mark within both members.

data sets may be better at discriminating between different approaches with most systems now being fairly competent on assessing easier pairs.[17]

6.4.1 Methods

Participating systems vary greatly in the approaches they take to solving STS. The overall winner, Samsung Poland NLP Team, proposes a textual similarity model that is a novel hybrid of recursive auto-encoders from deep learning with penalty and reward signals extracted from WordNet (Rychalska et al., 2016). To obtain even better performance, this model is combined in an ensemble with a number of other similarity models including a version of Sultan et al. (2015)'s very successful STS model enhanced with additional features found to work well in the literature.

The team in second place overall, UWB, combines a large number of diverse similarity models and features (Brychcin and Svoboda, 2016). Similar to Samsung, UWB includes both manually engineered NLP features (e.g., character n-gram overlap) with sophisticated models from deep learning (e.g., Tree LSTMs). The third place team, MayoNLPTeam, also achieves their best results using a combination of a more traditionally engineered NLP pipeline with a deep learning based model (Afzal et al., 2016). Specifically, MayoNLPTeam combines a pipeline that makes use of linguistic resources such as WordNet and well understood concepts such as the information content of a word (Resnik, 1995) with a deep learning method known as Deep Structured Semantic Model (DSSM) (Huang et al., 2013).

The next two teams in overall performance, ECNU and NaCTeM, make use of large feature sets, including features based on word embeddings. However, they did not incorporate the more sophisticated deep learning based models explored by Samsung, UWB and MayoNLPTeam (Tian and Lan, 2016; Przybyła et al., 2016).

The next team in the rankings, UMD-TTIC-UW, *only* makes use of a single deep learning model (He et al., 2016). The team extends a multi-perspective convolutional neural network (MPCNN) (He et al., 2015) with a simple word level attentional mecha-

---

[17]To see how much of this is related to the Q&A domain in particular, we will investigate including difficult non-Q&A evaluation data in future STS competitions.

nism based on the aggregate cosine similarity of a word in one text with all of the words in a paired text. The submission is notable for how well it performs without any manual feature engineering.

Finally, the best performing system on the postediting data, RICOH's Run-n, introduces a novel IR-based approach for textual similarity that incorporates word alignment information (Itoh, 2016).

6.5 Cross-lingual Spanish-English Subtask

The rankings for the cross-lingual Spanish-English STS subtask are provided in Table 7. Recall that the multi-source data is drawn from the same sources as the monolingual English STS pairs. It is interesting to note that the performance of cross-lingual systems on this evaluation set does not appear to be significantly worse than the monolingual submissions even though the systems are being asked to perform the more challenging problem of evaluating cross-lingual sentence pairs. While the correlations are not directly comparable, they do seem to motivate a more direct comparison between cross-lingual and monolingual STS systems.

In terms of performance on the manually culled news data set, the highest overall rank is achieved by an unsupervised system submitted by team UWB (Brychcin and Svoboda, 2016). The unsupervised UWB system builds on the word alignment based STS method proposed by Sultan et al. (2015). However, when calculating the final similarity score, it weights both the aligned and unaligned words by their inverse document frequency. This system is able to attain a 0.912 correlation on the news data, while ranking second on the multi-source data set. For the multi-source test set, the highest scoring submission is a supervised system from the UWB team that combines multiple signals originating from lexical, syntactic and semantic similarity approaches in a regression-based model, achieving a 0.819 correlation. This is modestly better than the second place unsupervised approach that achieves 0.808.

Approximately half of the submissions are able to achieve a correlation above 0.8 on the news data. On the multi-source data, the overall correlation trend is lower, but with half the systems still obtaining a score greater than 0.6. Due to the diversity of the material embedded in the multi-source data, it seems to amount to a more difficult testing scenario.

Nonetheless, there are cases of: 1) systems performing much worse on the news data set: the FBK HLT-MT systems experience an approximately 0.25 drop in correlation on the news data as compare to the multi-source setting; 2) systems performing evenly on both data sets.

6.5.1 Methods

In terms of approaches, most runs rely on a monolingual framework. They automatically translate the Spanish member of a sentence pair into English and then compute monolingual semantic similarity using a system developed for English. In contrast, the CNRC team (Lo et al., 2016) provides a true cross-lingual system that makes use of embedding space phrase similarity, the score from XMEANT, a cross-lingual machine translation evaluation metric (Lo et al., 2014), and precision and recall features for material filling aligned cross-lingual semantic roles (e.g., action, agent, patient). The FBK_HLT team (Ataman et al., 2016) proposes a model combining cross-lingual word embeddings with features from QuEst (Specia et al., 2013), a tool for machine translation quality estimation. The RTM system (Biçici, 2016) also builds on methods developed for machine translation quality estimation and is applicable to both cross-lingual and monolingual similarity. The GWU_NLP team (Aldarmaki and Diab, 2016) uses a shared cross-lingual vector space to directly assess sentences originating in different languages.[18]

7 Conclusion

We have presented the results of the 2016 STS shared task. This year saw a significant increase in participation. There are 119 submissions from 43 participating teams for the English STS subtask. This is a 45% increase in participating teams over 2015. The pilot cross-lingual Spanish-English STS subtask has 26 submissions from 10 teams, which is impressive given that this is the first year such a challenging subtask was attempted. Interestingly, the cross-lingual STS systems appear to perform competitively to monolingual systems on pairs drawn from the same sources. This suggests that it would be interesting to perform a more direct comparison between cross-lingual and monolingual systems.

---

[18]The GWU_NLP team includes one of the STS organizers.

Team	Run	News	Multi-Src	Mean	Run Rank	Team Rank
UWB	sup	0.90621	**0.81899**	**0.86311**	1	1
UWB	unsup	**0.91237**	0.80818	0.86089	2	
SERGIOJIMENEZ	run1	0.88724	0.81836	0.85321	3	2
SERGIOJIMENEZ	run3	0.89651	0.80737	0.85246	4	
DCU-SEManiacs	run2	0.89739	0.79262	0.84562	5	3
DCU-SEManiacs	run1	0.89408	0.76927	0.83241	6	
SERGIOJIMENEZ	run2	0.82911	0.81266	0.82098	7	
GWU_NLP	run2_xWMF	0.86768	0.73189	0.80058	8	4
GWU_NLP	run1_xWMF	0.86626	0.69850	0.78337	9	
GWU_NLP	run3_bWMF	0.83474	0.72427	0.78015	10	
CNRC	MT1	0.87562	0.64583	0.76208	11	5
CNRC	MT2	0.87754	0.63141	0.75592	12	
CNRC	EMAP	0.71943	0.41054	0.56680	13	
RTM	FS+PLS-SVR	0.59154	0.52044	0.55641	14	6
RTM	FS-SVR	0.53602	0.52839	0.53225	15	
RTM	SVR	0.49849	0.52935	0.51374	16	
FBK_HLT	MT-run3	0.25507	0.53892	0.39533	17	7
FBK_HLT	MT-run1	0.24318	0.53465	0.38720	18	
FBK_HLT	MT-run2	0.24372	0.51420	0.37737	19	
LIPM-IIMAS	sopa	0.08648	0.15931	0.12247	20	8
WHU_NLP	CNN10	0.03337	0.04083	0.03706	21	9
WHU_NLP	CNN5	0	0.05512	0.02724	22	
WHU_NLP	CNN20	0.02428	-0.06355	-0.01912	23	
JUNITMZ	backpropagation1	-0.05676	-0.48389	-0.26781	24	10
JUNITMZ	backpropagation2	-0.34725	-0.39867	-0.37266	25	
JUNITMZ	backpropagation3	-0.52951	-0.39891	-0.46498	26	

Table 7: STS 2016: Cross-lingual Spanish-English Rankings

Acknowledgments

This material is based in part upon work supported by DARPA-BAA-12-47 DEFT grant to George Washington University, by DEFT grant #12475008 to the University of Michigan, and by a MINECO grant to the University of the Basque Country (TUNER project TIN2015-65308-C5-1-R). Aitor Gonzalez Agirre is supported by a doctoral grant from MINECO (PhD grant FPU12/06243). Any opinions, findings, and conclusions or recommendations expressed in this material are those of the authors and do not necessarily reflect the views of the Defense Advanced Research Projects Agency.

References

Naveed Afzal, Yanshan Wang, and Hongfang Liu. 2016. MayoNLP at SemEval-2016 Task 1: Semantic textual similarity based on lexical semantic net and deep learning semantic model. In *Proceedings of the 10th International Workshop on Semantic Evaluation (SemEval 2016)*, San Diego, CA, USA.

Eneko Agirre, Daniel Cer, Mona Diab, and Aitor Gonzalez-Agirre. 2012. SemEval-2012 Task 6: A pilot on semantic textual similarity. In **SEM 2012: The First Joint Conference on Lexical and Computational Semantics – Volume 1: Proceedings of the main conference and the shared task, and Volume 2: Proceedings of the Sixth International Workshop on Semantic Evaluation (SemEval 2012)*, pages 385–393, Montréal, Canada.

Eneko Agirre, Daniel Cer, Mona Diab, Aitor Gonzalez-Agirre, and Weiwei Guo. 2013. *SEM 2013 shared task: Semantic Textual Similarity. In *Second Joint Conference on Lexical and Computational Semantics (*SEM), Volume 1: Proceedings of the Main Conference and the Shared Task: Semantic Textual Similarity*, pages 32–43, Atlanta, Georgia, USA.

Eneko Agirre, Carmen Banea, Claire Cardie, Daniel Cer, Mona Diab, Aitor Gonzalez-Agirre, Weiwei Guo, Rada Mihalcea, German Rigau, and Janyce Wiebe. 2014. SemEval-2014 Task 10: Multilingual semantic textual similarity. In *Proceedings of the 8th International Workshop on Semantic Evaluation (SemEval 2014)*, pages 81–91, Dublin, Ireland.

Eneko Agirre, Carmen Banea, Claire Cardie, Daniel Cer, Mona Diab, Aitor Gonzalez-Agirre, Weiwei Guo, Iñigo Lopez-Gazpio, Montse Maritxalar, Rada Mihalcea, German Rigau, Larraitz Uria, and Janyce Wiebe. 2015. SemEval-2015 Task 2: Semantic Textual Similarity, English, Spanish and Pilot on Interpretability. In *Proceedings of the 9th International Workshop on Semantic Evaluation (SemEval 2015)*, Denver, CO.

Hanan Aldarmaki and Mona Diab. 2016. GWU NLP at SemEval-2016 Shared Task 1: Matrix factorization for crosslingual STS. In *Proceedings of the 10th International Workshop on Semantic Evaluation (SemEval 2016)*, San Diego, CA, USA.

Duygu Ataman, Jose G. C. de Souza, and Marco Turchi1 Matteo Negri. 2016. FBK HLT-MT at SemEval-2016 Task 1: Cross-lingual semantic similarity measurement using quality estimation features and compositional bilingual word embeddings. In *Proceedings of the 10th International Workshop on Semantic Evaluation (SemEval 2016)*, San Diego, CA, USA.

Collin F. Baker, Charles J. Fillmore, and John B. Lowe. 1998. The Berkeley FrameNet Project. In *COLING*

'98 Proceedings of the 17th international conference on Computational linguistics - Volume 1.

Clive Best, Erik van der Goot, Ken Blackler, Teófilo Garcia, and David Horby. 2005. Europe Media Monitor - System description. In *EUR Report 22173-En*, Ispra, Italy.

Ergun Biçici. 2016. RTM at SemEval-2016 Task 1: Predicting semantic similarity with referential translation machines and related statistics. In *Proceedings of the 10th International Workshop on Semantic Evaluation (SemEval 2016)*, San Diego, CA, USA.

Tomas Brychcin and Lukas Svoboda. 2016. UWB at SemEval-2016 Task 1: Semantic textual similarity using lexical, syntactic, and semantic information. In *Proceedings of the 10th International Workshop on Semantic Evaluation (SemEval 2016)*, San Diego, CA, USA.

C. Christiane Fellbaum. 1998. *WordNet: An Electronic Lexical Database*. MIT Press.

Paul Clough and Mark Stevenson. 2011. Developing a corpus of plagiarised short answers. *Language Resources and Evaluation*, 45(1):5–24.

Ido Dagan, Bill Dolan, Bernardo Magnini, and Dan Roth. 2010. Recognizing textual entailment: Rational, evaluation and approaches. *Natural Language Engineering*, 16:105–105.

Günes Erkan and Dragomir R. Radev. 2004. LexRank: Graph-based lexical centrality as salience in text summarization. *J. Artif. Int. Res.*, 22(1):457–479.

Hua He, Kevin Gimpel, and Jimmy Lin. 2015. Multi-perspective sentence similarity modeling with convolutional neural networks. In *Proceedings of the 2015 Conference on Empirical Methods in Natural Language Processing*, pages 1576–1586, Lisbon, Portugal.

Hua He, John Wieting, Kevin Gimpel, Jinfeng Rao, and Jimmy Lin. 2016. UMD-TTIC-UW at SemEval-2016 Task 1: Attention-based multi-perspective convolutional neural networks for textual similarity measurement. In *Proceedings of the 10th International Workshop on Semantic Evaluation (SemEval 2016)*, San Diego, CA, USA.

Eduard Hovy, Mitchell Marcus, Martha Palmer, Lance Ramshaw, and Ralph Weischedel. 2006. OntoNotes: The 90% solution. In *Proceedings of the Human Language Technology Conference of the North American Chapter of the ACL*.

Po-Sen Huang, Xiaodong He, Jianfeng Gao, Li Deng, Alex Acero, and Larry Heck. 2013. Learning deep structured semantic models for web search using click-through data. ACM International Conference on Information and Knowledge Management (CIKM).

Hideo Itoh. 2016. RICOH at SemEval-2016 Task 1: Ir-based semantic textual similarity estimation. In *Proceedings of the 10th International Workshop on Semantic Evaluation (SemEval 2016)*, San Diego, CA, USA.

Philipp Koehn, Hieu Hoang, Alexandra Birch, Chris Callison-Burch, Marcello Federico, Nicola Bertoldi, Brooke Cowan, Wade Shen, Christine Moran, Richard Zens, Chris Dyer, Ondřej Bojar, Alexandra Constantin, and Evan Herbst. 2007. Moses: Open source toolkit for statistical machine translation. In *Proceedings of the 45th Annual Meeting of the ACL on Interactive Poster and Demonstration Sessions*, ACL '07.

Dekang Lin. 1998. An information-theoretic definition of similarity. In *Proceedings of the Fifteenth International Conference on Machine Learning*, ICML '98, pages 296–304, San Francisco, CA, USA.

Chi-kiu Lo, Meriem Beloucif, Markus Saers, and Dekai Wu. 2014. XMEANT: Better semantic MT evaluation without reference translations. In *Proceedings of the 52nd Annual Meeting of the Association for Computational Linguistics (Volume 2: Short Papers)*.

Chi-kiu Lo, Cyril Goutte, and Michel Simard. 2016. CNRC at SemEval-2016 Task 1: Experiments in crosslingual semantic textual similarity. In *Proceedings of the 10th International Workshop on Semantic Evaluation (SemEval 2016)*, San Diego, CA, USA.

Christopher D. Manning, Mihai Surdeanu, John Bauer, Jenny Finkel, Steven J. Bethard, and David McClosky. 2014. The Stanford CoreNLP natural language processing toolkit. In *Association for Computational Linguistics (ACL) System Demonstrations*, pages 55–60.

Tomas Mikolov, Kai Chen, Greg Corrado, and Jeffrey Dean. 2013. Efficient estimation of word representations in vector space. In *Proceedings of the International Conference on Learning Representations (ICLR)*, Scottsdale, AZ, USA.

George A. Miller. 1995. WordNet: A lexical database for english. *Commun. ACM*, 38(11):39–41.

Eugene W. Myers. 1986. Ano(nd) difference algorithm and its variations. *Algorithmica*, 1(1):251–266.

Jeffrey Pennington, Richard Socher, and Christopher D. Manning. 2014. GloVe: Global Vectors for Word Representation. In *Empirical Methods in Natural Language Processing (EMNLP)*, pages 1532–1543.

Piotr Przybyła, Nhung T. H. Nguyen, Matthew Shardlow, Georgios Kontonatsios, and Sophia Ananiadou. 2016. NaCTeM at SemEval-2016 Task 1: Inferring sentence-level semantic similarity from an ensemble of complementary lexical and sentence-level features. In *Proceedings of the 10th International Workshop on Semantic Evaluation (SemEval 2016)*, San Diego, CA, USA.

Philip Resnik. 1995. Using information content to evaluate semantic similarity in a taxonomy. In *Proceedings of the 14th International Joint Conference on Artificial Intelligence - Volume 1*, IJCAI'95, pages 448–453.

Barbara Rychalska, Katarzyna Pakulska, Krystyna Chodorowska, Wojciech Walczak, and Piotr Andruszkiewicz. 2016. Samsung Poland NLP Team at SemEval-2016 Task 1: Necessity for diversity; combining recursive autoencoders, wordnet and ensemble methods to measure semantic similarity. In *Proceedings of the 10th International Workshop on Semantic Evaluation (SemEval 2016)*, San Diego, CA, USA.

Lucia Specia, Kashif Shah, Jose G.C. de Souza, and Trevor Cohn. 2013. QuEst - a translation quality estimation framework. In *Proceedings of the 51st Annual Meeting of the Association for Computational Linguistics: System Demonstrations*.

Lucia Specia. 2011. Exploiting objective annotations for measuring translation post-editing effort. In *15th Conference of the European Association for Machine Translation*, EAMT, pages 73–80, Leuven, Belgium.

Stack Exchange, Inc. 2016. Stack exchange data dump. `https://archive.org/details/stackexchange`.

Md Arafat Sultan, Steven Bethard, and Tamara Sumner. 2015. DLS@CU: Sentence similarity from word alignment and semantic vector composition. In *Proceedings of the 9th International Workshop on Semantic Evaluation (SemEval 2015)*, Denver, CO, USA.

Junfeng Tian and Man Lan. 2016. ECNU at SemEval-2016 Task 1: Leveraging word embedding from macro and micro views to boost performance for semantic textual similarity. In *Proceedings of the 10th International Workshop on Semantic Evaluation (SemEval 2016)*, San Diego, CA, USA.

SemEval-2016 Task 2: Interpretable Semantic Textual Similarity

Eneko Agirre[*], **Aitor Gonzalez-Agirre, Iñigo Lopez-Gazpio**
Montse Maritxalar, German Rigau and **Larraitz Uria**
IXA NLP group, University of the Basque Country
Manuel Lardizabal 1, 20.018 Donostia, Basque Country
`montse.maritxalar@ehu.eus`

Abstract

The final goal of Interpretable Semantic Textual Similarity (iSTS) is to build systems that explain which are the differences and commonalities between two sentences. The task adds an explanatory level on top of STS, formalized as an alignment between the chunks in the two input sentences, indicating the relation and similarity score of each alignment. The task provides train and test data on three datasets: news headlines, image captions and student answers. It attracted nine teams, totaling 20 runs. All datasets and the annotation guideline are freely available[1]

1 Introduction

Semantic Textual Similarity (STS) (Agirre et al., 2015) measures the degree of equivalence in the underlying semantics of paired snippets of text. The idea of Interpretable STS (iSTS) is to explain *why* two sentences may be related/unrelated, by supplementing the STS similarity score with an explanatory layer.

Our final goal would be to enable interpretable systems, that is, systems that are able to explain which are the differences and commonalities between two sentences. For instance, let's assume the following two sentences drawn from a corpus of news headlines:

12 killed in bus accident in Pakistan
10 killed in road accident in NW Pakistan

---

[*] Authors listed in alphabetical order
[1]`http://at.qrci.org/semeval2016/task2/`

The output of such a system would be something like the following:

> The two sentences talk about accidents with casualties in Pakistan, but they differ in the number of people killed (12 vs. 10) and level of detail: the first one specifies that it is a *bus* accident, and the second one specifies that the location is *NW* Pakistan.

While giving such explanations comes naturally to people, constructing algorithms and computational models that mimic human level performance represents a difficult Natural Language Understanding (NLU) problem, with applications in dialogue systems, interactive systems and educational systems.

In the iSTS 2015 pilot task (Agirre et al., 2015), we defined a first step of such an ambitious system, which we follow in 2016. Given the input (a pair of sentences), participant systems need first to identify the chunks in each sentence, and then, align chunks across the two sentences, indicating the relation and similarity score of each alignment. The relation can be one of equivalence, opposition, specificity, similarity or relatedness, and the similarity score can range from 1 to 5. Unrelated chunks are left unaligned. An optional tag can be added to alignments for the cases where there is a difference in factuality or polarity. See Figure 1 for the manual alignment of the two sample sentences. The alignments between chunks in Figure 1 can be used to produce the kind of explanations shown in the previous example.

In previous work, Brockett (2007) and Rus et al. (2012) produced a dataset where corresponding

Proceedings of SemEval-2016, pages 512–524,
San Diego, California, June 16-17, 2016. ©2016 Association for Computational Linguistics

```
[12] <=> [10] : (SIMILAR 4)
[killed] <=> [killed] : (EQUIVALENT 5)
[in bus accident] <=> [in road accident] : (MORE-SPECIFIC 4)
[in Pakistan] <=> [in NW Pakistan] : (MORE-GENERAL 4)
```

Figure 1: Example of a manual alignment of two sentences: "12 killed in bus accident in Pakistan" and "10 killed in road accident in NW Pakistan". Each aligned pair of chunks included information on the type of alignment, and the score of alignment.

words (including some multiword expressions like named-entities) were aligned. Although this alignment is useful, we wanted to move forward to the alignment of segments, and decided to align chunks (Abney, 1991). Brockett (2007) did not provide any label to alignments, while Rus et al. (2012) defined a basic typology. In our task, we provided a more detailed typology for the aligned chunks as well as a similarity/relatedness score for each alignment. Contrary to the mentioned works, we first identified the segments (chunks in our case) in each sentence separately, and then aligned them.

In a different strand of work, Nielsen et al. (2009) defined a textual entailment model where the "facets" (words under some syntactic/semantic relation) in the response of a student were linked to the concepts in the reference answer. The link would signal whether each facet in the response was entailed by the reference answer or not, but would not explicitly mark which parts of the reference answer caused the entailment. This model was later followed by Levy et al. (2013). Our task was different in that we identified the corresponding chunks in both sentences. We think that, in the future, the aligned facets could provide complementary information to chunks.

The SemEval Semantic Textual Similarity (STS) task in 2015 contained a subtask on Interpretable STS (Agirre et al., 2015), showing that the task is feasible, with high inter-annotator agreement and system scores well above baselines. The datasets comprised news headlines and image captions.

For 2016, the pilot subtask has been updated into a standalone task. The restriction from the iSTS 2015 task to allow only one-to-one alignments has been now lifted, and we thus allow any number of chunks to be aligned to any number of chunks. Annotation guidelines have been revised accordingly, including an updated chunking criterium for subordinate clauses and a better explanation of the instruc-

tions.

The 2015 datasets were re-annotated and released as training data. New pairs from news headlines and image captions have been annotated and used for test. In addition, a new dataset of sentence pairs from the education domain has been produced, including train and test data.

The paper is organized as follows. We first provide the description of the task, followed by the evaluation metrics and the baseline system. Section 5 describes the participation, Section 6 the results, and Section 7 comments on the systems, tools and resources used.

2   Task Description

The dataset was produced using sentence pairs from news headlines, image captions and answers from students. Headlines have been mined from several news sources by European Media Monitor, and collected by us using their RSS feed[2]. We saw a pair of headlines from this corpus in the introduction.

The Image descriptions dataset is a subset of the Flickr dataset presented in (Rashtchian et al., 2010), which consisted of 8108 hand-selected images from Flickr, depicting actions and events of people or animals, with five captions per image. The image captions of the dataset are released under a Creative Commons Attribution-Share Alike license. This is a sample pair from this dataset:

> A man sleeps with a baby in his lap
> A man asleep in a chair holding a baby

The Answer-Students corpus consists of the interactions between students and the BEETLE II tutorial dialogue system. The BEETLE II system is an intelligent tutoring engine that teaches students in basic electricity and electronics. At first, students

---

[2]http://emm.newsexplorer.eu/NewsExplorer/home/en/latest.html

513

dataset	pairs	source	STS
HDL train	750	news headlines	2013
HDL test	375	news headlines	2014
Images train	750	image captions	2014
Images test	375	image captions	2015
Student train	333	student answers	2015
Student test	344	student answers	2015

Table 1: Details of the datasets, including number of pairs, source, and relation to STS datasets. HDL stands for Headlines, and Student to Student-Answers.

spend from three to five hours reading the material, building and observing circuits in the simulator and interacting with a dialogue-based tutor. They used the keyboard to interact with the system, and the computer tutor asked them questions and provided feedback via a text-based chat interface. The data from 73 undergraduate volunteer participants at south-eastern US university were recorded and annotated to form the BEETLE human-computer dialogue corpus (Dzikovska et al., 2010; Dzikovska et al., 2012), and later used in a SemEval 2015 task (Dzikovska et al., 2013). In the present corpus, we include sentence pairs composed of a student answer and the reference answer of a teacher. We have rejected those answers containing pronouns whose antecedent is not in the sentence (pronominal coreference), as the question is not included in the train data and, therefore, it is not possible to deduce which is the antecedent. There are also some dataset-specific details that are mentioned in the same section. The next pair sentences are an example of the Answer-Students corpus.

> because switch z is in bulb c's closed path
> there is a path containing both Z and C

All datasets have been previously used in STS tasks. Table 1 shows details of the datasets, including train-test splits. The Headlines and Images datasets are tokenized, as in the STS release. The Answer-Students dataset was not tokenized, and was used as in the STS release.

2.1 Annotation

The manual annotation has been performed following the annotation guidelines [3]. Please refer to those

---

[3] http://alt.qcri.org/
semeval2016/task2/data/uploads/

guidelines for further details. The general annotation procedure is as follows:

1. First identify the chunks in each sentence separately.

2. Align chunks in order, from the clearest and strongest correspondences to the most unclear or weakest ones.

3. For each alignment, provide a similarity/relatedness score.

4. For each alignment, choose one (or more) alignment label.

Chunk annotation was based on those used in the CoNLL 2000 chunking task (Tjong Kim Sang and Buchholz, 2000). The annotators were provided with the output of an automatic chunker[4] trained on the CoNLL corpora[5], which they corrected manually.

Independently of the labels, and before assigning any label, the annotators need to provide a similarity/relatedness score for each alignment from 5 (maximum similarity/relatedness) to 0 (no relation at all), as follows:

5 if the meaning of both chunks is equivalent

[4,3] if the meaning of both chunks is very similar or closely related

[2,1] if the meaning of both chunks is slightly similar or somehow related

0 (represented as NIL) if the meaning of the chunk is completely unrelated.

Note that 0 is not possible for an aligned pair, as that would mean that the two chunks would be left unaligned. Note also that if the score is 5, then the label assigned later should be equivalence (EQUI, see below). After assigning the label, the annotator should check for the following: if a chunk is not aligned it should have NIL score, equivalent chunks

---

annotationguidelinesinterpretablests2016v2.
2.pdf

[4] https://github.com/ixa-ehu/
ixa-pipe-chunk

[5] http://www.clips.ua.ac.be/conll2000/
chunking/

(EQUI) should have a 5 score. The rest of the labels should have a score larger than 0 but lower than 5.

We will now describe the alignment types, but first note that the interpretation of the whole sentence, including common sense inference, has to be taken into account. This means that we need to take into account the context in order to know whether the aligned chunks refer to the same instance (or set of instances) or not. Instances may refer to physical or abstract object instances (for NPs) or real world event instances (for verb chains):

- EQUI: both chunks have the same meaning, they are semantically equivalent in this context.
- OPPO: the meanings of the chunks are in opposition to each other, lying in an inherently incompatible binary relationship.
- SPE1: both chunks have similar meanings, but chunk in sentence 1 is more specific.
- SPE2: like SPE1, but it is the chunk in sentence 2 which is more specific.

In addition, the meaning of the chunks can be very close, either because they have a similar meaning, or because their meanings have some other relation. In those cases, we use SIMI or REL as follows:

- SIMI: both chunks have similar meanings, they share similar attributes and there is no EQUI, OPPO, SPE1 or SPE2 relation.
- REL: both chunks are not considered similar but they are closely related by some relation not mentioned above (i.e. no EQUI, OPPO, SPE1, SPE2, or SIMI relation).
- NOALI: this chunk has not any corresponding chunk in the other sentence. Therefore, it is left unaligned.

The above seven labels are exclusive, and each alignment should have one such label.

In addition to one of the labels above, there are two labels which can be used either in isolation or together, that is, you can use none, one or both:

- FACT: the factuality in the aligned chunks (i.e. whether the statement is or is not a fact or a speculation) is different.
- POL: the polarity in the aligned chunks (i.e. the expressed opinion, which can be positive, negative, or neutral) is different.

Note that NOALI can also be FACT or POL, meaning that the respective chunk adds a factuality or polarity nuance to the sentence.

Listing 1 shows the annotation format for a given sentence pair from the training set (note that each alignment is reported in one line as follows: token-id-sent1 <==> token-id-sent2 // label // score // comment).

Finally, there are some specific criteria related to the Answer-Students corpus that have been followed during the annotation process. For instance, in the Answer-Students example in the previous section, *switch z* (first sentence) and *Z* (second sentence) are considered equivalent as, in this dataset, X, Y, and Z always refer to switches X, Y, and Z. The same criteria is followed when annotating *bulb c* and *C* as equivalent, as A, B and C are always used to refer to bulb A, B and C. In the same way *closed path* and *a path* are equivalent, as paths are always considered to be closed. For further details related to such a corpus specific criteria refer to the annotation guidelines.

3 Evaluation Metrics

The official evaluation is based on (Melamed, 1998), which uses the F1 of precision and recall of token alignments (in the context of alignment for Machine Translation). Fraser and Marcu (2007) argue that F1 is a better measure than other alternatives such as the Alignment Error Rate. The idea is that, for each pair of chunks that are aligned, we consider that any pairs of tokens in the chunks are also aligned with some weight. The weight of each token-token alignment is the inverse of the number of alignments of each token (so-called fan out factor, Melamed, 1998). Precision is measured as the ratio of token-token alignments that exist in both system and gold standard files, divided by the number of alignments in the system. Recall is measured similarly, as the ratio of token-token alignments that exist in both system and gold-standard, divided by the number of alignments in the gold standard. Precision and recall are evaluated separately for all alignments of all pairs.

Participating runs were evaluated using four different metrics: F1 where alignment type and score are ignored (alignment F1, F for short); F1 where alignment types need to match, but scores are ignored (type F1, +T for short); F1 where alignment type is ignored, but each alignment is penalized

Listing 1: Annotation format

```
<sentence id="6" status="">
 12 killed in bus accident in Pakistan
 10 killed in road accident in NW Pakistan

 ...
<alignment>
 1 <==> 1 // SIMI // 4 // 12 <==> 10
 2 <==> 2 // EQUI // 5 // killed <==> killed
 3 4 5 <==> 3 4 5 // SPE1 // 4 // in bus accident <==> in road accident
 6 7 <==> 6 7 8 // SPE2 // 4 // in Pakistan <==> in NW Pakistan
</alignment>
</sentence>
```

when scores do not match[6] (score F1, +S for short); and, F1 where alignment types need to match, and each alignment is penalized when scores do not match (type and score F1, +TS for short). The type and score F1 is the main overall metric.

Note that our evaluation procedure does not explicitly evaluate the chunking results. The method implicitly penalizes chunking errors via the induced token-token alignments, using a soft penalty.

4 Baseline System

The baseline system consists of a cascade concatenation of several procedures. First, input sentences are tokenized using simple regular expressions. Additionally, we collect chunks coming either from the gold standard or from the chunking done by *ixa-pipes-chunk* (Agerri et al., 2014). This is followed by a lower-cased token aligning phase, which consists of aligning (or linking) identical tokens across the input sentences. Then we use chunk boundaries as token regions to group individual tokens into groups, and compute all links across groups. The weight of the link across groups is proportional to the number of links counted between within-group tokens. The next phase consists of an optimization step in which groups x,y that have the highest link weight are identified, as well as the chunks that are linked to either x or y but not with a maximum alignment weight (thus enabling us to know which chunks were left unaligned). Finally, in the

last phase, the baseline system uses a rule-based algorithm to directly assign labels and scores: to chunks with the highest link weight assign label = "EQUI" and score = 5, to the rest of aligned chunks (with lower weights) assign label = "NOALI" and score = NIL, and, to unaligned chunks assign label = "NOALI" and score = NIL.

5 Participation

The pilot task presented two scenarios: raw text and gold standard chunks. In the first scenario, given a pair of sentences, participants had to identify the composing chunks, and then align them; after that they would assign a relatedness tag and a similarity score to each alignment. In the gold standard scenario, participants were provided with the gold standard chunks.

In both scenarios the datasets were provided with tokenized text, with exception of Answer-Students, which was not tokenized[7].

The task allowed up to a total of three submissions for each team on each of the evaluation scenarios. The organizers provided a script to check if the run files are well formed.

Nine teams participated on the gold chunks scenario, and out of them six teams also participated in the system chunks scenario. Regarding the datasets, all the teams gave their results for the three datasets,

---

[6]The penalization is the difference between the scores divided by five.

[7]In fact The Answer-Students dataset was only partially tokenized. In order to be consistent with the gold standard, participants had to follow the partial tokenization, separating tokens at blanks alone.

516

except *Venseseval* who sent results only for Headlines and Images.

The iUBC team includes some of the organizers of the interpretable STS task. It is marked by the symbol $*$ in the result tables, and it is not taken into account in the rankings. The organizers took measures to prevent developers of that team to access the test data or any other information, so the team participated in identical conditions to the rest of participants.

6 Results

Table 2 provides the overall type and score (+TS) performance per dataset, and the mean accross the three datasets. Results for Headlines, Images and Answer-Students datasets are shown in the Appendix, tables 3, 4 and 5, respectively. Each row of the tables corresponds to a run configuration named *TeamID_RunID*. Note that task results are separately written with respect to the scenario. A unique baseline was used for both evaluation scenarios and its performance is jointly presented with the scores obtained by participants.

The results of the present edition corroborate last years' results regarding the difficulty of the system chunks scenario. Indeed, it is considerably more challenging than the gold chunks scenario.

With regard to the datasets, the Answer-Students ended up being more challenging than the other datasets for five out of eight teams, but FBK-HLT-NLP, IISCNLP and iUBC teams give their best results for such a scenario.

Compared to last year, the best results for Images and Headlines in the +TS metric have improved in both SYS and GS scenarios: 4 and 6 points for Headlines (in SYS and GS, respectively), and 5 and 7 points for Images (in SYS and GS, respectively). In order to check whether the datasets where easier this year, we checked the performance of the baseline. The differences are small: this year the Images dataset seems slightly easier (3 and 4 point difference for SYS and GS scenarios), and the Headlines dataset is only slightly more difficult (1 point difference for SYS and GS scenarios). The improvement in results for this year seems to be due to better system performance.

The complexity of the evaluation (cf. tables 3, 4 and 5) was incremental for the four available metrics, which obviously, were lower for the system chunks. Both type and score are bounded by the alignment results and it is thus natural that alignment results are higher. Comparing type and score results, the type results are generally lower, possibly due to the harder task of guessing the correct label. The final results are bounded by both type and score, and the systems doing best in type are the ones doing best overall. From the results we can see that labeling the type was the most challenging.

Regarding the overall test results for type and score (+TS) across datasets, UWB (Konopík et al., 2016) and DTSim (Banjade et al., 2016) obtained the best results for the gold chunks scenario, and DTSim and FBK-HLT-NLP (Magnolini et al., 2016) for the system chunks scenario. In addition, DTSim obtained the best overall results even though they have not good results for the Answer-Students dataset.

7 Systems, tools and resources

Most of the teams reported input text processing such as lemmatization and part of speech tagging, and in some cases named-entity recognition and syntactic parsing. Additional resources such as Word-Net, distributional embeddings, paraphrases from PPDB and global STS sentence scores were also used. Participants also revealed that most of their systems were built using some kind of distributional or knowledge-based similarity metrics. We noticed, for instance, that WordNet or word embeddings were used by several teams to compute word similarity.

Looking at the learning approaches, both supervised and unsupervised approaches have been applied, as well are mainly manual rule-based combinations.

Next, we briefly introduce the participant teams, whit slightly more details for the top performing systems.

- UWB (Konopík et al., 2016): UWB used three separate supervised classifiers to perform alignment, scoring and typing. They defined a similarity function based on a distribution similarity paradigm: vector composition, lexical semantic vectors and iDF weighting. They introduced a modified method to create word vectors, and

+TS Syschunks						+TS Goldchunks					
System	**I**	**H**	**AS**	**Mean**	**R**	**System**	**I**	**H**	**AS**	**Mean**	**R**
Baseline	.404	.438	.443	.428		Baseline	.480	.546	.557	.528	
DTSim_r3	.610	.545	.503	.552	1	UWB_r1	.667	.621	.625	.638	1
DTSim_r2	.599	.547	.507	.551	2	UWB_r3	.671	.630	.611	.637	2
DTSim_r1	.587	.538	.505	.543	3	DTSim_r2	.636	.649	.546	.610	3
FBK-HLT-NLP_r1	.548	.510	.542	.533	4	DTSim_r3	.648	.641	.537	.609	4
FBK-HLT-NLP_r3	.535	.505	.555	.532	5	Inspire_r1	.613	.696	.510	.606	5
FBK-HLT-NLP_r2	.497	.503	.541	.513	6	DTSim_r1	.624	.639	.543	.602	6
Inspire_r1	.563	.520	.452	.512	7	Inspire_r2	.588	.663	.479	.576	7
IISCNLP_r2	.487	.492	.520	.500	8	VRep_r3	.547	.597	.580	.575	8
IISCNLP_r3	.474	.469	.545	.496	9	VRep_r2	.543	.597	.579	.573	9
IISCNLP_r1	.474	.469	.540	.494	10	FBK-HLT-NLP_r3	.566	.562	.589	.572	10
Inspire_r2	.536	.495	.419	.483	11	FBK-HLT-NLP_r1	.574	.559	.581	.571	11
Inspire_r3	.450	.446	.338	.411	12	UWB_r2	.621	.601	.475	.566	12
Venseseval_r1	.462	.453	-	-		IISCNLP_r2	.509	.556	.617	.560	13
*iUBC_r2	.550	.476	.559	.528		IISCNLP_r1	.485	.551	.639	.558	14
*iUBC_r3	.516	.498	.559	.524		IISCNLP_r3	.492	.541	.639	.557	15
*iUBC_r1	.477	.423	.449	.450		VRep_r1	.548	.596	.523	.556	16
AVG	.525	.499	.497	.510		FBK-HLT-NLP_r2	.525	.555	.571	.551	17
MAX	.610	.547	.555	.552		Rev_r1	.493	.562	.410	.489	18
						Inspire_r3	.487	.579	.386	.484	19
						Venseseval_r1	.574	.573	-	-	
						*iUBC_r2	.612	.587	.644	.614	
						*iUBC_r3	.578	.592	.644	.604	
						*iUBC_r1	.513	.505	.499	.506	
						AVG	.570	.598	.549	.573	
						MAX	.671	.696	.639	.638	

Table 2: Overall test results for type and score (**+TS**) across datasets. Each row correspond to a system run, and each column to a dataset: (**I**) for Images, (**H**) for Headlines, (**AS**) for Answer-Students, **Mean** for the mean across the three datasets, and **R** for the rank. The "*" symbol denotes runs that include task organizers. Additionally, the table shows results for the baseline, average of participants (**AVG**) and maximum score of participants (**MAX**).

combine unique words from the chunks of both sentences into one single vocabulary which is then used to produce similarity measures. They claim that the following three differences have significant influence on the final results: modified lexical semantic vectors (+3% of the mean of T+S F1 scores), shared words (+2%) and POS tags difference (+2%).

- DTSim (Banjade et al., 2016): This team builds on the NeroSim system (Banjade et al., 2015), which participated in the 2015 task with good results using a system based on manual rules blended semantic similarity features. The team explored several chunking algorithms and in-cluded new rules. Concretely, they expanded the rules for SIMI and EQUI. They mainly improved the chunker and concluded that a Conditional Random Fields (CRFs) based chunking tool is the best approach for chunking. The input sequence to their chunking model are POS tags, and the chunker yielded the highest average accuracies on both the training and test datasets.

- FBK-HLT-NLP (Magnolini et al., 2016): This teams built a multi-layer perceptron to solve alignment, scoring and typing. The perceptron shares some layers for the three tasks, and other layers are separate. They use a variety of features, including WordNet and word embeddings. The system performs better in the system chunks scenario than in the gold chunks one. Therefore, there is no specific advantage of using chunked sentence pairs and their system is very powerful. The Answer-Students dataset has better performance than Headlines and Images. They obtain better results training a single system for the three datasets (compared to training a classifier separately for each dataset).

- Inspire (Kazmi and Schüller, 2016): The authors propose a system based on logic programming which extends the basic ideas of NeroSim (Banjade et al., 2015). The rule based system makes use of several resources to prepare the input and uses Answer Set Programming to determine chunk boundaries.

- IISCNLP (Tekumalla and Sharmistha, 2016): The system uses an algorithm, iMATCH, for the alignment of multiple non-contiguous chunks based on Integer Linear Programming (ILP). Similarity type and score assignment for pairs of chunks is done using a supervised multiclass classification technique based on Random Forest Classifier.

- Vrep (Henry and Sands, 2016): features are extracted to create a learned rule-based classifier to assign a label. It uses semantic and syntactic (form of the chunks) relationship features.

- Rev (Ping Ping et al., 2016): The system consists of rules based on the analysis of the Headlines dataset considering lexical overlapping, part of speech tags and synonymy.

- Venseseval: This system is an adaptation of a pre-existing textual entailment system, VENSES, which first performs a semantic analysis of the text including argument structure and then looks for bridging information between chunks using several knowledge resources.

- iUBC (Lopez-Gazpio et al., 2016): A two layer architecture is used to produce the similarity type and score of pairs of chunks. The top layer consists of two models: a classifier and a regressor. The bottom layer consists of a recurrent neural network that processes input and feeds composed semantic feature vectors to the top layer. Both layers are trained at the same time by propagating gradients.

8 Conclusions

Last year, the Interpretable STS task was introduced as a pilot subtask of the STS task. At the present edition, it has been presented as an independent task that has attracted nine teams. In addition to the image caption and news headlines datasets, this year participants were challenged with a new dataset from the Educational area. Concretely, the Answer-Students corpus, which consists of the interactions between students of electronics and the BEETLE II tutorial dialogue system.

Compared to the results last year (Agirre et al., 2015), the results have improved in the two datasets that happened both years, Images and Headlines. The Answer-Students dataset is the most challenging, and among the three subtasks (alignment, type and score) guessing the correct type of the aligned chunks is the most difficult one. Teams that did best on type get the best overall score.

All datasets and the annotation guideline are available in `http://alt.qcri.org/semeval2016/task2/`.

Acknowledgments

This material is based in part upon work supported a MINECO grant to the University of the Basque Country (TUNER project TIN2015-65308-C5-1-R). Aitor Gonzalez Agirre and Iñigo Lopez-Gazpio are by doctoral grants from MINECO. The IXA group is funded by the Basque Government (A type Research Group).

References

Steven Abney. 1991. Parsing by chunks. In *Principle-based parsing: Computation and psycholinguistics. Robert Berwick and Steven Abney and Carol Tenny(eds.)*, pages 257–278.

Rodrigo Agerri, Josu Bermudez, and German Rigau. 2014. Ixa pipeline: Efficient and ready to use multilingual NLP tools. In *Proceedings of the 9th Language Resources and Evaluation Conference (LREC 2014)*, pages 26–31.

Eneko Agirre, Carmen Banea, Claire Cardie, Daniel Cer, Mona Diab, Aitor Gonzalez-Agirre, Weiwei Guo,

Iñigo Lopez-Gazpio, Montse Maritxalar, Rada Mihalcea, German Rigau, Larraitz Uria, and Janyce Wiebe. 2015. SemEval-2015 Task 2: Semantic Textual Similarity, English, Spanish and Pilot on Interpretability. In *Proceedings of the 9th International Workshop on Semantic Evaluation (SemEval 2015)*, Denver, CO, June. Association for Computational Linguistics.

Rajendra Banjade, Nobal Bikram Niraula, Nabin Maharjan, Vasile Rus, Dan Stefanescu, Mihai Lintean, and Dipesh Gautam. 2015. Nerosim: A system for measuring and interpreting semantic textual similarity. In *Proceedings of the 9th International Workshop on Semantic Evaluation (SemEval 2015)*, pages 164–171, Denver, Colorado, June. Association for Computational Linguistics.

Rajendra Banjade, Nabin Maharjan, Nobal B. Niraula, and Vasile Rus. 2016. Dtsim at semeval-2016 task 2: Interpretable semantic textual similarity. In *Proceedings of the 10th International Workshop on Semantic Evaluation (SemEval 2016)*, San Diego, California, June. Association for Computational Linguistics.

Chris Brockett. 2007. Aligning the RTE 2006 corpus. *Microsoft Research*.

Myroslava O. Dzikovska, Diana Bental, Johanna D. Moore, Natalie B. Steinhauser, Gwendolyn E. Campbell, Elaine Farrow, and Charles B. Callaway, 2010. *Sustaining TEL: From Innovation to Learning and Practice: 5th European Conference on Technology Enhanced Learning, EC-TEL 2010, Barcelona, Spain, September 28 - October 1, 2010. Proceedings*, chapter Intelligent Tutoring with Natural Language Support in the Beetle II System, pages 620–625. Springer Berlin Heidelberg, Berlin, Heidelberg.

Myroslava O. Dzikovska, Rodney D. Nielsen, and Chris Brew. 2012. Towards effective tutorial feedback for explanation questions: A dataset and baselines. In *Proceedings of the 2012 Conference of the North American Chapter of the Association for Computational Linguistics: Human Language Technologies*, NAACL HLT '12, pages 200–210, Stroudsburg, PA, USA. Association for Computational Linguistics.

Myroslava O. Dzikovska, Rodney Nielsen, Chris Brew, Claudia Leacock, Danilo Giampiccolo, Luisa Bentivogli, Peter Clark, Ido Dagan, and Hoa Trang Dang. 2013. Semeval-2013 task 7: The joint student response analysis and 8th recognizing textual entailment challenge. In **SEM 2013: The First Joint Conference on Lexical and Computational Semantics*, Atlanta, Georgia, USA, 13-14 June. Association for Computational Linguistics.

Alexander Fraser and Daniel Marcu. 2007. Measuring word alignment quality for statistical machine translation. *Computational Linguistics*, 33(3):293–303.

Sam Henry and Allison Sands. 2016. Vrep at semeval-2016 task 1 and task 2. In *Proceedings of the 10th International Workshop on Semantic Evaluation (SemEval 2016)*, San Diego, California, June.

Mishal Kazmi and Peter Schüller. 2016. Inspire at semeval-2016 task 2: Interpretable semantic textual similarity alignment based on answer set programming. In *Proceedings of the 10th International Workshop on Semantic Evaluation (SemEval 2016)*, San Diego, California, June. Association for Computational Linguistics.

Miloslav Konopík, Ondřej Pražák, David Steinberger, and Tomáš Brychcín. 2016. Uwb at semeval-2016 task 2: Interpretable semantic textual similarity with distributional semantics for chunks. In *Proceedings of the 10th International Workshop on Semantic Evaluation (SemEval 2016)*, San Diego, California, June. Association for Computational Linguistics.

Omer Levy, Torsten Zesch, Ido Dagan, and Iryna Gurevych. 2013. Recognizing partial textual entailment. In *ACL (2)*, pages 451–455.

Iñigo Lopez-Gazpio, Eneko Agirre, and Montse Maritxalar. 2016. iubc at semeval-2016 task 2: Rnns and lstms for interpretable sts. In *Proceedings of the 10th International Workshop on Semantic Evaluation (SemEval 2016)*, San Diego, California, June. Association for Computational Linguistics.

Simone Magnolini, Anna Feltracco, and Bernardo Magnini. 2016. Fbk-hlt-nlp at semeval-2016 task 2: A multitask, deep learning approach for interpretable semantic textual similarity. In *Proceedings of the 10th International Workshop on Semantic Evaluation (SemEval 2016)*, San Diego, California, June. Association for Computational Linguistics.

I Dan Melamed. 1998. Manual annotation of translational equivalence: The blinker project. *arXiv preprint cmp-lg/9805005*.

Rodney D. Nielsen, Wayne Ward, and James H. Martin. 2009. Recognizing entailment in intelligent tutoring systems. *Natural Language Engineering*, 15(04):479–501.

Tan Ping Ping, Karin Verspoor, and Tim Miller. 2016. Rev at semeval-2016 task 2: Aligning chunks by lexical, part of speech and semantic equivalence. In *Proceedings of the 10th International Workshop on Semantic Evaluation (SemEval 2016)*, San Diego, California, June. Association for Computational Linguistics.

Cyrus Rashtchian, Peter Young, Micah Hodosh, and Julia Hockenmaier. 2010. Collecting image annotations using Amazon's Mechanical Turk. In *Proceedings of the NAACL HLT 2010 Workshop on Creating Speech and Language Data with Amazon's Mechanical Turk*, CSLDAMT 2010, pages 139–147.

Vasile Rus, Mihai Lintean, Cristian Moldovan, William
Baggett, Nobal Niraula, and Brent Morgan. 2012. The
SIMILAR corpus: A resource to foster the qualitative
understanding of semantic similarity of texts. In *Semantic Relations II: Enhancing Resources and Applications, The 8th Language Resources and Evaluation
Conference (LREC 2012), May*, pages 23–25.

Lavanya Sita Tekumalla and Sharmistha. 2016. IISC-
NLP at semeval-2016 task 2: Interpretable STS with
ILP based multiple chunk aligner. In *Proceedings of
the 10th International Workshop on Semantic Evaluation (SemEval 2016)*, San Diego, California, June. Association for Computational Linguistics.

Erik F. Tjong Kim Sang and Sabine Buchholz. 2000.
Introduction to the CoNLL-2000 shared task: Chunking. In *Proceedings of the 2nd workshop on Learning
language in logic and the 4th conference on Computational natural language learning-Volume 7 (CoNLL
2000)*, pages 127–132.

Headlines Syschunks					
System	**F**	**+T**	**+S**	**+TS**	**R**
Baseline	.649	.438	.591	.438	
DTSim_r2	.837	.561	.760	.547	1
DTSim_r3	.838	.560	.759	.545	2
DTSim_r1	.837	.561	.739	.538	3
Inspire_r1	.704	.526	.659	.520	4
FBK-HLT-NLP_r1	.808	.523	.737	.510	5
FBK-HLT-NLP_r3	.805	.519	.737	.505	6
FBK-HLT-NLP_r2	.797	.514	.731	.503	7
Inspire_r2	.759	.503	.691	.495	8
IISCNLP_r2	.821	.508	.740	.492	9
IISCNLP_r1	.811	.489	.723	.469	10
IISCNLP_r3	.811	.494	.721	.469	11
Venseseval_r1	.708	.468	.649	.453	12
Inspire_r3	.769	.455	.687	.446	13
*iUBC_r3	.809	.507	.739	.498	
*iUBC_r2	.809	.486	.738	.476	
*iUBC_r1	.809	.431	.714	.423	
AVG	.793	.514	.718	.499	
MAX	.838	.561	.760	.547	

Headlines Goldchunks					
System	**F**	**+T**	**+S**	**+TS**	**R**
Baseline	.846	.546	.761	.546	
Inspire_r1	.819	.703	.787	.696	1
Inspire_r2	.892	.673	.832	.663	2
DTSim_r2	.907	.665	.836	.649	3
DTSim_r3	.907	.658	.833	.641	4
DTSim_r1	.907	.665	.819	.639	5
UWB_r3	.899	.641	.838	.630	6
UWB_r1	.898	.632	.835	.621	7
UWB_r2	.890	.615	.815	.601	8
VRep_r3	.893	.602	.805	.597	9
VRep_r2	.901	.603	.808	.597	10
VRep_r1	.891	.602	.803	.596	11
Inspire_r3	.897	.589	.818	.579	12
Venseseval_r1	.873	.593	.810	.573	13
Rev_r1	.866	.571	.784	.562	14
FBK-HLT-NLP_r3	.885	.577	.809	.562	15
FBK-HLT-NLP_r1	.879	.574	.810	.559	16
IISCNLP_r2	.913	.576	.829	.556	17
FBK-HLT-NLP_r2	.886	.564	.802	.555	18
IISCNLP_r1	.914	.573	.820	.551	19
IISCNLP_r3	.914	.567	.821	.541	20
*iUBC_r3	.928	.602	.858	.592	
*iUBC_r2	.928	.600	.861	.587	
*iUBC_r1	.928	.512	.830	.505	
AVG	.892	.612	.816	.598	
MAX	.914	.703	.838	.696	

Table 3: Test results in Headlines for both scenarios. Each row correspond to a system run, and each column to one evaluation metric: F alignment (**F**), F alignment with type penalty (**+T**), F alignment with score penalty (**+S**) and F alignment with type and score penalty (**+TS**), and **R** for the rank. The "*" symbol denotes runs that include task organizers. Additionally, the table shows results for the baseline, average of participants (**AVG**) and maximum score of participants (**MAX**).

Images Syschunks						Images Goldchunks					
System	F	+T	+S	+TS	R	System	F	+T	+S	+TS	R
Baseline	.713	.404	.625	.404		Baseline	.856	.480	.746	.480	
DTSim_r3	.843	.628	.781	.610	1	UWB_r3	.892	.687	.841	.671	1
DTSim_r2	.843	.615	.781	.599	2	UWB_r1	.894	.683	.840	.667	2
DTSim_r1	.843	.615	.759	.587	3	DTSim_r3	.877	.668	.816	.648	3
Inspire_r1	.754	.564	.704	.563	4	DTSim_r2	.877	.653	.814	.636	4
FBK-HLT-NLP_r1	.843	.566	.786	.548	5	DTSim_r1	.877	.653	.796	.624	5
Inspire_r2	.817	.543	.742	.536	6	UWB_r2	.871	.635	.808	.621	6
FBK-HLT-NLP_r3	.842	.554	.785	.535	7	Inspire_r1	.797	.614	.748	.613	7
FBK-HLT-NLP_r2	.843	.518	.781	.497	8	Inspire_r2	.867	.596	.795	.588	8
IISCNLP_r2	.846	.499	.777	.487	9	FBK-HLT-NLP_r1	.873	.595	.815	.574	9
IISCNLP_r1	.834	.486	.765	.474	10	Venseseval_r1	.844	.579	.805	.574	10
IISCNLP_r3	.834	.486	.765	.474	11	FBK-HLT-NLP_r3	.879	.588	.819	.566	11
Venseseval_r1	.743	467	.695	.463	12	VRep_r1	.854	.552	.765	.548	12
Inspire_r3	.811	.453	.735	.450	13	VRep_r3	.855	.551	.765	.547	13
*iUBC_r2	.856	.561	.796	.550		VRep_r2	.857	.547	.763	.543	14
*iUBC_r3	.856	.523	.794	.516		FBK-HLT-NLP_r2	.879	.543	.818	.525	15
*iUBC_r1	.856	.489	.770	.477		IISCNLP_r2	.893	.525	.823	.509	16
AVG	.822	.538	.758	.525		Rev_r1	.831	.501	.740	.493	17
MAX	.846	.628	.786	.610		IISCNLP_r3	.893	.505	.826	.492	18
						Inspire_r3	.855	.489	.781	.487	19
						IISCNLP_r1	.893	.502	.829	.485	20
						*iUBC_r2	.908	.622	.855	.612	
						*iUBC_r3	.908	.587	.846	.578	
						*iUBC_r1	.908	.520	.816	.513	
						AVG	.868	.583	.800	.570	
						MAX	.894	.687	.841	.671	

Table 4: Test results in Images for both scenarios. Each row correspond to a system run, and each column to one evaluation metric: F alignment (**F**), F alignment with type penalty (**+T**), F alignment with score penalty (**+S**) and F alignment with type and score penalty (**+TS**), and **R** for the rank. The "*" symbol denotes runs that include task organizers. Additionally, the table shows results for the baseline, average of participants (**AVG**) and maximum score of participants (**MAX**).

Answer-Students Syschunks						Answer-Students Goldchunks					
System	**F**	**+T**	**+S**	**+TS**	**R**	**System**	**F**	**+T**	**+S**	**+TS**	**R**
Baseline	.619	.443	.5702	.443		Baseline	.820	.557	.746	.557	
FBK-HLT-NLP_r3	.817	.561	.757	.555	1	IISCNLP_r1	.868	.651	.825	.639	1
IISCNLP_run3	.756	.560	.710	.545	2	IISCNLP_r3	.868	.651	.825	.639	2
FBK-HLT-NLP_r1	.816	.548	.759	.542	3	UWB_r1	.864	.630	.809	.625	3
FBK-HLT-NLP_r2	.816	.543	.748	.541	4	IISCNLP_r2	.868	.627	.826	.617	4
IISCNLP_r1	.756	.553	.710	.540	5	UWB_r3	.859	.617	.804	.611	5
IISCNLP_r2	.745	.532	.700	.520	6	FBK-HLT-NLP_r3	.851	.598	.790	.589	6
DTSim_r2	.817	.516	.737	.507	7	FBK-HLT-NLP_r1	.878	.589	.810	.581	7
DTSim_r1	.817	.516	.725	.505	8	VRep_r3	.879	.582	.792	.580	8
DTSim_r3	.818	.511	.736	.503	9	VRep_r2	.870	.581	.785	.579	9
Inspire_r1	.690	.455	.640	.452	10	FBK-HLT-NLP_r2	.860	.576	.791	.571	10
Inspire_r2	.725	.424	.653	.419	11	DTSim_r2	.858	.555	.781	.546	11
Inspire_r3	.762	.343	.670	.338	12	DTSim_r1	.858	.555	.769	.543	12
*iUBC_r2	.796	.565	.748	.559		DTSim_r3	.861	.547	.780	.537	13
*iUBC_r3	.796	.565	.748	.559		VRep_r1	.772	.525	.701	.523	14
*iUBC_r1	.796	.450	.710	.449		Inspire_r1	.795	.513	.735	.510	15
AVG	.778	.505	.712	.497		Inspire_r2	.821	.483	.744	.479	16
MAX	.818	.561	.759	.555		UWB_r2	.875	.481	.783	.475	17
						Rev_r1	.846	.418	.727	.410	18
						Inspire_r3	.874	.391	.770	.386	19
						*iUBC_r2	.892	.651	.843	.644	
						*iUBC_r3	.892	.651	.843	.644	
						*iUBC_r1	.892	.502	.794	.499	
						AVG	.854	.556	.781	.549	
						MAX	.879	.651	.826	.639	

Table 5: Test results in Answer-Students for both scenarios. Each row correspond to a system run, and each column to one evaluation metric: F alignment (**F**), F alignment with type penalty (**+T**), F alignment with score penalty (**+S**) and F alignment with type and score penalty (**+TS**), and **R** for the rank. The "*" symbol denotes runs that include task organizers. Additionally, the table shows results for the baseline, average of participants (**AVG**) and maximum score of participants (**MAX**).

SemEval-2016 Task 3: Community Question Answering

Preslav Nakov Lluís Màrquez Alessandro Moschitti

Walid Magdy Hamdy Mubarak Abed Alhakim Freihat

ALT Research Group, Qatar Computing Research Institute, HBKU

James Glass

MIT Computer Science and Artificial Intelligence Laboratory

Bilal Randeree

Qatar Living

Abstract

This paper describes the SemEval–2016 Task 3 on Community Question Answering, which we offered in English and Arabic. For English, we had three subtasks: *Question–Comment Similarity* (subtask A), *Question–Question Similarity* (B), and *Question–External Comment Similarity* (C). For Arabic, we had another subtask: *Rerank the correct answers for a new question* (D). Eighteen teams participated in the task, submitting a total of 95 runs (38 primary and 57 contrastive) for the four subtasks. A variety of approaches and features were used by the participating systems to address the different subtasks, which are summarized in this paper. The best systems achieved an official score (MAP) of 79.19, 76.70, 55.41, and 45.83 in subtasks A, B, C, and D, respectively. These scores are significantly better than those for the baselines that we provided. For subtask A, the best system improved over the 2015 winner by 3 points absolute in terms of Accuracy.

1 Introduction

Building on the success of SemEval–2015 Task 3 "Answer Selection in Community Question Answering"[1] (Nakov et al., 2015), we run an extension in 2016, which covers a full task on *Community Question Answering* (CQA) and which is, therefore, closer to the real application needs. All the information related to the task, data, participants, results and publications can be found on the SemEval–2016 Task 3 website.[2]

CQA forums such as Stack Overflow[3] and Qatar Living[4], are gaining popularity online. These forums are seldom moderated, quite open, and thus they typically have little restrictions, if any, on who can post and who can answer a question. On the positive side, this means that one can freely ask any question and can then expect some good, honest answers. On the negative side, it takes effort to go through all possible answers and to make sense of them. For example, it is not unusual for a question to have hundreds of answers, which makes it very time-consuming for the user to inspect and to winnow through them all. The present task could help to automate the process of finding good answers to new questions in a community-created discussion forum, e.g., by retrieving similar questions in the forum and by identifying the posts in the comment threads of those similar questions that answer the original question well.

In essence, the main CQA task can be defined as follows: "given (*i*) a new question and (*ii*) a large collection of question-comment threads created by a user community, rank the comments that are most useful for answering the new question".

The test question is new with respect to the collection, but it is expected to be related to one or several questions in the collection. The best answers can come from different question-comment threads. In the collection, the threads are independent of each other and the lists of comments are chronologically sorted and contain some meta information, e.g., date, user, topic, etc.

---

[1]http://alt.qcri.org/semeval2015/task3
[2]http://alt.qcri.org/semeval2016/task3
[3]http://stackoverflow.com/
[4]http://www.qatarliving.com/forum

Proceedings of SemEval-2016, pages 525–545,
San Diego, California, June 16-17, 2016. ©2016 Association for Computational Linguistics

The comments in a particular thread are intended to answer the question initiating that thread, but since this is a resource created by a community of casual users, there is a lot of noise and irrelevant material, apart from informal language usage and lots of typos and grammatical mistakes. Interestingly, the questions in the collection can be semantically related to each other, although not explicitly.

Our intention was not to run just another regular Question Answering task. Similarly to the 2015 edition, we had three objectives: (*i*) to focus on semantic-based solutions beyond simple "bag-of-words" representations and "word matching" techniques; (*ii*) to study the new natural language processing (NLP) phenomena arising in the community question answering scenario, e.g., relations between the comments in a thread, relations between different threads and question-to-question similarity; and (*iii*) to facilitate the participation of non IR/QA experts to our challenge. The third point was achieved by explicitly providing the set of potential answers—the search engine step was carried out by us—to be (re)ranked and by defining two optional subtasks apart from the main CQA task. Subtask A (*Question-Comment Similarity*): given a question from a question-comment thread, rank the comments according to their relevance (similarity) with respect to the question; Subtask B (*Question-Question Similarity*): given the new question, rerank all similar questions retrieved by a search engine, assuming that the answers to the similar questions should be answering the new question too.

Subtasks A and B should give participants enough tools to create a CQA system to solve the main task. Nonetheless, one can approach CQA without necessarily solving the two tasks above. Participants were free to use whatever approach they wanted, and the participation in the main task and/or the two subtasks was optional. A more precise definition of all subtasks can be found in Section 3.

Keeping the multilinguality from 2015, we provided data for two languages: English and Arabic. For English, we used real data from the community-created Qatar Living forum. The Arabic data was collected from medical forums, with a slightly different procedure. We only proposed the main ranking CQA task on this data, i.e., finding good answers for a given new question.

Finally, we provided training data for all languages and subtasks with human supervision. All examples were manually labeled by a community of annotators in a crowdsourcing platform. The datasets and the annotation procedure are described in Section 4, and some examples can be found in Figures 3 and 4.

The rest of the paper is organized as follows: Section 2 introduces some related work. Section 3 gives a more detailed definition of the task. Section 4 describes the datasets and the process of their creation. Section 5 explains the evaluation measures. Section 6 presents the results for all subtasks and for all participating systems. Section 7 summarizes the main approaches and features used by these systems. Finally, Section 8 offers some further discussion and presents the main conclusions.

2   Related Work

Our task goes in the direction of passage reranking, where automatic classifiers are normally applied to pairs of questions and answer passages to derive a relative order between passages, e.g., see (Radlinski and Joachims, 2005; Jeon et al., 2005; Shen and Lapata, 2007; Moschitti et al., 2007; Severyn and Moschitti, 2015; Moschitti, 2008; Tymoshenko and Moschitti, 2015; Tymoshenko et al., 2016; Surdeanu et al., 2008). In recent years, many advanced models have been developed for automating answer selection, producing a large body of work. For instance, Wang et al. (2007) proposed a probabilistic quasi-synchronous grammar to learn syntactic transformations from the question to the candidate answers; Heilman and Smith (2010) used an algorithm based on Tree Edit Distance (TED) to learn tree transformations in pairs; Wang and Manning (2010) developed a probabilistic model to learn tree-edit operations on dependency parse trees; and Yao et al. (2013) applied linear chain CRFs with features derived from TED to automatically learn associations between questions and candidate answers. One interesting aspect of the above research is the need for syntactic structures; this is also corroborated in (Severyn and Moschitti, 2012; Severyn and Moschitti, 2013). Note that answer selection can use models for textual entailment, semantic similarity, and for natural language inference in general.

Using information about the thread is another important direction. In the 2015 edition of the task, the top participating systems used thread-level features, in addition to the usual local features that only look at the question–answer pair. For example, the second-best team, HITSZ-ICRC, used as a feature the position of the comment in the thread, whether the answer is first, whether the answer is last (Hou et al., 2015). Similarly, the third-best team, QCRI, used features that model a comment in the context of the entire comment thread, focusing on user interaction (Nicosia et al., 2015). Finally, the fifth-best team, ICRC-HIT, treated the answer selection task as a sequence labeling problem and proposed recurrent convolution neural networks to recognize good comments (Zhou et al., 2015b).

In a follow-up work, Zhou et al. (2015a) included long-short term memory (LSTM) units in their convolutional neural network to learn the classification sequence for the thread. In parallel, Barrón-Cedeño et al. (2015) exploited the dependencies between the thread comments to tackle the same task. This was done by designing features that look globally at the thread and by applying structured prediction models, such as Conditional Random Fields (Lafferty et al., 2001).

This research direction was further extended by Joty et al. (2015), who used the output structure at the thread level in order to make more consistent global decisions. For this purpose, they modeled the relations between pairs of comments at any distance in the thread, and they combined the predictions of local classifiers in a graph-cut and in an ILP frameworks.

Finally, Joty et al. (2016) proposed two novel joint learning models that are on-line and integrate inference within the learning process. The first one jointly learns two node- and edge-level MaxEnt classifiers with stochastic gradient descent and integrates the inference step with loopy belief propagation. The second model is an instance of fully connected pairwise CRFs (FCCRF). The FCCRF model significantly outperforms all other approaches and yields the best results on the task (SemEval-2015 Task 3) to date. Crucial elements for its success are the global normalization and an Ising-like edge potential.

3 Definition of the Subtasks

The challenge was structured as a set of four different and independent subtasks. Three of them (A, B and C) were offered for English, while the fourth one (D) was offered for Arabic. We describe them below in detail. In order to make the subtask definitions more clear, we also provide some high-level information about the datasets we used (they will be described in more detail later in Section 4).

The English data comes from the Qatar Living forum, which is organized as a set of seemingly independent question–comment threads. In short, for subtask A we annotated the comments in a question-thread as "Good", "PotentiallyUseful" or "Bad" with respect to the question that started the thread. Additionally, given original questions we retrieved related question–comment threads and we annotated the related questions as "PerfectMatch", "Relevant", or "Irrelevant" with respect to the original question (subtask B). We then annotated the comments in the threads of related questions as "Good", "PotentiallyUseful" or "Bad" with respect to the original question (subtask C).

For Arabic, the data was extracted from medical forums and has a different format. Given an original question, we retrieved pairs of the form (related_question, answer_to_the_related_question). These pairs were annotated as "Direct" answer, "Relevant" and "Irrelevant" with respect to the original question.

English subtask A *Question-Comment Similarity.* Given a question Q and its first ten comments[5] in the question thread $(c_1, \ldots, c_{10})$, the goal is to rank these ten comments according to their relevance with respect to the question.

Note that this is a ranking task, not a classification task; we use mean average precision (MAP) as an official evaluation measure. This setting was adopted as it is closer to the application scenario than pure comment classification. For a perfect ranking, a system has to place all "Good" comments above the "PotentiallyUseful" and "Bad" comments; the latter two are not actually distinguished and are considered "Bad" in terms of evaluation.

---

[5]We limit the number of comments we consider to the first ten only in order to spare some annotation efforts.

Note also that subtask A this year is the same as subtask A at SemEval-2015 Task 3, but with slightly different annotation and evaluation measure.

English subtask B *Question-Question Similarity.* Given a new question Q (aka original question) and the set of the first ten related questions from the forum $(Q_1, \ldots, Q_{10})$ retrieved by a search engine, the goal is to rank the related questions according to their similarity with respect to the original question.

In this case, we consider the "PerfectMatch" and "Relevant" questions both as good (i.e., we do not distinguish between them and we will consider them both "Relevant"), and they should be ranked above the "Irrelevant" questions. As in subtask A, we use MAP as the official evaluation measure. To produce the ranking of related questions, participants have access to the corresponding related question-thread.[6] Thus, being more precise, this subtask could have been named *Question — Question+Thread Similarity.*

English subtask C *Question-External Comment Similarity.* Given a new question Q (aka the original question), and the set of the first ten related questions $(Q_1, \ldots, Q_{10})$ from the forum retrieved by a search engine, each associated with its first ten comments appearing in its thread $(c_1^1, \ldots, c_1^{10}, \ldots, c_{10}^1, \ldots, c_{10}^{10})$, the goal is to rank the 100 comments $\{c_i^j\}_{i,j=1}^{10}$ according to their relevance with respect to the original question Q.

This is the main English subtask. As in subtask A, we want the "Good" comments to be ranked above the "PotentiallyUseful" and "Bad" comments, which will be considered just bad in terms of evaluation. Although, the systems are supposed to work on 100 comments, we take an application-oriented view in the evaluation, assuming that users would like to have good comments concentrated in the first ten positions. We believe users care much less about what happens in lower positions (e.g., after the 10th) in the rank, as they typically do not ask for the next page of results in a search engine such as Google or Bing. This is reflected in our primary evaluation score, MAP, which we restrict to consider only the top ten results in subtask C.

---

[6]Note that the search engine indexes entire Web pages, and thus, the search engine has compared the original question to the related questions together with their comment threads.

Arabic subtask D *Rank the correct answers for a new question.* Given a new question Q (aka the original question), the set of the first 30 related questions retrieved by a search engine, each associated with one correct answer $((Q_1, c_1) \ldots, (Q_{30}, c_{30}))$, the goal is to rank the 30 question-answer pairs according to their relevance with respect to the original question. We want the "Direct" and the "Relevant" answers to be ranked above the "Irrelevant" answers; the former two are considered "Relevant" in terms of evaluation. We evaluate the position of "Relevant" answers in the rank, therefore, this is again a ranking task.

Unlike the English subtasks, here we use 30 answers since the retrieval task is much more difficult, leading to low recall, and the number of correct answers is much lower. Again, systems were evaluated using MAP, restricted to the top-10 results.

4 Datasets

As we mentioned above, the task is offered for two languages, English and Arabic. Below we describe the data for each language.

4.1 English Dataset

We refer to the English data as the CQA-QL corpus; it is based on data from the Qatar Living forum.

The English data is organized with focus on the main task, which is subtask C, but it contains annotations for all three subtasks. It consists of a list of original questions, where for each original question there are ten related questions from Qatar Living, together with the first ten comments from their threads. The data is annotated with the relevance of each related question with respect to the original question (subtask B), as well as with the relevance of each comment with respect to the related (subtask A) and also with respect to the original question (subtask C).

To build the dataset, we first selected a set of questions to serve as original questions. In a real-world scenario those would be questions that were never asked before; however, here we used existing questions from Qatar Living. For the training and for the development datasets, we used questions from SemEval-2015 Task 3 (Nakov et al., 2015), while we used new Qatar Living questions for testing.

From each original question, we generated a query, using the question's subject (after some word removal if the subject was too long). Then, we executed the query in Google, limiting the search to the Qatar Living forum, and we collected up to 200 resulting question-comment threads as related questions. Afterwards, we filtered out threads with less than ten comments as well as those for which the question was more than 2,000 characters long. Finally, we kept the top-10 surviving threads, keeping just the first 10 comments in each thread.

We formatted the results in XML with UTF-8 encoding, adding metadata for the related questions and for their comments; however, we did not provide any meta information about the original question, in order to emulate a scenario where it is a new question, never asked before in the forum. In order to have a valid XML, we had to do some cleansing and normalization of the data. We added an XML format definition at the beginning of the XML file and made sure it validates.

We provided a split of the data into three datasets: training, development, and testing. A dataset file is a sequence of original questions (OrgQuestion), where each question has a subject, a body (text), and a unique question identifier (ORGQ_ID). Each such original question is followed by ten threads, where each thread has a related question (according to the search engine results) and its first ten comments.

Each related question (RelQuestion) has a subject and a body (text), as well as the following attributes:

- RELQ_ID: question identifier;

- RELQ_RANKING_ORDER: the rank of the related question in the list of results returned by the search engine for the original question;[7]

- RELQ_CATEGORY: the question category, according to the Qatar Living taxonomy;[8]

- RELQ_DATE: date of posting;

- RELQ_USERID: identifier of the user asking the question;

- RELQ_USERNAME: name of the user asking the question;

- RELQ_RELEVANCE2ORGQ: human assessement on the relevance this RelQuestion thread with respect to OrgQuestion. This label can take one of the following values:

    - *PerfectMatch*: RelQuestion matches OrgQuestion (almost) perfectly; at test time, this label is to be merged with Relevant;
    - *Relevant*: RelQuestion covers some aspects of OrgQuestion;
    - *Irrelevant*: RelQuestion covers no aspects of OrgQuestion.

Each comment has a body text,[9] as well as the following attributes:

- RELC_ID: comment identifier;

- RELC_USERID: identifier of the user posting the comment;

- RELC_USERNAME: name of the user posting the comment;

- RELC_RELEVANCE2ORGQ: human assessment about whether the comment is Good, Bad, or Potentially Useful with respect to the original question, OrgQuestion. This label can take one of the following values:

    - *Good*: at least one subquestion is directly answered by a portion of the comment;
    - *PotentiallyUseful*: no subquestion is directly answered, but the comment gives potentially useful information about one or more subquestions (at test time, this class will be merged with Bad);
    - *Bad*: no subquestion is answered and no useful information is provided (e.g., the answer is another question, a thanks, dialog with another user, a joke, irony, attack of other users, or is not in English, etc.).

---

[7]This is the rank of the thread in the original list of Google results, before the thread filtering; see above.

[8]Here are some examples of Qatar Living categories: Advice and Help, Beauty and Style, Cars and driving, Computers and Internet, Doha Shopping, Education, Environment, Family Life in Qatar, Funnies, Health and Fitness, Investment and Finance, Language, Moving to Qatar, Opportunities, Pets and Animals, Politics, Qatar Living Lounge, Qatari Culture, Salary and Allowances, Sightseeing and Tourist attractions, Socialising, Sports in Qatar, Visas and Permits, Welcome to Qatar, Working in Qatar.

[9]As most of the time the comment's subject is just "RE: <question subject>", we decided to drop it from the dataset.

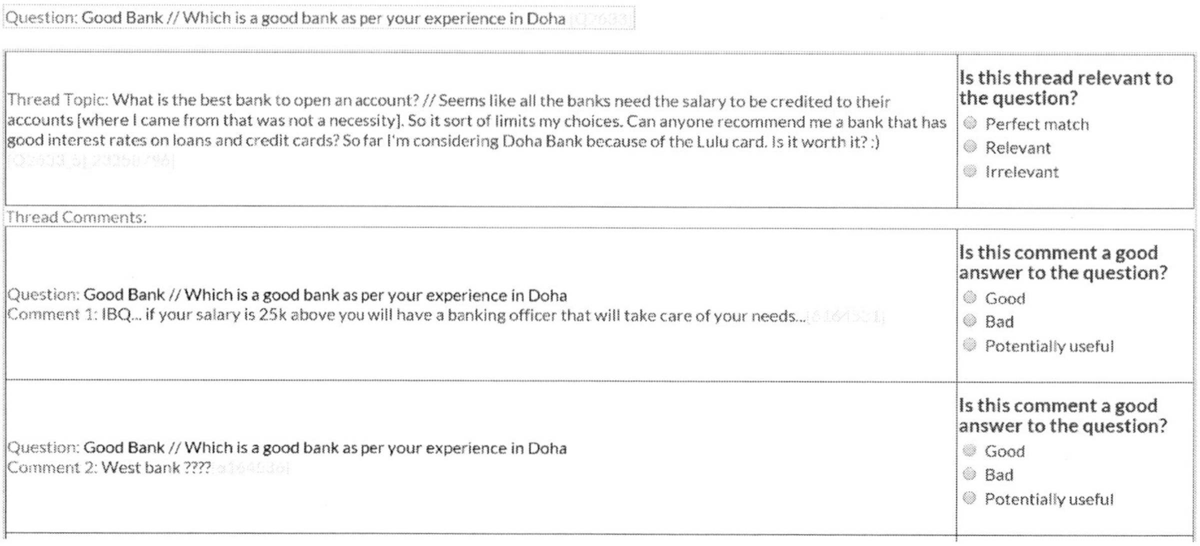

Question: Good Bank // Which is a good bank as per your experience in Doha

Thread Topic: What is the best bank to open an account? // Seems like all the banks need the salary to be credited to their accounts [where I came from that was not a necessity]. So it sort of limits my choices. Can anyone recommend me a bank that has good interest rates on loans and credit cards? So far I'm considering Doha Bank because of the Lulu card. Is it worth it? :)

Is this thread relevant to the question?
- Perfect match
- Relevant
- Irrelevant

Thread Comments:

Question: Good Bank // Which is a good bank as per your experience in Doha
Comment 1: IBQ... if your salary is 25k above you will have a banking officer that will take care of your needs...

Is this comment a good answer to the question?
- Good
- Bad
- Potentially useful

Question: Good Bank // Which is a good bank as per your experience in Doha
Comment 2: West bank ????

Is this comment a good answer to the question?
- Good
- Bad
- Potentially useful

Figure 1: Screenshot for the first English annotation job, collecting labels for subtasks B and C.

Question and Comments:

Question: massage oil // is there any place i can find scented massage oils in qatar?
Comment 1: Yes. It is right behind Kahrama in the National area.

Is this comment a good answer to the question?
- Good
- Bad
- Potentially useful

Question: massage oil // is there any place i can find scented massage oils in qatar?
Comment 2: whats the name of the shop?

Is this comment a good answer to the question?
- Good
- Bad
- Potentially useful

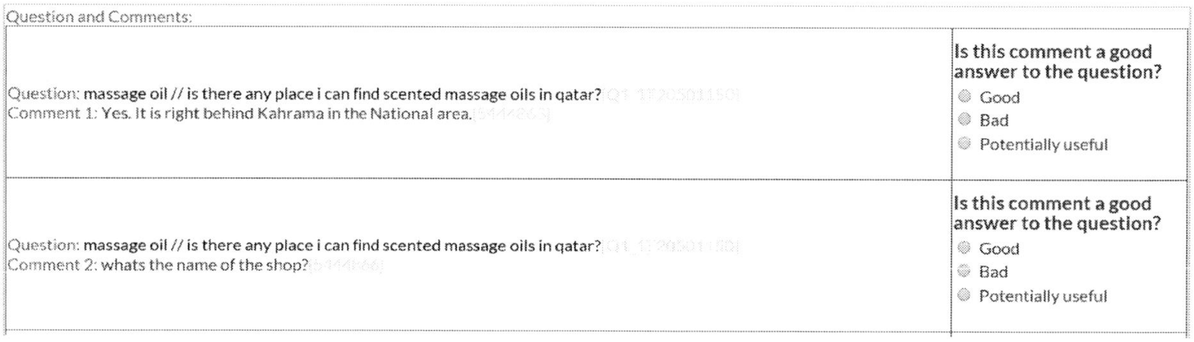

Figure 2: Screenshot of the second English annotation job, collecting labels for subtask A.

- RELC_RELEVANCE2RELQ: human assessment about whether the comment is Good, Bad, or PotentiallyUseful (again, the latter two are merged under Bad at test time) with respect to the related question, RelQuestion.

We used the CrowdFlower[10] crowdsourcing platform to annotate the gold labels for the three subtasks, namely RELC_RELEVANCE2RELQ for subtask A, RELQ_RELEVANCE2ORGQ for subtask B, and RELC_RELEVANCE2ORGQ for subtask C. We collected several annotations for each decision (there were at least three human annotators per example) and we resolved the discrepancies using the default mechanisms of CrowdFlower, which take into account the general quality of annotation for each annotator (based on the hidden tests).

Unlike SemEval-2015 Task 3 (Nakov et al., 2015), where we excluded comments for which there was a lot of disagreement about the labels between the human annotators, this time we did not eliminate any comments (but we controlled the annotation quality with hidden tests), and thus we guarantee that for each question thread, we have the first ten comments without any comment being skipped.

To gather gold annotation labels, we created two annotation jobs on CrowdFlower, screenshots of which are shown in Figures 1 and 2.

The first annotation job aims to collect labels for subtasks B and C. We show a screenshot in Figure 1. An annotation example consists of an original question, a related question, and the first ten comments for that related question.

---

[10]http://www.crowdflower.com

```
<OrgQuestion ORGQ_ID="Q1">
    <OrgQSubject>Massage oil</OrgQSubject>
    <OrgQBody>Where I can buy good oil for massage?</OrgQBody>

    <Thread THREAD_SEQUENCE="Q1_R1">
        <RelQuestion RELQ_ID="Q1_R1" RELQ_RANKING_ORDER="1" RELQ_CATEGORY="Qatar Living Lounge"
        RELQ_DATE="2010-08-27 01:38:59" RELQ_USERID="U1" RELQ_USERNAME="sognabodl"
        RELQ_RELEVANCE2ORGQ="PerfectMatch">
            <RelQSubject>massage oil</RelQSubject>
            <RelQBody>is there any place i can find scented massage oils in qatar?</RelQBody>
        </RelQuestion>

        <RelComment RELC_ID="Q1_R1_C1" RELC_DATE="2010-08-27 01:40:05" RELC_USERID="U2"
        RELC_USERNAME="anonymous" RELC_RELEVANCE2ORGQ="Good" RELC_RELEVANCE2RELQ="Good">
            <RelCText>Yes. It is right behind Kahrama in the National area.</RelCText>
        </RelComment>

        <RelComment RELC_ID="Q1_R1_C2" RELC_DATE="2010-08-27 01:42:59" RELC_USERID="U1"
        RELC_USERNAME="sognabodl" RELC_RELEVANCE2ORGQ="Bad" RELC_RELEVANCE2RELQ="Bad">
            <RelCText>whats the name of the shop?</RelCText>
        </RelComment>
```

Figure 3: Annotated English question from the CQA-QL corpus. Shown are the first two comments only.

We asked the annotators to judge the relevance of the thread with respect to the original question (RELQ_RELEVANCE2ORGQ, for subtask B), as well as the relevance of each comment with respect to the original question (RELC_RELEVANCE2ORGQ, for subtask C). Each example is judged by three annotators who must maintain 70% accuracy throughout the job, measured on a hidden set of 121 examples.[11] The average inter-annotator agreement on the training, development, and testing datasets is 80%, 74%, and 87% for RELQ_RELEVANCE2ORGQ, and 83%, 74%, and 88% for RELC_RELEVANCE2ORGQ.

The second CrowdFlower job collects labels for subtask A; a screenshot is shown in Figure 2. An annotation example consists of a question-comments thread, with ten comments, and we ask annotators to judge the relevance of each comment with respect to the thread question (RELC_RELEVANCE2RELQ). Again, each example is judged by three annotators who must maintain 70% accuracy throughout the job, measured on a hidden set of 150 examples. The average inter-annotator agreement on the training, development, and testing datasets is 82%, 89%, and 79% for RELC_RELEVANCE2RELQ.

A fully annotated example is shown in Figure 3. Statistics about the datasets are shown in Table 1.

Note that the training data is split into two parts, where part2 is noisier than part1. For part2, a different annotation setup was used,[12] which confused the annotators, and they often provided annotation for RELC_RELEVANCE2ORGQ while wrongly thinking that they were actually annotating RELC_RELEVANCE2RELQ. Note that the development data was annotated with the same setup as training part2; however, we manually double-checked and corrected it. Instead, the training part1 and testing datasets used the less confusing, and thus higher-quality annotation setup described above.

Note also that in addition to the above-described canonical XML format, we further released the data in an alternative uncleansed[13] multi-line format. We further released a simplified file format containing only the relevant information for subtask A, where duplicated related questions are removed.[14] Finally, we reformatted the training, development, and test data from SemEval-2015 Task 3 (Nakov et al., 2015), to match the subtask A format for this year.

<hr>

[11]The hidden tests for all subtasks were generated gradually. We started with a small number of initial tests, verified by two task coorganizers, and we gradually added more, choosing from those for which we had highest annotation agreement.

[12]Here are the annotation instructions we used for part2: http://alt.qcri.org/semeval2016/task3/data/uploads/annotation_instructions_for_part2.pdf

[13]In fact, minimally cleansed, so that the XML file is valid.

[14]The same question can be retrieved as related for different original questions. These are not repetitions for subtasks B and C, but they are such for subtask A.

Category	Train (1st part)	Train (2nd part)	Train+Dev+Test (from SemEval 2015)	Dev	Test	Total
Original Questions	**200**	**67**	-	**50**	**70**	**387**
Related Questions	**1,999**	**670**	**2,480+291+319**	**500**	**700**	**6,959**
– *Perfect Match*	*181*	*54*	-	*59*	*81*	*375*
– *Relevant*	*606*	*242*	-	*155*	*152*	*1,155*
– *Irrelevant*	*1,212*	*374*	-	*286*	*467*	*2,339*
Related Comments **(with respect to Original Question)**	**19,990**	**6,700**	**14,893+1,529+1,876**	**5,000**	**7,000**	**56,988**
– *Good*	*1,988*	*849*	*7,418+813+946*	*345*	*654*	*13,013*
– *Bad*	*16,319*	*5,154*	*5,971+544+774*	*4,061*	*5,943*	*38,766*
– *Potentially Useful*	*1,683*	*697*	*1,504+172+156*	*594*	*403*	*5,209*
Related Comments **(with respect to Related Question)**	**14,110**	**3,790**	-	**2,440**	**7,000**	**27,340**
– *Good*	*5,287*	*1,364*	-	*818*	*2,767*	*10,236*
– *Bad*	*6,362*	*1,777*	-	*1,209*	*3,090*	*12,438*
– *Potentially Useful*	*2,461*	*649*	-	*413*	*1,143*	*4,666*

Table 1: Main statistics about the English CQA-QL corpus.

We released this reformatted SemEval-2015 Task 3, subtask A data as additional training data. We further released a large unannotated dataset from Qatar Living with 189,941 questions and 1,894,456 comments, which is useful for unsupervised learning or for training domain-specific word embeddings.

4.2 Arabic Dataset

While at SemEval-2015 (Nakov et al., 2015) we used a dataset from the Fatwa website, this year we changed the domain to medical, which is largely ignored for Arabic. We will refer to the Arabic corpus as CQA-MD. We extracted data from three popular Arabic medical websites that allow visitors to post questions related to health and medical conditions, and to get answers by professional doctors. We collected 1,531 question-answer (QA) pairs from WebTeb,[15] 69,582 pairs from Al-Tibbi,[16] and 31,714 pairs from the medical corner of Islamweb.[17]

We used the 1,531 questions from WebTeb as our original questions, and we looked to find related QA pairs from the other two websites. We collected over 100,000 QA pairs in total from the other two websites, we indexed them in Solr, and we searched them trying to find answers to the WebTeb questions.

We used several different query/document formulations to perform 21 retrieval runs, and we merged the retrieved results, ranking them according to the reciprocal rank fusion algorithm (Cormack et al., 2009). Finally, we truncated the result list to the 30 top-ranked QA pairs, ending up with 45,164 QA pairs[18] for the 1,531 original questions. Next, we used CrowdFlower to obtain judgments about the relevance of these QA pairs with respect to the original question using the following labels:

- **"D"** (Direct): The QA pair contains a direct answer to the original question such that if the user is searching for an answer to the original question, the proposed QA pair would be satisfactory and there would be no need to search any further.

- **"R"** (Related): The QA pair contains an answer to the original question that covers some of the aspects raised in the original question, but this is not sufficient to answer it directly. With this QA pair, it would be expected that the user will continue the search to find a direct answer or more information.

- **"I"** (Irrelevant): The QA pair contains an answer that is irrelevant to the original question.

---

[15] http://www.webteb.com/
[16] http://www.altibbi.com/
[17] http://consult.islamweb.net/

[18] We had less than 30 answers for some questions.

```
<Question QID = "200215">
<Qtext>انا احاول الحمل. الدورة الشهرية الاخيرة حدثت عندي قبل شهر ونصف ثم توقفت عن اخذ حبوب منع الحمل.
ومنذ ذلك الحين لم تحدث عندي الدورة. اجريت فحص الدم لتشخيص الحمل وكان الجواب سلبي. طبيب امراض النساء
اوصاني باخذ حبوب اسمها Primolut-Nor لمدة خمسة ايام صباحا ومساء. هل يوجد لهذه الحبوب اثار جانبية هل
استطيع الحمل بعد الحيض الذي يحدث بسبب هذه الحبوب هل من الافضل الانتظار حتى تاتي الدورة بشكل طبيعي
لماذا هي لا تاتي قبل عامين توقفت عن اخذ الحبوب لمدة ستة اشهر وكانت الدورة تاتي في كل شهر. لماذا لم
يحدث هذا الان </Qtext>
<QApair QAID="319095" QArel="R" QAconf="1.0">
<QAquestion>السؤال أنا أستخدم حبوب منع الحمل (جينيرا) وبعد انتهاء العبوة الأولى جاءتني الدورة
الشهرية ثم لم تأتني فأجريت تحليل الحمل المنزلي وكانت النتيجة سلبية فاستمررت في تناول الحبوب وإلى
الآن لم تأتني الدورة الشهرية منذ أربعة أشهر.هل هذا الأمر طبيعي وهل أتوقف عن تناول الحبوب
</QAquestion>
<QAanswer>الإجابة بسم الله الرحمن الرحيم الأخت الفاضلة فاطمة حفظها الله. السلام عليكم ورحمة الله وبركاته
وبعد: تختلف النساء في تفاعلهن مع حبوب منع الحمل ولكن من المعروف أن حبوب منع الحمل تؤدي إلى
التقليل من دم الدورة أثناء تناولها وقد تنقطع الدورة عند بعض النساء كما حدث معك وطالما أنك تأخذين
الحبوب في موعدها وتتركين الحبوب فترة السبعة أيام التي بين انتهاء العبوة وبداية عبوة جديدة وطالما
أنك أجريت اختباراً للحمل ولم يظهر الحمل فلا خوف من عدم مجيء الدورة وإن كنت أفضل إعادة تحليل الحمل
مرةً أخرى للتأكد عن طريق الدم ويمكنك تغيير نوع الحبوب إلى نوع آخر ففي بعض ا؟ ?حالات يحصل الانقطاع
مع نوع من الحبوب ولا يحصل مع الأنواع الأخرى وذلك حتى تطمئني نفسياً عندما تنزل الدورة بانتظام.والله
الموفق. </QAanswer>
</QApair>
```

Figure 4: Annotated question from the Arabic CQA-MD corpus.

We controlled the quality of annotation using a hidden set of 50 test questions. We had three judgments per example, which we combined using the CrowdFlower mechanism. The average inter-annotator agreement was 81%.

Finally, we divided the data into training, development and testing datasets, based on confidence, where the examples in the test dataset were those with the highest annotation confidence. We further double-checked and manually corrected some of the annotations for the development and the testing datasets whenever necessary.

Figure 4 shows part of the XML file we generated. We can see that, unlike the English data, there are no threads here, just a set of question-answer pairs; moreover, we do not provide much meta data, but we give information about the confidence of annotation (for the training and development datasets only, but not for the test dataset).

Table 2 shows some statistics about the dataset size and the distribution of the three classes in the CQA-MD corpus.

Category	Train	Dev	Test	Total
Questions	**1,031**	**250**	**250**	**1,531**
QA Pairs	**30,411**	**7,384**	**7,369**	**45,164**
– Direct	*917*	*70*	*65*	*1,052*
– Related	*17,412*	*1,446*	*1,353*	*20,211*
– Irrelevant	*12,082*	*5,868*	*5,951*	*23,901*

Table 2: Main statistics about the CQA-MD corpus.

5 Scoring

The official evaluation measure we used to rank the participating systems is Mean Average Precision (MAP) calculated for the ten comments a participating system has ranked highest. It is a well-established in Information Retrieval. We further report the results for two unofficial ranking measures, which we also calculate for the top-10 results only: Mean Reciprocal Rank (MRR) and Average Recall (AvgRec). Additionally, we report the results for four standard classification measures, which we calculate over the full list of results: Precision, Recall, F_1 (with respect to the Good/Relevant class) and Accuracy.

We released a specialized scorer that calculates and reports all above-mentioned seven scores.

6 Participants and Results

The list of all participating teams can be found in Table 7. The results for subtasks A, B, C, and D are shown in Tables 3, 4, 5, and 6, respectively. In all tables, the systems are ranked by the official MAP scores for their primary runs[19] (shown in the third column). The following columns show the scores based on the other six unofficial measures; the ranking with respect to these additional measures are marked with a subindex (for the primary runs).

[19]Participants could submit one primary run, to be used for the official ranking, and up to two contrastive runs, which are scored but have unofficial status.

Eighteen teams participated in the challenge presenting a variety of approaches and features to address the different subtasks. They submitted a total of 95 runs (38 primary and 57 contrastive), which are broken down by subtasks in the following way: The English subtasks A, B and C attracted 12, 11, and 10 systems and 29, 25 and 28 runs, respectively. The Arabic subtask D got 5 systems and 13 runs. The best MAP scores varied from 45.83 to 79.19, depending on the subtask. The best systems in each subtask were able to beat the baselines we provided by sizeable margins.

6.1 Subtask A, English (Question-Comment Similarity)

Table 3 shows the results for subtask A, English, which attracted 12 teams, which submitted 29 runs: 12 primary and 17 contrastive. The last four rows of the table show the performance of four baselines. The first one is the chronological ranking, where the comments are ordered by their time of posting; we can see that all submissions outperform this baseline on all three ranking measures. The second baseline is a random baseline, which outperforms some systems in terms of F_1, primarily because of having very high Recall. Baseline 3 classifies all comments as Good, and it outperforms four of the primary systems in terms of F_1. Finally, baseline 4 classifies all comments as Bad; it outperforms one of the primary systems in terms of Accuracy.

The winning team is that of KeLP (Filice et al., 2016), which achieved the highest MAP of 79.19, outperforming the second best by a margin; they are also first on AvgRec and MRR, and second on Accuracy. They learn semantic relations between questions and answers using kernels and previously-proposed features from (Barrón-Cedeño et al., 2015). Their system is based on the KeLP machine learning platform (Filice et al., 2015), and thus the name of the team.

The second best system is that of ConvKN (Barrón-Cedeño et al., 2016) with MAP of 77.66; it is also first on Accuracy, second on F_1, and third on AvgRec. The system combines convolutional tree kernels and convolutional neural networks, together with text similarity and thread-specific features. Their contrastive1 run achieved even better results: MAP of 78.71.

The third best system is SemanticZ (Mihaylov and Nakov, 2016b) with MAP of 77.58. They use semantic similarity based on word embeddings and topics; they are second on AvgRec and MRR.

Note also the cluster of systems of very close MAP: ConvKN (Barrón-Cedeño et al., 2016) with 77.66, SemanticZ (Mihaylov and Nakov, 2016b) with 77.58, ECNU (Wu and Lan, 2016) with 77.28, and SUper_team (Mihaylova et al., 2016) with 77.16. The latter also has a contrastive run with MAP of 77.68, which would have ranked second.

6.2 Subtask B, English (Question-Question Similarity)

Table 4 shows the results for subtask B, English, which attracted 11 teams and 25 runs: 11 primary and 14 contrastive. This turns out to be a hard task. For example, the IR baseline (i.e., ordering the related questions in the order provided by the search engine) outperforms 5 of the 11 systems in terms of MAP; it also outperforms several systems in terms of MRR and AvgRec. The random baseline outperforms one system in terms of F_1 and Accuracy, again due to high recall. The all-Good baseline outperforms two systems on F_1, while the all-Bad baseline outperforms two systems on Accuracy.

The winning team is that of UH-PRHLT (Franco-Salvador et al., 2016), which achieved MAP of 76.70 (just 2 MAP points over the IR baseline). They use distributed representations of words, knowledge graphs generated with BabelNet, and frames from FrameNet. Their contrastive2 run is even better, with MAP of 77.33.

The second best system is that of ConvKN (Barrón-Cedeño et al., 2016) with MAP of 76.02; they are also first on MRR, second on AvgRec and F_1, and third on Accuracy.

The third best system is KeLP (Filice et al., 2016) with MAP of 75.83; they are also first on AvgRec, F_1, and Accuracy. They have a contrastive run with MAP of 76.28, which would have ranked second.

The fourth best, SLS (Mohtarami et al., 2016) is very close, with MAP of 75.55; it is also first on MRR and Accuracy, and third on AvgRec. It uses a bag-of-vectors approach with various vector- and text-based features, and different neural network approaches including CNNs and LSTMs to capture the semantic similarity between questions and answers.

6.3 Subtask C, English (Question-External Comment Similarity)

The results for subtask C, English are shown in Table 5. This subtask attracted 10 teams, and 28 runs: 10 primary and 18 contrastive. Here the teams performed much better than they did for subtask B. The first three baselines were all outperformed by all participating systems. However, due to severe class imbalance, the all-Bad baseline outperformed 9 out of the 10 participating teams in terms of Accuracy.

The best system in this subtask is that of the SUper_team (Mihaylova et al., 2016), which achieved MAP of 55.41; the system is also first on AvgRec and MRR. It used a rich set of features, grouped into three categories: question-specific features, answer-specific features, and question-answer similarity features. This includes more or less standard metadata, lexical, semantic, and user-related features, as well as some exotic ones such as features related to readability, credibility, as well as goodness polarity lexicons.[20] It is important to note that this system did not try to solve subtask C directly, but rather just multipled their predicted score for subtask A by the reciprocal rank of the related question in the list of related questions (as returned by the search engine, and as readily provided by the organizers as an attribute in the XML file) for the original question. In fact, this is not an isolated case, but an approach taken by several participants in subtask C.

The second best system is that of KeLP (Filice et al., 2016), with MAP of 52.95; they are also first on F_1, and second on AvgRec and MRR. KeLP also has a contrastive run with a MAP of 55.58, which would have made them first. This team really tried to solve the actual subtask C by means of stacking classifiers: they used their subtask A classifier to judge how good the answer is with respect to the original and with respect to the related question. Moreover, they used their subtask B classifier to judge the relatedness of the related question with respect to the original question. Finally, they used these three scores, together with some features based on them, to train a classifier that solves subtask C.

---

[20]These goodness polarity lexicons were at the core of another system, PMI-cool (Balchev et al., 2016), which did not perform very well as it limited itself to lexicons and ignored other important features.

In fact, we anticipated solutions like this when we designed the task, i.e., that participants would solve subtasks A and B, and use them as auxiliary tasks to attack the main task, namely subtask C. Unfortunately, subtask B turned out to be too hard, and thus many participants decided to skip it and just to use the search engine's reciprocal rank.

The third best system is SemanticZ (Mihaylov and Nakov, 2016b), with MAP of 51.68. Similarly to SUper_team, they simply multiply their predicted score for subtask A by the reciprocal rank of the related question in the list of related questions for the original question.

6.4 Subtask D, Arabic (Reranking the correct answers for a new question)

Finally, the results for subtask D, Arabic are shown in Table 6. It attracted 5 teams, which submitted 13 runs: 5 primary and 8 contrastive. As the class imbalance here is even more severe than for subtask C, the all-Bad baseline outperforms all participating systems in terms of Accuracy. In contrast, the all-Good baseline only outperforms one system in terms of F_1. Here the teams perform much better than for subtask B. The random baseline outperforms one system in terms of both MAP and AvgRec.

The clear winner here is SLS (Mohtarami et al., 2016), which is ranked first on all measures: MAP, AvgRec, MRR, F_1, and Accuracy. Yet, their MAP of 45.83 is only slightly better than that of ConvKN, 45.50, which ranks second on MAP, AvgRec, MRR and F_1, and third on Accuracy.

The third system is RDI (Magooda et al., 2016) with MAP of 43.80, which is ranked third also on AvgRec and MRR. The system combines a TF.IDF module with a recurrent language model and information from Wikipedia.

7 Features and Techniques

The systems that participated in several subtasks typically re-used some features for all subtasks, whenever possible and suitable. Such features include the following: (*i*) *similarity features* between questions and comments from their threads or between original questions and related questions, e.g., cosine similarity applied to lexical, syntactic and semantic representations or distributed representations, often derived using neural networks, *(ii) content features*, which are special signals that can clearly indicate a bad answer, e.g., when a comment contains "thanks", *(iii) thread level/meta features*, e.g., user ID, comment rank in the thread, and *(iv) automatically generated features* from syntactic structures using tree kernels.

Overall, most of the top positions are occupied by systems that used tree kernels, combined with similarity features. Regarding the machine learning approaches used, most systems chose SVM classifiers (often these were ranking versions such as SVM-Rank), or different kinds of neural networks. Below we look in more detail in the features and the used learning methods.

7.1 Feature Types

Participants preferred different kinds of features for different subtasks:

Subtask A. Similarities between question subject vs. comment, question body vs. comment, and question subject+body vs. comment.

Subtask B. Similarities between the original and the related question at different levels: subject vs. subject, body vs. body, and subject+body vs. subject+body.

Subtask C. The same from above, plus the similarities of the original question subject, body, and full levels with the comments from the thread of the related question.

The similarity scores to be used as features were computed in various ways, e.g., the majority of teams used dot product calculated over word n-grams (n=1,2,3), character 3-grams, or with TF-IDF weighting. Or simply using word overlap, i.e., the number of common words between two texts, often normalized, e.g., by question/comment length. Or overlap in terms of nouns or named entities.

Several systems, e.g., UH-PRHLT, KeLP, SLS, SemanticZ, ECNU, used additional similarities based on distributed representations. For example, using the continuous skip-gram model of word2vec or Glove, trained on Google News, on the English Wikipedia, or on the unannotated Qatar Living dataset.

In particular, UH-PRHLT used word alignments and distributed representations to align the words of the question with the words of the comment.

On the alignment topic, it is worth mentioned that MTE-NN applied a model originally defined for machine translation evaluation (Guzmán et al., 2015), e.g., based on features computed with BLEU, TER, NIST, and Meteor (Guzmán et al., 2016a). Similarly, ECNU used Spearman, Pearson, and Kendall Ranking Coefficients as similarity scores for question similarity estimation, whereas ICL00 used word-to-word translation probabilities, and UniMelb used convolutional neural networks (CNNs) fed with word embeddings and machine translation evaluation scores as input.

ConvKN used a CNN that also encodes relational links between the involved pieces of texts (Severyn and Moschitti, 2015). MTE-NN applied a simple neural network, ECNU and SLS used LSTM networks, and Overfitting applied Feedforward Neural Net Language Model (FNNLM).

It should be noted that ConvKN and KeLP used tree kernels with relational links (Tymoshenko and Moschitti, 2015; Tymoshenko et al., 2016), i.e., the questions are aligned with the comments (or with the other questions) by means of a special REL tag, directly annotated in the parse trees.

Regarding text structures, UH-PRHLT used Knowledge Graph Analysis, which consists in labeling, weighting, and expanding concepts in the text using a directed graph. They also used frames from FrameNet to generate semantic features.

Several teams, e.g., ConvKN, KeLP and SUper Team, used meta-features, such as the user ID. In particular, the SUper Team collected statistics about the users, e.g., the comments/questions they produced, time since their last activity, the number of good and bad comments in the training data, etc.

Other important features, which were used by most systems, are related to rank, e.g., rank of the comment in the question thread, or rank of the related question in the list of questions retrieved by the search engine for the original question.

Some exotic features by the SUper Team modeled readability, credibility, sentiment analysis, trollness (Mihaylov et al., 2015a; Mihaylov et al., 2015b; Mihaylov and Nakov, 2016a), and goodness polarity, e.g., based on PMI lexicons as for PMI-Cool.

Regarding Arabic, QU-IR and SLS used word2vec, whereas RDI_Team relied on language models. In particular, the winning SLS team used simple text- and vector-based features, where the text similarities are computed at the word- and the sentence-level. Most importantly, they computed two sets of features: one between the original and the related questions, and one between the original question and the related answer, which are then concatenated in one feature vector.

The ConvKN team combined some basic SLS features with tree kernels applied to syntactic trees, obtaining a result that is very close to that of the winning SLS team.

QU-IR used a standard Average Word Embedding and also a new method, Covariance Word Embedding, which computes a covariance matrix between each pair of dimensions of the embedding, thus considering vector components as random variables.

Finally, RDI used Arabic-Wikipedia to boost the weights of medical terms, which improved their ranking function.

7.2 Learning Methods

The most popular machine learning approach was to use Support Vector Machines (SVM) on the features described in the previous section. SVMs were used in three different learning tasks: classification, regression, and ranking. Note that SVMs allow the use of complex convolutional kernels such as tree kernels, which were used by two systems (which in fact combined kernels with other features).

Neural networks were also widely used, e.g., in word2vec to train word embeddings. As previously mentioned, there were also systems using CNNs, LSTMs and FNNLM. Overfitting also used Random Forests.

Comparing tree kernels vs. neural networks: approaches based on the former were ranked first and second in Subtask A, second and third in Subtask B, and second in Subtasks C and D, while neural network-based systems did not win any subtask, but neural networks contributed to the best systems in all subtasks, e.g., with word2vec. Yet, post-competition improvements have shown that NN-based systems can perform on par with the best (Guzmán et al., 2016a).

8 Conclusion

We have described SemEval-2016 Task 3 on Community Question Answering, which extended SemEval-2015 Task 3 (Nakov et al., 2015) with new subtasks (Question–Question similarity, Question–External Comment Similarity, and Reranking the correct answers for a new question), new evaluation metrics (based on ranking), new datasets, and new domains (biomedical for Arabic). The overall focus was on answering new questions that were not already answered in the target community forum.

The task attracted 18 teams, which submitted 95 runs; this is good growth compared to 2015, when 13 teams submitted 61 runs. The participants built on the lessons learned from the 2015 edition of the task, and further experimented with new features and learning frameworks. It was interesting to see that the top systems used both word embeddings trained using neural networks and syntactic kernels, which shows the importance of both distributed representations and linguistic analysis. It was also nice to see some new features being tried.

Apart from the new lessons learned from this year's edition, we believe that the task has another important contribution: the datasets we have created as part of the task (with over 7,000 questions and over 57,000 annotated comments), and which we have released for use to the research community, should be useful for follow up research beyond SemEval.

Finally, given the growth in the interest for the task, we plan a rerun at SemEval-2017 with data from a new domain.

Acknowledgements

This research was performed by the Arabic Language Technologies (ALT) group at the Qatar Computing Research Institute (QCRI), HBKU, part of Qatar Foundation. It is part of the Interactive sYstems for Answer Search (Iyas) project, which is developed in collaboration with MIT-CSAIL.

We would like to thank the anonymous reviewers for their constructive comments, which have helped us improve the paper.

References

Daniel Balchev, Yasen Kiprov, Ivan Koychev, and Preslav Nakov. 2016. PMI-cool at SemEval-2016 Task 3: Experiments with PMI and goodness polarity lexicons for community question answering. In *Proceedings of the 10th International Workshop on Semantic Evaluation*, SemEval '16, San Diego, CA.

Alberto Barrón-Cedeño, Simone Filice, Giovanni Da San Martino, Shafiq Joty, Lluís Màrquez, Preslav Nakov, and Alessandro Moschitti. 2015. Thread-level information for comment classification in community question answering. In *Proceedings of the 53rd Annual Meeting of the Association for Computational Linguistics and the 7th International Joint Conference on Natural Language Processing*, ACL-IJCNLP '15, pages 687–693, Beijing, China.

Alberto Barrón-Cedeño, Giovanni Da San Martino, Shafiq Joty, Alessandro Moschitti, Fahad A. Al Obaidli, Salvatore Romeo, Kateryna Tymoshenko, and Antonio Uva. 2016. ConvKN at SemEval-2016 Task 3: Answer and question selection for question answering on arabic and english fora. In *Proceedings of the 10th International Workshop on Semantic Evaluation*, SemEval '16, San Diego, CA.

Gordon V Cormack, Charles LA Clarke, and Stefan Buettcher. 2009. Reciprocal rank fusion outperforms condorcet and individual rank learning methods. In *Proceedings of the 32nd international ACM SIGIR conference on Research and development in information retrieval*, SIGIR '09, pages 758–759, Boston, MA.

Chang e Jia. 2016. ITNLP-AiKF at SemEval-2016 Task 3: Community question answering. In *Proceedings of the 10th International Workshop on Semantic Evaluation*, SemEval '16, San Diego, CA.

Yassine El Adlouni, Imane Lahbari, Horacio Rodríguez, Mohammed Meknassi, and Said Ouatik El Alaoui. 2016. UPC-USMBA at SemEval-2016 Task 3: UPC-USMBA participation in SemEval 2016 task 3, subtask d: CQA for Arabic. In *Proceedings of the 10th International Workshop on Semantic Evaluation*, SemEval '16, San Diego, CA.

Simone Filice, Giuseppe Castellucci, Danilo Croce, Giovanni Da San Martino, Alessandro Moschitti, and Roberto Basili. 2015. KeLP: a Kernel-based Learning Platform in java. In *Proceedings of the workshop on Machine Learning Open Source Software: Open Ecosystems*, Lille, France.

Simone Filice, Danilo Croce, Alessandro Moschitti, and Roberto Basili. 2016. KeLP at SemEval-2016 Task 3: Learning semantic relations between questions and answers. In *Proceedings of the 10th International Workshop on Semantic Evaluation*, SemEval '16, San Diego, CA.

Marc Franco-Salvador, Sudipta Kar, Thamar Solorio, and Paolo Rosso. 2016. UH-PRHLT at SemEval-2016 Task 3: Combining lexical and semantic-based features for community question answering. In *Proceedings of the 10th International Workshop on Semantic Evaluation*, SemEval '16, San Diego, CA.

Francisco Guzmán, Shafiq Joty, Lluís Màrquez, and Preslav Nakov. 2015. Pairwise neural machine translation evaluation. In *Proceedings of the 53rd Annual Meeting of the Association for Computational Linguistics and the 7th International Joint Conference on Natural Language Processing (Volume 1: Long Papers)*, ACL-IJCNLP '15, pages 805–814, Beijing, China.

Francisco Guzmán, Lluís Màrquez, and Preslav Nakov. 2016a. Machine translation evaluation meets community question answering. In *Proceedings of the 54th Annual Meeting of the Association for Computational Linguistics*, ACL '16, Berlin, Germany.

Francisco Guzmán, Preslav Nakov, and Lluís Màrquez. 2016b. MTE-NN at SemEval-2016 Task 3: Can machine translation evaluation help community question answering? In *Proceedings of the 10th International Workshop on Semantic Evaluation*, SemEval '16, San Diego, CA.

Michael Heilman and Noah A. Smith. 2010. Tree edit models for recognizing textual entailments, paraphrases, and answers to questions. In *Proceedings of the Human Language Technologies: The 2010 Annual Conference of the North American Chapter of the Association for Computational Linguistics*, NAACL-HLT '10, pages 1011–1019, Los Angeles, CA.

Doris Hoogeveen, Yitong Li, Huizhi Liang, Bahar Salehi, Timothy Baldwin, and Long Duong. 2016. UniMelb at SemEval-2016 Task 3: Identifying similar questions by combining a CNN with string similarity measures. In *Proceedings of the 10th International Workshop on Semantic Evaluation*, SemEval '16, San Diego, CA.

Yongshuai Hou, Cong Tan, Xiaolong Wang, Yaoyun Zhang, Jun Xu, and Qingcai Chen. 2015. HITSZ-ICRC: Exploiting classification approach for answer selection in community question answering. In *Proceedings of the 9th International Workshop on Semantic Evaluation*, SemEval '15, pages 196–202, Denver, CO.

Jiwoon Jeon, W. Bruce Croft, and Joon Ho Lee. 2005. Finding similar questions in large question and answer archives. In *Proceedings of the 14th ACM International Conference on Information and Knowledge Management*, CIKM '05, pages 84–90, Bremen, Germany.

Shafiq Joty, Alberto Barrón-Cedeño, Giovanni Da San Martino, Simone Filice, Lluís Màrquez,

538

Alessandro Moschitti, and Preslav Nakov. 2015. Global thread-level inference for comment classification in community question answering. In *Proceedings of the 2015 Conference on Empirical Methods in Natural Language Processing*, EMNLP '15, pages 573–578, Lisbon, Portugal.

Shafiq Joty, Lluís Màrquez, and Preslav Nakov. 2016. Joint learning with global inference for comment classification in community question answering. In *Proceedings of the 2016 Conference of the North American Chapter of the Association for Computational Linguistics: Human Language Technologies*, NAACL-HLT '16, San Diego, CA.

John Lafferty, Andrew McCallum, and Fernando Pereira. 2001. Conditional random fields: Probabilistic models for segmenting and labeling sequence data. In *Proceedings of the Eighteenth International Conference on Machine Learning*, ICML '01, pages 282–289, San Francisco, CA.

Ahmed Magooda, Amr Gomaa, Ashraf Mahgoub, Hany Ahmed, Mohsen Rashwan, Hazem Raafat, Eslam Kamal, and Ahmad Al Sallab. 2016. RDI at SemEval-2016 Task 3: RDI unsupervised framework for text ranking. In *Proceedings of the 10th International Workshop on Semantic Evaluation*, SemEval '16, San Diego, CA.

Rana Malhas, Marwan Torki, and Tamer Elsayed. 2016. QU-IR at SemEval-2016 Task 3: Learning to rank on Arabic community question answering forums with word embedding. In *Proceedings of the 10th International Workshop on Semantic Evaluation*, SemEval '16, San Diego, CA.

Todor Mihaylov and Preslav Nakov. 2016a. Hunting for troll comments in news community forums. In *Proceedings of the 54th Annual Meeting of the Association for Computational Linguistics*, ACL '16, Berlin, Germany.

Todor Mihaylov and Preslav Nakov. 2016b. SemanticZ at SemEval-2016 Task 3: Ranking relevant answers in community question answering using semantic similarity based on fine-tuned word embeddings. In *Proceedings of the 10th International Workshop on Semantic Evaluation*, SemEval '16, San Diego, CA.

Todor Mihaylov, Georgi Georgiev, and Preslav Nakov. 2015a. Finding opinion manipulation trolls in news community forums. In *Proceedings of the Nineteenth Conference on Computational Natural Language Learning*, CoNLL '15, pages 310–314, Beijing, China.

Todor Mihaylov, Ivan Koychev, Georgi Georgiev, and Preslav Nakov. 2015b. Exposing paid opinion manipulation trolls. In *Proceedings of the International Conference Recent Advances in Natural Language Processing*, RANLP '15, pages 443–450, Hissar, Bulgaria.

Tsvetomila Mihaylova, Pepa Gencheva, Martin Boyanov, Ivana Yovcheva, Todor Mihaylov, Momchil Hardalov, Yasen Kiprov, Daniel Balchev, Ivan Koychev, Preslav Nakov, Ivelina Nikolova, and Galia Angelova. 2016. SUper Team at SemEval-2016 Task 3: Building a feature-rich system for community question answering. In *Proceedings of the 10th International Workshop on Semantic Evaluation*, SemEval '16, San Diego, CA.

Mitra Mohtarami, Yonatan Belinkov, Wei-Ning Hsu, Yu Zhang, Tao Lei, Kfir Bar, Scott Cyphers, and Jim Glass. 2016. SLS at SemEval-2016 Task 3: Neural-based approaches for ranking in community question answering. In *Proceedings of the 10th International Workshop on Semantic Evaluation*, SemEval '16, San Diego, CA.

Alessandro Moschitti, Silvia Quarteroni, Roberto Basili, and Suresh Manandhar. 2007. Exploiting syntactic and shallow semantic kernels for question answer classification. In *Proceedings of the 45th Annual Meeting of the Association of Computational Linguistics*, ACL '07, pages 776–783, Prague, Czech Republic.

Alessandro Moschitti. 2008. Kernel methods, syntax and semantics for relational text categorization. In *Proceedings of the 17th ACM Conference on Information and Knowledge Management*, CIKM '08, pages 253–262, Napa Valley, California, USA.

Preslav Nakov, Lluís Màrquez, Walid Magdy, Alessandro Moschitti, Jim Glass, and Bilal Randeree. 2015. SemEval-2015 task 3: Answer selection in community question answering. In *Proceedings of the 9th International Workshop on Semantic Evaluation*, SemEval '15, pages 269–281, Denver, CO.

Massimo Nicosia, Simone Filice, Alberto Barrón-Cedeño, Iman Saleh, Hamdy Mubarak, Wei Gao, Preslav Nakov, Giovanni Da San Martino, Alessandro Moschitti, Kareem Darwish, Lluís Màrquez, Shafiq Joty, and Walid Magdy. 2015. QCRI: Answer selection for community question answering - experiments for Arabic and English. In *Proceedings of the 9th International Workshop on Semantic Evaluation*, SemEval '15, pages 203–209, Denver, CO.

Filip Radlinski and Thorsten Joachims. 2005. Query chains: Learning to rank from implicit feedback. In *Proceedings of the Eleventh ACM SIGKDD International Conference on Knowledge Discovery in Data Mining*, KDD '05, pages 239–248, Chicago, IL.

Aliaksei Severyn and Alessandro Moschitti. 2012. Structural relationships for large-scale learning of answer re-ranking. In *Proceedings of the 35th International ACM SIGIR Conference on Research and De-

velopment in Information Retrieval, SIGIR '12, pages 741–750, Portland, OR.

Aliaksei Severyn and Alessandro Moschitti. 2013. Automatic feature engineering for answer selection and extraction. In *Proceedings of the 2013 Conference on Empirical Methods in Natural Language Processing*, EMNLP '13, pages 458–467, Seattle, WA.

Aliaksei Severyn and Alessandro Moschitti. 2015. Learning to rank short text pairs with convolutional deep neural networks. In *Proceedings of the 38th International ACM SIGIR Conference on Research and Development in Information Retrieval*, SIGIR '15, pages 373–382, Santiago, Chile.

Dan Shen and Mirella Lapata. 2007. Using semantic roles to improve question answering. In *Proceedings of the 2007 Joint Conference on Empirical Methods in Natural Language Processing and Computational Natural Language Learning*, EMNLP-CoNLL '07, pages 12–21, Prague, Czech Republic.

Mihai Surdeanu, Massimiliano Ciaramita, and Hugo Zaragoza. 2008. Learning to rank answers on large online QA collections. In *Proceedings of the 46th Annual Meeting of the Association for Computational Linguistics and the Human Language Technology Conference*, ACL-HLT '08, pages 719–727, Columbus, Ohio, USA.

Kateryna Tymoshenko and Alessandro Moschitti. 2015. Assessing the impact of syntactic and semantic structures for answer passages reranking. In *Proceedings of the 24th ACM International on Conference on Information and Knowledge Management*, CIKM '15, pages 1451–1460, Melbourne, Australia.

Kateryna Tymoshenko, Daniele Bonadiman, and Alessandro Moschitti. 2016. Convolutional neural networks vs. convolution kernels: Feature engineering for answer sentence reranking. In *Proceedings of the 2016 Conference of the North American Chapter of the Association for Computational Linguistics: Human Language Technologies*, NAACL '16, San Diego, CA.

Mengqiu Wang and Christopher D. Manning. 2010. Probabilistic tree-edit models with structured latent variables for textual entailment and question answering. In *Proceedings of the 23rd International Conference on Computational Linguistics*, COLING '10, pages 1164–1172, Beijing, China.

Hujie Wang and Pascal Poupart. 2016. Overfitting at SemEval-2016 Task 3: Detecting semantically similar questions in community question answering forums with word embeddings. In *Proceedings of the 10th International Workshop on Semantic Evaluation*, SemEval '16, San Diego, CA.

Mengqiu Wang, Noah A. Smith, and Teruko Mitamura. 2007. What is the Jeopardy model? A quasi-synchronous grammar for QA. In *Proceedings of the 2007 Joint Conference on Empirical Methods in Natural Language Processing and Computational Natural Language Learning*, EMNLP-CoNLL '07, pages 22–32, Prague, Czech Republic.

Guoshun Wu and Man Lan. 2016. ECNU at SemEval-2016 Task 3: Exploring traditional method and deep learning method for question retrieval and answer ranking in community question answering. In *Proceedings of the 10th International Workshop on Semantic Evaluation*, SemEval '16, San Diego, CA.

Yunfang Wu and Minghua Zhang. 2016. ICL00 at SemEval-2016 Task 3: Translation-based method for cqa system. In *Proceedings of the 10th International Workshop on Semantic Evaluation*, SemEval '16, San Diego, CA.

Xuchen Yao, Benjamin Van Durme, Chris Callison-Burch, and Peter Clark. 2013. Answer extraction as sequence tagging with tree edit distance. In *Proceedings of the 2013 Conference of the North American Chapter of the Association for Computational Linguistics: Human Language Technologies*, NAACL-HLT '13, pages 858–867.

Xiaoqiang Zhou, Baotian Hu, Qingcai Chen, Buzhou Tang, and Xiaolong Wang. 2015a. Answer sequence learning with neural networks for answer selection in community question answering. In *Proceedings of the 53rd Annual Meeting of the Association for Computational Linguistics*, pages 713–718, Beijing, China.

Xiaoqiang Zhou, Baotian Hu, Jiaxin Lin, Yang Xiang, and Xiaolong Wang. 2015b. ICRC-HIT: A deep learning based comment sequence labeling system for answer selection challenge. In *Proceedings of the 9th International Workshop on Semantic Evaluation*, SemEval '15, pages 210–214, Denver, CO.

	Submission	MAP	AvgRec	MRR	P	R	F_1	Acc
1	**Kelp-primary**	**79.19_1**	88.82_1	86.42_1	76.96_1	55.30_8	64.36_5	75.11_2
	ConvKN-contrastive1	78.71	88.98	86.15	77.78	53.72	63.55	74.95
	SUper_team-contrastive1	77.68	88.06	84.76	75.59	55.00	63.68	74.50
2	**ConvKN-primary**	**77.66_2**	88.05_3	84.93_4	75.56_2	58.84_6	66.16_2	75.54_1
3	**SemanticZ-primary**	**77.58_3**	88.14_2	85.21_2	74.13_4	53.05_{10}	61.84_8	73.39_5
	ConvKN-contrastive2	77.29	87.77	85.03	74.74	59.67	66.36	75.41
4	**ECNU-primary**	**77.28_4**	87.52_5	84.09_6	70.46_6	63.36_4	66.72_1	74.31_4
	SemanticZ-contrastive1	77.16	87.73	84.08	75.29	53.20	62.35	73.88
5	**SUper_team-primary**	**77.16_5**	87.98_4	84.69_5	74.43_3	56.73_7	64.39_4	74.50_3
	MTE-NN-contrastive2	76.98	86.98	85.50	58.71	70.28	63.97	67.83
	SUper_team-contrastive2	76.97	87.89	84.58	74.31	56.36	64.10	74.34
	MTE-NN-contrastive1	76.86	87.03	84.36	55.84	77.35	64.86	65.93
	SLS-contrastive2	76.71	87.17	84.38	59.45	67.95	63.41	68.13
	SLS-contrastive1	76.46	87.47	83.27	60.09	69.68	64.53	68.87
6	**MTE-NN-primary**	**76.44_6**	86.74_7	84.97_3	56.28_9	76.22_1	64.75_3	66.27_8
7	**SLS-primary**	**76.33_7**	87.30_6	82.99_7	60.36_8	67.72_3	63.83_6	68.81_7
	ECNU-contrastive2	75.71	86.14	82.53	63.60	66.67	65.10	70.95
	SemanticZ-contrastive2	75.41	86.51	82.52	73.19	50.11	59.49	72.26
	ICRC-HIT-contrastive1	73.34	84.81	79.65	63.43	69.30	66.24	71.28
8	**ITNLP-AiKF-primary**	**71.52_8**	82.67_9	80.26_8	73.18_5	19.71_{12}	31.06_{12}	64.43_9
	ECNU-contrastive1	71.34	83.39	78.62	66.95	41.31	51.09	67.86
9	**ICRC-HIT-primary**	**70.90_9**	83.36_8	77.38_{10}	62.48_7	62.53_5	62.50_7	69.51_6
10	**PMI-cool-primary**	**68.79_{10}**	79.94_{10}	80.00_9	47.81_{12}	70.58_2	57.00_9	56.73_{12}
	UH-PRHLT-contrastive1	67.57	79.50	77.08	54.10	50.11	52.03	62.45
11	**UH-PRHLT-primary**	**67.42_{11}**	79.38_{11}	76.97_{11}	55.64_{10}	46.80_{11}	50.84_{11}	63.21_{10}
	UH-PRHLT-contrastive2	67.33	79.34	76.73	54.97	49.13	51.89	62.97
12	**QAIIIT-primary**	**62.24_{12}**	75.41_{12}	70.58_{12}	50.28_{11}	53.50_9	51.84_{10}	59.60_{11}
	QAIIIT-contrastive2	61.93	75.22	69.95	49.48	49.96	49.72	58.93
	QAIIIT-contrastive1	61.80	75.12	69.76	49.85	50.94	50.39	59.24
	Baseline 1 (chronological)	**59.53**	**72.60**	**67.83**	—	—	—	—
	Baseline 2 (random)	52.80	66.52	58.71	40.56	74.57	52.55	45.26
	Baseline 3 (all 'true')	—	—	—	40.64	100.00	**57.80**	40.64
	Baseline 4 (all 'false')	—	—	—	—	—	—	59.36

Table 3: **Subtask A, English (Question-Comment Similarity):** results for all submissions. The first column shows the rank of the primary runs with respect to the official MAP score. The second column contains the team's name and its submission type (primary vs. contrastive). The following columns show the results for the primary, and then for other, unofficial evaluation measures. The subindices show the rank of the primary runs with respect to the evaluation measure in the respective column.

	Submission	MAP	AvgRec	MRR	P	R	F_1	Acc
	UH-PRHLT-contrastive2	77.33	90.84	83.93	63.57	70.39	66.80	76.71
1	**UH-PRHLT-primary**	**76.70**$_1$	**90.31**$_4$	**83.02**$_4$	**63.53**$_7$	**69.53**$_3$	**66.39**$_3$	**76.57**$_4$
	UH-PRHLT-contrastive1	76.56	90.22	83.02	62.74	70.82	66.53	76.29
	Kelp-contrastive1	76.28	91.33	82.71	63.83	77.25	69.90	77.86
	Kelp-contrastive2	76.27	91.44	84.10	64.06	77.25	70.04	78.00
	SLS-contrastive1	76.17	90.55	85.48	74.39	52.36	61.46	78.14
	SLS-contrastive2	76.09	90.14	84.21	77.21	45.06	56.91	77.29
2	**ConvKN-primary**	**76.02**$_2$	**90.70**$_2$	**84.64**$_1$	**68.58**$_3$	**66.52**$_6$	**67.54**$_2$	**78.71**$_3$
3	**Kelp-primary**	**75.83**$_3$	**91.02**$_1$	**82.71**$_6$	**66.79**$_4$	**75.97**$_2$	**71.08**$_1$	**79.43**$_1$
	ConvKN-contrastive1	75.57	89.64	83.57	63.77	72.53	67.87	77.14
4	**SLS-primary**	**75.55**$_4$	**90.65**$_3$	**84.64**$_1$	**76.33**$_2$	**55.36**$_9$	**64.18**$_6$	**79.43**$_1$
	SUper_team-contrastive1	75.17	88.84	83.66	63.25	63.52	63.38	75.57
5	**ICL00-primary**	**75.11**$_5$	**89.33**$_5$	**83.02**$_4$	**33.29**$_{11}$	**100.00**$_1$	**49.95**$_9$	**33.29**$_{11}$
	ICL00-contrastive1	74.89	89.08	82.71	33.29	100.00	49.95	33.29
6	**SUper_team-primary**	**74.82**$_6$	**88.54**$_7$	**83.66**$_3$	**63.64**$_6$	**57.08**$_8$	**60.18**$_7$	**74.86**$_7$
	ICL00-contrastive2	74.05	89.11	82.79	33.29	100.00	49.95	33.29
7	**ECNU-primary**	**73.92**$_7$	**89.07**$_6$	**81.48**$_7$	**100.00**$_1$	**18.03**$_{11}$	**30.55**$_{11}$	**72.71**$_9$
	ECNU-contrastive1	73.25	88.55	80.81	100.00	18.03	30.55	72.71
	ECNU-contrastive2	71.62	86.55	80.88	54.61	71.24	61.82	70.71
8	**ITNLP-AiKF-primary**	**71.43**$_8$	**87.31**$_8$	**81.28**$_8$	**62.75**$_9$	**68.67**$_4$	**65.57**$_4$	**76.00**$_6$
9	**UniMelb-primary**	**70.20**$_9$	**86.21**$_9$	**78.58**$_{11}$	**63.96**$_5$	**54.08**$_{10}$	**58.60**$_8$	**74.57**$_8$
10	**overfitting-primary**	**69.68**$_{10}$	**85.10**$_{10}$	**80.18**$_9$	**63.20**$_8$	**67.81**$_5$	**65.42**$_5$	**76.14**$_5$
	QAIIIT-contrastive1	69.24	85.24	80.30	38.99	66.09	49.04	54.29
11	**QAIIIT-primary**	**69.04**$_{11}$	**84.53**$_{11}$	**79.55**$_{10}$	**39.53**$_{10}$	**64.81**$_7$	**49.11**$_{10}$	**55.29**$_{10}$
	QAIIIT-contrastive2	46.23	68.07	48.92	36.25	51.50	42.55	53.71
	Baseline 1 (IR)	**74.75**	**88.30**	**83.79**	—	—	—	—
	Baseline 2 (random)	46.98	67.92	50.96	32.58	73.82	45.20	40.43
	Baseline 3 (all 'true')	—	—	—	33.29	100.00	**49.95**	33.29
	Baseline 4 (all 'false')	—	—	—	—	—	—	**66.71**

Table 4: **Subtask B, English (Question-Question Similarity):** results for all submissions. The first column shows the rank of the primary runs with respect to the official MAP score. The second column contains the team's name and its submission type (primary vs. contrastive). The following columns show the results for the primary, and then for other, unofficial evaluation measures. The subindices show the rank of the primary runs with respect to the evaluation measure in the respective column.

	Submission	MAP	AvgRec	MRR	P	R	F_1	Acc
	Kelp-contrastive2	55.58	63.36	61.19	32.21	70.18	44.16	83.41
1	**SUper_team-primary**	**55.41$_1$**	**60.66$_1$**	**61.48$_1$**	**18.03$_7$**	**63.15$_4$**	**28.05$_4$**	**69.73$_8$**
	SUper_team-contrastive2	53.48	59.40	59.09	18.42	66.97	28.89	69.20
2	**Kelp-primary**	**52.95$_2$**	**59.27$_2$**	**59.23$_2$**	**33.63$_5$**	**64.53$_3$**	**44.21$_1$**	**84.79$_5$**
	Kelp-contrastive1	52.95	59.34	58.06	34.08	65.29	44.78	84.96
3	**SemanticZ-primary**	**51.68$_3$**	**53.43$_6$**	**55.96$_4$**	**17.11$_8$**	**57.65$_5$**	**26.38$_5$**	**69.94$_7$**
	SemanticZ-contrastive1	51.46	52.69	55.75	16.94	57.49	26.17	69.69
	MTE-NN-contrastive2	49.49	55.78	51.80	15.68	73.09	25.82	60.76
4	**MTE-NN-primary**	**49.38$_4$**	**55.44$_4$**	**51.56$_7$**	**15.26$_9$**	**76.15$_2$**	**25.43$_6$**	**58.27$_9$**
5	**ICL00-primary**	**49.19$_5$**	**51.07$_7$**	**53.89$_6$**	**9.34$_{10}$**	**100.00$_1$**	**17.09$_8$**	**9.34$_{10}$**
6	**SLS-primary**	**49.09$_6$**	**56.04$_3$**	**55.98$_3$**	**47.85$_2$**	**13.61$_8$**	**21.19$_7$**	**90.54$_2$**
	SemanticZ-contrastive2	48.76	50.72	53.85	16.92	57.34	26.13	69.71
	MTE-NN-contrastive1	48.52	54.71	50.51	15.13	76.61	25.27	57.67
7	**ITNLP-AiKF-primary**	**48.49$_7$**	**55.16$_5$**	**55.21$_5$**	**30.05$_6$**	**50.92$_6$**	**37.80$_2$**	**84.34$_6$**
	ECNU-contrastive1	48.49	53.17	53.47	68.75	8.41	14.99	91.09
	SUper_team-contrastive1	48.23	54.93	54.85	22.81	36.70	28.14	82.49
	ECNU-contrastive2	47.24	53.21	51.89	70.27	7.95	14.29	91.09
	ICL00-contrastive1	47.23	49.71	50.28	9.34	100.00	17.09	9.34
8	**ConvKN-primary**	**47.15$_8$**	**47.46$_{10}$**	**51.43$_8$**	**45.97$_3$**	**8.72$_{10}$**	**14.65$_{10}$**	**90.51$_3$**
	SLS-contrastive1	46.48	53.31	52.53	16.24	85.93	27.32	57.29
9	**ECNU-primary**	**46.47$_9$**	**50.92$_8$**	**51.41$_9$**	**66.29$_1$**	**9.02$_9$**	**15.88$_9$**	**91.07$_1$**
	SLS-contrastive2	46.39	52.83	51.17	16.18	85.63	27.22	57.23
	UH-PRHLT-contrastive1	43.37	48.01	48.43	38.56	32.72	35.40	88.84
	UH-PRHLT-contrastive2	43.32	47.97	48.45	38.21	32.72	35.26	88.77
	ConvKN-contrastive1	43.31	44.19	48.89	30.00	3.21	5.80	90.26
10	**UH-PRHLT-primary**	**43.20$_{10}$**	**47.96$_9$**	**47.79$_{10}$**	**37.65$_4$**	**34.25$_7$**	**35.87$_3$**	**88.56$_4$**
	ICL00-contrastive2	41.32	44.56	43.55	9.34	100.00	17.09	9.34
	ConvKN-contrastive2	41.12	38.89	44.17	33.55	32.11	32.81	87.71
	Baseline 1 (IR+chronological)	**40.36**	**45.97**	**45.83**	—	—	—	—
	Baseline 2 (random)	15.01	11.44	15.19	9.40	75.69	16.73	29.59
	Baseline 3 (all 'true')	—	—	—	9.34	100.00	**17.09**	9.34
	Baseline 4 (all 'false')	—	—	—	—	—	—	**90.66**

Table 5: **Subtask C, English (Question-External Comment Similarity):** results for all submissions. The first column shows the rank of the primary runs with respect to the official MAP score. The second column contains the team's name and its submission type (primary vs. contrastive). The following columns show the results for the primary, and then for other, unofficial evaluation measures. The subindices show the rank of the primary runs with respect to the evaluation measure in the respective column.

	Submission	MAP	AvgRec	MRR	P	R	F_1	Acc
1	**SLS-primary**	**45.83**$_1$	51.01$_1$	53.66$_1$	34.45$_1$	52.33$_3$	41.55$_1$	71.67$_1$
2	**ConvKN-primary**	**45.50**$_2$	50.13$_2$	52.55$_2$	28.55$_2$	64.53$_2$	39.58$_2$	62.10$_3$
	SLS-contrastive1	44.94	49.72	51.58	62.96	2.40	4.62	80.95
3	**RDI_team-primary**	**43.80**$_3$	47.45$_3$	49.21$_3$	19.24$_5$	100.00$_1$	32.27$_4$	19.24$_5$
	SLS-contrastive2	42.95	47.61	49.55	27.20	74.40	39.84	56.76
	RDI_team-contrastive1	42.18	47.03	47.93	19.24	100.00	32.27	19.24
	ConvKN-contrastive2	39.98	43.68	46.41	26.26	68.39	37.95	57.00
	QU-IR-contrastive2	39.07	42.72	44.14	24.90	44.08	31.82	63.66
	RDI_team-contrastive2	38.84	42.98	42.97	19.24	100.00	32.27	19.24
4	**QU-IR-primary**	**38.63**$_4$	44.10$_4$	46.27$_4$	25.50$_3$	45.13$_5$	32.59$_3$	64.07$_2$
	ConvKN-contrastive1	38.33	42.09	43.75	20.38	96.95	33.68	26.58
	QU-IR-contrastive1	37.80	40.96	44.39	23.54	41.89	30.14	62.64
5	**UPC_USMBA-primary**	**29.09**$_5$	30.04$_5$	34.04$_5$	20.14$_4$	51.69$_4$	28.99$_5$	51.27$_4$
	Baseline 1 (chronological)	**28.88**	28.71	30.93	—	—	—	—
	Baseline 2 (random)	29.79	31.00	33.71	19.53	20.66	20.08	68.35
	Baseline 3 (all 'true')	—	—	—	19.24	100.00	**32.27**	19.24
	Baseline 4 (all 'false')	—	—	—	—	—	—	80.76

Table 6: **Subtask D, Arabic (Reranking the correct answers for a new question):** results for all submissions. The first column shows the rank of the primary runs with respect to the official MAP score. The second column contains the team's name and its submission type (primary vs. contrastive). The following columns show the results for the primary, and then for other, unofficial evaluation measures. The subindices show the rank of the primary runs with respect to the evaluation measure in the respective column.

Team ID	Team Affiliation
ConvKN	Qatar Computing Research Institute, HBKU, Qatar; University of Trento, Italy
	(Barrón-Cedeño et al., 2016)
ECNU	East China Normal University, China
	(Wu and Lan, 2016)
ICL00	Institute of Computational Lingustics, Peking University, China
	(Wu and Zhang, 2016)
ICRC-HIT	Intelligence Computing Research Center, Harbin Institute of Technology, China
ITNLP-AiKF	Intelligence Technology and Natural Lang. Processing Lab., Harbin Institute of Technology, China
	(e Jia, 2016)
Kelp	University of Roma, Tor Vergata, Italy; Qatar Computing Research Institute, HBKU, Qatar
	(Filice et al., 2016)
MTE-NN	Qatar Computing Research Institute, HBKU, Qatar
	(Guzmán et al., 2016b)
overfitting	University of Waterloo, Canada
	(Wang and Poupart, 2016)
PMI-cool	Sofia University, Bulgaria
	(Balchev et al., 2016)
QAIIIT	IIIT Hyderabad, India
QU-IR	Qatar University, Qatar
	(Malhas et al., 2016)
RDI_team	RDI Egypt, Cairo University, Egypt
	(Magooda et al., 2016)
SemanticZ	Sofia University, Bulgaria
	(Mihaylov and Nakov, 2016b)
SLS	MIT Computer Science and Artificial Intelligence Lab, USA
	(Mohtarami et al., 2016)
SUper_team	Sofia University, Bulgaria; Qatar Computing Research Institute, HBKU, Qatar
	(Mihaylova et al., 2016)
UH-PRHLT	Pattern Recognition and Human Language Technologies Research Center,
	Universitat Politècnica de València; University of Houston
	(Franco-Salvador et al., 2016)
UniMelb	The University of Melbourne, Australia
	(Hoogeveen et al., 2016)
UPC_USMBA	Universitat Politècnica de Catalunya, Spain; Sidi Mohamed Ben Abdellah University, Morocco
	(El Adlouni et al., 2016)

Table 7: The participating teams and their affiliations.

SemEval-2016 Task 10:
Detecting Minimal Semantic Units and their Meanings (DiMSUM)

Nathan Schneider
School of Informatics
University of Edinburgh
Edinburgh, UK

Dirk Hovy **Anders Johannsen**
Center for Language Technology
University of Copenhagen
Copenhagen, Denmark

Marine Carpuat
Computer Science Dept.
University of Maryland
College Park, Maryland, USA

nschneid@inf.ed.ac.uk, krx628@hum.ku.dk, anders@johannsen.com, marine@cs.umd.edu

Abstract

This task combines the labeling of multiword expressions and supersenses (coarse-grained classes) in an explicit, yet broad-coverage paradigm for lexical semantics. Nine systems participated; the best scored 57.7% F_1 in a multi-domain evaluation setting, indicating that the task remains largely unresolved. An error analysis reveals that a large number of instances in the data set are either hard cases, which no systems get right, or easy cases, which all systems correctly solve.

1 Introduction

Grammatical analysis tasks, e.g., part-of-speech tagging, are rather successful applications of natural language processing (NLP). They are *comprehensive*, i.e., they operate under the assumption that all grammatically-relevant parts of a sentence will be analyzed: We do not expect a POS tagger to only know a subset of the tags in the language. Most POS tags accommodate unseen words and adapt readily to new text genres. Together, these factors indicate a representation which achieves *broad coverage*.

Explicit analysis of lexical semantics, by contrast, has been more difficult to scale to broad coverage owing to limited comprehensiveness and extensibility. The dominant paradigm of fine-grained word sense disambiguation, WordNet (Fellbaum, 1998), is difficult to annotate in corpora, results in considerable data sparseness, and does not readily generalize to out-of-vocabulary words. While the main corpus with WordNet senses, SemCor (Miller et al., 1993), does reflect several text genres, it is hard to expand SemCor-style annotations to new genres, such as social web text or transcribed speech. This severely limits the applicability of SemCor-based NLP tools and restricts opportunities for linguistic studies of lexical semantics in corpora.

To address this limitation, in the DiMSUM 2016 shared task,[1] we challenged participants to analyze the lexical semantics of English sentences with a tagset integrating **multiword expressions** and **noun and verb supersenses** (following Schneider and Smith, 2015), on multiple nontraditional genres of text. By moving away from fine-grained sense inventories and lexicalized, language-specific[2] annotation, we take a step in the direction of broad-coverage, coarse-grained lexical semantic analysis. We believe this departure from the classical lexical semantics paradigm will ultimately prove fruitful for a variety of NLP applications in a variety of genres.

The integrated lexical semantic representation (§2, §3) has been annotated in an extensive benchmark data set comprising several nontraditional domains (§4). Objective, controlled evaluation procedures (§5) facilitate a comparison of the 9 systems submitted as part of the official task (§6). While the systems range in performance, all are below 60% in our composite evaluation, suggesting that further work is needed to make progress on this difficult task.

2 Background

Multiword expressions. Most contemporary approaches to English syntactic and semantic analysis treat space-separated words as the basic units of structure. However, this fails to reflect the basic units of meaning for sentences with non-compositional or idiosyncratic expressions, such as:

(1) The staff leaves a lot to be desired .

(2) I googled restaurants in the area and Fuji Sushi came up and reviews were great so I made a carry out order of : L 17 .

---

[1] http://dimsum16.github.io/

[2] Though our data set is limited to English, the representation is applicable to other languages: see §2.

546

In these sentences, *a lot*, *leaves. . . to be desired*, *Fuji Sushi*, *came up*, *made. . . order*, and *carry out* are all **multiword expressions** (MWEs): their combined meanings can be thought of as "prepackaged" in a single lexical expression that happens to be written with spaces. MWEs such as these have attracted a great deal of attention within computational semantics; see Baldwin and Kim (2010) for a review. Schneider et al. (2014b) introduced an English corpus resource annotated for heterogenous MWEs, suitable for training and evaluating general-purpose MWE identification systems (Schneider et al., 2014a). Prior to that, most MWE evaluations were focused on particular constructions such as noun compounds (recently: Constant and Sigogne, 2011; Green et al., 2012; Ramisch et al., 2012; Vincze et al., 2013), though the corpus and identification system of Vincze et al. (2011) targets several kinds of MWEs.

Importantly, the MWEs in Schneider et al.'s (2014b) corpus are not required to be contiguous, but may contain **gaps** (viz.: *made. . . order*). The corpus also contains qualitative labels indicating the strength of MWEs, either **strong** (mostly non-compositional) or **weak** (compositional but idiomatic). For simplicity we only include strong MWEs in this task.

Supersenses. As noted above, relying on WordNet-like fine-grained, lexicalized **senses** creates problems for annotating at a large scale and covering new domains and languages. Named entity recognition (NER) does not suffer from these problems, as it uses a much smaller number of coarse-grained classes. However, these classes only apply to a subset of the nouns in a sentence and exclude verbs and adjectives. They therefore provide far from complete coverage in a corpus.

Noun and verb **supersenses** (Ciaramita and Altun, 2006) offer a middle ground in granularity: they generalize named entity classes to cover all nouns (with 26 classes), but also cover verbs (15 classes)—see table 1—and provide a human-interpretable high-level clustering. WordNet supersenses for adjectives and adverbs nominally exist, but are based on morphosyntactic rather than semantic properties. There is, however, recent work on developing supersense taxonomies for English adjectives and

N:TOPS	N:OBJECT	V:COGNITION
N:ACT	N:PERSON	V:COMMUNICATION
N:ANIMAL	N:PHENOMENON	V:COMPETITION
N:ARTIFACT	N:PLANT	V:CONSUMPTION
N:ATTRIBUTE	N:POSSESSION	V:CONTACT
N:BODY	N:PROCESS	V:CREATION
N:COGNITION	N:QUANTITY	V:EMOTION
N:COMMUNICATION	N:RELATION	V:MOTION
N:EVENT	N:SHAPE	V:PERCEPTION
N:FEELING	N:STATE	V:POSSESSION
N:FOOD	N:SUBSTANCE	V:SOCIAL
N:GROUP	N:TIME	V:STATIVE
N:LOCATION	V:BODY	V:WEATHER
N:MOTIVE	V:CHANGE	

Table 1: The 41 noun and verb supersenses in WordNet.

prepositions (Tsvetkov et al., 2014; Schneider et al., 2015).

The inventory for nouns and verbs originates from the top-level organization of WordNet, but can be applied directly to annotate new data—including out-of-vocabulary words in English or other languages (Schneider et al., 2012; Johannsen et al., 2014). Similar to NER, supersense tagging approaches have generally used statistical sequence models and have been evaluated in English, Italian, Chinese, Arabic, and Danish.[3]

Features based on supersenses have been exploited in downstream semantics tasks such as preposition sense disambiguation, noun compound interpretation, question generation, and metaphor detection (Ye and Baldwin, 2007; Hovy et al., 2010; Tratz and Hovy, 2010; Heilman, 2011; Hovy et al., 2013; Tsvetkov et al., 2013).

Relationship between MWEs and supersenses. We believe that MWEs and supersenses should be tightly coupled: idiomatic combinations such as MWEs are best labeled holistically, since their joint supersense category will often differ from that of the individual words. For example, *spill the beans* in its literal interpretation would receive supersenses V:CONTACT and N:FOOD, whereas the idiomatic interpretation, 'divulge a secret', is represented as an MWE holistically tagged as V:COMMUNICATION. Schneider and Smith (2015) develop this idea at

---

[3]Evaluations used English SemCor (Ciaramita and Altun, 2006; Paaß and Reichartz, 2009), English-Italian MultiSemCor (Picca et al., 2008, 2009; Attardi et al., 2010), the Italian Syntactic-Semantic Treebank and Italian Wikipedia (Attardi et al., 2010; Rossi et al., 2013), Chinese Cilin (Qiu et al., 2011), Arabic Wikipedia (Schneider et al., 2013), and the Danish CLARIN Reference Corpus (Martínez Alonso et al., 2015).

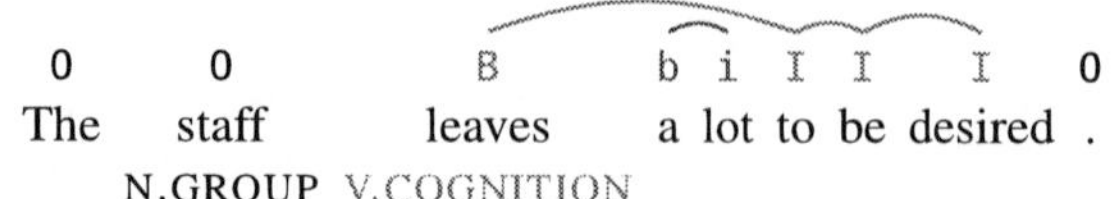

Figure 1: Illustration of the target representation. MWE positional markers are shown above the sentence and noun and verb supersenses below the sentence. Links illustrate the behavior of the MWE tags. The supersense labeling must respect the MWEs; thus, V.COGNITION applies to a four-word unit—*to*, *be*, and *desired* must not receive separate supersenses from *leaves*.

length, and provide a web reviews data set with the integrated annotation. Here, we expand the paradigm to additional domains and compare the performance of several systems.

3 Representation

The analysis for each sentence is represented as a sequence of paired MWE and supersense tags. Figure 1 illustrates the MWE part above the sentence and the supersense part below the sentence.

The MWE portion is a BIO-style (Ramshaw and Marcus, 1995) positional marker. Of the schemes discussed by Schneider et al. (2014a), we adopt the 6-tag scheme, which uses case to allow gaps in an MWE (lowercase tag variants mark tokens within a gap). The positions are thus O, o, B, b, I, i. Systems are expected to ensure that the full tag sequence for a sentence is valid: global validity can be enforced with first-order constraints to prohibit invalid bigrams such as O I and b I (see Schneider et al., 2014a for details).

Because strong MWEs receive a supersense as a unit (if at all), I and i are never accompanied by a supersense label. O or o indicates that the token is not part of any MWE, but many such tokens do bear a noun or verb supersense.

This task uses a CoNLL-style main **file format** consisting of one line per token, each line having 9 tab-delimited columns. Scripts to convert to and from the .sst format, which displays one sentence per line and contains annotations in a JSON data structure, are provided as well.

4 Data

The task built upon two existing data sets of social web text, which were harmonized to form the training data. Four new samples from three domains were newly annotated to form the test set. The train and test sets are summarized in tables 2 and 3 and are publicly available on the web.[4]

The domains covered are **online customer reviews**, **tweets**, and **TED talks**. This section describes, for each domain, how its component data sets were sampled, preprocessed, and annotated.

4.1 Annotation Process

We compiled data sets from various sources, with varying degrees of existing pre-annotation. Unless already provided, we added Universal POS tags as defined by the Universal Dependencies project (Nivre et al., 2015), and baseline supersenses (heuristically using the most frequent WordNet sense, and in some cases grouping sequences of proper nouns as MWEs). The pre-annotated supersenses were then manually corrected by a trained annotator, who simultaneously annotated the sentence for comprehensive MWEs.

The annotator (a linguist) was trained by the first author of this paper using Schneider and Smith's (2015) web interface and annotation guidelines. Prior to starting on the data sets for this task, the annotator devoted approximately 8 hours to training practice on a separate data set which already had a gold standard. Periodic feedback was given on initial annotations as the annotator grew accustomed to the conventions. The annotator spent approximately 50 hours on DiMSUM data (not including the initial training phase), which amounts to roughly 90 seconds per sentence.

In order to estimate inter-annotator agreement (IAA), the first author independently annotated a sample of Ritter tweets (§4.3) in 6 groups of 11 sentences, spaced out across the main annotator's annotation batches. IAA estimates for these sets ranged from 60% to 75% F_1 for MWEs, and 67%–80% accuracy for supersenses (on tokens which had supersenses in both annotations). Resources did not allow for more systematic double annotation and IAA estimation throughout the data.

The test set newly annotated for this task comprises exactly 1,000 sentences and exactly 16,500 words. 3,120 word tokens (19%) differ from the pre-annotation with respect to gold MWE boundaries

---

[4] https://github.com/dimsum16/dimsum-data

	Domain	Source corpus	UPOS (UD 1.2–style)	Docs	Sents	Words	w/s	#lemmas
Train	REVIEWS	STREUSLE 2.1 (Schneider and Smith, 2015)	Conv. from PTB parses	723	3,812	55,579	14.6	5,052
Train	TWEETS	Lowlands (tweets w/ URLs) (Johannsen et al., 2014)	Conv. from Petrov-style	N/A	200	3,062	15.3	1,201
Train	TWEETS	Ritter (Ritter et al., 2011; Johannsen et al., 2014)	Conv. from Petrov-style	N/A	787	15,185	19.3	3,819
		Train Total			4,799	73,826	15.4	7,988
Test	REVIEWS	Trustpilot (Hovy and Søgaard, 2015)	Conv. from Petrov-style	N.A.	340	6,357	18.7	1,365
Test	TWEETS	Tweebank (Kong et al., 2014)	Conv. from TweetNLP POS in FUDG parses	N/A	500	6,627	13.3	1,786
Test	TED	NAIST-NTT (⊂ IWSLT train) (Cettolo et al., 2012; Neubig et al., 2014)	Conv. from PTB parses	10	100	2,187	21.9	630
Test	TED	IWSLT test (Cettolo et al., 2012)	Auto	6	60	1,329	22.2	457
		Test Total			1,000	16,500	16.5	3,160
		REVIEWS Total			4,152	61,936	14.9	5,477
		TWEETS Total			1,487	24,874	16.7	5,464
		TED Total			160	3,516	22.0	900
		Grand Total			5,799	90,326	15.6	9,321

Table 2: Source datasets and preprocessing to obtain 17-tag Universal POS tags (UPOS) version 1.2. Most sources already contained some form of POS tags, which we automatically converted to UPOS. We added missing necessary distinctions—e.g., UD-style UPOS distinguishes auxiliaries from main verbs, but Petrov-style (Petrov et al., 2011), PTB (Marcus et al., 1993), or TweetNLP (Owoputi et al., 2013) POS tagsets do not. Disambiguation was done manually or via a gold parse, where available. We also modified the tokenization of the Tweebank data, to be consistent with UPOS conventions for English (e.g., separating clitics).

Only some portions of the data group sentences into documents: N/A = not applicable; N.A. = not available.

	Domain	Source corpus	MWEs+Supersenses	Words	MWEs	Gappy MWEs		% tokens in MWE	N SS units	MWE	V SS units	MWE
Train	REVIEWS	STREUSLE	Gold	55,579	3,117	397	13%	13%	9,112	13%	7,689	13%
Train	TWEETS	Lowlands	Gold—revised	3,062	276	5	2%	22%	741	31%	281	7%
Train	TWEETS	Ritter	Gold—revised	15,185	839	65	8%	13%	2,738	20%	1,893	10%
		Train Total		73,826	4,232	467	11%	13%	12,591	16%	9,863	12%
Test	REVIEWS	Trustpilot	Gold—new	6,357	327	13	4%	12%	1,055	23%	848	6%
Test	TWEETS	Tweebank	Gold—new	6,627	362	20	6%	13%	899	21%	911	8%
Test	TED	NAIST-NTT	Gold—new	2,187	93	2	2%	9%	373	16%	278	7%
Test	TED	IWSLT test	Gold—new	1,329	55	1	2%	9%	228	15%	153	3%
		Test Total		16,500	837	36	4%	12%	2,555	21%	2,190	7%
		REVIEWS Total		61,936	3,444	410	12%	13%	10,167	14%	8,537	12%
		TWEETS Total		24,874	1,477	90	6%	14%	4,378	22%	3,085	9%
		TED Total		3,516	148	3	2%	9%	601	16%	431	6%
		Grand Total		90,326	5,069	503	10%	13%	15,146	17%	12,053	11%

Table 3: Annotated datasets: status of lexical semantic annotations (retained, revised, or newly annotated for this task) per subcorpus; word token and MWE instance counts; number and proportion (out of all MWEs) that are gappy; proportion of tokens that belong to an MWE; number of units labeled with a noun supersense, and proportion that are MWEs; likewise for verb supersenses.

Additional statistics relatively consistent across domains: MWEs per word: mean/median .055 (lowest: TED, .044; highest: STREUSLE, .090). Supersenses per word: mean/median 0.3. Just 8 MWEs contain more than one gap (all in STREUSLE or Ritter).

and/or supersenses.[5] In addition, portions of the training data were reannotated for improved quality and consistency with the STREUSLE annotations, as explained below.

4.2 REVIEWS

Training. The REVIEWS part of the training data consists of the STREUSLE corpus (Schneider et al., 2014b; Schneider and Smith, 2015),[6] comprising comprehensive multiword expression and supersense annotations on a 55,000-token portion of the English Web Treebank (EWTB; Bies et al., 2012) made up of 723 online user reviews for services (such as restaurants and beauticians).

STREUSLE annotation was done by linguists, who took pains to establish conventions and resolve disagreements. Each sentence was annotated independently by at least 2 annotators; disagreements were resolved by negotiation.

The task release is based on version 2.1 of STREUSLE, with weak MWEs removed and Penn Treebank–style POS tags replaced with Universal POS tags.[7]

Test. The test portion comprises 340 sentences (6,357 tokens) from the online review site Trustpilot, a subset of the data used in Hovy and Søgaard (2015) (the website as a general resource was described in Hovy et al. (2015)). The reviews were chosen to obtain a demographic balance (by age, gender, and location), and contained gold POS tags.

4.3 TWEETS

Training. Johannsen et al. (2014) recently annotated two samples of 987 Twitter messages (18,000 words) with supersenses: (a) the POS+NER-annotated data set of Ritter et al. (2011), and (b) Plank et al.'s (2014) sample of 200 tweets.[8] Annotators were shown pre-annotations from a heuristic supersense chunking/tagging system (based on

the most frequent sense of each word) and asked to correct the boundaries and supersense labels. Though there was no explicit MWE annotation phase, many of the multiword chunks tagged with a noun or verb supersense would be considered MWEs.

We fully reannotated both data sets to match the conventions of the REVIEWS data from the STREUSLE corpus. The annotator examined every sentence and corrected any MWE or supersense decisions deemed to be inconsistent with the guidelines.

Test. Our test set consists of 500 tweets (6,627 tokens) taken from the Tweebank corpus (Kong et al., 2014),[9] which already contained some gold-standard MWEs. We converted the POS tags from gold ARK TweetNLP POS + FUDG dependencies to UPOS and had an annotator supply supersenses.

4.4 TED TALKS

Test. To test the broad-coverage aspect of the submitted systems, the test set contained a "surprise" domain. We opted to sample transcribed sentences from TED talks. Because individual TED talks tend to heavily repeat vocabulary, we took the first 10 sentences from each of 16 documents in order to achieve a lexically diverse sample. Specifically, we chose (a) 100 sentences (2,187 tokens) from the 10 talks in the NAIST-NTT Ted Talk Treebank[10] (Neubig et al., 2014) (which in turn is a subset of the IWSLT training data); and (b) 60 sentences (1,329 tokens) from the IWSLT test data (Cettolo et al., 2012).[11] The latter 6 documents were chosen to maximize language pair diversity.[12]

We induced parts of speech by conversion from the gold PTB trees for the NAIST-NTT data, and

---

[5]On the surface, this might be taken to mean that the accuracy of the heuristic baseline used for pre-annotation is 81%. However, because the annotator saw the pre-annotation, we expect that this agreement rate is higher than if the gold standard had been produced from scratch.

[6]http://www.ark.cs.cmu.edu/LexSem/

[7]The PTB-to-UPOS conversion script is available at: http://tiny.cc/ptb2upos

[8]The supersense-annotated tweets are available at https://github.com/coastalcph/supersense-data-twitter.

[9]http://www.cs.cmu.edu/~ark/TweetNLP/

[10]http://ahclab.naist.jp/resource/tedtreebank/

[11]https://wit3.fbk.eu/

[12]These 6 talks are known to have been translated from English into (at least) the following languages: {ar, de, es, fa, he, hi, it, ko, nl, th, vi, zh}. Additionally, we note that 4 of the documents have Czech (cs) translations, while the other 2 have French (fr) translations.

Neubig et al. (2014) report that all the 10 documents in the NAIST-NTT Treebank have been translated from English into the following 18 languages: {ar, bg, de, el, es, fr, he, it, ja, ko, nl, pl, pt-BR, ro, ru, tr, zh-CN, zh-TW}. Many additional languages are represented for subsets of the documents.

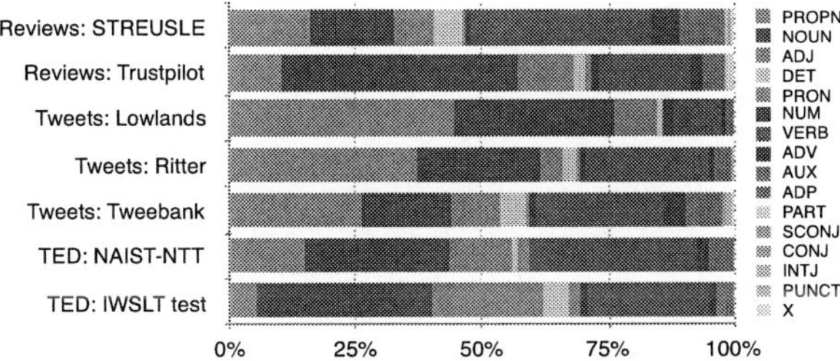

Figure 2: Counts of MWE occurrences, grouped by the POS of the first word in the MWE. Blue bars represent POSes that tend to start nominal MWEs; red bars roughly capture verbal MWEs.

for the remaining data, by automatic tagging with an averaged structured perceptron model (Rungsted[13]) trained on the English Universal Dependencies v1.2 treebank (Nivre et al., 2015).[14]

4.5 Comparing Domains

A natural question to ask about lexical semantic annotations is whether we observe strong differences between domains. For example, which kinds of multiword expressions and which kinds of supersenses occur more often in some domains than in others? In this section, we report our observations but do not make any strong claims about their generality, for the following reasons: the samples are not necessarily representative of their domains overall, and, in fact, may have been sampled in a biased way (e.g., the Lowlands sample was limited to tweets containing a URL, and as a result, most of these tweets are headlines and advertisements). Furthermore, the annotation procedures differed by subcorpus, likely biasing the results.

MWEs. Figure 2 summarizes MWEs in the seven subcorpora with respect to syntactic status. Colors represent the POS tag of the first word in the MWE. Starting with proper nouns, the blue bars indicate POS tags that tend to begin nominal MWEs (noun, adjective, determiner, etc.). Red bar POS tags are characteristic of verbal MWEs. The remaining bars are prepositional (dark green) and other miscellaneous tags, which collectively comprise no more than 10% of the MWEs in each subcorpus.

It is worth noting that in this plot, subcorpora within the same domain are sometimes more diver-

gent than subcorpora in different domains. Lowlands stands out as having a large share of proper noun MWEs—presumably due to the headline-oriented nature of the sample. STREUSLE has the smallest proportion of nominal MWEs, perhaps owing to the way it was annotated: initial rounds of STREUSLE annotation targeted MWEs only, with noun and verb supersenses added only later; whereas in the other data sets, MWE and supersense annotation were performed jointly, so annotator attention may have been focused on nominal and verbal expressions rather than other MWEs.

Supersenses. In the spirit of Schneider et al. (2012), we performed an analysis to see which supersenses were more characteristic of some domains than others. Figure 3 plots the relative frequency (out of all supersense-labeled units) of each supersense in each of the three domains. We use the REVIEWS domain as base frequency: relative to that, the x-axis is the supersense's occurrence rate in the TWEETS domain, and the y-axis represents the rate for the TED talks.

These plots show some clear outliers: among nouns (left plot), N.GROUP and N.FOOD are over-represented in REVIEWS relative to the other domains—unsurprising because restaurants and other businesses are prominent in this subcorpus. On the other hand, N.PERSON is underrepresented in REVIEWS. N.TIME and N.COMMUNICATION are more popular in the TWEETS domain than the others. Among verbs (right plot), V.STATIVE is underrepresented, apparently due to the relative rarity of the copula (which often can be safely omitted in headlines and other telegraphic messages without obscuring the meaning).

5 Evaluation

Submission conditions. We invited submissions in multiple data conditions. The **open** condition encouraged participants to make wide use of any and all available resources, including for distant or direct supervision. A **closed** condition encouraged controlled comparisons of algorithms by limiting their training to specific resources distributed for the task. Lastly, we allowed for a **semi-supervised closed** condition, in which use of a specific large unla-

---

[13] https://github.com/coastalcph/rungsted
[14] http://hdl.handle.net/11234/1-1548

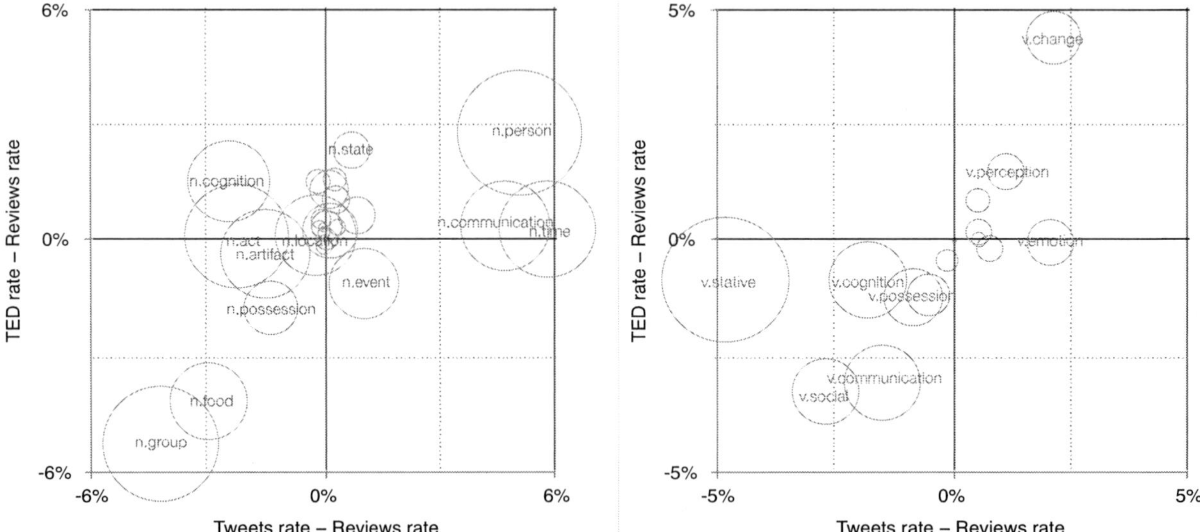

Figure 3: Supersense rate differences by domains, compared to reviews data set. Circle area proportional to the supersense's *total* frequency across all domains. Noun supersenses on the left, verb supersenses on the right. Each domain's rate is microaveraged across its subcorpora; thus, larger subcorpora weigh more heavily than smaller subcorpora in the same domain.

beled corpus—the Yelp Academic Dataset[15]—was permitted. Teams were permitted to submit no more than one run per condition. Only one team submitted a system in the semi-supervised closed condition.

All conditions had access to: 1) the annotated data we provided; 2) Brown clusterings (Brown et al., 1992) computed from large corpora of tweets and web reviews;[16] and 3) the English WordNet lexicon. The input at test time included POS tags.

No sentence-level metadata was provided in the input at test time: test set sentence IDs were obscured to hide the source domain, and the order of sentences was randomized to remove document structure. The training data, however, marked the domain from which the sentence was drawn (REVIEWS or TWEETS); systems were free to make use of this information, so long as it was not required as part of the input at test time.

Scoring. We provided an evaluation script to allow participants to check the format of system output and to compute all official scores.

The **MWE** measure looks at precision, recall, and F_1 of the identified MWEs. Tokens not involved in a

predicted or gold MWE do not factor into this measure. To award partial credit for partial overlap between a predicted MWE and a gold MWE, these scores are computed based on *links* between consecutive tokens in an expression (Schneider et al., 2014a). The tokens must appear in order but do not need to be adjacent. The precision is the proportion of predicted links whose words both belong to the same expression in the gold standard. Recall is the same as precision, but swapping the predicted and gold annotations.[17] Figure 4 defines this measure in detail and illustrates the calculations for an example.

To isolate the **supersense** classification performance, we compute precision, recall, and F_1 of the supersense-labeled word tokens. The numerator of both precision and recall is the number of tokens labeled with the correct supersense. (This interacts slightly with MWE identification, however, as supersenses are only marked on the first token of MWEs. We do not mark supersenses on all words of the MWE to avoid giving MWEs a disproportionate influence on the supersense score.)

Finally, **combined** precision, recall, and F_1 aggregate the MWE and supersense subscores. The combined precision ratio is computed from the MWE

---

[15]https://www.yelp.com/academic_dataset

[16]I.e., TweetNLP clusters (http://www.cs.cmu.edu/~ark/TweetNLP/) and the Yelp Academic Dataset clusters used in AMALGrAM (http://www.cs.cmu.edu/~ark/LexSem/).

[17]This computation on the basis of links is a slight simplification of the MUC coreference measure (Vilain et al., 1995).

> *MWE Precision:* The proportion of predicted links whose words both belong to the same expression in the gold standard.
>
> *MWE Recall:* Same as precision, but swapping the predicted and gold annotations.

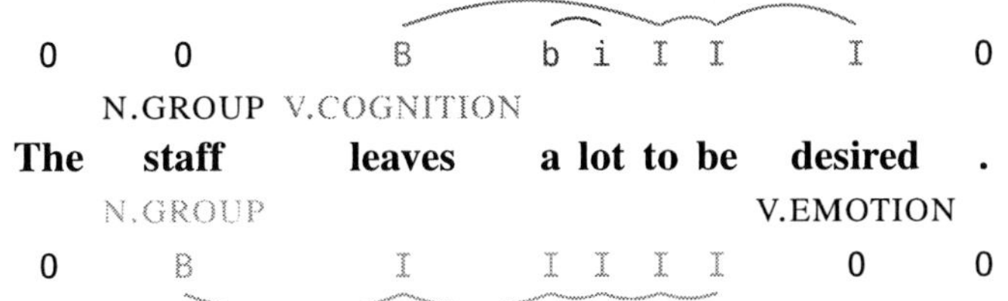

Figure 4: A REVIEWS sentence with MWE and supersense analyses: gold above and hypothetical prediction below. MWE precision of the bottom annotation relative to the top one is 2/5. (Note that a link between words w_1 and w_2 is "matched" if, in the other annotation, there is a path between w_1 and w_2.) The MWE recall value is 3/4. Supersense precision and recall are both 1/2. Combined precision/recall scores add the respective subscores' numerators and denominators: thus, combined precision is $\frac{2+1}{5+2}$ = 3/7, and combined recall is $\frac{3+1}{4+2}$ = 2/3. Combined F_1 is their harmonic mean, i.e. 12/23.

and supersense precision ratios by adding their numerators and denominators, and likewise for combined recall (see the example in figure 4).

Within each domain, scores are computed as microaverages. The official tri-domain scores reported here are domain macroaverages: per-domain measures are aggregated with the three domains weighted equally. The main score, tri-domain combined F_1, is the arithmetic mean of the three per-domain combined F_1 scores. (Some system papers report domain microaverages, which give less influence to the TED domain because it is the smallest of the domains in the test set.)

6   Entries and Results

Six teams[18] participated in the task, submitting a total of nine unique system entries prior to the deadline. We give an overview of these systems and analyze their performance.

6.1   Synopsis of approaches

From the **UFRGS&LIF** team (Cordeiro et al., 2016), S106 detects MWEs by heuristic pattern-matching against sequences in the training data, and predicts the most frequent supersense observed for each type in the training data.

From the **UTU** team (Björne and Salakoski, 2016), S211, S254, and S255 match word sequences against a variety of resources and then choose a

supersense with an ensemble of classifiers. The method performs reasonably well for supersenses, but is weak at detecting MWEs.

The **UW-CSE** team (Hosseini et al., 2016) experimented with a sequence CRF as well as a double-chained CRF, with separate chains for MWE tags and supersenses, and some parameters shared between them. The closed-condition and open-condition feature sets were drawn from AMALGrAM (Schneider and Smith, 2015). Of the official submissions, S248 used a single-chain CRF and S249 a double-chained CRF. A full comparison demonstrates that the double-chained CRF performs best on the combined measure in both the closed and open conditions.

From the **ICL-HD** team (Kirilin et al., 2016), S214 uses the AMALGrAM sequence tagger (Schneider and Smith, 2015) with an augmented feature set that leverages word embeddings and a knowledge base. The word embedding features, the knowledge base–derived features, and their union all improve over the condition with no new features, with respect to both MWE performance and supersense performance. The best results for the combined measure are obtained with the word embedding features (but not the knowledge base features). The word embeddings are shown to be somewhat complementary to AMALGrAM's Brown cluster features: ablating either reduces performance.

From the **WHUNlp** team (Tang et al., 2016), S108 uses a pipeline where a sequence CRF first identifies

---

[18]None of the teams included any DiMSUM organizers.

#	System	Team	Score	Resources
1	S214	ICL-HD	57.77	++
	S249	UW-CSE	57.71	++
	S248	UW-CSE	57.10	
2	S106	UFRGS&LIF	50.27	
3	S227	VectorWeavers	49.94	++
4	S255	UTU	47.13	++
5	S211	UTU	46.17	+
	S254	UTU	45.79	
6	S108	WHUNlp	25.71	

Table 4: Main results on the test set. Scores are tri-domain combined F_1 percentages. Resource conditions are described in §6.2.

MWEs, and a maximum entropy classifier then predicts a supersense independently for each lexical expression. Each of these models has a small number of feature templates recording words and POS tags.

From the **VectorWeavers** team (Scherbakov et al., 2016), S227 relies on neural network classifiers to detect MWE boundaries and label supersenses, using features based on word embeddings and syntactic parses. Results show that syntax helps identify MWE boundaries accurately, and that simple incremental composition functions can help construct useful MWE representations.

6.2 Overall results

The main results appear in table 4. The first column of table 4 gives the ranking of the systems. Several systems may share a rank if they do not produce significantly different predictions, as detailed below. The score is the combined supersense and MWE measure, macroaveraged over the three test set domains as described above. The final column indicates the resource condition: systems entered in the open condition (all resources allowed) are designated "++"; "+" indicates the more restricted semi-supervised closed condition, while the remaining systems are in the closed condition (most restrictive). Details of the resource conditions and scoring appear in §5.

Ranking and significance. The overall best scoring system, with a combined measure of 57.77%, is S214. The competition, however, is close: S249 scored 57.71%, and S248 obtained a combined score of 57.10%. To check whether the predictions of the systems are significantly different from each other,

Submission	REVIEWS	TED	TWEETS
Multiword expressions			
S106	49.57	56.76	51.16
S108	26.39	33.44	34.18
S211 +	9.07	18.28	15.76
S214 ++	53.37	**57.14**	59.49
S227 ++	36.18	41.76	39.32
S248	53.96	52.35	54.48
S249 ++	**54.80**	53.48	**61.09**
S254	7.05	16.30	6.34
S255 ++	8.68	20.11	15.50
Supersenses			
S106	50.93	49.61	49.20
S108	25.82	24.68	24.63
S211 +	52.00	51.40	49.95
S214 ++	**57.66**	**60.06**	55.99
S227 ++	51.36	52.00	51.70
S248	57.19	59.11	56.82
S249 ++	57.00	59.17	**57.46**
S254	52.68	51.44	49.66
S255 ++	51.98	53.28	51.11
Combined score			
S106	50.71	50.57	49.54
S108	25.86	25.39	25.87
S211 +	46.19	47.90	44.42
S214 ++	**56.98**	**59.71**	56.63
S227 ++	49.25	50.82	49.74
S248	56.66	58.26	56.38
S249 ++	56.61	58.33	**58.18**
S254	46.57	47.82	42.99
S255 ++	46.15	49.81	45.44

Table 5: Per-domain evaluation results. Figures are F_1 percentages. The best value in each section and column is in bold. Refer to table 4 for the identities of the systems.

we ran McNemar's test, a paired test that operates directly on the predicted system output. A consequence of this is that we do not directly test whether the computed *scores* are significantly different from each other, only whether the *predictions* are.

According to McNemar's test, the predictions of the highest-ranking and the next-highest-ranking system are not significantly different at $p < .05$. The third highest ranking system performs significantly worse than the top system, but is *not* significantly different from the second-place system. We therefore decided to rank all three systems together. In general, adjacent entries in the sorted scoring table are ranked together if the difference between them is not statistically significant according to the test.

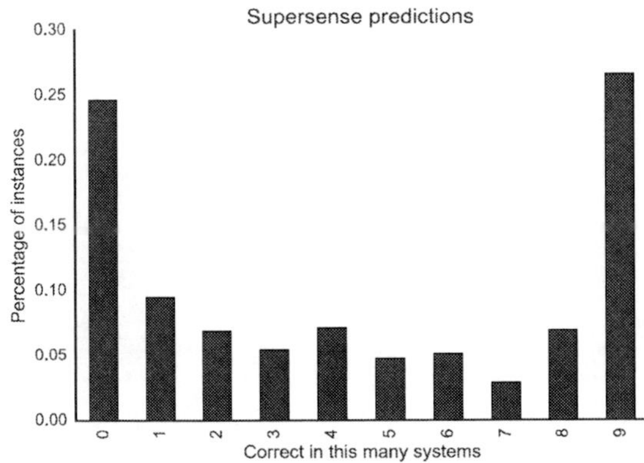

Figure 5: Number of systems predicting the correct supersense (for tokens where there is a gold supersense).

Drilling down. Table 5 offers a more detailed breakdown by domain and subscore (MWEs vs. supersenses vs. combined). The best scores are about 57% for both MWEs and supersenses. Systems S214 and S249 are the clear winners: the former is better in the surprise TED domain—particularly TED MWEs (by nearly 4 points). The latter is slightly better in TWEETS, and the systems are quite close in REVIEWS (the domain with the most training data).

S214 and S249 were in the open condition, taking advantage of additional resources. The best system in the closed condition is S248, which is very similar to S249—and recall that its predictions, overall, are not statistically worse. Table 5 reveals one striking difference, however: in MWE scores for TWEETS, S249 bests S248 by nearly 7 points.

When scores in the 3 domains are compared for each system, there is surprisingly little difference overall. We expected that the TED domain would be most difficult because it is not represented in the training data, but the scores in table 5 give no clear indication that this is the case. Perhaps systems escaped domain bias because the training data included two highly divergent genres; or perhaps other aspects of the data sets (e.g., topic) matter more for this task than differences in genre.

6.3 Easy and hard decisions

Overall, the results clearly show that the joint supersense and MWE tagging task is not yet resolved. Given the wide range of participating systems and previous work, it is reasonable to assume that the task itself is not easy. On the other hand, it is not

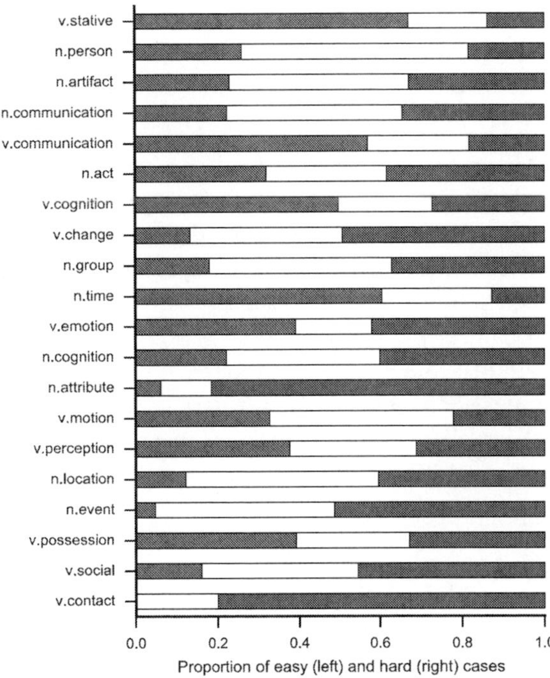

Figure 6: Easy and hard supersense decisions. Shown in blue in the left side of the plot is the proportion of instances of the given supersense type where at most one system gave the *wrong* answer. On the right side in red is the corresponding figure where at most one system gave the *right* answer. Supersenses are sorted by corpus frequency.

uniformly hard. In fact, some decisions are relatively easy, in the sense that most or all systems get them right; whereas others are hard, in that none or very few systems produce the correct answer. Figure 5 explores this for the supersense-tagging subtask. The tallest bars are near the left and right sides of the graph, representing the hard and easy instances, respectively. Hard instances account for about 25% of instances where the gold data has a supersense, which also puts an upper bound on any system combination. Even an oracle system allowed to choose the best prediction for each instance from among all the systems would still not push the accuracy above 75%.

The distribution of easy and hard instances varies a lot between labels, though. As shown for supersenses in figure 6, individual labels range from the fairly easy (e.g. V.STATIVE and V.COMMUNICATION) to the more difficult (e.g. N.ATTRIBUTE and V.CONTACT). The most common

555

supersense, V.STATIVE, is easy because it has few distinct lexical forms (the ten most common lemmas make up more than 77% of the instances). Examples of V.STATIVE lemmas include *be, have, use,* and *get.*

Supersenses may be difficult for more than one reason. For instance, V.CONTACT—e.g. *deliver, receive,* and *take*—has more distinct forms than V.STATIVE and also a more complex mapping between lemmas and supersenses. In contrast, person names, job titles, etc. that should be tagged as N.PERSON are rarely ambiguous with respect to supersense. The main challenge in that case is that the category is open-ended and not in general evident from syntactic structure.

6.4 System correlation

Finally, we examine whether the submitted approaches capture different aspects of the task. I.e., could we produce a better system by combining the individual systems? We cannot estimate this from the results tables, since, combinatorially, there are many ways to obtain a given score. However, we can estimate it from the prediction overlap between systems. The $N \times N$ labeled matrix in figure 7 shows how the N systems relate to each other. Each cell compares the predictions of two systems a and b in the joint supersense and MWE task. The value of a cell $T_{a,b}$ is the number of correct predictions made by a that were not correctly predicted by b. This is an asymmetric measure of predictive similarity. A single low number indicates one out of two things: either the systems are similar, or a is better than b. When the sum $T_{a,b} + T_{b,a}$ is small, the two systems make similar predictions.

Clustering the systems in figure 7 (shown on the left side of the plot) results in groups that correspond to the ranking in table 4. Inside the cluster of systems ranked at 1, the asymmetric predictive advantage ranges between 267 and 469. Lower-ranked systems all have a smaller predictive advantage with respect to the top-ranked systems. The best combination system would thus likely be between two of the rank-1 systems. However, the gains are small, and overall the systems seem to extract the same knowledge, or subsets of the same knowledge, out of the training data.

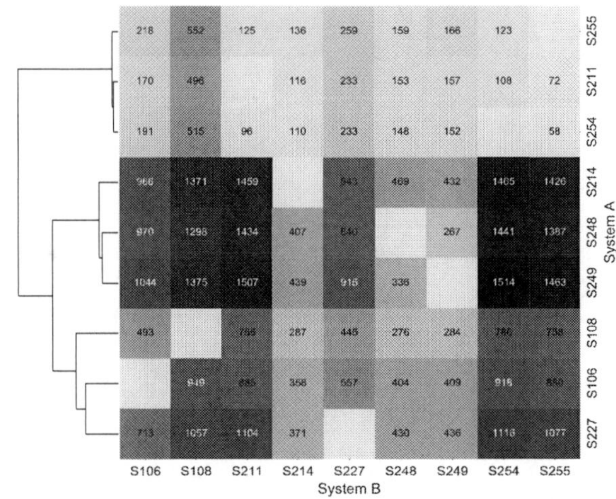

Figure 7: System clusters. Each cell compares the predictions of two systems i and j with respect to a gold standard. The value in the i,j-th cell is the number of predictions that i got right but j did not.

7 Conclusion

This task featured a broad-coverage lexical semantic analysis task that combines MWE identification and supersense tagging. The semantic tagset strikes a balance between the extremely difficult fine-grained distinctions in classical WSD, and the restrictiveness of the NER task. To guard against domain bias, we provided training data from two different genres, namely online reviews and tweets, as well as a test-only data set with TED talk transcripts. The training and test data sets are publicly available at `https://github.com/dimsum16/dimsum-data`.

The best scoring systems obtained 57.7% F_1 on a composite measure over the two subtasks of MWE and supersense tagging, averaged over the three test domains. This level of performance suggests that the task is not yet resolved. Furthermore, our error analysis suggests that the submitted systems arrived at similar generalizations from the training data. Substantially improving performance would thus seem to require novel approaches.

Acknowledgments

We are grateful to Sam Gibbon for the lexical semantic annotation, which was generously supported by Carlsberg infrastructure grant No. CF14-0694.

References

Giuseppe Attardi, Stefano Dei Rossi, Giulia Di Pietro,

Alessandro Lenci, Simonetta Montemagni, and Maria Simi. 2010. A resource and tool for super-sense tagging of Italian texts. In Nicoletta Calzolari, Khalid Choukri, Bente Maegaard, Joseph Mariani, Jan Odijk, Stelios Piperidis, Mike Rosner, and Daniel Tapias, editors, *Proc. of LREC*. Valletta, Malta.

Timothy Baldwin and Su Nam Kim. 2010. Multiword expressions. In Nitin Indurkhya and Fred J. Damerau, editors, *Handbook of Natural Language Processing, Second Edition*. CRC Press, Taylor and Francis Group, Boca Raton, FL.

Ann Bies, Justin Mott, Colin Warner, and Seth Kulick. 2012. English Web Treebank. Technical Report LDC2012T13, Linguistic Data Consortium, Philadelphia, PA. URL http://www.ldc.upenn.edu/Catalog/catalogEntry.jsp?catalogId=LDC2012T13.

Jari Björne and Tapio Salakoski. 2016. UTU at SemEval-2016 Task 10: Binary Classification for Expression Detection (BCED). In *Proc. of SemEval*. San Diego, California, USA.

Peter F. Brown, Peter V. deSouza, Robert L. Mercer, Vincent J. Della Pietra, and Jenifer C. Lai. 1992. Class-based n-gram models of natural language. *Computational Linguistics*, 18(4):467–479.

Mauro Cettolo, Christian Girardi, and Marcello Federico. 2012. WIT^3: Web Inventory of Transcribed and Translated Talks. In Mauro Cettolo, Marcello Federico, Lucia Specia, and Andy Way, editors, *Proc. of EAMT*, pages 261–268. Trento, Italy.

Massimiliano Ciaramita and Yasemin Altun. 2006. Broad-coverage sense disambiguation and information extraction with a supersense sequence tagger. In *Proc. of EMNLP*, pages 594–602. Sydney, Australia.

Matthieu Constant and Anthony Sigogne. 2011. MWU-aware part-of-speech tagging with a CRF model and lexical resources. In *Proc. of the Workshop on Multiword Expressions: from Parsing and Generation to the Real World*, pages 49–56. Portland, Oregon, USA.

Silvio Cordeiro, Carlos Ramisch, and Aline Villavicencio. 2016. UFRGS&LIF at SemEval-2016 Task 10: Rule-based MWE identification and predominant-supersense tagging. In *Proc. of SemEval*. San Diego, California, USA.

Christiane Fellbaum, editor. 1998. *WordNet: an electronic lexical database*. MIT Press, Cambridge, MA.

Spence Green, Marie-Catherine de Marneffe, and Christopher D. Manning. 2012. Parsing models for identifying multiword expressions. *Computational Linguistics*, 39(1):195–227.

Michael Heilman. 2011. *Automatic factual question generation from text*. Ph.D. dissertation, Carnegie Mellon University, Pittsburgh, Pennsylvania. URL http://www.ark.cs.cmu.edu/mheilman/questions/papers/heilman-question-generation-dissertation.pdf.

Mohammad Javad Hosseini, Noah A. Smith, and Su-In Lee. 2016. UW-CSE at SemEval-2016 Task 10: Detecting multiword expressions and supersenses using double-chained conditional random fields. In *Proc. of SemEval*. San Diego, California, USA.

Dirk Hovy, Anders Johannsen, and Anders Søgaard. 2015. User review sites as a resource for large-scale sociolinguistic studies. In *Proc. of WWW*, pages 452–461. Florence, Italy.

Dirk Hovy, Shashank Shrivastava, Sujay Kumar Jauhar, Mrinmaya Sachan, Kartik Goyal, Huying Li, Whitney Sanders, and Eduard Hovy. 2013. Identifying metaphorical word use with tree kernels. In *Proc. of the First Workshop on Metaphor in NLP*, pages 52–57. Atlanta, Georgia, USA.

Dirk Hovy and Anders Søgaard. 2015. Tagging performance correlates with author age. In *Proc. of ACL-IJCNLP*, pages 483–488. Beijing, China.

Dirk Hovy, Stephen Tratz, and Eduard Hovy. 2010. What's in a preposition? Dimensions of sense disambiguation for an interesting word class. In *Coling 2010: Posters*, pages 454–462. Beijing, China.

Anders Johannsen, Dirk Hovy, Héctor Martínez Alonso, Barbara Plank, and Anders Søgaard. 2014. More or less supervised supersense tagging of Twitter. In *Proc. of *SEM*, pages 1–11. Dublin, Ireland.

Angelika Kirilin, Felix Krauss, and Yannick Versley. 2016. ICL-HD at SemEval-2016 Task 10: Improving the detection of minimal semantic units and their meanings with an ontology and word embeddings. In *Proc. of SemEval*. San Diego, California, USA.

Lingpeng Kong, Nathan Schneider, Swabha Swayamdipta, Archna Bhatia, Chris Dyer, and Noah A. Smith. 2014. A dependency parser for tweets. In *Proc. of EMNLP*, pages 1001–1012. Doha, Qatar.

Mitchell P. Marcus, Beatrice Santorini, and Mary Ann Marcinkiewicz. 1993. Building a large annotated corpus of English: the Penn Treebank. *Computational Linguistics*, 19(2):313–330.

Héctor Martínez Alonso, Anders Johannsen, Sussi Olsen, Sanni Nimb, Nicolai Hartvig Sørensen, Anna Braasch, Anders Søgaard, and Bolette Sandford Pedersen. 2015. Supersense tagging for Danish. In Beáta Megyesi, editor, *Proc. of NODALIDA*, pages 21–29. Vilnius, Lithuania.

George A. Miller, Claudia Leacock, Randee Tengi, and Ross T. Bunker. 1993. A semantic concordance. In *Proc. of HLT*, pages 303–308. Plainsboro, NJ, USA.

Graham Neubig, Katsuhito Sudoh, Yusuke Oda, Kevin Duh, Hajime Tsukada, and Masaaki Nagata. 2014. The naist-ntt ted talk treebank. In *International Workshop on Spoken Language Translation*.

Joakim Nivre, Željko Agić, Maria Jesus Aranzabe, Masayuki Asahara, Aitziber Atutxa, Miguel Ballesteros, John Bauer, Kepa Bengoetxea, Riyaz Ahmad Bhat, Cristina Bosco, Sam Bowman, Giuseppe G. A. Celano, Miriam Connor, Marie-Catherine de Marneffe, Arantza Diaz de Ilarraza, Kaja Dobrovoljc, Timothy Dozat, Tomaž Erjavec, Richárd Farkas, Jennifer Foster, Daniel Galbraith, Filip Ginter, Iakes Goenaga, Koldo Gojenola, Yoav Goldberg, Berta Gonzales, Bruno Guillaume, Jan Hajič, Dag Haug, Radu Ion, Elena Irimia, Anders Johannsen, Hiroshi Kanayama, Jenna Kanerva, Simon Krek, Veronika Laippala, Alessandro Lenci, Nikola Ljubešić, Teresa Lynn, Christopher Manning, Cătălina Mărănduc, David Mareček, Héctor Martínez Alonso, Jan Mašek, Yuji Matsumoto, Ryan McDonald, Anna Missilä, Verginica Mititelu, Yusuke Miyao, Simonetta Montemagni, Shunsuke Mori, Hanna Nurmi, Petya Osenova, Lilja Øvrelid, Elena Pascual, Marco Passarotti, Cenel-Augusto Perez, Slav Petrov, Jussi Piitulainen, Barbara Plank, Martin Popel, Prokopis Prokopidis, Sampo Pyysalo, Loganathan Ramasamy, Rudolf Rosa, Shadi Saleh, Sebastian Schuster, Wolfgang Seeker, Mojgan Seraji, Natalia Silveira, Maria Simi, Radu Simionescu, Katalin Simkó, Kiril Simov, Aaron Smith, Jan Štěpánek, Alane Suhr, Zsolt Szántó, Takaaki Tanaka, Reut Tsarfaty, Sumire Uematsu, Larraitz Uria, Viktor Varga, Veronika Vincze, Zdeněk Žabokrtský, Daniel Zeman, and Hanzhi Zhu. 2015. Universal Dependencies 1.2. URL `https://lindat.mff.cuni.`
`cz/repository/xmlui/handle/11234/1-1548`, LINDAT/CLARIN digital library at Institute of Formal and Applied Linguistics, Charles University in Prague.

Olutobi Owoputi, Brendan O'Connor, Chris Dyer, Kevin Gimpel, Nathan Schneider, and Noah A. Smith. 2013. Improved part-of-speech tagging for online conversational text with word clusters. In *Proc. of NAACL-HLT*, pages 380–390. Atlanta, Georgia, USA.

Gerhard Paaß and Frank Reichartz. 2009. Exploiting semantic constraints for estimating supersenses with CRFs. In *Proc. of the Ninth SIAM International Conference on Data Mining*, pages 485–496. Sparks, Nevada.

Slav Petrov, Dipanjan Das, and Ryan McDonald. 2011. A universal part-of-speech tagset. *arXiv:1104.2086 [cs]*. URL `http://arxiv.org/abs/1104.2086`.

Davide Picca, Alfio Massimiliano Gliozzo, and Simone Campora. 2009. Bridging languages by SuperSense entity tagging. In *Proc. of NEWS*, pages 136–142. Suntec, Singapore.

Davide Picca, Alfio Massimiliano Gliozzo, and Massimiliano Ciaramita. 2008. Supersense Tagger for Italian. In Nicoletta Calzolari, Khalid Choukri, Bente Maegaard, Joseph Mariani, Jan Odjik, Stelios Piperidis, and Daniel Tapias, editors, *Proc. of LREC*, pages 2386–2390. Marrakech, Morocco.

Barbara Plank, Dirk Hovy, and Anders Søgaard. 2014. Learning part-of-speech taggers with inter-annotator agreement loss. In *Proc. of EACL*, pages 742–751. Gothenburg, Sweden.

Likun Qiu, Yunfang Wu, Yanqiu Shao, and Alexander Gelbukh. 2011. Combining contextual and structural information for supersense tagging of Chinese unknown words. In *Computational Linguistics and Intelligent Text Processing: Proceedings of the 12th International Conference (CICLing'11)*, volume 6608 of *Lecture Notes in Computer Science*, pages 15–28. Springer, Berlin.

Carlos Ramisch, Vitor De Araujo, and Aline Villavicencio. 2012. A broad evaluation of techniques for automatic acquisition of multiword expressions. In *Proc. of ACL 2012 Student Research Workshop*, pages 1–6. Jeju Island, Korea.

Lance A. Ramshaw and Mitchell P. Marcus. 1995. Text chunking using transformation-based learning. In

Proc. of the Third ACL Workshop on Very Large Corpora, pages 82–94. Cambridge, MA.

Alan Ritter, Sam Clark, Mausam, and Oren Etzioni. 2011. Named entity recognition in tweets: an experimental study. In *Proc. of EMNLP*, pages 1524–1534. Edinburgh, Scotland, UK.

Stefano Dei Rossi, Giulia Di Pietro, and Maria Simi. 2013. Description and results of the SuperSense tagging task. In Bernardo Magnini, Francesco Cutugno, Mauro Falcone, and Emanuele Pianta, editors, *Evaluation of Natural Language and Speech Tools for Italian*, number 7689 in Lecture Notes in Computer Science, pages 166–175. Springer Berlin Heidelberg.

Andreas Scherbakov, Ekaterina Vylomova, Fei Liu, and Timothy Baldwin. 2016. VectorWeavers at SemEval-2016 Task 10: From incremental meaning to semantic unit (phrase by phrase). In *Proc. of SemEval*. San Diego, California, USA.

Nathan Schneider, Emily Danchik, Chris Dyer, and Noah A. Smith. 2014a. Discriminative lexical semantic segmentation with gaps: running the MWE gamut. *Transactions of the Association for Computational Linguistics*, 2:193–206.

Nathan Schneider, Behrang Mohit, Chris Dyer, Kemal Oflazer, and Noah A. Smith. 2013. Supersense tagging for Arabic: the MT-in-the-middle attack. In *Proc. of NAACL-HLT*, pages 661–667. Atlanta, Georgia, USA.

Nathan Schneider, Behrang Mohit, Kemal Oflazer, and Noah A. Smith. 2012. Coarse lexical semantic annotation with supersenses: an Arabic case study. In *Proc. of ACL*, pages 253–258. Jeju Island, Korea.

Nathan Schneider, Spencer Onuffer, Nora Kazour, Emily Danchik, Michael T. Mordowanec, Henrietta Conrad, and Noah A. Smith. 2014b. Comprehensive annotation of multiword expressions in a social web corpus. In Nicoletta Calzolari, Khalid Choukri, Thierry Declerck, Hrafn Loftsson, Bente Maegaard, Joseph Mariani, Asuncion Moreno, Jan Odijk, and Stelios Piperidis, editors, *Proc. of LREC*, pages 455–461. Reykjavík, Iceland.

Nathan Schneider and Noah A. Smith. 2015. A corpus and model integrating multiword expressions and supersenses. In *Proc. of NAACL-HLT*, pages 1537–1547. Denver, Colorado.

Nathan Schneider, Vivek Srikumar, Jena D. Hwang, and

Martha Palmer. 2015. A hierarchy with, of, and for preposition supersenses. In *Proc. of The 9th Linguistic Annotation Workshop*, pages 112–123. Denver, Colorado, USA.

Xin Tang, Fei Li, and Donghong Ji. 2016. WHUNlp at SemEval-2016 Task 10: A pilot study in detecting minimal semantic units and their meanings using supervised models. In *Proc. of SemEval*. San Diego, California, USA.

Stephen Tratz and Eduard Hovy. 2010. ISI: Automatic classification of relations between nominals using a maximum entropy classifier. In *Proc. of SemEval*, pages 222–225. Uppsala, Sweden.

Yulia Tsvetkov, Elena Mukomel, and Anatole Gershman. 2013. Cross-lingual metaphor detection using common semantic features. In *Proc. of the First Workshop on Metaphor in NLP*, pages 45–51. Atlanta, Georgia, USA.

Yulia Tsvetkov, Nathan Schneider, Dirk Hovy, Archna Bhatia, Manaal Faruqui, and Chris Dyer. 2014. Augmenting English adjective senses with supersenses. In Nicoletta Calzolari, Khalid Choukri, Thierry Declerck, Hrafn Loftsson, Bente Maegaard, Joseph Mariani, Asuncion Moreno, Jan Odijk, and Stelios Piperidis, editors, *Proc. of LREC*, pages 4359–4365. Reykjavík, Iceland.

Marc Vilain, John Burger, John Aberdeen, Dennis Connolly, and Lynette Hirschman. 1995. A model-theoretic coreference scoring scheme. In *Proc. of MUC-6*, pages 45–52. Columbia, Maryland, USA.

Veronika Vincze, István Nagy T., and Gábor Berend. 2011. Detecting noun compounds and light verb constructions: a contrastive study. In *Proc. of the Workshop on Multiword Expressions: from Parsing and Generation to the Real World*, pages 116–121. Portland, Oregon, USA.

Veronika Vincze, János Zsibrita, and István Nagy T. 2013. Dependency parsing for identifying Hungarian light verb constructions. In *Proc. of the Sixth International Joint Conference on Natural Language Processing*, pages 207–215. Nagoya, Japan.

Patrick Ye and Timothy Baldwin. 2007. MELB-YB: Preposition sense disambiguation using rich semantic features. In *Proc. of SemEval*, pages 241–244. Prague, Czech Republic.

SemEval 2016 Task 11: Complex Word Identification

Gustavo Henrique Paetzold and **Lucia Specia**
Department of Computer Science
University of Sheffield, UK
`{ghpaetzold1,l.specia}@sheffield.ac.uk`

Abstract

We report the findings of the Complex Word Identification task of SemEval 2016. To create a dataset, we conduct a user study with 400 non-native English speakers, and find that complex words tend to be rarer, less ambiguous and shorter. A total of 42 systems were submitted from 21 distinct teams, and nine baselines were provided. The results highlight the effectiveness of Decision Trees and Ensemble methods for the task, but ultimately reveal that word frequencies remain the most reliable predictor of word complexity.

1 Introduction

Complex Word Identification (CWI) is the task of deciding which words should be simplified in a given text. It is commonly connected with the task of Lexical Simplification (LS), which has as goal to replace complex words and expressions with simpler alternatives. In the usual LS pipeline, which was first introduced by (Shardlow, 2014), CWI is the first step. An effective CWI strategy can prevent LS approaches from replacing simple words, and hence prevent them from making grammatical and/or semantic errors. Early LS approaches (Devlin and Tait, 1998; Carroll et al., 1999) do not include CWI. As shown in (Paetzold and Specia, 2013; Shardlow, 2014), ignoring this step can considerably decrease the quality of the output produced by a simplifier.

CWI has been gaining popularity in recent research. The LS approach in (Horn et al., 2014) employs an implicit CWI strategy in which a target word is only deemed complex if the LS model can find a candidate substitution which is simpler. Their results, however, show that the approach is unable to find simplifications for one third of the complex words in the dataset. (Shardlow, 2013b) presents the CW corpus: the first dataset for CWI. Although a relevant contribution, this dataset contains only 731 instances extracted automatically from the Simple English Wikipedia edits, which raises concerns about its reliability and applicability.

The results obtained by Shardlow (2013a) highlight some of the issues of the dataset. They use the CW corpus to compare the performance of three solutions to CWI: a Threshold-Based approach, a Support Vector Machine (SVM), and a "Simplify Everything" approach. In their experiments, the "Simplify Everything" approach achieves higher Accuracy, Recall and F-scores than all other systems, suggesting that simplifying all words in a sentence is the most effective approach for CWI. These results are clearly counter intuitive and conflicting with the conclusions drawn in (Paetzold and Specia, 2013; Paetzold, 2013; Shardlow, 2014).

In this paper we describe the first edition of the Complex Word Identification task, organized at SemEval 2016. This is an initiative that aims to provide reliable resources and new insights for CWI, as well as to establish the state of the art performance in CWI for English texts, and bring more visibility to the area of Text Simplification.

2 Task Description

The Complex Word Identification task of SemEval 2016 invited participants to create systems that,

Proceedings of SemEval-2016, pages 560–569,
San Diego, California, June 16-17, 2016. ©2016 Association for Computational Linguistics

given a sentence and a target word within it, can predict whether or not a non-native English speaker would be able to understand the meaning of the target word. We chose non-native speakers as a target audience because, unlike second language learners and those with low literacy levels or conditions such as Aphasia and Dyslexia, non-native speakers of English have not yet been explicitly assessed with respect to their simplification needs. In addition, the broad availability of such an audience makes data collection more feasible.

We have established main goals for the task:

1. To learn which words challenge non-native English speakers and to understand what their traits are.

2. To investigate how well one's individual vocabulary limitations can be predicted from the overall vocabulary limitations of others in the same category.

3. To introduce a new corpus to be used in Text Simplification and other tasks related to Topic Modelling and Semantics.

4. To evaluate the reliability of various resources commonly used in the creation of Lexical Simplification approaches.

5. To establish the state of the art performance in CWI for English texts.

6. To investigate and establish evaluation metrics for the task of CWI.

In order to achieve these objectives for the shared task, we started by creating a manually annotated dataset through a user study.

3   User Study

In the study, volunteers were asked to judge whether or not they could understand the meaning of each word in a given sentence. In the following we provide more details on the sentences used and the annotation process.

3.1   Data Sources

We selected 9,200 sentences to be annotated, after filtering out cases with spurious characters, HTML or CSS markup, or outside the 20-40 word-length range. These sentences were taken from three sources:

CW Corpus (Shardlow, 2013b): composed of 731 sentences from the Simple English Wikipedia in which exactly one word had been simplified by Wikipedia editors from the standard English Wikipedia. Commonly used for the training and evaluation of Complex Word Identification systems. 231 sentences that conformed to our criteria were extracted.

LexMTurk Corpus (Horn et al., 2014): composed of 500 sentences from the Simple English Wikipedia containing one target word that had been simplified from the standard English Wikipedia. Commonly used for the training and evaluation of Lexical Simplification systems. 269 sentences that conformed to our criteria were extracted.

Simple Wikipedia (Kauchak, 2013): composed of 167,689 sentences from the Simple English Wikipedia, each aligned to an equivalent sentence in the standard English Wikipedia. We selected a set of 8,700 sentences from the Simple Wikipedia version that conformed to our criteria and were aligned to an identical sentence in Wikipedia. The goal was to evaluate the ability of the Wikipedia (human) editors in identifying complex words for readers of the Simple Wikipedia.

3.2   Annotation Process

400 non-native speakers of English participated in the experiment, mostly university students or staff. Volunteers provided anonymous information about their native language, age, education level and English proficiency level according to CEFR (Common European Framework of Reference for Languages). They were asked to judge whether or not they could understand the meaning of each content word (nouns, verbs, adjectives and adverbs, as tagged by Freeling (Padr and Stanilovsky, 2012)) in a set of sentences, each of which was judged independently. Volunteers were instructed to annotate all words that they could not understand individually, even if they could comprehend the meaning of the sentence as a whole.

A subset of 200 sentences was split into 20 subsets of 10 sentences, and each subset was annotated by a total of 20 volunteers. The remaining 9,000 sentences were split into 300 subsets of 30 sentences, each of which was annotated by a single volunteer.

4 Analysis

A total of 35,958 distinct words were annotated (232,481 in total). Out of these, 3,854 distinct words (6,388 in total) were deemed as complex by at least one annotator. In the following sections, we discuss details of the data collected.

4.1 Profile of Annotators

Annotators are speakers of 45 languages. The most predominant languages were Portuguese (15.3%), Chinese (13%) and Spanish (11.3%). Annotators are between 18 and 66 years old (average 28.2). 63.7% of the volunteers were Postgraduate students, 32.3% Undergraduate, and 4% were in High School. 36.8% claimed to have Advanced (C2) English proficiency skills, 37.7% Pre-Advanced (C1), 16.6% Upper-Intermediate (B2), 6.4% Intermediate (B1), 2% Pre-Intermediate (A2) and 0.5% Elementary (A1).

By inspecting the data, we found interesting correlations between the number of complex words annotated and volunteers' age or English proficiency level. Figures 1 and 2 illustrate average and standard deviation values using 10-year age bands and proficiency levels, respectively.

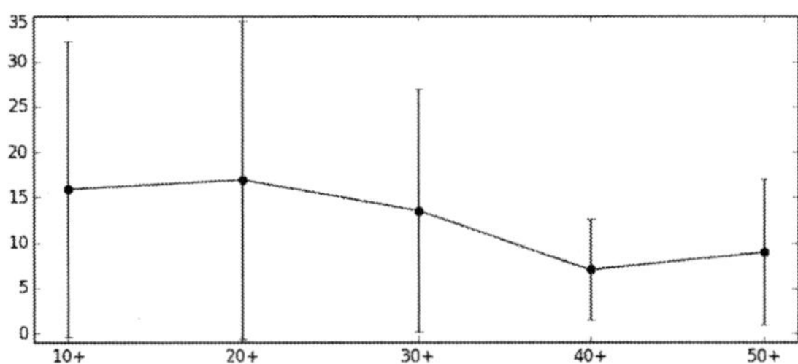

Figure 1: Age bands over number of complex words

Both graphs show that, although the average number of complex words drops as age and proficiency level increase, the variance within each group is very high, suggesting that such groups may not be significantly distinct from each other. By performing F-tests with $p = 0.05$, we found a significant difference between the band of 40+ years of age and the bands

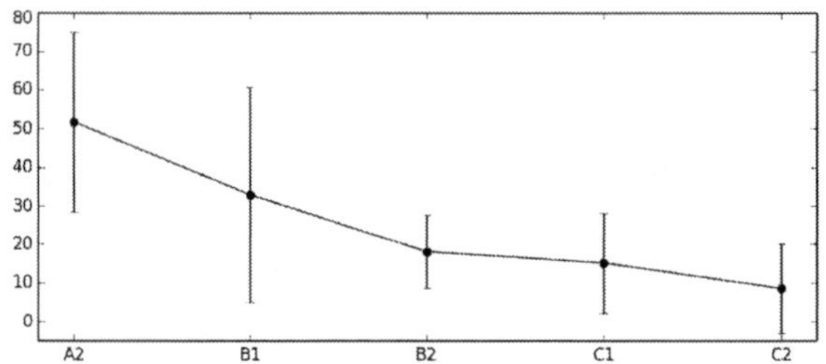

Figure 2: Proficiency levels over number of complex words

of 10+, 20+ and 30+ years of age, which suggests that one's English knowledge peaks at such age. We also found significant differences between almost all English proficiency levels above A2, except between B2 and C1. We did not find significant differences among education levels.

4.2 Analysis of Data Sources

Evaluating the data, we found that the words deemed complex by Wikipedia editors were marked as complex by our annotators in only 0.8% of the CW instances, and 19.7% of the LexMTurk instances. In contrast, 51.9% of the edited words in the CW corpus and 40.8% of those in the LexMTurk corpus were deemed complex by at least one of our annotators. As for the remaining Simple Wikipedia instances, we found that at least one word in 27.3% of the instances was deemed complex by an annotator, which shows that the simplified version of Wikipedia may still be challenging to non-native speakers.

We also inspected these and other datasets for the purposes of LS. In addition to the aforementioned CW and LeXMturk corpora, we took the dataset used in the English Lexical Simplification task of SemEval 2012, composed of 2,010 instances total, and LSeval, the LS evaluation dataset introduced by (De Belder and Moens, 2012), composed by 430 instances. Each instance in all these datasets contains a sentence and a target complex word. Table 1 shows the number of target words included in each dataset, how many of them appear in at least one of our 9,200 sentences, and the proportion of the latter that was deemed complex by at least one of our annotators.

The figures suggest that the aforementioned resources may not be ideal for the training or evaluation of CWI or LS approaches targeting non-native speakers, since they do not necessarily capture their

	Total	Appear in 9,200	Complex
CW	272	260	34.6%
LexMTurk	454	420	33.3%
SemEval	410	342	26.0%
LSeval	80	59	20.3%

Table 1: Results of dataset analysis

needs with respect to simplification.

4.3 Features of Complex Words

We collected statistics that highlight the differences between simple words and those deemed complex by at least one annotator. We consider words' log-probability in a trigram language model built from the Simple Wikipedia corpus (Kauchak, 2013), their length, number of syllables, and number of senses, synonyms, hypernyms and hyponyms registered in Wordnet (Fellbaum, 1998). Table 2 shows average values for these features. According to F-tests with $p = 0.01$, for all features considered, complex and simple words are significantly different. On average, complex words are less ambiguous, shorter, and occur less in Simple Wikipedia.

Feature	Complex	Simple
Length	7.490 ± 2.683	7.966 ± 2.724
Syllables	2.313 ± 1.101	2.557 ± 1.163
-Probability	5.974 ± 5.956	5.599 ± 3.784
Senses	4.169 ± 5.945	4.739 ± 5.649
Synonyms	10.501 ± 15.663	11.893 ± 14.889
Hypernyms	3.141 ± 4.732	3.586 ± 4.612
Hyponyms	10.389 ± 28.687	12.253 ± 30.989

Table 2: Mean and standard deviation for word features

We also noticed that the words most frequently deemed complex by annotators were nouns of technical nature, such as "undercroft", "malleus" and "chalybeatus".

4.4 Agreement Analysis

We calculated the Krippendorff's Alpha agreement coefficient (Hayes and Krippendorff, 2007) for each set of 10 sentences that were annotated by 20 volunteers. The Cohen's Kappa coefficient (Cohen, 1968) was not used due to the large disparity between the number of complex and simple words, which causes the likelihood of annotators agreeing by chance to be higher than the relative observed agreement. The sets have an average agreement coefficient of 0.244, and a standard deviation of 0.1. The relatively low agreement value highlights the expected heterogeneity among non-native speakers with different language backgrounds and proficiency levels.

5 Datasets

We have created two training datasets for the task: **joint** and **decomposed**. Both contain all instances which were annotated by 20 non-native speakers. The **joint** dataset contains a single label for each instance, which is 1 if at least one of the 20 annotators has deemed it complex, and 0 otherwise. Differently, the **decomposed** dataset contains one label for each of the 20 annotators, which is 1 if they have judged it to be complex, and 0 otherwise. Along with the labels, the dataset instances also include the sentence, target word and its position. Participants were allowed to use any additional external resources to build their models. A participant could, for an example, use other (not necessarily publicly available) datasets to complement the one provided.

The test set is composed by all the instances annotated by only one non-native speaker. While the training sets contain the data pertaining to the same 2,237 instances, the test set contains 88,221 instances. Using this setup, we are able to replicate a realistic scenario in Text Simplification, where the needs of many readers must be predicted based on the needs of a sample of the reader population.

Table 3 shows some examples of instances from our **joint** training set.

6 Systems

Each team was allowed to submit at most two systems. In total, 42 systems were submitted by 21 teams:

AI-KU Introduces two SVM classifiers trained with a Radial Basis Function over the joint dataset. While one of their systems use as features the word embeddings of the target word itself and its substrings (native), the other uses the embeddings of the surrounding words as well (native1).

AKTSKI Presents two SVM classifiers: one that weighs labels according to the annotators' judgements (wsys), and another that does not (svmbasic). Their systems use various semantic and morphological features, and were trained over the joint dataset.

Sentence	Word	Position	Label
Leo, on December 23, took an oath of purgation concerning the charges brought against him, and his opponents were exiled.	took	6	0
Leo, on December 23, took an oath of purgation concerning the charges brought against him, and his opponents were exiled.	oath	8	1
It resembles five deep spoons with the handles linked, or, alternately, the hammocks resemble five fig halves.	deep	3	0
It resembles five deep spoons with the handles linked, or, alternately, the hammocks resemble five fig halves.	halves	19	1
If the growth rate is known, the maximum lichen size will give a minimum age for when this rock was deposited.	growth	2	0
If the growth rate is known, the maximum lichen size will give a minimum age for when this rock was deposited.	lichen	9	1

Table 3: Dataset instances

Amrita-CEN Introduces two SVM classifiers trained over the joint dataset. While one of them uses word embeddings as well as various semantic and morphological features (w2vecSim), the other also includes POS tag information (w2vecSimPos).

BHASHA Presents two systems: an SVM (SVM) classifier and a Decision Tree (DECISIONTREE) classifier. The instances in the dataset are first pre-processed, then classified according to various lexical and morphological features. Finally, the results are post-processed with hand-crafted rules. Both systems are trained over the joint dataset.

ClacEDLK Uses Random Forests to train two classifiers over the joint dataset with semantic, morphological, lexical and psycholinguistic features. While one classifier uses a class-assignment threshold of 0.5 (RandomForest-0.5), the other uses a threshold of 0.6 (RandomForest-0.6).

CoastalCPH Introduces a Neural Networks and a Logistic Regression solution. Their Neural Networks system (NeuralNet) is trained over the joint dataset, and uses two hidden layers leading to a single activation node. Their Logistic Regression system (Concatenation) is trained over the decomposed dataset. Both systems use the same set of features, which include word frequency measures and word embedding values.

GARUDA Presents two solutions: a hybrid model (HSVM&DT) and an SVM classifier ensemble (SVMPP). HSVM&DT obtains predictions from various SVM models, which are then validated by Decision Tree classifiers trained specifically to judge whether the predictions are correct. The validated predictions are then combined into a final label. SVMPP trains a single SVM classifier for each of the 20 annotators of the decomposed dataset, then uses a weighted average to combine their predictions.

HMC Performs CWI through a Decision and a Regression Tree, both with a maximum depth of four. During training, their systems deem complex those words which were judged so by at least 25% (DecisionTree25) and 5% (RegressionTree05) of the first 19 annotators in the decomposed dataset. Their systems are then tuned based on the judgment of the 20th annotator.

IIIT Resorts to Nearest Centroid Classification to perform CWI. While one of their classifiers uses the Manhattan distance during training (NCC), the other uses the Euclidean distance (NCC2). As features, they use semantic and morphological features. Their systems are trained over the joint dataset.

JUNLP Presents a Random Forest (RandomForest) and a Naive Bayes (NaiveBayes) classifier trained over the joint dataset. Among the semantic, Lexicon-Based and morphological features used are the words' POS tag and Named Entity information.

LTG Uses a very simple setup of Decision Trees trained over the decomposed dataset. Both of their systems learn a Threshold Based on the number of complex judgments in the decomposed dataset. While one of them learns only one threshold (System1), the other combines various (System2).

MACSAAR Introduces a Random Forest (RFC) and an SVM (NNC) classifier. They use Zipfian features, such as the percentile ranking of the target word, and character n-gram features, such as the probability sum of all character n-grams in the sentence. For training, they use the joint dataset.

MAZA Employs ensemble methods over the joint dataset. They train a context-independent system (A) that uses various word frequency features, and a context-aware system (B) that also includes frequency of the previous and following words.

Melbourne Uses weighted Random Forest classifiers along with various lexical and semantic features. While one of their systems attributes weight 1.5 to the complex class (runw15), the other attributes weight 3 (runw3).

PLUJAGH Presents two Threshold-Based solutions to CWI. Their first system (SEWDF) judges a word to be complex if its frequency in Simple Wikipedia is lower than 147. Their other system learns the frequency threshold from the joint dataset that maximises the F-Score (SEWDFF).

Pomona Uses Threshold-Based bagged classifiers with bootstrap re-sampling. The thresholds of their classifiers are determined through brute-force over the target words' frequencies in a given corpus. They use bag sizes of 10 re-samplings selected through 10-fold cross validation, repeated 20 times. The corpora used are Wikipedia (NormalBag) and the Google Web Corpus (GoogleBag). Their systems are trained over the joint dataset.

Sensible Provides a solution that combines Recurrent Neural Networks and Ensemble Methods. Their Neural Networks are composed of Long Short-Term Memory layers leading to a single activation node. They predict that a word is only complex if the activation node outputs a value equal or bigger than 0.5. The architecture of their networks is determined through cross-validation over the joint dataset. While one of their systems consist of the best performing Neural Network architecture found (Baseline), the other combines the five best architectures using an eXtreme gradient boosted ensemble (Combined).

SV000gg Employs two System Voting techniques that combine various Lexicon-Based, Threshold-Based and Machine Learning voter sub-systems into one. Their first system (Hard) uses Hard Voting: it increases the prediction likelihood of a label by one for each voter that has predicted it for a given instance. Their second system (Soft) uses Performance-Oriented Soft Voting: instead of increasing it by one, they increase it by the systems' G-Score over a held-out portion of the joint dataset. Their voters use a total of 69 morphological, lexical, collocational and semantic features.

TALN Uses Random Forests to perform CWI. While one of their systems is trained over the joint dataset (RandomForest_SIM), the other is trained over the decomposed dataset (RandomForest_WEI), and includes the number of annotators that deemed the word to be complex as a feature. Both systems also include various lexical, morphological, semantic and syntactic features.

USAAR Presents two Bayesian Ridge classifiers. Their first system (Entropy) is trained based solely on a hand-crafted Word Sense Entropy metric, which is calculated for each target word in the joint dataset. Their other system (Entroplexity) combines Word Sense Entropy with perplexity measures calculated with a language model.

UWB Performs CWI with the help of Maximum Entropy classifiers. Both classifiers use only one feature: document frequencies of words in Wikipedia. While one of them is trained over the joint dataset (All), the other is trained over the decomposed dataset (Agg).

7 Baselines

Along with the submitted systems, we include eleven baselines:

- All Complex: Predicts that all words are complex.

- All Simple: Predicts that all words are simple.

- (TB) Simple Wiki: Threshold-Based approach that exploits the word's language model probabilities from the Simple Wikipedia.

- (TB) Wikipedia: Threshold-Based approach that exploits the word's language model probabilities from Wikipedia.

- (TB) Length: Threshold-Based approach that exploits the word's length.

- (TB) Senses: Threshold-Based approach that exploits the word's number of senses.

- (LB) Ogden: Lexicon-Based approach that classifies as simple words which are in the Ogden's vocabulary[1].

- (LB) Simple Wiki: Lexicon-Based approach that classifies as simple words which are in the Simple Wikipedia.

- (LB) Wikipedia: Lexicon-Based approach that classifies as simple words which are in Wikipedia.

We train 3-gram language models with SRILM (Stolcke, 2002). The Wikipedia and Simple Wikipedia corpora are the ones made available by (Kauchak, 2013). Sense counts were extracted from WordNet (Fellbaum, 1998).

For completion, we also assess the performance of two ensemble methods:

- (HV) All Systems: Ensemble approach that combines all systems submitted, including the aforementioned baselines, through Hard Voting, in which the final label of each instance is the one that was most frequently predicted by the systems.

- (HV) No Baselines: Identical to the previous baseline, except it does not include our baselines.

8   Evaluation

To assess the systems' performance, we choose to complement the typical F-score, which is the harmonic mean between Precision and Recall. Even though F-score is arguably the most frequently used evaluation metric to compare the performance of classifiers, we feel that, as far as the relationship between Complex Word Identification and Lexical

Simplification are concerned, it does not accurately capture the effectiveness of a solution for the task.

To motivate our decision, we must first outline the characteristics of a great lexical simplifier. In order to be both effective and reliable, it must accomplish two things simultaneously:

1. Not to make any replacements that compromise the sentences' grammaticality and/or meaning.

2. To make a text as simple as possible.

In order to help a simplifier achieve these goals, a complex word identifier must consequently:

1. Avoid labeling complex words as simple, and hence impede them from being simplified.

2. Avoid labeling simple words as complex, and hence allow for unnecessary, possibly erroneous simplifications.

3. To capture as many complex words as possible, and hence maximise the simplicity of a sentence.

Now that we have outlined what the ideal identifier must do, we can translate these objectives into typical evaluation expressions used in the context of classification problems. In this context, "positive" and "negative" decisions refer to labeling words as complex and simple, respectively.

While objectives number one and two state that the identifier must minimise the number of false negatives and false positives, item three states that it must maximise the number of true positives. One way to measure the proficiency of a classifier in achieving these goals is through **Accuracy** and **Recall**, respectively. In order to balance these two metrics, we have conceived the **G-score**, which measures the harmonic mean between Accuracy and Recall. For completion, we also report the systems' ranking according to **F-score**.

9   Results

The official G and F-score ranks obtained by each system are reported in the first two columns of Table 4 (G and F). The systems that have achieved the highest G-scores are the ones submitted by the

---

[1] http://ogden.basic-english.org/words.html

G	F	Team	System	Accuracy	Precision	Recall	F-score	G-score
1	13	SV000gg	Soft	0.779	0.147	0.769	0.246	0.774
2	16	SV000gg	Hard	0.761	0.138	0.787	0.235	0.773
3	9	TALN	RandomForest_WEI	0.812	0.164	0.736	0.268	0.772
4	10	UWB	All	0.803	0.157	0.734	0.258	0.767
4	11	PLUJAGH	SEWDF	0.795	0.152	0.741	0.252	0.767
4	15	JUNLP	NaiveBayes	0.767	0.139	0.767	0.236	0.767
5	7	HMC	RegressionTree05	0.838	0.182	0.705	0.290	0.766
6	5	HMC	DecisionTree25	0.846	0.189	0.698	0.298	0.765
7	12	JUNLP	RandomForest	0.795	0.151	0.730	0.250	0.761
8	8	MACSAAR	RFC	0.825	0.168	0.694	0.270	0.754
9	6	TALN	RandomForest_SIM	0.847	0.186	0.673	0.292	0.750
10	14	MACSAAR	NNC	0.804	0.146	0.660	0.240	0.725
11	21	Pomona	NormalBag	0.604	0.095	0.872	0.171	0.714
12	22	Melbourne	runw15	0.586	0.091	0.870	0.165	0.701
13	23	UWB	Agg	0.569	0.089	0.885	0.161	0.693
14	24	Pomona	GoogleBag	0.568	0.088	0.881	0.160	0.691
15	25	IIIT	NCC	0.546	0.084	0.880	0.154	0.674
16	2	LTG	System2	0.889	0.220	0.541	0.312	0.672
16	25	**Baseline**	**(TB) Wikipedia**	0.536	0.084	0.901	0.154	0.672
17	18	MAZA	A	0.773	0.115	0.578	0.192	0.661
18	28	**Baseline**	**(TB) Simple Wiki**	0.513	0.081	0.902	0.148	0.654
19	29	Melbourne	runw3	0.513	0.080	0.895	0.147	0.652
20	31	Sensible	Baseline	0.591	0.078	0.713	0.140	0.646
21	30	ClacEDLK	ClacEDLK-RF_0.6	0.688	0.081	0.548	0.141	0.610
22	1	PLUJAGH	SEWDFF	0.922	0.289	0.453	0.353	0.608
23	32	IIIT	NCC2	0.465	0.071	0.860	0.131	0.604
24	26	ClacEDLK	ClacEDLK-RF_0.5	0.751	0.090	0.475	0.152	0.582
25	33	**Baseline**	**(TB) Senses**	0.436	0.068	0.861	0.125	0.579
26	4	MAZA	B	0.912	0.243	0.420	0.308	0.575
27	35	AmritaCEN	w2vecSim	0.627	0.061	0.486	0.109	0.547
28	24	GARUDA	SVMPP	0.796	0.099	0.415	0.160	0.546
29	39	AIKU	native1	0.583	0.057	0.512	0.103	0.545
29	40	AIKU	native	0.555	0.056	0.535	0.101	0.545
30	41	AKTSKI	wsys	0.587	0.056	0.490	0.100	0.534
30	42	AKTSKI	svmbasic	0.512	0.053	0.558	0.097	0.534
31	19	BHASHA	DECISIONTREE	0.836	0.118	0.387	0.181	0.529
32	17	USAAR	entropy	0.869	0.148	0.376	0.212	0.525
33	34	Sensible	Combined	0.737	0.072	0.390	0.122	0.510
34	20	BHASHA	SVM	0.844	0.119	0.363	0.179	0.508
35	36	CoastalCPH	NeuralNet	0.693	0.063	0.398	0.108	0.506
36	37	**Baseline**	**(TB) Length**	0.332	0.057	0.852	0.107	0.478
36	3	LTG	System1	0.933	0.300	0.321	0.310	0.478
37	29	USAAR	entroplexity	0.834	0.097	0.305	0.147	0.447
38	41	AmritaCEN	w2vecSimPos	0.743	0.060	0.306	0.100	0.434
39	38	**Baseline**	**(LB) Ogdens**	0.248	0.056	0.947	0.105	0.393
40	27	GARUDA	HSVM&DT	0.880	0.112	0.226	0.149	0.360
41	35	CoastalCPH	Concatenation	0.869	0.080	0.171	0.109	0.285
42	43	**Baseline**	**(LB) Wikipedia**	0.047	0.047	1.000	0.089	0.090
43	43	**Baseline**	**All Complex**	0.047	0.047	1.000	0.089	0.089
44	44	**Baseline**	**(LB) Simple Wiki**	0.953	0.241	0.002	0.003	0.003
45	45	**Baseline**	**All Simple**	0.953	0.000	0.000	0.000	0.000
-	-	**Baseline**	**(HV) All Systems**	0.791	0.151	0.748	0.251	0.769
-	-	**Baseline**	**(HV) No Baselines**	0.880	0.204	0.539	0.296	0.668

Table 4: Final system ranks and scores. Baselines are in boldface.

SV000gg team, which combine various Threshold-Based, Lexicon-Based and Machine Learning approaches with minimalistic voting techniques. Similarly, the system from the TALN team, which has the third highest G-score, uses an ensemble method that combines various Decision Tree classifiers. Interestingly, the (HV) All Systems and (HV) No Baselines systems, which combine the submitted systems using the same Hard Voting strategy employed by the runner up SV000gg-Hard, did not manage to outperform it.

One of the most clearly highlighted phenomena in our results is the recurring effectiveness of Decision Trees and Random Forests in CWI: out of the systems with the 10 best G-scores, only three do not employ them. Their reliability is also highlighted by the variety of distinct feature sets used to train them, which range from morphological to syntactic. In contrast, the scores obtained by the BHASHA-DECISIONTREE and GARUDA-HSVM&DT systems reveal that these techniques can be much less effective when incorporated in more elaborate setups.

When it comes to F-score, Decision Trees and Random Forests remain dominant among the top 10 systems, but ultimately lose to a much more minimalistic Threshold-Based strategy. The PLUJAGH-SEWDFF system, which obtained the highest F-score, simply learns the threshold of word frequencies in Wikipedia that maximises the F-score over the joint dataset. Similarly, the LTG systems, which achieved the second and third highest F-scores, use Decision Trees to learn a threshold over the number of annotators that judged a word to be complex.

Another interesting finding refers to the difference between raw word frequencies and single-word language model probabilities. The systems submitted by the PLUJAGH team, which learn thresholds over raw word frequencies from Simple Wikipedia, have consistently outperformed the "(TB) Simple Wiki" baseline, which uses language model probabilities, in both G and F-scores.

Perhaps the biggest surprise from our results comes from to the overall performance of systems which employ Neural Networks and/or word embedding models: systems that do so – the ones submitted by AI-KU, AmritaCEN, CoastalCPH and Sensible – ranked no better than 20th in G-score and 31th in F-score. This comes as a surprise, given that these techniques have been employed in state of the art solutions to a range of tasks in recent years. We hypothesize that the small amount of training data available is the main cause for their unsatisfactory performance.

10   Conclusions

In this paper we have described the findings of the Complex Word Identification task of SemEval 2016. The task was framed as a simple, accessible and yet interesting challenge, such that researchers with any background can participate. It attracted a very large number of participants, particularly given that this was its first edition.

To create the task's dataset, we conducted a user study with 400 non-native English speakers, which resulted in a total of 158,624 individual annotations. By analyzing the data obtained we were able to confirm that, according to non-native speakers of English, there is a statistically significant difference between complex and simple words. We have also found a noticeable correlation between the number of complex words annotated and English proficiency level, which is positive evidence that our CWI datasets do, at least to some extent, capture the CWI needs of non-natives. In contrast, we have found that other available resources, such as the CW, LexMTurk and LSeval datasets, may not necessarily do so.

A total of 42 systems were submitted to the task. They reach upwards of impressive 77% in G-score, suggesting that predicting one's individual simplification needs based on the profile of a more diverse audience is feasible. The strategies used range from very simple Threshold-Based approaches to elaborate Ensemble methods that combine various Deep Recurrent Neural Networks and word embeddings. We have ranked systems according to two metrics: F-score and G-score. We found that, likely due to the nature of the task and the reduced number of training instances available, Decision Trees and Ensemble methods perform better than Neural Networks and word embedding models. Additionally, it remains very clear that the most effective way to determine a word's complexity is by searching for its frequency in corpora. The quality of the corpora plays an important role.

In the future, we plan to propose more SemEval tasks in the Text Simplification domain, so that we can continue to learn about word complexity, and hopefully further increase this topic's reach and popularity.

References

John Carroll, Guido Minnen, Darren Pearce, Yvonne Canning, Siobhan Devlin, and John Tait. 1999. Simplifying text for language-impaired readers. In *Proceedings of the 9th EACL*, pages 269–270.

Jacob Cohen. 1968. Weighted kappa: Nominal scale agreement provision for scaled disagreement or partial credit. *Psychological bulletin*, 70:213.

Jan De Belder and Marie-Francine Moens. 2012. A dataset for the evaluation of lexical simplification. In *Proceedings of the 13th CICLING*.

Siobhan Devlin and John Tait. 1998. The use of a psycholinguistic database in the simplification of text for aphasic readers. *Linguistic Databases*, pages 161–173.

Christiane Fellbaum. 1998. *WordNet: An Electronic Lexical Database*. Bradford Books.

Andrew F. Hayes and Klaus Krippendorff. 2007. Answering the call for a standard reliability measure for coding data. *Communication Methods and Measures*, 1.

Colby Horn, Cathryn Manduca, and David Kauchak. 2014. Learning a lexical simplifier using wikipedia. In *Proceedings of the 52nd ACL*, pages 458–463.

David Kauchak. 2013. Improving text simplification language modeling using unsimplified text data. In *Proceedings of the 51st ACL*, pages 1537–1546.

Llus Padr and Evgeny Stanilovsky. 2012. Freeling 3.0: Towards wider multilinguality. In *Proceedings of the 2012 LREC*.

Gustavo H. Paetzold and Lucia Specia. 2013. Text simplification as tree transduction. In *Proceedings of the 9th STIL*.

Gustavo H. Paetzold. 2013. *Um sistema de simplificação automática de textos escritos em inglês por meio de transduçao de árvores*. State University of Western Paraná.

Matthew Shardlow. 2013a. A comparison of techniques to automatically identify complex words. In *Proceedings of the 51st ACL Student Research Workshop*, pages 103–109.

Matthew Shardlow. 2013b. The cw corpus: A new resource for evaluating the identification of complex words. In *Proceedings of the 2nd Workshop on Predicting and Improving Text Readability for Target Reader Populations*, pages 69–77.

Matthew Shardlow. 2014. Out in the open: Finding and categorising errors in the lexical simplification pipeline. In *Proceedings of the 9th LREC*.

Andreas Stolcke. 2002. Srilm-an extensible language modeling toolkit. In *Proceedings of the International Conference on Spoken Language Processing*, pages 257–286.

FBK HLT-MT at SemEval-2016 Task 1: Cross-lingual Semantic Similarity Measurement Using Quality Estimation Features and Compositional Bilingual Word Embeddings

Duygu Ataman[1,2], José G. C. de Souza[1,2], Marco Turchi[1], Matteo Negri[1]

[1] HLT - MT

Fondazione Bruno Kessler, Trento, Italy

[2]Department of Information Engineering and Computer Science

University of Trento, Italy

{ataman,desouza,turchi,negri}@fbk.eu

Abstract

This paper describes the system by FBK HLT-MT for cross-lingual semantic textual similarity measurement. Our approach is based on supervised regression with an ensemble decision tree. In order to assign a semantic similarity score to an input sentence pair, the model combines features collected by state-of-the-art methods in machine translation quality estimation and distance metrics between cross-lingual embeddings of the two sentences. In our analysis, we compare different techniques for composing sentence vectors, several distance features and ways to produce training data. The proposed system achieves a mean Pearson's correlation of 0.39533, ranking 7th among all participants in the cross-lingual STS task organized within the SemEval 2016 evaluation campaign.

1 Introduction

Semantic textual similarity (STS) measures the degree of equivalence between the meanings of two text sequences (Agirre et al., 2015). The similarity of the text pair can be represented as a continuous or discrete-time value ranging from irrelevance to exact semantic equivalence (Agirre et al., 2015).

STS has been one of the official shared tasks in SemEval since 2013 and has attracted the participation of many researchers from the scientific community; enabling the evaluation of several different approaches in natural language processing with a common benchmark and the production of novel annotated data sets that can be used in future research. State-of-the-art monolingual STS methods make use of several approaches including word alignments and distributional semantics, which are typically employed in a machine learning scenario (Sultan et al., 2015; Hänig et al., 2015).

This is the first year in which SemEval has organized a cross-lingual STS (CL-STS) sub-task, for which a baseline system applicable to the problem has not been defined yet. Similar to the monolingual STS task, the cross-lingual task requires the interpretation of the semantic similarity of two cross-lingual sentences, one in English and another one in Spanish, with a score ranging from 0 to 5. CL-STS measurement could be extremely useful for achieving textual entailment, paraphrase identification, word-sense disambiguation or sentiment analysis at the cross-lingual level as well as providing new means for an adequacy-oriented evaluation of machine translation outputs.

A related task in natural language processing is quality estimation. Quality estimation (QE) is used for automatically predicting the quality of machine translation outputs with respect to the source sentences in the original language (Mehdad et al., 2012; Turchi et al., 2014; C. de Souza et al., 2014a; C. de Souza et al., 2014b; C. de Souza et al., 2015). One shortcoming of QE approaches is that the QE system may not capture all aspects of the semantic representations of sentences. For instance, from a QE perspective, under which the number of edit operations required to fix a translation is used as a proxy of quality, a fluent translation containing an unnecessary negation would likely be labelled as a "good" translation. Therefore, a better solution would be

570

Proceedings of SemEval-2016, pages 570–576,

San Diego, California, June 16-17, 2016. ©2016 Association for Computational Linguistics

geared to also capture the adequacy aspects of cross-lingual comparison of the sentences. In order to improve the quality of the comparison, the features used in a QE system can be improved using distributional semantics. Neural language models, such as CBOW or Skipgram (Mikolov et al., 2013a) have proved to be useful in the monolingual STS task before (Agirre et al., 2015). Recent studies have extended these models to create bilingual word embeddings such that the embeddings are mapped to a common cross-lingual vector space by using a parallel training corpus or a dictionary (Klementiev et al., 2012; Mikolov et al., 2013b; Luong et al., 2015).

In light of these considerations, our submission to the first SemEval CL-STS task combines features derived from QE with distance features obtained by applying cross-lingual word embeddings. These features are used to feed an Extremely Randomized Trees (ET) regressor (Geurts et al., 2006) trained to predict the similarity score of the two sentences.

The rest of this paper is organized as follows. Section 2 describes the components of our CL-STS system. The details of the experimental analysis carried out on different composition approaches, the characteristics of the system under the influence of each vector space feature and varying data distributions are presented in Section 3. The final ranking of our system can be found in Section 4 along with the conclusions of our study in Section 5.

2   System Description

This section describes the proposed CL-STS system. The data to be semantically compared is first pre-processed as described in Section 2.1. The embedding corresponding to each word is retrieved and composed to form a sentence embedding using one of the methods described in Section 2.2. The features to be used in the regression are extracted from the sentence embeddings using 8 different distance measures listed in Section 2.2. These features are combined with 79 more features obtained by QE (Section 2.3) to produce a final set of 87 features, which is used to predict the similarity score of the two sentences. The overall system is illustrated in Figure 1.

2.1   Pre-processing

The data used in training and testing the system are processed before feature extraction in the following way. First of all, a language identification package developed by Lui et al. (2012) is used to detect the order of English and Spanish sentences in each line of the data set. This step is meant as a first sanity check since some of the next processing steps are language-dependent and hence sensitive to the order in which the two sentences are presented. The data is then tokenized and lowercased before the extraction of features using the text processing system of Moses (Koehn et al., 2007).

2.2   Bilingual Embedding Features

To obtain word embeddings, we use the bilingual Skipgram model by Luong et al. (2015). The embeddings are trained using the default parameters described by the authors and with a dimension of 200. We constructed an English-Spanish parallel corpus from Europarl (Koehn, 2005), UN (Rafalovitch et al., 2009), data sets of the quality estimation shared task in WMT 2012 (Callison-Burch et al., 2012), as well as the training data of the monolingual STS task from previous years (See Subsection 3.1) and used this data to train our bilingual embeddings.

Sentence embeddings are then generated by averaging the word embeddings in each sentence. Averaging is a simple and powerful composition method for monolingual word embeddings which has not been outperformed yet by much more sophisticated schemes, such as the recurrent neural networks and long short-term memories (Blacoe and Lapata, 2012; Wieting et al., 2015). Moreover, the latter often requires language-specific syntactic parsers which are not available in all languages, thus are not generally suitable for cross-lingual applications.

In our system, we implement three different averaging strategies to see the influence of stop words or term frequencies in the final sentence embedding. Our approaches consist of:

1. Averaging with all the tokens in the sentence including punctuation;

2. Averaging after removing stop words and punctuation in the sentence;

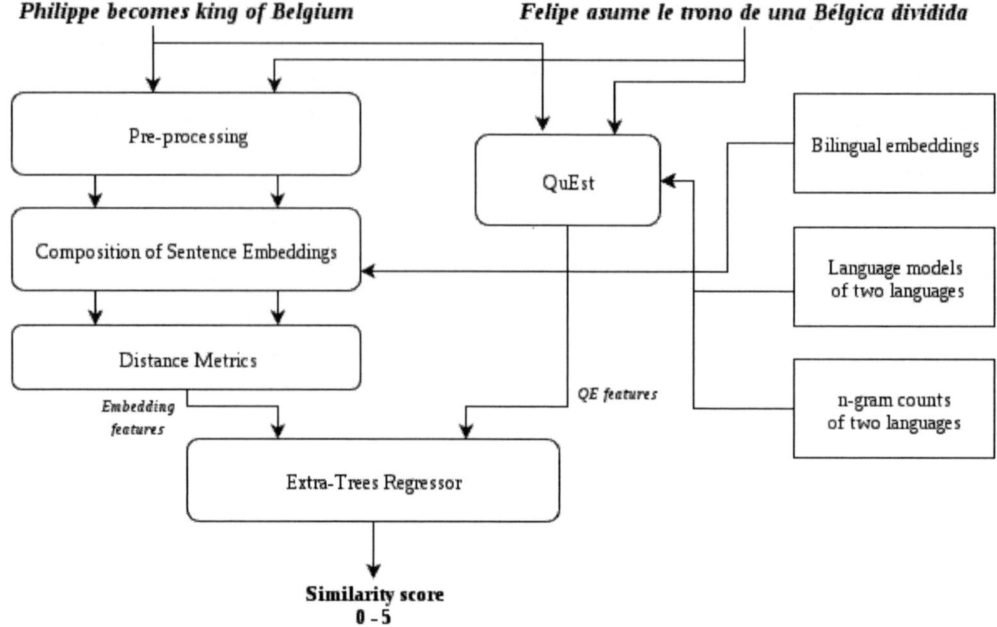

Figure 1: The schematic of the overall system for CL-STS

3. Averaging by weighting each word in the sentence by their inverse term frequencies.

During processing of the two sentences in English and Spanish, the words and punctuation in each corresponding sentence are averaged according to one of the methods above to generate one final embedding representing each sentence in the two languages.

In order to apply semantic comparison between the sentence embeddings, we select 8 distance measures that are defined in vector space. Given the two sentence vectors, the selected distance metrics include:

1. Cosine distance

2. Euclidean distance

3. Manhattan distance

4. Chebyshev distance

5. Canberra distance

6. Pearson's correlation

7. Ratio of number of words

8. Ratio of means

We further analyze the usefulness of these features through a set of experiments before using in the CL-STS task (Section 3).

2.3　Quality Estimation Features

The QE features used in our system are obtained by QuEst tool (Specia et al., 2013). The QuEst tool uses language models, POS-taggers or word aligners to extract many features that can represent complexity (*e.g.* language model probabilities or n-gram counts in the source segment) fluency (*e.g.* language model probabilities or number of tokens in the target segment), adequacy (*e.g.* word alignment features such as ratio of nouns/verbs/etc. in each sentence) or confidence (*e.g.* global scores or n-best lists) of a translation pair. For a more detailed description of each feature, we refer the reader to Specia et al. (2013). The language models used to extract the features are trained with the NY Times portion of English Gigaword (v.5) (Parker et al., 2011) and Spanish Gigaword (v.2) (Mendonca et al., 2009) and the same parallel data as described in the training of bilingual word embeddings (See Section 2.2)

Features	# Features	Pearson's correlation		
QE	79	0.5899		
Embeddings	8	0.4690		
QE + sentence embedding features				
		Composition method		
		Average	Average w/o stop words	ITF-weighted Average
+ Cosine	80	0.6106	0.6399	0.6017
+ Manhattan	81	0.6127	0.6429	0.5897
+ Euclidean	82	0.6152	$\mathbf{0.6445}^{run1}$	0.5906
+ Canberra	83	0.6149	0.6435	0.5962
+ Pearson's correlation	84	0.6145	0.6361	0.6039
+ Chebyshev	85	0.6136	0.6364	0.5907
+ Ratio of NumWords	86	0.6138	0.6366	0.5915
+ Ratio of Means	87	0.6154	$\mathbf{0.6375}^{run2}$	0.5996

Table 1: Pearson's correlation of system predictions using cross-validation. The first and second entries in the table indicate performance of the system using the two approaches separately. The second part indicates the system performance when the two approaches are combined, revealing the effect of each distance-based feature on the performance. Each column represents a different sentence composition method; including averaging, averaging after removing stop words and weighted averaging. Numbers in bold are the two runs, **[run1]** wth 82 and **[run2]** wth 87 features respectively, submitted to the SemEval 2016 - CL-STS shared task.

2.4 Ensemble Regression

An ET regressor is used as the learning method in the system. The ET regressor applies bagging to generate a number of random subsets of the training data and fits individual decision trees using different subsets of features and hyper parameters. The final prediction is produced by an ensemble average over all of the decision trees.

3 Experiments

3.1 Corpus

For this first round of the CL-STS task, training data was not released by the organizers. Therefore, the data for training the regressor was generated using those from the monolingual STS tasks organized in 2012, 2013, 2014 and 2015 (Agirre et al., 2012; Agirre et al., 2013; Agirre et al., 2014; Agirre et al., 2015). The data was translated to Spanish using the MateCat tool (Federico et al., 2014) to create a cross-lingual data set where one of the sentences is in English and the other is in Spanish. In order to compensate for the different characteristics of data which occur after translation, we generate three different sets as follows:

1. The first sentence in the data set is selected as the English sentence, the second sentence is translated to Spanish, denoted as: $s_1(en)$ - $\overline{s_2}(es)$.

2. The second sentence in the data set is selected as the English sentence, the first sentence is translated to Spanish, denoted as: $s_2(en)$ - $\overline{s_1}(es)$.

3. The first two data sets are concatenated, denoted as the *merged* set.

The size of each set is given in Table 2. The three data sets are evaluated during our experiments in terms of the capability to represent the true data distribution and used in the test phase with the selected settings (Section 3.3).

Data set	# sent	# src	# tgt
s1(en) - $\overline{s2}$(es)	18,105	233,141	250,359
s2(en) - $\overline{s1}$(es)	18,091	230,300	253,115
merged	36196	463441	503474

Table 2: Sizes of the training sets: number of sentence pairs and number of words in source and target languages

3.2 Cross-validation on the merged set

The performance of our ET regressor is evaluated using 10-fold cross-validation on the merged set. The results are presented in Table 1.

We run a detailed analysis to evaluate each individual distance metric according to their effect on the performance. For evaluating the performance of the system we use Pearson's correlation. The experiments show that QE features and embedding features perform poorly when used as two different groups, but the performance can be improved when they are integrated together. The best correlation is achieved when cosine, manhattan and euclidean distances are combined with the QE features. All distance metrics show a consistent improvement over the system trained only on QE features, except for the Pearson's correlation (Table 1).

The experiments also reveal that averaging after removing the stop words and punctuation is the best sentence composition method among the three averaging strategies. Compared to this method, inverse term-frequency weighted averaging aims to decrease the effect of stop words in a less greedy way. However, we see that this approach results in even poorer performance than straightforward averaging; suggesting that we may lose important information from word semantics necessary in composing the sentence meaning when we weight each word with their inverse term frequencies. Thus, we select averaging without stop words as the composition method to use in our system to participate in the SemEval 2016 CL-STS shared task.

3.3 Performance of different training data sets on the evaluation data

In the second phase, we compare the performance of our ET regressor in terms of three different training sets, as explained in Section 3.1. 30% of the training set is used for validation and the remaining 70% is used for training purposes. The regressor then performs predictions for the same validation set using the different sets. Finally, we implement an ensemble model which is an average of the predictions of the three subsystems. The results of these experiments can be seen in Table 3.

In light of these experiments, we choose the feature sets composing of 82 and 87 features and the merged set for training purposes (See Table 1). These two systems are submitted as our **[run1]** and **[run2]** to the CL-STS shared task. We contribute with the ensemble average system as shown in Ta-

Data set	Pearson's correlation
s1(en) - s2(es)	0.5499
s2(en) - s1(es)	0.5815
merged	0.6227
Average	**0.6131**^{run3}

Table 3: Pearson's correlation of system (run2) predictions using 30-70 split in the (merged) data set. Performance is shown according to three different training data distributions. Average indicates the performance of ensemble of the three approaches, and is the system chosen to be submitted as **[run3]** to the SemEval 2016 - CL-STS shared task.

ble 3 for **[run3]**.

System	News	Multi-source	Mean
run3	0.25507	0.53892	0.39533
run1	0.24318	0.53465	0.3872
run2	0.24372	0.5142	0.37737

Table 4: Official results of SemEval 2016 - CL-STS shared task

4   Results

The performance of our system in the SemEval 2016 - CL-STS task is given in Table 4. The test set of the CL-STS task contains two parts with different characteristics. The first set contains 301 sentence pairs in the news domain and the second set consists of 2973 sentence pairs drawn from different domains. By using these data sets to test our system, we achieve a Pearson's correlation of 0.539 on the multi-source test set and 0.255 on the news set between our predictions and the true labels (Table 4).

We observe that using **[run3]**, which combines the three systems trained on three data sets with different distributions, is the most successful approach. The decreased values of Pearson's correlation are consistent with the fact that test data of the task and our training set are sampled from different distributions. Moreover, our system performs better in the general domain and worse in the specific domain of news. However, this performance can be improved by extending the training corpus to a similar content with the test corpus. Other aspects to improve are the quality of bilingual word embeddings, which should also be trained with more data and parameters that are more suitable for the specific task, and addition of feature selection quality to the system.

The results also show that performance of the system using only QE features and the three distance metrics consisting of cosine, manhattan and euclidean distances provide better results than the system using all features. Therefore, one can see that these three features can provide significant information when comparing two sentence embeddings and could be reliably used in future applications.

5 Conclusion

We have presented the CL-STS measurement system with which we participated in the SemEval 2016 CL-STS shared task. Our system used QE and distance features based on bilingual word embeddings to train an ET regressor that predicts the cross-lingual semantic similarity between a pair of sentences. We used an ensemble method to generate and use training data for the task and saw that this approach improved the performance of our system. Our best performance achieves a Pearson's correlation of 0.53892 while placing FBK HLT-MT as the 7th out of 10 teams in the task.

Acknowledgments

This work has been partially supported by the EC-funded H2020 project QT21 (grant agreement no. 645452).

References

Eneko Agirre, Daniel Cer, Mona Diab, and Aitor Gonzalez-Agirre. 2012. Semeval-2012 task 6: A pilot on semantic textual similarity. In *SEM 2012: The First Joint Conference on Lexical and Computational Semantics – Volume 1: Proceedings of the main conference and the shared task, and Volume 2: Proceedings of the Sixth International Workshop on Semantic Evaluation (SemEval 2012)*, pages 385–393, Montréal, Canada, 7-8 June. Association for Computational Linguistics.

Eneko Agirre, Daniel Cer, Mona Diab, Aitor Gonzalez-Agirre, and Weiwei Guo. 2013. *sem 2013 shared task: Semantic textual similarity. In *Second Joint Conference on Lexical and Computational Semantics (*SEM), Volume 1: Proceedings of the Main Conference and the Shared Task: Semantic Textual Similarity*, pages 32–43, Atlanta, Georgia, USA, June. Association for Computational Linguistics.

Eneko Agirre, Carmen Banea, Claire Cardie, Daniel Cer, Mona Diab, Aitor Gonzalez-Agirre, Weiwei Guo, Rada Mihalcea, German Rigau, and Janyce Wiebe. 2014. Semeval-2014 task 10: Multilingual semantic textual similarity. In *Proceedings of the 8th international workshop on semantic evaluation (SemEval 2014)*, pages 81–91.

Eneko Agirre, Carmen Baneab, Claire Cardiec, Daniel Cerd, Mona Diabe, Aitor Gonzalez-Agirrea, Weiwei Guof, Inigo Lopez-Gazpioa, Montse Maritxalara, Rada Mihalceab, et al. 2015. Semeval-2015 task 2: Semantic textual similarity, english, spanish and pilot on interpretability. In *Proceedings of the 9th international workshop on semantic evaluation (SemEval 2015)*, pages 252–263.

William Blacoe and Mirella Lapata. 2012. A comparison of vector-based representations for semantic composition. In *Proceedings of the 2012 Joint Conference on Empirical Methods in Natural Language Processing and Computational Natural Language Learning*, pages 546–556. Association for Computational Linguistics.

José G. C. de Souza, Jesús González-Rubio, Christian Buck, Marco Turchi, and Matteo Negri. 2014a. FBK-UPV-UEdin participation in the WMT14 Quality Estimation shared-task. In *Proceedings of the Ninth Workshop on Statistical Machine Translation*, pages 322–328.

José G. C. de Souza, Marco Turchi, and Matteo Negri. 2014b. Machine translation quality estimation across domains. In *Proceedings of COLING 2014, the 25th International Conference on Computational Linguistics: Technical Papers*, pages 409–420.

José G. C. de Souza, Matteo Negri, Elisa Ricci, and Marco Turchi. 2015. Online Multitask Learning for Machine Translation Quality Estimation. In *Proceedings of the 53rd Annual Meeting of the Association for Computational Linguistics (Volume 1: Long Papers)*, pages 219–228, Beijing, China, July.

Chris Callison-Burch, Philipp Koehn, Christof Monz, Matt Post, Radu Soricut, and Lucia Specia. 2012. Findings of the 2012 workshop on statistical machine translation. In *Proceedings of the Seventh Workshop on Statistical Machine Translation*, pages 10–51, Montréal, Canada, June. Association for Computational Linguistics.

Marcello Federico, Nicola Bertoldi, Mauro Cettolo, Matteo Negri, Marco Turchi, Marco Trombetti, Alessandro Cattelan, Antonio Farina, Domenico Lupinetti, Andrea Martines, et al. 2014. The matecat tool. In *COLING (Demos)*, pages 129–132.

Pierre Geurts, Damien Ernst, and Louis Wehenkel. 2006. Extremely randomized trees. *Machine learning*, 63(1):3–42.

Christian Hänig, Robert Remus, and Xose de la Puente. 2015. Exb themis: Extensive feature extraction from word alignments for semantic textual similarity. In *Proceedings of the 9th International Workshop on Semantic Evaluation (SemEval 2015)*, pages 264–268, Denver, Colorado, June. Association for Computational Linguistics.

Alexandre Klementiev, Ivan Titov, and Binod Bhattarai. 2012. Inducing crosslingual distributed representations of words.

Philipp Koehn, Hieu Hoang, Alexandra Birch, Chris Callison-Burch, Marcello Federico, Nicola Bertoldi, Brooke Cowan, Wade Shen, Christine Moran, Richard Zens, et al. 2007. Moses: Open source toolkit for statistical machine translation. In *Proceedings of the 45th annual meeting of the ACL on interactive poster and demonstration sessions*, pages 177–180. Association for Computational Linguistics.

Philipp Koehn. 2005. Europarl: A parallel corpus for statistical machine translation. In *MT summit*, volume 5, pages 79–86.

Marco Lui and Timothy Baldwin. 2012. langid. py: An off-the-shelf language identification tool. In *Proceedings of the ACL 2012 system demonstrations*, pages 25–30. Association for Computational Linguistics.

Thang Luong, Hieu Pham, and Christopher D Manning. 2015. Bilingual word representations with monolingual quality in mind. In *Proceedings of the 1st Workshop on Vector Space Modeling for Natural Language Processing*, pages 151–159.

Yashar Mehdad, Matteo Negri, and Marcello Federico. 2012. Match without a Referee: Evaluating MT Adequacy without Reference Translations. In *Proceedings of the Machine Translation Workshop (WMT2012)*, pages 171–180, Montréal, Canada, June.

Angelo Mendonca, David Andrew Graff, Denise DiPersio, Linguistic Data Consortium, et al. 2009. *Spanish gigaword second edition*. Linguistic Data Consortium.

Tomas Mikolov, Kai Chen, Greg Corrado, and Jeffrey Dean. 2013a. Efficient estimation of word representations in vector space. *arXiv preprint arXiv:1301.3781*.

Tomas Mikolov, Quoc V Le, and Ilya Sutskever. 2013b. Exploiting similarities among languages for machine translation. *arXiv preprint arXiv:1309.4168*.

Robert Parker, David Graff, Junbo Kong, Ke Chen, and Kazuaki Maeda. 2011. English gigaword fifth edition, june. *Linguistic Data Consortium, LDC2011T07*.

Alexandre Rafalovitch, Robert Dale, et al. 2009. United nations general assembly resolutions: A six-language parallel corpus. In *Proceedings of the MT Summit*, volume 12, pages 292–299.

Lucia Specia, Kashif Shah, José G. C. de Souza, and Trevor Cohn. 2013. Questa translation quality estimation framework. In *Proceedings of the 51st Annual Meeting of the Association for Computational Linguistics*, pages 79–84.

Md Arafat Sultan, Steven Bethard, and Tamara Sumner. 2015. Dls@cu: Sentence similarity from word alignment and semantic vector composition. In *Proceedings of the 9th International Workshop on Semantic Evaluation (SemEval 2015)*, pages 148–153, Denver, Colorado, June. Association for Computational Linguistics.

Marco Turchi, Antonios Anastasopoulos, José G. C. de Souza, and Matteo Negri. 2014. Adaptive Quality Estimation for Machine Translation. In *Proceedings of the 52nd Annual Meeting of the Association for Computational Linguistics (Volume 1: Long Papers)*, pages 710–720, Baltimore, Maryland, USA, June.

John Wieting, Mohit Bansal, Kevin Gimpel, and Karen Livescu. 2015. Towards universal paraphrastic sentence embeddings. *arXiv preprint arXiv:1511.08198*.

VRep at SemEval-2016 Task 1 and Task 2: A System for Interpretable Semantic Similarity

Sam Henry and **Allison Sands**
Computer Science Department
Virginia Commonwealth University
Richmond, VA 23284, USA
henryst@vcu.edu
allisonsands1224@gmail.com

Abstract

VRep is a system designed for SemEval 2016 Task 1 - Semantic Textual Similarity (STS) and Task 2 - Interpretable Semantic Textual Similarity (iSTS). STS quantifies the semantic equivalence between two snippets of text, and iSTS provides a reason why those snippets of text are similar. VRep makes extensive use of WordNet for both STS, where the Vector relatedness measure is used, and for iSTS, where features are extracted to create a learned rule-based classifier. This paper outlines the VRep algorithm, provides results from the 2016 SemEval competition, and analyzes the performance contributions of the system components.

1 Introduction

VRep competed in SemEval 2016 Task 1 - Semantic Textual Similarity (STS) and Task 2 - Semantic Interpretable Textual Similarity (iSTS). Both of these tasks compute STS between two fragments of text. Task 2 expands upon Task 1 by requiring a reason for their similarity. VRep uses an STS measure based on the Vector relatedness measure (Pedersen et al., 2004), and a reasoning system based on JRIP (Cohen, 1995), an implementation of the iREP algorithm.

For Task 1, we are provided with paired sentences, and for each pair of sentences VRep assigns a number indicating their STS. The number ranges from 0 to 5, 0 indicating no similarity and 5 indicating equivalence.

For Task 2, we are provided with paired sentences and align the chunks of one sentence to the most similar chunks in the other sentence. Next, a reason and score are computed for that alignment. A chunk is a fragment of text that conveys a single meaning such as in the following example for which chunks are bracketed.

| [Black Cow] | [walking] | [in a pasture] |
| [Black and white Cow] | [sitting] | [in the grass] |

Alignment reasons are selected from a small list of possible labels created by the event organizers (Agirre et al., 2015):

1. Equivalent (EQUI) - the two chunks convey an equivalent meaning ("hot water", "scalding water")

2. Opposite (OPPO) - the two chunks convey an opposite meaning ("hot water", "cold water")

3. More General (SPE1) - this chunk conveys a more general meaning than the other chunk ("hot water", "water")

4. More Specific (SPE2) - this chunk conveys a more specific meaning than the other chunk "water", "hot water")

5. Similar (SIMI) - the two chunks convey a similar meaning ("sip water", "gulp water")

6. Related (REL) - the two chunks are somehow related ("boil water", "ocean water")

7. No Alignment (NOALI) - there are no chunks in the other sentence that are semantically similar to this chunk

Proceedings of SemEval-2016, pages 577–583,
San Diego, California, June 16-17, 2016. ©2016 Association for Computational Linguistics

As in Task 1 the scores range from 0 to 5, 0 indicating no similarity and 5 indicating equivalence. VRep makes extensive use of WordNet (Fellbaum, 2005) to compute STS and assign a label in iSTS. Vrep is written in Perl and is freely available for download[1].

2 Algorithm Description

The same measure of STS is used for both Task 1 and Task 2; however, the algorithm for Task 1 is simpler and consists of only the first two steps: Preprocessing and Semantic Textual Similarity. The steps are outlined below and are expanded on in subsequent subsections.

1. Preprocessing - text is standardized

2. Semantic Textual Similarity - the STS between two chunks or two sentences is computed. This is the final step for Task 1.

3. Chunk Alignment - align each chunk of one sentence to a chunk in another sentence. If no chunks are similar then no alignment (NOALI) is assigned.

4. Alignment Reasoning - assign a label to each aligned chunk pair

5. Alignment Scoring - assign an alignment score on a 0-5 scale

2.1 Preprocessing

In the first step, data is prepared for processing as outlined below:

1. Tokenization - spaces are used as a delimiter

2. Lowercase All Characters - standardizes string equivalence testing and prevents incorrect part of speech (POS) tagging. The POS tagger tends to tag most words that have a capital letter as a proper noun which is often incorrect. This is particularly problematic with the headlines data set.

3. Punctuation Removal - standardizes string equivalence testing

4. POS tagging - Lingua::EN::Tagger[2] is used. POS tags are used for stop word removal and for alignment reasoning.

5. Stop Word Removal - remove any words that are not tagged as a noun, verb, adjective, or adverb. This reduces chunks and sentences to content words.

2.2 Semantic Textual Similarity (STS)

STS is computed in the same way for both tasks; however it is computed between two sentences for Task 1 and between two chunks for Task 2. While describing the computation of STS we refer to chunks; for Task 1 a sentence can be conceptualized as a chunk. VRep's STS computation is shown in Equation (1) and is similar to the method described by NeRoSim (Banjade et al., 2015) and Stefanescu (Ştefănescu et al., 2014). $chunkSim$ takes two chunks (c_1, c_2) as input and computes the weighted sum of maximum word to word similarities, $sim(w_i, w_j)$. To do this, the $sim(w_i, w_j)$ is found for each word in c_2 against c_1, and the maximum is added to a running sum.

$$chunkSim(c_1, c_2) = \frac{\sum_{i=1}^{n} \max_{j=1}^{m} sim(w_i, w_j)}{min(n, m)} \quad (1)$$

where c_1 and c_2 are two chunks, n and m are the number of words in c_1 and c_2, w_i is word i of c_1, w_j is word j of c_2

$sim(w_i, w_j)$ is defined differently for words in WordNet and words not in WordNet. For words in WordNet, $sim(w_i, w_j)$ is the Vector relatedness measure[3] (Pedersen et al., 2004) with a threshold applied. The Vector measure was chosen for several reasons. Firstly it returns values scaled between 0 and 1 which is beneficial for applying thresholds in both chunk alignment and alignment reasoning. A known scale also allows for a direct mapping from the weighted sum to the answer space of Task 1 (scaled 0-5). Secondly the Vector measure works well when w_i and w_j are different parts of speech because it does not rely on WordNet hierarchies. When calculating $sim(w_i, w_j)$ all possible senses of both w_i and w_j are used, and $sim(w_i, w_j)$ is chosen as

---

[1] http://www.people.vcu.edu/ henryst/

[2] http://search.cpan.org/ acoburn/Lingua-EN-Tagger/
[3] WordNet::Similarity::Vector

the maximum value. This eliminates the need for word sense disambiguation (WSD). After computing the measure, a threshold is applied that reduces any value less than 0.9 to 0.0. This value was tuned separately using the training data for both tasks via a grid search and 0.9 was found to be optimum for both. The threshold prevents dissimilar terms from impacting the STS which improves the accuracy and prevents noisy chunk alignments.

For words not in WordNet, $chunkSim(w_i, w_j)$ is a binary value: 1 if all the characters in both words match, 0 otherwise. Words not in WordNet tend to be proper nouns, abbreviations, or short words such as "he" or "she", "is" or "in", all of which are generally spelled identically making this a suitable measure.

$chunkSim$ is defined as the sum of maximum word to word similarities normalized by the number of words in the shorter of the chunk pair. Normalization prevents similarity scores from increasing as chunk length increases. It also scales $chunkSim$ within a predictable range of about $0.0 - 1.0$.

$chunkSim$ is used directly in Task 1 where it is linearly scaled by 5 to produce final output. We experimented with multiple regression fits (linear, exponential, logarithmic, power, and polynomial) between our $chunkSim$ output and the provided gold standard values with little to no improvement, so the linear scaling of 5 was chosen for simplicity.

2.3 Chunk Alignment

$chunkSim$ is computed between each chunk of two aligned sentences and the chunk with the highest $chunkSim$ is selected for alignment. Multiple alignments are allowed for a single chunk. If all chunks have a similarity of 0, no alignment (NOALI) is assigned. Due to the high $sim(w_i, w_j)$ threshold, no threshold is required for $chunkSim$ as with NeRoSim(Banjade et al., 2015).

2.4 Alignment Reasoning

Alignment Reasoning takes as input a chunk pair and provides a reason why that chunk pair is aligned. VRep's alignment reasoning is inspired by NeRoSim (Banjade et al., 2015), and SVCTSTS (Karumuri et al., 2015). Both these systems classify a chunk pair using features extracted from the chunk pair itself. NeRoSim's features tend to focus more on the semantic relationship between chunk pairs, such as whether or not the two chunks contain antonyms, synonyms, etc. The features of SVCSTS focus more on the syntactic form of the chunks, such as the number of words or counts of parts of speech in a chunk pair. VRep combines the two approaches and extracts a total of 72 syntactic and semantic features for each chunk pair.

Gold Standard chunk pairs of the SemEval 2015 Task 2 Test Data[4] were used to train our classifier, WEKA's (Hall et al., 2009) JRIP algorithm (Cohen, 1995) which creates a decision list for classification. The classifier uses only 24 of original 72 features and a series of 10 rules.

JRIP was chosen as a classifier due to its performance (see Table 5), and its concision. The rules generated are human readable which provides insight into how the classification occurs and the types of features that are discriminative. Classifiers were trained with chunk pairs from every data set (student answers, headlines, and images), both individually and combined. The best performing classifier for each topic was generated from the combined data. The set of features used and classification rules are shown below. α and β designate the individual chunks in the chunk pair being classified, and $\vec{x_i}$ indicates a feature vector created from a chunk pair. i indicates the feature number in the feature list below.

Features used in Classification:
1 - unmatched content word percentage of α
2 - unmatched content word percentage of β
3 - 1 if α contains a location
4 - 1 if β contains a location
5 - 1 if α has a verb
6 - 1 if α has an adjective
7 - 1 if α has an adverb
8 - 1 if α and β contain antonyms
9 - 1 if α and β have a equivalent nouns
10 - 1 if α and β contain numeric quantities
11 - number of words in α (before stop word removal)
12 - number of words in β (before stop word removal)
13 - ratio of the number content words to all words in α (before stop word removal)

---

[4]http://alt.qcri.org/semeval2016/task2/data/uploads/train_2015_10_22.utf-8.tar.gz

14 - difference in number of content words in α and β

15 - difference in number of words in α and β (before stop word removal)

16 - absolute value of the difference in number of content words in α and β

17 - absolute value of the difference in number of words in α and β (before stop word removal)

18 - ratio of the number of content words in α to all words in α (before stop word removal) over the ratio of the number of content words in β to all words in β (before stop word removal)

19 - number of nouns in β

20 - ratio of the number of nouns in α to the number of content words in α

21 - ratio of the number of verbs in α to the number of content words in α

22 - ratio of the number of adjectives in α to the number of content words in α

23 - ratio of the number of conjunctions in α to the number of content words in α

24 - difference in the number of verbs in α and β

Algorithm 1 Alignment Reasoning Rules

1: **if** $\vec{x_8} \geq 1$ & $\vec{x_{22}} \geq 1$
2: **or** $\vec{x_8} \geq 1$ & $\vec{x_4} \geq 1$ & $\vec{x_5} \geq 1$ & $\vec{x_{16}} \geq 1$
3: **or** $\vec{x_8} \geq 1$ & $\vec{x_{23}} \geq \frac{1}{2}$ & $\vec{x_1} \geq \frac{1}{2}$
4: **or** $\vec{x_{21}} \geq \frac{1}{2}$ & $\vec{x_7} \geq 1$ & $\vec{x_{12}} \leq 1$
      return OPPO
5: **if** $\vec{x_2} \geq \frac{1}{3}$ & $\vec{x_{14}} \leq -1$ & $\vec{x_9} \geq 1$ & $\vec{x_{19}} \leq 0$
      & $\vec{x_{13}} \geq \frac{4}{7}$
      return SPE2
6: **if** $\vec{x_{14}} \geq 1$ & $\vec{x_9} \geq 1$ & $\vec{x_2} \leq 0$ & $\vec{x_6} \geq 1$
      & $\vec{x_{11}} \leq 4$ & $\vec{x_{24}} \leq 0$
7: **or** $\vec{x_{14}} \geq 1$ & $\vec{x_{17}} \geq 2$ & $\vec{x_{13}} \geq \frac{5}{7}$
8: **or** $\vec{x_{15}} \geq 1$ & $\vec{x_{18}} \geq \frac{8}{9}$ & $\vec{x_2} \leq 0$ & $\vec{x_3} \geq 1$
9: **or** $\frac{1}{4} \leq \vec{x_1} \leq \frac{2}{3}$ & $\vec{x_{14}} \geq 1$ & $\vec{x_5} \leq 0$
      & $\vec{x_{20}} \leq \frac{1}{5}$ & $\vec{x_{18}} \leq 1$ & $\vec{x_{13}} \geq \frac{2}{3}$
      return SPE1
10: **if** $\vec{x_2} \geq \frac{1}{2}$ & $\vec{x_1} \geq \frac{1}{3}$ & $\vec{x_{10}} \geq 1$
      return SIMI
11: **return** EQUI

It is interesting to note that there is no classifier for the REL class. The data set was heavily skewed towards the EQUI class which consisted of 60% of the total data, leaving a small percentage to be divided among the remaining 5 classes, with just around 5% being REL. With a larger training set we would ex-

pect a classifier for REL to be generated.

2.5 Alignment Scoring

Alignment scores are assigned as either the required scores, 0 for NOALI and 5 or EQUI, or the average alignment score for each class as in (Karumuri et al., 2015). The average alignment score for classes were computed both for each topic alone and for all topics combined. The best performing set of scores came for all topics, came from the images data set alone. Scores used for each class are as follows: EQUI = 5.00, OPPO = 4.00, SPE1 = 3.24, SPE2 = 3.69, SIMI = 2.975, REL = 3.00, NOALI = 0.00.

3 Results

The performance of VRep is shown below for SemEval 2016 Task 1 and Task 2 test data sets. The baseline described by the task organizers (Agirre et al., 2015) is shown for comparison for Task 2. Baseline results were not made available for Task 1.

3.1 Task 1 - Semantic Similarity

For Task 1 the Pearson Correlation Coefficient between VRep's results and Gold Standard results are reported for the 2016 Task 1 Test Data[5]. A value of 1.0 indicates perfect correlation, 0.0 indicates no correlation. We ran VRep on five data sets with the results of each data set shown in Table 1. More details on the data sets and evaluation metrics are described in the competition summary[6].

Data set	VRep
answers-answers	0.29487
headlines	0.68185
plagiarism	0.69730
post editing	0.72966
question-question	0.49029
Mean	0.578794

Table 1: Results of VRep on SemEval 2016 Task 1 Test Data

3.2 Task 2 - Interpretable Semantic Similarity

For Task 2, we report results for the Gold Chunks scenario (data is pre-chunked). Each data set is evaluated using the F1 score in four categories:

---

[5]http://alt.qcri.org/semeval2016/task1/data/uploads/sts2016-english-with-gs-v1.0.zip

[6]http://alt.qcri.org/semeval2016/task1/

(Ali) - Alignment - F1 score of the chunk alignment

(Type) - Alignment Type - F1 score of the alignment reasoning

(Score) - Alignment Scoring - F1 score of alignment scoring

(Typ+Scor) - Alignment Type and Score - a combined F1 score of alignment reasoning and scoring

F1 scores range from 0.0 to 1.0 with 1.0 being the best score. Data sets are available online[7] and evaluation metrics are described in more detail in the competition summary (Agirre et al., 2015).

Data set	Baseline	VRep
Answers-Students		
F1 Ali	0.8203	0.7723
F1 Type	0.5566	0.5249
F1 Score	0.7464	0.7014
F1 Typ+Scor	0.5566	0.5226
Headlines		
F1 Ali	0.8462	0.8908
F1 Type	0.5462	0.6015
F1 Score	0.7610	0.8027
F1 Typ+Scor	0.5461	0.5964
Images		
F1 Ali	0.8556	0.8539
F1 Type	0.4799	0.5516
F1 Score	0.7456	0.7651
F1 Typ+Scor	0.4799	0.5478

Table 2: Results of VRep on SemEval 2016 Task 2 Test Data

4 Component Analysis

In this section the contributions of system components and possible additions are evaluated. VRep can be split into two major components, STS and Alignment Reasoning, both of which have different evaluation criteria. Data used for this section comes from the SemEval 2015 Task 1[8] training data and SemEval 2016 Task 2[9] training data. Two-Tailed p-values are shown in the Tables 3 and 4.

---

[7]http://alt.qcri.org/semeval2016/task2/data/uploads/
test_goldstandard.tar.gz

[8]http://ixa2.si.ehu.es/stswiki/images/2/21/STS2015-en
-rawdata-scripts.zip

[9]http://alt.qcri.org/semeval2016/task2/data/uploads/train
_2015_10_22.utf-8.tar.gz

$$LevenshteinMeasure = \begin{cases} \frac{\beta - \delta}{\beta} & \delta < \beta \\ 0 & \delta \geq \beta \end{cases} \qquad (2)$$

where δ is the Levenshtein distance between the two words, and β is the threshold used

4.1 STS Component Analysis

Pearson Correlation Coefficients of STS scores of Task 1 and the F1 Ali Task 2 are used as evaluation metrics for the STS portion of VRep. Tables 3 and 4 show the effects of adding a component to the *Basic* system. Each component and the *Basic* system are described below:

1. As a baseline a *Basic* system which only applies Equation (1) is used. For Task 1 the result is scaled by 5. For Task 2 each chunk is aligned with the chunk with the highest $chunkSim$. No thresholding, or preprocessing is performed.

2. *Threshold* adds a threshold to $sim(w_i, w_j)$ in Equation (1). A modest threshold of 0.4 was used. The optimum threshold of 0.9 used in the final system was found with the system as a whole. We did not perform a grid search to optimize the threshold for all component tests.

3. *Stop Removal* adds stop word removal as described in subsection 2.1.

4. *Levenshtein* modifies $sim(w_i, w_j)$ for words not in WordNet. Rather than using a binary value for exact string matching the Levenshtein measure shown in Equation (2) is used. This allows for slight differences in spelling, plurality, tenses, etc. The measure requires a threshold parameter, β which limits the maximum Levenshtein distance (δ) and scales the Levenshtein Measure between 0.0 and 1.0. $\beta = 2.0$ was found via a grid search to perform best. The Levenshtein Measure is unnecessary for these tasks most likely because, as stated in section 1, words not in WordNet tend to be proper nouns or abbreviations for which the spelling is the same, and for short words such as "he" or "she", "is" or "in", even small edit distances can transform the word into a completely unrelated word.

	F1 Ali	p-value	significant
Basic	65.40	-	-
Threshold	0.7263	<0.0001	yes
Stop Removal	0.7349	<0.0001	yes
Levenshtein	0.6586	0.1445	no

Table 3: The effects of additional components to the core VRep system on Task 1

	F1 Ali	p-value	significant
Basic	0.7508	-	-
Threshold	0.8812	<0.0001	yes
Stop Removal	0.7511	0.9920	no
Levenshtein	0.7524	0.7795	no
WSD	0.7799	<0.0001	yes
Threshold + WSD	0.8216	<0.0001	yes

Table 4: The effects of components to the core VRep system on Task 2

5. Word Sense Disambiguation (*WSD*) should help to reduce noisy alignments by using the correct synset when computing the Vector relatedness measure. We used the entire sentence (all chunks) as input to SenseRelate::AllWords (Patwardhan et al., 2003). WSD improves results when used as a single component, but when used in combination with a threshold (*Threshold + WSD*) results are worse than a threshold alone. This is likely due to the fact that both WSD and thresholding aim to reduce noisy STS and chunk alignments. When used singularly they both achieve this task, but in combination WSD errors reduce performance.

Analysis of the test data indicated that the addition of these extra components was unnecessary, however to further analyze their contributions three runs were submitted for the both tasks 1 and 2. Run 1 used the *basic* system, run 2 eliminated the stop removal preprocessing step, and run 3 used the *basic* system with the *Levenshtein* measure described above. Test results were mixed and data set dependant, see the respective competition summaries (Agirre et al., 2016) for complete results.

4.2 Alignment Reasoning Component Analysis

For alignment reasoning, only the assignment of a label (Type) to a chunk pair is evaluated. We used the gold standard alignments provided for each data set, converted each gold standard chunk pair to the

	Answers	Headlines	Images
Baseline	67.9	61.4	54.2
Naive Bayes	23.9	41.5	35.1
Bayes Net	49.3	58.9	51.3
SMO	69.6	65.7	54.9
Decision Table	67.5	65.7	55.8
J48	66.1	64.9	52.7
Random Forest	68.4	65.8	53.6
JRip	68.9	65.4	56.2

Table 5: The performance of different classifiers on alignment reasoning

entire set of 72 features and tested multiple classification algorithms. All classifiers are WEKA (Hall et al., 2009) implementations; results are shown in Table 5. The baseline score is calculated as simply assigning the most common class, EQUI.

5 Conclusions and Future Work

In future iterations, more analysis should be done to refine the features used in classification. Using JRIP and other analysis criteria we can see see why certain features are discriminative, and develop more informative features.

Rather than relying solely on the *Levenshtein* measure for words outside of WordNet, additional metrics, such as word2vec (Mikolov et al., 2013) could be incorporated.

Additional data should be added for training classifiers. The top performing classifier was generated from all data combined indicating that additional samples are necessary. It is likely that given more data, topic specific classifiers will outperform the general classifier we evaluated. Additional data will also help to reduce the class imbalance and will likely result in a set of rules for the REL class.

Since VRep already makes use of WordNet, it could be easily expanded to compete in the polarity subtask by implementing a polarity classifier using SentiWordNet (Baccianella et al., 2010).

6 Acknowledgments

We would like to thank Dr. Bridget McInnes for her advice during the development of VRep, and Uzair Abbasi for his contributions to the initial development of the system.

References

Eneko Agirre, Carmen Banea, et al. 2015. Semeval-2015 task 2: Semantic textual similarity, english, spanish and pilot on interpretability. In *Proceedings of the 9th International Workshop on Semantic Evaluation (SemEval 2015), June*.

Eneko Agirre, Aitor Gonzalez-Agirre, Inigo Lopez-Gazpio, Montse Maritxalar, German Rigau, and Larraitz Uria. 2016. Semeval-2016 task 2: Interpretable semantic textual similarity. In *Proceedings of the 10th International Workshop on Semantic Evaluation (SemEval 2016)*, San Diego, California, June.

Stefano Baccianella, Andrea Esuli, and Fabrizio Sebastiani. 2010. Sentiwordnet 3.0: An enhanced lexical resource for sentiment analysis and opinion mining. In *LREC*, volume 10, pages 2200–2204.

Rajendra Banjade, Nobal B Niraula, Nabin Maharjan, Vasile Rus, Dan Stefanescu, Mihai Lintean, and Dipesh Gautam. 2015. Nerosim: A system for measuring and interpreting semantic textual similarity.

William W. Cohen. 1995. Fast effective rule induction. In *Twelfth International Conference on Machine Learning*, pages 115–123. Morgan Kaufmann.

Christiane Fellbaum. 2005. Wordnet and wordnets.

Mark Hall, Eibe Frank, Geoffrey Holmes, Bernhard Pfahringer, Peter Reutemann, and Ian H Witten. 2009. The weka data mining software: an update. *ACM SIGKDD explorations newsletter*, 11(1):10–18.

Sakethram Karumuri, Viswanadh Kumar Reddy Vuggumudi, and Sai Charan Raj Chitirala. 2015. Umduluthblueteam: Svcsts-a multilingual and chunk level semantic similarity system. *SemEval-2015*, page 107.

Tomas Mikolov, Ilya Sutskever, Kai Chen, Greg S Corrado, and Jeff Dean. 2013. Distributed representations of words and phrases and their compositionality. In *Advances in neural information processing systems*, pages 3111–3119.

Siddharth Patwardhan, Satanjeev Banerjee, and Ted Pedersen. 2003. Using measures of semantic relatedness for word sense disambiguation. In *Computational linguistics and intelligent text processing*, pages 241–257. Springer.

Ted Pedersen, Siddharth Patwardhan, and Jason Michelizzi. 2004. Wordnet::similarity: measuring the relatedness of concepts. In *Demonstration papers at hlt-naacl 2004*, pages 38–41. Association for Computational Linguistics.

Dan Ştefănescu, Rajendra Banjade, and Vasile Rus. 2014. A sentence similarity method based on chunking and information content. In *Computational Linguistics and Intelligent Text Processing*, pages 442–453. Springer.

UTA_DLNLP at SemEval-2016 Task 1: Semantic Textual Similarity: A Unified Framework for Semantic Processing and Evaluation

Peng Li
Computer Science and Engineering
University of Texas at Arlington
jerryli1981@gmail.com

Heng Huang[*]
Computer Science and Engineering
University of Texas at Arlington
heng@uta.edu

Abstract

In this paper, we propose a deep neural network based natural language processing system for semantic textual similarity prediction. We leverage multi-layer bidirectional LSTM to learn sentence representation. After that, we construct matching features followed by Highway Multilayer Perceptron to make predictions. Experimental results demonstrate that this approach can't get better results on standard evaluation datasets.

1 Introduction

Traditional approaches (Lai and Hockenmaier, 2014; Zhao et al., 2014; Jimenez et al., 2014) for semantic textual similarity prediction usually build the supervised model using a variety of hand crafted features. Hundreds of features generated at different linguistic levels are exploited to boost classification. With the success of deep learning in many machine learning related applications, there has been much interest in applying deep neural network based techniques to further improve the prediction tasks in natural language processing (NLP) (Socher et al., 2011b; Iyyer et al., 2014; Tai et al., 2015).

A key component of deep neural network is word embeddings which serves as a lookup table to get word representations. From low-level NLP tasks such as language modeling, POS tagging, name entity recognition, and semantic role labeling, to high-

level tasks such as machine translation, information retrieval and semantic analysis (Kalchbrenner and Blunsom, 2013; Socher et al., 2011a; Tai et al., 2015). Deep word representation learning has demonstrated its importance for these tasks. All the tasks get performance improvement via further learning either word level representations or sentence level representations.

In this work, we focus on deep neural network based semantic textual similarity prediction. We use multi-layer bidirectional LSTM (Long Short Term Memory) (Graves et al., 2013) to learn sentence representations. After that, we construct matching features followed by Highway Multilayer Perceptron to learn high-level hidden matching feature representations. Below, we will briefly introduce Multi-Layer Bidirectional LSTM.

2 Multi-Layer Bidirectional LSTM

2.1 RNN vs LSTM

Recurrent neural networks (RNNs) are capable of modeling sequences of varying lengths via the recursive application of a transition function on a hidden state. For example, at each time step t, an RNN takes the input vector $\mathbf{x}_t \in \mathbb{R}^n$ and the hidden state vector $\mathbf{h}_{t-1} \in \mathbb{R}^m$, then applies affine transformation followed by an element-wise nonlinearity such as hyperbolic tangent function to produce the next hidden state vector $\mathbf{h}_t$:

$$\mathbf{h}_t = \tanh(\mathbf{W}\mathbf{x}_t + \mathbf{U}\mathbf{h}_{t-1} + \mathbf{b}). \tag{1}$$

A major issue of RNNs using these transition functions is that it is difficult to learn long-range de-

---
[*] To whom all correspondence should be addressed. This work was partially supported by NSF-IIS 1117965, NSF-IIS 1302675, NSF-IIS 1344152, NSF-DBI 1356628, NIH R01 AG049371.

Proceedings of SemEval-2016, pages 584–587,
San Diego, California, June 16-17, 2016. ©2016 Association for Computational Linguistics

pendencies during training step because the components of the gradient vector can grow or decay exponentially (Bengio et al., 1994).

The LSTM architecture (Hochreiter and Schmidhuber, 1998) addresses the problem of learning long range dependencies by introducing a memory cell that is able to preserve state over long periods of time. Concretely, at each time step t, the LSTM *unit* can be defined as a collection of vectors in $\mathbb{R}^d$: an *input gate* $\mathbf{i}_t$, a *forget gate* $\mathbf{f}_t$, an *output gate* $\mathbf{o}_t$, a *memory cell* $\mathbf{c}_t$ and a hidden state $\mathbf{h}_t$. We refer to d as the *memory dimensionality* of the LSTM. One step of an LSTM takes as input $\mathbf{x}_t$, $\mathbf{h}_{t-1}$, $\mathbf{c}_{t-1}$ and produces $\mathbf{h}_t$, $\mathbf{c}_t$ via the following transition equations:

$$
\begin{aligned}
\mathbf{i}_t &= \sigma(\mathbf{W}^{(i)}\mathbf{x}_t + \mathbf{U}^{(i)}\mathbf{h}_{t-1} + \mathbf{b}^{(i)}), \\
\mathbf{f}_t &= \sigma(\mathbf{W}^{(f)}\mathbf{x}_t + \mathbf{U}^{(f)}\mathbf{h}_{t-1} + \mathbf{b}^{(f)}), \\
\mathbf{o}_t &= \sigma(\mathbf{W}^{(o)}\mathbf{x}_t + \mathbf{U}^{(o)}\mathbf{h}_{t-1} + \mathbf{b}^{(o)}), \\
\mathbf{u}_t &= \tanh(\mathbf{W}^{(u)}\mathbf{x}_t + \mathbf{U}^{(u)}\mathbf{h}_{t-1} + \mathbf{b}^{(u)}), \\
\mathbf{c}_t &= \mathbf{i}_t \odot \mathbf{u}_t + \mathbf{f}_t \odot \mathbf{c}_{t-1}, \\
\mathbf{h}_t &= \mathbf{o}_t \odot \tanh(\mathbf{c}_t),
\end{aligned}
\tag{2}
$$

where $\sigma(\cdot)$ and $\tanh(\cdot)$ are the element-wise sigmoid and hyperbolic tangent functions, $\odot$ is the element-wise multiplication operator.

2.2 Model Description

One shortcoming of conventional RNNs is that they are only able to make use of previous context. In semantic text similarity prediction task, the decision is made after the whole sentence pair is digested. Therefore, exploring future context would be better for sequence meaning representation. Bidirectional RNNs architecture (Graves et al., 2013) proposed a solution of making prediction based on future words. At each time step t, the model maintains two hidden states, one for the left-to-right propagation $\overrightarrow{\mathbf{h}}_t$ and the other for the right-to-left propagation $\overleftarrow{\mathbf{h}}_t$. The hidden state of the Bidirectional LSTM is the concatenation of the forward and backward hidden states. The following equations illustrate the main ideas:

$$
\begin{aligned}
\overrightarrow{\mathbf{h}}_t &= \tanh(\overrightarrow{\mathbf{W}}\mathbf{x}_t + \overrightarrow{\mathbf{U}}\,\overrightarrow{\mathbf{h}}_{t-1} + \overrightarrow{\mathbf{b}}) \\
\overleftarrow{\mathbf{h}}_t &= \tanh(\overleftarrow{\mathbf{W}}\mathbf{x}_t + \overleftarrow{\mathbf{U}}\,\overleftarrow{\mathbf{h}}_{t+1} + \overleftarrow{\mathbf{b}}),
\end{aligned}
\tag{3}
$$

Deep RNNs can be created by stacking multiple RNN hidden layer on top of each other, with the output sequence of one layer forming the input sequence for the next. Assuming the same hidden layer function is used for all N layers in the stack, the hidden vectors $\mathbf{h}^n$ are iteratively computed from $n = 1$ to N and $t = 1$ to T:

$$
\mathbf{h}_t^n = \tanh(\mathbf{W}\mathbf{h}_t^{n-1} + \mathbf{U}\mathbf{h}_{t-1}^n + \mathbf{b}). \tag{4}
$$

Multilayer bidirectional RNNs can be implemented by replacing each hidden vector $\mathbf{h}^n$ with the forward and backward vectors $\overrightarrow{\mathbf{h}^n}$ and $\overleftarrow{\mathbf{h}^n}$, and ensuring that every hidden layer receives input from both the forward and backward layers at the level below. Furthermore, we can apply LSTM memory cell to hidden layers to construct multilayer bidirectional LSTM.

Finally, we can concatenate sequence hidden matrix $\overrightarrow{\mathbf{M}} \in \mathbb{R}^{n \times d}$ and reversed sequence hidden matrix $\overleftarrow{\mathbf{M}} \in \mathbb{R}^{n \times d}$ to form the sentence representation. Here n is the number of layers, d is the *memory dimensionality* of the LSTM. In the next section, we will use the two matrices to generate matching feature planes via linear algebra operations.

3 Learning from Matching Features

Inspired by (Tai et al., 2015), we apply element-wise merge to first sentence matrix $M_1 \in \mathbb{R}^{n \times 2d}$ and second sentence matrix $M_2 \in \mathbb{R}^{n \times 2d}$. Similar to previous method, we can define two simple matching feature planes (*FPs*) with below equations:

$$
\begin{aligned}
FP_1 &= M_1 \odot M_2, \\
FP_2 &= |M_1 - M_2|,
\end{aligned}
\tag{5}
$$

where $\odot$ is the element-wise multiplication. The FP_1 measure can be interpreted as an element-wise comparison of the signs of the input representations. The FP_2 measure can be interpreted as the distance between the input representations.

3.1 Highway MLP

Inspired by (Kim et al., 2016), we build Highway Multilayer Perceptron (HMLP) layer to further enhance representation learning. Conventional MLP applies an affine transformation followed by a nonlinearity to obtain a new set of features:

$$
\mathbf{z} = g(\mathbf{W}\mathbf{y} + \mathbf{b}). \tag{6}
$$

One layer of a highway network does the following:

$$\mathbf{z} = \mathbf{t} \odot g(\mathbf{W}_H\mathbf{y} + \mathbf{b}_H) + (1 - \mathbf{t}) \odot \mathbf{y}, \quad (7)$$

where g is a nonlinearity, $\mathbf{t} = \sigma(\mathbf{W}_T\mathbf{y} + \mathbf{b}_T)$ is called as the transform gate, and $(1 - \mathbf{t})$ is called as the carry gate. Similar to the memory cells in LSTM networks, highway layers allow adaptively carrying some dimensions of the input directly to the input for training deep networks.

4 Experiments

We use all previous dataset to train our LSTM classifier. The total number of training examples is 12912, and the number of dev examples is 680. Note that we didn't use cross validation to find the best model. Table 1 shows the Pearson correlation results of STS task.

4.1 Hyperparameters and Training Details

We first initialize our word representations using publicly available 300-dimensional Glove word vectors [1]. LSTM memory dimension is 100, the number of layers is 2. Training is done through stochastic gradient descent over shuffled mini-batches with the AdaGrad update rule (Duchi et al., 2011). The learning rate is set to 0.05. The mini-batch size is 25. The model parameters were regularized with a per-minibatch L2 regularization strength of 10^{-4}. Note that word embeddings were fixed during training.

4.2 Objective Functions

The task of semantic similarity prediction tries to measure the degree of semantic similarity of a sentence pair by assigning a similarity score ranging from 1 (completely unrelated) to 5 (semantically equivalent). Inspired by (Tai et al., 2015), given a sentence pair, we wish to predict a real-valued similarity score in a range of $[1, K]$, where $K > 1$ is an integer. The sequence $1, 2, ..., K$ is the ordinal scale of similarity, where higher scores indicate greater degrees of similarity. We can predict the similarity score $\hat{y}$ by predicting the probability that the learned hidden representation x_h belongs to the ordinal scale. This is done by projecting an input representation onto a set of hyperplanes, each of which corresponds to a class. The distance from the input

---

[1] http://nlp.stanford.edu/projects/glove/

to a hyperplane reflects the probability that the input will located in corresponding scale.

Mathematically, the similarity score $\hat{y}$ can be written as:

$$
\begin{aligned}
\hat{y} &= r^T \cdot \hat{p}_\theta(y|x_h) \\
&= r^T \cdot softmax(W \cdot x_h + b) \\
&= r^T \cdot \frac{e^{W_i x_h + b_i}}{\sum_j e^{W_j x_h + b_j}}
\end{aligned}
\quad (8)
$$

where $r^T = [1\ 2 \ldots K]$ and the weight matrix W and b are parameters.

In order to introduce the task objective function, we define a sparse target distribution p that satisfies $y = r^T p$:

$$
p_i = \begin{cases}
y - \lfloor y \rfloor, & i = \lfloor y \rfloor + 1 \\
\lfloor y \rfloor - y + 1, & i = \lfloor y \rfloor \\
0 & otherwise
\end{cases}
\quad (9)
$$

where $1 \leq i \leq K$. The objective function then can be defined as the regularized KL-divergence between p and p_θ:

$$
J(\theta) = -\frac{1}{m}\sum_{k=1}^{m} KL(p^{(k)}\|p_\theta^k) + \frac{\lambda}{2}\|\theta\|_2^2, \quad (10)
$$

where m is the number of training pairs and the superscript k indicates the k-th sentence pair (Tai et al., 2015).

5 Conclusions and Discussions

In this paper, we propose a deep neural network architecture that leverages pre-trained word embeddings to learn sentence meanings. Our approach first generates word sequence representations as inputs into a multilayer bidirectional LSTM to learn sentence representations. After that, we construct matching features followed by highway MLP to learn high-level hidden matching feature representations. Experimental results on benchmark datasets demonstrate that our model didn't achieved the state-of-the-art performance compared with other approaches. Our approach is above the median scores only on question-question domain. We suspect our model have worse capability of domain adaption. Also the Highway MLP may increase the model complexity and lead to worse performance.

Method	All	answer-answer	headlines	plagiarism	postediting	question-question
Our Run: 100-1	0.64965	0.46391	0.74499	0.74003	0.71947	0.58083
Our Run: 150-1	0.64500	0.43042	0.72133	0.71620	0.74471	0.62006
Our Run: 150-3	0.63698	0.41871	0.72485	0.70296	0.69652	0.65543
Median	0.68923	0.48018	0.76439	0.78949	0.81241	0.57140
Best	0.77807	0.69235	0.82749	0.84138	0.86690	0.74705

Table 1: The pearson correlation score comparison on STS Task, Here 100 and 150 are LSTM memory dimension. 1 and 3 are the number of LSTM layers

References

Yoshua Bengio, Patrice Simard, and Paolo Fransconi. 1994. Learning long-term dependencies with gradient descent is difficult. In *IEEE Transactions on Neural Networks 5(2)*.

John Duchi, Elad Hazan, and Yoram Singer. 2011. Adaptive subgradient methods for online learning and stochastic optimization. *The Journal of Machine Learning Research*, 12:2121–2159.

Alex Graves, Navdeep Jaitly, and Abdel rahman Mohamed. 2013. Hybrid speech recognition with deep bidirectional lstm. In *IEEE Workshop on Au- tomatic Speech Recognition and Understanding (ASRU)*, pages 273–278.

Sepp Hochreiter and Jürgen Schmidhuber. 1998. Long short-term memory. In *Neural Computation 9(8)*.

Mohit Iyyer, Jordan Boyd-Graber, Leonardo Claudino, Richard Socher, and Hal Daumé III. 2014. A neural network for factoid question answering over paragraphs. In *Empirical Methods in Natural Language Processing*.

Sergio Jimenez, George Duenas, Julia Baquero, and Alexander Gelbukh. 2014. UNAL-NLP: Combining soft cardinality features for semantic textual similarity, relatedness and entailment. In *Proceedings of SemEval 2014: International Workshop on Semantic Evaluation*.

Nal Kalchbrenner and Phil Blunsom. 2013. Recurrent continuous translation models. In *Proceedings of the 2013 Conference on Empirical Methods in Natural Language Processing*, pages 1700–1709, Seattle, Washington, USA. Association for Computational Linguistics.

Yoon Kim, Yacine Jernite, David Sontag, and Alexander M Rush. 2016. Character-aware neural language models. In *Thirtieth AAAI Conference on Artificial Intelligence*.

Alice Lai and Julia Hockenmaier. 2014. Illinois-lh: A denotational and distributional approach to semantics. In *Proceedings of SemEval 2014: International Workshop on Semantic Evaluation*.

Richard Socher, Eric H Huang, Jeffrey Pennin, Christopher D Manning, and Andrew Y Ng. 2011a. Dynamic pooling and unfolding recursive autoencoders for paraphrase detection. In *Advances in Neural Information Processing Systems*, pages 801–809.

Richard Socher, Jeffrey Pennington, Eric H Huang, Andrew Y Ng, and Christopher D Manning. 2011b. Semi-supervised recursive autoencoders for predicting sentiment distributions. In *Proceedings of the Conference on Empirical Methods in Natural Language Processing*, pages 151–161. Association for Computational Linguistics.

Kai Sheng Tai, Richard Socher, and Christopher D Manning. 2015. Improved semantic representations from tree-structured long short-term memory networks. *arXiv preprint arXiv:1503.00075*.

Jiang Zhao, Tian Tian Zhu, and Man Lan. 2014. ECNU: One stone two birds: Ensemble of heterogenous measures for semantic relatedness and textual entailment. In *Proceedings of SemEval 2014: International Workshop on Semantic Evaluation*.

UWB at SemEval-2016 Task 1: Semantic Textual Similarity using Lexical, Syntactic, and Semantic Information

Tomáš Brychcín
NTIS – New Technologies
for the Information Society,
Faculty of Applied Sciences,
University of West Bohemia,
Technická 8, 306 14 Plzeň
Czech Republic
brychcin@kiv.zcu.cz

Lukáš Svoboda
Department of Computer
Science and Engineering,
Faculty of Applied Sciences,
University of West Bohemia,
Technická 8, 306 14 Plzeň
Czech Republic
svobikl@kiv.zcu.cz

Abstract

We present our UWB system for Semantic Textual Similarity (STS) task at SemEval 2016. Given two sentences, the system estimates the degree of their semantic similarity.

We use state-of-the-art algorithms for the meaning representation and combine them with the best performing approaches to STS from previous years. These methods benefit from various sources of information, such as lexical, syntactic, and semantic.

In the monolingual task, our system achieve mean Pearson correlation 75.7% compared with human annotators. In the cross-lingual task, our system has correlation 86.3% and is ranked first among 26 systems.

1 Introduction

Semantic Textual Similarity (STS) is one of the core disciplines in Natural Language Processing (NLP). Assume we have two textual fragments (word phrases, sentences, paragraphs, or full documents), the goal is to estimate the degree of their semantic similarity.

STS systems are usually compared with the manually annotated data. In the case of SemEval the data consist of pairs of sentences with a score between 0 and 5 (higher number means higher semantic similarity). For example, English pair

```
Two dogs play in the grass.
Two dogs playing in the snow.
```

has a score 2.8, i.e. the sentences are not equivalent, but share some information.

This year, SemEval's STS is extended with the Spanish-English cross-lingual subtask, where e.g. the pair

```
Tuve el mismo problema que tú.
I had the same problem.
```

has a score 4.8, which means nearly equivalent.

Each year STS belongs to one of the most popular tasks at SemEval competition. The best STS system at SemEval 2012 (Bär et al., 2012) used lexical similarity and Explicit Semantic Analysis (ESA) (Gabrilovich and Markovitch, 2007). In SemEval 2013, the best model (Han et al., 2013) used semantic models such as Latent Semantic Analysis (LSA) (Deerwester et al., 1990), external information sources (WordNet) and n-gram matching techniques. For SemEval 2014 and 2015 the best system comes from (Sultan et al., 2014a; Sultan et al., 2014b; Sultan et al., 2015). They introduced new algorithm, which align the words between two sentences. They showed that this approach can be efficiently used also for STS. Overview of systems participating in previous SemEval competitions can be found in (Agirre et al., 2012; Agirre et al., 2013; Agirre et al., 2014; Agirre et al., 2015).

The best performing systems from previous years are based on various architectures benefiting from lexical, syntactic, and semantic information. In this work we try to use the best techniques presented during last years, enhance them, and combine into a single model.

2 Semantic Textual Similarity

This section describes various techniques for estimating the text similarity.

Proceedings of SemEval-2016, pages 588–594,
San Diego, California, June 16-17, 2016. ©2016 Association for Computational Linguistics

2.1 Lexical and Syntactic Similarity

This section presents the techniques exploiting lexical and syntactic information in the text. Some of them have been successfully used by (Bär et al., 2012). Many of the following techniques benefit from the weighing of words in a sentence using *Term Frequency - Inverse Document Frequency* (TF-IDF) (Manning and Schütze, 1999).

- **Lemma n-gram overlaps:** We compare word n-grams in both sentences using *Jaccard Similarity Coefficient* (JSC) (Manning and Schütze, 1999). We do it separately for different orders $n \in \{1, 2, 3, 4\}$. *Containment Coefficient* (Broder, 1997) is used for orders $n \in \{1, 2\}$. We extend original metrics by weighing of n-grams. We define this weight as a sum of *IDF* values of words in n-gram. N-gram match is not counted as 1 but as the weight of this n-gram. According to our experiments, this weighing significantly improves performance.

  We also use information about the length of *Longest Common Subsequence* compared to the length of the sentences.

- **POS n-gram overlaps:** In similar way as for lemmas, we calculate *Jaccard Similarity Coefficient* and *Containment Coefficient* for n-grams of part-of-speech (POS) tags. Again, we use n-gram weighing and $n \in \{1, 2, 3, 4\}$. These features exploit syntactic similarity of the sentences.

- **Character n-gram overlaps:** Similarly to lemma or POS n-grams, we use *Jaccard Similarity Coefficient* and *Containment Coefficient* for comparing common substrings in both sentences. Here the *IDF* weights are computed on character n-gram level. We use n-gram weighing and $n \in \{2, 3, 4, 5\}$.

  We enrich these features also by *Greedy String Tiling*(Wise, 1996) allowing to deal with reordered text parts and by *Longest Common Substring* (LCS) measuring the ration between LCS and length of the sentences.

- **TF-IDF:** For each word in a sentence we calculate *TF-IDF*. Given the word vocabulary V, the sentence is represented as a vector of dimension $|V|$ with *TF-IDF* values of words present in the sentence. The similarity between two sentences is expressed as cosine similarity between corresponding *TF-IDF* vectors.

2.2 Semantic Similarity

In this section we describe in detail the techniques that are more semantically oriented and are based on *Distributional Hypothesis*. This principle states that we can induce (to some degree) the meaning of words from their distribution in the text. This claim has multiple theoretical roots in psychology, structural linguistics, or lexicography (Firth, 1957; Rubenstein and Goodenough, 1965; Miller and Charles, 1991).

- **Semantic composition:** This approach is based on *Frege's principle of compositionality*, which states that the meaning of a complex expression is determined as a composition of its parts, i.e. words. To represent the meaning of a sentence we use simple linear combination of word vectors, where weights are represented by the *TF-IDF* values of appropriate words. We use state-of-the-art word embedding methods, namely Continuous Bag of Words (CBOW) (Mikolov et al., 2013) and Global Vectors (GloVe) (Pennington et al., 2014). We use cosine similarity to compare vectors.

- **Paragraph2Vec:** Paragraph vectors were proposed in (Le and Mikolov, 2014) as an unsupervised method of learning text representation. Resulting feature vector has fixed dimension while the input text can be of any length. The paragraph vectors and word vectors are concatenated to predict the next word in a context. The paragraph token acts as a memory that remembers what information is missing from the current context. We use cosine similarity for comparing two paragraph vectors.

- **Tree LSTM**: Long Short-Term Memory (LSTM) is a type of Recurrent Neural Network (RNN) with a complex computational unit. We use tree-structured representation of LSTM presented in (Tai et al., 2015). Tree model represents the sentence structure. RNN processes input sentences of variable length via recursive application of a transition function on a hidden state vector h_t. For each sentence pair it creates sentence representations h_L and h_R using Tree-LSTM model. Given these representations, model predicts the similarity score using a neural network considering distance and angle between vectors.

- **Word alignment:** Method presented in (Sultan et al., 2014a; Sultan et al., 2014b; Sultan et al., 2015) has been very successful in last years. Given two sentence we want to compare, this method finds and aligns the words that have similar meaning and similar role in these sentences.

Unlike the original method, we assume that not all word alignments have the same importance for the meaning of the sentences. The weight of a set of words A is a sum of word's *IDF* values $\omega(A) = \sum_{w \in A} \text{IDF}(w)$, where w is a word. Then the sentence similarity is given by

$$\text{sim}(S_1, S_2) = \frac{\omega(A_1) + \omega(A_2)}{\omega(S_1) + \omega(S_2)}, \quad (1)$$

where S_1 and S_2 are input sentences (represented as sets of words). A_1 and A_2 denote the sets of aligned words for S_1 and S_2, respectively. The weighing of alignments improves our results significantly.

2.3 Similarity Combination

The combination of STS techniques is in fact a regression problem where the goal is to find the mapping from input space $x_i \in \mathbb{R}^d$ of d-dimensional real-valued vectors (each value $x_{i,a}$, where $1 \leq a \leq d$ represents the single STS technique) to an output space $y_i \in \mathbb{R}$ of real-valued targets (desired semantic similarity). These mapping are learned from the training data $\{x_i, y_i\}_{i=1}^N$ of size N. There exist a lot of regression methods. We experiment with several of them:

- **Linear Regression:** Linear Regression (LR) is probably the simplest regression method. It is defined as $y_i = \lambda x_i$, where λ is a vector of weights that can be estimated for example by the *least squares method*.

- **Gaussian processes regression:** Gaussian process regression (GPR) is nonparametric kernel-based probabilistic model for non-linear regression (Rasmussen and Williams, 2005).

- **SVM Regression:** We use Support Vector Machines (SVM) for regression with the radial basis functions (RBF) as a kernel. We use improved Sequential Minimal Optimization (SMO) algorithm for parameter estimation introduce in (Shevade et al., 2000).

- **Decision Trees Regression:** The output of the Decision Trees Regression (DTR) (Breiman et al., 1984) is predicted by the sequence of decisions organized in a tree.

- **Perceptron Regression:** Multilayer Perceptron (MLP) is feed-forward artificial neural network that uses back-propagation to classify instances.

3 System Description

This section describes the settings of our final STS system. For monolingual STS task we submitted two runs. First is based on supervised learning and the second is unsupervised system:

- **UWB sup:** Supervised system based on SVM regression with RBF kernel. We use all techniques described in 2 as features for regression. During the regression we also use the simple trick. We create another features represented as a product of each pair of features $x_{i,a} \times x_{i,b}$ for $a \neq b$. We do so to better model the dependencies between single features. Together, we have 301 STS features. The system is trained on all SemEval datasets from prior years (see Table 1).

- **UWB unsup:** Unsupervised system based only on weighted word alignment (Section 2.2).

We handled with the cross-lingual STS task with Spanish-English bilingual sentence pairs in two steps. Firstly, we translated Spanish sentences to English via *Google translator*. The English sentences

Corpora	Pairs
SemEval 2012 Train	2,234
SemEval 2012 Test	3,108
SemEval 2013 Test	1,500
SemEval 2014 Test	3,750
SemEval 2015 Test	3,000

Table 1: STS gold data from prior years.

	News	Multi-Source	Mean	RR	TR
UWB sup	0.9062	**0.8190**	**0.8631**	1	1
UWB unsup	**0.9124**	0.8082	0.8609	2	1

Table 4: Pearson correlations on cross-lingual STS task of SemEval 2016. *RR* denote the run (system) ranking and *TR* denote our team ranking.

were left untouched. Secondly, we used the same STS systems as for monolingual task.

For preprocessing pipeline we used Standford CoreNLP library (Manning et al., 2014), i.e. for tokenization, lemmatization and POS tagging. Most of our STS techniques (apart from word alignment and POS n-gram overlaps) work with lemmas instead of word forms (this leads to slightly better performance). Some of our STS techniques are based on unsupervised learning and thus they need large unannotated corpora to train. We trained Paragraph2Vec, GloVe and CBOW models on *One billion word benchmark* presented in (Chelba et al., 2014). Dimension of vectors for all these models was set to 300. TF-IDF values were also estimated on this corpus.

All regression methods mentioned in Section 2.3 are implemented in WEKA (Hall et al., 2009).

4   Results and Discussion

This section presents the results of our systems for both English monolingual and Spanish-English cross-lingual STS task of SemEval 2016. In addition we present detailed results on the test data from SemEval 2015. As an evaluation measure we use *Pearson correlation* between system output and human annotations.

In the tables we present the correlation for each individual test set. Column *Mean* represents the weighted sum of all correlations, where the weight

are given by the ratio of data set length compared to the full length of all datasets together. The mean value of Pearson correlations is also used as the main evaluation measure for ranking the system submissions.

In the Table 2 we show the results for the test data from 2015. We trained our systems on SemEval STS data from years 2012–2014. We provide comparison of individual STS techniques as well as of different types of regressions. Clearly, the SVM regression and Gaussian processes regression perform best and with our feature set it is 1% better than the winning system of SemEval 2015. The best performing single technique is indisputably the weighed word alignment correlated by 79.6% with gold data. Note that without weighing, we achieved only 74.2% on this data. The original result from authors of this approach was, however, 79.2%. This is probably caused by some inaccuracies in our implementation. Anyway, the weighing improves the correlation even if we compare it to the original results. Note that for estimating regression parameters we use the data from all years apart from 2015 (see Table 1).

The results for monolingual STS task of SemEval 2016 are shown in Table 3. In the time of writing this paper the ranks of submitted systems were not known. Thus we present only our correlations. We can see that our supervised system (SVM regression) performs approximately 3% better than the unsupervised one (weighed word alignment). On the data from SemEval 2015 this difference was not so significant (approximately 1.5%).

Finally, the results for cross-lingual STS task of SemEval 2016 are shown in Table 4. We achieved very high correlations. To be honest we must say that we expected much lower correlation through the fact that we use the machine translation via Google translator causing certainly some inaccuracies (at least in the syntax of the sentence). On the other hand, it proves that our model efficiently generalizes the learned patterns. Here, there is almost no difference in performance between supervised and unsupervised version of submitted systems. Our submitted runs finished first and second among 26 competing systems.

Model \Corpora	Answers-forums	Answers-students	Belief	Headlines	Images	Mean
Winner of SemEval 2015	0.7390	0.7725	0.7491	0.8250	0.8644	0.8015
Linear regression – all lexical	0.7053	0.7656	0.7190	0.7887	0.8246	0.7728
Linear regression – all syntactic	0.3089	0.3165	0.4570	0.2900	0.1862	0.2939
Tf-idf	0.5629	0.6043	0.6762	0.6603	0.7530	0.6593
Tree LSTM	0.4181	0.5490	0.5863	0.7324	0.8168	0.6501
Paragraph2Vec	0.5228	0.7017	0.6643	0.6562	0.7385	0.6725
CBOW composition	0.6216	0.6846	0.7258	0.6927	0.7831	0.7085
GloVe composition	0.5820	0.6311	0.7164	0.6969	0.7972	0.6936
Weighted word alignment	0.7171	**0.7752**	0.7632	0.8179	0.8525	0.7964
Linear regression	**0.7411**	0.7589	0.7739	0.8193	0.8568	0.7982
Gaussian processes regression	0.7363	0.7701	**0.7846**	0.8393	0.8749	0.8112
Decision trees regression	0.6700	0.6991	0.7281	0.7792	0.8206	0.7495
Perceptron regression	0.7060	0.7481	0.7467	0.8093	0.8594	0.7858
SVM regression	0.7375	0.7678	**0.7846**	**0.8398**	**0.8776**	**0.8116**

Table 2: Pearson correlations on SemEval 2015 evaluation data and comparison with the best performing system in this year.

Model \Corpora	Answer-answer	Headlines	Plagiarism	Postediting	Question-question	Mean
UWB sup	0.6215	**0.8189**	0.8236	**0.8209**	**0.7020**	**0.7573**
UWB unsup	**0.6444**	0.7935	**0.8274**	0.8121	0.5338	0.7262

Table 3: Pearson correlations on monolingual STS task of SemEval 2016.

5 Conclusion

In this paper we described our UWB system participating in SemEval 2016 competition in the task of Semantic Textual Similarity. We participated on both monolingual and cross-lingual parts of competition.

Our best results have been achieved by SVM regression of various STS techniques based on lexical, syntactic, and semantic information. This approach has been shown to work well for both subtasks.

Acknowledgments

This publication was supported by the project LO1506 of the Czech Ministry of Education, Youth and Sports and by Grant No. SGS-2016-018 Data and Software Engineering for Advanced Applications. Computational resources were provided by the CESNET LM2015042 and the CERIT Scientific Cloud LM2015085, provided under the programme "Projects of Large Research, Development, and Innovations Infrastructures".

References

Eneko Agirre, Mona Diab, Daniel Cer, and Aitor Gonzalez-Agirre. 2012. Semeval-2012 task 6: A pilot on semantic textual similarity. In *Proceedings of the First Joint Conference on Lexical and Computational Semantics - Volume 1: Proceedings of the Main Conference and the Shared Task, and Volume 2: Proceedings of the Sixth International Workshop on Semantic Evaluation*, SemEval '12, pages 385–393, Stroudsburg, PA, USA. Association for Computational Linguistics.

Eneko Agirre, Daniel Cer, Mona Diab, Aitor Gonzalez-Agirre, and Weiwei Guo. 2013. *sem 2013 shared task: Semantic textual similarity. In *Second Joint Conference on Lexical and Computational Semantics (*SEM), Volume 1: Proceedings of the Main Conference and the Shared Task: Semantic Textual Similarity*, pages 32–43, Atlanta, Georgia, USA, June. Association for Computational Linguistics.

Eneko Agirre, Carmen Banea, Claire Cardie, Daniel

Cer, Mona Diab, Aitor Gonzalez-Agirre, Weiwei Guo, Rada Mihalcea, German Rigau, and Janyce Wiebe. 2014. Semeval-2014 task 10: Multilingual semantic textual similarity. In *Proceedings of the 8th International Workshop on Semantic Evaluation (SemEval 2014)*, pages 81–91, Dublin, Ireland, August. Association for Computational Linguistics and Dublin City University.

Eneko Agirre, Carmen Banea, Claire Cardie, Daniel Cer, Mona Diab, Aitor Gonzalez-Agirre, Weiwei Guo, Inigo Lopez-Gazpio, Montse Maritxalar, Rada Mihalcea, German Rigau, Larraitz Uria, and Janyce Wiebe. 2015. Semeval-2015 task 2: Semantic textual similarity, english, spanish and pilot on interpretability. In *Proceedings of the 9th International Workshop on Semantic Evaluation (SemEval 2015)*, pages 252–263, Denver, Colorado, June. Association for Computational Linguistics.

Daniel Bär, Chris Biemann, Iryna Gurevych, and Torsten Zesch. 2012. Ukp: Computing semantic textual similarity by combining multiple content similarity measures. In *Proceedings of the 6th International Workshop on Semantic Evaluation, held in conjunction with the 1st Joint Conference on Lexical and Computational Semantics*, pages 435–440, Montreal, Canada, June.

Leo Breiman, Jerome Friedman, Charles J. Stone, and R.A. Olshen. 1984. *Classification and Regression Trees*. Wadsworth and Brooks, Monterey, CA.

Andrei Z. Broder. 1997. On the resemblance and containment of documents. In *SEQUENCES '97 Proceedings of the Compression and Complexity of Sequences*, pages 21–29, Jun.

Ciprian Chelba, Tomas Mikolov, Mike Schuster, Qi Ge, Thorsten Brants, Phillipp Koehn, and Tony Robinson. 2014. One billion word benchmark for measuring progress in statistical language modeling. In *Proceedings of the 15th Annual Conference of the International Speech Communication Association*, pages 2635–2639, Singapore, September.

Scott Deerwester, Susan T. Dumais, George W. Furnas, Thomas K. Landauer, and Richard Harshman. 1990. Indexing by latent semantic analysis. *Journal of the American Society for Information Science 41*, pages 391–407.

John R. Firth. 1957. A Synopsis of Linguistic Theory, 1930-1955. *Studies in Linguistic Analysis*, pages 1–32.

Evgeniy Gabrilovich and Shaul Markovitch. 2007. Computing semantic relatedness using wikipedia-based explicit semantic analysis. In *Proceedings of the 20th International Joint Conference on Artifical Intelligence*, IJCAI'07, pages 1606–1611, San Francisco, CA, USA. Morgan Kaufmann Publishers Inc.

Mark Hall, Eibe Frank, Geoffrey Holmes, Bernhard Pfahringer, Peter Reutemann, and Ian H. Witten. 2009. The weka data mining software: An update. *ACM SIGKDD Explorations Newsletter*, 11(1):10–18, November.

Lushan Han, Abhay L. Kashyap, Tim Finin, James Mayfield, and Jonathan Weese. 2013. Umbc_ebiquity-core: Semantic textual similarity systems. In *Second Joint Conference on Lexical and Computational Semantics (*SEM), Volume 1: Proceedings of the Main Conference and the Shared Task: Semantic Textual Similarity*, pages 44–52, Atlanta, Georgia, USA, June. Association for Computational Linguistics.

Quoc V. Le and Tomas Mikolov. 2014. Distributed representations of sentences and documents. In *Proceedings of the 31th International Conference on Machine Learning, ICML 2014, Beijing, China, 21-26 June 2014*, pages 1188–1196.

Christopher D. Manning and Hinrich Schütze. 1999. *Foundations of Statistical Natural Language Processing*. MIT Press, Cambridge, MA, USA.

Christopher D. Manning, Mihai Surdeanu, John Bauer, Jenny Finkel, Steven J. Bethard, and David McClosky. 2014. The Stanford CoreNLP natural language processing toolkit. In *Association for Computational Linguistics (ACL) System Demonstrations*, pages 55–60.

Tomas Mikolov, Kai Chen, Greg Corrado, and Jeffrey Dean. 2013. Efficient estimation of word representations in vector space.

George A. Miller and Walter G. Charles. 1991. Contextual correlates of semantic similarity. *Language and Cognitive Processes*, 6(1):1–28.

Jeffrey Pennington, Richard Socher, and Christopher D Manning. 2014. Glove: Global vectors for word representation. In *Proceedings of the 2014 Conference on Empirical Methods in Natural Language Processing (EMNLP)*, pages 1532–1543.

Carl Edward Rasmussen and Christopher K. I. Williams. 2005. *Gaussian Processes for Machine Learning (Adaptive Computation and Machine Learning)*. The MIT Press.

Herbert Rubenstein and John B. Goodenough. 1965. Contextual correlates of synonymy. *Communications of the ACM*, 8(10):627–633, October.

Shirish K. Shevade, Sathiya S. Keerthi, Chiru Bhattacharyya, and K.R.K. Murthy. 2000. Improvements to the smo algorithm for svm regression. *IEEE Transactions on Neural Networks*, 11(5):1188–1193, Sep.

Md Sultan, Steven Bethard, and Tamara Sumner. 2014a. Back to basics for monolingual alignment: Exploiting word similarity and contextual evidence. *Transactions of the Association for Computational Linguistics*, 2:219–230.

Md Arafat Sultan, Steven Bethard, and Tamara Sumner. 2014b. Dls@cu: Sentence similarity from word alignment. In *Proceedings of the 8th International Workshop on Semantic Evaluation (SemEval 2014)*, pages 241–246, Dublin, Ireland, August. Association for Computational Linguistics and Dublin City University.

Md Arafat Sultan, Steven Bethard, and Tamara Sumner. 2015. Dls@cu: Sentence similarity from word alignment and semantic vector composition. In *Proceedings of the 9th International Workshop on Semantic Evaluation (SemEval 2015)*, pages 148–153, Denver, Colorado, June. Association for Computational Linguistics.

Kai Sheng Tai, Richard Socher, and Christopher D. Manning. 2015. Improved semantic representations from tree-structured long short-term memory networks. In *Proceedings of the 53rd Annual Meeting of the Association for Computational Linguistics and the 7th International Joint Conference on Natural Language Processing (Volume 1: Long Papers)*, pages 1556–1566, Beijing, China, July. Association for Computational Linguistics.

Michael J. Wise. 1996. Yap3: Improved detection of similarities in computer program and other texts. In *Proceedings of the Twenty-seventh SIGCSE Technical Symposium on Computer Science Education*, SIGCSE '96, pages 130–134, New York, NY, USA. ACM.

HHU at SemEval-2016 Task 1: Multiple Approaches to Measuring Semantic Textual Similarity

Matthias Liebeck, Philipp Pollack, Pashutan Modaresi, Stefan Conrad
Institute of Computer Science
Heinrich Heine University Düsseldorf
D-40225 Düsseldorf, Germany
{liebeck,modaresi,conrad}@cs.uni-duesseldorf.de
philipp.pollack@hhu.de

Abstract

This paper describes our participation in the SemEval-2016 Task 1: *Semantic Textual Similarity* (STS). We developed three methods for the English subtask (STS Core). The first method is unsupervised and uses WordNet and word2vec to measure a token-based overlap. In our second approach, we train a neural network on two features. The third method uses word2vec and LDA with regression splines.

1 Introduction

Measuring semantic textual similarity (STS) is the task of determining the similarity between two different text passages. The task is important for various natural language processing tasks like topic detection or automated text summarization because languages are versatile and authors can express similar content or even the same content with different words. Predicting semantic textual similarity has been a recurring task in SemEval challenges (Agirre et al., 2015; Agirre et al., 2014; Agirre et al., 2013; Agirre et al., 2012). As in previous years, the purpose of the STS task is the development of systems that automatically predict the semantic similarity of two sentences in the continuous interval $[0, 5]$ where 0 represents a complete dissimilarity and 5 denotes a complete semantic equivalence between the sentences (Agirre et al., 2015).

The organizers provide sentence pairs whose semantic similarities have to be predicted by the contestants. The quality of a system is determined by calculating the Pearson correlation between the predicted values and a human gold standard that has been created by crowdsourcing. The data from previous STS tasks can be used for training supervised methods.

The test data consists of text content from different sources. In this year's shared task, the systems are tested on five different categories with different topics and varying textual characteristics like text length or spelling errors: *answer-answer*, *plagiarism*, *postediting*, *headlines*, and *question-question*

The remainder of the paper is structured as follows: Section 2 discusses related approaches to automatically determining semantic textual similarity. Section 3 describes our three methods in detail. We discuss their results in section 4. Finally, we conclude in chapter 5 and outline future work.

2 Related Work

In the last shared tasks, most of the teams used natural languages processing techniques like tokenization, part-of-speech tagging, lemmatization, named entity recognition and word embeddings. External resources like WordNet (Miller, 1995) and word2vec (Mikolov et al., 2013) are commonly used. In (Agirre et al., 2012) and (Agirre et al., 2013), the organizers provide a list and a comparison of the tools and resources used by the participants in the first two years, respectively.

In each year, the organizers provide a baseline value by calculating the cosine similarity of the binary bag-of-words vectors from both sentences in each sample. Since 2013, TakeLab (Šarić et al., 2012), the best ranked system in 2012, has also been used as another baseline value.

Most of the teams used machine learning in 2015

Proceedings of SemEval-2016, pages 595–601,
San Diego, California, June 16-17, 2016. ©2016 Association for Computational Linguistics

(Agirre et al., 2015). In 2014, the best two submitted runs were from unsupervised systems.

The work most closely related to our Overlap method is (Han et al., 2015), which uses a two-phased approach called *Align-and-Differentiate*. In the first phase, they compute an alignment score. Afterwards, they modify the alignment score in a differentiate phase by subtracting a penalty score for terms that can not be aligned. The idea behind the computation of our alignment scores is the same: For each sample, we average over the crosswise similarities between the sentences by aligning them, accumulating similarities between tokens and dividing by sentence lengths. The results of the alignment score in our Overlap method differ because (i) our alignment is different, (ii) we use another similarity function for tokens, and (iii) our preprocessing is different.

In (Vu et al., 2015), the similarity between LDA vectors calculated from documents is used together with syntactic and lexical similarity measures to compute the similarity between text fragments. This idea is also incorporated in our Deep LDA method. Moreover, both approaches use different flavors of regression analysis for the final model prediction. Regression analysis was also used in (Sultan et al., 2015), where the authors combine an unsupervised method with ridge regression analysis. Our approach differs in the sense that it introduces k-nearest neighbors as a lazy training layer before the regression analysis phase to decrease the effect of noisy data points.

3 Methods

In this section, we describe our three system runs. The ideas behind our methods are independent of the word order in a sentence. Our first method is unsupervised, whereas the other two methods are supervised. The first and second method share the same preprocessing.

3.1 Run 1: Overlap Method

Our first method is unsupervised. It measures the overlap between the tokens in sentence s_1 and the tokens in sentence s_2.

3.1.1 Preprocessing

For preprocessing the input text, we first process each sentence with Stanford CoreNLP (Manning et al., 2014). Afterwards, we use Hunspell[1] with the latest OpenOffice English dictionaries to suggest spelling corrections for tokens with at least two characters in length. For each token, we calculate the Levenshtein distance for all suggestions. If suggestions have the same lowest distance, we choose the longest word and replace the former misspelt word. Abbreviations are also replaced by their full forms. Afterwards, we process the corrected sentence with Stanford CoreNLP again. We use the WordnetStemmer from the *Java Wordnet Interface* (Finlayson, 2014) to look up lemmas with the help of WordNet (Miller, 1995). If the WordnetStemmer can not provide a lemma for a token, we use the predicted lemma from the Stanford CoreNLP.

Instead of accessing all tokens in a sentence, we start from the root token and recursively follow outgoing dependency edges and add all visited tokens to a list. This approach improves our results slightly because some tokens will be ignored. Furthermore, the tokens are filtered for stopwords[2].

3.1.2 Method

The Overlap method measures the token-based overlap between two sentences. Therefore, we need to define a similarity function for tokens: We first try to identify a textual similarity of 1 by comparing the lower case lemmas of both tokens or by checking if their most common WordNet synsets are the same. We assess their similarity as 0.5 if they share any synset. If this is not the case, we use word2vec (Mikolov et al., 2013) with the 300-dimensional *GoogleNews-vectors-negative300* model. We look up both words (or their lemmas if the words are not present in the model) and calculate the cosine similarity of their word embeddings. Otherwise, we return a default value.

This yields the following similarity function for two tokens:

---

[1] http://hunspell.github.io/
[2] http://xpo6.com/list-of-english-stop-words/

$$
\text{sim}(t_1, t_2) := \begin{cases} 1 & \text{if } t_1.\text{lemma} == t_2.\text{lemma} \\ 1 & \text{if } t_1 \text{ and } t_2 \text{ have the same} \\ & \text{most common synset} \\ 0.5 & \text{if } t_1 \text{ and } t_2 \text{ share any} \\ & \text{synset} \\ d(t_1, t_2) & \text{if } t_1 \text{ and } t_2 \text{ have word} \\ & \text{embeddings} \\ \textit{default} & \text{otherwise} \end{cases}
$$

where $d(t_1, t_2)$ denotes the cosine similarity between the two word embeddings of the tokens.

Given a token t from one sentence, we calculate its similarity to another sentence S by taking the maximum similarity between t and all tokens of S:

$$
\text{msim}(t, S) := \max_{t_2 \in S} \text{sim}(t, t_2)
$$

We define the similarity score between two sentences in $[0, 1]$ as follows:

$$
\text{ssim}(s_1, s_2) := \frac{\sum\limits_{t \in s_1} \text{msim}(t, s_2)}{2 \cdot |s_1|} + \frac{\sum\limits_{t \in s_2} \text{msim}(t, s_1)}{2 \cdot |s_2|}
$$

To predict the semantic similarity score in $[0, 5]$, we multiply ssim by 5, however, this does not change our evaluation results because the Pearson correlation is scale invariant:

$$
\text{STS}(s_1, s_2) := 5 \cdot \text{ssim}(s_1, s_2)
$$

We observed that some samples in the STS 2016 test data consist almost entirely of stopwords. For example, the STS 2016 evaluation data contained a sample with the sentences *"I think you should do both."* and *"You should do both."* before the final filtering. After filtering stop words, the first sentence would only contain the word *"think"* and the second sentence would be empty, which would result in a predicted score of zero. To avoid these extreme cases, we do not filter stop words if this would result in a sentence length of less than two tokens in both sentences.

3.2 Run 2: Same Word Neural Network Method

We train a neural network with 3 layers and a sigmoid activation function in Accord.NET (de Souza,

2014). Our network consists of 2 neurons in the input layer, 3 neurons in the hidden layer and 1 neuron in the output layer, as illustrated in Figure 1. The layer weights are initialized by the Nguyen-Widrow function (Nguyen and Widrow, 1990). We use the Levenberg-Marquardt algorithm (Levenberg, 1944; Marquardt, 1963) to train our network on the STS Core test data from 2015 and 2014.

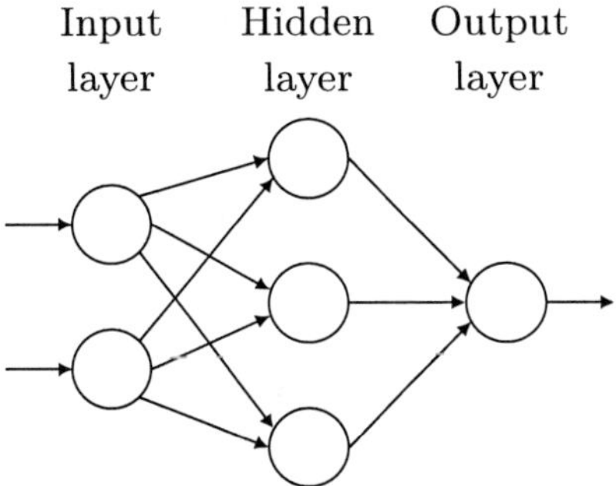

Figure 1: Architecture of our neural network

All samples are preprocessed as described in section 3.1.1. For each sample (s_1, s_2, gs) in the training set, we create a vocabulary list of the lowercase lemmas from both sentences. Lemmas that share a most common synset in WordNet are grouped together. Let n be the size of the vocabulary. We create two bag-of-words vectors bow_{s_1} and bow_{s_2}. For each lemma l, we calculate the minimum number of times l occurs in each sentence and the delta between the minimum and the maximum:

$$
\min_i := \min(\text{bow}_{s_1}[i], \text{bow}_{s_2}[i])
$$
$$
|\Delta_i| := |\text{bow}_{s_1}[i] - \text{bow}_{s_2}[i]|
$$

As input vectors for the neural net, we build two sums per sample and use them as the two dimensional feature vector (sameWords, notSameWords) for the expected output gs:

$$
\text{sameWords} := \sum_{i=1}^{n} \min_i
$$
$$
\text{notSameWords} := \sum_{i=1}^{n} |\Delta_i|
$$

Table 1 shows an example of the same word neural network method for the two input sentences *"Tim plays the guitar"* and *"Tim likes guitar songs"*, which have the input vector $(2, 3)$.

i	Lemma	bow_{s_1}	bow_{s_2}	$\min_i$	$|\Delta_i|$
1	tim	1	1	1	0
2	play	1	0	0	1
3	guitar	1	1	1	0
4	like	0	1	0	1
5	song	0	1	0	1
$\sum$				2	3

Table 1: An example for creating the two-dimensional feature vector for the *Same Word Neural Network* method

We trained the neural net until the error rate between two iterations did not change more than $\varepsilon = 10^{-5}$.

3.3 Run 3: Deep LDA Method

We represent the semantic similarity between two documents s_1 and s_2 by means of a vector $F = [f_1, f_2, f_3, f_4] \in \mathbb{R}^4$, where each component of F is responsible for modelling a different aspect of the semantic similarity, namely the *surface-level similarity*, *context similarity*, and the *topical similarity*.

Surface-level Similarity

The surface-level similarity can to some extent (although not entirely) capture the semantic similarity between documents. Let s_1 and s_2 be the reference and the candidate documents respectively. We compute the components $f_1, f_2 \in \mathbb{R}$ as follows:

$$f_1(s_1, s_2, N) = \frac{m_N}{l_N^{s_1}}$$

$$f_2(s_1, s_2, N) = \left(\prod_{n=1}^{N} \frac{m_N}{l_n^{s_2}} \right)^{\frac{1}{N}}$$

where m_N is the number of matched N-grams between s_1 and s_2, $l_N^{s_1}$ denotes the total number of N-grams in s_1 and $l_n^{s_2}$ is the total number of n-grams in s_2. f_1 is the common ROUGE (Lin, 2004) metric used in automatic text summarization and f_2 is a modified version of the BLEU (Papineni et al., 2002) metric (standard machine translation metric) where the brevity penalty is eliminated. Note that f_1 can be interpreted as the recall-oriented surface similarity and f_2 as the precision-oriented one.

Context Similarity

In order to model the context similarity between documents, we use word embeddings that learn semantically meaningful representations for words from local co-occurrences in sentences. More specifically we use *word2vec* (Mikolov et al., 2013) which seems to be a reasonable choice to model context similarity as the word vectors are trained to maximize the log probability of context words. We denote the context similarity of two documents s_1 and s_2 by $f_3 \in \mathbb{R}$ and compute it as follows:

$$f_3(s_1, s_2) = \cos(\tilde{v}_{s_1}, \tilde{v}_{s_2})$$
$$= \cos \left(\frac{\sum_{v \in s_1} v}{|s_1|}, \frac{\sum_{v' \in s_2} v'}{|s_2|} \right)$$

where v is the dense vector representation of a token and $\tilde{v}$ represents the centroid of the word vectors in a document.

Topical Similarity

To model the topical similarity between two documents, we use Latent Dirichlet Allocation (LDA) (Blei et al., 2003) to train models on the English Wikipedia. For both documents s_1 and s_2, we compute the topic distributions θ_1 and θ_2 and use the Hellinger distance to measure the similarity between the documents. This can be formally written as

$$f_4(s_1, s_2) = 1 - \frac{1}{\sqrt{2}} \sqrt{\sum_{i=1}^{k} \left(\sqrt{\theta_{1_i}} - \sqrt{\theta_{2_i}} \right)^2}$$

where k represents the number of learned LDA topics.

Similarity Prediction

In order to predict the semantic similarity between two documents, we use a combination of k-NN and Multivariate Adaptive Regression Splines (MARS) (Friedman, 1991).

Let $T = \{(s_1, s'_1, gs_1), \ldots, (s_m, s'_m, gs_m)\}$ be the training set consisting of m document pairs together with their corresponding gold standard semantic similarity and $(s_i, s'_i) \notin T$ be a document pair for which the semantic similarity has to be computed. We construct a set $\mathcal{F} = \{(F_1, gs_1), \ldots, (F_m, gs_m)\}$ where each F_j is the four-dimensional vector representation of the semantic similarity between s_j and s'_j. Moreover, we

Sentence 1	Sentence 2	gs	STS
Unfortunately the answer to your question is we simply do not know.	Sorry, I don't know the answer to your question.	4	4.05800
You should do it.	You can do it, too.	1	4.39817
Unfortunately the answer to your question is we simply do not know.	My answer to your question is "Probably Not".	1	3.70982
$P(A|B)$ is the conditional probability of A, given B.	$P(B|A)$ is the conditional probability of B given A.	3	4.32017

Table 2: Examples for the results of the Overlap method with the corresponding gold standards

compute the vector F_i. Next, we construct a set $\mathcal{F}_k$ containing the k-nearest neighbors to the vector F_i. In order to calculate the distances between the vectors, we use the Euclidean distance. Finally, we construct a vector gs_k containing the gold standard similarity values of the k-nearest neighbors and feed it into a MARS model to predict the semantic similarity of the pair (s_i, s'_i). The choice of MARS is due to its capability to automatically model non-linearities between variables.

4 Results

We report the results of our three approaches for the STS Core test from 2016 and 2015.

4.1 STS 2016 Results

In this years shared task, 117 runs were submitted. We achieved weighted mean Pearson correlations of 0.71134, 0.67502 and 0.62078. In this year's run, our best result was the Overlap method, followed by the Same Word Neural Network method and the Deep LDA approach. Table 2 shows examples of good and bad results of our Overlap method on the 2016 data. Detailed results of our runs are given in Table 3 per test set. Our three approaches achieved different results.

From a semantic point of view, the most obvious value for the default value in our Overlap method is 0. However, we have discovered that a default value 0.15 returned better results on the STS Core test data from 2015 and also chose this default value for our submission.

In the Deep LDA approach, we set the parameter $N = 2$, although the use of unigrams did not show any significant statistical difference in the results. We choose the number of topics in the LDA model to be 300. In the prediction phase of the al-

Data set	Run 1	Run 2	Run 3
answer-answer	0.50435	0.42673	0.47211
headlines	0.77406	0.75536	0.58821
plagiarism	0.83049	0.79964	0.62503
postediting	0.83846	0.84514	0.84743
question-question	0.60867	0.54533	0.57099
Weighted Mean	0.71134	0.67502	0.62078

Table 3: Pearson correlation of the 2016 test data

Data set	Run 1	Run 2	Run 3
answers-forums	0.74163	0.70387	0.79987
answers-students	0.73685	0.76658	0.76733
belief	0.74046	0.73319	0.78242
images	0.82032	0.80813	0.84747
headlines	0.75358	0.74363	0.76076
Weighted Mean	0.76295	0.75922	0.79168

Table 4: Pearson correlation of the 2015 test data

gorithm, we select $k = 100$ nearest neighbors from the data sets provided from 2012 to 2015.

4.2 STS 2015 Results

We list the results of our methods for the 2015 test data in Table 3 to discuss the effect of different evaluation sets. It is interesting to see that the Deep LDA method performed best out of our three systems on 2015. Its results on 2016 were surprisingly lower. We attribute this difference to the lack of domain specific training data for 2016. As an unsupervised approach, the Overlap method has fewer problems with the domain change.

It should be noted that the gold standard of the 2015 test data was available during the development of our methods. For the training phase, the Same Word Neural Network method used the STS Core test from 2014. The Deep LDA method was trained on the data from 2012 to 2014.

5 Conclusion and Future Work

We have presented three approaches to measure textual semantic similarity. This year, our unsupervised method achieved the best result. By comparing our result for 2016 and 2015, we showed that the approaches yielded different results in a different order.

In our future work, we will try to modify the Overlap method, by also using a penalty score and by applying certain similarity score shifters, for instance modifying the score by applying a date extraction with a specific distance function for dates. We tried to group words into phrases by using a sliding window approach with a shrinking window size and matching phrases in word2vec. In our initial attempt, this worsened the results for the Overlap method. We will adjust the similarity function to increase the weight of phrases in comparison to unigrams.

We aim to adapt the techniques for German and Spanish.

Acknowledgments

This work was partially funded by the PhD program *Online Participation*, supported by the North Rhine-Westphalian funding scheme *Fortschrittskollegs* and by the German Federal Ministry of Economics and Technology under the ZIM program (Grant No. KF2846504). The authors want to thank the anonymous reviewers for their suggestions and comments.

References

Eneko Agirre, Daniel Cer, Mona Diab, and Aitor Gonzalez-Agirre. 2012. SemEval-2012 Task 6: A Pilot on Semantic Textual Similarity. In *SEM 2012: The First Joint Conference on Lexical and Computational Semantics – Volume 1: Proceedings of the main conference and the shared task, and Volume 2: Proceedings of the Sixth International Workshop on Semantic Evaluation (SemEval 2012)*, pages 385–393. Association for Computational Linguistics.

Eneko Agirre, Daniel Cer, Mona Diab, Aitor Gonzalez-Agirre, and Weiwei Guo. 2013. *SEM 2013 shared task: Semantic Textual Similarity. In *Second Joint Conference on Lexical and Computational Semantics (*SEM), Volume 1: Proceedings of the Main Conference and the Shared Task: Semantic Textual Similarity*, pages 32–43. Association for Computational Linguistics.

Eneko Agirre, Carmen Banea, Claire Cardie, Daniel Cer, Mona Diab, Aitor Gonzalez-Agirre, Weiwei Guo, Rada Mihalcea, German Rigau, and Janyce Wiebe. 2014. SemEval-2014 Task 10: Multilingual Semantic Textual Similarity. In *Proceedings of the 8th International Workshop on Semantic Evaluation (SemEval 2014)*, pages 81–91. Association for Computational Linguistics and Dublin City University.

Eneko Agirre, Carmen Banea, Claire Cardie, Daniel Cer, Mona Diab, Aitor Gonzalez-Agirre, Weiwei Guo, Inigo Lopez-Gazpio, Montse Maritxalar, Rada Mihalcea, German Rigau, Larraitz Uria, and Janyce Wiebe. 2015. SemEval-2015 Task 2: Semantic Textual Similarity, English, Spanish and Pilot on Interpretability. In *Proceedings of the 9th International Workshop on Semantic Evaluation (SemEval 2015)*, pages 252–263. Association for Computational Linguistics.

David M. Blei, Andrew Y. Ng, and Michael I. Jordan. 2003. Latent Dirichlet Allocation. *Journal of Machine Learning Research*, 3:993–1022.

César Roberto de Souza. 2014. The Accord.NET Framework. http://accord-framework.net.

Mark Finlayson. 2014. Java Libraries for Accessing the Princeton Wordnet: Comparison and Evaluation. In *Proceedings of the Seventh Global Wordnet Conference*, pages 78–85.

Jerome H. Friedman. 1991. Multivariate Adaptive Regression Splines. *The Annals of Statistics*, 19(1):1–67.

Lushan Han, Justin Martineau, Doreen Cheng, and Christopher Thomas. 2015. Samsung: Align-and-Differentiate Approach to Semantic Textual Similarity. In *Proceedings of the 9th International Workshop on Semantic Evaluation (SemEval 2015)*, pages 172–177. Association for Computational Linguistics.

Kenneth Levenberg. 1944. A Method for the Solution of Certain Non-Linear Problems in Least Squares. *Quarterly Journal of Applied Mathmatics*, II(2):164–168.

Chin-Yew Lin. 2004. ROUGE: A Package for Automatic Evaluation of Summaries. In *Proceedings of the Workshop on Text Summarization Branches Out (WAS 2004)*, pages 74–81.

Christopher Manning, Mihai Surdeanu, John Bauer, Jenny Finkel, Steven Bethard, and David McClosky. 2014. The Stanford CoreNLP Natural Language Processing Toolkit. In *Proceedings of 52nd Annual Meeting of the Association for Computational Linguistics: System Demonstrations*, pages 55–60.

Donald W. Marquardt. 1963. An Algorithm for Least-Squares Estimation of Nonlinear Parameters. *SIAM Journal on Applied Mathematics*, 11(2):431–441.

Tomas Mikolov, Kai Chen, Greg Corrado, and Jeffrey Dean. 2013. Efficient Estimation of Word Representations in Vector Space. *ICLR Workshop*.

George A. Miller. 1995. WordNet: A Lexical Database for English. *Communications of the ACM*, 38(11):39–41.

Derrick Nguyen and Bernard Widrow. 1990. Improving the Learning Speed of 2-Layer Neural Networks by Choosing Initial Values of the Adaptive Weights. In *Proceedings of the International Joint Conference on Neural Networks (IJCNN)*, volume 3, pages 21–26. IEEE.

Kishore Papineni, Salim Roukos, Todd Ward, and Wei-Jing Zhu. 2002. BLEU: a Method for Automatic Evaluation of Machine Translation. In *Proceedings of the 40th Annual Meeting on Association for Computational Linguistics*, ACL '02, pages 311–318. Association for Computational Linguistics.

Md Arafat Sultan, Steven Bethard, and Tamara Sumner. 2015. DLS@CU: Sentence Similarity from Word Alignment and Semantic Vector Composition. In *Proceedings of the 9th International Workshop on Semantic Evaluation (SemEval 2015)*, pages 148–153. Association for Computational Linguistics.

Frane Šarić, Goran Glavaš, Mladen Karan, Jan Šnajder, and Bojana Dalbelo Bašić. 2012. TakeLab: Systems for Measuring Semantic Text Similarity. In **SEM 2012: The First Joint Conference on Lexical and Computational Semantics – Volume 1: Proceedings of the main conference and the shared task, and Volume 2: Proceedings of the Sixth International Workshop on Semantic Evaluation (SemEval 2012)*, pages 441–448. Association for Computational Linguistics.

Tu Thanh Vu, Quan Hung Tran, and Son Bao Pham. 2015. TATO: Leveraging on Multiple Strategies for Semantic Textual Similarity. In *Proceedings of the 9th International Workshop on Semantic Evaluation (SemEval 2015)*, pages 190–195. Association for Computational Linguistics.

Samsung Poland NLP Team at SemEval-2016 Task 1: Necessity for diversity; combining recursive autoencoders, WordNet and ensemble methods to measure semantic similarity.

Barbara Rychalska, Katarzyna Pakulska, Krystyna Chodorowska,
Wojciech Walczak and **Piotr Andruszkiewicz**

Samsung R&D Institute Poland
Polna 11
Warsaw, Poland
{b.rychalska, k.pakulska, k.chodorowsk,
w.walczak, p.andruszki2}@samsung.com

Abstract

This paper describes our proposed solutions designed for a STS core track within the SemEval 2016 English Semantic Textual Similarity (STS) task. Our method of similarity detection combines recursive autoencoders with a WordNet award-penalty system that accounts for semantic relatedness, and an SVM classifier, which produces the final score from similarity matrices. This solution is further supported by an ensemble classifier, combining an aligner with a bi-directional Gated Recurrent Neural Network and additional features, which then performs Linear Support Vector Regression to determine another set of scores.

1   Introduction

The tasks from the Semantic Textual Similarity (STS) contest have always attracted vivid interest from the NLP community. The goal is to measure the semantic similarity between two given sentences on a scale from 0 to 5, trying to emulate the idea of similarity degrees, thus replicating human language understanding.

After processing two pieces of text, semantic textual similarity software captures degrees of semantic equivalence. One of the goals of the STS task is to create a unified framework for extracting and measuring semantic similarity. Improvements achieved in the course of this task can be useful in many research areas, such as question answering (Marsi and Krahmer, 2005), machine translation (Callison-Burch, 2008), and plagiarism detection (Clough et al., 2002).

We present a solution designed to detect both the similarity between single words and longer, multiword phrases. It employs two important components: the unfolding recursive autoencoder (RAE) (Socher et al., 2011) and the penalty-award weight system based on WordNet (Miller et al., 2002). First, RAE is used to perform unsupervised learning on parse trees, then the WordNet module adjusts the distances of RAE vectors using awards and penalties based on semantic similarities of words. The complete pipeline includes a deep net (RAE) module, a WordNet module, a normalization module and a sentence similarity matrices computing module.

Another solution that ran in parallel to the RAE pipeline, was the monolingual word aligner (in some cases we used its corrected version with additional features, including a bag-of-words). Finally an ensemble classifier was used to perform Linear Support Vector Regression (Drucker et al., 1996) over the results from all the other classifiers. This included: the base word aligner (Sultan et al., 2015), bi-directional Gated Recurrent Neural Network (Cho et al., 2014; Chung et al., 2014), the RAE with WordNet features and the corrected aligner.

2   System Overview

This section describes the modules that constitute our three runs. Detailed information about the configuration of these runs can be found in Section 3.

2.1   RAE with WordNet Features

RAE with the WordNet module is composed of two major parts: a recursive autoencoder (RAE) for unsupervised training of sentence representations and

Proceedings of SemEval-2016, pages 602–608,
San Diego, California, June 16-17, 2016. ©2016 Association for Computational Linguistics

additional WordNet-based submodule for enhancing the performance of the RAE.

The RAE takes unlabeled parse trees and word vectors as input and learns phrase features for each node in the tree. The learned features can be used to recursively reconstruct the vectors at each node in the tree. The encoding part follows the Semantic Depencency Tree Recursive Neural Network (SDT-RNN) structure described in (Socher et al., 2014). In the decoding part, the tree structure used to encode the sentence is mirrored. The reconstruction error (the total error of the network) is counted for all subtrees as the summed Euclidean distance between a subtree's decoded terminal nodes and the original word vectors. The network learns to encode representations of meaningful phrases in tree nodes. We use the word representation vectors published by (Pennington et al., 2014).

The RAE is first trained in an unsupervised way on the Corpus of Contemporary American English (Davies, 2008) combined with SemEval STS training sets released before 2015 (only sentences without labels), then a sentence similarity matrices computing module (Section 2.1.2) is used to generate similarity scores for two candidate sentences. Our first experiment involved a procedure described in (Socher et al., 2011) with unmodified word representation vectors, using Euclidean distance as a measure of word-to-word similarity.

However, we noticed that some pairs of vectors representing related concepts (e.g., 'lady' and 'woman') were located surprisingly far from each other in the Euclidean space, while others were too close. As shown in (Cho et al., 2014), words and phrases which merely belong to the same class of concepts without being exact synonyms have a low distance in Euclidean space (e.g., phrases 'a few seconds' and 'two years' are grouped together). The representation vectors returned by the RAE do not amend this problem. For this reason, we created an additional module which uses WordNet (Miller, 1995) to enhance our word similarity measures in RAE trees. In Table 1 we show the influence of individual modules.

2.1.1 WordNet awards and penalties

The WordNet module adjusts the Euclidean distance between RAE vectors with awards and penal-ties based on the semantic similarity of pairs of words. We combined the following ideas:

- awarding pairs of words with positive semantic similarity;

- penalizing out-of-context words and disjoint similar concepts;

- propagating scores to higher nodes of the dependency trees.

The concept of semantic similarity reflects the work of (Han et al., 2013), while out-of-context words and disjoint similar concepts reflect the ideas presented in (Han et al., 2015), but there are differences in both implementation and usage.

Awards. WordNet is used to extract semantic relations between pairs of nouns, verbs, adjectives and adverbs. Semantic distance D is measured using the following conditions for two words:

- being equal or first-sense synonyms $(D(x,y) = 0)$, e.g. *car auto*;

- sharing common sense with WordNet frequency of at least 5 $(D(x,y) = 1)$ e.g. *track chase*;

- being hypernyms or two-link hypernyms (applicable for nouns and verbs) $(D(x,y) = 2)$, e.g. *orange citrus*;

- being similar due to satellite synsets (applicable for adjectives and adverbs) $(D(x,y) = 3)$, e.g. *soggy waterlogged*;

- sharing any common sense $(D(x,y) = 3)$, e.g. *grind mash*;

- being derivationally related $(D(x,y) = 4)$, e.g. *rocket missile*;

- being enclosed in the glosses of the other word's meanings $(D(x,y) = 5)$, e.g. *Florida Fla.*

If none of the conditions are met, the semantic distance D is set to a negative value, which facilitates the counting of an award A described below. Thus, effectively, the value of D is an integer such that $D(x,y) \in \{-1, 0, 1, 2, 3, 4, 5\}$.

The semantic distance $D(x, y)$ is transformed to an award A using the formula $e^{-\alpha D(x,y)}$ introduced by (Li et al., 2003), where α is set to 0.25, as this value seemed to yield the best results:

$$A(x, y) = \begin{cases} \beta e^{-\alpha D(x,y)}, & \text{if } D(x, y) \geq 0 \\ 0, & \text{otherwise} \end{cases} \quad (1)$$

where β is a positive number (5 by default) used to control the level of adjustment made by the WordNet-related score. If $\beta = 5$ the maximum score for $A(x, y)$ is 5. The Euclidean distances of RAE vectors are usually in the range of $[0, 10]$, thus the parameter ensures that the WordNet-related similarity is sufficiently important.

Penalties. The out-of-context penalty for word x, $OOC(x)$, is defined as a penalty for a word not paired in the second input sentence SS (Han et al., 2015). The word is not paired if its semantic similarity (or award) $A = 0$ with all the words (referenced below by the index i) in the second sentence:

$$OOC(x) = \begin{cases} -1, & \text{if } \sum_i A(x, SS(i)) = 0 \\ 0, & \text{otherwise} \end{cases} \quad (2)$$

We allow three strategies for out-of-context penalization: penalize all recognizable parts of speech (nouns, verbs, adjectives and adverbs), penalize only nouns, penalize only physical objects (i.e. words which have $physical\_object$ in their WordNet's hypernyms path). The third option is used by default, since both the original research of (Han et al., 2015) and ours suggest that it usually is the best option (although, in a minority of tests, the penalization of all out-of-context nouns yields better results).

We also penalize disjoint similar concepts. Disjoint similar concepts $DSC(x, y)$ are defined as 'special care antonyms' or words of disjoint meaning (i.e. *Monday Tuesday*). In our solution they are found using WordNet's hypernyms hierarchy. If two words have a common direct hypernym, they are disjoint similar concepts (e.g. both *Monday* and *Tuesday* have *weekday* as a common hypernym in the WordNet hierarchy). By default, the $DSC(x, y)$ function returns a penalty of -2 when two words are found to be antonyms or disjoint similar concepts, and 0 otherwise. Thus, the penalty P for two words x and y is:

$$P(x, y) = OOC(x) + OOC(y) + DSC(x, y) \quad (3)$$

A complete framework of WordNet-related awards and penalties is defined by:

$$sim_{WN} = \begin{cases} A(x, y), & \text{if } D(x, y) \geq 0 \\ P(x, y), & \text{if } P(x, y) < 0 \\ 0, & \text{otherwise} \end{cases} \quad (4)$$

Propagation. In the Sentence similarity matrices computing module 2.1.2, scores are calculated for all sentence subtrees, while WordNet's awards and penalties are calculated for words. Thus, to use WordNet's scores on all subtrees, the awards and penalties have to be propagated up, until they affect all nodes. To propagate WordNet's scores on a tree containing more than one word, we define a function:

$$sim_{WN}(subtree) = \sum_{i=1}^{n} \frac{sim_{WN}(i)}{depth(i)} \quad (5)$$

where i is an index for a single leaf in the subtree, and n is the total number of leaves in the subtree. $sim_{WN}(i)$ is a similarity score for a leaf i. The scores for particular leaves are divided by their depth $depth(i)$ relative to the root of the subtree to account for their importance in the more complex trees, and then the scores are summed up at the root. For example, if we have a leaf with a score of 0.75, then this score is added up at the root level with its full weight only if the leaf is a direct child of the root. If it is located deeper in the subtree, the score is divided by this leaf's depth relative to the root of the subtree. The same procedure applies to all the leaves in the current subtree. In Table 1 we compare the efficiency of the WordNet module with and without propagation.

An alternative strategy for incorporating the WordNet scores is to refine the vectors associated with particular leaves and then use these refined vectors to recompute complex tree nodes using RAE. For example, given the WordNet similarity ϵ for words 'woman' and 'lady', and the vectors A for 'woman' and B for 'lady', the vector A is refined using the following formula:

$$A_{refined} = \epsilon A + (1 - \epsilon)B. \quad (6)$$

The vector B stays the same. The tests have proven that the former strategy offers better results, so we decided to stick with it.

Table 1: The synergy of all parts of the solution (weighted mean presented).

Test set	RAE	RAE with Word-Net	RAE with Propa-gation	Final RAE based solu-tion
Answers forums	0.4724	0.4916	0.5404	0.6836
Answers students	0.7066	0.7185	0.7085	0.7679
Belief	0.6109	0.6002	0.6418	0.7517
Headlines	0.706	0.7115	0.7114	0.8315
Images	0.7469	0.7797	0.7952	0.8625
Weighted mean	0.6753	0.6889	0.7016	0.7949

2.1.2 Sentence Similarity Matrices Computing

As a first step in our full algorithm, the RAE computes vectors for every node in the dependency parse tree. Then the subtrees of these trees are used to create the distance matrix. The matrix is created in a number of steps: the trees are traversed in level order, the subtrees are then sorted by depth and the leaves representing stop words are removed[1]. The remaining subtrees are used to construct the distance matrix, which is then filled with Euclidean distance measures d between each pair of subtrees x and y.

$$D_{RAE} = d(x, y) - sim_{WN} \qquad (7)$$

The above score is further transformed in two ways: it is made certain that the score value falls within the range 0-5, and that the distance is set to 0 if the WordNet similarity sim_{WN} has a maximum value:

$$D'_{RAE} = \begin{cases} 0, & \text{if } sim_{WN} = max \\ 0, & \text{if } D_{RAE} < 0 \\ 5, & \text{if } D_{RAE} > 5 \\ D_{RAE}, & \text{otherwise} \end{cases} \qquad (8)$$

The original score D_{RAE} is replaced with the adjusted score D'_{RAE} in the distance matrix. Finally, we use dynamic pooling module as described in (Socher et al., 2011). The pooling module accounts for the varying lengths of the two trees.

---

[1] Stop words list contains about 60 most common words in training data set and all punctuation characters.

2.1.3 Final RAE-based solution

The final score was produced by Linear Support Vector Regression over cells from the distance matrices after pooling as well as 12 additional features:

- adjustment of roots (the Euclidean distance between WordNet-adjusted tree roots);

- cosine distance between vectors representing tree roots of sentences;

- information about the negation status of the two sentences (if both sentences contain/ do not contain negation = true, otherwise = false);

- mean out of context penalty over full tree;

- mean disjoint penalty over full tree;

- mean WordNet similarity score over full tree;

- score from aligner (Section 2.2);

- if both sentences agree on the numbers (true for no numbers or the same numbers; false otherwise);

- if both sentences have the same numbers (binary);

- the absolute difference in tokens between two sentences;

- if the numbers in one sentence contain the numbers from the second sentence (binary);

- the percentage of tokens similarity between two sentences.

A new SVM classifier was created for every test set, since for every test set a different subset of training sets was used[2]. Distance matrices for all classifiers were created and normalized independently.

$$norm_c = 0.4\left(\frac{\max(\min(\frac{c}{\mu}, 3\sigma), -3\sigma)}{3\sigma} + 1\right) + 0.1 \qquad (9)$$

First the normalization process was used to calculate mean μ and standard deviation σ for the matrix, next we performed calculations according to Equation 9 for every cell c of the matrix. The equation comes from (Socher et al., 2013) and normalizes the values to range $[0.1, 0.9]$.

---

[2] The training data contains all previous SemEval datasets from 2012 to 2015.

Table 2: Mapping training sets to test sets.

Test set	Training sets
Answer-answer	answers-students 2015, belief 2015.
Headlines	MSRpar 2012 (training and test set), SMTnews 2012, deft-news 2014, headlines 2013, headlines 2014, headlines 2015, images 2014, images 2015.
Plagiarism	MSRpar 2012 (training and test set), answers-students 2015.
Postediting	deft-news 2014, deft-forum 2014, SMTnews 2012.
Question-question	deft-news 2014, deft-forum 2014, belief 2015.

2.2 Aligner

As a monolingual word aligner we use two algorithms: a basic aligner and a corrected aligner. Both are based on the aligner described in (Sultan et al., 2014). The basic algorithm performs the following steps for the two sentences: align identical word sequences, align named entities, align content words using dependencies and align content words using surrounding words. Scoring is calculated according to (Sultan et al., 2015):

$$score(S^1, S^2) = \frac{n^a(S^1) + n^a(S^2)}{n(S^1) + n(S^2)},$$

where $n(S^i)$ and $n^a(S^i)$ are the number of content words and aligned content words in a sentence S^i, respectively.

An aligner using only the basic algorithm could not handle negations and antonyms well, so we modified it by adding two modules. The negation module checks whether there is a negation component present in only one sentence, and if so, the module reduces the score to 0. The antonym module verifies whether the two sentences contain at least one pair of antonyms from a list based on the WordNet, and if so, also reduces score to 0.

The corrected aligner is a Linear Support Vector Regression (Drucker et al., 1996) using the following features: the modified basic aligner feature, Bag of Words features inspired by (Han et al., 2015) (element-wise absolute value difference between vectors for words and bigrams, sentences' length

difference, percentage of exact lemma to lemma matches) and additional features used in (Hänig et al., 2015):

- length of the longest common subsequence of characters (some characters may be skipped),

- length of the longest common sequence of characters,

- cosine similarity between vectors of words,

- edit distance between sentences,

- WordNet word overlap (Šarić et al., 2012).

2.3 Ensemble

The ensemble classifier was actually a Linear Support Vector Regression over results from the other classifiers used for semantic similarity measurement. Each one of them returned score from 0 up to 5. The following classifiers were chosen for the ensemble approach:

- modified basic aligner, presented in Section 2.2;

- Bi-directional Gated Recurrent Neural Network (Cho et al., 2014; Chung et al., 2014) with the output neural network described in (Tai et al., 2015);

- RAE with WordNet Features, described in Section 2.1;

- corrected aligner, described in Section 2.2

The training data set was split into 75% vs 25%. All classifiers except the aligner (which does not need to be trained) were trained on the 75%. The ensemble classifier was trained on a subset of the remaining data set.

Scores returned by the above classifiers were used as features in the Linear Support Vector Regression. The final result was rescaled to get score from the $[0, 5]$ range.

3 Evaluation

In order to separately train models for each evaluation set, we created reference test sets that are similar to the evaluation sets, e.g. for headlines we used

Table 3: The results obtained over three runs in the evaluation period of SemEval 2016.

	Answer-answer	Headlines	Plagiarism	Postediting	Question-question	Weighted mean
RAE (AE)	0.6577	0.8180	0.8129	0.7885	0.5867	0.7357
Ensemble (EN1)	0.6924	0.8275	0.8414	0.8352	0.6870	0.7781
Merged (EN2)	0.6924	0.8275	0.8129	0.8352	0.5867	0.7547

Table 4: Comparison of our solutions with the 2015 winning system on SemEval 2015 evaluation datasets.

Run	Answers forums	Answers students	Belief	Headlines	Images	Weighted mean
RAE (AE)	0.6836	0.7747	0.7517	0.8363	0.8625	0.7949
Aligner (with our modifications)	0.6725	0.7715	0.7282	0.8223	0.8478	0.7854
BiGRU	0.5424	0.5925	0.5917	0.7947	0.8588	0.7032
Ensemble (EN1)	0.6489	0.7664	0.7549	0.854	0.8884	0.8027
Merged (EN2)	0.6836	0.7747	0.7549	0.8540	0.8884	**0.8091**
DLS@CU	0.7390	0.7725	0.7491	0.8250	0.8644	0.8015

30% of headlines 2015; for answer-answer we used 30% of answers-students 2015; for plagiarism 30% of MSRpar 2012 test set; for postediting 30% deft-news 2014 and for question-question 30% of deft-forum 2014. These randomly selected samples that constituted the test sets were removed from the training sets. We used these reference test sets to find the best parameters of our models and chose the best model for run EN2. The final model uses all samples from sets assigned to each evaluation set in Table 2. Our final results are presented in Table 3.

For the AE run, we used RAE with WordNet Features, as described in Section 2.1. For each test, a separate classifier was created with its own training set, as presented in Table 2. The mapping was based on the average number of words per sentence in the set.

For the EN1, run we used the ensemble model described in Section 2.3. In the EN2 model we chose either RAE or ensemble based on the results for test sets matched with evaluation sets.

As shown in Table 3, the ensemble model (EN1) yields better results than RAE (AE) for all sets. Thus, the merged model (EN2) falls between the two.

We also present the results (Table 4) of our solution for SemEval 2015 sets. Comparing them with the best run from SemEval 2015 competition (weighted mean), we concluded that bi-GRU yields the worst results. Second and third worst results came from the modified aligner and RAE respectively. The ensemble and merged model yield the best results that surpass the performance of the 2015 winning solution.

4 Conclusions and Future Work

Our solution combines a vector similarity feature derived from word embeddings without losing the information contained in lexical similarity relations. As it turned out, one of the primary limitations of our paraphrase detection system is its heavy reliance on word order, which makes the solution less universal in its application. The other drawback of converting words to word vectors is being unable to account for situations where the same information is formatted differently (for instance, units of measurement, time expressions, etc.) Thus, our future works include improving our preprocessing module, so that it would produce a unified input, e.g., all numbers written in words will be converted into numerals and all dates will be unified into one format. We will also use specifically designed training modes to prevent overfitting and create a new curriculum learning dataset to make RAE training easier.

References

Chris Callison-Burch. 2008. Syntactic constraints on paraphrases extracted from parallel corpora. In *Proceedings of the Conference on Empirical Methods in Natural Language Processing*, pages 196–205. Association for Computational Linguistics.

Kyunghyun Cho, Bart van Merrienboer, Çaglar Gülçehre, Fethi Bougares, Holger Schwenk, and Yoshua Bengio. 2014. Learning phrase representations using RNN encoder-decoder for statistical machine translation. *CoRR*, 1406.1078.

Junyoung Chung, Çaglar Gülçehre, KyungHyun Cho, and Yoshua Bengio. 2014. Empirical evaluation of gated recurrent neural networks on sequence modeling. *CoRR*, 1412.3555.

Paul Clough, Robert Gaizauskas, Scott SL Piao, and Yorick Wilks. 2002. Meter: Measuring text reuse. In *Proceedings of the 40th Annual Meeting on Association for Computational Linguistics*, pages 152–159. Association for Computational Linguistics.

Mark Davies. 2008. The Corpus of Contemporary American English: 520 million words, 1990-present. http://corpus.byu.edu/coca/.

Harris Drucker, Christopher J. C. Burges, Linda Kaufman, Alexander J. Smola, and Vladimir Vapnik. 1996. Support vector regression machines. In Michael Mozer, Michael I. Jordan, and Thomas Petsche, editors, *Advances in Neural Information Processing Systems 9, NIPS, Denver, CO, USA, December 2-5, 1996*, pages 155–161. MIT Press.

Lushan Han, Abhay Kashyap, Tim Finin, James Mayfield, and Jonathan Weese. 2013. Umbc ebiquity-core: Semantic textual similarity systems. In *Proceedings of the Second Joint Conference on Lexical and Computational Semantics*, volume 1, pages 44–52.

Lushan Han, Justin Martineau, Doreen Cheng, and Christopher Thomas. 2015. Samsung: Align-and-differentiate approach to semantic textual similarity. *SemEval-2015*, pages 172–177.

Christian Hänig, Robert Remus, and Xose de la Puente. 2015. Exb themis: Extensive feature extraction from word alignments for semantic textual similarity. In *Proceedings of the 9th International Workshop on Semantic Evaluation (SemEval 2015)*, pages 264–268, Denver, Colorado, June. Association for Computational Linguistics.

Yuhua Li, Zuhair A Bandar, and David McLean. 2003. An approach for measuring semantic similarity between words using multiple information sources. *Knowledge and Data Engineering, IEEE Transactions on*, 15(4):871–882.

Erwin Marsi and Emiel Krahmer. 2005. Explorations in sentence fusion. In *Proceedings of the European Workshop on Natural Language Generation*, pages 109–117. Citeseer.

George A Miller, C Fellbaum, R Tengi, P Wakefield, H LANGONE, and BR HASKELL. 2002. Wordnet: A lexical database for the english language. 2002. *Available from: http://wordnet.princeton.edu/.*

George A Miller. 1995. Wordnet: A lexical database for english. *Commun. ACM*, 38(11):39–41, nov.

Jeffrey Pennington, Richard Socher, and Christopher D. Manning. 2014. Glove: Global vectors for word representation. In *Empirical Methods in Natural Language Processing (EMNLP)*.

Richard Socher, Eric H. Huang, Jeffrey Pennington, Andrew Y. Ng, and Christopher D. Manning. 2011. Dynamic pooling and unfolding recursive autoencoders for paraphrase detection. In *Advances in Neural Information Processing Systems 24*.

Richard Socher, Chris Manning, and Yoshua Bengio. 2013. Naacl 2013 tutorial: Deep learning for nlp.

Richard Socher, Andrej Karpathy, Quoc V. Le, Christopher D. Manning, and Andrew Y. Ng. 2014. Grounded compositional semantics for finding and describing images with sentences. *TACL*, 2:207–218.

Md Arafat Sultan, Steven Bethard, and Tamara Sumner. 2014. Dls@cu: Sentence similarity from word alignment. In *Proceedings of the 8th International Workshop on Semantic Evaluation (SemEval 2014)*, pages 241–246, Dublin, Ireland, August. Association for Computational Linguistics and Dublin City University.

Md Arafat Sultan, Steven Bethard, and Tamara Sumner. 2015. Dls@cu: Sentence similarity from word alignment and semantic vector composition. In *Proceedings of the 9th International Workshop on Semantic Evaluation (SemEval 2015)*, pages 148–153, Denver, Colorado, June. Association for Computational Linguistics.

Kai Sheng Tai, Richard Socher, and Christopher D. Manning. 2015. Improved semantic representations from tree-structured long short-term memory networks. March.

Frane Šarić, Goran Glavaš, Mladen Karan, Jan Šnajder, and Bojana Dalbelo Bašić. 2012. Takelab: Systems for measuring semantic text similarity. In *SEM 2012: The First Joint Conference on Lexical and Computational Semantics – Volume 1: Proceedings of the main conference and the shared task, and Volume 2: Proceedings of the Sixth International Workshop on Semantic Evaluation (SemEval 2012)*, pages 441–448, Montréal, Canada, 7-8 June. Association for Computational Linguistics.

USFD at SemEval-2016 Task 1: Putting different State-of-the-Arts into a Box

Ahmet Aker, Frederic Blain, Andres Duque[*], Marina Fomicheva[+],
Jurica Seva, Kashif Shah and **Daniel Beck**

University of Sheffield, UK
University of Madrid, Spain[*]
Universitat Pompeu Fabra, Spain[+]

`ahmet.aker@ f.blain@ j.seva@ kashif.shah@`
`sheffield.ac.uk`
`andres.duq.fer@gmail.com, marina.fomicheva@upf.edu`
`debeck1@sheffield.ac.uk`

Abstract

In this paper we describe our participation in the STS Core subtask which is the determination of the monolingual semantic similarity between pair of sentences. In our participation we adapted state-of-the-art approaches from related work applied on previous STS Core subtasks and run them on the 2016 data. We investigated the performance of single methods but also the combination of them. Our results show that Convolutional Neural Networks (CNN) are superior to both the Monolingual Word Alignment and the Word2Vec approaches. The combination of all the three methods performs slightly better than using CNN only. Our results also show that the performance of our systems varies between the datasets.

1 Introduction

Semantic Textual Similarity (STS) is a metric which aims to determine the likeness between two short textual entities. Therefore, STS is widely used in many research areas such as Natural Language Processing, for a large amount of tasks like Information Retrieval (IR), Natural Language Understanding (NLU) or even Machine Translation (MT) evaluation, for which STS allows capturing more information than traditional metrics based on n-grams match like BLEU (Papineni et al., 2002).

Part of the SemEval campaign, STS competition benefits from a growing interest over the year (Agirre et al., 2012; Agirre et al., 2013; Agirre et al., 2014; Agirrea et al., 2015). In 2016, participants had the possibility to compete in two tasks: (i) STS split into 'STS Core' and 'Cross-lingual STS' which are respectively an English monolingual and English/Spanish bilingual subtasks; (ii) iSTS which focuses on the interpretable aspect of STS assessment. Introduced for the first time in 2015, iSTS became a standalone task this year.

This paper describes our participation in the STS Core subtask and is organised as follows: we first describe in Section 2 methods we have adapted to tackle the task. Next, we present and discuss our results (Section 3). Finally, Section 4 will conclude this system description paper with some remarks.

2 System description

For adressing monolingual semantic similarity between two sentences different methods have been proposed in related work. In our monolingual STS participation we have focused on some methods that were reported as state-of-

609

Proceedings of SemEval-2016, pages 609–613,
San Diego, California, June 16-17, 2016. ©2016 Association for Computational Linguistics

the-art systems. Given that those methods have been reported separately a natural question that arises from this is what the performance is when those methods are combined. This is exactly what we did and what we propose in this paper. We adapted methods from related work that have been applied on the monolingual STS task and used their combined version on the new 2016 monolingual task. Methods adapted and the strategy we used to combine them are described in the following sections.

2.1 Monolingual Alignment

We use an alignment-based approach, which was among the top-perfoming submissions in the past year's task (Sultan et al., 2015). Sentence similarity score is computed in two separate steps. First, an alignment between related words in the input sentences is established using Monolingual Word Aligner (MWA) (Sultan et al., 2014). Next, sentence similarity is calculated based on the proportion of aligned content words:

$$sim(S^1, S^2) = \frac{n_c^a(S^1) + n_c^a(S^2)}{n_c(S^1) + n_c(S^2)} \quad (1)$$

where $n_c(S^i)$ and $n_c^a(S^i)$ are the number of content words and the number of aligned content words in sentence i, respectively. MWA makes alignment decisions based on lexical similarity and contextual evidence. Lexical similarity component identifies word pairs that are possible candidates for alignment. Context words are considered as evidence for alignment if they are lexically similar and have the same or equivalent syntactic relations with the words to be aligned. Word pairs are aligned in decreasing order of a weighted sum of their lexical and contextual similarity.

2.2 Convolutional Neural Network Score

Another method adapted in our system is a Convolutional Neural Network (CNN), which generates a similarity score for each pair of sentences. More specifically, we replicated the system presented in (He et al., 2015), using previous SemEval data for training the network and generating similarity values between 0 and 5, for each of the test sentences given by the organizers. In the following subsections, we briefly summarize the CNN system, although specific details can be found in the cited paper.

Word Representation

Words in the sentences to be compared are first transformed into vectors using the GloVe word embeddings (Pennington et al., 2014). These embeddings are trained on 840 billion tokens, and the resulting vectors are 300-dimensional. Hence, each sentence $sent$ with n words will be transformed into a matrix $M_{sent} \in \mathbb{R}^{n \times 300}$. Hence, $sent_{i:j}$ denotes the word embeddings of words i to j inside the sentence, $sent_i^{[k]}$ denotes the k-th dimension of word embedding i and $sent_{i:j}^{[k]}$ the k-th dimension of words i to j inside the sentence.

Sentence modelling

The technique makes use of two different types of filters for extracting features from the sentences: holistic and per-dimension. Holistic filters generate a vector representing a "temporal" convolution, this is, complete regions of the word sequence. On the other hand, per-dimension filters perform spatial convolutions, limited to a predefined dimension k. After the application of those filters, the last step of the convolutional layer is to perform pooling operations over the vectors generated by the filters, in order to convert those vectors into scalar values. The system defines three types of pooling: max, min and $mean$. Finally, the system also defines a $group$ as a specific convolution layer (with either holistic or per-dimension filters) with width ws and a specific type of pooling, which operates over a sentence. A set of groups composed by convolution layers with the same width which explore different pooling functions is called a $block$.

Similarity Measurement Layer

Once that the sentence representation is done through the use of filters and pooling functions, a way to compare two sentences has to be defined. The comparison of two different sentences is made over local regions of the sentence representation. For this purpose, the system consider the output of the convolutional layers in order to perform both "horizontal" and "vertical" comparisons. Given two vectors, each of them representing the same region of an input sentence, a new output vector is created by measuring cosine distance, L_2 Euclidean distance and element-wise absolute difference. This output vector is added to an accumulated vector which stores the outputs of all the compared regions of the input sentences. The final output of the system generates an output similarity score through a final log-softmax layer, which receives the accumulated vector. System parameters (window size, number of filters, learning rate, regularization parameter, hidden units) are maintained with respect to the original work in which the system is presented.

2.3 Word2Vec

Word embeddings using Word2vec (Mikolov et al., 2013) have been extensively used to measure the semantic similarity between words. Our word embeddings comprise the vectors published by Baroni et al. (2014). To measure the similarity between a pair of sentences we first remove from each sentence stop-words as well as punctuations, query for each word its vector representation and create a averaged sum of the word vectors. The number of remaining words in each sentence is used to average that sentence. Finally, we use the resulting averaged sum vectors and determine their similarity using cosine.

2.4 Model Combination

In this section, we present the experiments to combine all methods described in previous sections. We formulated the problem as a regres-

sion task where we are given multiple features capturing different attributes of inputs along with gold labels and we predict the output for unseen examples. Support Vector Regression (SVR) (Chang and Lin, 2001) is the most commonly used algorithm for such tasks. We used the 3 features described in previous sections and trained SVR models to estimate a continuous score within [0,5]. We evaluated different settings of these models including various available kernels. Based on optimum performance, we used a radial basis function (RBF) kernel, which has been shown to perform very well in quality estimation tasks (Callison-Burch et al., 2012). Kernel parameters are optimised using grid search with 5-fold cross-validation. The correlation scores using SVR as learning algorithm are reported in Table 3. It can be seen that adding all features together improves the results in as compared to the individual scores for each of the methods.

Application on SemEval Data

The described system has been trained with data from previous Semantic Textual Similarity tasks of SemEval, more specifically data from 2012, 2013, 2014 and 2015. The final training dataset is composed by 13,560 sentence pairs.

3 Results

In SemEval STS Core Task the performance of each method (or system) is evaluated using Pearson Correlation that measures the linear correlation between the system's outputs and gold-standard data. A score of 1 indicates 100% correlation and 0 no correlation at all. Table 3 shows the individual results for methods adapted in this work as well as the result when all methods are combined together as a single system.

We can first observe that the best single performing method is CNN, with an overral achievement of 0.727 correlation score (see last column). The other two approaches achieve

Method	answer-answer	headlines	plagiarism	postediting	question-question	OverALL
CNN	0.510	0.818	**0.834**	0.792	0.685	0.727
MWA	0.436	0.704	**0.749**	0.587	0.579	0.611
Word2vec	<u>0.276</u>	0.642	**0.787**	0.750	0.688	0.622
Combination	0.508	0.820	**0.838**	0.794	0.689	0.728

Table 1: Pearson correlation between the prediction and gold standard data.

substantially lower correlation figures with a drop of about 0.10. Monolingual Word Alignment is the less performing method achieving 0.611, just behind Word2Vec with 0.622. From our results we can also remark that the combined version of all the three methods lead to 0.728 which is similar to the CNN method only.

Secondly, if we look at the results for each dataset individually, we can also remark that the performance of our system drastically change from one to another. While all approaches perform poorly on the answer-answer data, they achieve high correlation scores on the headlines, post-editing and plagiarism data sets. The latter being the data on which our approaches are the most efficient with a minimum of 0.749 correlation.

4 Conclusions and further studies

In this paper we described our participation to the STS Core Task for SemEval 2016. We adapted state-of-the-art methods from previous studies applied on the monolingual semantic similarity task and run them on the 2016 data. We investigated the performance of single methods individually but also combined altogether.

Overall, our results show that the CNN-based approach was the most effective compared to the others individual approaches. The combination of those methods achieves slightly better results than CNN only. We can also observe that results vary between the different dataset: they are highly satisfactory on both the headlines and plagiarism dataset, but perform poorly on the answer-answer data, especially Word2Vec with only 0.276 Pearson Correlation compared to gold-standard.

For the future work we aim to conduct a deeper analysis about the performance of our different systems. This will also include the understanding concerning their effectiveness over on diverse datasets. Finally, we would like to investigate the QuEst framework (Specia et al., 2013) as additional method to describe the semantic similarity between sentences:

QuEst framework

For our future work we aim to use the QuEst framework (Specia et al., 2013) and extract features to capture the semantic similarity between monolingual sentences. These features are used and have shown to perform well in the WMT shared tasks on QE. They include simple counts, e.g. number of tokens in the segments, language model probabilities and perplexities, number of punctuation marks in source and target segments, among other features reflecting the complexity and fluency of the given segments. Though these features are originally designed to estimate the quality of machine translation, we aim to adapt and explore their potential in addition to the methods discussed in previous sections.

Acknowledgements

The research leading to these results has received funding from the EU - Seventh Framework Program (FP7/2007-2013) under grant agreement n610916 SENSEI.

References

Eneko Agirre, Mona Diab, Daniel Cer, and Aitor Gonzalez-Agirre. 2012. Semeval-2012 task 6: A pilot on semantic textual similarity. In *Proceedings of the First Joint Conference on Lexical and Computational Semantics-Volume 1: Proceedings of the main conference and the shared task, and Volume 2: Proceedings of the Sixth International Workshop on Semantic Evaluation*, pages 385–393. Association for Computational Linguistics.

Eneko Agirre, Daniel Cer, Mona Diab, Aitor Gonzalez-Agirre, and Weiwei Guo. 2013. sem 2013 shared task: Semantic textual similarity, including a pilot on typed-similarity. In *In* SEM 2013: The Second Joint Conference on Lexical and Computational Semantics. Association for Computational Linguistics*. Citeseer.

Eneko Agirre, Carmen Banea, Claire Cardie, Daniel Cer, Mona Diab, Aitor Gonzalez-Agirre, Weiwei Guo, Rada Mihalcea, German Rigau, and Janyce Wiebe. 2014. Semeval-2014 task 10: Multilingual semantic textual similarity. In *Proceedings of the 8th international workshop on semantic evaluation (SemEval 2014)*, pages 81–91.

Eneko Agirrea, Carmen Baneab, Claire Cardiec, Daniel Cerd, Mona Diabe, Aitor Gonzalez-Agirrea, Weiwei Guof, Inigo Lopez-Gazpioa, Montse Maritxalara, Rada Mihalceab, et al. 2015. Semeval-2015 task 2: Semantic textual similarity, english, spanish and pilot on interpretability. In *Proceedings of the 9th international workshop on semantic evaluation (SemEval 2015)*, pages 252–263.

Marco Baroni, Georgiana Dinu, and Germán Kruszewski. 2014. Don't count, predict! a systematic comparison of context-counting vs. context-predicting semantic vectors. In *ACL (1)*, pages 238–247.

Chris Callison-Burch, Philipp Koehn, Christof Monz, Matt Post, Radu Soricut, and Lucia Specia, editors. 2012. *Proceedings of the Seventh Workshop on Statistical Machine Translation*. Association for Computational Linguistics, Montréal, Canada, June.

Chih-Chung Chang and Chuan-bi Lin. 2001. Training v-support vector classifiers: theory and algorithms. *Neural computation*, 13(9):2119–2147.

Hua He, Kevin Gimpel, and Jimmy Lin. 2015. Multi-perspective sentence similarity modeling with convolutional neural networks. In *Proceedings of the 2015 Conference on Empirical Methods in Natural Language Processing*, pages 1576–1586.

Tomas Mikolov, Ilya Sutskever, Kai Chen, Greg S Corrado, and Jeff Dean. 2013. Distributed representations of words and phrases and their compositionality. In *Advances in neural information processing systems*, pages 3111–3119.

Kishore Papineni, Salim Roukos, Todd Ward, and Wei-Jing Zhu. 2002. BLEU: a method for automatic evaluation of machine translation. In *Proceedings of the 40th Annual Meeting on Association for Computational Linguistics*, pages 311–318, Juillet.

Jeffrey Pennington, Richard Socher, and Christopher D Manning. 2014. Glove: Global vectors for word representation. In *EMNLP*, volume 14, pages 1532–1543.

Lucia Specia, Kashif Shah, Jose G. C. De Souza, Trevor Cohn, and Fondazione Bruno Kessler. 2013. Quest - a translation quality estimation framework. In *In Proceedings of the 51th Conference of the Association for Computational Linguistics (ACL), Demo Session*.

Md Arafat Sultan, Steven Bethard, and Tamara Sumner. 2014. Back to basics for monolingual alignment: Exploiting word similarity and contextual evidence. *Transactions of the Association for Computational Linguistics*, 2:219–230.

Md Arafat Sultan, Steven Bethard, and Tamara Sumner. 2015. Dls@ cu: Sentence similarity from word alignment and semantic vector composition. In *Proceedings of the 9th International Workshop on Semantic Evaluation*, pages 148–153.

NaCTeM at SemEval-2016 Task 1: Inferring sentence-level semantic similarity from an ensemble of complementary lexical and sentence-level features

Piotr Przybyła, Nhung T. H. Nguyen, Matthew Shardlow,
Georgios Kontonatsios and **Sophia Ananiadou**
National Centre for Text Mining
University of Manchester
Manchester, UK
{piotr.przybyla,nhung.nguyen,matthew.shardlow,
georgios.kontonatsios,sophia.ananiadou}@manchester.ac.uk

Abstract

We present a description of the system submitted to the Semantic Textual Similarity (STS) shared task at SemEval 2016. The task is to assess the degree to which two sentences carry the same meaning. We have designed two different methods to automatically compute a similarity score between sentences. The first method combines a variety of semantic similarity measures as features in a machine learning model. In our second approach, we employ training data from the Interpretable Similarity subtask to create a combined word-similarity measure and assess the importance of both aligned and unaligned words. Finally, we combine the two methods into a single hybrid model. Our best-performing run attains a score of 0.7732 on the 2015 STS evaluation data and 0.7488 on the 2016 STS evaluation data.

1 Introduction

If you ask a computer if two sentences are identical, it will return an accurate decision in a split-second. Ask it to do the same for a million sentence pairs and it will take a few seconds — far quicker than any human. But similarity has many dimensions. Ask a computer if two sentences mean the same and it will stall, yet the human can answer instantly. Now we have the edge. But what metrics do we use in our personal cognitive similarity-scoring systems? The answer is at the heart of the semantic similarity task. In our solution, we have incorporated several categories of features from a variety of sources. Our approach covers both low-level visual features such as length and edit-distance as well as high-level semantic features such as topic-models and alignment quality measures.

Throughout our approach, we have found it easier to consider similarity at the lexical level. This is unsurprising, as each lexeme may be seen as a semantic unit with the sentence's meaning built directly from a specific combination of lexemes. We have explored several methods for abstracting our lexical-level features to the sentence level as explained in Section 4. Our methods are built from both intuitive features as well as the results of error-analyses on our trial runs. We have combined multiple feature sources to build a powerful semantic-similarity classifier, discarding non-performing features as necessary.

2 Related Work

The presented system has been submitted to the Semantic Textual Similarity (STS) shared task at SemEval 2016, which has been organised since 2012 (Agirre et al., 2016). Existing approaches to the problem adopt a plethora of similarity measures including string-based, content-based and knowledge-based methods. String-based methods (Bär et al., 2012; Malakasiotis and Androutsopoulos, 2007; Jimenez et al., 2012) exploit surface features (e.g., character n-grams, lemmas) to compute a semantic similarity score between two sentences. Bär et al. (2012) showed that string-based features improve performance when using machine learning. Knowledge-based features (Mihalcea et al., 2006; Gabrilovich and Markovitch, 2007) estimate the semantic similarity of textual units using external

Proceedings of SemEval-2016, pages 614–620,
San Diego, California, June 16-17, 2016. ©2016 Association for Computational Linguistics

knowledge resources (e.g., WordNet). As an example, Liu et al. (2015) used the shortest path that links two words in the WordNet taxonomy as a similarity measure between words. To calculate a similarity score between sentences, the authors used the sum of the similarity scores of the constituent words. Content-based features are based upon the distributional similarity of words and sentences. Distributional semantics methods (Mikolov et al., 2013; Baroni et al., 2014) encode the lexical context of words into a vector representation. A vector representation of a sentence may be estimated as a function of the vectors of the constituent words (Mitchell and Lapata, 2010). The semantic relatedness between sentences is measured using the cosine of the angle of the composed sentence vectors.

3   Feature Sources

We have collected a variety of resources to help us create semantic similarity features. Some of these (Subsections 3.2 and 3.4) give features at the level of the sentence itself. Other resources (Subsections 3.1, 3.3, 3.5. 3.6 and 3.7) give features at the level of the individual words. We explain how we adapt these features to sentence-level metrics in Section 4.

3.1   Distributional semantics

We use a count-based distributional semantics model (Turney and Pantel, 2010) and the Continuous Bag-Of-Words (CBOW) model (Mikolov et al., 2013) to learn word vectors. The training corpus that we used is a combination of all monolingual texts provided by the organiser of the 2014 Machine Translation Shared Task[1], whose size is about 20 GB. Before training, we tokenised and transferred the corpus into lowercase text. The size of the context window is 5 for both of the models. The numbers of dimensions in the resulting vectors are 150,000 and 300 for the count-based and the CBOW models respectively.

3.2   Machine translation

A pair of input sentences can be considered as the input and output of a machine translation system. Therefore, we can apply machine translation (MT) metrics to estimate the semantic relatedness of the input pair. Specifically, we used three popular MT metrics: BLEU (Papineni et al., 2002), Translation Edit Rate (TER) (Snover et al., 2006), and METEOR (Denkowski and Lavie, 2014).

3.3   Lexical paraphrase scores

Another promising resource for similarity estimation is the lexical paraphrase database (PPDB) by Ganitkevitch et al. (2013). Each of the word pairs in the PPDB has a set of 31 different features (Ganitkevitch and Callison-Burch, 2014). In this work, we calculate the similarity of a word pair by using the formula that Ganitkevitch and Callison-Burch (2014) recommended to measure paraphrases' quality. However, for word pairs that have been seen very rarely, i.e., their rarity penalty score in PPDB is higher than 0.1, we simply set the similarity score at 0 instead of applying the formula.

3.4   Topic modelling

We induce a topic-based vector representation of sentences by applying the Latent Dirichlet Allocation (LDA) method (Blei et al., 2003). We hypothesise that a varying granularity of vector-representations provide complementary information to the machine learning system. Based upon this, we extract 26 different topic-based vector representations by varying the number of topics; starting from a small number of 5 topics which resulted in a coarse-grained topic-based representation to a larger number of 800 topics which produced a more fine-grained representation. In our experiments, we used the freely available MALLET toolkit (McCallum, 2002). Additionally, we performed hyper-parameter optimisation for every 10 Gibbs sampling iterations and set the total number of iterations to 2, 000.

3.5   WordNet

For WordNet-based similarity between a pair of words we have chosen Jiang-Conrath (Jiang and Conrath, 1997) similarity based on an evaluation by Budanitsky and Hirst (2006). To compute the score, we lemmatise the words using Stanford CoreNLP (Manning et al., 2014), find corresponding synsets in Princeton WordNet (Fellbaum, 1998) and obtain the Jiang-Conrath value using the WS4J library[2].

---

[1] http://www.statmt.org/wmt14/
translation-task.html#download

[2] https://code.google.com/archive/p/ws4j/

3.6 Character string

Sometimes semantically related words are very similar as sequences of characters, e.g. *cooperate* and *co-operate* or *recover* and *recovery*. To handle such cases we compute Levenshtein distance (Levenshtein, 1966) between words. To keep the similarity score x_l in the $[0, 1]$ range, we adjust the obtained distance d by computing $x_l = (l - d)/l$, where l denotes the length of the longer word.

3.7 Word importance measures

We calculated the combined probability of each word occurring in a given context. We used smoothed unigram and bigram probabilities taken from the Google Web1T data (Brants and Franz, 2006). We multiplied the smoothed unigram probability of a word together with the smoothed bigram probability of both the word itself and the word immediately before it to give the 2-word contextual probability of a word's appearance. Whilst this model could theoretically be extended to longer sequences, we found that memory resources limited our capacity to a sequence of 2 words.

$$p(w_i|w_{i-1}, w_i) = p(w_{i-1}, w_i) \times p(w_i)$$

We also investigated psycholinguistic properties as measures of word importance. We used the MRC Psycholinguistic norms (Wilson, 1988) to attain values for the 'familiarity', 'imagery' and 'concreteness' of each word. These metrics can be defined as follows:

Familiarity: This indicates how likely a word is to be recognised by a user. Words which occur very often such as *cat* are likely to be more familiar than less common words such as *feline*.

Concreteness: This indicates whether a reader perceives a word as referring to a physical entity. A conceptual phrase such as *truth* will have a lower value for concreteness than an object which is more easily relatable such as *house* or *man*.

Imagery: This metric indicates how easy it is to call-up images associated with a word. This is related to concreteness, but may differ in some cases. For example, some actions (*jumping, flying*) or common emotions (*joy, sadness, fear*) may have high imagery, but low concreteness.

4 Feature Generation

We found that the greatest challenge of the task was to combine different existing word-level relatedness cues into a sentence-level similarity measure. We have submitted three permutations of our system, as allowed by the task. The first system 'Aggregation (*Macro*)' passes a set of 36 features through a random forest classifier. The second system 'Alignment (*Micro*)' first aligns the sentences using word-level metrics and then calculates 49 features describing this alignment. Our final system '*Hybrid*' is simply the combination of the former two approaches.

4.1 Aggregation (Macro)

In this approach feature sources are used separately, each applied as a sentence similarity measure that is further represented as a single feature.

- *Compositional semantic vectors.* A sentence vector is simply calculated by cumulatively adding its component word vectors. The similarity of a sentence pair is then estimated by the cosine of the angle between the corresponding vectors.

- *Average maximum cosine.* Given a sentence pair of (s, t) whose number of words are m and n respectively, the similarity score is calculated as the average of the maximum cosine similarity of word pairs as follows:

$$score(s, t) = \frac{\sum_{i=1}^{m} \max_{j=1}^{n} \cos(\overrightarrow{w_i}, \overrightarrow{w_j})}{\max(m, n)}$$

- *MT metrics.* We apply MT metrics at the sentence level. We used smoothed BLEU-4 and TER implemented within Stanford Phrasal[3] while the METEOR score was provided using techniques from Denkowski and Lavie (2014).

- *Paraphrase DB.* To compute sentence similarity using PPDB, we find the most similar counterpart for each of the words and return an average of obtained similarity scores, weighted by word length.

---

[3] http://nlp.stanford.edu/phrasal/

- *Topic modelling metric.* Given that each sentence is represented by a topic-based vector, we can compute a similarity score for a sentence pair using the cosine similarity.

This leads to 36 features, each expected to be positively correlated with sentence similarity.

4.2 Alignment (Micro)

In this approach we combine different techniques of assessing relatedness to create a single word similarity measure, use it to align compared sentences, and compute features describing a quality of alignment.

4.2.1 Word-level similarity

We employ a machine learning model to create a measure of semantic similarity between words. The model uses four measures:

1. adjusted Levenshtein distance x_l,

2. word-vector cosine similarity x_{wv},

3. WordNet Jiang-Conrath similarity x_{wn},

4. paraphrase database score x_p.

Each measure returns values between 0 (no similarity) and 1 (identical words). As a training set, we have used all the data from the previous year's interpretable subtask (Agirre et al., 2015), which includes pairs of chunks with assigned similarity between 0 and 5. As this set contain pairs of chunks, not words, we extended these measures for multiword arguments. This has been done by (1) using the whole chunk for Levenshtein distance, (2) finding the best pair for WordNet similarity and (3) using solutions for sentence-level aggregation (described in the previous section) for word vectors and paraphrase database.

Negative examples have been created by selecting unaligned pairs and assigning to them a score equal to 0. In that way we obtain 19,673 training cases, from which the following linear regression model has been deduced:

$$y = -0.3285 + 1.3343 \times x_l + 0.8625 \times x_{wv}$$
$$+0.9875 \times x_{wn} + 2.1496 \times x_p$$

The coefficients of this model show that the word vectors and WordNet features have a lower influence on the final score output by the model, whereas the paraphrase database score has a greater influence. Although the final model was trained on all the data from last year's interpretable similarity subtask, we performed a separate evaluation on this data in which we partitioned the data into train and test subsets. The resulting correlation on the test subset was 0.8964, which we consider to be very reasonable.

4.2.2 Finding alignment

Having a universal similarity measure between words, we can compute an alignment of sentences. To do this, we tokenise each sentence and compute similarity value between every pair of words. Then we find an alignment in a greedy way, by pairing free words in order of decreasing similarity of pairs. This process stops when we reach 1 (in a 0-5 scale, see previous section), which usually leaves some of the words unaligned.

4.2.3 Features

The features generated in this approach describe the quality of the alignment of a pair of sentences. The simple measures are: mean similarity between aligned pairs, length of aligned parts as a proportion of sentence length (average from two sentences) and a number of crossings in permutation defined by the alignment, i.e. Kendall's tau (Kendall, 1955). Secondly, we also include sums of lengths of aligned and unaligned words with particular tags, using Stanford CoreNLP (Manning et al., 2014) with slightly simplified Brown tagset (19 tags). This follows our intuition that significance of success or failure of alignment of a particular word is different for different parts of speech (e.g proper nouns vs. determiners). Finally, we measure the importance of matched and unmatched words by their probability (sum of logarithms) and psycholinguistic metrics – familiarity, concreteness and imagery (sum of values). As a result of this process we get 49 features.

4.3 Hybrid

The hybrid approach simply combines outputs from the two feature generation solutions described above. This leads to 85 features, some of which may be redundant.

Feature	Impurity decrease
Paraphrase DB score	8082.91
METEOR	4611.94
Average max. cosine	2262.56
Compositional sem. cosine	1895.34
LDA (800 topics)	967.74
LDA (675 topics)	907.32
LDA (600 topics)	852.86
Smoothed BLEU	753.78
LDA (525 topics)	735.61
Translation Edit Rate	706.48

Table 1: Ten most useful variables from the aggregation approach according to random forest importance measure, i.e. mean decrease in residual sum of squares.

Feature	Impurity decrease
Alignment ratio	9350.65
Prob. of aligned words	4809.45
Mean similarity	2361.40
Unaligned nouns	1691.97
Prob. of unaligned words	1576.07
Aligned nouns	1258.54
Fam. of aligned words	1224.19
Im. of aligned words	1073.80
Fam. of unaligned words	905.14
Con. of unaligned words	874.51

Table 2: Ten most useful variables from the alignment approach according to random forest importance measure, i.e. mean decrease in residual sum of squares (*Prob.* – probability, *Fam.* – familiarity, *Im.* – imagery, *Con.* – concreteness).

5 Learning

Each of the three feature sets described above has been used to create a single regression model. For this purpose we explored different methods available in the R environment (R Core Team, 2013): linear regression, decision trees (Breiman et al., 1984), multivariate adaptive regression splines (Friedman, 1991) and generalised additive models (Hastie and Tibshirani, 1990), but internal evaluation has shown that random forests (Breiman, 2001) perform the best in this task. Since the dimensionality of the task is not very high, we have not performed any feature selection, leaving this to the random forests. They offer a useful measure of variable importance, namely the decrease in residual sum of squares averaged over all trees. Tables 1 and 2 show the ten most useful variables for this purpose from the aggregation and alignment approaches, respectively.

6 Evaluation

As explained in previous sections, we have used three features sets to create three classification models, called *Macro* (from aggregation-based features), *Micro* (from alignment-based features) and *Hybrid* (including both feature sets). According to the shared task guidelines, the performance has been measured by computing a correlation between predicted and gold standard (assigned by humans) scores in each data set, and then obtaining their average.

We have performed two main experiments. Firstly, we have used the data that have been available for training and testing in the 2015 competition (Agirre et al., 2015) to select the best approach. Then, we have created three final models on all available 2015 data and used them to label the test data provided by the organisers of the 2016 task. Table 3 shows the results of both experiments.

7 Discussion

What may seem the most surprising in the results is their diversity – some of the methods achieve correlation well over 0.8 for one data set and below 0.6 for another. In our opinion, that not only shows that there is room for improvement but also reveals a fundamental problem in this task, namely that training and test sets come from different sources. The distribution of features also differs. This situation simulates many real-world scenarios, but also impedes any ML-based approach. In this light, our drop in performance between development (2015) and evaluation (2016) sets seems satisfactorily small.

The data sets related to questions and answers have turned out to cause the most difficulties for our system. We have performed a post-hoc error analysis to understand why. We found that these sets expose weaknesses of our reliance on abstracting from word-level similarity to the sentence-level. For example, consider the following two questions: *What is the difference between Erebor and Moria?* and *What is the difference between splicing and superim-*

| | **Features set** | | |
Data set	Macro	Micro	Hybrid
2015			
images	0.8022	0.8129	0.8457
headlines	0.7963	0.8183	0.8263
belief	0.7107	0.7031	0.7455
answers-students	0.6994	0.7264	0.7378
answers-forum	0.6186	0.6797	0.7108
Mean	0.7254	0.7481	**0.7732**
2016			
headlines	0.7976	0.7914	0.8046
plagiarism	0.7895	0.8313	0.8148
postediting	0.8261	0.8266	0.8286
answer-answer	0.5848	0.5521	0.6024
question-question	0.6704	0.6124	0.6937
Mean	0.7337	0.7228	**0.7488**

Table 3: Correlations of predicted and actual similarity scores measured for datasets available in 2015 and 2016 shared task.

position? As you can see, they have the same structure and a lot of identical words, but the two remaining words create a wholly different meaning. This means that our approach, confirmed by the ranking of features (see table 2), deserves further work.

We may be able to boost our performance on the 2016 task by a few simple measures. Firstly, we could include semantic features from a wider variety of sources. Especially for the word-importance metrics. Secondly, we could consider pre-filtering the sentences for a list of stop-words which typically do not contain much semantic importance to a sentence. Finally, we could attempt to weight our word-level measures based on the semantic importance of each word in a sentence. For example, verbs and nouns are probably more important than adjectives and adverbs, which in turn are likely to be more important than conjunctions.

References

Eneko Agirre, Carmen Banea, Claire Cardie, Daniel Cer, Mona Diab, Aitor Gonzalez-Agirre, Weiwei Guo, Inigo Lopez-Gazpio, Montse Maritxalar, Rada Mihalcea, German Rigau, Larraitz Uria, and Janyce Wiebe. 2015. SemEval-2015 Task 2: Semantic Textual Similarity, English, Spanish and Pilot on Interpretability. In *Proceedings of the 9th International Workshop on Semantic Evaluation (SemEval 2015)*. Association for Computational Linguistics.

Eneko Agirre, Carmen Banea, Daniel Cer, Mona Diab, Aitor Gonzalez-Agirre, Rada Mihalcea, and Janyce Wiebe. 2016. SemEval-2016 Task 1: Semantic Textual Similarity - Monolingual and Cross-lingual Evaluation. In *Proceedings of the 10th International Workshop on Semantic Evaluation (SemEval 2016)*. Association for Computational Linguistics.

Daniel Bär, Chris Biemann, Iryna Gurevych, and Torsten Zesch. 2012. UKP: Computing semantic textual similarity by combining multiple content similarity measures. In *Proceedings of the First Joint Conference on Lexical and Computational Semantics (SemEval '12)*. Association for Computational Linguistics.

Marco Baroni, Georgiana Dinu, and Germán Kruszewski. 2014. Don't count, predict! A systematic comparison of context-counting vs. context-predicting semantic vectors. In *Proceedings of the 52nd Annual Meeting of the Association for Computational Linguistics*. Association for Computational Linguistics.

David M. Blei, Andrew Y. Ng, and Michael I. Jordan. 2003. Latent Dirichlet Allocation. *Journal of Machine Learning Research*, 3:993–1022.

Thorsten Brants and Alex Franz. 2006. Web 1T 5-gram corpus version 1.1. *Linguistic Data Consortium*.

Leo Breiman, Jerome H. Friedman, Richard A. Olshen, and Charles J. Stone. 1984. *Classification and Regression Trees*. Wadsworth & Brooks.

Leo Breiman. 2001. Random Forests. *Machine Learning*, 45(1):5–32.

Alexander Budanitsky and Graeme Hirst. 2006. Evaluating WordNet-based Measures of Lexical Semantic Relatedness. *Computational Linguistics*, 32(1):13–47.

Michael Denkowski and Alon Lavie. 2014. Meteor Universal: Language Specific Translation Evaluation for Any Target Language. In *Proceedings of the EACL 2014 Workshop on Statistical Machine Translation*. Association for Computational Linguistics.

Christiane Fellbaum. 1998. *WordNet: An Electronic Lexical Database*. MIT Press.

Jerome H. Friedman. 1991. Multivariate Adaptive Regression Splines. *The Annals of Statistics*, 19:1–67.

Evgeniy Gabrilovich and Shaul Markovitch. 2007. Computing semantic relatedness using Wikipedia-based explicit semantic analysis. In *Proceedings of the 20th International Joint Conference on Artifical Intelligence (IJCAI'07)*. Morgan Kaufmann Publishers.

Juri Ganitkevitch and Chris Callison-Burch. 2014. The Multilingual Paraphrase Database. In *Proceedings of the Ninth International Conference on Language Resources and Evaluation (LREC'14)*. European Language Resources Association.

Juri Ganitkevitch, Benjamin Van Durme, and Chris Callison-Burch. 2013. PPDB: The Paraphrase Database. In *The 15th Annual Conference of the North American Chapter of the Association for Computational Linguistics: Human Language Technologies (NAACL-HLT '13)*. Association for Computational Linguistics.

Trevor J. Hastie and Robert J. Tibshirani. 1990. *Generalized Additive Models*. Chapman & Hall/CRC.

Jay J. Jiang and David W. Conrath. 1997. Semantic Similarity Based on Corpus Statistics and Lexical Taxonomy. In *Proceedings of 10th International Conference on Research in Computational Linguistics (RO-CLING'97)*.

Sergio Jimenez, Claudia Becerra, and Alexander Gelbukh. 2012. Soft cardinality: A parameterized similarity function for text comparison. In *Proceedings of the First Joint Conference on Lexical and Computational Semantics (SemEval '12)*. Association for Computational Linguistics.

Maurice G. Kendall. 1955. *Rank correlation methods*. Hafner Publishing.

Vladimir Iosifovich Levenshtein. 1966. Binary codes capable of correcting deletions, insertions, and reversals. *Soviet Physics Doklady*, 10:707–710.

Yang Liu, Chengjie Sun, Lei Lin, and Xiaolong Wang. 2015. yiGou: A Semantic Text Similarity Computing System Based on SVM. *Proceedings of the 9th International Workshop on Semantic Evaluation (SemEval 2015)*.

Prodromos Malakasiotis and Ion Androutsopoulos. 2007. Learning textual entailment using SVMs and string similarity measures. In *Proceedings of the ACL-PASCAL Workshop on Textual Entailment and Paraphrasing*. Association for Computational Linguistics.

Christopher D. Manning, John Bauer, Jenny Finkel, Steven J. Bethard, Mihai Surdeanu, and David McClosky. 2014. The Stanford CoreNLP Natural Language Processing Toolkit. In *Proceedings of 52nd Annual Meeting of the Association for Computational Linguistics: System Demonstrations*. Association for Computational Linguistics.

Andrew Kachites McCallum. 2002. MALLET: A machine learning for language toolkit.

Rada Mihalcea, Courtney Corley, and Carlo Strapparava. 2006. Corpus-based and knowledge-based measures of text semantic similarity. In *Proceedings of the 21st National Conference on Artificial intelligence (AAAI '06)*. AAAI Press.

Tomas Mikolov, Kai Chen, Greg Corrado, and Jeffrey Dean. 2013. Efficient Estimation of Word Representations in Vector Space. *arXiv*.

Jeff Mitchell and Mirella Lapata. 2010. Composition in distributional models of semantics. *Cognitive Science*, 34(8):1388–1429.

Kishore Papineni, Salim Roukos, Todd Ward, and Wei-Jing Zhu. 2002. BLEU: a method for automatic evaluation of machine translation. In *Proceedings of the 40th Annual Meeting on Association for Computational Linguistics (ACL '02)*. Association for Computational Linguistics.

R Core Team. 2013. R: A Language and Environment for Statistical Computing.

Matthew Snover, Bonnie Dorr, Richard Schwartz, Linnea Micciulla, and John Makhoul. 2006. A study of translation edit rate with targeted human annotation. In *Proceedings of Association for Machine Translation in the Americas*, pages 223–231.

Peter D. Turney and Patrick Pantel. 2010. From frequency to meaning: vector space models of semantics. *Journal of Artificial Intelligence Research*, 37(1):141–188.

Michael Wilson. 1988. MRC Psycholinguistic Database: Machine-usable dictionary , version 2.00.

ECNU at SemEval-2016 Task 1: Leveraging Word Embedding from Macro and Micro Views to Boost Performance for Semantic Textual Similarity

Junfeng Tian[1], Man Lan[1,2]*
[1]Department of Computer Science and Technology,
East China Normal University, Shanghai, P.R.China
[2]Shanghai Key Laboratory of Multidimensional Information Processing
`51151201048@ecnu.cn, mlan@cs.ecnu.edu.cn`*

Abstract

This paper presents our submissions for semantic textual similarity task in SemEval 2016. Based on several traditional features (i.e., string-based, corpus-based, machine translation similarity and alignment metrics), we leverage word embedding from macro (i.e., first get representation of sentence, then measure the similarity of sentence pair) and micro views (i.e., measure the similarity of word pairs separately) to boost performance. Due to the various domains of training data and test data, we adopt three different strategies: 1) U-SEVEN: an unsupervised model, which utilizes seven straight-forward metrics; 2) S1-All: using all available datasets; 3) S2: selecting the most similar training sets for each test set. Results on test sets show that the unified supervised model (i.e., S1-All) achieves the best averaged performance with a mean correlation of 75.07%.

1 Introduction

Estimating the degree of semantic similarity between two sentences is the building block of many Natural Language Processing (NLP) applications, such as question answering, textual entailment, text summarization etc. Therefore, Semantic Textual Similarity (STS) has received an increasing amount of attention in recent years, e.g., the STS tasks in Semantic Evaluation Exercises have been held from 2012 to 2016.

To identify semantic similarity of sentence pairs, most existing works adopt at least one of the following feature types: 1) string based similarity (Bär et al., 2012; Jimenez et al., 2012) which employs common functions to calculate similarities over string sequences extracted from original strings, e.g., lemma, stem, or n-grams sequences; 2) corpus based similarity (Šarić et al., 2012) where distributional models such as Latent Semantic Analysis (LSA), are used to derive the distributional vectors of words from a large corpus according to their occurrence patterns, afterwards, similarities of sentence pairs are calculated using these vectors; 3) knowledge based method (Agirre et al., 2015b) which estimates the similarities with the aid of external resources, such as WordNet. Among them, Sultan et al. (2015) leverage different word alignment strategies to bring word-level similarity to sentence-level similarity.

Traditional NLP feature engineering often treat sentence as a bag of words or term frequency, and endeavor to evaluate the similarity according to the co-occurrence of words or other replacement words. For example, Zhao et al. (2014) built a supervised model using ensemble of heterogeneous features and achieved great performance on STS Task 2014. However, it is difficult to evaluate semantic relatedness if all the word in both sentences is unique. For example: *A storm will spread snow over Shanghai; The earthquakes have shaken parts of Oklahoma.* These sentences have no words in common, although they convey the similar information.

In this work, we first borrow the aforementioned effective types of similarity measurements including string-based, corpus-based, machine translation similarity and alignment measures to capture the semantic similarity between two sentences. Besides, we also present our highly interpretable and

Proceedings of SemEval-2016, pages 621–627,
San Diego, California, June 16-17, 2016. ©2016 Association for Computational Linguistics

hyper-parameter free word embedding features from macro and micro views to boost the performance. Then we adopt three different strategies of the usage of training data: 1) U-SEVEN: an unsupervised model, which utilizes seven straight-forward metrics (i.e., longest common sequence, alignment feature, corpus-based feature, and others are all from word embedding features); 2) S1-All: use all available datasets and train a unified regression model after deleting unnecessary features; 3) S2: select the most similar training sets for each test set, according to the source of the dataset, average sentence length, and similarity distance (i.e., word mover's distance, discussed in Section 2.3).

The rest of this paper is organized as follows. Section 2 describes various similarity measurements used in our systems. Section 3 gives the datasets and system setups. Results on training set and test set will show in Section 4 and 5 respectively, and finally conclusion is given in Section 6.

2　Semantic Similarity Measurements

Previous excellent work (Zhao et al., 2014; Sultan et al., 2015) have shown great performance for STS tasks. Following their works, we engineer the traditional widely used features for semantic similarity measurements (i.e., string-based, corpus-based, machine translation similarity and alignment measures). In this work, we also present our highly interpretable and hyper-parameter free word embedding features from macro and micro views to boost the performance.

2.1　Preprocessing

Several text preprocessing operations are performed before feature engineering: 1) Converting the contractions to their formal writing, e.g., *"doesn't"* is rewritten as *"does not"*. 2) The WordNet-based Lemmatizer implemented in Natural Language Toolkit[1] is used to lemmatize all words to their nearest based forms in WordNet, e.g., *"was"* is lemmatized to *"be"*. 3) Stanford CoreNLP (Manning et al., 2014) is adopted to get the Part-Of-Speech (POS) tag and Named Entity Recognition (NER) tag.

---

[1] http://www.nltk.org

2.2　Traditional NLP Feature Engineering

2.2.1　String-Based Similarity

Length Features (len): We record the length information of given sentence pairs using the following eight measure functions: $|A|, |B|, |A - B|, |B - A|, |A \cup B|, |A \cap B|, \frac{|A-B|}{|B|}, \frac{|B-A|}{|A|}$, where $|A|$ stands for the number of non-repeated words in sentence A.

Syntactic Features (pos): Since two sentences with similar syntax structure convey similar meaning, we estimate the similarities of syntax structure. We firstly use Stanford CoreNLP toolkit (Manning et al., 2014) to obtain the POS tags of each sentence. Afterwards, we use eight measure functions mentioned in the Length Features on the sets of POS tags to calculate Syntactic Features.

Longest Common Sequence (lcs): In consideration of the different length of sentence pairs, we divide the maximum length of the common subsequence of two sentences by the length of the shorter one.

***n*-grams Overlap Features (*n*-grams):** We obtain n-grams at three different level (i.e., the original word level, the lemmatized word level and the character level). Then Jaccard similarity is used for calculating the similarity of these n-grams pairs. In our experiments, $n = \{1, 2, 3\}$ are used for the word level whereas $n = \{2, 3, 4\}$ are used for the character level.

Named Entities Features (ner): Besides of the surface similarities between words, we also calculate the relatedness of named entities in two sentences using *lcs* function. Seven types of named entities (i.e., *location, organization, data, money, person, time, percent*), recognized by Stanford CoreNLP toolkit (Manning et al., 2014), are considered.

2.2.2　Machine Translation Similarity

Machine Translation (MT) evaluation metrics are designed to assess whether the output of a MT system is semantically equivalent to a set of reference translations. The two given sentences are viewed as one input and one output of a MT system, then we get two MT scores of each MT measure (i.e., *WER, TER, PER, NIST, ROUGE-L, GTM-1*). Two strategies is employed to get MT similarity features, 1).

average two MT scores in each MT measure; 2). concatenate two MT scores in each MT measure.

2.2.3 Corpus-based Features

WordNet Rank Features (wordnet): The above semantic similarities only consider the surface similarities rather than their relations in corpus. Hence, we use graph-based lexical relatedness, which performs with a pre-existing Knowledge Base (KB) (i.e., WordNet), to get the relations of words. Then Personalized PageRank is applied on the Lexical Knowledge Base (LKB) to rank the vertices of the LKB. The details of the method are described in A-girre et al. (2015b). It outputs a ranking vector of the sentence over KB nodes and the values of the weights are normalized so that all link weights of particular headword sum to one. Finally, we calculate the `Cosine`, `Manhattan`, `Euclidean`, `Jaccard` of the two sentence vectors.

Vector Space Sentence Similarity (lsa): This measure is motivated by the idea of compositionality of distributional vector (Mitchell and Lapata, 2008). we adopt two distributional word sets released by TakeLab (Šarić et al., 2012), where Latent Semantic Analysis (LSA) was performed on the New York Times Annotated Corpus (NYT)[2] and Wikipedia. Then two strategies are used to convert the distributional meaning of words to sentence level: 1). simply summing up. 2). using *tf* to weigh each word vector.

2.2.4 Alignment Measures

(Sultan et al., 2015) used delicate word aligner to compute proportion of aligned words across the two input sentences. It aligned words based on their semantic similarity in the two sentences, as well as the similarity between local semantic contexts, which relies on dependencies and surface-form neighbors. The paraphrase Database (PPDB) (Ganitkevitch et al., 2013) was used to identify semantically similar words. Word pairs are aligned with greedy strategy, in descending order of their similarity.

Global Alignment Features (global): Given sentences S_1 and S_2, single proportion over all words is computed over all words:

$$sim(S_1, S_2) = \frac{n_a(S_1) + n_a(S_2)}{n(S_1) + n(S_2)} \quad (1)$$

where $n(S_i)$ is the number of non-repeated words in S_i, while $n_a(S_i)$ is the number of aligned content words in S_i.

Specific Alignment Features (pos-specific): Taking weight of POS tag of aligned words into consideration, score of aligned *noun* word pair is surely higher than the *adjective*. Using this property, we propose the specific alignment feature, to calculate the aligned words proportion specifically according to POS tag (i.e., noun, verb, adjective, adverb).

2.3 Word Embedding Feature Engineering

Recently, the distributed representations of words (i.e., word embedding) learned by neural networks over a large raw corpus have been shown that they performed significantly better than Latent Semantic Analysis for preserving linear regularities among words (Mikolov et al., 2013). The training on very large datasets allows the model to learn complex word relationships such as $vec(Berlin) - vec(Germany) + vec(France) \approx vec(Paris)$ (Mikolov et al., 2013).

As discussed in Section 1, it is very hard to evaluate semantic similarity if no words in the sentence pair in common. Obviously, word embedding features supply the gap. For example, *A storm will spread snow over Shanghai; The earthquakes have shaken parts of Oklahoma.* while *storm* is similar to *earthquake* and *spread* is analogous to *shaken*, *Shanghai* and *Oklahoma* both are locations.

In order to evaluate semantic similarity of a sentence pair, we define the function *INFO* is the semantic information of a word or a sentence carried.

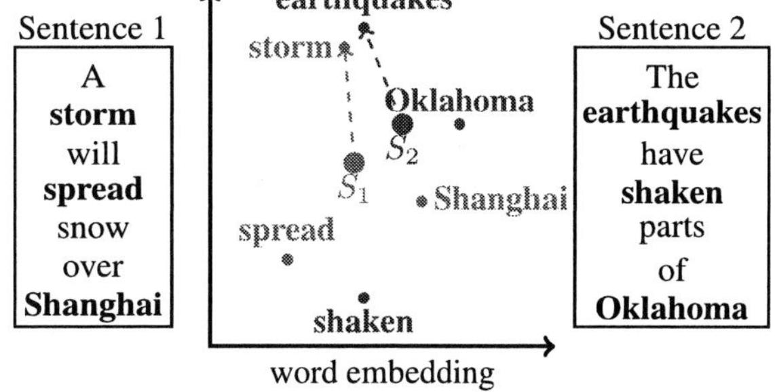

Figure 1: An illustration of the word centroid distance. Points in red is the word from sentence 1 (stopwords is ignored), while blue from sentence 2. S_i is the centroid of points from sentence i.

---

[2]https://catalog.ldc.upenn.edu/LDC2008T19

Thus the semantic similarity of sentence pair can be regarded as the distance between their *INFOs*. In other words, given sentence S_1 and S_2,

$$sts(S_1, S_2) = INFO(S_1) - INFO(S_2) \qquad (2)$$

where *INFO(S_i)* is the semantic information of sentence S_i. We study the above formula from macro and micro views.

Macro Information Distance: From macro view, we first get the *INFO* of each sentence (i.e., semantic information), and then calculate the distance between them. As follows:

$$sts(S_1, S_2) = INFO\left(f(w_1^{S_1}, w_2^{S_1}, \ldots, w_{len(S_1)}^{S_1})\right) - INFO\left(f(w_1^{S_2}, w_2^{S_2}, \ldots, w_{len(S_2)}^{S_2})\right) \qquad (3)$$

where $w_i^{S_j}$ is the word embedding of word i in sentence j and function f is to obtain the sentence representation from word embeddings, such as sum, average or convolution. Assuming that if two sentences are similar, one word in a sentence should have the similar meaning word with another, we use the centroid of word embedding to symbolise the macro *INFO* of the sentence. As showed in Figure 1, S_i represents for sentence i, and the distance between S_1 and S_2 represents for the similarity of the sentence pair. What is more, *storm* and *earthquakes* are the most important word in the sentence pair, we surely should give them more weight. As they are similar, the distance centroid tend to be close (the dashed lines). We use *idf* from datasets to weigh the importance.

Micro Information Distance: As for micro view, we first get the *INFO* of each word, and evaluate the distance between the sentence pair according to the

INFO of words. The formula is described as Equation 4.

$$\begin{aligned}
sts(S_1, S_2) =\, &INFO(w_1^{S_1}) + INFO(w_2^{S_1}) + \ldots + INFO(w_{len(S_1)}^{S_1}) \\
&- INFO(w_1^{S_2}) - INFO(w_2^{S_2}) - \ldots - INFO(w_{len(S_2)}^{S_2})
\end{aligned} \qquad (4)$$

Our goal is to incorporate the semantic similarity between each word pairs into the micro information distance of sentence. Here, we adopted word mover's distance (Kusner et al., 2015), the minimum cumulative distance that all word in sentence 1 need to travel to exactly match sentence 2, showed in Figure 2. For more details, see Kusner et al. (2015).

Word Embedding Features: Zhao et al. (2014) shows that heterogenous feature outperform a single feature, and we use three embeddings (Turian et al., 2010; Mikolov et al., 2013; Pennington et al., 2014) as our initial word vector input. Incidentally, the distance is substitutable, and we replace it with different measurements (i.e., *cosine distance, Manhanttan distance, Euclidean distance, Pearson coefficient, Spearman coefficient, Kendall tau coefficient*). Specially, because of the high time complexity of word mover's distance, we only train it on *word2vec* (Mikolov et al., 2013), although other embeddings are also plausible.

3 Experiments

3.1 Datasets

We collect all the datasets from 2012 to 2015 as training data. Each dataset consists of a number of sentence pairs and each pair has a human-assigned similarity score in the range[0,5] which increases with similarity. The datasets are collected from different but related domains. We briefly describe data in Table 1, Refer Agirre et al. (2015a) for details. We emphasize dataset with symbol * for that this dataset appears both in training and test sets, which is very useful to our third submission **S2** (see Section 3.4 for more details).

3.2 Evaluation Measurement

In order to evaluate the performance of different algorithms, we adopt the official evaluation measure, i.e, Pearson correlation coefficient for each individual test set, and a weighted sum of all correlations is used as final evaluation metric. It weights according to the number of gold sentence pairs. The weight of

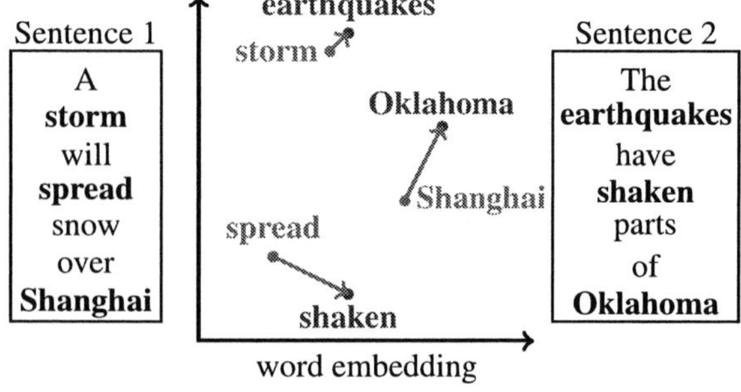

Figure 2: An illustration of the word mover's distance, an instance of micro information distance.

Training Set			Test Set		
Dataset	Input	Gold	Dataset	Input	Gold
MSRpar	1500	1500	answers-answers	1572	254
SMTeuroparl	1193	1193	plagiarism	1271	230
headlines*	3000	2250	headlines*	1498	249
SMTnews	399	399	postediting	3287	244
MSRvid	1500	1500	question-question	1555	209
OnWN	2061	2061	-	-	-
FNWN	189	189	-	-	-
images	2250	1500	-	-	-
deft-forum	450	450	-	-	-
deft-news	300	300	-	-	-
tweet-news	750	750	-	-	-
answers-forums	1500	375	-	-	-
answers-students	1500	750	-	-	-
belief	2000	375	-	-	-
All	19092	13592	All	9183	1186

Table 1: The statistics of all datasets for STS task. Dataset with symbol * represents that this dataset appears both in training and test sets.

a test set is equal to the rate of the gold sentences pairs in all the gold sentences.

3.3 Learning Algorithm

We conduct a series of experiments using all features discussed in Section 2.2 and 2.3 to obtain the optimized learning algorithm. Three supervised learning methods are explored: Support Vector Regression (SVR), Random Forest (RF) and Gradient Boosting (GB). These supervised learning algorithms are implemented using scikit-learn toolkit (Buitinck et al., 2013).we use all the datasets from STS Task 2015 as development data while others from STS Task 2012 to 2014 as training data.

To configure the parameters in the regression algorithm, i.e., the trade-off parameter c in SVR, the number of trees n_{RF} in RF and the number of boosting stages n_{GB} in GB, we make a grid search for c in $[0.01, 0.1, 1, 10]$, n_{RF} from 5 to 100 with step 5 and n_{GB} from 10 to 300 with step 10.

Regression	belief	answers -students	headlines	images	answers -forums	Weighted Mean
SVR(c=1)	0.7413	0.7359	0.8168	0.8660	0.7400	0.7898
RF(n=40)	0.7466	0.7100	0.8200	0.8534	0.7398	0.7816
GB(n=140)	**0.7655**	0.7484	**0.8439**	**0.8791**	**0.7469**	**0.8080**
DLSCU-S1	0.7491	**0.7725**	0.8250	0.8644	0.7390	0.8015

Table 2: Pearson coefficient of development data using different algorithms with different hyperparameter, as well as top rank results on STS 2015 test data.

Table 2 shows the best result of each algorithm , as well as the top runs on STS 2015 test data. GB(n=140) outperformed other algorithms on all datasets. We choose GB(n=140) as our final regression algorithm on our next series experiments. Al-

so, without any specific training dataset selections or choosing suitable features, we achieve the considerable results compare to the top runs on STS 2015 Task. Sultan et al. (2015) has shown that specific training datasets with similar domains and enough data will yield better results than an all-inclusive training datasets. And next we endeavor to select specific training sets and suitable features.

3.4 System Setups

We build three different systems according to the usage of training datasets as follows.

U-SEVEN: This is an unsupervised system based on the word aligner described in (Sultan et al., 2015) without any training data. We evaluate semantic similarity by adopting straight-forward measurements (i.e., longest common sequence, alignment feature, corpus-based feature, all four features from word embedding features), which are averaged to get the final score. We adopt *cosine distance, Pearson coefficient, Spearman coefficient* as the distance measurements, which perform better results on our preliminary experiments.

S1-All: We use all the training datasets and build a single global regression model regardless of domain information of different test datasets. In order to make better use of these features and improve the performance, we construct feature selection procedure on development set (i.e., test set of STS 2015 Task) and vote for the preserved feature sets. As for feature selection strategy, we adopt *hill climbing*: keep adding one type feature at a time until no further improvement can be achieved.

S2: Sultan et al. (2015) has shown that taking all the training datasets into consideration may hurt the performance since training and test sets are from different domains. Hence, for each test set, we select the datasets which are most similar, taking source, average length of sentences and word mover's distance (discussed in Section 2.3) into consideration. For the data set with symbol * (i.e., *headlines*), we use all *headlines* pairs. For *answers-answers* and *question-question*, we use *belief, deft-forums, answers-students, answers-forums* pairs. For postediting, we use *SMTeuropar* and *MSRpar* pairs. For plagiarism, we use *onWN* and *FNWN* pairs.

4 Results on Training Data

According to the above preliminary experimental results, we employ GB(n=140) algorithm as our final regression algorithm. In order to explore the influences of word embedding features and make better use of all the above features, we construct feature selection experiment on development set (i.e., test set of STS 2015 Task) and vote for the preserved feature sets.

Feature		belief	answers -students	headlines	image	answers -forums
String-based	len	-	-	✓	✓	-
	pos	-	-	✓	-	✓
	lcs	-	-	✓	✓	✓
	n-grams	-	✓	✓	✓	✓
	ner	-	✓	✓	-	-
Machine Translation	average	✓	-	✓	✓	-
	concat	-	-	-	-	-
Corpus-based	wordnet	✓	✓	✓	-	✓
	lsa	-	✓	✓	✓	✓
Alignment	global	-	✓	✓	✓	✓
	pos-specific	✓	✓	✓	✓	✓
Word Embedding (Macro)	word2vec	✓	✓	✓	✓	✓
	glove	-	-	-	-	-
	turian's	✓	✓	✓	✓	-
Word Embedding (Micro)	wmd	✓	✓	✓	✓	✓
Our Results		**0.7835**	0.7713	**0.8455**	**0.8808**	**0.7636**
Best Scores		0.7717	**0.7879**	0.8417	0.8713	0.7390

Table 3: Results of feature selection experiments on STS 2015 test data. The last row shows the the best scores of all submitted system on STS 2015 task.

Table 3 shows the results of feature selection experiments on STS 2015 test data. From the table, we find that 1) Word embedding features, the positive complementary of macro perspective and micro perspective, indeed improve results. 2) Specific alignment features can compensate for the weaknesses of global alignment features. 3) Since concatenate MT metrics and glove features does not perform well on all five data sets, we remove them from our feature sets and train our S1-All model with the preserved features.

5 Results on Test Data

Table 4 summarizes the results of our submitted runs on test datasets officially released by the organizers, as well as the top runs. In terms of weighted mean of Pearson measurement, system S1-All performs the best while our corpus-specific system **S2** performs the worst. We think the measurement to choose training data from the candidate datesets in main task are ill-suited. It is noteworthy that on plagiarism and postediting, our unsupervised model U-SEVEN achieves much better results than the supervised model (i.e., S1-All, S2), which indicates the efficiency of the ensemble of similar measurements.

Dataset	Runs			Best Score
	U-SEVEN	S1-All	S2	
answers-answers	0.4774	0.5697	**0.5715**	0.6923
plagiarism	**0.8301**	0.8250	0.7733	0.8413
headlines	0.7668	**0.8121**	0.7903	0.8274
postediting	**0.8423**	0.8234	0.7496	0.8669
question-question	0.7191	**0.7311**	0.6763	0.7470
weighted mean	0.7242	**0.7507**	0.7116	0.7780

Table 4: The results of our three runs on STS 2016 test datasets.The rightmost column shows the best score by any system. The last row shows the value of the officially evaluation metric.

On *answer-answer* set, the gap between top systems and our systems is about 12%. According to our investigations on this set, we find that certain sentence pairs are similar in syntactical structure but express different meanings. For example,

$\left\{ \begin{array}{l} \textit{You should do it.} \\ \textit{You can do it, too.} \end{array} \right.$ $\left\{ \begin{array}{l} \textit{It's pretty much up to you.} \\ \textit{It's much better to ask.} \end{array} \right.$

Our assumption (i.e., two sentences with similar syntax structure convey similar meaning) does not apply to the above condition.

6 Conclusion

We use the traditional NLP features including string-based features, corpus-based features and alignment features for textual similarity estimation, as well as efficient word embedding features. It is also worth pointing out that our word embedding features are highly interpretable and hyper-parameter free, as well as they are straight-forward to measure semantic textual similarity. The difference between top system and our best system is about 2.8%, which means our systems are promising. Noticing the gap between top system and our systems on *answer-answer* set, we will explore to find the central words of sentences in future work.

Acknowledgments

This research is supported by grants from Science and Technology Commission of Shanghai Municipality (14DZ2260800 and 15ZR1410700), Shanghai Collaborative Innovation Center of Trustworthy Software for Internet of Things (ZF1213).

References

Eneko Agirre, Carmen Banea, Claire Cardie, Daniel Cer, Mona Diab, Aitor Gonzalez-Agirre, Weiwei Guo, Inigo Lopez-Gazpio, Montse Maritxalar, Rada Mihalcea, German Rigau, Larraitz Uria, and Janyce Wiebe. 2015a. Semeval-2015 task 2: Semantic textual similarity, english, spanish and pilot on interpretability. In *Proceedings of the 9th International Workshop on Semantic Evaluation (SemEval 2015)*, pages 252–263, Denver, Colorado, June. Association for Computational Linguistics.

Eneko Agirre, Ander Barrena, and Aitor Soroa. 2015b. Studying the wikipedia hyperlink graph for relatedness and disambiguation. *CoRR*, abs/1503.01655.

Daniel Bär, Chris Biemann, Iryna Gurevych, and Torsten Zesch. 2012. Ukp: Computing semantic textual similarity by combining multiple content similarity measures. In *Proceedings of the First Joint Conference on Lexical and Computational Semantics-Volume 1: Proceedings of the main conference and the shared task, and Volume 2: Proceedings of the Sixth International Workshop on Semantic Evaluation*, pages 435–440. Association for Computational Linguistics.

Lars Buitinck, Gilles Louppe, Mathieu Blondel, Fabian Pedregosa, Andreas Mueller, Olivier Grisel, Vlad Niculae, Peter Prettenhofer, Alexandre Gramfort, Jaques Grobler, Robert Layton, Jake VanderPlas, Arnaud Joly, Brian Holt, and Gaël Varoquaux. 2013. API design for machine learning software: experiences from the scikit-learn project. In *ECML PKDD Workshop: Languages for Data Mining and Machine Learning*, pages 108–122.

Juri Ganitkevitch, Benjamin Van Durme, and Chris Callison-Burch. 2013. PPDB: The paraphrase database. In *Proceedings of NAACL-HLT*, pages 758–764, Atlanta, Georgia, June. Association for Computational Linguistics.

Sergio Jimenez, Claudia Becerra, and Alexander Gelbukh. 2012. Soft cardinality: A parameterized similarity function for text comparison. In *Proceedings of the First Joint Conference on Lexical and Computational Semantics-Volume 1: Proceedings of the main conference and the shared task, and Volume 2: Proceedings of the Sixth International Workshop on Semantic Evaluation*, pages 449–453. Association for Computational Linguistics.

Matt Kusner, Yu Sun, Nicholas Kolkin, and Kilian Q Weinberger. 2015. From word embeddings to document distances. In *Proceedings of the 32nd International Conference on Machine Learning (ICML-15)*, pages 957–966.

Christopher D. Manning, Mihai Surdeanu, John Bauer, Jenny Finkel, Steven J. Bethard, and David McClosky. 2014. The Stanford CoreNLP natural language processing toolkit. In *Proceedings of 52nd Annual Meeting of the Association for Computational Linguistics: System Demonstrations*, pages 55–60.

Tomas Mikolov, Ilya Sutskever, Kai Chen, Greg S Corrado, and Jeff Dean. 2013. Distributed representations of words and phrases and their compositionality. In *Advances in neural information processing systems*, pages 3111–3119.

Jeff Mitchell and Mirella Lapata. 2008. Vector-based models of semantic composition. In *Proceedings of ACL-08: HLT*, pages 236–244, Columbus, Ohio, June. Association for Computational Linguistics.

Jeffrey Pennington, Richard Socher, and Christopher D. Manning. 2014. Glove: Global vectors for word representation. In *Proceedings of the 2014 Conference on Empirical Methods in Natural Language Processing (EMNLP 2014)*, pages 1532–1543.

Md Arafat Sultan, Steven Bethard, and Tamara Sumner. 2015. Dls@cu: Sentence similarity from word alignment and semantic vector composition. In *Proceedings of the 9th International Workshop on Semantic Evaluation (SemEval 2015)*, pages 148–153, Denver, Colorado, June. Association for Computational Linguistics.

Joseph Turian, Lev Ratinov, and Yoshua Bengio. 2010. Word representations: a simple and general method for semi-supervised learning. In *Proceedings of the 48th annual meeting of the association for computational linguistics*, pages 384–394. Association for Computational Linguistics.

Frane Šarić, Goran Glavaš, Mladen Karan, Jan Šnajder, and Bojana Dalbelo Bašić. 2012. Takelab: Systems for measuring semantic text similarity. In *Proceedings of the Sixth International Workshop on Semantic Evaluation (SemEval 2012)*, pages 441–448, Montréal, Canada, 7-8 June. Association for Computational Linguistics.

Jiang Zhao, Tiantian Zhu, and Man Lan. 2014. Ecnu: One stone two birds: Ensemble of heterogeneous measures for semantic relatedness and textual entailment. In *Proceedings of the 8th International Workshop on Semantic Evaluation (SemEval 2014)*, pages 271–277, Dublin, Ireland, August. Association for Computational Linguistics and Dublin City University.

SAARSHEFF at SemEval-2016 Task 1:
Semantic Textual Similarity with
Machine Translation Evaluation Metrics
and (eXtreme) Boosted Tree Ensembles

Liling Tan[1], Carolina Scarton[2], Lucia Specia[2] and Josef van Genabith[1,3]

Universität des Saarlandes[1] / Campus A2.2, Saarbrücken, Germany
University of Sheffield[2] / Regent Court, 211 Portobello, Sheffield, UK
Deutsches Forschungszentrum für Künstliche Intelligenz[3] / Saarbrücken, Germany
`alvations@gmail.com,` `c.scarton@sheffield.ac.uk,`
`l.specia@sheffield.ac.uk,` `josef.van_genabith@dfki.de`

Abstract

This paper describes the SAARSHEFF systems that participated in the English Semantic Textual Similarity (STS) task in SemEval-2016. We extend the work on using machine translation (MT) metrics in the STS task by automatically annotating the STS datasets with a variety of MT scores for each pair of text snippets in the STS datasets. We trained our systems using boosted tree ensembles and achieved competitive results that outperforms he median Pearson correlation scores from all participating systems.

1 Introduction

Semantic Textual Similarity (STS) is the task of measuring the degree to which two texts have the same meaning (Agirre et al., 2014). For instance, given the two texts, *"the man is slicing the tape from the box."* and *"a man is cutting open a box."*, an STS system predicts a real number similarity score on a scale of 0 (no relation) to 5 (semantic equivalence).

This paper presents a collaborative submission between Saarland University and University of Sheffield to the STS English shared task at SemEval-2016. We have submitted three supervised models that predict the similarity scores for the STS task using Machine Translation (MT) evaluation metrics as regression features.

2 Related Work

Previous approaches have applied MT evaluation metrics for the STS task with progressively improv-ing results (Agirre et al., 2012; Agirre et al., 2013; Agirre et al., 2014; Agirre et al., 2015).

At the pilot English STS-2012 task, Rios et al. (2012) trained a Support Vector Regressor using the lexical overlaps between the surface strings, named entities and semantic role labels and the BLEU (Papineni et al., 2002) and METEOR (Banerjee and Lavie, 2005; Denkowski and Lavie, 2010) scores between the text snippets and their best system scored a Pearson correlation mean of 0.3825. The system underperformed compared to the organizers' baseline system[1] which scored 0.4356.

For the English STS-2013 task, Barrón-Cedeño et al. (2013) also used a Support Vector Regressor with an larger array of machine translation metrics (BLEU, METEOR, ROUGE (Lin and Och, 2004), NIST (Doddington, 2002), TER (Snover et al., 2006)) with measures that compute similarities of dependency and constituency parses (Liu and Gildea, 2005) and semantic roles, discourse representation and explicit semantic analysis (Gabrilovich and Markovitch, 2007) annotations of the text snippets. These similarity measures are packaged in the Asiya toolkit (Giménez and Màrquez, 2010). They scored 0.4037 mean score and performed better than the Takelab baseline (Šarić et al., 2012) at 0.3639.

At the SemEval-2014 Cross-level Semantic Similarity task (Jurgens et al., 2014; Jurgens et al., 2015), participating teams submitted similarity scores for text of different granularity. Huang and Chang (2014) used a linear regressor solely with MT evalu-

---

[1]Refers to the token cosine baseline system (`baseline-tokencos`) in STS-2012.

Proceedings of SemEval-2016, pages 628–633,
San Diego, California, June 16-17, 2016. ©2016 Association for Computational Linguistics

ation metrics (BLEU, METEOR, ROUGE) to compute the similarity scores between paragraphs and sentences. They scored 0.792 beating the lowest common substring baseline which scored 0.613.

In the SemEval-2015 English STS and Twitter similarity tasks, Bertero and Fung (2015) trained a neural network classifier using (i) lexical similarity features based on WordNet (Miller, 1995), (ii) neural auto-encoders (Socher et al., 2011), syntactic features based on parse tree edit distance (Zhang and Shasha, 1989; Wan et al., 2006) and (iii) MT evaluation metrics, viz. BLEU, TER, SEPIA (Habash and Elkholy, 2008), BADGER (Parker, 2008) and MEANT (Lo et al., 2012).

For the classic English STS task in SemEval-2015, Tan et al. (2015) used a range of MT evaluation metrics based on lexical (surface n-gram overlaps), syntactic (shallow parsing similarity) and semantic features (METEOR variants) to train a Bayesian ridge regressor. Their best system achieved 0.7275 mean Pearson correlation outperforming the `token-cos` baseline which scored 0.5871 while the top system (Sultan et al., 2015) achieved 0.8015.

Another notable mention of MT technology in the STS tasks is the use of referential translation machines to predict and derive features instead of using MT evaluation metrics (Biçici and van Genabith, 2013; Biçici and Way, 2014; Bicici, 2015).

3 Approach

Following the success of systems that use MT evaluation metrics, we train three regression models using an array of MT metrics based on lexical, syntactic and semantic features.

3.1 Feature Matrix

Machine translation evaluation metrics utilize various degrees of lexical, syntactic and semantic information. Each metric considers several features that compute the translation quality by comparing a translation against one or several reference translations.

We trained our system using the follow feature sets: (i) n-gram, shallow parsing and named entity overlaps (`Asiya`), (ii) BEER, (iii) METEOR and (iv) ReVal.

3.1.1 `Asiya` Features

Gonzàlez et al. (2014) introduced a range of language independent metrics relying on n-gram overlaps similar to the modified n--gram precisions of the BLEU metric (Papineni et al., 2002). Different from BLEU, Gonzàlez et al. (2014) computes n-gram overlaps using similarity coefficients instead of proportions. We use the `Asiya` toolkit (Giménez and Màrquez, 2010) to annotate the dataset with the similarity coefficients of n-gram overlap features described in this section.

We use 16 features from both cosine similarity and Jaccard Index coefficients of the character-level and token-level n-grams from the order of bigrams to 5-grams. Additionally, we use the Jaccard similarity of the pseudo-cognates and the ratio of n-gram length as the 17th and 18th features.

Adding a syntactic dimension to our feature set, we use 52 shallow parsing features described in (Tan et al., 2015); they measure the similarity coefficients from the n-gram overlaps of the lexicalized shallow parsing (aka chunking) annotations. As for semantics, we use 44 similarity coefficients from Named Entity (NE) annotation overlaps between two texts.

After some feature analysis, we found that 22 out of the 44 NE n-gram overlap features and 1 of the shallow parsing features have extremely low variance across all sentence pairs in the training data. We removed these features before training our models.

3.1.2 BEER Features

Stanojevic and Simaan (2014) presents an MT evaluation metric that uses character n-gram overlaps, the Kendall tau distance of the monotonic word order (Isozaki et al., 2010; Birch and Osborne, 2010) and abstract ordering patterns from tree factorization of permutations (Zhang and Gildea, 2007).

While Asiya features are agnostic to word classes, BEER differentiates between function words and non-function words when calculating its adequacy features.

3.1.3 METEOR Features

METEOR first aligns the translation to its reference, then it uses the unigram mapping to see whether they match based on their surface forms,

	answer-answer	headlines	plagiarism	postediting	question-question	All
Linear	0.31539	0.76551	0.82063	0.83329	0.73987	0.68923
Boosted	0.37717	0.77183	0.81529	0.84528	0.66825	0.69259
XGBoost	**0.47716**	**0.78848**	**0.83212**	**0.84960**	**0.69815**	**0.72693**
Median	0.48018	0.76439	0.78949	0.81241	0.57140	0.68923
Best	0.69235	0.82749	0.84138	0.86690	0.74705	0.77807

Table 1: Pearson Correlation Results for English STS Task at SemEval-2016

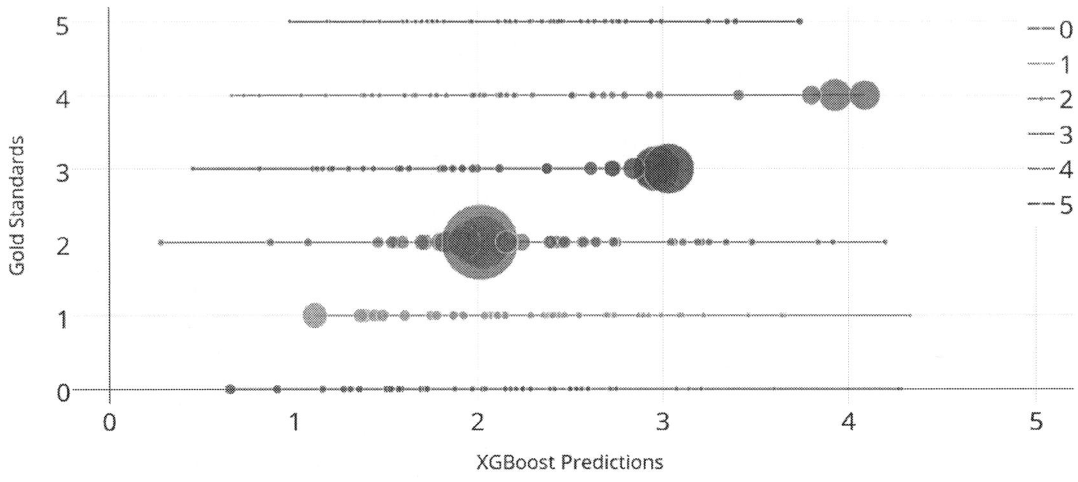

Figure 1: L1 Error Analysis on the answer-answer domain

word stems, synonyms and paraphrases (Banerjee and Lavie, 2005; Denkowski and Lavie, 2010).

Similar to BEER features, METEOR makes a distinction between content words and function words and its recall mechanism weights them differently. We use all four variants of METEOR: exact, stem, synonym and paraphrase.

3.1.4 `ReVal` Features

ReVal (Gupta et al., 2015) is a deep neural net based metric which uses the cosine similarity score between the Tree-based Long Short Term Memory (LSTM) (Hochreiter and Schmidhuber, 1997; Cho et al., 2014; Tai et al., 2015) dense vector space representations of two sentences.

3.2 Models

We annotated the STS 2012 to 2015 datasets with the features as described in Section 3.1 and submitted three models to the SemEval-2016 English STS Task using (i) a linear regressor (`Linear`), (ii) boosted tree regressor (`Boosted`) (Friedman, 2001) and (iii) eXtreme Gradient Boosted tree re-

gressor (`XGBoost`) (Chen and He, 2015; Chen and Guestrin, 2015). They were trained using all features described in Section 3.

We have released the MT metrics annotations of the STS data and implementation of systems on `https://github.com/alvations/stasis /blob/master/notebooks/ARMOR.ipynb`

4 Results

Table 1 presents the official results for our submissions to the English STS task. The bottom part of the table presents the median and the best correlation results across all participating teams for the respective domains.

Our baseline linear model outperforms the median scores for all domains except the *answer-answer* domain. Our boosted tree model performs better than the linear model and the extreme gradient boosted tree model performs the best of the three. We note that our correlation scores for all three models is lower than the median for the *answer-answer* domain.

Figure 1 shows the bubble chart of the L1 error analysis of our XGBoost model against the gold standard similarity scores for the answer-answer domain. The colored lines correspond to the integer annotations, e.g. the yellow line represents the data points where the gold-standard annotations are 1.0. The span of the line represents the span of predictions our model made for these texts. The size of the bubble represents the effect size of our predictions' contribution to the Pearson correlation score, i.e. how close our predictions are to the gold standards.

5 Discussion

As we see from Figure 1, the centroids of the bubbles represents our model's best predictions. Our predictions for texts that are annotated at 1 to 4 similarity scores are reasonably close to the gold standards but the model performs poorly for texts annotated with the 0 and 5 similarity scores.

Looking at the texts that are rated 0, we see that there are cases where the n-grams within these texts are lexically / syntactically similar but the meaning of the texts are disparate. For example, this pair of text snippets, *'You don't have to know'* and *'You don't have equipments/facilities'* are rated 0 in the gold standards but from a machine translation perspective, a translator would have to do little work to change *'to know'* to *'equipments/facilities'*.

Because of this, machine translation metrics would rate the texts as being similar and even suitable for post-editing. However, the STS task focuses only on the meaning of the text which corresponds more to the adequacy aspect of the machine translation metrics. Semantic adequacy is often overlooked in machine translation because our mass reliance on BLEU scores to measure the goodness of translation with little considerations for penalizing semantic divergence between the translation and its reference.

On the other end of the spectrum, machine translation metrics remain skeptical when text snippets are annotated with a score of 5 for being semantically analogous but syntactically the texts are expressed in a different form. For example, given the text snippets, *'There's not a lot you can do about that'* and *'I'm afraid there's not really a lot you can do'*, most machine translation metrics will not allocate full similarity scores due to the difference in lexical and stylistic ways in which the sentences are expressed.

Machine translation metrics' failure to capture similarity score extremes is evident in Figure 1 where there are no 0 and 5.0 predictions.

6 Conclusion

In this paper, we have described our submission to the English STS task for SemEval-2016. We have annotated the STS2012-2016 datasets with machine translation (MT) evaluation metric scores and trained a baseline linear regression and two tree ensemble models with the annotated data and achieved competitive results compared to the median pearson correlation scores from all participating systems.

Acknowledgments

The research leading to these results has received funding from the People Programme (Marie Curie Actions) of the European Union's Seventh Framework Programme FP7/2007-2013/ under REA grant agreement n° 317471.

References

Eneko Agirre, Daniel Cer, Mona Diab, and Aitor Gonzalez-Agirre. 2012. SemEval-2012 Task 6: A Pilot on Semantic Textual Similarity. In *First Joint Conference on Lexical and Computational Semantics (*SEM): Proceedings of the Main Conference and the Shared Task*, pages 385–393, Montréal, Canada.

Eneko Agirre, Daniel Cer, Mona Diab, Aitor Gonzalez-Agirre, and Weiwei Guo. 2013. SEM 2013 shared task: Semantic Textual Similarity. In *Second Joint Conference on Lexical and Computational Semantics (*SEM), Volume 1: Proceedings of the Main Conference and the Shared Task*, pages 32–43, Atlanta, Georgia.

Eneko Agirre, Carmen Banea, Claire Cardic, Daniel Cer, Mona Diab, Aitor Gonzalez-Agirre, Weiwei Guo, Rada Mihalcea, German Rigau, and Janyce Wiebe. 2014. SemEval-2014 Task 10: Multilingual Semantic Textual Similarity. In *Proceedings of the 8th International Workshop on Semantic Evaluation (SemEval 2014)*, pages 81–91, Dublin, Ireland.

Eneko Agirre, Carmen Banea, Claire Cardie, Daniel Cer, Mona Diab, Aitor Gonzalez-Agirre, Weiwei Guo, Inigo Lopez-Gazpio, Montse Maritxalar, Rada Mihalcea, German Rigau, Larraitz Uria, and Janyce Wiebe.

2015. SemEval-2015 Task 2: Semantic Textual Similarity, English, Spanish and Pilot on Interpretability. In *Proceedings of the 9th International Workshop on Semantic Evaluation (SemEval 2015)*, pages 252–263, Denver, Colorado, June.

Satanjeev Banerjee and Alon Lavie. 2005. METEOR: An Automatic Metric for MT Evaluation with Improved Correlation with Human Judgments. In *Proceedings of the ACL 2005 Workshop on Intrinsic and Extrinsic Evaluation Measures for MT and/or Summarization*, pages 65–72, Ann Arbor, Michigan.

Alberto Barrón-Cedeño, Lluís Màrquez, Maria Fuentes, Horacio Rodríguez, and Jordi Turmo. 2013. UPC-CORE: What Can Machine Translation Evaluation Metrics and Wikipedia Do for Estimating Semantic Textual Similarity? In *Second Joint Conference on Lexical and Computational Semantics (*SEM), Volume 1: Proceedings of the Main Conference and the Shared Task*, pages 143–147, Atlanta, Georgia.

Dario Bertero and Pascale Fung. 2015. Hltc-hkust: A neural network paraphrase classifier using translation metrics, semantic roles and lexical similarity features. In *Proceedings of the 9th International Workshop on Semantic Evaluation (SemEval 2015)*, pages 23–28, Denver, Colorado, June.

Ergun Biçici and Josef van Genabith. 2013. CNGL-CORE: Referential Translation Machines for Measuring Semantic Similarity. In *Second Joint Conference on Lexical and Computational Semantics (*SEM), Volume 1: Proceedings of the Main Conference and the Shared Task*, pages 234–240, Atlanta, Georgia.

Ergun Biçici and Andy Way. 2014. RTM-DCU: Referential Translation Machines for Semantic Similarity. In *Proceedings of the 8th International Workshop on Semantic Evaluation (SemEval 2014)*, pages 487–496, Dublin, Ireland.

Ergun Bicici. 2015. Rtm-dcu: Predicting semantic similarity with referential translation machines. In *Proceedings of the 9th International Workshop on Semantic Evaluation (SemEval 2015)*, pages 56–63, Denver, Colorado, June.

Alexandra Birch and Miles Osborne. 2010. Lrscore for evaluating lexical and reordering quality in mt. In *Proceedings of the Joint Fifth Workshop on Statistical Machine Translation and MetricsMATR*, pages 327–332.

Tianqi Chen and Carlos Guestrin. 2015. Xgboost: Reliable large-scale tree boosting system.

Tianqi Chen and Tong He. 2015. xgboost: extreme gradient boosting. *R package version 0.4-2*.

Kyunghyun Cho, Bart van Merrienboer, Caglar Gulcehre, Dzmitry Bahdanau, Fethi Bougares, Holger Schwenk, and Yoshua Bengio. 2014. Learning phrase representations using rnn encoder–decoder for statistical machine translation. In *Proceedings of the 2014 Conference on Empirical Methods in Natural Language Processing (EMNLP)*, Doha, Qatar, October.

Michael Denkowski and Alon Lavie. 2010. Extending the METEOR Machine Translation Evaluation Metric to the Phrase Level. In *Proceedings of the HLT: The 2010 Annual Conference of the North American Chapter of the Association for Computational Linguistics*, pages 250–253, Los Angeles, California.

George Doddington. 2002. Automatic evaluation of machine translation quality using n-gram co-occurrence statistics. In *Proceedings of the second international conference on Human Language Technology Research*, pages 138–145. Morgan Kaufmann Publishers Inc.

Jerome H Friedman. 2001. Greedy function approximation: a gradient boosting machine. *Annals of statistics*, pages 1189–1232.

Evgeniy Gabrilovich and Shaul Markovitch. 2007. Computing semantic relatedness using wikipedia-based explicit semantic analysis. In *Proceedings of Twentieth International Joint Conference on Artificial Intelligence*.

Jesús Giménez and Lluís Màrquez. 2010. Asiya: An Open Toolkit for Automatic Machine Translation (Meta-)Evaluation. *The Prague Bulletin of Mathematical Linguistics*, (94):77–86.

Meritxell Gonzàlez, Alberto Barrón-Cedeo, and Llus Màrquez. 2014. Ipa and stout: Leveraging linguistic and source-based features for machine translation evaluation. In *Ninth Workshop on Statistical Machine Translation*, page 8.

Rohit Gupta, Constantin Orasan, and Josef van Genabith. 2015. Reval: A simple and effective machine translation evaluation metric based on recurrent neural networks. In *Proceedings of the 2015 Conference on Empirical Methods in Natural Language Processing*, pages 1066–1072, Lisbon, Portugal, September.

Nizar Habash and Ahmed Elkholy. 2008. Sepia: surface span extension to syntactic dependency precision-based mt evaluation. In *Proceedings of the NIST metrics for machine translation workshop at the association for machine translation in the Americas conference, AMTA-2008. Waikiki, HI*.

Sepp Hochreiter and Jürgen Schmidhuber. 1997. Long short-term memory. *Neural computation*, 9(8):1735–1780.

Pingping Huang and Baobao Chang. 2014. SSMT:A Machine Translation Evaluation View To Paragraph-to-Sentence Semantic Similarity. In *Proceedings of the 8th International Workshop on Semantic Evaluation (SemEval 2014)*, pages 585–589, Dublin, Ireland.

Hideki Isozaki, Tsutomu Hirao, Kevin Duh, Katsuhito Sudoh, and Hajime Tsukada. 2010. Automatic evaluation of translation quality for distant language pairs. In *Proceedings of the 2010 Conference on Empirical Methods in Natural Language Processing*, pages 944–952.

David Jurgens, Mohammad Taher Pilehvar, and Roberto Navigli. 2014. Semeval-2014 task 3: Cross-level semantic similarity. In *Proceedings of the 8th International Workshop on Semantic Evaluation (SemEval 2014)*, pages 17–26, Dublin, Ireland, August. Association for Computational Linguistics and Dublin City University.

David Jurgens, Mohammad Taher Pilehvar, and Roberto Navigli. 2015. Cross level semantic similarity: an evaluation framework for universal measures of similarity. *Language Resources and Evaluation*, 50(1):5–33.

Chin-Yew Lin and Franz Josef Och. 2004. Automatic evaluation of machine translation quality using longest common subsequence and skip-bigram statistics. In *Proceedings of the 42nd Meeting of the Association for Computational Linguistics (ACL'04), Main Volume*, pages 605–612, Barcelona, Spain, July.

Ding Liu and Daniel Gildea. 2005. Syntactic features for evaluation of machine translation. In *Proceedings of the ACL Workshop on Intrinsic and Extrinsic Evaluation Measures for Machine Translation and/or Summarization*.

Chi-kiu Lo, Anand Karthik Tumuluru, and Dekai Wu. 2012. Fully automatic semantic mt evaluation. In *Proceedings of the Seventh Workshop on Statistical Machine Translation*, pages 243–252.

George A Miller. 1995. Wordnet: a lexical database for english. *Communications of the ACM*, 38(11):39–41.

Kishore Papineni, Salim Roukos, Todd Ward, and Wei jing Zhu. 2002. BLEU: A Method for Automatic Evaluation of Machine Translation. In *Proceedings of the 40th Annual Meeting of the Association for Computational Linguistics*, pages 311–318, Philadelphia, Pennsylvania.

Steven Parker. 2008. Badger: A new machine translation metric. pages 21–25.

Miguel Rios, Wilker Aziz, and Lucia Specia. 2012. UOW: Semantically Informed Text Similarity. In *First Joint Conference on Lexical and Computational Semantics (*SEM): Proceedings of the Main Conference and the Shared Task*, pages 673–678, Montréal, Canada.

Frane Šarić, Goran Glavaš, Mladen Karan, Jan Šnajder, and Bojana Dalbelo Bašić. 2012. Takelab: Systems for measuring semantic text similarity. In *Proceedings of the First Joint Conference on Lexical and Computational Semantics-Volume 1: Proceedings of the

main conference and the shared task, and Volume 2: Proceedings of the Sixth International Workshop on Semantic Evaluation*, pages 441–448. Association for Computational Linguistics.

Matthew Snover, Bonnie Dorr, Richard Schwartz, Linnea Micciulla, and John Makhoul. 2006. A study of translation edit rate with targeted human annotation. In *Proceedings of association for machine translation in the Americas*.

Richard Socher, Eric H Huang, Jeffrey Pennin, Christopher D Manning, and Andrew Y Ng. 2011. Dynamic pooling and unfolding recursive autoencoders for paraphrase detection. In *Advances in Neural Information Processing Systems*, pages 801–809.

Miloš Stanojevic and Khalil Simaan. 2014. Beer: Better evaluation as ranking. In *Proceedings of the Ninth Workshop on Statistical Machine Translation*, pages 414–419.

Md Arafat Sultan, Steven Bethard, and Tamara Sumner. 2015. Dls@cu: Sentence similarity from word alignment and semantic vector composition. In *Proceedings of the 9th International Workshop on Semantic Evaluation (SemEval 2015)*, pages 148–153, Denver, Colorado, June.

Kai Sheng Tai, Richard Socher, and Christopher D. Manning. 2015. Improved semantic representations from tree-structured long short-term memory networks. In *Proceedings of the 53rd Annual Meeting of the Association for Computational Linguistics and the 7th International Joint Conference on Natural Language Processing (Volume 1: Long Papers)*, pages 1556–1566, Beijing, China, July.

Liling Tan, Carolina Scarton, Lucia Specia, and Josef van Genabith. 2015. Usaar-sheffield: Semantic textual similarity with deep regression and machine translation evaluation metrics. In *Proceedings of the 9th International Workshop on Semantic Evaluation (SemEval 2015)*, pages 85–89, Denver, Colorado, June.

Stephen Wan, Mark Dras, Robert Dale, and Cécile Paris. 2006. Using dependency-based features to take the para-farce out of paraphrase. In *Proceedings of the Australasian Language Technology Workshop*, volume 2006.

Hao Zhang and Daniel Gildea. 2007. Factorization of synchronous context-free grammars in linear time. In *Proceedings of the NAACL-HLT 2007/AMTA Workshop on Syntax and Structure in Statistical Translation*, pages 25–32.

Kaizhong Zhang and Dennis Shasha. 1989. Simple fast algorithms for the editing distance between trees and related problems. *SIAM journal on computing*, 18(6):1245–1262.

WOLVESAAR at SemEval-2016 Task 1:
Replicating the Success of Monolingual Word Alignment and Neural Embeddings for Semantic Textual Similarity

Hanna Bechara, Rohit Gupta, Liling Tan,
Constantin Orăsan, Ruslan Mitkov, Josef van Genabith
University of Wolverhampton / UK,
Universität des Saarlandes / Germany
Deutsches Forschungszentrum für Künstliche Intelligenz / Germany
{hanna.bechara, r.gupta, corsasan, r.mitkov}@wlv.ac.uk,
liling.tan@uni-saarland.de, josef.van_genabith@dfki.de

Abstract

This paper describes the WOLVESAAR systems that participated in the English Semantic Textual Similarity (STS) task in SemEval-2016. We replicated the top systems from the last two editions of the STS task and extended the model using GloVe word embeddings and dense vector space LSTM based sentence representations. We compared the difference in performance of the replicated system and the extended variants. Our variants to the replicated system show improved correlation scores and all of our submissions outperform the median scores from all participating systems.

1 Introduction

Semantic Textual Similarity (STS) is the task of assigning a real number score to quantify the semantic likeness of two text snippets. Similarity measures play a crucial role in various areas of text processing and translation technologies ranging from improving information retrieval rankings (Lin and Hovy, 2003; Corley and Mihalcea, 2005) and text summarization to machine translation evaluation and enhancing matches in translation memory and terminologies (Resnik and others, 1999; Ma et al., 2011; Banchs et al., 2015; Vela and Tan, 2015).

The annual SemEval STS task (Agirre et al., 2012; Agirre et al., 2013; Agirre et al., 2014; Agirre et al., 2015) provides a platform where systems are evaluated on the same data and evaluation criteria.

2 DLS System from STS 2014 and 2015

For the past two editions of the STS task, the top performing submissions are from the DLS@CU team (Sultan et al., 2014b; Sultan et al., 2015).

Their STS2014 submission is based on the proportion of overlapping content words between the two sentences treating semantic similarity as a monotonically increasing function of the degree to which two sentences contain semantically similar units and these units occur in similar semantic contexts (Sultan et al., 2014b). Essentially, their semantic metric is based on the proportion of aligned content words between two sentences, formally defined as:

$$prop_{Al}^{(1)} = \frac{|\{i : [\exists j : (i,j) \in Al] \ and \ w_i^{(1)} \in C\}|}{|\{i : w_i^{(1)} \in C\}|} \tag{1}$$

where $prop_{Al}^{(1)}$ is the monotonic proportion of the semantic unit alignment from a set of alignments Al that maps the positions of the words (i, j) between sentences $S^{(1)}$ and $S^{(2)}$, given that the aligned units belong to a set of content words, C. Since the proportion is monotonic, the equation above only provides the proportion of semantic unit alignments for $S^{(1)}$. The Al alignments pairs are automatically annotated by a monolingual word aligner (Sultan et al., 2014a) that uses word similarity measures based on contextual evidence from the Paraphrase Database (PPDB) (Ganitkevitch et al., 2013) and syntactic dependencies.

The same computation needs to be made for $S^{(2)}$. An easier formulation of the equation without the formal logic symbols is:

Proceedings of SemEval-2016, pages 634–639,
San Diego, California, June 16-17, 2016. ©2016 Association for Computational Linguistics

$$prop_{Al}^{(1)} = \frac{sum(1 \; for \; w_i, w_j \; in \; Al^{(1,2)} \; if \; w_i \; in \; C)}{sum(1 \; for \; w_i \; in \; S^{(1)} \; if \; w_i \; in \; C)} \tag{2}$$

Since the semantic similarity between $(S^{(1)}, S^{(2)})$ should be a single real number, Sultan et al. (2014b) combined the proportions using harmonic mean:

$$sim(S^{(1)}, S^{(2)}) = \frac{2 * prop_{Al}^{(1)} * prop_{Al}^{(2)}}{prop_{Al}^{(1)} + prop_{Al}^{(2)}} \tag{3}$$

Instead of simply using the alignment proportions, Sultan et al. (2015) extended their hypothesis by leveraging pre-trained neural net embeddings (Baroni et al., 2014). They posited that the semantics of the sentence can be captured by the centroid of its content words[1] computed by the element-wise sum of the content word embeddings normalized by the number of content words in the sentence. Together with the similarity scores from Equation 3 and the cosine similarity between two sentence embeddings, they trained a Bayesian ridge regressor to learn the similarity scores between text snippets.

3 Our Replica of DLS for STS 2016

To replicate the success of Sultan et al. (2014b), we use the monolingual word aligner from Sultan et al. (2014a) to annotate the STS-2012 to STS-2015 datasets and computed the alignment proportions as in Equation 1 and 2.

In duplicating Sultan et al. (2015) work, we first have to tokenize and lemmatize text. The details of pre-processing choices was undocumented in their paper, thus we lemmatized the datasets with the NLTK tokenizer (Bird et al., 2009) and PyWSD lemmatizer (Tan, 2014). We use the lemmas to retrieve the word embeddings from the COMPOSES vector space (Baroni et al., 2014). Similar to Equation 2 (changing only the numerator), we sum the sentence embedding's centroid as follows:

$$v(S^{(1)}) = \frac{sum(v(w_i) \; for \; w_i \; in \; S^{(1)} \; if \; w_i \; in \; C)}{sum(1 \; for \; w_i \; in \; S^{(1)} \; if \; w_i \; in \; C)} \tag{4}$$

---

[1] In the implementation, they have used lemmas instead of words to reduce sparsity when looking up the pre-trained embeddings (personal communication with Arafat Sultan).

where $v(S^{(1)})$ refers to the dense vector space representation of the sentence $S^{(1)}$ and $v(w_i)$ refers to the word embedding of word i provided by the COMPOSES vector space. The same computation has to be done for $S^{(2)}$.

Intuitively, if either of the sentences contains more or less content words than the other, we can see the numerator changing but the denominator changes with it. The difference between $v(S^{(1)})$ and $v(S^{(2)})$ contributes to *distributional semantic distance.*

To calculate a real value similarity score between the sentence vectors, we take the dot product between the vectors to compute the cosine similarity between the sentence vectors:

$$sim(S^{(1)}, S^{(2)}) = \frac{v(S^{(1)}) \cdot v(S^{(2)})}{|v(S^{(1)})| \, |v(S^{(2)})|} \tag{5}$$

There was no clear indication of which vector space Sultan et al. (2015) have chosen to compute the similarity score from Equation 5. Thus we compute two similarity scores using both COMPOSES vector spaces trained with these configurations:

- 5-word context window, 10 negative samples, subsampling, 400 dimensions

- 2-word context window, PMI weighting, no compression, 300K dimensions

In this case, we extracted two similarity features for every sentence pair. With the harmonic proportion feature from Equation 3 and the similarity scores from Equation 5, we trained a boosted tree ensemble on the 3 features using the STS 2012 to 2015 datasets and submitted the outputs from this model as our baseline submission in the English STS Task in SemEval 2016.

3.1 Replacing COMPOSES with GloVe

Pennington et al. (2014) handles semantic regularities (Levy et al., 2014) explicitly by using a global log-bilinear regression model which combines the global matrix factorization and the local context vectors when training word embeddings.

Instead of using the COMPOSES vector space, we experimented with replacing the $v(w_i)$ component in Equation 4 with the GloVe vectors,[2] $v_{glove}(w_i)$ such that:

$$sim_{glove}(S^{(1)}, S^{(2)}) = \frac{v_{glove}(S^{(1)}) \cdot v_{glove}(S^{(2)})}{|v_{glove}(S^{(1)})| \, |v_{glove}(S^{(2)})|} \quad (6)$$

The novelty lies in the usage of the global matrix to capture corpus wide phenomena that might not be captured by the local context window. The model leverages on both the non-zero elements in the word-word co-occurence matrix (not a sparse bag-of-words matrix) and the individual context window vectors similar to the word2vec model (Mikolov et al., 2013).

3.2 Similarity Using Tree LSTM

Recurrent Neural Nets (RNNs) allow arbitrarily sized sentence lengths (Elman, 1990) but early work on RNNs suffered from the vanishing/exploding gradients problem (Bengio et al., 1994). Hochreiter and Schmidhuber (1997) introduced multiplicative input and output gate units to solve the vanishing gradients problem. While RNN and LSTM process sentences in a sequential manner, Tree-LSTM extends the LSTM architecture by processing the input sentence through a syntactic structure of the sentence. We use the ReVal metric (Gupta et al., 2015) implementation of Tree-LSTM (Tai et al., 2015) to generate the similarity score.

ReVal represents both sentences (h_1, h_2) using Tree-LSTMs and predicts a similarity score $\hat{y}$ based on a neural network which considers both distance and angle between h_1 and h_2:

$$
\begin{aligned}
h_\times &= h_1 \odot h_2 \\
h_+ &= |h_1 - h_2| \\
h_s &= \sigma \left(W^{(\times)} h_\times + W^{(+)} h_+ + b^{(h)} \right) \\
\hat{p}_\theta &= \text{softmax} \left(W^{(p)} h_s + b^{(p)} \right) \\
\hat{y} &= r^T \hat{p}_\theta
\end{aligned}
\quad (7)
$$

where, σ is a sigmoid function, $\hat{p}_\theta$ is the estimated probability distribution vector and $r^T = [1 \, 2...K]$. The cost function $J(\theta)$ is defined over probability distributions p and $\hat{p}_\theta$ using regularised Kullback-Leibler (KL) divergence.

$$J(\theta) = \frac{1}{n} \sum_{i=1}^{n} \text{KL} \left(p^{(i)} \middle\| \hat{p}_\theta^{(i)} \right) + \frac{\lambda}{2} ||\theta||_2^2 \quad (8)$$

In Equation 8, i represents the index of each training pair, n is the number of training pairs and p is the sparse target distribution such that $y = r^T p$ is defined as follows:

$$
p_j = \begin{cases}
y - \lfloor y \rfloor, & j = \lfloor y \rfloor + 1 \\
\lfloor y \rfloor - y + 1, & j = \lfloor y \rfloor \\
0 & \text{otherwise}
\end{cases}
$$

for $1 \leq j \leq K$, where, $y \in [1, K]$ is the similarity score of a training pair. This gives us a similarity score between [1, K] which is mapped between [0, 1].[3] Please refer to Gupta et al. (2015) for training details.

4 Submission

We submitted three models based on the original replication of the Sultan et al. (2014b) and Sultan et al. (2015) system and our variants and extensions of their approach.

Our `baseline` submission uses the similarity score from Equations 3 and 5 as features to train a linear ridge regression. Our `baseline` submission achieved an overall 0.69244 Pearson correlation score on all domains.

Extending the `baseline` implementation, we included the similarity score from Equations 6 and 8 to the feature set and trained a boosted tree ensemble (Friedman, 2001) to produce our `Boosted` submission. Finally, we use the same feature set to train an eXtreme Boosted tree ensemble (XGBoost) (Chen and He, 2015; Chen and Guestrin, 2015) model.

We annotated the STS 2012 to 2015 datasets with the similarity scores from Equations 2, 3, 5, 6, 8. The annotations and our open source implementation of the system are available at `https://github.com/alvations/stasis /blob/master/notebooks/STRIKE.ipynb`

---

[2] We use the 300 dimensions vectors from the GloVe model trained on the Commoncrawl Corpus with 840B tokens, 2.2M vocabulary.

[3] score = (score-1)/K

	answer-answer	headlines	plagiarism	postediting	question-question	All
`Baseline`	0.48799	0.71043	0.80605	0.84601	0.61515	0.69244
`Boosted`	0.49415	0.71439	**0.79655**	0.83758	**0.63509**	0.69453
`XGBoost`	**0.49947**	**0.72410**	0.79076	**0.84093**	0.62055	**0.69471**
`+Saarsheff`	0.50628	0.77824	0.82501	0.84861	0.70424	0.73050
Median	0.48018	0.76439	0.78949	0.81241	0.57140	0.68923
Best	0.69235	0.82749	0.84138	0.8669	0.74705	0.77807

Table 1: Pearson Correlation Results for English STS Task at SemEval-2016

5 Results

Table 1 shows the results of our submission to the English STS task in SemEval-2016; the median and best scores are computed across all participating teams in the task. Our baseline system performs reasonably well, outperforming the median scores in most domains.

Our extended variant of the baseline using boosted tree ensemble performs better in the answer-answer, headlines and postediting domains but performed worse in others. Comparatively, it improves the overall correlation score marginally by 0.002.

The system using XGBoost performs the best of the 3 models but it underperforms in the headlines and plagiarism domain when compared to the median scores.

Generally, we did not achieve the outstanding scores in the task as compared to the top performing team DLS@CU in the English STS 2015. Our XGBoost system performs far from the best scores from the top systems. However, overall our correlation scores are higher than the median scores across all submissions for the task.

As a post-hoc test, we have evaluated our baseline system by training on the STS 2012 to 2014 dataset and testing on the STS 2015 dataset and we achieved 0.76141 weighted mean Pearson correlation score on all domains. As compared to Sultan et al. (2015) results of 0.8015 we are 0.04 points short of their results which should technically rank our system at 20th out of 70+ submissions to the STS 2015 task[4].

Machine Translation (MT) evaluation metrics have shown competitive performance in previous STS tasks (Barrón-Cedeño et al., 2013; Huang and Chang, 2014; Bertero and Fung, 2015; Tan et al., 2015). Tan et al. (2016) annotated the STS datasets with MT metrics scores for every pair of sentence in the training and evaluation data. We extend our XGBoost model with these MT metric annotations and achieved a higher score for every domain leading to an overall Pearson correlation score of 0.73050 (`+Saarsheff` in Table 1).

6 Conclusion

In this paper, we have presented our findings on replicating the top system in the STS 2014 and 2015 task and evaluated our replica of the system in the English STS task of SemEval-2016. We have introduced variants and extensions to the replica system by using various state-of-art word and sentence embeddings. Our systems trained on (eXtreme) Boosted Tree ensembles outperform the replica system using linear regression. Although our replica of the previous best system did not achieve stellar scores, all our systems outperform the median scores computed across all participating systems.

Acknowledgments

The research leading to these results has received funding from the People Programme (Marie Curie Actions) of the European Union's Seventh Framework Programme FP7/2007-2013/ under REA grant agreement n° 317471.

References

Eneko Agirre, Daniel Cer, Mona Diab, and Aitor Gonzalez-Agirre. 2012. SemEval-2012 Task 6: A Pilot on Semantic Textual Similarity. In *First Joint Conference on Lexical and Computational Semantics (*SEM): Proceedings of the Main Conference and the Shared Task*, pages 385–393, Montréal, Canada.

---

[4]Our replication attempt obtained better results compared to our STS-2015 submission (`MiniExperts`) that used a Support Vector Machine regressor trained on a number of linguistically motivated features (Gupta et al., 2014); it achieved 0.7216 mean score (Béchara et al., 2015).

Eneko Agirre, Daniel Cer, Mona Diab, Aitor Gonzalez-Agirre, and Weiwei Guo. 2013. SEM 2013 shared task: Semantic Textual Similarity. In *Second Joint Conference on Lexical and Computational Semantics (*SEM), Volume 1: Proceedings of the Main Conference and the Shared Task*, pages 32–43, Atlanta, Georgia.

Eneko Agirre, Carmen Banea, Claire Cardic, Daniel Cer, Mona Diab, Aitor Gonzalez-Agirre, Weiwei Guo, Rada Mihalcea, German Rigau, and Janyce Wiebe. 2014. SemEval-2014 Task 10: Multilingual Semantic Textual Similarity. In *Proceedings of the 8th International Workshop on Semantic Evaluation (SemEval 2014)*, pages 81–91, Dublin, Ireland.

Eneko Agirre, Carmen Banea, Claire Cardie, Daniel Cer, Mona Diab, Aitor Gonzalez-Agirre, Weiwei Guo, Inigo Lopez-Gazpio, Montse Maritxalar, Rada Mihalcea, German Rigau, Larraitz Uria, and Janyce Wiebe. 2015. Semeval-2015 task 2: Semantic textual similarity, english, spanish and pilot on interpretability. In *Proceedings of the 9th International Workshop on Semantic Evaluation (SemEval 2015)*, pages 252–263, Denver, Colorado.

Rafael E Banchs, Luis F D'Haro, and Haizhou Li. 2015. Adequacy–fluency metrics: Evaluating mt in the continuous space model framework. *Audio, Speech, and Language Processing, IEEE/ACM Transactions on*, 23(3):472–482.

Marco Baroni, Georgiana Dinu, and Germán Kruszewski. 2014. Don't count, predict! a systematic comparison of context-counting vs. context-predicting semantic vectors. In *Proceedings of the 52nd Annual Meeting of the Association for Computational Linguistics (Volume 1: Long Papers)*, pages 238–247, Baltimore, Maryland.

Alberto Barrón-Cedeño, Lluís Màrquez, Maria Fuentes, Horacio Rodríguez, and Jordi Turmo. 2013. UPC-CORE: What Can Machine Translation Evaluation Metrics and Wikipedia Do for Estimating Semantic Textual Similarity? In *Second Joint Conference on Lexical and Computational Semantics (*SEM), Volume 1: Proceedings of the Main Conference and the Shared Task*, pages 143–147, Atlanta, Georgia.

Hanna Béchara, Hernani Costa, Shiva Taslimipoora, Rohit Guptaa, Constantin Orăsan, Gloria Corpas Pastorb, and Ruslan Mitkova. 2015. Miniexperts: An svm approach for measuring semantic textual similarity. In *Proceedings of the 9th International Workshop on Semantic Evaluation (SemEval 2015)*, pages 96–101.

Yoshua Bengio, Patrice Simard, and Paolo Frasconi. 1994. Learning long-term dependencies with gradient descent is difficult. *Neural Networks, IEEE Transactions on*, 5(2):157–166.

Dario Bertero and Pascale Fung. 2015. Hltc-hkust: A neural network paraphrase classifier using translation metrics, semantic roles and lexical similarity features. In *Proceedings of the 9th International Workshop on Semantic Evaluation (SemEval 2015)*, pages 23–28, Denver, Colorado.

Steven Bird, Ewan Klein, and Edward Loper. 2009. *Natural language processing with Python*. " O'Reilly Media, Inc.".

Tianqi Chen and Carlos Guestrin. 2015. Xgboost: Reliable large-scale tree boosting system.

Tianqi Chen and Tong He. 2015. xgboost: extreme gradient boosting. *R package version 0.4-2*.

Courtney Corley and Rada Mihalcea. 2005. Measuring the semantic similarity of texts. In *Proceedings of the ACL Workshop on Empirical Modeling of Semantic Equivalence and Entailment*, EMSEE '05, pages 13–18, Stroudsburg, PA, USA.

Jeffrey L Elman. 1990. Finding structure in time. *Cognitive science*, 14(2):179–211.

Jerome H Friedman. 2001. Greedy function approximation: a gradient boosting machine. *Annals of statistics*, pages 1189–1232.

Juri Ganitkevitch, Benjamin Van Durme, and Chris Callison-Burch. 2013. Ppdb: The paraphrase database. In *Proceedings of the 2013 Conference of the North American Chapter of the Association for Computational Linguistics: Human Language Technologies*, pages 758–764, Atlanta, Georgia.

Rohit Gupta, Hanna Béchara, Ismail El Maarouf, and Constantin Orăsan. 2014. Uow: Nlp techniques developed at the university of wolverhampton for semantic similarity and textual entailment. In *8th Int. Workshop on Semantic Evaluation (SemEval14)*, pages 785–789.

Rohit Gupta, Constantin Orăsan, and Josef van Genabith. 2015. Reval: A simple and effective machine translation evaluation metric based on recurrent neural networks. In *Proceedings of the 2015 Conference on Empirical Methods in Natural Language Processing*, pages 1066–1072, Lisbon, Portugal.

Sepp Hochreiter and Jürgen Schmidhuber. 1997. Long short-term memory. *Neural computation*, 9(8):1735–1780.

Pingping Huang and Baobao Chang. 2014. SSMT:A Machine Translation Evaluation View To Paragraph-to-Sentence Semantic Similarity. In *Proceedings of the 8th International Workshop on Semantic Evaluation (SemEval 2014)*, pages 585–589, Dublin, Ireland.

Omer Levy, Yoav Goldberg, and Israel Ramat-Gan. 2014. Linguistic regularities in sparse and explicit word representations. In *CoNLL*, pages 171–180.

Chin-Yew Lin and Eduard Hovy. 2003. Automatic evaluation of summaries using n-gram co-occurrence statistics. In *Proceedings of the 2003 Conference of the North American Chapter of the Association for Computational Linguistics on Human Language Technology-Volume 1*, pages 71–78.

Yanjun Ma, Yifan He, Andy Way, and Josef van Genabith. 2011. Consistent translation using discriminative learning: a translation memory-inspired approach. In *Proceedings of the 49th Annual Meeting of the Association for Computational Linguistics: Human Language Technologies-Volume 1*, pages 1239–1248.

Tomas Mikolov, Ilya Sutskever, Kai Chen, Greg S Corrado, and Jeff Dean. 2013. Distributed representations of words and phrases and their compositionality. In *Advances in neural information processing systems*, pages 3111–3119.

Jeffrey Pennington, Richard Socher, and Christopher Manning. 2014. Glove: Global vectors for word representation. In *Proceedings of the 2014 Conference on Empirical Methods in Natural Language Processing (EMNLP)*, pages 1532–1543, Doha, Qatar.

Philip Resnik et al. 1999. Semantic similarity in a taxonomy: An information-based measure and its application to problems of ambiguity in natural language. *J. Artif. Intell. Res.(JAIR)*, 11:95–130.

Md Arafat Sultan, Steven Bethard, and Tamara Sumner. 2014a. Back to basics for monolingual alignment: Exploiting word similarity and contextual evidence. *Transactions of the Association for Computational Linguistics*, 2:219–230.

Md Arafat Sultan, Steven Bethard, and Tamara Sumner. 2014b. Dls@ cu: Sentence similarity from word alignment. In *Proceedings of the 8th International Workshop on Semantic Evaluation (SemEval 2014)*, pages 241–246.

Md Arafat Sultan, Steven Bethard, and Tamara Sumner. 2015. Dls@ cu: Sentence similarity from word alignment and semantic vector composition. In *Proceedings of the 9th International Workshop on Semantic Evaluation*, pages 148–153.

Kai Sheng Tai, Richard Socher, and Christopher D. Manning. 2015. Improved semantic representations from tree-structured long short-term memory networks. In *Proceedings of the 53rd Annual Meeting of the Association for Computational Linguistics and the 7th International Joint Conference on Natural Language Processing (Volume 1: Long Papers)*, pages 1556–1566, Beijing, China.

Liling Tan, Carolina Scarton, Lucia Specia, and Josef van Genabith. 2015. Usaar-sheffield: Semantic textual similarity with deep regression and machine translation evaluation metrics. In *Proceedings of the 9th International Workshop on Semantic Evaluation (SemEval 2015)*, pages 85–89, Denver, Colorado.

Liling Tan, Carolina Scarton, Lucia Specia, and Josef van Genabith. 2016. Saarsheff at semeval-2016 task 1: Semantic textual similarity with machine translation evaluation metrics and (extreme) boosted tree ensembles. In *Proceedings of the 10th International Workshop on Semantic Evaluation (SemEval 2016)*, San Diego, California.

Liling Tan. 2014. Pywsd: Python implementations of word sense disambiguation (wsd) technologies [software]. https://github.com/alvations/pywsd.

Mihaela Vela and Liling Tan. 2015. Predicting machine translation adequacy with document embeddings. In *Proceedings of the Tenth Workshop on Statistical Machine Translation*, pages 402–410, Lisbon, Portugal.

DTSim at SemEval-2016 Task 1: Semantic Similarity Model Including Multi-Level Alignment and Vector-Based Compositional Semantics

Rajendra Banjade, Nabin Maharjan, Dipesh Gautam, Vasile Rus
Department of Computer Science / Institute for Intelligent Systems
The University of Memphis
Memphis, TN, USA
{rbanjade, nmharjan, dgautam, vrus}@memphis.edu

Abstract

In this paper we describe our system (DT-Sim) submitted at SemEval-2016 Task 1: Semantic Textual Similarity (STS Core). We developed Support Vector Regression model with various features including the similarity scores calculated using alignment based methods and semantic composition based methods. The correlations between our system output and the human ratings were above 0.8 in three datasets.

1 Introduction

The task of measuring the Semantic Textual Similarity (STS) is to quantify the degree of semantic similarity between the given pair of texts. For example, the similarity score of 0 means that the texts are not similar at all and 5 means that they have same meaning (Agirre et al., 2015; Banjade et al., 2015). In this paper, we describe our system DTSim and the submitted three different runs in this year's SemEval shared task on Semantic Textual Similarity English track (STS Core; Agirre et al. (2016)). We applied Support Vector Regression (SVR) with various features in order to predict the similarity score for the given sentence pairs. The features of the model included semantic similarity scores calculated using individual methods (described in Section 3) and other general features. The pipeline of components in DTSim is shown in Figure 1.

2 Preprocessing

Hyphens were replaced with whitespaces if they were not composite verbs (e.g. video-gamed). The

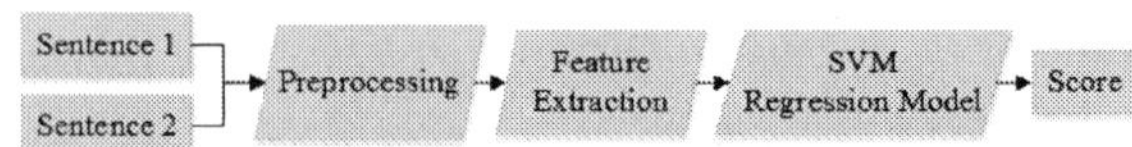

Figure 1: Pipeline of components in DTSim system.

composite verbs were detected based on the POS tag assigned by the POS tagger. Also, the words starting with co-, pre-, meta-, multi-, re-, pro-, al-, anti-, ex-, and non- were left intact. Then, the hyphen-removed texts were tokenized, lemmatized, POS-tagged and annotated with Named Entity tags using Stanford CoreNLP Toolkit (Manning et al., 2014). We also marked each word as whether it was a stop word. We also created chunks using our own Conditional Random Fields (CRF) based chunking tool (Maharjan et al., 2016) which outperforms OpenNLP chunker when evaluated with human annotated chunks provided in interpretable similarity shared task in 2015. We normalized texts using mapping data. For example, *pct* and % were changed to *percent*.

3 Feature Extraction

We used various features in our regression models including semantic similarity scores generated using individual methods. Before describing those individual methods, we present word similarity methods which were used for sentence similarity calculation.

3.1 Word-to-Word Similarity

We used vector based word representation models, PPDB 2.0 database (Pavlick et al., 2015), and Word-Net (Miller, 1995) in order to measure the similarity

640

Proceedings of SemEval-2016, pages 640–644,
San Diego, California, June 16-17, 2016. ©2016 Association for Computational Linguistics

between words as given below.

$$sim(w1, w2, m) = \begin{cases} 1, \text{ if w1 and w2 are synonyms} \\ 0, \text{ if w1 and w2 are antonyms} \\ ppdb(w1,w2), \text{ if m = ppdb} \\ \frac{\mathbf{X1.X2}}{|\mathbf{X1}||\mathbf{X2}|}, \text{ otherwise} \end{cases}$$

Where $m \in \{ppdb, LSAwiki, word2vec, GloVe\}$ **X1** and **X2** are vector representations of words *w1* and *w2* respectively.

We first checked synonyms and antonyms in WordNet 3.0. If the word pair was neither synonym nor antonym, we calculated the similarity score based on the model selected. The word representation models used are: word2vec (Mikolov et al., 2013)[1], Glove (Pennington et al., 2014)[2], and LSA Wiki (Stefanescu et al., 2014a)[3]. The cosine similarity was calculated between the word representation vectors. We also used the similarity score found in PPDB database[4].

Handling missing words: We checked for the representation of word in raw form as well as in base (lemma) form. If neither of them was found, we used vector representation of one of its synonyms in WordNet for the given POS category. The same strategy was used while using PPDB to retrieve similarity score.

3.2 Sentence-to-Sentence Similarity

3.2.1 Word Alignment Based Method

In this approach, all the content words (in lemma form) in two sentences (S1 and S2) were aligned optimally (OA) using Hungarian algorithm (Kuhn, 1955) as described in (Rus and Lintean, 2012) and implemented in SEMILAR Toolkit (Rus et al., 2013). The process is same as finding the maximum weight matching in a weighted bipartite graph. The nodes are words and the weights are the similarity scores between the word pairs. The sentence similarity is calculated as:

$$sim(S1, S2) = 2 * \frac{\sum_{(w1,w2) \in OA} sim(w1, w2)}{|S1| + |S2|}$$

---

[1] https://code.google.com/archive/p/word2vec/
[2] http://nlp.stanford.edu/projects/glove/
[3] http://semanticsimilarity.org
[4] http://paraphrase.org/

In order to avoid the noisy alignments, we reset the similarity score below 0.5 (empirically set threshold) to 0.

3.2.2 Chunk Alignment Based Method

We chunked texts (see Section 2) and aligned chunks optimally as described in (Ştefănescu et al., 2014b). The difference is that the chunks containing Named Entities were aligned using rules: (a) the chunks were treated as equivalent if both were named entities and at least one of the content words was matching, (b) they were treated as equivalent if one was the acronym of another. In other cases, chunk-to-chunk similarity was calculated using optimal word alignment method. The process is same as word alignment based method. First, the words in chunks were aligned to calculate chunk-to-chunk similarity. Finally, chunks in two sentences were aligned optimally for sentence level similarity. In order to avoid noisy alignments, we set similarity score to 0 below 0.5 for word alignment and 0.6 for chunk alignment. These thresholds were set empirically.

3.2.3 Interpretable Feature Based Method

We aligned chunks from one sentence to another and assigned semantic relations and similarity scores for each alignment. The semantic labels were EQUI, OPPO, SIMI, REL, SPE1, SPE2, and NOALI. For example, the semantic relation EQUI was assigned if the given two chunks were equivalent. The similarity score range from 0 (no similarity) to 5 (equivalent). We aligned chunks and assigned labels as described in (Maharjan et al., 2016). Once the chunks were aligned and semantic relation types and similarity scores were assigned, sentence level scores were calculated for each relation type as well as an overall score was calculated using all alignment types as shown next.

$$Norm\_count(alignment - type)$$
$$= \frac{(\text{\# alignments with type = alignment-type})}{\text{Total \# alignments including NOALI}}$$

$$Similarity(S1, S2)$$
$$= \frac{\sum_{(c1,c2) \in Alignments} sim(c1, c2)}{5 * (\text{Total \# alignments including NOALI})}$$

Where $c1 \in \{S1 \text{ chunks}\}$, $c2 \in \{S2 \text{ chunks}\}$, and alignment-type $\in$

$\{EQUI, OPPO, SIMI, REL, SPE1, SPE2, NOALI\}$.

3.2.4 Vector Algebra Based Method

In this approach, we combined vector based word representations to obtain sentence level representations through vector algebra as:

$$\mathbf{RV}(S) = \sum_{w \in W} \mathbf{V}_w$$

Where W is the set of content words in sentence S and $\mathbf{V}_w$ is the vector representation for word w. The cosine similarity was calculated between the resultant vectors - RV(S1) and RV(S2). Word representations from LSA Wiki, word2vec and GloVe models were used.

3.2.5 Similarity Matrix Based Method

The approach is similar to the word alignment based method and similarity scores for all pairs of words from given two sentences are calculated. However, a key difference is that all word-to-word similarities are taken into account, not just the maximally aligned word similarities as described in (Fernando and Stevenson, 2008).

3.3 Features

All or subset of the following features was used for three different runs as described in Section 4. We used word2vec representation and WordNet antonym and synonym for word similarity unless anything else is mentioned specifically.

1. Similarity scores generated using word alignment based methods where word-to-word similarity was calculated using methods described in Section 3.1.

2. Similarity score using optimal alignment of chunks where word-to-word similarity scores were calculated using representation from word2vec model.

3. Similarity scores using similarity matrix based methods. The similarities between words were calculated using different word similarity methods discussed in Section 3.1.

4. Similarity scores using chunk alignment types and alignment scores (interpretable features).

Data set	Count	Release time
SMTnews	351	STS2012-Test
Headlines	750	STS2014-Test
Headlines	742	STS2015-Test
Deft-forum	423	STS2014-Test
Deft-news	299	STS2014-Test
Answer-forums	375	STS2015-Test
Answer-students	750	STS2015-Test
Belief	375	STS2015-Test
Total	**4065**	

Table 1: Summary of training data.

5. Similarity scores using the resultant vector based method using word representations from word2vec, GloVe, and LSA Wiki models.

6. Noun-Noun, Adjective-Adjective, Adverb-Adverb, and Verb-Verb similarity scores and similarity score for other types of words using word alignment based method.

7. Multiplication of noun-noun similarity scores and verb-verb similarity scores.

8. $\frac{|C_{i1}-C_{i2}|}{C_{i1}+C_{i2}}$ where C_{i1} and C_{i2} are the counts of $i \in \{$all tokens, adjectives, adverbs, nouns, and verbs$\}$ for sentence 1 and 2 respectively.

9. Presence of adjectives and adverbs in first sentence, and in the second sentence.

10. Unigram overlap with synonym check, bigram overlap and BLEU score.

11. Number of EQUI, OPPO, REL, SIMI, and SPE relations in aligning chunks between texts relative to the total number of alignments.

12. Presence of antonym pair among all word pairs between given two sentences.

4 Building Models

Training Data: For building models, we used data released in previous shared tasks (summarized in Table 1). We selected datasets that included texts from different genres. However, some others, such as Tweet-news and MSRPar were not included. For instance, Tweet-news data were quite different from most other texts.

Models and Runs: Using the combination of features described in Section 3.3, we built three different Support Vector Regression (SVR) models corresponding to three runs (R1-3) submitted. In Run 1 (i.e. R1), all of the features except chunk alignment based features were used. The XL version of PPDB 2.0 was used. In Run 2, we selected the features using Weka's correlation based feature selection tool (Hall and Smith, 1998) which also included chunk alignment based similarity score. In Run 3, we took the representative features from all of the features described in Section 3.3. For example, alignment based similarity scores generated using word2vec model were selected as it performed relatively better in training set compared to GloVe and LSA Wiki models. Also, we used XXXL version of the PPDB 2.0 database (the precision maybe lower but the coverage is higher as compared to the smaller version of the database).

We used LibSVM library (Chang and Lin, 2011) in Weka 3.6.8[5] to develop SVR models. We evaluated our models in training data using 10-fold cross validation approach. The correlation scores in training set were 0.791, 0.773 and 0.800 for R1, R2, and R3 respectively. The best results in training set was obtained using RBF kernel. All other parameters were set to Weka's default.

5 Results

The test data contained 1186 sentence pairs as: Headlines (249), Plagiarism (230), Postediting (244), Question-question (209), and Answer-Answer (254). The further details about the test data can be found in (Agirre et al., 2016).

Table 2 shows the correlation (Pearson) of our system outputs with human ratings. The correlation scores of all three runs are 0.8 or above for three datasets - Headlines, Plagiarism, and Postediting. However, the correlations are comparatively lower for Question-question and Answer-answer datasets. One of the reasons is that these two datasets are quite different from the texts we used for the training (we could not include them as such type of datasets were not available during model building). For example, the question pair (#24 in Question-question dataset): *How to select a workout plan?* and *How to create a*

[5] http://www.cs.waikato.ac.nz/ml/weka/

Data set	R1	R2	R3
Headlines	0.815	0.795	0.812
Plagiarism	0.837	0.828	0.832
Postediting	0.823	0.815	0.815
Question-Question	0.614	0.608	0.591
Answer-Answer	0.578	0.550	0.562
Weighted Mean	0.735	0.720	0.724

Table 2: Results of our submitted runs on test data.

workout plan? have high lexical overlap but they are asking very different things. Analyzing the focus of the questions may be needed in order to distinguish the questions, i.e. the similarity between such pairs may need to be modeled differently. With the release of this type of dataset will foster the development of similarity models where the text pair consists of questions. It should to be noted that we used a single set of training data in all models without tailoring our models to specific test data.

Another interesting observation is that the results of three different runs are similar to each other. The most predictive feature was the word alignment based similarity using word2vec model. The correlation in full training set was 0.725. It is not surprising considering that the alignment based systems were top performing systems in the past shared tasks as well (Han et al., 2013; Sultan et al., 2015; Agirre et al., 2015). Selecting smaller set of features that best predict the similarity scores should be considered in the future which will reduce the complexity of the model and potential of overfitting.

6 Conclusion

This paper presented the DTSim system and three different runs submitted at SemEval 2016 task on STS English track. We developed support vector regression models with various features in order to predict the similarity score for the given pair of texts. The correlation of our system output were up to 0.83. However, the relatively lower scores for two datasets which were of new types (such as question-question) indicate that different datasets may need to be treated differently.

References

Eneko Agirre, Carmen Baneab, Claire Cardiec, Daniel Cerd, Mona Diabe, Aitor Gonzalez-Agirrea, Weiwei Guof, Inigo Lopez-Gazpioa, Montse Maritxalara, Rada Mihalceab, et al. 2015. Semeval-2015 task 2: Semantic textual similarity, english, spanish and pilot on interpretability. In *Proceedings of the 9th international workshop on semantic evaluation (SemEval 2015)*, pages 252–263.

Eneko Agirre, Carmen Baneab, Daniel Cer, Mona Diab, Aitor Gonzalez-Agirree, Rada Mihalceab, and Janyce Wiebe. 2016. Semeval-2016 task 1: Semantic textual similarity - monolingual and cross-lingual evaluation. In *Proceedings of the 10th international workshop on semantic evaluation (SemEval 2016)*.

Rajendra Banjade, Nobal B Niraula, Nabin Maharjan, Vasile Rus, Dan Stefanescu, Mihai Lintean, and Dipesh Gautam. 2015. Nerosim: A system for measuring and interpreting semantic textual similarity. *SemEval-2015*, page 164.

Chih-Chung Chang and Chih-Jen Lin. 2011. Libsvm: a library for support vector machines. *ACM Transactions on Intelligent Systems and Technology (TIST)*, 2(3):27.

Samuel Fernando and Mark Stevenson. 2008. A semantic similarity approach to paraphrase detection. In *Proceedings of the 11th Annual Research Colloquium of the UK Special Interest Group for Computational Linguistics*, pages 45–52. Citeseer.

Mark A Hall and Lloyd A Smith. 1998. Practical feature subset selection for machine learning.

Lushan Han, Abhay Kashyap, Tim Finin, James Mayfield, and Jonathan Weese. 2013. Umbc ebiquity-core: Semantic textual similarity systems. In *Proceedings of the Second Joint Conference on Lexical and Computational Semantics*, volume 1, pages 44–52.

Harold W Kuhn. 1955. The hungarian method for the assignment problem. *Naval research logistics quarterly*, 2(1-2):83–97.

Nabin Maharjan, Rajendra Banjade, Nobal Niraula, and Vasile Rus. 2016. Semaligner: A tool for aligning chunks with semantic relation types and semantic similarity scores. In *LREC*.

Christopher D Manning, Mihai Surdeanu, John Bauer, Jenny Rose Finkel, Steven Bethard, and David McClosky. 2014. The stanford corenlp natural language processing toolkit. In *ACL (System Demonstrations)*, pages 55–60.

Tomas Mikolov, Ilya Sutskever, Kai Chen, Greg S Corrado, and Jeff Dean. 2013. Distributed representations of words and phrases and their compositionality. In *Advances in neural information processing systems*, pages 3111–3119.

George A Miller. 1995. Wordnet: a lexical database for english. *Communications of the ACM*, 38(11):39–41.

Ellie Pavlick, Johan Bos, Malvina Nissim, Charley Beller, Ben Van Durme, and Chris Callison-Burch. 2015. Ppdb 2.0: Better paraphrase ranking, fine-grained entailment relations, word embeddings, and style classification. In *Proc. ACL*.

Jeffrey Pennington, Richard Socher, and Christopher D Manning. 2014. Glove: Global vectors for word representation. *Proceedings of the Empiricial Methods in Natural Language Processing (EMNLP 2014)*, 12:1532–1543.

Vasile Rus and Mihai Lintean. 2012. A comparison of greedy and optimal assessment of natural language student input using word-to-word similarity metrics. In *Proceedings of the Seventh Workshop on Building Educational Applications Using NLP*, pages 157–162. Association for Computational Linguistics.

Vasile Rus, Mihai C Lintean, Rajendra Banjade, Nobal B Niraula, and Dan Stefanescu. 2013. Semilar: The semantic similarity toolkit. In *ACL (Conference System Demonstrations)*, pages 163–168. Citeseer.

Dan Stefanescu, Rajendra Banjade, and Vasile Rus. 2014a. Latent semantic analysis models on wikipedia and tasa.

Dan Ştefănescu, Rajendra Banjade, and Vasile Rus. 2014b. A sentence similarity method based on chunking and information content. In *Computational Linguistics and Intelligent Text Processing*, pages 442–453. Springer.

Md Arafat Sultan, Steven Bethard, and Tamara Sumner. 2015. Dls@cu: Sentence similarity from word alignment and semantic vector composition. In *Proceedings of the 9th International Workshop on Semantic Evaluation*, pages 148–153.

ISCAS_NLP at SemEval-2016 Task 1: Sentence Similarity Based on Support Vector Regression using Multiple Features

Cheng Fu, Bo An
Institute of Software, Chinese Academy of
Sciences, Beijing, China
{fucheng,anbo}@nfs.iscas.ac.cn

Xianpei Han, Le Sun
State Key Laboratory of Computer Science,
Institute of Software, Chinese Academy of
Sciences, Beijing, China
{xianpei,sunle}@nfs.iscas.ac.cn

Abstract

This paper describes our system developed for English Monolingual subtask (STS Core) of SemEval-2016 Task 1: "Semantic Textual Similarity: A Unified Framework for Semantic Processing and Evaluation". We measure the similarity between two sentences using three different types of features, including word alignment-based similarity, sentence vector-based similarity and sentence constituent similarity. The best performance of our submitted runs is a mean 0.69996 Pearson correlation which outperforms the median score from all participating systems.

1 Introduction

Semantic Textual Similarity (STS) is the task of measuring the degree of semantic equivalence of a sentence pair (Agirre et al., 2012). STS was first held in SemEval 2012 and has drawn considerable attention in recent years. STS has been widely used in a lot of natural language processing tasks such as information retrieval, machine translation, question answering, text summarization, and so on.

Previous methods for this task could be roughly divided into three categories: alignment approaches, vector space approaches and machine learning approaches (Hänig et al., 2015). Alignment approaches align words or phrases in a sentence pair, and then take the quality or coverage of alignments as similarity measure (Sultan et al., 2014). Vector space approaches represent sentences as bag-of-words vectors and take vector similarity as their similarity measure (Meadow et al., 1992).

Machine learning approaches combine different similarity measures and features using supervised machine learning models (Bär et al., 2012).

In our system, we measure semantic text similarity by combining evidence from all above three categories. Specifically, we extract alignment-based similarity features, vector-based similarity features and sentence constituent similarity features from sentence pairs, and produce similarity scores between two sentences by combining these feature through a Support Vector Regression (SVR) model.

2 System Overview

To measure the similarity between two sentences, we first extract a series of features, including alignment-based similarity features, vector-based similarity features and sentence constituent similarity features. Then we combine all these features and get an overall similarity using a Support Vector Regression (SVR). In following we first describe how to extract different types of features. Then we describe how to train the SVR model.

2.1 Alignment-based Similarity Features

Sultan aligner is an open source unsupervised word alignment tool[1] whose core algorithm is described in (Sultan et al., 2014).

This aligner aligns related words in two sentences based on the following two properties of the words: firstly, whether they are semantically similar; secondly, whether they occur in similar semantic contexts in the respective sentences. As to the

---

[1] *https://github.com/ma-sultan/monolingual-word-aligner/*

Proceedings of SemEval-2016, pages 645–649,
San Diego, California, June 16-17, 2016. ©2016 Association for Computational Linguistics

former one, it mainly utilizes information provided by the Paraphrase Database (PPDB) (Ganitkevitch et al., 2013) to make decisions. In the case of the latter, contextual similarity for a word pair is computed as the sum of the word similarities for each pair of words in the context of them. The system based on Sultan aligner achieved the best performance at the SemEval 2014 STS task. And then at the SemEval 2015 English STS task, they constructed a top-performing system combining output of Sultan aligner and another vector-based feature.

In our system, we use the output result of Sultan aligner as follows:

- Given two input sentences, we compute their similarity score based on the produced word alignments, using a similarity function the same as the one described in (Sultan et al., 2015).

- The word aligner is used as the basis of subsequent feature extraction. Specifically, we use the word aligner to determine sentence major constituent similarity, named entity similarity and keyword similarity.

2.2 Vector-based similarity Features

In our system, we extract two vector-based similarity features based on two different types of word vectors. Given two sentences, we first generate two vector representations, and then compute a cosine similarity between these vectors as their similarity score.

The first type of word vectors used in our system comes from Baroni et al. (2014), which were learned by Skip-Gram framework in word2vec toolkit (Mikolov et al., 2013) from a corpus of about 2.8 billion tokens. Details on their approach can be found in (Baroni et al., 2014). We get the vector representation of a sentence by combining all the vectors of words in this sentence via element-wise addition.

The second type of word vectors we used is the multi-prototype word vectors come from (Liu Y et al., 2015). They assume that a word in different topic express different meanings. In our work, we employ Latent Dirichlet Allocation (LDA) (Ng and Jordan., 2003) framework to infer the topic distribution of text, and collapsed Gibbs sampling algorithm (Griffiths and Steyvers., 2004) to assign a topic to each word in the corpus. In our work, we use Wikipedia English Dump (2012.12 Version) to learn the LDA model and TWE-2 framework, which consider each word-topic pair $<w_i, z_i>$ as pseudo word to learn. To get the representation of a sentence, we first use LDA and collapsed Gibbs sampling algorithm to get the topic assignment for each word in this sentence, and combine these vectors by the same way as the first type of vectors.

2.3 Sentence constituent similarity Features

In our system, we extract the following sentence constituent similarity features:

- **Subject similarity:** If the subjects of two sentences are the same, we assign a subject similarity 1, otherwise 0.

- **Predicate similarity:** If the predicates of two sentences are the same, we assign a predicate similarity 1, otherwise 0.

- **Object similarity:** If the objects of two sentences are the same, we assign an object similarity 1, otherwise 0.

- **Complement similarity:** If the complements of two sentences are the same, we assign a complement similarity 1, otherwise 0.

- **Named entity similarity:** We extract three similarity features based on whether there are aligned time pairs, location pairs or person pairs between compared sentences. For instance, given two sentences, if there exist locations that could be aligned between them, we will assign a 1 to the according named entity similarity, otherwise 0.

- **Keyword similarity:** Given two sentences, we acquire a keyword set for each one from the output of the Stanford CoreNLP tools2 (Manning, Christopher D. et al., 2014). And then find out the keyword pairs that appear in the result of Sultan aligner. Finally, we get a real number between 0 and 1 as keyword similarity based on the proportion of aligned keywords in the above two sets.

---

2 *http://stanfordnlp.github.io/CoreNLP/*

Generally speaking, different words in a sentence belonging to different sentence constituents may have different contributions to the semantic of the whole sentence. Based on this assumption, we extract four features to capture the similarities between the four major constituents of two sentences, including subject, predicate, object and complement. In our implementation, we extract the above constituents from the syntactic parsing result of the Stanford CoreNLP tools, and then we use the alignment result provided by Sultan aligner to judge whether they could be aligned.

In some specific domains, named entities play important roles in sentence semantic similarity. For instance, two headlines usually will be regarded to have little similarity when some named entities such as times and locations are different, although the rest parts may be quite similar. Based on the above observation, we extract three named entity similarity features for our system, according to whether there exist aligned time pairs, location pairs or person pairs between compared sentences. Concretely, if there exist aligned named entities of the above three types between two sentences, we set their corresponding similarity to 1, otherwise set it to 0. When extracting these features, we take outputs of the Stanford CoreNLP tools and the Sultan aligner as input.

Finally, we also extract an additional feature based on the keyword sets outputted by the Stanford CoreNLP tools. It is obtained by measuring the overlap between the two keyword sets of the sentence pair. In detail, given two sentences $S^{(1)}$ and $S^{(2)}$, the keyword similarity feature is a real number between 0 and 1, which is computed as the following formula,

$$Sim_{key} = \frac{2 * N_{Ak}}{N_k^1 + N_k^2}$$

where N_{Ak} is the number of aligned keywords, N_k^i is the size of keyword set of $S^{(i)}$.

2.4 Support Vector Regression Model

Finally, we combine all the above features using a support vector regression model which is implemented in Scikit-learn (Pedregosa et al., 2011). We use its default SVR parameter settings(C=1.0, cache_size=200, coef0=0.0, degree=3, epsilon=0.1, gamma='auto', kernel='rbf', max_iter=-1, shrinking=True, tol=0.001, verbose=False) without further optimization.

3 Data

There are five test date sets in English Monolingual subtask (STS Core) of SemEval-2016 Task 1, which are Q&A Answer-Answer data set, Headlines data set, Plagiarism Detection data set, Post-Edited Machine Translations data set and Q&A Question-Question data set.

We trained our supervised systems using data from the past four years (2012-2015) of SemEval English STS task. For headlines we used all Headlines (2013), Headlines (2014), Deft-news(2014), SMTnews (2012) and Headlines (2015) sentence pairs. For the other four domains, we used all past annotation data.

4 Evaluation

We submitted three runs named S1, S2 and S3 before the deadline, but S3 is identical to S1 by mistake. So in this paper, we just discuss S1 and S2.

Table 1 lists the settings of run S1 and run S2. For run S1, we used all the features described in this paper. For run S2, we just used word alignment-based and sentence vector-based features.

Run	Settings
S1	Use all three different types of features
S2	Use alignment-based similarity features and vector-based similarity features

Table 1: Settings of our submitted runs for SemEval 2016

Data Set	Runs	
	S1	S2
Answer-Answer	0.4937	**0.4965**
Headlines	**0.7976**	0.7904
Plagiarism	**0.8193**	0.8121
Post-Edited	**0.8118**	0.8118
Question-Question	**0.5721**	0.5718
All	**0.6999**	0.6975

Table 2: Performances on STS 2016 test data. Each number in rows 1–5 is the correlation between system output and human annotations for the corresponding data set. The last row shows the values of the comprehensive results of each run.

Performances of our two runs on each of the STS 2016 test sets are shown in Table 2. Each bold number represents the best score on the corresponding test set. The weighted mean of correlations for each run is also shown. The results show that S1 performs equally or better than S2 in all the data sets but Answer-Answer.

Data Set	Align-Sim	Vector-Sim1	Vector-Sim2	S1
Answer-Answer	0.4776	0.1247	0.2339	0.4937
headlines	0.7938	0.6931	0.5785	0.7976
Plagiarism	0.8185	0.7919	0.6774	0.8193
Post-Edited	0.8179	0.8183	0.7740	0.8118
Question-Question	0.5696	0.6816	0.2287	0.5721

Table 3: Performance of three individual feature and our best run (S1) on STS 2016 test sets.

Table 3 shows the performance of our best run S1 and other three runs which only use one specific kind of features. *Align-Sim* uses only word alignment information, *Vector-Sim1* uses only sentence vector information and word vectors comes from (Baroni et al., 2014), *Vector-Sim2* uses only sentence vector information and word vectors coms from (Liu Y et al., 2015).

Results in table 3 show that our approach can achieve best performance by combining different types of features.

5 Conclusions and Future Work

At SemEval 2016, we present a supervised system for English Monolingual subtask of task1 using multiple features including alignment-based similarity features, vector-based similarity features and sentence constituent similarity features. Experimental results show that our approach can achieve better performance by combining more features.

For future work, we want to better measure the similarity between the major constituents of two sentences, rather than simply use 1 or 0 as their similarity values. We also want to get better sentence vector representation by developing better word composition models.

Acknowledgments

This work is supported by the National Natural Science Foundation of China under Grants no. 61433015, 61572477 and 61272324, and the National High Technology Development 863 Program of China under Grants no. 2015AA015405. Moreover, we sincerely thank the reviewers for their valuable comments.

References

Hänig, Christian, Robert Remus, and Xose De La Puente. "ExB Themis: Extensive Feature Extraction from Word Alignments for Semantic Textual Similarity." SemEval-2015 (2015): 264.

Bär, Daniel, et al. "Ukp: Computing semantic textual similarity by combining multiple content similarity measures." *Proceedings of the First Joint Conference on Lexical and Computational Semantics-Volume 1: Proceedings of the main conference and the shared task, and Volume 2: Proceedings of the Sixth International Workshop on Semantic Evaluation.* Association for Computational Linguistics, 2012.

Han L, Martineau J, Cheng D, et al. Samsung: Align-and-Differentiate Approach to Semantic Textual Similarity[J]. SemEval-2015, 2015: 172.

Pedregosa, Fabian, Gaël Varoquaux, Alexandre Gramfort, Vincent Michel, Bertrand Thirion, Olivier Grisel, Mathieu Blondel et al. "Scikit-learn: Machine learning in Python." The Journal of Machine Learning Research 12 (2011): 2825-2830.

Sultan M A, Bethard S, Sumner T. Back to basics for monolingual alignment: Exploiting word similarity and contextual evidence[J]. Transactions of the Association for Computational Linguistics, 2014, 2: 219-230.

Sultan M A, Bethard S, Sumner T. Dls@ cu: Sentence similarity from word alignment[C]//*Proceedings of the 8th International Workshop on Semantic Evaluation (SemEval 2014)*. 2014: 241-246.

Sultan M A, Bethard S, Sumner T. DLS@ CU: Sentence similarity from word alignment and semantic vector composition[C]//*Proceedings of the 9th International Workshop on Semantic Evaluation.* 2015: 148-153.

Manning, Christopher D., Mihai Surdeanu, John Bauer, Jenny Finkel, Steven J. Bethard, and David McClosky. 2014. The Stanford CoreNLP Natural Language Processing Toolkit In *Proceedings of the 52nd Annual Meeting of the Association for Computational Linguistics: System Demonstrations*, pp. 55-60.

Ganitkevitch J, Van Durme B, Callison-Burch C. PPDB: The Paraphrase Database[C]//HLT-NAACL. 2013: 758-764.

Baroni M, Dinu G, Kruszewski G. Don't count, predict! A systematic comparison of context-counting vs. context-predicting semantic vectors[C]//ACL (1). 2014: 238-247.

Liu Y, Liu Z, Chua T S, et al. Topical Word Embeddings[C]//AAAI. 2015: 2418-2424.

Zellig S. Harris. 1954. Distributional structure. Word, pages 10(23):146–162.

Blei, D. M., Ng, A. Y., & Jordan, M. I. 2003 . Latent dirichlet allocation. Journal of Machine Learning Research, 3: 993–1022

Griffiths, T. L., and Steyvers, M. 2004. Finding scientific topics. PNAS, 101:5228–5235.

DLS@CU at SemEval-2016 Task 1: Supervised Models of Sentence Similarity

Md Arafat Sultan[†]   **Steven Bethard**[‡]   **Tamara Sumner**[†]

[†]Institute of Cognitive Science and Department of Computer Science,
University of Colorado Boulder

[‡]Department of Computer and Information Sciences,
University of Alabama at Birmingham,

`arafat.sultan@colorado.edu`, `bethard@uab.edu`, `sumner@colorado.edu`

Abstract

We describe a set of systems submitted to the SemEval-2016 English Semantic Textual Similarity (STS) task. Given two English sentences, the task is to compute the degree of their semantic similarity. Each of our systems uses the SemEval 2012–2015 STS datasets to train a ridge regression model that combines different measures of similarity. Our best system demonstrates 73.6% correlation with average human annotations across five test sets.

1   Introduction

Identification of short-text semantic similarity is an important research problem with application in a multitude of NLP tasks: question answering (Yao et al., 2013; Severyn and Moschitti, 2013), short answer grading (Mohler et al., 2011; Ramachandran et al., 2015), text summarization (Dasgupta et al., 2013; Wang et al., 2013), evaluation of machine translation (Chan and Ng, 2008; Liu et al., 2011), and so on. The SemEval Semantic Textual Similarity (STS) task series (Agirre et al., 2012; Agirre et al., 2013; Agirre et al., 2014; Agirre et al., 2015) is a core platform for the task: a publicly available corpus of more than 14,000 sentence pairs have been developed over a span of four years with human annotations of similarity for each pair; and about 300 system runs have been evaluated.

In this article, we describe a set of systems that participated in the SemEval-2016 English Semantic Textual Similarity (STS) task. Given two English sentences, the objective is to compute their semantic similarity in the range [0, 5], where the score increases with similarity (i.e., 0 indicates no similarity and 5 indicates identical meanings). The official evaluation metric is the Pearson product-moment correlation coefficient with human annotations. Our systems leverage different measures of sentence similarity and train ridge regression models that learn to combine predictions from these different sources using past SemEval data. The best of our three system runs achieves 73.6% with human annotations among all submitted systems on five test sets (containing a total of 1186 test pairs).

Early work in sentence similarity (Mihalcea et al., 2006; Li et al., 2006; Islam and Inkpen, 2008) established the basic procedural framework under which most modern algorithms operate: computing sentence similarity as a mean of word similarities across the two input sentences. With no human annotated STS dataset available, these algorithms are unsupervised and were evaluated extrinsically on tasks like paraphrase detection and textual entailment recognition. The SemEval STS task series has made an important contribution through the large annotated dataset, enabling intrinsic evaluation of STS systems and making supervised STS systems a reality.

At SemEval 2012–2015, most of the top-performing STS systems used a regression algorithm to combine different measures of similarity (Bär et al., 2012; Šarić et al., 2012; Wu et al., 2013; Lynum et al., 2014; Sultan et al., 2015), with the notable exception of a couple of unsupervised systems that relied primarily on alignment of related words in the two sentences (Han et al., 2013; Sultan et al., 2014b).

Our models are based on the successful linear re-

650

Proceedings of SemEval-2016, pages 650–655,
San Diego, California, June 16-17, 2016. ©2016 Association for Computational Linguistics

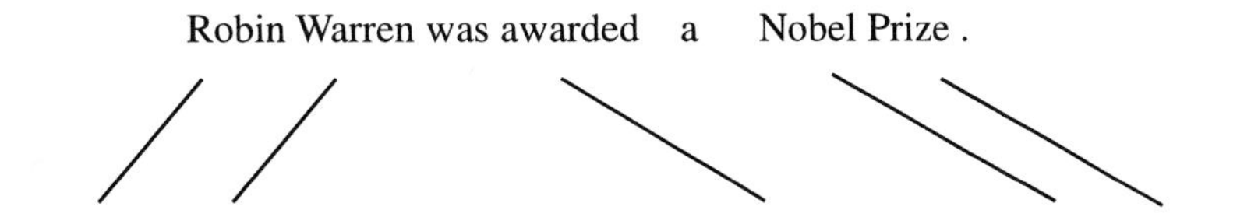

Figure 1: Words aligned by our aligner across two sentences taken from the MSR alignment corpus (Brockett, 2007). (We show only part of the second sentence.) Besides exact word/lemma matches, it identifies and aligns semantically similar word pairs using PPDB (`awarded` ↔ `received` in this example).

gression architecture of past SemEval systems in general, and the winning system of SemEval-2015 (Sultan et al., 2015) in particular. We use the features in the latter system unchanged in one of our runs and augment them with simple word and character n-gram overlap features in the other two runs.

2 System Description

Our system employs a ridge regression model (linear regression with L_2 error and L_2 regularization) to combine a set of similarity measures. The model is trained on SemEval 2012–2015 data. Our three runs differ in the subset of features drawn from the feature pool. We describe the feature set in this section; the individual runs will be discussed in Section 4.

2.1 Features

Word Alignment Proportion. This feature operationalizes the hypothesis that highly semantically similar sentences should also have a high degree of conceptual alignment between their semantic units, i.e., words and phrases. To that end, we apply the monolingual word aligner developed by Sultan et al. (2014a) to input sentence pairs.[1]

This aligner aligns words based on their semantic similarity and the similarity between their local semantic contexts in the two sentences. It uses the paraphrase database PPDB (Ganitkevitch et al., 2013) to identify semantically similar words, and relies on dependencies and surface-form neighbors of the two words to determine their contextual similarity. Word pairs are aligned in decreasing order of a weighted sum of their semantic and contextual similarity. Figure 1 shows an example set of alignments.

For more details, see (Sultan et al., 2014a).

Additionally, we also consider a Levenshtein distance[2] of 1 between a misspelled word and a correctly spelled word (of length > 2) to be a match.

Given sentences $S^{(1)}$ and $S^{(2)}$, the alignment-based similarity measure is computed as follows:

$$sim(S^{(1)}, S^{(2)}) = \frac{n_c^a(S^{(1)}) + n_c^a(S^{(2)})}{n_c(S^{(1)}) + n_c(S^{(2)})}$$

where $n_c(S^{(i)})$ and $n_c^a(S^{(i)})$ are the number of content words and the number of aligned content words in $S^{(i)}$, respectively.

Sentence Embedding. A fundamental limitation of the above feature is that it only relies on PPDB to identify semantically similar words; consequently, similar word pairs are limited to only lexical paraphrases. Hence it fails to utilize semantic similarity or relatedness between non-paraphrase word pairs (e.g., `sister` and `related`). In the current feature, we leverage neural word embeddings to overcome this limitation. We use the 400-dimensional vectors[3] developed by Baroni et al. (2014). They used the word2vec toolkit[4] to extract these vectors from a corpus of about 2.8 billion tokens. These vectors perform well across different word similarity datasets in their experiments. Details on their approach and findings can be found in (Baroni et al., 2014).

Instead of comparing word vectors across the two input sentences, we adopt a simple vector composition scheme to construct a vector representation of

---

[1] `https://github.com/ma-sultan/`
`monolingual-word-aligner`

[2] The minimum number of single-character edits needed to change one word into the other, where an edit is an insertion, a deletion or a substitution.

[3] `http://clic.cimec.unitn.it/composes/`
`semantic-vectors.html`

[4] `https://code.google.com/p/word2vec/`

Dataset	Source of Text	# of Pairs
answer-answer	Q&A forums	254
headlines	news headlines	249
plagiarism	plagiarised answers	230
postediting	post-edited MT pairs	244
question-question	Q&A forums	209

Table 1: Test sets at SemEval STS 2016.

each input sentence and then take the cosine similarity between the two sentence vectors as our second feature for this run. The vector representing a sentence is simply the sum of its content lemma vectors.

Word n-gram Overlap. This feature computes the proportion of word n-grams (lemmatized) that are in both $S^{(1)}$ and $S^{(2)}$. We employ separate instances of this feature for $n = 1, 2, 3$. The goal is to identify high local similarities in the two snippets and learn the influence that such local similarities might have on human judgment of sentence similarity.

Character n-gram Overlap. This feature computes the proportion of character n-grams that are in both $S^{(1)}$ and $S^{(2)}$ in their surface form. We employ separate instances of this feature for $n = 3, 4$. The goal is to identify and correct for spelling errors as well as incorrect lemmatizations.

Soft Cardinality. Soft Cardinality (Jimenez et al., 2012) is a measure of set cardinality where similar items in a set contribute less to its cardinality than dissimilar items. Jimenez et al. (2012) propose a parameterized measure of semantic similarity based on soft cardinality that computes sentence similarity from word similarity and the latter from character n-gram similarity. This measure was highly successful at SemEval-2012 (Agirre et al., 2012). We employ this measure with untuned parameter values as a feature for our model: $p = 1$, $bias = 0$, $\alpha = 0.5$, $bias_{sim} = 0$, $\alpha_{sim} = 0.5$, $q_1 = 2$, and $q_2 = 4$. (Please see the original article for a detailed description of these parameters as well as the similarity measure.)

3   Data

The 1186 test sentence pairs at SemEval-2016 are divided into five sets, each consisting of pairs from a particular domain. Each pair is assigned a similarity score in the range [0, 5] by human annotators (0: no similarity, 5: identicality). Test sets are discussed briefly in Table 1.

We train our supervised systems using data from the past four years of SemEval STS (Agirre et al., 2012; Agirre et al., 2013; Agirre et al., 2014; Agirre et al., 2015). The selections vary by test set, which we discuss in the next section.

4   Runs

We submit three runs at SemEval-2016. Each run employs a ridge regression model; we use Scikit-learn (Pedregosa et al., 2011) for model implementation. Different training data from SemEval 2012–2015 are used for different test sets. For *headlines*, we train the model on *headlines* (2013, 2014, 2015), *deft-news* (2014), *tweet-news* (2014), and *smtnews* (2012) pairs. For *postediting*, the model is trained on *smt* (2013), *smteuroparl* (2012) and *smtnews* (2012) pairs. These selections are based on the similarity between the source and the target domains— news data for *headlines*, machine translation data for *postediting*. For the other three test sets, all past annotations (except those for *fnwn* (2013)) are used, as we did not find any close matches for these test sets in the SemEval 2012–2015 data.

4.1   Run 1

Run 1 is a ridge regression model based only on the first two features—alignment and embeddings. The regularization strength parameter α is set using cross-validation on training data.

4.2   Run 2

Run 2 employs a model similar to the run 1 model, but uses the entire feature set described in Section 2.1. The same training sets are used for each test set and the model parameter α is again set using cross-validation on training data.

4.3   Run 3

Run 3 is identical to run 2, except that it assigns a lower value to the regularization parameter α (100 as opposed to 500 in run 2).

5   Evaluation

Table 2 shows the performances of the three runs (measured by Pearson's r, the official evaluation metric at SemEval STS) alongside the score for the

Dataset	Runs			Best Score
	1	**2**	**3**	
answer-answer	.5523	.5599	.5453	.6924
headlines	.8008	.8033	.8033	.8275
plagiarism	.8229	.8123	.8195	.8414
postediting	.8426	.8442	.8442	.8669
question-question	.6599	.6423	.6666	.7471
Weighted Mean	**.7356**	**.7330**	**.7355**	**.7781**

Table 2: Performance on STS 2016 data. Each number in rows 1–5 is the correlation (Pearson's r) between system output and human annotations for the corresponding test set. The rightmost column shows the best score by any system. The last row shows the value of the final evaluation metric for each run as well as the top-performing system.

Data Set	Run 1	Alignment	Embedding
answer-answer	.5523	.5196	.4972
headlines	.8008	.8013	.7240
plagiarism	.8229	.8149	.7813
postediting	.8426	.8226	.8214
question-question	.6599	.5767	.6833
Weighted Mean	.7356	.7084	.6994

Table 3: Performance of each individual feature of our best run (run 1) on STS 2016 test sets. Combining the two features improves performance on most test sets.

Runs	Pearson's r
1, 2	.9834
1, 3	.9952
2, 3	.9920

Table 4: Pairwise correlations between the three runs.

best performing system for each test set. The last row shows the official evaluation metric that computes a weighted sum of correlations over all test sets, where the weight of a test set is proportional to the number of sentence pairs it contains.

Runs 1 and 3 have very similar overall performances, slightly better than that of run 2. Among the different test sets, the models perform well on news headlines, plagiarism and machine translation data, but poorly on the Q&A forums data.

5.1 Ablation Study

From the overall performances in Table 2, it is clear that the three new features added to the Sultan et al. (2015) model do not improve performance. Therefore, we run a feature ablation study only on the run 1 model. Table 3 shows the results. Similar to the findings reported in (Sultan et al., 2015), the alignment-based feature performs better across test sets. However, the addition of the embedding feature improves performance on almost all test sets.

5.2 Relation between the Runs

We compute pairwise correlations between the predictions of our three runs to see how different they are. As Table 4 shows, the predictions are highly correlated, which is expected given the results in Table 2.

6 Conclusions and Future Work

We present three supervised models of sentence similarity based on the winning system at SemEval-2015 (Sultan et al., 2015). Our additional features

do not improve performance and results show similar influences of alignment and embedding features as in SemEval-2015.

Besides high performance, the run 1 model has the key advantage of simplicity and high replicability. All the major design components are also available for free download (links provided in Section 2).

A key limitation of the system is its inability to model semantics of units larger than words (phrasal verbs, idioms, and so on). This is an important future direction not only for our system but also for STS and text comparison tasks in general. Incorporation of stop word semantics is key to identifying similarities and differences in subtle aspects of sentential semantics like polarity and modality. Domain-specific learning of the word vectors can also improve results.

References

Eneko Agirre, Mona Diab, Daniel Cer, and Aitor Gonzalez-Agirre. 2012. SemEval-2012 Task 6: A Pilot on Semantic Textual Similarity. In *Proceedings of the Sixth International Workshop on Semantic Evaluation*, SemEval '12, pages 385–393, Montréal, Canada.

Eneko Agirre, Daniel Cer, Mona Diab, Aitor Gonzalez-Agirre, and Weiwei Guo. 2013. *SEM 2013 shared task: Semantic Textual Similarity. In *Second Joint Conference on Lexical and Computational Semantics*, *SEM '13, pages 32–43, Atlanta, Georgia, USA.

Eneko Agirre, Carmen Banea, Claire Cardie, Daniel Cer, Mona Diab, Aitor Gonzalez-Agirre, Weiwei Guo,

Rada Mihalcea, German Rigau, and Janyce Wiebe. 2014. SemEval-2014 Task 10: Multilingual Semantic Textual Similarity. In *Proceedings of the 8th International Workshop on Semantic Evaluation*, SemEval '14, pages 81–91, Dublin, Ireland.

Eneko Agirre, Carmen Banea, Claire Cardie, Daniel Cer, Mona Diab, Aitor Gonzalez-Agirre, Weiwei Guo, Inigo Lopez-Gazpio, Montse Maritxalar, Rada Mihalcea, German Rigau, Larraitz Uria, and Janyce Wiebe. 2015. SemEval-2015 Task 2: Semantic Textual Similarity, English, Spanish and Pilot on Interpretability. In *Proceedings of the 9th International Workshop on Semantic Evaluation*, SemEval '15, pages 252–263, Denver, Colorado.

Daniel Bär, Chris Biemann, Iryna Gurevych, and Torsten Zesch. 2012. UKP: Computing Semantic Textual Similarity by Combining Multiple Content Similarity Measures. In *Proceedings of the Sixth International Workshop on Semantic Evaluation*, SemEval '12, pages 435–440, Montréal, Canada.

Marco Baroni, Georgiana Dinu, and Germán Kruszewski. 2014. Don't count, predict! A systematic comparison of context-counting vs. context-predicting semantic vectors. In *Proceedings of the 52nd Annual Meeting of the Association for Computational Linguistics*, ACL '14, pages 238–247, Baltimore, Maryland.

Chris Brockett. 2007. Aligning the RTE 2006 Corpus. Technical Report MSR-TR-2007-77, Microsoft Research.

Yee Seng Chan and Hwee Tou Ng. 2008. MAXSIM: A Maximum Similarity Metric for Machine Translation Evaluation. In *Proceedings of ACL-08: HLT*, pages 55–62, Columbus, Ohio.

Anirban Dasgupta, Ravi Kumar, and Sujith Ravi. 2013. Summarization Through Submodularity and Dispersion. In *Proceedings of the 51st Annual Meeting of the Association for Computational Linguistics*, ACL '13, pages 1014–1022, Sofia, Bulgaria.

Juri Ganitkevitch, Benjamin Van Durme, and Chris Callison-Burch. 2013. PPDB: The Paraphrase Database. In *Proceedings of the 2013 Conference of the North American Chapter of the Association for Computational Linguistics – Human Language Technologies*, NAACL '13, pages 758–764, Atlanta, Georgia, USA.

Lushan Han, Abhay L. Kashyap, Tim Finin, James Mayfield, and Jonathan Weese. 2013. UMBC_EBIQUITY-CORE: Semantic Textual Similarity Systems. In *Second Joint Conference on Lexical and Computational Semantics*, *SEM '13, pages 44–52, Atlanta, Georgia, USA.

Aminul Islam and Diana Inkpen. 2008. Semantic Text Similarity Using Corpus-based Word Similarity and String Similarity. *ACM Transactions on Knowledge Discovery from Data*, 2(2):10:1–10:25.

Sergio Jimenez, Claudia Becerra, and Alexander Gelbukh. 2012. Soft Cardinality: A Parameterized Similarity Function for Text Comparison. In *Proceedings of the Sixth International Workshop on Semantic Evaluation*, SemEval '12, pages 449–453, Montréal, Canada.

Yuhua Li, David McLean, Zuhair A. Bandar, James D. O'Shea, and Keeley Crockett. 2006. Sentence Similarity Based on Semantic Nets and Corpus Statistics. *IEEE Transactions on Knowledge and Data Engineering*, 18(8):1138–1150.

Chang Liu, Daniel Dahlmeier, and Hwee Tou Ng. 2011. Better Evaluation Metrics Lead to Better Machine Translation. In *Proceedings of the 2011 Conference on Empirical Methods in Natural Language Processing*, EMNLP '13, pages 375–384, Edinburgh, Scotland, UK.

André Lynum, Partha Pakray, Björn Gambäck, and Sergio Jimenez. 2014. NTNU: Measuring Semantic Similarity with Sublexical Feature Representations and Soft Cardinality. In *Proceedings of the 8th International Workshop on Semantic Evaluation*, SemEval '14, pages 448–453, Dublin, Ireland.

Rada Mihalcea, Courtney Corley, and Carlo Strapparava. 2006. Corpus-based and Knowledge-based Measures of Text Semantic Similarity. In *Proceedings of the 21st National Conference on Artificial Intelligence*, AAAI '06, pages 775–780.

Michael Mohler, Razvan Bunescu, and Rada Mihalcea. 2011. Learning to Grade Short Answer Questions Using Semantic Similarity Measures and Dependency Graph Alignments. In *Proceedings of the 49th Annual Meeting of the Association for Computational Linguistics: Human Language Technologies*, ACL '11, pages 752–762, Portland, Oregon, USA.

Fabian Pedregosa, Gaël Varoquaux, Alexandre Gramfort, Vincent Michel, Bertrand Thirion, Olivier Grisel, Mathieu Blondel, Peter Prettenhofer, Ron Weiss, Vincent Dubourg, Jake Vanderplas, Alexandre Passos, David Cournapeau, Matthieu Brucher, Matthieu Perrot, and Édouard Duchesnay. 2011. Scikit-learn: Machine Learning in Python. *Journal of Machine Learning Research*, 12:2825–2830.

Lakshmi Ramachandran, Jian Cheng, and Peter Foltz. 2015. Identifying Patterns For Short Answer Scoring Using Graph-based Lexico-Semantic Text Matching. In *Proceedings of the Tenth Workshop on Innovative Use of NLP for Building Educational Applications*, NAACL-BEA '15, pages 97–106.

Aliaksei Severyn and Alessandro Moschitti. 2013. Automatic Feature Engineering for Answer Selection and Extraction. In *Proceedings of the 2013 Conference* on *Empirical Methods in Natural Language Processing*, EMNLP '13, pages 458–467, Seattle, Washington, USA.

Md Arafat Sultan, Steven Bethard, and Tamara Sumner. 2014a. Back to Basics for Monolingual Alignment: Exploiting Word Similarity and Contextual Evidence. *Transactions of the Association for Computational Linguistics*, 2:219–230.

Md Arafat Sultan, Steven Bethard, and Tamara Sumner. 2014b. DLS@CU: Sentence Similarity from Word Alignment. In *Proceedings of the 8th International Workshop on Semantic Evaluation*, SemEval '14, pages 241–246, Dublin, Ireland.

Md Arafat Sultan, Steven Bethard, and Tamara Sumner. 2015. DLS@CU: Sentence Similarity from Word Alignment and Semantic Vector Composition. In *Proceedings of the 9th International Workshop on Semantic Evaluation*, SemEval '15, pages 148–153, Denver, Colorado, USA.

Frane Šarić, Goran Glavaš, Mladen Karan, Jan Šnajder, and Bojana Dalbelo Bašić. 2012. TakeLab: Systems for Measuring Semantic Text Similarity. In *Proceedings of the Sixth International Workshop on Semantic Evaluation*, SemEval '12, pages 441–448, Montréal, Canada.

Lu Wang, Hema Raghavan, Vittorio Castelli, Radu Florian, and Claire Cardie. 2013. A Sentence Compression Based Framework to Query-Focused Multi-Document Summarization. In *Proceedings of the 51st Annual Meeting of the Association for Computational Linguistics*, ACL '13, pages 1384–1394, Sofia, Bulgaria.

Stephen Wu, Dongqing Zhu, Ben Carterette, and Hongfang Liu. 2013. MayoClinicNLP-CORE: Semantic Representations for Textual Similarity. In *Proceedings of the Second Joint Conference on Lexical and Computational Semantics*, *SEM '13, pages 148–154, Atlanta, Georgia, USA.

Xuchen Yao, Benjamin Van Durme, Chris Callison-Burch, and Peter Clark. 2013. Answer Extraction as Sequence Tagging with Tree Edit Distance. In *Proceedings of the 2013 Conference of the North American Chapter of the Association for Computational Linguistics – Human Language Technologies*, NAACL '13, pages 858–867, Atlanta, Georgia, USA.

DCU-SEManiacs at SemEval-2016 Task 1: Synthetic Paragram Embeddings for Semantic Textual Similarity

Chris Hokamp, Piyush Arora
ADAPT Centre
School of Computing
Dublin City University
Dublin, Ireland
`{chokamp,parora}@computing.dcu.ie`

Abstract

We experiment with learning word representations designed to be combined into sentence-level semantic representations, using an objective function which does not directly make use of the supervised scores provided with the training data, instead opting for a simpler objective which encourages similar phrases to be close together in the embedding space. This simple objective lets us start with high-quality embeddings trained using the Paraphrase Database (PPDB) (Wieting et al., 2015; Ganitkevitch et al., 2013), and then tune these embeddings using the official STS task training data, as well as synthetic paraphrases for each test dataset, obtained by pivoting through machine translation.

Our submissions include runs which only compare the similarity of phrases in the embedding space, directly using the similarity score to produce predictions, as well as a run which uses vector similarity in addition to a suite of features we investigated for our 2015 Semeval submission.

For the crosslingual task, we simply translate the Spanish sentences to English, and use the same system we designed for the monolingual task.

1 Introduction

We describe the work carried out by the DCU-SEManiacs team on the Semantic Textual Similarity (STS) task at SemEval-2016 (Agirre et al., 2013; Agirre et al., 2014; Nakov et al., 2015).

The main ideas we investigate in our systems are:

1. Using a margin-based objective function to train high-quality sentence embeddings without using supervised scores

2. Creating new synthetic training data using machine translation to generate artificial paraphrases

3. Using ensemble models to combine features generated by our embedding networks with features obtained from other sources

1.1 Task Description

The Semeval Semantic Textual Similarity (STS) task provides participants with training data consisting of pairs of sentences annotated with gold-standard semantic similarity scores. The crowd-sourced similarity scores are given on a scale from 0 (no relation) to 5 (semantic equivalence). Thus, our aim is to use the training data to learn a model which predicts a score between 0 and 5 for unseen input pairs (Nakov et al., 2015). The monolingual STS task has been organized each year since 2012, and most approaches have viewed the learning task as a regression problem, where real-valued model output is clipped to be $0 <= \hat{y} <= 5$ (Agirre et al., 2013; Agirre et al., 2014; Nakov et al., 2015).

For two of our three STS systems, we take a novel approach to this task, and directly use the similarity scores produced by the embedding networks as the predicted score. When training the embedding networks, we use the gold scores only to *reduce* the task-internal data to segments with a high-semantic similarity – embeddings are then learned using a simplified training objective which only makes use

Proceedings of SemEval-2016, pages 656–662,
San Diego, California, June 16-17, 2016. ©2016 Association for Computational Linguistics

of training pairs which are "perfect" paraphrases (see section 2.1). Interestingly, these models perform very well without access to the gold standard scores.

The 2016 edition of the STS task also introduced a pilot crosslingual STS task in addition to the monolingual STS task. The crosslingual task is similar to monolingual STS, except either member of each sentence pair may be in Spanish (language identification is *not* provided with the data). In order to use our monolingual STS system in the crosslingual task, we first automatically identify sentences which are probably in Spanish, use machine translation to translate Spanish sentences to English, then approach the crosslingual task as another monolingual task.

Although our systems performed well in both the crosslingual and monolingual STS tasks, we also discuss some possible shortcomings of our approach, and opportunities for improvement.

The rest of the paper is organized as follows: section 2 discusses the main novelties of our submissions, and presents the task-internal and external datasets we leverage for training our systems, section 3 gives a detailed discussion of each of our submitted systems, including information on hyperparameters and training configuration, section 4 gives a summary of experimental results, and section 5 discusses the advantages and disadvantages of our approach, and proposes avenues for future work.

2 Methodology

2.1 Paragram Vectors and PPDB

Wieting (2015) introduced Paragram-phrase embeddings, which use a novel training objective designed to learn robust sentence-level embeddings which are simple bag-of-words averages of the embeddings in each sequence. Wieting discusses several possible means of encoding a sequence into a vector using shallow and deep feedforward and recurrent networks. Surprisingly, the best performing model is a single-layer word embedding matrix, where sentence vectors are constructed by taking the mean of the token embeddings (equation 1).

In our preliminary experiments, we also experimented with deeper feedforward models, as well as mono-directional and bi-directional Long Short-Term Memory (LSTM) recurrent models (Hochreiter and Schmidhuber, 1997) in place of the simple averaging approach; however, we did not observe an improvement in performance, which supports the results presented by Wieting (2015).

We also experimented with objective functions that are more representative of the task objective, such as Kullback-Leibler Divergence (Tai et al., 2015; Wieting et al., 2015); however, we found that the simple margin-based training objective outperforms cost-functions which take the score into account. We hypothesize that this is because the notion of "partial-similarity" is mostly captured by the bag-of-words averaging of all token embeddings to compose the vector representation of a sequence, and because the semantic similarity scores for the STS task are sufficiently coarse that the bulk of their semantic content can be efficiently captured even when all structural information has been discarded.

Equation 2 shows the objective function for the Paragram-phrase model. This function pushes similar examples together, and dissimilar examples apart, driven by the margin δ. $\mathbf{g}(\mathbf{x})$ is some differentiable function which transforms a sequence of tokens into a fixed-size vector. This model is simple to implement, and very fast to train[1]. An additional advantage of the margin-based objective function is that the model can learn from any dataset containing pairs of phrases which are semantically equivalent, enabling the use of unsupervised paraphrase data during training. We exploit this flexibility to greatly improve the performance of our models by tuning the Paragram vectors with new data (section 3.2).

$$embedding(x) = \frac{1}{n} \sum_{i}^{n} W_{word}^{x^i} \qquad (1)$$

The word embeddings are the only parameters of this network. Intuitively, tokens whose embeddings have a high L2 norm in this space contribute more to the semantics of a sentence than those whose norm is low. This simple parameterization has the added advantage that it is very fast to train, relative to other possible architectures, such as mono- or bi-directional LSTMs or Gated Recurrent Units (GRUs) (Chung et al., 2015). However, the main

---

[1] our implementations will be made available at https://www.github.com/chrishokamp/synthetic-embeddings

$$\min_{W_w} \frac{1}{|X|} \sum_{\langle x_1, x_2 \rangle \in X} max(0, \delta - cos(g(x_1), g(x_2)) + cos(g(x_1), g(t_1)))$$

$$+ max(0, \delta - cos(g(x_1), g(x_2)) + cos(g(x_2), g(t_2)))$$

$$+ \lambda_w ||W_{w_{initial}} - W_w||^2 \qquad (2)$$

Dataset	DCU 2015 model	Paragram Raw	Paragram + DCU 2015
forums	**.673**	.647	.672
students	.682	**.773**	.732
belief	.708	**.774**	.762
headlines	.810	.748	**.816**
images	.840	.826	**.850**
ALL	.743	.754	**.766**

Table 1: Using the 2015 STS data as development data, a comparison of our 2015 model with raw results from paragram vectors trained on PPDB, and an ensemble system of our 2015 model with the paragram similarity included as a feature.

advantage of this objective function for our work is that models can now be trained with any dataset consisting of pairs of sequences which are semantically equivalent. Thus datasets such as PPDB can be used to train high-quality embeddings.

We start by using the 300-dimensional vectors provided by Wieting (2015). These vectors were trained using the XXL version of PPDB (Ganitkevitch et al., 2013). The sentence embeddings obtained by averaging the raw paragram vectors are used as the development baseline for our systems, and we look for ways to tune the model for the STS task without changing the training objective.

This training objective assumes that each pair is "sufficiently similar" – there is no explicit way to represent partial similarity, since the δ margin dictates that the model should predict a score of at least δ for positive training examples. Therefore, we filter the Semeval STS 2012-2014 training data to contain only those pairs whose similarity is $>= 3.8^2$.

3 System Descriptions

3.1 Generating Negative Examples

Wieting (2015) discusses two ways of selecting negative examples for the paragram vector training objective. The first is to compute the similarity of x_1

and x_2 with every segment in the training minibatch, choosing the most similar segment t_1 to x_1 and the most similar segment t_2 to x_2 that are *not* members of the current pair (x_1, x_2), and to use these as the negative training examples for the pair. The second is to alternate between choosing a random negative example and choosing the most similar phrase. Although the approach of choosing the most similar negative example is theoretically satisfying, there are heavy computational costs: this requires at least N vector comparisons for each example in each pair, where N is the size of the minibatch, and the comparisons must be repeated for each training epoch, since the most similar segment may have changed since the previous epoch. Due to the computational overhead associated with computing the most similar example for each example in each minibatch, we opt instead to use randomly chosen segments as the negative examples. Because the random negative examples are re-selected for each epoch, the model also views more data – each time a training pair is seen, the negative examples t_1 and t_2 selected for x_1 and x_2 are different. Intuitively, this should positively contribute to desirable invariance in the learned semantic embeddings; however, we did not validate this empirically.

3.2 Synthetic Data Generation

We believe that the requirement for human annotation is the major bottleneck for producing more training data for the STS task. Inspired by the

---

[2] This cutoff parameter was tuned between 3-4.5 with increments of 0.1, note that lowering this threshold results in more training data, but also lowers the quality of the paraphrases, since more partially-similar pairs are included

Dataset	task-internal	synthetic	fusion	*Median*	*Best System*
answer-answer	.627	**.688**	.583	.480	.692
headlines	.719	.687	**.764**	.764	.827
plagiarism	.808	**.819**	.814	.789	.841
postediting	.809	.809	**.847**	.812	.867
question-question	.516	.506	**.566**	.571	.747
ALL	.699	.7133	**.717**	0.689	.778

Table 2: Monolingual STS results by run, with median scores and best scores for reference. "fusion" indicates the ensemble system. Our best performing systems are bolded.

Dataset	task-internal	synthetic	*Best System*
News	.894	**.897**	.912
Multi-source	.769	**.793**	.819
Mean*	.832	**.846**	.863

Table 3: Crosslingual STS results by run, with best scores for reference. Our best performing systems are bolded.

methodology used to create PPDB (Ganitkevitch et al., 2013), we propose a novel means of producing paraphrases which combines domain-adaptation with paraphrase generation using two or more MT systems. For the experiments presented here, we translate every test sentence into Spanish, then back into English, and add the resulting "pseudo-instance" to the data provided by the task organizers. This method has the additional advantage that we can generate new paraphrases targeted at the sentences in the test data, allowing unsupervised domain adaptation of the model to the test datasets.

This approach is obviously dependent upon the quality of the machine translation output; however, if translation from $e \rightarrow f \rightarrow \hat{e}$ outputs exactly the input e, the new synthetic training example would be of little use. Therefore, the MT systems used for synthetic generation should ideally produce fluent output $\hat{e}$ which paraphrases the original input e, but is diverse with respect to the gold-standard reference translations.

In order to validate that adding synthetic data actually improves performance, we generated synthetic paraphrases for the 2015 Images dataset, and compared performance with respect to the Paragram baseline, and with respect to a model trained with only the task-internal data. These experiments confirmed that synthetic data generation can significantly improve performance. During development, we did not test performance on all of the 2015 data because the process of generating paraphrases is

time-consuming, and because we wanted to keep our usage of the Google Translate API within the free credit allocated for test usage of the API, to ensure that our results can be easily replicated.

3.3 Semantic Textual Similarity

We submit three systems to the monolingual STS task. The first system is an ensemble of features from our 2015 submission, together with two features produced by the embedding systems. The second system uses the task-internal data from Semeval 2012-2015 to tune the Paragram embeddings for the STS task. The third system includes one synthetic paraphrase for each sentence in each test dataset, generated by first translating the sentence into Spanish, then back into English. Note that, due to time constraints we did not tune a separate model for each test dataset, instead we used one model trained with all synthetic paraphrases from all test datasets. We believe that training a separate model for each test dataset with synthetic data for only that dataset would improve performance somewhat. Because the scores of the embedding models are in the range 0–1, we scale the outputs by a factor of 5 to match the Semeval scoring system.

3.4 Ensemble Model

In order to test the use of embedding model similarity scores as downstream features, we train an ensemble system with all features from our 2015 submission along with the similarity scores generated

Feature	Gini Coefficient	Description
paraphrase1	0.337	Vector similarity
paraphrase2	0.073	Vector similarity with synthetic data
cosine icf	0.054	Normalized cosine similarity
f15	0.049	Weighted Word Match
f14	0.042	WordNet match
f20	0.038	Relative length difference
product	0.036	Word2Vec based sentence similarity score
f2	0.033	F1-score of number match
nn1	0.028	Comparing only nouns using Word2Vec

Table 4: Ensemble model top 10 features in decreasing order

by both the task-internal and synthetic models. This ensemble, which we call "fusion" was our best system overall (see table 2). We used gradient boosting regressor[3] model trained over combined set of previous year's Semeval STS data sets from 2012-2015. The details of this system are described in (Arora et al., 2015).

3.5 Cross-lingual

For our submission to the cross-lingual STS task, we leverage the Google translate API[4] in three ways: the language identification API is used to detect which segments are in Spanish, the translation API is used to translate Spanish sentences into English, and the pivoting method for generating synthetic paraphrases discussed in section 3.2 is used to generate one new paraphrase for each segment in each test instance. We then apply our monolingual embedding methodology to the translated text with no modification.

3.6 Training Configuration

For the final systems, we use all existing task-internal training data from the Semeval STS task from 2012-2015. The 2015 datasets were used as validation data to find the best system settings, and then included in the training data for the final systems. δ from equation 2 is set to 0.8 for all of our experiments. Embedding dimensionality is 300. We use a minibatch size of 100, and use AdaDelta (Zeiler, 2012) as the gradient update

[3]http://scikit-learn.org/stable/modules/generated/sklearn.ensemble.GradientBoostingRegressor.html
[4]https://cloud.google.com/translate/

method. The regularization weight λ is set to 10^{-5} for all models.

Dataset	% Unknown
question-question	3.2
plagiarism	4.9
post-editing	4.2
headlines	4.86
answer-answer	0.81

Table 5: Total % unknown for each 2016 dataset

The pretrained paragram vectors have a size of 42091; we do not add any new tokens to the index. Table 5 gives the total percentage of each 2016 test dataset which is unknown with respect to our index. Because the baseline paragram vector index does not contain a special "UNKNOWN" token, we randomly choose a low-frequency token to assign as unknown. Some experimentation showed that using a rare token instead of a stopword results in a small performance improvement.

4 Results

Our monolingual STS systems all performed better than the median system, with the fusion system slightly outperforming the embedding model trained with synthetic data (see tables 2 and 3).

For all systems in both the monolingual and crosslingual STS tasks, we observe an overall improvement over the Paragram baseline when using task-internal training data, and a further improvement when we incorporate synthetic training examples. This result validates the utility of synthetic paraphrases generated by machine translation, and encourages us to explore this avenue further.

For our ensemble based approach, we analyzed the features using Gini importance[5] (Singh et al., 2010). Table 4 shows the importance of the top 10 features in our ensemble model. The relative impact of our two paraphrase features is very high, confirming the utility of the paragram embedding model for the STS task.

Our Features
task-internal paraphrases, synthetic paraphrases, cosine_icf, product_w2v, nn_w2v, vb_w2v, cosine, sum_w2v, det_1, det_2
TakeLab (Šarić et al., 2012) features
weighted_word_match, wn_sim_match, relative_len_difference, number_features, weighted_dist_sim, case_matches, relative_ic_difference

Table 6: Important features.

5 Conclusions

We have presented a method of fine-tuning Paragram-phrase vectors for the STS task using both task-internal and synthetic paraphrases. Our embedding models achieve surprisingly good performance on the STS task without directly taking advantage of the gold-standard scores during training. We have also introduced a novel method of generating synthetic paraphrases for test instances using machine translation. Finally we have shown that a combination of traditional features with the similarity score learned by our embedding models outperforms each individual system.

Future work will focus on increasing the diversity of the synthetic data, and on incorporating multiple objective functions into different stages of the training process.

Acknowledgments

This research was supported by the EXPERT (EU Marie Curie ITN No. 317471) project, and Science Foundation Ireland (SFI) as a part of the ADAPT Centre at Dublin City University (Grant No: 12/CE/I2267),

---

[5] http://scikit-learn.org/stable/ modules/generated/sklearn.tree. DecisionTreeClassifier.html

References

Eneko Agirre, Daniel Cer, Mona Diab, Aitor Gonzalez-Agirre, and Weiwei Guo. 2013. *SEM 2013 shared task: Semantic Textual Similarity. In *Second Joint Conference on Lexical and Computational Semantics (*SEM), Volume 1: Proceedings of the Main Conference and the Shared Task: Semantic Textual Similarity*, pages 32–43, Atlanta, Georgia, USA.

Eneko Agirre, Carmen Banea, Claire Cardie, Daniel Cer, Mona Diab, Aitor Gonzalez-Agirre, Weiwei Guo, Rada Mihalcea, German Rigau, and Janyce Wiebe. 2014. SemEval-2014 Task 10: Multilingual Semantic Textual Similarity. In *Proceedings of the 8th International Workshop on Semantic Evaluation (SemEval 2014)*, pages 81–91, Dublin, Ireland.

Piyush Arora, Chris Hokamp, Jennifer Foster, and Gareth Jones. 2015. Dcu: Using distributional semantics and domain adaptation for the semantic textual similarity semeval-2015 task 2. In *Proceedings of the 9th International Workshop on Semantic Evaluation (SemEval 2015)*, pages 143–147, Denver, Colorado, June. Association for Computational Linguistics.

Junyoung Chung, Caglar Gulcehre, Kyunghyun Cho, and Yoshua Bengio. 2015. Gated feedback recurrent neural networks. In *International Conference on Machine Learning*.

Juri Ganitkevitch, Benjamin Van Durme, and Chris Callison-Burch. 2013. Ppdb: The paraphrase database. In *Proceedings of the 2013 Conference of the North American Chapter of the Association for Computational Linguistics: Human Language Technologies*, pages 758–764, Atlanta, Georgia, June. Association for Computational Linguistics.

Sepp Hochreiter and Jürgen Schmidhuber. 1997. Long short-term memory. *Neural Comput.*, 9(8):1735–1780, November.

Preslav Nakov, Torsten Zesch, Daniel Cer, and David Jurgens, editors. 2015. *Proceedings of the 9th International Workshop on Semantic Evaluation (SemEval 2015)*. Association for Computational Linguistics, Denver, Colorado, June.

Sanasam Ranbir Singh, Hema A. Murthy, and Timothy A. Gonsalves. 2010. Feature selection for text classification based on gini coefficient of inequality. In *Proceedings of the Fourth International Workshop on Feature Selection in Data Mining, FSDM, held at PAKDD 2010, Hyderabad, India, June 21st, 2010*, pages 76–85.

Kai Sheng Tai, Richard Socher, and Christopher D. Manning. 2015. Improved semantic representations from tree-structured long short-term memory networks. In *Proceedings of the 53rd Annual Meeting of the Association for Computational Linguistics and the 7th*

International Joint Conference on Natural Language Processing of the Asian Federation of Natural Language Processing, ACL 2015, July 26-31, 2015, Beijing, China, Volume 1: Long Papers, pages 1556–1566.

Frane Šarić, Goran Glavaš, Mladen Karan, Jan Šnajder, and Bojana Dalbelo Bašić. 2012. TakeLab: Systems for Measuring Semantic Text Similarity. In *Proceedings of the First Joint Conference on Lexical and Computational Semantics - Volume 1: Proceedings of the Main Conference and the Shared Task, and Volume 2: Proceedings of the Sixth International Workshop on Semantic Evaluation*, SemEval '12, pages 441–448, Montréal, Canada.

John Wieting, Mohit Bansal, Kevin Gimpel, and Karen Livescu. 2015. Towards universal paraphrastic sentence embeddings. *CoRR*, abs/1511.08198.

Matthew D. Zeiler. 2012. Adadelta: An adaptive learning rate method. *CoRR*, abs/1212.5701.

GWU_NLP at SemEval-2016 Shared Task 1:
Matrix Factorization for Crosslingual STS

Hanan Aldarmaki and **Mona Diab**
Department of Computer Science
The George Washington University
{aldarmaki;mtdiab}@gwu.edu

Abstract

We present a matrix factorization model
for learning cross-lingual representations for
sentences. Using sentence-aligned corpora,
the proposed model learns distributed representations by factoring the given data into
language-dependent factors and one shared
factor. As a result, input sentences from both
languages can be mapped into fixed-length
vectors and then compared directly using the
cosine similarity measure, which achieves 0.8
Pearson correlation on Spanish-English semantic textual similarity.

1 Introduction

Semantic textual similarity (STS) is a measure of
relatedness in meaning between a pair of variable-
length textual snippets, such as sentences. Using
unsupervised vector space models, words and sentences can be mapped into dense vector representations that capture implicit syntactic and semantic
information. These representations can then be directly compared using well-known distance or sim-
ilairty measures, such as the Euclidean distance or
cosine similarity, which reflect their overall semantic relatedness.

Such distributed representations of words, or
word embeddings, can be learned using global word
co-occurrence statistics as in matrix factorization
models (Guo and Diab, 2012; Pennington et al.,
2014), or using local context as in neural probabilistic language models (Bengio et al., 2003; Collobert and Weston, 2008; Socher et al., 2013). A
variable-length sentence can be mapped into a fixed-
length vector either by combining word embeddings

or directly learning sentence representations as in
the paragraph vector model proposed in (Le and
Mikolov, 2014).

In crosslingual STS, the challenge is to compare
sentences from two different languages. We address
this problem by directly learning crosslingual vector
representations for words and sentences, which allows us to calculate the STS scores without the need
for explicit translation or mapping. Several models can be used for learning cross-lingual compositional representations (Klementieva et al., 2012; Shi
et al., 2015; Pennington et al., 2014; Cavallanti et al.,
2010; Mikolov et al., 2013; Coulmance et al., 2015;
Pham et al., 2015). We propose a relatively simple and nuanced unsupervised model inspired by the
monolingual weighted matrix factorization (WMF)
model proposed in (Guo and Diab, 2012), which we
extend to the cross-lingual setting.

The WMF model learns word representations by
decomposing a sparse tf-idf matrix into two low-
rank factor matrices representing words and sentences. The weights are adjusted to reflect the confidence levels in reconstructing observed vs. missing words in the original matrix. Representations
for variable-length sequences can be calculated by
minimizing the reconstruction error as described in
Section 2.1. In this paper, we propose to extend
this model to the cross-lingual setting by modeling
two languages in parallel to obtain shared semantic
representations. The proposed model has a simple
loss function and only uses sentence-aligned data for
learning the shared representations. We describe the
model in two variations in Section 2.2. This model
yields a performance of 0.8 Pearson correlation in

Proceedings of SemEval-2016, pages 663–667,
San Diego, California, June 16-17, 2016. ©2016 Association for Computational Linguistics

Semeval's English-Spanish crosslingual STS task.

2   Related Work

The weighted matrix factorization model we extend was first proposed in (Guo and Diab, 2012) to learn distributed vector representations for words in the monolingual space. The GloVe algorithm proposed (Pennington et al., 2014) is also a weighted matrix factorization method, but it includes additional word-specific bias terms and uses a different weighting scheme.

As mentioned above, we extend the WMF model proposed in (Guo and Diab, 2012) to bilingual and multilingual settings by forcing the two monolingual components to use a shared factor. (Shi et al., 2015) proposes a similar approach for learning bilingual embeddings. They extend GloVe (Pennington et al., 2014) to the bilingual case using a matrix of bilingual co-occurrence counts with word alignments in addition to the monolingual components. This model is similar in spirit to our model, but it has a different objective function that incorporates cross-lingual co-occurrence statistics or word alignments.

3   Proposed Approach

3.1   Background: Weighted Matrix Factorization (WMF)

In the WMF model proposed in (Guo and Diab, 2012), a large corpus is represented as an $m \times n$ matrix X, where each X_{ij} cell is the tf-idf weight of word i in sentence j. This sparse matrix is then factorized into a $k \times m$ matrix P and a $k \times n$ matrix Q, such that $X = P^T Q$. The factorization results in k-dimensional representations for words and sentences: the columns in P are latent k-dimensional representations for words, and the columns in Q are latent k-dimensional representations for the training sentences.

The values of P and Q can be calculated by minimizing the following weighted loss function:[1]

$$C = \sum_{i,j} W_{ij}(P_i^T Q_j - X_{ij})^2 + \lambda(\|P\|^2 + \|Q\|^2) \quad (1)$$

where λ is a regularization parameter to avoid overfitting, and W is an $m \times n$ weight matrix. The

weights reflect the confidence levels associated with the reconstruction errors of the corresponding items in X. A small weight is assigned to all missing words, $\{X_{ij} \in X | X_{ij} = 0\}$, to reflect some appropriate level of uncertainty:

$$W_{i,j} = \begin{cases} 1, & \text{if } X_{i,j} \neq 0 \\ w_m, & \text{if } X_{i,j} = 0 \end{cases}$$

where $w_m << 1$; In other words, we assign minimal confidence that each word in the vocabulary could legitimately appear in any given sentence, while the confidence level is highest for observed words.

By fixing P, the cost function becomes quadratic in Q and the global minimum is achieved using the matrix Q_{min} that satisfies $C'(Q_{min}) = 0$. The jth column in Q_{min} is calculated as follows:

$$Q_j = (PW^j P^T + \lambda I)^{-1} PW^j X_j \quad (2)$$

where W^j is a diagonal matrix with coefficients W_{ij} in row/column j (the jth column of W).

Similarly, the vectors in P_{min} are calculated by fixing Q and minimizing the cost function $P(Q)$:

$$P_i = (QW^i Q^T + \lambda I)^{-1} QW^i X^T_{i} \quad (3)$$

where W^i is a diagonal matrix with coefficients W_{ij} in row/column i (the ith row of W).

Thus, alternating least squares (ALS) is used to minimize $C(P,Q)$ by iteratively fixing P to calculate Q, then fixing Q to calculate P using equations (2) and (3).[2]

To generate vector representations for additional sentences after training, P is fixed and Q is calculated for the new sentences using equation (2). In other words, we calculate the representations that minimize the loss function (1), which is quadratic when P is fixed.

3.2   Cross-lingual WMF

Here we describe our proposed extension of the WMF model for learning bilingual semantic representations. Given a parallel corpus of n sentence pairs, we generate an $m \times n$ tf-idf matrix X for language 1 sentences, and an $l \times n$ tf-idf matrix Y for

---

[1] Single subscripts refer to column vectors in all equations.

[2] Details on similar calculations and speedup recommendations are found in (Hu et al., 2008).

language 2 sentences, where m and l are the number of words in the vocabulary of each language. The learning objective of the bilingual WMF model is to factorize both X and Y into two language-specific factors and one shared factor. More precisely, the desired factorization would result in a $k \times m$ matrix P, a $k \times l$ matrix A, and a $k \times n$ matrix Q, such that $X = P^T Q$ and $Y = A^T Q$. To achieve these bilingual objectives, we define two methods for calculating the loss function for both languages as detailed below: A global bilingual loss function (b-WMF), and a monolingual loss function with an explicit shared factor (x-WMF).

3.2.1 b-WMF: Bilingual Loss Function

We define a global loss function for both languages as follows:

$$C=\sum_{i,j} W_{ij}(P_i^T Q_j - X_{ij})^2 + \sum_{d,j} U_{dj}(A_d^T Q_j - Y_{dj})^2$$
$$+\lambda(\|P\|^2 + \|Q\|^2 + \|A\|^2) \quad (4)$$

where U is the weight matrix for Y, defined similar to W.

This objective function is convex if we fix two of the factor matrices and minimize with respect to the remaining factor. Alternating least squares can be used to estimate the factors iteratively using the following three equations:

$$Q_j = (PW^j P^T + AU^j A^T + \lambda I)^{-1}(PW^j X_j + AU^j Y_j)$$
$$P_i = (QW^i Q^T + \lambda I)^{-1} QW^i X^T{}_i$$
$$A_d = (QU^d Q^T + \lambda I)^{-1} QU^d Y^T{}_d$$
$$(5)$$

To generate vector representations for additional sentences in either language, the language-specific factors P and A are fixed, and the semantic vectors Q_j are calculated using equation (2) for language 1 and equation (6) for language 2.

$$Q_j = (AU^j A^T + \lambda I)^{-1} AU^j Y_j \quad (6)$$

In other words, the two models are independent once the training is complete, but the resultant representations are expected to reflect shared semantic components.

3.2.2 x-WMF: Monolingual Loss Functions

Alternatively, we can define two loss functions with a shared factor:

$$C_1 = \sum_{i,j} W_{ij}(P_i^T Q_j - X_{ij})^2 + \lambda(\|P\|^2 + \|Q\|^2)$$
$$C_2 = \sum_{d,j} U_{dj}(A_d^T Q_j - Y_{dj})^2 + \lambda(\|A\|^2 + \|Q\|^2)$$
$$(7)$$

Minimizing C_1 and C_2 separately is equivalent to training two separate monolingual models. To achieve the bilingual objective, we only train C_1 as a monolingual model, and then we use the learned factors P to find A. If we assume that the compositional representations generated by P are optimal, then we can use it to fix Q in C_2, and the loss function becomes quadratic in A; all we have to do is find the values of A that minimize C_2. Given a parallel corpus and word representations P, we calculate Q using equation (2), then calculate A using equation (5).

The training procedure is carried out as follows:

1. Independently train a monolingual WMF model for a pivot language.

2. Using a parallel corpus and the trained word representations P for the pivot language, generate sentence representations Q using equation (2)

3. Using the same parallel corpus, and fixing Q as calculated in step 2, calculate word representations A for the second language using equation (5).

Note that we only use the alternating least squares (ALS) algorithm for training the pivot model; the parameters of the second model, A, are calculated deterministically in one step. This method can be readily extended to more than two languages. Using one trained monolingual model, we can quickly learn representations for any number of languages using sentence-aligned data.

4 Empirical Evaluation

4.1 Data

Monolingual Data: For the monolingual English model, the training set consists of 700K sentences derived from various resources. We extract and combine the following sets: a random set of 150K sentences from LDC's English Gigaword fifth edition (Parker et al., 2011), a random set of 150K sentences from the English Wikipedia[3], the Brown Corpus (Francis, 1964), Wordnet (Miller, 1995) and Wiktionary[4] definitions appended with examples.

Bilingual Data: We extract training data for the bilingual models from WMT13 (Macháček and Bojar, 2013) sentence-aligned parallel corpora, specifically version 7 of the EuroParl parallel corpus (Koehn, 2005), the multiUN parallel corpus (Eisele and Chen, 2010), and news commentary data. We train the bilingual model using a sample of 1M sentence pairs from these datasets.

All sentences in our data are tokenized and stemmed, and number sequences are replaced with a special token as a normalization step. We use the Stanford CoreNLP toolkit (Manning et al., 2014) for English preprocessing, and Treetagger tools (Schmid, 1995) for Spanish. Words that appear less than 5 times in the training set are discarded from the vocabulary.

4.2 Parameter Settings

We train our bilingual b-WMF models strictly using the bilingual parallel data. On the other hand, we train the English pivot model used in x-WMF strictly using the English monolingual data, while the parallel corpora are only used for training the Spanish component of the x-WMF models. For the b-WMF models and the English monolingual model, we run the ALS algorithm for 20 iterations. We use the following parameters for all models: k=100, $w_m = 0.01$ and $\lambda = 20$.[5]

---

[3]http://en.wikipedia.org

[4]http://www.wiktionary.org

[5]These parameters are tuned empirically and we found these values to be robust across models.

Model	News	Multi Source	Mean
b-WMF	0.83	0.72	0.78
x-WMF	0.87	0.73	0.80
UWB	0.91	0.82	0.86

Table 1: Cross-lingual STS EN-SP Test results using Pearson Correlation Coefficient.

4.3 Cross-lingual Semantic Textual Similarity

Semantic Textual Similarity (STS) is a measure of the degree of similarity between two sentences. STS scores range from 0 to 5, where higher values indicate closer semantic content. In the crosslingual STS test sets, the sentences can either be English or Spanish. We use the TextCat (Cavnar and Trenkle, 1994) tool to identify the languages before processing.

Using the b-WMF and x-WMF cross-lingual models, we generate sentence vectors for the given pairs, then we calculate the cosine similarity between each pair. Since most of the output is positive, and negative values are generally very close to zero, we round up negative similarity values to 0.

Table 1 shows the results on the test data of Semeval 2016 EN-ES cross-lingual STS shared task. The evaluation metric is the Pearson Correlation Coefficient. The x-WMF models performs slightly better than b-WMF in this task, and we achieve rank 4 in the official STS semeval evaluation. We also show the results of the official first rank system UWB.

5 Discussion and Conclusions

We proposed a new unsupervised approach for generating cross-lingual semantic representations for variable-length sequences using a weighted matrix factorization model. The models successfully learned cross-lingual compositional representations as evident in the high correlation scores in the crosslingual STS task.

Learning a monolingual WMF model involves optimizing a non-convex loss function, but the loss function becomes quadratic once we fix one of the factors. As a result, learning any additional languages becomes trivial once we fix the sentence representations using a pivot model. The model naturally extends to several languages since the additional factors are calculated deterministically. Moreover, the model is simple and robust as we learned good representations using relatively small parallel datasets and without parameter optimization.

References

Yoshua Bengio, Réjean Ducharme, Pascal Vincent, and Christian Janvin. 2003. A neural probabilistic language model. *J. Mach. Learn. Res.*, 3:1137–1155, March.

Giovanni Cavallanti, Nicol Cesa-Bianchi, and Claudio Gentile. 2010. Linear algorithms for online multitask classification. *Journal of Machine Learning Research*, 11:2901–2934.

William B. Cavnar and John M. Trenkle. 1994. N-gram-based text categorization. In *In Proceedings of SDAIR-94, 3rd Annual Symposium on Document Analysis and Information Retrieval*, pages 161–175.

Ronan Collobert and Jason Weston. 2008. A unified architecture for natural language processing: Deep neural networks with multitask learning. In *Proceedings of the 25th International Conference on Machine Learning*, ICML '08, pages 160–167, New York, NY, USA. ACM.

Jocelyn Coulmance, Jean-Marc Marty, Guillaume Wenzek, and Amine Benhalloum. 2015. Trans-gram, fast crosslingual word embeddings. *Proceedings of the 2015 Conference on Empirical Methods in Natural Language Processing*, pages 1109–1113.

Andreas Eisele and Yu Chen. 2010. Multiun: A multilingual corpus from united nation documents. In Daniel Tapias, Mike Rosner, Stelios Piperidis, Jan Odjik, Joseph Mariani, Bente Maegaard, Khalid Choukri, and Nicoletta Calzolari (Conference Chair), editors, *Proceedings of the Seventh conference on International Language Resources and Evaluation*, pages 2868–2872. European Language Resources Association (ELRA), 5.

W. Nelson Francis. 1964. A standard sample of present-day english for use with digital computers. *Report to the U.S. Office of Education on Cooperative Research Project No. E-007.*

Weiwei Guo and Mona Diab. 2012. Modeling sentences in the latent space. In *Proceedings of the 50th Annual Meeting of the Association for Computational Linguistics: Long Papers - Volume 1*, ACL '12, pages 864–872, Stroudsburg, PA, USA. Association for Computational Linguistics.

Yifan Hu, Yehuda Koren, and Chris Volinsky. 2008. Collaborative filtering for implicit feedback datasets. In *Proceedings of the 2008 Eighth IEEE International Conference on Data Mining*, ICDM '08, pages 263–272, Washington, DC, USA. IEEE Computer Society.

Alexandre Klementieva, Ivan Titov, , and Binod Bhattarai. 2012. Inducing crosslingual distributed representations of words. *COLING.*

Philipp Koehn. 2005. Europarl: A Parallel Corpus for Statistical Machine Translation. In *Conference Proceedings: the tenth Machine Translation Summit*, pages 79–86, Phuket, Thailand. AAMT, AAMT.

Quoc Le and Tomas Mikolov. 2014. Distributed representations of sentences and documents. In Tony Jebara and Eric P. Xing, editors, *Proceedings of the 31st International Conference on Machine Learning (ICML-14)*, pages 1188–1196. JMLR Workshop and Conference Proceedings.

Matouš Macháček and Ondřej Bojar. 2013. Results of the WMT13 metrics shared task. In *Proceedings of the Eighth Workshop on Statistical Machine Translation*, pages 45–51, Sofia, Bulgaria, August. Association for Computational Linguistics.

Christopher D. Manning, Mihai Surdeanu, John Bauer, Jenny Finkel, Steven J. Bethard, and David McClosky. 2014. The Stanford CoreNLP natural language processing toolkit. In *Association for Computational Linguistics (ACL) System Demonstrations*, pages 55–60.

Tomas Mikolov, Quoc V. Le, and Ilya Sutskever. 2013. Exploiting similarities among languages for machine translation. *CoRR.*

George A. Miller. 1995. Wordnet: A lexical database for english. *Commun. ACM*, 38(11):39–41, November.

Robert Parker, David Graff, Junbo Kong, Ke Chen, and Kazuaki Maeda. 2011. English gigaword fifth edition ldc2011t07. *Wen download file.*

Jeffrey Pennington, Richard Socher, and Christopher D. Manning. 2014. Glove: Global vectors for word representation. In *Proceedings of the 2014 Conference on Empirical Methods in Natural Language Processing (EMNLP 2014)*, pages 1532–1543.

Hieu Pham, Thang Luong, and Christopher Manning. 2015. Learning distributed representations for multilingual text sequences. *NAACL.*

Helmut Schmid. 1995. Treetagger— a language independent part-of-speech tagger. *Institut für Maschinelle Sprachverarbeitung, Universität Stuttgart*, 43:28.

Tianze Shi, Zhiyuan Liu, Yang Liu, and Maosong Sun. 2015. Learning cross-lingual word embeddings via matrix co-factorization. In *Proceedings of the 53rd Annual Meeting of the Association for Computational Linguistics and the 7th International Joint Conference on Natural Language Processing (Volume 2: Short Papers)*, pages 567–572, Beijing, China, July. Association for Computational Linguistics.

Richard Socher, John Bauer, Christopher D. Manning, and Andrew Y. Ng. 2013. Parsing With Compositional Vector Grammars. In *ACL.*

CNRC at SemEval-2016 Task 1: Experiments in Crosslingual Semantic Textual Similarity

Chi-kiu Lo   **Cyril Goutte**   **Michel Simard**

National Research Council Canada

Multilingual Text Processing

1200 Montreal Road, Ottawa, Ontario K1A 0R6, Canada

`FirstName.LastName@nrc.ca`

Abstract

We describe the systems entered by the National Research Council Canada in the SemEval-2016 Task1: Crosslingual Semantic Textual Similarity. We tried two approaches: One computes a true crosslingual similarity based on features extracted from lexical semantics and shallow semantic structures of the source and target fragments, combined using a linear model. The other approach relies on Statistical Machine Translation, followed by a monolingual semantic similarity, relying again on syntactic and semantic features. We report our experiments using trial data, as well as official final results on the evaluation data.

1 Introduction

The SemEval-2016 Semantic Textual Similarity (STS) evaluation (task1) introduced a crosslingual track. Given a Spanish-English bilingual fragment pair, the goal is to compute the degree of equivalence between them. This offers additional challenges compared to the "STS Core" track, where both fragments are in the same language (English or Spanish in 2014-15). The crosslingual track requires potentially to detect which fragment is in which language, perform further language processing accordingly, and estimate lexical and semantic similarities across languages.

In our work, we investigated two approaches. In the first approach, we try to build a true crosslingual similarity based on a number of features computed from both fragments. One of these features projects Spanish words into an English embedding space in order to compute similarities in that space. Other features compute various kinds of syntactic and semantic overlap between the fragments. These features are combined in a linear model estimated on the trial data, and combined with an isotonic regression (de Leeuw et al., 2009) layer in order to account for non-linearity in the scores.

The second approach uses a Statistical Machine Translation system to map Spanish fragments to English, then relies on a monolingual semantic similarity between the translated fragment and the English fragment. Various monolingual similarity features, using embeddings, syntactic and semantic information, are computed and combined again using a linear model followed by an isotonic regression layer.

In the next section, we describe the two approaches and their components: SMT system, crosslingual and monolingual feature extraction, and the output layer fitting the features to the semantic similarity scores. We then describe the corpora used to fit the features to the output similarity score, and make various modeling choices (Section 3). We present our experimental results on the trial and test data in Section 4.

2 System description

We describe our two approaches: the direct crosslingual similarity using embedding mapping (`EMAP` run) and the use of Machine Translation followed by a monolingual semantic similarity (`MT1` and `MT2`).

2.1 Crosslingual Embedding Mapping

Feature Extraction: We evaluate the semantic similarity of the given text based on two levels: lex-

Proceedings of SemEval-2016, pages 668–673,

San Diego, California, June 16-17, 2016. ©2016 Association for Computational Linguistics

ical semantics and shallow semantic structure.

One of the trivial ways to evaluate the crosslingual lexical similarity is using the alignment probability of an alignment model trained with a large-scale parallel corpus.[1] However, the alignment model does not evaluate the meaning similarity of words as well as the vector space model which is explicitly trained to evaluate semantic similarity. We therefore propose to combine the two models: given a Spanish word, we first look up in the alignment model for a list of the most probable (5-best) aligned English word (the *mapping* step); we then evaluate the lexical similarity of each entry in the 5-best list against the target English word using a word embeddings model. In our experiments, we used pretrained `word2vec` (Mikolov et al., 2013) embeddings.[2] The resulting crosslingual lexical similarity of the targeted pair of Spanish and English words is the highest similarity between the 5 mapped words and the target English word. We then reconstruct the semantic phrasal similarity by averaging the English-idf-weighted crosslingual embeddings mapped lexical similarity according to the 1-1 maximal matching alignment of the lexicons in the two phrases.

In addition to the flat lexical semantic feature, we use XMEANT (Lo et al., 2014), the crosslingual semantic frame based machine translation evaluation metric, for generating shallow structural semantic features. We use MATE (Björkelund et al., 2009) for Spanish shallow semantic parsing and SENNA (Collobert et al., 2011) for English shallow semantic parsing. In evaluating machine translation quality, the confusion of semantic roles is a major source of errors due to reordering. However, in evaluating STS, confusion of semantic roles is less frequent while missing information in one of the test fragments is more frequent. This motivates a further simplification of the 12 semantic role types (Lo et al., 2014) into 5 semantic role types: action, agent, patient, beneficiary and others. The same phrasal semantic similarity function mentioned above is used for evaluating the role fillers similarity, instead of the ITG-constrained crosslingual phrasal similarity function (Lo et al., 2014).

As a result, for each pair of the test sentences,

Feature	Description
1	Embedding-based phrasal similarity
2	XMEANT score
3,4	p,r for semantic role: action
5,6	p,r for semantic role: agent
7,8	p,r for semantic role: patient
9,10	p,r for semantic role: beneficiary
11,12	p,r for semantic role: others

Table 1: Features used by the cross-lingual and monolingual semantic similarity. p,r stands for precision and recall.

we extracted 12 features (Table 1). The first feature is the simple phrasal similarity by considering the whole string of the testing sentences as one phrase. The second feature is the XMEANT score. The remaining 10 features are the precision and recall of the 5 semantic role types used in XMEANT.

Fitted Output Layer: Most of the extracted features are correlated with the gold standard semantic similarity score, by capturing various aspects of the similarity. In order to combine these features, we estimate a linear combination by fitting a least mean squares linear regression on the trial data gold standard similarity score.[3] Although it may be desirable to combine features in a non linear way, the amount of available annotated data severely limits our capacity to estimate non-linear models. We improve the modeling slightly by fitting a non-linear transformation of the estimated score produced by the linear combination, with the constraint that the transformation preserves the ordering of scores. This is done through isotonic regression, using the efficient implementation available in R (de Leeuw et al., 2009). In order to avoid overfitting to the limited number of training example, we use a 10-fold cross-validation estimator on the trial data to select the appropriate features and check the performance of the isotonic regression layer.

2.2 MT + Monolingual Similarity

Statistical Machine Translation. All Spanish text was translated to English using an SMT system based on *Portage*, the NRC's phrase-based SMT technology (Larkin et al., 2010). The system was

---

[1]Part of the MT system described in Section 2.2.

[2]`https://code.google.com/archive/p/word2vec/` [3]We use the `glm` function in R.

trained using standard resources – Europarl, Common Crawl (CC) and News & Commentary (NC) – totaling approximately 110M words in each language. Phrase extraction was done by aligning the corpora at the word level using HMM, IBM2 and IBM4 models, using the union of phrases extracted from these separate alignments for the phrase table, with a maximum phrase length of 7 tokens. Phrase pairs were filtered so that the top 30 translations for each source phrase were retained. The following feature functions are used in the log-linear model: three 5-gram language models with Kneser-Ney smoothing (Kneser and Ney, 1995), i.e. one for each of Europarl, CC and NC data, combined linearly (Foster and Kuhn, 2007) to best fit NC data; lexical estimates of the forward and backward translation probabilities obtained either by relative frequencies or using the method of (Zens and Ney, 2004); lexicalized distortion (Tillmann, 2004; Koehn et al., 2005); and word count. The parameters of the log-linear model were tuned by optimizing BLEU on the development set using the batch variant of MIRA (Cherry and Foster, 2012). Decoding uses the cube-pruning algorithm of (Huang and Chiang, 2007) with a 7-word distortion limit.

For any given input in Spanish, the SMT system produces the translation that is most likely with regard to its own training data; that translation may be arbitrarily distant from the English sentence to which it will be compared in the STS task. These arbitrary surface differences may complicate the task of measuring semantic similarity. To alleviate this problem, we bias the MT system to produce a translation that is as close as possible on the surface to the English sentence. This is done by means of log-linear model features that aim at maximizing n-gram precision between the MT output and the English sentence. The relative weights of these features are set to maximize BLEU on the trial data. This optimization is performed separately from that of the other features, using a simple grid-search approach. Systems MT1 and MT2 are the top-ranking systems in this regard: MT1 uses unigram/bigram/trigram weights 16/4/1, while MT2 uses 16/2/2.

Feature Extraction. The features extracted in this run are essentially the same as those in the crosslingual approach, except that the lexical semantic similarity is now directly evaluated using the monolingual word embeddings model. Similarly, the structural semantic similarity is now evaluated using MEANT (Lo et al., 2015) instead of XMEANT, and the semantic role similarity features are obtained by evaluating the semantic parses in the same languages.

Fitted Output Layer. This output layer is essentially the same as the one in the crosslingual approach, but estimated on the monolingual features. One key advantage here is that we rely on a monolingual semantic similarity. We can then fit the monolingual models on English trial and test data from previous STS tasks. We combine the 2012 to 2014 development and test sets totaling 10,662 examples, instead of the 103 trial bilingual pairs available for the crosslingual task.

3 Textual Similarity Data

Monolingual. In order to estimate parameters of the monolingual similarity, we use 10,662 English pairs from the 2012 to 2014 development and test sets. We test this similarity on the 2015 test data, comprising 3000 examples in 5 different test sets.

Crosslingual. We use the 103 Spanish-English pairs provided as trial data for the crosslingual task for two purposes. We estimate the crosslingual similarity output layer, and we compute performance estimates for all our runs. In order to tune the output layer (in particular to select the relevant features), we compute an unbiased estimator of the prediction performance using cross-validation on the data used for fitting (103 examples in crosslingual, 10,662 in monolingual).

4 Experimental results

4.1 Results on trial data

For the crosslingual embedding mapping (EMAP run), the only gold standard data available is the 103 trial set pairs. In order to get an unbiased estimate of the performance, we compute a 10-fold cross-validation estimator. We use it to select the best subset of features. Figure 1 shows that the choice of features has a large impact, with estimated performance ranging from 0.64 (for all features) to 0.71 with the four features with highest correlation with the gold

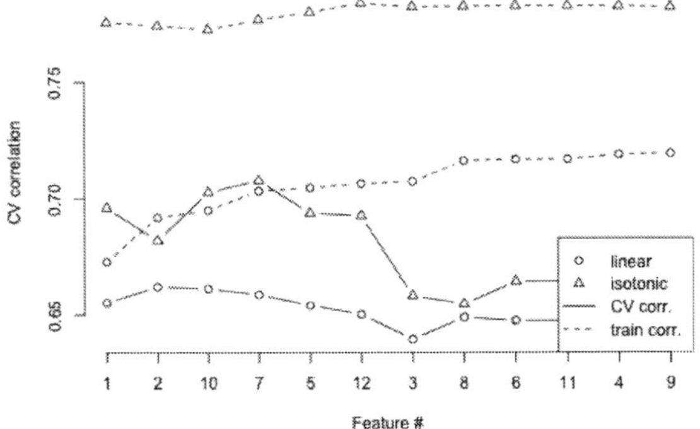

Figure 1: Cross-validated correlation when adding new features, ranked by individual correlation with the gold standard. The optimal CV estimate (solid+triangle curve) is obtained with four features (1, 2, 7 and 10).

	Top1	Linear	Isotonic
EMAP	.674	.659*	.708*
MT1	.714	.723	.731
MT2	.713	.720	.727

Table 2: Estimated results on the trial data (* estimates from 10-fold cross-validation).

Run	News (301)	MultiSource (294)	Mean
MT1	0.876	0.646	0.762
MT2	0.878	0.631	0.756
EMAP	0.719	0.411	0.567

Table 3: Official evaluation results for our three runs.

standard. These four features are: the crosslingual similarity score, the XMEANT score and two semantic role features. The cross-validated correlation for the linear model and isotonic regression are 0.659 and 0.708, respectively (Table 2). For our submitted run EMAP, we re-estimated the linear mode and isotonic regression on all 103 trial examples and used those models to estimate scores on the two test sets (301 and 2973 examples, respectively).

For the MT1 and MT2 runs, the monolingual similarity is trained on the available monolingual STS data from 2012 to 2014. In order to test the resulting similarity, we apply it to the 2015 test data, and obtain an average correlation of .713 on the five test sets, significantly below the best performing system at the 2015 task (.801 average). We also apply the monolingual STS to the trial data after forced decoding and feature extraction and obtain an estimated trial correlation of .727–.731 (Table 2).

4.2 Test results

Test results computed by the organizers are shown in Table 3. Average test results and results on the News part are significantly higher than estimated on the trial data. A large difference is not unexpected considering the test data was clearly very different from the trial data. The average fragment length is 3-4 times larger on News than on trial, for example. We can conjecture that the higher performance on the News test set may actually be due to the longer fragments providing more information to estimate the similarity. On the Multisource test set, on the other hand, all our runs perform poorly. We also note that the performance of the EMAP run is much worse, relative to the MT runs, than could be anticipated from the trial data performance (Table 2). We analyse these differences below.

4.3 Analysis

MT vs EMAP: As noted above, performance of EMAP was disappointing on the test set, and the gap with MT runs much larger than expected from the trial data. Two main reasons can explain this. First, MT uses monolingual word embeddings directly, and second, we could use 10,662 monolingual pairs with reference STS scores to fit and tune the feature combination model. By contrast, for lack of cross-lingual embedding vectors, the EMAP run had to rely on word alignment to map Spanish words to English embeddings, and the feature combination model could only use 103 cross-lingual pairs with reference STS scores.

MultiSource performance is lower than performance on the News part of the test set for almost all systems involved in the evaluation (FBK being the notable exception). The difference is particularly pronounced for our runs: our MT runs are only .035 below the top run on News, which is likely not significant on 301 examples;[4] our performance on MultiSource, on the other hand, is .17 to .40 below the top runs. Given that this gap is especially pronounced for our systems, we can not rule out formatting errors of inconsistencies on our side. Further investigation will be needed to clarify this.

Running Time: One attractive feature of both our approaches is that they rely on shallow semantic features which are easy and fast to obtain using semantic role labeling. The MT runs rely on a SMT system which is expensive to train, but this can be done offline. Once trained, producing translations is of the order of ten sentences per second. The linear feature combination model is also fast to train and apply, requiring a single dot product between the 12 features and a similarly-sized parameter vector.[5]

5 Conclusion

We described the systems used for the submissions of the National Research Council Canada to the crosslingual semantic textual similarity task. We experimented with two approaches. The first estimates a true crosslingual similarity combining lexical semantics and shallow semantic structure. The second uses Machine Translation in combination with a monolingual semantic similarity. We found that the latter outperforms the former. We conjecture that this may be due to the very limited amount of crosslingual data available. By contrast, there are very large corpora available for training a reasonably efficient MT system, and we can rely on a lot of data from previous STS tasks to build a monolingual semantic similarity. Test results indicate that our approach performs relatively well on the News test set, but suffers on the Multisource test set. In addition, the crosslingual approach performs much worse on average on the test data than estimated on the limited trial data. This suggests that it is hard to build a competitive, truly crosslingual approach from little reference data, when it is possible to rely on thousands to millions of examples to build a SMT+monolingual similarity pipeline.

---

[4]Assessing statistical significance would require access to the predictions of the best run.

[5]Prediction for the 301+2973 test examples takes 24ms.

References

Anders Björkelund, Love Hafdell, and Pierre Nugues. 2009. Multilingual semantic role labeling. In *Proceedings of the Thirteenth Conference on Computational Natural Language Learning: Shared Task*, pages 43–48. Association for Computational Linguistics.

Colin Cherry and George Foster. 2012. Batch Tuning Strategies for Statistical Machine Translation. In *Proceedings of the 2012 Conference of the North American Chapter of the Association for Computational Linguistics: Human Language Technologies*, pages 427–436, Montréal, Canada, June.

Ronan Collobert, Jason Weston, Léon Bottou, Michael Karlen, Koray Kavukcuoglu, and Pavel P. Kuksa. 2011. Natural language processing (almost) from scratch. *CoRR*, abs/1103.0398.

Jan de Leeuw, Kurt Hornik, and Patrick Mair. 2009. Isotone optimization in r: Pool-adjacent-violators algorithm (pava) and active set methods. *Journal of Statistical Software*, 32(1):1–24.

George Foster and Roland Kuhn. 2007. Mixture-Model Adaptation for SMT. In *Proceedings of the 45th Annual Meeting of the Association of Computational Linguistics*, pages 128–135, Prague, Czech Republic, June.

Liang Huang and David Chiang. 2007. Forest Rescoring: Faster Decoding with Integrated Language Models. In *Proceedings of the 45th Annual Meeting of the Association of Computational Linguistics*, pages 144–151, Prague, Czech Republic, June. Association for Computational Linguistics.

Reinhard Kneser and Hermann Ney. 1995. Improved backing-off for m-gram language modeling. In *Acoustics, Speech, and Signal Processing, 1995. ICASSP-95., 1995 International Conference on*, volume 1, pages 181–184. IEEE.

Philipp Koehn, Amittai Axelrod, Alexandra Birch Mayne, Chris Callison-Burch, Miles Osborne, and David Talbot. 2005. Edinburgh System Description for the 2005 IWSLT Speech Translation Evaluation. In *Proceedings of IWSLT-2005*, Pittsburgh, PA.

S. Larkin, B. Chen, G. Foster, U. Germann, E. Joanis, H. Johnson, and R. Kuhn. 2010. Lessons from NRC's Portage system at WMT 2010. In *the Joint Fifth Workshop on Statistical Machine Translation and Metrics-MATR*, pages 127–132.

Chi-kiu Lo, Meriem Beloucif, Markus Saers, and Dekai Wu. 2014. XMEANT: Better semantic MT evaluation without reference translations. In *52nd Annual Meeting of the Association for Computational Linguistics (ACL 2014)*, pages 765–771.

Chi-kiu Lo, Philipp C Dowling, and Dekai Wu. 2015. Improving evaluation and optimization of MT systems against MEANT. In *10th Workshop on Statistical Machine Translation (WMT 2015)*, page 434.

Tomas Mikolov, Ilya Sutskever, Kai Chen, Greg Corrado, and Jeffrey Dean. 2013. Distributed representations of words and phrases and their compositionality. *CoRR*, abs/1310.4546.

Christoph Tillmann. 2004. A Unigram Orientation Model for Statistical Machine Translation. In Daniel Marcu Susan Dumais and Salim Roukos, editors, *HLT-NAACL 2004: Short Papers*, pages 101–104, Boston, Massachusetts, USA, May 2 - May 7. Association for Computational Linguistics.

Richard Zens and Hermann Ney. 2004. Improvements in Phrase-Based Statistical Machine Translation. In Daniel Marcu Susan Dumais and Salim Roukos, editors, *HLT-NAACL 2004: Main Proceedings*, pages 257–264, Boston, Massachusetts, USA, May 2 - May 7. Association for Computational Linguistics.

MayoNLP at SemEval-2016 Task 1: Semantic Textual Similarity based on Lexical Semantic Net and Deep Learning Semantic Model

Naveed Afzal [*], Yanshan Wang[*], Hongfang Liu
Department of Health Sciences Research
Mayo Clinic, Rochester, MN
{Afzal.Naveed, Wang.Yanshan, Liu.Hongfang}@mayo.edu

Abstract

Given two sentences, participating systems assign a semantic similarity score in the range of 0-5. We applied two different techniques for the task: one is based on lexical semantic net (corresponding to run 1) and the other is based on deep learning semantic model (corresponding to run 2). We also combined these two runs linearly (corresponding to run 3). Our results indicate that the two techniques perform comparably while the combination outperforms the individual ones on four out of five datasets, namely *answer-answer, headlines, plagiarism,* and *question-question,* and on the overall weighted mean of STS 2016 and 2015 datasets.

1 Introduction

There is a growing need for an effective method to compute semantic similarity between two text snippets. Many natural language processing (NLP) applications can benefit from effective semantic textual similarity (STS) techniques such as paraphrase recognition (Dolan et al., 2004), textual summarization (Aliguliyev, 2009), automatic machine translation evaluation (Kauchak and Barzilay, 2006), tweets search (Sriram et al., 2010), and student answer assessment (Rus and Lintean, 2012; Niraula et al., 2013).

The SemEval STS task series (Agirre et al., 2012; Agirre et al., 2013; Agirre et al., 2014; Agirre et al., 2015) have provided a vital platform for this task by making available a huge collection of sentence pairs with manual annotation for each sentence pair. The objective of the task is to compute semantic similarity between a pair of sentences in the range [0, 5], and where 0 indicates no similarity and 5 indicates complete similarity.

The approaches for computing semantic similarity between text snippets can be broadly classified into three approaches: information retrieval vector space model (e.g. Meadow, 1992; Sahami and Heilman, 2006), text alignment on the basis of semantic equivalence (e.g. Mihalcea et al., 2006) and machine learning models on the basis of lexical, syntactic and semantic features (e.g. Saric et al., 2012).

In this paper, we describe two techniques for the SemEval 2016 English STS task: the first one adopts the text alignment technique on the basis of semantic equivalence by leveraging a semantic net and corpus statistics; and the second technique is a machine learning models where we utilize a deep learning semantic model.

In the following, we present our techniques in detail and provide the evaluation results of our systems on STS 2016 and 2015 datasets. Conclusions and future directions are also provided.

2 System Description

This section describes the data and our systems in detail.

2.1 Data

There are five datasets in the SemEval 2016 English STS task: *answer-answer, headlines, plagiarism, postediting* and *question-question* collected form different sources in this year's English STS task. Each dataset consists of sentence pairs with human-assigned similarity score in the range of 0-5.

* indicates joint first author's

Proceedings of SemEval-2016, pages 674–679,
San Diego, California, June 16-17, 2016. ©2016 Association for Computational Linguistics

2.2 Preprocessing

In the preprocessing phase, for each sentence, we use regular expressions in Python[1] to find and replace all text contractions with their respective complete text. For example, "wouldn't" is replaced with "would not" All the URLs, email addresses, and parenthetical expressions (in the cases for abbreviation definition) are removed. Then we normalize common abbreviations with their expansions by using synonyms of those abbreviations in a lexical database, WordNet[2], (for example, "USA" is replaced with "United States of America") and a manually crafted abbreviation list based on STS 2015 data (for example, "govt" is replaced with "government", "1.6lb" and "5m" are replaced with "1.6 pound" and "5 million"). Moreover, we replace all the negations such as 'not present' with 'absent' using WordNet antonyms, and correct misspelled words using an English dictionary provided by a dictionary module pyenchant[3] in Python. Stopwords are removed for datasets *headlines, plagiarism* and *postediting,* according to the Stanford stopwords list. For the datasets of *answer-answer* and *question-question,* stopwords are not removed since many pairs only contain stopwords, such as sentence pair *"Can you do this?" "You can do it, too", etc.* Finally, the remaining words in each sentence are lemmatized to their base forms using the lemmatizer provided by natural language toolkit (NLTK) in Python. The entire preprocessing workflow is illustrated in Figure 1.

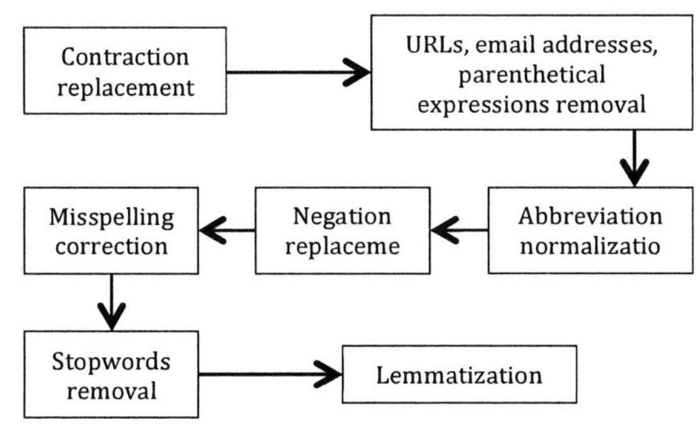

Figure 1: Workflow of preprocessing

[1] https://www.python.org/
[2] https://wordnet.princeton.edu/
[3] https://pypi.python.org/pypi/pyenchant/

2.3 Run 1

Our first technique (official run 1), illustrated in Figure 2, is inspired by the work of Li et al. (Li et al., 2006) where the textual similarity computation is based on both syntactic and semantic similarities.

The main differences of our technique comparing to theirs include preprocessing and synsets selection. We select the most similar pair of synsets from WordNet instead of just picking the first noun synset for each word.

After the preprocessing phase, the textual similarity is derived from the combination of semantic (semantic vectors) and syntactic information (syntactic vectors) present in a sentence pair as detailed in the following.

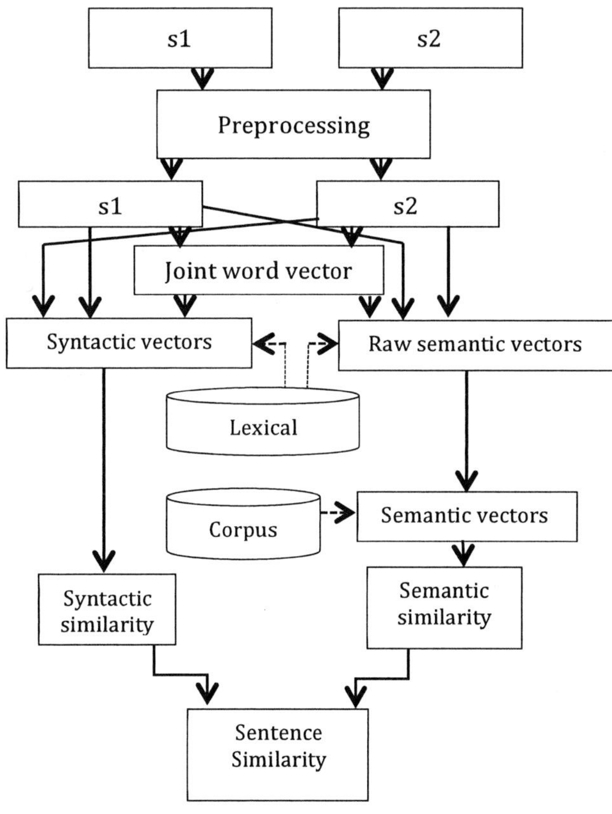

Figure 2: System architecture (Run 1)

We first form a joint word vector (JWV) by collecting unique words that occur in the sentence pair. The semantic similarity is computed by comparing the semantic meaning hidden in the sentences and the syntactic similarity is computed according to the word order in the two sentences.

To compute semantic similarity of the pair, each sentence is mapped to a vector: if ith word in JWV is present in the sentence, we assign a value 1 to the ith entry; otherwise, we calculate the semantic similarity score between the ith word and each word in the sentence and choose the highest score to be the ith entry with the aid of the WordNet using the following strategy.

For every two words in the WordNet, we use the path length and depth of two words in the WordNet to calculate ith entry:

$$s\left(w_i, w_j\right) = e^{\alpha l} \cdot \frac{e^{\beta h} - e^{-\beta h}}{e^{\beta h} + e^{-\beta h}},$$

where l is the length of the shortest path between words w_i and w_j, h returns a measure of depth in the WordNet, and α, β are constants (0.2 and 0.45 respectively in our experiment). α and β are dependent on the knowledge base and for WordNet we have used the values for alpha and beta found to be best by Li et al., (2003). The reason behind using depth along with the length of the shortest path is that in the WordNet, words at upper layers are more generic comparing to words at lower layers. If $s\left(w_i, w_j\right)$ is greater than a threshold (0.2 in our experiment) then we set the value to be the score, otherwise we set the value to 0.

The similarity score of the ith entry is then normalized by multiplying information content score of the ith word. The information content of word is defined by (Resnik, 1995):

$$I(w) = 1 - \frac{\log(n + 1)}{\log (N + 1)},$$

where N is the total number of words in the Brown corpus, n is the frequency of the word w in the corpus. According to this definition, the information content score is between 0 and 1. In our system, the information content of each word was computed using the Brown corpus (Francis and Kučera, 1979).

The semantic similarity is then defined as S_{sem}, which is the cosine similarity between the two vectors corresponding to the sentence pair.

Similarly, to compute syntactic similarity, each sentence is mapped to a syntactic vector. The dimension of the syntactic vector is identical as the size of the JWV. If the ith word in the JWV occurs at the jth position in the sentence, then the value of the ith entry in the vector is j. If the ith word does not exist in the sentence, the value of the ith entry is the position of the most similar word obtained from WordNet using $s\left(w1, w2\right)$. Different from the form of semantic similarity measure, syntactic similarity should take word order information into consideration. Therefore, the syntactic similarity is defined by:

$$s_{syn} = 1 - \frac{|o_1 - o_2|}{|o_1 + o_2|},$$

where o_1 and o_2 represent syntactic vector for sentences s1 and s2 respectively. From the definition of syntactic vector, we see that it contains the basic structural information of a sentence and measure the word order similarity between two sentences.

Since semantic similarity represents the lexical similarity while syntactic similarity contains information about the orders between words, both contribute in conveying the similarity of the sentences. Therefore, the final sentence pair similarity is defined by combining semantic similarity and syntactic similarity, i.e.

$$S\left(s_1, s_2\right) = \Omega\, s_{sem} + (1 - \Omega)s_{syn}$$

Since syntax plays a subordinate role for semantic processing of text we used Ω ($\Omega = 0.85$) in the final similarity.

2.4   Run 2

Our second system (run 2) is built upon a Deep Structured Semantic Model (DSSM) proposed by Huang et al., (2013). DSSM is a deep learning based technique that is proposed for semantic understanding of textual data. It maps short textual strings, such as sentences, to feature vectors in a low-dimensional semantic space. Then the vector representations are utilized for document retrieval by comparing the similarity between documents and queries. DSSM is reported to outperform other semantic models applying to document retrieval (Huang et al., 2013). However, the performance has not been evaluated to measure the degree of similarity in the underlying semantics of paired snippets of text.

DSSM uses the typical deep neural network (DNN) architecture to represent a sentence (document) in the semantic vector space. Unlike other DNN where bag-of-word (BoW) term vectors are used as input, DSSM employ a novel word hashing method to reduce the dimensionality of the BoW vectors. Specifically, each word (for example, 'girl') is attached with a word starting mark and an ending mark (i.e., '#girl#') and split into letter trigrams (i.e., #gi, gir, irl, rl#). By doing so, the dimension is reduced to the number of trigrams, which is 3073 in our system. Then, each word representing by a vector of letter trigrams is used as input to the DNN.

The layers in DNN consists of three parts, namely, word hashing layer, hidden layers, and top layer, where the layer functions are:

$$l_1 = W_1 x,$$
$$l_i = f(W_i l_{i-1} + b_i), i = 2, \ldots, N - 1,$$

and

$$y = f(W_N l_{N-1} + b_N),$$

where x is the input term vector, y the output vector, $l_i, i = 1, \ldots, N - 1$ the hidden layers, W_i the ith weight matrix, b_i the ith bias, and $f(\cdot)$ the *tanh* activation function. The feature vectors generated by the word-hashing layer are projected through the hidden layers, and formed as semantic feature vectors in the top layer.

After obtaining the semantic feature vectors for each paired snippets of text, cosine similarity is utilized to measure the semantic similarity between the pair. Since the elements of semantic vector are nonnegative and the range of cosine similarity is [0, 1], we used the simplest linear transformation to map the range into [0, 5].

Regarding the implementation of DSSM, we exploit the Sent2Vec tool. Sent2Vec provides DSSM and convolutional DSSM (C-DSSM) (Gao et al., 2014; Shen et al., 2014). Based on our experiments on the SemEval 2015 English STS datasets, the performance of DSSM is slightly superior to C-DSSM without statistical significance. Therefore, DSSM is utilized in the official run 2. In the DSSM, we used one hidden layer with 1000 hidden nodes in the neural networks. A larger number of hidden layers or hidden nodes may be applied though we used the simplest one due to the computational complexity.

2.5 Run 3

Our run 3 is a linear combination of run 1 and run 2, i.e.,

$$S_{run3} = \alpha \cdot S_{run1} + \beta \cdot S_{run2}$$

where the equal weights are assigned to run 1 and run 2, i.e., $\alpha = \beta = 0.5$

3 Evaluation

We submitted 3 runs at SemEval 2016 English STS task based on the Section 2.

Dataset	Run 1	Run 2	Run 3	Best
answer-answer (254 pairs)	0.58873	0.57739	0.61426	0.69235
headlines (249 pairs)	0.73458	0.75061	0.77263	0.82749
plagiarism (230 pairs)	0.76887	0.80068	0.80500	0.84138
postediting (244 pairs)	0.85020	0.82857	0.84840	0.86690
question-question (209 pairs)	0.69306	0.73035	0.74705	0.74705
Weighted Mean	0.72646	0.73569	0.75607	0.77807

Table 1: Official Results of evaluation on STS 2016 data

Table 1 shows the performance of each official run. This is reported as the Pearson correlation between the scores produced by our systems and the human annotations. The last row shows the value of weighted mean that is the sum of all datasets correlation scores. The weight assigned to a dataset is proportional to its number of pairs.

Our run 1 performed better than run 2 on the following datasets: *answer-answer* and *postediting* while run 2 performed better than run 1 on the following datasets: *headlines, plagiarism* and *question-question*. Our run 3 that is a linear combination of run 1 and run 2 is the best performing system in terms of weighted mean.

3.1 Performance on STS 2015 Data

We also applied our systems on the SemEval 2015 English STS task data. Table 2 shows the evaluation results on STS 2015 data. We can observe that mean run 3 outperforms run 1 and run 2 in terms of overall weighted mean. However, for *answers-students* dataset the performance of run 1 is better than other runs, and for datasets *belief* and *images* run 2 perform better than other two runs. The reason might be that run 1 considers word order information, which is crucial information when describing math or chemistry problems in dataset *answers-students*.

Dataset	Run 1	Run 2	Run 3	Best
answers-forums (375 pairs)	0.7049	0.6660	0.7246	0.7390
answers-students (750 pairs)	0.7422	0.6770	0.7416	0.7879
belief (375 pairs)	0.7287	0.7439	0.7389	0.7717
headlines (750 pairs)	0.7630	0.7749	0.7776	0.8417
images (750 pairs)	0.8198	0.8576	0.8367	0.8713
Weighted Mean	0.7604	0.7536	0.7719	0.8015

Table 2: Results of evaluation on STS 2015 data

4 Conclusions and Future Work

In this paper, we presented three systems for measuring the semantic similarity between two sentences. The systems will be released in the future at GitHub.[1] Our systems give promising results on both English STS datasets 2015 and 2016. Our first system relies on a lexical database and corpus statistics. A lexical database represents common human knowledge about a natural language while a corpus reflects the actual usage of language and words. Our second system utilizes deep learning semantic model while our third system is an ensemble of system 1 and 2.

In our future work, we would like to investigate the different contributions of syntactic similarity and semantic similarity in run 1 and improve the performance of run 1 by adding new corpora to increase the impact of corpus statistics. For the second system, we would like to test whether adding additional hidden layers into the deep neural net improves the performance. Currently, our third system is a linear combination of system 1 and 2 by using heuristic weights since no training data were given in the task and we concerned about over-fitting if the data from previous years were used to train our system. In the future we would like to investigate whether the performance could be improved by applying supervised or unsupervised machine learning algorithms to calculate the optimal weights based on the previous data sets. Moreover, we would like to extend our systems into the biomedical domain with the use of biomedical lexical databases and biomedical corpus.

Acknowledgments

Our participation of STS is partially supported by the grants received from NIGMS R01 GM102282 and from National Library of Medicine R01LM11934.

References

Bharath Sriram, Dave Fuhry, Engin Demir, Hakan Ferhatosmanoglu, and Murat Demirbas. 2010. Short text classification in twitter to improve information filtering. In Proceedings of the 33rd international ACM SIGIR conference on Research and development in information retrieval, pages 841–842.

Bill Dolan, Chris Quirk, and Chris Brockett. 2004. Unsupervised construction of large paraphrase corpora: exploiting massively parallel news sources. In Proceedings of the 20th international conference on Computational Linguistics , COLING '04.

C.T. Meadow. 1992. Text Information Retrieval Systems. Academic Press, Inc.

David Kauchak and Regina Barzilay. 2006. Paraphrasing for automatic evaluation. In HLT-NAACL '06 , pages 455–462.

Eneko Agirre, Daniel Cer, Mona Diab, and Aitor Gonzalez-Agirre. 2012. SemEval-2012 task 6: A Pilot on Semantic Textual Similarity. In Proceedings of the First Joint Conference on Lexical and

---

[1] https://github.com/naveedafzal/MayoClinic_SemEval_2016_Task-1

Computational Semantics, Volume 2: Proceedings of the Sixth International Workshop on Semantic Evaluation, SemEval '12, pages 385-393, Montreal, Canada.

Eneko Agirre, Daniel Cer, Mona Diab, Aitor Gonzalez-Agirre, and Weiwei Guo. 2013. *SEM 2013 Shared Task: Semantic Textual Similarity. In Proceedings of the Second Joint Conference on Lexical and Computational Semantics, *SEM '13, pages 32-43, Atlanta, Georgia, USA.

Eneko Agirre, Carmen Banea, Claire Cardie, Daniel Cer, Mona Diab, Aitor Gonzalez-Agirre, Weiwei Guo, Rada Mihalcea, German Rigau, and Janyce Wiebe. 2014. SemEval-2014 Task 10: Multilingual Semantic Textual Similarity. In Proceedings of the 8th International Workshop on Semantic Evaluation, SemEval '14, pages 81-91, Dublin, Ireland.

Eneko Agirre, Carmen Banea, Claire Cardie, Daniel Cer, Mona Diab, Aitor Gonzalez-Agirre,Weiwei Guo, I˜nigo Lopez-Gazpio, Montse Maritxalar, Rada Mihalcea, German Rigau, Larraitz Uria, and Janyce Wiebe. 2015. SemEval-2015 Task 2: Semantic Textual Similarity, English, Spanish and Pilot on Interpretability. In Proceedings of the 9th International Workshop on Semantic Evaluation, SemEval '15, Denver, Colorado, USA.

Frane Saric, G. Glavas, M. Karan, J. Snajder, B.D. Basic. 2012. TakeLab: systems for measuring semantic text similarity. In Proceedings of 1st Joint Conference on Lexical and Computational Semantics, pp. 441–448.

Jianfeng Gao, Patrick Pantel, Michael Gamon, Xiaodong He, Li Deng, Yelong Shen. 2014. Modeling interestingness with deep neural networks. In Proceedings of the Conference on Empirical Methods in Natural Language Processing, Doha, Qatar.

M Sahami, T.D Heilman. 2006. A web-based kernel function for measuring the similarity of short text snippets. In Proceedings of 15th International Conference on World Wide Web, pp. 377–386.

Nobal B. Niraula, Rajendra Banjade, Dan Stefanescu, and Vasile Rus. 2013. Experiments with semantic similarity measures based on lda and lsa. In Statistical Language and Speech Processing , pages 188–199. Springer.

Philip Resnik. 1995. Using information content to evaluate semantic similarity in a taxonomy. In Proceedings of the 14th international joint conference on Artificial intelligence, pages 448-453, Montreal, Quebec, Canada.

Po-Sen Huang, Xiaodong He, Jianfeng Gao, Li Deng. 2013. Learning deep structured semantic models for web search using clickthrough data. In Proceedings of the 22nd ACM international conference on Conference on information & knowledge management, pages. 2333-2338, San Francisco, CA, USA.

Rada Mihalcea, Courtney Corley, Carlo Strapparava. 2006. Corpus-based and knowledge-based measures of text semantic similarity. In Proceedings of 21st National Conference on Artificial Intelligence, pp. 775–780.

Ramiz M Aliguliyev. 2009. A new sentence similarity measure and sentence based extractive technique for automatic text summarization. Expert Systems with Applications, 36(4):7764–7772.

Vasile Rus and Mihai Lintean. 2012. A comparison of greedy and optimal assessment of natural language student input using word-to-word similarity metrics. In Proceedings of the Seventh Workshop on Building Educational Applications Using NLP, pages 157–162.

W. N. Francis and H. Kučera. 1964, 1971, 1979. A standard corpus of present-day edited American English, for use with digital computers (Brown). Compiled by Brown University. Providence, Rhode Island.

Yelong Shen, Xiaodong He, Jianfeng Gao, Li Deng, Gregoire Mesnil. 2014. A latent semantic model with convolutional-pooling structure for information retrieval. In Proceedings of the 23rd ACM International Conference on Information and Knowledge Management, Shanghai, China.

Yuhua. Li, Zuhair. A. Bandar, David McLean. 2003. An approach for measuring semantic similarity using multiple information sources. IEEE Trans. Knowledge and Data Engineering, vol. 15, no.4, pages 871-882.

Yuhua. Li, David McLean, Zuhair. A. Bandar, James D. O'Shea, and Keeley. Crockett. 2006. Sentence similarity based on semantic nets and corpus statistics. IEEE Trans. Knowledge and Data Engineering, vol. 18, no. 8, pages 1138–1150.

AUTHOR INDEX

AUTHOR INDEX

AUTHOR INDEX

AUTHOR INDEX

Association for Computational Linguistics
209 N. Eighth Street
Stroudsburg, Pennsylvania 18360

ISBN 978-1-5108-2607-6

10th International Workshop on Semantic Evaluation (SemEval 2016)

San Diego, California, USA
16 - 17 June 2016

Volume 2 of 2

10th International Workshop on Semantic Evaluation (SemEval 2016)

San Diego, California, USA
16 - 17 June 2016

Volume 2 of 2

ISBN: 978-1-5108-2607-6

SemEval-2016

The 10th International Workshop on Semantic Evaluation

Proceedings of the Workshop

June 16-17, 2016
San Diego, California, USA

Welcome to SemEval-2016

The Semantic Evaluation (SemEval) series of workshops focuses on the evaluation and comparison of systems that can analyse diverse semantic phenomena in text with the aim of extending the current state of the art in semantic analysis and creating high quality annotated datasets in a range of increasingly challenging problems in natural language semantics. SemEval provides an exciting forum for researchers to propose challenging research problems in semantics and to build systems/techniques to address such research problems.

SemEval-2016 is the tenth workshop in the series of International Workshops on Semantic Evaluation Exercises. The first three workshops, SensEval-1 (1998), SensEval-2 (2001), and SensEval-3 (2004), focused on word sense disambiguation, each time growing in the number of languages offered, in the number of tasks, and also in the number of participating teams. In 2007, the workshop was renamed to SemEval, and the subsequent SemEval workshops evolved to include semantic analysis tasks beyond word sense disambiguation. In 2012, SemEval turned into a yearly event. It currently runs every year, but on a two-year cycle, i.e., the tasks for SemEval-2016 were proposed in 2015.

SemEval-2016 was co-located with the 2016 Conference of the North American Chapter of the Association for Computational Linguistics: Human Language Technologies (NAACL-HLT'2016) in San Diego, California. It included the following 14 shared tasks organized in five tracks:

- Text Similarity and Question Answering Track

    - Task 1: Semantic Textual Similarity: A Unified Framework for Semantic Processing and Evaluation
    - Task 2: Interpretable Semantic Textual Similarity
    - Task 3: Community Question Answering

- Sentiment Analysis Track

    - Task 4: Sentiment Analysis in Twitter
    - Task 5: Aspect-Based Sentiment Analysis
    - Task 6: Detecting Stance in Tweets
    - Task 7: Determining Sentiment Intensity of English and Arabic Phrases

- Semantic Parsing Track

    - Task 8: Meaning Representation Parsing
    - Task 9: Chinese Semantic Dependency Parsing

- Semantic Analysis Track

    - Task 10: Detecting Minimal Semantic Units and their Meanings
    - Task 11: Complex Word Identification
    - Task 12: Clinical TempEval

- Semantic Taxonomy Track

    – Task 13: TExEval-2 – Taxonomy Extraction
    – Task 14: Semantic Taxonomy Enrichment

This volume contains both Task Description papers that describe each of the above tasks and System Description papers that describe the systems that participated in the above tasks. A total of 14 task description papers and 198 system description papers are included in this volume.

We are grateful to all task organisers as well as the large number of participants whose enthusiastic participation has made SemEval once again a successful event. We are thankful to the task organisers who also served as area chairs, and to task organisers and participants who reviewed paper submissions. These proceedings have greatly benefited from their detailed and thoughtful feedback. We also thank the NAACL 2016 conference organizers for their support. Finally, we most gratefully acknowledge the support of our sponsor, the ACL Special Interest Group on the Lexicon (SIGLEX).

The SemEval-2016 organizers,
Steven Bethard, Daniel Cer, Marine Carpuat, David Jurgens, Preslav Nakov and Torsten Zesch

Organizers:

Steven Bethard, University of Alabama at Birmingham
Daniel Cer, Google
Marine Carpuat, University of Maryland
David Jurgens, Stanford University
Preslav Nakov, Qatar Computing Research Institute, HBKU
Torsten Zesch, University of Duisburg-Essen

Steering Committee:

Eneko Agirre, University of the Basque Country (UPV/EHU)
Niranjan Balasubramanian, Stony Brook University
Timothy Baldwin, The University of Melbourne
Svetla Boytcheva, Bulgarian Academy of Sciences, IICT
Tommaso Caselli, VU Amsterdam
Kevin Cohen, Computational Bioscience Program, U. Colorado School of Medicine
Gerard de Melo, Tsinghua University
Mona Diab, GWU
Anna Divoli, Pingar Research
Nadir Durrani, QCRI
Judith Eckle-Kohler, Technische Universität Darmstadt
Stefano Faralli, University of Mannheim
Dimitris Galanis, Institute for Language and Speech Processing, Athena Research Center
Francisco Guzmán, Qatar Computing Research Institute
Nizar Habash, New York University Abu Dhabi
Valia Kordoni, Humboldt-Universität zu Berlin
Zornitsa Kozareva, Yahoo!
Maria Liakata, University of Warwick
Wei Lu, Singapore University of Technology and Design
Lluís Màrquez, Qatar Computing Research Institute
Vivi Nastase, University of Heidelberg
Ani Nenkova, University of Pennsylvania
Stephan Oepen, Universitetet i Oslo
Sebastian Padó, Stuttgart University
Haris Papageorgiou, Institute for Language and Speech Processing ILSP/ ATHENA R.C.
Marius Pasca, Google
Ted Pedersen, University of Minnesota, Duluth
Marco Pennacchiotti, eBay Inc
Mohammad Taher Pilehvar, University of Cambridge
Sameer Pradhan, cemantix.org
Carlos Ramisch, LIF, Aix-Marseille Université
Alan Ritter, The Ohio State University
Sara Rosenthal, Columbia University

Irene Russo, ILC CNR
Derek Ruths, McGill University
Hassan Sajjad, Qatar Computing Research Institute
Fabrizio Sebastiani Qatar Computing Research Institute,
Veselin Stoyanov, Facebook
Carlo Strapparava, FBK-irst
Mihai Surdeanu, University of Arizona
Stan Szpakowicz, EECS, University of Ottawa
Irina Temnikova, Qatar Computing Research Institute, HBKU
Tony Veale, University College Dublin
Marilyn Walker, University of California Santa Cruz
Diarmuid Ó Séaghdha, Apple

Table of Contents

Workshop Program

16 Jun 2016

09:00–09:15   **Welcome**

Opening Remarks
SemEval organizers

09:15–10:30   **Sentiment Analysis**

09:15–09:30   *SemEval-2016 Task 4: Sentiment Analysis in Twitter*
Preslav Nakov, Alan Ritter, Sara Rosenthal, Fabrizio Sebastiani and Veselin Stoyanov

09:30–09:45   *SemEval-2016 Task 5: Aspect Based Sentiment Analysis*
Maria Pontiki, Dimitris Galanis, Haris Papageorgiou, Ion Androutsopoulos, Suresh Manandhar, Mohammad AL-Smadi, Mahmoud Al-Ayyoub, Yanyan Zhao, Bing Qin, Orphee De Clercq, Veronique Hoste, Marianna Apidianaki, Xavier Tannier, Natalia Loukachevitch, Evgeniy Kotelnikov, Núria Bel, Salud María Jiménez-Zafra and Gülşen Eryiğit

09:45–10:00   *SemEval-2016 Task 6: Detecting Stance in Tweets*
Saif Mohammad, Svetlana Kiritchenko, Parinaz Sobhani, Xiaodan Zhu and Colin Cherry

10:00–10:15   *SemEval-2016 Task 7: Determining Sentiment Intensity of English and Arabic Phrases*
Svetlana Kiritchenko, Saif Mohammad and Mohammad Salameh

10:15–10:30   *Sentiment Analysis Discussion*
Task Organizers

10:30–11:00   ***Coffee Break***

11:00–12:30   Poster Session: Sentiment Analysis

CUFE at SemEval-2016 Task 4: A Gated Recurrent Model for Sentiment Classification
Mahmoud Nabil, Amir Atyia and Mohamed Aly

QCRI at SemEval-2016 Task 4: Probabilistic Methods for Binary and Ordinal Quantification
Giovanni Da San Martino, Wei Gao and Fabrizio Sebastiani

SteM at SemEval-2016 Task 4: Applying Active Learning to Improve Sentiment Classification
Stefan Räbiger, Mishal Kazmi, Yücel Saygın, Peter Schüller and Myra Spiliopoulou

I2RNTU at SemEval-2016 Task 4: Classifier Fusion for Polarity Classification in Twitter
Zhengchen Zhang, Chen Zhang, wu fuxiang, Dongyan Huang, Weisi Lin and Minghui Dong

LyS at SemEval-2016 Task 4: Exploiting Neural Activation Values for Twitter Sentiment Classification and Quantification
David Vilares, Yerai Doval, Miguel A. Alonso and Carlos Gómez-Rodríguez

TwiSE at SemEval-2016 Task 4: Twitter Sentiment Classification
Georgios Balikas and Massih-Reza Amini

ISTI-CNR at SemEval-2016 Task 4: Quantification on an Ordinal Scale
Andrea Esuli

aueb.twitter.sentiment at SemEval-2016 Task 4: A Weighted Ensemble of SVMs for Twitter Sentiment Analysis
Stavros Giorgis, Apostolos Rousas, John Pavlopoulos, Prodromos Malakasiotis and Ion Androutsopoulos

thecerealkiller at SemEval-2016 Task 4: Deep Learning based System for Classifying Sentiment of Tweets on Two Point Scale
Vikrant Yadav

12:30–02:00 *Lunch*

02:00–03:30   Textual Similarity, Question Answering and Semantic Analysis

02:00–02:15   *SemEval-2016 Task 1: Semantic Textual Similarity, Monolingual and Cross-Lingual Evaluation*
Eneko Agirre, Carmen Banea, Daniel Cer, Mona Diab, Aitor Gonzalez-Agirre, Rada Mihalcea, German Rigau and Janyce Wiebe

02:15–02:30   *SemEval-2016 Task 2: Interpretable Semantic Textual Similarity*
Eneko Agirre, Aitor Gonzalez-Agirre, Inigo Lopez-Gazpio, Montse Maritxalar, German Rigau and Larraitz Uria

02:30–02:45   *SemEval-2016 Task 3: Community Question Answering*
Preslav Nakov, Lluís Màrquez, Alessandro Moschitti, Walid Magdy, Hamdy Mubarak, abed Alhakim Freihat, Jim Glass and Bilal Randeree

02:45–03:00   *SemEval-2016 Task 10: Detecting Minimal Semantic Units and their Meanings (DiMSUM)*
Nathan Schneider, Dirk Hovy, Anders Johannsen and Marine Carpuat

03:00–03:15   *SemEval 2016 Task 11: Complex Word Identification*
Gustavo Paetzold and Lucia Specia

03:15–03:30   *Textual Similarity and Question Answering Discussion*
Task Organizers

03:30–04:00   *Coffee Break*

04:00–05:30   Poster Session: Textual Similarity, and Question Answering

FBK HLT-MT at SemEval-2016 Task 1: Cross-lingual Semantic Similarity Measurement Using Quality Estimation Features and Compositional Bilingual Word Embeddings
Duygu Ataman, Jose G. C. De Souza, Marco Turchi and Matteo Negri

VRep at SemEval-2016 Task 1 and Task 2: A System for Interpretable Semantic Similarity
Sam Henry and Allison Sands

UTA DLNLP at SemEval-2016 Task 1: Semantic Textual Similarity: A Unified Framework for Semantic Processing and Evaluation
Peng Li and Heng Huang

UWB at SemEval-2016 Task 1: Semantic Textual Similarity using Lexical, Syntactic, and Semantic Information
Tomáš Brychcín and Lukáš Svoboda

HHU at SemEval-2016 Task 1: Multiple Approaches to Measuring Semantic Textual Similarity
Matthias Liebeck, Philipp Pollack, Pashutan Modaresi and Stefan Conrad

Samsung Poland NLP Team at SemEval-2016 Task 1: Necessity for diversity; combining recursive autoencoders, WordNet and ensemble methods to measure semantic similarity.
Barbara Rychalska, Katarzyna Pakulska, Krystyna Chodorowska, Wojciech Walczak and Piotr Andruszkiewicz

USFD at SemEval-2016 Task 1: Putting different State-of-the-Arts into a Box
Ahmet Aker, Frederic Blain, Andres Duque, Marina Fomicheva, Jurica Seva, Kashif Shah and Daniel Beck

NaCTeM at SemEval-2016 Task 1: Inferring sentence-level semantic similarity from an ensemble of complementary lexical and sentence-level features
Piotr Przybyła, Nhung T. H. Nguyen, Matthew Shardlow, Georgios Kontonatsios and Sophia Ananiadou

ECNU at SemEval-2016 Task 1: Leveraging Word Embedding From Macro and Micro Views to Boost Performance for Semantic Textual Similarity
Junfeng Tian and Man Lan

17 Jun 2016

09:00–10:30 **Perspectives**

09:00–09:30 *SemEval-2017 Preview*
SemEval organizers

09:30–10:30 ***Invited Talk***

10:30–11:00 ***Coffee Break***

11:00–12:30 **Semantic Analysis, Semantic Parsing and Semantic Taxonomy**

11:00–11:15 *SemEval-2016 Task 12: Clinical TempEval*
Steven Bethard, Guergana Savova, Wei-Te Chen, Leon Derczynski, James Pustejovsky and Marc Verhagen

11:15–11:30 *SemEval-2016 Task 8: Meaning Representation Parsing*
Jonathan May

11:30–11:45 *SemEval-2016 Task 9: Chinese Semantic Dependency Parsing*
Wanxiang Che, Yanqiu Shao, Ting Liu and Yu Ding

11:45–12:00 *SemEval-2016 Task 13: Taxonomy Extraction Evaluation (TExEval-2)*
Georgeta Bordea, Els Lefever and Paul Buitelaar

12:00–12:15 *SemEval-2016 Task 14: Semantic Taxonomy Enrichment*
David Jurgens and Mohammad Taher Pilehvar

12:30–02:00 ***Lunch***

02:00–03:30   Best Of SemEval

02:00–02:15   *UMD-TTIC-UW at SemEval-2016 Task 1: Attention-Based Multi-Perspective Convolutional Neural Networks for Textual Similarity Measurement*
Hua He, John Wieting, Kevin Gimpel, Jinfeng Rao and Jimmy Lin

02:15–02:30   *Inspire at SemEval-2016 Task 2: Interpretable Semantic Textual Similarity Alignment based on Answer Set Programming*
Mishal Kazmi and Peter Schüller

02:30–02:45   *KeLP at SemEval-2016 Task 3: Learning Semantic Relations between Questions and Answers*
Simone Filice, Danilo Croce, Alessandro Moschitti and Roberto Basili

02:45–03:00   *SwissCheese at SemEval-2016 Task 4: Sentiment Classification Using an Ensemble of Convolutional Neural Networks with Distant Supervision*
Jan Deriu, Maurice Gonzenbach, Fatih Uzdilli, Aurelien Lucchi, Valeria De Luca and Martin Jaggi

03:00–03:15   *IIT-TUDA at SemEval-2016 Task 5: Beyond Sentiment Lexicon: Combining Domain Dependency and Distributional Semantics Features for Aspect Based Sentiment Analysis*
Ayush Kumar, Sarah Kohail, Amit Kumar, Asif Ekbal and Chris Biemann

03:15–03:30   *LIMSI-COT at SemEval-2016 Task 12: Temporal relation identification using a pipeline of classifiers*
Julien Tourille, Olivier Ferret, Aurélie Névéol and Xavier Tannier

03:30–04:00   *Coffee Break*

04:00–05:30   Poster Session: Semantic Analysis, Parsing, and Taxonomy

RIGA at SemEval-2016 Task 8: Impact of Smatch Extensions and Character-Level Neural Translation on AMR Parsing Accuracy
Guntis Barzdins and Didzis Gosko

DynamicPower at SemEval-2016 Task 8: Processing syntactic parse trees with a Dynamic Semantics core
Alastair Butler

M2L at SemEval-2016 Task 8: AMR Parsing with Neural Networks
Yevgeniy Puzikov, Daisuke Kawahara and Sadao Kurohashi

ICL-HD at SemEval-2016 Task 8: Meaning Representation Parsing - Augmenting AMR Parsing with a Preposition Semantic Role Labeling Neural Network
Lauritz Brandt, David Grimm, Mengfei Zhou and Yannick Versley

UCL+Sheffield at SemEval-2016 Task 8: Imitation learning for AMR parsing with an alpha-bound
James Goodman, Andreas Vlachos and Jason Naradowsky

CAMR at SemEval-2016 Task 8: An Extended Transition-based AMR Parser
Chuan Wang, Sameer Pradhan, Xiaoman Pan, Heng Ji and Nianwen Xue

The Meaning Factory at SemEval-2016 Task 8: Producing AMRs with Boxer
Johannes Bjerva, Johan Bos and Hessel Haagsma

UofR at SemEval-2016 Task 8: Learning Synchronous Hyperedge Replacement Grammar for AMR Parsing
Xiaochang Peng and Daniel Gildea

CLIP@UMD at SemEval-2016 Task 8: Parser for Abstract Meaning Representation using Learning to Search
Sudha Rao, Yogarshi Vyas, Hal Daumé III and Philip Resnik

UoB-UK at SemEval-2016 Task 1: A Flexible and Extendable System for Semantic Text Similarity using Types, Surprise and Phrase Linking

Harish Tayyar Madabushi, Mark Buhagiar, Mark Lee
School of Computer Science,
University of Birmingham,
Birmingham, United Kingdom.
H.T.Madabushi@cs.bham.ac.uk, Buhagiar.Mark.A@gmail.com, M.G.Lee@cs.bham.ac.uk

Abstract

We present in this paper a system for measuring Semantic Text Similarity (STS) in English. We introduce three novel techniques: the use of *Types*, methods of linking phrases, and the use of a *Surprise Factor* to generate 8,370 similarity measures, which we then combine using Support Vector and Kernel Ridge Regression. Our system out performs the State of the Art in SemEval 2015, and our best performing run achieved a score of .7094 on the 2016 test set as a whole, and over 0.8 on the majority of the datasets. Additionally, the use of Surprise, Types and phrase linking is not limited to STS and can be used across various Natural Language Processing tasks, while our method of combining scores provides a flexible way of combining variously generated Similarity Scores.

1 Introduction and Motivation

The goal of Semantic Text Similarity (STS) is to find the degree of overlap in the meaning of two pieces of text. This ranges from text fragments that are exact semantic equivalents, to others that have no semantic relation. STS has a wide variety of applications, including text summarisation (Aliguliyev, 2009), machine translation (Kauchak and Barzilay, 2006), and search optimisation (Sriram et al., 2010).

The STS task, which has been set by the SemEval conference for the past number of years (Agirre et al., 2014; Agirre et al., 2015), requires that submitted systems assign a score between 0 (the sentences are on different topics) and 5 (the sentences mean exactly the same thing) that reflects how similar two sentences are.

Most systems that tackled SemEval's STS task in previous years have involved three main approaches: The first is text alignment, based on the content words' meaning (Sultan et al., 2015; Sultan et al., 2014b). The second represents text as vectors, which are used to find the similarity score using a vector similarity metric (such as cosine). Third, machine learning approaches are used to compute multiple lexical, semantic, and syntactic features to classify each sentence pair's similarity.

We make use of both text alignments and vector representations, while limiting comparisons to words of the same *Type* (Section 4.1), a novel concept we introduce in addition to methods of phrase linking (Section 4.2) and establishing common noun importance (Section 4.3). These, combined with several different weight combinations we pick for each word Type, provide us with *8,370* semantic relation measures (Section 5). The overall algorithm for generating the several similarity measures is presented in Algorithm 1. We choose a subset of these measures using methods detailed in Section 6.1, combine them with a limited set of features and use Support Vector Regression and Kernel Ridge Regression to generate a Similarity Score (Section 6.2).

Our approach also handles definitions separately from arbitrary sentences, as we observed that their structure is significantly different. Since the test data provided this year did not contain a definition data set, this paper focuses on our generic approach, with definition similarity discussed briefly in Section 7.

Proceedings of SemEval-2016, pages 680–685,
San Diego, California, June 16-17, 2016. ©2016 Association for Computational Linguistics

2   Preprocessing

Due to the varied nature of the input presented we perform various data cleaning operations. We start by expansion of common contractions (e.g. "isn't") and informal contractions (e.g. "howz", "couldve"). We then perform a spell check and hyphen removal, which are conditional, in the sense that a word is not modified unless the modified form appears in the other sentence. All remaining hyphens are replaced by spaces, a method different from those that previously handled hyphens (Han et al., 2013).

We also perform case correction, as has been done previously (Hänig et al., 2015), since we observe several instances wherein sentence capitalisation is not suitable for parsing (e.g. headlines and forums).

3   Similarity Measures

We use two measures, which are boosted based on different parameters described in Section 4.

3.1   Alignments

The first measure makes use of the aligner developed by Sultan et al. (2014a), which was used to achieve State of the Art results in 2014 and 2015 (Sultan et al., 2014b; Sultan et al., 2015).

Our use of the aligner disregards sequences thus making use of the aligner more as a synonym finder, with the additional power of the Paraphrase Database (PPDB) (Ganitkevitch et al., 2013).

3.2   Word Embeddings

Word embeddings provide a method of mapping words or phrases to vectors, whose cosine distance represents semantic similarity. They have proved to be powerful in many NLP tasks, and have been used by top ranking systems at SemEval STS (Sultan et al., 2015; Hänig et al., 2015). We use word2vec[1], with the model trained by Google on the Google News dataset, through its Python interface Gensim[2]. We make use of word2vec in two distinct ways. The first is by extracting the mean of the vector representation of each word in a Type and finding its cosine similarity between the two sentences. The second is by adding the word2vec similarity scores of words not aligned within the same Type. We also

provide the option of disregarding word pairs that have a score of less than 0.3, a method similar to that by Hänig et al. (2015).

4   Boosting Similarity

In this section, we detail the variations used to generate different similarity measures. These variations are not used simultaneously, but are instead combined as described in Algorithm 1 (Section 5), which iterates through all possible variations to generate a different similarity score associated with each combination.

4.1   Type Specific Comparison

Given a sentence pair, we calculate their similarity based only on how similar corresponding Parts-of-Speech (POS) are, a method previous systems have made use of, either implicitly (Kashyap et al., 2014; Sultan et al., 2015) or explicitly (Hänig et al., 2015).

We extend this idea by defining what we call word *Types*, which further subdivide each POS. A Type represents an abstract concept that several words can share. Consider the sentence pair "A man is sitting on a stool", "A boy is sitting on a chair". Although the words "man", "boy", "stool" and "chair" are all nouns, an effective strategy for comparing these sentences would be to compare the first two and the last two words independently, before then adding up their similarity. To achieve this we categorise words into different Types, which are then compared across sentences. In this case, such a categorisation might place the first two into the Type "Person" and the others into the category "Artifact". This problem could very easily extend to the problem of Word Sense Disambiguation, which we avoid by use of a heuristic.

We calculate the Type of a noun by the use of WordNet (Miller, 1995) hypernyms: W_1 is considered a hypernym of W_2 if $\forall e \in W_2$, e is an instance of W_1. We recursively find hypernyms until we reach a manually selected set of concepts (such as food.n.02). We manually combine sets of such concepts to define a Type. As a concrete example, we combine the WordNet concepts "communication.n.02", "food.n.02" and other similar concepts into the Type "thing_r1". As a single word can be part of several Types, based on the particular sense

---

[1]https://code.google.com/p/word2vec/

[2]https://radimrehurek.com/gensim/models/word2vec.html

of the word, we pick the most frequently occurring Type for each word.[3]

4.2 Phrase Linking

Consider sentences with the the phrases "Prime Minister" and "Prime Number". Although the word "Prime" is present in both sentences, the context in which it is being used makes this irrelevant. In this particular case, the semantic similarity of the sentences is dependent on the head of the phrase that the word "Prime" is contained in (i.e. "Minister" and "Number"). This is also the case with phrases that contain adjectives and adverbs.

We address this by finding phrases that consist of adjectives, adverbs and nouns, and varying the importance of the semantic similarity between words that are not the head of that phrase. The similarity of each word, that is part of such a phrase, but not the head of the phrase, is additionally weighted in three different ways: The first assigns a zero or one weight based on whether or not the head of the phrase is aligned, the second provides a weight based on the number of words, following this word, that are aligned in the phrase and the third simply ignores the phrase structure.

4.3 Noun Importance

Consider the following sentence pairs with relations assigned by human annotators: "A *boy* is playing a guitar.", "A *man* is playing a guitar.", rel: 3.2; and "A man is cutting up a *potato*.", "A man is cutting up *carrots*.", rel: 2.4. Although both pairs of sentences differ by exactly one noun, the first pair was considered to be more closely associated than the second. We associate this to what we call the "Surprise" and assign a value to this, which we call the "Surprise Factor".

Surprise is based on the work by Dunning (1993), who observed that the assumption of normality of data is invalid as "simple word counts made on a moderate-sized corpus show that words that have a frequency of less than one in 50,000 words make up about 20-30% of typical English language newswire reports. This 'rare' quarter of English includes many of the content-bearing words ..."

We define the Surprise Factor of a noun or phrase to be proportional to the number of Web Search Hits for that phrase or term, while inversely proportional to the Search Hits in the case of proper nouns. Intuitively this makes sense, as words that are more common will generate less Surprise, carry less information, and will also be more widely used on the Internet.

We incorporate this idea of Surprise by adding the option of additionally weighting nouns by the total number of Web Search Hits or Results[4]. We define, H_i to be the the number of Web Search Hits for the noun i, HT the total number of hits for all nouns $HT = \sum_{i=0}^{N} H_i$, N_i the fraction of the Search Hits that noun i captures $N_i = \frac{H_n}{HT}$, and NT the normalised total of all nouns (C) in a given sentence $NT = \sum_{i=0}^{C} N_i$. We define the Surprise of word i in terms of the above in Equation 1.

$$S_i = \frac{N_i}{NT} \qquad (1)$$

5 System Overview

Algorithm 1 provides an overview of the system we use to generate the various Similarity Scores, We call each combination that generates a score a "Method". We use thirty weights for Types[3], while providing the option of dividing the scores by the number of WordNet Synsets (UseSSToWeight), which captures any dilution due to a word's different senses. We also scale word2vec scores by different values. This gives us a total of 8,370 "Methods".

In calculating the similarity score, we capture the fraction of each Type that is aligned and scale it by the weight of that Type. This is captured in Equation 2 where $score_t$ represents the Similarity Score assigned to Type t by either of the measures detailed in Section 3, $count_t$ represents the number of words of Type t in *both* sentences, w_t the weight of Type t in the current iteration, and T is the total number of Types.

$$5 \times \left(\frac{\sum_{t=0}^{T} score_t \times w_t \times 2}{\sum_{t=0}^{T} count_t \times w_t} \right) \qquad (2)$$

---

[3]The termination concepts, corresponding Types, definitions for non-noun types, and Weights are provided online at: www.harishmadabushi.com/SemEval2016/Appendix.pdf

[4]We use the Bing Web Search API: http://www.bing.com/toolbox/bingsearchapi

```
Data: Sentence Pairs
Result: List of Similarity Scores
Initialise list of similarity scores "SimScores" to empty list;
for w in Type-Weights do
    for n in NounHandleMethod do
        for av in Adjective-AdverbHandleMethod do
            for UseSearchHits in [True,False] do
                if UseSearchHits == True then
                    Calculate Similarity Score (SS) using
                    Alignments;
                    Append SS to SimScores;
                    Continue;
                for UseSSToWeight in [True, False] do
                    Calculate Similarity Score (SS) using
                    Alignments;
                    Append SS to SimScores;
                for UseWeightCutOff in [True,False] do
                    for VectorCombineMethod in
                    [UseAlignments, UseMeanVector] do
                        for ScaleVortorSimBy in [ 6, 5, 4, 3, 2,
                        1, "log" ] do
                            Calculate Similarity Score (SS)
                            using Word Embeddings;
                            Append SS to SimScores;
Return SimScores (the list of similarity scores);
```

Algorithm 1: Calculating Semantic Similarity Scores

6 Combining Similarity Scores

As described above, we use variations to generate thousands of Similarity Scores, each of which we call a "Method". Each Method's performance varies depending on the input. In this section, we detail the process for combining these Methods, which is performed using either Support Vector Regression (SVR) or Kernel Ridge Regression (KRR).

6.1 Picking a Subset of Methods

We first select a subset of the Methods, which are then passed on to either the SVR or KRR model. To do this, each of our Methods is ranked using three metrics with respect to the training set: The first is by use of the Pearson Correlation (a criterion we call "Method"), the second is by the sum of the absolute error between Similarity Scores (a criterion we call "Error"). The third metric aggregates the the rankings from the two criterion described above, and we call this criterion "Combine". We select the top 50 methods using one of the three selection criterion.

6.2 Generating Similarity Scores

In addition to using scores from the chosen Methods, we add the following features to some of our submitted runs: a) a binary value to represent whether each of the sentences were case corrected, b) the length of each of the sentences, c) the number of contin-

uous aligned or unaligned sequences, d) the maximum and minimum lengths of continuous aligned or unaligned sequences, and e) a binary value to represent alignments that are non-sequential.

It should be noted that the specific Methods we choose for use in the SVR or KRR will depend on the training data picked. We found, by testing our system using several different combinations of training data, that the best results were achieved when our system was trained on the headlines data from the years 2015, 2014 and 2013. The method selection criterion, regression model and parameters used for each of the runs submitted are detailed in Table 1. Although some of the settings are very similar (e.g. run2), we noticed that these minor changes translated to significant differences in performance.

Run	Headlines		Other Datasets	
	Model:	KRR	Model:	SVR
	Features:	False	Features:	False
	Train:	Headlines	Train:	Headlines
Run1	Picked:	Combine	Picked:	Combine
	Kernel:	Poly	C:	100
	Alpha:	50	Epsilon:	0.05
			Gamma:	9e-05
	Model:	SVR	Model:	SVR
	Features	True	Features:	True
	Train:	Headlines	Train:	Headlines
Run2	Picked:	Method	Picked:	Method
	C:	100	C:	100
	Epsilon:	0.01	Epsilon:	0.05
	Gamma:	9e-05	Gamma:	9e-06
	Model:	SVR	Model:	SVR
	Features	True	Features:	True
	Train:	Headlines	Train:	Headlines
Run3	Picked:	Method	Picked:	Combine
	C:	100	C:	100
	Epsilon:	0.01	Epsilon:	0.01
	Gamma:	9e-05	Gamma:	9e-06

Table 1: Parameters and models used for each run. The row Features represents if features were used, Train represents the training data used, and Picked represents the selection criterion (Method, Error or Combine).

7 Finding Similarities between Definitions

In order to find similarities between definitions, we first identify the word that a definition is defining. We achieve this by use of OneLook's reverse dictionary search[5], which returns a number of candidate

---

[5]http://www.onelook.com/reverse-dictionary.shtml

words for a given definition. For each definition, the similarity of the top 10 candidates is then computed using Word2Vec and five similarity metrics provided by WordNet: Path distance, Leacock-Chodorow, Wu and Palmer, Jiang-Conrath and Lin. The final score is scaled between 0 and 5 and averaged across the 10 candidates returned by OneLook.

We found this method of calculating similarities between definitions to be very good at telling if two definitions refer to the same word, but not ideally suited for measuring *how* similar they are. As a consequence, we found that results were clustered around 0 and 5. The system produced a Pearson correlation of 0.69 on the SemEval 2014 definitions data set.

8 Results and Analysis

Dataset	Best	Run1	Run2	Run3
Mean	.77807	.70940	.70168	.70911
postediting	.86690	.81272	.80835	.81333
ques-ques	.74705	.56040	.47904	.56451
headlines	.82749	.81894	.82352	.81894
plagiarism	.84138	.82066	.82406	.81958
ans-ans	.69235	.52460	.55217	.52028

Table 2: Performance on the 2016 STS Test Set

We list the performance of our system in Table 2. Our system's poor performance on the ans-ans and ques-ques datasets can be attributed to our choice of training data, which, although well suited for previous years, was not well suited for these datasets.

However, our system produces State of the Art results on the 2015 Test Sets. A breakdown of each of the run's performance against the 2015 STS data set is provided in Table 3. We note that the results we have reported for previous State of Art for individual data sources are not the results from just the winning system but the State of Art across all Systems for that data source. Our system also achieves comparable results (0.7793) to that presented by Sultan et al. (2015) (0.779) on the 2014 STS dataset. The weighted mean reported by us does not include definitions as we decided to consider them independently.

Table 4 provides a comparison of our system against the previous State of the Art for the STS 2014 data set. The overall State of Art across all data sets was reported by Sultan et al. (2015) based

Source	St. of Art	Run1	Run2	Run3
Mean	0.8015	0.8086	**0.8147**	0.8130
ans-std	0.7879	0.7919	**0.7965**	0.7953
ans-for	**0.739**	0.7184	0.7137	0.7090
belief	0.7717	0.7703	**0.7811**	0.7752
headlines	0.8417	0.8508	**0.8532**	**0.8532**
images	**0.8713**	0.8448	0.8617	0.8615

Table 3: Performance on the 2015 STS Test Set.

Source	St. of Art	Run1	Run2	Run3
Mean	0.779	0.7714	**0.7793**	0.7790
de-forum	0.504	0.5435	0.5630	**0.5636**
de-news	**0.785**	0.7718	0.7774	0.7756
headlines	0.765	**0.8082**	0.8055	0.8055
images	0.834	0.8340	0.8492	**0.8496**
OnWN	0.875	–	–	–
tweet-n	**0.792**	0.7551	0.7569	0.7573

Table 4: Performance on the 2014 STS Test Set.

on their 2015 System.

9 Conclusion and Future Work

In this paper we have described the system we used for participation in the SemEval STS Monolingual Task which made use of Types, Phrase Linking, and a method of establishing common noun importance.

In the future, we intend to experiment with including features for each of the Methods during the training phase, other kinds of phrases, and different Type definitions. We also intend to use the STS data for learning the weights of different Types for use in other NLP applications.

We believe that Types have significant potential and intend to explore them in greater detail. Our immediate objectives will be in better defining types, re-categorising common noun Types based on clearer instructions to manual annotators, including finer definitions of Types for proper nouns using named entity recognition, and exploring methods of defining Types for verbs, adverbs and adjectives. We also intend to explore the use of Types in Question Classification and Question Answering.

Acknowledgments

This work was supported, in part, by the EPSRC, U.K., under grant number 1576491, and is also partially funded by the ENDEAVOUR Scholarships Scheme, which may be part-financed by the European Union - European Social Fund.

References

Eneko Agirre, Carmen Banea, Claire Cardie, Daniel Cer, Mona Diab, Aitor Gonzalez-Agirre, Weiwei Guo, Rada Mihalcea, German Rigau, and Janyce Wiebe. 2014. Semeval-2014 task 10: Multilingual semantic textual similarity. In *Proceedings of the 8th International Workshop on Semantic Evaluation (SemEval 2014)*, pages 81–91.

Eneko Agirre, Carmen Banea, et al. 2015. Semeval-2015 task 2: Semantic textual similarity, english, s-panish and pilot on interpretability. In *Proceedings of the 9th International Workshop on Semantic Evaluation (SemEval 2015), June*.

Ramiz M Aliguliyev. 2009. A new sentence similarity measure and sentence based extractive technique for automatic text summarization. *Expert Systems with Applications*, 36(4):7764–7772.

Ted Dunning. 1993. Accurate methods for the statistics of surprise and coincidence. *Comput. Linguist.*, 19(1):61–74, March.

Juri Ganitkevitch, Benjamin Van Durme, and Chris Callison-Burch. 2013. Ppdb: The paraphrase database. In *HLT-NAACL*, pages 758–764.

Lushan Han, Abhay L. Kashyap, Tim Finin, James Mayfield, and Jonathan Weese. 2013. Umbc_ebiquity-core: . In *Second Joint Conference on Lexical and Computational Semantics (*SEM), Volume 1: Proceedings of the Main Conference and the Shared Task: Semantic Textual Similarity*, pages 44–52, Atlanta, Georgia, USA, June. Association for Computational Linguistics.

Christian Hänig, Robert Remus, and Xose de la Puente. 2015. Exb themis: Extensive feature extraction from word alignments for semantic textual similarity. In *Proceedings of the 9th International Workshop on Semantic Evaluation (SemEval 2015)*, pages 264–268, Denver, Colorado, June. Association for Computational Linguistics.

Abhay Kashyap, Lushan Han, Roberto Yus, Jennifer Sleeman, Taneeya Satyapanich, Sunil Gandhi, and Tim Finin. 2014. Meerkat mafia: Multilingual and cross-level semantic textual similarity systems. In *Proceedings of the 8th International Workshop on Semantic Evaluation (SemEval 2014)*, pages 416–423, Dublin, Ireland, August. Association for Computational Linguistics and Dublin City University.

David Kauchak and Regina Barzilay. 2006. Paraphrasing for automatic evaluation. In *Proceedings of the main conference on Human Language Technology Conference of the North American Chapter of the Association of Computational Linguistics*, pages 455–462. Association for Computational Linguistics.

George A Miller. 1995. Wordnet: a lexical database for english. *Communications of the ACM*, 38(11):39–41.

Bharath Sriram, Dave Fuhry, Engin Demir, Hakan Ferhatosmanoglu, and Murat Demirbas. 2010. Short text classification in twitter to improve information filtering. In *Proceedings of the 33rd international ACM SIGIR conference on Research and development in information retrieval*, pages 841–842. ACM.

Md Arafat Sultan, Steven Bethard, and Tamara Sumner. 2014a. Back to basics for monolingual alignment: Exploiting word similarity and contextual evidence. *Transactions of the Association for Computational Linguistics*, 2:219–230.

Md Arafat Sultan, Steven Bethard, and Tamara Sumner. 2014b. DLS@CU: Sentence similarity from word alignment. In *Proceedings of the 8th International Workshop on Semantic Evaluation (SemEval 2014)*, pages 241–246, Dublin, Ireland, August. Association for Computational Linguistics and Dublin City University.

Md Arafat Sultan, Steven Bethard, and Tamara Sumner. 2015. DLS@CU: Sentence similarity from word alignment and semantic vector composition. In *Proceedings of the 9th International Workshop on Semantic Evaluation (SemEval 2015)*, pages 148–153, Denver, Colorado, June. Association for Computational Linguistics.

BIT at SemEval-2016 Task 1: Sentence Similarity Based on Alignments and Vector with the Weight of Information Content

Hao Wu [1], Heyan Huang*[1], Wenpeng Lu [2]

[1]Beijing Engineering Research Center of High Volume Language Information Processing
and Cloud Computing Applications, School of Computer Science,
Beijing Institute of Technology, Beijing, 100081, China
[2]QiLu University of Technology
`wuhao123@bit.edu.cn`, `hhy63@bit.edu.cn`, `lwp@qlu.edu.cn`

Abstract

This paper describes three unsupervised systems for determining the semantic similarity between two short texts or sentences submitted to the SemEval 2016 Task 1, all of which make use of only off-the-shelf software and data making them easy to replicate. Two systems achieved a similar Pearson correlation coefficient (0.64661 by simple vector, 0.65319 by word alignments). We include experiments on using our alignment based system on evaluation data from the 2014 and 2015 STS shared task. The results suggest that beyond the core similarity algorithm, other factors such as data preprocessing and use of domain-specific knowledge are also important to similarity prediction performance.

1 Introduction

Given two short texts or sentences, similarity systems or models should output a score that reflects how similar the two texts are in meaning. Semantic textual similarity (STS) formalizes an operation that is an important component of many natural language processing systems and has generated substantial interest within the research community (Agirre et al., 2012; Agirre et al., 2013; Agirre et al., 2014; Agirre et al., 2015). STS methods can be applied in example-based machine translation, machine translation evaluation, information retrieval, text summarization, question answering, and recommendation systems.

---

*Corresponding author

2 System Overview

In STS 2016, we submitted three system runs, and all of which were unsupervised. They could be generally divided into two kinds: vector based and alignment based.

2.1 Run 1: Simple Vector Method

In this run, we use a sentence vector derived from word embeddings obtained from word2vec (Mikolov et al., 2013). Using these sentence level vector representations, the similarity between two texts can be computed using the cosine operation.

We train word embeddings by running the word2vec toolkit1 over the fifth edition of the Gigaword corpus (LDC2011T07). We preprocess the Gigaword data with the following tools from the Moses machine translation toolkit (Koehn et al., 2007): the data is tokenized using tokenizer.perl; truecase.perl4 is used to standardize capitalizing.

As illustrated in Equation (1), we construct the sentence vector $\vec{s}$ by simply summing together the word embeddings, $\vec{t_i}$, associated with each token in a sentence.

$$\vec{s} = \sum_{i=1}^{|s|} \vec{t_i} \,.　\tag{1}$$

Here $|s|$ is the number of tokens that the sentence contains.

The similarity between a pair of sentences is computed as the cosine of their associated sentence level embedding vectors.

Proceedings of SemEval-2016, pages 686–690,
San Diego, California, June 16-17, 2016. ©2016 Association for Computational Linguistics

2.2 Run 2: Weighted Vector Method

The above method weights all word embeddings e-
qually. We submitted an alternative run that weights
the word embeddings by the information content
(IC) of the concepts referenced by their word sense
tagged tokens (Resnik, 1995). Word sense disambiguation is performed using BabelNet (Navigli and Ponzetto, 2012) with the WordNet (Miller,
1995) sense inventory. NLTK (Bird, 2006) is used
to obtain the frequencies of words belongs to the
WordNet synset. The probability associated with
each concept is estimated over the BNC[1] using add
one smoothing. Following Resnik (1995), we then
compute the information content of each concept as
follows:

$$IC\left(c\right) = -\log P(c).\qquad(2)$$

Here $P(c)$ refers to the statistical frequency of
concept c.

This method allows us to compute IC based
weights only for the nouns and verbs covered
by WordNet. We heuristically set the weight of
adjectives and adverbs to 5 and other words to 2.

2.3 Run 3: Word Alignment Method

Our final run differs from the vector based methods
described above and follows a popular alternative
approach to assessing sentence similarity through
word alignments. We make use of Sultan et al.
(2014a)'s open-source monolingual word aligner
with default parameters and the similarity formula
proposed in Sultan et al. (2015). An unsupervised
system based on Sultan et al. (2015)'s similarity
formula above took fifth place at STS 2015. Its
predecessor, based on a similar formula, took 1st
place at STS 2014. As shown in Equation (3),
similarity is computed as

$$sts\left(S^{(1)}, S^{(2)}\right) = \frac{n_c^a\left(S^{(1)}\right) + n_c^a\left(S^{(2)}\right)}{n_c\left(S^{(1)}\right) + n_c\left(S^{(2)}\right)}.\qquad(3)$$

Here $n_c^a\left(S^{(i)}\right)$ and $n_c\left(S^{(i)}\right)$ are the number of
content words and the number of aligned content
words in sentence $S^{(i)}$, respectively.

---

[1] http://ota.ox.ac.uk/desc/2554

No.	Dataset	Total Pairs	Pairs with GS
1	answer-answer	1572	254
2	headlines	1498	249
3	plagiarism	1271	230
4	postediting	3287	244
5	question-question	1555	209
	Total	9183	1186

Table 1: Test sets at SemEval STS 2016.

3 Data

As shown in Table 1, the 2016 STS shared task
included 5 distinct datasets. Systems were required
to annotated between 1,498 and 3,287 pairs per
dataset. System performance was evaluated on a
subset of each dataset consisting of between 209 to
255 gold standard (GS) pairs.

The GS similarity scores for each pair range from
0 to 5, with the values having the corresponding
interpretations:

5 indicates completely equivalence; 4 expresses
mostly equivalent with differences only in some
unimportant details; 3 means roughly equivalent but
with differences in some important details; 2 means
non-equivalence but sharing some details; 1 means
the pairs only share the same topic; and 0 represents
no overlap in similarity.

We note that there is a big gap between 0 and 1 in
GS metric: Intuitively, within the range [1,5], scores
linearly represent the similarity between two texts.
However, there is a much larger conceptual range of
topical similarity that spans from pairs on the exact
same topic to those that are completely dissimilar.

4 Evaluation

The evaluation metric is the Pearson correlation
coefficient (PCC) (Brownlee, 1965) between system
output and the gold standard. PCC is used for
each individual test set, and the final evaluation is
measured by weighted mean of PCC on all datasets
(Agirre et al., 2012).

4.1 STS 2016 Results

Performances of our three systems on each of STS
2016 test sets are showed in Table 2, and the last two
columns show the results of the following modified
versions of Run 2 and Run 3.

Run 2': Word embedding vectors are normalized
to have length=1, and the heuristic IC weights are

No.	Run 1	Run 2	Run 3	Run 2'	Run 3'
1	.48863	.37565	**.54530**	.52210	**.64349**
2	.62804	.55925	**.78140**	.69421	**.80295**
3	.80106	.75594	**.80473**	.78410	**.81391**
4	**.79544**	.77835	.79456	.79666	**.79863**
5	**.51702**	.51643	.29972	**.58535**	.57826
Mean	.64661	.59560	**.65319**	.67668	**.73044**

Table 2: Performance on STS 2016. The last row shows weighted mean which is the final evaluation metric, and the last two columns describe modified versions of Run 2 and Run 3.

Dataset 2015	Run 3	DLS15u	Best15	Run 3'
answers-forums	.6404	.6821	.7390	.6675
answers-students	.7543	.7879	.7879	.7590
belief	.6724	.7325	.7717	.7189
headlines	.7671	.8238	.8417	.8009
images	.7927	.8485	.8713	.8496
Weighted Mean	.7426	.7919	.8015	.7757

Dataset 2014	Run 3	DLS14-2	Best14	Run 3'
deft-forum	.452	.483	.531	.484
deft-news	.608	.766	.781	.772
headlines	.734	.765	.784	.753
images	.794	.821	.834	.830
OnWN	.705	.859	.875	.824
tweet-news	.694	.764	.792	.723
Weighted Mean	.688	.761	.761	.746

Table 3: Table 3: Run 3 and Run 3 performance on STS 2014 and 2015. For each year, the third column shows the performance of the submitted unsupervised system with the best overall performance for that year. The forth column shows the best per dataset performance across submitted unsupervised systems.

adjusted as follows: 6 for adjectives and adverbs and 3 for other words.

Run 3': If there is no content word aligned, we make use of longest common substring algorithm to obtain the longest common consecutive words (LCCW) of the compared sentences. Similarity is computed as

$$sts\left(S^{(1)}, S^{(2)}\right) = \frac{2 \times \left|LCCW\left(S^{(1)}, S^{(2)}\right)\right|}{\left|S^{(1)}\right| + \left|S^{(2)}\right|}.$$

(4)

Here $\left|LCCW\left(S^{(1)}, S^{(2)}\right)\right|$ is the number of words that are present in the LCCW of $S^{(1)}$ and $S^{(2)}$.

Words are classified as content words if they are either nouns, verbs, adjectives or adverbs with a small number of exceptions. We elected to classify *think, know, want* and *act* as non-content words based on their IDF scores.

From Table 2, we make the following observations:

1. From our submitted systems, we obtain the best overall results from Sultan et al. (2015)'s word alignment based method (0.65319). However, the simple vector method (0.64661) is very close in performance with only a 0.00658 absolute difference in the overall correlation scores.

2. Weighting the raw word embeddings by their IC degraded performance on all of the datasets. Run 2' normalized the word embedding vectors before taking the IC weighted vector sum, resulting in significantly improved performance over both the submitted Run 2 as well as over Run 1's simple summation of the embedding vectors. This shows any reweighting of the word level embedding vectors needs to account for differences in the magnitude of the raw embeddings.

3. The best performance of all of our systems is achieved by Run 3', which included additional logic to handle pairs with no aligned content words. However, both Run 3 and Run 3 performed particularly badly on the question-question dataset. Inspecting the data reveals that some sentence pairs have a GS score of 0 even when there is some level of similarity between what is being asked, such as "What's the best way to store asparagus?" vs "What's the best way to store unused sushi rice?". We also observe that many pairs in this dataset set have similarly structured sentences with particular core words playing a decisive role.

4.2 Results on Past Test Sets

In order to better frame the performance of our systems, we examined the performance of Run 3 and Run 3', our word alignment base systems, on the STS shared task evaluation sets from 2014 to 2015. Recall that our method is unsupervised and most comparable to Sultan et al. (2015)'s unsupervised system submission. We contrast our results with both Sultan et al. (2014b)'s best shared task submission and to Sultan et al. (2015)'s supervised extension to the unsupervised system. The results are shown in Table 3.

At the SemEval 2014 STS task, unsupervised DLS@CU2014-run 2 (Sultan et al., 2014b) achieved the highest final PCC score across all 38 submitted systems runs. Sultan et al. (2015) submitted a supervised system that contained only two features: (1) the similarity score from the unsupervised Sultan et al. (2015) system; (2) a complementary feature based on the cosine of the sentence level vector representations obtained by averaging word-level embedding vectors. This system took first place in the 2015 shared task, with the unsupervised Sultan et al. (2015) system coming in 5th place. Our Run 3 and Run 3' systems are identical to Sultan et al. (2015)'s unsupervised system except for differences in text preprocessing. We observe that our performance may have been diminished by not performing the following preparation steps:

1. Our systems didn't use a spelling correction module, such as a levenshtein distance of 1 between a misspelt word and a correctly spelt word before running the aligner or finding word vectors.

2. Knowledge of domain-specific stop words was not taken into account in submitted systems.

We suspect these contributed to the performance gap between our system and even the very similar Sultan et al. (2014b) submission.

5   Conclusions and Future Work

At SemEval 2016, we submittted three unsupervised STS systems: simple vector method, weighted vector method and word alignment method. Two make use of sentence level embedding vectors and the other applies a known well performing method for calculating STS similarity scores that is based on monolingual word alignments. We observe that both types of systems are able to achieve a similar PCC. Based on observations obtained by running our system on evaluation sets from earlier years, we believe our system could have been improved by including more of the text preprocessing steps performed in prior work.

First, our systems should introduce a spelling correction module to deal with misspelt words, which is a good way to increase the recall of the input. Second, domain-specific knowledge should be taken into account, such as domain-specific stop words, which can adapt to requirements posed by different data domains and applications. In future work, we hope to investigate the use of domain-specific weights for words as well as other methods for term weighting such as TF-IDF.

Acknowledgments

The work described in this paper is mainly supported by State Key Program of National Natural Science Foundation of China under Grant 61132009, National Programs for Fundamental Research and Development of China (973 Program) under Grant 2013CB329303 and National Natural Science Foundation of China under Grant 61202244.

The authors would like to thank Daniel Cer for his insightful comments to the improvement in technical contents and paper presentation.

References

Eneko Agirre, Mona Diab, Daniel Cer, and Aitor Gonzalez-Agirre. 2012. SemEval-2012 task 6: A pilot on semantic textual similarity. In *Proceedings of the First Joint Conference on Lexical and Computational Semantics-Volume 1: Proceedings of the main conference and the shared task, and Volume 2: Proceedings of the Sixth International Workshop on Semantic Evaluation*, pages 385–393. Association for Computational Linguistics.

Eneko Agirre, Daniel Cer, Mona Diab, Aitor Gonzalez-Agirre, and Weiwei Guo. 2013. SemEval-2013 shared task: Semantic textual similarity, including a pilot on typed-similarity. In *In* SEM 2013: The Second Joint Conference on Lexical and Computational Semantics. Association for Computational Linguistics*. Citeseer.

Eneko Agirre, Carmen Banea, Claire Cardie, Daniel Cer, Mona Diab, Aitor Gonzalez-Agirre, Weiwei Guo, Rada Mihalcea, German Rigau, and Janyce Wiebe. 2014. SemEval-2014 task 10: Multilingual semantic textual similarity. In *Proceedings of the 8th International Workshop on Semantic Evaluation (SemEval 2014)*, pages 81–91.

Eneko Agirre, Carmen Banea, et al. 2015. SemEval-2015 task 2: Semantic textual similarity, English, Spanish and pilot on interpretability. In *Proceedings of the 9th International Workshop on Semantic Evaluation (SemEval 2015), June.*

Steven Bird. 2006. NLTK: the natural language toolkit. In *Proceedings of the COLING/ACL on Interactive presentation sessions*, pages 69–72. Association for Computational Linguistics.

Kenneth Alexander Brownlee. 1965. *Statistical theory and methodology in science and engineering*, volume 150. Wiley New York.

Philipp Koehn, Hieu Hoang, Alexandra Birch, Chris Callison-Burch, Marcello Federico, Nicola Bertoldi, Brooke Cowan, Wade Shen, Christine Moran, Richard Zens, et al. 2007. Moses: Open source toolkit for statistical machine translation. In *Proceedings of the 45th annual meeting of the ACL on interactive poster and demonstration sessions*, pages 177–180. Association for Computational Linguistics.

Tomas Mikolov, Kai Chen, Greg Corrado, and Jeffrey Dean. 2013. Efficient estimation of word representations in vector space. *arXiv preprint arXiv:1301.3781*.

George A Miller. 1995. WordNet: a lexical database for English. *Communications of the ACM*, 38(11):39–41.

Roberto Navigli and Simone Paolo Ponzetto. 2012. BabelNet: the automatic construction, evaluation and application of a wide-coverage multilingual semantic network. *Artificial Intelligence*, 193:217–250.

Philip Resnik. 1995. Using information content to evaluate semantic similarity in a taxonomy. *International Joint Conference on Artificial Intelligence(IJCAI)*.

Md Arafat Sultan, Steven Bethard, and Tamara Sumner. 2014a. Back to basics for monolingual alignment: Exploiting word similarity and contextual evidence. *Transactions of the Association for Computational Linguistics*, 2:219–230.

Md Arafat Sultan, Steven Bethard, and Tamara Sumner. 2014b. DLS@CU: sentence similarity from word alignment. In *Proceedings of the 8th International Workshop on Semantic Evaluation (SemEval 2014)*, pages 241–246.

Md Arafat Sultan, Steven Bethard, and Tamara Sumner. 2015. DLS@CU: sentence similarity from word alignment and semantic vector composition. In *Proceedings of the 9th International Workshop on Semantic Evaluation*, pages 148–153.

RICOH at SemEval-2016 Task 1: IR-based Semantic Textual Similarity Estimation

Hideo Itoh
RICOH Company, LTD.
Institute of Information and Communication Technology
16-1, Shinei, Tsuzuki, Yokohama, Japan
`hideo.itoh@nts.ricoh.co.jp`

Abstract

This paper describes our IR (Information Retrieval) based method for SemEval 2016 task 1, Semantic Textual Similarity (STS). The main feature of our approach is to extend a conventional IR-based scheme by incorporating word alignment information. This enables us to develop a more fine-grained similarity measurement. In the evaluation results, we have seen that the proposed method improves upon a conventional IR-based method on average. In addition, one of our submissions achieved the best performance for the "postediting" data set.

1 Introduction

Given two sentences, Semantic Textual Similarity (STS) measures their degree of semantic equivalence (Agirre et al., 2015). This fundamental functionality can be used for many applications such as text search, classification and clustering.

This paper describes our monolingual (English) STS system which participated in SemEval 2016 task 1. Our objective is to improve a conventional IR (Information Retrieval) based method for the STS task. In general, an IR-based method estimates semantic similarity between given sentences using similarity between document search results which are obtained using each sentence as a search query. This scheme allows us to utilize a large document database for handling diverse semantic phenomena. However, in our preliminary experiments using past SemEval test data, a conventional IR-based method was not so effective.

In failure analysis of the method, we found the following:

- It is not sufficient only to measure the commonality among sentences.
- It is necessary to measure the importance of the identified commonality in each sentence.

Based on these findings, we propose a new IR-based method for STS. In this method, word alignment techniques are applied to refine the assessment of commonality. The importance of the commonality in each sentence is measured using IR techniques.

2 Related Work

Let us define a conventional IR-based approach more formally and generally. For a given text T, a document retrieval is performed using T as a search query. The search target U is a set of documents. As a result, a document set $R(T, U)$ is obtained. Because U has been fixed in our research, we denote $R(T, U)$ as $R(T)$. The semantic similarity between two texts $T1$ and $T2$ is measured as the similarity between document sets $R(T1)$ and $R(T2)$.

Explicit Semantic Analysis (ESA) (Gabrilovich and Markovitch, 2007) is a well-known IR-based approach. In their research, Wikipedia articles are used as U. $R(T)$ is regarded as a vector of documents and the cosine similarity of vectors is used to measure the semantic similarity.

In previous STS competitions, we can find IR-based approaches in Buscaldi et al. (2013), more recently Buscaldi et al. (2015). In their research, $R(T)$ is regarded as a list of ranked documents with search scores. They defined an original similarity score using the rank and search score of each document.

Proceedings of SemEval-2016, pages 691–695,
San Diego, California, June 16-17, 2016. ©2016 Association for Computational Linguistics

3 Our Approach

Figure 1 both illustrates our approach and contrasts it with conventional IR-based methods.

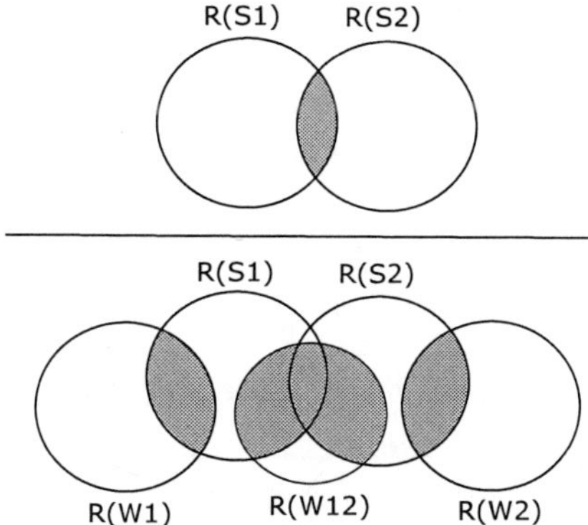

Figure 1: IR-based Semantic Similarity Measures

A conventional IR-based approach is shown at the top of the figure and is followed by our approach. Each of circles $R(T)$ represents documents retrieved for a query text T. Assuming the retrieved documents are ranked by search scores, the top-N documents are used as $R(T)$, where N is a constant. For the STS task, the conventional approach only uses the sentences $S1$ and $S2$ as search queries. The similarity between $S1$ and $S2$ is measured by calculating the ratio of the gray-colored set intersection to the union of $R(S1)$ and $R(S2)$. Specifically, the similarity function Sim is given by the Dice coefficient (Dice, 1945) expressed in Formula 1.

$$Sim(S1, S2) = \frac{2|R(S1) \cap R(S2)|}{|R(S1)| + |R(S2)|} \quad (1)$$

In our approach, additional document sets $R(W1)$, $R(W2)$ and $R(W12)$ are used, where $W12$ is a set of words which are aligned between sentence $S1$ and $S2$, while $W1$ and $W2$ are the set of words that are left unaligned in $S1$ and $S2$, respectively. Our method still computes the conventional $Sim(S1, S2)$ but then also calculate $Sim(S1, W1)$ and $Sim(S1, W12)$. Similarly, $Sim(S2, W2)$ and $Sim(S2, W12)$ are also obtained. All together, five similarity values are used as regression features within a model trained to generate the final similarity score. In other words, our approach extends a conventional IR-based scheme by incorporating word alignment information and this allows us to develop a more fine-grained similarity measurement.

$Sim(S1, W12)$ and $Sim(S2, W12)$ can be regarded as a measurement of the importance of $W12$, the aligned words, in sentence $S1$ and $S2$ respectively. When $Sim(S1, W1) > Sim(S1, W12)$, the aligned material $W12$ may not be central to the meaning of $S1$. Therefore, even if the value of $Sim(S1, S2)$ is large, the overall meaning of $S1$ and $S2$ may not be very similar to each other.

We use the Dice coefficient to keep our system simple. The optimal similarity function is left as an open question for future work.

4 System Description

4.1 System Overview

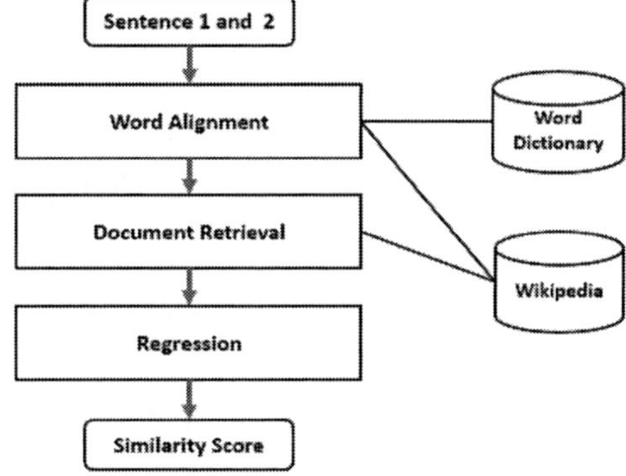

Figure 2: System Overview

We show an overview of our system in Figure 2. As data resources, we used the following:

- The Online Plain Text English Dictionary[1].
- English Wikipedia pages, snapshot on November 2nd, 2015[2].

For each pair of input sentences, we use a fuzzy word alignment procedure described later in this section to produce the following three sets of words:

W12: Aligned words in sentences 1 and 2.

W1: Unaligned words in sentence 1.

W2: Unaligned words in sentence 2.

Each of the word sets is used as a search query. The search target is a document database built from the Wikipedia data set. We used Apache Solr 5.3.1[3] as our IR system. Top-N document IDs returned by the IR system for a given query are used as the search

---

[1] http://www.mso.anu.edu.au/~ralph/OPTED/
[2] https://dumps.wikimedia.org/enwiki/20151102/
[3] http://lucene.apache.org/solr/

result. The Dice similarity scores obtained from the different query formulations are then used to construct regression features for a model that is trained to generate the final similarity score.

In the following subsections, we describe the details of each step.

4.2 Preprocessing

Each of the input sentences is converted to a word sequence. All non-alphanumeric characters are removed. Words are identified by splitting text using white space. In addition, within-word splitting is performed such as "50mm" to "50" and "mm" whenever the characters transition from numeric to alphabetic and vice versa. Stop words identified using a dictionary[4] are eliminated.

4.3 Spell Correction

Apache Solr 5.3.1 provides a function to suggest similar spellings for a query word. This is performed by fuzzy matching between a query word and words in a database index. The result is a list of words sorted by the degree of the similarity in spelling to the original query term. If a query word is found in a database index, its original spelling is always first ranked. We utilized this function for spell correction. Specifically, we replace each word with its top ranked suggested spelling whenever it is different from the original search term.

4.4 Use of Wikipedia Redirect Relations

The Wikipedia data includes information on redirection between pages. Most of the redirections are based on different names for the same underlying topic. For titles that correspond to a single word, we can use the redirection relations to identify synonymous words. For this purpose, a database of the redirect relations is constructed. A record within this database corresponds to one redirect relation and it includes the titles of source and target pages of the redirection. For each pair of words w1 and w2 from within sentences 1 and 2, we used the database to search for possible redirect relationships. When a redirect relationship is found to exist, the corresponding pair of words are aligned to each other and added to the aligned word set W12.

4.5 String Matching Based Alignment

Additional alignment pairs between words and phrases are extracted using string matching heuristics. The following alignments are handled.

- Word unigram to bigram alignment (e.g., "backstroke to back stroke"). The global alignment algorithm (Needleman and Wunsch, 1970) is used for this approximate matching.
- Acronym alignment (e.g., "GE" to "General Electric"). This is performed by matching consecutive capitalized letters with a phrase that can be used to construct the given sequence of capitalized letters as an acronym. We do not use a dictionary of acronym for this.

Aligned words or phrases are added to W12.

4.6 Dictionary Based Alignment

Using the English word dictionary mentioned in subsection 4.1, the system detects alignments between a word and its derivative forms such as "wear" versus "worn" or "America" versus "American". Semantic information such as synonyms in the dictionary are not used in order to avoid spurious alignments which would be only appropriate in specific contexts. All of the dictionary aligned words are added to W12.

4.7 Spell Expansion

Apache Solr has an API for word stemming. In addition, we can use the suggester mentioned in subsection 4.3, which provides a list of similar spellings for a given word. Both functions are used to compute spelling variations for the purposes of word alignment. Specifically, the built in Porter stemmer[5] (Porter, 1997) is used for English word stemming. Solr's FuzzySuggester mechanism[6] is called for each term and we retain the top-five suggested alternative spellings as candidates for matching by the aligner. If word w1 and w2 from sentence 1 and 2 share the same spelling in any of the expanded alignment candidates, they are aligned and added to W12.

4.8 IR-based Similarity Estimation

After the word alignment processes, the word set W1, W2, W12 are fixed. Using W1, W2, W12 and

---

[4]http://www.ranks.nl/stopwords

[5]http://wiki.apache.org/solr/LanguageAnalysis
[6]http://wiki.apache.org/solr/Suggester

sentence 1 and 2 as a natural language query (disjunctive word combination), a document search is performed. The BM25 relevance function provided by Apache Solr is used. The search target is the Wikipedia page abstracts[7]. The number of the pages in the database is around 12 million.

The search result is a list of ranked document IDs in descent order of the BM25 score. Top-N are used as $R(T)$ explained in section 3. The value of N is empirically set to 100 based on preliminary experiments on the STS 2015 data. This produces the document ID sets $R(S1)$, $R(S2)$, $R(W1)$, $R(W2)$ and $R(W12)$.

4.9 Scoring by Regression

The values of the features F1 – F5 are calculated using the expressions given below. The metric Sim is given by Formula 1 in section 3. The notation $|X|$ means the number of elements in a set X.

F1: $\{Sim(S1, W1) + Sim(S2, W2)\} / 2$
F2: $\{Sim(S1, W12) + Sim(S2, W12)\} / 2$
F3: $|W12| / (|W12| + |W1| + |W2|)$
F4: $Sim(S1, S2)$
F5: F3 value calculated including stop words.

The features F1 and F2 are newly introduced by our proposal explained in section 3. F3 roughly corresponds to a similar feature used in Sultan et al. (2014)'s well-known word alignment based STS method. F4 is the similarity measure used in conventional IR-based methods explained in section 3. F5 is introduced to handle the case that input sentences contain stop words only.

We used LIBSVM (Chang and Lin, 2011) for support vector regression to generate similarity scores using the training environment provided by the TakeLab tool (Šarić et al., 2012). We used the Radial Basis Function (RBF) kernel. Training on the STS 2015 test data was performed to identify the optimal regression parameters. Similarity scores generated by the regression were trimmed to a range 0.0 - 5.0 by setting similarity scores that are less than 0 or greater than 5 to be 0 and 5, respectively.

If the word set W12 is empty, we use the feature F4 only and directly convert it to a similarity score by $F4*c$, where c is a constant to adjust scale between the metric Sim and a similarity score with

range 0.0 - 5.0. The c value was empirically set to 70 using the STS 2015 test data.

5 Results

5.1 Evaluation

We submitted three variants of our system to the shared task evaluation. The three systems differed in how they used Wikipedia redirect relationships (explained in section 4.4) to aid in word alignment for each word w in input sentences.

RUN-b : Attempts to match w with the targets of the redirect relationships. If no matches are found, tries to match w with the titles of the redirection sources.

RUN-s : Attempts to match w with only the titles of the redirection sources.

RUN-n : Does not use Wikipedia redirection relationships.

The evaluation results (Pearson correlation with the gold standard data) of our three submitted runs are shown in Table 1. As a baseline, we also include the performance of our system when configured to operate as a conventional IR-based method. Specifically, the baseline system uses only the features F3, F4 and F5 (see section 4.9). As with Run-n, the baseline does not use the Wikipedia redirect relationships.

DATA SET	RUN-b	RUN-s	RUN-n	Baseline
answer-answer	0.5087	0.5129	0.5075	0.5287
headlines	0.7869	0.7800	0.7741	0.7701
plagiarism	0.8266	0.8299	0.8225	0.8212
postediting	0.8655	0.8625	0.8669	0.8480
question-question	0.5625	0.5232	0.5426	0.4566
MEAN	0.7116	0.7042	0.7047	0.6891

Table 1: Evaluation Results on SemEval 2016 Task 1

5.2 Discussion

Among the three submitted runs, Run-b has the best performance on average. However, in detailed analysis, we found that the contribution of the Wikipedia redirect relations is small and the differences mainly come from differences in the optimal parameter settings used for LIBSVM training with the parameters arrived at for Run-b resulting in better generalization to the test data. When the hyperparameters that were originally used to train Run-b (cost:10, gamma:1) are also used for Run-n, the mean performance of Run-n increases to 0.7104.

---

[7]The data file "enwiki-20151102-abstract.xml" was used.

Run-n outperforms the baseline system on all of the data sets except answer-answer. In failure analysis, we found that words in answer-answer typically have larger document frequencies as compare to the other data sets. In other words, answer-answer consists of more general and less topical words. This harms both the performance of our approach and the conventional IR-based baseline.

On the postediting data set, Run-n achieved the best performance of participating systems in the 2016 STS shared task. However, our performance on the question-question data set is relatively poor, lowering the mean performance of our system. Within the question-question data, many of the sentences share the words from common question formulations (e.g., "What is the best way to ..""). The alignment of such words puts too much focus on generic material that is less central to the core meaning of the question.

6 Conclusion

We proposed a new IR-based method for STS. The main feature is to extend a conventional IR-based scheme by incorporating word alignment information. The evaluation results show that the proposed method improves upon a conventional IR-based method on average. While we used the Dice coefficient for our IR-based similarity measure for simplicity, future work may see improved performance from alternative mechanisms for contrasting two different collections of ranked documents, such as Webber et al. (2010)'s Rank-Biased Overlap.

References

Eneko Agirre, Carmen Banea, Claire Cardie, Daniel Cer, Mona Diab, Aitor Gonzalez-Agirre, Weiwei Guo, Inigo Lopez-Gazpio, Montse Maritxalar, Rada Mihalcea, German Rigau, Larraitz Uria, and Janyce Wiebe. 2015. Semeval-2015 task 2: Semantic textual similarity, english, spanish and pilot on interpretability. In *Proceedings of the 9th International Workshop on Semantic Evaluation (SemEval 2015)*, pages 252–263, Denver, Colorado, June. Association for Computational Linguistics.

Davide Buscaldi, Joseph Le Roux, Jorge J. Garcia Flores, and Adrian Popescu. 2013. Lipn-core: Semantic text similarity using n-grams, wordnet, syntactic analysis, esa and information retrieval based features. In *Second Joint Conference on Lexical and Computational Semantics (*SEM), Volume 1: Proceedings of the Main Conference and the Shared Task: Semantic Textual Similarity*, pages 162–168, Atlanta, Georgia, USA, June. Association for Computational Linguistics.

Davide Buscaldi, Jorge Garcia Flores, Ivan V. Meza, and Isaac Rodriguez. 2015. Sopa: Random forests regression for the semantic textual similarity task. In *Proceedings of the 9th International Workshop on Semantic Evaluation (SemEval 2015)*, pages 132–137, Denver, Colorado, June. Association for Computational Linguistics.

Chih-Chung Chang and Chih-Jen Lin. 2011. LIBSVM: A library for support vector machines. *ACM Transactions on Intelligent Systems and Technology*, 2:27:1–27:27. Software available at http://www.csie.ntu.edu.tw/ cjlin/libsvm.

Lee R Dice. 1945. Measures of the amount of ecologic association between species. *Ecology*, 26(3):297–302.

Evgeniy Gabrilovich and Shaul Markovitch. 2007. Computing semantic relatedness using wikipedia-based explicit semantic analysis. In *Proceedings of The Twentieth International Joint Conference for Artificial Intelligence*, pages 1606–1611, Hyderabad, India.

Saul B Needleman and Christian D Wunsch. 1970. A general method applicable to the search for similarities in the amino acid sequence of two proteins. *Journal of molecular biology*, 48(3):443–453.

M. F. Porter. 1997. Readings in information retrieval. chapter An Algorithm for Suffix Stripping, pages 313–316. Morgan Kaufmann Publishers Inc., San Francisco, CA, USA.

Md Arafat Sultan, Steven Bethard, and Tamara Sumner. 2014. Dls@cu: Sentence similarity from word alignment. In *Proceedings of the 8th International Workshop on Semantic Evaluation (SemEval 2014)*, pages 241–246, Dublin, Ireland, August. Association for Computational Linguistics and Dublin City University.

Frane Šarić, Goran Glavaš, Mladen Karan, Jan Šnajder, and Bojana Dalbelo Bašić. 2012. Takelab: Systems for measuring semantic text similarity. In *Proceedings of the Sixth International Workshop on Semantic Evaluation (SemEval 2012)*, pages 441–448, Montréal, Canada, 7-8 June. Association for Computational Linguistics.

William Webber, Alistair Moffat, and Justin Zobel. 2010. A similarity measure for indefinite rankings. *ACM Trans. Inf. Syst.*, 28(4):20:1–20:38, November.

IHS-RD-Belarus at SemEval-2016 Task 1:
Multistage Approach for Measuring Semantic Similarity

Maryna Beliuha, Maryna Chernyshevich

IHS Inc. / IHS Global Belarus

131 Starovilenskaya St

220123, Minsk, Belarus

{Marina.Beliuga}@ihs.com,

{Marina.Chernyshevich}@ihs.com

Abstract

This paper describes the system for rating the degree of semantic equivalence between two text snippets developed by IHS-RD-Belarus for the SemEval 2016 STS shared task (Task 1). To predict the human ratings of text similarity we use a support vector regression model with multiple features representing similarity and difference scores calculated for each pair of sentences.

1 Introduction

Measuring semantic equivalence between two texts has become an emerging research subject in recent years. Graded textual similarity notion can be applied to a wide range of NLP tasks such as paraphrase recognition, automatic machine translation evaluation, question answering, text summarization, information retrieval, etc.

The SemEval STS shared task has been held annually since 2012 (Agirre et al., 2012; Agirre et al., 2013; Agirre et al., 2014, Agirre et al., 2015) attracting numerous participating teams with various approaches, such as alignment of related content word sequences (Sultan et al., 2015), measuring similarity between vector representations of texts and using machine learning algorithms for computing multiple lexical, syntactic and semantic features.

In this article, we present the system developed by IHS-RD-Belarus for automated measuring of semantic similarity between two sentences using support vector regression (SVR) implemented in LIBSVM toolbox[1] (Chang and Lin, 2011) with multiple features representing similarity and difference scores calculated for each pair of sentences.

The rest of the paper is structured as follows. In Section 2 we describe the task and the data used to train our system. Section 3 describes in detail the features used by our system. Results and a short conclusion are presented in Section 4 and 5, respectively.

2 Task description

Semantic Textual Similarity (STS) measures the degree of equivalence in the underlying semantics of paired snippets of text. It can range from complete unrelatedness to exact semantic equivalence (Agirre et al., 2015).

Given two sentences, participating systems are asked to return a continuous valued similarity score on a scale from 0 to 5, with 0 indicating that the semantics of the sentences are completely unrelated and 5 signifying semantic equivalence. For example, the sentence *"Military plane crashes in south France"* and the sentence *"Military plane crashes in southeastern Turkey, 1 dead"* have a very low similarity score despite many equal words, thus scored 1.0, while the sentence *"Sarkozy announces re-election bid"* and the sentence *"France's Nicolas Sarkozy makes his reelection bid official"* are scored 4.2, as they are considered very similar even though there are many word differences between them.

---

[1] https://www.csie.ntu.edu.tw/~cjlin/libsvm/

696

Proceedings of SemEval-2016, pages 696–701,
San Diego, California, June 16-17, 2016. ©2016 Association for Computational Linguistics

2.1 Dataset

The dataset used for training of our system consists of the datasets provided by the organizers of the STS shared task, specifically 1500 pairs of newswire headlines, 1500 pairs of image descriptions, 450 pairs of sentences from forum posts, 300 pairs of sentences from news summary, 750 pairs of students answers, 375 pairs of Q&A forum answers and 375 pairs of sentences from committed belief annotation. We excluded some of the datasets provided by the organizers from our training data as they had a negative influence on all the data we used for testing in preliminary experiments. As a development test set we used 20% of each dataset provided by the organizers as training data.

Our intention was to create a universal system, therefore we didn't use any domain specific features and didn't train separate models for predicting the similarity scores of the text snippets provided for evaluation depending on their domain. Thus, we used the same set of data listed above to train our SVR model and the same model was used to predict the similarity scores of all test datasets.

2.2 Evaluation

Gold standard scores are averaged over multiple human annotations. Performance of the systems is assessed by computing the Pearson correlation between machine assigned semantic similarity scores and gold standard scores.

3 System description

To predict the scores of the test set we use supervised machine learning, specifically a support vector regression model, to combine a large amount of features computed from pairs of sentences. Each feature represents either a similarity or difference score between two text snippets. To obtain the optimal values for SVR parameters C, g and p, we used grid search. The system we end up submitting had parameters $C = 10$, $g = 0.1$ and $p = 0.2$.

3.1 Semantic similarity features

The workflow for computing the similarity measures is based on a multistage aligner using various internal and external resources that align identical or similar words and phrases. As these resources have different degrees of reliability, we calculate similarity measures, described in Section 3.1.1, after each alignment step and use them as separate features.

The aligning steps performed by our system are illustrated in Figure 1.

Stage 1. First, to identify semantically similar words and phrases we use the Paraphrase Database (PPDB) (Ganitkevitch et al., 2013), which is a large database of lexical, phrasal and syntactic paraphrases.

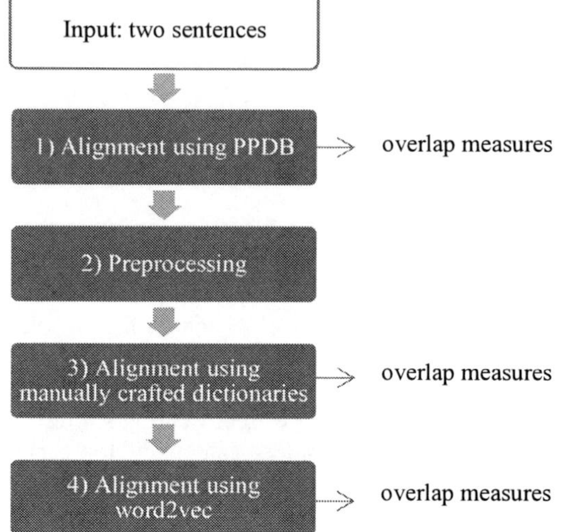

Figure 1: Aligning steps performed by the system

Stage 2. To obtain additional word alignments our system performs the following preprocessing steps:

- words are tokenized with IHS Goldfire[2] linguistic processor (Чеусов, 2006);
- words are POS tagged with IHS Goldfire linguistic processor;
- stop words, uninformative adverbs, discourse markers and words that do not contain at least one letter or number are deleted;
- words are lowercased;
- punctuation marks are removed.

On **Stage 3** we apply manually crafted domain independent wordlists such as 14870 pairs of synonymous adjectives, verbs and nouns *("wrong" – "incorrect", "link" – "connect", "seller" – "vendor")*, 1435 pairs of adjectives and adverbs derived from them *("clear" – "clearly")*, 2953 pairs of ac-

---

[2] https://www.ihs.com/products/design-standards-software-goldfire.html

tions and their agents (*"connect"* – *"connector"*), 17556 pairs of verbs and deverbal nouns (*"pulsate"* – *"pulsation"*), 563 pairs of nouns and denominal adjectives (*"sinusoid"* – *"sinusoidal"*). The lists were automatically generated using derivational affixes and then validated on random corpus of two million sentences (a derived synonym was considered valid if it appeared in the corpus more than 3 times). We also used Wikipedia lists of 264 paired country names and nationalities (*"british"* – *"uk"*) and 262 paired country names and capitals (*"uk"* – *"London"*).

During this stage we also align words having a Levenshtein distance of less than 1 to catch common misspellings.

On **Stage 4** we align words in the sentences using the GoogleNews vectors dataset, available on the word2vec web site[3], which has a 3,000,000 word vocabulary of 300-dimensional word vectors trained on about 100 billion words. We consider two words to be semantically similar if the cosine between the words is more than 0.7.

3.1.1 Word overlap measures

To calculate similarity scores we use two similarity measures which we apply after each alignment step described above.

Jaccard similarity coefficient. We measure the similarity score using Jaccard index, which is defined as the amount of word overlap normalized by the union of the sets of words present in the two sentences. It is calculated using the formula:

$$J(S_1, S_2) = \frac{|S_1 \cap S_2|}{|S_1 \cup S_2|}$$

where S_1 and S_2 are the vectors of the first and the second sentence, respectively. We consider the intersection of vectors S_1 and S_2 to be to be the words that are aligned to each other.

Similarity score using TF-IDF. A word's TF-IDF score reflects the importance of the word for the particular sentence offset by the frequency of the word in all sentences. It can be used as a weighting factor when calculating semantic similarity of the sentences. Therefore, as one of the features, we calculate the TF-IDF weighted proportion of aligned content words over the sum of the

TF-IDF scores for all words in the two sentences. In other words, given sentences S_1 and S_2,

$$sts(S_1, S_2) = \frac{\sum_{w \in (S_1^a \cup S_2^a)} tfidf(w)}{\sum_{w \in (S_1 \cup S_2)} tfidf(w)}$$

where $\sum_{w \in (S_1^a \cup S_2^a)} tfidf(w)$ is a sum of TF-IDF values of all the aligned words in S_1 and S_2, while $\sum_{w \in (S_1 \cup S_2)} tfidf(w)$ is a sum of TF-IDF values of all words in both sentences.

Intuitively, the lower is the sum of TF-IDF values of the aligned words, the less important the aligned words, which makes the total similarity score smaller and vice versa.

3.2 Cosine similarity measures

Similarity can also be defined by the cosine of the angle between two vectors. Cosine similarity is one of the most well-known similarity measures as has been broadly applied to numerous information retrieval tasks (Strehl, 2000). We calculated the similarity of pairs of text snippets using the following equation:

$$cos(A, B) = \frac{\sum_{i=1}^{n} A_i B_i}{\sqrt{\sum_{i=1}^{n} A_i^2} \sqrt{\sum_{i=1}^{n} B_i^2}}$$

where A and B are TF-IDF vectors. The cosine similarity score is non-negative and bounded between $[0,1]$.

Following our multi-stage principle we generate word vectors and calculate cosine similarity scores after each of 4 stages of original sentences transformation and use them as separate features. Each step aims to limit words diversity of text:

Stage 1. Normalization: change to a lowercase, removal of punctuation marks and stop words.

Stage 2. Grammatical transformation of words: nouns to singular form; verbs to infinitive form; adjectives and adverbs to positive degree.

Stage 3. Aligning, described in detail in section 3.1.

Stage 4. Words expansion: each word in a sentence is expanded with a vector of words with the word2vec similarity of more than 0.6, generated using word2vec and pre-trained Google vectors. We add only words having a zero entry in the vector. The TF-IDF scores of the added words are cal-

---

[3] https://code.google.com/archive/p/word2vec/

culated in the following way: the TF-IDF of the source word is multiplied by the word2vec similarity. The resulting vectors are approximately 4 times larger than the initial ones.

3.3 Syntactic similarity

Word overlap based measures may lead to discrepancies, because they do not capture syntactic relations. The similarity of the words or phrases having the same syntactic roles in two sentences may be indicative of their overall semantic similarity (Oliva et al., 2011) and vice versa. For example, in two expressions "the notebook of my mother" and "my mother cooks amazing" the word "mother" has different syntactic meaning: in the first expression it has just an attributive meaning, while in the second it is a subject. Similarly, if two sentences differ, for example, by their main predicates (e.g., "predict" and "walk"), it can indicate that they are more likely to have significant semantic differences.

To address this issue, we design features that compute similarity scores based on a syntactic analysis of the sentences.

Noun phrase similarity feature: To align noun phrases first we extracted all noun phrases from the first and the second sentence and calculated similarity between each pair of noun phrases. Noun phrase extraction was performed by IHS Goldfire linguistic processor that is based on shallow parsing but with support for head word identification.

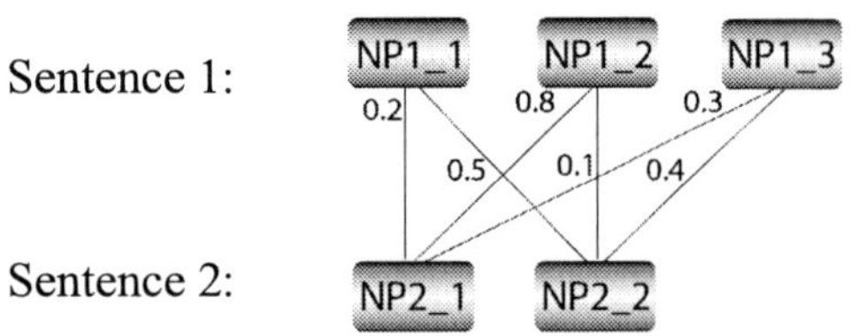

Figure 2: Example of noun phrase alignment

The similarity between two noun phrases is calculated using the WordNet path similarity provided by NLTK[4] and the Levenshtein distance. Path similarity scores denote how similar two word senses are based on the shortest path that connects the senses in the WordNet hypernym-hyponym taxonomy. The similarity between two noun phrases is the sum of the similarity between head words

---

[4] http://www.nltk.org/howto/wordnet.html

$Sim(mw)$ and the similarity of all attributes $Sim(att)$ divided by 2 in order to penalize the weight of attributes:

$$Sim(np_1, np_2) = Sim(mw) + \frac{Sim(att)}{2}$$

After calculating all pairwise similarity scores, we align each noun phrase from the first sentence with the noun phrase from the second one having the highest similarity score:

$$NP1\_1 : NP2\_2 \ (0.5),$$
$$NP1\_2 : NP2\_1 \ (0.8),$$
$$NP1\_3 : NULL \ (0)$$

The sentence level noun phrase similarity score is calculated as the averaged score of the individual aligned noun phrase similarities.

Parse trees comparison feature: At this level of analysis we compare binary verb-centric nodes (Subject-Action, Action-Object, etc.) of the trees extracted with IHS Goldfire linguistic processor while leaving aside the nodes of lesser importance (Main-Attribute, Main-Preposition, etc.). Complete or partial match within the contents of the important verb-centric compared nodes suggests various degrees of syntactic and semantic role equivalence.

We give a higher score to a pair of sentences if they have aligned words in the same or similar verb-centric nodes (the score then equals the count of the number of matching verb-centric nodes) and we give a penalty score if the sentences have no matching nodes or aligned words appear only in non-informative nodes (the score equals minus one). If any of the sentences has no verb-centric nodes at all and therefore the parse tree is not generated the score remains 0.

3.4 Differentiation features

Another set of features is used to reveal semantic differences between the sentences.

Part-of-speech feature: We assume sentences that differ by uninformative words to have a higher similarity score than sentences that differ by words that have informative POS-tags such as verbs or nouns. Compare a pair of sentences having different determiners "how is this possible?" – "how is that possible?" and a pair of sentences having different nouns "I love cats" – "I love dogs". Therefore, we calculate a weighted sum of weights of all non-matching words having informative POS-tags (i.e. verbs, nouns, adjectives, adverbs and numerals) based on an empirically determined informativeness weight of the POS-tags.

Named entity feature: Comparing, for example, the pair of sentences *"Ten people killed in twin blasts in Nigeria"* and *"Ten killed in new blast in Russia"*, we assume that the impact of named entities to semantic equivalence is disproportionately high. Therefore, we count the total number of non-matching named entities as another feature.

As matching named entities we considered two named entities that match:

- exactly: *Russia - Russia*;
- partially: *Bill Torn - Mr. Torn*;
- country name and nationality pairs list: *british – UK*;
- country name and capital pairs list: UK – London.

TF-IDF feature: We calculate TF-IDF of all words that differ in two sentences. Taking its mean value as a separate feature allows us to make a conclusion on how different the sentences are: the lower is the value of this feature, the higher is the degree of similarity, and vice versa.

4   Results

To assess system performance, the organizers provided five test sets from different domains. Table 1 illustrates the performance of the system developed by our team as compare to the top and median scores of the other systems that participated in the task.

Our system outperformed most other systems achieving very promising results. As seen below, it performed well above the median for all of the datasets and achieved results that are very close to the best performing system on headlines. However, note that most systems showed relatively poor performance on the answer-answer (ans-ans) and question-question (ques-ques) datasets which can be explained by significant differences between the provided training data and these particular test sets.

Dataset	Best	Median	Our system
plagiarism	.84138	.78949	.82634
ans-ans	.69235	.48018	.55322
postediting	.86690	.81241	.83761
headlines	.82749	.76439	.82539

ques-ques	.74705	.57140	.599
ALL	**.77807**	**.68923**	**.728312**

Table 1: Performance on the 2016 STS Test Set

5   Conclusion

In this paper we present our system for automatic rating of semantic textual similarity developed by our team for the SemEval 2016 STS shared task (Task 1). To measure semantic equivalence of two text snippets we use a supervised system based on a support vector regression model to combine multiple features representing similarity and difference scores calculated for each pair of sentences. Our system performed relatively well on all of the STS 2016 evaluation datasets. We believe that introducing additional features for deeper understanding of textual semantics might further improve performance on the task.

References

Alexander Strehl, Joydeep Ghosh, Raymond Mooney. 2000. Impact of Similarity Measures on Web-page Clustering. In Proceedings of the AAAI-2000: Workshop of Artificial Intelligence for Web Search, July 2000, 58-64

Chih-Chung Chang and Chih-Jen Lin. 2011. LIBSVM: A library for support vector machines. ACM Transactions on Intelligent Systems and Technology, 2:27:1–27:27.

Eneko Agirre, Daniel Cer, Mona Diab, Aitor Gonzalez-Agirre, WeiWei Guo. *SEM 2013 shared task: Semantic Textual Similarity. In Proceedings of the Second Joint Conference on Lexical and Computational Semantics, *SEM '13, pages 32-43, Atlanta,Georgia, USA.

Eneko Agirre, Daniel Cer, Mona Diab, Aitor Gonzalez-Agirre. SemEval-2012 Task 6: A Pilot on Semantic Textual Similarity. In Proceedings of the First Joint Conference on Lexical and Computational Semantics, Volume 2: Proceedings of the Sixth International Workshop on Semantic Evaluation, SemEval '12, pages 385-393, Montreal, Canada.

Eneko Agirre; Carmen Banea; Claire Cardie; Daniel Cer; Mona Diab; Aitor Gonzalez-Agirre; Weiwei Guo; Rada Mihalcea; German Rigau; Janyce Wiebe. SemEval-2014 Task 10: Multilingual Semantic Textual Similarity. In Proceedings of the 8th International Workshop on Semantic Evaluation, SemEval '14, Dublin, Ireland.

Eneko Agirre; Carmen Banea; Claire Cardie; Daniel Cer; Mona Diab; Aitor Gonzalez-Agirre; Weiwei

Guo; Inigo Lopez-Gazpio; Montse Maritxalar; Rada Mihalcea; German Rigau; Larraitz Uria; Janyce Wiebe. SemEval-2015 Task 2: Semantic Textual Similarity, English, Spanish and Pilot on Interpretability. Proceedings of the 9th International Workshop on Semantic Evaluation (SemEval 2015), Denver, CO, June.

James Todhunter, Igor Sovpel and Dzianis Pastanohau. System and method for automatic semantic labeling of natural language texts. *U.S. Patent 8 583 422, November 12, 2013*.

Jesús Oliva, José Ignacio Serrano, María Dolores del Castillo, Ángel Iglesias. 2011. SyMSS: A syntax-based measure for short-text semantic similarity. Data & Knowledge Engineering

Juri Ganitkevitch, Benjamin Van Durme, and Chris Callison-Burch. 2013. PPDB: The Paraphrase 152Database. In Proceedings of the 2013 Conference of the North American Chapter of the Association for Computational Linguistics. Association for Computational Linguistics, 758-764.

Md Arafat Sultan, Steven Bethard, and Tamara Sumner. 2015. DLS@CU: Sentence similarity from word alignment and semantic vector composition. In Proceedings of the 9th International Workshop on Semantic Evaluation (SemEval 2015), pages 148–153, Denver, Colorado, June. Association for Computational Linguistics.

Чеусов, А. В. Разработка лингвистических процессоров промышленной обработки текстовых документов / А. В. Чеусов // Искусственный ин-теллект. Интеллектуальные и многопроцессорные системы: материалы научно-технической конференции, п. Кацивели, 25-30 сентября 2006 г.; в 3 т. / Мин. обр-я и науки Рсн, Мин. обр-я и науки Украины, НАН Беларуси; ред. В.О. Бронзов. - Таганрог: ТРТУ, 2006. - Т. 2. - С. 366-370.

JUNITMZ at SemEval-2016 Task 1: Identifying Semantic Similarity Using Levenshtein Ratio

Sandip Sarkar
Computer Science and Engineering
Jadavpur University, Kolkata
sandipsarkar.ju@gmail.com

Dipankar Das
Computer Science and Engineering
Jadavpur University, Kolkata
dipankar.dipnil2005@gmail.com

Partha Pakray
Computer Science and Engineering
NIT Mizoram, Mizoram
parthapakray@gmail.com

Alexander Gelbukh
Center for Computing Research
Instituto Politcnico Nacional, Mexico
gelbukh@gelbukh.com

Abstract

In this paper we describe the JUNITMZ [1] system that was developed for participation in SemEval 2016 Task 1: Semantic Textual Similarity. Methods for measuring the textual similarity are useful to a broad range of applications including: text mining, information retrieval, dialogue systems, machine translation and text summarization. However, many systems developed specifically for STS are complex, making them hard to incorporate as a module within a larger applied system.

In this paper, we present an STS system based on three simple and robust similarity features that can be easily incorporated into more complex applied systems. The shared task results show that on most of the shared tasks evaluation sets, these signals achieve a strong (>0.70) level of correlation with human judgements. Our system's three features are: unigram overlap count, length normalized edit distance and the score computed by the METEOR machine translation metric. Features are combined to produces a similarity prediction using both a feedforward and recurrent neural network.

1   Introduction

Semantic similarity plays important role in many natural language processing (NLP) applications. The semantic textual similarity (STS) shared task has been held annually since 2012 in order to assess different approaches to computing textual similarity across a variety of different domains.

Research systems developed specifically for the STS task have resulted in a progression of systems that achieve increasing levels of performance but that are often also increasingly more complex. Complex approaches may be difficult if not impossible to incorporate as a component of larger applied NLP systems.

The system described in this paper explores an alternative approach based on three simple and robust textual similarity features. Our features are simple enough that they can be easily incorporated into larger applied systems that could benefit from textual similarity scores. The first feature simply counts the number of words common to the pair of sentences being assessed. The second provides the length normalized edit distance to transform one sentence into another. The final feature scores the two sentences using the METEOR machine translation metric. The latter allows the reuse of the linguistic analysis modules developed within the machine translation community to assess translation quality. METEOR's implementation of these modules is lightweight and efficient, making it not overly cumbersome to incorporate features based on METEOR into larger applied systems.

The remainder of this paper is structured as follows. Section 2 provides an overview of our system architecture and Section 3 describes our feature set. Section 4 reviews the neural network models we use to predict the STS scores. Section 5 describes the evaluation data followed by our results on the evaluation data in Section 6.

[1]This work was supported by the Project No. YSS/2015/000988 of National Institute of Technology Mizoram.

Proceedings of SemEval-2016, pages 702–705,
San Diego, California, June 16-17, 2016. ©2016 Association for Computational Linguistics

2 System Framework

As shown in Figure 1, our system performs on a neural network based regression over our three textual similarity features. As described in the next section, the three similarity features we use are: unigram overlap count, editdistance and the METEOR score from the machine translation evaluation metric research community. The three features are combined using a neural network in order to predict a pair's final STS score.

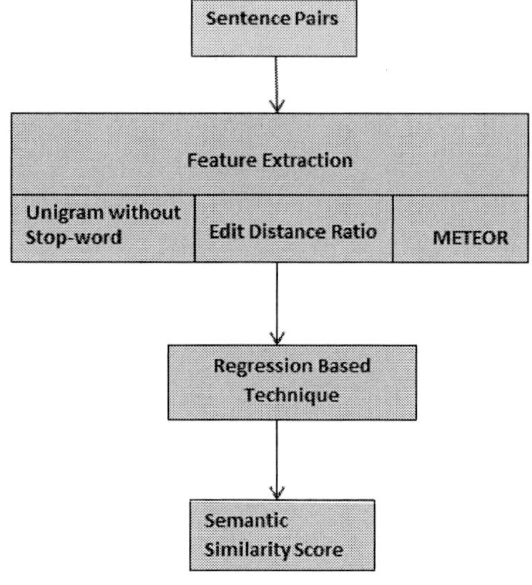

Figure 1: JUNITMZ STS System Architecture

3 Features

3.1 Unigram matching without stop-word

The unigram overlap count feature indicates the number of non stop-words that appear in both sentence pairs. [2] Table 1 illustrates the operation of this feature on an STS sentence pair.

The words "to" and "on" are present in both sentences, but we excluded them as stopwords for the purposes of the unigram overlap count.

3.2 Edit Distance Ratio

We compute the minimum number of edit operations involving the insertion, deletion or substitution

---

[2]We obtain our stop word list from http://www.nltk.org/book/ch02.html

Sentence Pair	Score
TSA drops effort to **allow small knives** on **planes**.	6
TSA drops plan to **allow small knives** on **planes**.	

Table 1: Unigram matching, ignoring stopwords

of individual characters that are required to transform one sentence into another. Commonly known as the Levenshtein distance (Levenshtein, 1966), this string similarity metric captures both similarity in the overall structure of the two sentences being compared as well as some similarity between different word forms (e.g., "California" vs. "Californian").

As shown in equation (1), we normalize the raw edit distance by the length of the two sentences. The score is then inverted such that a perfect match will have a score of 1.0, and completely dissimilar strings will be assigned a value of 0.0.

$$\text{EditRatio}(a, b) = 1 - \frac{\text{EditDistance}(a, b)}{|a| + |b|} \quad (1)$$

An example of the edit distance ratio feature is given in Table 2.

Sentence Pair	Levenshtein Distance	Edit Distance Ratio
TSA drops effort to allow small knives on planes.	6	.8958
TSA drops plan to allow small knives on planes.		

Table 2: Edit Distance Ratio

3.3 Meteor

METEOR is a well known evaluation metric from the machine translation community (Denkowski and Lavie, 2014). The method incorporates linguistic analysis modules but in a manner that is lightweight, efficient and robust to the noisy data generated by machine translation systems. The method operates by first computing an alignment between the individual words in a sentence pair. In additional to matching identical words with each other, METEOR also supports matching words based on synonymy relationships in WordNet, entries in a paraphrase database or by word stem. The metric then computes a weighted F score based on the unigram alignments that is then scaled by a word scrambling penalty. The synonym matching is computed using WordNet. We use the METEOR 1.5 system for our STS Task.

4 Neural Network Framework

We predict STS scores based on three similarity features as described above using Matlab toolkit containing modules for three different neural networks. The neural networks have been used with respect to each of the corresponding runs submitted by our team to the shared task. The inputs of those network were the feature set along with the gold standard similarity scores extracted from the training data whereas the outputs produce the semantic scores for the test dataset. In **Run1**, we use two-layer feedforward network with 10 neurons in the hidden layer and trained using the Levenberg-Marquardt algorithm. [3] **Run2** uses the same network but trained using Resilient Backpropagation algorithm (Riedmiller and Braun, 1992). [4] In case of **Run 3**, we use the framework of Layer Recurrent Network which can be seen as a generalization of simple recurrent networks (Elman, 1990). [5]. The inputs of this recurrent neural network were similar like the other 2 neural network with default parameter.

5 Dataset

The 2016 STS shared task includes sentence pairs from a number of different data sources organized into five evaluation sets: News Headlines, Plagiarism, Postediting, Q&A Answer-Answer and Q&A Question-Question. The sentence pairs are assigned similarity scores by multiple crowdsourced annotators on a scale ranging from 0 to 5 with the scores having the following interpretations: (5) complete equivalence, (4) equivalent but differing in minor details, (3) roughly equivalent but differing in important details (2) not equivalent but sharing some details (1) not equivalent but on the same topic (0) completely dissimilar. The individual crowdsourced

---

[3]we have used Matlab for regression http://nl.mathworks.com/help/nnet/ref/feedforwardnet.html

[4]http://nl.mathworks.com/help/nnet/ref/trainrp.html

[5]http://nl.mathworks.com/help/nnet/ug/design-layer-recurrent-neural-networks.html

Sentence Pairs	Score
Two green and white trains sitting on the tracks.	4.4
Two green and white trains on tracks.	
A cat standing on tree branches.	3.6
A black and white cat is high up on tree branches.	
A woman riding a brown horse.	3.8
A young girl riding a brown horse.	

Table 3: Examples of sentence pairs with their gold scores (on a 5-point rating scale)

Type	Sentence Pair
answer-answer	1572
headlines	1498
plagiarism	1271
postediting	3287
question-question	1555

Table 4: Statistics of STS-2016 Test Data

scores are aggregated to assign a final gold standard similarity score to each pair.

Table 3 provides example sentence pairs with their corresponding gold standard similarity scores. Systems are assessed on each data set based on the Pearson correlation between the scores they produce and the gold standard. The detailed statistics of the STS-2016 Test datasets are given in Table 4. For the training process we used all gold standard training and test data of year 2012 to 2015 resulting in 12500 sentence pairs.

6 Result

For our training dataset we use trail, training and test data from previous STS competitions. As shown in Table 5, we used different subsets of the data from prior STS evaluations to train different models for the 2016 evaluation sets.

Table 7 illustrates the performance of our three system submission on each of the STS 2016 evaluation sets as assessed by their correlation with the gold standard similarity scores. Overall performance is reported as the weighted mean correlation across all five data sets. The best overall correlation we obtain is 0.62708, which is achieved by run1, the LevenbergMarquardt trained feedforward network. For comparison, the best and mean scores achieved by all systems submitted to the 2016 STS shared task

Test Dataset	Training Dataset	Count
answer-answer	MSRpar, MSRvid, OnWN, image	5350
headlines	MSRpar, MSRvid, SMTnews, headline	4899
plagiarism	MSRpar, MSRvid, OnWN, tweet-news	5250
postediting	MSRpar, OnWN, SMTnews	4193
question-question	MSRpar,OnWN, SMTeuroparl	4093

Table 5: Training data used for the STS-2016 datasets

Dataset	Best	Median
ALL	0.77807	0.68923
answer-answer	0.69235	0.48018
headlines	0.82749	0.76439
plagiarism	0.84138	0.78949
postediting	0.86690	0.81241
question-question	0.74705	0.57140

Table 6: Top and median scores of SemEval-2016

Dataset	Run1	Run2	Run3
ALL	**0.62708**	0.58109	0.59493
answer-answer	**0.48023**	0.40859	0.44218
headlines	**0.70749**	0.66524	0.66120
plagiarism	0.72075	**0.76752**	0.73708
postediting	**0.77196**	0.66522	0.69279
question-question	**0.43751**	0.38711	0.43092

Table 7: System performance on SemEval STS-2016 data.

are provided by Table 6.

While our models are less accurate in their predictions than other systems, we note that our submission is based on simple and robust features that allow it to be more easily integrated into complex downstream applications. With our feature set, we still achieve a strong (>0.70) correlation with human judgements on 3 of the 5 shared task evaluation sets. However, our system struggles on both of the Q&A data sets, questionquestion and answeranswer, suggesting additional signals may be necessary in order to correctly handle pairs from this domain.

7 Conclusion and Future Work

We have presented an STS system based on three simple robust features. The results of the shared task evaluation show that our feature set is able to achieve a strong (>0.70) correlation on 3 of the 5 shared task evaluation sets. The simplicity of our feature set should make it easier to incorporate into downstream applications. We do note that, similar to submissions from other teams, our systems struggle on the two question answering datasets. We are optimistic that it is possible to also obtain strong correlations on this dataset without resorting to overly complex systems.

In future we plan to investigate using features directly based on resources such as WordNet as well as attempt to generalize our system to the crosslingual formulation of the STS task.

Acknowledgments

I am very thankful to JUNLP team member for their help in my SEMEVAL task. I am also thankful to the organizer for their support. This work was supported by the Project No. $YSS/2015/000988$ of National Institute of Technology Mizoram.

References

Michael Denkowski and Alon Lavie. 2014. Meteor universal: Language specific translation evaluation for any target language. In *Proceedings of the EACL 2014 Workshop on Statistical Machine Translation*.

Jeffrey L. Elman. 1990. Finding structure in time. *COGNITIVE SCIENCE*, 14(2):179–211.

V. I. Levenshtein. 1966. Binary Codes Capable of Correcting Deletions, Insertions and Reversals. *Soviet Physics Doklady*, 10:707, February.

M. Riedmiller and H. Braun. 1992. RPROP: A fast adaptive learning algorithm. In E. Gelenbe, editor, *International Symposium on Computer and Information Science VII*, pages 279 – 286, Antalya, Turkey.

Amrita_CEN at SemEval-2016 Task 1: Semantic Relation from Word Embeddings in Higher Dimension

Barathi Ganesh HB
Artificial Intelligence Practice
Tata Consultancy Services
Kochi - 682 042
Kerala, India
barathiganesh.hb@tcs.com

Anand Kumar M and **Soman KP**
Center for Computational Engineering
and Networking
Amrita School of Engineering, Coimbatore
Amrita Vishwa Vidyapeetham
Amrita University, India
m_anandkumar@cb.amrita.edu
kp_soman@.amrita.edu

Abstract

Semantic Textual Similarity measures similarity between pair of texts, even though the similar context is projected using different words. This work attempted to incorporate the context space of the sentence from that sentence alone. It proposes combination of Word2Vec and Non-Negative Matrix Factorization to represent the sentence as context embedding vector in context space. Distance and correlation values between context embedding vector pairs used as a features for Support Vector Regression to built the domain independent similarity measuring model. The proposed model yielding performance 0.41 in terms of correlation.

1 Introduction

Semantic Textual Similarity (STS) assess the degree to which two snippets of text mean the same thing (Agirrea et al., 2015). The modules developed for successful STS systems have a broad range of potential applications including: Discourse Analysis, Information Retrieval, Machine Reading, Machine Translation, Question Answering, Text Summarization and Plagiarism Detection.

Degree of dependence between sentences vary even-though there exist similar words present in them (Example 1) whereas the dependence remains unchanged when the context is being projected with different words (Example 2). For instance,

S1 : Boy chases the cat.
S2 : Cat chases the boy.
Example 1

S1 : The rat jumps inside the tub.
S2 : Mouse dives into the vessel.
Example 2

From the above example, representing sentence as context dependent vector in a context space is more informative than the traditional frequency based representation methods. Thus by considering this, the proposed approach measures the similarity between the sentences as prescribed in STS task, which is given in the Table 1.

From the Table 1 it is clear that simple frequency based representation will fail to achieve the objective. Our approach proposes measuring similarity based on contextual information provided by the other words in the sentences instead of measuring similarity using just the words. Words tends to have different meaning with respect to their appearance with context.

In this proposed approach, sentence embedding will be found from word embedding in which words are represented as word embedding vectors with respect to context they occurs. Thereafter the similarity measure is done by finding correlation of the features in the sentence embedding.

Remaining paper details about the related works done on STS in section 2, detailed mathematical explanation is given in section 3 and statistics about the data-set, experiment and observations are explained in section 4.

2 Related Works

In this section we discuss the related works carried on the STS and how the current proposal has been built from the previous works.

706

Proceedings of SemEval-2016, pages 706–711,
San Diego, California, June 16-17, 2016. ©2016 Association for Computational Linguistics

Score	Similarity	Similarity Description	Sentence Pair
0	Different Topic	Different topics	S1: As long as it's not completely sealed air will get in S2 : Covers are also there to prevent things from getting in
1	Not Equal	Same topic	S1 : Actor Mickey Rooney dies aged 93 S2 : Ariel Sharon dies aged 85
2	Not Equal	Share some details	S1 : Putin opens Paralympics as protest staged S2 : Putin opens Winter Paralympics
3	Roughly Equal	Important information missing	S1 : India Ink: Image of the Day: July 2 S2 : India Ink: Image of the Day: March 4
4	Mostly Equal	Unimportant information missing	S1 : U.S. retailers agree to Bangladesh plant safety pact S2 : 70 retailers agree to new Bangladesh factory safety pact
5	Completely Equal	Means same thing	S1 : CIA chief visits Israel for Syria talks S2 : CIA chief in Israel to discuss situation in Syria

Table 1: STS Score Level for Similarity

The objective of the work is to represent the context of the sentence embedding from the word embedding of the sentence. To achieve this most of the recent research and also previous years works on paraphrase detection were based on deep learning or dimensionality reduction for semantic representation. This in turn was followed by a classification or regression to get the similarity score (Agirrea et al., 2015). Most of the distributional semantic representation based on dimensionality reduction algorithms (Han et al., 2013; Kashyap et al., 2015) and word embedding models were based on deep learning (Kenter and de Rijke, 2015; Wu et al., 2014; Socher et al., 2011).

The knowledge of WordNet and Latent Semantic Analysis (LSA) was integrated in-order to develop features for STS model SemEval 2013. This was done using distributional semantics (based on word's co-occurrence in different context) and semantic relation between the words in sentences (Han et al., 2013; Kashyap et al., 2015). Web corpus from the Stanford WebBase[1] project utilized to build the distributional semantic word representation and then the model was enhanced by integrating POS with WordNet. Same system was then extended to the Multilingual Semantic Textual Similarity and Cross Level Semantic Similarity in SemEval 2014 with few external resources (Google translate[2], Wordnik[3], and bing[4]) and showed greater accuracy (Kashyap et al., 2015).

In order to represent the sentence pair, high quality word embedding was obtained using Word2Vec and Glove. Further feature vectors of length 60 computed using feature functions and evaluated on Microsoft Research Paraphrase Corpus (MSRP) (Kenter and de Rijke, 2015). As dealt with short text, similarity on long texts were found by computing non-linear semantic word representations on it. Thereafter it was fed to the Deep Semantic Embedding (DSE) to map long text into semantic space, where the semantic information was utilized to compute the similarity score (Wu et al., 2014).

Unfolding Recursive Auto encoder (U-RAE) along with dynamic pooling layer for fixed size representation was introduced for measuring the similarity between sentence pairs. Here it represents sentence as the parsed tree and words as word embedding. The pooled representation of sentences are then fed to the soft-max classifiers. The performance of this approach was evaluated using MSRP corpus and it attained the state of art accuracy (Socher et al., 2011).

In the above mentioned systems few tried to achieve the objective by using lexical information alone with high feature engineering, which seemed to have high manual effort and external resources. Other systems achieved greater accuracy by having context of the sentence either with the help of much external resources or with complex structure and computation. Finding mean or sum of the word embedding, are poor way to represent the context of the sentence. Our proposed approach simplifies the objective by relying only on word embedding and matrix factorization. This approach is able to represent the context of the sentence with fixed size, which serves to be the essential and complex part of the objective.

3 Mathematical Representation

This section details how the vector representation of the word gives context information of individual lexicon in semantic space with respect to their co-occurring lexicons (3.1). It also shows the methodology for fixed size representation of the sentence embedding (3.2). It then deals with the feature functions (3.3) that is fed to the regression analyser(3.4).

3.1 Distributional to Distributed Representation

The phrase, "Distributional Semantics" means, representing a word with respect to the context that occurs across the corpus. Typically it was derived from dimensionality reduction algorithms (Singular Value Decomposition and other matrix factorization methods) applied on word - word context matrix (Turian et al., 2010). The represented vector in high dimension is sparse and dimension of the representation depends on the vocabulary of the word. This led to the research on word embedding representation.

Word embedding (Distributed Representation) is a low dimensional vector, which represents the word with respect to the context it occurs(Turian et al., 2010). Recent works have focused and shown proven results on distributed representation in-order to attain greater accuracy(Socher et al., 2011; Kenter and de Rijke, 2015). This is because, the model represents word as dense-low dimensional vector through non-linearity learning and negative sample learning for syntax - semantic information (Mikolov et al., 2013). Mathematically,

$$P(w_t|c) = softmax(score(w_t, c)) \qquad (1)$$

$$= \frac{exp\{score(w_t, c)\}}{\sum_{w'} exp\{score(w', c)\}} \qquad (2)$$

w_t is the vector representation for the word t in the vocabulary and $score(w_t, c)$ computes the like-mindedness of word w_t with the context c, where c represents the remaining words co-occurring with w_t. w_t is the word embedding with d dimension length, which is used to find the context embedding.

3.2 Word Embedding to Context Embedding

As discussed in previous section, the objective is to find the fixed size vector representation of the context from the sentence. Sentences may vary in length but their representation need to be in same length for further similarity measure. Here this is achieved by concatenating word embedding (context matrix or word embedding matrix) of the words in the sentence followed by the Non - Negative Matrix Factorization (NMF) (Lee and Seung, 1999). Given non-negative matrix V, NMF will factorize it into the basis matrix W and mixture matrix H, which is also a non-negative matrix. Mathematically,

$$V \approx WH^T \qquad (3)$$

Where, V is $m \times n$ matrix, W is $m \times r$ basis matrix and H is $n \times r$ mixture matrix. Linear combination of basis vector (column vector) of W with weights of H gives the approximated context matrix (word embedding matrix) V. While factorizing, formerly random values are assigned to W and H then the optimization function is applied on it to compute appropriate W and H.

$$min f_r(W, H) \equiv \left\| V - WH^T \right\|_F^2 \qquad (4)$$

$$s.t. \ W, H \geq 0$$

Where, r is the reduced dimension and F is the Frobenius norm. Here r fixed as 1 to have $d \times 1$ context embedding, where d is the dimension of the word embedding.

Each column vector in V is represented by a basis vector W weighted by the elements of H. This basis vector considered as context embedding vector, which is linearly combined with elements in the H to recompute the word embedding vectors with respect to its context. The non-negativity constraints makes interpretability straight forward than the other factorization methods. The basis vector in context space is not constrained to be a orthogonal, which is not affordable by finding singular vectors or eigen vectors. (Xu et al., 2003)

3.3 Feature Function and Decision Algorithm

Feature function measures the distance, dissimilarity and correlation between the context embedding pairs. Distance is measured to know, how close the two context embeddings are in the context space, dissimilarity gives independence measure of context embeddings and correlation is carried over to know the dependency between context embeddings. Euclidean distance, BrayCurtis dissimilarity, City Block Distance, Chebyshev distance and Pearson correlation are considered in the feature function (Cha, 2007). For instance consider P and Q are the context embedding vectors of the two sentences and d is the dimension of the vector, then the measured functions given in the Table 2.

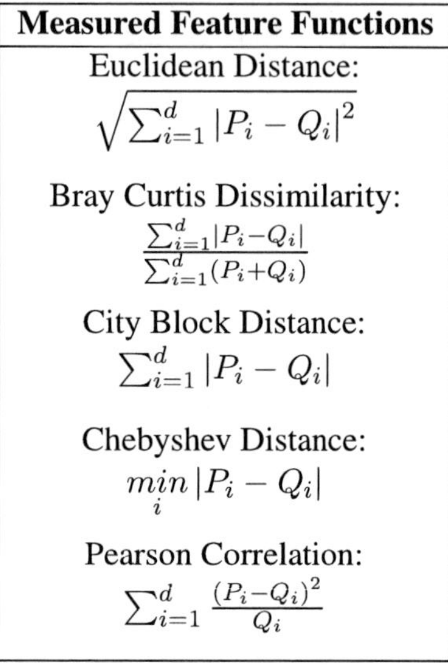

Measured Feature Functions
Euclidean Distance: $$\sqrt{\sum_{i=1}^{d}|P_i - Q_i|^2}$$
Bray Curtis Dissimilarity: $$\frac{\sum_{i=1}^{d}|P_i - Q_i|}{\sum_{i=1}^{d}(P_i + Q_i)}$$
City Block Distance: $$\sum_{i=1}^{d}|P_i - Q_i|$$
Chebyshev Distance: $$\min_{i}|P_i - Q_i|$$
Pearson Correlation: $$\sum_{i=1}^{d}\frac{(P_i - Q_i)^2}{Q_i}$$

Table 2: Measured Features

Attributes from the feature function is fed to the Support Vector Regression (SVR) to build the supervised similarity measure model. SVR is extended version of Support Vector Machine in-order to deal with regression problems (Welling, 2004). The advantages of the SVR here is, it doesn't make any assumption about data distribution, empirical risk minimization and has the ability to include non-linearity learning by changing the kernels.

4 Experiment

The Model diagram of the conducted experiment is given in Figure 1.

Statistics about the data-set are given in Table 3. Given data-set includes wide varieties of sentences in varying length and representation. This work is focused on building a unified model irrespective of domain. The training corpus for similarity measure involves shuffled sentence pairs from all the domains (i.e. single model for measuring similarity for Plagiarism, Answer-Answer, Post-editing, Headlines and Question-Question corpus).

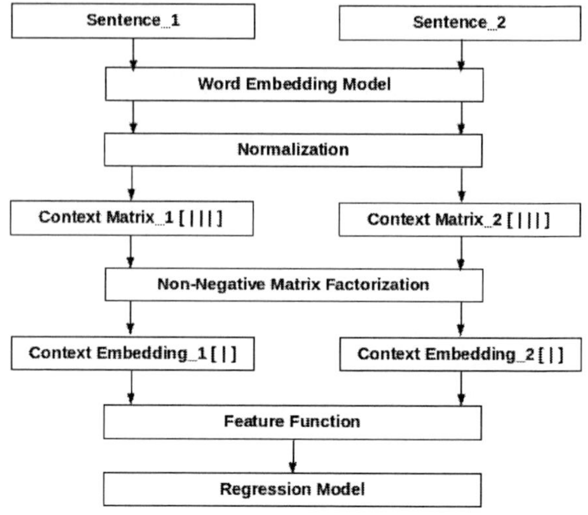

Figure 1: Model Diagram

To build the word embedding model, we use a snapshot of the articles in the English Wikipedia[5] (articles) has been utilized. After removing XML tags, special characters and unwanted spaces the corpus (size:12 GB) is fed to the Continuous Bag of Words (CBOW) model for processing (Mikolov et al., 2013). Window size, minimum occurrence and vector dimension are assigned as 5, 4, 400 respectively to create word embedding model (size:2.6 GB) using the Gensim package.[6]

The sentence pairs were fed to the word embedding model to represent the words in a sentence as vector of dimension 400. Word vectors in a sentence are concatenated to form a matrix (Context Matrix). Before concatenation the vectors are normalized (unity-based normalization) between 0 and 1, which forms dense positive vectors that are appropriate for further factorization. This is given by,

$$W' = \frac{W - min(W)}{max(W) - min(W)} \tag{5}$$

By equating the reduction rank to be one (r=1) the

---

[5]https://dumps.wikimedia.org/enwiki/latest/enwiki-latest-pages-articles.xml.bz2 Downloaded on December 2015 (size:49.9 GB).

[6]https://radimrehurek.com/gensim/.

DataPerformance	# Training Sentences	# Test Sentences	Best	Median	Amrita_CEN
Plagiarism	1271	230	0.84138	0.78949	0.63336
Answer-Answer	1572	254	0.69235	0.48018	0.30309
Post-editing	3287	244	0.86690	0.81241	0.66465
Headlines	1498	249	0.82749	0.76439	0.43164
Question-Question	1555	209	0.74705	0.57140	-0.03174

Table 3: Data-set Statistics and System Performance in terms of correlation

NMF is carried out using the Nimfa package[7] on the context matrix to get the basis vector. This resultant basis vector of NMF is considered as the context embedding. This is because the linear combination of basis matrix along with mixture matrix will reconstruct context matrix. This can be visualized by generating words based on its context.

Once the context embedding pairs are found, they are fed to the feature function to measure the distance and correlation between them. These are used as attributes to train the SVR. SVR has been trained using Python Scikit-learn[8]. Radial Basis Function (RBF) kernel used for the non-linearity learning. The typical C = 1.0 and gamma = 1/length(training set) parameters are used in SVR.

While training, the performance of the system is measured by 10-cross validation. Correlation coefficient between gold-standard and predicted vector are computed to validate the significance of the system. The average correlation value obtained out of 10-cross validation during the training phase is 0.4178.

Our final system was trained on entire training corpus (9183 pairs) and then submitted to the STS shared task for evaluation. The official evaluation results are reported in Table 3. Our model performed poorly on the Question-Question data, but performed better on all the others. The model did best on the Plagiarism and Post-editing pairs. The average score of the system is 0.4090, which is almost equal to the training accuracy (0.4178).

5   Conclusion

A novel method for SemEval-2016 Monolingual Semantic Textual Similarity task has been described in this paper. Without depending on any resources or hand crafted features, it represents a simplified and unsupervised feature learning model for similarity measure. Our method performs well on the 2016 evaluation data except for the Question - Question corpus, however there is still room for improvement. The future work will be focused on more research on and the justification of context embedding derivation.

References

Eneko Agirrea, Carmen Baneab, Claire Cardiec, Daniel Cer, Mona Diabe, Aitor Gonzalez-Agirrea, Weiwei Guof, Inigo Lopez-Gazpioa, Montse Maritxalara, Rada Mihalceab, et al. 2015. Semeval-2015 task 2: Semantic textual similarity, english, spanish and pilot on interpretability. In *Proceedings of the 9th international workshop on semantic evaluation (SemEval 2015)*, pages 252–263.

Sung-Hyuk Cha. 2007. Comprehensive survey on distance/similarity measures between probability density functions. *City*, 1(2):1.

Lushan Han, Abhay Kashyap, Tim Finin, James Mayfield, and Jonathan Weese. 2013. Umbc ebiquity-core: Semantic textual similarity systems. In *Proceedings of the Second Joint Conference on Lexical and Computational Semantics*, volume 1, pages 44–52.

Abhay Kashyap, Lushan Han, Roberto Yus, Jennifer Sleeman, Taneeya Satyapanich, Sunil Gandhi, and Tim Finin. 2015. Robust semantic text similarity using lsa, machine learning, and linguistic resources. *Language Resources and Evaluation*, pages 1–37.

Tom Kenter and Maarten de Rijke. 2015. Short text similarity with word embeddings. In *Proceedings of the 24th ACM International on Conference on Information and Knowledge Management*, pages 1411–1420. ACM.

Daniel D Lee and H Sebastian Seung. 1999. Learning the parts of objects by non-negative matrix factorization. *Nature*, 401(6755):788–791.

Tomas Mikolov, Kai Chen, Greg Corrado, and Jeffrey Dean. 2013. Efficient estimation of word representations in vector space. *arXiv preprint arXiv:1301.3781*.

Richard Socher, Eric H Huang, Jeffrey Pennin, Christopher D Manning, and Andrew Y Ng. 2011. Dynamic

---

[7]http://nimfa.biolab.si/.
[8]http://scikit-learn.org/stable/.

pooling and unfolding recursive autoencoders for paraphrase detection. In *Advances in Neural Information Processing Systems*, pages 801–809.

Joseph Turian, Lev Ratinov, and Yoshua Bengio. 2010. Word representations: a simple and general method for semi-supervised learning. In *Proceedings of the 48th annual meeting of the association for computational linguistics*, pages 384–394. Association for Computational Linguistics.

Max Welling. 2004. Support vector regression. *Department of Computer Science, University of Toronto, Toronto (Kanada)*.

Hao Wu, Martin Renqiang Min, and Bing Bai. 2014. Deep semantic embedding. In *SMIR@ SIGIR*, pages 46–52.

Wei Xu, Xin Liu, and Yihong Gong. 2003. Document clustering based on non-negative matrix factorization. In *Proceedings of the 26th annual international ACM SIGIR conference on Research and development in informaion retrieval*, pages 267–273. ACM.

NUIG-UNLP at SemEval-2016 Task 1: Soft Alignment and Deep Learning for Semantic Textual Similarity

John P. McCrae and **Kartik Asooja** and **Nitish Aggarwal** and **Paul Buitelaar**

Insight Centre for Data Analytics

National University of Ireland, Galway

IDA Business Park

Galway, Ireland

`{john.mccrae, katrik.asooja, nitish.aggarwal,`
`paul.buitelaar}@insight-centre.org`

Abstract

We present a multi-feature system for computing the semantic similarity between two sentences. We introduce the use of soft alignment for computing text similarity, and also evaluate different methods to produce it. The main features used by our system are based on alignment and Explicit Semantic Analysis. Our system was above the median scores for 4 out of the 5 datasets at SemEval 2016 STS Task 1.

1 Introduction

Semantic textual similarity is the task of deciding if two sentences express a similar or identical meaning and requires a deep understanding of a sentence and its meaning in order to achieve high performance. Recent successful approaches to this problem have been based on the idea of creating monolingual alignments (Sultan et al., 2014a) indicating which words in each of the two sentences correspond to each other. This is quite successful in many cases where many words have the same lemma, however when synonymous and semantically similar terms are used, it is much harder to construct alignment. For this reason, we propose the use of *soft alignments*, where instead of producing a hard linking between individual words in the sentence, we instead produce a score indicating how likely one word in a sentence is to be aligned to another word in the other sentence. We examine several methods that can be used to learn these alignments including word embeddings (Mikolov et al., 2013; Pennington et al., 2014) and models based on deep learn-

ing that have been suggested for machine translation (Bahdanau et al., 2014; Cho et al., 2014). In addition, we look into recent models for sentence and document similarity that can leverage the large amount of loosely aligned text in particular those based on Explicit Semantic Analysis (Gabrilovich and Markovitch, 2007) and recent extensions aimed at generating orthogonal representations (McCrae et al., 2013; Aggarwal et al., 2015). While these novel techniques alone can achieve high performance on the task, we note that simple metrics such as the number of overlapping terms can produce reasonable performance. For added robustness we combine features based on simple metrics with novel methods explored in this work as a multi-feature regression problem, which we solve by means of an M5 Decision tree (Wang and Witten, 1996; Quinlan, 1992). The rest of the paper is structured as follows: we present our system in Section 2. We then present both our internal evaluation results and the official Task 1 results in Section 3 and finally we conclude in Section 4.

2 Methods

For convenience we assume that semantic textual similarity consists of finding a function that maps two strings, $\mathbf{a}$ and $\mathbf{b}$, of length n_a, n_b, to a single value $y \in [0, 1]$. We will use A to denote the set of words in $\mathbf{a}$ and B for the words in $\mathbf{b}$. We assume we have a dataset D consisting of triples of the form $(\mathbf{a}_i, \mathbf{b}_i, y_i)$.

712

Proceedings of SemEval-2016, pages 712–717,

San Diego, California, June 16-17, 2016. ©2016 Association for Computational Linguistics

2.1 Baseline features

The basic level of our system is the construction of baseline features that can be quickly and easily evaluated to quickly find candidates that are likely to be highly similar, which may be useful in search applications. Our features were partially based on those of Hänig et al. (2015), but simplified such that we do not require a part-of-speech tagger. The features we used are as follows:

Longest Common Subsequence The length in tokens of the longest common subsequence between the two sequences

n-gram Overlap The number of n-grams that occur in both sentences divided by the length of the shorter sentence.

Jaccard The Jaccard Index of the sentences using a bag-of-words model ($|A \cap B|/|A \cup B|$).

Dice The Dice Co-efficient of the sentences using a bag-of-words model ($2|A \cap B|/(|A| + |B|)$).

Containment The containment of the sentences using a bag-of-words model ($|A \cap B|/\min(|A|, |B|)$).

Sentence Length Ratio The length of the sentence using the following symmetrized ratio: $\min(|\mathbf{a}|, |\mathbf{b}|)/\max(|\mathbf{a}|, |\mathbf{b}|)$.

Average Word Length Ratio The average length of the words, using the symmetric ratio as above.

Greedy String Tiling As in Wise (1993), we used Arun Kumar Jayapal's implementation[1], where similarity is given as follows, where coverage is the number of tokens covered by the tiling.

$$\frac{2 \times \text{coverage}}{|A| + |B|}$$

Source and Target Length The length (in tokens) of each of the two strings

Keypairs For each word pair (a, b) where $a \in A$ and $b \in B$, we calculated

$$\lambda_{a,b} = \sum_{(\mathbf{a}_i, \mathbf{b}_i, y_i) \in D, a \in \mathbf{a}_i, b \in \mathbf{b}_i} y_i - \bar{y}$$

Where $\bar{y} = \frac{\sum_D y_i}{|D|}$. We took only the word pairs with the 20 highest absolute values for $\lambda_{a,b}$. The feature consisted of the number of occurrences of these keypairs.

2.2 Hard alignment

As we believe that hard alignments are also useful, we included features from hard alignment, firstly using a model based on Sultan et al. (2014b)'s system. We simplified this method using only the Word Similarity Aligner (*wsAlign*) and Named Entity Aligner (*neAlign*) parts of Sultan's method, we found that this agreed with Sultan's implementation[2] to an F-Measure of 93.8% and our observations and internal results suggested that the differences in alignments did not correspond to obvious improvements in alignment accuracy.[3]

We also use the alignments given by Jacana aligner (Yao et al., 2013)[4] directly as further alignments in our system. Jacana is a discriminatively trained monolingual word aligner that uses Conditional Random Field (CRF) model to globally decode the best alignment. It uses features based on WordNet and part-of-speech tags.

2.3 Soft Alignment

2.3.1 WordSim

Semantic relatedness measures can be directly used to compute the soft alignments between the sentences. In this approach, we compare the pretrained neural word embeddings to compute the relatedness between words across both the sentences, thus producing the soft alignment matrix. We use cosine similarity for this purpose. We use the neural embeddings[5] developed by Baroni et al. (2014).

---

[1] https://github.com/arunjeyapal/GreedyStringTiling

[2] https://github.com/ma-sultan/monolingual-word-aligner

[3] For example in the pair "Being against nukes does not mean not wanting to use nukes" and "Being against using nukes means not wanting to use nukes" the systems differed in the alignment of the word "use"

[4] https://github.com/chetannaik/jacana

[5] Best predict vectors on http://clic.cimec.unitn.it/composes/semantic-vectors.html

| | | Dataset | | | | | | |
Method	Micro	DEFT forum	DEFT news	headlines	images	Onto-WordNet	Tweet News	Weighted Mean
Sultan Only (-DF)	N	0.456	0.699	0.682	0.790	0.619	0.655	0.607
Sultan Only	N	0.419	0.689	0.706	0.800	0.720	0.683	0.644
Sultan + Jacana	N	0.430	0.708	0.721	0.808	0.819	0.756	0.673
Sultan + WordSim	N	0.423	0.756	0.744	0.816	0.816	0.730	0.676
Sultan + WordSim + WordPairs	N	0.434	0.743	0.743	0.825	0.833	0.743	0.689
All aligners	N	0.464	0.713	0.732	0.821	0.834	0.733	0.686
All aligners + ESA	N	0.490	0.741	0.740	0.841	0.826	0.756	0.699
All aligners + ESA	Y	0.554	0.712	0.749	0.836	0.859	0.761	0.737
Sultan + WordSim	Y	0.555	0.733	0.747	0.827	0.844	0.753	0.728

Table 1: Pearson's Correlation achieved by configurations of our system during development on the SemEval 2014 dataset

For each word pair (a, b) where $a \in A$ and $b \in B$, lets consider $\vec{a}$ and $\vec{b}$ as neural word embeddings respectively for a and b. Thus, soft alignment can be defined formally as a matrix **S** of size n_a x n_b, where $s_{ij} = \vec{a}.\vec{b}$ giving similarity between the word vectors.

2.3.2 BiLSTM

Soft alignments based only on the word similarity do not consider the word context in the sentence. Therefore, with the help of bidirectional recurrent neural network (BiRNN), we produce context-dependent word representations. BiRNN consists of a forward recurrent neural network (RNN) and a separate backward RNN to read the sentence in forward and backward directions respectively. Figure 1 shows a BiRNN representation for encoding a sentence. Here, $\vec{a_i}$ refers to the pre-trained neural word embedding, and $\vec{h_i}$ refers to the BiRNN representation for i^{th} word in the sentence, produced by the concatenation of forward and backward RNN representations. The approach being followed here is the same used in order to produce variable length sentence representation for soft attention mechanism in neural machine translation (Bahdanau et al., 2014). However, here we just use the BiRNN representations of the words for producing the soft alignments. Such representations can be considered as context-dependent representation as they carry the sentence summary at the position of each word. After producing the BiRNN representations for both the sentences, we simply compute cosine similarities be-

tween these representations at each word position across both the sentences, to produce the soft alignment matrix. Similarly as above in section 2.3.1, soft alignment can be defined as a matrix **S** of size n_a x n_b, where $s_{ij} = \vec{h}.\vec{g}$ and $\vec{h}$ and $\vec{g}$ are the BiRNN based contextual word representations. We use long short-term memory (Hochreiter and Schmidhuber, 1997, LSTM) for our experiments using our own implementation. For learning the BiLSTM based representations, we use a collection of the sentences from the previous years Semantic Textual Similarity Task.

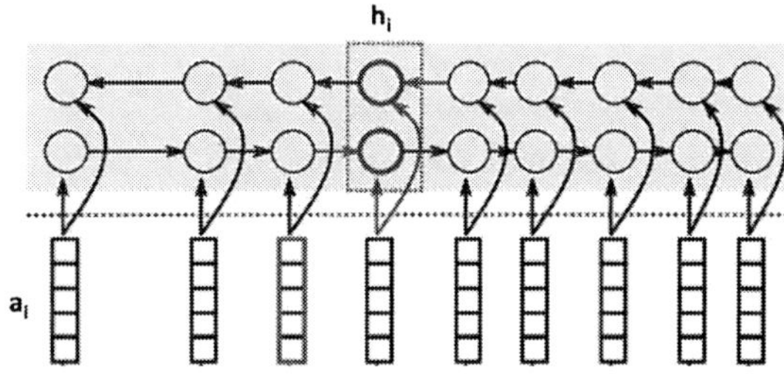

Figure 1: BiRNN representation for encoding a sentence

2.3.3 Features

In order to apply soft alignment in a machine learning setting, we wish to transform these alignments into a set of features. In particular, these features should be able to calculate a single value bounded in some range regardless of the relative size of the two target sentences. As we generate a non-square matrix of variable size, we hypothesize that good alignments should resemble hard alignments.

System	plagiarism	answer-answer	postediting	headlines	question-question	All
m5all3	0.80332	0.40165	0.81606	0.75400	0.72228	0.69528
m5dom1	0.75539	0.41211	0.80086	0.76778	0.69782	0.68368
m5dom2	0.74351	0.38303	0.76549	0.76485	0.57263	0.64520
Median	0.78949	0.48018	0.81241	0.76439	0.57140	0.68923
Best system on dataset	0.84138	0.69235	0.86690	0.82749	0.74705	0.77807

Table 2: Official results from SemEval, giving Pearson's correlation on each dataset

For hard alignments, we used the number of rows (i.e., tokens) that had at least one alignment, thus for the soft alignment we used the row max of the alignment as follows:

$$m_\phi = \frac{\sum_{i=1\ldots n_a} \frac{\max_{j=1\ldots n_b} |\alpha_{ij}|^\phi}{\sum_{j=1\ldots n_b} \alpha_{ij}^\phi}}{n_a}$$

For out experiments we calculated four features with the following values of $\phi = 0.1, 0.5, 1, 2$.

In addition, we experimented with other sparsity features proposed by Hurley and Rickard (2009) and included the H_G metric and a modified version of the $-l^p$ metric we call col-l^p as they gave good correlations with the sentence scores.

$$H_G = -\sum_{i=1,\ldots,n_a; j=1,\ldots,n_b} \log \alpha_{ij}^2$$

$$-l^p = \left(\sum_{i=1,\ldots,n_a; j=1,\ldots,n_b} \alpha_{ij}^p\right)^{\frac{1}{p}}$$

$$\text{col-}l^p = \frac{\sum_{i=1,\ldots,n_a} \left(\sum_{j=1,\ldots,n_b} \alpha_{ij}^p\right)^{\frac{1}{p}}}{n_a}$$

We used $p = 2, 10$ to give two features for col$-l^p$.

Finally, we noted that in many cases the most important alignments were those between low frequencies word, therefore we transformed our alignments by multiplying them with the inverse document frequency of the words, e.g.,

$$\alpha'_{ij} = \frac{\alpha_{ij}}{df(a_i) df(b_j)}$$

2.4 ESA Similarity

Gabrilovich and Markovitch (2007) introduced the ESA model that represents the semantics of a word with a distributional vector over the Wikipedia concepts. We use a snapshot of English Wikipedia from 1st October, 2013 which contains 13.9 million articles (concepts). We built an index of all Wikipedia articles using Lucene. We retrieve distributional vector of a sentence by searching over a Lucene index. Thus, a Lucene ranking score represents the magnitude of a vector dimension that corresponds to a retrieved Wikipedia article. We used Lucene's built-in scoring function to obtain the top $K = 1000$ articles and then to obtain the semantic relatedness between two sentences, we compute cosine similarity between their distributional vectors.

2.5 Classifying with M5 Trees

Finally, having baseline features, extracted features from the hard and soft alignments, and the ESA similarity, we combine all of our features into a single vector and thus transform the problem into that of a traditional regression task. We experimented with various classifiers using the Weka toolkit (Hall et al., 2009) and found that in nearly all experiments, the strongest performance was obtained using the M5 Decision Tree method (Wang and Witten, 1996; Quinlan, 1992) and so we adopted this for all our experiments.

3 Evaluation

3.1 Internal Evaluation

We conducted a series of evaluations using data from previous SemEval challenges (Agirre et al., 2014) as a baseline as shown in Table 1. These results present the following configurations using 10-fold cross-validation:

Sultan Only (-DF) Using baseline features, which are also used in all experiments, and Sultan et al.'s (2014a) aligner. Without accounting for term document frequency (see Section 2.3.3)

Sultan Only As above only with document frequency included as a feature

Sultan + Jacana Including the Jacana aligner (Section 2.2)

Sultan + WordSim Including the WordSim features (Section 2.3.3)

Sultan + WordSim + WordPairs Including keypairs features (Section 2.3.3)

All aligners Using Sultan, Jacana, WordSim and BiLSTM aligners

All aligners + ESA Also including the ESA method (Section 2.4)

In addition, we noticed that different datasets tended to have a different distribution of scores. As such we tried evaluating in two modes *macrotraining* where we trained the decision tree on all datasets simultaneously and *microtraining* where a decision tree was trained for each dataset and used only for this dataset. As the microtraining results are much stronger, for the task, we developed a lightweight domain classifier that found the nearest training dataset to the test dataset and used the classifier trained on the most appropriate dataset in our evaluation runs. This classifier used the size of the intersection of the set of 100 most frequent words in each dataset and we obtained 100% accuracy for this classifier in identifying datasets by 10-fold cross-validation, i.e., we choose the classifier trained on the training set T which maximizes the following similarity to the test set T':

$$|\text{top100words}(T) \cap \text{top100words}(T')|$$

3.2 SemEval results

We submitted three runs to the SemEval task and the results are reported in Table 2, the configurations were as follows:

m5all3 This run uses all the aligners (Sultan, Jacana, WordSim) including ESA, and trains a single decision tree on all datasets simultaneously, without using the domain classifier.

m5dom1 This run uses Sultan, WordSim as aligners including ESA, and trains a decision tree per test dataset on the nearest training datasets using the domain classifier.

m5dom2 This run uses all the aligners including ESA, and trains a decision tree per test dataset on the nearest training dataset using the domain classifier.

We notice that our system has above-median performance in most datasets however, we have significant difficulties in the *answer-answer*, this is because of the length and complexity of the sentences. We also see that while the domain classifier was helpful in a few cases, notably the headlines, it did not in general seem to improve the results. Finally, we find that the combination of all classifiers was helpful.

4 Conclusion

We propose a combination of different approaches and our internal results suggest that combining multiple approaches can improve overall system performance. However, we notice that for some datasets performance is still very low and we hypothesise that in this case a new approach is needed. We notice that adapting to the domain proved extremely effective in the cross-fold setting but not in the general case, however our proposed method was very simplistic and further improvement in the quality of the result may be achieved by a more sophisticated algorithm.

Acknowledgments

This research was supported in by funding from the Science Foundation Ireland under Grant Number SFI/12/RC/2289 (Insight).

References

Nitish Aggarwal, Kartik Asooja, Georgeta Bordea, and Paul Buitelaar. 2015. Non-orthogonal explicit semantic analysis. *Lexical and Computational Semantics (*SEM 2015)*, page 92.

Eneko Agirre, Carmen Banea, Claire Cardie, Daniel Cer, Mona Diab, Aitor Gonzalez-Agirre, Weiwei Guo, Rada Mihalcea, German Rigau, and Janyce Wiebe. 2014. Semeval-2014 task 10: Multilingual semantic textual similarity. In *Proceedings of the 8th international workshop on semantic evaluation (SemEval 2014)*, pages 81–91.

Dzmitry Bahdanau, Kyunghyun Cho, and Yoshua Bengio. 2014. Neural machine translation by jointly learning to align and translate. *arXiv preprint arXiv:1409.0473*.

Marco Baroni, Georgiana Dinu, and Germán Kruszewski. 2014. Don't count, predict! a systematic comparison of context-counting vs. context-predicting semantic vectors. In *Proceedings of the 52nd Annual Meeting of the Association for Computational Linguistics (Volume 1: Long Papers)*, pages 238–247, Baltimore, Maryland, June. Association for Computational Linguistics.

Kyunghyun Cho, Bart Van Merriënboer, Caglar Gulcehre, Dzmitry Bahdanau, Fethi Bougares, Holger Schwenk, and Yoshua Bengio. 2014. Learning phrase representations using rnn encoder-decoder for statistical machine translation. *arXiv preprint arXiv:1406.1078*.

Evgeniy Gabrilovich and Shaul Markovitch. 2007. Computing semantic relatedness using wikipedia-based explicit semantic analysis. In *IJCAI*, volume 7, pages 1606–1611.

Mark Hall, Eibe Frank, Geoffrey Holmes, Bernhard Pfahringer, Peter Reutemann, and Ian H Witten. 2009. The weka data mining software: an update. *ACM SIGKDD explorations newsletter*, 11(1):10–18.

Christian Hänig, Robert Remus, and Xose De La Puente. 2015. ExB Themis: Extensive feature extraction from word alignments for semantic textual similarity. *SemEval-2015*, page 264.

Sepp Hochreiter and Jürgen Schmidhuber. 1997. Long short-term memory. *Neural computation*, 9(8):1735–1780.

Niall Hurley and Scott Rickard. 2009. Comparing measures of sparsity. *Information Theory, IEEE Transactions on*, 55(10):4723–4741.

John McCrae, Philipp Cimiano, and Roman Klinger. 2013. Orthonormal explicit topic analysis for cross-lingual document matching. In *Proceedings of the 2013 Conference on Empirical Natural Language Processing*.

Tomas Mikolov, Ilya Sutskever, Kai Chen, Greg S Corrado, and Jeff Dean. 2013. Distributed representations of words and phrases and their compositionality. In *Advances in neural information processing systems*, pages 3111–3119.

Jeffrey Pennington, Richard Socher, and Christopher D Manning. 2014. Glove: Global vectors for word representation. In *EMNLP*, volume 14, pages 1532–1543.

John R Quinlan. 1992. Learning with continuous classes. In *5th Australian joint conference on artificial intelligence*, volume 92, pages 343–348. Singapore.

Md Arafat Sultan, Steven Bethard, and Tamara Sumner. 2014a. Back to basics for monolingual alignment: Exploiting word similarity and contextual evidence. *Transactions of the Association for Computational Linguistics*, 2:219–230.

Md Arafat Sultan, Steven Bethard, and Tamara Sumner. 2014b. Dls@ cu: Sentence similarity from word alignment. In *Proceedings of the 8th International Workshop on Semantic Evaluation (SemEval 2014)*, pages 241–246.

Yong Wang and Ian H Witten. 1996. *Induction of model trees for predicting continuous classes*. Department of Computer Science, University of Waikato.

Michael J Wise. 1993. String similarity via greedy string tiling and running Karp-Rabin matching. *Online Preprint, Dec*, 119.

Xuchen Yao, Benjamin Van Durme, Chris Callison-Burch, and Peter Clark. 2013. A lightweight and high performance monolingual word aligner. In *ACL (2)*, pages 702–707. The Association for Computer Linguistics.

NORMAS at SemEval-2016 Task 1: SEMSIM: A Multi-Feature Approach to Semantic Text Similarity

Adebayo Kolawole John and **Luigi Di Caro** and **Guido Boella**
University of Torino
Corso Svizzera 185
Torino, 10149, Italy
`kolawolejohn.adebayo@unibo.it, (dicaro, guido)@di.unito.it`

Abstract

This paper presents the submission of our team (NORMAS) to the SemEval 2016 semantic textual similarity (STS) shared task. We submitted three system runs, each using a set of 36 features extracted from the training set. The runs explore the use of the following three machine learning algorithms: Support Vector Regression, Elastic Net and Random Forest. Each run was trained using sentence pairs from the STS 2012 training data. Features extracted include lexical, syntactic and semantic features. This paper describes the features we designed for assessing the semantic similarity between sentence pairs, the models we build using these features and the performance obtained by the resulting systems on the 2016 evaluation data.

1   Introduction

Computationally assessing the semantic similarity of natural language data has gained the attention of researchers in the field of computational linguistics. Machines that are able to quantify the semantics of natural language have numerous important applications including: Document Similarity (Elsayed et al., 2008; Huang, 2008), Word Similarity (Resnik, 1995; Dagan, 2000; Bollegala et al., 2007; Pedersen et al., 2004), Text Summarization (Barzilay and El-hadad, 1999; Gong and Liu, 2001), Informtion Retrieval (Salton and Buckley, 1988; Manning et al., 2008), Plagiarism detection (Si et al., 1997), Paraphrase detection (Fernando and Stevenson, 2008) and especially Machine Translation (Brown et al., 1990).

The semantic textual similarity (STS) (Agirre et al., 2012) task measures the level of semantic equivalence between two approximately sentence sized snippets of texts on a graded scale from 0 (unrelated) to 5 (completely equivalent). This paper describes our participation in the SemEval 2016 STS shared task (Agirre et al., 2016). Our system explores 36 lexical and semantic features (e.g., string matching, WordNet similarity, word overlap) in combination with three very distinct learning algorithms (Support Vector Regression, Elastic Net and Random forest).

The remainder of this paper is organized as follows: *Section 2* describes our feature set in detail and our approach to feature selection. *Section 3* describes our machine learning models with section 4 presenting our results on the shared task evaluation data.

2   Feature Generation

We used a mixture of lexical, syntactic and semantic features extracted from text. Below, we describe each of the features provided to our model.

2.1   Lexical Features

String matching: String matching techniques compare words in two texts character by character and can be used to approximately capture morphological differences in the terms. Bär et al. (2012), one of the best performing systems in 2012, used variants of string matching algorithms. Our system made use of features computed using the following string matching methods:

1. ***Longest common Substring***: This obtains the longest sequences of words appearing in both

Proceedings of SemEval-2016, pages 718–725,
San Diego, California, June 16-17, 2016. ©2016 Association for Computational Linguistics

sentences (Gusfield, 1997).

2. *Levenshtein Distance*: This measures the number of basic edit-operations (insertions, deletions, and substitutions) required to change one text into the other.

3. *Jaccard Similarity*: This measures the number of words shared by two sentences in ratio with the total number of words in the sentences i.e. given sentences A and B, the ratio is defined as:

$$Jac = \frac{A \cap B}{A \cup B} \qquad (1)$$

Word Ordering: We use the union of all tokens in a pair of sentences to build a vocabulary of non-repeating terms. For each sentence, the position mapping of each word in the vocabulary is used to build a vector. To obtain the position mapping, a unique index number is assigned to each vocabulary term. To obtain the word order vector for a sentence, each term in the vocabulary is compared against terms in the sentence. If a vocabulary term is found in the sentence, the index number of that term in the vocabulary is added to the vector. Otherwise, similarity of the vocabulary term and each term in the sentence is calculated using a WordNet based word similarity algorithm. The index number of the sentence term with highest similarity score above a threshold is added. If the first two conditions does not hold, 0 is added to the vector. Consider two sentences S1 and S2,

S1: A panda bear

S2: A baby panda

Then the vocabulary is a list that contains the union of tokens in *S1* and *S2* as shown below:

Vocabulary = A, baby, bear, panda

Vocabulary-Index = A:1, baby:2, bear:3, panda:4

and the sentences are transformed to the vectors below:

S1 = 1,0,3,4

S2 = 1,2,4,4

In the example, the vocabulary term *bear* does not exist in *S2*. However, *bear* is closer to *panda* than all the terms in *S2*. The similarity score between them also exceeds the threshold. The index number of *panda* is thus assigned in place of *bear*. In

S1, the vocabulary term *baby* is not similar to any term, thus 0 is assigned. The word ordering feature is then computed as the cosine of the vectors after the WordNet based similarity transformation.

Word Overlap: We use the word n-gram overlap features of Šarić et al. (2012). The n-grams overlap is defined as the harmonic mean of the degree of mappings between the first and second sentence and vice versa, requiring an exact string match of n-grams in the two sentences.

$$\text{Ng(A,B)} = \left(2(\frac{|A|}{A \cap B} + \frac{|B|}{A \cap B})^{-1} \right) \qquad (2)$$

Where *A* and *B* are the set of n-grams in the two sentences. We computed three separate features using equation 2 for each of the following character n-grams: unigram, bigrams and trigrams. We also use weighted word overlap which uses information content (Resnik, 1995).

$$\text{wwo(A,B)} = \frac{\sum_{w \in A \cap B} ic(w)}{\sum_{w' \in B} ic(w')} \qquad (3)$$

$$\text{ic(w)} = \left(\ln \frac{\sum_{w' \in C} freq(w')}{freq(w)} \right) \qquad (4)$$

Where C is the set of words and *freq(w)* is the occurrence count obtained from the Brown corpus. Our weighted word overlap feature is computed as the harmonic mean of the functions *wwo(A,B)* and *wwo(B,A)*.

Entity Overlap: When two sentences have Named Entities (NEs) in common, a semblance of similarity is reflected. We extracted NEs from each sentence using the Stanford NER tagger (Finkel et al., 2005; Manning et al., 2014). The entity overlap feature is obtained as follows:

$$\text{EOV} = \frac{|A \tilde{\cap} B|}{|A \cup B|} \qquad (5)$$

Where *A* and *B* represent the set of named entities in the first and second sentences, respectively. The intersection, $\tilde{\cap}$, allows partial matches since the NEs are considered equivalent if either there is an exact match or if one NE is a substring of the other. For example, *'President Obama'* is not the same as *'Barack Obama'*, but *'Obama'* is considered a match for either of these.

2.2 Syntactic Features

POS Overlap: We used the Stanford POS-tagger to tag the words in each sentence with their POS categories. We group the words by the following coarse grained POS categories: nouns, verbs, adjectives and adverbs. We then compare the overlap between these classes of part of speech in each sentence, e.g., we compare the nouns in sentence 1 to the nouns in sentence 2 and vice versa across all 4 coarse grained POS categories. The POS overlap features are defined as the Jaccard similarity of the two sentences across just the words in a particular POS category:

$$POV_{pos} = \frac{|A_{pos} \cap B_{pos}|}{|A_{pos} \cup B_{pos}|} \quad (6)$$

Where A_{pos} and B_{pos} are the set of terms in POS class pos of sentences 1 and 2, respectively. This results in 4 unique POS overlap features.

Dependency Parsing: It is apt to assume that shared named entities can point to similarity in sentences. This assumption is more valid if sentences share the same *subject* and *object*. For example, if a named entity that is a *subject* in sentence1 is also the *subject* in sentence2 and vice versa the object. As an example, consider the two sentences below:

S1: Obama is the president of the United States

S2: Obama is the leader of the United States

In the first sentence, *Obama* is the subject (n-subj) of *President* while *State* modifies (nmod) the *President*. Also in the second sentence *Obama* is the subject of *leader* while *State* modifies the word *leader*.

We used the well-known *Stanford Parser* (Manning et al., 2014; De Marneffe et al., 2006) to extract the *subject-verb-object* triples from each sentence. In particular, the Neural Network-based dependency parser (Chen and Manning, 2014) was employed. We compare the *subject* and *object* of both sentences. If any of the objects or subjects in a sentence is a NE, we simply compare with the corresponding one from the other sentence by pure string matching.When the same word takes either the role of *subject* or *object* in the two sentences, we assign a flat score of 0.5. If both the *subject* and *object* in the two sentences correspond to the same NEs as in the example above, we assign a score of 1.0. Otherwise, we assign a score of 0.0.

2.3 Semantic Features

We extracted some semantic features using both information induced from corpus data as well as knowledge from existing semantic resources as described below:

Word Embedding Similarity: Word2Vec[1] (Mikolov et al., 2013b; Mikolov et al., 2013a) is an algorithm for inducing vector space representations of words, commonly known as word embeddings, that capture semantic relatedness and similarity. The method exploits the Distributional Hypothesis (Turney et al., 2010) and works best when trained on large corpora. We used the Gensim[2] implementation of the algorithm with specific parameter fine-tuning.[3] Gensim implements a variant of the algorithm known as *Skip-Gram*, which trains word representations using a model that when given a word will predict what words are likely to occur within a fixed window around it.[4] Once the word embeddings have been trained, the similarity of two words is computed as the cosine of the two embedding vectors.[5] Our word embeddings are trained on a combination of the Wikipedia dump of English language articles and the STS 2016 training data.[6]

For sentence level similarity scores, we compare each word in the first sentence to each word in the second sentence, obtaining a similarity score with the word2vec model. For each pair being compared, if the similarity score is less than < 0.25 then that similarity value is dropped. The final similarity is computed by summing the pair similarity values greater than 0.25 and dividing by the total count of these similarity scores. The aggregation function is

---

[1]Word2vec is available at https://code.google.com/p/word2vec/

[2]Gensim is a python library for an array of NLP tasks. It is available at https://radimrehurek.com/gensim/

[3]Parameters used: Context Window: 5, Neural Network layer size: 200, Minimum word count: 5.

[4]Skip-gram training generally performs better than an alternative Word2Vec model known as Continuous-Bag-of-Words (CBOW) that uses an alternative objective that tries to predict a word by conditioning on all of the words that surround it within a window.

[5]model.similarity(word1, word2) returns a similarity value from -1 to 1 between word1 and word2. Also model[word1] returns a numpy vector of word1

[6]The wikipedia dump was downloaded on July 30, 2015. It is accessible at https://dumps.wikimedia.org/enwiki/

given below:

$$\text{Sim} = \frac{\sum_{i,j}^{m,n} |S(w_i, w_j > x)|}{tCount} \qquad (7)$$

Where $S(w_i, w_j)$ is the similarity score for two words, *tCount* is the total number of the set of similarity scores that exceeds the threshold and *Sim* is the aggregating function combining all pairwise similarities.

WordNet similarity: The idea of pairing and aggregating similarity of words from two sentences being compared is not new and has been used both in textual entailment (Agichtein et al., 2008) and semantic textual similarity (Bär et al., 2012). To derive similarity from WordNet, we used both the path length between each word as well as the depth function. Usually, longer path length between two concepts signifies lower similarity. However, as pointed out by Li et al. (2006), this obviates the distance knowledge that can be easily observed from the hierarchical organization of some *semantic nets*. As a solution, the depth function was introduced, with the intuition that words at upper layer of a *semantic nets* contains general semantics and less similarity while those at lower layers are more similar. Thus, similarity should be a function of both the depth and the path length distances between concepts. If f1(h) is a function of the depth and f2(l) is a function of the length, then the similarity between two word is given by:

$$S(w_1, w_2) = f1(h).f2(l) \qquad (8)$$

The length function is a monotonically decreasing function with respect to the path length l between two concepts. This is captured by introducing a constant alpha.

$$f2(l) = e^{-\alpha l} \qquad (9)$$

Likewise, the depth function is monotonically increasing with respect to the depth h of concept in the hierarchy.

$$f1(h) = \frac{e^{\beta h} - e^{-\beta h}}{e^{\beta h} + e^{-\beta h}} \qquad (10)$$

The similarity between two concepts is then calculated by:

$$S(w_1, w_2) = e^{-\alpha l} . \frac{e^{\beta h} - e^{-\beta h}}{e^{\beta h} + e^{-\beta h}} \qquad (11)$$

Li et al. (2006) empirically discovered that for optimal performance in WordNet, alpha should be set to 0.2 and Beta set to 0.45. To aggregate the similarities, we used the formula in *equation 7* with a threshold of 0.25.

Vector Space based Similarity: We used the feature extraction module of the *scikit-learn* to extract the *TFIDF* weighted feature vectors for the two sentences and then calculated the cosine similarity between them:

$$\cos(A, B) = \frac{\sum_{t=1}^{n} TFIDF(w_{t,A})TFIDF(w_{t,B})}{\sqrt{\sum_{t=1}^{n} w_{t,A}^2 \sum_{t=1}^{n} w_{t,B}^2}} \qquad (12)$$

Where A and B are the two texts being compared for similarity. The term frequency *TF* and inverse document frequency *IDF* are computed solely from the compared sentence pairs.

Compositional Distributional Approach: A limitation of Distributional Hypothesis (Harris, 1954; Firth, 1957) is that it captures the meaning of words in isolation. However, the true meaning of a sentence must take into account the interplay between the words it contains (Mitchell and Lapata, 2008; Mitchell and Lapata, 2009; Grefenstette et al., 2014). To account for this, we perform vector composition of the words in each sentence, using both additive and multiplicative composition (Mitchell and Lapata, 2010; Baroni, 2013). We obtained the vectors from the Word2Vec model described earlier. For the additive model, the vectors of all the words in a sentence are summed together to get a single vector for that sentence. Likewise, in the multiplicative model, vectors of all words in a sentence are multiplied component-wise to obtain a single vector for the sentence. To obtain similarity scores for each composition method, i.e., additive and multiplicative, we take the cosine of the vector space representation of the two sentences being compared.

3 System Description

For each sentence pair, our system generates 36 lexical, syntactic and semantic features. We experiment with using three distinct learning algorithms to map our feature representation onto an STS similarity score for the pair. The three learning algorithms correspond to the three runs we submitted to the shared task: ***Normas-RF1***, was trained with *Random Forest*

Dataset	Run1	Run2	Run3	Mean	Baseline-Median	Baseline-Best
Answer	.160	**.365**	.276	.267	.480	.692
Question	.467	.613	**.653**	.577	.571	.747
Postediting	.720*	**.802***	.797*	.773	.812	.866
Plagiarism	.621	**.746**	.724	.697	.789	.841
Headlines	.588	.688	**.722**	.666	.764	.827
Runs Mean	.508	.640	.630	.596		

Table 1: Summary of Pearson Correlation Evaluation Of The Submitted System

(Breiman, 2001; Liaw and Wiener, 2002); **Normas-SV2**, uses *Support Vector Regression* (Chang and Lin, 2011; Basak et al., 2007); **Normas-ECV3**, is based on *Elastic Net* (Zou and Hastie, 2005). As training data, we used **2234** sentence pairs from the *2012* training data. Parameter fine-tuning[7] for each of the algorithms was done using *OnWN* dataset of the STS 2013 evaluation data as the development test set. We used the scikit-learn[8] implementation of the three algorithms.

4 Evaluation and Discussion

We conducted two experiments, *Pre-Submission* and *Post-Submission* experiments. Table 1 summarizes the result of the Runs submitted across the datasets for the first experiment (*Pre-Submission*). The scores in **bold** shows the best scores per dataset. The scores with *asterisk (*)* appended shows the best scores under each Run. We used the preliminary result of the 2016 STS task released by the organizers as the baseline for evaluation. The preliminary result includes the median scores (*Baseline-Median*) and best scores (*Baseline-Best*) of the participating systems on each dataset. The *Baseline Best* is the score of the top performing system for each dataset of the Semeval 2016 task(Agirre et al., 2016).

It can be seen from *Table 1* that our best scores were from #Run2 and #Run3. The Random Forest algorithm performed poorly compared to the other two Runs on all of the datasets. All three Runs performed best on the Post-Editing dataset. This conforms to the pattern observed from the Baseline

scores. Analysis of this dataset revealed that the sentences are longer and share more words.

Our worst performance across board is on the Answer-Answer dataset. Inspecting the data reveals that the sentences are both short and tend to share words that have little or no impact on their overall meaning. Our models may have been misguided by these spurious matching words.

Overall, our best systems, #Run2 and #Run3, have results very close to the *Baseline-Best* on three datasets and outclassed *Baseline-Median* on Question-question dataset. Our system performance may have been handicapped by the limited amount of data we used for training. Recall that we trained our system on only **2234** sentences of the 2012 training data. The tiny size of the dataset was necessitated by the complexity of computing some of the semantic features. Specifically, the WordNet similarity features used. Also, analysis of our training data shows that the sentences are of few words (short) and with high term overlap. Perhaps, our system could have performed better with more training data, especially if we had used a dataset with long sentences and also included more training data from previous STS evaluation tasks.

After the official evaluation, we reproduced our experiment using a larger training set. The new training data contains **9902** sentences drawn from the *2012-2014* evaluation datasets. Using more training data resulted in a notable improvement in performance. *Table 2* reports the results obtained by our (*post-submission*) systems. The *Percentage Gain* column shows the improvement in performance when the *Mean* result in the second experiment is compared to the one submitted initially (*pre-submission*).

The best improvement observed is from the *Answer-Answer* dataset with **38.0** % improvement

---

[7]For SVR, we used the LibSvm scikit implementation with RBF kernel. We set C=1.0, epsilon=0.2 and cache size=200. For Elastic Net we used alpha=0.5. Random Forest, we used 100 trees, max_depth=None and max_leaf_nodes=None. Grid search was used for hyperparameter optimization.

[8]http://scikit-learn.org/

Dataset	Run1	Run2	Run3	Mean	Percent Gain	Baseline-Median	Baseline-Best
Answer	.380	**.542**	.371	.431	38.0	.480	.692
Question	.698	.714	**.723**	.711	18.8	.571	.747
Postediting	.819*	**.852***	.809*	.826	6.80	.812	.866
Plagiarism	.797	**.821**	.784	.800	12.8	.789	.841
Headlines	**.805**	.789	.780	.791	15.8	.764	.827
Runs Mean	.699	.743	.693	.711	16.1	.683	.794

Table 2: Post-Submission Experiment With More Training Data (9902 sentence pairs)

across all Runs. The result from our top performing Runs across all datasets clearly surpass the *Baseline-Median* results. The top scores for each dataset were also very close to the *Baseline-Best* results. Our overall Mean of **0.711** surpasses the overall Mean of the *Baseline-Median (0.683)* and is far better than the 0.596 obtained by our submitted systems.

5 Conclusion

This paper has described our system submission to the SemEval 2016 STS shared task. We participated in the STS-Core (*Monolingual subtask*). We submitted three Runs using the same feature set but with models built by different machine learning algorithms. We obtained the best performance from the *Support Vector Regression* and *Elastic Net* based models and observed relatively poor performance from *Random Forests*.

The systems we submitted to the shared task obtained results that are very close to the best performing shared task system in 3 datasets and above the median mark on another dataset .

After the shared task, we reproduced our experiment on a bigger training dataset. We obtained a significant improvement (16.1%) when compared to the first experiment.

In future work, we plan to investigate the significance of all features so as to identify noisy or less important ones as well as to attempt to identify the optimal combination of features. Another improvement might be to build an *ensemble* combining individual systems built using variations in any one of the following: learning algorithm, feature set, or training data sampling (e.g., combining our best two systems).

References

Eugene Agichtein, Walt Askew, and Yandong Liu. 2008. Combining lexical, syntactic, and semantic evidence for textual entailment classification. *Proceedings of TAC*, 31.

Eneko Agirre, Mona Diab, Daniel Cer, and Aitor Gonzalez-Agirre. 2012. Semeval-2012 task 6: A pilot on semantic textual similarity. In *Proceedings of the First Joint Conference on Lexical and Computational Semantics-Volume 1: Proceedings of the main conference and the shared task, and Volume 2: Proceedings of the Sixth International Workshop on Semantic Evaluation*, pages 385–393. Association for Computational Linguistics.

Eneko Agirre, Carmen Banea, Daniel Cer, Mona Diab, Aitor Gonzalez-Agirre, Rada Mihalcea, and Janyce Wiebe. 2016. Semeval-2016 task 1: Semantic textual similarity, monolingual and cross-lingual evaluation. In *In* Proceedings of the 10th International Workshop on Semantic Evaluation (SemEval 2016)*, San Diego, USA, June. Association for Computational Linguistics.

Daniel Bär, Chris Biemann, Iryna Gurevych, and Torsten Zesch. 2012. Ukp: Computing semantic textual similarity by combining multiple content similarity measures. In *Proceedings of the First Joint Conference on Lexical and Computational Semantics-Volume 1: Proceedings of the main conference and the shared task, and Volume 2: Proceedings of the Sixth International Workshop on Semantic Evaluation*, pages 435–440. Association for Computational Linguistics.

Marco Baroni. 2013. Composition in distributional semantics. *Language and Linguistics Compass*, 7(10):511–522.

Regina Barzilay and Michael Elhadad. 1999. Using lexical chains for text summarization. *Advances in automatic text summarization*, pages 111–121.

Debasish Basak, Srimanta Pal, and Dipak Chandra Patranabis. 2007. Support vector regression. *Neural Information Processing-Letters and Reviews*, 11(10):203–224.

Danushka Bollegala, Yutaka Matsuo, and Mitsuru Ishizuka. 2007. Measuring semantic similarity between words using web search engines. *www*, 7:757–766.

Leo Breiman. 2001. Random forests. *Machine learning*, 45(1):5–32.

Peter F Brown, John Cocke, Stephen A Della Pietra, Vincent J Della Pietra, Fredrick Jelinek, John D Lafferty, Robert L Mercer, and Paul S Roossin. 1990. A statistical approach to machine translation. *Computational linguistics*, 16(2):79–85.

Chih-Chung Chang and Chih-Jen Lin. 2011. Libsvm: a library for support vector machines. *ACM Transactions on Intelligent Systems and Technology (TIST)*, 2(3):27.

Danqi Chen and Christopher D Manning. 2014. A fast and accurate dependency parser using neural networks. In *EMNLP*, pages 740–750.

Ido Dagan. 2000. Contextual word similarity. *Handbook of Natural Language Processing*, pages 459–475.

Marie-Catherine De Marneffe, Bill MacCartney, Christopher D Manning, et al. 2006. Generating typed dependency parses from phrase structure parses. In *Proceedings of LREC*, volume 6, pages 449–454.

Tamer Elsayed, Jimmy Lin, and Douglas W Oard. 2008. Pairwise document similarity in large collections with mapreduce. In *Proceedings of the 46th Annual Meeting of the Association for Computational Linguistics on Human Language Technologies: Short Papers*, pages 265–268. Association for Computational Linguistics.

Samuel Fernando and Mark Stevenson. 2008. A semantic similarity approach to paraphrase detection. In *Proceedings of the 11th Annual Research Colloquium of the UK Special Interest Group for Computational Linguistics*, pages 45–52. Citeseer.

Jenny Rose Finkel, Trond Grenager, and Christopher Manning. 2005. Incorporating non-local information into information extraction systems by gibbs sampling. In *Proceedings of the 43rd Annual Meeting on Association for Computational Linguistics*, pages 363–370. Association for Computational Linguistics.

John R Firth. 1957. {A synopsis of linguistic theory, 1930-1955}.

Yihong Gong and Xin Liu. 2001. Generic text summarization using relevance measure and latent semantic analysis. In *Proceedings of the 24th annual international ACM SIGIR conference on Research and development in information retrieval*, pages 19–25. ACM.

Edward Grefenstette, Mehrnoosh Sadrzadeh, Stephen Clark, Bob Coecke, and Stephen Pulman. 2014. Concrete sentence spaces for compositional distributional models of meaning. In *Computing Meaning*, pages 71–86. Springer.

Dan Gusfield. 1997. *Algorithms on strings, trees and sequences: computer science and computational biology*. Cambridge university press.

Zellig S Harris. 1954. Distributional structure. *Word*, 10(2-3):146–162.

Anna Huang. 2008. Similarity measures for text document clustering. In *Proceedings of the sixth new zealand computer science research student conference (NZCSRSC2008), Christchurch, New Zealand*, pages 49–56.

Yuhua Li, David McLean, Zuhair A Bandar, James D O'shea, and Keeley Crockett. 2006. Sentence similarity based on semantic nets and corpus statistics. *Knowledge and Data Engineering, IEEE Transactions on*, 18(8):1138–1150.

Andy Liaw and Matthew Wiener. 2002. Classification and regression by randomforest. *R news*, 2(3):18–22.

Christopher D Manning, Prabhakar Raghavan, Hinrich Schütze, et al. 2008. *Introduction to information retrieval*, volume 1. Cambridge university press Cambridge.

Christopher D Manning, Mihai Surdeanu, John Bauer, Jenny Rose Finkel, Steven Bethard, and David McClosky. 2014. The stanford corenlp natural language processing toolkit. In *ACL (System Demonstrations)*, pages 55–60.

Tomas Mikolov, Kai Chen, Greg Corrado, and Jeffrey Dean. 2013a. Efficient estimation of word representations in vector space. *arXiv preprint arXiv:1301.3781*.

Tomas Mikolov, Ilya Sutskever, Kai Chen, Greg S Corrado, and Jeff Dean. 2013b. Distributed representations of words and phrases and their compositionality. In *Advances in neural information processing systems*, pages 3111–3119.

Jeff Mitchell and Mirella Lapata. 2008. Vector-based models of semantic composition. In *ACL*, pages 236–244.

Jeff Mitchell and Mirella Lapata. 2009. Language models based on semantic composition. In *Proceedings of the 2009 Conference on Empirical Methods in Natural Language Processing: Volume 1-Volume 1*, pages 430–439. Association for Computational Linguistics.

Jeff Mitchell and Mirella Lapata. 2010. Composition in distributional models of semantics. *Cognitive science*, 34(8):1388–1429.

Ted Pedersen, Siddharth Patwardhan, and Jason Michelizzi. 2004. Wordnet:: Similarity: measuring the relatedness of concepts. In *Demonstration papers at HLT-NAACL 2004*, pages 38–41. Association for Computational Linguistics.

Philip Resnik. 1995. Using information content to evaluate semantic similarity in a taxonomy. *arXiv preprint cmp-lg/9511007*.

Gerard Salton and Christopher Buckley. 1988. Term-weighting approaches in automatic text retrieval. *Information processing & management*, 24(5):513–523.

Frane Šarić, Goran Glavaš, Mladen Karan, Jan Šnajder, and Bojana Dalbelo Bašić. 2012. Takelab: Systems for measuring semantic text similarity. In *Proceedings of the First Joint Conference on Lexical and Computational Semantics-Volume 1: Proceedings of the main conference and the shared task, and Volume 2: Proceedings of the Sixth International Workshop on Semantic Evaluation*, pages 441–448. Association for Computational Linguistics.

Antonio Si, Hong Va Leong, and Rynson WH Lau. 1997. Check: a document plagiarism detection system. In *Proceedings of the 1997 ACM symposium on Applied computing*, pages 70–77. ACM.

Peter D Turney, Patrick Pantel, et al. 2010. From frequency to meaning: Vector space models of semantics. *Journal of artificial intelligence research*, 37(1):141–188.

Hui Zou and Trevor Hastie. 2005. Regularization and variable selection via the elastic net. *Journal of the Royal Statistical Society: Series B (Statistical Methodology)*, 67(2):301–320.

LIPN-IIMAS at SemEval-2016 Task 1: Random Forest Regression Experiments on Align-and-Differentiate and Word Embeddings penalizing strategies

Oscar Lithgow

Centro de Ciencias Genómicas (CCG)
Universidad Nacional Autónoma de México (UNAM)
Ciudad Universitaria, DF, Mexico
`owl@turing.iimas.unam.mx`

Ivan V. Meza, Albert Orozco

Instituto de Investigaciones en Matemáticas Aplicadas y en Sistemas
Universidad Nacional Autónoma de México (UNAM)
Ciudad Universitaria, DF, Mexico
`{ivanvladimir,albert}@turing.iimas.unam.mx`

Jorge Gacia Flores, Davide Buscaldi

Laboratoire d'Informatique de Paris Nord, CNRS (UMR 7030)
Université Paris 13, Sorbonne Paris Cité, Villetaneuse, France
`{buscaldi,jgflores}@lipn.univ-paris13.fr`

Abstract

This paper describes the *SOPA-N* system used by the LIPN-IIMAS team in Semeval 2016 Semantic Textual Similarity (Task 1). We based our work on the *SOPA 2015* system. The *SOPA-2015* system used 16 similarity features (including Wordnet, Information Retrieval and Syntactic Dependencies) within a Random Forest learning model. We expanded this system with an Align and Differentiate based strategy, word embeddings and penalization, which showed 6.8% of improvement on the development set. However, we found that on the evaluation data for the 2016 STS shared task, the 2015 system outperformed our newer systems.

1 Introduction

The *SOPA* system combines a regression model with multi-level similarity measures, from very simple ones (like edit distance) to more sophisticated ones (like IR-based or Wordnet similarity) (Buscaldi et al., 2013). Our goal this year was to add an align-and-differentiate penalizing strategy based on (Han et al., 2015) to our 2015 system (*SOPA*) (Buscaldi

et al., 2015). The previous version consists on 16 similarity features which are regressed using a Random Forest learning algorithm. The rationale of the penalization was to account for cases when apparent distributional alignments are closer than their semantically equivalent (for instance, colors: while *black* and *white* are distributional close because are colors, but they are not semantically equivalent). We present two versions of the enhanced system SOPA 100 and 1000 which refers to the number of estimation trees used by the Random Forest algorithm.

We find that augmenting our 2015 model with an align and differentiate module boosts performance on the 2015 evaluation data. However, on the STS 2016 test data it only outperformed our previous approach on the plagiarism dataset. A closer error analysis showed that the gap between *SOPA* 100 and the gold standard (GS) scores are systematically positive, meaning that our new system overestimated the semantic similarity between phrases. Another interesting finding from the error analysis was that in those sentences where *SOPA* 100 outperform *SOPA*, it was also more accurate, given the fact that the *SOPA* 100 standard deviation from the gold standard annotation was smaller than the one of

726

SOPA.

Ablation tests for every feature were performed as well. Within our 2015 system, Sultan's alignment based similarity feature, Sultan et al. (2015)'s feature 18 , seems to be pulling down scores both for the headlines and question-question domains of 2016 dataset, despite the fact that 2015 train and test sets were used to train our 2016 system. Further analysis might be necessary in order to fully answer why *SOPA* 100 runs seemed to improve our scores for evaluation data from 2015, but they didn't for 2016 datasets.

2 SOPA

The SOPA system was built upon the idea on combining simple measures with a regression model to obtain a global, graded measure of textual similarity. Past experiences on this system have shown that the Random Forest (Breiman, 2001) outperforms other regression algorithms (like ν-Support Vector Regression or Multi-Layer Perceptron). Table 1 shows individual text similarity measures used as features for the global system, which have been described in more detail in (Buscaldi et al., 2013) and (Buscaldi et al., 2015).

2.1 Align-and-differentiate

This year we included a strategy that consists in two main steps:

1. Align words of both phrases

2. Differentiate or penalize those alignments that distributionally appear closer than they really are.

In the first step, the first word of phrase A is compared against each word of phrase B, and the pair which has the best similarity score is considered as an alignment pair and the words are removed from candidates. Then the process is repeated for the second word of phrase A and so on until all words are used.

The second step consists in inspecting each candidate alignment and penalizing those alignments that do not represent interchangeable concepts (synonyms). First, if an alignment score does not surpass a threshold, the alignment pair is discarded and those words are considered out-of-context. Second,

	Measure
1	N-gram Based Similarity
2	WordNet Conceptual Similarity (Wu Palmer)
3	Syntactic Dependencies
4	Edit Distance
5	Cosine tf-idf
6	Named Entity Overlap
7	WordNet Conceptual Similarity (Jiang-Corath)
8	Information Retrieval Similarity (AQUAINT)
9	Geographical Context Similarity
10	Rank-Biased Overlap Similarity
11	DBPedia named entity Similarity
12	IR-based similarity (UkWaC index)
13	Skip-gram similarity
14	Sphynx WER
15	Sultan Similarity
16	Sentence size similarity
17*	Sultan alignment with word2vec* (left-right)
18*	Sultan alignment with WordNet (left-right)
19*	Sultan alignment with word2vec* (right-left)
20*	Sultan alignment with WordNet (right-left)
21*	Word2vec simple alignment (left-right)
22*	Word2vec simple alignment (right-left)
23*	Average of word2vec alignments

Table 1: Similarity Measures (* new features for 2016.)

the words of each pair is searched in Wordnet and: if those words are antonyms the alignment is penalized; if both words are hyponyms of a Disjoint Similar Concept (DSC) (Han et al., 2015), the alignment is penalized as well.

We also included an alignment-shift-penalization. It is computed using Spearman correlation over the position in the phrase of the aligned words. The idea behind is to reduce the similarity score on those phrase alignments in which aligned pairs consist in words with a very different position in phrase A with respect phrase B.

2.2 Alignments

Two different alignment strategies were tried. A pure distributional based alignment in which words are aligned using *word2vec* (Mikolov et al., 2013) to measure the cosine similarity between the two words and aligned pairs are determined using the best local alignment. In this approach, a left-right alignment and a right-left alignment are combined in order to, in some way, alleviate the appearance of local maxima.

The second is a hybrid strategy that combines a syntactic based alignment produced by Sultan with a distributional alignment. This is, it uses the pairs given by Sultan aligner (Sultan et al., 2014) and those not aligned words of both phrases are submitted to a second alignment process (distributional) that in some sense complements the syntactic alignment.

3   Experimental setting

We used the following configurations for *SOPA* 100 and *SOPA* 1, 000 runs, they were applied to the features 17-23:

- Words identification and tokenization was done using a simple space-based regular expression.

- Similarity in WordNet was obtained using the *path_similarity* metric available in NLTK package (Loper and Bird, 2002).

- For the penalization by shift-external-alignment, the Spearman correlation between the positions of aligned words is computed and, if the correlation is above a threshold of 0.25, it is multiplied by the alignment score.

- When checking the aligned pairs of words in WordNet: if one word of the pair is listed as an antonym of the other, a penalty of 1.0 is applied.; if words are not antonyms, we search the lowest common hypernym for both synsets, then we walk the path from this hypernym to the root and if in this walk we visit one of the nodes considered DSC then a penalty of 0.5 is applied.

- We used cosine as the measure of distance among vectors. The vectors are extracted form the standard Google pretrained *word2vec* models with 300 dimensions.[1]

- We used the list of English stop-words available in the NLTK package to filter stop-words from sentences.

[1]`https://code.google.com/archive/p/word2vec/`

- We discarded alignments that are below an align-threshold of 0.3.

- Each unaligned word was considered out-of-context (OOC) and for each of those, a penalization of 1.0 was applied.

The code of our implementation and experimentation is openly available.[2]

4   Results

These year runs were:

SOPA The *SOPA* 2015 system (16 scores) trained with a random forest regressor set to 100 estimators (Buscaldi et al., 2015).

SOPA 100 This was the *SOPA* similarities plus the align-and-differentiate scores trained with a random forest regressor set to 100 estimators.

SOPA 1000 This was the *SOPA* similarities plus the align-and-differentiate features trained with a random forest regressor set to 1,000 estimators.

Table 2 shows the performance of each of these systems on the 2016 STS evaluation data. As it can be appreciated the *SOPA* outperforms the other runs in most domains and in the overall evaluation. The extracted scores using the align-and-differentiate strategy were not helpful for these datasets. This was contrary to our development experience in which the these scores contributed to improve the performance of the 2015 *SOPA* system (see Table 3 with 2015 test dataset).

The change of behavior from the developing to the testing stage was unexpected. With this in mind we proceed to do further experimentation. First we re-run the *SOPA* 100 and *SOPA* 1, 000 setting but only using the align-and-differentiate scores. Table 4 present these results, as expected this time the performance is quite poor. Effectively, the performances of the score were too poor, so that they bring down the full performance. These experiments confirms what we learn from Table 2. In order to gain a better insight on the scores we run an ablation experiment. In this case we suppress each the score and measure the loss in performance. Table 5 presents

[2]`https://github.com/rcln/SemEval`

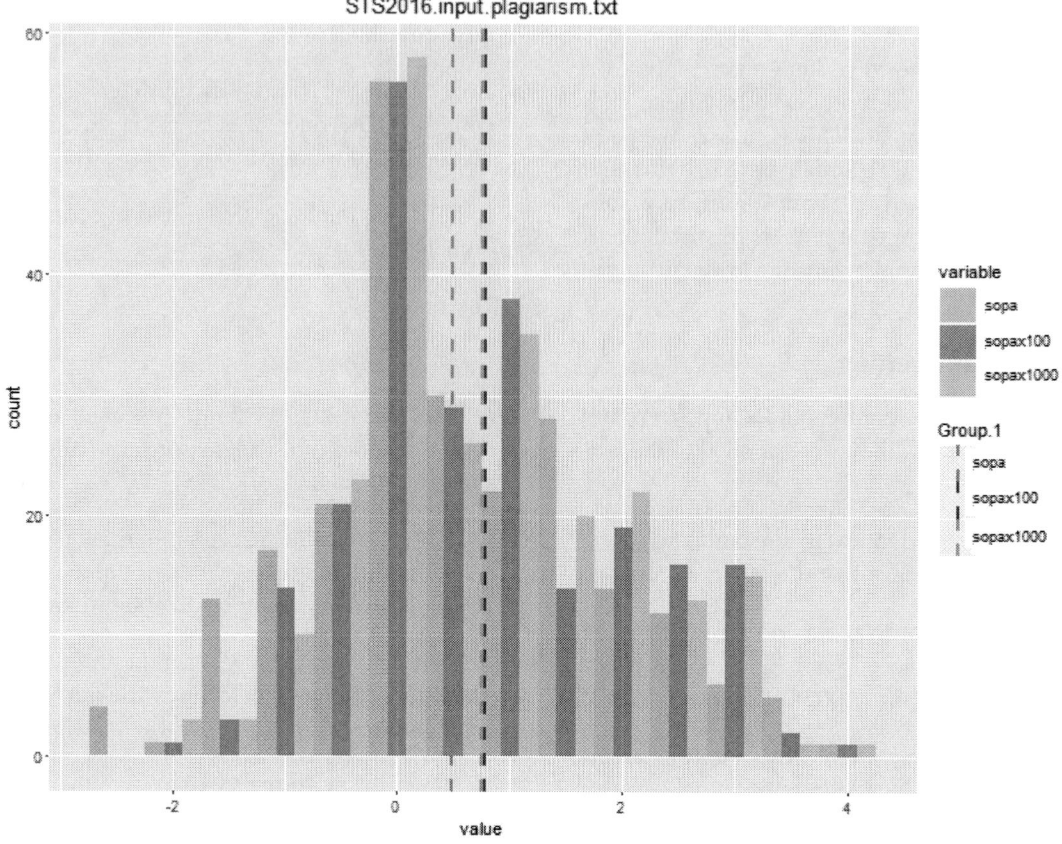

Figure 1: Distribution of the difference with plagiarism

these losses. The table marks with a star those score which have a negative loss, meaning that without them the performance will increase. However, we do not observe a general pattern. Similarity scores for some domains made them particularly worse, but not for others. The *headlines*, *plagiarism* and *question-question* has a larger amount of features that were not very useful. We identify 8 scores with a negative overall loss, however further experimentation without these features did not give a better performance for the *SOPA* 100 and *SOPA* 1, 000 settings.

Figure 2 shows the differences of the runs with the gold standard. The first thing to notice from this graph is that all systems tend to overestimate the score, this is they give a larger score than the gold standard. We also notice that the standard deviation is close to one for most of the runs. However, these graphs do not tell the whole story, for instance in the case of the *plagiarism* domain the distribution of the

Dataset	SOPA	100	1,000
answer-answer	**0.44901**	0.43216	0.44893
headlines	**0.62411**	0.58499	0.59721
plagiarism	0.69109	0.74727	**0.75936**
postediting	**0.79864**	0.75560	0.76157
question-question	**0.59779**	0.55310	0.56285
Overall	**0.63087**	0.61321	0.62466

Table 2: Final test results

difference is far from normal, Figure 1 shows the histogram of score differences, illustrating a slight positive skew in the predictions.

5 Conclusions and perspectives

In this paper we introduced the *SOPA-N* system used to calculate semantic similarity between sentence pairs for the Semeval STS 2016 Challenge. *SOPA-N* is based in a 23 similarity feature set and

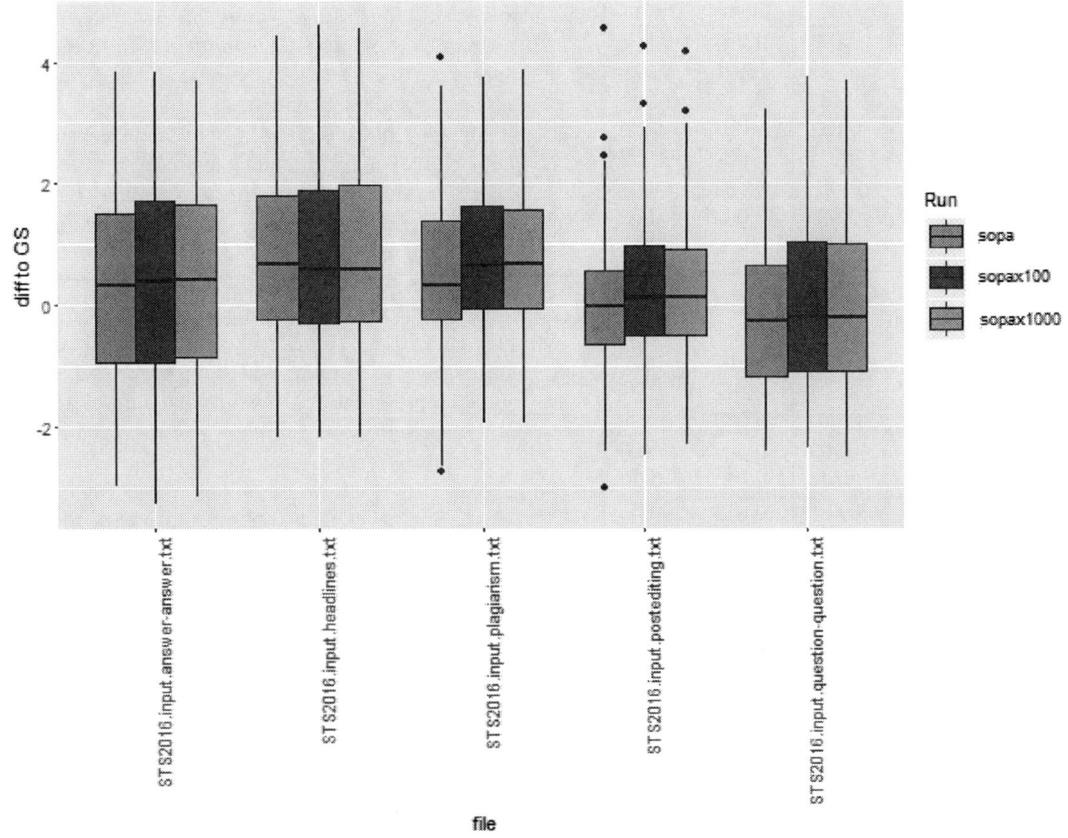

Figure 2: Distribution of the difference with GS for the plagiarism corpus

Dataset	SOPA	100	1000
answer-forums	0.63331	0.64814	**0.65398**
answers-students	0.63893	**0.70356**	0.70137
images	0.81768	0.84109	**0.84237**
headlines	0.81666	**0.8247**	0.82376
believe	0.59779	0.73149	**0.73179**
Overall	0.68232	0.74976	**0.75065**

Table 3: Development results (STS 2015)

Dataset	100	1000
answer-answer	0.40169	0.39145
headlines	0.50688	0.50928
plagiarism	0.70305	0.70814
postediting	0.6669	0.66366
question-question	0.37848	0.39587

Table 4: Re-run of **100** system with only align-and-differentiate scores

a Random Forest learning algorithm. New features for this year challenge included word embeddings based on Sultan et al. (2015)'s alignment and an Align-And-Differentiate strategy inspired by Han et al. (2015). These improvements allowed us to outperform our previous approach only for the *plagiarism* test corpus. Even if *SOPA-N* was more accurate for those sentences where its score gap between the gold standard was better than *SOPA*, further error analysis is needed.

We hypothesize that the addition of align based features was not appropriate for this year data. Particularly we plan to analyze alignment errors and expand the context to better guide the alignment. Also, future research will focus in a deeper characterization of 2016 test in terms of spelling correctness, typography profile POS-tag categories, semantic and discursive level in order to find correlation between these characteristics and the GS gap of our system.

	a.-a.	head.	pla.	post.	q.-q.
1	−0.01	−0.02	0.02	0.00	0.02
2	0.01	**-0.04**	0.02	−0.01	0.02
3*	0.00	**-0.03**	−0.02	0.01	−0.01
4	0.00	0.00	0.01	0.00	−0.01
5	0.02	0.00	0.01	0.00	−0.02
6	0.02	0.00	0.00	0.00	0.00
7	0.01	0.02	0.00	0.00	0.01
8	0.00	0.01	−0.01	0.00	0.01
9	0.00	0.00	0.02	0.00	0.02
10*	0.01	−0.02	−0.02	0.00	−0.01
11*	0.01	−0.02	−0.01	−0.01	0.01
12*	0.00	−0.01	0.00	0.00	−0.02
13*	0.01	0.01	−0.01	−0.01	−0.01
14	0.00	0.01	0.00	0.01	0.01
15*	0.00	**-0.04**	−0.01	0.00	**-0.05**
16	0.01	−0.01	0.01	0.02	−0.00
17*	0.01	0.00	0.01	0.01	**0.03**
18	0.01	0.01	−0.01	0.01	**-0.04**
19	0.02	0.01	0.01	0.01	0.01
20*	0.01	**-0.03**	0.00	0.00	−0.01
21	0.01	0.00	−0.02	0.00	0.02
22	0.02	0.01	0.00	0.00	0.02
23	0.00	−0.02	**0.03**	0.00	0.02

Table 5: Loss for each score for **100** run

6 Acknowledgments

Work by Oscar Lithgow was supported by the National Institute of Health (Award number: GM110597) through the Centro de Ciencias Computacionales, UNAM.

References

[Breiman2001] Leo Breiman. 2001. Random forests. *Machine learning*, 45(1):5–32.

[Buscaldi et al.2013] Davide Buscaldi, Joseph Le Roux, Jorge J. Garcia Flores, and Adrian Popescu. 2013. LIPN-CORE: Semantic Text Similarity using n-grams, WordNet, Syntactic Analysis, ESA and Information Retrieval based Features. In *Second Joint Conference on Lexical and Computational Semantics (*SEM), Volume 1: Proceedings of the Main Conference and the Shared Task: Semantic Textual Similarity*, pages 162–168, Atlanta, Georgia, USA, June.

[Buscaldi et al.2015] Davide Buscaldi, Jorge García Flores, Ivan V. Meza, and Isaac Rodríguez. 2015. SOPA: Random Forests Regression for the Semantic Textual Similarity task. In *SemEval 2015*, pages 132–137.

[Han et al.2015] Lushan Han, Justin Martineau, Doreen Cheng, and Christopher Thomas. 2015. Samsung: Align-and-differentiate approach to semantic textual similarity. In *Proceedings of the 9th International Workshop on Semantic Evaluation (SemEval 2015)*, pages 172–177, Denver, Colorado, June. Association for Computational Linguistics.

[Loper and Bird2002] Edward Loper and Steven Bird. 2002. Nltk: The natural language toolkit. In *Proceedings of the ACL-02 Workshop on Effective Tools and Methodologies for Teaching Natural Language Processing and Computational Linguistics - Volume 1*, ETMTNLP '02, pages 63–70, Stroudsburg, PA, USA. Association for Computational Linguistics.

[Mikolov et al.2013] Tomas Mikolov, Ilya Sutskever, Kai Chen, Greg S Corrado, and Jeff Dean. 2013. Distributed representations of words and phrases and their compositionality. In *Advances in neural information processing systems*, pages 3111–3119.

[Sultan et al.2014] Md Arafat Sultan, Steven Bethard, and Tamara Sumner. 2014. Back to Basics for Monolingual Alignment: Exploiting Word Similarity and Contextual Evidence.

[Sultan et al.2015] Md Arafat Sultan, Steven Bethard, and Tamara Sumner. 2015. Dls@cu: Sentence similarity from word alignment and semantic vector composition. In *Proceedings of the 9th International Workshop on Semantic Evaluation (SemEval 2015)*, pages 148–153, Denver, Colorado, June. Association for Computational Linguistics.

UNBNLP at SemEval-2016 Task 1: Semantic Textual Similarity: A Unified Framework for Semantic Processing and Evaluation

Milton King and **Waseem Gharbieh** and **SoHyun Park** and **Paul Cook**
Faculty of Computer Science, University of New Brunswick
Fredericton, NB E3B 5A3, Canada
{milton.king,waseem.gharbieh,sohyun.park,paul.cook}@unb.ca

Abstract

In this paper we consider several approaches to predicting semantic textual similarity using word embeddings, as well as methods for forming embeddings for larger units of text. We compare these methods to several baselines, and find that none of them outperform the baselines. We then consider both a supervised and unsupervised approach to combining these methods which achieve modest improvements over the baselines.

1 Introduction

Word embeddings (Mikolov et al., 2013) have recently led to improvements in a wide range of tasks in natural language processing. A number of approaches to forming embeddings for sentences, paragraphs, and documents have also recently been proposed (e.g., Le and Mikolov, 2014; Kiros et al., 2015). These methods seem particularly well suited to the task of predicting semantic textual similarity (STS), and indeed have been shown to work very well on similar tasks (Kiros et al., 2015).

This paper describes the system of UNBNLP at SemEval-2016 Task 1. We first implement several baseline approaches to STS based on cosine similarity of count-based vectors representing sentences, with a variety of approaches to term weighting. We then consider approaches drawing off of word2vec (Mikolov et al., 2013), paragraph vectors (Le and Mikolov, 2014), and skip-thoughts (Kiros et al., 2015). We find that none of these approaches improve over any of our baselines.

We then consider combining information from these individual methods to measuring STS. We consider an unsupervised approach based on the average of the predicted similarities for a number of these individual approaches. We further consider a supervised approach in which we train ridge regression with features corresponding to the similarities from these individual methods. Each of these methods for combining information achieves modest improvements over the baselines.

2 Measuring short text similarity

We present several methods for measuring STS in Section 2.1. We then present approaches to combining these methods in Section 2.2.

2.1 Individual methods

2.1.1 Baselines

We present three baseline methods. In all of these baselines, each sentence in a pair of sentences is represented as a vector, where each dimension corresponds to a word type (i.e., a word form).

In the first approach, referred to as BASELINE-BIN, the dimensions hold binary values indicating whether the corresponding type occurs in the sentence. In the second approach, BASELINE-FREQ, the dimensions hold the frequency of the corresponding type in the sentence. For the third approach, BASELINE-TF-IDF, each dimension holds the tf-idf weight for the corresponding type in the sentence. Idf values were calculated over a 2015 dump of English Wikipedia from 1 September 2015, which was pre-processed using wp2txt[1] to remove markup.

---

[1] https://github.com/yohasebe/wp2txt

732

Proceedings of SemEval-2016, pages 732–735,
San Diego, California, June 16-17, 2016. ©2016 Association for Computational Linguistics

For all baseline methods, the similarity between two sentences is calculated as the cosine between the vectors representing them. In these baseline methods, the documents are tokenized using an approach suggested by Speriosu et al. (2011) — the text is first split based on whitespace; for each token, if it contains at least one alphanumeric character, then all leading and trailing non-alphanumeric characters are stripped. Stopwords are removed based on a stopword list,[2] and case folding is applied.

2.1.2 Word2vec

We considered two methods based on word embeddings from word2vec (Mikolov et al., 2013). For each sentence, we formed a vector corresponding to the element-wise summation, and product, of the word embeddings for each token in that sentence. We then measure the similarity of two sentences as the cosine between their vector representations. We refer to these methods as WORD2VEC-SUM and WORD2VEC-PROD, respectively.

For this method, we used pre-trained word2vec vectors provided by Google.[3] These vectors have 300 dimensions, and were trained on a corpus of documents from Google News that contained approximately 100 billion tokens.

For this method, sentences were tokenized by splitting on whitespace, and then removing non-alphanumeric characters. The text was also case-folded.

2.1.3 Paragraph vectors

Paragraph Vectors (Le and Mikolov, 2014) is an extension of word2vec (Mikolov et al., 2013) to text of arbitrary length. In our implementation, we used the Distributed Memory Model of Paragraph Vectors (PV-DM) to represent each sentence as a vector. The similarity between two sentences was then computed as the cosine of their vector representations. We refer to this approach as PARAGRAPH-VECTORS.

The gensim[4] implementation of the PV-DM model was trained on a roughly 540 million token sample of English Wikipedia. To tokenize the Wikipedia corpus, the text was first split based on whitespace; then, all non-alphanumeric characters, except for +, -, $ and %, were removed. The remaining tokens wore case-folded. Tokens that did not have a Unicode encoding, or that occurred less than 5 times in the corpus were removed. During training, every paragraph in the corpus was treated as a separate paragraph in the model.[5]

The dimensionality of the word and paragraph representations was set to 400. A window size of 8 was used. The negative sampling parameter was set to 20. The subsampling parameter was set to 10^{-5}. After training the model, the vector representing each sentence was inferred.

2.1.4 Skip-thoughts

Skip-thoughts (Kiros et al., 2015) can be viewed as an extension of the word2vec skipgram model for obtaining vector representations of sentences. Skip-thoughts is primarily an encoder–decoder model composed of gated recurrent units (GRUs). A GRU (Cho et al., 2014) is a recurrent neural network used for sequence modeling (Chung et al., 2014). It is similar to long short-term memory (Hochreiter and Schmidhuber, 1997), but with a simplified gating architecture that does not include separate internal memory cells. The encoder receives a sequence of tokens from a sentence, and the decoder attempts to predict the sentence before the input sentence, and the sentence after it. Once the model has been trained, the vector representation of a sentence can be extracted from the learned encoder by inputting the sequence of tokens that makes up the sentence.

We used the pre-trained combine-skip model provided by Kiros et al. (2015) to build the vector representation of sentences. This produces a 4800 dimensional vector for each sentence by concatenating the vector representations from the uni-skip model and the bi-skip model. The uni-skip model is a unidirectional encoder that encodes the input tokens of a sentence in their original order, and outputs a 2400 dimensional vector. The bi-skip model is a bidirectional model that encodes the input tokens of a sentence in their original order, and in their reversed order, outputting a 1200 dimensional vector for each direction. The similarity between two sentences is

---

Method	Answer–answer	Headlines	Plagiarism	Post-editing	Question–question	All
BASELINE-BIN	0.50937	0.70636	**0.80108**	0.76370	0.61827	0.67881
BASELINE-FREQ	0.44204	**0.72754**	0.79604	0.79483	**0.65749**	0.68122
BASELINE-TF-IDF (Run 1)	0.45928	0.66593	0.75778	0.77204	0.61710	0.65271
WORD2VEC-PROD	0.39310	0.60667	0.71528	0.21306	0.10847	0.41322
WORD2VEC-SUM	0.13521	0.14328	0.23290	-0.02673	0.25153	0.14303
PARAGRAPH-VECTORS	0.41123	0.69169	0.60488	0.75547	-0.02245	0.50206
SKIP-THOUGTS	0.27148	0.23199	0.49643	0.48636	0.17749	0.33446
SKIP-THOUGTS-REG	0.28626	0.51019	0.66708	0.69947	0.40459	0.51299
AVERAGE (Run 2)	**0.58520**	0.69006	0.78923	**0.82540**	0.58605	0.69635
REGRESSION (Run 3)	0.55254	0.71353	0.79769	0.81291	0.62037	**0.69940**

Table 1: Pearson correlation for each method, on each dataset, as well as the weighted average correlation over all datasets ("All"). The best method on each dataset, and over all datasets, is shown in boldface.

then computed by taking the cosine similarity of their vector representations. This method is referred to as SKIP-THOUGTS.

We further considered a supervised approach based on skip-thought vectors. We again formed a vector representing each sentence using the pre-trained model provided by Kiros et al. Then, following Kiros et al., we represented each pair of sentences as a vector consisting of the concatenation of the componentwise product, and absolute difference, of the vectors representing the sentences. That is, if $\vec{u}$ and $\vec{v}$ are the d-dimensional skip-thought vectors representing two sentences, we represent this sentence pair as a $2d$-dimensional vector consisting of the concatenation of $\vec{u} \circ \vec{v}$ and $|\vec{u} - \vec{v}|$. We trained ridge regression using gold-standard STS data from 2012, 2013 and 2015, and then used this model to predict similarity for the test sentence pairs. We refer to this model as SKIP-THOUGTS-REG. We implemented this model after submitting our official runs.

2.2 Method combinations

We used two different methods — one unsupervised, and one supervised — to combine the individual methods in an effort to develop a stronger system.

For the unsupervised method, AVERAGE, we computed the average of BASELINE-BIN, BASELINE-TF-IDF, WORD2VEC-PROD, PARAGRAPH-VECTORS, and SKIP-THOUGTS. We did not consider BASELINE-FREQ here because it is quite similar to BASELINE-BIN, which performed better on development data.

For the supervised approach to combining individual methods, we trained ridge regression over the similarities produced by the following methods: BASELINE-BIN, BASELINE-TF-IDF, PARAGRAPH-VECTORS, and SKIP-THOUGTS. The ridge regression was trained using the gold standard data provided for STS tasks in 2012, 2013, and 2015; this model was then used to predict similarities for sentence pairs in the test data. We refer to this method as REGRESSION.

3 Results

Results for each method, on each dataset, are shown in Table 1. We first consider the baseline approaches. On development data from previous STS tasks, BASELINE-TF-IDF gave higher correlations than baselines based on word presence (BASELINE-BIN) or word frequency (BASELINE-FREQ). Moreover, this was a challenging baseline to beat, and was among the best methods we considered on the development data. It was therefore submitted as one of our official runs. However, on the test data, BASELINE-TF-IDF had the lowest average correlation of the three baseline approaches considered.

In terms of the methods based on word2vec, representing a sentence as the componentwise product of the vectors for the words in that sentence (WORD2VEC-PROD) performed much better than the approach based on vector addition (WORD2VEC-SUM). PARAGRAPH-VECTORS outperformed both word2vec approaches. However, none of these word embedding-based methods performed as well as any of the baselines.

Naively measuring similarity as the cosine between skip-thought vectors for the sentences in a pair (SKIP-THOUGTS) led to relatively poor performance. Training ridge regression based on features derived from skip-thought vectors (SKIP-THOUGTS-REG, described in Section 2.1.4) led to substantial improvements, although again this approach did not beat any of the baselines.

AVERAGE and REGRESSION — both submitted as official runs — combine several of the individual methods together, and both achieve correlations that are, overall, better than those of any of the baselines. However, the improvements are relatively modest. Although there is some variation across the datasets, AVERAGE and REGRESSION perform very similarly overall. AVERAGE, however, has an advantage, in that it is an unsupervised approach.

4   Conclusions

In this paper we first considered several baseline approaches to STS. We then considered approaches based on word2vec, paragraph vectors, and skip-thoughts. We found that none of these approaches improved over any of the baselines. We further considered combining these approaches via averaging, and a supervised approach based on regression, and achieved modest improvements over the baselines.

Acknowledgments

This work is financially supported by the Natural Sciences and Engineering Research Council of Canada, the New Brunswick Innovation Foundation, and the University of New Brunswick.

References

Kyunghyun Cho, Bart van Merriënboer, Dzmitry Bahdanau, and Yoshua Bengio. 2014. On the properties of neural machine translation: Encoder–decoder approaches. In *Proceedings of SSST-8, Eighth Workshop on Syntax, Semantics and Structure in Statistical Translation*. Doha, Qatar, pages 103–111.

Junyoung Chung, Caglar Gulcehre, KyungHyun Cho, and Yoshua Bengio. 2014. Empirical evaluation of gated recurrent neural networks on sequence modeling. In *Proceedings of Deep Learning and Representation Learning Workshop: NIPS 2014*. Montreal, Canada.

Sepp Hochreiter and Jürgen Schmidhuber. 1997. Long short-term memory. *Neural computation* 9(8):1735–1780.

Ryan Kiros, Yukun Zhu, Ruslan Salakhutdinov, Richard S. Zemel, Antonio Torralba, Raquel Urtasun, and Sanja Fidler. 2015. Skip-thought vectors. In C. Cortes, N. D. Lawrence, D. D. Lee, M. Sugiyama, and R. Garnett, editors, *Advances in Neural Information Processing Systems 28*, Curran Associates, Inc., pages 3276–3284.

Quoc Le and Tomas Mikolov. 2014. Distributed representations of sentences and documents. In *Proceedings of the 31st International Conference on Machine Learning*. Beijing, China.

Tomas Mikolov, Ilya Sutskever, Kai Chen, Greg S Corrado, and Jeff Dean. 2013. Distributed representations of words and phrases and their compositionality. In C. J. C. Burges, L. Bottou, M. Welling, Z. Ghahramani, and K. Q. Weinberger, editors, *Advances in Neural Information Processing Systems 26*, Curran Associates, Inc., pages 3111–3119.

Michael Speriosu, Nikita Sudan, Sid Upadhyay, and Jason Baldridge. 2011. Twitter polarity classification with label propagation over lexical links and the follower graph. In *Proceedings of the First workshop on Unsupervised Learning in NLP*. Edinburgh, Scotland, pages 53–63.

ASOBEK at SemEval-2016 Task 1: Sentence Representation with Character N-gram Embeddings for Semantic Textual Similarity

Asli Eyecioglu and **Bill Keller**
University of Sussex
Department of Informatics
Brighton, BN19QJ, UK
A.Eyecioglu@sussex.ac.uk,
billk@sussex.ac.uk

Abstract

A growing body of research has recently been conducted on semantic textual similarity using a variety of neural network models. While recent research focuses on word-based representation for phrases, sentences and even paragraphs, this study considers an alternative approach based on character n-grams. We generate embeddings for character n-grams using a continuous-bag-of-n-grams neural network model. Three different sentence representations based on n-gram embeddings are considered. Results are reported for experiments with bigram, trigram and 4-gram embeddings on the STS Core dataset for SemEval-2016 Task 1.

1 Introduction

This paper presents an approach for finding the degree of semantic similarity between sentence pairs. Semantic textual similarity (STS) is of relevance to many NLP applications. Recent tasks in recognizing textual entailment, sentence completion and paraphrase identification are closely related. The approach described here makes use of a neural network (NN) algorithm (word2vec) that is typically used to generate word embeddings (Mikolov et al., 2013a). Rather than generating vector representations for words however, we propose a character n-gram-to-vector approach. A sentence is then represented as a vector generated through a combination of character n-gram embeddings.

The use of character level vectors has been proposed in a number of recent studies. Subword language models that use the combination of characters, syllables and frequent words have been explored by Mikolov et al. (2012). Character-level language modeling has been performed for modeling OOV words, where using words as the atomic units of the model would not be sufficient to assign a probability score. In Ling et al. (2015), word representations are composed of vectors of characters, called character to word (C2W). The C2W vectors are used successfully for language modeling and POS tagging without any handcrafted features. The resulting model is competitive on English POS tagging with the Stanford POS tagger word look-up tables and also produces a notable improvement in results for morphologically rich languages such as Turkish. Kim et al. (2015) apply a simple convolutional neural network model, which uses character level inputs for word representations. Again, this method outperforms the models that use word/morpheme level features in morphologically rich languages, while also having competitive results in English. Huang et al. (2013) introduce a word hashing technique using character n-grams to scale up training of deep NN models for large-scale web search applications.

Our motivation for exploring character n-grams derives in part from previous work we have conducted on paraphrase identification (PI). The PI task is that of deciding whether two sentences have the same meaning. We have shown that sentence representations based on bags or sets of character n-gram features can perform well at this task (Eyecioglu and Keller, 2015). It is hypothesized that n-grams are useful for capturing lexical similarity and perform a role similar to lemmatization whilst preserving differences. Thus, sentence representations based on collections of n-grams as features may offer some advantages over representations based on words as features.

736

Proceedings of SemEval-2016, pages 736–740,
San Diego, California, June 16-17, 2016. ©2016 Association for Computational Linguistics

The current study aims to extend this earlier work by working with n-gram embeddings. (Mikolov et al., 2013a) introduced two new NN architectures that were applied to learning word embeddings: continuous-bag-of-words (CBOW) and skip grams (SG). These NN models have been shown to perform well in many NLP areas such as STS and PI (Zarrella et al., 2015; Yin and Schütze, 2015; He et al., 2015). Recent research has taken steps to extend these word vectors to sentences, paragraphs and documents (Le and Mikolov, 2014).

We introduce an alternative approach to obtaining sentence level embedding vectors that make use of character n-grams rather than words. We adopt a model architecture that is analogous to CBOW, which we call *continuous-bag-of-n-grams* and notate as CBO*n*G throughout the paper. In keeping with our earlier work on paraphrase identification (Eyecioglu and Keller, 2015), pre-processing is kept to a minimum and no use is made of any manually constructed semantic or syntactic processing tools or resources.

Operationally, STS is similar to paraphrase identification. The two tasks differ in that STS sentence pairs are assigned a degree of semantic equivalence instead of a binary paraphrase label. STS shared tasks have produced a sizable amount of research on sentence similarity (Agirre et al., 2012, 2013, 2014, 2015).

2   The Task

SemEval-2016 Task 1: Semantic Textual Similarity (Agirre et al., 2016) requires systems to determine the degree of semantic similarity between pairs of sentences. Similarity scores are on a scale from 0 (completely dissimilar) to 5 (semantically equivalent). We participated in the monolingual STS Core subtask. This subtask includes English language evaluation data from multiple sources organized into 5 distinct evaluation datasets: Plagiarism Detection, Q&A Question-Question, Q&A Answer-Answer, Post-Edited Machine Translations and Headlines. The evaluation data have a gold standard similarity score based on human judgements collected using Crowdsourcing. The Pearson correlation between similarity scores assigned by the systems and the human judgements is used to assess task performance.

3   Approach

The sentences within the STS pairs are split into character n-grams. No preprocessing is applied besides lowercasing of the text and removing punctuation.

Our training procedure was unsupervised, using only a large unlabelled dataset drawn from Wikipedia. These data are used to train a CBO*n*G model. We explore using three different methods for constructing sentence level vector representations from the character embeddings. STS scores for the sentence pairs are computed as the cosine similarity of the resulting sentence level embedding vectors. Three different cosine similarity scores, one from each representation, are obtained.

4   Wikipedia Dataset

We used a dump of English Wikipedia articles[1] that includes 3,831,719 articles and 8,179,596 unique words. Wikipedia provides a large and accessible collection of text consisting of well-formed sentences that is suitable for training purposes. We obtained a plain text representation of the documents by removing the data dump xml tags using the script provided in the Gensim package (Rehurek and Sojka, 2010). Matching the minimal pre-processing performed on the STS pairs, training data are only lowercased and cleared of punctuation. The Wikipedia dataset is split into adjacent n-grams and spaces between words replaced with the "-" symbol. For example, the following sequence of trigrams would be produced from the text *amazon gift*.

    -am ama maz azo zon on- n-g -gi gif ift ft-

4.1   Constructing a CBO*n*G Model

Our CBO*n*G is constructed and trained identically to a CBOW model (Mikolov et al., 2013a) but substituting character n-grams in place of words. The quality of such a model is affected by a number of hyper-parameters such as the size of the character n-gram vectors (embeddings), the size of the training window, and the cut-off point for less frequent n-grams. Although experiments by Mikolov et al. (2013b) describe how to choose the appropriate features for a word similarity task, the same fea-

---

tures might not be ideal here. Moreover, our model brings an additional new modeling parameter that defines the size of the character n-grams.

Embedding models scale linearly with the number of unique unfiltered tokens in the training data. Each token has a corresponding fixed size embedding vector. Mikolov et al. (2013a) explored using embedding vector sizes ranging from 20 to 600. In general, the results showed that increasing the dimensionality of vectors and the size of training data, improved the accuracy on semantic-syntactic word relationship task using otherwise identical features.

For our experiments, we make use of 400 dimension embedding vectors. Our CBOnG model was trained using surrounding n-grams within a window size of 5. Character n-grams that occur fewer than 5 times are filtered. Our model is trained using the Gensim package (Rehurek and Sojka, 2010) and its support for CBOW *(word-level)* models but over data tokenized into character n-grams.

4.2 Compositions of Vector Representations

The construction of embedding vectors for phrases and sentences directly from word embeddings is still an active area of research. As noted in Section 2, there have been various efforts to build good embedding representations of text beyond those tied to individual words. We believe the diversity of methods for constructing textual embedding representations beyond the word level is due to the fact the appropriateness of the various representations is very task dependent.

One simple approach is to construct textual embedding representations using either point-wise addition multiplication of the embedding vectors representing individual words and phrases. The resulting representations have been shown to work well for phrase similarity and PI tasks (Blacoe and Lapata, 2012).

We make use of a similar composition algorithm for our sentence level embeddings, but using character n-gram rather than word embeddings. We describe three different methods for combining n-gram embeddings. The first is formed by addition of the embeddings of the n-gram *tokens* in a sentence, effectively weighting the embeddings by their frequency. The second and third are based on n-gram *types*, and formed by concatenation and weighted addition, respectively.

4.3 Sentence Representations

For the STS task, the core experimental unit is a pair of sentences. A target sentence, S, consisting of some sequence of n tokens (i.e. character n-grams) $(t_{S_1}, t_{S_2}, ..., t_{S_n})$ is paired with another sentence, S' that consists of some sequence m of tokens $(t_{S'_1}, t_{S'_2}, ..., t_{S'_m})$. Note that the numbers of tokens for each sentence do not necessarily need to be equal. In the following, a vector embedding associated with a token t is notated by v_t. We consider three different vector based sentence representations built from n-gram embeddings.

For a given sentence S, the first representation is produced through element-wise addition of the vectors associated with each token in S. The result of this operation is a vector V_S^1 having the specified vector size of the token embeddings, as is defined in advance to building the models (i.e. 400 in this case).

For the second approach, S is represented as a matrix of size $400 \times d$, where d is the size of the model vocabulary (i.e. the number of unique n-grams using in training). Combining the d vectors in order forms a vector representation:

$$V_S^2 = \left[v^S_{t_1}, v^S_{t_2}, ..., v^S_{t_d} \right]$$

where $v^S_{t_i}$ is the embedding associated with the ith term t_i in the model vocabulary if t_i occurs in S, and is the null vector if the ith term does not occur in S.

Finally, for the third representation, element-wise addition of all of the embeddings in V^2_S is computed. We obtain a new vector of V^3_S the dimension of the embedding vector size, which is specified as 400:

$$V_S^3 = \left[v^S_{t_1} + v^S_{t_2} + \cdots + v^S_{t_d} \right]$$

We note that the difference between Run1 and Run3 is that for Run1, the contributions of the n-gram embeddings are weighted for frequency.

5 Experiments

To obtain semantic similarity scores for each pair of sentences S and S', the cosines of the corresponding vector representations are computed.

Run1: $Sim1(S, S') = cosine(V_S^1, V_{S'}^1)$
Run2: $Sim2(S, S') = cosine(V_S^2, V_{S'}^2)$
Run3: $Sim3(S, S') = cosine(V_S^3, V_{S'}^3)$

Previous work on the use of character n-grams for PI has shown that trigrams perform well. The three runs chosen for submission to SemEval 2016's STS task use sentence representations constructed from trigram embeddings. Wikipedia articles were pruned using the Gensim package with default parameters. A total of 108,452 articles are used to construct a character-trigram model for the experiments. The statistical properties of the Wikipedia-trained model using character trigrams are shown in Table 1 below.

Properties	Count
Total trigrams	1,068,456,094
Unique trigrams	91,686
Unique trigrams > 5	47,951

Table 1: Statistical properties of Wikipedia dataset used in our experiment.

Further experiments were conducted for sentence representations based on bigrams and 4-grams. Although these were not submitted for the task, the results are also reported in the following section.

6 Results

The Pearson Correlation results from our three different runs obtained using trigram embeddings are presented in Table 2. These results represent the ASOBEK submission to SemEval-2016 Task 1. It is noted that Run2 and Run3 generally appear to outperform Run1, with Run2 performing best overall. The best individual result is obtained on the Post-editing dataset. This result is ranked above the median for results reported on this sub-task. The correlation scores evidence variable performance across the individual datasets. Most notable is that the results from each of the runs applied on the Question-Question dataset are much lower relative to the other categories. In spite of this, the overall performance is 0.6178 with Run2.

Datasets (Trigrams)	Run1	Run2	Run3
Overall	*0.5956*	***0.6178***	*0.6143*
Answer-Answer	0.4269	**0.5228**	0.4792
Headlines	0.6790	0.6374	**0.6865**
Plagiarism	0.7572	**0.7852**	0.7778
Post-editing	0.8195	**0.8425**	0.8409
Question-Question	0.2618	**0.2635**	0.2480

Table 2: Pearson Correlation Results using character trigrams

Experiments were also conducted for bigrams and 4-grams. Results are shown in Table 3. Highlighted scores indicate cases where performance exceeds that obtained using trigram embeddings.

As for trigrams, better results are generally obtained for Run2 and Run3. For 4-grams, the overall performance of Run3 actually exceeds that based on trigrams. Across all of the systems, results on the Question-Question dataset depress the overall performance significantly. This is especially evident for Run2 of the 4-gram dataset, where there is little correlation evident between system scores and human judgements. In contrast, using bigrams Run2 produces our best result for this dataset. Examination of the data indicates that this may be due to the particular form of the questions. For example, character n-grams generated from the following pair will contain many tokens that are not informative in discriminating meaning:

What should I look for in a jump rope?
What should I look for in a running shoe?

Datasets (Bigrams)	Run1	Run2	Run3
Overall	*0.5340*	*0.5996*	*0.5784*
Answer-Answer	0.3869	0.4547	0.4520
Headlines	0.6422	0.6697	0.6668
Plagiarism	0.6204	0.7088	0.6582
Post-edit.	0.7439	0.8168	0.7879
Question-Question	0.2768	**0.3482**	0.3270
Datasets (4-grams)	**Run1**	**Run2**	**Run3**
Overall	*0.6088*	*0.5567*	***0.6183***
Answer-Answer	0.4587	**0.5375**	0.4927
Headlines	0.6757	0.6023	0.6831
Plagiarism	0.7743	0.7507	0.7796
Post-editing	0.8295	0.8356	0.8417
Question-Question	0.3057	0.0574	0.2943

Table 3: Pearson Correlation Results using character bigrams and 4-grams

7 Conclusions

A method for STS based on embeddings of character n-grams generated by a CBOnG model was introduced. This is the only study that we are aware of that utilizes embeddings of character n-grams to build representations of sentences. The study presents preliminary results showing that the approach can successfully help identify semantic similarity of sentence pairs.

Using our method, we observe significant variations in performance across the STS Core datasets. In particular, performance is generally poor for the

Question-Question dataset. This suggests that it may improve performance to weight the contributions of the embeddings according to the informativeness of the associated n-grams. We intend to consider this in future experiments.

Acknowledgements

We are grateful for the very constructive comments from the reviewers on an earlier draft of this paper.

References

Agirre, Eneko et al. (2014) 'SemEval-2014 Task 10: Multilingual Semantic Textual Similarity'. *Proceedings of the 8th International Workshop on Semantic Evaluation (SemEval 2014)*.

Agirre, Eneko et al. (2015) 'SemEval-2015 Task 2: Semantic Textual Similarity , English , Spanish and Pilot on Interpretability'. *SemEval2015*.

Agirre, Eneko et al. (2016) 'SemEval-2016 Task 1: Semantic Textual Similarity - Monolingual and Cross-lingual Evaluation'. *Proceedings of the 10th International Workshop on Semantic Evaluation (SemEval 2016)*. San Diego, USA.

Agirre, Eneko, Daniel Cer, Mona Diab, and Aitor Gonzalez-Agirre. (2012) 'Semeval-2012 task 6: A pilot on semantic textual similarity'. *Proceedings of the 6th International Workshop on Semantic Evaluation, in conjunction with the First Joint Conference on Lexical and Computational Semantics*.

Agirre, Eneko, Daniel Cer, Mona Diab, Aitor Gonzalez-Agirre, and Weiwei Guo. (2013) '*SEM 2013 shared task: Semantic Textual Similarity'. *The Second Joint Conference on Lexical and Computational Semantics (*SEM 2013)*, vol. 1.

Blacoe, William, and Mirella Lapata. (2012) 'A Comparison of Vector-based Representations for Semantic Composition'. *Proceedings of the 2012 Joint Conference on Empirical Methods in Natural Language Processing and Computational Natural Language Learning (EMNLP-CoNLL '12)*.

Eyecioglu, Asli, and Bill Keller. (2015) 'ASOBEK: Twitter Paraphrase Identification with Simple Overlap Features and SVMs'. *Proceedings of the 9th International Workshop on Semantic Evaluation (SemEval 2015)*. Denver, Colorado.

He, Hua, Kevin Gimpel, and Jimmy Lin. (2015) 'Multi-Perspective Sentence Similarity Modeling with Convolutional Neural Networks'. *Proceedings of the 2015 Conference on Empirical Methods in Natural Language Processing*. Lisbon, Portugal.

Huang, Po-sen et al. (2013) 'Learning Deep Structured Semantic Models for Web Search using Clickthrough Data'. *Conference on Information and Knwoledge Management (CIKM-2013)*.

Kim, Yoon, Yacine Jernite, David Sontag, and Alexander M. Rush. (2015) 'Character-Aware Neural Language Models'. *CoRR* 1508.06615. http://arxiv.org/abs/1508.06615.

Le, Qv, and Tomas Mikolov. (2014) 'Distributed Representations of Sentences and Documents'. *International Conference on Machine Learning - ICML 2014* 32:1188–1196.

Ling, Wang et al. (2015) 'Finding Function in Form: Compositional Character Models for Open Vocabulary Word Representation'. *CoRR* 1508.02096. http://arxiv.org/abs/1508.02096.

Mikolov, Tomas, Greg Corrado, Kai Chen, and Jeffrey Dean. (2013a) 'Efficient Estimation of Word Representations in Vector Space'. *Proceedings of the International Conference on Learning Representations (ICLR 2013)*.

Mikolov, Tomas, Ilya Sutskever, and Anoop Deoras. 2012. *Subword language modeling with neural networks*.

Mikolov, Tomas, Wen-tau Yih, and Geoffrey Zweig. (2013b) 'Linguistic regularities in continuous space word representations'. *Proceedings of NAACL-HLT* 746–751.

Rehurek, Radim, and Petr Sojka. (2010) 'Software framework for topic modelling with large corpora'. *Proceedings of the LREC 2010 Workshop on New Challenges for NLP Frameworks* 45–50.

Yin, Wenpeng, and Hinrich Schütze. (2015) 'Convolutional Neural Network for Paraphrase Identification'. *Naacl 2015*.

Zarrella, Guido, John Henderson, Elizabeth M Merkhofer, and Laura Strickhart. (2015) 'MITRE: Seven Systems for Semantic Similarity in Tweets'. *Proceedings of the 9th International Workshop on Semantic Evaluation (SemEval 2015)*. Denver, Colorado.

SimiHawk at SemEval-2016 Task 1: A Deep Ensemble System for Semantic Textual Similarity

Peter Potash*, **William Boag***, **Alexey Romanov***,
Vasili Ramanishka, Anna Rumshisky
Dept. of Computer Science
University of Massachusetts Lowell
198 Riverside St, Lowell, MA 01854
{ppotash,wboag,aromanov,vramanis,arum}@cs.uml.edu

Abstract

This paper describes the SimiHawk system submission from UMass Lowell for the core Semantic Textual Similarity task at SemEval-2016. We built four systems: a small feature-based system that leverages word alignment and machine translation quality evaluation metrics, two end-to-end LSTM-based systems, and an ensemble system. The LSTM-based systems used either a simple LSTM architecture or a Tree-LSTM structure. We found that of the three base systems, the feature-based model obtained the best results, outperforming each LSTM-based model's correlation by .06. Ultimately, the ensemble system was able to outperform the base systems substantially, obtaining a weighted Pearson correlation of 0.738, and placing 7th out of 115 participating systems. We find that the ensemble system's success comes largely from its ability to form a consensus and eliminate complementary noise from its base systems' predictions.

1 Introduction

The task of semantic textual similarity (STS) has been developed over the past several SemEval competitions with the idea of capturing the degree of similarity in the meaning conveyed by two snippets of text (usually two sentences). In that respect, the STS task can be seen as similar to such tasks as paraphrase detection (Xu et al., 2015), recognizing textual entailment (RTE) (Negri et al., 2012), and semantic relatedness (Marelli et al., 2014a). The

STS task captures different gradations of similarity, rather than a binary decision, and it is symmetric, rather than directed, as is the case with RTE (Agirre et al., 2012). It also aims to capture a more general notion of semantic similarity that does not focus solely on the semantic relatedness derived through compositional processes. In this paper, we describe the SimiHawk system submission for the core Semantic Textual Similarity (STS) task at the SemEval-2016 competition.

The STS task series (Agirre et al., 2012; Agirre et al., 2013; Agirre et al., 2014; Agirrea et al., 2015) has aggregated a sizable dataset of sentence pairs annotated with numeric similarity scores. The presence of this dataset allows for a shift from earlier work that mostly used unsupervised learning (Corley and Mihalcea, 2005; Mihalcea et al., 2006; Li et al., 2006), to the supervised approaches that leverage the labeled data (Sultan et al., 2015; Han et al., 2015; Hänig et al., 2015). The availability of labeled data from different genres also allows for a clearer evaluation and a better comparison across different approaches.

Specifically, the task of semantic similarity is defined as follows: given an input of two sentences, output a real number in the range [0,5] where 0 means lowest and 5 means highest similarity. The top-performing system from last year's task (Sultan et al., 2015) relied heavily on a hand-engineered word alignment tool (Sultan et al., 2014) (achieving 5th place with the aligner alone), combined with dense word embeddings (Baroni et al., 2014) to create a two-feature regression model. Other top-performing systems (Han et al., 2015; Hänig et al.,

---

*These three authors contributed equally to this work.

Proceedings of SemEval-2016, pages 741–748,
San Diego, California, June 16-17, 2016. ©2016 Association for Computational Linguistics

2015) follow this trend of exploiting word alignment and embedding similarity across textual pairs.

Recent work (Bowman et al., 2014; Bowman et al., 2015b; Tai et al., 2015) has shown the effectiveness of deep learning end-to-end architectures using recurrent and recursive neural networks on tasks similar to semantic similarity, such as semantic relatedness (Tai et al., 2015), natural language inference (Bowman et al., 2015a), and textual entailment (Marelli et al., 2014b), providing state-of-the-art performance. Since all of these tasks evaluate the relationship between the semantics of two input sentences, it stands to reason that systems with such architecture may perform well on the more general task of semantic similarity.

In our submission, we are interested in comparing an approach using hand-engineered features against the deep RNN-based architectures with Long Short-Term Memory (LSTM) cells. We therefore implemented a feature-based system over a small number of heavily engineered features, and two LSTM-based systems: one that uses a simple LSTM architecture and one that uses a Tree-LSTM architecture that mirrors the syntactic dependencies of the input in the LSTM model.

In the following section, we describe each system in detail. We then report and analyze the outcome of this bake-off. Not surprisingly, the ensemble system performs the best, obtaining a weighted Pearson correlation of 0.738. Of the three base systems, the feature-based model obtained the best results, outperforming the LSTM-based models by .06.

2 System Description

2.1 Feature-Based

Because of the impressive success of feature-based methods in previous STS shared tasks, we wanted to understand whether deep learning approaches were even necessary. The winning system for the 2015 shared task computed two features:

1. **alignment ratio** As part of their 1st place system, (Sultan et al., 2015) constructed a custom, open tool to align the words within a sentence pair[1]. The alignment ratio feature r is computed as:

$$r = \frac{a(s_1) + a(s_2)}{t(s_1) + t(s_2)} \qquad (1)$$

where s_1 and s_2 are sentences 1 and 2 respectively, $a()$ is the number of aligned content words in a sentence, and $t()$ is the total number of content words in a sentence.

2. **cosine of word2vec centroids** Since word2vec came out in 2013 (Mikolov et al., 2013), word embeddings have gained massive popularity. Though a naive form of compositionality, simple vector addition has been shown as a surprisingly effective way to represent phrases. Using the official word2vec skip-gram Google News embeddings[2], we compute the word2vec cosine feature w as follows:

$$w = \cos\left(\frac{\Sigma w_1^i}{N_1}, \frac{\Sigma w_2^i}{N_2}\right) \qquad (2)$$

where Σw_s^i is the sum of the embeddings of each word in sentence s and N_s is the sentence length.

We used this system as a starting point, but we added two additional feature classes. The two feature classes we added were:

1. **cosine of one-hot bag-of-words** Similar to word2vec centroids, we also computed a feature b as the cosine of binary bag-of-words encodings of each sentence:

$$b = \cos(\Sigma e_1^i, \Sigma e_2^j) \qquad (3)$$

where for a vocabulary (consisting of the union of the two sentences' sets of tokens) of size V, the one-hot vector e_s^i is a vector of size V consisting of $V - 1$ zero entries and a 1 at word i's entry in the vocabulary. Note that subscripts 1 and 2 signify one-hot vectors representing tokens from sentences 1 and 2, respectively.

2. **Machine Translation evaluation metrics** In 2012, an ensemble of various MT metrics was created to attain (at the time) state-of-the-art results in Paraphrase Identification (Madnani et

---

[1] https://github.com/ ma-sultan/monolingual-word-aligner

[2] https://code.google.com/archive/p/word2vec

al., 2012). We created features for each of the following metrics to compute the similarity between sentences 1 and 2:

- BLEU (Papineni et al., 2002)[3]
- NIST (Doddington, 2002)[4]
- METEOR (Lavie and Agarwal, 2005)[5]
- BADGER (Parker, 2008)[6]
- TER (Snover et al., 2006)[7]
- TERp (Snover et al., 2009)[8]

We combine these four feature classes using a fully-connected neural network with 2 layers of size 40. Similar to (Tai et al., 2015) (specifically equations (14) and (15)), the network produces a probability distribution over scores and is trained using categorical cross-entropy loss. To build the network, we use the Keras library (Chollet, 2015), a Python neural network library written on top of Theano (Bergstra et al., 2010; Bastien et al., 2012).

2.2 Deep End-to-End LSTM-Based Systems

Deep end-to-end systems are very enticing because they learn the representation for a given input, as opposed to manually constructing a feature space. We built two LSTM-based systems for this task. Although in principle these systems can be considered end-to-end, both systems make use of pre-trained word embeddings as input. We describe the two systems below, assuming a familiarity with regular LSTM cell structure. We begin by discussing Tree-LSTM because it recently achieved state-of-the-art performance on the semantic relatedness task (Tai et al., 2015).

2.2.1 Tree-LSTM

The architecture of Tree-LSTM is a generalization of LSTMs to tree-structured network topologies. The tree-structured LSTM composes its current state from an input vector, as well as the hidden

states of an arbitrary number of child units. As previously mentioned, the Tree-LSTM architecture has been used for the semantic relatedness task. For this task, the specific tree structure the authors use is a dependency tree, obtained via the Stanford Neural Network Dependency Parser (Chen and Manning, 2014). For the semantic relatedness task, the system takes as input two pieces of text, and outputs a real number in the range [1,5]. Therefore, one only needs to modify the original Tree-LSTM system to output a number in the range [0,5] in order to apply it to the task of semantic similarity.

The specific architecture we use is referred to by the original authors as Child-Sum Tree-LSTM (Tai et al., 2015). Using the authors' original notation, and using $C(j)$ to denote the set of children of node j, the hidden state at a given node is computed as follows:

$$\tilde{h}_j = \sum_{k \in C(j)} h_k \tag{4}$$

$$i_j = \sigma(W^i x_j + U^i \tilde{h}_j + b^i) \tag{5}$$

$$f_{jk} = \sigma(W^f x_j + U^f h_k + b^f) \tag{6}$$

$$o_j = \sigma(W^o x_j + U^o \tilde{h}_j + b^o) \tag{7}$$

$$u_j = tanh(W^u x_j + U^u \tilde{h}_j + b^u) \tag{8}$$

$$c_j = i_j \odot u_j + \sum_{k \in C(j)} f_{jk} \odot u_k \tag{9}$$

$$h_j = o_j \odot tanh(c_j) \tag{10}$$

where x_j is the input of node j (typically a word embedding vector), σ is the logistic sigmoid function, and $\odot$ is element-wise multiplication. Note here we refer to nodes instead of timesteps, since the the tree structure induced by the dependency parse alters the standard temporal flow of a normal LSTM. Consequently, the hidden state from the root node is then used as a representation for a given text input.

Given two input texts, the authors use a Tree-LSTM to generate a representation for each input, which we call h_L and h_R. These are then used to compute a final score, $\hat{y}$, as follows:

$$h_\times = h_L \odot h_R \tag{11}$$

$$h_+ = |h_L - h_R| \tag{12}$$

$$h_s = \sigma(W^\times h_\times + W^+ h_+ + b^h) \tag{13}$$

---

[3]ftp://jaguar.ncsl.nist.gov/mt/resources/mteval-v13a-20091001.tar.gz

[4]ftp://jaguar.ncsl.nist.gov/mt/resources/mteval-v13a-20091001.tar.gz

[5]http://www.cs.cmu.edu/ alavie/METEOR/download/meteor-1.5.tar.gz

[6]http://babblequest.org/badger

[7]http://www.cs.umd.edu/~snover/tercom/tercom-0.7.25.tgz

[8]https://github.com/snover/terp

$$\hat{p}_\theta = softmax(W^p h_s + b^p) \qquad (14)$$

$$\hat{y} = r^T \hat{p}_\theta \qquad (15)$$

Note how (14) creates a distribution over integer scores, and (15) converts the distribution into a real number in range $[a,b]$ by setting r equal to a vector of integer values $[a \dots b]$. For our system, we simply set r equal to the vector $[0\ 1\ 2\ 3\ 4\ 5]$, as opposed to the original values of $[1\ 2\ 3\ 4\ 5]$ for the semantic relatedness task. The inclusion of zero will better facilitate the output of scores less than one. This is because distributions that have their mass highly concentrated in the first index will have little remaining mass in the other indices that can then multiply by the non-zero integers.

For our implementation we used the code from the original authors[9], which uses Glove embeddings (Pennington et al., 2014) as input vectors x_j, hidden states (h_i) of size 200, and a similarity module of size 50 (h_s (13)). For training, we use a regularization strength of 0.0004, a minibatch size of 25, and a learning rate of 0.05. The model trained for 10 epochs. We also decided to disregard the use of a validation set, since our intermediate results showed that, if anything, the use of a validation set hurt performance.

2.2.2 LSTM

Despite the potential of the Tree-LSTM model for this task, (Bowman et al., 2015b) shows that even for text that is highly syntactically dependent, a standard LSTM architecture can perform as well as a Tree-LSTM architecture given enough training data. The authors also show that an LSTM can perform better on shorter sentences. Moreover, (Vinyals et al., 2015) successfully applied a sequence-to-sequence LSTM model with attention to the syntactic parsing task, achieving state-of-the-art results. Motivated by these results, we also produced a model that uses standard LSTM architecture.

The architecture of the LSTM model is represented in Figure 1. The model is very similar to the Tree-LSTM, but instead of using tree-structured LSTMs, it uses standard LSTM cells. The hidden states of the LSTMs are combined by concatenation

of element-wise multiplication, summation and cosine similarity, and the resulting vector serves as the input to the fully-connected layer. As in (Tai et al., 2015), the network produces a probability distribution over scores, which is in turn transformed into a real number over the specified range.

We used the Keras library to implement this model, creating LSTMs with hidden states of size 300, and fully-connected layers of size 50. For training, we use a regularization strength of 0.0004, mini-batch size of 25, and dropout of 0.1. The model was trained for 15 epochs. We also trimmed sentences to have a maximum length of 50 tokens. The LSTM system uses Glove embeddings (Pennington et al., 2014) as its pretrained word vectors. We chose to use Glove instead of word2vec because Glove had fewer out-of-vocabulary tokens for the dataset.

2.3 Ensemble

In order to hedge our bets, we created a ensemble system, using Feature-Based, Tree-LSTM, and LSTM systems as base systems. The ensemble model can be seen as a feature-based, stacking system because it uses the predictions of the three base systems as the features for a supervised model. Thus, the most basic stacking system has three features, one for each base system.

In order to train the stacking model, we need base predictions that are not 'dirty': the data used to train base systems to generate predictions (which in turn train our stacking system) must have an empty intersection with the data we use to make predictions. To overcome this, each base system performed 5-fold cross-validation on the training data. By doing this, we create predictions for each training example from 'clean' data. Next, we used the predictions on the held-out folds as the features to train the stacking model. We made sure to shuffle the training data prior to creating the folds to ensure that each fold would be statistically similar in terms of which domains are represented as well as the distributions over gold standard scores. To generate test scores for the stacking system, we allowed the base systems to train on all the training data and then make predictions on the test data, which become the test features for the stacking system.

We hypothesize that in certain scenarios, the stacking system should favor the scores from certain

---

[9]https://github.com/stanfordnlp/treelstm

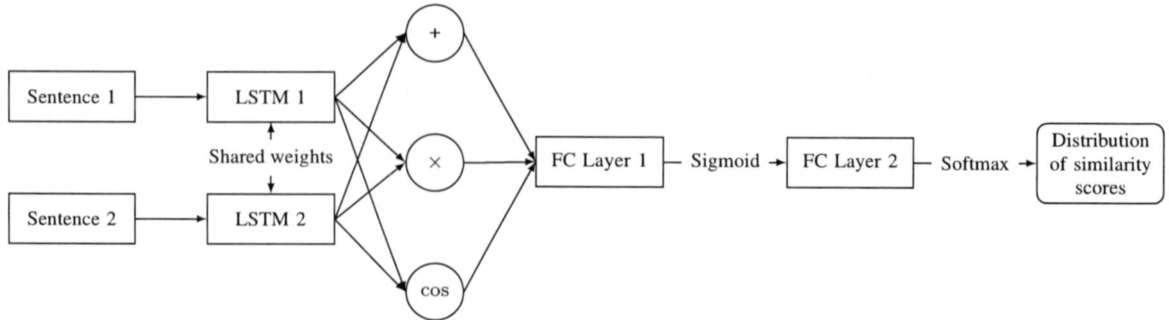

Figure 1: The architecture of the LSTM model

System	mean	answer-answer	headlines	plagiarism	postediting	question-question
Ensemble	**0.73774**	**0.59237**	**0.81419**	0.80566	**0.82179**	0.65048
Feature-based	0.70647	0.44003	0.77109	**0.81105**	0.81600	**0.71035**
LSTM	0.64840	0.44177	0.75703	0.71737	0.72317	0.60691
TreeLSTM	0.64140	0.52277	0.74083	0.67628	0.70655	0.55265
# Examples	-	254	249	230	244	209

Table 1: Results of our systems on the 2016 gold standard. The highest score from each column is in bold.

Features	Weighted Mean
All	0.7168
-average pronoun count	0.7178
-average length	0.7211
-embeddings similarity	0.7237
-edit distance	0.7164
-align ratio	0.6952
-sentence length	0.7116

Table 2: Feature ablation study for ensemble system. '-' denotes witholding a feature.

base systems. For example, (Bowman et al., 2015b) has shown that LSTM models can have difficulty on long sequences. Therefore, we performed a feature ablation study where we combined the three baseline predictions with several hand-picked features: length of sentence 1, length of sentence 2 (these two combined are called sentence length), alignment ratio (1), string edit distance, embedding similarity (2), average sentence length between the pair, and average pronoun count. We included average pronoun count because we found certain domains contain a larger frequency of pronouns. The ablation experiment was performed on 2015 evaluation data, and the results are shown in Table 2. It is visible in the table that the only feature absence that generated any significant drop-off is alignment ratio. Therefore, we decided to include alignment ratio as the fourth and final feature in our stacking system. For the stacking implementation, we use the same neural network as the feature-based system. However, we decided to use a three-layer network based on experimental results.

3 Results

All systems were trained using the training/evaluation data from previous years' tasks (Agirre et al., 2012; Agirre et al., 2013; Agirre et al., 2014; Agirrea et al., 2015). After filtering for duplicate examples, our training set contains a total of 13,061 examples.

Results of our systems on the 2016 gold standard are shown in Table 1. We report the performance, specifically Pearson correlation, across five different domains: Answer-Answer, Headlines, Plagiarism, Postediting, and Question-Question. We also report the weighted mean across all five domains. The last row of Table 1 also records the number of gold standard examples for each domain.

According to the official results, the overall performance of our ensemble system was .738, exceeding the performance of the base systems, although it is not the highest performing system for every domain. Specifically for the question-question domain, the feature-based system seems to outperform it substantially. The overall ranking of the ensemble system is 7 out of 115 submitted systems, while feature-based ranks 37, LSTM ranks 73, and TreeLSTM ranks 77.

System	Fold 1	Fold 2	Fold 3	Fold 4	Fold 5	mean
LSTM	0.802	0.806	0.805	0.795	0.790	0.800
Feature-based	0.790	0.800	0.813	0.823	0.799	0.805
TreeLSTM	0.772	0.797	0.793	0.806	0.794	0.792

Table 3: Results of our base systems on cross-validation folds

System	Ensemble	Features	LSTM	TreeLSTM	Reference
Ensemble	1.000	0.769	0.751	0.802	0.592
Feature-based	0.769	1.000	0.456	0.413	0.440
LSTM	0.751	0.456	1.000	0.608	0.442
TreeLSTM	0.802	0.413	0.608	1.000	0.523
Reference	0.592	0.440	0.442	0.523	1.000

Table 4: Pairwise correlation scores amongst systems' predictions and gold labels (Reference) on the answer-answer domain.

We also report five-fold cross-validation results for our three base systems (Table 3). These experiments used the training data, drawn from several domains. We shuffled the data for our cross-validation experiments so that each fold has a similar distribution of domain examples as well as scores. These results show that when the data is shuffled, and domains and scores are equally distributed, the overall correlation is much higher.

4 Discussion

The ensemble system's success can be attributed to its ability to form a consensus among the base systems and eliminate noise in the predictions. As we can see in Table 4, which shows the correlation between systems for the answer-answer domain, although the three base systems have low pairwise correlations (.456, .413, .608), they all have high correlations with the ensemble system (.769, .751, .802). We can also see that the ensemble system has its largest correlation with the highest-scoring base system for answer-answer, TreeLSTM. Since each base system had pairwise low correlation, they were capturing different views of the data, and the ensemble system was able to take the important parts of each view, while canceling out the noise. This allowed the ensemble system to outperform the base systems in answer-answer by .12, on average.

To further illustrate this point, take for example the following input pair: "There's not a lot you can do about that." and "There's not that much that you can do with a sourdough starter." with a gold label of 2. The baseline systems predict the following scores: 3.96 from the feature-based system, 0.31 from the LSTM system, and 1.39 from the TreeL-STM system. The TreeLSTM system provides the closest prediction, while the feature-based system provides the worst prediction, over-predicting the gold label by almost 2. However, the ensemble system is able to effectively leverage this higher prediction, producing a prediction of 1.76, which is the most accurate prediction out of all four systems.

In our experiments, we found that in three domains (answer-answer, headlines, question-question), the ensemble system had the highest correlation with TreeLSTM. It is likely that TreeLSTM's low score on question-question (.553), combined with a high correlation with the ensemble (.900), were what brought the ensemble system's score down enough for the feature-based system to outperform it. On the other two occasions (plagiarism and postediting), the base system with the highest correlation with ensemble system was the feature-based system. In both of these scenarios, the two systems produced very similar scores, within .01 of one another for both occasions.

Although the feature-based system was the highest scoring base system on 4 out of 5 domains, there is only one occasion where its correlation with another base system exceeds .79 (plagiarism with LSTM). This suggests that the shallow methods for feature extraction are not able to represent some important information that the deep LSTM-based models are able to capture. As a result, the ensemble system was able to outperform all three base systems in most cases, suggesting that none of the base systems were able to capture the whole picture individually.

References

Eneko Agirre, Mona Diab, Daniel Cer, and Aitor Gonzalez-Agirre. 2012. Semeval-2012 task 6: A pilot on semantic textual similarity. In *Proceedings of the First Joint Conference on Lexical and Computational Semantics-Volume 1: Proceedings of the main conference and the shared task, and Volume 2: Proceedings of the Sixth International Workshop on Semantic Evaluation*, pages 385–393. Association for Computational Linguistics.

Eneko Agirre, Daniel Cer, Mona Diab, Aitor Gonzalez-Agirre, and Weiwei Guo. 2013. sem 2013 shared task: Semantic textual similarity, including a pilot on typed-similarity. In *In* SEM 2013: The Second Joint Conference on Lexical and Computational Semantics. Association for Computational Linguistics*. Citeseer.

Eneko Agirre, Carmen Banea, Claire Cardie, Daniel Cer, Mona Diab, Aitor Gonzalez-Agirre, Weiwei Guo, Rada Mihalcea, German Rigau, and Janyce Wiebe. 2014. Semeval-2014 task 10: Multilingual semantic textual similarity. In *Proceedings of the 8th international workshop on semantic evaluation (SemEval 2014)*, pages 81–91.

Eneko Agirrea, Carmen Baneab, Claire Cardiec, Daniel Cerd, Mona Diabe, Aitor Gonzalez-Agirrea, Weiwei Guof, Inigo Lopez-Gazpioa, Montse Maritxalara, Rada Mihalceab, et al. 2015. Semeval-2015 task 2: Semantic textual similarity, english, spanish and pilot on interpretability. In *Proceedings of the 9th international workshop on semantic evaluation (SemEval 2015)*, pages 252–263.

Marco Baroni, Georgiana Dinu, and Germán Kruszewski. 2014. Don't count, predict! a systematic comparison of context-counting vs. context-predicting semantic vectors. In *ACL (1)*, pages 238–247.

Frédéric Bastien, Pascal Lamblin, Razvan Pascanu, James Bergstra, Ian J. Goodfellow, Arnaud Bergeron, Nicolas Bouchard, and Yoshua Bengio. 2012. Theano: new features and speed improvements. Deep Learning and Unsupervised Feature Learning NIPS 2012 Workshop.

James Bergstra, Olivier Breuleux, Frédéric Bastien, Pascal Lamblin, Razvan Pascanu, Guillaume Desjardins, Joseph Turian, David Warde-Farley, and Yoshua Bengio. 2010. Theano: a cpu and gpu math expression compiler. In *Proceedings of the Python for scientific computing conference (SciPy)*, volume 4, page 3. Austin, TX.

Samuel R Bowman, Christopher Potts, and Christopher D Manning. 2014. Recursive neural networks can learn logical semantics. *arXiv preprint arXiv:1406.1827*.

Samuel R Bowman, Gabor Angeli, Christopher Potts, and Christopher D Manning. 2015a. A large annotated corpus for learning natural language inference. *arXiv preprint arXiv:1508.05326*.

Samuel R Bowman, Christopher D Manning, and Christopher Potts. 2015b. Tree-structured composition in neural networks without tree-structured architectures. *arXiv preprint arXiv:1506.04834*.

Danqi Chen and Christopher D Manning. 2014. A fast and accurate dependency parser using neural networks. In *EMNLP*, pages 740–750.

Franois Chollet. 2015. Keras. https://github.com/fchollet/keras.

Courtney Corley and Rada Mihalcea. 2005. Measuring the semantic similarity of texts. In *Proceedings of the ACL workshop on empirical modeling of semantic equivalence and entailment*, pages 13–18. Association for Computational Linguistics.

G. Doddington. 2002. Automatic evaluation of machine translation quality using n-gram co-occurrence statistics. In *Proceedings of HLT*, pages 138–145.

Lushan Han, Justin Martineau, Doreen Cheng, and Christopher Thomas. 2015. Samsung: Align-and-differentiate approach to semantic textual similarity. *SemEval-2015*, page 172.

Christian Hänig, Robert Remus, and Xose De La Puente. 2015. Exb themis: Extensive feature extraction from word alignments for semantic textual similarity. *SemEval-2015*, page 264.

Alon Lavie and Abhaya Agarwal. 2005. Meteor: An automatic metric for mt evaluation with improved correlation with human judgments. In *Proceedings of the ACL 2005 Workshop on Intrinsic and Extrinsic Evaluation Measures for MT and/or Summarization*, pages 65–72.

Yuhua Li, David McLean, Zuhair A Bandar, James D O'shea, and Keeley Crockett. 2006. Sentence similarity based on semantic nets and corpus statistics. *Knowledge and Data Engineering, IEEE Transactions on*, 18(8):1138–1150.

Nitin Madnani, Joel Tetreault, and Martin Chodorow. 2012. Re-examining machine translation metrics for paraphrase identification. In *Proceedings of the 2012 Conference of the North American Chapter of the Association for Computational Linguistics: Human Language Technologies*, pages 182–190, Montréal, Canada, June. Association for Computational Linguistics.

Marco Marelli, Luisa Bentivogli, Marco Baroni, Raffaella Bernardi, Stefano Menini, and Roberto Zamparelli. 2014a. Semeval-2014 task 1: Evaluation of compositional distributional semantic models on full sentences through semantic relatedness and textual entailment. *SemEval-2014*.

Marco Marelli, Stefano Menini, Marco Baroni, Luisa Bentivogli, Raffaella Bernardi, and Roberto Zamparelli. 2014b. A sick cure for the evaluation of compositional distributional semantic models. In *LREC*, pages 216–223.

Rada Mihalcea, Courtney Corley, and Carlo Strapparava. 2006. Corpus-based and knowledge-based measures of text semantic similarity. In *AAAI*, volume 6, pages 775–780.

Tomas Mikolov, Ilya Sutskever, Kai Chen, Greg Corrado, and Jeffrey Dean. 2013. Distributed representations of words and phrases and their compositionality. *CoRR*, abs/1310.4546.

Matteo Negri, Alessandro Marchetti, Yashar Mehdad, Luisa Bentivogli, and Danilo Giampiccolo. 2012. Semeval-2012 task 8: cross-lingual textual entailment for content synchronization. In *Proceedings of the First Joint Conference on Lexical and Computational Semantics-Volume 1: Proceedings of the main conference and the shared task, and Volume 2: Proceedings of the Sixth International Workshop on Semantic Evaluation*, pages 399–407. Association for Computational Linguistics.

Kishore Papineni, Salim Roukos, Todd Ward, and Wei-Jing Zhu. 2002. Bleu: a method for automatic evaluation of machine translation. In *Proceedings of 40th Annual Meeting of the Association for Computational Linguistics*, pages 311–318, Philadelphia, Pennsylvania, USA, July. Association for Computational Linguistics.

Steven Parker. 2008. Badger: A new machine translation metric.

Jeffrey Pennington, Richard Socher, and Christopher D Manning. 2014. Glove: Global vectors for word representation. In *EMNLP*, volume 14, pages 1532–1543.

Matthew Snover, Bonnie Dorr, Richard Schwartz, Linnea Micciulla, and John Makhoul. 2006. A study of translation edit rate with targeted human annotation. In *In Proceedings of Association for Machine Translation in the Americas*, pages 223–231.

Matthew G. Snover, Nitin Madnani, Bonnie Dorr, and Richard Schwartz. 2009. Ter-plus: Paraphrase, semantic, and alignment enhancements to translation edit rate.

Md Arafat Sultan, Steven Bethard, and Tamara Sumner. 2014. Back to basics for monolingual alignment: Exploiting word similarity and contextual evidence. *Transactions of the Association for Computational Linguistics*, 2:219–230.

Md Arafat Sultan, Steven Bethard, and Tamara Sumner. 2015. Dls@ cu: Sentence similarity from word alignment and semantic vector composition. In *Proceedings of the 9th International Workshop on Semantic Evaluation*, pages 148–153.

Kai Sheng Tai, Richard Socher, and Christopher D Manning. 2015. Improved semantic representations from tree-structured long short-term memory networks. *arXiv preprint arXiv:1503.00075*.

Oriol Vinyals, Łukasz Kaiser, Terry Koo, Slav Petrov, Ilya Sutskever, and Geoffrey Hinton. 2015. Grammar as a foreign language. In *Advances in Neural Information Processing Systems*, pages 2755–2763.

Wei Xu, Chris Callison-Burch, and William B Dolan. 2015. Semeval-2015 task 1: Paraphrase and semantic similarity in twitter (pit). *Proceedings of SemEval*.

SERGIOJIMENEZ at SemEval-2016 Task 1: Effectively Combining Paraphrase Database, String Matching, WordNet and Word Embedding for Semantic Textual Similarity

Sergio Jimenez

Bogotá D.C., Colombia

`sergio.jimenez.vargas@gmail.com`

Abstract

In this paper, a system for semantic textual similarity, which participated in Task-1 in SemEval 2016 (monolingual and cross-lingual sub-tasks) is described. The system contains a preprocessing step that simplifies text using PPDB 2.0 and detects negations. Also, six lexical similarity functions were constructed using string matching, word embedding and synonyms-antonyms relations in WordNet. These lexical similarity functions are projected to sentence level using a new method called Polarized Soft Cardinality that supports negative similarities between words to model opposites. We also introduce a novel L^2-norm "cardinality" for vector space representations. The system extracts a set of 660 features from each pair of text snippets using the proposed cardinality measures. From this set, a subset of 12 features was selected in a supervised manner. These features are combined by SVR and, alternatively, by using the arithmetic mean to produce similarity predictions. Our team ranked second in the cross-lingual sub-task and got close to the best official results in the monolingual sub-task.

1 Introduction

Semantic Textual Similarity (STS) is a fundamental task in the field of natural language processing that has been addressed in SemEval competitions uninterruptedly since 2012 (Agirre et al., 2012; Agirre et al., 2013; Agirre et al., 2014; Agirre et al., 2015). The task is to compare two text fragments and produce a similarity score that is assessed according to human judgment. This year (Agirre et al., 2016), a new cross-lingual sub-task in English and Spanish is proposed in addition to the traditional monolingual English task. In SemEval 2015, the most popular approach among the best systems was the use of words alignments between sentences combining resources such as WordNet (Miller, George A., 1995), neural word embedding (Mikolov, Tomas et al., 2013) and the Paraphrase Database (Pavlick et al., 2015).

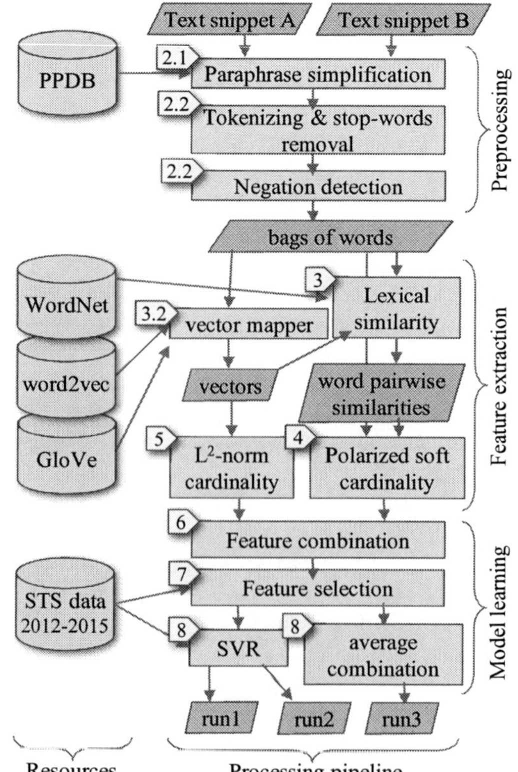

Figure 1: STS system architecture

Proceedings of SemEval-2016, pages 749–757,
San Diego, California, June 16-17, 2016. ©2016 Association for Computational Linguistics

This paper describes our system submission to STS 2016 that uses a cardinality-based approach (instead of word alignments) for combining the resources mentioned above. Several teams have used soft cardinality successfully in previous STS competitions from 2012 to 2014 (Jimenez et al., 2012; Jimenez et al., 2013a; Jimenez et al., 2013b; Jimenez et al., 2014; Lynum et al., 2014). For the proposed system, we extended the model of soft cardinality to allow the use of negative values in the lexical similarity component to model opposites due to antonymy and negation.

Figure 1 shows the overall architecture of the proposed system. Yellow labels in the upper left corner of each process component (blue squares) indicate the sections of this document where the module is discussed. In this figure, the processing pipeline is represented vertically in three stages: preprocessing, feature extraction and model learning. Red parallelograms represent the inputs and outputs of each process, from the pair of snippets of text for evaluation, through different intermediate representations (bag-of-words, vectors, etc.) and end on the predictions of similarity scores. The left side contains the used external resources linked to the process that makes use of each one.

2 Preprocessing

2.1 Paraphrase Simplification

The Paraphrase Database (PPDB) is a list of pairs of words, short phrases of syntactic rules where each pair is semantically equivalent in some degree (Pavlick et al., 2015). In PPDB, each paraphrases pair $\{e_1, e_2\}$ is obtained from translation models making use of the observation that if e_1 and e_2 are frequently translated to a same word or phrase in a foreign language, then there is a high probability of e_1 and e_2 being paraphrases of each other. In PPDB 2.0 each pair is labeled with $-\log(P(e_1|e_2))$ and $-\log(P(e_2|e_1))$ obtained from the translation models, where $P(e_2|e_1)$ is the inferred probability that the word or phrase e_1 is a good paraphrase for e_2, and the contrary for $P(e_1|e_2)$. The motivation for using this resource is that text pairs that can be paraphrased to simplified versions should be easier to analyze by downstream modules. For example, consider the paraphrase pair $e_1 =$"*interdisciplinary*"

and $e_2 =$"*cross-disciplinary*" labeled in PPDB with $-\log(P(e_2|e_1)) = 4.28$ and $-\log(P(e_1|e_2)) = 0.82$. Now, consider a pair of sentences for STS evaluation where these paraphrases occur: "The study was *interdisciplinary*." and "Our research is *cross-disciplinary*." Given that e_1 is higher scoring paraphrase for e_2 than the contrary (i.e. $-\log(P(e_2|e_1)) > -\log(P(e_1|e_2)))$, e_2 can be replaced by e_1 in the second sentence: "Our research is *interdisciplinary*". As a result, the pair of sentences now contains more frequent words and shares more words thereby facilitating subsequent STS analysis.

Let A and B be a pair of texts snippets for STS evaluation and e_1 and e_2 a pair of paraphrases from PPDB. Thus, $\{e_1, e_2\}$ occurs in $\{A, B\}$ if $e_1 \subset A \wedge e_2 \subset B$ or $e_2 \subset A \wedge e_1 \subset B$, being aware of the special cases when $e_1 \subset e_2$ or $e_2 \subset e_1$(whole words matching is used in those cases). The operator "$\subset$" means that the left argument is a sub-string of the right one. The input pairs of sentences for the STS task where preprocessed by looking for occurrences of paraphrases from PPDB and replacing the least probable paraphrase by the most probable paraphrase. For that, we used the top-ranked lexical paraphrases and phrasal paraphrases from the M-size version of the PPDB 2.0 [1] (syntactic rules were not used). We determined the number of top-ranking lexical and phrasal paraphrases to use experimentally by using the overall STS system described in this paper trained and tested with STS datasets from previous years. Consistent increases in the performance measured by mean correlation was observed as the number of used paraphrases increased. The average relative improvement stabilized around 2% using 150,000 lexical paraphrases and 3,000,000 phrasal paraphrases. Using these thresholds for the paraphrase database we assessed the 14 thousand sentence pairs in training data and found 3,294 occurrences of lexical paraphrases and 1,778 phrasal paraphrases.

2.2 Tokenizing, Stop-words Removal and Negation Detection

The preprocessing continues by tokenizing sentences, removing stop-words and labeling negated

---

[1] http://paraphrase.org/#/download

words. For this stage, we use the tokenizer and stop-words list from NLTK[2] augmented with the following words: *should, now, 's, 't, 've, something, would* and *also*. Once stop-words are removed from the text, each word preceded by a negation token is labeled as a negated word. The negation tokens we use are: *not, n't, nor, null, neither, barely, scarcely, hardly, no, none, nobody, nowhere, nothing, never* and *without*. The negation tagged tokens are used by subsequent modules for modeling oppositeness between negated and non-negated forms (e.g. "not running" and "running").

3   Lexical Similarity

The analysis of short texts based on soft cardinality relies only on a similarity function between lexical units (Jimenez et al., 2010). Therefore, the first component of the proposed STS system is composed of four lexical similarity functions that compare a pair of words and yield a numerical value in [-1,1] interval. Returning values of 1 means that the two words can be considered identical, 0 for unrelated words, negative values for representing opposition, and other values for representing intermediate degrees of similarity and opposition. In this section, the four lexical similarity functions we use are described.

3.1   Lexical String Matching Boosted with Synonyms and Antonyms

The NLP community has widely recognized that the use of lemmas or stems, instead of words, is desirable in many applications of automatic text processing. Therefore, before comparing any pair of words we reduced them to their stems using the Porter's algorithm (Porter, 1980). Let x and y be two stemmed words represented each as a sequence of characters. The first proposed lexical function replaces this basic word representation by the set of tri-grams and tetra-grams of characters on each word. This representation was used successfully for addressing the STS task with purely string-based approaches (Jimenez et al., 2012). For example, the word *country* is stemmed to $x =$*countri*. Next, its [3:4]-grams representation is $x =${*cou, oun, unt, ntr, tri, coun, ount, untr, ntri*}. Once x and y are represented as

---

[2]http://www.nltk.org/

described, they are compared with the following expression:

$$S_1(x, y) = \frac{|x \cap y|}{\sqrt{|x| \times |y|}}$$

The second lexical similarity function is the well-known Jaro-Winkler (Winkler, 1990) expression:

$$d(x, y) = \frac{1}{3}\left(\frac{m}{\text{len}(x)} + \frac{m}{\text{len}(y)} + \frac{m - t}{m}\right)$$

$$S_2 = \begin{cases} d(x, y) & \text{if } d(x, y) < b_t \\ d(x, y) + (lp \times (1 - d(x, y))) & \text{otherwise} \end{cases}$$

Where, $\text{len}(x)$ is the number of characters in word x, m is the number of matching characters between x and y, t is the number of transpositions between x and y, lp is the length of the common prefix, $p = 0.1$, and $b_t = 0.7$ is the "boost threshold". The number of matching characters m is the number of common characters between x and y whose occurrences are not farther than $\left\lfloor \frac{max[len(x),len(y)]}{2} \right\rfloor - 1$ positions. The number t of transpositions is the number of matching characters that occur in different sequence order on each string. Clearly, $m \leq \text{len}(x)$, $m \leq \text{len}(y)$, and $t \leq m$, therefore $d(x, y)$ is defined only in $[0, 1]$ interval (if $m = 0$, then $d(x, y)$ is set to 0). Similarly to S_1, S_2 was used to compare stems instead of words.

Both S_1 and S_2 returns 1 when x and y are identical, 0 when x and y do not have common characters, and intermediate values for other cases. To a certain extent, this stem string similarity reflects semantic similarity between words. To improve this property, a wrapper function $\mathring{S}$ was built over S_1 and S_2 to include information from the synonym and antonym relationships in WordNet and the negation feature extracted at preprocessing stage (see subsection 2.2). If x and y are synonyms in WordNet, then the wrapper function $\mathring{S}$ overwrites the results of S_1 and S_2 to 1 (identical meaning). For the case when x and y are antonyms, the wrapper function should return a negative value to represent the opposition between words x and y (opposite meaning). Unlike synonymy and identity, the relation between antonymy and numerical oppositeness is rather unclear because most antonym pairs also are semantically similar (e.g. *small-large*) (Mohammad et al.,

2008). The natural choice for this negative values is -1 (Yih et al., 2012)(Yih et al., 2012). However, instead of setting -1 to represent oppositions between two words, we decided to set this value as a parameter to be determined experimentally. For that, we used the overall STS system described in this paper with the STS datasets from previous years. The value that optimized the mean correlation was -0.2 in a search range from -1 to 1. The negation feature of the words is used to add negation logic to $\mathring{S}$. For example, if x and y are synonyms but x is negated, then they are considered antonyms. Some examples are: $\mathring{S}(car, auto) = 1$, $\mathring{S}(\neg car, \neg auto) = 1$, $\mathring{S}(\neg car, auto) = -0.2$, $\mathring{S}(love, hate) = -0.2$, $\mathring{S}(\neg love, \neg hate) = -0.2$ and $\mathring{S}(\neg love, hate) = 1$ ($\neg$ signify "negated word"). In the remaining cases, when x and y are neither synonyms nor antonyms, the wrapper function returns $S_i(x, y)$ except for the case when either x or y is negated. In that later case, the wrapper function returns $0.26 \times S_i(x, y)$, which is a scaling factor for modeling negation determined experimentally in the same way as the opposite value of 0.2. A couple of examples are: $\mathring{S}_1(skater, skateboard) = 0.489$, $\mathring{S}_1(\neg skater, skateboard) = 0.489 \times 0.26 = 0.127$. Henceforth, functions S_1 and S_2 are assumed to be overwritten by the described wrapper function.

3.2 Word Embedding

Two additional lexical similarity functions were built using word embedding representations. Let $\vec{x}$ and $\vec{y}$ be the vectorial representations of words x and y in $\mathbb{R}^n$. The used lexical similarity function between a pair of words is the cosine between these vectorial representations:

$$S_3(x, y) = \frac{\vec{x} \cdot \vec{y}}{\|\vec{x}\| \times \|\vec{y}\|}$$

Function S_3 is computed using the publicly available pre-trained Google News corpus word embedding [3] from the *word2vec* tool (Mikolov, Tomas et al., 2013). We also include a similar function S_4 that is defined identically to S_3 but uses pre-trained Twitter corpus word embedding [4] from *the GloVe*

---

[3] GoogleNews-vectors-negative300.bin downloaded from https://code.google.com/archive/p/word2vec/

[4] glove.twitter.27B.50d.txt downloaded from http://nlp.stanford.edu/projects/glove/

tool (Pennington, Jeffrey et al., 2014). These cosine based similarities produce scores in the range from -1 to 1.

4 Polarized Soft Cardinality

Lexical similarity can be leveraged to address sentence similarity by aggregating lexical similarity scores. One successful mechanism for doing this is soft cardinality (Jimenez et al., 2010), which is a generalization of the classic set cardinality that considers similarities between elements. Thus, the soft cardinality of a bag of words $A = \{a_1, a_2, \ldots, a_n\}$ (i.e. a sentence) and a similarity function between words $S(a_i, a_j)$ is defined by this expression:

$$|A|_S = \sum_{i=1}^{n} \left(\frac{1}{\sum_{j=1}^{n} S(a_i, a_j)^p} \right)$$

Where p is the softness-control parameter, which is positive and its default value is $p = 1$. Soft cardinality is a generalization of classic cardinality because as p increases, $|A|_S$ gets closer to $|A|$. The soft cardinality of the union of two bags of words $|A \cup B|_S$ is simply the soft cardinality of the concatenation of the bags. The soft cardinality of the intersection of two bag is defined as $|A \cap B|_S = |A|_S + |B|_S - |A \cup B|_S$. This model is restricted only to positive lexical similarity functions because negative values could lead to division-by-zero if $\sum_{j=1}^{n} S(a_i, a_j)^p = 0$ for any a_i.

Given that the lexical similarity functions S_1 to S_4 (described in Section 3) can return negative values for words with opposite semantics, a new soft cardinality model that supports such negative similarities between elements was proposed for this competition. The new *polarized soft cardinality* model is:

$$|A|_S = \sum_{i=1}^{n} \left(\frac{2 - \frac{1}{1 - \sum_{j=1}^{n} \mathrm{neg}(S(a_i, a_j), p)}}{\sum_{j=1}^{n} \mathrm{pos}(S(a_i, a_j), p)} \right)$$

$$\mathrm{neg}(s, p) = \begin{cases} (-s)^p & \text{if } s < 0 \\ 0 & \text{otherwise} \end{cases}$$

$$\mathrm{pos}(s, p) = \begin{cases} s^p & \text{if } s \geq 0 \\ 0 & \text{otherwise} \end{cases}$$

Functions $\mathrm{neg}(s, p)$ and $\mathrm{pos}(s, p)$ filter respectively negative and positive values of s, then raise them to p power ignoring the sign. Note that, if $S(a_i, a_j)$ is strictly positive, then this model is equivalent to soft cardinality . This new model inserts dummy or "ghost" elements in A if there are opposite elements in A. For example, consider $A = auto, love, hate$ and $S(auto, love) = S(auto, hate) = S(love, hate) = 0$. Clearly, $|A|_S = 3$. However, if $S(love, hate) = -1$, then $|A|_S = 4$. This increment in soft cardinality reflects the presence of a dummy element due to the fact that *love* and *hate* are opposites.

Using the lexical similarity functions presented in Section 3, four soft cardinality functions can be built: $|*|_{S_1}, |*|_{S_2}, |*|_{S_3}$ and $|*|_{S_4}$. Each of those has the following softness control parameter values: $p_{S_1} = 1.05, p_{S_2} = 0.85, p_{S_3} = 0.5$ and $p_{S_4} = 0.65$, which were obtained experimentally using STS data from previous SemEval campaigns. These soft cardinality functions are used to extract numerical features from each pair of sentences to be evaluated (see Section 6).

5 L^2-norm Cardinality

Given two sentences A and B represented as bag of words, the proposed L^2-*norm cardinality* is a measure of the amount of information in A, B, $A \cap B$ and $A \cup B$. L2-norm cardinality is analogous to soft cardinality but uses vectorial representations of the words and vector operations in its formulation. Instead of exploiting pairwise similarities between words as soft cardinality does, L^2-norm cardinality uses vectorial representations of the words in the "bag" to assess its cardinality. Let $A = \{\vec{a}_1, \vec{a}_2, \ldots, \vec{a}_p\}$ and $B = \{\vec{b}_1, \vec{b}_2, \ldots, \vec{b}_q\}$ be a bag of vector-represented words in $\mathbb{R}^n$, where p and q are the number of words in A and B respectively. Firstly, A and B obtain a representation in $\mathbb{R}^n$ by adding up the vectors in their respective bags, i.e. $\mathbf{A} = \sum_{i=1}^p \vec{a}_i$ and $\mathbf{B} = \sum_{i=1}^q \vec{b}_i$. L^2-norm cardinality is defined by the following expressions:

$$
\begin{aligned}
|A|_n &= \|\mathbf{A}\|^2 \\
|B|_n &= \|\mathbf{B}\|^2 \\
|A \cap B|_n &= \mathbf{A} \cdot \mathbf{B} \\
|A \cup B|_n &= |A|_n + |B|_n - |A \cap B|_n
\end{aligned}
$$

Two L^2-norm cardinality functions can be built

reusing the same word embedding used in S_3 and S_4. Thus, $|*|_{300}$ is obtained using the pre-trained word2vec vectors and $|*|_{50}$ is obtained from the pre-trained GloVe vectors. L^2-norm cardinalities $|*|_{300}$ and $|*|_{50}$ are added to the set of the four previously proposed soft cardinality functions to be used for extracting numerical features from sentence pairs.

6 Feature Extraction

The six cardinality functions proposed in Section 4 and Section 5 can be used to build a variety of similarity assessment measures for STS.. For example, for sentences A and B, the expression $sim(A, B) = \frac{|A \cap B|_{S_1}}{|A \cup B|_{S_1}}$ is a possible STS measure based on Jaccard's coefficient. However, the space of possible similarity functions that can be built from cardinalities $|A|_{S_1}, |B|_{S_1}, |A \cup B|_{S_1}$ and $|A \cap B|_{S_1}$ is huge. We explore a limited portion of this space by generating similarity function expressions from a set of 11 factors (see Table 1). Parameter c in Table 1 represents the sub-index for identifying the possible cardinality function, $c \in \{S_1, S_2, S_3, S_4, 300, 50\}$. The set of expressions used for combining these factors is heuristic but motivated by the formulations of existing cardinality-based similarity measures (e.g. Jaccard, Dice, matching, cosine among others). For each one of the six cardinality functions, these factors were combined into expressions that generate a total of $11 \times 10 = 110$ features of the form $\frac{f_i}{f_j}; i \neq j$.

7 Feature Selection

The feature selection process consists in selecting the k-best features from the set of 110 features for each cardinality function. We used the method *SelectKBest*[5] from the *Scikit-learn* machine learning kit (Pedregosa, Fabian et al., 2011). The data used for this selection process was the concatenation of 20 STS datasets labeled with gold standard from the past SemEval campaigns from the years 2012 to 2015 (14,437 sentence pairs with gold standard annotations). The process was performed using 10-fold cross-validation repeating the selection ten times with different randomly selected fold partitions. The k features that were selected the most

---

[5] http://scikit-learn.org/stable/modules/generated/ sklearn.feature_selection.SelectKBest.html

Factor	Expression†	Name
f_1	$|A \cap B|_c$	intersection
f_2	$|A \cup B|_c$	union
f_3	$|A \triangle B|_c$	symmetric diff.
f_4	$\min[|A|_c, |B|_c]$	minimum
f_5	$\max[|A|_c, |B|_c]$	maximum
f_6	$0.5 \times (|A|_c + |B|_c)$	mean
f_7	$\sqrt{|A|_c \times |B|_c}$	geometric mean
f_8	$\sqrt{0.5 \times (|A|_c^2 + |B|_c^2)}$	quadratic mean
f_9	$\sqrt[3]{0.5 \times (|A|_c^3 + |B|_c^3)}$	cubic mean
f_{10}	$\sqrt[4]{0.5 \times (|A|_c^4 + |B|_c^4)}$	4^{th}mean
f_{11}	1.0	1.0

$^\dagger\, c \in \{S_1, S_2, S_3, S_4, 300, 50\}$

Table 1: Factors for rational similarity functions based on cardinality functions

times in the k-best selection after all runs were retained for the final model. Preliminary experiments suggest a good value for k is two, as determined using the overall STS system with the same data. Table 2 shows the selected features for each cardinality function and their results on the mean correlation performance measure as assessed under previous STS shared task evaluation settings. Although, none of the features outperformed the best official results, results of $| * |_{S_1}$ and $| * |_{300}$ cardinality functions are highly competitive. It is important to note that, in spite that the feature selection procedure is supervised, the selected features by themselves are inherently un-supervised.

8   Feature Combination

The 12 selected features showed in Table 2 were combined to produce predictions for our three participating runs. *Run1* and *run2* were SVR (support-vector regression) models with RBF kernel (Drucker, Harris et al., 1997) built with the 14,437 sentence pairs available for training. The difference between *run1* and *run2* is the values of the used SVR parameters C and γ. For *run1*, we used $C = 0.6$ and $\gamma = 0.004$, which were obtained by optimizing the weighted average of Pearson correlations using each available STS dataset alternatively for testing and the remaining pairs for training. For *run2*, we used $C = 53$ and $\gamma = 0.012$, which were obtained using all 14,437 sentence pairs as a single dataset

and 5-folds cross-validation in 5 randomly selected division folds.

Unlike *run1* and *run2*, *run3* was effectively unsupervised and operated by simply averaging the 12 feature values after multiplying by -1 the values of the features with negative correlations in Table 2.

9   Cross-lingual Sub-task

The predictions of the three runs submitted to the STS cross-lingual sub-task were produced using the same systems that produced predictions for the STS monolingual sub-task (English). For that, the texts in Spanish were translated into English using Google's public translate service.[6]

10   Results

Table 3 shows results obtained with the same systems used to produce our runs 1, 2 and 3, but using datasets from STS competitions from 2012 to 2015. The results labeled as "held-out" were obtained by holding out each dataset for testing and using the remaining datasets for training including the three training datasets from 2012. The results labeled as "same-data" were otained using the same training data available during each historical STS evaluation. All "held-out" systems outperformed consistently the best official results obtained by a single system for each year using the performance measure of weighted mean correlation. For the "same-data" systems, the *run1* outperformed historical official results from 2013 to 2015, while *run2* and *run3* made it only for 2013 and 2014. Table 4 shows results of the same systems ("held-out" testing setting) and the best official results obtained on each dataset of the 20 individual evaluation datasets from prior STS competitions. In this tougher comparison, the proposed systems obtained state-of-the-art results in 10 out of the 20 individual datasets, and competitive results for the majority of the remaining datasets. Finally, Table 5 and Table 6 show the results obtained by our systems on the 2016 datasets along with the best official results of the competition. When comparing our three runs, none of them was consistently better with the three runs typically obtaining similar results. Therefore, it is possible to conclude that the

---

[6]https://translate.google.com/

Cardinality function	Feature	Expression	2012	2013	2014	2015
$\|*\|_{S_1}$	f_3/f_8	$\dfrac{\|A\triangle B\|_{S_1}}{\sqrt{0.5\times(\|A\|_{S_1}^2+\|B\|_{S_1}^2)}}$	**-0.6404**	-0.5994	-0.7538	**-0.7953**
SC+[3:4]grams	f_3/f_9	$\dfrac{\|A\triangle B\|_{S_1}}{\sqrt[3]{0.5\times(\|A\|_{S_1}^3+\|B\|_{S_1}^3)}}$	-0.6376	-0.5952	**-0.7534**	-0.7933
$\|*\|_{S_2}$	f_1/f_2	$\dfrac{\|A\cap B\|_{S_2}}{\|A\cup B\|_{S_2}}$	0.4327	0.3287	0.3793	0.4012
SC+Jaro-Winkler	f_3/f_2	$\dfrac{\|A\triangle B\|_{S_2}}{\|A\cup B\|_{S_2}}$	-0.4327	-0.3385	-0.3793	-0.4012
$\|*\|_{S_3}$	f_8/f_2	$\dfrac{\sqrt{0.5\times(\|A\|_{S_3}^2+\|B\|_{S_3}^2)}}{\|A\cup B\|_{S_3}}$	0.5671	0.4722	0.5572	0.5831
SC+word2vec	f_9/f_2	$\dfrac{\sqrt[3]{0.5\times(\|A\|_{S_3}^3+\|B\|_{S_3}^3)}}{\|A\cup B\|_{S_3}}$	0.5652	0.4702	0.5604	0.5804
$\|*\|_{S_4}$	f_{11}/f_1	$\dfrac{1.0}{\|A\cap B\|_{S_4}}$	-0.2195	-0.2331	-0.3014	-0.2961
SC+GloVe	f_3/f_2	$\dfrac{\|A\triangle B\|_{S_4}}{\|A\cup B\|_{S_4}}$	-0.4348	-0.2915	-0.3168	-0.3093
$\|*\|_{300}$	f_3/f_{11}	$\dfrac{\|A\triangle B\|_{300}}{1.0}$	-0.6389	**-0.6065**	-0.7334	-0.7509
L^2-norm+word2vec	$f_3,/f_5$	$\dfrac{\|A\triangle B\|_{300}}{\max[\|A\|_{300},\|B\|_{300}]}$	-0.6389	-0.6022	-0.7334	-0.7509
$\|*\|_{50}$	f_1/f_2	$\dfrac{\|A\cap B\|_{50}}{\|A\cup B\|_{50}}$	0.5377	0.4750	0.5808	0.5744
L^2-norm+GloVe	f_3/f_2	$\dfrac{\|A\triangle B\|_{50}}{\|A\cup B\|_{50}}$	-0.5377	-0.4750	-0.5808	-0.5744
Best official result at SemEval			**0.6773**	**0.6181**	**0.7610**	**0.8015**

Table 2: Results of mean correlation (official performance measure) of the 2-best features for each cardinality function in previous years STS data

System	2012	2013	2014	2015
run1.held-out	**0.6951**	**0.6393**	0.7842	**0.8101**
run2.held-out	0.6895	0.6367	0.7826	0.8013
run3.held-out	0.6945	0.6383	**0.7851**	0.8099
run1.same-data	**0.6771**	0.6322	**0.7692**	**0.8048**
run2.same-data	0.6696	0.6241	0.7677	0.7931
run3.same-data	0.6721	**0.6327**	0.7553	0.7925
best official result	0.6773	0.6181	0.7610	0.8015

Table 3: Results of our 2016 systems using data from previous STS SemEval competitions (mean correlation performance measure).

contribution of SVR was not considerable, with an exception for the *answer-answer* dataset.

11 Conclusion

The proposed STS system combined effectively the most popular resources used by the top systems during the SemEval 2015 for STS shared task. Results show that the proposed system outperformed all past systems in a per-system based comparison, and obtained state-of-the-art results in half of the datasets from past STS competitions at SemEval.

Yr.	Dataset	*run1*	*run2*	*run3*	best†
2012	MSRpar	0.6522	0.6549	0.5829	**0.7343**
	MSRvid	0.8520	0.8612	0.8494	**0.8803**
	SMTeurop.	0.5332	0.5285	0.5499	**0.5666**
	OnWN	0.7270	0.7120	0.7228	**0.7273**
	SMTnews	0.6068	0.5750	0.5965	**0.6085**
2013	FNWN	0.4705	0.3920	0.4721	**0.5818**
	headlines	**0.8006**	0.8020	0.7836	0.7838
	OnWN	0.7865	0.8057	0.7562	**0.8431**
	SMT	0.4105	0.4065	**0.4165**	0.4035
	deft-forum	**0.5512**	0.5307	0.5464	0.5305
	deft-news	**0.7925**	0.7757	0.7823	0.7850
2014	headlines	**0.7913**	0.7914	0.7768	0.7837
	OnWN	0.8367	0.8388	0.8224	**0.8745**
	tweet-news	0.8019	0.8027	**0.8148**	0.7921
	images	**0.8435**	0.8514	0.8324	0.8343
2015	ans.-forums	**0.7474**	0.7066	0.7364	0.7390
	ans.-studt.	0.7853	0.7698	**0.7900**	0.7879
	belief	0.7536	0.7464	0.7496	**0.7717**
	headlines	0.8307	0.8289	0.8183	**0.8417**
	images	0.8740	**0.8797**	0.8712	0.8713

†Official results of the best system for each dataset

Table 4: Results of our 2016 systems being compared against best official results in a comparison for each dataset.

2016 dataset	*run1*	*run2*	*run3*	best
answer-answer	0.5018	0.5526	0.4907	0.6924
headlines	0.7865	0.7830	0.7773	0.8275
plagiarism	0.8365	0.8151	0.8293	0.8414
postediting	0.8364	0.8163	0.8481	0.8669
question-quest.	0.6652	0.6663	0.6729	0.7471
ALL mean r	0.7241	0.7262	0.7222	0.7781†

†Best individual system submission

Table 5: Official results for our participating systems in the monolingual sub-task (English).

2016 dataset	*run1*	*run2*	*run3*	best
News	0.8872	0.8291	0.8965	0.9124
Multisource	0.8184	0.8127	0.8074	0.8190
ALL mean r	0.8532	0.8210	0.8525	0.8631
Run Rank	3rd	7th	4th	1st
Team Rank	2nd	2nd	2nd	1st

Table 6: Official results for our participating systems in the cross-lingual sub-task (English/Spanish).

Acknowledgments

I thank the anonymous reviewers and Daniel Cer for their constructive comments. In addition, I am indebted to my beloved Claudia Luisa, and Sara, who kindly conceded part of our time together for this participation.

References

Eneko Agirre, Daniel Cer, Mona Diab, and Gonzalez-Agirre Aitor. 2012. SemEval-2012 Task 6: A Pilot on Semantic Textual Similarity. In *First Joint Conference on Lexical and Computational Semantics (*SEM)*, pages 385–393, Montreal,Canada. ACL.

Eneko Agirre, Daniel Cer, Mona Diab, Aitor Gonzalez-Agirre, and Weiwei Guo. 2013. *SEM 2013 Shared Task: Semantic Textual Similarity, including a Pilot on Typed-Similarity. pages 32–43, Atlanta, Georgia, USA. ACL.

Eneko Agirre, Carmen Banea, Claire Cardie, Daniel Cer, Mona Diab, Aitor Gonzalez-Agirre, Weiwei Guo, Rada Mihalcea, German Rigau, and Janyce Wiebe. 2014. SemEval-2014 Task 10: Multilingual semantic textual similarity. In *Proceedings of the 8th International Workshop on Semantic Evaluation (SemEval 2014)*, pages 81–91, Dublin, Ireland. ACL.

Eneko Agirre, Carmen Banea, Claire Cardie, Daniel Cer, Mona Diab, Aitor Gonzalez-Agirre, Weiwei Guo,

Inigo Lopez-Gazpio, Montse Maritxalar, Rada Mihalcea, and others. 2015. Semeval-2015 task 2: Semantic textual similarity, english, spanish and pilot on interpretability. In *Proceedings of the 9th international workshop on semantic evaluation (SemEval 2015)*, pages 252–263. ACL.

Eneko Agirre, Carmen Banea, Daniel Cer, Mona Diab, and Aitor Gonzalez-Agirre. 2016. SemEval-2016 Task 1: Semantic Textual Similarity - Monolingual and Cross-lingual Evaluation. ACL.

Drucker, Harris, Burges, Chris J.C., Kaufman, Linda, Smola, Alex, and Vapnik, Vladimir. 1997. Support vector regression machines. *Advances in neural information processing systems*, 9:155–161.

Sergio Jimenez, Fabio Gonzalez, and Alexander Gelbukh. 2010. Text Comparison Using Soft Cardinality. In Edgar Chavez and Stefano Lonardi, editors, *String Processing and Information Retrieval*, volume 6393 of *LNCS*, pages 297–302. Springer, Berlin, Heidelberg.

Sergio Jimenez, Claudia Becerra, and Alexander Gelbukh. 2012. Soft Cardinality: A Parameterized Similarity Function for Text Comparison. In *First Joint Conference on Lexical and Computational Semantics (*SEM)*, pages 449–453, Montreal, Canada. ACL.

Sergio Jimenez, Claudia Becerra, and Alexander Gelbukh. 2013a. SOFTCARDINALITY-CORE: Improving Text Overlap with Distributional Measures for Semantic Textual Similarity. In *Second Joint Conference on Lexical and Computational Semantics (*SEM), Volume 1: Proceedings of the Main Conference and the Shared Task*, pages 194–201, Atlanta, Georgia, USA, June. ACL.

Sergio Jimenez, Claudia Becerra, and Alexander Gelbukh. 2013b. SOFTCARDINALITY: Learning to Identify Directional Cross-Lingual Entailment from Cardinalities and SMT. In *Second Joint Conference on Lexical and Computational Semantics (*SEM), Volume 2: Seventh International Workshop on Semantic Evaluation (SemEval 2013)*, pages 34–38, Atlanta, Georgia, USA, June. ACL.

Sergio Jimenez, George Duenas, Julia Baquero, and Alexander Gelbukh. 2014. UNAL-NLP: Combining soft cardinality features for semantic textual similarity, relatedness and entailment. In *Proceedings of the 8th International Workshop on Semantic Evaluation (SemEval 2014)*, pages 732–742, Dublin, Ireland. ACL.

André Lynum, Partha Pakray, Björn Gambäck, and Sergio Jimenez. 2014. NTNU: Measuring Semantic Similarity with Sublexical Feature Representations and Soft Cardinality. In *Proceedings of the 8th International Workshop on Semantic Evaluation (SemEval 2014)*, pages 448–453, Dublin, Ireland. ACL.

Mikolov, Tomas, Sutskever, Ilya, Chen, Kai, Corrado, Greg, and Dean, Jeff. 2013. Distributed representations of words and phrases and their compositionality. In *Advances in Neural Information Processing Systems (NIPS)*, pages 3111–3119.

Miller, George A. 1995. WordNet: A Lexical Database for English. *Communications of the ACM*, 38(11):39–41.

Saif Mohammad, Bonnie Dorr, and Graeme Hirst. 2008. Computing word-pair antonymy. In *Proceedings of the Conference on Empirical Methods in Natural Language Processing*, pages 982–991. Association for Computational Linguistics.

Ellie Pavlick, Johan Bos, Malvina Nissim, Charley Beller, Ben Van Durme, and Chris Callison-Burch. 2015. PPDB 2.0: Better paraphrase ranking, fine-grained entailment relations, word embeddings, and style classification. In *Proc. ACL*.

Pedregosa, Fabian, Varoquaux, Gaël, Gramfort, Alexandre, Michel, Vincent, Thirion, Bertrand, Grisel, Olivier, Blondel, Mathieu, Prettenhofer, Peter, Weiss, Ron, Doubourg, Vincent, Vanderplas, Jake, Passos, Alexandre, Cournapeau, David, Brucher, Matthieu, Perrot, Matthieu, and Duchesnay, Edouard. 2011. Scikit-learn: Machine Learning in {P}ython. *The Journal of Machine Learning Research*, 12:2825–2830.

Pennington, Jeffrey, Socher, Richard, and Manning, Christopher D. 2014. Glove: Global vectors for word representation. In *Proceedings of the Empiricial Methods in Natural Language Processing (EMNLP 2014)*, volume 12, pages 1532–1543, Doha, Qatar.

Martin Porter. 1980. An algorithm for suffix stripping. *Program*, 3(14):130–137, October.

William E. Winkler. 1990. String comparator metrics and enhanced decision Rules in the Fellegi-Sunter Model of Record Linkage. In *Proceedings of the Section on Survey Research Methods*, pages 354–359. American Statistical Association.

Wen-tau Yih, Geoffrey Zweig, and John C. Platt. 2012. Polarity inducing latent semantic analysis. In *Proceedings of the 2012 Joint Conference on Empirical Methods in Natural Language Processing and Computational Natural Language Learning*, pages 1212–1222. Association for Computational Linguistics.

RTM at SemEval-2016 Task 1: Predicting Semantic Similarity with Referential Translation Machines and Related Statistics

Ergun Biçici

ergunbicici@yahoo.com

bicici.github.com

Abstract

We use referential translation machines (RTMs) for predicting the semantic similarity of text in both STS Core and Cross-lingual STS. RTMs pioneer a language independent approach to all similarity tasks and remove the need to access any task or domain specific information or resource. RTMs become 14th out of 26 submissions in Cross-lingual STS. We also present rankings of various prediction tasks using the performance of RTM in terms of MRAER, a normalized relative absolute error metric.

1 Semantic Agreement

We participated in Semantic Textual Similarity task at SemEval-2016 (Bethard et al., 2016) with RTMs. RTMs identify translation acts between any two data sets with respect to interpretants, data close to the task instances, effectively judging monolingual and bilingual similarity. We use RTMs for predicting the semantic similarity of text. Interpretants are used to derive features measuring the closeness of the test sentences to the training data, the difficulty of translating them, and the presence of the acts of translation, which may ubiquitously be observed in communication.

Semantic Web's dream is to allow machines to share, exploit, and understand knowledge on the web. As more and more shared conceptualizations of domains emerge, we get closer to this goal. Semantic textual similarity (STS) task (Agirre et al., 2016) at SemEval-2016 (Bethard et al., 2016) is about quantifying the degree of similarity between two given sentences S_1 and S_2 in the same language (English) in STS Core (STS English) or in different languages (English or Spanish) in Cross-lingual STS (STS Spanish), with a real number in $[0, 5]$. S_1 and S_2 may be constructed using different models and with different conceptualizations of the world or different ontologies and different vocabulary. Even if two instances are categorized as same, they may have different implications for commonsense reasoning (both albatros and penguin are a bird) (Biçici, 2002).

The existence of a single ontology that can cover all the required conceptual information for reaching semantic understanding is questionable because it would presume an agreement among all ontology experts. Yet, semantic agreement using heterogeneous ontologies may not be possible as well since in the most extreme case, they would not use the same tokens. Therefore, semantic textual similarity is harder than the Chinese room thought experiment (Internet Encyclopedia of Philosophy, 2016) since we are not given any instructions about how to answer queries. Our goal is to quantify the level of semantic agreement between S_1 and S_2 and RTMs use interpretants, data close to the task instances for building prediction models for semantic similarity.

2 Referential Translation Machine

Each RTM model is a data translation prediction model between the instances in the training set and the test set and translation acts are indicators of the data transformation and translation. RTMs are powerful enough to be applicable in different domains and tasks while achieving top performance in both

Proceedings of SemEval-2016, pages 758–764,
San Diego, California, June 16-17, 2016. ©2016 Association for Computational Linguistics

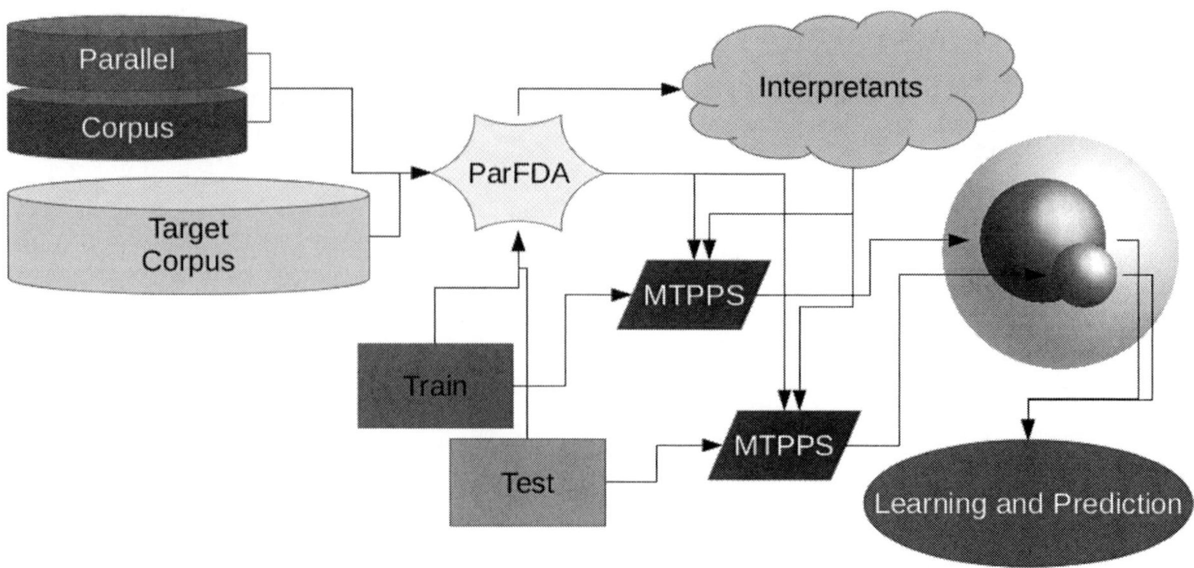

Figure 1: RTM depiction: ParFDA selects interpretants close to the training and test data using parallel corpus in bilingual settings and monolingual corpus in the target language or just the monolingual target corpus in monolingual settings; an MTPPS use interpretants and training data to generate training features and another use interpretants and test data to generate test features in the same feature space; learning and prediction takes place taking these features as input.

		ans.-ans.	headlines	plagiarism	postediting	que.-que.
STS	base	1572	1498	1271	3287	1555
English	eval.	254	249	230	244	209

		multisource	newswire
STS	base	2973	301
Spanish	eval.	294	301

Table 1: Number of instances in the STS test set. Only some of the instances are actually evaluated (eval. row).

monolingual (Biçici and Way, 2015) and bilingual settings (Biçici et al., 2015b). Our encouraging results in the semantic similarity tasks increase our understanding of the acts of translation we ubiquitously use when communicating and how they can be used to predict semantic similarity.

Figure 1 depicts RTMs and explains the model building process. Given a training set `train`, a test set `test`, and some corpus $\mathcal{C}$, preferably in the same domain, the RTM steps are:

1. select($\text{train}, \text{test}, \mathcal{C}) \rightarrow \mathcal{I}$
2. MTPP($\mathcal{I}, \text{train}) \rightarrow \mathcal{F}_{\text{train}}$
3. MTPP($\mathcal{I}, \text{test}) \rightarrow \mathcal{F}_{\text{test}}$
4. learn($M, \mathcal{F}_{\text{train}}) \rightarrow \mathcal{M}$
5. predict($\mathcal{M}, \mathcal{F}_{\text{test}}) \rightarrow \hat{y}$

RTMs use ParFDA (Biçici et al., 2015a) for instance selection and machine translation performance prediction system (MTPPS) (Biçici and Way, 2015) for generating features.

We use support vector regression (SVR) for building the predictor in combination with feature selection (FS) and partial least squares (PLS). Assuming that $\hat{y}, y \in \mathbb{R}^n$ are the prediction and the target respectively, evaluation metrics we use are defined in Equation (1) where metrics are Pearson's correlation (r), mean absolute error (MAE), relative absolute error (RAE), relative Pearson's correlation (r_R), MAER (mean absolute error relative), and MRAER (mean relative absolute error relative).

We use MAER and MRAER for easier replication and comparability. MAER is the mean absolute error relative to the magnitude of the target and MRAER is the mean absolute error relative to the absolute error of a predictor always predicting the target mean assuming that target mean is known (Biçici and Way, 2015). $\lfloor \,.\, \rfloor_\epsilon$ caps its argument from below to ϵ where $\epsilon = \text{MAE}(\hat{y}, y)/2$, which represents half of the score step with which a decision about a change in measurement's value can be made.

Model	Domain r						r	r_R	MAE	RAE	MAER	MRAER
	ans-ans.	headlines	plagiarism	postediting	que.-que.	Weighted r						
SVR	0.4486	0.6634	0.8038	0.8133	0.6237	0.6685	0.6506	0.7563	1.015	0.679	0.5819	0.726
PLS-SVR	0.344	0.6605	0.8064	0.8231	0.6454	0.6518	0.6386	0.7786	1.0228	0.684	0.5779	0.739
FS+PLS-SVR	0.3533	0.6529	0.8049	0.823	0.648	0.6524	0.6369	0.7733	1.0243	0.685	0.5766	0.742

Table 2: STS English test results for each domain.

Model	Domain r				r	r_R	MAE	RAE	MAER	MRAER
	Multisource r	News r	Weighted r	Rank						
FS+PLS-SVR	0.5204	0.5915	0.5564	14	0.5244	0.5291	1.241	0.809	0.8812	0.856
SVR	0.5294	0.4985	0.5137	16	0.4455	0.4075	1.3473	0.878	0.9933	0.924
FS-SVR	0.5284	0.536	0.5322	15	0.4691	0.444	1.3094	0.853	0.9441	0.891

Table 3: STS Spanish test results.

$$r = \frac{\sum\limits_{i=1}^{n}(\hat{y}_i - \bar{\hat{y}})(y_i - \bar{y})}{\sqrt{\sum\limits_{i=1}^{n}(\hat{y}_i - \bar{\hat{y}})^2}\sqrt{\sum\limits_{i=1}^{n}(y_i - \bar{y})^2}}$$

$$\text{MAE}(\hat{\mathbf{y}}, \mathbf{y}) = \frac{\sum\limits_{i=1}^{n}|\hat{y}_i - y_i|}{n}$$

$$\text{RAE}(\hat{\mathbf{y}}, \mathbf{y}) = \frac{\sum\limits_{i=1}^{n}|\hat{y}_i - y_i|}{\sum\limits_{i=1}^{n}|\bar{y} - y_i|}$$

$$r_R = \frac{\sum\limits_{i=1}^{n}\left(\frac{\hat{y}_i - \bar{\hat{y}}}{\lfloor|y_i|\rfloor_\epsilon}\right)\left(\frac{y_i - \bar{y}}{\lfloor|y_i|\rfloor_\epsilon}\right)}{\sqrt{\sum\limits_{i=1}^{n}\left(\frac{\hat{y}_i - \bar{\hat{y}}}{\lfloor|y_i|\rfloor_\epsilon}\right)^2}\sqrt{\sum\limits_{i=1}^{n}\left(\frac{y_i - \bar{y}}{\lfloor|y_i|\rfloor_\epsilon}\right)^2}}$$

$$\text{MAER}(\hat{\mathbf{y}}, \mathbf{y}) = \frac{\sum\limits_{i=1}^{n}\frac{|\hat{y}_i - y_i|}{\lfloor|y_i|\rfloor_\epsilon}}{n}$$

$$\text{MRAER}(\hat{\mathbf{y}}, \mathbf{y}) = \frac{\sum\limits_{i=1}^{n}\frac{|\hat{y}_i - y_i|}{\lfloor|\bar{y} - y_i|\rfloor_\epsilon}}{n} \tag{1}$$

We compare different tasks in Table 9 with evaluation results that are calculated relative to the magnitude of each target score instance. r multiplies distance of $\hat{y}_i$ and y_i to their own means (Equation (1)). We obtain normalized correlation, r_R, using $\epsilon = \sigma(\mathbf{y})/2$.

3 SemEval-16 STS Results

SemEval-2016 STS contains sentence pairs from different domains: answer-answer, headlines, plagiarism, postediting, question-question for English and multisource and newswire for Spanish. Official evaluation metric in STS is the Pearson's correlation score. Table 1 lists the number of instances in the test set where only some of the instances are actually evaluated.

We build individual RTM models for each subtask. Our team name is RTM. Interpretants are selected from the corpora distributed by the translation task of WMT16 (Bojar et al., 2016) and they consist of monolingual sentences used to build the LM and parallel sentence pair instances used by MTPPS to derive features and for word alignment features. We use monolingual corpora in English for STS English to select interpretants and also for STS Spanish shuffled dataset, which is the official format that was made available to the participants.

We used English-Spanish parallel corpus and English and Spanish monolingual corpora for our STS Spanish experiments in Section 4 after the challenge using the language identified version. We built RTM models using 200 thousand sentences for training data and 5 million sentences for the language model, which corresponds to the fixed training set size setting in (Biçici and Way, 2015). We identified numeric expressions using regular expressions as a preprocessing step, which replaces them with a label. For training RTM models for STS Spanish, we use STS English training data and STS Spanish data from SemEval-2015 after scaling the scores to range

Task	Setting		r	MAE	RAE	MAER	MRAER
train		SVR	0.74	0.8028	0.612	0.4745	0.69
	+numerics	SVR	0.73	0.8108	0.618	0.4758	0.698
test		SVR	0.65	1.0224	0.684	0.6074	0.719
	+numerics	SVR	**0.66**	**1.0052**	**0.673**	**0.5954**	0.719

Table 4: RTM top predictor results on STS English show that performance improve after identification of numerics on the test set.

Setting	Model	ans.-ans.	headlines	plagiarism	postediting	que.-que.	Weighted r	r	r_R	MAE	RAE	MAER	MRAER
				Domain % numerics									
		1.4	3.2	0.33	1.2	0.3	1.01 (% of total)						
				Domain r									
	SVR	0.4458	0.6813	0.8	0.7881	0.6218	0.6654	0.6549	0.7441	1.0224	0.684	0.6074	0.719
+numerics	SVR	**0.4978**	0.6767	0.7956	**0.7983**	0.6096	**0.6746**	**0.6632**	**0.7612**	**1.0052**	**0.673**	**0.5954**	**0.719**

Table 5: STS English test results for each domain from new experiments. Domain % numerics lists the percentage of tokens classified as numerics in each domain.

$[0, 5]$.

Table 2 and Table 3 list the results on the test set. Ranks are out of 26 submissions in STS Spanish. We also observe that r over all of the test set, which does not compute the weighted average of r according to the number of instances in each domain can differ from the weighted r scores.

4 Experiments After the Challenge

In this section, we detail the training performance of our model based on major modeling differences with our previous RTM models on SemEval tasks (Biçici and Way, 2015). This year, we identified numeric expressions using regular expressions as a preprocessing step, which mainly identifies integers and real numbers that can have exponents. After sending the test results, we further worked on the numeric expression identification to expand the types of identified expressions. We also experimented with language identification for STS Spanish. Language identification is done using the manually corrected results starting from the output of automatic language identification tool mguesser. [1] After language identification, corpora were split into English and Spanish rather than the shuffled format that was made available to the participants. We compare the performance after identification of numeric expressions and identification of the language using SVR. Both STS Spanish models use previous years' training data from both STS English and STS Spanish for training, which total to 13823 instances.

---

[1] http://www.mnogosearch.org

Table 4 and Table 5 presents the results before and after identification of numerics on STS English. We observe that identification of numerics improve the performance on the test set (**bolded** results).

Table 6 presents the results on STS Spanish with the default shuffled setting and with the setting where we model the prediction as machine translation performance prediction from English to Spanish after identifying the language of each sentence in the training set. STS Spanish training dataset contains English sentences in majority and shuffled +numerics setting only use English corpora even though Spanish sentences are shuffled in the test set and eventually, shuffled +numerics setting obtains better results than language identified +numerics setting on the training set. Even so, we observe that identification of the language improve the performance on the test set (**bolded** results). Training results on setting language identified +numerics is lower, which may be due to the RTM model using language identified test corpus and the same training corpus as the shuffled +numerics setting.

Table 8 plots the performance on the test set where instances are sorted according to the magnitude of the target scores. For STS English, we observe decreasing AER and a valley of absolute errors, which may be due to SVR preferring predictions close to the mean of train score distribution.

5 RTMs Across Tasks and Years

We compare the difficulty of various prediction tasks where RTMs participated (Biçici and Way, 2015) ac-

Task	Setting		r	MAE	RAE	MAER	MRAER
train	shuffled +numerics	SVR	0.72	0.8224	0.639	0.4864	0.718
	language identified +numerics	SVR	0.69	0.8567	0.666	0.5261	0.74
test	shuffled +numerics	SVR	0.3687	1.4589	0.951	1.0949	1.04
	language identified +numerics	SVR	**0.6739**	**1.0529**	**0.686**	**0.7087**	**0.729**

Table 6: RTM SVR results on STS Spanish show that performance improve after language identification on the test set.

Setting	Model	Domain r Multisource r	News r	Weighted r	Rank	r	r_R	MAE	RAE	MAER	MRAER
shuffled +numerics	SVR	0.5375	0.4498	0.4931	17	0.3687	0.3722	1.4589	0.951	1.0949	1.04
language identified +numerics	SVR	**0.6066**	**0.7225**	**0.6652**	13	**0.6739**	**0.6604**	**1.0529**	**0.686**	**0.7087**	**0.729**

Table 7: STS Spanish test results from new experiments.

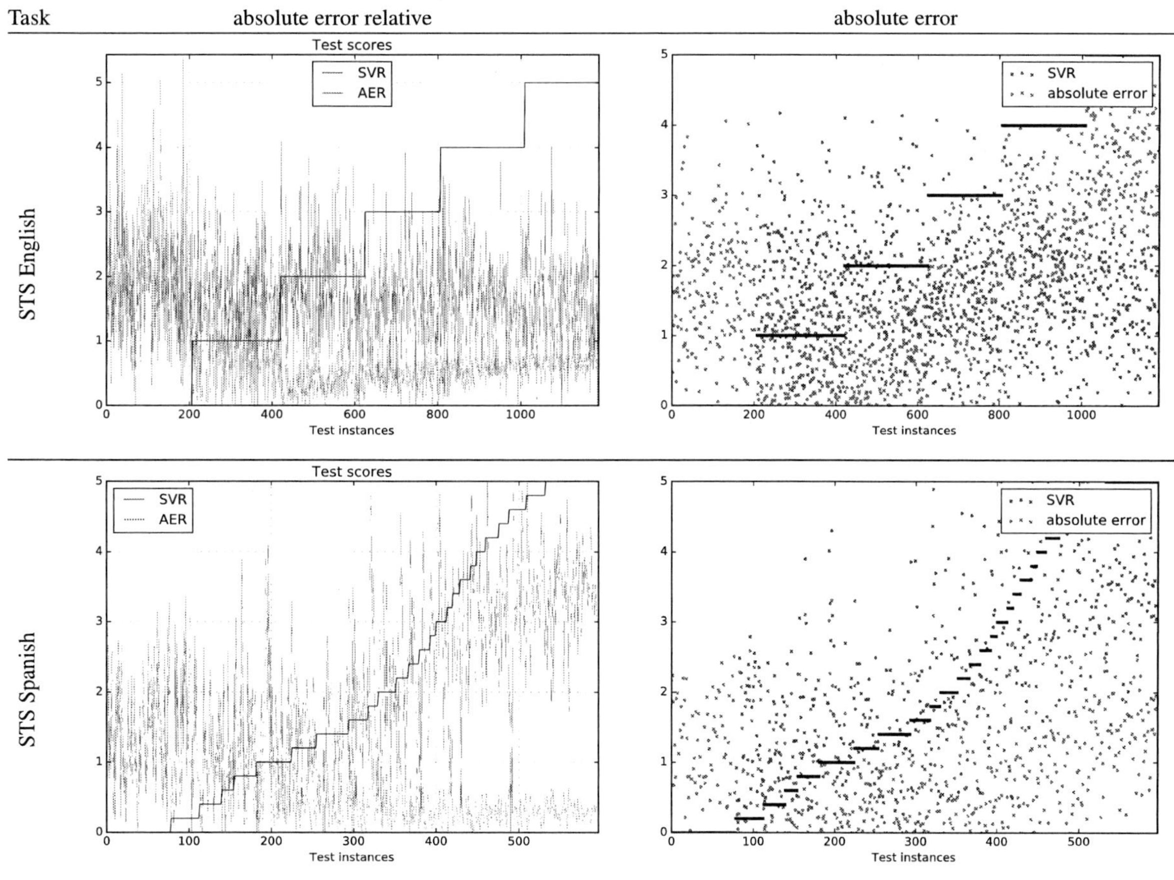

Table 8: RTM SVR performance on the test set in STS 2016. Left figure in each row is the absolute error relative to the magnitude of the target (AER) and the right figure is the absolute error.

cording to MRAER in Table 9. MAER and MRAER considers both the predictor's error and the fluctuations of the target scores at the instance level, which is at the sentence level in STS 2016. The best results are obtained for the CLSS 2014 paragraph-to-sentence subtask, which may be due to the larger contextual information that paragraphs can provide for the RTM models. We observe that the performance in STS improved in 2016 compared to STS in previous years. Table 9 can be used to evaluate the difficulty of various tasks and domains based on RTM. We separated the results having MRAER greater than 1 as in these tasks and subtasks RTM does not perform significantly better than the mean predictor, and fluctuations render these as tasks that may require more work. Our findings are negative towards re-use of those datasets and results obtained without further work. STS Spanish is able to achieve MRAER less than 1 in 2016. We also note that RTMs achieve the top result in both CLSS 2014 (Jurgens et al., 2014) and in all QET tasks in Table 9, including the QET 2015 German-English METEOR task (Bojar et al., 2015).

6 Contributions

Referential translation machines pioneer a clean and intuitive computational model for automatically measuring semantic similarity by measuring the acts of translation involved. We show that identification of numeric expressions in STS English and identification of the language in STS Spanish improve the performance on the test set. RTM test performance on various tasks sorted according to MRAER can identify which tasks and subtasks and the datasets provided are mature enough for further results.

Acknowledgments

We thank the reviewers for providing constructive comments.

References

Eneko Agirre, Carmen Banea, Daniel Cer, Mona Diab, Aitor Gonzalez-Agirre, Rada Mihalcea, and Janyce Wiebe. 2016. Semeval-2016 task 1: Semantic textual similarity, monolingual and cross-lingual evaluation. In *Proc. of the 10th International Workshop on Semantic Evaluation (SemEval 2016)*, San Diego, USA, June. Association for Computational Linguistics.

Steven Bethard, Marine Carpuat, Daniel Cer, David Jurgens, Preslav Nakov, and Torsten Zesch. 2016. Proc. of the 10th international workshop on semantic evaluation (semeval 2016). In *Proc. of the 10th International Workshop on Semantic Evaluation (SemEval 2016)*. Association for Computational Linguistics.

Ergun Biçici and Andy Way. 2015. Referential translation machines for predicting semantic similarity. *Language Resources and Evaluation*, pages 1–27.

Ergun Biçici, Qun Liu, and Andy Way. 2015a. ParFDA for fast deployment of accurate statistical machine translation systems, benchmarks, and statistics. In *Proc. of the Tenth Workshop on Statistical Machine Translation*, Lisbon, Portugal, September. Association for Computational Linguistics.

Ergun Biçici, Qun Liu, and Andy Way. 2015b. Referential translation machines for predicting translation quality and related statistics. In *Proc. of the Tenth Workshop on Statistical Machine Translation*, Lisbon, Portugal, September. Association for Computational Linguistics.

Ergun Biçici. 2002. Prolegomenon to commonsense reasoning in user interfaces. *ACM Crossroads*, 9(1).

Ondrej Bojar, Rajan Chatterjee, Christian Federmann, Barry Haddow, Chris Hokamp, Matthias Huck, Pavel Pecina, Philipp Koehn, Christof Monz, Matteo Negri, Matt Post, Carolina Scarton, Lucia Specia, and Marco Turchi. 2015. Findings of the 2015 workshop on statistical machine translation. In *Proc. of the Tenth Workshop on Statistical Machine Translation*, Lisbon, Portugal, September.

Ondrej Bojar, Christian Buck, Rajan Chatterjee, Christian Federmann, Liane Guillou, Barry Haddow, Matthias Huck, Antonio Jimeno Yepes, Aurélie Névéol, Mariana Neves Pavel Pacina, Martin Poppel, Philipp Koehn, Christof Monz, Matteo Negri, Matt Post, Lucia Specia, Karin Verspoor, Jörg Tiedemann, and Marco Turchi. 2016. Proc. of the 2016 workshop on statistical machine translation. In *Proc. of the Eleventh Workshop on Statistical Machine Translation*, Berlin, Germany, August.

Internet Encyclopedia of Philosophy. 2016. Chinese room thought experiment.

David Jurgens, Mohammad Taher Pilehvar, and Roberto Navigli. 2014. SemEval-2014 Task 3: Cross-level semantic similarity. In *Proc. of the 8th International Workshop on Semantic Evaluation (SemEval 2014)*, pages 17–26, Dublin, Ireland, August.

Task	Subtask	Domain	RAE	MAER	MRAER
CLSS 2014	Paragraph to Sentence	Mixed	0.458	0.5112	0.504
STS 2014	English	OnWN	0.558	0.7975	0.546
QET 2014	English-Spanish PEE	Europarl	1.079	0.304	0.614
STS 2015	English	Images	0.588	0.5424	0.623
STS 2015	English	Headlines	0.589	0.4844	0.638
CLSS 2014	Sentence to Phrase	Mixed	0.626	0.6857	0.644
QET 2015	English-German METEOR	Europarl	0.7279	0.3249	0.647
QET 2014	German-English PEE	Europarl	0.82	0.3575	0.679
QET 2014	English-German PEE	Europarl	0.86	0.3692	0.698
STS 2016	English	ALL	0.673	0.5954	0.719
STS 2014	English	Images	0.74	0.8338	0.725
STS 2016	Spanish	ALL	0.686	0.7087	0.729
QET 2014	Spanish-English PEE	Europarl	0.9	0.3798	0.749
STS 2014	English	ALL	0.745	0.7274	0.757
STS 2013	English	ALL	0.779	0.8494	0.77
QET 2014	English-Spanish PET	Europarl	0.722	0.4651	0.779
STS 2014	English	Headlines	0.784	0.6711	0.785
STS 2015	English	ALL	0.722	0.7379	0.788
STS 2014	English	Tweet-news	0.714	0.4225	0.797
SRE 2014	English	SICK	0.664	0.1827	0.818
STS 2015	English	Answers-students	0.782	0.5542	0.84
CLSS 2014	Phrase to Word	Mixed	0.949	1.1454	0.848
QET 2015	English-Spanish HTER	Europarl	0.896	0.8344	0.849
STS 2013	English	OnWN	0.826	1.2875	0.86
ParSS 2015	English	Tweets	0.788	0.6788	0.862
QET 2014	English-Spanish HTER	Europarl	0.853	0.7727	0.876
STS 2014	English	Deft-news	0.872	0.6271	0.881
QET 2015	German-English METEOR	Europarl	0.876	0.395	0.916
STS 2015	Spanish	News	0.898	0.3757	1.089
STS 2015	Spanish	ALL	0.889	0.3883	1.094
STS 2015	English	Answers-forums	1.06	1.3883	1.107
STS 2015	Spanish	Wikipedia	0.868	0.413	1.121
STS 2013	English	Headlines	1.023	1.0456	1.144
STS 2014	English	Deft-forum	1.091	0.7724	1.216
STS 2015	English	Belief	1.153	1.5882	1.224
STS 2013	English	FNWN	1.263	1.5087	1.405
STS 2014	Spanish	News	1.157	0.4773	1.492
QET 2013	English-Spanish HTER	Europarl	0.885	2.3738	1.643
STS 2014	Spanish	ALL	1.251	0.5345	1.657
STS 2014	Spanish	Wikipedia	1.358	0.65	1.661
STS 2013	English	SMT	1.613	0.1669	2.072

Table 9: Best RTM test results for different tasks and subtasks sorted according to MRAER.

DalGTM at SemEval-2016 Task 1: Importance-Aware Compositional Approach to Short Text Similarity

Jie Mei, Aminul Islam, Evangelos Milios

Faculty of Computer Science
Dalhousie University, Canada
{jmei,islam,eem}@cs.dal.ca

Abstract

This paper describes our system submission to the SemEval 2016 English Semantic Textual Similarity (STS) shared task. The proposed system is based on the compositional text similarity model, which aggregates pairwise word similarities for computing the semantic similarity between texts. In addition, our system combines word importance and word similarity to build an importance-similarity matrix. Three different word similarity measures are used in our three submitted runs. The evaluation results show that taking into account context dependent word importance information improves performance. However, the performance of the system varies drastically between different evaluation subsets. The best of our submitted runs achieves rank 60th with weighted mean Pearson correlation to human judgements of 0.6892.

1 Introduction

Semantic Textual Similarity (STS) measures the degree of equivalence in the underlying semantics of paired natural language texts. It is an extensively researched problem with applications widely used in many research areas including natural language processing, information retrieval, and text mining. The STS task has been held annually since 2012 (Agirre et al., 2012; Agirre et al., 2013; Agirre et al., 2014; Agirrea et al., 2015) to encourage research into understanding sentence-level semantics. Systems for this task compute semantic similarity scores for paired text snippets. Performance is evaluated by

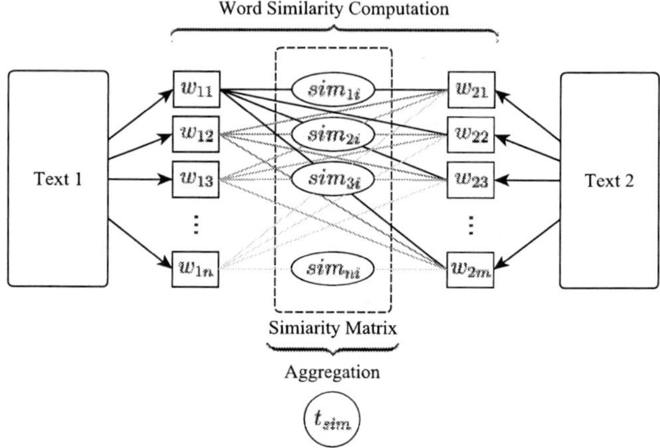

Figure 1: The general procedure of the compositional text similarity measures. They take three general steps: tokenize the input text, compute pairwise word similarities between all words, and aggregate the resulting scores to a sentence level textual similarity score. $\{w_{11}, w_{12}, \ldots, w_{1n}\}$ and $\{w_{21}, w_{22}, \ldots, w_{1m}\}$ are the tokenized words from Text 1 and Text 2, respectively. Each node in the middle represents a vector of pairwise similarity values computed by one word from Text 1 and all distinct words from Text 2.

the Pearson correlation between the system scores and human judgements.

This paper describes our system submission to the SemEval 2016 STS shared task (Agirre et al., 2016). The proposed system is based on the compositional text similarity model, which have been broadly researched in the literature by (Mihalcea et al., 2006; Li et al., 2006; Islam and Inkpen, 2006; Ho et al., 2010; Islam et al., 2012; Bär, 2013). The compositional text similarity model makes use of word-level

Proceedings of SemEval-2016, pages 765–770,
San Diego, California, June 16-17, 2016. ©2016 Association for Computational Linguistics

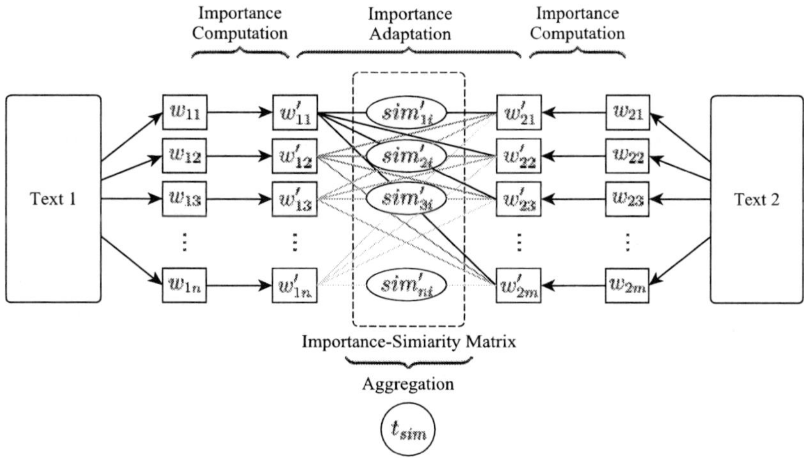

Figure 2: The procedure of the proposed importance-aware similarity measure. The general compositional procedure in Fig. 1 uses context independent similarity value. In addition, this measure takes into account context dependent word importance information. It first computes the word importance value w' using Eq. 3 and adapted into every entry sim' in the importance-similarity matrix using Eq. 4.

similarity values as the building blocks to compute sentence-level semantics. Computing textual similarity using this approach proceeds as follows: tokenize the input text, compute pairwise word similarities between all words, and aggregate the resulting scores to a sentence level textual similarity score. State-of-the-art word similarity measures can be used in this model to provide context independent word relatedness. However, words an be more or less important depending on the contexts in which they appear.

We extend traditional compositional models with an importance term for each word. Our three submitted runs use this extended model in combination with three different word similarity measures: Google Trigram Method (Islam et al., 2012), Skipgrams word embedding (Mikolov et al., 2013), and GloVe word embedding (Pennington et al., 2014). The evaluation results show that including matching importance information improves the performance of compositional models on most of the evaluation sets for STS 2015 and 2016. However, the relative performance of our systems varies dramatically when comparing against other systems submitted to the shared task. The best of our submitted runs achieves rank 60th with weighted mean Pearson correlation of 0.6892 with human judgements.

The rest of the paper is organized as follows: Section 2 describes the details of the submitted systems. Section 3 shows the experimental results for our three runs using evaluation data from SemEval 2015 and 2016. Section 4 summarizes our observations and concludes.

2 System Description

Our proposed approach takes advantage of the compositional model while also taking the importance of words into consideration. It first computes the matching importance, which characterizes the importance of a word in a particular text pair similarity computation. Instead of building the similarity matrix used by the traditional compositional approach (Fig. 1), we construct an alternative importance weighted similarity matrix. The importance weighted similarity values are then used when computing the overall textual similarity score.

2.1 Text Preprocessing

The input texts are tokenized using the Penn Treebank tokenization with additional rules from Google.[1] Punctuation and the 33 most common English words are filtered because these tokens contribute little to the semantic meaning of a text. Then, we lemmatized the remaining words taking into account their POS tags. The preprocessed input text

---

[1] Decribed in Section 2.2 on
https://catalog.ldc.upenn.edu/docs/LDC2006T13/readme.txt

is represented by these lemmas. POS tagging and lemmatization use NLTK toolkit.[2]

2.2 Word Similarity Computation

Word similarities are the core building blocks in compositional text similarity measures. Our three different runs each explore using a different word similarity algorithm.

Google Trigram Method (Islam et al., 2012) is an unsupervised statistical similarity measure that can be applied to word pairs. This word similarity method characterizes the co-occurrence feature using the frequencies of trigrams starting and ending with a word pair. It is computed using the following formula:

$$\varphi'(w_1, w_2) = \frac{\frac{\frac{1}{2}(f_n(w_1,w_2)+f_n(w_2,w_1))}{\min(f(w_1),f(w_2))}}{\frac{f(w_1)}{f_{\max}} \cdot \frac{f(w_2)}{f_{\max}}}, \quad (1)$$

where $f_n(w_1, w_2)$ indicates the total frequency of n-grams starting with w_1 and ending with w_2. $f(w)$ stands for the word (i.e. uni-gram) frequency of w and $f_{\max}$ is the largest word frequency in the corpus. Then, the following normalization function is applied to Eq. 1 to bound the word similarity values in range $[0, 1]$:

$$sim(w_1, w_2)$$

$$= \begin{cases} \frac{\log \varphi'(w_1,w_2)}{-2 \times \log \frac{\min(f(w_1),f(w_2))}{C_{\max}}} & \text{if } \log \varphi'(w_1,w_2) > 1 \\ \frac{\log 1.01}{-2 \times \log \frac{\min(f(w_1),f(w_2))}{f_{\max}}} & \text{if } \log \varphi'(w_1,w_2) \leq 1 \\ 0 & \text{if } f_n(w_1,w_2)+f_n(w_2,w_1)=0. \end{cases}$$

$$(2)$$

We use the efficient implementation of this method described in Mei et al. (2015).

Skip-grams (Mikolov et al., 2013) is a neural network model for learning word embeddings. Word embeddings are trained using a model that attempts to discriminatively predict word co-occurrences within a fixed context window. The resulting word embedding vectors have been shown to be effective at capturing word-level semantic information. We use the pre-trained vectors that were learned on a part of Google News dataset (about 100 billion words).[3]

GloVe (Pennington et al., 2014) is an unsupervised learning algorithm for word embeddings. The method learns word embedding vectors using a model that predicts global word co-occurrence statistics extracted from a corpus. We use the pre-trained vectors built using the Wikipedia 2014 dump and the English Gigaword Fifth Edition.[4]

For Skip-gram and GloVe, we use cosine similarity to compute pairwise similarity value.

2.3 Matching Importance Computation

We define matching importance as a function that characterizes the importance of a word in a particular textual similarity computation. Given w in one text and $w_1, w_2, \ldots, w_n$ in the other text, the matching importance of w is computed by this expression:

$$imp(w) = \alpha \cdot \mu(S) + \beta \cdot \sigma(S) \quad (3)$$

$$s.t. \quad S = \{s \mid s = sim(w, w_i), 1 \leq i \leq n\},$$

where function μ and ρ stands for the mean and standard deviation of a set of values. This expression is used in Islam et al. (2012) for selecting important matchings. The mean of similarities is an indicator of semantic relatedness, whereas the standard deviation indicates distinctiveness. We take the weighted sum of both features as the final importance score. In our system submissions, we set $\alpha = \beta = 1$.

2.4 Matching Importance Adaptation

To incorporate the importance information, we rescale the pairwise word-level similarity scores by the minimum of the context dependent importance scores for the words being compared:

$$sim'(w_i, w_j)$$
$$= sim(w_i, w_j) \cdot \min(imp(w_i), imp(w_j)). \quad (4)$$

2.5 Textual Similarity Computation

Given a preprocessed text pair, we count (δ) and remove the identical words in both texts. Let the

---

[2]http://www.nltk.org/
[3]https://code.google.com/archive/p/word2vec/
[4]http://nlp.stanford.edu/projects/glove/

Year	Subset Name	Description	#Pairs
2015	answer-forums	forums answers	375
	answer-students	student short answers	750
	belief	belief annotations	750
	headline	news headlines	750
	images	image descriptions	750
2016	answer-answer	stackexchange answers	254
	headline	news headline	249
	plagiarism	plagiarised short answers	230
	question-question	stackexchange questions	209
	postediting	machine translations with post-editions	244

Table 1: A brief description of SemEval 2015 and 2016 datasets. The SemEval 2015 and 2016 datasets contain test sentence pairs distributed across nine domains.

remaining words be $T_1 = \{w_{11}, \ldots, w_{1n}\}$ and $T_2 = \{w_{21}, \ldots, w_{2m}\}$, we construct an importance weighted similarity matrix $M_{n \times m}$. Prior work suggests that only using the most important entries in the matrix may suppress interference during semantic analysis. (Mihalcea et al., 2006; Islam and Inkpen, 2008; Islam et al., 2012) Thus, we set up a threshold t_i to filter the less important matchings in the ith row of the matrix:

$$t_i = \mu(S') + \rho(S') \tag{5}$$

$$s.t. \quad S' = \{s \mid s = sim'(w_{1i}, w_{2j}), 1 \le j \le m\}.$$

The textual similarity between two sentences is computed as follows in Eq. 6:

$$t_{sim} = \frac{(\delta + \sum_{1 \le i \le n} \mu(S))(n + m + 2\delta)}{2(n + \delta)(m + \delta)} \tag{6}$$

$$s.t. \quad S = \{s \mid s = sim'(w_{1i}, w_{2j}), s \ge t_i,$$
$$1 \le i \le n, 1 \le j \le m\}.$$

sim' is the importance weighted similarity from Eq. 4. $n + \delta$ and $m + \delta$ are the lengths of two preprocessed texts. The textual similarity score ranges within $[0, 1]$.

3 Evaluation

We evaluated our three system submissions using the STS 2015 and 2016 evaluation datasets. The SemEval 2015 and 2016 datasets contain test sentence pairs distributed across nine domains. Each

pair was assigned a similarity scores in the range [0, 5] by multiple human annotators. The performance of our three system submissions is shown in Table 2 and 3. Recall that our three systems only differ in the method they use for assessing lexical similarity: Google Trigram Method (*GTM*), Word2vec (*W2V*), and *GloVe*. Systems that make use of matching importance are tagged with +*IAC*. Otherwise, the system directly uses pairwise similarity values to compute the aggregate similarity score using Eq. 6. Note that systems with the proposed matching importance approach perform consistently better than the original compositional model in most of the domain subsets. This shows that adding an importance feature can effectively improve the performance of the compositional model. However, comparing against the average system performance in each domain, the performance of our submitted systems vary dramatically in their relative performance to systems submitted by other participating teams. For example, our systems perform well on the postediting dataset and dramatically worse, even relative to other systems, on the question-question data. This suggests that the proposed system may have an implicit domain specific bias.

4 Conclusions and Future Work

In this paper, we present an Importance-Aware Compositional Approach to STS and its evaluation during the SemEval 2016 STS shared task. Experimental results show that the proposed approach performs consistently better than matched compositional similarity models that do not take importance into account. In future work, it would be useful to investigate a more robust weighting scheme for word importance, incorporating syntactic analysis of texts and using external knowledge-bases for word sense disambiguation.

Acknowledgments

The research was funded in part by the Natural Sciences and Engineering Research Council of Canada (NSERC), and The Boeing Company.

References

Eneko Agirre, Mona Diab, Daniel Cer, and Aitor Gonzalez-Agirre. 2012. Semeval-2012 task 6: A pilot

system	answer-forums	answer-students	belief	headline	images	average
GloVe	0.4220	0.6959	0.5901	0.6998	0.7775	0.6371
GloVe+IAC	0.5301	0.7134	0.6893	0.6992	0.7928	0.6850
GTM	0.5963	0.7021	0.6837	0.6880	0.7676	0.6875
GTM+IAC	0.6065	0.7128	0.7203	0.6940	0.7841	0.7035
W2V	0.6033	0.7164	0.7181	0.6939	0.7932	0.7050
W2V+IAC	0.6116	0.7336	0.6961	0.7033	0.8150	0.7119
average official	0.5705	0.6599	0.6382	0.7220	0.7689	0.6888
best official	0.7390	0.7725	0.7491	0.8250	0.8644	0.8015

Table 2: Evaluation result for SemEval 2015 STS dataset. Both the compositional model and the proposed model (systems with *+IAC*) are implemented with three word similarity measures: *GTM, W2V*, and *GloVe*. In most of the comparison experiments, the proposed model gets higher Pearson correlation than the original compositional model with the same setting. However, the performance of our submitted systems varies dramatically comparing with the average system performance in different domain subsets.

system	answer-answer	headlines	plagiarism	question-question	postediting	average
GTM	0.4894	0.6717	0.7791	0.4271	0.8525	0.6440
GTM+IAC	0.5137	0.6907	0.7969	0.4331	0.8478	0.6564
W2V	0.5136	0.6791	0.8174	0.4739	0.8522	0.6672
W2V+IAC	0.5365	0.6855	0.8087	0.4710	0.8456	0.6695
GloVe	0.4745	0.6957	0.7994	0.5065	0.8301	0.6721
GloVe+IAC	0.5285	0.6961	0.7994	0.5480	0.8301	0.6804
average official	0.4802	0.7644	0.7895	0.5714	0.8124	0.6892
best official	0.6924	0.8275	0.8414	0.7471	0.8669	0.7781

Table 3: Evaluation results for SemEval 2016 STS dataset. It shows the same characteristics of the proposed model in both SemEval datasets.

on semantic textual similarity. In *Proceedings of the First Joint Conference on Lexical and Computational Semantics - Volume 1: Proceedings of the Main Conference and the Shared Task, and Volume 2: Proceedings of the Sixth International Workshop on Semantic Evaluation*, SemEval '12, pages 385–393, Stroudsburg, PA, USA. Association for Computational Linguistics.

Eneko Agirre, Daniel Cer, Mona Diab, Aitor Gonzalez-agirre, and Weiwei Guo. 2013. sem 2013 shared task: Semantic textual similarity, including a pilot on typed-similarity. In *In *SEM 2013: The Second Joint Conference on Lexical and Computational Semantics. Association for Computational Linguistics*.

Eneko Agirre, Carmen Banea, Claire Cardie, Daniel Cer, Mona Diab, Aitor Gonzalez-Agirre, Weiwei Guo, Rada Mihalcea, German Rigau, and Janyce Wiebe. 2014. Semeval-2014 task 10: Multilingual semantic textual similarity. In *Proceedings of the 8th international workshop on semantic evaluation (SemEval 2014)*, pages 81–91.

Eneko Agirre, Carmen Banea, Daniel Cer, Mona Diab, Aitor Gonzalez-Agirre, Rada Mihalcea, and Janyce Wiebe. 2016. Semeval-2016 task 1: Semantic textual similarity - monolingual and cross-lingual evaluation. In *Proceedings of the 10th International Workshop on Semantic Evaluation (SemEval 2016)*, San Diego, USA, June. Association for Computational Linguistics.

Eneko Agirrea, Carmen Baneab, Claire Cardiec, Daniel Cerd, Mona Diabe, Aitor Gonzalez-Agirrea, Weiwei Guof, Inigo Lopez-Gazpioa, Montse Maritxalara, Rada Mihalceab, et al. 2015. Semeval-2015 task 2: Semantic textual similarity, english, spanish and pilot on interpretability. In *Proceedings of the 9th international workshop on semantic evaluation (SemEval 2015)*, pages 252–263.

Daniel Bär. 2013. *A Composite Model for Computing Similarity Between Texts*. Ph.D. thesis, TU Darmstadt, TU Darmstadt, 10.

Chukfong Ho, Masrah Azrifah Azmi Murad, Rabiah Abdul Kadir, and Shyamala C. Doraisamy. 2010. Word sense disambiguation-based sentence similarity. In *Proceedings of the 23rd International Conference on Computational Linguistics: Posters*, COLING '10, pages 418–426, Stroudsburg, PA, USA. Association for Computational Linguistics.

Aminul Islam and Diana Inkpen. 2006. Second order co-occurrence pmi for determining the semantic similarity of words. In *Proceedings of the 21st International Conference on Language Resources and Evaluation*, pages 1033–1038, Genoa, Italy.

Aminul Islam and Diana Inkpen. 2008. Semantic text similarity using corpus-based word similarity and string similarity. *ACM Trans. Knowl. Discov. Data*, 2(2):10:1–10:25, July.

Aminul Islam, Evangelos Milios, and Vlado Kešelj. 2012. Text similarity using google tri-grams. In *Advances in Artificial Intelligence*, pages 312–317. Springer Berlin Heidelberg.

Y. Li, D. McLean, Z. A. Bandar, J. D. O'Shea, and K. Crockett. 2006. Sentence similarity based on semantic nets and corpus statistics. *IEEE Transactions on Knowledge and Data Engineering*, 18(8):1138–1150, Aug.

Jie Mei, Xinxin Kou, Zhimin Yao, Andrew Rau-Chaplin, Aminul Islam, Abidalrahman Moh'd, and Evangelos E. Milios. 2015. Efficient computation of co-occurrence based word relatedness. In *Proceedings of the 2015 ACM Symposium on Document Engineering*, DocEng '15, pages 43–46, New York, NY, USA. ACM.

Rada Mihalcea, Courtney Corley, and Carlo Strapparava. 2006. Corpus-based and knowledge-based measures of text semantic similarity. In *Proceedings of the 21st National Conference on Artificial Intelligence - Volume 1*, AAAI'06, pages 775–780. AAAI Press.

Tomas Mikolov, Kai Chen, Greg Corrado, and Jeffrey Dean. 2013. Efficient estimation of word representations in vector space. *CoRR*, abs/1301.3781.

Jeffrey Pennington, Richard Socher, and Christopher D. Manning. 2014. Glove: Global vectors for word representation. In *Empirical Methods in Natural Language Processing (EMNLP)*, pages 1532–1543.

iUBC at SemEval-2016 Task 2: RNNs and LSTMs for interpretable STS

Iñigo Lopez-Gazpio and **Eneko Agirre** and **Montse Maritxalar**
IXA NLP group. University of the Basque Country (UPV/EHU)
Manuel Lardizabal 1, 20.018, Donostia, Basque Country
inigo.lopez@ehu.eus

Abstract

This paper describes *iUBC*, a neural network based approach that achieves competitive results on the interpretable STS task (iSTS 2016). Actually, it achieves top performance in one of the three datasets. iUBC makes use of a jointly trained classifier and regressor, and both models work on top of a recurrent neural network. Through the paper we provide detailed description of the approach, as well as the results obtained in iSTS 2015 test, iSTS 2016 training and iSTS 2016 test.

1 Introduction

Semantic Textual Similarity (STS) aims to catch the degree of equivalence between a pair of text nuggets. *Interpretable STS* (iSTS) is beyond STS in that it adds fine-grained information when evaluating the equivalence between text snippets. This explanatory layer is achieved by **aligning text segments** pertaining to one sentence with the segments pertaining to the second sentence, and, for each alignment, indicating a **relation label** and a **similarity score**.

In sum, alignments consist of a similarity score and a relation label that are defined as follows. On the one hand, the relation label has to be chosen from a set of categorical values (*equivalence, opposition, specialization, similarity and other kind of relation*). On the other hand, the similarity score has to be a real number bounded by (0,5]. Apart from this, there is an extra label to handle *not aligned* text segments.

The present paper describes *iUBC* and its participation in the *International Workshop on Semantic Evaluation* (SemEval-2016) task 2: Interpretable Semantic Textual Similarity. To check the task in full detail please refer to Agirre et al. (2016). Note that some of the authors participated in the organization of the task. Organizers prevented developers from access to the test dataset, and only allowed to access the same data as the rest of participants.

The paper is organized as follows. Section 2 describes iUBC's components, section 3 describes development performance and run configurations, section 4 shows the results obtained in the iSTS 2016 task, and, finally, section 5 mentions the conclusions and future work directions.

2 System Description

iUBC is composed of **three components**. The first component, *Input handling and chunking* (section 2.1), is responsible for reading the input and identifying segments over sentences; the second component, *Alignment* (section 2.2), takes care of aligning segments; and, finally, the third component, *Joint classification and scoring* (section 2.3), handles the assignment of similarity scores and relation labels. The main contribution of this architecture resides in the third component, in which a classifier and a regressor have been **trained jointly** on top of a recurrent artificial neural network (*ANN*).

2.1 Input handling and chunking

The iSTS task offers *two different scenarios* as regards the input: the scenario known as *System chunks* (syschunks), where participant systems are responsible for identifying the segments contained in the raw sentence pairs; and the *Gold chunks* scenario (goldchunks), where participants are provided

771

Proceedings of SemEval-2016, pages 771–776,
San Diego, California, June 16-17, 2016. ©2016 Association for Computational Linguistics

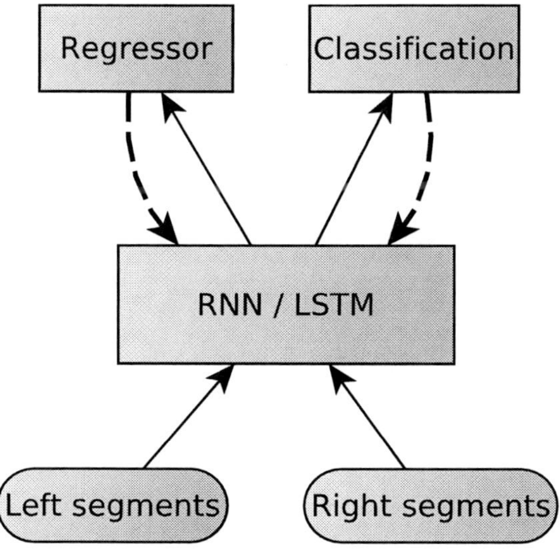

Figure 1: Joint model diagram. In the forward propagation (normal arrow) left and right segments are processed by a recurrent ANN producing as output a d-dimensional vector for each input segment. Features computed out of these vectors are then fed to both a regressor and a classifier that produce the similarity score and the relation label. In the backward propagation (stripped arrow) weights are adjusted in the recurrent ANN combining the gradients that propagate from the above models.

with gold standard segment marks over raw sentence pairs. The current component is only used in the syschunks scenario.

To identify and segment raw input sentences we use *python's NLTK library* (Bird, 2006) and the *ixa-pipes-chunker* (Agerri et al., 2014). Once the chunks are marked we use regular expressions to tune them according to the task's chunk definition. We developed four rules to optimize how conjunctions, punctuations and prepositions are handled. These rules aim to merge consequent chunks to form new chunks[1].

The output of the component are the same sentence pairs as the ones provided as input, but incorporating chunk marks to denote the start and end of segments.

2.2 Alignment

The alignment component focuses on making optimal segment connections for each sentence pair. The algorithm is as follows.

To begin with, the module constructs a token-token matrix in which each element (i,j) determines that there exists a connection between token i and token j[2]. The token-token matrix is populated using the weighted sum of the following metrics: lower-cased token overlap, stemmed or lemmatized token overlap, cosine similarity between Mikolov's pre-trained word vectors (Mikolov et al., 2013) and the alignment prediction provided by the monolingual word aligner described in Sultan et al. (2014).

Once the token-token matrix is built, the alignment component makes use of segment regions to group individual tokens. The strength of each segment connection is proportional to the weights of the interconnected tokens. By carrying out this operation over all segments in the pair the module obtains the chunk-chunk matrix[3]. Once the chunk-chunk matrix has been computed, the last step is to use the Hungarian-Munkres algorithm (Clapper, 2009) to discover the segments (x,y) that maximize the connection weights.

The alignment is done as follows: the segments that maximize the alignment strength are taken as *alignment main nodes*. Once the process is finished, the segments that are connected with lower weights to either one or the other of the main nodes are incorporated as *satellite nodes*. No many-to-many alignments are produced as we considered further analysis is necessary in order to obtain significant improvement.

2.3 Joint classification and scoring

iUBC uses a classification model and a regressor to predict the relation label and the similarity score for aligned segments.

The main picture of this component can be described as a **two layer architecture**, in which, a

---

[1]We found significant improvement if prepositional phrases followed by a nominal phrase are unified as a single chunk. The other three rules unify nominal phrases separated by punctuations, conjunctions, or a combination of them. The four rules are coded as regular expressions in Python.

[2]Token i being a token from the first sentence and token j being a token from the second sentence. Thus, the token-token matrix has a dimensionality of (#sentence1tokens x #sentence2tokens).

[3]This operation can be seen as pooling the token-token matrix by collapsing weights. The chunk-chunk matrix has a dimensionality of (#sentence1segments x #sentence2segments).

classifier and a regressor **work on top of a recurrent ANN**. While the models on the top layer are trained to produce scores and labels, the underlying recurrent net tries to capture the semantic representation of input segments and feed it upwards.

Both models on the top layer are trained in a supervised manner at the same time, and the delta error messages computed on them are used to train the net of the bottom layer. That is, **the gradient propagating from both models on the top layer** is used to train the weights of the ANN (Figure 1). A similar architecture with one top layer propagating gradients to an ANN has previously been used in Tai et al. (2015), which we use as motivation for our work.

The whole model works as follows: the ANN from the bottom layer processes segment words one at a time until there are no more words left. At each time step the net updates its *internal memory state* so that it keeps on capturing *the semantic representation of the segment*. Once the two segments have been processed the net outputs both segment representation d-dimensional vectors. These vectors are used to compute features for the models in the top layer.

Element wise *distance* ($|\vec{S1}^d - \vec{S2}^d|$) and *angle* ($\vec{S1}^d * \vec{S2}^d$) are computed as features, as proposed in Tai et al. (2015). The distance and angle concatenation yields a 2 * d-dimensional vector. This resulting vector is used as input in top layer models.

As regards the top layer models, feedforward neural networks are used for both. All the parameters of the models are summarized in Table 1. The scientific computing framework *Torch* has been used to build the whole component (Collobert et al., 2011). Note that this component doesn't use any type of lexicalized or domain specific feature but Pennington et al. (2014) word embeddings.

3 Development

Initial experiments (section 3.2) have been carried out using the official train and test splits from iSTS 2015 (Agirrea et al., 2015). The 2016 interpretable STS task released three train datasets: *Images*, *Headlines* and *Answer-Students*. These datasets have been used to train the models using 10-fold cross-validation.

In Section 3.1 we describe in detail the set up of

Bottom layer ANN: RNN or LSTM	
Input	Glove word embeddings
Output	Sentence representation
Input-dim	300
Memory-dim	150
Output-dim	150
Non linearity	Sigmoid function
Learning rate	0.05
Regularization	1e-4
Top layer - Regressor	
Input	Distance and angle
Output	Similarity score
Input-dim	2 * 150
Hidden-dim	50
Output-dim	1
Non linearity	Sigmoid function
Loss function	MSE criterion
Learning rate	0.05
Regularization	1e-4
Top layer - Classification model	
Input	Distance and angle
Output	Softmax pr among labels
Input-dim	2*150
Hidden-dim	50
Output-dim	5 (OPPO is not learnt)
Non linearity	Sigmoid function
Loss function	Multi-Class margin loss
Learning rate	0.05
Regularization	1e-4

Table 1: All parameters used in the Joint classification and scoring component.

iUBC for each run, Section 3.2 presents the results on iSTS 2015 data, and in Section 3.3 we present the training results from iSTS 2016.

3.1 Selection of runs

We developed three runs with the following specific settings: **iUBC_run1**, the simplest run, uses a 1-layer RNN trained separately on each dataset; **iUBC_run2**, is the same as run1 but instead of using a 1-layer RNN it employs a 1-layer LSTM; **iUBC_run3**, is the same as run2 but the datasets are perturbed so they include segments that are not part of the gold standard. To produce this perturbation or noise we combine the gold standard alignments with the system alignments. The aim of doing so is to incorporate some noise in the training data, which we think would be useful to prevent overfitting. Both ANN models (RNN and LSTM) are coded following the equations of Tai et al. (2015).

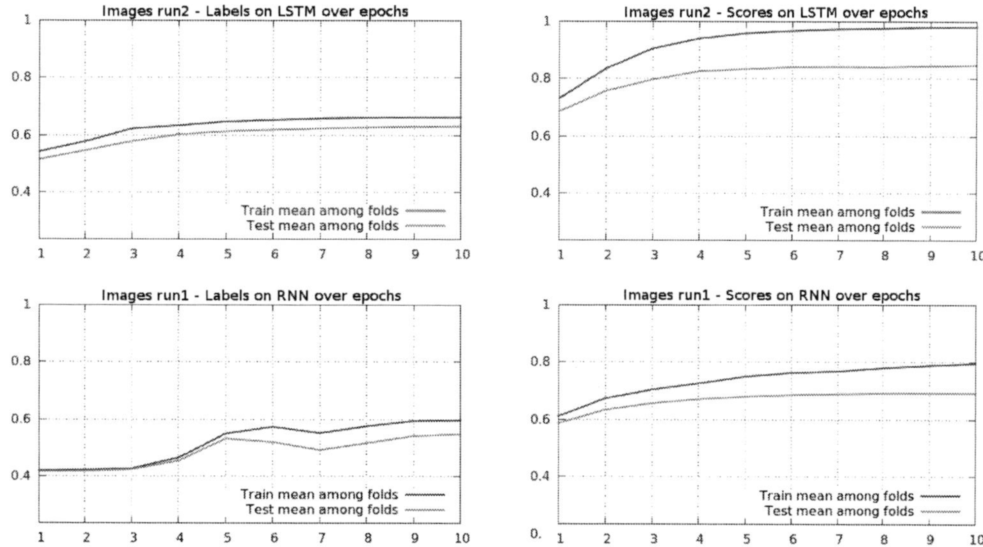

Figure 2: Cross-validation results for the *Joint classification and scoring* component over the iSTS 2015 training data. Figure describes run1 (RNN) and run2 (LSTM) results on the Images dataset. Micro F-score is used to evaluate labels and Pearson correlation coefficient is used to evaluate scores.

iSTS15	H syschunks				H gschunks			
	F	+T	+S	+TS	F	+T	+S	+TS
iUBC_r2	**0.78**	0.47	**0.71**	0.46	**0.91**	0.60	**0.83**	0.60
iUBC_r3	**0.78**	0.46	0.70	0.46	**0.91**	0.61	**0.83**	0.58
iUBC_r1	**0.78**	0.46	0.68	0.45	**0.91**	0.57	0.81	0.55
Baseline	0.67	0.46	0.60	0.46	0.84	0.56	0.76	0.56
AVG	0.69	0.45	0.61	0.43	0.84	0.56	0.75	0.54
MAX	**0.78**	**0.51**	0.70	**0.51**	0.90	**0.67**	**0.83**	**0.64**

	I syschunks				I gschunks			
	F	+T	+S	+TS	F	+T	+S	+TS
iUBC_r3	**0.85**	0.56	**0.78**	0.54	**0.90**	**0.61**	0.74	0.59
iUBC_r2	**0.85**	0.55	**0.78**	0.53	**0.90**	0.60	**0.84**	0.58
iUBC_r1	**0.85**	0.47	0.75	0.45	**0.90**	0.48	0.80	0.47
Baseline	0.71	0.37	0.61	0.37	0.84	0.43	0.72	0.43
AVG	0.67	0.41	0.59	0.39	0.82	0.50	0.72	0.47
MAX	0.83	**0.58**	0.75	**0.56**	0.89	**0.61**	0.80	**0.60**

Table 2: iSTS 2015 test results in Headlines and Images on both scenarios. Baseline, AVG and Max participants rows are taken from iSTS 2015. *F*, *+T*, *+S* and *+TS* stand for the official evaluation metrics F1 Alignment, F1 Type, F1 Score and F1 Type+Score.

3.2 Results on iSTS 2015 test

Results obtained using the described runs on iSTS 2015 test data are shown in Table 2. Comparing our runs to the published results, we think they perform competitively. According to the *F* evaluation metric, in both datasets we obtain equal or higher results than the maximum score among participants,

moreover, our second run also obtains the highest results on the *+S* evaluation metric. The *+T* and *+TS* evaluation metrics are the ones in which our runs don't outperform best published results. Yet, they are above participants average in all scenarios, in some cases by large margin.

As regards our runs, we conclude that run2 and run3 outperform run1, but they both perform quite similarly. It seems that the noise added in the third run helps very slightly in the *Images* dataset. We also noticed that the hardest scenario for our runs turns to be the *Headlines syschunks*, where we almost obtain the same results for all runs.

As the majority of the systems participating in the iSTS 2015 task used lexicalized and task specific features or rules, we think iUBC is rather a different approach. It contributes to the task by being a system that doesn't make use of domain specific features but word embeddings while remaining competitive. We also think that results on the iSTS 2016 task will be reasonable as the training data for the iSTS 2016 task duplicates the one of the 2015. Actually, the reduced size of the training data is a matter that worried us. Due to this, for iSTS 2016 we decided not to divide the training data in train and development splits but to use cross-validation.

3.3 Results on iSTS 2016 train

Figure 2 shows cross-validation results for the *Joint classification and scoring* component over the *Images* dataset. Due to space constraint we have only included figures for the first and second run.

Comparing the RNN (Figure 2 bottom images) with the LSTM (Figure 2 top images) we can observe that the LSTM is able to fit the dataset with better results in fewer iterations. Actually, the evolution over epochs for the LSTM is smoother than the evolution of the RNN, especially for the labeling task. It seems that the RNN needs more epochs than the LSTM to fit the dataset.

It is also observable the high fitting of the LSTM to the scores of the training data, which is almost reaching the 100% correctness. Yet, this over-fitting seems not to contribute badly towards test results, which are noticeably higher than the RNN's. On the contrary, for relation labels the fitting is not that high for neither of the networks, even the LSTM outperforms the RNN.

4 Results on iSTS 2016 test

Table 3 shows the results obtained by distinct runs respectively in *Headlines*, *Images* and *Answer-Students* datasets.

Overall, iUBC performs competitively being *Headlines* the most difficult dataset to fit in and *Answer-Students* the best. In addition, we can see that both run2 and run3 outperform run1 by a large margin. Actually, the results scored by run1 are not that good as it scores below the participants' average. The main conclusion drawn from these result tables as regards run1 is that RNNs are not able to fit these datasets as well as LSTMs do.

Concerning run2 and run3 we expected run3 to outperform run2 on *syschunk* scenarios because of the noise it has been trained with. Nevertheless, this behavior can only be observed in *Headlines*, as in *images* run2 scores better than run3 and in *Answer-Students* they both score equally. The noise also seems not to affect *gschunks* scenarios very badly as in *Headlines* and *Anser-students* both runs score equally. Even though, run3's performance worsens 3 points in *Images* dataset on this scenario.

As pointed out in section 3.2 the *F* evaluation metric and the +*S* evaluation metric continue to be the

iSTS16	H syschunks				H gschunks			
	F	+T	+S	+TS	F	+T	+S	+TS
iUBC_r3	0.81	0.51	0.74	0.50	**0.93**	0.60	**0.86**	0.59
iUBC_r2	0.81	0.49	0.74	0.48	**0.93**	0.60	**0.86**	0.59
iUBC_r1	0.81	0.43	0.71	0.42	**0.93**	0.51	0.83	0.50
Baseline	0.65	0.44	0.59	0.44	0.85	0.55	0.76	0.55
AVG	0.80	0.51	0.72	0.50	0.89	0.61	0.82	0.60
MAX	**0.84**	**0.56**	**0.76**	**0.55**	0.91	**0.70**	0.84	0.70
	I syschunks				I gschunks			
	F	+T	+S	+TS	F	+T	+S	+TS
iUBC_r2	**0.86**	0.56	**0.80**	0.55	**0.91**	0.62	**0.86**	0.61
iUBC_r3	**0.86**	0.52	**0.80**	0.52	**0.91**	0.59	0.85	0.58
iUBC_r1	**0.86**	0.49	0.77	0.48	**0.91**	0.52	0.82	0.51
Baseline	0.71	0.40	0.63	0.40	0.86	0.48	0.75	0.48
AVG	0.82	0.54	0.76	0.52	0.87	0.58	0.80	0.57
MAX	0.85	**0.63**	0.79	**0.61**	0.90	**0.69**	0.84	**0.67**
	AS syschunks				AS gschunks			
	F	+T	+S	+TS	F	+T	+S	+TS
iUBC_r3	0.80	**0.57**	0.75	**0.56**	**0.89**	**0.65**	**0.84**	**0.64**
iUBC_r2	0.80	**0.57**	0.75	**0.56**	**0.89**	**0.65**	**0.84**	**0.64**
iUBC_r1	0.80	0.45	0.71	0.45	**0.89**	0.50	0.79	0.50
Baseline	0.62	0.44	0.57	0.44	0.82	0.56	0.75	0.56
AVG	0.78	0.51	0.71	0.50	0.85	0.56	0.78	0.55
MAX	**0.82**	0.56	**0.76**	0.55	0.88	**0.65**	0.83	**0.64**

Table 3: iSTS 2016 test results in Headlines, Images and Answers-Students on both scenarios. Baseline, AVG and Max participants rows are taken from iSTS 2016. *F*, +*T*, +*S* and +*TS* stand for the official evaluation metrics F1 Alignment, F1 Type, F1 Score and F1 Type+Score.

ones in which iUBC scores best. Being sometimes (primarily on *gschunks* scenario) the top performing system above the participants' maximum. On the contrary, it is harder for the system to perform on the +*T* evaluation metric. This is related to what have been described in section 3.3. That is, the system finds it more difficult to fit the dataset labels than the scores. The main conclusion drawn from here could be that not only word embeddings, but also lexicalized features may be necessary in order to continue improving performance. Similar conclusions are achieved in Yin et al. (2015) regarding to the concatenation of word embedding based features and other kind of features.

5 Conclusions and Future Work

Throughout this paper we have described *iUBC*: a RNN and LSTM based system that has achieved reasonable results on the interpretable STS 2016 task. We have seen how the system works by **jointly training** a classifier and a regressor to produce the relation labels and the similarity scores. We have also described how the error gradient from this top layer propagates to the bottom recurrent net, which aims to capture the semantic representation of input sentences into d-dimensional vectors.

We have shown performance of the system in the iSTS 2016 test data and described that iUBC **performs especially well** in the *Answer-Students dataset*. In addition, we have mentioned that the RNN based run is not able to perform as well as **LSTMs based runs**. Moreover, we have seen that including **noise in the training** data helps improve performance in the *Headlines* dataset on the *syschunks* scenario. But, worsens results in the *Images* dataset on the *gschunks* scenario.

We have also discussed that the model is more suitable to produce **similarity scores** than relation labels. This could be a consequence of the reduced size of the training data and labeling being a more demanding task. As regards this issue, we have mentioned that further features might be necessary in order to continue improving the system's results. In any case, this will require some more analysis.

All in all, we can conclude by saying that the interpretable STS task is an **interesting challenge** whose aim is to share knowledge about building NLP systems able to provide valuable feedback.

Acknowledgments

This material is based in part upon work supported a MINECO grant to the University of the Basque Country (TUNER project TIN2015-65308-C5-1-R). Iñigo Lopez-Gazpio is supported by a doctoral grant from MINECO. The IXA group is funded by the Basque Government (A type Research Group).

References

Rodrigo Agerri, Josu Bermudez, and German Rigau. 2014. IXA pipeline: Efficient and ready to use multilingual NLP tools. In *LREC*, volume 2014, pages 3823–3828.

Eneko Agirre, Aitor Gonzalez-Agirre, Iñigo Lopez-Gazpio, Montse Maritxalar, German Rigau, and Larraitz Uria. 2016. Semeval-2016 task 2: Interpretable semantic textual similarity. In *Proceedings of the 10th International Workshop on Semantic Evaluation (SemEval 2016)*, San Diego, California, June.

Eneko Agirrea, Carmen Baneab, Claire Cardiec, Daniel Cerd, Mona Diabe, Aitor Gonzalez-Agirrea, Weiwei Guof, Inigo Lopez-Gazpioa, Montse Maritxalara, Rada Mihalceab, and others. 2015. Semeval-2015 task 2: Semantic textual similarity, english, spanish and pilot on interpretability. In *Proceedings of the 9th international workshop on semantic evaluation (SemEval 2015)*, pages 252–263.

Steven Bird. 2006. NLTK: the natural language toolkit. In *Proceedings of the COLING/ACL on Interactive presentation sessions*, pages 69–72. Association for Computational Linguistics.

BM Clapper. 2009. munkres: a python module implementing the hungarian method described by munkres (1957). version 1.0. 5.3.

Ronan Collobert, Koray Kavukcuoglu, and Clment Farabet. 2011. Torch7: A matlab-like environment for machine learning. In *BigLearn, NIPS Workshop*.

Tomas Mikolov, Kai Chen, Greg Corrado, and Jeffrey Dean. 2013. Efficient estimation of word representations in vector space.

Jeffrey Pennington, Richard Socher, and Christopher D Manning. 2014. Glove: Global vectors for word representation. In *EMNLP*, volume 14, pages 1532–1543.

Md Arafat Sultan, Steven Bethard, and Tamara Sumner. 2014. Back to basics for monolingual alignment: Exploiting word similarity and contextual evidence. 2:219–230.

Kai Sheng Tai, Richard Socher, and Christopher D. Manning. 2015. Improved semantic representations from tree-structured long short-term memory networks.

Wenpeng Yin, Hinrich Schtze, Bing Xiang, and Bowen Zhou. 2015. ABCNN: Attention-based convolutional neural network for modeling sentence pairs.

Rev at SemEval-2016 Task 2: Aligning Chunks by Lexical, Part of Speech and Semantic Equivalence

Tan Ping Ping and **Karin Verspoor** and **Tim Miller**
Department of Computing and Information System
University of Melbourne
Australia
{pingt@student., karin.verspoor@, tmiller@}unimelb.edu.au

Abstract

We present the description of our submission to SemEval-2016 Task 2, for the sub-task of aligning pre-annotated chunks between sentence pairs and providing similarity and relatedness labels for the alignment. The objective of the task is to provide interpretable semantic textual similarity assessments by adding an explanatory layer to aligned chunks. We analysed the provided datasets, considering lexical overlap, the part of speech tags and the synonyms of the words in the chunks, and developed a rule-based system reflecting that analysis. Our system performance indicates that when sentence pairs are similar, alignment of chunks can be performed fairly well using lexical information alone without syntactic or semantic analysis. The advantage of our system is that we can easily trace when chunks are aligned.

1 Introduction

We developed a system for SemEval-2016 Task 2: "Interpretable Semantic Textual Similarity" (Agirre et al., 2016), which requires the development of a system that labels aligned chunks of a sentence pair, in terms of their similarity or relatedness. Our approach is based on a detailed analysis of the provided annotation guidelines for the task and the annotated training data.

The annotation guidelines for the task indicate how to align the chunks of two sentence pairs and how to label the similarity or relatedness types and assign scores. Annotations are provided for three different training sets: headlines, images and student responses to questions. Chunks consist of a word or contiguous words. The training sets come in the form of sentence pairs, pre-annotated chunks with their alignment and alignment labels.

The number of sentence pairs for the training and test sets supplied is, respectively: headlines – 726 and 375; images – 750 and 375; and student answers – 330 and 344. The test sets come with the pre-annotated chunks but without alignments or labels. Participants of the sub-task are required to align the pre-annotated chunks and provide the similarity and relatedness assessment for the alignment, which is considered as an explanatory layer that enriches measurement of similarity between the sentence pairs.

The alignment types are semantically equivalent (EQUI), opposite in meaning (OPPO), similar in meaning but specific to the chunk in the first sentence (SPE1), similar in meaning but specific to the chunk in second sentence (SPE2), similar in meaning (SIMI) and related in meaning (REL). Additional types, are factuality (FACT) and polarity (POL). For chunks with no alignment, the label is NOALI. The similarity and relatedness scores are 5 for equivalent (i.e. EQUI//5), [4, 3] for very similar or closely related, [2, 1] for slightly similar or somehow related and 0 for completely unrelated (i.e. NOALI//0).

In order to demonstrate that the relationship between chunks are based on lexical selection, Abney (1991) uses context-free grammar to describe the structure of chunks, providing a definition of a chunk from a linguistic perspective, which he hypothesizes is closer to how humans parse texts. His

Proceedings of SemEval-2016, pages 777–782,
San Diego, California, June 16-17, 2016. ©2016 Association for Computational Linguistics

definition provided room for computational implementation. Thus, for this SemEval sub-task, we attempt to understand how lexical overlap, syntactic (more precisely, Part of Speech (PoS) categories), and word synonyms can be used to align chunks, as this information is not provided. Even though string, substring and approximate string matching have been well studied (Yu et al., 2006; Chang and Lawler, 1990; Cole and Hariharan, 2002; Gusfield, 1997), there have been fewer attempts to assess similarity based on not only lexical/character-level overlap but also incorporating other linguistic characteristics. Therefore we attempt to explore the use of this more linguistic information in chunk alignment. We manually examined the annotation guidelines and training set supplied to understand how the chunks are aligned and how the similarity and relatedness labels may be assigned based on this information. Our objective is to develop rules for an automatic system that can effectively align and label the chunks between sentence pairs.

2 Data Analysis

We perform manual data analysis considering lexical matches, part of speech (PoS) categories and synonyms on the headlines training set and derived the rules based on our observation. Through an iterative process, we observed how well the rules derived generalise to the other two training sets (i.e., images and student-answers) and refined the rules. Due to time constraints, the rules were derived mostly from headlines training set and tested on the other two datasets with limited rule refinement iterations from the other two datasets. We summarise our rules below according to the type of lexical match, noting how they correspond to alignment label and score.

[**Punctuations**], such as full stop and comma, which are pre-annotated as individual chunks, do not align. [**Identical string**] Two identical chunks align directly, and indicate equivalence with relatedness of 5. For example, injured $\iff$ injured; in Iraq $\iff$ in Iraq. Although the label EQUI//5 is provided, its interpretation as direct lexical matching is confirmed. [**Sub-string**] Lexical overlap where the chunk from

one sentence is a proper sub-string of another generally results in alignment to create similar meaning, with one chunk being more specific than the other (SPE1 or SPE2). For example: SPE1//gay marriage bill $\iff$ gay marriage; SPE2//airstrike $\iff$ new airstrike. The following generalisations are also made:

- [Verb and verb agreement] If the PoS tag for the words in the chunks is a verb, direct matching with an addition of 's' on any of the chunks will produce alignment of EQUI//5. For example: kill $\iff$ kills; recognizes $\iff$ recognize. This captures the situation that not all EQUI//5 cases are direct matching; in this case the verb is aligned and the variation reflects only verb agreement.

- [Plural and singular] If the PoS for the words in both the chunks is a noun, direct lexical overlap, with an addition of 's' on each side will produce alignment SIMI//4. For example: Suicide bomber $\iff$ Suicide Bombers; despite concession $\iff$ despite concessions. This occurs when the chunks are the same noun, but plural/singular variants.

- [Syntactic function 'to'] Direct matching of 'to' on either side of the chunks will create alignment of EQUI//5. For example: to vote $\iff$ vote; to NZ same-sex marriage $\iff$ New Zealand same-sex marriage

[**Number**] For chunks containing numbers, several subcases apply.

- [Same value]. Two chunks containing the same number results in EQUI//5. For example: at 91 $\iff$ aged 91; Boeing 787 Dreamliner $\iff$ on 787 Dreamliner

- Otherwise, chunks with digits are aligned to produce alignment label of SIMI. The Relatedness score depends on the differences of the digits extracted from the chunks. We have identified the following heuristics:

- If the difference is greater than 100,
  alignment will produce Relatedness of 1
  (e.g., `to 35 years` $\Longleftrightarrow$ `to 1,000
  years`)

- If the difference is between 30 and 100,
  assign Relatedness 2 (e.g., `At least
  45` $\Longleftrightarrow$ `At least 13`)

- If the difference is between 7 and 10, assign Relatedness 3 (e.g., `17` $\Longleftrightarrow$ `10`)

- if the difference is less than 7, assign Relatedness 4 (e.g., `17` $\Longleftrightarrow$ `15`)

[**Single word match**] Generally, if a single word in a chunk is string equivalent to a word in another multi-word chunk, they will align. For example: `in bus accident` $\Longleftrightarrow$ `in road accident`. The following related generalisations are also made:

- [Synonymous] If the two chunks contain a synonymous word rather than an identical word, the chunks are aligned and given labels of EQUI//5. For example: `China stocks` $\Longleftrightarrow$ `Chinese stocks`; `From Soccer` $\Longleftrightarrow$ `from football`.

- [PP - modifier to head noun] If the words in the chunks are prepositional phrases (PP) with the same head noun but different modifiers, the chunks are aligned with a label of SIMI//4. For example: `as legitimate representative` $\Longleftrightarrow$ `as sole representative`.

- [NP - different head noun] If both the words in the chunks are noun phrases (NP) and the matching word is an adjective, the chunks are aligned as REL. For example: `economic traps` $\Longleftrightarrow$ `economic growth`; `French train` $\Longleftrightarrow$ `French train passengers`.

Through stemming, individual words in the chunks are converted to root word.

[**Same root word**] Chunks that can be converted to same root word, are aligned as EQUI//5. For example: `detained` $\Longleftrightarrow$ `detains`; `summoned` $\Longleftrightarrow$ `summons`.

[**Synonymous root word**] If the root words are synonymous, aligned as EQUI//5 (for example: `to permit` $\Longleftrightarrow$ `Allowed`)

[**Misc**] A few recurrent cases appeared in training set like OPPO//5 (e.g.: `higher` $\Longleftrightarrow$ `lower`) and OPPO//4 (e.g.: `close` $\Longleftrightarrow$ `open`); these chunks are matched as antonyms.

3 Methodology

In order to understand the effect of lexical overlap in aligning chunks between sentences, we developed two separate systems: LexiM and Rev, although we only submitted one run for this sub-task, which is the Rev system. Both systems are implemented in Java and strictly rule-based systems. LexiM, a system purely based on lexical overlap contained 13 rules. The rules are based on string or sub-string matches, which follow the category of our data analysis but excluding cases that considers PoS or word synonym, or the rules that require conversion to root word. We performed error analysis on the other training sets but the overall performance is compared to the baseline approach supplied by the organiser (Table 1).

Rev extends LexiM by adopting the rules of LexiM as outlined in Section 2 (excluding the Misc rule), with addition of string distance and semantic similarity-based strategies. LexiM works to align chunks which have lexical overlap, while string similarity and semantic distance work in two ways. The first way is to align chunks that that cannot be handled with those rules and follow by assining labels to the aligned chunks. The second way is for the chunks that are aligned through LexiM, the string distance and semantic similarity rule will provide similarity and relatedness labels. There are existing tools which perform tasks such as string distance measurement like SecondString (Cohen et al., 2003) and stringmetric (Madden, 2013), PoS taggers like Stanford Parser (Klein and Manning, 2003), and dictionary for synonymous words like Word-Net (Fellbaum, 1998). Cohen et al. (2003) shows that Jaro-Winkler is an effective string distance metric for name matching task. Liu et al. (2010) has shown that TESLA, a similarity metric that considers both PoS tags and semantic equivalence (based on WordNet synsets), is effective in the task of automatic evaluation of machine translation in English language. We used Jaro-Winkler proximity (SecondString implementation) for string distance measurement, and TESLA for semantic similarity measurement.

We analyzed the chunks in terms of their string distance and semantic similarity scores, relating the scores to the similarity and relatedness types and scores in the annotated data. We identified the lowest, average and highest values for the string distance and semantic similarity measures for each association type and score, for example: REL//1 corresponds to {string distance: 0.0, 0.19, 0.43} and {semantic similarity: 0.04, 0.18, 0.5}. Subsequently, we developed rules for alignment using string distance and semantic similarity where both ranges must be satisfied in order for the rules to be applied. Chunks that do not fulfill any of the rules or similarity criteria will be assigned as NOALI//0.

4 Results and Discussion

The evaluation method determined by the organiser is F_1-score (Powers, 2011). As shown in our results tables (Table 1 and 2), F_1-score is calculated separately for the aligned chunks (Ali), the alignment type (Type), the similarity and relatedness score (Score) and combination of alignment type and score (Typ+Sco).

The performance of LexiM helps to understand the effect of lexical overlap and sub-string matches in aligning chunks between sentence pairs. We compared the results to the baseline approach (Agerri et al., 2014) provided (Table 1, the Student-Answers baseline is not provided (NS)). The baseline approach is a multilingual Natural Language Processing (NLP) tool that can perform tokenization and segmentation, statistical POS tagging and lemmatization, Named Entity Recognition tagger, probabilistic chunker and constituent parser for several languages, including English. LexiM, although consists of lexical overlap and sub-string matches rules, outperformed the baseline (Table 1). This demonstrates that alignment of chunks can be performed purely using lexical matching; the lexical information was useful for identifying overlaps between the chunks, especially in the case of similar sentences.

Some of the examples where LexiM produces

Dataset	Baseline	LexiM	Rev
Headlines	F_1-Score	F_1-Score	F_1-Score
Ali	0.8354	0.8519	0.8573
Type	0.5392	0.5494	0.5611
Score	0.7409	0.7638	0.7691
Typ+Sco	0.5391	0.5352	0.5464
Images	F_1-Score	F_1-Score	F_1-Score
Ali	0.8364	0.7949	0.8318
Type	0.4444	0.4636	0.4951
Score	0.7186	0.6711	0.7487
Typ+Sco	0.4442	0.4636	0.4854
Student-Answers	F_1-Score	F_1-Score	F_1-Score
Ali	NS	0.7764	0.8513
Type	NS	0.3118	0.3952
Score	NS	0.6210	0.7232
Typ+Sco	NS	0.3060	0.3879

Table 1: Results on Different Training Sets

correct alignment with the wrong type and score: `a baby` $\Longleftrightarrow$ `holding a baby`; `sitting` $\Longleftrightarrow$ `sit`; `is not connected` $\Longleftrightarrow$ `are not connected`; `at the negative connection.` $\Longleftrightarrow$ `the battery.` There are cases where the alignment by LexiM is interpretable. For example in the images dataset, LexiM produced SPE1//4//`in front of yellow flowers` $\Longleftrightarrow$ `in a field`, while gold standard labels is SIMI//2. Another case, LexiM produced SPE2//4//`sheep` $\Longleftrightarrow$ `A sheep` while the standard labels are EQUI//5. Even if only two sentences with the chunks are provided, the system is able to produce a reasonable alignment of the chunks.

We observed slight improvement in F_1-scores between LexiM and Rev. The difference between LexiM and Rev is additional lexical information like PoS and synonym. We performed error analysis on the output of LexiM and Rev with comparison to the baseline approach which uses probabilistic approach. We performed error analysis to understand this better: Rev produced correct alignment and labels EQUI//5//`sleeps` $\Longleftrightarrow$ `asleep` considering the both words are synonymous, while LexiM is able to align the chunks lexically with wrong labels and the baseline approach fails to align the chunks; Rev is able to align `standing` $\Longleftrightarrow$ `grazing` but with wrong labels, while LexiM and the baseline approach fails to align the chunks. This shows that adding additional information like PoS and syn-

Testing Set	F_1-Score	Rev	Baseline
Headlines	Ali	0.8662	0.8462
(Rank 14 out of 20)	Type	0.5705	0.5462
	Score	0.7844	0.761
	Typ+Sco	0.5624	0.5461
Images	Ali	0.831	0.8556
(Rank 17 out of 20)	Type	0.5014	0.4799
	Score	0.7399	0.7456
	Typ+Sco	0.4929	0.4799
Student-Answers	Ali	0.8458	0.8203
(Rank 18 out of 19)	Type	0.4179	0.5566
	Score	0.7265	0.7464
	Typ+Sco	0.4104	0.5566

Table 2: Official Results

onym can assist in alignment and labelling of the aligned chunks.

The overall performance of Rev using the test sets is presented in Table 2. As stated previously, the rules are derived mostly from the headlines dataset. Therefore it is unsurprising that Rev exhibits the best performance over the headlines test set. Indeed, it performs slightly better on the headlines test set than on the corresponding training set; although the reasons for this are unclear, it suggests that the rules captured in Rev have indeed captured reasonable generalizations.

Unfortunately, Rev did not perform well for the other two datasets because the rules are too specific to the headlines dataset. There are many more other potential rules which could be derived from the other datasets; more targeted effort in rule development for those data sets would improve the performance of Rev. It is also clear from the results that the current rules in Rev are quite brittle; they did not perform well in comparison to other submissions for the task.

Using the chunk alignments produced by Rev, we can easily provide an explanation for the alignment by highlighting the rule that facilitated the alignment. Here are some examples of this, concentrating on cases without direct lexical matching:

[Synonymous root word] `a set of stairs` $\Longleftrightarrow$ `steps`.

[Synonymous root word] `jumps` $\Longleftrightarrow$ `leaps`.

[Number] `22 Dead` $\Longleftrightarrow$ `89 dead`.

[Plural and singular] `The dog` $\Longleftrightarrow$ `Three dogs`.

The weakness of Rev is that the rules are limited to the direct observations of the training set, and only consider a narrow set of linguistic characteristics. Clearly, other linguistic rules could be incorporated. For instance, an antonym dictionary could be consulted; this would directly benefit the OPPO label included in the task.

5 Conclusion

Based on the observation that pairs of chunks that align are often lexically very similar, we have concentrated on alignment using a lexical approach. Although deriving and iteratively refining rules manually is a time consuming process, this process is helpful to build an interpretable semantic textual similarity system.

As future work, we plan to directly include an indication of the rule that produced the alignment as an additional explanation in the output, beyond the similarity and relatedness scores and types alone. There are many other types of linguistic analysis that can be performed and we will consider incorporating these as future enhancements to our system.

References

Steven P Abney. 1991. *Parsing by chunks*. Springer.

Rodrigo Agerri, Josu Bermudez, and German Rigau. 2014. Ixa pipeline: Efficient and ready to use multilingual nlp tools. In *LREC*, volume 2014, pages 3823–3828.

Eneko Agirre, Aitor Gonzalez-Agirre, Iigo Lopez-Gazpio, Montse Maritxalar, German Rigau, and Larraitz Uria. 2016. Semeval-2016 task 2: Interpretable semantic textual similarity. In *Proceedings of the 10th International Workshop on Semantic Evaluation (SemEval 2016)*, San Diego, California, June.

William I Chang and Eugene L Lawler. 1990. Approximate string matching in sublinear expected time. In *Foundations of Computer Science, 1990. Proceedings., 31st Annual Symposium on*, pages 116–124. IEEE.

William W Cohen, Pradeep D Ravikumar, Stephen E Fienberg, et al. 2003. A comparison of string distance metrics for name-matching tasks. In *IIWeb*, volume 2003, pages 73–78.

Richard Cole and Ramesh Hariharan. 2002. Approximate string matching: A simpler faster algorithm. *SIAM Journal on Computing*, 31(6):1761–1782.

Christiane Fellbaum. 1998. A semantic network of english verbs. *WordNet: An electronic lexical database*, 3:153–178.

Dan Gusfield. 1997. *Algorithms on strings, trees and sequences: computer science and computational biology*. Cambridge university press.

Dan Klein and Christopher D Manning. 2003. Accurate unlexicalized parsing. In *Proceedings of the 41st Annual Meeting on Association for Computational Linguistics-Volume 1*, pages 423–430. Association for Computational Linguistics.

Chang Liu, Daniel Dahlmeier, and Hwee Tou Ng. 2010. Tesla: Translation evaluation of sentences with linear-programming-based analysis. In *Proceedings of the Joint Fifth Workshop on Statistical Machine Translation and MetricsMATR*, pages 354–359. Association for Computational Linguistics.

Rocky Madden. 2013. stringmetric @ONLINE.

David Martin Powers. 2011. Evaluation from precision, recall and f-measure to roc, informedness, markedness and correlation.

Fang Yu, Zhifeng Chen, Yanlei Diao, TV Lakshman, and Randy H Katz. 2006. Fast and memory-efficient regular expression matching for deep packet inspection. In *Proceedings of the 2006 ACM/IEEE symposium on Architecture for networking and communications systems*, pages 93–102. ACM.

FBK-HLT-NLP at SemEval-2016 Task 2: A Multitask, Deep Learning Approach for Interpretable Semantic Textual Similarity

Simone Magnolini
Fondazione Bruno Kessler
University of Brescia
Brescia, Italy
magnolini@fbk.eu

Anna Feltracco
Fondazione Bruno Kessler
University of Pavia
Pavia, Italy
feltracco@fbk.eu

Bernardo Magnini
Fondazione Bruno Kessler
Povo-Trento, Italy
magnini@fbk.eu

Abstract

We present the system developed at FBK for the SemEval 2016 Shared Task 2 "Interpretable Semantic Textual Similarity" as well as the results of the submitted runs. We use a single neural network classification model for predicting the alignment at chunk level, the relation type of the alignment and the similarity scores. Our best run was ranked as first in one the subtracks (i.e. raw input data, Student Answers), among 12 runs submitted, and the approach proved to be very robust across the different datasets.

1 Introduction

The Semantic Textual Similarity (STS) task measures the degree of equivalence between the meaning of two texts, usually sentences. In the Interpretable STS (iSTS) (Agirre et al., 2016) the similarity is calculated at chunk level, and systems are asked to provide the type of the relationship between two chunks, as an interpretation of the similarity. Given an input pair of sentences, participant systems were asked to: (i) identify the chunks in each sentence; (ii) align chunks across the two sentences; (iii) indicate the relation between the aligned chunks and (iv) specify the similarity score of each alignment.

The iSTS task has already been the object of an evaluation campaign in 2015, as a subtask of the SemEval-2015 Task 2: Semantic Textual Similarity (Agirre et al., 2015). More in general, shared tasks for the identification and measurement of STS were organized in 2012 (Agirre et al., 2012), 2013 (Agirre et al., 2013) and 2014 (Agirre et al., 2014).

Data provided to participants include three datasets: image captions (Images), pairs of sentences from news headlines (Headlines), and a question-answer dataset collected and annotated during the evaluation of the BEETLE II tutorial dialogue system (Student Answers) (Agirre et al., 2015). For each dataset, two subtracks were released: the first with raw input data (SYS), the second with data split in gold standard chunks (GS). Given these input data, participants were required to identify the chunks in each sentence (for the first subtrack only), align chunks across the two sentences, specify the semantic relation of the alignment - selecting one of the following: EQUI for equivalent, OPPO for opposite, SPE1 and SPE2 if chunk in sentence1 is more specific than chunk in sentence2 and vice versa, SIMI for similar meanings, REL for chunks that have related meanings, and NOALI for chunk has no corresponding chunk in the other sentence (Agirre et al., 2015)-, and provide a similarity score for each alignment, from 5 (maximum similarity/relatedness) to 0 (no relation at all). In addition, an optional tag for alignments showing factuality (FACT) or polarity (POL) phenomena, can be specified. The evaluation is based on (Melamed, 1998), which uses the F1 of precision and recall of token alignments.

We participate in the iSTS shared task with a system that combines different features - including word embedding and chunk similarity - using a Multilayer Perceptrons (MLP). Our main contribution was focused on the optimization of a Neural Network setting (i.e. topology, activation function, multi-task training) for the iSTS task. We show that

Proceedings of SemEval-2016, pages 783–789,
San Diego, California, June 16-17, 2016. ©2016 Association for Computational Linguistics

even with a relatively small and unbalanced training dataset, a neural network classifier can be built that achieves results very close to the best system. Particularly, our system makes use of a single model for the different training sets of the task, proving to be very robust to domain differences.

The paper is organized as follows. Section 2 presents the system we built; Section 3 reports the results we obtained and an evaluation of our system. Finally, Section 4 provides some conclusions.

2 System Description

Our system is built combining different linguistic features in a classification model for predicting chunk-to-chunk alignment, relation type and STS score. We decide to use the same features for all these three subtasks and to use a unique multitask MLP with shared layers for all the subtasks. The system is expandable and scalable for adopting more useful features aiming at improving the accuracy.

In this Section, we describe the pre-processing of the data, the features we used, the MLP structure, its training, its output and, finally, the difference between the three submitted runs.

2.1 Data Pre-processing

The input data undergo a data pre-processing in which we use a Python implementation of MBSP (Daelemans and Van den Bosch, 2005), a library providing tools for tokenization, sentence splitting, part of speech tagging, chunking, lemmatization and prepositional phrase attachment. The MBSP chunker is used in the SYS subtrack, which requires participants to identify the chunks in each sentence. For both subtracks, we pre-processed the initial datasets of sentence pairs by pairing all the chunks in the first sentence with all the chunks in the second sentence. Henceforth, we will refer to the two chunks in each of the obtained pairs as *chunk1* and *chunk2*, being *chunk1* a chunk of the first sentence and *chunk2* a chunk of the second sentence.

2.2 Feature Selection

To compute the chunk-to-chunk alignment, the relation type and the STS score we use a total of 245 features.

Chunk tags. A total of 18 features (9 for *chunk1* and 9 for *chunk2*) are related to chunk tags (e.g. noun phrase, prepositional phrase, verb phrase).

For each chunk in the SYS datasets -chunked with MBSP- the system takes into consideration the chunk tags as identified by that library. [1]

For the GS datasets -already chunked datasets- the system first re-chunks the datasets with MBSP and than evaluates if chunks in the GS corresponds to chunks as identified in MBSP. If this is the case, chunk tag is extracted; otherwise the systems does the same operation (i.e. re-chunking and tag extraction) using *pattern.en* (De Smedt and Daelemans, 2012), a regular expressions-based shallow parser for English that uses a part-of-speech tagger extended with a tokenizer, lemmatizer and chunker. [2]

If no corresponding chunk is found, no chunk tag is assigned.

Token and lemma overlap. Four further features are related to tokens and lemmas overlap between a pair of chunks. In particular, the system considers the percentage of (i) tokens and (ii) lemmas in *chunks1* that are present also in *chunk2* and viceversa (iii - iv).

WordNet based features. Another group of features concerns lexical and semantic relations between words extracted from WordNet 3.0 (Fellbaum, 1998). As such, we evaluate the type of relation between chunks by considering all the lemmas in the two chunks and checking whether a lemma in *chunk1* is a synonym, antonym, hyponym, hyperonym, meronym or holonym of a lemma in *chunk2*. The relations between all the combinations of the lemmas in the two chunks are extracted. The presence or absence of a relation is consider a feature at chunk level (for a total of 6 features for *chunk1* and 6 features for *chunk2*).

Furthermore, we consider as a feature the synset similarity existing in the WordNet hierarchy between each lemma in the two chunks, as calculated

---

[1] The chunk tags are the following: noun phrase (NP), prepositional phrase (PP), verb phrase (VP), adverb phrase (ADVP), adjective phrase (ADJP), subordinating conjunction (SBAR), particle (PRT), interjection (INTJ), prepositional noun phrase (PNP).

[2] The two chunkers use the same set of chunk tags.

by *pattern.en*. We calculate the average of the best alignments for each lemma in the two chunks. For example, consider the chunk pair: *chunk1* "the animal" and *chunk2* "the sweet dog". For each lemma in *chunk1*, for which a synset can be retrieved from WordNet, ("animal"), we calculate the maximum similarity with lemmas in *chunk2*. Thus, for this pair of chunks the resulting maximum similarity is between "animal-dog" = 0.299 (being equal to 0.264 for "animal-sweet"). The chunk similarity score is 0.299. With the same strategy we calculate similarity between lemmas in *chunk2* towards *chunk1*, i.e. "sweet-animal" = 0.264 , "dog-animal" = 0.299 resulting in a chunk similarity score of [(0.264 + 0.299)/ 2] = 0.281. If lemmas were not found in WordNet, the synset similarity is considered 0.

Word embedding. We use a distributional representation of the chunk for a total of 200 features (100 for chunk1 and 100 for chunk2) by first calculating word embedding and then combining the vectors of the words in the chunk (i.e. by calculating the element wise mean of each vector). We use Mikolov word2vec (Mikolov et al., 2013) with 100 dimensions using ukWaC, GigaWords (NYT), Europarl V.7, Training Set (JRC) corpora.

The system computes the chunk-to-chunk similarity by calculating the cosine similarity between the two chunk vectors with three different models: the first uses the already described vectors (one feature); the second uses vectors representations extracted with a different corpus and a different parametres -i.e. Google News, with 300 dimensions of the vectors- (one feature); the third uses GloVe vectors (Pennington et al., 2014) with 300 dimensions (one feature).

Baseline feature. The baseline output - provided by the organizers (Agirre et al., 2016) - was also exploited, i.e. we consider if the chunks are evaluated as aligned, if *chunk1* is not aligned, if *chunk2* is not aligned (3 features).

Composition of the input data. The last three features refer to the datasets. The system takes into consideration if the chunks are extracted from Headline, Images, or Student Answers dataset.

	#features
Chunk tags	18
Token and lemma overlap	4
WordNet relations and similarity	14
Word embedding	200
Cosine Similarity	3
Baseline feature	3
Composition of the input data	3
Total	245

Table 1: Feature Selection.

2.3 Neural Network

We use a multitask MLP (see Figure 1) to classify chunk pairs, implemented with the TensorFlow library (Abadi et al., 2015). The system uses three classifiers: one for the chunk alignment, one for alignment type, one for STS score. The input layer has 245 entities, so we use fully connected hidden layers with 250 nodes. During the test we observed that smaller (200 nodes) or bigger (300 nodes) layers reduce the performances. The system is composed by two layers (i.e. L1 and L2) shared between the three classifiers. On the top of them there are other two layers: the former (L3a) used only for the alignment classifier and the latter (L3b) shared among the score classifier and the type classifier. At the very end of L3b, there are other two layers one for the score (L4a) and one for the type (L4b). In synthesis for alignment there are three hidden layers, two shared (L1 and L2) and one private (L3a), for STS score there are four hidden layers, three shared (L1, L2, L3b) and one private (L4a) and the same for the type labeling (L1, L2, L3b + L4b). Every output layers is a softmax; during the training the system has a dropout layer that remove nodes from the layer with a probability of 50% to avoid overfitting.

We use sigmoid as activation function as it results the best one during the development test among all the activation function available in the library. Finally, we train our MLP using three different optimizers; each of them reduces the softmax error on a subtasks (i.e. alignment, type labeling or STS score). For the optimization we use the Adam algorithm (Kingma and Ba, 2014) with different learning rates: 0.00006 for the first classifier and 0.00004 for

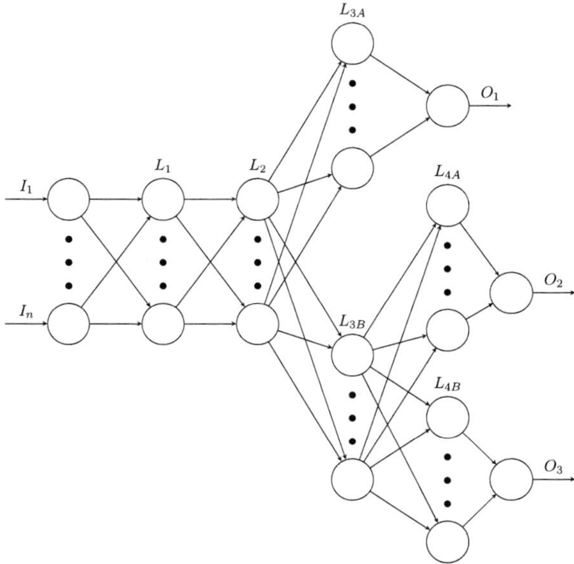

Figure 1: Multitask learning Neural Network.

the other ones.

We train the classifiers for three cycles. This training strategy is driven by learning curves analysis: we keep training the classifiers until the learning curves keep growing. We notice that the alignment classifier stops learning earlier, followed by the relation type classifier, and, at the end, the STS score classifier. Under these findings, to train all the classifiers in the same way overfits the training data. Furthermore, the training data are very unbalanced (most of the pairs are not aligned); thus, we use random mini-batches with a fix proportion between aligned pairs and unaligned pairs. To do so, we use the unaligned pairs more than once in a single training epoch. In particular, first we train the alignment classifier with the following proportion: 2/5 of aligned examples and 3/5 of not aligned pairs, for 8 training epochs (i.e. every aligned pair is used as training data at least 8 times). The second training cycle optimizes relation type labeling and STS score, with the proportion of 9/10 aligned and 1/10 not aligned for other 8 training epochs. Finally, in the third training cyle, we train only for STS score with a proportion of 9/10 aligned and 1/10 not aligned pairs.

2.4 Output

We combine the output of the three classifiers (alignment, relation type and similarity score) organized in a pipeline. First, we label as "not aligned" all the punctuation chunks (i.e. those defined as "not alignable" by the baseline); then we label as "aligned" all the chunks aligned by the first classifier, allowing multiple alignments for each chunk. For every aligned chunk pair we add the type label and the STS score. We do not take into consideration chunk pairs classified as "not aligned" by the first classifier even if they are classified with a label different from NOTALI or with an STS score higher than 0.

2.5 Submitted Runs

We submitted three runs, with different training settings. In the first run we use all the training data with a mini-batch of 150 elements. In the second run we train and evaluate separately each dataset with a mini-batch of 150 elements. Finally, in the third run we use all the training data with a mini-batch of 200 elements. We choose these settings in order to evaluate how in-domain data and different sizes of the mini-batch influence the classification results.

3 Results and Evaluation

Table 2 compares the results of our runs with the baseline and the best system for each subtrack of the three datasets, showing:

- F1 on alignment classification (F);
- F1 on alignment classification plus relation alignment type (+T);
- F1 on alignment classification plus STS score (+S);
- F1 on alignment classification plus relation alignment type and STS score (+TS);
- Ranked position over the runs submitted: i.e. 13 runs for Images and Headlines SYS, 12 for Student Answer SYS, 20 for Images and Headlines GS and 19 for Student Answer GS (RANK)

Table 2 shows that for all the six subtracks run1 and run3 register better results. In particular, for what concerns GS subtasks (with already chunked sentences), run2 is ranked at least two positions lower with respect to the other two runs. Since the difference between run2 and the other runs lays on the data used for training, these results seem to

	IMAGES SYS					IMAGE GS				
	F	+T	+S	+TS	RANK	F	+T	+S	+TS	RANK
Baseline	0.7127	0.4043	0.6251	0.4043		0.8556	0.4799	0.7456	0.4799	
OurSystem-Run1	0.8427	0.5655	*0.7862*	0.5475	5	0.8728	0.5945	0.8147	0.5739	9
OurSystem-Run2	0.8427	0.5179	0.7807	0.4969	8	0.8789	0.543	0.8178	0.525	15
OurSystem-Run3	0.8418	0.5541	*0.7847*	0.5351	7	0.8786	0.5884	0.8193	0.5656	11
BestSystem	0.8429	0.6276	0.7813	0.6095	1	0.8922	0.6867	0.8408	0.6708	1

	HEADLINES SYS					HEADLINES GS				
	F	+T	+S	+TS	RANK	F	+T	+S	+TS	RANK
Baseline	0.6486	0.4379	0.5912	0.4379		0.8462	0.5462	0.761	0.5461	
OurSystem-Run1	0.8078	0.5234	0.7374	0.5099	5	*0.879*	0.5744	*0.8096*	0.5591	16
OurSystem-Run2	0.7973	0.5138	0.7369	0.5028	7	*0.8859*	0.5643	*0.8019*	0.5554	18
OurSystem-Run3	0.805	0.5185	0.7374	0.5054	6	*0.8853*	0.5771	*0.8089*	0.562	15
BestSystem	0.8366	0.5605	0.7595	0.5467	1	0.8194	0.7031	0.7865	0.696	1

	STUDENT ANSWERS SYS					STUDENT ANSWERS GS				
	F	+T	+S	+TS	RANK	F	+T	+S	+TS	RANK
Baseline	0.6188	0.4431	0.5702	0.4431		0.8203	0.5566	0.7464	0.5566	
OurSystem-Run1	0.8162	0.5479	*0.7589*	0.542	3	*0.8775*	0.5888	0.8102	0.5808	7
OurSystem-Run2	0.8161	0.5434	*0.7481*	0.5405	4	0.859	0.5758	0.791	0.5714	10
OurSystem-Run3	**0.8166**	**0.5613**	**0.7574**	**0.5547**	**1**	0.8505	0.5984	0.7896	0.589	6
BestSystem						0.8684	0.6511	0.8245	0.6385	1

Table 2: Results for the Baseline, Our System three runs and the Best System for the two subtracks split in the three datasets.

suggest that the system takes advantage of a bigger training set with different domain data. Instead, the size of the mini-batch (that is the difference between run1 and run3) does not seem to have a clear influence on the system performance, since in some cases run1 is higher ranked while in other cases run3 is higher ranked.

Furthermore, Table 2 shows that results for Alignment classification (F) and for Alignment plus STS score (+S) frequently approach the Best System (being the major deficit for F equal to 0.0393 in Headline SYS for run3 and equal to 0.0349 for +S in Student Answwer GS dataset for run3) and in a few cases outperform it (e.g. in Headlines GS for F results and in Images SYS for +S results). On the other hand, when also relation type classification is considered (i.e. +T and +TS) we register worse performances, being the minimum difference with the Best System equals to 0.0371 for +T results and of 0.0368 for +TS results (both in Headlines SYS) and

the maximum difference equals to 0.1437 for +T and to 0.1458 for +TS (both in Images GS). This indicates that type labelling is the hardest subtask for our system, probably because the subtask requires to identify a higher number of classes (i.e. 7 types).

By comparing the rank of the two subtracks SYS and GS, we notice that our system performs much better in the SYS subtrack (being the worst ranking 8 out of 13 for SYS and 18 out of 20 for GS). This fact indicates that our system does not benefit from having already chunked sentence pairs.

Table 3 presents the final rank calculated by considering the mean of +TS results for the three datasets. As previously mentioned, our system performs relatively better when chunk identification is required. Also, it evidences again that run2 performs worse and that run1 and run3 are similar. Overall our system ranked second among 4 systems (+1 by the authors) in the SYS subtrack.

	SYS		GS	
	MEAN F + TS	**RANK**	**MEAN F + TS**	**RANK**
Baseline	0.428433		0.527533	
Run1	0.533133	4	0.571266	11
Run2	0.5134	6	0.5506	17
Run3	0.531733	5	0.5722	10
BestSystem	0.552333	1	0.637733	1

Table 3: Mean of the F+TS results in the two subtracks for the Baseline, Our System three runs and the Best System and final rank.

4 Conclusion and Further Work

Considering the obtained results, in particular the difference between the runs, we expect our system to be robust also in situation where data from different domains are provided (e.g. training data from several domains and test data on one of them). In fact, for domain adaptation our system seems to require few data of the target domain.

In any case, the system perform better with more training data, independently on the domains involved. As such, further work may include the use of silver data extracted from other datasets, e.g. SICK dataset (Marelli et al., 2014).

In addition, we believe that a deep analysis of the distribution of the type labels and of the STS scores can improve significantly the performance of the system.

Finally, an ablation test can be helpful in identifying the most salient features for the systems, helping to reduce the complexity of the MLP or to develop better topologies.

Acknowledgments

We are grateful to José G. C. de Souza, Matteo Negri, and Marco Turchi for their suggestions.

References

Martín Abadi, Ashish Agarwal, Paul Barham, Eugene Brevdo, Zhifeng Chen, Craig Citro, Greg S. Corrado, Andy Davis, Jeffrey Dean, Matthieu Devin, Sanjay Ghemawat, Ian Goodfellow, Andrew Harp, Geoffrey Irving, Michael Isard, Yangqing Jia, Rafal Jozefowicz, Lukasz Kaiser, Manjunath Kudlur, Josh Levenberg, Dan Mané, Rajat Monga, Sherry Moore, Derek Murray, Chris Olah, Mike Schuster, Jonathon Shlens, Benoit Steiner, Ilya Sutskever, Kunal Talwar, Paul Tucker, Vincent Vanhoucke, Vijay Vasudevan, Fernanda Viégas, Oriol Vinyals, Pete Warden, Martin Wattenberg, Martin Wicke, Yuan Yu, and Xiaoqiang Zheng. 2015. TensorFlow: Large-scale machine learning on heterogeneous systems. Software available from tensorflow.org.

Eneko Agirre, Mona Diab, Daniel Cer, and Aitor Gonzalez-Agirre. 2012. Semeval-2012 task 6: A pilot on semantic textual similarity. In *Proceedings of the First Joint Conference on Lexical and Computational Semantics-Volume 1: Proceedings of the main conference and the shared task, and Volume 2: Proceedings of the Sixth International Workshop on Semantic Evaluation*, pages 385–393. Association for Computational Linguistics.

Eneko Agirre, Daniel Cer, Mona Diab, Aitor Gonzalez-Agirre, and Weiwei Guo. 2013. sem 2013 shared task: Semantic Textual Similarity, including a Pilot on Typed-Similarity. In *In*SEM 2013: The Second Joint Conference on Lexical and Computational Semantics. Association for Computational Linguistics*. Citeseer.

Eneko Agirre, Carmen Banea, Claire Cardie, Daniel Cer, Mona Diab, Aitor Gonzalez-Agirre, Weiwei Guo, Rada Mihalcea, German Rigau, and Janyce Wiebe. 2014. Semeval-2014 task 10: Multilingual Semantic Textual Similarity. In *Proceedings of the 8th International Workshop on Semantic Evaluation (SemEval 2014)*, pages 81–91.

Eneko Agirre, Carmen Baneab, Claire Cardiec, Daniel Cerd, Mona Diabe, Aitor Gonzalez-Agirrea, Weiwei Guof, Inigo Lopez-Gazpioa, Montse Maritxalara, Rada Mihalceab, et al. 2015. Semeval-2015 task 2: Semantic Textual Similarity, English, Spanish and Pilot on Interpretability. In *Proceedings of the 9th International Workshop on Semantic Evaluation (SemEval 2015)*, pages 252–263.

Eneko Agirre, Aitor Gonzalez-Agirre, Iñigo Lopez-Gazpio, Montse Maritxalar, German Rigau, and Larraitz Uria. 2016. Semeval-2016 task 2: Interpretable semantic textual similarity. In *Proceedings of the 10th International Workshop on Semantic Evaluation (SemEval 2016)*, San Diego, California, June.

Walter Daelemans and Antal Van den Bosch. 2005. *Memory-based language processing*. Cambridge University Press.

Tom De Smedt and Walter Daelemans. 2012. Pattern for python. *The Journal of Machine Learning Research*, 13(1):2063–2067.

Christiane Fellbaum. 1998. *WordNet*. Wiley Online Library.

Diederik Kingma and Jimmy Ba. 2014. Adam: A

method for stochastic optimization. *arXiv preprint arXiv:1412.6980*.

Marco Marelli, Stefano Menini, Marco Baroni, Luisa Bentivogli, Raffaella Bernardi, and Roberto Zamparelli. 2014. A sick cure for the evaluation of compositional distributional semantic models. In *Proceeding of Language Resources and Evaluation Conference (LREC 2014)*, pages 216–223.

I. Dan Melamed. 1998. Manual annotation of translational equivalence: The blinker project. Technical Report 98-07, Institute for Research in Cognitive Science, Philadelphia.

Tomas Mikolov, Ilya Sutskever, Kai Chen, Greg S Corrado, and Jeff Dean. 2013. Distributed representations of words and phrases and their compositionality. In *Advances in neural information processing systems*, pages 3111–3119.

Jeffrey Pennington, Richard Socher, and Christopher D Manning. 2014. Glove: Global vectors for word representation. In *Proceedings of Empirical Methods in Natural Language Processing (EMNLP 2014)*, pages 1532–1543.

IISCNLP at SemEval-2016 Task 2: Interpretable STS with ILP based Multiple Chunk Aligner

Lavanya Sita Tekumalla and **Sharmistha**

lavanya.tekumalla@gmail.com sharmistha.jat@gmail.com

Indian Institute of Science, Bangalore, India

Abstract

Interpretable semantic textual similarity (iSTS) task adds a crucial explanatory layer to pairwise sentence similarity. We address various components of this task: chunk level semantic alignment along with assignment of similarity type and score for aligned chunks with a novel system presented in this paper. We propose an algorithm, iMATCH, for the alignment of multiple non-contiguous chunks based on Integer Linear Programming (ILP). Similarity type and score assignment for pairs of chunks is done using a supervised multiclass classification technique based on Random Forrest Classifier. Results show that our algorithm iMATCH has low execution time and outperforms most other participating systems in terms of alignment score. Of the three datasets, we are top ranked for answer-students dataset in terms of overall score and have top alignment score for headlines dataset in the gold chunks track.

1   Introduction and Related Work

Semantic Textual Similarity (STS) refers to measuring the degree of equivalence in underlying semantics(meaning) of a pair of text snippets. It finds applications in information retrieval, question answering and other natural language processing tasks. Interpretable STS (iSTS) adds an explanatory layer, by measuring similarity across chunks of segmented text, leading to an improved interpretability. It involves aligning multiple chunks across sentences with similar meaning along with similarity score(0-5) and type assignment.

Interpretable STS task was first introduced as a pilot task in 2015 Semeval STS task. Several approaches were proposed including NeRoSim (Banjade et al., 2015), UBC-Cubes (Agirre et al., 2015) and Exb-Thermis (Hänig et al., 2015). For the task of alignment, these submissions used approaches based on monolingual aligner using word similarity and contextual features (Md Arafat Sultan and Summer, 2014), JACANA that uses phrase based semi-markov CRFs (Yao and Durme, 2015) and Hungarian Munkers algorithm (Kuhn and Yaw, 1955). Other popular approaches for mono-lingual alignment include two-stage logistic-regression based aligner (Md Arafat Sultan and Summer, 2015), techniques based on edit rate computation such as (lien Maxe Anne Vilnat, 2011) and TER-Plus (Snover et al., 2009). (Bodrumlu et al., 2009) used ILP for word alignment problem. The iSTS task in 2016 introduced problem of many-to-many chunk alignment, where multiple non-contiguous chunks of the source can align with multiple-non-contiguous chunks of the target sentence, that previous mono-lingual alignment techniques cannot handle. We propose iMATCH, a new technique for monolingual alignment for many-to-many alignment at the chunk level, that can combine non-contiguous chunks based on integer linear programming (ILP). We also explore several features to define a similarity score between chunks to define the objective function for our optimization problem, similarity type and score classification modules. To summarize our contributions:

- We propose a novel algorithm for monolingual alignment : iMATCH that handles many-to-

Proceedings of SemEval-2016, pages 790–795,
San Diego, California, June 16-17, 2016. ©2016 Association for Computational Linguistics

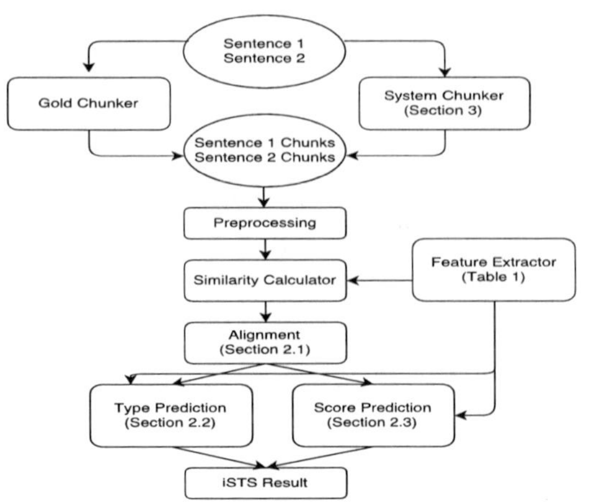

Figure 1: Flow diagram of proposed iSTS system

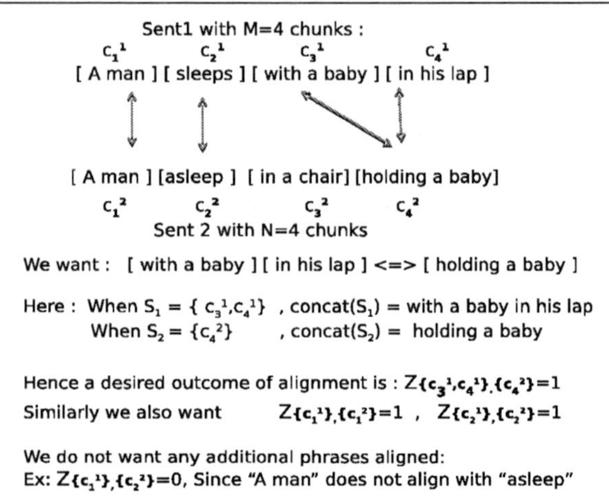

Figure 2: iMatch: An example illustrating notation

many chunk level alignment, based on Integer Linear Programming.

- We propose a system for Interpretable Semantic Textual Similarity: In the Gold-chunks track, our system is the top performer for the students-dataset and our alignment score is in that of the best two teams for all datasets.

2 System for Interpretable STS

Our system comprises of (a) alignment module, iMATCH (section 2.1), (2) Type prediction module (section 2.2) and (3) Score prediction module (section 2.3). In the case of system chunks, there is an additional chunking module for segmenting input sentences into chunks. Figure 1 shows the block diagram of proposed system.

Problem Formulation: Following is the formal definition of our problem. Consider source sentence ($Sent_1$) with M chunks and target sentence ($Sent_2$) with N chunks. Consider sets $C^1 = \{c_1^1, \ldots, c_M^1\}$, the chunks of sentence $Sent_1$ and $C^2 = \{c_1^2, \ldots, c_N^2\}$, the chunks of sentence $Sent_2$. Consider sets $\mathscr{S}_1 \subset PowerSet(C^1) - \phi$ and $\mathscr{S}_2 \subset PowerSet(C^2) - \phi$. Note that $\mathscr{S}_1$ and $\mathscr{S}_2$ are subsets of the power set (set of all possible combinations of sentence chunks) of C^1 and C^2 respectively. Consider sets $S_1 \in \mathscr{S}_1$ and $S_2 \in \mathscr{S}_2$, which denotes a specific subset of chunks that are likely to be combined during alignment. Let $concat(S_1)$ denote the phrase resulting from concatenation of chunks in S_1 and $concat(S_2)$ denote the phrase resulting from concatenation of chunks of S_2. Consider a binary

variable Z_{S_1,S_2} that takes value 1 if $concat(S_1)$ is aligned with $concat(S_2)$ and 0 otherwise.

The goal of *alignment module* is to determine the decision variables (Z_{S_1,S_2}), which are non-zero. S_1 and S_2 can have more than one chunk (multiple alignment), that are not necessarily contiguous. Aligned chunks are further classified using Type classifier and Score classifier. *Type prediction module* identifies a pair of aligned chunks ($concat(S_1), concat(s_2)$)) with a relation type like EQUI (equivalent), OPPO (opposite) etc. *Score classifier module* assigns a similarity score ranging between 0-5 for a pair of chunks. For the system chunks track, the *chunking module*, converts sentences $Sent_1, Sent_2$ to sentence chunks C_1, C_2.

2.1 iMATCH: ILP based Monolingual Aligner for Multiple-Alignment at the Chunk Level

We approach the problem of multiple alignment (permitting non-contiguous chunk combinations) by formulating it as an Integer Linear Programming (ILP) optimization problem. We construct the objective function as the sum of all $Z_{S_1,S_2}, \forall S_1, S_2$ weighed by the similarity between $concat(S_1)$ and $concat(S_2)$, subject to constraints to ensure that each chunk is aligned only a single time with any other chunk. This leads to the following optimization problem based on Integer linear programming

(Nemhauser and Wolsey, 1988):

$$\max_{Z} \quad \sum_{S_1 \in \mathcal{S}_1, S_2 \in \mathcal{S}_2} Z_{S_1,S_2} \, \alpha(S_1, S_2) \, Sim(S_1, S_2)$$

$$\text{S.T} \quad \sum_{\bar{S}_1 = \{S : c^1 \in S, S \in \mathcal{S}_1\}, S_2 \in \mathcal{S}_2} Z_{S_1,S_2} \leq 1, \forall 1 \leq c^1 \leq M$$

$$\sum_{S_1 \in \mathcal{S}_1, \bar{S}_2 = \{S : c^2 \in S, S \in \mathcal{S}_2\}} Z_{S_1,S_2} \leq 1, \forall 1 \leq c^2 \leq N$$

$$Z_{S_1,S_2} \in \{0,1\}, \forall S_1 \in \mathcal{S}_1, S_2 \in \mathcal{S}_2$$

Optimization constraints ensure that a particular chunk c appears in an alignment a single time with any subset of chunks in the other sentence. Therefore, one chunk can be part of alignment only once. We note that all possible multiple alignments are explored by this optimization problem when $\mathcal{S}_1 = PowerSet(C^1) - \phi$ and $\mathcal{S}_2 = PowerSet(C^2) - \phi$. However, this leads to a very high number of decision variables Z_{S_1,S_2}, not suitable for realistic use. Hence we consider a restricted usecase

$$\mathcal{S}_1 = \{C_1^1\}, \ldots, \{C_M^1\} \cup \{\{C_i^1, C_j^1\} : 1 \leq i < j \leq M\}$$

$$\mathcal{S}_2 = \{C_1^2\}, \ldots, \{C_N^2\} \cup \{\{C_i^2, C_j^2\} : 1 \leq i < j \leq N\}$$

This leads to many-to-many alignment where at most two chunks are combined to align with two other chunks. For iSTS task submission, we restrict our experiments to this setting (since this worked well for the iSTS task), but can relax sets S_1 and S_2 to cover combinations of 3 or more chunks. For efficiency, it should be possible to consider a subset of chunks based on adjacency information, existence of a dependency using dependency parsing techniques. $Sim(S_1, S_2)$, the similarity score, that measures desirability of aligning $concat(S_1)$ with $concat(S_2)$, plays an important role in finding the optimal solution for the monolingual alignment task. We compute this similarity score by taking the maximum of similarity scores obtained from a subset of features F1, F2, F3, F8, F10 and F11 given in Table 1 as follows: $max(F1, F2, F3, F8, F10, F11)$. During implementation, the weighting term, $\alpha(S_1, S_2)$ is set as a function of the cardinality of S_1 and cardinality of S_2 to ensure aligning fewer individual chunks (for instance, single alignment tends to increase objective function value more due to more aligned pairs, since similarity scores are normalized to lie between

-1 and 1) does not get an undue advantage over multiple alignment. This is a hyper-parameter whose value is set using simple grid search. We solve the actual ILP optimization problem using PuLP (Mitchell et al., 2011), a python toolkit for linear programming. Our system achieved the best alignment score for headlines datasets in the gold chunks track.

2.2 Type Prediction Module

We use a supervised approach for multiclass classification based on the training data of 2016 and that of previous years (for some submitted runs) to learn the similarity type between aligned pair of chunks based on various features derived from the chunk text. We train a one-vs-rest random forest classifier (Pedregosa et al., 2011) with various features mentioned in Table 1. We perform normalization on the input phrases as a preprocessing step before extracting features for classification. Normalisation step includes various heuristic steps to convert similar words to the same form, for example 'USA' and 'US' were mapped to 'U.S.A'. Empirical results suggested that features F1, F2, F3, F5, F7, F8, F9, F12 along with unigram and bigram features give good accuracy with decision tree classifier. Feature vector normalisation is done before training and prediction. We note that our type classification module performed well for the answer-students dataset, while it did not generalize as well for the headlines and images. We are exploring other features to improve performance on these datasets as future work.

2.3 Score Prediction Module

Similar to type classifier, we designed the Score classifier to do multiclass classification using one-vs-rest random forest classifier (Pedregosa et al., 2011). Each score 1-5 is considered as a class. '0' score is assigned by default for 'not-aligned' chunks. Word normalization (US, USA, U.S.A are mapped to U.S.A string) is performed as a preprocessing step. Features F1, F2, F3, F5, F7, F8, F9, F12 along with unigram and bigram features (refer Table 1) were used in training the multi-class classifier. Feature normalization was performed to improve results. Our score classifier works well on all datasets. The system achieved highest score on the gold-chunks track for answer-students dataset and

Table 1: Feature Extraction as used in various modules of iSTS system

No.	Feature Name	Description
F1	Common Word Count	$v1\_words = \{\text{words1 from sentence 1}\}$ $v2\_words = \{\text{words2 from sentence 2}\}$ feature value $= \frac{\{|v1\_words \cap v2\_words|\}}{0.5*(sentence1\_length + sentence2\_length)}$
F2	Wordnet Synonym Count	$v1 = \{\text{words1}\} \cup \{\text{wordnet synsets, similar\_tos, hypernms and hyponyms of words in sentence 1}\}$ $v2 = \{\text{words2}\} \cup \{\text{wordnet synsets, similar\_tos, hypernms and hyponyms of words in sentence 2}\}$ feature value $= \frac{|v1 \cap v2|}{0.5*(sentence1\_length + sentence2\_length)}$
F3	Wordnet Antonym Count	$v1\_words = \{\text{words1}\}, v1\_anto = \{\text{wordnet antonyms of words in sentence 1}\}$ $v2\_words = \{\text{words2}\}, v2\_anto = \{\text{wordnet antonyms of words in sentence 2}\}$ feature value $= \frac{\{|v1\_words \cap v2\_anto|\} + \{|v2 - words \cap v1\_anto|\}}{0.5*(sentence1\_length + sentence2\_length)}$
F4	Wordnet IsHyponym & IsHypernym	$v1\_syn = \{\text{synonyms of words in sentence 1}\}, v1\_hyp = \{\text{hypo\{/hyper\}nyms of words in v1\_syn}\}$ $v2\_syn = \{\text{synonyms of words in sentence 2}\}, v2\_hyp = \{\text{hypo\{/hyper\}nyms of words in v2\_syn}\}$ feature value = 1 if $|v1\_syn \cap v2\_hyp| \geq 1$
F5	Wordnet Path Similarity	$v1\_syn = \{\text{synonyms of words in sentence 1}\}$ $v2\_syn = \{\text{synonyms of words in sentence 2}\}$ feature value $= \frac{\{\sum w1.path\_similarity(w2)\}}{(sentence1\_length + sentence2\_length)}, w1 \in v1\_syn, w2 \in v2\_syn$
F6	Has Number	feature value = 1 if phrase contains a number
F7	Is Negation	feature value = 1 if one phrase contains a 'not' or 'n't' or 'never' and other phrase does not contain those terms.
F8	Edit Score	$v1 = \text{words in sentence 1}$ $v2 = \text{words in sentence 2}$ value $= \sum [\max(1 - \frac{EditDistance(w1, w2)}{(max(len(sentence1), len(sentence2)))}), \forall w2 \in v2] \, \forall w1 \in v1.$ feature value $= \frac{value}{sentence1\_length}$ For phrasal score, sum editscore of sentence 1 words with the closest sentence 2 words. Compute the average over scores for words in source.
F9	PPDB Similarity	$v1 = \text{words in sentence 1}$ $v2 = \text{words in sentence 2}$ feature value $= \sum [ppdb\_similarity\{w1, w2\}], w1 \in v1, w2 \in v2$
F10	W2V Similarity	$v1 = \text{words in sentence 1}, v1\_vec = \sum \text{word2vec embedding}\{w1\}, w1 \in v1$ $v2 = \text{words in sentence 2}, v2\_vec = \sum \text{word2vec embedding}\{w2\}, w2 \in v2$ feature value $= cosine\_distance(v1\_vec, v2\_vec)$
F11	Bigram Similarity	$v1 = \text{bigrams in sentence 1,}$ $v2 = \text{bigrams in sentence 2,}$ feature value $= cosine\_distance(v1, v2)$
F12	Length Difference	feature value $= len(sentence1) - len(sentence2)$

headlines dataset and is within 2% of the top score for all other datasets.

2.4 System Chunks Track: Chunking Module

When gold chunks are not given, we perform an additional chunking step. We use two methods for chunking: (1) With OpenNLP Chunker(Apache, 2010) (2) With stanford-core-nlp (Manning et al., 2014) API for generating parse trees and using the chunklink (Buchholz, 2000) tool for chunking based on the parse trees.

For chunking, we do preprocessing to remove punctuations unless the punctuation is space separated (therefore constitutes an independent word). We also convert unicode characters to ascii characters. Output of chunker is further post-processed to combine each single preposition phrase with the preceding phrase. We noted that the OpenNLP chunker ignored last word of a sentence, in which case, we concatenated the last word as a separate chunk. In the case of chunking based on stanford-core-nlp parser, we noted that in several instances, particularly in the student answer dataset, a conjunction such as 'and' was consistently being separated into an independent chunk in most cases, and therefore improved chunking can be realized by potentially combining chunks around a conjunction. These processing heuristics are based on observations from gold chunks data. We observe that quality of chunking has a huge impact on the overall score in system chunks track. As future work, we are exploring ways to improve the chunking with custom algorithms.

3 Experimental Results

In this section, we present our results, in both the gold standard and the system chunks tracks. We submitted 3 runs for each track. In *gold chunks track,*

Table 2: Gold Chunks Images

RunName	Align	Type	Score	T+S	Rank
IIScNLP R2	0.8929	0.5247	0.8231	0.5088	15
IIScNLP R3	0.8929	0.505	0.8264	0.4915	17
IIScNLP R1	0.8929	0.5015	0.8285	0.4845	19
UWB R3	0.8922	0.6867	**0.8408**	0.6708	1
UWB R1	**0.8937**	0.6829	0.8397	0.6672	2

Table 3: Gold Chunks headlines

RunName	Align	Type	Score	T+S	Rank
IIScNLP R2	0.9134	0.5755	**0.829**	0.5555	16
IIScNLP R1	**0.9144**	0.5734	0.82	0.5509	18
IIScNLP R3	0.9144	0.567	0.8206	0.5405	19
Inspire R1	0.8194	0.7031	0.7865	0.696	1

Table 4: Gold Chunks Answer Students

RunName	Align	Type	Score	T+S	Rank
IIScNLP R1	0.8684	**0.6511**	0.8245	**0.6385**	**1**
IIScNLP R2	0.8684	0.627	**0.8263**	0.6167	4
IIScNLP R3	0.8684	0.6511	0.8245	0.6385	2
V-Rep R2	**0.8785**	0.5823	0.7916	0.5799	8

Table 5: Gold Chunks Overall

RunName	Images	Headline	Answer Student	Mean	Rank
IISCNLP r2	0.5088	0.5555	0.6167	0.560	13
IIScNLP R1	0.4845	0.5509	**0.6385**	0.558	14
IIScNLP R3	0.4915	0.5405	0.6385	0.557	15
UWB R1	0.6672	0.6212	0.6248	0.637	1

Table 6: System Chunks Images

RunName	Align	Type	Score	T+S	Rank
IIScNLP R2	**0.8459**	0.4993	0.777	0.4872	9
IIScNLP R3	0.8335	0.4862	0.7654	0.4744	11
IIScNLP R1	0.8335	0.4862	0.7654	0.4744	10
DTSim R3	0.8429	0.6276	0.7813	0.6095	1
Fbk-Hlt-Nlp R1	0.8427	0.5655	**0.7862**	0.5475	5

Table 7: System Chunks Headlines

RunName	Alignment	Type	Score	T+S	Rank
IIScNLP R2	0.821	0.508	0.7401	0.4919	9
IIScNLP R1	0.8105	0.4888	0.723	0.4686	10
IIScNLP R3	0.8105	0.4944	0.721	0.4685	11
DTSim R2	0.8366	0.5605	**0.7595**	0.5467	1
DTSim R3	**0.8376**	0.5595	0.7586	0.5446	2

Table 8: System Chunks Answer Students

RunName	Align	Type	Score	T+S	Rank
IIScNLP R3	0.7563	0.5604	0.71	0.5451	2
IIScNLP R1	0.756	0.5525	0.71	0.5397	5
IIScNLP R2	0.7449	0.5317	0.6995	0.5198	6
Fbk-Hlt-Nlp R3	**0.8166**	0.5613	0.7574	0.5547	1
Fbk-Hlt-Nlp R1	0.8162	0.5479	**0.7589**	0.542	3

Table 9: System Chunks Overall

RunName	Image	Headline	Answer Student	Mean	Rank
IISCNLP-R2	0.4872	0.4919	0.5198	0.499	8
IISCNLP-R3	0.4744	0.4685	**0.5451**	0.496	9
IISCNLP-R1	0.4744	0.4686	0.5397	0.494	10
DTSim R3	0.6095	0.5446	0.5029	0.552	1

all three runs used the same algorithm, with different training data for the supervised prediction of type and score. While, in system chunks track, we submitted different algorithm and data combination for various runs. Detailed run information follows:

– *Gold Chunks - Run 1* uses training data from

2015+2016 for the headlines and images dataset and 2016 data for answer-students dataset.

– *Gold Chunks - Run 2* uses training data of all datasets combined from 2015 and 2016 for headlines and images and 2016 data for answer-students.

– *Gold Chunks - Run 3* uses 2016 training data alone for each dataset.

–*System Chunks - Run 1* uses OpenNLP chunker with supervised training of type and score with data of all datasets combined for years 2015,2016.

– *System Chunks - Run 2* we use chunker based on stanford nlp parser and chunklink with training data of all datasets combined for years 2015,2016.

– *System Chunks - Run 3*, we use the OpenNLP chunker, with training data of 2016 alone.

Results of our system compared to the best performing systems in each track are listed in Tables 2-9. In both gold and system chunks track, run2 performs best owing to more data during training. Our system performed well for the answer-students dataset owing to our edit-distance feature that enables handling noisy data without any preprocessing for spelling correction. Our alignment score is best or close to the best in the gold chunks track, thus validating that our novel and simple approach based on ILP can be used for high quality monolingual multiple alignment at the chunk level. Our system took only 5.2 minutes for a single threaded execution on a Xeon 2420, 6 core system for the headlines dataset. Therefore, our technique is fast to execute. We observe that the quality of chunking has a huge impact on alignment and thereby the final score. We are actively exploring other chunking strategies that could improve results. Code for our alignment module is available at `https://github.com/lavanyats/iMATCH.git`

4 Conclusion and Future

We have proposed a system for Interpretable Semantic Textual Similarity (task 2- Semeval 2016) (Agirre et al., 2016). We introduce a novel monolingual alignment algorithm iMATCH for multiple-alignment at the chunk level based on Integer Linear Programming(ILP) that leads to the best alignment score in several cases. Our system uses novel features to capture dataset properties. For example, we designed edit distance based feature for answer-students dataset which had considerable number of spelling mistakes. This feature helped our system perform well on the noisy data of test set without any preprocessing in the form of spelling-correction.

As future work, we are actively exploring features to improve our classification accuracy for type classification, which could help us improve out mean score. Some exploration in the techniques for simultaneous alignment and chunking could significantly boost the performance in sys-chunk track.

Acknowledgment We thank Prof. Partha Pratim Talukdar, IISc for guidance during this research.

References

[Agirre et al.2015] Eneko Agirre, Aitor Gonzalez-Agirre, Inigo Lopez-Gazpio, Montse Maritxalar, German Rigau, and Larraitz Uria. 2015. Ubc: Cubes for english semantic textual similarity and supervised approaches for interpretable sts. In *Proceedings of the 9th International Workshop on Semantic Evaluation (SemEval 2015)*, pages 178–183, Denver, Colorado, June. Association for Computational Linguistics.

[Agirre et al.2016] Eneko Agirre, Aitor Gonzalez-Agirre, Inigo Lopez-Gazpio, Montse Maritxalar, German Rigau, and Larraitz Uria. 2016. Semeval-2016 task 2: Interpretable semantic textual similarity. In *Proceedings of the 10th International Workshop on Semantic Evaluation (SemEval 2016)*, San Diego, California, June.

[Apache2010] Apache. 2010. Opennlp.

[Banjade et al.2015] Rajendra Banjade, Nobal Bikram Niraula, Nabin Maharjan, Vasile Rus, Dan Stefanescu, Mihai Lintean, and Dipesh Gautam. 2015. Nerosim: A system for measuring and interpreting semantic textual similarity. In *Proceedings of the 9th International Workshop on Semantic Evaluation (SemEval 2015)*, pages 164–171, Denver, Colorado, June. Association for Computational Linguistics.

[Bodrumlu et al.2009] Tugba Bodrumlu, Kevin Knight, and Sujith Ravi. 2009. A new objective function for word alignment. In *Proceedings of the Workshop on Integer Linear Programming for Natural Langauge Processing*, ILP '09, pages 28–35, Stroudsburg, PA, USA. Association for Computational Linguistics.

[Buchholz2000] Sabine Buchholz. 2000. Chunklink perl script. http://ilk.uvt.nl/team/sabine/chunklink/README.html.

[Hänig et al.2015] Christian Hänig, Robert Remus, and Xose de la Puente. 2015. Exb themis: Extensive feature extraction from word alignments for semantic textual similarity. In *Proceedings of the 9th International Workshop on Semantic Evaluation (SemEval 2015)*, pages 264–268, Denver, Colorado, June. Association for Computational Linguistics.

[Kuhn and Yaw1955] H. W. Kuhn and Bryn Yaw. 1955. *The Hungarian method for the assignment problem*. Naval Research Logistics Quarterly 2: 8397. doi:10.1002/nav.3800020109.

[lien Maxe Anne Vilnat2011] Houda Bouamor Aur lien Maxe Anne Vilnat. 2011. *Monolingual Alignment by Edit Rate Computation on Sentential Paraphrase Pairs*. ACL.

[Manning et al.2014] Christopher D. Manning, Mihai Surdeanu, John Bauer, Jenny Finkel, Steven J. Bethard, and David McClosky. 2014. The Stanford CoreNLP natural language processing toolkit. In *Association for Computational Linguistics (ACL) System Demonstrations*, pages 55–60.

[Md Arafat Sultan and Summer2014] Steven Bethard Md Arafat Sultan and Tamara Summer. 2014. *Back to basics for Monolingual Alignment, Exploiting word Similarity and Contextual Evidence*. ACL.

[Md Arafat Sultan and Summer2015] Steven Bethard Md Arafat Sultan and Tamara Summer. 2015. *Feature-Rich Two-Stage Logistic Regression for Monolingual Alignment*. EMNLP.

[Mitchell et al.2011] Mitchell, Stuart Michael OSullivan, and Iain Dunning. 2011. Pulp: a linear programming toolkit for python. The University of Auckland, Auckland, New Zealand, http://www. optimization-online. org/DB-FILE/2011/09/3178.

[Nemhauser and Wolsey1988] George L. Nemhauser and Laurence A. Wolsey. 1988. *Integer and combinatorial optimization*. Wiley. ISBN 978-0-471-82819-8.

[Pedregosa et al.2011] F. Pedregosa, G. Varoquaux, A. Gramfort, V. Michel, B. Thirion, O. Grisel, M. Blondel, P. Prettenhofer, R. Weiss, V. Dubourg, J. Vanderplas, A. Passos, D. Cournapeau, M. Brucher, M. Perrot, and E. Duchesnay. 2011. Scikit-learn: Machine learning in Python. *Journal of Machine Learning Research*, 12:2825–2830.

[Snover et al.2009] Matthew G. Snover, Nitin Madnani, Bonnie Dorr, and Richard Schwartz. 2009. *TER-Plus: paraphrase, semantic, and alignment enhancements to Translation Edit Rate*. Machine Translation 23.2-3 (2009): 117-127.

[Yao and Durme2015] X Yao and B Van Durme. 2015. *A Lightweight and High Performance Monolingual Word Aligner: Jacana based on CRF Semi-Markov Phrase-based Monolingual Alignment*. EMNLP.

VENSESEVAL at Semeval-2016 Task 2: iSTS - with a full-fledged rule-based approach

Rodolfo Delmonte

Department of Language Studies and Comparative Cultures &
Department of Computer Science - Ca' Foscari University of Venice
Ca' Bembo – Dorsoduro 1075 - 30123 VENEZIA
Email:delmont@unive.it - Website: http//project.cgm.unive.it

Abstract

In our paper we present our rule-based system for semantic processing. In particular we show examples and solutions that may be challenge our approach. We then discuss problems and shortcomings of Task 2 – iSTS. We comment on the existence of a tension between the inherent need to on the one side, to make the task as much as possible "semantically feasible". Whereas the detailed presentation and some notes in the guidelines refer to inferential processes, paraphrases and the use of commonsense knowledge of the world for the interpretation to work. We then present results and some conclusions.

1   Introduction

In this presentation we will focus on Task 2, Interpretable Semantic Textual Similarity. We will comment on the way in which the task has been defined and what is eventually made available to participants to the task. In the section below we will present our system created for RTE – Recognizing Textual Entailment - challenges, and how it has been reorganized to suit the new current task. We discuss examples that suit or challenge our approach. We then comment in detail problems and shortcoming related to issues related to the annotations and the choice of semantic relations. In a final section we will present our results and a discussion.

2   The system *VENSESEVAL*

The system is an adaptation of *VENSES* Venice team system used for RTE (Recognizing Text Entailment) challenges (see Delmonte et al. 2009).

In fact Venses was only partially adaptable to the new task, and so we had to partly recast it. In particular, the semantic evaluation module which was used to issue a binary (or ternary) decision in RTE challenges, in iSTS scenario works in a totally different manner. RTE required a Text - which could be constituted by a single simple or complex sentence - to be compared to an Hypothesis, this usually a simple sentence. From a purely theoretic and abstract point of view, measuring semantic similarity between two sentences (snippets) resembles very closely RTE as indicated in the paper accompanying 2015 challenge, (see Agirre et al. 2015). As the authors comment, iSTS can be defined as a graded similarity notion. In iSTS the comparison is between chunks which must be aligned first.

We find this approach certainly very useful and adequate for the task of semantic similarity checking. However, we had to reorganize and partly rewrite the modules for semantic matching. This has taken a lot of time and in fact the module hasn't been fully completed. So we assume that next year challenge will see a better – or at least complete - version of *VENSESEVAL*.

In the current challenge, we used only part of the original RTE system for various reasons. *Venses* was created to allow for semantic matching at different levels of complexity and representations. In particular, the task allowed semantic composition over different sentences, not necessarily adjacent to one another. It required anaphoric processes to be part of the semantic interpretation, again over a span of text made up of a number of different but referentially related sentences. For that reason, we used a complete system for semantic interpretation that not only had a level of anaphora and coreference resolution, it also ended up by creating a logical form representation which was then used for deep

Proceedings of SemEval-2016, pages 796–802,
San Diego, California, June 16-17, 2016. ©2016 Association for Computational Linguistics

semantic matching[1].

Venseseval has a different structure and less components. iSTS task seems much more a word or chunk level interpretation process. It does not require anaphora/coreference resolution because it is bound at sentence level. It does not require a logical form to be computed, or at least we haven't found a real motivation to do that. In fact, we then found good reasons for computing predicate-argument structures, but only after the deadline expired – more on this below. Eventually we decided to limit ourselves to produce syntactic constituency structure which could then be used to produce non-embedded chunks. The pipeline we used is then fairly simple:
- a tokenizer + a sentence splitter
- a tagger + an augmented recursive transition network
- a chunker extracting simple chunks - in the same fashion in which they have been characterized in the task - from sentence level constituency.

The system had to be reorganized around the gold chunk option which is what we wanted to experiment with. In order to allow chunk alignment to work correctly, sentences have been tokenized without introducing any further computation which could modify the order of the tokens. We just wanted to use tagged tokens with the gold chunks options, and chunked structures with the system option of the task.

In particular, in our original system, NP chunks were organized internally as a list to show the Head of the chunk in first position: all modifiers were moved to the right of the head. This was no longer possible, given the fact that we had to preserve the word order of the input sentence. No multiwords have been created, and this is something that may have contributed to decrease our tagger accuracy and as a consequence also chunks have a lower level of accuracy. The final system used the Named Entity Recognition module which however was only activated at chunk level, all other cases have been neglected. The reason for not producing multiwords was also related to the fact that we wanted to keep matching procedures as simple as possible. But we intend to reintroduce it in a future reimplementation of the system.

The first pass into the sentence pair is done with

the aim to produce a general similarity evaluation based on tagged words only. To do this, we use part of the matching procedures explained below which erase function or stop words, and evaluate identity and similarity between content words without however issuing any score. Then we pass to the chunk-based analysis which is similar to the algorithm proposed in the Annotation Guidelines that can be taken as a starting point also for our module. For instance, as specified in the Procedure at pag.11, 3.d where it says "proceed from strongest to weakest 1:1 alignments". This is exactly what our system does, as specified in the algorithm below:

```
- given one sentence pair,
  - select first chunk in sentence one
    - recursively try to match chunk
      one to each of the chunks in
      sentence two
      - start matching procedures
        from EQUIvalence/OPPOsite
        - succeed, move to second
          chunk in sentence one
      - repeat
      - fail
      - move to matching procedures
        for SPE1/SPE2
        - succeed, move to second
          chunk in sentence one
      - fail
      - move to matching procedures
        for SIMI, REL
        - succeed, move to second
          chunk in sentence one
      - fail
      - assign NOALI label to chunk
      - move to second chunk in
        sentence one
      - repeat until end of chunks
        in sentence one
  - end
```

The main algorithm is a depth first attempt at finding the best match: we always select the first candidate available at each similarity level. We don't try all possible matches, in a breadth-first approach where we should score them and then choose the best candidate. At the end of the main recursion, the algorithm looks for possible recovery actions, by collecting all NOALI marked chunks and searching for possible matches with the already matched chunks except for the ones computed as EQUI. This is done trying to match

---

[1] A version of the RTE system is still working on our website, http://project.cgm.unive.it/cgi-bin/venses/venses.pl

the head of the NOALI chunk with the head of the companion chunk. In case of match, it substitutes the other chunk with the current one and turns it into a NOALI.

In the Annotation Guidelines we find two secondary features - Polarity and Factuality, appearing as extensions to main features, which are scarcely commented. We didn't implement these extensions because there were no clear instructions to do so in the guidelines. In the case of POLarity we only found four cases so labeled in the training gold standard for headlines – none in the images gold standard. As to FACTuality extensions we only implemented NOALI_FACT for all those cases in which a communication verb was labeled. Also in this case, however, there was no clear definition of the task in the guidelines, but we found 29 labeled cases in the headlines gold standard, none in the images. 13 examples were cases of NOALI_FACT which gave us sufficient confidence in assigning the label. The remaining cases were split between EQUI and SIMI with two SPE1 cases, and it was fairly hard to establish a rule that could fit with them all. SPE cases are individuated by matching the head of the two chunks which must be equal in the sense provided by EQUIvalence algorithm.

SIMI on the contrary requires some inferential step – but see section below. In particular we used a specialized label SIMI-2 to classify all chunk-pairs which involved differences in numbers, simple integers but also dates. Integers were then measured to check the distance in value and decide a score to associate to SIMI, which could vary from, 2 to 4. We used it also to indicate difference in country names, i.e. Locations recognized by the NER algorithm.

Problems arise for all those cases of paraphrases included in the corpus. There's a few examples in the training corpus of Headlines, in sentence 214,

//Iran says it captures drone ; U.S. denies losing one.
//Iran says it has seized U.S. drone ; U.S. says it 's not true
8 <==> 10 12 13 14 // EQUI // 5 // denies <==> says 's not true

Another such case is present in sentence 402,

//Egypt 's main opposition rejects president 's call for dialogue.
//Egypt opposition mulls response to Morsi dialogue

call.
5 <==> 3 4 // SPE1 // 3 // rejects <==> mulls response
Finally, consider the example in sentence n.670 again from Headlines,

//No plan to shut petrol pumps at night Moily.
//India govt rejects proposal to shut petrol pumps at night
1 2 <==> 3 4 // SIMI // 4 // No plan <==> rejects proposal

We set up a specialized algorithm for cases like the one in 214. But the other two cases we found are not computable: "no plan" can be paraphrased in an infinite number of different ways. The same applies to "mulls response".

Coming now to the need to compute predicate-argument structures, we have been convinced of its usefulness only after discovering poor performance of the system in total NOALI classification. In all those cases in which the sentence pair did not share any chunk, the system was still trying to relate far-fetched similarities, despite the fact that the overall meaning was not compatible with that interpretation. Take for instance the pair from the test-set, sentence no.9:

// Many dead as asylum boat sinks off Australia
// Mandela spends third day in hospital
3 4 5 <==> 5 6 // SIMI // 2 // as asylum boat <==> in hospital

Our system wrongly found some similarity between two chunks, where "asylum" and "hospital" share meaning components. However, the two sentences are clearly talking about totally different topics so the apparent meaning similarity should not apply. Preventing this from happening could only take place in case predicate argument structures were made available. Main predicates SINK and SPEND would then be judged not to share any meaning nor would the SUBJect "asylum" and "Mandela". Argumenthood could then be used to prevent a SUBJect "asylum boat" from being made to share semantic similarity components with a locative adjunct "in hospital", where the sinking event doesn't find any correspondence.

2.1   Matching procedures

Matching is applied at different levels using different resources. We use WordNet[2] for EQUI relations by searching non identical predicates in the same synset. Again WordNet is used for SIMI by searching up and down the path one level only, for all non identical predicates; we also use an extended version of VerbOcean[3] for entailment relations between verbs, where we added some 250 new relations. For more general REL relations we use Roget's Thesaurus[4]. And of course there's a great number of gazeteers and lexica for NER that is made available, in particular, the ones by JRC made available by Ralph Steinberg[5].

For more complex semantic similarity relations, we have reconstructed our Finite State Automaton that we introduced in our last participation in RTE n.5. We report it here below. It requires tagged words and a number of linguistic rules to be implemented. The current version of the algorithm is made up of 86 different rules.

The procedure takes as input the tagged list of words making up the current chunk pairs and tries to match it, by the predicate match_template(Chunk1, Chunk2). If the match succeeds the semantic evaluation outputs a value that is indicative of the type of decision taken. This matching procedure is reached by the analysis only after EQUI have failed. Consider the example below where we highlight the portion of the chunk pair relevant for the semantic evaluation:

T: Trains, trams, cars and buses ground to a halt on Monday after a shoot-out between 18:00 CET and 19:00 CET in the historical *city of Basel in Switzerland.*
H: *Basel is a European city.*

In more detail, Augmented Finite State Automata mean that in addition to equality matching that is at the basis of the whole algorithm, the system looks for inferences and other lexical information to authorize the match. In fact, these procedures as a whole allow the matching to become more general though introducing some constraints. The instructions reported below are expressed in Prolog

which treats capitalized words as variables. Constants on the contrary are written with lower case letter, as for instance the words "of" and "in" below.

```
match_template([A,Is-_,T-_,F_,G|Hyp],
[G,of-_,A,in-_,L-_|Text])
:-
lightverbs(Is),
high_rank(T,Lex),
locwn(L),
is_in(L,F1),
(natl(F1,F,_);natl(F1,_,F)), !.
```

where the procedure "lightverbs" looks for copulative verbs, i.e. the verb of the Chunk1 must be a copulative verb; "high_rank" looks for high frequency words like articles; "locwn" verifies that the word present in the variable "L" is a location. Then there are two inferences: the first one is fired by the call "is_in" that recovers the name of the continent to which "L" belongs, thus implicitly requiring "L" to be the name of a nation. Then the second inference looks for the corresponding nationality adjective. Values for all above variables (L,A,F,F1,T,G,Is), are then as follows:

L --> Switzerland, F1 --> Europe, F --> European
A = Basel-np, Is = is, T = a, G = city-n

3 Analysing iSTS Annotation Criteria

As said above, measuring semantic similarity between two sentences (snippets) resembles very closely TE. However, differences are clearer seen that iSTS imposes an additional first step - chunk alignment - which is finding the chunk pair that is semantically closer and then assigning a type and a score. In this sense, it is intuitively limited to what pertains to semantics, while TE had no such limitation and the word Entailment was understood as possessing a much wider import than just semantics. In fact, if we read the annotation guidelines carefully, we discover at pag. 2 that the subdivision into chunks is defined as follows: "Chunks are aligned in context, taking into account the interpretation of the whole sentence, including common sense." Common sense has no reference whatsoever to SEMANTICS being rather based on knowledge of the world. The same we find at pag. 3, "Note that the interpretation of the whole sentence, including common sense inference, has

[2] https://wordnet.princeton.edu/wordnet/
download/current-version/
[3] http://demo.patrickpantel.com/demos/
verbocean/
[4] http://www.gutenberg.org/ebooks/10681
[5] http://langtech.jrc.it/RS.html

to be taken into account." Then in the annotation guidelines, we find other elements that indicate a need to go beyond semantics: "B. When aligning, take into account the deep meaning of the chunk in context, beyond the surface."

In fact, we expected task data to pertain to so-called "literal" and direct meaning decomposition subset of sentences and not to contain any "non-literal" or "indirect" interpretable data. We also didn't expect to find unexpressed or implicit meaning components that had to be reconstructed while interpreting chunks. As we will see, this is only partially confirmed. The task itself has been organized so as to favour semantic decomposition operations to be applicable to chunks which should be at first paired by the system and then interpreted and "semantically explained". Semantic explanation is to be carried out by choosing among a small number of semantic relational label, including:
- EQUI(valent) SIMI(lar) OPPO(site) SPE(cific)1 SPE(cific)2 REL(ation) NOALI(gnment)
but also additional labels with further semantic content:
-      EQUI_FACT   EQUI_POL   SIMI_FACT SPE1_FACT SPE2_FACT NOALI_FACT SIMI-2
In particular label SIMI-2 is not explained in the guidelines. As to the other additional labels, FACT stands for factuality and POL for polarity, i.e. these two extensions should be used in case the sentence contains elements of one or the other phenomenon. The 2016 version of the task introduces then some further difficulty, when it allows chunks to match not just in a 1:1 but also 2:1. As to this procedure, in our system we check for a possible match already in the first recursive search and at the end of the recursive matching procedure.

We will now look into semantic relation labels first and see whether they are adequate and consistent. The first label, EQUIvalent covers all cases of full identity between wordforms in the two chunks. Equivalence without full orthographic identity is very frequent and includes all cases where the system matching algorithm has to put up with capitalized, or fully upper case words, and sometimes dashed version of the same unique word. But certainly the most frequent cases of equivalence-not-identity are where the two wordforms have different morphology and lemmata have to be matched. During EQUI matching procedures, we transform head words into their corresponding lemmata and try a match.

More difficult cases include named entity recognition processes, whenever an institution or a person is present with the abbreviated wordform in one chunk and the fully expressed name in the other; or when the name is used in one chunk and the other contains name and surname. Eventually, in some cases, the nationality has to match the word for the nation in the other chunk. Differentiating between SIMI and SPE is certainly hard[6].

In all these definitions, we find the same words "similar meanings" except for REL where the word "relation" is used instead. Now differences between SPE and SIMI can only be found in the presence of "attributes" in the definition of SIMI, whereas in SPE we find reference to specificity, which we may assume can be related to the presence of "attributes" but in different measure. It would seem then that SPE relations are more "similar" than SIMI relations, where semantic relations are less close. Let's now look at the examples presented in the guidelines. The second one poses already a problem:

[Red double decker bus][driving][through the streets]
[Double decker passenger bus][driving][with traffic]
Alignment: 1<==>1(SPE1   4),   2<==>2(EQUI   5), 3<==>3(REL 3)

The first two chunks have been interpreted as entertaining a SPE1 relation, which means that the first chunk "Red double decker bus" is more SPEcific than the second one. But the second one also contains a specification which is not present in the first chunk, "double decker passenger bus", constituted by the noun modifier "passenger". The choice of regarding chunk 1 more specific is driven by the fact that the colour specification adds a more relevant information to the common "double decker bus" than the noun "passenger", which is regarded of no import to the identification of the semantic reference realized by the multiword head double_decker_bus. So it would seem that in order to decide whether to use SPE1 or SPE2 a system for semantic evaluation should be equipped with "commonsense" knowledge that would weigh the two attributes accordingly. However, it may be

---

[6] The guidelines defines it as follows (pag.3/4) very vaguely.

disputable to define reference to "colour" as a less relevant attribute than reference to "passenger", for the simple reason that this decision eventually depends on the spatial location of the event. If it is England the location, then it is a commonplace notion that double decker buses are just red. But suppose the location was Lisbon, where double decker are sometimes red sometimes multicoloured, these latter being used by tourists to tour the city. In that case colour would have been more relevant than passenger. Even though "passenger" constitutes a more general attribute than "tourist" bus. So eventually, in order to use commonsense knowledge, at least time/place location must be made available.

Similar problems may be raised in another example (pag.6), where the semantic relation is expressed by predicates:

[Hundreds]1[of Bangladesh clothes factory workers]2 [ill]3
[Hundreds]1[fall]2[sick]3[in Bangladesh factory]4
Alignment: 1<==>1 (EQUI 5), 2<==>4 (SPE1 3), 3 <==> 2,3 (EQUI 5)

Here the adjective "ill" is make to relate to "fall sick" by EQUI. However, (TO BE) "ill" where the verb to be is simply left implicit in the nominalized title, is interpretable as a STATE; whereas TO "fall sick" is clearly an EVENT. So maybe the two predicates are not EQUI but SIMI and in order to align FALL to the missing BE some inference is required. This goes against what is being affirmed under 2b, as to the fact that two events are (weakly) relatable but cannot be aligned because they "refer to different events". However the reference to different events is not clearly inferrable.

[Saudis]1 [to permit]2 [women]3 [to compete]4 [in Olympics]5
[Women]1 [are confronting]2 [a glass ceiling]3
Alignment: 1<==>Ø(NOALI), 2<==>Ø(NOALI), 3<==>1(SPE1 4), 4<==>Ø(NOALI), 5<==>Ø(NOALI), Ø<==>2(NOALI), Ø<==>3 (NOALI)

In one sentence we are told that women are in Saudi Arabia, but nothing is said in the second sentence, and since spatio-temporal locations can be left implicit we are unable to separate the two events and the two references to women. So we find it hard to consider the semantic relation

intervening between the two chunks as SIMI.

4   Results

We report here below results for two of the three corpora only. As to the corpus for student-answer, it was filled with typos and spelling errors, and this was regarded part of the task. We were unable to compute any reasonable semantic similarity match for an extended number of sentences. So we decided to abandon it. As to the other two texts, results for test texts are very similar to those we already obtained for training ones, so we only show test results.

	Ali	Type	Score	TypSco
Venseval	0.7428	0.4667	0.6949	0.4624
Baseline	0.7100	0.4043	0.6251	0.4043

Table 1: Results compared to Baseline for IMAGES SYS – Rank 12 over 13

	Ali	Type	Score	TypSco
Venseval	0.8443	0.5789	0.8046	0.5735
Baseline	0.8556	0.4799	0.7456	0.4799

Table 2: Results compared to Baseline for IMAGES GS – Rank 10 over 20

As can be noticed by comparing results in SYS and GS tables, in the analysis of Images corpus the decrease of performance of the system is higher than the difference between baselines. Here below results for Headlines.

	Ali	Type	Score	TypSco
Venseval	0.7081	0.4679	0.6493	0.4531
Baseline	0.6486	0.4379	0.5912	0.4379

Table 3: Results compared to Baseline for HEADLINES SYS – Rank 12 over 13

	Ali	Type	Score	TypSco
Venseval	0.8731	0.5927	0.8099	0.5729
Baseline	0.8462	0.5462	0.7610	0.5461

Table 4: Results compared to Baseline for HEADLINES GS – Rank 13 over 20

In the Headlines corpus analysis differences in performance between SYS and GS are comparable. If we look closer at results in terms of number of teams we see that they are only 8, and our rank is now fifth, both in Images and Headlines results. In conclusion, we favoured a rule-based approach because we assume it can account for differences in text structures. However, rules require fine-tuning which cannot be completed in a short time. This is clearly born out by differences in performance between the two corpora analysed, Images and Headlines, where the first one should have been much easier to process than the second.

References

Agirre, E. and Banea, C. and Cardie, C. and Cer, D. and Diab, M. and Gonzalez-Agirre, A. and Guo, W. and Lopez-Gazpio, I. and Maritxalar, M. and Mihalcea, R. and Rigau, G. and Uria, L. and Wiebe, J. (2015). SemEval-2015 task 2: Semantic textual similarity, English, Spanish and pilot on interpretability. In Proceedings of the 9th International Workshop on Semantic Evaluation (SemEval 2015), June.

Chklovski, Timothy & Patrick Pantel. 2004. VERBOCEAN: Mining the Web for Fine-Grained Semantic Verb Relations. In Proceedings of Conference on Empirical Methods in Natural Language Processing (EMNLP-04). Barcelona, Spain.

Delmonte R., S.Tonelli, R. Tripodi, 2009. Semantic Processing for Text Entailment with VENSES, in Proceedings of Text Analysis Conference (TAC) 2009 Workshop - Notebook Papers and Results, NIST, Gaithersburg MA, pp. 453-460.

Fellbaum, Christiane (ed.), 1998. WordNet: An Electronic Lexical Database. Cambridge, MA: MIT Press.

Levy, Omer, Torsten Zesch, Ido Dagan, and Iryna Gurevych. 2013. Recognizing Partial Textual Entailment. In *ACL (2)*, pages 451–455.

UWB at SemEval-2016 Task 2: Interpretable Semantic Textual Similarity with Distributional Semantics for Chunks

Miloslav Konopík and **Ondřej Pražák** and **David Steinberger** and **Tomáš Brychcín**
NTIS – New Technologies for the Information Society,
Department of Computer Science and Engineering,
Faculty of Applied Sciences, University of West Bohemia, Technická 8, 306 14 Plzeň
Czech Republic
{konopik,brychcin}@ntis.zcu.cz,
{ondfa,fenic}@kiv.zcu.cz

Abstract

We introduce a system focused on solving SemEval 2016 Task 2 – Interpretable Semantic Textual Similarity. The system explores machine learning and rule-based approaches to the task. We focus on machine learning and experiment with a wide variety of machine learning algorithms as well as with several types of features. The core of our system consists in exploiting distributional semantics to compare similarity of sentence chunks. The system won the competition in 2016 in the "Gold standard chunk scenario". We have not participated in the "System chunk scenario".

1 Introduction

The goal of the *Interpretable Semantic Textual Similarity* task is to go deeper with the assessment of semantic textual similarity of sentence pairs. It is requested to add an explanatory layer that offers a deeper insight into the sentence similarities. The sentences are split into chunks and the first goal is to find corresponding chunks (with respect to their meanings) among the compared sentences. When the corresponding chunks are known, the chunks are annotated with their similarity scores and their relation types (e.g. equivalent, more specific, etc).

The task follows a pilot task from the preceding SemEval 2015 competition (Agirre et al., 2015). The best performing systems adopted various approaches, (Banjade et al., 2015) relied on hand-crafter rules, (Karumuri et al., 2015) employed a classifier for relation types and they associated each relation with a precomputed similarity score and

(Hänig et al., 2015) extended their word alignment algorithm for the task.

1.1 Math notation

The data consist of sentence pairs $\mathbf{S}_i^a$ and $\mathbf{S}_i^b$, where a denotes the first item of the pair, b denotes the second item of the pair and i indexes the sentences (for simiplicity we further omit i for sentences). We perceive a sentence $\mathbf{S}^a$ to be an ordered set of chunks $\mathbf{CH}_j^a \in \mathbf{S}^a$ and the chunks to be ordered sets of words $w_k \in \mathbf{CH}_j^a$ (and analogically for sentence $\mathbf{S}^b$).

Next we define two functions: $\mathrm{sim}(\mathbf{CH}_i^a, \mathbf{CH}_j^b) \in \{0, 1, 2, 3, 4, 5\}$ for chunk similarity and $\mathrm{rel}(\mathbf{CH}_i^a, \mathbf{CH}_j^b) \in \mathbf{TYPE}$ for chunk relation type.

The possible types are: $\mathbf{TYPE} = \{EQUI, OPPO, SPE1, SPE2, SIMI, REL\}$. These are the main types. All these types can have two modifiers (*FACT*, *POL*). The modifiers are optionally attached to the main types. For example, you can generate *SPE1_FACT*. For more information, please see the annotation guidelines[1].

2 System Overview

2.1 Preprocessing

As a first step of our approach we perform the following text preprocessing:

- *Stopwords removal* – we mark the words found in a predefined list of 32 stopwords.

---

[1] http://alt.qcri.org/
semeval2016/task2/data/uploads/
annotationguidelinesinterpretablests2016v2.
2.pdf

Proceedings of SemEval-2016, pages 803–808,
San Diego, California, June 16-17, 2016. ©2016 Association for Computational Linguistics

- *Special character removal* we remove special characters that violate the tokenization. E.g. in one of the datasets, dots, commas, quotation marks and other punctuation characters were present in tokens.

- *Lowercasing* – we remove casing from the words.

- *Lemmatization* – we find lemmas with the Stanford CoreNLP tool (Manning et al., 2014).

Our preprocessing rather adds new information and does not modify the original information. Thus, the original word and all the generated variants are always available. In this way, we can generate the output file with identical words (including the special characters) from the input. The dataset are already tokenized.

2.2 Chunk Semantic Similarity

The core of our system is based upon computing semantic similarity of sentence chunks. More precisely, we are looking for the best estimation of $\mathrm{sim}(\mathbf{CH}_i^a, \mathbf{CH}_j^b)$. The sim score should describe semantic similarity of a given chunk pair – the higher score the more easily both chunks can be replaced with each other without chaining the meaning of both sentences. The similarity score ranges from 0 to 5, where 0 is the lowest similarity and 5 is the highest similarity. Eg. the sim("a new laptop", "a new notebook") $= 5$ and sim("a new laptop", "an old rock") $= 0$. We use the chunk similarity as a feature in our machine learning approach (Section 3) and as a metric in our unsupervised approach (Section 4).

Our attempts to estimate the sim function are based upon estimating semantic similarity of individual words and compiling them into one number for a given chunk pair. We experiment with Word2Vec (Mikolov et al., 2013) and GloVe (Pennington et al., 2014) for estimating similarity of words. We compile all the word similarities in one number that reflects semantic similarity of whole chunks via the following methods: 1) the *vector composition* method and 2) an adapted method for constructing vectors called *lexical semantic vectors*.

Vector composition requires that the semantics of words is described by vectors. E.g. we have vectors for all words $\vec{m}_i : \forall w_i \in \mathbf{CH}_j^a$ and $\vec{n}_i : \forall w_i \in \mathbf{CH}_k^b$ in two given chunks $\mathbf{CH}_j^a$ and $\mathbf{CH}_k^b$. The vectors for words in each chunk are summed (or averaged) to obtain one vector for each chunk: $\vec{m} = \sum_i (\vec{m}_i)$ and $\vec{n} = \sum_j (\vec{n}_j)$. The vectors are then compared with cosine distance: $\mathrm{sim}(\mathbf{CH}_j^a, \mathbf{CH}_k^b) = \cos(\theta) = \frac{\vec{m} \cdot \vec{n}}{\|\vec{m}\|\|\vec{n}\|}$.

Lexical semantic vectors were originally introduced in (Li et al., 2006). We have made two modifications. We do not weight words with their information content and we use methods for distributional semantics (Word2Vec and GloVe) rather than semantic networks. The modified method is explained here. First of all, we create a combined vocabulary of all unique words from chunks $\mathbf{CH}_k^a$ and $\mathbf{CH}_l^b$: $\mathbf{L} = \mathrm{unique}(\mathbf{CH}_k^a \cup \mathbf{CH}_l^b)$. Then we take all words from vocabulary $\mathbf{L}$: $w_i \in \mathbf{L}$ and look for maximal similarities with words from chunks a and b, respectively. This way we get vectors $\vec{m}$ and $\vec{n}$ containing maximal similarities of chunk words and words from the combined vocabulary:

$$
\begin{aligned}
m_i &= \max_{j:1 \leq j \leq |\mathbf{CH}_k^a|} \mathrm{sim}(w_i, w_j) : \quad \forall w_i \in \mathbf{L} \\
n_i &= \max_{j:1 \leq j \leq |\mathbf{CH}_l^b|} \mathrm{sim}(w_i, w_j) : \quad \forall w_i \in \mathbf{L}
\end{aligned}
\tag{1}
$$

where m_i and n_i are elements of vectors $\vec{m}$ and $\vec{n}$.

In order to obtain similarity of a chunk pair we compare their respective vectors with the cosine similarity similarly to the previous approach. The principle of the method is illustrated by the example in figure 1.

iDF weighting. We assume that some words are more important than others. In order to reflect this assumption, we try to weight the vectors with iDF weighting. We compute the iDF weights on the articles from English wikipedia text data (Wikipedia dump from March 7, 2015).

3 Machine Learning Approach

The main effort of our team was focused on the machine learning approach to the task. We divided the task into to three classification / regression tasks:

sim("a new laptop", "a new notebook"):

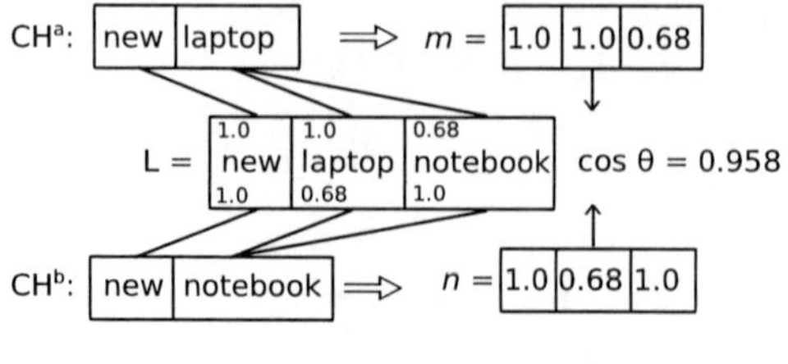

sim("a new laptop", "an old rock"):

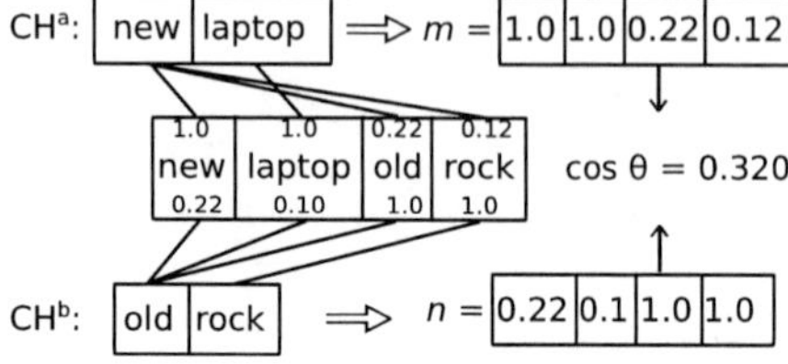

Figure 1: An example of the modified lexical semantic vectors method.

- *Alignment binary classification* – we decide whether two given chunks should be aligned with each other.

- *Score classification / regression* – we experiment with both classification and regression of the chunks similarity score.

- *Type classification* – we classify all aligned pairs of chunks into a predefined set of types – see Section 1.1.

3.1 Classifiers

We experiment with the following classifiers: *Maximum Entropy Classifier* (Berger et al., 1996), *Support Vector Machines Classifier* (Cortes and Vapnik, 1995), *Multilayer perceptron* and *Voted perceptron neural networks* (Freund and Schapire, 1999) and with *Decision / regression tree learning* (Breiman et al., 1984).

We employ the following two frameworks: *Brainy* (Konkol, 2014) and *Weka* (Hall et al., 2009).

3.2 Features

We divide the employed features into four categories: lexical, syntactic, semantic, external.

Lexical features consist of the following features: word base form overlap, word lemma overlap, chunk length difference, word sentence positions difference.

Syntactic features contains closest common parent comparison (we compute the closest common parent of all words for each chunk in the parse tree and retrieve the name of the parent node), parse tree path comparison (we compute the path from the root of the sentence to the chunk). POS (Part Of Speech) count difference (e.g. differences in counts of nouns, adjectives, verbs, etc). POS tagging and syntactic parsing are performed with Stanford CoreNLP (Manning et al., 2014).

Semantic features are described in Section 2.2. Additionally, some members of our team participated in the STS task (task 1) of the SemEval 2016 (Brychcín and Svoboda, 2016) and they annotated the semantic similarity of the whole sentences with their system for us. This score is used as one feature.

External features consist of the WordNet – Lin similarity metric (Lin, 1998) and the paraphrase database (Ganitkevitch et al., 2013) feature.

3.3 Post-processing

The alignment of chunks is generated by the binary classification of all possible chunk pairs. If one chunk is aligned with multiple chunks in the other sentence, these chunks should be merged into one chunk. Also, impossible multiple chunks to multiple chunks alignments are generated in some cases (e.g. two chunks from the first sentence belong a chunk in the second sentence but one of the two chunks from the first sentence belong also to a different chunk in the second sentence). These cases are resolved with few hand crafted rules.

4 Rule-based Approach

We attempt to solve the task with a rule-based approach as well. First, we define the similarity of chunks as described in Section 2.2. The similarity is then used for the chunk alignment. We employ an algorithm inspired by the IBM word model II for machine translation (Brown et al., 1993). We iterate over all chunks from sentence S_a and find the chunk with maximal similarity from sentence S_b. More chunks from sentence S_a can be aligned to one chunk in the sentence S_b. In this way, we obtain N:1 mapping. Then, we do the same with the reversed order of sentences and get the 1:M mapping. Then, we compare the mappings and take the one with the highest overall similarity. In this way, it is ensured that we generate only valid mappings (unlike in the previous case of machine learning – see Section 3.3).

The relation types are then determined by an extremely simple algorithm:

- If the similarity is 5, then the relation type is *EQUI*.

- If the similarity is 4 or 3 and chunks contain the same amount of words, then the relation is *SIMI*.

- If the similarity is 4 or 3, then chunk with more words is more specific.

- If the similarity is 2 or 1, then the relation is *SIMI*.

- If the similarity is 0, then the relation type is *NOALI*.

5 Results

5.1 Experimental setup

Machine learning approach We employ the following classifiers and classification frameworks:

- *Alignment binary classification* – Voted perceptron (Weka).

- *Score classification* – Maximum entropy (Brainy).

- *Type classification* – Support vector machines (Brainy).

These classifiers perform best on the evaluation datasets.

We achieved the best results for estimating chunk similarity with Word2Vec and the modified lexical semantic vectors – see Section 2.2.

We experimented with reduced feature set (word overlap, word positions difference, POS tags difference, semantic similarity, global semantic similarity, paraphrase database) – run 1 and with all features – run 3. The run 1 contains the optimal combination of features. Since this combination is established on evaluation datasets it does not need to be optimal for the test datasets. To increase our chances in the

completion, we also run the system with all features – run 3.

We use the provided annotated evaluation dataset (*Images, Headlines, Answer students*) for training the models. We train three models, each for one dataset. For development, we use the 10-fold cross-validation. For final test runs, we train the three models on evaluation datasets and run the system on the corresponding test datasets (e.g. *Images* evaluation dataset based model is used to annotate *Images* test data). We do not neither modify the original datasets nor annotate any additional data.

Rule-based approach There are little options in this approach. Again, we have achieved the best results for estimating chunk similarity with Word2Vec and the modified lexical semantic vectors – see Section 2.2. We set the threshold for the similarity score to 2.5. All lower values are set to 0. This is the run 2.

Individual setting for different dataset We restrained from setting individual configurations for different datasets. The setup is completely identical for all datasets.

5.2 Results

In this section, we summarize the official results for the SemEval 2016 competition – see table 1. The results are calculated for the following dataset: *Headlines, Images* and *Answer students*. The results show F1 scores for chunk alignment (*Ali*), determination of the relation type (*Type*), chunk similarity score (*Score*) and combination of relation type and score similarity (*T+S*). The bold numbers are the overall best scores. We participated only in the gold standard chunk scenario.

The results clearly show that the unsupervised run 2 perform much worse than the supervised runs 1 and 3. We expected that. However, it is worth of noticing that the unsupervised alignment algorithm inspired by machine translation alignment placed quite well. In fact, it is newer looses more than 3% from the best alignment score in all datasets. The overall rank of the run 2 places in the top half among all system with exception of the *answer student* dataset. The poor performance of the run 2 on this dataset is most likely caused by the fact that the hand-crafted rules were prepared for the *images* and

Run	Ali	Type	Score	T+S	Rank
	Images dataset (756 sentence pairs)				
3	0.8922	**0.6867**	0.8408	**0.6708**	1
1	**0.8937**	0.6829	0.8397	0.6672	2
2	0.8713	0.6346	0.8083	0.6206	6
	Headlines dataset (750 sentence pairs)				
3	0.8987	0.6412	**0.8382**	0.6296	6
1	0.8979	0.6319	0.8346	0.6212	7
2	0.8897	0.6146	0.815	0.6013	8
	Answer students dataset (330 sentence pairs)				
1	0.8644	0.6299	0.8089	0.6248	3
3	0.8588	0.6167	0.8038	0.6114	5
2	0.8752	0.4806	0.7826	0.4748	17
	Overall results (mean)				
1	0.6672	0.6212	0.6248	0.6377	1
3	**0.6708**	0.6296	0.6114	0.6373	2
2	0.6206	0.6013	0.4748	0.5656	12

Table 1: Official system evaluation.

headlines datasets and they are clearly not applicable on the *answer student* which is substantially different.

The runs 1 and 3 perform very similarly. The optimized feature set of the run 1 helps especially in the *answer student* dataset. However, the differences between these runs are too small and they can be caused by chance. It is worth of noticing that the run 1 is not the best one in any of the datasets and it still wins in the overall results table. The reason is that it provides the most consistent results among all other runs of all systems in the competition.

In order to provide additional information about the features effectiveness, we have evaluated them on the final test datasets. In many cases, the obtained results are not conclusive. On some datasets, the features help slightly on others they even decrease the performance. However, the following three features have significant influence on the final results: modified lexical semantic vectors (+3% of the mean of T+S F1 scores), shared words (+2%), POS tags difference (+2%). The modified lexical semantic vectors method performed better than vector composition by 1% for the machine learning approach and by 2% for the rule-based approach in average. By optimizing the feature set, we were able to increase the mean score to 0.6484 of T+S F1 measure.

6 Conclusion

The machine learning approach with combination of methods for the distributional semantics (Word2Vec and GloVe) proved to be very capable of solving the advanced task of Interpretable Semantic Textual Similarity. We have chosen not to tune the system for individual datasets but to tune it for the task as a whole. The modified lexical semantic vectors approach seems to be an attractive alternative to the more traditional vector composition.

Acknowledgments

This publication was supported by the project LO1506 of the Czech Ministry of Education, Youth and Sports and by Grant No. SGS-2016-018 Data and Software Engineering for Advanced Applications. Computational resources were provided by the CESNET LM2015042 and the CERIT Scientific Cloud LM2015085, provided under the programme "Projects of Large Research, Development, and Innovations Infrastructures".

References

Eneko Agirre, Carmen Banea, Claire Cardie, Daniel Cer, Mona Diab, Aitor Gonzalez-Agirre, Weiwei Guo, Inigo Lopez-Gazpio, Montse Maritxalar, Rada Mihalcea, German Rigau, Larraitz Uria, and Janyce Wiebe. 2015. Semeval-2015 task 2: Semantic textual similarity, english, spanish and pilot on interpretability. In *Proceedings of the 9th International Workshop on Semantic Evaluation (SemEval 2015)*, pages 252–263, Denver, Colorado, June. Association for Computational Linguistics.

Rajendra Banjade, Nobal Bikram Niraula, Nabin Maharjan, Vasile Rus, Dan Stefanescu, Mihai Lintean, and Dipesh Gautam. 2015. Nerosim: A system for measuring and interpreting semantic textual similarity. In *Proceedings of the 9th International Workshop on Semantic Evaluation (SemEval 2015)*, pages 164–171, Denver, Colorado, June. Association for Computational Linguistics.

Adam L. Berger, Vincent J. Della Pietra, and Stephen A. Della Pietra. 1996. A maximum entropy approach to natural language processing. *Computational Linguistics*, 22(1):39–71, March.

Leo Breiman, Jerome Friedman, Richard A. Olshen, and Charles Stone. 1984. *Classification and Regression Trees*. Wadsworth and Brooks, Monterey, CA.

Peter F. Brown, Vincent J. Della Pietra, Stephen A. Della Pietra, and Robert L. Mercer. 1993. The mathematics of statistical machine translation: Parameter estimation. *Computational Linguistics*, 19(2):263–311, June.

Tomáš Brychcín and Lukáš Svoboda. 2016. Uwb at semeval-2016 task 1: Semantic textual similarity using lexical, syntactic, and semantic information. In *Proceedings of the 10th International Workshop on Semantic Evaluation (SemEval 2016)*, San Diego, California, June.

Corinna Cortes and Vladimir Vapnik. 1995. Support-vector networks. *Mach. Learn.*, 20(3):273–297, September.

Yoav Freund and Robert E. Schapire. 1999. Large margin classification using the perceptron algorithm. *Machine Learning*, 37(3):277–296, December.

Juri Ganitkevitch, Benjamin Van Durme, and Chris Callison-Burch. 2013. PPDB: The paraphrase database. In *Proceedings of NAACL-HLT*, pages 758–764, Atlanta, Georgia, June. Association for Computational Linguistics.

Mark Hall, Eibe Frank, Geoffrey Holmes, Bernhard Pfahringer, Peter Reutemann, and Ian H. Witten. 2009. The weka data mining software: An update. *SIGKDD Explorations Newsletter*, 11(1):10–18, November.

Christian Hänig, Robert Remus, and Xose de la Puente. 2015. Exb themis: Extensive feature extraction from word alignments for semantic textual similarity. In *Proceedings of the 9th International Workshop on Semantic Evaluation (SemEval 2015)*, pages 264–268, Denver, Colorado, June. Association for Computational Linguistics.

Sakethram Karumuri, Viswanadh Kumar Reddy Vuggumudi, and Sai Charan Raj Chitirala. 2015. Umduluthblueteam: Svcsts - a multilingual and chunk level semantic similarity system. In *Proceedings of the 9th International Workshop on Semantic Evaluation (SemEval 2015)*, pages 107–110, Denver, Colorado, June. Association for Computational Linguistics.

Michal Konkol. 2014. Brainy: A machine learning library. In Leszek Rutkowski, Marcin Korytkowski, Rafa Scherer, Ryszard Tadeusiewicz, Lotfi A. Zadeh, and Jacek M. Zurada, editors, *Artificial Intelligence and Soft Computing*, volume 8468 of *Lecture Notes in Computer Science*, pages 490–499. Springer International Publishing.

Yuhua Li, David McLean, Zuhair A. Bandar, James D. O'Shea, and Keeley Crockett. 2006. Sentence similarity based on semantic nets and corpus statistics. *IEEE Trans. on Knowl. and Data Eng.*, 18(8):1138–1150, August.

Dekang Lin. 1998. Extracting collocations from text corpora. In *First Workshop on Computational Terminology*.

Christopher D. Manning, Mihai Surdeanu, John Bauer, Jenny Finkel, Steven J. Bethard, and David McClosky. 2014. The Stanford CoreNLP natural language processing toolkit. In *Proceedings of 52nd Annual Meeting of the Association for Computational Linguistics: System Demonstrations*, pages 55–60.

Tomas Mikolov, Kai Chen, Greg Corrado, and Jeffrey Dean. 2013. Efficient estimation of word representations in vector space. *CoRR*, abs/1301.3781.

Jeffrey Pennington, Richard Socher, and Christopher Manning. 2014. Glove: Global vectors for word representation. In *Proceedings of the 2014 Conference on Empirical Methods in Natural Language Processing (EMNLP)*, pages 1532–1543. Association for Computational Linguistics.

DTSim at SemEval-2016 Task 2: Interpreting Similarity of Texts Based on Automated Chunking, Chunk Alignment and Semantic Relation Prediction

Rajendra Banjade,* **Nabin Maharjan***, **Nobal B. Niraula, Vasile Rus**
Department of Computer Science / Institute for Intelligent Systems
The University of Memphis
Memphis, TN, USA
{rbanjade, nmharjan, nbnraula, vrus}@memphis.edu

Abstract

In this paper we describe our system (DTSim) submitted at SemEval-2016 Task 2: Interpretable Semantic Textual Similarity (iSTS). We participated in both gold chunks category (texts chunked by human experts and provided by the task organizers) and system chunks category (participants had to automatically chunk the input texts). We developed a Conditional Random Fields based chunker and applied rules blended with semantic similarity methods in order to predict chunk alignments, alignment types and similarity scores. Our system obtained F1 score up to 0.648 in predicting the chunk alignment types and scores together and was one of the top performing systems overall.

1 Introduction

Measuring the semantic similarity of texts is to quantify the degree of semantic similarity between a given pair of texts, such as two words or two sentences (Rus et al., 2008; Agirre et al., 2015). For example, a similarity score of 0 means that the texts are not similar at all and 5 means that they have same meaning. While useful, such quantitative or even qualitative assessments are hard to interpret because they do not provide details, i.e. they do not explain or justify why the similarity score was assigned high or low. One way to provide an explanatory layer to text similarity assessment methods is to align chunks between texts and assigning semantic relation to each alignment. To this end, Brockett (2007) and Rus et al. (2012) produced datasets

where corresponding words (or multiword expressions) were aligned and in the latter case their semantic relations were explicitly labeled

In interpretable Semantic Textual Similarity (iSTS) tasks (Agirre et al., 2016), participants had first to identify the chunks in each sentence (sys chunks) or use the chunks given by the task organizers (gold chunks), and then, align chunks across the two sentences indicating the semantic relation and similarity score of each alignment. The chunk alignment types were EQUI (semantically equivalent), OPPO (opposite in meaning), SPE (one chunk is more specific than other), SIMI (similar meanings, but not EQUI, OPPO, SPE), REL (related meanings, but not SIMI, EQUI, OPPO, SPE), and NOALI (has no corresponding chunk in the other sentence). The relatedness/similarity scores were assigned in the range of 0 to 5.

A pilot on iSTS task was organized in 2015 (Agirre et al., 2015). In 2016, the iSTS allowed many-to-many chunk alignment while in the pilot task of 2015 they only allowed one-to-one or no alignment. Also, a new dataset consisting of student answers given to a tutoring system was added in 2016. For further details about the task, please see Agirre et al. (2016).

We participated in both categories: system chunks and gold chunks. Our system first preprocesses texts, creates chunks (in sys chunks category) using our own chunking tool, and performs alignments and labels them with semantic relations and similarity scores. In this paper, we describe our system DTSim[1] and the submitted three different runs in the

---

* These authors contributed equally to this work

[1] Available for download from http://semanticsimilarity.org

Proceedings of SemEval-2016, pages 809–813,
San Diego, California, June 16-17, 2016. ©2016 Association for Computational Linguistics

shared task. Our system was one of the top perform-ing systems.

2   Preprocessing

Hyphens were replaced with whitespaces if they were not composite words (e.g. video-gamed). Also, the words starting with co-, pre-, meta-, multi-, re-, pro-, al-, anti-, ex-, and non- were left in-tact. Then, the texts were tokenized, lemmatized, POS-tagged and annotated with Named Entity (NE) tags using Stanford CoreNLP Toolkit (Manning et al., 2014). We also marked each word as whether it was a stop word. In the system chunks category, we had plain texts and we created chunks using our own Conditional Random Fields (CRF) based chunking tool (see Section 3). We normalized texts using map-ping data. For example, *pct* and *%* were changed to *percent*. These preprocessing steps were performed for both gold chunks and system chunks category.

In student-answers dataset which consists of stu-dent answers given to a computer based logic tu-tor (Agirre et al., 2016), we replaced symbol *A/B/C* with *bulb A/B/C*. Similarly, *X/Y/Z* was replaced by *switch X/Y/Z*. We used this domain knowledge based on the notes found in student-answers training data description file.

3   Chunking

We developed a CRF based chunker[2] using both CoNLL-2000 shared task training and test data[3]. This data consists of a Wall Street Journal corpus: sections 15-18 as training data (211727 tokens) and section 20 as test data (47377 tokens). We gener-ated shallow parsing features such as previous and next words from current word, current word itself, current word POS tag, previous and next word POS tags and their different combinations as described in Tjong Kim Sang and Buchholz (2000). We used CRF++ tool[4] to build the CRF models.

Furthermore, we analyzed its output (i.e. chunks) and added the following rules in the system to merge some of the chunks, resulting in chunks that make more sense and are consistent with iSTS gold chunks.

---

[2]Our chunker is available at http://semanticsimilarity.org
[3]http://www.cnts.ua.ac.be/conll2000/chunking/
[4]https://taku910.github.io/crfpp/

DataSet	Chunker	CL	SL
Training data			
Headlines	O-NLP	53.74	13.49
	EO-NLP	80.67	59.39
	CRF	**82.60**	**62.56**
Image	O-NLP	52.35	5.06
	EO-NLP	89.13	72.66
	CRF	**89.74**	**74.13**
Test data			
Headlines	O-NLP	53.88	16.13
	EO-NLP	80.96	60.18
	CRF	**83.32**	**63.23**
Image	O-NLP	52.71	5.33
	EO-NLP	89.30	72.13
	CRF	**90.29**	**74.93**

Table 1: Comparison of chunking accuracies of the various chunkers at chunk level (CL) and at sentence level (SL) with iSTS 2015 gold data.

(a) PP + NP => PP
(b) VP + PRT => VP
(c) NP + CC + NP => NP

For example, it merges chunks [on] and [Friday] to form single PP chunk [on Friday] using rule (a).

We evaluated the chunking accuracy of the CRF chunker by comparing its output against the gold chunks of iSTS 2015 data: the training and test data sets each consist of 375 pairs of Images anno-tation data and 378 pairs of Headlines texts. This chunker yielded the highest average accuracies on both the training and test datasets compared to other chunkers which are described next. The accuracies on the training dataset were 86.20% and 68.34% at chunk level and sentence level respectively. For the test dataset, the accuracies were 86.81% and 69% at chunk and sentence level, respectively. The results are presented in Table 1.

We also chunked the input texts using the Open-NLP chunking tool (O-NLP). The average (of Im-ages and Headlines data) accuracies were 53.04% at chunk level and a modest 9.27% at sentence level for the training dataset. It yielded similar results on test data. We extended Open-NLP chunker (EO-NLP) using the rules described before. The results were improved and resulted in 84.% chunk level and 66.02% sentence level average accuracies on the training dataset, respectively. The accuracy on the test data was comparable at 85.13% chunk level and 66.15% at sentence level. However, the results of our CRF based chunker were superior in all cases.

4 Chunk Alignment System

For a given sentence pair, the chunks of the first sentence were mapped to those from the second by assigning different semantic relations and scores based on a set of rules, similarity functions, and lookup resources. Before preforming alignments, we preprocessed texts as described in Section 2.

We built upon a previous system called NeRoSim (Banjade et al., 2015). The limitation of their system was that the alignments were restricted to 1:1. We modified it to support many to many alignments as well. Also, the NeRoSim system was able to process only gold chunks (i.e., chunks provided by the organizers). Now, the system can take input in the form of plain texts as well and create chunks on the fly. In addition to the chunking feature described in Section 3, the updates made to the systems are described below.

Many-to-Many Alignments:
MULTI1: If there is any ALIC chunk (i.e., chunk which does not have any corresponding chunk in the other sentence because of the 1:1 alignment restriction) in sentence A whose content words are subsumed by the content words of any already aligned chunk (C) in another sentence B, merge ALIC chunk with the chunk in A paired with C. If the content words of merged chunk and those of C are same/equal, realign chunk C with merged chunk as EQUI and update the score to 5.0.
For example:
// [Iran] [hopes] [nuclear talks] [. . .].
// [Iran Nuclear Talks] [spur] [. . .].
Step 1:
nuclear talks <=> Iran Nuclear Talks // SPE2
Iran <=> //ALIC
Step2:
Iran nuclear talks <=> Iran Nuclear Talks // EQUI

MULTI2: In *MULTI1*, if all the content words of merged chunk and those of C are not matching

completely, then realign chunk C with merged chunk but keep the previous alignment type and score.

Furthermore, we have expanded the rules for SIMI and EQUI.
EQx: If unmatched words are morphological inflections of each other and all other words in the chunks are already matched, assign the EQUI relation.
E.g. *Korean Air <=> Air Korea*
SIMIx: If nouns are matching but not the adjective or vice-versa, assign SIMI label.
E.g. *red carpet <=> brown carpet*

Runs
R1: We included many-to-many alignment in NeRoSim (i.e., MULTI1 and MULTI2 were added).
R2: Same as R1 in alignment but the alignment scores were assigned based on the average scores for each alignment type in the full training data.
R3: Same as R2 but SIMIx and EQx rules added.

5 Results

The test data consisted of 1,094 sentence pairs which included texts from headlines (375), image annotations (375), and student-answers (344). The results (F1 scores)[5] on test datasets are presented in Table 2 and Table 3. Further details about the test data and the evaluation metrics can be found in Agirre et al. (2016).

Table 2 presents the results in terms of F1 scores on test set with gold chunks. We can see that the alignment scores are higher compared to the baseline system and are very close to the best results from all submissions in those categories. However, the alignment type score in each case is relatively lower than the alignment-only score and it ultimately impacted the F1 score calculated for type and score together (i.e. T+S).

Similar to Table 2, the Table 3 presents the results on the test set but this time with system chunks. In image and headlines data, our system obtained the best results. However, following the same pattern as in gold chunk results, the F1 scores for alignments

---

[5]Based on (Melamed, 1998) which was proposed in the context of alignment for Machine Translation.

System	A	T	S	T+S
Headlines				
Baseline	0.8462	0.5462	0.7610	0.5461
R1	0.9072	0.6650	0.8187	0.6385
R2	0.9072	0.6650	0.836	**0.6487**
R3	0.9072	0.6583	0.8329	0.6405
Max	0.9278	0.7031	0.8382	0.6960
Image				
Baseline	0.8556	0.4799	0.7456	0.4799
R1	0.8766	0.6530	0.7955	0.6238
R2	0.8766	0.6530	0.8144	0.6362
R3	0.8766	0.6675	0.8156	**0.6483**
Max	0.9077	0.6867	0.8552	0.6708
Student-answers				
Baseline	0.8203	0.5566	0.7464	0.5566
R1	0.8584	0.5552	0.7686	0.5432
R2	0.8584	0.5552	0.7809	**0.5458**
R3	0.8614	0.5468	0.7798	0.5374
Max	0.8922	0.6511	0.8433	0.6385

Table 2: F1 scores on test data with gold chunks. A, T and S refer to Alignment, Type, and Score, respectively. Max score is the best score for each metric given by any of the participating systems in the shared task including the system submitted by the team involved in organizing the task.

System	A	T	S	T+S
Headlines				
Baseline	0.6486	0.4379	0.5912	0.4379
R1	0.8366	0.5605	0.7394	0.5384
R2	0.8366	0.5605	0.7595	**0.5467**
R3	0.8376	0.5595	0.7586	0.5446
Max	0.8366	0.5605	0.7595	0.5467
Image				
Baseline	0.7127	0.4043	0.6251	0.4043
R1	0.8429	0.6148	0.7591	0.5870
R2	0.8429	0.6148	0.7806	0.5990
R3	0.8429	0.6276	0.7813	**0.6095**
Max	0.8557	0.6276	0.7961	0.6095
Student-answers				
Baseline	0.6188	0.4431	0.5702	0.4431
R1	0.8165	0.5157	0.7248	0.5049
R2	0.8165	0.5157	0.7367	**0.5074**
R3	0.8181	0.5112	0.7360	0.5029
Max	0.8166	0.5651	0.7589	0.5547

Table 3: Results on test data with system chunks.

are high but the scores for predicting the alignment types are relatively lower. It indicates that the systems overall performance will be improved greatly if improvements can be made in predicting the alignment types. Also, the scores for student-answers are lower than headlines and image texts and it requires further analysis to fully understand why this is the case. One of the reasons might be that we did not use this dataset while developing the system and no prior information about such dataset was modeled. Additionally, more errors might have been introduced in our NLP pipeline as the texts in this dataset were not standard written texts.

In addition to the difficulty of the task of aligning the chunks and assigning relation types, we found some discrepancies in the annotation which we think induced some errors. For example, *on a sofa <=> on a blue sofa* (#65 in image data), the human annotated label is SIMI but arguably the SPE2 label best describes the relation. Similarly, *in a field <=> in a green field* (#693 in image data), the SPE1 label has

been found in the training set but it should be SPE2. In another example (#193 in image data), *A young boy <=> A young blonde girl* has been assigned a label SPE2 in the training data. Though the second chunk gives some additional details, the question is whether we should really compare them (and decide which one is more specific) because these two chunks are referring to different objects and therefore it sounds more like comparing apples and oranges.

6 Conclusion

This paper presented the system DTSim and three different runs submitted in SemEval 2016 Shared Task on Interpretable Textual Semantic Similarity (iSTS). We described our chunking tool and results on gold chunks as well as on system chunks categories. Our system was one of the best systems submitted in the shared task. However, there is room for improvement particularly on assigning alignment labels which we intend to address in future work. Furthermore, the annotated dataset is now quite big and it will certainly be useful in applying alternative approaches to predict chunk alignments and alignment types.

References

Eneko Agirre, Carmen Baneab, Claire Cardiec, Daniel Cerd, Mona Diabe, Aitor Gonzalez-Agirrea, Weiwei Guof, Inigo Lopez-Gazpioa, Montse Maritxalara, Rada Mihalceab, et al. 2015. Semeval-2015 task 2: Semantic textual similarity, english, spanish and pilot on interpretability. In *Proceedings of the 9th international workshop on semantic evaluation (SemEval 2015)*, pages 252–263.

Eneko Agirre, Aitor Gonzalez-Agirre, (Iñigo) Lopez-Gazpio, Montse Maritxalar, German Rigau, and Larraitz Uria. 2016. Semeval-2016 task 2: Interpretable semantic textual similarity. In *Proceedings of the 10th International Workshop on Semantic Evaluation (SemEval 2016)*, San Diego, California, June.

Rajendra Banjade, Nobal B Niraula, Nabin Maharjan, Vasile Rus, Dan Stefanescu, Mihai Lintean, and Dipesh Gautam. 2015. Nerosim: A system for measuring and interpreting semantic textual similarity. *SemEval-2015*, page 164.

Chris Brockett. 2007. Aligning the rte 2006 corpus. *Microsoft Research*.

Christopher D Manning, Mihai Surdeanu, John Bauer, Jenny Rose Finkel, Steven Bethard, and David McClosky. 2014. The stanford corenlp natural language processing toolkit. In *ACL (System Demonstrations)*, pages 55–60.

I Dan Melamed. 1998. Manual annotation of translational equivalence: The blinker project. *arXiv preprint cmp-lg/9805005*.

Vasile Rus, Philip M McCarthy, Mihai C Lintean, Danielle S McNamara, and Arthur C Graesser. 2008. Paraphrase identification with lexico-syntactic graph subsumption. In *FLAIRS conference*, pages 201–206.

Vasile Rus, Mihai Lintean, Cristian Moldovan, William Baggett, Nobal Niraula, and Brent Morgan. 2012. The similar corpus: A resource to foster the qualitative understanding of semantic similarity of texts. In *Semantic Relations II: Enhancing Resources and Applications, The 8th Language Resources and Evaluation Conference (LREC 2012), May*, pages 23–25.

Erik F Tjong Kim Sang and Sabine Buchholz. 2000. Introduction to the conll-2000 shared task: Chunking. In *Proceedings of the 2nd workshop on Learning language in logic and the 4th conference on Computational natural language learning-Volume 7*, pages 127–132. Association for Computational Linguistics.

UH-PRHLT at SemEval-2016 Task 3:
Combining Lexical and Semantic-based Features for
Community Question Answering

Marc Franco-Salvador[1], **Sudipta Kar**[2], **Thamar Solorio**[2], and **Paolo Rosso**[1]

[1] Pattern Recognition and Human Language Technology (PRHLT) research center
Universitat Politècnica de València, Spain
[2] Department of Computer Science
University of Houston, United States
`mfranco@prhlt.upv.es, skar3@uh.edu,`
`tsolorio@uh.edu, prosso@prhlt.upv.es`

Abstract

In this work we describe the system built for the three English subtasks of the SemEval 2016 Task 3 by the Department of Computer Science of the University of Houston (UH) and the Pattern Recognition and Human Language Technology (PRHLT) research center - Universitat Politècnica de València: UH-PRHLT. Our system represents instances by using both lexical and semantic-based similarity measures between text pairs. Our semantic features include the use of distributed representations of words, knowledge graphs generated with the BabelNet multilingual semantic network, and the FrameNet lexical database. Experimental results outperform the random and Google search engine baselines in the three English subtasks. Our approach obtained the highest results of subtask B compared to the other task participants.

1 Introduction

The key role that the Internet plays today for our society benefited the dawn of thousands of new Web social activities. Among those, forums emerged with special relevance following the paradigm of the Community Question Answering (CQA). These type of social networks allow people to post a question to other users of that community. The usage is simple, without much restrictions, and infrequently moderated. The popularity of CQA is a strong indicator that users receive some good and valuable answers.

However, there are several issues related to that type of community. First is the large amount of answers received that makes it difficult and time-consuming for users to search and distinguish the good ones. This is exacerbated with the amount of noise that these questions contain. It is not uncommon to have wrong or misguiding answers that produce more unrelated answers, discussions and sub-threads. Finally, there is a lot of redundancy, questions may be repeated or closely related to previously asked questions.

Details of the SemEval 2016 Task 3 on CQA can be found in the overview paper (Nakov et al., 2016). In this work we evaluate the three English-related Task 3 subtasks on CQA. We first represent each instance to rank — question versus (vs.) comments, question vs. related questions, or question vs. comments of related questions — with a set of similarities computed at two different levels: lexical and semantic. This representation allows us to estimate the relatedness between text pairs in terms of what is explicitly stated and what it means. Our lexical similarities employ representations such as word and character n-grams, and bag-of-words (BOW). The semantic similarities include the use of distributed word bidirectional alignments, distributed representations of text, knowledge graphs, and frames from the FrameNet lexical database (Baker et al., 1998). This type of dual representations have been successfully employed for question answering by the highest performing system in the previous edition of this Se-

Proceedings of SemEval-2016, pages 814–821,
San Diego, California, June 16-17, 2016. ©2016 Association for Computational Linguistics

mEval task (Tran et al., 2015). Other Natural Language Processing (NLP) tasks such as cross-language document retrieval and categorization also benefited from similar representations (Franco-Salvador et al., 2014). In this task, if the question or comment includes multiple text fields, e.g. body and subject, similarities are estimated using all possible combinations (see Section 3.2). Finally, the ranking of instances is performed using a state-of-the-art machine-learned ranking algorithm: SVM$_{rank}$.

2   Related Work

Automatic question answering has been a popular interest of research in NLP from the beginning of the Internet to more recently where voice interfaces have been incorporated (Rosso et al., 2012). The use of BOW representations allowed to correctly answer 60% of the questions of the first large-scale question answering evaluation at the TREC-8 Question Answering track (Voorhees, 1999). More complex systems used inference rules to connect expressions between questions and answers (Lin and Pantel, 2001). Similarly, Ravichandran and Hovy (2002) employed bootstrapping to generate surface text patterns in order to successfully answer questions. Other works such as Buscaldi et al. (2010) are based on the redundancy of n-grams in order to find one or more text fragments that include tokens of the original question and the answer. Jeon et al. (2005) studied the semantic relatedness between texts for question answering. They used translation obfuscation to paraphrase the text and to detect which terms are closer in context. Probabilistic topic models have been also useful for detecting the semantics in this task. Celikyilmaz et al. (2010) used Latent Dirichlet Allocation (LDA) (Blei et al., 2003) for representing questions by means of latent topics.

The previous edition of the SemEval CQA task included two English subtasks (Nakov et al., 2015). The first one was focused on classifying answers as *good, bad,* or *potentially relevant* with respect to one question. The second subtask answered a question with *yes, no,* or *unsure* based on the list of all answers. In addition, the first subtask was also available in Arabic. Several teams experimented with complex solutions that included meta-learning, external resources, and linguistic features such as syntactic relations and distributed word representations. Similarly to our work, the highest performing approach employed a combination of lexical and semantic-based similarity measures (Tran et al., 2015). Its semantic features included the use of probabilistic topic models, translation obfuscation-based alignments, and pre-computed distributed representations of words both generated with the word2vec[1] and GloVe[2] toolkits. Their lexical features included BOW, word alignments, and noun matching. They employed a regression model for classification. Another interesting approach, Hou et al. (2015), included textual features — word lengths and punctuation — in addition to syntactical-based features — Part-of-Speech (PoS) tags.

In this work we aim at differentiating from the other approaches by enhancing our ranking model with new similarity measures. These include the use of knowledge graphs obtained using the largest multilingual semantic network — BabelNet — frames from the FrameNet lexical database, and bidirectional distributed word alignments.

3   Lexical and Semantic-based Community Question Answering

In this section we detailed the system that we designed for this CQA task. First in Section 3.1 we described our set of lexical features and semantic-based ones. Next, in Section 3.2 we detail the specific adaptation that we employed for each subtask and the ranking algorithm that we used. We note that all our features are similarity scores obtained with different text similarity measures. More details and examples can be found in their respective papers.

3.1   Feature Description

Our system exploits both the verbatim and the contextual similarities between texts, i.e., questions and comments. In Section 3.1.1 we

---

[1] https://code.google.com/archive/p/word2vec/
[2] http://nlp.stanford.edu/projects/glove/

detailed our lexical and in Section 3.1.2 our semantic-based features.

3.1.1 Lexical Features

The lexical features that we employed are the following:

- **Cosine Similarity.** We used cosine similarity to measure lexical similarity between two text snippets. We calculated cosine similarity based on word n-grams(n=1,2), character 3-grams and tf-idf (Salton and McGill, 1986) scores of words.

- **Word Overlap.** We used the count of common words between two texts. This count was normalized by the length.

- **Noun Overlap.** We used NLTK[3] to part-of-speech tag the text and computed the normalized count of overlapping nouns in two texts as a similarity measure.

- **N-gram Overlap.** We computed the normalized count of common n-grams(n=1,2,3) between two texts.

3.1.2 Semantic Features

The semantic features that we employed are the following:

- **Distributed representations of texts.** We used the continuous Skip-gram model (Mikolov et al., 2013) of the word2vec toolkit to generate distributed representations of the words of the complete English Wikipedia.[4] Next, for each text, e.g. question or comment, we averaged its word vectors in order to have a single representation of its content as this setting has shown good results in other NLP tasks (e.g. for language variety identification (Franco-Salvador et al., 2015a) and discriminating similar languages (Franco-Salvador et al., 2015b)). Finally, the similarity between texts, e.g. question vs. comment, is estimated using the cosine similarity.

- **Distributed word alignments.** The use of word alignment strategies has been employed in the past for textual semantic relatedness (Hassan and Mihalcea, 2011). Tran et al. (2015) employed distributed representations to align the words of the question with the words of the comment. A more recent work introduced the Continuous Word Alignment-based Similarity Analysis (CWASA) (Franco-Salvador et al., 2016a). CWASA uses distributed representations to measure the similarity by double-direction aligning words of texts. In this work we selected as feature the similarity provided by CWASA between questions and comments.

- **Knowledge graphs.** A knowledge graph is a labeled, weighted, and directed graph that expands and relates the concepts belonging to a text. Knowledge Graph Analysis (KGA) (Franco-Salvador et al., 2016b) measures semantic relatedness between texts by means of their knowledge graphs. In this work we used the Babel-Net (Navigli and Ponzetto, 2012) multilingual semantic network to generate knowledge graphs from questions and comments, and measured their similarity using KGA.

- **Common frames.** We used Framenet (Baker et al., 1998) to extract the frames associated with the lexical items in the text. For each frame present in the text, we calculated the common lexical items between sentences associated with this frame. The goal is to allow inference of similarity at the level of semantic roles.

As additional feature, for Subtasks A and C we also used the ranking provided by the Google search engine for the questions related to the original questions.

3.2 Data Representation and Ranking

Due to the representation of questions — composed by *subject* and *body* fields — and answers — a *comment* field — we adapted our system for the different English subtasks:

---

[3]http://www.nltk.org/

[4]We used 200-dimensional vectors, context windows of size 10, and 20 negative words for each sample.

- **Subtask A (question-comment similarity ranking):** we used the aforementioned similarity-based features at three levels: question subject vs. comment, question body vs. comment, and full question vs. comment.

- **Subtask B (question-related question similarity ranking):** for this subtask we measured the similarities at body, subject, and full question level.

- **Subtask C (question-external comment similarity ranking):** we employed all the features of Subtasks A and B, plus the similarities of the original question — subject, body, and full levels — with the related question comments.

In order to rank the questions and comments, we selected a variant of Support Vector Machines (SVM) (Hearst et al., 1998) optimized for ranking problems: SVM_{rank} (Joachims, 2002). In our evaluation of Section 4, we call our system as the combination of the acronyms of our member institutions: UH-PRHLT.

Preproscessing steps included stopword removal, lemmatization, and stemming. However, for the distributed representation and knowledge graph-based features we did not employ stemming. These decisions were motivated for performance reasons during our prototyping.

Note that each subtask allows to submit three runs per team: primary, contrastive 1 (contr. 1), and contrastive 2 (contr. 2). We used a linear kernel and optimized the cost factor parameter using Bayesian optimization[5] (Snoek, 2013). Our three runs differ only in the value for that parameter and correspond with the three best — and considerably distant — values. In addition to the ranking, the task requires also to provide with a label for each instance that reflects if the question or comment is relevant to the compared question. For each subtask we optimized a threshold to determine the relevance of each instance that is based on our predicted relevance ranking. In other words, we binarize our ranking.

---

[5]We used the Spearmint toolkit: `https://github.com/HIPS/Spearmint`

4 Evaluation

This section presents the evaluation of the SemEval 2016 Task 3 on CQA. Details about this task, the datasets, and the three subtasks can be found in the task overview (Nakov et al., 2016). Note that for our system we did not use data from SemEval 2015 CQA as we did not observe gains in performance.

We compared the results of our approach with those provided by the random baseline and the Google search engine when ranking the questions and comments.[6] The official measure of the task is the Mean Average Precision (MAP), but we included also two alternative ranking measures: Average Recall (AvgRec) and Mean Reciprocal Rank (MRR). In addition, we included four classification measures: Accuracy (acc.), Precision (P), Recall (R), and F1-measure (F1).

4.1 Results and Discussion

The best results per partition and subtask are highlighted in bold. In addition, we always refer to the run with the highest performance. Finally, our percentage comparisons use always absolute values. We can see the results of Subtask A (question-comment similarity ranking) in Table 1. In terms of ranking measures, our system outperformed both the random and the search engine baseline. Using the development set, we observed a MAP improvement of 9.4% compared with the results obtained by the search engine. We can see similar differences with respect to the other two ranking measures. Classification results are also superior. We obtain improvements in accuracy and F1 of 24.9% and 5.2% respectively. These results manifest the potential of the selected lexical and semantic-based features for this subtask.

Similar to Subtask A, the performance of our approach has been also superior in Subtask B

---

[6]Some considerations about the evaluation: these subtasks employed binary classification. At testing time, *Bad* and *PotentiallyUseful* are both considered *false*. The same occurs with *PerfectMatch* and *Relevant*, which are both considered *true*. In addition, following the rules of the task, the employed measures used only the top 10 ranked instances.

	Model	Ranking measures			Classification measures			
		MAP	**AvgRec**	**MRR**	**Acc.**	**P**	**R**	**F1**
	Development set results							
(a)	Random baseline	0.456	0.654	0.535	0.433	0.344	**0.764**	0.475
	Search engine	0.538	0.728	0.631	n/a	n/a	n/a	n/a
(b)	UH-PRHLT (primary)	**0.632**	**0.812**	**0.725**	**0.682**	**0.526**	0.500	0.513
	UH-PRHLT (contr. 1)	0.630	0.811	0.722	0.672	0.510	0.545	**0.527**
	UH-PRHLT (contr. 2)	0.630	0.810	0.722	0.674	0.514	0.522	0.518
	Test set results							
(a)	Random baseline	0.528	0.665	0.587	0.525	0.452	0.405	0.428
	Search engine	0.595	0.726	0.678	n/a	n/a	n/a	n/a
(b)	UH-PRHLT (primary)	0.674	0.794	0.770	**0.632**	**0.556**	0.468	0.508
	UH-PRHLT (contr. 1)	**0.676**	**0.795**	**0.771**	0.624	0.541	**0.501**	**0.520**
	UH-PRHLT (contr. 2)	0.673	0.793	0.767	0.630	0.550	0.491	**0.520**

Table 1: Results of **Subtask A: English Question-Comment Similarity**. (a) Baselines; (b) proposed approach.

	Model	Ranking measures			Classification measures			
		MAP	**AvgRec**	**MRR**	**Acc.**	**P**	**R**	**F1**
	Development set results							
(a)	Random baseline	0.559	0.732	0.622	0.488	0.443	**0.766**	0.562
	Search engine	0.713	0.861	0.766	n/a	n/a	n/a	n/a
(b)	UH-PRHLT (primary)	**0.759**	**0.911**	**0.830**	**0.762**	**0.721**	0.724	**0.723**
	UH-PRHLT (contr. 1)	0.757	**0.911**	**0.830**	0.758	0.712	0.729	0.721
	UH-PRHLT (contr. 2)	0.755	0.910	0.817	0.758	0.714	0.724	0.719
	Test set results							
(a)	Random baseline	0.470	0.679	0.510	0.452	0.404	0.326	0.361
	Search engine	0.747	0.883	0.838	n/a	n/a	n/a	n/a
(b)	UH-PRHLT (primary)	0.767	0.903	0.830	0.766	0.635	0.695	0.664
	UH-PRHLT (contr. 1)	0.766	0.902	0.830	0.763	0.627	**0.708**	0.665
	UH-PRHLT (contr. 2)	**0.773**	**0.908**	**0.840**	**0.767**	**0.636**	0.704	**0.668**

Table 2: Results of **Subtask B: English Question-Question Similarity**. (a) Baselines; (b) proposed approach.

	Model	Ranking measures			Classification measures			
		MAP	**AvgRec**	**MRR**	**Acc.**	**P**	**R**	**F1**
	Development set results							
(a)	Random baseline	0.138	0.096	0.160	0.284	0.070	**0.759**	0.128
	Search engine	0.306	0.346	0.360	n/a	n/a	n/a	n/a
(b)	UH-PRHLT (primary)	**0.383**	0.413	0.420	0.894	0.242	0.252	0.247
	UH-PRHLT (contr. 1)	**0.383**	**0.421**	0.425	0.897	**0.252**	0.249	**0.250**
	UH-PRHLT (contr. 2)	**0.383**	0.419	**0.435**	0.899	0.251	0.232	0.241
	Test set results							
(a)	Random baseline	0.150	0.114	0.152	0.167	0.296	0.094	0.143
	Search engine	0.404	0.460	0.459	n/a	n/a	n/a	n/a
(b)	UH-PRHLT (primary)	0.432	**0.480**	0.478	0.886	0.376	**0.342**	**0.359**
	UH-PRHLT (contr. 1)	**0.434**	**0.480**	**0.484**	**0.888**	**0.386**	0.327	0.354
	UH-PRHLT (contr. 2)	0.433	**0.480**	**0.484**	**0.888**	0.382	0.327	0.353

Table 3: Results of **Subtask C: English Question-External Comment Similarity**. (a) Baselines; (b) proposed approach.

(question-related question similarity ranking). As we can see in Table 2, using the development set, the improvement of MAP, AvgRec, and MRR has been of 4.6%, 5%, and 6.4% respectively compared to the search engine baseline. In this case, the similarity between questions was easier to estimate — also for the baselines — and the improvements in performance were slightly reduced. With respect to the classification measures, we outperformed the random baseline with 27.4% and 16.1 % of accuracy and F1-measure respectively.

In Table 3 we can see the results of the Subtask C (question-external comment similarity ranking). In this case, we are ranking 100 comments (10 times more compared to the other subtasks). Therefore, this has been the most difficult subtask. However, we obtained improvements in line with those reported for the other subtasks. Compared to the search engine baseline, the MAP, AvgRec, and MRR improved 8.7%, 8.5%, and 7.5% respectively when using the development partition. The accuracy and F1-measure improved 61.5% and 12.2% respectively. The largest number of comments to rank, and the use of top 10 results when measuring results, benefited our approach with this especially high difference in accuracy.

After the analysis of results in the three English subtasks, we highlight that the combination of lexical and semantic-based features that we employ in this work offers a competitive performance for the CQA task. This is true also when comparing results with other task participants. Our approach obtained the highest results — with considerable margin (1.04%) — for subtask B. It is worth mentioning that we designed our system for the subtask B and adapted it later for the other tasks. However, for the other two subtasks, we obtained a low ranking position. At this point we have not discovered any coding error that could explain this difference. In addition, we analysed the information gain ratio of the features for the three subtasks. That results showed an average decrease of ~66% for subtasks A and C. Therefore, we conclude that our approach is more adequate for tasks of similarity rather than question answering. That analysis also manifests that the most relevant features are the word n-gram ones followed by the CWASA, distributed representation-based, and knowledge-graph-based ones. The comparison of results of all the submitted systems and task participants can be found in the task overview (Nakov et al., 2016).

5 Conclusions

In this work we evaluated the three English subtasks of the SemEval 2016 Task 3 on CQA. In order to measure similarities, our proposed approach combined lexical and semantic-based features. We included simple — and effective — representations based on BOW, character and word n-grams. We also employed semantic features which used distributed representations of words to represent documents or to directly measure similarity by means of distributed word bidirectional alignments. The use of knowledge graphs generated with the BabelNet multilingual semantic network has been exploited too. Experimental results showed that our system was able to outperform — with considerably differences — the random and Google search engine baselines in all the evaluated subtasks. In addition, our approach obtained the highest results in subtask B compared to the other task participants. This fact manifests the potential of our combination of lexical and semantic features for the CQA subtask.

As future work we will continue studying how to approach CQA with knowledge graphs and distributed representations. In addition, we will further explore how to employ this type of lexical and semantic-based representations for other NLP tasks such as plagiarism detection.

Acknowledgments

The work of the authors of the PRHLT research center was supported by the SomEMBED TIN2015-71147-C2-1-P MINECO research project and by the Generalitat Valenciana under the grant ALMAMATER (PrometeoII/2014/030). We thank Joan Puigcerver (PRHLT) for his support and comments.

References

Collin F Baker, Charles J Fillmore, and John B Lowe. 1998. The berkeley framenet project. In *Proceedings of the 17th international conference on Computational linguistics-Volume 1*, pages 86–90. Association for Computational Linguistics.

David M Blei, Andrew Y Ng, and Michael I Jordan. 2003. Latent dirichlet allocation. *the Journal of machine Learning research*, 3:993–1022.

Davide Buscaldi, Paolo Rosso, José Manuel Gómez-Soriano, and Emilio Sanchis. 2010. Answering questions with an n-gram based passage retrieval engine. *Journal of Intelligent Information Systems*, 34(2):113–134.

Asli Celikyilmaz, Dilek Hakkani-Tur, and Gokhan Tur. 2010. Lda based similarity modeling for question answering. In *Proceedings of the NAACL HLT 2010 Workshop on Semantic Search*, pages 1–9. Association for Computational Linguistics.

Marc Franco-Salvador, Paolo Rosso, and Roberto Navigli. 2014. A knowledge-based representation for cross-language document retrieval and categorization. In *Proceedings of the 14th Conference of the European Chapter of the Association for Computational Linguistics*, pages 414–423. Association for Computational Linguistics.

Marc Franco-Salvador, Francisco Rangel, Paolo Rosso, Mariona Taulé, and M. Antònia Martí. 2015a. Language variety identification using distributed representations of words and documents. In *Proceeding of the 6th International Conference of CLEF on Experimental IR meets Multilinguality, Multimodality, and Interaction (CLEF 2015)*, volume LNCS(9283), page n/a. Springer-Verlag.

Marc Franco-Salvador, Paolo Rosso, and Francisco Rangel. 2015b. Distributed representations of words and documents for discriminating similar languages. In *Proceeding of the Joint Workshop on Language Technology for Closely Related Languages, Varieties and Dialects (LT4VarDial), RANLP*.

Marc Franco-Salvador, Parth Gupta, Paolo Rosso, and Rafael E. Banchs. 2016a. Cross-language plagiarism detection over continuous-space representations of language. *Pre-print submitted to journal*.

Marc Franco-Salvador, Paolo Rosso, and Manuel Montes y Gómez. 2016b. A systematic study of knowledge graph analysis for cross-language plagiarism detection. *Information Processing & Management*.

Samer Hassan and Rada Mihalcea. 2011. Semantic relatedness using salient semantic analysis. In *AAAI*.

Marti A. Hearst, Susan T Dumais, Edgar Osman, John Platt, and Bernhard Scholkopf. 1998. Support vector machines. *Intelligent Systems and their Applications, IEEE*, 13(4):18–28.

Yongshuai Hou, Cong Tan, Xiaolong Wang, Yaoyun Zhang, Jun Xu, and Qingcai Chen. 2015. Hitszicrc: Exploiting classification approach for answer selection in community question answering. In *Proceedings of the 9th International Workshop on Semantic Evaluation, SemEval*, volume 15 of *SemEval '15*, pages 196–202. Association for Computational Linguistics.

Jiwoon Jeon, W Bruce Croft, and Joon Ho Lee. 2005. Finding similar questions in large question and answer archives. In *Proceedings of the 14th ACM international conference on Information and knowledge management*, pages 84–90. ACM.

Thorsten Joachims. 2002. Optimizing search engines using clickthrough data. In *Proceedings of the eighth ACM SIGKDD international conference on Knowledge discovery and data mining*, pages 133–142. ACM.

Dekang Lin and Patrick Pantel. 2001. Discovery of inference rules for question-answering. *Natural Language Engineering*, 7(04):343–360.

Tomas Mikolov, Ilya Sutskever, Kai Chen, Greg S Corrado, and Jeff Dean. 2013. Distributed representations of words and phrases and their compositionality. In *Advances in Neural Information Processing Systems 26*, pages 3111–3119.

Preslav Nakov, Lluís Màrquez, Walid Magdy, and Alessandro Moschitti. 2015. Semeval-2015 task 3: Answer selection in community question answering. In *Proceedings of the 9th International Workshop on Semantic Evaluation*, SemEval '15, pages 269–281. Association for Computational Linguistics.

Preslav Nakov, Lluís Màrquez, Walid Magdy, Alessandro Moschitti, Jim Glass, and Bilal Randeree. 2016. SemEval-2016 task 3: Community question answering. In *Proceedings of the 10th International Workshop on Semantic Evaluation*, SemEval '16, San Diego, California, June. Association for Computational Linguistics.

Roberto Navigli and Simone Paolo Ponzetto. 2012. Babelnet: The automatic construction, evaluation and application of a wide-coverage multilingual semantic network. *Artificial Intelligence*, 193:217–250.

Deepak Ravichandran and Eduard Hovy. 2002. Learning surface text patterns for a question answering system. In *Proceedings of the 40th annual meeting on association for computational linguistics*, pages 41–47. Association for Computational Linguistics.

Paolo Rosso, Lluís-F Hurtado, Encarna Segarra, and Emilio Sanchis. 2012. On the voice-activated question answering. *IEEE Transactions on Systems, Man, and Cybernetics–Part C*, 42(1):75–85.

Gerard Salton and Michael J. McGill. 1986. *Introduction to Modern Information Retrieval*. McGraw-Hill, Inc.

Jasper Snoek. 2013. *Bayesian Optimization and Semiparametric Models with Applications to Assistive Technology*. Ph.D. thesis, University of Toronto.

Quan Hung Tran, Vu Tran, Tu Vu, Minh Nguyen, and Son Bao Pham. 2015. Jaist: Combining multiple features for answer selection in community question answering. In *Proceedings of the 9th International Workshop on Semantic Evaluation*, volume 15 of *SemEval '15*, pages 215–219. Association for Computational Linguistics.

Ellen M. Voorhees. 1999. The trec-8 question answering track report. In *Trec*, volume 99, pages 77–82.

RDI_Team at SemEval-2016 Task 3: RDI Unsupervised Framework for Text Ranking

Ahmed Magooda[1,§], Amr M. Sayed[2,§], Ashraf Y. Mahgoub[1, §], Hany Ahmed[1, §], Mohsen Rashwan[1], Hazem Raafat[3], Eslam Kamal[4], Ahmad A. Al Sallab[5]

[1] RDI, Cairo, Egypt.

[2]Computer Science Department, Faculty of Computers and Information, Cairo University, Egypt.

[3]Computer Science Department, Kuwait University, Kuwait

[4]Microsoft Research, Cairo, Egypt.

[5]Valeo Inter-branch Automotive Software, Cairo, Egypt.

§ These four authors contributed equally to this work.

ahmed.ezzat.gawad@gmail.com, amr@fci-cu.edu.eg, ashraf.youssef.mahgoub@gmail.com, hanyahmed@aucegypt.edu, mrashwan@rdi-eg.com, hazem@cs.ku.edu.kw, eskam@microsoft.com, ahmad.el-sallab@valeo.com

Abstract

Ranking is an important task in the field of information retrieval. Ranking may be used in different modules in natural language processing such as search engines. In this paper, we introduce a competitive ranking system which combines three different modules. The system participated in SemEval 2016 question ranking task for the Arabic language. The task is a ranking task that targets reordering results retrieved from search engine. Results reordering is done based on relevancy between search result and the original query issued. The data provided in the competition is in the form of question (query) and 30 question answer pairs retrieved from search engine. For each question retrieved from the search engine the system generates a relevancy score that is to be used for ranking. The proposed system came in the third position in the Competition. Since the majority of modules are unsupervised the unsupervised naming was used.

1 Introduction

This paper describes RDI System, the system participated in SemEval 2016 Community question ranking shared task for the Arabic language (Nakov et al., 2016). The task is a ranking task for medical community questions, whenever a new user wants to submit a new question, the system should retrieve similar questions that are previously answered. Questions retrieved by the search engine are then to be ordered by its relevancy to query question in order to reduce redundancy.

The task proceeds as follows, for each query question 30 previously answered question answer pairs are retrieved through a search engine. The aim of the task is to reorder the retrieved 30 question answer pairs based on its relevancy to the query question.

As query expansion and results re-ranking are two major paradigms for search engine enhancements, (Mahgoub et al., 2014) used Google synonyms and Arabic Wikipedia to expand search queries, on the other hand (Abouenour et al., 2010) proposed a system that uses Arabic WordNet to expand queries. In this paper we are going to propose a

Proceedings of SemEval-2016, pages 822–827,
San Diego, California, June 16-17, 2016. ©2016 Association for Computational Linguistics

ranking system which consists of three modules merged with each other to produce a relevancy score. The proposed system managed to achieve the third position in the SemEval 2016 Community question ranking shared task for the Arabic. The 3 modules presented in this system are:

1- TF-IDF based module
2- Language model (LM) based module
3- Wikipedia-based module

The paper is organized as follows: Section 2 introduces some related work. Section 3 introduces data used. Section 4 contains proposed system. Section 5 contains Results obtained. In Section 6, some conclusions and perspective are discussed. Section 7 contains future work.

2   Related Work

The community question ranking problem is different than ordinary question answering system that aims to generate a satisfactory answer for a specific question. Community question ranking problem aims to find the most suitable answer for a question within a closed set of question answers pool.

(Zongcheng et al. 2012) argued that a question and answer can be considered the same topic distribution written in two different languages or written by two different writers. So they proposed extracting the latent topics from question and answer, they used the extracted topics to represent the question and answer, alongside measuring how much question and answer share topics.

(Jeon et al. 2006) used some non-textual features to cover the contextual information of questions and answers, and proposed using language modeling to process these features in order to predict the quality of answers collected from a specific CQA service. (Blooma et al. 2008) used regression to combine textual and non-textual features to generate predictive score to identify the best answer.

(Ko et al. 2007) proposed using probabilistic answer ranking model to calculate the answer relevance and answer similarity. They used logistic regression to calculate the correctness score for an answer using its relevancy to the question. The authors then improved their work by using probabilistic graphical model so that the correlation between all the answers can be taken into consideration.

3   Data

During the development of the proposed system 4 sets of data were used.

A) Training data provided by SemEval

This data consists of 1030 search queries, each query is accompanied with 30 search engine retrieved results. Data is manually annotated with relevancy score and is marked as relevant or irrelevant. Where relevant annotated questions are questions that are actually relevant to the query question, and irrelevant annotated questions are irrelevant to the query question.

B) Development data provided by SemEval

This data consists of 250 search queries, each query is accompanied with 30 search engine retrieved results. Data is manually annotated as relevant or irrelevant. Where relevant annotated questions are questions that are actually relevant to the query question, and irrelevant annotated questions are irrelevant to the query question.

C) Test data provided by SemEval

This data consists of 250 search queries, each query is accompanied with 30 search engine retrieved results. In this case, data has no annotation provided.

D) Crawled data

This data is in the form of question-answer pairs crawled from http://www.altibbi.com. 170,000 question answer pairs were crawled, all of these data samples were considered relevant samples as we considered relevancy between answer text and question text.

4   Proposed System

This section describes the proposed system in details. As shown in figure 1, three different modules are proposed. First, relevancy between search results retrieved from the search engine and the search query are calculated using three modules. The three relevancy values calculated are then converted into one relevancy score using weighted summation.

Retrieved documents are then re-ordered based on the new weighted sum scores. The best weights used for weighting the three modules (α, β and γ) were inferred through tuning over development set.

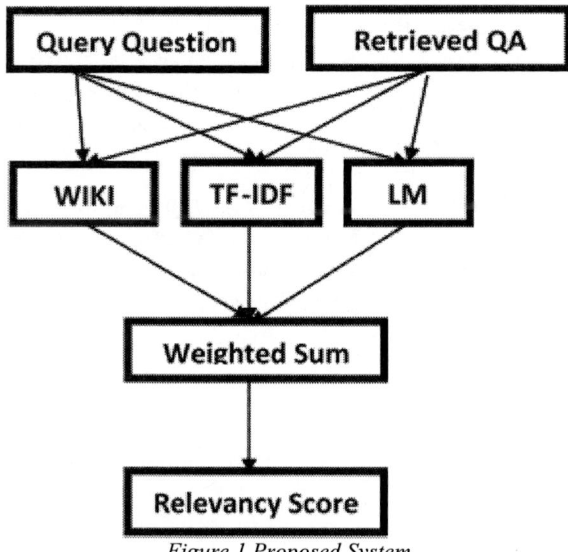

Figure 1.Proposed System

4.1 TF-IDF Module

This module uses the crawled data as background corpora to calculate the relevancy between the query question and each of the 30 retrieved question answer pairs.

The main idea of the algorithm is that for each query question, cluster the background data into relevant and irrelevant classes. The two constructed classes are then used to calculate how much the retrieved 30 question answer pairs are relevant to the query question. The algorithm flows as follows:

- Crawled data and query question are normalized by removing (non-Arabic words, Numbers, Punctuations and Stop words).
- For the query question, cluster the crawled data into two classes; 1- Relevant and 2- Irrelevant. This can be done by counting the number of common words between the query question and each question answer pair of the crawled data. If the number of common words is more than or equal 3, then this pair is considered relevant, otherwise is considered irrelevant.
- For each pair of the retrieved question answer pairs, unigrams, bigrams and trigrams are extracted. For each unigram, bigram and trigram TF-IDF is calculated twice, once using IDF extracted from the relevant class question answer pairs and once using the IDF extracted from the irrelevant class question answer pairs.

- The TF-IDF for the question pair is calculated by weighting the unigram TF-IDF by ω_1, bigrams by ω_2 and trigrams by ω_3.
- The TF-IDF with relevant class and TF-IDF with irrelevant class are normalized into probability values.
- The relevant probability is then used as the final score for the current question answer pair.

4.2 Language Model Module

This module utilizes the concept of language modeling into the ranking task. A language model was trained using the crawled data alongside the training data provided for the competition that was annotated as relevant question answer pair. In our experiments, we used the provided training data to reform new training samples as shown in figure.2.

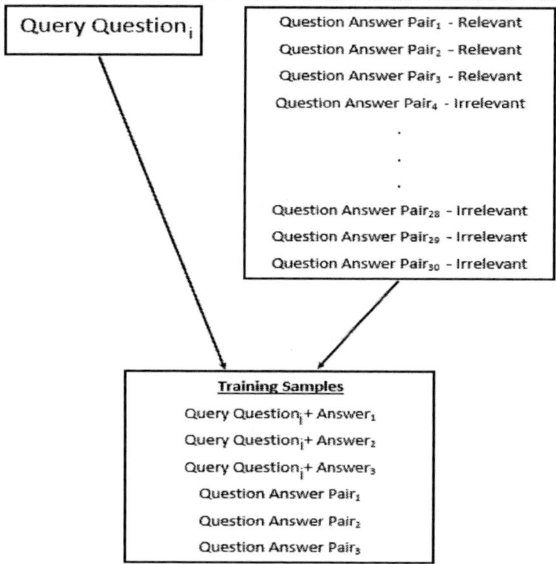

Figure 2. Generating LM training samples

As shown in figure.2, for each query question and its 30 retrieved question answer pairs, to form new text samples, query question text has been appended to answer text of pairs which are annotated as relevant. The main idea behind using language model is that, a sentence formed from question and its answer is coherent, so using the answer with the query question in case the answer is annotated as relevant; will lead to coherent sentence too.

By using the previous algorithm, we generated new training samples which represent the relevancy between questions and answers. Those training samples are essential to feed the language model with more coherent training samples.

Using the previous generated samples a recurrent neural network for language modeling (Mikolov et al., 2011) with the following characteristics was trained;

- 1-hidden layer of size 200 neuron and sigmoid activation function.
- Hierarchical Softmax output layer over the whole vocabulary.

This module is the only supervised module used within the system, since human annotation was employed within this module.

4.3   Wikipedia-based module

This module uses medical information provided by Arabic-Wikipedia in order to provide better scoring methodology. The intuition behind using Wikipedia's medical terms is to provide higher matching score for those terms present in Wikipedia's medical tree over other matched terms.

Using the categorization system provided by Wikipedia, about 250,000 medical subcategories where extracted from the Medical category, the list is available for download from the author's website[1]. These extracted terms are then separated into three categories: unigrams, bigrams, or more, where each category weighted by a different matching factor.

To assign a total matching score between a query question and a question answer pair, the following steps are applied for each of the 30 retrieved question answer pairs:
- Top 1500 Most frequent words generated by (Zahran et al., 2015) were removed from both query question and the questions answer pairs.
- Find matching terms between the question and the question answer pair.
- For each matching term:
  - If the matching term is a unigram which exists in Wikipedia extracted terms, then increment the total matching score by *Uni_Wiki_Factor*
  - Else if the matching term is a unigram which doesn't exists in Wikipedia extracted terms, then increment the total matching score by *Uni_Factor*.
  - Repeat the previous two steps for both: bigrams and higher n-grams using (*Bi_Wiki_Factor, Bi_Factor*) for bigrams and (*N_Wiki_Factor, N_Factor*) for higher order n-grams.

Moreover, values of these matching factors are tuned over a subset of the provided training set and then validated on the development set. The optimum values of the matching factors are

- Uni_Wiki_Factor = 1.5
- Uni_Factor = 1
- Bi_Wiki_Factor = 2
- Bi_Factor = 1
- N_Wiki_Factor = 2
- N_Factor = 1

5   Results

The proposed system achieved the 3rd position in the Arabic subtask of SemEval 2016 task3.

Follows a detailed analysis of the system performance on development data set, alongside the performance of each module on the same data:

- **TF-IDF Module:**

Data	System	MAP	AvgRec	MRR
Dev	**TF-IDF Module**	**40.6**	**0.42**	**47**

Table 1.Performance of TFIDF module

- **Language Model Module:**

Data	System	MAP	AvgRec	MRR
Dev	**Language Model**	**35.8**	**0.374**	**40**

Table 2.Performance of Language Model module

- **Wikipedia Module:**

Data	System	MAP	AvgRec	MRR
Dev	**Wikipedia Module**	**42.6**	**0.46**	**48.3**

Table 3.Performance of Wikipedia module

The best parameters used to combine the three modules were inferred from tuning the system over the development data set, the best weights are

α (TF-IDF) = 0.3

β (Language Model) = 0.05

---

[1] https://drive.google.com/file/d/0B0FhtCSJsoyoeT-Jkd1FUQksxRmM/view

γ (Wikipedia) = 0.75

Table 4 shows the performance of the combined system on the development data set:

Data	System	MAP	AvgRec	MRR
Dev	**Combined System**	**44.8**	**0.48**	**51.1**

Table 4.Performance of combined system on development data

Simple as it may seem, the Wikipedia module achieved the best results on development data set compared to the other two modules. This behavior is due to the ability of the Wikipedia module to highlight medical terms and assign it higher weights compared to other matched terms, on the other hand the other two modules neglect this property, as both modules focus on detecting similarity between sentences regardless of the domain.

The proposed system also achieved 43.80 Mean Average Precision (MAP) on test set. Follows the final scores achieved on the test set alongside the scores achieved by the other four participants.

Data	System	MAP	AvgRec	MRR
Train	**RDI**	**78.3**	**81.2**	**83.3**
Dev	**RDI**	**44.8**	**47.9**	**51.1**
Test	SLS	45.83	51.01	53.66
	ConvKN	45.50	50.13	52.55
	RDI	**43.80**	**47.45**	**49.21**
	QU-IR	38.63	44.10	46.27
	UPC US-MBA	29.09	30.04	34.04
	Baseline	**28.88**	**28.71**	**30.93**

Table 5.Results achieved in SemEval 2016 task 3

We can see that the proposed system achieved very good results compared to the baseline system. The system also achieved comparable results to the systems that achieved first and second positions

6 Conclusion

In this paper, we have introduced a combination of different algorithms which can be used in ranking problems. The performance of different systems has been studied. The paper also presented a comparison with other systems, and the results show that the proposed system is efficient. The results achieved by the proposed system are very promising compared with other systems in the competition.

7 Future work

Future work includes the enhancement of the system using sentence representation in vector space, as well as the combination of this system with other types of features.

We are planning to try sentence representation models like recursive auto encoder (RAE) (Socher et al., 2011) to represent the whole sentence in a vector. Using a model like RAE can facilitate measuring similarity between 2 sentence using vector representations for sentences.

The use of weighted sum for merging the proposed three modules is a very naive method that also suffers from over fitting. So We are planning to merge the proposed modules by means of machine learning (SVR, Neural Network, etc..) instead of using the naïve weighted sum. We are also planning to invest some effort to perform more experiments on the language model module since it has contributed the less within the three modules.

References

Socher, R., Pennington, J., Huang, E. H., Ng, A. Y., & Manning, C. D. (2011, July). Semi-supervised recursive autoencoders for predicting sentiment distributions. In Proceedings of the Conference on Empirical Methods in Natural Language Processing (pp. 151-161). Association for Computational Linguistics.

Zahran, M. A., Magooda, A., Mahgoub, A. Y., Raafat, H., Rashwan, M., & Atyia, A. (2015). Word Representations in Vector Space and their Applications for Arabic. In Computational Linguistics and Intelligent Text Processing (pp. 430-443). Springer International Publishing.

Mikolov, T., Karafiát, M., Burget, L., Cernocký, J., & Khudanpur, S. (2010, September). Recurrent neural network based language model. In *INTERSPEECH* (Vol. 2, p. 3).

Mikolov, T., Kombrink, S., Burget, L., Černocký, J. H., & Khudanpur, S. (2011, May). Extensions of recurrent neural network language model. In Acoustics, Speech and Signal Processing (ICASSP), 2011 IEEE International Conference on (pp. 5528-5531). IEEE.

Nakov, P., Marquez, L., Magdy, W., Moschitti, A., Glass, J. & Randeree, B. (2016). SemEval-2016 Task 3: Community Question Answering. In Proceedings of the 10th International Workshop on Semantic Evaluation. San Diego, California. Association for Computational Linguistics.

Abouenour, L., Bouzouba, K., & Rosso, P. (2010). An evaluated semantic query expansion and structure-based approach for enhancing Arabic question/answering. International Journal on Information and Communication Technologies

Mahgoub, A. Y., Rashwan, M. A., Raafat, H., Zahran, M. A., & Fayek, M. B. (2014). Semantic query expansion for Arabic information retrieval. ANLP 2014

Ji, Z., Xu, F., Wang, B. and He, B., 2012, October. Question-answer topic model for question retrieval in community question answering. In Proceedings of the 21st ACM international conference on Information and knowledge management.

J. Jeon, W. Croft, and etc. . a framework to predict the quality of answers with non-textual features. In Proc. SIGIR, 2006.

J. Ko, L. Si, and E. Nyberg. A probabilistic framework for answer selection in question answering. In Proc. NAACL/HLT, 2007.

M. Blooma, A. Chua, and D. Goh. A predictive framework for retrieving the best answer. In Proc. SAC, 2008.

SLS at SemEval-2016 Task 3: Neural-based Approaches for Ranking in Community Question Answering

Mitra Mohtarami, Yonatan Belinkov, Wei-Ning Hsu, Yu Zhang
Tao Lei, Kfir Bar[†], Scott Cyphers, James Glass
MIT Computer Science and Artificial Intelligence Laboratory
[†]Tel Aviv University
{mitra, belinkov, wnhsu, yzhang87, taolei, cyphers, glass}@csail.mit.edu [†]kfirbar@post.tau.ac.il

Abstract

Community question answering platforms need to automatically rank answers and questions with respect to a given question. In this paper, we present the approaches for the *Answer Selection* and *Question Retrieval* tasks of SemEval-2016 (task 3). We develop a bag-of-vectors approach with various vector- and text-based features, and different neural network approaches including CNNs and LSTMs to capture the semantic similarity between questions and answers for ranking purpose. Our evaluation demonstrates that our approaches significantly outperform the baselines.

1 Introduction

Community Question Answering (cQA) forums are rapidly growing, resulting in an urgent need to automatically search for relevant answers among many responses provided for a given question (Answer Selection), and search for relevant questions to reuse their existing answers (Question Retrieval). In this paper, we aim to address the SemEval 2016 tasks (Nakov et al., 2016) that are designed for Answer Selection (AS) and Question Retrieval (QR). These tasks are briefly described as follows:

A **Question-Comment Similarity**: given a question and its first 10 comments in the question thread, rerank these 10 comments according to their relevance with respect to the question.

B **Question-Question Similarity**: given a new question (named *original* question) and the set of the first 10 related questions retrieved by a search engine, rerank the related questions according to their similarity regarding the original question.

C **Question-External Comment Similarity**: given a new question (*original* question) and the set of the first 10 related questions retrieved by a search engine, each associated with its first 10 comments appearing in its thread, rerank the 100 comments (10 questions x 10 comments) according to the new question.

D **Question-External Question-Comment Pair Similarity**: Given a new question and a set of 30 related questions retrieved by a search engine, each associated with one correct answer, rerank the 30 question-comment pairs according to their relevance with respect to the original question.

Task B is considered as QR and the others as AS problems. The first three tasks are evaluated on an English dataset and the fourth on an Arabic dataset. Several factors make all these tasks more challenging. First, cQA forums contain *open-domain* and *non-factoid* questions and answers, resulting in high variance Q&A quality (Màrquez et al., 2015). A second factor is that the Q&A are *long* and their length may vary from several words to several hundred words. The third factor concerns the relatively close relation between some annotation labels; the comments in the tasks *A* and *C* are labeled as *Relevant*, *Potential* and *Irrelevant*, and the *Relevant* comments need to be ranked above the *Potential* and *Irrelevant* comments. From a natural language processing perspective, it is difficult to define a clear distinction between the relevant and potential labels.

Proceedings of SemEval-2016, pages 828–835,
San Diego, California, June 16-17, 2016. ©2016 Association for Computational Linguistics

To address these tasks, we first present a bag-of-vectors (BOV) approach in which various vector- and text-based features are designed and passed through a linear SVM classifier to compute the degree of relatedness between the Q&As. Then, we present different NN-based approaches including CNNs and LSTMs to compute the representations of the Q&As. We evaluate our models on the cQA corpus provided by SemEval. The results demonstrate that our approaches outperform the baselines.

2 Method

Given a question q, a list of answers A for AS, and a list of questions Q for QR, we aim to rank the lists A and Q with respect to q. To address these problems, we present a bag-of-vectors (BOV) approach to compute various vector- and text-based features for a classifier. Furthermore, we present NN-based approaches (LSTM with attention, CNN and RCNN) for learning the vector representations of the questions and answers to be used for capturing their semantic similarity. The degree of similarity between the Q&A is used for their ranking.

2.1 Bag-of-Vectors (BOV)

Previous work presented a BOV approach to address the classification tasks in cQA (Belinkov et al., 2015). In this paper, we aim to extend the previous approach for the ranking tasks by updating the feature sets and developing new models. The features are categorized into text, vector and meta-data based features that are briefly explained below (in the experiments section below we detail the features chosen for each task). Then, we explain our approach to shorten the length of Q&As in the Arabic data.

Text-based features These features are mainly computed using text similarity metrics, word clustering and topic modeling. As the first set of text-based features, we use various text similarity metrics that measure string overlap between Q&As: *Longest Common Substring* (Gusfield, 1997), *Longest Common Subsequence* (Allison and Dix, 1986), *Longest Common Subsequence Norm, Greedy String Tiling* (Wise, 1996), *Monge Elkan Second String* (Monge and Elkan, 1997), *Jaro Second String* (Jaro, 1989), *Jaccard coefficient* (Lyon et al., 2004) and *Containment* measures (Broder,

1997). These metrics are explained in (Belinkov et al., 2015).

Another set of text-based features are computed using word clustering that has been useful in many supervised NLP approaches. We use Brown clustering (Brown et al., 1992; Liang, 2005) that creates word clusters such that they are hierarchical in a binary tree. In the tree, each word is assigned to a bitstring depending on its tree path, and the prefixes of the bitstring are the ancestor clusters used as additional features. We use an implementation of Brown clustering,[1] that is designed as an HMM-based algorithm which partitions words into a base set of N (=500) clusters. Given a question or an answer as a document, its clusters are determined based on its word clusters. This captures the global clusters.

Topic modeling approaches can also be used to automatically identify topics of documents. We use Non-negative Matrix Factorization (NMF) for topic modeling. A document-term matrix is constructed with TF-IDF weights. This matrix is factored into a term-topic and a topic-document matrix. The N (=100) topics are derived from the contents of the documents, and the topic-document matrix describes topics of related documents. We use each column of the topic-document matrix as features for each individual document. The entire train, development and test datasets provided by SemEval 2015 and 2016 are employed to compute the word clustering and topic modeling features.

Vector-based features The concatenation of the normalized Q&A representations is used as vector-based features for a (q, a) pair. The question or answer representation is obtained with the average of its word representations computed from `Word2Vec` vectors (Mikolov et al., 2013a; Mikolov et al., 2013b; Mikolov et al., 2013c). For English word vectors we use the `GoogleNews` vectors dataset.[2] For Arabic word vectors we use `Word2Vec` to train 100-dimensional vectors on either the general domain Arabic Gigaword (Linguistic Data Consortium, 2011) or the domain-specific raw data provided with the task. We select the word vector set based on the performance of the development set.

---

[1] `https://github.com/percyliang/brown-cluster`.

[2] `https://code.google.com/p/word2vec`.

Furthermore, for the Arabic the pair of sentence vectors in the question and answer with the highest cosine similarity is used as features.

We use a zero vector if the question or answer contains only out-of-vocabulary words. To make it easier for the classifier to ignore the vectors in these cases, we design two boolean features to identify whether the question and answer are zero vectors.

Metadata-based features We use a metadata-based feature that identifies whether the user who posted the question is the same user who wrote the answer. This feature is useful to identify irrelevant dialogue answers, and used for the tasks A and C.

Shrinking the sentence length Some of the questions and answers in the community forum are very long. In fact, in the Arabic dataset questions and answers have an average length of 50 and 120 words, respectively. Therefore, we preprocess the texts using `TextRank` (Mihalcea and Tarau, 2004), a graph-based keyword extraction algorithm, for finding the most meaningful words within every thread. Once the meaningful words are found, we filter all other words from each thread instance, and build the subsequent feature representation based on the shortened texts.

Given a document, `TextRank` builds a graph representation, where nodes stand for word types, connected by undirected links representing co-occurrence within a window of size N. An importance weight is then calculated for each node, using an iterative formula introduced by `PageRank` (Brin and Page, 1998). We use our implementation of `TextRank`, in which we select a certain percentage of the words, defined as P, sorted top-down by importance weight, as the final keywords.

We treat each thread, including all its question-answer pairs, as an individual document for `TextRank`. We preprocess each document with MADA 3.1 (Habash et al., 2009), a context-sensitive lemmatizer, for finding word lemmas and part-of-speech tags. Finally, our `TextRank` graphs include only lemmas of content words, Latin-script words and words with no lemmas. Content words in this sense are defined as nouns, verbs, adjectives and adverbs. All other `TextRank` parameters are assigned with values according to (Mihalcea and Tarau, 2004).

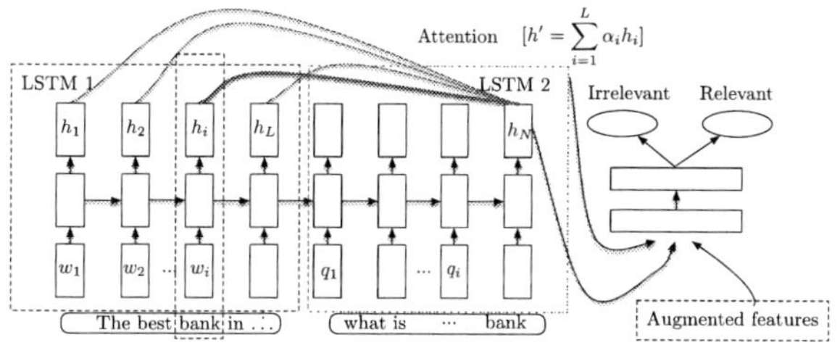

Figure 1: The Architecture of the LSTM with attention for cQA

2.2 Long Short-Term Memory (LSTM) Networks with Attention

LSTMs have shown great success in many different fields, such as textual entailment (Rocktäschel et al., 2015), language modeling (Sundermeyer et al., 2012), and acoustic modeling (Graves et al., 2013). The recurrent structure as well as the ability to store long-term information make LSTMs suitable for encoding sequences of variable length into fixed-length representations.

However, for very long sequences, such as the comments in cQA tasks (~hundreds of words), an LSTM may still fail to compress all information into this representation. Recently, a neural attention model (Bahdanau et al., 2014) has been proposed to alleviate this issue by enabling the network to attend to all past outputs. The attention mechanism along with an LSTM is ideal for cQA tasks.

Following (Mohtarami et al., 2016), as illustrated in Figure 1, we apply two LSTMs to encode (q, q') or (q, a) respectively. The first LSTM reads one object, and passes information through hidden units to the second LSTM. The second LSTM then reads the other object and generates its representation biased by the first object after finishing reading.

By augmenting an attention mechanism to the encoder, we allow the second LSTM to attend to the sequence of output vectors from the first LSTM, and hence generate a weighted representation of the first object according to both objects. Let h_N be the last output of the second LSTM and $M = [h_1, h_2, \cdots, h_L]$ be the sequence of output vectors of the first object. The weighted representation of the first object is

$$h' = \sum_{i=1}^{L} \alpha_i h_i \tag{1}$$

Embedding	**init** or random, fix or **update**
Two LSTM	shared or **not**
#cells for LSTM	64, **128**, 256
# nodes for MLP	128, **256**
Optimizer	**AdaGrad**, AdaDelta, SGD
learning rate	0.001,**0.01**,0.1
Regularizer	**Dropout**, L2 regularization
Dropout rate	0.0, 0.2, 0.3, **0.4**, 0.5
L2	0, 0.001, **0.0001**, 0.00001

Table 1: Hyper-parameters of the LSTM model. The bold value is the selected parameter.

The weight is computed by

$$\alpha_i = \frac{exp(a(h_i, h_N))}{\sum_{j=1}^{L} exp(a(h_j, h_N))} \tag{2}$$

where $a()$ is the importance model that produces a higher score for (h_i, h_N) if h_i is useful for determining the object pair's relationship. We parametrize this model using a feed-forward neural network.

To classify the relationship of this pair, another feed-forward neural network is built on top of the LSTMs that takes the representations of both objects, h_N and h', as input. Note that in our framework, we can use the augmented features f to enhance the classifier. In this case, the final input to the classifier will become h_N, h', and f. The details of this model are explained in (Mohtarami et al., 2016).

Our system is based on Theano (Bastien et al., 2012; Bergstra et al., 2010). Table 1 gives a list of hyperparameters we tried. As suggested by (Greff et al., 2015), the hyperparameters for an LSTM can be tuned independently. We tune each parameter separately on a dev set and pick the best one.

2.3 Convolutional Neural Network (CNN)

Convolutional Neural Networks (CNNs) are useful in many NLP tasks, such as language modeling (Kalchbrenner et al., 2014), semantic role labeling (Collobert and Weston, 2008) and semantic parsing (Yih et al., 2014). Our reason for using a CNN for cQA is that it can capture both features of n-grams and long-range dependencies (Yu et al., 2014), and can extract discriminative word sequences that are common in the training instances (Severyn and Moschitti, 2015). These traits make CNNs useful for dealing with long questions.

Following (Mohtarami et al., 2016), as illustrated in Figure 2, we employ a CNN-based model to first

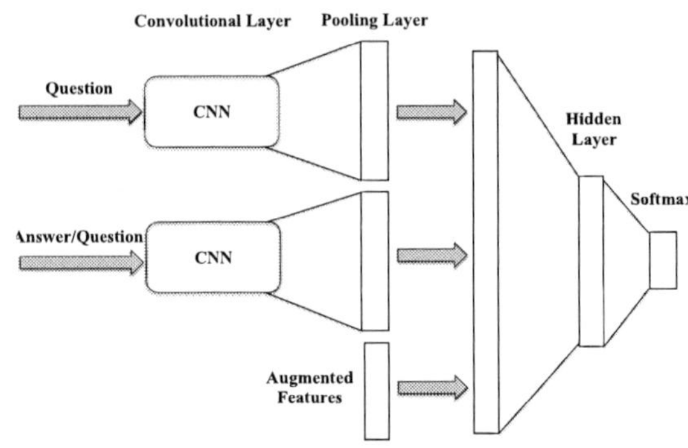

Figure 2: The Architecture of the CNN for cQA

compute a relatedness score for each pair, (q, a) or (q, q), and then rank the lists based on the resulting scores. In the model, for a given pair, the embedding vectors of q and a are considered as input. The CNN convolution and pooling layers then generate the convolutional vector representations. These vectors are concatenated with other additional feature vectors and used as input to a fully connected Multi-Layer Perceptron (MLP) whose softmax layer generates a probability score $P(y|q, a)$ over the labels $y \in \{0, 1\}$, where 1 means *relevant*, and 0 means *irrelevant*. The hyperparameter configuration of the CNN model is shown in Table 3, and the details of this model are explained in (Mohtarami et al., 2016).

2.4 Recurrent Convolutional Neural Network (RCNN)

For task B, we also apply the recurrent convolutional neural network model, which has been recently proposed and successfully applied to a similar question retrieval problem (Lei et al., 2015). Unlike traditional CNNs which only extract local n-gram features, RCNNs extract and aggregate all possible n-grams within the input sequence, including ones that are not consecutive. Similar to LSTMs and Gated Recurrent Units (GRUs), which have internal "memory" states, RCNNs maintain aggregated vectors to store the weighted average of n-gram features. These vectors are updated in a recurrent fashion when the input tokens are successively read into the network.

Following the set-up in (Lei et al., 2015), we take the last state vector as the final representation of the question. The parameters of RCNN encoder are trained in a max-margin fashion, maximizing the

Embedding	Glove vector, fixed
Hidden dimension	200
Filter width	2
Optimizer	Adam
Learning rate	0.01
Dropout rate	0.1
L2	0.00001

Table 2: The hyper-parameters of RCNN model.

Embedding	word2vec, fixed
Hidden dimension	300
Filter width	5
Optimizer	AdaDelta
Learning rate	0.95
Dropout rate	0.5
L2	0.00001

Table 3: The hyper-parameters of CNN model.

(cosine) similarity difference between positive question pairs and negative pairs. The hyperparameter configuration of the model is shown in Table 2.

3 Experimental Results

We evaluate our approaches on all the cQA tasks. We use the cQA datasets provided by SemEval 2016. The English data were collected from the Qatar Living forum.[3] and the Arabic data were collected from medical forums. Table 4 provides statistics for the datasets. As evaluation metrics, we use F1-score for a global assessment of the approaches in addition to the following ranking metrics: Mean Average Precision (MAP), Average Recall (AveRec) and Mean Reciprocal Rank (MRR). For the MAP, we use the average of MAP@1 to MAP@10.

Baselines For a baseline, we use the Information Retrieval (IR) ranking score that is computed as follows: given a q, the top 100 threads retrieved by Google from the Qatar Living forum are considered and the order of each thread is used as its IR ranking score. As another baseline, we use a system that randomly ranks a given list of Q or A.

Question-comment similarity The results for this task are shown in Table 5(a). The first two rows are the IR and random baseline results, and the next two rows are the best two performances among all SemEval submissions for this task. The other three rows are the results of our approaches and respectively submitted to SemEval as *primary*, *con-*

[3]http://www.qatarliving.com/forum.

	A	B	C	D
Original questions	-	317	317	1,281
Related questions	6,398	3,169	3,169	37,795
Comments	40,288	-	31,690	37,795

Table 4: Statistics of the dataset through the tasks.

trastive1 and *contrastive2* results. As shown in the table, our results are significantly higher than the baselines and comparable with the best results over all performance metrics, and there is no significant difference between the results of our approaches for this task. We use various combinations of our BOV, LSTM and CNN approaches, then select the best ones with respect to the development set. The combination of the approaches is computed by $1/(R_1 + R_2 + ... + R_i)$ where R_i is the ranking of the ith approach.

In this task, the BOV includes all the features except for the NMF features, and we employ the order of the answers in their threads as augmented features for our NN-based approaches. The structure of the threads (e.g., answer order) can help to extract relevant answers (Barrón-Cedeño et al., 2015).

Question-question similarity Table 5(b) shows the results for this task. The first two rows are the results for IR and random baselines, and the next two are the best two performances of SemEval. The other three results are related to our approaches and respectively submitted to SemEval as *primary*, *contrastive1* and *contrastive2* results. The table shows that our results are significantly better than the baselines. While there is no significant difference between our *contrastive1* and *contrastive2* results with the best result, these results are higher than the second best SemEval result on MAP, and the highest result is obtained with our primary result on accuracy. With respect to our results, the combination of BOV, LSTM and RCNN achieves the highest result on MAP and the combination of BOV and RCNN is the best on F1.

In this task, the combination of the approaches is computed using a linear SVM with the feature vector $R_1, R_2, ..., R_i$ where R is the ranking of the ith approach. Furthermore, in this experiment, the BOV includes all the features except the word clustering features, and we employ the ranking order of the IR as augmented features for our NN-based approaches.

Task A (a)							
Method	**MAP**	**AveRec**	**MRR**	**P**	**R**	**F1**	**Acc**
IR	59.53	72.60	67.83	-	-	-	-
Random	52.80	66.52	58.71	45.26	40.56	74.57	52.55
Kelp (first)	79.19	88.82	86.42	76.96	55.30	64.36	75.11
ConvKN (second)	77.66	88.05	84.93	75.56	58.84	66.16	75.54
BOV+LSTM+CNN (primary)	76.33	87.30	82.99	60.36	67.72	63.83	68.81
BOV+CNN (contrastive1)	76.46	87.47	83.27	60.09	69.68	64.53	68.87
BOV+LSTM (contrastive2)	76.71	87.17	84.38	59.45	67.95	63.41	68.13

Tast B (b)							
Method	**MAP**	**AveRec**	**MRR**	**P**	**R**	**F1**	**Acc**
IR	74.75	88.30	83.79	-	-	-	-
Random	46.98	67.92	50.96	40.43	32.58	73.82	45.20
UH-PRHLT (first)	76.70	90.31	83.02	63.53	69.53	66.39	76.57
ConvKN (second)	76.02	90.70	84.64	68.58	66.52	67.54	78.71
BOV+RCNN (primary)	75.55	90.65	84.64	76.33	55.36	64.18	79.43
BOV+LSTM+RCNN (contrastive1)	76.17	90.55	85.48	74.39	52.36	61.46	78.14
RCNN (contrastive2)	76.09	90.14	84.21	77.21	45.06	56.91	77.29

Task C (c)							
Method	**MAP**	**AveRec**	**MRR**	**P**	**R**	**F1**	**Acc**
IR	40.36	45.97	45.83	-	-	-	-
Random	15.01	11.44	15.19	29.59	9.40	75.69	16.73
SUper-team (first)	55.41	60.66	61.48	18.03	63.15	28.05	69.73
Kelp (second)	52.95	59.27	59.23	33.63	64.53	44.21	84.79
LSTM+BOV+IR (primary)	49.09	56.04	55.98	47.85	13.61	21.19	90.54
BOV+IR+LSTM+CNN (contrastive1)	46.48	53.31	52.53	16.24	85.93	27.32	57.29
BOV+CNN+IR (contrastive2)	46.39	52.83	51.17	16.18	85.63	27.22	57.23

Tast D (d)							
Method	**MAP**	**AveRec**	**MRR**	**P**	**R**	**F1**	**Acc**
IR	28.88	28.71	30.93	-	-	-	-
Random	29.79	31.00	33.71	19.53	20.66	20.08	68.35
ConvKN (second)	45.50	50.13	52.55	28.55	64.53	39.58	62.10
RDI_team (third)	43.80	47.45	49.21	19.24	100.00	32.27	19.24
BOV (primary; first)	45.83	51.01	53.66	34.45	52.33	41.55	71.67
BOV (contrastive1)	44.94	49.72	51.58	62.96	2.40	4.62	80.95
BOV (contrastive2)	42.95	47.61	49.55	27.29	74.40	39.84	56.76

Table 5: Results on **test** data for answer selection and question retrieval tasks

Question-external comment similarity The results for this task are shown in Table 5(c). The first two rows are the IR and random baseline results and the next two rows are the best two SemEval results. The other three rows are our results that respectively are *primary*, *contrastive1* and *contrastive2* results. As shown in the table, our results are significantly higher than the baselines but lower than the best SemEval results. We use a similar combination approach to task A for our contrastive results and the *primary* is computed using the BOV and IR features as the augmented features for LSTM. In this task, the BOV includes all the features except for the word clustering and NMF features, and we employ both the ranking order of the IR and answer order as augmented features for our NN-based models.

Question-external question-comment pair similarity This task is only available for Arabic. Our feature set for this task is somewhat simplified compared to the English tasks: we only use our BOV approach with simple text- and vector-based features. Similarities are computed only on word- and sentence-level, and not on chunk-level as in (Belinkov et al., 2015). We do not use word clustering or topic modeling features and we note that the Arabic dataset has no associated metadata. Furthermore, in this dataset every original question has a number of related question-answer pairs. To fully exploit this information we compute two sets of features: one between the original and related questions, and one between the original question and the related answer. We then concatenate the two sets as the final feature representation to the classifier.

Our *primary* submission is a uniform combination of scores from four different settings of shrinking the length: (i) no shrinking (all words are kept as is);[4] (ii) only keeping content lemmas (iii) only content lemmas and TextRank with $N = 3$, $P = 5$; (iv) only content lemmas and TextRank with $N = 4$, $P = 1$. We also submit (i) as *contrastive1* and (iii) as *contrastive2*. These settings were chosen based on the performance on the development set.

As Table 5(d) shows, our *primary* submission ranks first on all ranking metrics and on F1. Our *contrastive* submissions are also very competitive.

Finally, we experimented with two sets of word vectors, either trained from the general domain Gigaword corpus ($\sim$1B words) or the domain-specific unsupervised data provided with the task ($\sim$26M words). Despite the very different sizes of the raw corpora, we found mixed results: the general domain vectors were useful with no shrinking (i) while the domain-specific ones were more beneficial with shrinking (ii-iv); we used these settings for the submission. Using word vectors trained on a combined corpus from both raw datasets did not result in additional improvement.

4   Conclusion

We developed bag-of-vectors and neural network approaches, and demonstrated their effectiveness on the cQA tasks for ranking a list of questions or answers for a given question. We evaluated our approaches on the SemEval-2016 corpus and our results significantly outperform the baselines. In addition, our results are comparable to the result of the best submission to SemEval-2016 for English and achieved the first place for Arabic.

Acknowledgments

This research was supported by the Qatar Computing Research Institute (QCRI). We would like to thank Alessandro Moschitti, Preslav Nakov, Lluís Màrquez, and other members of the QCRI Arabic Language Technologies group for their collaboration on this project.

---

[4]In this setting we found it useful to omit all "Relevant" question-answer pairs from training and only keep "Direct" and "Irrelevant" pairs. This helps probably due to annotation issues.

References

Lloyd Allison and Trevor I. Dix. 1986. A bit-string longest-common-subsequence algorithm. *Information Processing Letters*, 23(5):305 – 310.

Dzmitry Bahdanau, Kyunghyun Cho, and Yoshua Bengio. 2014. Neural machine translation by jointly learning to align and translate. *arXiv preprint arXiv:1409.0473*.

Alberto Barrón-Cedeño, Simone Filice, Giovanni Da San Martino, Shafiq R. Joty, Lluís Màrquez, Preslav Nakov, and Alessandro Moschitti. 2015. Thread-level information for comment classification in community question answering. In *ACL (2)*, pages 687–693. The Association for Computer Linguistics.

Frédéric Bastien, Pascal Lamblin, Razvan Pascanu, James Bergstra, Ian J. Goodfellow, Arnaud Bergeron, Nicolas Bouchard, and Yoshua Bengio. 2012. Theano: new features and speed improvements. Deep Learning and Unsupervised Feature Learning NIPS 2012 Workshop.

Yonatan Belinkov, Mitra Mohtarami, Scott Cyphers, and James Glass. 2015. VectorSLU: A Continuous Word Vector Approach to Answer Selection in Community Question Answering Systems. In *Proceedings of the 9th International Workshop on Semantic Evaluation (SemEval 2015)*, pages 282–287, Denver, Colorado, June. Association for Computational Linguistics.

James Bergstra, Olivier Breuleux, Frédéric Bastien, Pascal Lamblin, Razvan Pascanu, Guillaume Desjardins, Joseph Turian, David Warde-Farley, and Yoshua Bengio. 2010. Theano: a CPU and GPU math expression compiler. In *Proceedings of the Python for Scientific Computing Conference (SciPy)*, June. Oral Presentation.

Sergey Brin and Lawrence Page. 1998. The anatomy of a large-scale hypertextual web search engine. *Comput. Netw. ISDN Syst.*, 30(1-7):107–117, April.

Andrei Z. Broder. 1997. On the Resemblance and Containment of Documents. In *Proceedings of the Compression and Complexity of Sequences 1997*, SEQUENCES '97, pages 21–, Washington, DC, USA.

Peter F. Brown, Peter V. deSouza, Robert L. Mercer, Vincent J. Della Pietra, and Jenifer C. Lai. 1992. Class-based N-gram Models of Natural Language. *Comput. Linguist.*, 18(4):467–479, December.

Ronan Collobert and Jason Weston. 2008. A unified architecture for natural language processing: Deep neural networks with multitask learning. In *Proceedings of the 25th International Conference on Machine Learning*, ICML '08, pages 160–167, New York, NY, USA. ACM.

Alan Graves, Abdel-rahman Mohamed, and Geoffrey Hinton. 2013. Speech recognition with deep recurrent neural networks. In *Acoustics, Speech and Signal*

Processing (ICASSP), 2013 IEEE International Conference on*, pages 6645–6649. IEEE.

Klaus Greff, Rupesh Kumar Srivastava, Jan Koutník, Bas R. Steunebrink, and Jürgen Schmidhuber. 2015. LSTM: A search space odyssey. *CoRR*, abs/1503.04069.

Dan Gusfield. 1997. *Algorithms on Strings, Trees, and Sequences: Computer Science and Computational Biology*. Cambridge University Press, New York, NY, USA.

Nizar Habash, Owen Rambow, and Ryan Roth. 2009. Mada+ tokan: A toolkit for arabic tokenization, diacritization, morphological disambiguation, pos tagging, stemming and lemmatization. In *Proceedings of the 2nd international conference on Arabic language resources and tools (MEDAR), Cairo, Egypt*, pages 102–109.

Matthew A. Jaro. 1989. Advances in Record-Linkage Methodology as Applied to Matching the 1985 Census of Tampa, Florida. *Journal of the American Statistical Association*, 84(406):414–420.

Nal Kalchbrenner, Edward Grefenstette, and Phil Blunsom. 2014. A convolutional neural network for modelling sentences. In *Proceedings of the 52nd Annual Meeting of the Association for Computational Linguistics (Volume 1: Long Papers)*, pages 655–665, Baltimore, Maryland, June. Association for Computational Linguistics.

Tao Lei, Hrishikesh Joshi, Regina Barzilay, Tommi Jaakkola, Katerina Tymoshenko, Alessandro Moschitti, and Lluis Marquez. 2015. Denoising bodies to titles: Retrieving similar questions with recurrent convolutional models. *arXiv preprint arXiv:1512.05726*.

Percy Liang. 2005. Semi-supervised learning for natural language. In *MASTERS THESIS, MIT*.

Linguistic Data Consortium. 2011. Arabic Gigaword Fifth Edition. `https://catalog.ldc.upenn.edu/LDC2011T11`.

Caroline Lyon, Ruth Barrett, and James Malcolm. 2004. A theoretical basis to the automated detection of copying between texts, and its practical implementation in the ferret plagiarism and collusion detector. In *Plagiarism: Prevention, Practice and Policies 2004 Conference*.

Lluís Màrquez, James Glass, Walid Magdy, Alessandro Moschitti, Preslav Nakov, and Bilal Randeree. 2015. SemEval-2015 Task 3: Answer Selection in Community Question Answering. In *Proceedings of the 9th International Workshop on Semantic Evaluation (SemEval 2015)*.

Rada Mihalcea and Paul Tarau. 2004. Textrank: Bringing order into texts. In Dekang Lin and Dekai Wu, editors, *Proceedings of EMNLP 2004*, pages 404–411, Barcelona, Spain, July. Association for Computational Linguistics.

Tomas Mikolov, Kai Chen, Greg Corrado, and Jeffrey Dean. 2013a. Efficient Estimation of Word Representations in Vector Space. *CoRR*, abs/1301.3781.

Tomas Mikolov, Ilya Sutskever, Kai Chen, Greg Corrado, and Jeffrey Dean. 2013b. Distributed Representations of Words and Phrases and their Compositionality. *CoRR*, abs/1310.4546.

Tomas Mikolov, Wen-tau Yih, and Geoffrey Zweig. 2013c. Linguistic Regularities in Continuous Space Word Representations. In *Human Language Technologies: Conference of the North American Chapter of the Association of Computational Linguistics, Proceedings, June 9-14, 2013, Westin Peachtree Plaza Hotel, Atlanta, Georgia, USA*, pages 746–751.

Mitra Mohtarami, Wei-Ning Hsu, Yu Zhang, and James Glass. 2016. Answer Selection and Question Retrieval with Neural Networks. *Under review*.

Alvaro Monge and Charles Elkan. 1997. An Efficient Domain-Independent Algorithm for Detecting Approximately Duplicate Database Records.

Preslav Nakov, Lluís Màrquez, Walid Magdy, Alessandro Moschitti, Jim Glass, and Bilal Randeree. 2016. SemEval-2016 task 3: Community question answering. In *Proceedings of the 10th International Workshop on Semantic Evaluation*, SemEval '16, San Diego, California, June. Association for Computational Linguistics.

Tim Rocktäschel, Edward Grefenstette, Karl Moritz Hermann, Tomáš Kočiský, and Phil Blunsom. 2015. Reasoning about entailment with neural attention. *arXiv preprint arXiv:1509.06664*.

Aliaksei Severyn and Alessandro Moschitti. 2015. Learning to rank short text pairs with convolutional deep neural networks. In *Proceedings of the 38th International ACM SIGIR Conference on Research and Development in Information Retrieval*, SIGIR '15, pages 373–382, New York, NY, USA. ACM.

Martin Sundermeyer, Ralf Schlüter, and Hermann Ney. 2012. Lstm neural networks for language modeling. In *INTERSPEECH*, pages 194–197.

Michael J. Wise. 1996. YAP3: Improved Detection Of Similarities In Computer Program And Other Texts. In *SIGCSEB: SIGCSE Bulletin (ACM Special Interest Group on Computer Science Education)*, pages 130–134.

Wen-tau Yih, Xiaodong He, and Christopher Meek. 2014. Semantic parsing for single-relation question answering. In *Proceedings of ACL*. Association for Computational Linguistics, June.

Lei Yu, Karl Moritz Hermann, Phil Blunsom, and Stephen Pulman. 2014. Deep learning for answer sentence selection. *CoRR*, abs/1412.1632.

SUper Team at SemEval-2016 Task 3:
Building a Feature-Rich System for Community Question Answering

Tsvetomila Mihaylova, Pepa Gencheva, Martin Boyanov, Ivana Yovcheva,
Todor Mihaylov, Momchil Hardalov, Yasen Kiprov, Daniel Balchev, Ivan Koychev
FMI, Sofia University "St. Kliment Ohridski", Sofia, Bulgaria

Preslav Nakov
ALT Research Group, Qatar Computing Research Institute, HBKU, Doha, Qatar

Ivelina Nikolova, Galia Angelova
IICT, Bulgarian Academy of Sciences, Sofia, Bulgaria (`iva@lml.bas.bg`)

Abstract

We present the system we built for participating in SemEval-2016 Task 3 on Community Question Answering. We achieved the best results on subtask C, and strong results on subtasks A and B, by combining a rich set of various types of features: semantic, lexical, metadata, and user-related. The most important group turned out to be the metadata for the question and for the comment, semantic vectors trained on QatarLiving data and similarities between the question and the comment for subtasks A and C, and between the original and the related question for Subtask B.

1 Introduction

SemEval-2016 Task 3 on Community Question Answering[1] (Nakov et al., 2016) aims to solve a real-life application problem. The main **subtask C (Question-External Comment Similarity)** asks to find an answer in the forum that will be appropriate as a response to a newly posted question. This is achieved by retrieving similar questions and ranking their answers with respect to the new question. Two additional supporting subtasks are defined:

Subtask A (Question-Comment Similarity): Given a question from a question-comment thread, rank the comments within the thread based on their relevance with respect to the question.

Subtask B (Question-Question Similarity): Given a new question, re-rank the similar questions retrieved by a search engine with respect to that question.

2 Related Work

We build our preprocessing and feature extraction pipeline based on the system of Zamanov et al. (2015), which was developed by a subset of our 2016 team for SemEval-2015 Task 3 on Answer Selection in Community Question Answering (Nakov et al., 2015). The task in 2015 was to classify comments in a thread as *relevant, potentially useful,* or *bad* with respect to the thread question. This year's Community Question Answering subtask A is similar to subtask A in 2015, but now it is a ranking task, asking to rank the answers in a thread based on their relevance with respect to the thread's question. Given this similarity, most of the techniques used by participants in the 2015 subtask A are potentially valuable for this year's subtask A as well. Below we mention just the few most relevant among them.

In their 2015 system, Belinkov et al. (2015) used vectors of the question and of the comment, metadata features, and text-based similarities. Nicosia et al. (2015) used similarity measures, URLs in the comment text and statistics about the user profile: number of good, bad, and potentially useful comments. Similarly, we use the number of posts by the same user in the thread, the ID of the question's author, topic model-based feature, special words, etc.

Determing the overall sentiment of the question can also be useful, and it was used in 2015 (Nicosia et al., 2015). One way to do it is to build a sufficiently large question taxonomy as described in (Li and Roth, 2006). This may help determine the quality of the answer, but it requires significant efforts in order to build such a taxonomy.

---

[1] http://alt.qcri.org/semeval2016/task3/

Proceedings of SemEval-2016, pages 836–843,
San Diego, California, June 16-17, 2016. ©2016 Association for Computational Linguistics

3   Data

For training and testing, we used data provided by the SemEval-2016 Task 3 organizers. The datasets consist of 6,398 questions and 40,288 comments for Subtask A, 317 original + 3,169 related questions for Subtask B, and 317 original questions + 3,169 related questions + 31,690 comments for Subtask C.

For subtask A, the comments in a question-answer thread are annotated as *Good*, *PotentiallyUseful* and *Bad*. A good ranking is one that ranks all *Good* comments above *PotentiallyUseful* and *Bad* ones (without distinguishing between the latter two).

For subtask B, the potentially relevant questions are annotated as *PerfectMatch*, *Relevant* and *Irrelevant* with respect to the original question. A good ranking is one where the *PerfectMatch* and the *Relevant* questions (without distinguishing between them) are both ranked above the *Irrelevant* ones.

We also used semantic vectors (Mikolov et al., 2013a) pretrained on Google News data: 300-dimensional vectors, available for three million words and phrases.

For all subtasks, we further trained semantic vectors using Gensim (Řehůřek and Sojka, 2010) on 200,000 questions and two million comments from the Qatar Living Forum,[2], which were provided by the task organizers.

Finally, using this same data, and following (Mihaylov et al., 2015a; Mihaylov et al., 2015b), we scraped information about the users from the forum and we extracted for each of them the time in the forum, the active period, the number of questions, the comments in the forum, etc.

4   Method

We build our system on top of the framework developed by our colleagues (Zamanov et al., 2015). In particular, we approach the task as a classification problem similarly to the approach we took for SemEval 2015 Task 3 (Nakov et al., 2015). However, unlike 2015, this year we have a ranking problem for all subtasks, e.g., for subtask A we have to rank the comments depending on how likely the classifier thinks they are to be *Good* vs. them being *Bad* or *PotentiallyUseful*.

---

[2]Qatar Living: http://www.qatarliving.com/forum

We use variety of features like question and comment metadata; question and comment lexical features; distance measures between the question and the comment; text readability measures applied to the question and to the comment; lexical semantics vectors for the question and for the comment; features modeling the likelihood of a user being a troll.

These features proved quite useful for ranking comments with respect to a given question (Subtask A and C), but they did not achieve as high results when ranking questions with respect to other questions (Subtask B).

4.1   Features

Metadata Features

These features are based on surface observations of the thread's structure and properties. From the comments' attributes we extract whether the comment is written by the author of the question. We further extract the comment's position in the thread, and the ID of the author of the comment. Next, we tokenize the text and we calculate the ratio of the comment length and of the question length (in terms of number of tokens). In terms of the threads we measure, the number of comments from the same user in a particular thread and the order in which they are written by the user, i.e., first, second, etc. comment by the same user. In terms of the whole QatarLiving forum, we calculate the number of questions in a category.

Another family of metadata features explores the presence and the number of links in the question and in the comment. We counted both inbound (i.e., to `qatarliving.com`) and outbound links. Our hypothesis was that the presence of a reference to another resource is indicative of a relevant comment. Investigations on the training set showed that a relevant comment was more likely to contain such a link. Unfortunately, less than 10% of the comments had links, and ultimately these features did not have a very high impact on the results.

Lexical Features

These features represent the lexical content of questions and comments. They are obtained with the help of the GATE (Cunningham et al., 2011; Cunningham et al., 2002) preprocessing pipeline with some hand-crafted rules and various statistics.

We use token-, NP-, and sentence-based features as well as features based on the following entities: Person, Location, Organisation and Address. The latter ones are used to mark whether the comment contains an answer to a **wh**-question (**where**, **who**, **wh**at, etc.), e.g., if the question contains the word "where". We further add a boolean feature modeling whether the comment contains a Location or an Address. We tagged the named entities using the high-quality named entity recognition pipeline of Ontotext.[3] We further extracted statistics about the number of verbs, nouns, pronouns, and adjectives in the question and in the comment, as well as the number of question marks in the comments, and the number of question words in the question and in the comment.

Another group of lexical features are extracted from the comment text only and show whether it contains smileys, currency units, e-mails, phone numbers, only laughter, "thank you" phrases, personal opinions, or disagreement.

Other lexical features relate to spelling and include number of misspelled words that are within edit distance of 1 from a word in our vocabulary and number of offensive words from a predefined list.

We also borrow a dictionary from the PMI-cool system (Balchev et al., 2016), which is based on unigram and bigram occurrences across the classes. We use it to compute the *Pointwise Mutual Information* (PMI) between a dictionary entry and a class. Based on it, we add features that sum the PMI for all tokens in a given comment. This family of features are weighed most heavily by the classifier.

We further computed lexical similarity between a question and a comment using *SimHash* (Sadowski and Levin, 2007), which is a near-duplicate similarity measure but it did not help much.

We also apply a set of statistical scores to measure the **level of readability** and complexity of the text (Aluisio et al., 2010). The standard readability measures include Automated Readability Index, Coleman-Liau Index, Flesch Reading Ease, Gunning Fog Index, Flesch-Kincaid Grade Level, LIX, SMOG grade. We also employ statistics about the average number of words per sentence in the comment or question, and type-to-token ratios.

---

[3]http://ontotext.com/

Semantic Features

Our semantic features try to capture the proximity between the meanings encoded in the word sequences of the questions and of the answers.

One of the semantic features uses **Mallet topic modelling** (McCallum, 2002). We build a topic model with 100 topics. Then we measure the cosine distance between the topics in the first text and the topics in the second text, i.e., in the question and in the answer (Subtasks A and C), or in the original and in the related question (Subtask B).

We also used **semantic vectors** trained with word2vec (Mikolov et al., 2013b). We performed experiments to select the best vectors for the task. We tried pre-trained vectors from Google News. We further trained vectors from the unannotated data from the QatarLiving forum. We used the latter vectors in our system as they yielded better results.

We experimented with training vectors of different sizes and different minimal word counts. Because of the many common misspelled words, the smaller word count yields better results. We tried different tokenizations for the words. To capture the specifics of the forum language, we added identifiers for numbers, smileys, URLs and images. For each question-comment pair, we calculated the centroid vectors of the question and of the comment and we used the components of the resulting vectors as features for the classifier. We used Gensim (Řehůřek and Sojka, 2010) for building the vectors.

User Features

We downloaded and used characteristics about the users from the QatarLiving forum, such as number of questions, comments, classifieds; time since registration, time since last activity in the forum, time of the day in which the user was active, etc. We also added as user characteristics the number of good and bad comments from the annotated training data. However, the user features did not improve the results. We noticed that over time, the number of both good and bad comments for a user in the forum grew, and the number of good and bad comments for most of the users was similar.

We also used troll user features, e.g., number of mentions of the user as troll and troll behavior characteristics as described in (Mihaylov et al., 2015a; Mihaylov et al., 2015b; Mihaylov and Nakov, 2016a).

Features	Dev-2016 as test set		Test-2016 as test set	
	MAP	Accuracy	MAP	Accuracy
All	69.89	76.60	77.83	74.43
All − semantic vectors	65.93	73.11	74.61	70.76
All − metadata	65.51	74.96	74.30	72.91
All − comment characteristics	69.30	75.49	77.38	73.30
All − distances	68.22	76.19	76.90	73.70
All − URLs	69.96	76.27	77.84	74.04
All − User stats	70.08	76.48	78.34	74.31
All − Wh-words in Q and C	69.55	76.56	77.72	74.80
All − Wh-words in Q	69.73	76.97	77.66	74.40
All − Wh-words in C	69.98	76.48	77.88	74.28
All − Loc/Org in Comment	69.95	76.56	77.82	74.28
All − POS count in Q	69.85	76.07	77.36	74.50
All − POS count in C	69.61	76.02	77.62	74.22
All − POS and Wh-words in Q	70.02	76.43	77.81	74.59
Primary	70.67	77.62	77.16	74.50
Contrastive-1	70.06	76.84	77.68	74.50
Contrastive-2	——	——	76.97	74.34

Table 1: Subtask A: Experiments with all features and excluding some feature groups.

Credibility Features

We further added some of the credibility features described in (Castillo et al., 2013). We trained a prediction model on tweets from the dataset described in that paper. We used **linear Support Vector Machines** (linear SVMs) with Stochastic Gradient Descent (SGD) and L2 regularization. We used an off-the-shelf implementation of SVM, provided in the **Apache Spark** library (Apache Software Foundation Team, 2015).

For each answer we extracted the following features: length of the answer (characters); does the answer contain special punctuation, like question marks, exclamation marks, etc.; is there an emoticon in the text; is there a first person singular (*I, me, my, mine, we*) or plural pronoun (*our, ours, we, us*); is there a third person singular (*he, she, it, his, hers, him, her*) or plural pronoun (*they, them, their*); does the answer contain a user mention (@user); does the text contain URLs in it.

Based on these features we trained an SVM model to classify items as credible or not. For our submission, we used all the features used to train the credibility module as well as the predicted label and the probability it is predicted with.

4.2 Classifier

Using the above features, we formed vectors associated with each question-answer pair. Those vectors are a concatenation of the extracted features, including the centroid of the semantic vectors for the question and for the comment.

We then used an SVM classifier as implemented in LibSVM (Chang and Lin, 2011) for classification. We experimented with different kernels (Hsu et al., 2003), and we achieved the best results with the RBF kernel, which we use to train the model for our submissions. The ranking score for a question-comment pair in Subtask A is the calculated probability of the pair to be classified as *Good*.

For Subtask C, we used the same approach as in Subtask A. We first ranked the comments with respect to the relevant question. For the final ranking, we multiplied the probability of the pair "relevant question – comment" being *Good* by the reciprocal rank of the related question as given by Google.

For subtask B, we passed to the classifier characteristics of the pair "original question – relevant question". For ranking, we used the probability of the pair to be classified as *Good*.

| | Dev-2016 as test set | | Test-2016 as test set | |
Features	MAP	Accuracy	MAP	Accuracy
All	41.46	69.32	55.62	70.21
All − semantic vectors	35.57	71.52	52.51	71.04
All − metadata	39.90	69.08	54.58	71.10
All − comment characteristics	40.57	68.92	56.20	70.50
All − distances	40.96	69.66	52.97	70.64
All − URLs	40.31	69.44	56.20	70.57
All − User stats	41.30	69.22	55.57	70.07
All − Wh-words in Q and C	39.20	68.76	53.58	70.40
All − Wh-words in Q	40.19	69.12	54.61	70.50
All − Wh-words in C	39.83	69.16	55.01	70.69
All − Loc/Org in Comment	40.14	69.24	55.70	70.34
All − POS count in Q	40.62	69.12	54.70	70.47
All − POS count in C	40.09	69.26	56.47	70.31
All − POS and Wh-words in Q	41.57	69.14	54.62	70.44
Primary	42.42	68.46	55.41	69.73
Contrastive-1	42.54	81.38	48.23	82.49
Contrastive-2	42.56	68.64	53.48	69.20

Table 2: **Subtask C.** Experiments with all features and excluding some feature groups.

| | Dev-2016 as test set | | Test-2016 as test set | |
Features	MAP	Accuracy	MAP	Accuracy
Only semantic vectors	71.17	67.20	74.91	68.71
Semantic vectors + cosine distance	71.76	69.00	74.43	72.43
Above + topic distance	72.34	70.80	75.22	74.43
Above + metadata	72.84	70.20	74.82	74.86
Above + text distance	72.39	72.00	75.17	75.57
All − semantic vectors	71.98	71.20	74.43	77.14

Table 3: **Subtask B.** Experiments with the different feature sets for the related and the original question.

5 Experiments and Evaluation

We grouped our features in several groups and we ran experiments by excluding some of them in order to identify the most important types of features. In particular, we used the LibSVM `fselect` script for feature selection. We achieved the best results by combining the features with the semantic vectors of the question and of the comment trained on Qatar-Living data.

In Table 1, we present the results for Semeval-2016 Task 3, Subtask A using all features, as well as when excluding individual feature groups. Our primary submission includes the top-rated features and semantic vectors. We selected our primary submission as it achieved higher score on Dev than Contrastive1 and Contrastive2.

Compared to Contrastive-1, our Primary has some additional features: number of user comments in the thread, cosine between the comment text with question subject and category, more locations and organizations. Our Contrastive-1 submission included the top-rated features and semantic vectors, and our Contrastive-2 submission included the same features as our Primary submission, but used Dev-2016 as additional training set.

In Table 2, we show the results for Semeval-2016 Task 3, Subtask C using all features, as well as when excluding individual feature groups. Our Primary submission includes all features excluding user statistics and troll features. Our Contrastive-1 submission includes all features, including PMI, while Contrastive-2 includes all features, excluding PMI.

Features	Dev-2016 as test	
	MAP	Accuracy
Vectors from Google News		
Nouns	54.95	68.52
Nouns + verbs	55.21	69.06
Nouns + verbs + adjectives	54.97	68.48
Vectors from QatarLiving		
Nouns + verbs	61.48	70.82
Nouns + verbs + adjectives	60.43	70.37
MWC=40; words only	58.95	71.27
MWC=40; + special symbols	59.65	71.27
All words; MWC=5	62.68	71.80
Included cosine distance	63.88	72.99

Table 4: **Selection of semantic vectors.** Experiments with different sources, vector size, and minimum word count.

Tables 1 and 2 have shown that the most important feature groups are the metadata characteristics, the distance measures between the question and the comment, and the semantic vectors. Other features that `fselect` scored highly are the credibility score, text readability measures and the number of tokens of some parts of speech in the comment text (namely, number of adjectives and nouns). The least useful features are statistics about the forum users and characteristics of the question: question length and number of tokens of different parts of speech in the question text. In all above reported results, we used vectors for which we achieved the best results on the development dataset.

In Table 4, we present the results from experiments with semantic vectors. We experimented with pre-trained vectors from Google News and we also trained vectors with word2vec on the unannotated Qatar Living forum data. When training vectors on Qatar Living data, we experimented with different vector sizes and minimum word frequencies. We also added the following entities as words: numbers, images, URLs, smileys (referred to in the table as "special symbols"). We achieved best results with vectors from QatarLiving, vector size 100, and minimum word frequency of 5. Including special symbols as words also improved the results. We experimented with calculating the centroids of the question and of the comment using specific parts of speech only; however, ultimately we found that using all words from all parts of speech worked best.

For **Subtask B**, we used a similar approach as for Subtask A: we passed to the classifier the semantic vectors of the original and of the related question, some metadata and distance features. However, we could not experiment much with this subtask, and thus our results are not as strong, as Table 3 shows.

6 Conclusion

We have presented the system developed by our team for participating in SemEval-2016 Task 3 on Community Question Answering. We achieved the best results on subtask C, and strong results on subtasks A and B, by combining a rich set of various types of features: semantic, lexical, metadata, and user-related. The most important group turned out to be the metadata for the question and for the comment, semantic vectors trained on QatarLiving data and similarities between the question and the comment for subtasks A and C, and between the original and the related question for Subtask B.

In future work, we would like to experiment with new, interesting features, e.g., based on various word embeddings as in the SemanticZ system (Mihaylov and Nakov, 2016b). We also want to use our features in a deep learning architecture, e.g., as in the MTE-NN system (Guzmán et al., 2016a; Guzmán et al., 2016b), which borrowed an entire neural network framework and architecture from previous work on machine translation evaluation (Guzmán et al., 2015).

We further plan to use information from entire threads to make better predictions, as using thread-level information for answer classification has already been shown useful for SemEval-2015 Task 3, subtask A, e.g., by using features modeling the thread structure and dialogue (Nicosia et al., 2015; Barrón-Cedeño et al., 2015), or by applying thread-level inference using the predictions of local classifiers (Joty et al., 2015; Joty et al., 2016). How to use such models efficiently in the ranking setup of 2016 is an interesting research question.

Finally, we would like to address subtask C in a more solid way, making good use of the data, the gold annotations, the features, the models, and the predictions for subtasks A and B.

Acknowledgments

This research was performed by a team of students from MSc programs in Computer Science in the Sofia University "St Kliment Ohridski".

It is also part of the Interactive sYstems for Answer Search (Iyas) project, which is developed by the Arabic Language Technologies group at the Qatar Computing Research Institute, HBKU, part of Qatar Foundation in collaboration with MIT-CSAIL.

We would also like to thank Ontotext for providing us with their high-quality NER pipeline.

References

Sandra Aluisio, Lucia Specia, Caroline Gasperin, and Carolina Scarton. 2010. Readability assessment for text simplification. In *Proceedings of the NAACL HLT 2010 Fifth Workshop on Innovative Use of NLP for Building Educational Applications*, pages 1–9, Los Angeles, California, USA.

Apache Software Foundation Team. 2015. Spark programming guide.

Daniel Balchev, Yasen Kiprov, Ivan Koychev, and Preslav Nakov. 2016. PMI-cool at SemEval-2016 Task 3: Experiments with PMI and goodness polarity lexicons for community question answering. In *Proceedings of the 10th International Workshop on Semantic Evaluation*, SemEval '16, San Diego, California, USA.

Alberto Barrón-Cedeño, Simone Filice, Giovanni Da San Martino, Shafiq Joty, Lluís Màrquez, Preslav Nakov, and Alessandro Moschitti. 2015. Thread-level information for comment classification in community question answering. In *Proceedings of the 53rd Annual Meeting of the Association for Computational Linguistics and the 7th International Joint Conference on Natural Language Processing*, ACL-IJCNLP '15, pages 687–693, Beijing, China.

Yonatan Belinkov, Mitra Mohtarami, Scott Cyphers, and James Glass. 2015. VectorSLU: A continuous word vector approach to answer selection in community question answering systems. In *Proceedings of the 9th International Workshop on Semantic Evaluation*, SemEval '15, pages 282–287, Denver, Colorado, USA.

Carlos Castillo, Marcelo Mendoza, and Barbara Poblete. 2013. Predicting information credibility in time-sensitive social media. *Internet Research*, 23(5):560–588.

Chih-Chung Chang and Chih-Jen Lin. 2011. LIBSVM: A library for support vector machines. *ACM Transactions on Intelligent Systems and Technology*, 2:27:1–27:27.

Hamish Cunningham, Diana Maynard, Kalina Bontcheva, and Valentin Tablan. 2002. GATE: an architecture for development of robust HLT applications. In *Proceedings of 40th Annual Meeting of the Association for Computational Linguistics*, ACL '12, pages 168–175, Philadelphia, Pennsylvania, USA.

Hamish Cunningham, Diana Maynard, Kalina Bontcheva, Valentin Tablan, Niraj Aswani, Ian Roberts, Genevieve Gorrell, Adam Funk, Angus Roberts, Danica Damljanovic, Thomas Heitz, Mark A. Greenwood, Horacio Saggion, Johann Petrak, Yaoyong Li, and Wim Peters. 2011. *Text Processing with GATE (Version 6)*.

Francisco Guzmán, Shafiq Joty, Lluís Màrquez, and Preslav Nakov. 2015. Pairwise neural machine translation evaluation. In *Proceedings of the 53rd Annual Meeting of the Association for Computational Linguistics and the 7th International Joint Conference on Natural Language Processing (Volume 1: Long Papers)*, ACL-IJCNLP '15, pages 805–814, Beijing, China.

Francisco Guzmán, Lluís Màrquez, and Preslav Nakov. 2016a. Machine translation evaluation meets community question answering. In *Proceedings of the 54th Annual Meeting of the Association for Computational Linguistics*, ACL '16, Berlin, Germany.

Francisco Guzmán, Lluís Màrquez, and Preslav Nakov. 2016b. MTE-NN at SemEval-2016 Task 3: Can machine translation evaluation help community question answering? In *Proceedings of the 10th International Workshop on Semantic Evaluation*, SemEval '16, San Diego, California, USA.

Chih-Wei Hsu, Chih-Chung Chang, and Chih-Jen Lin. 2003. A practical guide to support vector classification. Technical report, Department of Computer Science, National Taiwan University.

Shafiq Joty, Alberto Barrón-Cedeño, Giovanni Da San Martino, Simone Filice, Lluís Màrquez, Alessandro Moschitti, and Preslav Nakov. 2015. Global thread-level inference for comment classification in community question answering. In *Proceedings of the 2015 Conference on Empirical Methods in Natural Language Processing*, EMNLP '15, pages 573–578, Lisbon, Portugal.

Shafiq Joty, Lluís Màrquez, and Preslav Nakov. 2016. Joint learning with global inference for comment classification in community question answering. In *Proceedings of the 2016 Conference of the North American Chapter of the Association for Computational Linguistics: Human Language Technologies*, NAACL-HLT '16, San Diego, California, USA.

Xin Li and Dan Roth. 2006. Learning question classifiers: The role of semantic information. *Nat. Lang. Eng.*, 12(3):229–249, September.

Andrew Kachites McCallum. 2002. Mallet: A machine learning for language toolkit. http://mallet.cs.umass.edu.

Todor Mihaylov and Preslav Nakov. 2016a. Hunting for troll comments in news community forums. In *Proceedings of the 54th Annual Meeting of the Association for Computational Linguistics*, ACL '16, Berlin, Germany.

Todor Mihaylov and Preslav Nakov. 2016b. SemanticZ at SemEval-2016 Task 3: Ranking relevant answers in community question answering using semantic similarity based on fine-tuned word embeddings. In *Proceedings of the 10th International Workshop on Semantic Evaluation*, SemEval '16, San Diego, California, USA.

Todor Mihaylov, Georgi Georgiev, and Preslav Nakov. 2015a. Finding opinion manipulation trolls in news community forums. In *Proceedings of the Nineteenth Conference on Computational Natural Language Learning*, CoNLL '15, pages 310–314, Beijing, China.

Todor Mihaylov, Ivan Koychev, Georgi Georgiev, and Preslav Nakov. 2015b. Exposing paid opinion manipulation trolls. In *Proceedings of the International Conference Recent Advances in Natural Language Processing*, RANLP '15, pages 443–450, Hissar, Bulgaria.

Tomas Mikolov, Ilya Sutskever, Kai Chen, Greg S Corrado, and Jeff Dean. 2013a. Distributed representations of words and phrases and their compositionality. In C. J. C. Burges, L. Bottou, M. Welling, Z. Ghahramani, and K. Q. Weinberger, editors, *Advances in Neural Information Processing Systems 26*, NIPS '13, pages 3111–3119. Curran Associates, Inc.

Tomas Mikolov, Wen-tau Yih, and Geoffrey Zweig. 2013b. Linguistic regularities in continuous space word representations. In *Proceedings of the 2013 Conference of the North American Chapter of the Association for Computational Linguistics: Human Language Technologies*, NAACL-HLT '13, pages 746–751, Atlanta, Georgia, USA.

Preslav Nakov, Lluís Màrquez, Walid Magdy, Alessandro Moschitti, Jim Glass, and Bilal Randeree. 2015. SemEval-2015 task 3: Answer selection in community question answering. In *Proceedings of the 9th International Workshop on Semantic Evaluation*, SemEval '15, pages 269–281, Denver, Colorado, USA.

Preslav Nakov, Lluís Màrquez, Alessandro Moschitti, Walid Magdy, Hamdy Mubarak, Abed Alhakim Freihat, Jim Glass, and Bilal Randeree. 2016. SemEval-2016 task 3: Community question answering. In *Proceedings of the 10th International Workshop on Semantic Evaluation*, SemEval '16, San Diego, California, USA.

Massimo Nicosia, Simone Filice, Alberto Barrón-Cedeño, Iman Saleh, Hamdy Mubarak, Wei Gao, Preslav Nakov, Giovanni Da San Martino, Alessandro Moschitti, Kareem Darwish, Lluís Màrquez, Shafiq Joty, and Walid Magdy. 2015. QCRI: Answer selection for community question answering - experiments for Arabic and English. In *Proceedings of the 9th International Workshop on Semantic Evaluation*, SemEval '15, pages 203–209, Denver, Colorado, USA.

Radim Řehůřek and Petr Sojka. 2010. Software Framework for Topic Modelling with Large Corpora. In *Proceedings of the LREC 2010 Workshop on New Challenges for NLP Frameworks*, pages 45–50, Valletta, Malta.

Caitlin Sadowski and Greg Levin. 2007. Simihash: Hash-based similarity detection. Technical Report UCSC-SOE-11-07, University of California, Santa Cruz, USA.

Ivan Zamanov, Marina Kraeva, Nelly Hateva, Ivana Yovcheva, Ivelina Nikolova, and Galia Angelova. 2015. Voltron: A hybrid system for answer validation based on lexical and distance features. In *Proceedings of the 9th International Workshop on Semantic Evaluation*, SemEval '15, pages 242–246, Denver, Colorado, USA.

PMI-cool at SemEval-2016 Task 3: Experiments with PMI
and Goodness Polarity Lexicons for Community Question Answering

Daniel Balchev, Yasen Kiprov, Ivan Koychev
Faculty of Mathematics and Informatics
Sofia University "St. Kliment Ohridski"
Sofia, Bulgaria
{dblachev,yasen.kiprov}@gmail.com
koychev@fmi.uni-sofia.bg

Preslav Nakov
Qatar Computing Research Institute
HBKU, P.O. box 5825
Doha, Qatar
pnakov@qf.org.qa

Abstract

We describe our submission to SemEval-2016 Task 3 on Community Question Answering. We participated in subtask A, which asks to rerank the comments from the thread for a given forum question from good to bad. Our approach focuses on the generation and use of goodness polarity lexicons, similarly to the sentiment polarity lexicons, which are very popular in sentiment analysis. In particular, we use a combination of bootstrapping and pointwise mutual information to estimate the strength of association between a word (from a large unannotated set of question-answer threads) and the class of good/bad comments. We then use various features based on these lexicons to train a regression model, whose predictions we use to induce the final comment ranking. While our system was not very strong as it lacked important features, our lexicons contributed to the strong performance of another top-performing system.

1 Introduction

Online forums have been gaining a lot of popularity in recent years. In these forums, one can ask a question, and based on the wisdom of the crowd, expect to get some good answers. In practice, unless there is strong moderation, most such forums get populated with bad answers, which can be annoying for users as it takes time to read through all answers in a long thread. As the importance of the problem was recognized in the research community, this gave rise to two shared tasks on Community Question Answering at SemEval-2015 (Nakov et al., 2015) and SemEval-2016 (Nakov et al., 2016).

Here we describe the PMI-cool system, which we developed to participate in SemEval-2016 Task 3, subtask A, which asks to rerank the answers in a question-answer thread, ordering them from good to bad (Nakov et al., 2016). As the name of our system suggests, our approach is heavily based on pointwise mutual information (PMI), which we use to estimate the association strength between a word and a class, e.g., the class of good or the class of bad comments. Based on this association strength, we perform bootstrapping in a large unannotated set of question-answer threads to generate specialized *goodness polarity* lexicons. We then use various features based on these lexicons to train a regression model, whose predictions we use to induce the final comment ranking.

While our PMI-cool system did not perform very well at the competition as it lacked important features and as we found a bug in our submission, our goodness polarity lexicons proved useful and contributed to the strong performance of another top-performing system at SemEval-2016 Task 3: SUper_team (Mihaylova et al., 2016).

2 Method

Our solution can be separated into two phases: (*i*) feature extraction, and (*ii*) machine learning. The feature extraction phase consists of extracting various PMI-based and other features, which we describe in the following sections. In the second phase, we apply a support vector machine (SVM) regression model (Drucker et al., 1997), taking the features as an input and returning the similarity score for each question-answer pair as an output.

844

Proceedings of SemEval-2016, pages 844–850,
San Diego, California, June 16-17, 2016. ©2016 Association for Computational Linguistics

At test time, we generate regression scores for each answer in a question-answer thread and we rerank the answers accordingly. Before exploring our features, we will first introduce PMI and how we use it to generate goodness polarity lexicons.

3 Pointwise Mutual Information and Strength of Association

The pointwise mutual information (PMI) is a notion from the theory of information: given two random variables A and B, the mutual information of A and B is the "amount of information" (in units such as bits) obtained about the random variable A, through the random variable B (Church and Hanks, 1990).

Let a and b be two values from the sample space of A and B, respectively. The *pointwise* mutual information between a and b is defined as follows:

$$pmi(a; b) = \log \frac{P(A = a, B = b)}{P(A = a) \cdot P(B = b)} \quad (1)$$

$$= \log \frac{P(A = a|B = b)}{P(A = a)} \quad (2)$$

$pmi(a; b)$ takes values between $-\infty$, which is when $P(A = a, B = b) = 0$, and $\min\{-\log P(A = a), -\log P(B = b)\}$, when $P(A = a|B = b) = P(B = b|A = a) = 1$.

The mutual information between A and B is the expected value of $pmi(a; b)$:

$$MI(A, B) = \sum_{a \in A} \sum_{b \in B} pmi(a; b) \quad (3)$$

PMI is central to a popular approach for bootstrapping sentiment lexicons proposed by Turney (2002). The idea is to start with a small set of seed positive (e.g., *excellent*) and negative words (*bad*), and then to use these words to induce sentiment polarity orientation for new words in a large unannotated set of texts (in his case, product reviews). The idea is that words that co-occur in the same text with positive seed words are likely to be positive, while those that tend to co-occur with negative words are likely to be negative. To quantify this intuition, Turney defines the notion of semantic orientation (SO) for a term w as follows:

$$SO(w) = pmi(w, pos) - pmi(w, neg)$$

where *pos* and *neg* stand for any positive and negative seed word, respectively.

The idea was later used by other researchers, e.g., Mohammad et al. (2013) built several lexicons based on PMI between words and tweet categories. Here the categories (positive and negative) were defined by a seed set of emotional hashtags, e.g., #happy, #sad, #angry, etc. or by simple positive and negative smileys, e.g., ;) , :) , ; (, : (. In this case, the resulting lexicons included not only words, but also bigrams and discontinuous pairs of words.

Another related work is that of Severyn and Moschitti (2015), who proposed an approach to lexicon induction, which, instead of using PMI for SO, assigns positive/negative labels to the unlabeled tweets (based on the seeds), and then trains an SVM classifier on them, using word n-grams as features. These n-grams are then used as lexicon entries with the learned classifier weights as polarity scores. While this is an interesting approach, in our experiments below, we will stick to PMI as a more established method to estimate SO.

Finally, there is a related task at SemEval-2016 on predicting the out-of-context sentiment intensity of phrases (Kiritchenko et al., 2016), but there the focus is on multiword phrases.

4 Building Goodness Polarity Lexicons

We use SO to build goodness polarity lexicons for good/bad comments in the forum. Instead of using positive and negative sentiment words as seeds, we start with seed words that are associated with good or bad comments. Unlike the work above, we do not do pure bootstrapping, but rather we use a semi-supervised approach, which works in two steps.

Step 1: In order to come up with a list of words that signal a good/bad comment (which is not as easy as it is to come up with such words manually), we look for words that are strongly associated with good vs. bad comments in the annotated training dataset, using SO. We then select the top 5% of the words with the most extreme positive/negative values of SO, which corresponds to the most extreme good/bad comment words.

Step 2: We then apply the SO again, but this time using the seed words that we selected in Step 1, in order to build the final large-scale goodness polarity lexicon, as in the above-described work.

5 Features

We used a variety of features based on the textual content of the question and of the answer and on metadata about the question and about the question-answer pair.

5.1 Metadata features

All the metadata features we used are included with their SO with the good/bad class. We used the following features:

- *SameAuthor.* This feature checks whether the target answer is given by the same user who asked the question. The assumption here is that the author of the question is unlikely to provide a good answer to his/her own question. We do not use this boolean feature directly, but we use the SO between it and the good/bad classes.

- *AnswerNumber.* This is the rank of the answer (e.g., first, second, third, ..., tenth). The assumption is that most discussions tend to degenerate and to lose focus over time. This is also visible in the baseline that ranks the answers based on their chronologicak rank, which performs better than random (Nakov et al., 2016). The feature value is the SO of the answer rank and of the good/bad classes.

- *AnswerAuthor.* This is the ID of the person who gave the answer. The idea is that some users might tend to give mostly good/bad answers. Thus, the SO between the author ID and the good/bad classes is useful for user modeling.

5.2 Word PMI

The main feature of our PMI-cool system is based on the lexicon constructed by computing the SO of each word, used in all the answers in the training corpus. Using this technique, we identify words commonly used in good versus bad answers in general, regardless of the question; we used words without stemming as stemming lowered the performance. For instance, bad answers often contain variants of thanks statements, insults, words generally used in off-topic comments and interjections, etc. Table 1 shows some of the top words that are most strongly associated with bad answers in terms of SO.

5.3 Sentiment Lexicon

Another resource we used is the Sentiment140 lexicon, which was constructed by Mohammad et al. (2013) using SO for word weighting, as we mentioned above. Our assumption here is that good/bad sentiment expressed in the answer suggests good/bad answers, as previously suggested in (Nicosia et al., 2015). The feature we calculate is the sum of the sentiment scores of the sentiment-bearing words in the answer.

5.4 Bootstrapped PMI

As explained above, we used bootstrapping to induce larger goodness polarity lexicons from the large unnanotated corpus provided for the task. For this purpose, we first used PMI to build a lexicon from the labeled training data, removing rarely mentioned words and taking the top and the bottom 5% of the rest, based on the SO score. Then, we used PMI again, using these words as good/bad seeds to generate the large lexicon. Unfortunately, due to implementation issues before the submission deadline, this feature was not included in the submitted system's feature set.

6 Ineffective Features

We further used some features that turned out to be ineffective. Still, we describe them here as we believe this might be useful for other researchers.

6.1 Personality Trait Features

We used the lexicons of Schwartz et al. (2013), which were designed to measure a user's big-five personality traits: openness to experience, conscientiousness, extraversion, agreeableness, and neuroticism. These lexicons were also computed using PMI and SO metrics between words in a large set of user-generated content on social media: 75,000 Facebook user profiles with personality values and 700 million words, phrases, and topic instances. There are two lexicons for each trait, with the 100 most and the 100 least characteristic words for the target trait.

We calculated a personality score for each of the five traits by summing the scores of all matching words in all answers written by the author of the answer, thus modeling his/her personality profile. However, this feature, did not yield improvements.

Word	SO
thanx	-2.1962458411
wk	-2.1638105653
tnx	-2.0627144485
thanks	-2.0458352035
thx	-1.965984822
thank	-1.9291830558
lols	-1.8324534294
colt	-1.8324534294
khanan	-1.7960857852
md	-1.7090744082
richard	-1.6989220368
khattak	-1.6783027496
huh	-1.6783027496
appreciate	-1.6643165076
avatar	-1.5798626767
joking	-1.5798626767
hahaha	-1.5798626767
tinker	-1.5798626767
gun	-1.5447713569
dracula	-1.5157838201
lp	-1.4959811928
idiot	-1.4234104999
bach	-1.4234104999
weird	-1.4141511745
valuable	-1.3906206771
illusions	-1.3906206771
ah	-1.3906206771
wonder	-1.375353205
silly	-1.3418305129
wow	-1.3334622633
fs	-1.3334622633

Table 1: Words with the smallest SO.

6.2 Topic Features

The text features used in PMI-cool are based on words only. We also tried to build a Latent Dirichlet Allocation (LDA) model (Blei et al., 2003) on the question and on the answers and to add the resulting topic distributions as features. However, this did not help on the development dataset, and thus we did not use it in our final submission.

7 Experiments and Evaluation

For training the prediction model for good versus bad answers, we used an SVM with a linear kernel as implemented in LibLinear (Fan et al., 2008). We treated each answer as a separate instance with all the above features, merging the PotentiallyUseful and the Bad labels under the *bad* class, and we ranked the answers based on the SVM score.

Features	MAP
MAX possible score	0.865
All features	0.638
All − metadata	0.620
All − personality	0.638
All − sentiment	0.636
All − word PMI	0.572
Baseline (chronological)	0.595
Baseline (random)	0.535

Table 2: Ablation results on the development dataset.

Here is a list of the useful features we experimented with:

- *SO SameAuthor*;

- *SO AnswerNumber*;

- *SO AnswerAuthor*;

- sum of $SO(w)$ for the answer words;

- sum of the sentiment for the answer words;

- one feature for each personality trait: sum of the scores of the lexicon words for that trait in all posts by the answer author;

- number of words with positive $BootstrapedSO$ in the answer;

- number of words with negative $BootstrapedSO$ in the answer;

- fraction of words with positive $BootstrapedSO$ in the answer;

- fraction of words with negative $BootstrapedSO$ in the answer;

- sum of the positive $BootstrapedSO$ scores for the answer words;

- sum of the negative $BootstrapedSO$ scores for the answer words;

- maximum value of $BootstrapedSO$ for a word in the answer;

- minimum value of $BootstrapedSO$ for a word in the answer;

- sum of $BootstrapedSO$ scores for all answer words.

The MAP scores resulting from our experiments on the development dataset are shown in Table 2. The first row shows the maximum possible score: it is lower than 1, as 33 of the 244 dev threads had no good answers. Next, we show the MAP score when all features are enabled; we can see that it outperforms both the chronological and the random baseline, by 4 and 10 MAP points absolute, respectively. The following four rows show results with some class of features disabled. We can see that the personality features had virtually no impact on the results, sentiment had a minimal impact (0.2 MAP points), metadata had a real impact (1.8 MAP points), while the word PMI features had the largest impact (6.6 MAP points).

8   Post-Submission Analysis

After the competition ended, we fixed a bug in the bootstrapped lexicon construction, which resulted in sizable improvements. We further replaced the uniting SVR with SVC, and we excluded the PotentiallyUseful comments from training. These changes collectively yielded a boost in MAP to 74.67 on the test dataset. As Table 3 shows, this is 6 MAP points absolute higher than the score for the system we submitted to the competition. It is also only 4.5 MAP points behind the best, and only 3 points behind the second-best team.

9   Conclusion and Future Work

We have described our PMI-cool system for SemEval-2016, Task 3 on Community Question Answering, subtask A, which asks to rerank the comments from the thread for a given forum question from good to bad. Our approach relied on using SO scores based on PMI to construct various features, the most important of which were our goodness polarity lexicons, which are based on an idea we borrowed from sentiment analysis. In particular, we used a combination of bootstrapping and pointwise mutual information to estimate the strength of association between a word (from a large unannotated set of question-answer threads) and the class of good/bad comments. We then used various features based on these lexicons to train a regression model, whose predictions we used to induce the final comment ranking.

While our PMI-cool system did not perform very well at the competition as it lacked important features and as we had a bug at submission time, our goodness polarity lexicons proved useful and contributed to the strong performance of another top-performing system at SemEval-2016 Task 3: SUper_team (Mihaylova et al., 2016).

In future work, we plan to strengthen our system with more features. In particular, we would like to incorporate rich knowledge sources, e.g., semantic similarity features based on fine-tuned word embeddings and topics similarities as in the SemanticZ system (Mihaylov and Nakov, 2016b). There are also plenty of interesting features to borrow from the SUper_Team system (Mihaylova et al., 2016), including veracity, text complexity, and troll user features as inspired by (Mihaylov et al., 2015a; Mihaylov et al., 2015b; Mihaylov and Nakov, 2016a). It would be interesting to combine these in a deep learning architecture, e.g., as in the MTE-NN system (Guzmán et al., 2016a; Guzmán et al., 2016b), which borrowed an entire neural network framework and achitecture from previous work on machine translation evaluation (Guzmán et al., 2015).

We further plan to use information from entire threads to make better predictions, as using thread-level information for answer classification has already been shown useful for SemEval-2015 Task 3, subtask A, e.g., by using features modeling the thread structure and dialogue (Nicosia et al., 2015; Barrón-Cedeño et al., 2015), or by applying thread-level inference using the predictions of local classifiers (Joty et al., 2015; Joty et al., 2016). How to use such models efficiently in the ranking setup of 2016 is an interesting research question.

Acknowledgments.

This research was performed by Daniel Balchev, a student in Computer Science in the Sofia University "St Kliment Ohridski", as part of his MSc thesis.

This research is also part of the Interactive sYstems for Answer Search (Iyas) project, which is developed by the Arabic Language Technologies (ALT) group at the Qatar Computing Research Institute (QCRI), HBKU, part of Qatar Foundation in collaboration with MIT-CSAIL.

	Submission	MAP	AvgRec	MRR	P	R	F1	Acc
1	SemEval 1st	79.19_1	88.82_1	86.42_1	76.96_1	55.30_8	64.36_5	75.11_2
2	SemEval 2nd	77.66_2	88.05_3	84.93_4	75.56_2	58.84_6	66.16_2	75.54_1
3	SemEval 3rd	77.58_3	88.14_2	85.21_2	74.13_4	53.05_{10}	61.84_8	73.39_5
...	...	...	...	...	...	...	...	...
	PMI-cool-improved	*74.67*	*85.28*	*83.54*	*76.43*	*33.18*	*46.27*	*68.69*
...	...	...	...	...	...	...	...	...
10	**PMI-cool-primary**	$\mathbf{68.79_{10}}$	79.94_{10}	80.00_9	47.81_{12}	70.58_2	57.00_9	56.73_{12}
...	...	...	...	...	...	...	...	...
12	SemEval 12th	62.24_{12}	75.41_{12}	70.58_{12}	50.28_{11}	53.50_9	51.84_{10}	59.60_{11}
	Baseline 1 (chronological)	**59.53**	**72.60**	**67.83**	—	—	—	—
	Baseline 2 (random)	52.80	66.52	58.71	40.56	74.57	52.55	45.26
	Baseline 3 (all 'true')	—	—	—	40.64	100.00	**57.80**	40.64
	Baseline 4 (all 'false')	—	—	—	—	—	—	**59.36**

Table 3: **Comparison to the official results on SemEval-2016 Task 3, subtask A.** The first column shows the rank of the primary runs with respect to the official MAP score. The second column contains the team's name and its submission type. The following columns show the results for the primary, and then for other, unofficial evaluation measures. The subindices show the rank of the primary runs with respect to the evaluation measure in the respective column.

References

Alberto Barrón-Cedeño, Simone Filice, Giovanni Da San Martino, Shafiq Joty, Lluís Màrquez, Preslav Nakov, and Alessandro Moschitti. 2015. Thread-level information for comment classification in community question answering. In *Proceedings of the 53rd Annual Meeting of the Association for Computational Linguistics and the 7th International Joint Conference on Natural Language Processing*, ACL-IJCNLP '15, pages 687–693, Beijing, China.

David M. Blei, Andrew Y. Ng, and Michael I. Jordan. 2003. Latent dirichlet allocation. *J. Mach. Learn. Res.*, 3:993–1022, March.

Kenneth Ward Church and Patrick Hanks. 1990. Word association norms, mutual information, and lexicography. *Comput. Linguist.*, 16(1):22–29, March.

Harris Drucker, Christopher J. C. Burges, Linda Kaufman, Alex J. Smola, and Vladimir Vapnik. 1997. Support vector regression machines. In M. I. Jordan and T. Petsche, editors, *Advances in Neural Information Processing Systems 9*, pages 155–161. MIT Press.

Rong-En Fan, Kai-Wei Chang, Cho-Jui Hsieh, Xiang-Rui Wang, and Chih-Jen Lin. 2008. LIBLINEAR: A library for large linear classification. *Journal of Machine Learning Research*, 9:1871–1874.

Francisco Guzmán, Shafiq Joty, Lluís Màrquez, and Preslav Nakov. 2015. Pairwise neural machine translation evaluation. In *Proceedings of the 53rd Annual Meeting of the Association for Computational Linguistics and the 7th International Joint Conference on Natural Language Processing (Volume 1: Long Papers)*, ACL-IJCNLP '15, pages 805–814, Beijing, China.

Francisco Guzmán, Lluís Màrquez, and Preslav Nakov. 2016a. Machine translation evaluation meets community question answering. In *Proceedings of the 54th Annual Meeting of the Association for Computational Linguistics*, ACL '16, Berlin, Germany.

Francisco Guzmán, Lluís Màrquez, and Preslav Nakov. 2016b. MTE-NN at SemEval-2016 Task 3: Can machine translation evaluation help community question answering? In *Proceedings of the 10th International Workshop on Semantic Evaluation*, SemEval '16, San Diego, California, USA.

Shafiq Joty, Alberto Barrón-Cedeño, Giovanni Da San Martino, Simone Filice, Lluís Màrquez, Alessandro Moschitti, and Preslav Nakov. 2015. Global thread-level inference for comment classification in community question answering. In *Proceedings of the 2015 Conference on Empirical Methods in Natural Language Processing*, EMNLP '15, pages 573–578, Lisbon, Portugal.

Shafiq Joty, Lluís Màrquez, and Preslav Nakov. 2016. Joint learning with global inference for comment classification in community question answering. In *Proceedings of the 2016 Conference of the North American Chapter of the Association for Computational Linguistics: Human Language Technologies*, NAACL-HLT '16, San Diego, California, USA.

Svetlana Kiritchenko, Saif M Mohammad, and Mohammad Salameh. 2016. SemEval-2016 task 7: Determining sentiment intensity of English and Arabic phrases. In *Proceedings of the 10th International Workshop on Semantic Evaluation*, SemEval '16, San Diego, California, USA.

Todor Mihaylov and Preslav Nakov. 2016a. Hunting for troll comments in news community forums. In *Proceedings of the 54th Annual Meeting of the Association for Computational Linguistics*, ACL '16, Berlin, Germany.

Todor Mihaylov and Preslav Nakov. 2016b. SemanticZ at SemEval-2016 Task 3: Ranking relevant answers in community question answering using semantic similarity based on fine-tuned word embeddings. In *Proceedings of the 10th International Workshop on Semantic Evaluation*, SemEval '16, San Diego, California, USA.

Todor Mihaylov, Georgi Georgiev, and Preslav Nakov. 2015a. Finding opinion manipulation trolls in news community forums. In *Proceedings of the Nineteenth Conference on Computational Natural Language Learning*, CoNLL '15, pages 310–314, Beijing, China.

Todor Mihaylov, Ivan Koychev, Georgi Georgiev, and Preslav Nakov. 2015b. Exposing paid opinion manipulation trolls. In *Proceedings of the International Conference Recent Advances in Natural Language Processing*, RANLP '15, pages 443–450, Hissar, Bulgaria.

Tsvetomila Mihaylova, Pepa Gencheva, Martin Boyanov, Ivana Yovcheva, Todor Mihaylov, Momchil Hardalov, Yasen Kiprov, Daniel Balchev, Ivan Koychev, Preslav Nakov, Ivelina Nikolova, and Galia Angelova. 2016. SUper Team at SemEval-2016 Task 3: Building a feature-rich system for community question answering. In *Proceedings of the 10th International Workshop on Semantic Evaluation*, SemEval '16, San Diego, California, USA.

Saif Mohammad, Svetlana Kiritchenko, and Xiaodan Zhu. 2013. NRC-Canada: Building the state-of-the-art in sentiment analysis of tweets. In *Proceedings of the Second Joint Conference on Lexical and Computational Semantics (*SEM), Volume 2: Proceedings of the Seventh International Workshop on Semantic Evaluation*, SemEval '13, pages 321–327, Atlanta, Georgia, USA.

Preslav Nakov, Lluís Màrquez, Walid Magdy, Alessandro Moschitti, Jim Glass, and Bilal Randeree. 2015. SemEval-2015 task 3: Answer selection in community question answering. In *Proceedings of the 9th International Workshop on Semantic Evaluation*, SemEval '15, pages 269–281, Denver, Colorado, USA.

Preslav Nakov, Lluís Màrquez, Alessandro Moschitti, Walid Magdy, Hamdy Mubarak, Abed Alhakim Freihat, Jim Glass, and Bilal Randeree. 2016. SemEval-2016 task 3: Community question answering. In *Proceedings of the 10th International Workshop on Semantic Evaluation*, SemEval '16, San Diego, California, USA.

Massimo Nicosia, Simone Filice, Alberto Barrón-Cedeño, Iman Saleh, Hamdy Mubarak, Wei Gao, Preslav Nakov, Giovanni Da San Martino, Alessandro Moschitti, Kareem Darwish, Lluís Màrquez, Shafiq Joty, and Walid Magdy. 2015. QCRI: Answer selection for community question answering - experiments for Arabic and English. In *Proceedings of the 9th International Workshop on Semantic Evaluation*, SemEval '15, pages 203–209, Denver, Colorado, USA.

H Andrew Schwartz, Johannes C Eichstaedt, Margaret L Kern, Lukasz Dziurzynski, Stephanie M Ramones, Megha Agrawal, Achal Shah, Michal Kosinski, David Stillwell, Martin EP Seligman, and Lyle H Ungar. 2013. Personality, gender, and age in the language of social media: The open-vocabulary approach. *PLOS ONE*, page e73791.

Aliaksei Severyn and Alessandro Moschitti. 2015. On the automatic learning of sentiment lexicons. In *Proceedings of the 2015 Conference of the North American Chapter of the Association for Computational Linguistics: Human Language Technologies*, NAACL-HLT '15, pages 1397–1402, Denver, Colorado, USA.

Peter D Turney. 2002. Thumbs up or thumbs down?: semantic orientation applied to unsupervised classification of reviews. In *Proceedings of the 40th annual meeting on association for computational linguistics*, ACL '02, pages 417–424.

UniMelb at SemEval-2016 Task 3: Identifying Similar Questions by Combining a CNN with String Similarity Measures

Doris Hoogeveen[1,2]
dhoogeveen@student.unimelb.edu.au
Huizhi Liang[2]
oklianghuizi@gmail.com
Long Duong[1,2]
lduong@student.unimelb.edu.au

Yitong Li[2]
yitongl4@student.unimelb.edu.au
Bahar Salehi[1,2]
bsalehi@student.unimelb.edu.au
Timothy Baldwin[2]
tb@ldwin.net

[1]NICTA
[2]Department of Computing and Information Systems
The University of Melbourne
VIC, Australia

Abstract

This paper describes the results of the participation of The University of Melbourne in the community question-answering (CQA) task of SemEval 2016 (Task 3-B). We obtained a MAP score of 70.2% on the test set, by combining three classifiers: a NaiveBayes classifier and a support vector machine (SVM) each trained over lexical similarity features, and a convolutional neural network (CNN). The CNN uses word embeddings and machine translation evaluation scores as features.

1 Introduction

In this paper we present the system we submitted for the community question-answering (CQA) task of the SemEval 2016 workshop (Task 3-B: Nakov et al. (2016)). By finding an automatic way to answer new questions based on existing ones, we unlock an enormous wealth of information stored in online CQA archives. In the task as specified for the SemEval workshop, we were given 70 query questions. Each question had at most ten candidate questions, which we were to re-rank according to their similarity to the query question. Each question consisted of a title and a description. The data was taken from the Qatar Living forum.[1] The training data set was small: 267 queries, with ten candidate duplicate questions each. The candidate questions were originally labelled according to the three classes: RELEVANT, PERFECT-MATCH and IRRELEVANT. Subsequently, however, RELEVANT and PERFECTMATCH were merged into a single class. In an ideal ranking, documents with

relevant labels were to be ranked higher than the IR-RELEVANT documents.

The system we submitted combines the predictions of three different classifiers through simple voting. The first two classifiers (naive Bayes and SVM) made use of semantic similarity measures as features, and the third one was a convolutional neural network (CNN) that used word embeddings and machine translation evaluation scores as input. The combined system achieved a MAP score of 70.2% on the test set.

2 Approach

Our system combined the scores of three different classifiers based on simple voting. If at least two of the three classifiers considered a candidate question relevant to a query question, it was considered to be relevant. The candidate questions were then ranked according to this judgement, with the relevant ones on top (in any order, since this was not taken into account in the official evaluation). In this section we will describe the details of the three classifiers.

2.1 String Similarity Features (SS1)

Our first set of features consisted of string similarity measures, which we selected based on our recent success in applying these features to measure the compositionality of multiword expressions (Salehi and Cook, 2013), to estimate semantic textual similarity (Gella et al., 2013), and to detect cross-lingual textual entailment (Graham et al., 2013).

To measure the string similarity between two questions, the titles and the descriptions of the questions were lemmatized using NLTK (Bird, 2006).

---

[1]http://www.qatarliving.com/forum

851

We used two string similarity measures in this study: longest common substring and the Smith-Waterman algorithm.[2] The output of each measure was normalized to the range of $[0, 1]$, where 0 indicated that the questions were completely different, while 1 showed that they were identical. More details on the string similarity measures and how we normalise the scores are described in Salehi and Cook (2013).

Our primary experiments showed that measuring string similarity between the titles of questions led to a higher accuracy than using the question descriptions. Therefore, we only considered the titles in our final run. Ultimately, in order to combine all string similarity measures into one score, we used the linear kernel SVM as implemented in the scikit-learn package[3], using the default parameters.

2.2 String Similarity Features 2 (SS2)

For our second model, we used five more lexical similarity measures as features: the Jaccard similarity, cosine similarity calculated over binary term vectors, the overlap coefficient, de Sørensen-Dice coefficient, and Kullback-Leibler (KL) divergence. With these features we obtained the best results by using both the title and the description of the question. In contrast to our first classifier, no stemming or lemmatization was applied because it was found not to make any difference. The classifier we used was naive Bayes.[4]

2.3 Convolutional Neural Network (CNN)

The third classifier we used was a convolutional neural network ("CNN"). CNN structures have been shown to be very successful in speech recognition and computer vision tasks (Graves et al., 2013; Krizhevsky et al., 2012). Recently, they have also been applied to natural language tasks, and again, have achieved good results (Collobert and Weston, 2008; Yin and Schütze, 2015).

Kalchbrenner et al. (2014) developed a CNN-based model that can be used for sentence modelling

---

[2]We also experimented with Levenshtein and modified Levenshtein, but we did not observe any improvement when using these features.

[3]http://scikit-learn.org

[4]We used the version implemented in the Weka toolkit: http://www.cs.waikato.ac.nz/ml/weka/, using the default settings.

problems. With several combinations of convolutional filters and dynamic k-max pooling filters, the model is very good at capturing features on both the local word level and the global sentence level. The word-level features are combined in several stages to model sentences. This characteristic of capturing meaning at different levels is particularly attractive for the target domain, as two questions with similar meaning may have a very different surface form. A neural network that can model meaning at the sentence level may recognise two questions as being similar even though they have very little lexical overlap. This is the reason we decided to use Kalchbrenner's CNN for our task, enhanced with some aspects of Yin and Schütze (2015)'s model, who used a CNN for Paraphrase Identification (PI).

In our approach, we used the CNN to compare two sentences at different levels in the model. The similarity scores obtained in this way were combined with several machine translation evaluation scores and fed into a multi-Layer perceptron (MLP) classifier to get a final similarity score. We decided to make this final classifier a neural network too so that we could get a non-linear output for the newly added features. The expectation is that this will improve the classification.

In the following subsections we explain the details of the CNN: how to model sentences on different levels and how to generate the features using sentence embeddings. We also explain some other features that we added, and how we trained the model.

2.3.1 Model Overview

Figure 1 show the CNN model. Each tokenised input sentence $\mathbf{S}$ consists of n words $\{w_1, w_2, \cdots, w_n\}$, where n denotes the length of the sentence. Each word has a word vector $e_n \in \mathbb{R}^d$, where d is the dimension of the word vector. All the word vectors combined form a sentence matrix embedding $\mathbf{E} \in \mathbb{R}^{d \times n}$, which is used as the input to our CNN model. Different input sentences will have different lengths, but this is not a problem at this stage. We deal with this issue when comparing the sentences to obtain features, as explained in Section 2.3.2.

For each convolutional level l, we convolved the input matrix with a wide one-dimensional convolution filter, and generated a convolutional matrix

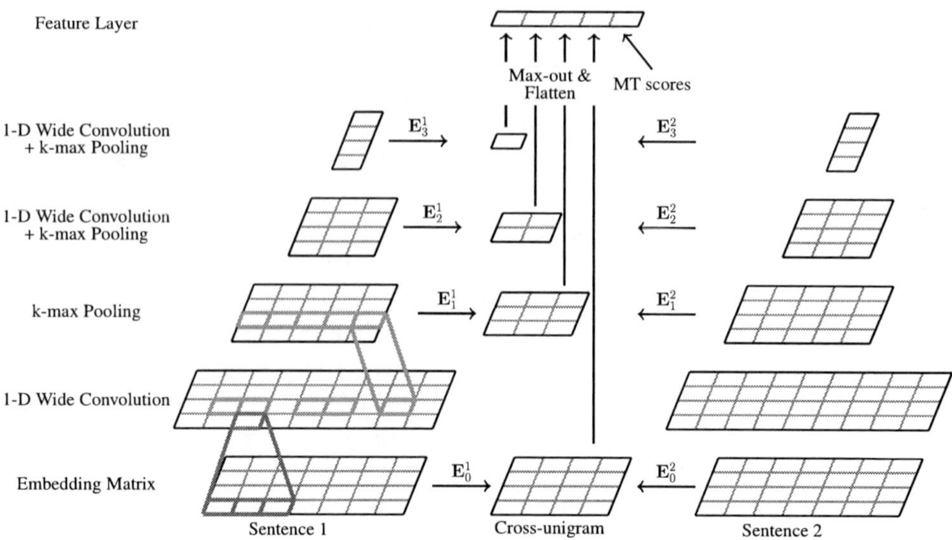

Figure 1: The Convolutional Neural Network.

$\mathbf{C} \in \mathbb{R}^{d \times (n+m-1)}$, where m is the filter width, which is set to 3 (see the red highlighting in Figure 1). We then applied a non-linear function (rectified linear units (ReLU)) to get the convolutional layer $\mathbf{C}\prime = ReLU(\mathbf{C})$. C and $C\prime$ are combined in Figure 1 and shown as "1-D Wide Convolution". Next, we applied Kalchbrenner et al. (2014)'s dynamic k-max pooling approach on $\mathbf{C}'$. For each dimension of $\mathbf{C}'$, we extracted a maximum of k features and calculated the pooling layer. The output of the pooling layer is $\mathbf{E}_l \in \mathbb{R}^{d \times k_l}$. $\mathbf{E}_l$ is the sentence embedding of level l and is used as the input for the next level $(l + 1)$ of the CNN.

After a series of such convolution operations, we get a deep CNN structure as a representation of each question.

2.3.2 Features

As explained in the previous section, the input features to the CNN consisted of word embeddings. We used constant word embeddings directly from Mikolov et al. (2013)'s pre-trained word embeddings model, with dimension $d = 300$.

After applying the convolution operations on a question pair $(\mathbf{S}_1, \mathbf{S}_2)$, we obtained an embedding set for each question: $\{\mathbf{E}_0^1, \mathbf{E}_1^1, \cdots, \mathbf{E}_l^1\}$ and $\{\mathbf{E}_0^2, \mathbf{E}_1^2, \cdots, \mathbf{E}_l^2\}$, where l is the number of levels in our CNN structure. Different embeddings represent the semantics of the question with a different granularity. $\mathbf{E}_0$ corresponds to the input word embeddings, which represent the semantics of the question at the word level. Each increase in subscript represents a convolutional level in the model. The higher up we get, the more convolved the features will be, until we end up with $\mathbf{E}_l$, which represents the document-level meaning of the question.

To obtain the features for the final classifier, we determined the similarity of the embedding matrices $\mathbf{E}_l^1$ and $\mathbf{E}_l^2$ for each level, by comparing each vector in $\mathbf{E}_l^1$ to each vector in $\mathbf{E}_l^2$; a process known on the word level as cross-unigram comparison. The similarity of the vectors was calculated using both cosine similarity and Euclidean distance. This resulted in two matrices per question pair per level, which we concatenated. To reduce the size of these low-level matrices we applied a two-dimensional maxout filter on them. The height and width of the filter were adjusted for different sentence lengths of the questions $\mathbf{S}_1$ and $\mathbf{S}_2$, to ensure that the output always had the same length. Next we flattened the matrix into a vector and used this as our sentence embedding similarity features that formed part of the input to our final classifier.

Apart from the sentence embedding similarity features, we also used several machine translation evaluation measures as extra features before applying the final classifier. Machine translation evaluation measures are designed to detect whether two sentences have a similar meaning or not. They have

	Training Set	Development Set	Test Set
query questions	267	50	70
archived questions	2,669	500	700

Table 1: The number of query and archived question pairs in the SemEval-2016 dataset

been shown to be useful features for paraphrase identification (Madnani et al., 2012), a task very similar to ours. The measures we used were BLEU (Papineni et al., 2002), NIST (Doddington, 2002), METEOR (Banerjee and Lavie, 2005), Ter (Snover et al., 2006), Ter-Plus (Snover et al., 2009), and MaxSim (Chan and Ng, 2008). After adding these additional features to the sentence embedding similarity features, we fed our feature vectors into a Multiple Layer Perceptron (MLP) classifier to get a final similarity score.

2.3.3 Training the model

In this section we will explain how we trained our model. Our CNN consisted of three convolutional layers, with a MLP classifier at the top. The MLP combined three fully-connected hidden layers, which contained 512 nodes each and ReLU as its activation function, with a softmax layer on the top.

For the network training, we used AdaDelta (Zeiler, 2012) to update the weights of the model, and set the initial learning rate to $\alpha = 10^{-4}$. Dropout (Srivastava et al., 2014) was added to the input layer of the MLP, with L_2-regularization. The dropout rate was set to 0.5.

3 Experiments

In this section, we will describe the experimental setup and the results of our experiments.

3.1 Dataset

Table 1 presents basic statistics for the SemEval-2016 Task 3-B dataset. Each query question was paired up with at most ten archived questions, which we had to re-rank according to relevance. The dataset was partitioned into three components: (1) a training set, (2) a development set, and (3) a test set.

3.2 Results

To evaluate the effectiveness of the different feature sets, we report on the results of both the combined model and the separate classifiers in Tables 2 and 3. Baselines 1 and 2 are the official baselines as given by the SemEval organisers. The information retrieval (IR) baseline was produced using Google to rank the candidate questions.

We use the Mean Average Precision (MAP) as our primary evaluation metric,[5] but also report the Average Recall (AvgRec), Mean Reciprocal Rank (MRR), Precision (P), Recall (R), F1-measure (F1), and Accuracy (Acc) scores.

On the development set, we obtained the best MAP score with the majority voting model, but on the test set we did not see the same result. On the test set, the CNN model by itself obtained the best results. It is interesting to see that all three models separately performed better on the test set than on the development set, but the combined model did not.

Although models SS1 and SS2 both make use of string similarity measures, they produced different classification outputs for 60.2% of the development set queries. SS1's predictions differed from the CNN's in 54.8% of the development queries, and SS2's predictions differed from the CNN's in 72.6% of the development queries. The fact that the three models produced such different results, while each performed reasonably well, was the motivation for combining them.

One reason for the different results on the test and development sets might be the difference in the class balance. In the development set, 43% of the candidate questions were labeled as relevant, and 57% as irrelevant. In the test set this was 33% and 67% respectively. The training data resembled the development set more than the test set, with 45% relevant and 55% irrelevant candidate questions. We suspect that more training data is needed to obtain consistent results.

It would be interesting to see whether the scores improve when we add the string similarity features to the CNN directly (thereby losing the majority voting component), in the same way as we added the

---

[5]This is also what the official ranking of the participating systems is based on.

Test Set

Model	MAP(%)	AvgRec(%)	MRR	Acc(%)	P(%)	R(%)	F1(%)
Baseline 1(IR)	74.75	88.30	83.79	-	-	-	-
Baseline 2 (random)	46.98	67.92	50.96	45.20	40.43	32.58	73.82
SS1	71.11	85.71	81.20	70.00	55.02	54.08	54.55
SS2	72.95	88.51	82.26	70.29	55.92	50.64	53.15
CNN	**73.04**	87.72	82.21	73.43	60.09	60.09	60.09
Majority voting	70.20	86.21	78.58	74.57	63.96	54.08	58.60

Table 2: The official evaluation results for the SemEval-2016 Test Set

Development Set

Model	MAP(%)	AvgRec(%)	MRR	Acc(%)	P(%)	R(%)	F1(%)
Baseline 1(IR)	71.35	86.11	76.67	-	-	-	-
Baseline 2 (random)	55.95	73.23	62.23	48.80	44.42	76.64	56.16
SS1	70.06	85.95	77.33	68.80	68.35	50.47	58.06
SS2	68.96	85.58	74.00	64.60	64.12	39.25	48.70
CNN	72.71	87.86	79.33	75.20	76.47	60.75	67.71
Majority voting	**73.13**	88.93	80.00	72.20	64.48	78.04	70.61

Table 3: The official evaluation results for the SemEval-2016 Development Set

machine translation evaluation features. We leave this for future work.

4 Summary

In this paper, we proposed a method based on the combination of three different classifiers for the task of duplicate question ranking, in the context of Se-mEval 2016 Task 3-B. The classifiers we combined were a CNN using word embeddings and machine translation evaluation metrics, and two classifiers that used lexical similarity features: a naive Bayes classifier and a support vector machine (SVM). The results we obtained on the test set were quite different from the results on the development set, which may be explained by the small size of the training data set.

References

Satanjeev Banerjee and Alon Lavie. 2005. METEOR: An Automatic Metric for MT Evaluation with Improved Correlation with Human Judgments. In *Proceedings of the 2005 ACL Workshop on Intrinsic and Extrinsic Evaluation Measures for Machine Translation and/or Summarization*, volume 29, pages 65–72.

Steven Bird. 2006. NLTK: The Natural Language Toolkit. In *Proceedings of the 2006 International Conference on Computational Linguistics (COLING), Interactive Presentation Sessions*, pages 69–72.

Yee Seng Chan and Hwee Tou Ng. 2008. MAXSIM: A Maximum Similarity Metric for Machine Translation Evaluation. In *Proceedings of the 46th Human Language Technology Conference of the North American Chapter of the Association for Computational Linguistics (HLTNAACL)*, pages 55–62.

Ronan Collobert and Jason Weston. 2008. A Unified Architecture for Natural Language Processing: Deep Neural Networks with Multitask Learning. In *Proceedings of the 25th International Conference on Machine Learning*, pages 160–167.

George Doddington. 2002. Automatic Evaluation of Machine Translation Quality Using N-Gram Co-occurrence Statistics. In *Proceedings of the 2nd Human Language Technology Conference (HLT)*, pages 138–145.

Spandana Gella, Bahar Salehi, Marco Lui, Karl Grieser, Paul Cook, and Timothy Baldwin. 2013. UniMelb NLP-CORE: Integrating Predictions from Multiple Domains and Feature Sets for Estimating Semantic Textual Similarity. *Proceedings of the 2nd Joint Conference on Lexical and Computational Semantics (*SEM)*, pages 207–216.

Yvette Graham, Bahar Salehi, and Timothy Baldwin. 2013. Umelb: Cross-lingual Textual Entailment with Word Alignment and String Similarity Features. *Proceedings of the 2nd Joint Conference on Lexical and Computational Semantics (*SEM)*, page 133.

Alan Graves, Abdel-rahman Mohamed, and Geoffrey Hinton. 2013. Speech Recognition with Deep Recurrent Neural Networks. In *Proceedings of the 2013 IEEE International Conference on Acoustics, Speech and Signal Processing (ICASSP)*, pages 6645–6649.

Nal Kalchbrenner, Edward Grefenstette, and Phil Blunsom. 2014. A Convolutional Neural Network for Modelling Sentences. In *Proceedings of the 52nd Annual Meeting of the Association for Computational Linguistics (ACL)*, pages 655–665.

Alex Krizhevsky, Ilya Sutskever, and Geoffrey E Hinton. 2012. ImageNet Classification with Deep Convolutional Neural Networks. In *Advances in Neural Information Processing Systems*, pages 1097–1105.

Nitin Madnani, Joel Tetreault, and Martin Chodorow. 2012. Re-Examining Machine Translation Metrics for Paraphrase Identification. In *Proceedings of the 50th Human Language Technology Conference of the North American Chapter of the Association for Computational Linguistics (HLTNAACL)*, pages 182–190.

Tomas Mikolov, Ilya Sutskever, Kai Chen, Greg S Corrado, and Jeff Dean. 2013. Distributed Representations of Words and Phrases and Their Compositionality. In *Advances in Neural Information Processing Systems*, pages 3111–3119.

Preslav Nakov, Lluís Màrquez, Walid Magdy, Alessandro Moschitti, Jim Glass, and Bilal Randeree. 2016. SemEval-2016 Task 3: Community Question Answering. In *Proceedings of the 10th International Workshop on Semantic Evaluation (SemEval)*.

Kishore Papineni, Salim Roukos, Todd Ward, and Wei-Jing Zhu. 2002. BLEU: A Method for Automatic Evaluation of Machine Translation. In *Proceedings of the 40th Annual Meeting of the Association for Computational Linguistics (ACL)*, pages 311–318.

Bahar Salehi and Paul Cook. 2013. Predicting the Compositionality of Multiword Expressions Using Translations in Multiple Languages. In *Proceedings of the 2nd Joint Conference on Lexical and Computational Semantics (*SEM)*, pages 266–275.

Matthew Snover, Bonnie Dorr, Richard Schwartz, Linnea Micciulla, and John Makhoul. 2006. A Study of Translation Edit Rate with Targeted Human Annotation. In *Proceedings of the Association for Machine Translation in the Americas*, pages 223–231.

Matthew G Snover, Nitin Madnani, Bonnie Dorr, and Richard Schwartz. 2009. TER-Plus: Paraphrase, Semantic, and Alignment Enhancements to Translation Edit Rate. *Machine Translation*, 23(2-3):117–127.

Nitish Srivastava, Geoffrey Hinton, Alex Krizhevsky, Ilya Sutskever, and Ruslan Salakhutdinov. 2014. Dropout: A Simple Way to Prevent Neural Networks from Overfitting. *Journal of Machine Learning Research*, 15(1):1929–1958.

Wenpeng Yin and Hinrich Schütze. 2015. Convolutional Neural Network for Paraphrase Identification. In *Proceedings of the 53rd Human Language Technology Conference of the North American Chapter of the Association for Computational Linguistics (HLTNAACL)*, pages 901–911.

Matthew D Zeiler. 2012. ADADELTA: An Adaptive Learning Rate Method. *arXiv:1212.5701*.

ICL00 at SemEval-2016 Task 3: Translation-Based Method for CQA System

Minghua Zhang   Yunfang Wu
Institute of Computational Linguistics, Peking University

Abstract

We participate in the English subtask B and C at SemEval-2016 Task 3 "Community Question Answering". This paper is concerned with the description of our participating system. We propose a ranking model that combines a translation model with the cosine similarity-based method. Compared to the traditional bag of words method, the proposed model is more effective because the relationships between words can be explicitly modeled through word-to-word translation probabilities. Experiments conducted on the official test data demonstrate that our proposed ranking method obtains promising results.

1 Introduction

The SemEval-2016 Task 3 (Nakov et al., 2016) Community Question Answering (CQA) covers a full task on CQA and which is, therefore, closer to a real application. To facilitate the participation of non IR/QA scholar to the task, the search engine step is already carried out which means that the task organizers explicitly provides the set of potential answers to be reranked. That is to say, given a new question (aka original question) and the set of the first 10 related questions (retrieved by a search engine) in subtask B, our system will focus on reranking the related questions according to their similarity with the original question. Similar to subtask B, in subtask C that is the main English subtask, Given a new question and the set of the first 10 related questions, each associated with its first 10 comments appearing in its thread, we will rerank the 100 comments (10 questions * 10 comments) according to their relevance with respect to the original question.

Note that the subtask B will give us enough tools to solve the main subtask. And therefore, our paper will give an overall description of the system based on subtask B. In section 2, we will briefly discuss an important difference between the subtask C and subtask B in the course of reranking.

However, the major challenge for subtask B, as for most of CQA systems, is the word mismatch between the original question and the related question. For example, "Where I can buy good oil for massage?" and "Is there any place I can find scented massage oils in Qatar?" are two very similar questions, but they only have a few words in common. To solve the word mismatch problem, we focus on translation-based approaches in this paper.

The remainder of this paper is organized as follows. Section 2 introduces the methods used in the ranking model clearly. Section 3 presents the translation probabilities Estimation. We will talk about an overview of the system in section 4. Section 5 presents the experimental results. In Section 6, we conclude with ideas for future research.

2 Ranking Approach

In SemEval-2016 Task 3, the dataset file is a sequence of question pair instances. Each instance contain an original question and a thread which consists of a potentially related question, together with 10 comments for it. Next, let Q-Q denotes the set of all original-related question pairs in the archive, Q-Q = {…, [(org$_i$, rel$_1$), (org$_i$, rel$_2$), ..., (org$_i$, rel$_j$), …, (org$_i$, rel$_{10}$)], …}. So, the goal of subtask B is to re-rank the related questions according to the Score(org$_i$, rel$_j$). Typically, this score can be modeled by the probability that org$_i$ is generated by rel$_j$. Thus, the following part of this section focus on how to calculate P(org$_i$|rel$_j$).

Proceedings of SemEval-2016, pages 857–860,
San Diego, California, June 16-17, 2016. ©2016 Association for Computational Linguistics

However, the job of subtask C is to rerank the 100 comments according to their relevance with respect to each original question. For clarity, let Q-C denotes the set of all question-comment pairs, Q-C = {…, [(org$_i$, rel$_j$, C$_{ij1}$), (org$_i$, rel$_j$, C$_{ij2}$), …, (org$_i$, rel$_j$, C$_{ijk}$), …, (org$_i$, rel$_j$, C$_{ij100}$)], …}. To begin the process, we apply the tool which is designed for subtask B to calculate the relevance between original question and related question, then regard it as a weight. In the next step, we make use of translation model to obtain the relevance between original question and comment. Finally, we will rerank the comments according to the Score(org$_i$, C$_{ijk}$) which can be written as:

$$Weight_j = \frac{P(org_i|rel_j)}{\sum_{j'=1}^{n} P(org_i|rel_{j'})} \tag{1}$$

$$Score(org_i, C_{ijk}) = Weight_j * P_{trans}(org_i|C_{ijk}) \tag{2}$$

where org$_i$ is the original question, rel$_j$ is the related question, and C$_{ijk}$ is the comment for rel$_j$.

2.1 Word-Based Translation Model

Previous work (Jeon et al., 2005) were the first to apply the translation based method to CQA, subsequent work (Xue et al., 2008) proposed to linearly combine language model and word-based translation model into a unified framework. The experiments show that this model gains better performance than both the language model and the word-based translation model. Following Xue et al. (2008), this model can be written as:

$$Score(org_i, rel_j) = \prod_{w \in org_i} P(w|rel_j) \tag{3}$$

$$P(w|rel_j) = \alpha \frac{\#(w, rel_j)}{|rel_j|} + \beta \sum_{t \in rel_j} P(w|t) \frac{\#(t, rel_j)}{|rel_j|} +$$
$$\gamma \frac{\#(w, B)}{|B|} \tag{4}$$

where $\#(w, rel_j)$ and $\#(t, rel_j)$ is the frequency of term w and t in rel$_j$ respectively, B denotes the whole archive, |rel$_j$| and |B| denote the length of rel$_j$ and B respectively, P(w|t) denotes the translation probability from word t to word w.

2.2 Combination of Cosine similarity and Translation Method

We compared the performances of a unigram language model and a cosine similarity-based method on the development dataset, which demonstrated that the cosine similarity method outperforms the language model. Therefore, we propose to linearly combine the cosine similarity and translation model into a ranking model, which can be written as:

$$Score(org_i, rel_j) = \alpha P_{cos}(org_i, rel_j) +$$
$$\beta P'_{trans}(org_i|rel_j) \tag{5}$$

$$P_{trans}(org_i|rel_j) = \prod_{w \in org_i} (\sum_{t \in rel_j} P(w|t) \frac{\#(t, rel_j)}{|rel_j|}) \tag{6}$$

$$P'_{trans}(org_i|rel_j) = {10}/{-\log_2 P_{trans}(org_i|rel_j)} \tag{7}$$

where $P_{cos}(org_i, rel_j)$ denotes the cosine similarity. $P_{trans}(org_i|rel_j)$ denotes the translation probabilities. The two parts are not in an order of magnitude. So when we obtained the two similarity scores, the translation probabilities have to be transformed according to the formula (7).

3 Translation Probabilities Estimation

3.1 Parallel Corpus Collection

The performance of the proposed ranking model heavily depends on the quality of the translation probabilities. Therefore, besides designing translation based ranking method, another important problem is how to learn good word-to-word translation probabilities.

In the given training dataset, the similarity relationship between the related question and original question can be accessed from the attribute "RELQ_RELEVANCE2ORGQ" belonging to the tag "RelQuestion", which can be PerfectMatch, Relevant and Irrelevant. When the attribute value takes PerfectMatch or Relevant, there's a strong possibility that the original question and relevant question express similar meanings with different words. So, it is natural to use the matching original-relevant question pairs as the "parallel corpus" to estimate word-to-word translation probabilities. Furthermore, it is easy to realize that if one original question is similar with two different relevant questions simultaneously, then the two relevant questions would also express similar meanings. As an example, from the initial parallel corpus {[org$_1$, rel$_1$], [org$_1$, rel$_2$], [org$_1$, rel$_3$], [org$_2$, rel$_4$], [org$_2$, rel$_5$]}, we can obtain the new big parallel corpus {[org$_1$, rel$_1$], [org$_1$, rel$_2$], [org$_1$, rel$_3$], [rel$_1$, rel$_2$], [rel$_1$, rel$_3$], [rel$_2$, rel$_3$], [org$_2$, rel$_4$], [org$_2$, rel$_5$], [rel$_4$, rel$_5$]} through the simple extension method.

In the IBM translation model 1, sentences are normally translated from one language into another language. But in our task, the similar sentence pairs are written in the same language, the correspondence of words is not as strong as in the bilingual sentence pair. The word-to-word translation probabilities can be learned with either part as the source language and the other part as the target. Accordingly, the training data is doubled. When there is a parallel corpus consisting of the similar sentence pairs, the training module will utilize IBM translation model 1 incorporating an EM-based algorithm to learn the word-to-word translation probabilities.

3.2 Consolidation Method

The parallel sentence pairs are written in the same language. If source sentences contain word "wi" and target sentences contain word "wj", we can obtain the word-to-word translation probabilities $P(wj|wi)$. Conversely, the word "wi" can also appear in target sentences and the word "wj" appear in source sentences. So, we can obtain the reverse translation probabilities $P(wi|wj)$ through the same training process. Then we assume that the reverse translation probabilities are additional information to improve the word-to-word translation probabilities, and the combination of both will be consolidation beneficial. So we linearly combine the trained word-to-word translation probabilities:

$$P_{lin}(wi|wj) = \gamma P(wi|wj) + (1 - \gamma)P(wj|wi) \qquad (8)$$

To see how much the consolidation strategy benefits the rerank task, we introduce two baseline methods for comparison. The first method denotes the initial word-to-word translation probabilities, and the second denote the reverse translation probabilities. Table 1 reports the experimental results of Subtask B on the development dataset. We can see that the consolidation strategy outperforms the two baseline methods in our task. From the experimental result, we can see that the reverse translation probabilities do have some positive effects.

Model	Trans Prob	MAP
$Score(org_i, rel_j)$	$P(wj\|wi)$	0.7312
	$P(wi\|wj)$	0.7376
	$P_{lin}(wi\|wj)$	0.7415

Table 1: The impact of consolidation strategy.

4 System overview

In the following part, we will introduce the details of the implementation. The whole calculation process can be divided into two main modules: Pre-processing and Estimate.

Pre-processing. This module tries to extract the subject text and the main body of questions from the XML-formatted input file first of all, then combine the two parts together to form the original question and related question. Next, the system makes word segmentation for each pairs of original question and related question, and removes stop words at the same time. Furthermore, Porter stemmer is employed to extract stem, which will be beneficial to learn good word-to-word translation probabilities. For the sake of saving the evaluation times, we execute statistical calculations on the word list which represents the original question and related question after segmentation. For example, there is a words list [massage, oil, where, buy, good, oil, massage], we'll obtain a dictionary {massage:2, oil:2, where:1, buy:1, good:1} after statistics, and we also know that the length of list is seven.

Estimate: In this stage, the system loads the word-to-word translation probability table, which we select defaultdict[1] as its storage structure. Finally, we compute the similarity score of original question and related question according to our ranking model which linearly combines the cosine similarity and translation model. In subtask B, the labels PerfectMatch and Relevant should be regarded as equal, so our goal is to rank the PerfectMatch and Relevant candidates at the top, in any order, and the Irrelevant candidates at the bottom, also in any order.

5 Experiments

In this section, experiments are conducted on DEV

---

[1] Defaultdict is a subclass of the dict that calls a factory function to supply missing values in Python.

dataset to demonstrate the performance of our proposed ranking model.

5.1 Data Set and Evaluation Metrics

The official dataset contains TRAIN, DEV and TEST. The development dataset is intended to be used as a development-time evaluation dataset as we develop our systems. However, when submitting prediction results, we will add the development dataset to training data as well. The total available data of the TRAIN part is made up of 267 original questions and 2669 related questions for Subtask B, plus 26690 related comments for Subtask C. DEV dataset which were manually double-checked and are very reliable consist of 50 original questions, 500 related questions, and 5,000 comments. As far as the TEST is concerned, the task organizers provide participants with 70 original questions, so, there would be 700 predictions for subtask B and 7,000 predictions for subtask C. The official scorer will provide a number of evaluation measures to assess the quality of the output of a system, but the official evaluation measure towards which all systems will be evaluated and ranked is Mean Average Precision (MAP).

5.2 Results

Five types of baselines are used to compare with our proposed ranking model. Table 2 presents the MAP performance comparison of different methods on DEV dataset in subtask B. Row 1 to row 5 are the IR engine default ordering, Language Model, Cosine Similarity-based method, Translation Model and Translation-based Language model. Row 5 is our proposed translation-based reranking method. Compared with other baselines approaches, our proposed model received good results. Finally, the competition result for our primary submissions are 0.7511 against 0.7475 baseline in Subtask B, and 0.4919 against 0.4036 baseline in Subtask C.

6 Conclusions and Future Work

In this paper, we propose a ranking model that combines a translation model with the cosine-based similarity method to solve the rerank task in CQA. Experiments on test data demonstrate the effectiveness of our method.

There are some ways in which this research could be continued. First, we plan to apply neural machine

#	Methods	MAP
1	IR-engine	0.7135
2	LM	0.7248
3	Cosine	0.7287
4	Trans	0.7342
5	Trans-LM	0.7360
6	Trans-Cosine	0.7415

Table 2: Comparison of different methods in subtask B.

translation (Bahdanau et al., 2014) to learn good translation probabilities. In addition, phrase-based translation model for question retrieval (Zhou et al., 2011) have shown superior performance compared to word-based translation models. So it is necessary to try this method to further improve the performance.

Acknowledgments

This work is supported by National Natural Science Foundation of China (61371129), National High Technology Research and Development Program of China (2015AA015403), Key Program of Social Science foundation of China (12&ZD227).

References

Bahdanau D, Cho K, Bengio Y. *Neural Machine Translation by Jointly Learning to Align and Translate[J]*. Eprint Arxiv, 2014.

J. Jeon, W. B. Croft, and J. H. Lee. *Finding similar questions in large question and answer archives*. In *Proceedings of the 14th ACM Conference on Information and Knowledge Management*, pages 84–90, 2005.

Preslav Nakov, Llu\'{i}s M\`{a}rquez, Alessandro Moschitti, Walid Magdy, Hamdy Mubarak, Abed Alhakim Freihat, Jim Glass, and Bilal Randeree. 2016. SemEval-2016 task 3: Community Question Answering. In *Proceedings of the 10th International Workshop on Semantic Evaluation*, SemEval '16, San Diego, CA.

X. Xue, J. Jeon, and W. B. Croft. 2008. *Retrieval models for question and answer archives*. In *Proceedings of SIGIR*, pages 475-482.

Zhou G, Cai L, Zhao J, et al. *Phrase-Based Translation Model for Question Retrieval in Community Question Answer Archives[C]// Proceedings of the 49th Annual Meeting of the Association for Computational Linguistics*: Human Language Technologies - Volume 1. Association for Computational Linguistics, 2011:653-662.

Overfitting at SemEval-2016 Task 3: Detecting Semantically Similar Questions in Community Question Answering Forums with Word Embeddings

Hujie Wang
University of Waterloo
200 University Ave W
Waterloo, ON N2L 3G1, Canada
h3wang@uwaterloo.ca

Pascal Poupart
University of Waterloo
200 University Ave W
Waterloo, ON N2L 3G1, Canada
ppoupart@uwaterloo.ca

Abstract

This paper presents an approach for estimating the question-question similarity of an English dataset specified in Shared Task 3, subtask B of SemEval-2016. Given a new question and a set of the first 10 related questions retrieved by a search engine, participants are asked to produce a binary relevant/irrelevant judgement and rerank the related questions according to their similarity with respect to the original question. Our submitted system uses a 2-layer feed-forward neural network with the averages of word embedding vectors to predict the semantic similarity score of two questions. We also evaluate the results of Random Forests and Support Vector Machine in comparison to the Neural Network. Results on the test dataset show that the model achieves a Mean Average Precision 69.681.

1 Introduction

Finding semantically related questions is a difficult task due to two main factors: (1) paraphrasing, which can appear at different levels, e.g., lexical, phrasal, sentential (Madnani and Dorr, 2010); and (2) two questions could be asking different things but look for the same solution. Thus, traditional surface similarity measures such as Edit Distance, Jaccard, Dice and Overlap coefficient and their variations are not able to capture many cases of semantic relatedness. To preserve the semantic meaning of a question, we use weighted average word embedding vectors to model questions. We evaluate several algorithms that take the weighted average word embedding vectors of two questions as inputs and predict whether two questions are related or not.

To provide a benchmark so as to compare and develop question-question similarity measuring models in Community Question Answering forums, the Question-Question Similarity task in SemEval-2016 Task 3, Subtask B (Nakov et al., 2016) requires the participants to determine whether two questions are sementically related and given a new question, rerank all similar questions retrieved by a search engine. **Table 1** presents an example of a pair of semantically related questions.

We perform an extensive number of experiments using data from Shared Task 3 and compare three types of classifiers: Neural Network (NN), Support Vector Machine (SVM) and Random Forests (RF), as well as the impact of different weighting schemes for averaging word embedding vectors and different word embedding dimensions. The results show that 2-layer Feedforward Neural Network with Idf weighting scheme and in-domain word embeddings outperforms the rest of models.

Title: Best Bank
Body: Which is a good bank as per your experience in Doha
Title: Good Bank
Body: Hi Guys; I need to open a new bank accoount. Which is the best bank in Qatar ? I assume all of them will roughly be the same; but stll which has a slight edge (Money transfer; benifits etc) Thanks !!!

Table 1: An example of semantically related questions

Proceedings of SemEval-2016, pages 861–865,
San Diego, California, June 16-17, 2016. ©2016 Association for Computational Linguistics

2   Word Embedding Features

Recently (Mikolov et al., 2013) introduced word2vec, a novel word-embedding procedure. Their model is able to learn continuous vector representations of words from a very large dataset by using a feedforward Neural Net Language Model (NNLM). Specifically, The CBOW architecture predicts the current word based on the context, and the Skip-gram architecture predicts surrounding words given the current word. Learning the word embedding is entirely unsupervised and it can be computed on the text corpus of interest.

Each word is encoded by a column vector in an embedding matrix $W_e \in \mathbb{R}^{d \times |V|}$ learnt by using word2vec, where V is a fixed-sized vocabulary. Each column of the matrix represents the word embedding vector of the i-th word in V. Each word w is transformed into its vector representations v_w by using a matrix-vector product:

$$v_w = W_e b_w \tag{1}$$

where b_w is a one-hot encoding vector of size $|V|$ which has value 1 at the index of the word w and zero in all other positions. Let X_t and X_b be the set of word tokens of a question's title and body, then the vector representations of the question's title and body are the weighted vector average of the word embeddings associated with tokens in X_t and X_b:

$$Q_t = \frac{1}{|X_t|} \sum_{w \in X_t} v_w c_w \tag{2}$$

$$Q_b = \frac{1}{|X_b|} \sum_{w \in X_b} v_w c_w \tag{3}$$

where c_w denotes the weight of the word w. We also investigate the impact of different weighting schemes:

1. $c_w = 1$
2. $c_w = IDF(w)$ where IDF denotes inverse document frequency (Sparck Jones, 1972). Specifically,

$$IDF(w) = \log(1 + \frac{N}{n_w + 1}) \tag{4}$$

N is the total number of documents in the corpus and n_w is the number of documents where the term w appears. In our case, we define each question's body in the training dataset as a document.

Given a pair of questions $(Q^{(1)}, Q^{(2)})$, we compute $Q_t^{(1)}$, $Q_b^{(1)}$, $Q_t^{(2)}$ and $Q_b^{(2)}$ by using the above transformations. Given vectors u and v, we denote the similarity features $sim_{(u,v)}$ as the concatenation of $u \cdot v$ (component-wise product of u and v) and $|u - v|$. These two features were also used by (Tai et al., 2015). The final vector representations or features for the input pair of questions $(Q^{(1)}, Q^{(2)})$ is defined as the concatenation of $sim_{(Q_t^{(1)}, Q_t^{(2)})}$ and $sim_{(Q_b^{(1)}, Q_b^{(2)})}$. Those features are then fed into a classifier to predict a binary True/False label.

3   Experiments and Results

3.1   Datasets

In our experiments we use data from the community-created Qatar Living Forums[1] collected for SemEval-2016 task 3, subtask B. There are 317 original questions and 3,169 related questions. The dataset is pre-splitted into 264 original questions and 2669 related question for training, as well as 50 original questions and 500 related question for validation. Each data point is a pair of questions (an original question and a related question) and a similarity label, which is either "PerfectMatch", "Relevant" or "Irrelevant". According to the task description, we need to predict a binary label where "True" covers "PerfectMatch" and "Relevant", and "False" covers "Irrelevant", and rerank a set of related questions according to their similarity with respect to the original question.

3.2   Preprocessing

Several text preprocessing operations are performed before we extract features. We first transform all words into lowercase, filter out stop words, remove all punctuations and replace numbers with the token "NUMBER". Then the Phrase Detection Toolkit implemented in Gensim is used to group tokens together if they form a phrase. After that, all unique words and phrases are selected from the training set as our vocabulary which has a size of 11990. We deal with unseen words in the test set by marking them as "UNK".

---

[1] www.qatarliving.com/forum

Model	Classifier	Weighting Scheme	Word Embedding Dimension
NN-Idf-100	NN	$c_w = Idf(w)$	100
RF-Idf-30	RF	$c_w = Idf(w)$	30
NN-Avg-30	NN	$c_w = 1$	30
RF-Avg-30	RF	$c_w = 1$	30
SVM-Avg-80	SVM	$c_w = 1$	80
SVM-Avg-30	SVM	$c_w = 1$	30

Table 2: Description of models

3.3 Word Embedding Features

We perform pre-training using the skip-gram NN architecture (Mikolov et al., 2013) available in the Gensim Word2vec tool[2]. We use in-domain word embeddings vectors trained on the Community Question Answering dataset provided by SemEval-2016 Task 3 with the following parameter settings: (1) 30, 80 and 100 dimensional embedding vectors; (2) the maximum distance between the current and predicted word within a sentence is set to 5; (3) ignoring all words with total frequency lower than 5; (4) for each positive sample, 5 negative samples are drawn for negative sampling; (5) the number of iterations is set to 30.

3.4 Models

Several classification algorithms are explored on development dataset including Feedforward Neural Network (NN), Support Vector Machine (SVM) and Random Forests (RF). Due to the lack of the time, we only submitted the predictions from one of our NN classifiers. Configuration details of each model are presented in **Table 2**.

3.4.1 Feedforward Neural Network

We consider a two-layer Feedforward Neural Network with 64 sigmoid activation hidden units as our classifier. Weights are initialized with random orthogonal conditions (Saxe et al., 2013). We apply Dropout (Srivastava et al., 2014) with a fixed dropping probability of 0.9 for the input layer and 0.5 for the hidden layer. Our network is trained by minimizing the categorical cross entropy error over the training set using Adam (Kingma and Ba, 2014), a first-order gradient-based optimization method. We use the backpropagation algorithm (Rumelhart et al.,

1988) to compute gradients of the network. In our experiments, we implement the NN and the backpropagation algorithm using Keras[3].

3.4.2 Support Vector Machine

We use the (Gaussian) radial basis function kernel

$$K(x, x') = \exp(-\gamma|x - x'|^2) \qquad (5)$$

with $\gamma = \frac{1}{4d}$, where d is the dimension of word embedding vectors. We set the regularization parameter C of soft margin cost function to 1.

3.4.3 Random Forests

We explored a large set of parameter values by doing randomized search and selecting only the best set of parameters for our RF models. Specifically, we use the following fine-tuned parameters:

- The number of trees: 382
- Measurement of the quality of a split: entropy
- The maximum depth of the tree: 33
- The minimum number of samples required to split an internal node: 5
- The minimum number of samples in newly created leaves: 2
- The number of features to consider when looking for the best split: 116

3.5 Results and Discussion

Table 3 summarizes the performance of our systems, along with the baseline systems provided by the organizers and the top three systems (UH-PRHLT-primary, ConvKN-primary and Kelp-primary). The results show that models with Idf weighting scheme outperform models using naive word embedding averages. The performance differences between different models using the same weighting scheme and the same word embedding

---

Model	Rank	MAP	AvgRec	MRR	Precision	Recall	F1	Accuracy
NN-Idf-100	—	**71.55**	**86.21**	**81.76**	56.84	57.08	56.96	71.29
RF-Idf-30	—	70.67	85.43	79.25	62.69	54.08	58.06	74.00
NN-Avg-30*	10	69.68	85.10	80.18	**63.20**	**67.81**	**65.42**	**76.14**
RF-Avg-30	—	68.65	84.43	78.37	60.71	51.07	55.48	72.71
SVM-Avg-80	—	67.06	82.55	78.80	55.91	60.94	58.32	71.00
SVM-Avg-30	—	61.39	78.20	71.91	61.59	43.35	50.88	72.14
UH-PRHLT-primary	1	76.70	90.31	83.02	63.53	69.53	66.39	76.57
ConvKN-primary	2	76.02	90.70	84.64	68.58	66.52	67.54	78.71
Kelp-primary	3	75.83	91.02	82.71	66.79	75.97	71.08	79.43
Baseline 1 (IR)	—	74.75	88.30	83.79	—	—	—	—
Baseline 2 (random)	—	46.98	67.92	50.96	32.58	73.82	45.20	40.43
Baseline 3 (all true)	—	—	—	—	33.29	100.00	49.95	33.29
Baseline 4 (all false)	—	—	—	—	—	—	—	66.71

Table 3: Performance of out top 6 systems and baseline systems on test dataset, as well as top ranking systems. The second column shows the rank of the primary runs with respect to the official MAP score. NN-Avg-30 is the model we used for the official submission. MAP and MRR stand for Mean Average Precision and Mean Reciprocal Rank, respectively.

dimension are not significant, which shows that the type of the classifier is not the bottleneck of overall performance. Also, we find that RF and NN perform slightly better than SVM. We also observe that using a large word embedding dimension (≥ 80) results in severe overfitting on the development dataset since we have a small dataset. Applying strong regularization such as Dropout with high dropping probability reduces overfitting and helps our NN models achieve high performance. Our best classifier (NN-Idf-100) achieves the highest Mean Average Precision among our classifiers.

4 Conclusion

In this paper, we address the Question-Question Similarity task by building three types of supervised classifiers. The results show that classifiers without heavy feature engineering are able to outperform the random baseline by a large margin. It also demonstrates that using the proposed features based on word embeddings is effective and able to capture semantic meanings of a question.

References

Diederik Kingma and Jimmy Ba. 2014. Adam: A method for stochastic optimization. *arXiv preprint arXiv:1412.6980*.

Nitin Madnani and Bonnie J Dorr. 2010. Generating phrasal and sentential paraphrases: A survey of data-driven methods. *Computational Linguistics*, 36(3):341–387.

Tomas Mikolov, Kai Chen, Greg Corrado, and Jeffrey Dean. 2013. Efficient estimation of word representations in vector space. *arXiv preprint arXiv:1301.3781*.

Preslav Nakov, Lluís Màrquez, Alessandro Moschitti, Walid Magdy, Hamdy Mubarak, Abed Alhakim Freihat, Jim Glass, and Bilal Randeree. 2016. SemEval-2016 task 3: Community question answering. In *Proceedings of the 10th International Workshop on Semantic Evaluation*, SemEval '16, San Diego, California, June. Association for Computational Linguistics.

David E Rumelhart, Geoffrey E Hinton, and Ronald J Williams. 1988. Learning representations by back-propagating errors. *Cognitive modeling*, 5(3):1.

Andrew M Saxe, James L McClelland, and Surya Ganguli. 2013. Exact solutions to the nonlinear dynamics of learning in deep linear neural networks. *arXiv preprint arXiv:1312.6120*.

Karen Sparck Jones. 1972. A statistical interpretation of term specificity and its application in retrieval. *Journal of documentation*, 28(1):11–21.

Nitish Srivastava, Geoffrey Hinton, Alex Krizhevsky, Ilya Sutskever, and Ruslan Salakhutdinov. 2014. Dropout: A simple way to prevent neural networks from overfitting. *J. Mach. Learn. Res.*, 15(1):1929–1958, January.

Kai Sheng Tai, Richard Socher, and Christopher D Manning. 2015. Improved semantic representations from tree-structured long short-term memory networks. *arXiv preprint arXiv:1503.00075*.

QU-IR at SemEval 2016 Task 3: Learning to Rank on Arabic Community Question Answering Forums with Word Embedding

Rana Malhas and **Marwan Torki** and **Tamer Elsayed**

Qatar University

Department of Computer Science & Engineering

Doha, Qatar

`{rana.malhas,mtorki,telsayed}@qu.edu.qa`

Abstract

Resorting to community question answering **(CQA)** websites for finding answers has gained momentum in the past decade with the explosive rate at which social media has been proliferating. With many questions left unanswered on those websites, automatic and smart question answering systems have seen light. One of the main objectives of such systems is to harness the plethora of existing answered questions; hence transforming the problem to finding good answers to newly posed questions from similar previously-answered ones. As SemEval 2016 Task 3 "Community Question Answering" has focused on this problem, we have participated in the Arabic Subtask. Our system has adopted a supervised learning approach in which a learning-to-rank model is trained over data (questions and answers) extracted from Arabic CQA forums using word2vec features generated from that data. Our primary submission achieved a 29.7% improvement over the MAP score of the baseline. Post submission experiments were further conducted to integrate variations of the word2vec features to our system. Integrating covariance word embedding features has raised the the improvement over the baseline to 37.9%.

1 Introduction

The ubiquitous presence of community question answering (CQA) websites has motivated research in the direction of building automatic question answering (QA) systems that can benefit from previously-answered questions to answer newly-posed ones (Shtok et al., 2012). A core functionality of such systems is their ability to effectively rank previously-suggested answers with respect to their degree/probability of relevance to a posted question. The ranking functionality is vital to push away irrelevant and low quality answers, which is commonplace in CQA as they are generally open with no restrictions on who can post or answer questions.

Question: ما هي الدوالي وما هي اسبابها

Candidate question-answer pairs (QApairs):

Q : هل لدوالي القدم اعراض يوجد معي دوالي في القدم ولكن اطلب منكم تزويدي باعراض الدوالي والمشاكل التي يسببها

A : العرض الأكثر شيوعا هو ظهور الأوردة منتفخة على واجهة الساق واالتشخيص يكون من خلال الفحص الطبي المباشر والعلاج سيكون وفق السبب

Q : ماهى دوالي الدرجه الثالثه وما اسبابها وكيف يتم الوقايه منها

A : الدوالي هي عباره عن توسع في الاورده العلويه للمنطقه المصابه ولها الكثير من الاسباب كالحمل والسمنه والجلوس لمده طويله جدا ويتم الوقايه منها عن طريق عدم الوقوف لمده طويله وممارسة الرايضه بشكل اكبر ولبس جوارب مخصصه لهذه الحالات لمنع التفاقم

Q: هل العروق الملتويه بشكل واضح في القدم تعتبر من الدوالي وهل الدوالي لها اخطار اذا لم يتم علاجها

A: يمكن أن تنفجر الدوالي تحت الجلد وتؤدى إلى كدمات وترسبات دموية وتصبغات تحت الجلد ويمكن أن تؤدي إلى تقرحات. قد يشمل علاج دوالي الساقين عدد من التدابير التي تهدف الى التخفيف من حدة الأعراض أو الحد من تطورها

Q: انا شاب عمري ٣٧سنة وأعاني من من دوالي الأوردة في الساقين فكيف أزيلها

A: الغالب أنه بحاجة لاستئصال إذا كانت كبيرة ومزعجة راجع اختصاصي جراحة عامة أو جراحة الأوعية الدموية لتقييم الحالة

Figure 1: A question and 4 of its given 30 candidate QApairs

To this effect, SemEval 2016 Task 3 "Community Question Answering" has emphasized the ranking component in the main task of the challenge. We have participated in Task 3-Subtask D (Arabic Subtask) which is confined to the main task of ranking answers; given a new question and a set of 30 question-answer pairs (QApairs) retrieved by a

Proceedings of SemEval-2016, pages 866–871,
San Diego, California, June 16-17, 2016. ©2016 Association for Computational Linguistics

search engine, re-rank those QApairs by their degree/probability of relevance to the new question. Figure 1 shows an example of a question and four of its 30 given candidate question-answer pairs.

The Arabic training, development and test datasets provided by the organizers were extracted from Arabic medical forums (webteb[1], altibbi[2]), and "Consult Islamweb"[3]. Further details about SemEval 2016 Task 3 can be found in (Nakov et al., 2016).

In this paper, we describe the system we developed to participate in SemEval-2016 Task 3 (Arabic Subtask). The system has leveraged a supervised learning approach over word2vec features extracted from a collection of questions and their candidate question-answer pairs to build a ranking model. The functionality of the developed system is confined to the answers re-ranking task described by SemEval 2016 Task 3. With the MAP (Mean Average Precision) being the official measure for evaluation, our efforts were mainly focused on optimizing this measure. Our developed system has achieved a MAP score improvement of 29.7% over the baseline via our primary submission, and an improvement of 37.9% via our post-submission enhancements and experiments.

The rest of the paper is organized as follows; the approach and the generated features are introduced in section 2; the experimental evaluation and setup followed by our submissions to the Arabic Subtask and their results are presented in section 3. Enhancements and further experiments conducted are also presented in section 3 before concluding with final remarks.

2   Approach

We tackled the answer ranking task with a supervised learning approach that leveraged learning-to-rank models. The features used in training are mainly semantic, where vectorized word embedding representations were used as features in different alternatives, as explained below. An overview of our system is depicted in Figure 2. Details regarding the specific models and features used in our primary and

contrastive submissions are presented in section 3.

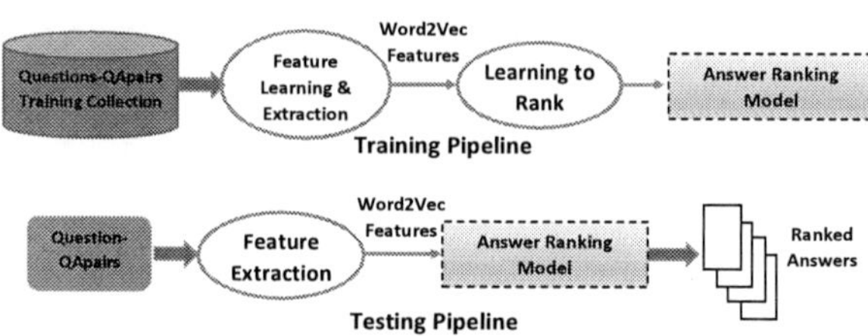

Figure 2: System overview

2.1   Data Setup

We are given a set of questions Q; each is associated with P question-answer pairs. To compute our features, we define a document according to three setups:

- **QQA:** We consider the concatenation of an original question q and one **pair** p of its associated question-answer pairs as a document d.

- **QA:** We consider the concatenation of an original question q and one **answer** of its associated question-answer pairs as a document d.

- **QQ:** We consider the concatenation of an original question q and one **question** of its associated question-answer pairs as a document d.

We have extracted features for the above data setups seeking those with the most discriminating power against our ranking problem; this is further elaborated in section 3.

2.2   Features

Every document $d_n \in D$, where $n \in \{ 1, \cdots, N \}$, has a set of words. Each word has a fixed-length word embedding representation, $w \in \mathbb{R}^{Dim}$, where Dim is the dimensionality of the word embedding. Thus for every document d_n in the set D, we define $d_n = \{w_1, \cdots, w_{k_n}\}$, where k_n is the number of words in the document d_n. The word embedding representation is computed offline following Mikolov et al approach (Mikolov et al., 2013).

To enable learning, we represent each document by a feature vector; different alternatives for feature representations are adopted as described next.

867

2.2.1 Average Word Embedding

For a document that has k_n words, we compute the average vector as follows:

$$\mu_n = \frac{\sum_{i=1}^{k_n}(w_i)}{k_n} \qquad (1)$$

Notice that $\mu_n \in \mathbb{R}^{Dim}$. For our primary and contrastive submissions, we only used the average vector μ_n to represent its respective document.

2.2.2 Covariance Word Embedding

Instead of computing the average vector, we can compute a covariance matrix $C \in \mathbb{R}^{Dim \times Dim}$. The covariance matrix C is computed by treating each dimension as a random variable and every entry in $C_{n_{u,v}}$ is the covariance between the pair of variables (u, v). The covariance between two random variables u and v is computed as in eq. 2, where k_n is the number of observations (words).

$$C_{n_{u,v}} = \frac{\sum_{i=1}^{k_n}(u_i - \bar{u})(v_i - \bar{v})}{k_n - 1} \qquad (2)$$

The matrix $C_n \in \mathbb{R}^{Dim \times Dim}$ is a symmetric matrix. We compute a vectorized representation of the matrix C_n as the stacking of the lower triangular part of matrix C_n as in eq. 3. This process produces a vector $v_n \in \mathbb{R}^{Dim \times (Dim+1)/2}$

$$\mathbf{vect}(C_n) = \left\{ C_{n_{u,v}} : u \in \{\,1, \cdots, Dim\}, v \in \{\,u, \cdots, Dim\} \right\} \qquad (3)$$

In our post submission experiments we used the covariance descriptors v_n in comparison to the basic μ_n average vectors.

2.2.3 Unigrams and tf-idf weighting

In our post submission experiments, we also used the standard unigram representation with tf-idf weighting. We have chosen the most frequent 5000 unigrams from the training data to represent every document as a sparse vector of 5000 dimensions.

2.3 Ranking Models

A learning-to-rank (L2Rank) setup was adopted that is similar to (Chen et al., 2015; Surdeanu et al., 2008). The L2Rank models were trained over the labeled Arabic data provided by the SemEval 2016 Task 3 organizers. The data constituted 1,031 original questions and their potentially related 30,411

question-answer pairs (QApairs); i.e. about 30 QApairs per original question. Each QApair is labeled by either being *Direct*, *Relevant* or *Irrelevant* with respect to the original question; the distribution of these labels are 3.0%, 57.0% and 40.0%, respectively (Nakov et al., 2015).

Two algorithms were used to train our learning-to-rank models, namely the MART (Multiple Additive Regression Trees, a.k.a. Gradient boosted regression tree) algorithm and the Random Forests algorithm.

3 Experimental Evaluation

In this section we present the experimental setup and results of our primary, contrastive-1 and contrastive-2 submissions, in addition to our post-submission experiments.

3.1 Experimental Setup

We have used the Arabic collection of questions and their potentially related question-answer pairs provided by Task3 organizers for training our models. We evaluated those models using the development dataset of 7,355 question-QApairs instead of the full provided dataset of 7,385 question-QApairs; one question (out of the 250) and its potentially related 30 QApairs were not properly formed and thus excluded. Another data preprocessing step was to parse and transform the XML files into flat files for easier data processing/tracking of question-answers.

The Gensim[4] tool was used to generate the word2vec model from training data[5]. We used the learned model to compute our features as described in section 2.2. Features were generated for the three data setups described in section 2.1.

RankLib[6] was used to create and evaluate our learning-to-rank models. Although we have experimented with a number of pairwise and listwise learning-to-rank algorithms, we adopted pointwise L2Rank algorithms in our submissions as they exhibited a relatively better performance than the other two categories.

---

[4]http://radimrehurek.com/gensim/

[5]Testing data are held out during the computation of the word2vec model.

[6]http://sourceforge.net/p/lemur/wiki/RankLib/

3.2 Evaluation Measures

Since MAP (Mean Average Precision) is the official evaluation measure to evaluate Task 3-Subtask D submissions, we focused our experiments and evaluations to optimize this measure. Time constraints have withheld us from optimizing the other evaluation measures that are also adopted by the task's official scorer, such as F1 measure, accuracy, etc.

3.3 Submissions and Results

Table 1 below summarizes the official results of our submissions which are discussed in the context of the following sub-sections.

3.3.1 Primary and Contrastive Submissions

The average word embedding features were used in all three submissions. We used $Dim = 100$ for the word2vec model we learned from training data. The differences among submissions lie in the data setup (QQA, QA or QQ) used in generating the features; and the algorithm deployed in training the L2Rank model that ranks the answers.

Submission	MAP
Primary	38.63
Contrastive-1	37.80
Contrastive-2	39.07
Baseline	29.79

Table 1: The official MAP scores attained by our primary and contrastive submissions to SemEval 2016 Task 3-SubTask D

Primary submission. The QQA data setup was used in generating the average word embedding features; and the MART algorithm (Multiple Additive Regression Trees, a.k.a. Gradient boosted regression tree) was used to train the L2Rank model. This submission has attained a MAP score of 38.63 which placed it in the fourth position among the other primary submissions of other participating teams. It achieved a 29.7% improvement over the baseline (29.79).

Contrastive-1 submission. The QA data setup was used in generating the features; and the Random Forests algorithm was deployed in training the L2Rank model. This submission has attained a MAP score of 37.80 which is lower than our other two submissions (Table 1). This suggests that using the QA data setup in feature generation (i.e. using the original question and **answers** of the QApairs while leaving out the questions of the QApairs), is not as good as using the QQA data setup (i.e. using the original questions and their **QApairs**). Further experiments might be needed to assert this finding.

Contrastive-2 submission. The QQA data setup was used in generating the features, and again the Random Forests algorithm was deployed in training the L2Rank model. Another difference in the setup of this submission was using 20% of the training data in validating the trained model while using the remaining 80% for training. This submission has performed better than our primary and contrastive-1 submissions; it attained a MAP score of 39.07 and an improvement of 31.3% over the baseline.

It is worth noting that feature values in the primary and contrastive-1 submissions were normalized using zscore and sum, respectively. In the primary submission, each feature was normalized by its *mean/standard deviation*, while in the contrastive-1 submission, each feature was normalized by the *sum* of all its values.

Although Subtask D at the surface is a re-ranking task, it has also embedded a classification task where answers need to be ranked and labeled with either *true* or *false*; the former designates a *Direct* or *Relevant* answer, and the latter designates an *Irrelevant* answer. In all submissions, we have adopted a simple heuristic of labeling the top 10 ranked answers with the label *true*, and the remaining answers with *false* otherwise. Alternatively, a supervised classifier can be used to predict the answer labels, or find a good cutoff threshold point (such as the average or median of answers rank scores) to label those exceeding that threshold with *true*, and *false* otherwise.

3.3.2 Post-Submission Experiments

Further experiments were conducted to explore the performance of Covariance Word Embedding (CovWE) and unigram features as compared to the Average Word Embedding (AvgWE) features. In Table 2, we report the MAP scores achieved by these features using a dimensionality of 50 and 100, respectively, for representing the vectors of word embeddings. In our post-submission experiments, we only extracted features using the QQA data setup.

As such, we only include the results of our primary and contrastive-2 submissions in Table 2 because their features were also extracted using the QQA data setup, unlike the contrastive-1 submission.

Experiment/Features	Normalization	MAP
AvgWE-50	-	36.01
AvgWE-100 (primary)	Zscore	38.63
AvgWE-100 (contrastive-2)	-	39.07
AvgWE-100 and Unigrams	-	37.71
CovWE-50	Linear	**41.07**
CovWE-100	Linear	**40.68**
CovWE-100 and Unigrams	-	37.51
Baseline	-	29.79

Table 2: Post-submission experiments comparing the performance of Covariance Word Embedding (CovWE) features and Unigrams to that of Average Word Embedding (AvgWE) features. The suffix numbers 50 and 100 designate the dimensionality of the vectors representing the word embeddings. Best scoring features are boldfaced.

In most of the experiments reported in Table 2, the MART algorithm was used for training the L2Rank models; whereas, for the AvgWE-100 and Unigrams experiment, the Random Forests algorithm was used. In general, the MART algorithm performed better in the majority of our experiments that we have conducted but have not reported. The main observations worth mentioning regarding the experiments in Table 2 are:

- Using tf.idf weighted uni-grams of the most frequent 5000 words along with word2vec features (AvgWE and CovWE) did not mark an improvement over using word2vec features solely.

- Normalization of feature values seem to have a tendency of enhancing the achieved MAP scores when applied. For this reason, we include in Table 2 the normalization scheme (if any) that was adopted in each experiment.

- The discriminant potential of the covariance word embedding features seem to be relatively stronger than that of average word embedding features. For example, the features CovWE-50 and CovWE-100 have achieved relatively higher MAP scores than AvgWE-50 and

AvgWE-100, respectively. With their 41.07 and 40.68 MAP scores, CovWE features have achieved an improvement of about 37.9% over the baseline. AvgWE-100 and AvgWE-50 followed with the MAP scores of 38.63 (primary submission score) and 36.01, respectively; hence, attaining lower improvements (29.7% and 20.9%) over the baseline.

- The covariance word embedding features CovWE-50 and CovWE-100 have attained comparable MAP scores of 41.07 and 40.68, respectively. Interestingly, the CovWE-50 experiment consumed 44.5 minutes to learn the L2Rank model, while the CovWE-100 experiment consumed 5.27 hours. This finding is also suggesting that covariance word embedding features seem to have a relatively higher discriminating potential even with lower dimensions.

More rigorous benchmarking experiments might be needed to further verify the merit of the above implications.

4 Conclusion

This paper describes the system we have developed to participate in SemEval-2016 Task 3 on Community Question Answering. Our system has focused on the Arabic Subtask which is confined to Answer Selection in Community Question Answering, i.e. finding good answers for a given new question. The training data provided by the organizers were extracted from Arabic medical forums (*webteb* and *al-tibbi*) and *consult islamweb*.

We have adopted a supervised learning approach where learning-to-rank models were trained over word2vec features generated from the training data. In our primary submission, average word embedding features were used; our system ranked fourth among the other participating teams. It achieved a 29.7% improvement over the baseline. Post-submission experiments were further conducted to enhance the system and integrate covariance word embedding features. The enhanced system marked an improvement of 37.9% over the baseline.

Our experiments have provided preliminary evidence regarding the discriminant potential of the covariance word embedding features over the average word embedding features; the former type of word2vec features enabled the learned model to attain a relatively better MAP score.

Furthermore, the highly comparable MAP scores attained by the covariance word embedding features for 50 and 100 dimensions (Table 2) suggest another interesting finding: the covariance word embedding features seem to have a relatively higher discriminating potential even with lower dimensions.

In future work, we intend to integrate more semantic features extracted from richer and larger semantic Arabic resources.

Acknowledgments

This work was made possible by NPRP grant# NPRP 6-1377-1-257 from the Qatar National Research Fund (a member of Qatar Foundation).

References

Ruey-Cheng Chen, Damiano Spina, W Bruce Croft, Mark Sanderson, and Falk Scholer. 2015. Harnessing semantics for answer sentence retrieval. In *Proceedings of the Eighth Workshop on Exploiting Semantic Annotations in Information Retrieval*, pages 21–27. ACM.

Tomas Mikolov, Kai Chen, Greg Corrado, and Jeffrey Dean. 2013. Efficient estimation of word representations in vector space. *arXiv preprint arXiv:1301.3781*.

Preslav Nakov, Lluís Màrquez, Walid Magdy, Alessandro Moschitti, Jim Glass, and Bilal Randeree. 2015. SemEval-2015 task 3: Answer selection in community question answering. In *Proceedings of the 9th International Workshop on Semantic Evaluation*, SemEval '2015, pages 269–281, Denver, Colorado, June. Association for Computational Linguistics.

Preslav Nakov, Lluís Màrquez, Alessandro Moschitti, Walid Magdy, Hamdy Mubarak, Abed Alhakim Freihat, Jim Glass, and Bilal Randeree. 2016. SemEval-2016 task 3: Community question answering. In *Proceedings of the 10th International Workshop on Semantic Evaluation*, SemEval '16, San Diego, California, June. Association for Computational Linguistics.

Anna Shtok, Gideon Dror, Yoelle Maarek, and Idan Szpektor. 2012. Learning from the past: answering new questions with past answers. In *Proceedings of the 21st international conference on World Wide Web*, pages 759–768. ACM.

Mihai Surdeanu, Massimiliano Ciaramita, and Hugo Zaragoza. 2008. Learning to rank answers on large online qa collections. In *ACL*, volume 8, pages 719–727.

ECNU at SemEval-2016 Task 3: Exploring Traditional Method and Deep Learning Method for Question Retrieval and Answer Ranking in Community Question Answering

Guoshun Wu[1], Man Lan[1,2]*
[1]Department of Computer Science and Technology,
East China Normal University, Shanghai, P.R.China
[2]Shanghai Key Laboratory of Multidimensional Information Processing
`51141201064@ecnu.cn, mlan@cs.ecnu.edu.cn`*

Abstract

This paper describes the system we submitted to the task 3 (Community Question Answering) in SemEval 2016, which contains three subtasks, i.e., Question-Comment Similarity (subtask A), Question-Question Similarity (subtask B), and Question-External Comment Similarity (subtask C). For subtask A, we employed three different methods to rank question-comment pair, i.e., supervised model using traditional features, Convolutional Neural Network and Long-Short Term Memory Network. For subtask B, we proposed two novel methods to improve semantic similarity estimation between question-question pair by integrating the rank information of question-comment pair. For subtask C, we implemented a two-step strategy to select out the similar questions and filter the unrelated comments with respect to the original question.

1 Introduction

The purpose of Community Question Answering task in SemEval 2016 (Nakov et al., 2016) is to provide a platform for finding good answers to new questions in a community-created discussion forum, where the main task (subtask C) is defined as follows: given a new question and a large collection of question-comment threads created by a user community, participants are required to rank the comments that are most useful for answering the new question. Obviously, this main task consists of two optional subtasks, i.e., Question-Comment Similarity (subtask A, also known as *answer ranking*), which is to re-rank comments/answers according to their relevance with respect to the question, and Question-Question Similarity (i.e., subtask B, also known as *question retrieval*), which is to retrieve the similar questions according to their semantic similarity with respect to the original question.

To address subtask A, we explored a traditional machine learning method which uses multiple types of features, e.g., Word Match Features, Translation-based Features, and Lexical Semantic Similarity Features. Additionally, for subtask A, we also built a Convolutional Neural Network (CNN) model and a bidirectional Long Short-Term Memory (BLSTM) model to learn joint representation for question-comment (Q-C) pair. For subtask B, besides IR method and traditional machine learning method, we also proposed two novel methods to improve semantic similarity estimation between question-question (Q-Q) pairs by integrating the rank information of Q-C pairs. Since subtask C can be regarded as a joint work of the two above-mentioned subtasks, we implemented a two-step strategy to first select out similar questions and then to filter out the unrelated comments with respect to the original question.

The rest of this paper is organized as follows. Section 2 describes our system. Section 3 describes experimental setting. Section 4 and 5 report results on training and test sets. Finally, Section 6 concludes this work.

2 System Description

For subtask A, we presented three different methods i.e., using traditional linguistic features, learning a CNN model and a bidirectional LSTM model to represent question and comment sentences. For sub-

Proceedings of SemEval-2016, pages 872–878,
San Diego, California, June 16-17, 2016. ©2016 Association for Computational Linguistics

task B, besides traditional methods, we proposed two novel methods to improve semantic similarity estimation between Q-Q pairs by integrating the rank information of Q-C pairs. The first is to adopt general ranking evaluation metrics of Q_0-C and Q_1-C (i.e., Spearman, Pearson, and Kendall Coefficient) as additional ranking scores or features of Q_0-Q_1 where Q_0 and Q_1 represent original question and its related question, respectively. The second is to extract features on Q_0-C and Q_1-C and to regard the cosine values which are calculated on these two feature vectors as additional features for Q_0-Q_1.

2.1 Features Engineering

All three subtasks can be regarded as an estimation task of sentence semantic measures which can be modeled by various types of features. In this work, we employed the following four types of features borrowed from previous work, i.e., Word Match Features, Translation Based Features, Topic Model Based Features, and Lexical Semantic Similarity Features. The details of these four types of features are described as follows. Note that the following four feature types are adopted in both Q-Q and Q-C pairs, here we took the Q-Q pair for example.

Word Matching Feature (WM): This feature records the proportions of co-occurred words between a given sentence pair. Given a Q-Q pair, this feature type is calculated using five measures: $|Q_0 \cap Q_1|, |Q_0 \cup Q_1|/|Q_0|, |Q_0 \cap Q_1|/|Q_1|, |Q_1 - Q_0|/|Q_1|, |Q_0 - Q_1|/|Q_0|$, where $|Q_0|$ and $|Q_1|$ denote the number of the words of Q_0 and Q_1.

Translation Based Feature (TB): The above WM feature only considers the overlapped words between Q_0 and Q_1 and thus it may fail to "bridge the lexical gap" between Q-Q pair. One possible solution is to regard this task as a statistic machine translation problem between question and answer by using the IBM Model 1(Brown et al., 1993) to learn the word-to-word probabilities. Following (Xue et al., 2008; Surdeanu et al., 2011), we regarded $P(Q_0|Q_1)$, i.e., the translation probability of Q_1 when given Q_0, as a translation based feature. The probabilities are calculated as:

$$P(Q_0|Q_1) = \prod_{w \in Q_0} P(w|Q_1)$$

$$P(w|Q_1) = (1 - \lambda)P_{tr}(w|Q_1) + \lambda P_{ml}(w|C)$$

$$P_{ml}(w|Q_1) = \sum_{a \in Q_1} P(w|a)P_{ml}(a|Q_1)$$

where $P(Q_0|Q_1)$ is the probability that the Q_0 word w is generated from Q_1, λ is a smoothing parameter, C is a background collection. $P_{ml}(w|C)$ is computed by maximum likelihood estimator. $P(w|a)$ denotes the translation probability from Q_1 word a to Q_0 word w. The GIZA++ Toolkit[1] is used to compute these probabilities.

Topic Model Based Feature (TMB): We used the LDA (Blei et al., 2003) model to transform Q_0 and Q_1 into topic-based vectors and then took the *cosine* value of two topic vectors as feature. We use the *GibbsLDA++* (Phan and Nguyen, 2007) Toolkit to train the topic model.

Lexical Semantic Similarity Feature (LSS): Inspired by (Yih et al., 2013), we included the lexical semantic similarity features in our model. We used three different word vectors to represent LSS feature, i.e., the 300-dimensional version of word2vec (Mikolov et al., 2013) vectors, 300-dimensional Glove vectors (Pennington et al., 2014) and 300-dimensional vectors which are pre-trained with the unsupervised neural language model (Mikolov et al., 2013) on the Qatar Living data [2]. Words not present in the set of pre-trained words are initialized randomly. There are two ways to calculate the LSS features. One is to calculate the cosine similarity by summing up all word vectors in Q_0 and Q_1. Another is to adopt averaged pairwise cosine similarity between each word in Q_0 and Q_1.

Besides above four types of features, for Q-Q pair, we also extracted following two question information features (**QI**) to describe the informativeness of related question Q_1: (1) the number of words in Q_1 (2) the position of Q_1 in all related questions. For Q-C pair, we also extracted following two comment information features (**CI**) to measure the informativeness of a comment text: (1) the number of words in comment (2) the number of nouns, verbs and adjectives in comment.

2.2 Two Methods to address subtask A

2.2.1 Method 1: CNN

We proposed a convolutional neural network to model question-comment sentence. As illustrated in

---

[1] http://www.statmt.org/moses/giza/GIZA++.html

[2] http://alt.qcri.org/semeval2015/task3/index.php?id=data-and-tools

Figure 1, we first input word embeddings (here we used 300-dimensional Glove vectors in (Pennington et al., 2014)) of question and comment words and then learn the meaning (i.e., feature vector) of question and comment through convolution and pooling operation. After a simple concatenation layer connecting question and comment vectors, we final obtain a relevant score through a softmax operation.

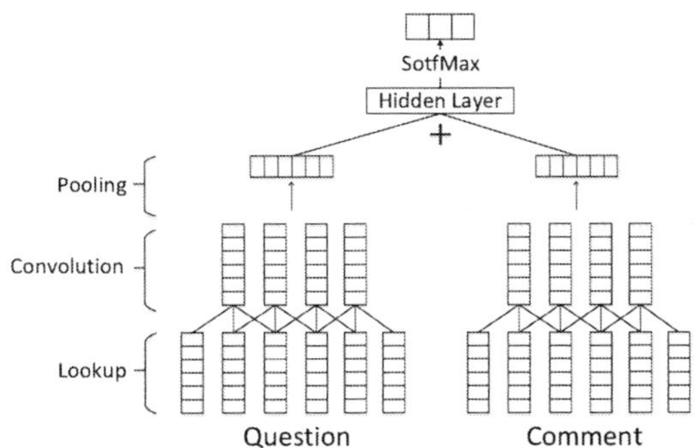

Figure 1: An illustration of CNN for question-comment similarity estimation.

2.2.2 Method 2: BLSTM

Figure 2 shows a multiple-layer BLSTM network model we used for question and comment sentences modeling. The procedure of BLSTM is similar to that of CNN. The words of question and comment sentences are first converted into vectors by looking up publicly available 300-dimensional Glove vectors. Then they are sequentially read by BLSTM from both directions. In this way, the contextual information across words in both question and comment sentences is modeled by employing temporal recurrence in BLSTM. Like CNN, finally it outputs a relevant score between question and comment by a simple concatenation operation on these two output vectors and a softmax operation.

2.3 Two Methods for subtask B

To calculate semantic similarity between Q_0 and Q_1 pair, previous work extracted features only from the Q-Q sentence pair. We stated that the comment set C and its rank with respect to Q_1 also provide useful information for question-question similarity. To address it, we propose two novel methods to improve

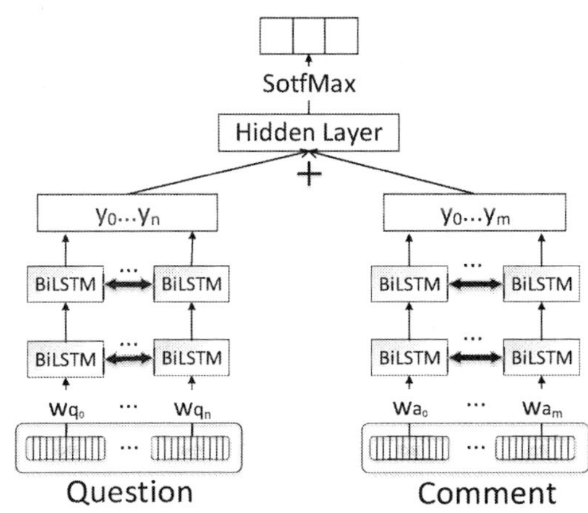

Figure 2: An illustration of BLSTM model for question-comment similarity estimation.

semantic similarity estimation between Q-Q pair by integrating the rank information of Q-C pair.

2.3.1 Method 1: adopt Q-C Ranking Evaluation Metrics as Similarity Score

The first method is to adopt rank evaluation metrics, i.e., *Spearman*, *Pearson*, and *Kendall* Ranking Coefficient directly as similarity scores for question similarity estimation.

Generally, these three nonparametric metrics are to measure the statistical dependence between two variables and to assess how similar between two variables. In comment ranking, they are used to measure how similar the two rankings Q_0-C and Q_1-C are. Based on our consideration, given one comment set C, if the two ranks of Q_0-C and Q_1-C are similar, the semantic similarity between Q_0-Q_1 is high. These three ranking correlation coefficients (i.e., *Spearman*, *Pearson*, and *Kendall* Coefficient) can be used directly as question similarity scores or used as additional ranking scores in combination with other features (described in Section 2.1) extracted from Q_0-Q_1 pair.

2.3.2 Method 2: add new features extracted from Q-C pair

We presented two methods to add new features extracted from Q-C pair. The first is to extract the features from Q_0-C and Q_1-C pair and then use the *cosine* scores calculated on the two feature vectors as additional features for Q_0-Q_1. We extracted traditional NLP features described in Section 2.1 from Q_0-C and Q_1-C pairs, respectively, denoted as two feature vectors, i.e., F_0 and F_1. Then we calculated the *cosine* similarity on these two vectors respectively, and obtain two *cosine* scores, i.e., $cos(Q_0$-$C)$, and $cos(Q_1$-$C)$. After that, we calculated the absolute difference between these two *cosine* scores. Finally, the obtained scores (denoted as $[cos_1, cos_2, ...]$) are ranked as additional features.

The second is to calculate the ranking scores of Q_0-C and Q_1-C by using comment ranking model firstly, then use the *Manhattan Distance* of two lists of ranked scores as an additional feature.

2.4 A Two-Step Filtering for Subtask C

To overcome the error propagation from question-question similarity step to question-comment similarity step, we employed a two-step filtering strategy for subtask C. The first step is to choose the top N similar questions with the aid of the Q-C ranking. The second step is to re-rank the comment and choose the top M comments with integration of the previous Q-Q results.

3 Experimental Setting

3.1 Datasets

Table 1 shows the statistics of training, development and test data sets, where the #_original, #_related, and #_answers represent the number of original questions, related questions and answers, respectively. The types of comments with respect to original question and related question fall into three classes: *Good*, *PotentiallyUseful* and *Bad*. The types of related question with respect to original question fall into three classes: *PerfectMatch*, *Relevant* and *Irrelevant*.

Subtask	Data	#_original	#_related	#_answers
A	train	–	5,898	37,848
	dev	–	500	5,000
	test	–	327	3,270
B	train	267	2,669	26,690
	dev	50	500	5,000
	test	70	700	7,000
C	train	267	2,669	26,690
	dev	50	500	5,000
	test	70	700	7,000

Table 1: Statistics of datasets.

3.2 Preprocessing

We first removed stop words and punctuation, and changed all words to lowercase. After that, we performed tokenization and stemming using NLTK[3] Toolkit.

3.3 Evaluation Metrics

To evaluate performance of the tasks, the *Mean Average Precision* (MAP) is adopted as official evaluation measure by the organizers which the MAP is defined as the mean of the averaged precision scores for queries.

3.4 Learning Algorithm

We compared two ranking strategies in traditional method. One is to train a pairwise-based ranking model, i.e., *Learning-to-rank* (Trotman, 2005), and use the output of model as a ranking score directly. Another is to first train a supervised classification model and then use the confidence score of probability as a ranking score. To train a supervised classifier, two algorithms implemented in SKLearn[4] have been examined, i.e., Logistic Regression (LR) and Support Vector Machine (SVM). Finally, Logistic Regression classifier (penalized argument $c = 1$) is adopted for all three subtasks for its good performance in preliminary experiments.

4 Experiments on Training Data

4.1 Results on Subtask A

For the experiments of subtask A, the hyperparameters of CNN model are set as follows: the number of filter windows is 2, feature maps are set to 100, learning rate is set to 0.01. And the hyperparameters of BLSTM model are set as follows: memory size is set to 500 and the learning rate is 0.01. Table 2 shows the results of subtask A with three different methods.

Firstly, all CI, TB, TMB, and LSS features significantly over WM baseline. Since CI is a measure of the informativeness of comment text, this indicates that users trend to choose the comment with more information. TB can learn word alignment between different words. Unlike the surface word matching features which only consider the surface word, the

---

[3]http://www.nltk.org/
[4]http://scikit-learn.org/stable/

Methods	Features	MAP(%)
Traditional NLP Features	WM	57.13
	.+TB	58.91
	.+TMB	61.37
	.+CI	63.03
	.+LSS	**65.37**
CNN	–	65.04
BLSTM	–	65.13
Tra + CNN + BLSTM	–	**66.84**

Table 2: Results of subtask A using different methods. ".+" means to add current feature to the previous feature set.

LSS features are obtained by integrating context of the word. Therefore, the LSS features show that this particular word embedding seems to complement the surface word matching information. Secondly, the combination of five types of features achieve the best performance for traditional method. Thirdly, the model based CNN and BLSTM achieve comparable performance with traditional method. Finally, the combination of three methods achieve the best performance which shows that CNN and BLSTM catch complementary information for Q-C pair with traditional method.

4.2 Results on Subtask B

Table 3 summarizes the results of subtask B with NLP features and integrating the rank information of Q-C pair. Here *Lucene* represents using Lucene

Method	Features	MAP(%)
Lucene	BM25	69.95
Traditional NLP Features	WM	69.91
	.+TB	70.72
	.+TBM	71.05
	.+LSS	72.13
	.+QI	**74.03**
Method 1	*Pearson*	61.18
	Spearman	62.86
	Kendall	62.95
	Pearson + NLP	68.15
	Spearman + NLP	68.49
	Kendall + NLP	**68.95**
Method 2	NLP	74.03
	.+ARC	74.25
	.+ARR	**75.04**

Table 3: Results of subtask B using different methods.

Toolkit[5] with the original question as query with B-M25 ($K_1 = 1.2$ and $B = 0.75$). *ARC* and *ARR*

---

are the first and second methods presented in Section 2.3.2. According to the results of Table 3, we can make following three observations:

(1) Traditional NLP features significantly improve the performance of question-question similarity over *Lucene* baseline.

(2) The *Pearson*, *Spearman*, and *Kendall* get similar performance and do not perform well versus traditional NLP method. The three rank correlations all take down the performance of traditional NLP method when combined with it. The possible reason is that the ranked scores of comments are obtained by pre-trained comment ranking model which has a limitation of performance.

(3) Both *ARC* and *ARR* make contributions to the performance which means combining the information of Q-C pair is helpful to find related questions.

4.3 Results on Subtask C

Table 4 depicts the results on subtask C, where *WMQ*, *TMBQ* and *TBQ* represent extracting word matching, topic model based and translation based features on original question and related question. From Table 4, we observe the similar results with those in subtask A, i.e., traditional features make contribution to comment ranking. Moreover, the performance is improved by adding features extracted from Q-Q pair, which indicates that the information extracted from Q-Q pair makes significant contribution to answer ranking subtask.

Method	Features	MAP(%)
Lucene	BM25	24.59
Traditional NLP Features	WM	30.15
	.+CI	33.13
	.+TB	34.27
	.+TMB	35.80
	.+LSS	**36.82**
Q-Q Features	NLP	36.82
	.+WMQ	38.14
	.+TMBQ	38.51
	.+TBQ	**39.39**

Table 4: Results of subtask C with different traditional NLP features.

However, above results are evaluated using MAP on top 10 comments. Therefore the errors introduced in question retrieval (subtask B) would be prorogated to answer ranking (subtask A) and finally reduce the whole performance of CQA (subtask C).

To solve this problem, we investigated a two-step method to first filter unrelated comments and then filter unrelated answers. Figure 3 shows the results of two filtering methods on MAP metric, where N represents the number of top related questions and M represents the number of top ranked answers.

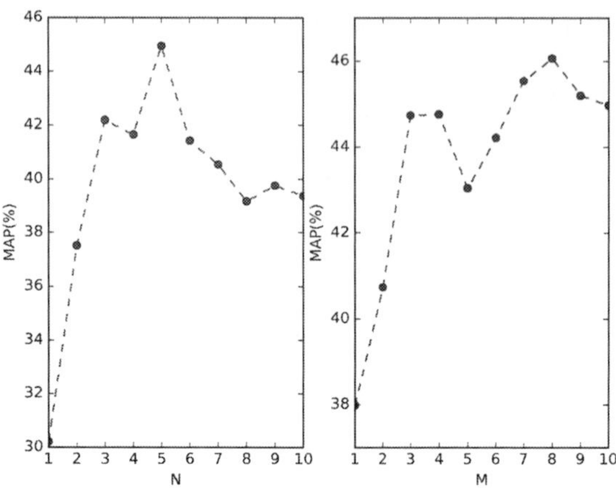

Figure 3: The results of subtask C using two-step filtering operation.

From left subplot of the Figure 3, we see that the best performance with filtering operation are much higher than the best score ($MAP = 39.39\%$) without any filtering. The best performance 44.97% is obtained when $N = 5$ and $M = 10$. The reason may be that the filtering operation of unrelated questions can take away many unrelated comments for original question. The right subplot of the Figure 3 shows the performance curve ($N = 5$) when increasing the values of M. Similarly, the performance increases with M increasing from 7 to 9 and it achieves the best score of 46.07% when $N = 5$ and $M = 8$.

4.4 System Configuration

Based on above experimental analysis, the three system configurations are as followings:

(1) subtask A: We used the combination of traditional method, CNN and BLSTM as the primary run in the test set. Traditional method and BLSTM serve as contrastive1 run and contrastive2 run.

(2) subtask B: Traditional method with Method 2 is used as primary run in the test set. The combination of traditional method with Method 2 and *Lucene* is contrastive1 run and traditional method alone is

contrastive2 run.

(3) subtask C: The two-step filtering operation with $N = 5$ and $M = 8$ serves as primary run in the test set. The two-step filtering operation with $N = 4$ and $M = 7$ is contrastive1 run. Traditional features adding Q-Q pair information is used as contrastive2 run.

5   Results on Test Data

Table 5 shows the results on test set which are released by the organizers.

subtask	run(rank)	MAP(%)
A	ECNU-primary(4)	77.28
	ECNU-contrastive1	71.34
	ECNU-contrastive2	75.71
	Kelp-primary(1)	79.19
B	ECNU-primary(7)	73.92
	ECNU-contrastive1	73.25
	ECNU-contrastive2	71.62
	UH-PRHLT-primary(1)	76.70
C	ECNU-primary(7)	46.47
	ECNU-contrastive1	48.49
	ECNU-contrastive2	47.24
	SUper team-primary(1)	55.41

Table 5: Our results and the best results on three subtask test sets.

From the results, we find: (1) In subtask A, the combination of three methods significantly improve the performance over the traditional method and BLSTM, which is consistent with the results on training data as our expectation. (2) In subtask B, the result using traditional features is higher than *Lucene* but still has a certain gap with the best result. The possible reason may be because several traditional features do not work well in the test set. (3) In subtask C, beyond our expectation, the method using two-step filtering operation does not make obvious contribution. The possible reason may be that the values of M and N are not suitable for test set.

6   Conclusion

In this paper, we proposed multiple strategies (i.e., traditional method of extracting features and deep learning models) to address Community Question Answering task in SemEval 2016. For subtask A, we trained a classifier and learned the question-comment representation based CNN and BLSTM. The combination of three models obtains the best results. For subtask B, we proposed two novel methods to improve semantic similarity estimation between Q-Q pairs by utilizing the information of Q-C ranking. For subtask C, we employed a two step filtering strategy to reduce the noise which taking from unrelated comments. The results on test set show the effectiveness of our methods.

Acknowledgments

This research is supported by grants from Science and Technology Commission of Shanghai Municipality (14DZ2260800 and 15ZR1410700), Shanghai Collaborative Innovation Center of Trustworthy Software for Internet of Things (ZF1213).

References

David M Blei, Andrew Y Ng, and Michael I Jordan. 2003. Latent dirichlet allocation. *the Journal of machine Learning research*, 3:993–1022.

Peter F. Brown, Vincent J. Della Pietra, Stephen A. Della Pietra, and Robert L. Mercer. 1993. The mathematics of statistical machine translation: Parameter estimation. *Comput. Linguist.*, 19(2):263–311, June.

Tomas Mikolov, Ilya Sutskever, Kai Chen, Greg S Corrado, and Jeff Dean. 2013. Distributed representations of words and phrases and their compositionality. In C.J.C. Burges, L. Bottou, M. Welling, Z. Ghahramani, and K.Q. Weinberger, editors, *Advances in Neural Information Processing Systems 26*, pages 3111–3119. Curran Associates, Inc.

Preslav Nakov, Lluís Màrquez, Walid Magdy, Alessandro Moschitti, Jim Glass, and Bilal Randeree. 2016. Semeval-2016 task 3: Community question answering. In *Proceedings of the 10th International Workshop on Semantic Evaluation (SemEval 2016)*, Berlin, Germany, August. Association for Computational Linguistics.

Jeffrey Pennington, Richard Socher, and Christopher D. Manning. 2014. Glove: Global vectors for word representation. In *Proceedings of the 2014 Conference on Empirical Methods in Natural Language Processing (EMNLP 2014)*, pages 1532–1543.

Xuan-Hieu Phan and Cam-Tu Nguyen. 2007. Gibbslda++: Ac/c++ implementation of latent dirichlet allocation (lda).

Mihai Surdeanu, Massimiliano Ciaramita, and Hugo Zaragoza. 2011. Learning to rank answers to non-factoid questions from web collections. *Computational Linguistics*, 37(2).

Andrew Trotman. 2005. Learning to rank. *Information Retrieval*, 8(3):359–381.

Xiaobing Xue, Jiwoon Jeon, and W. Bruce Croft. 2008. Retrieval models for question and answer archives. In *Proceedings of the 31st Annual International ACM SIGIR Conference on Research and Development in Information Retrieval*, SIGIR '08, pages 475–482, New York, NY, USA. ACM.

Wen-tau Yih, Ming-Wei Chang, Christopher Meek, and Andrzej Pastusiak. 2013. Question answering using enhanced lexical semantic models. In *Proceedings of the 51st Annual Meeting of the Association for Computational Linguistics (Volume 1: Long Papers)*, pages 1744–1753, Sofia, Bulgaria, August. Association for Computational Linguistics.

SemanticZ at SemEval-2016 Task 3:
Ranking Relevant Answers in Community Question Answering
Using Semantic Similarity Based on Fine-tuned Word Embeddings

Todor Mihaylov
Research Training Group AIPHES
Institute for Computational Linguistics
Heidelberg University
mihaylov@cl.uni-heidelberg.de

Preslav Nakov
Qatar Computing Research Institute, HBKU
P.O. box 5825
Doha, Qatar
pnakov@qf.org.qa

Abstract

We describe our system for finding good answers in a community forum, as defined in SemEval-2016, Task 3 on Community Question Answering. Our approach relies on several semantic similarity features based on fine-tuned word embeddings and topics similarities. In the main Subtask C, our primary submission was ranked third, with a MAP of 51.68 and accuracy of 69.94. In Subtask A, our primary submission was also third, with MAP of 77.58 and accuracy of 73.39.

1 Introduction

Posting questions that have already been asked and answered in a community forum is annoying to users as it usually ends up with them being referred to a previously asked question. The SemEval-2016 Task 3 on Community Question Answering[1] (Nakov et al., 2016) aims to solve this real-life problem. The main subtask (Subtask C) asks to find an answer that already exists in the forum and will be appropriate as a response to a newly-posted question. There is also a secondary, Subtask A, which focuses on Question-Comment Similarity and asks to rank the comments within a question-comment thread based on their relevance with respect to the thread's question.

Here, we examine the performance of using different word embeddings obtained with the Word2Vec tool (Mikolov et al., 2013), which we use to build vectors for the questions and the answers. We train classifiers using features derived from these embeddings to solve subtasks A and C.

---

[1] http://alt.qcri.org/semeval2016/task3/

Our contribution is in producing good word embeddings based on empirical evaluation of different configurations working in the Community Question Answering domain; as they perform well, we make them freely available to the research community.[2]

2 Related Work

This year's SemEval-2016 Task 3 is a follow up of SemEval-2015 Task 3 on Answer Selection in Community Question Answering (Nakov et al., 2015). The 2015 subtask A asked to determine whether an answer was relevant, potentially useful, or bad, while this year this is about ranking.

Here we focus on features that use semantic knowledge such as word embeddings, various features extracted from word embeddings, and topic models. Word embeddings and word embeddings similarities have been used by teams in the 2015 edition of the task (Belinkov et al., 2015; Zamanov et al., 2015; Tran et al., 2015; Nicosia et al., 2015). LDA topic have also been used (Tran et al., 2015).

Many other features have been tried for the task. For example, Tran et al. (2015) used metadata about the question and the comment. User profile statistics such as number of *Good*, *Bad* and *Potentially Useful* comments by a given user have been used to model user likelihood of posting different types of comment (Nicosia et al., 2015). Vo et al. (2015) and Nicosia et al. (2015) used syntactic tree similarities to compare questions to comments. The problem of selecting relevant answers has even been approached as a spam filtering task (Vo et al., 2015).

---

[2] https://github.com/tbmihailov/
semeval2016-task3-cqa

Proceedings of SemEval-2016, pages 879–886,
San Diego, California, June 16-17, 2016. ©2016 Association for Computational Linguistics

3 Data

In our experiments, we used annotated training, development and testing datasets, as well as a large unannotated dataset, all provided by the SemEval-2016 Task 3 organizers. We further collected some additional unannotated in-domain data from some other sources, as explained below; finally, we used some models pretrained on out-of-domain data.

Training, development, and testing data. For Subtask A, there are 6,398 questions and 40,288 comments from their question-answer threads, and for Subtask C, there are 317 original questions, 3,169 related questions, and 31,690 comments. For both subtasks, the comments are annotated as *Good*, *PotentiallyUseful* and *Bad*; for subtask A, the annotation is with respect to the question in whose thread the comment appeared, while for subtask C, it is with respect to a new question. For both subtasks, a successful ranking is one that ranks all *Good* comments before all *PotentiallyUseful* and *Bad* ones (without distinguishing between the latter two).

Unannotated data. We performed experiments with Word2Vec embeddings trained on different unannotated data sources. We wanted to find the best performing embeddings and to use them in our system. In Table 1, we list the various data sources we used for training our Word2Vec models, and their vocabulary size.

Qatar Living Forum is the original Qatar Living.[3] unannotated data containing 189,941 questions and 1,894,456 comments. It is limited to the forums section of the Qatar Living website.

Qatar Living Forum + Ext includes the *Qatar Living Forum* dataset, i.e., the forums, but also some other sections of Qatar Living: Jobs, Classifieds, Pages, Wiki and Events posts.

Doha News is a dataset that we built by crawling about 7,000 news publications about the life in Doha, Qatar from the DohaNews website.[4]

We also used an out-of-domain, general model, which is readily-pretrained using Word2Vec on *Google News*,[5] as provided by Mikolov et al. (2013).

---

[3] www.qatarliving.com is an online community for everyone living in or interested in the State of Qatar.

[4] dohanews.co covers breaking news, politics, business, culture and more in and around Qatar.

[5] code.google.com/archive/p/word2vec/

Features	Train size	Vocab
Qatar Living Forum	61.84M	104K
Qatar Living Forum+Ext	90M	126K
Google News	100B	3M
Doha News	1.45M	17K

Table 1: **Data used for training word embedding vectors.** Shown are training source size (word tokens) and vocabulary size (word types).

4 Method

Below we focus our explanation on subtask A; for subtask C, we combine the predictions for subtask A with the Google's reciprocal rank for the related question (see below).

We approach subtask A as a classification problem. For each comment, we extract variety of features from both the question and the comment, and we train a classifier to label comments as Good or Bad with respect to the thread question. We rank the comments in each question according to the classifier's score of being classified as Good with respect to the question.

We first train several word embedding vector models and we fine-tune them using different configurations. For fine-tuning the parameters of the word embeddings training configuration, we setup a simple baseline system and we evaluate it on the official MAP score. We then use the best-performing embeddings in our further experiments. Our main features are semantic similarity based on word embeddings and topics, but we also use some metadata features.

4.1 Preprocessing

Before extracting features, we preprocessed the input text using several steps. We first replaced URLs in text with TOKEN_URL, numbers with TOKEN_NUM, images with TOKEN_IMG, and emoticons with TOKEN_EMO. We then tokenized the text by matching only continuous alphabet characters including _(underscore). Next, we lowercased the result. For the training, the development, and the test datasets, we removed the stopwords using the English stopwords lexicon from the NLTK toolkit (Bird and Loper, 2004).

4.2 Features

We used several semantic vector similarity and metadata feature groups. For the similarity measures mentioned below, we used cosine similarity:

$$1 - \frac{u.v}{\|u\| . \|v\|} \tag{1}$$

Semantic Word Embeddings. We used semantic word embeddings obtained from Word2Vec models trained on different unannotated data sources including the QatarLiving and DohaNews. We also used a model pre-trained on Google News text. For each piece of text such as comment text, question body and question subject, we constructed the centroid vector from the vectors of all words in that text (excluding stopwords).

$$centroid(w_{1..n}) = \frac{\sum\limits_{i=1}^{n} w_i}{n} \tag{2}$$

We built centroid vectors (2) from the question body and the comment text. We then examined different Word2Vec models in terms of training source and training configuration including word vector size, training window size, minimum word occurrence in the corpus, and number of skip-grams.

Semantic Vector Similarities. We used various similarity features calculated using the centroid word vectors on the question body, on the question subject and on the comment text, as well as on parts thereof:

Question to Answer similarity. We assume that a relevant answer should have a centroid vector that is close to that for the question. We used the question body to comment text, and question subject to comment text vector similarities.

Maximized similarity. We ranked each word in the answer text to the question body centroid vector according to their similarity and we took the average similarity of the top N words. We took the top 1,2,3 and 5 words similarities as features. The assumption here is that if the average similarity for the top N most similar words is high, then the answer might be relevant.

Aligned similarity. For each word in the question body, we chose the most similar word from the comment text and we took the average of all best word pair similarities as suggested in (Tran et al., 2015).

Part of speech (POS) based word vector similarities. We performed part of speech tagging using the Stanford tagger (Toutanova et al., 2003), and we took similarities between centroid vectors of words with a specific tag from the comment text and the centroid vector of the words with a specific tag from the question body text. The assumption is that some parts of speech between the question and the comment might be closer than other parts of speech.

Word clusters (WC) similarity. We clustered the word vectors from the Word2Vec vocabulary in 1,000 clusters (with 200 words per cluster on average) using K-Means clustering. We then calculated the cluster similarity between the question body word clusters and the answer text word clusters. For all experiments, we used clusters obtained from the Word2Vec model trained on QatarLiving forums with vector size of 100, window size 10, minimum words frequency of 5, and skip-gram 1.

LDA topic similarity. We performed topic clustering using Latent Dirichlet Allocation (LDA) as implemented in the *gensim* toolkit (Řehůřek and Sojka, 2010) on Train1+Train2+Dev questions and comments. We built topic models with 100 topics. For each word in the question body and for the comment text, we built a bag-of-topics with corresponding distribution, and calculated similarity. The assumption here is that if the question and the comment share similar topics, they are more likely to be relevant to each other.

Metadata. In addition to the semantic features described above, we also used some common sense metadata features:

Answer contains a question mark. If the comment has an question mark, it may be another question, which might indicate a bad answer.

Answer length. The assumption here is that longer answers could bring more useful detail.

Question length. If the question is longer, it may be more clear, which may help users give a more relevant answer.

Question to comment length. If the question is long and the answer is short, it may be less relevant.

The answer's author is the same as the corresponding question's author. If the answer is posted by the same user who posted the question and it is relevant, why has he/she asked the question in the first place?

Answer rank in the thread. Earlier answers could be posted by users who visit the forum more often, and they may have read more similar questions and answers. Moreover, discussion in the forum tends to diverge from the question over time.

Question category. We took the category of the question as a sparse binary feature vector (a feature with a value of 1 appears if question is in the category). The assumption here is that the question-comment relevance might depend on the category of the question.

4.3 Classifier

For each Question+Comment pair, we extracted the features explained above from the *Question* body and the subject text fields, and from the *Comment* text; we also extracted the relevant metadata. We concatenated the extracted features in a bag of features vector, scaling them in the 0 to 1 range, and feeding them to a classifier. In our experiments, we used different feature configurations. We used L2-regularized logistic regression classifier as implemented in Liblinear (Fan et al., 2008). For most of our experiments, we tuned the classifier with different values of the C (cost) parameter, and we took the one that yielded the best accuracy on 5-fold cross-validation on the training set. We used binary classification *Good* vs. *Bad* (including both *Bad* and *Potentially Useful* original labels). The output of the evaluation for each test example was a label, either *Good* or *Bad*, and the probability of being *Good* in the 0 to 1 range. We then used this output probability as a relevance rank for each *Comment* in the *Question* thread.

5 Experiments and Evaluation

As explained above, we rely mainly on semantic features extracted from Word2Vec word embeddings. Thus, we ran several experiments looking for the best embeddings for the task.

Table 2 shows experiments with Word2Vec models trained on the unannotated datasets described above. The Google News Word2Vec model comes pretrained with vector size of 300, window 10, minimum word frequency of 10 and skip-gram 1. We started with training our three Word2Vec models using the same parameters.

Dataset	Dev2016	
	MAP	Accuracy
Qatar Living Forum	**0.6311**	0.7078
Qatar Living Forum+Ext	0.6269	**0.7131**
Google News	0.6113	0.6996
Doha News	0.5769	0.6844

Table 2: Semantic vectors trained on different unannotated datasets as the only features for subtask A: training on train2016-part1, testing on dev2016.

Vector size	Test2016	
	MAP	Accuracy
800	**78.45**	74.22
700	78.12	73.98
600	77.31	73.15
500	77.61	73.30
400	78.36	74.19
300	77.25	74.50
200	77.90	73.88
100	77.08	**74.53**
50	77.22	73.85
20	75.44	72.42
Baseline	59.53	-

Table 3: Semantic vectors of different vector sizes, trained on Qatar Living Forum+Ext as features for subtask A (together with all other features): training on train2016-part1, testing on test2016.

Table 2 shows results using raw word vectors as features, together with an extra feature for question body to comment cosine similarity. We can see that training on *Qatar Living Forum* data performs best followed by using *Qatar Living Forum+Ext*, *Google News*, and *Doha News*. This is not surprising as the first two datasets are in-domain, while the latter two cover more topics (as they are news) and more formal language. Overall, Doha News contains topics that largely overlap with the topics discussed in the Qatar Living forum; yet, it uses more formal language and contains very little conversational word types (mostly in quotations and interviews); moreover, being smaller in size, it covers much less vocabulary. Based on these preliminary experiments on Dev2016, we concluded that the domain-specific word vectors trained on *Qatar Living Forum* were the best for this task, and we used them further in our experiments.

After we have selected the best dataset for training our semantic vectors, we continued with various experiments to select the best training parameters for Word2Vec. Below we present the results of these experiments on Test2016, but we experimented with Dev2016 when developing our system.

In Table 3, we present experiments with different vector sizes. We trained our classifier with all features mentioned above, extracted for the corresponding word vector model. We can see that word vectors of size 800 perform best followed by sizes 400 and 700. However, we should note that using word vectors of size 800 generates more than 1,650 features (800+800+other features), which slows down training and evaluation. Moreover, in our experiments, we noticed that using large word vectors blurs the impact of the other, non-vector features.

Thus, next we tried to achieve the MAP for the 800-size vector by using better parameters for smaller vector sizes. Table 4 shows the results, where we used vectors of size 100 and 200. We can see that the configuration with word vector size 200, window size 5, minimum word frequency 1 and skip-gram 3 performed best improving the 200 vectors MAP by 0.31 (compared to Table 3). However, the experiments with word vector size 100 improved its MAP score by 0.85, which suggests that there might be potential for improvement when using vectors of smaller size. We also tried to use Doc2Vec (Le and Mikolov, 2014) instead of Word2Vec, but this led to noticeably lower performance.

We further experimented with Word2Vec models trained with different configurations and different feature groups. Tables 5 and 6 show the results for ablation experiments using the best-performing configuration for Subtask A and C, respectively.

For Subtask A we achieved the best score with semantic vectors of size 200, trained with window size 5, minimum word frequency 1 and skip-grams 3. The best score we achived (MAP 78.52) is slightly hbetter than the best score from Table 3 (MAP 78.45), which means that it may be a good idea to use smaller word vectors in combination with other features. We can see that the features that contribute most (the bottom features are better) are the raw word centroid vectors and metadata features, followed by various similarities such as LDA topic similarity and POS-tagged-word similarity.

| | | | | Test2016 | |
Size	Window	Freq	Skip	MAP	Acc
200	5	1	3	**78.21**	74.25
200	5	5	1	78.19	73.49
200	5	5	3	78.13	74.01
200	5	1	1	78.01	**74.53**
100	5	1	1	77.93	74.19
200	10	5	1	77.90	73.88
100	5	1	3	77.81	73.94
100	10	1	1	77.72	74.43
200	10	1	1	77.58	74.25
100	5	5	1	77.53	74.07
200	10	1	3	77.43	73.73
100	10	10	1	77.18	73.79
100	10	5	1	77.08	**74.53**

Table 4: **Exploring Word2Vec training parameters on Qatar Living Forum+Ext:** word vector size (Size), context window (Window), minimum word frequency (Freq), and skip-grams (Skip). Vectors used as features for subtask A (together with all other features): training on train2016-part1, testing on test2016.

| Train2016-part1 as training | Test2016 | |
Features	MAP	Acc
All − Quest. to Comment sim	**78.52**	74.31
All − Maximized similarity	78.38	74.59
All − Word Clusters similarity	78.29	74.25
All − WC sim & Meta cat	78.22	74.04
All − Meta categories	78.21	74.25
All	78.21	74.25
All − Meta cat & LDA sim	78.18	73.88
All − Ext POS sim & WC sim	78.10	74.28
All − Aligned similarity	77.97	74.16
All − Cat & WC & LDA sim	77.95	74.19
All − WC & LDA sims	77.92	74.25
All − Ext POS sim	77.92	74.43
All − LDA sim	77.85	74.37
All − POS sim	77.77	**74.80**
All − Metadata full	74.50	70.31
All − Word Vectors	74.35	70.80
Primary	77.58	73.39
Contrastive 1	77.16	73.88
Contrastive 2	75.41	72.26
Baseline (IR)	59.53	−

Table 5: **Subtask A. Using all features without some feature groups.** Word2Vec is trained with word vector size 200, context window 5, minimum word frequency 1, and skip-grams 3.

Train2016-part1 as training	Test-2016	
Features	**MAP**	**Acc**
All − Q to C sim	**53.39**	69.87
All − Meta categories	53.06	69.81
All − WC sim & Meta cat	52.91	69.54
All − WC sim & LDA sim	52.84	70.06
All − Meta cat & LDA sim	52.83	69.87
All − Ext POS sim & WC sim	52.82	70.21
All	52.78	69.43
All − Aligned similarity	52.76	70.10
All − Word Clusters similarity	52.58	69.63
All − Maximized similarity	52.47	69.27
All − Cat & WC & LDA sim	52.44	69.51
All − Exr POS sim	52.23	69.91
All − LDA sim	52.08	69.97
All − POS sim	51.57	69.96
All − Word Vectors	49.57	70.13
All − Metadata full	46.03	**71.06**
Primary	51.68	69.94
Contrastive 1	51.46	69.69
Contrastive 2	48.76	69.71
Baseline (IR)	28.88	−

Table 6: Subtask C. Using all features without some feature groups. Word2Vec is trained with word vector size 100, context window 5, minimum word frequency 1, and skip-grams 1.

For Subtask C, we achieved the best score with vectors of size 100, trained with window size 5, minimum word frequency 1, and skip-grams 1. The features that contributed most were mostly the same as for Subtask A. One difference is the maximized similarity features group, which now yields worse results when excluded, which indicates its importance.

Our *Primary*, *Contrastive 1* and *Contrastive 2* submissions were built with the same feature set: *All features - POS similarity & Meta Category*, but were trained with fixed C=0.55 on different datasets: *Primary* was trained on Train2016-part1, *Contrastive 1* was trained on Train2016-part1 + Train2016-part2, and *Contrastive 2* was trained on Train2016-part2.

6 Conclusion and Future Work

We have described our system for SemEval-2016, Task 3 on Community Question Answering. Our approach relied on several semantic similarity features based on fine-tuned word embeddings and topics similarities.

In the main Subtask C, our primary submission was ranked third, with a MAP of 51.68 and accuracy of 69.94. In Subtask A, our primary submission was also third, with MAP of 77.58 and accuracy of 73.39. After the submission deadline, we improved our MAP score to 78.52 for Subtask A, and to 53.39 for Subtask C, which would rank our system second.

In future work, we plan to use our best performing word embeddings models and features in a deep learning architecture, e.g., as in the MTE-NN system (Guzmán et al., 2016a; Guzmán et al., 2016b), which borrowed an entire neural network framework and achitecture from previous work on machine translation evaluation (Guzmán et al., 2015). We also want to incorporate several rich knowledge sources, e.g., as in the SUper Team system (Mihaylova et al., 2016), including troll user features as inspired by (Mihaylov et al., 2015a; Mihaylov et al., 2015b; Mihaylov and Nakov, 2016), and PMI-based goodness polarity lexicons as in the PMI-cool system (Balchev et al., 2016), as well as sentiment polarity features (Nicosia et al., 2015).

We further plan to use information from entire threads to make better predictions, as using thread-level information for answer classification has already been shown useful for SemEval-2015 Task 3, subtask A, e.g., by using features modeling the thread structure and dialogue (Nicosia et al., 2015; Barrón-Cedeño et al., 2015), or by applying thread-level inference using the predictions of local classifiers (Joty et al., 2015; Joty et al., 2016). How to use such models efficiently in the ranking setup of 2016 is an interesting research question.

Finally, we would like to address subtask C in a more solid way, making good use of the data, the gold annotations, the features, the models, and the predictions for subtasks A and B.

Acknowledgments. This work is partly supported by the German Research Foundation as part of the Research Training Group "Adaptive Preparation of Information from Heterogeneous Sources" (AIPHES) under grant No. GRK 1994/1. It is also part of the Interactive sYstems for Answer Search (Iyas) project, which is developed by the Arabic Language Technologies (ALT) group at the Qatar Computing Research Institute (QCRI), Hamab bin Khalifa University (HBKU), part of Qatar Foundation in collaboration with MIT-CSAIL.

References

Daniel Balchev, Yasen Kiprov, Ivan Koychev, and Preslav Nakov. 2016. PMI-cool at SemEval-2016 Task 3: Experiments with PMI and goodness polarity lexicons for community question answering. In *Proceedings of the 10th International Workshop on Semantic Evaluation*, SemEval '16, San Diego, California, USA.

Alberto Barrón-Cedeño, Simone Filice, Giovanni Da San Martino, Shafiq Joty, Lluís Màrquez, Preslav Nakov, and Alessandro Moschitti. 2015. Thread-level information for comment classification in community question answering. In *Proceedings of the 53rd Annual Meeting of the Association for Computational Linguistics and the 7th International Joint Conference on Natural Language Processing*, ACL-IJCNLP '15, pages 687–693, Beijing, China.

Yonatan Belinkov, Mitra Mohtarami, Scott Cyphers, and James Glass. 2015. VectorSLU: A continuous word vector approach to answer selection in community question answering systems. In *Proceedings of the 9th International Workshop on Semantic Evaluation*, SemEval '15, pages 282–287, Denver, Colorado, USA.

Steven Bird and Edward Loper. 2004. NLTK: The natural language toolkit. In *The Companion Volume to the Proceedings of 42st Annual Meeting of the Association for Computational Linguistics*, pages 214–217, Barcelona, Spain.

Rong-En Fan, Kai-Wei Chang, Cho-Jui Hsieh, Xiang-Rui Wang, and Chih-Jen Lin. 2008. LIBLINEAR: A library for large linear classification. *Journal of Machine Learning Research*, 9:1871–1874.

Francisco Guzmán, Shafiq Joty, Lluís Màrquez, and Preslav Nakov. 2015. Pairwise neural machine translation evaluation. In *Proceedings of the 53rd Annual Meeting of the Association for Computational Linguistics and the 7th International Joint Conference on Natural Language Processing (Volume 1: Long Papers)*, ACL-IJCNLP '15, pages 805–814, Beijing, China.

Francisco Guzmán, Lluís Màrquez, and Preslav Nakov. 2016a. Machine translation evaluation meets community question answering. In *Proceedings of the 54th Annual Meeting of the Association for Computational Linguistics*, ACL '16, Berlin, Germany.

Francisco Guzmán, Lluís Màrquez, and Preslav Nakov. 2016b. MTE-NN at SemEval-2016 Task 3: Can machine translation evaluation help community question answering? In *Proceedings of the 10th International Workshop on Semantic Evaluation*, SemEval '16, San Diego, California, USA.

Shafiq Joty, Alberto Barrón-Cedeño, Giovanni Da San Martino, Simone Filice, Lluís Màrquez, Alessandro Moschitti, and Preslav Nakov. 2015. Global thread-level inference for comment classification in community question answering. In *Proceedings of the 2015 Conference on Empirical Methods in Natural Language Processing*, EMNLP '15, pages 573–578, Lisbon, Portugal.

Shafiq Joty, Lluís Màrquez, and Preslav Nakov. 2016. Joint learning with global inference for comment classification in community question answering. In *Proceedings of the 2016 Conference of the North American Chapter of the Association for Computational Linguistics: Human Language Technologies*, NAACL-HLT '16, San Diego, California, USA.

Quoc V. Le and Tomas Mikolov. 2014. Distributed representations of sentences and documents. *CoRR*, abs/1405.4053.

Todor Mihaylov and Preslav Nakov. 2016. Hunting for troll comments in news community forums. In *Proceedings of the 54th Annual Meeting of the Association for Computational Linguistics*, ACL '16, Berlin, Germany.

Todor Mihaylov, Georgi Georgiev, and Preslav Nakov. 2015a. Finding opinion manipulation trolls in news community forums. In *Proceedings of the Nineteenth Conference on Computational Natural Language Learning*, CoNLL '15, pages 310–314, Beijing, China.

Todor Mihaylov, Ivan Koychev, Georgi Georgiev, and Preslav Nakov. 2015b. Exposing paid opinion manipulation trolls. In *Proceedings of the International Conference Recent Advances in Natural Language Processing*, RANLP '15, pages 443–450, Hissar, Bulgaria.

Tsvetomila Mihaylova, Pepa Gencheva, Martin Boyanov, Ivana Yovcheva, Todor Mihaylov, Momchil Hardalov, Yasen Kiprov, Daniel Balchev, Ivan Koychev, Preslav Nakov, Ivelina Nikolova, and Galia Angelova. 2016. SUper Team at SemEval-2016 Task 3: Building a feature-rich system for community question answering. In *Proceedings of the 10th International Workshop on Semantic Evaluation*, SemEval '16, San Diego, California, USA.

Tomas Mikolov, Wen-tau Yih, and Geoffrey Zweig. 2013. Linguistic regularities in continuous space word representations. In *Proceedings of the 2013 Conference of the North American Chapter of the Association for Computational Linguistics: Human Language Technologies*, NAACL-HLT '13, pages 746–751, Atlanta, Georgia, USA.

Preslav Nakov, Lluís Màrquez, Walid Magdy, Alessandro Moschitti, Jim Glass, and Bilal Randeree. 2015. SemEval-2015 task 3: Answer selection in community question answering. In *Proceedings of the 9th International Workshop on Semantic Evaluation*, SemEval '15, pages 269–281, Denver, Colorado, USA.

Preslav Nakov, Lluís Màrquez, Alessandro Moschitti, Walid Magdy, Hamdy Mubarak, Abed Alhakim Freihat, Jim Glass, and Bilal Randeree. 2016. SemEval-2016 task 3: Community question answering. In *Proceedings of the 10th International Workshop on Semantic Evaluation*, SemEval '16, San Diego, California, USA.

Massimo Nicosia, Simone Filice, Alberto Barrón-Cedeño, Iman Saleh, Hamdy Mubarak, Wei Gao, Preslav Nakov, Giovanni Da San Martino, Alessandro Moschitti, Kareem Darwish, Lluís Màrquez, Shafiq Joty, and Walid Magdy. 2015. QCRI: Answer selection for community question answering - experiments for Arabic and English. In *Proceedings of the 9th International Workshop on Semantic Evaluation*, SemEval '15, pages 203–209, Denver, Colorado, USA.

Radim Řehůřek and Petr Sojka. 2010. Software Framework for Topic Modelling with Large Corpora. In *Proceedings of the LREC 2010 Workshop on New Challenges for NLP Frameworks*, pages 45–50, Valletta, Malta.

Kristina Toutanova, Dan Klein, Christopher D. Manning, and Yoram Singer. 2003. Feature-rich part-of-speech tagging with a cyclic dependency network. In *Proceedings of the 2003 Conference of the North American Chapter of the Association for Computational Linguistics on Human Language Technology - Volume 1*, NAACL-HLT '03, pages 173–180, Edmonton, Canada.

Quan Hung Tran, Vu Tran, Tu Vu, Minh Nguyen, and Son Bao Pham. 2015. JAIST: Combining multiple features for answer selection in community question answering. In *Proceedings of the 9th International Workshop on Semantic Evaluation*, SemEval '15, pages 215–219, Denver, Colorado, USA.

Ngoc Phuoc An Vo, Simone Magnolini, and Octavian Popescu. 2015. FBK-HLT: An application of semantic textual similarity for answer selection in community question answering. In *Proceedings of the 9th International Workshop on Semantic Evaluation*, SemEval '15, pages 231–235, Denver, Colorado, USA.

Ivan Zamanov, Marina Kraeva, Nelly Hateva, Ivana Yovcheva, Ivelina Nikolova, and Galia Angelova. 2015. Voltron: A hybrid system for answer validation based on lexical and distance features. In *Proceedings of the 9th International Workshop on Semantic Evaluation*, SemEval '15, pages 242–246, Denver, Colorado, USA.

MTE-NN at SemEval-2016 Task 3: Can Machine Translation Evaluation Help Community Question Answering?

Francisco Guzmán, **Lluís Màrquez** and **Preslav Nakov**
Arabic Language Technologies Research Group
Qatar Computing Research Institute, HBKU
{fguzman,lmarquez,pnakov}@qf.org.qa

Abstract

We present a system for answer ranking (SemEval-2016 Task 3, subtask A) that is a direct adaptation of a pairwise neural network model for machine translation evaluation (MTE). In particular, the network incorporates MTE features, as well as rich syntactic and semantic embeddings, and it efficiently models complex non-linear interactions between them. With the addition of lightweight task-specific features, we obtained very encouraging experimental results, with sizeable contributions from both the MTE features and from the pairwise network architecture. We also achieved good results on subtask C.

1 Introduction

We present a system for SemEval-2016 Task 3 on Community Question Answering (cQA), subtask A (English). In that task, we are given a question from a community forum and a thread of associated text comments intended to answer the question, and the goal is to rank the comments according to their appropriateness to the question. Since cQA forum threads are noisy, as many comments are not answers to the question, the challenge lies in learning to rank all *good* comments above all *bad* ones.[1]

In this work, we approach subtask A from a novel perspective: by using notions of machine translation evaluation (MTE) to decide on the *quality* of a comment. In particular, we extend the MTE neural network framework from Guzmán et al. (2015).

We believe that this neural network is interesting for the cQA problem because: (*i*) it works in a pairwise fashion, i.e., given two translation hypotheses and a reference translation to compare to, the network decides which translation hypothesis is better; this is appropriate for a ranking problem; (*ii*) it allows for an easy incorporation of rich syntactic and semantic embedded representations of the input texts, and it efficiently models complex non-linear relationships among them; (*iii*) it uses a number of MT evaluation measures that have not been explored for the cQA task (e.g., TER, Meteor and BLEU).

The analogy we apply to adapt the neural MTE architecture to the cQA problem is the following: given two comments c_1 and c_2 from the question thread—which play the role of the two translation hypotheses—we have to decide whether c_1 is a better answer than c_2 to question q—which plays the role of the translation reference.

The two tasks seem similar: both reason about the similarity of two competing texts against a reference text, to decide which one is better. However, there are some profound differences. In MTE, the goal is to decide whether a hypothesis translation conveys the same meaning as the reference translation. In cQA, it is to determine whether the comment is an appropriate answer to the question. Furthermore, in MTE we can expect shorter texts, which are much more similar among them. In cQA, the question and the intended answers might differ significantly both in length and in lexical content. Thus, it is not clear a priori whether the MTE network can work well for cQA. Here, we show that the analogy is convenient, allowing to achieve competitive results.

---

[1]More detail and examples can be found on the task website (http://alt.qcri.org/semeval2016/task3/) and in the associated task description paper (Nakov et al., 2016).

887

Proceedings of SemEval-2016, pages 887–895,
San Diego, California, June 16-17, 2016. ©2016 Association for Computational Linguistics

At competition time, we achieved the sixth best result on the task from a set of twelve systems. Right after the competition we introduced some minor improvements and extra features, without changing the fundamental architecture of the network, which improved the MAP result by almost two points. We also performed a more detailed experimental analysis of the system, checking the contribution of several features and parts of the NN architecture. We observed that every single piece contributes important information to achieve the final performance. While task-specific features are crucial, other aspects of the framework are relevant too: syntactic embeddings, MT evaluation measures, and pairwise training of the network.

Finally, we used our system for subtask A to solve subtask C, which asks to find good answers to a new question that was not asked before in the forum by reranking the answers to related questions. For the purpose, we weighted the subtask A scores by the reciprocal rank of the related questions (following the order given by the organizers, i.e., the ranking by Google). Without any subtask C specific addition, we achieved the fourth best result in the task.

2 Related Work

Recently, many neural network (NN) models have been applied to cQA tasks: e.g., *question-question similarity* (Zhou et al., 2015; dos Santos et al., 2015; Lei et al., 2016) and *answer selection* (Severyn and Moschitti, 2015; Wang and Nyberg, 2015; Shen et al., 2015; Feng et al., 2015; Tan et al., 2015). Also, other participants in the SemEval 2016 Task 3 applied NNs to solve some of the subtasks (Nakov et al., 2016). However, our goal was different: we were interested in extending an existing pairwise NN framework from a different but related problem.

There is also work that uses scores from machine translation models as a features for cQA (Berger et al., 2000; Echihabi and Marcu, 2003; Jeon et al., 2005; Soricut and Brill, 2006; Riezler et al., 2007; Li and Manandhar, 2011; Surdeanu et al., 2011; Tran et al., 2015), e.g., a variation of IBM model 1, to compute the probability that the question is a "translation" of the candidate answer. Unlike that work, here we use machine translation *evaluation* (MTE) instead of machine translation models.

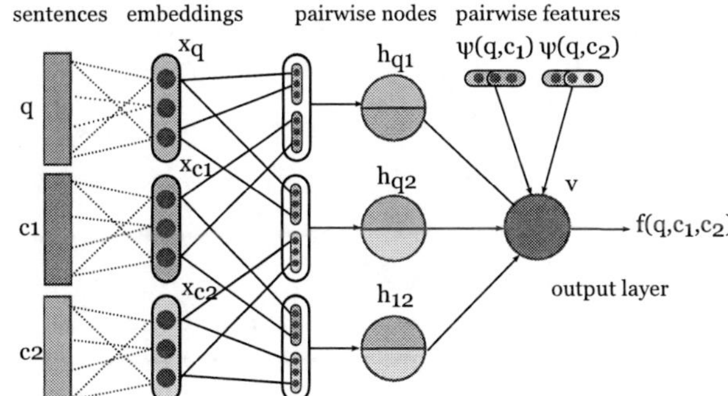

Figure 1: Overall architecture of the NN.

Another relevant work is that of Madnani et al. (2012), who applied MTE metrics as features for paraphrase identification. However, here we have a different problem: cQA. Moreover, instead of using MTE metrics as features, we port an entire MTE framework to the cQA problem.

3 Neural Model for Answer Ranking

The NN model we use for answer ranking is depicted in Figure 1. It is a direct adaptation of the feed-forward NN for MTE described in (Guzmán et al., 2015). Technically, we have a binary classification task with input (q, c_1, c_2), which should output 1 if c_1 is a better answer to q than c_2, and 0 otherwise.[2] The network computes a sigmoid function $f(q, c_1, c_2) = \mathrm{sig}(\mathbf{w_v^T}\phi(q, c_1, c_2) + b_v)$, where $\phi(x)$ transforms the input x through the hidden layer, $\mathbf{w_v}$ are the weights from the hidden layer to the output layer, and b_v is a bias term.

We first map the question and the comments to a fixed-length vector $[\mathbf{x}_q, \mathbf{x}_{c_1}, \mathbf{x}_{c_2}]$, using syntactic and semantic embeddings. Then, we feed this vector as input to the neural network, which models three types of interactions, using different groups of nodes in the hidden layer. There are two *evaluation* groups $\mathbf{h_{q1}}$ and $\mathbf{h_{q2}}$ that model how good each comment c_i is to the question q. The input to these groups are the concatenations $[\mathbf{x}_q, \mathbf{x}_{c_1}]$ and $[\mathbf{x}_q, \mathbf{x}_{c_2}]$, respectively. The third group of hidden nodes $\mathbf{h_{12}}$, which we call *similarity* group, models how close c_1 and c_2 are. Its input is $[\mathbf{x}_{c_1}, \mathbf{x}_{c_2}]$. This might be useful as highly similar comments are likely to be comparable in appropriateness, irrespective of whether they are good or bad answers in absolute terms.

---

[2]In this work, we do not learn to predict ties.

In summary, the transformation $\phi(q, c_1, c_2) = [\mathbf{h_{q_1}}, \mathbf{h_{q_2}}, \mathbf{h_{12}}]$ can be written as follows:

$$\mathbf{h_{qi}} = g(\mathbf{W_{qi}}[\mathbf{x_q}, \mathbf{x_{c_i}}] + \mathbf{b_{qi}}), \; i = 1, 2$$
$$\mathbf{h_{12}} = g(\mathbf{W_{12}}[\mathbf{x_{c_1}}, \mathbf{x_{c_2}}] + \mathbf{b_{12}}),$$

where $g(.)$ is a non-linear activation function (applied component-wise), $\mathbf{W} \in \mathbb{R}^{H \times N}$ are the associated weights between the input layer and the hidden layer, and $\mathbf{b}$ are the corresponding bias terms. We use tanh as an activation function, rather than sig, to be consistent with how parts of our input vectors (the word embeddings) are generated.

The model further allows to incorporate external sources of information in the form of *skip arcs* that go directly from the input to the output, skipping the hidden layer. These arcs represent pairwise *similarity* feature vectors between q and either c_1 or c_2. In these feature vectors, we encode MT evaluation measures (e.g., TER, Meteor, and BLEU), cQA task-specific features, etc. See Section 4.3 for details about the features implemented as skip arcs. In the figure, we indicate these pairwise external feature sets as $\psi(q, c_1)$ and $\psi(q, c_2)$. When including the external features, the activation at the output is $f(q, c_1, c_2) = \text{sig}(\mathbf{w_v^T}[\phi(q, c_1, c_2), \psi(q, c_1), \psi(q, c_2)] + b_v)$.

4 Learning Features

We experiment with three kinds of features: (*i*) input embeddings, (*ii*) features motivated by previous work on Machine Translation Evaluation (MTE) (Guzmán et al., 2015) and (*iii*) task-specific features, mostly proposed by participants in the 2015 edition of the task (Nakov et al., 2015).

4.1 Embedding Features

We use the following vector-based embeddings of (q, c_1, c_2) as input to the NN:

- GOOGLE_VEC: We use the pre-trained, 300-dimensional embedding vectors, which Tomas Mikolov trained on 100 billion words from Google News (Mikolov et al., 2013).

- SYNTAX_VEC: We parse the entire question/comment text using the Stanford neural parser (Socher et al., 2013), and we use the final 25-dimensional vector that is produced internally as a by-product of parsing.

Moreover, we use the above vectors to calculate pairwise similarity features. More specifically, given a question q and a pair of comments c_1 and c_2 for it, we calculate the following features: $\psi(q, c_1) = cos(q, c_1)$ and $\psi(q, c_2) = cos(q, c_2)$.

4.2 MTE features

MTFEATS (in MTE-NN-improved only). We use (as skip-arc pairwise features) the following six machine translation evaluation features, to which we refer as MTFEATS, and which measure the similarity between the question and a candidate answer:

- BLEU: This is the most commonly used measure for machine translation evaluation, which is based on n-gram overlap and length ratios (Papineni et al., 2002).

- NIST: This measure is similar to BLEU, and is used at evaluation campaigns run by NIST (Doddington, 2002).

- TER: Translation error rate; it is based on the edit distance between a translation hypothesis and the reference (Snover et al., 2006).

- METEOR: A measure that matches the hypothesis and the reference using synonyms and paraphrases (Lavie and Denkowski, 2009).

- PRECISION: measure, originating in information retrieval.

- RECALL: another measure coming from information retrieval.

BLEUCOMP. Following (Guzmán et al., 2015), we further use as features various components that are involved in the computation of BLEU: n-gram precisions, n-gram matches, total number of n-grams (n=1,2,3,4), lengths of the hypotheses and of the reference, length ratio between them, and BLEU's brevity penalty. We will refer to the set of these features as BLEUCOMP.

4.3 Task-specific features

QL_VEC (in MTE-NN-improved only). Similarly to the GOOGLE_VEC, but on task-specific data, we train word vectors using WORD2VEC on all available cQA training data (Qatar Living) and use them as input to the NN.

QL+IWSLT_VEC (in MTE-NN-{primary, contrastive1/2} only). We also use trained word vectors on the concatenation of the cQA training data and the English portion of the IWSLT data, which consists of TED talks (Cettolo et al., 2012) and is thus informal and somewhat similar to cQA data.

TASK_FEAT. We further extract various task-specific skip-arc features, most of them proposed for the 2015 edition of the task (Nakov et al., 2015). This includes some comment-specific features:

- number of URLs/images/emails/phone numbers;

- number of occurrences of the string *thank*;[3]

- number of tokens/sentences;

- average number of tokens;

- type/token ratio;

- number of nouns/verbs/adjectives/adverbs/pronouns;

- number of positive/negative smileys;

- number of single/double/triple exclamation/interrogation symbols;

- number of interrogative sentences (based on parsing);

- number of words that are not in word2vec's Google News vocabulary.[4]

And also some question-comment pair features:

- question to comment count ratio in terms of sentences/tokens/nouns/verbs/adjectives/adverbs/pronouns;

- question to comment count ratio of words that are not in word2vec's Google News vocabulary.

We also have two meta features:

- is the person answering the question the one who asked it;

- reciprocal rank of the comment in the thread.

---

[3]When an author thanks somebody, this post is typically a bad answer to the original question.

[4]Can detect slang, foreign language, etc., which would indicate a bad answer.

5 Experiments and Results

Below we explain which part of the available data we used for training, as well as our basic settings. Then, we present in detail our experiments and the evaluation results.

5.1 Data and Settings

We experiment with the data from SemEval-2016 Task 3 (Nakov et al., 2016). The task offers a higher quality training dataset TRAIN-PART1, which includes 1,412 questions and 14,110 answers, and a lower-quality TRAIN-PART2 with 382 questions and 3,790 answers. We train our model on TRAIN-PART1 with hidden layers of size 3 for 63 epochs with minibatches of size 30, regularization of 0.0015, and a decay of 0.0001, using stochastic gradient descent with adagrad (Duchi et al., 2011); we use Theano (Bergstra et al., 2010) for learning. We normalize the input feature values to the $[-1; 1]$ interval using minmax, and we initialize the network weights by sampling from a uniform distribution as in (Bengio and Glorot, 2010). We train the model using all pairs of good and bad comments, ignoring ties. At test time we get the full ranking by scoring all possible pairs, and accumulating the scores at the comment level.

We evaluate the model on TRAIN-PART2 after each epoch, and ultimately we keep the model that achieves the highest Kendall's Tau (τ); in case of a tie, we prefer the parameters from a later epoch. We selected the above parameter values on the DEV dataset (244 questions and 2,440 answers) using the full model, and we use them for all experiments below, where we evaluate on the official TEST dataset (329 questions and 3,270 answers).

For evaluation, we use mean average precision (MAP), which is the official evaluation measure. We further report scores using average recall (AvgRec), mean reciprocal rank (MRR), Precision (P), Recall (R), F-measure (F_1), and Accuracy (Acc). Note that the first three are ranking measures, to which we directly give our ranking scores. However, the latter four measures require Good vs. Bad categorical predictions. We generate them based on the ranking scores using a threshold: if the score is above 0.95 (chosen on the DEV set), we consider the comment to be Good, otherwise it is Bad.

5.2 Contrastive Runs

We submitted two contrastive runs, which differ from the general settings above as follows:

- MTE-NN-contrastive1: a different network architecture with 50 units in the hidden layer (instead of 3 for each of h_{q1}, h_{q2}, h_{12}) and higher regularization (0.03, i.e., twenty times bigger). On the development data, it performed very similarly to those for the primary run, and we wanted to try a bigger NN.

- MTE-NN-contrastive2: the same architecture as the primary but different training. We put together TRAIN-PART1 and DEV and randomly split them into 90% for training and 10% for model selection. The idea here was to have some training examples from development, which was supposed to be a cleaner dataset (and so more similar to the test set).

5.3 Official Results

Table 1 shows the results for our submissions for subtask A. Our primary submission was ranked sixth out of twelve teams on MAP. Note, however, that it was third on MRR and F_1. It is also 3 and 14 points above the average and the worst systems, respectively, and well above the baselines. Both our contrastive submissions performed slightly better, but neither of them is strong enough to change the overall ranking if we had chosen one of them as primary.

For subtask C, we multiplied (*i*) our scores for subtask A for the related question by (*ii*) the given reciprocal rank of the related question in the list of related questions. That is, we did not try to address question-question similarity (subtask B). We achieved 4th place with a MAP of 49.38, which is well above the baseline of 40.36. Our contrastive2 run performed slightly better at 49.49.

5.4 Post-submission Analysis on the Test Set

After the competition, we produced a refined version of the system (**MTE-NN-improved**) where the settings changed as follows: (*i*) using QL_VEC instead of QL+IWSLT_VEC, (*ii*) adding MTFEATS to the set of features, (*iii*) optimizing accuracy instead of Kendall's tau, (*iv*) training for 100 epochs instead of 63, and (*v*) regularization of 0.005 instead of 0.0015.

System	MAP	AvgRec	MRR	Δ_{MAP}
MTE-NN-improved	**78.20**	**88.01**	**86.93**	
−TASK_FEATS	72.91	84.06	78.73	-5.29
−COMMENT_RANK	76.08	86.41	84.42	-2.12
−SAME_AUTHOR	76.60	86.75	83.71	-1.60
−QL_VEC	75.83	86.57	83.90	-2.37
−GOOGLE_VEC	76.96	87.66	84.72	-1.24
−SYNTAX_VEC	77.65	87.65	85.85	-0.55
−COSINES	76.97	87.28	85.03	-1.23
−MTFEATS	77.75	87.76	86.01	-0.45
−BLEUCOMP	77.83	87.85	86.32	-0.37

Table 2: Ablation study of our improved system on the test data.

Note that the training and development set remained unchanged. **MTE-NN-improved** showed notable improvements on the DEV set over our primary submission. In Table 2, we present the results on the TEST set. To gain additional insight about the contribution of various features and feature groups to the performance of the overall system, we also present the results of an ablation study where we removed different feature groups one by one. For this purpose, we study Δ_{MAP}, i.e., the absolute change in MAP when the feature or feature group is excluded from the full system. Not surprisingly, the most important turn out to be the TASK_FEATS (contributing over 5 MAP points) as they handle important information sources that are not available to the system from other feature groups, e.g., the reciprocal rank of the comment in the comment thread, which alone contributes 2.12 MAP points, and the feature checking whether the person who asked the question is the one who answered, which contributes 1.60 MAP points. Next in terms of importance come word embeddings, QL_VEC (contributing over 2 MAP points), trained on text from the target forum, Qatar-Living. Then come the GOOGLE_VEC (contributing over 1 MAP point), which are trained on 100 billion words, and thus are still useful even in the presence of the domain-specific QL_VEC, which are in turn trained on four orders of magnitude less data. Interestingly, the MTE-motivated SYNTAX_VEC vectors contribute half a MAP point, which shows the importance of modeling syntax for this task. Next, we can see that using just the vectors is not enough, and adding cosines as pairwise features for the three kinds of vectors contributes over one MAP point.

	Submission	MAP	AvgRec	MRR	P	R	F1	Acc
1	SemEval 1st	79.19_1	88.82_1	86.42_1	76.96_1	55.30_8	64.36_5	75.11_2
	MTE-NN-improved	*78.20*	*88.01*	*86.93*	*57.08*	*76.75*	*65.47*	*67.09*
2	SemEval 2nd	77.66_2	88.05_3	84.93_4	75.56_2	58.84_6	66.16_2	75.54_1
3	SemEval 3rd	77.58_3	88.14_2	85.21_2	74.13_4	53.05_{10}	61.84_8	73.39_5
4	SemEval 4th	77.28_4	87.52_5	84.09_6	70.46_6	63.36_4	66.72_1	74.31_4
5	SemEval 5th	77.16_5	87.98_4	84.69_5	74.43_3	56.73_7	64.39_4	74.50_3
	MTE-NN-contrastive2	*76.98*	*86.98*	*85.50*	*58.71*	*70.28*	*63.97*	*67.83*
	MTE-NN-contrastive1	*76.86*	*87.03*	*84.36*	*55.84*	*77.35*	*64.86*	*65.93*
6	**MTE-NN-primary**	$\mathbf{76.44_6}$	$\mathbf{86.74_7}$	$\mathbf{84.97_3}$	$\mathbf{56.28_9}$	$\mathbf{76.22_1}$	$\mathbf{64.75_3}$	$\mathbf{66.27_8}$
…	…	…	…	…	…	…	…	…
	SemEval Average	73.54	84.61	81.54	64.80	57.03	58.77	68.45
…	…	…	…	…	…	…	…	…
12	SemEval 12th	62.24_{12}	75.41_{12}	70.58_{12}	50.28_{11}	53.50_9	51.84_{10}	59.60_{11}
	Baseline 1 (IR)	**59.53**	**72.60**	**67.83**	—	—	—	—
	Baseline 2 (random)	52.80	66.52	58.71	40.56	74.57	52.55	45.26
	Baseline 3 (all 'true')	—	—	—	40.64	100.00	**57.80**	40.64
	Baseline 4 (all 'false')	—	—	—	—	—	—	**59.36**

Table 1: **Comparison to the official results on SemEval-2016 Task 3, subtask A.** The first column shows the rank of the primary runs with respect to the official MAP score. The subindices in the results columns show the rank of the primary runs with respect to the evaluation measure in the respective column.

Finally, the two MTE features, MTFEATS and BLEUCOMP, together contribute 0.8 MAP points. It is interesting that the BLEU components manage to contribute on top of the MTFEATS, which already contain several state-of-the-art MTE measures, including BLEU itself. This is probably because the other features we have do not model n-gram matches directly.

We further used the output of our MTE-NN-improved system to generate predictions for subtask C, as explained above. This yielded improvements from 49.38 to 49.87 on MAP, from 55.44 to 56.08 on AvgRec, and from 51.56 to 52.16 on MRR.

6 Conclusion

We have explored the applicability of machine translation evaluation metrics to answer ranking in community Question Answering, a seemingly very different task (compared to MTE). In particular, with ranking in mind, we have adopted a pairwise neural network architecture, which incorporates MTE features, as well as rich syntactic and semantic embeddings of the input texts that are non-linearly combined in the hidden layer.

Our post-competition improvements have shown state-of-the-art performance (Guzmán et al., 2016), with sizeable contribution from both the MTE features and from the network architecture. This is an encouraging result as it was not a priori clear that an MTE approach would work well for cQA.

In future work, we plan to incorporate fine-tuned word embeddings as in the SemanticZ system (Mihaylov and Nakov, 2016b), and information from entire threads (Nicosia et al., 2015; Barrón-Cedeño et al., 2015; Joty et al., 2015; Joty et al., 2016). We also want to add more knowledge sources, e.g., as in the SUper Team system (Mihaylova et al., 2016), including veracity, sentiment, complexity, troll user features as inspired by (Mihaylov et al., 2015a; Mihaylov et al., 2015b; Mihaylov and Nakov, 2016a), and PMI-based goodness polarity lexicons as in the PMI-cool system (Balchev et al., 2016).

We further plan to explore the application of our NN architecture to subtasks B and C, and to study the interactions among the three subtasks in order to solve the primary subtask C. Furthermore, we would like to try a similar neural network for other semantic similarity problems, such as textual entailment.

Acknowledgments

This research was performed by the Arabic Language Technologies (ALT) group at the Qatar Computing Research Institute (QCRI), HBKU, part of Qatar Foundation. It is part of the Interactive sYstems for Answer Search (Iyas) project, which is developed in collaboration with MIT-CSAIL.

References

Daniel Balchev, Yasen Kiprov, Ivan Koychev, and Preslav Nakov. 2016. PMI-cool at SemEval-2016 Task 3: Experiments with pmi and goodness polarity lexicons for community question answering. In *Proceedings of the 10th International Workshop on Semantic Evaluation*, SemEval '16, San Diego, California, USA.

Alberto Barrón-Cedeño, Simone Filice, Giovanni Da San Martino, Shafiq Joty, Lluís Màrquez, Preslav Nakov, and Alessandro Moschitti. 2015. Thread-level information for comment classification in community question answering. In *Proceedings of the 53rd Annual Meeting of the Association for Computational Linguistics and the 7th International Joint Conference on Natural Language Processing*, ACL-IJCNLP '15, pages 687–693, Beijing, China.

Yoshua Bengio and Xavier Glorot. 2010. Understanding the difficulty of training deep feedforward neural networks. In *Proceedings of the 13th International Conference on Artificial Intelligence and Statistics*, volume 9 of *AISTATS '10*, pages 249–256, Chia Laguna Resort, Sardinia, Italy.

Adam Berger, Rich Caruana, David Cohn, Dayne Freitag, and Vibhu Mittal. 2000. Bridging the lexical chasm: Statistical approaches to answer-finding. In *Proceedings of the 23rd Annual International ACM Conference on Research and Development in Information Retrieval*, SIGIR '00, pages 192–199, Athens, Greece.

James Bergstra, Olivier Breuleux, Frédéric Bastien, Pascal Lamblin, Razvan Pascanu, Guillaume Desjardins, Joseph Turian, David Warde-Farley, and Yoshua Bengio. 2010. Theano: a CPU and GPU math expression compiler. In *Proceedings of the Python for Scientific Computing Conference*, SciPy '10, Austin, Texas, USA.

Mauro Cettolo, Christian Girardi, and Marcello Federico. 2012. WIT^3: Web inventory of transcribed and translated talks. In *Proceedings of the 16th Conference of the European Association for Machine Translation*, EAMT '12, pages 261–268, Trento, Italy.

George Doddington. 2002. Automatic evaluation of machine translation quality using n-gram co-occurrence statistics. In *Proceedings of the Second International Conference on Human Language Technology Research*, HLT '02, pages 138–145, San Diego, California, USA.

Cicero dos Santos, Luciano Barbosa, Dasha Bogdanova, and Bianca Zadrozny. 2015. Learning hybrid representations to retrieve semantically equivalent questions. In *Proceedings of the 53rd Annual Meeting of the Association for Computational Linguistics and the 7th International Joint Conference on Natural Language Processing (Volume 2: Short Papers)*, ACL-IJCNLP '15, pages 694–699, Beijing, China.

John Duchi, Elad Hazan, and Yoram Singer. 2011. Adaptive subgradient methods for online learning and stochastic optimization. *Journal of Machine Learning Research*, 12:2121–2159.

Abdessamad Echihabi and Daniel Marcu. 2003. A noisy-channel approach to question answering. In *Proceedings of the 41st Annual Meeting of the Association for Computational Linguistics - Volume 1*, ACL '03, pages 16–23, Sapporo, Japan.

Minwei Feng, Bing Xiang, Michael R Glass, Lidan Wang, and Bowen Zhou. 2015. Applying deep learning to answer selection: A study and an open task. In *Proceedings of the 2015 IEEE Automatic Speech Recognition and Understanding Workshop*, ASRU '15, Scottsdale, Arizona, USA.

Francisco Guzmán, Shafiq Joty, Lluís Màrquez, and Preslav Nakov. 2015. Pairwise neural machine translation evaluation. In *Proceedings of the 53rd Annual Meeting of the Association for Computational Linguistics and the 7th International Joint Conference on Natural Language Processing (Volume 1: Long Papers)*, ACL-IJCNLP '15, pages 805–814, Beijing, China.

Francisco Guzmán, Lluís Màrquez, and Preslav Nakov. 2016. Machine translation evaluation meets community question answering. In *Proceedings of the 54th Annual Meeting of the Association for Computational Linguistics*, ACL '16, Berlin, Germany.

Jiwoon Jeon, W. Bruce Croft, and Joon Ho Lee. 2005. Finding similar questions in large question and answer archives. In *Proceedings of the 14th ACM International Conference on Information and Knowledge Management*, CIKM '05, pages 84–90, Bremen, Germany.

Shafiq Joty, Alberto Barrón-Cedeño, Giovanni Da San Martino, Simone Filice, Lluís Màrquez, Alessandro Moschitti, and Preslav Nakov. 2015. Global thread-level inference for comment classification in community question answering. In *Proceedings of the 2015 Conference on Empirical Methods in Natural Language Processing*, EMNLP '15, pages 573–578, Lisbon, Portugal.

Shafiq Joty, Lluís Màrquez, and Preslav Nakov. 2016. Joint learning with global inference for comment classification in community question answering. In *Proceedings of the 2016 Conference of the North American Chapter of the Association for Computational Linguistics: Human Language Technologies*, NAACL-HLT '16, San Diego, California, USA.

Alon Lavie and Michael Denkowski. 2009. The METEOR metric for automatic evaluation of machine translation. *Machine Translation*, 23(2–3):105–115.

Tao Lei, Hrishikesh Joshi, Regina Barzilay, Tommi S. Jaakkola, Kateryna Tymoshenko, Alessandro Moschitti, and Lluís Màrquez. 2016. Denoising bodies to titles: Retrieving similar questions with recurrent convolutional models. In *Proceedings of the 15th Annual Conference of the North American Chapter of the Association for Computational Linguistics: Human Language Technologies*, NAACL-HLT '16, San Diego, California, USA.

Shuguang Li and Suresh Manandhar. 2011. Improving question recommendation by exploiting information need. In *Proceedings of the 49th Annual Meeting of the Association for Computational Linguistics: Human Language Technologies - Volume 1*, HLT '11, pages 1425–1434, Portland, Oregon, USA.

Nitin Madnani, Joel Tetreault, and Martin Chodorow. 2012. Re-examining machine translation metrics for paraphrase identification. In *Proceedings of the 2012 Conference of the North American Chapter of the Association for Computational Linguistics: Human Language Technologies*, NAACL-HLT '12, pages 182–190, Montréal, Canada.

Todor Mihaylov and Preslav Nakov. 2016a. Hunting for troll comments in news community forums. In *Proceedings of the 54th Annual Meeting of the Association for Computational Linguistics*, ACL '16, Berlin, Germany.

Todor Mihaylov and Preslav Nakov. 2016b. SemanticZ at SemEval-2016 Task 3: Ranking relevant answers in community question answering using semantic similarity based on fine-tuned word embeddings. In *Proceedings of the 10th International Workshop on Semantic Evaluation*, SemEval '16, San Diego, California, USA.

Todor Mihaylov, Georgi Georgiev, and Preslav Nakov. 2015a. Finding opinion manipulation trolls in news community forums. In *Proceedings of the Nineteenth Conference on Computational Natural Language Learning*, CoNLL '15, pages 310–314, Beijing, China.

Todor Mihaylov, Ivan Koychev, Georgi Georgiev, and Preslav Nakov. 2015b. Exposing paid opinion manipulation trolls. In *Proceedings of the International Conference Recent Advances in Natural Language Processing*, RANLP '15, pages 443–450, Hissar, Bulgaria.

Tsvetomila Mihaylova, Pepa Gencheva, Martin Boyanov, Ivana Yovcheva, Todor Mihaylov, Momchil Hardalov, Yasen Kiprov, Daniel Balchev, Ivan Koychev, Preslav Nakov, Ivelina Nikolova, and Galia Angelova. 2016. SUper Team at SemEval-2016 Task 3: Building a feature-rich system for community question answering. In *Proceedings of the 10th International Workshop on Semantic Evaluation*, SemEval '16, San Diego, California, USA.

Tomas Mikolov, Wen-tau Yih, and Geoffrey Zweig. 2013. Linguistic regularities in continuous space word representations. In *Proceedings of the 2013 Conference of the North American Chapter of the Association for Computational Linguistics: Human Language Technologies*, NAACL-HLT '13, pages 746–751, Atlanta, Georgia, USA.

Preslav Nakov, Lluís Màrquez, Walid Magdy, Alessandro Moschitti, Jim Glass, and Bilal Randeree. 2015. Semeval-2015 task 3: Answer selection in community question answering. In *Proceedings of the 9th International Workshop on Semantic Evaluation*, SemEval '15, pages 269–281, Denver, Colorado, USA.

Preslav Nakov, Lluís Màrquez, Alessandro Moschitti, Walid Magdy, Hamdy Mubarak, Abed Alhakim Freihat, Jim Glass, and Bilal Randeree. 2016. SemEval-2016 task 3: Community question answering. In *Proceedings of the 10th International Workshop on Semantic Evaluation*, SemEval '16, San Diego, California, USA.

Massimo Nicosia, Simone Filice, Alberto Barrón-Cedeño, Iman Saleh, Hamdy Mubarak, Wei Gao, Preslav Nakov, Giovanni Da San Martino, Alessandro Moschitti, Kareem Darwish, Lluís Màrquez, Shafiq Joty, and Walid Magdy. 2015. QCRI: Answer selection for community question answering - experiments for Arabic and English. In *Proceedings of the 9th International Workshop on Semantic Evaluation*, SemEval '15, pages 203–209, Denver, Colorado, USA.

Kishore Papineni, Salim Roukos, Todd Ward, and Wei-Jing Zhu. 2002. BLEU: a method for automatic evaluation of machine translation. In *Proceedings of 40th Annual Meting of the Association for Computational Linguistics*, ACL '02, pages 311–318, Philadelphia, Pennsylvania, USA.

Stefan Riezler, Alexander Vasserman, Ioannis Tsochantaridis, Vibhu Mittal, and Yi Liu. 2007. Statistical machine translation for query expansion in answer retrieval. In *Proceedings of the 45th Annual Meeting of the Association of Computational Linguistics*, ACL '07, pages 464–471, Prague, Czech Republic.

Aliaksei Severyn and Alessandro Moschitti. 2015. Learning to rank short text pairs with convolutional deep neural networks. In *Proceedings of the 38th International ACM SIGIR Conference on Research and Development in Information Retrieval*, SIGIR '15, pages 373–382, Santiago, Chile.

Yikang Shen, Wenge Rong, Nan Jiang, Baolin Peng, Jie Tang, and Zhang Xiong. 2015. Word embedding based correlation model for question/answer matching. *arXiv preprint arXiv:1511.04646*.

Matthew Snover, Bonnie Dorr, Richard Schwartz, Linnea Micciulla, and John Makhoul. 2006. A study of translation edit rate with targeted human annotation. In *Proceedings of the 7th Biennial Conference of the Association for Machine Translation in the Americas*, AMTA '06, pages 223–231, Cambridge, Massachusetts, USA.

Richard Socher, John Bauer, Christopher D. Manning, and Ng Andrew Y. 2013. Parsing with compositional vector grammars. In *Proceedings of the 51st Annual Meeting of the Association for Computational Linguistics (Volume 1: Long Papers)*, ACL '13, pages 455–465, Sofia, Bulgaria.

Radu Soricut and Eric Brill. 2006. Automatic question answering using the web: Beyond the factoid. *Inf. Retr.*, 9(2):191–206, March.

Mihai Surdeanu, Massimiliano Ciaramita, and Hugo Zaragoza. 2011. Learning to rank answers to non-factoid questions from web collections. *Comput. Linguist.*, 37(2):351–383, June.

Ming Tan, Bing Xiang, and Bowen Zhou. 2015. Lstm-based deep learning models for non-factoid answer selection. *arXiv preprint arXiv:1511.04108*.

Quan Hung Tran, Vu Tran, Tu Vu, Minh Nguyen, and Son Bao Pham. 2015. JAIST: Combining multiple features for answer selection in community question answering. In *Proceedings of the 9th International Workshop on Semantic Evaluation*, SemEval '15, pages 215–219, Denver, Colorado, USA.

Di Wang and Eric Nyberg. 2015. A long short-term memory model for answer sentence selection in question answering. In *Proceedings of the 53rd Annual Meeting of the Association for Computational Linguistics and the 7th International Joint Conference on Natural Language Processing (Volume 2: Short Papers)*, ACL-IJCNLP '15, pages 707–712, Beijing, China.

Guangyou Zhou, Tingting He, Jun Zhao, and Po Hu. 2015. Learning continuous word embedding with metadata for question retrieval in community question answering. In *Proceedings of the 53rd Annual Meeting of the Association for Computational Linguistics and the 7th International Joint Conference on Natural Language Processing (Volume 2: Short Papers)*, ACL-IJCNLP '15, pages 250–259, Beijing, China.

ConvKN at SemEval-2016 Task 3: Answer and Question Selection for Question Answering on Arabic and English Fora

Alberto Barrón-Cedeño[†], Daniele Bonadiman[‡], Giovanni Da San Martino[†],
Shafiq Joty[†], Alessandro Moschitti[†], Fahad A. Al Obaidli[†],
Salvatore Romeo[†], Kateryna Tymoshenko[‡], Antonio Uva[‡]

[†]ALT group, Qatar Computing Research Institute, Hamad Bin Khalifa University, Qatar
[‡]Department of Computer Science and Information Engineering, University of Trento, Italy
{albarron,gmartino,sjoty,faalobaidli,amoschitti,sromeo}@qf.org.qa
{d.bonadiman,kateryna.tymoshenko,antonio.uva}@unitn.it

Abstract

We describe our system, ConvKN, participating to the SemEval-2016 Task 3 "Community Question Answering". The task targeted the reranking of questions and comments in real-life web fora both in English and Arabic. ConvKN combines convolutional tree kernels with convolutional neural networks and additional manually designed features including text similarity and thread specific features. For the first time, we applied tree kernels to syntactic trees of Arabic sentences for a reranking task. Our approaches obtained the second best results in three out of four tasks. The only task we performed averagely is the one where we did not use tree kernels in our classifier.

1 Introduction

SemEval-2016 Task 3 challenged the participants on the different steps of the full task of Community Question Answering (cQA).[1] Given a set of existing forum questions Q, where each existing question $q \in Q$ is associated with a set of answers C_q, and a new user question q', the ultimate task is to determine whether a comment $c \in C_q$ represents a pertinent answer to q' or not. This task can be subdivided into three tasks, namely: (A) to assign a relevance (*goodness*) score to each answer $c \in C_q$ with respect to the existing question q; (B) to re-rank the set of questions Q according to their relevance against the new question q'; and finally (C) to predict the appropriateness of the answers $c \in C_q$ against q'.

Task 3 included these three tasks for English, whereas an adaptation of Task C was proposed for Arabic (Task D). The reader can refer to (Nakov et al., 2016) for a more detailed description of the tasks. Task A was also proposed in the SemEval-2015 edition (Nakov et al., 2015).[2]

We designed systems for all tasks. We used the feature vectors designed by Barrón-Cedeño et al. (2015) and Nicosia et al. (2015) for tasks A, B and C, whereas we just used a basic feature vector derived from the system of Belinkov et al. (2015) for Task D.

Most importantly, for tasks A, B and D, we combined feature vectors with tree kernels (Moschitti, 2006) for relational learning from short text (Moschitti et al., 2007; Moschitti, 2008). In particular, we used the improved models that have been successful applied for several tasks and datasets in standard QA, see for example, (Severyn and Moschitti, 2012; Severyn and Moschitti, 2013; Severyn et al., 2013b; Severyn et al., 2013a; Tymoshenko et al., 2014; Tymoshenko and Moschitti, 2015).

Additionally, we used Convolutional Neural Networks (CNNs) (Severyn and Moschitti, 2015) and combined them with vectors and tree kernels for Task A as we did in (Tymoshenko et al., 2016).

We acknowledge that the automatic feature engineering of tree kernels was very useful to tackle the new challenges of the SemEval-2016 Task 3. Indeed, all our three systems using relational models based on tree kernels achieved the second official

---

[1]http://alt.qcri.org/semeval2016/task3

[2]Note that in that paper the naming convention is slightly different. The fresh user question and the forum question are called "original" and "related", respectively.

Proceedings of SemEval-2016, pages 896–903,
San Diego, California, June 16-17, 2016. ©2016 Association for Computational Linguistics

position. In contrast, for Task C, we did not have time for using the relational model in our submitted system, this has probably caused our average performance in such task, i.e., our system was ranked at the eighth position. For similar reasons, we could apply CNNs to only Task A.

The rest of the paper is organized as follows. Section 2 describes the four CQA tasks and gives a brief overview of the corpora. Section 3 describes the features used. Section 4 discusses our models and our official results. Section 6 presents final remarks.

2 Tasks Description

In this section we sketch the four proposed tasks.

Task A: Question–Comment Similarity. Given a user question and a thread of ten comments associated with it, re-rank the comments in the thread according to their pertinence. Three classes exist in this case: (*i*) `good`: the comment is definitively relevant; (*ii*) `potentially useful`: the comment is not good, but it still contains related information worth checking; and (*iii*) `bad`: the comment is irrelevant (e.g., it is part of a dialogue or unrelated to the topic). For evaluation purposes, both `potentially useful` and `bad` comments were considered as `bad`.

Task B: Question–Question Similarity. Given a new question and a set of ten forum questions, re-rank the forum questions by assessing if they are (*i*) `perfect match`: the new and forum questions request roughly the same information, (*ii*) `relevant`: the new and forum questions ask for similar information, or (*iii*) `irrelevant`: the new and forum questions are completely unrelated. For evaluation purposes, both `perfect match` and `relevant` forum questions are considered as `relevant`.

Task C: New Question–Comment Similarity. Similar to task A, but in this case the relevance of one-hundred comments is assessed against a new out-of-the-forum question. Same evaluation considerations as in task A apply.

Task D: Question–{Forum Question+Comment}. A new question and a set of thirty forum question–answer pairs are provided (it is known in advance that the answer is correct with respect to the forum question). Re-rank the question+comment pairs according to three classes: (*i*) `direct`: a direct answer to the new question; (*ii*) `relevant`: not a direct answer to the question but with information related to the topic; and (*iii*) `irrelevant`: an answer to another question, not related to the topic. For evaluation purposes, both `direct` and `relevant` forum questions are considered as `good`.

Tasks A, B, and C use English instances extracted from *Qatar Living*, a forum for people to pose questions on multiple aspects of daily life in Qatar.[3] Task D uses Arabic instances extracted from three medical fora: *webteb*, *altibbi*, and *consult islamweb*.[4]

As this is a reranking task, mean average precision (MAP) is the referring evaluation metric. We also evaluate our models in terms of average Recall (AvgRec), Precision (P), Recall (R), F-measure (F_1), and Accuracy.

Further details about the corpora, evaluation and other settings can be found in (Nakov et al., 2016).

3 Approach

In order to re-rank the comments according to their relevance, either against the forum questions or against the new questions, we train a binary SVM classifier and use its score as a measure of relevance. The classifier uses partial tree kernels (Moschitti, 2006) defined over shallow syntactic trees, along with other numeric features.

We used the DKPro Core toolkit (Eckart de Castilho and Gurevych, 2014)[5] for pre-processing the texts in English. More precisely, we used OpenNLP's tokenizer, POS-tagger and chunk annotator[6], and Stanford's lemmatizer (Manning et al., 2014), all accessible through DKPro Core.

We used the MADAMIRA toolkit (Pasha et al., 2014) for segmenting Arabic texts. In order to split the texts into sentences, we used the Stanford splitter.[7] For parsing Arabic texts into syntactic trees, we

---

[3]http://www.qatarliving.com/forum

[4]https://www.webteb.com/, http://www.altibbi.com/, and http://consult.islamweb.net.

[5]https://dkpro.github.io/dkpro-core/

[6]https://opennlp.apache.org/

[7]http://stanfordnlp.github.io/CoreNLP

used the Berkeley parser (Petrov and Klein, 2007). Following, we briefly describe the numeric features used in different tasks.

3.1 SemEval-2015 Features

For English texts, we consider three kinds of similarity measures: lexical, syntactic, and semantic (Barrón-Cedeño et al., 2015; Nicosia et al., 2015)

In the case of Task A, the context of a comment is a relevant factor. Comments are organized sequentially according to the time line of the comment thread. Important factors to assess the value of a comment is whether the thread includes further comments by the person who originally asked the question, if the same user is behind various comments in the thread, or what forum category the thread belongs to. Therefore, we consider a set of features that try to describe a comment in the context of the entire thread. Other Boolean context features characterize different situations including the identification of potential dialogues, which usually represent a bunch of `bad` comments, or the position of the comment in the thread. We also considered the categories of the questions in the forum (as some of them tend to include more open-ended questions and even invite for discussion on ambiguous topics), as well as the occurrence of specific strings or the length of a comment. In-depth descriptions of these features are available in (Nicosia et al., 2015).

For Arabic texts, we utilize the embedding vectors as obtained by Belinkov et al. (2015): employing word2vec (Mikolov et al., 2013) on the Arabic Gigaword corpus (Parker et al., 2011). More specifically, we concatenate the vectors representing a new question and an existing question in the question–answer pair, which is then fed to the SVM classifier.

3.2 Rank Feature

The meta-information in the English corpus includes the position of the forum threads in the rank generated by the Google search engine for a given new question. We exploit this information in tasks B and C. We employ the inverse of such position as a feature and refer to it as the rank feature.

3.3 Tree Kernels

Tree kernels are similarity functions that measure the similarity between tree structures. We con-

structed a syntactic tree for each comment or question. Each task involves a pair of trees, question and comment (tasks A and C) and new and forum questions (tasks B and D). Replicating Severyn and Moschitti (2012), we link the two trees by connecting (i) part-of-speech nodes with a lexical match between the corresponding non-stop words; and (ii) chunk nodes such as NP, PP, VP, when there is a link above between POS-tags. Such links are marked with the presence of a specific tag. We then apply the partial tree kernel (PTK) or the syntactic tree kernels[8] (STK) both defined in (Moschitti, 2006) on the pairs as:

$$K((t_1, t_2), (u_1, u_2)) = TK(t_1, u_1) + TK(t_2, u_2),$$
(1)

where t and u are parse trees extracted from the text pair, i.e., either question and comment for task A or question and question for tasks B and D.

4 Submissions and Results

We describe our primary submissions for the four tasks in Section 4.1. The contrastive submissions are discussed in Section 4.2. Table 1 shows our official competition results for both primary and contrastive submissions.

In all submissions we employed Support Vector Machines (SVM) (Joachims, 1999) using either SVM-Light (Joachims, 1999), KeLP[9] (Filice et al., 2015), or SVM-light-TK[10] (Moschitti, 2006) (only the last two can handle tree kernels).

4.1 Primary Submissions

Task A. The submission consists in an SVM operating on two kernels: (*i*) the tree kernel described in Section 3.3, applied to the structures described by Tymoshenko and Moschitti (2015) without question and focus classification; (*ii*) a polynomial kernel of degree 3 applied to the feature vector that is a concatenation of the feature vector described in Section 3.1, and question and answer embeddings learned on the training set by the Convolutional Neural Network (CNN) described in (Severyn and Moschitti, 2015). More details about the used

---

[8]Also called SST.

[9]https://github.com/SAG-KeLP

[10]http://disi.unitn.it/moschitti/Tree-Kernel.htm

A	MAP	AvgRec	MRR	P	R	F_1	Acc
primary[2]	77.66	88.05	84.93	75.56	58.84	66.16	75.54
cont_1	78.71	88.98	86.15	77.78	53.72	63.55	74.95
cont_2	77.29	87.77	85.03	74.74	59.67	66.36	75.41
best	79.19	88.82	86.42	76.96	55.30	64.36	75.11
baseline	59.53	72.60	67.83				
B							
primary[2]	76.02	90.70	84.64	68.58	66.52	67.54	78.71
cont_1	75.57	89.64	83.57	63.77	72.53	67.87	77.14
best	76.70	90.31	83.02	63.53	69.53	66.39	76.57
baseline	74.75	88.30	83.79				
C							
primary[8]	47.15	47.46	51.43	45.97	8.72	14.65	90.51
cont_1	43.31	44.19	48.89	30.00	3.21	5.80	90.26
cont_2	41.12	38.89	44.17	33.55	32.11	32.81	87.71
best	55.41	60.66	61.48	18.03	63.15	28.05	69.73
baseline	40.36	45.97	45.83				
D							
primary[2]	45.50	50.13	52.55	28.55	64.53	39.58	62.10
cont_1	38.33	42.09	43.75	20.38	96.95	33.68	26.50
cont_2	39.98	43.68	46.41	26.26	68.39	37.95	57.00
best	45.83	51.01	53.66	34.45	52.33	41.55	71.67
baseline	28.88	28.71	30.93				

Table 1: Performance of our official primary and contrastive submissions to SemEval-2016 Task 3 for tasks A, B, C, and D. Best-performing and baseline systems included for comparison. The super-index in the primary submission stands for the position in the challenge ranking. The baselines are as provided by the task organizers; they are based on search engine rankings (except for task D, which is random).

embeddings and the resulting kernels can be seen in (Tymoshenko et al., 2016). The SVM was trained on the union of both training and development sets.

Task B. The submission consists in an SVM operating on three kernels: (*i*) an RBF kernel on the features described in Section 3.1, (*ii*) an RBF kernel on the features described in Section 3.2; and (*iii*) the tree kernel described in Section 3.3. The C parameter of the SVM was set to 1. Both the tree and the RBF kernels use default values for the parameters. The SVM was trained on the union of the training and development sets.

Task C. The submission consists in an SVM operating on two RBF kernels (with default parameter values): the first one is on the features described in Section 3.1. The second one is on the features described in Section 3.2 plus the score obtained from the prediction of a comment according to a classifier built for task A, computed by cross-validation. The SVM is trained on the union of the training part 2 and development sets.

Task D. The submission consists in an SVM operating on two kernels: (*i*) the syntactic tree kernel (SST) (Moschitti, 2006), applied as described in Section 3.3, to the constituency trees of the question texts; (*ii*) a linear kernel applied to the features in (Belinkov et al., 2015). In tasks A and B we used PTK, which is slower but more accurate. However, the trees of the Arabic data were rather large and very noisy. Thus we used SST, which is faster and uses less features. The value 0.1 for parameter L served the purpose of removing noise. The SVM was trained on the union of the training and development sets.

4.2 Contrastive Submissions

Task A. We submitted a contrastive run (cont$_1$), where we use a joint learning and inference approach based on a Fully-connected Conditional Random Field (FCCRF) (Joty et al., 2016) to classify all the comments in a thread collectively. We used the numeric (non-tree) features used previously in (Joty et al., 2015; Barrón-Cedeño et al., 2015), and also the predictions of the SVM used in our primary run. The FCCRF model uses an Ising-like edge potential, which distinguishes between only *same* and *different* (as opposed to all four possibilities) state transitions to model all pair dependencies.

The second contrastive run (cont$_2$) is as the primary submission, but without tree kernels.

Task B. We submitted one contrastive submission which is identical to the primary one, with the only exception that SVM is trained on the training part 2 and development sets only.

Task C. We submitted one contrastive submission which is identical to the primary one, with the exception that SVM is trained on all training and development sets.

The second contrastive submission consists of a rule-based system which relies on the outputs from tasks A and B. A comment is labeled as `good` if it is considered `good` with respect to the related question (Task A) and the related question is considered `relevant` with respect to the new question (Task B). The comment is considered `bad` otherwise.

Task D. The contrastive systems did not use tree kernels. Our first contrastive run used only feature vectors. Our second contrastive run also used additional features borrowed from machine translation evaluation: BLEU (Papineni et al., 2002), TER (Snover et al., 2006), Meteor (Lavie and Denkowski, 2009), NIST (Doddington, 2002), Precision and Recall, and length ratio between the question and the comment.

5 Results and Discussion

Table 1 shows the results obtained in the four tasks. We achieved the second position for tasks A, B, and D. In Task A, tree kernels give no major boost, but without them our model would be cont$_2$, which

achieved the third position on the test set. The joint model cont$_1$, run on top of our primary system, was able to improve it by more than one point. We were not sure about the outcome of this model, thus we preferred not to use it as our primary submission, even though we got an improvement also on the development set.

Our cont$_1$ system for Task B, trained only on the train part 2 and development sets, scored less than our primary one. Even if our preliminary observations had suggested that the distributions of the different training and development sets were too different and potentially damaging the model learning, having more diverse data ended up as a better solution to the task.

Our submission for Task C is very limited as it does not include tree kernel models. The use of our feature vectors only (the same used for tasks A and B), results in an average performance in the challenge.

Regarding Task D, cont$_1$, using embedding features from (Belinkov et al., 2015), is an average system. When we add the machine translation evaluation (MTE) features the MAP increases from 38.33 to 39.98. We did not trust the MTE features as in the development set they obtained a lower result than the simple embedding features. This resulted to be a mistake from the competition viewpoint as they could have been combined with tree kernels. Indeed, our Primary system just combines tree kernels with the embedding features improving them by more than 7 absolute points, achieving the second position with a MAP of 45.50, very close to the best system, i.e., 45.83.

6 Conclusions

In this paper, we have presented the systems developed by the teams of the Qatar Computing Research Institute (QCRI) and the University of Trento for participating in SemEval-2016 Task 3 on Community Question Answering.

We used supervised machine learning approaches based on various combinations of the convolution tree kernels, text embedding features, including those learned by the convolutional neural networks, and a number of task-specific features from our previous work for SemEval-2015, Task 3.

For each task we submitted one primary and two contrastive runs incorporating various combinations of the above components. Our primary runs scored second for tasks A, B and D and eighth for task C. Finally, we analyzed the performance of our runs and discussed which components are more beneficial for a specific task/language.

In future work, we plan to devise better ways of combining convolution tree kernels with CNNs, e.g. by embedding the CNN similarities into the structural kernels, and encoding more complex relations into the structural representations of the text snippets.

Acknowledgments

This research is developed by the Arabic Language Technologies (ALT) group at the Qatar Computing Research Institute (QCRI), HBKU, Qatar Foundation in collaboration with MIT. It is part of the Interactive sYstems for Answer Search (IYAS) project. This work has been partially supported by the EC project CogNet, 671625 (H2020-ICT-2014-2, Research and Innovation action) and by an IBM Faculty Award.

References

Alberto Barrón-Cedeño, Simone Filice, Giovanni Da San Martino, Shafiq Joty, Lluís Màrquez, Preslav Nakov, and Alessandro Moschitti. 2015. Thread-level information for comment classification in community question answering. In *Proceedings of the 53rd Annual Meeting of the Association for Computational Linguistics and the 7th International Joint Conference on Natural Language Processing (Volume 2: Short Papers)*, pages 687–693, Beijing, China, July. Association for Computational Linguistics.

Yonatan Belinkov, Mitra Mohtarami, Scott Cyphers, and James Glass. 2015. Vectorslu: A continuous word vector approach to answer selection in community question answering systems. In *Proceedings of the 9th International Workshop on Semantic Evaluation (SemEval 2015)*, pages 282–287, Denver, Colorado, June. Association for Computational Linguistics.

George Doddington. 2002. Automatic evaluation of machine translation quality using n-gram co-occurrence statistics. In *Proceedings of the Second International Conference on Human Language Technology Research*, HLT '02, pages 138–145, San Francisco, CA, USA. Morgan Kaufmann Publishers Inc.

Richard Eckart de Castilho and Iryna Gurevych. 2014. A broad-coverage collection of portable nlp components for building shareable analysis pipelines. In *Proceedings of the Workshop on Open Infrastructures and Analysis Frameworks for HLT*, pages 1–11, Dublin, Ireland, August. Association for Computational Linguistics and Dublin City University.

Simone Filice, Giuseppe Castellucci, Danilo Croce, and Roberto Basili. 2015. Kelp: a kernel-based learning platform for natural language processing. In *Proceedings of ACL-IJCNLP 2015 System Demonstrations*, pages 19–24, Beijing, China, July. Association for Computational Linguistics and The Asian Federation of Natural Language Processing.

Thorsten Joachims. 1999. Making Large-scale Support Vector Machine Learning Practical. In Bernhard Schölkopf, Christopher J. C. Burges, and Alexander J. Smola, editors, *Advances in Kernel Methods*, pages 169–184. MIT Press, Cambridge, MA, USA.

Shafiq Joty, Alberto Barrón-Cedeño, Giovanni Da San Martino, Simone Filice, Lluís Màrquez, Alessandro Moschitti, and Preslav Nakov. 2015. Global thread-level inference for comment classification in community question answering. In *Proceedings of the 2015 Conference on Empirical Methods in Natural Language Processing*, pages 573–578, Lisbon, Portugal, September. Association for Computational Linguistics.

Shafiq Joty, Llus Mrquez, and Preslav Nakov. 2016. Joint learning with global inference for comment classification in community question answering. In *Proceedings of the 2016 Conference of the North American Chapter of the Association for Computational Linguistics: Human Language Technologies*, pages xx–xx, San Diego, California, June. Association for Computational Linguistics.

Alon Lavie and Michael Denkowski. 2009. The METEOR metric for automatic evaluation of machine translation. *Machine Translation*, 23(2–3):105–115.

Christopher D. Manning, Mihai Surdeanu, John Bauer, Jenny Finkel, Steven J. Bethard, and David McClosky. 2014. The Stanford CoreNLP natural language processing toolkit. In *Association for Computational Linguistics (ACL) System Demonstrations*, pages 55–60.

Tomas Mikolov, Wen-tau Yih, and Geoffrey Zweig. 2013. Linguistic Regularities in Continuous Space Word Representations. In *Proceedings of the 2013 Conference of the North American Chapter of the Association for Computational Linguistics: Human Language Technologies*, NAACL-HLT '13, pages 746–751, Atlanta, GA, USA.

Alessandro Moschitti, Silvia Quarteroni, Roberto Basili, and Suresh Manandhar. 2007. Exploiting syntactic and shallow semantic kernels for question answer classification. In *Proceedings of the 45th Annual Meeting of the Association of Computational Linguistics*, pages 776–783, Prague, Czech Republic, June. Association for Computational Linguistics.

Alessandro Moschitti. 2006. Efficient Convolution Kernels for Dependency and Constituent Syntactic Trees. In Johannes Fürnkranz, Tobias Scheffer, and Myra Spiliopoulou, editors, *Machine Learning: ECML 2006*, volume 4212 of *Lecture Notes in Computer Science*, pages 318–329. Springer Berlin Heidelberg.

Alessandro Moschitti. 2008. Kernel Methods, Syntax and Semantics for Relational Text Categorization. In *Proceeding of ACM 17th Conf. on Information and Knowledge Management (CIKM'08)*, Napa Valley, CA, USA.

Preslav Nakov, Lluís Màrquez, Walid Magdy, Alessandro Moschitti, Jim Glass, and Bilal Randeree. 2015. Semeval-2015 task 3: Answer selection in community question answering. In *Proceedings of the 9th International Workshop on Semantic Evaluation (SemEval 2015)*, pages 269–281, Denver, Colorado, June. Association for Computational Linguistics.

Preslav Nakov, Lluís Màrquez, Alessandro Moschitti, Walid Magdy, Hamdy Mubarak, Abed Alhakim Freihat, Jim Glass, and Bilal Randeree. 2016. SemEval-2016 task 3: Community question answering. In *Proceedings of the 10th International Workshop on Semantic Evaluation*, SemEval '16, San Diego, California, June. Association for Computational Linguistics.

Massimo Nicosia, Simone Filice, Alberto Barrón-Cedeño, Iman Saleh, Hamdy Mubarak, Wei Gao, Preslav Nakov, Giovanni Da San Martino, Alessandro Moschitti, Kareem Darwish, Lluís Màrquez, Shafiq Joty, and Walid Magdy. 2015. QCRI: Answer selection for community question answering - experiments for Arabic and English. In *Proceedings of the 9th International Workshop on Semantic Evaluation*, SemEval '15, Denver, Colorado, USA.

Kishore Papineni, Salim Roukos, Todd Ward, and Wei-Jing Zhu. 2002. BLEU: a method for automatic evaluation of machine translation. In *Proceedings of 40th Annual Meting of the Association for Computational Linguistics*, ACL '02, pages 311–318, Philadelphia, Pennsylvania, USA.

Robert Parker, David Graff, Ke Chen, Junbo Kong, and Kazuaki Maeda. 2011. *Arabic Gigaword Fifth Edition*. Linguistic Data Consortium (LDC), Philadelphia.

Arfath Pasha, Mohamed Al-Badrashiny, Mona Diab, Ahmed El Kholy, Ramy Eskander, Nizar Habash, Manoj Pooleery, Owen Rambow, and Ryan Roth. 2014. Madamira: A fast, comprehensive tool for morphological analysis and disambiguation of arabic. In Nicoletta Calzolari (Conference Chair), Khalid Choukri, Thierry Declerck, Hrafn Loftsson, Bente Maegaard, Joseph Mariani, Asuncion Moreno, Jan Odijk, and Stelios Piperidis, editors, *Proceedings of the Ninth International Conference on Language Resources and Evaluation (LREC'14)*, Reykjavik, Iceland, may. European Language Resources Association (ELRA).

Slav Petrov and Dan Klein. 2007. Improved inference for unlexicalized parsing. In *Human Language Technologies 2007: The Conference of the North American Chapter of the Association for Computational Linguistics; Proceedings of the Main Conference*, pages 404–411, Rochester, New York, April. Association for Computational Linguistics.

Aliaksei Severyn and Alessandro Moschitti. 2012. Structural relationships for large-scale learning of answer re-ranking. In *Proceedings of the 35th International ACM SIGIR Conference on Research and Development in Information Retrieval*, SIGIR '12, pages 741–750, New York, NY, USA. ACM.

Aliaksei Severyn and Alessandro Moschitti. 2013. Automatic feature engineering for answer selection and extraction. In *EMNLP*, pages 458–467. ACL.

Aliaksei Severyn and Alessandro Moschitti. 2015. Learning to rank short text pairs with convolutional deep neural networks. In *Proceedings of the 38th International ACM SIGIR Conference on Research and Development in Information Retrieval*, pages 373–382. ACM.

Aliaksei Severyn, Massimo Nicosia, and Alessandro Moschitti. 2013a. Building structures from classifiers for passage reranking. In *Proceedings of the 22nd ACM international conference on Conference on information & knowledge management*, CIKM '13, pages 969–978, New York, NY, USA. ACM.

Aliaksei Severyn, Massimo Nicosia, and Alessandro Moschitti. 2013b. Learning adaptable patterns for passage reranking. In *Proceedings of the Seventeenth Conference on Computational Natural Language Learning*, CoNLL '13, pages 75–83, Sofia, Bulgaria.

Matthew Snover, Bonnie Dorr, Richard Schwartz, Linnea Micciulla, and John Makhoul. 2006. A study of translation edit rate with targeted human annotation. In *Proceedings of the 7th Biennial Conference of the Association for Machine Translation in the Americas*, AMTA '06, Cambridge, Massachusetts, USA.

Kateryna Tymoshenko and Alessandro Moschitti. 2015. Assessing the impact of syntactic and semantic structures for answer passages reranking. In *Proceedings of the 24th ACM International on Conference on In-*

formation and Knowledge Management, CIKM '15, pages 1451–1460, New York, NY, USA. ACM.

Kateryna Tymoshenko, Alessandro Moschitti, and Aliaksei Severyn. 2014. Encoding semantic resources in syntactic structures for passage reranking. In *14th Conference of the European Chapter of the Association for Computational Linguistics 2014, EACL 2014*, pages 664–672, Gothenburg, Sweden, April. Association for Computational Linguistics (ACL).

Kateryna Tymoshenko, Daniele Bonadiman, and Alessandro Moschitti. 2016. Convolutional neural networks vs. convolution kernels: Feature engineering for answer sentence reranking. In *Proceedings of the 2016 Conference of the North American Chapter of the Association for Computational Linguistics: Human Language Technologies*, NAACL '16, San Diego, CA, USA, June. Association for Computational Linguistics.

ITNLP-AiKF at SemEval-2016 Task 3: a question answering system using community QA repository

Chang'e Jia[1], Xinkai Du[2], Chengjie Sun[1] and Lei Lin[1]
[1]Harbin Institute of Technology, Harbin Heilongjiang 150001, China
[2]Beijing Huilan Technology Co.,Ltd.
{cejia, cjsun, linl}@insun.hit.edu.cn
duxk@huilan.com

Abstract

Community Question Answering (CAQ) systems play an important role in people's lives due to the huge knowledge accumulated in them. In order to take full advantage of the huge knowledge, the target of semeval2016 task3 is to find the best answers to a new question in CQA. This work proposes to use rich semantic text similarity (STS) features to complete the task. We address the task as a ranking problem and Support Vector Regression (SVR) model is chosen to combine rich semantic similarity features and context features. Finally, we used genetic algorithm to do feature selection. Our method achieves an MAP (mean average precision) of 71.52%, 71.43% and 48.49% in subtask A, B and C respectively. It ranked 8th in subtask A and subtask B, and 7th in subtask C.

1 Introduction

The CQA system with interactive and open character, can better adapt to the diversity of needs of users. With the growth of the number of users, community question answering system has accumulated a lot of QA pair archives. It has presented new challenges to analyze user's requirement and recommends high-quality answers to users.

In response to this problem, Semeval2015 Task3 - "Answer Selection in Community Question Answering"[1] (Nakov et al., 2015) proposed a task to divide the answers into three levels in accordance with the relevance of the question. However, the classification system does not fully comply with the question requirement, as it does not implement the recommending function.

Semeval2016 Task3 - "Community Question Answering"[2] (Nakov et al., 2016) puts forward new requirements to automate the process of finding good answers to new questions in a community-created discussion forum based on the Semeval2015 Task3. The task is divided into three parts: subtask A - "Question-Comment Similarity", subtask B - "Question-Question Similarity" and subtask C - "Question-External Comment Similarity".

In our work, we focus on using features that employ STS knowledge, such as extracting text similarity features from word vectors, structured resource and topic models, to deal with the task. Word vectors has been used in (Liu, Sun, Lin, Zhao, & Wang, 2015) and (Nicosia et al., 2015) to compute STS, and (Jin, Sun, Lin, & Wang, 2014) has evaluated word-phrase semantic similarity with structured resource.

2 Feature

The main idea of our method is to find the similarity between most similar words in two sentences to estimate sentence similarity. Our features include the following categories: WordNet-based features, vector features, word matching features, topic features and answer features.

904

Proceedings of SemEval-2016, pages 904–909,
San Diego, California, June 16-17, 2016. ©2016 Association for Computational Linguistics

2.1 Vector Features

There are three approaches that we are applying to measure sentence similarity with word vector.

The first one uses the sum of all the words' vectors in sentence s as the representative of s, and calculate the distance of two sentences' vector.

$$vec(s) = \sum_{w_i \in s} vec(w_i) \qquad (1)$$

$$sim(s_1, s_2) = c\_sim(vec(s_1), vec(s_2)) \qquad (2)$$

Where s is a sentence, $vec(w)$ is the vector of word w, and $c\_sim(v,u)$ is cosine similarity which will be mentioned below.

$$c\_sim(v,u) = \frac{\sum_i^n v_i \times u_i}{\sqrt{\sum_i^n (v_i)^2} \times \sqrt{\sum_i^n (u_i)^2}} \qquad (3)$$

Where v and u are two $N\text{-}dimensional$ vectors. v_i is the $i\text{-}th$ element of v.

The second and the third are similar to each other. The procedure that computing sentence pair similarity includes the following three steps.

First, given two sentences s_1 and s_2, and for each word v in sentence s_1, we find the most similarity word u in sentence s_2, to word v. And we do the same to sentence s_2.

$$sc(v, u \in s_1) = \max_{u \in s_2}(sim(v,u)) \qquad (4)$$

Second, we calculate the similarity of a sentence-sentence pair based on each sentence respectively:

$$sim(s) = \frac{\sum_{w \in s} sc(w)}{l} \qquad (5)$$

$$idfsim(s) = \frac{\sum_{w \in s} sc(w) \times idf(w)}{\sum_{w \in s} idf(w)} \qquad (6)$$

Where l is the number of the words with stopwords removed from sentence s, and $idf(w)$ is the inverse document frequency (Sparck Jones, 1972) of word w in the Wikipedia data.

Third, the value is averaged over the two sentence:

$$sim\_ag(s_1, s_2) = \frac{sim(s_1) + sim(s_2)}{2} \qquad (7)$$

$$idfsim\_ag(s_1, s_2) = \frac{idfsim(s_1) + idfsim(s_2)}{2} \qquad (8)$$

We trained two word2vec[3] models using Gensim toolkit[4] (Řehůřek & Sojka, 2010). The first one is trained on the training data, and the second one on Wikipedia data[5]. Only these latter two ways are used in both models.

In addition, we also make use of existing word vectors mentioned by earlier researchers (Nicosia et al., 2015), Glove[6] (Pennington, Socher, & Manning, 2014) and COMPOSES[7] (Baroni, Dinu, & Kruszewski, 2014), which have been proved to be helpful in many NLP applications.

2.2 WordNet-based Features

WordNet (Fellbaum, 2005) is widely used in semantic similarity computing in the field of natural language processing. WordNet provides six ways to calculate the similarity of words depending on the meanings: path-similarity (Resnik, 1999), Leacock-Chodorow Similarity (Leacock & Chodorow, 1998), Wu-Palmer Similarity (Wu & Palmer, 1994), Resnik Similarity (Resnik, 1995), Jiang-Conrath Similarity (Jiang & Conrath, 1997) and Lin Similarity (Lin, 1998).

In our systems, the six methods are all used to measure word similarity. The WordNet-based features are computed using the same formulas as the last two methods of vector features.

2.3 Word Match Features

Longest Common Subsequence (Allison & Dix, 1986) can retain the words' position information when computing the sentence similarity:

$$sim(s_1, s_2) = \frac{\dfrac{lcs(s_1, s_2)}{l_1} + \dfrac{lcs(s_1, s_2)}{l_2}}{2} \qquad (9)$$

Where $lcs(s_1, s_2)$ is the length of the longest common subsequence, l_1 and l_2 are the numbers of the words in s_1 and s_2.

We also use the bag of word to search the hidden relationship between words and sentences,

---

[3] The size is 400.
[4] http://scikit-learn.org/stable/index.html
[5] https://dumps.wikimedia.org
[6] http://nlp.stanford.edu/projects/glove/
[7] http://clic.cimec.unitn.it/composes/semantic-vectors.html

and the cosine similarity is used to be the measure of vector similarity.

Besides, we use Stanford CoreNLP toolkit (Finkel, Grenager, & Manning, 2005) to get the two sentences' nouns and measure their similarity by bag of word.

2.4 Topic Features

All the features mentioned above are based on lexical similarity. In order to overcome the limitation of the lexical features, we build Latent Dirichlet Allocation (Blei, Ng, & Jordan, 2003) model and Latent Semantic Analysis (Hofmann, 2001) model using the Gensim toolkit (Řehůřek & Sojka, 2010), which are both trained on Wikipedia data.

The topic models[8] can get sentence vector directly, and we calculate the vector distance by cosine similarity.

2.5 Answer Features

Closely analyzing the train data, we noticed that many "Good" comments would like to suggest questioners to visit a web site or ask further questions by email, and many "Good" comments prefer to contain pictures or numbers to explain themselves more clearly. Moreover, "Good" comments' sentence length is much longer than "PotentiallyUserful" comments and "Bad" comments'.

In addition, respondents themselves have a great influence on the quality of the answers. It may lead to a "Bad" comment if the respondent is also the questioner, and if the respondent is not the questioner but asks a question, it may also lead to a "Bad" comment. If a respondent was accustomed to submit high-quality comments, he/she has a high likelihood of offering a "Good" suggestion in the current question. So, we have voted the accuracy and error rates of comments for all users.

The answer features are only applied in subtask A.

3 Method and Result

3.1 Feature generation

Each question has brief description and detailed description. Take the following question as an example:

OrgQSubject: *What is the purpose of heaven?*

OrgQBody: *What is the point? What is in it for the ones that get there? Let's leave the purpose of hell for another thread. I invite you to ponder. You can quote scripture or Sura's etc if you want but you must expand upon them with your own thoughts.*

As we can see, people can get a broad understanding on the question by reading the brief description, and experiments show that the features of brief description lead to a better result.

Features	F1 score
Sub	0.4898
Body	0.4476
Sub+Body	0.5316

Table 1: Experiments for subtask B. A classification model is trained on training dataset and tested on development dataset.

We assume that if the features come off well on a classification model, they would do a good job on ranking model.

So, we extracted eigenvalue from both brief description and detailed description for subtask B. The subtask A is trained models with all the characteristics mentioned above. We multiply the subtask A's results by the subtask B's as subtask C's. And eventually we got 38 features for subtask A and 56 features for subtask B. Table 2 lists all the features.

3.2 Feature Selection

Considering that there may be a feature subset performing better than other subset of all features, we designed a genetic algorithm (Renna, 2000) to find the best one. The genetic algorithm (GA) can be described as follows:

Encoding: Assuming that there are n features, n-bit binary will be needed to encode a chromosome then. The process of feature selection is as the Figure 1 shows.

---

[8] The size of both models are 100.

	Category	Feature
Subtask A and Subtask B	Vector features	W2V_wiki, W2V_wiki_idf, W2V_qatar, W2V_qatar_idf, Glove_sp, Glove_w2w, Glove_w2w_idf, COMPOSES_sp, COMPOSES_w2w, COMPOSES_w2w_idf
	WordNet-based features	PATH_sim, LCH_sim, WUP_sim, RES_sim, JCN_sim, LIN_sim, PATH_sim_idf, LCH_sim_idf, WUP_sim_idf, RES_sim_idf, JCN_sim_idf, LIN_sim_idf
	Topic features	LDA_sim, LSA_sim
	Word match features	LCS_sim, BagOfW_sim, NOUN_sim, NOUN_sim_idf
Subtask A	Answer features	IS_QUsr, IS_Thank, IS_Ask, IS_Other_Ask, IS_Email, IS_URL, U_BestRate, U_GoodRate, U_BadRate, Sen_Lenght, IS_NUM, IS_IMG,

Table 2: The features we extracted

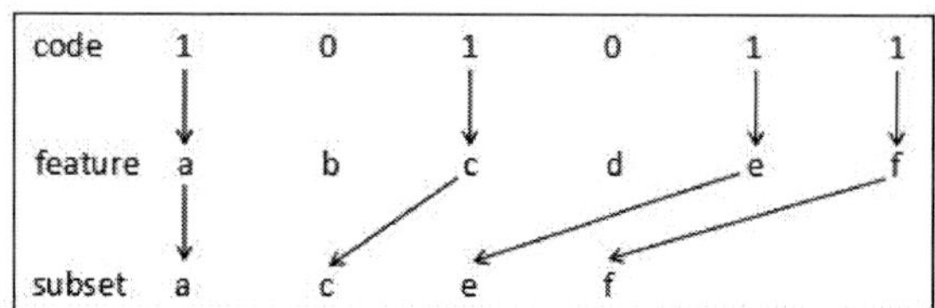

Figure 1: Feature subset selection. If the *i-th* feature is added into the subset, the value of the *i-th* binary is 1, and if not is 0.

Individual creation: Relying on the hypothesis that a feature can make a feature subset work better if it is added to the current feature subset, we increase the probability[9] that each feature is selected.

Fitness: We employ SVR as the evaluation function of feature selection.

Selection: The reproduction operator just selects the top individuals of fitness as a part of the next generation, instead of adopting a probability selection algorithm to select superior individuals.

Crossover: Here we use the single-point crossover.

Mutation: Get a probability, and if the value is less than the preset threshold, an individual will be selected and a binary will be changed randomly. In order to retain the best feature subset, all operations mentioned above are among the superiors, and the aberration rate is set to a larger value[10] to escape the local minimum.

Figure 2 is the flowchart of GA. Where n is quorum, m is selection scale, and *thresh* is fitness-threshold.

GA can lead to different results for each run, so we run the selection function several times and choose the best one. Table 3 and Table 4 show the results of subtask A and subtask B in 20 runs of GA respectively. All experiments below train models on training dataset, and test them on development dataset.

Operation	Statistics	Result
Undo selection	—	0.5263
Do selection	max	0.6182
	min	0.6121
	average	0.6163
	Standard deviation	0.0014

Table 3: 20 runs' results of GA for subtask A.

Operation	Statistics	Result
Undo selection	—	0.5889
Do selection	max	0.7801
	min	0.7320
	average	0.7627
	Standard deviation	0.0137

Table 4: 20 runs' results of GA for subtask B.

---

[9] The value is 0.75.

[10] The value we set is 0.3.

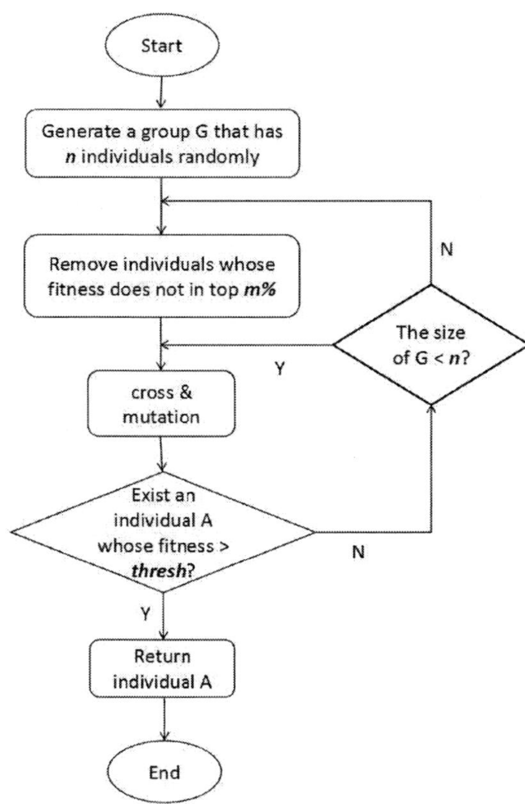

Figure 2: genetic algorithm

3.3 Training Model

We trained a Maximum Entropy Modeling using the maxent toolkit (Le, 2004) and a SVR model (Smola & Schölkopf, 2004) using scikit-learn toolkit (Pedregosa et al., 2011).

Table 5 and Table 6 show the results of different models.

Runs	MAP
random baselines	0.4556
IR baselines	0.5384
Maxent	0.5826
SVR	**0.6179**

Table 5: Experiments for Subtask A

Runs	MAP
random baselines	0.5595
IR baselines	0.7135
Maxent	0.7135
SVR	**0.7801**

Table 6: Experiments for Subtask B

3.4 Result

We just submit one time, and our system perform better in subtask A and subtask C than subtask B.

	IR	SYS
MAP	0.5953	**0.7152**
AvgRec	0.7260	0.8267
MRR	67.83	80.26

Table 7: System performance for subtask A.

	IR	SYS
MAP	0.7475	**0.7143**
AvgRec	0.8830	0.8731
MRR	83.79	81.28

Table 8: System performance for subtask B.

	IR	SYS
MAP	0.4036	**0.4849**
AvgRec	0.4597	0.5516
MRR	45.83	55.21

Table 9: System performance for subtask C

4 Conclusion and Future Work

We have tested the system by taking part in Semeval2016 Task 3 on English sub tasks, and our system works better on subtask A and subtask C than the IR system provided by organizers.

Aware our method's shortcomings that the features center on lexical similarity, we will pay attention to process long sentence similarity in further work.

Acknowledgments

We thank reviewers for their helpful comments on an earlier version of this work. This work is supported by National Natural Science Foundation of China (61572151 and 61300114).

References

Allison, L., & Dix, T. I. (1986). A bit-string longest-common-subsequence algorithm. *Information Processing Letters, 23*(5), 305-310.

Baroni, M., Dinu, G., & Kruszewski, G. (2014). *Don't count, predict! A systematic comparison of context-counting vs. context-predicting semantic vectors.* Paper presented at the ACL (1).

Blei, D. M., Ng, A. Y., & Jordan, M. I. (2003). Latent dirichlet allocation. *the Journal of machine Learning research, 3*, 993-1022.

Fellbaum, C. (2005). WordNet and wordnets.

Finkel, J. R., Grenager, T., & Manning, C. (2005). *Incorporating non-local information into information extraction systems by gibbs sampling.* Paper presented at the Proceedings of the 43rd Annual Meeting on Association for Computational Linguistics.

Hofmann, T. (2001). Unsupervised learning by probabilistic latent semantic analysis. *Machine learning, 42*(1-2), 177-196.

Jiang, J. J., & Conrath, D. W. (1997). Semantic similarity based on corpus statistics and lexical taxonomy. *arXiv preprint cmp-lg/9709008.*

Jin, X., Sun, C., Lin, L., & Wang, X. (2014). Exploiting Multiple Resources for Word-Phrase Semantic Similarity Evaluation *Chinese Computational Linguistics and Natural Language Processing Based on Naturally Annotated Big Data* (pp. 46-57): Springer.

Le, Z. (2004). Maximum entropy modeling toolkit for Python and C++. *Natural Language Processing Lab, Northeastern University, China.*

Leacock, C., & Chodorow, M. (1998). Combining local context and WordNet similarity for word sense identification. *WordNet: An electronic lexical database, 49*(2), 265-283.

Lin, D. (1998). *An information-theoretic definition of similarity.* Paper presented at the ICML.

Liu, Y., Sun, C., Lin, L., Zhao, Y., & Wang, X. (2015). Computing Semantic Text Similarity Using Rich Features.

Nakov, P., Marquez, L., Magdy, W., Moschitti, A., Glass, J., & Randeree, B. (2015). *SemEval-2015 Task 3: Answer Selection in Community Question Answering.*

Nakov, P., Marquez, L., Magdy, W., Moschitti, A., Mubarak, H., Freihat, A. A., Glass, J., & Randeree, B. (2016). *SemEval-2016 Task 3: Community question answering.*

Nicosia, M., Filice, S., Barrón-Cedeno, A., Saleh, I., Mubarak, H., Gao, W., . . . Darwish, K. (2015). *QCRI: Answer selection for community question answeringexperiments for Arabic and English.* Paper presented at the Proceedings of the 9th International Workshop on Semantic Evaluation, SemEval.

Pedregosa, F., Varoquaux, G., Gramfort, A., Michel, V., Thirion, B., Grisel, O., . . . Dubourg, V. (2011). Scikit-learn: Machine learning in Python. *the Journal of machine Learning research, 12*, 2825-2830.

Pennington, J., Socher, R., & Manning, C. D. (2014). *Glove: Global Vectors for Word Representation.* Paper presented at the EMNLP.

Řehůřek, R., & Sojka, P. (2010). Software framework for topic modelling with large corpora.

Renna, J. (2000). *Genetic algorithm viewer: Demonstration of a genetic algorithm.* Ph. D. May.

Resnik, P. (1995). Using information content to evaluate semantic similarity in a taxonomy. *arXiv preprint cmp-lg/9511007.*

Resnik, P. (1999). Semantic similarity in a taxonomy: An information-based measure and its application to problems of ambiguity in natural language. *J. Artif. Intell. Res.(JAIR), 11*, 95-130.

Smola, A. J., & Schölkopf, B. (2004). A tutorial on support vector regression. *Statistics and computing, 14*(3), 199-222.

Sparck Jones, K. (1972). A statistical interpretation of term specificity and its application in retrieval. *Journal of documentation, 28*(1), 11-21.

Wu, Z., & Palmer, M. (1994). *Verbs semantics and lexical selection.* Paper presented at the Proceedings of the 32nd annual meeting on Association for Computational Linguistics.

UFRGS&LIF at SemEval-2016 Task 10: Rule-Based MWE Identification and Predominant-Supersense Tagging

Silvio Ricardo Cordeiro[1,2] and **Carlos Ramisch**[2] and **Aline Villavicencio**[1]

[1] Universidade Federal do Rio Grande do Sul, Porto Alegre, Brazil

[2]Aix Marseille Université, CNRS, LIF UMR 7279

{srcordeiro,avillavicencio}@inf.ufrgs.br

carlos.ramisch@lif.univ-mrs.fr

Abstract

This paper presents our approach towards the SemEval-2016 Task 10 – Detecting Minimal Semantic Units and their Meanings. Systems are expected to provide a representation of lexical semantics by (1) segmenting tokens into words and multiword units and (2) providing a supersense tag for segments that function as nouns or verbs. Our pipeline rule-based system uses no external resources and was implemented using the mwetoolkit. First, we extract and filter known MWEs from the training corpus. Second, we group input tokens of the test corpus based on this lexicon, with special treatment for non-contiguous expressions. Third, we use an MWE-aware predominant-sense heuristic for supersense tagging. We obtain an F-score of 51.48% for MWE identification and 49.98% for supersense tagging.

1 Introduction

Accurate segmentation and semantic disambiguation of minimal text units is a major challenge in the general pipeline of NLP applications. A machine translation system, for example, needs to decide what is the intended meaning for a given word or phrase in its context, so that it may translate it into an equivalent meaning in the target language.

While determining the meaning of single words is a difficult task on its own, the problem is compounded by the pervasiveness of Multiword Expressions (MWEs). MWEs are semantic units that span over multiple lexemes in the text (e.g. dry run, look up, fall flat). Their meaning cannot be inferred by applying regular composition rules on the meanings

of their component words. The task of semantic tagging is thus deeply intertwined with the identification of multiword expressions.

This paper presents our solution to the DiMSUM shared task (Schneider et al., 2016), where the evaluated systems are expected to perform both semantic tagging and multiword identification. Our pipeline system first detects and groups MWEs and then assigns supersense tags, as two consecutive steps. For MWE identification, we use a task-specific instantiation of the mwetoolkit (Ramisch, 2015), handling both contiguous and non-contiguous MWEs with some degree of customization (Cordeiro et al., 2015). Additionally, MWE type-level candidates are extracted without losing track of their token-level occurrences, to guarantee that all the MWE occurrences learned from the training data are projected onto the test corpus. For semantic tagging we adopted a predominant-sense heuristic.

In the remainder of this paper, we present related work (§ 2), then we present and discuss the results of the MWE identification subsystem (§ 3) and of the supersense tagging subsystem (§ 4). We then conclude and share ideas for future improvements (§ 5).

2 Related Work

Practical solutions for rule-based MWE identification include tools like jMWE (Kulkarni and Finlayson, 2011), a library for direct lexicon projection based on preexisting MWE lists. Finite-state transducers can also be used to take into account the internal morphology of component words and perform efficient tokenization based on MWE dictionaries (Savary, 2009). The problem of MWE identification

Proceedings of SemEval-2016, pages 910–917,
San Diego, California, June 16-17, 2016. ©2016 Association for Computational Linguistics

has also been modeled using supervised machine learning. Probabilistic MWE taggers usually encode the data using a begin-inside-outside scheme and learn CRF-like taggers on it (Constant and Sigogne, 2011; Schneider et al., 2014). The `mwetoolkit` (Ramisch, 2015) provides command-line programs that allow one to discover new MWE candidate lists, filter them and project them back on text according to some parameters. Our system uses the latter as basis for MWE identification.

Word sense disambiguation (WSD) methods can be roughly classified into knowledge-based, supervised and unsupervised. Knowledge-based methods use lexico-semantic taxonomies like WordNet to calculate the similarity between context and target words (Lesk, 1986). Supervised approaches generally use context-sensitive classifiers (Cabezas et al., 2001). Unsupervised approaches using clustering and distributional similarity (Brody and Lapata, 2008; Goyal and Hovy, 2014) can also be employed for WSD. Both supervised and unsupervised WSD techniques have also been used to distinguish literal from idiomatic uses of MWEs (Fazly et al., 2009; Diab and Bhutada, 2009). Nonetheless, systematically choosing the most frequent sense is a surprisingly good baseline, not always easy to beat (McCarthy et al., 2007; Navigli, 2009). This was also verified for MWE disambiguation (Uchiyama et al., 2005). Thus, in this work, we implemented a simple supervised predominant-sense heuristic and will investigate more sophisticated WSD techniques as future work.

3 MWE Identification

Our MWE identification algorithm uses 6 different rule configurations, targeting different MWE classes. Three of these are based on data from the training corpus, while the other three are unsupervised. The parameters of each configuration are optimized on a held-out development set, consisting of ⅑ of the training corpus. The final system is the union of all configurations.[1]

For the 3 supervised configurations, annotated MWEs are extracted from the training data and then filtered: we only keep combinations that have been annotated often enough in the training corpus. In other words, we keep MWE candidates whose proportion of annotated instances with respect to all occurrences in the training corpus is above a threshold t, discarding the rest. The thresholds were manually chosen based on what seemed to yield better results on the development set. Finally, we project the resulting list of MWE candidates on the test data, that is, we segment as MWEs the test token sequences that are contained in the lexicon extracted from the training data. These configurations are:

CONTIG Contiguous MWEs annotated in the training corpus are extracted and filtered with a threshold of $t = 40\%$. That is, we create a lexicon containing all contiguous lemma+POS sequences for which at least 40% of the occurrences in the training corpus were annotated. The resulting lexicon is projected on the test corpus whenever that contiguous sequence of words is seen.

GAPPY Non-contiguous MWEs are extracted from the training corpus and filtered with a threshold of $t = 70\%$. The resulting MWEs are projected on the test corpus using the following rule: an MWE is deemed to occur if its component words appear sequentially with at most a total of 3 gap words in between them.

NOUN^2-KN Collect all noun-noun sequences in the test corpus that also appear at least once in the training corpus (known compounds), and filter them with a threshold of $t = 70\%$. The resulting list is projected onto the test corpus.

We further developed 3 additional configurations based on empirical findings. We identify MWEs in the test corpus based on POS-tag patterns, without any filtering (and thus without looking at the training corpus)[2]:

NOUN^2-UKN Collect all noun-noun sequences in the test corpus that never appear in the training corpus (unknown compounds), and project all of them back on the test corpus.

PROPN$^{2..\infty}$ Collect sequences of two or more contiguous words with POS-tag PROPN and project all of them back onto the test corpus.

---

[1] When there is an overlap, we favor longer MWEs.

[2] For NOUN^2-UKN, we exclude known compounds, as otherwise that would undo the filtering work done by NOUN^2-KN.

VP Collect verb-particle candidates and project them back onto the test corpus. A verb-particle candidate is a pair of words under these constraints: the first word must have POS-tag VERB and cannot have lemma *go* or *be*. The two words may be separated by a N[3] or PROPN. The second word must be in a list of frequent non-literal particles[4]. Finally, the particle must be followed by a word with one of these POS-tags: ADV, ADP, PART, CONJ, PUNCT. Even though we might miss some cases, this final delimiter avoids capturing regular verb-PP sequences.

Table 1 presents the results for each isolated configuration (evaluated on the test corpus, with all MWEs). These results are calculated based on the fuzzy metrics of the shared task (Schneider et al., 2014), where partial MWE matches are taken into account. Our final MWE identification system is the union of all rule configurations described above. The final recall of the system is not the sum of coverage values because MWE candidate lexicons may overlap (multiple configurations may have identified the same MWE).

Configuration	Precision	Coverage
CONTIG	57.9%	11.6%
GAPPY	36.0%	0.9%
NOUN^2-KN	100.0%	1.6%
NOUN^2-UKN	80.2%	18.9%
PROPN$^{2..\infty}$	96.0%	8.5%
VP	71.2%	4.2%

Table 1: Precision and coverage per MWE annotation. Coverage is the recall of each configuration applied independently.

3.1 Error Analysis

Table 2 presents the system results for the most common POS-tag sequences in the test corpus, using an exact match (a MWE is either correct or incorrect). Overall results are presented in both exact and fuzzy metrics.

N_N errors Since our system looks for all occurrences of adjacent noun-noun pairs, we obtain a high

---

[3] In the remainder of the paper, we abbreviate the POS tag NOUN as N.

[4] The 13 most frequent non-literal particles: *about, around, away, back, down, in, into, off, on, out, over, through, up* (Sinclair, 2012).

POS-tags	Precision		Recall		F_1
N_N	$^{170}/_{278} =$	61%	$^{170}/_{181} = 94\%$		74.0%
VERB_ADP	$^{43}/_{60} =$	72%	$^{43}/_{73} = 59\%$		64.9%
ADJ_N	$^{5}/_{6} =$	83%	$^{5}/_{69} =$ 7%		12.9%
PROPN_PROPN	$^{65}/_{82} =$	79%	$^{65}/_{66} = 98\%$		87.5%
VERB_PART	$^{31}/_{37} =$	84%	$^{31}/_{49} = 63\%$		72.0%
PROPN_N	$^{1}/_{1} = 100\%$		$^{1}/_{34} =$ 3%		5.8%
N_N_N	$^{0}/_{0} = 100\%$		$^{0}/_{22} =$ 0%		0.0%
ADP_N	$^{10}/_{14} =$	71%	$^{10}/_{22} = 45\%$		55.1%
VERB_N	$^{1}/_{5} =$	20%	$^{1}/_{16} =$ 6%		9.2%
DET_N	$^{4}/_{23} =$	17%	$^{4}/_{16} = 25\%$		20.2%
ADJ_N_N	$^{0}/_{0} = 100\%$		$^{0}/_{11} =$ 0%		0.0%
Overall (exact)	$^{364}/_{613} =$	59%	$^{364}/_{837} = 43\%$		50.2%
Overall (fuzzy)	$^{460}/_{635} =$	72%	$^{461}/_{1115} = 41\%$		52.6%

Table 2: MWE identification results on test set per POS-tag.

recall for N_N compounds. The most common false positive errors are presented below.

- **Not in the same phrase** In 19 cases, our system has identified two Ns that are not in the same phrase; e.g. *when I have a <u>problem customer services</u> don't want to know.* In order to realize that these nouns are not related, we would need parsing information. Nonetheless, it is not clear whether an off-the-shelf parser could solve these ambiguities in the absence of punctuation.

- **Partial N_N_N** 17 cases have been missed due to only the first two nouns in the MWE being identified; e.g. *Try the <u>memory foam</u> pillows!* – instead of *<u>memory foam pillows</u>*.

- **Partial ADJ_N_N** 10 cases have been missed; e.g. *My sweet <u>pea plants</u> arrived 00th May completely dried up and dead!* – instead of *<u>sweet pea plants</u>*. These cases are a consequence of the fact that we do not look for adjective-noun pairs (see ADJ_N errors below).

- **Compositional N_N** In 24 cases, our system identified a compositional compound; e.g. *<u>Quality gear</u> guys, excellent!* Semantic features would be required to filter such cases out.

- **Questionable N tags** 10 false noun compounds were found due to words such as *today* being tagged as nouns (e.g. *I'm saving <u>gas today</u>*). Another 5 cases had adjectives classified as nouns: *Maybe this is a kind of an <u>artificial way</u> to read an e-book.*

VERB_ADP errors Most of the VERB_ADP expressions were caught by the VP configuration, but we still had some false negatives. In 7 cases, the underlying particle was not in our list (e.g. *I regret ever going near their store*), while in 9 other cases, the particle was followed by a noun phrase (e.g. *Givin out Back shots*). 5 of the missed MWEs could have been found by accepting the particle to be followed by a SCONJ, or to be followed by the end of the line as delimiters. Most of the false positives were due to the verb being followed by an indirect object or prepositional phrase. We believe that disambiguating these cases would require valency information, either from a lexicon or automatically acquired from large corpora (Preiss et al., 2007).

ADJ_N errors While the few ADJ_N pairs that our system identified were usually correct MWEs, most of the annotated cases were missed. This is because we do not specifically look for adjective-noun pairs, due to the high likelihood of them being compositional. For example, a simple ADJ_N annotation scheme (as performed in NOUN^2-UKN) would have achieved a precision of only $69/505 = 14\%$.

Out of all annotated sentences, in 23 cases the noun is transparent, and we could replace the adjective by a synonym; e.g. *I guess people are going again next week, do you think you'll go?* (which could be replaced by *the following week*). In another 17 cases, the noun is transparent and the adjective suggestive of the global meaning, even though it is fixed; e.g. *23 is the lucky number* (but not **fortunate number*, albeit related to *luck*).

These cases could be dealt with using fixedness tests such as substitution and permutation (Fazly et al., 2009; Ramisch et al., 2008).

PROPN_PROPN errors Since our system looks for all occurrences of adjacent PROPN pairs, we obtain near-perfect recall for PROPN_PROPN compounds. Most false positives were caused by possessives or personal titles, which were annotated as part of the MWE in the gold standard.

VERB_PART errors The results for VERB_PART are similar to the ones found for VERB_ADP: 3 false negatives are due to the particle not being in our list, and in another 7 cases they are followed by a noun phrase. Additionally, in 6 cases the particle was followed by a verb (e.g. *Stupid Kilkenny didn't get to meet @Royseven*). 4 false positives were CONTIG cases of *go to* being identified as a MWE (e.g. **In my mother's day, she didn't go to college*). In the training corpus, this MWE had been annotated 57% of the time, but in future constructions (e.g. *Definitely not going to purchase a car from here*). Canonical forms would be easy to model with a specific contextual rule of the form *going to* verb.

PROPN_N errors While the few PROPN_N pairs we found were all correct MWEs, most of the annotated cases were missed. These cases did not earn special attention during the development of the system due to an incorrectly perceived infrequency. However, using only an annotation scheme such as NOUN^2-UKN, we could have achieved a precision of 72% for these MWEs.

N_N_N errors The occurrence of N_N_N sequences is rare in the training corpus, and we did not specifically look for them, which explains our recall of 0%. By annotating the longest sequence of Ns in the corpus ($\text{NOUN}^{2..\infty}$), we could have obtained a precision of 56% and recall of 91% for N_N_N. The precision of N_N would also increase to 70% (with a recall of 93%). If we then replace NOUN^2 by $\text{NOUN}^{2..\infty}$, the full-system's F-score increases to 56.23%.

ADP_N errors The false positives were ambiguous determinerless PPs that can be compositional or not according to the context. For instance, the system identified **Try them all, in order* after seeing *The Big Lebowski is in order tonight*. False negatives were mainly due to threshold-based filters, like *at all* and *in peace*. Unsupervised MWE discovery on large corpora using context-sensitive association measures could have helped in these cases.

VERB_N errors We only generated 4 false positives, which look like light-verb constructions missed by the annotators (*give ride, place order*) False negatives include 8 cases of gerunds POS-tagged as verbs (e.g. *to listen to flying saucers*), which are actualy similar to ADJ_N cases discussed above. We also found 7 false negatives, mainly light-verb constructions, that were not present in the training corpus (*take place, take control*).

DET_N errors 8 false negatives were compositional time adjuncts (e.g. *this morning, this season*). False positives are mainly cases that seem inconsistent between training and test data concerning frequent quantifiers (e.g. *a lot, a bit, a couple*).

Noun compounds (two or more Ns in a row) account for a significant proportion of MWEs in the training corpus ($^{601}/_{4232} = 14\%$) and an even larger amount of the testing corpus ($^{203}/_{837} = 24\%$). The NOUN^2 rule sets were essential to obtaining good results. If we remove NOUN^2 from our system, its global performance would drop to a fuzzy $F_1 = 33.79\%$.

The domain of the corpus does not seem to have a great influence on our method's performance. Our lowest performance is on the Reviews subcorpus (fuzzy $F_1 = 49.57\%$) and our best performance is on TED (fuzzy $F_1 = 56.76\%$).

Some of the missed MWEs are questionable and we feel that our system should not annotate them. These include regular verbal chains (*shouldn't have, have been*), infinitival and selected preposition *to* (*to take, go to*) and compositional noun phrases (*this Saturday*). Fortunately, these cases correspond to a small proportion of the data.

4 Supersense Tagging

Supersense tagging takes place after MWE identification. Sense tags are coarse top-level Wordnet synsets. The tagset for nouns and verbs has respectively 26 and 15 supersense tags. We use a predominant-sense heuristic to perform WSD.

Before tagging the test data, our system collects all annotated supersense tags from MWEs in the training corpus. We create a mapping with entries of the form $(w_1, w_2, \ldots, w_N) \mapsto S$, where each MWE component $w_i = (\mathrm{lemma}_i, \mathrm{POStag}_i)$. This mapping indicates the most frequent tag S associated a given MWE. Single words are treated as length-1 MWEs and are also added to this mapping.

The supersense tagging algorithm then goes through all segmented units (MWEs or single words) in the test corpus and annotates them according to the most common tag seen in the training set. If a tag has not been seen for a given word or MWE, we do not tag it at all. This heuristic is very simple and not very realistic. Nonetheless, it allowed us to

have a minimal supersense tagger quickly and then focus on accurate MWE identification as the main contribution of our system.

4.1 Error Analysis

Tables 3 and 4 show the confusion matrices of our system for the 10 most common tags. Each row corresponds to a gold tag and contains the distribution of predicted tags. The perfect system would have numbers only in the main diagonal and zeros everywhere else. The skewed distribution of supersense tags makes our simple heuristic quite effective when the MWE/word has been observed in the training data.

Known nouns seem easy to tag. Most of our errors come from the fact that we did not observe instances of a noun in the training data, and thus did not assign it any tag (column "skipped"). Some distinctions seem harder than others due to similar semantic classes: attributive/cognition and event/time.

The occurrence of verbs in the training data is less of a problem than their polysemy. Stative verbs correspond to the large majority of verbs in the dataset. This is magnified by the nature of the corpus: reviews tend to use stative verbs to talk about product characteristics, tweets often use them to describe the state of the author. While very frequent, stative verbs are also difficult to disambiguate: most false negatives were tagged as change verbs while most false positives were tagged as social verbs. Some distinctions seem extremely hard to make, specially for less frequent supersense tags like contact/motion and perception/cognition.

5 Conclusions and Future Work

We developed a simple rule-based system that was able to obtain competitive results. Its main advantage is that it was very quick to implement in the context of the generic framework of the `mwetoolkit`. The system is freely available as part of the official `mwetoolkit` release.[5] The main limitation of our system is that it cannot properly take unseen MWEs into account and generalize from seen instances. Moreover, most of our rule sets are highly language dependent.

Ideas for future improvements include:

---

[5] `http://mwetoolkit.sourceforge.net`

Gold tag	PERS	ARTI	COMM	ACT	GROU	TIME	COGN	ATTR	LOCA	EVEN	skipped	total
n.person	157	1			8			3			238	413
n.artifact	2	103	6	3	6		5	3	8		187	337
n.communic	2	4	128	4	2	1	6	2	2	1	119	284
n.act	1	9	5	111	4	1	9			14	83	256
n.group	6	4	2	1	54				2	1	130	205
n.time				1		114	2			6	56	180
n.cognition	1	4	3	3			48	1		5	51	130
n.attribute	3		1	3	1		30	10			53	130
n.location		5		2	9	7	2		23	1	45	99
n.event	1					16	1			28	31	84
not-a-noun	123	18	23	12	44	39	25	138	8	87		587

Table 3: Confusion matrix for noun supersense tagging. Skipped segments are those absent in training data.

Gold tag	STAT	COMM	COGN	CHAN	EMOT	MOTI	PERC	POSS	SOCI	CONT	skipped	total
v.stative	617	5	21	3	3	14		4	47	1	53	769
v.communic	8	201	3	2		7	1	4	14	4	36	280
v.cognition	14	14	158	1	1	2	11		22	1	25	250
v.change	49	5	2	67		12		6	22	6	39	210
v.emotion	2	7	44	1	72				3	1	12	143
v.motion	5		2	9		77			8		20	122
v.perception		1	16	1	2	1	69		8	1	10	109
v.possession	17	5	1	1		1		43	5		5	79
v.social	16	2	3	2		5			29		18	75
v.contact	10	4	1	2	2	14		4	3	10	15	70
not-a-verb	355	9	9	12	7	7			4			405

Table 4: Confusion matrix for verb supersense tagging. Skipped segments are those absent in training data.

- Adding specific rules for verb-particle constructions, probably based on a lexicon of idiomatic combinations.

- Replacing the CONTIG method by a sequence tagger for contiguous MWEs (e.g. using a CRF), in order to identify unknown MWEs based on generalizations made from known MWEs (Constant and Sigogne, 2011; Schneider et al., 2014).

- Taking parse trees into account to distinguish MWEs from accidental cooccurrences (Nasr et al., 2015).

- Using semantic-based association measures and semantic-based features based on word embeddings to target idiomatic MWEs (Salehi et al., 2015).

- Using fixedness features to identify and disambiguate very productive patterns like ADJ_N (Ramisch et al., 2008; Fazly et al., 2009).

- Developing a more realistic WSD algorithm for supersense tagging, able to tag unseen words and MWEs and to take context into account.

Acknowledgments

This work has been funded by the French Agence Nationale pour la Recherche through projects PARSEME-FR (ANR-14-CERA-0001) and ORFEO (ANR-12-CORP-0005), and by French-Brazilian cooperation projects CAMELEON (CAPES-COFECUB #707/11) and AIM-WEST (FAPERGS-INRIA 1706-2551/13-7). Part of the results presented in this paper were obtained through research on a project titled "Simplificação Textual de Expressões Complexas", sponsored by Samsung Eletrônica da Amazônia Ltda. under the terms of Brazilian federal law No. 8.248/91.

References

Samuel Brody and Mirella Lapata. 2008. Good neighbors make good senses: Exploiting distributional similarity for unsupervised WSD. In *Proceedings of the 22nd International Conference on Computational Linguistics (Coling 2008)*, pages 65–72, Manchester, UK, August. Coling 2008 Organizing Committee.

Clara Cabezas, Philip Resnik, and Jessica Stevens. 2001. Supervised sense tagging using support vector machines. In *Proceedings of SENSEVAL-2 Second International Workshop on Evaluating Word Sense Disambiguation Systems*, pages 59–62, Toulouse, France, July. Association for Computational Linguistics.

Matthieu Constant and Anthony Sigogne. 2011. MWU-aware part-of-speech tagging with a CRF model and lexical resources. In *Proceedings of the Workshop on Multiword Expressions: from Parsing and Generation to the Real World*, pages 49–56, Portland, Oregon, USA, June. Association for Computational Linguistics.

Silvio Ricardo Cordeiro, Carlos Ramisch, and Aline Villavicencio. 2015. Token-based MWE identification strategies in the mwetoolkit. In *PARSEME's 4th general meeting*.

Mona Diab and Pravin Bhutada. 2009. Verb noun construction MWE token classification. In *Proceedings of the Workshop on Multiword Expressions: Identification, Interpretation, Disambiguation and Applications*, pages 17–22, Singapore, August. Association for Computational Linguistics.

Afsaneh Fazly, Paul Cook, and Suzanne Stevenson. 2009. Unsupervised type and token identification of idiomatic expressions. *Computational Linguistics*, 35(1):61–103.

Kartik Goyal and Eduard Hovy. 2014. Unsupervised word sense induction using distributional statistics. In *Proceedings of COLING 2014, the 25th International Conference on Computational Linguistics: Technical Papers*, pages 1302–1310, Dublin, Ireland, August. Dublin City University and Association for Computational Linguistics.

Nidhi Kulkarni and Mark Alan Finlayson. 2011. jMWE: A java toolkit for detecting multi-word expressions. In *Proceedings of the Workshop on Multiword Expressions: from Parsing and Generation to the Real World*, pages 122–124. Association for Computational Linguistics.

Michael Lesk. 1986. Automatic sense disambiguation using machine readable dictionaries: How to tell a pine cone from an ice cream cone. In *Proceedings of the Fifth International Conference on Systems Documentation (SIGDOC 86)*, pages 24–26, Toronto, Canada.

Diana McCarthy, Rob Koeling, Julie Weeds, and John Carroll. 2007. Unsupervised acquisition of predominant word senses. *Computational Linguistics*, (4):553–590, dec.

Alexis Nasr, Carlos Ramisch, José Deulofeu, and André Valli. 2015. Joint dependency parsing and multiword expression tokenization. In *Proceedings of the 53rd Annual Meeting of the Association for Computational Linguistics and the 7th International Joint Conference on Natural Language Processing (Volume 1: Long Papers)*, pages 1116–1126, Beijing, China, July. Association for Computational Linguistics.

Roberto Navigli. 2009. Word sense disambiguation: A survey. *ACM Comput. Surv.*, 41(2):10:1–10:69.

Judita Preiss, Ted Briscoe, and Anna Korhonen. 2007. A system for large-scale acquisition of verbal, nominal and adjectival subcategorization frames from corpora. In *Proceedings of the 45th Annual Meeting of the Association of Computational Linguistics*, pages 912–919, Prague, Czech Republic, June. Association for Computational Linguistics.

Carlos Ramisch, Paulo Schreiner, Marco Idiart, and Aline Villavicencio. 2008. An Evaluation of Methods for the Extraction of Multiword Expressions. In *Proceedings of the LREC Workshop Towards a Shared Task for Multiword Expressions (MWE 2008)*, pages 50–53, Marrakech, Morocco, June.

Carlos Ramisch. 2015. *Multiword Expressions Acquisition: A Generic and Open Framework*, volume XIV of *Theory and Applications of Natural Language Processing*. Springer. 230 p.

Bahar Salehi, Paul Cook, and Timothy Baldwin. 2015. A word embedding approach to predicting the compositionality of multiword expressions. In *Proceedings of the 2015 Conference of the North American Chapter of the Association for Computational Linguistics: Human Language Technologies*, pages 977–983, Denver, Colorado, May–June. Association for Computational Linguistics.

Agata Savary. 2009. Multiflex: A Multilingual Finite-State Tool for Multi-Word Units. In Sebastian Maneth, editor, *CIAA*, volume 5642 of *Lecture Notes in Computer Science*, pages 237–240. Springer.

Nathan Schneider, Emily Danchik, Chris Dyer, and Noah A. Smith. 2014. Discriminative lexical semantic segmentation with gaps: running the MWE gamut. *Transactions of the Association for Computational Linguistics*, 2:193–206, April.

Nathan Schneider, Dirk Hovy, Anders Johannsen, and Marine Carpuat. 2016. SemEval 2016 Task 10: Detecting Minimal Semantic Units and their Meanings (DiMSUM). In *Proc. of SemEval*, San Diego, California, USA, June.

John Sinclair, editor. 2012. *Collins COBUILD phrasal verbs dictionary*. Harper Collins, Glasgow, UK, third edition. 528 p.

Kiyoko Uchiyama, Timothy Baldwin, and Shun Ishizaki. 2005. Disambiguating japanese compound verbs. *Computer Speech and Language*, 19(4):497 – 512.

WHUNlp at SemEval-2016 Task DiMSUM: A Pilot Study in Detecting Minimal Semantic Units and their Meanings using Supervised Models

Xin Tang and **Fei Li** and **Donghong Ji**
Computer School, Wuhan University, Wuhan, China
`1648706227@qq.com`, `lifei_csnlp` and `dhji@whu.edu.cn`

Abstract

This paper describes our approach towards the SemEval-2016 Task 10: Detecting Minimal Semantic Units and their Meanings (DiMSUM). We consider that the two problems are similar to multiword expression detection and supersense tagging, respectively. The former problem is formalized as a sequence labeling problem solved by first-order CRFs, and the latter one is formalized as a classification problem solved by Maximum Entropy Algorithm. To carry out our pilot study quickly, we extract some simple features such as words or part-of-speech tags from the training set, and avoid using external resources such as Word-Net or Brown clusters which are allowed in the supervised closed condition. Experimental results show that much further work on feature engineering and model optimization needs to be explored.

1 Introduction

In the community of natural language processing, multiword expressions (MWEs) detection (Schneider et al., 2014b; Schneider et al., 2014a) and supersense tagging (Ciaramita and Johnson, 2003; Ciaramita and Altun, 2006) have received much research attention due to their various applications such as syntactic parsing (Candito and Constant, 2014; Bengoetxea et al., 2014), semantic parsing (Banarescu et al., 2013), and machine translation (Carpuat and Diab, 2010). However, not much attention has been paid to the relationship between MWEs and supersenses (Piao et al., 2005; Schneider and Smith, 2015).

Input: Security$_{NOUN}$ increased$_{VERB}$ in$_{ADP}$ Mumbai$_{PROPN}$ amid$_{ADP}$ terror$_{NOUN}$ threats$_{NOUN}$ ahead$_{ADP}$ of$_{ADP}$ Ganeshotsav$_{PROPN}$
Output: Security$_{n.state}$ increased$_{v.change}$ in Mumbai$_{n.location}$ amid terror_threats$_{n.communication}$ ahead of Ganeshotsav$_{n.event}$

Figure 1: An DiMSUM Example. Given a tokenized and POS-tagged sentence, outputs will be a representation annotated with MWEs and supersenses. Noun and verb supersenses start with "n." and "v.", respectively. "_" joins tokens within a MWE.

The DiMSUM shared task (Schneider et al., 2016) at SemEval 2016 aims to predict a broad-coverage representation of lexical semantics giving an English sentence. This representation consists of two facets: a segmentation into minimal semantic units, and a labeling of some of those units with semantic classes. Based on the task descriptions, we consider the concepts of minimal semantic units and semantic classes are identical to those of MWEs and supersenses, respectively. Figure 1 shows an input example and its corresponding outputs of DiMSUM task.

Prior work on MWE detection using unsupervised methods includes lexicon lookup (Bejček et al., 2013), statistical association measures (Ramisch et al., 2012), parallel corpora (Tsvetkov and Wintner, 2010), or hybrid methods (Tsvetkov and Wintner, 2011). More sophisticated methods use supervised techniques such as conditional random fields (CRFs) (Shigeto et al., 2013; Constant et al., 2012; Vincze et al., 2013) or structured perceptron

Proceedings of SemEval-2016, pages 918–924,
San Diego, California, June 16-17, 2016. ©2016 Association for Computational Linguistics

(Schneider et al., 2014a), and usually achieve better performance. Compared to most aforementioned systems, MWEs in the DiMSUM task may be not contiguous or restricted by syntactic construction, which increases the detection difficulty.

Supersense tagging has been studied on diverse languages such as English (Ciaramita and Johnson, 2003; Ciaramita and Altun, 2006; Johannsen et al., 2014; Schneider and Smith, 2015), Italian (Attardi et al., 2010), Chinese (Qiu et al., 2011) and Arabic (Schneider et al., 2012). It is usually formalized as a multi-classification problem solved by supervised approaches such as perceptron. In the DiMSUM task, both single-word and multiword expressions that holistically function as noun or verb, can be considered as units for supersense tagging.

Following prior work using supervised approaches, we divide DiMSUM task into two subtasks: first, MWEs detection is treated as a sequence labeling task using first-order CRFs; second, supersense tagging is treated as a multi-classification task using Maximum Entropy Algorithm. We focus on the supervised closed condition, so only the training set are used for training both submodels separately. Then results generated on the test set are submitted for official evaluation. The evaluation results show that our system performance are not as good as those of other teams, since we leverage only some simple features such as words, POS, etc. Syntactic features and semantic resources such as WordNet (Miller, 1995) and Brown clusters (Brown et al., 1992) are not used. This suggests that further work needs to be done on feature engineering and model optimization.

2 Multiword Expression Detection

In the training set, sentences are tokenized into words, and every word has been annotated with POS and lemma. We formalize MWE detection as a sequence labeling problem, so Mallet (McCallum, 2002), Off-the-shelf implementation of CRFs, is used to handle this task. All the labels of our CRF model, extracted from the training set, are listed as follows:

- O, which indicates that the current word does not belong to a MWE.

1	current word w_i
2	whether current word w_i is in the beginning of a sentence
3	whether current word w_i is in the end of a sentence
4	previous word w_{i-1}
5	next word w_{i+1}
6	POS of current word t_i
7	POS of previous word t_{i-1}
8	POS of next word t_{i+1}
9	whether current word w_i is the only word of a sentence

Table 1: Feature templates for MWE Detection.

- B, which indicates that the current word is the first token of a MWE.

- I, which denotes that the current word continues a MWE.

- o, which indicates that the current word does not belong to a MWE, but inside the gap of another MWE.

- b, which denotes that the current word is the first token of a MWE and inside the gap of another MWE.

- i, which indicates that the current word continues a MWE and inside the gap of another MWE.

Compared with prior work on MWE detection, one difference in DiMSUM is that gaps may exist in MWEs, which increases difficulty to recognize them correctly. For example, given "Bramen Honda was a bit of a hassle ." as input, the output labels will be "Bramen$_B$ Honda$_I$ was$_B$ a$_b$ bit$_i$ of$_o$ a$_I$ hassle$_I$.$_O$". Tag "B" and tag "I" can be discontinuous and there may be several "b", "i" or "o" between them.

In order to implement a system for our pilot study quickly, we only use some simple features which are shown in Table 1. The values of these features are discrete, namely 0 or 1. The motivation of Feature 7 and 8 is to help our model to generate correct label sequences which satisfy some constraints. For example, only "B" and "O" can be located in the beginning of a sentence, and "b", "i" and "o" cannot be in the end of a sentence. Feature 9 is added since most of words which is the only one of a sentence, are tagged as "O" in the training set.

3 Supersense Tagging

We treat supersense tagging as a multi-classification problem using Maximum Entropy Algorithm, and

noun	verb
act, animal, artifact	body, change
attribute, body, cognition	cognition, social
communication, event	communication
food, group, location	competition
motive, natural_object	consumption
other, person, phenomenon	contact, weather
plant, possession, process	creation, motion
quantity, relation, shape	emotion, stative
state, substance, time	perception
feeling	possession

Table 2: Supersense Categories.

1	$w_1 w_2 ... w_n$ of mwe_i or swe_i
2	$w_1 w_2 ... w_n$ of mwe_{i-1} or swe_{i-1}
3	$w_1 w_2 ... w_n$ of mwe_{i+1} or swe_{i+1}
4	$t_1 t_2 ... t_n$ of mwe_i or swe_i
5	$t_1 t_2 ... t_n$ of mwe_{i-1} or swe_{i-1}
6	$t_1 t_2 ... t_n$ of mwe_{i+1} or swe_{i+1}

Table 3: Feature templates for Supersense Tagging. *swe* or *mwe* denotes a single or multiple word expression. mwe_i, mwe_{i-1} and mwe_{i+1} denote current, previous and next multiple word expressions, respectively. $w_1 w_2 ... w_n$ and $t_1 t_2 ... t_n$ denote word and POS combinations, respectively.

Mallet is also used to implement our supersense tagging subsystem. Based on the task description, single-word or multiword expressions can receive supersenses, so both of them are treated as classification units. This suggests that supersense tagging does not totally depend on the results of MWE detection. According to Schneider and Smith (2015), supersense categories are listed as Table 2.

Given "Bramen$_B$ Honda$_I$ was$_B$ a$_b$ bit$_i$ of$_o$ a$_I$ hassle$_I$.$_O$" as input, our model will firstly transform it into classification units based on the labels, "[Bramen Honda], [was a hassle], [a bit], [of], [.]". Since the span of "[was a hassle]" includes "[a bit]" and "[of]", it is located before "[a bit]" and "[of]". Then these units will be classified into supersense categories and an empty class which receives the units which do not belong to any category.

Supersense tagging features are shown in Table 3. The values of these features are also discrete.

Features	F_1
Baseline	28.9
+4	36.5
+5	31.4
+6	51.5
+7	50.4
+8	19.9
+9	34.8

(a)

Features	F_1
Baseline	50.3
+2	42.2
+3	40.1
+4	55.5
+5	50.7
+6	52.2

(b)

Table 4: Subtable (a) and (b) dennote contributions of features in Table 1 and 3, respectively. "+" denotes that only the feature in the current line is added. The numbers in the first column correspond to the ones in Table 1 and 3, respectively.

4 Experiments

4.1 Experimental Settings

There are three conditions in the DiMSUM[1] shared task at SemEval 2016. In the supervised closed condition, only the training set, WordNet and Brown clusters are allowed to be used. In the semi-supervised closed condition, all of the above are permitted, plus the Yelp Academic Dataset. In the open condition, all available resources can be used. We carry out our experiments according to the demands in the supervised closed condition, but WordNet and Brown clusters are not used. The test set consists of 16,500 words in 1,000 English sentences which are drawn from the following sources: reviews from the TrustPilot corpus (Hovy et al., 2015), tweets from the Tweebank corpus (Kong et al., 2014), TED talks from the WIT3 archive (Cettolo et al., 2012).

During the development period, we split 30% data from the training set as our development set and use the remainder for training. The maximum training iteration is set as 500. The evaluation scripts (v1.5) released by task organizers are used for tuning parameters and features. During the official evaluation period, we use all the training set to train our CRF and Maximum Entropy models, and prediction results on the test set are submitted.

4.2 Development Results

The contributions of features are shown in Table 4. The baseline in Table 4a does not only use Feature 1

---

[1]http://dimsum16.github.io/

Team	Condition	μ-M	μ-S	μ-C	Tw-M	Tw-S	Tw-C	R-M	R-S	R-C	TED-M	TED-S	TED-C	Macro-C
ICL-HD	open	56.66	57.55	57.41	59.49	55.99	56.63	53.37	57.66	56.98	57.14	60.06	59.71	57.77
VectorWeavers	open	38.49	51.62	49.77	39.32	51.70	49.74	36.18	51.36	49.25	42.76	52	50.82	49.94
UW-CSE	open	57.24	57.64	57.57	61.09	57.46	58.18	54.80	57	56.61	53.48	59.17	58.33	57.71
BCED	open	13.48	51.93	46.64	15.50	51.11	45.44	8.68	51.98	46.15	20.11	53.28	49.81	47.13
BCED	semi-closed	13.46	51.11	45.86	15.76	49.95	44.42	9.07	52	46.19	18.28	51.40	47.90	46.17
UFRGS	super-closed	51.48	49.98	50.22	51.16	49.20	49.54	49.57	50.93	50.71	56.76	49.61	50.57	50.27
WHUNlp	super-closed	**30.98**	**25.14**	**25.76**	**34.18**	**24.63**	**25.87**	**26.39**	**25.82**	**25.86**	**33.44**	**24.68**	**25.39**	**25.71**
UW-CSE	super-closed	53.93	57.47	56.88	54.48	56.82	56.38	53.96	57.19	56.66	52.35	59.11	58.26	57.10
BCED	super-closed	8.20	51.29	45.47	6.34	49.66	42.99	7.05	52.68	46.57	16.30	51.44	47.82	45.79
UW-CSE	open(late)	56.71	57.72	57.54	61.96	57.65	58.51	52.09	57.22	56.31	54.09	58.78	58.16	57.66

Table 5: Official Evaluation Results (in %) of DiMSUM 2016.

in Table 1, but also Feature 2 and 3 since they help to generate correct label sequences. The baseline in Table 4b uses only Feature 1 in Table 3. It can be seen that Feature 8 in Table 1, Feature 2 and 3 in Table 3 lead to decreases of F_1 scores, so they should be excluded[2].

4.3 Final Results

Table 5 shows official evaluation results. The columns "μ-M", "μ-S" and "μ-C" denote microaverages of F1 scores for MWEs (-M), supersenses (-S) and combined (-C), respectively. "Tw", "R" and "TED" indicate F1 scores for tweets, reviews and TED talks, respectively. The results in the last column denote macroaverages of F1 scores across three domains. Compared with other supervised closed condition systems, the performance of our system is not good. This suggests that that there is substantial work to be done on exploring more features to improve our system.

Apart from using simple features, another reason that leads to poor performance of our system is that we use a pipeline model. Since errors generated in the first step are inherited by the second step, the performance of supersense tagging further decreases. Error propagation can be reduced by leveraging joint models. Previous work (Schneider and Smith, 2015) has already leveraged joint models on this issue, so we plan to follow this approach in our future work.

Moreover, it is worth noting that UW-CSE system in the supervised closed condition, achieves competitive results compared with the best scoring systems in the open condition. This suggests that good performance can still be obtained without too much external resources or data.

---

[2]In the official evaluation, these features are included due to our coding problems, so this may be one of the reasons due to poor performance.

MWE Features	Improved F_1
prefix of w_i	11.2
suffix of w_i	10.4
whether the first character of w_i is uppercase	12.1
whether w_i contains non-alpha or non-numeric characters	7.4
context POS bigram ($t_i t_{i+1}$)	21.4
word + context POS ($t_{i-1} w_i t_{i+1}$)	11.4
Supersense Features	**Improved F_1**
whether swe_i is a noun	2.9
whether swe_i is a verb	5.1
first character and POS combinations of swe_i or mwe_i	6

Table 6: Expanded Feature templates and their improved performance on the development set. w_i denotes the current word and t_i denotes the POS of current word. swe_i or mwe_i denotes the current single or multiple word expression.

4.4 Feature Enrichment

After the evaluation results are released, we expand our feature templates to improve the performance. Table 6 shows the contributions of these expanded features evaluated on the development set and some of them are inspired by (Schneider et al., 2014a). Compared with the performance improvements of MWE detection, the performance of supersense tagging increases less. On the test set, "μ-M", "μ-S" and "μ-C" can achieve 45.6%, 46.1% and 46.0% using all the features proposed in this paper.

4.5 Error Analysis

We calculate false positive (FP) and false negative (FN) errors on the test set. For MWE detection errors in Table 7, a MWE is counted as FP if its boundary is incorrectly identified, and a MWE is counted as FN if it has not been recognized. Table 7 shows that "***_NOUN" is the most difficult pattern to be

False Positive		False Negative	
POS Pattern	Count	POS Pattern	Count
NOUN_NOUN	25	NOUN_NOUN	100
VERB_NOUN	20	ADJ_NOUN	59
DET_NOUN	17	VERB_ADP	34
VERB_ADP	16	NOUN_NOUN_NOUN	19
ADP_NOUN	14	PROPN_NOUN	15
ADJ_NOUN	12	DET_NOUN	15
ADJ_ADP	11	VERB_NOUN	14
VERB_PART	10	PROPN_PROPN	13
ADV_ADV	8	ADJ_NOUN_NOUN	11
VERB_ADP_NOUN	7	ADP_NOUN	11

Table 7: Top 10 false positive and false negative patterns for MWE detection.

False Positive		False Negative	
Supersense	Count	Supersense	Count
n.artifact	783	n.person	216
v.stative	629	n.communication	172
n.person	499	n.artifact	168
n.cognition	493	v.change	165
v.social	441	n.act	161
v.cognition	373	v.stative	154
v.communication	303	n.group	136
n.group	269	n.attribute	117
n.communication	253	v.cognition	98
n.time	237	n.location	82

Table 8: Top 10 false positive and false negative supersenses.

recognized. One reason might be that noun phrases often consist of weak MWEs, while weak MWEs are harder to be detected since their vocabularies are more flexible and their meanings are more ambiguous than those of strong MWEs.

For supersense tagging errors in Table 8, a predicted supersense is counted as FP if it is not identical to its corresponding gold supersense, and a gold supersense is counted as FN if it has not been recognized. The single or multiple word expression without a supersense is not taken into account. Table 8 shows that "n.artifact" and "n.person" are more difficult to be tagged. One reason might be "n.artifact" is usually associated with abstract nouns such as "thing" or polyscmous words such as "watch". "n.person" recognition might be difficult since various person names lead to many out-of-vocabulary words. This problem may be more serious in the supervised closed condition. In addition, stative verbs are very frequent and also difficult to be disambiguated.

5 Conclusion

We attend the DiMSUM shared task at SemEval 2016 which aims to predict MWEs and supersenses when an English sentence is given. Two submodels, namely CRFs and Maximum Entropy, are explored to detect multiword expressions and supersenses, respectively. Experimental results in the official evaluation suggest that there is substantial work to be done to improve the performance of our system.

In future work, we plan to extend our work in two directions. Firstly, feature templates need to be further expanded and finetuned. Secondly, joint models, which may not only reduce error propagation, but also utilize relations between MWEs and supersenses, can be used to facilitate both subtasks.

References

Giuseppe Attardi, Stefano Dei Rossi, Giulia Di Pietro, Alessandro Lenci, Simonetta Montemagni, and Maria Simi. 2010. A resource and tool for super-sense tagging of italian texts. In *Proceedings of the Seventh conference on LREC*, may.

Laura Banarescu, Claire Bonial, Shu Cai, Madalina Georgescu, Kira Griffitt, Ulf Hermjakob, Kevin Knight, Philipp Koehn, Martha Palmer, and Nathan Schneider. 2013. Abstract meaning representation for sembanking. In *Proceedings of the 7th Linguistic Annotation Workshop and Interoperability with Discourse*, pages 178–186, August.

Eduard Bejček, Pavel Stranak, and Pavel Pecina. 2013. Syntactic identification of occurrences of multiword expressions in text using a lexicon with dependency structures. In *Proceedings of the 9th Workshop on Multiword Expressions*, pages 106–115, June.

Kepa Bengoetxea, Eneko Agirre, Joakim Nivre, Yue Zhang, and Koldo Gojenola. 2014. On wordnet semantic classes and dependency parsing. In *Proceedings of the 52nd Annual Meeting of ACL*.

Peter F. Brown, Peter V. deSouza, Robert L. Mercer, T. J. Watson, Vincent J. Della Pietra, and Jenifer C. Lai. 1992. Class-based n-gram models of natural language. *Computational Linguistics*, 18:467–479.

Marie Candito and Matthieu Constant. 2014. Strategies for contiguous multiword expression analysis and dependency parsing. In *Proceedings of the 52nd Annual Meeting of ACL*, pages 743–753, June.

Marine Carpuat and Mona Diab. 2010. Task-based evaluation of multiword expressions: a pilot study in statistical machine translation. In *Human Language Technologies: The 2010 Annual Conference of NAACL*, pages 242–245, June.

Mauro Cettolo, Christian Girardi, and Marcello Federico. 2012. Wit^3: Web inventory of transcribed and translated talks. In *Proceedings of the 16th Conference of the European Association for Machine Translation (EAMT)*, pages 261–268, Trento, Italy, May.

Massimiliano Ciaramita and Yasemin Altun. 2006. Broad-coverage sense disambiguation and information extraction with a supersense sequence tagger. In *Proceedings of the 2006 Conference on EMNLP*.

Massimiliano Ciaramita and Mark Johnson. 2003. Supersense tagging of unknown nouns in WordNet. In Michael Collins and Mark Steedman, editors, *Proceedings of the 2003 Conference on EMNLP*.

Matthieu Constant, Anthony Sigogne, and Patrick Watrin. 2012. Discriminative strategies to integrate multiword expression recognition and parsing. In *Proceedings of the 50th Annual Meeting of ACL*.

Dirk Hovy, Anders Johannsen, and Anders Søgaard. 2015. User review sites as a resource for large-scale sociolinguistic studies. In *Proceedings of the 24th International Conference on World Wide Web*, WWW '15, pages 452–461, New York, NY, USA. ACM.

Anders Johannsen, Dirk Hovy, Héctor Martínez Alonso, Barbara Plank, and Anders Søgaard. 2014. More or less supervised supersense tagging of twitter. In *Proceedings of the Third Joint Conference on Lexical and Computational Semantics (*SEM 2014)*, pages 1–11.

Lingpeng Kong, Nathan Schneider, Swabha Swayamdipta, Archna Bhatia, Chris Dyer, and Noah A. Smith. 2014. A dependency parser for tweets. In *Proceedings of the 2014 Conference on Empirical Methods in Natural Language Processing (EMNLP)*, pages 1001–1012, Doha, Qatar, October. Association for Computational Linguistics.

Andrew Kachites McCallum. 2002. Mallet: A machine learning for language toolkit. http://mallet.cs.umass.edu.

G. A. Miller. 1995. Wordnet: A lexical database for english. *Communications of the ACM*, 38:39–41.

Scott Songlin Piao, Paul Rayson, Dawn Archer, and Tony McEnery. 2005. Comparing and combining a semantic tagger and a statistical tool for mwe extraction. *Computer Speech & Language*, 19(4):378–397.

Likun Qiu, Yunfang Wu, and Yanqiu Shao. 2011. Combining contextual and structural information for supersense tagging of chinese unknown words. In *12th International Conference Computational Linguistics and Intelligent Text Processing*.

Carlos Ramisch, Vitor De Araujo, and Aline Villavicencio. 2012. A broad evaluation of techniques for automatic acquisition of multiword expressions. In *Proceedings of ACL 2012 Student Research Workshop*, pages 1–6, July.

Nathan Schneider and Noah A. Smith. 2015. A corpus and model integrating multiword expressions and supersenses. In *Proceedings of the 2015 Conference of the North American Chapter of ACL*, pages 1537–1547, May–June.

Nathan Schneider, Behrang Mohit, Kemal Oflazer, and Noah A. Smith. 2012. Coarse lexical semantic annotation with supersenses: An arabic case study. In *Proceedings of the 50th Annual Meeting of ACL*, pages 253–258, July.

Nathan Schneider, Emily Danchik, Chris Dyer, and Noah Smith. 2014a. Discriminative lexical semantic segmentation with gaps: Running the mwe gamut. *Transactions of the Association for Computational Linguistics*, 2:193–206.

Nathan Schneider, Spencer Onuffer, Nora Kazour, Emily Danchik, Michael T. Mordowanec, Henrietta Conrad, and Noah A. Smith. 2014b. Comprehensive annotation of multiword expressions in a social web corpus. In *Proceedings of LREC'14*, pages 455–461, May.

Nathan Schneider, Dirk Hovy, Anders Johannsen, and Marine Carpuat. 2016. SemEval 2016 Task 10: Detecting Minimal Semantic Units and their Meanings (DiMSUM). In *Proc. of SemEval*, June.

Yutaro Shigeto, Ai Azuma, Sorami Hisamoto, Shuhei Kondo, Tomoya Kouse, Keisuke Sakaguchi, Akifumi Yoshimoto, Frances Yung, and Yuji Matsumoto. 2013. Construction of English MWE dictionary and its application to POS tagging. In *Proceedings of the 9th Workshop on Multiword Expressions*, pages 139–144.

Yulia Tsvetkov and Shuly Wintner. 2010. Extraction of multi-word expressions from small parallel corpora. In *Coling 2010: Posters*, pages 1256–1264, August.

Yulia Tsvetkov and Shuly Wintner. 2011. Identification of multi-word expressions by combining multiple linguistic information sources. In *Proceedings of the 2011 Conference on EMNLP*, pages 836–845, July.

Veronika Vincze, Istvn Nagy T., and Jnos Zsibrita. 2013. Learning to detect english and hungarian light verb constructions. *TSLP*, 10(2):6.

UTU at SemEval-2016 Task 10: Binary Classification for Expression Detection (BCED)

Jari Björne and Tapio Salakoski

Department of Information Technology, University of Turku

Turku Centre for Computer Science (TUCS)

Faculty of Mathematics and Natural Sciences, FI-20014, Turku, Finland

`firstname.lastname@utu.fi`

Abstract

The SemEval 2016 DiMSUM Shared Task concerns the detection of minimal semantic units from text and prediction of their coarse lexical categories known as supersenses. Our approach is to define this task as a binary classification problem approachable by straightforward machine learning methods.

We start by detecting semantic units by matching text spans against several large dictionaries, including the English WordNet, expressions derived from the Yelp Academic Dataset and concepts from the English Wikipedia, generating a set of potential supersenses for each matched span. For each potential supersense and text span pair a binary machine learning example is defined. We classify these examples using an ensemble method, taking as the final predicted supersense the one with the highest confidence score.

Our system achieves good performance on the supersense classification task but has limited performance for detection of multi-word semantic units. We show that the task of supersense prediction can be effectively defined as a binary classification task.

1 Introduction

The SemEval 2016 DiMSUM Shared Task[1] concerns the detection of *minimal semantic units* and their semantic classification using *supersenses* (Schneider et al., 2016). The minimal semantic units can consist of either single words or *multiword expressions (MWE)* in cases where multiple words

form a lexical item. The concept of MWE as used in the DiMSUM task is described in detail in Schneider et al. (2014). The *supersenses* are broad-coverage, coarse lexical categories, 26 for nouns and 15 for verbs. These supersenses mostly correspond to the WordNet lexicographer files. A detailed description of the supersenses is in Schneider and Smith (2015). Automated supersense tagging has previously been explored by e.g. Curran (2005), Ciaramita and Altun (2006) and Johannsen et al. (2014).

In the DiMSUM task systems must both detect the minimal semantic units and assign correct supersenses for them. The final metric of the shared task is the averaged performance on these tasks, which are also evaluated independently. The systems can approach these tasks either independently (e.g. in a pipeline) or through a joint model.

We approach the DiMSUM task as a machine learning classification task where examples are generated for all semantic units found in a pre-defined dictionary. These semantic units are classified into one of the 41 supersenses by generating an example for each possible semantic unit + supersense pair, turning the task of assigning one of many supersenses into a binary classification problem. In this manner, the task becomes a generalized machine learning task for which almost any classifier can be used.

The DiMSUM shared task defines three subtasks or data conditions in which the systems can participate, varying in the amount of resources that are allowed to be used. The *supervised closed* condition defines the most limited case where participants can use the labeled training corpus, the English Word-

---

[1] `http://dimsum16.github.io/`

925

Proceedings of SemEval-2016, pages 925–930,
San Diego, California, June 16-17, 2016. ©2016 Association for Computational Linguistics

Net lexicon and two sets of Brown word clusters. In the *semi-supervised closed* condition the Yelp Academic Dataset can also be used, and in the *open* condition systems may use any and all resources available.

2 Data and Methods

2.1 Datasets

The DiMSUM corpus and evaluation tools, version 1.5, were provided by the task organizers. The corpus consists of a training and test set. The training set is a unified combination of the STREUSLE 2.1 corpus of web reviews, and the Ritter and Lowlands Twitter datasets, and consists of 4,799 sentences with tokenization, POS, MWE and supersense annotation. The test set consists of 1,000 sentences from online reviews, tweets and TED talk transcripts, with only tokenization and POS annotation.

The Yelp's Academic Dataset[2], which consists of JSON objects describing 13,490 businesses, 330,071 reviews and 130,873 users, was used with permission from Yelp Inc. WordNet version 3.0 (Fellbaum, 1998) was used through NLTK version 3.1 (Bird et al., 2009). For the English Wikipedia, the dump of titles in the main namespace *enwiki-20160113-all-titles-in-ns0.gz* was used[3]. Wikipedia page categories were downloaded using the Wikipedia Python library[4] by Jonathan Goldsmith.

2.2 System Overview

Our system follows a straightforward machine learning approach where examples are first generated and then classified using a standard classifier library. The task specific code is in the example generation part, which consists of two steps: 1) detection of minimal semantic units and 2) assignment of candidate supersenses for these units.

The detection of minimal semantic units is a rule-based step consisting mostly of dictionary matching. One sentence is processed at a time, one token at a time. For each token, the token itself and the following five tokens are first tested for a match, then the

token and the next four tokens, and so on until just the token on its own. A set of *taggers* are applied for each span of tokens, and if any of the taggers finds a match, one or more examples are generated.

All tokens that are part of the matched set are then "consumed" and example generation continues from the next free token. In this manner, each token is assigned to the longest matched minimal semantic unit. As a consequence, each token may belong to a maximum of one candidate semantic unit. We do not attempt to detect disjoint MWEs.

A tagger will provide for each positive match a list of potential supersenses. A feature vector is built for each combination of the matched span of tokens and potential supersenses, with the example containing the correct supersense labeled as a positive and the rest as negatives.

2.3 Taggers

In our system taggers are the modules that detect minimal semantic units among the tokens in the sentence. For each set of consecutive tokens each tagger can generate zero or more candidate supersenses. Each unique candidate supersense will then be used to produce one example for classification.

The *WordNet tagger* is used in all three conditions as the primary tagger. Tested tokens are joined to a span by first using their lemmas and if no match is found by using their exact words. For the joined span all synsets are retrieved from WordNet and for each synset the corresponding lexicographer file name is added as a potential supersense. In the case of the *noun.Tops* file name the span itself is added as a supersense if it directly matches a known supersense.

The *Out-of-Vocabulary (OoV) tagger* is used in all three conditions to match semantic units not detected by the other taggers, providing a fuzzy matching system for common positive spans not included in any of the dictionaries. It detects such constructs as Twitter @-codes (*n.person*), possessive suffix tokens starting with an apostrophe (*v.stative*) and words whose DiMSUM supersense differs from their WordNet lexicographer file name, commonly businesses such as "restaurant", "store" or "hotel" (*n.group*). Cases for the OoV tagger were determined manually using the DiMSUM training corpus.

---

[2] https://www.yelp.com/academic_dataset
[3] https://dumps.wikimedia.org/enwiki/
[4] https://github.com/goldsmith/Wikipedia

2.3.1 The Yelp Tagger

The *Yelp tagger* is used in the *semi-supervised closed* and *open* conditions. First, three types of information are extracted from the Yelp Academic Dataset. For business objects the name of the business itself is used, but businesses also contain information on nearby schools and neighborhoods, and these are likewise added to the dictionary. When matching token sets, the businesses provide the *n.group* supersense and schools and neighborhoods the *n.location* supersense. Exact matches are tested for all of these cases.

Many business names have a common last noun, as in "Harvard Square Cafe" or "Minami Sushi". Thus, for token sets consisting only of nouns and proper nouns (POS tags *NOUN* or *PROPN*) a match is generated if the last token in the set matches the last token of any Yelp business or location. Candidate supersenses are generated based on all Yelp objects in which a token from the set is found in a corresponding position (first, middle or last). In addition to the *n.group* and *n.location* supersenses the additional supersense *n.food* is generated for the token "Restaurants".

Yelp user objects contain the first name and the last initial of the user. All first names are added to a dictionary. When detecting potential matches, first names of more than two characters are used as matches for the *n.person* supersense, tested against the first token in sets of no more than two upper-cased tokens.

2.3.2 The Wikipedia Tagger

The *Wikipedia tagger* is used only in the *open* condition. All token sets for which a match cannot be provided by the WordNet tagger are compared against the list of Wikipedia page titles. Before matching the parenthesized disambiguation parts are removed from the titles. For matching titles, potential supersenses are provided according to the categories of that page. A page category can match zero or more DiMSUM supersenses.

Common Wikipedia page categories, present in pages for titles matching the DiMSUM training set, are manually assigned to supersenses if they are relevant for the DiMSUM task. For example, a category ending in "births" (e.g. "1968 births") corresponds to the *n.person* supersense, common media categories such as "album", "game", "television" or "comics" correspond to *n.communication* and any category ending in "companies" to *n.group*.

Based on these rules, the page categories of all matched Wikipedia titles are automatically mapped to supersenses. This mapping is done only for the subset of Wikipedia page titles found in the entire DiMSUM corpus, as processing the large Wikipedia dataset is quite time consuming. In this way, the resulting subset of 1,110 page titles and categories linked to corresponding DiMSUM supersenses can also be easily distributed alongside our source code.

2.4 Feature Representation

For each candidate token set + supersense pair a feature vector is built for machine learning. The same feature representation is used in all three DiMSUM task conditions.

For each token in the set a feature is built for the *lemma*, *POS* and *word* values. For the first and last tokens in the set, additional copies of these features are built, marked with the token's position. If the set consists of only a single token, an additional copy of these features is likewise built, marking that they come from a single-token example.

For the whole set of tokens, the consecutive *lemma*, *POS* and *word* values of the entire set are catenated together as features. The supersense of the token set + supersense pair is added as a feature. The supersenses of all the other examples generated for the same token set are also added as features distinct from the supersense feature of the current pair.

2.5 Machine Learning

For machine learning we use the scikit-learn library version 0.16.1 (Pedregosa et al., 2011). After examples are generated for each token set + supersense pair a binary classifier is used to classify them as either positives or negatives. We classify the examples with the Extra Trees Classifier ensemble method (Geurts et al., 2006) using its *predict_proba* function which gives probability estimates. For each token set, the final prediction is the supersense with the highest probability estimate among all supersenses predicted as positive for that token set.

3 Results and Discussion

The official results for the six teams participating in the DiMSUM shared task are shown in Table 1. Using the primary metric of the shared task, macro-averaged performance over both the minimal semantic unit detection and supersense assignment tasks, our system (BCED) was ranked third out of four participants in the *supervised closed* condition, fourth out of four participants in the *open* condition and was the only participating system in the *semi-supervised closed* condition.

3.1 Minimal Semantic Units

Compared to the other systems, the major limitation in our system was in the detection of the minimal semantic units. Our approach of detecting known MWEs, even using a very large dictionary such as the Wikipedia, was not sufficient to cover the scope of the DiMSUM MWEs, which consist of not only compound words and common idioms, but also more generalized noun phrases.

The numbers of generated examples are shown in Table 2. The vast majority of examples are detected by the WordNet tagger. It's notable how few additional positives are detected with the Wikipedia and Yelp dictionaries, even though the Wikipedia tagger considers only examples missed by the WordNet tagger. The number of examples detected by the OoV tagger doesn't change much between the conditions, as it mostly matches special cases not in any of the dictionaries.

The primary issue with the dictionary matching approach is that approximately a third of real positive examples are missed in all three conditions. The addition of first the Yelp and then the Wikipedia taggers decreases this number by 392 examples but compared to the total missed this is a relatively small improvement. Looking at the categories of the missed examples, MWEs that are *too long* (longer than six tokens) and those with *gaps* fall outside the scope of the system. Inclusion of the Yelp and Wikipedia taggers reduces the token sets for which *no match* is found by a considerable 718 examples, but there is a corresponding increase of 64 missing *type* examples for which a correct candidate supersense was not found.

Finally, the *nested* category highlights an inter-

	Super	Semi	Open
WordNet +	14435	14363	14294
WordNet −	78007	77045	76229
Wikipedia +	-	-	348
Wikipedia −	-	-	2635
Yelp +	-	334	329
Yelp −	-	675	640
OoV +	856	848	848
OoV −	756	751	751
total +	15203	15408	15595
total −	78714	78400	80158
too long	6	6	6
no match	3206	2876	2488
gaps	426	426	426
type	2783	2768	2847
nested	830	970	1092
total missed	7251	7046	6859

Table 2: Example generation for the training corpus. Each column corresponds to one of the conditions. The uppermost rows show the positive and negative examples generated by each of the four taggers, followed by the combined totals. After these are shown the five categories of false negative examples followed by their totals.

esting issue in example generation. Even while the Yelp and Wikipedia taggers provide more matches, at the same time the number of examples that are undetectable due to being nested within a false, longer MWE increases by 262. The issue of missing nested examples could be solved by generating examples for matched nested spans, but the corpus annotation might not be compatible with this approach, as each token can belong to a maximum of one annotated semantic unit. In the case of strong MWEs, for example in the idiom "close call", it is not clear what, if any, supersense the "call" token alone could be assigned (Schneider et al., 2014). However, in an MWE such as "cricket bat" (*n.artifact*) it is clear what the meaning of "bat" is, and likewise, "cricket" refers to the sport. Nevertheless, there is no annotation within MWEs, so while "cricket" alone has the supersense *n.act*, nested in "cricket bat" it has no supersense of its own. Thus, examples generated for nested spans would be inconsistent with non-nested examples.

3.2 Supersense classification

While MWE detection performance was very low due to the issues in example generation, supersense

SYS	Team	Condition	μ-M	μ-S	μ-C	Macro-C	extra resources
214	ICL-HD	open	56.66	57.55	57.41	57.77	Yago3, GloVe embeddings
227	VectorWeavers	open	38.49	51.62	49.77	49.94	Google News EB, TurboParser
249	UW-CSE	open	57.24	57.64	57.57	57.71	Schneider MWE lexicons
255	BCED	open	13.48	51.93	46.64	47.13	English Wikipedia
211	BCED	semi-closed	13.46	51.11	45.86	46.17	
106	UFRGS	super-closed	51.48	49.98	50.22	50.27	
108	WHUNlp	super-closed	30.98	25.14	25.76	25.71	
248	UW-CSE	super-closed	53.93	57.47	56.88	57.10	
254	BCED	super-closed	8.20	51.29	45.47	45.79	
263	UW-CSE	open (late)	56.71	57.72	57.54	57.66	Schneider MWE lexicons

Table 1: The results of the DiMSUM 2016 shared task (provided by task organizers). Micro- and macro-averaged F-scores are shown for (M) MWE detection, (S) supersense assignment and (C) their combination. EB refers to embeddings.

assignment worked quite well (See Table 1). For supersenses, our approach reached F-scores of around 51% while the best performing systems were at 57%. Thus, our system placed 2nd and 3rd in terms of supersenses in the *supervised closed* and *open* conditions. As only 19% of all annotated minimal semantic units have more than one token the impact of MWE detection on supersense classification is limited.

The supersense classification is the only machine learning step in our system. Like most classifiers, the parameters of the Extra Trees Classifier must be optimized on known data for best performance. For parameter optimization, we used three-fold cross-validation on the training corpus, using one of the STREUSLE, Ritter and Lowlands datasets for performance estimation at a time and the other two for training.

Parameter optimization highlighted a conflict in using one binary classification step for both detecting MWEs and assigning the supersenses. Generally, the performance of the Extra Trees Classifier can be increased by increasing the ensemble size, and we noticed such increases while testing sizes from the default of 10 estimators up to 100. However, while the overall classification performance increased, the classifier became increasingly likely to not take any chances with MWE examples, assigning them all as negative. Only by decreasing ensemble size to 2 it became possible to detect at least some MWEs, albeit at the cost of slightly reduced performance on supersense assignment.

4 Conclusions

We developed a binary classification system for the DiMSUM 2016 task of detecting minimal semantic units and their supersenses. Our system consists of a customizable dictionary matching step for example generation, followed by a classification step.

The main advantage of this system is its simplicity. Standard machine learning systems can be applied for the classification of the generalized binary examples. As only one machine learning step is used, parameter optimization can likewise be performed in a standard cross-validation loop. The dictionary matching step can be quickly extended by adding new taggers for different vocabularies.

The primary shortcoming of the system is its low performance on MWE detection. This is largely a result of the dictionary matching approach being only partially applicable for the task of detecting the DiMSUM corpus MWEs. We speculate that using machine learning to follow the annotated scope of the MWEs would be a better approach for this part of the task.

Nevertheless, our system achieved good performance on supersense classification, indicating that binarizing this multi-class task is a valid approach. Moreover, even with a simple feature representation consisting only of token attributes and their combinations, comparatively high performance could be achieved.

We publish all of our experimental code, our Wikipedia derived datasets and our detailed results as an open source project [5].

---

[5] https://github.com/jbjorne/DiMSUM2016

References

Steven Bird, Ewan Klein, and Edward Loper. 2009. *Natural language processing with Python*. O'Reilly Media, Inc.

Massimiliano Ciaramita and Yasemin Altun. 2006. Broad-coverage sense disambiguation and information extraction with a supersense sequence tagger. In *Proceedings of the 2006 Conference on Empirical Methods in Natural Language Processing*, pages 594–602. Association for Computational Linguistics.

James R. Curran. 2005. Supersense tagging of unknown nouns using semantic similarity. In *Proceedings of the 43rd Annual Meeting on Association for Computational Linguistics*, ACL '05, pages 26–33, Stroudsburg, PA, USA. Association for Computational Linguistics.

Christiane Fellbaum. 1998. *WordNet*. Wiley Online Library.

Pierre Geurts, Damien Ernst, and Louis Wehenkel. 2006. Extremely randomized trees. *Machine learning*, 63(1):3–42.

Anders Johannsen, Dirk Hovy, Héctor Martínez Alonso, Barbara Plank, and Anders Søgaard. 2014. More or less supervised supersense tagging of twitter. *Proc. of* SEM*, pages 1–11.

F. Pedregosa, G. Varoquaux, A. Gramfort, V. Michel, B. Thirion, O. Grisel, M. Blondel, P. Prettenhofer, R. Weiss, V. Dubourg, J. Vanderplas, A. Passos, D. Cournapeau, M. Brucher, M. Perrot, and E. Duchesnay. 2011. Scikit-learn: Machine learning in Python. *Journal of Machine Learning Research*, 12:2825–2830.

Nathan Schneider and Noah A Smith. 2015. A corpus and model integrating multiword expressions and supersenses. In *NAACL HLT 2015, The 2015 Conference of the North American Chapter of the Association for Computational Linguistics: Human Language Technologies, Denver, Colorado, USA, May 31 - June 5, 2015.*

Nathan Schneider, Spencer Onuffer, Nora Kazour, Emily Danchik, Michael T Mordowanec, Henrietta Conrad, and Noah A Smith. 2014. Comprehensive annotation of multiword expressions in a social web corpus. In *Proceedings of the Ninth International Conference on Language Resources and Evaluation (LREC-2014), Reykjavik, Iceland, May 26-31, 2014.*

Nathan Schneider, Dirk Hovy, Anders Johannsen, and Marine Carpuat. 2016. SemEval 2016 Task 10: Detecting Minimal Semantic Units and their Meanings (DiMSUM). In *Proc. of SemEval*, San Diego, California, USA, June.

UW-CSE at SemEval-2016 Task 10: Detecting Multiword Expressions and Supersenses using Double-Chained Conditional Random Fields

Mohammad Javad Hosseini   Noah A. Smith   Su-In Lee
Computer Science and Engineering
University of Washington
Seattle, WA 98195, USA
`{hosseini,nasmith,suinlee}@cs.washington.edu`

Abstract

We describe our entry to SemEval 2016 Task 10: Detecting Minimal Semantic Units and their Meanings. Our approach uses a discriminative first-order sequence model similar to Schneider and Smith (2015). The chief novelty in our approach is a factorization of the labels into multiword expression and supersense labels, and restricting first-order dependencies within these two parts. Our submitted models achieved first place in the closed competition (CRF) and second place in the open competition (2-CRF).

1   Introduction

Schneider and Smith (2015) argued that the problems of segmenting a piece of text into minimal semantic units, and of labeling those units with semantic classes (e.g., supersenses), are intimately connected.

We propose to use a double-chained conditional random field (which we refer to as "2-CRF," an example of a factorial CRF; §3.4) for joint multiword expression identification and supersense tagging. Like other CRFs, 2-CRF is a feature-rich probabilistic model that can represent probabilistic dependencies between features and labels and between the labels of the consecutive words. The 2-CRF models local dependencies between MWE and supersense sequences with two parallel chains of labels, restricting direct interaction between the two to local, single-word positions. Label constraints on tag bigrams ensure a globally consistent tagging.

Our experiments show that 2-CRF outperforms a zero-order baseline, the structured perceptron used by Schneider and Smith (2015), and a conventional CRF (§4). For SemEval 2016 Task 10: Detecting Minimal Semantic Units and their Meanings, we submitted a CRF for the closed condition and a 2-CRF (incompletely trained) for the open condition, achieving first and second place, respectively.

2   Task Description

For completeness, we briefly review the shared task. The shared task training dataset, called "Detecting Minimal Semantic Units and their Meanings" (DiMSUM) (Schneider et al., 2016),[1] consists of sentences with multiword expression (MWE) and supersense annotations. The data combine and harmonize the STREUSLE 2.1 corpus of web reviews (Schneider and Smith, 2015)[2] and Ritter and Lowlands Twitter datasets (Johannsen et al., 2014).[3]

Similar to prior work (Schneider and Smith, 2015), the annotation for MWEs extends the conventional BIO scheme (Ramshaw and Marcus, 1995) to include gappy MWEs with one level of nesting.[4] Segmentations are represented using six tags; the lower-case variants indicate that an expression is within another MWE's gap.

- O and o: single word expression

- B and b: the first word of a MWE

---

[1] `https://github.com/dimsum16/`
`dimsum-data/blob/1.5/README.md`

[2] `http://www.cs.cmu.edu/~ark/LexSem`

[3] `https://github.com/coastalcph/`
`supersense-data-twitter`

[4] Unlike in Schneider and Smith (2015), there is no notion of weak and strong MWEs.

Proceedings of SemEval-2016, pages 931–936,
San Diego, California, June 16-17, 2016. ©2016 Association for Computational Linguistics

- *I* and *i*: a word continuing a MWE

We call a tag sequence *valid* if it matches the regular expression *(O|B(o|bi⁺|I)*I⁺)⁺*. Validity can be ensured using label constraints on tag bigrams (Schneider, 2014).

Each noun or verb expression is also annotated with a supersense; there are 26 supersenses for nouns and 15 for verbs. Only the first word of a MWE receives a supersense tag.

One approach to encoding the MWE and supersense tags is to define an extended label set containing both tags (Schneider and Smith, 2015). This will result in 170 potential labels: *I*, *i*, and each of *B*, *b*, *O* and *o* paired with one of the 41 supersenses and no supersense ($2 + 4 \times 42 = 170$). Only 110 of these are attested in the training data, and these are the combinations our approach considers.

There are 4,799 sentences in the training data. For each token, the dataset provides its offset in the sentence, lemma, POS tag, MWE tag, offset of parent, and supersense label (if applicable).

The blind test set consists of 1,000 sentences from three sources: online reviews from the Trust-Pilot corpus (Hovy et al., 2015), tweets from the Tweebank corpus (Kong et al., 2014) and TED talk transcripts from the IWSLT MT evaluation campaigns, obtained from the WIT[3] archive (Cettolo et al., 2012).

The shared task has three data conditions: supervised closed, semi-supervised closed, and open. In the supervised closed condition, only the labeled data, the English WordNet lexicon, a provided Brown clustering (Brown et al., 1992) on the 21-million-word Yelp Academic Dataset[5] (Schneider et al., 2014), and any of the ARK Tweet NLP clusters[6] are allowed. The semi-supervised closed condition adds the Yelp Academic Dataset to the resources. The open condition allows the use of any available resources. We have participated in the supervised closed and open conditions. The evaluation is based on F_1 score for MWE identification, supersense labeling, and their combination.[7]

---

3 Models

3.1 Input Features

For the open condition, we use all features introduced in Schneider and Smith (2015): a.) Basic MWE features used by Schneider et al. (2014), including lemma, POS tags, word shapes and features indicating whether the token matches entries in any of several multiword lexicons (WordNet, SemCor, SAID, WikiMwe, English Wiktionary and Multiword Entries on the Phrases.net website), b.) the provided Brown clusters and c.) capitalization features, an auxiliary verb vs. main verb feature and unlexicalized WordNet supersense features. Based on the model, these features are conjoined with the MWE, supersense, or extended label set to form zero-order features. For the closed condition, we exclude the features based on multiword lexicons.

3.2 Baseline: Multinomial Logistic Regression

As a baseline, we predict the label of each word based on the features of the word within a sentence. The multinomial logistic regression models the conditional probability of the label of the ith word, denoted by Y_i, in a sentence $\boldsymbol{x}$ as:

$$p(Y_i = y \mid \boldsymbol{x}, i; \boldsymbol{\lambda}) = \frac{\exp \boldsymbol{\lambda}^\top \mathbf{h}(\boldsymbol{x}, y, i)}{\sum_{y'} \exp \boldsymbol{\lambda}^\top \mathbf{h}(\boldsymbol{x}, y', i)}, \quad (1)$$

where $\mathbf{h}$ denotes a feature vector that contains features that describe the token i, and its relationships with some of its adjacent words in $\boldsymbol{x}$ conjoined with the label y. $\boldsymbol{\lambda}$ denotes a vector of feature weights and is learned from data.

Constraints on labels are not taken into account during training. We incorporated these constraints during testing in a greedy manner: For the ith word, we considered only the labels that make it valid with respect to the bigram label constraints based on the predicted label for the $(i - 1)$th word.

3.3 Conditional Random Field

In the linear chain CRF (Lafferty et al., 2001), the conditional probability of a valid label sequence $\boldsymbol{y}$ of words in a sentence $\boldsymbol{x}$ is modeled as:

$$p(\boldsymbol{y} \mid \boldsymbol{x}; \boldsymbol{\lambda}) = \frac{\exp \boldsymbol{\lambda}^\top \sum_{i=1}^{|\boldsymbol{x}|} \mathbf{h}(\boldsymbol{x}, y_i, y_{i-1}, i)}{\sum_{\boldsymbol{y}'} \exp \boldsymbol{\lambda}^\top \sum_{i=1}^{|\boldsymbol{x}|} \mathbf{h}(\boldsymbol{x}, y_i', y_{i-1}', i)},$$

$$(2)$$

where $\boldsymbol{\lambda}$ is a vector of feature weights shared across all positions (i.e., words) and sentences. The feature vector $\mathbf{h}$ contains the zero-order features described above and the first-order features. The first-order features model the dependencies between the label of ith word and that of $(i + 1)$th word. We assume a dummy label y_0 for notational convenience.

In both training and testing, we ensure that the constraints on the consecutive labels are satisfied. The label of the ith word only depends on the token sequence, its offset in the sentence and the labels of $(i-1)$th and $(i+1)$th words. Dynamic programming is used for exact inference; runtime is quadratic in the size of the label set and linear in the sequence length. We maximize ℓ_2-regularized log-likelihood using L-BFGS to learn the feature weights $\boldsymbol{\lambda}$:

$$\sum_{(\boldsymbol{x}, \boldsymbol{y} \in \mathcal{D})} \log p(\boldsymbol{y} \mid \boldsymbol{x}; \boldsymbol{\lambda}) - \alpha_1 \|\boldsymbol{\lambda}_1\|_2^2 - \alpha_2 \|\boldsymbol{\lambda}_2\|_2^2,$$

$$(3)$$

where $\mathcal{D}$ contains all training instances, $\boldsymbol{\lambda}_1$ ($\boldsymbol{\lambda}_2$) corresponds to the parameters for zero-order (first-order) features, and α_1 (α_2) is the regularization strength for zero-order (first-order) feature weights. In our preliminary experiments, we found that using different regularization strengths for zero-order and first-order features can benefit accuracy.

3.4 Double-Chained CRF

We propose a double-chained CRF (2-CRF) that factors the labels into separate MWE and supersense annotations. Such a model has been used for joint POS tagging and noun-phrase chunking by Sutton et al. (2007). The model is illustrated in Fig. 1; the heart of the difference lies in restricting first-order dependencies within MWE or supersense labels, not the combination of the two.

Concretely, the 2-CRF separates the zero-order features for MWE and for supersense tags. Second, while the traditional chain-structured CRF has a feature for each pair of labels in the extended label set, the 2-CRF introduces first-order features capturing each consecutive pair of MWE labels, and (separately) each consecutive pair of supersense labels. This model removes some repetitive parameters. For example, instead of having parameters to capture the relation between consecutive B and I tags paired with all supersenses, 2-CRF will have only one parameter. Moreover, if the feature weights $\boldsymbol{\lambda}$ for all the features between m_i and s_i pairs are zero, the 2-CRF model is equivalent to two separate CRFs for the two tasks. Therefore, it has a flexibility to learn the parameters for the two tasks jointly or separately. Due to this kind of flexibility, we expect that the 2-CRF model has a better generalization ability.

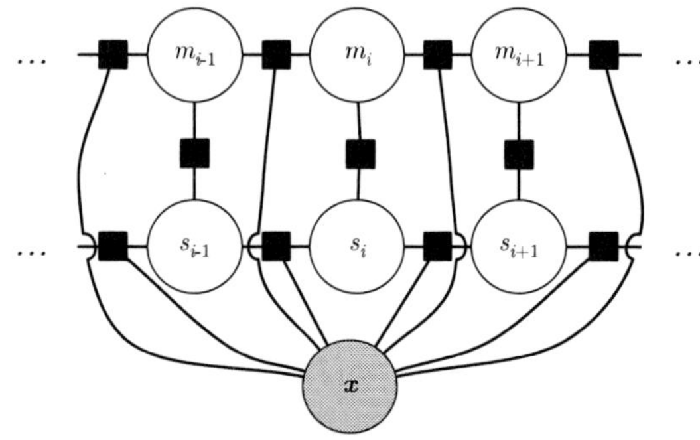

Figure 1: Double-chained CRF expressed as a factor graph: $\boldsymbol{x}$ is the whole sentence. For a token in position i, its MWE label is m_i and its supersense tag is s_i.

For a sentence $\boldsymbol{x}$ with a valid label sequence $\boldsymbol{y} = (\boldsymbol{m}, \boldsymbol{s})$, where $\boldsymbol{m}$ denotes the MWE tag sequence and $\boldsymbol{s}$ denotes supersense tag sequence, the conditional probability of $(\boldsymbol{m}, \boldsymbol{s})$ given $\boldsymbol{x}$ is defined as:

$$p(\boldsymbol{m}, \boldsymbol{s} \mid \boldsymbol{x}) =$$

$$\frac{\exp \boldsymbol{\lambda}^\top \sum_{i=1}^{|\boldsymbol{x}|} \mathbf{h}(\boldsymbol{x}, m_i, s_i, m_{i-1}, s_{i-1}, i)}{\sum_{\boldsymbol{m}', \boldsymbol{s}'} \exp \boldsymbol{\lambda}^\top \sum_{i=1}^{|\boldsymbol{x}|} \mathbf{h}(\boldsymbol{x}, m_i', s_i', m_{i-1}', s_{i-1}', i)},$$

$$(4)$$

where the feature vector function $\mathbf{h}$ can be written as:

$$\mathbf{h}(\boldsymbol{x}, m_i, s_i, m_{i-1}, s_{i-1}, i) =$$
$$\langle \mathbf{h}^m(\boldsymbol{x}, m_i, i); \mathbf{h}^s(\boldsymbol{x}, s_i, i); \qquad (5)$$
$$\mathbf{h}^{mm}(m_i, m_{i-1}); \mathbf{h}^{ss}(s_i, s_{i-1}); \mathbf{h}^{ms}(m_i, s_i) \rangle.$$

$\mathbf{h}$ contains the following features: two copies of the zero-order features conjoined with the MWE tag m_i and supersense tag s_i, first-order features between m_i and m_{i-1}, s_i and s_{i-1} and m_i and s_i.

Similar to the CRF, we enforce label constraints on the MWE label sequence both at training and prediction time.

Inference can be carried out exactly using similar dynamic programming algorithms to those used for the CRF. Training is carried out as for the CRF (i.e., ℓ_2-regularized log-likelihood; see Eq. 3).[8]

4 Experiments

4.1 Experimental Setup

We compare the performance of the following four models that use exactly the same input features §3.1:

- Multinomial logistic regression (MLR) as described in §3.2 (a zero-order model)

- Structured perceptron as used by Schneider and Smith (2015) with the same set of features (first-order, similar to our CRF)

- CRF as described in §3.3

- Double-chained CRF as described in §3.4

We used the AMALGrAM[9] code base for feature extraction (Schneider and Smith, 2015). For hyperparameter tuning, we hold out 30% randomly selected training samples of the DiMSUM dataset as validation data. Using preliminary experiments on validation data, we set the number of L-BFGS iterations for multinomial logistic regression, CRF, and 2-CRF as 100, 120, and 120, respectively. We set the number of iterations of averaged perceptron algorithm for structured percepron as 10. We also impose a percept cutoff of 3 on the minimum number of occurrences for a zero-order percept to be considered in the models. We use validation data to tune α_1 and α_2 (where applicable) hyperparameters. After tuning the parameters, we use the whole DiMSUM training dataset to train the models.

4.2 Results and Discussion

Tables 1 and 2 show the results for the closed and open conditions. The selected hyperparameters α_1 and α_2 are shown for each model. In each table, we show the results on our held-out validation data and on the DiMSUM test datasets.

The official submitted systems are marked with * in the tables.[10] For the closed condition, the 2-CRF had not completed training, so our entry was the CRF; it achieved first place.

For the open condition, training of 2-CRF had only completed 80 iterations at the submission deadline, so that is what was entered (it achieved second place). We report those scores, as well as the slightly improved scores obtained after 120 iterations.

Across the board, there is roughly a 9% decrease in the F_1 score when we move from validation to DiMSUM test datasets. This is not surprising because the validation and DiMSUM datasets represent different text genres and styles.

We measured the statistical significance of the difference between the structured perceptron (SP) and the other methods. We used a randomization test (Yeh, 2000) at the sentence level to estimate the confidence level of the difference (p-value < 0.05). We indicate in Tables 1 and 2 in italics the cases where the improvement over the structured perceptron is significant.

In the closed condition, the 2-CRF model leads to the highest F_1 scores for all evaluation metrics. Interestingly, the structured perceptron improves on MWE but suffers on supersenses, relative to the zero-order MLR model.[11] CRF and 2-CRF show improvements against MLR on both tasks, with the latter winning overall on validation and (slightly) on test data.

In the open condition, we see similar patterns except a few cases: structured perceptron has the highest F_1 score in MWE identification on validation data and MLR slightly outperforms 2-CRF in supersense tagging on test data. However, the differences are not statistically significant over 2-CRF, and it has the highest combined score.

Finally, we observe that adding the features based

---

[8]An open source efficient cython implementation of our method will be made publicly available at: `https://github.com/mjhosseini/2-CRF-MWE`.

[9]`http://www.cs.cmu.edu/~ark/LexSem`

[10]The official results of the shared task are based on the macroaverages of the per-domain scores, while we have done the detailed analysis based on microaverage scores of the whole dataset. Our system got combined macroaverage F_1 score of 57.10% for the closed condition and 57.71% for the open condition.

[11]The MLR model could potentially be improved with dynamic programming instead of greedy prediction.

	# iter.	α_1	α_2	Validation Data			DiMSUM Data		
				MWE	SST	Combined	MWE	SST	Combined
MLR	100	1.6	-	58.68	*66.24*	64.96	49.84	*57.14*	*56.04*
SP	10	-	-	63.39	65.15	64.83	52.37	55.85	55.29
CRF*	120	1.6	0.32	60.76	*66.66*	*65.57*	53.93	*57.47*	*56.88*
2-CRF	120	1.6	0.12	**64.13**	***67.02***	***66.46***	**54.02**	*57.89*	*57.23*

Table 1: Closed condition: Results on validation (left) and DiMSUM data (right) for multinomial logistic regression (MLR), structured perceptron (SP), CRF, and 2-CRF models. The hyperparameters and F_1 scores for identifying MWEs, supersenses, and their combination are reported. The best result in each column is bolded. The results that are significant over SP (p-value < 0.05) are italicized. The system denoted by * is our official submission for the supervised closed condition.

	# iter	α_1	α_2	Validation Data			DiMSUM Data		
				MWE	SST	Combined	MWE	SST	Combined
MLR	100	2.4	-	62.75	*66.40*	65.76	51.71	***58.04***	*57.08*
SP	10	-	-	**69.21**	65.72	66.37	56.79	55.93	56.08
CRF	120	1.2	0.12	66.78	*66.74*	66.75	56.61	*57.62*	*57.44*
2-CRF	120	1.6	0.2	67.30	***67.29***	***67.29***	56.42	*57.87*	***57.61***
2-CRF*	80	1.6	0.2	67.37	*66.78*	66.89	**57.24**	*57.64*	*57.57*

Table 2: Open condition: Results on validation (left) and DiMSUM data (right) for multinomial logistic regression (MLR), structured perceptron, CRF, and 2-CRF models. The hyperparameters and F_1 scores for identifying MWEs, supersenses, and their combination are reported. In the open condition, we have added features using the following lists of English MWEs based on: WordNet, SemCor, SAID, WikiMwe, English Wiktionary, Multiword Entries on the Phrases.net website (Schneider et al., 2014). The best result in each column is bolded. The results that are significant over SP are italicized. The system denoted by * is our official submission for the open condition.

on multiword lexicons (moving from supervised closed to open condition) improves MWE identification, without harming supersense tagging performance. The increase in the performance of MWE identification is statistically significant across all methods and test datasets.

5 Conclusions

We presented the results of four models for the joint prediction of MWE annotations and supersense annotations: multinomial logistic regression, structured perceptron, CRF and double-chained CRF. We found that double-chained CRF performs well on both tasks. We showed that, consistent with past work, adding features based on multiword lexicons improves the performance of all models.

Acknowledgments

We are grateful to Nathan Schneider for helping us use his feature extraction codebase. We also thank Lingpeng Kong and the reviewers for helpful feedback. This research was supported in part by DARPA DEFT (FA8750-12-2-0342), National Science Foundation (DBI-1355899), the American Cancer Society (127332-RSG-15-097-01-TBG), and Solid Tumor Translational Research.

References

Peter F. Brown, Peter V. Desouza, Robert L. Mercer, Vincent J Della Pietra, and Jenifer C. Lai. 1992. Class-based n-gram models of natural language. *Computational Linguistics*, 18(4):467–479.

Mauro Cettolo, Christian Girardi, and Marcello Federico. 2012. Wit3: Web inventory of transcribed and translated talks. In *Proceedings of EAMT*.

Dirk Hovy, Anders Johannsen, and Anders Søgaard. 2015. User review sites as a resource for large-scale sociolinguistic studies. In *Proceedings of WWW*.

Anders Johannsen, Dirk Hovy, Héctor Martinez, Barbara Plank, and Anders Sgaard. 2014. More or less supervised super-sense tagging of Twitter. In *Proceedings of *SEM*.

Lingpeng Kong, Nathan Schneider, Swabha

Swayamdipta, Archna Bhatia, Chris Dyer, and Noah A. Smith. 2014. A dependency parser for tweets. In *Proc. of EMNLP*.

John Lafferty, Andrew McCallum, and Fernando C.N. Pereira. 2001. Conditional random fields: Probabilistic models for segmenting and labeling sequence data. In *Proc. of ICML*.

Lance A. Ramshaw and Mitchell P. Marcus. 1995. Text chunking using transformation-based learning. arXiv preprint cmp-lg/9505040.

Nathan Schneider and Noah A. Smith. 2015. A corpus and model integrating multiword expressions and supersenses. In *Proc. of NAACL*.

Nathan Schneider, Emily Danchik, Chris Dyer, and Noah A. Smith. 2014. Discriminative lexical semantic segmentation with gaps: running the mwe gamut. *Transactions of the Association for Computational Linguistics*, 2:193–206.

Nathan Schneider, Dirk Hovy, Anders Johannsen, and Marine Carpuat. 2016. SemEval 2016 Task 10: Detecting Minimal Semantic Units and their Meanings (DiMSUM). In *Proc. of SemEval*, San Diego, California, USA, June.

Nathan Schneider. 2014. *Lexical Semantic Analysis in Natural Language Text*. Ph.D. thesis, Carnegie Mellon University.

Charles Sutton, Andrew McCallum, and Khashayar Rohanimanesh. 2007. Dynamic conditional random fields: Factorized probabilistic models for labeling and segmenting sequence data. *The Journal of Machine Learning Research*, 8:693–723.

Alexander Yeh. 2000. More accurate tests for the statistical significance of result differences. In *Proceedings of COLING*.

ICL-HD at SemEval-2016 Task 10: Improving the Detection of Minimal Semantic Units and their Meanings with an Ontology and Word Embeddings

Angelika Kirilin and **Felix Krauss** and **Yannick Versley**

Institute for Computational Linguistics
Ruprecht-Karls-University
Heidelberg

{kirilin,krauss,versley}@cl.uni-heidelberg.de

Abstract

This paper presents our system submitted for SemEval 2016 Task 10: Detecting Minimal Semantic Units and their Meanings (DiM-SUM; Schneider, Hovy, et al., 2016). We extend AMALGrAM (Schneider and Smith, 2015) by tapping two additional information sources. The first information source uses a semantic knowledge base (YAGO3; Suchanek et al., 2007) to improve supersense tagging (SST) for named entities. The second information source employs word embeddings (GloVe; Pennington et al., 2014) to capture fine-grained latent semantics and therefore improving the supersense identification for both nouns and verbs. We conduct a detailed evaluation and error analysis for our features and come to the conclusion that both our extensions lead to an improved detection for SST.

1 Introduction

The SemEval 2016 Task 10 on Detecting Minimal Semantic Units of Meaning (DiMSUM) is concerned with the identification of semantic classes called supersenses for single words as well as multi-word expressions (MWEs).

Identifying supersenses in text allows for abstractions that characterize word meanings beyond superficial orthography (Schneider and Smith, 2015) as well as inferring representations that move towards language independence (Schneider, Mohit, et al., 2013). It has been used to extend named entity recognition (Ciaramita and Johnson, 2003) and to support supervised word sense disambiguation as it

provides partial disambiguation (Ciaramita and Altun, 2006; Ciaramita and Johnson, 2003) as well as in syntactic parse re-ranking (Koo et al., 2005) as latent semantic features.

The addition of MWEs - idiosyncratic interpretations that cross word boundaries (Sag et al., 2002) - takes into account that the supersense of a MWE is usually not predictable from the meaning of the individual lexemes. The Task moreover distinguishes between continuous MWEs like "$high\_school_{\text{n.group}}$" and discontinuous (*gappy*) MWEs like "*track* people $down_{\text{v.social}}$". The inventory of supersenses used for the task - 41 supersense classes, consisting of 26 noun and 15 verb supersenses - is derived from WordNet's top-level hypernyms in the taxonomy. They are designed to be broad enough to encompass all nouns and verbs (Miller, 1990; Fellbaum, 1990).

2 Related Work

Schneider and Smith (2015) are the first to approach SST and MWE detection jointly with a discriminative model. Most of the previous work focuses on each of the tasks in separate. Sag et al. (2002) tried to raise attention for the issue of MWEs in general and analyzed different types of MWE. Baldwin et al. (2003) employed latent semantic analysis to determine the decomposability of MWEs. Finally many MWE lexicons have been built for different purposes which is why Schneider et al. picked up the issue to address MWE annotation for general purposes (Schneider, Danchik, et al., 2014; Schneider, Onuffer, et al., 2014).

Ciaramita and Johnson (2003) first trained and tested a discriminative model for SST of unambigu-

Proceedings of SemEval-2016, pages 937–945,
San Diego, California, June 16-17, 2016. ©2016 Association for Computational Linguistics

ous nouns on data extracted from different versions of WordNet and achieved an accuracy of slightly over 52%. Curran (2005) applied an unsupervised approach based on vector-space word similarity and achieved 63% accuracy on the same data used by Ciaramita and Johnson (2003). When revisiting the task Ciaramita and Altun (2006) achieved between 70% and 77% F-score using a HMM sequence tagger.

3 System Description

3.1 Baseline System

We use AMALGrAM 2.0 (Schneider and Smith, 2015) as our baseline system. The model uses a first-order structured perceptron (Collins, 2002) with averaging. It involves a linear scoring function, a Viterbi algorithm that chooses the highest-scoring valid output tag sequence and an online learning algorithm that determines the best tagging given the current model.

We contrast four feature sets for full SST: Schneider and Smith (2015) most effective feature set which is further described in section 3.2, those baseline features plus YAGO feature (3.3), baseline features plus GloVe word embeddings (3.4), and finally a feature set that combines all the above mentioned.

3.2 Baseline Features

The feature set incorporates three components: the first is Schneider, Danchik, et al. (2014) basic MWE features, second is Brown clusters and the last component is WordNet synset features (Schneider and Smith, 2015). Basic MWE features analyze word n-grams, character pre- and suffixes, and POS tags, as well as lexicon entries that match lemmas of MWE in the sentence. We use four of the ten available lookup lexicons: *semcor_mwes* including all MWEs in SemCor (Miller et al., 1993), *WordNet_mwes* containing all MWEs from WordNet (Fellbaum, 1998), *phrases_dot_net* which is a phrase idiom lexicon[1], *wikimwe* which is mined from English Wikipedia (Hartmann et al., 2012), and *enwikt* consisting of all MWE entries in English Wiktionary. The second component of the baseline feature set provides un-supervised distributional word clusters in the form

of Brown clusters (Brown et al., 1992). Those clusters reflect lexical generalizations that are useful for syntactic and semantic analysis tasks and are therefore suitable for our task. The last component of the feature set helps predicting supersenses by creating possible supersense candidates from WordNet synsets.

3.3 YAGO Feature

We implement a YAGO lookup component that provides semantic information as an additional feature for the AMALGrAM system with the purpose of improving SST for named entities. YAGO (Yet Another Great Anthology; Suchanek et al., 2007) is a knowledge resource that combines the structural benefits from the WordNet taxonomy with the richness of Wikipedia's categories system. This renders it ideal for our task by enabling us to retrieve WordNet hypernyms for many different named entities. The following part describes how we look up potential concepts in YAGO, how we find potential names of YAGO concepts within the text and how we encode the returned results as a feature for AMALGrAM.

There is no guarantee that the named entities contained in training or test data appear in the same surface form as they are stored in YAGO (e.g. *"Elvis"* vs. *"Elvis_Presley"*). We apply some heuristics should an initial query with a potential named entity not yield a result:

1. Capitalize the initial character of each token [2]

2. Try to retrieve the exact entry via Wikipedias "redirectedFrom" links that are included in YAGO (e.g. $\langle Elvis\_Presley \rangle$, $\langle redirectedFrom \rangle$, $\langle$ *"Elvis"* @eng$\rangle$)

3. Drop all tokens except the first and repeat the previous steps (only applicable for sequences)

For the detection of named entities during feature extraction we rely on the gold POS tag annotation in the provided data. Whenever a token appears with a "PROPN" tag (e.g. Germany $_{PROPN}$) we query it on YAGO. If the token is followed by a continuous sequence of further "PROPN" tagged tokens (e.g.

---

[1]http://www.phrases.net/

[2]We found that we get the best results when capitalizing every candidate expression.

athlete	fullback	physical_entity
back	living_thing	player
causal_agent	object	preserver
contestant	organism	running_back
defender	person	whole
football_player		

Table 1: WordNet hypernyms contained in the YAGO-Entry: "Jérôme_Boateng".

FC$_{\text{PROPN}}$ Bayern$_{\text{PROPN}}$ Munich$_{\text{PROPN}}$) the whole sequence linked with underscores is used as the search query.

The feature extraction is done in the following way: In a first step we iterate over all supersense bearing singleton and MWE nouns in our training data and try to query them in YAGO. If we have a match we extract the WordNet hypernyms for the found entity. An example for a successful query can be seen in Table 1. We accumulate a count of observed WordNet hypernyms for each supersense. From the count we calculate a tf-idf whereby the supersenses are seen as the "documents" and the WordNet hypernyms as "words". What we obtain from this procedure is a tf-idf index that tells us the significance of a WordNet hypernym for a given supersense based on our training data. We require that a WordNet hypernym has to appear at least three times with a supersense otherwise its tf-idf is set to zero for this supersense. During feature extraction we provide the information from extracted WordNet hypernyms in two ways: The straightforward way is to provide each WordNet hypernym as is. With the second feature we make use of our precomputed tf-idf index by calculating a supersense ranking whenever we find a candidate entity in YAGO. For each supersense we add up the tf-idf values of the WordNet hypernyms found with the current candidate entity. If the entity is linked to many WordNet hypernyms with high tf-idf values for a certain supersense the respective supersense will receive a high rank. [3]

3.4 GloVe Feature

The second novel feature we provide is based on word embeddings which are representations of the meaning of words in terms of real-valued vectors in a low-dimensional vector space. Because such embeddings provide generalizations over the meaning of words, including words that do not occur in the training data, they are often used as a general way to improve accuracy in the form of extra word features (Turian et al., 2010). Two of the most popular methods to create such a mapping include: global matrix factorization and the local context window method. Pennington et al. (2014) combine both methods in the GloVe word embeddings. The available word vectors are derived from a 2014 Wikipedia[4] dump and the Gigaword 5 corpus[5]. Both sources together comprise 400,000 word types and there are four versions available that differ in the size of their dimensions: 50, 100, 200 and 300. GloVe word embeddings capture fine-grained semantic and syntactic regularities using a global log-bilinear regression model with a weighted least-squares objective. The training objective of GloVe is to learn word vectors such that their dot product equals the logarithm of the words' probability of co-occurrence.

We incorporate our feature set using a similar method to the lookup lexicons. GloVe word embeddings are essentially a dictionary where each entry consists of a word type and their word vector. If a given lowercase token matches a GloVe lexicon entry then we extend the feature vector of that token with its corresponding word embeddings. Turian et al. (2010) mention that the weights in word embeddings are not necessarily in a bounded range. If the range of the word embeddings is too large, they will exert more influence than the remaining features. To prevent the word embeddings from exerting too much influence on the prediction when they consist of an unbounded range of real numbers we adopt Turian et al.'s (2010) method of scaling the word vectors. Assuming that all word embeddings are represented in a matrix E: Each row E_i contains the word embeddings of a token, each column E_j represents one dimension of the word embeddings and each cell contains a word embedding E_{ij}. We scale each word vector dimension by a scaling constant σ and the inverse of the standard deviation over

---

[3]We achieve the best results when using the top ranked supersense as well as all additional supersenses that receive at least half of the top ranked supersense's tf-idf score.

[4]http://dumps.wikimedia.org/enwiki/20140102/
[5]https://catalog.ldc.upenn.edu/LDC2011T07

the values across all words:

$$w_{new} = \frac{\sigma * E_{ij}}{stdev(E_j)} \tag{1}$$

4 Experiments

In the following section we present the data we used, then the tools and parameters and finally the results of our experiments.

4.1 Data

Our training and test data consists of the data made available for SemEval 2016 Task 10. The training data includes three harmonized data-sets: STREUSLE 2.1 (Schneider and Smith, 2015), Ritter and Lowlands Twitter dataset (Johannsen et al., 2014). The test set also consists of three sources: online reviews from the TrustPilot corpus (Hovy et al., 2015), tweets from the Tweebank corpus (Kong et al., 2014) and TED talk transcripts (Cettolo et al., 2012; Neubig et al., 2014). All datasets use the 17 Universal POS categories and the extended BIO scheme from Schneider and Smith, 2015. For feature development we used a shuffled held-out portion of the train set.

4.2 Experimental Setup

We conduct the experiments on the aforementioned DiMSUM data sets. We use the AMALGrAM 2.0 tagger as baseline system with the following parameters:[6] four training iterations, features that appeared less than five times were cutoff, a constraint for the decoding process that asserts that the "O" label is never followed by an "I", including loss term and a cost penalty of 100 for errors against recall. Furthermore we use brown clusters and five MWE lexica mentioned in section 3.2. Additionally we create a new tagset that suits the DiMSUM tags. We only consider tags occurring in the DiMSUM training set, yielding $|Y| = 170$ tags.

$$\underbrace{|\{BbOo\}|}_{4} \times \underbrace{(|N| + |V| + |\emptyset|)}_{26+15+1} + \underbrace{|\{Ii\}|}_{2} = 170$$

All evaluation scores where obtained using the evaluation script for SemEval 2016 Task 10.

---

[6]We have been orienting ourselves towards the parameters used in Schneider and Smith (2015).

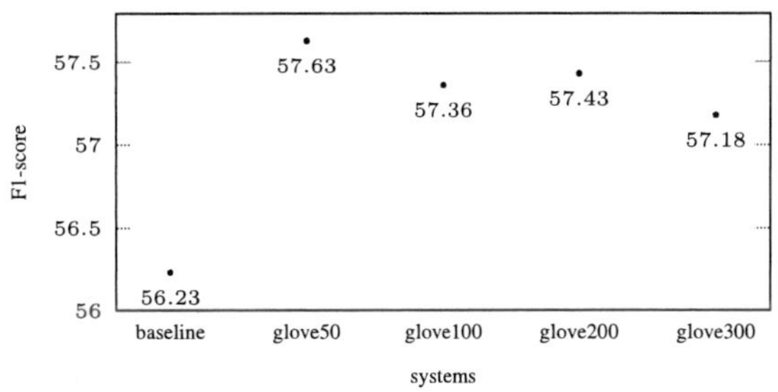

Figure 1: Evaluation of the influence of high dimensional word embeddings on the performance of the baseline system using combined F1-scores.

4.3 YAGO Feature Experiments

The effects of the YAGO feature on AMALGrAM can be seen in Table 5. Compared to the baseline (BL) the WordNet hypernyms have almost no effect on MWE detection (+0.02) while improving SST (+0.64). The supersense rankings improve MWE detection (+0.49) as well as SST (+0.62). Combining the features further improves the detection for MWEs (+0.59) and SST (+1.13).

4.4 GloVe Feature Experiments

The first experiment involves the evaluation of different word embedding dimensions. Figure 1 shows a comparison between the baseline system (BL) which uses no word embeddings and our system adopting GloVe word embeddings with four dimension sizes: 50, 100, 200 and 300. This experiment uses word embeddings in their given real-valued form without scaling them. All systems using word embeddings show improved performance and are approximately one percent higher than the baseline. In this experiment the system performs best with 50 dimensional word embeddings, after which the performance shows a slight decrease with growing vector dimensionality.

The second experiment evaluates the influence of unscaled versus scaled word embeddings using the method of Turian et al. (2010) which we described in section 3.4. Table 2 compares the F1-scores of four systems: the first - *Glove50* - uses unscaled word embedding whereas the remaining three systems scale those word embeddings with varying σ-values (0.01, 0.1 and 1). According to Turian et al. (2010) their method works best with a σ-value that scales the standard derivation to 0.1. With our data

	Glove50	σ=0.01	σ=0.1	σ=1
MWE	57.52	**58.49**	57.71	58.38
SST	57.65	57.14	57.04	**57.98**
combined	57.63	57.36	57.15	**58.05**

Table 2: Influence of unscaled (Glove50) versus scaled word embeddings for MWE, SST and both tags (combined) using F1-score. Last three columns use Turian et al.'s 2010 scaling method with varying σ-values.

	-brown		+brown	
	BL	**Best**	**BL**	**Best**
MWE	58.13	57.69	58.10	**58.38**
SST	56.28	57.43	55.87	**57.98**
combined	56.59	57.47	56.23	**58.05**

Table 3: Comparison of baseline (BL) and our most successful system (Best) with (+brown) and without (-brown) Brown cluster.

that value is $\sigma = 0.1$. However our results contradict Turian et al. (2010) as our experiment shows that $\sigma = 0.01$ is more successful in predicting MWEs whereas $\sigma = 1$ is more suitable for the detection of supersenses as well as both combined.

The third experiment evolves around the interaction between Brown clusters and word embeddings. As both methods have a similar aim - capturing the semantic representation of words - it is of interest to distinguish their influence on the system performance. To accomplish this we train the baseline system (BL) and our most successful system (Glove50, $\sigma = 1$) with (+brown) and without using Brown clusters (-brown). Table 3 represents the resulting F1-scores. Our system profits from the Brown clusters as the F1-scores for all categories (MWE, SST and combined) improves.

4.5 Final System Comparison

Finally we evaluate the combined impact of our features on the performance of the baseline system. Table 5 compares the baseline system plus YAGO, baseline plus GloVe and our combined system using both YAGO and GloVe features (final)[7] with var-

---

[7]This is a revised version of our submitted system for SemEval 2016 where we used our YAGO combined and unscaled

	system	Acc	P	R	F1
MWE	YAGO	91.70	70.43	**50.31**	**58.69**
	GloVe	**91.99**	**73.47**	48.43	58.38
	final	91.70	71.74	47.35	57.05
SST	YAGO	85.02	55.96	58.08	57.00
	GloVe	**85.34**	**56.82**	**59.20**	**57.98**
	final	85.15	56.52	59.09	57.78
combined	YAGO	81.29	57.98	56.60	57.28
	GloVe	**81.81**	**58.97**	**57.15**	**58.05**
	final	81.57	58.49	56.86	57.66

Table 4: Accuracy (Acc), precision (P), recall (R) and F1-score (F1) for MWE detection, SST and both (combined) for the baseline system (BL) + YAGO, BL + GloVe and BL + YAGO + GloVe (final).

ious measurements. Our GloVe feature produces the overall best results except for the detection of MWEs due to a decrease in recall. In this case the YAGO feature improves all measures which leads to the highest performance. Although the combination of both features (final) results in an improvement of the baseline the performance mostly ranges in between the results for the individual GloVe and YAGO features.

5 Feature Analysis

To get a deeper understanding of the impact and benefit of our features we conduct the following analyzes. First we compare the coverage of our YAGO lookup with NLTK's WordNet component and examine the accuracy of our ranking feature. Then we analyze the coverage of GloVe on the provided data set and give a detailed recall analysis for each tag.

5.1 YAGO coverage

For the coverage comparison we extract all supersense bearing nouns from the whole gold annotated DiMSUM data set. We query the extracted nouns and count the ones that are found exclusively with the lookup component of the YAGO feature and not by NLTK-WordNet. Figure 2 (see Appendix A) displays the results for each supersense that has at

---

GloVe100 features. The results of our submitted system were slightly better (combined F1-score 57.77%), but could not be reproduced after revising our system.

	BL	Hyp	Rank	H+R
MWE	58.10	58.12	58.59	**58.69**
SST	55.87	56.61	56.49	**57.00**
combined	56.23	56.86	56.84	**57.28**

Table 5: Evaluation of the YAGO feature with F1-score comparing baseline (BL), baseline + WordNet hypernym features (Hyp), baseline + ranking features (Rank) and baseline + both additional features combined (H+R).

least 100 associated nouns. Looking at the results we observe a decreased coverage of the WordNet lookup for nouns associated to supersenses that tend to have an increased proportion of named entities, e.g. "n.location", "n.group" or "n.person". For the YAGO lookup this correlation is inverted resulting in an increased amount of additionally found supersense bearing nouns for the previously described supersenses.

We also investigate the YAGO feature's ranking component. First we extract a tf-idf index from the DiMSUM training data set. We use the index to generate a ranking for each expression that we are able to detect with our YAGO feature on the test data set. Figure 3 (see Appendix A) shows the relative distribution of gold supersenses for the first five ranking positions. In this evaluation, the correct supersense is present in the first two ranks for the majority of cases. This experiment also indicates how well the detection of supersense bearing nouns performs. E.g. out of 413 nouns in the DiMSUM test set that are marked with the "n.person" supersense, 146 were detected and received a rank.

5.2 GloVe errors

We conduct two experiments to assess our GloVe feature: The first experiment examines the number of tokens for both the train and test set for which there is a GloVe word vector. As described in section 3.4 we use lowercase tokens and match them to their corresponding GloVe word embeddings if possible. With this method we get a coverage of 97.35% for the train set and 94.32% for the test set. Which means that almost every word of the DiMSUM data set is represented by GloVe word embeddings.

To fully assess our GloVe feature we investigate the improvement and deterioration of each tag with our second experiment. To accomplish this we compare the difference between the F1-score of our system and the F1-score of the baseline (F1-score discrepancy) for each tag. Since there are two types of tags - MWE and supersenses - we conduct an analysis for each type. We provide separate evaluations for tokens that have already been seen in the training set (seen) and tokens that have never been seen before (unseen). Firstly we examine the F1-score discrepancy for all supersenses. Figure 4 (see Appendix A) shows the result for all supersenses that occur more than 50 times in the test data set having a F1-score discrepancy that is higher than |0.5|. Most supersenses - whether they have been previously seen in the training set or not - improve with the use of the GloVe feature. An exception is "n.event" - a supersense whose F1-score decreases by -8.2% for seen tokens. The average F1-score discrepancy of all noun and verb supersense tags is +0.59; this further confirms our claim that the majority of the supersenses improve with the adoption of the GloVe feature. Lastly we examine the F1-score discrepancy for all MWE tags that occur more than 50 times in the test set. The results can be seen in Figure 5 (see Appendix A). The detection of "I" on seen tokens decreases by 13.2%, whereas the detection of "B" improves for unseen tokens by +8.2%. Overall the GloVe feature has a slightly positive influence on MWE detection.

6   Conclusion

Both YAGO and GloVe are effective in improving the performance for SST and MWE detection. Our experiments show that the GloVe word embeddings provide information in addition to Brown clusters that help the system further distinguish between tags. Unfortunately the benefits of our features don't add up but instead balance each other out. Learning the reason for this could be subject to future work. One could also replace the heuristics we employed for the detection of named entities in the text with more sophisticated named entity resolution techniques. Another possibility would be the comparison of the effect of different word embeddings on the performance. It might also be advantageous to further research the scaling of word embeddings.

References

Baldwin, Timothy, Colin Bannard, Takaaki Tanaka, and Dominic Widdows (2003). "An Empirical Model of Multiword Expression Decomposability". In: *Proceedings of the ACL 2003 Workshop on Multiword Expressions: Analysis, Acquisition and Treatment - Volume 18*. MWE '03. Sapporo, Japan: Association for Computational Linguistics, pp. 89–96.

Brown, Peter F, Peter V Desouza, Robert L Mercer, Vincent J Della Pietra, and Jenifer C Lai (1992). "Class-based n-gram models of natural language". In: *Computational linguistics* 18.4, pp. 467–479.

Cettolo, Mauro, Christian Girardi, and Marcello Federico (2012). "Wit3: Web inventory of transcribed and translated talks". In: *Proceedings of the 16th Conference of the European Association for Machine Translation (EAMT)*, pp. 261–268.

Ciaramita, Massimiliano and Yasemin Altun (2006). "Broad-coverage sense disambiguation and information extraction with a supersense sequence tagger". In: *Proceedings of the 2006 Conference on Empirical Methods in Natural Language Processing*. Association for Computational Linguistics, pp. 594–602.

Ciaramita, Massimiliano and Mark Johnson (2003). "Supersense tagging of unknown nouns in WordNet". In: *Proceedings of the 2003 conference on Empirical methods in natural language processing*. Association for Computational Linguistics, pp. 168–175.

Collins, Michael (2002). "Discriminative training methods for Hidden Markov Models: Theory and experiments with perceptron algorithms". In: *Proceedings of the ACL-02 conference on Empirical methods in natural language processing-Volume 10*. Association for Computational Linguistics, pp. 1–8.

Curran, James R (2005). "Supersense tagging of unknown nouns using semantic similarity". In: *Proceedings of the 43rd Annual Meeting on Association for Computational Linguistics*. Association for Computational Linguistics, pp. 26–33.

Fellbaum, Christiane (1990). "English verbs as a semantic net". In: *International Journal of Lexicography* 3.4, pp. 278–301.

– (1998). *WordNet: An Electronic Lexical Database*. MIT Press.

Hartmann, Silvana, György Szarvas, and Iryna Gurevych (2012). "Mining multiword terms from Wikipedia". In: *Semi-Automatic Ontology Development: Processes and Resources*, pp. 226–258.

Hovy, Dirk, Anders Johannsen, and Anders Søgaard (2015). "User review sites as a resource for large-scale sociolinguistic studies". In: *Proceedings of the 24th International Conference on World Wide Web*. International World Wide Web Conferences Steering Committee, pp. 452–461.

Johannsen, Anders, Dirk Hovy, Héctor Martinez, Barbara Plank, and Anders Søgaard (2014). "More or less supervised super-sense tagging of Twitter". In: *The 3rd Joint Conference on Lexical and Computational Semantics (*SEM)*. Dublin, Ireland.

Kong, Lingpeng, Nathan Schneider, Swabha Swayamdipta, Archna Bhatia, Chris Dyer, and Noah A Smith (2014). "A dependency parser for tweets". In: *Proceedings of Conference on Empirical Methods In Natural Language Processing (EMNLP)*, pp. 1001–1012.

Koo, Terry and Michael Collins (2005). "Hidden-variable models for discriminative reranking". In: *Proceedings of the conference on Human Language Technology and Empirical Methods in Natural Language Processing*. Association for Computational Linguistics, pp. 507–514.

Miller, George A (1990). "Nouns in WordNet: a lexical inheritance system". In: *International journal of Lexicography* 3.4, pp. 245–264.

Miller, George A, Claudia Leacock, Randee Tengi, and Ross T Bunker (1993). "A semantic concordance". In: *Proceedings of the workshop on Human Language Technology*. Association for Computational Linguistics, pp. 303–308.

Neubig, Graham, Katsuhito Sudoh, Yusuke Oda, Kevin Duh, Hajime Tsukada, and Masaaki Nagata (2014). "The NAIST-NTT Ted Talk Treebank". In: *International Workshop on Spoken Language Translation*.

Pennington, Jeffrey, Richard Socher, and Christopher D Manning (2014). "GloVe: Global Vectors for Word Representation." In: *EMNLP*. Vol. 14, pp. 1532–1543.

Sag, Ivan A, Timothy Baldwin, Francis Bond, Ann Copestake, and Dan Flickinger (2002). "Multiword expressions: A pain in the neck for NLP". In: *Computational Linguistics and Intelligent Text Processing*. Springer, pp. 1–15.

Schneider, Nathan, Emily Danchik, Chris Dyer, and Noah A Smith (2014). "Discriminative lexical semantic segmentation with gaps: running the MWE gamut". In: *Transactions of the Association for Computational Linguistics* 2, pp. 193–206.

Schneider, Nathan, Dirk Hovy, Anders Johannsen, and Marine Carpuat (2016). "SemEval 2016 Task 10: Detecting Minimal Semantic Units and their Meanings (DiMSUM)". In: *Proc. of SemEval*. San Diego, California, USA.

Schneider, Nathan, Behrang Mohit, Chris Dyer, Kemal Olflazer, and Noah A Smith (2013). "Supersense tagging for Arabic: the MT-in-the-middle attack". In: Association for Computational Linguistics.

Schneider, Nathan, Spencer Onuffer, Nora Kazour, Emily Danchik, Michael T Mordowanec, Henrietta Conrad, and Noah A Smith (2014). "Comprehensive annotation of multiword expressions in a social web corpus". In: *Proceedings of the Language Resources and Evaluation Conference (LREC)*.

Schneider, Nathan and Noah A Smith (2015). "A corpus and model integrating multiword expressions and supersenses". In: *Proceedings of the Conference of the North American Chapter of the Association for Computational Linguistics: Human Language Technologies*, pp. 1537–1547.

Suchanek, Fabian M, Gjergji Kasneci, and Gerhard Weikum (2007). "Yago: a core of semantic knowledge". In: *Proceedings of the 16th international conference on World Wide Web*. ACM, pp. 697–706.

Turian, Joseph, Lev Ratinov, and Yoshua Bengio (2010). "Word representations: a simple and general method for semi-supervised learning". In: *Proceedings of the 48th annual meeting of the association for computational linguistics*. Association for Computational Linguistics, pp. 384–394.

Appendix A

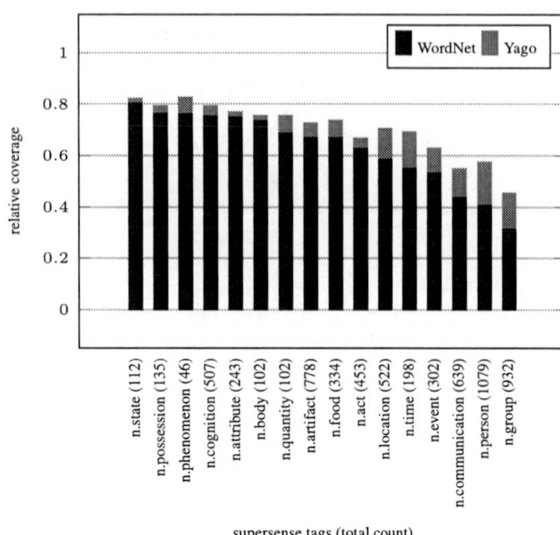

Figure 2: Additional nouns from the DiMSUM dataset found with the YAGO feature.

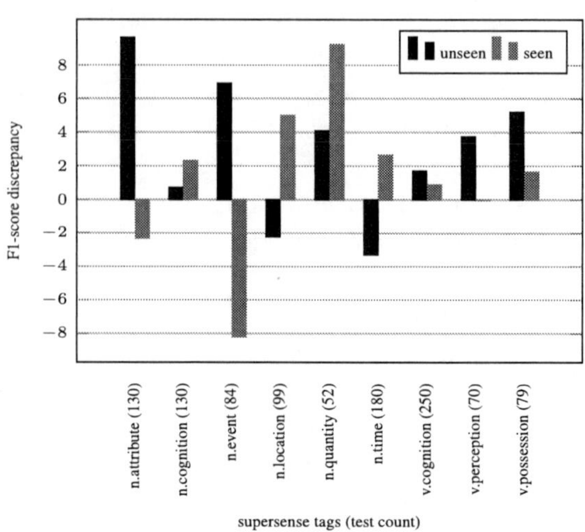

Figure 4: F1-score discrepancy higher than |0.5| between baseline and best system using GloVe feature for supersense tags that occur more than 50 times in the test set distinguishing between seen and unseen tokens.

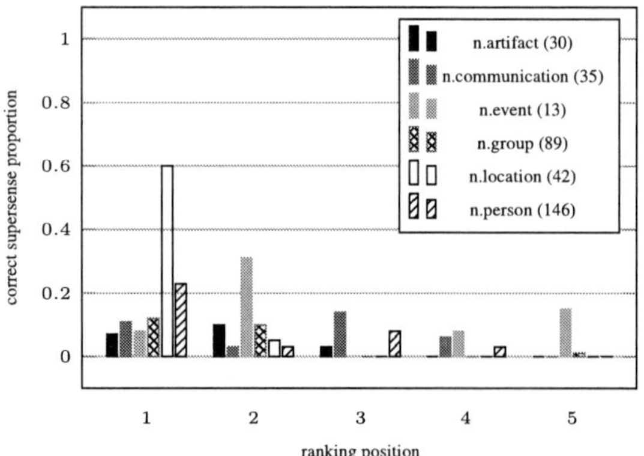

Figure 3: Normalized distribution of gold supersenses over first five ranks on test set.

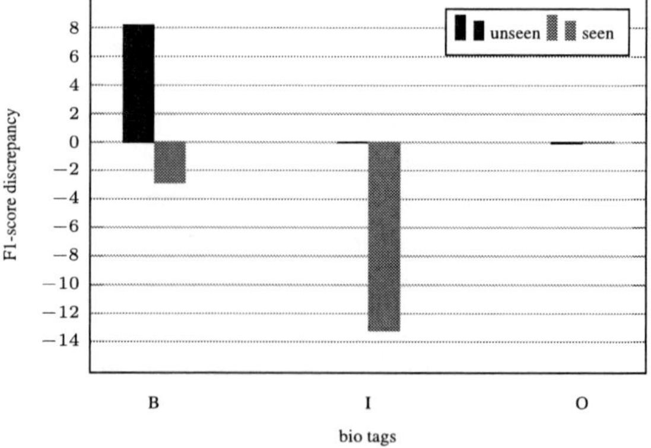

Figure 5: F1-score discrepancy between baseline and best system using GloVe feature for BIO tags that occur more than 50 times in the test set distinguishing between seen and unseen tokens.

VectorWeavers at SemEval-2016 Task 10: From Incremental Meaning to Semantic Unit (phrase by phrase)

Andreas Scherbakov   **Ekaterina Vylomova**   **Fei Liu**   **Timothy Baldwin**

andreas@softwareengineer.pro, evylomova@gmail.com,
fliu3@student.unimelb.edu.au, tb@ldwin.net

The University of Melbourne
VIC 3010, Australia

Abstract

This paper describes an experimental approach to Detection of Minimal Semantic Units and their Meaning (DiMSUM), explored within the framework of SemEval'16 Task 10. The approach is primarily based on a combination of word embeddings and parser-based features, and employs unidirectional incremental computation of compositional embeddings for multiword expressions.

1 Motivation

This paper proposes an approach to the segmentation of POS-tagged English sentences into minimal semantic units along with labelling of units with semantic classes ("supersenses"). Supersenses are "lightweight semantic annotation[s] of text originating in WordNet" (Schneider et al., 2012). Here, we investigate two major ideas, as follows.

First, inspired by Salehi et al. (2015) we hypothesise that word embeddings (WEMBs), e.g. from word2vec (Mikolov et al., 2013a), could be an extremely valuable resource of knowledge for guessing the sense of the word. WEMBs have been shown to represent distinguishable sense components learnt from large training corpora. Many papers have described experiments with word meaning extraction from word embeddings, and demonstrated that it's possible to detect semantic relations between words based on them. Additionally, they may be used to simulate various types of relations between words with simple linear operations over word vectors, and for capturing morphological properties of words (Mikolov et al., 2013b; Vylomova et al., 2015).

However, more generally, they lack any coherent sense-to-value correspondence. According to this, it's natural to attempt to use WEMBs as a source of word meaning information in predicting the senses of semantic units, as part of the larger task of simultaneously detecting minimal semantic units and assigning them meaning. It should be noted that the general term "multiword expression" (MWE) embraces expressions of different types (Baldwin and Kim, 2010). Some of them are meaning-based and the meaning may be preserved under substitution with synonyms, e.g.; other kinds, on the other hand, are semantically idiomatic word combinations, where we would expect WEMBs to have less utility. This first approach is thus an examination of the use of WEMBs in analysing semantic units of mixed semantic compositionality.

Our second hypothesis is that parser-based features will positively impact on the identification of MWEs. Our preliminary explorations showed that the syntactic structure of a text is closely related to the probability of an MWE occurring. For instance, in almost all cases an MWE is fully subsumed within a single clause; in the DiMSUM training set, e.g., there is just one sentence (out of 4800) where this condition is violated. Additionally, all of the components of an MWE tend to be directly connected within a dependency graph. As we observe strong correlation between the distance between two words in a parse tree and their likelihood of forming an MWE, we decided to employ parse trees as a source of features. It may be noted that we initially attempted to create a system where an MWE is treated as a special kind of clause: we modified

946

Proceedings of SemEval-2016, pages 946–952,
San Diego, California, June 16-17, 2016. ©2016 Association for Computational Linguistics

the syntactic tree using knowledge of MWE boundaries in the training corpus and then trained a special version of the parser aware of such modified trees. That special parser version was used to directly produce MWE-labeled clauses over an arbitrary text. Although such a direct approach didn't yield good results, we believe that directly incorporating MWE identification as part of the parsing process is a promising and fruitful direction for future work.

In our submission, we intentionally avoided the use of any pre-existing lexical resources, including multiword lexicons, to better focus our attention on WEMBs.

Our source code is available at:

https://github.com/andreas-softwareengineer-pro/dimsum-semeval2016.

2 Overview

An overall architecture of our system is shown in Figure 1. The neural network consists of three blocks: (1) an *incremental vector (recurrency)* calculator for a candidate MWE; (2) a two-layer perceptron for sense classification; and (3) a (somewhat wider) two-layer perceptron for MWE classification. An incremental vector produced by the first block is used as a source of feature vectors by each of the latter blocks.

The incremental vector calculator produces a vector $v_n \in \mathbb{R}^{D_v}$ for a n-word semantic unit expression:

$$v_n = \tanh \left(\begin{array}{l} W_v(P_n) \times wordvec(w_n) + \\ W_h(P_n) \times hash(w_n) + \\ W_f \times wordfeat(w_n) + \\ W_c(P_n) \times \left\{ \begin{array}{ll} v_{n-1}, & n > 0 \\ seed, & n = 0 \end{array} \right\} \end{array} \right)$$

where $W_v \in \mathbb{R}^{D_v \times M}$, $W_h \in \mathbb{R}^{D_h \times M}$, $W_f \in \mathbb{R}^{D_f \times M}$ and $W_c \in \mathbb{R}^{D_c \times M}$ are parameter matrices, D_v, D_h, D_f and D_c are their respective feature vector sizes, M is the incremental vector size, w_n and P_n are the nth word and its part of speech, respectively, *wordvec* is a word embedding lookup, *hash* is a hash function over characters of the word (used as a means of generating embeddings for unknown words and preserve the ability to distinguish

concrete words), and *wordfeat* produces a vector of various word-wise features (see Table 2), in the spirit of approaches like Drahomíra johanka Spoustová et al. (2009). When calculating v_1 (for a single word), an initial *seed* vector of parameters learnt through backpropagation is used. The motivation behind using the $n = 1$ stage for every MWE (rather than simply starting with $n = 2$ and two word vectors) is based on an intention to avoid switching between word embeddings (that play the role of features) and internally calculated v_i that we expect to better capture the structure of the MWE based on the WEMBs (including following their dimension counts). Also, this technique makes the vector composition learning cycle more frequent w.r.t. the amount of training data, improving the learning rate and the final penalty. This evaluation schema is inspired by the work of Socher et al. (2011; 2010; 2014). It's actually a recursive neural network (RNN) but, in contrast to previously used techniques, the recursion is based on candidate MWEs rather than the whole content of the sentence.

The incremental vector is used as an input to two two-layer perceptrons: one for MWE classification and one for one-hot sense vector learning. Back propagation processing of these two also drives the training of the incremental vector calculator, as described above.

We calculate distance-based features based on positions of two adjacent words in an MWE. A *position* here may mean a position in a sentence, in a parse tree, or, say, inside or outside a quoted phrase. The distance feature vector is supplied as input to the MWE classifier. As an alternative, it may be supplied to the incremental vector calculator input (shown by the dotted line at Figure 1, although no significant difference in performance was observed when we did this).

3 Learning

As briefly mentioned above, our procedure considers n-word expressions incrementally, starting with single words.

3.1 MWE boundary

The system learns a single scalar output value of $+1$ for every extension from $(n-1)$-word prefix to a n-

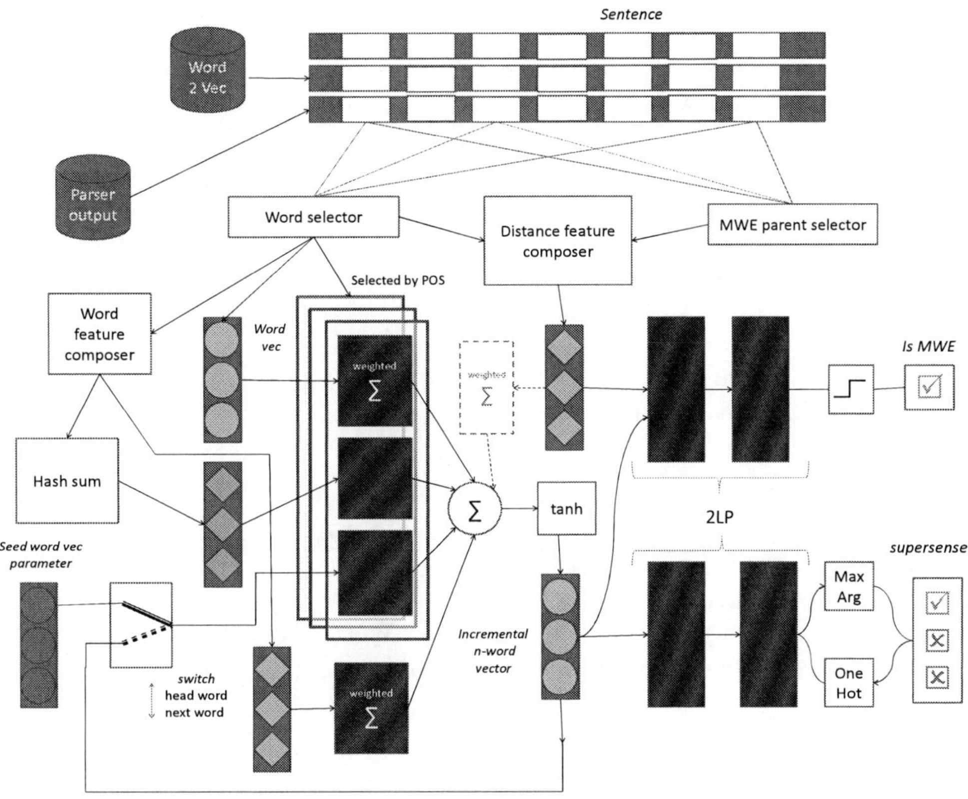

Figure 1: An outline of the system architecture

word MWE (either complete or incomplete), where $n \geq 2$. In such a way, every n-word expression finally yields $n - 1$ incremental positive samples.

Also, for every word, regardless of whether it is a standalone word or a member of MWE, it learns a -1 value (i.e. a negative sample) for its (unobserved) extension to an MWE with a random word. Such a random word is chosen of the L words ahead in the same sentence, not involved in the same MWE with the current word.[1]

During the learning process (and, correspond-

ingly, during the prediction), recursive computations of the incremental vector are solely fed by members of the same MWE, and are restarted for each semantic unit.

3.2 Senses

We learn a sense once per complete n-word expression, including $n = 1$. We have a distinct output per sense, including "unknown" (42 in total in the DiMSUM data set). We factorise sense classification error by the number of senses in order to balance the backpropagation of two perceptrons to the incremental vector calculator.

4 Prediction

We use a greedy procedure for MWE prediction in a text. An *outer* loop iterates through all words of a sentence. It selects each word (not yet consumed by some previously predicted MWE) as the head

---

[1]We limit L to 9 words, and also limit the probability of every word selection to < 0.25 (by randomly down-weighting the sample processing for $L < 4$) in order to prevent possible bias to the distribution of inter-word offsets occurring while processing the last few words of a sentence. We solely pick the same sentence words as negative samples in order to make learning more focused on prediction environment patterns rather than noise, as we use a small training corpus, and at the same time to keep an approximate balance in count between negative and positive samples.

word of a possible new MWE and restarts the incremental vector computation. An *inner* loop iterates through (up to L) remaining words in the sentence following the current head word. Each time, a probability for such a second word to be a continuation of the MWE is evaluated. Once a new MWE or an MWE extension is predicted, it consumes the right hand word and designates it to be the next word of the MWE; the incremental vector is updated respectively with the new MWE member. Such a procedure is able to generate a deep stack of nested MWEs with gaps, but we restrict the depth to be compliant to the DiMSUM data format.

5 Features

5.1 Word Embeddings

We utilised a publicly available pre-trained CBOW word2vec model, with 300-dimensional word vectors based on the Google News corpus. Out-of-vocabulary words are represented with zero-filled vectors.

We use the following search strategy when looking up a word in the word2vec dictionary (until the first successful lookup returns the final embedding):[2].

1. strip off leading "#" and "@"

2. if the word is a number then replace by "NUM"

3. lowercase the word

4. (optionally) lemmatize

5. remove all non-alpha characters

6. return the word embedding associated with the word OR if no match, return a zero vector

5.2 Word Hash Sum

We produce a 64-dimensional $+1/-1$ hash sum vector for words where the embedding vector is unknown; a zero vector was supplied for words (somehow) found in the Google News WEMB database.

---

[2]We tried using light spelling correction to reduce the rate of unknown words (a simple substitution of one character and then selecting the most probable word according to its frequency ranking). However it didn't seem to be effective, as the number of mispredicted words was greater then the number of correctly predicted ones, in particular due to the absence of a great number of frequent words ("stop-words") in the Google News vectors DB. Thus, a more sophisticated system would be needed if one wants to correct typos.

Feature	Range	Description
Gap	$\frac{n}{8}, n \in Z_{\geq 0}$	gap between word positions (divided by 8)
Par$_{Dist}$	$\{2; 0; -\frac{3}{2}\}$	hierarchical distance between words in a parse tree; three gradations for distances of $1, 2, \geq 3$
Par$_{Parent}$	$\{-1, 1\}$	two words are head word and child word of the same clause, according to the parser output
InterQt	$\{-1, 1\}$	double-quotes anywhere between given words?

Table 1: Distance features

Only alphabetic characters were counted in the hash sum.

5.3 Word Distance features

Table 1 displays inter-word distance-based features.

We used a parser prediction file created for the source text in order to evaluate a hierarchical distance between two candidate words. The hierarchical distance here means the maximum of two counts of edges that connect two given words to the nearest clause they share. For instance, two sibling nodes have the hierarchical distance value of one. The same is also true of a phrase head word and its immediate dependent word (that case is indicated by a distinct feature). We employed TurboParser v.2.0.0 (Martins and Almeida, 2014) and trained it on a Penn TreeBank data collection (some conversion was needed to match with the part-of-speech tagset used in the DiMSUM task).

5.4 Heuristic word features

The full list of miscellaneous word features (concerning capitalization, punctuation characters, lookup success etc.) is presented in Table 2.

6 Results

The system configuration which was used as our official run for the SemEval 2016 task was parameterized as follows: wide layer 1 in MWE prediction perceptron = 1024 nodes; hash sum size = 16bit, calculated both for known and unknown word, using all characters in a word (alpha + non-alpha); a

Feature	Value range	Description
$\text{Cap}_{\text{First}}$	$\{-1, 1\}$	Word starts with a capital letter
Cap_{Norm}	$[0, 1]$	Word starts with a capital letter, a value normalized by dividing by the sentence word count
$\text{Cap}_{\text{Ratio}}$	$[0, 1]$	Ratio of uppercase letters in the word
$\text{Has}_{\text{NAlpha}}$	$\{-1, 1\}$	Word has non-alpha characters
Has_{Num}	$\{-1, 1\}$	Word has any digit inside
$\text{Has}_{\text{Prime}}$	$\{-1, 1\}$	Word has an apostrophe
Is_{At}	$\{-1, 1\}$	Word starts with "@"
Is_{Hash}	$\{-1, 1\}$	Word starts with "#"
Is_{Num}	$\{-1, 1\}$	Word is num (integer, float or "NUM" keyword)
Is_{Punct}	$\{-1, 1\}$	Word contains punctuation character(s) (one or more of "!?.,:;[]()/")
Is_{Unk}	$\{-1, 1\}$	word2vec out-of-vocabulary word, including stop words
Is_{Url}	$\{-1, 1\}$	Word is "URL"
$\text{Log}_{\text{Range}}$	$[0, 12]$	Smoothed logarithm of the word's frequency range found in the word2vec dictionary, $\log(0.1 \times \text{range} + 1)$; the more frequent the word, the lower the value
Quot_{Pre}	$\{-1, 1\}$	A double-quote is located at the previous word position
$\text{Quot}_{\text{Post}}$	$\{-1, 1\}$	A double-quote is found at the next word position

Table 2: Word Features

mean vector of word embeddings over the sentence was included as extra feature; distance features are supplied to the composed vector evaluator (as shown with the dotted line in Figure 1); a confidence level of -0.15 was applied to the MWE perceptron when predicting a two-word MWE prefix (but not when expanding it to the third and next words, encouraging an MWE to start). The whole DiMSUM training

Type	Prec	Recall	F1
Experiments			
MWEs	0.4697	0.4655	46.76%
Supersenses	0.5320	0.5138	52.27%
Combined	0.5194	0.5046	51.19%
Official			
MWE	0.6122	0.2807	38.49%
Supersenses	0.5009	0.5326	51.62%
Combined	0.5114	0.4846	49.77%
Macro			49.94%

Table 3: Results

set was used to train the system.

Table 3 displays the results, measured with the DiMSUM evaluation script.

Table 4 represents a brief ablation study with feature vector disabled. Word embeddings seem to be the critical source of supersense information, and they are also one of the important contributors to MWE recall. The incremental n-word vector is critical for MWE precision, and Distance features are of great importance both for precision and recall in MWE detection, but especially for the recall. Word hash and, surprisingly, heuristic word features are of much less significance than other feature vectors.

7 Findings & Conclusions

The system captures supersenses rather well (when we consider the large number of senses, small size of the training data, and ambiguity in the sense assignments). However, it frequently admits harsh mispredictions that are probably caused by the lack of global sense coherence in WEMBs (Qu et al., 2015). Also, it suffers from the lack of (other than MWE-related) context information in cases of ambiguity. Improving context awareness may be the most obvious next step. Unsurprisingly, the most frequent supersenses have the best recall, up to 80% for V.STATIVE. The mean recall value for senses is around 50–60%, and there are senses (like N.WEATHER) that are never correctly predicted. Exceptions are N.ATTRIBUTE, N.LOCATION, and V.CHANGE, where recall is below 30% despite them being reasonably frequent. Some of the most frequent mispredictions are the following: N.PERSON $\rightarrow$ N.GROUP; N.COMMUNICATION $\rightarrow$

Ablated	MWEs			Supersenses			Combined		
features	Prec	Recall	F1	Prec	Recall	F1	Prec	Recall	F1
—Recurrency	0.2125	0.4960	29.75%	0.4638	0.3581	40.41%	0.3591	0.3843	37.13%
—Heuristic	0.4230	0.5821	48.99%	0.5033	0.4797	49.12%	0.4822	0.4991	49.05%
—Distance	0.3246	0.2771	29.90%	0.4494	0.4575	45.34%	0.4281	0.4232	42.56%
—Word hash	0.3640	0.6350	46.27%	0.5133	0.4811	49.67%	0.4674	0.5104	48.80%
—word2vec	0.3204	0.5193	39.63%	0.1898	0.1766	18.29%	0.2293	0.2418	23.54%

Table 4: Feature ablation results

N.ARTEFACT; N.ATTRIBUT $\rightarrow$ N.COGNITION; N.ACT $\rightarrow$ N.EVENT; and V.EMOTION $\rightarrow$ V.COGNITION.

MWE identification looks generally reasonable for all principal types of MWEs (even, surprisingly, ones of an idiomatic nature), but the overall accuracy is low.

Hysteresis bias pattern. The MWE classifier tends to be biased toward *not* joining two words into a MWE[3]; at the same time, once an MWE is predicted, it tends to be extended excessively to include a third and subsequent words, often selecting a non-relevant word with some gap.[4] This probably means that the proposed sampling schema is not balanced enough to work for small amounts of training data.

Lookahead. The method obviously lacks the ability to model context when predicting MWEs. In cases of expressions like *John , Mary & Company*, for example, our system will predict *John Mary Company* with all the punctuation missing. Some bidirectional, attentional (Bahdanau et al., 2014; Cohn et al., 2016) or lookahead-based approach is needed, as we may not have a reasonable isolated rule for whether *John* should be joined to the comma. A similar situation may also occur in punctuation-less contexts.

Parsing. The use of parsing results in markedly better precision and recall. Taking into account the strong correlation between parser-based features and MWE boundaries, further investigation of the parser-based approach is warranted.

Multiword-to-Sense Collision. A shared n-word incremental vector computation both for MWE and sense learning imposes a collision. It may be observed that for better MWE training, the distance features should be supplied to the computation input (as shown with the dotted line in Figure 1), but this will decreases the sense prediction score.

Needs a deeper network. The training dynamics observed in the experiments show that the neural networks (especially the one used for MWE prediction) need to be deeper (use more than two layers, as suggested in Sutskever et al. (2014)).

References

[Bahdanau et al.2014] Dzmitry Bahdanau, Kyunghyun Cho, and Yoshua Bengio. 2014. Neural machine translation by jointly learning to align and translate. *arXiv preprint arXiv:1409.0473*.

[Baldwin and Kim2010] Timothy Baldwin and Su Nam Kim. 2010. Multiword expressions. In Nitin Indurkhya and Fred J. Damerau, editors, *Handbook of Natural Language Processing*. CRC Press, Boca Raton, USA, 2nd edition.

[Cohn et al.2016] Trevor Cohn, Cong Duy Vu Hoang, Ekaterina Vymolova, Kaisheng Yao, Chris Dyer, and Gholamreza Haffari. 2016. Incorporating structural alignment biases into an attentional neural translation model. *arXiv preprint arXiv:1601.01085*.

[Drahomíra johanka Spoustová et al.2009] Jan Drahomíra johanka Spoustová, Hajič, Jan Raab, Miroslav Spousta, et al. 2009. Semi-supervised training for the averaged perceptron pos tagger. In *Proceedings of the 12th Conference of the European Chapter of the Association for Computational Linguistics*, pages 763–771. Association for Computational Linguistics.

[Martins and Almeida2014] André FT Martins and Mariana SC Almeida. 2014. Priberam: A turbo semantic parser with second order features. In *Proceedings of the 8th International Workshop on Semantic Evaluation (SemEval 2014)*, pages 471–476.

---

[3]An example from the DiMSUM test data: *English speaking advisor* produces an MWE predicted to be *English advisor* (not including *speaking*

[4]As a very rough compensation of such an effect, one may use two confidence levels, one (negative) at $n = 2$, another (positive) at $n \geq 3$.

[Mikolov et al.2013a] Tomas Mikolov, Ilya Sutskever, Kai Chen, Greg S Corrado, and Jeff Dean. 2013a. Distributed representations of words and phrases and their compositionality. In *Advances in neural information processing systems*, pages 3111–3119.

[Mikolov et al.2013b] Tomas Mikolov, Wen-tau Yih, and Geoffrey Zweig. 2013b. Linguistic regularities in continuous space word representations. In *Proceedings of the 2013 Conference of the North American Chapter of the Association for Computational Linguistics: Human Language Technologies (NAACL HLT 2013)*, pages 746–751, Atlanta, USA.

[Qu et al.2015] Lizhen Qu, Gabriela Ferraro, Liyuan Zhou, Weiwei Hou, Nathan Schneider, and Timothy Baldwin. 2015. Big data small data, in domain out-of-domain, known word unknown word: The impact of word representation on sequence labelling tasks. *arXiv preprint arXiv:1504.05319*.

[Salehi et al.2015] Bahar Salehi, Paul Cook, and Timothy Baldwin. 2015. A word embedding approach to predicting the compositionality of multiword expressions. In *Proceedings of the 2015 Conference of the North American Chapter of the Association for Computational Linguistics: Human Language Technologies*, pages 977–983.

[Schneider et al.2012] Nathan Schneider, Behrang Mohit, Kemal Oflazer, and Noah A Smith. 2012. Coarse lexical semantic annotation with supersenses: an arabic case study. In *Proceedings of the 50th Annual Meeting of the Association for Computational Linguistics: Short Papers-Volume 2*, pages 253–258. Association for Computational Linguistics.

[Socher et al.2010] Richard Socher, Christopher D Manning, and Andrew Y Ng. 2010. Learning continuous phrase representations and syntactic parsing with recursive neural networks. In *Proceedings of the NIPS-2010 Deep Learning and Unsupervised Feature Learning Workshop*, pages 1–9.

[Socher et al.2011] Richard Socher, Cliff C Lin, Chris Manning, and Andrew Y Ng. 2011. Parsing natural scenes and natural language with recursive neural networks. In *Proceedings of the 28th international conference on machine learning (ICML-11)*, pages 129–136.

[Socher2014] Richard Socher. 2014. *Recursive Deep Learning for Natural Language Processing and Computer Vision*. Ph.D. thesis, Citeseer.

[Sutskever et al.2014] Ilya Sutskever, Oriol Vinyals, and Quoc V Le. 2014. Sequence to sequence learning with neural networks. In *Advances in neural information processing systems*, pages 3104–3112.

[Vylomova et al.2015] Ekaterina Vylomova, Laura Rimell, Trevor Cohn, and Timothy Baldwin. 2015. Take and took, gaggle and goose, book and read: Evaluating the utility of vector differences for lexical relation learning. *CoRR*, abs/1509.01692.

PLUJAGH at SemEval-2016 Task 11:
Simple System for Complex Word Identification

Krzysztof Wróbel

Jagiellonian University

ul. Golebia 24

31-007 Krakow, Poland

AGH University of Science and Technology

al. Mickiewicza 30

30-059 Krakow, Poland

`kwrobel@agh.edu.pl`

Abstract

This paper presents the description of a system which detects complex words. It solely uses information regarding the presence of a word in a prepared vocabulary list. The system outperforms multiple more advanced systems and is ranked fourth for the shared task, with minimal loss to the best system. F-score optimization guaranteed the first place in this measurement. Different features are considered and evaluated. Maximal bounds are predicted. The rule "the simplest methods give the best results" is confirmed.

1 Introduction

The goal of Complex Word Identification (CWI) is to detect words in a text that are complex (not easy to understand) for some group of people. CWI is one of the tasks of SemEval-2016 (Paetzold and Specia, 2016).

CWI can be treated as the first step of Lexical Simplification (LS). LS was a task of SemEval-2012 (Specia et al., 2012). Complex words were identified using n-grams, the length of the word, and the number of syllables (Ligozat et al., 2012; De Belder et al., 2010; Biran et al., 2011). The resources exploited in this task include Wikipedia, WordNet, Google Web 1T corpus (Sinha, 2012; Paetzold and Specia, 2015). Additional annotation of input sentences was performed by: a part-of-speech tagger, and word sense disambiguation (Amoia and Romanelli, 2012; Jauhar and Specia, 2012).

A similar task is the prediction of the readability of a whole text. In comparison, in CWI, each word has to be scored. The applied methods are summarized in (Dębowski et al., 2015).

This paper presents findings regarding the necessary data and the performed experiments. For the final submission, a simple system was chosen, which scored at fourth place.

2 Task Data Analysis

It is important to notice the difference between training and test data. Each sentence in the training set was annotated by 20 annotators. If at least one of them classified a word in a sentence as complex, it was marked as complex. The training data consists of 2237 classified words. On the other hand, each sentence in the test data (88221 classified words) was annotated by only one annotator.

Complex words represent 31.56% of the words in the training data. Fortunately, organizers published the unaggregated annotations – every word in a sentence has 20 annotations. In this scenario, only 4.55% instances are classified as complex.

A priori probability of the word being complex is important knowledge for the classification task.

What is more, the organizers shared the baseline results for test data (Table 1). It shows that complex words represent 4.7% of instances in the test data – similar to training.

3 Resources and Methods

Knowledge bases are essential to this task. Wikipedia is one of the most popular sources of text used in NLP. Using the cycloped.io (Smywiński-Pohl and Wróbel, 2014) framework the English and Simple English Wikipedia were preprocessed. The

Proceedings of SemEval-2016, pages 953–957,
San Diego, California, June 16-17, 2016. ©2016 Association for Computational Linguistics

Table 1: Scores for baseline systems on the test data. 1) All complex – all words are classified as complex, 2) All simple: all words are classified as simple, 3) Ogden's lexicon: words present in Ogden's Basic English vocabulary are classified as simple, others as complex. G-score is defined as a harmonic mean of accuracy and recall.

System	Accuracy	Recall	G-score
All complex	0.047	1.000	0.089
All simple	0.953	0.000	0.000
Ogden's lexicon	0.248	0.947	0.393

text extracted from articles allowed the calculation of term frequency (TF) and document frequency (DF). TF represents the total number of times a word appears in the corpora; DF is the number of documents in which the word occurred at least once.

It was required to apply the same tokenization of corpora as in the data from the organizers.

For every word which needed classification, many features were created:

- TF and DF for the word and its lemma use,
  - English Wikipedia,
  - Simple English Wikipedia,
  - corpora created from training and test sentences,
- length of sentence (number of words),
- length of word (number of characters),
- position of word in sentence,
- GloVe word embedding (Pennington et al., 2014).

For quick development, sklearn (Pedregosa et al., 2011) was used. Many supervised machine-learning algorithms were tested using cross-validation:

- decision trees with maximum depth from 1 to 6,
- linear classifier with stochastic gradient descent (SGD) training,
- k-nearest neighbors classifiers for k=3,5,10,20,
- random forest,
- extremely randomized trees,
- AdaBoost,
- GradientBoostingClassifier,
- LinearSVC.

Table 2: Ranking of features in terms of G-score. The last position presents the score for all features used in one model.

Feature	G-score
DF of Simple English Wikipedia	0.781
lemma TF of Simple English Wikipedia	0.781
TF of Simple English Wikipedia	0.780
lemma TF of English Wikipedia	0.778
TF of training corpus	0.774
TF of English Wikipedia	0.767
GloVe word embeddings	0.767
TF of CHILDES Parental Corpus	0.738
length of word	0.618
position of word in sentence	0.556
length of sentence	0.505
all features	0.784

4 Evaluation

All experiments were conducted by employing cross-validation on raw vote data. Training data were aggregated – a word is labeled as complex if at least two annotators marked it accordingly.

4.1 Metrics

The results are scored using a harmonic mean of accuracy and recall (marked as G-score). In comparison to F-score (a harmonic mean of precision and recall), it is higher if more instances are predicted as complex.

4.2 Experiments

Tree-based classifiers achieved the best results (except for word embeddings). Table 2 presents the G-scores obtained by training a classifier with each of the features. Combining features gives only a slightly better score.

4.2.1 Upper Bounds

Complex word identification is a subjective task. The understanding of a word depends on the knowledge of a particular person. Therefore, 100% G-score is impossible to achieve. Due to the fact that the training data was annotated by multiple annotators, it was possible to measure the inter-annotator agreement. Two theoretical systems were scored on the training data. Both systems have knowledge regarding the annotators' assessment of the words in

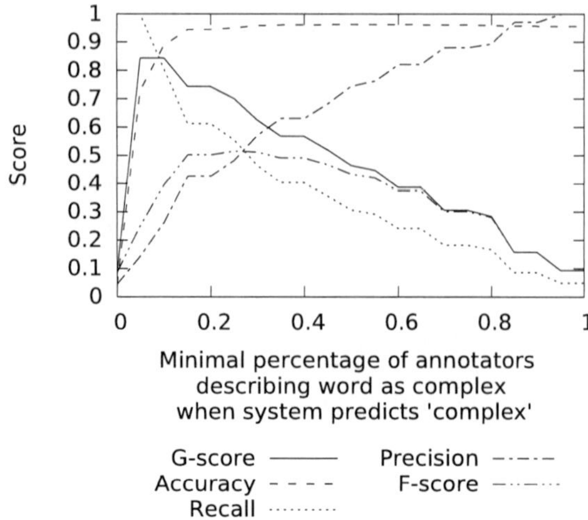

Figure 1: Results for the first theoretical system using classification with information about context.

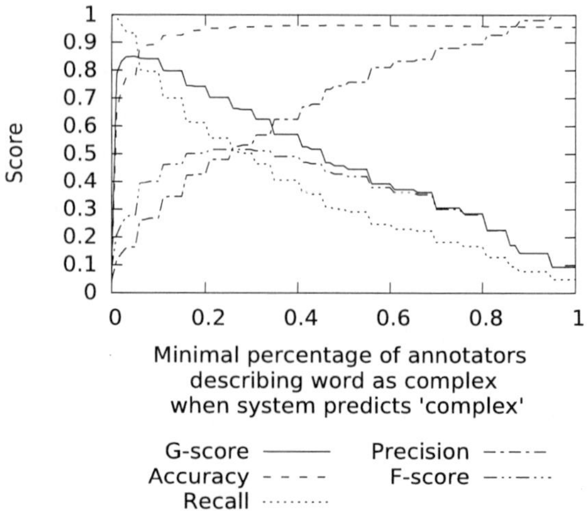

Figure 2: Results for the second theoretical system using classification without information about context.

sentences. The first one has information regarding the context (whole sentence) – for each sentence, it knows how many annotators recognized each word as complex. The second one knows how many times each word was assessed as complex (without context).

1. The problem can be treated as simple classification and not sequence labeling. For every word in every sentence, the system predicts words as complex if at least X people annotated it as complex. The maximum G-score is 84.54% for X=10% and the F-score is 51.66% for X=25%. This system has information regarding the word and the sentence. However, it is still not sequence classification – it has no information regarding the predictions of the other words in the sentence. Figure 1 presents results in a function of X.

2. Going further input data can be solely words, without the sentence, so that we can aggregate annotations for the same words, but in different sentences. The system describes a word as complex if at least X people annotated it as complex (this system has no information regarding the context of the sentence). The maximum G-score is 85.04% for X from 4% to 5%, and the F-score is 51.71% for X from 26% to 27%. This system has information only about the word. Figure 2 presents results in a function of X.

The results above show that a G-score of 86% can

not be exceeded on this data.

4.2.2 Final Submission

The experiments showed a minimally increased score for more advanced classifiers using more features in comparison to the simple one-rule algorithm with one feature. Simple models are usually more difficult to overfit. The complexity of this algorithm is $\mathcal{O}(1)$ for every word using hashing.

The final submission uses DF of Simple English Wikipedia. The scores, as a function of threshold, are presented in Figure 3.

The main submission is optimized for G-score, and its threshold is 147. Words with a DF exceeding this threshold are considered simple, and others are considered complex. A set of simple words contains almost 11 thousand tokens (without sanitization). The size of the model is 78 kilobytes.

The second submission was optimized for F-score and the threshold was 18.

5 Results and Discussion

Table 3 shows the top 10 results of the systems on the test data in terms of G-score. The system placed fourth with two other systems.

The best system, SV000gg, ensembles 23 distinct systems using 69 morphological, lexical, semantic, collocation, and nominal features. The system is much more advanced than the one presented in this

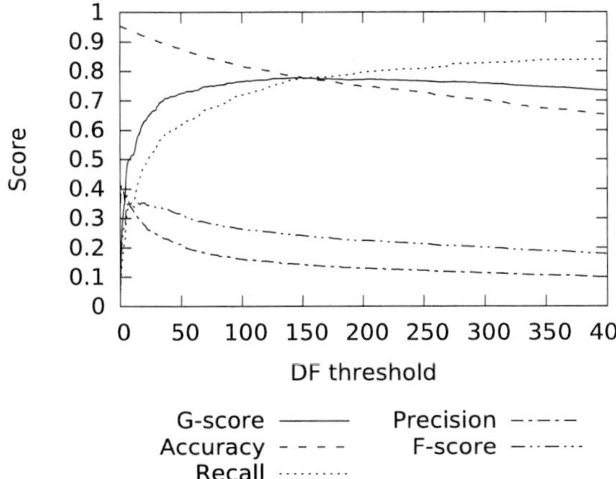

Figure 3:

Table 3: Top 10 systems in terms of G-score. Additionally, the average scores of all systems and their standard deviations are provided.

System	Accuracy	Recall	G-score
SV000gg-Soft	0.779	0.769	0.774
SV000gg-Hard	0.761	0.787	0.773
TALN-WEI	0.812	0.736	0.772
UWB-All	0.803	0.734	0.767
PLUJAGH-SEWDF	0.795	0.741	0.767
JUNLP-NaiveBayes	0.767	0.767	0.767
HMC-RegressionTree	0.838	0.705	0.766
HMC-DecisionTree	0.846	0.698	0.765
JUNLP-RandomForest	0.795	0.730	0.761
MACSAAR-RFC	0.825	0.694	0.754
TALN-SIM	0.847	0.673	0.750
MACSAAR-NNC	0.804	0.660	0.725
Average	0.737	0.591	0.620
Standard deviation	0.130	0.202	0.123

Table 4: Top 3 systems in terms of F-score. Additionally, the average scores of all systems and their standard deviations are provided.

System	Precision	Recall	F-score
PLUJAGH-SEWDFF	0.289	0.453	0.353
LTG-System2	0.220	0.541	0.312
LTG-System1	0.300	0.321	0.310
Average	0.123	0.590	0.193
Standard deviation	0.061	0.202	0.073

paper. Its result is higher by almost one percentage point.

The next system in the ranking, TALN-WEI, uses external resources, i.e. WordNet, simple/complex word lists, tools, i.e. part-of-speech tagger, and a dependency parser. A random forest classifier is then trained.

JUNLP-NaiveBayes employs word sense disambiguation and features extracted from an ontology. Also, a random forest classifier is used. Additional word lists are developed, i.e. scientific, geographical, and non-English.

Surprisingly, UWB-ALL is almost the same as the one presented in this article (the English version of Wikipedia is used, not Simple English).

The presented system took first place in terms of F-score. The higher score is probably due to this submission being optimized for F-score with no other teams doing this.

Beating 85% G-score is not possible without more information. It is possible that having the possibility to model every person's knowledge would improve the results. However, this approach needs historic data annotated by a specified user and the predictions would be only relevant for this user.

References

Marilisa Amoia and Massimo Romanelli. 2012. Sb: mmsystem-using decompositional semantics for lexical simplification. In *Proceedings of the First Joint Conference on Lexical and Computational Semantics- Volume 1: Proceedings of the main conference and the shared task, and Volume 2: Proceedings of the Sixth International Workshop on Semantic Evaluation*, pages 482–486. Association for Computational Linguistics.

Or Biran, Samuel Brody, and Noémie Elhadad. 2011. Putting it simply: a context-aware approach to lexical simplification. In *Proceedings of the 49th Annual Meeting of the Association for Computational Linguistics: Human Language Technologies: short papers-Volume 2*, pages 496–501. Association for Computational Linguistics.

Jan De Belder, Koen Deschacht, and Marie-Francine Moens. 2010. Lexical simplification. In *Proceedings of ITEC2010: 1st international conference on interdisciplinary research on technology, education and communication*.

Łukasz Dębowski, Bartosz Broda, Bartłomiej Nitoń, and Edyta Charzyńska. 2015. Jasnopis – a program to compute readability of texts in Polish based on psycholinguistic research. In *Natural Language Processing and Cognitive Science. Proceedings 2015*, pages 51–61.

Sujay Kumar Jauhar and Lucia Specia. 2012. Uow-shef: Simplex–lexical simplicity ranking based on contextual and psycholinguistic features. In *Proceedings of the First Joint Conference on Lexical and Computational Semantics-Volume 1: Proceedings of the main conference and the shared task, and Volume 2: Proceedings of the Sixth International Workshop on Semantic Evaluation*, pages 477–481. Association for Computational Linguistics.

Anne-Laure Ligozat, Anne Garcia-Fernandez, Cyril Grouin, and Delphine Bernhard. 2012. Annlor: a naïve notation-system for lexical outputs ranking. In *Proceedings of the First Joint Conference on Lexical and Computational Semantics-Volume 1: Proceedings of the main conference and the shared task, and Volume 2: Proceedings of the Sixth International Workshop on Semantic Evaluation*, pages 487–492. Association for Computational Linguistics.

Gustavo Henrique Paetzold and Lucia Specia. 2015. Lexenstein: A framework for lexical simplification. *ACL-IJCNLP 2015*, 1(1):85–90.

Gustavo H. Paetzold and Lucia Specia. 2016. Semeval 2016 task 11: Complex word identification. In *Proceedings of the 10th International Workshop on Semantic Evaluation (SemEval 2016)*.

F. Pedregosa, G. Varoquaux, A. Gramfort, V. Michel, B. Thirion, O. Grisel, M. Blondel, P. Prettenhofer, R. Weiss, V. Dubourg, J. Vanderplas, A. Passos, D. Cournapeau, M. Brucher, M. Perrot, and E. Duchesnay. 2011. Scikit-learn: Machine learning in Python. *Journal of Machine Learning Research*, 12:2825–2830.

Jeffrey Pennington, Richard Socher, and Christopher D. Manning. 2014. Glove: Global vectors for word representation. In *Empirical Methods in Natural Language Processing (EMNLP)*, pages 1532–1543.

Ravi Sinha. 2012. Unt-simprank: Systems for lexical simplification ranking. In *Proceedings of the First Joint Conference on Lexical and Computational Semantics-Volume 1: Proceedings of the main conference and the shared task, and Volume 2: Proceedings of the Sixth International Workshop on Semantic Evaluation*, pages 493–496. Association for Computational Linguistics.

Aleksander Smywiński-Pohl and Krzysztof Wróbel. 2014. The importance of cross-lingual information for matching Wikipedia with the Cyc ontology. In *9th International Workshop on Ontology Matching*, pages 176–177.

Lucia Specia, Sujay Kumar Jauhar, and Rada Mihalcea. 2012. Semeval-2012 task 1: English lexical simplification. In *Proceedings of the First Joint Conference on Lexical and Computational Semantics - Volume 1: Proceedings of the Main Conference and the Shared Task, and Volume 2: Proceedings of the Sixth International Workshop on Semantic Evaluation*, SemEval '12, pages 347–355, Stroudsburg, PA, USA. Association for Computational Linguistics.

USAAR at SemEval-2016 Task 11:
Complex Word Identification with
Sense Entropy and Sentence Perplexity

José Manuel Martínez Martínez and Liling Tan
Universität des Saarlandes
Campus, Saarbrücken, Germany
`j.martinez@mx.uni-saarland.de`
`liling.tan@uni-saarland.de`

Abstract

This paper describes an information-theoretic approach to complex word identification using a classifier based on an entropy based measure based on word senses and sentence-level perplexity features. We describe the motivation behind these features based on information density and demonstrate that they perform modestly well in the complex word identification task in SemEval-2016. We also discuss the possible improvements that can be made to future work by exploring the subjectivity of word complexity and more robust evaluation metrics for the complex word identification task.

1 Introduction

Complex Word Identification (CWI) is the task of automatically identifying difficult words in a sentence.

It is an important subtask *prior to* the textual/lexical simplification task that *pertains to* the *substitution* of *abstruse* words with *lucid* variants which can be *apprehended* by a wider *gamut* of readers (Siddharthan, 2006; Specia et al., 2012; Shardlow, 2013).

The aim of the CWI task is to annotate the difficult words as shown in the underlined examples in the previous paragraph, such that a lexical simplification system can produce the following sentence:

It is an important subtask *before* the textual/lexical simplification task that *concerns* the *replacement* of *difficult* words with *simpler* variants which can be *understood* by a *wider* range of readers.

Lexical simplification is a specific case of lexical substitution where the complex words in a sentence are replaced with simpler words.

Historically, lexical substitution was conceived as a means to examine the issue of the appropriateness of a fixed word sense inventory in the word sense disambiguation task the "sense" of a polysemous word is correctly identified given a context sentence (Kilgarriff, 1997; Palmer, 2000; Hanks, 2000; Ide and Wilks, 2007; McCarthy and Navigli, 2009). By allowing fluidity in the "sense" inventory and by quantifying how much the systems were able to generate good substitutes, these lexical substitutes would have built a word sense cluster of words that may not be covered by a set of pre-defined words in a sense inventory, e.g. Princeton WordNet (Miller, 1995) and Open Multilingual WordNet (Bond and Paik, 2012).

2 Entropy and Perplexity

Entropy is an information-theoretical measure of the degree of indeterminacy of a random variable[1]. In simpler words, entropy measures how unpredictable an event is likely to occur (Shannon, 1951).

For the case of complex word , we can also assume that the degree of word ambiguity contributes to its level of unpredictability which determines its complexity. We define the degree of word ambiguity as the number of possible senses a word can have,

---

[1] https://www.encyclopediaofmath.org/index.php/Entropy

958

Proceedings of SemEval-2016, pages 958–962,
San Diego, California, June 16-17, 2016. ©2016 Association for Computational Linguistics

more specially the number of synsets of a lemma of the target word as recorded in the Princeton Word-Net. Formally, we define the ***sense entropy*** of a word, $H(word)$, as such:

$$H(word) = -\sum_{k=1}^{n} p(sense_k) \log p(sense_k) \quad (1)$$

where n is the number of possible sense of a word and $p(sense_k)$ is the probability of sense given the context sentence where the word occurs. We assume a uniform distribution across all senses of a word, thus we assign $1/n$ to the $p(sense_k)$ variable.

Perplexity is inverse measure of entropy that measures how predictable an event is likely to occur. Intuitively, if a complex word appears in a sentence, the sentence would become less common and less predictable, yielding a higher sentence perplexity score. Mathematically, we define the ***sentence perplexity***, $2^{H(sentence)}$ as follows:

$$2^{H(sentence)} = 2^{-\sum_{i=1}^{N} p(word_i) \log p(word_i)}$$

$$(2)$$

where N is the number of words in the sentence and $p(word_i)$ is the unigram probability of the word generated from a modified Kneser-Ney language model (Chen and Goodman, 1999).

3   Experimental Setup

The dataset for the CWI task in SemEval-2016 is annotated at word level with binary labels; 1 for complex and 0 for non-complex.

	Train	Test
# Sentences	200	8,929
# Labels	2,237	88,221
# Lemma	1,903	20,016
# Synsets	1,617	12,989
% WN Cover	84.97	64.89
% Complex	31.86	4.68

Table 1: CWI Task Dataset for SemEval-2016.

Table 1 presents the corpus statistics of the dataset provided for the CWI Task. The organizers have decided to emulate the limited human language capacity with a small training set and a large testing set that reflects the relatively larger proportion of text that a human will encounter in reality. However, we do note the stark difference between the percentage of complex words in the training and test data; it skews towards words being annotated with the non-complex labels.

To compute the sense entropy, we annotated the dataset with lemmas using the PyWSD lemmatizer (Tan, 2014) and reference the lemmas to the Princeton WordNet. The training and testing set comprise 2,237 and 88,221 words respectively. Of the annotated words, the training and testing set has 1,903 and 20,016 unique lemmas and the WordNet covers 84.97% and 64.89% of these lemmas respectively. When a lemma is not covered by WordNet, we assign an entropy of 0 that indicates that the lemma's complexity is easily predictable and the classifier would assign the majority label to the word.

To compute the sentence perplexity as presented in the previous section, we use the English Wikipedia section of the SeedLing corpus (Emerson et al., 2014) and the news articles from the DSL Corpus Collection (Tan et al., 2014) to train the language model using the KenLM tool (Heafield et al., 2013). On average, there are 11 annotated words per sentence and every word in the same sentence shares the same sentence perplexity.

Using both the sense entropy and sentence perplexity as features, we train a boosted tree binary classifier (Friedman, 2002) using the Graphlab Create[2] machine learning toolkit to identify the word complexity.

Interestingly, when we use the raw number of senses instead of sense entropy as a feature on various machine learning classifiers, the number of senses were uninformative and the classifiers either labels all words as complex or all words as non-complex.

4   Results

We submitted 2 systems to the CWI task in SemEval-2016 (Paetzold and Specia, 2016), one using only the sense entropy (`sentropy`) and another that includes the sentence perplexity feature (`entroplexity`).

The complex word classification would be evaluated based on classic (i) `accuracy`, (ii) `precision`, (iii) `recall`, (iv) `F-score`. In ad-

---

[2]https://dato.com/products/create/

dition to the harmonic F-score between the precision and recall, the organizers reported the harmonic mean between the accuracy and recall, dubbed `G-score`[3].

Since the accuracy score computes the percentage of true positive labels globally, it might be more indicative to read the accuracy scores given the highly skewed dataset ($<5\%$ of the test set is labelled as complex).

Table 2 presents the comparative results between our systems, 4 systems that ranked top in F-score and G-score and 2 baseline systems that uses threshold frequencies that best separate complex from simple words learned from the English and Simple English Wikipedias.

PLUJAGH-SEWDFF uses frequency thresholding techniques, they consider any word that occurs less than 147 times in the simple English Wikipedia to be complex. LTG-System2 uses a decision tree classifier trained using similar threshold features. SV000gg uses a soft and hard voting ensemble to combine 23 different systems that includes threshold-based and lexicon-based techniques and machine learning classifiers based on 69 distinct morphological, lexical, semantic, collocational and nominal features.

Compared to the top systems, our system has performed modestly and our `Sentropy` system outperforms the thresholding baselines. We note that our accuracy and precision scores are relatively competitive as compared to the top systems but our recall is distinctly lower which affects the F- and G-scores. Possibly, we could improve the system by using a word sense disambiguation tool that provide the sense probabilities instead of assuming uniform probabilities across all senses, especially when word senses are often dictated by the most common sense of the word given the context sentence.

Intuitively, we can expect the `Entroplexity` system with sentence-level perplexity to underperform in this particular test set because the variance of the perplexity measures are low since all words within the same sentence attain the same sentence perplexity. For a dataset where there are more training sentences, the feature could perform better.

---

[3]This should not be confused with the G-Measure that is used to measure cluster similarities (Fowlkes and Mallows, 1983).

5   Discussion

5.1   Subjectivity of Word Complexity

From the example in the introduction, we see the subjectivity of word complexity and how it may vary from speaker to speaker. Arguably *substitution* and *replacement* could have been of equal word complexity depending on the speaker's level of English proficiency. Although the word *variant* could easily be considered simple for a native French/German speaker learning English where the equivalence *Variante* exists in his/her native language, it might have been considered a complex word for other second English language speaker.

The annotations from the CWI task training set were collected from 20 annotators over a set of 200 sentences. A word is labelled complex if any one of the annotator deems it to be complex, while testing set was annotated by 1 annotator.

To explore the reader-based subjectivity in word complexity identification, we suggest that future work on CWI explores reader-specific annotations and models user-specific annotations. In this respect, readers' meta-data such as their native and non-native languages, country of residence, etc. could potentially be more telling in predicting their English proficiency and identifying complex word catered to specific readers or groups of readers.

5.2   Evaluation Metrics

Complex Word Identification is a novel task and possibly the standard F-score and accuracy measures might not be reflective of the task difficulty or the system efficiency. Given the binary nature of the classification task, we suggest the use of Matthews correlation coefficient (Matthews, 1975) that measures the measures the correlation coefficient between the observed and predicted binary labels, which can be viewed as a variant of the chi-square coefficient[4].

It measures the discordant relations between the true and false positives and negatives and avoids the need to optimize the systems based on either accuracy or precision but a healthy fusion of both. The coefficient value ranges from -1 to +1 where +1, 0

---

[4]http://scikit-learn.org/stable/modules/generated/sklearn. metrics.matthews_corrcoef.html

Teams-System	Accuracy	Precision	Recall	F-Score	G-Score
PLUJAGH-SEWDFF	**0.922**	**0.289**	0.453	**0.353**	0.608
LTG-System2	0.889	0.220	0.541	0.312	0.672
SV000gg-Soft	0.779	0.147	0.769	0.246	**0.774**
SV000gg-Hard	0.761	0.138	**0.787**	0.235	0.773
USAAR-Sentropy	0.869	0.148	0.376	0.212	0.525
Baseline-Wiki Threshold	0.536	0.084	0.901	0.154	0.672
Baseline-SimpleWiki Threshold	0.513	0.081	0.902	0.148	0.654
USAAR-Entroplexity	0.834	0.097	0.305	0.147	0.447

Table 2: Comparative Results between our Systems, the Top Systems and Threshold-based Baselines in SemEval-2016 CWI Task.

and -1 respectively represents perfect, random and inverse predictions.

6 Related Work

Although the lexical simplification/substitution task is well-studied, the complex word identification task has mostly been discussed as an anterior subtask.

Devlin and Tait (1998) implemented a lexical substitution system that ***considers all words as complex words*** and generated the simpler variant of the words by referencing the most frequent synonym of the word from the WordNet synsets and SUBTLEX corpus (Brysbaert and New, 2009).

Another method to identify complex words is to use the Zipfian nature of language by ***thresholding frequencies and classify words that occurs below a certain threshold as complex***. Zeng et al. (2005) and Elhadad (2006) applied the thresholding method to the medical domain to identify technical terms that non-experts would find it difficult to read, the complex terms and varying frequencies correlate with the word difficulty scores elicited from questionnaires (Zeng-Treitler et al., 2008). Similarly, (Zampieri and Tan, 2014) used n-gram based frequency threshold to identify complex words that has caused second language Chinese learners to make errors in their essays.

Other than the heuristics described above, previous studies had also used **supervised machine learning algorithms** and data annotated with binary labels for each words in the training corpus. Malmasi et al. (2016) use Zipfian word ranks and character n-grams features to train a random forest, an SVM and a nearest neighbour classifier to predict word complexity.

Shardlow (2013) compared various techniques to identify complex words, viz. (i) treating every word as complex, (ii) thresholding frequency using the mean of the thresholds discovered through the highest accuracies achieved across cross-validations folds of the training and (iii) an SVM classifier using word-level and character-level (orthographic and phonemic) frequencies and the number of synsets of each words.

While the *'everything is complex'* technique achieved the highest recall, the SVM classifier scored the best precision[5]. The coefficients in his SVM classifier presented the sense feature as the weakest while the frequency features indicated higher correlations with the binary label distribution[6]. In comparison, our sense entropy system is based solely on the number of senses per word reported modest results in the CWI task.

7 Conclusion

In this paper, we presented our systems submitted to the complex word identification task in SemEval-2016. We introduced the notion of sense entropy that measures the unpredictability of a word based on its number of senses and used it as a feature to identify complex word . The implementation of our system is released as an open source tool available on `https://github.com/alvations/entroplexity`.

---

[5]The SVM outputs were significantly different from the other two techniques.

[6]Although coefficient values indicates a feature 'strength' anecdotally and the coefficients does not necessarily explain the true effect on the label decision because each coefficient is influenced by other variables.

Acknowledgments

The research leading to these results has received funding from the People Programme (Marie Curie Actions) of the European Union's Seventh Framework Programme FP7/2007-2013/ under REA grant agreement n° 317471.

References

Francis Bond and Kyonghee Paik. 2012. A survey of wordnets and their licenses. In *GWC 2012 6th International Global Wordnet Conference*, volume 8, page 64.

Marc Brysbaert and Boris New. 2009. Moving beyond kučera and francis: A critical evaluation of current word frequency norms and the introduction of a new and improved word frequency measure for american english. *Behavior research methods*, 41(4):977–990.

Stanley F Chen and Joshua Goodman. 1999. An empirical study of smoothing techniques for language modeling. *Computer Speech & Language*, 13(4):359–393.

Siobhan Devlin and John Tait. 1998. The use of a psycholinguistic database in the simplification of text for aphasic readers. *Linguistic databases*, pages 161–173.

Noémie Elhadad. 2006. Comprehending technical texts: predicting and defining unfamiliar terms. In *AMIA Annual Symposium, pp. 239-243. Washington, DC.*

Guy Emerson, Liling Tan, Susanne Fertmann, Alexis Palmer, and Michaela Regneri. 2014. Seedling: Building and using a seed corpus for the human language project. In *Proceedings of the 2014 Workshop on the Use of Computational Methods in the Study of Endangered Languages*, pages 77–85, Baltimore, Maryland, USA.

Edward B Fowlkes and Colin L Mallows. 1983. A method for comparing two hierarchical clusterings. *Journal of the American statistical association*, 78(383):553–569.

Jerome H Friedman. 2002. Stochastic gradient boosting. *Computational Statistics & Data Analysis*, 38(4):367–378.

Patrick Hanks. 2000. Do word meanings exist? *Computers and the Humanities*, 34(1):205–215.

Kenneth Heafield, Ivan Pouzyrevsky, Jonathan H. Clark, and Philipp Koehn. 2013. Scalable modified Kneser-Ney language model estimation. In *Proceedings of the 51st Annual Meeting of the Association for Computational Linguistics*, pages 690–696, Sofia, Bulgaria.

Nancy Ide and Yorick Wilks. 2007. Making sense about sense. In *Word sense disambiguation*, pages 47–73. Springer.

Adam Kilgarriff. 1997. I dont believe in word senses. *Computers and the Humanities*, 31(2):91–113.

Shervin Malmasi, Marcos Zampieri, and Liling Tan. 2016. Macsaar: Zipfian and character-level features for complex word identification. In *Proceedings of the 10th International Workshop on Semantic Evaluation*.

Brian W Matthews. 1975. Comparison of the predicted and observed secondary structure of t4 phage lysozyme. *Biochimica et Biophysica Acta (BBA)-Protein Structure*, 405(2):442–451.

Diana McCarthy and Roberto Navigli. 2009. The english lexical substitution task. *Language resources and evaluation*, 43(2):139–159.

George A Miller. 1995. Wordnet: a lexical database for english. *Communications of the ACM*, 38(11):39–41.

Gustavo Henrique Paetzold and Lucia Specia. 2016. Complex word identification. In *Proceedings of the 10th International Workshop on Semantic Evaluation (SemEval 2016)*.

Martha Palmer. 2000. Consistent criteria for sense distinctions. *Computers and the Humanities*, 34(1-2):217–222.

Claude E Shannon. 1951. Prediction and entropy of printed english. *Bell system technical journal*, 30(1):50–64.

Matthew Shardlow. 2013. A comparison of techniques to automatically identify complex words. In *51st Annual Meeting of the Association for Computational Linguistics Proceedings of the Student Research Workshop*, pages 103–109, Sofia, Bulgaria.

Advaith Siddharthan. 2006. Syntactic simplification and text cohesion. *Research on Language and Computation*, 4(1):77–109.

Lucia Specia, Sujay Kumar Jauhar, and Rada Mihalcea. 2012. Semeval-2012 task 1: English lexical simplification. In *Proceedings of the Sixth International Workshop on Semantic Evaluation*, pages 347–355.

Liling Tan, Marcos Zampieri, Nikola Ljubešic, and Jörg Tiedemann. 2014. Merging comparable data sources for the discrimination of similar languages: The dsl corpus collection. In *Proceedings of The 7th Workshop on Building and Using Comparable Corpora*.

Marcos Zampieri and Liling Tan. 2014. Grammatical error detection with limited training data: The case of chinese. In *Proceedings of the 1st Workshop on Natural Language Processing Techniques for Educational Applications (NLPTEA'14), Nara, Japan*.

Qing Zeng, Eunjung Kim, Jon Crowell, and Tony Tse. 2005. A text corpora-based estimation of the familiarity of health terminology. In *Biological and Medical Data Analysis*, pages 184–192. Springer.

Qing Zeng-Treitler, Sergey Goryachev, Tony Tse, Alla Keselman, and Aziz Boxwala. 2008. Estimating consumer familiarity with health terminology: a context-based approach. *Journal of the American Medical Informatics Association*, 15(3):349–356.

Sensible at SemEval-2016 Task 11:
Neural Nonsense Mangled in Ensemble Mess

Nat Gillin

Gillin Inc.

36 Natchez Street, Seahaven, USA

gillin.nat@gmail.com

Abstract

This paper describes our submission to the Complex Word Identification (CWI) task in SemEval-2016. We test an experimental approach to blindly use neural nets to solve the CWI task that we know little/nothing about. By structuring the input as a series of sequences and the output as a binary that indicates 1 to denote complex words and 0 otherwise, we introduce a novel approach to complex word identification using Recurrent Neural Nets (RNN). We also show that it is possible to simply ensemble several RNN classifiers when we are unsure of the optimal hyper-parameters or the best performing models using eXtreme gradient boosted trees classifiers. Our systems submitted to the CWI task achieved the highest accuracy and F-score among the systems that uses neural networks.

1 Introduction

The *Deep Learning Tsunami* has hit the Natural Language Processing (NLP) and Computational Linguistics field (Manning, 2016). Deep neural nets has shown to be the ultimate hammer in various NLP shared tasks, systems trained on neural nets often emerge as the top systems and/or beat state-of-the-art performance (Collobert et al., 2011; Mikolov et al., 2013; Pennington et al., 2014; Levy et al., 2014; Shazeer et al., 2016; Gupta et al., 2015; Jean et al., 2015; Kreutzer et al., 2015; Sultan et al., 2014; Sultan et al., 2015)

In the concluding remarks of the Google's Deep Learning course on Udacity[1], Vincent Vanhoucke

---

[1] https://www.udacity.com/course/deep-learning–ud730

said, *"What's really cool about those [neural net application] examples is that you don't have to know much about the problem you're trying to solve"*. Armed with basic knowledge of deep learning and neural nets and almost zero familiarity of the problem, we attempt to treat the Complex Word Identification (CWI) task as a binary classification task using Long Short-Term Memory (LSTM) Recurrent Neural Nets (RNN) with Gated Recurrent Units (GRU).

2 Neural Network and Deep Learning

Neural Networks are powerful at modelling various modalities, e.g. signals, text, images, videos. As the name suggests, neural network is inspired by the brain's synaptic transmission mechanism that transmits signalling molecules (aka neurotransmitters) to different signal receptors (aka neurons) throughout our body. Metaphorically, we can emulate a neuron as a computational unit and consider the neurotransmitters as real number inputs and outputs that pass from a neuron to another. Each input to a neuron comes with a associated weight and the neuron will process the different inputs (often by summing them) and passing it to a non-linear function which will provide an output value.

For instance, we can think of a neuron as a typical AND/OR logic gate. Given two binary inputs x_1 and x_2 and a *bias* unit with input 1 and a varying weights, we pass it to a neuron that sums the product of the weights and input and passes the sum to a non-linear function that outputs a boolean y value of 0 if the sum is below 0 and 1 if the sum is above 0.

From the left graph and table in Figure 1, we see

Proceedings of SemEval-2016, pages 963–968,
San Diego, California, June 16-17, 2016. ©2016 Association for Computational Linguistics

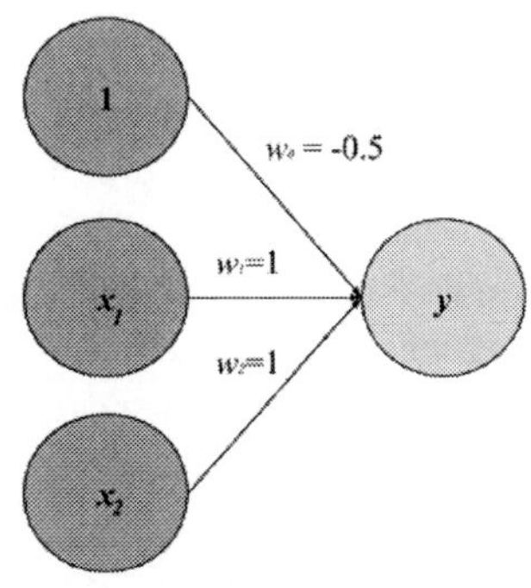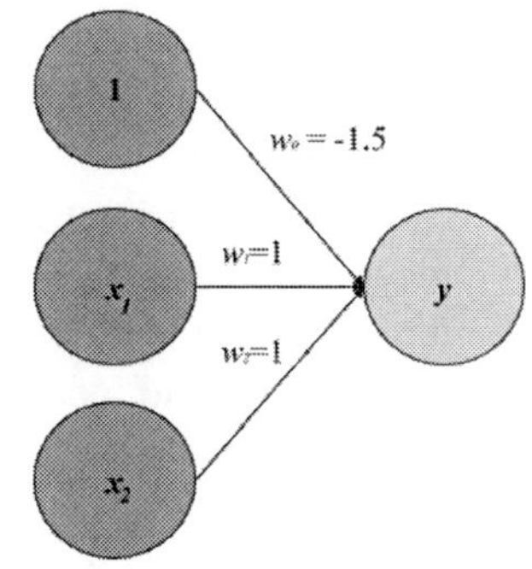

x_1	x_2	$sum = w_0*1 + w_1*x_1 + w_2*x_2$	$y = 1$ if $sum > 0$ $y = 0$ if $sum <= 0$
0	0	-0.5*1 + 1*0 + 1*0 = -0.5	0
0	1	-0.5*1 + 1*0 + 1*1 = 0.5	1
1	0	-0.5*1 + 1*1 + 1*0 = 0.5	1
1	1	-0.5*1 + 1*1 + 1*1 = 1.5	1

x_1	x_2	$sum = w_0*1 + w_1*x_1 + w_2*x_2$	$y = 1$ if $sum > 0$ $y = 0$ if $sum <= 0$
0	0	-1.5*1 + 1*0 + 1*0 = -1.5	0
0	1	-1.5*1 + 1*0 + 1*1 = -0.5	0
1	0	-1.5*1 + 1*1 + 1*0 = -0.5	0
1	1	-1.5*1 + 1*1 + 1*1 = 0.5	1

Figure 1: Single Neuron to Emulate an OR Gate (left) and AND Gate (right)

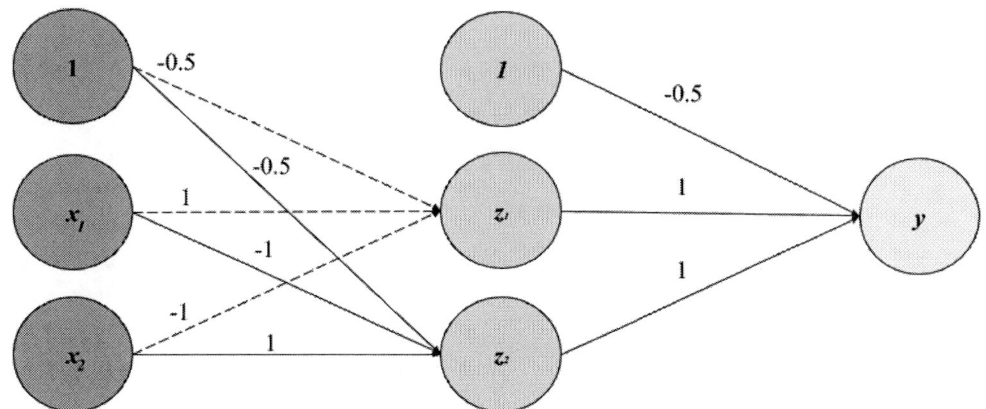

x_1	x_2	$sum_1 = w_0*1 + w_1*x_1 + w_2*x_2$	z_1	$sum_2 = w_0*1 + w_1*x_1 + w_2*x_2$	z_2
0	0	-0.5*1 + 1*0 + -1*0 = -0.5	0	-0.5*1 + -1*0 + 1*0 = -0.5	0
0	1	-0.5*1 + 1*0 + -1*1 = -1.5	0	-0.5*1 + -1*0 + 1*1 = 0.5	1
1	0	-0.5*1 + 1*1 + -1*0 = 0.5	1	-0.5*1 + -1*1 + 1*0 = -1.5	0
1	1	-0.5*1 + 1*1 + -1*1 = -0.5	0	-0.5*1 + -1*1 + 1*1 = -0.5	0

z_1	z_2	$sum_3 = w_0*1 + w_1*x_1 + w_2*x_2$	y
0	0	-0.5*1 + 1*0 + 1*0 = -0.5	0
0	1	-0.5*1 + 1*0 + 1*1 = 0.5	1
1	0	-0.5*1 + 1*1 + 1*0 = 0.5	1
0	0	-0.5*1 + 1*0 + 1*0 = -0.5	0

Figure 2: Emulate an XOR Gate with Feed-forward Network

that the neuron emulates an OR logic gate where it outputs 1 when either of the input is a positive input and outputs 0 when both inputs are 0s. Similarly, right graph and table in Figure 1 presents a neural depiction of a AND logic gate.

If we consider the 2nd row in the left table of Figure 1, the *bias* with the value of 1 and inputs $x_1 = 0$ and $x_1 = 1$ are fed into neuro to produce the y output. Within the neuron, it first sums the inputs and the associated weights up (i.e. $w_0 * bias + w_1 * x_1 + w_1 * x_1$). Then using a non-linear thresholding function, the neuron outputs $y = 1$ since the sum is larger than 0. Thus the neuron fulfils the function of an OR that accepts a 1 and 0 input bit to produce a positive bit.

The problem gets more complicated when we want to use neurons to emulate an exclusive OR XOR logic gate, to get a positive binary output, only one of the inputs can be positive and XOR returns a negative output when there are more than one or less than one positive input(s).

We can split the XOR problem into small logical expressions:

$$\text{XOR} = [x_1 \text{ AND NOT } x_2] \text{ OR } [\text{NOT } x_1 \text{ AND } x_2]$$

As shown in Figure 2, we can emulate an XOR gate by stacking two layers of neurons. On the first layer, we solve for

(i) z_1 to represent $[x_1 \text{ AND NOT } x_2]$ with weights -0.5, 1 and -1 attached to the *bias*, x_1 and x_2

(ii) z_2 to represent $[\text{NOT } x_1 \text{ AND } x_2]$ with weights -0.5, -1 and 1 attached to the *bias*, x_1 and x_2.

At the second layer, we apply the same weights we use for the OR gates and feed z_1 and z_2 as the input to produce the XOR outputs. Interestingly, if we look at the first layer, we notice that the z_1 and z_2 will never both be 1s. Often the network architecture we use to solve the XOR example is referred to as a *feed-forward multi-layered network*.

The logic gates examples motivate the simple use of single neurons and the effect of stacking layers of neurons to produce the desired outcome[2]. Hence the notion, *"Deep Learning"*.

---

[2]The logic gates examples are taken from Emily Fox and Carlos Guestrin machine learning course on Coursera, https://www.coursera.org/learn/ml-foundations

In all the logic gate examples we have manually assigned the weights that are associated with the neurons and it perfectly predicts the desired XOR outputs. In practice, these weights has to be trained using pairs of input bits and their respective outputs.

The rest of the paper will not go through the neural network architecture used in our submission in the same level of detail as this section. Goldberg (2015) and Cho (2015) provides a great read on using deep learning and neural networks for NLP tasks and the formal mathematical descriptions of how to train the networks.

3 Recurrent Neural Net

A Recurrent Neural Net (RNN) is an architecture of deep neural network that chains up neurons in a sequential manner. The Elman Network is the simplest formulation of RNN; it allow arbitrarily sized structured inputs to be represented by a fixed-size vector observing the structured properties of the input (Elman, 1990).

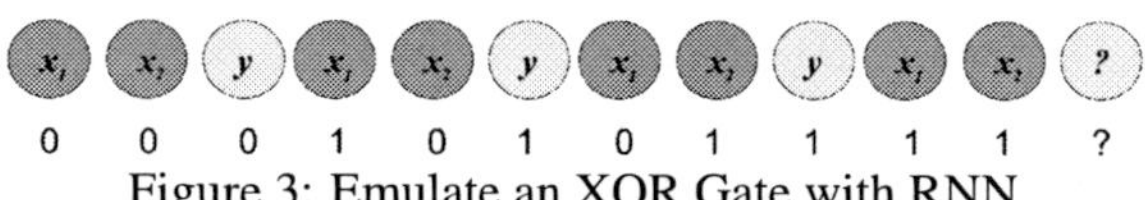

Figure 3: Emulate an XOR Gate with RNN

Returning to the XOR problem, instead of using a feed-forward multi-layered network, we can change the problem into a sequential one. Figure 3 shows how the inputs can be chained in a sequential manner in candence, $x_1, x_1, y, x_1, x_1, y, ...$ (*input input output, input input output, ...*). And at the end of the sequence, the network can predict the output of the last set of inputs without an output.

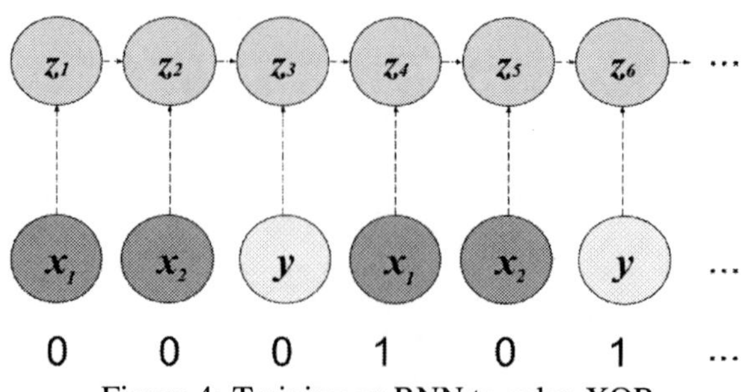

Figure 4: Training an RNN to solve XOR

Figure 4 presents a naive method to chain the inputs x_i, outputs y and hidden units z_i to train an RNN and the dotted lines presents trainable weights.

965

Despite its simplicity, RNN produces competitive results for sequence tagging (Xu et al., 2015) and language modelling (Mikolov et al., 2010). However, it is hard to train effectively due to the vanishing gradient problem; the gradients in the later steps of the sequence quickly diminishes during back-propagation (Rumelhart et al., 1988) and they don't reach the earlier inputs.

To solve the vanishing gradients problem, Hochreiter and Schmidhuber (1997) introduced the Long Short-Term Memory (LSTM). The intuition is to introduce a "memory cell" to preserve the gradients; at every input state, a gate is used to control how much of the new input should be kept in the memory cell how much it should forget. Cho et al. (2014) proposed a similar "memory" device, Gated Recurrent Unit (GRU), to control that add extra weight matrices to learn what long-distance relationships to remember or forget.

4   Complex Word Identification

Complex Word Identification (CWI) is task of identifying difficult words in a text automatically. Usually, it is structured as a subtask prior to lexical simplification where a difficult words from a text is substituted to simpler ones (Specia et al., 2012; Shardlow, 2013). The inputs of the task is a target word and the context sentence in which it occurs. For example, given the underlined word and the context sentence,

> *The short words math or maths are often used for <u>arithmetic</u> , geometry or basic algebra by young student and their schools.*

The desired output for the inputs would either be a 1 to indicate that the target word is complex and 0 if the target word is not.

4.1   Complex Word Identification with RNN

Neural network has opened a Pandora box where engineers can stack the network in different architectures to train their desired models for almost any NLP task. The sequential nature of language production fits the recurrent structure of the RNN and engineers can easily redesign any NLP task into a sequence prediction task.

Knowing little about the task, we lemmatize and lowercase the sentence[3] and restructure the CWI inputs as a sequence where the target word is separated by a placeholder symbol $< s >$ followed by the context sentence, e.g.

> *arithmetic $< s >$ the short word math or math are often use for arithmetic , geometry or basic algebra by young student and their school .*

Then we fit all the training instances into an RNN network with GRU to output the binary labels. However, we are unsure of the optimal hyper-parameters for the model, so we trained 180 models with varying *embedding sizes* (10, 20, 50, 100, 200, 1000), *GRU sizes* (10, 20, 50, 100, 200, 1000) and *no. of epoch* (1, 3, 5, 7, 10).

We select the top model with the lowest labelling error on the training labels as our `Baseline` submission. Since we do not know the variance between the training and evaluation data, we select outputs from the top 5 models with the lowest training error and train an eXtreme Boosted Trees regressor (Friedman, 2001; Chen and Guestrin, 2016) to produce a single output label.

The open-source implementation of our system can be found on `https://github.com/alvations/stubboRNNess`. It is based on the Passage RNN[4] and XGBoost[5] Ensemble libraries.

5   Results

Table 1 presents the results of the best systems and the neural network systems from the CWI task in SemEval-2016 (Paetzold and Specia, 2016). We have submitted our systems under the team name, *Sensible*.

The CWI task was evaluated based on classic accuracy, precision recall and F-score metric. Additionally, the organizers decided to account for the harmonic mean between the accuracy and recall and they called it the G-Score.

The top teams used a variety of heuristics and classificatoin based techniques. PLUJAGH-SEWDFF uses frequency thresholding where they

---

[3]Using lemmatizer from `PyWSD` (Tan, 2014)
[4]https://github.com/IndicoDataSolutions/Passage
[5]https://github.com/dmlc/xgboost

Team	Submission	Accuracy	Precision	Recall	F-Score	G-Score
PLUJAGH	SEWDFF	**0.922**	**0.289**	0.453	**0.353**	0.608
LTG	System2	0.889	0.22	0.541	0.312	0.672
SV000gg	Soft	0.779	0.147	0.769	0.246	**0.774**
SV000gg	Hard	0.761	0.138	**0.787**	0.235	0.773
Sensible	Baseline	0.591	0.078	0.713	0.140	0.646
Sensible	Combined	0.737	0.072	0.390	0.122	0.510
AmritaCEN	w2vecSim	0.627	0.061	0.486	0.109	0.547
CoastalCPH	NeuralNet	0.693	0.063	0.398	0.108	0.506
AmritaCEN	w2vecSimPos	0.743	0.060	0.306	0.100	0.434

Table 1: Results of Best (Upper) and Neural Network Systems (Lower) in the SemEval-2016 CWI Task

consider any word that occurs less than 147 times in the simple English Wikipedia to be complex. Similarly, LTG-System2 uses threshold features to train a decision tree classifier. SV000gg combines 23 different systems uses soft and hard voting ensemble, their pre-ensembled systems includes threshold- and lexicon-based heuristics and machine learning classifiers trained on 69 distinct linguistic features.

CoastalCPH's NeuralNet system extracted an array of features (including parts-of-speech, frequencies, character perplexity and embeddings) and they train a deep neural network with 2 hidden layers. AmritaCEN's w2vecSim trained an SVM classifier using Word2Vec embeddings and the similarity between the target word, in addition, they used character and token based features to train the classifier. Their w2vecSimPossystem added a POS feature to train the classifier.

Among the neural network systems, our baseline system achieved the highest F- and G-score. We are also the only team that restructured the target word and sentence to train recurrent neural net to predict the output label. One possible reason for the poor performance of our systems is due to the training data size of the task. The training data contains 2,237 labelled instances while the test data contains 88,221 instances. Given more data, we believe that our system can scale towards accuracies comparative to the top systems.

Although our ensemble system performed poorly in the harmonic scores, we see that it achieves reasonably high accuracy close to the top systems. Our ensemble system was penalized due to the low recall and rate. Provided that we have more training data, the recall should proportionally increase and improve our ensemble system.

6 Conclusion

In this paper, we motivated the use of deep learning and neural nets in NLP applications and introduced basic notions of feed-forward and recurrent neural nets through the XOR example. And as expected, we can easily build a relatively competitive system with little understanding of the task by restructuring the inputs as a sequence to train an RNN classifier.

We have introduced a novel approach using RNN to solve the complex word identification task and showed that we can easily ensemble several RNN classifiers if we are unsure of the optimal hyperparameters or the best performing models using extreme gradient boosted trees classifiers.

Acknowledgments

We thank Jimmy Callin, Jon Dehdari and Yoav Goldberg for the pointers on the literature review sections on (Recurrent) Neural Nets.

References

T. Chen and C. Guestrin. 2016. XGBoost: A Scalable Tree Boosting System. *ArXiv e-prints*.

Kyunghyun Cho, Bart Van Merriënboer, Caglar Gulcehre, Dzmitry Bahdanau, Fethi Bougares, Holger Schwenk, and Yoshua Bengio. 2014. Learning phrase representations using rnn encoder-decoder for statistical machine translation. *arXiv preprint arXiv:1406.1078*.

Kyunghyun Cho. 2015. Natural language understanding with distributed representation. *arXiv preprint arXiv:1511.07916*.

Ronan Collobert, Jason Weston, Léon Bottou, Michael Karlen, Koray Kavukcuoglu, and Pavel Kuksa. 2011. Natural language processing (almost) from scratch. *The Journal of Machine Learning Research*, 12:2493–2537.

Jeffrey L Elman. 1990. Finding structure in time. *Cognitive science*, 14(2):179–211.

Jerome H Friedman. 2001. Greedy function approximation: a gradient boosting machine. *Annals of statistics*, pages 1189–1232.

Yoav Goldberg. 2015. A primer on neural network models for natural language processing. *arXiv preprint arXiv:1510.00726*.

Rohit Gupta, Constantin Orasan, and Josef van Genabith. 2015. Reval: A simple and effective machine translation evaluation metric based on recurrent neural networks. In *Proceedings of the 2015 Conference on Empirical Methods in Natural Language Processing*, pages 1066–1072, Lisbon, Portugal, September.

Sepp Hochreiter and Jürgen Schmidhuber. 1997. Long short-term memory. *Neural computation*, 9(8):1735–1780.

Sébastien Jean, Orhan Firat, Kyunghyun Cho, Roland Memisevic, and Yoshua Bengio. 2015. Montreal neural machine translation systems for wmt15. In *Proceedings of the Tenth Workshop on Statistical Machine Translation*, pages 134–140, Lisbon, Portugal, September.

Julia Kreutzer, Shigehiko Schamoni, and Stefan Riezler. 2015. Quality estimation from scratch (quetch): Deep learning for word-level translation quality estimation. In *Proceedings of the Tenth Workshop on Statistical Machine Translation*, pages 316–322, Lisbon, Portugal, September. Association for Computational Linguistics.

Omer Levy, Yoav Goldberg, and Israel Ramat-Gan. 2014. Linguistic regularities in sparse and explicit word representations. In *CoNLL*, pages 171–180.

Christopher D Manning. 2016. Computational linguistics and deep learning. *Computational Linguistics*.

Tomáš Mikolov, Martin Karafiát, Lukáš Burget, Jan Černocký, and Sanjeev Khudanpur. 2010. Recurrent neural network based language model. In *Proceedings of the 11th Annual Conference of the International Speech Communication Association (INTERSPEECH 2010)*, volume 2010, pages 1045–1048.

Tomas Mikolov, Ilya Sutskever, Kai Chen, Greg S Corrado, and Jeff Dean. 2013. Distributed representations of words and phrases and their compositionality. In *Advances in neural information processing systems*, pages 3111–3119.

Gustavo Henrique Paetzold and Lucia Specia. 2016. Complex word identification. In *Proceedings of the 10th International Workshop on Semantic Evaluation (SemEval 2016)*, San Diego, California.

Jeffrey Pennington, Richard Socher, and Christopher D Manning. 2014. Glove: Global vectors for word representation. In *EMNLP*, volume 14, pages 1532–1543.

David E Rumelhart, Geoffrey E Hinton, and Ronald J Williams. 1988. Learning representations by back-propagating errors. *Cognitive modeling*, 5(3):1.

Matthew Shardlow. 2013. A comparison of techniques to automatically identify complex words. In *51st Annual Meeting of the Association for Computational Linguistics Proceedings of the Student Research Workshop*, pages 103–109, Sofia, Bulgaria, August.

Noam Shazeer, Ryan Doherty, Colin Evans, and Chris Waterson. 2016. Swivel: Improving embeddings by noticing what's missing. *arXiv preprint arXiv:1602.02215*.

Lucia Specia, Sujay Kumar Jauhar, and Rada Mihalcea. 2012. Semeval-2012 task 1: English lexical simplification. In *Proceedings of the Sixth International Workshop on Semantic Evaluation*, pages 347–355.

Md Arafat Sultan, Steven Bethard, and Tamara Sumner. 2014. DLS@CU: Sentence Similarity from Word Alignment. In *Proceedings of the 8th International Workshop on Semantic Evaluation (SemEval 2014)*, pages 241–246, Dublin, Ireland, August.

Md Arafat Sultan, Steven Bethard, and Tamara Sumner. 2015. DLS@CU: Sentence Similarity from Word Alignment and Semantic Vector Composition. In *Proceedings of the 9th International Workshop on Semantic Evaluation (SemEval 2015)*, pages 148–153, Denver, Colorado, June.

Liling Tan. 2014. Pywsd: Python implementations of word sense disambiguation (wsd) technologies [software]. https://github.com/alvations/pywsd.

Wenduan Xu, Michael Auli, and Stephen Clark. 2015. Ccg supertagging with a recurrent neural network. In *Proceedings of the 53rd Annual Meeting of the Association for Computational Linguistics and the 7th International Joint Conference on Natural Language Processing (Volume 2: Short Papers)*, pages 250–255, Beijing, China, July.

SV000gg at SemEval-2016 Task 11:
Heavy Gauge Complex Word Identification with System Voting

Gustavo Henrique Paetzold and **Lucia Specia**
Department of Computer Science
University of Sheffield, UK
{ghpaetzold1,l.specia}@sheffield.ac.uk

Abstract

We introduce the SV000gg systems: two Ensemble Methods for the Complex Word Identification task of SemEval 2016. While the SV000gg-Hard system exploits basic Hard Voting, the SV000gg-Soft system employs Performance-Oriented Soft Voting, which weights votes according to the voter's performance rather than its prediction confidence, allowing for completely heterogeneous systems to be combined. Our performance comparison shows that our voting techniques outperform traditional Soft Voting, as well as other systems submitted to the shared task, ranking first and second overall.

1 Introduction

In Complex Word Identification (CWI), the goal is to find which words in a given text may challenge the members of a given target audience. It is part of the usual Lexical Simplification pipeline, which is illustrated in Figure 1. As shown by the results obtained by (Paetzold and Specia, 2013) and (Shardlow, 2014), ignoring the step of Complex Word Identification in Lexical Simplification can lead simplifiers to neglect challenging words, as well as to replace simple words with inappropriate alternatives.

Various strategies have been devised to address CWI and most of them are very simple in nature. For example, to identify complex words, the lexical simplifier for the medical domain in (Elhadad and Sutaria, 2007) uses a Lexicon-Based approach that exploits the UMLS (Bodenreider, 2004) database: if a medical expression is among the technical terms registered in UMLS, then it is complex.

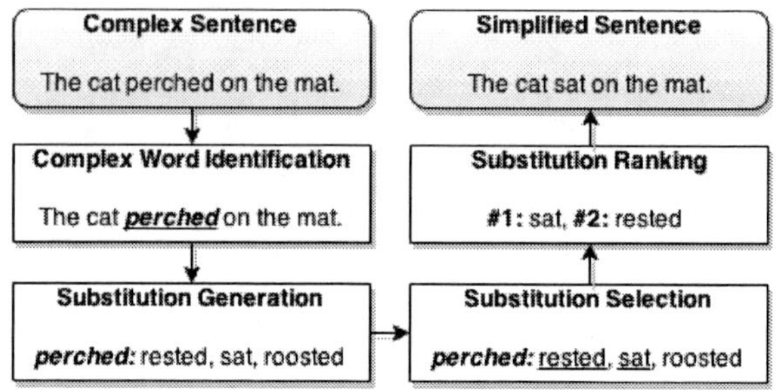

Figure 1: Lexical Simplification pipeline

The complexity identifier for the lexical simplifier in (Keskisärkkä, 2012), for Swedish, uses a threshold over word frequencies to distinguish complex from simple words. Recently, however, more sophisticated approaches have been used. (Shardlow, 2013) presents a CWI benchmarking that compares the performance of a Threshold-Based strategy, a Support Vector Machine (SVM) model trained over various features, and a "simplify everything" baseline.

(Shardlow, 2013)'s SVM model has shown promising results, but CWI approaches do not tend to explore Machine Learning techniques and, in particular, their combination. As an effort to fill this gap, in this paper we describe our contributions to the Complex Word Identification task of SemEval 2016. We introduce two systems, SV000gg-Hard and SV000gg-Soft, both of which use straightforward Ensemble Methods to combine different predictions for CWI. These come from a variety of models, ranging from simple Lexicon-Based approaches to more elaborate Machine Learning classifiers.

Proceedings of SemEval-2016, pages 969–974,
San Diego, California, June 16-17, 2016. ©2016 Association for Computational Linguistics

2 Dataset and Evaluation

In the CWI task of SemEval 2016, participants were asked to submit predictions on the complexity of words based on the needs of non-native English speakers. The setup of the task is as follows: given a target word in a sentence, predict whether or not a non-native English speaker would be able to understand it. For training, a **joint** and a **decomposed** dataset were provided. Both datasets consist in $2,237$ instances containing a sentence, a target word, its position in the sentence, and complexity label(s). The **decomposed** dataset contains 20 binary complexity labels, provided by 20 annotators, while the **joint** dataset contains only one label: 1 if at least one of the 20 annotators did not understand it (complex), and 0 otherwise (simple). Participants were allowed to train their systems over either, both or none of the datasets, as well as use any external resources.

The test set contains $88,221$ instances and follows the same format of the joint dataset, but was generated using only one word complexity label. The difference between the training and test sets is that while each instance in the training set was annotated by 20 people, each instance in the test set was annotated by only one person. The goal with this setup was that of replicating a realistic scenario in Text Simplification, where systems must predict the individual preferences of a target audience based on the overall needs of a population sample.

For evaluation, common metrics – Accuracy, Precision, Recall and F-score – are used, along with a new metric designed specifically for CWI: the **G-score**. The G-score consists of the harmonic mean between Accuracy and Recall, and aims at capturing the performance of a CWI approach to be used within a Lexical Simplification system. The reasoning behind the metric is that an ideal CWI system should avoid both false negatives and false positives, which is measured through Accuracy, and at the same time capture as many complex words as possible, which is measured through Recall. High values on these two metrics would prevent a lexical simplifier from making unnecessary and possibly erroneous word replacements and from neglecting words which should be simplified.

3 System Overview

Our strategy explores the idea behind the popular saying *"two heads are better than one"* for the CWI problem. We believe that combining the "opinion" of various distinct approaches to a given task can yield better results than any of the individual approaches. This idea is not new for classification tasks like ours, and have been thoroughly explored in several ways. Strategies that combine multiple Machine Learning classifiers are often referred to as Ensemble Methods. Such methods range from very simple solutions, such as Hard Voting, in which labels are determined based on how many times they were predicted by the classifiers, to very elaborate approaches, such as Random Forests (Breiman, 2001) and Gradient Boosting (Friedman, 2001).

The strategy we employ consists of a variant of Soft Voting, in which the class of a given instance is determined as in Equation 1.

$$c_f = \arg\max_c \sum_{s \in S} T(s, c) \qquad (1)$$

In traditional Soft Voting, c_f is the selected class, c is one of the possible classes in a classification problem, S the collection of systems considered, and T a confidence estimate, i.e. a function that expresses how confident system s is that c is the correct class. Its goal is to increment Hard Voting by incorporating the systems' classification confidence in the decision process, hopefully making for a more reliable way of exploiting their strengths and weaknesses.

Although sensible in principle, Soft Voting might not be able to effectively combine systems if they do not have a reasonably uniform way of determining the confidence on their predictions. The presence of over-optimistic or over-pessimistic systems may skew the results severely, and hence make the resulting classifier have worse performance than that of the best system among those considered in the voting. Another clear limitation of traditional Soft Voting is that it cannot include systems which simply cannot estimate the confidence level of their prediction. Lexicon-Based CWI approaches such as the ones of (Elhadad and Ph, 2006) and (Elhadad and Sutaria, 2007), for example, predict that a word is simple if it is present in a certain vocabulary. These approaches tend to be very effective in certain contexts, but can only produce binary confidence estimates: if the word is in the vocabulary, then it is 100% sure the word is simple, if not, it is 100% sure the word is complex.

In order to address these limitations, we exploit Performance-Oriented Soft Voting (Georgiou and Mavroforakis, 2013). Instead of using the systems' summed confidence to predict a label, it uses their performance score over a certain validation dataset. Formally, we decompose function T from Equation 1 into the two functions illustrated in Equation 2.

$$c_f = \arg\max_c \sum_{s \in S} P(s, d) * D(s, c) \qquad (2)$$

In Equation 2, P represents the score of system s over a certain dataset d given a certain performance metric, such as Precision, Recall, F1, Accuracy, etc. Function D, on the other hand, outputs value 1 if system s has predicted c for the classification problem in question, and 0 otherwise.

This setup works under the assumption that the systems' performance under a validation dataset is a reliable surrogate for confidence predictions, and allows for any type of systems to be combined, whether or not they are homogeneous in their way of predicting classes.

In what follows, we described the features and settings used in the creation of our two CWI systems: SV000gg-Hard and SV000gg-Soft. While SV000gg-Hard uses basic Hard Voting, SV000gg-Soft uses Performance-Oriented Soft Voting. Since both of them combine a series of sub-systems, to avoid confusion, we henceforth refer to these sub-systems as "voters".

3.1 Features

Our voters use a total of 69 features. They can be divided in four categories:

- **Binary:** If a target word is part of a certain vocabulary, then it receives label 1, otherwise, 0. We extract vocabularies from Simple Wikipedia (Kauchak, 2013), Ogden's Basic English (Ogden, 1968) and SubIMDB (Paetzold, 2015).

- **Lexical:** Includes word length, number of syllables, number of senses, synonyms, hypernyms and hyponyms in WordNet (Fellbaum, 1998), and language model probability in Wikipedia (Kauchak and Barzilay, 2006), Simple Wikipedia and SubIMDB.

- **Collocational:** Language model probabilities of all n-gram combinations with windows $w < 3$ to the left and right of the target complex word in Wikipedia, SUBTLEX (Brysbaert and New, 2009), Simple Wikipedia and SubIMDB.

- **Nominal:** Includes the word itself, its POS tag, both word and POS tag n-gram combinations with windows $w < 3$ to the left and right, and the word's language model backoff behavior (Uhrik and Ward, 1997) according to a 5-gram language model trained over Simple Wikipedia with SRILM (Stolcke and others, 2002).

In order for language model probabilities to be calculated, we train a 5-gram language model for each of the aforementioned corpora using SRILM (Stolcke and others, 2002). Nominal features were obtained with the help of LEXenstein (Paetzold and Specia, 2015).

3.2 Voters

We train a total of 21 voters which we have grouped in three categories:

- **Lexicon-Based (LB):** If a word is present in a given vocabulary of simple words, then it is simple, otherwise, it is complex. We train one Lexicon-Based voter for each binary feature described in the previous Section.

- **Threshold-Based (TB):** Given a certain feature, learns the threshold t which best separates complex and simple words. In order to learn t, it first calculates the feature value for all instances in the training data and obtains its minimum and maximum. It then divides the interval into $10,000$ equally sized parts, and performs a brute force search over all $10,000$ values to find the one which yields the highest G-score over the training data. We train one Threshold-Based voter for each lexical feature described in the previous Section.

System	Accuracy	Precision	Recall	F-score	G-score
All Complex	0.047	0.047	1.000	0.089	0.089
All Simple	0.953	0.000	0.000	0.000	0.000
(LB) SubIMDB	0.913	0.217	0.332	0.262	0.487
(LB) Ogden's	0.248	0.056	0.947	0.105	0.393
(LB) Wikipedia	0.047	0.047	1.000	0.089	0.090
(LB) Simple Wikipedia	0.953	0.241	0.002	0.003	0.003
(TB) Probability: Wikipedia	0.536	0.084	0.901	0.154	0.672
(TB) Probability: Simple Wiki	0.513	0.081	0.902	0.148	0.654
(TB) Number of Hypernyms	0.572	0.076	0.728	0.137	0.641
(TB) Probability: SUBTLEX	0.492	0.077	0.896	0.142	0.636
(TB) Probability: SubIMDB	0.445	0.072	0.912	0.133	0.598
(TB) Number of Senses	0.436	0.068	0.861	0.125	0.579
(TB) Number of Hyponyms	0.384	0.065	0.906	0.121	0.539
(TB) Length	0.332	0.057	0.852	0.107	0.478
(ML) Decision Trees	0.805	0.158	0.733	0.260	0.767
(ML) Adaptive Boosting	0.799	0.153	0.728	0.253	0.762
(ML) Random Forests	0.826	0.170	0.698	0.273	0.756
(ML) Gradient Boosting	0.802	0.147	0.672	0.241	0.731
(ML) Multi-Layer Perceptron	0.691	0.105	0.741	0.183	0.715
(ML) Passive Aggressive Learning	0.852	0.171	0.562	0.262	0.677
(ML) Conditional Random Fields	0.534	0.076	0.808	0.140	0.643
(ML) Stochastic Gradient Descent	0.648	0.057	0.423	0.101	0.512
(ML) Support Vector Machines	0.715	0.061	0.357	0.105	0.476
TALN-RandomForest_WEI	0.812	0.164	0.736	0.268	0.772
UWB-All	0.803	0.157	0.734	0.258	0.767
PLUJAGH-SEWDF	0.795	0.152	0.741	0.252	0.767
JUNLP-NaiveBayes	0.767	0.139	0.767	0.236	0.767
HMC-RegressionTree05	0.838	0.182	0.705	0.290	0.766
HMC-DecisionTree25	0.846	0.189	0.698	0.298	0.765
JUNLP-RandomForest	0.795	0.151	0.730	0.250	0.761
MACSAAR-RFC	0.825	0.168	0.694	0.270	0.754
TALN-RandomForest_SIM	0.847	0.186	0.673	0.292	0.750
MACSAAR-NNC	0.804	0.146	0.660	0.240	0.725
Pomona-NormalBag	0.604	0.095	0.872	0.171	0.714
Melbourne-runw15	0.586	0.091	0.870	0.165	0.701
UWB-Agg	0.569	0.089	0.885	0.161	0.693
Pomona-GoogleBag	0.568	0.088	0.881	0.160	0.691
IIIT-NCC	0.546	0.084	0.880	0.154	0.674
LTG-System2	0.889	0.220	0.541	0.312	0.672
MAZA-A	0.773	0.115	0.578	0.192	0.661
Melbourne-runw3	0.513	0.080	0.895	0.147	0.652
Sensible-Baseline	0.591	0.078	0.713	0.140	0.646
ClacEDLK-ClacEDLK-RF_0.6	0.688	0.081	0.548	0.141	0.610
PLUJAGH-SEWDFF	0.922	0.289	0.453	**0.353**	0.608
IIIT-NCC2	0.465	0.071	0.860	0.131	0.604
ClacEDLK-ClacEDLK-RF_0.5	0.751	0.090	0.475	0.152	0.582
MAZA-B	0.912	0.243	0.420	0.308	0.575
AmritaCEN-w2vecSim	0.627	0.061	0.486	0.109	0.547
Soft Voting	0.780	0.125	0.615	0.207	0.688
SV000g-Soft	0.779	0.147	0.769	0.246	**0.774**
SV000g-Hard	0.761	0.138	0.787	0.235	0.773

Table 1: Performance scores. Separated by double horizontal lines are three system groups: our voters, other systems submitted to the SemEval task, and our Ensemble solutions.

- **Machine-Learning-Assisted (ML):** Learn a binary classification model from the training data using a Machine Learning algorithm. We build models using the following seven algorithms in the scikit-learn toolkit (Pedregosa et al., 2011):

  1. Support Vector Machines
  2. Passive Aggressive Learning
  3. Stochastic Gradient Descent
  4. Decision Trees
  5. Ada Boosting
  6. Gradient Boosting
  7. Random Forests

Additionally, we use Keras[1] to otrain a Multi-Layer Perceptron voter. Its architecture, including number and size of hidden-layers, was decided through 5-fold cross-validation over the training set. The aforementioned models use as input all binary, lexical and collocational features. Finally, we also train a Conditional Random Field model using CRFSuite (Okazaki, 2007). It uses as input all nominal features described in the previous Section. The hyper-parameters of all Machine Learning-assisted voters are determined through 5-fold cross-validation over the G-score.

We select the number of the top G-score systems to be considered through 5-fold cross-validation over the joint dataset. For completion, we also include a traditional Soft Voting system that combines Machine Learning approaches only, given that the others do not have well-established ways of calculating prediction probability estimates.

4 Results

Table 1 illustrates the performance scores of all individual voters, along with the 25 best performing systems in the CWI task, a standard Soft Voting approach, and our two SV000gg systems. Despite their simplicity, our system voting strategies are the two most effective CWI solutions submitted to SemEval 2016, having both obtained considerably higher G-scores than traditional Soft Voting. These results

---

[1] http://keras.io

show the importance of finding clever ways to combine distinct strategies for a task, since, by not considering Lexicon and Threshold-Based voters, the traditional soft voter suffered a considerable loss in G-score.

The results of the individual voters reveal that Decision Trees and Ensemble Methods achieve noticeably higher performance than the Multi-Layer Perceptron, which have been used as state-of-the-art solutions to various tasks. Another surprise comes with the scores of Threshold-Based voters, which offer competitive performance in comparison to Machine Learning techniques. The performance of our Conditional Random Field voter suggest that nominal features are not as reliable as numeric features in predicting word complexity.

The effectiveness of Ensemble Methods is further highlighted by the scores of ours' and others' solutions for the SemEval task: precisely 50% of the top 10 systems use some type of Ensemble.

5 Conclusions

We have presented our contributions to the Complex Word Identification task of SemEval 2016: the SV000gg systems, which exploit two types of system Ensemble voting schemes. Along with the typical Hard Voting, we employ Performance-Oriented Soft Voting, which diverges from traditional Soft Voting by weighting votes not by their prediction confidence, but rather by overall system performance.

Our performance comparison shows how effective our voting strategies can be: they top the rankings in the SemEval task, outperforming even elaborate Ensemble strategies. We hope that our approach will serve as a reliable alternative to other problems in Natural Language Processing and beyond.

In the future, we also intend to explore the use of Gaussian Processes and Multi-Task Learning for Complex Word Identification.

References

O. Bodenreider. 2004. The unified medical language system (umls): integrating biomedical terminology. *Nucleic acids research*, 32.

Leo Breiman. 2001. Random forests. *Machine Learning*, 45:5–32.

Marc Brysbaert and Boris New. 2009. Moving beyond kucera and francis: a critical evaluation of current word frequency norms and the introduction of a new and improved word frequency measure for american english. *Behavior research methods*, 41(4):977–90, December.

Noemie Elhadad and D Ph. 2006. Comprehending technical texts : Predicting and defining unfamiliar terms. pages 239–243.

Noemie Elhadad and Komal Sutaria. 2007. Mining a lexicon of technical terms and lay equivalents. pages 49–56.

Christiane Fellbaum. 1998. *WordNet: An Electronic Lexical Database*. Bradford Books.

Jerome H Friedman. 2001. Greedy function approximation: a gradient boosting machine. *Annals of statistics*, pages 1189–1232.

Harris V Georgiou and Michael E Mavroforakis. 2013. A game-theoretic framework for classifier ensembles using weighted majority voting with local accuracy estimates. *arXiv preprint arXiv:1302.0540*.

David Kauchak and Regina Barzilay. 2006. Paraphrasing for automatic evaluation. In *Proceedings of the 2006 NAACL*, pages 455–462.

David Kauchak. 2013. Improving text simplification language modeling using unsimplified text data. In *Proceedings of the 51st ACL*, pages 1537–1546.

R Keskisärkkä. 2012. Automatic text simplification via synonym replacement.

Charles Kay Ogden. 1968. *Basic English: international second language*. Harcourt, Brace & World.

Naoaki Okazaki. 2007. CRFsuite: a fast implementation of conditional random fields. http://www.chokkan.org/software/crfsuite/.

Gustavo H. Paetzold and Lucia Specia. 2013. Text simplification as tree transduction. In *Proceedings of the 9th STIL*.

Gustavo Henrique Paetzold and Lucia Specia. 2015. Lexenstein: A framework for lexical simplification. In *Proceedings of The 53rd ACL*.

Gustavo Henrique Paetzold. 2015. Reliable lexical simplification for non-native speakers. In *Proceedings of the 2015 NAACL Student Research Workshop*.

F. Pedregosa, G. Varoquaux, A. Gramfort, V. Michel, B. Thirion, O. Grisel, M. Blondel, P. Prettenhofer, R. Weiss, V. Dubourg, J. Vanderplas, A. Passos, D. Cournapeau, M. Brucher, M. Perrot, and E. Duchesnay. 2011. Scikit-learn: Machine learning in Python. *Journal of Machine Learning Research*, 12:2825–2830.

Matthew Shardlow. 2013. A comparison of techniques to automatically identify complex words. In *Proceedings of the 51st ACL Student Research Workshop*, pages 103–109.

Matthew Shardlow. 2014. Out in the open: Finding and categorising errors in the lexical simplification pipeline. In *Proceedings of the 9th LREC*.

Andreas Stolcke et al. 2002. Srilm - an extensible language modeling toolkit. In *Interspeech*.

C Uhrik and W Ward. 1997. Confidence metrics based on n-gram language model backoff behaviors. In *Proceedings of EUROSPEECH*.

Melbourne at SemEval 2016 Task 11: Classifying Type-level Word Complexity using Random Forests with Corpus and Word List Features

Julian Brooke　　**Timothy Baldwin**
Computing and Info Systems
The University of Melbourne
jabrooke@unimelb.edu.au
tb@ldwin.net

Alexandra L. Uitdenbogerd
Computer Science and Info Technology
RMIT University
sandrau@rmit.edu.au

Abstract

SemEval 2016 task 11 involved determining whether words in a sentence were complex or simple for a cohort of people with English as a second language. Training data consisted of 200 annotated sentences, representing the combined judgements of 20 human annotators, such that if any annotator of the group labelled a word as complex, then it was considered to be complex. Testing was based on single annotator judgements. Our system used a random forest classifier with a variety of features, the most important of which were term frequency statistics garnered from four large corpora, and style lexicons built on two large corpora. Minor features in the final system include the presence or absence of words in various readability word lists; many other features we tried were not successful. Our ranking amongst submitted systems did not reflect the strength of our system, due to submitting a far from optimal weighting between complex and simple, but we show that when a more appropriate weighting is used, our system ranks amongst the best submitted systems.

1　Introduction

Most work related to readability measurement (Chall and Dale, 1995) focuses on text-level assessment, but it is clear that being able to determine the difficulty of individual words is important to both that task as well as related ones such as lexical text simplification (Shardlow, 2014). Although some words can be considered conceptually difficult — that is, a level of intellectual sophistication is required to grasp its meaning — for language learners,

it is more common for words to be considered difficult (or complex) simply because a reader has had little or no exposure to them. This exposure may depend on many different external factors related to the person's background, some of which may generalize across other similar readers, while others may be entirely idiosyncratic to the reader in question. For example, those who study academic English, or operate in an academic environment, have a different vocabulary exposure to those who specialize in hospitality English. Therefore, there is value in not only trying to predict some prior difficulty of a word, but also trying to generalize across readers in a similar cohort. Task 11 of the 2016 SemEval competition (Complex Word Identification) is aimed at addressing this challenge.

This paper describes our system for the task. We commenced with previous work in word readability scoring (Brooke et al., 2012) and stylistic lexicon creation (Brooke and Hirst, 2013; Brooke and Hirst, 2014). For features, we drew on a diverse set of corpus-based and human-derived metrics, and built a random forest-based classifier. While a mistake related to the proper distribution of complex versus simple words prevented us from scoring amongst the top teams in either of the evaluations metrics used in this task, we show that by appropriate class weighting with the same classifier and features, we can obtain results on either metric that are competitive or better than the best teams.

2　Background

The motivation for SemEval 2016 Task 11 was the need to automatically identify complex

975

Proceedings of SemEval-2016, pages 975–981,
San Diego, California, June 16-17, 2016. ©2016 Association for Computational Linguistics

words (Shardlow, 2013) for the task of automated text simplification (Shardlow, 2014). However, the modelling of word complexity and text complexity has a long history, much of it using the term *readability*, and intended for finding reading material of an appropriate level of difficulty for children and language learners (Chall and Dale, 1995). The measurement of word readability, or lexical complexity, is a fundamental component for a range of techniques and their applications beyond automated text simplification: text readability measurement is used as a basis for automatically recommending reading to language learners (Collins-Thompson and Callan, 2004a); lexical complexity measurement can also allow the automatic glossing of reading material presented electronically (Walmsley, 2011), or the display of text comprising a mixture of two languages (Uitdenbogerd, 2014).

Early work on readability resulted in a large number of measures being developed, typically based on tests given to school-aged native speakers of English (Klare, 1974). The majority of these measures had two recognizable components: grammatical difficulty and word difficulty. The word difficulty component of the measures had the following varieties: inclusion in a list of generally known words, such as the Dale-Chall measure (Chall and Dale, 1995); word length in letters, such as the Automated Readability Index (Senter and Smith, 1967) and Coleman-Liau formulae (Coleman and Liau, 1975); word length in syllables, such as the Flesch and Kincaid formulae (Kincaid et al., 1975); the proportion of words exceeding a word length threshold in characters, such as Lix; and proportion of words exceeding a length threshold in syllables, such as the SMOG formula (Klare, 1974). Criticism of these early readability measures included their inability to capture conceptual difficulty (Gordon, 1980), leading the field to be abandoned to some extent until the current millennium, in which corpus-based techniques, language models, and classifiers became popular, and large-scale corpora became readily available (Collins-Thompson and Callan, 2004b; François, 2009).

For second language learners, it has been observed that higher frequency of exposure increases the chance that a word is known, leading to a typical vocabulary knowledge profile in which the percentage of known words per 1000 in a ranked list by frequency, monotonically decreases (Meara, 1992). When language learning is optimized based on word frequency, as is often recommended by researchers of language acquisition (Sinclair and Renouf, 1988), the effect may even be exaggerated.

3   Data

The training data released for this task included about 200 sentences, in which each word token that was not a proper noun was annotated as either complex or simple. A word was considered complex if any one annotator from a set of 20 annotators marked it as such. We found many sentences being tagged entirely or almost entirely as complex, for no obvious reason; for training, we excluded any sentence where the number of complex words was greater than or equal to the number of tagged words minus 2, leading to 29 sentences being removed. We also excluded from training any appearances of a set of 140 closed-class function words, which we always classified as simple; both test and training data have words from our list that were tagged as complex, but these appear to be mostly errors, and in general we didn't want our classifier focusing on classifying extremely common words.

After applying these two filters, the total number of tokens tagged complex in the training set was 427, and the total number of tokens tagged simple was 1234, or roughly a 3 to 1 ratio of simple to complex. By contrast, the test set, which was the result of annotation by individual annotators of about 9000 sentences, had a ratio of simple to complex of almost 18 to 1 (after the common words are removed), which is an extreme difference in class distribution; though we expected to see this effect, when we prepared our system we had no good way of estimating its magnitude. Late in the competition, the organizers released individual annotations which allowed for a more accurate estimate of the expected class distribution, but we became aware of that only after the competition was over, and our work here is based on optimizing using the initial class distribution.

4   Lists of Features

We divide our feature lists into three categories: major features, minor features, and unused features.

Major features are those which we believe are essential to the good performance of the model; minor features were helpful in the version of the classifier we used here, based on 20-fold cross-validation in the training set, but the effect was fairly modest; and unused features were not found to be helpful, but we include them for completeness to give a full sense of everything we tried. There are too many features (and too many combinations) to offer up individual numerical analysis of what worked and what didn't. Our features were selected by optimizing G-score (see Section 6) with a 20-fold cross-validation of the training set.

4.1 Major Features

Term frequency statistics We collected term frequency statistics from four large corpora: the British National Corpus ("BNC": Burnard (2000)), the Gigaword corpus (Graff and Cieri, 2003), the International Conference on Web and Social Media (ICWSM) blog corpus (Burton et al., 2009), and Project Gutenberg (read using the GutenTag tool (Brooke et al., 2015)). We consciously chose corpora that had significant variety with respect to their genre, with the intent of allowing the classifier to focus in on particular kinds of words that certain groups might have trouble with. Note that we typically used the count for the specific word type, but where it didn't exist in the corpus we substituted the lemma count, rather than giving a count of zero. All of the corpora were of benefit to the final model.

Six style lexicons For the ICWSM and the Project Gutenberg corpora, we built lexicons for six lexical styles using the co-occurrence information in these corpora. The six styles are: literary, abstract, objective, colloquial, concrete, and subjective; each style for each corpus is an individual feature. We used the seed set for the six styles from Brooke et al. (2013), and the co-occurrence profile ranking approach from Brooke and Hirst (2014). We chose these two corpora because they are extremely large, varied in content, and we have used and evaluated them in other work; highly constrained language like the newswire text in the Gigaword corpus is unlikely to be of much use for building stylistic lexicons in this fashion.

4.2 Minor Features

Dale-Chall List The presence or absence of the word in the Dale-Chall list, a list of 3000 common words used in the Dale-Chall readability metric (Chall and Dale, 1995).

Academic Word List The ranking of the word on the 570-word Academic Word List, which divides academic language into 10 frequency categories (Coxhead, 2000).

Beginner List A list of 4636 beginner words, including words from the Dolch list (Dolch, 1936), previously used as a training/test set in earlier lexical readability work (Brooke et al., 2012).

Is Lemma A boolean feature indicating whether a word is its lemma or not. For instance *run* is a lemma but *ran* is not.

4.3 Unused Features

Document Frequency We tested document frequency as a complement or alternative to term frequency for the various corpora.

Average Sentence Length The average sentence length of the documents the word appears in, for the 4 corpora used for term frequency. It was a useful feature in our earlier work on lexical readability (Brooke et al., 2012), and is an excellent readability feature generally (Uitdenbogerd, 2005).

Word Length The length of the word, in characters, was useful in early iterations but not in the final model.

Average Word Length The average word length in the documents that the word appears in, for the 4 corpora, is another feature from Brooke et al. (2012).

Formality lexicon The formality lexicon built from the ICWSM corpus in Brooke and Hirst (2014). We believe the information in it overlaps considerably with the 6-style lexicon.

Readability rank The readability rank of words as given by the model from Brooke et al. (2012).

Complexity lexicon Using the words from the training set, we attempted to build a complexity dictionary using the method of Brooke and Hirst (2014). The results were not competitive when the six-style lexicon was included.

Latinate affixes A boolean feature which indicates the presence or absence of a Latinate affix, which can indicate increased formality (Brooke et al., 2010).

Number of Senses The number of senses of the lemma of the word in WordNet (Fellbaum, 1998).

Hyphen fix For hyphenated words, derive all other statistics using the first word in the hyphenation, instead of the whole word.

Bigram style lexicon The features we use do not distinguish between the word type in different contexts, so we cannot distinguish between word senses. We saw examples of this in the data, such as the word *tried* in the legal sense in *was tried for murder*. We made an initial attempt at integrating this information by building a bigram style lexicon, using the same method as the regular method, averaging the styles of the two possible contexts, and either replacing the word style or including it as a different feature. However, performance was worse.

Is Cognate While not actually implemented, we considered the possibility of using cognates, which might allow us to discount otherwise complex words which are easy for L2 speakers coming from European language backgrounds because there is a very similar word in other languages (Uitdenbogerd, 2005). However, the results of our early investigation suggested that cognates were not appearing with greater frequency among the simple words than expected, and that therefore the language background of the participants was probably not uniformly European.

5   Classifier

Though rarely competitive on large feature sets, a decision-tree-based classifier has several advantages, being considered by some as the only true off-the-shelf classifier (Hastie et al., 2008), in part because it does not require the feature scaling that is typical in linear classification models, and naturally mixes boolean, ordinal and continuous features without having to convert one to the other. If the number of examples and features is low enough, Random Forests — an ensemble classifier that builds multiple decision trees using subsets of the examples and features and then combining the individual votes — is a powerful classifier with all the advantages of the basic decision tree (except interpretability). On the basis of 20-fold cross-validation over the training set, we found that it was the best classifier among a wide range of options (including all the other ensemble classifiers) that we tested in Sci-kit learn (Pedregosa et al., 2011). We tuned the parameters with an initial feature set, carried out feature selection, and then tuned the parameters again, with very little further effect. The only two parameters that were different to the default were the number of estimators (50); and the maximum depth (3). We also tested with different class weights to improve our performance with regard to G-score, which is discussed in the next section. Having class weights penalizes errors for a particular class more, which effectively forces the classifier to guess that class more often, shifting the class distribution.

6   Evaluation Metrics

The evaluation for this task includes 3 basic metrics (precision, recall, and accuracy) and two combined metrics based on them (F-score and G-score). For precision and recall, the positive class is COM-PLEX, and this is the basis for calculating F-score. G-score, the primary evaluation metric for this competition, is the harmonic mean of precision and accuracy, putting extra emphasis on recall for the COM-PLEX class beyond that which is built into the accuracy score. Relevant to this task, the effect of G-score is opposite to the class imbalance problem mentioned earlier: when training on a set where the positive class is over-represented, the resulting classifier will do better on G-score than F-score because it will tend to overestimate the instances of the positive class, improving recall.

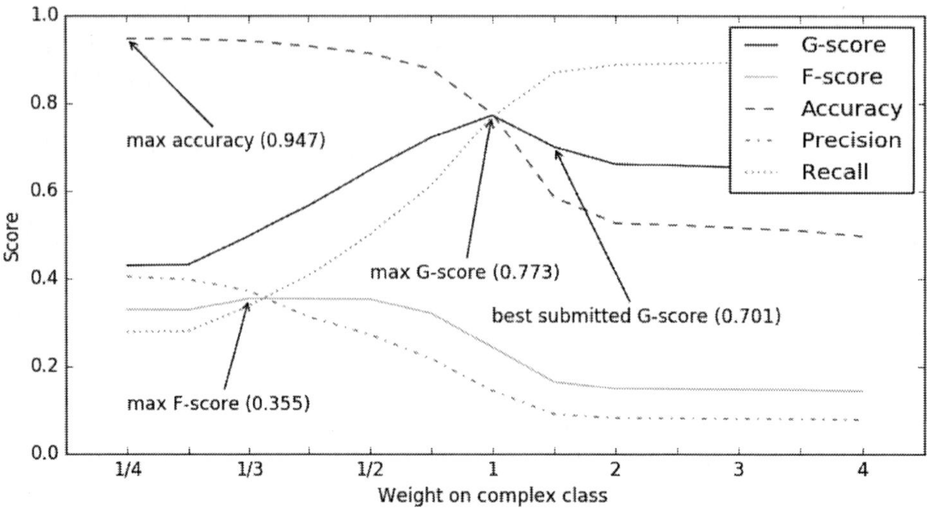

Figure 1: Scores for various metrics for different weightings of the COMPLEX class

7 Results

Figure 1 shows the performance of our system for the various metrics across different weightings of the COMPLEX class. With regard to G-score and F-score, our best submitted system is far from optimal, since we overestimated the effect of G-score, and underestimated the influence of the class imbalance between the training and test sets; we incorrectly put too much weight on the COMPLEX class, which resulted in a G-score of 0.701 (12th ranked) for the 1.5 weighting of COMPLEX, and 0.647 (19th ranked) for the 3.0 weighting of COMPLEX. However, across all possible weightings, our best G-score (0.773), which is our system without any weighting at all, is tied with the second best G-score in the competition (the best score was 0.774). If we put more weight on simple words, we reach the maximum F-score of 0.355 when the ratio is (roughly) 3 to 1 in favor of simple words; this F-score is better than any other reported F-score (the best F-score of a submitted system is 0.353), though we note that teams might have been more focused on optimizing G-score, since it was the primary metric. Accuracy is maximized simply by minimizing the number of COMPLEX guesses, and in fact guessing only SIMPLE will net an accuracy of 0.953, which is impossible for our system to beat.

Table 1 shows the results of a small feature ab-

Features	G-score	F-score
All Features	0.773	0.355
No term frequency	0.550	0.001
No 6-style lexicon	0.748	0.349
No minor features	0.772	0.347

Table 1: Feature ablation

lation study using the best system with regard to each the two combined metrics (no weighting for G-score, 1/3 weighting for F-score); results were erratic for less than optimal values. Term frequency information is clearly the most important source of information for deciding complexity, but we also see improvements due to the stylistic lexicons built using co-occurrence information, and the minor features. The effects are not consistent with respect to degree across the two metrics, likely because different feature sets result in substantially different class distributions, which in turn have very different effects on G-score and F-score.

8 Discussion

Our results using the unweighted model put us among the best teams in the competition, though in fact there are 6 other teams with G-scores within 0.01 of each other, and what we know about the effects of weighting should make us cautious about coming to any strong conclusion about which of these systems (or other systems, for that matter) are better. From our perspective, it is unfortunate for us that the organizers created a situation where the class distribution in the test set was very unclear. As it happens, the use of G-score almost exactly counters the effect of the class imbalance (in fact, it seems as if G-score may have been selected exactly for this purpose), such that a classifier built on the training data with an eye to F-score will do well with regard to G-score over the testing data (though not the training data), but it didn't seem obvious to us that this would be the case. More generally, we wonder whether some kind of ROC metric might not be more appropriate for this task. In our opinion, the quality of a model of complexity is orthogonal to producing a class distribution which optimizes a particular metric, and collapsing the two just creates confusion and might lead us to overlook otherwise good approaches.

Most of our performance seems to be due to term frequency and word co-occurrence information from a set of four large corpora. Although using multiple corpora was helpful, we actually rather doubt that our model is learning much that is particular to the group of people involved; more likely it is learning a more general model of word difficulty. Choosing the correct proficiency level is primarily a matter of choosing the best class distribution (via weighting); if one has individual annotations of the target population (which we didn't use, but were eventually made available), this is relatively straightforward. What would have been more interesting is if the task had involved multiple groups with very distinct characteristics (for example, two very different L1 language backgrounds, or L1 children versus L2 adults), so that a good model would have had to truly adapt to the specific characteristics of different groups to be successful. It would also be interesting to see if we could build models that can adapt to individuals, predicting words that a reader would or wouldn't know based on a small sample of words tagged by them only. Such a setup might bring us closer to the goals that motivate the task.

References

J. Brooke and G. Hirst. 2013. Hybrid models for lexical acquisition of correlated styles. In *Proceedings of the 6th International Joint Conference on Natural Language Processing (IJCNLP '13)*, pages 82–90, Nagoya, Japan.

J. Brooke and G. Hirst. 2014. Supervised ranking of co-occurrence profiles for acquisition of continuous lexical attributes. In *Proceedings of The 25th International Conference on Computational Linguistics (COLING 2014)*, pages 2172–2183, Dublin, Ireland.

J. Brooke, T. Wang, and G. Hirst. 2010. Automatic acquisition of lexical formality. In *Proceedings of the 23rd International Conference on Computational Linguistics: Poster Volume (COLING '10)*, pages 90–98, Beijing, China.

J. Brooke, V. Tsang, D. Jacob, F. Shein, and G. Hirst. 2012. Building readability lexicons with unannotated corpora. In *Proceedings of the 1st Workshop on Predicting and Improving Text Readability for target reader populations*, pages 26–35, Montreal, Canada.

J. Brooke, A. Hammond, and G. Hirst. 2015. GutenTag: An NLP-driven tool for digital humanities research in the Project Gutenberg corpus. In *Proceedings of the 4nd Workshop on Computational Literature for Literature (CLFL '15)*, pages 42–47, Denver, USA.

L. Burnard. 2000. User reference guide for British National Corpus. Technical report, Oxford University.

K. Burton, A. Java, and I. Soboroff. 2009. The ICWSM 2009 Spinn3r Dataset. In *Proceedings of the Third Annual Conference on Weblogs and Social Media (ICWSM '09)*, San Jose, USA.

J. S. Chall and E. Dale. 1995. *Readability revisited: the new Dale-Chall readability formula*. Brookline Books, Massachusetts, USA.

M. Coleman and T. L. Liau. 1975. A computer readability formula designed for machine scoring. *Journal of Applied Psychology*, 60(2):283.

K. Collins-Thompson and J. Callan. 2004a. Information retrieval for language tutoring: An overview of the REAP project. In *Proc. ACM-SIGIR International Conference on Research and Development in Information Retrieval*, Sheffield, UK. Poster.

K. Collins-Thompson and J. Callan. 2004b. A language modeling approach to predicting reading difficulty. In *Proceedings of the HLT/NAACL 2004 Conference*, pages 193–200, Boston, USA.

A. Coxhead. 2000. A new academic word list. *TESOL quarterly*, 34(2):213–238.

E. W. Dolch. 1936. A basic sight vocabulary. *The Elementary School Journal*, 36(6):456–460.

C. Fellbaum, editor. 1998. *WordNet: An Electronic Lexical Database*. The MIT Press.

T. L. François. 2009. Combining a statistical language model with logistic regression to predict the lexical and syntactic difficulty of texts for FFL. In *Proceedings of the EACL Student Research Workshop*, pages 19–27, Athens, Greece.

R. M. Gordon. 1980. The readability of unreadable text. *English Journal*, pages 60–61, March.

D. Graff and C. Cieri. 2003. *English Gigaword*. Linguistic Data Consortium, Philadelphia, PA.

T. Hastie, R. Tibshirani, and J. Friedman. 2008. *The Elements of Statistical Learning: Data Mining, Inference and Prediction*. Springer, 2 edition.

J. Peter Kincaid, Robert. P. Fishburne Jr., Richard L. Rogers, and Brad. S. Chissom. 1975. Derivation of new readability formulas for Navy enlisted personnel. Research Branch Report 8-75, Millington, TN: Naval Technical Training, U. S. Naval Air Station, Memphis, USA.

G. R. Klare. 1974. Assessing readability. *Reading Research Quarterly*, X:62–102.

P. Meara. 1992. *EFL vocabulary tests*. ERIC Clearinghouse.

F. Pedregosa, G. Varoquaux, A. Gramfort, V. Michel, B. Thirion, O. Grisel, M. Blondel, P. Prettenhofer, R. Weiss, V. Dubourg, J. Vanderplas, A. Passos, D. Cournapeau, M. Brucher, M. Perrot, and E. Duchesnay. 2011. Scikit-learn: Machine learning in Python. *Journal of Machine Learning Research*, 12:2825–2830.

R. J. Senter and E. A. Smith. 1967. Automated readability index. Technical report, DTIC Document.

M. Shardlow. 2013. A comparison of techniques to automatically identify complex words. In *ACL 2013 Student Research Workshop*, pages 103–109, Sofia, Bulgaria.

M. Shardlow. 2014. A survey of automated text simplification. *International Journal of Advanced Computer Science and Applications*, 4(1).

J. M. Sinclair and A. Renouf. 1988. A lexical syllabus for language taching. In R. Carter and M. McCarthy, editors, *Vocabulary and language teaching*. Longman, London, UK.

A. L. Uitdenbogerd. 2005. Readability of French as a foreign language and its uses. In *Australasian Document Computing Symposium*, Sydney, Australia.

A. L. Uitdenbogerd. 2014. Tools for supporting language acquisition via extensive reading. In *First Workshop on Natural Language Processing Techniques for Educational Applications (NLP-TEA 1)*, pages 35–41, Nara, Japan.

M. Walmsley. 2011. Automatic glossing for second language reading. In *New Zealand Computer Science Research Student Conference 2011*, Palmerston North, New Zealand.

CLaC at SemEval-2016 Task 11: Exploring linguistic and psycho-linguistic Features for Complex Word Identification

Elnaz Davoodi and **Leila Kosseim**

Concordia University

Department of Computer Science and Software Engineering

Montréal, Québec, Canada H3G 2W1

{e_davoo, kosseim}@encs.concordia.ca

Abstract

This paper describes the system deployed by the CLaC-EDLK team to the *SemEval 2016, Complex Word Identification task*. The goal of the task is to identify if a given word in a given context is *simple* or *complex*. Our system relies on linguistic features and cognitive complexity. We used several supervised models, however the Random Forest model outperformed the others. Overall our best configuration achieved a G-score of 68.8% in the task, ranking our system 21 out of 45.

1   Introduction

Text simplification involves reducing the complexity of a text in order to make it more accessible to a larger audience or to a specific audience such as children, second language learners, the elderly, etc.

Research efforts on text simplification have mostly focused on either lexical (Devlin and Tait, 1998; Carroll et al., 1998; Biran et al., 2011) or syntactic simplification (Chandrasekar and Srinivas, 1997; Siddharthan, 2006; Kauchak, 2013). Lexical simplification involves replacing specific words in order to reduce lexical complexity, while still conveying the same information. Lexical simplification is still a challenging task as identifying and simplifying complex words in a given context is not straightforward. Complex word identification is the first step towards lexical simplification.

For the challenge, we experimented with a number of features that we suspected would be correlated with a word's complexity level and selected five that were the most discriminating on the given training data set. Using a Random Forest classifier, we built two models that we deployed to the Sem-Eval 2016 Complex Word Identification Task. These models achieved better than average ranking compared to the other participating systems. We believe that the approach proposed in this paper can link linguistic features and cognitive complexity together in order to improve lexical simplification.

2   Complex Word Identification Task Setup

The SemEval 2016 Complex Word Identification Task required participating systems to automatically classify words as *simple* or *complex* in a given context. For training, participants were given 2247 instances. Each instance consisted of a target word W, its offset in the sentence and a class label (0 if W was considered *simple* in the sentence, or 1 if W was *complex* in the sentence). For example, given the training instance 1 below, the target word *happened* is classified as simple; however in training instance 2, the same word is classified as complex.

Training instance 1: There are several stories about Mozart 's final illness and death , and it is not easy to be sure what happened . happened 21 0

Training instance 2: Although anoxic events have not happened for millions of years , the geological record shows that they happened many times in the past . happened 5 1

Given the above, the task was to identify if a word is *complex* or *simple* in a test set of 88,221 instances.

3   Methodology

We experimented with various supervised models for this binary classification task; however Random

Forest outperformed the others. We also experimented with various features and retained the five features described below.

3.1 Feature Set

In our final complex word identification system, we used as features: the frequency of the target word in the Web1T Google N-gram Corpus, its Part of Speech (POS) tag, the number of synonyms it has in WordNet, the inverse of its length and a psycholinguistic feature indicating its "abstract" level. These features were selected based on their discriminating power on the training data.

3.1.1 Frequency in the Web1T Google N-gram Corpus

The Google N-gram corpus (Michel et al., 2011) is a collection of English one- to five-grams with their frequencies from different sources and from different years. This corpus contains approximately 1 trillion words from the Web. In order to focus on the more recent usage of the words and reduce the size of the corpus, we considered the frequency of the target words in sources which were indexed after year 2000. This way, we reduced the influence of frequent but obsolete words. We used this feature based on the assumption that simpler words are more frequently used.

3.1.2 Part of Speech Tag

We suspected that a word's POS tag may influence its complexity level. As a word may be tagged with different parts-of-speech, we suspected that a particular usage may be more complex than another depending on how common that usage is. For example, the word *highlight* may be used as a noun or, less frequently, as a verb. Hence, *highlight* as noun may be more likely to be considered *simple* and *highlight* as verb may be more likely to be considered *complex*. As a feature, we used the POS tags of target words given in the training and test data sets. The words in each sentence are tagged using Stanford POS tagger (Toutanova et al., 2003).

3.1.3 Number of Synonyms in WordNet

Another linguistic feature that we suspected may be correlated with the complexity of a word is the number of synonyms it has. Based on our statistical analysis of the training set, complex words have fewer synonyms than simpler words. For instance, the probability that a complex word has less than 4 synonyms is 33.65% on the training set; while this number is 24.10% for simple words. This can be explained by the fact that complex words tend to denote specific entities or concepts and therefore tend to have less synonyms. Thus, we considered the number of synonyms of the target word as one of our features.

3.1.4 Inverse of Word Length

Based on the work of traditional text complexity measures such as the Flesch index (Kincaid et al., 1975), we took into account the length of a word as a feature to determine its simplicity level.

3.1.5 Psycholinguistic Feature

We suspected that the more abstract a word, the more complex it will be perceived. To investigate the correlation between the degree of abstractness of a word and its complexity, we used the MRC psycholinguistic database (Wilson, 1988). This electronic resource contains the score of 26 psycholinguistic features for 150,834 words. One such feature indicates the level of abstraction associated with the entity or concept denoted by the word. This concreteness feature is available for 8,228 words and is indicated by an integer value ranging from 100 (very abstract) to 700 (very concrete). For this psycholinguistic feature, if the target word had a concreteness value in the MRC, we used its value as a feature. However, using this feature has a drawback since it does not cover all the words. For now, we deal with this problem by considering the value of out-of-database words as 0.

3.2 Feature Selection

In order to evaluate the effectiveness of these five features, we used two feature selection methods: (1) information gain (a filter-based method) and (2) subset selection (a wrapper method). Table 1 shows the features ranked using information gain. For example, WordNet synonyms are the most discriminating features; whereas word length is the least.

On the other hand, using the subset selection method, the best subset of features was determined to be the frequency in the Web1T Google N-gram Corpus + the number of synonyms in WordNet +

Feature	Information Gain
Number of Synonyms in WordNet	0.048
Psycholinguistic Feature	0.024
Part of Speech Tag	0.015
Frequency in Web1T Google N-gram Corpus	0.007
Inverse of Word Length	0.006

Table 1: Information gain of each feature.

Learning Model	Precision	Recall	F-Measure	Class
Naïve Bayes	0.680	0.978	0.803	0 (Simple)
Naïve Bayes	0.267	0.017	0.032	1 (Complex)
Naïve Bayes	0.548	0.672	0.557	Weighted Average
Neural Network	0.707	0.913	0.797	0 (Simple)
Neural Network	0.509	0.193	0.280	1 (Complex)
Neural Network	0.644	0.684	0.632	Weighted Average
Decision Tree (J48)	0.715	0.919	0.804	0 (Simple)
Decision Tree (J48)	0.551	0.212	0.306	1 (Complex)
Decision Tree (J48)	0.662	0.694	0.645	Weighted Average
Random Forest	0.738	0.815	0.775	0 (Simple)
Random Forest	0.491	0.383	0.430	1 (Complex)
Random Forest	0.660	0.677	0.667	Weighted Average

Table 2: Performance of various learning models evaluated using 10-fold cross-validation on the training set.

the psycholinguistic feature. It is interesting to note that both methods identify the psycholinguistic feature and the number of synonyms in WordNet as two of the most discriminating features; and word length as less useful.

4 Results and Discussion

We experimented with various learning models trained on the features described above. As a baseline, we used a Naïve Bayes classifier. Table 2 shows the weighted average precision, recall and F-measure on the training set evaluated using 10 fold cross-validation. As can be seen in Table 2, all learning models perform significantly better in classifying simple words rather than complex words. Based on the weighted average of the learning models, we submitted two Random Forest models: CLaC-EDLK-RF_0.6 and CLaC-EDLK-RF_0.5. The only difference between these submissions is the threshold for class assignment. In the first submission, we used the threshold of 0.5, and in the second we used 0.6. Our official ranking at the shared task ranked our CLaC-EDLK-RF_0.6 as 21st and CLaC-EDLK-RF_0.5 as 24th out of 45 systems using the G-score. However, based on the F-score, CLaC-EDLK-RF_0.5 ranked 26th and CLaC-EDLK-RF_0.6 ranked 30th.

5 Future Work

For future work, we plan to investigate the use of other linguistic and psycholinguistic features. Because the MRC database contained a concreteness score for only 8,228 words, we plan to combine more psycholinguistic features from the same database. In addition, it would be interesting to investigate the influence of context on the readers' understanding of a target word. To do this, we could examine a window-based approach to consider the surrounding words which may affect the complexity of a word.

Acknowledgement

The authors would like to thank the anonymous reviewers for their feedback on the paper. This work was financially supported by NSERC.

References

Or Biran, Samuel Brody, and Noémie Elhadad. 2011. Putting it simply: A context-aware approach to lexical simplification. In *Proceedings of the 49th Annual Meeting of the Association for Computational Linguistics: Human Language Technologies: short papers-Volume 2*, pages 496–501.

John Carroll, Guido Minnen, Yvonne Canning, Siobhan Devlin, and John Tait. 1998. Practical simplification of English newspaper text to assist aphasic readers. In *Proceedings of the AAAI-98 Workshop on Integrating Artificial Intelligence and Assistive Technology*, pages 7–10.

Raman Chandrasekar and Bangalore Srinivas. 1997. Automatic induction of rules for text simplification. *Knowledge-Based Systems*, 10(3):183–190.

Siobhan Devlin and John Tait. 1998. The use of a psycholinguistic database in the simplification of text for aphasic readers. *Linguistic Databases*, pages 161–173.

David Kauchak. 2013. Improving text simplification language modeling using unsimplified text data. In *Proceeding of ACL (Volume 1: Long Papers)*, pages 1537–1546.

J Peter Kincaid, Robert P Fishburne Jr, Richard L Rogers, and Brad S Chissom. 1975. Derivation of new readability formulas (automated readability index, fog count and flesch reading ease formula) for navy enlisted personnel. Technical report, DTIC Document.

Jean-Baptiste Michel, Yuan Kui Shen, Aviva Presser Aiden, Adrian Veres, Matthew K Gray, Joseph P Pickett, Dale Hoiberg, Dan Clancy, Peter Norvig, Jon Orwant, et al. 2011. Quantitative analysis of culture using millions of digitized books. *Science*, 331(6014):176–182.

Advaith Siddharthan. 2006. Syntactic simplification and text cohesion. *Research on Language & Computation*, 4(1):77–109.

Kristina Toutanova, Dan Klein, Christopher D Manning, and Yoram Singer. 2003. Feature-rich part-of-speech tagging with a cyclic dependency network. In *Proceedings of the 2003 Conference of the North American Chapter of the Association for Computational Linguistics on Human Language Technology-Volume 1*, pages 173–180.

Michael Wilson. 1988. MRC psycholinguistic database: Machine-usable dictionary, version 2.00. *Behavior Research Methods, Instruments, & Computers*, 20(1):6–10.

JU_NLP at SemEval-2016 Task 11: Identifying Complex Words in a Sentence

Niloy Mukherjee, Braja Gopal Patra, Dipankar Das, and **Sivaji Bandyopadhyay**
Department of Computer Science and Engineering, Jadavpur University
Kolkata, India
{niloymukherjee93,brajagopal.cse,dipankar.dipnil2005}@gmail.com
sivaji_cse_ju@yahoo.com

Abstract

The complex word identification task refers to the process of identifying difficult words in a sentence from the perspective of readers belonging to a specific target audience. This task has immense importance in the field of lexical simplification. Lexical simplification helps in improving the readability of texts consisting of challenging words. As a participant of the SemEval-2016: Task 11 shared task, we developed two systems using various lexical and semantic features to identify complex words, one using Naïve Bayes and another based on Random Forest Classifiers. The Naïve Bayes classifier based system achieves the maximum G-score of 76.7% after incorporating rule based post-processing techniques.

1 Introduction

Extensive research has been performed in the field of lexical simplification (Specia et al., 2012; Rello et al., 2013; Paetzold, 2015). Lexical simplification refers to identifying complex words and replacing them with lexically simple substitutes (Specia et al., 2012). The English lexical simplification task[1] was organized in the year 2012, in which the complex words were provided by the organizers.

The complex word (CW) identification is the first step towards the lexical simplification task. Understanding words which are not frequently used in any language is very difficult for non-native speakers. It may be challenging for a reader to interpret a particular word because it might be absent in his vocabulary. Also it may so happen that he knows the word but cannot comprehend it as he fails to capture the context it is used in. Generally, it is observed that the frequent use of complex words decreases the readability of the document. Thus, the complex word identification (CWI) task aims to classify those challenging words in a sentence with respect to a particular target audience.

For example, in the following sentence, the words in italics are complex words. These words are related to biology and are rarely used in our daily life. e.g. "The first *amniotes*, such as *Casineria*, resembled small lizards and evolved from *amphibian reptiliomorphs* about 340 million years ago."

Some research has been performed in CWI task in comparison to the lexical simplification (Shardlow, 2013; Paetzold, 2015). The important features which have been used previously in the CWI task are frequency thresholding and lexical matching etc. (Shardlow, 2013).

Some motivations of the CWI task are to understand the defining characteristics of the words which are challenging for non-native speakers to interpret. Another is assessing an individual's vocabulary limitations from the group he is a part of.

We have participated in the SemEval 2016-Task 11: Complex Word Identification[2] (Paetzold and Specia, 2016). The main goal of this task is to identify the complex words from English sentences. We identified highly correlated features and performed the classification using Naïve Bayes and Random Forest classifiers. After the classification, we used post-processing techniques with deterministic features to improve the F-Score of our system.

---

[1]https://www.cs.york.ac.uk/semeval-2012/task1.html

[2]http://alt.qcri.org/semeval2016/task11/

Proceedings of SemEval-2016, pages 986–990,
San Diego, California, June 16-17, 2016. ©2016 Association for Computational Linguistics

2   Dataset Description

Participants were provided with training and test datasets by the organizers of CWI task. A subset of words of a sentence are tagged as complex or non-complex. The training and test datasets comprise of 2,237 and 88,221 instances respectively. The numbers of complex and noncomplex words are 706 and 1531 for the training dataset, whereas the number of complex and noncomplex words are 4,131 and 84,090 in the test dataset.

The training dataset was collected through a survey, in which 400 annotators were presented with 200 sentences. They were asked to select the words which they did not understand in terms of the meaning. Each of the words in the training dataset have been annotated by 20 distinct annotators. Even if one of the 20 annotators judged the word to be complex it has been tagged as complex. The test set has annotations made over 9,000 sentences by only one annotator (Paetzold and Specia, 2016).

3   Features

3.1   Data Pre-processing

The Stanford Parser[3] was used to get the lemma of the tagged words in the training dataset. Further, the lemmas of these words have been used to identify various features. The R (version 3.1.0)[4] software is used to collect various statistics and identifying the features which have high correlation with the complex or noncomplex class.

3.2   Part-of-Speech (POS)

We used POS tags of the words as a feature. The frequencies of corresponding POS tags of complex and noncomplex words are given in Table 1.

3.3   Hypernym and Hyponym

The main idea of the present approach is to find out the position of the words in the tree constructed by the WordNet.[5] Our hypothesis is that generic words being easier to understand are present at the top of the WordNet tree. Alternately specialized words which are difficult to understand are at the bottom of

<hr>

[3]http://stanfordnlp.github.io/CoreNLP/

[4]https://www.r-project.org/

[5]https://rednoise.org/rita/reference/RiWordNet.html

POS	Complex	Noncomplex
NN	263	413
NNS	101	198
JJ	93	247
VBN	46	99
RB	45	103
VBD	40	101
Others	116	358

Table 1: POS tagging statistics

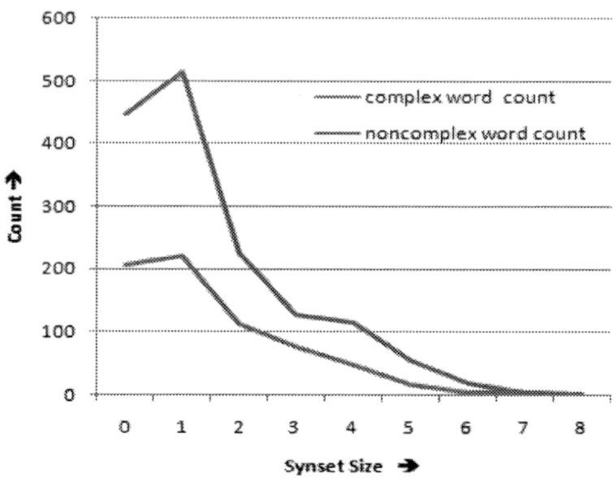

Figure 1: Statistics of synset size

the tree. We used the number of hypernym and hyponym as features. For example, the word 'car' has no hypernym and is tagged as noncomplex, whereas the word 'resemble' has eight hypernyms and therefore is tagged as complex. We observed that 762 out of 1531 (around 50%) noncomplex words have no hypernyms in the training dataset.

3.4   Synset Size

The synset size is one of the important features which has been used to identify CWs in previous related work (Shardlow, 2013). We observed that the words with larger synset sizes have several senses and are generally ambiguous in nature. These words may be confusing for the readers and are considered complex. For example, approximately 73% of the words having synset size greater than equal to five were marked as complex in the training dataset. It can be observed from Figure 1 that the probability of a word being noncomplex is high when the synset size of that word is low.

3.5 Named Entity (NE)

Generally, NEs are understood by the non-native speakers. They are aware of currencies or nationalities, e.g. Dollars or British. We found 54 out of 78 (approximately 70%) NEs are noncomplex in the training data. We used the 7 class model of Stanford NER[6] to identify the NEs in the tagged words of the training and test dataset. We used NEs as a feature and for the post-processing as well.

3.6 Stopwords

We observed that determiners like a/an/the or conjunctions like or/and/but have a low probability of being complex. Thus, we used stopwords as a feature.

3.7 Syllable count

The words with a high number of syllables are difficult to pronounce and onerous to read too. The syllable count was calculated by the number of consonants present between contiguous chunks of vowels. We used syllable count as a feature to identify the CWs.

3.8 Most frequently used English words

We collected a list of most frequently used words in English language from the web.[7] Two lists were prepared, one containing top 2,000 words and the other containing top 5,000 words. We observed that the words present in the list of 'most frequently used words' have a lower chance of being complex.

3.9 Index of words

The index of each tagged word in a sentence is used as a feature.

Negative features: The length of the word was not used as a feature because a lot of noncomplex words in the training dataset were hyphenated and hence had higher length. The hyphenated words which are individually understandable should be considered as noncomplex.

4 System Framework

The Naïve Bayes and Random Forest classifiers were implemented using the Weka tool.[8]

4.1 Evaluation

The performance of the systems was calculated using Accuracy, Precision, Recall, F-Score, and G-Score (Paetzold and Specia, 2016). The accuracy is calculated as:

Accuracy = (correctly classified instances) / (total instances).

The G-Score metric has been used to rank the systems. The G-score is the harmonic mean of Accuracy and Recall (Paetzold and Specia, 2016).

4.2 Post-Processing

Crawler: The specialized words of any particular subject are not generally understood by readers and are found to be complex. Thus, we prepared word lists of three specific topics (Biology, Geography, and Physics).

A web crawler was developed to collect specialized words from the glossaries of Biology,[9] Geography,[10] and Physics.[11] A total of 1327, 1689, and 273 number of words were collected for Biology, Geography and Physics, respectively. We observed that there are 48 CWs in the training dataset belong to the above glossaries. Thus, a word is tagged as complex, if it is found in any three of these glossaries.

Dictionary Module: We observed that the words not present in the English dictionary are tagged as complex. A python dictionary module *pyenchant*[12] (both US and UK) was used to identify the non-English words. If a word was not found in either of them, then it was tagged as complex.

Most frequently used English words: If a word is not found in the 5,000 word list, then it was tagged as complex.

Named Entity as noncomplex: The NEs which are identified as CWs by our system are re-annotated as noncomplex words. We also tagged positional words (such as 2nd/3rd/4th) as noncomplex.

---

[6]http://nlp.stanford.edu/software/CRF-NER.shtml

[7]http://functional-programming.it.jyu.fi/resources/word_list.txt

[8]http://www.cs.waikato.ac.nz/ml/weka/

[9]http://www.phschool.com/science/biology_place/glossary/

[10]http://www.physicalgeography.net/glossary.html

[11]http://www.etutorphysics.com/glossary.html

[12]https://pypi.python.org/pypi/pyenchant

4.3 Results

We performed the 10-fold cross validation on the training dataset using the Random Forests classifier and achieved a F-Score of 0.53. Again, we applied the post-processing on the results obtained by the above system and observed an improvement of 0.04 in the F-Score. Thus, we presented all the results on the test dataset after implementing the post-processing techniques.

The Naïve Bayes and Random Forest classifiers based systems achieved the maximum accuracies of 0.767 and 0.795 respectively. However, the precision of both the systems are quite low (0.139 and 0.151). One of the main reasons is that the number of CWs in test dataset are quite low as compared to CWs in the training dataset (4.69% and 31.6% for test and training dataset, respectively). This happened because 20 annotators have annotated the training dataset and a word is tagged as complex if any one of the annotator annotated so. Whereas, a word in the test dataset is annotated by only one annotator.

The maximum recalls achieved by Naïve Bayes and Random Forest based systems are 0.767 and 0.73 respectively. Both the systems achieved almost similar recalls and accuracies because all the features used are biased towards complex words. The maximum F-Score achieved for the Naïve Bayes based system is 0.236 and that for Random Forest based system is 0.25. The detailed statistics of the system performances are given in Table 2. The confusion matrix for the above systems are given in Table 3.

The team **SV000gg** has achieved the first and second positions with G-scores of 0.774 and 0.773, respectively. The team **TALN** which came third with the maximum G-Score of 0.772 has used Random Forest classifier. They included the number of annotators who marked a particular word complex as a feature.

Our Naïve Bayes and Random Forest based systems achieved fourth and seventh position with the maximum G-scores of 0.767 and 0.761 respectively. There are two other systems namely **UWB** and **PLUJAGH** who have also achieved the fourth position. The team **UWB** uses Maximum Entropy classifiers and uses document frequencies of words in

	Acc.	Prec.	Rec.	F-Score	G-Score
NB	0.767	0.139	0.767	0.236	**0.767**
RF	0.795	0.151	0.730	0.250	0.761

Table 2: System performance (NB: Naïve Bayes, RF: Random Forest, Acc.: Accuracy, Prec.: Precision, Rec.: Recall)

		Predicted			
		NB		**RF**	
		0	**1**	**0**	**1**
Actual	**0**	64493	19597	67132	16958
	1	964	3167	1115	3016

Table 3: Confusion Matrix for systems

Wikipedia as the only feature. They obtain higher accuracy of 0.803, but have the same G-Score as our system. The team **PLUJAGH** achieved the same G-Score as our system, but they achieved the higher accuracy of 0.795. Their system learns the threshold of word frequencies in Wikipedia that maximizes the F-score over the joint dataset. Another system of the team **PLUJAGH** achieved the maximum F-Score of 0.353, but got quite low G-Score of 0.608 and obtained 22nd position.

5 Conclusion and Future Work

In this paper, we have presented two systems for identifying the complex words in English. We believe that this problem will become increasingly important for lexical simplification. Our Naïve Bayes based system obtained the fourth position with the maximum G-score of 0.767.

In the training dataset, various stopwords within complex phrases were tagged as complex, because the annotator could not understand the context of that phrase. Thus, capturing complex phrase in a sentence is an interesting task and it would require context and n-gram level features. Apart from this, the feature set can be extended to build a model to identify the persons suffering from dyslexia.

Acknowledgments

The present work is supported by a grant from the project "CLIA System Phase II" funded by Department of Electronics and Information Technology (DeitY), Ministry of Communications and Information Technology (MCIT), Government of India. The second author is supported by "Visvesvaraya Ph.D.

Fellowship" funded by DeitY, Government of India.

References

Gustavo H. Paetzold and Lucia Specia. 2016. Semeval 2016 task 11: Complex word identification. In *Proceedings of the International Workshop on Semantic Evaluation*, SemEval'16, San Diego, California.

Gustavo H. Paetzold. 2015. Reliable lexical simplification for non-native speakers. In *Proceedings of the NAACL-HLT 2015 Student Research Workshop (SRW)*, pages 9–16.

Luz Rello, Ricardo A. Baeza-Yates, and Horacio Saggion. 2013. The impact of lexical simplification by verbal paraphrases for people with and without dyslexia. In *Proceedings of the 14th International Conference on Intelligent Text Processing and Computational Linguistics (CICLing-2013)*, pages 501–512.

Matthew Shardlow. 2013. A comparison of techniques to automatically identify complex words. In *ACL (Student Research Workshop)*, pages 103–109. Citeseer.

Lucia Specia, Sujay K. Jauhar, and Rada Mihalcea. 2012. Semeval-2012 task 1: English lexical simplification. In *Proceedings of the Sixth International Workshop on Semantic Evaluation*, pages 347–355.

MAZA at SemEval-2016 Task 11: Detecting Lexical Complexity Using a Decision Stump Meta-Classifier

Shervin Malmasi
Macquarie University
Sydney, NSW, Australia
shervin.malmasi@mq.edu.au

Marcos Zampieri
Saarland Unviersity
Saarbrücken, Germany
marcos.zampieri@dfki.de

Abstract

This paper describes team *MAZA* entries for the 2016 SemEval Task 11: Complex Word Identification (CWI). The task is a binary classification task in which systems are trained to predict whether a word in a sentence is considered to be complex or not. We developed our two systems for this task based on classifier stacking using decision stumps and decision trees. Our best system, using contextual features, frequency information, and word and sentence length, achieved 91.2% accuracy and 30.8% F-Score. The system ranked 4th among the 38 entries in the CWI task in terms of F-Score.

1 Introduction

Lexical simplification is a popular task in natural language processing and it was the topic of a successful SemEval task in 2012 (Specia et al., 2012). It consists of applying computational methods to substitute words or short phrases for simpler ones to improve text readability and comprehension aimed at a given target population (e.g. children, language learners, people with reading impairment, etc.). Lexical simplification is considered to be the sub-task of text simplification that deals with the lexicon while other sub-tasks address, for example, complex syntactic structures (Siddharthan, 2014).

To perform lexical simplification efficiently, computational methods should be first applied to identify which words in a text pose more difficulty to readers and they therefore good candidates for substitution (Shardlow, 2013). This task is called complex word identification (CWI) and it is the topic of the 2016 SemEval Task 11 with the same name.

The CWI shared task is modeled as a binary text classification task. Participants are provided with training data containing sentences and a label for each word in them containing a value of either 1 (for complex words) or 0 (for simple words). The label was attributed according to the judgment of human annotators that were required to indicate which words in the sentences could not be easily understood. Below, an example can be found of a sentence from the training set. Complex words are marked in bold.

(1) The name 'kangaroo mouse' refers to the species' **extraordinary** jumping ability, as well as its habit of **bipedal locomotion**.

In the example presented above, the CWI systems should label *extraordinary, bipedal* and *locomotion* as complex words.[1] To accomplish this task, the *MAZA* team applied a decision stump meta-classifier and a wide set of features that we will describe here.

2 Data

Organizers of the SemEval CWI task provided a training and test set comprising English sentences with each word annotated with a complex or simple label. According to the CWI task website[2]: '400 annotators were presented with several sentences and asked to select which words they did not understand

---

[1] Note that participants are free to consider *bipedal locomotion* as single words or as a multiword expression.

[2] http://alt.qcri.org/semeval2016/task11/

Proceedings of SemEval-2016, pages 991–995,
San Diego, California, June 16-17, 2016. ©2016 Association for Computational Linguistics

their meaning'. There was no scale or gradation, all words should be assigned as simple or complex.

The training set was composed of 2,237 sentences. It contains judgments made by 20 annotators over a set of 200 sentences. A word is considered to be complex if at least one of the 20 annotators assigned them as complex. Subsequently a test set with the same format was released containing 88,221 sentences. According to the organizers, the test set contains by judgments made over 9,000 sentences by a single annotator.

The proportion of training vs. test instances of 1:40 should also be noted as it represents and additional challenge to participants. This data split is different from other similar text classification shared tasks which provide much more training than test instances (at least 10:1) (Tetreault et al., 2013; Zampieri et al., 2015). Given the amount of training data, participating teams should employ efficient algorithms able to perform generalizations on a much larger test set.[3]

3   Features

We experimented with two types of features in our submissions. Each of these two classes, as described below, contains several features which we combine using a meta-classifier.

3.1   Frequency and Length Features

These are features based on the occurrence of the target word in a given reference corpus and its length. The idea is inspired by the Zipfian frequency distribution of words that indicate that the most frequent words in any language tend to be shorter (e.g. in English some of the most frequent words are: *it, the, an, and*). If we consider that frequent words are also likely to be short, our assumption is that complex words are likely to be, on average, both less frequent and longer than simple ones (Zipf, 1949). This assumption is also related to text readability and it has been tested in an experiment with dyslexic readers concluding that frequent words tend to improve readability while shorter words help text comprehension (Rello et al., 2013).

The reference corpus we used was the English section of the DSL corpus collection (DSLCC) (Tan et al., 2014). This corpus seems to be an appropriate choice for our task as it was designed for language variety discrimination. For this reason, it contains English texts from both England and the United States. This ensures a desired variability in terms of spelling and word combination between the two most representative English varieties.

The frequency and length features we use are:

- **Word Probability**: The probability of the word occurring in the reference corpus.

- **Word Length**: The number of characters in the word. Our aforementioned intuition is that longer words tend to be both less frequent and more complicated to readers (Zipf, 1935; Zipf, 1949).

- **Sentence Length**: The number of characters in the sentence to which the target word belongs.

3.2   Context Features

This set of features is based on estimating the likelihood of the target word within its context in a sentence. For a given target word w_i, we calculate six different types of probability, as described here.

The probabilities were extracted using the Microsoft Web N-gram service[4] which is based on web-scale data.

- **Conditional Probabilities:** We estimate the conditional probability of w_i, given its preceding context. Two probabilities are calculated: the probability of w_i given the previous word and the probability of w_i given the previous two words.

- **Joint Probabilities** Additionally, we also extract the joint probability of w_0 and its surrounding words. We derived such joint probabilities for $\{w_{i-2}, w_{i-1}, w_i\}$, $\{w_{i-1}, w_i\}$, $\{w_i, w_{i+1}\}$ and $\{w_i, w_{i+1}, w_{i+2}\}$.

---

[3]As noted by Zampieri and Tan (2014) in the Chinese Error Correction Shared Task (Yu et al., 2014)

[4]http://research.microsoft.com/en-us/ collaboration/focus/cs/web-ngram.aspx

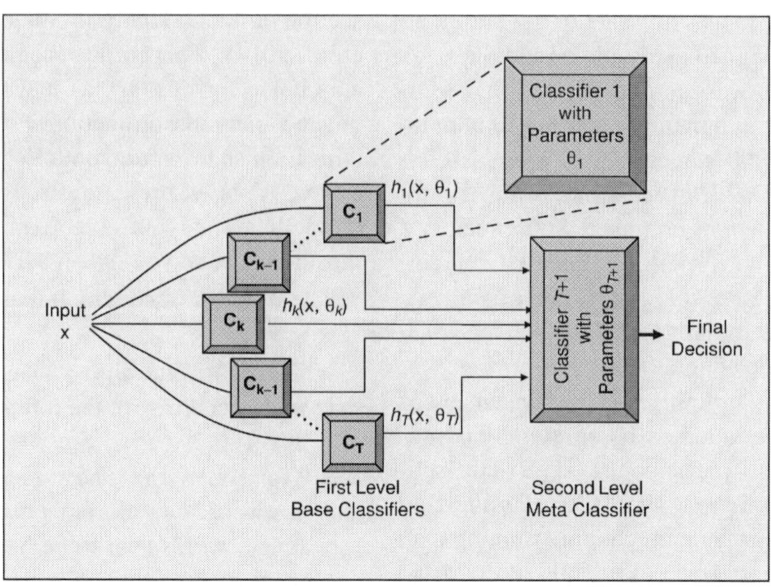

Figure 1: An illustration of a meta-classifier architecture. Image reproduced from Polikar (2006).

4 Experimental Setup

We employed a meta-classifier for our entry, also referred to as classifier stacking. A meta-classifier architecture is generally composed of an ensemble of base classifiers that each make predictions for all of the input data. Their individual predictions, along with the gold labels are used to train a second-level meta-classifier that learns to predict the final decision for an input, given the decisions of the individual classifiers.

This setup is illustrated in Figure 1. This meta-classifier attempts to learn from the collective knowledge represented by the ensemble of local classifiers. The first step in such a setup is to create the set of base classifiers that form the first layer of the architecture. We describe this process below.

4.1 Ensemble Construction

Our ensemble was created using a set of decision stump classifiers. A decision stump is a decision tree trained using only a single feature (Iba and Langley, 1992); it is usually considered a weak learner.

We used the features listed in Section 3 to create an ensemble of 9 classifiers. Each classifier predicts every input and assigns a probability output to each of the two possible labels.

Classifiers ensembles have proved to an efficient and robust alternative in other text classification tasks such as language identification (Malmasi and Dras, 2015a) and grammatical error detection (Xiang et al., 2015). This motivated us to try this approach in the CWI SemEval task.

4.2 Meta-classifier

For our meta-classifier, we adopted a decision tree with bootstrap aggregating (bagging). The inputs to each decision tree are the two probability outputs from each decision stump in our ensemble, along with the original gold label. 200 bagged decision trees were created using this input. The final label was selected through a plurality voting process over the entire set of bagged decision trees.

4.3 Systems

Using the methods described so far, we created two different systems for the shared task. They are summarized next:

- **MAZA A:** Our first system used only the frequency and length features described in Section 3.1.

- **MAZA B:** The second system we created combined the frequency and length features used in *MAZA A* with the addition of the contextual features we described in Section 3.2.

Rank	Team	System	Accuracy	Precision	Recall	F-score	G-score
1	PLUJAGH	SEWDFF	0.922	0.289	0.453	0.353	0.608
2	LTG	System2	0.889	0.220	0.541	0.312	0.672
3	LTG	System1	0.933	0.300	0.321	0.310	0.478
4	**MAZA**	B	0.912	0.243	0.420	0.308	0.575
5	HMC	DecisionTree25	0.846	0.189	0.698	0.298	0.765
6	TALN	RandomForest_SIM.output	0.847	0.186	0.673	0.292	0.750
7	HMC	RegressionTree05	0.838	0.182	0.705	0.290	0.766
8	MACSAAR	RFC	0.825	0.168	0.694	0.270	0.754
9	TALN	RandomForest_WEI.output	0.812	0.164	0.736	0.268	0.772
10	UWB	All	0.803	0.157	0.734	0.258	0.767
11	PLUJAGH	SEWDF	0.795	0.152	0.741	0.252	0.767
12	JUNLP	RandomForest	0.795	0.151	0.730	0.250	0.761
13	SV000gg	Soft	0.779	0.147	0.769	0.246	0.774
14	MACSAAR	NNC	0.804	0.146	0.660	0.240	0.725
15	JUNLP	NaiveBayes	0.767	0.139	0.767	0.236	0.767
16	SV000gg	Hard	0.761	0.138	0.787	0.235	0.773
17	USAAR	entropy	0.869	0.148	0.376	0.212	0.525
18	**MAZA**	A	0.773	0.115	0.578	0.192	0.661
19	BHASHA	DECISIONTREE	0.836	0.118	0.387	0.181	0.529
20	BHASHA	SVM	0.844	0.119	0.363	0.179	0.508

Table 1: The top 20 systems submitted to the shared task, ranked by their F-score.

We expected the system *B* to perform better, but we were interested in quantifying the impact of the contextual features on the test set results by the comparing the two systems.

5 Results

We present in Table 1 the best 20 out of 38 systems ranked by their F-score. We present the results obtained in terms of Accuracy, Recall, Precision, F-Score, and G-Score.[5] The complete results and more information about the evaluation can be found in the CWI shared task report paper (Paetzold and Specia, 2015).

As expected, our second system, *MAZA B* that incorporated contextual features along with frequency and length features performed better, ranking in 4th place overall. Our first system, *MAZA A* obtained performance more than 11 percentage points worse than the *B* system, coming in 18th place.

Our results show that the contextual features we applied in the *MAZA B* submission are very informative for this task. This suggests that the complexity of a word is strongly tied to the context in which it

is being used and it cannot be solely determined by how frequent or how long the word is.

6 Conclusion

In this paper we described our systems for SemEval 2016 Task 11: Complex Word Identification (CWI). Our best system, *MAZA B* was ranked 4th in terms of F-Score among 38 entries in the shared task. We consider the results we obtained to be very positive given the amount of teams participating in the task.

We applied a meta-classifier approach where each target word is classified by several base classifiers, and another classifier learns to predict the final label using the outputs of those classifiers. Our system's competitive performance in task suggests that this is a promising approach for this task.

Future work could look at how additional language resources could be used for this task. Analyzing the language produced by learners could provide insight into the limitations of learners' vocabulary. Learner corpora, widely used in the task of Native Language Identification (Malmasi and Dras, 2014; Malmasi and Dras, 2015b) could be useful here.

---

[5]According to the organizers, the G-score is the harmonic mean between Accuracy and Recall.

Acknowledgments

We would like to thank the SemEval CWI organizers, Gustavo Paetzold and Lucia Specia, for organizing this event. We also thank the anonymous reviewers for their constructive comments.

References

Wayne Iba and Pat Langley. 1992. Induction of one-level decision trees. In *Proceedings of the ninth international conference on machine learning*, pages 233–240.

Shervin Malmasi and Mark Dras. 2014. Chinese Native Language Identification. In *Proceedings of EACL*.

Shervin Malmasi and Mark Dras. 2015a. Language identification using classifier ensembles. In *Proceedings of the LT4VarDial Workshop*.

Shervin Malmasi and Mark Dras. 2015b. Multilingual Native Language Identification. In *Natural Language Engineering*.

Gustavo Henrique Paetzold and Lucia Specia. 2015. Semeval 2016 task 11: Complex word identification. In *Proceedings of SemEval*.

Robi Polikar. 2006. Ensemble based systems in decision making. *Circuits and Systems Magazine, IEEE*, 6(3):21–45.

Luz Rello, Ricardo Baeza-Yates, Laura Dempere-Marco, and Horacio Saggion. 2013. Frequent words improve readability and short words improve understandability for people with dyslexia. In *Proceedings of INTER-ACT*.

Matthew Shardlow. 2013. A comparison of techniques to automatically identify complex words. In *Proceedings of the ACL Student Research Workshop*.

Advaith Siddharthan. 2014. A survey of research on text simplification. *ITL-International Journal of Applied Linguistics*, 165(2):259–298.

Lucia Specia, Sujay Kumar Jauhar, and Rada Mihalcea. 2012. Semeval-2012 task 1: English lexical simplification. In *Proceedings of SemEval*.

Liling Tan, Marcos Zampieri, Nikola Ljubešic, and Jörg Tiedemann. 2014. Merging comparable data sources for the discrimination of similar languages: The dsl corpus collection. In *Proceedings of the BUCC workshop*.

Joel Tetreault, Daniel Blanchard, and Aoife Cahill. 2013. A report on the first native language identification shared task. In *Proceedings of the BEA Workshop*.

Yang Xiang, Xiaolong Wang, Wenying Han, and Qinghua Hong. 2015. Chinese grammatical error diagnosis using ensemble learning. In *Proceedings of the NLP-TEA Workshop*.

Liang-Chih Yu, Lung-Hao Lee, and Li-Ping Chang. 2014. Overview of grammatical error diagnosis for learning chinese as a foreign language. In *Proceedings of ICCE*.

Marcos Zampieri and Liling Tan. 2014. Grammatical error detection with limited training data: The case of chinese. In *Proceedings of ICCE*.

Marcos Zampieri, Liling Tan, Nikola Ljubešic, Jörg Tiedemann, and Preslav Nakov. 2015. Overview of the DSL shared task 2015. In *Proceedings of the LT4VarDial Workshop*.

George Kingsley Zipf. 1935. *The Psychobiology of Language*. Houghton Mifflin.

George Kingsley Zipf. 1949. *Human behavior and the principle of least effort*. Addison-wesley Press.

LTG at SemEval-2016 Task 11: Complex Word Identification with Classifier Ensembles

Shervin Malmasi[1]   **Mark Dras[1]**   **Marcos Zampieri[2,3]**

[1]Macquarie University, Sydney, NSW, Australia
[2]Saarland University, Germany
[3]German Research Center for Artificial Intelligence, Germany
{first.last}@mq.edu.au, marcos.zampieri@dfki.de

Abstract

We present the description of the LTG entry in the SemEval-2016 Complex Word Identification (CWI) task, which aimed to develop systems for identifying complex words in English sentences. Our entry focused on the use of contextual language model features and the application of ensemble classification methods. Both of our systems achieved good performance, ranking in 2nd and 3rd place overall in terms of F-Score.

1 Introduction

Complex Word Identification (CWI) is the task of identifying complex words in texts using computational methods (Shardlow, 2013). The task is usually carried out as part of lexical and text simplification systems. Shardlow (2014) considers CWI as the first processing step in lexical simplification pipelines. Complex or difficult words should first be identified so they can be later substituted by simpler ones to improve text readability.

CWI has gained more importance in the last decade as lexical and text simplification systems have been developed or tailored for a number of purposes. They have been applied to make texts more accessible to language learners (Petersen and Ostendorf, 2007); other researchers have explored text simplification strategies targeted at populations with low literacy skills (Aluísio et al., 2008). Finally, another relevant application of text simplification are people with dyslexia (Rello et al., 2013).

The SemEval 2016 Task 11: Complex Word Identification (CWI) provides an interesting opportunity to evaluate methods and approaches for this task. The organizers proposed a binary text classification task in which participants were required label words in English sentences as either complex (1) or simple (0). The task organizers provided participants with a training set containing sentences annotated with this information, followed by an unlabeled test set for evaluation. The assessment of whether words in a sentence are complex or simple was performed by human annotators required to label the data.[1]

2 Data

Based on the information available at the shared task's website[2]: "400 annotators were presented with several sentences and asked to select which words they did not understand their meaning."

The CWI task dataset was divided as follows:

- **Training set:** 2,237 judgments by 20 annotators over 200 sentences. A word is considered complex if at least one of the 20 annotators assigned it as so.

- **Test set:** 88,221 judgments made over 9,000 sentences (1 annotator per sentence).

---

[1]Here the term *complex* is used as a synonym for difficult. Unlike the Morphology term *complex* (antonym of *simplex*) that defines compound words or words composed of multiple morphs (Adams, 2001).

[2]http://alt.qcri.org/semeval2016/task11/

Proceedings of SemEval-2016, pages 996–1000,
San Diego, California, June 16-17, 2016. ©2016 Association for Computational Linguistics

3 Methodology

The primary focus of our team's entry was the use of judgements from different annotators to create training data. We looked at how adjusting the threshold for inter-annotator agreement would affect the results and whether the combination of data created using different threshold values could improve performance.

Initially, the training data released by the organizers was labeled in a way that a word was marked as complex if any annotator judged it so. During the course of the shared task the organizers released additional information about the training data, chiefly the individual judgements of the 20 annotators that were used to derive the final labels for each word.

We attempted to use this data in our system. During development we noted that by increasing this threshold to two, the performance of our system under cross-validation improved by a small amount. Accordingly, we pursued this direction as the main focus of our experiments.

3.1 Classifiers

We utilize a decision tree classifier, which we found to perform better than Support Vector Machine (SVM) and Naïve Bayes classifiers for this data.

3.2 Features

Our core set of features are based on estimating n-gram probabilities using web-scale language models. More specifically, this data was sourced from the Microsoft Web N-Gram Service[3], although we should note that this service has been deprecated and replaced since the shared task.[4] These language models are trained on web-scale corpora collected by Microsoft's Bing search engine from crawling English web pages.

Given a target word w_t, we extract several probability estimates to use as classification features. These estimates, which we describe below, use the target word as well its preceding and following words, as shown in Figure 1.

---

[3]http://weblm.research.microsoft.com/
[4]It has been replaced by Microsoft's Project Oxford: https://www.projectoxford.ai/weblm

3.2.1 Word Probability

This is an estimate of how likely the target word is to occur in the language model:

$$P\left(w_t\right)$$

Rarer words would be assigned lower values and thus this feature can help quantify word frequency for the classifier.

3.2.2 Conditional Probability

We calculate the bigram probability of w_t:

$$P\left(w_t \mid w_{t-1}\right)$$

Similarly, we estimate the trigram probability:

$$P\left(w_t \mid w_{t-1}, w_{t-2}\right)$$

These values estimate the likelihood of the target word occurring given the previous one or two words. They can help quantify if the word is being used in a common or less frequent context.

3.2.3 Joint Probability

We also use the following joint probability estimates of the target word and its surrounding words:

$$P\left(w_{t-1}, w_{t-2}, w_t\right)$$
$$P\left(w_{t-1}, w_t\right)$$
$$P\left(w_{t-1}, w_t, w_{t+1}\right)$$
$$P\left(w_t, w_{t+1}\right)$$
$$P\left(w_t, w_{t+1}, w_{t+2}\right)$$

The intuition underlying the use of all of these n-gram language model features is that the understanding of certain words depends on the context they appear in. A large number of English words are polysemous and their classification, without taking into account the specific sense being use, could lead to misclassifications. This can occur in scenarios where a learner knows the most frequently used sense of a polysemous word, but is confronted with a different sense that they have not encountered before. Additionally, even if a known word is used in an unusual context, it could be a cause of confusion for learners.

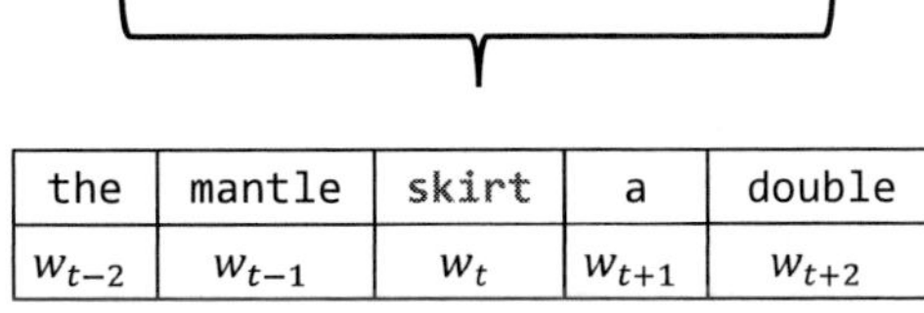

the	mantle	skirt	a	double
w_{t-2}	w_{t-1}	w_t	w_{t+1}	w_{t+2}

Figure 1: An example of the context extracted for a target word, which is "skirt" in this example.

3.2.4 Word Length

Guided by the intuition that the most frequent words in a language are usually shorter, we use the length of a word as a classification feature.

4 Ensemble Classifiers

Classifier ensembles are a way of combining different classifiers or experts with the goal of improving accuracy through enhanced decision making. They have been applied to a wide range of real-world problems and shown to achieve better results compared to single-classifier methods (Oza and Tumer, 2008). Through aggregating the outputs of multiple classifiers in some way, their outputs are generally considered to be more robust. Ensemble methods continue to receive increasing attention from researchers and remain a focus of much machine learning research (Woźniak et al., 2014; Kuncheva and Rodríguez, 2014).

Such ensemble-based systems often use a parallel architecture, as illustrated in Figure 2, where the classifiers are run independently and their outputs are aggregated using a fusion method. For example, *Bagging* (bootstrap aggregating) is a commonly used method for ensemble generation (Breiman, 1996) that can create multiple base classifiers.

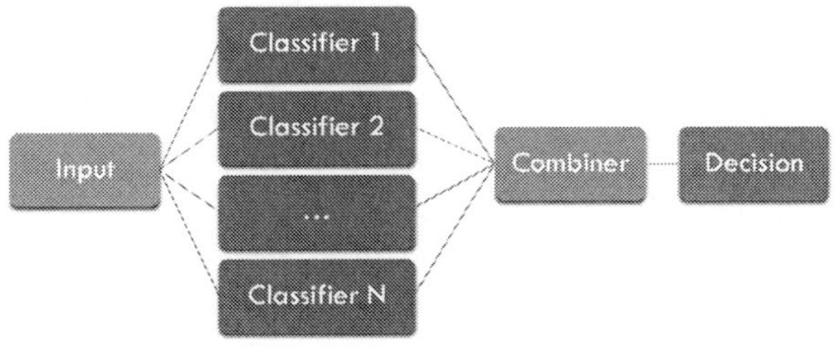

Figure 2: An example of parallel classifier ensemble architecture where N independent classifiers provide predictions which are then fused using an ensemble combination method.

It works by creating multiple bootstrap training sets from the original training data and a separate classifier is trained from each one of these sets. The generated classifiers are said to be diverse because each training set is created by sampling with replacement and contains a random subset of the original data.

Other, more sophisticated, ensemble methods that rely on meta-learning may employ a stacked architecture where the output from a first set of classifiers is fed into a second level meta-classifier and so on.

The first part of creating an ensemble is generating the individual classifiers. Various methods for creating these ensemble elements have been proposed. These involve using different algorithms, parameters or feature types; applying different preprocessing or feature scaling methods and varying (*e.g.* distorting or resampling) the training data.

5 Systems

In this section we describe the two systems we created and entered in the shared task.

5.1 System 1

Our first system was based on decision tree classifier trained on data where the minimum threshold for inter-annotator agreement was set to 3. Given that the testing data was only annotated by a single rater, we did not want to pick a value that was too high, even though this could improve cross-validation performance on the training data.

Additionally, we converted this setup to an ensemble by creating 100 randomized decision tree classifiers by using bagging, which we described earlier. The decisions of these learners were fused via plurality voting to yield the final label for an instance.

Rank	Team	System	Accuracy	Precision	Recall	F-score	G-score
1	PLUJAGH	SEWDFF	0.922	0.289	0.453	0.353	0.608
2	LTG	System2	0.889	0.220	0.541	0.312	0.672
3	LTG	System1	0.933	0.300	0.321	0.310	0.478
4	MAZA	B	0.912	0.243	0.420	0.308	0.575
5	HMC	DecisionTree25	0.846	0.189	0.698	0.298	0.765
6	TALN	RandomForest_SIM.output	0.847	0.186	0.673	0.292	0.750
7	HMC	RegressionTree05	0.838	0.182	0.705	0.290	0.766
8	MACSAAR	RFC	0.825	0.168	0.694	0.270	0.754
9	TALN	RandomForest_WEI.output	0.812	0.164	0.736	0.268	0.772
10	UWB	All	0.803	0.157	0.734	0.258	0.767

Table 1: The top 10 systems in task, ranked by their F-score.

5.2 System 2

For our second system we extended the threshold-based approach to an ensemble of decision trees trained on different data.

We created four individual classifiers, each trained with a different minimum threshold[5] ranging between 1–4. The outputs of these classifiers, a binary prediction, were then combined using a plurality voting combiner. It should also be noted that having an even number of base classifiers also introduces the possibility of ties occurring.

6 Results

The top 10 task submissions, ranked by the F-score, are shown in Table 1 with our systems highlighted. Both of our systems achieved very competitive results, ranking in second and third place overall.

Our second system, an ensemble of classifiers trained on distinct data derived using different levels of inter-rater agreement, performed slightly better than the first system. This could be interpreted as this evidence the second approach is slightly better, and we hypothesize that combining annotations from different combinations of annotators may help the classifier learn reliable models of the phenomenon, since individual annotations (as well as the original combined annotation) were noisy. However, determining this requires further experiments. This is due to the fact that with four classifiers in the ensemble, voting resulted in a tie for some 6% of the testing data. These ties were broken arbitrarily, introducing an element of stochasticity to our results.

In hindsight this does not appear to have been the most intuitive or robust way of dealing with such ties since the distribution of classes is not balanced. In fact, this distribution is highly skewed, as we discuss in the next section.

6.1 Conclusion

We developed two ensemble-based systems for this task, both of which achieved competitive results in the final rankings. Our results indicate that the use of contextual features, as well as language models, are promising for this task.

Analysis of the gold standard labels release after the task shows that only 4.7% of the 88k samples belonged to the positive class. This is a very highly skewed distribution that can make it hard to train effective classifiers. It also means that accuracy cannot be used as the sole evaluation metric here; a balanced measure of precision and recall like the F-score is required. Alternatively, the balanced accuracy measure (Brodersen et al., 2010) could also be used. Such a high data imbalance can result in training classifiers that are biased towards the majority class. This bias can be more problematic if the distribution of classes is different in the test set. Accordingly, future work in this area could look at the use of methods for dealing with unbalanced datasets (He and Garcia, 2009). The application of such methods, in conjunction with ensembles, could potentially result in greater performance.

Future work could attempt to integrate additional language resources for this task. Analyzing the text produced by learners could provide insight into the limitations of learner vocabulary. Learner corpora, widely used in the task of Native Language Identification (Malmasi and Dras, 2014; Malmasi and Dras, 2015) could be useful here.

---

[5] Setting the threshold to 1 is equivalent to using the original training data.

Acknowledgments

We would like to thank the CWI task organizers for managing the organization of this event. We also thank the anonymous reviewers for their insightful comments.

References

Valerie Adams. 2001. *Complex words in English*. Routledge.

Sandra M Aluísio, Lucia Specia, Thiago AS Pardo, Erick G Maziero, and Renata PM Fortes. 2008. Towards brazilian portuguese automatic text simplification systems. In *Proceedings of DocEng*.

Leo Breiman. 1996. Bagging predictors. In *Machine Learning*, pages 123–140.

Kay H Brodersen, Cheng Soon Ong, Klaas E Stephan, and Joachim M Buhmann. 2010. The balanced accuracy and its posterior distribution. In *Proceedings of ICPR*.

Haibo He and Edwardo A Garcia. 2009. Learning from Imbalanced Data. *IEEE Transactions on Knowledge and Data Engineering,*, 21(9):1263–1284.

Ludmila I Kuncheva and Juan J Rodríguez. 2014. A weighted voting framework for classifiers ensembles. *Knowledge and Information Systems*, 38(2):259–275.

Shervin Malmasi and Mark Dras. 2014. Chinese Native Language Identification. In *Proceedings of EACL*.

Shervin Malmasi and Mark Dras. 2015. Multilingual Native Language Identification. In *Natural Language Engineering*.

Nikunj C Oza and Kagan Tumer. 2008. Classifier ensembles: Select real-world applications. *Information Fusion*, 9(1):4–20.

Sarah E Petersen and Mari Ostendorf. 2007. Text simplification for language learners: a corpus analysis. In *Proceedings of SLaTE*.

Luz Rello, Ricardo Baeza-Yates, Stefan Bott, and Horacio Saggion. 2013. Simplify or help?: text simplification strategies for people with dyslexia. In *Proceedings of W4A*.

Matthew Shardlow. 2013. A comparison of techniques to automatically identify complex words. In *Proceedings of the ACL Student Research Workshop*.

Matthew Shardlow. 2014. A survey of automated text simplification. *International Journal of Advanced Computer Science and Applications (IJACSA)*, (Special Issue on Natural Language Processing).

Michał Woźniak, Manuel Graña, and Emilio Corchado. 2014. A survey of multiple classifier systems as hybrid systems. *Information Fusion*, 16:3–17.

MacSaar at SemEval-2016 Task 11: Zipfian and Character Features for Complex Word Identification

Marcos Zampieri[1,2], Liling Tan[1], Josef van Genabith[1,2]
[1]Saarland University, Germany
[2]German Research Center for Artificial Intelligence, Germany
{first.last}@uni-saarland.de

Abstract

This paper presents the *MacSaar* system developed to identify complex words in English texts. *MacSaar* participated in the SemEval 2016 task 11: Complex Word Identification submitting two runs. The system is based on the assumption that complex words are likely to be less frequent and on average longer than words considered to be simple. We report results of 82.5% accuracy and 27% F-Score using a Random Forest Classifier. The best *MacSaar* submission was ranked 8th in terms of F-Measure among 45 entries.

1 Introduction

Complex Word Identification (CWI) is the task of automatically identifying complex words in texts. It is considered a sub-task carried out in most lexical simplification pipelines (Paetzold and Specia, 2015). In this step, complex words, which are likely to be difficult words for readers and language learners, are identified so they can be substituted for simpler ones (Specia et al., 2012; Shardlow, 2013). Lexical simplification methods are usually integrated into text simplification systems developed for a particular target population (e.g. people with reading impairment or dyslexia, language learners, etc.) (Siddharthan, 2014).

Given a sentence, a CWI system is trained to identify words which are considered by readers to be complex. To give an example, let us consider the following sentence extracted from the SemEval CWI task training set:

(1) Leo took an <u>oath</u> of <u>purgation</u> concerning the <u>charges</u> brought against him , and his opponents were <u>exiled</u>.

Taking Example 1 into account, the task of the CWI system is to assign as complex the four underlined words, namely: *oath, purgation, charges*, and *exiled*. But what makes these words complex and not, for example, *opponents* or *took*?

In the lexical simplification literature, the term *complex* is a synonym for difficult or complicated. For practical purposes, we consider as complex words those that were assigned by a pool of human annotators, provided by the organizers of the CWI task, as difficult to be understood due to several factors that we will discuss in this paper. This is a readability notion that is not necessarily related to intrinsic linguistic phenomena (e.g. word formation).[1]

1.1 Motivation

MacSaar participated in the CWI SemEval task interested in two aspects of complex words. The first one is related to communication principles, or in other words, what makes words complex or simple to readers. One of our assumptions is that complex words tend to be less frequent in general language corpora than simple words. The second aspect is language learning. Lexical and text simplification methods are very important to produce simpler texts

---

[1]It is important to note that the definition of *complex* used here is different from that used in Morphology, where complex words are defined as compound words or words composed of multiple morphs as opposed to *simplex* words which are words with no affixes and not part of compounds (e.g. *happy* is a simplex word and *unhappiness* is a complex one) (Adams, 2001).

Proceedings of SemEval-2016, pages 1001–1005,
San Diego, California, June 16-17, 2016. ©2016 Association for Computational Linguistics

targeted at language learners which facilitate reading comprehension.

In communication theory, the *cooperative principle* states that interlocutors cooperate and mutually accept one another to be understood in a particular way to optimize each interaction (Grice, 1975). Interactions should take what Grice describes as the four maxims into account: *quality, quantity, relevance*, and *manner*.

We relate the *maxim of manner* to the usage of simple words that a learner will hear more frequently than complex words. Therefore, it should be possible to determine whether a word is complex or simple by observing Zipfian frequency distributions computed from suitable text corpora (Zipf, 1949). Another aspect to consider is the length of the words. Words that are more frequent tend to be shorter as noted by Zipf: *'the magnitude of words tends, on the whole, to stand in an inverse (not necessarily proportionate) relationship to the number of occurrences'* (Zipf, 1935). That said, our approach takes both frequency and word length into account to determine whether a word is complex or not.

Finally, another aspect that we take into account is the difficulty in vocabulary acquisition that is related to the spelling of complex words (Xu et al., 2011; Dahlmeier et al., 2013). Educational applications that are tailored towards non-native speakers use character-level n-grams to identify possible spelling errors that language learner make. Thus making character combinations another interesting aspect to be consider in this task.

2 Related Work

CWI is a sub-task included in many lexical and text simplification systems. Lexical simplification, as the name suggests, focuses only on the substitution of complex words for simpler words in texts whereas text simplification comprises also the modification of syntactic structures to improve readability. Most text simplification systems also contain a lexical simplification module or component which often relies on the accurate identification of complex words for subsequent substitution. The three tasks are therefore inseparable.

Both lexical and text simplification approaches have been widely investigated. They have been applied to different languages, examples include: Basque (Aranzabe et al., 2012), Italian (Barlacchi and Tonelli, 2013), Portuguese (Aluísio et al., 2008), Spanish (Bott et al., 2012), and the SemEval lexical simplification task for English (Specia et al., 2012).

To the best of our knowledge, very few methods have focused solely on complex word identification prior to the CWI shared task. An exception is the work by Shardlow (2013) which compared different techniques to identify complex words.

3 Methods

3.1 Task and Data

The SemEval 2016 Task 11, Complex Word Identification (CWI) is a binary text classification task at the word level. Systems are trained to attribute a label of either 1 (for complex words) or 0 (for simple words) to each word in a given sentence. There are no borderline cases or gradation, all words are either complex of simple.

A tokenized data set containing English sentences annotated with the complex or simple label for each word was provided. The training set contained 2,237 sentences, and the test set contained 88,221 sentences. The shared task website[2] states that: 'the data was collected through a survey, in which 400 annotators were presented with several sentences and asked to select which words they did not understand their meaning'. There was no information of whether annotators were English native speakers.

The proportion of training vs. test instances makes the task more challenging than other similar shared tasks which provide much more training than test instances (Tetreault et al., 2013; Zampieri et al., 2015), a common practice in text classification tasks.[3]

3.2 Approach

Given the motivation described in Section 1.1, we approach the CWI task using word frequency and character-level n-gram features.[4] To emulate a language learner exposure to English, we use newspa-

---

[2]http://alt.qcri.org/semeval2016/task11/

[3]The Chinese grammatical error diagnosis (CGED) shared task (Yu et al., 2014) is an exception. See the discussion in Zampieri and Tan (2014).

[4]Our implementation is open source and it can be found on: https://github.com/alvations/MacSaar-CWI

pers text from the English subsection of the DSL Corpus Collection (Tan et al., 2014) to compute the word frequencies and n-gram probability used to train our classifier.

The features used are explained in detail in the following sections and summarized in Table 1.

Type	Feature
Zipfian	Zipfian Frequncy (ZipfFreq)
	True Frequncy (TrueFreq)
Orthographic Difficulty	Word Length (no. of chars)
	Word-level Trigrams Density
	Sentence Length (no. of words)
	Sentence-level Trigram Density

Table 1: Features used in *MacSaar*

3.2.1 Zipfian Features

We model the language learners perspicuity by using insights from Zipfian properties of human language. Zipf (1949) predicts that the frequency of an element from a population of n elements, *ZipfFreq*, is defined as follows:

$$ZipfFreq(word) = \frac{1}{k^s H_{n,s}} = \frac{1}{k_{word}} \quad (1)$$

where k is the rank of the word sorted by most frequent first, s is the exponent characterizing the distribution, n is the vocabulary and size $H_{n,s}$ is the generalized harmonic number i.e. the sum of the reciprocals of the size of vocabulary. In the simplest case, where we assume that the harmonic number and exponent to be 1, we compute *ZipfFreq* by taking the inverse of the the rank of a word.[5]

The Zipfian frequency is a hypothetical estimate of the nature of word frequency in natural language. To account for the true frequency of the word, we calculate the non-smoothed probabilities of the count of a word divided by the number of tokens in the corpus. Formally:

$$TrueFreq(word) = \frac{count(word)}{N} \quad (2)$$

where N is the number of (non-unique) words in the corpus.

3.2.2 Character-based Features

To measure orthographic difficulty, we model word complexity by computing its (i) word length and (ii) sum probability of the character trigrams (normalized by the sum of all possible trigrams within the word). Intuitively, we could skip the normalization of the n-grams since we can assume that longer words are more complex. But we have the word length feature to account for the length of words, so the normalization of the n-grams probabilities would account for density of the n-gram probabilities independent of the length of the word.

Additionally, we computed (iii) sentence length and (iv) sum probability of the character trigrams of the sentence to account for contextual orthographic complexity with respect to the word-level spelling complexity. These sentence-level features are similar to those used in Native Language Identification (Gebre et al., 2013; Malmasi and Dras, 2015; Malmasi et al., 2015b).

As a meta-feature that captures both word and sentential level spelling complexity, we use the proportion of word to sentence orthographic difficulty by taking the ratio of the aforementioned features (ii) and (iv).

3.2.3 Classifiers

We trained 3 different classifiers using the features described in Table 1: a (i) Random Forest Classifier (RFC), (ii) Nearest Neighbor Classifier[6] (NNC) and (iii) Support Vector Machine[7] (SVM).

Nearest neighbor classifiers usually work well when the distribution between the training set data points are dense and similar to (or representative) of test set. Since there is a limitation of two official submissions, we only submitted the output generated by RFC and SVM.[8]

4 Results

The shared task organizers reported 45 submissions to the CWI task (including baseline systems). An overview of the task containing the complete scores

---

[5]In the actual implementation of our submission, we have taken the percentile of the word rank, i.e. the product of the rank of the word and the inverse of number of words in the vocabulary, $|n|$. Empirically, they have the same effect in a classification since $|n|$ is a constant.

[6]RFC and NNC trained using Graphlab Create https://dato.com/products/create/ with default parameters (without tuning)

[7]SVM trained using Scikit-Learn (Pedregosa et al., 2011)

[8]SVM has been shown to perform well for large text classification tasks (Malmasi and Dras, 2014; Malmasi et al., 2015a).

Rank	Team	System	Accuracy	Precision	Recall	F-score	G-score
1	PLUJAGH	SEWDFF	**0.922**	0.289	0.453	**0.353**	0.608
2	LTG	System2	0.889	0.220	0.541	0.312	0.672
3	LTG	System1	0.933	**0.300**	0.321	0.310	0.478
4	MAZA	B	0.912	0.243	0.420	0.308	0.575
5	HMC	DecisionTree25	0.846	0.189	0.698	0.298	0.765
6	TALN	RandomForest_SIM	0.847	0.186	0.673	0.292	0.750
7	HMC	RegressionTree05	0.838	0.182	0.705	0.290	0.766
8	**MACSAAR**	RFC	0.825	0.168	0.694	0.270	0.754
9	TALN	RandomForest_WEI	0.812	0.164	0.736	0.268	0.772
10	UWB	All	0.803	0.157	0.734	0.258	0.767
11	PLUJAGH	SEWDF	0.795	0.152	0.741	0.252	0.767
12	JUNLP	RandomForest	0.795	0.151	0.730	0.250	0.761
13	SV000gg	Soft	0.779	0.147	**0.769**	0.246	**0.774**
14	**MACSAAR**	SVM	0.804	0.146	0.660	0.240	0.725
15	JUNLP	NaiveBayes	0.767	0.139	0.767	0.236	0.767

Table 2: The top 15 out of 45 systems in the shared task, ranked by their F-score.

obtained by all participants is available in the shared task report (Paetzold and Specia, 2016).

In Table 2 we include the top 15 submissions ranked by F-Score. We report results in terms of Accuracy, Precision, Recall, F-score, and G-score. The best scores for each metric are presented in bold.[9] Our best performing system (RFC) achieved 82.5% accuracy and 27% F-Score. Our second system (SVM), scored 2.1 percentage points accuracy and 3.0 percentage points less than the one using RFC.[10] Our best submission was ranked 8th in the CWI task in terms of both F-Score and G-Score.

We observed that some systems were trained to obtain good Recall and G-Score, for example the system ranked 13th by team SV000gg, while others obtained high Accuracy, for example the systems by teams LTG (System1), PLUJAGH, and MAZA which obtained accuracy scores higher than 90%. No system delivered a balanced combination of both scores which confirms the difficulty of this task.

Finally, as to the performance of the NNC system, we tested the NNC model on the gold data and this system achieved 75.9% accuracy and 11% F-score. As expected, it did not perform well because of the split between training and test set.

5 Conclusion and Future Work

The two *MacSaar* submissions were ranked on the top half of the table, among the top 15 out of 45 entries, in the SemEval-2016 Task 11: Complex Word Identification (CWI). Our best system using a Random Forest Classifier was ranked 8th in terms of both F-score and G-Score. This indicates that the performance we obtained can be comparable to other state-of-the-art systems for this task.

More than a good performance, we showed that the use of Zipfian features are a good source of information for this task. The frequency of occurrence and word length in complex and simple words are two interesting variables to be investigated in future work. By looking at the relationship between word frequencies and word length Piantadosi et al. (2011) states that word lengths are optimized for efficient communication and that 'information content is a considerably more important predictor of word length than frequency'. In our approach we did not take information content into account and we would like to investigate this in the future.

Another interesting, and to a certain extent surprising, outcome is that the SVM classifier did not outperform RFC using the same set of features. Due to its architecture, SVM is well-known for performing well in binary classification tasks and we would like to look analyse the most informative features and to perform error analysis to investigate the reasons for SVM's poor performance in this task.

---

[9]G-score is the harmonic mean between Accuracy & Recall.

[10]In the official CWI task scores (Paetzold and Specia, 2016), our second system is referred to as NNC even though it used an SVM. This occurred because we substituted the output of the NNC for the SVM but were unable to change the entry's name.

Acknowledgments

We would like to thank Gustavo Paetzold and Lucia Specia for organizing the CWI shared task. We also thank the anonymous reviewers and Shervin Malmasi for their feedback.

Liling Tan is supported by the People Programme (Marie Curie Actions) of the European Union's Seventh Framework Programme FP7/2007-2013/ under REA grant agreement n° 317471.

References

Valerie Adams. 2001. *Complex words in English*. Routledge.

Sandra M Aluísio, Lucia Specia, Thiago AS Pardo, Erick G Maziero, and Renata PM Fortes. 2008. Towards brazilian portuguese automatic text simplification systems. In *Proceedings of DocEng*.

María Jesús Aranzabe, Arantza Dıaz de Ilarraza, and Itziar Gonzalez-Dios. 2012. First approach to automatic text simplification in basque. In *Proceedings of the NLP4ITA Workshop*.

Gianni Barlacchi and Sara Tonelli. 2013. Ernesta: A sentence simplification tool for childrens stories in Italian. In *Proceedings of CICLing*.

Stefan Bott, Luz Rello, Biljana Drndarevic, and Horacio Saggion. 2012. Can spanish be simpler? lexsis: Lexical simplification for spanish. In *Proceedings of Coling*.

Daniel Dahlmeier, Hwee Tou Ng, and Siew Mei Wu. 2013. Building a large annotated corpus of learner english: The nus corpus of learner english. In *Proceedings of the BEA Workshop*.

Binyam Gebrekidan Gebre, Marcos Zampieri, Peter Wittenburg, and Tom Heskes. 2013. Improving native language identification with tf-idf weighting. In *Proceedings of the BEA Workshop*.

Paul Grice. 1975. Logic and conversation. In *Syntax and Semantics*, pages 41–58. Academic Press, New York.

Shervin Malmasi and Mark Dras. 2014. Language Transfer Hypotheses with Linear SVM Weights. In *Proceedings of EMNLP*.

Shervin Malmasi and Mark Dras. 2015. Multilingual Native Language Identification. In *Natural Language Engineering*.

Shervin Malmasi, Eshrag Refaee, and Mark Dras. 2015a. Arabic Dialect Identification using a Parallel Multidialectal Corpus. In *PACLING*.

Shervin Malmasi, Joel Tetreault, and Mark Dras. 2015b. Oracle and Human Baselines for Native Language Identification. In *Proceedings of the BEA Workshop*.

Gustavo Henrique Paetzold and Lucia Specia. 2015. LEXenstein: A framework for lexical simplification. In *Proceedings of ACL*.

Gustavo Henrique Paetzold and Lucia Specia. 2016. Semeval 2016 task 11: Complex word identification. In *Proceedings of SemEval*.

F. Pedregosa, G. Varoquaux, A. Gramfort, V. Michel, B. Thirion, O. Grisel, M. Blondel, P. Prettenhofer, R. Weiss, V. Dubourg, J. Vanderplas, A. Passos, D. Cournapeau, M. Brucher, M. Perrot, and E. Duchesnay. 2011. Scikit-learn: Machine learning in Python. *Journal of Machine Learning Research*, 12:2825–2830.

Steven T Piantadosi, Harry Tily, and Edward Gibson. 2011. Word lengths are optimized for efficient communication. *Proceedings of the National Academy of Sciences*, 108(9):3526–3529.

Matthew Shardlow. 2013. A comparison of techniques to automatically identify complex words. In *Proceedings of the ACL Student Research Workshop*.

Advaith Siddharthan. 2014. A survey of research on text simplification. *ITL-International Journal of Applied Linguistics*, 165(2):259–298.

Lucia Specia, Sujay Kumar Jauhar, and Rada Mihalcea. 2012. Semeval-2012 task 1: English lexical simplification. In *Proceedings of SemEval*.

Liling Tan, Marcos Zampieri, Nikola Ljubešic, and Jörg Tiedemann. 2014. Merging comparable data sources for the discrimination of similar languages: The dsl corpus collection. In *Proceedings of BUCC*.

Joel Tetreault, Daniel Blanchard, and Aoife Cahill. 2013. A report on the first native language identification shared task. In *Proceedings of the BEA Workshop*.

Wei Xu, Joel Tetreault, Martin Chodorow, Ralph Grishman, and Le Zhao. 2011. Exploiting syntactic and distributional information for spelling correction with web-scale n-gram models. In *Proceedings of EMNLP*.

Liang-Chih Yu, Lung-Hao Lee, and Li-Ping Chang. 2014. Overview of grammatical error diagnosis for learning chinese as a foreign language. In *Proceedings of ICCE*.

Marcos Zampieri and Liling Tan. 2014. Grammatical error detection with limited training data: The case of chinese. In *Proceedings of ICCE*.

Marcos Zampieri, Liling Tan, Nikola Ljubešic, Jörg Tiedemann, and Preslav Nakov. 2015. Overview of the DSL shared task 2015. In *Proceedings of the LT4VarDial Workshop*.

George Kingsley Zipf. 1935. *The Psychobiology of Language*. Houghton Mifflin.

George Kingsley Zipf. 1949. *Human behavior and the principle of least effort*. Addison-wesley Press.

Garuda & Bhasha at SemEval-2016 Task 11: Complex Word Identification Using Aggregated Learning Models

Prafulla Kumar Choubey and **Shubham Pateria**
System Software
Samsung R & D Institute India Bangalore Pvt Ltd
Bangalore, Karanataka, India -560037
`prafulla.ch, s.pateria@samsung.com`

Abstract

This paper describes aggregated learning models for Complex Word Identification (CWI) task in SemEval 2016. The work focused on selecting the features that determine complexity of words and used different combinations of support vector machine (SVM) and decision tree (DT) techniques for classification. These classifiers were pipelined with pre-processing and post-processing blocks which helped improving accuracy of systems, though had little impact on recall. Four systems were evaluated on the test set; SVM and DT systems by team Bhasha achieved G score of 0.529 and 0.508 respectively and SVM&DT and SVMPP systems by team Garuda achieved G scores of 0.360 and 0.546 respectively.

1 Introduction

CWI constitutes the first stage in lexical simplification (LS) pipeline (Specia et al., 2012). Performance of any LS system highly relies on accurate identification of complex words. (Shardlow, 2014) categorized errors in LS into six types and two of them (type 2A and 2B) are reflections of recall and precision of CWI system. The author concluded that type 2B errors occur with highest frequency, nearly 0.54, followed by type 2A (0.11). Also only 0.1 of simplifications were free from error. Thus, designing a robust CWI system impacts LS task the most.

CWI has long been researched and used in LS systems. (Paetzold, 2015) named some of the approaches used inclusive to LS task, like lexicon based approaches, frequency thresholding based approaches, word length thresholding and user driven approaches. Trained classifiers have also been proposed in literature like, (Shardlow, 2013) used SVM as classifier on feature sets comprising of frequency, length, synonym counts etc.

This work is extension to the method proposed by (Shardlow, 2013). The proposed systems are built on broader set of features and multiple classifiers have been used individually or in aggregation to know trade-off between precision and recall. These systems are trained solely on the training data released by task organizers and no external resource has been used, except the WordNet (Miller, 1995; Fellbaum, 1998).

The rest of paper is organized as follows, section 2 describes the feature sets used. Section 3 describes the approaches used and submitted systems performance w.r.t other participants. Finally, section 4 presents the conclusions and outlines some directions of future work.

2 Feature Sets

Selection of relevant feature is key to better performance of a machine learning model. While in some tasks, feature extraction is an obvious process, in tasks like CWI its hard to determine features aptness. So, in this work all the feature sets whose inclusion improves any of recall, precision or accuracy were used. These features have been described below.

Proceedings of SemEval-2016, pages 1006–1010,
San Diego, California, June 16-17, 2016. ©2016 Association for Computational Linguistics

2.1 Characters n-grams Frequency

These features are based on an assumption that character sequences that are frequently used should be easier to be recognized compared to rarely used sequences. For instance, if it is required to choose between Quixotic and Idealistic, idealistic would be easier to remember. Probably, because ideal, deal, idea are very commonly observed sequences, while quix is a rarely used character sequence in English dictionary. Given infinite possible character sequences, this work limited the sequences to 300 most frequently used uni, bi and tri-grams of characters.

2.2 Word's Features

In most of the LS tasks, word frequency thresholding has been used to determine its complexity (Brysbaert and New, 2009). In our systems, we have also included frequencies of words at positions [-2,-1,1,2] relative to the word, which is accounted only to observed higher accuracy.

We have also used Parts-of-Speech tag of target word and the words at position [-2,-1,1,2] relative to it as features. Brown corpus (Francis and Kucera, 1979) tagged with pos-tags used in the Penn treebank (Marcus et al., 1993) project was used to calculate trigram and emission probabilities for words and their parts of speech. Using Viterbi algorithm (Jurafsky and Martin, 2000) and probabilities calculated above, training and test sentences were tagged. Inclusion of pos-tags as features are again accounted to higher accuracy observed on validation set. The pos-tags are quantized as their occurrence frequency in combined training and testing datasets, table 1 contains the values.

Other word level features used are- word length (Keskisärkkä, 2012), words position, ratio of vowels and consonants, words stem length and frequency of stemmed words.

2.3 WordNet

The objective of LS is to find an alternative to complex word which is supposedly more common to target user. The words which have simpler synonyms available are more likely to be recognized as complex. For instance, succumb is likely to be complex provided yield is used more frequently. To intro-

Pos-tags	Values	Pos-tags	Values
{PRP$}	0.000645	{WP}	0.000227
{VBG}	0.039401	{VBZ}	0.001063
{VBD}	0.005699	{DT}	0.001253
{VBN}	0.047874	{NN}	0.537558
{VBP}	0.000189	{FW}	0.000113
{WDT}	0. 000152	{TO}	0.000008
{JJ}	0.075610	{PRP}	0.000873
{RB}	0.024962	{Other}	0.0

Table 1: Pos-tags and the corresponding numerical values used in Classifiers

duce this into our system, we used WordNet to find synonyms of word and used word frequency relative to its SynSets as an input feature. Like in case of succumb, yield, succumb and yield have frequency counts of 4 and 0 respectively. So the input feature will be 0 [0 / (0+4)] for succumb and 1 [4 / (0+4)] for yield.

3 Proposed Systems

We are proposing three stage pipelined systems for CWI task, comprising of pre-processing, classification by one or ensemble of trained models, and post-processing stages. These stages are described below.

3.1 Pre-processing

This stage comprises of four preliminary checks that directly classify words based on rules.

1. All the named entities are classified as non-complex.

2. The words which dont belong to English are classified as complex. We have used words available in various corpora provided by nltk package and English word list (Lawler, 1999) for this.

3. Words with length less than 2 are classified as non-complex.

4. Words with pos-tags CD, DT and TO as per UPenn tag-sets are classified as non-complex.

3.2 Trained Classifiers

This stage consists of a trained classifier based on features described in section 2. We submitted four systems with classifiers trained using different classification algorithms. Systems submitted

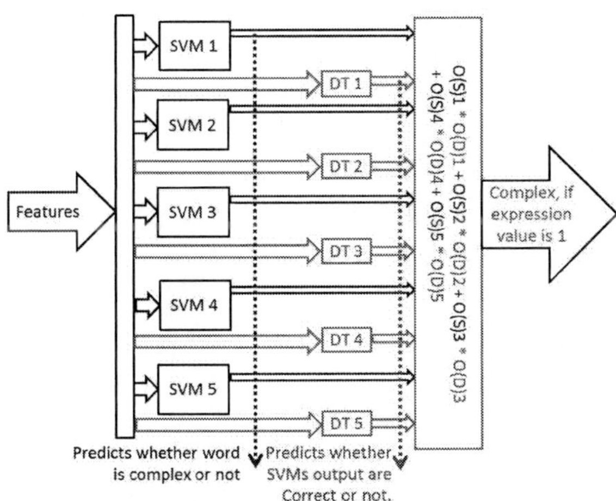

Figure 1: HSVM&DT Architecture for CWI.

by team Bhasha were based on support vector machines (SVM) and decision tree (DT). We used standard classifiers available in scikit-learn package (Pedregosa et al., 2011). Systems submitted by Garuda team were based on hybrid of classifiers. They are described below.

HSVM&DT: This is a hybrid model, inspired by bagging ensembles, comprising of multiple SVMs and DT for classifying words. We have used 5 SVMs with different training parameters (gamma, kernel and C values) and 5 different DT classifiers. SVMs perform classification of words as complex or non-complex, while DTs classify the predictions of SVM as correct or incorrect. Figure 1 explains the architecture.

A pair of SVM and DT model works together to classify the words. For each pair, training data is divided into two sets; first set is used to train the SVM and on second set, trained SVM is used to predict the output. In second set, if predicted output of SVM is same as the actual word label, we define target output as 1 for DT classifier and other wise 0. With this new target output and input features same as SVM, DT model is trained. Five such pairs were trained, each trained on randomly sampled training data. Random sampling allows learning more generalized. This algorithm is described in figure 2. One clear distinction of this aggregated model from conventional bagging is in terms of combining methodology. Output of only those SVM classifiers are used for which corresponding DT predicts 1.

SVMPP: This model is built on CWI_training_allannotations data. Twenty separate SVMs were trained on each annotation available in training data. It was designed with a belief that this system would achieve higher recall, though precision may be substantially low. In training data, a word was defined as complex, if any of the annotation was complex. However in our design, we have calculated coefficients for all 20 classifiers that define the contribution of each SVM classifier in final output. Also, output label for this model was modified as $\{-1,1\}$ instead of $\{0, 1\}$. Detailed algorithm is described in figure 3.

HSVM&DT Algorithm

Given: Training Data S
for i = 1 to 5:
   Divide data in two sets S_λ, S_μ in ratio 3:2
   Train an SVM Classifier on S_λ
   Predict class of $X_\mu \in S_\mu$ by trained SVM: Y'_μ
   Generate training data for DT classifier:
     if $Y'_\mu == Y_\mu$:
      $Y_{\mu,DT}=1$
     else:
      $Y_{\mu,DT}=0$
   Train DT Classifier with $X_\mu, Y_{\mu,DT} \in S_\mu$
Output Hypothesis: $0 \iff \Sigma O_{S[i]} * O_{D[i]} = 0$
              1, otherwise.

Figure 2: HSVM&DT Algorithm.

SVMPP Algorithm

Given: Training Data S_i, i=1..20 #20 annotators
Output Pre-processing: Y'= -1, if Y=0
                      Y'= 1, if Y=1
for i = 1 to 20:
   Train SVM Classifier SVC_i, on S_i.
   Calculate λ_i & μ_i coefficients for classifier:
   λ_i = T.P./(T.P. + F.P.) μ_i = T.N./(T.N. + F.N.)
   T.P.$\rightarrow$ True Positive   F.P.$\rightarrow$ False Positive
   T.N.$\rightarrow$ True Negative F.N.$\rightarrow$ False Negative
Output Hypothesis:
$0 \iff \Sigma f * O_{SVC_i} < 0$;
1, otherwise.
where, f = λ_i, when $O_{SVC_i} == 1$
        f = μ_i, when $O_{SVC_i} == -1$

Figure 3: SVMPP Algorithm.

As described in Figure 3, each SVM classifier has two associated coefficients $\{\lambda, \mu\}$. λ defines the precision of classifier in predicting non-complex words and μ defines precision for identifying complex words.

3.3 Post-Processing

This stage comprises of final check to remove highly probable miss-classifications.

1. Character bigrams (402 character bigrams were present in training set) which were not observed in training data but is present in test data and has occurrence frequency less than 0.00005 are classified as complex (Ex: zt, kz etc.).

2. Words with occurrence frequency above 0.001 and labelled as non-complex (if label available) in training data but vice versa by trained model, are classified non-complex.

3.4 Performance Comparison

Table 2 compares the performance of our systems with respect to performance statistics of all submitted systems, including baselines. From the analysis, it can be easily concluded that none of our systems are very effective in deciding complexity of words. Three of our systems- SVMPP, DT and SVM could reach around average performances and were ranked 31, 38 and 41 based on G-Score among 52 systems. The performances of SVM and SVMPP are almost comparable to other SVM based submitted systems and SVM seems to be less effective for CWI. But our DT system failed in achieving performance scores comparable to other DT and RFC based systems.

System HSVM&DT performed even worse than individual SVM and DT classifiers and was ranked 48 among all the systems. To determine the reasons, we analyzed the system's performance on only two features- word's frequency and word's length and plotted the decision boundaries. And it was observed that the system failed to achieve its objective of using multiple classifiers to predict the complexity of word and then deciding a classifier that has highest confidence on its prediction. The main reason for its failure was that all SVMs had almost overlapping decision boundaries. And the error in DTs prediction further worsened the prediction.

Systems	Precision	Recall	Fscore	Gscore
maximum	0.299	1	0.353	0.774
sv000gg	0.147	0.769	0.246	0.774
plujagh	0.289	0.453	0.353	0.608
average	0.114	0.606	0.173	0.560
s.d. [σ]	0.065	0.252	0.081	0.194
svmpp	0.099	0.415	0.160	0.546
dt	0.118	0.387	0.181	0.529
svm	0.119	0.363	0.179	0.508
hsvm&dt	0.112	0.226	0.149	0.360
minimum	0.0	0.0	0.0	0.0

Table 2: Systems Performance Measures

HSVM&DT, however, can be a very effective classifier for any task if we can manage to generate non-overlapping decision boundaries for all SVMs or any other constituent classifier. The performance of this system, though, is open for examination and needs to be explored further.

4 Conclusion

We tried several combinations of SVM and DT classifiers, but they could only achieve average of G-scores of all the submitted systems. As concluded by (Paetzold and Specia, 2016) in the CWI task description paper, DT and RFC perform better than most of the submitted systems. Also, the authors concluded that frequency measure possesses the highest confidence in deciding complexity of words. In our later study, we tried reducing the number of features and it was found that by merely including word-frequency, pos-tags, word-length and WordNet features, and training a DT model on same training set, system was able to achieve better G score on the test set. So, average performance of our systems can be mainly accounted to improper selection of features for the task. Inclusion of too many features shadowed the impact of frequency feature. In our future study, we plan to work on finding a suitable feature selection method for CWI and than work on classifier. Also as discussed before, failure of HSVM&DT model in this task is mainly accounted to lack of diversity in classifiers. We will continue our work on an ensemble classifier based on the principle of this model.

References

Marc Brysbaert and Boris New. 2009. Moving beyond kucera and francis: a critical evaluation of current word frequency norms and the introduction of a new and improved word frequency measure for american english. *BEHAVIOR RESEARCH METHODS*, 41(4):977–990.

Christiane Fellbaum, editor. 1998. *WordNet An Electronic Lexical Database*. The MIT Press, Cambridge, MA ; London, May.

W. N. Francis and H. Kucera. 1979. Brown corpus manual. Technical report, Department of Linguistics, Brown University, Providence, Rhode Island, US.

Daniel Jurafsky and James H. Martin. 2000. *Speech and Language Processing: An Introduction to Natural Language Processing, Computational Linguistics, and Speech Recognition*. Prentice Hall PTR, Upper Saddle River, NJ, USA, 1st edition.

Robin Keskisärkkä. 2012. Automatic text simplification via synonym replacement.

Mitchell P. Marcus, Mary Ann Marcinkiewicz, and Beatrice Santorini. 1993. Building a large annotated corpus of english: The penn treebank. *Comput. Linguist.*, 19(2):313–330, June.

George A. Miller. 1995. Wordnet: A lexical database for english. *Commun. ACM*, 38(11):39–41, November.

Gustavo H. Paetzold and Lucia Specia. 2016. Semeval 2016 task 11: Complex word identification. In *Proceedings of the 10th International Workshop on Semantic Evaluation (SemEval 2016)*.

Gustavo Paetzold. 2015. Reliable lexical simplification for non-native speakers. In *Proceedings of the 2015 Conference of the North American Chapter of the Association for Computational Linguistics: Student Research Workshop*, pages 9–16, Denver, Colorado, June. Association for Computational Linguistics.

F. Pedregosa, G. Varoquaux, A. Gramfort, V. Michel, B. Thirion, O. Grisel, M. Blondel, P. Prettenhofer, R. Weiss, V. Dubourg, J. Vanderplas, A. Passos, D. Cournapeau, M. Brucher, M. Perrot, and E. Duchesnay. 2011. Scikit-learn: Machine learning in Python. *Journal of Machine Learning Research*, 12:2825–2830.

Matthew Shardlow. 2013. A comparison of techniques to automatically identify complex words. In *ACL (Student Research Workshop)*, pages 103–109. The Association for Computer Linguistics.

Matthew Shardlow. 2014. Out in the open: Finding and categorising errors in the lexical simplification pipeline. In Nicoletta Calzolari (Conference Chair), Khalid Choukri, Thierry Declerck, Hrafn Loftsson, Bente Maegaard, Joseph Mariani, Asuncion Moreno, Jan Odijk, and Stelios Piperidis, editors, *Proceedings of the Ninth International Conference on Language Resources and Evaluation (LREC'14)*, Reykjavik, Iceland, may. European Language Resources Association (ELRA).

Lucia Specia, Sujay Kumar Jauhar, and Rada Mihalcea. 2012. Semeval-2012 task 1: English lexical simplification. In *Sixth International Workshop on Semantic Evaluation*, *SEM, pages 347–355, Montréal, Canada.

TALN at SemEval-2016 Task 11: Modelling Complex Words by Contextual, Lexical and Semantic Features

Francesco Ronzano, Ahmed Abura'ed, Luis Espinosa-Anke, Horacio Saggion
Department of Information and Communication Technologies (DTIC)
Universitat Pompeu Fabra
Tangèr 122, Barcelona (08018), Spain
{francesco.ronzano,ahmed.aburaed,luis.espinosa,horacio.saggion}@upf.edu

Abstract

This paper presents the participation of the TALN team in the Complex Word Identification Task of SemEval-2016 (Task 11). The purpose of the task was to determine if a word in a given sentence can be judged as complex or not by a certain target audience. To experiment with word complexity identification approaches, Task organizers provided a training set of 2,237 words judged as complex or not by 20 human evaluators, together with the sentence in which each word occurs. In our contribution we modelled each word to evaluate as a numeric vector populated with a set of lexical, semantic and contextual features that may help assess the complexity of a word. We trained a Random Forest classifier to automatically decide if each word is complex or not. We submitted two runs in which we respectively considered unweighted and weighted instances of complex words to train our classifier, where the weight of each instance is proportional to the number of evaluators that judged the word as complex. Our system scored as the third best performing one.

1 Introduction

Approaches to automatically identify if a target audience will perceive a certain word as complex or not constitute a core component in several language-related areas of research, including *Lexical Simplification* (Bott et al., 2012) and *Readability Assessment* (Collins-Thompson, 2014).

The Complex Word Identification Task of SemEval-2016 proposes a shared framework for evaluating complex word identification systems. Task participants were provided with a set of sentences where, for each sentence, one or more words have been rated as complex or not by 20 human evaluators. An example sentence from this dataset is:

If the growth rate is known , the maximum lichen size will give a minimum age for when this rock was deposited.

In this sentence, the words 'lichen' and 'deposited' were classified as complex by at least one out of the 20 evaluators, unlike e.g. 'growth', which did not received this label by any of them.

In our participation in Task 11, we cast the identification of complex words as a binary classification problem in which each word is evaluated as complex or not, given the sentence in which it occurs. We modelled each word by a set of lexical, semantic and contextual features and evaluated distinct binary classification algorithms. Our approach to Task 11 obtained good performance: our team ranked as the second best performing one and one of the two systems we proposed scored as the third best performing system according to the G-score official evaluation metric (harmonic mean between Accuracy and Recall).

In Section 2 we provide an overview of relevant research related to Complex Word Identification. Section 3 and 4 respectively introduce the Task 11 dataset and present the text analysis tools and resources we exploited to characterize complex words. In Section 5 we describe the word features we used to build our complex word classifier. In Section 6 we present and discuss the performance of our Task 11 system. Finally, in Section 7 we formulate our

Proceedings of SemEval-2016, pages 1011–1016,
San Diego, California, June 16-17, 2016. ©2016 Association for Computational Linguistics

conclusions and outline future venues of research.

2   Related work

The identification of complex words constitutes a key aspect of *Lexical Simplification* (Bott et al., 2012). It can be defined as the problem of replacing difficult words by their simpler synonyms taking into account the specific context in which each word is used. Several techniques have been applied so far to identify complex words. In the context of the PSET Project (Devlin and Tait, 1998), the first lexical simplification system for English was developed, aimed at people with aphasia. It relies on a word difficulty assessment based on psycholinguistic evidence (Quinlan, 1992) in order to decide whether to simplify a word. Recent work exploited the availability of comparable corpora of original documents (e.g. English Wikipedia) and their 'simplified' versions (e.g. Simple English Wikipedia pages) to induce measures which can be used to compare and rank 'quasi-synonymic' word pairs (Yatskar et al., 2010). (Shardlow, 2013) compares three techniques to identify complex words in English: a psycholinguistic approach (Devlin and Tait, 1998), frequency thresholding (i.e. words with low frequency are considered complex), and a machine learning algorithm trained only on word features (frequency, syllable count, ambiguity, etc.). In this work, a corpus of complex words is created based on edit histories from the Simple Wikipedia. The authors conclude that the three tested methods perform similarly in terms of F-measure. (Saggion et al., 2016) use the combined evidence of word frequency and word length to assess the word complexity of a list of synonyms so as to select the simpler one in an Spanish lexical simplification system. (Rello et al., 2013) argue that word frequency and length are two important factors affecting readability and understanding for people with dyslexia.

Besides lexical simplification, the identification of complex words constitutes a core component of *readability assessment* (Collins-Thompson, 2014), the problem of quantifying the readability of a given text. The presence of complex words usually penalizes readability. Lists of easy words (Dale and Chall, 1948), word characteristics (Kincaid et al., 1975; Gunning, 1952; Mc Laughlin, 1969), or word use in context (e.g. language models) (Si and Callan, 2001) are all techniques or resources which have been used to support the assessment of text readability: these approaches could also be adapted to evaluate word complexity.

3   Dataset

The organizers of SemEval-2016 Task 11 released a *training dataset* composed of 2,236 words together with the sentence in which each word occurs. For each word, the binary complexity judgements of 20 human evaluators were provided (complex word or not complex word). Similarly, Task 11 *testing dataset* consisted of 88,221 words together with the sentence in which each word occurs. In this case, for each word, the binary complexity judgement of only one human annotator was collected.

4   Resources and Tools

In order to identify complex words, we characterize each word by means of a set of lexical, semantic and contextual features. To this purpose, we analyze both the word and the sentence in which it occurs by means of the language resources and text analysis tools described in what follows.

4.1   Language Resources

Information about the frequency of use is important to assess word complexity. Therefore, in our complex word identification approach we exploit the word frequency data of two large corpora: (i) a 2014 English Wikipedia Dump and (ii) the British National Corpus (Leech and Rayson, 2014). We also use WordNet (Miller, 1995) to model semantic word features by relying on word senses and synset relations (e.g. hypernymy). Moreover, we use the Dale & Chall list of 3,000 simple words (Dale and Chall, 1948) in order to incorporate the text readability dimension, as this list contains words which 4th grade students considered understandable.

4.2   Text Analysis Tools

We analyze the sentences in which a word to evaluate occurs by means of the Mate dependency parser (Bohnet, 2010). As a result, we obtain a lemmatized and Part-Of-Speech (POS) tagged version of the sentence, along with its syntactic dependencies. Both POS tags and dependency information are used to compute several features as described in the following Section.

We also processed each sentence by the UKB graph-based Word Sense Disambiguation algorithm (Agirre and Soroa, 2009). Specifically, we benefited from the UKB implementation integrated in the Freeling workbench (Padró and Stanilovsky, 2012). In this way, we may disambiguate single or multiword expressions against WordNet 3.0.

5 Method

In order to evaluate the complexity of a word, we modelled each word as a feature vector. Then, we used such word representation to enable the training and evaluation of distinct binary classification algorithms tailored to determine whether a word is complex or not. To this end, we relied on the Weka machine learning framework (Witten and Frank, 2000). We evaluated the performance of four classification algorithms: Support Vector Machine (with linear kernel), Naïve Bayes, Logistic Regression and Random Forest. For each algorithm, we experimented the effectiveness of the following two training approaches:

- *Simple*: in which complex and non complex word training instances have the same relevance (weight);

- *Weighted*: in which we weighted each non complex word with weight 1 and each complex word with a weight ranging from 1 to 20 with respect to the number of human annotators (over 20) that evaluated the word as complex.

In the remainder of this Section we describe the set of word features we used, and motivate their relevance with respect to the characterization of complex words. When presenting word features, we group subsets of related features in the same subsection (Shallow features, Dependency Tree features, etc.). It is important to note that some of the word features presented are computed by considering, besides the target word, also context words in a $[-3, 3]$ window, where position 0 refers to the target word. If the context word at a specific position cannot be

determined, the value of the related feature is set to *undefined*.

5.1 Shallow Features

We exploited the following set of shallow word features:

- **Word length** (CharNumber): the length of the target word (number of characters).

- **Position of the word** (WordPosition): the position of the target word in the sentence. The value of this feature is normalized in the interval $[0, 1]$ by dividing the the position of the target word in the sentence by the length of the same sentence (number of words). The position of the first word of a sentence is 0.

- **Words in sentence** (NumSentenceWords): the number of tokens in the sentence.

5.2 Dependency Tree Features

The following set of features is derived by processing the dependency tree of the sentences that include the word to evaluate:

- **Word depth in the dependency tree** (DepthInTree_*position* - 7 features): we considered the depth in the dependency tree of the target word (*position* equal to 0), the three previous words and the three following words.

- **Parent word length** (ParentCharNumber): the length (number of characters) of the parent of the current (target) word in the dependency tree.

5.3 Corpus-based Features

Word frequency data derived from the British National Corpus and the 2014 English Wikipedia was used to compute the following set of features:

- **British National Corpus frequency** (BNCFrequency_*position* - 7 features): we considered the BNC frequency[1] of the target word lemma (*position* equal to 0), the three previous word lemmas and the three following word lemmas.

---

[1] http://ucrel.lancs.ac.uk/bncfreq/lists/1_1_all_fullalpha.txt.Z

- **English Wikipedia frequency** (ENwikiFrequency_*position* - 7 features): we considered the 2014 English Wikipedia frequency of the target word (*position* equal to 0), the three previous words and the three following words. Word frequencies were computed over a tokenized and lower-cased version of the English Wikipedia.

- **Simple word list** (Dale_Chall): a binary feature to point out the presence of the target word in the Dale & Chall list.

5.4 WordNet features

We used WordNet 3.0 to compute the following features. Given a target word, we refer as *target-word-synsets* the set of synsets that have the same POS of the target word and include the target word among their lexicalizations (all the senses of the target word). Note that this set of features is computed without relying on Word Sense Disambiguation.

- **Number of Synsets** (WNSynsetN): the number of synsets in *target-word-synsets* (i.e. number of senses of the target word).

- **Number of Senses** (WNSenseN): the sum of the number of word senses (i.e. the number of lexicalizations) of each *target-word-synset*.

- **Depth in the hypernym tree** (WNDepth): the average depth in the WordNet hypernym hierarchy among all the *target-word-synsets*.

- **Number of Lemmas** (WNLemma): the average number of synset lexicalizations among all the *target-word-synsets*.

- **Gloss length** (WNGloss): the average length of synset Glosses among all the *target-word-synsets*, in terms of number of tokens.

- **Number of relations** (WNRelation): the average number of semantic relations among all the *target-word-synsets*.

- **Number of Distinct POSs** (WNDistinctPOS): the number of distinct POS represented by at least one *target-word-synset*.

- **Part of Speech** (WN_*POS* - 4 features): for each WordNet POS (*POS* equal to Noun, Verb, Adjective and Adverb) we counted the number of synsets with that POS among the *target-word-synsets*, thus generating four features.

5.5 WordNet and corpus frequency features

The following set of features was computed by combining WordNet data, the word frequencies of the British National Corpus (BNC) and the results of the UKB WordNet-based Word Sense Disambiguation algorithm applied to the sentences where complex words appear. Thanks to the UKB algorithm, we identify the WordNet 3.0 synset that characterizes the sense of each target word (*WSD-synset*). Besides the target word, each *WSD-synset* usually has other lexicalizations, i.e. other synonyms. We retrieve the BNC frequency of all the lexicalizations of the *target-word-WSD-synset* and compute the following features:

- **Percentage of lexicalizations with higher / lower frequency than target word** (Lexic*Higher/Lower*FreqWSD - 2 features): the percentage of the lexicalizations of the *WSD-synset* with a BNC frequency higher / lower than the target word BNC frequency.

- **Ratio of total lexicalizations' frequencies related to lexicalizations with higher / lower frequency than target word** (Lexic*Higher/Lower*SumFreqWSD - 2 features): the ratio between the sum of BNC frequencies of the lexicalizations of the *WSD-synset* with a frequency higher / lower than the target word frequency and the sum of BNC frequencies of all the lexicalizations of the *WSD-synset*.

We also computed the previous set of 4 features without relying on the results of the UKB Word Sense Disambiguation algorithm: we considered for each target word all the lexicalizations of all the synsets that represent possible senses and have the same POS of the same target word. Similarly to the UKB based features, these features are referred to as: Lexic*Higher/Lower*FreqALL and Lexic*Higher/Lower*SumFreqALL.

6   Experiment and results

In order to identify the best approach to classify words as complex or not, we compared four classifiers by training on both the *Simple* and *Weighted* datasets. We evaluated the classification performance by means of a 10-fold cross-validation. Results are summarized in Table 1.

Classifier	Dataset	Precision	Recall	G-Score	F-Score
Random	Simple	0.746	0.756	0.582	**0.735 (run 1)**
Forest	Weighted	0.836	0.823	0.780	**0.824 (run 2)**
Support Vector	Simple	0.685	0.707	0.707	0.650
Machine	Weighted	0.728	0.718	0.718	0.719
Logistic	Simple	0.667	0.697	0.476	0.659
Regression	Weighted	0.733	0.734	0.745	0.733
Naïve	Simple	0.654	0.613	0.594	0.626
Bayes	Weighted	0.706	0.708	0.750	0.705

Table 1: Comparison of the performance of four complex word binary classifiers by a 10-fold cross-validation over the Task 11 training dataset.

Table 1 shows that the best performance in terms of F-Score was achieved by the Random Forest classifier for both approaches (*Simple* and *Weighted*). As a consequence, the two systems we submitted to Task 11 relied on a Random Forest model respectively trained on *Simple* (unweighted, run 1) and *Weighted* (run 2) instances. Our run based on *Weighted* instances performed quite well, ranking as the third best system in Task 11 with a G-Score of 0.772, where the G-Score of the best performing system is 0.774. With respect to F-Score our best performing run was the one based on *Simple* instances that ranked as sixth.

In Table 2 we show the top 10 features in our feature set in terms of information gain.

Info-gain	Feature name
0.37865	ENwikiFrequency_position_0
0.33303	BNCFrequency_position_0
0.18752	WNSynsetN
0.18439	WNGloss
0.14452	Dale_Chall
0.13596	LemmaLowerFreqALL
0.10567	WNdepth
0.10558	LemmaLowerSumFreqALL
0.08037	WNDistinctPOS
0.06244	WNSenseN

Table 2: Top 10 features with respect to information gain.

We can see that the frequencies of the word to evaluate in the two corpora we considered (English Wikipedia and British National Corpus) constitute the two most informative features. Five of the top 10 features are computed by relying on WordNet, without performing Word Sense Disambiguation: among them we can find the number of synsets (senses) of the word to evaluate (WNSynsetN), the average length of the glosses of these synsets (WNGloss) and the average depth of these synsets in the hypernym tree (WNDepth). Other useful indicators of word complexity are the presence of the word in the simple words list of Dale & Chall and the set of lexicalizations (of the synsets associated to the word) characterized by a frequency in the British National Corpus lower than the frequency of the word to evaluate (LexicLowerFreqALL and LexicLowerSumFreqALL).

In Table 3 we show the performance of the four classification algorithms we considered by training them on the whole *training dataset* (with *Simple* or *Weighted* instances) and testing them on the *testing dataset*. The best performance in terms of both F-Score and G-Score are achieved by the two Random Forest classifiers that were trained respectively on *Simple* (unweighted) and *Weighted* instances. In general, when we train the classifiers on *Weighted* instances in place of *Simple* ones, on the one hand both recall and accuracy improve, thus resulting in a higher G-Score, on the other hand the precision decreases, thus resulting in a lower F-Score.

Classifier	Dataset	Precision	Recall	G-Score	F-Score
Random	Simple	0.186	0.673	0.750	0.292 +
Forest	Weighted	0.164	0.736	0.772 *	0.268
Support Vector	Simple	0.132	0.406	0.549	0.199
Machine	Weighted	0.103	0.720	0.706	0.180
Logistic	Simple	0.131	0.454	0.588	0.203
Regression	Weighted	0.086	0.804	0.682	0.156
Naïve	Simple	0.083	0.769	0.670	0.151
Bayes	Weighted	0.079	0.787	0.656	0.144

Table 3: Comparison of the performance of four complex word binary classifiers. Each classifier is trained on the whole *training dataset* and tested on the annotated *testing dataset*. The asterisk symbol (*) points out the best performing classifier by G-Score while the plus symbol (+) the best performing classifier by F-Score.

7 Conclusions

In this paper, we described our participation to SemEval-2016 Task 11 concerning Complex Word Identification. We presented and evaluated our system based on both the characterization of words by means of contextual, lexical and semantic features and the exploitation of a Random Forest classifier to decide if a word is complex or not.

As future work we are planning to expand the feature set that we consider to characterize words by relying on new corpora and lexical resources. Moreover, we would like to explore complementary approaches to take advantage of distributional representations of words (i.e. word embeddings) or other language models to determine words complexity.

Acknowledgments

This work is partly supported by the Spanish Ministry of Economy and Competitiveness under the Maria de Maeztu Units of Excellence Programme (MDM-2015-0502) and the ABLE-TO-INCLUDE Project (Competitivity and Innovation Programme of the European Commission, CIP-ICT-PSP-2013-7/621055).

References

Eneko Agirre and Aitor Soroa. 2009. Personalizing Pagerank for Word Sense Disambiguation. In *Proceedings of the 12th Conference of the European Chapter of the Association for Computational Linguistics*, pages 33–41. Association for Computational Linguistics.

Bernd Bohnet. 2010. Very High Accuracy and Fast Dependency Parsing is not a Contradiction. In *Proceedings of the 23rd International Conference on Computational Linguistics (Coling 2010)*, pages 89–97, Beijing, China, August.

Stefan Bott, Luz Rello, Biljana Drndarevic, and Horacio Saggion. 2012. Can Spanish Be Simpler? LexSiS: Lexical Simplification for Spanish. In *Proceedings of the 24th International Conference on Computational Linguistics (CoLing 2012)*, December.

Kevyn Collins-Thompson. 2014. Computational Assessment of Text Readability. A Survey of Current and Future Research. *ITL - International Journal of Applied Linguistics 165:2*, 165(2):97–135.

Edgar Dale and Jeanne S. Chall. 1948. The Concept of Readability. *Elementary English*, 23(24).

Siobhan Devlin and John Tait. 1998. The Use of a Psycholinguistic Database in the Simplification of Text for Aphasic Readers. *Linguistic Databases*, pages 161–173.

Robert Gunning. 1952. *The Technique of Clear Writing*. McGraw-Hill.

J. Peter Kincaid, Robert P. Fishburne Jr., Richard L. Rogers, and Brad S. Chissom. 1975. Derivation of New Readability Formulas for Navy Enlisted Personnel. Technical report, Naval Technical Training Command.

Geoffrey Leech and Paul Rayson. 2014. *Word Frequencies in Written and Spoken English: Based on the British National Corpus*. Routledge.

G. Harry Mc Laughlin. 1969. SMOG Grading - a new Readability Formula. *Journal of Reading*, pages 639–646, May.

George A. Miller. 1995. WordNet: a Lexical Database for English. *Communications of the ACM*, 38(11):39–41.

Lluis Padró and Evgeny Stanilovsky. 2012. FreeLing 3.0: Towards Wider Multilinguality. In *Proceedings of the Language Resources and Evaluation Conference (LREC 2012)*, Istanbul, Turkey, May. ELRA.

Philip T. Quinlan. 1992. *The Oxford Psycholinguistic Database*. Oxford University Press.

Luz Rello, Ricardo Baeza-Yates, Laura Dempere-Marco, and Horacio Saggion. 2013. Frequent Words Improve Readability and Short Words Improve Understandability for People with Dyslexia. In *Human-Computer Interaction - INTERACT 2013*, pages 203–219.

Horacio Saggion, Stefan Bott, and Luz Rello. 2016. Simplifying Words in Context. Experiments with Two Lexical Resources in Spanish. *Computer Speech & Language*, 35:200–218.

Matthew Shardlow. 2013. A Comparison of Techniques to Automatically Identify Complex Words. In *ACL (Student Research Workshop)*, pages 103–109. The Association for Computer Linguistics.

Luo Si and Jamie Callan. 2001. A Statistical Model for Scientific Readability. In *Proceedings of the Tenth International Conference on Information and Knowledge Management*, CIKM '01, pages 574–576, New York, NY, USA. ACM.

Ian H. Witten and Eibe Frank. 2000. *Data Mining: Practical Machine Learning Tools and Techniques with Java Implementations*. Morgan Kaufmann Publishers Inc., San Francisco, CA, USA.

Mark Yatskar, Bo Pang, Cristian Danescu-Niculescu-Mizil, and Lillian Lee. 2010. For the Sake of Simplicity: Unsupervised Extraction of Lexical Simplifications from Wikipedia. In *Proceedings of the Proceedings of the 49th Annual Meeting of the Association for Computational Linguistics*, pages 365–368.

IIIT at SemEval-2016 Task 11: Complex Word Identification using Nearest Centroid Classification

Ashish Palakurthi and **Radhika Mamidi**
Kohli Center on Intelligent Systems
IIIT-Hyderabad, India.
`ashish.palakurthi@research.iiit.ac.in`
`radhika.mamidi@iiit.ac.in`

Abstract

This paper describes the system that was submitted to SemEval2016 Task 11: *Complex Word Identification*. It presents a preliminary investigation into exploring word difficulty for non-native English speakers. We developed two systems using Nearest Centroid Classification technique to distinguish complex words from simple words. Optimized over G-score, the presented solution obtained a G-score of 0.67, while the winner achieved a G-score of 0.77 and the average G-score of all the submitted systems in the task was 0.56.

1 Introduction

Lexical Simplification aims at improving the readability and comprehensibility of text by transforming complex text into simple text. Lexical Simplification (Specia et al., 2012; Belder et al., 2010; Horn et al., 2014) is the process of replacing a word in a given context with its simplest substitute to enhance the readability of the text. The process should make sure that while replacing words with other variants, the meaning of the text is preserved. Lexical Simplification (Siddharthan, 2014) is useful to a wide variety of target audience like people with aphasia, children and also non-native speakers. Complex Word Identification (Shardlow 2013; Paetzold 2015) is considered to be the first step in the pipeline of Lexical Simplification. The overall performance of a Lexical Simplification system is thus crucially dependent upon Complex Word Identification. The problem of Complex Word Identification is relatively new in the field of Natural Language

Processing. However, a few approaches have been previously proposed for this task. The simplicity score (Bott et al., 2012) of a word is computed by integrating both, frequency and length of a word. They consider a threshold value and simplify words only if the word's frequency is lower than the fixed threshold. Matthew Shardlow (2013) explores the frequency thresholding to differentiate between simple and complex words by experimenting with each threshold value on a particular corpus. However, this approach is not practically convincing. The same author also frames the problem as a machine learning classification problem by designing a few features. We approach the problem at hand on similar lines.

The Complex Word Identification (CWI) task is framed as a binary classification problem. Given a word in a sentence, the task is to predict whether the word is simple or complex. A word is tagged with 0 if it is simple and 1 if the word is found to be complex. [1]

$$c(w) = \begin{cases} 1 & if \ w \in C \\ 0 & if \ w \in S \end{cases}$$

C is the set of complex words, S is the set of simple words and $c(w)$ represents the class of the word. Here is an example of a sentence taken from the training dataset provided by the organizers.

⋄ A **frenulum** is a small fold of tissue that secures or **restricts** the **motion** of a mobile organ in the body.

---

[1] Complex: In the context of this shared task, complex words are the words which are difficult to understand for a non-native English speaker.

Proceedings of SemEval-2016, pages 1017–1021,
San Diego, California, June 16-17, 2016. ©2016 Association for Computational Linguistics

In the above example, the task requires a system to spae the words in bold as complex. The remainder of this paper is structured as follows. In Section 2, we describe our systems and Section 3 discusses experiments and results. We conclude in Section 4.

2 System Description

We use the Nearest Centroid Classification technique (Manning et al., 2008) for the classification of words using Manhattan and Standardised Euclidean distance metrics. This classification method is widely used in Information Retrieval tasks. In this method, each class is represented by the mean of all the training samples belonging to that class in the training data. A new observation is assigned a class label, whose mean is closest to the observation. Given below are the labeled training samples:

$$(\vec{x_1}, y_1), ..., (\vec{x_n}, y_n), y_i \in Y$$

$$\vec{\mu_c} = \frac{1}{|N_c|} \sum_{i \in N_c} \vec{x_i}$$

$$\hat{y} = arg\ min_{c \in Y} ||\vec{\mu_c} - \vec{x_i}||$$

where Y is the set of classes,
$|N_c|$ is the number of samples in class $c \in$ Y,
μ_c is the centroid of all samples belonging to class c,
$\hat{y}$ is the class assigned to the new observation.

We submitted two systems for this shared task. Our first system uses the Manhattan distance metric for the Nearest Centroid Classification. The Manhattan distance function computes the distance to be travelled to get from one data point to another point in a grid-like path. The Manhattan distance between two points is the sum of the differences of their corresponding components. Manhattan distance between two points $A(x,y)$ and $B(x,y)$ is defined as:

$$d(A, B) \equiv |A_x - B_x| + |A_y - B_y|$$

The distance metric used by System 2 in the training algorithm of the Nearest Centroid Classification was Standardised Euclidean, which is a slight variant of Euclidean distance. Euclidean distance between two points is defined as the sum of the squares of the differences between the corresponding components of the points. The Standardised Euclidean

distance between two points $A(x,y)$ and $B(x,y)$ is defined as:

$$d(A, B) \equiv \frac{\sqrt{(A_x - B_x)^2 + (A_y - B_y)^2}}{V}$$

where, V is the 1-D array of component variances and the numerator is the Euclidean distance between two points $A(x,y)$ and $B(x,y)$.

Both, System 1 and System 2 rely on 5 features to classify the target word as simple or complex. An almost similar set of features was previously employed by Matthew Shardlow (2013) to identify complex words using Support Vector Machines. The features we considered for the classification of words are:

- **Unigram Word Probability:** We used the Google Books Ngram Viewer[2] to obtain the word probability of the target word in the sentence. This information was considered only for the year 2000.

- **Length:** We considered length of the target word as a feature because longer words are likely to be complex.

- **Number of Senses:** A word with higher number of senses is relatively more ambiguous in comparison to a word with fewer senses. Number of senses of a word was obtained using WordNet[3] from NLTK[4] package.

- **Syllable Count:** A word with higher number of syllables[5] is likely to be more difficult to be read.

- **CD Count:** The number of films in which the target word had appeared was obtained from the SUBTLEX[6] corpus.

3 Experiments and Discussions

3.1 Data

We used the joint dataset provided by the task organizers for training. The training and test data consisted of 2,237 and 88,221 instances, respectively.

---

[2]https://books.google.com/ngrams
[3]http://www.nltk.org/howto/wordnet.html
[4]http://www.nltk.org/
[5]http://www.syllablecount.com/syllables.
[6]http://zipf.ugent.be/open-lexicons/interfaces/subtlex-uk/

Also, the training and test data comprised 200 and 8,929 unique sentences respectively.

3.2 Discussions

We discuss our experiments with respect to the training dataset. Experiments were run with a variety of machine learning algorithms using the Scikit-learn toolkit (Pedregosa et al., 2011). However, the Nearest Centroid Classification algorithm was found to outperform other algorithms like Random Forest and Support Vector Machines significantly over 5-fold cross-validation of the training dataset. We tried numerous combinations of features and finalized on the feature set described in the previous section.

There are a few features that we tried during our experimentation but did not include in the final system, as the results turned comparatively lower with their inclusion during cross-validation. We believe that the features are still worth discussing. They are:

1. *Average Word Length of Synonyms:* If the length of the given word is greater than the average length of all its synonyms, then the word is tagged as 1, else 0. This gives us a relative estimate on whether people would prefer to use a word more regularly in comparison to its synonyms. A similar feature could be tried using frequency or syllables in addition to length of the word. But for our experiments, we only used the length feature.

2. *Rank of a Sense:* We use the Lesk algorithm from Wordnet to find the sense of a word in the given sentence. We find the corresponding sense and the rank of the sense based on frequency using Wordnet. A lower rank of a sense suggests higher frequency of usage of that sense (Christiane Fellbaum, 1998). A higher frequency of a sense indicates that the word is likely to be inferred as simple. The rank of a sense is divided by the total number of senses of the word to get a normalized measure of the feature.

3. *Number of Synonyms:* Number of synonyms of a given word was considered. This information was obtained using Wordnet.

4. *Collocation Score:* Collocations are a set of words which occur together frequently. We find collocations for the target word in each sentence. We calculate a collocation score (C-score) defined as

$$C\text{-}score = \frac{C}{N}$$

where, C is the number of collocations matched in the sentence and N is the total number of tokens in the sentence. A higher C-score value indicates that the word usage is less ambiguous. Collocations[7] include Noun, Verb, Adjective, Adverb and Conjunction collocations.

We believe that the first two features are very critical in differentiating simple words from complex ones as words should be inspected in a relative frame with respect to their synonyms and senses. *A complex word may have higher number of senses but it does not necessarily imply that a word with higher number of senses is always complex.* It is fairly possible that a word (with many senses) in the given sentence may turn out to be the most frequently used sense and hence appear to be simple.

Thresholding based on frequency of a word is a common and effective way to identify complex words. The PLUJAGH team submitted a frequency threshold-based system and it stood first in this shared task when evaluated on F-score. In addition to simple thresholding, it is essential to consider relative frequencies of a word with respect to their synonyms. For example, consider the words *eldest* and *oldest*. From a manual experiment, we found that *eldest* is a complex word and *oldest* is a simple word. The frequency of *oldest* is higher than the frequency of *eldest*. However, the word *unused* (from the training dataset provided by organizers) which is less frequent (google ngrams) than *eldest* is a simple word. We found 110 words in the training dataset whose frequency is lower than *eldest* and are still simple. We claim that this may be due to the relatively higher frequency/usage of *oldest* with respect to the frequency/usage of *eldest*.

In conclusion, it becomes important to speculate words in a relative frame (of frequency/senses/length) with respect to their synonyms, to improve complex word identification.

---

[7]Collocations were collected from http://prowritingaid.com/free-online-collocations-dictionary.aspx

The effectiveness of this hypothesis could have been empirically better visible with the availability of a larger training dataset.

3.3 Evaluation Metric

The official evaluation metric of the task is G-score. It is the harmonic mean of Accuracy (A) and Recall (R).

$$G\text{-}score = \frac{2 * A * R}{A + R}$$

3.4 Results

Table 1 shows the average G-score obtained using different classifiers for 5-fold cross-validation on the training data. For experiments using the Nearest Centroid Classification, we explored 24 different distance metrics, of which Manhattan and Standardised Euclidean metrics performed the best. Based on G-score, our systems were ranked 15th and 23rd in the task. Our first system was able to beat all the baseline systems including the threshold-based and the lexicon-based systems. Table 2 shows the performance of System 1 and System 2 on the test data.

System	G
System 1	0.65
System 2	0.63
Decision Tree	0.54
Naive Bayes	0.61
AdaBoost	0.58
Gradient Boost	0.54
SVM	0.44
Random Forest	0.53

Table 1: Cross-validation results on Training Data

System	A	R	G
System 1	0.546	0.879	0.674
System 2	0.465	0.860	0.603
Decision Tree	0.734	0.613	0.668
Naive Bayes	0.404	0.924	0.562
AdaBoost	0.767	0.777	**0.772**
Gradient Boost	0.826	0.705	0.761
SVM	0.837	0.546	0.661
Random Forest	0.794	0.641	0.709

Table 2: Results on Test Data

The reason for choosing the Nearest Centroid Classifier was its consistent and comprehensive dominance over other classifiers tuned over various parameters and different feature combinations during the 5-fold cross-validation on the joint dataset. The results shown in Table 2 pertain only to the finalized feature set discussed in Section 3. Table 2 also shows the results obtained on the test data using different classifiers with the same set of features employed for System 1 and System 2. At this point of time, we are not sure about why few classifiers like AdaBoost and Random Forest performed way better than System 1 and System 2 on the test data. A possible reason for the poor performance of the Nearest Centroid Classifier in comparison to other systems could be the imbalance between the training and the test data size. The test data being highly skewed could probably be another reason. AdaBoost[8] classifier (Table 2) was found to achieve a G-score of 0.772 on test data. This suggests that both, the proposed feature set and the approach presented are competent.

4 Conclusion and Future Work

In this paper, we described a promising approach for identifying complex words for non-native English speakers using Nearest Centroid Classification technique. Our approach is simple in terms of both, features and the learning algorithms.

We emphasized that words should be inspected in a relative frame with respect to their synonyms and senses. Testing this supposition in depth will be the subject of future work. We further look to improve the system by incorporating phonetic and semantic features. We also look to explore the problem at sentence level, as the complexity of the sentence can influence a person in comprehending a word's meaning in that sentence.

Acknowledgment

We would like to thank the SemEval-2016 Task 11 organizers, Henry Gustavo Paetzold and Lucia Specia for conducting this interesting shared task. In addition, we thank the anonymous reviewers for their

---

[8]For the AdaBoost classifier, the number of estimators used was 10.

constructive comments and insights that helped us in improving this manuscript. We are grateful to Himani Chaudhry and Himanshu Sharma.

References

Jan De Belder, Koen Deschacht, and Marie-Francine Moens. 2010. Lexical simplification. In *Proceedings of ITEC2010: 1st international conference on interdisciplinary research on technology, education and communication.*

Stefan Bott, Luz Rello, Biljana Drndarevic, Horacio Saggion. 2012. Can Spanish Be Simpler? LexSiS: Lexical Simplification for Spanish. In *Proceedings of COLING, Mumbai, India* .

Colby Horn, Cathryn Manduca and David Kauchak. 2014. Learning a Lexical Simplifier Using Wikipedia. In *Proceedings of the ACL 2014*, page pp. 458-463.

Christiane Fellbaum. 1998. Wordnet: An Electronic Lexical Database. Cambridge: MIT Press.

Fabian Pedregosa, Gael Varoquaux, Alexandre Gramfort, Vincent Michel, Bertrand Thirion, Olivier Grisel, Mathieu Blondel, Peter Prettenhofer, Ron Weiss, Vincent Dubourg, Jake Vanderplas , Alexandre Passos, David Cournapeau, Matthieu Brucher, Matthieu Perrot, Edouard Duchesnay. 2011. Scikit-learn: Machine Learning in Python In *Journal of Machine Learning Research, 12*, pages 2825–2830.

Michel Jean-Baptiste, Yuan Kui Shen, Aviva P. Aiden, Adrian Veres, Matthew K. Gray, Joseph P. Pickett, Dale Hoiberg, Dan Clancy, Peter Norvig, Jon Orwant, Steven Pinker, Martin A. Nowak, and Erez Lieberman Aiden. 2011. Quantitative analysis of culture using millions of digitized books, science, 331(6014), pp.176-182.

Christopher Manning, Prabhakar Raghavan, & Hinrich Schutze. 2008. Introduction to information retrieval. Vol. 1. No. 1. Cambridge: Cambridge university press.

Gustavo Henrique Paetzold. 2015. Reliable Lexical Simplification for Non-Native Speakers. In *Proceedings of the NAACL-HLT 2015 Student Research Workshop (SRW)*, page p9.

Gustavo Henrique Paetzold and Lucia Specia. 2016. SemEval 2016 Task 11: Complex Word Identification. In *Proceedings of the 10th International Workshop on Semantic Evaluation (SemEval 2016)*.

Matthew Shardlow. 2013. A Comparison of Techniques to Automatically Identify Complex Words. In *Proceedings of the ACL (Student Research Workshop)*, page pp103-109.

Advaith Siddharthan. 2014. A Survey of Research on Text Simplification. In *ITL-International Journal of Applied Linguistics*, page pp165(2):259-298.

Lucia Specia, Sujay Kumar Jauhar and Rada Mihalcea. 2012. SemEval-2012 Task 1:English Lexical Simplification. In *Proceedings of the First Joint Conference on Lexical and Computational Semantics-Volume 1: Proceedings of the main conference and the shared task, and Volume 2: Proceedings of the Sixth International Workshop on Semantic Evaluation. Association for Computational Linguistics.*

AmritaCEN at SemEval-2016 Task 11: Complex Word Identification using Word Embedding

Sanjay S.P and **Anand Kumar M** and **Soman K P**
Centre for Computational Engineering & Networking (CEN)
Amrita School of Engineering, Coimbatore
Amrita Vishwa Vidyapeetham
Amrita University
India
sanjay.poongs@gmail.com, m_anandkumar@cb.amrita.edu, kp_soman@amrita.edu

Abstract

Complex word identification task focuses on identifying the difficult word from English sentence for a Non-Native speakers. Non-Native speakers are those who don't have English as their native language. It is a sub-task for lexical simplification. We have experimented with word embedding features, orthographic word features, similarity features and POS tag features which improves the performance of the classification. In addition to the SemEval 2016 results we have evaluated the training data by varying the vector dimension size and obtained the best possible size for producing better performance. The SVM learning algorithm will attains constant and maximum accuracy through linear classifier. We achieve a G-score of 0.43 and 0.54 on computing complex words for two systems.

1 Introduction

Complex Word Identification (CWI) is the task of identifying difficult words for a Non-Native speaker. The main objective of Complex Word Identification is to simplify and enhance the perplexing words in the sentences for Non-Native speakers. Complex Word Identification is used in Lexical Simplification (LS). The Lexical Simplification is important for all Text Simplification (Gustavo Henrique Paetzold, 2006). The perspective of each user is different therefore the task Complex Word Identification have been demanding one. For distinguish complex words for individual user will be a tedious task, therefore the CWI task is a difficult one, so we are identifying the complex words for a group of users.

CWI could be used in summarization of stories or generate abstract of a book. Shortening a paragraph would be difficult without removing the complex words, since the shortened text with complex words would be very difficult or confusing for non-native users to read and understand. We can make a story more simple for kids to read by replacing complex words with most common words (Tomoyuki Kajiwara et al., 2013). The main ways to identify the complex words are Threshold-based and Classification-based approches (Gustavo Henrique Paetzold, 2006). In Threshold-based approach, length, number of syllables, count of ambiguity and word frequency are considered as features. If the values are above the threshold, then the word is said to be a complex word. In the Classifier-based approach, the word features are trained and the word features which are similar to the trained word features are considered to be a complex word.

2 Complex Word Identification (CWI) - Task Description

The SemEval-2016 organizers have released three files *cwi_training, cwi_training_allannotations, and cwi_testing*. The first two files are training files and the third file is a testing file. Our task is to find the words in the testing file and label each one as 1 if the given word is a complex word, or 0 if the word is not a complex word.

The *training_allannotations* file contains tags of 20 authors for given sentences. The training file contains a single tag for the sentences representing the group of 20 authors in allannotations file. Each word is tagged complex if any of the author tagged it as 1.

Proceedings of SemEval-2016, pages 1022–1027,
San Diego, California, June 16-17, 2016. ©2016 Association for Computational Linguistics

If the all authors tagged it as non-complex then it is tagged as 0. We trained a binary classifier on the *cwi_training* data to identify the complex words in the testing data.

3 Neural word embedding

From the given sentences, unique words are converted into a more meaningful mathematical vector representation called a Neural word embedding (Tomas Mikolov et al., 2013). For a given word, the vector formed by the word is related to the semantic and syntactic contexts of the word, and also related to the the neighboring occurrence of the word. To produce the maximum vector of given size. The w_0 is the given word where the conditional probability is given in the Figure 1, where j is the index of actual output in the output layer.

3.1 Gensim - Implementation

The Gensim word2vec uses skip-gram and CBOW models. The word2vec run two passes to the training data. The first pass will collect the required unique words and build the tree structure. The second pass will train the neural model (Tomas Mikolov et al., 2013). We can vary the dimensions of the vector space model.

4 Methodology

The input data to our system is in the form of sentences but the output requires only word to tagged, so we cannot train the classifier with sentence features. The sentence with the word to be identified are tokenized. We have given the tokenized data into a word embedding models, it produced vectors for each words. we have acquired similarity features with nearby words. The other features like POS tagging and orthographic word features are obtained from the word and these features does not depend on the sentence. All the features are incorporated and saved in a text file. The text file is given to a SVM classifier which compares with the trained model and generates the result. The working process is given in Figure 1.

5 Feature Extraction

The features, are extracted from the given word in the testing data. We have extracted four types of features, namely orthographic features, similarity features, word embedding features and POS tag features. In these four types of features the orthographic feature based on the word itself, it provides the shape features of the word. The other two features namely similarity features and word embedding features are extracted from the word2vec model which is mentioned above. The Part Of Speech (POS) tag features is obtained with the help of NLTK tool kit and all the features are incorporated for training.

5.1 Orthographic features

Orthographic word features do not depend on the sentence. They are generic features of a given word like length of the word, number of syllables, ambiguity count and frequency. The count of the characters in the corresponding target word which provides the length of the word. The syllable feature gives the number of syllables present in the word, using the pyhyphen package we have retrieved the features. We used NLTK WordNet synsets (Steven Bird, 2006) for obtaining the ambiguity of the word. WordNet has an built-in dictionary from which number of ambiguity present for the word is obtained (George A. Miller, 1995; ?). The ambiguity is defined as the number of words that have similar meaning. A word is said to be more familiar if the word has more meaning. In the frequency feature, we count occurrences of the word in both training and testing data. These word features improve the accuracy.

5.2 Similarity features

These features represent how similar the word occurs to the neighboring words. We have derived four similarity values. Let us assume that the given word is represented as w_0 then the similarity values are attained as $[w_0 \& w_{-2}][w_0 \& w_{-1}][w_0 \& w_1][w_0 \& w_2]$. The similarity values are acquired from the word2vec model using Gensim.

5.3 Word embedding features

All the training and testing data were combined and passed into word2vec model. In word2vec, the unique words are obtained and its corresponding vector representations are created for all the words. We can vary the size of the vector while creating the

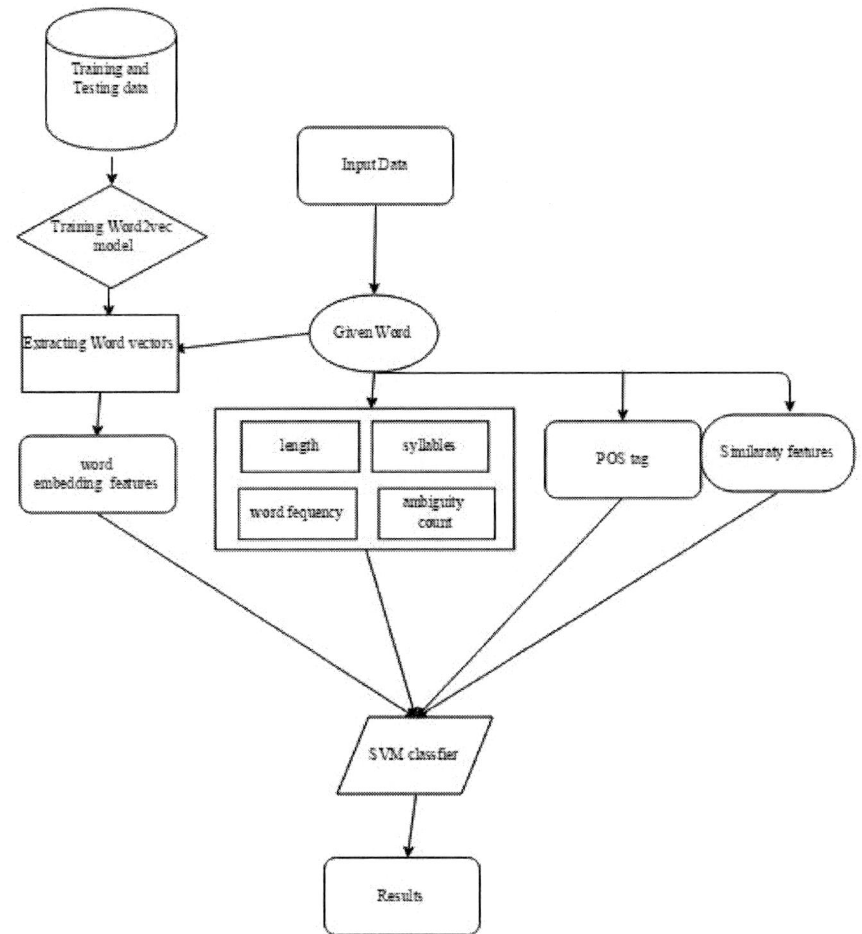

Figure 1: Working model

Accuracy

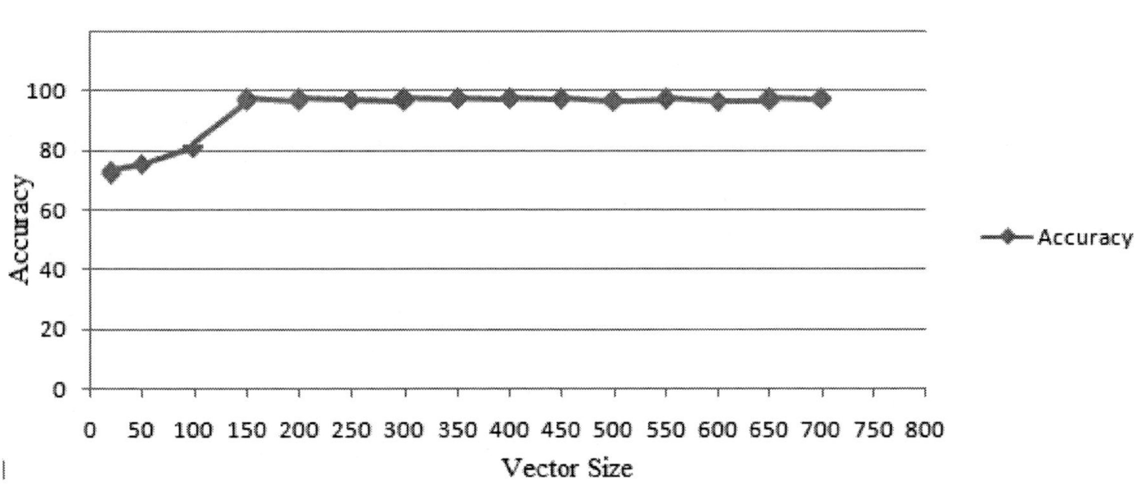

Figure 2: Training accuracy

vector representation model. We have obtained various results by varying the vector size. We varied the vector size, getting good accuracy after a vector size of 150, as shown in Figure 3. Finally concluded the best vector size as 500 at which we have obtained reasonable results for all other features. The curve tends to decrease after vector size of 500.

5.4 POS tag features

The Part Of Speech tag is taken for five words, by assuming the current word as w_0, then the POS tagging is taken for $w_{-2}, w_{-1}, w_0, w_1, w_2$. We are using NLTK (Natural Language Tool Kit) for POS tagging. The NLTK is an open source tool kit for python[3]. We implemented 2 systems. The first system trained an SVM without including the POS tagging. In the second system, POS tagging with other features has been included. The POS tag increases the accuracy of the data but it might reduce the recall.

6 Classifier

The SVM classifier is used for classification. The data is classified based on the features of the test data. For a given training point (x^i, y^i) it finds out the hyper plane $w^t(x) + b = 0$. Here we have used LIBSVM (Chang and Lin, 2011), which is integrated tool for Support Vector Classification (SVC) with regression and distributed estimation [1]. Python LIBSVM supports cross-validation. It is built on the C/C++ core SVM performance.

7 Data set:

We were provided with 2,237 training words and 88,221 testing words. In the training data there are 706 (31.56%) complex words and 1531 (68.4%) non complex words. The training file is in the format of <sentences> <word> <position> <1 or 0>. 1 indicates if the word is complex and 0 indicates if the word is not complex. The test data is in the format of <sentences> <word> <position>.

8 Experimental results

The Figure 3 gives our system's precision, recall, and F-score on the CWI training data. We tried varying the vector size in the word2vec model. Word features include length, number of syllables, ambiguity

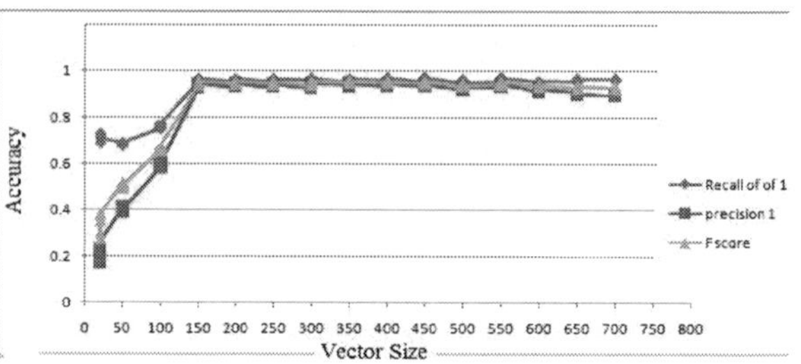

Figure 3: F-score accuracy

count, and frequency. We have four possible combinations and the test results are been tabled in Table 1. The first combination includes word2vec features. The second combination includes word2vec and word features. The third combination includes word2vec and similarity features. The fourth combination includes word2vec, similarity and word features. By varying the size and features the precision and recall tend to combine at a point called break though point. After the break though point the F-score becomes steady. The break through point for data is 150. Above which the accuracy tends to be linear, After the break through point the curve tends to decrease after 500. Therefore, we have concluded at a vector size of 500 and including all the features we have achieved the maximum accuracy. From the Figure 3 we can clearly see the F-score gradually decreasing at 550.

The accuracy graph steadily increases and reaches a maximum at 500 then accuracy tends to steadily decreases. Table 1, provides the additional results experimented by us.

8.1 SemEval Results:

We have submitted 2 files w2vecSimPos and w2vecSim. The first file w2vecSimPos is extracted by including all the four features mentioned namely word embedding, similarity, special word features, and POS tag features. The second file consist of word embedding, similarity and special word features. In the second file we have not included POS tag features. From the table, we can clearly see by including POS tag features there is in an improvement in the accuracy of the system. F-score denotes harmonic mean between precision and recall. G-score denotes harmonic mean between accuracy and recall. By including the POS tag as a feature the ac-

Table 1: Additional Results

Embedding Size	Word2vec	Word2vec + Orthographic	Word2vec + Similarity	Word2vec + Orthographic+ Similarity
20	0.27721	0.35542	0.30112	0.38263
50	0.511586453	0.513227513	0.495495495	0.505829596
100	0.657097289	0.657643312	0.669316375	0.679904686
150	**0.941852118**	**0.951833214**	**0.949466192**	**0.954903364**
200	0.943287868	0.94751977	0.950537634	0.955587393
250	0.944723618	0.954154728	0.946543122	0.953471725
300	0.943042538	0.951149425	0.95149786	0.955523673
350	0.948497854	0.949567723	0.955777461	0.955587393
400	0.948424069	0.950395399	0.955714286	0.95764537
450	0.946236559	0.951079137	0.951428571	0.95764537
500	**0.946599424**	**0.951516245**	**0.954960686**	**0.952101501**
550	0.944723618	0.949640288	0.953604568	0.957706093
600	0.93410572	0.93487699	0.935158501	0.940836941
650	0.932016353	0.933913358	0.930656314	0.934688976
700	0.927825678	0.928478303	0.927098887	0.928424859

curacy is improved but the recall is decreased therefore G-score is also decreased.

Table 2: SemEval Results.

System	W2VecSimPos	W2VecSim
Accuracy	0.743	0.627
Precision	0.060	0.061
Recall	0.306	0.486
F-Score	0.100	0.109
G-Score	0.434	0.547

9 Conclusion

The proposed model with features specially derived for identifying complex words produced good results. The word embedding features played a major role compared with other features. By increasing the size of vectors our accuracy increased constantly. We tried all possible combinations with the four features mentioned in the Table 1 and conclude that the word embedding features alone also have a good accuracy. Our systems have generated a good precision compared with the baseline. Among 45 systems, we ranked 27th position for G-score evaluation. Although, the frequency counts and embedding features are reasonable for a given resource-constraint task, if we have provided for English language in general it might have provide with better accuracy.

References

Chih-Chung Chang and Chih-Jen Lin. (2011). *LIB-SVM: a library for support vector machines.* ACM Transactions on Intelligent Systems and Technology (TIST).2(3), p.27.

Christiane Fellbaum. (1998). *WordNet: An Electronic Lexical Database. Cambridge, MA: MIT Press.*

Daniel Ferres, Montserrat Marimon, Horacio Saggion. (2015). *A Web-based Text Simplification System for English.* Procesamiento del Lenguaje Natural, 55, 191-194.

Dany Amiot. (2004). *Between compounding and derivation Elements of word-formation corresponding.* Morphology and its demarcations: Selected papers from the 11th Morphology meeting, Vienna, Vol. 264.

George A. Miller. (1995). *WordNet: A Lexical Database for English.* Communications of the ACM Vol. 38, No. 11: 39-41.

Gustavo Henrique Paetzold. (2015). *Reliable Lexical Simplification for Non-Native Speakers.* NAACL-HLT 2015 Student Research Workshop (SRW).

La Pointe, Linda B and Randall W. Engle. (1990). *Simple and complex word spans as measures of working memory capacity.* Journal of Experimental Psychology: Learning, Memory, and Cognition 16.6 (1990): 1118.

Lucia Specia, Dhwaj Raj, Marco Turchi. (2010). *Machine translation evaluation versus quality estimation.* Machine translation, 24(1), pp.39-50.

Or Biran, Samuel Brody, Noemie Elhadad. (2011). *Putting it simply: a context-aware approach to lexical simplification*. Proceedings of the 49th Annual Meeting of the Association for Computational Linguistics: Human Language Technologies: short papers-Volume 2. Association for Computational Linguistics.

Radim Rehurek and Petr Sojra. (2010). *Software framework for topic modelling with large corpora*. Proceedings of the LREC 2010 Workshop on New Challenges for NLP Frameworks, ELRA, p.45-50

Edward Loper and Steven Bird. (2006). *NLTK: the natural language toolkit*. Proceedings of the ACL-02 Workshop on Effective tools and methodologies for teaching natural language processing and computational linguistics-Volume 1. Association for Computational Linguistics, 2002.

Tomas Mikolov, Kai Chen, Greg Corrado, Jeffrey Dean. (2010). *Efficient estimation of word representations in vector space*. rXiv preprint arXiv:1301.3781.

Tomoyuki Kajiwara, Hiroshi Matsumoto, Kazuhide Yamamoto. (2013). *Selecting Proper Lexical Paraphrase for Children*. Proceedings of the Twenty-Fifth Conference on Computational Linguistics and Speech Processing (ROCLING 2013).

William Snyder. (2001). *On the nature of syntactic variation: Evidence from complex predicates and complex word-formation*. Language Vol. 77, No. 2, pp. 324-342.

CoastalCPH at SemEval-2016 Task 11:
The importance of designing your Neural Networks right

Joachim Bingel and **Natalie Schluter**
Centre for Language Technology
University of Copenhagen (Denmark)
{bingel,natschluter}@hum.ku.dk

Héctor Martínez Alonso
Alpage
INRIA & University Paris 7 (France)
hector.martinez-alonso@inria.fr

Abstract

We present two methods for the automatic detection of complex words in context as perceived by non-native English readers, for the SemEval 2016 Task 11 on *Complex Word Identification* (Paetzold and Specia, 2016). The submitted systems exploit the same set of features, but are highly disparate in (i) their learning algorithm and (ii) their angle on the learning objective, where especially the latter presents an effort to account for the sparsity of positive instances in the data as well as the large disparity between the distributions of positive instances in the training and test data.

We further present valuable insights that we gained during intensive and extensive post-task experiments. Those revealed that despite poor results in the task, our neural network approach is competitive with the systems achieving the best results. The central contribution of this paper is therefore a demonstration of the aptitude of deep neural networks for the task of identifying complex words.

1 Introduction

The identification of complex words plays an important role in the development of simplified reading resources. In particular, accurate automatic complex word identification strongly benefits lexical simplification (LS) as a first step in an LS pipeline (Paetzold and Specia, 2013; Shardlow, 2014). As such, accurate complex word identification may also be critical to higher-level tasks in text simplification, e.g. sentence compression, where the overall readability of a text is at least partly influenced by the difficulty of its vocabulary.

However, the perceived difficulty of words does not generalise across different groups of readers. That is, a system trained on manual annotations of word difficulty among second-language learners does not necessarily perform well in predicting words that are particularly difficult to persons of reduced literacy. The 2016 SemEval Task 11 puts its focus on the identification of complex words for second-language learners of English.

We chose to explore supervised methods for the task, employing a simple feed-forward neural network as well as a logistic regression classifier for two separate system submissions. Both systems take as input a single list of word and context features that we deemed to potentially indicate the complexity of words themselves and with respect to their context in the sentence.

In this system description paper, we focus specifically on our neural network model. As noted in the task description paper (Paetzold and Specia, 2016), systems based on neural networks generally performed rather weakly in the task, which the organisers speculate to be a consequence of the small amount of training data. However, we show in post-hoc experiments how careful network design may lead to performance figures close to those of the task-winning system. We make our revised system publicly available.[1]

---

[1]https://github.com/jbingel/cwi2016

Proceedings of SemEval-2016, pages 1028–1033,
San Diego, California, June 16-17, 2016. ©2016 Association for Computational Linguistics

2   Related work

The identification of complex words in context has in the past been embedded, often implicitly, into broader (lexical) simplification endeavours (Yatskar et al., 2010; Medero and Ostendorf, 2011; Horn et al., 2014). These models usually employ lexicons or corpus frequencies to determine candidates for lexical substitution. In a corpus study of the standard/Simple English Wikipedia, Medero and Ostendorf (2009) identify a number of word-level features that are indicative of texts with more difficult vocabulary. One of their findings is that words that are typical of simple texts tend to have longer definitions and more user-entered translations in Wiktionary. They also tend to be more ambiguous with respect to word class membership.

Research explicitly dedicated to complex word identification in context, however, has only appeared recently. Shardlow (2013a) presents experiments based on his complex word dataset mined from edit histories in Simple Wikipedia (Shardlow, 2013b); his classification system uses an SVM over a small number of features, achieving an F-score above 0.8 on the named dataset, where one word per sentence is a positive instance.

3   Task data

The data for the task was collected in a survey with 400 non-native speakers of English, such that it may in particular serve the identification of words that pose problems to language learners.

The organisers chose to have each of the 200 sentences in the training set annotated by 20 individuals, while in the test set each of the 9,000 sentences was only seen by one annotator. This presents an effort to model "how well one's individual vocabulary limitations can be predicted from the overall limitations of a group which they are part of" (Paetzold and Specia, 2016). The training data is released in two versions, once with the *individual* votings for each of the 20 annotators, and once with a *combined* vote that is defined as positive if at least annotator deems the word to be complex, negative otherwise. For both train training and the testing set, only a subset of the words in each sentence are annotated, resulting in 2,237 instances for training and 88,221 instances for testing, corresponding to roughly 40%

and 39% of the overall number of tokens, respectively.

The challenge of the data.   The task at hand poses two major challenges with regard to the data, *sparsity* of positive examples and *disparity* between train and test data. Regarding sparsity, combining the individual votings as described above results in roughly one third of the train data being marked positive. A one-to-two proportion is not too skewed, but if one considers each annotator in the training set separately, a mere 4.5% of the individual votings were positive.

Regarding disparity, the share of complex examples is very different between the train and test instances (31.9% vs. 4.7%). Furthermore, the perception of word complexity shows great variation across annotators, with more than half of the complex examples in the training data (360 out of 716) marked as such by only one of the 20 annotators, and only 5.4% being perceived as difficult by the majority of the annotators.

4   Features

Both systems that we describe in Section 5 use the same set of features. We preprocessed the data using the Stanford NLP tools (Manning et al., 2014), obtaining for every sentence lemma forms, part-of-speech tags, name-entity types, and a dependency parse. We make use of Wikipedia and Simple Wikipedia for features based on corpus frequencies.

For a word w in a sentence s, we thus collect features from the following classes:

1. SIMPLE This feature group contains simple word properties such as length of w in characters, its named-entity type (if any) and its part-of-speech. Our feature model is delexicalised and we do not use word forms or lemmas as features.

2. POSITION This feature group contains the relative position of the w in s, and the number of commas as well as the number of verbs before or after w.

3. MORPH This feature group describes whether w has a Latin root, the length difference in characters between w and its lemma and stem, and the number of steps the Porter stemmer spends

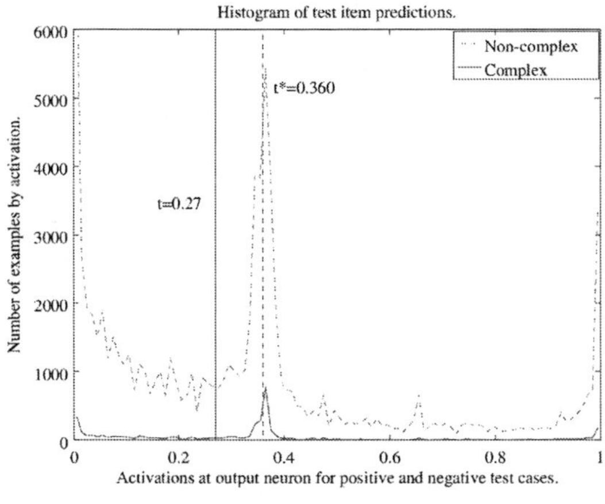

(a) Submitted predictions

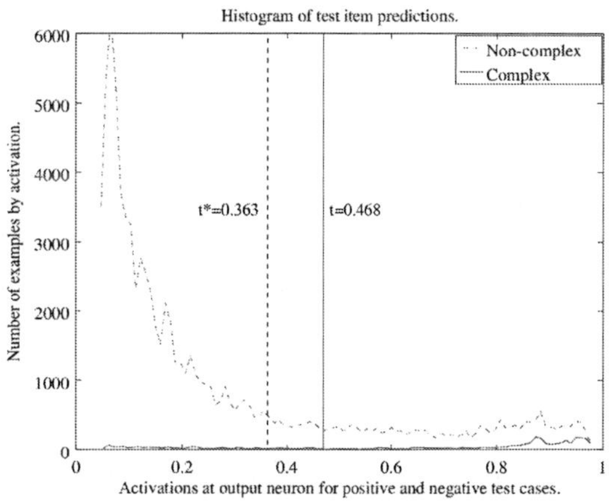

(b) Revised predictions

Figure 1: Histograms of submitted (left) and revised (right) Neural Network predictions. Solid vertical lines indicate the learned threshold at which we classify targets into simple and complex. The dashed vertical lines indicate the thresholds that would optimise the G-scores (cf. also Figure 3).

on w (Porter, 2001), which we use as a proxy for the number of inflectional morphemes that w has. We use the NLTK Porter for the latter and the Etymological WordNet (De Melo, 2014) for detecting Latin roots.

4. SYNTAX This class contains the distance (in tokens) between w and the root of the dependency tree, the dependency relation connecting w and its head, the distance to its head, and the number of dependents of w and its head.

5. PROB This group contains the probability of w in the English Wikipedia, in the Simple Wikipedia, and their ratio.

6. CHARCOMPLEXITY The feature group contains the character-level unigram and bigram probability of the word based on frequencies in Wikipedia and Simple Wikipedia, as well as the respective ratios. This is motivated by the observation that "words with simple grapheme-to-phoneme ratios [are] easier to learn than more phonetically complex words" (Dela Rosa and Eskenazi, 2011). Finally, this group includes the share of vowels in the word.

7. BROWN This feature group includes the Brown cluster of w, as well as height and depth of the cluster in the hierarchical clustering tree (Brown et al., 1992). We use the default 1000 clusters generated by Percy Liang's implementation.[2]

8. EMBS This feature group contains the 300-dimensional GloVe embeddings of w, calculated using Word2Vec over a Wikipedia dump.[3]

9. WORDNET This feature reflects the semantic complexity of w as measured by its number of WordNet synsets (Fellbaum, 1998).

5 Our systems

System 1: NeuralNet. We train a deep neural network with 2 hidden layers of 150 and 50 units, respectively, using PyCnn.[4] At every hidden layer, we perform $L2$-regularisation.

The network has a single output unit that yields a value between 0 and 1, which we map to binary complexity judgements after applying a threshold. If our neural network learned a perfect fit to the data, i.e. if it assigned a value close to 0 to every negative example and a value close to 1 to every positive

---

example, the natural decision boundary of 0.5 would be a good classification threshold to binarise the predicted values. However, as the model fit is far from perfect, the learning problem extends to finding an appropriate threshold (see below).

System 2: Information Sieve. Departing from the observation that different language learners consider different words as complex, the motivation for this system is to prevent our classifier from learning idiosyncratic annotator behaviour. To achieve this, we take an *information sieve* approach, which is meant to filter out idiosyncratic information. We train a logistic regression classifier based on the *concatenation* of all individual votings in the training set, such that every instance is seen 20 times during training, namely one per annotator. The intention behind this training method is to expose the learning algorithm to all individual annotator decisions, acquiring a preference for annotation decisions that are more consistent across annotators. We retrieve the probability outputs from the classifier and predict as positive the top decile.[5]

Hyperparameter optimisation All hyperparameter tuning for the neural network, including its architecture and the classification threshold, is based on 10-fold cross-validation over the training set. For each fold, we test the respectively trained model on each of the 20 individual votings in the test split, rather than on the combined votings. We do this in order to account for the mentioned disparity in the share of positive examples that we expect to find in the training and final testing data. Evaluating the performance of a single hyperparameter configuration thus involves training 10 models and testing on 200 sets of individual annotations.

For optimising the classification threshold, we compare the system's predictions to the respective train/test split annotations at every cross-validation fold (again testing on the individual votings of 20 annotators), and record the decision boundary that best separates negative and positive instances. For each of the 10 cross-validation folds, we thus get an array of 20 annotator-wise optimal thresholds. We finally compute the best threshold for a single fold

---

[5]The decision to predict the top 10% as positive was based on our expectation of the positive share in the test data.

System	G-score	Recall	Acc.	Rank
NeuralNet	.506	.398	.693	35
InfoSieve	.285	.171	.869	41
SV000gg	.774	.769	.779	1
Revised NN	.756	.725	.791	(8)

Table 1: Test set results for the two submitted systems, the winning system and our revised system.

as the median over these values, and the best overall threshold as the average over the per-fold medians.

6 Results and System Revision

Table 1 shows the performance of our systems as measured by the G-score[6] as well as recall and accuracy. As suggested by a post-hoc experiment on the combined training examples, the poor result obtained by the InfoSieve system is due to its sampling strategy much more than the training and inference algorithm or any hyperparameters. We therefore discard this strategy and focus on the neural network in our following analysis.

In order to get a better understanding of the neural network's performance, Figure 1a visualises the distribution of the submitted predictions that we obtain in the original set-up. With a threshold at 0.27, we correctly discard only 43.8% of the non-complex examples, while identifying 69.3% of all complex instances. We observe that, relatively independent of the threshold, the model fails to clearly separate simple and complex instances.

With these numbers, the neural network is very far from the results achieved by the best systems in the task, which we generally observe to employ some variant of ensemble methods, most notably random forests. In the remainder of this section, we reconsider some design decisions for our neural network and introduce a revised model, which we demonstrate to obtain results on the test set that place it in the region of the mentioned ensemble systems.

Neural network library and architecture In a first post-task experiment, we exchange the PyCnn

---

[6]The task organisers define G as the harmonic mean between recall and accuracy. In using this metric to gauge system performance, the organisers reward systems that primarily maximise the number of true positives, while giving less weight to minimising false positives.

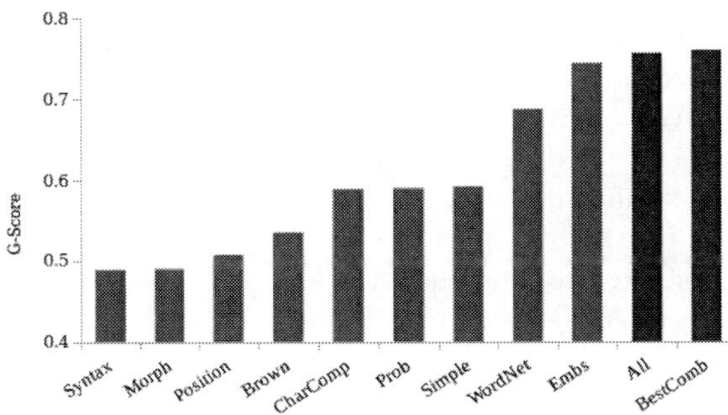

Figure 2: Contribution of feature classes in a deep neural network with three hidden layers of 50 computational units each.

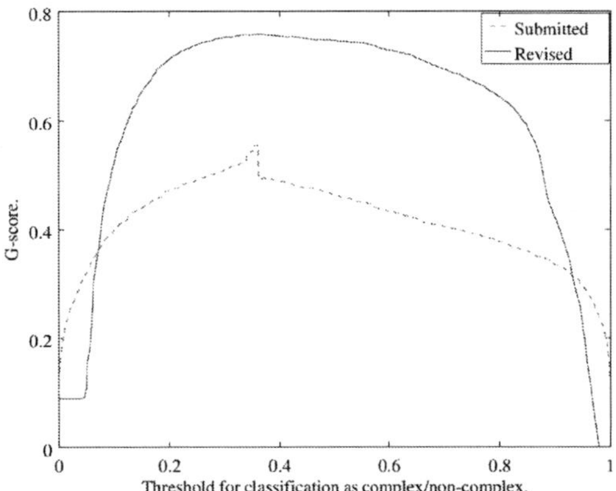

Figure 3: G-score curves in dependence of the threshold t for the submitted (red dashed) and the revised (blue solid) system.

implementation of deep NNs with Keras.[7] Surprisingly, we observe a tremendous increase in performance when using Keras: with the same set of features and the same basic network architecture, we reach a G-score that exceeds the 0.70 mark.[8] Subsequently, we evaluate different network architectures, including different rates of dropout after the hidden layers as an alternative way of regularising the model (Srivastava et al., 2014). Note that all hyperparameter optimisation is still performed in cross-validation experiments.

We finally find that we achieve a good fit to the data with a network of three hidden layers, each of which comprises 50 computational units, and a moderate dropout rate of 10% after every hidden layer.

Feature contribution To gain insights into which features are salient for our system, we train models on the individual feature classes listed in Section 4, as well as combinations of the classes. As Figure 2 shows, word embeddings are by far the most important single feature class, and they also contribute to the best combination of feature types, which is WORDNET+PROB+MORPH+EMBS. In the remainder of the paper, we refer to the system trained on this feature combination as the 'revised system.'

Threshold For the submitted as well as for the revised system, there is a certain discrepancy between the G-scores that we obtain from setting the thresholds to the value computed in the cross-validation and the figures we could achieve with optimal threshold setting. Concretely, this difference pertains to .05 in G-score (.506 vs. .556) for the submitted system and .002 (.756 vs. .758) for the revised system (cf. Figure 3).

While in Figure 1b it appears that we have missed the optimal threshold by a wide margin for the revised system, the actual difference in performance (as measured by G) is rather small. In fact, as Figure 3 illustrates, finding the optimal threshold is considerably less critical for the revised system due to a much flatter curve between threshold values 0.2 and 0.8.

Optimal result In conclusion, a G-score of .758 poses an upper bound for our system architecture (a neural network with three hidden layers of 50 units and a dropout rate of 10% after each hidden layer). How closely this figure can be approximated depends on the optimisation of the threshold.

---

[7]https://github.com/fchollet/keras. Keras is a Python neural networks library running on top of Theano and TensorFlow.

[8]The great performance differences between the two libraries are actually more than surprising. The differences are consistent across several experiments, which is why an infelicitous random initialisation or local optima can be ruled out as possible explanations. Other intuitions as to what might the reason for the different results touch on possible errors in the implementation of one of the libraries, but this is clearly very speculative.

7   Conclusion

This paper presented our submissions to the Sem-Eval 2016 Shared Task 11, *Complex Word Identification*, which we approached with two very disparate systems: a deep neural network trained on the combined votings from 20 annotators, and a logistic regression classifier trained on each annotator separately. While neither of these systems reaches competitive performance figures, we re-design our neural network approach to train a revised system, which shows that neural networks do have the potential to successfully identify complex words.

Specifically, we find that 300-dimensional word embeddings carry a strong signal for word complexity, such that our revised system finally reaches a G-score that would place it in the top quartile of the task submissions. The strong contribution of word embeddings is not easily explained, but we suspect that certain distributional features may encode the presence of a complex word in more specific contexts such as technical jargon.

Our results contrast with the observation that task submissions which employed neural networks and/or word embeddings generally achieved rather poor results, and it shows that competitive performance figures can be reached with neural networks despite a relatively small amount of training data.

References

Peter F. Brown, Peter V. deSouza, Robert L. Mercer, Vincent J. Della Pietra, and Jenifer C. Lai. 1992. Class-based n-gram models of natural language. *Computational linguistics*, 18(4):467–479.

Gerard De Melo. 2014. Etymological wordnet: Tracing the history of words. In *LREC*, pages 1148–1154. Citeseer.

Kevin Dela Rosa and Maxine Eskenazi. 2011. Effect of Word Complexity on L2 Vocabulary Learning. In *Proc Workshop on Innovative Use of NLP for Building Educational Applications*, pages 76–80, Portland, OR, USA.

Christiane Fellbaum. 1998. *WordNet*. Wiley Online Library.

Colby Horn, Cathryn Manduca, and David Kauchak. 2014. Learning a lexical simplifier using wikipedia. In *ACL 2014*, pages 458–463.

Christopher D. Manning, Mihai Surdeanu, John Bauer, Jenny Finkel, Steven J. Bethard, and David McClosky. 2014. The Stanford CoreNLP natural language processing toolkit. In *Association for Computational Linguistics (ACL) System Demonstrations*, pages 55–60.

Julie Medero and Mari Ostendorf. 2009. Analysis of vocabulary difficulty using wiktionary. In *SLaTE*, pages 61–64.

Julie Medero and Mari Ostendorf. 2011. Identifying targets for syntactic simplification. In *SLaTE*, pages 69–72.

Gustavo H. Paetzold and Lucia Specia. 2013. Text simplification as tree transduction. In *Proceedings of the 9th Brazilian Symposium in Information and Human Language Technology*, pages 116–125.

Gustavo H. Paetzold and Lucia Specia. 2016. SemEval 2016 Task 11: Complex Word Identification. In *Proceedings of the 10th International Workshop on Semantic Evaluation (SemEval 2016)*.

Martin F. Porter. 2001. Snowball: A language for stemming algorithms.

Matthew Shardlow. 2013a. A Comparison of Techniques to Automatically Identify Complex Words. In *ACL 2013 Student Research Workshop*, pages 103–109. Citeseer.

Matthew Shardlow. 2013b. The CW Corpus: A New Resource for Evaluating the Identification of Complex Words. *ACL 2013*, page 69.

Matthew Shardlow. 2014. Out in the open: Finding and categorising errors in the lexical simplification pipeline. In *LREC*, pages 1583–1590.

Nitish Srivastava, Geoffrey Hinton, Alex Krizhevsky, Ilya Sutskever, and Ruslan Salakhutdinov. 2014. Dropout: A simple way to prevent neural networks from overfitting. *The Journal of Machine Learning Research*, 15(1):1929–1958.

Mark Yatskar, Bo Pang, Cristian Danescu-Niculescu-Mizil, and Lillian Lee. 2010. For the sake of simplicity: Unsupervised extraction of lexical simplifications from Wikipedia. In *Human Language Technologies: The 2010 Annual Conference of the North American Chapter of the Association for Computational Linguistics*, pages 365–368. Association for Computational Linguistics.

HMC at SemEval-2016 Task 11: Identifying Complex Words Using Depth-limited Decision Trees

Maury Quijada and **Julie Medero**
Harvey Mudd College
340 E Foothill Blvd
Claremont, CA, 91711, USA
{mquijada, jmedero}@hmc.edu

Abstract

We present two systems created for SemEval-2016s Task 11: Complex Word Identification. Our two systems, a regression tree and decision tree, were trained with a word's unigram and lemma word counts, average age-of-acquisition, and a measure of concreteness. The systems ranked 5th and 6th, respectively, on the test set by G-score (the harmonic mean between accuracy and recall). With the regression tree's predictions earning a G-score of 0.766, and the decision tree's earning 0.765, the two systems scored within 1 percent of the score of the best-performing system in the task.

1 Introduction

Text simplification is the process of reducing the complexity of a text while preserving the original meaning. Text simplification may include syntactic or pragmatic aspects (Siddharthan, 2014), but much of the work that has been done has focused on lexical simplifications. In lexical simplification, difficult words or phrases are replaced to make a text more accessible. This kind of simplification can benefit several reader populations, including second-language learners (Petersen and Ostendorf, 2009).

One important first step in lexical simplification is complex word identification. This step predicts which words in a text will be difficult for a reader so that they can then be targeted for simplification.

The International Workshop on Semantic Evaluation for 2016 (SemEval-2016) hosted Task 11: Complex Word Identification (CWI), which asked participants to identify words that would be challenging for non-native English speakers (Paetzold and Specia, 2016). Task participants were given 2,237 training examples. Each example contained a word, the sentence containing the word, and the word's index in the sentence. In addition, each word was labeled as *complex* or *not complex* (or *simple*) by 20 human annotators, and each word was given a binary label of *complex* if at least one annotator thought the word was hard to read. The individual labels of the 20 annotators were also made available to participants.

Submissions were evaluated on a test set of 88,221 words. Test set items had the same format as the training set, except that they were only annotated by one person, so the labels indicated whether that annotator alone labeled it *complex*.

2 Previous Work

This is the first year of the CWI Task, so no previous work has been done on exactly the same task. However, substantial work has been done previously in the general area of characterizing word difficulty.

Traditional readability measures like Flesch-Kincaid (Kincaid and others, 1975) and Gunning Fog (Gunning, 1952) rely primarily on word length, while the Lexile framework considers word length and unigram frequency. More recent work has incorporated n-grams and part of speech information (Petersen and Ostendorf, 2009; Graesser and others, 2004), word clusters (Deane and others, 2006) to improve the accuracy of reading level predictions, while other work has used orthographic and phonemic features (Mostow and others, 2002) to predict where children would have reading difficulty.

Proceedings of SemEval-2016, pages 1034–1037,
San Diego, California, June 16-17, 2016. ©2016 Association for Computational Linguistics

3   Methodology

For each word in the training set, we extracted features that we predicted would be good indicators of a word's complexity. We also used the labels from the individual annotators to generate continuous-valued labels for each of the training words. Finally, we trained several machine learning models as implemented using Python's `scikit-learn` package (Pedregosa and others, 2011).

3.1   Features

We investigated several potential features for the CWI Task, based on metrics across various features for words in the training set (see Table 1).

1. **Unigram** and **lemma frequency** from the Corpus of Contemporary American English (COCA) (Davies, 2008), using the WordNet lemmatizer in Python's `nltk` package (Loper and Bird, 2002). *Complex* words are, on average, less frequent than *simple* words.

2. **Word age-of-acquisition** according to the average age-of-acquisition (AoA) for a word in a list of roughly 30,000 English words (Kuperman and others, 2012). *Complex* words, have a higher mean AoA.

3. **Word concreteness**, on a scale of 1 to 5, according to a list of roughly 40,000 English words (Brysbaert and others, 2013). *Complex* words have higher scores, possibly due to the inclusion of technical words.

4. **Word length**, **stem length**, and **lemma length** in characters. For all three, *complex* words are longer on average than *simple* words.

5. **Number of word pronunciations** in Carnegie Mellon University's Pronouncing dictionary (Lenzo, 2007), accessed through `nltk`. *Complex* words have a lower number of pronunciations on average, possibly because these words tend to be more technical.

6. **Probability of the word's sequence of characters** according to a character-based trigram language model created with SRILM and trained on the COCA dataset (Stolcke and

Feature	Simple	Complex
Unigram Count	443k (1M)	151k (597k)
Lemma Count	183k (742k)	68k (290k)
Age of Acquisition	8.9 (3.2)	9.8 (3.0)
Concreteness	2.8 (0.9)	3.0 (1.0)
Word Length	6.0 (2.5)	6.7 (2.5)
Pronunciation Count	1.4 (0.7)	1.2 (0.5)
Synset Count	9.5 (8.7)	6.7 (8.3)

Table 1: Summary of feature means and standard deviations.

others, 2002). *Complex* words have lower log-probabilities. This may be because *complex* words have more "unlikely" character sequences that are hard to decode.

7. **Number of synsets** in WordNet. *Complex* words belong to a lower number of synsets, possibly because they are more likely to be unique and domain-specific.

8. **Part-of-speech** (POS) given by `nltk`'s part-of-speech tagger. Nouns are more likely to be *complex* words, and verbs are more likely to be *simple* words. For models that do not support categorical features, we performed a one-hot encoding of the most common tags: NN, NNS, JJ, RB, and VBD.

We experimented with different combinations of features, but only five features were used in the predictions given by our models: unigram and lemma frequency, age-of-acquisition, concreteness, and word length. Therefore, those were the features that we used in our sybmitted system.

3.1.1   Labels

Originally, the training set included binary labels that correspond to whether at least one annotator thought a word was *complex*. However, because these labels are binary, they are not indicative of the extent to which the annotators agreed each word was difficult. It is useful to learn the difference, for example, between a word that almost all of the annotators agree is difficult, and one that 19/20 annotators felt was *simple*, but one annotator thought was *complex*.

To help with this, we replaced every binary label with a continuous label representing the percentage of annotators who found the word to be complex.

Description	Regression Tree	Decision Tree
Accuracy	0.838	0.846
Precision	0.182	0.189
Recall	0.705	0.698
F_1-score	0.290	0.298
G-score	0.766	0.765

Table 2: Summary of system performance on the CWI test set

We used thresholding to convert the continuous labels back to binary labels as needed.

3.2 Models

We experimented with Support Vector Machines, Logisitic Regression, and Perceptrons, but got the best results from `scikit-learn`'s implementation of depth-limited regression and decision trees with our features and a maximum depth of 3. These models gave the best performance on average in terms of cross-validation accuracy, F_1-score, and G-score. Regression trees and decision trees have the added benefit of providing a level of model interpretability that the other models do not.

Since decision trees requires discrete categories for training, we used a threshold of 0.25 when providing the labels to the model for training. That is to say, all examples in training were labeled *complex* if at least 25 percent of annotators marked it *complex*. For each cross-validation fold, we used the proportion of the first 19 annotators who labeled a word complex as labels during training, then evaluated our model on the labels provided by the 20th annotator.

We also trained our regression tree on the proportion of the first 19 annotators who labeled each word *complex*. But since regression trees train on and predict continuous-valued labels, we used the percent of annotators directly as labels during training, then thresholded the model's prediction for each word at test time. We got best results with a threshold of 0.05: words were interpreted as *complex* if the model predicted its measure of complexity to be 0.05 or greater. These thresholds were chosen because they gave the best G-score for 5-fold cross-validation on the training set.

4 Results

On the CWI test set, our regression tree and decision tree ranked 5th and 6th on G-score, respectively, out of the 40 system submissions (Paetzold and Specia,

2016). Table 2 breaks down the precision, recall, and G-score of each model. The models had G-scores of 0.765 and 0.766. By comparison, the top scoring system had a G-score of 0.774, and overall the average G-score was 0.620 with a standard deviation of 0.123 (Paetzold and Specia, 2016).

		Prediction	
		Complex	**Not Complex**
Truth	**Complex**	2913	1218
	Not Complex	13059	71031

Figure 1: Regression tree confusion matrix on the CWI test set.

		Prediction	
		Complex	**Not Complex**
Truth	**Complex**	2884	1247
	Not Complex	12355	71735

Figure 2: Decision tree confusion matrix on the CWI test set

Figures 1 and 2 depict the confusion matrices generated from comparing the trees' predictions to the testing labels. Over 90% of the misclassifications given by both trees were false positives. This indicates that the models tended to overpredict complex words, which is also seen in the relatively low precision of both systems.

5 Analysis

Our models relied most heavily on unigram and lemma frequency features. Even when the AoA, concreteness, and lemma length features are excluded, the regression tree and decision tree obtain a G-score of 0.735 and 0.770, respectively, on the test set. This indicates that corpus frequency alone is an extremely good indicator of a word's complexity.

Despite our submitted models' success with corpus-based features, we obtained low precision scores of 0.18 for each model. These scores were consistent with results for many of the other systems participating in the task. The average precision score was 0.123 with a standard deviation of 0.06 (Paetzold and Specia, 2016).

We posit that this problem is due in part to the difference in distribution between the training and testing sets for our models. Namely, our models must train on labels that are representative of the judgments of multiple annotators, but also be tested

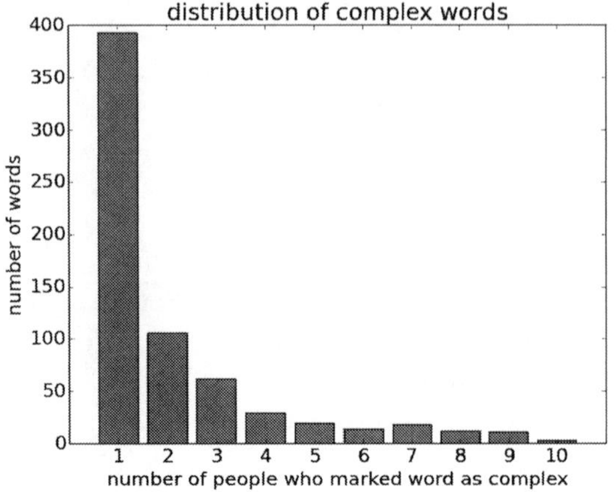

Figure 3: Distribution of how often a certain number of annotators marked a word *complex*.

on labels that are representative of the judgment of *only one* annotator. The difference in distribution between the training and testing set means that the model learns to predict word complexity for a group, but is evaluated on one person's judgments. This problem is exacerbated by the low agreement between annotators. Figure 3 shows that most words marked *complex* are labeled so by only one person.

In addition, some of the labels in the test set are possibly counterintuitive. For example, in:

> The Plan of Management is the main policy document for the Park and strives to balance strategic or long-term goals and tactical or day to day goals.

the word *strives* and both instances of the word *goals* were labeled *complex*. Intuitively, those words seem less difficult to us than the words *strategic* and *tactical*, which were both labeled *not complex* by the same annotator. This example illustrates what makes the task so difficult: not only are the testing and training set distributions different, but the labels for each are subjective and possibly conflicting.

6 Conclusion

This paper details our submission to SemEval-2016's Task 11: Complex Word Identification. We explored several potential features, eventually submitting a regression tree and decision tree based on unigram and lemma frequency, age-of-acquisition, concreteness, and word length. By incorporating annotator disagreement into our models through continuous-valued labels during training and testing, our models ranked 5th and 6th overall in the Task. Error analysis reveals that our models had trouble generalizing the judgments of multiple annotators in the training set to the judgment of one annotator in the test set, leading to low precision.

References

M Brysbaert et al. 2013. Concreteness ratings for 40 thousand generally known english word lemmas. *Behavior Research Methods*, 46(3):904–911.

M Davies. 2008. The corpus of contemporary american english: 520 million words, 1990-present.

P Deane et al. 2006. Differences in Text Structure and Its Implications for Assessment of Struggling Readers. *Scientific Studies of Reading*, 10(3):257–275, July.

A C Graesser et al. 2004. Coh-Metrix:Analysis of text on cohesion and language. *Behavior Research Methods, Instruments, and Computers*, 36:193–202.

R Gunning. 1952. *The Technique of Clear Writing*. McGraw-Hill.

J. P. Jr. Kincaid et al. 1975. Derivation of new readability formulas for Navy enlisted personnel. *Research Branch Report 8-75*.

V Kuperman et al. 2012. Age-of-acquisition ratings for 30,000 english words. *Behavior Research Methods*, 44(4):978–990.

K Lenzo. 2007. The cmu pronouncing dictionary.

E Loper and S Bird. 2002. Nltk: The natural language toolkit. In *Proc. ACL-02 Workshop on Effective Tools and Methodologies for Teaching NLP and Comp. Linguistics*, ETMTNLP '02, pages 63–70, Stroudsburg, PA, USA. Association for Computational Linguistics.

J Mostow et al. 2002. Predicting Oral Reading Miscues. In *Proc. ICSLP*.

G Paetzold and L Specia. 2016. Semeval2016, task 11: Complex word identification. In *Proc. Sem-Eval 20016 Shared Task 11: Complex Word Identification*.

F Pedregosa et al. 2011. Scikit-learn: Machine learning in Python. *Journal of Machine Learning Research*, 12:2825–2830.

S Petersen and M Ostendorf. 2009. A machine learning approach to reading level assessment. *Computer, Speech and Language*, 23(1):89–106.

A Siddharthan. 2014. A survey of research on text simplification. *ITL-International Journal of Applied Linguistics*, 165(2):259–298.

A Stolcke et al. 2002. Srilm-an extensible language modeling toolkit. In *Proc. INTERSPEECH*.

UWB at SemEval-2016 Task 11:
Exploring Features for Complex Word Identification

Michal Konkol

NTIS – New Technologies for the Information Society &
Department of Computer Science and Engineering,
Faculty of Applied Sciences,
University of West Bohemia,
Univerzitní 8, 306 14 Plzeň
Czech Republic
`konkol@kiv.zcu.cz`

Abstract

In this paper, we present our system developed for the SemEval 2016 Task 11: Complex Word Identification. Our team achieved the 3rd place among 21 participants. Our systems ranked 4th and 13th among 42 submitted systems. We proposed multiple features suitable for complex word identification, evaluated them, and discussed their properties. According to the results of our experiments, our final system used maximum entropy classifier with a single feature – document frequency.

1   Introduction

This paper describes our participation in the Complex Word Identification (CWI) shared task of SemEval 2016. CWI is a subtask of text simplification. Text simplification changes the structure, grammar, and vocabulary of the text to make it easier to understand without losing information. CWI looks for the words that should be simplified. The task is motivated and described in detail by the organizers (Paetzold and Specia, 2016).

In this paper we apply a machine learning approach to CWI. Our main goal is to explore suitable features.

The paper has the following structure. Section 2 introduces the task in more detail. Section 3 presents the design of our system. In Section 4, we choose the optimal parameters and features for our final system. In Section 5, we discuss overall results of the task. Section 6 summarizes our contribution.

2   Task

The task is defined as a binary classification with classes *complex* and *simple*. The complex class represents words that should be simplified. Given a word in a sentence, a system decides whether the word is complex or not.

Paetzold and Specia (2016) prepared two training data sets. The first data set contains 20 decisions from unique annotators; we call it *all*. Second data set aggregates the annotations – the word becomes complex if at least one annotator considers it complex; we call it *aggregated*. Both data sets have 2 237 sentences (i.e. the all data set has 44 740 training examples, the aggregated set has only 2 237). The organizers announced that the test data set has 9 200 sentences annotated by a single annotator.

The task was evaluated using *G-score*: a harmonic mean of accuracy and recall of the complex class. Each team could submit two systems for evaluation.

3   System

CWI is a binary classification task. We chose the maximum entropy classifier for our system, but we believe the choice of classifier has only a small impact compared with the choice of features.

We propose features that may be suitable for the CWI task and motivate them in the following list.

Word frequency – A ratio of occurrences of the current token to the number of all tokens in the corpus. We expect less frequent words to be more likely complex. Also extended to n-grams.

Proceedings of SemEval-2016, pages 1038–1041,
San Diego, California, June 16-17, 2016. ©2016 Association for Computational Linguistics

Document frequency – A ratio of documents that contain the current token to the number of all documents. The motivation is the same as for word frequency. Also extended to n-grams.

Character n-gram frequency – The frequency of character n-grams of the current word. We expect that some character n-grams are typical for complex words.

Language model word probability – The probability of the current word given by a language model. The more probable words are not likely to be complex.

Part of speech – Part of speech tag of the current word. Some word categories are used less often by non-native speakers.

Word length – Length of the current word. Common words are usually shorter.

WordNet synset size – The size of WordNet synsets which contain the current word. Large synsets might be highly ambiguous and thus harder for a non-native speaker.

WordNet frequency ratio – The ratio between the current word and the most frequent word in a synset. If there is a lot more frequent word with the same meaning, the non-native speaker usually uses this word instead of the current word.

WordNet number of synsets – The number of synsets that contain the current word. Word with many meanings may be harder.

Language model sentence probability – The probability of the whole sentence. The overall probability of a sentence may indicate the sentence complexity. A complex sentence may affect the difficulty of the current word.

Average n-gram frequency – The average n-gram frequency of the sentence. If the sentence contains a higher number of complex words, then even a common word may become complex.

3.1 G-score decision boundary

A standard maximum entropy classifier is trained so that all types of errors have the same weight. This is

not the case when G-score is used as an evaluation metric. With G-score and a skewed data set, it is necessary to give higher priority to errors where complex class is incorrectly classified as simple class. This type of errors lowers the recall of the system.

To deal with it, we propose an altered decision criterion (1) for the standard classifier, where y^* is the class chosen by the system, $p(y = c|d)$ is the probability of the complex class given the data, and t is the threshold.

$$y^* = \begin{cases} \text{complex} & p(y = c|d) > t \\ \text{simple} & \text{otherwise} \end{cases} \quad (1)$$

4 Optimizing parameters

Each team could submit two systems. We decided to submit two versions of the same system with different parametrization – the first one trained on the *aggregated* data and the second one on the *all* data.

4.1 Experimental setup

We estimated the n-gram frequencies from Wikipedia. We used the language model from (Brychcín and Konopík, 2015), Stanford CoreNLP for part-of-speech tags (Toutanova et al., 2003), the MIT Java Wordnet Interface (Finlayson, 2014), and the Brainy implementation of maximum entropy classifier (Konkol, 2014).

4.2 Procedure

We measure the improvement of our system with 5-fold cross-validation on the training data.

First, we optimized hyper-parameters (e.g. thresholds, discretization) of individual features.

Second, we iteratively added more features to the (initially empty) feature set. At each step we included the feature that improved G-score the most. We stopped if G-score decreased.

For each evaluation, we chose the optimal threshold t from (1).

4.3 Results

Table 1 shows the results for individual features (i.e. first iteration) on the *aggregated* data. We compare the features to a baseline that marks all words as complex.

We found that the unigram document and word frequencies predicted the complex words best from

System	Accuracy	Recall	G-score
all complex	31.6%	100.0%	48.0%
1-gram freq	69.5%	65.0%	67.2%
2-gram freq	54.6%	77.9%	64.2%
3-gram freq	51.1%	71.8%	59.7%
1-gram doc freq	64.2%	72.5%	68.1%
2-gram doc freq	52.5%	80.9%	63.7%
3-gram doc freq	36.2%	96.9%	52.7%
char 3-gram freq	58.2%	63.6%	60.8%
char 4-gram freq	50.5%	83.4%	62.9%
char 5-gram freq	58.5%	66.7%	62.3%
lang model	61.0%	61.0%	61.0%
pos	47.8%	67.0%	55.8%
word length	48.3%	80.7%	60.4%
WN synset size	46.9%	67.8%	55.5%
WN freq ratio	47.3%	56.4%	51.5%
WN num synsets	54.7%	62.2%	58.2%
global lang model	42.6%	91.8%	58.2%
avg word freq	45.1%	84.5%	58.8%

Table 1: Results for individual features with 5-fold cross-validation on the aggregated training data. The official metric for evaluation is called G-score and it is a harmonic mean of accuracy and recall of the complex class.

all the proposed features. The unigram document frequency performed slightly better. We believe document frequency better reflected the real frequency of the words. For example the word YouGov appears almost 3000 times at a single Wikipedia page, thus we overestimated the word frequency of YouGov.

We are ambivalent about the role of the context. The global language model and the average word frequency features show that the overall complexity of a sentence affected the complexity of its words. It suggests that the context of the word plays a role. However, unigrams performed better than higher order n-grams for document and word frequencies. The complexity of the word may be thus affected by some words in the sentence but not necessarily the closest words. We believe this phenomenon requires further research.

The WordNet features revealed that the number of meanings and number of synonyms influenced the complexity of the word.

The character n-gram features might indicate that some combinations of letters were typical for com-

plex words, but it might also only identify the shorter words (and their frequencies). The latter option is supported by better scores of higher order character n-grams, because they could recognize longer words.

The word length feature showed that such a simple feature can be relatively good predictor of complex words.

The part-of-speech feature proves that some types of words are more complex than others, e.g. adverbs are more complex than verbs.

Even though all the features improved the all complex baseline, we found that adding more features to the unigram document frequency (best individual feature) did not improve the G-score. We did not expect this behavior, because the features represent different information sources. This might have many reasons, we elaborate two of them. First, we might get close to the inter-annotator agreement as the task seems to be highly subjective. Second, we use a heuristic procedure for finding the optimal feature set. This procedure might be flawed, especially choosing the discretization before we combined the features.

The final system used only the unigram document frequency. As we used only one feature, it might be better to drop the classifier and simply find a threshold for unigram document frequency. We believe the results would be the same, but the system could be even simpler.

5 Shared task evaluation

Paetzold and Specia (2016) presented complete results for all systems. 21 teams participated in the task and submitted 42 systems. The results show that the top 9 systems were over 76%, so they performed almost as good as the winner (77.4%).

We provide a summarized results of our systems in Table 2. Our team ranked third with systems on 4th (*all* data) and 13th (*aggregated* data) place. The system trained on the aggregated data predicts complex words for the worst English speakers (among the annotators); the other one for average speakers. The difference between the systems (7.4%) suggest that the difference between worst and average speakers (regarding vocabulary) is not that high.

TR	SR	System	Accuracy	Recall	G-score
1.	1.	SV000gg soft	77.9%	76.9%	77.4%
3.	4.	UWB All	80.3%	73.4%	76.7%
3.	13.	UWB Agg	56.9%	88.5%	69.3%
—	—	Average	73.69%	59.1%	62.0%

Table 2: The official comparison with other systems. TR stands for team rank, SR for system rank. There were 21 teams and 42 systems. The official metric for evaluation is called G-score and it is a harmonic mean of accuracy and recall of the complex class.

6 Conclusion

We proposed a set of features that might be suitable for the CWI task. We showed that most of the features had some information value, even though their combination may not lead to an improvement. We can conclude that the word frequency and document frequency were the best predictors for complex words.

Our final system used a maximum entropy classifier with a single feature – document frequency. We ended up as the third best team (with the 4th best system). It proves that it is possible to achieve a state-of-the-art G-score in the CWI task with a very simple system.

Acknowledgments

This publication was supported by the project LO1506 of the Czech Ministry of Education, Youth and Sports.

References

Tomáš Brychcín and Miloslav Konopík. 2015. Latent semantics in language models. *Computer Speech & Language*, 33(1):88 – 108.

Mark Finlayson. 2014. Java libraries for accessing the princeton wordnet: Comparison and evaluation. In Heili Orav, Christiane Fellbaum, and Piek Vossen, editors, *Proceedings of the Seventh Global Wordnet Conference*, pages 78–85, Tartu, Estonia.

Michal Konkol. 2014. Brainy: A machine learning library. In Leszek Rutkowski, Marcin Korytkowski, Rafa Scherer, Ryszard Tadeusiewicz, Lotfi A. Zadeh, and Jacek M. Zurada, editors, *Artificial Intelligence and Soft Computing*, volume 8468 of *Lecture Notes in Computer Science*, pages 490–499. Springer International Publishing.

Gustavo H. Paetzold and Lucia Specia. 2016. Semeval 2016 task 11: Complex word identification. In *Proceedings of the 10th International Workshop on Semantic Evaluation (SemEval 2016)*.

Kristina Toutanova, Dan Klein, Christopher D. Manning, and Yoram Singer. 2003. Feature-rich part-of-speech tagging with a cyclic dependency network. In *Proceedings of the 2003 Conference of the North American Chapter of the Association for Computational Linguistics on Human Language Technology - Volume 1*, NAACL '03, pages 173–180, Stroudsburg, PA, USA. Association for Computational Linguistics.

AI-KU at SemEval-2016 Task 11: Word Embeddings and Substring Features for Complex Word Identification

Onur Kuru

Artificial Intelligence Laboratory

Koc University

Istanbul, Turkey

`okuru13@ku.edu.tr`

Abstract

We investigate the usage of word embeddings, namely Glove and SCODE, along with substring features on Complex Word Identification task. We introduce two systems: the first system utilizes the word embeddings of the target word and its substrings as features while the other considers the context information by using the embeddings of the surrounding words as well. Although the proposed representations perform below the average with nonlinear models, we show that word embeddings with substring features is an effective representation choice when employed with linear classifiers.

1 Introduction

Complex Word Identification (CWI) is the task of determining which words in a given sentence should be simplified. CWI is often considered as the first step in Lexical Simplification (LS) where the goal is to identify and replace complex words with simpler substitutes. Although CWI is considered as a vital component of Lexical Simplification pipeline, there is not a lot of work done for identifying word complexity in the context of Lexical Simplification. Horn et al. (2014) describes an LS model in which they employ a Complex Word identifier implicitly. However, their results show that the method is not able to capture complex words very accurately.

Paetzold and Specia (2016) organizes the Complex Word Identification task of SemEval 2016 with the goal of attracting systems that are able to detect complex words in given a sentence. This work investigates the usage of word embeddings along with substrings as features to build a Complex Word Identifier. Word embeddings are unsupervised word representations which map each word to a dense, real valued, low dimensional vector. These vectors are able to capture semantic and syntactic similarities between words and proven useful as features in a variety of applications, such as, document classification (Sebastiani, 2002), named entity recognition (Turian et al., 2010), and parsing (Socher et al., 2013).

GloVe (Pennington et al., 2014) is an unsupervised learning algorithm for obtaining vector representations for words which is essentially a log-bilinear model with a weighted least-squares objective. Pennington et al. (2014) shows that the word embeddings produced by the model achieves state-of-the-art performance in Word Analogy task. Moreover, they also illustrate that Glove embeddings outperform embeddings induced by other methods on several word similarity tasks.

Another work (Yatbaz et al., 2012) represents the context of a word by its probable substitutes. Words with their probable substitutes are fed to a co-occurrence modeling framework (SCODE) (Maron et al., 2010). Words co-occurring in similar context are closely embedded on a sphere. These word embeddings are effective at modeling syntactic features and they achieve state-of-the-art results in inducing part-of-speech.

We conducted several experiments to examine the usage of word embeddings. First, we investigated whether pretrained word embeddings improve random embedding baseline. Second, we tried concate-

Proceedings of SemEval-2016, pages 1042–1046,
San Diego, California, June 16-17, 2016. ©2016 Association for Computational Linguistics

nations of word embeddings with different types and dimensions. Next, we examined context-aware representations of target words by incorporating embeddings of neighbouring words. After the release of test set annotations, we scrutinize how a linear model benefits from increasing the size of the training set.

This paper is organized as follows: Section 2 details the proposed dataset and evaluation metric, Section 3 analyzes the utilization of word embeddings for CWI, Section 4 presents results and discusses the performance of our work and Section 5 concludes the paper.

2 Dataset and Evaluation

Complex Word Identification task of SemEval 2016 (Paetzold and Specia, 2016) prepares a dataset with 200 sentences for training and 9000 for testing. The training set is composed of 5,362 tokens with 2,237 instances annotated, and the test set is composed of 217,902 tokens with 88,221 instances annotated. Dataset properties are summarized in Table 1.

9,200 sentences were annotated through a survey, in which 400 volunteers were presented with several sentences and asked to judge whether or not they could understand the meaning of each word in a given sentence. A set of 200 sentences is separated for training and split into 20 subsets of 10 sentences, and each subset was annotated by a total of 20 volunteers. In the training set, a word is considered as complex if at least one of the 20 annotators judged them so. To compose the test set, remaining 9,000 sentences were split into 300 subsets of 30 sentences, each of which was annotated by a single volunteer.

	Training	Test
Annotated	2237	88221
Tokens	5362	217902
Sentences	200	9000

Table 1: Dataset Properties

Notably, training set is extremely small compared to test set. As a result of this, 92% of test set vocabulary is unknown to training set.

In the context of Lexical Simplification, a CW identifier is expected to accomplish two things. First, it should predict the complexity of words

as proficiently as possible (Accuracy). Second, it should capture as many of the complex words as possible (Recall) to maximize the simplicity of a sentence. Therefore, instead of F-Score (harmonic mean of Precision and Recall), CWI task defines and uses G-Score which measures the harmonic mean between Accuracy and Recall.

3 Experiments

3.1 Word Embeddings

To illustrate the effect of word embeddings on CWI task, we conducted several experiments. For Glove word embeddings, we used the publicly available word vectors[1] pretrained on a 2014 Wikipedia dump[2] with 1.6 billion tokens merged with Gigaword 5 which has 4.3 billion tokens. We use a sample from Wikipedia dump with approximately 150 million tokens to induce SCODE word embeddings[3]. For each word embedding experiment, we used Support Vector Machines with linear kernel as our classifier. We utilized scikit-learn (Buitinck et al., 2013) as our machine learning arsenal. We applied 5-fold cross validation on training set and report the result at the optimum C (penalty parameter of the error term) from a grid search in $e^{-20}, e^{-19}, ..., e^6, e^7$.

Embedding	Dimensions	G-Score
Random	50	0.5526
Glove	50	0.6357
Glove	100	0.6171
Glove	200	0.6084
SCODE	50	0.6013
SCODE	100	0.6044
SCODE	200	0.6098

Table 2: Random Embedding Baseline, Comparison of Glove and SCODE.

Firstly, each annotated word in a sentence represented with its corresponding dense real valued embedding and fed to the classifier. As a simple baseline we assigned a random embedding to each annotated word. A random embedding consists of 50 dimensions and each component is drawn from uniform distribution $U(0, 1)$. Table 2 holds the results

---

[1]http://nlp.stanford.edu/projects/glove/
[2]http://dumps.wikimedia.org/enwiki/
[3]https://github.com/ai-ku/wvec/

for each experiment. We observe that both SCODE and Glove outperforms the random embedding baseline and Glove (trained on a much generous corpus) yields better results in general. Increasing the number of dimensions improves the performance slightly for SCODE but it hurts the performance of Glove embeddings.

		Glove		
		50	100	200
	50	**0.6559**	0.6317	0.6185
SCODE	100	0.6514	0.6310	0.6174
	200	0.6531	0.6323	0.6189

Table 3: Embedding Concatenations.

Subsequently, we took the cartesian product of both embeddings and experimented with concatenations. Instead of representing a word with only one embedding, we employed the concatenation of embeddings as features for each target word. Results are presented in Table 3. Experiments yield the best results when we use 50 dimensional embeddings of both methods. We show that concatenating embeddings yields better results.

		k=0	k=1	k=2	k=3
S-50	G-50	0.6559	0.6393	0.6260	0.6206
S-100	G-50	0.6514	0.6394	0.6260	0.6204
S-200	G-50	0.6531	0.6399	0.6264	0.6207

Table 4: Context-Aware Representations. S and G denotes SCODE and Glove respectively. k is the number of left and right neighbors.

Moreover, we took the surrounding words into account to make the representation of a target word context-aware. In this setup, each target word is represented not only by its own embedding but also with embeddings of surrounding words. As candidates, we selected the best performing concatenated embeddings from Table 3. Table 4 lists the results for context-aware representations where k is the number of left and right neighbors. Results imply that context-aware representations do not yield any improvements.

3.2 Final System

We submitted two systems[4] for the Complex Word Identification task. Both systems use SVM classifier

---

[4]Code is available at: https://github.com/kuruonur1/cwi

trained with Radial Basis Function. While first system (native) use the word embedding of the target word and its substrings as features, the second system (native1) uses the embeddings of preceding and following words as well. For target and surrounding words, we used the concatenation of SCODE and Glove with 50 dimensions which performed best for word embedding experiments. As substring features of the target word, we used prefixes, suffixes and character n-grams which are of length 3 and 4. We applied chi-squared test between each substring feature and class to reveal which ones are more relevant to classification and we kept the p percentile of highest scoring substring features.

	C	γ	p	G-Score
native	0.2705	0.1370	17	**0.6800**
native1	0.0595	0.0251	20	0.6500

Table 5: Best performed hyperparameters and 5-fold cross validation results on training set. C is the penalty parameter of the error term for SVM, γ is the coefficient of RBF kernel. p denotes the percentile of substrings utilized with feature selection.

Either system has 3 parameters: the coefficient of RBF kernel (γ), penalty parameter of the error term (C), percentile (p) of substring features. In order to tune the hyperparameters, we ran a random search (Bergstra and Bengio, 2012) using Hyperopt (Bergstra et al., 2013). For each hyperparameter configuration, we drawn C and γ from $e^{U(-15,5)}$, p from $U(5, 30)$. For each system, we tried 100 hyperparameter configurations and applied 5-fold cross validation. We selected the best performed hyperparameters (see Table 5) and trained our final models on the whole training set.

4 Results and Discussion

Complex Word Identification task has 9 baselines, 3 of which announced before system results and 6 baselines announced with system results. We have selected highest scoring 5 baselines to compare our systems' results. Baselines are either threshold-based (TB) or lexicon-based (LB). Two of the baselines, (TB) Wikipedia and (TB) Simple Wiki exploits language model probabilities. (TB) Senses and (TB) Length exploits words' number of senses and word lengths respectively. (LB) Ogdens baseline is released before system results and classifies a word as complex only if it is not in the Ogdens vocabulary[5]. We present our final systems' results on test set with baselines scores in Table 6.

Best Result[6]	0.7740
nativeLin[7]	0.7328
(TB) Wikipedia	0.6720
(TB) Simple Wiki	0.6540
(TB) Senses	0.5790
native1	0.5450
native	0.5450
(TB) Length	0.4780
(LB) Ogdens	0.3930

Table 6: Final system results on test set along with baselines

First and foremost, we see that both of our submitted systems perform equally well on test set. Therefore, taking the surrounding words into account does not yield any improvements as we observed while validating our model on training set. Although the threshold-based baselines simply look at the frequency of a word in a corpus, they outperform our rather sophisticated systems significantly.

One may hypothesize that the small amount of training set available is the main cause of this unsatisfactory performance. After the release of annotated test set, we examined the effect of amount of training set available to our system.

# of sentences	G-Score
training set	0.7451
+200	0.7475
+400	0.7512
+800	0.7559
+1600	0.7588
+3200	0.7638
+6400	0.7670

Table 7: G-Scores on held out test set while number of sentences in training set increasing.

We held out 1000 sentences from test set as our new test set. We started with the original training set and added sentences from annotated test set. We used the same configuration as *native* system except

<hr>

[5]http://ogden.basic-english.org/words.html

[6]Best scoring system on SemEval-2016 CWI task

[7]This model is evaluated on test set after official results are announced

we used a linear kernel instead of nonlinear RBF kernel to speed up experiments. For each training set we cross validated the penalty parameter of the error term (C) and evaluated it on held out test set. For each experiment, we report the mean G-Score of 5 random runs where the extra training set and held out test set splits selected from different shuffles. Table 7 illustrates that as the amount of training set increases our model performs better on held-out test set. Another key observation is that albeit our system is trained on the original training set with linear kernel, it has a high G-Score. Moreover, all other participants of CWI task which utilize word embeddings use nonlinear models. This scrutiny refutes the hypothesis that small amount of training set is the primary cause of word embeddings' unsatisfactory performance. Finally we trained *native* system with linear kernel using only the original training set and evaluated on whole test set. Native system with linear kernel (*nativeLin*) achieves a G-Score of *0.7328* on whole test set.

5 Conclusion

We investigated the utilization of word embeddings along with substrings as features on Complex Word Identification task. We showed that instead of representing a word with only one embedding type, word embedding concatenations yield better results. Moreover we considered context information by incorporating the embeddings of surrounding words which did not improve overall performance. Although the proposed representations perform below the average with nonlinear models, we conclude that word embeddings with substring features is an effective representation choice when employed with linear classifiers.

References

James Bergstra and Yoshua Bengio. 2012. Random search for hyper-parameter optimization. *The Journal of Machine Learning Research*, 13(1):281–305.

James Bergstra, Daniel Yamins, and David Daniel Cox. 2013. Making a science of model search: Hyperparameter optimization in hundreds of dimensions for vision architectures.

Lars Buitinck, Gilles Louppe, Mathieu Blondel, Fabian Pedregosa, Andreas Mueller, Olivier Grisel, Vlad Niculae, Peter Prettenhofer, Alexandre Gramfort, Jaques

Grobler, Robert Layton, Jake VanderPlas, Arnaud Joly, Brian Holt, and Gaël Varoquaux. 2013. API design for machine learning software: experiences from the scikit-learn project. In *ECML PKDD Workshop: Languages for Data Mining and Machine Learning*, pages 108–122.

Colby Horn, Cathryn Manduca, and David Kauchak. 2014. Learning a lexical simplifier using wikipedia. In *ACL (2)*, pages 458–463.

Yariv Maron, Elie Bienenstock, and Michael James. 2010. Sphere embedding: An application to part-of-speech induction. In *Advances in Neural Information Processing Systems*, pages 1567–1575.

Gustavo H. Paetzold and Lucia Specia. 2016. Semeval 2016 task 11: Complex word identification. In *Proceedings of the 10th International Workshop on Semantic Evaluation (SemEval 2016)*.

Jeffrey Pennington, Richard Socher, and Christopher D Manning. 2014. Glove: Global vectors for word representation. In *EMNLP*, volume 14, pages 1532–1543.

Fabrizio Sebastiani. 2002. Machine learning in automated text categorization. *ACM computing surveys (CSUR)*, 34(1):1–47.

Richard Socher, John Bauer, Christopher D Manning, and Andrew Y Ng. 2013. Parsing with compositional vector grammars. In *ACL (1)*, pages 455–465.

Joseph Turian, Lev Ratinov, and Yoshua Bengio. 2010. Word representations: a simple and general method for semi-supervised learning. In *Proceedings of the 48th annual meeting of the association for computational linguistics*, pages 384–394. Association for Computational Linguistics.

Mehmet Ali Yatbaz, Enis Sert, and Deniz Yuret. 2012. Learning syntactic categories using paradigmatic representations of word context. In *Proceedings of the 2012 Joint Conference on Empirical Methods in Natural Language Processing and Computational Natural Language Learning*, pages 940–951. Association for Computational Linguistics.

Pomona at SemEval-2016 Task 11:
Predicting Word Complexity Based on Corpus Frequency

David Kauchak
Computer Science Department
Pomona College
Claremont, CA
david.kauchak@pomona.edu

Abstract

We introduce a word frequency-based classifier for the SemEval 2016 complex word identification task (#11). Words with lower frequency are predicted as complex based on a threshold optimized for G-score. We examine three different corpora for calculating frequencies and find English Wikipedia to perform best (ranked 13th on the SemEval task), followed by the Google Web Corpus and lastly Simple English Wikipedia. Bagging is also shown to slightly improve the performance of the classifier. Overall, we find word frequency to be a strong predictor of complexity. On the SemEval "test" set, a frequency classifier that uses the optimal frequency threshold performs on-par with the best submitted system and a system trained using only 500 labeled examples split from the test set achieves results that are only slightly below the best submitted system.

1 Introduction

Text simplification aims to transform text into more accessible versions while retaining the original meaning. A frequent subproblem of the general simplification problem is complex word identification: identify words in a text that are difficult to understand for the reader. Complex word identification is critical in lexical simplification algorithms where the simplification process is done a word at a time; frequently, simplification is broken into two steps, first identifying the complex words that need simplifying and, second, determining substitutions for these words (Shardlow, 2014). Even for simplifi-

cation systems that make sentence-level transformations (Siddharthan, 2014) complex word identification can be used as an additional feature function in the model and as a development tool to help measure progress. Additionally, in some domains such as health and medicine, accuracy is critical and semi-automated simplification tools are common (Leroy et al., 2012). In these domains, complex word identification is useful to help guide the simplification process by both identifying which words need to be simplified and filtering/ranking possible candidate substitutions (Leroy et al., 2013).

In this paper, we explore the use of word frequency as a predictor of the complexity of that word. Corpus studies have shown that simpler texts contain more frequent words than more complicated texts (Breland, 1996; Pitler and Nenkova, 2008; Leroy et al., 2012). User studies have also shown a correlation between word frequency and whether users know the definition of a word (Leroy and Kauchak, 2013). In semi-automated text simplification approaches, replacing less frequent words with higher frequency synonyms has been shown to produce text that people view as simpler and is easier to understand (Leroy et al., 2013).

2 Bagged Frequency Classifier

Given a sentence $S = s_1 s_2 ... s_m$ and a word in that sentence, s_j, the complex word identification task is to predict whether that word is complex (1) or not (0). Labeled examples are triples consisting of the sentence, the word and the label, i.e. $\langle S, s_j, \{0, 1\} \rangle$, and unlabeled examples consist only of the sentence and word $\langle S, s_j \rangle$. We view the problem as a super-

Proceedings of SemEval-2016, pages 1047–1051,
San Diego, California, June 16-17, 2016. ©2016 Association for Computational Linguistics

vised classification problem: given a collection of training examples, the goal is to learn a classifier to predict the label of unlabeled examples. See the SemEval Task 11 description for more details (Paetzold and Specia, 2016).

We utilize bagging (bootstrap resampling) to learn and combine multiple basic classifiers that predict by thresholding the frequency of occurrence of the word in question (s_j) in an external corpus. Classification is then done by majority vote of these classifiers. The subsections below provide more details.

2.1 Basic frequency classifier

The basic frequency classifier predicts the word complexity using only a single feature, the frequency of the word in question (s_j) in a corpus. Given an unlabeled example, the classifier predicts based on a learned threshold, α:

$$predict(\langle S, s_j \rangle) = \begin{cases} 1 & \text{if } freq(s_j) < \alpha \\ 0 & \text{otherwise} \end{cases}$$

with the assumption that words that occur less frequently in a corpus are more complex.

To train the basic classifier, we select α in an exhaustive fashion by considering all possible frequencies of seen in the training examples as candidate thresholds. Specifically, for each training example $\langle S, s_j, \{0, 1\} \rangle$, we consider using $\alpha = freq(s_j)$. We select the α that maximizes the G-score on the training set, where the G-score is defined as:

$$\frac{2 * accuracy * recall}{accuracy + recall}$$

We chose to optimize the G-score since it was the metric used for evaluation in the SemEval task (Paetzold and Specia, 2016), though other metrics could be used instead.

2.2 Word frequencies

Word frequencies can be pre-calculated from any corpus. For this paper we examined three corpora: articles from Simple English Wikipedia[1], articles from English Wikipedia[2] and the Google Web Corpus (Brants and Franz, 2006). For the Wikipedia articles we used the document aligned data set created

---

[1]https://simple.wikipedia.org/
[2]https://en.wikipedia.org/

by Kauchak (2013) consisting of approximately 60K articles on the same topics from each Wikipedia.

To collect word frequencies for the two Wikipedia variants, tokenization was first performed using the Stanford CoreNLP PTBTokenizer (Manning et al., 2014) and then frequencies were calculated. For the Google Web Corpus, we used the unigram counts. In all corpora, all capitalization variants were aggregated, e.g. occurrences of "natural" and "Natural" would both be counted towards the same word form.

2.3 Bagging

To improve classifier performance and reduce variance we investigated the use of bagging (Breiman, 1996), also referred to as bootstrap resampling. An ensemble classifier is learned by training multiple basic frequency classifiers. Specifically, let $train$ be a training set consisting of $size(train)$ labeled examples and b be the number of basic classifiers to be learned and combined. The bagged classifier is trained by repeatedly

1) generating a new training sample $S \subseteq train$ containing $size(train)$ labeled examples by randomly sampling with replacement from $train$ and then

2) training a new basic frequency classifier on S.

These two steps are repeated b times resulting in b different classifiers. To classify a new, unlabeled example, each of the b classifiers makes a prediction and the final label is the label with the majority vote, with ties going to not complex (0), since this was the more frequent class.

3 Experiments

We submitted two systems to the SemEval Complex Word Identification challenge (Task 11), which used the same parameter settings and only differed in where the corpus frequencies were collected, English Wikipedia (NormalBag) and the Google Web Corpus (GoogleBag). Both systems used $b = 10$ rounds of bagging, which was shown experimentally to have the best scoring value, using repeated rounds of 10-fold validation. We also discuss results here for a system which used Simple English Wikipedia word frequencies, though we did not submit it to the challenge (for consistency, we denote it SimpleBag).

System	Test			Train		
	G-score	Accuracy	Recall	G-score	Accuracy	Recall
NormalBag	0.714	0.603	0.872	0.684	0.665	0.705
GoogleBag	0.691	0.568	0.881	0.675	0.648	0.704
SimpleBag	0.674	0.542	0.891	0.674	0.630	0.725

Table 1: Results for the bagged systems ($b = 10$) with word frequencies calculated on the three different corpora. Results are shown for the test and training sets for systems trained on the training data.

The task consisted of a training data set ($N = 2{,}237$), which was available during development, and a test data set ($N = 88{,}221$) on which the competition was scored and the labels were only released after the competition (Paetzold and Specia, 2016). We use both data sets here to analyze the performance of the classifiers.

3.1 The impact of corpus choice

Table 1 shows the results for the classifiers trained using bagging with word frequencies calculated from the three different corpora. English Wikipedia performed the best, followed by Google Web Corpus and finally Simple English Wikipedia. The top two entries were entered into the SemEval competition and ranked 13th and 16th respectively out of 51 systems (42 team submitted systems and 9 baseline systems). We hypothesize that English Wikipedia represents a good compromise between size/coverage and corpus quality; even though NormalBag had slightly lower recall than the other two, it was able to achieve that recall with a significantly higher accuracy.

To verify that the differences in performance between the three systems were significant, we used bootstrap resampling with a paired sample t-test (Koehn, 2004). Based on 100 random samples, all differences between all metrics and all systems were significant ($p < 0.0001$, with Bonferroni correction to correct for testing multiple different comparisons).

Overall, relative to other systems that were submitted for the SemEval task, these frequency-based classifiers biased towards recall, e.g. the Google frequency and English Wikipedia frequency systems ranked 3rd and 5th with respect to recall (of the 42 team submitted systems).

Corpus	Train	
	basic G-score	bagged G-score
Normal	0.677	**0.680**
Google	0.668	0.667
Simple	0.665	**0.669**

Table 2: Comparison of the basic frequency classifiers and their bagged counterparts with $b = 10$ on the training data averaged over 100 random 10-fold samples. Systems that were significantly different between the basic and bagged are in bold.

3.2 The impact of bagging

To measure the impact of bagging on the prediction performance of the systems, for each corpus source, we compared the basic frequency classifier to the bagged variant. We generated 100 random 10-fold partitions of the training data and performed 10-fold cross validation on each for each system variant. We averaged the results across the each 10-fold set resulting in 100 scores for each of the systems.

Table 2 shows the averages over these 100 scores. For both of the Wikipedia variants (Normal and Simple) bagging provided a small increase in performance ($p < 0.0001$ based on a paired t-test). For the Google frequencies the performance actually decreased, though this decrease was not significant.

To understand the effect that b (the number of bootstrap samples) has on the performance of the classifier, we compared the performance of the classifier with $b = 1, 2, ..., 100$. Figure 1 shows a plot of the G-score versus the number of bags used by the classifier for the NormalBag classifier on the training set. As with the previous experiment, to partially mitigate noise, we generated 100 randomly 10-fold sets and averaged the results across all of these to generate the data.

For small b, increasing the number of classifiers voting does increase the performance of the classifier. However, after around $b = 10$ adding more

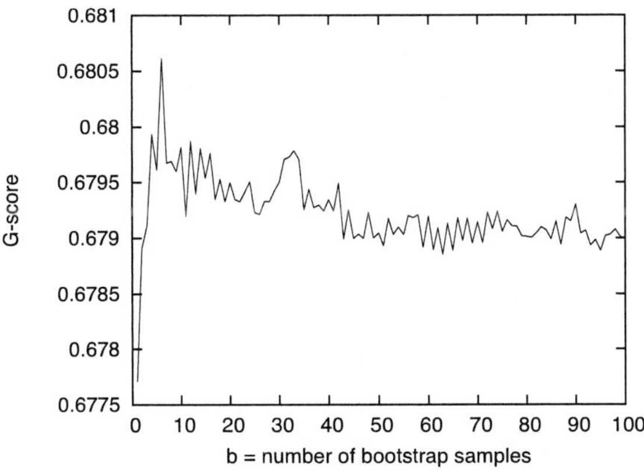
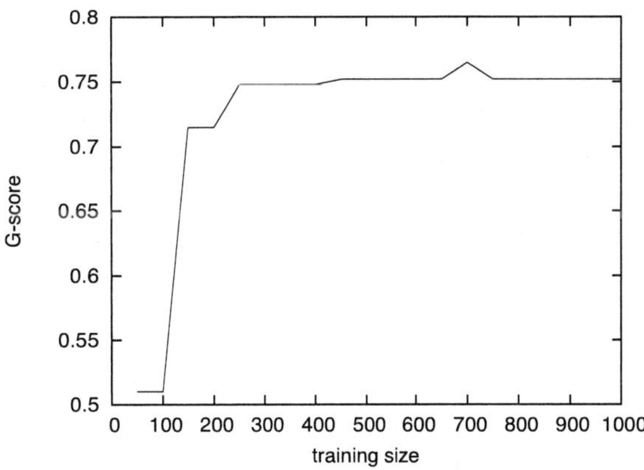

Figure 1: G-score for the NormalBag classifier with varying number of boostrap samples. Results are averages over 100 random 10-fold samples of the training data.

Figure 2: G-score for the basic threshold classifier using English Wikipedia frequencies for increasing training data size. Here the training data is a subset of the SemEval "test" set.

classifiers degrades the performance with the classifier. Although the difference is small for $b = 1$ vs. $b = 10$ (0.677 vs. 0.680), the difference is statistically significant.

3.3 Limits of frequency-based classification

Using English Wikipedia frequencies and the optimal frequency threshold (i.e. α), the basic threshold classifier achieves a G-score of 0.779 on the test data set. This is slightly higher than the best scoring SemEval system, which achieved 0.774. Clearly frequency provides a strong signal for word complexity.

The previous experiment assumes an unreasonable scenario where we know the labels and can pick the optimal value. To better understand the impact of frequency, we split the test data into 10-folds and performed 10-fold cross-validation analysis using the basic threshold classifier, training the threshold on 90% of the SemEval "test" data and then testing on the remaining 10%. In this scenario, the threshold classifier still achieves a G-score of 0.764, only slightly less than the score achieved using the optimal threshold.

0.764 is still significantly higher than the score achieved by the system when trained on the SemEval "training" set. Two possible differences exist between the training and testing data. First, the test data is two orders of magnitude larger than the original training data. This additional data could result in a more reliable classifier. Alternatively, train and test were generated in different ways and could have different characteristics.

To investigate this, we held out 10% of the "test" data set as testing data and trained the basic threshold classifier on increasing amounts of the remaining 90%. Figure 2 shows the G-score for training sizes up to 1,000 (the G-score mostly stabilized beyond 1,000 with only minor variation). Even with only 250 training examples, the classifier already achieves a G-score of 0.748 and with 500 training examples, it achieves 0.752, only a little less than the final score using all of the training data of 0.760. For the frequency classifier, more the data domain, and less the size, accounts for the differences in performance seen.

4 Conclusion

In this paper, we described our entry for the complex word identification SeEval 2016 task (#11). We utilize word frequency to classify complexity, with less frequent words being classified as complex. As has been seen in previous corpus studies, frequency is a very strong predictor of the complexity of a word. However, the corpus where those frequencies are measured does play a role in performance. We found that English Wikipedia performed best for this particular task. Future research is needed to investigate this phenomena more broadly.

References

Thorsten Brants and Alex Franz. 2006. Web 1T 5-gram version 1. Linguistic Data Consortium, Philadelphia.

Leo Breiman. 1996. Bagging predictors. *Machine learning*.

Hunter M Breland. 1996. Word frequency and word difficulty: A comparison of counts in four corpora. *Psychological Science*.

William Coster and David Kauchak. 2011. Simple English Wikipedia: A new text simplification task. In *Proceedings of ACL*.

David Kauchak. 2013. Improving text simplification language modeling using unsimplified text data. In *Proceedings of ACL*.

Philipp Koehn. 2004. Statistical significance tests for machine translation evaluation. In *EMNLP*.

Gondy Leroy and David Kauchak. 2013. The effect of word familiarity on actual and perceived text difficulty. *Journal of American Medical Informatics Association*.

Gondy Leroy, James Endicott, Obay Mouradi, David Kauchak, and Melissa Just. 2012. Improving perceived and actual text difficulty for health information consumers using semi-automated methods. In *American Medical Informatics Association (AMIA) Fall Symposium*.

Gondy Leroy, James E. Endicott, David Kauchak, Obay Mouradi, and Melissa Just. 2013. User evaluation of the effects of a text simplification algorithm using term familiarity on perception, understanding, learning, and information retention. *Journal of Medical Internet Research (JMIR)*.

Christopher D Manning, Mihai Surdeanu, John Bauer, Jenny Rose Finkel, Steven Bethard, and David McClosky. 2014. The stanford corenlp natural language processing toolkit. In *ACL (System Demonstrations)*.

Courtney Napoles and Mark Dredze. 2010. Learning simple Wikipedia: A cogitation in ascertaining abecedarian language. In *Proceedings of HLT/NAACL Workshop on Computation Linguistics and Writing*.

Gustavo H. Paetzold and Lucia Specia. 2016. Semeval 2016 task 11: Complex word identification. In *Proceedings of the 10th International Workshop on Semantic Evaluation (SemEval 2016)*.

Emily Pitler and Ani Nenkova. 2008. Revisiting readability: A unified framework for predicting text quality. In *Proceedings of the conference on empirical methods in natural language processing*. Association for Computational Linguistics.

Matthew Shardlow. 2014. A survey of automated text simplification. *International Journal of Advanced Computer Science and Applications*.

Advaith Siddharthan. 2014. A survey of research on text simplification. *ITL-International Journal of Applied Linguistics*.

SemEval-2016 Task 12: Clinical TempEval

Steven Bethard
University of Alabama at Birmingham
Birmingham, AL 35294, USA
bethard@cis.uab.edu

Guergana Savova
Harvard Medical School
Boston, MA 02115, USA
Guergana.Savova@childrens.harvard.edu

Wei-Te Chen
University of Colorado Boulder
Boulder, CO 80309
weite.chen@colorado.edu

Leon Derczynski
University of Sheffield
Sheffield, S1 4DP, UK
leon.derczynski@sheffield.ac.uk

James Pustejovsky
Brandeis University
Waltham, MA 02453, USA
jamesp@cs.brandeis.edu

Marc Verhagen
Brandeis University
Waltham, MA 02453, USA
marc@cs.brandeis.edu

Abstract

Clinical TempEval 2016 evaluated temporal information extraction systems on the clinical domain. Nine sub-tasks were included, covering problems in time expression identification, event expression identification and temporal relation identification. Participant systems were trained and evaluated on a corpus of clinical and pathology notes from the Mayo Clinic, annotated with an extension of TimeML for the clinical domain. 14 teams submitted a total of 40 system runs, with the best systems achieving near-human performance on identifying events and times. On identifying temporal relations, there was a gap between the best systems and human performance, but the gap was less than half the gap of Clinical TempEval 2015.

1 Introduction

The TempEval shared tasks have, since 2007, provided a focus for research on temporal information extraction (Verhagen et al., 2007; Verhagen et al., 2010; UzZaman et al., 2013). Participant systems compete to identify critical components of the timeline of a text, including time expressions, event expressions and temporal relations. However, the TempEval campaigns to date have focused primarily on in-document timelines derived from news articles. In recent years, the community has moved toward testing such information extraction systems on clinical data (Sun et al., 2013; Bethard et al., 2015) to broaden our understanding of the language of time beyond newswire expressions and structure.

Clinical TempEval focuses on discrete, well-defined tasks which allow rapid, reliable and repeatable evaluation. Participating systems are expected to take as input raw text, for example:

> April 23, 2014: The patient did not have any postoperative bleeding so we'll resume chemotherapy with a larger bolus on Friday even if there is slight nausea.

The systems are then expected to output annotations over the text, for example, those shown in Figure 1. That is, the systems should identify the time expressions, event expressions, attributes of those expressions, and temporal relations between them.

Clinical TempEval 2016 addressed one of the major challenges in Clinical TempEval 2015: data distribution. Because Clinical TempEval is based on real patient notes from the Mayo Clinic, participants go through a lengthy authorization process involving a data use agreement and an interview. For Clinical TempEval 2016, we streamlined this process and were able to authorize data access for more than twice as many participants as Clinical TempEval 2015. And since all the training and evaluation data distributed for Clinical TempEval 2015 was used as the training data for Clinical TempEval 2016, participants had more than a year to work on their systems. The result was that four times as many teams participated.

1052

Proceedings of SemEval-2016, pages 1052–1062,
San Diego, California, June 16-17, 2016. ©2016 Association for Computational Linguistics

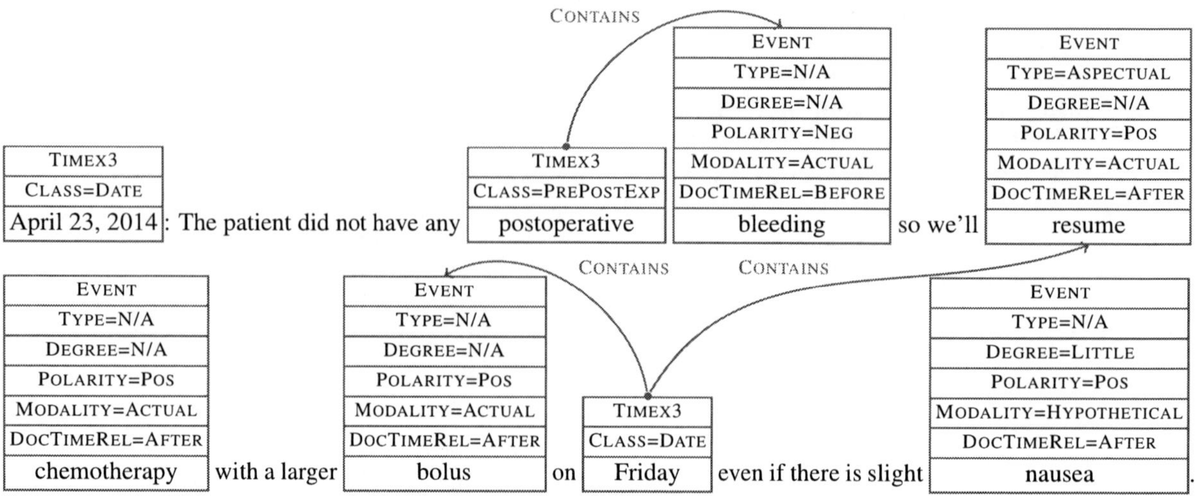

Figure 1: Example Clinical TempEval annotations

2 Data

The Clinical TempEval corpus was based on a set of 600 clinical notes and pathology reports from cancer patients at the Mayo Clinic. These notes were manually de-identified by the Mayo Clinic to replace names, locations, etc. with generic placeholders, but time expressions were not altered. The notes were then manually annotated by the THYME project (thyme.healthnlp.org) using an extension of ISO-TimeML for the annotation of times, events and temporal relations in clinical notes (Styler et al., 2014b). This extension includes additions such as new time expression types (e.g., PREPOSTEXP for expressions like *postoperative*), new EVENT attributes (e.g., DEGREE=LITTLE for expressions like *slight nausea*), and an increased focus on temporal relations of type CONTAINS (a.k.a. INCLUDES).

The annotation procedure was as follows:

1. Annotators identified time and event expressions, along with their attributes
2. Adjudicators revised and finalized the time and event expressions and their attributes
3. Annotators identified temporal relations between pairs of events and events and times
4. Adjudicators revised and finalized the temporal relations

More details on the corpus annotation process are documented in a separate article (Styler et al., 2014a).

Because the data contained incompletely de-

identified clinical data (the time expressions were retained), participants were required to sign a data use agreement with the Mayo Clinic to obtain the raw text of the clinical notes and pathology reports.[1] The event, time and temporal relation annotations were distributed separately from the text, in an open source repository[2] using the Anafora standoff format (Chen and Styler, 2013).

The corpus was split into three portions: Train (50%), Dev (25%) and Test (25%). Patients were sorted by patient number (an integer arbitrarily assigned by the de-identification process) and stratified across these splits. The Train and Dev portions were released to participants for training and tuning their systems. The Test portion was reserved for evaluation of the systems. Table 1 shows the number of documents, event expressions (EVENT annotations), time expressions (TIMEX3 annotations) and narrative container relations (TLINK annotations with TYPE=CONTAINS attributes) in the Train, Dev, and Test portions of the corpus.

3 Tasks

Nine tasks were included (the same as those of Clinical TempEval 2015), grouped into three categories:

- Identifying time expressions (TIMEX3 annotations in the THYME corpus) consisting of the

---

[1]Details on the process: http://thyme.healthnlp.org/
[2]https://github.com/stylerw/thymedata

	Train	Dev	Test
Documents	293	147	151
TIMEX3s	3833	2078	1952
EVENTs	38890	20974	18990
TYPE=CONTAINS TLINKs	11176	6173	5894

Table 1: Number of documents, event expressions, time expressions and narrative container relations in Train, Dev, and Test portions of the THYME data. Both Train and Dev were released as part of Clinical TempEval 2015.

following components:

- The span (character offsets) of the expression in the text
- Class: DATE, TIME, DURATION, QUANTIFIER, PREPOSTEXP or SET

- Identifying event expressions (EVENT annotations in the THYME corpus) consisting of the following components:
  - The span (character offsets) of the expression in the text
  - Contextual Modality: ACTUAL, HYPOTHETICAL, HEDGED or GENERIC
  - Degree: MOST, LITTLE or N/A
  - Polarity: POS or NEG
  - Type: ASPECTUAL, EVIDENTIAL or N/A

- Identifying temporal relations between events and times, focusing on the following types:
  - Relations between events and the document creation time (BEFORE, OVERLAP, BEFORE-OVERLAP or AFTER), represented by DOCTIMEREL annotations.
  - Narrative container relations (Pustejovsky and Stubbs, 2011), which indicate that an event or time is temporally contained in (i.e., occurred during) another event or time, represented by TLINK annotations with TYPE=CONTAINS.

The evaluation was run in two phases:

1. Systems were provided access only to the raw text, and were asked to identify time expressions, event expressions and temporal relations
2. Systems were provided access to the raw text and the manual event and time annotations, and were asked to identify only temporal relations

4 Evaluation Metrics

All of the tasks were evaluated using the standard metrics of precision (P), recall (R) and F_1:

$$P = \frac{|S \cap H|}{|S|} \quad R = \frac{|S \cap H|}{|H|} \quad F_1 = \frac{2 \cdot P \cdot R}{P + R}$$

where S is the set of items predicted by the system and H is the set of items annotated by the humans. Applying these metrics only requires a definition of what is considered an "item" for each task.

- For evaluating the spans of event expressions or time expressions, items were tuples of (begin, end) character offsets. Thus, systems only received credit for identifying events and times with exactly the same character offsets as the manually annotated ones.
- For evaluating the attributes of event expressions or time expressions – Class, Contextual Modality, Degree, Polarity and Type – items were tuples of (begin, end, value) where begin and end are character offsets and value is the value that was given to the relevant attribute. Thus, systems only received credit for an event (or time) attribute if they both found an event (or time) with the correct character offsets and then assigned the correct value for that attribute.
- For relations between events and the document creation time, items were tuples of (begin, end, value), just as if it were an event attribute. Thus, systems only received credit if they found a correct event and assigned the correct relation (BEFORE, OVERLAP, BEFORE-OVERLAP or AFTER) between that event and the document creation time. In the second phase of the evaluation, when manual event annotations were provided as input, only recall (which in this case is equivalent to standard classification accuracy) is reported.
- For narrative container relations, items were tuples of (($begin_1$, end_1), ($begin_2$, end_2)), where the begins and ends corresponded to the character offsets of the events or times participating in the relation. Thus, systems only received credit for a narrative container relation if they found both events/times and correctly assigned a CONTAINS relation between them.

For event and time attributes, we also measure how accurately a system predicts the attribute values on just those events or times that the system predicted. The goal here is to allow a comparison across systems for assigning attribute values, even when different systems produce different numbers of events and times. This metric is calculated by dividing the F_1 on the attribute by the F_1 on identifying the spans:

$$A = \frac{\text{attribute } F_1}{\text{span } F_1}$$

For narrative container relations, the P and R definitions were modified to take into account *temporal closure*, where additional relations are deterministically inferred from other relations (e.g., A CONTAINS B and B CONTAINS C, so A CONTAINS C):

$$P = \frac{|S \cap \text{closure}(H)|}{|S|} \quad R = \frac{|\text{closure}(S) \cap H|}{|H|}$$

Similar measures were used in prior work (UzZaman and Allen, 2011) and TempEval 2013 (UzZaman et al., 2013), following the intuition that precision should measure the fraction of system-predicted relations that can be verified from the human annotations (either the original human annotations or annotations inferred from those through closure), and that recall should measure the fraction of human-annotated relations that can be verified from the system output (either the original system predictions or predictions inferred from those through closure).

5 Baseline Systems

Two rule-based systems were used as baselines to compare the participating systems against.

memorize For all tasks but the narrative container task, a memorization baseline was used.
To train the model, all phrases annotated as either events or times in the training data were collected. All exact character matches for these phrases in the training data were then examined, and only phrases that were annotated as events or times greater than 50% of the time were retained. For each phrase, the most frequently annotated type (event or time) and attribute values for instances of that phrase were determined.
To predict with the model, the raw text of the test data was searched for all exact character

matches of any of the memorized phrases, preferring longer phrases when multiple matches overlapped. Wherever a phrase match was found, an event or time with the memorized (most frequent) attribute values was predicted.

closest For the narrative container task, a proximity baseline was used. Each time expression was predicted to be a narrative container, containing only the closest event expression to it in the text.

6 Participating Systems

14 research teams submitted a total of 40 runs:

brundlefly (Fries, 2016) submitted 1 run for phase 1 based on recurrent neural networks, word embeddings, and logistic regression, and 1 run for phase 2 run based on the DeepDive framework (`http://deepdive.stanford.edu`).

CDE-IIITH (Chikka, 2016) submitted 2 runs for each phase, the first based on deep learning models, and the second based on conditional random fields and support vector machines.

Cental (Hansart et al., 2016) submitted 1 run for phase 1, based on conditional random fields and lexical resources.

GUIR (Cohan et al., 2016) submitted 2 runs for phase 1 and 1 run for phase 2, based on conditional random fields and logistic regression with lexical, morphological, syntactic, dependency, and domain specific features, combined with pattern matching rules.

HITACHI (Sarath P R et al., 2016) submitted 2 runs for the time portion of phase 1, based on ensembles of rule-based and machine learning systems with lexical, syntactic and morphological features. The second run included 50% more training data than the first.

KULeuven-LIIR (Leeuwenberg and Moens, 2016) submitted 2 runs for phase 2, based on the cTAKES-temporal machine-learning model (Lin et al., 2015), with additional features.

LIMSI (Grouin and Moriceau, 2016) submitted 2 runs for each phase, based on conditional random fields with lexical, morphological, and word cluster features, and the rule-based Heidel-Time (Strötgen and Gertz, 2013).

LIMSI-COT (Tourille et al., 2016) submitted 2 runs for phase 2, the first based on support vector machines with lexical, syntactic, structural, and UMLS features, and the second based on replacing the lexical features with word embeddings.

ULISBOA (Barros et al., 2016) submitted 2 runs for each phase, based on the IBEnt framework's support vector machines with lexical and morphological features (`https://github.com/AndreLamurias/IBEnt`), and rule-based extensions to Stanford CoreNLP (Manning et al., 2014). The runs differed on how rules were incorporated for each subtask.

UtahBMI (Velupillai and Meystre, 2016) submitted 2 runs for each phase, the first based on conditional random fields and the second based on support vector machines. Both runs used lexical, morphological, syntactic, shape, character pattern, character n-gram, section type, and gazetteer features.

UTA-MLNLP (Li and Huang, 2016) submitted 2 runs for each phase, based on a neural network with a different window size for each run.

UTHealth (Lee et al., 2016) submitted 2 runs for each phase, based on linear and structural (HMM) support vector machines using lexical, morphological, syntactic, discourse, and word representation features. The runs differed on the features included.

VUACLTL (Caselli and Morante, 2016) submitted 2 runs for each phase, based on conditional random fields with morpho-syntactic, lexical, UMLS, and DBpedia features. The first run was a two-step approach to temporal relations, the second, a one step approach.

7 Human Agreement

We also provide two types of human agreement on the task, measured with the same evaluation metrics as the systems:

ann-ann Inter-annotator agreement between the two independent human annotators who annotated each document. This is the most commonly reported type of agreement, and often considered to be an upper bound on system performance.

adj-ann Inter-annotator agreement between the adjudicator and the two independent annotators. This is usually a better bound on system performance in adjudicated corpora, since the models are trained on the adjudicated data, not on the individual annotator data.

Precision and recall are not reported in these scenarios since they depend on the arbitrary choice of one annotator as human (H) and the other as system (S).

Note that since temporal relations between events and the document creation time were annotated at the same time as the events themselves, agreement for this task is only reported in phase 1 of the evaluation. Similarly, since narrative container relations were only annotated after events and times had been adjudicated, agreement for this task is only reported in phase 2 of the evaluation.

8 Evaluation Results

8.1 Time Expressions

Table 2 shows results on the time expression tasks. The UTHealth systems achieved the best results on almost all time-related tasks. For finding times, while one system had comparable precision to UTHealth (0.836 UTHealth vs. 0.840 LIMSI), no system had competitive recall (0.757 UTHealth vs. 0.714 from the next best, UtahBMI), and thus the UTHealth system consistently outperformed the other systems in F_1. The results were similar for jointly finding times and assigning them a time class, though a couple systems (HITACHI, GUIR) did have more accurate predictions for the time class when scored only on the times that they were able to find (0.971 UTHealth vs. 0.975 HITACHI vs. 0.989 GUIR).

Compared to human agreement, the UTHealth and UtahBMI systems exceeded the inter-annotator agreement on times of 0.731, but even UTHealth's F_1 of 0.795 did not reach the annotator-adjudicator agreement of 0.830, and the results were similar for jointly finding times and assigning their classes (0.772 vs. 0.807). Nonetheless, these 0.025 and 0.035 gaps between the top system and the human agreement are smaller than the 0.051 and 0.038 gaps observed in Clinical TempEval 2015 (Bethard et al., 2015).

8.2 Event Expressions

Table 3 shows results on the event expression tasks. Again, UTHealth dominated the field, achieving the highest score on almost every event-related task. However, the gap to the second place team was much smaller for events than it was for times: only a 0.011

Team	span			span + class			
	P	R	F1	P	R	F1	A
UTHealth-1	0.836	**0.757**	**0.795**	0.812	**0.735**	**0.772**	0.971
UTHealth-2	0.826	0.758	0.790	0.800	0.734	0.765	0.968
UtahBMI-crf	0.798	0.714	0.754	0.771	0.690	0.729	0.967
UtahBMI-svm	0.810	0.690	0.745	0.792	0.674	0.728	0.977
HITACHI-1	0.781	0.685	0.730	0.759	0.671	0.712	0.975
HITACHI-2	0.781	0.668	0.720	0.758	0.654	0.702	0.975
Cental-crf	0.777	0.564	0.653	0.752	0.545	0.632	0.968
LIMSI-2	0.830	0.518	0.638	0.804	0.503	0.619	0.970
LIMSI-1	**0.840**	0.510	0.635	**0.815**	0.495	0.616	0.970
CDE-IIITH-crf	0.752	0.515	0.612	0.644	0.439	0.522	0.853
CDE-IIITH-dl	0.614	0.560	0.586	0.468	0.426	0.446	0.761
brundlefly	0.686	0.415	0.517	0.639	0.387	0.482	0.932
VUACLTL-1	0.660	0.372	0.476	0.638	0.363	0.462	0.971
VUACLTL-2	0.660	0.372	0.476	0.638	0.363	0.462	0.971
GUIR-2	0.649	0.256	0.367	0.640	0.253	0.362	0.986
GUIR-1	0.486	0.273	0.349	0.480	0.269	0.345	**0.989**
Baseline: memorize	0.774	0.428	0.551	0.746	0.413	0.532	0.966
GUIR†	0.802	0.678	0.735	0.775	0.655	0.710	0.966
ULISBOA-2†	0.776	0.692	0.732	-	-	-	-
ULISBOA-1†	0.623	0.065	0.118	-	-	-	-
Agreement: ann-ann	-	-	0.731	-	-	0.688	0.941
Agreement: adj-ann	-	-	0.830	-	-	0.807	0.972

Table 2: System performance and annotator agreement on TIMEX3 tasks: identifying the time expression's span (character offsets) and class (DATE, TIME, DURATION, QUANTIFIER, PREPOSTEXP or SET). The best system score from each column is in bold. Systems marked with † were submitted after the competition deadline and are not considered official.

gap between UTHealth's 0.903 F_1 and UtahBMI's 0.892. The gap was even smaller if we look at precision and recall separately: a 0.007 gap between UTHealth's 0.915 precision and UTA's 0.908, and a 0.005 gap between UTHealth's 0.891 precision and UtahBMI's 0.886. The results were similar for most of the attributes, though the precision gaps were larger (1.1-1.4) and the recall gaps were smaller (0.3-0.7).

Compared to human agreement, UTHealth, UtahBMI, Cental, GUIR, and UTA all exceeded inter-annotator agreement on identifying events, and UTHealth and UtahBMI exceeded inter-annotator agreement on all of the attributes. None of the systems reached the level of annotator-adjudicator agreement: even UTHealth's F_1 on events of 0.903 had a gap of 0.019 from the annotator-adjudicator agreement of 0.922, and the results were similar for event attributes: 0.049 for modality, 0.021 for degree, 0.029 for polarity, 0.024 for type. These gaps are almost all bigger than the gaps observed in Clinical TempEval 2015: 0.005 for event spans, 0.031 for modality, 0.007 for degree, 0.012 for polarity, 0.030 for type. However, Clinical TempEval 2016's human agreement was substantially higher, with all annotator-adjudicator agreement above 0.90, while in Clinical TempEval 2015, annotator-adjudicator agreement ranged from 0.853 to 0.880.

8.3 Temporal Relations

Table 4 shows performance on the temporal relation tasks. In both phase 1 (where systems were provided only the raw text) and phase 2 (where systems were provided the manually annotated events and times), the UTHealth system was again the top system for most tasks. For relating events to the document creation time, the UTHealth system had the best precision, recall, and F_1 (0.766, 0.746, and 0.756) in phase

Team	span			span + modality				span + degree			
	P	R	F1	P	R	F1	A	P	R	F1	A
UTHealth-1	**0.915**	**0.891**	**0.903**	**0.866**	**0.843**	**0.855**	**0.947**	**0.911**	**0.887**	**0.899**	0.996
UTHealth-2	0.903	0.886	0.895	0.855	0.839	0.847	0.946	0.899	0.883	0.891	0.996
UtahBMI-svm	0.897	0.886	0.892	0.841	0.831	0.836	0.937	0.892	0.881	0.887	0.994
UtahBMI-crf	0.902	0.883	0.892	0.850	0.832	0.841	0.943	0.898	0.879	0.889	**0.997**
Cental-crf	0.892	0.878	0.885	-	-	-	-	-	-	-	-
GUIR-2	0.887	0.872	0.880	0.836	0.822	0.829	0.942	0.883	0.868	0.875	0.994
GUIR-1	0.886	0.872	0.879	0.830	0.817	0.824	0.937	0.882	0.868	0.875	0.995
UTA-4	0.908	0.842	0.874	0.842	0.780	0.810	0.927	0.904	0.838	0.869	0.994
UTA-5	0.900	0.850	0.874	0.837	0.790	0.813	0.930	0.896	0.845	0.870	0.995
VUACLTL-1	0.868	0.828	0.847	0.795	0.758	0.776	0.916	0.864	0.824	0.844	0.996
VUACLTL-2	0.868	0.828	0.847	0.795	0.758	0.776	0.916	0.864	0.824	0.844	0.996
LIMSI-1	0.885	0.808	0.845	0.811	0.742	0.775	0.917	0.880	0.805	0.841	0.995
LIMSI-2	0.869	0.816	0.842	0.798	0.749	0.772	0.917	0.865	0.812	0.838	0.995
CDE-IIITH-crf	0.835	0.797	0.815	0.764	0.729	0.746	0.915	0.830	0.793	0.811	0.995
CDE-IIITH-dl	0.838	0.786	0.811	0.779	0.731	0.754	0.930	0.834	0.783	0.807	0.995
brundlefly	0.883	0.660	0.755	0.819	0.612	0.701	0.928	0.878	0.657	0.752	0.996
Baseline: memorize	0.878	0.834	0.855	0.810	0.770	0.789	0.923	0.874	0.831	0.852	0.996
GUIR†	0.891	0.872	0.881	0.836	0.818	0.827	0.939	0.887	0.868	0.877	0.995
ULISBOA-1†	0.881	0.745	0.807	-	-	-	-	-	-	-	-
ULISBOA-2†	0.879	0.739	0.803	-	-	-	-	-	-	-	-
Agreement: ann-ann	-	-	0.864	-	-	0.833	0.964	-	-	0.861	0.997
Agreement: adj-ann	-	-	0.922	-	-	0.904	0.980	-	-	0.920	0.998

Team	span + polarity				span + type			
	P	R	F1	A	P	R	F1	A
UTHealth-1	**0.900**	**0.875**	**0.887**	0.982	**0.894**	**0.870**	**0.882**	**0.977**
UTHealth-2	0.888	0.872	0.880	**0.983**	0.880	0.863	0.871	0.973
UtahBMI-svm	0.879	0.869	0.874	0.980	0.854	0.843	0.849	0.952
UtahBMI-crf	0.885	0.867	0.876	0.982	0.875	0.857	0.866	0.971
Cental-crf	0.870	0.857	0.864	0.976	-	-	-	-
GUIR-2	0.871	0.856	0.864	0.982	0.864	0.850	0.857	0.974
GUIR-1	0.869	0.855	0.862	0.981	0.863	0.850	0.857	0.975
UTA-4	0.876	0.812	0.842	0.963	0.877	0.813	0.844	0.966
UTA-5	0.861	0.813	0.836	0.957	0.869	0.820	0.844	0.966
VUACLTL-1	0.780	0.743	0.761	0.898	0.839	0.800	0.819	0.967
VUACLTL-2	0.780	0.743	0.761	0.898	0.839	0.800	0.819	0.967
LIMSI-1	0.867	0.792	0.828	0.980	0.825	0.754	0.788	0.933
LIMSI-2	0.851	0.799	0.824	0.979	0.811	0.761	0.785	0.932
CDE-IIITH-crf	0.750	0.716	0.733	0.899	0.806	0.769	0.787	0.966
CDE-IIITH-dl	0.813	0.764	0.788	0.972	0.814	0.765	0.789	0.973
brundlefly	0.856	0.640	0.733	0.971	0.829	0.620	0.709	0.939
Baseline: memorize	0.812	0.772	0.792	0.926	0.855	0.813	0.833	0.974
GUIR†	0.875	0.856	0.866	0.983	0.868	0.849	0.858	0.974
Agreement: ann-ann	-	-	0.852	0.986	-	-	0.835	0.966
Agreement: adj-ann	-	-	0.916	0.993	-	-	0.906	0.983

Table 3: System performance and annotator agreement on EVENT tasks: identifying the event expression's span (character offsets), contextual modality (ACTUAL, HYPOTHETICAL, HEDGED or GENERIC), degree (MOST, LITTLE or N/A), polarity (POS or NEG) and type (ASPECTUAL, EVIDENTIAL or N/A). The best system score from each column is in bold. Systems marked with † were submitted after the competition deadline and are not considered official.

	To document time			Narrative containers		
	P	R	F1	P	R	F1
Phase 1: systems are provided only the raw text						
UTHealth-1	**0.766**	**0.746**	**0.756**	0.488	**0.471**	**0.479**
UTHealth-2	0.757	0.743	0.750	0.479	0.466	0.472
UtahBMI-crf	0.753	0.737	0.745	0.502	0.215	0.301
UtahBMI-svm	0.741	0.732	0.736	0.498	0.215	0.300
GUIR-2	0.719	0.707	0.713	-	-	-
GUIR-1	0.712	0.701	0.706	-	-	-
VUACLTL-1	0.655	0.624	0.639	**0.531**	0.244	0.334
VUACLTL-2	0.655	0.624	0.639	0.493	0.268	0.347
CDE-IIITH-dl	0.643	0.604	0.623	0.285	0.225	0.252
LIMSI-1	0.635	0.580	0.607	-	-	-
LIMSI-2	0.624	0.585	0.604	-	-	-
CDE-IIITH-crf	0.481	0.460	0.470	0.431	0.167	0.241
brundlefly	0.389	0.290	0.332	-	-	-
UTA-4	0.340	0.315	0.327	-	-	-
UTA-5	0.336	0.317	0.326	-	-	-
Baseline: memorize / closest	0.620	0.589	0.604	0.403	0.067	0.115
GUIR†	0.719	0.704	0.711	-	-	-
ULISBOA-1†	-	-	-	0.122	0.009	0.017
ULISBOA-2†	-	-	-	0.108	0.009	0.017
Agreement: ann-ann	-	-	0.721	-	-	-
Agreement: adj-ann	-	-	0.844	-	-	-
Phase 2: systems are provided manually annotated EVENTs and TIMEX3s						
UTHealth-1	-	0.835	-	0.588	**0.559**	**0.573**
UTHealth-2	-	0.833	-	0.568	0.564	0.566
LIMSI-COT-lexical	-	0.769	-	0.704	0.436	0.538
GUIR-1	-	0.813	-	0.546	0.471	0.506
LIMSI-COT-embedding	-	0.807	-	**0.751**	0.320	0.449
KULeuven-LIIR-1	-	-	-	0.714	0.428	0.536
KULeuven-LIIR-2	-	-	-	0.715	0.429	0.536
VUACLTL-2	-	0.701	-	0.589	0.368	0.453
VUACLTL-1	-	0.701	-	0.642	0.345	0.449
UtahBMI-crf+svm	-	**0.843**	-	0.562	0.254	0.350
CDE-IIITH-dl	-	0.705	-	0.348	0.284	0.313
UtahBMI-svm	-	0.571	-	0.605	0.230	0.333
ULISBOA-1	-	-	-	0.273	0.255	0.264
brundlefly	-	0.742	-	-	-	-
uta-5	-	0.788	-	-	-	-
uta-6	-	0.786	-	-	-	-
LIMSI-1	-	0.687	-	-	-	-
CDE-IIITH-crf	-	0.588	-	0.493	0.185	0.269
LIMSI-2	-	0.679	-	-	-	-
ULISBOA-2	-	-	-	0.823	0.056	0.105
Baseline: memorize / closest	-	0.675	-	0.459	0.154	0.231
UtahBMI-crf+svm†	-	0.843	-	0.693	0.425	0.527
UtahBMI-svm†	-	0.571	-	0.711	0.372	0.489
Agreement: ann-ann	-	-	-	-	-	0.651
Agreement: adj-ann	-	-	-	-	-	0.817

Table 4: System performance and annotator agreement on temporal relation tasks: identifying relations between events and the document creation time (DOCTIMEREL), and identifying narrative container relations (CONTAINS). The best system score from each column is in bold. Systems marked with † were submitted after the competition deadline and are not considered official.

1, and the second best score (0.835 vs. UtahBMI's 0.843) in phase 2. For finding narrative container relations, the UTHealth system had the best recall (0.471 in phase 1, 0.559 in phase 2), and though other systems (UtahBMI, VUACLTL, LIMSI-COT, and KULeuven-LIIR) had higher precisions, the recall gap from UTHealth to the next system was large (0.203 in phase 1 and 0.088 in phase 2) and thus UTHealth had the best F_1 in both phases (0.479 in phase 1, 0.573 in phase 2).

Compared to human agreement, UTHealth and UtahBMI exceeded inter-annotator agreement on relations to the document time (while still leaving a gap of 0.088 to the annotator-adjudicator agreement), but no participant system was near the human agreement for narrative containers (a gap of 0.078 from inter-annotator agreement and a gap of 0.244 from annotator-adjudicator agreement). For relations to the document time, the 0.088 gap between systems and annotator-adjudicator agreement is slightly larger than the 0.059 of Clinical TempEval 2015, but for narrative container relations the 0.244 gap is much smaller than the 0.412 of Clinical TempEval 2015. As with other tasks, human agreement is higher this year (0.844 and 0.817 in 2016 vs. 0.761 and 0.672 in 2015), which may explain the larger gap for document time relations. The smaller gap for narrative container relations despite the increased human agreement suggests that major improvements have been made to the systems for this task.

9   Discussion

The results of Clinical TempEval 2016 suggest that current state-of-the-art systems are close to solving most event and time related tasks. For all of these tasks, the gap between system performance and human performance was less than 0.05, and for half the tasks (time spans, event spans, event degree, event type) it was 0.025 or less.

The temporal relation tasks were more difficult. Systems trying to predict the temporal relation between an event and the time at which the document was written lagged about 0.09 behind human performance. And systems trying to predict narrative containers (whether one event or time contains another) lagged about 0.25 behind human performance, even when provided human-annotated events and times.

Nonetheless, the latter result was a major improvement over Clinical TempEval 2015, where the gap on narrative containers was more than 0.4.

While there was variability across the subtasks in the rankings of teams, UTHealth and UtahBMI were always at the top of the lists. Both of these systems relied on structured learning models (UTHealth used HMM support vector machines; UtahBMI used conditional random fields) with a wide variety of features (lexical, morphological, syntactic, and many others). We can thus infer that such approaches hold promise for temporal information extraction. However, these two teams were also among the first to make it through the data use agreement process, so their success may in part reflect the advantage of having more time for experimentation and feature engineering on the training data.

Overall, Clinical TempEval 2016 represented a major step forward from Clinical TempEval 2015. It saw a much greater breadth of participating systems (14 teams in 2016 vs. 3 teams in 2015), with the top systems maintaining 2015's high performance on the event and time tasks, while making major progress on the harder temporal relation tasks. Future plans for Clinical TempEval target the robustness of these systems: instead of testing on only colon cancer notes from the Mayo Clinic (the same domain as the training set), systems will be tested on other types of medical conditions and notes from other institutions.

Acknowledgements

The project described was supported in part by R01LM010090 (THYME) from the National Library Of Medicine. The content is solely the responsibility of the authors and does not necessarily represent the official views of the National Institutes of Health.

References

Marcia Barros, André Lamúrias, Gonçalo Figueiró, Marta Antunes, Joana Teixeira, Alexandre Pinheiro, and Francisco Couto. 2016. ULISBOA at SemEval-2016 Task 12: Extractions of temporal expressions, clinical events and relations using IBEnt. In *Proceedings of the 10th International Workshop on Semantic Evaluation (SemEval 2016)*, San Diego, California, June. Association for Computational Linguistics.

Steven Bethard, Leon Derczynski, Guergana Savova, James Pustejovsky, and Marc Verhagen. 2015.

Semeval-2015 task 6: Clinical tempeval. In *Proceedings of the 9th International Workshop on Semantic Evaluation (SemEval 2015)*, pages 806–814, Denver, Colorado, June. Association for Computational Linguistics.

Tommaso Caselli and Roser Morante. 2016. VUACLTL at SemEval-2016 Task 12: A crf pipeline to clinical temporal. In *Proceedings of the 10th International Workshop on Semantic Evaluation (SemEval 2016)*, San Diego, California, June. Association for Computational Linguistics.

Wei-Te Chen and Will Styler. 2013. Anafora: A web-based general purpose annotation tool. In *Proceedings of the 2013 NAACL HLT Demonstration Session*, pages 14–19, Atlanta, Georgia, June. Association for Computational Linguistics.

Veera Raghavendra Chikka. 2016. CDE-IIITH at SemEval-2016 Task 12: Extraction of temporal information from clinical documents using machine learning techniques. In *Proceedings of the 10th International Workshop on Semantic Evaluation (SemEval 2016)*, San Diego, California, June. Association for Computational Linguistics.

Arman Cohan, Kevin Meurer, and Nazli Goharian. 2016. GUIR at SemEval-2016 Task 12: Temporal information extraction from clinical narratives. In *Proceedings of the 10th International Workshop on Semantic Evaluation (SemEval 2016)*, San Diego, California, June. Association for Computational Linguistics.

Jason Fries. 2016. Brundlefly at SemEval-2016 Task 12: Recurrent neural networks vs. joint inference for clinical temporal information extraction. In *Proceedings of the 10th International Workshop on Semantic Evaluation (SemEval 2016)*, San Diego, California, June. Association for Computational Linguistics.

Cyril Grouin and Véronique Moriceau. 2016. LIMSI at SemEval-2016 Task 12: machine-learning and temporal information to identify clinical events and time expressions. In *Proceedings of the 10th International Workshop on Semantic Evaluation (SemEval 2016)*, San Diego, California, June. Association for Computational Linguistics.

Charlotte Hansart, Damien De Meyere, Patrick Watrin, André Bittar, and Cédrick Fairon. 2016. Cental at SemEval-2016 Task 12: A linguistically fed CRF model for medical and temporal information extraction. In *Proceedings of the 10th International Workshop on Semantic Evaluation (SemEval 2016)*, San Diego, California, June. Association for Computational Linguistics.

Hee-Jin Lee, Hua Xu, Jingqi Wang, Yaoyun Zhang, Sungrim Moon, Jun Xu, and Yonghui Wu. 2016. UTHealth at SemEval-2016 Task 12: Temporal information extraction from clinical notes - uthealth's system for the 2016 clinical tempeval challenge. In *Proceedings of the 10th International Workshop on Semantic Evaluation (SemEval 2016)*, San Diego, California, June. Association for Computational Linguistics.

Artuur Leeuwenberg and Marie-Francine Moens. 2016. KULeuven-LIIR at SemEval-2016 Task 12: Detecting narrative containment in clinical records. In *Proceedings of the 10th International Workshop on Semantic Evaluation (SemEval 2016)*, San Diego, California, June. Association for Computational Linguistics.

Peng Li and Heng Huang. 2016. UTA_MLNLP at SemEval-2016 Task 12. In *Proceedings of the 10th International Workshop on Semantic Evaluation (SemEval 2016)*, San Diego, California, June. Association for Computational Linguistics.

Chen Lin, Dmitriy Dligach, Timothy A Miller, Steven Bethard, and Guergana K Savova. 2015. Multilayered temporal modeling for the clinical domain. *Journal of the American Medical Informatics Association*.

Christopher Manning, Mihai Surdeanu, John Bauer, Jenny Finkel, Steven Bethard, and David McClosky. 2014. The Stanford CoreNLP natural language processing toolkit. In *Proceedings of 52nd Annual Meeting of the Association for Computational Linguistics: System Demonstrations*, pages 55–60, Baltimore, Maryland, June. Association for Computational Linguistics.

James Pustejovsky and Amber Stubbs. 2011. Increasing informativeness in temporal annotation. In *Proceedings of the 5th Linguistic Annotation Workshop*, pages 152–160, Portland, Oregon, USA, June. Association for Computational Linguistics.

Sarath P R, Manikandan R, and Yoshiki Niwa. 2016. Hitachi at SemEval-2016 Task 12: Extraction of temporal information for the 2016 clinical tempeval challenge. In *Proceedings of the 10th International Workshop on Semantic Evaluation (SemEval 2016)*, San Diego, California, June. Association for Computational Linguistics.

Jannik Strötgen and Michael Gertz. 2013. Multilingual and cross-domain temporal tagging. *Language Resources and Evaluation*, 47(2):269–298.

William F. Styler, IV, Steven Bethard, Sean Finan, Martha Palmer, Sameer Pradhan, Piet de Groen, Brad Erickson, Timothy Miller, Chen Lin, Guergana Savova, and James Pustejovsky. 2014a. Temporal annotation in the clinical domain. *Transactions of the Association for Computational Linguistics*, 2:143–154.

William F. Styler, IV, Guergana Savova, Martha Palmer, James Pustejovsky, Tim O'Gorman, and Piet C. de Groen. 2014b. THYME annotation guidelines, 2.

Weiyi Sun, Anna Rumshisky, and Ozlem Uzuner. 2013. Evaluating temporal relations in clinical text: 2012 i2b2 challenge. *Journal of the American Medical Informatics Association*, 20(5):806–813.

Julien Tourille, Olivier Ferret, Aurélie Névéol, and Xavier Tannier. 2016. LIMSI-COT at SemEval-2016 Task 12: Temporal relation identification for the clinical tempeval challenge. In *Proceedings of the 10th International Workshop on Semantic Evaluation (SemEval 2016)*, San Diego, California, June. Association for Computational Linguistics.

Naushad UzZaman and James Allen. 2011. Temporal evaluation. In *Proceedings of the 49th Annual Meeting of the Association for Computational Linguistics: Human Language Technologies*, pages 351–356, Portland, Oregon, USA, June. Association for Computational Linguistics.

Naushad UzZaman, Hector Llorens, Leon Derczynski, James Allen, Marc Verhagen, and James Pustejovsky. 2013. SemEval-2013 Task 1: TempEval-3: Evaluating Time Expressions, Events, and Temporal Relations. In *Second Joint Conference on Lexical and Computational Semantics (*SEM), Volume 2: Proceedings of the Seventh International Workshop on Semantic Evaluation (SemEval 2013)*, pages 1–9, Atlanta, Georgia, USA, June. Association for Computational Linguistics.

Sumithra Velupillai and Stephane Meystre. 2016. UtahBMI at SemEval-2016 Task 12: Extracting temporal information from clinical text. In *Proceedings of the 10th International Workshop on Semantic Evaluation (SemEval 2016)*, San Diego, California, June. Association for Computational Linguistics.

Marc Verhagen, Robert Gaizauskas, Frank Schilder, Mark Hepple, Graham Katz, and James Pustejovsky. 2007. SemEval-2007 Task 15: TempEval Temporal Relation Identification. In *Proceedings of the Fourth International Workshop on Semantic Evaluations (SemEval-2007)*, pages 75–80, Prague, Czech Republic, June. Association for Computational Linguistics.

Marc Verhagen, Roser Sauri, Tommaso Caselli, and James Pustejovsky. 2010. SemEval-2010 Task 13: TempEval-2. In *Proceedings of the 5th International Workshop on Semantic Evaluation*, pages 57–62, Uppsala, Sweden, July. Association for Computational Linguistics.

SemEval-2016 Task 8: Meaning Representation Parsing

Jonathan May
Information Sciences Institute
University of Southern California
jonmay@isi.edu

Abstract

In this report we summarize the results of the
SemEval 2016 Task 8: Meaning Representation Parsing. Participants were asked to generate Abstract Meaning Representation (AMR)
(Banarescu et al., 2013) graphs for a set of
English sentences in the news and discussion
forum domains. Eleven sites submitted valid
systems. The availability of state-of-the-art
baseline systems was a key factor in lowering the bar to entry; many submissions relied
on CAMR (Wang et al., 2015b; Wang et al.,
2015a) as a baseline system and added extensions to it to improve scores. The evaluation
set was quite difficult to parse, particularly due
to creative approaches to word representation
in the web forum portion. The top scoring systems scored 0.62 F1 according to the Smatch
(Cai and Knight, 2013) evaluation heuristic.
We show some sample sentences along with
a comparison of system parses and perform
quantitative ablative studies.

1 Introduction

Abstract Meaning Representation (AMR) is a compact, readable, whole-sentence semantic annotation (Banarescu et al., 2013). It includes entity
identification and typing, PropBank semantic roles
(Kingsbury and Palmer, 2002), individual entities
playing multiple roles, as well as treatments of
modality, negation, etc. AMR abstracts in numerous
ways, e.g., by assigning the same conceptual structure to *fear* (v), *fear* (n), and *afraid* (adj). Figure 1
gives an example.

With the recent public release of a sizeable corpus of English/AMR pairs (LDC2014T12), there has

```
(f / fear-01
   :polarity "-"
   :ARG0 ( s / soldier )
   :ARG1 ( d / die-01
          :ARG1  s ))
```

The soldier was not afraid of dying.
The soldier was not afraid to die.
The soldier did not fear death.

Figure 1: An Abstract Meaning Representation
(AMR) with several English renderings. Example
borrowed from Pust et al. (2015).

been substantial interest in creating parsers to recover this formalism from plain text. Several parsers
were released in the past couple of years (Flanigan et
al., 2014; Wang et al., 2015b; Werling et al., 2015;
Wang et al., 2015a; Artzi et al., 2015; Pust et al.,
2015). This body of work constitutes many diverse
and interesting scientific contributions, but it is difficult to adequately determine which parser is numerically superior, due to heterogeneous evaluation decisions and the lack of a controlled blind evaluation.
The purpose of this task, therefore, was to provide a
competitive environment in which to determine one
winner and award a trophy to said winner.

2 Training Data

LDC released a new corpus of AMRs
(LDC2015E86), created as part of the DARPA
DEFT program, in August of 2015. The new corpus, which was annotated by teams at SDL, LDC,
and the University of Colorado, and supervised by
Ulf Hermjakob at USC/ISI, is an extension of pre-

Proceedings of SemEval-2016, pages 1063–1073,
San Diego, California, June 16-17, 2016. ©2016 Association for Computational Linguistics

vious releases (LDC2014E41 and LDC2014T12). It contains 19,572 sentences (subsuming, in turn, the 18,779 AMRs from LDC2014E41 and the 13,051 AMRs from LDC2014T12), partitioned into training, development, and test splits, from a variety of news and discussion forum sources.

The AMRs in this corpus have changed somewhat from their counterparts in LDC2014E41, consistent with the evolution of the AMR standard. They now contain wikification via the `:wiki` attribute, they use new (as of July 2015) PropBank framesets that are unified across parts of speech, they have been deepened in a number of ways, and various corrections have been applied.

3   Other Resources

We made the following resources available to participants:

- The aforementioned AMR corpus (LDC2015E86), which included automatically generated AMR-English alignments over tokenized sentences.

- The tokenizer (from Ulf Hermjakob) used to produce the tokenized sentences in the training corpus.

- The AMR specification, used by annotators in producing the AMRs.[1]

- A deterministic, input-agnostic trivial baseline 'parser' courtesy of Ulf Hermjakob.

- The JAMR parser (Flanigan et al., 2014) as a strong baseline. We provided setup scripts to process the released training data but otherwise provided the parser as is.

- An unsupervised AMR-to-English aligner (Pourdamghani et al., 2014).

- The same Smatch (Cai and Knight, 2013) scoring script used in the evaluation.

- A Python AMR manipulation library, from Nathan Schneider.

---

[1] https://github.com/kevincrawfordknight/amr-guidelines/blob/master/amr.md.

Description	Code	Sents
Agence France-Presse news	afp	23
Associated Press news	apw	52
BOLT discussion forum	bolt	257
New York Times news	nyt	471
Weblog	web1	232
Xinhua news	xin	18

Table 1: Split by domain of evaluation data.

System	Prec.	Rec.	F1
Brandeis/cemantix.org/RPI	0.57	0.67	**0.62**
CLIP@UMD	0.40	0.48	0.44
CMU	0.53	0.61	0.56
CU-NLP	0.58	0.63	0.61
DynamicPower	0.34	0.40	0.37
ICL-HD	0.54	0.67	0.60
M2L	0.54	0.66	0.60
RIGA	0.57	0.68	**0.62**
Meaning Factory	0.46	0.48	0.47
UCL+Sheffield	0.56	0.65	0.60
UofR	0.49	0.51	0.50
Determ. baseline	0.23	0.26	0.24
JAMR baseline	0.43	0.58	0.50

Table 2: Main Results: Mean of five runs of Smatch 2.0.2 with five restarts per run is shown; Standard deviation of F1 was about 0.0002 per system.

4   Evaluation Data

For the specific purposes of this task, DEFT commissioned and LDC released an additional set of English sentences along with AMR annotations[2] that had not been previously seen. This blind evaluation set consists of 1,053 sentences in a roughly 50/50 discussion forum/newswire split. The distribution of sentences by source is shown in Table 1.

5   Task Definition

We deliberately chose a single, simple task. Participants were given English sentences and had to return an AMR graph (henceforth, 'an AMR') for each sentence. AMRs were scored against a gold AMR with the Smatch heuristic F1-derived tool and metric. Smatch (Cai and Knight, 2013) is calculated

---

[2] LDC2015R33 for just the sentences, and LDC2015R36 for sentences with their AMRs.

by matching instance, attribute, and relation tuples to a reference AMR (See Section 7.2). Since variable naming need not be globally consistent, heuristic hill-climbing is done to search for the best match in sub-exponential time. A trophy was given to the team with the highest Smatch score under consistent heuristic conditions.[3]

6 Participants and Results

11 teams participated in the task.[4] Their systems and scores are shown in Table 2. Below are brief descriptions of each of the various systems, based on summaries provided by the system authors. Readers are encouraged to consult individual system description papers for more details.

6.1 CAMR-based systems

A number of teams made use of the CAMR system from Wang et al. (2015a). These systems proved among the highest-scoring and had little variance from each other in terms of system score.

6.1.1 Brandeis / cemantix.org / RPI
(Wang et al., 2016)

This team, the originators of CAMR, started with their existing AMR parser and experimented with three sets of new features: 1) rich named entities, 2) a verbalization list, and 3) semantic role labels. They also used the RPI Wikifier to wikify the concepts in the AMR graph.

6.1.2 ICL-HD
(Brandt et al., 2016)

This team attempted to improve AMR parsing by exploiting preposition semantic role labeling information retrieved from a multi-layer feed-forward neural network. Prepositional semantics was included as features into CAMR. The inclusion of the features modified the behavior of CAMR when creating meaning representations triggered by prepositional semantics.

6.1.3 RIGA
(Barzdins and Gosko, 2016)

Besides developing a novel character-level neural translation based AMR parser, this team also

extended the Smatch scoring tool with the C6.0 rule-based classifier to produce a human-readable report on the error patterns frequency observed in the scored AMR graphs. They improved CAMR by adding to it a manually crafted wrapper fixing the identified CAMR parser errors. A small further gain was achieved by combining the neural and CAMR+wrapper parsers in an ensemble.

6.1.4 M2L
(Puzikov et al., 2016)

This team attempted to improve upon CAMR by using a feed-forward neural network classification algorithm. They also experimented with various ways of enriching CAMR's feature set. Unlike ICL-HD and RIGA they were not able to benefit from feed-forward neural networks, but were able to benefit from feature enhancements.

6.2 Other Approaches

The other teams either improved upon their existing AMR parsers, converted existing semantic parsing tools and pipelines into AMR, or constructed AMR parsers from scratch with novel techniques.

6.2.1 CLIP@UMD
(Rao et al., 2016)

This team developed a novel technique for AMR parsing that uses the Learning to Search (L2S) algorithm. They decomposed the AMR prediction problem into three problems—that of predicting the concepts, predicting the root, and predicting the relations between the predicted concepts. Using L2S allowed them to model the learning of concepts and relations in a unified framework which aims to minimize the loss over the entire predicted structure, as opposed to minimizing the loss over concepts and relations in two separate stages.

6.2.2 CMU
(Flanigan et al., 2016)

This team's entry is a set of improvements to JAMR (Flanigan et al., 2014). The improvements are: a novel training loss function for structured prediction, new sources for concepts, improved features, and improvements to the rule-based aligner in Flanigan et al. (2014). The overall architecture of the system and the decoding algorithms for con-

---

[3]Four random restarts.

[4]A twelfth team, CUCLEAR, participated but produced invalid AMRs that could not be scored.

	Full AMR	Instances	Attributes	Relations
Brandeis/cemantix.org/RPI	**0.6195**	0.7433	0.6043	0.5494
CLIP@UMD	0.4370	0.6097	0.4013	0.3712
CMU	0.5636	0.7288	0.5433	0.4960
CU-NLP	0.6060	0.7338	0.6141	0.5323
DynamicPower	0.3706	0.4088	0.3560	0.3955
ICL-HD	0.6005	0.7161	0.5361	**0.5517**
M2L	0.5952	0.7245	0.5099	0.5378
RIGA	**0.6196**	0.7298	**0.6288**	0.5507
Meaning Factory	0.4702	0.5596	0.5400	0.4120
UCL+Sheffield	0.5983	**0.7545**	0.5914	0.5155
UofR	0.4985	0.7054	0.5586	0.4203
Determ. baseline	0.2440	0.2269	0.0014	0.3556
JAMR baseline	0.4965	0.6970	0.3089	0.4562

Table 3: Ablation of instances, attributes, and relations.

cept identification and relation identification are unchanged from Flanigan et al. (2014).

6.2.3 Dynamic Power
(Butler, 2016)

No use was made of the training data provided by the task. Instead, existing components were combined to form a pipeline able to take raw sentences as input and output meaning representations. The components are a part-of-speech tagger and parser trained on the Penn Parsed Corpus of Modern British English to produce syntactic parse trees, a semantic role labeler, and a named entity recognizer to supplement obtained parse trees with word sense, functional and named entity information. This information is passed into an adapted Tarskian satisfaction relation for a Dynamic Semantics that is used to transform a syntactic parse into a predicate logic based meaning representation, followed by conversion to the required Penman notation.

6.2.4 The Meaning Factory
(Bjerva et al., 2016)

This team employed an existing open-domain semantic parser, Boxer (Curran et al., 2007), which produces semantic representations based on Discourse Representation Theory. As the meaning representations produced by Boxer are considerably different from AMRs, the team used a hybrid conversion method to map Boxer's output to AMRs. This process involves lexical adaptation, a conversion from DRT-representations to AMR, as well as post-processing of the output.

6.2.5 UCL+Sheffield
(Goodman et al., 2016)

This team developed a novel transition-based parsing algorithm using exact imitation learning, in which the parser learns a statistical model by imitating the actions of an expert on the training data. They used the imitation learning algorithm DAGGER to improve the performance, and applied an alpha-bound as a simple noise reduction technique.

6.2.6 UofR
(Peng and Gildea, 2016)

This team applied a synchronous-graph-grammar-based approach for string-to-AMR parsing. They applied Markov Chain Monte Carlo (MCMC) algorithms to learn Synchronous Hyperedge Replacement Grammar (SHRG) rules from a forest that represents likely derivations consistent with a fixed string-to-graph alignment (extracted using an automatic aligner). They make an analogy of string-to-AMR parsing to the task of phrase-based machine translation and came up with an efficient algorithm to learn graph grammars from string-graph pairs. They proposed an effective approximation strategy to resolve the complexity issue of graph compositions. Then they used the Earley algorithm with cube-pruning for AMR parsing given new sentences and the learned SHRG.

6.2.7 CU-NLP
(Foland and Martin, 2016)

This parser does not rely on a syntactic pre-parse, or heavily engineered features, and uses five recurrent neural networks as the key architectural components for estimating AMR graph structure.

7 Result Ablations

We conduct several ablations to attempt to empirically determine what aspects of the AMR parsing task were more or less difficult for the various systems.

7.1 Impact of Wikification

The AMR standard has recently been expanded to include wikification and the data used in this task reflected that expansion. Since this is a rather recent change to the standard and requires some kind of global external knowledge of, at a minimum, Wikipedia's ontology, we suspected performance on `:wiki` attributes would suffer. To measure the effect of wikification, we performed two ablation experiments, the results of which are in Figure 2. In the first ("no wiki"), we removed `:wiki` attributes and their values from reference and system sets before scoring. In the second ("bad wiki"), we replaced the value of all `:wiki` attributes with a dummy entry to artificially create systems that did not get any wikification correct.

The "no wiki" ablations show that the inclusion of wikification into the AMR standard had a very small impact on overall system scores. No system's score changed by more than 0.01 when wikification was removed, indicating that systems appear to wikify about as well as they handle the rest of AMR's attributes. The "bad wiki" ablations show performance drop when wikification is corrupted of around 0.02 to 0.03 for six of the systems, and a negligible performance drop for the remaining systems. This result indicates that the systems with a performance drop are doing a fairly good job at wikification.

7.2 Performance on different parts of the AMR

In this set of ablations we examine systems' relative performance on correctly identifying *instances*, *attributes*, and *relations* of the AMRs. Instances are the labeled nodes of the AMR. In the example AMR of Figure 1, the instances are `fear-01`, `soldier`, and `die-01`. To match an instance one must simply match the instance's label.[5]

Attributes are labeled string properties of nodes. In the example AMR, there is a **polarity** attribute attached to the `fear-01` instance with a value of "-." There is also an implicit attribute of "TOP" attached to the root node of the graph, with the node's instance as the attribute value. To match an attribute one must match the attribute's label and value, and the attribute's instance must be aligned with the corresponding instance in the reference graph.

Relations are labeled edges between two instances. In the example AMR, the relations (`f`, `s`, `ARG0`), (`f`, `d`, `ARG1`), and (`d`, `s`, `ARG1`) exist. To match a relation, the labeled edge between two nodes of the hypothesis must match the label of the edge between the correspondingly aligned nodes of the reference graph.

It should not be surprising that systems tend to perform best at instance matching and worst at relation matching. Note, however, that the best performing systems on instances and relations were not the overall best performing systems. Ablation results can be seen in Table 3.

7.3 Performance on different data sources

As discussed in Section 8, less formal sentences, sentences with misspellings, and sentences with non-standard representations of meaning were the hardest to parse. We ablate the results by domain of origin in Table 4. While the strongest-performing systems tended to perform best across ablations, we note that the machine-translated and informal corpora were overall the hardest sections to parse.

8 Qualitative Comparison

In this section we examine some of the sentences that the systems found particularly easy or difficult to parse.

---

[5]That is, correctly generating a multi-set of instances with the same labels as those in the reference is sufficient for a perfect score. The task of correctly generating instances that are in proper relation to each other is handled by the relations.

8.1 Easiest Sentences

The easiest sentence to parse in the eval corpus was the sentence "I was tempted."[6]

It has a gold AMR of:

```
(t / tempt-01
      :ARG1 (i / i))
```

The mean score for this sentence was 0.977. All submitted systems except one parsed it perfectly.

Another sentence that was quite easy to parse was the sentence "David Cameron is the prime minister of the United Kingdom."[7] Two systems parsed it perfectly and a third omitted wikification but was otherwise perfect. Figure 3 shows a detailed comparison of each system's performance on the sentence. In general we see that shorter sentences from the familiar and formal news domain are parsed best by the submitted systems.

8.2 Hardest Sentences

Five sentences were unable to be parsed in any way by any system.[8] They are shown below, along with their AMRs:

```
E-mail: mward(at)statesman.com.
(e / email-address-entity
  :value "mward@statesman.com")
x
(s / string-entity :value "x")
*sigh*
(s / sigh-01)
Yes_it_is.
(y / yes)
M E D I A A D V I S O R Y
(a / advise-01
      :ARG1 (m / media))
```

Data noise was another confounding factor. In the next example,[9] which had an average score of 0.17, parsers were confused both by the misspelling ("lie" for "like") and by the quoted title, which all systems except UCL+Sheffield, tried to parse for meaning.

```
Why not a title lie "School Officials Screw over Rape Victim?"
(t / title-01 :polarity -
   :ARG1-of (r / resemble-01
      :ARG2 (t2 / title-01 :wiki "A_Rape_on_Campus"
               :name (n2 / name :op1 "School" :op2 "Officials"
                               :op3 "Screw" :op4 "Over"
                               :op5 "Rape" :op6 "Victim")))
   :ARG1-of (c / cause-01
      :ARG0 (a / amr-unknown))))
```

We note that all of these difficult sentences are not conceptually hard for humans to parse. Humans have far less difficulty in resolving errors or processing non-standard tokenization than do computers.

9 There Can Be Only One?

We intended to award a single trophy to the single best system, according to the narrow evaluation conditions (balanced F1 via Smatch 2.0.2 with 5 restarts, to two decimal places). However, the top two systems, Brandeis/cemantix.org/RPI and RIGA, scored identically according to that metric. Hoping to elicit some consistent difference between the systems, we ran Smatch with 20 restarts, looked at four decimal places, and re-ran five times. Each system scored a mean of 0.6214 with standard deviation of 0.00013. We thus capitulate in the face of overwhelming statistics and award the inaugural trophy to both teams, equally.[10]

10 Conclusion

The results of this competition and the interest in participation in it demonstrate that AMR parsing is a difficult, competitive task. The large number of systems using released code lowered the bar to entry significantly but may have led to a narrowing of diversity in approaches. Low-level irregularities such as creative tokenization and misspellings befuddled the systems. We hope to conduct another AMR parsing competition in the future, in the biomedical domain, and also conduct a generation competition.

---

[6] nyt_eng_20130426_0143.23.

[7] bolt-eng-DF-200-192446-3811676_0094.5.

[8] nyt_eng_20131029_0042.18, web1-eng-DF-225-195996-5376307_0002.3, web1-eng-DF-233-195474-1207335_0002.1, web1-eng-DF-233-195474-1207335_0010.2, and web1-eng-DF-183-195729-5441907_0001_3.

[9] bolt-eng-DF-170-181122-8787556_0049_6.

---

[10] Funding for trophies graciously provided by the Jelinek-Mercer Institute for Semantic Translation.

	With wiki	No wiki	Bad wiki
Brandeis/cemantix.org/RPI	0.6195	0.6264	0.5991
CLIP@UMD	0.4370	0.4477	0.4369
CMU	0.5636	0.5660	0.5337
CU-NLP	0.6060	0.5948	0.5813
DynamicPower	0.3706	0.3790	0.3704
ICL-HD	0.6005	0.6157	0.6004
M2L	0.5952	0.6092	0.5954
RIGA	0.6196	0.6247	0.6042
Meaning Factory	0.4702	0.4718	0.4512
UCL+Sheffield	0.5983	0.6077	0.5812
UofR	0.4985	0.4887	0.4990

(a) Comparison of regular systems ('With wiki'), systems and references with all wikification removed ('No wiki'), and systems with wikification corrupted ('Bad wiki').

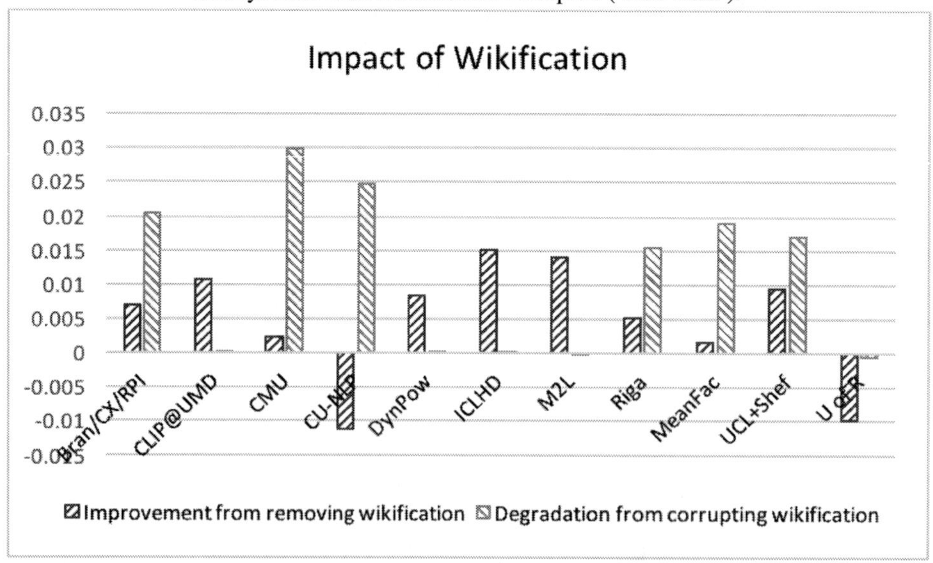

(b) Removing wikification from hypothesis and reference raises scores by less than 0.01 Smatch in seven systems. Corrupting wikification in the hypothesis lowers scores by 0.015 or more in six systems.

Figure 2: Ablations of `:wiki` attribute.

	afp	apw	bolt	nyt	web1	xin	all
# Sentences	23	52	257	471	232	18	1053
Brandeis/cemantix.org/RPI	0.6287	**0.6829**	**0.6052**	0.6285	0.5933	0.5703	**0.6195**
CLIP@UMD	0.4334	0.4723	0.4211	0.446	0.4223	0.3879	0.437
CMU	0.6303	0.6747	0.5954	0.5354	0.572	0.57	0.5636
CU-NLP	0.6136	0.6510	0.5917	0.6088	0.5974	**0.6181**	0.6060
DynamicPower	0.3249	0.3847	0.3765	0.3715	0.3702	0.3366	0.3706
ICL-HD	0.6136	0.6572	0.581	0.6111	0.573	0.5615	0.6005
M2L	0.5987	0.6409	0.5788	0.603	0.5789	0.5456	0.5952
RIGA	**0.6611**	0.6715	0.6004	**0.6292**	**0.598**	0.5603	**0.6196**
The Meaning Factory	0.5019	0.5542	0.4679	0.4611	0.4566	0.5281	0.4702
UCL+Sheffield	0.611	0.6672	0.5942	0.596	0.5891	0.5936	0.5983
UofR	0.5248	0.5475	0.5022	0.4938	0.4908	0.5039	0.4985
mean	0.5709	0.6132	0.5493	0.5538	0.5419	0.5388	0.5542
Determ. baseline	0.2791	0.2799	0.2095	0.2589	0.2279	0.2562	0.2440
JAMR baseline	0.5422	0.5714	0.5302	0.4722	0.5027	0.5049	0.4965

Table 4: Ablation of Smatch scores by text source. AP wire ('apw') data was the easiest to parse, Web forum ('web1') and Xinhua ('xin') were the hardest.

```
(h / have-org-role-91
  :ARG0 (p / person
      :wiki "David_Cameron"
      :name (n / name :op1 "David"
                      :op2 "Cameron"))
  :ARG1 (c / country
      :wiki "United_Kingdom"
      :name (n2 / name :op1 "United"
                       :op2 "Kingdom"))
  :ARG2 (m / minister
      :mod (p2 / prime)))
```

(a) Gold / CMU / RIGA (1.0)
(M2L = 0.95; missing wiki)

```
(x6 / have-org-role-91
  :ARG0 (x1 / person
      :wiki "David_Cameron"
      :name (n / name :op1 "David"
                      :op2 "Cameron"))
  :ARG1 (x9 / country
      :wiki "United_Kingdom"
      :name (n1 / name :op1 "United"
                       :op2 "Kingdom"))
  :ARG2 (m / minister)
  :mod (x5 / prime))
```

(b) Brandeis / cemantix.org / RPI (0.95)
(prime not mod of minister)

```
(c3 / minister
  :mod (c1 / prime)
  :ARG0 (c2 / have-org-role-91
            :ARG2 c3)
  :mod (c0 / person
      :name (n0 / name :op1 "David"
                       :op2 "Cameron"))
  :ARG1 (c4 / country
      :name (n1 / name :op1 "United"
                       :op2 "Kingdom")))
```

(c) CLIP@UMD (0.77)
(minister is root; wrong ARG0 direction, no
wiki)

```
( EVENT-4 / copula
  :ARG0 ( PERSON-david_cameron / PERSON
      :name ( n-1 / name :op1 "david"
                         :op2 "cameron"))
  :ARG1 ( ENTITY-1 / minister
      :mod ( ATTRIB-3 / prime)
      :poss ( LOCATION-united_kingdom / LOCATION
      :name ( n-2 / name :op1 "united"
                         :op2 "kingdom"))))
```

(d) DynamicPower (.68)
(wrong frame, no wiki)

```
(x1 / person
  :name (n / name :op1 "David"
                  :op2 "Cameron")
  :ARG0-of (x6 / have-org-role-91
      :ARG2 (m / minister
          :mod (x5 / prime))
      :ARG1 (x9 / country
          :name (n1 / name :op1 "United"
                           :op2 "Kingdom"))))
```

(e) ICL-HD (.89)
(no wiki, wrong root)

```
(c / country
  :ARG0-of (h / have-org-role-91
      :ARG1 (p / person
          :name (n / name :op1 "David"
                          :op2 "Cameron")
          :wiki "David_Cameron")
      :ARG2 (m / minister
          :mod (p2 / prime)))
  :name (n2 / name :op1 "United"
                   :op2 "Kingdom")
  :wiki "United_Kingdom")
```

(f) UofR (.85)
(ARG swap, wrong root)

```
(e1 / thing
  :name (n5 / name :op1 "prime"
                   :op2 "minister")
  :wiki "Prime_Minister_of_the_United_Kingdom"
  :domain (x1 / person
      :name (n3 / name :op1 "david"
                       :op2 "cameron")
      :wiki "David_Cameron" )
  :poss (x2 / country
      :name (n7 / name :op1 "united"
                       :op2 "kingdom")
      :wiki "United_Kingdom" ))
```

(g) The Meaning Factory (.59)
(wrong frame, errant wiki)

```
( n / person
  :wiki "-"
  :name ( m / name :op1 "David"
                   :op2 "Cameron")
  :UNKNOWN ( f / minister
      :mod ( e / prime )
      :mod ( l / country
          :wiki "United_Kingdom"
          :name ( k / name :op1 "United"
                           :op2 "Kingdom"))))
```

(h) UCL+Sheffield (.74)
(no frame, wiki missing, wrong relations)

```
(n1.2 / have-org-role-91
  :ARG0 (n1.1000 / person
      :wiki "David_Cameron"
      :name (n1.0 / name :op1 david
                         :op2 cameron ) )
  :ARG2 (n1.5 / minister
      :mod (n1.4 / prime )
      :ARG2-of (n1.6 / have-org-role-91
          :ARG1 (n1.1008 / country
              :wiki "United_Kingdom"
              :name (n1.8 / name :op1 united
                                 :op2 kingdom )))))
```

(i) CU-NLP (.71)
(capitalization, extra role, attachment)

Figure 3: A comparison of parser performance on the sentence "David Cameron is the Prime Minister of the United Kingdom."

Acknowledgments

Many thanks to the AMR creation team: Kira Griffitt, Ulf Hermjakob, Kevin Knight, and Martha Palmer. Thanks also to the SemEval organizers: Steven Bethard, Daniel Cer, Marine Carpuat, David Jurgens, Preslav Nakov, and Torsten Zesch. We also gratefully acknowledge the participating teams' efforts. This work was sponsored by DARPA DEFT (FA8750-13-2-0045).

Erratum

Subsequent to the camera-ready deadline for this document it was determined that changes between Smatch versions 2.0 and 2.0.2 led to quoted and non-quoted items in AMRs being judged non-identical; in previous versions they were judged identical and the change in 2.0.2 was not intended to alter this behavior. CU-NLP saw a significant increase in overall F1 as a result of the fix, while the other systems were not affected. Thanks to William Foland for identifying the bug. This version also fixes some attribution errors.

References

Yoav Artzi, Kenton Lee, and Luke Zettlemoyer. 2015. Broad-coverage CCG semantic parsing with AMR. In *Proceedings of the 2015 Conference on Empirical Methods in Natural Language Processing*, pages 1699–1710, Lisbon, Portugal, September. Association for Computational Linguistics.

Laura Banarescu, Claire Bonial, Shu Cai, Madalina Georgescu, Kira Griffitt, Ulf Hermjakob, Kevin Knight, Philipp Koehn, Martha Palmer, and Nathan Schneider. 2013. Abstract Meaning Representation for sembanking. In *Proceedings of the 7th Linguistic Annotation Workshop and Interoperability with Discourse*, pages 178–186, Sofia, Bulgaria, August. Association for Computational Linguistics.

Guntis Barzdins and Didzis Gosko. 2016. RIGA at SemEval-2016 task 8: Impact of Smatch extensions and character-level neural translation on AMR parsing accuracy. In *Proceedings of the 10th International Workshop on Semantic Evaluation (SemEval 2016)*, San Diego, California, June. Association for Computational Linguistics.

Johannes Bjerva, Johan Bos, and Hessel Haagsma. 2016. The Meaning Factory at SemEval-2016 task 8: Producing AMRs with Boxer. In *Proceedings of the 10th International Workshop on Semantic Evaluation (SemEval 2016)*, San Diego, California, June. Association for Computational Linguistics.

Lauritz Brandt, David Grimm, Mengfei Zhou, and Yannick Versley. 2016. ICL-HD at SemEval-2016 task 8: Meaning representation parsing - augmenting AMR parsing with a preposition semantic role labeling neural network. In *Proceedings of the 10th International Workshop on Semantic Evaluation (SemEval 2016)*, San Diego, California, June. Association for Computational Linguistics.

Alastair Butler. 2016. DynamicPower at SemEval-2016 task 8: Processing syntactic parse trees with a dynamic semantics core. In *Proceedings of the 10th International Workshop on Semantic Evaluation (SemEval 2016)*, San Diego, California, June. Association for Computational Linguistics.

Shu Cai and Kevin Knight. 2013. Smatch: an evaluation metric for semantic feature structures. In *Proceedings of the 51st Annual Meeting of the Association for Computational Linguistics (Volume 2: Short Papers)*, pages 748–752, Sofia, Bulgaria, August. Association for Computational Linguistics.

James Curran, Stephen Clark, and Johan Bos. 2007. Linguistically motivated large-scale NLP with C&C and Boxer. In *Proceedings of the 45th Annual Meeting of the Association for Computational Linguistics Companion Volume Proceedings of the Demo and Poster Sessions*, pages 33–36, Prague, Czech Republic, June. Association for Computational Linguistics.

Jeffrey Flanigan, Sam Thomson, Jaime Carbonell, Chris Dyer, and Noah A. Smith. 2014. A discriminative graph-based parser for the Abstract Meaning Representation. In *Proceedings of the 52nd Annual Meeting of the Association for Computational Linguistics (Volume 1: Long Papers)*, pages 1426–1436, Baltimore, Maryland, June. Association for Computational Linguistics.

Jeffrey Flanigan, Chris Dyer, Noah A. Smith, and Jaime Carbonell. 2016. CMU at SemEval-2016 task 8: Graph-based AMR parsing with infinite ramp loss. In *Proceedings of the 10th International Workshop on Semantic Evaluation (SemEval 2016)*, San Diego, California, June. Association for Computational Linguistics.

William Foland and James H. Martin. 2016. CU-NLP at SemEval-2016 task 8: AMR parsing using LSTM-based recurrent neural networks. In *Proceedings of the 10th International Workshop on Semantic Evaluation (SemEval 2016)*, San Diego, California, June. Association for Computational Linguistics.

James Goodman, Andreas Vlachos, and Jason Naradowsky. 2016. UCL+Sheffield at SemEval-2016 task

8: Imitation learning for AMR parsing with an alphabound. In *Proceedings of the 10th International Workshop on Semantic Evaluation (SemEval 2016)*, San Diego, California, June. Association for Computational Linguistics.

Paul Kingsbury and Martha Palmer. 2002. From Treebank to Propbank. In *In Language Resources and Evaluation*.

Xiaochang Peng and Daniel Gildea. 2016. UofR at SemEval-2016 task 8: Learning synchronous hyperedge replacement grammar for AMR parsing. In *Proceedings of the 10th International Workshop on Semantic Evaluation (SemEval 2016)*, San Diego, California, June. Association for Computational Linguistics.

Nima Pourdamghani, Yang Gao, Ulf Hermjakob, and Kevin Knight. 2014. Aligning English strings with Abstract Meaning Representation graphs. In *Proceedings of the 2014 Conference on Empirical Methods in Natural Language Processing (EMNLP)*, pages 425–429, Doha, Qatar, October. Association for Computational Linguistics.

Michael Pust, Ulf Hermjakob, Kevin Knight, Daniel Marcu, and Jonathan May. 2015. Parsing English into Abstract Meaning Representation using syntax-based machine translation. In *Proceedings of the 2015 Conference on Empirical Methods in Natural Language Processing*, pages 1143–1154, Lisbon, Portugal, September. Association for Computational Linguistics.

Yevgeniy Puzikov, Daisuke Kawahara, and Sadao Kurohashi. 2016. M2L at SemEval-2016 task 8: AMR parsing with neural networks. In *Proceedings of the 10th International Workshop on Semantic Evaluation (SemEval 2016)*, San Diego, California, June. Association for Computational Linguistics.

Sudha Rao, Yogarshi Vyas, Hal Daumé III, and Philip Resnik. 2016. Clip@umd at SemEval-2016 task 8: Parser for Abstract Meaning Representation using learning to search. In *Proceedings of the 10th International Workshop on Semantic Evaluation (SemEval 2016)*, San Diego, California, June. Association for Computational Linguistics.

Chuan Wang, Nianwen Xue, and Sameer Pradhan. 2015a. Boosting transition-based AMR parsing with refined actions and auxiliary analyzers. In *Proceedings of the 53rd Annual Meeting of the Association for Computational Linguistics and the 7th International Joint Conference on Natural Language Processing (Volume 2: Short Papers)*, pages 857–862, Beijing, China, July. Association for Computational Linguistics.

Chuan Wang, Nianwen Xue, and Sameer Pradhan. 2015b. A transition-based algorithm for AMR parsing. In *Proceedings of the 2015 Conference of the North American Chapter of the Association for Computational Linguistics: Human Language Technologies*, pages 366–375, Denver, Colorado, May–June. Association for Computational Linguistics.

Chuan Wang, Nianwen Xue, Sameer Pradhan, Xiaoman Pan, and Heng Ji. 2016. CAMR at SemEval-2016 task 8: An extended transition-based AMR parser. In *Proceedings of the 10th International Workshop on Semantic Evaluation (SemEval 2016)*, San Diego, California, June. Association for Computational Linguistics.

Keenon Werling, Gabor Angeli, and Christopher D. Manning. 2015. Robust subgraph generation improves Abstract Meaning Representation parsing. In *Proceedings of the 53rd Annual Meeting of the Association for Computational Linguistics and the 7th International Joint Conference on Natural Language Processing (Volume 1: Long Papers)*, pages 982–991, Beijing, China, July. Association for Computational Linguistics.

SemEval-2016 Task 9: Chinese Semantic Dependency Parsing

Wanxiang Che[†]   **Yanqiu Shao**[‡]   **Ting Liu**[†]   **Yu Ding**[†]

[†]`{car, tliu, yding}@ir.hit.edu.cn`   [‡]`yqshao@blcu.edu.cn`
School of Computer Science and Technology   School of Information Science
Harbin Institute of Technology   Beijing Language and Culture University
Harbin, China, 150001   Beijing, China, 100083

Abstract

This paper describes the SemEval-2016 Shared Task 9: *Chinese semantic Dependency Parsing*. We extend the traditional tree-structured representation of Chinese sentence to directed acyclic graphs that can capture richer latent semantics, and the goal of this task is to identify such semantic structures from a corpus of Chinese sentences. We provide two distinguished corpora in the NEWS domain with 10,068 sentences and the TEXT-BOOKS domain with 14,793 sentences respectively. We will first introduce the motivation for this task, and then present the task in detail including data preparation, data format, task evaluation and so on. At last, we briefly describe the submitted systems and analyze these results.

1 Introduction

This task is a rerun of the task 5 at SemEval 2012 (Che et al., 2012), named Chinese semantic dependency parsing (SDP). In the previous task, we aimed at investigating "deep" semantic relations within sentences through tree-structured dependencies. As traditionally defined, syntactic dependency parsing results are connected trees defined over all words of a sentence and language-specific grammatical functions. On the contrary, in semantic dependency parsing, each head-dependent arc instead bears a semantic relation, rather than grammatical relation. In this way, semantic dependency parsing results can be used to answer questions directly, like *who did what to whom when and where*.

However, according to the *meaning-text linguistic theory* (Mel'čuk and Žolkovskij, 1965), a theoretical framework for the description of natural languages, it is said that trees are not sufficient to express the complete meaning of sentences in some cases, which has been proven undoubted in our practice of corpus annotation. This time, not only do we refine the easy-to-understand meaning representation in Chinese in order to decrease ambiguity or fuzzy boundary of semantic relations on the basis of Chinese linguistic knowledge, we extend the dependency structure to directed acyclic graphs that conform to the characteristics of Chinese, because Chinese is an parataxis language with flexible word orders, and rich latent information is hidden in facial words.

Figure 1 illustrates an example of semantic dependency graph. Here, "她 (she)" is the argument of "脸色 (face)" and at the same time it is an argument of "病 (disease)". Researchers in dependency parsing community realized dependency parsing restricted in a tree structure is still too shallow, so they explored semantic information beyond tree structure in task 8 at SemEval 2014 (Oepen et al., 2014) and task 18 at SemEval 2015 (Oepen et al., 2015). They provided data in similar structure with what we are going to provide, but in distinct semantic representation systems. Once again we propose this task to promote research that will lead to deeper understanding of Chinese sentences, and we believe that freely available and well annotated corpora which can be used as common testbed is necessary to promote research in data-driven statistical dependency parsing.

Proceedings of SemEval-2016, pages 1074–1080,
San Diego, California, June 16-17, 2016. ©2016 Association for Computational Linguistics

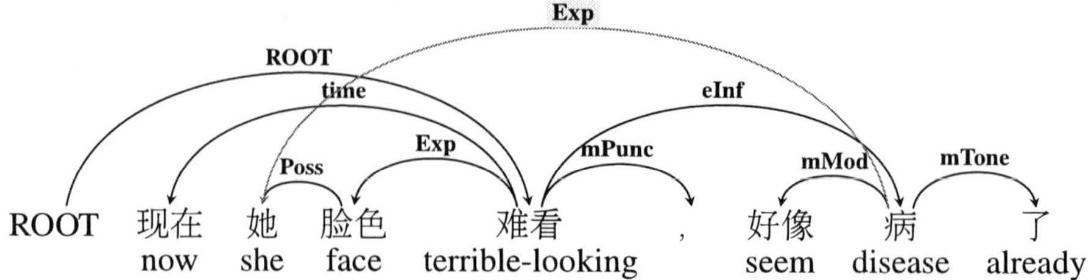

Figure 1: An example of our proposed DAG-based semantic dependency representation.

The rest of the paper is organized as follows. Section 2 gives an overview of semantic dependency parsing, with specific focus on the proposed DAG semantic representation. Section 3 describes the technical details of the task. Section 4 presents the participating systems, and Section 5 compares and analyzes the results. Finally, Section 6 concludes the paper.

2 Semantic Dependency Parsing

Given a complete sentence, semantic dependency parsing (SDP) aims at determining all the word pairs related to each other semantically and assigning specific predefined semantic relations. Semantic dependency analysis represents the meaning of sentences by a collection of dependency word pairs and their corresponding relations. This procedure survives from syntactic variations.

In this paper, we define a Chinese semantic dependency scheme based on Chinese-specific linguistic knowledge, which represents the meaning of sentences in graphic formats (Figure 1).

2.1 Structure of Chinese Semantic Dependency Graph

We used semantic dependency graphs to represent the meanings of sentences, which contain dependency relations between all the word pairs with direct semantic relations. Predicates includes most predicative constituents (i.e. most verbs and a small number of nouns and adjectives), and arguments are defined as all the possible participants in the real scene corresponding to a certain predicate (e.g. the eater, food, tool, location, time in the scene related to "eat"). One principle of building dependency arcs is to find arguments for predicates in content words preferentially because they are the ones that related

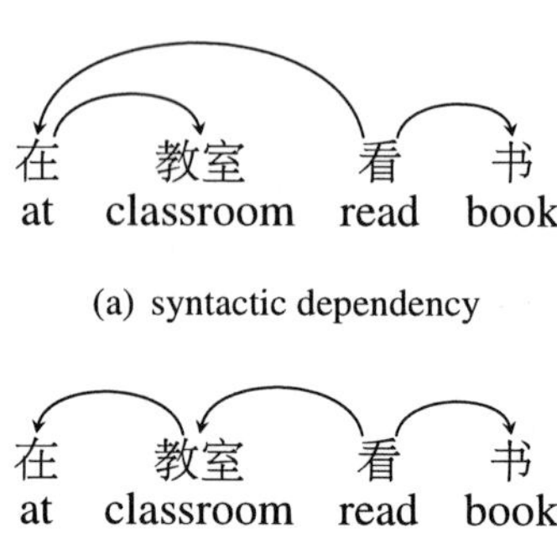

(a) syntactic dependency

(b) semantic dependency

Figure 2: Difference between syntactic and semantic dependency on preposition

to predicates directly. Unlike syntactic dependency, which inserts non-content words between predicate and its "real arguments" (Figure 2). Due to the completeness of the representation of relations between words, some words have relations with more than one other word (some words have more than one child, and some have more than one father), which forms direct acyclic graphs finally. We define a set of labels to describe dependency relations between words.

2.2 Semantic Dependency Relations

On the basis of SemEval 2012 task 5, we refined the semantic relation set in terms of more solid Chinese linguistic theories, except for the reference of HowNet (Dong and Dong, 2006), a popular Chinese semantic thesaurus. We mainly referred to the idea of semantic network of Chinese grammar defined by Lu (2001). He adapted semantic network to Chinese, which is the formal network for "semantic composition systems" by distinguishing the hierarchies of "semantic relations", "semantic alignment" and "semantic orientation". We borrowed his ideas of semantic unit classification and semantic combination, and integrated them with the dependency grammar to re-divided boundary for each semantic relation and re-organized the total label set for clarity and definiteness.

Semantic units are divided from high to low into event chains, events, arguments, concepts and markers. Arguments refer to noun phrases related to certain predicates. Concepts are simple elements in basic human thought or content words in syntax. Markers represent the meaning attached to entity information conveyed by speakers (e.g., speakers' tones or moods). These semantic units correspond to compound sentences, simple sentences, chunks, content words and function words. The meaning of sentences is expressed by event chains. Event chains consist of multiple simple sentences. The meaning of simple sentences is expressed by arguments, while arguments are reflected by predicate, referential or defining concepts. Markers are attached to concepts.

The meaning of sentences consists of the meaning of semantic units and their combinations, including semantic relations and attachments. Semantic attachments refer to markers on semantic units. Semantic relations are classified into symmetric and asymmetric types. Symmetric relations include coordination, selection, and equivalence relations, while asymmetric relations include:

Collocational relations occur between core and non-core roles. For example, in "工人 (worker) 修理 (repair) 地下 (pipeline) 管道 (pipeline)" serves as a non-core role, and is the patient of "修理 (repair)," which is a verb and core role. Relations between predicates and nouns belong to collocational relations. Semantic roles usually refer to collocational relations, Table 1 presents the 32 semantic roles we defined, divided into eight small categories. Additional relations refer to the modifying relations among concepts within an argument; all semantic roles are available, e.g. in "地下 (underground) 的 (de) 管道 (pipeline)", "地下 (underground)" is the modifier of "管道 (pipeline)", which refers to location relation. Connectional relations are bridging relations between two events that are neither symmetric nornested relation. For example, for "如果 (If) 天气 (weather)好 (good)，(,) 我 (I) 就 (will) 去 (go) 故宫 (the Summer Palace)," the former event

is the hypothesis of the latter. Events in Chinese semantic dependency have 15 relations. According to the above classification of sentence hierarchies, we can get to know how each sentence component constitutes the entire meaning of sentences. We design semantic dependency relations in terms of this theoretical basis.

2.3 Special Situations

On the analysis of the nature of Chinese language, two special situations need special handling. we list them here and describe their annotation strategies.

- Reverse relations. When a verb modifies a noun, a reverse relation is assigned with the label r-XX (XX refers to a single-level semantic relation). Reverse relation is designed because a word pair with the same semantic relation appears in different sentences with different modifying orders. Reverse relation is used to distinguish them. For example, the verb "打 (play)" modifies the kernel word "男孩 (boy)" in (a) of Figure 3, so r-agent is assigned; while in (b) "打 (play)" is a predicate and "男孩 (boy)" is the agent role with the label agent.

- Nested events. We define another kind of special relation–nested relation to mark that one sentence is degraded as a constituent for another sentence.Two events have a nested relation, i.e., one event is degraded as a grammatical item of the other, which belong to two semantic hierarchies. For example, in the sentence in Figure 4, the event "小 (little) 孙女 (granddaughter) 在 (be) 玩 (play) 电脑 (computer)" is degraded as a content of the action of "看见 (see)". A prefix "d" is added to single-level semantic relations as distinctive label.

Finally, we got 45 labels to describe relations between main semantic roles and relations within arguments, 19 labels for relations between different predicates. We also defined 17 labels to mark the auxiliary information of predicates. The total semantic relation set is shown in Table 1.

3 Task Description

This task contains two tracks, which are closed track and open track. People participating in closed track

Semantic roles	
Subject roles	Agt(Agent), Exp(Experiencer), Aft(Affection), Poss(Possessor)
Object roles	Pat(Patient), Cont(Content), Prod(Product), Orig(Origin), Comt(Comitative), Comp(Comparison)
Copula roles	Belg(Belongings), Clas(Classification), Accd(According)
Cause roles	Reas(Reason), Int(Intention), Cons(Consequence)
Condition roles	Mann(Manner), Tool, Matl(material)
Space-time roles	Time, Loc(Location), Dir(Direction), Proc(Process), Sco(Scope)
Measurement roles	Quan(Quantity), Qp(Quantity-phrase), Freq(Frequency), Seq(Sequence)
Special attribute roles	Desc(Description), Host, Nmod(Name-modifier), Tmod(Time-modifier)
Reverse relations	r + semantic roles
Nested relations	d + semantic roles
Event relations	
Symmetric relations	eCoo(Coordination), eSelt(Selection), eEqu(Equivalent)
Consecutive relations	ePrec(Precedent), eSucc(Successor), eProg(Progression), eCau(Cause), eAdvt(adversative), eResu(Result), eInf(Inference), eCond(Condition), eSupp(Supposition), eConc(Concession), eAban(Abandonment), eMetd(Method), ePurp(Purpose), ePref(Preference), eSum(Summary), eRect(Recount)
Semantic markers	
Relation markers	mConj(Conjection), mAux(Auxiliary), mPrep(Preposition)
Attachment markers	mTone, mTime, mRang(Range), mDegr(Degree), mMod(Modal), mFreq(Frequency), mDir(Direction), mPars(Parenthesis), mNeg(Negation)
Auxiliary markers	mMaj(Majority), mSepa(Separation), mRept(Repetition), mVain, mPunc(Punctuation)

Table 1: Label set of the semantic relation of BH-SDP-v2

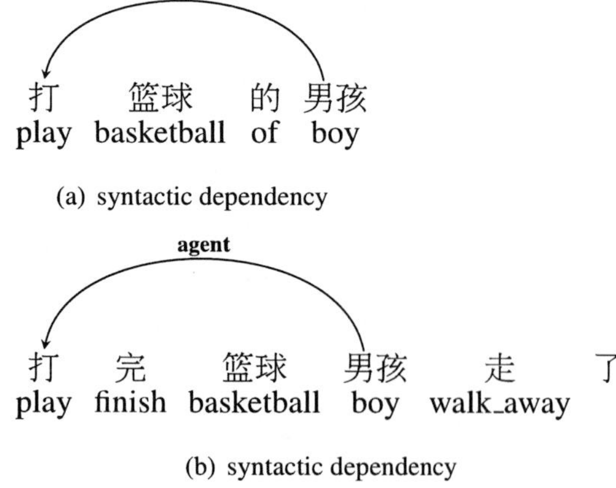

(a) syntactic dependency

(b) syntactic dependency

Figure 3: Reverse relations.

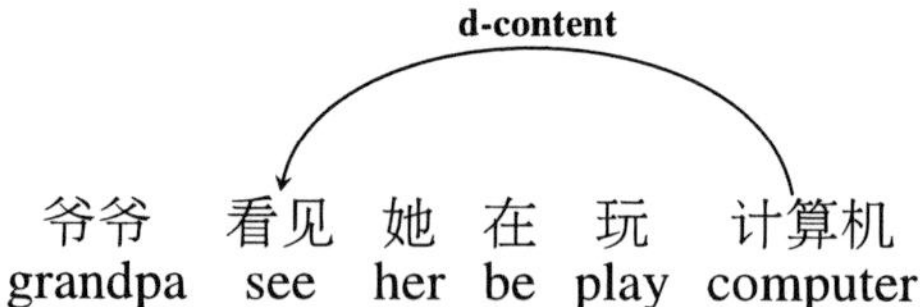

Figure 4: Nested relations.

parsing systems on graphs and the open track stimulates researchers to try how to integrate linguistic resource and world knowledge into semantic dependency parsing. The two tracks will be ranked separately. We provide two training files containing sentences in each domain. There is no rules for the use of these two training data.

3.1 Corpus Statistics

Since texts in rich categories have different linguistic properties with different communication purpose. This task provides two distinguished corpora in appreciable quantity respectively in the domain

could use only the given training data to train their systems and any other additional resource is forbidden. While any knowledge beyond training data is allowed in open track. The closed track encourages participates to focus on building dependency

of NEWS and TEXTBOOKS (from primary school textbooks). Each corpus contains particular linguistic phenomena. We provide 10,068 sentences of NEWS and 14,793 sentence of TEXTBOOKS. The sentences of news keep the same with the data in task 5 at SemEval 2012, which come from the Chinese PropBank 6.01 (Xue and Palmer, 2003) as the raw corpus to create the Chinese semantic dependency corpus. Sentences were selected by index: 1-121, 1001-1078, 1100-1151. TEXTBOOKS refer to shorter sentences with various ways of expressions, i.e., colloquial sentences (3,000), primary school texts (11,793). Detailed statics are described in Table 2.

		Train	Dev	Test
NEWS	#sent	8,301	534	1,233
	#word	250,249	15,325	34,305
TEXT	#sent	10,817	1,546	3,096
	#word	128,095	18,257	36,097

Table 2: Statics of the corpus.

3.2 Data Format

All data provided for the task uses a column-based file format, similar to the one of the 2006 CoNLL Shared Task (Table 3). Each training/developing/testing set is a text file, containing sentences separated by a blank line. Each sentence consists of more than one tokens, and each token is represented on one line consisting of 10 fields. Buchholz and Marsi (2006) provide more detailed information on the format. It's worth noting that if one word has more than one heads, it will appear in more than one lines in the training/developing/testing files continuously. Fields are separated from each other by a tab. Only five of the 10 fields are used: token id, form, pos tagger, head, and deprel. Head denotes the semantic dependency of each word, and deprel denotes the corresponding semantic relations of the dependency. In the data, the lemma column is filled with the form and the cpostag column with the postag.

3.3 Evaluation

During the phase of evaluation, each system should propose parsing results on the previously unseen testing data. Similar with training phase, testing

files containing sentences in two domains will be released separately. The final rankings will refer to the average results of the two testing files (taking training data size into consideration). We compare predicted dependencies (predicate-role-argument triples, and some of them contain roots of the whole sentences) with our human-annotated ones, which are regarded as gold dependencies.

Our evaluate measures are on two granularity, dependency arc and the complete sentence. Labeled and unlabeled precision and recall with respect to predicted dependencies will be used as evaluation measures. Since non-local dependencies (following Sun et al. (2014), we call these dependency arcs making dependency trees collapsed non-local ones) discovery is extremely difficult, we will evaluate non-local dependencies separately. For sentences level, we will use labeled and unlabeled exact match to measure sentence parsing accuracy. Following Task 8 at SemEval 2014, below and in other task-related contexts, we abbreviate these metrics as:

- Labeled precision (LP), recall (LR), F1 (LR) and recall for non-local dependencies (NLR);

- Unlabeled precision (UP), recall (UR), F1 (UF) and recall for non-local dependencies (NUR);

- Labeled and unlabeled exact match (LM, UM).

When ranking systems participating in this task, we mainly refer to the average F1 (LF) on the two testing sets.

4 Participating Systems

Fifteen organizations were registered to participate in this task. Finally, five systems were received from three organizations. These systems are as follows:

1. IHS-RD-Belarus. This system applied transition-based dependency parsing with online reordering, in order to deal with non-projective dependency arcs. The model is trained with both gold training instances and auto-parsed training instances, referred to as *bootstrapping*. Additional semantic features extracted from the IHS Goldfile Question-Answering system are utilized and demonstrated to be effective. It also used graph

ID	FORM	LEMMA	CPOS	PPOS	FEAT	HEAD	REL	PHEAD	PREL
1	现在	现在	NT	NT	_	4	Time	_	_
2	她	她	PN	PN	_	3	Poss	_	_
2	她	她	PN	PN	_	7	Exp	_	_
3	脸色	脸色	NN	NN	_	4	Exp	_	_
4	难看	难看	VA	VA	_	7	eCau	_	_
5	，	，	PU	PU	_	4	mPunc	_	_
6	好像	好像	AD	AD	_	7	mMod	_	_
7	病	病	VV	VV	_	0	ROOT	_	_
8	了	了	SP	SP	_	7	mTone	_	_

Table 3: Data format.

pre- and post-processing to handle ambiguities of some specific semantic relations (i.e., *eCoo*).

2. OCLSP (lbpg, lbpgs, lbpg75). This system proposed a bottom-up neural parser using long short-term memory (LSTM) networks. Since the basic neural parser (lbpg) has no guarantee to produce a dependency graph, they applied Chu-Liu-Edmond's algorithm (Chu and Liu, 1965) to generate the minimal spanning directed graph (lbpgs). To further address the multi-head annotation in this task, a threshold of δ is set on the probabilities to decide whether an extra arc exists (lbpg75).

3. OSU_CHGCG. This system proposed to use parsers trained with Chinese Generalized Categorial Grammar (GCG) (Bach, 1981) annotations to obtain the syntactic structures of a sentence. Then the GCG features, along with traditional features (e.g., word, POS, etc.) are fed into a multinomial classifier for semantic dependency classification.

5   Results & Analysis

We use LF, UF and NLF, NUF as the main evaluation metrics here. Table 4 shows the results of all participating systems. Note that all of the submitted systems used additional resource beyond training data provided in the task. IHS-RD-Belarus used semantic features extracted from the output of IHS Goldfire Question-Answering system, and both OCLSP and OSU_CHGCG used GCG features. Therefore, the results reported in Table 4 are all in the open track.

Overall, the IHS-RD-Belarus system achieves the best results in both NEWS and TEXT domain. However, it didn't perform well on the prediction of non-local labeled dependencies. OSU_CHGCG instead behaves more promising in the prediction of non-local dependencies. OCLSP (lbpg75) achieves remarkable results in the non-local labeled dependencies of the TEXT domain (57.51 of NLF).

From the perspective of methodology, IHS-RD-Belarus is a tree-structure prediction system, lacking the ability of revealing multi-head structures; while both OCLSP and OSU_CHGCG deal with graph structure, with either post-processing or classification-based models. From the perspective of resource, all the systems demonstrated that features extracted from a syntactic or semantic source are helpful for the SDP task, which is expected.

In general, some novel methods and ideas were proposed for this task, providing evidences for future research on both model design and feature selection of semantic dependency parsing.

6   Conclusion

We described the Chinese Semantic Dependency Parsing task for SemEval-2016, which is designed to analyze the graph-structured semantic representation of Chinese sentences. Five systems were submitted by three organizations. The systems explored the semantic dependency parsing problem along different directions, which will significantly push forward the research on SDP. We also note that the performance of SDP is still far from promising, especially for labeled dependencies and non-local dependencies. Challenges still remain in designing more effective and efficient parsing algorithms for graph-

	System	LP	LR	LF	UP	UR	UF	NLF	NUF	LM	UM
NEWS	IHS-RD-Belarus	**58.78**	**59.33**	**59.06**	**77.28**	**78.01**	**77.64**	40.84	60.20	**12.73**	**20.60**
	OCLSP (lbpg)	55.64	58.89	57.22	72.87	77.11	74.93	45.57	58.03	12.25	18.73
	OCLSP (lbpgs)	58.38	57.25	57.81	76.28	74.81	75.54	41.56	54.34	12.57	20.11
	OCLSP (lbpg75)	57.88	57.67	57.78	75.55	75.26	75.40	48.89	58.28	12.57	19.79
	OSU_CHGCG	55.52	55.85	55.69	73.51	73.94	73.72	**49.23**	**60.71**	5.03	11.35
	AVG	*57.24*	*57.80*	*57.51*	*75.10*	*75.83*	*75.45*	*45.22*	*58.31*	*11.03*	*18.12*
TEXT	IHS-RD-Belarus	**68.71**	**68.46**	**68.59**	**82.56**	**82.26**	**82.41**	50.57	64.58	**16.82**	**40.12**
	OCLSP (lbpg)	63.34	67.89	65.54	76.73	82.24	79.39	51.75	63.21	11.49	27.60
	OCLSP (lbpgs)	67.35	65.11	66.21	81.22	78.52	79.85	47.79	55.51	12.82	33.29
	OCLSP (lbpg75)	66.43	66.43	66.38	79.97	79.85	79.91	**57.51**	63.87	12.56	32.09
	OSU_CHGCG	65.36	64.98	65.17	79.06	78.60	78.83	54.70	**65.71**	11.36	32.02
	AVG	*66.24*	*66.57*	*66.38*	*79.91*	*80.29*	*80.08*	*52.46*	*62.58*	*13.01*	*33.02*

Table 4: Results of the submitted systems.

structured semantics. The annotation standard of semantic dependencies and the quality of our proposed corpus may also be further improved, which we leave to future work.

Acknowledgments

This work was supported by the National Key Basic Research Program of China via grant 2014CB340503 and the National Natural Science Foundation of China (NSFC) via grant 61133012 and 61370164.

References

Emmon W Bach. 1981. Discontinous constituents in generalized categorial grammar.

Sabine Buchholz and Erwin Marsi. 2006. Conll-x shared task on multilingual dependency parsing. In *Proceedings of the Tenth Conference on Computational Natural Language Learning (CoNLL-X)*, pages 149–164, New York City, June. Association for Computational Linguistics.

Wanxiang Che, Meishan Zhang, Yanqiu Shao, and Ting Liu. 2012. Semeval-2012 task 5: Chinese semantic dependency parsing. In **SEM 2012: The First Joint Conference on Lexical and Computational Semantics – Volume 1: Proceedings of the main conference and the shared task, and Volume 2: Proceedings of the Sixth International Workshop on Semantic Evaluation (SemEval 2012)*, pages 378–384, Montréal, Canada, 7-8 June. Association for Computational Linguistics.

Yoeng-Jin Chu and Tseng-Hong Liu. 1965. On shortest arborescence of a directed graph. *Scientia Sinica*, 14(10):1396.

Zhendong Dong and Qiang Dong. 2006. *HowNet and the Computation of Meaning*. World Scientific.

Chuan Lu. 2001. *The Semantic Network of Chinese Grammar*. The Commercial Printing house.

Igor Mel'čuk and AK Žolkovskij. 1965. O vozmožnom metode i instrumentax semantičeskogo sinteza. *Naučno-texničeskaja informacija*, (5):23–28.

Stephan Oepen, Marco Kuhlmann, Yusuke Miyao, Daniel Zeman, Dan Flickinger, Jan Hajic, Angelina Ivanova, and Yi Zhang. 2014. Semeval 2014 task 8: Broad-coverage semantic dependency parsing. In *Proceedings of the 8th International Workshop on Semantic Evaluation (SemEval 2014)*, pages 63–72, Dublin, Ireland, August. Association for Computational Linguistics and Dublin City University.

Stephan Oepen, Marco Kuhlmann, Yusuke Miyao, Daniel Zeman, Silvie Cinkova, Dan Flickinger, Jan Hajic, and Zdenka Uresova. 2015. Semeval 2015 task 18: Broad-coverage semantic dependency parsing. In *Proceedings of the 9th International Workshop on Semantic Evaluation (SemEval 2015)*, pages 915–926, Denver, Colorado, June. Association for Computational Linguistics.

Weiwei Sun, Yantao Du, Xin Kou, Shuoyang Ding, and Xiaojun Wan. 2014. Grammatical relations in chinese: Gb-ground extraction and data-driven parsing. In *ACL (1)*, pages 436–456.

Nianwen Xue and Martha Palmer. 2003. Annotating the propositions in the penn chinese treebank. In *Proceedings of the Second SIGHAN Workshop on Chinese Language Processing*.

SemEval-2016 Task 13: Taxonomy Extraction Evaluation (TExEval-2)

Georgeta Bordea*, Els Lefever, Paul Buitelaar***
*Insight Centre for Data Analytics
National University of Ireland, Galway
`name.surname@insight-centre.org`
**LT3, Language and Translation Technology Team,
Ghent University, Belgium
`name.surname@ugent.be`

Abstract

This paper describes the second edition of the shared task on Taxonomy Extraction Evaluation organised as part of SemEval 2016. This task aims to extract hypernym-hyponym relations between a given list of domain-specific terms and then to construct a domain taxonomy based on them. TExEval-2 introduced a multilingual setting for this task, covering four different languages including English, Dutch, Italian and French from domains as diverse as environment, food and science. A total of 62 runs submitted by 5 different teams were evaluated using structural measures, by comparison with gold standard taxonomies and by manual quality assessment of novel relations.

1 Introduction

Taxonomies are useful tools for content organisation, navigation, and retrieval, providing valuable input for semantically intensive tasks such as question answering (Harabagiu et al., 2003) and textual entailment (Geffet and Dagan, 2005). In general, a hierarchical relation is any asymmetrical relation that indicates subordination between two terms, but in this task we focus on hyponym-hypernym relations. Taxonomy learning from text is a challenging task that can be divided in several subtasks, including term extraction, hypernym identification and taxonomy construction. Existing approaches for hypernym identification from text rely on lexico-syntactic patterns (Hearst, 1992; Lefever et al., 2014), cooccurrence information (Grefenstette, 2015), substring inclusion, or exploit semantic relations provided in textual definitions (Velardi et al., 2013). This stage usually produces a large number of noisy, inconsistent relations, which assign multiple parents to a node and contain cycles. Hence, the third stage of taxonomy learning, taxonomy construction, focuses on the overall structure of the resulting graph and aims to organise terms in a hierarchical structure, more specifically a directed acyclic graph (Velardi et al., 2013; Kozareva and Hovy, 2010).

More recently, the hypernym identification subtask has attracted an increased interest from the distributional semantics community (Santus et al., 2014; Rei and Briscoe, 2014; Roller et al., 2014; Yu et al., 2015), as part of a wider effort to distinguish between different semantic relations which exist between distributional similar words (Weeds et al., 2014; Levy et al., 2015). Although this is a promising direction of research, that addresses some of the limitations of pattern-based approaches, including low coverage of domain-specific terms, most participants in this shared task opted for traditional approaches for hypernym identification, with the exception of one system (Pocostales, 2016).

TexEval-2 is mainly concerned with automatically extracting hierarchical relations from text and subsequent taxonomy construction, therefore we make the assumption that a list of terms is readily available. This simplifies evaluation by providing a common ground for all the systems, but participants are allowed to add additional nodes, i.e. terms, in the hierarchy as they consider appropriate. To avoid the need for term extraction, terms are extracted from existing taxonomies, providing participants with a domain lexicon that has to be organised in a hierarchical structure.

Proceedings of SemEval-2016, pages 1081–1091,
San Diego, California, June 16-17, 2016. ©2016 Association for Computational Linguistics

2 Task Description

The first TExEval shared task (Bordea et al., 2015), organised as part of SemEval 2015, introduced a monolingual dataset that covers terms and hierarchical relations from four domains that were not previously considered for this task. Performance was evaluated across domains, considering common sense knowledge as well as technical domains gathered from WordNet and other well known taxonomies. The second TExEval shared task aimed to extend this experimental setting to a multilingual setting, covering English, French, Italian and Dutch. A main challenge faced by the participants in the first TExEval was that no corpus was provided by the task organisers. We address this issue by providing participants with instructions for downloading and preparing a Wikipedia-based corpus. Depending on the selected approach, a system may or may not require large amounts of text to extract relations between terms, therefore participants are allowed to extend this corpus as they consider appropriate. The task is structured in several subtasks, including monolingual subtasks for hypernym identification and taxonomy construction in English, as well as two corresponding multilingual subtasks that cover Dutch, French and Italian.

3 Dataset Creation

We selected three target domains (i.e. Environment, Food and Science) with three root concepts (i.e. "environment", "food" and "science", respectively). Then, for each domain we considered different sources for gathering gold standard taxonomies, including a multilingual thesaurus, Eurovoc[1], a large lexical database of English, WordNet, and a general purpose resource, the Wikipedia Bitaxonomy (Flati et al., 2014). We also considered other domain-specific resources including "The Google product taxonomy" [2] for Food, and the "Taxonomy of Fields and their Subfields" [3] for Science.

English taxonomies The English gold standard taxonomies are collected from each of the sources

described above as follows. Gold standards are gathered from WordNet by selecting concepts and relationships in the hypernym-hyponym hierarchy rooted on the corresponding root concept for each domain. Relations extracted from Wikipedia are combined together with relations extracted from domain-specific resources, to obtain high-coverage domain-specific taxonomies. Hierarchical relations from Eurovoc were used integrally without any modification, but currently Eurovoc covers only the Environment and Science domains. It is worth nothing that the English gold standard taxonomies gathered from WordNet and from combined resources were also used as test data in the previous edition of this shared task (Bordea et al., 2015).

Multilingual taxonomies For the three other languages, the collected English gold standards were manually translated by six linguists (two computational linguists and four master students of the Ghent University Translation, Communication and Interpreting department). In a first step, the English term lists were translated in Excel by one annotator per language. The first annotator was allowed to mark entries that needed to be revised by a second annotator. In addition, the annotators could make remarks in an additional column. Some of the English terms could not be properly translated in the specific domain (e.g. "center" in the food domain) and were left out. In a second step, the translated term lists were used to automatically replace the English terms in the gold standard taxonomies with their corresponding translation.

The translation of English gold standards revealed a number of issues. First of all, some of the translations were near-synonyms in the other language, which eventually lead to cycles in the taxonomy. Examples in Italian are for instance "cibo" (English: food) and "vitto" (English: fare) which are in Italian almost synonymous, whereas their English counterparts have a more distinctive meaning. Another problematic example are the Italian words "condimento" (English: seasoning, sauce, dressing) and "salsa" (English: dressing, sauce), which can be hypernyms of each other, depending on the exact meaning of the word. The translated taxonomies also revealed errors in the original English taxonomy, such as for instance "conserve" is a kind of "confiture", which is incorrect.

Language	Domain	Source	$|V|$	$|E|$	#i.i.	#c.c.	Cycles
English	Environment	Eurovoc	261	261	60	1	no
	Food	Combined	1556	1587	70	1	no
		WordNet	1486	1576	302	1	no
	Science	Combined	453	465	54	1	no
		Eurovoc	125	124	31	1	no
		WordNet	429	452	117	1	no
Dutch	Environment	Eurovoc	267	267	59	1	no
	Food	Combined	1429	1446	66	**3**	no
		WordNet	1299	1340	259	**3**	no
	Science	Combined	445	449	54	1	no
		Eurovoc	125	124	32	1	no
		WordNet	399	399	105	1	no
French	Environment	Eurovoc	267	266	61	1	no
	Food	Combined	1418	1441	64	1	no
		WordNet	1329	1358	263	**2**	no
	Science	Combined	449	451	54	1	no
		Eurovoc	125	124	31	1	no
		WordNet	390	389	101	1	no
Italian	Environment	Eurovoc	267	266	59	1	no
	Food	Combined	1274	1304	60	**3**	no
		WordNet	1277	1332	254	1	**yes**
	Science	Combined	442	444	54	1	no
		Eurovoc	125	124	32	1	no
		WordNet	396	396	105	1	no

Table 1: Structural measures of gold standard taxonomies, including number of vertices ($|V|$), edges ($|E|$), intermediate nodes (#i.i), connected components (#c.c.) and cycles.

Table 1 shows the resulting number of vertices $|V|$ and edges $|E|$ of the produced gold standard taxonomies for each considered domain, source and language. We also report structural information about the number of intermediate nodes (#i.i), the number of connected components (#c.c.) and the number of cycles. Test data for this task consists of six lists of domain-specific terms for each language that were provided to participants as a shared basis to construct the taxonomies. The initial English taxonomies provide connections from the root node to all the other nodes, as they form one connected component. As some of the terms did not have a correspondent in all the other languages, some of the translated taxonomies have several components. This is specifically the case for the food domain that is highly dependent on the language and that shows the largest variation in number of nodes. For example, 127 terms from the Combined English taxonomy for Food could not be translated into Dutch

and 279 terms could not be translated into Italian. Additionally, four cycles are erroneously introduced for the WordNet Italian taxonomy for Food, including "cibo"-"vitto"-"cibo" and "piatto principale"-"piatto"-"piatto principale". Slight differences exist between the Eurovoc taxonomies constructed for different languages as well, and these taxonomies underwent a thorough review process.

4 Evaluation Approach

The construction of taxonomies is a challenging task even for humans but evaluating a taxonomy is not a trivial task either. In this shared task, taxonomies are evaluated through comparison with gold standard relations collected from WordNet and other well known, freely available taxonomies. This is complemented by a manual evaluation of relations that are not covered by the gold standard and through quantitative and qualitative structural analysis of the resulting graph. The evaluation methodology is sim-

Domain	Source	System	$|V|$	$|E|$	#i.i.	#c.c.	cycles
Environment	Eurovoc	Baseline	123	112	27	17	**no**
		JUNLP	**321**	**463**	123	19	**no**
		TAXI	148	207	50	**1**	**no**
		NUIG-UNLP	312	456	**176**	58	yes
		USAAR	57	47	10	10	**no**
		QASSIT	261	365	88	**1**	**no**
Food	Combined	Baseline	636	627	130	40	**no**
		JUNLP	1802	3015	**581**	48	yes
		TAXI	781	1118	132	**1**	**no**
		NUIG-UNLP	-	-	-	-	-
		USAAR	**3716**	**4347**	323	217	**no**
		QASSIT	-	-	-	-	-
Food	WordNet	Baseline	826	812	205	79	**no**
		JUNLP	**1748**	**3607**	**866**	123	yes
		TAXI	1122	2067	259	**1**	**no**
		NUIG-UNLP	-	-	-	-	-
		USAAR	675	540	146	135	**no**
		QASSIT	-	-	-	-	-
Science	Combined	Baseline	232	214	41	28	**no**
		JUNLP	**602**	1046	255	24	**no**
		TAXI	294	418	73	**1**	**no**
		NUIG-UNLP	595	**1656**	**409**	99	yes
		USAAR	371	312	60	59	**no**
		QASSIT	452	708	58	**1**	yes
Science	Eurovoc	Baseline	50	42	11	9	**no**
		JUNLP	**186**	**342**	**133**	15	yes
		TAXI	100	139	25	**1**	**no**
		NUIG-UNLP	97	218	72	13	yes
		USAAR	37	30	7	7	**no**
		QASSIT	125	164	25	**1**	**no**
Science	WordNet	Baseline	217	174	52	48	**no**
		JUNLP	**424**	690	**304**	90	**no**
		TAXI	290	459	88	**1**	**no**
		NUIG-UNLP	251	**929**	195	9	yes
		USAAR	136	104	32	32	**no**
		QASSIT	370	647	67	**1**	**no**

Table 2: Structural analysis of the submitted taxonomies and the string-based baseline for the monolingual setting

ilar to the approach introduced in the first edition of TExEval, with the main difference that we also report separate overall rankings of the participant systems for each of the subtasks.

Let $S = (V_S, E_S)$ be an output taxonomy produced by a system for a given domain, where V_S includes the set of domain concepts initially provided by the task organizers and E_S is the set of taxonomy edges extracted by the system. To broadly analyze the quality of the produced set of hypernymy relationships E_S, these results are benchmarked against the string-based baseline described in Section 4.1, using the following evaluation approaches: i) analyse the graph structure and check if the produced taxonomy is a Directed Acyclic Graph (DAG); ii) compare the edges E_S, against the set of relations from each type of gold standard; iii) manually validate a sample of novel relationships produced by the system that are not contained in the gold standard.

The final ranking of the systems takes into consideration these three types of evaluation by aggregating the achieved ranks using a voting scheme. First, the output taxonomies are ranked on the basis of the average performance obtained for each evaluated aspect and for each domain. The resulting ranks are simply summed up, favoring systems at the top of the ranked list and penalizing systems at the lower end.

4.1 Baseline

Simple string-based approaches that exploit term compositionality as a main property to hierarchically relate terms are known to be highly effective (Bordea et al., 2015). In this task, we implement the following baseline approach for hypernym extraction and taxonomy construction that is used to benchmark the evaluated systems. The baseline accounts for relations between compound terms such as *(science, network science)* and is implemented as follows:

$$B = (V_B, E_B) \tag{1}$$

where $E_B = \{(a, b)|\ b$ starts with a or ends with a and $|b| > |a|\}$. In this equation a is a term and b is a compound term that includes a as a substring. This baseline approach takes as input only a list of terms and does not require any external corpora or other structured information. It is worth noting that the same approach was applied in the multilingual setting, without any language-specific modification.

4.2 Structural Analysis

In this task, the structural evaluation quantifies the size of a taxonomy under investigation in terms of nodes and edges, evaluating whether the overall graph generated by hypernym-hyponym relations provides connections between the root of the taxonomy and all the other nodes. This is an important property of taxonomies that are used for search because it ensures that all the nodes are findable when exploring the taxonomy from the root. Another structural property of taxonomies is the absence of cycles, which are inconsistent with the semantics of hierarchical relations. Additionally, we highlight the number of nodes located on higher levels of a taxonomy, called intermediate nodes. Finding these nodes is more important than connecting a large number of leaves, as they generate taxonomies with a deeper and richer structure.

Based on these considerations, structural evaluation is performed by computing the cardinality of $|V_S|$ and $|E_S|$. We use an algorithm that finds all the elementary circuits of a simple directed graph (Johnson, 1975) to establish if the taxonomy S contains simple directed cycles (self loop excluded). We then use an approach based on the Tarjan algorithm (Tarjan, 1972) to calculate the number of connected components in S. Finally, we compute the number of intermediate nodes as the number of nodes $|V_S| - |L_S|$ where L_S is the set of leaf nodes in S, where a leaf node is defined as a node with the out-degree zero.

4.3 Gold Standard Comparison

While initial gold standard datasets for evaluating taxonomy extraction were mainly based on relations extracted from WordNet (Kozareva and Hovy, 2010), more recent work (Velardi et al., 2013) focuses on specialized domains such as artificial intelligence. The dataset introduced in this shared task brings together gold standards collected from Word-Net together with gold standards extracted from domain-specific taxonomies and from Wikipedia, a collaborative resource.

Given a gold standard taxonomy $G = (V_G, E_G)$, the comparison between a target taxonomy and a gold standard taxonomy is quantified using the following measures:

- Edge precision: $P = |E_S \cap E_G|/|E_S|$
- Edge recall: $R = |E_S \cap E_G|/|E_G|$
- F-score: $F = 2(P * R)/(P + R)$

Additionally, we consider the Cumulative Fowlkes&Mallows (Cumulative F&M) measure (Velardi et al., 2013), denoted as $B_{S,G}$, and defined as a value between 0.0 and 1.0 which measures level by level how well a target taxonomy S clusters similar nodes compared to a gold standard taxonomy G. $B_{S,G}$ is calculated as follows: let k be the maximum depth of both S and G, and H_{ij} a cut of the hierarchy, where $i \in \{0, ..., k\}$ is the cut level and $j \in \{G, S\}$ selects the clustering of interest.

Then, for each cut i, the two hierarchies can be seen as two flat clusterings C_{iS} and C_{iG} of the n concepts. When $i = 0$ the cut is a single cluster incorporating all the objects, and when $i = k$ we obtain n singleton clusters. Now let: n_{11} be the number of object pairs that are in the same cluster in both C_{iS} and C_{iG}; n_{00} be the number of object pairs that are in different clusters in both C_{iS} and C_{iG}; n_{10} be the number of object pairs that are in the same cluster in C_{iS} but not in C_{iG}; n_{01} be the number of object pairs that are in the same cluster in C_{iG} but not in C_{iS}.

The generalized Fowlkes&Mallows measure of cluster similarity for the cut i ($i \in \{0, ..., k\}$), as reformulated in (Wagner and Wagner, 2007), is defined as:

$$B^i_{S,G} = \frac{n^i_{11}}{\sqrt{(n^i_{11} + n^i_{10}) \cdot (n^i_{11} + n^i_{01})}}. \quad (2)$$

And the Cumulative Fowlkes&Mallows Measure:

$$B_{S,G} = \frac{\sum_{i=0}^{k-1} \frac{i+1}{k} B^i_{S,G}}{\sum_{i=0}^{k-1} \frac{i+1}{k}} = \frac{\sum_{i=0}^{k-1} \frac{i+1}{k} B^i_{S,G}}{\frac{k+1}{2}}. \quad (3)$$

4.4 Manual Evaluation

Even the most complete and up to date taxonomy can be extended with additional nodes and relations, therefore it is possible for systems to identify correct relations that are not covered by the gold standard. A problem faced by gold standard evaluation is that these relations are considered incorrect when relying on a direct comparison with the gold standard taxonomy. This is why we additionally evaluate by hand a subset of new relations proposed by each system to estimate the number of relations in E_S that do not belong to E_G. Due to limited resources, we extract only a random sample of novel relations from each submission and manually annotate them to compute precision P as: $|correctISA|/|sample|$. At most 100 relations were evaluated by one annotator for each system, domain, and language for a total of 6200 term pairs. Two different annotators were tasked to evaluate submissions for the monolingual subtask (English) and for the multilingual subtask (Dutch, French, Italian).

The annotators were provided with a list of term pairs organized by domain and were asked if the relation was a correct ISA relation, if the relation and the terms were domain specific, and if the relation was too generic. Overall, a relation is considered correct only if it is considered a correct hypernym-hyponym relation, if it is relevant for the given domain and not over-generic. Take for example the following edges from the food domain: *(linguine, pasta)* and *(lemon, food)*. Both edges are correct ISA relations and are domain specific, but the second edge is over-generic because lemons can be categorized more precisely as fruits.

5 Participants and Results

A total of five teams participated in the shared task, but only two systems participated in the multilingual subtasks. Two of the systems that participated in the monolingual subtask alone did not submit runs for the food domain, which has the largest number of nodes. Overall, 62 system runs were submitted by the five teams, 36 for the multilingual subtasks and 26 for the monolingual subtasks. Next, we provide a short description of each approach starting with the two systems that participated in the multilingual subtasks.

JUNLP The JUNLP system makes use of an external linguistic resource for hypernym identification (Maitra and Das, 2016). This resource is the BabelNet semantic network that connects concepts and named entities in a very large network of semantic relations, called Babel synsets (Navigli and Ponzetto, 2010). To make sure that no relations that were used to construct the gold standards are considered, only relations that mention Wikipedia as a source were selected, discarding relations from all the other sources. Additionally, the system makes use of two string inclusion heuristics. The first heuristic checks if any of the terms provided by the organisers is included as a substring in another term. The second heuristic considers terms that have a considerable overlap, for instance *Chocolate Pudding* and *Vanilla Pudding* although their hypernym (i.e., *Pudding*) is not mentioned in the list of terms. A limitation of this approach is that stopwords are also considered as hypernyms, but this can be easily avoided by using a stopword list.

TAXI The methods for hypernym identification used in the TAXonomy Induction system (TAXI) rely on two sources of evidence: substring matching

Domain	Source	Measure	B	JUNLP	TAXI	NUIG-UNLP	USAAR	QASSIT
Environment	Eurovoc	Fscore	**0.3003**	0.1658	0.2992	0.2008	0.2468	0.1725
		F&M	0.0	0.0814	0.2384	0.0007	0.0007	**0.4349**
Food	Combined	Fscore	0.2665	0.1730	**0.2787**	-	0.0883	-
		F&M	0.0019	**0.2608**	0.2021	-	0.0	-
Food	WordNet	Fscore	0.34	0.2053	0.2932	-	**0.3601**	-
		F&M	0.0022	0.1925	**0.3260**	-	0.0021	-
Science	Combined	Fscore	**0.3947**	0.1906	0.3669	0.1537	0.3063	0.2165
		F&M	0.0163	0.1774	0.3634	0.0090	0.0020	**0.5757**
Science	Eurovoc	Fscore	**0.3133**	0.1931	0.3118	0.1696	0.2468	0.2431
		F&M	0.0056	0.1373	**0.3893**	0.1517	0.0023	**0.3893**
Science	WordNet	Fscore	**0.3834**	0.2487	0.3776	0.2361	0.3058	0.2384
		F&M	0.0016	0.0494	**0.2255**	0.0027	0.0008	**0.2255**

Table 3: Gold standard comparison using Fscore and Cumulative F&M measure for the monolingual setting, where B stands for the string-based baseline

Domain	Source	JUNLP	TAXI	NUIG-UNLP	USAAR	QASSIT
Environment	Eurovoc	0.02	0.11	0.08	**0.22**	0.07
Food	Combined	0.2	0.36	-	**0.73**	-
Food	WordNet	0.18	0.32	-	**0.81**	-
Science	Combined	0.06	0.14	0.09	**0.71**	0.07
Science	Eurovoc	0.02	0.02	0.04	0.0	**0.05**
Science	WordNet	0.06	0.22	0.05	**0.47**	0.22

Table 4: Manual evaluation of 100 (at most) randomly selected novel relations based on precision for English

and Hearst-like patterns (Panchenko et al., 2016). The Hearst patterns for all languages are extracted from Wikipedia and from focused crawls with seed pages that are Wikipedia pages. In addition, for English, several additional corpora are used including GigaWord, ukWaC, a news corpus and the CommonCrawl. For French, Italian and Dutch the method is completely unsupervised and relies on KNN approach. For English, an SVM classifier is trained on the trial data. For all languages the features are the same: substrings and ISA relations extracted with lexico-syntactic patterns. No databases or linguistic resources beyond trial data and raw text corpora mentioned above are used. For the taxonomy construction subtasks, the system makes use of an unsupervised graph pruning approach based on the Tarjan algorithm, connecting the resulting disconnected components to the root of the graph.

NUIG-UNLP The system implements a semi-supervised method that finds hypernym candidates for the provided noun phrases by representing them as distributional vectors. Roughly, this method assumes that hypernyms may be induced by adding a vector offset (Mikolov et al., 2013; Rei and Briscoe, 2014) to the corresponding hyponym representation generated by GloVe over a Wikipedia dump. The vector offset is obtained as the average offset between 200 pairs of hyponym-hypernym in the same vector space selected from trial data.

USAAR This system introduces hypernym endocentricity as a useful property for hypernym identification (Tan, 2016). Often multi-word hyponyms are endocentric constructions which contains a word that fulfills the same function as one part of its word. E.g. an "apple pie" is essentially a "pie". The number of multi-words terms that are endocentric in English is investigated and whether this endocentric property can be used to generate entity links to connect terms in the Wikipedia list of list.

QASSIT A semi-supervised methodology is used for the acquisition of lexical taxonomies based on genetic algorithms (Cleuziou and Moreno, 2016). It is based on the theory of pretopology that offers a powerful formalism to model semantic relations and transforms a list of terms into a structured term space by combining different discriminant criteria.

In particular, rare but accurate pieces of knowledge are used to parameterize the different criteria defining the pretopological term space. Then, a structuring algorithm is used to transform the pretopological space into a lexical taxonomy.

5.1 Monolingual Subtasks (English)

Table 2 presents the results of the structural analysis for English, giving an overview of the structural measures presented in Section 4.2 for each of the submitted runs. The taxonomies constructed by the TAXI and QASSIT systems are the only taxonomies that provide a path from the root to all the other nodes, as the corresponding graphs have a single connected component. All the other submissions have more than ten disconnected components. The string-based baseline is also producing several disconnected components. The TAXI and USAAR systems are the only systems that produce directed acyclic graphs across all the domains. The QASSIT system generates two cycles in the case of the combined taxonomy for Science. Overall, only the TAXI system consistently produces well-structured taxonomies across domains. The systems that output taxonomies with a large number of nodes, edges and intermediate nodes (e.g., JUNLP and NUIG-UNLP) tend to do so at the cost of introducing cycles in the graph.

In Table 3 we summarize the results of the comparison with gold standards in terms of Fscore and the Cumulative F&M measure. The string-based baseline is relatively strong compared to the other systems in terms of Fscore, providing the best results for all the domains with the exception of the food domain. A reason why the baseline is weaker in this domain is that a much larger number of food terms are single-word terms that are not compositional, but in absolute terms the results are still comparative with the results of the best system coming second on the overall ranking. In terms of the Cumulative F&M measure that quantifies structural similarity with the gold standards, the QASSIT system takes the lead for all the domains where a taxonomy was submitted. In the case of the Food domain, it is the TAXI system that achieves the best results for the Combined gold standard and the USAAR system for the WordNet gold standard. The string-based baseline captures only a small part of the structure of the

gold standard, as shown by the poor results for the Cumulative F&M measure.

The results of the manual evaluation of a sample of novel relations is presented in Table 4. It is worth noting that not all the systems had at least one hundred novel relations to analyse, therefore in some cases a smaller number of relations was manually evaluated. The USAAR submissions introduce the largest number of correct novel relations, with precision higher than 70% for Food taxonomies and the Science taxonomy gathered from Combined sources. The TAXI system comes second for all the domains with the exception of the Science taxonomy gathered from Eurovoc, where the QASSIT system achieves the best results.

The final ranking of the systems is produced by using a voting approach based on the averaged scores of selected measures that cover the main properties of a well-formed taxonomy. For this shared task all the properties are considered to be equally important, but a weighted approach could also be considered depending on the intended purpose of a taxonomy. These properties include (1) cyclicity, measured in terms of the number of submissions that have cycles; (2) structural similarity with gold standard taxonomies, measured with Cumulative F&M measure; (3) categorization, measured in number of intermediate nodes #i.i. that can be interpreted as taxonomical categories; (4) connectivity, measured in number of connected components #c.c.; (5) overlap of edges with the gold standard taxonomy, measured by Fscore; (6) number of covered domains; (7) precision of novel relations from manual evaluation of sample relations. Table 5 presents the averaged results for each of these measures across domains.

Take for example the best ranked system TAXI, where none of the submitted taxonomies had any cycles, which resulted in an overall score of 0 for cyclicity and a rank 1 in the overall ranking, as this is a desirable feature for a taxonomy. In the case of the structure property, measured by averaging the Cumulative F&M measure over all the submitted taxonomies, the TAXI system achieved the second highest score. This score is below the score achieved by the QASSIT system for the same feature, which brings the TAXI system on the second position in the final ranking for the structure property. Cyclicity

Measure	Baseline	JUNLP	TAXI	NUIG-UNLP	USAAR	QASSIT
Cyclicity	**0**	3	**0**	4	**0**	1
Structure (F&M)	0.01	0.15	0.29	0.04	0.00	**0.4**
Categorisation (#i.i.)	77.67	**377**	104.5	213	96.33	59.5
Connectivity (#c.c.)	36.83	53.17	**1**	44.75	76.67	**1**
GS Fscore	**0.33**	0.20	0.32	0.19	0.26	0.22
Domains	**6**	**6**	**6**	4	**6**	4
Manual Precision	n.a.	0.09	0.20	0.07	**0.49**	0.10

Table 5: Average scores achieved by the systems for the monolingual subtasks.

Subtask	Measure	JUNLP	TAXI	NUIG-UNLP	USAAR	QASSIT
TC	Cyclicity	3	**1**	4	**1**	2
	Structure (F&M)	3	2	4	5	**1**
	Categorisation (#i.i.)	**1**	3	2	4	5
	Connectivity (#c.c.)	3	**1**	2	4	**1**
TC & HI	GS Fscore	4	**1**	5	2	3
	Domains	**1**	**1**	2	**1**	2
	Manual Precision	4	2	5	**1**	3
TC	Ranking	4	**1**	5	3	2
HI		3	**1**	4	**1**	2

Table 6: Overall ranking of the systems for the monolingual subtasks on Taxonomy Construction (TC) and Hypernym Indentification (HI).

and connectivity are the only two properties where low scores are preferable, while for the structure, categorisation, gold standard Fscore, domains, and manual precision higher values are preferred.

The averaged scores shown in Table 5 are directly used to obtain the final ranking of the system for the monolingual subtasks presented in Table 6. The scores used to generate the rankings for the Hypernym Identification (HI) subtask are mainly the last three properties, namely the Fscore with the gold standard, the number of domains, and the precision from manual evaluation. All the seven taxonomical properties described above are used for ranking systems for the Taxonomy Construction (TC) subtask. The TAXI system achieves the best results based on most of these measures, coming third only for the categorization property. This brings the system to the first place both for the Hypernym Identification and the Taxonomy Construction subtasks, in the monolingual setting. There is a tie with the USAAR system, but only for the Hypernym Identification subtask. The second placed system is the QASSIT system, that is ranked on the top three positions for most of the properties with the exception of the categorization property, where it is ranked on the second last place. This is due to the fact that the QASSIT system produces a relatively flat structure, with a smaller number of intermediate nodes.

5.2 Multilingual Subtasks (Dutch, French, Italian)

The results for the multilingual subtasks cover a much smaller number of systems, as only two out of the five participants submitted multilingual taxonomies. The same properties are used for the final rankings of the systems as in the previous section, as can be seen in Table 7. This table shows the average scores of the two systems and of the string-based baseline across domains. Both systems submitted runs for all the domains, therefore in the multilingual subtask the number of domains was not used for ranking the systems. Table 8 presents the final ranking of the systems for the multilingual Taxonomy Construction subtask and the multilingual Hypernym Identification subtask. The TAXI system achieves the best results across all the metrics, with the exception of the categorisation property where JUNLP system introduces a larger number of in-

Measure	Baseline	JUNLP	TAXI
Cyclicity	**0**	**0**	**0**
Structure (F&M)	0.01	0.02	**0.19**
Categorisation (#i.i.)	64.28	**178.22**	64.94
Connectivity (#c.c.)	40.5	34.89	**1**
GS Fscore	**0.31**	0.19	0.28
Manual Precision	n.a.	0.30	**0.63**

Table 7: Average scores of the systems for the multilingual subtasks.

Subtask	Measure	JUNLP	TAXI
TC	Cyclicity	**1**	**1**
	Structure (F&M)	2	**1**
	Categorisation (#i.i.)	**1**	2
	Connectivity (#c.c.)	2	**1**
TC & HI	GS Fscore	2	**1**
	Manual Precision	2	**1**
TC	Ranking	2	**1**
HI		2	**1**

Table 8: Overall ranking of the systems for the multilingual subtasks on Taxonomy Construction (TC) and Hypernym Indentification (HI).

termediate nodes. Again, the string-based baseline achieves the best Fscore results in comparison with the gold standards. The TAXI system achieves the best results for English, with a 12.5% decrease in Fscore for Dutch and French and a 9.4% decrease for Italian. JUNLP performance is more stable across languages, with only a 5% drop in Fscore for Dutch and Italian compared to English, and the same Fscore for French.

6 Conclusion

This paper provides an overview of the SemEval 2016 task on Taxonomy Extraction, that introduced a multilingual dataset for evaluating hypernym extraction and taxonomy construction. The constructed dataset covers three domains including Environment, Food, and Science. The task attracted 62 submissions from five teams that were automatically evaluated against gold standards collected from WordNet, Eurovoc, Wikipedia and other domain-specific resources. We also reported the results of an extensive structural analysis of the submitted taxonomies and a manual evaluation of a sample of edges that are not covered by the gold standards.

The best results were obtained by an approach based on Hearst patterns that makes use of a large web-based corpus including Wikipedia. All the systems could benefit from addressing the taxonomy construction subtask, by paying attention to the overall structure of the taxonomy not just the task of extracting pairs of terms. Compared to the previous edition of TExEval, there are two systems that submitted proper taxonomies compared to just one system last year. In this edition, it is also worthy of mention the introduction of methods that make use of purely distributional approaches. These approaches leave a lot of place for improvement, achieving a competitive recall but lagging behind pattern-based approaches in terms of precision.

A possible improvement of this shared task is to analyse system performance in relation to word polysemy. This could be measured by example based on Wikipedia disambiguation pages or on the number of WordNet senses. It is reasonable to assume that hypernym/hyponym pairs between polysemous words are more difficult to connect without using disambiguation methods to identify the appropriate sense for a domain.

Acknowledgments

This work has been funded in part by a research grant from Science Foundation Ireland (SFI) under Grant Number SFI/12/RC/2289 (INSIGHT).

References

Georgeta Bordea, Paul Buitelaar, Stefano Faralli, and Roberto Navigli. 2015. Semeval-2015 task 17: Taxonomy extraction evaluation (TExEval). *SemEval-2015*, 452(465):902.

Guillaume Cleuziou and Jose G. Moreno. 2016. QAS-SIT at SemEval-2016 Task 13: On the integration of semantic vectors in pretopological spaces for lexical taxonomy acquisition. In *Proceedings of the 10th International Workshop on Semantic Evaluation (SemEval 2016)*, San Diego, California, June. Association for Computational Linguistics.

Tiziano Flati, Daniele Vannella, Tommaso Pasini, and Roberto Navigli. 2014. Two Is Bigger (and Better) Than One: the Wikipedia Bitaxonomy Project. In *Proceedings of the 52nd Annual Meeting of the Association for Computational Linguistics (ACL 2014)*, pages

945–955, Baltimore, Maryland. Association for Computational Linguistics.

Maayan Geffet and Ido Dagan. 2005. The distributional inclusion hypotheses and lexical entailment. In *Proceedings of the 43rd Annual Meeting on Association for Computational Linguistics*, ACL '05, pages 107–114, Stroudsburg, PA, USA. Association for Computational Linguistics.

Gregory Grefenstette. 2015. INRIASAC: Simple hypernym extraction methods. In *Proceedings of the Ninth International Workshop on Semantic Evaluation (SemEval 2015)*.

Sanda M. Harabagiu, Steven J. Maiorano, and Marius Pasca. 2003. Open-domain textual question answering techniques. *Natural Language Engineering*, 9(3):231–267.

Marti A Hearst. 1992. Automatic acquisition of hyponyms from large text corpora. In *Proceedings of the 14th conference on Computational linguistics-Volume 2*, pages 539–545. Association for Computational Linguistics.

Donald B Johnson. 1975. Finding all the elementary circuits of a directed graph. *SIAM Journal on Computing*, 4(1):77–84.

Zornitsa Kozareva and Eduard Hovy. 2010. A semi-supervised method to learn and construct taxonomies using the web. In *Proceedings of the 2010 Conference on Empirical Methods in Natural Language Processing*, EMNLP '10, pages 1110–1118, Stroudsburg, PA, USA. Association for Computational Linguistics.

Els Lefever, Marjan Van de Kauter, and Veronique Hoste. 2014. HypoTerm: Detection of hypernym relations between domain-specific terms in Dutch and English. *Terminology*, 20(2):250–278.

Omer Levy, Steffen Remus, Chris Biemann, Ido Dagan, and Israel Ramat-Gan. 2015. Do supervised distributional methods really learn lexical inference relations. *Proceedings of NAACL, Denver, CO*.

Promita Maitra and Dipankar Das. 2016. JUNLP at SemEval-2016 Task 13: A language independent approach for hypernym identification. In *Proceedings of the 10th International Workshop on Semantic Evaluation (SemEval 2016)*, San Diego, California, June. Association for Computational Linguistics.

Tomas Mikolov, Wen-tau Yih, and Geoffrey Zweig. 2013. Linguistic regularities in continuous space word representations. In *HLT-NAACL*, pages 746–751.

Roberto Navigli and Simone Paolo Ponzetto. 2010. Babelnet: Building a very large multilingual semantic network. In *Proceedings of the 48th annual meeting of the association for computational linguistics*, pages 216–225. Association for Computational Linguistics.

Alexander Panchenko, Stefano Faralli, Eugen Ruppert, Steffen Remus, Hubert Naets, Cedrick Fairon, Simone Paolo Ponzetto, and Chris Biemann. 2016. TAXI at SemEval-2016 Task13: a taxonomy induction method based on lexico-syntactic patterns, substrings and focused crawling. In *Proceedings of the 10th International Workshop on Semantic Evaluation (SemEval 2016)*. Association for Computational Linguistics.

Joel Pocostales. 2016. NUIG-UNLP at SemEval-2016 Task 13: A simple word embedding-based approach for taxonomy extraction. In *Proceedings of the 10th International Workshop on Semantic Evaluation*, San Diego, California, June. Association for Computational Linguistics.

Marek Rei and Ted Briscoe. 2014. Looking for hyponyms in vector space. In *CoNLL*, pages 68–77.

Stephen Roller, Katrin Erk, and Gemma Boleda. 2014. Inclusive yet selective: Supervised distributional hypernymy detection. In *COLING*, pages 1025–1036.

Enrico Santus, Alessandro Lenci, Qin Lu, and Sabine Schulte Im Walde. 2014. Chasing hypernyms in vector spaces with entropy. In *EACL*, pages 38–42.

Liling Tan. 2016. USAAR at SemEval-2016 Task 13: Hyponym endocentricity. In *Proceedings of the 10th International Workshop on Semantic Evaluation (SemEval 2016)*, San Diego, California, June. Association for Computational Linguistics.

Robert Tarjan. 1972. Depth-first search and linear graph algorithms. *SIAM Journal on Computing*, 1:146–160.

Paola Velardi, Stefano Faralli, and Roberto Navigli. 2013. OntoLearn Reloaded: A Graph-Based Algorithm for Taxonomy Induction. *Computational Linguistics*, 39(3):665–707.

Silke Wagner and Dorothea Wagner. 2007. Comparing clusterings an overview. Technical Report 2006-04, Faculty of Informatics, Universität Karlsruhe (TH).

Julie Weeds, Daoud Clarke, Jeremy Reffin, David Weir, and Bill Keller. 2014. Learning to distinguish hypernyms and co-hyponyms. In *Proceedings of COLING 2014, the 25th International Conference on Computational Linguistics: Technical Papers*, pages 2249–2259.

Zheng Yu, Haixun Wang, Xuemin Lin, and Min Wang. 2015. Learning term embeddings for hypernymy identification. In *Proceedings of the 24th International Conference on Artificial Intelligence*, IJCAI'15, pages 1390–1397. AAAI Press.

SemEval-2016 Task 14: Semantic Taxonomy Enrichment

David Jurgens
Stanford University
jurgens@cs.stanford.edu

Mohammad Taher Pilehvar
University of Cambridge
mp792@cam.ac.uk

Abstract

Manually constructed taxonomies provide a crucial resource for many NLP technologies, yet these resources are often limited in their lexical coverage due to their construction procedure. While multiple approaches have been proposed to enrich such taxonomies with new concepts, these techniques are typically evaluated by measuring the accuracy at identifying relationships between words, e.g., that a dog is a canine, rather relationships between specific concepts. Task 14 provides an evaluation framework for automatic taxonomy enrichment techniques by measuring the placement of a new concept into an existing taxonomy: Given a new word and its definition, systems were asked to attach or merge the concept into an existing WordNet concept. Five teams submitted 13 systems to the task, all of which were able to improve over the random baseline system. However, only one participating system outperformed the second, more-competitive baseline that attaches a new term to the first word in its gloss with the appropriate part of speech, which indicates that techniques must be adapted to exploit the structure of glosses.

1 Introduction

Semantic networks and ontologies are key resources in Natural Language Processing. Of these resources, WordNet (Fellbaum, 1998), the de facto standard lexical database of English, has remained in widespread use over the past two decades, with a broad range of applications such as Word Sense Disambiguation (Navigli, 2009), Query expansion and Information Retrieval (Varelas et al., 2005; Fang, 2008), sentiment analysis (Esuli and Sebastiani, 2006), and semantic similarity measurement (Budanitsky and Hirst, 2006a; Pilehvar et al., 2013). The performances of these WordNet-based techniques are directly affected by the lexical coverage of WordNet's vocabulary, especially if applied to specific domains and social media texts. However, the manual maintenance of WordNet is an expensive endeavour which requires significant effort and time. As a result, WordNet is not updated frequently and omits many lemmas and senses, such as those from domain specific lexicons (e.g., DNA replication, regular expression, and long shot), creative slang usages (e.g., homewrecker), or those for technology or entities that came into recent existence (e.g., selfie, mp3).

Hence, a variety of techniques have tried to tackle the coverage limitation of WordNet, often by drawing new word senses from other domain-specific or collaboratively-constructed dictionaries and adding the new word senses to the WordNet hierarchy (Poprat et al., 2008; Snow et al., 2006; Toral et al., 2008; Yamada et al., 2011; Jurgens and Pilehvar, 2015). However, these approaches have usually been tested on relatively small datasets, often testing for word-level relationships without precisely measuring integration accuracy at the concept level. Similarly, other techniques have been proposed for automatically discovering novel senses of words (Lau et al., 2012); however, these senses were not re-integrated into the taxonomy.

Given the availability of large-scale dictionaries such as Wiktionary, Task 14 is designed to inspire

Proceedings of SemEval-2016, pages 1092–1102,
San Diego, California, June 16-17, 2016. ©2016 Association for Computational Linguistics

new automated approaches for using the definitions in these resource to expand WordNet with new concepts. Accordingly, the task provides a high-quality dataset of one thousand definitions from a wide range of domains to be added to the WordNet hierarchy, either by adding them as new concepts or integrating them as new lemmas of an existing concept. The task provides a robust evaluation framework for measuring the accuracy of ontology expansion techniques. More broadly, the techniques developed as a part of Task 14 can play an important role in the construction of new automatically-built ontologies.

2 Task Description

The goal of Task 14 is to evaluate systems that enrich semantic taxonomies with new word senses drawn from other lexicographic resources. The task provides systems with a set of word senses that are not defined in WordNet.[1] Each word sense comprises three parts: a lemma, part of speech tag, and definition. For example, the noun *geoscience* is a word sense in our dataset which is associated with the definition "Any of several sciences that deal with the Earth". The word sense is drawn from Wiktionary.[2] For each of these word senses, a system's task is to identify a point in the WordNet's subsumption (i.e., is-a) hierarchy which is the most plausible point for placing the new word sense. In other words, a system's task is to find the most semantically similar WordNet synset to the given new word sense.

Operations   Once the target synset is identified, a system has to decide how to integrate the new word sense. For a given new word sense s and a target synset S we define two possible operations:

- MERGE: when s refers to the same concept that is conceptualized by the synset S. As a result of this operation s is added to the set of synonymous word senses in S.

- ATTACH: when s refers to a more specific concept than S. In other words, S is a generalization of the new word sense s (i.e., its hypernym). This operation creates a new synset containing the sole word sense s and attaches

the new synset as a hyponym of S in the WordNet's subsumption hierarchy.

Table 1 shows example new word senses together with the target synset and the operation. Note that after both these operations, the polysemy of the lemma of s is increased by one. Also, the total number of synsets in the enriched WordNet increases by one after an ATTACH operation whereas it remains unchanged after MERGE, since in the latter case, a new word sense is added to an existing synset. Our datasets contain instances from noun and verb parts of speech.

2.1 Subtasks

For each item in our datasets, we provide the source dictionary from which the corresponding word sense (i.e., a word and its definition) is obtained. The participating systems were allowed to use the source dictionary in order to draw additional information or exploit its structural properties. Based on their usage of the source dictionary, we classify the participating systems into two categories:

- Resource-aware: the participating systems could use the URLs provided in the dataset to gather additional information (e.g., hyperlinks, wiki-markup) for performing the integration and may use additional information from any dictionary, including the one from which the target word sense had been obtained, e.g., Wiktionary.

- Constrained: the system might use any resource other than dictionaries.

We allowed each team to submit up to three runs per system type to let them explore different configurations, features, or parameter settings in the official rankings.

2.2 Related Tasks

Task 14 directly relates to three branches of prior tasks in SemEval.   First, two recent tasks have evaluated automatic methods for constructing taxonomies (Bordea et al., 2015; Bordea et al., 2016). In these tasks, participants are presented with word pairs –but no glosses– and tasked with organizing the words into hypernym relationships. Task 14 provides the next step in such evaluations by explicitly

---

[1] We use WordNet 3.0.
[2] http://www.wiktionary.org

Lemma	POS	Definition	Target synset	Operation
geoscience	noun	Any of several sciences that deal with the Earth	earth_science – (any of the sciences that deal with the earth or its parts)	MERGE
mudslide	noun	A mixed drink consisting of vodka, Kahlua and Bailey's.	cocktail – a short mixed drink	ATTACH
euthanize	verb	To submit (a person or animal) to euthanasia.	destroy, put down – put (an animal) to death	MERGE
changing_room	noun	A room, especially in a gym, designed for people to change their clothes.	dressing_room – a room in which you can change clothes	MERGE
Apple	noun	An American multinational technology company headquartered in Cupertino, California, that designs, develops, and sells consumer electronics, computer software, online services, and personal computers.	corporation, corp – (a business firm whose articles of incorporation have been approved in some state)	ATTACH
own	verb	To illicitly obtain "super-user" or "root" access into a computer system thereby having access to all of the user files on that system.	crack – gain unauthorized access computers with malicious intentions.	ATTACH

Table 1: Sample instances from Task 14's datasets. A system's task is to identify, for a new word sense, the target synset and the corresponding operation.

incorporating polysemy into the task by requiring systems to specify a concept, rather than a word, as a hypernym. For example, when recognizing the relationships that a dog is a canine, the system would be required to specify that the concept should be attached to the animal sense of canine, not the tooth sense.

Second, the task of comparing a gloss associated with a new concept is closely related to the recent tasks on semantic similarity, i.e., Semantic Textual Similarity (Agirre et al., 2012; Agirre et al., 2013, STS) and Cross-Level Semantic Similarity (Jurgens et al., 2014, CLSS). Indeed, prior STS tasks included gloss pairs from OntoNotes in the datasets (Hovy et al., 2006) and CLSS had, among its four different evaluation types, an evaluation for systems measuring the similarity between word senses and words. However, while textual similarity is likely to be core component of Task 14 systems, the data is often richer than raw text by containing (a) regular linguistic structure where the parent concept is likely to be introduced first and (b) contextual features from where the gloss appears such as hyperlinks or example usages, which may help to disambiguate.

Third, prior tasks on Word Sense Induction (WSI)

have evaluated methods that automatically discover the different meanings of a word (Manandhar et al., 2010; Jurgens and Klapaftis, 2013; Navigli and Vannella, 2013). However, the new senses discovered by these methods were never integrated into any taxonomy, making them difficult to use and relate to existing concepts. Task 14 provides a natural next step for WSI pairs, should any novel induced senses be matched with a gloss describing it.

3 Task Data

Given that WordNet 3.0 offers wide coverage of common concepts, the majority of novel concepts to be integrated are likely to come from topical domains, informal expressions, and neologisms. Therefore, the dataset for Task 14 was constructed to contain concepts from a wide variety of domains and to include glosses typical of those seen if performing an automated integration from online sources, such as those from heavily-curated sources such as Wiktionary and more idiosyncratic online glossaries with a single author. Table 3 shows the distribution of instances in the Task 14's training and test datasets across different genres. The dataset consists of a total of 1000 items, split into training and test datasets containing 400 and 600 items, respectively.

	Training			Test		
	M	A	Total	M	A	Total
Noun	27	322	349	26	490	516
Verb	6	45	51	6	78	84
Total	33	367	400	32	568	600

Table 2: The distribution of items in the task's datasets according to the part of speech and the target operation, i.e., Merge (M) and Attach (A).

Novel concepts were limited to nouns and verbs, as only these parts of speech have fully-developed taxonomies in WordNet.[3] Table 2 shows the distribution of training and test items according to their parts of speech and the intended operation, highlighting the fact that most new items are novel concepts that require a new synset to be added, rather than new lemmas to be included in an existing synset.

For each item, in addition to the target synset and the operation, we also provide the resource from which the new word sense was obtained. Glosses were provided as purely text data, with the hope was that systems may use the source URL provided with each gloss to identify additional page structure that could prove useful for concept integration (e.g., hyperlinks, wiki-markup, page topics).

3.1 Annotation Process

The two authors independently annotated each of the 1000 items, identifying the appropriate synset and operation. In a small number of cases, neither author could determine an appropriate integration for an item; such items were discarded and replaced with more-easily annotated items. Ultimately, all disagreements were discussed and adjudicated to determine the final dataset.

Annotators initially agreed on the annotation for 37.5% of the items. While this rate seems low at first glance, most disagreements were due to one annotator finding a more refined integration of the item, e.g,. DNA vs. Mutant Gene, which is expected given the large search space of over 82K noun and 13.7K verb synsets from which to find the appropriate hypernym or synonym synset. Indeed, most disagreements were very close in meaning; in fact, dis-

³We do note that Tsvetkov et al. (2014) have proposed a taxonomy for adjectives, for which our methodology could be applied.

agreements had an average semantic similarity between their synsets of 0.74 according to the Wu and Palmer (1994) measure. Hence, the moderate exact-match agreement is an underestimate of the true semantic agreement between annotators. Furthermore, several of the remaining dissimilar pairs were instances where similar concepts were distantly located in WordNet's structure.

The annotation proved difficult for three categories of concepts, not all of which were successfully integrated. First, many technical domains include unique processes and techniques specific to their field, e.g.,

> Lautering (noun) – The process of separating the sweet wort (pre-boil) from the spent grains in a lauter tun or with other straining apparatus.

However, some techniques and processes do not have a correspondence to any existing synsets, leaving their closest appropriate hypernym as a sense of process or technique. This difficulty is reflected in the current structure of WordNet, where *process#n#1* already has the dissimilar concepts of "fingerprinting," "computation," and "modus operandi" all as direct hyponyms, highlighting the challenge of placing some concepts. Where possible, we opted to avoid attaching new concepts to general senses, either by finding a more specific concept or leaving them out of the dataset entirely.

Second, in rare occasions, WordNet does not contain an intermediate concept necessary for the appropriate integration. For example, integrating the new concept

> Root (noun) – The administrative account (UID 0) on a *nix system that has all privileges; cf. superuser.

requires first having a concept of a computer account, which is not currently present in WordNet. These gaps are particularly evident for action nouns, where most verbs do not have a corresponding noun gerund. While the novel concept may still be attached to a more-distant hypernym of the appropriate location, this situation points to the need for an iterative integration process where intermediary concepts are first inserted.

Third, concepts that express a negated or partial state often do not have associated concepts in the more-specific depths of the taxonomy. For example, annotators had difficulty finding appropriate synsets that were not too general for the following two concepts:

> NaN (noun) – Not a number; applied to numeric values that represent an undefined or unrepresentable value, such as zero divided by itself

> Neomort (noun) – A brain-dead human being that could be kept on life support for organ transplantation, medical and nursing education, and drug research.

Without additional synsets for representing partial or negated state, these concepts would need to be attached to very general synsets such as *value#n#1* or *person#n#1*.

The challenge of agreeing upon a specific location for a new concept underscores the need for automated approaches developed as a part of this task. As an ontology grows in size, it becomes less obvious where a new concept could be integrated, despite an annotator's familiarity with the concepts contained therein. Our annotation process relied on two annotators whose collective experience was necessary to identify the appropriate location. However, for larger ontologies such as BabelNet (Navigli and Ponzetto, 2012), which contains several orders of magnitude more concepts than WordNet, automated integration approaches will be necessary as it is infeasible for a single human annotator to recall the appropriate insertion point among millions of concepts.

3.2   Evaluation Metrics

We evaluated the performance of the participating system according to two criteria: (1) the accuracy by which the placements were performed, and (2) the percentage of items for which a decision was made (Recall).

3.2.1   Accuracy (Wu&P)

Our first criteria verifies the ability of a system to correctly identify the attachment or merge point in the WordNet hierarchy. Checking for exact matches would penalize equally both a placement in the near proximity of the intended synset and a random placement far in the network. A system's automatically-made attachment to the WordNet hierarchy is expected to be as close as possible to the correct attachment point given by the gold-standard data. We therefore evaluate the systems according to a fuzzy measure of accuracy which is sensitive to the distance between the intended target synset and the one outputted by the system. However, we recognize that links in the taxonomy do not necessarily represent uniform semantic distances, since siblings that are deep in the hierarchy tend to be more related to one another. Hence, a direct edge-counting approach might not provide a reliable basis for the evaluation of the attachment accuracy. Interestingly, the attachment accuracy evaluation can be cast as a WordNet-based semantic similarity measurement in which the goal is to compute the similarity between two concepts based on the structural properties of WordNet (Budanitsky and Hirst, 2006b), most important of which is the distance between the two. Therefore, we measure accuracy using the Wu and Palmer (1994, Wu&P) semantic similarity measure, defined as:

$$\frac{2 \cdot depth_{LCS}}{depth_1 + depth_2} \tag{1}$$

where $depth_1$ and $depth_2$ are the depths of the two concepts in WordNet's subsumption hierarchy (hypernymy/hyponymy relations) and $Depth_{LCS}$ is the depth of their least common subsumer, i.e., the most specific concept which is an ancestor of both the concepts. For each instance in the test set for which the system made a prediction, we measure the Wu&P similarity of the output attachment and the corresponding correct synset. An accurate system is expected to have a high similarity score when aggregated over all instances in the test set. Please note that picking the correct target synset with an incorrect operation is analogous to increasing the distance by one edge.

3.2.2   Lemma Match

A key challenge in the integration task is identifying the appropriate word in the gloss that denotes the hypernym (if it exists) and then disambiguating which sense of that word is the appropriate concept for attachment or merger. For example, given the

Genre	Subgenre	Training	Testing	Subgenre Total	Genre Total
Medical	UMLS	7	-	7	200
	Genomics	69	-	69	
	Virology	10	-	10	
	Dental	8	-	8	
	Healthcare	6	8	14	
	Immunology	-	24	24	
	Physiology	-	12	12	
	Homeopathy	-	6	6	
	Toxicology	-	3	3	
	Surgery	-	32	32	
	Veterinary medicine	-	4	4	
	Ophthalmology	-	5	5	
	Embryology	-	6	6	
Technical Language	Linux Glossary	20	5	25	200
	Mathematics	20	5	25	
	Narratology	10	14	24	
	Earth Science	10	16	26	
	Music	-	41	41	
	Brewing	-	35	35	
	Neuroscience	-	14	14	
	Architecture	-	10	10	
Sports domains	Gridiron football	25	-	25	100
	Cycling	25	-	25	
	Golf	-	13	13	
	Sailing	-	8	8	
	Weightlifting	-	5	5	
	Climbing	-	9	9	
	Volleyball	-	15	15	
Legal Language	American Law	-	100	100	100
Slang	American Slang	30	35	60	150
	British Slang	5	5	10	
	Online Slang/jargon	25	15	40	
	Military Slang	10	10	20	
Jargon	Computer	20	50	50	50
Idioms	American Idioms	20	25	50	50
Religious Language	Islam	15	10	25	100
	Hinduism	15	10	25	
	Judaism	20	5	25	
	Catholicism	15	10	25	
Financial Language	Banking	15	10	25	50
	Stocks	-	25	25	
Total		400	600	1000	1000

Table 3: The distribution of instances across different genres in the training and test data sets of Task 14.

item

> Grief (verb) – To deliberately harass and
> annoy or cause grief to other players of a
> game in order to interfere with their enjoy-
> ment of it

a system may correctly identify that the verb *harass*
is the hypernym but select the wrong sense to which
grief should be attached. Such a mistake would be
penalized heavily according to the Wu&P measure
and mask that the system is accurate at identifying
hypernyms in glosses. Therefore, we include a second unofficial metric, lemma match, that measures
the percentage of items for which the system has selected a synset with at least one word in common
with the correct synset where the item should be integrated; i.e., how often the system picked the right
word but wrong sense.

3.2.3 Recall

Some word senses may be more difficult to place
in the WordNet hierarchy than others due to a variety
of reasons, such an entry with a gloss that contains
many out of vocabulary words. Therefore, we allow
a system to decline to place these senses in order to
avoid making placements with low confidence. As
an evaluation metric, we report Recall as the percentage of items for which a decision was made by
the system.

3.3 System ranking

A system's performance is computed by the F1 score
of Wu&P and Recall. The official ranking of the
systems was done according to their F1 scores.

4 Systems

Five teams submitted 13 systems, where each team's
systems were variations on a common architecture.
No system utilized resource-specific features beyond the gloss (e.g., the Wiktionary markup) and
so all systems were ultimately submitted in the constrained category. Systems were compared against
two baselines.

4.1 Participants

The **MSejrKU** systems build definitional representations based on skip-gram vectors trained on
Wikipedia data and incorporates syntactic features.

Words in a candidate gloss are disambiguated using
the method of Agirre and Soroa (2009) and then a
classifier predicts the goodness of fit for a candidate
attachment synset related to those in the gloss.

The **Duluth** systems perform string matching to
compare a definition with each of the glosses in
WordNet. Given a new definition, systems differ in
which words are included from the WordNet synset
for comparison: Duluth2 uses only the words in the
definition after stopword removal, while Duluth1 extends Duluth2 by including words from the hypernyms of the compared synset. Duluth3 extends Du-
luth1 with words from the hyponyms but also takes
the step of breaking each definition into character
tri-grams to capture surface-form regularities. The
UMNDuluth team performs a similar approach but
weights gloss similarity by favoring specific kinds
of terms, such as those that are longer and those that
appear in WordNet.

The **TALN** systems project the definition of the
novel term into a vector space using SENSEMBED
(Iacobacci et al., 2015). Then this vector is compared with the vectors for senses in WordNet to find
the closest match. System variations address issues
when words have no associated vectors and how to
select between candidate attachments.

The **JRC** system uses a form of second-order similarity by representing each definition as a vector
over the synsets that contain its words. New terms
are attached by finding the WordNet synset whose
definition has maximal cosine similarity.

The **VCU** systems adopt multiple approaches
based on textual similarity. Run1 uses a second-
order expansion by representing a definition using
frequency of words related to those in the definition.
Run2 compares glosses using Lesk relatedness measure. Run3 performs no pre-processing and compares the words in the glosses directly as first-order
vectors.

4.2 Baselines

The first baseline, **Random synset** captures the expected performance of a system at chance when attaching the new concept to a randomly picked synset
from WordNet with the appropriate part of speech.
This baseline provides the lower bound in expected
similarity for an attachment.

The second baseline captures our observation that

Rank	Team	System	LM	Wu&P	Recall	F1
1	MSejrKU	System2	0.428	0.523	0.973	0.680
2	MSejrKU	System1	0.432	0.518	0.968	0.675
3	TALN	test_cfgRun1	0.360	0.476	1.000	0.645
4	TALN	test_cfgRunPickerHypos	0.240	0.472	1.000	0.641
5	TALN	test_cfgRun2	0.353	0.464	1.000	0.634
6	VCU	Run3	0.161	0.432	0.997	0.602
7	VCU	Run2	0.171	0.419	0.997	0.590
8	VCU	Run1	0.124	0.408	0.997	0.579
9	Duluth	Duluth2	0.043	0.347	1.000	0.515
10	JRC	MainRun	0.066	0.347	0.987	0.513
11	Duluth	Duluth3	0.017	0.345	1.000	0.513
12	UMNDuluth	Run1	0.098	0.340	0.998	0.507
13	Duluth	Duluth1	0.023	0.331	1.000	0.498
Baseline: First word, first sense			0.415	0.514	1.000	0.679
Baseline: Random synset			0.000	0.227	1.000	0.370

Table 4: Evaluation results showing the Lemma Match (LM), Wu&P, and Recall measures.

glosses are reasonably well structured such that the word expressing the hypernym concept appears early in the gloss (if at all). Therefore, given new word sense s with definition d_s and part of speech tag p, the **First word, first sense** (FWFS) baseline picks the first occurring word w in d_s with part of speech p as the hypernym (i.e., the first noun if the word sense to be attached is a noun and the first verb otherwise).

The new word sense is then attached to the synset containing the first sense of w. For example, given the item

> Immunoglobin (noun) – Any protein that functions as an antibody

the FWFS baseline attaches the item to the first sense of the noun protein in WordNet, i.e., *protein#n#1*. Despite the wide variety of domains seen in the data, 65% of all integrations in the gold standard data connect the first sense of the target word, suggesting that in the absence of specific information to disambiguate a word in the gloss, its first (most frequent) sense is relatively high precision back-off strategy.

For the FWFS baseline, glosses are POS-tagged using CoreNLP (Manning et al., 2014) and we include a minimal heuristic that prevents attaching to "a" or "an," both of which are nouns in WordNet. In the rare event that no word can be found with the same part of speech, the item is attached to either the

general concepts of *entity#n#1* or *be#v#1*, depending on the part of speech.

5 Results

All of the thirteen participating systems improved over the Random synset baseline. Table 4 shows the evaluation results for Task 14's participating systems. However, only one of the systems, System2 of MSejrKU, could slightly outperform the FWFS baseline, showing the competitiveness of this simple baseline, which takes advantage of the inherent structure of definitions. Indeed, the lower ranked systems frequently performed holistic comparisons between gloss texts, which frequently include terms from later in the gloss that do not aid in identifying the closest meaning.

While its performance is relatively high among participants, the FWFS baseline should not be mistaken for a satisfactory solution; many of the attachments made by the baseline are overly general and do not take advantage of the remainder of the gloss's content, which can identify the correct, more-specific concept to which the item should be attached. For example, with the item

> Hot reactor (noun) – A person whose blood pressure and heart rate increase abnormally in response to stress

the baseline naively attaches to *person#n#1*, while a

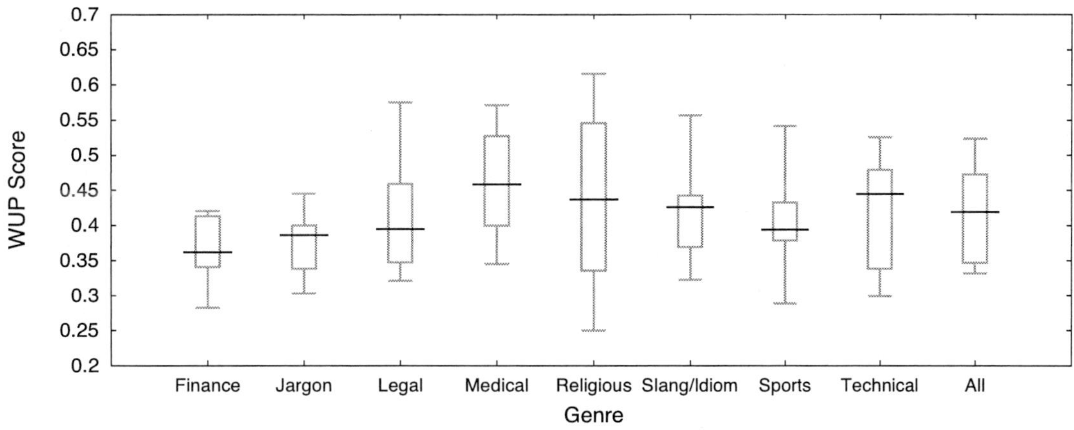

Figure 1: The distribution of Wu&P scores of the participating systems per genre. Whiskers show minimum and maximum scores and lines denote the median.

more sophisticated solution could use the additional text in gloss to identify an appropriate hyponym of *person#n#1* to which the item may be attached, e.g., *sick_person#n#1*. Thus, we speculate that the gloss similarity used by participants may still prove highly useful by first identifying the appropriate general concept in the gloss (e.g., as the baseline does) and then searching its hyponyms for a better match.

Examining the performances of systems in Table 4, we see that no system performed significantly better on the Lemma Match measure than Wu&P, with both measures being highly correlated at r=0.96. This suggests that when the appropriate hypernym lemma was present in a gloss, systems struggled most with selecting it as the correct candidate lemma in the gloss, rather than identifying which synset of that lemma was the correct attachment.

Given the variety of genres and sources from which new definitions were drawn, we performed a follow-up analysis to examine the impact of the genre on system performance. Figure 1 shows the distribution of scores per genre. Surprisingly, Religious definitions cause the most variance among systems and also saw the highest and lowest system scores per genre. Religious definitions were drawn from more sources beyond just Wiktionary and thus, such variance may reflect systems' robustness to different writing styles. Systems performed worst on the Finance and Jargon domains; however, both genres had little training data relative to testing data, suggesting that systems had difficulty generalizing

from few examples. Nevertheless, systems still performed well for the Legal genre which was held out as a surprise dataset with no training data.

6 Conclusion

Semantic taxonomies are core components of many NLP systems and multiple approaches have been proposed for how to extend such taxonomies automatically with new concepts. We have introduced SemEval-2016 Task 14 as a framework and dataset for evaluating the accuracy of systems at integrating new definitions as concepts into an ontology using WordNet 3.0 as a base resource. Five teams submitted 13 systems for participation, with all teams performing better than chance but only one team surpassing a simple baseline that leverages knowledge of the expected word order in a definition to guess the correct hypernym concept. Our results point towards significant opportunity for improving taxonomy enrichment. In future work, we intend to integrate the best insights of this task into the next version of CROWN,[4] an automatically constructed extension of WordNet with concepts from online glossaries and lexicographic resources.

References

Eneko Agirre and Aitor Soroa. 2009. Personalizing pagerank for word sense disambiguation. In *Proceed-*

______
[4]https://github.com/davidjurgens/crown

ings of the 12th Conference of the European Chapter of the Association for Computational Linguistics, pages 33–41. Association for Computational Linguistics.

Eneko Agirre, Mona Diab, Daniel Cer, and Aitor Gonzalez-Agirre. 2012. SemEval-2012 task 6: A pilot on semantic textual similarity. In *Proceedings of the First Joint Conference on Lexical and Computational Semantics-Volume 1: Proceedings of the main conference and the shared task, and Volume 2: Proceedings of the Sixth International Workshop on Semantic Evaluation*, pages 385–393. Association for Computational Linguistics.

Eneko Agirre, Daniel Cer, Mona Diab, Aitor Gonzalez-Agirre, and Weiwei Guo. 2013. sem 2013 shared task: Semantic textual similarity, including a pilot on typed-similarity. In *In* SEM 2013: The Second Joint Conference on Lexical and Computational Semantics. Association for Computational Linguistics*. Association for Computational Linguistics.

Georgeta Bordea, Paul Buitelaar, Stefano Faralli, and Roberto Navigli. 2015. SemEval-2015 task 17: Taxonomy extraction evaluation (texeval). In *Proceedings of the 9th International Workshop on Semantic Evaluation*. Association for Computational Linguistics.

Georgeta Bordea, Els Lefever, and Paul Buitelaar. 2016. SemEval-2016 task 13: Taxonomy extraction evaluation (texeval-2). In *Proceedings of the 10th International Workshop on Semantic Evaluation*. Association for Computational Linguistics.

Alexander Budanitsky and Graeme Hirst. 2006a. Evaluating WordNet-based measures of Lexical Semantic Relatedness. *Computational Linguistics*, 32(1):13–47.

Alexander Budanitsky and Graeme Hirst. 2006b. Evaluating WordNet-based measures of lexical semantic relatedness. *Computational Linguistics*, 32(1):13–47.

Andrea Esuli and Fabrizio Sebastiani. 2006. SENTI-WORDNET: A publicly available lexical resource for opinion mining. In *In Proceedings of the 5th Conference on Language Resources and Evaluation*, pages 417–422.

Hui Fang. 2008. A re-examination of query expansion using lexical resources. In *Proceedings of ACL-08: HLT*, pages 139–147, Columbus, Ohio.

Christiane Fellbaum, editor. 1998. *WordNet: An Electronic Database*. MIT Press, Cambridge, MA.

Eduard Hovy, Mitchell Marcus, Martha Palmer, Lance Ramshaw, and Ralph Weischedel. 2006. OntoNotes: the 90% solution. In *Proceedings of the human language technology conference of the NAACL, Companion Volume: Short Papers*, pages 57–60. Association for Computational Linguistics.

Ignacio Iacobacci, Mohammad Taher Pilehvar, and Roberto Navigli. 2015. SensEmbed: learning sense embeddings for word and relational similarity. In *Proceedings of ACL*, pages 95–105.

David Jurgens and Ioannis Klapaftis. 2013. SemEval-2013 task 13: Word sense induction for graded and non-graded senses. In *Second joint conference on lexical and computational semantics (* SEM)*, volume 2, pages 290–299.

David Jurgens and Mohammad Taher Pilehvar. 2015. Reserating the awesometastic: An automatic extension of the WordNet taxonomy for novel terms. In *Proceedings of the 2015 Conference of the North American Chapter of the Association for Computational Linguistics: Human Language Technologies*, pages 1459–1465, Denver, Colorado.

David Jurgens, Mohammad Taher Pilehvar, and Roberto Navigli. 2014. SemEval-2014 task 3: Cross-level semantic similarity. In *Proceedings of the 8th International Workshop on Semantic Evaluation (SemEval 2014), in conjunction with COLING 2014*, pages 17–26, Dublin, Ireland.

Jey Han Lau, Paul Cook, Diana McCarthy, David Newman, and Timothy Baldwin. 2012. Word sense induction for novel sense detection. In *Proceedings of the 13th Conference of the European Chapter of the Association for Computational Linguistics*, pages 591–601. Association for Computational Linguistics.

Suresh Manandhar, Ioannis P Klapaftis, Dmitriy Dligach, and Sameer S Pradhan. 2010. SemEval-2010 task 14: Word sense induction & disambiguation. In *Proceedings of the 5th international workshop on semantic evaluation*, pages 63–68. Association for Computational Linguistics.

Christopher D Manning, Mihai Surdeanu, John Bauer, Jenny Rose Finkel, Steven Bethard, and David McClosky. 2014. The stanford corenlp natural language processing toolkit. In *ACL (System Demonstrations)*, pages 55–60.

Roberto Navigli and Simone Paolo Ponzetto. 2012. BabelNet: The automatic construction, evaluation and application of a wide-coverage multilingual semantic network. *Artificial Intelligence*, 193:217–250.

Roberto Navigli and Daniele Vannella. 2013. SemEval-2013 task 11: Word sense induction and disambiguation within an end-user application. In *Second Joint Conference on Lexical and Computational Semantics (* SEM)*, volume 2, pages 193–201.

Roberto Navigli. 2009. Word Sense Disambiguation: A survey. *ACM Computing Surveys*, 41(2):1–69.

Mohammad Taher Pilehvar, David Jurgens, and Roberto Navigli. 2013. Align, Disambiguate and Walk: a Unified Approach for Measuring Semantic Similarity. In *Proceedings of the 51st Annual Meeting of the Association for Computational Linguistics (ACL)*, pages 1341–1351, Sofia, Bulgaria.

Michael Poprat, Elena Beisswanger, and Udo Hahn. 2008. Building a BioWordNet by using WordNet's data formats and WordNet's software infrastructure: a failure story. In *Proceedings of the Workshop on Software Engineering, Testing, and Quality Assurance for Natural Language Processing*, pages 31–39, Columbus, Ohio.

Rion Snow, Dan Jurafsky, and Andrew Ng. 2006. Semantic taxonomy induction from heterogeneous evidence. pages 801–808.

Antonio Toral, Rafael Muoz, and Monica Monachini. 2008. Named Entity WordNet. In *Proceedings of the Sixth International Conference on Language Resources and Evaluation (LREC)*, pages 741–747.

Yulia Tsvetkov, Nathan Schneider, Dirk Hovy, Archna Bhatia, Manaal Faruqui, and Chris Dyer. 2014. Augmenting English adjective senses with supersenses. In *LREC*. European Language Resources Association.

Giannis Varelas, Epimenidis Voutsakis, Paraskevi Raftopoulou, Euripides G.M. Petrakis, and Evangelos E. Milios. 2005. Semantic similarity methods in WordNet and their application to information retrieval on the web. In *Proceedings of the 7th Annual ACM International Workshop on Web Information and Data Management*, pages 10–16.

Zhibiao Wu and Martha Palmer. 1994. Verbs semantics and lexical selection. In *Proceedings of the 32Nd Annual Meeting on Association for Computational Linguistics*, pages 133–138.

Ichiro Yamada, Jong-Hoon Oh, Chikara Hashimoto, Kentaro Torisawa, Junichi Kazama, Stijn De Saeger, and Takuya Kawada. 2011. Extending WordNet with hypernyms and siblings acquired from wikipedia. In *Proceedings of the 5th International Joint Conference on Natural Language Processing*, pages 874–882.

UMD-TTIC-UW at SemEval-2016 Task 1: Attention-Based Multi-Perspective Convolutional Neural Networks for Textual Similarity Measurement

Hua He[1], John Wieting[2], Kevin Gimpel[2], Jinfeng Rao[1], and Jimmy Lin[3]

[1] Department of Computer Science, University of Maryland, College Park
[2] Toyota Technological Institute at Chicago
[3] David R. Cheriton School of Computer Science, University of Waterloo

{huah,jinfeng}@umd.edu, {jwieting,kgimpel}@ttic.edu, jimmylin@uwaterloo.ca

Abstract

We describe an attention-based convolutional neural network for the English semantic textual similarity (STS) task in the SemEval-2016 competition (Agirre et al., 2016). We develop an attention-based input interaction layer and incorporate it into our multi-perspective convolutional neural network (He et al., 2015), using the PARAGRAM-PHRASE word embeddings (Wieting et al., 2016) trained on paraphrase pairs. Without using any sparse features, our final model outperforms the winning entry in STS2015 when evaluated on the STS2015 data.

1 Introduction

Measuring the semantic textual similarity (STS) of two pieces of text remains a fundamental problem in language research. It lies at the core of many language processing tasks, including paraphrase detection (Xu et al., 2014), question answering (Lin, 2007), and query ranking (Duh, 2009).

The STS problem can be formalized as: given a query sentence S_1 and a comparison sentence S_2, the task is to compute their semantic similarity in terms of a similarity score $sim(S_1, S_2)$. The SemEval Semantic Textual Similarity tasks (Agirre et al., 2012; Agirre et al., 2013; Agirre et al., 2014; Agirre et al., 2015; Agirre et al., 2016) are a popular evaluation venue for the STS problem. Over the years the competitions have made more than $15,000$ human annotated sentence pairs publicly available, and have evaluated over 300 system runs.

Traditional approaches are based on hand-crafted feature engineering (Wan et al., 2006; Madnani et al., 2012; Fellbaum, 1998; Fern and Stevenson, 2008; Das and Smith, 2009; Guo and Diab, 2012; Sultan et al., 2014; Kashyap et al., 2014; Lynum et al., 2014). Competitive systems in recent years are mostly based on neural networks (He et al., 2015; Tai et al., 2015; Yin and Schütze, 2015; He and Lin, 2016), which can alleviate data sparseness with pre-training and distributed representations.

In this paper, we extend the multi-perspective convolutional neural network (MPCNN) of He et al. (2015). Most previous neural network models, including the MPCNN, treat input sentences separately, and largely ignore context-sensitive interactions between the input sentences. We address this problem by utilizing an attention mechanism (Bahdanau et al., 2014) to develop an attention-based input interaction layer (Sec. 3). It converts the two independent input sentences into an inter-related sentence pair, which can help the model identify important input words for improved similarity measurement. We also use the strongly-performing PARAGRAM-PHRASE word embeddings (Wieting et al., 2016) (Sec. 4) trained on phrase pairs from the Paraphrase Database (Ganitkevitch et al., 2013).

These components comprise our submission to the SemEval-2016 STS competition (shown in Figure 1): an attention-based multi-perspective convolutional neural network augmented with PARAGRAM-PHRASE word embeddings. We provide details of each component in the following sections. Unlike much previous work in the SemEval competitions (Šarić et al., 2012; Sultan et al., 2014), we do not use sparse features, syntactic parsers, or external resources like WordNet.

Proceedings of SemEval-2016, pages 1103–1108,
San Diego, California, June 16-17, 2016. ©2016 Association for Computational Linguistics

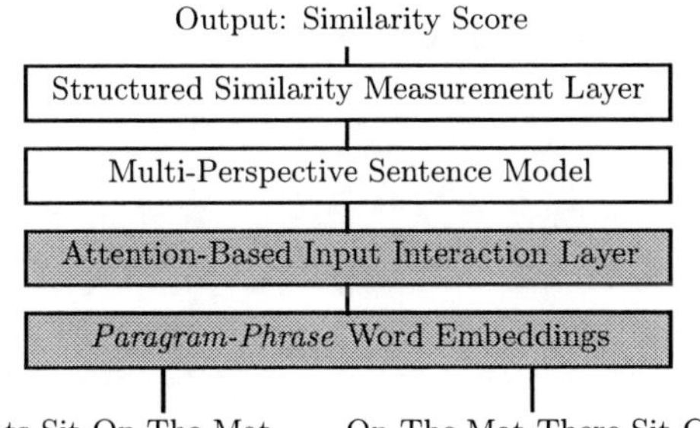

Figure 1: Model overview. Input sentences are processed by the attention-based input interaction layer and multi-perspective convolutional sentence model, then compared by the structured similarity measurement layer. The shaded components are our additions to the MPCNN model for the competition.

2 Base Model: Multi-Perspective Convolutional Neural Networks

We use the recently-proposed multi-perspective convolutional neural network model (MPCNN) of He et al. (2015) due to its competitive performance.[1] It consists of two major components:

1. A **multi-perspective sentence model** for converting a sentence into a representation. A convolutional neural network captures different granularities of information in each sentence using multiple types of convolutional filters, types of pooling, and window sizes.

2. A **structured similarity measurement layer** with multiple similarity metrics for comparing local regions of sentence representations.

The MPCNN model has a *Siamese* structure (Bromley et al., 1993), with a multi-perspective sentence model for each of the two input sentences.

Multiple Convolutional Filters. The MPCNN model applies two types of convolutional filters: 1-d per-dimension filters and 2-d holistic filters. The holistic filters operate over sliding windows while considering the full dimensionality of the word embeddings, like typical *temporal* convolutional filters. The per-dimension filters focus on information at a finer granularity and operate over sliding windows of each dimension of the word embeddings. Per-dimension filters can find and extract information

from individual dimensions, while holistic filters can discover broader patterns of contextual information. We use both kinds of filters for a richer representation of the input.

Multiple Window Sizes. The window size denotes how many words are matched by a filter. The MPCNN model uses filters with different window sizes ws in order to capture information at different n-gram lengths. We use filters with ws selected from $\{1, 2, 3\}$, so our filters can find unigrams, bigrams, and trigrams in the input sentences. In addition, to retain the raw information in the input, ws is also set to ∞ where pooling layers are directly applied over the entire sentence embedding matrix without the use of convolution layers in-between.

Multiple Pooling Types. For each output vector of a convolutional filter, the MPCNN model converts it to a scalar via a pooling layer. Pooling helps a convolutional model retain the most prominent and prevalent features, which is helpful for robustness across examples. One widely adopted pooling layer is *max pooling*, which applies a max operation over the input vector and returns the maximum value. In addition to max pooling, The MPCNN model uses two other types of pooling, min and mean, to extract different aspects of the filter matches.

Similarity Measurement Layer. After the sentence models produce representations for each sentence, we use a module that performs comparisons between the two sentence representations to output a final similarity score. One simple way to do this would be to flatten each sentence representation into a vector and then apply a similarity function such as cosine similarity. However, this discards important information because particular regions of the sentence representations come from different underlying sources. Therefore, the MPCNN model performs structured similarity measurements over particular local regions of the sentence representations.

The MPCNN model uses rules to identify local regions whose underlying components are related. These rules consider whether the local regions are: (1) from the same filter type; (2) from the convolutional filter with the same window size ws; (3) from the same pooling type; (4) from the same specific filter of the underlying convolution filter type.

---

[1] https://github.com/hohoCode

Only feature vectors that share at least two of the above are compared. There are two algorithms using three similarity metrics to compare local regions: one works on the output of holistic filters only, while the other uses the outputs of both the holistic and per-dimension filters.

On top of the structured similarity measurement layer, we stack two linear layers with a tanh activation layer in between, followed by a log-softmax layer. More details are provided in He et al. (2015).

3 Attention-Based Input Interaction Layer

The MPCNN model treats input sentences separately with two neural networks in parallel, which ignores the input contextual interaction information. We instead utilize an attention mechanism (Bahdanau et al., 2014) and develop an attention-based interaction layer that converts the two independent input sentences into an inter-related sentence pair.

We incorporate this into the base MPCNN model as the first layer of our system. It is applied over raw word embeddings of input sentences to generate re-weighted word embeddings. The attention-based re-weightings can guide the *focus* of the MPCNN model onto important input words. That is, words in one sentence that are more relevant to the other sentence receive higher weights.

We first define input sentence representation $S^i \in \mathbb{R}^{\ell_i \times d}$ ($i \in \{0, 1\}$) to be a sequence of ℓ_i words, each with a d-dimensional word embedding vector. $S^i[a]$ denotes the embedding vector of the a-th word in S^i. We then define an *attention matrix* $D \in \mathbb{R}^{\ell_0 \times \ell_1}$. Entry (a, b) in the matrix D represents the pairwise word similarity score between the a-th word embedding of S^0 and the b-th word embedding of S^1. The similarity score uses cosine distance:

$$D[a][b] = cosine(S^0[a], S^1[b])$$

Given the attention matrix D, we generate the attention weight vector $A^i \in \mathbb{R}^{\ell_i}$ for input sentence S^i ($i \in \{0, 1\}$). Each entry $A^i[a]$ of the attention weight vector can be viewed as an attention-based relevance score of one word embedding $S^i[a]$ with respect to all word embeddings of the other sentence $S^{1-i}[:]$. Attention weights $A^i[:]$ sum to one due to

the *softmax* normalization:

$$E^0[a] = \sum_b D[a][b]$$

$$E^1[b] = \sum_a D[a][b]$$

$$A^i = softmax(E^i)$$

We finally define updated embeddings $attenEmb \in \mathbb{R}^{2d}$ for each word as a concatenation of the original and attention-reweighted word embeddings:

$$attenEmb^i[a] = concat(S^i[a], A^i[a] \odot S^i[a])$$

where $\odot$ represents element-wise multiplication.

Our input interaction layer is inspired by recent work that incorporates attention mechanisms into neural networks (Bahdanau et al., 2014; Rush et al., 2015; Yin et al., 2015; Rocktäschel et al., 2016). Many of these add parameters and computational complexity to the model. However, our attention-based input layer is simpler and more efficient. Moreover, we do not introduce any additional parameters, as we simply use cosine distance to create the attention weights. Nevertheless, adding this attention layer improves performance, as we show in Section 5.

4 Word Embeddings

We compare several types of word embeddings to represent the initial sentence matrices (S^i). We use the PARAGRAM-SL999 embeddings from Wieting et al. (2015) and the PARAGRAM-PHRASE embeddings from Wieting et al. (2016). These were both constructed from the Paraphrase Database (PPDB) (Ganitkevitch et al., 2013) by training on *noisy* paraphrase pairs using a hinge-based loss with negative sampling. However, they were trained on two different types of data.

The PARAGRAM-SL999 embeddings were trained on the lexical section of PPDB, which consists of word pairs only. The PARAGRAM-PHRASE embeddings were trained on the phrasal section of PPDB, which consists of phrase pairs. The representations for the phrases were created by simply averaging word embeddings, which was found to outperform more complicated compositional architectures like LSTMs (Hochreiter and Schmidhuber, 1997)

STS2016	Domain	Pairs
answer-answer	Q&A forums	254
headlines	news headlines	249
plagiarism	short answer corpus	230
postediting	machine translation	244
question-question	Q&A forums	209
Test Total	-	**1,186**
Train Total	STS2012-2015	**14,342**

Table 1: Data statistics for STS2016.

STS2016	1st run	2nd run	3rd run
answer-answer	**0.6607**	0.6443	0.6432
headlines	**0.7946**	0.7871	0.7780
plagiarism	**0.8154**	0.7989	0.7816
postediting	**0.8094**	0.7934	0.7779
question-question	**0.6187**	0.5947	0.5586
Wt. Mean	**0.7420**	0.7262	0.7111

Table 2: Pearson's r on all five test sets. We show our three submission runs.

Ablation Study on STS2015	Pearson's r
Full System	**0.8040**
- Remove the attention layer (Sec. 3)	0.7948
- Replace PARAGRAM-PHRASE with GloVe (Sec. 4)	0.7622
- Replace PARAGRAM-PHRASE with PARAGRAM-SL999	0.7721
Winning System of STS2015	0.8015

Table 3: Ablation study on STS2015 test data.

when evaluated on out-of-domain data.[2] The resulting word embeddings yield sentence embeddings (via simple averaging) that perform well across STS tasks without task-specific tuning. Their performance is thought to be due in part to how the vectors for less important words have smaller norms than those for information-bearing words.

5 Experiments and Results

Datasets. The test data of the SemEval-2016 English STS competition consists of five datasets from different domains. We tokenize all data using Stanford CoreNLP (Manning et al., 2014). Each pair has a similarity score $\in [0, 5]$ which increases with similarity. We use training data from previous STS competitions (2012 to 2015). Table 1 provides a brief description.

Experimental Settings. We largely follow the same experimental settings as He et al. (2015), e.g., we perform optimization with stochastic gradient descent using a fixed learning rate of 0.01. We use the 300-dimensional PARAGRAM-PHRASE XXL word embeddings ($d = 300$).

Results on STS2016. We provide results of three runs in Table 2. The three runs are from the same system, but with models of different training epochs.

Ablation Study on STS2015. Table 3 shows an ablation study on the STS2015 test sets which consist of $3,000$ sentence pairs from five domains. Our training data for the ablation study is from previous test sets in STS2012-2014 following the rules of the STS2015 competition (Agirre et al., 2015). We remove or replace one component at a time from the full system and perform re-training and re-testing.

We observe a significant drop when the attention-based input interaction layer (Sec. 3) is removed. We also find that the PARAGRAM-PHRASE word embeddings are highly beneficial, outperforming both GloVe word embeddings (Pennington et al., 2014) and the PARAGRAM-SL999 embeddings of Wieting et al. (2015). Our full system performs favorably compared to the winning system (Sultan et al., 2015) at the STS2015 SemEval competition.

6 Conclusion

Our submission to the SemEval-2016 STS competition uses our multi-perspective convolutional neural network model as the base model. We develop an attention-based input interaction layer to guide the convolutional neural network to focus on the most important input words. We further improve performance by using the PARAGRAM-PHRASE word embeddings, yielding a result on the 2015 test data that surpasses that of the top system from STS2015.

Acknowledgments

This work was supported by NSF awards IIS-1218043 and CNS-1405688. The views expressed here are those of the authors and do not necessarily reflect those of the sponsor. We thank Mohit Bansal and Karen Livescu for helpful comments and NVIDIA for additional hardware support.

---

[2] For in-domain evaluation, LSTMs outperformed averaging.

References

Eneko Agirre, Mona Diab, Daniel Cer, and Aitor Gonzalez-Agirre. 2012. SemEval-2012 task 6: A pilot on semantic textual similarity. In *Proceedings of the First Joint Conference on Lexical and Computational Semantics*, pages 385–393.

Eneko Agirre, Daniel Cer, Mona Diab, Aitor Gonzalez-Agirre, and Weiwei Guo. 2013. SEM 2013 shared task: Semantic textual similarity. In *Proceedings of the Main Conference and the Shared Task: Semantic Textual Similarity*, pages 32–43.

Eneko Agirre, Carmen Banea, Claire Cardie, Daniel Cer, Mona Diab, Aitor Gonzalez-Agirre, Weiwei Guo, Rada Mihalcea, German Rigau, and Janyce Wiebe. 2014. SemEval-2014 task 10: Multilingual semantic textual similarity. In *Proceedings of the 8th International Workshop on Semantic Evaluation*, pages 81–91.

Eneko Agirre, Carmen Banea, Claire Cardie, Daniel Cer, Mona Diab, Aitor Gonzalez-Agirre, Weiwei Guo, Inigo Lopez-Gazpio, Montse Maritxalar, Rada Mihalcea, German Rigau, Larraitz Uria, and Janyce Wiebe. 2015. SemEval-2015 task 2: Semantic textual similarity, English, Spanish and pilot on interpretability. In *Proceedings of the 9th International Workshop on Semantic Evaluation*, pages 252–263.

Eneko Agirre, Carmen Banea, Daniel Cer, Mona Diab, Aitor Gonzalez-Agirre, Rada Mihalcea, and Janyce Wiebe. 2016. SemEval-2016 task 1: Semantic textual similarity - monolingual and cross-lingual evaluation. In *Proceedings of the 10th International Workshop on Semantic Evaluation*.

Dzmitry Bahdanau, Kyunghyun Cho, and Yoshua Bengio. 2014. Neural machine translation by jointly learning to align and translate. *CoRR*, abs/1409.0473.

Jane Bromley, James W Bentz, Léon Bottou, Isabelle Guyon, Yann LeCun, Cliff Moore, Eduard Säckinger, and Roopak Shah. 1993. Signature verification using a "Siamese" time delay neural network. *International Journal of Pattern Recognition and Artificial Intelligence*, 7(4):669–688.

Dipanjan Das and Noah A. Smith. 2009. Paraphrase identification as probabilistic quasi-synchronous recognition. In *Proceedings of the 47th Annual Meeting of the Association for Computational Linguistics*, pages 468–476.

Kevin K. Duh. 2009. *Learning to Rank with Partially-Labeled Data*. Ph.D. thesis, University of Washington.

Christiane Fellbaum. 1998. *WordNet: An Electronic Lexical Database*. MIT Press.

Samuel Fern and Mark Stevenson. 2008. A semantic similarity approach to paraphrase detection. In *Proceedings of the 11th Annual Research Colloquium of the UK Special-Interest Group for Computational Linguistics*, pages 45–52.

Juri Ganitkevitch, Benjamin Van Durme, and Chris Callison-Burch. 2013. PPDB: The Paraphrase Database. In *Proceedings of the 2013 Conference of the North American Chapter of the Association for Computational Linguistics: Human Language Technologies*, pages 758–764.

Weiwei Guo and Mona Diab. 2012. Modeling sentences in the latent space. In *Proceedings of the 50th Annual Meeting of the Association for Computational Linguistics*, pages 864–872.

Hua He and Jimmy Lin. 2016. Pairwise word interaction modeling with deep neural networks for semantic similarity measurement. In *Proceedings of the 2016 Conference of the North American Chapter of the Association for Computational Linguistics: Human Language Technologies*.

Hua He, Kevin Gimpel, and Jimmy Lin. 2015. Multiperspective sentence similarity modeling with convolutional neural networks. In *Proceedings of the 2015 Conference on Empirical Methods in Natural Language Processing*, pages 1576–1586.

Sepp Hochreiter and Jürgen Schmidhuber. 1997. Long short-term memory. *Neural Computation*, 9(8):1735–1780.

Abhay Kashyap, Lushan Han, Roberto Yus, Jennifer Sleeman, Taneeya Satyapanich, Sunil Gandhi, and Tim Finin. 2014. Meerkat mafia: Multilingual and cross-level semantic textual similarity systems. In *Proceedings of the 8th International Workshop on Semantic Evaluation*, pages 416–423.

Jimmy Lin. 2007. An exploration of the principles underlying redundancy-based factoid question answering. *ACM Transactions on Information Systems*, 25(2):1–55.

André Lynum, Partha Pakray, Björn Gambäck, and Sergio Jimenez. 2014. NTNU: Measuring semantic similarity with sublexical feature representations and soft cardinality. In *Proceedings of the 8th International Workshop on Semantic Evaluation*, pages 448–453.

Nitin Madnani, Joel Tetreault, and Martin Chodorow. 2012. Re-examining machine translation metrics for paraphrase identification. In *Proceedings of the 2012 Conference of the North American Chapter of the Association for Computational Linguistics: Human Language Technologies*, pages 182–190.

Christopher D. Manning, Mihai Surdeanu, John Bauer, Jenny Finkel, Steven J. Bethard, and David McClosky. 2014. The Stanford CoreNLP natural language processing toolkit. In *Proceedings of 52nd Annual Meeting of the Association for Computational Linguistics: System Demonstrations*, pages 55–60.

Jeffrey Pennington, Richard Socher, and Christopher D. Manning. 2014. GloVe: Global vectors for word representation. In *Proceedings of the 2014 Conference on Empirical Methods in Natural Language Processing*, pages 1532–1543.

Tim Rocktäschel, Edward Grefenstette, Karl Moritz Hermann, Tomáš Kočiský, and Phil Blunsom. 2016. Reasoning about entailment with neural attention. In *Proceedings of the 4th International Conference on Learning Representations*.

Alexander M. Rush, Sumit Chopra, and Jason Weston. 2015. A neural attention model for abstractive sentence summarization. In *Proceedings of the 2015 Conference on Empirical Methods in Natural Language Processing*, pages 379–389.

Frane Šarić, Goran Glavaš, Mladen Karan, Jan Šnajder, and Bojana Dalbelo Bašić. 2012. TakeLab: systems for measuring semantic text similarity. In *Proceedings of the First Joint Conference on Lexical and Computational Semantics*, pages 441–448.

Md Arafat Sultan, Steven Bethard, and Tamara Sumner. 2014. DLS@CU: Sentence similarity from word alignment. In *Proceedings of the 8th International Workshop on Semantic Evaluation*, pages 241–246.

Md Arafat Sultan, Steven Bethard, and Tamara Sumner. 2015. DLS@CU: Sentence similarity from word alignment and semantic vector composition. In *Proceedings of the 9th International Workshop on Semantic Evaluation*, pages 148–153.

Kai Sheng Tai, Richard Socher, and Christopher D. Manning. 2015. Improved semantic representations from tree-structured long short-term memory networks. In *Proceedings of the 53rd Annual Meeting of the Association for Computational Linguistics*, pages 1556–1566.

Stephen Wan, Mark Dras, Robert Dale, and Cecile Paris. 2006. Using Dependency-based Features to Take the "Para-farce" out of Paraphrase. In *Australasian Language Technology Workshop*, pages 131–138.

John Wieting, Mohit Bansal, Kevin Gimpel, Karen Livescu, and Dan Roth. 2015. From paraphrase database to compositional paraphrase model and back. *Transactions of the Association for Computational Linguistics*, 3:345–358.

John Wieting, Mohit Bansal, Kevin Gimpel, and Karen Livescu. 2016. Towards universal paraphrastic sentence embeddings. In *Proceedings of the 4th International Conference on Learning Representations*.

Wei Xu, Alan Ritter, Chris Callison-Burch, William B. Dolan, and Yangfeng Ji. 2014. Extracting lexically divergent paraphrases from Twitter. *Transactions of the Association for Computational Linguistics*, 2:435–448.

Wenpeng Yin and Hinrich Schütze. 2015. Convolutional neural network for paraphrase identification. In *Proceedings of the 2015 Conference of the North American Chapter of the Association for Computational Linguistics: Human Language Technologies*, pages 901–911.

Wenpeng Yin, Hinrich Schütze, Bing Xiang, and Bowen Zhou. 2015. ABCNN: attention-based convolutional neural network for modeling sentence pairs. *CoRR*, abs/1512.05193.

Inspire at SemEval-2016 Task 2: Interpretable Semantic Textual Similarity Alignment based on Answer Set Programming

Mishal Kazmi
Sabanci University
Istanbul, Turkey
mishalkazmi@sabanciuniv.edu

Peter Schüller
Marmara University
Istanbul, Turkey
peter.schuller@marmara.edu.tr

Abstract

In this paper we present our system developed for the SemEval 2016 Task 2 - Interpretable Semantic Textual Similarity along with the results obtained for our submitted runs. Our system participated in the subtasks predicting chunk similarity alignments for gold chunks as well as for predicted chunks. The Inspire system extends the basic ideas from last years participant NeRoSim, however we realize the rules in logic programming and obtain the result with an Answer Set Solver. To prepare the input for the logic program, we use the PunktTokenizer, Word2Vec, and WordNet APIs of NLTK, and the POS- and NER-taggers from Stanford CoreNLP. For chunking we use a joint POS-tagger and dependency parser and based on that determine chunks with an Answer Set Program. Our system ranked third place overall and first place in the Headlines gold chunk subtask.

1 Introduction

Semantic Textual Similarity (STS), refers to the degree of semantic equivalence between a pair of texts. This helps in explaining how some texts are related or unrelated. In Interpretable STS (iSTS) systems, further explanation is provided as to why the two texts are related or unrelated. Finding these detailed explanations helps in gathering a meaningful representation of their similarities.

The competition at SemEval 2016 was run on three different datasets: Headlines, Images and Student-Answers. Each dataset included two files containing pairs of sentences and two files containing pairs of gold-chunked sentences. Either the gold chunks provided by the organizers or chunks obtained from the given texts would be used as input to the system. The expected outputs of the system are m:n chunk-chunk alignments, corresponding similarity scores between 0 (unrelated) and 5(equivalent), and a label indicating the type of semantic relation. Possible semantic relations are EQUI (semantically equal), OPPO (opposite), SPE1/SPE2 (chunk 1/2 is more specific than chunk 2/1), SIMI (similar but none of the relations above), REL (related but none of the relations above), and NOALI (not aligned, e.g., punctuation). All relations shall be considered in the given context. For details see the companion paper (Agirre et al., 2016).

Similarity alignment in the Inspire system is based on ideas of previous year's NeRoSim (Banjade et al., 2015) entry, however we reimplemented the system and realize the rule engine in Answer Set Programming (ASP) (Lifschitz, 2008; Brewka et al., 2011) which gives us flexibility for reordering rules or applying them in parallel. To account for differences in datasets we detect the type of input with a Naive Bayes classifier and use different parameter sets for each of the datasets.

Chunking in the Inspire system is based on a joint POS-tagger and dependency parser (Bohnet et al., 2013) and an ASP program that determines chunk boundaries.

Proceedings of SemEval-2016, pages 1109–1115,
San Diego, California, June 16-17, 2016. ©2016 Association for Computational Linguistics

In Section 2 we give preliminaries of ASP, Section 3 describes how we represented semantic alignment in ASP, in Section 5 we explain parameter sets used for different datasets, Section 4 briefly outlines our chunking approach, and we give evaluation results in Section 6.

2 Answer Set Programming (ASP)

Answer Set Programming (ASP) (Lifschitz, 2008; Brewka et al., 2011) is a logic programming paradigm based on rules of the form:

$$a \leftarrow b_1, \ldots, b_m, \mathbf{not}\ b_{m+1}, \ldots, \mathbf{not}\ b_n$$

where a, b_i are atoms from a first-order language, a is the head and $b_1, \ldots, \mathbf{not}\ b_n$ is the body of the rule, and **not** is negation as failure. Variables start with capital letters, facts (rules without body condition) are written as 'a.' instead of '$a \leftarrow$'. Intuitively a is true if all positive body atoms are true and no negative body atom is true. ASP is declarative, i.e., the order of rules and the order of body atoms in rules does not matter (different from Prolog), a popular usage pattern of ASP is to create three program modules called Generate, Define, and Test, which (i) generate a space of potential solutions, (ii) define auxiliary concepts, and (iii) eliminate invalid solutions using constraints, respectively. ASP allows encoding of nondeterministic polynomial time (NP)-hard problems, solver tools usually first instantiate the given program and then find solutions of the variable-free theory using adapted Satisfiability (SAT) solvers. Apart from normal atoms and rules, ASP supports aggregates and other constructions, for details we refer to the ASP-Core-2 standard (Calimeri et al., 2012). In this work we use the ASP solvers Gringo and Clasp (Gebser et al., 2011) as a Python library.

3 Alignment based on ASP

For each sentence pair, we align chunks in the following architecture:

- Chunked input sentence pairs are preprocessed (POS, NER, Word2Vec, WordNet) and represented as a set of ASP facts (3.1).
- A generic set of rules represents how alignments can be defined and changed (3.2).

- We represent alignments based on the description of the NeRoSim engine (3.3).
- We evaluate the above components in an ASP solver, obtaining answers sets containing a representation of alignments. From this we create the system output file (3.4).

3.1 Preprocessing

In this step we create facts that represent the input, including lemmatization via NLTK (Bird, 2006), POS- and NER-tagging from Stanford CoreNLP (Manning et al., 2014), lookups in WordNet (Miller, 1995), and similarity values obtained using Word2Vec (Mikolov et al., 2013).

We explain the input representation of the following sentence pair:

[A tan puppy] [being petted] [.]
[A tan puppy] [being held and petted] [.]

We first represent sentences, chunks, and words in chunks with POS-tags, NER-tags, and lowercase versions of words as follows:

$sentence(1)$.
$chunk(sc(1,0))$.
$chunk(sc(1,1))$.
$chunk(sc(1,2))$.
$mword(cw(sc(1,0),1),"A","a","DT","O")$.
$mword(cw(sc(1,0),2),"tan",$
$\qquad\qquad\qquad "tan","NN","O")$.
$mword(cw(sc(1,0),3),"puppy",$
$\qquad\qquad\qquad "puppy","NN","O")$.
$\ldots$
$sentence(2)$.
$chunk(sc(2,0))$.
$\ldots$

Intuitively a sentence ID is an integer, a chunk ID is a composite $sc(sentenceID, chunkIdx)$, and a word ID is a composite $cw(chunkID, wordIdx)$.

We detect punctuation, cardinal numbers, and dates/times using regular expressions and represent this as facts $punct(\cdot)$, $cardinalnumber(\cdot)$, and $datetime(\cdot)$, resp., e.g.,

$$punct(cw(sc(1,2),0)).$$

We lookup synonyms, hypernyms, and antonyms in WordNet and add the respective facts.

$synonym("a", "a")$.

$synonym("a", "vitamin\ a")$.

$synonym("tan", "burn")$.

$hypernym("puppy", "dog")$.

$hypernym("puppy", "domestic\_dog")$.

$hypernym("puppy", "canis\_familiaris")$.

$\ldots$

We use distributional similarity with the Word2Vec tool (Mikolov et al., 2013) trained on the One Billion Word[1] benchmark (Chelba et al., 2014) with SkipGram context representation, window size 10, vector dimension 200, and pruning below frequency 50. Word-word similarity $sim(v, w)$ is computed using cosine similarity from scikit-learn (Pedregosa et al., 2011), between vectors of words v and w. We compute chunk-chunk similarity as

$$\frac{best(1, 2) + best(2, 1)}{2\min(n_1, n_2)}, \text{ where} \tag{1}$$

$$best(x, y) = \sum_{i=1}^{n_x} \max_{j=1}^{n_y} sim(w_i^x, w_j^y)$$

with n_x the number of words in chunk x and w_b^x the word of index b in chunk x. This is based on (Banjade et al., 2015, Section 2.2.2).

We represent chunk-chunk similarity as atoms $chunksimilarity(chunk1Id, chunk2Id, S)$. In our example this creates, e.g., the following facts.

$chunksimilarity(sc(1, 0), sc(2, 0), 101)$.

$chunksimilarity(sc(1, 0), sc(2, 1), 22)$.

$chunksimilarity(sc(1, 0), sc(2, 2), 2)$.

$chunksimilarity(sc(1, 1), sc(2, 0), 34)$.

$\ldots$

Note that similarity can be above 100 due to dividing by the shorter chunk length.

3.2 Rule Engine

To make POS, NER, word, and lowercase words more accessible, we project them to new facts

---

[1]http://www.statmt.org/lm-benchmark/

with the following rules

$$word(Id, W) \leftarrow mword(Id, W, \_, \_, \_).$$
$$lword(Id, L) \leftarrow mword(Id, \_, L, \_, \_).$$
$$pos(Id, P) \leftarrow mword(Id, \_, \_, P, \_).$$
$$ner(Id, N) \leftarrow mword(Id, \_, \_, \_, N).$$

where the arguments of $mword$ are word ID, word, lowercase word, POS and NER tag.

Variables of the form '$\_$' are anonymous, intuitively these values are projected away before applying the rule.

We interpret POS and NER tags, and mark nouns, verbs, contentwords, proper nouns, cardinal numbers and locations based on tags from the Penn Treebank (Marcus et al., 1993).

$$noun(Id) \leftarrow pos(Id, "NNS").$$
$$noun(Id) \leftarrow pos(Id, "NNP").$$
$$verb(Id) \leftarrow pos(Id, "VB").$$
$$verb(Id) \leftarrow pos(Id, "VBD").$$
$$\ldots$$
$$location(Id) \leftarrow ner(Id, "LOCATION").$$

We ensure symmetry of chunk similarity, synonyms and antonyms, and transitivity of the synonym relation.

$$chunksimilarity(C_2, C_1, S) \leftarrow$$
$$chunksimilarity(C_1, C_2, S).$$
$$synonym(W, W') \leftarrow synonym(W', W).$$
$$antonym(W, W') \leftarrow antonym(W', W).$$
$$synonym(W_1, W_3) \leftarrow synonym(W_1, W_2),$$
$$synonym(W_2, W_3).$$

We define pairs of chunks that can be matched together with their sentence indices. This is useful because this way we can define conditions on potential alignments without specifying the direction of alignment (1 to 2 vs. 2 to 1).

$$chpair(S_1, S_2, sc(S_1, C_1), sc(S_2, C_2)) \leftarrow$$
$$chunk(sc(S_1, C_1)), chunk(sc(S_2, C_2)), S_1 \neq S_2.$$

We represent alignments as follows:

(i) alignment happens in steps that have an order defined by atoms $nextStep(S, S')$ which indicates that S happens before S',

(ii) a chunk can be aligned to one or more chunks only within one step, afterwards alignment cannot be changed,

(iii) program modules can define atoms of form $chalign(C_1, R, Sc, C_2, St)$ which indicates that chunks C_1 and C_2 should be aligned with label R (e.g., "EQUI") and score Sc (e.g., 5) in step St.

Defining an alignment is possible if the chunks are not yet aligned, it marks both involved chunks as aligned, and they stay aligned.

$$aligned(C, S') \leftarrow \textbf{not } aligned(C, S),$$
$$chalign(C, \_, \_, \_, S), nextStep(S, S').$$
$$aligned(C, S') \leftarrow \textbf{not } aligned(C, S),$$
$$chalign(\_, \_, \_, C, S), nextStep(S, S').$$
$$aligned(C, S') \leftarrow aligned(C, S), nextStep(S, S').$$

Final alignments (that are interpreted by Python) are represented using predicate $final$, these atoms include raw chunk similarity (for experimenting with other ways to define the similarity score). Moreover only steps that are used (in $nextStep(\cdot, \cdot)$) are included.

$$usedStep(S) \leftarrow nextStep(S, \_).$$
$$usedStep(S') \leftarrow nextStep(\_, S').$$
$$final(C_1, Rel, Score, C_2, S, Simi) \leftarrow$$
$$chalign(C_1, Rel, Score, C_2, S),$$
$$\textbf{not } aligned(C_1, S), \textbf{not } aligned(C_2, S),$$
$$usedStep(S), chunksimilarity(C_1, C_2, Simi).$$

This system gives us flexibility for configuring the usage and application of the order of rules by defining $nextStep$ accordingly (see Section 5).

3.3 NeRoSim Rules

All that remains is to realize the NeRoSim rules, labeled with individual steps, and add them to the program.

In the following we give an example of how we realize NeRoSim's condition C_1 (one chunk has a conjunction and other does not).

$$cond_1(C_1, C_2) \leftarrow chpair(\_, \_, C_1, C_2),$$
$$\#count\{W_1 : conjunction(cw(C_1, W_1))\} = 0,$$
$$\#count\{W_2 : conjunction(cw(C_2, W_2))\} \geq 1.$$

Intuitively, the $\#count$ aggregates become true if the appropriate number of atoms in the set becomes true.

As a second example, our adaptation of rule SP_1 for SPE1/SPE2 alignments defines $sp1(C_1, C_2)$ if $cond_1$ holds between C_2 and C_1 and if C_1 contains all content words of C_2. Note that $contentword\_subset(A, B)$ is defined separately for chunks A, B if B contains all content words of A.

$$sp1(C_1, C_2) \leftarrow chpair(\_, \_, C_1, C_2),$$
$$cond_1(C_2, C_1), contentword\_subset(C_2, C_1).$$

We use $sp1$ in our stepwise alignment engine by defining $chalign$ with SPE1 and SPE2 according to which $sentence$ is more specific.

$$chalign(C_1, "SPE1", 4, C_2, sp1) \leftarrow$$
$$chpair(1, 2, C_1, C_2), sp1(C_1, C_2).$$
$$chalign(C_1, "SPE2", 4, C_2, sp1) \leftarrow$$
$$chpair(1, 2, C_1, C_2), sp1(C_2, C_1).$$

For reasons of space we are unable to list all NeRoSim rules and their ASP realization. For the description of rules NOALIC, EQUI(1–5), OPPO, SPE1/2(1–3), SIMI(1–5), REL, we refer to (Banjade et al., 2015).

The full ASP code is publicly available.[2]

3.4 Interpretation of Answer Sets

After the evaluation of the above rules with the facts that describe the input sentences (Section 3.1) the solver returns a set of answer sets (in our case a single answer set). This answer set contains all true atoms and we are interested only in the $final$ predicates.

$$word(cw(sc(1, 1), 4), "being").$$
$$word(cw(sc(1, 1), 5), "petted").$$
$$word(cw(sc(2, 1), 4), "being").$$
$$word(cw(sc(2, 1), 5), "held").$$
$$word(cw(sc(2, 1), 6), "and").$$
$$\dots$$
$$final(sc(1, 0), "EQUI", 5, sc(2, 0), equi1, 101).$$

---

[2]https://bitbucket.org/snippets/knowlp/yrjqr

final(sc(1, 1), "SPE2", 4, sc(2, 1), sp1, 106).

From these predicates we create the required output which is a single continous line of the following form:

```
4 5 6 <==> 4 5 6 7 // SPE2 // 4 //
   being petted <==> being held and petted
```

4   Chunking based on ASP

For this subtrack, the system has to identify chunks and align them. The Inspire system realizes chunking as a preprocessing step: sentences are tokenized and processed by a joint POS-tagger and parser (Bohnet et al., 2013). Tokens, POS-tags, and dependency relations are represented as ASP facts and processed by a program that roughly encodes the following:

- chunks extend to child tokens until another chunk starts, and
- chunks start at (i) prepositions, except 'of' in 'in front of'; (ii) determiners, unless after a preposition; (iii) punctuations (where they immediately end); (iv) adverbs; (v) nodes in an appositive relation; and (vi) nodes having a subject.

These rules were created manually to obtain a result close to (Abney, 1991).

5   Experiments and Parameters

Our system does not require training, so we tested and optimized it on the training data for Headlines (H), Images (I), and Student-Answers (S) datasets. As a criteria for accuracy the competition used the F1 score based on alignments (A), alignments and alignment type (AT), alignments and alignment score (AS), and full consideration of alignment, type, and score (ATS).

Our optimization experiments showed us, that there are significant differences in annotations between datasets. In particular S contains spelling mistakes, verbs are often singleton chunks in H, and 'to' and ''s' often start a new chunk in H, while they are annotated as part of the previous chunk in I and S.

Therefore we decided to configure our system differently for each dataset, based on a Multinomial Naive Bayes Classifier trained on input unigrams and bigrams implemented using scikit-learn (Pedregosa et al., 2011). F1-score obtained on training data with 10-fold cross-validation was 0.99.

Our dataset configuration is as follows: we exclude stopwords from the calculation of similarity (1) for datasets H and I by using the NLTK corpus of stopwords; we remove non-singleton punctuation for dataset S; and we add rules to handle verb types (VBP, VBZ) as punctuation and ''s' as a preposition in chunking.

We optimized parameters for 3 runs according to different criteria.

Run 1 is optimized for the full label (ATS). We used our implementation of NeRoSim rules in the same order, except SI4, SI5, and RE1, which we excluded. In ASP this is configured by defining facts for $nextStep(s, s')$ where

$$(s, s') \in \{(noalic, equi1), (equi1, equi2),$$
$$(equi2, equi3), (equi3, equi4), (equi4, equi5),$$
$$(equi5, oppo), (oppo, sp1), (sp1, sp2), (sp2, sp3),$$
$$(sp3, simi1), (simi1, simi2), (simi2, simi3),$$
$$(simi3, result)\}.$$

Run 2 is optimized for prediction of alignment (A), this is done by using all NeRoSim rules in their original order: we define $nextStep(s, s')$ for

$$(s, s') \in \{(noalic, equi1), (equi1, equi2),$$
$$(equi2, equi3), (equi3, equi4), (equi4, equi5),$$
$$(equi5, oppo), (oppo, sp1), (sp1, sp2).(sp2, sp3),$$
$$(sp3, simi1), (simi1, simi2), (simi2, simi3),$$
$$(simi3, simi4), (simi4, simi5), (simi5, rel1),$$
$$(rel1, result)\}.$$

In addition, for dataset S we perform automated spelling correction using Enchant.[3]

Run 3 is based the observation, that the scorer tool does not severely punish overlapping alignments in the F1-score of A. Hence we allow SIMI4, SIMI5, and REL1 to be applied simultaneously by defining $nextStep(s, s')$ for

$$(s, s') \in \{(noalic, equi1), (equi1, equi2),$$

---

[3] `http://www.abisource.com/projects/enchant/`

$(equi2, equi3), (equi3, equi4), (equi4, equi5),$
$(equi5, oppo), (oppo, sp1), (sp1, sp2), (sp2, sp3),$
$(sp3, simi1), (simi1, simi2), (simi2, simi3),$
$(simi3, simi4), (simi3, simi5), (simi3, rel1),$
$(simi4, result), (simi5, result), (rel1, result)\}.$

Accordingly, we expected Run 1 to perform best with respect to the ATS (and AT) metric, Run 2 to perform best with respect to A (and AS) metrics, and Run 3 to sometimes perform above other runs. These expectations were confirmed by the results shown in the next section.

6 Results and Conclusion

The results of the competition, obtained with the above parameter sets, are shown in Table 1.

The Inspire system made use of a rule-based approach using Answer Set Programming for determining chunk boundaries (based on a representation obtained from a dependency parser) and for aligning chunks and assigning alignment type and score (based on a representation obtained from POS, NER, and distributed similarity tagging). In team ranking, our system is among the top three systems for Headlines and Images datasets, and in overall ranking (both for system and gold chunks). In terms of runs (each team could submit three runs), our system obtains first and second place for Headlines with gold standard chunks. For Student-Answers dataset our system performs worst. The configuration of Run 1 performs best in all categories.

In future work we want to represent semantic knowledge in ASP externals (Eiter et al., 2015), and use ASP guesses, constraints, and optimization as outlined in (Lierler and Schüller, 2013).

Acknowledgments

This research has been supported by the Scientific and Technological Research Council of Turkey (TUBITAK) Grant 114E777.

References

Steven P Abney. 1991. *Parsing by chunks*. Springer.

Data	Run	A	AT	AS	ATS	R
		Gold-Standard Chunks				
H	Base	0.85	0.55	0.76	0.55	-
	1	0.82	**0.70**	0.79	**0.70**	1
	2	0.89	0.67	**0.83**	0.66	2
	3	**0.90**	0.59	0.82	0.58	12
I	BL	0.86	0.48	0.75	0.48	-
	1	0.80	**0.61**	0.75	**0.61**	7
	2	**0.87**	0.60	**0.79**	0.59	8
	3	0.86	0.49	0.78	0.49	19
S	BL	0.82	**0.56**	0.75	**0.56**	-
	1	0.80	0.51	0.73	0.51	15
	2	0.82	0.48	0.74	0.48	16
	3	**0.87**	0.39	**0.77**	0.39	19
		System Chunks				
H	BL	0.65	0.48	0.59	0.44	-
	1	0.70	**0.53**	0.66	**0.52**	4
	2	0.76	0.50	**0.69**	0.50	8
	3	**0.77**	0.46	**0.69**	0.45	13
I	BL	0.71	0.40	0.63	0.40	-
	1	0.75	**0.56**	0.70	**0.56**	4
	2	**0.82**	0.54	**0.74**	0.54	6
	3	0.81	0.45	0.73	0.45	13
S	BL	0.62	0.44	0.57	0.44	-
	1	0.69	**0.46**	0.64	**0.45**	10
	2	0.72	0.42	0.65	0.42	11
	3	**0.76**	0.34	**0.67**	0.34	12

Table 1: System Performance results (F1-score). BL is the baseline, R gives the rank in the respective competition category. Abbreviations are explained in Section 5.

Eneko Agirre, Aitor Gonzalez-Agirre, Iñigo Lopez-Gazpio, Montse Maritxalar, German Rigau, and Larraitz Uria. 2016. SemEval-2016 Task 2: Interpretable semantic textual similarity. In *Proceedings of the 10th International Workshop on Semantic Evaluation (SemEval 2016)*, San Diego, California, June.

Rajendra Banjade, Nobal B Niraula, Nabin Maharjan, Vasile Rus, Dan Stefanescu, Mihai Lintean, and Dipesh Gautam. 2015. NeRoSim: A system for measuring and interpreting semantic textual similarity. In *SemEval 2015*, pages 164–171.

Steven Bird. 2006. NLTK: the natural language toolkit. In *Proceedings of the COLING/ACL on Interactive presentation sessions*, pages 69–72. Association for Computational Linguistics.

Bernd Bohnet, Joakim Nivre, Igor Boguslavsky, Richárd Farkas, Filip Ginter, and Jan Hajič. 2013.

Joint morphological and syntactic analysis for richly inflected languages. *Transactions of the Association for Computational Linguistics*, 1:415–428.

Gerhard Brewka, Thomas Eiter, and Mirosław Truszczyński. 2011. Answer set programming at a glance. *Communications of the ACM*, 54(12):92–103.

Francesco Calimeri, Wolfgang Faber, Martin Gebser, Giovambattista Ianni, Roland Kaminski, Thomas Krennwallner, Nicola Leone, Francesco Ricca, and Torsten Schaub. 2012. ASP-Core-2 Input language format. Technical report.

Ciprian Chelba, Tomas Mikolov, Mike Schuster, Qi Ge, Thorsten Brants, Phillipp Koehn, and Tony Robinson. 2014. One billion word benchmark for measuring progress in statistical language modeling. Technical report.

Thomas Eiter, Michael Fink, Giovambattista Ianni, Thomas Krennwallner, Christoph Redl, and Peter Schüller. 2015. A model building framework for Answer Set Programming with external computations. *Theory and Practice of Logic Programming*, FirstView:1–47.

Martin Gebser, Benjamin Kaufmann, Roland Kaminski, Max Ostrowski, Torsten Schaub, and Marius Schneider. 2011. Potassco: The Potsdam Answer Set Solving Collection. *AI Communications*, 24(2):107–124.

Yuliya Lierler and Peter Schüller. 2013. Towards a tight integration of syntactic parsing with semantic disambiguation by means of declarative programming. In *International Conference on Computational Semantics (IWCS)*, pages 383–389.

Vladimir Lifschitz. 2008. What is answer set programming?. In *AAAI*, volume 8, pages 1594–1597.

Christopher D Manning, Mihai Surdeanu, John Bauer, Jenny Rose Finkel, Steven Bethard, and David McClosky. 2014. The Stanford CoreNLP natural language processing toolkit. In *ACL (System Demonstrations)*, pages 55–60.

Mitchell P Marcus, Mary Ann Marcinkiewicz, and Beatrice Santorini. 1993. Building a large annotated corpus of english: The penn treebank. *Computational linguistics*, 19(2):313–330.

Tomas Mikolov, Ilya Sutskever, Kai Chen, Greg S Corrado, and Jeff Dean. 2013. Distributed representations of words and phrases and their compositionality. In *Advances in neural information processing systems*, pages 3111–3119.

George A Miller. 1995. WordNet: a lexical database for English. *Communications of the ACM*, 38(11):39–41.

Fabian Pedregosa, Gaël Varoquaux, Alexandre Gramfort, Vincent Michel, Bertrand Thirion, Olivier Grisel, Mathieu Blondel, Peter Prettenhofer, Ron Weiss, Vincent Dubourg, et al. 2011. Scikit-learn: Machine learning in python. *The Journal of Machine Learning Research*, 12:2825–2830.

KeLP at SemEval-2016 Task 3:
Learning Semantic Relations between Questions and Answers

Simone Filice[1], **Danilo Croce**[2],
Alessandro Moschitti[3] and **Roberto Basili**[2]
[1] DICII, University of Roma, Tor Vergata
[2] DII, University of Roma, Tor Vergata
[3] ALT, Qatar Computing Research Institute, HBKU
{filice,croce,basili}@info.uniroma2.it
amoschitti@qf.org.qa

Abstract

This paper describes the KeLP system participating in the SemEval-2016 Community Question Answering (cQA) task. The challenge tasks are modeled as binary classification problems: kernel-based classifiers are trained on the SemEval datasets and their scores are used to sort the instances and produce the final ranking. All classifiers and kernels have been implemented within the Kernel-based Learning Platform called KeLP. Our primary submission ranked first in Subtask A, third in Subtask B and second in Subtask C. These ranks are based on MAP, which is the referring challenge system score. Our approach outperforms all the other systems with respect to all the other challenge metrics.

1 Introduction

This paper describes the KeLP system participating in the SemEval-2016 cQA challenge. In this task, participants are asked to automatically provide good answers in a cQA setting (Nakov et al., 2016). In particular, the main task is: given a *new question* and a large collection of *question-comment threads* created by a user community, rank the most useful comments on the top.

We participated in all English subtasks: the datasets were extracted from *Qatar Living*[1], a web forum where people pose questions about multiple aspects of their daily life in Qatar. Three subtasks are associated with the English challenge:

Subtask A: Given a question q and its first 10 comments $c_1, \ldots, c_{10}$ in its question thread, re-rank these 10 comments according to their relevance with respect to the question, i.e., the *good* comments have to be ranked above *potential* or *bad* comments.

Subtask B: Given a new question o and the set of the first 10 related questions $q_1, \ldots, q_{10}$ (retrieved by a search engine), re-rank the related questions according to their similarity with respect to o, i.e., the *perfect match* and *relevant* questions should be ranked above the *irrelevant* ones.

Subtask C: Given a new question o, and the set of the first 10 related questions, $q_1, \ldots, q_{10}$, (retrieved by a search engine), each one associated with its first 10 comments, $c_1^q, \ldots, c_{10}^q$, appearing in its thread, re-rank the 100 comments according to their relevance with respect to o, i.e., the *good* comments are to be ranked above *potential* or *bad* comments.

All the above subtasks have been modeled as binary classification problems: kernel-based classifiers are trained and the classification score is used to sort the instances and produce the final ranking. All classifiers and kernels have been implemented within the Kernel-based Learning Platform[2] (KeLP) (Filice et al., 2015b), thus determining the team's name. The proposed solution provides three main contributions: (*i*) we employ the approach proposed in (Severyn and Moschitti, 2012), which applies tree kernels directly to question and answer texts modeled as pairs of linked syntactic trees. We further improve the methods using the kernels proposed in (Filice et al., 2015c). (*ii*) we extended the features developed in (Barrón-Cedeño et al., 2015), by adopting several features (also derived from Word Embeddings (Mikolov et al., 2013)). (*iii*) we propose

---

[1] http://www.qatarliving.com/forum

[2] https://github.com/SAG-KeLP

Proceedings of SemEval-2016, pages 1116–1123,
San Diego, California, June 16-17, 2016. ©2016 Association for Computational Linguistics

a stacking schema so that classifiers for Subtask B and C exploit the inferences obtained in the previous subtasks.

Our primary submission ranked first in Subtask A, third in Subtask B and second in Subtask C, demonstrating that the proposed method is very accurate and adaptable to different learning problems. These ranks are based on the MAP metric. However, if we consider the other metrics also adopted in the challenge (e.g., F_1 or Accuracy) our approach outperforms all the remaining systems.

In the remaining, Section 2 introduces the system, Sections 3 and 4 describe the feature and kernel modeling, while Section 5 reports official results.

2 The KeLP system: an overview

In the three subtasks, the underlying problem is to understand if two texts are related. Thus, in subtasks A and C, each pair, (question, comment), generates a training instance for a binary Support Vector Machine (SVM) (Chang and Lin, 2011), where the positive label is associated with a *good* comment and the negative label includes the *potential* and *bad* comments. In Subtask B, we evaluated the similarity between two questions. Each pair generates a training instance for SVM, where the positive label is associated with the *perfect match* or *relevant* classes and the negative label is associated with the *irrelevant*; the resulting classification score is used to rank the question pairs.

In KeLP, the SVM learning algorithm operates on a linear combination of kernel functions, each one applied over a specific representation of the targeted examples: (*i*) feature vectors containing linguistic similarities between the texts in a pair; (*ii*) shallow syntactic trees that encode the lexical and morpho-syntactic information shared between text pairs; (*iii*) feature vectors capturing task-specific information; (*iv*) in subtasks B and C, feature vectors encoding stacked information derived by applying the classifiers obtained in the previous subtasks.

While (*i*) and (*ii*) use linguistic information that can be applied in any semantic processing task defined over text pairs (see Sec. 3), the information derived via (*iii*) and (*iv*) is task specific (see Sec. 4).

3 Learning from Text Pairs with Kernels

The problem of deciding whether two questions are related or whether a comment answers a question, can be somehow connected to the problems of recognizing textual entailment, and paraphrase identification. From a machine learning perspective, in these tasks, an example is a pair of texts, instead of a single entity. Conventional approaches convert input text pairs into feature vectors where each feature represents a score corresponding to a certain type of shared information or similarity between the elements within a pair. These intra-pair similarity approaches cannot capture complex relational pattern between the elements in the pair, such as a rewriting rule characterizing a valid paraphrase, or a question-answer pattern. Such information might be manually encoded into specific features, but it would require a complex feature engineering and a deep knowledge of the linguistic involved phenomena.

To automatize relational learning between pairs of texts, e.g., in case of QA, one of the early works is (Moschitti et al., 2007; Moschitti, 2008). This approach was improved in several subsequent researches (Severyn and Moschitti, 2012; Severyn et al., 2013a; Severyn et al., 2013b; Severyn and Moschitti, 2013; Tymoshenko et al., 2014; Tymoshenko and Moschitti, 2015), exploiting relational tags and linked open data. In particular, in (Filice et al., 2015c), we propose new inter-pair methods to directly employ text pairs into a kernel-based learning framework. In the proposed approach, we integrate the information derived from simple intra-pair similarity functions (Section 3.1) and from the structural analogies (Section 3.2).

3.1 Intra-pair similarities

In subtasks A and C, a *good* comment is likely to share similar terms with the question. In subtask B a question that is relevant to another probably shows common words. Following this intuition, given a text pair (either question/comment or question/question), we define a feature vector whose dimensions reflect the following similarity metrics:

- *Cosine similarity*, *Jaccard coefficient* (Jaccard, 1901) and *containment measure* (Broder, 1997) of n-grams of word lemmas. It captures lexical information and word ordering information ($n = 1, 2, 3, 4$ was used in all experiments).

- *Cosine similarity* of n-grams of part-of-speech tags. It considers a shallow syntactic similarity ($n = 1, 2, 3, 4$ was used in all experiments).

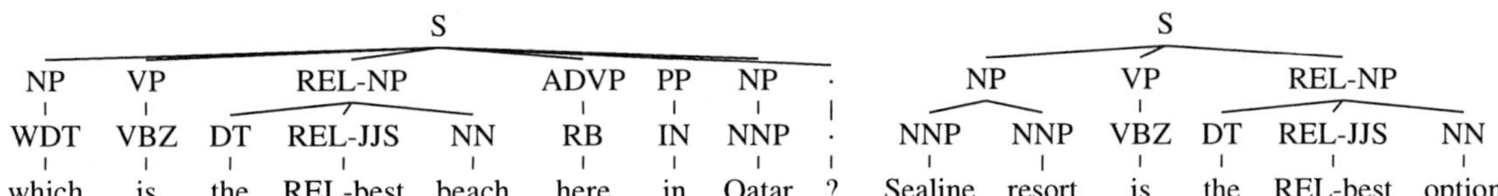

Figure 1: Structural Representation of a question-answer pair.

- *Partial tree kernel* (Moschitti, 2006) between the parse tree of the sentences. It performs a deep syntactic comparison.

- *Longest common substring measure* (Gusfield, 1997) determines the length of the longest contiguous sequence of characters shared by two text segments.

- *Longest common subsequence measure* (Allison and Dix, 1986) drops the contiguity requirement of the previous measure and allows to detect similarity in case of word insertions/deletions.

- *Greedy String Tiling* (Wise, 1996) provides a similarity between two sentences by counting the number of shuffles in their subparts.

- *Cosine similarity* between additive representations of word embeddings generated by applying word2vec (Mikolov et al., 2013) to the entire Qatar Living corpus from SemEval 2015[3]. We derived 250 dimensional vectors for 37,000 words by applying the settings min-count=50, window=5, iter=10 and negative=10. Five features are derived considering (*i*) only nouns, (*ii*) only adjectives, (*iii*) only verbs, (*iv*) only adverbs and (*v*) all the above words.

These metrics are computed in all the subtasks between the two elements within a pair, i.e., q and c_i for subtask A, q and o for subtask B, o and c_i for subtask C. In addition, in subtasks B and C, the similarity metrics (except the Partial Tree Kernel similarity) are computed between o and the entire thread of q, concatenating q with its answers. Similarities between q and o are also employed in subtask C.

3.2 Inter-pair kernel methods

The kernels we proposed in (Filice et al., 2015c) can be directly applied to Subtask B and to subtasks A and C for learning question/question and question/answer similarities, respectively. As shown in

Figure 1, a pair of sentences is represented as pair of their corresponding shallow parse trees, where common or semantically similar lexical nodes are linked using a tagging strategy (which is propagated to their upper constituents). This method discriminates aligned sub-fragments from non-aligned ones, allowing the learning algorithm to capture relational patterns, e.g., *the REL-best beach* and *the REL-best option*. Thus, given two pairs of sentences $p_a = \langle a_1, a_2 \rangle$ and $p_b = \langle b_1, b_2 \rangle$, some tree kernel combinations can be defined:

$$
\begin{aligned}
\mathrm{TK}^+(p_a, p_b) &= \ \mathrm{TK}(a_1, b_1) + \mathrm{TK}(a_2, b_2) \\
\mathit{All}^\times_{\mathrm{TK}}(p_a, p_b) &= \ \mathrm{TK}(a_1, b_1) \times \mathrm{TK}(a_2, b_2) \\
&+ \ \mathrm{TK}(a_1, b_2) \times \mathrm{TK}(a_2, b_1),
\end{aligned}
$$

where TK is a generic tree kernel, such as the Partial Tree Kernel (PTK) (Moschitti, 2006), or the Smoothed Partial Tree Kernel (SPTK) (Croce et al., 2011). Tree kernels, computing the shared substructures between parse trees, are effective in evaluating the syntactic similarity between two texts. The proposed tree kernel combinations extend such reasoning to text pairs, and can capture emerging pairwise patterns. Therefore this method can be effective in recognizing valid question/answer pairs, or similar questions, even in those cases in which the two texts have few words in common that would cause the failure of any intra-pair approach.

4 Task Specific Features

In this section, we describe features specifically developed for cQA. A single feature vector is generated for each of the following group of features.

4.1 Ranking Features

The ten questions related to an original question are retrieved using a search engine. We use their absolute and relative ranks[4] as features for subtasks B

---

[3] http://alt.qcri.org/semeval2015/task3

[4] Some of the results retrieved by the search engine were filtered out, because they were threads with less than 10 comments, or documents out of Qatar Living. Therefore, the threads in the dataset may have an associated rank higher than 10. The relative rank maps such absolute values into [1;10].

and C (for the latter the question rank is given to all the comments within the related question thread).

4.2 Heuristics

We adopt the heuristic features described in (Barrón-Cedeño et al., 2015), which can be applied to subtasks A and C. In particular forty-four boolean features express whether a comment: (*i*) includes URLs or emails (2 feats.). (*ii*) contains the word "yes", "sure", "no", "can", "neither", "okay", and "sorry", as well as symbols '?' and '@' (9 feats.); (*iii*) starts with "yes" (1 feat.); (*iv*) includes a sequence of three or more repeated characters or a word longer than fifteen characters (2 feats.); (*v*) belongs to one of the categories of the forum (*Socializing*, *Life in Qatar*, etc.) (26 feats.); (*vi*) has been posted by the same user who posted the question, such a comment can include a question (i.e., it contains a question mark), and acknowledgment (e.g., it contains *thank**, *acknowl**), or none of them (4 feats.);

An additional feature captures the length of the comment (as longer —*good*— comments usually contain detailed information to answer a question).

4.3 Thread-based features

In cQA, comments in a thread typically reflect an underlying concrete discussion, which contains more information than in a sequence of independent answers retreived from different documents. For instance, users replicate to each other, ask for further details, or can tease other users. Therefore, as discussed in (Barrón-Cedeño et al., 2015), comments in a common thread are strongly interconnected. To exploit such thread-level dependencies, we used some specific features for subtasks A and C. The following notation will be adopted: q is the question posted by user u_q, c is a comment from user u_c, in the comment thread.

The first four features indicate whether c appears in the proximity of a comment by u_q. The assumption is that an acknowledgment or further questions by u_q in the thread could signal a *good* answer. More specifically, they test if among the comments following c there is one by u_q (*i*) containing an acknowledgment, (*ii*) not containing an acknowledgment, (*iii*) containing a question, and, (*iv*) if among the comments preceding c there is one by u_q containing a question. These four features depend on the distance k, in terms of the number of comments,

between c and the closest comment by u_q:

$$f(c) = \begin{cases} 1.1 - 0.1k \\ 0 \text{ if no comments by } u_q \text{ exist,} \end{cases}$$

that is, the closer the comment to u_q, the higher the value assigned to this feature. Other features try to model potential dialogues, which at the end represent *bad* comments, by identifying interlacing comments between two users. These dialogue features are identifying conversation chains:

$$u_i \to \ldots \to u_j \to \ldots \to u_i \to \ldots \to [u_j]$$

Comments by other users can appear in between the nodes of this "pseudo-conversation" chain. Three features consider whether a comment is at the beginning, in the middle, or at the end of such a chain. Three more features are defined when $u_j = u_q$, i.e., the user who asked the question is one of the participants of these pseudo-conversations.

Another interesting aspect is whether a user u_i has been particularly active in a question thread. One boolean feature captures whether u_i wrote more than one comment in the current thread. Three more features identify the first, the middle and the last comments by u_i. One extra feature counts the total number of comments written by u_i. Moreover, it can be empirically observed that the likelihood of a comment being *good* decreases with its position in the thread. Therefore, another real-valued feature was included: $i/10$, where i represents the position of the comment in the thread.

4.4 Stacking classifiers across subtasks

The three subtasks are interconnected: the predictions from a subtask can provide useful information to carry out the other subtasks. This suggests the use of a stacking strategy.

Stacking classifiers in Subtask B. If the comments in the question thread of q are *good* answers for an original question o, we can suppose that o and q are strongly related. In Subtask B, we thus exploit the model trained on Subtask A. In particular, given the original question o, and the related question q with its comments, $c_1 \ldots c_n$, we use the model from Subtask A to classify the question/comment pairs, $\langle q, c_i \rangle$ and $\langle o, c_i \rangle$, obtaining respectively the scores p_{q,c_i} and p_{o,c_i}. We consider these scores as distributions and derive the following features: (*i*) *mean squared* *error* (MSE) = $\sum_i (p_{q,c_i} - p_{o,c_i})^2$; (*ii*) *Pearson correlation coefficient* between the $p_{q,c_1}, \ldots, p_{q,c_n}$ and the $p_{o,c_1}, \ldots, p_{o,c_n}$; (*iii*) ten features corresponding to the sorted differences between p_{q,c_i} and p_{o,c_i}; (*iv*) *agreement percentage*, i.e., percentage of times $sign(p_{q,c_i}) = sign(p_{o,c_i})$; (*v*) *max score* = $\max_i(p_{o,c_i})$; (*vi*) *mean score* = $\frac{1}{n}\sum_i p_{o,c_i}$; (*vii*) *positive percentage*, i.e., percentage of times $p_{o,c_i} > 0$; (*viii*) *normalized positive percentage*, i.e., percentage of times $p_{o,c_i} > 0$ when $p_{q,c_i} > 0$.

Stacking classifiers in Subtask C. A *good* comment for a question q should be also *good* for an original question o if q and o are strongly related, i.e., q is *relevant* or a *perfect match* to o. We thus developed a stacking strategy for Subtask C that uses the following scores in the classification step, w.r.t. an original question o and the comment c_i from the thread of q:

- p_{q,c_i}, which is the score of the pair $\langle q, c_i \rangle$ provided by the model trained on Subtask A;

- p_{o,c_i}, which is the score of the pair $\langle o, c_i \rangle$ provided by the model trained on Subtask A;

- $p_{o,q}$, which is the score of the pair $\langle o, q \rangle$ provided by the model trained on Subtask B.

Starting from these scores, we built the following features: (*i*) values and signs of p_{q,c_i}, p_{o,c_i} and $p_{o,q}$ (6 feats); (*ii*) a boolean feature indicating whether both p_{q,c_i} and $p_{o,q}$ are positive; (*iii*) *min value* = $min(p_{q,c_i}, p_{o,q})$; (*iv*) *max value* = $max(p_{q,c_i}, p_{o,q})$; (*v*) *average value* = $\frac{1}{2}(p_{q,c_i} + p_{o,q})$.

5 Submission and Results

We chose parameters using a 10 fold cross validation (cv) on the official train and development sets[5]. In Subtask B, some features depend on the scores provided on Subtask A, while in Subtask C the dependency is from both Subtasks A and B. Such scores are generated with the 10-fold cv. We used the OpenNLP pipeline for lemmatization, POS tagging and chunking to generate the tree representations described in Section 3.2. All the kernel-based learning models are implemented in KeLP (Filice et al., 2015b). For all the tasks, we used the C-SVM learning algorithm (Chang and Lin, 2011). The MAP@10 was the official metric. In addition, results are also reported in Average Recall (AvgR),

---

[5]We merged the official Train1, Train2 and Dev sets.

		MAP	AvgR	MRR	P	R	F$_1$	Acc
CV	IR	57.70	72.75	66.82	-	-	-	-
	KeLP	**74.76**	88.24	80.90	69.64	61.51	65.32	76.02
test	IR	59.53	72.60	67.83	-	-	-	-
	KeLP	**79.19**	88.82	86.42	76.96	55.30	64.36	75.11

Table 1: Results on Subtask A on a 10 fold CV on the training and development and on the official test set. IR is the baseline system based on the search engine results

Mean Reciprocal Rank (MRR), Precision (P), Recall (R), F$_1$, and Accuracy (Acc).

5.1 Subtask A

Model: The learning model operates on question-comment pairs $p = \langle q, c \rangle$. The kernel is $\text{PTK}^+(p_a, p_b) + \text{LK}_A(p_a, p_b)$. Such kernel linearly combines $\text{PTK}^+(p_a, p_b) = \text{PTK}(q_1, q_2) + \text{PTK}(c_1, c_2)$ (see Section 3.2) with a linear kernel LK_A that operates on feature vectors including: (*i*) the similarity metrics between q and c described in Section 3.1; (*ii*) the heuristic features introduced in Section 4.2; (*iii*) the thread-based features discussed in Section 4.3. PTK uses the default parameters (Moschitti, 2006), while the best SVM regularization parameter we estimated during cv is $C = 1$.

Results: Table 1 reports the outcome on Subtask A. The good results on the 10 fold cross validations are confirmed on the official test set: the model is very accurate and achieved the first position among 12 systems, with the best MAP. In this task the data distribution among classes is quite balanced and the accuracy is also a good performance indicator. In this case we achieved the second position.

5.2 Subtask B

Model: The proposed system operates on question-question pairs $p = \langle o, q \rangle$. The kernel is $All^{\times}_{\text{SPTK}}(p_a, p_b) + \text{LK}_B(p_a, p_b)$, by adopting the kernels defined in Section 3.2. This task is close to Paraphrase Identification, which is inherently symmetric. Therefore, in our primary submission, we adopted a tree kernel combination that exploits such characteristic, performing cross comparisons between the questions within pairs: $All^{\times}_{\text{SPTK}}(p_a, p_b) = \text{SPTK}(o_1, o_2) \times \text{SPTK}(q_1, q_2) + \text{SPTK}(o_1, q_2) \times \text{SPTK}(q_1, o_2)$. Such combination is based on the SPTK with standard parameters and a word similarity derived from the word embeddings described in Section 3.1. LK_B is a linear kernel that oper-

		MAP	AvgR	MRR	P	R	F$_1$	Acc
CV	IR	66.27	83.14	73.87	-	-	-	-
	KeLP	**70.37**	87.50	77.44	71.47	75.71	**73.53**	**77.69**
	KC1	69.97	87.22	76.71	70.19	75.87	72.92	76.93
	KC2	70.06	87.26	76.92	68.96	75.02	71.86	75.95
test	IR	74.75	88.30	83.79	-	-	-	-
	KeLP	75.83	91.02	82.71	66.79	75.97	**71.08**	**79.43**
	KC1	**76.28**	91.33	82.71	63.83	77.25	69.90	77.86
	KC2	76.27	91.44	84.10	64.06	77.25	70.04	78.00

Table 2: Results on Subtask B on a 10 fold Cross-Validation (CV) and on the official test set. KeLP is our primary submission, while KC1 and KC2 are the contrastive ones. IR is the baseline system based on the search engine results

		MAP	AvgR	MRR	P	R	F$_1$	Acc
dev	IR	30.65	34.55	35.97	-	-	-	-
	KeLP	**38.57**	44.09	41.28	21.55	64.64	32.32	81.32
	KC1	38.00	43.74	41.18	21.97	64.64	32.79	81.72
	KC2	37.22	42.63	42.80	22.30	71.30	33.98	80.88
test	IR	40.36	45.97	45.83	-	-	-	-
	KeLP	52.95	59.27	59.23	33.63	64.53	44.21	84.79
	KC1	52.95	59.34	58.06	34.08	65.29	**44.78**	**84.96**
	KC2	**55.58**	63.36	61.19	32.21	70.18	44.16	83.41

Table 3: Results on Subtask C on the official development set, and on the official test set. KeLP is our primary submission, while KC1 and KC2 are the contrastive ones. IR is the baseline system based on the search engine results

ates on feature vectors including: (*i*) the similarity metrics between o and q, and between o and the entire answer thread of q, as described in Section 3.1; (*ii*) ranking features discussed in Section 4.1; (*iii*) the features derived from the Subtask A scores (see Section 4.4). The best SVM regularization parameter estimated during the tuning stage is $C = 5$.

We made two additional submissions in which the model has minor variations: in the Contrastive 1 (KC1), we substituted $All_{\text{SPTK}}^{\times}$ with SPTK$^+$ whereas in the contrastive 2 (KC2) we do not include the features derived from the Subtask A scores.

Results: Table 2 shows the results on Subtask B. On the official test set, our primary submission achieved the third position w.r.t. MAP among 11 systems. Differently from what observed in the tuning stage, on the official test set the contrastive systems achieve a higher MAP and would have ranked second. The primary system achieves the highest F$_1$ and accuracy on both tuning and test stages. Considering these two metrics, our primary submission is overall the best model.

5.3 Subtask C

Model: The learning model operates on the triplet, $\langle o, q, c \rangle$, using the kernel, PTK$^+(p_a, p_b)$ + LK$_C(t_a, t_b)$, where PTK$^+(p_a, p_b)$ = PTK(o_1, o_2) + PTK(c_1, c_2) (see Section 3.2) and LK$_C$ is a linear kernel operating on feature vectors, which include: (*i*) the similarity metrics between o and c, between o and q, and between o and the entire thread of q, as described in Section 3.1; (*ii*) the heuristic features introduced in Section 4.2; (*iii*) the thread-based features discussed in 4.3; (*iv*) the ranking features (see Section 4.1); (*v*) the features derived from the scores of subtasks A and B, described in Section 4.4.

PTK uses the default parameters. The subtask data is rather imbalanced, as the number of negative examples is about 10 times the positive ones. We took this into account by setting the regularization parameter for the positive class, $C_p = \frac{\#negatives}{\#positives} C$, as in (Morik et al., 1999). The best SVM regularization parameter estimated during the tuning stage is $C = 5$. We also submitted a Contrastive 1 (KC1) with PTK$^+$ using $All_{\text{PTK}}^{\times}$ and a Constrastive 2 (KC2) identical as KC1 but with C set to 2.

Results: Table 3 shows the results for Subtask C. The organizers reported that the training labels were affected by noise, while the development labels were double-checked. Therefore, we decided to perform parameter tuning applying cv to the development set only. Our primary submission achieved the second highest MAP, while our Contrastive 2 is the best result. It should be also noted that the F$_1$ our system is the best among 10 primary submissions. In this subtask, accuracy is not a reliable measure, as the data is significantly imbalanced.

In a future work we would like to change the learning paradigm from classification, e.g., demonstrated in (Filice et al., 2015a) for several NLP applications, to a learning to rank problem. This can be enabled by the preference kernel (Severyn and Moschitti, 2012) and should have a positive impact on the MAP metric since the SVM classification algorithm we used optimizes accuracy.

Acknowledgements

This work has been partially supported by the EC project CogNet, 671625 (H2020-ICT-2014-2, Research and Innovation action), the PROGRESS-IT project (FILAS-CR-2011-1089) and by an IBM Faculty Award.

References

Lloyd Allison and Trevor I. Dix. 1986. A bit-string longest-common-subsequence algorithm. *Inf. Process. Lett.*, 23(6):305–310, December.

Alberto Barrón-Cedeño, Simone Filice, Giovanni Da San Martino, Shafiq Joty, Lluís Màrquez, Preslav Nakov, and Alessandro Moschitti. 2015. Thread-level information for comment classification in community question answering. In *Proceedings of the 53rd Annual Meeting of the Association for Computational Linguistics and the 7th International Joint Conference on Natural Language Processing (Volume 2: Short Papers)*, pages 687–693, Beijing, China, July.

A. Broder. 1997. On the resemblance and containment of documents. In *Proceedings of the Compression and Complexity of Sequences 1997*, SEQUENCES '97, pages 21–, Washington, DC, USA. IEEE Computer Society.

Chih-Chung Chang and Chih-Jen Lin. 2011. LIBSVM: A library for support vector machines. *ACM Transactions on Intelligent Systems and Technology*, 2:27:1–27:27.

Danilo Croce, Alessandro Moschitti, and Roberto Basili. 2011. Structured lexical similarity via convolution kernels on dependency trees. In *Proceedings of the Conference on Empirical Methods in Natural Language Processing*, EMNLP '11, pages 1034–1046, Stroudsburg, PA, USA. Association for Computational Linguistics.

Simone Filice, Giuseppe Castellucci, Danilo Croce, and Roberto Basili. 2015a. Kelp: a kernel-based learning platform for natural language processing. In *Proceedings of ACL-IJCNLP 2015 System Demonstrations*, pages 19–24, Beijing, China, July. Association for Computational Linguistics and The Asian Federation of Natural Language Processing.

Simone Filice, Giuseppe Castellucci, Danilo Croce, Giovanni Da San Martino, Alessandro Moschitti, and Roberto Basili. 2015b. KeLP: a Kernel-based Learning Platform in java. In *The workshop on Machine Learning Open Source Software (MLOSS): Open Ecosystems*, Lille, France, July. International Conference of Machine Learning.

Simone Filice, Giovanni Da San Martino, and Alessandro Moschitti. 2015c. Structural representations for learning relations between pairs of texts. In *Proceedings of the 53rd Annual Meeting of the Association for Computational Linguistics and the 7th International Joint Conference on Natural Language Processing (Volume 1: Long Papers)*, pages 1003–1013, Beijing, China, July.

Dan Gusfield. 1997. *Algorithms on Strings, Trees, and Sequences: Computer Science and Computational Biology*. Cambridge University Press, New York, NY, USA.

Paul Jaccard. 1901. Étude comparative de la distribution florale dans une portion des Alpes et des Jura. *Bulletin del la Société Vaudoise des Sciences Naturelles*, 37:547–579.

Tomas Mikolov, Kai Chen, Greg Corrado, and Jeffrey Dean. 2013. Efficient estimation of word representations in vector space. *CoRR*, abs/1301.3781.

Katharina Morik, Peter Brockhausen, and Thorsten Joachims. 1999. Combining statistical learning with a knowledge-based approach - a case study in intensive care monitoring. In *ICML*, pages 268–277, San Francisco, CA, USA. Morgan Kaufmann Publishers Inc.

Alessandro Moschitti, Silvia Quarteroni, Roberto Basili, and Suresh Manandhar. 2007. Exploiting syntactic and shallow semantic kernels for question answer classification. In *Proceedings of the 45th Annual Meeting of the Association of Computational Linguistics*, pages 776–783, Prague, Czech Republic, June. Association for Computational Linguistics.

Alessandro Moschitti. 2006. Efficient convolution kernels for dependency and constituent syntactic trees. In *ECML*, pages 318–329, Berlin, Germany, September. Machine Learning: ECML 2006, 17th European Conference on Machine Learning, Proceedings.

Alessandro Moschitti. 2008. Kernel Methods, Syntax and Semantics for Relational Text Categorization. In *Proceeding of ACM 17th Conf. on Information and Knowledge Management (CIKM'08)*, Napa Valley, CA, USA.

Preslav Nakov, Lluís Màrquez, Alessandro Moschitti, Walid Magdy, Hamdy Mubarak, Abed Alhakim Freihat, Jim Glass, and Bilal Randeree. 2016. SemEval-2016 task 3: Community question answering. In *Proceedings of the 10th International Workshop on Semantic Evaluation*, SemEval '16, San Diego, California, June. Association for Computational Linguistics.

Aliaksei Severyn and Alessandro Moschitti. 2012. Structural relationships for large-scale learning of answer re-ranking. In *Proceedings of the 35th International ACM SIGIR Conference on Research and Development in Information Retrieval*, SIGIR '12, pages 741–750, New York, NY, USA. ACM.

Aliaksei Severyn and Alessandro Moschitti. 2013. Automatic feature engineering for answer selection and extraction. In *EMNLP*, pages 458–467. ACL.

Aliaksei Severyn, Massimo Nicosia, and Alessandro Moschitti. 2013a. Building structures from classifiers for passage reranking. In *Proceedings of the 22nd ACM international Conference on Information and Knowledge Management*, CIKM '13, pages 969–978, New York, NY, USA. ACM.

Aliaksei Severyn, Massimo Nicosia, and Alessandro Moschitti. 2013b. Learning adaptable patterns for passage reranking. In *Proceedings of the Seventeenth Conference on Computational Natural Language Learning*, pages 75–83, Sofia, Bulgaria, August. Association for Computational Linguistics.

Kateryna Tymoshenko and Alessandro Moschitti. 2015. Assessing the impact of syntactic and semantic structures for answer passages reranking. In *Proceedings of the 24th ACM International on Conference on Information and Knowledge Management*, CIKM '15, pages 1451–1460, New York, NY, USA. ACM.

Kateryna Tymoshenko, Alessandro Moschitti, and Aliaksei Severyn, 2014. *Encoding semantic resources in syntactic structures for passage reranking*, pages 664–672. Association for Computational Linguistics (ACL), 1.

Michael J. Wise. 1996. Yap3: Improved detection of similarities in computer program and other texts. In *Proceedings of the Twenty-seventh SIGCSE Technical Symposium on Computer Science Education*, SIGCSE '96, pages 130–134, New York, NY, USA. ACM.

SwissCheese at SemEval-2016 Task 4: Sentiment Classification Using an Ensemble of Convolutional Neural Networks with Distant Supervision

Jan Deriu[*]
ETH Zurich
Switzerland
jderiu@student.ethz.ch

Maurice Gonzenbach[*]
ETH Zurich
Switzerland
mauriceg@student.ethz.ch

Fatih Uzdilli
Zurich University of Applied Sciences
Switzerland
uzdi@zhaw.ch

Aurelien Lucchi
ETH Zurich
Switzerland
alucchi@inf.ethz.ch

Valeria De Luca
ETH Zurich
Switzerland
vdeluca@vision.ee.ethz.ch

Martin Jaggi
ETH Zurich
Switzerland
jaggi@inf.ethz.ch

Abstract

In this paper, we propose a classifier for predicting message-level sentiments of English micro-blog messages from Twitter. Our method builds upon the convolutional sentence embedding approach proposed by (Severyn and Moschitti, 2015a; Severyn and Moschitti, 2015b). We leverage large amounts of data with distant supervision to train an ensemble of 2-layer convolutional neural networks whose predictions are combined using a random forest classifier. Our approach was evaluated on the datasets of the SemEval-2016 competition (Task 4) outperforming all other approaches for the *Message Polarity Classification* task.

1 Introduction

Sentiment analysis is a fundamental problem aiming to give a machine the ability to understand the emotions and opinions expressed in a written text. This is an extremely challenging task due to the complexity of human language, which makes use of rhetorical devices such as sarcasm or irony. Deep neural networks have shown great promises at capturing salient features for these complex tasks (Mikolov et al., 2013b; Severyn and Moschitti, 2015a). Particularly successful for sentiment classification were Convolutional Neural Networks (CNN) (Kim, 2014; Kalchbrenner et al., 2014; Severyn and Moschitti, 2015a; Severyn and Moschitti, 2015b; Johnson and Zhang, 2015), on which our work builds upon.

These networks typically have a large number of parameters and are especially effective when trained on large amounts of data. In this work, we use a distant supervision approach to leverage large amounts of data in order to train a 2-layer CNN [1], extending the 1-layer architecture proposed by (Severyn and Moschitti, 2015a). More specifically, we train a neural network using the following three-phase procedure: i) creation of word embeddings for initialization of the first layer; ii) distant supervised phase, where the network weights and word embeddings are trained to capture aspects related to sentiment; and iii) supervised phase, where the network is trained on the provided supervised training data. We also combine the predictions of several neural networks using a random forest meta-classifier. The proposed approach was evaluated on the datasets of the SemEval-2016 competition, Task 4 (Nakov et al., 2016)[2] for which it reaches state-of-the-art results.

2 System Description

2.1 Convolutional Neural Networks

We combine the outputs of two 2-layer CNNs having similar architectures but differing in the choice of certain parameters (such as the number of convolutional filters). These two networks were also initialized using different word embeddings and used slightly different training data for the distant supervised phase. The common architecture of the two

---

* These authors contributed equally to this work

[1] We here refer to a layer as one convolutional and one pooling layer.

[2] http://alt.qcri.org/semeval2016/

Proceedings of SemEval-2016, pages 1124–1128,
San Diego, California, June 16-17, 2016. ©2016 Association for Computational Linguistics

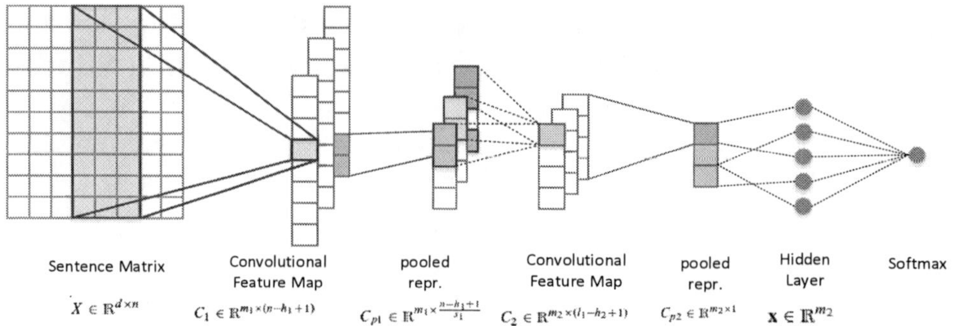

Figure 1: The architecture of the CNNs used in our approach.

CNNs is shown in Figure 1 and described in details below.

Sentence model. Each word is associated to a vector representation, which consists in a d-dimensional vector. A sentence (or tweet) is represented by the concatenation of the representations of its n constituent words. This yields a matrix $\mathbf{X} \in \mathbb{R}^{d \times n}$, which is used as input to the convolutional neural network.

Convolutional layer. In this layer, a set of m filters is applied to a sliding window of length h over each sentence. Let $\mathbf{X}_{[i:i+h]}$ denote the concatenation of word vectors $\mathbf{x}_i$ to $\mathbf{x}_{i+h}$. A feature c_i is generated for a given filter $\mathbf{F}$ by:

$$c_i := \sum_{k,j} (\mathbf{X}_{[i:i+h]})_{k,j} \cdot \mathbf{F}_{k,j} \qquad (1)$$

A concatenation of all vectors in a sentence produces a feature vector $\mathbf{c} \in \mathbb{R}^{n-h+1}$. The vectors $\mathbf{c}$ are then aggregated over all m filters into a feature map matrix $\mathbf{C} \in \mathbb{R}^{m \times (n-h+1)}$. The filters are learned during the training phase of the neural network using a procedure detailed in the next section.

Max pooling. The output of the convolutional layer is passed through a non-linear activation function, before entering a pooling layer. The latter aggregates vector elements by taking the maximum over a fixed set of non-overlapping intervals. The resulting pooled feature map matrix has the form: $\mathbf{C}_{\mathbf{pooled}} \in \mathbb{R}^{m \times \frac{n-h+1}{s}}$, where s is the length of each interval. In the case of overlapping intervals with a stride value s_t, the pooled feature map matrix has the form $\mathbf{C}_{\mathbf{pooled}} \in \mathbb{R}^{m \times \frac{n-h+1-s}{s_t}}$. Depending on whether the borders are included or not, the result of the fraction is rounded up or down respectively.

Hidden layer. A fully connected hidden layer computes the transformation $\alpha(\mathbf{W} * \mathbf{x} + \mathbf{b})$, where $\mathbf{W} \in \mathbb{R}^{m \times m}$ is the weight matrix, $\mathbf{b} \in \mathbb{R}^m$ the bias, and α the rectified linear ($relu$) activation function (Nair and Hinton, 2010). The output vector of this layer, $\mathbf{x} \in \mathbb{R}^m$, corresponds to the sentence embeddings for each tweet.

Softmax. Finally, the outputs of the final pooling layer $\mathbf{x} \in \mathbb{R}^m$ are fully connected to a soft-max regression layer, which returns the class $\hat{y} \in [1, K]$ with largest probability. i.e.,

$$\hat{y} := \arg\max_j P(y = j | \mathbf{x}, \mathbf{w}, \mathbf{a})$$
$$= \arg\max_j \frac{e^{\mathbf{x}^\mathsf{T} \mathbf{w}_j + a_j}}{\sum_{k=1}^{K} e^{\mathbf{x}^\mathsf{T} \mathbf{w}_k + a_j}}, \qquad (2)$$

where $\mathbf{w}_j$ denotes the weights vector of class j and a_j the bias of class j.

Network parameters. Training the neural network consists in learning the set of parameters $\Theta = \{\mathbf{X}, \mathbf{F}_1, \mathbf{b}_1, \mathbf{F}_2, \mathbf{b}_2, \mathbf{W}, \mathbf{a}\}$, where $\mathbf{X}$ is the sentence matrix, with each row containing the d-dimensional embedding vector for a specific word; $\mathbf{F}_i, \mathbf{b}_i (i = \{1, 2\})$ the filter weights and biases of the first and second convolutional layers; $\mathbf{W}$ the concatenation of the weights $\mathbf{w}_j$ for every output class in the soft-max layer; and $\mathbf{a}$ the bias of the soft-max layer.

2.2 Ensemble of classifiers

We combine the results of the two 2-layer CNN described in Section 2.1 with the intent of increasing the generalizability of the final classifier. This is achieved relying on two systems trained using different procedures as well as different word embeddings. The network parameters of the two CNNs are summarized in Table 1. The preprocessing and training phases of the two systems are described below.

2.2.1 System I

Preprocessing and word embeddings. The word embeddings are initialized using word2vec (Mikolov et al., 2013a) and then trained using an unlabelled corpus of 200M tweets. We apply a skipgram model of window size 5 and filter words that occur less than 5 times (Severyn and Moschitti, 2015b). The dimensionality of the vector representation is set to $d = 52$.

Training. During a first distant-supervised phase, we use emoticons to infer the polarity of a balanced set of 90M tweets (Read, 2005; Go et al., 2009). The resulting dataset contains 45M tweets for both the positive and negative class. The neural network is trained on these 90M tweets for one epoch, before training for 10 to 15 epochs on the labelled data provided by SemEval-2016. The word-embeddings $\mathbf{X} \in \mathbb{R}^{d \times n}$, are updated during both the distant and the supervised training phases, as back-propagation is applied through the entire network.

2.2.2 System II

Preprocessing and word embeddings. A corpus of 90M tweets[3] (30M contain positive emoticons, 30M negative ones and 30M contain none) is employed to create embedding vectors of $d = 50$ dimensions using *GloVe* (Pennington et al., 2014). Words which appear less than 5 times are discarded. Additionally, special flags $\in \{0, 1\}$ are assigned to some words, by appending a flag vector to their word embeddings. Four different flags can be set, marking *(i)* words that belong to hashtags, *(ii)* words that have been elongated (e.g. 'hellooo', which is mapped to the same vector as 'hello'), *(iii)* words in which all characters are capitalized, and *(iv)* punctuations that are repeated more than three times (e.g. '!!!!' and '!!!' being mapped to the same vector).

Training. In the distant supervised phase, the network is trained for one epoch on a set of 60M tweets,

containing an equal amount of samples with positive and negative emoticons. Similarly to System I, this pre-trained network is further refined by supervised training for about 15 epochs on the SemEval-2016 data. We apply L_2 regularization to reduce overfitting to the cost function (negative log likelihood) by adding a penalty of the form of $\lambda \|\theta\|_2^2$, with regularization strength[4] λ, where $\theta \in \Theta$ are the network parameters of each layer.

2.2.3 Optimization

The network parameters are learned using *AdaDelta* (Zeiler, 2012), which adapts the learning rate for each dimension using only first order information. We used the hyper-parameters $\epsilon = 1e{-}6$ and $\rho = 0.95$ as suggested by (Zeiler, 2012).

2.2.4 Meta-Classifier

Each aforementioned system outputs three real values $\hat{y}$ corresponding to the three sentiment classes. In addition, it outputs the categorical value for the predicted sentiment class. The meta-classifier uses these values (sentiment class and categorical value of systems I and II) as input features. We trained a random forest using the `Weka` (Hall et al., 2009) library on the training data. We selected the number of trees (300), maximum depth of the forest (2) and the number of features used per random selection (18) as to obtain the best overall performance over the previous years' test sets.

2.3 Computing Resources

The core routines are written in `Python`, making heavy use of mathematical routines in `Theano` (Bergstra et al., 2010) that exploits GPU acceleration. For further performance improvement, we used the `CuDNN` library (Chetlur and Woolley, 2014). The framework requires approximately 10 hours for the distant supervised phase and only 20-30 minutes for the supervised phase.

Experiments were conducted on g2.2xlarge instances of *Amazon Web Services* (AWS), which offer a *GRID K520* GPU with 3072 CUDA cores and 8 GB of GDDR5 RAM.

---

[3]This set differs to the 90M set used in System I, but is drawn from the same larger corpus of tweets

[4]$\mathbf{X}: \lambda = 1^{-6}$, $\mathbf{F}_1: \lambda = 1^{-5}$, $\mathbf{F}_2: \lambda = 1^{-5}$, $\mathbf{W}: \lambda = 1^{-7}$.

	SYSTEM I	SYSTEM II
Number of convolutional filters	$m = 200$	$m = 300$
Filter window size h	$h_1 = 6, h_2 = 3$	$h_1 = 6, h_2 = 4$
Size of first max-pooling interval	width = 6, striding = 2	width = 3, striding = 3
Activation function α	$relu$	$relu$

Table 1: Summary of the parameters used in System I and II

3 Data

The training and development datasets used in our experiments were provided by the SemEval-2016 competition. A fraction of the tweets (10-15%) from the period 2013-2015 were no longer available on Twitter, which made the results of this year competition not directly comparable to the ones of previous years. For testing, in addition to last year's data (tweets, SMS, LiveJournal), new tweets were accessible. An overview of the data available for download is given in Table 2.

Table 2: Overview of datasets and number of tweets (or sentences) provided in SemEval-2016. The data was divided into training, development and testing sets.

Dataset	Total	Posit.	Negat.	Neutr.
Train 2013 (Tweets)	8224	3058	1210	3956
Dev 2013 (Tweets)	1417	494	286	637
Train 2016 (Tweets)	5355	2749	762	1844
Dev 2016 (Tweets)	1269	568	214	487
DevTest 2016 (Tweets)	1779	883	276	620
Test: *Twitter2016*	20632	7059	3231	10342
Test: *Twitter2015*	2390	1038	365	987
Test: *Twitter2014*	1853	982	202	669
Test: *Twitter2013*	3813	1572	601	1640
Test: *SMS2013*	2093	492	394	1207
Test: *LiveJournal2014*	1142	427	304	411
Test: *Tw2014Sarcasm*	86	33	40	13

Data preparation. Before extracting features, the tweets were preprocessed using the following procedure:

- URLs and usernames were substituted by a replacement token
- The text was lowercased
- The NLTK twitter tokenizer was employed in System I and a customized version of the *CMU ARK Twitter Part-of-Speech Tagger* (Gimpel et al., 2011) in System II.

4 Results

The F-1 score was computed by the competition organizers as evaluation measure. As a result, the presented system was ranked 1st out of 34 participants, with an F1-score of 63.30 on the Twitter-2016 test set. See (Nakov et al., 2016) for further details.

Table 4 summarizes the results of individual subsystems, as well as the final system on each test set. For each test set the best score is marked in bold face. In case of the *Twitter2016* and *Twitter2015* test sets we marked the best performing subsystem in italics. For System I (S1), we observed that during the supervised phase, the F-1 scores measured on the different test sets presented large deviations. Hence, to improve robustness, we considered six different models of S1 (S1a, ..., S1f), varying the number of epochs between 12 and 25 during the supervised phase, stopping determined by the validation score on different sets. For System II (S2), the number of epochs, equal to 12, is determined by the one achieving the highest score on the *DevTest2016* set.

The final system (FS) using the meta-classifier trained on the outputs of systems S1a-f and S2, achieves the highest accuracy on the 2016 test set with the competition-winning F1-score of 63.30%. These results improve the score of the best performing subsystem (S1b) by 0.57 points. For the 2015 test set, FS shows an improvement of 0.35 points with respect to the score of the best subsystem (S1f).

	S1a	S1b	S1c	S1d	S1e	S1f	S2	FS
Twitter2016	60.47	62.73	61.89	60.58	57.19	62.20	62.36	**63.30**
Twitter2015	64.26	65.80	64.80	64.20	61.02	66.70	66.63	**67.05**
Twitter2014	73.98	74.60	**75.70**	74.15	69.12	72.00	72.45	71.55
Twitter2013	**71.52**	70.10	70.90	71.50	67.00	68.00	70.05	70.01
LiveJournal2014	73.86	70.57	72.54	**74.00**	71.32	68.00	70.86	69.51
Tw2014Sarcasm	57.84	52.04	51.50	57.84	62.00	57.30	**62.74**	56.63

Table 3: Overall results of the proposed subsystems. S1: System(s) I; S2: System II; FS: Final system, using the meta-classifier. Best (second-best) results are highlighted in bold (underlined) face.

5 Conclusion

We described a deep learning framework to predict the sentiment polarity of short phrases, such as tweets. The proposed approach is based on an ensemble of Convolution Neural Networks and relies on a significantly large amount of data for the distant-supervised phase. The final random forest classifier resulted in state-of-the-art performance, ranking 1st in the SemEval-2016 competition for the task of Message Polarity Classification.

Acknowledgments. We thank Aliaksei Severyn and Mark Cieliebak for fruitful discussions.

References

James Bergstra, Olivier Breuleux, Frederic Frédéric Bastien, Pascal Lamblin, Razvan Pascanu, Guillaume Desjardins, Joseph Turian, David Warde-Farley, and Yoshua Bengio. 2010. Theano: a CPU and GPU math compiler in Python. *Proceedings of the Python for Scientific Computing Conference (SciPy)*, (Scipy):1–7.

Sharan Chetlur and Cliff Woolley. 2014. cuDNN: Efficient Primitives for Deep Learning. *arXiv preprint*.

Kevin Gimpel, Nathan Schneider, Brendan O'Connor, Dipanjan Das, Daniel Mills, Jacob Eisenstein, Michael Heilman, Dani Yogatama, Jeffrey Flanigan, and Noah A. Smith. 2011. Part-of-Speech Tagging for Twitter: Annotation, Features, and Experiments. In *HLT '11 - Proceedings of the 49th Annual Meeting of the Association for Computational Linguistics: Short-papers*, number 2, pages 42–47.

Alec Go, Richa Bhayani, and Lei Huang. 2009. Twitter sentiment classification using distant supervision. *CS224N Project Report, Stanford*, 1:12.

Mark Hall, Eibe Frank, Geoffrey Holmes, Bernhard Pfahringer, Peter Reutemann, and Ian H. Witten. 2009. The WEKA Data Mining Software: An Update. In *SIGKDD Explorations*.

Rie Johnson and Tong Zhang. 2015. Semi-supervised Convolutional Neural Networks for Text Categorization via Region Embedding. In *NIPS 2015 - Advances in Neural Information Processing Systems 28*, pages 919–927.

Nal Kalchbrenner, Edward Grefenstette, and Phil Blunsom. 2014. A Convolutional Neural Network for Modelling Sentences. In *ACL - Proceedings of the 52nd Annual Meeting of the Association for Computational Linguistics*, pages 655–665, Baltimore, Maryland, USA.

Yoon Kim. 2014. Convolutional Neural Networks for Sentence Classification. In *EMNLP 2014 - Empirical Methods in Natural Language Processing*, pages 1746–1751.

Tomas Mikolov, Quoc V Le, and Ilya Sutskever. 2013a. Exploiting Similarities among Languages for Machine Translation. *arXiv*.

Tomas Mikolov, Ilya Sutskever, Kai Chen, Greg S Corrado, and Jeff Dean. 2013b. Distributed representations of words and phrases and their compositionality. In *NIPS 2013 - Advances in Neural Information Processing Systems 26*, pages 3111–3119.

Vinod Nair and Geoffrey E Hinton. 2010. Rectified linear units improve restricted boltzmann machines. In *ICML 2010 - Proceedings of the 27th International Conference on Machine Learning*, pages 807–814.

Preslav Nakov, Alan Ritter, Sara Rosenthal, Veselin Stoyanov, and Fabrizio Sebastiani. 2016. SemEval-2016 task 4: Sentiment analysis in Twitter. In *Proceedings of the 10th International Workshop on Semantic Evaluation*, SemEval '16, San Diego, California, June. Association for Computational Linguistics.

Jeffrey Pennington, Richard Socher, and Christopher D Manning. 2014. GloVe: Global Vectors for Word Representation. *Proceedings of the 2014 Conference on Empirical Methods in Natural Language Processing*, pages 1532–1543.

Jonathon Read. 2005. Using emoticons to reduce dependency in machine learning techniques for sentiment classification. In *Proceedings of the ACL student research workshop*, pages 43–48. Association for Computational Linguistics.

Aliaksei Severyn and Alessandro Moschitti. 2015a. Twitter Sentiment Analysis with Deep Convolutional Neural Networks. In *38th International ACM SIGIR Conference*, pages 959–962, New York, USA, August. ACM.

Aliaksei Severyn and Alessandro Moschitti. 2015b. UNITN: Training Deep Convolutional Neural Network for Twitter Sentiment Classification. In *SemEval 2015 - Proceedings of the 9th International Workshop on Semantic Evaluation*.

Matthew D. Zeiler. 2012. ADADELTA: An Adaptive Learning Rate Method. *arXiv preprint*.

IIT-TUDA at SemEval-2016 Task 5: Beyond Sentiment Lexicon: Combining Domain Dependency and Distributional Semantics Features for Aspect Based Sentiment Analysis

Ayush Kumar
IIT Patna, India
Dept. of Computer Science
ayush.cs12@iitp.ac.in

Sarah Kohail
TU Darmstadt, Germany
Computer Science Dept,
Language Technology Group
kohail@lt.informatik.tu-darmstadt.de

Amit Kumar
IIT Patna, India
Dept. of Computer Science
amit.mtmc14@iitp.ac.in

Asif Ekbal
IIT Patna, India
Dept. of Computer Science
asif@iitp.ac.in

Chris Biemann
TU Darmstadt, Germany
Computer Science Dept,
Language Technology Group
biem@cs.tu-darmstadt.de

Abstract

This paper reports the IIT-TUDA participation in the SemEval 2016 shared Task 5 of Aspect Based Sentiment Analysis (ABSA) for subtask 1. We describe our system incorporating domain dependency graph features, distributional thesaurus and unsupervised lexical induction using an unlabeled external corpus for aspect based sentiment analysis. Overall, we submitted 29 runs, covering 7 languages and 4 different domains. Our system is placed first in sentiment polarity classification for the English laptop domain, Spanish and Turkish restaurant reviews, and opinion target expression for Dutch and French in restaurant domain, and scores in medium ranks for aspect category identification and opinion target extraction.

1 Introduction

The advent of web technologies has made an unprecedented opportunity for online users to share and explain their views and opinions. The correlation between the views expressed by the users and the market strategies by the organizations strikes the importance of analyzing such reviews. But, valuable as they are, user-generated review texts are unstructured and very noisy. Major research studies adopted Natural Language Processing (NLP) and text mining techniques to better understand and process various types of information in user-generated reviews. Such efforts have come to be known as opinion mining, sentiment analysis or review mining (Pang and Lee, 2008).

Aspect level analysis performs a finer-grained sentiment analysis by addressing three subproblems: extracting aspects from the review text, identifying the entity that is referred to by the aspect, and finally classifying the opinion polarity towards the aspect (Liu, 2012). For example, a review of the "entity" laptop is likely to discuss distinct "aspects" like size, processing unit, and memory, and a single product can trigger a positive "opinion" about one feature, and a negative "opinion" about another.

In an attempt to support the efforts on Aspect Based Sentiment Analysis (ABSA), the SemEval 2016 shared Task 5 ABSA (Pontiki et al., 2016) offers the opportunity to experiment and evaluate on benchmark datasets (reviews) across various domains and languages through three subtasks. Subtask 1 covers the three sub-problems mentioned above, namely: aspect category identification (Slot 1), opinion target expression (OTE) (Slot 2) and sentiment polarity classification (Slot 3). We participated in Slot 1 and Slot 3 for English, Spanish, Dutch, French, Turkish, Russian and Arabic language for all available domains except telecoms. We also conducted experiments for Slot 2 for English, Spanish, Dutch and French. Overall, we submitted 29 runs, covering 7 languages and 4 different domains.

Proceedings of SemEval-2016, pages 1129–1135,
San Diego, California, June 16-17, 2016. ©2016 Association for Computational Linguistics

2 Method for Aspect Based Sentiment Analysis

In this section, we describe our data preprocessing and feature extraction. We also introduce an unsupervised approach for expanding the coverage of existing lexical resources based on the notion of distributional thesaurus. We use Support Vector Machine (SVM) (Cortes and Vapnik, 1995) as the baseline classifier for aspect category detection and sentiment polarity classification, and Conditional Random Fields (CRF) (Lafferty et al., 2001) for opinion target expression identification.

2.1 Preprocessing

We tokenize the data using Stanford tokenizer, normalize all digits to 'num' and remove stop words for tf-idf computation. For opinion target expression, we run Stanford CoreNLP[1] suite in order to extract information such as lemma, Part-of-Speech (PoS) and named entity (NE) in English language. For languages other than English, we use the universal parser[2] for tokenization and parsing. Since we deal with the OTE as a sequence labelling problem, it is necessary to identify the boundary of OT properly. We follow the standard BIO notation, where 'B-ASP', 'I-ASP' and 'O' represent the beginning, intermediate and outside tokens of a multi-word OTE respectively. e.g. In, *'Chow (B-ASP) fun (I-ASP) was (O) very (O) dry (O) . (O)'*, 'Chow Fun' is the OTE.

2.2 Features for Aspect Category Detection

- Domain Dependency Graph: We use the aspects list produced by Domain Dependency Graph (DDG) for each domain by (Kohail, 2015). The idea is to detect topics underlying a mixed-domain dataset, aggregate individual dependency relations between domain-specific content words, weigh them with tf-idf and produce a DDG by selecting the highest-ranked words and their dependency relations. Since the domains are already given, no topic modeling is required. However, only one domain was provided for French and Spanish, we used ex-

Token	DT Expansion
drinks	beers, wines, coffee, liquids, beverage
price	prices, pricing, cash, cost, pennies
fresh	fresher, new, refreshing, clean, frozen
laptop	pc, computer, notebook, tablet, imac
toshiba	samsung, sony, acer, asus, dell
touchpad	mouse, trackball, joystick, trackpad

Table 1: Example of DT expansions for frequent aspects.

ternal reviews dataset to compute tf-idf. We use movies reviews[3] for Spanish; and books, music and DVD reviews[4] for French. The resulting graphs were filtered and only 'amod' (adjective modifying a noun) and 'nsubj' (nominal subjects of predicates) relations were selected. For each extracted aspect from the opinion-aspect pairs, we determine the existence or absence of this aspect using a binary feature.

- Distributional Thesaurus: A Distributional Thesaurus (DT) is an automatically computed lexical resource that ranks words according to the semantic similarity. We employ an open source implementation of DT computation as described in (Biemann and Riedl, 2013). For every top five significant words based on tf-idf score in each aspect category (for example: 'overpriced', '$', 'pricey', 'cheap', 'expensive' are the most significant terms in 'food#price' category), we find ten most similar words according to DT. The presence or absence of these words in the review is used as a feature for aspect category identification. Examples from the distributional thesaurus are presented in Table 1.

- Tf-Idf Score: Each aspect category has some discriminative aspect terms. We extract a maximum of top five distinguishing words in each category based on tf-idf score. Presence or absence of each token in the review denotes the feature.

- Bag of Words: This feature denotes the number of occurrences of each word in the review.

---

[1] nlp.stanford.edu/software/corenlp.shtml
[2] http://www.undl.org/unlsys/uparser/UP.htm

[3] http://www.lsi.us.es/~fermin/index.php/Datasets
[4] http://www.uni-weimar.de/en/media/chairs/webis/corpora/corpus-webis-cls-10/

2.3 Features for Opinion Target Expression

- Word and Local Context: We use the current token, its lowercase form and the context tokens in a window of [-5..5] as features.

- Part-of-Speech (PoS) Information: We use PoS information of the current, preceding two and following two tokens as the features.

- Head Word and its PoS: We use the head word of the noun phrase and PoS information of the head word.

- Prefix and Suffix: We use prefix and suffix of length up to four characters.

- Frequent Aspect Term: We build a list of frequently occurring OTEs from the training set. An OTE is considered to be frequent if it appears at least four times in the training corpus. We define a binary feature for the presence or absence of extracted OTEs.

- Dependency Relations: In English language, features are defined in line with (Toh and Wang, 2014). For other languages, feature is defined by considering whether the current token is present in dependency relations 'nsubj', 'dep', 'amod', 'nmod' and 'dobj' or not.

- Character N-grams: We use all substrings up to length 5 of the current token as features.

- Orthographic feature: This feature checks whether the current token starts with the capitalized letter or not.

- DT features: We use the top 5 DT expansions of current token as the features.

- Expansion Score: OTEs have opinion around them. Opinions are regularly lexicalized with words found in sentiment lexicons. We calculate sentiment score based on SentiWordNet[5] (Esuli and Sebastiani, 2006) in English language. For Non-English language, we use our induced lexicons. We calculate sentiment score by considering the window size of 10 (preceding 5 and following 5 tokens of the target one).

We additionally extract the following features only for English language.

- Chunk information: To identify the boundaries of multi-word OTEs, we use chunk information of the current token as the features.

- Lemma: Lemmatization trims the inflectional forms and derivationally related forms of a token to a common base form.

- WordNet: We use top 4 noun synsets of current token from WordNet as the features.

- Named entity information: We extract named entity information of the current token with Stanford CoreNLP tool, and use the NER-sequence labels in BIO-scheme as features.

2.4 Features for Sentiment Polarity Classification

- Lexical Acquisition: We use lexical expansion for inducing sentiment words based on distributional hypothesis. We observe that for rare words, unseen instances and limited coverage of available lexicons, the distributional expansion can provide a useful backoff technique, also cf. (Govind et al., 2014).

For all languages, we construct a polarity lexicon using an external corpus and seed sentiment lexicon. For seed lexicons, we use English (Salameh et al., 2015) and Arabic (Salameh et al., 2015) versions of Bing Liu's lexicon (Hu and Liu, 2004) for English and Arabic respectively, VU sentiment lexicon[6] for French, Dutch and Spanish, a lexicon by (Panchenko, 2014) for Russian, and Senti-TurkNet (Dehkharghani et al., 2015) and NRC Emotion for Turkish[7]. For inducing a lexicon, we obtain the top 100 DT expansion of each word in the seed lexicon. Next we accept candidate terms that a) occur in the expansions of at least 10 seed terms, b) have a corpus frequency

---

[5]http://sentiwordnet.isti.cnr.it/

[6]https://github.com/opener-project/
VU-sentiment-lexicon
[7]http://saifmohammad.com/WebPages/
NRC-Emotion-Lexicon.htm

Language	Seed Lexicon			Induced Lexicon	Common Entries
	Positive	Negative	Neutral		
English	2005	4789	-	12953	4120
Dutch	3314	5923	-	8496	2992
French	9338	10339	5993	18308	7636
Spanish	2175	1737	7869	12480	4306
Russian	3217	8849	-	7697	2945
Turkish	1900	2515	1382	6547	1838
Arabic	1916	4467	-	9077	1447

Table 2: Expansion statistics for induced lexicons. Common entries denote the number of words which are present both in the seed lexicon and the induced lexicon.

of more than 50 in the background corpus (English[8], French[9], Spanish[10], Dutch[11], Russian[12], Arabic[13]). Finally, we compute the normalized positive, negative and neutral score for each word similar to (Kumar et al., 2015), and inspired by (Hatzivassiloglou and McKeown, 1997). The core assumption is that words tend to be semantically more similar to words of same sentiment. Hence, words appearing more in the expansions of positive (negative/neutral) words get assigned a higher positive (negative/neutral) sentiment score, Here, in difference to (Kumar et al., 2015), we compute normalized positive, negative and neutral scores rather than assigning one of the polarity class to the words. It should be noted that the volume of induced lexicon depends on two factors: (i) number of words in the seed lexicon that have expansions and (ii) pruning threshold for obtaining the induced lexicon. The unavailability of expansions for all words in the seed lexicon and higher threshold on conditions for accepting candidate terms reduces the volume of induced lexicon. Expansion statistics for the induced lexicons are provided in Table 2.

We compute the sum of positive, negative and

neutral scores of tokens using induced lexicon for that language as features. In addition, scores as given in the seed lexicon are also used as features. For English, we also computed these features from different lexicons: AFINN (Nielsen, 2011), NRC Hashtag, Sentiment 140 (Zhu et al., 2014), NRC Emotion (Mohammad and Turney, 2013) and Bing Liu (Hu and Liu, 2004).

- Word N-gram: All unigrams and bigrams tokens are extracted from the training set are used as a binary feature, where 1 and 0 indicates the presence and absence of n-grams in the review.

- Entity-Attribute Pair: We use E#A pair as a binary feature for sentiment classification.

3 Datasets, Experimental Results and Discussions

For feature selection and hyperparameter tuning, we perform five-fold cross-validation on the training set. For Slot 1 and Slot 3, we use supervised classification using Support Vector Machine (SVM)[14]. Based on cross-validation results, we set the probability threshold of 0.185, 0.13 and 0.145 for restaurants, laptops and phones, respectively, for predicting aspect categories in the review. All E#A pairs having predicted probability greater than the threshold are enlisted as aspect categories. For Slot 2, we use CRFSuite[15] with default parameters. CRF-

---

[8] https://snap.stanford.edu/data/web-Amazon.html

[9] http://wacky.sslmit.unibo.it/doku.php?id=corpora

[10] http://corporafromtheweb.org/escow14/

[11] http://corporafromtheweb.org/nlcow14/

[12] lib.ruc.ecebooks

[13] http://corpora2.informatik.uni-leipzig.de

[14] https://github.com/bwaldvogel/liblinear-java

[15] http://www.chokkan.org/software/crfsuite/

Language	Domain	Slot 1: F1/#Entries	Slot 2: F1/#Entries	Slot 3: Acc./#Entries
English	Restaurants	63.0 (U, 17), 61.2 (C, 20) / 30	42.6 (U, 18) / 19	86.7 (U, 2) / 29
Dutch	Restaurants	55.2 (U, 3), 54.9 (C, 4) / 6	56.9 (U, 1) / 3	76.9 (U, 2) / 4
Spanish	Restaurants	59.8 (U, 6), 59.0 (C, 7) / 9	64.3 (U, 3) / 5	83.5 (U, 1) / 5
French	Restaurants	57.8 (U, 2), 57.0 (C, 3) / 6	66.6 (U, 1) / 3	72.2 (U, 5) / 6
Russian	Restaurants	62.6 (C, 3), 58.1 (C, 4) / 7	-	73.6 (U, 3) / 6
Turkish	Restaurants	56.6 (U, 3), 55.7 (C, 4) / 5	-	84.2 (U, 1) / 3
Dutch	Phones	45.4 (U, 2), 45.0 (C, 3) / 4	-	82.5 (U, 2) / 3
English	Laptops	43.9 (U, 12), 42.6 (C, 14) / 22	-	82.7 (U, 1) / 22
Arabic	Hotels	-	-	81.7 (U, 2) / 3

Table 3: Evaluation result for Subtask 1. Mode of submission (C-constrained, U-unconstrained) and rank is given in the parenthesis. F1 and Acc. denote F1-Score and Accuracy. #Entries is the total number of submissions for respective slot and domains.

Dataset	All Features	All w/o E#A Pair	All w/o Induced Lexicon
English Restaurants	86.729	86.224	86.390
English Laptops	82.772	82.310	82.457
Dutch Restaurants	76.998	76.250	74.228
Dutch Phones	82.576	82.058	80.896
Russian Restaurants	73.615	73.158	70.657
French Restaurants	72.222	71.898	70.154
Spanish Restaurants	83.582	82.920	79.589
Turkish Restaurants	84.277	83.650	80.788
Arabic Hotels	81.720	80.650	78.680

Table 4: Feature Ablation Experiment for Sentiment Polarity Classification

Suite is a fast implementation of Conditional Random Field (CRFs) for segmenting and labelling sequential data.

Teams were allowed to submit their systems in two modes: constrained and unconstrained modes. In constrained mode, the participants are allowed to use only the resources and dataset provided by the organizers whereas in unconstrained submission, participants can use any external resource. For Slot 2 and Slot 3, we only sent unconstrained submission, while for Slot 1 we sent constrained as well as unconstrained submissions except for Russian restaurants.

Our system achieves the best results in sentiment polarity classification for reviews about English laptops, Spanish restaurants and Turkish restaurants. We score second for English restaurants. We also produce the maximum F1-score value for opinion target expression for French and Dutch restaurants. Our evaluation results across all domains and languages are given in Table 3.

The results show that our system performs comparably well for sentiment polarity classification and opinion target expression. A feature ablation experiment given in Table 4 shows the effectiveness of induced lexicon for Slot 3 task. We get a significant improvement on adding information from the induced lexicons in each language. This holds especially for languages other than English, where existing sentiment lexicons are less comprehensive. We also note that entity-attribute pairs also help in resolving conflicting sentiments (for example: *cheap food (positive)* to *cheap service (negative)*).

We score in medium ranks for Slot 1 task. Distributional thesaurus based expansion for discriminative terms and aspects obtained through domain dependency graph results in marginal increments. This could be attributed to conflict in very fine grained aspect categories (for example: Restaurant#Prices, Food#Prices, Drink#Prices)

Language	F1-measure
English	68.45
Dutch	64.37
Spanish	69.73
French	69.64

Table 5: Result on Slot 2 task after modification

which may not have been captured explicitly by the external features. For the Slot 2 task, we have found some inconsistencies in our extraction pipeline, unfortunately were not able to correct them in time for the submission.

After the evaluation period, we revised our feature representation to ensure that it matches the correct input format for CRF. We also added two new features including unsupervised PoS tags (Biemann, 2009) as the feature for all the languages and SentiWordNet score for English language. For the current token, we use PoS tag, distributional thesaurus, lexical expansion score, unsupervised PoS tag, SentiWordNet score of context tokens [-2, -1, 0, 1, 2], prefix (upto 3-character), suffix (upto 3-character) and chunk information of context tokens [-1, 0, 1]. The updated results of after modification are shown in Table 5. If we had incorporated these changes earlier, we would have scored third for English and first for the other three languages.

4   Conclusions and Future Work

In this paper, we report our work on the task of Aspect Based Sentiment Analysis, which covers three slots: aspect identification, opinion target extraction and sentiment polarity classification. By leveraging a distributional thesaurus, we expand the existing domain specific aspect list and sentiment lexicons for different languages to reach a higher coverage on sentiment words. Our system was ranked first in five out of 29 submitted runs. While performance is satisfactory for Slot 3 and Slot 2 (after correction), our setup compares infavorably to others for Slot 1. We will continually improve our system in future work.

References

Chris Biemann and Martin Riedl. 2013. Text: Now in 2D! a framework for lexical expansion with contextual similarity. *Journal of Language Modelling*, 1(1):55–95.

Chris Biemann. 2009. Unsupervised Part-of-Speech Tagging in the Large. *Research on Language and Computation*, 7(2):101–135.

Corinna Cortes and Vladimir Vapnik. 1995. Support vector machine. *Machine learning*, 20(3):273–297.

Rahim Dehkharghani, Yucel Saygin, Berrin Yanikoglu, and Kemal Oflazer. 2015. SentiTurkNet: a Turkish polarity lexicon for sentiment analysis. *Language Resources and Evaluation*, pages 1–19.

Andrea Esuli and Fabrizio Sebastiani. 2006. SentiWordNet: A publicly available lexical resource for opinion mining. In *In Proceedings of the 5th Conference on Language Resources and Evaluation*, pages 417–422, Genoa, Italy.

Govind, Asif Ekbal, and Chris Biemann. 2014. Multiobjective optimization and unsupervised lexical acquisition for named entity recognition and classification. In *Proceedings the 11th International Conference on Natural Language Processing (ICON)*, Goa, India.

Vasileios Hatzivassiloglou and Kathleen R McKeown. 1997. Predicting the semantic orientation of adjectives. In *Proceedings of the 35th annual meeting of the Association for Computational Linguistics and Eighth Conference of the European Chapter of the Association for Computational Linguistics*, pages 174–181, Madrid, Spain.

Minqing Hu and Bing Liu. 2004. Mining and summarizing customer reviews. In *Proceedings of the 10th ACM SIGKDD International Conference on Knowledge Discovery and Data Mining*, pages 168–177, Seattle, WA.

Sarah Kohail. 2015. Unsupervised topic-specific domain dependency graphs for aspect identification in sentiment analysis. In *Student Research Workshop Associated with the International Conference Recent Advances in Natural Language Processing (RANLP 2015)*, pages 16–23, Hissar, Bulgaria.

Ayush Kumar, Sarah Kohail, Asif Ekbal, and Chris Biemann. 2015. IIT-TUDA: System for sentiment analysis in indian languages using lexical acquisition. In *Mining Intelligence and Knowledge Exploration*, pages 684–693. Hyderabad, India.

John D Lafferty, Andrew McCallum, and Fernando C N Pereira. 2001. Conditional random fields: Probabilistic models for segmenting and labeling sequence data. In *Proceedings of the Eighteenth International Conference on Machine Learning*, ICML '01, pages 282–289, Williamstown, MA, USA.

Bing Liu. 2012. *Sentiment Analysis and Opinion Mining*. Synthesis Lectures on Human Language Technologies. Morgan & Claypool Publishers.

Saif M Mohammad and Peter D Turney. 2013. Crowd-sourcing a word–emotion association lexicon. *Computational Intelligence*, 29(3):436–465.

Finn Årup Nielsen. 2011. A new anew: Evaluation of a word list for sentiment analysis in microblogs. In *Proceedings of the ESWC2011 Workshop on 'Making Sense of Microposts': Big things come in small packages*, pages 93–98, Heraklion, Greece.

Alexander Panchenko. 2014. Sentiment index of the Russian speaking Facebook. In *In Proceedings of International Conference on Computational Linguistics. Dialogue 2014*, pages 506–517, Moscow, Russia.

Bo Pang and Lillian Lee. 2008. Opinion mining and sentiment analysis. *Foundations and Trends in Information Retrieval*, 2(1-2):1–135.

Maria Pontiki, Dimitrios Galanis, Haris Papageorgiou, Ion Androutsopoulos, Suresh Manandhar, Mohammad AL-Smadi, Mahmoud Al-Ayyoub, Yanyan Zhao, Bing Qin, Orphée De Clercq, Véronique Hoste, Marianna Apidianaki, Xavier Tannier, Natalia Loukachevitch, Evgeny Kotelnikov, Nuria Bel, Salud María Jiménez-Zafra, and Gülşen Eryiğit. 2016. SemEval-2016 Task 5: Aspect Based Sentiment Analysis. In *Proceedings of the 10th International Workshop on Semantic Evaluation*, SemEval '16, San Diego, California. Association for Computational Linguistics.

Mohammad Salameh, Saif M Mohammad, and Svetlana Kiritchenko. 2015. Sentiment after translation: A case-study on Arabic social media posts. In *Proceedings of the 2015 Conference of the North American Chapter of the Association for Computational Linguistics: Human Language Technologies*, pages 767–777, Denver, Colorado.

Zhiqiang Toh and Wenting Wang. 2014. Dlirec: Aspect term extraction and term polarity classification system. In *Proceedings of the 8th International Workshop on Semantic Evaluation (SemEval 2014)*, pages 235–240, Dublin, Ireland.

Xiaodan Zhu, Svetlana Kiritchenko, and Saif M Mohammad. 2014. NRC-Canada-2014: Recent improvements in the sentiment analysis of tweets. In *Proceedings of the 8th International Workshop on Semantic Evaluation (SemEval 2014)*, pages 443–447, Dublin, Ireland.

LIMSI-COT at SemEval-2016 Task 12:
Temporal relation identification using a pipeline of classifiers

Julien Tourille
LIMSI, CNRS,
Univ. Paris-Sud,
Université Paris-Saclay
julien.tourille@limsi.fr

Olivier Ferret
CEA, LIST,
Gif-sur-Yvette, F-91191 France.
olivier.ferret@cea.fr

Aurélie Névéol
LIMSI, CNRS,
Université Paris-Saclay
aurelie.neveol@limsi.fr

Xavier Tannier
LIMSI, CNRS,
Univ. Paris-Sud,
Université Paris-Saclay
xtannier@limsi.fr

Abstract

SemEval 2016 Task 12 addresses temporal reasoning in the clinical domain. In this paper, we present our participation for relation extraction based on gold standard entities (subtasks DR and CR). We used a supervised approach comparing plain lexical features to word embeddings for temporal relation identification, and obtained above-median scores.

1 Introduction

SemEval 2016 Task 12 offers 6 subtasks addressing temporal reasoning in the clinical domain using the THYME corpus (Styler IV et al., 2014). This corpus provides annotated clinical and pathological notes from colon cancer patients. The first group of subtasks concerns the identification of time and event expressions within raw text. The second group of subtasks deals with the identification of temporal relations. The latter consists of two subtasks. In the *Document Creation Time Relation* subtask (DR), participants are challenged to identify relations between the events and the document creation time. For the *Container Relation* subtask (CR), participants have to identity container relations between entities. Participants may submit either a complete system extracting entities and relations or focus on either the entity extraction or relation extraction (using the gold standard entities provided by the organizers). More details about the task and the definition of each subtask can be found in Bethard et al. (2016).

In this paper, we present our submission for the CR and DR subtasks based on gold-standard entities (phase 2). Our global approach, which is illustrated in Figure 1, tackles the identification of temporal relations as a set of supervised classification tasks. We submitted two runs, one using plain lexical features and one using word embeddings computed on a large clinical corpus. We obtained scores well above the median scores in both subtasks.

The remainder of this paper is organized as follows. Section 2 presents our system for the DR subtask while Section 3 describes our system for the CR subtask. Section 4 gives an overview of the system implementation. Finally, Section 5 presents our results.

2 Document Creation Time Relation (DR) Subtask

We treated the subtask as a supervised classification problem where each EVENT entity was classified into four categories (*Before, Before-Overlap, Overlap, After*).

We extracted lexical, contextual and structural features from the texts. Regarding the lexical features of EVENT entities, we took their surface forms, their gold standard attributes (*type, modality, degree* and *polarity*), their lemma(s)[1], as well as their Part-Of-Speech (POS) and Coarse Part-Of-Speech (CPOS) tags. We also extracted the semantic types

---

[1] The span of an EVENT entity can overlap with several tokens.

Proceedings of SemEval-2016, pages 1136–1142,
San Diego, California, June 16-17, 2016. ©2016 Association for Computational Linguistics

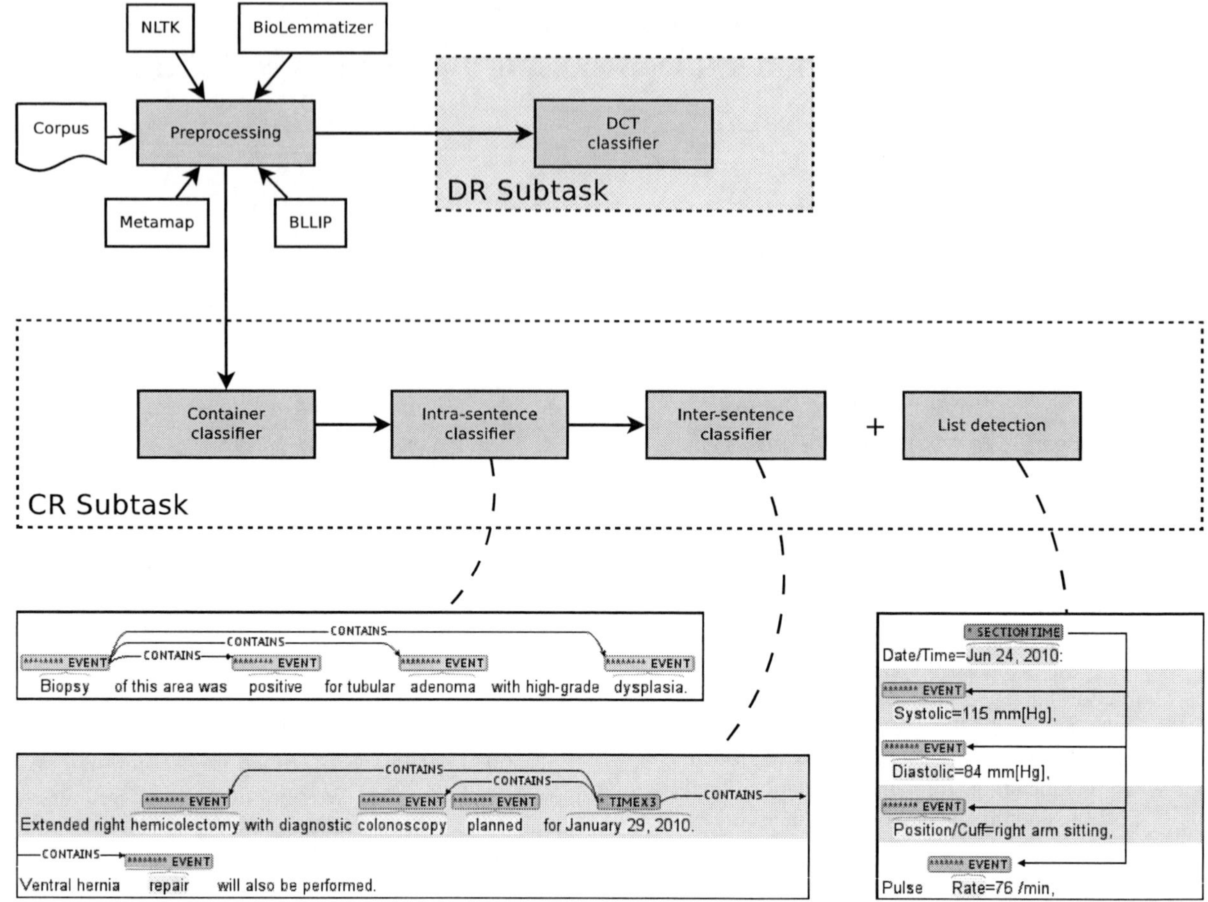

Figure 1: Overview of the processing chain

and semantic groups of the medical entities that have been detected by Metamap (Aronson and Lang, 2010) and that share a span overlap with the EVENT entities.

Concerning the contextual features, we extracted the gold standard entities that were present in the right and left contexts[2] within the sentence. We added the corresponding lemmas, surface forms, types, POS and CPOS tags, as well as the corresponding semantic groups and semantic types. We also added the lemmas of the tokens occurring in both left and right contexts. At the section level, we added entities occurring before and after the EVENT entity within the section. We used the same set of features as the one we used for the intra-sentence context: surface forms, lemmas, types, POS and CPOS tags, semantic types and semantic groups. We

also added the gold standard attributes of these entities.

Regarding the structural features, we used the position of the sentence within the section and the position of the section within the document. We added the number of tokens and entities occurring before and after the EVENT entity within the section, and the number of entities figuring before and after the EVENT entity at the document level.

3 Container Relation (CR) Subtask

3.1 Principles

Similarly to the DR subtask, we treated the CR subtask as a supervised classification problem and more particularly, as a binary classification task applied to pairs of EVENT and/or TIME entities in documents. However, considering all possible pairs of such entities for building the training set without any scope

---

[2] There is no size restriction on the contexts

1137

restriction would lead to unbalanced training examples where the negative examples largely outnumber the positive examples. Hence, some choices have been made to reduce the number of training examples.

The analysis of the training corpus shows that a large majority – around 76% – of the CONTAINS relations are intra-sentence relations, which means that the problem of their scope actually occur for one quarter only. The remaining relations, called inter-sentence relations, spread over at least two sentences. Given this context, we have built two separate classifiers, the first one for the intra-sentence relations, the second one for the inter-sentence relations. This distinction has two main advantages: first, it reduces drastically the number of negative examples, which produces better results as we observed on our development set; second, the intra-sentence classifier can benefit from a larger and richer set of features coming from sentence-level linguistic analyzers.

Concerning the inter-sentence relations, considering all pairs of EVENT and/or TIME entities would still give us a very large amount of negative examples. We first observed that all of them were contained within sections (no relation overlaps section boundaries). Within the scope of a section, we further noticed that inter-sentence relations within a 3-sentence window covered approximately 89% over all existing relations. A wider window would bring too much noise while giving us a very small bump on coverage. Table 1 shows the number of covered relations according to the size of the window, expressed in the number of sentences. The first line corresponds to the intra-sentence level (window=1).

To further reduce the number of candidates for both inter- and intra-sentence classifiers, we transformed the 2-category problem (*contains vs. no-relation*) into a 3-category classification problem (*contains*, *is-contained* or *no-relation*). Instead of considering all permutations of events within a sentence or a sentence-window, we considered all pairs of events from left to right, changing when necessary the *contains* relations into *is-contained* relations. This strategy allowed us to divide by a factor of two the number of candidates. We obtained 111,349 pairs for the intra-sentence classifier and 311,284 pairs for the inter-sentence classifier.

win.[a]	nb. of rel.[b]	total[c]
1	13,304	13,304 (76.30%)
2	1,463	14,767 (84.69%)
3	752	15,519 (89.00%)
4	497	16,016 (91.85%)
5	364	16,380 (93.94%)
6	151	16,531 (94.80%)

[a] Sentence window
[b] Number of CONTAINS relations
[c] Cumulative count of CONTAINS relations

Table 1: CONTAINS relations according to sentence window size. Window of size 1 corresponds to the intra-sentence level.

Some entities are more likely to be containers. By example, SECTIONTIME and TIMEX entities are, by nature, potential containers. This is also the case for some medical events. For instance, a *surgical operation* may contain other events such as *bleeding* or *suturing*. It will not be the same with the two latter in most cases. Following this observation, we have built a model to classify entities as being a potential *container* or *not*. As we will show in Section 5, this classifier obtain a high accuracy. We used its output as feature for our intra- and inter-sentence classifiers.

Finally, we developed a rule-based module to capture specific CONTAINS relations. There are some strong regularities in the handling of laboratory results where the first SECTIONTIME contains all the results, which are expressed with EVENT entities (see an example in Figure 1). The module we have built aims at capturing these inter-sentential regularities with the use of rules.

To summarize, our system is composed of four modules:

1. **Container detection module**: entities are classified according to whether or not they are the source of one or more CONTAINS relations;

2. **Intra-sentence relation module**: combinations of entities within sentences are considered (relations *contains*, *is-contained* or *no-relation*);

3. **Inter-sentence relation module**: combinations of entities within a 3-sentence window are

considered. We use the same relation classes as those used for intra-sentence relations;

4. **List detection module**: specific laboratory results written as lists are handled via manual rules.

3.2 Feature Extraction

For the container classifier, we used the form and the type of the considered entity, as well as its gold standard attributes. We extracted the semantic types and semantic groups of the entities that have been detected by Metamap and that share an overlap with the considered entity. We also extracted its lemma(s), POS and CPOS tags. Concerning the contextual features, we extracted the entities that are present in both left and right contexts within the sentence boundaries. Similarly to the DR subtask, we used entity forms, types, semantic groups and semantic types, POS and CPOS tags and lemmas. We also added the tokens from both left and right contexts. We used the corresponding lemmas, POS and CPOS tags. Finally, we added the number of entities within the sentence and the number of entities before and after the considered entity within the sentence.

For the intra-sentence classifier, we extracted the forms, semantic types and semantic groups, and the gold standard attributes of the two considered entities. We added their lemmas and their POS and CPOS tags. We added the number of tokens occurring between the two entities. We also extracted the entities occurring between the two considered entities. We used their entity types, gold standard attributes, semantic groups and semantic types. We added the number of entities that have been classified as containers by our container classification model and the number of entities that appear between the pair of entities. Finally, we added the syntactic paths[3] between the two entities (from left to right). We also added the results of our contain classification model for the two considered entities.

For the inter-sentence classifier, we used similar features. We extracted the forms, types, gold standard attributes and semantic groups and semantic types of the two considered entities. We also extracted features from the results of the intra-sentence

classifier. We specified whether the considered entities are intra-sentence containers or are contained by other entities at the intra-sentence level. We also extracted entities that are positioned between the two considered entities. We used entity types, gold-standard attributes, semantic groups and semantic types. We also added a feature specifying if these entities are containers at the intra-sentence level and the number of entities between the considered pair of entities. Finally we added the positions, at the section level, of the sentences in which the considered events are embedded.

4 System Implementation

4.1 Strategies

We implemented two strategies to represent the lexical features in both the DR and CR subtasks. In the first one, we used the plain forms of the different lexical attributes we mentioned (Strategy 1). In the second strategy, we substituted the lemmas and forms with word embeddings (Strategy 2). These embeddings have been computed on the Mimic 2 corpus (Saeed et al., 2011) using the word2vec tool with a CBOW model[4] (Mikolov et al., 2013). We used the mean of the vectors for multi-word units. Lexical contexts are thus represented by 200-dimensional vectors. When several contexts are considered e.g. right and left, several vectors are used.

4.2 Algorithm Selection

A grid search strategy was applied to select the most appropriate machine learning algorithm and its parameters. For Strategy 1, three algorithms were considered in our search: Random Forests, Linear Support Vector Machine (liblinear) and Support Vector Machine with a RBF kernel (libsvm). For Strategy 2, we only considered the Linear Support Vector Machine for the CR task and Random Forests for the DR task.

In both cases, 5-fold cross-validation was used to choose the algorithm and its parameters. We also implemented statistical feature selection as part of the grid search for Strategy 1 reducing progressively the number of attributes, using ANOVA F-test.

---

[3]Several paths are considered when the entities spread over more that one token.

[4]Parameters used during computation: min-count: 5; vector size: 200; window: 20; number of word classes: 1000; frequency threshold: 1e-3.

Run	Classifier	Algorithm	Parameters	% feat.[a]
1[c]	CONTAINER	SVM (RBF)	C=10, gamma=0.01	60
	INTRA	SVM (RBF)	C=10, gamma=0.01	60
	INTER	SVM (RBF)	C=1000, gamma=0.01	100
	DCT	SVM (Linear)	C=1, tol[b]=0.0001, normalization=l2, loss function=hinge	100
2[d]	CONTAINER	LinearSVM	C=1, tol=0.01, normalization=l2, loss function=hinge	100
	INTRA	SVM (Linear)	C=1, tol=0.01, normalization=l2, loss function=squared hinge	100
	INTER	SVM (Linear)	C=1000, tol=0.01, normalization=l2, loss function=hinge	100
	DCT	Random Forests	max features=auto, criterion=entropy, estimators=100	100

[a] Percentage of feature space kept for final submission (using ANOVA F-test)
[b] Tolerance for stopping criteria
[c] Using plain text features
[d] Using word embeddings

Table 2: Machine learning algorithms and parameters used for the final submission

The machine learning algorithms used for the final submission are presented in Table 2 together with their parameters and the percentage of the feature space kept after statistical feature selection. We used the Scikit-learn machine learning library (Pedregosa et al., 2011) for both implementing our classification models and performing statistical feature selection.

4.3 Corpus Preprocessing

We applied a four-step preprocessing on the 440 texts that were provided for the subtasks. First, we used NLTK (Loper and Bird, 2002) to segment the texts into sentences with the *Punkt Sentence Tokenizer* pre-trained model for English provided within the framework.

The second step consisted of parsing the resulting sentences. For this task, we used the BLLIP Reranking Parser (Charniak and Johnson, 2005) and a pre-trained biomedical parsing model (McClosky, 2010).

In the third step, we lemmatized the corpus using BioLemmatizer (Liu et al., 2012), a tool built for processing the biomedical literature. We used the Part-Of-Speech tags from the previous step as parameters for the lemmatization.

The last step consisted in using Metamap (Aronson and Lang, 2010) to detect biomedical events and linking them, after disambiguation, to their related UMLS® (Unified Medical Language System) concept. We chose to keep biomedical entities that had a span overlapping with at least one entity of the gold standard.

5 Results and Discussion

In Table 3, we present the cross-validation accuracies of our DCT and Container models over the development corpus. For DCT, we obtain high performance with Strategy 1, which is based on plain lexical features. Strategy 2, which exploits words embeddings, gives lower performance. Concerning the Container model, we obtain high performance with both strategies.

Model	plain text	word embeddings
DCT	0.873	0.778
CONTAINER	0.917	0.924

Table 3: DCT and CONTAINER model accuracies

We submitted two runs with our system, one for each strategy. The results for both subtasks are presented in Tables 4 and 5.

Concerning the DR subtask, we obtained above-median scores (median score: 0.724) for both runs. The second run, which relies on word embeddings to represent the lexical features of the EVENT entities, achieves better performance. These results are consistent with what was expected during the cross-validation process using the development set. The fact that the second strategy achieves the best performance is however in contradiction with the scores obtained during cross-validation, where Strategy 1 performed best.

In the CR subtask, we obtained above-median F1 for the first run and median scores for the second run (median score: 0.449). Using plain lexical features gives us a more balanced system than using word embeddings. With a F1 of 0.538, our system achieves performance close to the best system (0.573), thus validating our modeling choices. These results are consistent with those we obtained when testing against the development part of the corpus. The reasons for the decrease in recall when using the second strategy are however unclear and need further investigation.

Run	ref[a]	pred[b]	corr[c]	P	R	F1
1[d]	18,990	18,989	14,603	0.769	0.769	0.769
2[e]	18,990	18,989	15,317	0.807	0.807	**0.807**

[a] Number of gold standard relations
[b] Number of predicted relations
[c] Number of correct predictions
[d] Using plain text features
[e] Using word embeddings

Table 4: DR subtask - Evaluation script output

Run	ref[a]	pred[b]	corr[c]	P	R	F1
1[d]	5,894	3,755	2,642 2,570	0.704	**0.436**	**0.538**
2[e]	5,894	2,544	1,911 1,889	**0.751**	0.320	0.449

[a] Number of gold standard relations
[b] Number of predicted relations
[c] Number of correct relations (without and with temporal closure)
[d] Using plain text features
[e] Using word embeddings

Table 5: CR subtask - Evaluation script output

Acknowledgments

We would like to thank the Mayo Clinic for granting us the permission to use the THYME corpus. This work has been funded by Labex Digicosme, operated by the Foundation for Scientific Cooperation (FSC) Paris-Saclay. This work was supported in part by the French National Agency for Research under grant CABeRneT, ANR-13-JS02-0009-01.

References

Alan R Aronson and François-Michel Lang. 2010. An overview of MetaMap: historical perspective and recent advances. *Journal of the American Medical Informatics Association*, 17(3):229–236.

Steven Bethard, Guergana Savova, Wei-Te Chen, Leon Derczynski, James Pustejovsky, and Marc Verhagen. 2016. SemEval-2016 Task 12: Clinical TempEval. In *Proceedings of the 10th International Workshop on Semantic Evaluation (SemEval 2016)*, San Diego, California, June. Association for Computational Linguistics.

Eugene Charniak and Mark Johnson. 2005. Coarse-to-Fine n-Best Parsing and MaxEnt Discriminative Reranking. In *Proceedings of the 43rd Annual Meeting of the Association for Computational Linguistics (ACL'05)*, pages 173–180, Ann Arbor, Michigan, June. Association for Computational Linguistics.

Haibin Liu, Tom Christiansen, William A Baumgartner Jr, and Karin Verspoor. 2012. BioLemmatizer: a lemmatization tool for morphological processing of biomedical text. *Journal of Biomedical Semantics*, 3(3).

Edward Loper and Steven Bird. 2002. NLTK: The Natural Language Toolkit. In *Proceedings of the ACL-02 Workshop on Effective Tools and Methodologies for Teaching Natural Language Processing and Computational Linguistics*, pages 63–70, Philadelphia, Pennsylvania. Association for Computational Linguistics.

David McClosky. 2010. *Any Domain Parsing: Automatic Domain Adaptation for Natural Language Parsing*. Ph.D. thesis, Department of Computer Science, Brown University.

Tomas Mikolov, Ilya Sutskever, Kai Chen, Greg S Corrado, and Jeff Dean. 2013. Distributed Representations of Words and Phrases and their Compositionality. In C. J. C. Burges, L. Bottou, M. Welling, Z. Ghahramani, and K. Q. Weinberger, editors, *Advances in Neural Information Processing Systems 26*, pages 3111–3119. Curran Associates, Inc.

F. Pedregosa, G. Varoquaux, A. Gramfort, V. Michel, B. Thirion, O. Grisel, M. Blondel, P. Prettenhofer, R. Weiss, V. Dubourg, J. Vanderplas, A. Passos, D. Cournapeau, M. Brucher, M. Perrot, and E. Duchesnay. 2011. Scikit-learn: Machine Learning in Python. *Journal of Machine Learning Research*, 12:2825–2830.

Mohammed Saeed, Mauricio Villarroel, Andrew T. Reisner, Gari Clifford, Li-Wei Lehman, George Moody, Thomas Heldt, Tin H. Kyaw, Benjamin Moody, and Roger G. Mark. 2011. Multiparameter Intelligent Monitoring in Intensive Care II (MIMIC-II): A public-access intensive care unit database. *Critical Care Medicine*, 39:952–960, May.

William Styler IV, Steven Bethard, Sean Finan, Martha Palmer, Sameer Pradhan, Piet de Groen, Brad Erickson, Timothy Miller, Chen Lin, Guergana Savova, and James Pustejovsky. 2014. Temporal Annotation in the Clinical Domain. *Transactions of the Association for Computational Linguistics*, 2:143–154.

RIGA at SemEval-2016 Task 8: Impact of Smatch Extensions and Character-Level Neural Translation on AMR Parsing Accuracy

Guntis Barzdins, Didzis Gosko

University of Latvia, IMCS and LETA

Rainis Blvd. 29, Riga, LV-1459, Latvia

`guntis.barzdins@lu.lv, didzis.gosko@leta.lv`

Abstract

Two extensions to the AMR smatch scoring script are presented. The first extension combines the smatch scoring script with the C6.0 rule-based classifier to produce a human-readable report on the error patterns frequency observed in the scored AMR graphs. This first extension results in 4% gain over the state-of-art CAMR baseline parser by adding to it a manually crafted wrapper fixing the identified CAMR parser errors. The second extension combines a per-sentence smatch with an ensemble method for selecting the best AMR graph among the set of AMR graphs for the same sentence. This second modification automatically yields further 0.4% gain when applied to outputs of two nondeterministic AMR parsers: a CAMR+wrapper parser and a novel character-level neural translation AMR parser. For AMR parsing task the character-level neural translation attains surprising 7% gain over the carefully optimized word-level neural translation. Overall, we achieve smatch F1=62% on the SemEval-2016 official scoring set and F1=67% on the LDC2015E86 test set.

1 Introduction

Abstract Meaning Representation (AMR) (Banarescu et al., 2013) initially was envisioned as an intermediate representation for semantic machine translation, but has found applications in other NLP fields such as information extraction.

For SemEval-2016 Task 8 on Meaning Representation Parsing we took a dual approach: besides developing our own neural AMR parser, we also extended the AMR smatch scoring tool (Cai and Knight, 2013) with a rule-based C6.0 classifier[1] to guide development of an accuracy-increasing wrapper for the state-of-art AMR parser CAMR (Wang et al., 2015a; 2015b). A minor gain was also achieved by combining these two approaches in an ensemble.

The paper starts with the description of our smatch extensions, followed by the description of our AMR parser and wrapper, and concludes with the results section evaluating the contributions of described techniques to our final SemEval result.

2 Smatch Extensions

We describe two extensions[2] to the original AMR smatch scoring script. These extensions do not change the smatch algorithm or scores produced, but they extract additional statistical information helpful for improving results of any AMR parser, as will be illustrated in Section 3.

2.1 Visual Smatch with C6.0 Classifier Rules

The original AMR smatch scoring metric produces as output only three numbers: precision, recall and F1. When developing an AMR parser, these three numbers alone do not reveal the actual mistakes in the AMR parser output (we call it *silver* AMR) when compared to the human-annotated *gold* AMR.

---

[1] Available at http://c60.ailab.lv

[2] Available at https://github.com/didzis/smatchTools

Proceedings of SemEval-2016, pages 1143–1147,

San Diego, California, June 16-17, 2016. ©2016 Association for Computational Linguistics

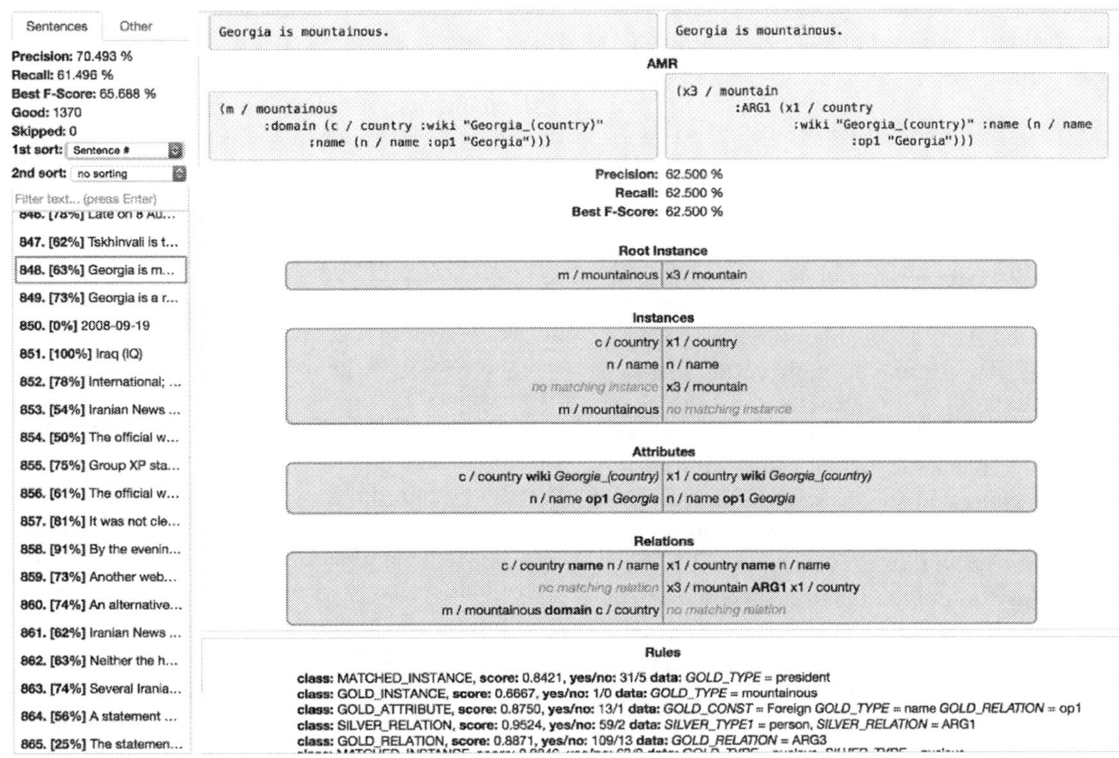

Figure 1. Visual smatch with Rules. Left pane shows the document content and statistics. Right pane shows single sentence gold AMR (left) and silver AMR (right) along with smatch aligned instance, attribute, relation AMR graph edges. The bottom pane shows C6.0 classifier generated rules describing the common error patterns found in the document.

The first step in alleviating this problem is visualizing the mappings produced by the smatch algorithm as part of the scoring process. Figure 1 shows such smatch alignment visualization where gold and silver AMR graphs are first split into the edges, which are further aligned through variable mapping. The smatch metric measures success of such alignment – perfect alignment results in F1 score 100% while incomplete alignment produces lower scores.

The visualization in Figure 1 is good for manual inspection of incomplete AMR alignments in individual sentences. But it still is only marginally helpful for AMR parser debugging, because the data-driven parsers are expected to make occasional mistakes due to the training data incompleteness rather than due to a bug in the parser.

Telling apart the repetitive parser bugs from the occasional training data incompleteness induced errors is not easy and to invoke the required statistical mechanisms we resorted to a rule-based C6.0 classifier (Barzdins et al., 2014; 2015), a modification of the legacy C4.5 classifier (Quinlan, 1993). The

classifier is asked to find most common patterns (rules) leading to some AMR graph edges to appear mostly in the gold, silver, or matched class after the smatch alignment. The bottom part of Figure 1 illustrates few such rules found by C6.0. For example, the second rule relates to the visualized sentence and should be read as "if the instance has type *mountainous*, then it appears 1 time in the gold graphs and 0 times in the silver graphs of the entire document". Similarly the third rule should be read as "word *Foreign* appears 13 times as :op1 of name in the gold graphs, but only 1 time in the silver graphs of the entire document" – such 13 to 1 ratio likely points to some capitalization error in the parser pipeline. The generated rules can be sorted by their statistical impact score calculated as Laplace ratio $(p+1)/(p+n+2)$ from the number of correct p and wrong n predictions made by this rule.

Classifier generated rules were the key instrument we used to create a bug-fixing wrapper for the CAMR parser, described in Section 3.1. We fixed only bugs triggering error-indicating-rules with the impact scores above 0.8, because Laplace ratio strongly correlates with the smatch score impact of the particular error.

2.2 Smatch Extension for Ensemble Voting

The original smatch algorithm is designed to compare only two AMR documents. Meanwhile CAMR parser is slightly non-deterministic in the sense that it produces different AMRs for the same test sentence, if trained repeatedly. Randomly choosing one of the generated AMRs is a suboptimal strategy. A better strategy is to use an ensemble voting inspired approach: among all AMRs generated for the given test sentence, choose the AMR which achieves the highest average pairwise smatch score with all the other AMRs generated for the same test sentence. Intuitively it means that among the non-deterministic options we choose the "prevalent" AMR.

Multiple AMRs for the same test sentence can be generated also from different AMR parsers with substantially different average smatch accuracy. In this case all AMRs still can participate in the scoring, but weights need to be assigned to ensure that only AMRs from the high-accuracy parser may win.

3 AMR Parsers

We applied the smatch extensions described in the previous Section to two very different AMR parsers.

3.1 CAMR Parser with Wrapper

We applied the debugging techniques from Section 2.1 to the best available open-source AMR parser CAMR[3]. The identified bug-fixes were almost entirely implemented as a CAMR parser wrapper[4], that runs extra pre-processing (normalization) step on input data and extra post-processing step on output data. Only minor modifications to CAMR code itself were made[5] to improve the performance on multi-core systems and to fix date normalization problems.

Our CAMR wrapper tries to normalize the input data to the format recognized well by CAMR and to fix some systematic discrepancies of annotation style between the actual CAMR output and the expected gold AMRs. The overall gain from our wrapper is about 4%.

The following normalization actions are taken during pre-processing step, together accounting for about 2% gain:

1. number normalization from a lexical (e.g. "seventy-eight"), semi-lexical (e.g. "5 million") or multi-token digital (e.g. "100,000" or "100 000") format to a single token digital format (e.g. "100000");

2. currency normalization from a number (any format mentioned in previous step) together with a currency symbol (e.g. "$ 100") to a single token digital number with the lexical currency name (e.g. "100 dollars");

3. date normalization from any number and lexical mix to an explicit eight-digit dash separated format "yyyy-mm-dd".

Small modifications had to be made to the baseline JAMR (Flanigan et al., 2014) aligner used by CAMR to reliably recognize the "yyyy-mm-dd" date format and to correctly align the date tokens to the graph entries (by default JAMR uses "yymmdd" date format that is ambiguous regarding century and furthermore can be misinterpreted as a number).

The rules for date normalization were extracted from the training set semi-automatically using C6.0 classifier by mapping date-entities in the gold AMR graphs and corresponding fragments in input sentences.

Additionally, all wiki edges were removed from the AMR graphs prior to training, because CAMR does not handle them well; this step ensures that CAMR is trained without wiki edges and therefore will not insert any wiki entries in the generated AMR. Instead, we insert wiki links deterministically during the post-processing step.

During post-processing step the following modifications are applied to the CAMR parser generated AMR graphs, together accounting for about 2% gain:

1. nationalities are normalized (e.g. "Italian" to "Italy");

2. some redundant graph leafs not carrying any semantic value are removed (e.g. "null-edge");

3. wiki links are inserted deterministically next to "name" edges using gazetteer extracted from the training data and extended with the complete list of countries and nationalities (wiki value is selected

---

[3] https://github.com/Juicechuan/AMRParsing
[4] https://github.com/didzis/CAMR/tree/wrapper

[5] Modified CAMR at https://github.com/didzis/CAMR

based on the parent concept and content of the "name" instance);

About 1% additional gain comes from the observation that CAMR parser suffers from overfitting: it achieves optimal results when trained for only 2 iterations and with empty validation set.

3.2 Neural AMR Parser

For neural translation based AMR parsing we used simplified AMRs without wiki links and variables. Prior to deleting variables, AMR graphs were converted into trees by duplicating the co-referring nodes. Such AMR simplification turned out to be nearly loss-less, as a simple co-reference resolving script restores the variables with average F1=0.98 smatch accuracy.

We trained a modified TensorFlow seq2seq neural translation model[6] with attention (Abadi et al., 2015; Sutskerev et al., 2014; Bahdanau et al., 2015) to "translate" plain English sentences into simplified AMRs. For the test sentence in Figure 1 it gives following parsing result:

```
(mountain-01
  :ARG1 (country
    :name (name :op1 "Georgia"))
```

Apart from a missing bracket this is a valid (although slightly incorrect) simplified AMR. Note that this translation has been learned in "closed task" and "end-to-end" manner only from the provided AMR training set without any external knowledge source. This explains overall lower accuracy of the neural AMR parser compared to CAMR, which uses external knowledge from wide coverage parsing models of BLLIP[7] parser (Charniak and Johnson, 2005). The neural AMR parser accuracy is close to CAMR accuracy for short sentences up to 100 characters, but degrades considerably for longer sentences.

We optimized TensorFlow seq2seq model hyperparameters within the constraints of the available GPU memory: 1 layer or 400 neurons, single bucket of size 480, each input and output character tokenized as a single "word", vocabulary size 120 (number of distinct characters), batch size 4, trained for 30 epochs (4 days on TitanX GPU).

Operating seq2seq model on the character-level (Karpathy, 2015; Chung et al., 2016; Luong et al., 2016) rather than standard word-level improved smatch F1 by notable 7%. Follow-up tests (Barzdins

Parser	F1 on LDC2015E86 test set	F1 on the official eval set
JAMR (baseline)	0.576	
CAMR (baseline)	0.617	
CAMR (no valid.set, 2 iter.)	0.630	
Neural AMR (word-level)	0.365	
Neural AMR (char-level)	0.433	0.376
CAMR+ wrapper	0.667	0.616
Ensemble of CAMR+ wrapper and NeuralAMR (char-level)	0.672	**0.620**

Table 1: Smatch scores.

et al., 2016) revealed that character-level translation with attention improves results only if the output is a syntactic variation of the input (as is the case for AMR parsing), but for e.g. English-Latvian translation gives inferior results due to attention mechanism failing to establish character-level mappings between the English and Latvian words.

4 Results

Table 1 shows smatch scores for various combinations of parsers and thus quantifies the contributions of all methods described in this paper. We improved upon CAMR rather than JAMR parser due to better baseline performance of CAMR, likely due to its reliance on the wide coverage BLLIP parser.

The CAMR parser wrapper (result of Sections 2.1 and 3.1) is the largest contributor to our results. The weighed ensemble of 3 runs of CAMR+wrapper and 1 run of neural AMR parser (Sections 2.2 and 3.2) gave an additional boost to the results. Including the neural AMR parser in the ensemble doubled the gain – apparently it acted as an efficient tiebreaker between the similar CAMR+wrapper outputs.

5 Conclusions

Although our results are based on CAMR parser, the described debugging and ensemble approaches are likely applicable also to other AMR parsers.

Acknowledgments

This work was supported in part by the Latvian National research program SOPHIS under grant agreement Nr.10-4/VPP-4/11 and in part by H2020 SUMMA project under grant agreement 688139/H2020-ICT-2015.

---

[6] https://github.com/didzis/tensorflowAMR

[7] https://github.com/BLLIP/bllip-parser

References

Martín Abadi, Ashish Agarwal, Paul Barham, Eugene Brevdo, Zhifeng Chen, Craig Citro, Greg S. Corrado, Andy Davis, Jeffrey Dean, Matthieu Devin, Sanjay Ghemawat, Ian Goodfellow, Andrew Harp, Geoffrey Irving, Michael Isard, Rafal Jozefowicz, Yangqing Jia, Lukasz Kaiser, Manjunath Kudlur, Josh Levenberg, Dan Mané, Mike Schuster, Rajat Monga, Sherry Moore, Derek Murray, Chris Olah, Jonathon Shlens, Benoit Steiner, Ilya Sutskever, Kunal Talwar, Paul Tucker, Vincent Vanhoucke, Vijay Vasudevan, Fernanda Viégas, Oriol Vinyals, Pete Warden, Martin Wattenberg, Martin Wicke, Yuan Yu, and Xiaoqiang Zheng. 2015. TensorFlow: Large-scale machine learning on heterogeneous systems. *Google Research whitepaper*. Software available from tensorflow.org.

Dzmitry Bahdanau, Kyunghyun Cho, and Yoshua Bengio. 2015. Neural machine translation by jointly learning to align and translate. In *ICLR'2015*.

Laura Banarescu, Claire Bonial, Shu Cai, Madalina Georgescu, Kira Griffitt, Ulf Hermjakob, Kevin Knight, Philipp Koehn, Martha Palmer, and Nathan Schneider, 2013. Abstract Meaning Representation for Sembanking. In *Proceedings of the 7th Linguistic Annotation Workshop and Interoperability with Discourse*, pages 178–186. Association for Computational Linguistics.

Guntis Barzdins, Didzis Gosko, Laura Rituma, and Peteris Paikens. 2014. Using C5.0 and Exhaustive Search for Boosting Frame-Semantic Parsing Accuracy. In: *Proceedings of the 9th Language Resources and Evaluation Conference (LREC-2014)*, pages 4476-4482.

Guntis Barzdins, Peteris Paikens and Didzis Gosko. 2015. Riga: from FrameNet to Semantic Frames with C6.0 Rules. In *Proceedings of the 9th International Workshop on Semantic Evaluation (SemEval 2015)*, pages 960–964. Association for Computational Linguistics.

Guntis Barzdins, Steve Renals and Didzis Gosko. 2016. Character-Level Neural Translation for Multilingual Media Monitoring in the SUMMA Project. In: *Proceedings of the 10th Language Resources and Evaluation Conference (LREC-2016)*, (to appear).

Shu Cai and Kevin Knight. 2013. Smatch: an evaluation metric for semantic feature structures. In *Proceedings of the 51st Annual Meeting of the Association for Computational Linguistics (Volume 2: Short Papers)*, pages 748–752. Association for Computational Linguistics.

Eugene Charniak and Mark Johnson. 2005. Coarse- tofine n-best parsing and maxent discriminative reranking. In *Proceedings of the 43rd Annual Meet- ing on Association for Computational Linguistics*, ACL '05, pages 173–180, Stroudsburg, PA, USA. Association for Computational Linguistics.

Junyoung Chung, Kyunghyun Cho, Yoshua Bengio. 2016. A Character-Level Decoder without Explicit Segmentation for Neural Machine Translation. *arXiv preprint* arXiv:1603:06147

Jeffrey Flanigan, Sam Thomson, Jaime Carbonell, Chris Dyer, and Noah A. Smith. 2014. A discriminative graph-based parser for the abstract meaning representation. In *Proceedings of the 52nd Annual Meeting of the Association for Computational Linguistics (Volume 1: Long Papers)*, pages 1426–1436, Baltimore, Maryland, June. Association for Computational Linguistics.

Andrej Karpathy. The unreasonable effectiveness of recurrent neural networks. Blog post, http://karpathy.github.io/2015/05/21/rnn-effectiveness/, 2015.

Minh-Thang Luong and Christopher D. Manning. 2016. Achieving Open Vocabulary Neural Machine Translation with Hybrid Word-Character Models. *arXiv preprint* arXiv:1604.00788

Ross J. Quinlan. 1993. *C4.5: Programs for Machine Learning*. Morgan Kaufmann Publishers.

Ilya Sutskever, Oriol Vinyals, and Quoc V. Le. Sequence to sequence learning with neural networks. In *NIPS, 2014*.

Chuan Wang, Nianwen Xue, and Sameer Pradhan. 2015a. A transition-based algorithm for AMR parsing. In *Proceedings of the 2015 Conference of the North American Chapter of the Association for Computational Linguistics: Human Language Technologies*, pages 366–375. Association for Computational Linguistics.

Chuan Wang, Nianwen Xue, and Sameer Pradhan. 2015b. Boosting Transition-based AMR Parsing with Refined Actions and Auxiliary Analyzers. In *Proceedings of the 53rd Annual Meeting of the Association for Computational Linguistics and the 7th International Joint Conference on Natural Language Processing (Short Papers)*, pages 857-862. Association for Computational Linguistics.

DynamicPower at SemEval-2016 Task 8: Processing syntactic parse trees with a Dynamic Semantics core

Alastair Butler

National Institute for Japanese Language and Linguistics

`ajb129@hotmail.com`

Abstract

This is a system description paper for a submission to Task 8 of SemEval-2016: Meaning Representation Parsing. No use was made of the training data provided by the task. Instead existing components were combined to form a pipeline able to take raw sentences as input and output meaning representations. Components are a part-of-speech tagger and parser trained on the Penn Parsed Corpus of Modern British English to produce syntactic parse trees, a semantic role labeller and a named entity recogniser to supplement obtained parse trees with word sense, functional and named entity information, followed by an adapted Tarskian satisfaction relation for a Dynamic Semantics that is used to transform a syntactic parse into a predicate logic based meaning representation, followed by conversion to penman/AMR notation required for the task appraisal.

1 Introduction

This is a system description paper for a submission to Task 8 of SemEval-2016: Meaning Representation Parsing. Syntactic structures are first obtained by parsing raw language input, from which meaning representations are derived by printing off information accumulated with an adapted Tarskian satisfaction relation for a Dynamic Semantics (Dekker, 2012). This is akin to compositional approaches of formal semantics that view the task of reaching a semantic value as being rooted in first obtaining a syntactic parse. Key advantages are modularity and domain independence.

This paper is structured as follows. Section 2 sketches the method used to obtain a syntactic parse. Section 3 covers reaching a semantic representation. Section 4 outlines conversion to penman/AMR notation. Section 5 reports experiment results. Section 6 is a conclusion. An appendix details how to run the available implementation.

2 Obtaining a syntactic parse

The approach first needs a way to obtain syntactic parse trees. Major components used were the Stanford Log-linear Part-Of-Speech Tagger[1] (Toutanova et al., 2003) and the Berkeley Parser[2] (Petrov and Klein, 2003), both trained on data from the years of 1840–1908 of the Penn Parsed Corpus of Modern British English[3] (Kroch et al., 2010). The particular setup followed suggestions of pre-processing and post-processing made by Kulick et al. (2014) and used tools, notably `create_stripped`, from the system of Fang, Butler and Yoshimoto (2014).[4]

Dating from over one hundred years ago, training data for the syntactic parser was not chosen for suitability to a potential task domain, but instead for the practical benefit that parse results would conform to the scheme proposed in the *Annotation manual for the Penn Historical Corpora and the Parsed Corpus of Early English Correspondence (PCEEC)* (Santorini, 2010). This scheme is exceptionally consistent, especially with regards to facilitating identi-

---

[1] http://nlp.stanford.edu/software/tagger.html
[2] https://github.com/slavpetrov/berkeleyparser
[3] http://www.ling.upenn.edu/hist-corpora/PPCMBE-RELEASE-1/index.html
[4] http://www.compling.jp/haruniwa/index.html

Proceedings of SemEval-2016, pages 1148–1153,
San Diego, California, June 16-17, 2016. ©2016 Association for Computational Linguistics

fication of construction types (small clause, comparative, cleft, etc.) and for its handling of coordination, offering the least obstacle for a robust conversion to the structures fed to the semantic component (seen in the next section).

As an example, consider:

(1) Upon turning 80, Mao Zedong felt that he would die soon.

A parse in tree form returned looks like:

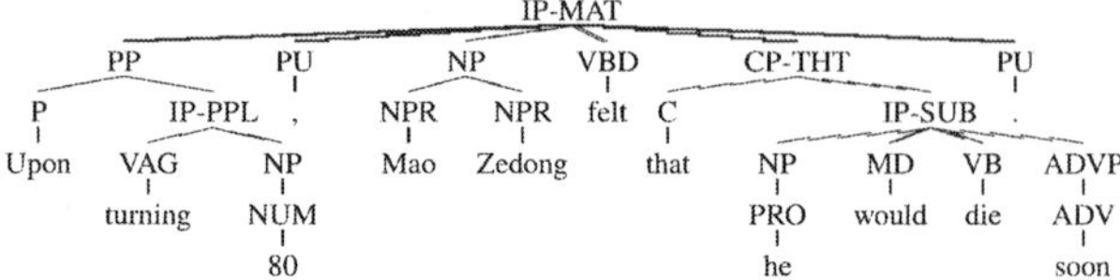

All words are part-of-speech labelled. Clause structure is generally flat with multiply branching nodes and no specified VP level, except with VP coordination. Phrasal nodes (NP, PP, ADVP, etc.) immediately dominate the phrase head (N, P, ADV, etc.) which has as sisters both modifiers and complements.

marked PERSON. From (1) as input, the combination of these tools collects the following information:

```
upon      TMP    _         O
turn      PMOD   turn.02    O
80        OBJ    _          O
,         P      _          O
mao       NAME   _          PERSON
zedong    SBJ    _          PERSON
felt      ROOT   feel.01    O
that      OBJ    _          O
he        SBJ    _          PERSON
would     SUB    _          O
die       VC     die.01     O
soon      TMP    _          O
.         P      _          O
```

The first column gives word lemmas, the second contains functional information to identify syntactic subjects (SBJ) and objects (OBJ) as well as adjunct roles such as LOC, MSR and TMP, the third column provides word sense information related to PropBank (Bonial et al., 2010) semantic frames ('turn.02', 'feel.02', 'die.01'), and the fourth column provides entity information. This column information is integrated with the parse to return:

IP-MAT tree (see figure)

Despite such flat clause and phrase structure, extended phrase labels marking function enable distinguishing the presence of modifiers (participial clauses (IP-PPL), adverbial clauses (CP-ADV), relative clauses (CP-REL), etc.) from complements (infinitive complements (IP-INF), that-complements (CP-THT), embedded questions (CP-QUE), etc.).

To arrive at a more complete parse for the task, word sense and functional information was obtained with mateplus[5] (Roth and Woodsend, 2014), which is an extended version of the mate-tools semantic role labeller (Björkelund et al., 2009). In addition, named entity information was gathered with the Stanford Named Entity Recognizer[6] (Finkel et al., 2005) using the MUC model that labels e.g., PERSON, ORGANIZATION, and LOCATION. Furthermore, pronouns, e.g., *he*, *she*, *they*, are default

The tree now includes extended phrase labels marking function (e.g., NP-SBJ=subject, NP-OB1=direct object, ADVP-TMP=temporal modifier). Terminal nodes are either word lemmas or, whenever available, PropBank word senses. Furthermore entity information is integrated with a BIND tag.

3 Obtaining semantic analysis

Having syntactic structures, the next step is to reach a level of semantic analysis. This is derived by printing off information accumulated with an adapted Tarskian satisfaction relation for a Dynamic Semantics (Dekker, 2012). Specifically, use is made of the Treebank Semantics implementation,[7] with syntactic structures converted into expressions of a formal language (Scope Control Theory or SCT) with a number of primitive operations (notably, among

---

[5] https://github.com/microth/mateplus
[6] http://nlp.stanford.edu/software/CRF-NER.html
[7] http://www.compling.jp/ts

others: `Namely` to make available fresh bindings, `T` to create bound arguments, `At` to allocate semantic roles, `Close` to bring about quantificational closures, `Rel` to establish predicate or connective relations, and `If` to conditionalise how calculation of a semantic value proceeds based on assignment state). The full list of operations and details are given in Butler (2015). Operations access or possibly alter a sequence based information state (Vermeulen, 2000) that retains binding information by assigning (possibly empty) sequences of values to binding names. This can be demonstrated with `Rel` creating an `"and"` relation with four arguments, each of which are processed against a different assignment state determined by instances of `Namely` embedded in occurrences of *Someone*:

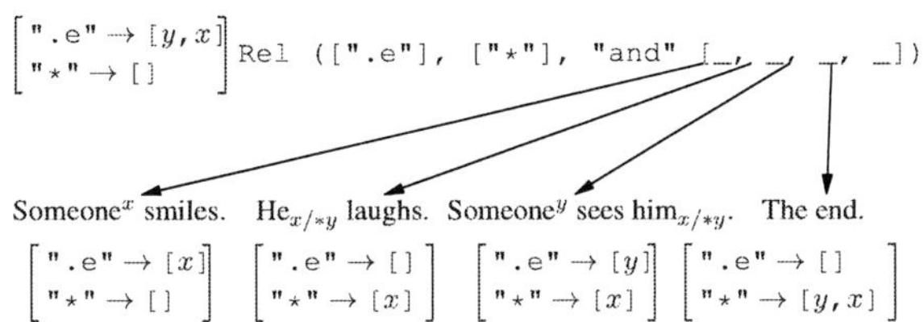

$$\begin{bmatrix} \texttt{".e"} \to [y,x] \\ \texttt{"*"} \to [] \end{bmatrix} \texttt{Rel ([".e"], ["*"], "and"} \underbrace{\quad}_{} , \; \_)$$

Someone^x smiles. He$_{x/*y}$ laughs. Someone^y sees him$_{x/*y}$. The end.

$$\begin{bmatrix} \texttt{".e"} \to [x] \\ \texttt{"*"} \to [] \end{bmatrix} \begin{bmatrix} \texttt{".e"} \to [] \\ \texttt{"*"} \to [x] \end{bmatrix} \begin{bmatrix} \texttt{".e"} \to [y] \\ \texttt{"*"} \to [x] \end{bmatrix} \begin{bmatrix} \texttt{".e"} \to [] \\ \texttt{"*"} \to [y,x] \end{bmatrix}$$

Pronouns are able to link to `"*"` bindings, which are accessible bindings that have reached the discourse context because of prior indefinites, while indefinites take bindings from `".e"`, which is a source for fresh bindings. This approach gives a handle on discourse, and more generally governs the interaction of quantification to capture the empirical results of accessibility from Discourse Representation Theory (Kamp and Reyle, 1993), as well as intra-sentential binding conditions (Butler, 2010).

Regarding the running example, the tree for (1) is converted to the following:

```
val ex1 =
( fn fh =>
  ( fn lc =>
    ( npr "PERSON" "mao_zedong" "ARG0"
      ( ( someFact fh ( gensym "TIME") ".e" "FACT"
          ( control lc
            ( ( fn lc =>
                ( some lc fh ( gensym "ENTITY") ".e"
                  ( someClassic lc fh ( gensym "ATTRIB") ".e" nil
                    ( adj lc "80") "CARDINAL"
                    ( nn lc "")) "ARG1"
                    ( verb lc ( gensym "EVENT") ".event" ["ARG1"] "turn.02")))
              [ "CARDINAL", "ARG1", "ARG0", "h"]))) "TMP"
        ( past ".event"
          ( embVerb lc ( gensym "EVENT") ".event" ["TMP", "ARG0"] "feel.01"
            ( THAT lc
              ( ( fn lc =>
                  ( pro ["*"] fh ["PERSON"] ( gensym "PERSON") ".e" "he" "ARG0"
                    ( md fh "would" free
                      ( advp lc fh ".event"
                        ( adv lc "TMP_soon")
                        ( verb lc ( gensym "EVENT") ".event" ["ARG0"] "die.01")))))
                [ "FACT", "ARG0", "ARG1", "h"]))))))))
      [ "TMP", "ARG0", "ARG1", "h"])
[ "@e", ".e", ".event"]
```

Such an expression is built exploiting the input syntactic structure by locating any complement for the phrase head to scope over, and adding modifiers with scope over the head. During construction information about binding names is gathered and integrated at clause levels with `fn fh =>` and `fn lc =>` acting as lambda abstractions.

With conversion to `ex1`, part of speech tags transform to operations (`some` (indefinite), `nn` (noun predicate), `verb` (predicate with an event argument), `pro` (pronoun), `gensym` (trigger to create a fresh binding), `free` (ensures no quantificational closure), etc.). Also, constructions can bring about the inclusion of operations (e.g., `someFact` with the participial clause, and `THAT` with the that-complement). Conversion also adds (i) information about local binding names (e.g., `"ARG0"` (logical subject role) and `"ARG1"` (logical object role)) and (ii) information about sources for fresh bindings from quantificational closures (`"@e"`, `".e"` and `".event"`). Once built `ex1` reduces to primitives of the SCT language, the start of which is as follows:

```
Sct.Close ("∃",["@e", ".e", ".event"],
 Sct.Clean (0, ["ARG0"], "*",
  Sct.Namely (Lang.C ("mao_zedong", "PERSON"),"@e",
   Sct.Lam ("@e", "ARG0",
    Sct.Clean (0, ["TMP"], "*",
     Sct.QuantThrow (Lang.X (1, "TIME"),".e",
      Sct.Lam (".e", "TMP",
       Sct.Rel (["@e", ".e", ".event"], ["*", "*", "*"], "", [
        Sct.Throw (".e",
         Sct.Rel ([], [], "FACT", [Sct.At (Sct.T ("TMP", 0), "FACT"),
          Sct.At (
           Sct.Lam ("TMP", "",
            Sct.Clean (0, ["ARG1", "LGS", "ARG2"], "ARG0",
             Sct.Clean (0, ["TMP", "ARG1", "h"], "*",
              Sct.If (fn,
               Sct.Clean (0, ["ARG1", "LGS", "ARG2"], "ARG0",
                Sct.Clean (0, ["TMP", "ARG1", "h"], "*", ...
```

Such an expression is given to the adapted Tarskian satisfaction procedure which, instead of returning a semantic value (e.g., `true` or `false` with respect to a model), is used to produce a meaning representation by printing accumulated information, thus:

```
∃ PERSON[6] ATTRIB[3] TIME[1] EVENT[4] EVENT[7]
  EVENT[5] ENTITY[2] (
 80(ATTRIB[3]) ∧ is_CARDINAL(ENTITY[2], ATTRIB[3]) ∧
   is_FACT_THAT(TIME[1],
     turn.02(EVENT[4], PERSON[mao_zedong], ENTITY[2])) ∧
   PERSON[6] = he{PERSON[mao_zedong]} ∧
   TMP_soon(EVENT[7]) ∧ past(EVENT[5]) ∧
      feel.01(EVENT[5], PERSON[mao_zedong],
        MD_would(die.01(EVENT[7], PERSON[6]))) ∧
      is_contained_in(TMP(EVENT[5]), TIME[1]))
```

This gives a Davidsonian representation (Davidson, 1967) in which verbs are encoded with minimally an event argument. All bindings are existentially quantified over at the highest level, which is a convenience for reaching penman/AMR notation and not an approach limitation. Also note the pronoun is resolved to the only accessible PERSON antecedent.

4 Conversion to penman/AMR notation

Conversion to penman/AMR notation (Matthiessen and Bateman, 1991; Banarescu et al., 2015) involves transforming obtained semantic structures into trees with explicit argument role information. An argument of each predicate (e.g., '@EVENT' if present, or the sole argument of a one-place predicate) is made the parent of the predicate. Also, binding is made implicit with the removal of quantification levels. Thus, the running example becomes:

'-of'). The latter is seen with the modal (*would*), but also serves to compact long distance dependencies that arise with relative clauses, comparatives, clefts, etc. There is also expansion of name information and some reordering of role placement.

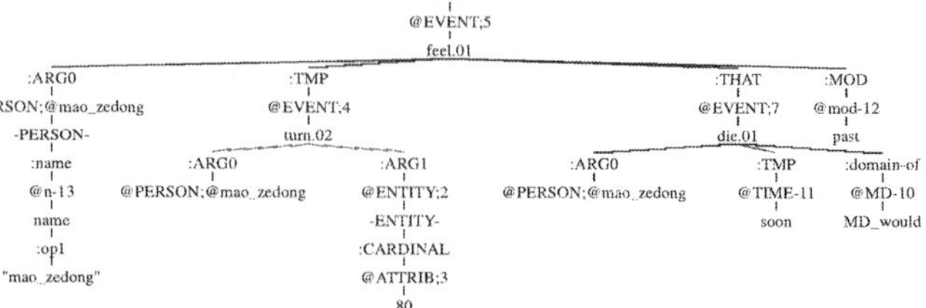

The final step involves pretty printing the assembled tree into the penman/AMR format, as well as the removal of tense information and remapping role names, e.g., :THAT changes to :ARG1, :TMP to :time, :ON to :prep-on, :CARDINAL to :quant, :ATTRIBUTE to :mod, and :POS to :poss.

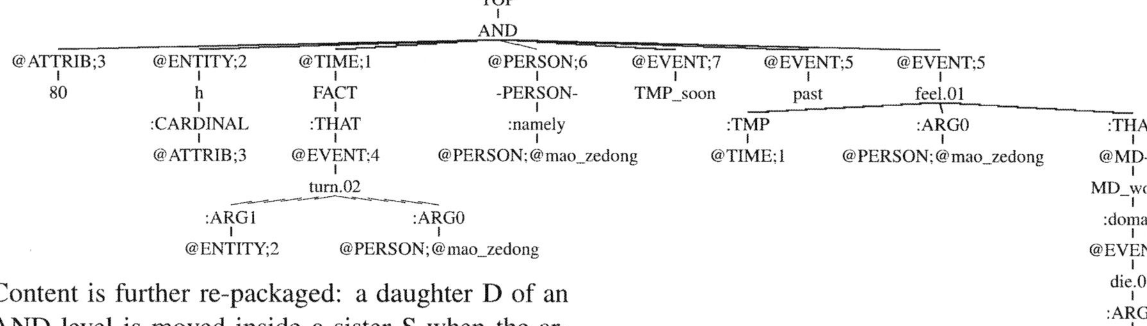

Content is further re-packaged: a daughter D of an AND level is moved inside a sister S when the argument name at the root of D is contained as an argument within S. Movement is to only one location.

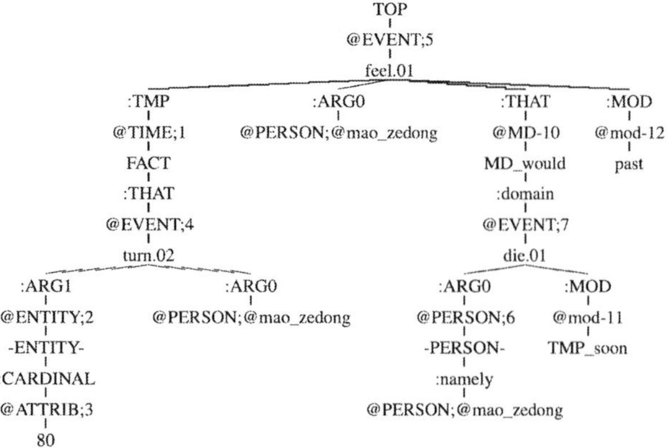

In addition, flatter structures are arrived at by excising redundant linking information, e.g., @TIME;1 FACT :THAT and folding tree material around inverse roles (signalled by ending the role name with

```
( EVENT-5 / feel-02
    :ARG0 ( PERSON-mao_zedong / PERSON
        :name ( n-13 / name :op1 "mao" :op2 "zedong"))
    :ARG1 ( EVENT-7 / die-01
        :ARG0 PERSON-mao_zedong
        :time ( TIME-11 / soon))
    :time ( EVENT-4 / turn-02
        :ARG0 PERSON-mao_zedong
        :ARG1 ( ENTITY-2 / ENTITY
            :quant ( ATTRIB-3 / 80)))))
```

For comparison, the gold analysis from the task training data for the running example is as follows:

```
( f / feel-02
    :ARG0 ( p / person
        :wiki "Mao_Zedong"
        :name ( n / name :op1 "Mao" :op2 "Zedong"))
    :ARG1 ( d / die-01
        :ARG1 p
        :time ( s / soon))
    :time ( t / turn-02
        :ARG1 p
        :ARG2 ( t2 / temporal-quantity
            :quant 80
            :unit ( y / year)))))
```

Table 1: Parsing results on the evaluation data of SemEval-2016 Task 8 and test data of LDC2015E86

	Precision	Recall	F-score
Task 8 eval	-	-	0.47
Test	0.37	0.39	0.38

It can be seen that gaps remain. In particular, there is no wikification to ground terms, and there is a lack of named entity information. Establishment of arguments as well as multiple roles for the same entity is largely successful, although there are mismatches with `die-01` and `turn-02`, reflecting that the semantic analysis stage lacks information for how PropBank roles for arguments should be allocated.

5 Experiments

The method of this paper is evaluated on the shared task evaluation data, which includes 1053 sentences. The smatch score on the evaluation data is 0.47. Table 1 also reports smatch score on the LDC2015E86 dataset, which includes 1371 test sentences. The scores are calculated with Smatch v2.0.2 (Cai and Knight, 2013), which evaluates the precision, recall, and $F1$ of the concepts and relations all together. The score for Task 8 is higher than the performance on the LDC2015E86 test data. Reasons for the difference include parser performance being better on the evaluate data, and there being fewer non-compositional aspects of representation in the evaluate data.

6 Conclusion

To sum up, this paper has described a modularised approach for building meaning representations, with a key role for an adapted Tarskian satisfaction relation for a Dynamic Semantics as the method to integrate and connect information sourced from a syntactic parser, semantic role labeller and named entity recogniser. Task performance was limited by not using the training data provided by the task, in particular: lacking information to allocate PropBank roles, neglecting wikification, and missing entity information to replicate non-compositional aspects of the Abstract Meaning Representation (AMR) specification (Banarescu et al., 2015). Nevertheless, this contribution indicates that AMRs are not far removed from what a compositional semantics can achieve, which is of interest for connecting to results from the formal semantics literature, such as gaining a treatment for quantification, as well as for relating to "Sembank" resources built with Discourse Representation Theory/Dynamic Semantics, such as the Groningen Meaning Bank[8] (Basile et al., 2012) and Treebank Semantics Corpus[9] (Butler and Yoshimoto, 2012).

Appendix: Implementation[10]

Assuming `text` is some original (multi-)sentence segmented data, `text.psd` contains the output from a parser trained on the PPCMBE, `text.mate` is output from mateplus, and `text.ner` is output from the Stanford Named Entity Recognizer, the following pipeline creates fully parsed data as described in section 2.

```
cat text.psd | add_functional text.mate |
add_sense text.mate | add_tsv_ner text.ner
| add_lemma text.mate | tree_select_word_2
> fullparse.psd
```

A script to recover the potentially multiple sentence segmentation of `text` obscured by parsing is achieved thus:

```
cat fullparse.psd | parse_discourse_split
text > segment.sh
```

The following pipeline achieves the semantic analysis of section 3, as well as the conversion to penman/AMR notation of section 4.

```
cat fullparse.psd | prepare_PPCMBE |
segment.sh | parse_normalize -propbank
-free -bind | see_sct -free -reset |
run_sct -penman | penman_like_amr |
pretty_penman
```

Acknowledgements

This paper has benefitted from the comments of three anonymous reviewers, discussions with Pascual Martínez-Gómez, Masaaki Nagata, and Kei Yoshimoto, and most particularly advice from the SemEval Task 8 organiser Jonathan May, all of

---

[8]http://gmb.let.rug.nl
[9]https://github.com/ajb129/tscorpus
[10]All pipeline programs are from: https://github.com/ajb129

which is very gratefully acknowledged. This research is supported by the Japan Society for the Promotion of Science (JSPS), Research Project Number: 15K02469.

References

Laura Banarescu, Claire Bonial, Shu Cai, Madalina Georgescu, Kira Griffitt, Ulf Hermjakob, Kevin Knight, Philipp Koehn, Martha Palmer, and Nathan Schneider. 2015. Abstract Meaning Representation (AMR) 1.2.2 Specification. https://github.com/amrisi/amr-guidelines/blob/master/amr.md.

V. Basile, J. Bos, K. Evang, and N.J. Venhuizen. 2012. Developing a large semantically annotated corpus. In *Proceedings of the 8th Int. Conf. on Language Resources and Evaluation.* Istanbul, Turkey.

Claire Bonial, Olga Babko-Malaya, Jinho D. Choi, Jena Hwang, and Martha Palmer. 2010. *PropBank Annotation Guidelines.* Center for Computational Language and Education Research, Institute of Cognitive Science, University of Colorado at Boulder, 3rd edn.

Anders Björkelund, Love Hafdell, and Pierre Nugues. 2014. Multilingual semantic role labeling. In *Proceedings of The Thirteenth Conference on Computational Natural Language Learning (CoNLL),* pages 43–48. Boulder, Colorado.

Alastair Butler. 2010. *The Semantics of Grammatical Dependencies,* vol. 23 of *Current Research in the Semantics/Pragmatics Interface.* Bingley: Emerald.

Alastair Butler. 2015. *Linguistic Expressions and Semantic Processing: A Practical Approach.* Heidelberg: Springer-Verlag.

Alastair Butler and Kei Yoshimoto. 2012. Banking meaning representations from treebanks. *Linguistic Issues in Language Technology - LiLT* 7(1):1–22.

Shu Cai and Kevin Knight. 2013. Smatch: an evaluation metric for semantic feature structures. In *Proc. of the ACL 2013.*

Donald Davidson. 1967. The logical form of action sentences. In N. Rescher, ed., *The Logic of Decision and Action.* Pittsburgh: University of Pittsburgh Press. Reprinted in: D. Davidson, 1980. *Essays on Actions and Events.* Claredon Press, Oxford, pages 105–122.

Paul Dekker. 2012. *Dynamic Semantics,* vol. 91 of *Studies in Linguistics and Philosophy.* Dordrecht: Springer Verlag.

Tsaiwei Fang, Alastair Butler, and Kei Yoshimoto. 2014. Parsing Japanese with a PCFG treebank grammar. In *Proceedings of the Twentieth Annual Meeting of the Association of Natural Language Processing,* pages 432–435. Sapporo, Japan.

Jenny Finkel, Trond Grenager, and Christopher Manning. 2005. Incorporating non-local information into information extraction systems by gibbs sampling. In *Proceedings of the 43nd Annual Meeting of the Association for Computational Linguistics (ACL 2005),* pages 363–370.

Hans Kamp and Uwe Reyle. 1993. *From Discourse to Logic: Introduction to Model-theoretic Semantics of Natural Language, Formal Logic and Discourse Representation Theory.* Dordrecht: Kluwer.

Anthony Kroch, Beatrice Santorini, and Ariel Diertani. 2010. *The Penn-Helsinki Parsed Corpus of Modern British English (PPCMBE).* Department of Linguistics, University of Pennsylvania. CD-ROM, second edition, (http://www.ling.upenn.edu/hist-corpora).

Seth Kulick, Anthony Kroch, and Beatrice Santorini. 2014. The Penn Parsed Corpus of Modern British English: First parsing results and analysis. In *Proceedings of the 52nd Annual Meeting of the Association for Computational Linguistics (Short Papers),* pages 662–667. Baltimore, Maryland, USA: Association for Computational Linguistics.

Christian Matthiessen and John A Bateman. 1991. *Text generation and systemic-functional linguistics: experiences from English and Japanese.* Pinter Publishers.

Slav Petrov and Dan Klein. 2007. Improved inference for unlexicalized parsing. In *Proceedings of NAACL HLT 2007,* pages 404–411.

Michael Roth and Kristian Woodsend. 2014. Composition of word representations improves semantic role labelling. In *Proceedings of the 2014 Conference on Empirical Methods in Natural Language Processing (EMNLP),* pages 407–413. Doha, Qatar.

Beatrice Santorini. 2010. Annotation manual for the Penn Historical Corpora and the PCEEC (Release 2). Tech. rep., Department of Computer and Information Science, University of Pennsylvania, Philadelphia. (http://www.ling.upenn.edu/histcorpora/annotation).

Kristina Toutanova, Dan Klein, Christopher Manning, and Yoram Singer. 2003. Feature-rich part-of-speech tagging with a cyclic dependency network. In *Proceedings of HLT-NAACL 2003,* pages 252–259.

C. F. M. Vermeulen. 2000. Variables as stacks: A case study in dynamic model theory. *Journal of Logic, Language and Information* 9:143–167.

M2L at SemEval-2016 Task 8:
AMR Parsing with Neural Networks

Yevgeniy Puzikov, Daisuke Kawahara, Sadao Kurohashi
Graduate School of Informatics, Kyoto University
Yoshida-honmachi, Sakyo-ku
Kyoto, 606-8501, Japan
`puzikov@nlp.ist.i.kyoto-u.ac.jp`
`{kuro,dk}@i.kyoto-u.ac.jp`

Abstract

This paper describes our contribution to the SemEval 2016 Workshop. We participated in the Shared Task 8 on Meaning Representation parsing using a transition-based approach, which builds upon the system of Wang et al. (2015a) and Wang et al. (2015b), with additions that utilize a Feedforward Neural Network classifier and an enriched feature set. We observed that exploiting Neural Networks in Abstract Meaning Representation parsing is challenging and we could not benefit from it, while the feature enhancements yielded an improved performance over the baseline model.

1 Introduction

Abstract Meaning Representation (AMR) (Banarescu et al., 2013; Dorr et al., 1998) is a semantic formalism which represents sentence meaning in a form of a rooted directed acyclic graph. AMR graph nodes represent concepts, labelled directed edges between the nodes show the relationships between concepts. The AMR formalism was created in order to explore the semantics behind natural language units for further analysis and application in various tasks.

At the time of writing this paper two AMR parsers are publicly available: graph-based JAMR (Flanigan et al., 2014) and transition-based CAMR (Wang et al., 2015a; Wang et al., 2015b). The latter has served as our baseline model, which we tried to improve by incorporating additional features defined for a wider conditioning context and a neural network (NN) classifier.

Inspired by the results of Chen and Manning (2014) and Weiss et al. (2015), who obtained state-of-the-art results in transition-based dependency parsing using Feedforward Neural Networks (FFNN), and taking into account the transition nature of the CAMR model, we performed a series of experiments in the same direction. Neural networks have been successfully applied to many NLP fields and we were curious to examine their potential in the task of AMR parsing. Specifically, we investigated the possibility of constraining the averaged perceptron algorithm (Collins, 2002) predictions by those of an FFNN at the initial step of the inference process.

2 Preprocessing

We used the Stanford CoreNLP v3.6.0 toolkit (Manning et al., 2014) to get named entity (NE) and dependency information, the latter in the form of Stanford dependencies was obtained from the NN dependency parser (Chen and Manning, 2014).

We used a publicly available semantic role labelling (SRL) system with a predicate disambiguation module (Björkelund et al., 2009). The system is a part of MATE tools[1], which also include a lemmatizer, a part of speech (POS) tagger, and a dependency parser. We use them to obtain lemmas and POS tags. All the tools were used with the pretrained models.

Using MALT dependencies instead of or in tandem with Stanford dependencies did not change the

---

[1] `https://storage.googleapis.com/ google-code-archive-downloads/v2/code. google.com/mate-tools`

1154

Proceedings of SemEval-2016, pages 1154–1159,
San Diego, California, June 16-17, 2016. ©2016 Association for Computational Linguistics

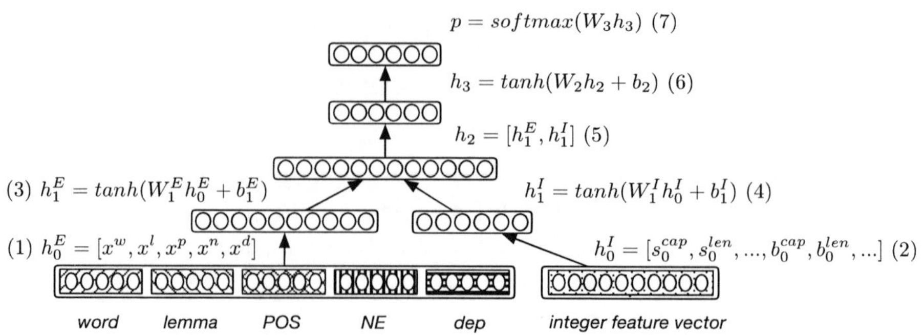

Figure 1: Schematic view of our NN model.

overall performance of the AMR parser. Due to time limitations, we did not perform a full analysis of the accuracy of both tools, which would be an interesting and important point to investigate further.

All information extracted after the preprocessing step was combined into one CoNLL-format file (Hajič et al., 2009). Finally, we used an AMR graph-to-sentence aligner of Flanigan et al. (2014) to map word spans to concept fragments in the AMR graph.

3   Parsing Algorithm

We use the same set of transitions and a parsing algorithm as Wang et al. (2015b). We skip the full description due to space limitations and refer to the original paper. It forms a quadruple $Q = (S, T, s_0, S_t)$, where S is a set of parsing states (or configurations), T is a set of parsing transitions (or actions), s_0 is the initial state and S_t is a set of terminal states of the parser. Each state is a triple (σ, β, G), where σ denotes a stack, storing indices of the nodes which have not been processed yet; it's top element is σ_0. β is a buffer, storing the children of σ_0. Finally, G is a partially built AMR graph aligned with the sentence tokens.

At the beginning of the parsing procedure, σ is initialized with a post-order traversal of the input dependency tree with topmost element σ_0; β is initialized with σ_0's children or set to null if σ_0 is a leaf node. G is initialized with the nodes and edges of the dependency tree, but all node and edge labels are set to null. The parser processes all nodes and their outgoing edges in the tree in a bottom-up left-right manner, applying some transition to the current node or edge. Parsing terminates when both σ and β are empty.

There are nine basic transitions (*NEXT-EDGE, SWAP, REATTACH, REPLACE-HEAD, REEN-TRANCE, MERGE, NEXT-NODE, DELETE-NODE, INFER*), some of which result in assigning either a concept label or an edge label. The sets of concept labels for aligned nodes, unaligned nodes and edge labels ($S_{aligned\_tag}$, $S_{unaligned\_tag}$, S_{edge}, respectively) are constructed during the preprocessing stage and are later used to provide candidate concept tags or edge labels for the respective transitions. Let's also introduce a set $S_{total} = S_{aligned\_tag} \bigcup S_{unaligned\_tag} \bigcup S_{edge}$. $|S_{total}|$ determines the number of classes for our classification algorithm to choose from.

We propose a parsing strategy which first uses an NN classifier to constrain the space of candidate transitions by choosing an unlabelled version of a transition, and then forces the perceptron algorithm to make a prediction only on the label of the chosen transition. We have also tried to completely substitute the averaged perceptron algorithm with an NN, experimenting with various types and architectures of the latter, but experimental results were unsatisfactory. This question is yet to be analysed in full, but presumably we failed to provide our NN classifiers with a sufficiently rich input representation: we used a very simple technique of concatenating embedding vectors (Section 4), which apparently did not capture enough information for an NN to make accurate predictions.

4   Neural Network Architecture

During preprocessing, we create a vocabulary V which stores all unique words, lemmas, POS tags, NE tags and dependency labels from the training set.

Perceptron model features	
Singular features	**Feature combination**
$\{\sigma_0, \beta_0, \beta_0^{head+}\}.\{w, l, n, p, d, brown4, brown6, brown10, brown20\}$	$\{\sigma_0.w, \sigma_0.l, \sigma_0.p, \sigma_0.n, \sigma_0.d, \sigma_0.len\} + t.tag$
$\sigma_0^{head}.\{w, l, p, n, d\}, \sigma_0.tag$	$\sigma_0.d + \beta_0.brown20, \sigma_0.brown4 + \beta_0.brown20, \sigma_0.brown20 + \beta_0.brown4, \sigma_0.brown20 + \beta_0.d$
$\sigma_0.isnom, \beta_0.len, \beta_0.rph$	$\sigma_0.n + \beta_0.n, \sigma_0.d + \beta_0.l, \sigma_0.p + \beta_0.l, \sigma_0.l + \beta_0.d, \sigma_0.l + \beta_0.p$
$dist_{\sigma_0,\beta_0}, dist_{\beta_0,\beta_0^{head+}}$	$\beta_0.l + \beta_0^{rsb}.d, \beta_0.l + \beta_0.numswp, \beta_0.l + \beta_0^{head+}.d, \beta_0.l + \beta_0^{head+}.p$
$\{\beta_0, \beta_0^{head+}\}.\{arglabel, prdlabel\}, \sigma_0.verb\_sense \star$	$\beta_0.n + \beta_0^{head+}.n, \beta_0.tag + \beta_0^{head+}.tag, \beta_0.n + \beta_0^{head+}.tag, \sigma_0.l + \beta_0.tag + \beta_0^{head+}.tag$
$\sigma_0.eq\_verb\_sense, \{\beta_0, \beta_0^{head+}\}.\{isarg, isprd\} \star$	$path_{\beta_0,\sigma_0} + \beta_0.l + \sigma_0.l, path_{\beta_0,\beta_0^{head+}} + \beta_0.l + \beta_0^{head+}.l$
$\{\sigma_0, \sigma_0^p, \sigma_0^{lsb}, \sigma_0^{rsb}, \sigma_0^{rsb2}, \sigma_0^{prs1}, \sigma_0^{prs2}\}.\{w, l, p, n, d\} \bullet$	$dist_{\sigma_0,\beta_0} + path_{\sigma_0,\beta_0}, dist_{\sigma_0,\beta_0} + path_{\beta_0^{head+},\beta_0}$
$\{\beta_0, \beta_0^p, \beta_0^{lsb}, \beta_0^{rsb}, \beta_0^{rsb2}, \beta_0^{prs1}, \beta_0^{prs2}\}.\{w, l, p, n, d\} \bullet$	$\sigma_0.p + t_{is\_verb}, \beta_0.d + \beta_0.arglabel \star$
NN model features	
Embedding features: $\{\sigma_0, \sigma_0^p, \sigma_0^{lsb}, \sigma_0^{rsb}, \sigma_0^{rsb2}, \sigma_0^{prs1}, \sigma_0^{prs2}\}.\{w, l, p, n, d\}$	**Numerical features:** $\{\sigma_0, \beta_0\}.\{cap, arg0, arg1, arg2, len, nech, isnom, isleaf\}$
$\{\beta_0, \beta_0^p, \beta_0^{lsb}, \beta_0^{rsb}, \beta_0^{rsb2}, \beta_0^{prs1}, \beta_0^{prs2}\}.\{w, l, p, n, d\}$	

Table 1: Feature sets. σ_0^{head} is the head of σ_0 in the dependency tree; β_0^{head+} is the node, to which β_0 could be attached to as a result of either reentrance or reattachment transition; t is a transition under consideration – during feature extraction we consider the tag which might be assigned as a result of transition ($t.tag$) or whether this candidate is a verb sense tag ($t.tag_{is\_verb}$). The *isnom* feature checks whether the lemma of a corresponding element is in the NomBank dictionary. *nech* is the number of an element's children which have an NE label from the set {"PERSON", "LOCATION", "ORGANIZATION", "MISC"}. Other features are self-explanatory.

Each of them is mapped to the same D-dimensional vector space ($e_i^w, e_i^l, e_i^p, e_i^n, e_i^d \in \mathbb{R}^D$). We create one embedding matrix $E \in \mathbb{R}^{|V| \times D}$, where $|V|$ is the total size of the vocabulary and D is the dimensionality of dense embedding vectors.

In each parsing configuration we consider a set of elements which might be useful in the prediction task. These elements are σ_0, β_0 and their neighbouring nodes, which for σ_0 include σ_0^p (the parent of σ_0 in the dependency tree), σ_0^{lsb} (the left sibling), $\sigma_0^{rsb}, \sigma_0^{rsb2}$ (the first and the second right siblings), $\sigma_0^{prs1}, \sigma_0^{prs2}$ (the first and the second previous tokens in the sentence); neighbouring nodes for β_0 are defined in a similar manner. Thus, the total number of relevant elements is $n_{elem} = 14$.

The overall architecture of the network is depicted in Figure 1. The input layer of the network consists of two components. The first one is formed by concatenating all the corresponding embedding vectors for each element's feature (Figure 1 (1)). Each of the x components is, in turn, a concatenation of the embeddings of the configuration elements for a particular type of annotation. For example, x^w is an $\mathbb{R}^N$ vector, where $N = d \times n_{elem}$. We form x^l, x^p, x^n, x^d in a similar manner and concatenate x^w, x^l, x^p, x^n, x^d to form the input vector h_0^E. The second component of the input vector is h_0^I (Figure 1 (2)), a concatenation of vectors, representing non-embedding numerical features (see Table 1).

We separately map two parts of the input layer to hidden layers using the *tanh* activation function: h_0^E to h_1^E, h_0^I to h_1^I (Figure 1 (3) and (4)). We then con-

catenate layers h_1^E and h_1^I (Figure 1 (5)) and pass the resultant vector to the last hidden layer h_3, applying the *tanh* function again (Figure 1 (6)). Finally, a softmax layer is added on top of h_3 in order to calculate probabilities of the output classes (Figure 1 (7)).

5   Feature Sets

We have designed two separate feature sets for the NN and perceptron classifiers. The feature set for the latter is roughly the same as in (Wang et al., 2015b) (Table 1). Following the authors of CAMR, we also make use of the NomBank 1.0 dictionary (Meyers et al., 2004) [2]. Unfortunately, we could not obtain the copy of the same SRL system which was used by the authors. Therefore, we also measure accuracy improvement from incorporating the semantic features defined in the original paper but extracted after processing the data with a different SRL system (marked with a $\star$).

We also measure the improvement from incorporating the features extracted from a wider configuration context – they were not included into the baseline model and are marked with a $\bullet$.

In the case of the NN classifier we follow a standard feature extraction procedure and discard transition-specific features. Apart from the embedding features, we also include a number of numerical features, which proved to be useful in our exper-

---

[2] http://nlp.cs.nyu.edu/meyers/NomBank.html

iments.

6 Training Procedure and Parsing Policy

We trained the perceptron with a weight-averaging procedure, described in (Collins, 2002).

For the NN classifier we first prepared a training set $\{(x_i, y_i)\}_{i=1}^{n}$, where x_i denotes a feature representation of configuration i and y_i is the unlabelled version of the correct transition. The training objective is to minimize L2-regularized negative log-likelihood of the model:

$$L(\theta) = -\sum_{i=1}^{n} \log P(y_i | x_i, \theta) + \lambda ||\theta||_2^2,$$

$$\theta = [E, W_1^E, W_1^I, W_2, W_3].$$

We randomly initialized the embeddings within $(-0.01, 0.01)$ and fixed their dimensionality at 32. All weight matrices were initialized using the normalized initialization technique of Glorot and Bengio (2010). Hidden layer sizes were fixed as follows: $h_0^E = 2,240, h_0^I = 32, h_1^E = 100, h_1^I = 16, h_2 = 116, h_3 = 64$. All the biases were set to 0.02.

We train our network using mini-batches of size 200 under the early stopping settings with RMSprop[3] as an optimization algorithm. The learning rate of 5×10^{-4} and $\lambda = 1.5 \times 10^{-5}$ were found to perform best on the validation set.

Given a feature representation of the current configuration s, the parsing algorithm first provides a pool of legal transitions $\mathcal{T} \in S_{total}$, $|\mathcal{T}| \ll |S_{total}|$. We compute the probabilities of nine unlabelled transitions using the NN. If the network is confident about its prediction (we set an empirically chosen probability threshold of 0.9), we choose the highest scoring candidate and force the perceptron to predict the label of the transition, if it is a transition which assigns a concept tag or edge label. Each candidate $t \in \mathcal{T}$ is being scored by a linear scoring function $score(t, s) = \omega \cdot \phi(t, s)$, where ω denotes a weight vector for a particular candidate transition and $\phi(t, s)$ is a feature function mapping a (t, s) pair to a real-valued feature vector. The best scoring transition is chosen and applied to the configuration. If the NN chooses a transition which does not assign

Model	P	R	F_1
Perceptron (baseline)	0.56	0.66	0.60
Perceptron + SRL	0.57	0.68	0.62
Perceptron + wide context	**0.58**	**0.69**	**0.63**
Perceptron + SRL + wide context	0.58	0.68	0.63
NN + Perceptron	0.56	0.66	0.60
NN + Perceptron + SRL + wide context	0.58	0.68	0.63

Table 2: Experimental results.

labels, we apply this transition without asking for the perceptron prediction. Finally, if the network is not confident about the prediction – that is, if the probability for the highest scoring candidate is lower than 0.9 – we disregard the NN prediction and choose the prediction given by the perceptron algorithm.

7 Experiments

All the experiments were performed on the LDC2015E86 dataset, provided by the organizers. In our experiments we followed the standard train/dev/test split ($16, 833$, $1, 368$ and $1, 371$ sentences, respectively). Parser performance was evaluated with the Smatch (Cai and Knight, 2013) scoring script v2.0.2 [4] (Table 2).

As expected, using SRL features resulted in better performance compared to the baseline model (roughly a 2 F_1 points gain). Conditioning on a wider context was also beneficial – widening the context to include more configuration elements is often a good feature expansion technique (Toutanova et al., 2003; Chen et al., 2014). In contrast to our expectations, the NN classifier did not improve the parser performance. This might be due to the higher complexity of the AMR parsing task or the peculiarities of the underlying parsing algorithm (as mentioned in Section 3, we discarded some action-specific features due to the difficulty of their integration into the NN model). Further investigation on this matter is required to draw ground conclusions.

8 Conclusion

We have performed a range of experiments which resulted in improving the performance of the baseline AMR parsing system. The results show that a richer feature set is very likely to lead to more accurate predictions. Unfortunately, our attempts to further im-

---

[3] http://www.cs.toronto.edu/~tijmen/
csc321/slides/lecture_slides_lec6.pdf

[4] http://alt.qcri.org/semeval2016/task8/
index.php?id=data-and-tools

prove the system using NN were not that successful. This goes against the hypothesis that a small number of dense vector embedding features are sufficient to capture the information necessary for accurate inference, which in traditional approaches is achieved by using a large amount of sparse hand-crafted features (Chen and Manning, 2014). The obtained results will be used in our further investigation on this matter.

Acknowledgments

We thank the anonymous reviewers for their insightful comments and suggestions. The first author is supported by a Japanese Government (MEXT) research scholarship.

References

Laura Banarescu, Claire Bonial, Shu Cai, Madalina Georgescu, Kira Griffitt, Ulf Hermjakob, Kevin Knight, Philipp Koehn, Martha Palmer, and Nathan Schneider. 2013. Abstract meaning representation for sembanking. In *Proceedings of the 7th Linguistic Annotation Workshop and Interoperability with Discourse*, pages 178–186.

Anders Björkelund, Love Hafdell, and Pierre Nugues. 2009. Multilingual semantic role labeling. In *Proceedings of the Thirteenth Conference on Computational Natural Language Learning: Shared Task*, CoNLL '09, pages 43–48, Stroudsburg, PA, USA. Association for Computational Linguistics.

Shu Cai and Kevin Knight. 2013. Smatch: an evaluation metric for semantic feature structures. In *Proceedings of the 51st Annual Meeting of the Association for Computational Linguistics (Volume 2: Short Papers)*, pages 748–752, Sofia, Bulgaria, August. Association for Computational Linguistics.

Danqi Chen and Christopher Manning. 2014. A fast and accurate dependency parser using neural networks. In *Proceedings of the 2014 Conference on Empirical Methods in Natural Language Processing (EMNLP)*, pages 740–750, Doha, Qatar, October. Association for Computational Linguistics.

Wenliang Chen, Yue Zhang, and Min Zhang. 2014. Feature embedding for dependency parsing. In *Proceedings of COLING 2014, the 25th International Conference on Computational Linguistics: Technical Papers*, pages 816–826, Dublin, Ireland, August. Dublin City University and Association for Computational Linguistics.

Michael Collins. 2002. Discriminative training methods for hidden markov models: Theory and experiments with perceptron algorithms. In *Proceedings of the ACL-02 Conference on Empirical Methods in Natural Language Processing - Volume 10*, EMNLP '02, pages 1–8, Stroudsburg, PA, USA. Association for Computational Linguistics.

Bonnie Dorr, Nizar Habash, and David Traum. 1998. A thematic hierarchy for efficient generation from lexical-conceptual structure. In *Proceedings of the Third Conference of the Association for Machine Translation in the Americas, AMTA-98, in Lecture Notes in Artificial Intelligence*, pages 333–343.

Jeffrey Flanigan, Sam Thomson, Jaime Carbonell, Chris Dyer, and A. Noah Smith. 2014. A discriminative graph-based parser for the abstract meaning representation. In *Proceedings of the 52nd Annual Meeting of the Association for Computational Linguistics (Volume 1: Long Papers)*, pages 1426–1436.

Xavier Glorot and Yoshua Bengio. 2010. Understanding the difficulty of training deep feedforward neural networks. In *Proceedings of the International Conference on Artificial Intelligence and Statistics (AISTATS10). Society for Artificial Intelligence and Statistics*.

Jan Hajič, Massimiliano Ciaramita, Richard Johansson, Daisuke Kawahara, Maria Antònia Martí, Lluís Màrquez, Adam Meyers, Joakim Nivre, Sebastian Padó, Jan Štěpánek, Pavel Straňák, Mihai Surdeanu, Nianwen Xue, and Yi Zhang. 2009. The conll-2009 shared task: Syntactic and semantic dependencies in multiple languages. In *Proceedings of the Thirteenth Conference on Computational Natural Language Learning: Shared Task*, CoNLL '09, pages 1–18, Stroudsburg, PA, USA. Association for Computational Linguistics.

Christopher D. Manning, Mihai Surdeanu, John Bauer, Jenny Finkel, Steven J. Bethard, and David McClosky. 2014. The Stanford CoreNLP natural language processing toolkit. In *Association for Computational Linguistics (ACL) System Demonstrations*, pages 55–60.

A. Meyers, R. Reeves, C. Macleod, R. Szekely, V. Zielinska, B. Young, and R. Grishman. 2004. The nombank project: An interim report. In A. Meyers, editor, *HLT-NAACL 2004 Workshop: Frontiers in Corpus Annotation*, pages 24–31, Boston, Massachusetts, USA, May 2 - May 7. Association for Computational Linguistics.

Kristina Toutanova, Dan Klein, Christopher D. Manning, and Yoram Singer. 2003. Feature-rich part-of-speech tagging with a cyclic dependency network. In *Proceedings of the 2003 Conference of the North American Chapter of the Association for Computational Linguistics on Human Language Technology - Volume 1*, NAACL '03, pages 173–180, Stroudsburg, PA, USA. Association for Computational Linguistics.

Chuan Wang, Nianwen Xue, and Sameer Pradhan. 2015a. A transition-based algorithm for amr parsing. In *Proceedings of the 2015 Conference of the North American Chapter of the Association for Computational Linguistics: Human Language Technologies*, pages 366–375, Denver, Colorado, May–June. Association for Computational Linguistics.

Chuan Wang, Nianwen Xue, and Sameer Pradhan. 2015b. Boosting transition-based amr parsing with refined actions and auxiliary analyzers. In *Proceedings of the 53rd Annual Meeting of the Association for Computational Linguistics and the 7th International Joint Conference on Natural Language Processing (Volume 2: Short Papers)*, pages 857–862, Beijing, China, July. Association for Computational Linguistics.

David Weiss, Chris Alberti, Michael Collins, and Slav Petrov. 2015. Structured training for neural network transition-based parsing. In *Proceedings of the 53rd Annual Meeting of the Association for Computational Linguistics and the 7th International Joint Conference on Natural Language Processing (Volume 1: Long Papers)*, pages 323–333, Beijing, China, July. Association for Computational Linguistics.

ICL-HD at SemEval-2016 Task 8: Meaning Representation Parsing - Augmenting AMR Parsing with a Preposition Semantic Role Labeling Neural Network

Lauritz Brandt and **David Grimm** and **Mengfei Zhou** and **Yannick Versley**

Institute for Computational Linguistics
Ruprecht-Karls-Universität
Heidelberg

`{brandt, grimm, zhou, versley}@cl.uni-heidelberg.de`

Abstract

We describe our submission system to the SemEval-2016 Task 8 on Abstract Meaning Representation (AMR) Parsing. We attempt to improve AMR parsing by exploiting preposition semantic role labeling information retrieved from a multi-layer feed-forward neural network. Prepositional semantics is included as features into the transition-based AMR parsing system CAMR (Wang, Xue, and S. Pradhan 2015a). The inclusion of the features modifies the behavior of CAMR when creating meaning representations triggered by prepositional semantics. Despite the usefulness of preposition semantic role labeling information for AMR parsing, it does not have an impact to the parsing F-score of CAMR, but reduces the parsing recall by 1%.

1 Introduction

Progress in Natural Language Processing has led to a multitude of well-motivated tasks that each represent part of a sentence's meaning but result in a meaning description spread over separate, unconnected descriptions. These separate levels of semantic annotation, like co-reference or named entities, and the lack of simple human-readable corpora where whole sentence meanings are encoded led to the Abstract Meaning Representation (AMR) formalism (Banarescu et al. 2013). AMR structures capture sentence meanings with rooted, directed and labeled graphs where sentences with the same meaning receive the same AMR. These graphs are encoded in a bracketed format and can be visually represented in a human-understandable way (see Figure 1). AMR structures are organized with nodes representing concepts and the semantic relationships that hold between these concepts[1]. Hence, AMRs can be useful for every NLP component that relies on or exploits semantic meaning resources. Particular application areas are, among others, entity linking (Pan et al. 2015), event detection (Li et al. 2015) and machine translation. An example for a AMR graph is given in Figure 1: there is a concept RECOMMEND-01 which is the root of the graph and there is a concept OFFER-01 that stands in semantic relationship to RECOMMEND-01 with the edge ARG1.

We augment the existing AMR parser CAMR (Wang, Xue, and S. Pradhan 2015a) with a preposition semantic role labeling (prepSRL) neural network with the intention to improve the AMR graph creation accuracy. Prepositions in conjunction with their arguments make a crucial contribution to the meaning of sentences and are therefore a very intuitive supplement to AMR parsing. For example, see how in Figure 2 the meaning of the preposition *in* is involved in the creation of the AMR edge :LOCATION. *in* semantically expresses the *agency*'s spatial location and therefore triggers the identically named AMR edge :LOCATION. Prepositional semantics is a knowledge resource that has not yet been exploited for the domain of AMR parsing. Moreover, CAMR has problems in correctly creating AMR edges triggered by prepositional relations.

---

[1]Concepts can be PropBank framesets, English words or special words standing for quantities, entity types or logical expressions.

1160

Proceedings of SemEval-2016, pages 1160–1166,
San Diego, California, June 16-17, 2016. ©2016 Association for Computational Linguistics

```
(R / RECOMMEND-01
    :ARG1 (O / OFFER-01
        :ARG0 (W / WE)
        :ARG1 (U / UNDERSTAND-01
            :ARG0 W
            :MOD (F / FULL))
        :ARG3 (P / PERSON
            :ARG0-OF (W2 / WORK-01
            :MOD (E / EARTHQUAKE)))))
```

Figure 1: Example of an AMR visualization

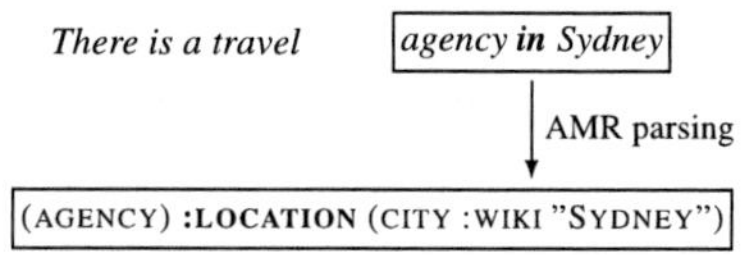

Figure 2: AMR edge activated by prepositional semantics

2 Related Work

The first attempt to automatically generate AMR structures from sentences was the work of Flanigan et al. (2014). They used a graph-based structured prediction algorithm with two stages: the first stage is a semi-Markov model concerned with identification of concepts, the second stage connects these concepts by finding the maximum spanning connected subgraph from a graph where all possible relations between concepts are realized. They achieve an F-score of 0.58 on the LDC2013E117 corpus. Werling, Angeli, and Manning (2015) improve the AMR parsing concept of Flanigan et al. (2014) by supporting the critical task of concept identification with a predefined set of actions for concept subgraph generation that are evoked after a statistical classification procedure. Besides graph-based approaches, there exist also other strategies on AMR parsing: Peng, Song, and Gildea (2015) learn synchronous hyperedge replacement grammar rules from string-

(a) Gold parse

```
(S3 / SAD
    :DOMAIN (N2 / NOTHING)
    :TOPIC (S2 / SHELL
        :MOD (O / OLD)))
```

(b) CAMR parse

```
(X3 / NOTHING
    :MOD (X4 / SAD
        :COMPARED-TO (X7 / SHELL
            :MOD (X6 / OLD))))
```

Figure 3: Examples of where CAMR's edge construction for prepositional phrases fails.

graph pairs. An Earley algorithm with cube-pruning then performs string-to-AMR parsing with these rules. Pust et al. (2015) treat English and AMR as a language pair and use a machine translation approach to parse AMRs from sentences. They convert AMRs into into a grammar of string-to-tree rules that can be handled by syntax-based machine translation formalisms and use these rules with a bottom-up chart decoder to parse AMRs with given local features and a language model. Wang, Xue, and S. Pradhan (2015a) use a transition-based system that transforms dependency graphs into AMR structures by evoking specific actions at each reached state while traversing the dependency tree. As can be seen, there are many different point of views on AMR parsing.

2.1 Motivation

The motivation for our system design comes from the error analysis of the transition-based AMR parser CAMR of Wang, Xue, and S. Pradhan (2015a). It turns out that the parser has difficulties on correctly identifying AMR relations which involve prepositional semantics. Therefore, we have chosen to aid CAMR with preposition semantic role labeling (prepSRL) in order to improve AMR parsing results.

2.2 Error Analysis of CAMR

Figure 3 shows a CAMR parse error: (b) should indicate a :TOPIC edge label for the edge between the concepts SAD and SHELL. This relation is semantically expressed by the preposition *about*. As can be seen in Table 1, parsing precision and parsing recall is low for certain relations that can be evoked by prepositional semantics. Where the :LOCATION edge shows an arguably good CAMR performance, other relations like :TOPIC and :DESTINATION fail to be correctly parsed at all. We aim to improve CAMR's action selection for prepositions by introducing features representing prepositional semantics.

Relation	Gold	Parser	Corr.	Prec.	Rec.
:LOCATION	394	371	131	35.31%	33.25%
:PURPOSE	130	118	14	11.86%	10.77%
:TOPIC	70	44	6	13.64%	8.57%
:SOURCE	55	27	2	7.41%	3.64%
:DESTINATION	11	7	0	0.0%	0.0%
:INSTRUMENT	10	9	0	0.0%	0.0%

Table 1: Error analysis of CAMR based on parses of sentences taken from the *DEFT* corpus for 6 common AMR edges. **Gold**, **Parser**: # of relations in CAMR parse and Gold standard. **Corr.**: # of correctly parsed CAMR relations. **Prec./Rec.**: Precision/Recall.

3 System Description

3.1 Baseline System

We used the AMR parser CAMR of Wang, Xue, and S. Pradhan (2015a) as a starting point for our idea of supporting AMR parsing with prepSRL. It converts dependency trees into AMR graphs with a transition-based technique by evoking certain tree transforming actions at reached transition states. In the training procedure, the tokens of the input sentence are first aligned with the nodes of its gold AMR graph using the JAMR aligner (Flanigan et al. 2014). Such aligned AMR graphs are represented as span graphs storing token spans for AMR concept nodes. With these span graphs, a greedy transition-based mechanism learns to rewrite the dependency trees into AMR graphs. In order to learn these transformations, a transition system processes the nodes of the input dependency graphs in a bottom-up left-to-right fashion. It decides at each reached configurations which action to perform next in transforming the dependency graph into an AMR span graph. Configurations are defined as a tuple of buffers holding unprocessed nodes and unprocessed edges and the partial span graph parses for the current input sentence. While traversing the dependency tree, an

- **NEXT-EDGE-l_r:** assigns relation label to current edge and steps on to the next edge

- **SWAP-l_r:** swaps dependency relation between nodes (head transforms to dependent and vice versa)

- **REATTACH$_k$-l_r:** removes an arc, reattaches the former dependent to another node and assigns a label to the new arc

- **REPLACE HEAD:** replaces a head with its dependent

- **REENTRANCE$_k$-l_r:** links a node to another node in the subgraph and therefore has the ability to convert trees into graphs

- **MERGE:** merges two nodes into one node

- **NEXT-NODE-l_c:** assigns a concept label to current node and proceeds to next element in buffer

- **DELETE-NODE:** deletes a node and all its connections

- **INFER-l_c:** inserts a concept node between current node and parent

Figure 4: Possible actions for the transition system

averaged perceptron algorithm decides the actions to take by computing scores for all possible actions given specific features[2] and a weight vector. During test time, always the highest scoring action is chosen before moving on to the next state. During training, the algorithm will update the weight vector if it has chosen the wrong action and proceeds parsing with the correct one[3]. The core of the system are the set of actions that can be taken at states by the algorithm. Figure 4 shows an overview and a short description of the eight possible action types[4]. Actions alter the dependency tree by deleting or inserting nodes, merging two nodes into one, assigning relation labels and creating or modifying arcs. Therefore, the averaged perceptron can learn to do the right transformations to end up with a AMR span graph.

3.2 Semantic Role Labeling Features

Wang, Xue, and S. Pradhan (2015b) successfully improve their base system described in chapter 3.1

---

[2]Feature contexts vary from action type to action type and can include lemmas, words, named entities, POS tags, dependency labels and node span lengths. For a full list of features see (Wang, Xue, and S. Pradhan 2015a).

[3]I.e. the action that is necessary to build the gold span graph.

[4]For more detailed information about the action types see (Wang, Xue, and S. Pradhan 2015a).

by adding SRL features to their model[5]. We also included these features and added our prepSRL information in a similar way. The first SRL feature encodes an action's compatibility with the predicted frameset from the SRL system. For each action that predicts a concept label (*NEXT-NODE-l_c*), the predicted SRL frameset is compared to the candidate concept labels. If both match, the value of the feature is set to *true*. Therefore, the system will bias towards choosing the predicted SRL frameset as concept label[6]. The second feature encodes predicted SRL argumenthood for an action's current edge. For each action that predicts edge labels, the parser has access to the information whether current action's dependent is predicted by the semantic role labeler. Hence, the system will favor edges that are congruent with the semantic role labeler's edges.

3.3 Preposition Semantic Role Labels

The prepSRL information consists of an attachment according to a dependency parse and a semantic role label for the prepositional phrase head predicted by a neural network. The neural network is trained on data annotated with semantic role labels. A simple feed-forward neural network with one hidden layer is trained in a softmax regression framework on the role labels of Penn Treebank (PTB), the SemEval 2007 Task 6 corpus and the DEFT corpus[7][8]. Additionally a 'multi-task' neural network was trained on all three corpora simultaneously. The network architecture is sketched in Figure 5. All three prediction models share the same two hidden layers. As labels and number of labels vary, softmax regression is performed for each corpus separately.

The neural networks are fed a combination of word embedding[9] and a subset of the hand-crafted

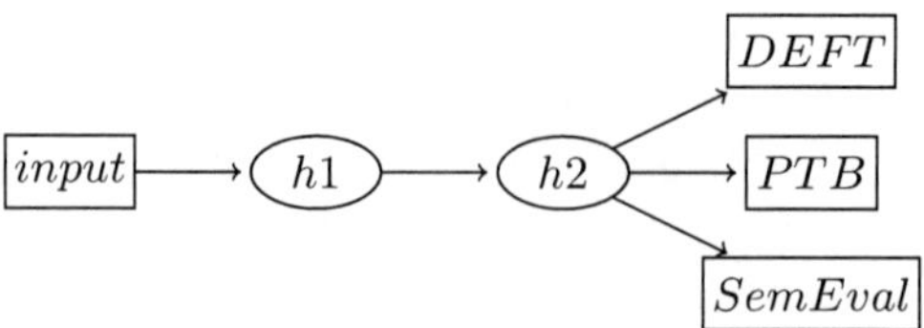

Figure 5: 'Multi-Task' neural network architecture. Each arrow represents a fully connected link to the next layer. Ellipsoid nodes are subject to non-linear activation, square nodes are subject to softmax regression. The three targets are trained alternating on mini-batches of 20 samples.

features proposed by (D. Hovy, Tratz, and E. H. Hovy 2010). These features include a binary indicator for token capitalization and a binary vector representation of both, the token's POS-tag and the supersense label according to WordNet[10]. For each sample, these features are extracted for the following tokens: the *preposition token*, the *previous token*, the *preceding verb*, the *preceding verb/adjective/noun*, the *dependency head*, the *dependency child* and a *heuristic child*, for which we choose the ensuing token. All corpora are parsed with the ClearNLP parser[11] to obtain POS-Tags and tokenization. For reasons of compatibility with the AMR-Parsing task, the dependency trees were extracted from parses by the BLLIP parser[12]. Corpus sizes and accuracy measures for the simple neural network can be seen in Table 2.

The neural network predicts a semantic role label for every prepositional phrase head. Comparing the different models by accuracy on these labels is difficult, as the target spaces and number of samples available differ. A list of valid target labels for each corpus can be seen in Table 3. The SemEval corpus comes with a total of 155 labels, where each preposition has a number of senses. These sense labels are reduced in number to create more meaningful target labels for the prepSRL task. The mapping scheme of Srikumar and Roth (2013) was implemented for this reduction. The DEFT corpus comes with a total

---

[5]They used the ASSERT SRL system described in (S. S. Pradhan et al. 2004).

[6]Remember that concept labels in AMR can be PropBank framesets.

[7]Used version: LDC2015E86: DEFT Phase 2 AMR Annotation R1

[8]All neural networks are trained with 200 hidden nodes per layer, a learning rate of 0.01 in a gradient descent batch learning environment. The weights are randomly initialized in $\left[\pm \sqrt{6/(input_{dim} + output_{dim})} \right]$. *Tanh* is used as non-linear activation function.

[9]The word embeddings are taken from (Pennington, Socher, and Manning 2014). For unknown words, a null vector is used

instead.

[10]For unavailable information, a null vector is used instead for POS-tags, whereas for supersenses a 'unknown' supersense was introduced.

[11]For detailed information, see `https://github.com/clir/clearnlp`.

[12]For detailed information see (McClosky, Charniak, and Johnson 2006) and (Charniak 2000).

	PTB	**SemEval**	**DEFT**
Corpus Size	$35,298$	$16,534$	$8,023$
simple accuracy	91.69%	82.47%	72.69%
simple* accuracy	90.67%	80.12%	72.95%
multi-task accuracy	92.19%	72.28%	72.18%

Table 2: Preposition Semantic Role Labeling results. *Corpus size* is given in samples. Accuracy is measured on a test set from a random train/dev/test-split containing 90%/10%/10% of the samples respectively, where *simple accuracy* uses the simple neural network, *simple* accuracy* uses the simple neural network with an additional hidden layer and *multi-task accuracy* uses the 'multi-task' neural network, with the respective corpus' label set as output space and the corpus' test set.

They are creating traffic congestion in new places.

```
(C / CREATE-01
    :ARG0 (T / THEY)
    :ARG1 (C2 / CONGEST-01
        :ARG2 (T2 / TRAFFIC)
    :ARG3 (P / PLACE
        :MOD (N / NEW)))))
```

Figure 6: Example of how an edge could be wrongly created.

PTB	LOC TMP DIR MNR PRP EXT BNF
DEFT	location manner mod name op1 op2 part-of poss purpose quant source time topic
SemEval	Activity Agent Attribute Beneficiary Cause Co-Participants Destination Direction EndState Experiencer Instrument Location Manner MediumOfCommunication Numeric ObjectOfVerb Opponent/Contrast Other Participant/Accompanier PartWhole PhysicalSupport Possessor ProfessionalAspect Recipient Separation Purpose Species Source StartState Temporal Topic Via

Table 3: Valid *prepSRL* target labels for each corpus. In total there are 7/13/32 labels for the PTB/DEFT/SemEval corpus respectively.

of 82 labels. We remove all labels with less than 200 samples from the corpus to ensure training quality.

Given this prepSRL system, the AMR parsing results are expected to be improved in the following way. In the AMR of Figure 6 currently the concept PLACE is the ARG3 of CREATE-01 but it should be the :LOCATION of CONGEST-01. Because the prepSRL feature has the ability to influence the edge creation and labeling actions of the transition system, the AMR parser can decide for the correct actions to take.

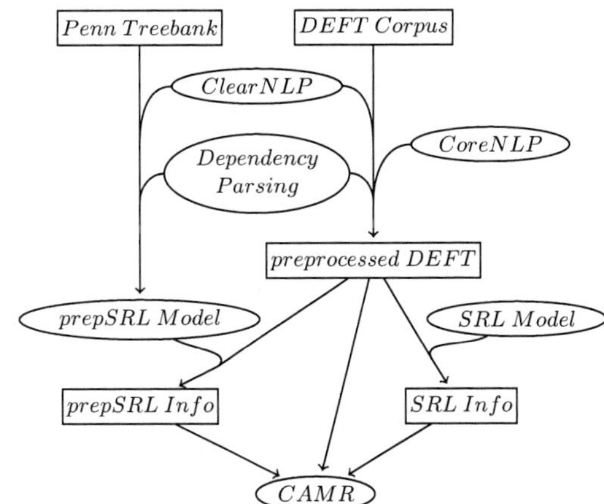

Figure 7: Preprocessing pipeline for our system. Round nodes depict models, rectangular nodes depict data.

4 Experiments

4.1 Experimental Setup

We first preprocessed the $16,831$ sentences of the DEFT corpus training section (Knight et al. 2014) that we used for training CAMR with the prepSRL features. Preprocessing information for the AMR parser includes lemmas, POS tags, named entities and dependency parses[13]. In addition, we preprocessed the training sentences with the ClearNLP toolkit for the training of the neural network. We used the tokenization and POS tag components of ClearNLP and replaced the generated dependencies for compatibility reasons with the dependencies generated by the BLLIP parser.

After preprocessing, the alignments between the AMR graphs and their sentences were created with the JAMR aligner. ASSERT-generated SRL files were provided to us by Sameer Pradhan for the training and test inputs, enabling us to run CAMR with the SRL features. Separately, the neural network for prepSRL is trained with PTB-style preposition labels. We parsed our training corpora with the resulting model and generated the feature files for the prepSRL information. We trained CAMR in four different feature settings that are shown in Figure 8. The generated models were tested on the DEFT corpus test set that contains 1371 sentences.

---

[13]Lemmas, POS tags and named entities are generated by the CoreNLP toolkit (Manning et al. 2014). The dependency parses were generated with the BLLIP parser ((McClosky, Charniak,

(a)	CAMR
(b)	(a) + SRL features
(c)	(a) + prepSRL features
(d)	(b) + prepSRL features

Figure 8: Overview of the used training settings

Model	Prec.	Rec.	F-Score
(a): CAMR	67%	58%	62
(b): (a) +SRL	68%	58%	62
(c): (a) +prepSRL	67%	57%	62
(d): (b) +prepSRL	68%	57%	62

Table 4: Evaluation results

Relation	Gold	Parser	Corr.	Prec.	Rec.
:LOCATION	394	374	135	36.10%	34.26%
:PURPOSE	130	109	9	8.26%	6.92%
:TOPIC	70	46	4	8.70%	5.71%
:SOURCE	55	39	2	5.12%	3.63%
:DESTINATION	11	4	0	0.0%	0.0%
:INSTRUMENT	10	9	0	0.0%	0.0%

Table 5: Error analysis of our parser (CAMR + SRL + prepSRL features) based on parses of sentences taken from the DEFT corpus test set. **Gold**, **Parser**: # of relations in CAMR parse and Gold standard. **Corr.**: # of correctly parsed CAMR relations. **Prec./Rec.**: Precision/Recall.

4.2 Results

We evaluated our approach of augmenting AMR parsing with a prepSRL system by using the standard evaluation measure for AMR parsing which is the Smatch evaluation metric to date[14]. Smatch uses semantic overlap between AMR parses to measure parsing accuracy. Results of the evaluation are given in Table 4. They reveal that the prepSRL features have a slightly negative influence on the parsing accuracy of CAMR. The Smatch F-score remains the same over all trained models, but the recall is reduced by 1% when adding the prepSRL features. The model with prepSRL achieves a Smatch score of 0.60 on the SemEval-2016 Task 8 test data. One possible explanation for the prepSRL results could be the ambiguity concerned with prepositions:

(1) *Establishing Models **in** Industrial Innovation.*

(2) *There is a travel agency **in** Sydney.*

In (1), *in* does not indicate an AMR :LOCATION relation, in contrast to its occurrence in (2). At the moment, our system cannot disambiguate between the two appearances of *in* according to the features used.

4.3 Error Analysis

A quantitative error analysis of our parser's output is shown in Table 5. If compared with the previous results in Table 1, the :LOCATION relation shows a minor improvement of precision and recall, where all other relations either show no difference or are parsed worse than before.

5 Conclusion

We extended the AMR parser CAMR (Wang, Xue, and S. Pradhan 2015a) with a neural network for prepSRL but did not reach improved AMR results using this method. In fact, the combination with prepSRL slightly reduced the recall of the system. This could be due to the fact that our prepSRL neural network generates parses for all preposition occurrences without disambiguating ambiguous prepositions. Future work has to find a better way to integrate prepSRL information into the architecture of CAMR. One possibility of this could be the refinement of the neural network where only prepositions receive a SRL parse that are likely to produce an AMR relation. Despite our results, we nevertheless think that the inclusion of prepositional semantics could improve AMR parsing results if used in an appropriate way.

Acknowledgments

We would like to thank Sameer Pradhan for providing us with SRL parses of all task data. Furthermore we would like to thank Chuan Wang for assisting us with detailed questions about CAMR code and parsing pipelines.

References

Banarescu, Laura, Claire Bonial, Shu Cai, Madalina Georgescu, Kira Griffitt, Ulf Hermjakob, Kevin Knight, Philipp Koehn, Martha Palmer, and Nathan Schneider (2013). "Abstract Meaning Representation for Sembanking". In: *Proceedings of the 7th Linguistic Annotation Workshop and Interoperability with Discourse*, pp. 178–186.

---

and Johnson 2006) and (Charniak 2000))

[14]see (Cai and Knight 2012)

Cai, Shu and Kevin Knight (2012). *Smatch: an evaluation metric for semantic feature structures. submitted.*

Charniak, Eugene (2000). "A Maximum-entropy-inspired Parser". In: *Proceedings of the 1st North American Chapter of the Association for Computational Linguistics Conference*. NAACL 2000. Seattle, Washington, pp. 132–139.

Flanigan, Jeffrey, Sam Thomson, Jaime G. Carbonell, Chris Dyer, and Noah A. Smith (2014). "A Discriminative Graph-Based Parser for the Abstract Meaning Representation". In: *Proceedings of the 52nd Annual Meeting of the Association for Computational Linguistics (Volume 1: Long Papers)*, pp. 1426–1436.

Hovy, Dirk, Stephen Tratz, and Eduard H. Hovy (2010). "What's in a Preposition? Dimensions of Sense Disambiguation for an Interesting Word Class". In: *COLING 2010, 23rd International Conference on Computational Linguistics, Posters Volume, 23-27 August 2010, Beijing, China*, pp. 454–462.

Knight, Kevin, Laura Baranescu, Claire Bonial, Madalina Georgescu, Kira Griffitt, Ulf Hermjakob, Daniel Marcu, Martha Palmer, and Nathan Schneider (2014). *Abstract Meaning Representation (AMR) Annotation Release 1.0.*

Li, Xiang, Thien Huu Nguyen, Kai Cao, and Ralph Grishman (2015). "Improving Event Detection with Abstract Meaning Representation". In: *Proceedings of the First Workshop on Computing News Storylines*. Beijing, China: Association for Computational Linguistics, pp. 11–15.

Manning, Christopher D., Mihai Surdeanu, John Bauer, Jenny Finkel, Steven J. Bethard, and David McClosky (2014). "The Stanford CoreNLP Natural Language Processing Toolkit". In: *Association for Computational Linguistics (ACL) System Demonstrations*, pp. 55–60.

McClosky, David, Eugene Charniak, and Mark Johnson (2006). "Effective Self-training for Parsing". In: *Proceedings of the Main Conference on Human Language Technology Conference of the North American Chapter of the Association of Computational Linguistics*. HLT-NAACL '06. New York, New York, pp. 152–159.

Pan, Xiaoman, Taylor Cassidy, Ulf Hermjakob, Heng Ji, and Kevin Knight (2015). *Unsupervised Entity Linking with Abstract Meaning Representation.*

Peng, Xiaochang, Linfeng Song, and Daniel Gildea (2015). *A Synchronous Hyperedge Replacement Grammar based approach for AMR parsing.*

Pennington, Jeffrey, Richard Socher, and Christopher D. Manning (2014). "GloVe: Global Vectors for Word Representation". In: *Empirical Methods in Natural Language Processing (EMNLP)*, pp. 1532–1543.

Pradhan, Sameer S, Wayne H Ward, Kadri Hacioglu, James H Martin, and Dan Jurafsky (2004). "Shallow Semantic Parsing using Support Vector Machines". In: *HLT-NAACL 2004: Main Proceedings*. Ed. by Daniel Marcu Susan Dumais and Salim Roukos. Boston, Massachusetts, USA: Association for Computational Linguistics, pp. 233–240.

Pust, Michael, Ulf Hermjakob, Kevin Knight, Daniel Marcu, and Jonathan May (2015). "Parsing English into Abstract Meaning Representation Using Syntax-Based Machine Translation". In: *Proceedings of the 2015 Conference on Empirical Methods in Natural Language Processing*. Lisbon, Portugal: Association for Computational Linguistics, pp. 1143–1154.

Srikumar, Vivek and Dan Roth (2013). "Modeling Semantic Relations Expressed by Prepositions". In: 1, pp. 231–242.

Wang, Chuan, Nianwen Xue, and Sameer Pradhan (2015a). "A Transition-based Algorithm for AMR Parsing". In: *Proceedings of the 2015 Conference of the North American Chapter of the Association for Computational Linguistics: Human Language Technologies*. Denver, Colorado: Association for Computational Linguistics, pp. 366–375.

– (2015b). "Boosting Transition-based AMR Parsing with Refined Actions and Auxiliary Analyzers". In: *Proceedings of the 53rd Annual Meeting of the Association for Computational Linguistics and the 7th International Joint Conference on Natural Language Processing (Volume 2: Short Papers)*. Beijing, China: Association for Computational Linguistics, pp. 857–862.

Werling, Keenon, Gabor Angeli, and Christopher D. Manning (2015). "Robust Subgraph Generation Improves Abstract Meaning Representation Parsing". In: *CoRR abs/1506.03139.*

UCL+Sheffield at SemEval-2016 Task 8: Imitation learning for AMR parsing with an α-bound

James Goodman[*] **Andreas Vlachos**[#] **Jason Naradowsky**[*]
[*] Computer Science Department, University College London
`james@janigo.co.uk, jason.narad@gmail.com`
[#] Department of Computer Science, University of Sheffield
`a.vlachos@sheffield.ac.uk`

Abstract

We develop a novel transition-based parsing algorithm for the abstract meaning representation parsing task using exact imitation learning, in which the parser learns a statistical model by imitating the actions of an expert on the training data. We then use the imitation learning algorithm DAGGER to improve the performance, and apply an α-bound as a simple noise reduction technique. Our performance on the test set was 60% in F-score, and the performance gains on the development set due to DAGGER was up to 1.1 points of F-score. The α-bound improved performance by up to 1.8 points.

1 Introduction

In abstract meaning representation parsing (Banarescu et al., 2013), the goal is to parse natural language in a domain-independent graph-based meaning representation (AMR). In the first AMR parsing work, Flanigan et al. (2014) split the task into two sub-tasks; *concept identification* and *graph creation*. The sub-tasks are learned independently, and exact inference is used to find highest-scoring maximum spanning connected acyclic graph that contains all the concepts identified in the first stage. Later work by Wang et al. (2015b) adopted a different strategy based on the similarity between the dependency parse of a sentence and the semantic AMR graph. They start from the dependency parse and learn a transition-based parser that converts it into an AMR graph. To learn the parser, Wang et al. (2015b) define an algorithm that for each instance in the training data infers the action sequence that convert the

input dependency tree into the corresponding AMR graph and train a classifier to predict the actions to be taken during testing. This strategy is also referred to as exact imitation learning, while the algorithm that infers the action sequence in the training instances is commonly referred to as the expert policy.

In our submission to SemEval Task 8 on AMR parsing, we follow the transition-based paradigm of Wang et al. (2015b) with modifications to the parsing algorithm, and also use the DAGGER imitation learning algorithm (Ross et al., 2011) to generalise better to unseen data. The central idea of DAGGER is that the distribution of states encountered by the expert policy during training may not be a good approximation to those seen in testing by the trained policy. Previous work by Rao et al. (2015) used SEARN, a similar imitation learning algorithm, on the AMR problem, with an algorithm that constructs the AMR graph directly from the sentence tokens. Imitation learning has also been used successfully in other semantic parsing tasks (Vlachos and Clark, 2014; Berant and Liang, 2015).

In imitation learning approaches such as DAGGER the previous actions become features for classification learning. However the partial graphs in AMR parsing are rather complex to represent in this way, and combined with the finite amount of training data different actions can be chosen by the expert even though the feature representations for them can be very similar. These decisions appear as noisy outliers in classification learning. To control noise we experiment with the α-bound discussed by Khardon and Wachman (2007), which excludes a training example from future training once it has been misclas-

Proceedings of SemEval-2016, pages 1167–1172,
San Diego, California, June 16-17, 2016. ©2016 Association for Computational Linguistics

Action Name	Param.	Pre-conditions	Outcome of action
NextEdge	l_r	β non-empty	Set label of edge (σ_0, β_0) to l_r. Pop β_0.
NextNode	l_c	β empty	Set concept of node σ_0 to l_c. Pop σ_0, and initialise β.
Swap		β non-empty	Make β_0 parent of σ_0 (reverse edge) and its sub-graph. Pop β_0 and insert β_0 as σ_1.
ReplaceHead		β non-empty	Pop σ_0 and delete it from the graph. Parents of σ_0 become parents of β_0. Other children of σ_0 become children of β_0. Insert β_0 at the head of σ and re-initialise β.
Reattach	κ	β non-empty	Pop β_0 and delete edge (σ_0, β_0). Attach β_0 as a child of κ. If κ has already been popped from σ then re-insert it as σ_1.
DeleteNode		β empty; leaf σ_0	Pop σ_0 and delete it from the graph.
Insert	l_c		Insert a new node δ with AMR concept l_c as the parent of σ_0, and insert δ into σ.
InsertBelow	l_c		Insert a new node δ with AMR concept l_c as a child of σ_0.
Reentrance	κ	Phase 2	Insert edge (σ_0, κ). Then apply NextEdge action.
Wikify	ω	Phase 2	See main text

Table 1: Action Space for the transition-based graph parsing algorithm

sified α times in training. Khardon and Wachman (2007) do not report any experimental results for this, and we are not aware of any previous use of this method.

2 System description

In the following subsections we focus on the differences from previous work and in particular that of Wang et al. (2015b) who introduced the transition-based dependency-to-AMR paradigm we follow. We initialise the main algorithm with a stack of the nodes in the dependency tree, root node first. This stack is termed σ. A second stack, β is initialised with all children of the top node in σ. The state at any time is described by σ, β, and the current graph (which starts as the dependency tree). Each action manipulates the top nodes in each stack, σ_0 and β_0. We reach a terminal state when σ is empty. [1]

2.1 The Expert Policy

The expert policy used in training applies heuristic rules to determine the next action from a given state. It uses the training alignments to construct a mapping between nodes in the dependency tree, and nodes in the target AMR. Any unmapped nodes in the dependency tree will be deleted by the expert, and any unmapped nodes in the AMR graph will be

---

inserted. All our experiments use node alignments from the system of Pourdamghani et al. (2014).

2.2 Action Space

Flanigan et al. (2014) and Wang et al. (2015b), both use AMR fragments as their smallest unit, which may consist of more than one AMR concept. Instead, we always work with the individual AMR nodes, and rely on Insert actions to learn how to build common fragments, such as country names. The main adaptations to the actions, summarised in Table 1, stem from this. NextNode and NextEdge form the core action set, labelling nodes and edges respectively without changing the graph structure. Swap, Reattach and ReplaceHead change this structure, but always retain a tree structure. Replace-Head covers two distinct actions in Wang et al. (2015b); ReplaceHead and Merge. Their Merge action merges σ_0 and β_0 into a composite node; this is not required without composite nodes and retention of a 1:1 mapping between nodes and AMR concept. Unlike Wang et al. (2015b) we do not parameterise Swap or Reattach actions with a label. We leave that decision to a later NextEdge action. We permit a Reattach action to use parameter κ equal to any node within six edges from σ_0, excluding any that would disconnect the graph or creating a cycle.

The Insert action inserts a new node as a parent of the current σ_0. Wang et al. (2015a) later introduced an 'Infer' action similar to our Insert action. Infer inserts an AMR concept node above the current node as Insert does, but is restricted to nodes that occur outside of AMR 'fragments', which continue to be the base building block.

Reentrance is the one action that will turn a Tree into a non-Tree. We only consider Reentrance actions during a second pass ("Phase Two") through the AMR graph once the first pass has reached a terminal state. In this second pass we consider each node as σ_0 in turn, and each nearby node as a possible κ to insert a new edge (σ_0, κ). We follow any Reentrance action with a NextEdge action to label the new arc. This approach simplifies the first pass, during which the graph is guaranteed to be a Tree. Reentrance makes only a small difference in the final F-Score, and was turned off for our final submission.

Also during Phase Two we decide whether to Wikify σ_0. This adds a new leaf node with a relation of `wiki`. There are three parameter values for ω that determine the wiki concept. In turn these use "-"; a concatenation of all child concepts in original word order; a dictionary look-up keyed on a concatenation of the child nodes if these were seen in the training data. An example of the third option is if a `name` node with a single child node of "Michael" is seen in the training data with a `wiki` relation of "Michael_Jackson". This wikification is held in the dictionary, and will be used for any `name` node with a single child node of "Michael" in test. If instead in test the `name` node had two children; "Michael", and "Jackson", then during ω would either add a wiki node of "-", or one of "Michael_Jackson" by concatenating the two child concepts in the order they appear in the sentence.

Figure 1 shows a parse of a sentence fragment. The current σ_0 node is shown dashed and in red. From the top the actions are Insert(date-entity); NextNode(WORD); NextEdge(year); *second diagram*; NextNode(WORD); ReplaceHead to remove "in"; *third diagram*; NextNode(WORD); NextEdge(mod); Reattach to move "date-entity"; *fourth diagram*; NextNode(VERB); ReplaceHead to remove "by"; NextEdge(ARG0); NextEdge(time); NextNode(strike-01).

Wang et al. (2015b) use all AMR concepts and relations that appear in the training set as possible parameters (l_c and l_r) if they appear in any sentence containing the same lemma as σ_0 and β. We reduce this to just concepts that have been aligned to the

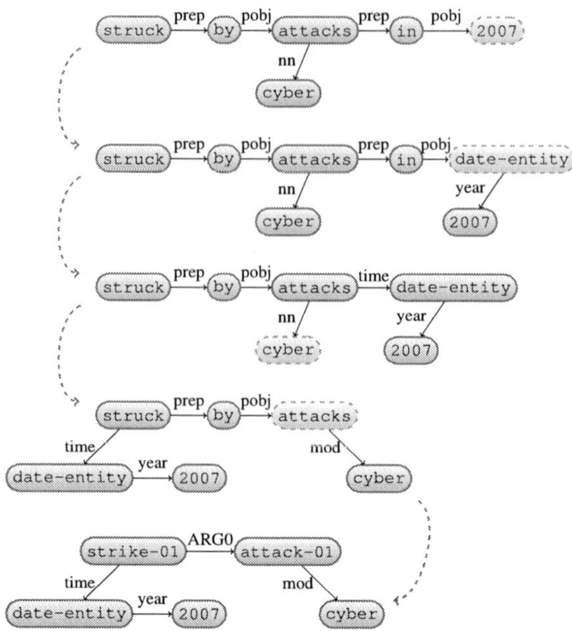

Figure 1: Example parse from dependency tree to AMR of the sentence fragment "... struck by cyber attacks in 2007."

current lemma. We initially run the expert policy over the training set, and track the AMR concept assigned for each lemma. These provide the possible l_c that will be used for NextNode actions. Similarly we track the lemmas at head and tail of each expert-assigned AMR relation, and compile possible l_r from these. There is no direct generalisation between different concepts and relations; so `ARG0` and `ARG0-of` are independently learned relations for example, although they represent the same semantic relationship.

AMR concepts/relations will never be considered during test if they were not aligned to that lemma in the training data. To relax this restriction we allow l_c to take the values `WORD`, `LEMMA`, `VERB`, which respectively use the word, lemma, or the lemma concatenated with '-01' as the AMR concept. This is inspired by Werling et al. (2015), who use a similar set of actions in a concept identification phase. These options improve performance (by 0.5 to 1.0 points on a validation set) by generalising to unseen tokens in test data, which otherwise would have no mapped AMR concepts. For the l_c parameters on Insert (InsertBelow) actions, we use all AMR concepts that the expert inserted above (below) any node in the training set with the same lemma as σ_0.

2.3 Additional action constraints

Transition-based parsing algorithms have classically relied on a fixed length of trajectory T for guarantees on performance, or at least a bounded T (Goldberg and Elhadad, 2010; Honnibal et al., 2013; Sartorio et al., 2013; McDonald and Nivre, 2007). In our approach T is theoretically unbounded and the algorithm could Insert, or Reattach *ad infinitum.*

We impose constraints to prevent these situations. A Swap action cannot be applied to a previously Swapped edge; once a node has been moved by Reattach, then it cannot be Reattached again; an Insert action is only permissible if no previous Insert action has been used with that node as σ_0; an Insert action is not permissible if it would insert an AMR concept already in use as any of the parent, children, grand-parents or grand-children of σ_0.

Any action that would create a cycle is prohibited. We do not prevent duplication of argument relations so that a concept could have two outgoing `ARG1` edges. We start with a fully connected graph (the dependency tree), and preserve full connectivity as none of the actions will disconnect a graph.

2.4 Imitation Learning

In the first iteration we only use the expert policy to generate a trajectory for each training sentence, and train a classifier π_1 from the collected data. At each step in the ith iteration we randomly choose the expert (with probability β_i) or else π_{i-1}. The full set of collected data from all iterations is then used to train π_{i-1} to obtain π_i. $\beta_1 = 1$ and we set $\beta_i = 0.7\beta_{i-1}$. Hence each iteration uses the expert policy less and less, with the training trajectories increasingly approximating the states the classifier would encounter without expert knowledge of the target. Formally the DAGGER algorithm is online (Ross et al., 2011), while we use it in a batch mode as described above. We use an averaged AROW classifier for all our experiments, with parameter $r = 100$ (Crammer et al., 2009). After each batch DAGGER iteration we use 3 iterations of (on-line) AROW training using all the collected data.

As well as the α-bound for noise reduction, we tried two additional modifications to DAGGER and AROW. Firstly, we considered reducing the num-

ber of actions explored at each stage. The currently trained classifier evaluates all possible actions, and discards any that exceed the best scoring action by some threshold. Only this smaller set, plus the expert action, are included in the training example. This speeds up classifier training. In the first iteration we choose three to five actions randomly. Ross and Bagnell (2014) use a random set of exploratory actions in their AGGREVATE algorithm, but do not use the classifier to focus the exploration.

Secondly, we used only the smallest training sentences in the first iteration, as measured by number of AMR nodes. At each further iteration the AMR size threshold for the training set was increased. The motivation was to train the classifier on 'easy' sentences, before introducing more complex ones. We start with up to 30 nodes, and increase this by 10 each iteration. Rao et al. (2015) similarly use the smallest sentences for training, but do not increase the size threshold as training proceeds.

2.5 Features

All features used are detailed in Table 2, largely based on Wang et al. (2015b). All are 0-1 indicator functions. *inserted* is 1 if the node was inserted by the parser; *dl* is the dependency label in the original dependency tree; *ner* the named entity tag; *POS* the part-of-speech tag; *prefix* is the string before the hyphen if word is hyphenated; *suffix* is the string after the hyphen; *brown* is the 100-class Brown cluster id with cuts at 4, 6, 10 and 20 [2]; *deleted* is the lemma of any child node previously deleted by the parser; *merged* is the lemma of any node merged into this node by a ReplaceHead action; *distance* is the distance between the tokens in the sentence; *path* concatenates lemmas and dls between the tokens in the dependency tree; *POSpath* concatenates POS tags between the tokens; *NERpath* concatenates NER tags between the tokens.

The key differences to Wang et al. (2015b) are the inclusion of the brown, POSpath, NERpath, prefix and suffix feature types.

2.6 Pre-processing

Pre-processing steps on the training sentences were to: pass the full sentence through the Stanford De-

---

[2]From `http://metaoptimize.com/projects/wordreprs/` and the code of Liang (2005)

Context	Features
σ_0	lemma, dl, ner, POS, inserted, prefix, suffix, brown, deleted, lemma-dl
σ_{0P}	inserted, lemma, brown
σ_{0C}	label, ner, label-brown
β_0	inserted, POS, lemma, brown, ner, dl, prefix, suffix, merged
κ	ner, POS, lemma, brown, label
$\sigma_0 \to \beta_0$	label, path, lemma-path-lemma, POSpath, inserted-inserted, lemma-POS, POS-lemma, dl-lemma, lemma-dl, lemma-label, label-lemma, ner-ner, distance
$\beta_0 \to \kappa$	path, lemma-path-lemma, NERpath, POSpath, distance, lemma-POS, dl-lemma, ner-ner
$\sigma_0 \to \kappa$	distance, lemma-path-lemma, brown-brown, NERpath, POSpath, lemma-dl, lemma-label
$\sigma_{0P} \to \sigma_0$	label, POS-lemma, dl-lemma, ner-ner
$\sigma_{0PP} \to \sigma_{0P} \to \sigma_0$	lemma-lemma-lemma
$\sigma_0 \to \sigma_{0C}$	POS-lemma, lemma-POS, dl-lemma, ner-ner

Table 2: Features used by context. σ_{0P} is the parent of σ_0, σ_{0PP} the parent of σ_{0P}, and σ_{0C} a child of σ_0.

pendency Parser v3.3.1 to construct a dependency tree (Manning et al., 2014); remove punctuation tokens; "/" characters are treated as token separators, but hyphenated words are kept as single tokens; simple regex expressions are applied to find common date formats, and convert these to numeric sequences (e.g. 03-Jan-72 to 3 1 1972); similar regex conversions of common numeric expressions e.g. "two thousand" becomes "2000". The parser was then able to learn to construct `date-entity`, `temporal-quantity` and similar AMR moieties.

3   Results

In all experiments, the training data was the union of all training and dev sets in the task data, and the union of all test sets was used for validation. Table 3 shows the F-Score of the validation set with and without the Reentrance action (Reent, NoR), and with combinations of reduced search (Red), and incremental data (Inc). All of these give the same result of 0.65 to 2 dp, and the bold entry was submitted. The Baseline entry uses only a single iteration, and the DAGGER experiments report the highest F-Score achieved over 10 iterations (usually reached between the 3rd to 5th iterations).

The reduced information in the first iterations for incremental data and reduced search lead to lower initial performance here, but they still achieve the 0.65 result in time and each iteration is faster. DAGGER provides a gain of 0.6 and 1.1 points of F-Score for experiments with and without Reentrance.

Table 4 shows that the α-bound helps signifi-

Table 3: F-Score results on validation set ($\alpha = 1$).

Parameter settings	NoR	Reent.
Baseline	0.642	0.640
DAGGER	0.648	0.651
DAGGER & Inc	0.653	0.655
DAGGER & Red	0.648	0.653
DAGGER & Inc & Red	**0.651**	0.649

cantly, with a gain of 1.8 points of F-Score in this example. We found consistently that the most extreme setting of α=1 worked best.

Table 4: Alpha-bound results with DAGGER, Inc and Red

Alpha-bound	F-Score
1	0.655
2	0.649
None	0.637

4   Conclusion

Imitation Learning algorithms like DAGGER help in the AMR task, as in other structured prediction problems. Performance is improved using the α-bound to reduce the impact of noise in the training examples, and future work could investigate the impact in similar tasks.

The reduction in search space and incremental growth of the training set do not have a significant impact on the results. The speed improvements they provide make little difference here, but could benefit more computationally demanding loss functions than the 0-1 expert loss used in DAGGER.

Acknowledgments

Andreas Vlachos is supported by the EPSRC grant Diligent (EP/M005429/1) and Jason Naradowsky by a Google Focused Research award.

References

Laura Banarescu, Claire Bonial, Shu Cai, Madalina Georgescu, Kira Griffitt, Ulf Hermjakob, Kevin Knight, Phillip Koehn, Martha Palmer, and Nathan Schneider. 2013. Abstract Meaning Representation for Sembanking. *Proceedings of the 7th Lingustic Annotation Workshop & Interoperability with Discourse*, pages 178–186.

Jonathan Berant and Percy Liang. 2015. Imitation learning of agenda-based semantic parsers. *Transactions of the Association for Computational Linguistics (TACL)*, 3:545–558.

Koby Crammer, Alex Kulesza, and Mark Dredze. 2009. Adaptive regularization of weight vectors. In *Advances in neural information processing systems*, pages 414–422.

Jeffrey Flanigan, Sam Thomson, Jaime Carbonell, Chris Dyer, and Noah A Smith. 2014. A discriminative graph-based parser for the abstract meaning representation.

Yoav Goldberg and Michael Elhadad. 2010. An efficient algorithm for easy-first non-directional dependency parsing. In *Human Language Technologies: The 2010 Annual Conference of the North American Chapter of the Association for Computational Linguistics*, pages 742–750. Association for Computational Linguistics.

Matthew Honnibal, Yoav Goldberg, and Mark Johnson. 2013. A non-monotonic arc-eager transition system for dependency parsing. In *Proceedings of the Seventeenth Conference on Computational Natural Language Learning*, pages 163–172. Citeseer.

Roni Khardon and Gabriel Wachman. 2007. Noise tolerant variants of the perceptron algorithm. *The journal of machine learning research*, 8:227–248.

Percy Liang. 2005. *Semi-supervised learning for natural language*. Ph.D. thesis, Citeseer.

Christopher D. Manning, Mihai Surdeanu, John Bauer, Jenny Finkel, Steven J. Bethard, and David McClosky. 2014. The Stanford CoreNLP natural language processing toolkit. In *Proceedings of 52nd Annual Meeting of the Association for Computational Linguistics: System Demonstrations*, pages 55–60.

Ryan T McDonald and Joakim Nivre. 2007. Characterizing the errors of data-driven dependency parsing models. In *EMNLP-CoNLL*, pages 122–131.

Nima Pourdamghani, Yang Gao, Ulf Hermjakob, and Kevin Knight. 2014. Aligning english strings with abstract meaning representation graphs. In *Proceedings of the 2014 Conference on Empirical Methods in Natural Language Processing (EMNLP)*, pages 425–429.

Sudha Rao, Yogarshi Vyas, Hal Daume III, and Philip Resnik. 2015. Parser for abstract meaning representation using learning to search. *arXiv preprint arXiv:1510.07586*.

Stephane Ross and J Andrew Bagnell. 2014. Reinforcement and imitation learning via interactive no-regret learning. *arXiv preprint arXiv:1406.5979*.

Stéphane Ross, Geoffrey J Gordon, and J Andrew Bagnell. 2011. A reduction of imitation learning and structured prediction to no-regret online learning.

Francesco Sartorio, Giorgio Satta, and Joakim Nivre. 2013. A transition-based dependency parser using a dynamic parsing strategy. In *ACL (1)*, pages 135–144.

Andreas Vlachos and Stephen Clark. 2014. A new corpus and imitation learning framework for context-dependent semantic parsing. *Transactions of the Association for Computational Linguistics*, 2:547–559.

Chuan Wang, Nianwen Xue, and Sameer Pradhan. 2015a. Boosting transition-based amr parsing with refined actions and auxiliary analyzers. In *Proceedings of the 53rd Annual Meeting of the Association for Computational Linguistics and the 7th International Joint Conference on Natural Language Processing (Volume 2: Short Papers)*, pages 857–862, Beijing, China, July. Association for Computational Linguistics.

Chuan Wang, Nianwen Xue, and Sameer Pradhan. 2015b. A transition-based algorithm for amr parsing. *North American Association for Computational Linguistics, Denver, Colorado*.

Keenon Werling, Gabor Angeli, and Christopher D. Manning. 2015. Robust subgraph generation improves abstract meaning representation parsing. In *Proceedings of the 53rd Annual Meeting of the Association for Computational Linguistics and the 7th International Joint Conference on Natural Language Processing (Volume 1: Long Papers)*, pages 982–991, Beijing, China, July. Association for Computational Linguistics.

CAMR at SemEval-2016 Task 8:
An Extended Transition-based AMR Parser

Chuan Wang
Brandeis University
cwang24@brandeis.edu

Sameer Pradhan
`cemantix.org`
Boulder Learning Inc.
pradhan@cemantix.org

Nianwen Xue
Brandeis University
xuen@brandeis.edu

Xiaoman Pan
Rensselaer Polytechnic Institute
panx2@rpi.edu

Heng Ji
Rensselaer Polytechnic Institute
jih@rpi.edu

Abstract

This paper describes CAMR, the transition-based parser that we use in the SemEval-2016 Meaning Representation Parsing task. The main contribution of this paper is a description of the additional sources of information that we use as features in the parsing model to further boost its performance. We start with our existing AMR parser and experiment with three sets of new features: 1) rich named entities, 2) a verbalization list, 3) semantic role labels. We also use the RPI Wikifier to wikify the concepts in the AMR graph. Our parser achieves a Smatch F-score of 62% on the official blind test set.

1 Introduction

AMR parsing is the task of taking a sentence as input and producing as output an Abstract Meaning Representation (AMR) that is a rooted, directed, edge-labeled and leaf-labeled graph that is used to represent the meaning of a sentence (Banarescu et al., 2013). AMR parsing has drawn an increasing amount of attention recently. The first published AMR parser, JAMR (Flanigan et al., 2014), performs AMR parsing in two stages: concept identification and relation identification. Flanigan et al. (2014) treat concept identification as a sequence labeling task and utilize a semi-Markov model to map spans of words in a sentence to concept graph fragments. For relation identification, they adopt graph-based techniques similar to those used in dependency parsing (McDonald et al., 2005). Instead of finding maximum spanning trees (MST) over words, they propose an algorithm that

finds the maximum spanning connected subgraph (MSCG) over concept fragments identified in the first stage.

Wang et al. (2015b) describes a transition-based parser that also involves two stages. In the first step, an input sentence is parsed into a dependency tree with a dependency parser. In the second step, it transforms the dependency tree into an AMR graph by performing a series of actions. Note that the dependency parser used in the first step can be any off-the-shelf dependency parser and does not have to trained on the same data set as used in the second step.

There are also approaches which utilize grammar induction to parse the AMR. Artzi et al. (2015) presents a model that first use Combinatory Categorial Grammar (CCG) to construct the lambda-calculus representations of the sentence, then further resolve non-compositional dependencies using a factor graph. Peng et al.(2015) and Pust et al.(2015) formalize parsing AMR as a machine translation problem by learning string-graph/string-tree rules from the annotated data.

Although the field of AMR parsing is growing and several systems (Wang et al., 2015a; Artzi et al., 2015; Pust et al., 2015; Flanigan et al., 2014) have substantially advanced the state of the art, the overall performance of existing AMR parsers is far less accurate than syntactic parsers (Charniak and Johnson, 2005). This makes it difficult to use in downstream NLP tasks. In this paper, we aim to boost the AMR parsing performance by introducing additional features. We mainly experiment with three sets of features derived from: 1) rich named entities, 2) a verbalization list provided by ISI, and 3) semantic role

1173

Proceedings of SemEval-2016, pages 1173–1178,
San Diego, California, June 16-17, 2016. ©2016 Association for Computational Linguistics

labels produced by an automatic SRL system.

The rest of the paper is organized as follows. In Section 2 we briefly describe CAMR, and in Section 3 we describe our extensions for the SemEval shared task. In Section 4 we describe the different AMR releases available with some salient characteristics. We report experimental results in Section 5 and conclude the paper in Section 6.

2 CAMR Overview

2.1 Basic Configuration

CAMR first uses a dependency parser to parse an input sentence, and then performs a small number of highly general actions to transform the resulting dependency tree to an AMR graph. The transition actions are briefly described below but due to the limited space, we cannot provide the full details of these actions here, and the reader is referred to previous work (Wang et al., 2015b) for a detailed description of these actions with illustrating examples. CAMR uses three types of actions: actions performed when an edge is visited, actions performed when a node is visited, and actions used to infer abstract concepts in AMR that does not correspond to any word or word sequence in the sentence.

CAMR performs one of the following six actions when an edge is visited:

- NEXT-EDGE-l_r (ned): Assign the current edge with edge label l_r and go to next edge.
- SWAP-l_r (sw): Swap the current edge, make the current dependent as the new head, and assign edge label l_r to the swapped edge.
- REATTACH$_k$-l_r (reat): Reattach current dependent to node k and assign edge label l_r.
- REPLACE-HEAD (rph): Replace current head node with current dependent node.
- REENTRANCE$_k$-l_r (reen): Add another head node k to current dependent and assign label l_r to edge between k and current dependent.
- MERGE (mrg): Merge two nodes connected by the edge into one node.

From each node in the dependency tree, CAMR performs the following two actions:

- NEXT-NODE-l_c (nnd): Assign the current node with concept label l_c and go to next node.

- DELETE-NODE (dnd): Delete the current node and all edges associated with current node.

Finally CAMR infers **abstract concepts** that are not aligned to any tokens in sentence with an INFER-l_c action. The INFER-l_c action works as follows: when the parser visits an node in dependency tree, it inserts an abstract node with concept label l_c right between the current node and its parent. For example in Figure 1, after applying action INFER-have-org-role-91 on node *minister*, the abstract concept is recovered and subsequent actions can be applied to transform the subgraph to its correct AMR.

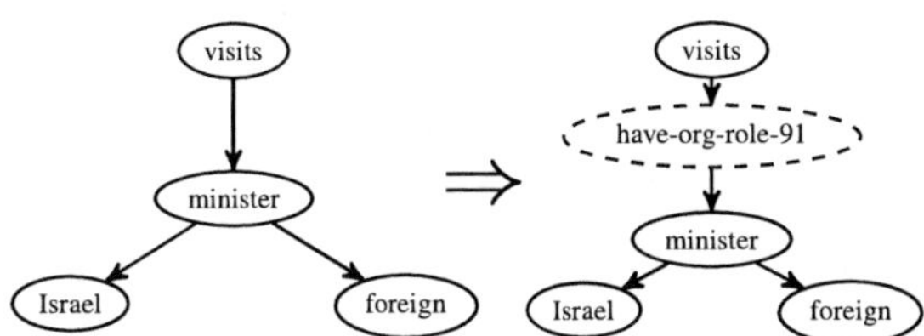

Figure 1: INFER-have-org-role-91 action

3 CAMR Extensions

3.1 Feature Enrichment

Rich named entity tags Since named entity types in AMR are much more fine-grained than the named entity types defined in a typical named entity tagging system, we assume that using a richer named entity tagger could improve concept identification in parsing. Here we use the 18 named entity types defined in the OntoNotes v5.0 Corpus (Weischedel et al., 2011; Pradhan et al., 2013).

The ISI verbalization list A large proportion of AMR concepts are "normalized" English words. This typically involves cases where the verb form of a noun or an adjective is used as the AMR concept. For example, the AMR concept "attract-01" is used for the adjective "attractive". Similarly, the noun "globalization" would invoke the AMR concept "globalize-01". To help CAMR produce these AMR concepts correctly, we use the verbalization-list provided by ISI[1] to improve the word-to-AMR-concepts alignment. If any alignment is missed by the JAMR aligner and left un-aligned, we simply add

---

[1] http://amr.isi.edu/download/lists/verbalization-list-v1.01.txt

an alignment to map the unaligned concept to its corresponding word token if the word token in the input sentence is in the verbalization list.

semantic role labeling:
wants, want-01,
ARG0: the boy, ARG1: the girl to believe him

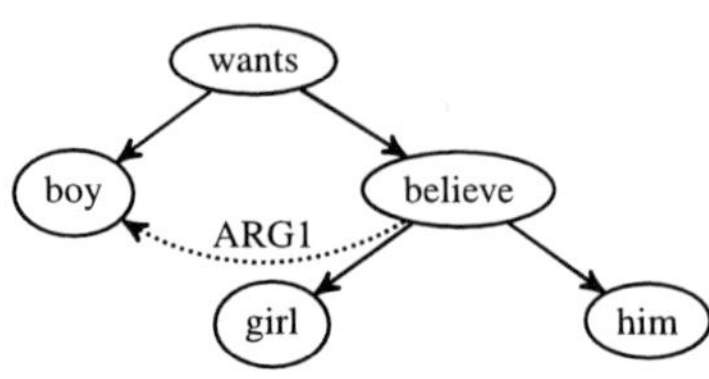

For action NEXT-NODE-want-01
EQ_FRAMESET: true

Figure 2: An example of semantic role labeling feature in partial parsing graph of sentence,"The boy wants the girl to believe him."

Semantic role labeling features We use the following semantic role labeling features: 1) EQ_FRAMESET. For actions that predict the concept label (NEXT-NODE-l_c), we check whether the candidate concept label l_c matches the frameset predicted by ASSERT (Pradhan et al., 2004). For example, in the partial graph in Figure 2, when we examine node *wants*, one of the candidate actions would be NEXT-NODE-want-01. Since the candidate concept label want-01 is equal to node *wants*'s frameset want-01 as predicted by AS-SERT, the value of feature EQ_FRAMESET is set to true. 2) IS_ARGUMENT. For actions that predict the edge label, we check whether ASSERT predicts that the current dependent is an argument of the current head. Note that arguments output by the semantic role labeler are typically constituents in a syntactic tree. We find the head of the argument and match it against the dependent. If the argument predicted by ASSERT matches the dependent, the value of the IS_ARGUMENT is set to true.

Word Clusters For the semi-supervised word cluster feature, we use Brown clusters, more specifically, the 1000-class word clusters trained by Turian et al. (2010). We use prefixes of lengths 4, 6, 10 and 20 of the word's bit-string as features.

3.2 Wikification

We apply an AMR based wikification system (Pan et al., 2015) which utilizes AMR to represent semantic information about entity mentions expressed in their textual context. Given an entity mention m, this system first constructs a Knowledge Graph $g(m)$ with m at the hub and leaf nodes obtained from entity mentions reachable by AMR graph traversal from m. A subset of the leaf nodes are selected as collaborators of m. Mentions connected by AMR conjunction relations are grouped into sets of coherent mentions. For each entity mention m, an initial ranked list of entity candidates $E = (e_1, \ldots, e_n)$ is generated based on a salience measure (Medelyan and Witten, 2008). Then a Knowledge Graph $g(e_i)$ is generated for each entity candidate e_i in m's entity candidate list E. The entity candidates are then re-ranked according to Jaccard Similarity, which computes the similarity between $g(m)$ and $g(e_i)$: $J(g(m), g(e_i)) = \frac{|g(m) \cap g(e_i)|}{|g(m) \cup g(e_i)|}$. Finally, the entity candidate with the highest score is selected as the appropriate entity for wikifying m. Moreover, the Knowledge Graphs of coherent mentions will be merged and wikified collectively.

4 Data

Research on AMR parsing so far has reported on two releases of the annotated data. This SemEval evaluation adds another release. The main difference between the SemEval release and the previous two releases is that the SemEval release contains wikification information which was absent from the previous two releases. Since the Smatch scorer uses this information as part of its scoring algorithm, we cannot make comparisons between results on the SemEval release and results previously reported by other systems. We summarize the characteristics of these three releases below.

   a. **LDC2013E117**—This is a non-public release that was used to report the very first results on AMR parsing. The first results were reported only on a subset of the test partition— The newswire proxy section. We do not report performance on this release in this paper.

   b. **LDC2014T12**—This was the first public release of the AMR data through LDC. Comparable numbers have been reported on this release for the same newswire proxy section as in (a.) as well as the entire test set.

c. **LDC2015E86**—This is the release specifically made available for the SemEval evaluation. One main difference between this version and the two previous versions is the addition of wikification information. Thus, the performance numbers on the full test set of this release are not directly comparable with previously published results on either of the other two releases.

In the following sections, we will report experiments primarily on the Semeval release (c.). In Section 5.3 we also use the full test set of release (b.) to evaluate the performance improvement made to CAMR as part of the SemEval evaluations against previously reported performance.

Syntactic Parser	P	R	F_1
Charniak (ON)	70.76	60.57	65.27
Charniak (WSJ)	69.88	60.24	64.70

Table 1: AMR parsing performance on the SemEval development set (LDC2015E86) across two Charniak parser models

5 Experiments

We use the official release dataset and standard train/dev/test split of SemEval Task 8 for experiments. All the sentences are preprocessed using Stanford CoreNLP (Manning et al., 2014) to get tokenization, lemma, named entity tag, POS tag. And we use the aligner that comes with JAMR (Flanigan et al., 2014) to align the sentence with its AMR graph. We then parse the tokenized sentences using Charniak parser (Charniak and Johnson, 2005)(Its phrase structure output is converted to dependency structure using a slightly modified version of the Stanford CoreNLP converter). Rich named entity tags are generated using Stanford named entity tagger. The semantic role labels are generated using ASSERT—a semantic role labeler (Pradhan et al., 2005), including a frameset disambiguator trained using a word sense disambiguation system—IMS (Zhong and Ng, 2010). All these components viz., the Charniak parser, Stanford named entity tagger, ASSERT, and IMS word sense disambiguator were retrained on the OntoNotes v5.0 training

data[2] (Pradhan et al., 2013)[3]. We use the version of CAMR described in (Wang et al., 2015a) (without the feature extensions) as the baseline. We evaluate our parser with Smatch v2.0.2 (Cai and Knight, 2013) on all the experiments. It should be noted that all the rows in Table 2 except for the last one get implicitly penalized by the scorer for lack of wikification information.

5.1 SemEval Development Set

As discussed in (Wang et al., 2015a), the performance of the syntactic parser in the first stage has a high impact on the AMR parsing accuracy. We first do a sanity check to choose the best first stage parser. Here we only consider two scenarios: the Charniak parser trained on WSJ and OntoNotes, as shown in Table 1. As using the Charniak parser trained on OntoNotes yields slightly better AMR parsing result, we will use this set-up for the following experiments.

In Table 2 we present results from extending CAMR. All experiments are conducted on the SemEval development set. we can see that the three major improvements are given by adding the verbalization list, semantic role labels and wikification separately. Rich named entities also yield a 0.4% point improvement, indicating that the more fine-grained named entity tagger is helpful to concept identification. In contrast, Brown cluster features actually hurt the overall performance. Therefore we did not use them in the configuration used for the official run.

5.2 SemEval Test Set and Blind Test Set

We evaluate our parser on the SemEval test set and also report the evaluation result on the SemEval blind test set with the best configuration obtained from §5.1, as shown in Table 3.

---

[2]Details of the training data and the trained models can be found at http://cemantix.org/data/ontonotes.html and https://github.com/ontonotes/conll-formatted-ontonotes-5.0/releases/tag/v12

[3]We excluded documents from the OntoNotes v5.0 training and development partitions that overlapped with the SemEval AMR data. List of overlapping document IDs is available at http://cemantix.org/ontonotes/ontonotes-amr-document-overlap.txt

Feature configuration	P	R	F_1
Baseline	70.76	60.57	65.27
+VERB	71.52	60.96	65.82
+VERB+BROWN	71.85	60.38	65.62
+VERB+RNE	71.89	61.02	66.01
+VERB+RNE+SRL	72.33	61.40	66.56
+VERB+RNE+SRL+WIKI	71.17	63.89	67.33

Table 2: AMR parsing performance on the official SemEval development set (LDC2015E86). VERB: ISI verbalization list. BROWN: Brown cluster features. RNE: Rich (OntoNotes) named entities. SRL: semantic role labeling features. WIKI: Addition of wikification of named entities in AMR.

Dataset	P	R	F_1
Test Set	70.36	63.12	66.54
Blind Test Set	67.44	57.39	62.01

Table 3: AMR parsing performance on full SemEval Test Set and the Blind Test Set

CAMR version	P	R	F_1
This paper	**71.35**	**62.29**	**66.51**
Wang et al. (2015a)	70.29	62.01	65.89

Table 4: CAMR parsing performance on the full test set of release LDC2014T12.

From Table 3 we can see that our parser remain relatively stable on the SemEval test set. However, the evaluation result on blind test set dropped by around 4 points, indicating the blind test set is much harder and we plan to do further error analysis to gain more insight on the difference.

5.3 Previous Release—LDC2014T12

Since the official dataset of SemEval is annotated with wiki relations that previous releases of the AMR Corpus do not have, we conduct additional experiments on the AMR annotation release 1.0 (LDC2014T12) to gain a clear understanding of the impact of the additional feature. We use the training/development/test split recommended in the release: 10,312 sentences for training, 1,368 sentences for development and 1,371 sentences for testing. We re-train the parser on the LDC2014T12 training set with the best parser configuration given in §5.1 — except for the wikification pass— and test the parser on the full test set. The result is shown in Table 4. For comparison, we include the result of our parser in (Wang et al., 2015a) which are also trained on the same dataset. The results show that the new features yield a modest improvement over our (Wang et al., 2015a) parser.

6 Conclusion

We build our system by taking our existing AMR parser and enriching it with three sets of features: 1) rich named entities, 2) a verbalization list, and 3) semantic role labels. We also use a wikifier to resolve the wiki relation in AMR graph. Our results show that the additional features are helpful to the AMR parsing task and a well-designed wikifier could be a helpful post-processing step to AMR parsing.

References

Yoav Artzi, Kenton Lee, and Luke Zettlemoyer. 2015. Broad-coverage ccg semantic parsing with amr. In *Proceedings of the 2015 Conference on Empirical Methods in Natural Language Processing*, pages 1699–1710, Lisbon, Portugal, September. Association for Computational Linguistics.

Laura Banarescu, Claire Bonial, Shu Cai, Madalina Georgescu, Kira Griffitt, Ulf Hermjakob, Kevin Knight, Philipp Koehn, Martha Palmer, and Nathan Schneider. 2013. Abstract meaning representation for sembanking. In *Proceedings of the 7th Linguistic Annotation Workshop and Interoperability with Discourse*, pages 178–186. Association for Computational Linguistics.

Shu Cai and Kevin Knight. 2013. Smatch: an evaluation metric for semantic feature structures. In *Proceedings of the 51st Annual Meeting of the Association for Computational Linguistics (Volume 2: Short Papers)*, pages 748–752. Association for Computational Linguistics.

Eugene Charniak and Mark Johnson. 2005. Coarse-to-fine n-best parsing and maxent discriminative reranking. In *Proceedings of the 43rd Annual Meeting on Association for Computational Linguistics*, ACL '05, pages 173–180, Stroudsburg, PA, USA. Association for Computational Linguistics.

Jeffrey Flanigan, Sam Thomson, Jaime Carbonell, Chris Dyer, and Noah A. Smith. 2014. A discriminative graph-based parser for the abstract meaning representation. In *Proceedings of the 52nd Annual Meeting of the Association for Computational Linguistics (Volume 1: Long Papers)*, pages 1426–1436, Baltimore, Maryland, June. Association for Computational Linguistics.

Christopher D. Manning, Mihai Surdeanu, John Bauer, Jenny Finkel, Steven J. Bethard, and David McClosky. 2014. The Stanford CoreNLP natural language processing toolkit. In *Proceedings of 52nd Annual Meeting of the Association for Computational Linguistics: System Demonstrations*, pages 55–60.

Ryan McDonald, Fernando Pereira, Kiril Ribarov, and Jan Hajič. 2005. Non-projective dependency parsing using spanning tree algorithms. In *Proceedings of the Conference on Human Language Technology and Empirical Methods in Natural Language Processing*, HLT '05, pages 523–530, Stroudsburg, PA, USA. Association for Computational Linguistics.

Olena Medelyan and Ian H Witten. 2008. Domain-independent automatic keyphrase indexing with small training sets. *Journal of the American Society for Information Science and Technology*, 59(7):1026–1040.

Xiaoman Pan, Taylor Cassidy, Ulf Hermjakob, Heng Ji, and Kevin Knight. 2015. Unsupervised entity linking with abstract meaning representation. In *Proceedings of the 2015 Conference of the North American Chapter of the Association for Computational Linguistics: Human Language Technologies*, pages 1130–1139, Denver, Colorado, May–June. Association for Computational Linguistics.

Xiaochang Peng, Linfeng Song, and Daniel Gildea. 2015. A synchronous hyperedge replacement grammar based approach for AMR parsing. In *Proceedings of the Nineteenth Conference on Computational Natural Language Learning*.

Sameer Pradhan, Wayne Ward, Kadri Hacioglu, James Martin, and Dan Jurafsky. 2004. Shallow semantic parsing using support vector machines. In *Proceedings of the Human Language Technology Conference/North American chapter of the Association of Computational Linguistics (HLT/NAACL)*, Boston, MA, May.

Sameer Pradhan, Kadri Hacioglu, Valerie Krugler, Wayne Ward, James Martin, and Dan Jurafsky. 2005.

Support vector learning for semantic argument classification. *Machine Learning Journal*, 60(1):11–39.

Sameer Pradhan, Alessandro Moschitti, Nianwen Xue, Hwee Tou Ng, Anders Björkelund, Olga Uryupina, Yuchen Zhang, and Zhi Zhong. 2013. Towards robust linguistic analysis using OntoNotes. In *Proceedings of the Seventeenth Conference on Computational Natural Language Learning*, pages 143–152, Sofia, Bulgaria, August.

Michael Pust, Ulf Hermjakob, Kevin Knight, Daniel Marcu, and Jonathan May. 2015. Parsing english into abstract meaning representation using syntax-based machine translation. In *Proceedings of the 2015 Conference on Empirical Methods in Natural Language Processing*, pages 1143–1154, Lisbon, Portugal, September. Association for Computational Linguistics.

Joseph Turian, Lev Ratinov, and Yoshua Bengio. 2010. Word representations: a simple and general method for semi-supervised learning. In *Proceedings of the 48th annual meeting of the association for computational linguistics*, pages 384–394. Association for Computational Linguistics.

Chuan Wang, Nianwen Xue, and Sameer Pradhan. 2015a. Boosting transition-based amr parsing with refined actions and auxiliary analyzers. In *Proceedings of the 53rd Annual Meeting of the Association for Computational Linguistics and the 7th International Joint Conference on Natural Language Processing (Volume 2: Short Papers)*, pages 857–862, Beijing, China, July. Association for Computational Linguistics.

Chuan Wang, Nianwen Xue, and Sameer Pradhan. 2015b. A transition-based algorithm for amr parsing. In *Proceedings of the 2015 Conference of the North American Chapter of the Association for Computational Linguistics: Human Language Technologies*, pages 366–375, Denver, Colorado, May–June. Association for Computational Linguistics.

Ralph Weischedel, Eduard Hovy, Mitchell Marcus, Martha Palmer, Robert Belvin, Sameer Pradhan, Lance Ramshaw, and Nianwen Xue. 2011. OntoNotes: A large training corpus for enhanced processing. Springer.

Zhi Zhong and Hwee Tou Ng. 2010. It makes sense: A wide-coverage word sense disambiguation system for free text. In *Proceedings of the ACL 2010 System Demonstrations*, pages 78–83, Uppsala, Sweden.

The Meaning Factory at SemEval-2016 Task 8: Producing AMRs with Boxer

Johannes Bjerva
CLCG
University of Groningen
j.bjerva@rug.nl

Johan Bos
CLCG
University of Groningen
johan.bos@rug.nl

Hessel Haagsma
CLCG
University of Groningen
hessel.haagsma@rug.nl

Abstract

We participated in the shared task on meaning representation parsing (Task 8 at SemEval-2016) with the aim of investigating whether we could use Boxer, an existing open-domain semantic parser, for this task. However, the meaning representations produced by Boxer, Discourse Representation Structures, are considerably different from Abstract Meaning Representations, AMRs, the target meaning representations of the shared task. Our hybrid conversion method (involving lexical adaptation as well as post-processing of the output) failed to produce state-of-the-art results. Nonetheless, F-scores of 53% on development and 47% on test data (50% unofficially) were obtained.

1 Introduction

With the currently increasing interest in semantic parsing, and the diversity of the meaning representations being used, an important challenge is to adapt existing semantic parsers for different semantic representations. Shared Task 8 of the SemEval-2016 campaign for semantic evaluation is an interesting venue for this, where a system is given an English sentence and has to produce an Abstract Meaning Representation (AMR) for it.

We participated in this shared task with a system rooted in formal semantics based on Discourse Representation Theory (DRT). In particular, we were interested in finding out whether the representations from DRT (Kamp, 1984; Kamp and Reyle, 1993), Discourse Representation Structures (DRSs), could be easily converted into AMRs. In this paper we

outline our method, which is based on the semantic parser Boxer (Bos, 2008; Bos, 2015), and then present and discuss our results.

2 Background

Before we outline our method, we will say a little about the open-domain semantic parser that we used in this shared task. We also give an overview of the differences between the meaning representations produced by Boxer and those that are required for the shared task. To get a first taste of these differences, compare the analysis of *'All equipment will be completely manufactured'* carried out by Boxer (Figure 1) and that of the gold-standard AMR (Figure 2).

```
 _____________________________________________
|                                             |
|............................................ |
| ____________   _________________            |
| |x1        |   |e1 s1          |          | |
| |..........|   |...............|          | |
| |equipment(x1)|>|manufacture(e1)|          | |
| |__________|   |Manner(e1,s1)  |          | |
|                |Theme(e1,x1)   |          | |
|                |complete(s1)   |          | |
|                |_______________|          | |
|_____________________________________________|
```

Figure 1: DRS, as produced by Boxer.

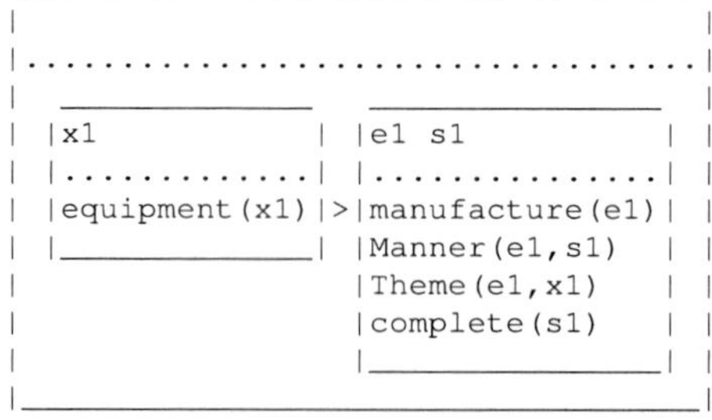

```
(m / manufacture-01
   :ARG1 (e2 / equipment
              :mod (a2 / all))
   :ARG1-of (c / complete-02))
```

Figure 2: Gold-standard AMR.

Proceedings of SemEval-2016, pages 1179–1184,
San Diego, California, June 16-17, 2016. ©2016 Association for Computational Linguistics

2.1 Boxer

The semantic parser that we employed is Boxer (Bos, 2008; Bos, 2015). It is the last component in the C&C tools pipeline (Curran et al., 2007), comprising a tokenizer (Evang et al., 2013), POS-tagger, lemmatizer (Minnen et al., 2001), and a robust parser for CCG, Combinatory Categorial Grammar (Steedman, 2001). Overall, this parsing framework shows many points of contact with the recent work by Artzi et al. (2015), who also use CCG coupled with a formal compositional semantics.

Boxer produces semantic representations based on Discourse Representation Theory (Kamp and Reyle, 1993), known as Discourse Representation Structures (DRSs), as Figure 1 shows. A DRS is a first-order representation, i.e., expressible with first-order logic. Various notations are possible, but widely used are the box-like representations shown in Figure 1. Boxes display scopes of discourse referents and contain properties of and relations between discourse referents. They are recursive structures, hence a box may contain other boxes.

2.2 Abstract Meaning Representations

At first glance, an AMR looks quite different from a DRS. Usually, an AMR is displayed as a directed graph with a unique root (Figure 2). However, it is also possible to view an AMR as a recursive structure, and then DRS and AMR have more in common than one perhaps would initially realize (Bos, 2016).

The variables in an AMR correspond to discourse referents in a DRS. The colon-prefixed symbols in an AMR are similar to the two-place relation symbols in a DRS. And the forward slashes in an AMR correspond to one-place predicates in a DRS. So the main commonalities between a DRS (as produced by Boxer) and an AMR (as used at the SEMEVAL-2016 shared task) are:

- both use a neo-Davidsonian event semantics;

- both are recursive meaning representations;

- both expect normalization of date expressions.

There are also some obvious differences between DRS and AMR. Some of them are theoretical and have to do with the expressive power of the chosen formalism. Others have to do with relatively arbitrary choice of labels and encoding of meanings. The most important differences are:

- AMR has no explicit structures for universal quantification and negation;

- AMR expects different labels for thematic roles (Boxer uses the VerbNet inventory);

- AMR assigns no scope for propositional meanings;

- AMR is strongly event-oriented (verbalization);

- AMR has flat lists of coordinated structures;

- AMR has symbol grounding by wikification (for named entities).

These are substantial differences posing a serious challenge when mapping DRSs to AMRs. In the next section we describe how we go about doing this.

3 Method

3.1 Pre-processing and Tokenisation

All input texts were normalized prior to semantic processing by our pipeline. First of all, double quotes were removed from sentences because they do not contribute to AMR components but they might give rise to suboptimal syntactic parses. Secondly, brackets containing unit conversions were removed (i.e., *30 yards (27 meters)* became *30 yards*) because the converted information does not show in gold-standard AMRs.

Tokenization was done using the Elephant tokenizer (Evang et al., 2013). Some of the documents that were supplied for the shared task had already undergone tokenization, however. Therefore, prior to tokenization, we determine per document whether or not tokenization is needed. This is done with a simple heuristic, applying tokenization if the document does not contain a full stop or comma with whitespace on both sides.

3.2 Lexical anticipation

Our key idea was to map DRSs as output by Boxer to AMR, and doing so in a systematic, principled way. However, during the implementation process it became clear that this mapping would become much easier when certain conversions would have been already made in Boxer's semantic lexicon. An obvious case is determiners, which receive an elaborate analysis in DRS but a minimal treatment in AMR. Anticipating this in the lexicon saves error-prone conversion steps later in the processing pipeline.

Apart from determiners, lexical conversion (i.e., altering the lexical semantics in order to get closer to AMR structures) was carried out for certain punctuation symbols (question and exclamation marks), all cases of coordination, for some non-logical symbols (for instance, contrastive discourse relations and conditionals), there-insertion, personal and possessive pronouns, demonstratives and quantifiers, comparatives and superlatives, certain temporal modifiers, and copula constructions.

3.3 From DRS to AMR

The conversion from DRS to AMR was implemented using a recursive translation function. Apart from some core translation rules mapping DRS to AMR constructs, there is also a set of rules that work on specific phenomena: modal operators in DRSs are mapped to events (recommend-01 and possible-01); the negation operator is mapped to `polarity-`, and disjunction to an `or`-instance with `op1` and `op2` relations.

Boxer's thematic roles are mapped to ARG0 (Actor) ARG1 (Theme, Topic) or ARG2 (recipient). In addition, we took advantage of Ulf Hermjakob's lists of `have-rel-role` and `have-org-role` predicates to rewrite roles when needed. A similar resource was used to cope with deverbalizations.

The outcome of the mapping is an AMR with possibly more than one root. Therefore the conversion also involves inversion of AMR roles until an AMR with a unique root is obtained. This is a non-trivial process and does not always succeed. In such cases only parts of the AMR are produced as output.

3.4 Re-labelling

An additional post-processing step consisted of changing labels where our output AMRs consistently differed from those in the training data. After processing each document in the training data with Boxer, Smatch (v 2.0.2) was used to obtain all matching triples for each AMR parse pair. Using these triples, we calculate counts of (BOXER-RELATION, GOLD-RELATION, COUNT). If Boxer consistently outputs a relation erroneously, we replace all occurrences of that label with the correct label from the training data.

Examples of phenomena that require re-labelling are: intensifiers, locative adjectives, ordinals, temporal adverbs, morphological mappings of symbols (for instance, historical $\to$ history), temporal roles, putting names together, time expressions, units of measurement, nationalities, modal adverbs, verbalizations, negation affixes, and abbreviations.

3.5 Wikification

Wikification was done as a post-processing step: each name-relation produced by boxer was initialized with an empty wiki (`:wiki -`). The value of the wiki was acquired by wikifying the whole sentence and then matching the wikification output to the name. One exception to this regards demonyms, which were assigned the correct wikification by Boxer already.

Wikification was done using DBPedia Spotlight (Daiber et al., 2013) through the web service[1], because of its high coverage and ease-of-use. Since we used Spotlight only for wikification, and not for NER, a high recall was more important than a high precision. The confidence parameter was optimized on the development set, and the optimal value turned out to be 0.3. This is a low value, which yields a large number of annotations for each sentence, a large proportion of which are incorrect.

The wikification output was then matched to the names in the sentence by using exact string matching, and if that failed, by matching on prefixes. Performance was high, with accuracy of wikification only, tested with the gold-standard AMRs at around 76%. In terms of AMR-parsing F-scores, wikification yielded gains of 2% to 4% on the development set, depending on the nature of the data and the quality of Boxer's NER. We also experimented with the Illinois Wikifier (Ratinov et al., 2011), but this did not yield any improvements over DBPedia Spotlight.

---

[1] http://spotlight.sztaki.hu:2222/rest/annotate

Table 1: F-scores on the *test* part of the released training data.

	DFA	Xinhua	Consensus	Bolt	Proxy
Boxer	39.9	**57.2**	45.8	47.0	56.0
JAMR	**47.5**	52.8	**49.6**	**48.7**	**60.2**

4   Results and Discussion

4.1   Overall Results

We obtained an F-score of 47% in the official scoring. Due to an error early in our pipeline script, a large amount of our parsing mistakes were caused by erroneous tokenization. Correcting this bug results in an F-score of 50% on the official evaluation data (calculated with Smatch v2.0.2 using 4 restarts).

Table 1 shows the F-scores we obtained on the *test* portion of the data set released for system development for this task. We compare our system with the JAMR parser, trained following released instructions on the *training* portion of the released data. Although our parser obtains a lower score on most sub-corpora, we are able to outperform the JAMR parser on the Xinhua sub-corpus.

4.2   Error Analysis

An analysis of the mistakes made on the gold test set reveals that some mistakes can be attributed to annotation mistakes. Figure 3 shows an example in which our AMR is arguably better than the gold AMR. In the sentence *'They are thugs and deserve a bullet.'*, the ones deserving a bullet should not be *all thugs* as in the gold parse, but the referent of *they*, as in our output. Figure 4 shows a similar instance, in which *A protester* is incorrectly assigned the modifier :quant 1 in the gold parse. (An anonymous reviewer of an earlier version of this article noted that "the AMR gold seems correct, even though I would have probably accepted the Boxer output as correct, at least without knowing more about the pragmatic context of the sentence.". We don't agree here, as many similar cases in the corpus are not annotated with the same attribute, and since there is no context, it is impossible to infer the less likely specific-indefinite reading.)

Another portion of the mistakes made by our system can be attributed to wrong choices of senses, arguments and coordination mistakes. Figure 5 shows an example in which we make a coordination mis-

take with the noun-noun compound *security force*, and interpret this as a possessive. We further also make a labelling mistake, interpreting *america* as an organization. Figure 6 also contains such a labelling mistake, in which we fail to resolve *take part* to `participate-01`. In the example in Figure 7 the wrong sense is chosen for *fall*.

A quantitative analysis of this type of mistake shows that there is quite some room for improvement to be made by correcting these. Assuming perfect Smatch alignment of triples, 18.5% of relations are mislabelled (for instance, `ARG1` when `ARG2` would be appropriate), and 42.8% of instances are mislabelled (for example, `fall-01` when `fall-07` would be appropriate).

5   Conclusion

In this paper we wanted to investigate how feasible it is to map DRSs to AMRs. DRSs and AMRs have a lot of points in common, but there are also significant differences. We approached the problem with a three-fold strategy: lexical adaptation (changing lexical entries of the Boxer system to match AMR), a recursive translation function from DRS to AMR, and a post-processing step (needed because of the differences in verbalization and symbol labelling in AMR).

On the one hand, the overall results are perhaps disappointing. The obtained F-score does not match that of state-of-the-art semantic parsers that are trained on gold-standard AMR datasets. On the other hand, with relatively little effort reasonable output is produced. For notoriously hard constructions such as control and coordination Boxer performs well.

The question remains whether this is a promising way of producing different semantic representations (i.e., AMRs instead of DRSs). It would be interesting for future research to investigate the possibility to make Boxer's syntax-semantics interface more transparent and transform the three-step process into two phases, eliminating the need for translating DRS to AMR. Needless to say, AMR is not a replacement for DRS, as it has less expressive power, but the ability to switch between the two formats would be a welcome feature.

```
(e6 / and                              (a / and
 :op1 (k1 / thug                         :op1 (t / thug
    :domain (x1 / they))                    :domain (t2 / they))
 :op2 (k2 / deserve-01                   :op2 (d / deserve-01
    :ARG0 x1                                :ARG0 t
    :ARG1 (x2 / bullet)))                   :ARG1 (b / bullet)))
```

Figure 3: They are thugs and deserve a bullet. (#111, F-score: 90.9, Boxer left, gold right)

```
(e1 / arrest-01                        (a / arrest-01
 :ARG1 (x1 / person                     :ARG1 (p / person :quant 1
   :ARG0-of (v1002 / protest-01)))         :ARG0-of (p2 / protest-01)))
```

Figure 4: A protester was arrested. (#710, F-score: 92.3, Boxer left, gold right)

```
(e1 / create-01                        (c3 / create-01
 :ARG1 (x1 / force                       :ARG0 (a / and
    :mod (s1 / country                      :op1 (c2 / country
       :name (p1002 / name                     :wiki "United_States"
        :op1 "afghanistan")                     :name (n2 / name :op1 "US"))
        :wiki "afghanistan" )              :op2 (c4 / coalition))
    :poss (x2 / security))               :ARG1 (f / force
 :ARG0 (x3 / and                           :purpose (s / security)
    :op1 (x4 / organization                :mod (c / country
       :name (n3 / name                       :wiki "Afghanistan"
        :op1 "us")                            :name (n / name
        :wiki "United_States" )                :op1 "Afghanistan")))))
    :op2 (x5 / coalition)))
```

Figure 5: The Afghan security force was created by the US and the coalition. (#300, F-score: 90.9, Boxer left, gold right)

```
(e1 / tell-01                          (t / tell-01
 :ARG0 (x1 / they)                       :ARG0 (t2 / they)
 :ARG1 (p1 / and                         :ARG1 (a / and
    :op1 (k1 / avoid-01                     :op1 (a2 / avoid-01
    :ARG0 (x2 / she)                        :ARG0 s
    :ARG1 (x3 / cafeteria))                 :ARG1 (c / cafeteria))
    :op2 (k2 / take-01                    :op2 (p / participate-01
    :ARG0 x2                                :polarity -
    :ARG1 (x4 / part)                       :ARG0 s
    :polarity -                             :ARG1 (h / homecoming)))
    :in (x5 / homecoming)))             :ARG2 (s / she))
 :ARG2 x2)
```

Figure 6: They told her to avoid the cafeteria and not take part in homecoming. (#151, F-score: 85.0, Boxer left, gold right)

```
(e1 / fall-01                          (f / fall-07
 :ARG0 (x1 / man                         :ARG1 (m / man
    :mod (s1 / innocent))                   :ARG1-of (i / innocent-01)
 :ARG1 (x2 / victim)                        :mod (a / another))
 :to (x3 / machine))                     :ARG2 (v / victimize-01
                                            :ARG0 (m2 / machine)
                                            :ARG1 m))
```

Figure 7: Another innocent man falls victim to the Machine. (#1024, F-score: 26.1, Boxer left, gold right)

Acknowledgments

We would like to thank the three anonymous reviewers for their helpful comments. We also thank Jon May for the splendid organization of the shared task. This work was partially funded by the NWO-VICI grant "Lost in Translation – Found in Meaning" (288-89-003).

References

Yoav Artzi, Kenton Lee, and Luke Zettlemoyer. 2015. Broad-coverage CCG semantic parsing with AMR. In *Proceedings of the 2015 Conference on Empirical Methods in Natural Language Processing, EMNLP 2015*, pages 1699–1710.

Johan Bos. 2008. Wide-Coverage Semantic Analysis with Boxer. In J. Bos and R. Delmonte, editors, *Semantics in Text Processing. STEP 2008 Conference Proceedings*, volume 1 of *Research in Computational Semantics*, pages 277–286. College Publications.

Johan Bos. 2015. Open-domain semantic parsing with boxer. In Beáta Megyesi, editor, *Proceedings of the 20th Nordic Conference of Computational Linguistics (NODALIDA 2015)*, pages 301–304.

Johan Bos. 2016. Expressive Power of Abstract Meaning Representations. *Computational Linguistics*, 42.

James Curran, Stephen Clark, and Johan Bos. 2007. Linguistically Motivated Large-Scale NLP with C&C and Boxer. In *Proceedings of the 45th Annual Meeting of the Association for Computational Linguistics Companion Volume Proceedings of the Demo and Poster Sessions*, pages 33–36, Prague, Czech Republic.

Joachim Daiber, Max Jakob, Chris Hokamp, and Pablo N. Mendes. 2013. Improving Efficiency and Accuracy in Multilingual Entity Extraction. In *Proceedings of the 9th International Conference on Semantic Systems (I-Semantics 2013)*, pages 121–124.

Kilian Evang, Valerio Basile, Grzegorz Chrupała, and Johan Bos. 2013. Elephant: Sequence labeling for word and sentence segmentation. In *Proceedings of the 2013 Conference on Empirical Methods in Natural Language Processing*, pages 1422–1426.

Hans Kamp and Uwe Reyle. 1993. *From Discourse to Logic; An Introduction to Modeltheoretic Semantics of Natural Language, Formal Logic and DRT*. Kluwer, Dordrecht.

Hans Kamp. 1984. A Theory of Truth and Semantic Representation. In Jeroen Groenendijk, Theo M.V. Janssen, and Martin Stokhof, editors, *Truth, Interpretation and Information*, pages 1–41. FORIS, Dordrecht – Holland/Cinnaminson – U.S.A.

Guido Minnen, John Carroll, and Darren Pearce. 2001. Applied morphological processing of english. *Journal of Natural Language Engineering*, 7(3):207–223.

Lev Ratinov, Dan Roth, Doug Downey, and Mike Anderson. 2011. Local and global algorithms for disambiguation to wikipedia. In *Proceedings of the 49th Annual Meeting of the Association for Computational Linguistics: Human Language Technologies - Volume 1*, pages 1375–1384.

Mark Steedman. 2001. *The Syntactic Process*. The MIT Press.

UofR at SemEval-2016 Task 8: Learning Synchronous Hyperedge Replacement Grammar for AMR Parsing

Xiaochang Peng and **Daniel Gildea**
Department of Computer Science
University of Rochester
Rochester, NY 14627

Abstract

In this paper, we apply a synchronous-graph-grammar-based approach to SemEval-2016 Task 8, Meaning Representation Parsing. In particular, we learn Synchronous Hyperedge Replacement Grammar (SHRG) rules from aligned pairs of sentences and AMR graphs. Then we use Earley algorithm with cube-pruning for AMR parsing given new sentences and the learned SHRG. Experiments on the evaluation dataset demonstrate that competitive results can be achieved using a SHRG-based approach.

1 Introduction

Abstract Meaning Representation (AMR) (Banarescu et al., 2013) is a semantic formalism where the meaning of a sentence is encoded as a rooted, directed graph. Figure 1 shows an example of the edge-labeled representation of an AMR graph, where the edges are labeled while the nodes are not. AMR utilizes PropBank frames, non-core semantic roles, coreference, named entity annotations and other semantic phenomena to represent the semantic structure of a sentence and abstracts away its syntax form. These properties render AMR representation useful in applications like question answering and semantics-based machine translation.

SemEval-2016 Task 8 is the task of recovering this type of semantic formalism for plain text. A large corpus of annotated English/AMR pairs is provided to learn this mapping. Hyperedge replacement grammar (HRG) is a context-free rewriting formalism for generating graphs (Drewes et al., 1997). Its

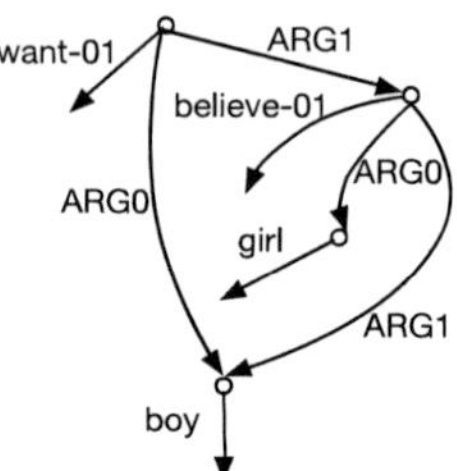

Figure 1: An example of AMR graph representing the meaning of: "The boy wants the girl to believe him"

synchronous counterpart, SHRG, can be used for transforming a graph from/to another structured representation such as a string or tree structure. Therefore, an SHRG-based approach can be used for AMR parsing. Previous approaches usually first map the components of the sentence to components of the graph. Then different supervised algorithms are used to assemble these graph components to generate a complete AMR graph (Flanigan et al., 2014; Wang et al., 2015b; Wang et al., 2015a).

Previously, we have developed a system that learns SHRG rules from sentence/AMR graph pairs (Peng et al., 2015), with automatic alignments extracted from JAMR (Flanigan et al., 2014). During the decoding procedure, we also use the concept identification results from Flanigan et al. (2014). The system is evaluated on the newswire section of LDC2013E117, which has around 4000 sentence-AMR pairs as training data.

In this paper, we extend this system by using the alignments from Ulf Hermjakob's automatic aligner and building a perceptron-based concept identifier where the boundary information of the mapped frag-

Proceedings of SemEval-2016, pages 1185–1189,
San Diego, California, June 16-17, 2016. ©2016 Association for Computational Linguistics

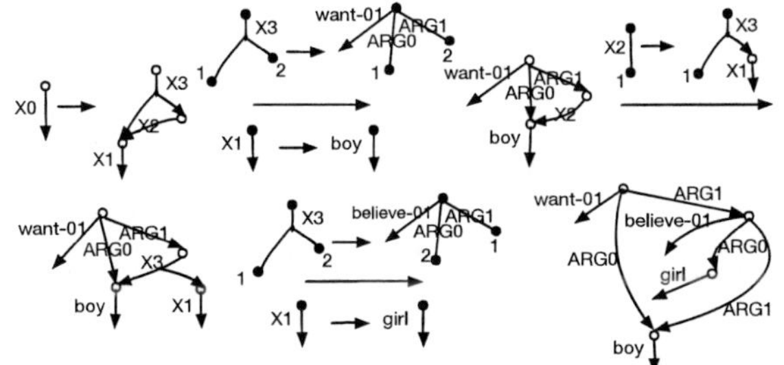

Figure 2: The series of HRG rules applied to derive the AMR graph of "The boy wants the girl to believe him". The first rule is directly shown. The other HRG rules are either above or below each right arrow. The white circle shows the root of each hyperedge. The indexes in each rule show the one-to-one mapping between the attachment nodes of l.h.s. nonterminal edges and the external nodes of the r.h.s. subgraph

ments is captured. We first introduce the overall pipeline of our parser. Then we describe the SHRG learning and the AMR parsing procedure in detail in Section 4 and Section 5. Finally we show the experimental results on the SemEval-2016 evaluation datasets.

2 Overall System Description

Our system is divided into two major components: SHRG learning and AMR parsing. Given English/AMR pairs and the automatic alignments from Ulf Hermjakob, we build a derivation forest representation of possible derivations. Markov Chain Monte Carlo (MCMC) algorithms are applied to sample a series of SHRG rules that generate each sentence/AMR pair.

Given the extracted SHRG and new sentences, we first identify the component spans on the string side. Then we use a perceptron classifier to find the graph fragment aligned to each of these spans. Finally, we use a decoder similar to those used for Synchronous Context-Free Grammar (SCFG) in machine translation, where the graph-side derivation is composed using HRG derivation instead of CFG, to get the AMR graphs for these sentences.

3 Hyperedge Replacement Grammar

HRG is similar to CFG in that it rewrites nonterminals independently. While CFG generates natural language strings by successively rewriting nonter-

minal tokens, the nonterminals in HRG are hyperedges, and each rewriting step in HRG replaces a hyperedge nonterminal with a subgraph instead of a span of a string.

The rewriting mechanism replaces a nonterminal hyperedge with the graph fragment specified by a production's righthand side (r.h.s.), attaching each external node of the r.h.s. to the corresponding attachment node of the lefthand side. Take Figure 2 as an example. Starting from our initial hypergraph with one edge labeled with the start symbol "$X0$", we select one edge with a nonterminal label in our current hypergraph, and rewrite it using a rule in our HRG. The first rule rewrites the start symbol with a subgraph shown on the r.h.s. We continue the rewriting steps until there are no more nonterminal-labeled edges.

We use the synchronous counterpart of HRG where the source side is a CFG and the target side is an HRG. Given such a synchronous grammar and a string as input, we can parse the string with the CFG side and then derive the counterpart graph by deduction from the derivation. The benefit of parsing with SHRG is that the complexity is bounded by that of CFG parsing. Table 2 shows the rule format of our SHRG. For each nonterminal $Xi\text{-}b_1 \cdots b_i$, i defines the type of the nonterminal, while each b_i indicates whether the i-th external node will have a concept edge in the rewriting result. This design guarantees that there is exactly one concept edge going out of each node.

4 Learning Synchronous Hyperedge Replacement Grammar

The **fragment decomposition forest** represents all possible ways to decompose the sentence-AMR pairs into component-level alignments. It also encodes a compact representation of possible SHRG derivations that are consistent with the alignments.

Therefore, starting with the component-level alignment pairs, we keep composing large span/fragment pairs from bottom up to build the derivation forest. Then we use Gibbs sampling to sample one derivation from the forest representation.

	JAMR	Ulf Hermjakob
string side	span, can be multiple	single token
graph side	concept fragments	single concept/relation
prepositions	usually not aligned	relation edges
mapping type	one-to-one	multiple-to-multiple

Table 1: Comparisons of English-AMR alignments from JAMR and Ulf Hermjakob

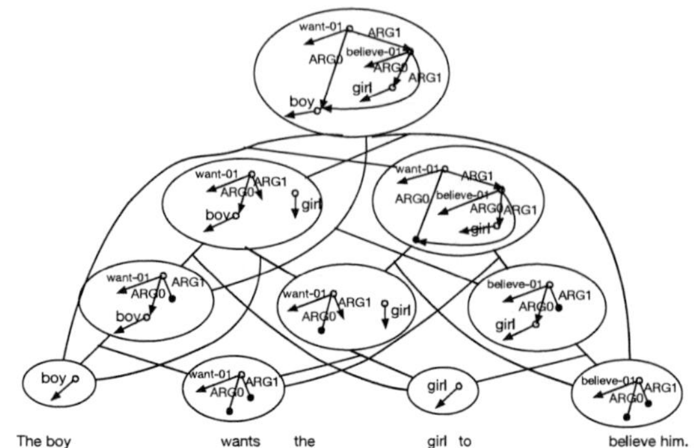

Figure 3: The fragment decomposition forest for the (sentence, AMR graph) pair for "The boy wants the girl to believe him"

4.1 Constructing Derivation Forests

We use the alignments from Ulf Hermjakob's aligner, which are provided for the training data. Some differences between this alignment and the alignment from JAMR (Flanigan et al., 2014) are summarized in Table 1. As the alignment is between a single token and a single concept/relation, we first heuristically identify the mappings of name entities by tracing the *:op* and *:name* relations. For each of the other aligned tokens, we compose its aligned concept or fragment.[1] There are also situations where multiple tokens are aligned to the same concept or relation. If they are adjacent, we compose them on the string side to form a larger span. Otherwise we delete the alignment of the shorter span to make the alignment one-to-one. We additionally use lemma information to retrieve some mappings from unaligned tokens to unaligned concepts.[2]

After we have extracted these alignments, we build the fragment decomposition forest from bottom up and left to right, gradually composing larger

---

[1]Our parser currently does not support multi-root graph fragments, so for alignments that align one token to multiple disconnected fragments, we only choose the largest fragment as the aligned fragment.

[2]Following Peng et al. (2015), we attach *:ARGs* and *:ops* to their head concepts and *:ARGx-of*s to their tail concepts.

(span, fragment) pairs from smaller ones until we have reached the root of the forest: the whole sentence-AMR pair. We maintain an ordered list of external nodes for each fragment, which will be used to track the order of the external nodes during the rule extraction phase. Figure 3 shows an example of a fragment decomposition forest. The forest construction procedure is described in detail in Peng et al. (2015).

Each node in the forest represents a span-fragment pair. We extract all span-fragment pairs of length smaller than 7 to construct a span to fragments alignment table Φ, which will be used during the concept identification procedure in Section 5.1

4.2 SHRG Learning Using MCMC

The fragment decomposition forest represents possible derivations of the sentence/AMR pairs in terms of minimal rules extracted from the alignments. We use an MCMC algorithm to learn a grammar of larger rules, by sampling both which minimal rules are used, and how minimal rules combine to form larger composed rules.

We sample two types of variables: an edge variable e_n representing which incoming hyperedge is chosen at a given node n in the forest (allowing us to sample one tree from a forest) and a cut variable z_n representing whether node n in the forest is a boundary between two SHRG rules or is internal to an SHRG rule (allowing us to sample rules/fragments from a tree). We use an MCMC algorithm to sample from top-down and one variable at a time (Peng and Gildea, 2014). Sampling tree fragments from forests is described in detail in Chung et al. (2014). Table 2 shows some examples of the sampled SHRG rules.

5 AMR parsing

In Section 4 we have described how we extract the SHRG from the training data. Now given a new sentence, we first use the perceptron algorithm to identify the graph fragments each span in the sentence aligns to. Then we use the Earley algorithm to decode the sentence and recover its AMR graph.

5.1 Concept Identification

First we identify the segmentation of the sentence. We use the Illinois Named Entity Tagger (NER) (Ratinov and Roth, 2009) to identify all the

| [A1-1] → ordinary people \| (. :p/person :mod (. :o/ordinary)) |
| [A0-1] → [A1-1,1] say that [A1-1,2] \| |
| (. :s/say-01 :ARG0 (. :[A1-1,1]) :ARG1 (. :[A1-1,2])) |
| [A0-1] → Do [A1-1,1] ? \| (. :[A1-1,1] :mode (. :interrogative)) |

Table 2: Some example of learned rules

	Precision	Recall	F-score
Dev	0.57	0.55	0.56
Test	0.56	0.55	0.55
Task 8 eval	-	-	0.50

Table 3: Parsing results on dev and test LDC2015E86 and the evaluation data of SemEval-2016 Task 8

named entities. We also use heuristic rules to identify dates, time expressions etc. We heuristically build the AMR fragments for these spans and add the mappings to Φ.[3] The other spans are of length 1. Then we use the perceptron algorithm to predict the AMR fragment for each span:

$$\hat{g}[e] = \arg\max_{g \in \Phi(e)} w^T f(e, g, c) \qquad (1)$$

where w is the weights, and f is the feature function. e is the current span, g is a candidate graph fragment from the span to fragment table Φ or matched using regular expressions. c is the context of span e. We use the following context features:

1. 3 words, pos tags, lemmas before and after the current span
2. 3 word, pos tag or lemma bigrams before and after the current span
3. the words, pos tags and lemmas in the current span
4. Length of the span

Our concept identification result is different from Flanigan et al. (2014) in that we are predicting not only the graph fragments but also the external nodes of each fragment. Therefore, each identified mapping is essentially a lexical SHRG rule at the leaf-level of the derivation tree. We add these identified lexical rules to the extracted SHRG locally before decoding each sentence. For lexical rules in Φ that cover more than 1 span of the sentence on the string side, we also add them to the SHRG locally.[4]

5.2 Decoding

Given the learned SHRG, we are simply parsing on the string side. We use the Earley algorithm with cube-pruning (Chiang, 2007) for the string-to-AMR

---

[3]As the named entity labels from Illinois NER is only a few, we predict their entity label from an entity label set built on the training data.

[4]We filter some rules that have non-content words on the left or right because such rules introduce a lot of errors from the alignments.

parsing. For each synchronous rule with N nonterminals on its l.h.s., we build an $N + 1$ dimensional cube and generate the top K candidates. Out of all the hypotheses generated by all satisfied rules within each span (i, j), we keep at most K candidates for this span. Our glue rules generate a pseudo *m/multisentence* concept and use *ARG* relations to connect disconnected components to make the result graph connected. The features used are described in Peng et al. (2015).

6 Experiments

We evaluate our parser on the LDC2015E86 dataset, which includes 16833 training, 1368 dev, and 1371 test sentences.

During the sampling procedure, all the cut variables in the derivation forest are initialized as 1 and an incoming hyperedge is sampled uniformly for each node. We run the sampler for 160 iterations and combine the grammar dumped every 10th iteration.

The performance of our SHRG-based parser is evaluated using Smatch v2.0.2 (Cai and Knight, 2013), which evaluates the precision, recall, and $F1$ of the concepts and relations all together. Table 3 shows the results on the dev and test set. We also report smatch score on the shared task evaluation data, which includes 1053 sentences. The smatch score on the evaluation data is 0.50. This score is much lower than the performance on the dev and test data. The reason might be that the evaluation data is much harder and includes more noise, which can break down the structure of the learned grammar.

The results show that SHRG-based parsing can be a viable approach for AMR parsing. Currently our system only uses a few simple features and all the weights are tuned by hand. The performance could be improved by using more complicated features and tuning their weights automatically. It would also be helpful to use external resources such as the common organizational roles, relational roles and the verbalization lists [5] and use fallback techniques to deal with unknown words.

7 Conclusion

In this paper, we have presented our SHRG-based AMR parsing system for SemEval-2016 Task 8. Our system extends from the work of Peng et al. (2015) and has shown some competitive results for a graph-grammar-based approach for AMR parsing. Currently our system only uses local features for decoding; it would be interesting to extend this system to incorporate a language model on the graph side and use discriminative models to incorporate more global features and tune the weights automatically.

Acknowledgments

Funded in part by NSF IIS-1446996, and a Google Faculty Research Award.

References

Laura Banarescu, Claire Bonial, Shu Cai, Madalina Georgescu, Kira Griffitt, Ulf Hermjakob, Kevin Knight, Philipp Koehn, Martha Palmer, and Nathan Schneider. 2013. Abstract meaning representation for sembanking. In *Proceedings of the 7th Linguistic Annotation Workshop and Interoperability with Discourse*.

Shu Cai and Kevin Knight. 2013. Smatch: an evaluation metric for semantic feature structures. In *ACL (2)*, pages 748–752.

David Chiang. 2007. Hierarchical phrase-based translation. *Computational Linguistics*, 33(2):201–228.

Tagyoung Chung, Licheng Fang, Daniel Gildea, and Daniel Štefankovič. 2014. Sampling tree fragments from forests. *Computational Linguistics*, 40(1):203–229.

Frank Drewes, Hans-Jörg Kreowski, and Annegret Habel. 1997. Hyperedge replacement, graph grammars. In *Handbook of Graph Grammars*, volume 1, pages 95–162. World Scientific, Singapore.

Jeffrey Flanigan, Sam Thomson, Jaime Carbonell, Chris Dyer, and Noah A Smith. 2014. A discriminative graph-based parser for the abstract meaning representation. In *Proc. of ACL*, pages 1426–1436.

Xiaochang Peng and Daniel Gildea. 2014. Type-based MCMC for sampling tree fragments from forests. In *Conference on Empirical Methods in Natural Language Processing (EMNLP-14)*.

Xiaochang Peng, Linfeng Song, and Daniel Gildea. 2015. A synchronous hyperedge replacement grammar based approach for amr parsing. In *Proceedings of the Nineteenth Conference on Computational Natural Language Learning*, pages 32–41, Beijing, China.

Lev Ratinov and Dan Roth. 2009. Design challenges and misconceptions in named entity recognition. In *Proceedings of the Thirteenth Conference on Computational Natural Language Learning (CoNLL-2009)*, pages 147–155, Boulder, Colorado, June. Association for Computational Linguistics.

Chuan Wang, Nianwen Xue, and Sameer Pradhan. 2015a. Boosting transition-based AMR parsing with refined actions and auxiliary analyzers. In *Proceedings of the 53rd Annual Meeting of the Association for Computational Linguistics and the 7th International Joint Conference on Natural Language Processing (Volume 2: Short Papers)*, pages 857–862, Beijing, China, July. Association for Computational Linguistics.

Chuan Wang, Nianwen Xue, and Sameer Pradhan. 2015b. A transition-based algorithm for AMR parsing. In *Proceedings of the 2015 Conference of the North American Chapter of the Association for Computational Linguistics: Human Language Technologies*, pages 366–375, Denver, Colorado, May–June. Association for Computational Linguistics.

---

[5]http://amr.isi.edu/download.html

CLIP@UMD at SemEval-2016 Task 8: Parser for Abstract Meaning Representation using Learning to Search

Sudha Rao[1,3]*, **Yogarshi Vyas**[1,3]*, **Hal Daumé III**[1,3], **Philip Resnik**[2,3]
[1]Computer Science, [2]Linguistics, [3]UMIACS
University of Maryland
{raosudha,yogarshi,hal}@cs.umd.edu, resnik@umd.edu

Abstract

In this paper we describe our approach to the Abstract Meaning Representation (AMR) parsing shared task as part of SemEval 2016. We develop a novel technique to parse English sentences into AMR using Learning to Search. We decompose the AMR parsing task into three subtasks - that of predicting the concepts, the relations, and the root. Each of these subtasks are treated as a sequence of predictions. Using Learning to Search, we add past predictions as features for future predictions, and define a combined loss over the entire AMR structure.

1 Introduction

This paper describes our submission to the Abstract Meaning Representation (AMR) Parsing Shared Task at SemEval 2016. The goal of the task is to generate AMRs automatically for English sentences. We develop a novel technique for AMR parsing that uses Learning to Search (L2S) (Ross et al., 2011; Daumé III et al., 2009; Collins and Roark, 2004).

L2S is a family of approaches that solves structured prediction problems. These algorithms have proven to be highly effective for problems in NLP like part-of-speech tagging, named entity recognition (Daumé III et al., 2014), coreference resolution (Ma et al., 2014), and dependency parsing (He et al., 2013). Briefly, L2S attempts to do structured prediction by (1) decomposing the production of the structured output in terms of an explicit search space (states, actions, etc.); and (2) learning hypotheses

---

The first two authors contributed equally to this work.

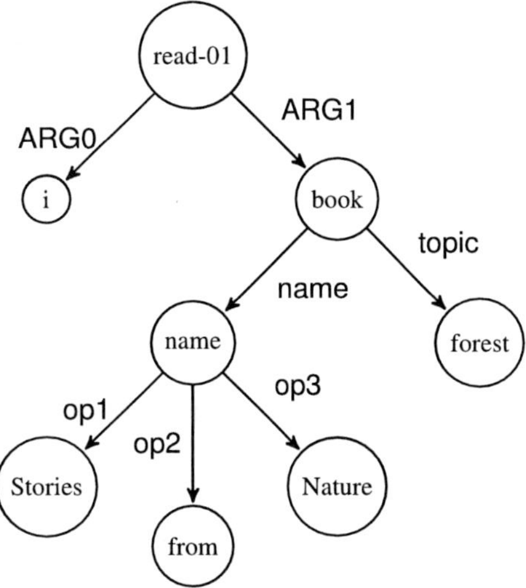

Figure 1: AMR graph for the sentence *"I read a book, called Stories from Nature, about the forest."*

that control a policy that takes actions in this search space. AMR (Banarescu et al., 2013), in turn, is a structured semantic representation which is a rooted, directed, acyclic graph. The nodes of this graph represent concepts in the given sentence and the edges represent relations between these concepts. As such, the task of predicting AMRs can be naturally placed in the L2S framework. This allows us to model the learning of concepts and relations in a unified setting which aims to minimize the loss over the entire predicted structure.

In the next section, we briefly review DAGGER and explain its various components with respect to our AMR parsing task. Section 3 describes our main algorithm along with the strategies we use to deal with the large search space of the search problem.

Proceedings of SemEval-2016, pages 1190–1196,
San Diego, California, June 16-17, 2016. ©2016 Association for Computational Linguistics

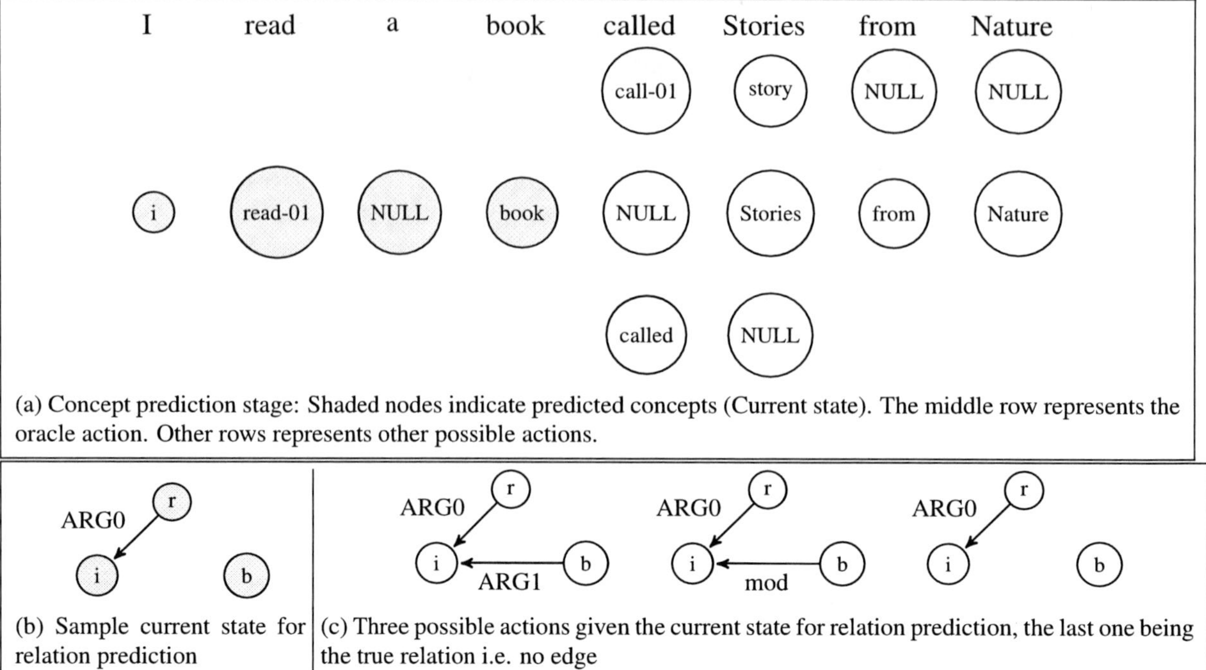

(a) Concept prediction stage: Shaded nodes indicate predicted concepts (Current state). The middle row represents the oracle action. Other rows represents other possible actions.

(b) Sample current state for relation prediction

(c) Three possible actions given the current state for relation prediction, the last one being the true relation i.e. no edge

Figure 2: Using DAGGER for AMR parsing

We then describe our experiments and results (Section 4).

2 Using L2S for AMR Parsing

L2S works on the notion of a policy which can be defined as "what is the best next action (y_i) to take" in a search space given the current state. It starts with an initial policy on a trajectory (called rollin policy), takes a one-step deviation and completes the trajectory with another policy (called the rollout policy). The different variations of L2S are defined based on what kind of policies it uses during rollin and rollout. For example DAGGER uses rollin=learned policy and rollout=reference policy, SEARN uses rollin=rollout=stochastic mixture of reference and learned policy, LOLS uses rollin=learned policy and rollout=stochastic mixture of reference and learned policy.

Next, we describe how we use L2S for AMR parsing. We decompose the full AMR parsing task into three subtasks - that of predicting the concepts, predicting the root, and predicting the relations between the predicted concepts (explained in more detail under section 3). The search space for concept and relation prediction consists of a state $s = (x_1, x_2, ..., x_m, y_1, y_2, .., y_{i-1})$, where the input $(x_1, x_2, ..., x_m)$ are the m words of a sentence.

- During concept prediction, the labels $(y_1, y_2, .., y_{i-1})$ are the concepts predicted up to the index $(i - 1)$ and the next action y_i is the concept for word x_i from a k-best list of concepts. In Figure 2a, the current state corresponds to the concepts {'i', 'read-01', 'book'} and the next action is assigning one of {'call-01', 'called', NULL} to the word 'called'.

- During relation prediction, the labels are the relations predicted for pairs of concepts obtained during the concept prediction stage. In Figure 2c, the current state corresponds to the relation 'ARG0' predicted between 'r' and 'i' and the next action is assigning one of {'ARG1', 'mod', NO-EDGE} to the pair of concept 'b' and 'i'.

For the root prediction subtask we train a multiclass classifier which makes a single prediction - that of choosing the root concept from all the predicted concepts.

Next, we need to define how we learn a policy for AMR parsing. When the reference policy is optimal, it has been shown that it is effective to rollout using the reference policy (Ross and Bagnell, 2014; Chang et al., 2015). This is true for our task and hence we use DAGGER. Below, we explain how we use DAGGER, with a running example in Figure 2.

At training time, DAGGER operates in an iterative fashion. It starts with an initial policy and given an input x, makes a prediction $y = y_1, y_2, ..., y_m$ using the current policy. For each prediction y_i it generates a set of multi-class classification examples each of which correspond to a possible action the algorithm can take given the current state. Each example can be defined using local features and features that depend on previous predictions. We use a one-against-all classifier to make the multi-class classification decisions.

During training, DAGGER has access to the reference policy. The reference policy during concept prediction is to predict the concept that was aligned to a given span using the JAMR aligner (explained in Section 3.4) For e.g. in Figure 2a, the reference policy is to predict NULL since the span "called" was aligned to NULL by the aligner. The reference policy during relation prediction is to predict the gold edge between two concepts. For e.g. in Figure 2c, the reference policy is to predict NO-EDGE.

DAGGER then calculates the loss between the predicted action and the best action using a pre-specified loss function. It then computes a new policy based on this loss and interpolates it with the current policy to get an updated policy, before moving on to the next iteration. At test time, predictions are made greedily using the policy learned during training.

3 Methodology

3.1 Learning technique

We use DAGGER as described in Section 2 to learn a model that can successfully predict the AMR y for a sentence x. The sentence x is composed of a sequence of spans $(s_1, s_2, ..., s_n)$ each of which can be a single word or a span of words (We describe how we go from a raw sentence to a sequence of spans

---

Algorithm 1

1: **for** *each span s_i* **do**
2:    $c_i = predict\_concept(s_i)$
3: **end for**
4: $c_{root} = predict\_root([c_1, ..., c_n])$
5: **for** *each concept c_i* **do**
6:    **for** *each $j < i$* **do**
7:       $r_{(i,j)} = predict\_relation(c_i, c_j)$
8:       $r_{(j,i)} = predict\_relation(c_j, c_i)$
9:    **end for**
10: **end for**

---

in Section 3.4). Given that our input has n spans, we first decompose the structure into a sequence of $n^2 + 1$ predictions $\mathbf{D} = (\mathbf{C}, \mathbf{ROOT}, \mathbf{R})$, where

$\mathbf{C} = c_1, c_2, ..., c_n$ - where c_i is the concept predicted for span s_i

$\mathbf{ROOT}$ is the decision of choosing one of the predicted concepts as the root (c_{root}) of the AMR

$\mathbf{R} = r_{2,*}, r_{*,2}, r_{3,*}, r_{*,3}, ..., r_{n,*}, r_{*,n}$ - where $r_{i,*}$ are the predictions for the directed relations from c_i to c_j $\forall j < i$, and $r_{*,i}$ are the predictions for the directed relations from c_j to c_i $\forall j < i$. We constrain our algorithm to not predict any incoming relations to c_{root}.

During training time, the possible set of actions for each prediction is given by the k-best list (Section 3.2). We use Hamming Loss as our loss function. Under Hamming Loss, the reference policy is simply choosing the right action for each prediction i.e. choosing the correct concept (relation) during the concept (relation) prediction phase. This loss is defined on the entire predicted output, and hence the model learns to minimize the loss for concepts and relations jointly.

Algorithm 1 describes the sequence of predictions to be made in our problem. We learn three different policies corresponding to each of the functions *predict_concept*, *predict_root* and *predict_relation*. The learner in each stage uses features that depend on predictions made in the previous stages. Tables 1, 2 and 3 describe the set of features we use for the concept prediction, relation prediction and root prediction stages respectively.

Feature label	Description
$w_{i-2}, w_{i-i}, w_i, w_{i+1}, w_{i+2}$	Words in s_i and context
$p_{i-2}, p_{i-i}, p_i, p_{i+1}, p_{i+2}$	POS tags of words in s_i and context
NE_i	Named entity tags for words in s_i
s_i	Binary feature indicating whether w_i is(are) stopword(s)
dep_i	All dependency edges originating from words in w_i
b_c	Binary feature indicating whether c is the most frequently aligned concept with s_i or not
c_{i-2}, c_{i-1}	Predicted concepts for two previous spans
c	Concept label and its conjunction with all previous features
$frame_i$ and $sense_i$	If the label is a PropBank frame (e.g. 'see-01', use the frame ('see') and the sense('01') as additional features.

Table 1: Concept prediction features for span s_i and concept label c_i

Feature label	Description
$c_i, c_j, c_i \wedge c_j$	The two concepts and their conjunction
$w_i, w_j, w_i \wedge w_j$	Words in the corresponding spans and their conjunction
$p_i, p_j, p_i \wedge p_j$	POS tags of words in spans and their conjunction
dep_{ij}	All dependency edges with tail in w_i and head in w_j
dir	Binary feature which is true iff $i < j$
r	Relation label and its conjunction with all other features

Table 2: Relation prediction features for concepts c_i and c_j and relation label r

Feature label	Description
c_i	Concept label. If the label is a PropBank frame (e.g. 'see-01', use the frame ('see') and the sense('01') as additional features.
w_i	Words in s_i, i.e. the span corresponding to c_i
p_i	POS tags of words in s_i
$is\_dep\_root_i$	Binary feature indicating whether one of the words in s_i is the root in the dependency tree of the sentence

Table 3: Root prediction features for concept c_i

3.2 Selecting k-best lists

For predicting the concepts and relations using DAG-GER, we need a candidate-list (possible set of actions) to make predictions from.

Concept candidates: For a span s_i, the candidate-list of concepts, CL-CON$_{s_i}$ is the set of all concepts that were aligned to s_i in the entire training data. If s_i has not been seen in the training data, CL-CON$_{s_i}$ consists of the lemmatized span, PropBank frames (for verbs) obtained using the Unified Verb Index (Schuler, 2005) and the NULL concept.

Relation candidates: The candidate list of relations for a relation from concept c_i to concept c_j, CL-REL$_{ij}$, is the union of the following three sets:

- $pairwise_{i,j}$ - All directed relations from c_i to c_j when c_i and c_j occurred in the same AMR,
- $outgoing_i$ - All outgoing relations from c_i, and
- $incoming_j$ - All incoming relations into c_j.

In the case when both c_i and c_j have not been seen in the training data, CL-REL$_{ij}$ consists of all relations seen in the training data. In both cases, we also provide an option NO-EDGE which indicates that there is no relation between c_i and c_j.

3.3 Pruning the search space

To prune the search space of our learning task, and to improve the quality of predictions, we use two observations about the nature of the edges of the AMR of a sentence, and its dependency tree (obtained using the Stanford dependency parser (De Marneffe et al., 2006)), within our algorithm.

First, we observe that a large fraction of the edges in the AMR for a sentence are between concepts whose underlying spans (more specifically, the words in these underlying spans) are within two edges of each other in the dependency tree of the sentence. Thus, we refrain from calling the *predict_relation* function in Algorithm 1 between concepts c_i and c_j if each word in w_i is three or more edges away from all words in w_j in the dependency tree of the sentence under consideration, and vice versa. This implies that there will be no relation r_{ij} in the predicted AMR of that sentence. This doesn't affect the number of calls to *predict_relation* in the worst case ($n^2 - n$, for a sentence with n spans), but practically, the number of calls are far fewer. Also, to make sure that this method does not filter out too many AMR edges, we calculated the percentage of AMR edges that are more than two edges away in dependency tree. We found this number to be only about 5% across all our datasets.

Secondly, and conversely, we observe that for a large fraction of words which have a dependency edge between them, there is an edge in the AMR between the concepts corresponding to those two words. Thus, when we observe two concepts c_i and c_j which satisfy this property, we force our *predict_relation* function to assign a relation r_{ij} that is not NULL.

3.4 Preprocessing

JAMR Aligner: The training data for AMR parsing consists of sentences paired with corresponding AMRs. To convert a raw sentence into a sequence of spans (as required by our algorithm), we obtain alignments between words in the sentence and concepts in the AMR using the automatic aligner of JAMR. The alignments obtained can be of three types (Examples refer to Figure 1):

- *A single word aligned to a single concept*: E.g., word 'read' aligned to concept 'read-01'.
- *Span of words aligned to a graph fragment*: E.g., span 'Stories from Nature' aligned to the graph fragment rooted at 'name'. This usually happens for named entities and multiword ex-

pressions such as those related to date and time.
- *A word aligned to* NULL *concept*: Most function words like 'about', 'a', 'the', etc are not aligned to any particular concept. These are considered to be aligned to the NULL concept.

Forced alignments: The JAMR aligner does not align all concepts in a given AMR to a span in the sentence. We use a heuristic to forcibly align these leftover concepts and improve the quality of alignments. For every unaligned concept, we count the number of times an unaligned word occurs in the same sentence with the unaligned concept across all training examples. We then align every leftover concept in every sentence with the unaligned word in sentence with which it has maximally coocurred.

Span identification: During training time, the aligner takes in a sentence and its AMR graph and splits each sentence into spans that can be aligned to the concepts in the AMR. However, during test time, we do not have access to the AMR graph. Hence, given a test sentence, we need to split the sentence into spans, on which we can predict concepts. We consider each word as a single span except for two cases. First, we detect possible multiword spans corresponding to named entities, using a named entity recognizer (Lafferty et al., 2001). Second, we use some basic regular expressions to identify time and date expressions in sentences.

3.5 Connectivity

Algorithm 1 does not place explicit constraints on the structure of the AMR. Hence, the predicted output can have disconnected components. Since we want the predicted AMR to be connected, we connect the disconnected components (if any) using the following heuristic. For each component, we find its roots (i.e. concepts with no incoming relations). We then connect the components together by simply adding an edge from our predicted root c_{root} to each of the component roots. To decide what edge to use between our predicted root c_{root} and the root of a component, we get the k-best list (as described in section 3.2) between them and choose the most frequent edge from it.

Dataset	Training	Dev	Test
BOLT DF MT	1061	133	133
Broadcast conversation	214	0	0
Weblog and WSJ	0	100	100
BOLT DF English	6455	210	229
Guidelines AMRs	689	0	0
2009 Open MT	204	0	0
Proxy reports	6603	826	823
Weblog	866	0	0
Xinhua MT	741	99	86

Table 4: Dataset statistics. All figures represent number of sentences.

3.6 Acyclicity

The post-processing step described in the previous section ensures that the predicted AMRs are rooted, connected, graphs. However, an AMR, by definition, is also acyclic. We do not model this constraint explicitly within our learning framework. Despite this, we observe that only a very small number of AMRs predicted using our fully automatic approach have cycles in them. Out of the total AMRs predicted in all test sets, less than 5% have cycles in them. Besides, almost all cycles that are predicted consist of only two nodes, i.e. both r_{ij} and r_{ji} have non-NO-EDGE values for concepts c_i and c_j. To get an acyclic graph, we can greedily select one of r_{ij} or r_{ji}, without any loss in parser performance.

4 Experiments and Results

The primary corpus for this shared task is the AMR Annotation Release 1.0 (LDC2015E86). This corpus consists of datasets from varied domains such as online discussion forums, blogs, and newswire, with about 19,000 sentence-AMR pairs. All datasets have a pre-specified training, dev and test split (Table 4).

We trained three systems. The first was trained on all available training data. The two other systems were trained using data from a single domain. Specifically, we chose *BOLT DF English* and *Proxy reports* since these are the two largest training datasets individually. The system trained on the *Proxy reports* dataset performed the best when evaluated on the dev set. Hence we used this system as our primary system for the task. Additionally, we use DAGGER as implemented in the Vowpal Wab-

bit machine learning library (Langford et al., 2007; Daumé III et al., 2014).

The evaluation of predicted AMRs is done using Smatch (Cai and Knight, 2013) [1], which compares two AMRs using precision, recall and F_1. Our system obtained a Smatch F_1 score of 0.46 with a *Precision* of 0.51 and a *Recall* of 0.43 on the test set in the Shared Task (We made a tokenization error during the actual semeval submission and so reported an F_1 score of 0.44 instead). The mean F_1 score of all systems submitted to the shared task was 0.55 and the standard deviation was 0.06.

5 Conclusion and Future work

We have presented a novel technique for parsing English sentences into AMR using DAGGER, a Learning to Search algorithm. We decompose the AMR parsing task into subtasks of concept prediction, root prediction and relation prediction. Using Learning to Search allows us to use past predictions as features for future predictions and also define a combined loss over the entire AMR structure. Additionally, we use a k-best candidate list constructed from the training data to make predictions from. To prune the large search space, we incorporate useful heuristics based on the dependency parse of the sentence. Our system is available for download [2].

Currently we ensure various properties of AMR, such as connectedness and acyclicity using heuristics. In the future, we plan to incorporate these as constraints in our learning technique.

References

Laura Banarescu, Claire Bonial, Shu Cai, Madalina Georgescu, Kira Griffitt, Ulf Hermjakob, Kevin Knight, Philipp Koehn, Martha Palmer, and Nathan Schneider. 2013. Abstract meaning representation for sembanking.

Shu Cai and Kevin Knight. 2013. Smatch: an evaluation metric for semantic feature structures. In *Proceedings of the 51st Annual Meeting of the Association for Computational Linguistics, ACL 2013, 4-9 August 2013, Sofia, Bulgaria, Volume 2: Short Papers*, pages 748–752.

---

[1] http://amr.isi.edu/download/smatch-v2.0.tar.gz

[2] http://cs.umd.edu/~yogarshi/amr_parser.zip

Kai-Wei Chang, Akshay Krishnamurthy, Alekh Agarwal, Hal Daumé III, and John Langford. 2015. Learning to search better than your teacher. In *Proceedings of the 32nd International Conference on Machine Learning, ICML 2015, Lille, France, 6-11 July 2015*, pages 2058–2066.

Michael Collins and Brian Roark. 2004. Incremental parsing with the perceptron algorithm. In *Proceedings of the 42nd Annual Meeting on Association for Computational Linguistics*, page 111. Association for Computational Linguistics.

Hal Daumé III, John Langford, and Daniel Marcu. 2009. Search-based structured prediction. *Machine learning*, 75(3):297–325.

Hal Daumé III, John Langford, and Stephane Ross. 2014. Efficient programmable learning to search. *arXiv preprint arXiv:1406.1837*.

Marie-Catherine De Marneffe, Bill MacCartney, Christopher D Manning, et al. 2006. Generating typed dependency parses from phrase structure parses. In *Proceedings of LREC*, volume 6, pages 449–454.

He He, Hal Daumé III, and Jason Eisner. 2013. Dynamic feature selection for dependency parsing. In *Proceedings of the 2013 Conference on Empirical Methods in Natural Language Processing, EMNLP 2013, 18-21 October 2013, Grand Hyatt Seattle, Seattle, Washington, USA, A meeting of SIGDAT, a Special Interest Group of the ACL*, pages 1455–1464.

John Lafferty, Andrew McCallum, and Fernando CN Pereira. 2001. Conditional random fields: Probabilistic models for segmenting and labeling sequence data.

John Langford, Lihong Li, and Alexander Strehl. 2007. Vowpal wabbit online learning project.

Chao Ma, Janardhan Rao Doppa, J Walker Orr, Prashanth Mannem, Xiaoli Fern, Tom Dietterich, and Prasad Tadepalli. 2014. Prune-and-score: Learning for greedy coreference resolution. In *Proceedings of Conference on Empirical Methods in Natural Language Processing (EMNLP)*.

Stephane Ross and J Andrew Bagnell. 2014. Reinforcement and imitation learning via interactive no-regret learning. *arXiv preprint arXiv:1406.5979*.

Stéphane Ross, Geoff J. Gordon, and J. Andrew Bagnell. 2011. A reduction of imitation learning and structured prediction to no-regret online learning. In *Proceedings of the Workshop on Artificial Intelligence and Statistics (AIStats)*.

Karin Kipper Schuler. 2005. Verbnet: A broad-coverage, comprehensive verb lexicon.

CU-NLP at SemEval-2016 Task 8: AMR Parsing using LSTM-based Recurrent Neural Networks

William R. Foland Jr.
OK Robot Go, Ltd.
5345 Dunraven Circle
Golden, Co, 80403, USA
bill.foland@okrobotgo.com

James H. Martin
Department of Computer Science and
Institute of Cognitive Science
University of Colorado
Boulder, CO 80309
James.Martin@colorado.edu

Abstract

We describe the system used in our participation in the AMR Parsing task for SemEval-2016. Our parser does not rely on a syntactic pre-parse, or heavily engineered features, and uses five recurrent neural networks as the key architectural components for estimating AMR graph structure.

1 Introduction

Abstract Meaning Representation, or AMR (Banarescu et al., 2012) is a graph-based representation of the meaning of sentences which incorporates linguistic phenomena such as semantic roles, coreference, negation, and more.[1]

The process of creating AMR's for sentences is called AMR Parsing. We used an early version of the system described in this paper to generate our submission to the Semeval-2016 Meaning Representation Parsing Task.[2]

The details of our system will be explained using this example sentence: *France plans further nuclear cooperation with numerous countries .* A graphical depiction is shown in Figure 1.

The system extracts features from the sentence which are processed by a form of recurrent neural network called BDLSTM to create a set of AMR concepts. Features from these concepts are processed by a pair of BDLSTM networks to compute relation probabilities. All concepts are then connected using an iterative, greedy algorithm to compute the set of relations in the AMR. Another two

---

[1]http://amr.isi.edu/language.html
[2]http://alt.qcri.org/semeval2016/task8/#

BDLSTM networks compute attribute and name categories to complete the estimation of AMR element probabilities.

2 Related Work

Most current AMR parsers assume input that has undergone varying degrees of syntactic analysis, ranging from simple part-of-speech tagging to more complex dependency or phrase-structure analysis. (Wang et al., 2015; Vanderwende et al., 2015; Peng et al., 2015; Pust et al., 2015; Artzi et al., 2015; Flanigan et al., 2014; Werling et al., 2015). In contrast, we follow the spirit of minimal feature extraction using pre-trained word embeddings, as in (Collobert et al., 2011) and a recurrent network architecture similar to that described in (Zhou and Xu, 2015).

3 System Architecture

3.1 Feature Extraction

In our system, all features are represented by embedding vectors, trained and stored in lookup tables. Word feature embeddings are mapped from the words in the sentence, and are trained with back propagation just like other parameters in the network. They are initialized with vectors which are pre-trained on large corpora of english text, we use the word embeddings from (Collobert et al., 2011).

The only explicit features not derived from the raw input are features based on named entity recognition (NER). We first use the Univ. of Illinois Wikifier to find and classify named entities and then encode these features as embeddings.

Proceedings of SemEval-2016, pages 1197–1201,
San Diego, California, June 16-17, 2016. ©2016 Association for Computational Linguistics

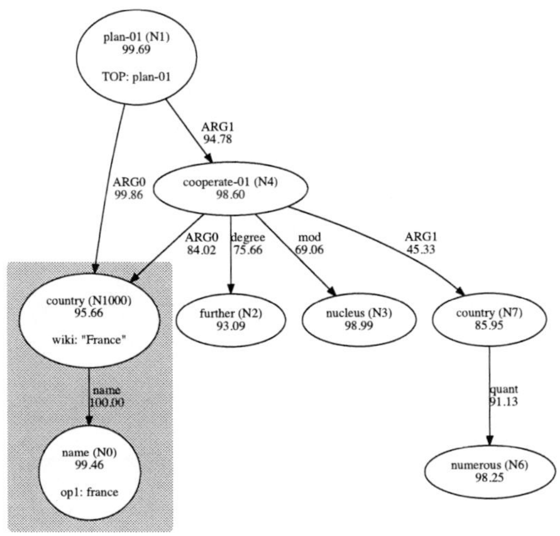

Figure 1: Graphical Representation of the Reference AMR (annotated with probabilities expressed as percentage.)

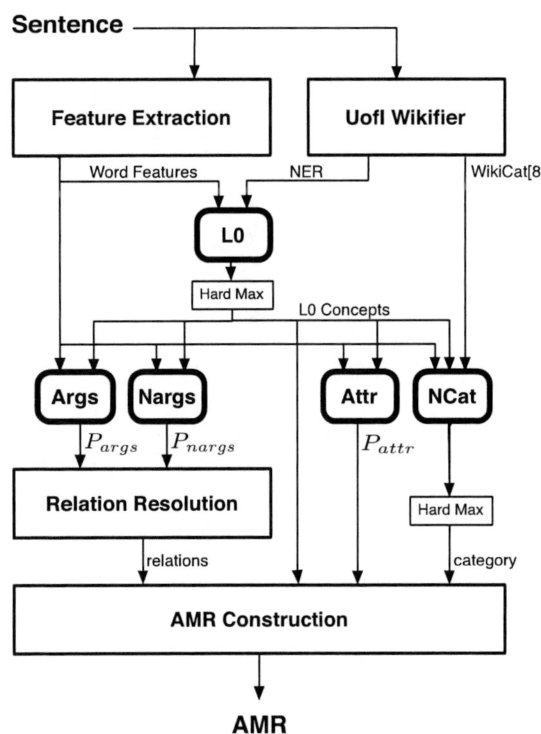

Figure 2: AMR Parser Architecture, BDLSTM networks in bold.

3.2 Neural Networks

Unlike relatively simple sequence processing tasks like part-of-speech tagging and NER, semantic analysis requires the ability to keep track of relevant information that may be arbitrarily far away from the words currently under consideration. Fortunately, recurrent neural networks (RNNs) are a class of neural architecture that use a form of short-term memory in order to solve this semantic distance problem. Basic RNN systems have been enhanced with the use of special memory cell units, referred to as Long Short-Term Memory neural networks, or LSTM's (Hochreiter and Schmidhuber, 1997). Such systems can effectively process information dispersed over hundreds of words (Schmidhuber et al., 2002; Gers et al., 2001).

Bidirectional LSTMs (BDLSTM) networks are LSTMs that are connected so that both future and past words in the sentence can be examined. We use the LSTM cell as described in (Graves et al., 2013), Figure 3, configured in a Bi-directional structure, called BDLSTM (Zhou and Xu, 2015), shown in Figure 4 as the core network in our system. Five BDLSTM Neural Networks comprise our parser.

3.2.1 Level 0 Concepts BDLSTM Network (L0)

The first step in our process is to create the set of concepts (nodes) that form the basis for any AMR representation; we call these Level 0, or L0, concepts. For the most part in current AMR training data, these concepts are in a direct relationship to words and sequences of words in a sentence. The task of the L0 network is, therefore, to take the input sequence of words and produce an output sequence of IOB tags that identify and classify the concepts in the AMR output.

For training, AMR concepts are first aligned to words using an AMR-to-word alignment algorithm. We used the alignment provided in the SemEval dataset. In cases where multiple concepts are associated with the same word, we use only the lower level concept and ignore upper level concept(s).

The system classifies each L0 concept as predicate or non-predicate, and predicts the PropBank sense for the predicates. AMR concepts are either

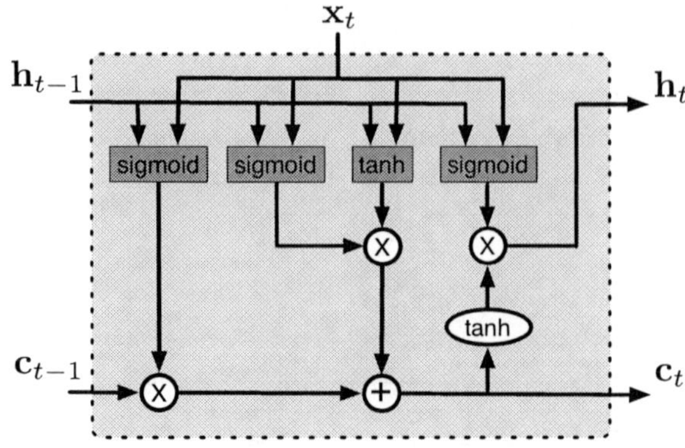

Figure 3: LSTM Cell.
An "unrolled" representation of an LSTM Cell. Rectangles represent linear layers followed by the labelled non-linearity. Each cell learns how to weigh, or gate, the input, previous cell memory, and output.

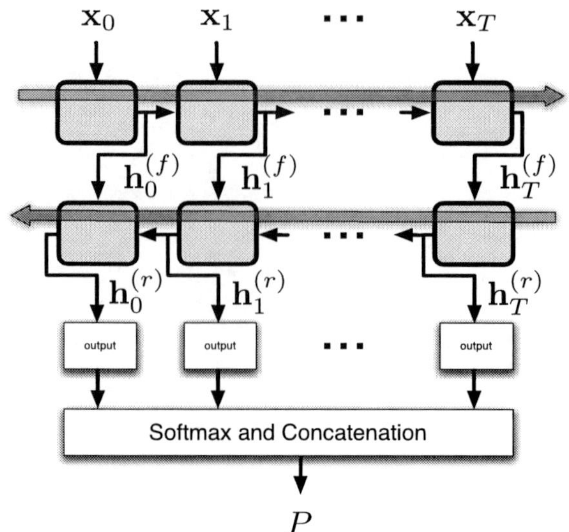

Figure 4: Bi-Directional LSTM.
A general diagram of a BDLSTM network, showing the feature input vectors x_i, the forward layer (f) and the reverse layer (r). The network generates vectors of log likelihoods which are converted to an array of probabilities.

English words (boy), PropBank framesets (plan-01), or special keywords. A translation table was created from training data by calculating the most probable AMR concept, given the sentence word and the general concept identifier.

The most common multilevel cases, a subgraph composed of a named entity, its related category, and a wiki link when available, are identified as exceptions and tagged as name concepts, which will be expanded.[3]

The features used in the L0 nework are:

- word: 130Kx50, the word embedding
- suffix: 430x5, embedding based on the final two letters of each word.
- caps: 5x5, embedding based on the capitalization pattern of the word.
- NER: 5x5, indexed by NER from the Wikifier, 'O', 'LOC', 'ORG', 'PER' or 'MISC'.

The L0 Network produces probabilities for 19 BIOES tagged concept types, and the highest probability tag is chosen for each word, as shown for the example sentence in Table 1.

3.2.2 Predicate Argument Relations BDLSTM Network (Args)

The Args Network is run once for each predicate concept, and produces a matrix P_{args} which defines

the probability of a type of predicate argument relation from an L0 predicate concept to any other L0 concept. (See, for example, ARG0 and ARG1 relations in Figure 1.), prior to the identification of any relations.[4] The matrix has dimensions a by c, where a is the number of non-arg relations to be identified, and c is the total number of concepts.

The Args features, calculated for each source predicate concept, are:

---

[4]relation probabilities change as hard decisions are made, see section 3.4

words	BIOES	Prob	kind
France	S_Named	0.995	txNamed
plans	S_Pred-01	0.997	plan-01
further	S_NonPred	0.931	further
nuclear	S_NonPred	0.990	nucleus
cooperation	S_Pred-01	0.986	cooperate-01
with	O	1.000	O
numerous	S_NonPred	0.982	numerous
countries	S_NonPred	0.860	country
.	O	0.999	O

Table 1: L0 Network Example Output

---

[3]For example *France* in the shaded section of Figure 1.

- Word, Suffix and Caps as in the L0 network.
- L0: 19x5, indexed by the L0 network identified concept.
- PredWords[5], 130Kx50: The word embeddings of the word and surrounding 2 words associated with the source predicate concept.
- PredL0[5], 19x10: The L0 embedding of the word and surrounding 2 words associated with the source predicate concept.
- regionMark: 21x5, indexed by the distance in words between the word and the word associated with the source predicate concept.

3.2.3 Non-Predicate Relations BDLSTM Network (Nargs)

The Nargs Network uses features similar to the Args network, is run once for each concept, and produces a matrix P_{nargs} which defines the probability of a type of relation from an L0 concept to any other L0 concept, prior to the identification of any relations.[5] The matrix has dimensions a_n by c, where a_n is the number of non-arg relations to be identified, and c is the total number of concepts.

3.2.4 Attributes BDLSTM Network (Attr)

The Attr Network determines a primary attribute for each concept, if any.[6] The attributes (op words) associated with named entities are determined directly during L0 concept identification. This network is simplified to detect only one attribute (there could be many) per concept, and only computes probabilities for the most common attributes: TOP, polarity, and quant.

3.2.5 Named Category BDLSTM Network (NCat)

The NCat Network uses features similar to the L0 Network, along with the suggested categories (up to eight) from the Wikifier, and produces probabilities for each of 68 :instance roles, or categories, for named entities identified in the training set AMR's.

- Word, Suffix and Caps as in the L0 network.
- WikiCat[8]: 108 x 5, indexed by suggested categories from the Wikifier.

---

[5]Degree, mod, or quant are examples of narg relations in Figure 1.

[6](TOP: plan-01) and (op1: france) are attribute examples shown in Figure 1.

Semeval Task 8 Dataset	Smatch F1
Test	66.1%
Evaluation	56.0%

Table 2: Smatch F1 results for Test and Eval Datasets

3.3 Wikifier

Named entities in AMR are annotated with a canonical form, using Wikipedia as the standard (see *France* in Figure 1). A :wiki role, or link, should be provided if an appropriate wikipedia page exists, root category (or top-level :instance role) should also be provided. To determine these fields, prior to running the L0 network, we run the sentences through the University of Illinois Wikifier (Ratinov et al., 2011; Cheng and Roth, 2013) which provides a wiki link and a list of possible categories. We insert the link directly as a :wiki role, and use the possible categories as feature inputs to the NCat Network.

3.4 Relation Resolution

The generated P_{args} and P_{nargs} for each L0 identified concept are processed to determine the most likely relation connections, using the constraints:

1. AMR's are single component graphs without cycles.
2. AMR's are simple directed graphs, a max of one relation between concepts is allowed.
3. Outgoing predicate relations are limited to one of each kind (i.e. can't have two ARG0's)

We apply a greedy algorithm which repeatedly selects the most probable edge from P_{args} and P_{nargs}, then adjusts P_{args} and P_{nargs} based on the constraints (hard decisions change the probabilities), until all edge probabilities are below a threshold. From then on, only the most probable edges which span subgraphs are chosen, until the graph contains a single component.

4 Results

Semeval task 8 provides aligned, split datasets. Our Smatch F1 result for the test dataset was 66.1%, and 56.0% for the eval dataset (Table 2). Reportedly, the eval dataset is more challenging than the provided test dataset. The mean of all task 8 results for the eval dataset is 55% with a standard deviation of 6%, more detail is not yet available.

5 Conclusion

In this paper, we have described our submission to the AMR Parsing task for SemEval-2016. Our parser does not make use of a syntactic pre-parse, and avoids the use of heavily engineered features. Future work will include expanding the identification of concepts and exploring the use of more sophisticated alignments and word embeddings.

References

Yoav Artzi, Kenton Lee, and Luke Zettlemoyer. 2015. Broad-coverage ccg semantic parsing with amr. In *Proceedings of the 2015 Conference on Empirical Methods in Natural Language Processing. Màrquez, Adam Meyers, Joakim Nivre, Sebastian Padó, Jan Štepánek, Pavel Stranák, Mihai Surdeanu, Nianwen Xue, and Yi Zhang.*

Laura Banarescu, Claire Bonial, Shu Cai, Madalina Georgescu, Kira Griffitt, Ulf Hermjakob, Kevin Knight, Philipp Koehn, Martha Palmer, and Nathan Schneider. 2012. Abstract meaning representation (amr) 1.0 specification. In *Parsing on Freebase from Question-Answer Pairs. In Proceedings of the 2013 Conference on Empirical Methods in Natural Language Processing. Seattle: ACL*, pages 1533–1544.

X. Cheng and D. Roth. 2013. Relational inference for wikification. In *EMNLP*.

Ronan Collobert, Jason Weston, Léon Bottou, Michael Karlen, Koray Kavukcuoglu, and Pavel Kuksa. 2011. Natural language processing (almost) from scratch. *The Journal of Machine Learning Research*, 12:2493–2537.

Jeffrey Flanigan, Sam Thomson, Jaime G Carbonell, Chris Dyer, and Noah A Smith. 2014. A discriminative graph-based parser for the abstract meaning representation.

Felix A Gers, Douglas Eck, and Jürgen Schmidhuber. 2001. Applying lstm to time series predictable through time-window approaches. In *Artificial Neural NetworksICANN 2001*, pages 669–676. Springer.

Alex Graves, Abdel-rahman Mohamed, and Geoffrey E. Hinton. 2013. Speech recognition with deep recurrent neural networks. *CoRR*, abs/1303.5778.

Sepp Hochreiter and Jürgen Schmidhuber. 1997. Long short-term memory. *Neural computation*, 9(8):1735–1780.

Xiaochang Peng, Linfeng Song, and Daniel Gildea. 2015. A synchronous hyperedge replacement grammar based approach for amr parsing. *CoNLL 2015*, page 32.

Michael Pust, Ulf Hermjakob, Kevin Knight, Daniel Marcu, and Jonathan May. 2015. Parsing english into abstract meaning representation using syntax-based machine translation. *Training*, 10:218–021.

L. Ratinov, D. Roth, D. Downey, and M. Anderson. 2011. Local and global algorithms for disambiguation to wikipedia. In *ACL*.

Jürgen Schmidhuber, F Gers, and Douglas Eck. 2002. Learning nonregular languages: A comparison of simple recurrent networks and lstm. *Neural Computation*, 14(9):2039–2041.

Lucy Vanderwende, Arul Menezes, and Chris Quirk. 2015. An amr parser for english, french, german, spanish and japanese and a new amr-annotated corpus. In *Proceedings of NAACL-HLT*, pages 26–30.

Chuan Wang, Nianwen Xue, Sameer Pradhan, and Sameer Pradhan. 2015. A transition-based algorithm for amr parsing. In *Proceedings of the 2015 Conference of the North American Chapter of the Association for Computational Linguistics: Human Language Technologies*, pages 366–375.

Keenon Werling, Gabor Angeli, and Christopher Manning. 2015. Robust subgraph generation improves abstract meaning representation parsing. *arXiv preprint arXiv:1506.03139*.

Jie Zhou and Wei Xu. 2015. End-to-end learning of semantic role labeling using recurrent neural networks. In *Proceedings of the Annual Meeting of the Association for Computational Linguistics*.

CMU at SemEval-2016 Task 8:
Graph-based AMR Parsing with Infinite Ramp Loss

Jeffrey Flanigan♠ **Chris Dyer**♠ **Noah A. Smith**♡ **Jaime Carbonell**♠
♠School of Computer Science, Carnegie Mellon University, Pittsburgh, PA, USA
♡Computer Science & Engineering, University of Washington, Seattle, WA, USA
{jflanigan,cdyer,jgc}@cs.cmu.edu, nasmith@cs.washington.edu

Abstract

We present improvements to the JAMR parser
as part of the SemEval 2016 Shared Task 8 on
AMR parsing. The major contributions are:
improved concept coverage using external resources and features, an improved aligner, and
a novel loss function for structured prediction
called infinite ramp, which is a generalization
of the structured SVM to problems with unreachable training instances.

1 Introduction

Our entry to the SemEval 2016 Shared Task 8 is a set
of improvements to the system presented in Flanigan
et al. (2014). The improvements are: a novel training loss function for structured prediction, which we
call "infinite ramp," new sources for concepts, improved features, and improvements to the rule-based
aligner in Flanigan et al. (2014). The overall architecture of the system and the decoding algorithms
for concept identification and relation identification
are unchanged from Flanigan et al. (2014), and we
refer readers seeking a complete understanding of
the system to that paper.

2 New Concept Fragment Sources and Features

The concept identification stage relies on a function
called *clex* in Section 3 of Flanigan et al. (2014)
to provide candidate concept fragments. In that
work, *clex* has three sources of concept fragments:
a lexicon extracted from the training data, rules for
named entities identified by the named entity tagger,

and rules for time expressions. We augment these
sources with five additional sources:

- **Frame file lookup**: for every word in the input
  sentence, if the lemma matches the name of a
  frame in the AMR frame files (with sense tag
  removed), we add the lemma concatenated with
  "-01" as a candidate concept fragment.

- **Lemma**: for every word in the input sentence,
  we add the lemma of the word as a candidate
  concept fragment.

- **Verb pass-through**: for every word in the input sentence, if the word is a verb, we add the
  lemma concatenated with "-00" as a candidate
  concept fragment.

- **Named entity pass-through**: for every span of
  words of length 1 until 7 in the input, we add
  the concept fragment "(thing :name (name :op1
  word1 ... :opn word$n$)" as a candidate concept
  fragment, where n is the length of the span,
  and "word1" and "word$n$" are the first and last
  words in the fragment.

We use the following features for concept identification:

- **Fragment given words**: Relative frequency
  estimates of the probability of a concept fragment given the sequence of words in the span.

- **Length** of the matching span (number of tokens).

- **Bias**: 1 for any concept graph fragment.

Proceedings of SemEval-2016, pages 1202–1206,
San Diego, California, June 16-17, 2016. ©2016 Association for Computational Linguistics

- **First match**: 1 if this is the first place in the sentence that matches the span.

- **Number**: 1 if the span is length 1 and matches the regular expression "[0-9]+".

- **Short concept**: 1 if the length of the concept fragment string is less than 3 and contains only upper or lowercase letters.

- **Sentence match**: 1 if the span matches the entire input sentence.

- **; list**: 1 if the span consists of the single word ";" and the input sentence is a ";" separated list.

- **POS**: the sequence of POS tags in the span.

- **POS and event**: same as above but with an indicator if the concept fragment is an event concept (matches the regex ".*-[0-9][0-9]").

- **Span**: the sequence of words in the span if the words have occurred more than 10 times in the training data as a phrase with no gaps.

- **Span and concept**: same as above concatenated with the concept fragment in PENMAN notation.

- **Span and concept with POS**: same as above concatenated with the sequence of POS tags in the span.

- **Concept fragment source**: indicator for the source of the concept fragment (corpus, NER tagger, date expression, frame files, lemma, verb-pass through, or NE pass-through).

- **No match from corpus**: 1 if there is no matching concept fragment for this span in the rules extracted from the corpus.

The new sources of concepts complicate concept identification training. The new sources improve concept coverage on held-out data but they do not improve coverage on the training data since one of the concept sources is a lexicon extracted from the training data. Thus correctly balancing use of the training data lexicon versus the additional sources to prevent overfitting is a challenge.

To balance the training data lexicon with the other sources, we use a variant of cross-validation. During training, when processing a training example in the training data, we exclude concept fragments extracted from the same section of the training data. This is accomplished by keeping track of the training instances each phrase-concept fragment pair was extracted from, and excluding all phrase-concept fragment pairs within a window of the current training instance. In our submission the window is set to 20.

While excluding phrase-concept fragment pairs allows the learning algorithm to balance the use of the training data lexicon versus the other concept sources, it creates another problem: some of the gold standard training instances may be unreachable (cannot be produced), because of the phrase-concept pair need to produce the example has been excluded. This can cause problems during learning. To handle this, we use a generalization of structured SVMs which we call "infinite ramp." We discuss this in the general framework of structured prediction in the next section.

3 Infinite Ramp Loss

The infinite ramp is a new loss function for structured prediction problems. It is useful when the training data contains outputs that the decoder cannot produce given their inputs (we refer to these as **"unreachable examples"**). It is a direct generalization of the SVM loss and latent SVM loss.

Let x be the input, $\mathcal{Y}(x)$ be the space of all possible outputs given the input x, and $\hat{y}$ be the predicted output. Let $\mathbf{f}(x, y')$ denote the feature vector for the output y' with the input x, which is the sum of the local features. (In concept identification, the local features are the features computed for each span, and $\mathbf{f}$ is the sum of the features for each span.) Let $\mathbf{w}$ be the parameters of a linear model, used to make predictions as follows:

$$\hat{y} = \arg\max_{y' \in \mathcal{Y}(x)} \mathbf{w} \cdot \mathbf{f}(x, y')$$

To train the model parameters $\mathbf{w}$, a function of the training data is minimized with respect to $\mathbf{w}$. This function is a sum of individual training examples' losses L, plus a regularizer:

$$L(\mathcal{D}; \mathbf{w}) = \sum_{(x_i, y_i) \in \mathcal{D}} L(x_i, y_i; \mathbf{w}) + \lambda \|\mathbf{w}\|^2$$

$$L(x_i, y_i; \mathbf{w}) = - \left(\lim_{\alpha \to \infty} \max_{y \in \mathcal{Y}(x_i)} \left(\mathbf{w} \cdot \mathbf{f}(x_i, y) + \alpha \cdot \left[\overbrace{\min_{y'' \in \mathcal{Y}(x_i)} cost(y_i, y'')}^{C(x_i, y_i)} - cost(y_i, y) \right] \right) \right)$$
$$+ \max_{y' \in \mathcal{Y}(x_i)} \left(\mathbf{w} \cdot \mathbf{f}(x_i, y') + cost(y_i, y') \right) \tag{1}$$

Figure 1: Infinite ramp loss.

Typical loss functions are the **structured perceptron loss** (Collins, 2002):

$$L(x_i, y_i; \mathbf{w}) = -\mathbf{w} \cdot \mathbf{f}(x_i, y_i) + \max_{y \in \mathcal{Y}(x_i)} \mathbf{w} \cdot \mathbf{f}(x_i, y) \tag{2}$$

and the **structured SVM loss** (Taskar et al., 2003; Tsochantaridis et al., 2004), which incorporates margin using a cost function:[1]

$$L(x_i, y_i; \mathbf{w}) = -\mathbf{w} \cdot \mathbf{f}(x_i, y_i)$$
$$+ \max_{y \in \mathcal{Y}(x_i)} \left(\mathbf{w} \cdot \mathbf{f}(x_i, y) + cost(y_i, y) \right) \tag{3}$$

Both (2) and (3) are problematic if example i is unreachable, i.e., $y_i \notin \mathcal{Y}(x_i)$, due to imperfect data or an imperfect definition of $\mathcal{Y}$. In this case, the model is trying to learn an output it cannot produce. In some applications, the features $\mathbf{f}(x_i, y_i)$ cannot even be computed for these examples. This problem is well known in machine translation: some examples cannot be produced by the phrase-table or grammar. It also occurs in AMR parsing.

To handle unreachable training examples, we modify (3), introducing the **infinite ramp loss**, shown in Eq. 1 in Fig. 1. The term labeled $C(x_i, y_i)$ is present only to make the limit well-defined in case $\min_{y \in \mathcal{Y}(x_i)} cost(y_i, y) \neq 0$. In practice, we set α to be a very large number (10^{12}) instead of taking a proper limit, and set $C(x_i, y_i) = 0$.

The intuition behind Eq. 1 is the following: for very large α, the first max picks a y that minimizes $cost(y_i, y)$, using the model score $\mathbf{w} \cdot \mathbf{f}(x_i, y)$ to break any ties. This is what the model updates *towards* in subgradient descent-style updates, called the "hope derivation" by Chiang (2012). The second max is the usual cost augmented decoding that gives

---

[1] $cost(y_i, y)$ returns the cost of mistaking y for correct output y_i.

a margin in the SVM loss, and is what the model updates *away from* in subgradient descent, called the "fear derivation" by Chiang (2012).

Eq. 1 generalizes the structured SVM loss. If y_i is reachable and the minimum over $y \in \mathcal{Y}(x_i)$ of $cost(y, y_i)$ occurs when $y = y_i$, then the first max in Eq. 1 picks out $y = y_i$ and Eq. 1 reduces to the structured SVM loss.

The infinite ramp is also a generalization of the latent structured SVM (Yu and Joachims, 2009), which is a generalization of the structured SVM for hidden variables. This loss can be used when the output can be written $y_i = (\tilde{y}_i, h_i)$, where $\tilde{y}_i$ is observed output and h_i is latent (even at training time). Let $\tilde{\mathcal{Y}}(x_i)$ be the space of all possible observed outputs and $\mathcal{H}(x_i)$ be the hidden space for the example x_i. Let $\tilde{c}$ be the cost function for the observed output. The **latent structured SVM loss** is:

$$L(x_i, y_i; \mathbf{w}) = - \max_{h \in \mathcal{H}(x_i)} \left(\mathbf{w} \cdot \mathbf{f}(x_i, \tilde{y}_i, h) \right)$$
$$+ \max_{\tilde{y} \in \tilde{\mathcal{Y}}(x_i)} \max_{h' \in \mathcal{H}(x_i)} \left(\mathbf{w} \cdot \mathbf{f}(x_i, \tilde{y}, h) + \tilde{c}(\tilde{y}_i, \tilde{y}) \right) \tag{4}$$

If we set $cost(y_i, y) = \tilde{c}(\tilde{y}_i, \tilde{y})$ in Eq. 1, and the minimum of $\tilde{c}(\tilde{y}_i, \tilde{y})$ occurs when $\tilde{y} = \tilde{y}_i$, then minimizing Eq. 1 is equivalent to minimizing Eq. 4.

Eq. 1 is related to **ramp loss** (Collobert et al., 2006; Chapelle et al., 2009; Keshet and McAllester, 2011):

$$L(x_i, y_i; \mathbf{w}) =$$
$$- \max_{y \in \mathcal{Y}(x_i)} \left(\mathbf{w} \cdot \mathbf{f}(x_i, y) - \alpha \cdot cost(y_i, y) \right)$$
$$+ \max_{y' \in \mathcal{Y}(x_i)} \left(\mathbf{w} \cdot \mathbf{f}(x_i, y') + cost(y_i, y') \right) \tag{5}$$

The parameter α is often set to zero, and controls the "height" of the ramp, which is $\alpha + 1$. Taking

$\alpha \to \infty$ in Eq. 5 corresponds roughly to Eq. 1, hence the name "infinite ramp loss". However, Eq. 1 also includes $C(x_i, y_i)$ term to make the limit well defined even when $\min_{y \in \mathcal{Y}(x_i)} cost(y_i, y) \neq 0$. Like infinite ramp loss, ramp loss also handles unreachable training examples (Gimpel and Smith, 2012), but we have found ramp loss to be more difficult to optimize than infinite ramp loss in practice due to local minima. Both loss functions are non-convex. However, infinite ramp loss is convex if $\arg \min_{y \in \mathcal{Y}(x_i)} cost(y_i, y)$ is unique.

4   Training

We train the concept identification stage using infinite ramp loss (1) with AdaGrad (Duchi et al., 2011). We process examples in the training data $((x_1, y_1), \ldots, (x_N, y_N))$ one at a time. At time t, we decode with the current parameters and the cost function as an additional local factor to get the two outputs:

$$h^t = \arg \max_{y' \in \mathcal{Y}(x_t)} \left(\mathbf{w}^t \cdot \mathbf{f}(x_t, y') - \alpha \cdot cost(y_i, y) \right) \quad (6)$$

$$f^t = \arg \max_{y' \in \mathcal{Y}(x_t)} \left(\mathbf{w}^t \cdot \mathbf{f}(x_t, y') + cost(y_i, y) \right) \quad (7)$$

and compute the subgradient:

$$\mathbf{s}^t = \mathbf{f}(x_t, h^t) - \mathbf{f}(x_t, f^t) - 2\lambda \mathbf{w}^t$$

We then update the parameters and go to the next example. Each component i of the parameters gets updated as:

$$w_i^{t+1} = w_i^t - \frac{\eta}{\sqrt{\sum_{t'=1}^{t} s_i^{t'}}} s_i^t$$

5   Experiments

We evaluate using Smatch (Cai and Knight, 2013). Following the recommended train/dev./test split of LDC2015E86, our parser achieves 70% precision, 65% recall, and 67% F_1 Smatch on the LDC2015E86 test set. The JAMR baseline on this same dataset is 55% F_1 Smatch, so the improvements are quite substantial. On the SemEval 2016 Task 8 test set, our improved parser achieves 56% F_1 Smatch.

We hypothesize that the lower performance of the parser on the SemEval Task 8 test set is due to drift in the AMR annotation scheme between the production of the LDC2015E86 training data and the SemEval test set. During that time, there were changes to the concept senses and the concept frame files. Because the improvements in our parser were due to boosting recall in concept identification (and using the frame files to our advantage), our approach does not show as large improvements on the SemEval test set as on the LDC2015E86 test set.

6   Conclusion

We have presented improvements to the JAMR parser as part of the SemEval 2016 Shared Task on AMR parsing, showing substantial improvements over the baseline JAMR parser. As part of these improvements, we introduced infinite ramp loss, which generalizes the structured SVM to handle training data with unreachable training examples. We hope this loss function will be useful in other application areas as well.

Acknowledgments

This work is supported by the U.S. Army Research Office under grant number W911NF-10-1-0533. Any opinion, findings, and conclusions or recommendations expressed in this material are those of the author(s) and do not necessarily reflect the view of the U.S. Army Research Office or the United States Government.

References

Shu Cai and Kevin Knight. 2013. Smatch: an evaluation metric for semantic feature structures. In *Proc. of ACL*.

Olivier Chapelle, Chuong B. Do, Choon H Teo, Quoc V. Le, and Alex J. Smola. 2009. Tighter bounds for structured estimation. In *NIPS*.

David Chiang. 2012. Hope and fear for discriminative training of statistical translation models. *JMLR*, 13(1):1159–1187.

Michael Collins. 2002. Discriminative training methods for hidden Markov models: Theory and experiments with perceptron algorithms. In *Proc. of EMNLP*.

Ronan Collobert, Fabian Sinz, Jason Weston, and Léon Bottou. 2006. Trading convexity for scalability. In *Proc. of ICML*.

John Duchi, Elad Hazan, and Yoram Singer. 2011. Adaptive subgradient methods for online learning and stochastic optimization. *JMLR*, 12:2121–2159.

Jeffrey Flanigan, Sam Thomson, Jaime Carbonell, Chris Dyer, and Noah A. Smith. 2014. A discriminative graph-based parser for the abstract meaning representation. In *Proc. of ACL*.

Kevin Gimpel and Noah A. Smith. 2012. Structured ramp loss minimization for machine translation. In *Proc. of NAACL*.

Joseph Keshet and David A McAllester. 2011. Generalization bounds and consistency for latent structural probit and ramp loss. In *Advances in Neural Information Processing Systems*.

Ben Taskar, Carlos Guestrin, and Daphne Koller. 2003. Max-margin markov networks. In *NIPS*.

Ioannis Tsochantaridis, Thomas Hofmann, Thorsten Joachims, and Yasemin Altun. 2004. Support vector machine learning for interdependent and structured output spaces. In *Proc. of ICML*.

Chun-Nam John Yu and Thorsten Joachims. 2009. Learning structural SVMs with latent variables. In *Proc. of ICML*.

IHS-RD-Belarus at SemEval-2016 Task 9: Transition-based Chinese Semantic Dependency Parsing with Online Reordering and Bootstrapping.

Artsiom Artsymenia
IHS Inc. / IHS Global Belarus
Minsk, Belarus

Palina Dounar
IHS Inc. / IHS Global Belarus
Minsk, Belarus

Maria Yermakovich
IHS Inc. / IHS Global Belarus
Minsk, Belarus

`{Artsiom.Artsymenia,Polina.Dovnar,Maria.Yermakovich}@ihs.com`

Abstract

This paper is a description of our system developed for SemEval-2016 Task 9: Chinese Semantic Dependency Parsing. We have built a transition-based dependency parser with on-line reordering, which is not limited to a tree structure and can produce 99.7% of the necessary dependencies while maintaining linear algorithm complexity. To improve parsing quality we used additional techniques such as pre- and post-processing of the dependency graph, bootstrapping and a rich feature set with additional semantic features.

1 Introduction

Dependency parsing is one of the core tasks in natural language processing, as it provides useful information for other NLP tasks. Traditional syntactic parsing usually represents a sentence as a tree-shape structure and this restriction is essential for most of efficient algorithms developed in the past years. Semantic dependency parsing, on the other hand, deals with acyclic graphs, where words may have multiple incoming dependencies. It significantly complicates the task and requires development of the new algorithms or special adoption of the old ones.

There are two main approaches to dependency parsing (Nivre and McDonald, 2008). The first one is a graph-based approach, for example, spanning tree algorithms (McDonald et al., 2005), where the goal is to find the highest scoring tree from a complete graph of dependencies between words in the sentence. The second approach is transition-based, which, instead of searching for global optimum, greedily finds local optimum with a chain of actions that lead to a parsing tree. The main advantage of the transition-based parsers is that they are in general faster than graph-based ones because of the linear complexity of the algorithm (Nivre, 2003).

As we move from syntactic parsing to semantic parsing, and instead of projective trees have to deal with acyclic graphs, exact inference becomes NP-hard, so some strong independence assumptions or heuristics are needed. A lot of modifications have been proposed for transition-based parsers to support non-projective structures. Nivre and Nilsson (2005) proposed a pseudo-projective parsing technique which consists in modifying the input into a projective dependency tree with extended labels, performing the projective parsing and then applying an approximate back transformation. Attardi (2006) introduced additional actions that add dependencies between the roots of non-adjacent subtrees. Both techniques maintain linear algorithm complexity at the expense of incomplete coverage of all possible dependency trees. Complete coverage of all non-projective trees is achieved by Nivre (2009) with a technique called *on-line reordering* but it increases the worst-case complexity from linear to quadratic.

2 System Description

The core of our system is a transition-based dependency parser with on-line reordering in style of Titov et al, (2009). It continues the tradition of At-

Proceedings of SemEval-2016, pages 1207–1211,
San Diego, California, June 16-17, 2016. ©2016 Association for Computational Linguistics

tardi (2006) by extending the action-set of the model, but adds only one new action. While this model is not enough to parse any arbitrary structure, it still can successfully reproduce 99.72% of the dependencies in the "sdpv2" corpus and 99.78% of the dependencies in the "text" corpus.

2.1 Parsing Algorithm

The state of the parser is defined by the current stack S, the queue I of remaining input sentence words, and partial dependency graph constructed by previous actions. The parser starts with artificial TOP node in S and all input words in I. The processing terminates when a state with an empty queue is reached. Parser can change its state with one of the five possible actions:

- Action *Left-Arc* adds a dependency arc from the first word in queue to the word on top of the stack

- Action *Right-Arc* adds a dependency arc from the word on top of the stack to the first word in queue

- Action *Reduce* removes the word from the top of the stack

- Action *Shift* moves the first word from the queue to the stack.

- Action *Swap* swaps two words at the top of the stack.

With additional limitation on the number of times *Swap* operation can be performed for each node, parser with this action set has a linear time complexity.

To convert gold dependencies into gold actions, the following algorithm is used for each state of the parser:

- If stack is empty, perform *Shift* action.

- If the word on the top of the stack has no incoming or outcoming dependencies or the rightmost dependency is located to the left of the first word in the queue, perform *Reduce* action.

- If the rightmost dependency of the word on top of the stack is equal to the first word in queue, but this dependency is already present in the partial dependency graph, perform *Reduce* action.

- If there is a dependency arc between the top of the stack and the first word in queue and it is not present in the partial dependency graph, perform *Left-Arc* or *Right-Arc* action according to the direction of dependency.

- If the size of the stack is less than two, or two top words in the stack in the same order were already swapped, perform *Shift* action.

- If there is a dependency arc between the second word in stack and the first word in the queue, and it is not present in the partial dependency graph, perform *Swap* action

- Otherwise, perform *Shift* action.

After that, the obtained gold actions are used to train a log-linear classifier with the following set of features:

- Words in stack and queue: W(S0), W(S1), W(S2), W(I0), W(I1), W(I2)

- POS tags: T(S0), T(S1), T(S2), T(I0), T(I1), T(I2)

- Words of the last left child(LC), last right child(RC) and last parent(P) in the partial dependency graph for words in stack and queue: W(LC_S0), W(RC_S0), W(P_S0), W(LC_S1), W(RC_S1), W(P_S1), W(LC_I0), W(P_I0)

- POS tags of LC, RC and P: T(LC_S0), T(RC_S0), T(P_S0), T(LC_S1), T(RC_S1), T(P_S1), T(LC_I0), T(P_I0)

- The number of left children, right children and parents: N(LC_S0), N(RC_S0), N(P_S0), N(LC_I0), N(P_I0)

- Previous action: PA

- Information about existing arcs in partial dependency graph: A(S0,I0), A(S1,I0)

- Distance between words: D(S0,I0), D(S1,S0)

- Various combinations of the above features, for example: W(I0)+T(I0), W(S0)+W(I0), T(S3)+T(S2)+T(S1)+T(I0)+T(I1) and other.

One more log-linear classifier is used to set a semantic label to the dependency. The feature set is similar to the one described above, but instead of words in the stack and the queue this model uses a parent and a child of the dependency arc in question.

2.2 Bootstrapping

Transition-based parsers use history to predict the next action. In our system the words in the stack, queue and partial dependency graph are used as features of the log-linear classifier. While it is the source of useful information (when past actions are correct), it is also the source of errors (when past actions are incorrect). If statistical model is trained only on gold parses, it has little possibility to recover from mistakes, because it will have to predict next decisions from a state that was never encountered during training. To reduce the gap between gold and real-life parser configurations, Choi and Palmer (2011) proposed to use bootstrapping on automatic parses. In this approach a model trained on gold configurations is used to parse training corpus and generate new training instances, where the current configuration is achieved by automatic parsing.

In our system we split training corpus into 10 parts and parse each part with a model trained with other 9 parts to be as close to real-life as possible. After that a new model is trained with both gold training instances and bootstrapped training instances.

2.3 Semantic Features

To analyze the influence of different semantic dependencies on each other, we used some additional features produced from the output of IHS Goldfire Question-Answering system (Todhunter et al., 2013). This system has its own Semantic Processor, which performs complete linguistic analysis of text documents, such as lexical, part-of-speech, syntactic, and semantic analysis and other. The Q-A system is built on top of the semantic labeling of words with basic knowledge types (e.g., objects/classes of objects, cause-effect relations,

whole-part relations etc.). A matching procedure makes use of the aforementioned types of semantic labels to determine the exact answers to the questions and present them to the user in the form of the fragments of sentences or a newly synthesized phrase in the natural language.

For example, one of such semantic labels, originally extracted by Goldfire system from one of the sentences in the training data, looked this way:

我六点钟出门，以便赶上火车

I left home at six, (in order) to catch the train.

出门 (left) –*Effect*→ 赶上火车 (catch the train)

In order to convert semantic labels into semantic dependencies, we extracted the main word of the answer and corrected differences in word segmentation. After transformations the example above is represented as the following semantic dependency:

6 赶上 VV 3(出门) Effect

Although the semantic labels, extracted by Goldfire, are different from the ones that should be extracted in SemEval-2016 Task 9 (in the example above the label is supposed to be *ePurp*), we expected them to provide additional information in cases when the context of words in stack and queue is not sufficient.

2.4 Dependencies Pre-processing and Post-processing

Error analysis of the base model showed that incorrect extraction of the *eCoo* dependency is one of the most frequent mistakes. It turned out that *eCoo* connections may have different direction: from left to right and from right to left. Further analysis revealed that in most cases the direction correlates with the position of the parent node of *eCoo* chain: if the parent is to the left, the direction is more likely to be from left to right, and if the parent is to the right, the direction is more likely to be from right to left.

The intuition is that the parser is confused with the different direction of the *eCoo* connections. That is why we converted all *eCoo* dependencies into right-to-left direction in the training corpus, and added a post-processing procedure which converts *eCoo* connections in the output dependency graph into left-to-right direction if the parent of the top node of *eCoo* chain is to the left.

model	LP	LR	LF	NLF
Base	61.61	60.91	61.26	49.16
PP	**62.79**	62.07	**62.43**	49.89
PP_BS	62.25	62.32	62.29	47.12
PP_SEM	62.68	62.13	62.40	**52.71**
PP_BS_SEM	62.37	**62.47**	62.42	46.88

Table 1: evaluation on sdpv2 (labeled)

model	UP	UR	UF	NUF
Base	78.20	77.30	77.75	62.77
PP	**79.87**	78.96	**79.41**	63.64
PP_BS	78.99	79.07	79.03	61.99
PP_SEM	79.55	78.85	79.20	**64.27**
PP_BS_SEM	79.33	**79.45**	79.39	60.42

Table 2: evaluation on sdpv2 (unlabeled)

model	LP	LR	LF	NLF
Base	66.79	65.74	66.26	51.48
PP	67.23	66.18	66.70	51.79
PP_BS	67.32	66.87	67.09	49.04
PP_SEM	68.42	67.55	67.98	**53.45**
PP_BS_SEM	**68.46**	**68.28**	**68.37**	50.94

Table 3: evaluation on text (labeled)

model	UP	UR	UF	NUF
Base	81.08	79.82	80.44	64.56
PP	81.67	80.40	81.03	64.66
PP_BS	81.44	80.90	81.17	63.18
PP_SEM	**82.60**	81.56	82.08	**65.77**
PP_BS_SEM	82.46	**82.25**	**82.35**	65.60

Table 4: evaluation on text (unlabeled)

model	LP	LR	LF	NLF
Our system	**58.78**	**59.33**	**59.06**	40.84
a1	55.52	55.85	55.69	**49.23**
a2	55.65	56.04	55.84	47.80
lbpg	55.64	58.89	57.22	45.57
lbpgs	58.38	57.25	57.81	41.56
lbpg75	57.88	57.67	57.78	48.89

Table 5: SemEval results on sdpv2 (labeled)

model	UP	UR	UF	NUF
Our system	**77.28**	**78.01**	**77.64**	60.20
a1	73.51	73.94	73.72	**60.71**
a2	73.79	74.30	74.04	59.69
lbpg	72.87	77.11	74.93	58.03
lbpgs	76.28	74.81	75.54	54.34
lbpg75	75.55	75.26	75.40	58.28

Table 6: SemEval results on sdpv2 (unlabeled)

model	LP	LR	LF	NLF
Our system	**68.71**	**68.46**	**68.59**	50.57
a1	65.36	64.98	65.17	54.70
a2	65.37	64.92	65.15	54.62
lbpg	63.34	67.89	65.54	51.75
lbpgs	67.35	65.11	66.21	47.79
lbpg75	66.43	66.33	66.38	**57.51**

Table 7: SemEval results on text (labeled)

model	UP	UR	UF	NUF
Our system	**82.56**	**82.26**	**82.41**	64.58
a1	79.06	78.60	78.83	**65.71**
a2	78.89	78.35	78.62	64.93
lbpg	76.73	82.24	79.39	63.21
lbpgs	81.22	78.52	79.85	55.51
lbpg75	79.97	79.85	79.91	63.87

Table 8: SemEval results on text (unlabeled)

3 Experiments

In order to evaluate the influence of the methods described above on parsing quality, we have built five different systems and tested them on the development set. The labeled and unlabeled results for 2 types of corpus ("sdpv2" and "text") are presented in tables from 1 to 4. LP, LR and LF are labeled precision, recall and F1-score for predicted dependencies (parent-child-dependency label triples). NLF is F1-score for non-local dependencies. UP, UR, UF and NUF are unlabeled counterparts. The *base* system is built with the algorithm described in 2.1. BS is bootstrapping (2.2), Sem – Semantic Features (2.3) and PP is pre- and post-processing (2.4). Pre- and post-processing procedures proved to be the most useful, especially on the "sdpv2" corpus. Bootstrapping improves recall, but harms precision and non-local dependencies. Semantic Features, on the other hand, help to ex-

tract non-local dependencies. The PP_BS_SEM system, with all features included, performed better than all other on the "text" corpus and has comparable results on the "sdpv2" corpus. That is why the output of this system was submitted to SemEval-2016 Task 9. The results of our system, compared to other submissions, are represented in tables 5-8. Our submitted system has shown the highest precision, recall and F1-score values for all dependencies, but did not perform well on non-local labeled dependencies, which may be an effect of bootstrapping or shortcomings of the selected model in general.

4   Conclusion

We have built a transition-based semantic dependency parser with online reordering, bootstrapping, additional semantic features and graph pre- and post-processing that achieved the best results in SemEval-2016 Task 9. All features proved to improve the overall performance, but some details may need further improvement. Bootstrapping requires a better balance to avoid its bad influence on precision and non-local dependencies. Also some additional restrictions to the base algorithm may be needed, because now it is allowed for some words to have no parent at all, and while it may be normal for semantic dependency parsing in general, it is not the thing for the task at hand. We leave these details for a future work.

References

Giuseppe Attardi. 2006. *Experiments with a multilanguage non-projective dependency parser*. In Proceedings of the 10th Conference on Computational Natural Language Learning (CoNLL), pages 166–170.

Jinho D. Choi and Martha Palmer. 2011. *Getting the most out of transition-based dependency parsing*. In Proceedings of the 49th Annual Meeting of the Association for Computational Linguistics: Human Language Technologies, pages 687–692.

Ryan McDonald, Fernando Pereira, Kiril Ribarov, and Jan Hajic. 2005. *Non-projective dependency parsing using spanning tree algorithms*. In Proceedings of the Conference on Human Language Technology and Empirical Methods in Natural Language Processing (HLT-EMNLP'05), pages 523–530.

Joakim Nivre. 2003. *An Efficient Algorithm for Projective Dependency Parsing*. In Proceedings of the 8th International Workshop on Parsing Technologies, IWPT'03, pages 149–160.

Joakim Nivre and Jens Nilsson. 2005. *Pseudo-projective dependency parsing*. In Proc. of ACL, 99–106.

Joakim Nivre and Ryan McDonald. 2008. *Integrating graph-based and transition-based dependency par ers*. In Proceedings of ACL, pages 950–958.

Joakim Nivre. 2009. *Non-projective dependency parsing in expected linear time*. In Proceedings of ACL-IJCNLP.

Ivan Titov and James Henderson. 2007. *A latent variable model for generative dependency parsing*. In Proceedings of the 10th International Conference on Parsing Technologies (IWPT), pages 144–155.

Todhunter, J., Sovpel, I., and Pastanohau, D. 2013. *System and method for automatic semantic labeling of natural language texts*. U.S. Patent 8 583 422.

OCLSP at SemEval-2016 Task 9: Multilayered LSTM as a Neural Semantic Dependency Parser

Lifeng Jin   Manjuan Duan   William Schuler
Department of Linguistics
The Ohio State University
{jin,duan,schuler}@ling.osu.edu

Abstract

Semantic dependency parsing aims at extracting arcs and semantic role labels for all words in a sentence. In this paper, we propose a semantic dependency parser which is based on Long Short-term Memory and makes heavy use of embeddings of words and POS tags. We describe in detail the implementation of the neural parser, including preprocessing, postprocessing and various input features, and show that the neural parser performs close to the top system in the shared task and is very good at capturing non-local dependencies. We also discuss some issues related to the parser and how to improve it.

1 Introduction

Semantic dependency parsing is a form of semantic analysis where semantic roles for all words in a sentence are analyzed and specific semantic relations are assigned to each word pair (Che et al., 2012). Chinese semantic dependency parsing is especially of interest as there is a remarkable difference between syntactic and semantic dependencies in Chinese (Che et al., 2012). In the SemEval 2016 Task 9 Chinese Semantic Dependency Parsing shared task, semantic dependency parsing for two text genres, TEXT, which includes sentences from conversations and primary school textbooks, and NEWS, which contains newswire text, is explored. We propose a neural parser with LSTM as the basic units and make heavy use of vectorial representations of basic linguistic units like words and POS tags. In this paper, we give a detailed description of the neural parser and discuss a few issues related to the current implementation.

2 Long Short-term Memory

Recurrent Neural Networks, or RNNs, are good for sequential prediction, but the problem of exploding or vanishing gradients makes learning long distance dependencies very difficult for them (Hochreiter, 1998). The LSTM architecture is proposed to address this problem (Hochreiter and Schmidhuber, 1997). In this paper, we follow the version defined in Graves et al. (2013b).

$$i_t = \sigma(W_{xi}x_t + W_{hi}h_{t-1} + W_{ci}c_{t-1} + b_i) \quad (1)$$

$$f_t = \sigma(W_{xf}x_t + W_{hf}h_{t-1} + W_{cf}c_{t-1} + b_f) \quad (2)$$

$$c_t = f_t c_{t-1} + i_t \tanh(W_{xc}x_t + W_{hc}h_{t-1} + b_c) \quad (3)$$

$$o_t = \sigma(W_{xo}x_t + W_{ho}h_{t-1} + W_{co}c_{t-1} + b_o) \quad (4)$$

$$h_t = o_t \tanh(c_t) \quad (5)$$

where σ is the sigmoid function, and i, f, o and c are the input gate, forget gate, output gate and the cell respectively. x_t is the input at time step t, and h_t is the hidden state or the output of the LSTM unit at time step t. With various gates and a cell, the LSTM unit may learn to store and release information inside the cell over many time steps. LSTMs have recently been used for various NLP tasks such as machine translation (Bahdanau et al., 2014; Sutskever et al., 2014), syntactic parsing (Vinyals et al., 2015) and semantic relatedness prediction and

Proceedings of SemEval-2016, pages 1212–1217,
San Diego, California, June 16-17, 2016. ©2016 Association for Computational Linguistics

sentiment classification (Tai et al., 2015). In this paper we apply the LSTM architecture to semantic dependency parsing and show that to use LSTM as a semantic dependency parser is both very powerful and very promising.

3 Overview of the System

3.1 Parsing Typology

For a sentence $S = \langle w_1, w_2, ...w_i, ...w_n \rangle$, the proposed parser traverses the whole parse chart linearly through all possible pairwise combinations of the elements in the sequence to predict the dependency labels. For example, the parser will first consider the word pair $\langle w_1, w_1 \rangle$ for dependency label prediction, treating the first in the pair to be the dependent and the second the head in a dependency relation, and then the word pair $\langle w_1, w_2 \rangle$, and so on. When it gets to $\langle w_i, w_n \rangle$, it proceeds to parse $\langle w_{i+1}, w_1 \rangle$, until the final pair $\langle w_n, w_n \rangle$ is parsed. For cases like $\langle w_i, w_i \rangle$, because there is no dependency arc that connects the same word in the same position, we use this for predicting the root of the sentence. Therefore the actual input to the parser is quadratic on the length of the input sequence, making the complexity of the parser $O(n^2)$.

3.2 Architecture of the Neural Parser

The neural parser is shown in figure 1. It consists of two main parts: the lower level which has a bidirectional LSTM as its main component and the upper level which has an LSTM and an output layer as its main component.

Lower Level: The main component of the lower level system is a bidirectional LSTM (Graves et al., 2013a). The bidirectional LSTM takes the same input sequence with n time-steps, and runs both forward and backward in time to generate hidden states for each time-step, and concatenates the two hidden states for a single time step to form a single hidden state of the whole system. For example, for a time sequence $X = \langle x_1, x_2, ...x_t, ...x_n \rangle$, the input to the bidirectional LSTM is x_t, and the output from it is the concatenation of the hidden state from the forward LSTM h_t and the hidden state of the backward LSTM h'_t. This bidirectional fea-

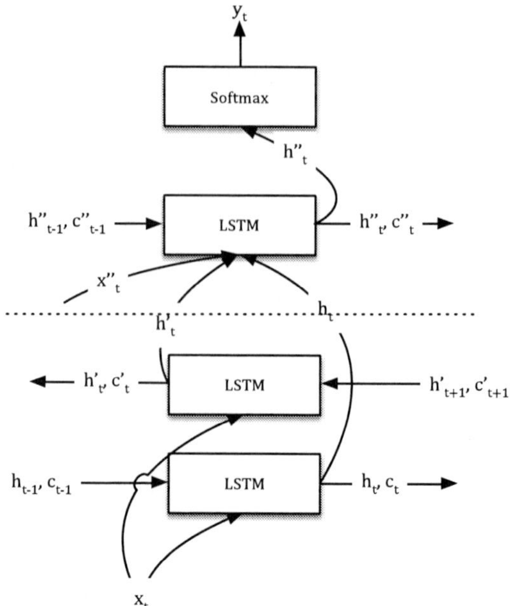

Figure 1: The OCLSP neural parser. x, h, c and y are the model input, hidden state of a LSTM, cell state of a LSTM and the model output respectively.

ture, which is also exploited by Bahdanau et al. (2014) for neural machine translation, provides information for the current time step with information gathered both from the beginning of the sentence and the end of the sentence in terms of cell states and the hidden states.

Upper Level: The main component of the upper level system is an LSTM. The LSTM takes in the output from the lower level (h_t, h'_t) as well as a secondary input x''_t the system and generates a hidden state h''_t which is then fed into a softmax layer to transform into a probability distribution. If $x_t = f(w_i, w_j)$ where w is a word in a sentence, f is the function from words to input vectors and i and j are the indexes of the words, then the final output of the upper level of the system can be viewed as $p(label_{i,j} | f(w_1, w_1), ..., f(w_i, w_j), ..., f(w_n, w_n), \theta)$, where θ is the model parameters.

3.3 Input Features

The input to the parser consists of two parts: the primary input x_t which is the input fed to the lower level system and the secondary input x_t'' which is fed to the upper level system. In development, different kinds of input features are added to the model incrementally to help feature selection. The f function mentioned in the model description translates word pairs to concatenation of different feature vectors.

The system makes heavy use of vectorial representations trained with *word2vec* (Mikolov et al., 2013). There are two kinds of embeddings used by the parser: word embeddings and Part-Of-Speech embeddings. The word embeddings are all trained with the full Chinese Wikipedia, [1] the Chinese Gigaword (Graff and Chen, 2003) as well as the training and development datasets from both genres in this task. The POS embeddings are trained with the POS tag sequences from training and development datasets from both genres in this task. The embeddings are fixed during training and test.

Basic features: The basic features for the lower level system are 300-dimension word embeddings for the current word pair $\langle w_i, w_j \rangle$. The basic features for the upper level system are 50-dimension word embeddings for the context words of the current word pair with a window size of 4, i.e. $\langle w_{i-3}, w_{i-2}, w_{i-1}, w_{i+1}, w_{i+2}, w_{i+3}, w_{j-3}, w_{j-2}, w_{j-1}, w_{j+1}, w_{j+2}, w_{j+3} \rangle$. The 50 dimensional word embeddings are used because we want the word embeddings at the upper level of the same length as the word embeddings in the lower level, and also we want to keep the number of parameters of the upper level inside a practical range for training. Whenever there is no word at a certain position of the window, an all-zero vector is used to indicate that there is no information from that position for the system to use.

POS features: The POS features for the lower level system are 50 dimensional POS embeddings for the current word pair, and for the upper level system, the 50 dimensional POS embeddings are also used for the context words of the current word pair. The all-zero vector is also used whenever a position inside the window has

[1] https://zh.wikipedia.org

Model	Labeled F	Unlabeled F
TEXT		
basic	61.26%	75.31%
basic+pos	65.58%	78.98%
basic+pos+gcg	67.68%	81.12%
NEWS		
basic+pos	57.94%	74.42%
basic+pos+gcg	58.95%	75.44%

Table 1: Results of models with different feature combinations on development dataset. The performance of the model with only basic features on NEWS is not reported here because it became evident that it never outperformed the other two models with more features.

no word.

Predicate-argument features: In previous work, non-local dependencies expressed using a generalized categorial grammar (Bach, 1981; Nguyen et al., 2012) have been used to train an off-the-shelf PCFG parser (Petrov and Klein, 2007) to accurately parse Chinese (Duan and Schuler, 2015). Predicate-argument dependency features were extracted from parsed training sentences using this representation and the trained parser, which gives directed dependencies with 16 different labels, like *arg-1* and *Nmod*, for some pairs of the words. These dependencies are transformed first into undirected dependencies with the original labels. This transform mitigates some problems with arbitrary arc direction discrepancies between two dependency schemes. Then the labels of these dependencies are converted into one hot vectors for the upper level system to use. For the word pairs without a predicate-argument dependency, an all-zero vector of length 16 is used.

Table 1 shows the labeled and unlabeled F scores for models trained with different feature sets on the development dataset. The POS embeddings are good indicators of semantic dependencies as it improves the scores on TEXT by about 4 percent, and the predicate-argument features further improve the F score by another 2 percent on TEXT, and 1 percent on NEWS. The submitted systems use all three feature categories to train and test.

3.4 Preprocessing and postprocessing

There are a few preprocessing and postprocessing steps that are adopted in the system to generate better results.

Word Segmentation: The datasets provided in the task come pre-segmented, but the training data used by *word2vec* need to be segmented first to produce embeddings. We use NLPIR 2015 (Zhang et al., 2003) for segmentation with all words in training and development datasets put into the user dictionary for segmentation. This guarantees that there is no out-of-vocabulary word in development, which also increases parser performance on development data.

OOV Replacement: The OOV words are processed in the following way. Suppose there is a large dataset D_1 for training word embeddings. The vocabulary of D_1 is the set V_1. Suppose there is a new dataset D_2 which has the vocabulary set V_2. The OOV words from D_2 are $V_{oov} = V_2 - V_1$. We first train an embedding model W_1 for D_1 and W_2 for D_2, and then for each word v_{oov} in V_{oov}, we find the word v in V_1 which has the highest similarity score by cosine to v_{oov} in W_2, and replace the v_{oov} with v in V_2. This procedure essentially replaces all the OOV words with the most similar words in the current semantic space of the word embeddings. By doing this, the models do not have to be retrained every time the semantic space of all word embeddings is shifted from W_1 to W_2 with addition of new embeddings. Also the replaced embeddings have more semantic information of the OOV words than a general UNK symbol.

Graph Generation: The proposed parser has no guarantee to produce a dependency graph with all nodes connected to the root. In practice, the raw output of the parser is often not a graph. The parser is generally over-conservative, so many words do not have a dependency arc at all. Therefore the Chu-Liu/Edmond's algorithm[2] is applied to the probability matrix for a complete parse chart of a sentence with the reciprocals of the probability values as costs of edges between nodes, and the

---

[2] https://github.com/mlbright/edmonds

minimal spanning directed graph is generated for the sentence. This guarantees that all final outputs are directed graphs.

The Chu-Liu/Edmond's algorithm outputs a directed graph with no reentrance, but semantic dependency graphs in the task have reentrant nodes. In order to produce reentrant dependencies, we set a threshold of σ on the probabilities for the arcs of a head word. When the parser decides there are multiple heads for a dependent, and the probabilities of the extra arcs are higher than σ, these arcs will be incorporated into the dependency graph. Two submitted systems use this method to generate final results. One system uses the direct output from the parser and generates an arc for any word without a head by adding an arc with the highest probability between the word and any candidate head.

3.5 Training

The loss function of the parser is set to be Negative Log-likelihood function and the training objective is to maximize the log-likelihood of the dependency labels given all word pairs. We use mini-batch update and Adagrad (Duchi et al., 2011) to optimize the parameter learning. Each sentence is a mini-batch. The models used for different datasets are trained separately. We used the F score on the development dataset as the metric to measure convergence. For TEXT, there are in total 10754 sentences in training and for NEWS there are 8301 sentences in training. There are in theory 171 possible dependency labels and 1 no-dependency label in training, but in practice we only observe 158 different semantic dependency labels and 1 no-dependency label in training and development. The models for TEXT are trained for 12 epochs, and the models for NEWS are trained for 8 epochs.

4 Task Evaluation Results

Three systems with slightly different configurations for the Graph Generation process were submitted for test. The results are shown in Table 2. The *lbpg* system does not use the Chu-Liu/Edmond's algorithm for graph generation. Instead it just generates an arc for a word without a head by adding an arc with the highest

Model	LF	NLF	UF	NUF
TEXT				
lbpg	65.54%	**57.51%**	79.39%	63.21%
lbpgs	66.21%	47.79%	79.85%	55.51%
lbpg75	66.38%	**57.51%**	79.91%	63.87%
TOP	**68.59%**	50.57%	**82.41%**	**64.58%**
NEWS				
lbpg	57.22%	45.57%	74.93%	58.03%
lbpgs	57.81%	41.56%	75.54%	54.34%
lbpg75	57.78%	**48.89%**	75.40%	58.28%
TOP	**59.06%**	40.84%	**77.64%**	**60.20%**

Table 2: Results of the submitted models on test dataset. LF, NLF, UF and NUF are respectively Labeled F, Non-local Labeled F, Unlabeled F and Non-local Unlabeled F scores.

probability between the word and any candidate head. It is the worst performing model among the three in terms of F scores. The *lbpgs* and *lbpg75* are both models with the graph generation algorithm. The difference between them is that *lbpgs* uses a σ value of 100, which means that all words have only one head in its output, whereas *lbpg75* uses a σ value of 75 meaning that the extra arcs of a word must have a probability over 0.75.

For the *lbpgs* system, it is interesting to see that only allowing one head per word does not seem to have a huge impact on the F scores. It actually performs better on the NEWS dataset in terms of LF and UF. This indicates that the systems do not perform very well on the extra arcs, either predicting the wrong labels for the arcs or predicting the wrong arcs altogether. However, the non-local scores see a big drop.

For the *lbpg75* system, it is clear that by choosing a high threshold of extra arc probability, in TEXT at least, we get slightly higher F scores. In both datasets, the non-local scores are the highest with this model, meaning that for the arcs with high confidence, the non-local dependency arcs within them are relatively accurate.

5 Discussion and Future Work

Negative Training Cases: One of the most obvious drawbacks of systems like this is that there is a disproportional amount of negative training cases in the training data. In training, the whole parse chart needs to be filled with labels. However, most of the time the number of arcs in a sentence does not exceed $2n$. Therefore the number of word pairs with the no-dependency label, or the number of negative cases, is $n^2 - 2n$. When n gets big, for example for some sentences in NEWS n can be over 200, the number of negative cases gets very large compared to the number of positive cases. It is interesting to see that the parser still captures fairly well the information from positive cases, which are few compared to the negative ones. However, but it may be even better if the number of negative cases can be greatly reduced, the information from positive cases can be even more accessible and the training time can be shorter.

OOV Words: The parser relies on word embeddings and POS embeddings to make dependency predictions. Due to different segmentation schemes used by the automatic segmenter and the annotators, about 10% of the vocabulary in test is OOV words even when the word embeddings are trained with Chinese Wikipedia and Chinese Gigaword combined. The OOV strategy adopted in this paper is shown to be better than just replacing all OOVs with a uniform vector like all-ones or all-zeros, in which case the parser just treats all OOVs as punctuation. However the relation between the OOV words and the replacement words do not seem to correspond to any linguistic or world knowledge for most of the replacement-OOV word pairs. For example, the most similar word for replacement of the OOV word "马来语" (Malay language) is "910129", and the most similar word for "税改" (tax reform) is "面谈成绩" (interview performance). OOVs are a challenge to all parsers, but it is especially important to parsers like the one in this paper, where its performance depends crucially on the quality of the embeddings.

Parsing Typology: The parsing typology used in this paper alleviates problems like reentrant nodes and crossing arcs, but at a cost of efficiency and accuracy. Only about 3% of all the dependency arcs are extra arcs, i.e. they are second or third dependency heads for a given dependent. Such dependencies are very hard to predict, and the typology used here, although able to generate such dependencies naturally, is less than ideal in different ways described above. More research needs to be done for a better parsing typology for neural parsers which addresses these issues without losing the ability to predict extra arcs.

6 Conclusion

We present a neural parser with LSTM in this paper for the task of Chinese semantic dependency parsing. We have shown that such a parser may perform close to the top performer in the task with minimal feature engineering. We also discussed places where potential improvements can be made.

References

Emmon Bach. 1981. Discontinuous constituents in generalized categorial grammars. *Proceedings of the Annual Meeting of the Northeast Linguistic Society (NELS)*, 11:1–12.

Dzmitry Bahdanau, Kyunghyun Cho, and Yoshua Bengio. 2014. Neural machine translation by jointly learning to align and translate. In *ICLR*, pages 1–15.

Wanxiang Che, Meishan Zhang, Yanqiu Shao, and Ting Liu. 2012. Semeval-2012 task 5 : Chinese semantic dependency parsing. In *SemEval*, pages 378–384.

Manjuan Duan and William Schuler. 2015. Parsing chinese with a generalized categorial grammar. In *Proceedings of Grammar Engineering Across Frameworks 2015*, pages 25–32.

John Duchi, Elad Hazan, and Yoram Singer. 2011. Adaptive subgradient methods for online learning and stochastic optimization. *Journal of Machine Learning Research*, 12:2121–2159.

David Graff and Ke Chen. 2003. Chinese gigaword ldc 2003t09.

Alex Graves, Navdeep Jaitly, and Abdel Rahman Mohamed. 2013a. Hybrid speech recognition with deep bidirectional lstm. *2013 IEEE Workshop on Automatic Speech Recognition and Understanding, ASRU 2013 - Proceedings*, pages 273–278.

Alex Graves, Abdel-rahman Mohamed, and Geoffrey Hinton. 2013b. Speech recognition with deep recurrent neural networks. *IEEE International Conference on Acoustics, Speech and Signal Processing (ICASSP)*, (3):6645–6649.

Sepp Hochreiter and Jürgen Schmidhuber. 1997. Long short-term memory. *Neural Comput.*, 9(8):1735–1780.

Sepp Hochreiter. 1998. The vanishing gradient problem during learning recurrent neural nets and problem solutions. *Int. J. Uncertain. Fuzziness Knowl.-Based Syst.*, 6(2):107–116.

Tomas Mikolov, Kai Chen, Greg Corrado, and Jeffrey Dean. 2013. Efficient estimation of word representations in vector space. *CoRR*, abs/1301.3:1–12.

Luan Nguyen, Marten van Schijndel, and William Schuler. 2012. Accurate unbounded dependency recovery using generalized categorial grammars. In *Proceedings of the 24th International Conference on Computational Linguistics (COLING '12)*, pages 2125–2140.

Slav Petrov and Dan Klein. 2007. Improved inference for unlexicalized parsing. In *Proceedings of {NAACL HLT} 2007*, pages 404–411. Association for Computational Linguistics, 4.

Ilya Sutskever, Oriol Vinyals, and Quoc V Le. 2014. Sequence to sequence learning with neural networks. *NIPS*, pages 3104–3112.

Kai Sheng Tai, Richard Socher, and Christopher D Manning. 2015. Improved semantic representations from tree-structured long short-term memory networks. *ACL*, pages 1556–1566.

Oriol Vinyals, Lukasz Kaiser, Terry Koo, Slav Petrov, Ilya Sutskever, and Geoffrey Hinton. 2015. Grammar as a foreign language. In *NIPS*.

Hua-Ping Zhang, Hong-Kui Yu, Xiong De-Yi, and Qun Liu. 2003. Hhmm-based chinese lexical analyzer ictclas. In *Proceedings of the Second SIGHAN Workshop on Chinese Language Processing*, volume 17, pages 184–187. Association for Computational Linguistics.

OSU_CHGCG at SemEval-2016 Task 9: Chinese Semantic Dependency Parsing with Generalized Categorial Grammar

Manjuan Duan   **Lifeng Jin**   **William Schuler**
Department of Linguistics
The Ohio State University
{duan,jin,schuler}@ling.osu.edu

Abstract

This paper introduces our Chinese semantic dependency parsing system for Task 9 of SemEval 2016. Our system has two components: a parser trained using the Berkeley Grammar Trainer on the Penn Chinese Treebank reannotated in a Generalized Categorial Grammar, and a multinomial logistic regression classifier. We first parse the data with the automatic parser to obtain predicate-argument dependencies and then we use the classifier to predict the semantic dependency labels for the predicate-argument dependency relations extracted. Although our parser is not trained directly on the task training data, our system yields the best performance for the non-local dependency recovery for the news data and comparable overall results.

1 Introduction

Semantic dependency parsing is an important language processing task which is useful in information extraction and question answering. In this paper, we introduce a Chinese semantic dependency parsing system which is built upon a categorial analysis of the Chinese language.

Categorial grammar annotations are attractive because they have a transparent syntactic-semantic interface and provide a natural account of long-distance dependencies in a language. For this system, we adopt a Generalized Categorial Grammar framework, GCG, (Bach, 1981), for our language

analysis. GCG annotations, compared with other Categorial Grammars, have a larger set of language-specific rules and a smaller set of lexical categories, which on the one hand retains the desirable features of a categorial grammar, such as straightforward compositionality of its syntactic derivations and elegant analysis of filler-gap phenomenon, and on the other hand, mitigates the sparse data problem faced by any heavily lexicalized annotations. Parsers trained with English GCG annotations have been shown to have state-of-the-art parsing performance and better long-distance dependency recovery (Rimell et al., 2009; Nguyen et al., 2012). Parsers trained with Chinese GCG annotations have been shown to achieve better parsing accuracy than the parser trained with Chinese Combinatory Categorial Grammar, CCG, (Steedman, 2000; Steedman, 2012) annotations (Tse and Curran, 2010; Tse and Curran, 2012) for those trees which both grammar annotations assign the same tree structures (Duan and Schuler, 2015).

The current experiment is our first experiment with dependency relations generated from the Chinese GCG annotations. We evaluate them against the manually annotated semantic dependencies in the current SemEval task. Since the purpose of the system is to verify the semantic dependencies generated by the Chinese GCG parser are reasonable, we adopt a minimalist machine learning scheme for this system to accomplish the evaluation. We first train the Berkeley parser (Petrov and Klein, 2007) with GCG annotations converted from the currently

Proceedings of SemEval-2016, pages 1218–1224,
San Diego, California, June 16-17, 2016. ©2016 Association for Computational Linguistics

reannotated protion of around 71% of the Chinese Treebank (Xue et al., 2005) sentences. With this parser, we parse the sentences from training sets of the SemEval task and extract dependencies from the parses. Since the dependency labels are more fine-grained in the SemEval task, we train a multinomial logistic regression classifier to predict the dependency labels for the extracted dependencies, using lexical, POS and other position features.

Even though the parser is not directly trained on the gold GCG annotations of the training sentences, this system still yields respectable results compared with other more task dependent systems. Also the official evaluation of the task shows that the current system yields the best non-local dependency parsing accuracy for the newspaper corpus, which supports the findings in English that GCG annotations yield superior performance in long-distance dependency recovery (Nguyen et al., 2012).

2 Chinese GCG Parser

This experiment used the Berkeley parser trained on Chinese GCG reannotated trees.

2.1 Chinese GCG framework

A generalized categorial grammar (Bach, 1981; Nguyen et al., 2012)[1] is a tuple $\langle P, O, R, W, M \rangle$ (Oehrle, 1994) consisting of a set P of primitive category types, a set O of type-constructing operators, a set R of inference rules, a set W of vocabulary items, and a mapping M from vocabulary items to syntactic categories. A set of complex syntactic categories C may then be defined as: $P \subset C$; $C \times O \times C \subset C$; nothing else is in C.

The reannotation of Chinese Treebank into GCG annotations is still an on-going project. So far, we have identified the following set of primitive syntactic categories P for Mandarin Chinese:

---

[1]Nguyen et al (2012) notate the '//' and '\\' operators of Bach (1981) as **-g** and **-h**, mnemonic for 'gap' and 'heavy shift'.

V: verb-headed clause
N: noun-headed phrase or clause
D: *de*-clause headed by 的
C: cardinal number
Q: quantificational phrase
A: adjectival phrase or nominal modifier
R: adverbial phrase or verbal modifier
B: verbal complement of in *ba*-construction
E: verbal complement of in passive voice

The set of type-constructing operators O for Mandarin Chinese includes **-a** and **-b** operators for unsatisfied requirements of preceding or succeeding arguments, **-c** and **-d** operators for unsatisfied requirements of preceding or succeeding conjuncts, and a **-g** operator for unsatisfied requirements of gap categories.[2]

A GCG category consists of a primitive category followed by one or more unsatisfied dependencies, each consisting of an operator followed by another category. For example the category for a transitive verb is 'V-aN-bN' , since it is headed by a verb and has unsatisfied dependencies for noun phrases preceding and following it, i.e., the subject and direct object respectively.

As in other categorial grammars, inference rules for local argument attachment apply functors of category $\varphi_{1...n\text{-}1}$**-ac** or $p\phi_{1...n\text{-}1}$**-bc** to initial or final arguments of category c, where $c \in C$, $p \in P$ and each $\varphi \in \{\textbf{-a}, \textbf{-b}\} \times C$:

$$c{:}g \quad p\varphi_{1..n\text{-}1}\textbf{-ac}{:}h \Rightarrow p\varphi_{1..n\text{-}1}{:}\lambda_x\, g\,(\mathbf{f}_n\, x) \wedge (h\, x) \quad \text{(Aa)}$$

$$p\varphi_{1..n\text{-}1}\textbf{-bc}{:}g \quad c{:}h \Rightarrow p\varphi_{1..n\text{-}1}{:}\lambda_x\,(g\, x) \wedge h\,(\mathbf{f}_n\, x) \quad \text{(Ab)}$$

These two inference rules stipulate the argument of category c is the n-th argument of the head. Inference rules for modifier composition apply preceding or succeeding modifiers of category p**-bd** to modificands of category c, where $p \in \{\mathbf{A}, \mathbf{R}\}$, $d \in \{\mathbf{N}, \mathbf{V}\}$:

$$p\textbf{-bd}{:}g \quad c{:}h \Rightarrow c{:}\lambda_x\, \exists_y\,(g\, y) \wedge (h\, x) \wedge (\mathbf{f}_1\, y){=}x \quad \text{(Ma)}$$

$$c{:}g \quad p\textbf{-bd}{:}h \Rightarrow c{:}\lambda_x\, \exists_y\,(g\, x) \wedge (h\, y) \wedge (\mathbf{f}_1\, y){=}x \quad \text{(Mb)}$$

Separate modifier composition rules makes it possible to assign the same syntactic category to the modifier regardless of its occurring position. The modifier composition rules Ma and Mb establish a '1'-labeled dependency from the modifier to the modificand. For example, for the sentence '小猫吃了

---

[2]Following Nguyen et al (2012), directional operators such as forward and backward slashes ('\' and '/') are not used because some operators, such as gap operators in tough constructions, are undirected.

鱼 *The little cat ate the fish*', we have the derivation and the dependencies extracted from the derivation as follows.

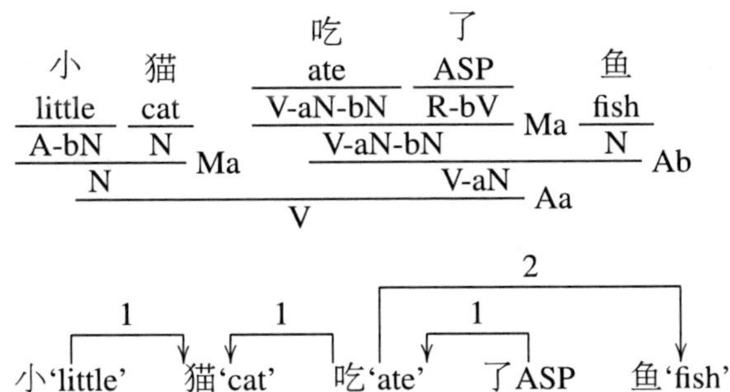

Inference rules for gap composition are:

$$p\varphi_{1..n-1}oc \Rightarrow p\varphi_{1..n-1}\text{-}\mathbf{g}c{:}\lambda_{vx}\,(g\,x) \wedge (\mathbf{f}_n\,x)=v \quad \text{(Ga)}$$

$$c{:}g \Rightarrow c\text{-}\mathbf{g}d{:}\lambda_{vx}\,(g\,x) \wedge (\mathbf{f}_1\,v)=x \quad \text{(Gb)}$$

$$\text{N}{:}g \Rightarrow \text{N-}\mathbf{g}\text{N}{:}\lambda_{vx}\,(g\,x) \wedge \exists_e\,(\mathbf{de\text{-}asso}\,e\,x\,v) \quad \text{(Gc)}$$

where $p \in P$, $o \in \{\text{-a, -b}\}$, $c \in C$, $d \in \{\mathbf{A\text{-}bN}, \mathbf{R\text{-}bV}\}$ and $\varphi \in \{\text{-a, -b}\} \times C$.

Rule Ga hypothesizes a gap as a preceding or succeeding argument, rule Gb hypothesizes an adjectival or adverbial modifier gap and rule Gc hypothesizes a gap which is associated with the subject in the topicalization construction which does not involve movement.

Non-local arguments, each consisting of a non-local operator and argument category $\psi \in \{\text{-g}\} \times C$, are then propagated to consequents from all possible combinations of antecedents. For $d{:}g \;\; e{:}h \Rightarrow c{:}(f\,g\,h) \in \{\text{Aa–b, Ma–b}\}$:

$$d\psi_{1..m}{:}g \;\; e\psi_{m+1..n}{:}h$$
$$\Rightarrow c\psi_{1..n}{:}\lambda_{v_{1..n}}\,f\,(g\,v_{1..m})\,(h\,v_{m+1..n})$$
$$\text{(Ac–d, Mc–d)}$$

Rules Ac–d and Mc–d stipulate non-local propagation through argument and modifier composition.

Inference rules for filler attachment apply gapped clauses to topicalized phrases as fillers. For $c \in C$, and $p \in P$:

$$p{:}g \;\; c\text{-}\mathbf{g}p{:}h \Rightarrow c{:}\lambda_x \exists_y\,(g\,y) \wedge (h\,y\,x) \quad \text{(Fa)}$$

For example, for a topicalized sentence such as "鱼，小猫吃了。 *The fish, the little cat ate.*", we can extract the dependencies as follows.

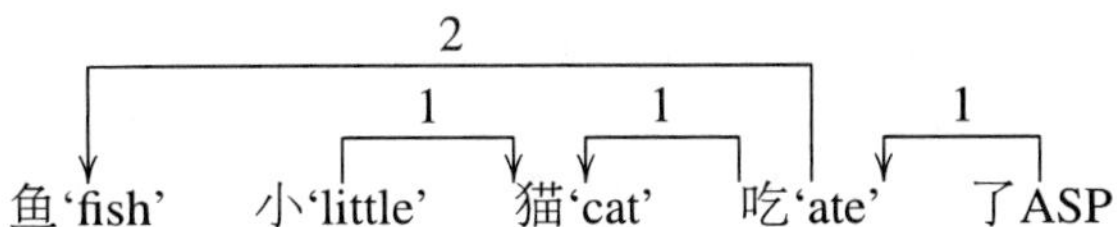

In Mandarin relative clauses, the particle 的 'de' takes a preceding clause containing a gap to form a relative clause modifying a succeeding noun. The modified noun is the filler of the gap in the relative clause. The inference rules for relative clauses apply the gapped *de*-clause to the modificand as a filler. For $c \in C$:

$$\mathbf{D\text{-}g}c{:}g \;\; \mathbf{N}{:}h \Rightarrow \mathbf{N}{:}\lambda_x\,(h\,x) \wedge \exists_y\,(g\,x\,y) \quad \text{(R)}$$

For a noun phrase such as "小猫吃的鱼 *the fish that the little cat ate*", we can extract the following dependencies.

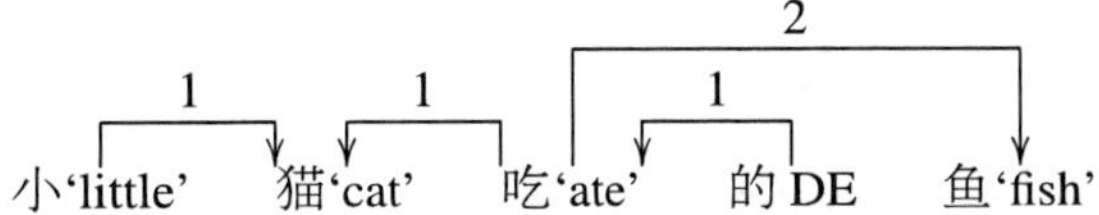

Ba constructions in Mandarin Chinese require the affected patients of certain verbs to occur before the verb. In our analysis, we propose that the particle *ba* takes a *ba*-verb as its complement. *Ba*-verbs can be derived from transitive verbs with the type conversion rule, or some verbs, such as some resultative verbs, have *Ba*-verb categories.

The particle 把 *ba* is assigned the category **V-aN-b(B-aN)**, with coindexation between the referent of its subject ($\mathbf{f}_1\,x$) and the referent of the subject of its complement ($\mathbf{f}_1\,(\mathbf{f}_2\,x)$).

$$把 \text{ 'ba' } \mapsto \mathbf{V\text{-}aN\text{-}b(B\text{-}aN)}{:}$$
$$\lambda_x\,(\mathbf{f}_0\,x)=\text{ba} \wedge (\mathbf{f}_1\,x)=(\mathbf{f}_1\,(\mathbf{f}_2\,x))$$

The lexical entry of *ba* gives the following dependencies for the sentence '猫把鱼吃了 *The cat ate the fish*.

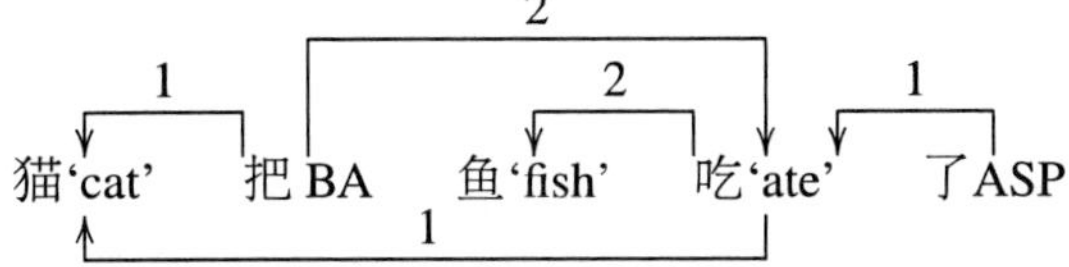

Mandarin Chinese uses the particle 被 *bei* to construct passive sentences. In *bei* constructions, the patient argument of a verb, usually the second argument of a transitive verb or a *ba*-verb, is moved to the subject position of the clause. We propose the particle 被 *bei* takes a *bei*-verb as its complement, which is converted from a transitive verb with a missing object. Here is the lexical entry we propose for the *bei* particle.

被 'bei' ↦ **V-aN-b(E-aN-gN)-bN**:

$$\lambda_x \, (\mathbf{f}_0 \, x) = \text{bei} \wedge (\mathbf{f}_3 \, x) = (\mathbf{f}_1 \, (\mathbf{f}_2 \, x))$$

For example, the sentence '鱼被猫吃了 *The fish was eaten by the cat* gives us the following dependencies.

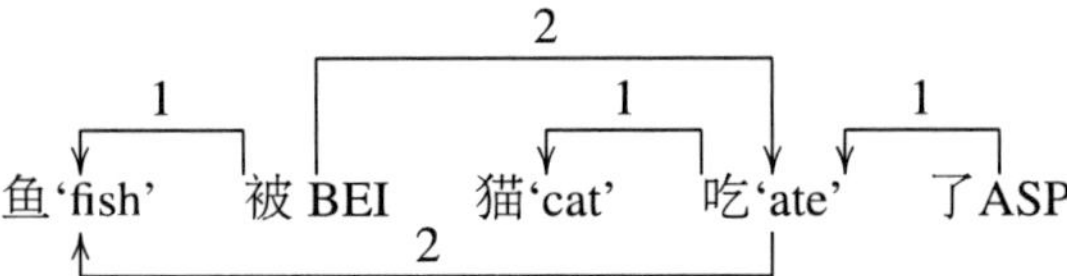

2.2 Training Chinese GCG Parser

The syntactic parser we used for the current semantic dependency parsing is trained by the latent variable PCFG trainer (Petrov and Klein, 2007) on Chinese GCG annotations. Converting Penn Chinese Treebank 5 and 6 into GCG annotations is still an on-going project. We use a set of reannotation rules similar to those described by Nguyen et al. (2012) to reannotate the Penn Chinese Treebank into GCG trees. We currently have fully annotated 71% of sentences (18,505 out of 26,062 sentences) from the Penn Chinese Treebank 5 and 6.[3] With these 18,505, we have trained the Chinese GCG parser which is used for the current semantic dependency parsing task. From the parses, we extracted the raw dependences as the input for the multinomial classifier in the next stage.

3 Multinomial Dependency Label Classifier

As shown in the examples above, the predicate-argument dependencies extracted from GCG derivations do not have fine-grained labels as those dependencies annotated for the task. Also the dependencies identified by the parser sometimes have different directions than those annotated in the task.

Therefore, in order to increase the coverage, for each dependency identified by the parser, we also add a dependency which has the reverse direction. For example, if the parser predicts that a dependency such as *1(eat, cat)*, in which the head is *eat*, the dependent is *cat*, the dependency label is '1', we would add another dependency with inversed direction: *1-inv(cat, eat)*. By doing so, we can increase the coverage of the annotated dependencies to around 83%. However, it also doubles the dependencies predicted by the parser and potentially hurts the recall of the accuracy later on.

There are totally 157 semantic dependency labels used in the task. Since the classifier also needs to decide whether a dependency relation exists between each pair of words, we add a "NoRel" label for those pairs of words which, according to the gold annotation, do not hold any dependency relation between them.

We train a one-vs-all multiclass classifier from the Vowpal Wabbit machine learning package.[4] We use the following features to predict the dependency labels:

Lexical features: the 300-dimensional word embeddings of the head and dependent words trained with *word2vec* (Mikolov et al., 2013) on the full Chinese Wikipedia, the Chinese Gigaword as well as the training and test datasets in this task;

POS features: the 50-dimensional vector representations of the POS tags of the head and dependent trained with the POS tag sequences from training and test datasets in this task;

Linear distance: the linear distance of the head and the dependent in the sentence;

Path distance: the distance of the nodes of the head and the dependent in the syntactic tree;

Syntactic categories: the GCG syntactic categories of the head and the dependent;

Pred-arg dependency labels: the dependency labels predicted by the parser, such as '1' or '2';

Repetition penalty: the reciprocal of the number of heads that the dependent word has, to penalize proposing too many heads for one word;

Joint features: two-way combinational features between GCG syntactic categories of the two words

---

[3]The reannotation rules for generating the training set for current parser are available at `http://www.sourceforge.net/projects/modelblocks`.

[4]`https://github.com/JohnLangford/vowpal_wabbit/wiki`

	LF	NLF	UF	NUF
News	58.99	54.99	76.64	63.51
Text	65.31	56.74	78.19	66.61

Table 1: Results of development set where LF is the F1 score of the labeled dependency, NLF is the F1 score of the non-local dependency, UF is the F1 score of the unlabeled dependency and NUF is the F1 score the non-local unlabeled dependency.

		LF	NLF	UF	NUF
News	GCG	55.69	**49.23**	73.72	**60.71**
	TOP	**58.78**	40.84	**77.64**	60.20
Text	GCG	65.17	**54.70**	78.83	**65.71**
	TOP	**68.59**	50.57	**82.41**	64.58

Table 2: Results of the test set compared with the best system where GCG is the current system and TOP is the system with the best labeled F1 score.

and the dependency label, such "V-aN_1" or "N_1";

4   Results and Discussion

This Chinese semantic dependency parsing task comes in two domains, the newspaper articles (News) and texts selected from Chinese textbooks (Text). In our experiment, we found the combining the two training sets yields better accuracy for the textbook corpus and a slightly worse performance for the newspaper corpus. Therefore the News results reported in Table 1 and 2 are obtained by a classifier only trained on the newspaper corpus, and the Text results are obtained by a classifier trained on the combined training set of the newspaper corpus and the textbook corpus.

The results in Table 1 show that newspaper text is more difficult to parse, even though the GCG parser is trained on a newspaper corpus. However, it also shows that the parser trained on the newspaper corpus can generalize nicely to another domain such as the textbook corpus, where more diverse syntactic constructions are found.

Table 2 shows the results on the test set compared with the system yielding the highest labeled F1 score. We can see that the current system is around 3 percentage lower than the top system in terms of the labeled F1 score. Considering the fact that the parser is not directly trained on the task-specific dependency annotations and gold POS tags, these results look reasonably good with the rather simplistic machine learning architecture. Table 2 also shows that the current system achieves the best performance on non-local dependencies according to the official evaluation, which supports the corresponding findings in English where parsers trained on GCG English annotations achieve the state-of-the-art performance in long distance dependency recovery (Nguyen et al., 2012).

5   Error Analysis

We randomly inspected around 20 sentences from each domain where the predictions of the current system are different from the gold annotations to examine the reason, and we identified the following sources of errors.

Parsing errors: Parsing errors caused around half of the wrong predictions we inspected. One type of mistake that we notice the parser often makes is wrong predictions about the internal structure of complex noun phrases. For example, for the noun phrase '国际货币基金组织 *International Monetary Fund Organization*', the parser proposes all first three nouns to be modifiers of the head noun '组织 *organization*', while '货币 *monetary*' actually modifies '基金 *fund*' in gold annotations. The parser also often makes mistakes when parsing questions, since there are not many questions in the Treebank.

Uncovered linguistic phenomena: the gold dependency annotations issued by the task contain dependencies involving co-reference.

(1) 我 觉得 自己   是 世界上   最幸福
     I think myself is in the world happiest
    的 人   了。
    DE person ASP.
    'I think I am the happiest person in the world.'

(2) 鲁肃 问   他： "你 叫   我 来   做
    Lusu asked him: "you asked me come do
    什么？"
    what?   "
    'Lusu asked him: "Why did you ask me to come?"'

In (1), '我 *I*' is annotated to have a *eEqu* relation with '自己 *myself*'. In (2), '鲁肃 *Lusu*' has a *eEqu* relation with '我 *me*'. Dependencies like these, especially the one in (2), cannot be resolved easily by a syntactic parser, which means we might need an extra layer of post-processing to do co-reference inference based on discourse information.

Ambiguous constructions: In some cases, a sentence can be analyzed in more than one way. All of them are reasonable analyses but each gives different dependencies.

(3) 我 爱 他 有 志气。
I love he have aspiration.
'I love he has aspiration.' or 'I love him to have aspiration.'

(4) 这里 一定 有 人 来 过。
here must have people come TENSE.
'Someone must have come here before'

The current parser parses both (3) and (4) as object control sentences. In (3) '他 *he*' is the object of '爱 *love*' and the subject of '有志气 *have aspiration*'. In the gold annotation of (3), '爱 *love*' takes a sentential complement '*he has aspiration*'. Therefore, for (3), our system proposes a dependency between '爱 *love*' and '他 *he*', while in the gold annotations, the dependency is between '爱 *love*' and '有 *have*'. In (4), our parser parses '人 *person*' as the object of '有 *have*' and the subject of '来过 *came*'. '有 *have*', therefore, is the root of the sentence. In gold annotations, '来 *come*' is the root of the sentence.

Inconsistent annotations: There are some cases where our predictions are systematically different from the gold annotations. For example, the current system is consistently different from the gold annotations on the identification of root where some adverbial clauses are involved.

(5) 万一 明天 下雨, 则 推迟 野游 日期。
If tomorrow rain, then postpone trip data.
'If it rains tomorrow, postpone the date of trip'

(6) 既然 她 讨厌 伦敦, 为什么 他 还 在 那里 买 了 房子?
Given she dislike London, why he still at there buy ASP house?
'Given that she does not like London, why did he buy a house there?'

We think both (5) and (6) contain a conditional subordinate clause, and the root of the sentence should

be '推迟 *postpone*' in (5) and '买 *buy*' in (6). In gold annotations, '下雨 *rain*' is annotated to be the root of (5) and '讨厌 *dislike*' the root of (6). Our assumption is that those clauses are handled as conjunctions in gold annotations.

Our predictions also do not agree with the gold annotations in some relative clauses.

(7) 这 正是 杰里米 喜欢 做 的 事情。
This is Jimmy like do DE thing.
'This is the thing that Jimmy likes to do'

Our system predicts the follow dependencies for the noun phrase 杰里米喜欢做的事情 *things that Jimmy likes to do*.

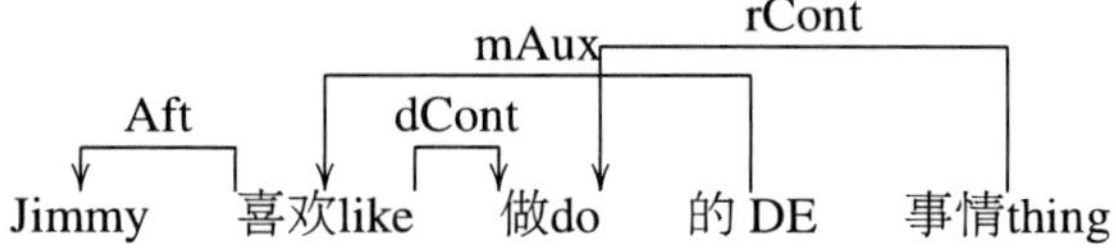

For the same noun phrase, the gold annotation is

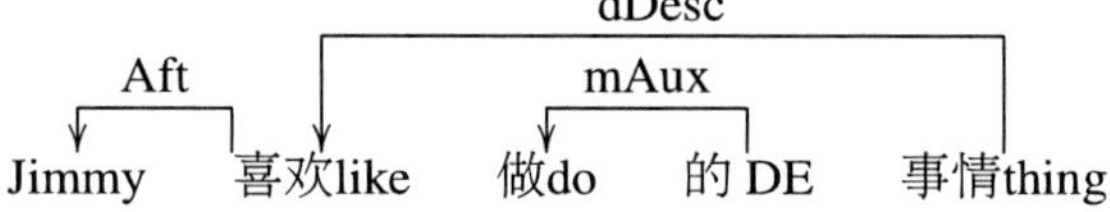

For (7), we think there is a dependency between '做 *do*' and '事情 *thing*', rather than '喜欢 *like*' and '事情 *thing*'.

6 Conclusion

This paper introduces the Chinese semantic dependency parsing system based on the predicate-argument dependencies predicted by a Berkeley parser trained on Chinese GCG trees reannotated from the Penn Chinese Treebank. This system achieves comparable performance for the overall labeled dependency prediction and superior performance for the non-local dependency recovery. Our error analysis shows that many dependency parsing errors can be attributed to the syntactic parsing errors. In the future, we will expand the training set of the parser to cover more diverse syntactic constructions such as questions. We will also consider including corpora from different domains to make the parser more adaptable to data from new domains.

References

Emmon Bach. 1981. Discontinuous constituents in generalized categorial grammars. *Proceedings of the Annual Meeting of the Northeast Linguistic Society (NELS)*, 11:1–12.

Manjuan Duan and William Schuler. 2015. Parsing Chinese with a Generative Categorial Grammar. In *Proceedings of Grammar Engineering Across Frameworks*, pages 25–32.

Tomas Mikolov, Kai Chen, Greg Corrado, and Jeffrey Dean. 2013. Efficient estimation of word representations in vector space. *CoRR*, abs/1301.3781:1–12.

Luan Nguyen, Marten van Schijndel, and William Schuler. 2012. Accurate unbounded dependency recovery using generalized categorial grammars. In *Proceedings of COLING '12*, pages 2125–2140, Mumbai, India.

Richard T. Oehrle. 1994. Term-labeled categorial type systems. *Linguistics and Philosophy*, 17(6):633–678.

Slav Petrov and Dan Klein. 2007. Improved inference for unlexicalized parsing. In *Proceedings of NAACL HLT 2007*, pages 404–411, Rochester, New York, April. Association for Computational Linguistics.

Laura Rimell, Stephen Clark, and Mark Steedman. 2009. Unbounded dependency recovery for parser evaluation. In *Proceedings of EMNLP 2009*, volume 2, pages 813–821.

Mark Steedman. 2000. *The syntactic process*. MIT Press/Bradford Books, Cambridge, MA.

Mark Steedman. 2012. *Taking Scope - The Natural Semantics of Quantifiers*. MIT Press.

Daniel Tse and James R. Curran. 2010. Chinese CCGbank: extracting CCG derivations from the penn chinese treebank. In *Proceedings of COLING '10*, pages 1083–1091.

Daniel Tse and James R. Curran. 2012. The Challenges of Parsing Chinese with Combinatory Categorial Grammar. In *Proceedings of NAACL-HLT '12*, pages 295–304, Montréal, Canada.

Nianwen Xue, Fei Xian, Fu-Dong Chiou, and Martha Palmer. 2005. The Penn Chinese Treebank: Phrase Structure annotation of a large corpus. *Natural Language Engineering*, 11:207–238.

LIMSI at SemEval-2016 Task 12: machine-learning and temporal information to identify clinical events and time expressions

Cyril Grouin

LIMSI, CNRS, Université Paris-Saclay

Bât 508, rue John von Neumann, Campus Universitaire, F-91405 Orsay

`cyril.grouin@limsi.fr`

Véronique Moriceau

LIMSI, CNRS, Univ. Paris-Sud, Université Paris-Saclay

Bât 508, rue John von Neumann, Campus Universitaire, F-91405 Orsay

`veronique.moriceau@limsi.fr`

Abstract

Our experiments rely on a combination of machine-learning (CRF) and rule-based (HeidelTime) systems. First, a CRF system identifies both EVENTS and TIMEX3, along with polarity values for EVENT and types of TIMEX. Second, the HeidelTime tool identifies DOCTIME and TIMEX3 elements, and computes DocTimeRel for each EVENT identified by the CRF. Third, another CRF system computes DocTimeRel for each previously identified EVENT, based on DocTimeRel computed by HeidelTime. In the first submission, all EVENTS and TIMEX3 are identified through one general CRF model while in the second submission, we combined two CRF models (one for both EVENT and TIMEX3, and one only for TIMEX3) and we applied post-processing rules on the outputs.

1 Introduction

In this paper, we present the methods we used while participating in the 2016 Clinical TempEval task as part of the SemEval-2016 challenge. A few recent NLP challenges focused on temporal expressions within clinical records, such as the 2014 i2b2/UTHealth[1] challenge (Stubbs et al., 2015) or the second task from the 2014 ShARe/CLEF eHealth[2] evaluation lab (Mowery et al., 2014).

2 Task description

2.1 Presentation

The 2016 Clinical TempEval track[3] proposed six tasks (Bethard et al., 2016). We participated in the first five tasks which concern the identification of: (i) spans of time expressions (TS task), (ii) spans of event expressions (ES task), (iii) the attribute of time expressions (TA task), (iv) attributes of event expressions (EA task), and (v) the relation between each event and the document creation time (DR task). We did not participate in the narrative container relation task (CR).

In both TS and ES tasks, spans of time and event expressions are represented using start and end offsets of characters. In the TA task, time expressions are related to the attribute "class" which specifies the type of time expressions among six possible values: *date, duration, prepostexp, quantifier, set, time*. In the EA task, event expressions are related to four attributes: "polarity" (either *positive* or *negative*), "modality" (*actual, hedged, hypothetical* or *generic*), "degree" (*most, little* or *N/A*) and "type" (*aspectual, evidential* or *N/A*).

Two phases were proposed. In the first phase, all tasks were proposed, based on raw texts. We thus participated to TS ES TA EA and DR tasks. In the second phase, reference annotations were given for tasks TS ES TA and EA, and participants were expected to identify the relations from DR and CR tasks. We also participated in this DR task.

---

[1]`https://www.i2b2.org/NLP/TemporalRelations/`

[2]`http://clefehealth2014.dcu.ie/task-2`

[3]`http://alt.qcri.org/semeval2016/task12/`

Proceedings of SemEval-2016, pages 1225–1230,

San Diego, California, June 16-17, 2016. ©2016 Association for Computational Linguistics

2.2 Corpora

The given training corpus was divided into two sub-corpora called *train* and *dev*. Table 1 shows the distribution of each category and its attributes in this corpus. The most frequent ones are in bold font.

	Attributes	Train	Dev	TOTAL
	Class			
TIMEX	Date	2588	1422	**4010**
	Duration	434	200	634
	PrePostExp	313	172	485
	Set	218	116	334
	Quantifier	162	109	271
	Time	118	59	177
	Type			
	N/A	36185	19414	**55599**
	Evidential	2206	1314	3520
	Aspectual	546	246	792
	Polarity			
	POS	34832	18795	**53627**
	NEG	4105	2179	6284
	Degree			
	N/A	38698	20864	**59562**
	Little	143	65	208
EVENT	Most	96	45	141
	Modality			
	Actual	35781	22647	**58428**
	Hypothetical	1656	829	2485
	Hedged	889	443	1332
	Generic	611	299	910
	DocTimeRel			
	Overlap	18297	9812	**28109**
	Before	14291	7896	22187
	After	4189	2138	6327
	Before/overlap	2160	1128	3288

Table 1: Statistics on the training data.

Corpora are composed of files of two types: "clinic" and "path" files. According to the organizers, annotations are of better quality for "clinic" files than for "path" files. Moreover, adjudication of annotations has been made only for "clinic" files.

3   Methods

Our methods mainly rely on machine-learning. We used the Wapiti (Lavergne et al., 2010) toolkit, based on the linear-chain CRFs framework (Lafferty et al., 2001). We considered this challenge as a classification task, where we have to classify each token from a file into a TIMEX or an EVENT category.

Due to the unbalanced distribution of attribute values in the training corpus (see Table 1), we decided not to automatically process three EVENT attributes ("modality", "degree", and "type"). For those attributes, we used the most frequent value as a default value: *Actual* for "modality" (89.5%), *N/A* for both "degree" (99.4%) and "type" (92.8%) attributes. As a consequence, we only processed the "polarity" and "doctimerel" EVENT attributes using our CRF systems.

3.1   Tasks TS, ES, TA, EA

CRF system   We merged all tasks of spans and attributes identification into a single task. This process consists in identifying the main category and the related attribute value in one step (e.g., EVENT-POS and EVENT-NEG to identify *positive* and *negative* EVENT expressions).

Since annotations are of better quality in "clinic" files, we compared the results we achieved (ES and TS tasks) on the whole development set (i.e., both "clinic" and "path" files) whether we trained our CRF model on both "clinic" and "path" files from the training set or on the "clinic" files from this training set only. Table 2 presents those results. We observed the CRF model only trained on the "clinic" files outperforms results globally and for each category. As a consequence, we decided to train our CRF models on the "clinic" files only.

Training set	Category	P	R	F
ClinPath (293 files)	EVENT	**.877**	.710	.785
	TIMEX	.801	.517	.629
	Overall	**.872**	.693	.773
Clin (195 files)	EVENT	.845	**.869**	**.857**
	TIMEX	**.810**	**.551**	**.656**
	Overall	.843	**.842**	**.843**

Table 2: Results on the development set whether the CRF model was trained on both "clinic" and "path" files (ClinPath) from the training set or "clinic" files only (Clin) (P=Precision, R=Recall, F=F-measure). Black font highlights the best results

We thus created three CRF models:

- a first model to identify both spans of EVENT expressions and the associated value of the attribute of polarity: model EVENT/Polarity;

- a second model to identify both spans of

TIMEX expressions and the associated value of the "class" attribute: model TIMEX/Class;

- and a last global model to identify both EVENT and TIMEX expressions (i.e., spans) with the associated values of "polarity" and "class" attributes: model EVENT/Polarity TIMEX/Class.

The following features were used to produce all CRF models: (i) the token itself; (ii) token length, typographic case of the token, presence of punctuation marks in the token, and presence of digits in the token; (iii) part-of-speech tag of the token, provided by the Tree Tagger POS tagger (Schmid, 1994); (iv) cluster ID of each token through an automatic unsupervised clustering of all tokens from the training corpus into 120 clusters,[4] using the algorithm designed by Brown et al. (1992) and implemented by Liang (2005).

Rule-based post-processing In order to correct predictions made by the CRF system, we designed a basic post-processing based on rules. This post-processing consists in identifying additional EVENT expressions from a list of 69 most frequent EVENT expressions we collected from the training set. For all EVENT expressions found in this list, we set the "Polarity" value to *positive* as a default value.

3.2   Task DR

HeidelTime tool HeidelTime (Strötgen and Gertz, 2010; Strötgen and Gertz, 2013) allows to extract and normalize temporal expressions in texts according to the TIMEX3 standard. For the normalization of relative temporal expressions, the document creation time (DCT) is used. In this task, HeidelTime considers the expression indicated as *start date* in the text files as the DCT. Once all TIMEX are normalized, we assigned to each of them one of the four temporal relations: *before, after, overlap, before/overlap* w.r.t the DCT.

---

[4]We used five distinct versions of each cluster ID: the original cluster ID (e.g., "01011") and four generalization of each ID, removing the last digit to produce a more generic version from the previous one for each iteration ("0101", "010", "01" and "0"). We gave the CRF all those versions.

CRF system We considered this relation task as a classification task, where we have to classify each EVENT into a relational class. In order to perform this classification, we gave the CRF additional features, namely the temporal features previously computed by the HeidelTime tool on each TIMEX.

4   Design of experiments

Figure 1 presents the design of experiments we followed for the official submissions for the first phase. The grey boxes represent the distinct CRF models we used and the type of expressions processed by each model.

4.1   Task TS, TA, ES, EA (phase 1)

We considered two configurations, based on the results we achieved on the development corpus:

- application of the global model to identify all elements (EVENT/Polarity and TIMEX/Class). In our experiments, we noticed this model allows us to achieve higher values for both precision and F-measure. This constitutes our first submission (run #1.1);

- application of both global model (i.e., EVENT/Polarity and TIMEX/Class) and TIMEX/Class specific model to identify all elements. We merged outputs from both models, giving priority to predictions from the specific model for the TIMEX/Class category, and applied our post-processing. This configuration allows us to obtain higher values for recall. This constitutes our second submission (run #1.2).

4.2   Task DR

4.2.1   Task DR (phase 1)

For the first phase, we designed a new CRF model to predict the value of the "DocTimeRel" attribute associated with each EVENT we previously identified. In order to improve the quality of predictions made by our CRF system, we added as features the temporal relations computed by HeidelTime (see Section 3.2): the relations computed by HeidelTime are mapped to TIMEX expressions detected by the CRF models used in phase 1. When the CRF model detects a TIMEX expression that is not extracted by HeidelTime, the default value is used (*overlap*).

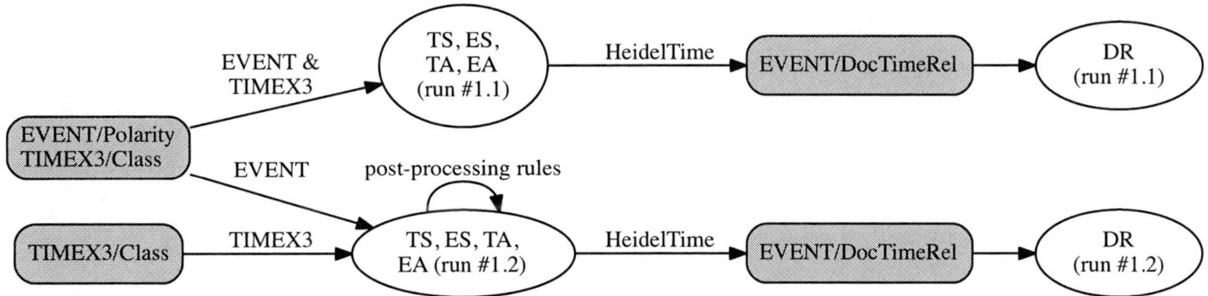

Figure 1: Design of experiments for phase 1. Grey boxes represent our distinct CRF models

We applied this model on outputs from runs #1.1 and #1.2. In this experiment, we tested how performs our DR CRF model depending on the quality of the outputs from the previous TS/ES/TA/EA tasks. Additionally, we considered the relations computed by HeidelTime and associated with each TIMEX expression would be useful.

4.2.2 Task DR (phase 2)

For the second phase, since gold standard annotations for TIMEX and EVENT expressions were given by the organizers, we trained two CRF models based on two different inputs:

- run #2.1: temporal relations computed by HeidelTime are mapped to the TIMEX entities from the gold standard annotations. If a TIMEX is not extracted by HeidelTime, the default value is used (*overlap*);

- run #2.2: only TIMEX and temporal relations extracted by HeidelTime are used.

5 Results and discussion

5.1 Official results (test set)

In this section, we present the official results we achieved on the test set. Outputs are evaluated through classical metrics used in information retrieval tasks: precision (positive predictive value), recall (true positive rate), and F-measure (weighted harmonic mean of precision and recall). In order to make the comparison between the results we obtained among our two submissions easier, the bold font pinpoints our best results.

5.1.1 Phase 1

Table 3 presents the official results we achieved on the test set for the tasks TS, ES, TA, EA and DR based on our first submission (run #1.1) from phase 1.

Task	Category	P	R	F
TS	TIMEX	**.840**	.510	.635
ES	EVENT	**.885**	.808	**.845**
TA	TIMEX/Class	**.815**	.495	.616
EA	EVENT/Degree	**.880**	.805	**.841**
	EVENT/Modality	**.811**	.742	**.775**
	EVENT/Polarity	**.867**	.792	**.828**
	EVENT/Type	**.825**	.754	**.788**
DR	EVENT/DocTimeRel	**.635**	.580	**.607**

Table 3: Official results on the test set (run #1.1) for tasks TS, ES, TA, EA and DR (P = Precision, R = Recall, F = F-measure). Bold font pinpoints best results

Table 4 presents the official results we achieved on the test set for the tasks TS, ES, TA, EA and DR based on our second submission (run #1.2) from phase 1.

Task	Category	P	R	F
TS	TIMEX	.830	**.518**	**.638**
ES	EVENT	.869	**.816**	.842
TA	TIMEX/Class	.804	**.503**	**.619**
EA	EVENT/Degree	.865	**.812**	.838
	EVENT/Modality	.798	**.749**	.772
	EVENT/Polarity	.851	**.799**	.824
	EVENT/Type	.811	**.761**	.785
DR	EVENT/DocTimeRel	.624	**.585**	.604

Table 4: Official results on the test set (run #1.2) for tasks TS, ES, TA, EA and DR (P = Precision, R = Recall, F = F-measure). Bold font pinpoints best results

We achieved our best results in our first submission, which is based on a global CRF model for tasks TS, ES, TA and EA, and a second CRF global model for task DR. As expected in our experimental setup, our first submission allows us to maximize the precision values, and generally obtains the higher F-measure values, while the second submission maximizes the recall values for all category and attribute.

In comparison with submissions from other participants from this first phase, we succeed to obtain better results than the median F-measure value for tasks TS (median=.637 vs. F=.638 in run #1.2) and ES (median=.830 vs. F=.845 and .842 respectively in runs #1.1 and #1.2). On TA, EA and DR tasks, we obtained lower results w.r.t. the median values. Our system only succeeds to obtain better results than the organizers' baseline on tasks TS (baseline F=.551) and DR (baseline=.604 vs. F=.607 in run #1.1).

5.1.2 Phase 2

Table 5 presents the official results we achieved on the test set for the task DR based on our first submission (run #2.1) from phase 2.

Task	Category	P	R	F
DR	EVENT/DocTimeRel	.687	.687	.687

Table 5: Official results on the test set (run #2.1) for task DR (P = Precision, R = Recall, F = F-measure)

Table 6 presents the official results we achieved on the test set for the task DR based on our second submission (run #2.2) from phase 2.

Task	Category	P	R	F
DR	EVENT/DocTimeRel	.679	.679	.679

Table 6: Official results on the test set (run #2.1) for task DR (P = Precision, R = Recall, F = F-measure)

On both submissions from phase 2, we did not succeed to obtain better results than the median value (F=.724). Nevertheless, our system obtained better results than the organizers' baseline (F=.675 vs. F=.687 in run #2.1 and .679 in run #2.2). This observation is consistent with the results we achieved on the DR task in phase 1.

5.2 Error analysis

Lack of robustness Since we trained our CRF models on "clinic" files only (see section 3.1), most of false negatives concern EVENT expressions that are only used in "path" files (e.g., *Description, nodes, orientation*, etc.). As the CRF failed to identify those expressions, we can consider that our model failed to generalize the properties of EVENT expressions, despite other features, and experienced difficulties to process unknown elements.

Similarly, due to the differences of structure between "clinic" and "path" files, most of false positives concern predictions made by our CRF system on "path" files exclusively (e.g., our system considered *Hematoxylin* to be annotated as an EVENT in all "path" files). This observation highlights the lack of robustness of our CRF systems on files being of different type.

Table 7 presents the results we achieved on the test set for each "clinic" and "path" files sub-set. Bold font highlights the best results. As expected, results are better on the "clinic" files sub-set than on the "path" files sub-set (on average 4 points more on the EVENT category for each metric).

Test sub-set	Category	P	R	F
Clinic (102 files)	EVENT	**.871**	**.891**	**.881**
	TIMEX	**.811**	**.663**	**.730**
	Overall	**.866**	**.867**	**.866**
Path (51 files)	EVENT	.828	.853	.840
	TIMEX	.000	.000	.000
	Overall	.828	.848	.838

Table 7: Results on the test set for each "clinic" and "path" files sub-set (P=Precision, R=Recall, F=F-measure)

Additionally, we observed that our CRF model failed to identify any TIMEX expressions on the "path" files from the test set.

TIMEX extraction with HeidelTime Evaluation of HeidelTime on TIMEX extraction of the test set gives the following results: P=.479, R=.586 and F=.527. The best scores are obtained for type *date* (P=.687, R=.677 and F=.682) whereas scores are very low for *quantifier* (F=.043), *set* (F=.065) and *time* (F=.083). This can be explained by the fact that some TIMEX annotations in the gold data are not compliant with the TimeML standard as used in HeidelTime. For example, the expression *12-MAY-2001 21:11* is annotated as a date (*12-MAY-2001*) and a time (*21:11*) in the gold data whereas the whole expression should be annotated as a time according to the TimeML standard. These low scores also explain why only 75% of TIMEX expressions in the gold data are mapped with a temporal relation computed by HeidelTime in run #2.1.

6   Conclusion

In this paper, we presented the methods we used while participating in the 2016 Clinical TempEval task as part of the SemEval-2016 challenge. We considered each task from the challenge as a classification task using machine-learning approaches. Our CRF systems allow us to predict both the offsets of each expression (TS and ES tasks) and the attribute of expressions (TA and EA tasks) as well as the temporal relations (DR task). Due to an unbalanced distribution of some EVENT attributes (namely "degree", "modality" and "type"), we gave the most frequent used value in the training corpus as a default value.

We designed two experiments. The first one is based on a single CRF model which identifies all expressions and attributes at the same time. The second one is based on a merge of two CRF models (one for EVENT, the other for TIMEX) and postprocessing rules to identify new EVENT expressions.

We achieved our best results through the first experiment (higher precision values for all tasks and the best F-measure values for all EVENT related tasks, F=.845 on ES) while the second experiment allows us to obtain higher recall values for all tasks and the best F-measure values for all TIMEX related tasks (F=.638 on TS). Our systems succeed to identify more correctly EVENT expressions than TIMEX expressions.

Our system achieved better results on the "clinic" files sub-set rather than on the "path" files sub-set. Future work is thus needed, first to improve the generalization of features used (in order to predict unknown expressions based on features), and second to ensure the robustness of our system (in order to process different files, namely "path" files).

References

Steven Bethard, Guergana Savova, Wei-Te Chen, Leon Derczynski, James Pustejovsky, and Marc Verhagen. 2016. Semeval-2016 task 12: Clinical tempeval. In *Proceedings of the 10th International Workshop on Semantic Evaluation (SemEval 2016)*, San Diego, California, June. Association for Computational Linguistics.

Peter F Brown, Vincent J Della Pietra, Peter V de Souza, Jenifer C Lai, and Robert L Mercer. 1992. Class-based n-gram models of natural language. *Computational Linguistics*, 18(4):467–79.

John D. Lafferty, Andrew McCallum, and Fernando C. N. Pereira. 2001. Conditional Random Fields: Probabilistic models for segmenting and labeling sequence data. In *Proc of ICML*, pages 282–9, Williamstown, MA.

Thomas Lavergne, Olivier Cappé, and François Yvon. 2010. Practical very large scale CRFs. In *Proc of ACL*, pages 504–13, Uppsala, Sweden, July.

Percy Liang. 2005. Semi-supervised learning for natural language. Master's thesis, Massachusetts Institute of Technology.

Danielle L Mowery, Sumithra Velupillai, Brett R South, Lee Christiensen, David Martinez, Liadh Kelly, Lorraine Goeuriot, Noémie Elhadad, Sameer Pradhan, Guergana K Savova, and Wendy W Chapman. 2014. Task 2: ShARe/CLEF eHealth evaluation lab 2014. In *CLEF2014 Working Notes*, volume 1180, Sheffield, UK.

Helmut Schmid. 1994. Probabilistic part-of-speech tagging using decision trees. In *Proc of International Conference on New Methods in Language*.

Jannik Strötgen and Michael Gertz. 2010. Heideltime: high quality rule-based extraction and normalization of temporal expressions. In *Proc of SemEval*.

Jannik Strötgen and Michael Gertz. 2013. Multilingual and cross-domain temporal tagging. *Language Resources and Evaluation*, 47(2):269–298.

Amber Stubbs, Christopher Kotfila, Hua Xu, and Özlem Uzuner. 2015. Identifying risk factors for heart disease over time: Overview of 2014 i2b2/UTHealth shared task track 2. *J Biomed Inform*, 58:S67–S77.

Hitachi at SemEval-2016 Task 12: A Hybrid Approach for Temporal Information Extraction from Clinical Notes

Sarath P R[1]**, Manikandan R**[1]**, Yoshiki Niwa**[2]

[1]Research & Development Center, Hitachi India Pvt Ltd, India
[2]Hitachi Ltd, Center for Exploratory Research, Japan

`{sarath,manikandan}@hitachi.co.in`
`yoshiki.niwa.tx@hitachi.com`

Abstract

This paper describes the system developed for the task of temporal information extraction from clinical narratives in the context of 2016 Clinical TempEval challenge. Clinical TempEval 2016 addressed the problem of temporal reasoning in clinical domain by providing annotated clinical notes and pathology reports similar to Clinical TempEval challenge 2015. The Clinical TempEval challenge consisted of six subtasks. Hitachi team participated in two time expression based subtasks: time expression span detection (TS) and time expression attribute identification (TA) for which we developed hybrid of rule-based and machine learning based methods using Stanford TokensRegex framework and Stanford Named Entity Recognizer and evaluated it on the THYME corpus. Our hybrid system achieved a maximum F-score of 0.73 for identification of time spans (TS) and 0.71 for identification of time attributes (TA).

1 Introduction

Temporal information extraction has been a trending topic of research interest in the field of information extraction. It is crucial for improvement of systems used in number of applications ranging from question answering, search engines, text classification etc. to the systems that establish timelines and explicitly ground events that occurs in clinical narratives.

This work focuses on the automatic identification of time expressions from clinical texts. Time expressions are words and phrases that correspond to points or spans on a timeline, such as Dates, Time, Durations, Quantifiers, Set, and PrepostExp. Table 1 shows the time expression clas ses used in this work, with examples given for each class.

Time Class	Example
Date	February 2 2010, Friday morning
Time	5:30 PM, 20 minutes ago
Duration	For the next 24 hours, nearly 2 weeks
Quantifier	twice, three times
Prepost	postoperatively, post-surgery
Set	twice daily, weekly

Table 1: Examples of time expressions.

Research work on temporal information extraction has been carried out in both general NLP domain (Verhagen et al., 2007; Verhagen et al., 2010; UzZaman et al., 2013) and in clinical domain (Raghavan et al., 2012; Sun et al., 2013; Miller et al.,2013; Bethard et al., 2015; Velupillai et al 2015). In clinical domain, temporal information extraction has seen much research interest with assignment of medical events to time bins (Raghavan et al, 2012), i2b2 (Informatics for Integrating Biology and the Bedside) shared task (Sun et al., 2013) with the best performing system (Xu et al., 2013) using CRF (Conditional Random Field) and SVM (Support Vector Machines) and development of a hybrid system (Kovacevic et al., 2013) that used CRF and rule-based methods. Further tasks similar to i2b2 that involve temporal reasoning were also attempted in ShARe CLEF 2013/2014 eHealth challenges (Pradhan et al., 2015) and Clinical TempEval 2015 (Bethard et al., 2015; Velupillai et al., 2015).

Clinical TempEval 2016 continues with the task of temporal information extraction from clinical notes in similar lines to previously described

Proceedings of SemEval-2016, pages 1231–1236,
San Diego, California, June 16-17, 2016. ©2016 Association for Computational Linguistics

works. The 2016 Clinical TempEval challenge consisted of six subtasks (i) identification of spans of the time expression (TS) (ii) identification of spans of the event expression (ES) (iii) identification of attributes of time expression (TA) (iv) identification of attributes of event expression (EA) (v) identification of relation between an event and document creation time (DR) and (vi) identification of narrative container relation (CR). Participants were provided with THYME corpus (Styler et al., 2014) which consisted of de-identified clinical notes and pathology reports of cancer patients from Mayo clinic and corresponding annotation files. The participating systems were compared against two rule-based systems namely Memorize and Closest (only for CR task) which were used as baseline. The evaluation was done in two phases. In phase-1, only raw clinical text documents were given and participants were asked to identify time expressions, event expressions and temporal relations. In phase-2, access to raw text documents as well as manual event and time annotations was given and participants were asked to identify only temporal relations.

The 2015 Clinical TempEval results and discussion reveals that top results were mostly dominated by machine learning based systems (Bethard et al., 2015). However historical works on temporal extraction have achieved success using rule-based systems (Tang et al., 2012; Kovacevic et al., 2013). Thus in this work we developed a hybrid system leveraging the best out of machine learning and rule-based systems and evaluated this hybrid system against the THYME corpus.

The rest of the paper is organized as follows. In section 2 we describe the clinical TempEval 2016 data set and our approach to identify time expression. Section 3 and 4 explains results, describing the limitations of the methods used and issues that were present in the given THYME corpus.

2   Data and Method

The THYME corpus released for TempEval 2016 totaled 600 records which were divided into three sets namely train dataset, dev dataset and test dataset with 297, 150 and 153 records in each set respectively.

We tackled the tasks as named entity recognition (NER) problem with the aim to identify relevant text spans and assign classes to texts corresponding to the identified spans for which we developed a hybrid system that combines a rule-based method and a machine learning based method that relies on simple lexical, syntactic features and domain specific words. The rule-based system was developed using the Stanford TokensRegex framework (Chang et al., 2014) and the machine learning based system employed Stanford CRF classifier (Finkel et al., 2005), which are both available as part of the Stanford CoreNLP (Manning et al., 2014) tool set.

2.1   Rule-based approach

The rules for the rule-based approach were designed using combination of dictionaries and lexical formation formats of sentences. We started development of the rule-based system by evaluating the THYME corpus against existing Stanford SUTime (Chang et al., 2012) rule based tagger which is built on top of Stanford TokensRegex framework to understand its performance and shortcomings on THYME corpus. The obtained result showed that SUTime gave good result for Date when compared to other temporal classes. Hence we retained some of the rules for identification of Date from SUTime, while the rules for Time, Duration, and Quantifier and Set classes were developed as explained.

- **Time rules**: For time rules we manually crafted dictionaries that consisted of constituents of time expressions that were present as part of the given Time class annotations namely the word "time", times of a day, time period qualifiers like "am", "pm" etc. and common time expression references (today, yesterday, previously, earlier, later, future etc.). Most of the annotations for Time class were phrases that contained word "time" or a time expression references prefixed by words such as "this", "that" etc. and suffixed with time period qualifiers. All in all 16 different rules were developed to identify the time expressions using above said dictionaries.

- **Duration rules**: The duration rules used manually crafted dictionaries that consist of different constituents that were present as part of the annotations of duration class, namely weekdays and months, times of a day and common time expression references (today, yesterday, previously, earlier, later, future etc.). In addition we created a dictionary of words that refers to time periods like (hours, minutes etc.) and their equivalent short forms and words that signify time references such as (since, dating back etc.). Totally we designed 43 different rules for identifying duration expressions using above said dictionaries.

- **Quantifier rules**: Most of the quantifier terms had an explicit dependency on words pertaining to domain specific or general events within in the same sentence where they are present .For example, in sentence "Four cups of coffee in the morning" the term "Four" is the quantifier that quantifies the event "cups of coffee". Similar to previous cases we handcrafted dictionaries that consist of domain specific and general events. Additionally a dictionary of commonly occurring suffixes such as "pack-year", "pack-a-day" etc. that is part of the word that contained the quantifier value was created. Totally we created 15 unique rules for the quantifiers using above said dictionaries.

- **Prepost rules**: Prepost expressions had a common characteristics where each expressions begin with words such as "pre", "post", "intra", "prior" etc. followed by a domain specific event term such as "operative" etc. Further we observed very few variants of prepost expressions being present in dev dataset. However to avoid unseen words that might follow the above mentioned prefixes in test dataset, we extracted domain specific words that commonly follow these prefixes by mining ICD9 website and in addition we also created a dictionary of various words that is related to surgical procedures by mining Wikipedia. Using above said dictionaries and prefix words we created 5 rules to extract prepost expressions. Once the quantifiers and prepost expressions were extracted we have set of post processing modules that were designed to improve the spans by removing certain words from extracted expressions.

- **Set rules**: The set rules used previously handcrafted dictionaries for time rules. In addition we created a dictionary containing words such as "annual", "weekly", "monthly", "daily" etc. that qualifies a Set. Most of the set expressions were either single words from previously described dictionary or a simple sentence of form "XX-times-a-{time period qualifier}","XX-{ time period qualifier }" etc. where XX is numeric quantifier. Totally 20 different rules were designed for identifying set expressions.

The results of the rule-based system that was developed using above mentioned rules on test dataset are as shown in Table 2.

Subtask	P	R	F1
TIMEX3	0.415	0.629	0.500
TIMEX3: Span	0.433	0.655	0.522
TIMEX3: Class	0.415	0.629	0.500
TIMEX3: Date	0.457	0.690	0.550
TIMEX3: Duration	0.298	0.455	0.360
TIMEX3: Prepost	0.986	0.637	0.774
TIMEX3: Quantifier	0.256	0.348	0.295
TIMEX3: Set	0.536	0.541	0.538
TIMEX3: Time	0.110	0.378	0.171

Table 2: Results for TS and TA tasks on the test dataset using rule-based system.

2.2 Machine learning approach

We created separate models for all six types of time classes using Stanford CRF classifier which is an implementation of arbitrary order linear chain conditional random field classifier. The data for training consisted of 447 records (train and dev datasets) which were preprocessed by tokenizing using the Penn Tree bank tokenizer and BIO encoding each of the tokens.

We used simple features such as N-Grams, word shape features, word window of size ± 1, sequence words from Stanford NER Feature factory for creating the model and tested using 153 records from test dataset. The results that were obtained are as shown in Table 3.

Subtask	P	R	F1
TIMEX3	0.79	0.655	0.720
TIMEX3: Span	0.821	0.669	0.737
TIMEX3: Class	0.798	0.655	0.720
TIMEX3: Date	0.823	0.749	0.784
TIMEX3: Duration	0.650	0.455	0.535
TIMEX3: Prepost	0.969	0.832	0.895

TIMEX3: Quantifier	0.500	0.167	0.250
TIMEX3: Set	0.732	0.369	0.491
TIMEX3: Time	0.385	0.167	0.233

Table 3: Results for TS and TA tasks on the test dataset using machine learning system (CRF).

3   Results

During system development phase we were able to see that rule based system performed well for Quantifier and Set while CRF performed well for the rest of the classes. Hence for the submission runs we used a hybrid of our rule-based and machine learning based systems (CRF) with the test data. For Quantifier and Set classes we used rule-based systems and for Date, PrepostExp, Duration, and Time class we used CRF classifier models.

Subtask	P	R	F1
TIMEX3	0.759	0.671	0.712
TIMEX3: Span	0.781	0.685	0.73
TIMEX3: Class	0.759	0.671	0.712
TIMEX3: Date	0.823	0.749	0.784
TIMEX3: Duration	0.65	0.455	0.535
TIMEX3: Prepost	0.969	0.832	0.895
TIMEX3: Quantifier	0.256	0.348	0.295
TIMEX3: Set	0.536	0.541	0.538
TIMEX3: Time	0.385	0.167	0.233

Table 4: Hitachi team results (run-1) for TS and TA tasks in Clinical TempEval 2016.

For run-1 we used 447 records (train & dev datasets) for training our hybrid system and the result which was obtained when evaluated on test data is shown in Table 4. For run-2 we decided to do an estimation of how well the CRF model has been trained and its property: accuracy dependency on number of training records. Hence we replaced the CRF classifier with models trained only on 297 records (train dataset). The results on test data for run-2 were similar to run-1 except a drop in overall F-score of 0.1.

4   Discussion

Our hybrid system outperformed the baseline systems for TS and TA tasks. We also obtained results that were above the median result of the challenge as shown in Table 5.

Subtask	P	R	F1
TIMEX3: Span (Hitachi run-1)	0.781	0.685	0.730

TIMEX3: Span (Hitachi run-2)	0.781	0.668	0.720
TIMEX3: Span (TempEval 16 baseline)	0.744	0.428	0.551
TIMEX3: Span (TempEval 16 top score)	0.84	0.75	0.795
TIMEX3: Span (TempEval 16 median score)	0.779	0.539	0.637
TIMEX3: Class (Hitachi run-1)	0.759	0.671	0.712
TIMEX3: Class (Hitachi run-2)	0.758	0.654	0.702
TIMEX3: Class (TempEval 16 baseline)	0.746	0.413	0.532
TIMEX3: Class (TempEval 16 top score	0.815	0.735	0.772
TIMEX3: Class (TempEval 16 median score)	0.755	0.499	0.618

Table 5: Comparison of Clinical TempEval 2016 results.

Table 2 shows the results of our rule-based system on test data for which we observe an F-score of 0.50 with date, prepost and set expression having recall higher than 0.5. During the system development we tuned the rule-based components towards the patterns of temporal expressions that were pre-identified in the training and dev dataset, but there were words such as "time" for Time class and "MO", "hrs" etc. for Duration class which led to increase in the number false positives thereby reducing the precision and overall F-score. Furthermore, the rule-based method, extracted many time expressions like "7:45 AM"," 24-May-2010 15:12:00", "10 Units" etc. that were valid but not present in the annotations which led again to reduction in F-scores.

Table 3 shows the results of our machine learning system (CRF) on test data. The result obtained using CRF classifier is consistent with the previous works that is based on CRF. CRF gave an average F score of 0.72 on test data. In fact CRF gave very good results for all classes except those belonging to Time and Quantifier class. For instance when tested with the test data for Duration class, CRF predicted 140 patterns out of which 91 were correct leading to a precision of 0.65. For the same attribute rule-based system extracted

305 patterns out of which only 91 were correct giving a low precision of 0.298.

We started our system development to understand how rule-based method and CRF performs individually for extraction of time expression present in the dev dataset of the THYME corpus. We were able to observe that the rule-based and machine learning systems gave good results only on subset of time expressions when used individually which can also be observed with the result on test dataset shown in Table 2 and 3. Further, based on results from Table 3 and 4 we can say that CRF alone has higher performance than the hybrid system, however we observed opposite results during system development process using dev dataset. Thus for the final submission we developed a hybrid system of rule-based and CRF by combining top performing systems on dev data, which lead to the results shown in Table 5.

Adaptation of Stanford TokensRegex framework for rule-based system performed fairly well giving an average F-score 0.5 for test data. Yet our rule-based method of the hybrid system had major limitation where our rules were highly syntax dependent which was unavoidable. Simple lexical features were useful for CRF classification approaches on TS and TA tasks. Further, the overall impact of reduction in training data for run-2 was negligible which is evident from the result. Also we observed that performance of CRF for classes like Quantifier remained unimproved even with addition of higher level syntactic features, which is evident from results in Table 3. Thus our aim of evaluating our hybrid system against THYME corpus which was developed using Stanford TokensRegex Framework and Stanford CRF Classifier was successful. As a future work we plan to evaluate performance of our hybrid system on other similar corpora and explore various strategies to combine rule-based and machine learning methods.

Acknowledgements

We thank Mayo clinic and clinical TempEval organizers for providing access to THYME corpus and other helps provided for our participation in the competition.

References

Aleksandar Kovačević, Azad Dehghan, Michele Filannino, John A Keane, and Goran Nenadic. 2013. Combining rules and machine learning for extraction of temporal expressions and events from clinical narratives. *Journal of the American Medical Informatics Association, 20(5):859– 866.*

Angel X. Chang, and Christopher Manning. 2012. SUTime: A library for recognizing and normalizing time expressions. *Proceedings of the Eight International Conference on Language Resources and Evaluation (LREC'12).*

Chang, Angel X., and Christopher D. Manning. TokensRegex: Defining cascaded regular expressions over tokens. 2014. *Technical Report CSTR 2014-02, Department of Computer Science, Stanford University.*

Jenny Rose Finkel, Trond Grenager, and Christopher Manning. 2005. Incorporating Non-local Information into Information Extraction Systems by Gibbs Sampling. *Proceedings of the 43nd Annual Meeting of the Association for Computational Linguistics (ACL 2005), pp. 363-370.*

Manning, Christopher D., Mihai Surdeanu, John Bauer, Jenny Finkel, Steven J. Bethard, and David McClosky. 2014. The Stanford CoreNLP Natural Language Processing Toolkit. In *Proceedings of the 52nd Annual Meeting of the Association for Computational Linguistics: System Demonstrations, pp. 55-60.*

Marc Verhagen, Robert Gaizauskas, Frank Schilder, Mark Hepple, Graham Katz, and James Pustejovsky. 2007. Semeval-2007 task 15: Tempeval temporal relation identification. In *Proceedings of the Fourth International Workshop on Semantic Evaluations (SemEval- 2007), pages 75–80, Prague, Czech Republic, 90 June. Association for Computational Linguistics.*

Marc Verhagen, Roser Sauri, Tommaso Caselli, and James Pustejovsky. 2010. Semeval-2010 task 13: Tempeval-2. In *Proceedings of the 5th International Workshop on Semantic Evaluation, pages 57–62, Uppsala, Sweden, July. Association for Computational Linguistics.*

Naushad UzZaman, Hector Llorens, Leon Derczynski, James Allen, Marc Verhagen, and James Pustejovsky. 2013. Semeval-2013 task 1: Tempeval-3: Evaluating time expressions, events, and temporal relations. In *Second Joint Conference on Lexical and Computational Semantics (*SEM), Volume 2: Proceedings of the Seventh International Workshop on Semantic Evaluation (SemEval 2013), pages 1–9, Atlanta, Georgia, USA, June. ACL*

Preethi Raghavan, Eric Fosler-Lussier, and Albert M Lai. 2012. Temporal classification of medical events. In *Proceedings of the 2012 Workshop on Biomedical Natural Language Processing, pages 29–37. Association for Computational Linguistics.*

Steven Bethard, Leon Derczynski, Guergana Savova, and James Pustejovsky. 2015. SemEval-2015 Task 6: Clinical TempEval. *Proceedings of the 9th International Workshop on Semantic Evaluation (SemEval 2015), pages 806-814.*

Sumithra Velupillai, Danielle L Mowery, Samir Abdelrahman, Lee Christensen, and Wendy W Chapman. 2015. BluLab: Temporal Information Extraction for the 2015 Clinical TempEval Challenge. *Proceedings of the 9th International Workshop on Semantic Evaluation (SemEval 2015), pages-815-819.*

Tang B, Wu Y, Jiang M, Chen Y, Denny JC, Xu H. A hybrid system for temporal information extraction from clinical text. *Journal of the American Medical Informatics Association : JAMIA.* 2013;20(5):828-835. doi:10.1136/amiajnl-2013-001635.

Timothy Miller, Steven Bethard, Dmitriy Dligach, Sameer Pradhan, Chen Lin, and Guergana Savova. 2013. Discovering temporal narrative containers in clinical text. In *Proceedings of the 2013 Workshop on Biomedical Natural Language Processing, pages 18–26, Sofia, Bulgaria, August. Association for Computational Linguistics.*

Weiyi Sun, Anna Rumshisky, and Ozlem Uzuner. 2013. Evaluating temporal relations in clinical text: 2012 i2b2 challenge. *Journal of the American Medical Informatics Association, 20(5):806– 813.*

William Styler, Steven Bethard, Sean Finan, Martha Palmer, Sameer Pradhan, Piet de Groen, Brad Erickson, Timothy Miller, Chen Lin, Guergana Savova, and James Pustejovsky. 2014. Temporal Annotation in the Clinical Domain. *Transactions of the Association for Computational Linguistics, 2:143–154.*

Yan Xu, Yining Wang, Tianren Liu, Junichi Tsujii, and Eric I-Chao Chang. 2013. An end-to-end system to identify temporal relation in discharge summaries: 2012 i2b2 challenge. *Journal of the American Medical Informatics Association : JAMIA.*

CDE-IIITH at SemEval-2016 Task 12: Extraction of Temporal Information from Clinical documents using Machine Learning techniques

Veera Raghavendra Chikka
Center For Data Engineering
International Institute of Information Technology
Hyderabad, India
`raghavendra.ch@research.iiit.ac.in`

Abstract

In this paper, we demonstrate our approach for identification of events, time expressions and temporal relations among them. This work was carried out as part of SemEval-2016 Challenge Task 12: Clinical TempEval. The task comprises six sub-tasks: identification of event spans, time spans and their attributes, document time relation and the narrative container relations among events and time expressions. We have participated in all six sub-tasks. We have provided with a manually annotated dataset which comprises of training dataset (293 documents), development dataset (147 documents) and 151 documents as test dataset. We have submitted our work as two systems for the challenge. One system is developed using machine learning techniques, Conditional Random Fields (CRF) and Support Vector machines (SVM) and the other system is developed using deep neural network (DNN) techniques. The results show that both systems have given relatively same performance on these tasks.

1   Introduction

The interest on extracting temporal information is well versed from the creation of time bank corpus (Pustejovsky et al., 2003b) in 2003. A specification language has been developed, TimeML (Markup Language for Temporal and Event Expressions) (Pustejovsky et al., 2003a) to conceptualize the events, time expressions and temporal relations using tags (EVENT, TIMEX, TLINKS, ALINKS, SLINKS). Various algorithms have been developed to tag events and time expressions on time bank corpus. Initial works used machine learning algorithms with manually extracted features (Mani et al., 2006), syntax and clausal features on inter-sentential events. Later, automated feature selection were used for extracting events and finding the temporal relation(Chambers et al., 2007; Lapata and Lascarides, 2006). TARSQI (Verhagen and Pustejovsky, 2008) is a project employed by the creators of TimeML to develop algorithms for tagging these tags in text.

A series of challenges have been organized on TempEval comprising evaluation tasks on events, time expressions and temporal relations on news data. I2b2 2012 (Sun et al., 2013) is the first conference to study the temporal information extraction in clinical domain using THYME corpus. It is followed by Clinical TempEval tasks in semEval2015. Most of the participants of these challenges used CRF and SVM for event extraction with features including the information gathered from different resources like UMLS (Unified Medical Language System), output of TARSQI toolkit, Brown Clustering, Wikipedia and Metamap (Aronson and Lang, 2010). For time expression extraction, various existing tools like SUTIME (Chang and Manning, 2012), HeidelTime (Strötgen and Gertz, 2010) and GUTIME were used. And for temporal relation extraction various machine learning methods ranging from MaxEnt, Bayesian and SVM to CRF were used incorporating the heuristics and rule based components. Out of many participants of these challenges/workshops, the top performing systems used hybrid approaches with machine learning techniques and rule based tools.

Proceedings of SemEval-2016, pages 1237–1240,
San Diego, California, June 16-17, 2016. ©2016 Association for Computational Linguistics

2 Methods

The SemEval 2016 Clinical TempEval challenge (Bethard et al., 2016) is on identification of event spans (ES), time spans (TS) and their attirbutes (EA and TA), document time relation (DR) and narrative container relations (CR) among events and time expressions. In this paper, we describe two approaches using machine learning techniques for these tasks. First, we broadly classify the tasks into three tasks:

1. Sequence labeling tasks: These tasks involves tagging the sequence of words with the output tags. For example, tasks like part of speech tagging (POS), Named Entity recognition (NER) are sequence labeling tasks.

2. Classification tasks: Classification tasks focuses on classifying the entities into one of the output classes.

3. Relation Extraction Tasks : These tasks involves extracting relation of the entities with the other entities. That is, identifying temporal relations among event/time expressions.

In the following sections, we group the SemEval tasks into one of the above three tasks and provide the methodology dealt with each of these tasks.

Table 1: Event and Time attributes and their values

Attributes	Values
EVENT:Modality	ACTUAL, HEDGED, HYPOTHETICAL or GENERIC
EVENT:Degree	N/A, MOST or LITTLE
EVENT:Polarity	POS or NEG
EVENT:Type	N/A, ASPECTUAL, EVIDENTIAL
TIMEX:Class	DATE, TIME, DURATION, QUANTIFIER, PREPOSTEXP or SET

Identification of events spans (ES) and Time Spans (TS)

Identifying events spans and time spans comes under sequence labeling. We use Conditional Random Field (CRF) which is a popularly used probabilistic graphical model for sequence labelling to extract event spans and time expressions. We use CRF++ suite (CRFPP,) tool for training conditional

random field model with the features:

Term feature: The word itself and its stem are used as features.

POS and Chunk tags: Parts of speech and chunk tags of the word. OpenNLP tagger is used for POS and Chunk tagging (Baldridge, 2005).

Orthographic features: Orthographic features like AlphaNumeric, IsNumeral, isUpperCase, startsWithUpperCase, etc.

Stopword: We use our custom English and Medical stopword list to tag this binary feature.

Train Events Dictionary: Dictionary of events build from the training dataset is used as a feature to check an event has already occurred in training dataset.

In addition to the above features, HeidelTime and HeidelTime Class are used as features for the identification of time expression.

Identifying Events Attributes (EA) and Time Attributes (TA)

Table 1 shows the Event and Time attributes and their classes. Assigning these attributes to one of its values is an classification task. We train a separate Support Vector Machine (SVM) (Chang and Lin, 2011) for each of the attributes to classify in to their respective classes. We use word representations or word embeddings as the features for training the SVM classifier. The word representations are generated based on the co-occurrence count modeling using Stanford Glove tool (Pennington et al., 2014). We trained this count-based model on a text window size of 5, to obtain words vector representations of dimension 25. These word representations are used to train separate SVM classifier for each attribute.

Identify Document Time Relation (DR) and Narrative Container Relation (CR)

Document Time Relation (DR) is the temporal relation of the entities with respect to the document create time. The document relations can take BEFORE, OVERLAP, BEFORE-OVERLAP or AFTER temporal relations.

Temporal links are used to identify the temporal ordering of the events in the timeline. These links are only provided for the events that happen within a temporal bucket, called narrative container, to avoid

Table 2: Phase 1 Evaluation on events, times and temporal relations

Task	Approach 1 (CRF and SVM)			Approach 2 (DNN)		
	Precision	Recall	F-Score	Precision	Recall	F-Score
EVENT:<span> (ES)	0.835	0.797	0.815	0.838	0.786	0.811
EVENT:Modality	0.764	0.729	0.746	0.779	0.731	0.754
EVENT:Degree	0.830	0.793	0.811	0.834	0.783	0.807
EVENT:Polarity	0.750	0.716	0.733	0.813	0.764	0.788
EVENT:Type	0.806	0.769	0.787	0.814	0.765	0.789
TIMEX3:<span> (TS)	0.752	0.515	0.612	0.614	0.560	0.586
TIMEX3:Class	0.644	0.439	0.522	0.468	0.426	0.446
EVENT:DocTimeRel (DR)	0.481	0.460	0.470	0.643	0.604	0.623
TLINK:Type (CR)	0.431	0.167	0.241	0.285	0.225	0.252

Table 3: Phase 2 Evaluation on temporal relations

Task	Approach1 (CRF and SVM)			Approach2 (DNN)		
	Precision	Recall	F-Score	Precision	Recall	F-Score
EVENT:<span>	0.935	0.912	0.923	0.994	0.994	0.994
EVENT:DocTimeRel (DR)	0.724	0.705	0.714	0.588	0.588	0.588
TIMEX3:<span>	0.965	0.794	0.871	0.999	0.999	0.999
TLINK:Type (CR)	0.348	0.284	0.313	0.493	0.185	0.269

the heap of links between all possible events in the document (Styler IV et al., 2014). In an example sentence, "When *compared* with *ECG* of yesterday no significant change is found.". Here, temporal link "BEFORE" is used to notify the event "*ECG*" is occurred BEFORE the event "*compared*". The temporal relations BEFORE, OVERLAP, BEGINS-ON and CONTAINS are used for Narrative Container Relation (CR). We train CRF model similar to that of event span (ES) model to identify DR and CR.

Another Approach using Deep Neural Networks (DNN)

Recent advances in deep learning architecture made us to try an another approach for this challenge. We have used deep neural networks (DNN) for all of the six sub-tasks of the challenge. Given a input sentence and output tags, the neural network learns the weights of nodes of each word of the sentence. The input words are represented as word embeddings which are same as that of word representations used for SVM classifier. A separate neural network is trained for each of the tasks using *deepnl* (Attardi, 2015) library. This neural network architecture follows the convolution method used for natural language processing (Collobert et al., 2011).

3 Results

The dataset used for the challenge comprises of de-identified cancer patient records from the Mayo Clinic with train dataset (195 clinical notes and 98 pathology reports), development dataset (98 clinical notes and 49 pathology reports) and test dataset (100 clinical notes and 51 pathology reports). All of the above described machine learning models are trained on the train and development dataset (340 documents) of THYME-corpus. The evaluation of the task is carried out in two phases. In the first phase, only plain clinical documents are provided. In the second phase, events and time expressions of clinical document are provided and the task is to find the document creation relation and narrative container relation. The results on extracting event, attributes and temporal relations on the test dataset (151 documents) are given in Table 2. Even though the values of DocTime Relation and Container relation are relatively less, they are comparable with the top performing system of SemEval challenge (Bethard et al., 2015). As the phase 2 of evaluation, we are provided with events, time expressions and their attributes, the results on extracting temporal relations are shown in Table 3.

4 Conclusion

In this paper, we present our work on Clinical TemEval task of SemEval 2016 challenge. We have used two approaches, first approach is based on CRF and SVM, and the second approach uses deep neural network to solve the tasks of the challenge. The results show that both approaches relatively same performance on the provided train and test datasets of the challenge.

References

Alan R Aronson and François-Michel Lang. 2010. An overview of metamap: historical perspective and recent advances. *Journal of the American Medical Informatics Association*, 17(3):229–236.

Giuseppe Attardi. 2015. Deepnl: a deep learning nlp pipeline. In *Proceedings of NAACL-HLT*.

Jason Baldridge. 2005. The opennlp project. *URL: http://opennlp. apache. org/index. html,(accessed 2 February 2012)*.

Steven Bethard, Leon Derczynski, James Pustejovsky, and Marc Verhagen. 2015. Semeval-2015 task 6: Clinical tempeval. In *Proceedings of the 9th International Workshop on Semantic Evaluation (SemEval 2015). Association for Computational Linguistics*.

Steven Bethard, Guergana Savova, Wei-Te Chen, Leon Derczynski, James Pustejovsky, and Marc Verhagen. 2016. Semeval-2016 task 12: Clinical tempeval. In *Proceedings of the 10th International Workshop on Semantic Evaluation (SemEval 2016)*, San Diego, California, June. Association for Computational Linguistics.

Nathanael Chambers, Shan Wang, and Dan Jurafsky. 2007. Classifying temporal relations between events. In *Proceedings of the 45th Annual Meeting of the ACL on Interactive Poster and Demonstration Sessions*, pages 173–176. Association for Computational Linguistics.

Chih-Chung Chang and Chih-Jen Lin. 2011. Libsvm: a library for support vector machines. *ACM Transactions on Intelligent Systems and Technology (TIST)*.

Angel X Chang and Christopher D Manning. 2012. Sutime: A library for recognizing and normalizing time expressions. In *LREC*, pages 3735–3740.

Ronan Collobert, Jason Weston, Léon Bottou, Michael Karlen, Koray Kavukcuoglu, and Pavel Kuksa. 2011. Natural language processing (almost) from scratch. *The Journal of Machine Learning Research*.

CRFPP. Crf++: Yet another crf toolkit.

Maria Lapata and Alex Lascarides. 2006. Learning sentence-internal temporal relations. *J. Artif. Intell. Res.(JAIR)*, 27:85–117.

I. Mani, M. Verhagen, B. Wellner, C.M. Lee, and J. Pustejovsky. 2006. Machine learning of temporal relations. In *Proceedings of the 21st International Conference on Computational Linguistics*, page 760. ACL.

Jeffrey Pennington, Richard Socher, and Christopher D Manning. 2014. Glove: Global vectors for word representation. *Proceedings of the Empiricial Methods in Natural Language Processing (EMNLP 2014)*, 12:1532–1543.

James Pustejovsky, José M Castano, Robert Ingria, Roser Sauri, Robert J Gaizauskas, Andrea Setzer, Graham Katz, and Dragomir R Radev. 2003a. Timeml: Robust specification of event and temporal expressions in text. *New directions in question answering*, 3:28–34.

James Pustejovsky, Patrick Hanks, Roser Sauri, Andrew See, Robert Gaizauskas, Andrea Setzer, Dragomir Radev, Beth Sundheim, David Day, Lisa Ferro, et al. 2003b. The timebank corpus. In *Corpus linguistics*, volume 2003, page 40.

Jannik Strötgen and Michael Gertz. 2010. Heideltime: High quality rule-based extraction and normalization of temporal expressions. In *Proceedings of the 5th International Workshop on Semantic Evaluation*, pages 321–324. Association for Computational Linguistics.

William F Styler IV, Steven Bethard, Sean Finan, Martha Palmer, Sameer Pradhan, Piet C de Groen, Brad Erickson, Timothy Miller, Chen Lin, Guergana Savova, et al. 2014. Temporal annotation in the clinical domain. *Transactions of the Association for Computational Linguistics*, 2:143–154.

Weiyi Sun, Anna Rumshisky, and Ozlem Uzuner. 2013. Evaluating temporal relations in clinical text: 2012 i2b2 challenge. *Journal of the American Medical Informatics Association*, 20(5):806–813.

Marc Verhagen and James Pustejovsky. 2008. Temporal processing with the tarsqi toolkit. In *22nd International Conference on on Computational Linguistics: Demonstration Papers*, pages 189–192. Association for Computational Linguistics.

VUACLTL at SemEval 2016 Task 12: A CRF Pipeline to Clinical TempEval

Tommaso Caselli and **Roser Morante**
CLTL Lab - Vrije Univeristeit Amsterdam
De Boelelaan 1105
1081 HV Amsterdam, The Netherlands
{t.caselli,r.morantevallejo}@vu.nl

Abstract

This paper describes VUACLTL, the system the CLTL Lab submitted to the SemEval 2016 Task Clinical TempEval. The system is based on a purely data-driven approach based on a cascade of seven CRF classifiers which use generic features and little domain knowledge. The challenge consisted in six subtasks related to temporal processing clinical notes from raw text (event and temporal expression detection and attribute classification, temporal relation classification between events and the Document Creation Time, and narrative container detection). The system was initially developed to process newswire texts and then re-trained to process clinical notes. This had an impact on the results, which are not equally competitive for all the subtasks.

1 Introduction

Temporal Processing is becoming more and more important for improving access to content. The availability of timelines (either event-centric or entity-centric) can help improving more complex semantically-focused tasks such as Question Answering, Text Summarization, and Textual Entailment, among others. Furthermore, timelines can be further exploited for monitoring the development in time of different phenomena, e.g. the opinions in debates. Temporal Processing research has mainly focused on the newswire domain (Verhagen et al., 2007; Verhagen et al., 2010; UzZaman et al., 2013) in the framework of several shared tasks where systems were challenged to extract the relevant components of a document timeline: temporal expressions, event mentions, and temporal relations. Several evaluations have shown the capabilities and limits of both the annotated resources and the systems. For instance, the best system in TempEval-3 (Bethard, 2013) reports 0.398 F1 on Temporal Relation Detection and Classification from raw text. The development of temporally annotated corpora has boosted research in languages other than English such as Italian (Caselli et al., 2014), French (Arnulphy et al., 2015), and Spanish (Llorens et al., 2010), among others. Recently, interest in temporal processing has moved forward in two directions: cross-document timeline extraction (Minard et al., 2015) and domain adaptation (Sun et al., 2013; Bethard et al., 2015).

The setting of the 2015 and 2016 SemEval Clinical TempEval Tasks is similar to previous TempEval campaigns, with the two main differences: i.) the domain , i.e. (colon) cancer clinical notes; and ii.) the annotation scheme, i.e. the THYME annotation scheme (Styler IV et al., 2014), an extended version of TimeML (Pustejovsky et al., 2003a). Similarly to the previous edition, the SemEval 2016 Clinical TempEval task (Bethard et al., 2016) consists of the following six subtasks: temporal expression detection (TS) and attribute classification (TA), event detection (ES) and attribute classification (EA), temporal relation detection and classification of an event with respect to the Document Creation Time (DR), and, finally, narrative container relation identification (CR). Systems are evaluated in two phases: Phase 1, which addressed all six subtasks from raw data, and Phase 2, where target entities, such as events and temporal expressions (including their attributes), were given and the systems were evaluated

Proceedings of SemEval-2016, pages 1241–1247,
San Diego, California, June 16-17, 2016. ©2016 Association for Computational Linguistics

only against the temporal relation subtasks (DR, and CR). Our team participated in all subtasks and in both submission phases. Our main goals were:

- To test how our full system for temporal processing (from raw text to temporal relations) developed for the newswire domain would perform in another domain using minimal domain specific knowledge, both in terms of lexical resources and tools could achieve a competitive performance;
- To test the robustness of a system that uses simple morpho-syntactic features provided by a standard NLP pipeline(s);

The remainder of the paper is structured as follows: in Section 2, we provide an extensive description of the system and the features we have used.[1] Section 3 reports the results of the submitted runs and their comparison with respect to the baseline system, the median, and the maximum values as provided by the organizers. In Section 4 we perform an error analysis in order to better understand the limits of our system and gain insights for future improvements. Finally, Section 5 puts forward some conclusions.

2 System Description

The task organizers provided 293 training reports, 147 development reports for system development, and 151 testing reports for blind system evaluation. The training and development data had been used in the previous edition of the task.

The general structure of our system can be described as a pipeline of basic NLP tools on top of which we apply several Conditional Random Field (CRF) classifiers (Lafferty et al., 2001). We have used the CRF++ tool with default settings for the regularization algorithm (L2)[2] for all tasks. The final output is obtained by converting the output of 7 different classifiers into the task representation format, i.e. anafora xml files. In the following subsections, we describe the preprocessing steps, which is common for all subtasks, and the specific system for each subtask.

2.1 Preprocessing

All text files have been preprocessed by using two different tools: the IXA-pipeline (Agerri et al., 2014)[3] and the Stanford CoreNLP tool (Manning et al., 2014). From the IXA pipeline, we used the tokenization, offset and sentence splitting modules. We then passed the tokenized data to the Stanford CoreNLP tool in order to extract additional basic annotation layers such as lemmatization, part-of-speech tagging, and dependency parsing. The preprocessing step outputs the texts in a tab separated column format.

After preprocessing the text files, we merged the preprocessed text with the gold annotations, which were exported from the anafora xml files into a tab-column separated files.

2.2 Span Detection (ES, TS) and Attributes Classification (EA, TA) Tasks

We addressed the ES and TS task as a sequence labeling problem. As for the ES subtask, given an input text, each token is classified as being at the beginning of an event (B-event), inside an event (I-event), or outside an event (O). For this subtask, we have minimally adapted an event classifier developed for the newswire domain (NewsC), by adding domain specific features. We then developed a dedicated classifier for the EA subtasks. The TS and TA tasks have been addressed in a similar way to the ES and EA subtasks though, in this case, the temporal expression detection (TS) and type classification (TA) have been performed in one step by classifying all tokens in a text as being at the beginning or inside of a specific type (B-DATE or B-DURATION, I-DATE, I-DURATION, ...) or outside a temporal expression (O).

The ES and TS/TA subtasks share a set of basic morphosyntactic, namely:

- Token's word, lemma, part-of speech, and dependency relation.
- Full dependency syntax path from the token to the root token.
- A combination of the token's part-of-speech, dependency relation and dependency syntax path to the root token.

---

[1]For obtaining scripts and trained models contact the authors.

[2]https://taku910.github.io/crfpp/#links

[3]https://github.com/ixa-ehu/
vmc-from-scratch

The specific features for ES are the following:

- Lemma and part-of-speech of the token's head in the dependency tree.
- Semantic features (PropBank classes, FrameNet frames, and WordNet classes).
- A context window of size +/-2 for word, lemma, and part-of-speech.
- Domain specific feature 1: UMLS entity types [4]. The UMLS types have been assigned by means of a dictionary look-up. The dictionary has been created by means of the manually UMLS annotation from the training and development data.
- Domain specific feature 2: DBPedia "disease" class. Similarly to the UMLS, the DBPedia "disease" class has been assigned by means of a dictionary look-up. The dictionary has been created by extracting all mentions belonging to the class "disease" from DBpedia. [5]

As for the TS/TA specific features we have selected:

- A combination of the token's dependency relation, lemma of its head, and part-of-speech.
- Semantic information (WordNet class and UMLS entity type, only).
- A context window of size +/-5 for token word, lemma, and part-of-speech.
- A context window of size +/-1 with a combination of the token's dependency relation, head's lemma and governor's part-of-speech.

As for the EA subtask, we focused only on the EA:type. We have used a reduced set of lexical features with respect to the ES task along with new features from the IXA pipeline, namely:

- The token's word, lemma, and part-of speech;
- A combination of the token's part-of-speech, dependency relation and dependency syntax path to the root.

- Semantic features (PropBank class, FrameNet frame, WordNet class, UMLS entity types and DBpedia "disease").
- The predicate-argument structure from the IXA pipeline.[6]

As for the other EA values, we have assigned to each predicted event the most frequent attribute value as obtained from the training and development data.

2.3 Relation between Event and Document Creation Time Relation (DR)

The DR task was addressed as a multi-class classification task by considering pairs of [*event, time*] where each event was paired with the Document Creation Time (DCT). Following the THYME annotation guidelines, we set the DCT to the temporal expression in the first line of the document with the expression "`head start date`". To represent the DCT, we have used only one feature, the predicted class. For each predicted event (as described above), the following features where used :

- The event word, lemma, and part-of-speech;
- The event's dependency relation, the event's head lemma and part-of-speech.
- A combination of the event part-of-speech, dependency relation, and the event's head part-of-speech.
- The predicted class of the event (as described above).
- A context window of +/-2 consisting of lemma, part-of-speech, and whether the token has been predicted either as an event or as a temporal expression.
- Semantic features (PropBank class, FrameNet frame, WordNet class, UMLS entity types, and DBpedia "disease").

2.4 Identifying Narrative Container Relations (CR)

Similarly to the DR task, the CR task was addressed as a classification task involving pairs of [*event, event*] and pairs of [*time, event*]. We restricted the pairs to intrasentential relations.

[4]https://www.nlm.nih.gov/research/umls/META3_current_semantic_types.html

[5]http://web.informatik.uni-mannheim.de/DBpediaAsTables/DBpediaClasses.htm

[6]https://github.com/newsreader/ixa-pipe-srl

We developed two different approaches. The first approach (CLTLVUA-run1) addresses the problem of CR identification and classification in two steps: first, it automatically identifies candidate events or temporal expressions which can be eligible for being containers, and then it uses this information to create the candidate pairs, i.e. [*event, event*] and [*time, event*], to detect the presence of a CR relation. On the other hand, the second approach (CLTLVUA-run2) detects and classifies CR relations in a single step. In both approaches the classifiers use the same set of features. The CR detection and classification tasks have been performed with two classifiers: one for [*event, event*] pairs and another for [*time, event*] pairs.

We used basic morpho-syntactic and semantic features for the container detection model, namely:

- The event/temporal expression's word, lemma and part-of-speech.

- Semantic features (PropBank class, FrameNet frame, WordNet class, UMLS entity types, and DBpedia "disease").

- The temporal expression's class;

- A context window of +/-2 consisting of lemmas and parts-of-speech.

- A combination of the token's part-of-speech, dependency relation and syntactic path to the root.

The CR classifier for [*event, event*] pairs uses three sets of features:

- Basic morpho-syntactic and semantic features for each event in the pair (text, lemma, part-of-speech, a combination of part-of-speech, dependency relation and head's part-of-speech, PropBank class, FrameNet frame, WordNet class, UMLS entity types, and DBpedia "disease").

- The syntactic path connecting the two events in the relations (enriched with parts-of-speech).

- Contextual features: temporal prepositions connecting the two events, temporal preposition at the beginning of the sentence and the presence of other events between the element in the pair.

The CR classifier for [*time, event*] pairs uses the same set of features as for the [*event, event*] classifier plus the temporal expressions class and the textual order of the pair.

3 Results

We report the results on the test set for all subtasks. For clarity's sake we will illustrate in different tables the results for all subtasks. Results have been computed in terms of Precision (P), Recall (R) and F1. For comparison we will also report the baseline provided by the organizers (Bethard et al., 2015), and the median and maximum scores of the participating systems.

Table 1 contains the system scores for ES and EA:type for Phase 1 of the evaluation. As for EA:type we will report only the F1 score. We also report the results obtained by our system on the newswire domain (test set of the TempEval-3 evaluation).

ES System	P	R	F1	type-F1
VUACLTL	0.868	0.828	**0.847**	0.819
Baseline	0.878	0.834	0.855	0.833
Median	0.887	0.846	0.874	0.844
Maximum	0.915	0.891	0.903	0.882
VUACLTL - NewsC	0.861	0.858	0.859	n.a.

Table 1: VUACLTL Results for ES and EA:type subtasks - Phase 1.

The results obtained are below the baseline (-0.017 for P and -0.006 for R) and median scores (-0.019 for P and -0.018 for R). In absolute terms, the results are not much different from the NewsC version of the system.

The results for TS and TA are reported in Table 2. We include also an out-of-competition version (VUACLTL_OC), with a bug correction in the conversion script for the final format. The VUACLTL_OC has a lower score for P for the baseline (-0.013) and median (-0.018), while R outperforms baseline and basically equals the median score.

TS System	P	R	F1	class-F1
VUACLTL	0.660	0.372	0.476	0.462
VUACLTL_OC	0.761	0.540	**0.632**	0.619
Baseline	0.774	0.428	0.551	0.532
Median	0.779	0.539	0.637	0.618
Maximum	0.840	0.758	0.795	0.772

Table 2: VUACLTL Results for TS and TA subtasks - Phase 1.

Table 3 reports the results for the DR for Phase 1 and Phase 2. For Phase 2 the organizers provided only R scores. In Phase 1 the system scores median results, while in Phase 2 the system R scores above baseline and below median.

DR System	P	R	F1
VUACLTL phase 1	**0.655**	**0.624**	**0.639**
Baseline - phase 1	0.620	0.589	0.604
Median - phase 1	0.655	0.624	0.639
Maximum - phase 1	0.766	0.746	0.756
VUACLTL phase 2	0.724	**0.701**	0.712
Baseline - phase 2	-	0.675	-
Median - phase 2	-	0.724	-
Maximum - phase 2	-	0.843	-

Table 3: VUACLTL Results for DR - Phase 1 and 2.

Finally, Table 4 reports the results for the CR subtask for Phase 1 and 2. In both evaluation phases, both runs of the systems outperform the baseline and median scores for P and R. The VUA-CLTL_OC also obtains competitive score for P with respect to the maximum score (-0.008). Similar observations hold for Phase 2 of the evaluation where VUACLTL-run1, though performing below the maximum scores, obtains the median scores for R and F1, and a higher P. On the other hand, VUACLTL-run2 tends to maximize R with a minor downgrading of P.

CR System	P	R	F1
VUACLTL-run1 phase 1	**0.497**	0.241	0.325
VUACLTL-run2 phase 1	0.493	**0.268**	**0.347**
VUACLTL_OC-run1 phase 1	**0.523**	0.253	0.341
Baseline - phase 1	0.403	0.067	0.115
Median - phase 1	0.491	0.235	0.318
Maximum - phase 1	0.531	0.471	0.479
VUACLTL-run1 phase 2	**0.642**	0.345	0.449
VUACLTL-run2 phase 2	0.589	**0.368**	**0.453**
Baseline - phase 2	0.459	0.154	0.231
Median - phase 2	0.589	0.345	0.449
Maximum - phase 2	0.823	0.564	0.573

Table 4: VUACLTL Results for CR - Phase 1 and 2.

4 Discussion

Overall, our system obtains competitive scores only in the DR and and CR subtasks while in the other substasks the performances are low.

As for the ES and EA:type subtasks, our approach was clearly not the best solution as our system cannot outperform the baseline. We have identified at least three different sources of errors: i) wrong output of the pre-processing modules, especially the tokenization module; ii) limitations of the features selected; and iii) lack of domain specific knowledge (i.e. semantics) and rules to add robustness to the data-driven approach (Valenzuela-Escárcega et al., 2015).

A per-document evaluation of the ES subtask has shown that out of the 151 testing reports half of them have an F1 equal or higher than the median score, 13 have an F1 between the baseline and the median score and 75 have an F1 below the baseline. In this latter group, we have a subset of 7 files with F1 below or equal 0.50. A detailed analysis of these subset has shown that the source of errors (between 46% - 67%) is due to wrong offsets. Different problems, such as lack of domain specific knowledge, errors in parsing[7], and lack of post-processing rules, affect the other 68 files. In particular, an analysis of a subset of the 47 files with P and R below the baseline shows that the false negatives represent between 20% and 37% of the system errors while false positives are only between 8% and 26%. Most of the false negatives are mentions of events that are illnesses (e.g. *tumor*, *adenocarcinoma*) or events with a limited number of annotated examples in the training and development data (e.g. *Grossed* 9 annotated cases out of 32 mentions; *labeled* 15 annotated cases out of 34 mentions). We have also noticed that errors derived from wrong tokenization (and offset) are still present with percentages ranging between 1% to 9%.

Despite the modest performance of the system, it is interesting to observe that features which work for the newswire domain[8] can be easily used to obtain good results also in other domains for this task. It is clear that the results of the ES subtask affects the performance on the EA:type subtask. Furthermore, the lack of rules and good domain specific knowledge have also affected the robusteness of the system.

A main factor that affects the performance of the system in the TS and TA subtasks is the choice of tackling span and class identification in one step, instead of two. Nevertheless, the VUACLTL_OC version obtains comparable results for TS for R and F1

---

[7]For some sentences, the Stanford CoreNLP parser was not able to provide a dependency output.

[8]See the performance of the NewsC system in Table 1.

with respect to the baseline and the median score, but not for P (-0.013 for the baseline, -0.018 for the median) and has a higher F1 score (+0.001 point) for the TA subtask.

In the DR subtask, the system achieved the median score in Phase 1 and obtained a lower R in Phase 2, but in both cases it performs better than baseline. A detailed evaluation by DR type shows that the system performs better for OVERLAP (0.643 F1) and BEFORE (0.736 F1), which is logical, since these types are more frequent than the other two types, AFTER (0.675 F1) and BEFORE/OVERLAP (0.438 F1). The system tends to overpredict BEFORE, which has the highest recall (0.823) while it obtains the highest precision for OVERLAP (0.809). In order to improve the results for this task, different features might be needed related to the section where the event occurs, temporal expressions surrounding the event, and tense and aspect features of the predicates in the event context.

As for the CR subtask, the two versions of our system perform well outperforming both baseline and median scores in both evaluation phases. The low R values are in part due to the fact that we paired *time* and *event* expressions within the same sentence only, ignoring cross-sentence relations. The two-step strategy implemented in VUACLTL-run1 clearly pays in terms of P with a minor impact on R. Notice that the bug in the final format conversion for temporal expressions has an impact also on the overall evaluation of the CRs. The P results of the VUACLTL_OC-run1 version show that the two-step approach scores only -0.008 with respect to the maximum score. Although the difference between the two approaches is not statistically significant ($\chi^2 > 0.05$), the VUACLTL-run1 (and VUACLTL_OC-run1) approach is to be preferred over VUACLTL-run2 because of the way it identifies narrative containers. The method focuses on [*event, event*] pairs for CRs in order to narrow down the search of possible pair relations and identify semantic properties of candidate containers. The set of features used to identify CRs is a valid one as the results on Phase 2 show (P and R are higher or equal to the median score for both version of the system).

Looking back at our initial goals, we can conclude that the temporal processing system developed for the newswire domain is portable to the clinical domain, although to achieve a top performance it is necessary to use domain specific tools and lexical resources to improve the feature generation. The system proved to be more robust for the CR and DR tasks, than for the ES and TS tasks.

5 Conclusions

We have described the VUACLTL system for the SemEval-2016 Clinical TempEval. The system is based on a combination of different CRFs classifiers, trained with basic morphosyntactic features and domain specific knowledge. Performances for the basic tasks, although competitive, leave room for improvement. Lack of domain specific knowledge and lack of postprocessing rules have affected the system robustness. However, the system has obtained competitive results for the CR task. Although the performances of the two versions of the system are not statistically significant, we prefer the two-step approach (VUACLTL-run1) because it is more precise and it reflects a more linguistically informed notion of narrative container.

There are many options to improve the system, ranging from fine tuning the pre-processing phase in order to avoid offset misalignments, to the generation of better features for the ES and DR subtasks, or the extension of the CR relations to cross-sentence relations. Very important is to integrate more domain specific knowledge.

As future work, we plan to implement all the improvements mentioned above, and additional improvements that might arise from the in-depth error analysis that we are carrying out in order to gain insight into the limitations of the system and to make informed decisions in the engineering of new features.

Acknowledgments

This work has been supported by EU NewsReader Project (FP7-ICT-2011-8 grant 316404), the NWO Spinoza Prize project Understanding Language by Machines (sub-track 3).

References

Rodrigo Agerri, Josu Bermudez, and German Rigau. 2014. Ixa pipeline: Efficient and ready to use multilingual nlp tools. In *LREC*, volume 2014, pages 3823–3828.

Béatrice Arnulphy, Vincent Claveau, Xavier Tannier, and Anne Vilnat. 2015. Supervised machine learning techniques to detect timeml events in french and english. In *Natural Language Processing and Information Systems*, pages 19–32. Springer.

Steven Bethard, Leon Derczynski, Guergana Savova, Guergana Savova, James Pustejovsky, and Marc Verhagen. 2015. Semeval-2015 task 6: Clinical tempeval. *Proceedings of the 9th International Workshop on Semantic Evaluation (SemEval 2015)*.

Steven Bethard, Guergana Savova, Wei-Te Chen, Leon Derczynski, James Pustejovsky, and Marc Verhagen. 2016. Semeval-2016 task 12: Clinical tempeval. In *Proceedings of the 10th International Workshop on Semantic Evaluation (SemEval 2016)*, San Diego, California, June. Association for Computational Linguistics.

Steven Bethard. 2013. Cleartk-timeml: A minimalist approach to tempeval 2013. In *Second Joint Conference on Lexical and Computational Semantics (* SEM)*, volume 2, pages 10–14.

Tommaso Caselli, Rachele Sprugnoli, Manuela Speranza, and Monica Monachini. 2014. EVENTI: EValuation of Events and Temporal INformation at Evalita 2014. In *Proceedings of the First Italian Conference on Computational Linguistics CLiC-it 2014 & and of the Fourth International Workshop EVALITA 2014*, pages 27–34. Pisa University Press.

John Lafferty, Andrew McCallum, and Fernando CN Pereira. 2001. Conditional random fields: Probabilistic models for segmenting and labeling sequence data. In *Proceedings of the 18th ICML*, pages 282–289.

Hector Llorens, Estela Saquete, and Borja Navarro. 2010. Tipsem (english and spanish): Evaluating crfs and semantic roles in tempeval-2. In *Proceedings of the 5th International Workshop on Semantic Evaluation*, pages 284–291. Association for Computational Linguistics.

Christopher Manning, Mihai Surdeanu, John Bauer, Jenny Finkel, Steven J. Bethard, and David McClosky. 2014. The Stanford CoreNLP Natural Language Processing Toolkit. In *Proceedings of the 52nd Annual Meeting of the Association for Computational Linguistics. System Demonstrations*, pages 55–60.

Anne-Lyse Minard, Manuela Speranza, Eneko Agirre, Itziar Aldabe, Marieke van Erp, Bernardo Magnini, German Rigau, Ruben Urizar, and Fondazione Bruno Kessler. 2015. Semeval-2015 task 4: Timeline: Cross-document event ordering. In *Proceedings of the 9th International Workshop on Semantic Evaluation (SemEval 2015)*, pages 778–786.

James Pustejovsky, José Castao, Robert Ingria, Roser Saurì, Robert Gaizauskas, Andrea Setzer, and Graham Katz. 2003a. TimeML: Robust Specification of Event and Temporal Expressions in Text. In *Fifth International Workshop on Computational Semantics (IWCS-5)*.

William F Styler IV, Steven Bethard, Sean Finan, Martha Palmer, Sameer Pradhan, Piet C de Groen, Brad Erickson, Timothy Miller, Chen Lin, Guergana Savova, et al. 2014. Temporal annotation in the clinical domain. *Transactions of the Association for Computational Linguistics*, 2:143–154.

Weiyi Sun, Anna Rumshisky, and Ozlem Uzuner. 2013. Evaluating temporal relations in clinical text: 2012 i2b2 challenge. *Journal of the American Medical Informatics Association*, 20(5).

Naushad UzZaman, Hector Llorens, Leon Derczynski, James Allen, Marc Verhagen, and James Pustejovsky. 2013. Semeval-2013 task 1: Tempeval-3: Evaluating time expressions, events, and temporal relations. In *Second Joint Conference on Lexical and Computational Semantics (*SEM), Volume 2: Proceedings of the Seventh International Workshop on Semantic Evaluation (SemEval 2013)*, pages 1–9, Atlanta, Georgia, USA, June. Association for Computational Linguistics.

Marco A Valenzuela-Escárcega, Gus Hahn-Powell, Thomas Hicks, and Mihai Surdeanu. 2015. A domain-independent rule-based framework for event extraction. In *Association for Computational Linguistics (ACL)*.

Marc Verhagen, Robert Gaizauskas, Frank Schilder, Mark Hepple, Graham Katz, and James Pustejovsky. 2007. Semeval-2007 task 15: Tempeval temporal relation identification. In *Proceedings of the 4th International Workshop on Semantic Evaluations*, pages 75–80. Association for Computational Linguistics.

Marc Verhagen, Roser Sauri, Tommaso Caselli, and James Pustejovsky. 2010. Semeval-2010 task 13: Tempeval-2. In *Proceedings of the 5th international workshop on semantic evaluation*, pages 57–62. Association for Computational Linguistics.

GUIR at SemEval-2016 task 12: Temporal Information Processing for Clinical Narratives

Arman Cohan, Kevin Meurer and **Nazli Goharian**
Information Retrieval Lab
Department of Computer Science
Georgetown University
{arman, nazli}@ir.cs.georgetown.edu, kam346@georgetown.edu

Abstract

Extraction and interpretation of temporal information from clinical text is essential for clinical practitioners and researchers. SemEval 2016 Task 12 (Clinical TempEval) addressed this challenge using the THYME[1] corpus, a corpus of clinical narratives annotated with a schema based on TimeML[2] guidelines. We developed and evaluated approaches for: extraction of temporal expressions (TIMEX3) and EVENTs; TIMEX3 and EVENT attributes; document-time relations; and narrative container relations. Our approach is based on supervised learning (CRF and logistic regression), utilizing various sets of syntactic, lexical and semantic features with addition of manually crafted rules. Our system demonstrated substantial improvements over the baselines in all the tasks.

1 Introduction

SemEval-2016 Task 12 (Clinical TempEval) is a direct successor to 2015 Clinical TempEval (Bethard et al., 2015) and the past I2b2 temporal challenge (Sun et al., 2013). Clinical TempEval is designed to address the challenge of understanding clinical timeline in medical narratives and it is based on the THYME corpus (Styler IV et al., 2014) which includes temporal annotations.

Researchers have explored ways to extract temporal information from clinical text. Velupillai et al. (2015) developed a pipeline based on ClearTK[3] and SVM with lexical features to extract TIMEX3 and EVENT mentions. In I2b2 2012 temporal challenge, all top performing teams used a combination of supervised classification and rule based methods for extracting temporal information and relations (Sun et al., 2013). Besides THYME corpus, there have been other efforts in clinical temporal annotation including works by Roberts et al. (2008), Savova et al. (2009) and Galescu and Blaylock (2012). Previous work has also investigated extracting temporal relations. Examples of these efforts include: classification by SVM (Chambers et al., 2007), Integer Linear Programming (ILP) for temporal ordering (Chambers and Jurafsky, 2008), Markov Logic Networks (Yoshikawa et al., 2009), hierarchical topic modeling (Alfonseca et al., 2012), and SVM with Tree Kernels (Miller et al., 2013).

Clinical TempEval 2016 was focused on designing approaches for timeline extraction in the clinical domain. There were 6 different tasks in the TempEval 2016, which are listed in Table 1. Per TimeML specifications (Pustejovsky et al., 2003), we refer to temporal expressions as TIMEX3 and events as EVENT throughout the paper. Attributes of TIMEX3 and EVENTs are outlined according to the THYME annotations (Styler IV et al., 2014). 16 teams participated in TempEval 2016 (Bethard et al., 2016).

For extracting temporal information from clinical text, we utilize supervised learning algorithms

---

[1]Temporal Histories of Your Medical Event. https://clear.colorado.edu/TemporalWiki/index.php/Main_Page
[2]TimeML is a standard specification language for events and temporal expressions in natural language. http://www.timeml.org/

Proceedings of SemEval-2016, pages 1248–1255,
San Diego, California, June 16-17, 2016. ©2016 Association for Computational Linguistics

Task	Description
TS	TIMEX3 spans
ES	EVENT spans
TA	Attributes of TIMEX3
Class	⟨DATE, TIME, DURATION, QUANTIFIER, PREPOSTEXP, SET⟩
EA	Attributes of EVENTs
Modality	⟨ACTUAL, HYPOTHETICAL, HEDGED, GENERIC⟩
Degree	⟨MOST, LITTLE, N/A⟩
Polarity	⟨POS, NEG⟩
Type	⟨ASPECTUAL, EVIDENTIAL, N/A⟩
DR	Relation between EVENT and document time ⟨BEFORE, OVERLAP, BEFORE/OVERLAP, AFTER⟩
CR	Narrative container relations

Table 1: Tasks of clinical TempEval 2016

Features	lowercase; token letter case; if token is title; if token is numeric; if token is stopword; POS tag; brown cluster; prefix; suffix; noun chunk shape of the token; lemma

Table 2: Base feature set for supervised algorithms

(Conditional Random Fields (CRF) and logistic regression) with diverse sets of features for each task. We also utilize manually-crafted rules to improve the performance of the classifiers, when appropriate. We show the effectiveness of the designed features and the rules for different tasks. Our system outperforms the baselines across all tasks, and is above the median results of all the teams in all tasks but one (CR in precision)[1].

2 Methodology

Our approach to all tasks is based on supervised learning using lexical, syntactic and semantic features extracted from the clinical text. We also designed custom rules for some tasks when appropriate. Details are outlined below:

2.1 TIMEX3 and EVENT Span Detection (TS, ES)

To extract TIMEX3 and EVENT spans (TS and ES), we use a combination of linear-chain CRFs (Lafferty et al., 2001) with manually-crafted rules[1]. Linear-chain CRFs are one of the most robust structured prediction approaches in natural language processing. We train the CRF for detecting TIMEX3s and EVENTs using BIO (Begin Inside Outside) labeling. That is, for the TIMEX3 classifier, after tokenizing the text, each token is labeled as

either "O," "B-TIMEX3," or "I-TIMEX3". Similarly, the event classifier labels the tokens as either "O" or "B-EVENT," as virtually all EVENT annotations are only one token long. We use the CRF-Suite toolkit (Okazaki, 2007) for our experiments.

The main features that we use for CRF in TS and ES tasks are outlined in Table 2. Among these features is Brown clustering (Brown et al., 1992) which is a form of hierarchical clustering based on the contexts in which the words appear. Brown clusters mitigate lexical sparsity issues by considering the words in their related cluster. We constructed fifty clusters across the the train and test datasets and passed the binary identifier of a token's cluster as the feature.

In addition to these features, we use domain specific features for EVENT span detection. Our domain feature extraction is based on the Unified Medical Language System (UMLS) ontology (Bodenreider, 2004). We use MetaMap[2] (Aronson and Lang, 2010), a tool for mapping text to UMLS concepts, for extracting the concepts. The semantic types of the extracted concepts are then used as features. Since UMLS is very comprehensive, considering all the semantic types causes drift. Thus, we limit semantic types to those indicative of clinical events (e.g. diagnostic procedure, disease or syndrome, and therapeutic procedure). For each feature set, we expand the features by considering a context window of +/- 3 tokens (The context window of size 3 yielded the best results on the development set).

For EVENT spans, we supplement the CRF output spans with manually crafted rules designed to capture EVENT spans. Particularly, we add rules to automatically identify EVENTs relating to standard patient readings. For example in: *"Diastolic=55 mm[Hg]"*, using simple regular expressions, we isolate the word "Diastolic" as an EVENT span.

For TIMEX3 spans, we use regular expressions that were designed to capture standard formatted

---

[1]The official ranking of participating teams is unknown at the time of writing and would be announced at the SemEval workshop.

[2]https://metamap.nlm.nih.gov/; we used the 2014 version

	Features
Set 1	UMLS semantic type; tense of the related verb in dependency tree; dependency root of the sentence
Set 2	class, text and brown cluster of closest DATE, PREPOSTEXP and TIMEX3; comparison with section time; comparison with document time; sentence tense and modals

Table 3: Additional feature sets used for document-time relation (DR) extraction.

dates. These rules improved the results of ES and TS considerably, as shown in Section 3.2.1.

2.2 Time and Event Attribute Detection

The main attribute for TIMEX3 mentions is their "class," which can be one of the following six types: DURATION, DATE, QUANTIFIER, PREPOSTEXP, SET, or TIME. EVENTs have four attributes each of which includes different types (Table 1). Full description of the types of the attributes are described by Styler IV et al. (2014). To properly classify each TIMEX3 and EVENT attribute, we train a separate logistic regression classifier[1] for each TIMEX3 and EVENT attribute value. These classifiers are trained on the TIMEX3 and EVENT spans that were previously extracted from the span CRFs (Section 2.1), and employ a similar feature set as the others.

In addition to the base feature set, we also incorporate rules as features in our classifier. We consider words that are indicative of certain EVENT attributes. For example, words such as "complete" or "mostly" indicate DEGREE:MOST, "possibly" indicates MODALITY:HEDGED and "never" shows POLARITY:NEG. We add such contextual features for DEGREE, MODALITY, and POLARITY.

In addition to the rules mentioned above, we further devise rules that lead to immediate classification as a specific class or attribute value. For example, TIMEX3 annotations in the format "[number] per [number]" are classified as SET automatically. We use the most probable predicted class as the final assigned label.

---

[1] We used the scikit-learn implementation. With L1 regularization and Liblinear solver.

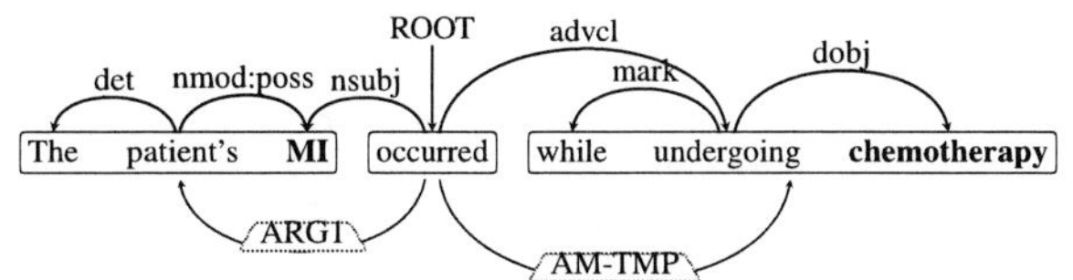

Figure 1: Example of dependency parse tree and semantic roles in the sentence. Dependency relations are shown by arrows above the sentence and semantic roles below it. The boldface terms in the sentence are event mentions. Per human annotation, the following relation exists in this sentence: *[MI]CONTAINS[chemotherapy]*.

2.3 Document-time Relation (DR)

Document-time relations (DR) are specific attributes of EVENTs indicating their temporal relation with the document creation time. There are 4 different types of DRs, namely, BEFORE, AFTER, OVERLAP, and BEFORE/OVERLAP. For identifying the DR attribute types, we use the same general classification approach as EVENT and TIMEX3 attributes; we train separate classifiers for each DR type using an extended set of features to what was used for EVENT attributes detection.

Table 3 describes the additional features that we use for DR extraction. In addition to the base features, we consider features specific to the EVENT annotation. These features are illustrated as Set 1 in table 3. We furthermore expanded the features by considering contextual features from the sentence and nearby time and date mentions (Set 2 in Table 3). Medical narratives often follow a chronological order. Therefore, nearest TIMEX3 mentions, and their comparison with the section timestamp or document timestamp can be good indicators of DRs. Similarly, verb tense and the modals in the sentence are also indicative of the sentence tense and can help in identifying the document-time relation. These additional features improved the results, as shown in Section 3.2.3.

2.4 Narrative Container Relations (CR)

Narrative containers (Pustejovsky and Stubbs, 2011) are TIMEX3s or EVENTs that subsume other EVENTs in a section of the text. They serve as temporal buckets into which other EVENTs fall. For example in the sentence: *"The patient recovered well after her first [surgery] on [December 16th]"*, [December 16th] is the narrative container and the

Evaluation	Phase 1																						
Task	TS			ES			TA			EA												DR		
							CLASS			MODALITY			DEGREE			POLARITY			TYPE					
Metric	P	R	F1	P	R	F1	P	R	F1	P	R	F1	P	R	F1	P	R	F1	P	R	F1	P	R	F1
Baseline	.774	.428	.551	.878	.834	.855	.746	.413	.532	.810	.770	.789	.874	.831	.852	.812	.772	.792	.885	.813	.833	.620	.589	.604
Median	.779	.539	.637	.887	.846	.874	.755	.499	.618	.830	.780	.810	.882	.838	.869	.868	.813	.839	.854	.813	.844	.655	.624	.639
Our system	.802	.678	.735	.891	.872	.881	.775	.655	.710	.836	.818	.827	.887	.868	.877	.875	.856	.866	.868	.849	.858	.719	.704	.711

Table 4: Phase 1 evaluation results on test set for the tasks Time Span (TS), Event Span (ES), Time Attribute (TA), Event Attribute (EA) and Document-time Relation (DR). Baseline refers to the *memorize* baseline described in Section 3.1

following containment relation exists: "{December 16th} CONTAINS [surgery]".

To extract narrative container relations, we use the semantic frames of the sentences. We only consider the intra-sentence containment relations (appearing in the same sentence) and do not handle inter-sentence relations (crossing sentences). According to the THYME annotation guidelines (Styler IV et al., 2014), both EVENTs and TIMEX3s can provide boundaries of narrative containers. The first step in identifying narrative container relations is to identify the *anchor*, the EVENT or TIMEX3 span which contains all the other related EVENTs (*targets*). To learn the *anchor*, *target* and containment relation, in addition to the base features for *anchor* and *target*, we use Semantic Role Labeling (SRL) and dependency parse tree features of the sentence.

SRL assigns semantic roles to different syntactic parts of the sentence. Specifically, according to PropBank guidelines (Palmer et al., 2005), SRL identifies the semantic arguments (or predicates) in a sentence. If the *anchor* or the *target* fall in a semantic argument of the sentence, we assign the argument label as the feature to the associated *anchor* or the *target*. Using semantic roles, we extract the semantics of constituent parts of the sentence in terms of features which help to identify the container relations. For SRL, we use Collobert et al. (2011) neural model[1]. An example of semantic role labels is outlined in figure 1, in which labels below the sentence indicate the semantic labels.

Next, we consider the dependency parse tree of the sentence. Given the *anchor* and the *target* we traverse the dependency parse tree of the sentence to identify if they are related through a same root. In the sample sentence shown in figure 1,

chemotherapy is the *anchor* and MI is another event which is the *target*. As shown, they are connected through the root of the sentence ("occurred").

Per annotation guidelines, TIMEX3 spans should receive higher priority over EVENTs for being labeled as the *anchor*. Therefore, we also consider the type of the expression (TIMEX3 or EVENT) as feature. Additional features such as UMLS semantic types, POS tags, dependency relations and verb tense of the sentence's root are also considered. To extract POS, syntactic and dependency-based features, we use the Spacy toolkit (Honnibal and Johnson, 2015).

3 Experiments

The 2016 Clinical TempEval task consisted of two evaluation phases. In phase 1, only the plain text was given and the TIMEX3 and EVENT mentions were unknown. In phase 2, which was only for DR and CR tasks, the TIMEX3 and EVENT mentions were revealed. In phase 1, we participated in all tasks, except for CR. In phase 2, we participated in both the DR and CR tasks.

3.1 Baselines

The baselines are two rule-based systems (Bethard et al., 2015) that are provided along with the corpus. The *memorize* baseline, which is the baseline for all tasks except for narrative containers, memorizes the EVENT and TIMEX3 mentions and attributes based on the training data. Then, it uses the memorized model to extract temporal information from new data. For narrative containers, the *closest match* baseline, predicts a time expression to be narrative container, if it is the closest EVENT expression.

3.2 Results

Our system's results on test set for all tasks are presented in Table 4 (phase 1) and Table 5 (phase 2).

---

[1]SENNA implementation: http://ml.nec-labs.com/senna/

Evaluation phase	Phase 2					
Task	DR			CR		
Metric	P	R	F1	P	R	F1
Baseline	-	.675	-	.459	.154	.231
Median	-	.724	-	.589	.345	.449
Our results	.816	.813	.815	.546	.471	.506

Table 5: Phase 2 evaluation results for Document-time Relation (DR) and narrative Containment Relations (CR) (The values indicated by (-) were not reported in SemEval official results). Baseline for DR is the *memorize* baseline and for CR is the *closest match* baseline (Section 3.1).

Model	P	R	F1
CRF	.758	.616	.679
CRF + rules	.777	.654	.710

Table 6: Effect of manually-crafted rules for TIMEX3 span (TS) on development set.

Our results in all tasks outperform the baselines, and in all but one case (CR-Precision) are above the median of all the participating teams.

3.2.1 TIMEX3 and EVENT spans (TS, ES)

For TS and ES, our system achieved F1 scores of 0.735 and 0.881 (on the test set) which gives +33.4% and +3.0% improvement over the baseline. While the improvement for TS is much larger, we observed less improvement on the ES task. For ES, Table 6 shows the effect of incorporating manually crafted rules to the output of CRF. These rules improved the F1 performance by 4.6%. In addition, as illustrated in Table 7, adding domain specific features (UMLS semantic types) improved the performance of base features (+2% F1). Adding manual rules to the output of CRF resulted in further improvement (additional +1% F1).

3.2.2 TIMEX3 and EVENT attributes (TA, EA)

For TA and EA, our system achieved an F1 of 0.710 and an average F1 of 0.856, respectively (Table 4). Our results improve over the baseline by 33.5% in TA and 4.8% in EA, respectively (for baseline, the average F1 of EA over all attribute types is 0.817). For EA, while performance of all types of attributes is comparable, the best performance relates to DEGREE attribute class with F1 of .887. The results of the TA and EA tasks for development set are also reported in Table 8. Generally, our results on the test set are marginally higher than on the development set which shows

Model	P	R	F1
base features	.863	.836	.849
+ UMLS	.879	.854	.866
+ rules	.886	.864	.875

Table 7: EVENT span (ES) results on development set based on different features.

Category	P	R	F1
TA:CLASS	.752	.632	.687
EA:MODALITY	.832	.816	.824
EA:DEGREE	.879	.863	.871
EA:POLARITY	.864	.848	.856
EA:TYPE	.854	.838	.846

Table 8: Results of the TIMEX3 and EVENT attributes (TA and EA) on the development set.

that we have successfully avoided over-fitting on the training and development sets.

3.2.3 Document-time relation (DR)

The DR task was included in both evaluation phases. Its F1 score in phase 1 was 0.711 and in phase 2 was 0.815. Naturally, since in phase 1, the spans of EVENTs were unknown, lower performance is expected in comparison with phase 2. The DR results in both phases show substantial improvements over the baseline (+17.7% F1 in phase 1 and +20.4% recall in phase 2).

The effect of context window size on DR performance on development set is reported in Table 9. As the window size increases, more contextual features are added and therefore performance increases. However, after a certain point, when the window becomes excessively large, the performance decreases. We attribute this to overfitting the training data because of too many features. The optimal context window size is 6 which we used for our final submission. As far as features, we evaluated three primary feature sets (using a window of 6), the results of which are outlined in Table 10. The features are defined in tables 2 and 3. As illustrated, the addition of Set 1 and Set 2 features resulted in improvements in all DR types.

Error analysis for DR showed that many of the misclassified examples were for the BEFORE/OVERLAP relations, as also reflected in the low relative performance of BEFORE/OVERLAP relations (Table 10). In many cases, these relations are wrongly classified as either BEFORE or OVERLAP categories. For some cases, it is

w (+/-)	P	R	F1
1	.781	.780	.781
2	.790	.789	.790
3	.794	.793	.794
4	.799	.798	.798
5	.801	.800	.801
6	.804	.802	.803
7	.802	.801	.802
8	.795	.793	.794

Table 9: DR results on development set by window size.

Features	DR Type				
	All	After	Bef.	B/O	Over.
Base	.785	.725	.791	.536	.820
+ Set 1	.792	.751	.796	.545	.823
+ Set 2	.803	.756	.812	.538	.833

Table 10: DR Results breakdown by type based on different features on the development set. Base features are defined in Table 2, Set 1 and 2 features are defined in Table 3.

not clear even for human whether the EVENTs had happened before the creation time of the document or they continued at document creation time. For example in the following: *"Resected rectal [adenocarcinoma], with biopsy-proven local [recurrence]"*, the EVENT [adenocarcinoma] is of document relation type BEFORE/OVERLAP whereas our classifier wrongly classified them as BEFORE.

3.2.4 Narrative Container relations (CR)

The CR results are presented in Table 5. Our approach substantially improves over the baseline, especially in terms of recall (+2.06 times recall improvement). This demonstrates that using semantic frames of the sentences as well as their dependency structure can be effective in identifying container relations. However, F1 score of 0.506 shows that there is still plenty of room for improvement on this task. Error analysis showed that many of the false negatives relate to the inter-sentence relations. Our approach is designed for capturing only intra-sentence container relations. Similarly, some other false negatives were due to the dates that were not syntactically part of the sentence. An example is: *"{June 14, 2010}: His first [colonoscopy] was positive for [polyp]"*. In this example, {June 14, 2010} is the anchor and *[colonoscopy]* and *[polyp]* are the targets. However, the designated date is not any syntactic part of the sentence and consequently, our approach is unable to capture that as the correct anchor of the narrative container.

4 Discussion and conclusions

SemEval 2016 task 12 (Clinical TempEval) was focused on temporal information extraction from clinical narratives. We developed and evaluated a system for identifying TIMEX3 and EVENT spans, TIMEX3 and EVENT attributes, document-time relations, and narrative container relations. Our system employed machine learning classification scheme for all the tasks based on various sets of syntactic, lexical, and semantic features. In all tasks, we showed improvement over the baseline and, in all but one case (CR-Precision) we placed above the median of all participants (The official ranking of the systems were not announced at the time of writing).

While we showed the effectiveness of diverse set of features along with supervised classifiers, we also illustrated that incorporating manually crafted extraction rules improves results. However, manual rules should be constrained as some rules interfere with the learning algorithm and negatively affect the results. The strongest rules were those based on consistent patterns, such as dates in the standard format (e.g. MM-DD-YYYY). On the other hand, while some other rules improved the recall, they led to much lower precision and F1 score. For example, a rule that matches the word "time" as TIMEX3 span, improved our TS recall considerably but at the expense of overall precision and therefore was not included in the final submission.

For narrative containment relations, we showed that semantic frames and dependency structure of the sentence are helpful in identifying the relations. However, our approach is limited to intra-sentence relations and we are not detecting relations that are cross-sentences. In future work, we aim to expand our approach to detect inter-sentence container relationships.

Acknowledgments

We thank the reviewers for their comments. This work was partially supported by National Science Foundation through grant CNS-1204347 and REU award IIP-1362046.

References

Enrique Alfonseca, Katja Filippova, Jean-Yves Delort, and Guillermo Garrido. 2012. Pattern learning for relation extraction with a hierarchical topic model. In *Proceedings of the 50th Annual Meeting of the Association for Computational Linguistics: Short Papers-Volume 2*, pages 54–59. Association for Computational Linguistics.

Alan R Aronson and François-Michel Lang. 2010. An overview of metamap: historical perspective and recent advances. *Journal of the American Medical Informatics Association*, 17(3):229–236.

Steven Bethard, Leon Derczynski, Guergana Savova, Guergana Savova, James Pustejovsky, and Marc Verhagen. 2015. Semeval-2015 task 6: Clinical tempeval. *Proc. SemEval*.

Steven Bethard, Guergana Savova, Wei-Te Chen, Leon Derczynski, James Pustejovsky, and Marc Verhagen. 2016. Semeval-2016 task 12: Clinical tempeval. In *Proceedings of the 10th International Workshop on Semantic Evaluation (SemEval 2016)*, San Diego, California, June. Association for Computational Linguistics.

Olivier Bodenreider. 2004. The unified medical language system (umls): integrating biomedical terminology. *Nucleic acids research*, 32(suppl 1):D267–D270.

Peter F Brown, Peter V Desouza, Robert L Mercer, Vincent J Della Pietra, and Jenifer C Lai. 1992. Class-based n-gram models of natural language. *Computational linguistics*, 18(4):467–479.

Nathanael Chambers and Dan Jurafsky. 2008. Jointly combining implicit constraints improves temporal ordering. In *Proceedings of the Conference on Empirical Methods in Natural Language Processing*, pages 698–706. Association for Computational Linguistics.

Nathanael Chambers, Shan Wang, and Dan Jurafsky. 2007. Classifying temporal relations between events. In *Proceedings of the 45th Annual Meeting of the ACL on Interactive Poster and Demonstration Sessions*, pages 173–176. Association for Computational Linguistics.

Ronan Collobert, Jason Weston, Léon Bottou, Michael Karlen, Koray Kavukcuoglu, and Pavel Kuksa. 2011. Natural language processing (almost) from scratch. *The Journal of Machine Learning Research*, 12:2493–2537.

Lucian Galescu and Nate Blaylock. 2012. A corpus of clinical narratives annotated with temporal information. In *Proceedings of the 2nd ACM SIGHIT International Health Informatics Symposium*, pages 715–720. ACM.

Matthew Honnibal and Mark Johnson. 2015. An improved non-monotonic transition system for dependency parsing. In *Proceedings of the 2015 Conference on Empirical Methods in Natural Language Processing*, pages 1373–1378, Lisbon, Portugal, September. Association for Computational Linguistics.

John D. Lafferty, Andrew McCallum, and Fernando C. N. Pereira. 2001. Conditional random fields: Probabilistic models for segmenting and labeling sequence data. In *Proceedings of the Eighteenth International Conference on Machine Learning*, ICML '01, pages 282–289, San Francisco, CA, USA. Morgan Kaufmann Publishers Inc.

Timothy Miller, Steven Bethard, Dmitriy Dligach, Sameer Pradhan, Chen Lin, and Guergana Savova, 2013. *Proceedings of the 2013 Workshop on Biomedical Natural Language Processing*, chapter Discovering Temporal Narrative Containers in Clinical Text, pages 18–26. Association for Computational Linguistics.

Naoaki Okazaki. 2007. Crfsuite: a fast implementation of conditional random fields (crfs).

Martha Palmer, Daniel Gildea, and Paul Kingsbury. 2005. The proposition bank: An annotated corpus of semantic roles. *Computational linguistics*, 31(1):71–106.

James Pustejovsky and Amber Stubbs. 2011. Increasing informativeness in temporal annotation. In *Proceedings of the 5th Linguistic Annotation Workshop*, pages 152–160. Association for Computational Linguistics.

James Pustejovsky, Patrick Hanks, Roser Sauri, Andrew See, Robert Gaizauskas, Andrea Setzer, Dragomir Radev, Beth Sundheim, David Day, Lisa Ferro, et al. 2003. The timebank corpus. In *Corpus linguistics*, volume 2003, page 40.

Angus Roberts, Robert Gaizauskas, Mark Hepple, George Demetriou, Yikun Guo, Andrea Setzer, and Ian Roberts. 2008. Semantic annotation of clinical text: The clef corpus. In *Proceedings of the LREC 2008 workshop on building and evaluating resources for biomedical text mining*, pages 19–26.

Guergana Savova, Steven Bethard, F William IV, IV Styler, James H Martin, Martha Palmer, James J Masanz, and Wayne Ward. 2009. Towards temporal relation discovery from the clinical narrative. In *AMIA*.

William F Styler IV, Steven Bethard, Sean Finan, Martha Palmer, Sameer Pradhan, Piet C de Groen, Brad Erickson, Timothy Miller, Chen Lin, Guergana Savova, et al. 2014. Temporal annotation in the clinical domain. *Transactions of the Association for Computational Linguistics*, 2:143–154.

Weiyi Sun, Anna Rumshisky, and Ozlem Uzuner. 2013. Evaluating temporal relations in clinical text: 2012 i2b2 challenge. *Journal of the American Medical Informatics Association*, 20(5).

Sumithra Velupillai, Danielle L Mowery, Samir Abdelrahman, Lee Christensen, and Wendy W Chapman. 2015. Blulab: Temporal information extraction for the 2015 clinical tempeval challenge. Association for Computational Linguistics.

Katsumasa Yoshikawa, Sebastian Riedel, Masayuki Asahara, and Yuji Matsumoto. 2009. Jointly identifying temporal relations with markov logic. In *Proceedings of the Joint Conference of the 47th Annual Meeting of the ACL and the 4th International Joint Conference on Natural Language Processing of the AFNLP: Volume 1-Volume 1*, pages 405–413. Association for Computational Linguistics.

UtahBMI at SemEval-2016 Task 12:
Extracting Temporal Information from Clinical Text

Abdulrahman Khalifa
University of Utah
abdulrahman.aal@utah.edu

Sumithra Velupillai
KTH, Stockholm/King's College, London
sumithra@kth.se

Stephane Meystre
University of Utah
stephane.meystre@hsc.utah.edu

Abstract

The 2016 Clinical TempEval continued the 2015 shared task on temporal information extraction with a new evaluation test set. Our team, UtahBMI, participated in all subtasks using machine learning approaches with ClearTK (LIBLINEAR), CRF++ and CRF-suite packages. Our experiments show that CRF-based classifiers yield, in general, higher recall for multi-word spans, while SVM-based classifiers are better at predicting correct attributes of TIMEX3. In addition, we show that an ensemble-based approach for TIMEX3 could yield improved results. Our team achieved competitive results in each subtask with an F1 75.4% for TIMEX3, F1 89.2% for EVENT, F1 84.4% for event relations with document time (DocTimeRel), and F1 51.1% for narrative container (CONTAINS) relations.

1 Introduction

Extracting temporal information from unstructured clinical narratives is an important step towards the accurate construction of a patient timeline over the course of clinical care (Savova et al., 2009), identifying and tracking patterns of care that are crucial for decision making (Augusto, 2005; Wang et al., 2008) and identifying cases or cohorts with temporal criteria for medical research (Raghavan et al., 2014). In the medical domain, more emphasis has been placed on utilizing temporal information from structured databases (Combi et al., 2010). However, recent developments in Medical Natural Language Processing (NLP) research has stimulated work in ex-tracting information from unstructured clinical text (Meystre et al., 2008; Velupillai et al., 2015a) and facilitated future directions to extracting temporal information (Zhou and Hripcsak, 2007).

The i2b2 series of NLP challenges focused in 2012 on extracting events (problems, treatments and tests), time expressions (date, duration, time and frequency) and temporal relations (before, after, overlap) from a set of annotated discharge summaries. The best performing systems used supervised machine learning approaches, except for time expression identification and normalization where rule-based followed by hybrid approaches were most successful (Sun et al., 2013b; Sun et al., 2013a).

In 2015, the SemEval challenge included a Clinical TempEval task (Bethard et al., 2015) with similar objectives to the 2012 i2b2 challenge. The TimeML event and temporal expressions specification language (Pustejovsky et al., 2010) was adapted to define events, time expressions and relation annotations suitable for the clinical domain (Styler et al., 2014). The THYME (Temporal Histories of Your Medical Event) corpus is used in the Clinical TempEval challenge. The annotations in this corpus introduce the use of narrative containers concept (Pustejovsky and Stubbs, 2011) to reduce the complexity of finding temporal relations between every possible pair, and allow rapid discovery through automatic inferences. Each event and time expression is, when possible, assigned a narrative container that defines their temporal span. Groups of events and times within a narrative container can then be linked as one unit with other containers; eliminating the need to explicitly link every pair of events and times.

Proceedings of SemEval-2016, pages 1256–1262,
San Diego, California, June 16-17, 2016. ©2016 Association for Computational Linguistics

The additional pairs can be derived easily from minimal links between pairs within different narrative containers.

We present in this paper the methods used and results obtained from experiments with SVM-based linear classifiers and CRF-based sequential classifiers for the Clinical TempEval task. We complement the paper with a discussion and insights that potentially could help future efforts in this domain.

2 Methods

2.1 Task & Materials

The 2016 Clinical TempEval challenge included 6 subtasks: TIMEX3 1) span detection and 2) attribute classification, EVENT 3) span detection and 4) attribute classification, 5) relation between each event and document creation time classification (known as DocTimeRel), and narrative container or 6) CONTAINS relations between pairs of events and times classification. Our team participated in both phases provided in the challenge (phase 1: plain text only of the test set and phase 2: reference annotations for TIMEX3 and EVENTS including attributes were given for the relation classification subtasks) For a detailed description of the subtasks and evaluation metrics we refer the reader to (Bethard et al., 2015; Bethard et al., 2016).

The THYME corpus used in this task consists of treatment and pathology notes for colon cancer patients from the Mayo clinic. Three datasets were provided: *train* (=293 documents), *dev* (=147) and *test* (=151). We used the dev set to benchmark different approaches during system development and as a guideline to manually select the best performing features. All final models used for predictions were trained using the combined *train+dev* datasets. The test set was used for the final evaluation. Each subtask was addressed separately using a machine learning classifier and groups of almost similar features with slight changes such as surrounding context window sizes. cTAKES (Savova et al., 2010) was used to pre-process each clinical note to generate morphological, lexical and syntactic-level annotations, which were used as features for training the classifiers. The ClearTK machine learning package (Bethard et al., 2014) was used to build Support Vector Machine (SVM) LIBLINEAR (Fan

et al., 2008) classifiers, while CRFsuite (Okazaki, 2007) and CRF++ (Kudo, 2005) were used to build Conditional Random Field (CRF) sequential classifiers. Both cTAKES and ClearTK utilize the Apache Unstructured Information Management Applications (UIMA) framework (Ferrucci and Lally, 2004) which makes it easy to integrate modules from both applications and pipeline output from cTAKES to ClearTK using the XML Metadata Interchange (XMI) format.

2.2 Input Preparation/Feature Extraction

Each clinical note in the corpus was previously segmented into sections with a [start section id=...] and [end section id=...] markers that were easy to identify and annotate using regular expressions. Therefore, we built a UIMA module to segment each clinical note into section boundaries; each annotated with their respective section ID. cTAKES clinical pipeline (version 3.2.2) was used to extract lexical and syntactic features. These include sentence boundaries, tokens, lemmas, part-of-speech tags, syntactic chunk tags (e.g. Verb Phrase-VP, Noun Phrase-NP), token type as defined by cTAKES (see figure 1), as well as dependency parse and semantic role labels used for relation classification. Furthermore, ClearTK feature extractors were used to generate word shape features (e.g. capital, lower, numeric), character patterns and character N-gram features for the linear classifiers. The CRFsuite package comes with built-in feature extractor functions for word shapes, character patterns and N-gram which were used for the TIMEX3, EVENT and DocTimeRel CRF classifiers. Table 1 outlines the features used in each subtask.

For the CRF packages, the features had to be transformed into a flat, tab-separated structure with columns of tokens and associated features each placed in one line. Sentences are designated by empty lines following a sequence of lines of tokens (see Figure 1 for an example).

2.3 SVM-based Approach

The LIBLINEAR package within ClearTK was used to train all linear classifiers with default settings (C=1.0; s=1; Loss=dual L2-regularized) except for TIMEX3 (grid search performed on the training set indicated a better value for C=0.5). We re-used

Feature Type	CRFsuite			CRF++	LIBLINEAR			
	TIMEX3	EVENT	DocTimeRel	DocTimeRel	TIMEX3	EVENT	DocTimeRel	CONTAINS
Window Size (preceding, following)	$-2, +2$	$-2, +2$	$-2, +2$	$-5, +5$	$-5, +5$	$-2, +2$	$-5, +5$	$-5, +5$
Token	*	*	*	*	*	*	*	*
Token (lowercased)	*	*	*		*	*		
Lemma	*	*	*	*			*	
Part of Speech (POS)	*	*	*	*	*	*	*	*
Chunk Type	*	*	*	*				
Token Type (WORD, NUMERIC, . . .)	*	*	*	*	*			
Word Shape (ALL-CAP, INITIAL-CAP, . . .)	*	*	*		*			
Section ID	*	*	*	*	*	*	*	*
Character Pattern	*	*	*		*			
Character Ngram	*	*	*		*			
EVENT and attributes Tags							*	*
TIMEX3 and attributes Tags							*	*
HeidelTime Token					*			
TIMEX position in sentence								*
Number of tokens between relation pair								*
Semantic role arguments								*
C Parameter	1.0	1.0	1.0	1.0	0.5	1.0	1.0	1.0

Table 1: List of features used (indicated with asterisk) for each subtask with different machine learning approaches.

```
token    lemma    pos chunk   token_type      section_ID   ...
#        #        NN  B-NP    SymbolToken     20112        ...
1        1        LS  I-NP    NumToken        20112        ...
Dilated  dilat    JJ  I-NP    WordToken       20112        ...
```

Figure 1: Example of the flat input used for the CRF approaches: features in columns separated by tabs.

the approach taken in the 2015 Clinical TempEval (Velupillai et al., 2015c) for TIMEX3, EVENT and DocTimeRel subtasks, with minor changes in the used features. For TIMEX3, one separate classifier was created for each class (e.g., DATE, TIME). For EVENT, one classifier was created for detecting the text span, and one separate classifier for each attribute (i.e., MODALITY, DEGREE, POLARITY and TYPE). In addition, we added a classifier in this pipeline, for event relations with the document time (DocTimeRel). The main feature additions in this year's challenge were a section ID feature for all classifiers; and a binary feature— whether or not a token was classified as temporal expression of an adapted version of HeidelTime (Strötgen and Gertz, 2010) — for the TIMEX3 subtask.

For the narrative container (CONTAINS) relations subtask, we trained four models to predict relations between pairs of 1) event-event and 2) event-time within a sentence; and 3) event-event and 4) event-time across consecutive sentences. This approach has been previously shown to be most effective in predicting temporal relations (Xu et al., 2013). The candidate pairs were selected[1] using

---

[1] cTAKES Temporal module was very useful in facilitating experiments for the TLINK relations.

the following strategy: All possible combinations of pairs between events and events-times within a sentence were generated for training and classification. For event-event pairs across consecutive sentences; only the first and last event from the current sentence were paired with the first and last from next (or subsequent) sentence. For event-time pairs across sentences; each time phrase in the current sentence is paired with the first and last events from the preceding and following sentences. This approach suffers from the limitation of allowing many examples with the negative class (i.e., pairs without a relation) to be selected; and hence causes class imbalance that may affect classifier training. (Tang et al., 2013) demonstrated that using heuristics to select candidates that are more likely to be part of a relation could produce superior results for temporal relation classification. Another possible remedy is to introduce scaling parameters to adjust the weight of each class during training, such that data samples from the positive class get more weight while the negative class samples get less weight (Lin et al., 2015). Due to time constraints, we were unable to experiment with either of these approaches.

2.4 CRF-based Approach

For the sequential classification, we used the CRFsuite for TIMEX3, EVENT and DocTimeRel subtasks in phase 1, and CRF++ for the DocTimeRel subtask in phase 2. All CRF trained models used default settings (C=1.0; algorithm=L-BFGS). During phase 1, we employed a cascaded approach: we trained CRFsuite models to 1) predict textual spans of TIMEX3 and EVENT tokens separately; 2) pre-

	span			span+class		
	P	R	F1	P	R	F1
MAX	0.840	0.758	0.795	0.815	0.735	0.772
CRFsuite	0.798	0.714	0.754	0.771	0.690	0.729
LIBLINEAR	**0.810**	0.690	0.745	**0.792**	0.674	0.728
CRFsuite+LIBLINEAR	0.761	**0.769**	**0.765**	0.733	**0.741**	**0.737**
memorize (Baseline)	0.774	0.428	0.551	0.746	0.413	0.532

Table 2: TIMEX3 subtask results on the test set.

dict TIMEX3 and EVENT attributes using the predictions in step 1), and 3) predict DocTimeRel and CONTAINS relations using the predictions in steps 1-2. The prediction labels were encoded using the standard IOB2 format of **I**nside, **B**egin, and **O**utside. For instance, prediction labels for the phrase "see him this afternoon ." will be encoded as "O O B-TIME I-TIME O" where "this afternoon" is a TIMEX3 expression in this context. CRF classifiers are probabilistic graphical models that take into account a previous window of prediction labels and assign the most likely sequence of labels based on estimates obtained from the training data. Therefore, they usually perform better in tasks that require assigning labels to sequential data. This is particularly true for the TIMEX3 subtask where the majority of time phrases span multiple tokens.

3 Results

The performance we obtained for the various subtasks on the test set are shown in Tables 2, 3, 4. We also include the results from two baseline systems (**memorize** — for EVENT, TIMEX3 and DocTimeRel, and **closest** — for CONTAINS relations) provided by the workshop organizers, as well as the maximum score achieved in each subtask from all submissions (Bethard et al., 2016). Note that for the narrative container subtask, we report the official score and corrected score we obtained after discovering and correcting a bug affecting the LIBLINEAR models that prevented predictions of event-time relations.

CRF achieved a better performance (F1 %75.4) than the linear classifier (F1 %74.5) when detecting TIMEX3 spans because of higher recall (R %71.4). The LIBLINEAR model resulted in higher precision (P %81). Our initial analysis indicates that this is partly due to many CRF predictions overlapping with the reference annotations rather than matching exactly. When using a strict match evaluation approach, these overlaps are counted as false

positives. For example, the CRF approach generated TIMEX3 labels for expressions like "at the time" and "in the past" while the reference standard included TIMEX3 annotations for only "the time" and "past", respectively. Combining the predictions from both models (by taking the union set of outputs and discarding duplicated predictions) allowed for improved performance (F1 %76.5) suggesting that an ensemble-based strategy could yield superior results for this subtask. Additional analysis will be needed to understand which class of TIMEX3 phrases each model is better at predicting and apply a more sophisticated ensemble method such as weighted average.

The results for the EVENT subtasks were almost identical between the two approaches (CRF or LIBLINEAR), except when classifying the *modality* and *type* attributes where CRF performed better. Combining the predictions from both models did not allow for any performance improvements. Note also that the baseline results for this subtask are very high.

For the DocTimeRel subtask, the CRFsuite model reached an F1 of %74.5 in phase 1, while the CRF++ model reached an F1 of %84.4 in phase 2; allowing for significant improvement over the performance of the LIBLINEAR model (F1 %81.8). For the CONTAINS relations classification subtask, the LIBLINEAR models achieved an F1 of %42.2 in phase 1 when using CRF predictions of TIMEX3 and EVENT; and F1 of %51.1 in phase 2. Note that for phase 2 we also included the prediction of DocTimeRel relations from CRF as an input feature to the LIBLINEAR models.

4 Discussion

Several important issues need to be addressed for future improvement in this task or other similar tasks. We outline some of these issues below, along with an analysis from the reference standard annotations and the system prediction errors.

The CRF-based classifiers detected TIMEX3 mentions with higher accuracy. As mentioned previously, many of these mentions were overlapping with the reference standard annotations. Our output included 352 false positive errors when using a strict match evaluation. Among these errors, about

	span			span+modality			span+degree			span+polarity			span+type		
	P	R	F1	P	R	F1	P	R	F1	P	R	F1	P	R	F1
MAX	0.915	0.891	0.903	0.866	0.843	0.855	0.911	0.887	0.899	0.900	0.875	0.887	0.894	0.870	0.882
CRFsuite	0.902	0.883	0.892	0.850	0.832	0.841	0.898	0.879	0.889	0.885	0.867	0.876	0.875	0.857	0.866
LIBLINEAR	0.897	0.886	0.892	0.841	0.831	0.836	0.892	0.881	0.887	0.879	0.869	0.874	0.854	0.843	0.849
memorize (Baseline)	0.878	0.834	0.855	0.810	0.770	0.789	0.874	0.831	0.852	0.812	0.772	0.792	0.855	0.813	0.833

Table 3: EVENT subtask results on the test set.

	DocTimeRel			CONTAINS		
	P	R	F1	P	R	F1
Phase 1: End-to-End with plain text only						
MAX	0.766	0.746	0.756	0.531	0.471	0.479
CRFsuite	0.753	0.737	0.745	-	-	-
LIBLINEAR	0.741	0.732	0.736	0.553	0.341	0.422
LIBLINEAR†	-	-	-	0.502	0.215	0.301
memorize/closest (baseline)	0.620	0.589	0.604	0.403	0.067	0.115
Phase 2: Includes manual annotations of TIMEX3 and EVENT						
MAX	-	0.843	-	0.823	0.564	0.573
CRF++	0.844	0.843	0.844	-	-	-
LIBLINEAR	0.818	0.818	0.818	0.657	0.418	0.511
LIBLINEAR†	-	-	-	0.562	0.254	0.350
memorize/closest (baseline)	-	0.675	-	0.459	0.154	0.231

Table 4: Relation classification results on the test set.
†Indicates official scores before bug correction.

228 were overlapping (but not matching perfectly) with reference annotations, and the remaining 124 errors were due to other reasons. If counting these overlapping errors as true positives instead of false positives, as in a partial match evaluation, significant accuracy improvements could be observed (P: 0.929, R: 0.833, F1: 0.878)[2]. Contributions from last year's TempEval task have pointed out the issue of TIMEX3 annotations inconsistency in the reference standard (Tissot et al., 2015). After examining the 228 overlapping false positive errors further, we noticed through empirical analysis that many were due to either missing or added prepositions (e.g., 'at', 'in', 'for', 'about') and determiners ('a', 'the'). Further examination revealed that, as pointed out by the previous authors, there is an inconsistent trend in the reference standard annotations. For example, the reference standard contains the following TIMEX3 phrases (underlined words indicate words not annotated in the reference standard): "in the past", "in the last three days", "for many years", "for two years", "at this time", "at this time", "about 27 years ago" and "about 30 years ago". These irregularities will make it difficult for any machine learning model to generalize well beyond the given dataset and most likely will indicate overfitting for higher performance models (Velupil-

lai et al., 2015b). The reported inter-annotator agreement for TIMEX3 span annotations of F1 77.4% (Bethard et al., 2015) further supports these assumptions. Therefore, future work should focus on creative ways to deal with this inconsistency and enable more generalizable solutions. Apart from the overlapping errors due to reference standard inconsistencies; other types of errors may indicate room for future improvement. We believe that training multiple classifiers and combining the outputs using ensemble-based approach could yield superior results as manifested from combining predictions of CRF and LIBLINEAR models.

For the DocTimeRel subtask, the CRF-based classification approach also allowed for significant improvements, particularly in phase 2. Table 5 shows the confusion matrix and evaluation scores obtained on the dev set for each category of DocTimeRel relation using CRF++ model when trained on the training set. The final scores achieved (R 83.3%) on the dev set, are comparable to the scores achieved (R 84.3%) on the test set. This allows us to make consistent conclusions about classifier performance on one set (dev) that can be expected to apply on the other set (test). The lowest accuracy (R 48.6%) was observed with the BEFORE/OVERLAP category. A possible explanation for this lower accuracy is the small number of training samples available in this category (2160 instances in the training set out of 38885). The confusion matrix shows that this category gets almost a balanced error rate between the BEFORE (297) and OVERLAP (271) categories. In addition, the highest number of misclassified instances occur in OVERLAP (972) and BEFORE (858) categories where one category is confused for the other. Future work should focus on improving classification in the BEFORE and OVERLAP categories.

The performance achieved using LIBLINEAR models in the CONTAINS relations subtask (F1 42.2%–51.1%) is a significant improvement over last year's attempt using a CRF model (F1 12.3%–

---

[2]This score was obtained using the `--overlap` option from the official evaluation script.

		SYSTEM			
		AFTER	BEFORE	BEFORE/OVERLAP	OVERLAP	TOTAL
REFERENCE	AFTER	**1686**	157	5	289	2137
	BEFORE	110	**6667**	145	972	7894
	BEFORE/OVERLAP	12	297	**548**	271	1128
	OVERLAP	231	858	145	**8579**	9813
	TOTAL	2039	7979	843	10111	20972
	SCORE (P/R/F1)	0.827/0.789/0.807	0.836/0.845/0.840	0.650/0.486/0.556	0.848/0.874/0.861	0.831/0.833/0.831

Table 5: Confusion matrix and scores for each category of DocTimeRel relation obtained on the dev set using CRF++ classifier.

26.0%) (Velupillai et al., 2015c). We think that studying different strategies for candidate pair selection or experimenting with different class weights to reduce effects of negative class predictions could allow for improvement in this subtask. In addition, although we used two separate models to predict relations between event pairs within and between consecutive sentences, we restricted the way we chose candidates across sentences (first and last from current sentence are paired with first and last from next sentence). This restriction was used to avoid an increase in the number of pairs without a relation (i.e., negative class pairs); in addition to the increased computational runtime penalty. However, this means that any candidate pairs spanning across many sentences will be missed by our classifier. This is especially true for some event and time phrases that are usually at the beginning of a sentence (mostly introducing a section header) and act as narrative containers for many events in the next few sentences. For instance, our classifier missed the 'HISTORY' narrative container appearing as part of the section header "PAST MEDICAL HISTORY", which is usually a relation source for many events discussed within the section. One example from the dev set shows that the 'HISTORY' event CONTAINS following events (e.g., medical conditions in a numbered list) spanning from the next first sentence down to the eleventh sentence. Future work could focus on using carefully hand-crafted rules to capture these pairs to increase recall. We think that the most successful approach for this subtask could use hybrid approaches combining rules and machine learning classifiers to improve recall and retain high precision, respectively.

5 Conclusion

Temporal information extraction and reasoning from clinical text remains a challenging task. Our analysis of different machine learning approaches have been informative, and resulted in competitive results for the 2016 Clinical TempEval subtasks. We plan to develop hybrid and ensemble-based approaches in the future to further improve performance on this, and other clinical corpora.

Acknowledgments

We would like to thank the Mayo clinic and the 2016 Clinical TempEval challenge organizers for providing access to the clinical corpus, and arranging NLP shared task.

References

Juan Carlos Augusto. 2005. Temporal reasoning for decision support in medicine. *Artificial intelligence in medicine*, 33(1):1–24, jan.

Steven Bethard, Philip V Ogren, and Lee Becker. 2014. Cleartk 2.0: Design patterns for machine learning in uima. In *LREC*, pages 3289–3293.

Steven Bethard, Leon Derczynski, Guergana Savova, Guergana Savova, James Pustejovsky, and Marc Verhagen. 2015. SemEval-2015 Task 6 : Clinical TempEval. pages 806–814.

Steven Bethard, Guergana Savova, Wei-Te Chen, Leon Derczynski, James Pustejovsky, and Marc Verhagen. 2016. Semeval-2016 task 12: Clinical tempeval. In *Proceedings of the 10th International Workshop on Semantic Evaluation (SemEval 2016)*, San Diego, California, June. Association for Computational Linguistics.

Carlo Combi, Elpida Keravnou-Papailiou, and Yuval Shahar. 2010. *Temporal information systems in medicine*. Springer Science & Business Media.

Rong-En Fan, Kai-Wei Chang, Cho-Jui Hsieh, Xiang-Rui Wang, and Chih-Jen Lin. 2008. LIBLINEAR: A Library for Large Linear Classification. *The Journal of Machine Learning*, 9(2008):1871–1874.

David Ferrucci and Adam Lally. 2004. UIMA: an architectural approach to unstructured information processing in the corporate research environment. *Natural Language Engineering*, 10(3-4):327–348.

Taku Kudo. 2005. Crf++: Yet another crf toolkit (2005). *Software available at http://crfpp. sourceforge. net.* Accessed: 2010-02-25.

Chen Lin, Dmitriy Dligach, Timothy A. Miller, Steven Bethard, and Guergana K. Savova. 2015. Multilayered temporal modeling for the clinical domain. *Journal of the American Medical Informatics Association*, page ocv113.

S M Meystre, G K Savova, K C Kipper-Schuler, and J F Hurdle. 2008. Extracting information from textual documents in the electronic health record: a review of recent research. *Yearbook of medical informatics*, pages 128–44, jan.

Naoaki Okazaki. 2007. Crfsuite: a fast implementation of conditional random fields (crfs), 2007. *URL http://www. chokkan. org/software/crfsuite.* Accessed: 2016-02-25.

James Pustejovsky and Amber Stubbs. 2011. Increasing Informativeness in Temporal Annotation. *Law*, (June):23–24.

James Pustejovsky, Kiyong Lee, Harry Bunt, and Laurent Romary. 2010. ISO-TimeML: An International Standard for Semantic Annotation. In *Proceedings of the Seventh International Conference on Language Resources and Evaluation (LREC'10)*, Valletta, Malta, may. European Language Resources Association (ELRA).

Preethi Raghavan, James L Chen, Eric Fosler-Lussier, and Albert M Lai. 2014. How essential are unstructured clinical narratives and information fusion to clinical trial recruitment? *AMIA Joint Summits on Translational Science proceedings AMIA Summit on Translational Science*, 2014:218–23.

Guergana Savova, Steven Bethard, Will Styler, James Martin, Martha Palmer, James Masanz, and Wayne Ward. 2009. Towards temporal relation discovery from the clinical narrative. *AMIA ... Annual Symposium proceedings / AMIA Symposium. AMIA Symposium*, 2009:568–72, jan.

Guergana K Savova, James J Masanz, Philip V Ogren, Jiaping Zheng, Sunghwan Sohn, Karin C Kipper-Schuler, and Christopher G Chute. 2010. Mayo clinical Text Analysis and Knowledge Extraction System (cTAKES): architecture, component evaluation and applications. *Journal of the American Medical Informatics Association : JAMIA*, 17:507–513.

Jannik Strötgen and Michael Gertz. 2010. Heideltime: High quality rule-based extraction and normalization of temporal expressions. In *Proceedings of the 5th International Workshop on Semantic Evaluation*, pages 321–324. Association for Computational Linguistics.

William F Styler, Steven Bethard an Sean Finan, Martha Palmer, Sameer Pradhan, Piet C de Groen, Brad Erickson, Timothy Miller, Chen Lin, Guergana Savova, and

James Pustejovsky. 2014. Temporal Annotation in the Clinical Domain. *Transactions of Computational Linguistics*, 2(April):143–154.

Weiyi Sun, Anna Rumshisky, and Ozlem Uzuner. 2013a. Evaluating temporal relations in clinical text: 2012 i2b2 Challenge. *Journal of the American Medical Informatics Association : JAMIA*, 20(5):806–13.

Weiyi Sun, Anna Rumshisky, and Ozlem Uzuner. 2013b. Temporal reasoning over clinical text: the state of the art. *Journal of the American Medical Informatics Association : JAMIA*, 20(5):814–9.

Buzhou Tang, Yonghui Wu, Min Jiang, Yukun Chen, Joshua C Denny, and Hua Xu. 2013. A hybrid system for temporal information extraction from clinical text. *Journal of the American Medical Informatics Association : JAMIA*, 20(5):828–35.

Hegler Tissot, Genevieve Gorrell, Angus Roberts, Leon Derczynski, Marcos Didonet, and Del Fabro. 2015. UFPRSheffield : Contrasting Rule-based and Support Vector Machine Approaches to Time Expression Identification in Clinical TempEval. *Proc. SemEval*, (SemEval):835–839.

Sumithra Velupillai, D Mowery, BR South, M Kvist, and H Dalianis. 2015a. Recent advances in clinical natural language processing in support of semantic analysis. *Yearbook of medical informatics*, 10(1):183.

Sumithra Velupillai, D. L. Mowery, S. Abdelrahman, L. Christensen, and W. W. Chapman. 2015b. Towards a Generalizable Time Expression Model for Temporal Reasoning in Clinical Notes. In *AMIA 2015 Proceedings*, pages 1252–1259, San Francisco, USA, November. American Medical Informatics Association.

Sumithra Velupillai, Danielle L Mowery, Samir Abdelrahman, Lee Christensen, and Wendy W Chapman. 2015c. BluLab : Temporal Information Extraction for the 2015 Clinical TempEval Challenge. *Proc. SemEval*, (SemEval):815–819.

Taowei David Wang, Catherine Plaisant, Alexander J Quinn, Roman Stanchak, and Shawn Murphy. 2008. Aligning Temporal Data by Sentinel Events : Discovering Patterns in Electronic Health Records. *CHI 2008 Proceedings Health and Wellness*, pages 457–466.

Yan Xu, Yining Wang, Tianren Liu, Junichi Tsujii, and Eric I-Chao Chang. 2013. An end-to-end system to identify temporal relation in discharge summaries: 2012 i2b2 challenge. *Journal of the American Medical Informatics Association : JAMIA*, 20(5):849–58.

Li Zhou and George Hripcsak. 2007. Temporal reasoning with medical data–a review with emphasis on medical natural language processing. *Journal of biomedical informatics*, 40(2):183–202, apr.

ULISBOA at SemEval-2016 Task 12: Extraction of temporal expressions, clinical events and relations using IBEnt

Marcia Barros, Andre Lamurias, Gonçalo Figueiro, Marta Antunes
Joana Teixeira, Alexandre Pinheiro and Francisco M. Couto
LaSIGE, Faculdade de Ciências, Universidade de Lisboa, Portugal
`mbarros@lasige.di.fc.ul.pt`

Abstract

This paper describes our approach to participate on SemEval2016 Task12: Clinical TempEval. Our system was based on IBEnt, a framework to identify chemical entities and their relations in text using machine learning techniques. This system has two modules, one to identify chemical entities, and other to identify the pairs of entities that represent a chemical interaction in the same text. In this work we adapted both IBEnt modules to extract temporal expressions, event expressions and relations, by creating new CRF classifiers, lists and rules. The top result of our system was in phase2 for the identification of narrative container relations where it obtained the maximum score of precision (0.823) from all participants.

1 Introduction

In this paper we present our approach to participate on SemEval 2016 Task12: Clinical TempEval (Bethard et al., 2016) challenge. In phase1, participants had only access to the raw text, and they were asked to identify and classify time expressions (TIMEX3), event expressions (EVENT) and relations between expressions (RELATION), and in phase2 participants had access to the raw text and the manual EVENT and TIMEX3 annotations, and they were asked to identify only RELATION annotations. Our team participated in TS (identify the span of TIMEX3 expressions), ES (identify the span of EVENT expressions) and CR (identify narrative container RELATION) subtasks in phase1, and in

phase2 we participated in the CR subtask. Our system was based on IBEnt (Lamurias et al., 2015), a framework that identifies chemical entities and their relations in text using machine learning techniques. Although IBEnt has been designed to extract chemical entities, we wanted to find out its potential to deal with other type of expressions. IBEnt has two modules: module one, an improvement of the tool developed by (Grego and Couto, 2013), recognizes chemical entities based on the Stanford NER software (Finkel et al., 2005) to train Conditional Random Field (CRF) classifiers using labelled data as input; module two identifies the pairs of entities that represent a chemical interaction in a given text based on machine learning techniques and domain knowledge. In particular, this latter module uses a nonlinear kernel, the Shallow Language kernel (Giuliano et al., 2006) taking into account both the global and local context of each entity to determine if they are interacting or not. The Shallow Language Kernel uses the word, lemma, POS and tag of each token to train a classifier. One instance was generated for each candidate pair, whose elements were identified with a specific tag. In our system we modified both modules in order to extract the relevant expressions and relations. We used module one to extract the span of TIMEX3 and EVENT expressions, and module two to extract the RELATION between expressions. For each subtask we modify IBEnt differently. To extract TIMEX3 expression, the features of the CRF classifier were changed, as well as some specific rules and lists. To extract EVENT expressions we modified the features of the CRF classifier and we added some rules. For TIMEX3 and EVENT

Proceedings of SemEval-2016, pages 1263–1267,
San Diego, California, June 16-17, 2016. ©2016 Association for Computational Linguistics

expressions we used n-gram features, lemma, context and word shape. Identifying the RELATION between expressions required a more complex scheme, with the training of four CRF classifiers and the creations of specific rules, addressed to find relations between near entities. For RELATION we used as features the word, lemma, POS and NER tag. Thus, the aim of our system was to identify the span of temporal expressions (TIMEX3) and clinical events (EVENT), and find relations between them (RELATION).

2   Methods

To train our system we used the data set provided by Clinical TempEval organization, with 439 raw text clinical notes from Maio Clinics and the respective manual annotations, and 153 raw text clinical notes to test the system. Some adaptations were made to IBEnt framework with the intent of identifying TIMEX3 and EVENT expressions. The manual annotated data set was divided into train and development sets. We used the train set to train the CRF classifiers and the development set to evaluate and tune the performance. First, as a pre-processing step, the raw text was split into sentences using the Genia Sentence Splitter (Sætre et al., 2007).Each sentence was then processed by Stanford CoreNLP to obtain basic synthetic information to be used by the algorithms.

For TIMEX3 expressions extraction, Stanford NER already had a library for recognizing and normalizing TIMEX3 expressions, named SUTime. The problem with SUTime was that it does not recognize temporal expressions related with clinical terms, such as "postoperative". To solve this inconvenience, our team created a manual list, with approximately 200 temporal clinical terms, such as "post-op", "pre-surgery" and "peritreatment", using different combinations of words, based on temporal medical concepts from Unified Medical Language System (UMLS) (Bodenreider, 2004). To complement this list, we trained a CRF classifier with the manual annotations and we created post-processing rules to improve the results. These rules were to exclude sections that were not supposed to be annotated, such as patient medication, allergies and education; to divide dates the CRF classifier was an-

notating together, for example "10-06-2010 10-06-2011" thus the system could consider this as two separated entities instead of just one entity; and to exclude invalid characters, such as quotation marks, commas and parenthesis. These rules were heuristically created, based in the observation of the clinical notes raw text.

For EVENT expressions extraction we trained a CRF classifier with the training set provided. We also created rules to solve problems the classifier was not able to identify and fix. One of the rules was about the number of words an event can have (we considered that an event had just one word, which is nearly always the case). For example, "tumor demonstrated" should be considered by the system as two entities. The other rule was to exclude expressions with numbers, once the CRF classifier was annotating, for example, "T4" and "N2" as EVENT expressions.

Regarding RELATION extraction, our approach was slightly different from the ones used to extract TIMEX3 and EVENT. For this subtask, we trained four different CRF classifiers, according with the relation type: EVENT EVENT; EVENT TIMEX3; TIMEX3 TIMEX3 and TIMEX3 EVENT. Each candidate pair was considered if the two entities appear in the same or adjacent sentences. A couple of rules were also created to find relations in the raw text. First rule: if there is a TIMEX3 expression and in the next four words there is an EVENT expression, the system points a relation between both expressions (TIMEX3 and EVENT). The second rule is about the patients history: every TIMEX3 or EVENT below the EVENT HISTORY will have a relation with it. These rules were determined empirically in order to reduce the number of potential relations, since any two entities mentioned in the same document could constitute a relation.

3   Results submission

The original submitted results for phase1 had a bug. Entities, which should always have different IDs, had the same ID for EVENT and RELATION. Thus, the evaluation script provided by the organization (Chen and Styler, 2013) was unable to evaluate our system. To fix this problem, we sent the same results again but with the corrected IDs. For both phase1 and phase2, we submitted two runs. Table1 shows the differences in our system between runs for each subtask. For TIMEX3 expressions, Phase1 Run1 (P1R1) was submitted only with the annotations obtained with the manual list of temporal concepts, without any expression obtained with the CRF classifier. On the other hand, Phase1 Run2 (P1R2) was submitted with the annotations obtained with the CRF classifier and the manual list of temporal concepts previously explained in Methods section. P1R1 and P1R2 for EVENT expressions just differ in the Stanford NER features used to train the CRF classifier, for example, MaxNGramLeng, maxLeft and useTypeSeqs. Regarding RELATION, in phase1 the main difference between runs was the input used, i.e., for this phase we used the TIMEX3 and EVENT expressions extracted from the raw text using our system. We submitted the RELATION annotated with the classifiers and with the rules (see Methods section). Phase2 submission had a greater difference between each run. Beside the fact the input was the manual annotations for TIMEX3 and EVENT provided by the organization, for Phase2 Run1 (P2R1) we submitted the RELATION obtained with either the CRF classifiers or rules, and for Phase2 Run2 (P2R2) we submitted the relations obtained with both the CRF classifiers and rules.

		TIMEX3	EVENT	RELATION
Phase1 with bugfix	Run1(P1R1)	List	Features	TIMEX3 and EVENT from P1R1
	Run2(P1R2)	List and CRF classifier	Features	TIMEX3 and EVENT from P1R2
Phase2	Run1(P2R1)	-	-	CRF classifier or Rules
	Run2(P2R2)	-	-	CRF classifier and Rules

Table 1: Main differences between run1 and run2 for phases 1 and 2. List: list of manually curated temporal expressions; Features: optimized features for precision/F1-measure; CRF classifier: CRF classifier trained with different training sets.

4   Results and Discussion

In this section we exhibit the results of ULISBOA for the participating subtasks and we discuss these results. In Table 2 we present ULISBOA results for both phases 1 and 2, and the maximum scores obtained in the competition for each subtask.

4.1   TS identifying the spans of time expressions(TIMEX3)

For TIMEX3 expressions extraction there is a major difference in the results of P1R1 and P1R2. For this subtask we intended to modify Stanford NER features, focusing P1R1 for a better recall and P1R2 for a better precision. Instead, and due to a misunderstanding, P1R1 was submitted only with the TIMEX3 annotations obtained through the manual list of temporal concepts, which justifies the low recall. However, after a deeper analysis of this problem, we concluded that precision should be higher, once it was assumed that all the terms in the list are always a TIMEX3 expression. With a posterior revision of the list (after the deadline of submission), we tested it again. Terms included in the list, like "at this time" and "at that time", were removed and we added all terms that were already in the list with the first letter in uppercase, with this obtaining a higher precision (0.933). This test suggest that the temporal list we have created is a good complement to our system. For P1R2, the score achieved is near the maximum for precision (-0.064), recall (-0.066) and F1-measure (-0.063). There are some words our system did not annotate as TIMEX3 expression, for example, "time" and "date". We also observed that there was some ambiguity on the annotations regarding the spans of expressions with more than one words. For example, there were cases where "at this time" was annotated, and others where only "this time" was annotated. These inconsistencies made it more difficult to train a CRF classifier and to generate a list of TIMEX3 expressions. Another issue was about our manual list of temporal concepts, which did not consider uppercases words, so the system did not annotate terms such as "Intraop" as TIMEX3.

4.2   ES identifying the spans of event expressions(EVENT)

P1R1 and P1R2 scores were similar in EVENT expressions extraction, with a difference between runs of 0.002 for precision, 0.006 for recall and 0.004 for F1-measure. For both runs we used different Stanford NER features, not achieving significant differences in results. However, P1R1 was the closest to the maximum score, especially regarding to precision (-0.034). Once this differences are not statisti-

		TIMEX3			EVENT			RELATIONS		
		P	**R**	**F1**	**P**	**R**	**F1**	**P**	**R**	**F1**
Phase1 with bugfix	Run1(P1R1)	0.623	0.065	0.118	0.881	0.745	0.807	0.122	0.009	0.017
	Run2(P1R2)	0.776	0.692	0.732	0.879	0.739	0.803	0.108	0.009	0.017
	Max	**0.840**	**0.758**	**0.795**	**0.915**	**0.891**	**0,903**	**0.531**	**0.471**	**0.479**
Phase2	Run1(P2R1)	-	-	-	-	-	-	0.273	0.255	0.264
	Run2(P2R2)	-	-	-	-	-	-	**0.823**	0.056	0.105
	Max	-	-	-	-	-	-	**0.823**	**0.564**	**0.573**

Table 2: ULISBOA results for phase1 (TIMEX3, EVENT and RELATION) and phase2 (RELATION). P=precision; R=Recall; F1=F1-measure; Max=maximum score obtained in the challenge.

cally significant, we are going to focus our discussion in P1R1. For this subtask, we trained a CRF classifier and combined the results with the rules explained in Methods sections. We did not use any ontology or dictionary which explains why some basic terms were not annotated (False Negatives), such as "scan" and "normal", or which were incorrectly annotated (False Positives), such as "CT-scan" and "plan". Our system achieved a score of 0.80 to F1-measure in the aforementioned subtask, i.e., a considerable part of the expressions was correctly classified as EVENT. However, classifying an expression as EVENT depends on its surrounding context. In the previous example, "scan", as the action of doing an exam, should be annotated as an EVENT, and "CT-scan", as X-Ray Computed Tomography machine, should not be annotated. Thus, there is an increased demand to develop new semantic techniques, such as semantic similarity, to complement our system (Couto and Pinto, 2013). Another problem was about the rule that considers the EVENT only as one word, because instead of separate the entity in two different entities, this rule excluded these entities from the results, so we were losing one entity and lowering the recall.

4.3 CR identifying narrative container relations(RELATION)

For Clinical TempEval phase1, our system RELATION results were much lower than the maximum scores, for both P1R1 (precision -0.409; recall -0.471; F1-measure -0.462) and P1R2 (precision -0.423; recall -0.471; F1-measure -0.462). The variances in the system between each run in phase1 were only the input, TIMEX3 and EVENT expressions extracted from the raw text with our system.

In phase2, our results were improved when compared with phase1 (see Table2). For example, in phase1, the same clinical note had 3 RELATIONS identified, compared with 109 RELATIONS identified in phase2. A better recall was obtained in phase2, for both runs. For P2R1 we considered relations identified either by the classifiers or rules, which is why we got a better recall for this run. For P2R2, we considered relations identified both by the classifiers and rules, i.e., we only accepted relations as positive if the same relation was identified by both the classifier and the rules. For example, in the sentence "the oncologist today would attempt to quantify", in P2R1 the relation between "today" and "quantify" was detected by the rules, but not by the classifier, showing in the final results as a false positive. In P2R2 this did not happen, being this relation excluded from final results because only the rules had detected it. In P2R2 our system achieved a maximum score of 0.823 for precision. However, the recall was lower than P2R1, since we limited the number of relations to be considered. Thus, we can affirm that our system in P2R2 found less relations, but with much higher precision.

5 Conclusions and Future Work

In SemEval Clinical TempEval we participated in three of the six subtasks: TS (TIMEX3 span extraction), ES (EVENT span extraction) and CR (RELATION extraction). Our system, based on machine learning and rules, achieved the maximum precision score for RELATIONS in Phase2. However, more work is necessary to understand how we can improve the recall without a significant decrease in precision. Despite the fact that we had limited time to work for this challenge, our scores for TIMEX3 and EVENT expressions extraction were acceptable and near the maximum scores achieved for other systems. For future work, we intend to correct errors already found and test the system again, and for EVENT expressions we want to test several ontologies, such as SNOMED-CT (Cornet and de Keizer, 2008), to improve our results. Due to the ambiguity of clinical notes, we must understand the real impact manual rules have in final results, so we may have the opportunity to create a greater number and more accurate rules in order to be applied in a larger number of cases. One technique that can be used is distant learning (Mintz et al., 2009). This technique uses a knowledge base, such as an ontology, to automatically generate training data, requiring less manual effort. Another approach is to extend our domain knowledge about the problem in hand by for example collecting and exploring semantic web medical resources (Machado et al., 2015). Furthermore, we want to create an open source framework for our system, after we make it stable. Next SemEval Clinical TempEval edition, we hope to participate in the remaining subtasks and to improve our results, especially for RELATION, where much work remains to be done.

Acknowledgments

This work was supported by FCT through funding LaSIGE Research Unit, ref. UID/CEC/00408/2013.

References

Steven Bethard, Guergana Savova, Wei-Te Chen, Leon Derczynski, James Pustejovsky, and Marc Verhagen. 2016. Semeval-2016 task 12: Clinical tempeval. June.

Olivier Bodenreider. 2004. The unified medical language system (umls): inte-grating biomedical terminology. *Nucleic acids research*, 32(1):267–270.

Wei-Te Chen and Will Styler. 2013. Anafora: A web-based general purpose annotation tool. pages 14–19, June.

Ronald Cornet and Nicolette de Keizer. 2008. Forty years of snomed: a literature review. *BMC medical informatics and decision making*, 8(1):S1:S2.

Francisco M Couto and Sofia Pinto. 2013. The next generation of similarity measures that fully explore the semantics in biomedical ontologies. *Journal of bioinformatics and computational biology*, 11(05):1371001.

Jenny Rose Finkel, Trond Grenager, and Christopher Manning. 2005. Incorporating non-local information into information extraction systems by gibbs sampling.

Proceedings of the 43nd Annual Meeting of the Association for Computational Linguistics, pages 363–370.

Claudio Giuliano, Alberto Lavelli, and Lorenza Romano. 2006. Exploiting shallow linguistic information for relation extraction from biomedical literature. *EACL*, 18:401–408.

Tiago Grego and Francisco M. Couto. 2013. Enhancement of chemical entity identification in text using semantic similarity validation. *PloS one*, 8(5):e62984.

Andre Lamurias, Joao D. Ferreira, and Francisco M. Couto. 2015. Improving chemical entity recognition through h-index based semantic similarity. *Journal of Cheminformatics*, 7:S–1: S13.

Catia Machado, Dietrich Rebholz-Schuhmann, Ana Freitas, and Francisco M Couto. 2015. The semantic web in translational medicine: current applications and future directions. *Briefings in bioinformatics*, 16(1):89–103.

Mike Mintz, Steven Bills, Rion Snow, and Dan Jurafsky. 2009. Distant supervision for relation extraction without labeled data. *Association for Computational Linguistics*, 2.

Rune Sætre, Kazuhiro Yoshida, Akane Yakushiji, Yusuke Miyao, Yuichiro Matsubayashi, and Tomoko Ohta. 2007. Akane system: protein-protein interaction pairs in biocreative2 challenge, ppi-ips subtask. In *Proceedings of the Second BioCreative Challenge Workshop*, pages 209–212.

UTA_DLNLP at SemEval-2016 Task 12: Deep Learning Based Natural Language Processing System for Clinical Information Identification from Clinical Notes and Pathology Reports

Peng Li
Computer Science and Engineering
University of Texas at Arlington
`jerryli1981@gmail.com`

Heng Huang[*]
Computer Science and Engineering
University of Texas at Arlington
`heng@uta.edu`

Abstract

We propose a deep neural network based natural language processing system for clinical information (such as time information, event spans, and their attributes) extraction from raw clinical notes and pathology reports. Our approach uses the context words and their part-of-speech tags and shape information as features. We utilize the temporal (1D) convolution neural network to learn the hidden feature representations. In prediction step, we use the Multilayer Perceptron (MLP) to predict event spans. The empirical evaluation demonstrates that our approach significantly outperforms baseline methods.

1 Introduction

In past several years, there has been much interest in applying neural network based deep learning techniques to solve many natural language processing (NLP) tasks. From low-level tasks such as language modeling, POS tagging, named entity recognition, and semantic role labeling (Collobert et al., 2011; Mikolov et al., 2013), to high-level tasks such as machine translation, information retrieval, semantic analysis (Kalchbrenner and Blunsom, 2013; Socher et al., 2011a; Tai et al., 2015) and sentence relation modeling tasks such as paraphrase identification and question answering (Socher et al., 2011b; Iyyer et al., 2014; Yin and Schutze, 2015). Deep representation learning has demonstrated its importance for

____

To whom all correspondence should be addressed. This work was partially supported by NSF-IIS 1117965, NSF-IIS 1302675, NSF-IIS 1344152, NSF-DBI 1356628, NIH R01 AG049371.

these tasks. All the tasks get performance improvement via learning either word level representations or sentence level representations.

In this work, we introduce the deep representation learning technologies to the electronic medical record research. Specifically, we focus on clinical information extraction, using clinical notes and pathology reports from the Mayo Clinic. Our system is designed to identify event expressions consisting of the following components:

- The spans (character offsets) of the expression in the raw text

- Contextual Modality: ACTUAL, HYPOTHETICAL, HEDGED or GENERIC

- Degree: MOST, LITTLE or N/A

- Polarity: POS or NEG

- Type: ASPECTUAL, EVIDENTIAL or N/A

The input of our system consists of raw clinical notes or pathology reports. The following is an example:

> *April 23, 2014: The patient did not have any postoperative bleeding so we will resume chemotherapy with a larger bolus on Friday even if there is slight nausea.*

The output annotations over the text capture the key information such as event mentions and attributes. Table 1 illustrates the output of clinical information extraction in details.

To solve this task, the major challenge is how to precisely identify the spans (character offsets) of

Proceedings of SemEval-2016, pages 1268–1273,
San Diego, California, June 16-17, 2016. ©2016 Association for Computational Linguistics

Clinical Note	Event Mention	Event Attribute	
April 23, 2014: The patient did not have any postoperative bleeding so we will resume chemotherapy with a larger bolus on Friday even if there is slight nausea.	bleeding	type=N/A polarity=NEG degree=N/A modality=ACTUAL	
	resume	type=ASPECTUAL polarity=POS degree: N/A modality=ACTUAL	
	chemotherapy	type=ASPECTUAL polarity=POS degree=N/A modality=ACTUAL	
	bolus	type=ASPECTUAL polarity=POS degree=N/A modality=ACTUAL	
	nausea	type=ASPECTUAL polarity=POS degree=N/A modality=HYPOTHETICAL	

Table 1: An example of information extraction from clinical note.

the event expressions from raw clinical notes. Traditional machine learning approaches usually build a supervised classifier with features generated by the Apache clinical Text Analysis and Knowledge Extraction System (cTAKES) [1]. For example, BluLab system (Velupillai et al., 2015) extracted morphological (lemma), lexical (token), and syntactic (part-of-speech) features encoded from cTAKES. Although using the domain specific information extraction tools can improve the performance, learning how to use this software well for clinical domain feature engineering is still very time-consuming. In short, a simple and effective method that only leverages basic NLP modules and achieves high extraction performance is desired for regular users.

To address this challenge, we propose a deep neural networks based method, especially convolution neural network (Collobert et al., 2011), to learn hidden feature representations directly from raw clinical notes. More specifically, one method first extracts a window of surrounding words for the candidate word. Then, we attach each word with their part-of-speech tag and shape information as extra features. After that, our system deploys a temporal convolution neural network to learn hidden feature representations. Finally, our system uses Multilayer Perceptron (MLP) to predict event spans. Note that we use the same model to predict event attributes.

2 Constructing High Quality Training Dataset

The major advantage of our system is that we only leverage NLTK [2] tokenization and a POS tagger to preprocess our training dataset. When implementing our neural network based clinical information extraction system, we found it is not easy to construct high quality training data due to the noisy format of clinical notes. Choosing the proper tokenizer is quite important for span identification. After conducting experiments, we found that "RegexpTokenizer" can match our needs. This tokenizer can generate spans for each token via sophisticated regular expression such as:

```
nltk.tokenize.RegexpTokenizer
("\w+|\$[\d\.]+|\S+")
```

We then use "PerceptronTagger" as our part-of-speech tagger due to its fast tagging speed. Note that when extracting context words, please make sure you deploy the same tokenization module instead of just splitting strings by space.

3 Neural Network Classifier

Event span identification is the task of extracting character offsets of the expression in raw clinical notes. This subtask is quite important due to the fact that the event span identification accuracy will affect the accuracy of attribute identification. We first run our neural network classifier to identify event spans. Then, given each span, our system tries to identify attribute values.

---

[1] Apache cTAKES is a natural language processing system for extraction of information from electronic medical record clinical free-text

[2] http://www.nltk.org

3.1 Temporal Convolutional Neural Network

The way we use temporal convolution neural network for event span and attribute classification is similar with the approach proposed by (Collobert et al., 2011). Generally speaking, we consider a word as represented by K discrete features $w \in D^1 \times \cdots \times D^K$, where D^K is the dictionary for the kth feature. In our scenario, we just use three features such as token mention, pos tag, and word shape. Note that word shape features are used to represent the abstract letter pattern of the word by mapping lower-case letters to "x", upper-case to "X", numbers to "d", and retaining punctuation. We associate to each feature a lookup table. Given a word, a feature vector is then obtained by concatenating all lookup table outputs. Then a clinical snippet is transformed into a word embedding matrix. The matrix can be fed to further 1-dimension convolutional neural network and max pooling layers. Below we will briefly introduce core concepts of Convolutional Neural Network (CNN).

Temporal Convolution

Temporal Convolution applies one-dimensional convolution over the input sequence. The one-dimensional convolution is an operation between a vector of weights $\mathbf{m} \in \mathbb{R}^m$ and a vector of inputs viewed as a sequence $\mathbf{x} \in \mathbb{R}^n$. The vector $\mathbf{m}$ is the *filter* of the convolution. Concretely, we think of $\mathbf{x}$ as the input sentence and $\mathbf{x}_i \in \mathbb{R}$ as a single feature value associated with the i-th word in the sentence. The idea behind the one-dimensional convolution is to take the dot product of the vector $\mathbf{m}$ with each m-gram in the sentence $\mathbf{x}$ to obtain another sequence $\mathbf{c}$:

$$\mathbf{c}_j = \mathbf{m}^T \mathbf{x}_{j-m+1:j} \,. \tag{1}$$

Usually, $\mathbf{x}_i$ is not a single value, but a d-dimensional word vector so that $\mathbf{x} \in \mathbb{R}^{d \times n}$. There exist two types of 1d convolution operations. One was introduced by (Waibel et al., 1989) and also known as Time Delay Neural Networks (TDNNs). The other one was introduced by (Collobert et al., 2011). In TDNN, weights $\mathbf{m} \in \mathbb{R}^{d \times m}$ form a matrix. Each row of $\mathbf{m}$ is convolved with the corresponding row of $\mathbf{x}$. In (Collobert et al., 2011) architecture, a sequence of length n is represented as:

$$\mathbf{x}_{1:n} = \mathbf{x}_1 \oplus \mathbf{x}_2 \cdots \oplus \mathbf{x}_n \,, \tag{2}$$

where $\oplus$ is the concatenation operation. In general, let $\mathbf{x}_{i:i+j}$ refer to the concatenation of words $\mathbf{x}_i, \mathbf{x}_{i+1}, \ldots, \mathbf{x}_{i+j}$. A convolution operation involves a filter $\mathbf{w} \in \mathbb{R}^{hk}$, which is applied to a window of h words to produce the new feature. For example, a feature c_i is generated from a window of words $\mathbf{x}_{i:i+h-1}$ by:

$$c_i = f(\mathbf{w} \cdot \mathbf{x}_{i:i+h-1} + b)\,, \tag{3}$$

where $b \in \mathbb{R}$ is a bias term and f is a non-linear function such as the hyperbolic tangent. This filter is applied to each possible window of words in the sequence $\{\mathbf{x}_{1:h}, \mathbf{x}_{2:h+1}, \ldots, \mathbf{x}_{n-h+1:n}\}$ to produce the feature map:

$$\mathbf{c} = [c_1, c_2, \ldots, c_{n-h+1}]\,, \tag{4}$$

where $\mathbf{c} \in \mathbb{R}^{n-h+1}$.

We also employ dropout on the penultimate layer with a constraint on ℓ_2-norms of the weight vector. Dropout prevents co-adaptation of hidden units by randomly dropping out a proportion p of the hidden units during forward-backpropagation. That is, given the penultimate layer $\mathbf{z} = [\hat{c}_1, \ldots, \hat{c}_m]$, instead of using:

$$y = \mathbf{w} \cdot \mathbf{z} + b \tag{5}$$

for output unit y in forward propagation, dropout uses:

$$y = \mathbf{w} \cdot (\mathbf{z} \circ \mathbf{r}) + b\,, \tag{6}$$

where $\circ$ is the element-wise multiplication operator and $\mathbf{r} \in \mathbb{R}^m$ is a masking vector of Bernoulli random variables with probability p of being 1. Gradients are backpropagated only through the unmasked units. At test step, the learned weight vectors are scaled by p such that $\hat{\mathbf{w}} = p\mathbf{w}$, and $\hat{\mathbf{w}}$ is used to score unseen sentences. We additionally constrain l_2-norms of the weight vectors by re-scaling $\mathbf{w}$ to have $||\mathbf{w}||_2 = s$ whenever $||\mathbf{w}||_2 > s$ after a gradient descent step.

4 Experimental Results

4.1 Dataset

We use the Clinical TempEval corpus [3] as the evaluation dataset. This corpus was based on a set of

---

[3] http://alt.qcri.org/semeval2016/task12/index.php?id=data

Category	Train	Dev	Test
Documents	293	147	151
Events	38872	20973	18989

Table 2: Number of documents, event expressions in the training, development and testing portions of the THYME data

600 clinical notes and pathology reports from cancer patients at the Mayo Clinic. These notes were manually de-identified by the Mayo Clinic to replace names, locations, *etc.* with generic placeholders, but time expression were not altered. The notes were then manually annotated with times, events, and temporal relations in clinical notes. These annotations include time expression types, event attributes, and an increased focus on temporal relations. The event, time, and temporal relation annotations were distributed separately from the text using the Anafora standoff format. Table 2 shows the number of documents, event expressions in the training, development and testing portions of the 2016 THYME data.

4.2 Evaluation Metrics

All of the tasks were evaluated using the standard metrics of precision (P), recall (R), and F_1:

$$P = \frac{|S \cap H|}{|S|}$$
$$R = \frac{|S \cap H|}{|H|} \tag{7}$$
$$F_1 = \frac{2 \cdot P \cdot R}{P + R}$$

where S is the set of items predicted by the system and H is the set of items manually annotated by the humans. Applying these metrics of the tasks only requires a definition of what is considered an "item" for each task. For evaluating the spans of event expressions, items were tuples of character offsets. Thus, system only received credit for identifying events with exactly the same character offsets as the manually annotated ones. For evaluating the attributes of event expression types, items were tuples of (begin, end, value) where begin and end are character offsets and value is the value that was given to the relevant attribute. Thus, systems only received credit for an event attribute if they both found

an event with correct character offsets and then assigned the correct value for that attribute (Bethard et al., 2015).

4.3 Hyperparameters and Training Details

Objective Function

We want to maximize the likelihood of the correct class. This is equivalent to minimizing the negative log-likelihood (NLL). More specifically, the label $\hat{y}$ given the inputs x_h is predicted by a softmax classifier that takes the hidden state h_j as input:

$$\hat{p}_\theta(y|x_h) = softmax(W \cdot x_h + b)$$
$$\hat{y} = \underset{y}{\operatorname{argmax}} \, \hat{p}_\theta(y|x_h) \tag{8}$$

After that, the objective function is the negative log-likelihood of the true class labels y^k:

$$J(\theta) = -\frac{1}{m} \sum_{k=1}^{m} \log \hat{p}_\theta(y^k|x_h^k) + \frac{\lambda}{2}||\theta||_2^2, \tag{9}$$

where m is the number of training examples and the superscript k indicates the k-th example.

Hyperparameters

We use Lasagne [4] deep learning framework. We first initialize our word representations using publicly available 300-dimensional Glove word vectors [5]. We deploy CNN model with kernel width of 2, a filter size of 300, sequence length is $2 * windows\_size+1$, number filters is $seqlen-kw+1$, stride is 1, pool size is $seqlen - filter\_size + 1$, cnn activation function is tangent, MLP activation function is sigmoid. MLP hidden dimension is 50. We initialize CNN weights using a uniform distribution. Finally, by stacking a softmax function on top, we can get normalized log-probabilities. Training is done through stochastic gradient descent over shuffled mini-batches with the AdaGrad update rule (Duchi et al., 2011). The learning rate is set to 0.05. The mini-batch size is 100. The model parameters were regularized with a per-minibatch L2 regularization strength of 10^{-4}.

---

[4] https://github.com/Lasagne/Lasagne
[5] http://nlp.stanford.edu/projects/glove/

4.4 Results and Discussions

Table 3 shows results on the event expression tasks. Our initial submits RUN 4 and 5 outperformed the memorization baseline on every metric on every task. The precision of event span identification is close to the max report. However, our system got lower recall. The reason of lower recall values is that the word2vec may not cover more domain specific words. Table 4 shows results on the phase 2 subtask.

Methods	DocTimeRel		
	P	R	F1
Memorize	–	0.675	–
Ours RUN5	0.788	0.788	0.788
Ours RUN6	0.786	0.786	0.786
Median report	–	0.724	–
Max report	–	0.843	–

Table 4: Phase 2: DocTimeRel

5 Conclusions

In this paper, we introduced a new clinical information extraction system that only leverages deep neural networks to identify event spans and their attributes from raw clinical notes. We trained deep neural networks based classifiers to extract clinical event spans. Our method attached each word to their part-of-speech tag and shape information as extra features. We then hire temporal convolution neural network to learn hidden feature representations. The entire experimental results demonstrate that our approach consistently outperforms the existing baseline methods on standard evaluation datasets.

Our research proved that we can get competitive results without the help of a domain specific feature extraction toolkit, such as cTAKES. Also we only leverage basic natural language processing modules such as tokenization and part-of-speech tagging. With the help of deep representation learning, we can dramatically reduce the cost of clinical information extraction system development. Due to the recall values are still low, we will consider use domain specific tools to enhance feature engineering.

References

Steven Bethard, Leon Derczynski, Guergana Savova, Guergana Savova, James Pustejovsky, and Marc Verhagen. 2015. Semeval-2015 task 6: Clinical tempeval. *Proc. SemEval.*

Ronan Collobert, Jason Weston, Léon Bottou, Michael Karlen, Koray Kavukcuoglu, and Pavel Kuksa. 2011. Natural language processing (almost) from scratch. *The Journal of Machine Learning Research*, 12:2493–2537.

John Duchi, Elad Hazan, and Yoram Singer. 2011. Adaptive subgradient methods for online learning and stochastic optimization. *The Journal of Machine Learning Research*, 12:2121–2159.

Mohit Iyyer, Jordan Boyd-Graber, Leonardo Claudino, Richard Socher, and Hal Daumé III. 2014. A neural network for factoid question answering over paragraphs. In *Empirical Methods in Natural Language Processing.*

Nal Kalchbrenner and Phil Blunsom. 2013. Recurrent continuous translation models. In *Proceedings of the 2013 Conference on Empirical Methods in Natural Language Processing*, pages 1700–1709, Seattle, Washington, USA. Association for Computational Linguistics.

Tomas Mikolov, Ilya Sutskever, Kai Chen, Greg S Corrado, and Jeff Dean. 2013. Distributed representations of words and phrases and their compositionality. In *Advances in Neural Information Processing Systems*, pages 3111–3119.

Richard Socher, Eric H Huang, Jeffrey Pennin, Christopher D Manning, and Andrew Y Ng. 2011a. Dynamic pooling and unfolding recursive autoencoders for paraphrase detection. In *Advances in Neural Information Processing Systems*, pages 801–809.

Richard Socher, Jeffrey Pennington, Eric H Huang, Andrew Y Ng, and Christopher D Manning. 2011b. Semi-supervised recursive autoencoders for predicting sentiment distributions. In *Proceedings of the Conference on Empirical Methods in Natural Language Processing*, pages 151–161. Association for Computational Linguistics.

Kai Sheng Tai, Richard Socher, and Christopher D Manning. 2015. Improved semantic representations from tree-structured long short-term memory networks. *arXiv preprint arXiv:1503.00075.*

Sumithra Velupillai, Danielle L Mowery, Samir Abdelrahman, Lee Christensen, and Wendy W Chapman. 2015. Blulab: Temporal information extraction for the 2015 clinical tempeval challenge. Association for Computational Linguistics.

Alexander Waibel, Toshiyuki Hanazawa, Geoffrey Hinton, Kiyohiro Shikano, and Kevin J Lang. 1989. Phoneme recognition using time-delay neural networks. *Acoustics, Speech and Signal Processing, IEEE Transactions on*, 37(3):328–339.

Methods	span			modality			degree			polarity			type		
	P	R	F1	P	R	F1	P	R	F1	P	R	F1	P	R	F1
Memorize	0.878	0.834	0.855	0.810	0.770	0.789	0.874	0.831	0.852	0.812	0.772	0.792	0.855	0.813	0.833
Ours RUN4	0.908	0.842	0.874	0.842	0.780	0.810	0.904	0.838	0.869	0.876	0.812	0.842	0.877	0.813	0.844
Ours RUN5	0.900	0.850	0.874	0.837	0.790	0.813	0.896	0.845	0.870	0.861	0.813	0.836	0.869	0.820	0.844
Median report	0.887	0.846	0.874	0.830	0.780	0.810	0.882	0.838	0.869	0.868	0.813	0.839	0.854	0.813	0.844
Max report	0.915	0.891	0.903	0.866	0.843	0.855	0.911	0.887	0.899	0.900	0.875	0.887	0.894	0.870	0.882

Table 3: System performance comparisons. Note that Run4 means the window size is 4, and Run5 means the window size is 5

Wenpeng Yin and Hinrich Schutze. 2015. Multigrancnn: An architecture for general matching of text chunks on multiple levels of granularity. In *Proceedings of th 53rd Annual Meeting of the Association for Computational Linguistics*, pages 63–73.

Brundlefly at SemEval-2016 Task 12:
Recurrent Neural Networks vs. Joint Inference
for Clinical Temporal Information Extraction

Jason Alan Fries
Stanford University
Mobilize Center
`jason-fries@stanford.edu`

Abstract

We submitted two systems to the SemEval-2016 Task 12: Clinical TempEval challenge, participating in Phase 1, where we identified text spans of time and event expressions in clinical notes and Phase 2, where we predicted a relation between an event and its parent document creation time.

For temporal entity extraction, we find that a joint inference-based approach using structured prediction outperforms a vanilla recurrent neural network that incorporates word embeddings trained on a variety of large clinical document sets. For document creation time relations, we find that a combination of date canonicalization and distant supervision rules for predicting relations on both events and time expressions improves classification, though gains are limited, likely due to the small scale of training data.

1 Introduction

This work discusses two information extraction systems for identifying temporal information in clinical text, submitted to SemEval-2016 Task 12 : Clinical TempEval (Bethard et al., 2016). We participated in tasks from both phases: (1) identifying text spans of time and event mentions; and (2) predicting relations between clinical events and document creation time.

Temporal information extraction is the task of constructing a timeline or ordering of all events in a given document. In the clinical domain, this is a key requirement for medical reasoning systems as well as longitudinal research into the progression of disease. While timestamps and the structured nature of the electronic medical record (EMR) directly capture some aspects of time, a large amount of information on the progression of disease is found in the unstructured text component of the EMR where temporal structure is less obvious.

We examine a deep-learning approach to sequence labeling using a vanilla *recurrent neural network* (RNN) with word embeddings, as well as a joint inference, structured prediction approach using Stanford's knowledge base construction framework DeepDive (Zhang, 2015). Our DeepDive application outperformed the RNN and scored similarly to 2015's best-in-class extraction systems, even though it only used a small set of context window and dictionary features. Extraction performance, however lagged this year's best system submission. For document creation time relations, we again use Deep-Dive. Our system examined a simple temporal distant supervision rule for labeling time expressions and linking them to nearby event mentions via inference rules. Overall system performance was better than this year's median submission, but again fell short of the best system.

2 Methods and Materials

Phase 1 of the challenge required parsing clinical documents to identify TIMEX3 and EVENT temporal entity mentions in text. TIMEX3 entities are expressions of time, ranging from concrete dates to phrases describing intervals like "the last few months." EVENT entities are broadly defined as anything relevant to a patient's clinical timeline, e.g., diagnoses, illnesses, procedures. Entity mentions

Proceedings of SemEval-2016, pages 1274–1279,
San Diego, California, June 16-17, 2016. ©2016 Association for Computational Linguistics

are tagged using a document collection of clinic and pathology notes from the Mayo Clinic called the THYME (Temporal History of Your Medical Events) corpus (Styler IV et al., 2014).

We treat Phase 1 as a sequence labeling task and examine several models for labeling entities. We discuss our submitted tagger which uses a vanilla RNN[1] and compare its performance to a DeepDive-based system, which lets us encode domain knowledge and sequence structure into a probabilistic graphic model.

For Phase 2, we are given all test set entities and asked to identify the temporal relationship between an EVENT mention and corresponding document creation time. This relation is represented as a classification problem, assigning event attributes from the label set {BEFORE, OVERLAP, BEFORE/OVERLAP, AFTER}. We use DeepDive to define several inference rules for leveraging neighboring pairs of EVENT and TIMEX3 mentions to better reason about temporal labels.

2.1 Recurrent Neural Networks

2.1.1 Overview

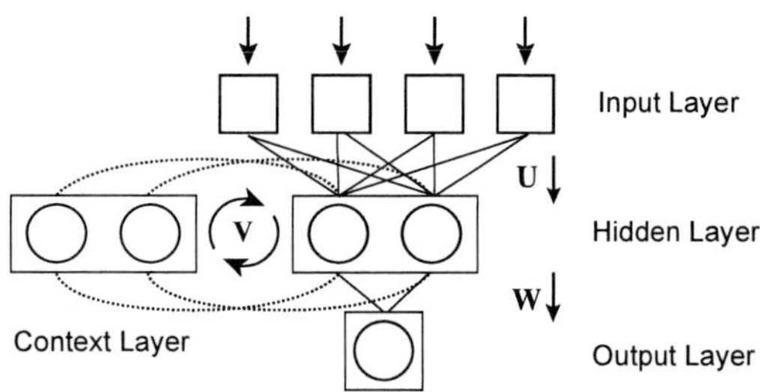

Figure 1: Simple Recurrent Neural Network. $\mathbf{U}$ is the input × hidden layer weight matrix. $\mathbf{V}$ is the context layer × hidden layer matrix, and $\mathbf{W}$ is the output weight matrix. Dotted lines indicate recurrent edge weights.

Vanilla (or Elman-type) RNNs are recursive neural networks with a linear chain structure (Elman, 1990). RNNs are similar to classical feedforward neural networks, except that they incorporate an additional hidden context layer that forms a time-lagged, recurrent connection (a directed cycle) to the

---

[1]There was a bug in our original RNN submission that dramatically lowered recall. We report the original and corrected test set scores in order to better characterize the contributions of this work.

primary hidden layer. In the canonical RNN design, the output of the hidden layer at time step $t - 1$ is retained in the context layer and fed back into the hidden layer at t; this enables the RNN to explicitly model some aspects of sequence history. (see Figure 1).

Each word in our vocabulary is represented as an n-dimensional vector in a lookup table of $|vocab|$ × n parameters (i.e., our learned embedding matrix). Input features then consist of a concatenation of these embeddings to represent a context window surrounding our target word. The output layer then emits a probability distribution in the dimension of the candidate label set. The lookup table is shared across all input instances and updated during training.

Formally our RNN definition follows (Mesnil et al., 2013):

$$h(t) = f(\mathbf{U}x(t) + \mathbf{V}h(t - 1))$$

where $x(t)$ is our concatenated context window of word embeddings, $h(t)$ is our hidden layer, $\mathbf{U}$ is the input-to-hidden layer matrix, $\mathbf{V}$ is the hidden layer-to-context layer matrix, and $f(x)$ is the activation function (logistic in this work).

$$f(x) = \frac{1}{1+e^{-x}}$$

The output layer $y(t)$ consists of a softmax activation function $g(x)$

$$y(t) = g(\mathbf{W}h(t)) \qquad g(x_i) = \frac{e^{x_i}}{\sum_k e^{x_k}}$$

where $\mathbf{W}$ is the output layer matrix. Training is done using batch gradient descent using one sentence per batch. Our RNN implementation is based on code available as part of Theano v0.7 (Bastien et al., 2012).

2.1.2 Word Embeddings

For baseline RNN models, all embedding parameters are initialized randomly in the range [-1.0, 1.0]. For all other word-based models, embedding vectors are initialized or *pre-trained* with parameters trained on different clinical corpora. Pre-training generally improves classification performance over random initialization and provides a mechanism to leverage large collections of unlabeled data for use in semi-supervised learning (Erhan et al., 2010).

We create word embeddings using two collections of clinical documents: the MIMIC-III database

Corpus	Note Type	Tokens	|Vocab|
MIMIC-III	Mixed (15 types)	758M	260K
UIHC-ALL	Mixed (41 types)	6.5B	899K
UIHC-CN	Clinic Notes	2.3B	378K
UIHC-PN	Progress Notes	1.8B	378K

Table 1: Summary statistics for embedding corpora.

containing 2.4M notes from critical care patients at Beth Israel Deaconess Medical Center (Saeed et al., 2011); and the University of Iowa Hospitals and Clinics (UIHC) corpus, containing 15M predominantly inpatient notes (see Table 1). All word embeddings in this document are trained with word2vec (Mikolov et al., 2013) using the Skipgram model, trained with a 10 token window size. We generated 100 and 300 dimensional embeddings based on prior work tuning representation sizes in clinical domains (Fries, 2015).

2.1.3 RNN Taggers

We train RNN models for three tasks in Phase 1: a character-level RNN for tokenization; and two word-level RNNs for POS tagging and entity labeling. Word-level RNNs are pre-trained with the embeddings described above, while character-level RNNs are randomly initialized. All words are normalized by lowercasing tokens and replacing digits with N, e.g., `01-Apr-2016` becomes `NN-apr-NNNN` to improve generalizability and restrict vocabulary size. Characters are left as unnormalized input. In the test data set, unknown words/characters are represented using the special token `<UNK>` . All hyperparameters were selected using a randomized grid search. [2]

Tokenization: Word tokenization and sentence boundary detection are done simultaneously using a character-level RNN. Each character is assigned a tag from 3 classes: `WORD (W)` if a character is a member of a token that does not end a sentence; `END (E)` for a token that does end a sentence, and whitespace `O`. We use IOB2 tagging to encode the range of token spans.

Models are trained using THYME syntactic annotations from colon and brain cancer notes. Training

---

[2]RNN parameter space: hidden units: [48 - 384]; L/R context window [2 - 6]; learning rate: (0.001, 0.01, 0.1, 0.25). Character-level RNN parameters: dim: (16, 32); sentence padding [0 - 5].

data consists of all sentences, padded with 5 characters from the left and right neighboring sentences. Each character is represented by a 16-dimensional embedding (from an alphabet of 90 characters) and an 11 character context window. The final prediction task input is one, long character sequence per-document. We found that the tokenizer consistently made errors conflating E and W classes (e.g., `B-W`, `I-E`, `I-E`) so after tagging, we enforce an additional consistency constraint on `B-*` and `I-*` tags so that contiguous BEGIN/INSIDE spans share the same class.

Part-of-speech Tagging: We trained a POS tagger using THYME syntactic annotations. A model using 100-dimensional UIHC-CN embeddings (clinic notes) and a context window of $\pm$ 2 words performed best on held out test data, with an accuracy of 97.67% and $F_1 = 0.973$.

TIMEX3 and EVENT Span Tagging: We train separate models for each entity type, testing different pre-training schemes using 100 and 300-dimensional embeddings trained on our large, unlabeled clinical corpora. Both tasks use context windows of $\pm$ 2 words (i.e., concatenated input of 5 n-d word embeddings) and a learning rate of 0.01. We use 80 hidden units for 100-dimensional embeddings models and 256 units for 300-dimensional models. Output tags are in the IOB2 tagging format.

2.2 DeepDive

DeepDive developers build domain knowledge into applications using a combination of *distant supervision rules*, which use heuristics to generate noisy training examples, and inference rules which use *factors* to define relationships between random variables. This design pattern allows us to quickly encode domain knowledge into a probabilistic graphical model and do joint inference over a large space of random variables.

For example, we want to capture the relationship between EVENT entities and their closest TIMEX3 mentions in text since that provides some information about when the EVENT occurred relative to document creation time. TIMEX3s lack a class `DocRelTime`, but we can use a distant supervision rule to generate a noisy label that we then leverage to predict neighboring EVENT labels. We also know that the set of all EVENT/TIMEX3 mentions within a given note section, such as patient history, provides discriminative information that should be shared across labels in that section. DeepDive lets us easily define these structures by linking random variables (in this case all entity class labels) with factors, directly encoding domain knowledge into our learning algorithm.

2.2.1 TIMEX3 and EVENT Spans

Phase 1: Our baseline tagger consists of three inference rules: logistic regression, conditional random fields (CRF), and skip-chain CRF (Sutton and McCallum, 2006). In CRFs, factor edges link adjoining words in a linear chain structure, capturing label dependencies between neighboring words. Skip-chain CRFs generalize this idea to include skip edges, which can connect non-neighboring words. For example, we can link labels for all identical words in a given window of sentences. We use DeepDive's feature library, ddlib, to generate common textual features like context windows and dictionary membership. We explored combinations of left/right windows of 2 neighboring words and POS tags, letter case, and entity dictionaries for all vocabulary identified by the challenge's baseline memorization rule, i.e., all phrases that are labeled as true entities $\geq 50\%$ of the time in the training set.

Feature Ablation Tests We evaluate 3 feature set combinations to determine how each contributes predictive power to our system.

Run 1: dictionary features, letter case

Run 2: dictionary features, letter case, context window ($\pm$ 2 normalized words)

Run 3: dictionary features, letter case, context window ($\pm$ 2 normalized words), POS tags

2.2.2 Document Creation Time Relations

Phase 2: In order to predict the relationship between an event and the creation time of its parent document, we assign a `DocRelTime` random variable to every TIMEX3 and EVENT mention. For EVENTs, these values are provided by the training data, for TIMEX3s we have to compute class labels. Around 42% of TIMEX3 mentions are simple dates ("12/29/08", "October 16", etc.) and can be naively canonicalized to a universal timestamp. This is done using regular expressions to identify common date patterns and heuristics to deal with incomplete dates.

The missing year in "October 16", for example, can be filled in using the nearest preceding date mention; if that isn't available we use the document creation year. These mentions are then assigned a class using the parent document's `DocTime` value and any revision timestamps. Other TIMEX3 mentions are more ambiguous so we use a distant supervision approach. Phrases like "currently" and "today's" tend to occur near EVENTs that overlap the current document creation time, while "ago" or "X-years" indicate past events. These dominant temporal associations can be learned from training data and then used to label TIMEX3s. Finally, we define a logistic regression rule to predict entity `DocRelTime` values as well as specify a linear skip-chain factor over EVENT mentions and their nearest TIMEX3 neighbor, encoding the baseline system heuristic directly as an inference rule.

3 Results

3.1 Phase 1

Word tokenization performance was high, F_1=0.993 while sentence boundary detection was lower with $F_1 = 0.938$ (document micro average $F_1 = 0.985$). Tokenization errors were largely confined to splitting numbers and hyphenated words ("ex-smoker" vs. "ex - smoker") which has minimal impact on upstream sequence labeling. Sentence boundary errors were largely missed terminal words, creating longer sentences, which is preferable to short, less informative sequences in terms of impact on RNN minibatches.

Tables 2 and 3 contain results for all sequence labeling models. For TIMEX3 spans, the best RNN ensemble model performed poorly compared to the winning system (0.706 vs. 0.795). DeepDive runs 2-3 performed as well as 2015's best system, but also fell short of the top system (0.730 vs. 0.795). EVENT spans were easier to tag and RNN models compared favorably with DeepDive, the former scoring higher recall and the latter higher precision. Both approaches scored below this year's best system (0.885 vs. 0.903).

3.2 Phase 2

Finally, Table 4 contains our DocRelTime relation extraction. Our simple distant supervision rule leads

Method	Span		
	P	**R**	**F$_1$**
Baseline: memorize	0.774	0.428	0.551
BluLab (2015) [1]	0.797	0.664	0.725
Median System (2016)	*0.779*	*0.539*	*0.637*
Best (2016):	***0.840***	***0.758***	***0.795***
DeepDive: run 1	0.655	0.566	0.607
DeepDive: run 2	0.795	0.675	**0.730**
DeepDive: run 3	**0.798**	0.665	0.725
RNN+randinit-100	0.694	0.679	0.686
RNN+MIMIC-III-100	0.706	0.695	0.701
RNN+UIHC-CN-100	0.699	0.688	0.693
RNN+UIHC-PN-100	0.701	0.670	0.685
RNN+UIHC-ALL-100	0.708	0.688	0.698
RNN+randinit-300	0.713	0.657	0.684
RNN+UIHC-CN-300	0.704	0.702	0.703
RNN+UIHC-PN-300	0.700	0.697	0.698
RNN Best Ensemble	0.708	**0.704**	0.706
Phase 1 RNN Submission	0.686	0.415	0.517

Table 2: TIMEX3 spans extraction performance for the test set (mean of 5 runs) [1] Baseline and BluLab scores are provided in (Bethard et al., 2015)

Method	Span		
	P	**R**	**F$_1$**
Baseline: memorize	0.878	0.834	0.855
BluLab (2015)	0.887	0.864	0.875
Median System (2016)	*0.887*	*0.846*	*0.874*
Best (2016):	***0.915***	***0.891***	***0.903***
DeepDive: run 1	0.864	0.836	0.850
DeepDive: run 2	**0.900**	0.864	0.882
DeepDive: run 3	**0.900**	0.866	0.883
RNN+randinit-100	0.864	0.869	0.866
RNN+MIMIC-III-100	0.861	0.877	0.869
RNN+UIHC-CN-100	0.873	0.887	0.880
RNN+UIHC-PN-100	0.878	0.882	0.880
RNN+UIHC-ALL-100	0.878	0.880	0.879
RNN+randinit-300	0.862	0.859	0.861
RNN+UIHC-CN-300	0.880	0.879	0.879
RNN+UIHC-PN-300	0.864	**0.892**	0.878
RNN Best Ensemble	0.882	0.889	**0.885**
Phase 1 RNN Submission	0.883	0.660	0.755

Table 3: EVENT spans extraction performance.

to better performance than then median system submission, but also falls substantially short of current state of the art.

4 Discussion

Randomly initialized RNNs generally weren't competitive to our best performing structured prediction

Attribute	P	R	F$_1$
Baseline: memorize / closest	-	-	0.675
BluLab (2015)	-	-	0.791
Median System (2016)	-	-	0.724
Best (2016)	-	-	***0.843***
Logistic Regression (LR)	0.738	0.737	0.737
LR+Skip-chain	0.743	0.742	**0.743**

Table 4: Phase 2: EVENT Document Creation Time Relation extraction measures (baseline precision/recall scores not provided).

models (DeepDive runs 2-3) which isn't surprising considering the small amount of training data available compared to typical deep-learning contexts. There was a statistically significant improvement for RNNs pre-trained with clinical text word2vec embeddings, reflecting the consensus that embeddings capture some syntactic and semantic information that must otherwise be manually encoded as features. Performance was virtually the same across all embedding types, independent of corpus size, note type, etc. While embeddings trained on more data perform better in semantic tasks like synonym detection, its unclear if that representational strength is important here. Similar performance might also just reflect the general ubiquity with which temporal vocabulary occurs in all clinical note contexts. Alternatively, vanilla RNNs rarely achieve state-of-the-art performance in sequence labeling tasks due to well-known issues surrounding the vanishing or exploding gradient effect (Pascanu et al., 2012). More sophisticated recurrent architectures with gated units such as Long Short-Term Memory (LSTM), (Hochreiter and Schmidhuber, 1997) and gated recurrent unit (Chung et al., 2014) or recursive structures like Tree-LSTM (Tai et al., 2015) have shown strong representational power in other sequence labeling tasks. Such approaches might perform better in this setting.

DeepDive's feature generator libraries let us easily create a large space of binary features and then let regularization address overfitting. In our extraction system, just using a context window of ± 2 words and dictionaries representing the baseline memorization rules was enough to achieve median system performance. POS tag features had no statistically significant impact on performance in either EVENT/TIMEX3 extraction.

For classifying an EVENT's document creation time relation, our DeepDive application essentially implements the joint inference version of the baseline memorization rule, leveraging entity proximity to increase predictive performance. A simple distant supervision rule that canonicalizes TIMEX3 timestamps and predicts nearby EVENT's lead to a slight performance boost, suggesting that using a larger collection of unlabeled note data could lead to further increases.

While our systems did not achieve current state-of-the-art performance, DeepDive matched last year's top submission for TIMEX3 and EVENT tagging with very little upfront engineering – around a week of dedicated development time. One of the primary goals of this work was to avoid an over-engineered extraction pipeline, instead relying on feature generation libraries or deep learning approaches to model underlying structure. Both systems explored in this work were successful to some extent, though future work remains in order to close the performance gap between these approaches and current state-of-the-art systems.

Acknowledgments

This work was supported by the Mobilize Center, a National Institutes of Health Big Data to Knowledge (BD2K) Center of Excellence supported through Grant U54EB020405.

References

Frédéric Bastien, Pascal Lamblin, Razvan Pascanu, James Bergstra, Ian J. Goodfellow, Arnaud Bergeron, Nicolas Bouchard, and Yoshua Bengio. 2012. Theano: new features and speed improvements. Deep Learning and Unsupervised Feature Learning NIPS 2012 Workshop.

Steven Bethard, Leon Derczynski, Guergana Savova, Guergana Savova, James Pustejovsky, and Marc Verhagen. 2015. Semeval-2015 task 6: Clinical tempeval. *Proc. SemEval*.

Steven Bethard, Guergana Savova, Wei-Te Chen, Leon Derczynski, James Pustejovsky, and Marc Verhagen. 2016. Semeval-2016 task 12: Clinical tempeval. In *Proceedings of the 10th International Workshop on Semantic Evaluation (SemEval 2016)*, San Diego, California, June. Association for Computational Linguistics.

Junyoung Chung, Çaglar Gülçehre, KyungHyun Cho, and Yoshua Bengio. 2014. Empirical evaluation of gated recurrent neural networks on sequence modeling. *CoRR*, abs/1412.3555.

Jeffrey L Elman. 1990. Finding structure in time. *Cognitive science*, 14(2):179–211.

Dumitru Erhan, Yoshua Bengio, Aaron Courville, Pierre-Antoine Manzagol, Pascal Vincent, and Samy Bengio. 2010. Why does unsupervised pre-training help deep learning? *The Journal of Machine Learning Research*, 11:625–660.

Jason Fries. 2015. *Modeling Words for Online Sexual Behavior Surveillance and Clinical Text Information Extraction*. Ph.D. thesis, University of Iowa.

Sepp Hochreiter and Jürgen Schmidhuber. 1997. Long short-term memory. *Neural computation*, 9(8):1735–1780.

Grégoire Mesnil, Xiaodong He, Li Deng, and Yoshua Bengio. 2013. Investigation of recurrent-neural-network architectures and learning methods for spoken language understanding. In *INTERSPEECH*, pages 3771–3775.

Tomas Mikolov, Kai Chen, Greg Corrado, and Jeffrey Dean. 2013. Efficient estimation of word representations in vector space. *arXiv preprint arXiv:1301.3781*.

Razvan Pascanu, Tomas Mikolov, and Yoshua Bengio. 2012. On the difficulty of training recurrent neural networks. *arXiv preprint arXiv:1211.5063*.

Mohammed Saeed, Mauricio Villarroel, Andrew T Reisner, Gari Clifford, Li-Wei Lehman, George Moody, Thomas Heldt, Tin H Kyaw, Benjamin Moody, and Roger G Mark. 2011. Multiparameter intelligent monitoring in intensive care ii (mimic-ii): a public-access intensive care unit database. *Critical care medicine*, 39(5):952.

William F Styler IV, Steven Bethard, Sean Finan, Martha Palmer, Sameer Pradhan, Piet C de Groen, Brad Erickson, Timothy Miller, Chen Lin, Guergana Savova, et al. 2014. Temporal annotation in the clinical domain. *Transactions of the Association for Computational Linguistics*, 2:143–154.

Charles Sutton and Andrew McCallum. 2006. An introduction to conditional random fields for relational learning. *Introduction to statistical relational learning*, pages 93–128.

Kai Sheng Tai, Richard Socher, and Christopher D Manning. 2015. Improved semantic representations from tree-structured long short-term memory networks. *arXiv preprint arXiv:1503.00075*.

Ce Zhang. 2015. *DeepDive: A Data Management System for Automatic Knowledge Base Construction*. Ph.D. thesis, UW-Madison.

KULeuven-LIIR at SemEval 2016 Task 12:
Detecting Narrative Containment in Clinical Records

Artuur Leeuwenberg and **Marie-Francine Moens**
Department of Computer Science
KU Leuven, Belgium
{tuur.leeuwenberg, sien.moens}@cs.kuleuven.be

Abstract

In this paper, we describe the KULeuven-LIIR system at the Clinical TempEval 2016 Shared Task for the narrative container relation sub-task (CR). Our approach is based on the cTAKES Temporal system (Lin et al., 2015). We explored extending this system with different features. Moreover, we provide an error analysis of the submitted system, and report on some additional experiments done after submission.

1 Introduction

We describe the KULeuven-LIIR submissions for the Clinical TempEval 2016 shared task (Bethard et al., 2016). Our motivation for this first participation is to gain insight into the task, and the data, as a basis for future work. We participated in the narrative container relation (CR) task. In the CR task narrative containment relations between events, and events and temporal expressions are to be extracted. Two examples of such relations are given in Sentence 1.

(1) A *colonoscopy* on *27 September 2008* revealed a circumferential *lesion*.

The relations that are to be extracted are

- CONTAINS(*27 September 2008*, *colonoscopy*)

- CONTAINS(*colonoscopy*, *lesion*)

In the shared task, the clinical records on colon cancer from the THYME corpus are used (Styler IV et al., 2014). We participated in phase 2 evaluation,

which means that manually annotated EVENT and TIMEX3 spans with their attributes are provided as part of the input. We submitted two runs that are both based on the cTAKES-Temporal system (Lin et al., 2015). For the first run, we used cTAKES-Temporal with a set of already provided features. We further explain the cTAKES-Temporal system and the features that we used in Section 2. For the second run, we added new features, that are based on an error analysis of a small sample from the results of running the first system on the development set. These additional features are described in Section 3. Moreover, we describe a more elaborate error analysis of the second system in Section 4, and some experiments that we performed with the aim to handle these errors in Section 5.

2 The cTAKES Temporal System (run 1)

The first version of the temporal module in cTAKES[1], an extensive open source information extraction system for clinical free-texts (Savova et al., 2010), is described by (Lin et al., 2015). We used the currently available version in our experiments. The current version of cTAKES Temporal consists of two SVM classifiers to detect containment. One for containment between events (EE), and one for containment between temporal expressions and events (TE), each using different features, as the nature of the two types of relations is quite different. The features we used for each classifier are described in Table 2, and will be explained further in the next paragraph. Note that with entity we refer to either an EVENT or TIMEX3 expression, which can con-

---

[1] ctakes.apache.org/

1280

Proceedings of SemEval-2016, pages 1280–1285,
San Diego, California, June 16-17, 2016. ©2016 Association for Computational Linguistics

sist of several tokens (words, numbers, punctuation etc.). The search space, or the entity-pairs that the system considers are all EE and TE pairs in each sentence or line, in each document for their respective classifier (the EE SVM, or the ET SVM).

As in the THYME corpus only the heads of events are annotated, cTAKES-Temporal expands these heads to their full phrase (e.g., the annotated head *cancer* expands to *ascending colon cancer*). Afterwards it creates extra training data by not only considering the pairs of entity phrases, but also the sub-phrases (e.g., *cancer, colon cancer*, and *ascending colon cancer*).

The precision, recall, and F-measure that our first submission scored on the test set is reported in Table 5. What can be noticed from the top-part of Table 5 is that the cTAKES Temporal system (run 1) gives reasonable results, scoring ∼9% higher than the median F-measure of all systems evaluated in Clinical TempEval 2016, and ∼4% short compared to the best system.

2.1 Features

The features used in run 1 correspond to those described by (Lin et al., 2015), and feature extraction is included within the (open source) cTAKES Temporal module. In this module, tokenization is done following the Penn Treebank rules (Mott et al., 2009). Sentence boundaries, parts-of-speech, chunks, and constituency parses (for finding heads) are obtained using the corresponding cTAKES modules. Dependency paths are extracted using the ClearNLP dependency parser model in cTAKES. UMLS types are extracted by means of direct token or chunk matches, and by creation of lexical variants using the UMLS Lexical Variant Generation package [2].

3 Additional Features (run 2)

Our motivations for the additional features come from analyzing a small sample of errors (small due to time constraints at the moment of submission) of the first system on the development set, from which we concluded that especially long distance and sometimes also short distance relations characterized by prepositions (especially *of* and *with*) were not found by the system. An example of

---

[2]https://www.nlm.nih.gov/research/umls

such a relation missed by the system is CON-TAINS(*colonoscopy, polypectomy*) in the fragment given in Figure 3.

The first added feature is a modified version of the dependency path (MDP). We include part of speech tags in the path for nouns, personal pronouns, numbers, adjectives and determiners. For other parts of speech we include the words themselves. In the original dependency path feature of cTAKES Temporal, only parts of speech are included. The second

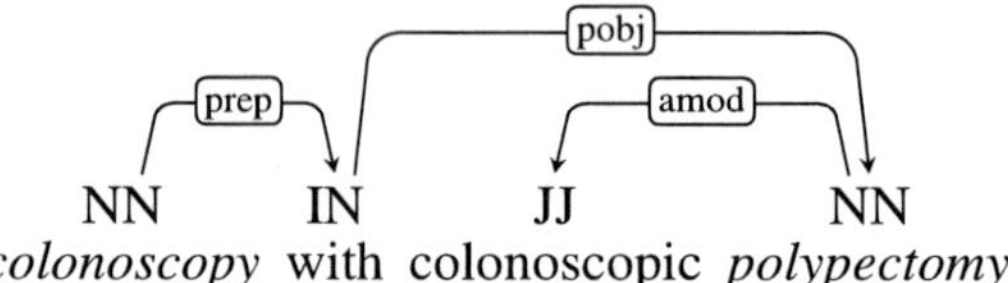

Figure 1: Sentence fragment, with its POS, and dependencies.

feature consists of the sequence in-between the two entities (IBS), i.e., the words in-between connected by an underscore. We replace the same categories as for the MDP by their respective POS in the sequence. The modified dependency path, and the in-between sequence (IBS) feature for the small fragment in Figure 3, where we consider *colonoscopy*, and *polypectomy* are:

MDP: `<NN>prep<with>pobj<NN>`

IBS: `with_JJ`

The precision, recall, and F-measure on the test set for the second run are shown in Table 5. Adding these features resulted only in a tiny increase in both precision and recall (0.001). From this we conclude that our error sample might not have been representative enough for the rest of the corpus, or that the features do not cover the errors made. Also, there is probably overlap between the MDP feature and the existing dependency path feature, and between the IBS feature and the existing Tokens feature explaining why adding the MDP and IBS features do not help much.

4 Error Analysis

4.1 Error Categories

We also ran the system of the second run on the development set of the THYME corpus (but now only trained on the train set) and analyzed its errors with

Feature	Description	Extraction
1. Tokens	String features for the tokens within each entity, the entity's first and last token, and the tokens in-between the two entities.	cTAKES-Temporal module, with Penn Treebank tokenization rules (Mott et al., 2009)
2. POS	String features for the parts of speech of the tokens of both entities.	cTAKES' POS tagger
3. Event Attributes	String features for each event modality, polarity, and event type of both entities.	Part of the input (phase 2 evaluation)
4. UMLS	Boolean flags for the semantic UMLS type of each entity, and as a paired feature ($type_1$-$type_2$).	cTAKES-Temporal module, with UMLS Lexical Variant Generation
5. Dependency Path	The dependency path between the entities, comprised of edge-labels, and POS tags.	cTAKES dependency parser (clinical ClearNLP model)
6. Overlapped Head	Consists of a string feature for each overlapping head word, and numerical features for the count and ratio of overlapping words.	cTAKES Temporal module, where heads are found by means of the cTAKES Constituency Parses
7. Nearest Flag	Boolean flag on if two entities are the closest candidates of each other.	cTAKES Temporal module
8. Conjunction Flag	Boolean flag for conjunctions in-between the entities only *CC*, *COMMA*, or *IN* POS tags are considered.	cTAKES Temporal module (using cTAKES's POS tagger)
9. Special Word Relation	Boolean feature for special phrase types in-between the entities (e.g., *starts out*: STARTING).	Manually constructed list by (Lin et al., 2015)
10. Temporal Attributes	String features for EVENT modality, and TIMEX3 class.	Part of the input (phase 2 evaluation)

Table 1: Feature descriptions for the EVENT-EVENT classifier, using features 1, 2, 3, 4, 5, 6 and the TIMEX3-EVENT classifier, using features 1, 3, 5, 7, 8, 9, 10.

category	count	percentage
Correct	22	44%
Questionable	10	20%
Negation	5	10%
Other	13	26%

Table 2: Categories of **false positives** for the run 2 system on the THYME development set.

regard to predicting the correct CONTAINER relations. Around 69% of the errors were false negatives, and around 31% false positives. We then randomly sampled 50 errors of both types and categorized them (∼1.5 % of false negatives, and ∼3.3% of false positives). For the false positives, we found four frequent categories: (1) predictions that we judge to be *correct* positive predictions, (2) predictions that we judge the correctness to be *questionable*, (3) incorrect predictions caused by an unprocessed *negation*.

In Table 2 the statistics of the categories are shown. What can be noticed is that many of the false positives are questionable or correct. This indicates that the actual precision of the system might be higher. On the other hand, the consistent errors

that the system makes result from ignoring negations or negating verbs (e.g., *to quit*). The errors in the category 'other' had various causes, such as wrong tokenization, mistakes in event annotation, or sometimes the cause was unclear.

A bigger, and maybe more interesting, source for improvement are the false negatives, i.e., the relations missed by the system. Here we found the following major (non-mutually exclusive) categories: (1) *cross-sentence* relations, (2) *unknown tokens (UNKS)* are tokens that appear in the dev-set as argument of the relation, but not in the train-set. Categories (1) and (2) appear to be a common source of false negatives. Another frequent error category is (3) the relation *crosses a newline*[3], (4) the relation is part of a data *table*, as shown in Figure 2, (5) one of the arguments of the relation is part of a within-sentence enumeration (usually comma-separated), (6) some false negatives we judge to be *correctly* predicted as negative. The proportions of these categories are shown in Table 3. In our notion of UNK errors, we exclude unseen dates (e.g.,

---

[3]Note that sentence boundaries are given by the sentence boundary detection, and new lines by the newline token ('\n').

category	count	percentage
Cross-sentence	13	26%
UNKs (excl. dates)	13	26%
Cross-newline	11	22%
Table	9	18%
Enumeration	6	12%
Correct	4	8%
Other	10	20%

Table 3: Categories of **false negatives** for the run 2 system on the THYME development set.

February 2, 2008) as they include digits, resulting in many (rather predictable) UNK tokens.

4.2 Examples of Errors

The UNK tokens from the false negatives seem a mix of more domain specific and general terms. More domain-specific terms are *CK5-6*, *seepage*, *mesh*, and *Mumps*. The more general are *outline*, *QUALITY*, *function*, and *question*. The cross-newline and table error categories have some overlap. An example of the cross-newline category is shown in Figure 2, where the missed relation in our random sample is CONTAINS(*HISTORY*, *affected*). But also the containment between *HISTORY* and *Polio*, *Obesity*, *equivalency*, *hyperlipidemia*, *Hypertension*, *PVD*, *stenosis*, and *disease* are missed by the system. A table-error would look similar, but with test measurement reports, such as for example patient height, weight, or body mass index.

```
PAST MEDICAL HISTORY
1) Polio at age 15. RUE affected.
2) Obesity.
3) CAD equivalency with hyperlipidemia ...
4) Hypertension, well-controlled.
5) PVD of left leg. Stable and asymptomatic.
6) Moderate aortic stenosis.
7) Non-alcoholic fatty liver disease.
```

Figure 2: An example of the cross-newline error category, where the CONTAINS(*HISTORY*, *affected*) relation is missed by the system (and many more).

The enumeration error category contains within sentence enumerations. An example sentence is given in sentence (2).

(2) We have discussed the *characteristics* of the cancer, including the type of malignancy, size,

grade, lymph node *status*, and stage of the cancer.

Here, CONTAINS(*characteristics*, *status*) is the missed error in our sample. One reason for this type of errors might be that the currently used dependency parser chains the parts of such enumerations, resulting in a long dependency path between the two entities, which is less likely to occur frequently in the training data.

4.3 Token Frequency

We also looked at token diversity in the training set for event-event containment, and time-event containment. What can be noticed from Table 4 is that there are slightly more EE container relations, than TE container relations. It is also striking that the source (first argument of the containment relation, i.e., the container) of the TE relations have a relatively low average token frequency, and a high percentage of UNKs, compared to the source of the EE relations. The explanation for this is that for the TE pairs the source category (TIMEX3) of tokens includes dates, containing numbers, causing big token diversity (each date is a new token). To get a better idea of token diversity without considering each number as a different token we conflated the digits in TE source tokens (e.g., *February 2, 2008* becomes *February 5, 5555*). In-between the brackets the percentage of UNKs is shown, after digit conflation of these tokens. Furthermore, the source of both the TE and the EE relations, i.e., the container, seems to be less diverse compared to the target, i.e., the event that is contained. We conclude that this is because of the relatively low vocabulary size of this category, and low percentage of UNKs, i.e., there are less different containers (container EVENT or TIMEX3 expressions) than containees (contained EVENTS).

5 Out-of-Competition Experiments

We conducted two sets of experiments, one set to address the UNK-related errors, and one to address the cross-newline errors.

To tackle the UNK token category, without adding extra resources, we experimented with adding subword features, in particular character 3-grams of the entities. We also experimented with adding word embeddings to the event-event SVM. We trained

	Event-Event		Time-Event	
	source	target	source	target
|train-tokens|	5931	5931	5093	5093
|train-vocabulary|	637	1417	1268 (839)	1198
avg. token-freq.	9.3	4.2	4.0 (6.0)	4.3
UNK percentage	0.10	0.18	0.43 (0.17)	0.15

Table 4: Token-frequency statistics. The 'source' of the containment relation refers to the container, and taget to the containee. For TE sources we also calculated statistics after digit conflation, shown in-between brackets.

the embeddings on 10 million words of crawled web data from the oncology/colon cancer domain[4] plus the THYME training data. To construct the word vectors we used the continuous bag-of-words (CBOW), and Skip-gram model (SG) by (Mikolov et al., 2013). The vectors are of dimension 250, and were trained using the default settings in the word2vec toolkit[5]. What can be noticed from Table 5 is that adding these features did not significantly improve the F-measure.

System	P	R	F
clinical tempeval 2016 – median	0.589	0.345	0.449
clinical tempeval 2016 – best	**0.823**	**0.564**	**0.573**
run 1	0.714	0.428	0.536
run 2	0.715	0.429	0.536
run 2 + character 3-grams	0.706	0.428	0.533
run 2 + CBOW^{EE}	0.701	0.438	0.539
run 2 + SG^{EE}	0.708	0.433	0.537
run 2 + newline extension	**0.714**	0.441	0.545
run 2 + newline ext. + CBOW^{EE}	0.706	0.452	0.551
run 2 + newline ext. + CBOW^{EE} + SG^{EE}	0.705	**0.452**	**0.551**

Table 5: THYME test set performance of different system settings. The lower part of the table comes from experiments done out-of-competition.

With the goal to handle errors caused by separation by a newline, we extended the search space by adding candidate pairs (either EE, or ET) that were separated by a new line, but for which the end of the line consisted of a comma, or colon symbol. This increased recall (by 2%), and thus F-measure slightly as well (by 1%). This small increase in performance does not match with the relative size of the cross-newline error category, so there is still much room for improvement.

---

[4] `emedicine.medscape.com`, Pubmed Central & Pubmed
[5] `code.google.com/archive/p/word2vec/`

6 Conclusions & Future Work

In this paper we described the first participation of KULeuven-LIIR in the Clinical TempEval Shared Task 2016 (Bethard et al., 2016). Our motivation to participate was to gain insight into the CONTAINER relation extraction task, and the data for future research. We started from the cTAKES-Temporal system (Lin et al., 2015) and experimented with adding various features. From our experiments we conclude that adding the modified dependency path feature, or in-between sequence features does not improve the performance of the system. Furthermore, from our cTAKES Temporal module, we noticed that cross-sentence relations, cross-newline relations, and UNKs are an important source of error. Also, false negatives seem a bigger problem than false positives. To tackle the problem of UNKs, we experimented with adding word embeddings, trained on in-domain web crawled text, as a feature, and adding a character n-gram feature. These features did not seem to contribute significantly. For future research it could be interesting to explore alternative methods to deal with UNKs. To tackle the cross-newline mistakes the system made, we extended the scope of the candidate pair creation across new lines, which improved recall on the test set slightly, but still leaves much room for improvement.

Acknowledgments

The authors would like to thank the reviewers for their constructive comments which helped us improve the paper. Also, we would like to thank the Mayo Clinic for permission to use the THYME corpus. This work was funded by the KU Leuven C22/15/16 project "MAchine Reading of patient recordS (MARS)", and by the IWT-SBO 150056 project "ACquiring CrUcial Medical information Using LAnguage TEchnology" (ACCUMULATE).

References

Steven Bethard, Leon Derczynski, James Pustejovsky, and Marc Verhagen. 2014. Clinical TempEval. *arXiv preprint arXiv:1403.4928*.

Steven Bethard, Leon Derczynski, Guergana Savova, Guergana Savova, James Pustejovsky, and Marc Verhagen. 2015. Semeval-2015 task 6: Clinical Tempeval. *Proceedings of the 9th International Workshop on Semantic Evaluation (SemEval 2015)*.

Steven Bethard, Guergana Savova, Wei-Te Chen, Leon Derczynski, James Pustejovsky, and Marc Verhagen. 2016. SemEval-2016 task 12: Clinical TempEval. In *Proceedings of the 10th International Workshop on Semantic Evaluation (SemEval 2016)*, San Diego, California, June. Association for Computational Linguistics.

Quynh Thi Ngoc Do, Steven Bethard, and Marie-Francine Moens. 2015. Domain adaptation in semantic role labeling using a neural language model and linguistic resources. *IEEE/ACM Transactions on Audio, Speech, and Language Processing*, 23(11):1812–1823, November.

Chen Lin, Dmitriy Dligach, Timothy A Miller, Steven Bethard, and Guergana K Savova. 2015. Multilayered temporal modeling for the clinical domain. *Journal of the American Medical Informatics Association: JAMIA*.

Alexa T McCray, Suresh Srinivasan, and Allen C Browne. 1994. Lexical methods for managing variation in biomedical terminologies. In *Proceedings of the Annual Symposium on Computer Application in Medical Care*, page 235. American Medical Informatics Association.

Tomas Mikolov, Stefan Kombrink, Anoop Deoras, Lukar Burget, and Jan Cernocky. 2011. RNNLM-Recurrent neural network language modeling toolkit. In *Proc. of the 2011 ASRU Workshop*, pages 196–201.

Tomas Mikolov, Kai Chen, Greg Corrado, and Jeffrey Dean. 2013. Efficient estimation of word representations in vector space. *arXiv preprint arXiv:1301.3781*.

Justin Mott, Ann Bies, Colin Warner, and Ann Taylor. 2009. Supplementary guidelines for ETTB 2.0. *University of Pennsylvania*.

Guergana K Savova, James J Masanz, Philip V Ogren, Jiaping Zheng, Sunghwan Sohn, Karin C Kipper-Schuler, and Christopher G Chute. 2010. Mayo clinical text analysis and knowledge extraction system (cTAKES): architecture, component evaluation and applications. *Journal of the American Medical Informatics Association*, 17(5):507–513.

William F Styler IV, Steven Bethard, Sean Finan, Martha Palmer, Sameer Pradhan, Piet C de Groen, Brad Erickson, Timothy Miller, Chen Lin, Guergana Savova, et al. 2014. Temporal annotation in the clinical domain. *Transactions of the Association for Computational Linguistics*, 2:143–154.

CENTAL at SemEval-2016 Task 12:
A linguistically fed CRF model for medical
and temporal information extraction

Charlotte Hansart   Damien De Meyere   Patrick Watrin
André Bittar   Cédrick Fairon

CENTAL
Université catholique de Louvain
Place Blaise Pascal 1, 1348 Louvain-la-Neuve, Belgium

Abstract

In this paper, we describe the system developed for our participation in the Clinical TempEval task of SemEval 2016 (task 12). Our team focused on the subtasks of span and attribute identification from raw text and proposed a system that integrates both statistical and linguistic approaches. Our system is based on Conditional Random Fields with high-precision linguistic features.

1   Introduction

Extracting and linking temporal and medical information from medical documents is a highly useful task for many clinical applications and plays an important role in health care assessment and patient safety (Sun et al., 2013). Since 2007, the SemEval competition includes a temporal information extraction task which is now transposed onto the medical domain.

This year, the twelfth task included six subtasks that are described in (Bethard et al., 2016). Our team focused on the first four of these (Phase 1 submission), i.e. identification of entity spans and attribute values from raw text[1].

We present an approach combining linguistic rules and machine learning methods. The tools presented here were initially developed for French to extract information (temporal expressions, Named Entities, etc.) from newspaper corpora, a text genre which is quite different from medical documents.

[1]For the event attributes, only the "polarity" attribute is handled by our system.

This challenge was thus a good opportunity for us to evaluate the scalability of our tools for both a language other than French and a new text genre.

2   Data

We received three different sets of medical documents: two for the development of our system, and one for testing purposes. The documents are clinical notes and pathology reports. The *Train* dataset comprises 297 clinical reports. The *Dev* dataset, used for testing our developments, contains 150 reports. Finally, the *Test* dataset, available only for the evaluation of our model, includes 153 documents.

All the documents are manually de-identified by the Mayo Clinic and annotated according to an extension of the ISO-TimeML standard (Pustejovsky et al., 2010): the THYME Annotation Guidelines, developed for the THYME project (Styler et al., 2014).

3   Methodology

The originality of our approach comes from the simultaneous consideration of both terminological and linguistic resources which feed a statistical model based on the Conditional Random Fields paradigm (Lafferty et al., 2001).

In our opinion, this strategy allowed us to take full advantage of the precision inherent to symbolic approaches while enabling us to benefit from the flexibility of supervised statistical modeling methods. Such a hybrid methodology has proven useful in previous research dealing with part-of-speech tagging (Constant and Sigogne, 2011).

1286

Proceedings of SemEval-2016, pages 1286–1291,
San Diego, California, June 16-17, 2016. ©2016 Association for Computational Linguistics

3.1 Statistical analysis

Models such as Conditional Random Fields (CRF) are able to learn quickly and effectively from a large amount of observed data represented by features that are identified during the preprocessing step. Such systems typically use a set of language-independent and generic features, such as the prefix of the token or the characters that compose each token (letters, digits, hyphens, etc.).

Such a model has many advantages, the most important being its sequentiality, i.e. the fact that the CRF takes into account the context of an observation. But this approach also has its limitations. First, it is language- and domain-independent. Consequently, some generic features can be irrelevant for the concerned language or domain. Likewise, a standard CRF learns from its training corpus. Consequently, its knowledge is proportional to the variety of the corpus: if a word, a pattern, a structure is not in the corpus, the model will not recognise it and this might generate errors. In the case of textual data, this may also result in limited (lexical) coverage over unseen data.

To address the weaknesses of CRF learning, we used the CRF presented in (Watrin et al., 2014), which allows us to leverage external linguistic knowledge and resources, that will be presented in the next section. We looked at the span and attribute identification task as a sequence labelling task: a single model tags each token into the documents as being or not a relevant entity and the assigned tags capture the spans and the type of the recognised entities. The possible entity tags follow the pattern $\langle TYPE \rangle + \langle ATTRIBUTE \rangle$, so our tagset contains tags such as TIMEX3+DATE, TIMEX3+DURATION or EVENT+NEG. The O tag is assigned to tokens outside of any entity. In short, the sequence labelling tagging allows us to identify in a single run the boundaries, the type and the attribute of an entity.

The CRF model is developed with the CRFsuite package (Okazaki, 2007). Regarding its parameterisation, we used the default parameters proposed by the library (graphical model: first-order Markov CRF with dyad features; training algorithm: L-BFGS; see the library documentation for more information). The set of features remains unchanged against our original model (Watrin et al., 2014) and

Feature	explanation
Lexical item	token to be labeled
lowercase	token in lowercase
hasHyphen	does the token contain hyphen?
hasDigit	does the token contain digits?
allUpperCase	is the token uppercase only?
shape	token in a Xxx form
prefix*(n)*	*n* first letters of the token
suffix*(n)*	*n* last letters of the token

Table 1: Language-independent features

Feature	explanation
pos	token part-of-speech tag
containsFeature*(x)*	does the token belong to the semantic class *x* ?
sac	semantic class ambiguity (all possible classes for the token)

Table 2: Lexical features

is reproduced in Table 1 and 2. As we will show in section 3.2, we tuned the *containsFeature(x)* feature according to the particularities of medical language.

3.2 Language resources

We combine two kinds of language-dependent resources: terminological and linguistic resources.

Terminological resources The language used in medical health records is characterized by a specific terminology. As this challenge focuses on English texts, we were able to reuse the numerous existing terminologies that are distributed throughout the *Unified Medical Language System* (UMLS). The UMLS brings together more than 150 vocabularies covering various aspects of healthcare (ICD-9-CM, ICD-10-CM, SNOMED-CT, MeSH, etc.) which were compiled into a dictionary of nearly 6 million terms. These entries were automatically classified into five generic categories, i.e. *procedures*, *diagnoses*, *anatomical terms*, *organisms* and *other* by simplifying the categories system of the UMLS. These categories were used as additional features for learning. As a word can be ambiguous, each category is considered as a separate feature in the CRF.

The training corpus being quite limited in size, these resources are necessary to overcome the problem of data sparseness as far as the medical terminology is concerned. As the UMLS already has an extensive coverage, we limited ourselves to importing its terminological components without any further linguistic processing, i.e. splitting into smaller units, stemming, etc. However, it has been shown that terminological components are only partially representative of the medical language in use (De Meyere et al., 2015). For example, terms in the UMLS can be affected by syntagmatic and paradigmatic variation to varying degrees (e.g. *incomplete bladder emptying = the emptying function of the bladder is incomplete*) or may be too precise or complex to actually be used in electronic health records (e.g. *Histologically confirmed intracranial glioblastoma multiforme (GBM) or gliosarcoma*). The use of approximate string matching, generation of lexical variants and cleaning up of the dictionary would certainly improve the performance for this step and have a beneficial influence on the subsequent processes. We will discuss some points of further improvement in section 4.

Linguistic resources Besides terminological resources, we also developed linguistic rules for the detection of negated sequences (e.g. *Patient does not show any signs of dehydration*) and temporal expressions (e.g. *In 2006 and 2009*). These two types of information can be expressed in a large variety of ways and may be split into more than one part. We therefore formalized our rules into local grammars as implemented by the text processing framework Unitex (Paumier, 2003).

Concretely, these graphs model generic patterns that are manually constructed to extract relevant sequences. Figure 1 represents an example of graphs for the extraction of time points (e.g. *in 1998 and 2001*, *three years ago*, etc.) and duration (e.g. *during the last few weeks*). Grey boxes represent subgraphs that model days of the month, month names (and possible abbreviations), years, etc. Such grammars (or transducers) are able to capture complex entities and to consider the linguistic context of sequences. For instance, a duration expression is often preceded by a preposition such as *over*, *during* or *for*. The Unitex grammars allow us to specify this requirement more easily than with regular expressions[2].

We designed two graphs for the detection of negation markers that occur either on the left (e.g. *His work-up **ruled out** an <u>acute coronary event</u>*) or on the right (e.g. *<u>Genetic testing</u> **has not yet been performed***)

---

[2]The star in Figure 1 indicates the end of the left context, meaning that this part of the grammar is used for computing matches but is not extracted (i.e. a preposition such as *over* must precede the article *the* but will not be included in the TIMEX3+DURATION entity).

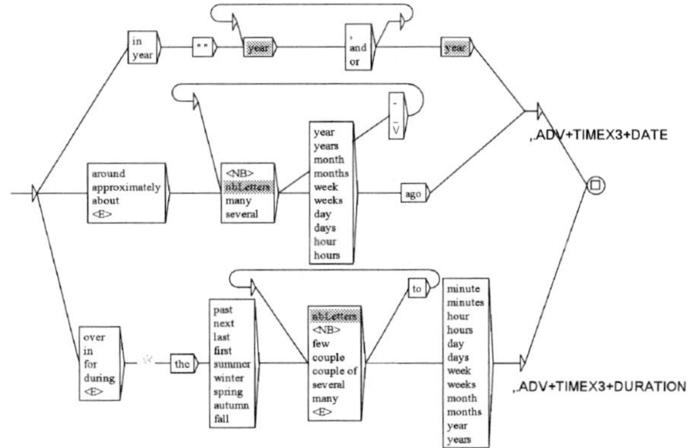

Figure 1: Example of Unitex transducer for the extraction of TIMEX3+DATE and TIMEX3+DURATION expressions

Events	P	R	F1
Max	0.915	0.891	0.903
ES:⟨*span*⟩	0.892	0.878	0.885
Median	0.887	0.846	0.874
Max	0.900	0.875	0.887
EA:Polarity	0.870	0.857	0.864
Median	0.868	0.813	0.839

Table 3: Results for the EVENT subtasks

formed) of a medical entity and five graphs identifying each TIMEX3 attribute. Each transducer produces a lexically relevant output that is integrated as features into our CRF model.

4   Results

In this section, we present our results on the final test data. We trained two different models: one was trained on the "Train" subcorpus, the other one on the "Train" and "Dev" datasets. We expected better results with the second model, given the larger training corpus. As the performance gain was quite limited between the two models, we do not mention here the performances of the first model.

In order to provide some context to these results, we also report the median and maximum results. Table 3 shows results for the EVENT tasks (ES, EA:polarity) and results for the TIMEX3 tasks (TS, TA) are reported in Table 4.

There are many more EVENT entities than TIMEX3 entities in the whole corpus (Train, Dev and Test). Consequently, we assume that if a class is more represented in the training corpus, the per-

Timex3	P	R	F1
Max	0.840	0.758	0.795
TS:⟨*span*⟩	0.777	0.564	0.653
Median	0.779	0.539	0.637
Max	0.815	0.735	0.772
TA:Class	0.752	0.545	0.632
Median	0.755	0.499	0.618

Table 4: Results for TIMEX3 subtasks

TA:attributes	P	R	F1
TA:date	0.768	0.573	0.656
TA:time	0.481	0.144	0.222
TA:prepostexp	0.979	0.814	0.889
TA:quantifier	0.594	0.288	0.388
TA:set	0.742	0.441	0.554

Table 5: Detailed results for TIMEX3 attributes

Error type	Percent
Positional errors	14.6%
Improvable resources	13.5%
Graph inconsistency	5.3%
Corpora inconsistencies	49.1%
Other	17.5%

Table 6: Error analysis (TIMEX3)

formances obtained on this class tend to be better: as we observed, the performances obtained for the EVENT class are higher than the ones for the TIMEX3 class.

In Table 5, we detail our results for each of the TIMEX3 attributes. Our system obtained very good results for the PREPOSTEXP attribute, probably because the lexical variation in this class is quite limited. By contrast, the results for the TIME and QUANTIFIER attributes remain low: this is partially explained by their low representation in the training corpus – the lowest among all the TIMEX3 attributes.

5 Discussion

A careful error analysis of 20% of the test corpus enabled us to pinpoint strategies for further improvement. We only considered TIMEX3 entities for this analysis. We identified four main types of issues that we can easily fix. We report the proportions of the various types of errors in Table 6.

Positional errors First, we noticed that some "easy" temporal expressions such as *Spring 2010* or *September 14, 2010* are not tagged by our system, even if they are detected by our linguistic rules and are thus inserted into the CRF's matrix of features. In a significant number of cases, the expressions are at the beginning of the sentence. The tuning of the tagger according to a specific type of documents (newspapers) may partially explain these er-

rors, and weighting the CRF's features would be a simple way of addressing this issue. Indeed, theses weights could favour some features instead of others. For instance, if we apply a greater weight onto the feature reporting the linguistic information given by the grammars, this feature will have a greater influence than the feature "position in the sentence" and the errors explained in this paragraph will be reduced.

Improvable linguistic resources Secondly, our system missed some entities because they are neither in the training corpus nor in our linguistic resources, for e.g. *in childhood* (TIMEX3+DATE), *QID* (TIMEX3+SET) and *short number* (TIMEX3+QUANTIFIER). One issue highlighted here is that our lexical coverage is still too narrow, and we thus need to further expand our linguistic resources. On the one hand, the Unitex grammars for TIMEX3 entities need to be extended in order to detect more – and more complex – expressions. For this purpose, a more detailed linguistic study of a medical corpus in English is needed. On the other hand, it would be beneficial to preprocess our terminological resources so that they would better reflect authentic medical texts. Some processes may consist in cleaning up UMLS entries with phrasings typical of classificatory systems (e.g. *not otherwise specified*), splitting long terms into smaller units and generation of lexical variants (e.g. *varices of the esophagus → esophageal varices*)[3].

Graph inconsistency Thirdly, some linguistic rules do not fit with the annotation scheme used in the reference corpora. Our DATE grammar, for example, is able to detect a date followed by a time (e.g. *September 2, 2010 at 18:45*) and associates the

---

[3]In this error class, we only quantified the errors due to the lack of completeness of our graphs, while the terminological resources are used for EVENT identification.

tag DATE to the whole sequence. However, it appeared that such sequences are actually split into a DATE entity and a TIME entity in the corpus. Fortunately, such minor problems can easily be corrected.

Corpora inconsistency We also noted repeated inconsistencies in the corpora that were provided. This is not surprising as the corpus was manually annotated and obtaining a satisfactory inter-annotator agreement can be complicated for such a task, due to the fastidious and time-consuming nature of manual annotation in general; for details, see the TimeBank Documentation (Pustejovsky et al., 2006). However, we believe that some inconsistencies tend to lower our results and we will discuss two of them.

The first one concerns incoherent annotation between the training and the test corpora and accounts for about 30% of the total error rate. For example, some sequences are tagged in the training corpus but not in the test corpus: consider the sequence *recently-diagnosed*, where the adverb *recently* was tagged as a DATE about 15 times in the training corpus, but is never annotated in the test corpus. This has an influence on our results as our system extracts all these kinds of sequences.

This class also includes errors rather due to a difference in perspectives. It seems that the human annotators have tried to capture relevant but maximally succinct entities. Indeed, few annotated sequences contain more than 2 words for the EVENT class, 3 for the TIMEX3 class. On the contrary, our rules are designed to recognize the longest sequences possible. As a consequence, they always capture modifiers like *approximately* or *at least* when occurring before a SET entity, i.e. *approximately 4 times a day* or *at least 3 months ago*. Such a delimitation is actually considered as incorrect during the evaluation procedure.

The second type of inconsistencies concerns the annotation of prepositions and determiners and also affects all the corpora; these errors represent about 20% of the total error rate. During the development phase, we noted that the boundaries of two identical entities are sometimes different because the preposition and/or the determiner is not always considered. For example, we observed three different annotations in the data for the sequence "at the same time", namely, *at the same time*, *the same time*

and *same time*. We made the same observation for other prepositions introducing temporal expressions, i.e. *for*, *over* (DURATION) and *in*, which were inconsistently annotated. For consistency, we adjusted our system to include the determiner in the entity, but not the preposition. Since the evaluation only considered as correct entities with the same offsets as those of the manually annotated entities, such a variation among the reference annotations inevitably had a negative impact on our score.

Nonetheless, we think that establishing a common definition of the temporal adverbial before the annotation phase is needed. Indeed, the preposition is structurally and semantically important for the adverbial (Gross, 1990): *in September*, for example, has a DATE attribute, but *since September* is a DURATION expression. Moreover, adopting this adverbial configuration would address issues at higher levels of linguistic analysis. Thus, such a definition step seems to be really important.

Finally, the *Other* category contains occasional errors. For instance, the sequence *in less than 6-weeks* is tagged as a DATE in the reference corpus, but as a DURATION by our system: this tag is incorrect given the semantic context of the expression. We consider these cases as learning errors due to a lack of occurrences of such constructions. One way to minimize this problem would be to increase the number of texts used for training.

6   Conclusion

This paper presents a hybrid approach for medical and temporal information extraction. Our objective was to evaluate the scalability of tools that have been previously developed to process French news articles. Our methodology relies on a single CRF model enriched by linguistic knowledge, and has been slightly adapted. We reused the terminological component of the UMLS and designed high-precision linguistic rules that feed the statistical model. The results are encouraging given the time constraints, but could definitely be improved using different strategies, some of which are detailed regarding major classes of errors.

References

S. Bethard, G. Savova, W.-T. Chen, L. Derczynski, J. Pustejovsky, and M. Verhagen. 2016. Semeval-2016 task 12: Clinical tempeval. In *Proceedings of the 10th International Workshop on Semantic Evaluation (SemEval 2016)*, San Diego, California, June. Association for Computational Linguistics.

M. Constant and A. Sigogne. 2011. Mwu-aware part-of-speech tagging with a crf model and lexical resources. In *Proceedings of the Workshop on Multiword Expressions: From Parsing and Generation to the Real World*, MWE '11, pages 49–56, Stroudsburg, PA, USA. Association for Computational Linguistics.

D. De Meyere, T. Klein, T. François, B. Fauquert, J.-C. Debongnie, C. Radulescu, N. Mbengo, M. Ouro Koura, Y. Coppieters 't Wallant, and C. Fairon. 2015. Automatic annotation of medical reports using SNOMED-CT: a flexible approach based on medical knowledge databases. In *Proceedings of the 7th Language Technology Conference (LTC2015)*, pages 519–523.

M. Gross. 1990. *Syntaxe de l'adverbe*, volume 3 of *Grammaire transformationnelle du français*. AS-STRIL.

J. D. Lafferty, A. McCallum, and F. C. N. Pereira. 2001. Conditional random fields : probabilistic models for segmenting and labeling sequence data. pages 282–289.

Naoaki Okazaki. 2007. Crfsuite: a fast implementation of conditional random fields (crfs).

Sébastien Paumier. 2003. *De la reconnaissance des formes linguistiques à l'analyse syntaxique*. Ph.D. thesis, Marne-la-Vallée.

J. Pustejovsky, J. Littman, R. Saurí, and M. Verhagen. 2006. Timebank 1.2 documentation.

J. Pustejovsky, K. Lee, H. Blunt, and L. Romary. 2010. Iso-timeml: An international standard for semantic annotation. *Proceedings of the 7th International Conference on Language Resources and Evaluation (LREC'10)*.

W. Styler, S. Bethard, S. Finan, M. Palmer, S. Pradhan, P. de Groen, B. Erickson, T. Miller, C. Lin, G. Savova, and J. Pustejovsky. 2014. Temporal annotation in the clinical domain. *Transactions of the Association for Computational Linguistics*, 2:143–154.

W. Sun, A. Rumshisky, and O. Uzuner. 2013. Annotating temporal information in clinical narratives. *Journal of Biomedical Informatics*, 46, Supplement:S5 – S12.

P. Watrin, L. de Viron, D. Lebailly, M. Constant, and S. Weiser. 2014. Named entity recognition for german using conditional random fields and linguistic resources. *Workshop Proceedings of the 12th KONVENS 2014*.

UTHealth at SemEval-2016 Task 12: an End-to-End System for Temporal Information Extraction from Clinical Notes

Hee-Jin Lee, Yaoyun Zhang, Jun Xu, Sungrim Moon, Jingqi Wang,
Yonghui Wu, and Hua Xu

University of Texas Health Science Center at Houston

Houston, TX, USA

`hee.jin.lee@uth.tmc.edu`, `{firstname.lastname}@uth.tmc.edu`

Abstract

The 2016 Clinical TempEval challenge addresses temporal information extraction from clinical notes. The challenge is composed of six sub-tasks, each of which is to identify: (1) event mention spans, (2) time expression spans, (3) event attributes, (4) time attributes, (5) events' temporal relations to the document creation times (DocTimeRel), and (6) narrative container relations among events and times. In this article, we present an end-to-end system that addresses all six sub-tasks. Our system achieved the best performance for all six sub-tasks when plain texts were given as input. It also performed best for narrative container relation identification when gold standard event/time annotations were given.

1 Introduction

Temporality is crucial in understanding the course of clinical events from a patient's electronic health records. Since a large part of the information on temporality resides in narrative clinical notes, automatic extraction of temporal information from clinical notes using natural language processing (NLP) techniques has received much attention. Over the years, research community challenges on clinical temporal information extraction have been organized; i.e., the 2012 Informatics for Integrating Biology and the Bedside (i2b2) challenge (Sun et al., 2013), the 2013/2014 CLEF/ShARe challenge (Mowery et al., 2014), and the 2015 Clinical TempEval challenge (Savova et al., 2015). These challenges provide annotated corpora on temporal entities and relations, which facilitate comparisons

of multiple systems and expedite the development of clinical temporal information extraction methodologies.

The 2016 Clinical TempEval challenge is the most recent community challenge that addresses temporal information extraction from clinical notes. Following the 2015 Clinical TempEval challenge, the 2016 challenge consists of six sub-tasks, each of which is to identify: (1) spans of event mentions, (2) spans of time expressions, (3) attributes of events, (4) attribute of times, (5) events' temporal relations to the document creation times (DocTimeRel), and (6) narrative container relations among events and times (TLINK:Contains). 440 annotated clinical notes from Mayo Clinic, or the THYME corpus (Styler IV et al., 2014), were provided as the training data set, and 153 plain text clinical notes were provided as the test set. The participating systems were evaluated through two phases. In phase 1, the systems were evaluated on their results for all six sub-tasks given plain texts as inputs. In phase 2, system predictions on DocTimeRel and TLINK:Contains were evaluated given the gold-standard event annotations (EVENT) and time annotations (TIMEX3).

In this article, we describe a comprehensive system that addresses all six sub-tasks. We designed the system by adapting state-of-the-art techniques from previous work on named entity recognition (Tang et al., 2013a; Jiang et al., 2011) and temporal relation identification (Tang et al., 2013b; Lin et al., 2015) in the medical domain. Our end-to-end system achieved top performance for all six sub-tasks in the phase 1 and the TLINK:Contains identification task in the phase 2 stages of the challenge.

1292

Proceedings of SemEval-2016, pages 1292–1297,
San Diego, California, June 16-17, 2016. ©2016 Association for Computational Linguistics

2 Methods

Our temporal information extraction system consists of four modules: the first module identifies the spans of event mentions and time expressions along with their types; the second module identifies attributes of events and times; the third module predicts DocTimeRel; and the last module identifies TLINK:Contains among events and times. The output results from previous modules are utilized by the latter modules. We describe those modules in detail in the following sections.

Please note that we utilized the following tools to construct our system: 1) CLAMP toolkit (`http://clinicalnlptool.com/index.php`) for tokenization, 2) OpenNLP toolkit (`http://opennlp.sourceforge.net/`) for Part-Of-Speech (POS) tagging and consitituency parsing, and 3) ClearNLP toolkit (`https://code.google.com/p/clearnlp/`) for dependency parsing. We utilized wrappers provided by cTAKES (Savova et al., 2010).

2.1 Event mentions and temporal expressions recognition

As the first step, our system identifies the spans of event mentions and time expressions along with their types.

According to our observations of the corpus, different types of event mentions and time expressions may show characteristics different from one another. For instance, events with EVIDENTIAL type are usually represented with verbs such as 'showed', 'reported', 'confirms', in contrast to the events with N/A type that are usually represented with medical terms such as 'nausea', 'chemotherapy' or 'colonoscopy'. Similarly, times with DATE type appear more often with the preposition 'on', while times with DURATION type appear more often with 'during' or 'since'. Such variations in the characteristics may limit the system's performance, if one tries to identify event mentions or time expressions of all types at once and then identify their types. Therefore, our system identifies the spans of events and times as well as their types simultaneously.

An HMM-SVM sequence tagger (Joachims et al., 2009) is employed to tag each token in the clinical notes as either O (outside of an event mention), B-*type* (beginning of an event mention of *type*), or I-*type* (inside of an event mention of *type*), where *type* can be any of the three event types defined by the Clinical TempEval challenge (i.e, N/A, ASPECTUAL, and EVIDENTIAL). Another HMM-SVM tagger is used in a similar manner to identify spans and types of time expressions.

We use various features that have been successfully used for many entity recognition tasks in the clinical domain (Tang et al., 2013b; Lin et al., 2015). In addition, we incorporate the results of SUTime (Stanford temporal tagger) (Chang and Manning, 2012) into our system as a feature. SUTime is a rule-based tagger that identifies time expressions as defined by the TimeML (Mani and Pustejovsky, 2004). The features used are as follows:

Lexical features: n-gram (uni-, bi-, and tri-) of nearby words (window size of +/- 2), character n-gram (bi- and tri-) of each word, prefix and suffix of each word (up to three characters), and orthographic forms of each word (obtained by normalizing numbers, uppercase letters, and lowercase letters to '#', 'A', and 'a', respectively, and by regular expression matching)

Syntactic features: POS n-gram (uni-, bi-, and tri-) of nearby words (window size of +/- 2)

Discourse level features: sentence length, sentence type (e.g., whether the sentence ends with a colon or starts with an enumeration mark such as '1.'), and section information

Word representation features: features derived from Brown clustering (Brown et al., 1992), random indexing (Lund and Burgess, 1996) and word embedding (Tang et al., 2014) (trained on MiPACQ (Albright et al., 2013) and MIMIC II (Saeed et al., 2011) corpora)

Features from external resources: dictionary matching results using customized dictionaries of medical/temporal terms, and the temporal expression prediction results from SUTime (TIMEX3 only).

2.2 Event attribute identification

Given spans and types of event mentions, our system further identifies three attributes of the events, i.e., *modality*, *degree*, and *polarity*. We trained three SVM classifiers for each of the three attributes using LIBLINEAR SVM package (Fan et al., 2008). We used features similar to those described in Section 2.1, where the features are extracted from a window size of +/- 5 tokens around each event mention. Additionally, we used the attribute-specific features (described below) for event attribute identification.

Attribute-specific features: existence of conditionality/possibility keywords (e.g., 'if', 'unless', 'could', and 'likely') in the window size of +/-5 tokens

2.3   DocTimeRel identification

Our system identifies DocTimeRel of each event mention in a manner similar to which it identifies event attributes. An SVM classifier was trained using the LIBLINEAR package, where the features are extracted from the window of +/- 5 tokens around each event mention. In addition to the set of features similar to the ones described in Section 2.1, the following features are used:

DocTimeRel-specific features: tense information of the verbs in the same sentence, event attributes, and information on time expressions in the same sentence (token/POS of time expressions before/after the event mention, token/POS of words between the closest time expression and the event mention)

2.4   TLINK:Contains identification

We divide the task of narrative container relation identification into six sub-problems based on two criteria: (1) whether the target narrative container relation is between two events or between an event and a time and (2) whether the two event/time mentions are within one sentence, within two adjacent sentences, or across more than two sentences. For each sub-problem, we trained an SVM classifier that identifies whether an ordered pair of two events/times (or a *candidate pair*) forms a TLINK of Contains type, using the LINLINEAR SVM package.

Before training the classifiers, we apply the following steps in order to take into account the data distribution characteristics. First, in the gold standard dataset, a large number of implicit temporal relations are left unannotated intentionally. Since providing implicit relations as negative instances to the SVM learners may harm the learning process, we extended the gold standard set of TLINK:Contains to its transitive closure, and used the extended set as the positive instances for training. The transitive closure was generated by applying Floyd-Warshall algorithm (Floyd, 1962) on the gold standard TLINK set based on the transitivity of the TLINK:Contains relation (i.e, A contains B $\wedge$ B contains C $\rightarrow$ A contains C).

Second, since any two events/times can be a candidate pair to train a classifier, the number of candidate pairs becomes huge with small portion of positive instances among them. This may not be ideal for training a classifier. In order to reduce the number of prospective negative instances, we filtered out some of the candidate pairs that are highly unlikely to form a TLINK:Contains relation based on the THYME corpus annotation guideline[1]. We removed a candidate pair either 1) when the two event/time mentions are not in the same section, or 2) when one event has ACTUAL modality while the other has HYPOTHETICAL modality, or 3) when one event has BEFORE DocTimRel while the other has AFTER DocTimeRel. For candidate pairs whose event/time mentions are across more than two sentences, we further filtered out the pairs based on heuristic rules, in order to keep only the candidate pairs that are higly likely to form a TLINK:Contains relation. We kept a candidate pair only when an event/time among the two events/times is mentioned in a section header that includes the keywords 'history' or 'evaluation' or in a section header that ends with a time expression.

We also applied cost-sensitive learning in order to counterbalance the effect of dominating number of negative instances. To each class, we assigned weight that is inversely proportional to the class frequency, adjusting the penalty factor in SVM training (Ben-Hur and Weston, 2009). For instance, if there were 20 positive pairs among 100 candidate pairs, we would assign the weight 5 (100/20) to the positive class and the weight 1.25 (100/80) to the negative class.

---

[1] `http://clear.colorado.edu/compsem/documents/THYME\%20Guidelines.pdf`

sub-task	P	R	F
ES (t)	0.915	0.891	0.903
TS (t)	0.840	0.758	0.795
ES (s)	**0.915**	**0.891**	**0.903**
TS (s)	0.836	0.757	**0.795**
ES (m)	0.887	0.846	0.874
TS (m)	0.779	0.539	0.637

Table 1: Test set results on EVENT span (ES) and TIMEX3 span (TS) identification. Bold faces signify the cases where our system showed the top performance.

The features used for the six classifiers are as follows. Note that an event mention was expanded to its covering noun phrase before the feature extraction:

Common features: event/time attributes, token and POS features on event/time mentions (as provided by cTAKES), punctuation between event/time mentions, other event/time mentions within the same sentence as the two event/time mentions, number of other event/time mentions between the two event/time mentions, tense of the verbs in the same sentence, section information, sentence type (the same as in Section 2.1), and word embedding representations of the head words of event/time mentions

Feaures for single-sentence cases: dependency path linking the two event/time mentions (as provided by cTAKES)

Features for multi-sentence cases: line distance between the two event/time mentions, and tokens that are common to the two event/time mentions

3 Results

In this section, we present our system's performance on test set along with the top and the median results from the challenge. Table 1, 2, and 3 show the results on event/time span identification, event/time attribute identification, and DocTimeRel and TLINK:Contains identification, respectively. In the tables, (t) and (m) stand for the top and median results of the 2016 challenge, while (s) stands for our system's results. Our system showed top F1 scores for event/time span, for event/time attribute, for DocTimeRel (phase 1 only), and for TLINLK:Contains identification.

sub-task	P	R	F	A
TA:type (t)	0.815	0.735	0.772	0.989
EA:type (t)	0.894	0.870	0.882	0.977
EA:modality (t)	0.866	0.843	0.855	0.947
EA:degree (t)	0.911	0.887	0.899	0.997
EA:polarity (t)	0.900	0.875	0.887	0.983
TA:type (s)	0.812	**0.735**	**0.772**	0.971
EA:type (s)	**0.894**	**0.870**	**0.882**	**0.977**
EA:modality (s)	**0.866**	**0.843**	**0.855**	**0.947**
EA:degree (s)	**0.911**	**0.887**	**0.899**	0.996
EA:polarity (s)	**0.900**	**0.875**	**0.887**	0.982
TA:type (m)	0.755	0.499	0.618	0.970
EA:type (m)	0.854	0.813	0.844	0.967
EA:modality (m)	0.830	0.780	0.810	0.930
EA:degree (m)	0.882	0.838	0.869	0.995
EA:polarity (m)	0.868	0.900	0.875	0.887

Table 2: Test set results on EVENT attribute (EA) and TIMEX3 attribute (TA) identification. Bold faces signify the cases where our system showed the top performance.

(a)

sub-task	P	R	F
DR (t)	0.766	0.746	0.756
CR (t)	0.531	0.471	0.479
DR (s)	**0.766**	**0.746**	**0.756**
CR (s)	0.488	**0.471**	**0.479**
DR (m)	0.655	0.624	0.639
CR (m)	0.491	0.235	0.318

(b)

sub-task	P	R	F	Acc.
DR (t)	-	-	-	0.843
CR (t)	0.823	0.564	0.573	-
DR (s)	-	-	-	0.835
CR (s)	0.588	0.559	**0.573**	-
DR (m)	-	-	-	0.724
CR (m)	0.589	0.345	0.449	-

Table 3: Test set results on DocTimeRel (DR) and TLINK:Contains (CR) identification. (a) phase 1 results. (b) phase 2 results. Bold faces signify the cases where our system showed the top performance.

DocTimeRel value	# EVENTs (%)	Acc.
AFTER	2073 (10.9%)	81.3%
OVERLAP	8983 (47.3%)	90.1%
BEFORE	6984 (36.8%)	79.9%
BEFORE/OVERLAP	952 (5.0%)	51.5%

Table 4: DocTimeRel identification accuracy on each Doc-TimeRel value. # EVENTs represents the number of event annotations from the gold standard with the specified DocTimeRel value in the test set.

4 Conclusion and discussion

In this article, we describe a system that shows the top performance in the 2016 Clinical TempEval challenge. We adapted the state-of-the-art techniques for entity recognition and temporal relation identification in the clinical domain, and show that those techniques are effective for the Clinical TempEval challenge as well.

For time expression identification, we found some error cases in which the system's prediction differs with the gold standard annotation only on the inclusion or exclusion of a preposition. For example, while a DURATION type time is annotated for the phrase "for the past 40 years" in the gold set, our system predicted a DURATION for the phrase "the past 40 years" omitting the preposition 'for' from the gold standard annotation.

Table 4 shows the DocTimeRel identification accuracy on each DocTimeRel value. Accuracy on the value OVERLAP is the highest, which might come from the abundance of the training data. Surprisingly, the classifier worked better for the value AFTER than the value BEFORE, even though there were three times more events with BEFORE DocTimeRel than those with AFTER. We conjecture that explicit keywords that indicate the future tense such as "will" and "potential" played key roles in identifying AFTER DocTimeRel.

Table 5 shows the 10-fold cross validation results of the six classifiers for TLINK:Contains identification. Temporal relations between an event and a time were predicted more accurately than the relations between two events. Classifiers for pairs across more than two sentences showed the best F1 scores, due to the heuristic filtering steps in which we kept only the candidate pairs that are highly likely to form a narrative container relation.

sub-problem	F
EVENT-EVENT-1	66.9%
EVENT-EVENT-2	69.1%
EVENT-EVENT-3	76.2%
EVENT-TIMEX3-1	79.9%
EVENT-TIMEX3-2	76.3%
EVENT-TIMEX3-3	84.3%

Table 5: F1 scores of the six classifiers for TLINK:Contains identification (10-fold cross validation on the training set). EVENT-EVENT and EVENT-TIMEX represent the sub-problems regarding the candidate pairs between two events, and the sub-problems regarding the pairs between an event and a time, respectively. The suffixes '-1', '-2' and '-3' indicate that the pairs should be within one sentence, within two adjacent sentences, and across more than two sentences, respectively.

We plan to further improve our system to show higher performance based on the observations above.

Acknowledgments

We would like to thank the Mayo Clinic for permission to use the THYME corpus. This study was supported in part by NIGMS grant 1 R01 GM103859.

References

Daniel Albright, Arrick Lanfranchi, Anwen Fredriksen, William F Styler, Colin Warner, Jena D Hwang, Jinho D Choi, Dmitriy Dligach, Rodney D Nielsen, James Martin, Wayne Ward, Martha Palmer, and Guergana K Savova. 2013. Towards comprehensive syntactic and semantic annotations of the clinical narrative. *Journal of the American Medical Informatics Association*, 20(5).

Asa Ben-Hur and Jason Weston. 2009. A User's Guide to Support Vector Machines. In *Data Mining Techniques for the Life Sciences*, pages 223–239. Humana Press, Totowa, NJ.

Peter F Brown, Peter V deSouza, Robert L Mercer, Vincent J Della Pietra, and Jenifer C Lai. 1992. Class-based n -gram models of natural language. *Computational Linguistics*, 18(4):467–479.

Angel X Chang and Christopher D Manning. 2012. SU-TIME: A Library for Recognizing and Normalizing Time Expressions. In *Proceedings of 8th International Conference on Language Resources and Evaluation LREC (LREC 2012)*.

Rong-En Fan, Kai-Wei Chang, Cho-Jui Hsieh, Xiang-Rui Wang, and Chih-Jen Lin. 2008. LIBLINEAR: A Library for Large Linear Classification. *The Journal of Machine Learning Research*, 9:1871–1874.

Robert W Floyd. 1962. Algorithm 97: Shortest path. *Communications of the ACM*, 5(6):345.

Min Jiang, Yukun Chen, Mei Liu, S Trent Rosenbloom, Subramani Mani, Joshua C Denny, and Hua Xu. 2011. A study of machine-learning-based approaches to extract clinical entities and their assertions from discharge summaries. *Journal of the American Medical Informatics Association*, 18(5):601–606.

Thorsten Joachims, Thomas Finley, and Chun-Nam John Yu. 2009. Cutting-Plane Training of Structural SVMs. *Machine Learning Journal*, 77(1):27–59.

Chen Lin, Dmitriy Dligach, Timothy A Miller, Steven Bethard, and Guergana K Savova. 2015. Multilayered temporal modeling for the clinical domain. *Journal of the American Medical Informatics Association*, pages ocv113–9.

Kevin Lund and Curt Burgess. 1996. Producing high-dimensional semantic spaces from lexical co-occurrence. *Behavior Research Methods, Instruments, & Computers*, 28(2):203–208.

Inderjeet Mani and James Pustejovsky. 2004. Temporal discourse models for narrative structure. In *Proceedings of ACL Workshop on Discourse Annotation*, pages 57–64. Association for Computational Linguistics.

Danielle L Mowery, Sumithra Velupillai, Brett R South, Lee Christensen, David Martinez, Liadh Kelly, Lorraine Goeuriot, Noémie Elhadad, Sameer Pradhan, Guergana Savova, and Wendy Chapman. 2014. Task 2: ShARe/CLEF eHealth Evaluation Lab 2014. In *Proceedings of CLEF 2014*, Sheffield.

Mohammed Saeed, Mauricio Villarroel, Andrew T Reisner, Gari Clifford, Li-Wei Lehman, George Moody, Thomas Heldt, Tin H Kyaw, Benjamin Moody, and Roger G Mark. 2011. Multiparameter Intelligent Monitoring in Intensive Care II (MIMIC-II): A public-access intensive care unit database. *Critical care medicine*, 39(5):952–960.

Guergana K Savova, James J Masanz, Philip V Ogren, Jiaping Zheng, Sunghwan Sohn, Karin C Kipper-Schuler, and Christopher G Chute. 2010. Mayo clinical Text Analysis and Knowledge Extraction System (cTAKES): architecture, component evaluation and applications. *Journal of the American Medical Informatics Association*, 17(5):507–513.

Guergana Savova, Marc Verhagen, Steven Bethard, Leon Derczynski, and James Pustejovsky. 2015. Semeval-2015 task 6: Clinical tempeval. In *Proceedings of the 9th International Workshop on Semantic Evaluation*.

William F Styler IV, Steven Bethard, Sean Finan, Martha Palmer, Sameer Pradhan, Piet C de Groen, Brad Erickson, Timothy Miller, Chen Lin, Guergana Savova, and

James Pustejovsky. 2014. Temporal Annotation in the Clinical Domain. *Transactions of the Association for Computational Linguistics*, 2(0):143–154.

Weiyi Sun, Anna Rumshisky, and Ozlem Uzuner. 2013. Evaluating temporal relations in clinical text: 2012 i2b2 Challenge. *Journal of the American Medical Informatics Association*, 20(5):806–813.

Buzhou Tang, Hongxin Cao, Yonghui Wu, Min Jiang, and Hua Xu. 2013a. Recognizing clinical entities in hospital discharge summaries using Structural Support Vector Machines with word representation features. *BMC Medical Informatics and Decision Making*, 13(Suppl 1):S1.

Buzhou Tang, Yonghui Wu, Min Jiang, Yukun Chen, Joshua C Denny, and Hua Xu. 2013b. A hybrid system for temporal information extraction from clinical text. *Journal of the American Medical Informatics Association*, 20(5):828–835.

Buzhou Tang, Hongxin Cao, Xiaolong Wang, Qingcai Chen, and Hua Xu. 2014. Evaluating Word Representation Features in Biomedical Named Entity Recognition Tasks. *BioMed Research International*, 2014(2):1–6.

NUIG-UNLP at SemEval-2016 Task 13: A Simple Word Embedding-based Approach for Taxonomy Extraction

Joel Pocostales

Insight Centre for Data Analytics

National University of Ireland, Galway

`name.surname@insight-centre.org`

Abstract

This paper describes the NUIG-UNLP system submitted to SemEval-2016, Task 13. We implement a semi-supervised method that extracts hypernym candidates for the terms provided in the test list. The main assumption of our system is that hypernyms may be induced by adding a vector offset to the corresponding hyponym word embedding. The vector offset is obtained as the average offset between 200 pairs of hyponym-hypernym in the same vector space. Our approach ranked second on connectivity (c.c.) and categorisation (i.i.) for the English taxonomy construction, and fifth on the overall ranking. Despite of these modest results, our system achieved comparable evaluations scores with the other participants.

1   Introduction

Hyponyms and hypernyms (sometimes called subordinate and superordinate terms, respectively) describe a type of relation which, in general, can be defined in terms of asymmetric entailment: given the hyponym of feline, cat, and its hypernym, feline, we can state that all cats are felines, but not that all felines are cats.

Likewise, the relations that hyponyms and hypernyms signal can also be characterized as a isa relation between a hyponym X and hypernym Y: for nouns, X is a Kind of Y or X is a type of Y (Saint-Dizier and Viegas, 1995). These particular *type /
kind-of* relations form the backbone of the construction of Lexical Taxonomies and Ontologies (Buitelaar et al., 2004; Navigli et al., 2011), and those

in turn plays a essential role in many Natural Language Processing applications: Question Answering, Textual Entailment, Natural Language Inference, or Text Summarization (Bordea et al., 2015).

In this regard, despite the fact that taxonomy construction can be addressed from a diversity of approaches, the lexico-syntactic patterns-based are still the most widely used. Nevertheless, in the last years some vector space-based approaches have emerged for learning semantic hierarchies (Saxe et al., 2013; Khashabi, 2013; Fu et al., 2014; Rei and Briscoe, 2014; Tan et al., 2015; Nayak, 2015). In the next sections we will mainly turn our attention to this type of approaches.

1.1   Task Definition

The five participating teams in SemEval-2016 Task 13 were provided with six datasets in four languages (English, Dutch, French and Italian)[1]. The datasets can be divided in three domains (science, environment and food). Additionally, this year the TExEval-2 task has a focus in four subtasks related to taxonomy construction:

1. Taxonomy construction

2. Hypernym identification

3. Multilingual taxonomy construction

4. Multilingual hypernym identification

However, due to lack of time, we decided to address only the English monolingual subtasks.

---

[1]The corresponding system description papers can be found in Cleuziou and Moreno (2016), Panchenko et al. (2016) and Tan (2016).

Proceedings of SemEval-2016, pages 1298–1302,
San Diego, California, June 16-17, 2016. ©2016 Association for Computational Linguistics

The key idea behind TExEval tasks is the creation and evaluation of systems capable of automatically extracting hierarchical relations from text and then constructing taxonomies. Following (Fu et al., 2014), ideally, the construction of those hierarchies can be seen as a directed acyclic graph DAG with a finite set of nodes (words) and edges representing the *asymmetric* and *transitive* hyponym-hypernym relations. This is formally defined by Fu et al. (2014) as follows:

- $\forall x, y \in L : x \xrightarrow{H} y \Rightarrow \neg \left(y \xrightarrow{H} x \right)$

- $\forall x, y, z \in L : \left(x \xrightarrow{H} z \wedge z \xrightarrow{H} y \right) \Rightarrow x \xrightarrow{H} y$

where in our case x, y and z denote the terms in the domain list $L_d \in L$, and the hyponym-hypernym relation is represented by $\xrightarrow{H}$. Therefore, the aim of the task was to return a list of pairs $x \xrightarrow{H} y$ for each term in the six different domains L_d.

2   Experimental Setup

We describe in this section our taxonomy extraction system.

2.1   Training Data

Since TExEval-2 organizers did not provide any specific corpus for the task, we used the latest Wikipedia dump[2]. We preprocessed it using the WikiExtractor tool[3], which generates a plain text from a Wikipedia database dump discarding markup tags and any other element different than text, such as tables, references, lists and images. On the other hand, in order to generate a single word embedding for each entry in the test list, we underscore all the entries containing open compound words:

civil engineering $\Rightarrow$
civil_engineering

2.2   Word Embeddings Generation

We use the log-bilinear model GloVe (Pennington et al., 2014) trained over the above-mentioned Wikipedia corpus to generate vector space representations of words. Following the analogy task results presented in their paper and some pre-experimental

test, we set a windows size of 10 and 300 dimensions word embeddings. The number of iterations of the model was set to 20.

2.3   Offset Model

Mikolov et al. (2013) and subsequently Levy and Golberg (2014) demonstrated that word embeddings generated by neural nets (and also other traditional distributional methods) preserve some syntactic and semantic information. Some of this encoded information, such as relational similarities between pairs of words, can be recovered by simple vector offsets between the vector embeddings of each word. Thus, as Mikolov et al. (2013) and Levy and Golberg (2014) showed, given two pairs of words that share a relation, $a : a^*, b : b^*$, the relation between those two words can be represented by their vector offset, as follows:

$$a^* - a \approx b^* - b \tag{1}$$

Therefore, the vector of the word b^* should be similar to the proxy vector y'

$$y' = b - a + a^* \tag{2}$$

where y', ideally, corresponds to the vector representation of b^*. Since y' will rarely match the exact position of the word b^*, different similarity measures may be applied to find the most similar word to y'. In this paper we will focus only in Cosine similarity (4) and Euclidean distance (5):

$$\cos(b^*, y) = \frac{b^* \cdot y'}{\parallel b^* \parallel \parallel y' \parallel} \tag{3}$$

maximizing the function:

$$\underset{b^* \in V}{\arg\max} \left(\cos(b^*, y') \right) \tag{4}$$

where V is the vocabulary.

And given the Euclidean distance formula, subsequently we obtain the following function:

$$d(b^*, y') = \parallel b^* - y' \parallel^2 \Rightarrow \underset{b^* \in V}{\arg\min} \parallel b^* - y' \parallel^2 \tag{5}$$

---

[2] We used the English snapshot of 17-Nov-2015
[3] https://github.com/attardi/wikiextractor

2.4 Offset Model for Hypernym-Hyponym Relation

Mikolov et al. (2013) and Levy and Golberg (2014) have only tested the vector offset method for simple symmetric relations such a capital-country, gender inflections, adjective-to-adverbs, etc. However, as Rei and Briscoe (2014) pointed out, hypernym-hyponyms relations are conceivable much more difficult to represent by simple vector offsets, as their relations rarely are symmetric.

Rei and Briscoe (2014) in their paper first assess how word embeddings perform in hypernym-hyponym detection and generation, and second, propose a new directional similarity measure (WeightedCosine) based on two new properties to detecting these relations.

In our submitted system, though, we finally decided not to implement this new measure due to lack of time.

2.5 Offset Model for the Hypernym-Hyponym Relation

We first generate a random list of 200 pairs of hypernym-hyponyms. This training list was extracted from the trial data provided in Bordea et al. (2015) and WordNet (Miller, 1995; Fellbaum, 1998) covering different domains.

Using the Gensim library[4] (Řehůřek and Sojka, 2010) we compute the vector offset as the average offset of all the pairs generated in the above-mentioned training data (Mikolov et al., 2013; Nayak, 2015):

$$v_{offset} = \frac{1}{n} \sum_{i=1}^{n} \left(v_{hyper(i)} - v_{hypo(i)} \right) \quad (6)$$

where $n = 200$, as the number of pairs of hypernym-hyponym in our training data.

Once the v_{offset} has been obtained, we add it to the target terms in the test list:

$$y' \approx v_{term} + v_{offset} \quad (7)$$

where we assume that the addition of the vectors v_{offset} and v_{term} projects y' close enough to the hidden hypernym representation b^*. Thus, we apply either the measure similarity (4) or (5) and we rank

---

[4]http://radimrehurek.com/gensim/

either the top 10 or 5 candidates, discarding those terms not included in the test list. We also implement a substring inclusion approach based on regexp (Nevill-Manning et al., 1999) so that

$$\text{civil engineering} \xrightarrow{H} \text{engineering}$$
$$\text{social psychology} \xrightarrow{H} \text{psychology}$$

In other words, given an open compound word such *civil engineering*, we assume that the second term *engineering* is the most likely hypernym of *civil engineering*.

3 Evaluation Metrics

In this section we present the results obtained in the second task on Taxonomy Extraction Evaluation as part of SemEval-2016. The metrics correspond to the structural analysis and the comparison against the Gold Standard effectuated by Bordea et al. (2016). The best results among all the systems appear in a bold font (note that Euclidean 5 and Cosine 5 have been excluded as they were not submitted on time).

3.1 Results

Table 1 shows the structural analysis of our system and the corresponding results when compared to Gold Standard. We were only able to submit the first system (Euclidean 10), and we had to exclude the food domains due to time limitations. However, we will also present here metrics beyond the official system submission, i.e, Euclidean 5 and Cosine 5 covering all domains provided on the test data.

The hyphen (-) is used in cases when the number of cycles could not be computed due to hardware limitations. This outcome should be interpreted as negative, as the presence of cycles goes against Directed Acyclic Graph (DAG) definition.

As per the structural analysis, the main goal is to evaluate the number of correct nodes and edges in comparison with the Gold Standard. Thus, the quantifying metrics in the left block (|V| ... i.n.) cannot really be considered aside of the Golden Standard evaluation. Therefore, in this section we will mainly focus on the qualifying metrics instead of the quantifying ones.

We observe that, likely, due to the restrictions imposed in our algorithm not allowing hypernym can-

Euclidean 10	|V|	|E|	#c.c	cycles	i.n.	#VC	%VC	:VN	#EC	%EC	:EN
Enviro_Eu.	312	456	58	347	**176**	221	0.8467	0.2917	72	0.2758	1.4713
Science	596	**1656**	99	-	**409**	422	0.9336	0.2907	163	0.3505	3.2107
Science_Eu.	97	218	13	269	72	83	0.6620	0.1443	29	0.2339	1.5242
Science_WN	251	**929**	9	-	195	241	0.6513	0.0398	163	0.3602	1.6947

Euclidean 5	|V|	|E|	#c.c	cycles	i.n.	#VC	%VC	:VN	#EC	%EC	:EN
Enviro_Eu.	329	944	58	310	192	221	0.8467	0.3283	134	0.5134	3.1034
Science	594	1366	94	-	396	417	0.9226	0.2980	132	0.2839	2.6538
Science_Eu.	98	212	13	239	72	83	0.6640	0.1531	26	0.2097	1.5000
Science_WN	246	748	9	1175180	188	236	0.6378	0.0406	127	0.2810	0.1374

Cosine 5	|V|	|E|	#c.c	cycles	i.n.	#VC	%VC	:VN	#EC	%EC	:EN
Enviro_Eu.	246	294	48	71	136	177	0.6781	0.2804	56	0.2145	0.9118
Food	909	888	206	84	460	679	0.4383	0.2530	190	0.1197	0.4398
Food_WN	983	1160	181	157	520	813	0.5471	0.1729	332	0.2106	0.5253
Science	403	835	45	1173	281	316	0.6991	0.2159	118	0.2538	1.5419
Science_Eu.	76	106	14	13	46	63	0.5040	0.1710	22	0.1774	0.6774
Science_WN	200	353	16	89	137	190	0.5135	0,0500	99	0.2190	0.5619

Table 1: Official Evaluation metrics for Euclidean measure top 10, 5 and Cosine measure 5 with substring inclusion. Number of nodes and edges |V|), |E|, connected components (c.c.), cycles, intermediate nodes (i.n.), number of vertices, vertices coverage and vertex novelty (#VC, %VC, VN), number of edges, edge coverage and edge novelty (#EC, %EC and EN)

	Euclidean 10			Euclidean 5			Cosine 5		
	Precision	Recall	F-Score	Precision	Recall	F-Score	Precision	Recall	F-Score
Enviro_Eu.	0.1579	**0.2759**	0.2008	0.1419	0.5134	0.2224	0.1905	0.2145	0.2018
Food	N/A	N/A	N/A	N/A	N/A	N/A	0.2140	0.1197	0.1535
Food_WN	N/A	N/A	N/A	N/A	N/A	N/A	0.2862	0.2106	0.2427
Science	0.0984	**0.3505**	0.1537	0.0967	0.2839	0.0144	0.1413	0.2537	0.1815
Science_Eu.	0.1330	0.2339	0.1695	0.1226	0.2097	0.1548	0.2075	0.1774	0.1913
Science_WN	0.1754	0.3606	0.2360	0.1698	0.2810	0.2117	0.2804	0.2190	0.2460
AVERAGE	0.1412	0.3052	0.1900	0.1327	0.3220	0.1508	0.2200	0.1100	0.2028

Table 2: Precision, Recall and F-Score for Euclidean Distance 10, 5 and Cosine 5

didates out of the test list, there are no significant differences between Euclidean top 10 and 5.

We also note that the number of cycles was considerably higher on the euclidean approaches, in fact, exceeding the computer memory capacities for some domains, namely, Science, Science_WordNet (see the surprisingly high figure for Euclidean 5, Science_WN). On the other hand, unlike our initial assumptions, the cosine approach did not perform much better than the Euclidean ones. Our system obtained comparable recall values with the other systems, at the expenses, though, of the precision. Therefore, the results achieved by our systems are in general modest, especially taking into consideration that our algorithm also included a substring inclusion module (as described in section 2.5).

3.2 Conclusion and Discussion

Although there is still room for improvement in our system, we conclude that the diversity involved in the complex hypernym-hyponym relations cannot easily be captured by a simple vector offset mean. As direction for future work, it might be worth considering domain specific vectors as well as incrementing the number of training pairs for the vector offset mean.

Our system ranked second on connectivity (c.c.) and categorisation (i.i.) for the English taxonomy construction, and fifth on the overall ranking (see Bordea et al. (2016) for further details on the evaluation metrics).

Acknowledgments

This work has been funded by a research grant from Science Foundation Ireland (SFI) under Grant Number SFI/12/RC/2289 (INSIGHT).

References

Georgeta Bordea, Paul Buitelaar, Stefano Faralli, and Roberto Navigli. 2015. Semeval-2015 task 17: Taxonomy Extraction Evaluation (TExEval). In *Proceedings of the 9th International Workshop on Semantic Evaluation*. Association for Computational Linguistics.

Georgeta Bordea, Els Lefever, and Paul Buitelaar. 2016. Semeval-2016 task 13: Taxonomy Extraction Evaluation (TExEval-2). In *Proceedings of the 10th International Workshop on Semantic Evaluation*. Association for Computational Linguistics.

Paul Buitelaar, Philipp Cimiano, and Bernardo Magnini. 2004. Ontology Learning from Text : An Overview. *Learning*, pages 1–10.

Guillaume Cleuziou and Jose G. Moreno. 2016. QAS-SIT at SemEval-2016 Task 13: On the integration of Semantic Vectors in Pretopological Spaces for Lexical Taxonomy Acquisition. In *Proceedings of the 10th International Workshop on Semantic Evaluation (SemEval 2016)*. Association for Computational Linguistics.

Christiane Fellbaum. 1998. WordNet: An Electronic Lexical Database.

Ruiji Fu, Jiang Guo, Bing Qin, Wanxiang Che, Haifeng Wang, and Ting Liu. 2014. Learning Semantic Hierarchies via Word Embeddings. *Association for Computational Linguistics*, pages 1199–1209.

Daniel Khashabi. 2013. In *On the Recursive Neural Networks for Relation Extraction and Entity Recognition Authors*. Technical report, may.

Omer Levy and Yoav Goldberg. 2014. Linguistic Regularities in Sparse and Explicit Word Representations. In *Proceedings of the 18th Conference on Computational Natural Language Learning (CoNLL 2014)*, pages 171–180.

Tomas Mikolov, Wen-tau Yih, and Geoffrey Zweig. 2013. Linguistic regularities in continuous space word representations. In *Proceedings of the 2013 Conference of the North American Chapter of the Association for Computational Linguistics: Human Language Technologies*, number June, pages 746–751.

George A. Miller. 1995. WordNet: A Lexical Database for English. *Commun. ACM*, 38(11):39–41, November.

Roberto Navigli, Paola Velardi, and Stefano Faralli. 2011. A graph-based algorithm for inducing lexical taxonomies from scratch. In *IJCAI International Joint Conference on Artificial Intelligence*, pages 1872–1877.

Neha Nayak. 2015. In *Learning Hyperonyms over Word Embeddings*. Student technical report.

Craig G. Nevill-Manning, Ian H. Witten, and Gordon W. xc Paynter. 1999. Lexically-generated subject hierarchies for browsing large collections. *International Journal on Digital Libraries*, 2(2-3):111.

Alexander Panchenko, Stefano Faralli, Eugen Ruppert, Steffen Remus, Hubert Naets, Cedrick Fairon, Simone Ponzetto, Paolo, and Chris Biemann. 2016. TAXI at SemEval-2016 Task 13: a Taxonomy Induction Method based on Lexico-Syntactic Patterns, Substrings and Focused Crawling. In *Proceedings of the 10th International Workshop on Semantic Evaluation (SemEval 2016)*. Association for Computational Linguistics.

Jeffrey Pennington, Richard Socher, and Christopher D Manning. 2014. GloVe: Global Vectors for Word Representation. In *Proceedings of the 2014 Conference on Empirical Methods in Natural Language Processing*.

Radim Řehůřek and Petr Sojka. 2010. Software Framework for Topic Modelling with Large Corpora. In *Proceedings of the LREC 2010 Workshop on New Challenges for NLP Frameworks*, pages 45–50, Valletta, Malta, May. ELRA.

Marek Rei and Ted Briscoe. 2014. Looking for Hyponyms in Vector Space. In *Proceedings of the Eighteenth Conference on Computational Natural Language Learning*, pages 68–77.

Patrick Saint-Dizier and Evelyne Viegas. 1995. Computational lexical semantics. *Studies in natural language processing*, pages ix, 447 p.

Andrew M. Saxe, James L McClelland, and Surya Ganguli. 2013. Learning hierarchical category structure in deep neural networks. *Proceedings of the 35th annual meeting of the Cognitive Science Society*, pages 1271–1276.

Liling Tan, Rohit Gupta, and Josef van Genabith. 2015. USAAR-WLV: Hypernym Generation with Deep Neural Nets. In *Proceedings of the 9th International Workshop on Semantic Evaluation (SemEval 2015)*, pages 932–937, Denver, Colorado. Association for Computational Linguistics.

Liling Tan, Francis Bond, and Josef van Genabith. 2016. USAAR at SemEval-2016 Task 13: Hyponym Endocentricity. In *Proceedings of the 10th International Workshop on Semantic Evaluation (SemEval 2016)*. Association for Computational Linguistics.

Liling Tan[1], Francis Bond[2] and Josef van Genabith[1]
Universität des Saarlandes[1] / Campus, Saarbrücken, Germany
Nanyang Technological University[2] / 14 Nanyang Drive, Singapore
`liling.tan@uni-saarland.de, bond@ieee.org`
`josef.van_genabith@dfki.de`

Abstract

This paper describes our submission to the SemEval-2016 Taxonomy Extraction Evaluation (TExEval-2) Task. We examine the endocentric nature of hyponyms and propose a simple rule-based method to identify hypernyms at high precision. For the food domain, we extract lists of terms from the Wikipedia lists of lists by using the name of each list as the endocentric head and treating all terms in the extracted tables as the hyponym of the endocentric head.

Our submission achieved competitive results in taxonomy construction and ranked top in hypernym identification when evaluated against gold standard taxonomies and also in manual evaluation of novel relations not covered by the gold standard taxonomies.

1 Introduction

Semantic taxonomies provide structured world knowledge to Artificial Intelligence (AI) and Natural Language Processing (NLP) systems. Traditional broad-coverage taxonomies such as CYC (Lenat, 1995), SUMO (Pease et al., 2002; Miller, 1995), YAGO (Suchanek et al., 2007) and Freebase (Bollacker et al., 2008) have been manually created or curated with much effort.

With the rapid technological evolution, it is more feasible to construct a domain-specific taxonomy that caters to domain or company specific terminology (Lefever, 2015). This motivated the move towards unsupervised approaches to taxonomy extraction (Berland and Charniak, 1999; Lin and Pantel,

2001; Snow et al., 2006) and specifically focused towards particular domains (Velardi et al., 2013; Bordea et al., 2015).

The aim of the Taxonomy Extraction Evaluation (TExEval) task is to automatically find lexical relations between pairs of terms within several specified domains. Previously, we have developed a hypernym extraction system using word embeddings by exploiting the frequent occurrence of the '*X is a Y*' pattern in encyclopedic text (Tan et al., 2015).

We have achieved competitive results in SemEval-2015 and as a follow up to our study, we would like to explore the endocentric nature of hyponyms that contributed substantially to the system performance in the previous TExEval task.

Below, we will briefly (i) describe related work on different approaches to taxonomy induction, (ii) explain the linguistic phenomenon of endocentricity, (iii) present our endocentric hypo-hypernym identification system and the results of our submission to the TExEval-2 task in SemEval-2016.

2 Related Work

The hierarchical structure of domain concepts is made of hypo-hypernymy relations between terms. Different approaches have been proposed to induce these relations automatically ranging from pattern/rule-based approaches (Hearst, 1992; Girju, 2003; Kozareva et al., 2008; Ceesay and Hou, 2015) to clustering and frequency based approaches (Lin, 1998; Caraballo, 2001; Pantel and Ravichandran, 2004; Grefenstette, 2015), classification approaches (Snow et al., 2004; Ritter et al., 2009; Espinosa Anke et al., 2015) and graph-based ap-

Proceedings of SemEval-2016, pages 1303–1309,
San Diego, California, June 16-17, 2016. ©2016 Association for Computational Linguistics

proaches (Kozareva and Hovy, 2010; Navigli et al., 2011; Fountain and Lapata, 2012; Tuan et al., 2014; Cleuziou et al., 2015).

More recently, there is a resurgence of vector space or distributional approaches (Van Der Plas, 2005; Lenci and Benotto, 2012; Santus et al., 2014) primarily because of the renaissance of deep learning and neural networks.

Semantic knowledge can be thought of as a vector space where each word is presented by a point and the proximity between words in this space quantifies their semantic association. The vector space is usually constructed from the distribution of words across contexts such that similar meanings tend to be found close to each other within the vector space (Mitchell and Lapata, 2010).

With the present advancement in neural nets and word embeddings (Mikolov et al., 2013; Pennington et al., 2014; Levy et al., 2014; Shazeer et al., 2016), neural space models are gaining popularity in taxonomy induction and relation extraction tasks (Saxe et al., 2013; Fu et al., 2014; Tan et al., 2015).

3   Endocentricity

Early research in theoretical linguistics discussed the idea of *endocentric* vs. *exocentric* constructions (Brugmann, 1886; Aleksandrov, 1886; Brockelmann, 1908; Bloomfield, 1983).

A grammatical construction is *endocentric* when it fulfills the same linguistic function as one of its part(s). For instance, the word *goldfish* is an endocentric compound noun as syntactically it functions as a noun just as its component part *fish* and semantically the compound denotes a type of *fish*.

Conversely, when a grammatical construction made of two or more parts is *exocentric*, no part component carries the linguistic function or meaning assigned to the complex construction. Intuitively, we would expect that there are many endocentric hyponyms in a taxonomy where part of the term conveys its main meaning and usually that part of term would be its hypernym.

The endo/exocentricity feature of a lexical term assumes that the term can be split into two or more parts. For example, *fish* is a single noun that cannot be split, thus it cannot be endo- or exocentric.

While experimenting with ways to weight a term

for information retrieval, Jones (1979) observed that compound nouns often follow the head-modifier principle where the meaning of the term can be conveyed by part(s) of the compound. Approaching endocentricity from a different angle, Nichols et al. (2005) identified the semantic head(s) of a term as its hypernym using the lowest scoping element of the Robust Minimal Recursion Semantics (RMRS) (Copestake et al., 2005) structure of the dictionary definition of the term.

In the first TExEval task in SemEval-2015, both Lefever (2015) and Tan et al. (2015)[1] independently developed string-based systems that exploit the endocentric nature of hyponyms.

In our submission to the TExEval-2 task (Bordea et al., 2016), we seek to answer the question of exactly *"how many hyponyms within a taxonomy are endocentric?"*. Additionally, we exploit the endocentric nature of the hyponyms to extend the taxonomy by crawling and cleaning Wikipedia's *List of Lists of Lists*.[2] Often these lists of terms are found in Wikipedia marked up as tables or in bullet forms.

4   Identifying Endocentric Parts

The main implementation of the rule-based identifier[3] checks *if a term T1 is a substring of another term T2 and if so, assign T1 as a hypernym of T2*. Examples of hypo-hypernym pairs captured by this rule includes are (*psycholinguistics, linguistics*), (*kobe beef, beef*), (*sauce gribiche, sauce*).

Our implementation is simpler than the three part morpho-syntactic analyzer component of the multi-modular taxonomy constructor in Lefever (2015). She implemented rules for three different syntactic constructions which check for suffixes and treat single-word terms and multi-word terms differently while our implementation is agnostic to the single and multi-word distinction.

In addition to the first rule, *if a term contains the "of" preposition, we swap the assignment and check that T2 starts with T1 then assign T2 as a hypernym of T1*. Examples of hypo-hypernym pairs

---

[1] https://github.com/alvations/USAAR-SemEval-2015/tree/master/task17-USAAR-WLV

[2] https://en.wikipedia.org/wiki/List_of_lists_of_lists

[3] Our open-source implementation can be found at https://github.com/alvations/Endocentricity

captured by this swap rule are (*elixir of life, elixir*), (*sociology of education, sociology*).

To improve the precision of the identifier, we set a threshold of a minimum character length of three when identifying a term as a hypernym.

5 Extending a Taxonomy with Wikipedia List of Lists of Lists

The Wikipedia List of Lists of Lists (LOLOL) is a crowdsourced list of lists of terms. We adapted the customized crawler[4] (Tan et al., 2014; Tan and Ordan, 2015) to crawl for tables or bullet points in the Wikipedia subpages of the LOLOL for the food domain. We started the crawl from these seed pages under the bullet point of `https://en.wikipedia.org/wiki/List_of_lists_of_lists#Food_and_drink`.

When the crawler lands on each List of Lists (LOL) page, it will ***treat the URL suffix as the hypernym*** and ***find words in the bullet points or tables that contain endocentric hyponyms***.

If an endocentric hyponym exists, it will extract either (i) all the terms in bold font if the LOL page is bulleted or (ii) all terms in the first column if the LOL page is in table form. The choice of the first column is based on the fact that often LOL tables are bi-column, one containing the terms and the other the gloss or/and description of the term.

5.1 Limitations of LOLOL Trawler

There are a number of issues with this ***trawling*** (*crawl+clean*) approach to extend the taxonomy.

LOL pages are not standardized: The way the crawler cleans the bullets or tables on each LOL page is not standardized because there is no constraint put on the format of the Wikipedia's LOL page. Our trawler only managed to crawl and clean less than 30 LOL pages when extracting the new terms for the food domain.

LOL pages are inceptive: The depth of how nested the LOLs are is undefined. Our trawler can start with a `List_of_foods` page and it leads to the `List_of_breads` page and then the `List_of_American_breads` page and it contin-

---

[4]It was built for crawling translations and diachronic texts in previous SemEval tasks

ues. For sanity, we had to break our trawler at the second page depth and return to the main LOLOL page to move on to the next LOL that we have not previously trawled.

6 Results

Table 1 presents the overview results of our submissions to the TExEval-2 task. Only the results for the food domain contains the hypo-hypernym pairs extracted by our trawler. The rest of the domains comprise of the outputs solely generated by our endocentric hypo-hypernym identifier.

Although it is counter-intuitive to think that endocentric hypo-hypernym pairs can be wrong, this example aptly demonstrates the limitation: (*honey bunches of oats, honey*). In this case, neither '*honey bunches of oats*' can be a hypernym of '*honey*' nor vice versa.

When compared against the gold standard taxonomies, our submission achieved the highest precision in the environment, food (WordNet), science (Eurovoc) and science (WordNet) domains.

As for the Food domain, we expected the fall in precision due to the additional terms that we introduced from the Wikipedia LOLOL outside of the gold standard taxonomy. Thus, we are also unable to determine the true "correctness" of these terms (indicated by the dash in Table 1).

Looking at the proportion of the number of hypo-hypernym pairs that our system correctly identified, we can approximate that *15-25% of the hypernyms in a taxonomy can be easily identified through their endocentric hyponyms* by taking the ratio of #Correct / #Terms.

However, the proportions presented in Table 1 exclude the correct hypo-hypernym pairs that are identified but are not currently in the gold-standard taxonomy. Table 2 presents the results of the manual evaluation for the precision of 100 randomly selected hypo-hypernym pairs that are not in the gold standard taxonomy. Our system achieved top precision in all domains other than science (Eurovoc).

If we consider the precision scores from Table 2 as the precision of the remaining identified but not correct hypo-hypernym pairs in Table 1, we would be able to add to the 15-25% hypononym endocentricity in taxonomies. However, the aggregation of

	Environment (Eurovoc)	Food (WordNet)	Food	Science (Eurovoc)	Science (WordNet)	Science
#Terms	261	1486	1555	370	125	452
#Relations	261	1576	1587	452	124	465
#Correct / Identified	38 / 47	381 / 540	– / 4347*	66 / 104	25 / 30	119 / 312
Precision	**0.8085**	**0.7056**	0.0603	**0.6333**	**0.8173**	0.3814
Recall	0.1456	0.2418	0.1651	0.1532	0.1881	0.2559
F-score	0.2468	**0.3601**	0.0883	0.2468	0.3058	0.3063
F&M	0.0007	0.0021	0.0	0.0023	0.0008	0.0020

Table 1: Results of our Endocentric Hypo-Hypernym Identifier Against the Gold Standard Taxonomy (**#Terms** refers to the no. of terms in the domain and **#Relations** refers to the no. of hypo-hypernym pairs found in the gold-standard taxonomy. **#Correct / #Identified** refers to the proportion of hypo-hypernym pairs our system has correctly identified. **Bold** items indicates that it is highest score among the participating teams in TExEval-2. The asterisk * indicates that the trawler was used to produce submissions for this domain.)

Domain	JUNLP	TAXI	NUIG-UNLP	USAAR	QASSIT
Environment (Eurovoc)	0.02	0.11	0.08	**0.22**	0.07
Food	0.20	0.36	–	**0.73***	–
Food (Wordnet)	0.18	0.32	–	**0.81**	–
Science	0.06	0.14	0.09	**0.71**	0.07
Science (Eurovoc)	0.02	0.02	**0.04**	0.00	0.05
Science (Wordnet)	0.06	0.22	0.05	**0.47**	0.22

Table 2: Results of Manual Evaluation on 100 Random Novel Hypo-Hypernym Pairs for Participating Teams In TExEval-2

the manual evaluation results should only be considered if the novel hypo-hypernym relations are curated and added to the standard taxonomies.

		Baseline	TAXI	USAAR
Food	P	0.5000	0.3388	**0.7056**
(WordNet)	R	0.2576	**0.2932**	0.2418
Science	P	0.6897	0.3747	**0.8173**
(WordNet)	R	0.2655	**0.3805**	0.1881

Table 3: Comparison of String-based Methods

Comparing against the TExEval-2 organizers baseline string-based method and the TAXI lexico-syntactic substring approach (Panchenko and Biemann, 2016) for the WordNet taxonomies, our system achieved highest precision but underperfomed in recall as shown in Table 3.

Since our main implementation of our hypernym identifier is language independent, in retrospect, we can easily remove the swap rule that is attached to the English '*of*' and apply the identifier to other languages in the TExEval-2 task.

6.1 Other Participating Systems

Table 2 presents a summary of the results of novel hypo-hypernym pairs identified by the participating systems in TExEval-2. A detailed overview of the results of TExEval-2 is presented in Bordea et al. (2016).

JUNLP relied on substrings and relations extracted from BabelNet (Navigli and Ponzetto, 2012) to identify hyper-hyponym pairs. Although it is sensible to approach the task using an existing ontology, their system achieved relatively low precision on the manual evaluation of novel hyper-hyponym pairs. The NUIG-UNLP team extended previous work on vector space approaches to taxonomy induction by comparing the similarity between the dense word embeddings of the hyponyms and their candidate hypernyms. They system achieved high recall but attained low precision (Pocostales, 2016).

Similar to our endocentric-based approach, the TAXI team extended the substring-based approach by filtering the hypernym candidates based on corpora statistics of lexico-syntactic patterns. Additionally, they applied pruning methods to improve the ontological structure which resulted in high Fowlkes and Mallows (F&M) Measure (Panchenko and Biemann, 2016). QASSIT used lexical patterns to extract hypernym candidates and applied the pretopological space graph optimization technique that is based on genetic algorithm to achieve the desired taxonomy structure (Cleuziou and Moreno, 2016).

TAXI and QASSIT ranked first and second in the taxonomy construction criterion of the TExEval task. Both teams used graph pruning techniques to improve the taxonomy structure and implicitly improve the F&M scores[5] of their taxonomy. Although our endocentricity based hypo-hypernym extraction system ranked first in hypernym identification of TExEval task, we ranked third in taxonomy construction with an overall F&M score of 0.0013.

7 Conclusion

In this paper, we have described our submission to the Taxonomy Extraction Evaluation (TExEval-2) Task for SemEval-2016. We have empirically shown that 15-25% of the hypernyms in a taxonomy can be easily identified through their endocentric hyponyms and we briefly discuss the intuitions and limitations of the approach.

We have achieved competitive results in taxonomy construction and achieved top precision score for hypernym identification in most domains involved in the task.

Acknowledgments

The research leading to these results has received funding from the People Programme (Marie Curie Actions) of the European Union's Seventh Framework Programme FP7/2007-2013/ under REA grant agreement no 317471.

References

Alexander Aleksandrov. 1886. *Sprachliches aus dem Nationaldichter Litauens Donalitius. T. 1, Zur Semasiologie : Inaugural-Dissertation zur Erlangung des Grades eines Magisters der vergleichenden Sprachkunde*. Schnakenburg.

Matthew Berland and Eugene Charniak. 1999. Finding Parts in Very Large Corpora. In *Proceedings of the 37th annual meeting of the Association for Computational Linguistics on Computational Linguistics*, pages 57–64.

Leonard Bloomfield. 1983. *An Introduction to the Study of Language*. 2. Benjamins.

Kurt Bollacker, Colin Evans, Praveen Paritosh, Tim Sturge, and Jamie Taylor. 2008. Freebase: A collaboratively created graph database for structuring human knowledge. In *Proceedings of the 2008 ACM SIGMOD International Conference on Management of Data*, SIGMOD '08, pages 1247–1250, New York, NY, USA. ACM.

Georgeta Bordea, Paul Buitelaar, Stefano Faralli, and Roberto Navigli. 2015. Semeval-2015 task 17: Taxonomy extraction evaluation (texeval). In *Proceedings of the 9th International Workshop on Semantic Evaluation (SemEval 2015)*, pages 902–910, Denver, Colorado.

Georgeta Bordea, Els Lefever, and Paul Buitelaar. 2016. Semeval-2016 task 13: Taxonomy extraction evaluation (texeval-2). In *Proceedings of the 10th International Workshop on Semantic Evaluation*.

Carl Brockelmann. 1908. *Grundriss der vergleichenden Grammatik der semitischen Sprachen*, volume 1. Reuther & Reichard.

Karl Brugmann. 1886. *Vergleichende Grammatik der indogermanischen Sprachen*. Walter de Gruyter.

Sharon Ann Caraballo. 2001. *Automatic Construction of a Hypernym-labeled Noun Hierarchy from Text*. Ph.D. thesis, Providence, RI, USA. AAI3006696.

Bamfa Ceesay and Wen Juan Hou. 2015. Ntnu: An unsupervised knowledge approach for taxonomy extraction. In *Proceedings of the 9th International Workshop on Semantic Evaluation (SemEval 2015)*, pages 938–943, Denver, Colorado.

Guillaume Cleuziou and Jose G. Moreno. 2016. Qassit at semeval-2016 task 13: On the integration of semantic vectors in pretopological spaces for lexical taxonomy acquisition. In *Proceedings of the 10th International Workshop on Semantic Evaluation (SemEval 2016)*, San Diego, California. Association for Computational Linguistics.

Guillaume Cleuziou, Davide Buscaldi, Gaël Dias, Vincent Levorato, and Christine Largeron. 2015. Qassit: A pretopological framework for the automatic construction of lexical taxonomies from raw texts. In *Proceedings of the 9th International Workshop on Semantic Evaluation (SemEval 2015)*, pages 955–959, Denver, Colorado.

Ann Copestake, Dan Flickinger, Carl Pollard, and Ivan A Sag. 2005. Minimal recursion semantics: An introduction. *Research on Language and Computation*, 3(2-3):281–332.

---

[5]Overall F&M scores for TAXI and QASSIT are 0.4064 and 0.2908

Luis Espinosa Anke, Horacio Saggion, and Francesco Ronzano. 2015. Taln-upf: Taxonomy learning exploiting crf-based hypernym extraction on encyclopedic definitions. In *Proceedings of the 9th International Workshop on Semantic Evaluation (SemEval 2015)*, pages 949–954, Denver, Colorado.

Trevor Fountain and Mirella Lapata. 2012. Taxonomy Induction using Hierarchical Random Graphs. In *Proceedings of the 2012 Conference of the North American Chapter of the Association for Computational Linguistics: Human Language Technologies*, pages 466–476.

Ruiji Fu, Jiang Guo, Bing Qin, Wanxiang Che, Haifeng Wang, and Ting Liu. 2014. Learning Semantic Hierarchies via Word Embeddings. In *Proceedings of the 52nd Annual Meeting of the Association for Computational Linguistics (Volume 1: Long Papers)*, pages 1199–1209.

Roxana Girju. 2003. Automatic Detection of Causal Relations for Question Answering. In *Proceedings of the ACL 2003 workshop on Multilingual summarization and question answering-Volume 12*, pages 76–83.

Gregory Grefenstette. 2015. Inriasac: Simple hypernym extraction methods. In *Proceedings of the 9th International Workshop on Semantic Evaluation (SemEval 2015)*, pages 911–914, Denver, Colorado.

Marti A Hearst. 1992. Automatic Acquisition of Hyponyms from Large Text Corpora. In *Proceedings of the 14th conference on Computational linguistics-Volume 2*, pages 539–545.

Karen Sparck Jones. 1979. Experiments in relevance weighting of search terms. *Information Processing & Management*, 15(3):133–144.

Zornitsa Kozareva and Eduard Hovy. 2010. A Semi-Supervised Method to Learn and Construct Taxonomies using the Web. In *Proceedings of the 2010 Conference on Empirical Methods in Natural Language Processing*, pages 1110–1118.

Zornitsa Kozareva, Ellen Riloff, and Eduard Hovy. 2008. Semantic Class Learning from the Web with Hyponym Pattern Linkage Graphs. In *Proceedings of ACL-08: HLT*, pages 1048–1056, Columbus, Ohio.

Els Lefever. 2015. Lt3: A multi-modular approach to automatic taxonomy construction. In *Proceedings of the 9th International Workshop on Semantic Evaluation (SemEval 2015)*, pages 944–948, Denver, Colorado.

Douglas B Lenat. 1995. CYC: A large-scale investment in knowledge infrastructure. *Communications of the ACM*, 38(11):33–38.

Alessandro Lenci and Giulia Benotto. 2012. Identifying hypernyms in distributional semantic spaces. In *Proceedings of the First Joint Conference on Lexical and Computational Semantics-Volume 1: Proceedings of the main conference and the shared task, and Volume 2: Proceedings of the Sixth International Workshop on Semantic Evaluation*, pages 75–79.

Omer Levy, Yoav Goldberg, and Israel Ramat-Gan. 2014. Linguistic regularities in sparse and explicit word representations. In *CoNLL*, pages 171–180.

Dekang Lin and Patrick Pantel. 2001. Discovery of Inference Rules for Question-Answering. *Natural Language Engineering*, 7(04):343–360.

Dekang Lin. 1998. Automatic Retrieval and Clustering of Similar Words. In *Proceedings of the 17th international conference on Computational linguistics-Volume 2*, pages 768–774.

Tomas Mikolov, Ilya Sutskever, Kai Chen, Greg S Corrado, and Jeff Dean. 2013. Distributed representations of words and phrases and their compositionality. In *Advances in neural information processing systems*, pages 3111–3119.

George A. Miller. 1995. WordNet: A Lexical Database for English. *Commun. ACM*, 38(11):39–41.

Jeff Mitchell and Mirella Lapata. 2010. Composition in Distributional Models of Semantics. *Cognitive Science*, 34(8):1388–1439.

Roberto Navigli and Simone Paolo Ponzetto. 2012. Babelnet: The automatic construction, evaluation and application of a wide-coverage multilingual semantic network. *Artificial Intelligence*, 193:217–250.

Roberto Navigli, Paola Velardi, and Stefano Faralli. 2011. A Graph-Based Algorithm for Inducing Lexical Taxonomies from Scratch. In *IJCAI 2011, Proceedings of the 22nd International Joint Conference on Artificial Intelligence, Barcelona, Catalonia, Spain, July 16-22, 2011*, pages 1872–1877.

Eric Nichols, Francis Bond, and Dan Flickinger. 2005. Robust ontology acquisition from machine-readable dictionaries. In *IJCAI-05, Proceedings of the Nineteenth International Joint Conference on Artificial Intelligence*, pages 1111–1116.

Stefano Ruppert Eugen Remus Steffen Naets Hubert Fairon Cedrick Ponzetto Simone Paolo Panchenko, Alexander Faralli and Chris Biemann. 2016. Taxi at semeval-2016 task 13: a taxonomy induction method based on lexico-syntactic patterns, substrings and focused crawling. In *Proceedings of the 10th International Workshop on Semantic Evaluation*. Association for Computational Linguistics.

Patrick Pantel and Deepak Ravichandran. 2004. Automatically Labeling Semantic Classes. In *Proceedings of the Human Language Technology Conference of the North American Chapter of the Association for Computational Linguistics: HLT-NAACL 2004*.

Adam Pease, Ian Niles, and John Li. 2002. The Suggested Upper Merged Ontology: A Large Ontology for the Semantic Web and its Applications. In *In Working Notes of the AAAI-2002 Workshop on Ontologies and the Semantic Web*.

Jeffrey Pennington, Richard Socher, and Christopher D Manning. 2014. Glove: Global vectors for word representation. In *EMNLP*, volume 14, pages 1532–1543.

Joel Pocostales. 2016. Nuig-unlp at semeval-2016 task 13: A simple word embedding-based approach for taxonomy extraction. In *Proceedings of the 10th International Workshop on Semantic Evaluation*.

Alan Ritter, Stephen Soderland, and Oren Etzioni. 2009. What is this, anyway: Automatic hypernym discovery. In *AAAI Spring Symposium: Learning by Reading and Learning to Read*, pages 88–93.

Enrico Santus, Alessandro Lenci, Qin Lu, and Sabine Schulte im Walde. 2014. Chasing hypernyms in vector spaces with entropy. In *Proceedings of the 14th Conference of the European Chapter of the Association for Computational Linguistics, volume 2: Short Papers*, pages 38–42, Gothenburg, Sweden.

Andrew M. Saxe, James L. McClelland, and Surya Ganguli. 2013. Learning Hierarchical Category Structure in Deep Neural Networks. pages 1271–1276.

Noam Shazeer, Ryan Doherty, Colin Evans, and Chris Waterson. 2016. Swivel: Improving embeddings by noticing what's missing. *arXiv preprint arXiv:1602.02215*.

Rion Snow, Daniel Jurafsky, and Andrew Y Ng. 2004. Learning syntactic patterns for automatic hypernym discovery. *Advances in Neural Information Processing Systems 17*.

Rion Snow, Daniel Jurafsky, and Andrew Y Ng. 2006. Semantic Taxonomy Induction from Heterogenous Evidence. In *Proceedings of the 21st International Conference on Computational Linguistics and the 44th annual meeting of the Association for Computational Linguistics*, pages 801–808.

Fabian M. Suchanek, Gjergji Kasneci, and Gerhard Weikum. 2007. Yago: A Core of Semantic Knowledge. In *Proceedings of the 16th International Conference on World Wide Web*, WWW '07, pages 697–706, New York, NY, USA. ACM.

Liling Tan and Noam Ordan. 2015. Usaar-chronos: Crawling the web for temporal annotations. In *Proceedings of the 9th International Workshop on Semantic Evaluation (SemEval 2015)*, pages 846–850, Denver, Colorado.

Liling Tan, Anne Schumann, Jose Martinez, and Francis Bond. 2014. Sensible: L2 translation assistance by emulating the manual post-editing process. In *Proceedings of the 8th International Workshop on Semantic Evaluation (SemEval 2014)*, pages 541–545, Dublin, Ireland.

Liling Tan, Rohit Gupta, and Josef van Genabith. 2015. Usaar-wlv: Hypernym generation with deep neural nets. In *Proceedings of the 9th International Workshop on Semantic Evaluation (SemEval 2015)*, pages 932–937, Denver, Colorado.

Luu Anh Tuan, Jung-jae Kim, and Kiong See Ng. 2014. Taxonomy construction using syntactic contextual evidence. In *Proceedings of the 2014 Conference on Empirical Methods in Natural Language Processing (EMNLP)*, pages 810–819.

Lonneke Van Der Plas. 2005. Automatic acquisition of lexico-semantic knowledge for qa. In *Proceedings of the IJCNLP workshop on Ontologies and Lexical Resources*, pages 76–84.

Paola Velardi, Stefano Faralli, and Roberto Navigli. 2013. OntoLearn Reloaded: A Graph-based Algorithm for Taxonomy Induction. *Computational Linguistics*, 39(3):665–707.

JUNLP at SemEval-2016 Task 13: A Language Independent Approach for Hypernym Identification

Promita Maitra and **Dipankar Das**

Department of Computer Science Engineering, Jadavpur University

Kolkata, India

`promita.maitra@gmail.com` and `dipankar.dipnil2005@gmail.com`

Abstract

This paper describes our approach to build a language-independent hypernym extraction system, based on two modules for the SemEval-2016 Task 13 on Taxonomy Extraction Evaluation (TExEval-2). This task focuses only on the hypernym-hyponym relation extraction from a list of terms collected from various domains and languages. The first module of our system is built on the state-of-the-art system using BabelNet while the second one deals with the parts found within terms and which are useful to establish a hierarchical relation among them. Our system performed well in terms of *recall* in most of the domains irrespective of the languages; however, the precision scores indicate a scope of improvement. In case of overall ranking, our present system stands fourth in monolingual (i.e. English) evaluation and second in multilingual (i.e. Dutch, Italian, French) setup.

1 Introduction

The rapid growth in terms of digitalized texts in the recent years (specially, in the fields including scientific, clinical, enterprise, legal, and personal information management) has made the management of textual information increasingly important. In order to fulfill the need of having more structured data, ontologies, taxonomy or hierarchical relations between ontological concepts are considered as useful tools for content organization, navigation, and retrieval, as well as to provide valuable input for semantically intensive tasks such as question answering and textual entailment. This task specifically focuses on the identification of hypernym-hyponym relation among terms in four different languages (English, Dutch, Italian and French) and different domains. Typically, taxonomy construction has three basic steps: entity or concept identification, discover different relations among different entities and taxonomy construction. The challenge organizers have made it easy by already providing us with a list of extracted entities (also called concepts/terms) for each of the domains in each of the languages. Our approach was to build a system that fits a multilingual setup and significantly reduces the computational time and complexity by taking existing resources into consideration.

The rest of the paper is organized as follows: Section 2 describes the task at hand in brief along with the main challenges. Section 3 gives a brief overview of the work already done in this field. Section 4 contains the details of the modules we have used to address the problem. Section 5 presents the analysis of results and finally, the conclusion and future scopes are discussed in Section 6.

2 Problem Description

SemEval-2016 Task 13: Taxonomy Extraction Evaluation (TExEval-2) has its main focus on hypernym-hyponym relation extraction from given lists of terms collected from multiple domains like Food, Environment and Science (Bordea et al., 2016). This year, the task organizers have extended the problem setup to address the multilingual structure. Along with English, there were terms in French, Dutch and Italian as well for all the domains. For this particular task, we did not have to go through the complexities of entity identification from a text

Proceedings of SemEval-2016, pages 1310–1314,
San Diego, California, June 16-17, 2016. ©2016 Association for Computational Linguistics

as the lists of terms were already given.

- i. One of the main challenges was that we were not provided with any annotated or plaintext corpus that we can use as training. However, the organizers suggested that it would be helpful if we explore the Wikipedia dump for the same.

- ii. Second big challenge was to develop a system that will work for languages we do not understand. Ontology development being such a task where some basic domain knowledge is inevitable, this multilingual setup was indeed a great concern for us.

- iii. We were specifically asked not to use the resources we most frequently use in this kind of tasks as they were used to construct the gold standard. The list of the resources that were prohibited is:

    - hypernym-hyponym relations from the Word-Net [1],

    - skos:broader and skos:narrower relations from EuroVoc [2],

    - the Google product taxonomy [3],

    - the Taxonomy of fields and their subfields provided for the National Academies of Sciences, Engineering, and Medicine [4].

However, in contrast, we were free to add more terms if needed to the term lists that were provided by the organizers.

3 Related Work

Hypernym detection from text is one of the most popular hierarchical relation extraction tasks in ontology learning for which research work dates back to at least 1984 (Calzolari, 1984). Hypernym can be described as a linguistic term for a word whose meaning includes the meanings of other words, which are known as hyponyms. For instance, *flower* is a hypernym of *daisy* and *rose*. On the other hand,

daisy and *rose* are some of the hyponyms of *flower*. In simple words, this relation deals with identifying the concepts and finding the particular superclass they fit in. Manually constructing these kind of relations from text is a time-consuming and labour-intensive procedure. Hence, the researchers felt the need to make this process automatic. The methods proposed can broadly be categorized into two: supervised and unsupervised. While the unsupervised methods can identify and extract semantic relations from plain text without the need of any pre-annotated text corpora, the supervised methods often find it difficult to find an annotated corpora in similar domain. A major part of the previous researches on automatic semantic classification of words was developed based on the method first proposed by Hearst, that the presence of certain lexico-syntactic patterns can indicate a particular semantic relationship between two noun phrases (Hearst, 1992). This paper introduced six basic lexical patterns. This rule based approach was further extended in subsequent works bringing out more valid patterns, either handcrafted or learned from training corpus for semantic relation extraction (Berland and Charniak, 1999) (Kozareva et al., 2008) (Widdows and Dorow, 2002). Pattern based results are effective and reliable, scores high on precision measure. However, these methods suffer in terms of recall. Later, a few distributional approaches were proposed by different authors making use of the large corpora present in (Guido Boella, 2014) (Navigli and Velardi, 2010). Machine learning based methods make use of features like term co-occurrence, semantic similarity or other syntantic information from text collection. Precision of these machine learning based approaches is lower compared to pattern based approach. The simple morpho-syntactic approach also proved to yield a decent result (Lefever, 2015) (Sang et al., 2011). In recent years, several researches are being carried out to extract semantic relations from texts in other languages.

4 System Description

In the present challenge, we had to keep three main points in mind. We wanted to make a single system appropriate for a multilingual setup (Dutch, French, Italian and English). However, it became

---

[1] https://wordnet.princeton.edu/

[2] http://eurovoc.europa.eu/

[3] https://www.google.com/basepages/producttype/taxonomy.en-US.txt

[4] http://sites.nationalacademies.org/PGA/Resdoc/PGA_044522

more difficult as we were not allowed to use any of the widely used resources like WordNet, EuroVoc, Google Product Taxonomy etc. Building a taxonomy which would provide structured information about semantic relations between words is an extremely slow and labor-intensive process. Therefore, we kept our focus on building a system which would be simple and significantly light in terms of computation time.

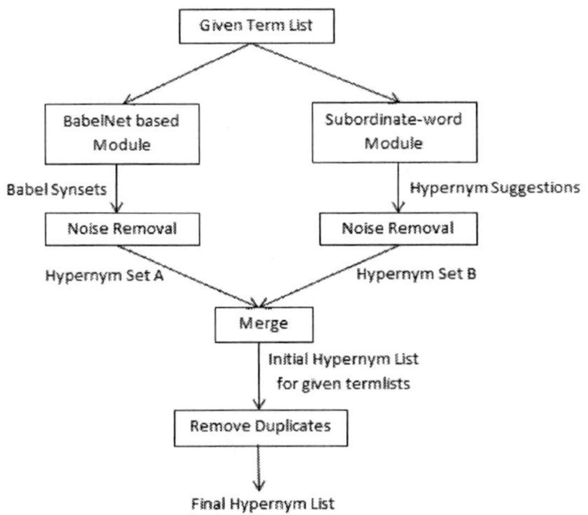

Figure 1: Basic system diagram

Our system has two main modules, as shown in Figure 1:

- i. Extracting semantic relations from BabelNet.

- ii. Analyzing the terms to find a subterm suitable to become a hypernym.

4.1 BabelNet Based Module

BabelNet[5] is an open source resource containing both multilingual dictionary with lexicographic and encyclopedic coverage of terms, and a network of concepts and named entities connected in a very large network of semantic relations, called Babel synsets (Navigli and Ponzetto, 2012). Each of the Babel synsets represents a given meaning and contains all the synonyms which express that meaning in a range of different languages. BabelNet 3.5 covers 272 languages, which also include our task related languages like English, French, Dutch and Italian.

---

[5]http://babelnet.org/

Finding out semantic relations from the entire Wikipedia dump with a pattern based approach proved to be quite a long process and computationally expensive as there can be numerous types of valid patterns that can hold a hypernym-hyponym relation. On the other hand, it would take days to initially start with a few patterns and then search for more with a bootstrapping approach. On the other hand, BabelNet already provides a variety of semantic relations for a large number of concepts using knowledge from various resources available including Wikipedia. So, our system execution time gets significantly reduced if we just use the semantic relation set available in BabelNet instead of extending the Wikipedia corpus and analyzing it for the pattern search. Secondly, we wanted to have a system that would fit into the multilingual setup that the task intends to have this year. The facts were that we do not have a satisfactory amount of knowledge required for identifying the valid patterns for hypernym-hyponym relations in languages other than English, and we also do not have an annotated training data to learn those patterns via a bootstrapping method for those languages. Therefore, it was essential for us to have a tool that could automatically extract such knowledge from corpus.

For each term that appears in each domain, we obtain a synset from the BabelNet for hypernym relations found over the Wikipedia articles in different languages. As the task organizers specifically asked not to use resources like WordNet, only the Wikipedia source is taken into account while obtaining hypernym relations, skipping the others like WordNet, VerbNet, Microsoft Terminology etc. This is done to make the system computionally light and reduce the huge time needed to process the Wikipedia articles searching for patterns. We consider the terms for their NOUN POS tag sense, with the language mentioned in the query. We only considered the NOUN POS tags because it was seen from our observation of term lists, that they contain terms which are mostly nouns. We get the synset for each term which contains a lot of noise such as repetitive sense words, out-of-domain senses, senses in different morphological form than the existing terms, etc. We fed the raw synset output to a cleansing module which would give us only the unique in-domain terms in their correct morphological form as given in the term-list.

We further extended this module to find the synsets of the terms present in the cleansed output in order to obtain the entire hypernym tree for the given term which helps to increase the recall of our system.

4.2 Subordinate-word Module

This module deals with finding appropriate parts of given terms that can possibly be the hypernym of the original term. For example, *Fruit Custard* is a type of *Custard*. Now these subordinate-words which are potential hypernyms can be of the following two types.

- The subordinate-word can itself be an independent term present in the term-list given. For example, if we have both the terms *Biochemistry* and *Chemistry* in the term-list, we can just analyze the term *Biochemistry* and identify *Chemistry* as its possible hypernym.

- There might be multiple terms for which no common part is an independent term but significant overlap exists among those, even more than once. In such cases we have introduced that overlapped part as our new term in the term-list. For example, we have *Chocolate Pudding* and *Vanilla Pudding* as two terms in our list but no entry for *Pudding*. Since we get overlapping in previous two terms with *Pudding*, we can consider *Pudding* as the possible hypernym of *Chocolate Pudding* and *Vanilla Pudding*.

However, the problem is that we were getting some noise in the input due to the stopwords present in the list. For example, University of PlaceA and University of PlaceB will have University and of as the subordinate-word hypernyms. Of cannot be a hypernym to some term. So we remove those subordinate-words which has only stopwords in them. Again, we had to deal with different morphological forms of the same word as hypernyms, for example science and sciences. For such instances, we checked if any one form is the part of our term list. If yes, we keep that form and remove others or we keep the lemmatized form otherwise.

5 Analysis of Results

Just as construction of suitable ontology from text, evaluation of an extracted ontology is not a simple

Language	Precision	Recall	Fscore
English	0.15	0.30	0.20
Dutch	0.16	0.22	0.19
French	0.17	0.25	0.20
Italian	0.13	0.20	0.19

Table 1: Average Precision, Recall, Fscore for Gold standard evaluation across all domains.

task either. For this particular task, structural evaluation was done which includes the presence of cycles, the number of intermediate nodes compared to leaf nodes, and the number of over generic relations with the root node. The output relations were also evaluated against collected gold standards collected from WordNet and other well known, openly available taxonomies using evaluation measures like standard precision, recall and Fscore.

Table1 shows the average result of our system with respect to the gold standard evaluation for each language taking an average over all the domains. We had our focus on generating a hypernym tree for each term by providing the hypernyms of a term as next input to the system. This resulted in better recall but the precision of our system showed a visible decline compared to the baseline system for all the languages.

Table 2 shows the structural evaluation of the output produced by our system for different domains in English and other languages. The structural measures used for the evaluation are as follows:

- V: number of distinct vertices;

- E: number of distinct edges;

- c.c.: number of connected components;

- i.i.: intermediate nodes = V - L where L is the set of leaves

- cycles: YES = the taxonomy contains cycles, NO = the taxonomy is a Directed Acyclic Graph (DAG)

- Cumulative Fowlkes and Mallows Measure (FM): cumulative measure of the similarity of two taxonomies.

As we can see, though we have cycles present in relations of English language, all other language-output is a DAG. We achieved better score in categorization due to high number of distinct vertices, edges and intermediate nodes obtained by our system.

Measure	English	Multilingual
Cyclicity	3	0
Structure (FM)	0.1498	0.0155
Categorisation (i.i.)	377	178.22
Connectivity (c.c.)	53.17	34.89

Table 2: Structural Evaluation for English and other languages.

6   Conclusion and Future Scope

In this paper we have discussed in brief our approach to address the Taxonomy Extraction and Evaluation task of SemEval 2016. We have kept our focus mainly on keeping the computation time optimal and building a system suitable for multilingual setup. We took a completely unsupervised approach without directly considering a text corpora. Both of our modules need only the terms to be fed as input and generates possible hypernym candidate for each term in a short span of time compared to the huge amount of time and knowledge needed to manually craft the lexico-syntactic pattern/regular expressions in each domain and then analyzing the large corpora for possible matches. The results were good in terms of recall, but the precision score suffered due to our approach of generating as many possible in-domain hypernyms of a term as we can.

We can try to improve our system's performance by making use of information available with Wikipedia dump other than the article texts such as infobox properties, redirect links, article titles, categories or other meta-information available. Also, provided a training set, we believe a bag-of-word model constructed within a specific context window can yield better overall results.

References

Matthew Berland and Eugene Charniak. 1999. Finding parts in very large corpora. In *In Proceedings of the 37th annual meeting of the Association for Computational Linguistics on Computational Linguistics*, page 57. Association for Computational Linguistics.

Georgeta Bordea, Els Lefever, and Paul Buitelaar. 2016. Semeval-2016 task 13: Taxonomy extraction evaluation (texeval-2). In *Proceedings of the 10th International Workshop on Semantic Evaluation*. Association for Computational Linguistics.

Nicoletta Calzolari. 1984. Detecting patterns in a lexical data base. In *10th International Conference on Computational Linguistics and 22Nd Annual Meeting on Association for Computational Linguistics*, page 170. Association for Computational Linguistics.

Alice Ruggeri Livio Robaldo Guido Boella, Luigi Di Caro. 2014. Learning from syntax generalizations for automatic semantic annotation. *Journal of Intelligent Information Systems*, page 1.

Marti A. Hearst. 1992. Automatic acquisition of hyponyms from large text corpora. In *Proc. of the Fourteenth International Conference on Computational Linguistics*, Nantes, France.

Zornitsa Kozareva, Ellen Riloff, and Eduard Hovy. 2008. Semantic class learning from the web with hyponym pattern linkage graphs. In *In Proceedings of ACL-08*, volume 8, page 1048. Association for Computational Linguistics.

Els Lefever. 2015. Lt3: A multi-modular approach to automatic taxonomy construction. In *In Proceedings of the 9th International Workshop on Semantic Evaluation (SemEval 2015)*, page 944. Association for Computational Linguistics.

Roberto Navigli and Simone Paolo Ponzetto. 2012. The automatic construction, evaluation and application of a wide-coverage multilingual semantic network. *Elsevier*, page 217.

Roberto Navigli and Paola Velardi. 2010. Learning word-class lattices for definition and hypernym extraction. In *In Proceedings of the 48th Annual Meeting of the Association for Computational Linguistics,ACL 10*, page 1318. Association for Computational Linguistics.

Erik Tjong Kim Sang, Katja Hofmann, and Maarten de Rijke. 2011. *Extraction of Hypernymy Information from Text*.

Dominic Widdows and Beate Dorow. 2002. A graph model for unsupervised lexical acquisition. In *In Proceedings of the 19th international conference on Computational linguistics*, volume 1, page 1. Association for Computational Linguistics.

QASSIT at SemEval-2016 Task 13: On the Integration of Semantic Vectors in Pretopological Spaces for Lexical Taxonomy Acquisition

Guillaume Cleuziou
Université d'Orléans,
INSA Centre Val de Loire,
LIFO EA 4022, France
cleuziou@univ-orleans.fr

Jose G. Moreno
LIMSI, CNRS,
Université Paris-Saclay,
F-91405 Orsay
moreno@limsi.fr

Abstract

This paper presents our participation to the SemEval "Task 13: Taxonomy Extraction Evaluation (TExEval-2)" (Bordea et al., 2016). This year, we propose the combination of recent semantic vectors representation into a methodology for semisupervised and auto-supervised acquisition of lexical taxonomies from raw texts. In our proposal, first similarities between concepts are calculated using semantic vectors, then a pretopological space is defined from which a preliminary structure is constructed. Finally, a genetic algorithm is used to optimize two different functions, the quality of the added relationships in the taxonomy and the quality of the structure. Experiments show that our proposal has a competitive performance when compared with the other participants achieving the second position in the general rank.

1 Introduction

The task of automatic taxonomy extraction consists in the generation of hierarchical relations between pairs of terms from a given initial set of terms. In this paper, we describe the second participation of QASSIT team to the "Taxonomy Extraction Evaluation (TExEval)" task. In this opportunity, we were interested in re-examining our proposed algorithm (Cleuziou and Dias, 2015)(Cleuziou et al., 2015), but with an improved range of information as input. Our algorithm is based on Pretopological Spaces combined with patterns and collocations counts. Patterns are a useful way to capture knowledge form huge corpus (Hearst, 1992), but its performance could be influence by the size of the corpus or the use of a fixed vocabulary. This is a main drawback of the previous version of the algorithm (Cleuziou et al., 2015), the requirement of non-zero mentions in a corpus of the input terms in the specific chosen patterns. For example, to an optimal performance our algorithm requires that the term "computational biology" appears at least once in one of the used patters. However, when searching in wikipedia with the query "*computational biology is a ...*" then we obtain results such as "PLOS **Computational Biology** is a peer-reviewed computational biology journal", "The Journal of **Computational Biology** is a monthly peer-reviewed scientific journal", "Cancer **computational biology** is a field that aims to determine the future mutations in" and "**Computational biology** is a specialized domain that often requires knowledge of computer programming"[1]. The first three results include the desired term as a part of another more specific term (in this case journal titles) and only the last result could be considered as relevant information. Moreover, neither "domain" or "computer programming" are part of the input terms for the taxonomy. This situation makes difficult the direct use of patterns with our algorithm for the taxonomy construction task.

In order to overcome this difficulty, we have redefined our algorithm to exclusively use as input information gathered from the corpus without the use of specific query patterns. Additionally, we have explored the integration of recent techniques in words representation known as semantic vectors (Mikolov

---

[1] Only journal titles are obtained when the pattern is replaced by "is an ".

Proceedings of SemEval-2016, pages 1315–1319,
San Diego, California, June 16-17, 2016. ©2016 Association for Computational Linguistics

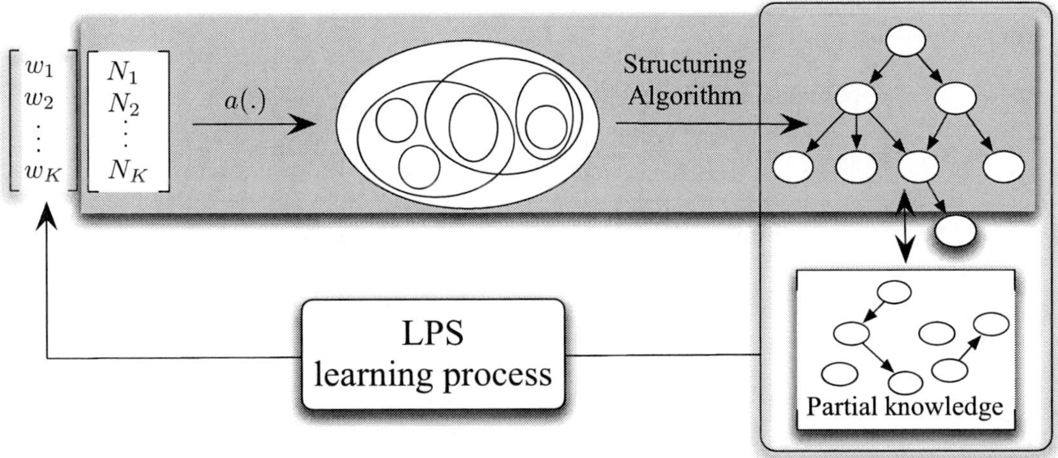

Figure 1: The LPS process uses partial knowledge on the expected structure in order to improve the parameterization of the pretopological space.

et al., 2013). This technique allows us to calculate similarities of the input terms if they are present in a corpus, avoiding the requirement of explicit patterns of the previous versions. Additionally, these vectors allow semantic similarity calculation of concepts that are not found together, but that their context does. The remainder of this paper includes a brief description of our pretopological spaces algorithm and their modifications for the integration of semantic vectors (Section 2). Experiments and results are presented in Section 3 and finally, discussion and conclusions are presented in Sections 4 and 5 respectively.

2 Pretopological Spaces for Lexical Taxonomy Acquisition

We used the learning pretopological spaces framework (LPS) proposed in our previous participation in the TExEval task and fully described in (Cleuziou and Dias, 2015). The general LPS framework is illustrated in Figure 1, and a brief description is presented below. This algorithm considers as input a set of non-symmetric binary relations $\{N_1, \ldots, N_K\}$ over a set of terms E and a partial knowledge S used as true partial information to structure E; LPS aims to find a $Space\ w$ which induces a good subsumption propagation function $a()$ for structuring E; the fitness function that guides the learning process is

defined by:

$$Score(w, S) = F_{meas.}(w, S) \times I_{struct.}(w) \quad (1)$$

where F and I are two terms quantifying respectively the satisfactions about:

- the matching with the partial knowledge S and

- a taxonomy structural property expected as output (e.g. a tree-like structure).

The score defined in Equation 1 is used to guide the exploration of the space of solutions through a learning strategy based on a Genetic Algorithm (GA).

2.1 Sources used for LPS Taxonomy Acquisition

In our previous algorithm, we have used patterns and collocation measures as piece of information to model the subsumption propagation between terms. In this version, we abandon the use of patterns due the additional extra task it requires to avoid noisy information. However, we introduce another source of information with low manual requirements in order to have a more automatic version of our algorithm. The three main sources of information we use are described bellow.

First, we have integrated a new robust semantic representation called semantic vectors or word

Table 1: Comparative automatic evaluation of the proposed taxonomies.

Dataset (Domain)	Measure	Best	QASSIT	Rank
Environment (Eurovoc)	Fscore	**0.2992**	0.1725	4/5
	F&M	0.2384	**0.4349**	1/5
Science	Fscore	**0.3669**	0.2165	3/5
	F&M	0.3634	**0.5757**	1/5
Science (Eurovoc)	Fscore	**0.3118**	0.2431	3/5
	F&M	**0.3893**	0.3893	1/5
Science (Wordnet)	Fscore	**0.3776**	0.2384	4/5
	F&M	**0.2255**	**0.2255**	1/5

embedding (Mikolov et al., 2013). These vectors are extracted using an unsupervised framework from large amounts of text information. The main characteristic of these vectors are their ability to encode semantic similarities in a rather small vector (300 dimensions) for each word or multi-word present in the corpus. In our experiments we have used a set of pre-trained vectors over an open domain collection [2]. We have searched by each corresponding term and assigned only one vector to it. If the term is a composed term and it is not found in the pre-trained set them the sum of vectors related to each word that compose the term is used. Following this strategy near to 95% of the terms have an assigned vector. Similarities between vectors are computed using the cosine similarity.

Second, we have extracted the collocation values between terms, to do so we have used the english subpart of wikipedia.org for frequency counts extraction. For each pair of terms (x, y), we retrieve the number of wikipedia pages where both terms occur (hits(x, y)). For example, hits(memory, politics) is retrieved with the following query ["memory" AND "politics"].

Finally, the partial knowledge[3] has been obtained by first extracting a list of candidate subsumption pairs observing suffix matching and then by manually correcting the candidate list and/or adding new pairs of subsumptions with the aim to reach at least two hundreds subsumption relations into S.

Each of the three previous sources led to a couple of (non-symetric) binary relations over the set of terms E. Finally, sixteen binary relations are given as input of the LPS framework in order to learn a relevant pretopological space.

3 Experiments and results

Manual and automatic evaluation were performed using four datasets[4]. Further details could be found in (Bordea et al., 2016). The automatic evaluation is based on the comparison of the proposed taxonomy against the respective gold standard. Several automatic metric were used by the task organizers. However, we have focused on more robust metrics such as $Fscore = 2(P * R)/(P + R)$ and $F\&M$. Results for the best[5] participant (Best column) and ours (QASSIT column) are reported in Table 1. Similarly, manual quality evaluation is performed over a random selection of hundred ISA relationships found in the proposed taxonomies. Each of these hundred relationship is binary evaluated as relevant or not. The used metric is $P_m = |correctISA|/100$ which calculates the accuracy of the taxonomies. Results for the best participant (Best column) and ours (QASSIT column) are presented in Table 2. In both tables the column *Rank* correspond to the obtained rank when compared with the other participants.

4 Discussion

In the general ranking our algorithm achieves the second position over the five participants in the Taxonomy Extraction Evaluation task; full results are

---

[2]Publicly available at https://code.google.com/archive/p/word2vec/ .

[3]Note that this is an expensive manual task. In future version we plan to eliminate this stage.

[4]The task include six datasets, however we have participated only in four of them.

[5]Best from the results obtained by (Tan et al., 2016), (Pocostales, 2016), JUNLP and (Panchenko and Biemann, 2016).

Table 2: Comparative manual evaluation over 100 randomly selected candidates.

Dataset (Domain)	Best	QASSIT	Rank
Environment (Eurovoc)	**0.22**	0.07	4/5
Science	**0.71**	0.07	4/5
Science (Eurovoc)	0.04	**0.05**	1/5
Science (Wordnet)	**0.47**	0.22	2/5

included in (Bordea et al., 2016), but it can be partially observed in Table 1. Our results outperform other participants in terms of F&M, but fails to obtain a similar performance in terms of $Fscore$. Note that the average of the column rank is 2,25 indicating that if only these metrics where considered our position remains the same. Indeed, in the evaluation many others factor were evaluated such as: Cyclicity, Categorisation (i.i.), Connectivity (c.c.) and domains. Our results are also good in all them where we obtain first or second best performance, except for Categorisation (i.i.) where we are the least performing team. Indeed, this can be explained by our choice of these objective functions that are driven by the partial knowledge. Due to the cost required to generate this partial knowledge, the manual annotators tend to relate one concept to many concepts which force some flatness in our taxonomy. However, the $I_{structure}$ objective criteria tends to force the acquisition of a hierarchical structure. In future experiments we plan to include additional objectives to avoid this situation.

In terms of manual evaluation, we obtain good results only for the *Science (Eurovoc)* dataset where our algorithm get the best performance. One explanation is the random selection of only hundred relationships to evaluate. Note that this sample is small compared with the actual number of terms in each dataset. However, only one of the participants manage to get good results in the manual evaluation. For the *Science dataset*, the ordered results of all participants are: 0.71, 0.14, 0.09, 0.07 and 0.06. Note that our performance, 0.07, is not very far from 3th and 5th position, but clearly far form the first one. This situation is quite similar for the *Enviromment (Eurovoc)* dataset, where the missing values of Table 2 are 0.02, 0.08 and 0.11. Note that, again, the best performance is clearly far from the other participants. A deeper analysis over the selection of the

sample for manual annotation or a full manual evaluation[6] must be performed to grasp a better understanding of these differences.

5 Conclusion

In this paper we presented the participation of the QASSIT team in the "Taxonomy Extraction Evaluation (TExEval-2)" task. Our strategy is based on a semi-supervised pretopological framework that learns a subsumption propagation process over a set of terms described by association measures and semantic vectors as input. Our results achieve the best performances in terms of $F\&M$ metric over the four datasets. In the general ranking, our algorithm achieved the second position. In terms of the manual evaluation, we obtained the first position for the Science (Eurovoc) dataset, second position for the Science (Wordnet) and fourth position for the remaining two datasets. Results encourage us to continue the exploration of strategies based on the theory of pretopoly and their combination with external resources. However, in future versions of our algorithm we plan to eliminate or automatize the partial knowledge extraction to have a fully automatic taxonomy construction framework.

References

Georgeta Bordea, Els Lefever, and Paul Buitelaar. 2016. Semeval-2016 task 13: Taxonomy extraction evaluation (texeval-2). In *Proceedings of the 10th International Workshop on Semantic Evaluation*. Association for Computational Linguistics.

Guillaume Cleuziou and Gaël Dias. 2015. Learning pretopological spaces for lexical taxonomy acquisition. In *Machine Learning and Knowledge Discovery in Databases: European Conference, ECML PKDD 2015, Porto, Portugal, September 7-11, 2015, Proceedings, Part II*, pages 493–508.

Guillaume Cleuziou, Davide Buscaldi, Vincent Levorato, Gaël Dias, and Christine Largeron. 2015. QASSIT: A Pretopological Framework for the Automatic Construction of Lexical Taxonomies from Raw Texts. In *International Workshop on Semantic Evaluation (SEMEVAL 2015)*, Denver, United States.

Marti A. Hearst. 1992. Automatic acquisition of hyponyms from large text corpora. In *Proceedings of the*

---

[6]This clearly increases the annotation cost for the task organizers.

14th Conference on Computational Linguistics - Volume 2, COLING '92, pages 539–545.

Tomas Mikolov, Ilya Sutskever, Kai Chen, Greg S Corrado, and Jeff Dean. 2013. Distributed representations of words and phrases and their compositionality. In *Advances in Neural Information Processing Systems 26*, pages 3111–3119.

Stefano Ruppert Eugen Remus Steffen Naets Hubert Fairon Cedrick Ponzetto Simone Paolo Panchenko, Alexander Faralli and Chris Biemann. 2016. TAXI at SemEval-2016 Task 13: a Taxonomy Induction Method based on Lexico-Syntactic Patterns, Substrings and Focused Crawling. In *Proceedings of the 10th International Workshop on Semantic Evaluation*. Association for Computational Linguistics.

Joel Pocostales. 2016. NUIG-UNLP at SemEval-2016 Task 13: A Simple Word Embedding-based Approach for Taxonomy Extraction. In *Proceedings of the 10th International Workshop on Semantic Evaluation*. Association for Computational Linguistics.

Liling Tan, Francis Bond, and Josef van Genabith. 2016. USAAR at SemEval-2016 Task 13: Hyponym Endocentricity. In *Proceedings of the 10th International Workshop on Semantic Evaluation (SemEval 2016)*. Association for Computational Linguistics.

TAXI at SemEval-2016 Task 13: a Taxonomy Induction Method based on Lexico-Syntactic Patterns, Substrings and Focused Crawling

Alexander Panchenko[1], Stefano Faralli[2], Eugen Ruppert[1], Steffen Remus[1], Hubert Naets[3], Cédrick Fairon[3], Simone Paolo Ponzetto[2] and Chris Biemann[1]

[1]TU Darmstadt,   [2]Mannheim University,   [3]UCLouvain,
LT Group, Germany   Web and Data Science, Germany   CENTAL, Belgium
panchenko@lt.informatik.tu-darmstadt.de

Abstract

We present a system for taxonomy construction that reached the first place in all subtasks of the SemEval 2016 challenge on Taxonomy Extraction Evaluation. Our simple yet effective approach harvests hypernyms with substring inclusion and Hearst-style lexico-syntactic patterns from domain-specific texts obtained via language model based focused crawling. Extracted taxonomies are evaluated on English, Dutch, French and Italian for three domains each (Food, Environment and Science). Evaluations against a gold standard and by human judgment show that our method outperforms more complex and knowledge-rich approaches on most domains and languages. Furthermore, to adapt the method to a new domain or language, only a small amount of manual labour is needed.

1 Introduction

In this paper, we describe TAXI – a taxonomy induction method first presented at the SemEval 2016 challenge on Taxonomy Extraction Evaluation (Bordea et al., 2016). We consider taxonomy induction as a process that should – as much as possible – be driven solely on the basis of raw text processing. While some labeled examples might be utilized to tune the extraction and induction process, we avoid relying on structured lexical resources such as WordNet (Miller, 1995) or BabelNet (Navigli and Ponzetto, 2010). We rather envision a situation where a taxonomy shall be induced in a new domain or a new language for which such resources do not

exist. In this paper, we demonstrate our methodology based on hyponym extraction from substrings and general-domain and domain-specific corpora for four languages and three domains.

2 Related Work

The extraction of taxonomic relationships from text is a long-standing challenge in ontology learning, see e.g. Biemann (2005) for a survey. The literature on hypernym extraction offers a high variability of methods, from simple lexical patterns (Hearst, 1992; Oakes, 2005), similar to those used in our method, to complex statistical techniques (Agirre et al., 2000; Ritter et al., 2009).

Snow et al. (2004) use sentences that contain two terms which are known to be hypernyms. They parse sentences and extract patterns from the parse trees. Finally, they train a hypernym classifier based on these features and applied to text corpora.

Yang and Callan (2009) presented a semi-supervised taxonomy induction framework that integrates co-occurrence, syntactic dependencies, lexical-syntactic patterns and other features to learn an ontology metric, calculated in terms of the semantic distance for each pair of terms in a taxonomy. Terms are incrementally clustered on the basis of their ontology metric scores.

Snow et al. (2006) perform incremental construction of taxonomies using a probabilistic model. They combine evidence from multiple supervised classifiers trained on large training datasets of hyponymy and co-hyponymy relations. The taxonomy learning task is defined as the problem of finding the taxonomy that maximizes the probability of individ-

Proceedings of SemEval-2016, pages 1320–1327,
San Diego, California, June 16-17, 2016. ©2016 Association for Computational Linguistics

ual relations extracted by the classifiers.

Kozareva and Hovy (2010) start from a set of root terms and use Hearst-like lexico-syntactic patterns to harvest hypernyms from the Web. The extracted hypernym relation graph is subsequently pruned.

Veraldi et al. (2013) proposed a graph-based algorithm to learn a taxonomy from textual definitions, extracted from a corpus and the Web. An optimal branching algorithm is used to induce a taxonomy.

Finally, Bordea et al. (2015) introduced the first shared task on Taxonomy Extraction Evaluation to provide a common ground for evaluation. Six systems participated in the competition. The top system in this challange used features based on substrings and co-occurrence statistics (Grefenstette, 2015). Lefever et al. (2015) reached the second place gathered hypernyms from patterns, substrings and Word-Net. Tan et al. (2015) used word embeddings, reaching the third place.

3 Taxonomy Induction Method

Our approach is characterized by scalability and simplicity, assuming that being able to process larger input data is more important than the sophisticated extraction inference. Our approach to taxonomy induction takes as input a set of domain terms and general-domain text corpora and outputs a taxonomy. It consists of four steps. Firstly, we crawl domain-specific corpora based on terminology of the target domain (see Section 3.1). These complement general-purpose corpora, like texts of Wikipedia articles. Secondly, candidate hypernyms are extracted based on substrings and lexico-syntactic patterns (see Section 3.2). Thirdly, the candidates are pruned so that each term has only a few most salient hypernyms (see Section 3.3). The last step performs optimization of the overall taxonomy structure removing cycles and linking disconnected components to the root (see Section 3.4).

3.1 Corpora for Taxonomy Induction

To build domain-specific taxonomies we use both general and domain-specific corpora.

General Domain Corpora. We use three general purpose corpora in our approach presented in Table 1: Wikipedia, 59G and CommonCrawl[1].

---

[1] https://commoncrawl.org

	EN	FR	NL	IT
Wikipedia	11.0	3.2	1.4	3.0
59G	59.2	–	–	–
CommonCrawl	168000.0 ‡	–	–	–
FocusedCrawl Food	22.8	7.9	3.4	3.6
FocusedCrawl Environment	23.9	8.9	2.0	7.1
FocusedCrawl Science	8.8	5.4	6.6	5.1

Table 1: Corpora sizes used in our system in GB, where ‡is the size of the crawl archive.

The second corpus is a concatenation of the English Wikipedia, Gigaword (Parker et al., 2009), ukWaC (Ferraresi et al., 2008) and a news corpora from the Leipzig Collection (Goldhahn et al., 2012).

Domain-Specific Corpora. Lefever (2015) showed the usefulness for taxonomy extraction of domain dependent corpora crawled from the Web using *BootCat* (Baroni and Bernardini, 2004). This method takes terms as input, which are randomly combined into sequences of a pre-defined length, and sent to a Web search engine. The search results, i.e. the returned URLs, compose a domain-dependent corpus. The number of input terms, the number of queries and the amount of desired URLs impact the size of the corpus. With 1,000 web queries and 10 URLs per query, the expected size of the resulting corpus is around 300 MB. While Lefever (2015) shows that such small in-domain corpora can be already useful for taxonomy extraction, we assumed that better results can be obtained if bigger domain-specific corpora are used.

We therefore follow a different approach based on *focused crawling*, where *BootCat* is used only for initialization of seed URLs. We use the provided taxonomy terms as input for the *BootCat* method, generate 1,000 random triples, and use the retrieved URLs as a starting point for further crawling. Focused crawling is an extension to standard web crawling where URLs, expected to point to relevant web documents, are prioritized for download (Chakrabarti et al., 1999).

Remus and Biemann (2016) introduced a focused crawling approach based on language modeling. The idea is that relevant web documents refer to other relevant web documents, where the relevance of a web document is computed by considering a statistical n-gram language model of a small, initially provided, domain-defining corpus. We provide a domain-defining corpus for each category by using Wikipedia articles, that are directly contained in the matching Wikipedia category. For example, for the the Food domain we used the Wikipedia articles of *Category:Foods* to build a language model of the Food domain. The language models for each domain were created using the 5-gram with the Kneser-Ney (1995) smoothing.

Using this technique, we are able to iteratively follow promising URLs and download web pages until a specified stopping criterion (no more pages with desired perplexity or timeout). Each domain and language was crawled for about one week on a single server machine with 24 cores and 32GB RAM, and harvested between 130 and 800 GB raw content, which results in 2 to 23 GB of unique plaintext sentences (c.f. Table 1). Note, that these sentences might contain cross-domain content.

3.2 Candidate Hypernyms via Substrings

A simple yet precise method for hypernym extraction is based on substring matching, c.f. the baseline system in Table 3 and (Lefever, 2015). For instance, "biomedical science" is a "science", "microbiology" is a "biology" and so on. We calculate the following substring-based hypernymy score $\sigma(t_i, t_j)$ between a pair of candidate terms t_i, t_j:

$$\sigma(t_i, t_j) = \begin{cases} \frac{length(t_j)}{length(t_i)} & \text{if } m(t_i, t_j) \wedge \neg m(t_j, t_i) \\ 0 & \text{otherwise} \end{cases}$$

Here $m(t_i, t_j)$ is a function that returns true in case of a match of the term t_i inside the term t_j. Such match happens if $length(t_i)$ is greater than 3. For English and Dutch, the hypernym t_i should match in the end of hyponym t_j, e.g. "natural science" is a "science". For French and Italian a match of hypernym should be in the beginning of hyponym e.g. "algèbre linéaire" is a "algèbre", not "linéaire". The same holds for English and Dutch if a hyponym contains a preposition e.g.: "toast with bacon" is a "toast", not "bacon" or "brood van gekiemd graan" is "brood", not "graan". Finally, if no match is found, we lemmatize terms t_i and t_j and retry matching. The precision-recall curve of the substring score calculated on the trial dataset is presented in Figure 1. As one can observe, precision of the substring score is constantly high, reaching 0.91 at the recall level of 0.29 with AUC of 0.61. There-

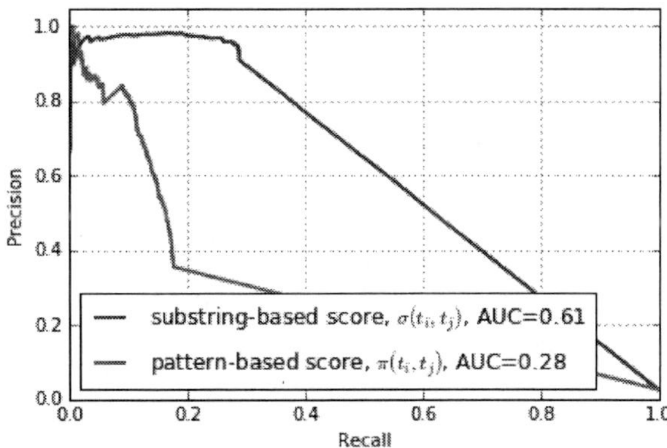

Figure 1: Precision-Recall plots of substring-based and pattern-based features of the TAXI approach measured on the trial dataset.

fore, this score is able to retrieve a significant number of high-quality hypernyms. Yet, only hypernyms of compound words can be retrieved via substrings.

3.3 Candidate Hypernyms via Patterns

To extract candidate hypernym relations from texts we used three systems listed below. All of them rely on lexico-syntactic patterns in the fashion of (Hearst, 1992; Klaussner and Zhekova, 2011). We used several systems to filter noise via complementary signals. Besides, not all the systems support all the four languages of the SemEval task. Porting of Hearst patterns to a new European language is a straightforward and relatively quick procedure. Yet, due to a dense SemEval schedule, we decided to implement new rules only for two languages not supported by any available system, namely Italian and Dutch and reuse extraction rules for other languages.

PattaMaika. This system was used to process English, Italian and Dutch corpora. It implements patterns using UIMA Ruta (Kluegl et al., 2014). First, part-of-speech information is used to assign noun phrase (NP) chunk annotations to nominal phrases. Next, we use patterns to identify hypernym relations between NP chunks. We adapted the 9 English rules to the target languages, resulting in 9 patterns for Italian and 8 patterns for Dutch.

PatternSim. This system was used to process English and French corpora. It encodes patterns in the form of finite state transducers implemented with the Unitex corpus processor.[2] PatternSim relies on 10 English patterns yielding average precision of top 5 extracted semantic relations per word of 0.69 (Panchenko et al., 2012). For French, 9 hypernym extraction patterns are used providing precision at top 5 of 0.63 (Panchenko et al., 2013).

WebISA. In addition to *PattaMaika* and *PatternSim*, we used a publicly available database of English hypernym relations extracted from the CommonCrawl corpus (Seitner et al., 2016). We used 108 million hypernym relations with frequency above one. This collection of relations was harvested using a regexp-based implementation of 59 patterns collected from the literature.

Combination of hypernyms. Result of the extraction are 18 collections of hypernym relations listed in Table 2. Even the huge *WebISA* collection extracted from tens of terabytes of text does not provide hypernyms for all rare taxonomic terms, such as "ground and whole bean coffee" and "black sesame rice cake". On the other hand, most of the collections contain many noisy relations. For instance, frequent relations for hypernyms often go in both directions, e.g. "history" is a "science", but also "science" is a "history". Therefore, we introduced an asymmetric pattern-based hypernymy score $\pi(t_i, t_j)$ between terms t_i and t_j. It combines information from different hypernym collections to filter noisy extractions. To compute the score, first we normalize extraction counts on the per word basis: $\pi^k(t_i, t_j) = \frac{freq^k(t_i, t_j)}{\max_j freq^k(t_i, t_j)}$, where $freq^k(t_i, t_j)$ is the number of relations extracted between terms t_i and t_j by the k-th extractor. These normalized scores are averaged across all extractors per language-domain pair: $\bar{\pi}(t_i, t_j) = \frac{1}{|LD|} \sum_{k \in LD} \pi^k(t_i, t_j)$, where LD is a set of hypernym collections relevant for a given language-domain pair. For instance, for the language-domain pair "English-Food", the LD contains four collections: general relations extracted by *PatternSim*, *PattaMaika* and *WebISA* plus domain-specific relations extracted by *PatternSim* (see Table 2). Finally, to get the pattern-based score, we subtract averaged scores of two terms in both directions: $\pi(t_i, t_j) = \bar{\pi}(t_i, t_j) - \bar{\pi}(t_j, t_i)$. This way, we downrank symmetrical relations like synonyms and co-hyponyms.

---

[2]http://www-igm.univ-mlv.fr/~unitex

	EN ‡, †,§	FR‡	NL†	IT†
General	27.6‡, 4.9†, 118.9§	3.2	2.22	0.13
Food	24.1‡	3.8	0.47	0.05
Environment	26.3‡	4.5	0.32	0.95
Science	9.3‡	2.7	0.97	0.05

Table 2: Number of hypernyms in millions of relations. Systems used to extract respective hypernym collections are denoted with ‡for *PatternSim*, †for *PattaMaika* and § for *WebISA*.

The precision-recall curve of the pattern-based score on the trial data is presented in Figure 1. This plot is calculated on general corpora as we did not crawl domain specific corpora for the trial dataset domains. As one can see, precision of 0.80 is achieved at recall of 0.15 or less and drops to 0.36 at recall of 0.19. AUC of 0.28 of is less than half of the substring-based score of 0.61. Thus, patterns are a less reliable source of hypernyms than the substrings. Yet, they can capture relations between words with different spelling like "apple" and "fruit", while the substring-based score need a character overlap, like in "grapefruit" and "fruit".

3.4 Pruning of Hypernyms

Patterns and substrings together yield up to several hundreds of hypernym candidates per term. This step prunes hypernym candidates, ranking them with an unsupervised and supervised combinations of the $\sigma(t_i, t_j)$ and $\pi(t_i, t_j)$ scores.

Unsupervised Pruning. In this pruning strategy, used for French, Dutch and Italian languages, a term t_i is a hypernym of term t_j if their substring score $\sigma(t_i, t_j)$ is greater than zero or if rank of the term t_i according to the pattern-based score $\pi(t_i, t_j)$ equals to one or two. Thus a term t_i obtains all hypernyms extracted by substrings and up to two hypernyms extracted by patterns.

Supervised Pruning. This pruning strategy used for English relies on a supervised classifier trained on the trial dataset (Bordea et al., 2016). [3] This pruning approach uses 3,249 hypernymy relations from the trial taxonomies as positive training samples, e.g. hypernym relation ("biology", "science") and 128,183 automatically generated relations as negatives samples coming from two sources: 3,249 in-

---

[3]We did not submit to SemEval both supervised and unsupervised versions of the system for English as only one run was allowed per language-domain pair.

verted hypernyms, such as ("science", "biology") plus 124,934 co-hyponyms from the trial taxonomy, for instance ("biology", "mathematics").

The classifier used in the competition had two features that characterize a word pair (t_i, t_j), namely substring-, and pattern-based scores $\sigma(t_i, t_j)$ and $\pi(t_i, t_j)$. Note, that the same features were used in the unsupervised approach. We applied an SVM classifier with RBF kernel (Vert et al., 2004), tuning kernel meta-parameters within an internal loop cross-validation procedure.

We tested multiple alternative configurations with extra features, including term frequency, out/in degree of terms in the hypernym graph, term length, expansions of hypernyms based on term clustering and shortest paths in the graph of candidate hypernyms as well as other classifiers including Logistic Regression, Gradient Boosted Trees, and Random Forest. However, none of the above mentioned configurations yielded consistently better results on the trial data than the two feature-based SVM.

To identify hypernyms among a set of terms T, we classify using a model trained on the trial data all possible word pairs except identical ones: $\{(t_i, t_j) : i \neq j; (t_i, t_j) \in T \times T\}$. The pairs classified using the positive class are added to the taxonomy.

3.5 Taxonomy Construction

At this point of the taxonomy construction, we obtained a noisy graph, which may contain cycles and disconnected components. To remove cycles and to obtain a directed acyclic graph taxonomy we used the unsupervised graph pruning approach of Faralli et al. (2015), which searches for a cycle C using topological sorting of Tarjan (1972) and then removes a random edge of C until no cycles are detected in the graph.

Besides, to improve connectivity of the taxonomy we connect all the nodes of each disconnected component with zero out degree to the taxonomy root.

4 Evaluation

To assess quality of the taxonomies several complementary measures were used. The first type of measurements are structural measures, such as the number of connected components (c.c.), the number of intermediate nodes (i.i.), i.e. the number of

nodes with out degree equal to zero, and the presence of cycles. Second, system outputs were compared against the corresponding domain gold standards and performances are evaluated in terms of F-score. Here precision and recall are based on the number of edges in common with the gold standard taxonomy over the number of system edges and over the number of gold standard edges respectively. To better compare against gold standard taxonomies the task included the evaluation of a cumulative measure (Velardi et al., 2013), namely Cumulative Fowlkes & Mallows Measure (F&M), where the similarity between the system and the reference taxonomies are measured as the combination of the hierarchical cluster similarities. Finally, the organizers performed manual quality assessment to estimate the precision of the hypernyms. To compute this measure, annotators labeled a sample of 100 hypernym relations as correct or wrong. The taxonomy extraction was evaluated on four languages, namely English, Dutch, French and Italian, and three different domains (Food, Science and Environment). A detailed description of the evaluation settings and metrics can be found in (Bordea et al., 2016).

5 Results

Table 3 presents a summary of evaluation of our method on the SemEval 2016 Task 13 dataset. Overall 5 systems participated in the challenge: JUNLP, TAXI, NUIG-UNLP, USAAR and QASITT. We represent the respective best scores across our four competitors in the *BestComp* column.

Gold Standard Comparison. The organizer-provided *Baseline* system implemented a string inclusion approach that covers relations between compound terms. A similar mechanism was used by the USAAR system (Tan et al., 2016), which improved over the baseline in terms of precision at the cost of recall. USAAR achieved the highest precision scores for English, as they used substring-based methods that yield high precision (c.f. Figure 1). Yet substrings cannot retrieve hypernyms of non-compound terms.

The main mechanisms we added in TAXI with regard to the substring-based methods are statistics over pattern-based extractions over large domain specific corpora and our taxonomy construction step

	Monolingual (EN)			Multilingual (NL, FR, IT)		
Measure	**Baseline**	**BestComp**	**TAXI**	**Baseline**	**BestComp**	**TAXI**
Cyclicity	*0*	**0**	**0**	*0*	**0**	**0**
Structure (F&M)	*0.005*	**0.406**	0.291	*0.009*	0.016	**0.189**
Categorisation (i.i.)	*77.67*	**377.00**	104.50	*64.28*	**178.22**	64.94
Connectivity (c.c.)	*36.83*	44.75	**1 .00**	*40.50*	34.89	**1.00**
Gold standard comparison (Fscore)	*0.330*	0.260	**0.320**	*0.009*	0.016	**0.189**
Manual Evaluation (Precision)	*n.a.*	**0.490**	0.200	*n.a.*	0.298	**0.625**

Table 3: Overall scores obtained by averaging the results over domains (Environment, Science, Food) and languages (NL, FR, IT) for the multilingual setting. The *BestComp* lists the respective best scores across four our competitors. The best scores excluding the baseline are set in boldface. Definitions of the measures are available in Section 4.

that improves structure of the resource. These united mechanisms are not used in other submissions to the challenge. The NUIG-UNLP team (Pocostales, 2016) relies on vector directionality in dense word embedding spaces. Such approximation of patterns based on distributional similarity provided good recall, but attained low precision.

The QASSIT team (Cleuziou and Moreno, 2016), who ranked second in the competition, uses patterns to extract hypernym candidates, but they rely solely on the Wikipedia. Subsequently, an optimization technique based on genetic algorithms is used to learn the parametrization of a so-called pre-topological space, which leads to desired structural properties of the resulting taxonomy. While we use simpler optimization procedure based on supervised learning, TAXI outperforms QASSIT in terms of comparisons with the gold standard. Possible reasons why our method performs better are (1) QASSIT use no substring features, (2) this team relies on smaller general-purpose corpora, while we use larger domain-specific corpora.

Finally, JUNLP relies on substrings and relations extracted from BabelNet. We find the latter to be undesirable for taxonomy extraction. Indeed, a rich lexical resource, such as BabelNet can be considered as a taxonomy in itself. Interestingly, even with the BabelNet-based features the system did not always reach the top precision and recall.

Manual Evaluation. Our system was ranked first in terms of manual judgments for the Dutch, Italan and French reaching the average precision across languages and domains of 0.625. Precision for different language-domain pairs ranged from 0.90 for the Italian-Science pair to 0.23 for the French-Environment pair. For English, our system was ranked second with the average score of 0.20, while the substring-based USAAR system obtained the score of 0.49 and the third-ranked system obtained the score of 0.09. We attribute lower precision in the English run to absence in the supervised ranking scheme of a limit on the number of extracted hypernyms per word.

Further detailed comparisons with other systems with breakdowns with regard to different languages, domains and evaluation schemes are presented by Bordea et al. (2016) and on SemEval website.[4]

Discussion. One shortcoming of our method is its coverage: for instance 774 terms of 1,555 of the English food domain are still not attached to any node, which is a typical issue with pattern-based approaches since not all taxonomic relationships are spelled out explicitly in corpora. To tackle this shortcoming, we plan to use hypernym expansion based on distributional semantics (Biemann and Riedl, 2013).

6 Conclusion

We presented a technique for taxonomy induction from a domain vocabulary. It extracts hypernyms from substrings and large domain-specific corpora bootstrapped from the input vocabulary. Multiple evaluations based on the SemEval taxonomy extraction datasets of four languages and three domains show state-of-the-art performance of our approach. An implementation of our method featuring all language resources, is available for download.[5]

Acknowledgments

We acknowledge the support of the Deutsche Forschungsgemeinschaft under the JOIN-T project.

---

[4] http://alt.qcri.org/semeval2016/task13
[5] http://tudarmstadt-lt.github.io/taxi

References

Eneko Agirre, Olatz Ansa, Eduard H. Hovy, and David Martínez. 2000. Enriching very large ontologies using the WWW. In *ECAI Workshop on Ontology Learning*, pages 28–33, Berlin, Germany.

Marco Baroni and Silvia Bernardini. 2004. BootCaT: Bootstrapping corpora and terms from the web. In *Proceedings of the 4th International Conference on Language Resources and Evaluation (LREC)*, pages 1313–1316, Lisbon, Portugal.

Chris Biemann and Martin Riedl. 2013. Text: Now in 2D! a framework for lexical expansion with contextual similarity. *Journal of Language Modelling*, 1(1):55–95.

Chris Biemann. 2005. Ontology Learning from Text: A Survey of Methods. *LDV Forum*, 20(2):75–93.

Georgeta Bordea, Paul Buitelaar, Stefano Faralli, and Roberto Navigli. 2015. Semeval-2015 task 17: Taxonomy extraction evaluation (TExEval). *SemEval-2015*, 452(465):902–910.

Georgeta Bordea, Els Lefever, and Paul Buitelaar. 2016. Semeval-2016 task 13: Taxonomy extraction evaluation (TExEval-2). In *Proceedings of the 10th International Workshop on Semantic Evaluation*, San Diego, CA, USA.

Soumen Chakrabarti, Martin van den Berg, and Byron Dom. 1999. Focused crawling: a new approach to topic-specific web resource discovery. *Computer Networks*, 31(11–16):1623–1640.

Guillaume Cleuziou and Jose G. Moreno. 2016. QASSIT at SemEval-2016 Task 13: On the integration of Semantic Vectors in Pretopological Spaces for Lexical Taxonomy Acquisition. In *Proceedings of the 10th International Workshop on Semantic Evaluation (SemEval 2016)*. Association for Computational Linguistics, June.

Stefano Faralli, Giovanni Stilo, and Paola Velardi. 2015. Large scale homophily analysis in twitter using a twixonomy. In *Proceedings of the Twenty-Fourth International Joint Conference on Artificial Intelligence, IJCAI 2015*, pages 2334–2340, Buenos Aires, Argentina.

Adriano Ferraresi, Eros Zanchetta, Marco Baroni, and Silvia Bernardini. 2008. Introducing and evaluating ukWaC, a very large web-derived corpus of English. In *Proceedings of the 4th Web as Corpus Workshop (WAC-4) Can we beat Google*, pages 47–54, Marakech, Morocco.

Dirk Goldhahn, Thomas Eckart, and Uwe Quasthoff. 2012. Building Large Monolingual Dictionaries at the Leipzig Corpora Collection: From 100 to 200 Languages. In *Proceedings of the Eight International Conference on Language Resources and Evaluation (LREC'12)*, pages 759–765, Istanbul, Turkey.

Gregory Grefenstette. 2015. INRIASAC: Simple hypernym extraction methods. *SemEval-2015*, pages 911–914.

Marti A Hearst. 1992. Automatic acquisition of hyponyms from large text corpora. In *Proceedings of the 14th conference on Computational linguistics-Volume 2*, pages 539–545.

Carmen Klaussner and Desislava Zhekova. 2011. Lexico-syntactic patterns for automatic ontology building. In *Student Research Workshop at RANLP 2011*, pages 109–114.

Peter Kluegl, Martin Toepfer, Philip-Daniel Beck, Georg Fette, and Frank Puppe. 2014. UIMA Ruta: Rapid development of rule-based information extraction applications. *Natural Language Engineering*, 22(1):1–40.

Reinhard Kneser and Hermann Ney. 1995. Improved backing-off for m-gram language modeling. In *Acoustics, Speech, and Signal Processing, 1995. ICASSP-95., 1995 International Conference on*, volume 1, pages 181–184. IEEE.

Zornitsa Kozareva and Eduard Hovy. 2010. Learning arguments and supertypes of semantic relations using recursive patterns. In *Proceedings of the 48th Annual Meeting of the Association for Computational Linguistics (ACL)*, pages 1482–1491, Uppsala, Sweden.

Els Lefever. 2015. LT3: a multi-modular approach to automatic taxonomy construction. *SemEval-2015*, pages 944–948.

George A Miller. 1995. Wordnet: a lexical database for english. *Communications of the ACM*, 38(11):39–41.

Roberto Navigli and Simone Paolo Ponzetto. 2010. BabelNet: building a very large multilingual semantic network. In *Proceedings of the 48th Annual Meeting of the Association for Computational Linguistics (ACL)*, pages 216–225, Uppsala, Sweden.

Michael P. Oakes. 2005. Using Hearst's rules for the automatic acquisition of hyponyms for mining a pharmaceutical corpus. In *RANLP Text Mining Workshop'05*, pages 63–67, Borovets, Bulgaria.

Alexander Panchenko, Olga Morozova, and Hubert Naets. 2012. A semantic similarity measure based on lexico-syntactic patterns. In Jeremy Jancsary, editor, *Proceedings of KONVENS 2012*, pages 174–178, Vienna, Austria. ÖGAI. Main track: poster presentations.

Alexander Panchenko, Hubert Naets, Laetitia Brouwers, Pavel Romanov, and Cédrick Fairon. 2013. Recherche et visualisation de mots sémantiquement liés. In *Proceedings of the TALN-RÉCITAL 2013*, pages 747–754, Les Sables d'Olonne, France.

Robert Parker, David Graff, Junbo Kong, Ke Chen, and Kazuaki Maeda. 2009. *English gigaword fourth edition*. Linguistic Data Consortium, Philadelphia, USA.

Joel Pocostales. 2016. NUIG-UNLP at SemEval-2016 Task 13: A Simple Word Embedding-based Approach for Taxonomy Extraction. In *Proceedings of the 10th International Workshop on Semantic Evaluation*. Association for Computational Linguistics.

Steffen Remus and Chris Biemann. 2016. Domain-specific corpus expansion with focused webcrawling. In *Proceedings of the 10th International Conference on Language Resources and Evaluation (LREC)*, Portorož, Slovenia.

Alan Ritter, Stephen Soderland, and Oren Etzioni. 2009. What is this, anyway: Automatic hypernym discovery. In *Proceedings of the 2009 AAAI Spring Symposium on Learning by Reading and Learning to Read*, pages 88–93, Palo Alto, California.

Julian Seitner, Christian Bizer, Kai Eckert, Stefano Faralli, Robert Meusel, Heiko Paulheim, and Simone Ponzetto. 2016. A Large DataBase of Hypernymy Relations Extracted from the Web. In *Proceedings of the 10th edition of the Language Resources and Evaluation Conference*, Portorož, Slovenia.

Rion Snow, Daniel Jurafsky, and Andrew Y. Ng. 2004. Learning syntactic patterns for automatic hypernym discovery. In Lawrence K. Saul, Yair Weiss, and Léon Bottou, editors, *Proc. of NIPS 2004*, pages 1297–1304, Cambridge, Mass. MIT Press.

Rion Snow, Dan Jurafsky, and Andrew Ng. 2006. Semantic taxonomy induction from heterogeneous evidence. In *Proceedings of COLING-ACL 2006*, pages 801–808, Sydney, Australia.

Liling Tan, Rohit Gupta, and Josef van Genabith. 2015. USAAR-WLV: hypernym generation with deep neural nets. *SemEval-2015*, pages 932–937.

Liling Tan, Francis Bond, and Josef van Genabith. 2016. USAAR at SemEval-2016 Task 13: Hyponym Endocentricity. In *Proceedings of the 10th International Workshop on Semantic Evaluation (SemEval 2016)*. Association for Computational Linguistics.

Robert Tarjan. 1972. Depth-first search and linear graph algorithms. *SIAM Journal on Computing*, 1:146–160.

Paola Velardi, Stefano Faralli, and Roberto Navigli. 2013. Ontolearn reloaded: A graph-based algorithm for taxonomy induction. *Computational Linguistics*, 39(3):665–707.

Jean-Philippe Vert, Koji Tsuda, and Bernhard Schölkopf. 2004. A primer on kernel methods. In Bernhard Schlkopf, Koji Tsuda, and Jean-Philippe Vert, editors, *Kernel Methods in Computational Biology*, pages 35–70. Cambridge, MA: MIT Press.

Hui Yang and Jamie Callan. 2009. A metric-based framework for automatic taxonomy induction. In *Proceedings of the Joint Conference of the 47th Annual Meeting of the Association for Computational Linguistics (ACL) and the 4th International Joint Conference on Natural Language Processing of the Asian Federation of Natural Language Processing (IJCNLP)*, pages 271–279, Suntec, Singapore.

Duluth at SemEval–2016 Task 14 :
Extending Gloss Overlaps to Enrich Semantic Taxonomies

Ted Pedersen
Department of Computer Science
University of Minnesota
Duluth, MN, 55812 USA
tpederse@d.umn.edu

Abstract

This paper describes the Duluth systems that participated in Task 14 of SemEval 2016, Semantic Taxonomy Enrichment. There were three related systems in the formal evaluation which are discussed here, along with numerous post–evaluation runs. All of these systems identified synonyms between Word-Net and other dictionaries by measuring the gloss overlaps between them. These systems perform better than the random baseline and one post–evaluation variation was within a respectable margin of the median result attained by all participating systems.

1 Introduction

The goal of Task 14 in SemEval–2016 was to enrich a semantic taxonomy with new word senses. In particular, this task sought to augment WordNet[1] with senses that are present in another dictionary. Task 14 drew glosses of words not found in WordNet from a variety of sources that will collectively be referred to as OtherDict in this paper.

The method the Duluth systems took was based on scoring overlaps between WordNet and Other-Dict glosses. A OtherDict sense was assigned to the WordNet sense with the highest overlapping score. Overlaps are defined to be exact matches between words and phrases in the glosses. Each overlap is assigned a score that is the square of the number of words in the overlap, and then all the overlaps between a pair of glosses is summed to provide the final score.

___
[1]http://wordnet.princeton.edu

The premise of relying on overlaps is that senses that are defined using many of the same words are certainly related, and indeed if they are defined using the same words they are likely synonyms. This is a well established and reliable intuition that goes back at least to (Lesk, 1986). Closely related words that may not be synonyms (such as hyponyms or hypernyms) will use many of the same words in their definitions, but then have specific differentia that distinguishes among them.

Task 14 asked participants to distinguish between merging a OtherDict sense into an existing Word-Net synset (i.e, a synonym) or attaching it as a hyponym (i.e., a more specific example) of a WordNet sense. However, our systems only merge OtherDict senses into WordNet synsets. It seems clear though that this merge versus attach problem can be tackled by setting some kind of threshold for the amount of overlap, where more significant degrees of overlap should result in a synonym merge whereas less overlap could indicate a hyponym attach. As yet we have not been successful in determining a reliable method for finding such a threshold. As a result we simply assumed every OtherDict sense would attach to its closest (most overlapping) WordNet sense.

Each Duluth system carried out the same preprocessing on both the WordNet and OtherDict glosses. In addition, the WordNet glosses were extended using additional information from WordNet such as the glosses of its hypernyms, hyponyms, derived forms, and meronyms. This follows naturally from the structure of WordNet and the intuitions that underlie the Extended Gloss Overlap measure (Banerjee and Pedersen, 2003b), which is

Proceedings of SemEval-2016, pages 1328–1331,
San Diego, California, June 16-17, 2016. ©2016 Association for Computational Linguistics

implemented in WordNet::Similarity (Pedersen et al., 2004) and UMLS::Similarity (McInnes et al., 2009). Unfortunately there was not time to expand the OtherDict glosses in similar ways, although this is at least a possibility since some other dictionaries (such as Wiktionary) provide hyponyms and hypernyms, among other relations.

Task 14 allowed two kinds of systems to participate : *resource–aware* that only used dictionary content, and *constrained* that used other resources beyond dictionaries. The Duluth systems are considered resource–aware since they only use information from WordNet and OtherDict.

2 Systems

All the Duluth systems start by pre–processing both WordNet and OtherDict glosses. This consists of removing any character that is not alphanumeric, and then converting all remaining characters to lower case. Compounds known to WordNet are identified in the WordNet glosses, but not as it turns out in the OtherDict glosses. This very likely reduced the number of overlaps we found since a WordNet compound such as *light_year* will not match *light year*, which is the form that would occur in OtherDict.

In the following sections we describe the Duluth systems. Since the only distinction between them is how they reconstruct WordNet glosses we will provide a running example to illustrate each system. We will use the noun feline#n#1 for this purpose. The original WordNet entry for this sense (prior to pre–processing) is shown here :

- feline#n#1 – (any of various lithe-bodied roundheaded fissiped mammals, many with retractile claws)

- hypernym : carnivore – (a terrestrial or aquatic flesh-eating mammal; "terrestrial carnivores have four or five clawed digits on each limb")

- hyponym1 : cat, true cat – (feline mammal usually having thick soft fur and no ability to roar: domestic cats; wildcats)

- hyponym2 : big cat, cat – (any of several large cats typically able to roar and living in the wild)

- meronym : feline – (a clawed foot of an animal especially a quadruped)

- derived : feline#a#1 – (of or relating to cats; "feline fur")

The Duluth systems build upon each other to some extent, so they are presented in an order that more easily illustrates those connections rather than their numeric order (which has no particular significance).

2.1 Duluth2

Duluth2 is the most basic of the Duluth systems. Each WordNet sense is represented by its gloss where all stop words and single character words have been removed. The stoplist comes from the Ngram Statistics Package (Banerjee and Pedersen, 2003a) and includes 392 words[2].

To continue our example, the first noun sense of feline is represented by Duluth2 as shown below - it has simply gone through pre–processing and then had stop words removed.

- feline#n#1 : lithe bodied roundheaded fissiped mammals retractile claws

This system represents a baseline for the overlap measures, since we are comparing the original WordNet and OtherDict glosses after having done minimal pre–processing.

2.2 Duluth1

Duluth1 is a natural extension of Duluth2, where each WordNet gloss is expanded by concatenating to it (in the following order) : the glosses of the hypernyms of the sense[3], the glosses of all the hyponyms of the sense, the glosses of any derived form of the sense, and the glosses of all the meronyms of the sense. This significantly expands the size of each WordNet gloss, to the point where our initial attempts to simply use these extended glosses in matching took too much time to finish during the available window of time for the evaluation. We were also concerned about the significant disparities in size among WordNet glosses, and of course with the unexpanded OtherDict glosses.

---

[2]http://cpansearch.perl.org/src/TPEDERSE/Text-NSP-1.31/bin/utils/stoplist-nsp.regex

[3]In general each sense has only one hypernym, although this is not always true in WordNet.

As a result we decided to shorten the WordNet glosses in Duluth1 by removing any word that is made up of four characters or less (rather than using a stoplist), and then only taking the first nine words in the expanded gloss. For many words this means that just the original gloss and the gloss of the hypernym and perhaps part of the gloss of a hyponym would be included. The OtherDict glosses were processed in a similar fashion, where any word with 4 or fewer characters was removed.

Our running example is shown below. Note that this is quite similar to Duluth2, except that *various* is included below (but was excluded in Duluth2 since it is in the stoplist), and that *terrestrial* is included (since it is the first word in the gloss of the hyponym).

- feline#n#1 : various lithe bodied roundheaded fissiped mammals retractile claws terrestrial

2.3   Duluth4

Note that Duluth4 was not included in our official evaluation. Rather this was run after the evaluation period, and it proved to be our most accurate result. Duluth4 is similar to Duluth1 in that it expands the WordNet glosses, but only does so with the glosses of its hypernyms and hyponyms (and does not include the derivational forms or meronyms, as Duluth1 does). Stop words are removed using the same list as Duluth2.

We can see in our running example that this provides a larger gloss, but it is not as large as what Duluth1 provided (before pruning it back to just the first nine words).

- feline#n#1 : lithe bodied roundheaded fissiped mammals retractile claws terrestrial aquatic flesh eating mammal terrestrial carnivores four five clawed digits limb feline mammal having thick soft fur ability roar domestic cats wildcats several large cats typically able roar living wild

2.4   Duluth3

There are many minor variations between words in WordNet and OtherDict glosses, and it is difficult to normalize the glosses in order to eliminate them. Instead, we decided to have one system that relied

	Wu & Palmer	Lemma Match	Recall	F1
First Word	.5140	.4150	1.00	.6790
Median				.5900
Duluth4(*)	.3810	.0550	1.00	.5518
Duluth2	.3471	.0433	1.00	.5153
Duluth3	.3452	.0167	1.00	.5132
Duluth1	.3312	.0233	1.00	.4976
Random	.2269	.0000	1.00	.3699

Table 1: Task 14 results, (*) indicates post–evaluation run.

on character tri-grams, since that could allow for matches between portions of words, rather than requiring the exact matches that all the other Duluth systems insist upon.

Duluth3 expands each WordNet gloss with the gloss of its hypernyms and its hyponyms (like Duluth4, although stop words are not eliminated in Duluth3). Then all spaces are removed from each expanded gloss, and it is broken into three character ngrams. Glosses were limited to 250 of these trigrams, mainly so that they could finish running in the available time during the evaluation.

If one studies the running example carefully you can reconstruct the gloss, which is similar to Duluth4 except that it includes stop words.

- feline#n#1 : any ofv ari ous lit heb odi edr oun dhe ade dfi ssi ped mam mal sma nyw ith ret rac til ecl aws ate rre str ial ora qua tic fle she ati ngm amm alt err est ria lca rni vor esh ave fou ror fiv ecl awe ddi git son eac hli mbf eli nem amm alu sua lly hav ing thi cks oft fur and noa bil ity tor oar dom est icc ats wil dca tsa nyo fse ver all arg eca tst ypi cal lya ble tor oar and liv ing int hew ild

3   Results and Discussion

Despite seemingly significant differences in how the WordNet glosses were expanded, Table 1 reveals that there were only minor differences in results among Duluth1, Duluth2, and Duluth3. This seems to support the conclusion that gloss overlaps provide a reliable and robust starting point for this problem. Indeed, the simplest of our approaches (Duluth2, which used WordNet glosses minus stop words) was slightly more effective than two more elaborate variations (Duluth1 and Duluth3). Recall that Duluth1

gloss size	token count	Wu & Palmer	Lemma Match	F1
1	195,242	0.3033	0.0050	0.4654
5	973,463	0.3336	0.0183	0.5003
9	1,701,884	0.3312	0.0233	0.4976
10	1,866,198	0.3278	0.0200	0.4937
20	3,023,538	0.3296	0.0200	0.4958
30	3,575,586	0.3476	0.0300	0.5159
40	3,871,786	0.3471	0.0383	0.5153
50	4,059,495	0.3444	0.0400	0.5123
100	4,466,581	0.3511	0.0400	0.5197

Table 2: Duluth 1 post–evaluation variations.

normalized gloss lengths by taking only the first nine words in the expanded glosses, and that Duluth3 attempted a kind of poor man's stemming by using character trigrams.

Duluth4 is an obvious extension of Duluth2, in that it expands glosses with their hypernym and hyponyms. This results in a modest but significant improvement on the systems submitted for the formal evaluation, and suggests that focusing on expanded gloss content in relatively straightforward ways can pay dividends. This system at least begins to approach the median score attained by the systems participating in the task. That said, even this result considerably lags the baseline First Word (Jurgens and Pilehvar, 2015) provided by the organizers.

Table 2 shows the results of additional experiments were carried out with Duluth1. Here the gloss sizes were varied from 1 to 100, where 9 is the value used during the formal evaluation. Note that the size of the OtherDict glosses was always 5,533 (tokens) and that the recall attained was always 1.00.

Table 2 shows that generally speaking increasing the number of words in the WordNet glosses results in a small but steady improvement in performance. However, it is important to keep in mind that as the WordNet glosses are growing, the OtherDict glosses are fixed at the same size. This seems to make it clear that the most important avenue moving forward is to expand the OtherDict glosses with additional content, comparable to that with which WordNet is expanded.

4 System Implementation Details

The Duluth systems are implemented using UMLS::Similarity, which provides measures of semantic relatedness and similarity for the Unified Medical Language System. In addition, it also allows a user supplied dictionary to be automatically included and utilized by the Lesk measure. Thus, the Duluth systems created dictionaries from OtherDict and WordNet suitable for use by the Lesk measure in UMLS::Similarity (via the –dict option). WordNet was accessed using the Perl module WordNet::QueryData[4].

References

Satanjeev Banerjee and Ted Pedersen. 2003a. The design, implementation, and use of the Ngram Statistics Package. In *Proceedings of the Fourth International Conference on Intelligent Text Processing and Computational Linguistics*, pages 370–381, Mexico City, February.

Satanjeev Banerjee and Ted Pedersen. 2003b. Extended gloss overlaps as a measure of semantic relatedness. In *Proceedings of the Eighteenth International Joint Conference on Artificial Intelligence*, pages 805–810, Acapulco, August.

David Jurgens and Mohammad Taher Pilehvar. 2015. Reserating the awesometastic: An automatic extension of the wordnet taxonomy for novel terms. In *Proceedings of the 2015 Conference of the North American Chapter of the Association for Computational Linguistics: Human Language Technologies*, pages 1459–1465, Denver, Colorado, May–June. Association for Computational Linguistics.

M.E. Lesk. 1986. Automatic sense disambiguation using machine readable dictionaries: how to tell a pine cone from an ice cream cone. In *Proceedings of the 5th annual international conference on Systems documentation*, pages 24–26. ACM Press.

B. McInnes, T. Pedersen, and S. Pakhomov. 2009. UMLS-Interface and UMLS-Similarity : Open source software for measuring paths and semantic similarity. In *Proceedings of the Annual Symposium of the American Medical Informatics Association*, pages 431–435, San Francisco.

T. Pedersen, S. Patwardhan, and J. Michelizzi. 2004. Wordnet::Similarity - Measuring the relatedness of concepts. In *Proceedings of Fifth Annual Meeting of the North American Chapter of the Association for Computational Linguistics*, pages 38–41, Boston, MA.

---

[4] http://search.cpan.org/WordNet-QueryData

TALN at SemEval-2016 Task 14: Semantic Taxonomy Enrichment Via Sense-Based Embeddings

Luis Espinosa-Anke, Horacio Saggion and **Francesco Ronzano**

TALN - Department of Information and Communication Technologies

Universitat Pompeu Fabra

Carrer Tànger 122-134, 08018 Barcelona (Spain)

{luis.espinosa, horacio.saggion, francesco.ronzano}@upf.edu

Abstract

This paper describes the participation of the TALN team in SemEval-2016 Task 14: Semantic Taxonomy Enrichment. The purpose of the task is to find the best point of attachment in WordNet for a set of Out of Vocabulary (OOV) terms. These may come, to name a few, from domain specific glossaries, slang or typical jargon from Internet forums and chatrooms. Our contribution takes as input an OOV term, its part of speech and its associated definition, and generates a set of WordNet synset candidates derived from modelling the term's definition as a sense embedding representation. We leverage a BabelNet-based vector space representation, which allows us to map the algorithm's prediction to WordNet. Our approach is designed to be generic and fitting to any domain, without exploiting, for instance, HTML markup in source web pages. Our system performs above the median of all submitted systems, and rivals in performance a powerful baseline based on extracting the first word of the definition with the same part-of-speech as the OOV term.

1 Introduction

Semantic knowledge, expressed in terms of concepts and relations holding among them, is an essential enabling component of NLP applications (Jurgens and Pilehvar, 2015). One of the best known semantic repository is WordNet (Miller et al., 1990), a manually created semantic network with a coverage of over 200k English senses and 155k word forms. However, as knowledge domains advance and expand, novel terms beyond the coverage of Word-

Net are coined on a regular basis. Thus, the need for automatic approaches which are able to gather information from unstructured online sources and structure them is in high demand. In this context, WordNet has become the reference semantic network in previous attempts to formalize novel knowledge. The SemEval-2016 Task 14: Semantic Taxonomy Enrichment (Jurgens and Pilehvar, 2016) aims at providing an experimental ground on the task of, given an Out-of-Vocabulary (OOV) term, and an associated definition and part of speech, find the best point of attachment in WordNet (its most similar synset). This is a challenging problem because an OOV term may be defined without any explicit mention to its closest WordNet synset. For instance, for the OOV term (from training data) "lectionary", the associated definition is "The book that contains all the readings from the Scriptures for use in the celebration of the liturgy", and the best point of attachment is sacred_text#n#01. However, if one was to simply obtain the first head word of the definition and retrieve its first sense, the result would be book#n#01, with a score of 0.125/1 according to the official evaluation metric (see Section 4).

In this paper we describe our approach to such task. We base our method on the intuition that unseen terminology may be *understood* in terms of how terms are defined. Hence, we propose an algorithm which, for each definition, performs part-of-speech tagging and parsing, generates a set of noun and verb phrases, and then takes advantage of a vector space representation of word and phrase senses for modelling the definition. Our algorithm produces several WordNet attachment candidates as

1332

Proceedings of SemEval-2016, pages 1332–1336,
San Diego, California, June 16-17, 2016. ©2016 Association for Computational Linguistics

the modelling takes place, e.g. by obtaining the definition's centroid and mapping it to WordNet, or by parsing the OOV term and searching for a mapping between its head and WordNet. For this task, we submitted the three runs of our system with the highest scores on the training data. Moreover, the task organizers provided two baselines: One which selected a random WordNet synset, and one which extracted the first word in the definition with the same part-of-speech, and assigned it its first sense in WordNet (*BaselineFirst*). The experimental results suggest that the baseline was a very strong competitor, ranking way above the median of the participating systems. Our best run was 3 points below the baseline and 5 points above the median according to a metric designed to compute the distance between two nodes in a hierarchical cluster (see Section 4).

The rest of this paper is structured as follows: After presenting an overview of related work (Section 2), we describe in detail the methodology followed for our submission (Section 3), then we provide evaluation results as compared with baseline systems and the participants' median score, along with a discussion of a few interesting cases. Finally, we outline directions of future work in a novel and exciting task, which opens a very interesting research problem to be tackled in the future.

2   Related Work

Expanding current semantic knowledge is a task that may be approached either by expanding WordNet with knowledge derived from structured or semi-structured repositories, or by learning hyponym-hypernym hierarchies separately in order to obtain novel knowledge. Within the former group, we find projects like BABELNET (Navigli and Ponzetto, 2012), a very large multilingual semantic network, or pairwise lexical resources alignments (Miller and Gurevych, 2014; Pilehvar and Navigli, 2014). These approaches, however, are not designed to capture novel terminology due to the fact that, for an alignment to occur, there must exist a direct correspondence between lemmas. This is addressed in projects belonging to the latter group, starting from (Snow et al., 2006), and following more recently with extraction of information from the web (Velardi et al., 2013; Luu Anh et al., 2014) or from BABELNET's

glosses (Espinosa-Anke et al., 2016). These approaches, however, do not perform a direct mapping against WordNet, but rather separate taxonomies with their own hierarchical structure.

3   Method

Our approach to finding the best match in WordNet for an OOV term is based on transforming the associated textual definition into a representative vector. However, performing this action over plain text would introduce an ambiguity problem due to the occurrence of polysemic entities and specific lexical and syntactic formulations within the definition. Therefore, we leveraged SENSEMBED (Iacobacci et al., 2015), a state of the art vector space representation of word senses designed with BABELNET as a reference sense inventory. In SENSEMBED, each vector includes a concatenation of lemma and BABELNET synset. We exploit the mapping BABELNET→WordNet in order to find the best candidate for the given OOV term.

Let t be an OOV term, and d its associated definition, our sense-finding algorithm aims at extracting a suitable WordNet sense for t. To attain this goal, we perform a set of steps which generate a candidate set $\mathcal{C}$, which we will afterwards rank according to certain criteria. The different candidate rankings that we obtain constitute the three runs of our submission. Let us explain how each candidate is obtained.

Candidate Retrieval

First, we parse both t and d using the parser described in (Bohnet, 2010). Note that t may be a multiword term including prepositional phrases (e.g. "margin of error") and hence simply tagging and retrieving the last token would not suffice. We traverse the parse trees obtained in both cases in a depth-first-fashion until a lemma with a WordNet synset with the same part-of-speech as t is found. This generates two candidate WordNet synsets c_t^{wn}, and c_d^{wn}, which correspond to the first sense of the matching lemma. After completing this first step, $\mathcal{C} = \{c_t^{wn}, c_d^{wn}\}$.

The process of retrieving these candidates is inspired by the baseline *BaselineFirst* provided by the task organizers, which retrieved the first word in the definition with the same part-of-speech as the novel term. We evaluated a (non-submitted) *baseline* version of our system, which only considers c_t^{wn} and c_d^{wn}. We obtained slightly worse performance than the organizers' baseline on both trial and training data, mostly due to parsing errors.

The second step of the algorithm aims at finding optimal candidate synsets for t by modeling d in terms of its vector representation. We proceed as follows. First, after stopword removal, we apply a shallow parsing technique over part-of-speech tags in order to isolate both single and multiword NPs and VPs. Specifically, we group all textual chunks that match the following regular expressions:

```
NP  =  <JJ|NN.*>+

VP  =  <VB.*><NP>?
```

This step results in d_{ch}, the set of noun and verb phrases identified in a definition. We did not consider multiword expressions including a prepositional phrase, as these introduced a considerable amount of noise. For example, for d = "Genetic drift is a mechanism of evolution", d_{ch} = {genetic_drift, drift, mechanism, evolution}. Then, for each $ch \in d_{ch}$, we obtain, where possible, all its available senses in SENSEMBED and store them in two separate sets. The first one, denoted as D_{Senses}, contains all senses extracted from all $ch \in d_{ch}$ without distinguishing the original chunk from which they come from. It is simply a set of senses. The second set, denoted as $D_{chSenses}$, isolates all available senses corresponding to each chunk in an individual set, and thus constitutes a set of sets.

We use these two sets for obtaining (1) A *centroid sense* μ over the definition's associated senses D_{Senses}, and (2) The set containing only the *best sense* for each chunk. For the former case, $\mu(D_{Senses})$ is obtained as follows:

$$\mu = \frac{1}{|D_{Senses}|} \sum_{s \in D_{Senses}} \frac{s}{\|s\|} \qquad (1)$$

As for the latter, *best sense* refers to the closest sense to μ by cosine score obtained from the set of senses retrieved for each chunk, namely $d_{chSen} \in D_{chSenses}$, which is computed as follows:

$$bestS(d_{chSen}) = \mathrm{argmax}_{s \in d_{chSen}} \frac{s \cdot \mu}{\|s\| \, \|\mu\|} \qquad (2)$$

The set of best senses per chunk is simply $D_{bestS} = \{bestS(d_{chSen}), d_{chSen} \in D_{chSenses}\}$, and will be used to generate the last candidate in our process.

At this stage, we obtain three more candidates to our candidate set, namely (1) The closest vector to the centroid from of all available senses in SENSEMBED, μ^{wn}; (2) The sense $bestS(d_{chSen})$ appearing at the first position of the sentence, denoted as $firstBest$; and (3) The sense in D_{Senses} with highest cosine similarity with μ, denoted as $highestBest$. In our sample sentence, μ^{wn} = branching_ratio$_{bn}$[1], $firstBest$ = drift$_{syn}$, and $highestBest$ = drift$_{syn}$.

Finally, we introduce one last additional candidate to our candidate pool. We observed that μ may not be an optimal centroid for the sentence as it is computed by considering all possible senses for each extracted chunk. For this reason, we take advantage of the fact that we have an available set of best senses for each chunk, namely D_{bestS}, and create a *sense-aware centroid*, denoted as μ_{best}^{wn}. Finally, $\mathcal{C} = \mathcal{C} \cup \{\mu^{wn}, firstBest, highestBest, \mu_{best}^{wn}\}$.

Ranking Candidates

Having obtained a set of candidate WordNet synsets $\mathcal{C}$ for an OOV term t, we propose a ranking scheme aimed at providing three possible outcomes for our system. Note that we may not have all candidates available from all the previously described steps, as there may be BABELNET synsets without a direct WordNet mapping, definitions may be very short (even one word), or there may be no available candidate with the same part-of-speech as t's head.

We submitted three runs of our system, which we describe as follows:

- **RunHeads** The baseline *BaselineFirst*, provided by the organizers, performed well, i.e. it found the exact correct attachment for almost half of the training instances. Based on this observation, in this submission we prioritized those cases in which there was a direct mapping between the first sense of the definition root and a WordNet synset (c_d). If

<hr>

[1]We denote with subscript *syn* those WordNet senses obtained via direct mapping from SENSEMBED, and with subscript *bn* those only found in BABELNET.

this was not the case, we searched for the mapping of t's head (c_t), as we found that in many cases, when t was a multiword expression, an optimal point of attachment could be found thanks to its head word. If none of these attempts were successful, we opted for selecting candidates in the following order: μ_{best}^{wn}, μ^{wn}, $firstBest$, and $highestBest$.

- **RunSenses** This run first incorporated a voting scheme based on candidates in $\mathcal{C}$ providing one same answer. If this was the case across three or more candidates, this was the synset selected by the system. However, if agreement across candidates was below three, priority was given to candidates coming from the definition modeling via SENSEMBED, and if no candidate was found, the system searched for mappings in c_d^{wn} and c_t^{wn}.

- **RunHyps** This run of our system was the most conservative approach. From all possible candidates extracted either via SENSEMBED, or from c_d and c_t, we computed the number of hyponyms each candidate had in the WordNet hierarchy. Then, our system selected as answer the most general synset, i.e. the one with the highest number of hyponyms. Our hypothesis was that by including the most generic terms possible (upper in the hierarchy) we would be less likely to incur in wrong senses of highly specific terms, where different senses may be placed more sparsely than in more generic ones.

4 Evaluation

Evaluation is performed over several criteria. First, the distance between the selected point of attachment and the gold standard is computed via the Wu & Palmer similarity (**W&P**) (Wu and Palmer, 1994). Second, a Recall measure (**R**), aimed at allowing systems to not provide an answer in doubtful cases, where the chances of an incorrect attachment would be high. It is simply computed as the percentage of items answered by the system. Finally, a score on *lemma match* (**LM**) is provided, in order to cover cases where the system identifies a correct lemma but selects the wrong sense of the lemma.

4.1 System Performance

We observe in the results shown in Table 1 that the three runs performed similarly, with only a few noticeable differences which we comment as follows. First, *RunHeads* and *RunSenses* seem to perform similarly. This may be due to the fact that in some cases no candidate was obtained from the sense-based modeling and hence the system resorted to direct matching from definition and term heads[2]. Another reason can be found in cases in which the definition is semantically very compact, i.e. all its extracted chunks belong to a similar semantic field and therefore the centroid vector we obtain is the same as the definition head, and also the first synset of the definition. This is the case, for instance, the term "complex disease", with definition "A complex disease is caused by the interaction of multiple genes and environmental factors". Here, the gold synset was *disease#n#01*, and this answer was provided by c_t, $firstBest$, and μ_{best}.

Another interesting discussion can be derived from observing the difference between scores in **LM** by the first two systems, on one hand, and *RunHyps* on the other. While *RunHyps* ranks 2nd in our local rank, its **LM** score is more than 10 points below its closest competitor. This is due to the fact that, since *RunHyps* is a conservative approach more aimed at providing generic answers rather than matches, it shows a reasonable performance in terms of **W&P**, but falls short in **LM** as it almost never will find the correct point of attachment at the top of WordNet's hierarchy.

In terms of comparative evaluation, all our submitted systems rank below the baseline *Baseline-First*, which shows that a simpler approach based on majority class (selecting the first WordNet synset for a given lemma, which usually corresponds to the most generic or widespread sense) is difficult to beat. However, in comparison with the median of all participating systems, all our submissions achieve **F1** scores between 4 and 5 points higher.

---

[2] In general we were reasonably satisfied with the coverage of SENSEMBED, as with our approach, we found at least one candidate BABELNET synset with WordNet mapping in the vast majority of cases. For instance, our run *RunHeads* missed only two nouns and four verbs. In these cases we set a default point of attachment *entity#n#01* and *breathe#v#01* respectively.

Subm	W&P	LM	R	F1
RunHeads	0.476	0.36	1	0.645
RunSenses	0.463	0.353	1	0.635
RunHyps	0.471	0.24	1	0.641
BaselineFirst	0.513	0.415	1	**0.678**
Median	-	-	-	0.590

Table 1: Evaluation summary for our submission

5 Future Work

We computed an *upper bound* on the training data, i.e. the score we would have achieved if, for each case, we had selected the best of the candidates proposed by our system. This artificial upper bound reached a **W&P** score of almost 0.70, which suggests that our approach has clear and well defined room for improvement. We are currently investigating potential ways to address this issue in order to surpass the baseline scores.

Acknowledgments

This work was partially funded by Dr. Inventor (FP7-ICT-2013.8.1611383), and by the Spanish Ministry of Economy and Competitiveness under the Maria de Maeztu Units of Excellence Programme (MDM-2015-0502).

References

Bernd Bohnet. 2010. Very High Accuracy and Fast Dependency Parsing is not a Contradiction. In *COLING*, pages 89–97.

Luis Espinosa-Anke, Horacio Saggion, Francesco Ronzano, and Roberto Navigli. 2016. ExTaSem! Extending, Taxonomizing and Semantifying Domain Terminologies. In *AAAI*.

Ignacio Iacobacci, Mohammad Taher Pilehvar, and Roberto Navigli. 2015. SENSEMBED: Enhancing Word Embeddings for Semantic Similarity and Relatedness. In *Proceedings of ACL*, Beijing, China, July. Association for Computational Linguistics.

David Jurgens and Mohammad Taher Pilehvar. 2015. Reserating the awesometastic: An automatic extension of the WordNet taxonomy for novel terms. In *Proceedings of the 2015 conference of the North American chapter of the association for computational linguistics: Human language technologies, Denver, CO*, pages 1459–1465.

David Jurgens and Mohammad Taher Pilehvar. 2016. Semeval-2016 Task 14: Semantic Taxonomy Enrichment. In *Semeval 2016*.

Tuan Luu Anh, Jung-jae Kim, and See Kiong Ng. 2014. Taxonomy Construction Using Syntactic Contextual Evidence. In *EMNLP*, pages 810–819, October.

Tristan Miller and Iryna Gurevych. 2014. WordNet - Wikipedia - Wiktionary: Construction of a Three-Way Alignment. In *LREC*, pages 2094–2100.

George A. Miller, R.T. Beckwith, Christiane D. Fellbaum, D. Gross, and K. Miller. 1990. WordNet: an Online Lexical Database. *International Journal of Lexicography*, 3(4):235–244.

Roberto Navigli and Simone Paolo Ponzetto. 2012. BabelNet: The Automatic Construction, Evaluation and Application of a Wide-Coverage Multilingual Semantic Network. *Artificial Intelligence*, 193:217–250.

Mohammad Taher Pilehvar and Roberto Navigli. 2014. A Robust Approach to Aligning Heterogeneous Lexical Resources. In *Proceedings of the 52nd Annual Meeting of the Association for Computational Linguistics, ACL 2014, June 22-27, 2014, Baltimore, MD, USA, Volume 1: Long Papers*, pages 468–478.

Rion Snow, Daniel Jurafsky, and Andrew Y Ng. 2006. Semantic taxonomy induction from heterogenous evidence. In *Proceedings of COLING/ACL 2006*, pages 801–808. Association for Computational Linguistics.

Paola Velardi, Stefano Faralli, and Roberto Navigli. 2013. Ontolearn Reloaded: A graph-Based Algorithm for Taxonomy Induction. *Computational Linguistics*, 39(3):665–707.

Zhibiao Wu and Martha Palmer. 1994. Verbs Semantics and Lexical Selection. In *Proceedings of the 32nd annual meeting on Association for Computational Linguistics*, pages 133–138. Association for Computational Linguistics.

MSejrKu at SemEval-2016 Task 14: Taxonomy Enrichment by Evidence Ranking

Michael Sejr Schlichtkrull
University of Copenhagen (Denmark)
`michael.sejr@gmail.com`

Héctor Martínez Alonso
Univ. Paris 7 - INRIA (France)
`hector.martinez-alonso@inria.fr`

Abstract

Automatic enrichment of semantic taxonomies with novel data is a relatively unexplored task with potential benefits in a broad array of natural language processing problems. Task 14 of SemEval 2016 poses the challenge of designing systems for this task. In this paper, we describe and evaluate several machine learning systems constructed for our participation in the competition. We demonstrate an f1-score of 0.680 for our submitted systems — a small improvement over the 0.679 produced by the hard baseline.

1 Introduction

This article describes our systems submitted for Se-mEval2016, task 14 on taxonomy enrichment. [1] The two submitted runs are based on Gaussian-kernel SVMs, and fall respectively under the constrained and the unconstrained condition of the shared task, namely using only WordNet and the training data, or incorporating outside sources. We chose our submitted models by evaluation on the trial data in lieu of a development set. Our runs perform better than the very hard baseline with a small 2% margin, while the best-performing heuristic outperforms the baseline by a 5% margin.

2 Related Work

Existing methods for taxonomy enrichment can roughly be divided into two categories: relying on alignment between multiple taxonomies, or relying on machine learning-based rating of subgraphs.

In (Jurgens and Pilehvar, 2015), Wordnet is extended with technical terms and rare lemmas from Wiktionary. In (Suchanek et al., 2007), relation-extraction is used to unify WordNet and Wikipedia. (Navigli and Ponzetto, 2012) further automates the alignment process itself. In (Toral et al., 2008), named entities are brought from Wikipedia to Word-Net through pattern matching.

In (Snow et al., 2006), the probabilities of taxonomies are evaluated based on evidence vectors associated to edges. A similar approach formulated in terms of factor graphs can be seen in (Bansal et al., 2013). Finally, (Yamada et al., 2011) employ a hybrid strategy, scoring edges by likelihood of appearance in Wikipedia. Our approach also falls in the second category, relying on a machine learning process to rank hypernym-hyponym edges.

3 Data

There are three data splits: *train*, *trial*, and *test*, described in Table 1. We use the trial data for model selection. Notice that attach-actions represent the vast majority of instances. We therefore focus exclusively on finding correct integrations and disregard the merge-attach distinction.

Several observations can be made from the distribution of the labels in the training set. First, we define the *closest* synset $s_c(t, g)$ of a term t with gold standard g as the synset such that a lemma of that synset is represented in some description sentence $d \in D(t)$ and the shortest path $\delta(g, s_c(t, g))$ in the taxonomy is minimized. Here, $D(t)$ is the set of description sentences corresponding to t. In Figure 1, we plot $\delta(g, s_c(t, g))$ versus number of instances.

---

[1] http://alt.qcri.org/semeval2016/task14/

Proceedings of SemEval-2016, pages 1337–1341,
San Diego, California, June 16-17, 2016. ©2016 Association for Computational Linguistics

Dataset	# Nouns	# Verbs	# Total	Sentences / instance	Tokens / sentence	# Attach	# Merge
Train	349	51	400	1.69	17.73	367	33
Trial	93	34	127	1.02	12.18	71	56
Test	512	82	600	1.21	18.45	569	31

Table 1: Overview of the datasets, showing the composition of nouns and verbs, merge-action and attach-actions, and the mean number of description sentences per term and number of tokens per description sentence.

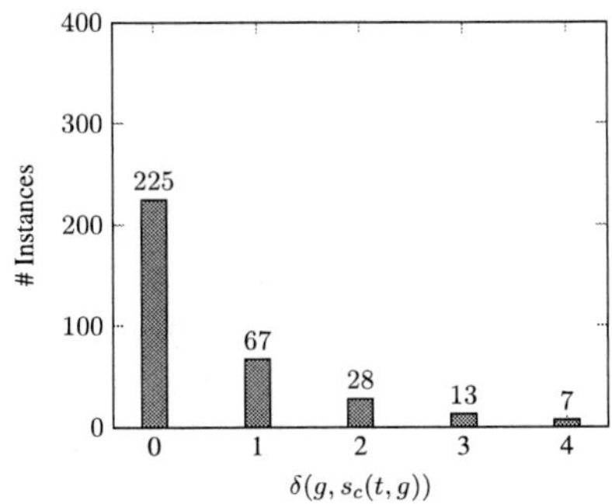

Figure 1: Number of instances in the training set such that $\delta(g, s_c(t, g))$ corresponds respectively to $0, 1, 2, 3,$ and 4.

As is apparent from the Zipfian-like distribution, s_c constitutes an excellent guess for g. Defining $w_c(t, d, g)$ for each $d \in D(t)$ in similar fashion as the synset minimizing $\delta(g, w_c(t, g))$, an analogous observation can be made for each description sentence. The result can be seen in Figure 2 below:

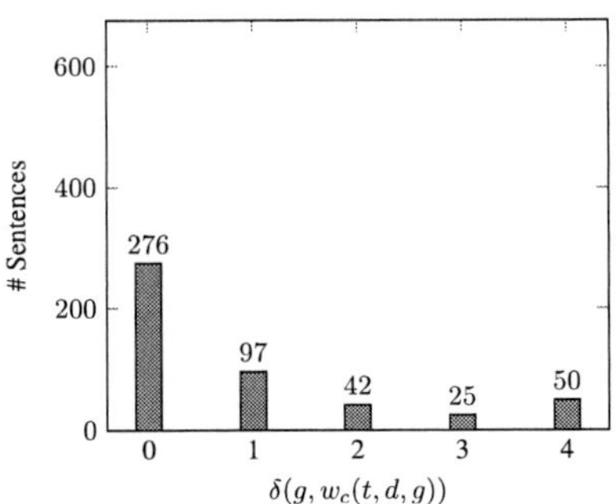

Figure 2: Number of sentences in the training set such that $\delta(g, w_c(t, d, g))$ corresponds respectively to $0, 1, 2, 3,$ and 4.

We again observe a Zipfian-like distribution, suggesting that each $w_c(t, d, g)$ represents a good candidate for $s_c(t, g)$. As terms often have multiple description sentences, we therefore have for each term several good guesses for $s_c(t, g)$ and therefore g. These observations form the basis of the strategies discussed in Section 5.2.

4 Features

Our systems use both lexical and syntactic features, with distributional features included in the second run. As a first step, we POS-tag and dependency parse the description sentences using the Mate parser in (Bohnet et al., 2013).[2] Additionally, we apply the unsupervised word sense disambiguation algorithm described in (Agirre and Soroa, 2009).[3]

4.1 Constrained Features

Description words are represented through features based on position, word shape, morphology, POS-tag, and dependency structure. Word senses are incorporated through the depths defined in (Devitt and Vogel, 2004). Morphological and shape features derived from the candidate term are also included, along with a binary feature representing the description word appearing in the target term.

For the direct classification strategies, we also use features derived from the candidate synset. These include POS-tag, overlap between synset- and term-description, and the length of the shortest path to the description. For the ranking systems, we also utilize pairwise features: the relative distance and position in the description sentence, the relative distance and position in the dependency tree, and the difference in number of overlapping lemmas between the description sentence and the most likely senses.

4.2 Embedding Features

We extend the features defined above with Skip-Gram embeddings as discussed in (Mikolov et al., 2013). We train the Gensim model (Řehůřek and Sojka, 2010) on a corpus consisting of the description sentences and the Wikipedia entries for each term, padded with the English part of the PolyGlot corpus presented in (Al-Rfou et al., 2013).

---

[2]Available at: https://code.google.com/archive/p/mate-tools/wikis/ParserAndModels.wiki .

[3]Available at: http://ixa2.si.ehu.es/ukb/ .

Word-level features are extended with embeddings for the word itself and the dependency head. Term-level features are extended with the sum of the embedding vectors of each word in the n-gram. Synset-level features are extended with the mean of the embedding vectors for each lemma. Finally, all pairwise features are extended with cosine distances.

5 Experiments

In this section, we explain the strategies we attempted. In all cases, we discount the merge action, focusing only on attaching.

5.1 Direct Classification

For comparison, we first attempt direct classification: Given a term and a candidate synset, predict whether that synset is a correct integration for the term. Enrichment is done by ranking all synsets according to prediction probability. We tried a linear logistic regression classifier, and a non-linear neural network classifier with a single hidden layer containing 100 units.

5.2 Right Word Classifier

As shown in Section 3, one can narrow down the search space by a large margin through finding $w_c(t, d, g)$. We propose to determine w_c through a machine learning process. Then, we estimate $s_c(t, g)$ by taking a majority vote over sentences. We experiment with four versions of the strategy.

We consider letting each sentence vote for the most likely sense of the best candidate for $w_c(t, d, g)$ with a weight of 1. Secondly, we consider including votes for the second-best candidate and the second-most likely senses, weighted by hyperparameters α and β. We determine the values for α and β through crossvalidation on the training set. We perform word sense disambiguation either through most frequent sense, or through Personalized Pagerank.

Ranking problems can be approached as pointwise regression, or as pairwise classification. Ranking by classification probability as discussed in the previous section corresponds to a pointwise regression with logistic loss. Following (Hang, 2011), transforming a pointwise problem into a pairwise problem can improve performance, especially when training data is scarce.

To transform the training set into a pairwise training set $\mathcal{L}_{pairwise}$, we combine for each description sentence d with content words of appropriate POS-tag $W_{t,d}$ every pair $(w_1, w_2) \in W_{t,d} \times W_{t,d}$ such that one equals $w_c(t, d, g)$ and the other does not. If w_1 is the match and w_2 is not, we add (w_1, w_2) to $\mathcal{L}_{pairwise}$ with the positive label. Else, we add (w_1, w_2) to $\mathcal{L}_{pairwise}$ with the negative label. We train a classifier on this dataset, observing that a relation $\prec_{t,d}$ is induced as positive and negative predictions on w_1 and w_2 correspond respectively to $w_1 \succ_{t,d} w_2$ and $w_1 \prec_{t,d} w_2$.

We experiment with various classifiers and parameter settings through cross-validation. As $(w_1, w_2) \in \mathcal{L}_{pairwise} \Leftrightarrow (w_2, w_1) \in \mathcal{L}_{pairwise}$, the dataset is balanced and chance performs at an accuracy of 0.5. The best-performing classifier was the Gaussian kernel SVM, with an accuracy of 0.81.

Through this classification, we learn for each term t a relation $\prec_{t,d}$ on the words $w \in W_{t,d}$ of each description sentence $d \in D(t)$. This relation, however, is asymmetric and therefore does not constitute an ordering. We therefore define a new ordering $\prec_{t,d}^*$ averaging over both directions of $\prec_{t,d}$:

$$p(w_1 \prec_{t,d}^* w_2) = \frac{p(w_1 \prec_{t,d} w_2) + p(w_2 \succ_{t,d} w_1))}{2}$$

We then let $w_1 \prec_{t,d}^* w_2$ if and only if $p(w_1 \prec_{t,d}^* w_2) > 0.5$. As $\prec_{t,d}^*$ is an ordering on the words of each description sentence, we let the largest element with respect to $\prec_{t,d}^*$ be our guess for w_c.

6 Results

The results for each system can be seen in Table 2. We provide results on the training data, the test data, and the trial data which was used as a development set in the model selection process. Apart from the submitted runs, all systems have a perfect recall of 1.0. For the submitted runs, a software error caused recall to drop to 0.97 as description words containing underscores were incorrectly processed.

The best-performing system on the trial data under both conditions is the vote-based ranking without sense disambiguation, outperforming the *first word, first sense*-baseline by a small margin. Following this observation, we chose to submit the constrained and unconstrained variants of this system - marked in bold in Table 2.

System	Train		Trial		Test	
	F1	Lemma M.	F1	Lemma M.	F1	Lemma M.
Random	0.35	0.00	0.39	0.00	0.37	0.00
First-word fist-sense	0.64	0.33	0.66	0.25	0.68	0.42
Logistic Regression	0.53	0.17	0.46	0.15	0.47	0.15
NN-classification	0.53	0.18	0.46	0.14	0.50	0.17
Rank-FS	0.69	0.43	0.66	0.28	0.68	0.42
Rank-WSD	0.72	0.42	0.65	0.29	0.70	0.42
Rank-vote-FS	0.70	0.42	0.67	0.27	**0.67**	**0.43**
Rank-vote-WSD	0.72	0.43	0.66	0.27	0.70	0.41
Rank-embed-FS	0.69	0.39	0.67	0.28	0.68	0.41
Rank-embed-WSD	0.73	0.42	0.67	0.28	0.68	0.42
Rank-embed-vote-FS	0.70	0.42	0.67	0.28	**0.68**	**0.43**
Rank-embed-vote-WSD	0.73	0.42	0.67	0.28	0.69	0.41

Table 2: Performance reported as the f1 of Wu & Palmer-score and recall, along with Lemma Matches. Results are shown for the baselines, the direct classifiers, and the constrained and unconstrained versions of the ranking-based systems. The submitted runs are marked in bold. Recall is 1.00 for all systems except for the submitted runs, where a software error caused a recall of 0.97.

7 Discussion

Investigating the errors made by the voting-based first-sense systems, we see a pattern in which hypernyms of the correct integration mistakenly are chosen. Examples include *steroid* instead of *anabolic steroid*, *drug* instead of *opiate*, and *person* instead of *woman*. Although these errors occur under both conditions, they are slightly more frequent in the constrained system. In (Levy et al., 2015), evidence is presented that distributional embeddings mainly encode hierarchical *level* rather than hierarchical *branch*. Our findings seem to support this conclusion. Refining the usage of the embeddings may well resolve this particular source of error.

In Table 1, we see how the training dataset not only on the average has more description sentences per term, but also longer description sentences. As the Personalized Pagerank algorithm relies on a context created from these sets of tokens, this may be the source of the poor performance of sense disambiguation compared to most frequent sense on the trial data seen in Table 2.

Similarly, the voting component was observed to have almost no effect on the test and trial data, while improving the performance on the training data by a wide margin. When the number of description sentences is smaller, it follows naturally that the number of candidates for s_c drops, thus reducing the effectiveness of voting.

Examining the difference between the predictions made by our systems and the baseline, we notice that no terms exist where we our prediction is equal to the gold standard, and the baseline is not. Rather, the improvement demonstrated by our systems comes in the form of wrongful guesses being closer to the gold than is the case for the baseline. This is further supported by the Zipfian observed in Section 3: our guesses mostly fall within a distance of 0–2 edges of the gold standard.

8 Conclusion

We have described several strategies for taxonomy enrichment, showing F1-scores of respectively 0.68 and 0.70 for the submitted and the best-performing systems. Our results show much better performance on the training data, even for the unsupervised sense disambiguation component. We have argued that the difference in number of description sentences and number of tokens per description sentence accounts partially for this difference, and therefore propose the gathering of additional evidence from outside sources to be added to the descriptions as the natural next step for future work. As our system demonstrates high performance for candidate generation and low performance for candidate selection, another possibility for future work would be to combine our approach with a filtering strategy in an ensemble or pipeline.

References

Eneko Agirre and Aitor Soroa. 2009. Personalizing pagerank for word sense disambiguation. In *Proceedings of the 12th Conference of the European Chapter of the Association for Computational Linguistics*, pages 33–41. Association for Computational Linguistics.

Rami Al-Rfou, Bryan Perozzi, and Steven Skiena. 2013. Polyglot: Distributed word representations for multilingual nlp. In *Proceedings of the Seventeenth Conference on Computational Natural Language Learning*, pages 183–192, Sofia, Bulgaria, August.

Mohit Bansal, David Burkett, Gerard De Melo, and Dan Klein. 2013. Structured learning for taxonomy induction with belief propagation.

Bernd Bohnet, Joakim Nivre, Igor Boguslavsky, Richárd Farkas, Filip Ginter, and Jan Hajič. 2013. Joint morphological and syntactic analysis for richly inflected languages. *Transactions of the Association for Computational Linguistics*, 1:415–428.

Ann Devitt and Carl Vogel. 2004. The topology of wordnet: Some metrics.

LI Hang. 2011. A short introduction to learning to rank. *IEICE TRANSACTIONS on Information and Systems*, 94(10):1854–1862.

David Jurgens and Mohammad Taher Pilehvar. 2015. Reserating the awesometastic: An automatic extension of the wordnet taxonomy for novel terms.

Omer Levy, Steffen Remus, Chris Biemann, Ido Dagan, and Israel Ramat-Gan. 2015. Do supervised distributional methods really learn lexical inference relations?

Tomas Mikolov, Ilya Sutskever, Kai Chen, Greg S Corrado, and Jeff Dean. 2013. Distributed representations of words and phrases and their compositionality. In *Advances in neural information processing systems*, pages 3111–3119.

Roberto Navigli and Simone Paolo Ponzetto. 2012. Babelnet: The automatic construction, evaluation and application of a wide-coverage multilingual semantic network. *Artificial Intelligence*, 193:217–250.

Radim Řehůřek and Petr Sojka. 2010. Software Framework for Topic Modelling with Large Corpora. In *Proceedings of the LREC 2010 Workshop on New Challenges for NLP Frameworks*, pages 45–50, Valletta, Malta, May. ELRA.

Rion Snow, Daniel Jurafsky, and Andrew Y Ng. 2006. Semantic taxonomy induction from heterogenous evidence. In *Proceedings of the 21st International Conference on Computational Linguistics and the 44th annual meeting of the Association for Computational Linguistics*, pages 801–808. Association for Computational Linguistics.

Fabian M Suchanek, Gjergji Kasneci, and Gerhard Weikum. 2007. Yago: a core of semantic knowledge. In *Proceedings of the 16th international conference on World Wide Web*, pages 697–706. ACM.

Antonio Toral, Rafael Munoz, and Monica Monachini. 2008. Named entity wordnet.

Ichiro Yamada, Jong-Hoon Oh, Chikara Hashimoto, Kentaro Torisawa, Jun'ichi Kazama, Stijn De Saeger, and Takuya Kawada. 2011. Extending wordnet with hypernyms and siblings acquired from wikipedia. In *IJCNLP*, pages 874–882.

Deftor at SemEval-2016 Task 14: Taxonomy Enrichment using Definition Vectors

Hristo Tanev
Joint Research Centre, EC
via Enrico Fermi 2749
Ispra, Italy
hristo.tanev@jrc.ec.europa.eu

Agata Rotondi
Universita' Ca' Foscari
Venezia, Italy
rotondiagata@gmail.com

Abstract

In this paper we describe the participation of the Joint Research Centre, EC, in task 14 - Semantic Taxonomy Enrichment at SemEval 2016. The algorithm which we propose transforms each candidate definition into a term vector, where each dimension represents a term and its value is calculated by TF.IDF. We attach the candidate term as a hyponym to the WordNet synset with the most similar definition. The results we obtained are encouraging, considering the simplicity of our approach. The obtained F measure is below the average, but above one of the baselines.

1 Introduction

In this paper we describe the participation of the Joint Research Centre, EC, in task 14 - Semantic Taxonomy Enrichment at SemEval 2016. We participate for the first time in a similar task. We opted for a relatively simple method for searching of relevant synsets, which does not exploit any external dictionary or another semantic resource. We called our system Deftor (DEFinition vecTOR). Deftor is a system which represents the definitions (glosses) as lexical vectors and finds the most similar one for each new lemma.

Automatic enrichment of taxonomies and knowledge bases is very important especially for rapidly changing domain. The taxonomy enrichment task is quite challenging, mostly because of the many possibilities when attaching a new term to an existing taxonomy: First, a new word can be attached as a hyponym to different concepts, which describe it at different levels of abstraction. For example, in WordNet the *hurricane* is a hyponym of *cyclone*, which is a hyponym of *windstorm*, which itself is a hyponym of *storm* and the *storm* is a hyponym of *atmospheric phenomenon*. It is not always easy to decide where to attach a concept: in the above mentioned case the definition of *storm* and *windstorm* are not very different. In this case, it is also difficult to decide if a new concept should be merged with a similar concept from WordNet or it should be attached as a hyponym. Another problem are the multiple aspects from which a concept can be perceived. For example, one can consider *hurricane* to be a *natural disaster*. It is also a *weather condition* or *cause of death*. All these considerations unfortunately make taxonomy enrichment task quite ambiguous and difficult to tackle. In some cases, the right attachment of a new concept will be difficult also for a human expert. Although the task is quite complicated, as we have pointed out, we applied a simple approach which is based on comparison of the lexical content of the definitions of the new concepts and the WordNet synsets.

Our approach to the taxonomy enrichment task represents each synset from WordNet and the candidate new terms as word vectors from their definitions and then attaches each new term as a hyponym to the synset for which the cosine similarity of its definition vector and the definition vector of the new term is the highest.

The algorithm which we propose transforms each candidate definition into a *definition vector*, a term vector, where each dimension represents a term and its weight is calculated by TF.IDF. In this way we

Proceedings of SemEval-2016, pages 1342–1345,
San Diego, California, June 16-17, 2016. ©2016 Association for Computational Linguistics

represent each WordNet definition, as well as the definitions of the new terms for inclusion in WordNet. Moreover, we expanded each definition vector with the definitions of the words from this vector.

We then calculated the cosine similarity between each WordNet synset definition and the definition of the candidate term whose place in the WordNet hierarchy is to be identified. Then, we attach the candidate term as a hyponym to the synset with the most similar definition.

Using this method we obtained results which are encouraging, considering the simplicity of our method - it relies solely on WordNet and no additional dictionaries or other resources were used. The results we obtained are somehow below the average, but above the weaker baseline.

2   Related Work

There are plenty of scientific papers, which address the taxonomy/ontology enrichment task and in particular the automatic enrichment of WordNet. See among the others (Haridy et al., 2010), (Navigli et al., 2004) and (Nimb et al., 2013). Existing work falls in one of the following categories: 1. Adding new semantic relations in an existing ontology (Montoyo et al., 2001). 2. Adding new senses for existing terms, e.g. (Nimb et al., 2013) 3. Adding new terms (Jurgens and Pilehvar, 2015). The new terms which are added may belong to already existing terminology (Stankovic et al., 2014), to a particular domain (e.g. biomedical (Poprat et al., 2008), medical (Smith and Fellbaum, 2004), or architectural (Bentivogli et al., 2004)), or they can belong to one well defined class like in (Toral and Monachini, 2008) who adds proper nouns to WordNet. The new terms may be taken from dictionaries or extracted from a corpus. In several cases the exploited resource is Wikipedia, like (Ruiz-Casado et al., 2005) and (Ponzetto and Navigli, 2009). Most of the work based on Wikipedia are limited mainly to the noun concepts; to overcome this limitation (Jurgens and Pilehvar, 2015) proposed to extend WordNet with novel lemmas from Wiktionary. For the WordNet enrichment task different resources have been exploited and different approaches have been experimented: distributional similarity techniques (Snow et al., 2006), structured based approaches

(Ruiz-Casado et al., 2005), creation of a new ontology and its merging with the existing one by alignment based methods (Pilehvar and Navigli, 2014) or considering the attributes distribution (Reisinger and Paşca, 2009).

The taxonomy enrichment task can be considered as a specific case of the ontology learning and population task, (Buitelaar and Cimiano, 2008), whose purpose is automatic learning of semantic classes and relations. Ontology population is about finding instances, which belong to certain ontological classes, like *Paris* is an instance of the class *city*.

3   Algorithm

As we pointed out earlier our method is based on similarity of *definition vectors*. In order to create a definition vector for a word sense, we perform part-of-speech tagging of its gloss and we represent each gloss as a list of lemmas of its non-stop words. Words are downcased. After that, as a second step, each definition vector is being expanded with the lemmas from the glosses of its words, obtained on the first step. For example, if the WordNet definition for *computer* is *a machine for performing calculations automatically*, then our algorithm creates a first version of the definition vector with the non-stop lemmas *machine, perform, calculation* and the TF.IDF values of these words. Then, the algorithm takes the glosses of all the WordNet senses of the words in the first version of the vector. In this particular case, we will add to the definition vector of *computer* the words from the glosses of all the senses of *machine, perform*, and *calculation*. Moreover, part-of-speech tags of these words are known, since we perform part of speech tagging of the glosses. As an additional step of pre-processing we extract the genus from the gloss - usually the first word which defines the more generic concept under which is the defined term

We have processed all the WordNet synsets, where each synset is represented as a definition vector. Then an inverted index was created for each definition vector, in which a word points to the definition vectors in which it appears. Then, for each new term t, we do the following

1. Find the definition vector d of t.

2. For each word w from d we find via the inverted index all the synsets whose definition vectors contain w and whose part-of-speech is the same as the one of t. Let's denote the set of definition vectors of these synsets as D.

3. We find the similarity of d and each vector $d_i \in D$. The similarity is being calculated as $d.d_i.cos(d, d_i)$, this formula was empirically derived from the training data.

4. If the part of speech of t is verb, we add to the above-calculated similarity score the similarity of the glosses of the genus of t and the genus of the synset under consideration

5. The synset with highest similarity is taken and then the new term is attached as its hyponym. If the similarity of the best synset is found to be under a certain threshold, then we do not attach the new term and we skip it

4   Evaluation

The evaluation shows that our system can be improved significantly, but still results are encouraging considering the simplicity of our approach. The F1 of our only run was found to be 0.5132, which is below the baseline First word, first sense, but much above the baseline Random synset, which shows the feasibility of our approach.

It goes without saying that our results can be improved, nevertheless we propose an approach whose main advantage is its simplicity and it is independent of external resources. Our method is potentially multilingual and can be applied on taxonomies in languages other than English. Our system Deftor does not rely on any external knowledge and it uses only part-of-speech tagging and lemmatization as a pre-processing step. Since P.O.S. taggers and lemmatizers are available in different languages, we can easily adapt Deftor between languages and between domains, since the exploited algorithm does not depend on the taxonomy domain. Moreover, the simplicity of our approach make it quite efficient and easy to implement.

References

Luisa Bentivogli, Andrea Bocco, and Emanuele Pianta. 2004. Archiwordnet: integrating wordnet with domain-specific knowledge. In *Proceedings of the 2nd International Global Wordnet Conference*, pages 39–47.

Paul Buitelaar and Philipp Cimiano. 2008. *Ontology learning and population: bridging the gap between text and knowledge*, volume 167. Ios Press.

Shaimaa Haridy, Nagwa L Badr, Omar H Karam, and Tarek F Gharib. 2010. Enriching ontologies using coarse-grained word senses in the case of: Wordnet. *Egyptian Computer Science Journal*, 34(2).

David Jurgens and Mohammad Taher Pilehvar. 2015. Reserating the awesometastic: An automatic extension of the wordnet taxonomy for novel terms. In *Proceedings of the 2015 conference of the North American chapter of the association for computational linguistics: Human language technologies, Denver, CO*, pages 1459–1465.

Andrés Montoyo, Manuel Palomar, and German Rigau. 2001. Wordnet enrichment with classification systems. In *Proceedings of WordNet and Other Lexical Resources: Applications, Extensions and Customisations Workshop.(NAACL-01) The Second Meeting of the North American Chapter of the Association for Computational Linguistics*, pages 101–106.

Roberto Navigli, Paola Velardi, Alessandro Cucchiarelli, Francesca Neri, and Ro Cucchiarelli. 2004. Extending and enriching wordnet with ontolearn. In *Proc. 2nd Global WordNet Conf.(GWC)*, pages 279–284.

Sanni Nimb, Bolette S Pedersen, Anna Braasch, Nicolai H Sørensen, and Thomas Troelsgård. 2013. Enriching a wordnet from a thesaurus. *Lexical Semantic Resources for NLP*, page 36.

Mohammad Taher Pilehvar and Roberto Navigli. 2014. A robust approach to aligning heterogeneous lexical resources. *A A*, 1:c2.

Simone Paolo Ponzetto and Roberto Navigli. 2009. Large-scale taxonomy mapping for restructuring and integrating wikipedia. In *IJCAI*, volume 9, pages 2083–2088.

Michael Poprat, Elena Beisswanger, and Udo Hahn. 2008. Building a biowordnet by using wordnets data formats and wordnets software infrastructurea failure story. *Software Engineering, Testing, and Quality Assurance for Natural Language*, page 31.

Joseph Reisinger and Marius Paşca. 2009. Latent variable models of concept-attribute attachment. In *Proceedings of the Joint Conference of the 47th Annual Meeting of the ACL and the 4th International Joint Conference on Natural Language Processing of the*

AFNLP: Volume 2-Volume 2, pages 620–628. Association for Computational Linguistics.

Maria Ruiz-Casado, Enrique Alfonseca, and Pablo Castells. 2005. Automatic assignment of wikipedia encyclopedic entries to wordnet synsets. In *Advances in web intelligence*, pages 380–386. Springer.

Barry Smith and Christiane Fellbaum. 2004. Medical wordnet: a new methodology for the construction and validation of information resources for consumer health. In *Proceedings of the 20th international conference on Computational Linguistics*, page 371. Association for Computational Linguistics.

Rion Snow, Daniel Jurafsky, and Andrew Y Ng. 2006. Semantic taxonomy induction from heterogenous evidence. In *Proceedings of the 21st International Conference on Computational Linguistics and the 44th annual meeting of the Association for Computational Linguistics*, pages 801–808. Association for Computational Linguistics.

Staša Vujicic Stankovic, Cvetana Krstev, and Duško Vitas. 2014. Enriching serbian wordnet and electronic dictionaries with terms from the culinary domain. *Volume editors*, page 127.

Antonio Toral and Monica Monachini. 2008. Named entity wordnet. In *In Proceedings of the 6th International Conference on Language Resources and Evaluation*. Citeseer.

UMNDuluth at SemEval-2016 Task 14:
WordNet's Missing Lemmas

Jon Rusert & Ted Pedersen
Department of Computer Science
University of Minnesota
Duluth, MN USA
{ruse0008,tpederse}@d.umn.edu

Abstract

This paper presents a solution to Semeval 2016 Task 14 which asks for a system that is able to insert new lemmas into WordNet. Our system aims to do this by overlapping words in the definitions of the to-be-inserted lemma and all senses in WordNet. This paper includes the results of our system and also includes the baseline provided by Task 14, with our system scoring higher than the random baseline, and lower than the first word baseline.

1   Introduction

Semeval 2016 Task 14 called for a system that could help enrich the WordNet taxonomy with new words and their senses. This translates to inserting new lemmas and senses that were previously not in WordNet into their (human perceived) correct place. The system was also to determine whether a sense would merge into the chosen synset or attach itself as a new hyponym. Task 14 allowed for one of two types of systems:

1. A resource-aware system, which could use any dictionary, or

2. Constrained, which used any resource other than a dictionary.

We opted with the former, resource-aware. While any dictionary could be used, we chose to use the definitions provided in the data set from Wiktionary, along with definitions from WordNet.

2   Methods

Our system solves the given problem in four steps:

1. Pre-processing: Acquire all necessary data from WordNet and store it in one step. The data needed includes each word's definitions, hypernyms, hyponyms, and synsets.

2. Overlaps: Score each sense on how well it matches each new lemma.

3. Refining chosen sense: Verify that the sense chosen in overlaps was more deserving than the other senses of the same lemma.

4. Determining attach or merge: Decide whether or not the new lemma should be attached to the synset of the chosen sense, or merged into it.

2.1   Pre-processing

As the implementation of our system was underway, it was clear that the system would be making a large amount of calls to WordNet. As we accessed more and more data from WordNet[1], our program took longer to finish each time which created a problem for testing out changes quickly. In response, the pre-processing method was created.

Pre-processing aims to consolidate all calls to WordNet in the beginning of the program, so no duplicate calls need to be made. It does this by first obtaining all nouns and verbs from WordNet and storing them in their respective arrays (one array for nouns and one for verbs). Pre-processing

---

[1] http://search.cpan.org/dist/WordNet-QueryData/QueryData.pm

Proceedings of SemEval-2016, pages 1346–1350,
San Diego, California, June 16-17, 2016. ©2016 Association for Computational Linguistics

then iterates through each word and retrieves each sense of each word, since the senses are what will determine which synset the new lemma will be merged or attached to later on. The senses are stored in a separate array, which is iterated through, one by one, in the Overlap step to obtain a score for each sense. Next, it iterates through each sense and obtains that senses gloss. Pre-processing cleans each gloss by making all letters into lower-case, removing punctuation, and also removing this list of common stop words *(the—is—at—which—on—a—an—and—or—up)* from each gloss. This list of stop words was determined by finding common, less helpful words in the trial/test data. These stop words were found by outputting what words were being overlapped, and these appeared the most frequently even though they rarely added positively to the overlaps scores. It then stores the cleaned gloss in a hash that maps the gloss to the corresponding sense. Finally, Pre-processing obtains the hypernyms, hyponyms, and synsets for each sense and stores them in their respective hashes (hypernyms, hyponyms, and synsets).

2.2 Overlap

The Overlap step is the main step in our system for determining where the new lemmas would be inserted into WordNet. Ideas were borrowed from both (Lesk, 1986) and Extended Gloss Overlaps (Banerjee and Pedersen, 2003).

2.2.1 Lesk

Lesk overlaps work by comparing two words' definitions and seeing if words in those definitions overlap onto one another. Words that share more overlaps score higher with the Lesk algorithm and therefore are more similar. However, one weakness with the Lesk algorithm is that different dictionaries might define even the same word differently, which means the number of overlaps is highly dependent on the dictionary used.

2.2.2 Extended Gloss Overlaps

To address the room for error in the Lesk over-laps, Extended Gloss Overlaps (EGO) incorporate not only the definitions of each word being com-pared, but also the definitions of the hypernyms and hyponyms of each word. EGOs use WordNet to re-trieve the hypernyms/hyponyms and their respective definitions for scoring. It was after EGOs that our system of scoring and calculating overlaps is based on.

2.2.3 Overlap Step

Our Overlap step works by iterating through each sense obtained from WordNet and creating an ex-panded sense by adding information from each sense. The expanded sense is then compared to the to-be-inserted lemmas creating a score to determine how alike the terms are. It should be noted that only corresponding parts of speech were compared as to improve time and not cause nouns to be mapped to verbs and vice versa.

For each sense to be compared, the expanded sense was created. First the sense's gloss was ob-tained from the hash initialized in pre-processing. Next the sense's immediate hypernyms and their glosses were retrieved and added to the expanded sense. Likewise, the sense's immediate hyponyms and their glosses were retrieved and added to the expanded sense. Finally, the sense's correspond-ing synset and their corresponding glosses were re-trieved and added to the expanded sense. Next be-fore any word overlaps could be processed, the new lemma's gloss needed to be cleaned up.

To provide clarity, we will act as if *ink* (taken from provided trial data) is being inserted into WordNet. For reference *ink*'s provided definition was "Tattoo work." The lemma was cleaned up following the same steps as the WordNet glosses followed in the pre-processing step. *Ink*'s definition would now be-come "tattoo work", since all letters are made low-ercase. However, since *ink* did not contain any stop words on the list, none were removed.

Now the system steps through each word in the lemma's gloss and checks for overlaps in the glosses of the expanded sense's gloss, each hyper-nym's gloss, each hyponym's gloss, and finally each synset's gloss. If the word being checked is part of the lemma of each sense, it receives a bonus score. The bonus score was originally set to (10 * the length of the lemma) but was later changed to (2 * the length of the lemma). This bonus was limited to compound words of at most two words. The decision to limit the length of compound words was arrived at since larger compounds like *Standing-*

on-top-of-the-world would score higher than *Worldwide* just because they were much longer compounds, even though they occur less often.

Since *ink*'s definition contains the word *tattoo*, any sense with *tattoo* in its lemma will receive the bonus. This means that *tattoo#n#:.* (i.e. any noun sense of *tattoo*) would receive a bonus. The same holds true for *work#n#:.* (i.e. any noun sense of *work*). The overlapping of words were also weighted by the number of characters present in those words (or more simply length of those words), so longer words carried a heavier weight in the score than shorter ones. As with *ink*, when the word *tattoo*, in the definition of ink, overlaps with another compared word it adds 6 to the score since *tattoo* contains 6 letters, whereas *work* would only add 4 to the score.

The final score of the sense was calculated by dividing the number of overlaps by the total length of words from the new term.

$$score = (SenseLaps + HypeLaps$$
$$+ HypoLaps + SynsLaps$$
$$+ BonusLapsTotal)/GlossLength$$
$$(1)$$

The sense with the highest score at the end was presumed to be the chosen sense to either attach or merge to.

Our system determined that *ink* belonged to *tattoo#n#3* whose definition from WordNet was, "the practice of making a design on the skin by pricking and staining". Since *ink* had a short definition provided from Wiktionary, the largest score came from the fact that *tattoo* gained the bonus score from overlapping with the definition. The correct answer provided in the key was *tattoo#n#2*, the reason for the differences was most likely the fact that our system did not identify present participle words, since *tattoo#n#2* contained the word "tattooing".

2.3 Refining the chosen sense

Now that the sense had been chosen, a new measure was implemented to make sure that, in fact, the correct sense had been chosen. This step was added since it was often the case that the first sense of a word was a better choice, however, a different sense of the same word would tie causing it to replace the first sense. When refining the sense, the system starts by assuming the first sense of the chosen word was the correct sense. This means that even though the system chooses *tattoo#n#3* for *ink*, Refine sense resets it to *tattoo#n#1* until evidence shows that *tattoo#n#3* is more deserving.

The system then performs a mini overlap, similar to the one above, limiting to just the senses of the chosen lemma and their glosses. If a sense other than the first one, had more words similar to the new term than the first one, then it would become the chosen sense of the word. The chosen sense is then cemented as the correct sense and the system moves on to merging or attaching.

2.4 Merge or Attach

The smallest amount of time (in developing this program) was spent on the problem of merging or attaching. This was due to the limited amount of time, and that time being focused more on determining the correct word over whether it should be merged or attached. Our system determines whether the term should be merged or attached by looking at the frequency of the chosen sense as obtained from the WordNet frequency() function. If the frequency was low (if it was equal to zero), then it was assumed to be a rarer sense so the program would attach the new term. If it was higher (greater than zero), then the opposite was assumed and merge was chosen. Our test data results are shown in the following contigency table.

		system		
		merge	attach	
key	merge	7	25	32
	attach	121	447	568
		128	472	600

ink was chosen to be attached to *tattoo#n#3* which means the frequency was greater than zero.

3 Results

On the 600 word test data set that was provided for SemEval Task 14, our system (*UMNDuluth Sys 1*) scored as shown in Table 1.

The SemEval14 organizers also included a baseline score on the data set, which is in the table under *baseline*. As mentioned in the methods section,

System	Wu & Palmer	Lemma Match	Recall	F1
UMNDuluth Sys 1 (2 bonus)	0.3395	0.0984	0.9983	0.5067
UMNDuluth Sys 2 (10 bonus)	0.3857	0.1467	1	0.5567
UMNDuluth Sys 3 (25 bonus)	0.3802	0.2117	1	0.5509
UMNDuluth Sys 4 (50 bonus)	0.3809	0.2100	1	0.5517
UMNDuluth Sys 5 (100 bonus)	0.3735	0.0517	1	0.5439
UMNDuluth Sys 6 (500 bonus)	0.3791	0.2083	1	0.5498
Baseline: First word, first sense	0.5139	0.415	1	0.6789
Baseline: Random synset	0.2269	0	1	0.3699
Median of Task14 Systems				0.5900

Table 1: SemEval Task 14 Scores

originally, our system weighted definitions that overlapped with senses' words as 10 times the length of the word. This was changed close to the end of development as it looked as it might give compound words too high of a score to reach with non-compound words. The 2 times amount was what was submitted and scored above. However, the 10 times amount was run against the same data and scored labeled by *UMNDuluth Sys 2*.

The Wu & Palmer Similarity, as defined by SemEval16 Task 14 task organizers[2], is calculated by finding the "similarity between the synset locations where the correct integration would be and where the system has placed the synset." This score is between 0 and 1. The Lemma Match, again defined by the task organizers, is scored by, "the percentage of answers where the operation is correct and the correct and system-provided synsets share a lemma." Recall refers to the percentage of lemmas attempted by the system. If 600 were attempted out of 600, then recall equals one.

4 Discussion

As the system was being built, we had the idea to originally use more information from Wiktionary[3]. However, when calls to Wiktionary were added in the system, the system slowed down to a halt, taking sometimes over 5 minutes per new lemma, even with the pre-processing. Since it was very impractical to wait this long, additional calls to Wiktionary were taken out of the program.

Another functionality that was thought to be used was the idea of adding in the level of the word in WordNet to the calculations. The level of each word in WordNet was thought to be used in the calculation of merge/attach. Unfortunately, the calls for this information to WordNet slowed the system to a halt at times, this meant the same fate as extra Wiktionary calls.

As seen in Table 1, our submitted system had a recall of less than one. This error most likely occurred because of time constraints. Since the system had to process 600 words, the 600 word file was split four ways to allow four instances of the system to process the data at once. In the splitting of the word file, a word was most likely lost.

Time constraints also was the reason of the difference between UMNDuluth Sys 1 and Sys 2. As stated in the results, Sys 1 had a bonus overlap multiplier of two while Sys 2 had a bonus of 10. The two multiplier was tested only on a small set of words, and little to no difference appeared between Sys 1 and Sys 2. However, it was discovered after the test data was turned in that the bonus multiplier scores higher when it is set to 10 as it is in Sys 2.

When seeing the improvement that occurred between Sys 1 and Sys 2, more tests were run by increasing the bonus. These are shown in Sys 3-6, which appear to peak between the 25 and 50 multiplier.

In the future, it would be interesting to see how additional Wiktionary data could help improve the choice of the system.

[2] http://alt.qcri.org/semeval2016/task14

[3] http://search.cpan.org/~clbecker/
Wiktionary-Parser-0.11/README.pod

References

Satanjeev Banerjee and Ted Pedersen. 2003. Extended gloss overlaps as a measure of semantic relatedness. In *Proceedings of the 18th International Joint Conference on Artificial Intelligence*, IJCAI'03, pages 805–810, San Francisco, CA, USA. Morgan Kaufmann Publishers Inc.

Michael Lesk. 1986. Automatic sense disambiguation using machine readable dictionaries: How to tell a pine cone from an ice cream cone. In *Proceedings of the 5th Annual International Conference on Systems Documentation*, SIGDOC '86, pages 24–26, New York, NY, USA. ACM.

VCU at Semeval-2016 Task 14: Evaluating similarity measures for semantic taxonomy enrichment

Bridget T. McInnes
Department of Computer Science
Virginia Commonwealth University
Richmond, VA 23284
btmcinnes@vcu.edu

Abstract

This paper describes the VCU systems that participated in the Semantic Taxonomy Enrichment task of SemEval 2016. The three systems are unsupervised and relied on dictionary-based similarity measures. The first two runs used first-order measures (Lesk and First-order vector), and the third run used a second-order measure (Second-order vector). The first-order measures obtained a higher Wu & Palmer score than the second-order measure on the test data. All three runs obtained a higher Wu & Palmer and F1 score than the random baseline but not the first-word first-sense baseline.

1 Introduction

Semantic knowledge bases are used in a number of NLP applications, e.g. Word Sense Disambiguation ((Agirre et al., 2014) (Agirre et al., 2010)) and Information Retrieval (Uddin et al., 2013). These knowledge bases span across a number of domains, e.g. WordNet, Gene Ontology, and Medical Subject Headings. Building and maintaining these knowledge bases is expensive and manually intensive (Martinez-Gil, 2015). Semantic taxonomy enrichment aims to aid in the maintenance process by automatically placing new terms into an existing taxonomy.

The Semantic Taxonomy Enrichment task (SemEval 2016 Task 14) objective was to automatically incorporate new word senses into WordNet [1], a lexical dictionary of English terms that are linked together based on a number of relations (e.g. is-a).

In this task, systems were provided a list of *out-of-vocabulary* terms (OOVs), their part-of-speech (POS), and a brief description of the term (OOV description). The goal of this task was to automatically identify which WordNet synset the OOV should be associated with and whether the association was synonymous ($merge$) or the OOV is a hyponym of the synset ($attach$).

Semantic similarity measures have been shown useful in the development of terminologies and ontologies (Vizenor et al., 2009). These measures quantify how related two terms are. The measures that we focus on for this task rely on definitional information extracted from knowledge sources such as WordNet. Our approach to the shared task is a modification of these measures relying on Word-Net's gloss information, and the OOV descriptions.

We categorize the measures we evaluated as first-order and second-order measures. The first-order measures conduct a direct comparison between the words in the WordNet synset's gloss and the words in the OOV description. Second-order measures incorporate additional context by creating a vector for each word in the synset's gloss (or OOV description) containing words that co-occur with it from an external corpus. These word vectors are then averaged to create a single co-occurrence vector for the OOV or synset.

The VCU systems were implemented using the freely available, open source UMLS-Similarity package (McInnes et al., 2009) (version 1.45), which includes support for user-defined dictionaries and corpora, in addition to the first-order and second-order measures.

---

[1] https://wordnet.princeton.edu/

Proceedings of SemEval-2016, pages 1351–1355,
San Diego, California, June 16-17, 2016. ©2016 Association for Computational Linguistics

The paper is organized as follows. First, we describe the details of the three VCU systems that participated in this task. Second, we discuss the evaluation metrics. Lastly, we discuss the results of the systems.

2 VCU Systems

There were three VCU systems. VCU-Run-1 uses the *Lesk* measure; VCU-Run-2 uses the *First-order vector* measure; and VCU-Run-3 uses the *Second-order vector* measure. Our goal was to compare the different measures on the task of identifying the appropriate placement for an OOV in WordNet. The measure used to identify the appropriate WordNet synset for a given OOV is the only difference between the three runs.

In the VCU systems, an OOV, its POS and text description is taken as input. First, the WordNet synsets are filtered based on their POS (see POS Filtering). Second, a score is assigned to each WordNet synset (see Measures). Third, the synset with the highest score is assigned to the OOV; if the score is greater than 0.7 it is labeled *merge* (the two terms are synonymous), otherwise *attach* (the OVV is a hyponym of the synset). The 0.7 score was set at development time and more work is required to determine what threshold should be used.

2.1 Measures

The VCU systems explored using three dictionary-based measures to identify the degree to which the OOV was similar to a WordNet synset for placement in the taxonomy. The first-order measure referred to as Lesk and First-order vector; and the third is a second-order measure referred to as Second-order vector. This subsection describes these measures.

2.1.1 Lesk

The Lesk measure, initially proposed by (Lesk, 1986), quantifies the relatedness between two terms by counting the number of overlaps between their two definitions. An overlap is defined as the longest sequence of one or more consecutive words that occur in both definitions. The length of the overlap is squared to give a greater weight to longer overlaps. For example, given the definitions *a very large number* and *a very large indefinite number*. The overlap *very large* would be given the score 4, the overlap

number would be given a score of 1, and the total Lesk score would be 5.

2.1.2 First-order vector

First-order vector is a modification of the Lesk measure. It treats each word in the definition as an element in a vector. A vector is created for the WordNet synset and the OOV where the element in the vector is the number of times the associated word occurred in their respective definitions. The cosine similarity is then used to quantify the degree to which the two terms are similar. Figure 1 shows a simple example where the OOV definition is *a very large number* and the WordNet definition is *a very large indefinite number*.

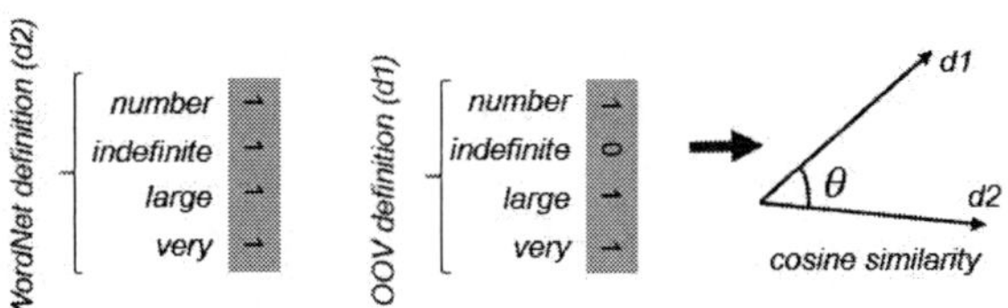

Figure 1: First-order vector example

2.1.3 Second-order vector

One of the disadvantages to first-order measures is that they rely on the exact matching of the words in the definitions. Therefore, *a humongous sum* would obtain a Lesk and First-order vector score of zero when compared to a *a very large number* even though both descriptions are clearly associated. The Second-order vector measure was introduced by (Patwardhan and Pedersen, 2006) to alleviate this.

In this measure, a vector is created for each word in the definition containing the words that co-occur with words from an external corpus. These word vectors are averaged to create a single co-occurrence vector for the OOV or synset. The similarity between the OOV and synset is then calculated by taking the cosine between their respective second-order vectors. Figure 2 shows a simple example using the "very large number" example again from above.

2.2 Definition Creation

The *definitions* we use in the VCU systems consist of: 1) the OOV description and 2) the WordNet synset's gloss.

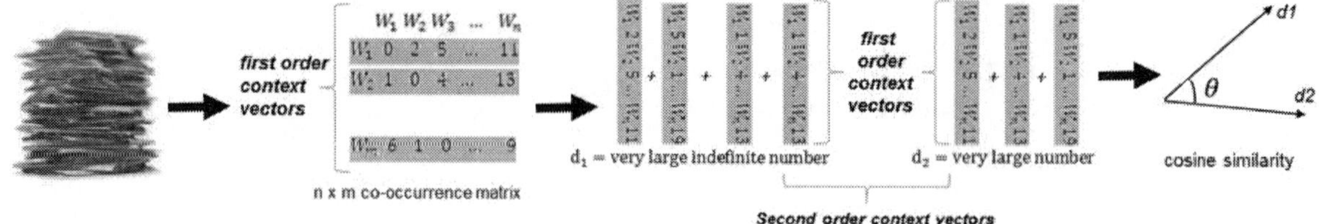

Figure 2: Second-order vector example

When implementing Lesk in WordNet, (Banerjee and Pedersen, 2002) found that the WordNet glosses were short, and did not contain enough overlaps to distinguish between multiple synsets, therefore, they extended this measure to include the glosses of the related concepts. This modification has been shown to improve the performance of both Lesk and Second-order vectors on the tasks of Word Sense Disambiguation (Banerjee and Pedersen, 2002) and Semantic Similarity (Patwardhan, 2003) (McInnes and Pedersen, 2013). The VCU Systems included the glosses of the following Word-Net relations: holonyms ($holo$), hypernyms ($hype$), hyponyms ($hypo$), and meronyms ($mero$). Therefore, our WordNet synset $definition$ contains not only the gloss of the synset but also the glosses of the related synsets.

The stop words were removed from the OOV descriptions and WordNet glosses prior to processing using the stoplist from the Ngram Statistics Package [2] (NSP), and all of the words were lower cased. No additional pre-processing (e.g. stemming) was conducted.

2.3 Matrix for second-order measure

In the VCU system, the second-order co-occurrence matrix was created using bigram counts obtained from the GigaWord Corpus 2nd Edition Agence France-Presse, English Service (afp_eng) data. We selected only those bigrams based on the following criteria: (1) neither word in the bigram was a stop word in the NSP stoplist; and (2) the bigram occurred at least twice in the corpus. The Ngram Statistics Package (Banerjee and Pedersen, 2003) was used to collect the bigram and their frequency counts.

The resulting matrix contained 59,217 rows and 70,726 columns, representing 4,487,663 unique bigrams. The matrix is not symmetric because the co-occurrences are bigrams. Therefore, the number of times *school bus* was seen in the text is different than the number of times *bus school*. All the words in the corpus were lower cased prior to processing.

2.4 Part-of-Speech Filters

Due to the number of synsets in WordNet, we filtered them based on two criteria: (1) the WordNet synset has the same POS as the OOV; and (2) the WordNet synset contained a word of the same POS as a word in the OOV description. These criteria were adaptations of the first-word/first-sense baseline that was provided by the organizers to reduce the number of possible synset choices. To obtain the POS of the words in the OOV descriptions, we used the OpenNLP POS Tagger (Baldridge et al., 2002).

3 Evaluation Metrics

The VCU system was evaluated using four metrics: WuP, Lemma Match, Recall and F1. WuP is based on the similarity metric proposed by (Wu and Palmer, 1994). It was used to evaluate how close the system came to identifying the correct synset. In this metric, the similarity is twice the depth of the two synsets ($synset_{sys}$ and $synset_{gold}$) Least Common Subsumer (LCS) divided by the sum of the depths of the individual synsets as defined in Equation 1. The LCS is the most specific ancestor shared by two synsets using WordNet's hypernymy/hyponymy relations.

$$\text{WuP} = \frac{2 * \text{depth}(\text{lcs}(synset_{sys}, synset_{gold}))}{\text{depth}(synset_{sys}) + \text{depth}(synst_{gold})} \tag{1}$$

---

[2] https://sourceforge.net/projects/ngram/

System	Measure	WuP	Lemma Match	Recall	F1
VCU-Run-1	First-order Lesk	0.4190	0.1706	0.9967	0.5900
VCU-Run-2	First-order vector	0.4317	0.1605	0.9967	0.6024
VCU-Run-3	Second-order vector	0.4076	0.1237	0.9967	0.5786
Baseline	Random	0.2269	0.0000	1.000	0.3699
Baseline	First word/sense	0.5134	0.4150	1.000	0.6790

Table 1: VCU System Test Results

Recall determines how many of the OOV terms were assigned to a WordNet synset. The F1 score is the F-measure (harmonic mean) of WuP and Recall. The Lemma Match is the percentage of system synsets that exactly matched the gold standard.

4 Results and Discussion

Table 1 shows the VCU system results for the Semantic Taxonomy Enrichment task, and the two baselines provided by the organizers (Random and First-word First-sense). The Random baseline chooses a random synset of the appropriate POS. The First-word First-sense (First word/sense) assigns the first synset whose word is also the first head word in the OOV description with the same POS.

The Recall results show that the VCU systems did not assign all of the OOVs to a WordNet synset. Investigation into this found that the POS filter (see Section 2.4) was too aggressive and no WordNet synset met the filtering criteria. The WuP and Lemma Match results show that the VCU systems obtained a higher score than the random baseline but not the First word/sense baseline.

The results between the three VCU system runs show that the First-order measures obtained a higher Lemma Match, WuP and F1 score than the Second-order vector measure. This indicates that the additional contextual information from the corpus did not provide useful information, hurting the performance. The co-occurrence matrix created for the Second-order vector measure was based on text from the GigaWord corpus. Looking back, we believe that utilizing a more up-to-date text such as Wikipedia, or using WordNet as a corpus itself as (Pedersen, 2014) may increase the performance the results.

The results between the first-order measures show Lesk obtained a lower WuP score than First-order vector, but a higher Lemma Match. Analysis of the mappings found that Lesk was merging all of the OOVs to the WordNet synsets rather than attaching them as a hyponym. When assigning *attach* rather than *merge* to each of the mappings, the WuP score for Lesk increased to 0.4461 (higher than First-order vector's 0.4317). This indicates that additional work is required to determine whether the attachment of the OOV to the synset should be a *merge* or an *attach*.

5 Conclusion and Future Work

In this paper, we described the VCU systems that participated in the Semantic Taxonomy Enrichment task of SemEval 2016. The three systems are unsupervised and relied on dictionary-based similarity measures. The first two runs used First-order measures (Lesk and First-order vector), and the third run used a second-order measure (Second-order vector). The first-order measures obtained a higher Wu & Palmer score than the second-order measure.

Analysis of the OOV mappings to WordNet synsets by the measures highlighted three areas of future work. First, more attention needs to be paid in determining whether the new term should be merged as a synonym or attached as a hyponym to the synset. Second, a more indepth analysis of the definitions used to represent the context of the new terms and the WordNet synsets needs to be conducted. Lastly, although the Second-order vector did not perform as well as the First-order measures, the type of the corpus used to create the second-order vectors needs to be explored.

Acknowledgments

WordNet was accessed using WordNet–QueryData [3]. The VCU systems were implemented using UMLS-Similarity [4]. I would like to thank Ted Pedersen for help in understanding the task, and useful brainstorming discussions.

---

[3] http://search.cpan.org/WordNet-QueryData
[4] http://search.cpan.org/UMLS-Similarity

References

E. Agirre, A. Soroa, and M. Stevenson. 2010. Graph-based word sense disambiguation of biomedical documents. *Bioinformatics*, 26(22):2889–2896.

E. Agirre, O.L. de Lacalle, and A. Soroa. 2014. Random walks for knowledge-based word sense disambiguation. *Computational Linguistics*, 40(1):57–84.

J. Baldridge, T. Morton, and G. Bierner. 2002. The opennlp maximum entropy package. *tech. rep., SourceForge*.

S. Banerjee and T. Pedersen. 2002. An Adapted Lesk Algorithm for Word Sense Disambiguation Using Word-Net. In *Proceedings of the Third Intl. Conf. on Intell. Text Process. and Comp. Ling.*, pages 136–145, Mexico City, Mexico, February. Springer.

Satanjeev Banerjee and Ted Pedersen. 2003. The design, implementation, and use of the ngram statistics package. In *Computational Linguistics and Intelligent Text Processing*, pages 370–381. Springer.

O. Bodenreider and A. Burgun. 2004. Aligning knowledge sources in the UMLS: methods, quantitative results, and applications. In *Proceedings of the 11th World Congress on MEDINFO*, pages 327–331, San Fransico, CA, November.

M. Lesk. 1986. Automatic sense disambiguation using machine readable dictionaries: how to tell a pine cone from an ice cream cone. In *Proc. of the 5th Annual Intl. Conf. on Sys. Doc.*, pages 24–26, Toronto, Canada, June.

J. Martinez-Gil. 2015. Automated knowledge base management: A survey. *Computer Science Review*, 18:1–9.

B.T. McInnes and T. Pedersen. 2013. Evaluating measures of semantic similarity and relatedness to disambiguate terms in biomedical text. *Journal of Biomedical Informatics*, 46(6):1116–1124.

B.T. McInnes, T. Pedersen, and S.V. Pakhomov. 2009. UMLS-Interface and UMLS-Similarity: Open source software for measuring paths and semantic similarity. In *Proc. of the AMIA Symposium*, pages 431–435, San Fransico, CA, November.

S. Patwardhan and T. Pedersen. 2006. Using WordNet-based context vectors to estimate the semantic relatedness of concepts. In *Proceedings of the EACL 2006 Workshop Making Sense of Sense - Bringing Computational Linguistics and Psycholinguistics Together*, pages 1–8, Trento, Italy, April.

S. Patwardhan. 2003. Incorporating dictionary and corpus information into a context vector measure of semantic relatedness. *Master's thesis, University of Minnesota, Duluth*.

Ted Pedersen. 2014. Duluth: Measuring cross–level semantic similarity with first and second–order dictionary overlaps. *SemEval 2014*, page 247.

M.N. Uddin, T.H. Duong, N.T. Nguyen, X. Qi, and G.S. Jo. 2013. Semantic similarity measures for enhancing information retrieval in folksonomies. *Expert Systems with Applications*, 40(5):1645–1653.

Lowell T Vizenor, Olivier Bodenreider, and Alexa T Mc-Cray. 2009. Auditing associative relations across two knowledge sources. *Journal of biomedical informatics*, 42(3):426–439.

Z. Wu and M. Palmer. 1994. Verbs semantics and lexical selection. In *Proc. of the 32nd Meeting of ACL*, pages 133–138, Las Cruces, NM, June.

AUTHOR INDEX

AUTHOR INDEX

AUTHOR INDEX

AUTHOR INDEX

Association for Computational Linguistics
209 N. Eighth Street
Stroudsburg, Pennsylvania 18360

ISBN 978-1-5108-2607-6